THEORIES

OF

SOCIETY

Edited by

TALCOTT PARSONS

EDWARD SHILS

KASPAR D. NAEGELE

JESSE R. PITTS

Fp

THEORIES

OF

SOCIETY

Foundations of Modern Sociological Theory

TWO VOLUMES IN ONE

THE FREE PRESS
A Division of Macmillan Publishing Co., Inc.
NEW YORK

COLLIER MACMILLAN
LONDON

THE FREE PRESS
A DIVISION OF MACMILLAN PUBLISHING CO., INC.
866 Third Avenue, New York, N.Y. 10022

Collier Macmillan Canada Ltd.

Library of Congress Catalog Card Number: 61–9171

Printed in the United States of America

printing number
9   10

CONTENTS—AN OVERVIEW

PREFACE   *xxi*

GENERAL INTRODUCTION   *1*

Part One   HISTORICAL AND ANALYTICAL FOUNDATIONS   *81*

    A. *The Interpretation of Action in the History of Social Thought*   *83*
    B. *The Elements of Social Interaction: Roles and Collectivities*   *145*
    C. *The Modes of the Institutionalization of Action*   *179*

Part Two   DIFFERENTIATION AND VARIATION IN SOCIAL STRUCTURES   *237*

    A. *Ascriptive Solidarities*   *265*
    B. *Occupation and Economy*   *405*
    C. *Stratification and Mobility*   *515*
    D. *Political Organization and Authority*   *577*
    E. *Religion and Social Structure*   *643*

Part Three   PERSONALITY AND THE SOCIAL SYSTEM   *683*

    A. *The Definition of the Situation and the Internalization of Objects*   *717*
    B. *The Elements of Learned Motivation*   *745*
    C. *Processes of Socialization*   *819*
    D. *Social Structure and the Motivation of Deviant and Conforming Behavior*   *867*

Part Four   CULTURE AND THE SOCIAL SYSTEM   *961*

    A. *Symbolic Processes and the Cultural Heritage*   *995*
    B. *Value and Belief Patterns*   *1051*
    C. *Expressive Symbolism*   *1163*

Part Five   SOCIAL CHANGE   *1205*

    A. *Factors of Change*   *1223*
    B. *Processes of Stabilization and Change*   *1285*
    C. *Patterns of Change and Development*   *1327*

EPILOGUE   *1403*

BIBLIOGRAPHY   *1449*

INDEX   *1481*

CONTENTS

LIST OF SELECTIONS, BY AUTHOR   *xvii*

PREFACE   *xxi*

GENERAL INTRODUCTION

  I. *Some Observations on the Scope of Sociological Analysis,* BY KASPAR D. NAEGELE   *3*

 II. *An Outline of the Social System,* BY TALCOTT PARSONS   *30*

Part One HISTORICAL AND ANALYTICAL FOUNDATIONS

A. *The Interpretation of Action in the History of Social Thought*

    Editorial Foreword, BY TALCOTT PARSONS   *85*

  1. *On Hatreds and Dissensions in the Republic,* BY NICCOLO MACHIAVELLI   *98*

  2. *Of the Natural Condition of Mankind,* BY THOMAS HOBBES   *99*

  3. *Of the State of Nature,* BY JOHN LOCKE   *101*

  4. *Of the Principle Which Gives Occasion to the Division of Labour,* BY ADAM SMITH   *104*

  5. *Of Systems of Equality,* BY THOMAS R. MALTHUS   *106*

  6. *The Civic Community,* BY GEORG W. F. HEGEL   *112*

  7. *The Functions of Government in General,* BY JOHN STUART MILL   *117*

  8. *On the Social Contract,* BY JEAN JACQUES ROUSSEAU   *119*

  9. *Society and Government,* BY AUGUSTE COMTE   *125*

  10. *The Material Forces and the Relations of Production,* BY KARL MARX   *136*

  11. *On Status and Contract,* BY SIR HENRY SUMNER MAINE   *138*

  12. *The Nature of Society,* BY HERBERT SPENCER   *139*

B. *The Elements of Social Interaction: Roles and Collectivities*

    Editorial Foreword, BY KASPAR D. NAEGELE   *147*

  1. *The Sociology of Sociability,* BY GEORG SIMMEL   *157*

2. *The I and the Me,* BY GEORGE H. MEAD   *163*

3. *Reciprocity,* BY MARCEL MAUSS   *168*

4. *Social Action and Its Types,* BY MAX WEBER   *173*

C. *The Modes of the Institutionalization of Action*

Editorial Foreword, BY KASPAR D. NAEGELE   *183*

1. *Gemeinschaft and Gesellschaft,* BY FERDINAND TOENNIES   *191*

2. *Status and Role,* BY RALPH LINTON   *202*

3. *On Mechanical and Organic Solidarity,* BY EMILE DURKHEIM   *208*

4. *Types of Suicide,* BY EMILE DURKHEIM   *213*

5. *Types of Social Organization,* BY MAX WEBER   *218*

6. *Legitimate Order and Types of Authority,* BY MAX WEBER   *229*

Part Two DIFFERENTIATION AND VARIATION IN SOCIAL STRUCTURES

Introduction, BY TALCOTT PARSONS   *239*

A. *Ascriptive Solidarities*

Editorial Foreword, BY TALCOTT PARSONS   *267*

I. KINSHIP

1. *Systems of Consanguinity,* BY LEWIS H. MORGAN   *269*

2. *Classificatory Systems of Relationship,* BY ALFRED L. KROEBER *271*

3. *The Complex of Mother-Right,* BY BRONISLAW MALINOWSKI   *276*

4. *The Study of Kinship Systems,* BY A. R. RADCLIFFE-BROWN   *278*

5. *The Household Community,* BY MAX WEBER   *296*

II. ETHNIC SOLIDARITIES

1. *Ethnic Groups,* BY MAX WEBER   *305*

2. *The Problem of Minority Groups,* BY LOUIS WIRTH   *309*

III. PRIMARY GROUPS

1. *Primary Groups,* BY CHARLES H. COOLEY   *315*

2. *Secrecy and Group Communication,* BY GEORG SIMMEL   *318*

3. *The Sociological Category of Communion,* BY HERMAN SCHMALENBACH *331*

4. *The Organization of the Primary Working Group,* BY F. J. ROETHLISBERGER
AND WILLIAM J. DICKSON   *348*

5. *The Solidarity of Occupational Groups,* BY EMILE DURKHEIM   *356*

IV. TERRITORIAL COMMUNITY

1. *On the Origins of the State*, BY ROBERT H. LOWIE   364

2. *The Village Community*, BY SIR HENRY SUMNER MAINE   370

3. *The Urban Community*, BY MAX WEBER   380

4. *European Feudalism*, BY MARC BLOCH   385

5. *Nationality*, BY LORD ACTON   392

B. *Occupation and Economy*

Editorial Foreword, BY TALCOTT PARSONS   407

I. GENERAL CONSIDERATIONS

Wants in Relation to Activities, BY ALFRED MARSHALL   409

II. ECONOMIC INSTITUTIONS

1. *Capitalists and Laborers*, BY ADAM SMITH   411

2. *The Division of Society into Classes*, BY THOMAS R. MALTHUS   415

3. *Types of Division of Labor*, BY MAX WEBER   418

4. *Ownership and Possession*, BY SIR FREDERICK POLLACK AND FREDERICK W.
   MAITLAND   422

5. *On Contract*, BY SIR HENRY SUMNER MAINE   429

6. *Organic Solidarity and Contract*, BY EMILE DURKHEIM   436

III. ORGANIZATION OF THE ECONOMY

1. *The Market*, BY MAX WEBER   443

2. *The Principal Modes of Capitalistic Orientation*, BY MAX WEBER   446

3. *The Essential Properties of Interest and Money*, BY JOHN MAYNARD KEYNES 447

4. *The Economic Organization*, BY FRANK H. KNIGHT   454

IV. UNITS OF THE ECONOMY

1. *Household Economy*, BY FRÉDÉRIC LE PLAY   457

2. *The Social Organization of Production*, BY MAX WEBER   460

3. *Budgetary Management and Profit Making*, BY MAX WEBER   470

4. *Industrial Organization*, BY ALFRED MARSHALL   478

V. ECONOMIC DEVELOPMENT

1. *A Historical Survey of Industrial Systems*, BY KARL BÜCHER   493

2. *The Fundamentals of Economic Development*, BY JOSEPH A. SCHUMPETER   505

C. *Stratification and Mobility*

Editorial Foreword, BY TALCOTT PARSONS   517

1. *Of Wages and Profit in the Different Employments of Labor and Stock*, BY
   ADAM SMITH   518

2. *The Class Struggle,* BY KARL MARX   529

3. *Class and Occupations,* BY EDMOND GOBLOT   535

4. *On Superordination and Subordination,* BY GEORG SIMMEL   540

5. *The Circulation of Elites,* BY VILFREDO PARETO   551

6. *Conspicuous Consumption,* BY THORSTEIN VEBLEN   558

7. *Social Stratification,* BY PITIRIM A. SOROKIN   570

8. *Social Stratification and Class Structure,* BY MAX WEBER   573

D. *Political Organization and Authority*

Editorial Foreword, BY TALCOTT PARSONS   579

I. POWER AND INEQUALITY

1. *The Withering Away of the State,* BY NICOLAI LENIN   580

2. *The Use of Force in Society,* BY VILFREDO PARETO   589

3. *On the Ruling Class,* BY GAETANO MOSCA   598

4. *The Sociological Character of Political Parties,* BY ROBERTO MICHELS 603

II. SOME PATTERNS OF POLITICAL ORGANIZATION AND AUTHORITY

1. *The Idea of Corporation,* BY OTTO VON GIERKE   611

2. *The Types of Authority,* BY MAX WEBER   626

3. *The Theory of Authority,* BY CHESTER I. BARNARD   632

E. *Religion and Social Structure*

Editorial Foreword, BY TALCOTT PARSONS   645

1. *The Theological Stage,* BY AUGUSTE COMTE   646

2. *Of Superstition and Enthusiasm,* BY DAVID HUME   656

3. *The Gods of the City,* BY FUSTEL DE COULANGES   659

4. *Jehovah and the Prophets,* BY W. ROBERTSON SMITH   661

5. *Church and Sect,* BY ERNST TROELTSCH   664

6. *Trends in Western Monasticism,* BY ADOLF VON HARNACK   670

7. *Religion and Society,* BY EMILE DURKHEIM   677

Part Three PERSONALITY AND THE SOCIAL
SYSTEM

    Introduction, BY JESSE R. PITTS   685

A. *The Definition of the Situation and the Internalization of
    Objects*

    Editorial Foreword, BY JESSE R. PITTS   719

    1. *Society and Individual Consciousness*, BY EMILE DURKHEIM   720

    2. *Ideas and Religious Interests*, BY MAX WEBER   724

    3. *The Libido's Attachment to Objects*, BY SIGMUND FREUD   729

    4. *The Ego and the Superego*, BY SIGMUND FREUD   733

    5. *Taking the Role of the Other*, BY GEORGE H. MEAD   739

    6. *The Four Wishes and the Definition of the Situation*, BY WILLIAM I. THOMAS   741

B. *The Elements of Learned Motivation*

    Editorial Foreword, BY JESSE R. PITTS   747

I. THE NATURE OF LEARNING

    1. *The Principal Instincts of Man*, BY WILLIAM MC DOUGALL   751

    2. *On Behaviorism*, BY JOHN P. WATSON   758

    3. *The Law of Effect*, BY EDWARD L. THORNDIKE   762

    4. *On Conditioned Reflexes*, BY IVAN P. PAVLOV   764

    5. *On Drive*, BY CLARK L. HULL   770

    6. *On Insight*, BY WOLFGANG KÖHLER   772

    7. *A Summary Discussion of Purposive Behavior*, BY EDWARD C. TOLMAN   777

II. THE ORGANIZATION OF MOTIVATIONAL SYSTEMS

    1. *Combinations and Group Persistence*, BY VILFREDO PARETO   780

    2. *Faithfulness and Gratitude*, BY GEORG SIMMEL   787

    3. *On Valence*, BY KURT LEWIN   794

    4. *Anxiety as Motivation*, BY SIGMUND FREUD   799

    5. *Mechanisms of Defense*, BY SIGMUND FREUD   808

C. *Processes of Socialization*

    Editorial Foreword, BY JESSE R. PITTS   821

    1. *The Social Self*, BY CHARLES H. COOLEY   822

2. *Internalized Others and the Self,* BY GEORGE H. MEAD   829

3. *On Intellectual Growth,* BY JEAN PIAGET   830

4. *Moral Realism,* BY JEAN PIAGET   835

5. *On Object-Relations and Psycho-Sexual Stages,* BY SIGMUND FREUD   838

6. *On the Internalization of the Sex Role: The Feminine Case,* BY SIGMUND FREUD 852

7. *On the Learning of Discipline,* BY EMILE DURKHEIM   860

D. *Social Structure and the Motivation of Deviant and Conforming Behavior*

   Editorial Foreword, BY JESSE R. PITTS   869

I. THE ELEMENTS OF DEVIANCE AND SOCIAL CONTROL

1. *On the Normality of Crime,* BY EMILE DURKHEIM   872

2. *The Psychology of Punitive Justice,* BY GEORGE H. MEAD   876

3. *The Psychopathology of Everyday Life,* BY SIGMUND FREUD   887

4. *Analytic Therapy and Transference,* BY SIGMUND FREUD   896

5. *Analysis Terminable and Interminable,* BY SIGMUND FREUD   903

II. THE STRUCTURE OF DEVIANT BEHAVIOR

1. *Anomic Suicide,* BY EMILE DURKHEIM   916

2. *Social Patterns and the Gang,* BY FREDERIC M. THRASHER   929

III. THE MOTIVATION OF DEVIANCE

1. *Three Types of Personality,* BY WILLIAM I. THOMAS AND FLORIAN ZNANIECKI 934

2. *Internal Sources of Behavioral Instability and Their Control,* BY SIGMUND FREUD 940

3. *Cultural Conflict and the Marginal Man,* BY ROBERT E. PARK   944

IV. THE MAINTENANCE OF CONFORMITY

1. *Death and the Reintegration of the Group,* BY BRONISLAW MALINOWSKI   947

2. *On the Rites of Passage,* BY ARNOLD VAN GENNEP   950

3. *On Taboo,* BY A. R. RADCLIFFE-BROWN   951

4. *On Communal Ritual,* BY EMILE DURKHEIM   959

Part Four   CULTURE AND THE SOCIAL SYSTEM

   Introduction, BY TALCOTT PARSONS   963

A. *Symbolic Processes and the Cultural Heritage*

   Editorial Foreword, BY TALCOTT PARSONS   997

Contents xiii

I. SYMBOLISM AND COMMUNICATION

1. *From Gesture to Symbol*, BY GEORGE H. MEAD 999
2. *Ideational Contents of the Sign*, BY ERNST CASSIRER 1004
3. *On Sacred Objects as Symbols*, BY EMILE DURKHEIM 1008
4. *Dream-Work*, BY SIGMUND FREUD 1010
5. *How Words Change Their Meanings*, BY ANTOINE MEILLET 1013
6. *Symbolism*, BY EDWARD SAPIR 1018

II. PATTERNS OF CULTURE

1. *The Factors of Social Phenomena*, BY HERBERT SPENCER 1021
2. *On Biological and Cultural Factors*, BY FRANZ BOAS 1024
3. *On Culture*, BY ALFRED L. KROEBER 1032
4. *On the Mores*, BY WILLIAM GRAHAM SUMNER 1037
5. *On the Patterns of Culture*, BY RUTH BENEDICT 1047

B. *Value and Belief Patterns*

    Editorial Foreword, BY TALCOTT PARSONS 1053

I. KNOWLEDGE AND RATIONALITY

1. *Rational Mastery of the Environment*, BY BRONISLAW MALINOWSKI 1056
2. *On Logical and Non-Logical Action*, BY VILFREDO PARETO 1061
3. *Types of Rationality*, BY MAX WEBER 1063
4. *Social Structure and the Structure of Thought*, BY EMILE DURKHEIM AND MARCEL MAUSS 1065
5. *On the Origins of the Idea of Force*, BY EMILE DURKHEIM 1068
6. *The Positive Role of the Sociology of Knowledge*, BY KARL MANNHEIM 1070

II. RELIGION AND MAGIC

1. *Types of Magic*, BY SIR JAMES G. FRAZER 1077
2. *On Magic and the Unknown*, BY MARCEL MAUSS AND H. HUBERT 1088
3. *On the Social Functions of Religion*, BY BRONISLAW MALINOWSKI 1091
4. *On Sacrifice*, BY W. ROBERTSON SMITH 1096
5. *The Tao*, BY MARCEL GRANET 1098
6. *Confucianism and Puritanism*, BY MAX WEBER 1101
7. *On Eastern and Western Christianity*, BY ADOLF HARNACK 1111
8. *On Religious Rejections of the World*, BY MAX WEBER 1120
9. *Religion and Social Status*, BY MAX WEBER 1138

C. *Expressive Symbolism*

    Editorial Foreword, BY TALCOTT PARSONS 1165
1. *Expression in Reference to the Body*, BY SIR CHARLES BELL 1167

2. *The Expression of the Emotions,* BY CHARLES DARWIN   *1168*

3. *Language in the Phase of Sensuous Expression,* BY ERNST CASSIRER   *1170*

4. *Life-Symbols: The Roots of Sacrament,* BY SUZANNE LANGER   *1179*

5. *The Art of Magic and the Power of Faith,* BY BRONISLAW MALINOWSKI   *1189*

6. *The Nature and Functions of Ceremonials,* BY A. R. RADCLIFFE-BROWN   *1191*

7. *An Incongruous Assortment of Incongruities,* BY KENNETH BURKE   *1200*

Part Five   SOCIAL CHANGE

Introduction, BY KASPAR D. NAEGELE   *1207*

A. *Factors of Change*

Editorial Foreword, BY KASPAR D. NAEGELE   *1225*

1. *On the Accumulation of Capital,* BY KARL MARX   *1226*

2. *On Protestantism and Capitalism,* BY MAX WEBER   *1253*

3. *On Psychology and History,* BY SIGMUND FREUD   *1265*

4. *The Hypothesis of Cultural Lag,* BY WILLIAM F. OGBURN   *1270*

5. *Fundamentals of Culture-Sociology,* BY ALFRED WEBER   *1274*

B. *Processes of Stabilization and Change*

Editorial Foreword, BY KASPAR D. NAEGELE   *1287*

1. *On the Equilibrium of the Social System,* BY VILFREDO PARETO   *1288*

2. *On Disorganization and Reorganization,* BY W. I. THOMAS AND FLORIAN

    ZNANIECKI   *1292*

3. *The Routinization of Charisma,* BY MAX WEBER   *1297*

4. *On the Process of Change in Social Values,* BY EMILE DURKHEIM   *1305*

5. *The Principle of Immanent Change,* BY PITIRIM SOROKIN   *1311*

6. *On Configurations of Culture Growth,* BY ALFRED L. KROEBER   *1321*

7. *On Conflict,* BY GEORG SIMMEL   *1324*

C. *Patterns of Change and Development*

Editorial Foreword, BY KASPAR D. NAEGELE   *1329*

1. *On the Three Stages of Social Evolution,* BY AUGUSTE COMTE   *1332*

2. *On the Style-Patterns of Culture,* BY OSWALD SPENGLER   *1343*

3. *The Disintegrations of Civilizations,* BY ARNOLD TOYNBEE   *1355*

4. *The Reality of Social Evolution,* BY ROBERT M. MAC IVER   *1364*

5. *Diffusion,* BY RALPH LINTON   *1371*

6. *Cycles of Interdependence,* BY VILFREDO PARETO   *1381*

7. *The Social Psychology of the World Religions,* BY MAX WEBER   *1385*

EPILOGUE

The Calling of Sociology, BY EDWARD SHILS   1405

BIBLIOGRAPHY   1451

INDEX FOLLOWS PAGE 1480   I

LIST OF SELECTIONS BY AUTHOR

LORD ACTON
Nationality — 392

CHESTER I. BARNARD
The Theory of Authority — 632

SIR CHARLES BELL
Expression in Reference to the Body — 1167

RUTH BENEDICT
On the Patterns of Culture — 1047

MARC BLOCH
European Feudalism — 385

FRANZ BOAS
On Biological and Cultural Factors — 1024

KARL BÜCHER
A Historical Survey of Industrial Systems — 493

KENNETH BURKE
An Incongruous Assortment of Incongruities — 1200

ERNST CASSIRER
Ideational Content of the Sign — 1004
Language in the Phase of Sensuous Expression — 1170

AUGUSTE COMTE
Society and Government — 125
The Theological Stage — 646
On the Three Stages of Social Evolution — 1332

CHARLES H. COOLEY
Primary Groups — 315
The Social Self — 822

CHARLES DARWIN
The Expression of the Emotions — 1168

WILLIAM J. DICKSON (AND F. J. ROETHLISBERGER)
The Organization of the Primary Working Group — 348

EMILE DURKHEIM
Anomic Suicide — 916
On Communal Ritual — 959
On the Learning of Discipline — 860
On Mechanical and Organic Solidarity — 208
On the Normality of Crime — 872
Organic Solidarity and Contract — 436
On the Origins of the Idea of Force — 1068
On the Process of Change in Social Values — 1305
Religion and Society — 677
On Sacred Objects as Symbols — 1008
Society and Individual Consciousness — 720
The Solidarity of Occupational Groups — 356
Types of Suicide — 213
(AND MARCEL MAUSS) Social Structure and the Structure of Thought — 1065

FRIEDRICH ENGELS (AND KARL MARX)
The Class Struggle — 529

SIR JAMES G. FRAZER
Types of Magic — 1077

SIGMUND FREUD
Analysis Terminable and Interminable — 903
Analytic Therapy and Transference — 896
Anxiety as Motivation — 799
Dream-Work — 1010
The Ego and the Superego — 733
On the Internalization of the Sex Role: The Feminine Case — 852
Internal Sources of Behavioral Instability and Their Control — 940
The Libido's Attachment to Objects — 729
Mechanisms of Defense — 808
On Object-Relations and Psycho-Sexual Stages — 838
On Psycholgy and History — 1265
The Psychopathology of Everyday Life — 887

N. D. FUSTEL DE COULANGES
The Gods of the City — 659

ARNOLD VON GENNEP
On the Rites of Passage — 950

OTTO VON GIERKE
The Idea of Corporation — 611

EDMOND GOBLOT
Class and Occupations — 535

MARCEL GRANET
The Tao — 1098

ADOLF VON HARNACK
On Eastern and Western Christianity — 1111
Trends in Western Monasticism — 670

GEORG W. F. HEGEL
The Civic Community — 112

THOMAS HOBBES
Of the Natural Condition of Mankind — 99

HENRI HUBERT (AND MARCEL MAUSS)
On Magic and the Unknown — 1088

CLARK L. HULL
On Drive — 770

DAVID HUME
    Of Superstition and Enthusiasm   656
JOHN MAYNARD KEYNES
    The Essential Properties of Interest and
       Money   447
FRANK H. KNIGHT
    The Economic Organization   454
WOLFGANG KÖHLER
    On Insight   772
ALFRED L. KROEBER
    Classificatory Systems of Relationship   271
    On Configurations of Culture Growth   1321
    On Culture   1032
SUZANNE LANGER
    Life-Symbols: The Roots of Sacrament   1179
NICOLAI LENIN
    The Withering Away of the State   580
FRÉDÉRIC LE PLAY
    Household Economy   457
KURT LEWIN
    On Valence   794
RALPH LINTON
    Diffusion   1371
    Status and Role   202
JOHN LOCKE
    Of the State of Nature   101
ROBERT H. LOWIE
    On the Origins of the State   364
NICCOLO MACHIAVELLI
    On Hatreds and Dissensions in the
       Republic   98
WILLIAM MC DOUGALL
    The Principal Instincts of Man   751
ROBERT M. MAC IVER
    The Reality of Social Evolution   1364
SIR HENRY SUMNER MAINE
    On Contract   429
    On Status and Contract   138
    The Village Community   370
FREDERIC W. MAITLAND (WITH SIR FRED-
    ERICK POLLOCK)
    Ownership and Possession   422
BRONISLAW MALINOWSKI
    The Art of Magic and the Power of Faith   1189
    The Complex of Mother-Right   276
    Death and the Reintegration of the Group   947
    Rational Mastery of the Environment   1056
    On the Social Functions of Religion   1091
THOMAS R. MALTHUS
    The Division of Society into Classes   415
    Of Systems of Equality   106
KARL MANNHEIM
    The Positive Role of the Sociology of
       Knowledge   1070
ALFRED MARSHALL
    Industrial Organization   478

    Wants in Relation to Activities   409
KARL MARX
    On the Accumulation of Capital   1226
    The Material Forces and the Relations of
       Production   136
    The Class Struggle   529
MARCEL MAUSS
    Reciprocity   168
    (AND H. HUBERT) *On Magic and the Un-*
       known   1088
    (AND EMILE DURKHEIM) *Social Structure*
       and the Structure of Thought   1065
GEORGE H. MEAD
    From Gesture to Symbol   999
    The I and the Me   163
    Internalized Others and the Self   829
    The Psychology of Punitive Justice   876
    Taking the Role of the Other   739
ANTOINE MEILLET
    How Words Change Their Meanings   1013
ROBERT MICHELS
    The Sociological Character of Political
       Parties   603
JOHN STUART MILL
    The Functions of Government in General   117
LEWIS H. MORGAN
    Systems of Consanguinity   269
GAETANO MOSCA
    On the Ruling Class   598
WILLIAM F. OGBURN
    The Hypothesis of Cultural Lag   1270
VILFREDO PARETO
    The Circulation of Elites   551
    Combinations and Group Persistence   780
    Cycles of Interdependence   1381
    On the Equilibrium of the Social System   1288
    On Logical and Non-Logical Action   1061
    The Use of Force in Society   589
ROBERT E. PARK
    Cultural Conflict and the Marginal Man   944
IVAN P. PAVLOV
    On Conditioned Reflexes   764
JEAN PIAGET
    On Intellectual Growth   850
    Moral Realism   835
SIR FREDERICK POLLOCK (AND FREDERICK
    W. MAITLAND)
    Ownership and Possession   422
A. R. RADCLIFFE-BROWN
    The Nature and Functions of Ceremonials   1191
    The Study of Kinship Systems   278
    On Taboo   951
JEAN JACQUES ROUSSEAU
    On the Social Contract   119
F. J. ROETHLISBERGER (AND WILLIAM J.
    DICKSON)

The Organization of the Primary Working Group 348

EDWARD SAPIR
Symbolism 1018

HERMAN SCHMALENBACH
The Sociological Category of Communion 331

JOSEPH A. SCHUMPETER
The Fundamentals of Economic Development 505

GEORG SIMMEL
On Conflict 1324
Faithfulness and Gratitude 787
Secrecy and Group Communication 318
The Sociology of Sociability 157
On Superordination and Subordination 540

ADAM SMITH
Capitalists and Laborers 411
Of the Principle Which Gives Occasion to the Division of Labour 104
Of Wages and Profit in the Different Employments of Labor and Stock 518

W. ROBERTSON SMITH
Jehovah and the Prophets 661
On Sacrifice 1096

PITIRIM A. SOROKIN
The Principle of Immanent Change 1311
Social Stratification 570

HERBERT SPENCER
The Factors of Social Phenomena 1021
The Nature of Society 139

OSWALD SPENGLER
On the Style-Patterns of Culture 1343

WILLIAM GRAHAM SUMNER
On the Mores 1037

WILLIAM I. THOMAS
The Four Wishes and the Definition of the Situation 741
(AND FLORIAN ZNANIECKI) *On Disorganization and Reorganization* 1292
Three Types of Personality 934

EDWARD L. THORNDIKE
The Law of Effect 762

FERDINAND TOENNIES
Gemeinschaft and Gesellschaft 191

EDWARD C. TOLMAN
A Summary Discussion of Purposive Behavior 777

ARNOLD TOYNBEE
The Disintegrations of Civilizations 1355

FREDERIC M. THRASHER
Social Patterns and the Gang 929

ERNST TROELTSCH
Church and Sect 664

THORSTEIN VEBLEN
Conspicuous Consumption 558

JOHN B. WATSON
On Behaviorism 758

ALFRED WEBER
Fundamentals of Culture-Sociology 1274

MAX WEBER
Budgetary Management and Profit-Making 470
Confucianism and Puritanism 1101
The Social Psychology of the World Religion 1385
Ethnic Groups 305
The Household Community 296
Ideas and Religious Interests 724
Legitimate Order and Types of Authority 229
The Market 443
The Principal Modes of Capitalistic Orientation 446
On Protestantism and Capitalism 1253
On Religious Rejections of the World 1120
The Routinization of Charisma 1297
Social Action and Its Types 173
The Social Organization of Production 460
Social Stratification and Class Structure 573
The Types of Authority 626
Types of Division of Labor 418
Types of Rationality 1063
Types of Social Organization 218
The Urban Community 380

LOUIS WIRTH
The Problem of Minority Groups 309

FLORIAN ZNANIECKI (AND W. I. THOMAS)
On Disorganization and Reorganization 1292
Three Types of Personality 934

Preface

"But I believe in Natural Selection, not because I can prove in any single case that it has changed one species into another, but because it groups and explains well (as it seems to me) a host of facts in classification, embryology, morphology, rudimentary organs, geological succession and distribution."

CHARLES DARWIN, 1861

THUS IN A LETTER, ADDRESSED to an unidentified critic of the *Origin of Species,* Charles Darwin,[1] just a century ago, struck a keynote for the appraisal of his central concept of Natural Selection. This interpretation of the significance of his theory—that "it groups and explains well a host of facts"—can, we believe, be adapted to the contents of these volumes.

The selections we have brought together document what we believe to constitute a major revolution in scholarly and professional thinking about the nature and determinants of human conduct in society. It is a revolution that may well turn out to be as crucial as was the crystallization of the biological theory of evolution a century ago. Like the theory of evolution it was centered in one scientific discipline, but its repercussions have begun to ramify through a major part of the whole intellectual world. Most important, however, like the theory of evolution, the critical contribution has not been the "discovery" of highly specific explanations of highly specific phenomena, comparable to the change of one species into another. There has been a great deal of advance in our knowledge of many social and behavioral phenomena on these more specific levels, during the generation with which our selections deal and even more subsequently, as the Epilogue makes clear. The most important event, however, has been a new kind of *ordering* of our knowledge, of the sort Darwin refers to when he speaks of the principle of

natural selection as "grouping and explaining well a host of facts."

In our case the relevant "host of facts" is not in the fields of embryology, morphology, and the like, but of political, economic, religious, social and legal history, of economic and political theory and various branches of philosophy, psychology, anthropology and sociology itself. The intellectual movement we document established the central framework within which sociology as a discipline has found a strategic place in the family of academic disciplines. This framework we have become accustomed to calling the "theory of action."

There is no single principle, organizing the "host of facts," as striking as that of natural selection. We believe, however, that analyses of the *patterning* of the phenomena of social interaction, of their *coherence* as social systems, and of the *establishment* of these systems through the internalization of normative culture within the personality of the individual, together constitute a mode of "grouping and explaining" social facts. This is the main theoretical basis of the new perspective previously mentioned. We have therefore treated interaction and institutionalization as our two central ideas, devoting two main sections of Part One to the principal originators of these ideas, along with a section on the main historical antecedents of this intellectual development.

Our conviction of the importance of this new ordering of facts and perspectives has informed our selection among the multitudinous writings that might be considered relevant to a collection of Readings on *Theories of Society,* as well as the way

---

1. This letter is in the British Museum manuscript collection, Additional Ms 37725, ff. 6–9.

in which we have put these selections together and the interpretive discussions we ourselves have contributed by way of introduction and epilogue.

In this light we have followed the implications of two further convictions. First the generation from about 1890 to 1935, in both Europe and America, produced a major turning point in thought about man in society and culture.[2] Out of this the discipline of sociology as it has now taken shape was born. Secondly, despite the immense variety of works and interests feeding into it, this new set of ideas constitutes in the most fundamental sense a unified movement, one that makes obsolete the older conception of an unending diversity of discrete, competing "schools" of thought. Very important antecedents of this movement occurred in the period preceding it. Classical economic theory—in our opinion, the first clearly articulated theoretical system in the study of society—was mainly articulated early in the nineteenth century. Political theory had a long tradition, and the work of many historians, particularly in legal and institutional fields, contained crucially important theoretical elements whose significance should not be underestimated.

This generation, however, saw the establishment of a number of new lines of work on the borders of sociology. One was the systematic study of non-Western societies—both the anthropological studies of non-literate societies, and the beginnings of much more substantial study of Oriental and Middle Eastern civilizations, by historians, linguists, archaeologists, students of comparative religion, and others. During the same period, systematic experimental psychology developed, bringing animal and, in some respects, human behavior within the scope of the laboratory. In the background lay the biological sciences' rise to prominence in the latter half of the nineteenth century, tremendously stimulated by the Darwinian synthesis. Finally, this period witnessed the beginnings of a type of study of segments of Western societies that departed from the established documentary methods of the historian. It was clearly, over a wide area, a generation of active advance.

As sociologists, we are primarily concerned with human societies, or, more generally, in a theoretical sense, with social systems. With the immense acceleration, in our period, of the accumulation of descriptive knowledge through interviewing and ob-

servation, and of knowledge and practice in methods of obtaining and verifying such data, a new form of generalized interpretation of known facts, and hence of ideas which could guide the search for new facts, has also been attained.

This movement has cut across the bounds of discipline and nation. At the central core of the theory of social systems, Pareto performed a special feat of synthesis relating economic, political, and "institutional, non-rational" components. Durkheim pursued the analysis of these problems more deeply. Max Weber carried the comparative analysis of the differences among societies and the interrelations of their constituent spheres to an entirely new level of sophistication. Finally, in the study of the individual's motivation, Freud, though his sociology was much weaker, provided an unprecedented perspective on the articulation of human personality within the system of social interaction. A more "collegial" than individual movement in the United States—involving particularly C. H. Cooley, G. H. Mead, and W. I. Thomas—mediated, in the name of "social psychology," between the more strictly sociological and the more psychological positions.

Selected on the basis of a particular interest, these are the barest highlights of a very complicated pattern of intellectual development. This interest defines the objective of this collection, drawn from the sources which lead to and constitute contemporary sociological theory. The contemporary student of human society will, unless he has devoted prolonged study to this phase of intellectual history, have considerable difficulty in orienting himself to the complex background from which his field of specialized concern has grown. No general history —certainly none which could claim to be complete and definitive—has been written in this field; to attempt to do so would probably be premature. The relevant literature is enormous, and the problems of its interpretation formidable.

However, the student need not be left entirely without guidance. From the very extensive literature, we have brought together a set of selections, with historical and analytical commentaries, that, though filling two large volumes, still comprise only a tiny fraction of the possibly relevant material. We do not consider the reading of these selections, particularly the large proportion presented in translation, as an adequate substitute for reading both the original works of which they are parts, and many other works not represented at all. For certain limited purposes reading the selections may be considered adequate; certainly it is better than no direct acquaintance with the primary sources. But we hope that our anthology will be treated more as an introduction and a guide to the literature—a guide which

2. The most comprehensive single treatment of the European phase of this movement, from the point of view of general intellectual history rather than of sociology, is H. Stuart Hughes, *Consciousness and Society* (New York: Alfred A. Knopf, 1958). For an interpretation stressing schools, cf. P. A. Sorokin, *Contemporary Sociological Theory* (New York: Harper & Brothers, 1928).

will help students to acquaint themselves with it much more fully.

The literature as a whole is too extensive for any individual—particularly one with more specialized interests—to investigate thoroughly. Different people will approach it with different special interests. We hope that bringing the different writers together in the way we have will provide common starting points for a variety of these more specialized excursions; thus someone interested in the relation of personality development to kinship structure would not study many of the same sections as the person interested in the relations between major religious movements and the larger societies within which they occurred.

By the nature of this enterprise, the editors must exercise a very drastic selectivity. They are hence subject to a whole range of possible objections to the policies followed in their selection and organization—no policies could satisfy all critics on this score. The best we can do is to make our own criteria as explicit as possible.

First, within the assumptions stated above, our primary concern has been with the more generalized framework for the theoretical analysis of social systems. We feel that a larger proportion of explicit contributions to this theme have been made at the more "macrosocial" levels dealing with total societies or bearing on their analysis. Hence, though maintaining that general theory in this field is applicable at all levels in the macroscopic-microscopic range, from the total society to the small experimental group, we have tended to select according to our more macroscopic interest. Furthermore, our interest in general theory has led to a certain favoring of writers and passages stressing this analytical level, rather than accumulations of highly detailed fact.

We feel, as we have said, that the major trends in the theory of social systems have been convergent rather than divergent, that the contributions which enrich a common conceptual scheme outweigh those which delineate the positions of divergent schools. For those who, however, tend to stress the divergence, we hope we have included a sufficient variety of points of view so that we are not guilty of a narrow parochialism in selecting only the writings which fit our own predilections, and omitting those which might be construed as incompatible with or inconvenient to our own point of view. In this respect, it is important to note that, though we continue to share the common convictions with which we began, the editors are not in fully detailed agreement among themselves; certain compromises have been necessary. In the introductory materials and commentaries, each author has naturally tended to stress his own interests and evaluations. The fact that all matter written by the editors is the responsibility of each individual editor testifies to the limitations on editorial consensus, far-reaching though the consensus is.

A second very important consideration in our policy of selection is that we have attempted to balance concentration on our interest in the social system as such with comprehensiveness in the inclusion of more concrete analysis. Some sociologists may feel that we have gone too far in the extent to which we have included materials ordinarily classified in psychology, anthropology, history, economics, political science, law, and the humanistic disciplines. Our basic justification for this is our belief that the theory of social systems is a product of the complex intellectual currents of the modern age. We can speak of a central core of theorists whose primary concern has been with social systems as such. However, the most fruitful efforts to understand society have never been a monopoly of professional sociologists; and in the period concerned, none of the greatest figures limited his attention to this discipline. Thus Durkheim was trained in philosophy and jurisprudence, Weber in jurisprudence and economics, Cooley in economics, and Mead in philosophy. We feel that if we confined our materials to "sociology" in a narrow sense we would, considering the intellectual history of the period, be excessively and injuriously parochial.

Within this catholic policy of judgments of relevance, however, certain standards in our decisions may well be controversial. Clearly, we have not included everything bearing on the topic of "human social behavior"; within this immense field, we have had to be highly selective.

Three beliefs have provided the main criteria of selection. First, we have conceived the development of theory as in part a process of the differentiation of a cognitive interest. Hence, we have, in Part One, discussed and illustrated certain fundamental problems in terms which are relatively independent of the differentiations which in our own times have come to constitute domains of particular disciplines. Second, we have attempted to treat the social system as an "open" system interacting with others on its "boundaries." We have, therefore, related social systems to the psychological and biological individual, and also to the culture, as major axes of the organization of our materials. We do not conceive biology and psychology, or the theory of culture, to be, as such, parts of the theory of social systems. We do, however, think that the *relations* of these spheres or systems to the social are crucial, and these relations must be systematically analyzed, not considered in an arbitrary *ad hoc* fashion. Finally, within our general interest in the *social system,* we have attempted to emphasize systematically the study of the *institutional* aspect. In other words, we have attempted to recognize a systemic set of relations to the concerns of the two adjacent disciplines of economics and political science, but to avoid any suggestion that they ought simply to be incorporated into sociology. It is, for example, no more possible to treat problems of social morphology in the economic sphere without reference to materials ordinarily allocated to economics, than to deal with the motivation of social behavior without using psychological materials. Our major criteria have been the same in all three of these cases.

We might have chosen to allow the selections to "speak for themselves"; limiting introductory materials to the bare essentials of editorial identification. This, however, would have imposed a heavy burden on readers not already familiar with the literature from which the selections are drawn, and hence made the selections less valuable to them. We also feel that we would have been missing an important opportunity. One of the most effective ways of estimating the state of theoretical analysis in sociology is to attempt to show, in considerable detail, the continuity between current ideas and problems and the most important contributions of our forebears. We have been particularly concerned with showing the continuity of contemporary views with those in the relatively recent past which, however, are far enough past to permit a certain perspective on the nature and importance of their work. The introductory material and the epilogue are designed to contribute to the understanding of this continuity, and thereby to help define a perspective for better evaluating the work of the many authors represented in the selections.

The editors' material falls into four main categories. The General Introduction has two parts. The first, by Kaspar Naegele, is an essay on the scope of theory in the social science field, and some of the problems involved in the construction of theory. The second, by Talcott Parsons, is an essay on the theory of social systems in what he conceived at the time of writing to be its current state. It is deliberately couched on the plane of the conceptual scheme rather than attempting to formulate empirical generalizations. It is intended as a review of general theoretical problems and some of the more specific problems which contemporary sociology must face, whether or not individual sociologists find the directions indicated for their solution congenial.

A second type of editorial material consists in the Introductions to four of the five main parts of the Reader, i.e., all except Part One. These attempt to review the theoretical problems underlying our selection and classification of materials in more detail for the particular area than was possible in the General Introduction. In each case, we have directly used and stated our own conceptions of the present state of knowledge in some of the most important aspects of the particular field. We have tried to link present problems with the principal themes represented in the selections themselves. We have not, however, in these Introductions, attempted to comment in detail on the selections or on literature we have not included.

This task, so far as we have attempted it at all, has been reserved for the much briefer Editorial Forewords to the sections within each part. These contain very brief statements of the relevance of the selections themselves to the plan of these volumes and their setting in the development of the problem under consideration. Sometimes brief comments on other literature are included.

Part One has been treated as a special case, because of the diversity of the materials included in its three divisions. All are fundamental prolegomena to the theory of social systems, the first in terms of its historical background, the other two in the critical substantive fields of the analysis of social interaction as such and the problem of the foundations of the motivational commitments involved in institutionalization. We have, therefore, not provided a general introduction to Part One as a whole, but have included considerably fuller Editorial Forewords to each Section than is the case with Sections of the other Parts. The Forewords to Sections in Part One contain both a good deal of our own independent theoretical analysis and specific references to the selections and their places in the development of theory.

The fourth element of editorial material is the Epilogue, written by Edward Shils. This essentially treats, in more connected fashion than in the more scattered Introductions, the major themes in the development of sociological theory since the generation primarily represented in the selections, and their general cultural significance. It is one man's point of view, a comprehensive commentary on the problems presented by the selections themselves and by the other introductory materials.

We have also included a Bibliography. This comprises all the principal works of the writers represented in the list of selections that were published in book form. The complete Index for both volumes will be found at the end of each volume. It is confined to proper names, since a full subject index would present a formidable task and seems unnecessary in the light of the detailed table of contents.

Perhaps a word about the history of the project and the division of labor between the editors is in order. The original plan for these volumes was developed in 1952, at the suggestion of Jeremiah Kaplan of The Free Press, by Talcott Parsons and Edward Shils, who also worked out the first tentative list of selections. The list has, however, been revised many times. Because of the pressure of other commitments, progress was slow; the combination of Shils's prospective absence from the country for a year and realization of the magnitude of the task led to the addition, in 1954, of Kaspar Naegele and Jesse Pitts to the "editorial committee." Since then the work on the selections has been carried on by Parsons, Naegele, and Pitts.

Any enterprise of the present magnitude owes debts to many different people and agencies, indeed too many to be acknowledged. It has not as such received direct financial support from any source except The Free Press of Glencoe, but it should be acknowledged that three of the editors did important parts of their work on it during the periods that they were Fellows of the Center for Advanced Study in the Behavioral Sciences. We also severally have used funds from various sources which were either entirely free or where their purposes overlapped so much with this one that the two uses could not be disentangled. A number of people gave important advice, both on the general

policy governing selections, and on particular problems in this field. Among these it seems appropriate to mention particularly Robert K. Merton of Columbia University, Francis X. Sutton of the Ford Foundation, Nicholas Grauer of the University of Copenhagen, Robert N. Bellah, Winston R. White, and Daniel J. Levinson of Harvard University, Claude Levi-Strauss of the College de France, Elliott Mishler of the Massachusetts Mental Health Center, and Bertram D. Cohen of Wayne State University and the Lafayette Clinic. Advice in these respects concerning selections has shaded into criticism of drafts of our introductions and editorial forewords. Dr. Anne Parsons of McLean Hospital and Dr. Mark Field of Harvard University gave valuable advice regarding some of the French translations. Finally there has of course been an immense amount of processing of manuscript material. Among the most important contributions here have been those of two successive secretaries of the senior editor, Mrs. Carolyn Cooper and Mrs. Sarah E. Hampson.

Talcott Parsons
Edward Shils
Kaspar D. Naegele
Jesse R. Pitts

April, 1961

GENERAL
INTRODUCTION

I. *Some Observations on the Scope of Sociological Analysis*

BY KASPAR D. NAEGELE

THE STUDY OF SOCIETY AS A cumulative and, therefore, scientific, enterprise, is under way. We may bemoan the fact or enjoy it. We may argue about how society can be studied and how its study should be divided among old and new intellectual disciplines. Yet we can no longer deny the possibility of reliable discoveries concerning life in society. Instead we can ask: How is society possible? How does it persist? Or we can ask a myriad of questions about intended or unintended events. We can probe into the ways people vote or slide down some social scale. We can try to unravel any order that may lie behind their decisions to buy or not to buy, to join an army or some club, to emigrate or to stay. We can see what happens when large organizations or small groups change their size, when new weapons in military spheres become noticed in the diplomatic spheres, or when several people want to talk at the same time.

As adults we cannot escape—unless we take deliberate measures to do so—some reflection about all this. We cannot live without society. Yet to participate in society is to take cognizance of other people. Such cognizance includes some anticipation, some inner rehearsal of part of the future. By the same token, as members of society and of the many circles that help constitute it, we also rehearse the past. We "go over again" what happened. Indeed, the greatest, if not the best part of our conversations, in North American society at least, probably consists of various kinds of selections from some immediate or more distant past. In that respect, the endless telephone conversations of certain adolescents, nourished on the slim morsels of what "he said to her and she to him," are just a caricature of the chronic properties of social arrangements.

This book is devoted to the study of the properties of social arrangements. It proceeds from recognizing that social arrangements have always been subject to observation and comment, but that their systematic study is rather young.

On the one hand, the world is full of writings or other symbolic accomplishments, like music and sculpture, that are to some extent direct commentaries on the social world itself. After all, that world—as this Reader documents—contains the necessary (though not sufficient) characteristic of being constituted by an endless process of mutual observation, reflection, confirmation, and transformation of the thoughts and apprehensions of men. On the other hand, cumulative and confirmed knowledge regarding it is scarce. This fact, if properly interpreted, is as much a lack as a source of further enlightenment. It reminds us that social orders are "open" systems. To be sure, they have their determinacy. They are intelligible. Yet they are not organisms, and they are certainly not machines. Still, they have a status as systems—both in the vivid personal sense of the discovered connectedness of the apparently disparate facts of immediate experience, and in the more abstract sense of allowing the growth of a consensus of related terms with which to study "the social."

The "openness" of social systems is ambiguous, the more so since any specific example, be it a tribe or a nation, a political party or the Daughters of the Nile, seems anything but "open," especially if it no longer exists. One must be careful, too, not to confuse our ignorance with openness. At the moment we cannot fully predict how a social gathering will go or what the social structure of Western Germany will be like in 1984. Such inability has several sources, including the fact that all concrete social arrangements are complicated. Each of them is a mixture of constraint on its participants to act in certain ways or to engender, between them, certain results, and of rights and opportunities to improvise or find some ways of their own. The balance shifts. From the perspective of some systems, with their cherished balances, others seem primarily coercive and hence "closed." Besides, the "same" system is not equally open to its constituent members. Furthermore, belief and fact diverge. A man may have more freedom than he thinks—or less. Moreover, the very terms by which we seek to translate our varied experience with the constraint and scope of the social arrangements around (and within) us into communicable, if not testable, accounts, are themselves subject to controversy. Freedom, necessity, determination, order, choice among alternatives—these are among the bedevilled terms and issues which are alike part of the drama of society itself, of the disagreements and agreements that bind and divide groups, and, sooner or later, of the thought necessary to study society, even in the name of science.

These thoughts may appear both too obvious and too aimless; certainly they have every appearance of being a start in the middle. This corresponds with the persistent intention of these volumes: they are concerned with presenting a background from which can grow that part of the systematic study of society that falls within the shifting borders of sociology. Once it has formally begun this is an endless enterprise, provided of course political and social events at least permit the continuity of this undertaking. We are concerned with the proper cultivation of this continuity. We wish to document the growth of sociology considered under the aspects of the major ideas and questions, and their relations, through which sociology is now continuously—though not evenly—being created as a discipline of inquiry, and hence as a field of knowledge.

Growth must have sources and resources. These are not of one piece. In a science, they include the craft and techniques of research. The division of labor among books and readers (and limitations of length) rules out here any consideration of techniques as devices for finding answers to questions or selecting the relevant meaning from gathered facts. We are confining ourselves to that range of ideas, proposals, and controversies without which sociology would be impossible. We hope thereby to help in the strenuous effort of enlarging the range of possible and viable ideas required for sociological analysis. We have no illusion that this is "merely" a matter of the addition of ideas. Sociology depends for its identity on its *difference* from

literature, philosophy, and theology. But we are certain, as, logically, any scientific inquirer must be, that this does not mean that sociology can leave unattended the task of clarifying the ideas, and their relations, that constitute its questions. Facts, after all, are like the moon: they derive their light, and hence their import, from an external source. They do not speak for themselves; they merely reply as part of an exchange of question and answer. This exchange, in turn, requires some pattern of ideas to begin. Once having started, the pattern must change. It is also likely to give rise to rival patterns and to become specialized "within" itself. Besides, "difference" does not exclude links; literature, philosophy, and theology are also necessary for the study of society.

This part of the Introduction is confined to some observations on the growth of the patterns of questions and answers that are sociology. It is not possible to forget the present and to present, even roughly or through personal observation, a succession of the strategic ideas and discoveries that preceded what surrounds us now in the name of sociology. We must start with some notion of the minimal characteristics of sociological analysis; we can then turn to some considerations on the timing of its birth, continue with questions about alternative directions in sociology's development, and end with some restatement of available images for the study of society. This is a deliberately limited undertaking. There would have been other alternatives. These were ruled out either by lack of sufficient knowledge on the authors' part or by the nature of this enterprise.

This is not the first effort of its kind. There are histories of sociology, and this is not an attempt to provide another one—even one confined to sociological theory. Nor are we interested in providing a museum for all sociologically relevant proposals that have ever found their way into print. We sought, instead, to provide a convenient reminder of distinctions and proposals necessary for the adequate pursuit of sociology. We believe that such a pursuit involves commitment to *some* pattern of thought; we could only follow the one that held most meaning and promise for us. Such a commitment includes the hope of the continuous revision and improvement of the pattern. There are other patterns which differ from ours, more in part than as a whole, and certainly there are other vocabularies. It is never really easy to know how to evaluate the difference between them. Indeed, there are a number of other collected readings in sociological theory. We cannot judge whether we have accomplished our end: to make strategic selections written before the mid-nineteen-thirties (with some very few exceptions) and after 1600; and to present these with the help of an arrangement of headings and subheadings testifying to our concept of the strategic issues within the discipline of sociology. At the same time, we hope to have presented enough of the data, or of reminders of further data that can be read "in the original," so that others, now and later, can come to different perspectives—and are, in fact, goaded on to seek new perspectives.

But what are "our conceptions of the strategic issues"?

Some Essential Sociological Notions

Strategy concerns the link between positions of departure and positions of arrival. Sociology, like any human enterprise (and the many acts composing any enterprise), is suspended between several notions at once.

It confronts the world (within and without) in order to make discoveries. (The uses of sociology cannot concern us here. Even the most avid "applied" sociologist must discover a link between knowledge, a given situation, and some desired state of change or persistence. Nor can we delay now to debate the validity of the famous proposition that nothing is so practical as a good theory.) Discoveries, however, are not made about the world "as a whole." The world, after all, is full of a number of things. Even its fullness is an impression that reminds us of the discrepancy between what we can say (or feel) and all of what might be said (or felt). Sociology, then, involves a characteristic image, or alternative set of images, concerning one part of the larger order of "the world," that can be increasingly known. Simply put, this is the social order. The other part of this General Introduction is in fact a detailed explication and differentiation of that view of the social order which seems to us, as editors, to be most consistent with the incontrovertible formulations of the past and the gathering volume of the present sociological findings. Similarly, sociology involves a logical as well as a concrete sense of the *difference* (and link) between the actual and the possible within the social order. This difference becomes important to the degree to which one remains alive to the "created," as distinct from the "given and unalterable," aspects of social arrangements and their relativity. As a scientific enterprise, sociology is finally concerned with the discovery of proposals that define or explain regularities characterizing the mutual relations, and the products to which they give rise, among human beings.

This may all seem rather abstract, particularly in view of the fact that sociology is an empirical inquiry, and as such involves a view of the coherence of events. For anyone seeking to be a sociologist, it proceeds through the elaboration of an initially more or less simple (or too grand) sense of orderliness. As a discipline, since its birth, it has had to proceed by fighting alike against oversimple and early grand schemes, and against the claim that the events it seeks to explain are too complicated—or, at least, that their complexity requires primarily the gifts and skills of historians, theologians, philosophers, and artists.

A sociologist must construct his rebuttal in part from the work of those who would question the necessity or the possibility of his existence. Good sociology is inevitably haunted by the labyrinthine immensity of human affairs; it is also always within reach of a governing assumption—without which science itself would be impossible—that this immensity exhibits intelligible and communicable regularities, and that these, at least for the time being, are of several kinds.

Some Features of Social Orders

This *severalness* repeatedly accompanies the study of society. There are various reasons for this, whose examination can provide a reminder of the growing scope of sociological theory, both in range and in depth. Such a reminder will move us closer to answering the questions: What distinctions and proposals help constitute sociological theory; and how, if at all, do these differ from the ideas about society that men must hold in order to live in it?

Social coherence is one possible form of coherence. Music, logic, atoms, and living organisms are other forms. The single form of social coherence—marked by the structure of reciprocal expectations, acts, and their intended and unintended consequences—is, as we all know, magnificently rich and inclusive. Our knowledge of it, studied or experienced, is varied. Such variation is part of the very social phenomena we seek to know. These phenomena, as a rule, combine obviousness with hiddenness. They are all about us. Yet it is the mark of complex societies—and it is in these that sociologists are born and shaped, even if they do not necessarily confine their studies to them—that they are constituted by reservoirs of "anonymous" other persons, whom one has various accidental and deliberate opportunities of meeting "for the first time." For all its dependence on routine and familiarity, society engenders an interminable succession of situations and "other people" who become associated with secrecy or the not-yet-known. These add one kind of severalness to the structure of social life: the severalness of what we have comprehended and what we have yet to unravel as presented by the immediate or distant presence of others. Sociology thus finds its puzzles along a huge line of occasions. Two men loading a haycart, saying nothing; some children in winter, skating on a tennis court; a black market or a grey one; mothers sitting on a bench; a panic and a dance; a slum, Mayfair, or Fire Island —all these are samples of social cohesion. Similarly, the rise of Social Credit as a political movement in Canada, the expulsion of Tito from the Cominform, fluctuations in the birth rate and in longevity, or the shifts in emphasis within the dogma of the Roman Catholic Church—all are samples of society considered as a succession of arrangements. It belongs to the office of sociology, as we would prefer to conceive it, to comprehend within its distinctions the whole range of possible social arrangements, and to be alive to human society as such. A sociology that cannot naturally and logically take into account the alternate modes of social stratification of Russia, India, the United States, and Peru, for instance, or the differences imposed on social reciprocity by differences in age and sex, is, of course, provincial and inappropriately narrow. Yet as a discipline, sociology cannot escape an appropriate narrowness—appropriate to the extent that it is preceded by some general commitment concerning the systematic study of human arrangements.

The growth of sociological theory seems to have proceeded from such commitments, while also helping to create them. These commitments are surrounded by debate. Part of this debate binds and fills the materials of this Reader. Parts of the debate concerning the "proper study of mankind" have been omitted, as settled. We know now that "theory" and "research" are, not alternatives for a scientific discipline, but different sides of one coin. We also know that, in any particular man's active work, there are choices to be made. Some people prefer to spend their life in an enduring effort to build a series of specific studies or to elaborate a set of techniques. Others prefer the equally hard work of formulating patterns of propositions that can do justice to a growing accumulation of established information, and transcend this information for the sake of its greater illumination and its continued growth. Yet the division of labor within a field cannot be taken as a logical description of alternative directions for the field as such. A division of labor combines individual differences, or differences of "position," within a single direction of effort. In sociology, the effort has gone in the direction of formulations concerning social relations, concerning the arrangement of social relations into various kinds of groupings or aggregations, and concerning the directions and conditions of development that

can be found within single, or some range of associated, social arrangements. Talcott Parsons has proposed in much more detail, in the following section, a way of ordering, on different levels, our sense of the structure of society.

The Unity and Diversity of Sociology

The inspection of the titles of the three hundred papers that are usually read at an annual meeting of the American Sociological Society, for instance, or of the hundreds of courses that are annually taught in the name of sociology at institutions of higher learning throughout the world, seems to belie this formal claim of unity and replace it with a sense of bewildering confusion. The apparently assured and single-minded inclusiveness of a Max Weber or a Durkheim, a Vilfredo Pareto or a Sigmund Freud, then looms reassuringly large as a refuge. Yet fleeing to them, to avoid the confusion of tongues that lets many people studying the same subject talk past each other, would be to misunderstand their work. We now have a Catholic and a non-Catholic sociology; the "jargons" current at Chicago, Columbia, Harvard, Michigan, Frankfurt, and in many other places; the fads of interest and the resurrections of older lines; the undigestible output of non-cumulative efforts; and the vague sense of a persistent discrepancy between what we do and what we feel to be the strategic issues. Yet this state of affairs is like society itself. There, too, people speak past and with each other, do one thing and mean another, find themselves at loggerheads with their own awareness of their ideals. Experience, and its accompanying multiplication of common sense and common error, then cease to be sufficient, though experience always remains necessary.

It is virtually impossible to keep these contradictions—between consensus and divergence, between the necessity of traditional experience and the insufficiency of it—appropriately in mind simultaneously. Each of the two introductory essays, with its respective emphasis, tends to stress one of the two sides. They should, then, be read as a whole. The present essay emphasizes the *variety* of views through which people studying the "same" phenomena have gone about their work. Similarly, it stresses the "experiential" component in the categories and questions constituting sociology. The following essay is more systematic. It differentiates a comprehensive point of view and proposes patterns of categories—such as values, norms, collectivities, and roles. It is concerned with matters of clarity and consistency.

The Realms of Society

Sociology is concerned with coherence of some meaning, to both its direct participants and its observers, that provides it with yet another kind of "severalness." First, a realm of meaning involves some exclusion and some unevenness. Even the simplest social encounters, like shaking someone's hand, involve the use of a mode of communication, of acknowledgment by another. Yet communication can assume many modes, of which language is only one; their advantages and possibilities differ. Still, any one social occasion, though its character would differ as the mode of talk within it varies, can, in theory, proceed in one of several languages. It cannot proceed at all in the absence of any language. *Language* includes the gestures of the deaf and dumb, the looks of the married, or the salutes of some military occasion. Social occasions, then, in including a mode of communication, also exclude many others.

As occasions, they also represent articulate or vague notions of importance. To eat now is to give up something else for this time; to talk of the weather is not to talk of politics. The actual both excludes many other possible events and comes to represent some sense of inequality of all possibilities. In other words, social coherence always has an economic dimension: it requires decisions of allocation and associated conceptions of relative importance. The social world is always uneven; it always has some features that between and within themselves appear under the aspects of "more or less." In this sense, society is a comparative phenomenon: it always contains some who are "older," luckier, shorter, livelier, or healthier than others.

Meaning, then, differentiates the world. It produces the severalness of question and answer. Relative to social arrangements, questions confront what is so both with speculations about what else could be—thereby reminding us of the created quality of social affairs—and with considerations of appropriateness. The social, after all, always contains evaluation. It implies various kinds of agreements about the ways of responding to the apparent imperatives of being alive and of managing the issues that such response successively engenders. Evaluation is a form of confrontation; it implies some matching of standards to what was, in fact, done. Often it involves balancing standards amongst themselves. Sociology must comprehend a host of confrontations, occurring within and between people. Confrontations within ourselves are an aspect of the differentiation of society itself. Part of our inner conversations reflect our simultaneous involvement in a variety of different spheres demanding from us a severalness of efforts, at times even of standards of work.

Sociology has come to refer to this phenomenon as a conflict of and in roles. Through roles, we participate as persons in social arrangements. For its members, a society engenders a succession and pattern of roles in accordance with its division of labor and of the spheres by which it seeks to keep going. A multiplicity of undertakings are carried on with the help of more or less large populations. The constituent individuals are all suspended between birth and death, but confront the society with the fact that they stand at different positions within this cycle. The spheres are easier to recognize than to analyze.

Any sociology that we have has been created by people whose experience has been confronted and constituted by the fact that, in our society, there are recognizable separations of several kinds. We cohere, for different purposes, into circles of mutual exclusion. Families and kinship are one form and principle of such coherence and exclusion. Friendship, involving different principles of exclusion, is another example. We are also irrevocably part of a process of aging robbed of its continuity by the social divisions of generational differences. These are joined by the radical and inescapable confrontations of the *two* sexes. We know now that this is not just a biological matter. Societies vary sharply in their notions of maleness and femaleness, and of the appropriate relations between them.

These divisions, furthermore, are associated with the distinctions between "realms." Religion, the economy, the polity, work, family, the educational system, the legal system, or the armed forces—these stand for divergent realms of endeavor, each carried forward by its own complement of institutions. Even a child knows that a church and a department store, a doctor's office and a wading pool, a home and a hotel, stand for characteristically different courses of conduct. Sociology has grown up in societies whose very growth is measured precisely by the proliferation of spheres. To a degree, one particular conflict between (or within) societies—engaging the ideological and military resources and loyalties of people, sometimes to the point of death—has become a great issue: how separate should these spheres be? What walls of independence or of privacy should be allowed to whom?

The growth of society, and of sociology, involves proliferation (or differentiation, as we have called it elsewhere in this Introduction). Yet to speak of a society, or of a discipline whose object is its study, is to acknowledge that proliferation is reciprocally related to coherence. Sociology thrives on the simple insight that separation of *I* and *You*, of the economy and the polity, of the church and the state, involves a coherence—in the form of inclusive agreements—that links what is separated.

Ultimately, the very aloneness of the self is thus a social phenomenon. Only because we become human in the company of others, and have to become human to be in their company, are we able to evolve the sense of being different from them. The common sense, in our society, of the strains between individuals and society, thus becomes an experienced confrontation which sociology must take seriously but not literally. In constituting society, the wish to oppose what appears as constraint contributes as much as the wish to carry out outer or inner dictates. It is socially important, however, that what is sociologically co-relative is presented by variously committed groups as an ideological antithesis. The phenomena which sociological theory must unravel include, in other words, the beliefs and moral commitments of people.

The presence of sociology among people creates a further discrepancy. Beliefs and commitments guide their holders in making decisions or justifying decisions made. To a sociological theorist, they appear as constituent facts within the structure and function of social arrangements. As such they are necessary, but not sufficient, for a valid account of what is to be explained. A theorist sees society as transcending the intentions and beliefs of people without being independent of them. He sees it as a deposited order that cannot be comprehended only by knowledge of its constituent members taken singly; nor can it be comprehended as a self-contained system of impersonal forces. Its comprehension constitutes a divergence from the common sense of any circle of society. The divergence itself varies, since the differences among circles and societies lie partially in the variation governing ways of regarding human affairs and assigning importance to the elements that are known or believed to constitute them.

Sociological theory, then, studies the divergence and coherence that make social arrangements. It is driven on by the confrontations of an I and a You and between a We and a They, as well as by the emergent divergences between people's intentions and the issues arising from the arrangements they make to implement these intentions. As part of knowledge, the theory and practice of sociology help differentiate knowledge itself. Moreover, sociology augments—in varying degrees of reliability—our chances to make deliberate changes within social arrangements themselves. The following essay, however, proposes a four-fold set of requirements defining the generic issues that arise for and within the arrangements by which people live with or

against one another. A technical exposition of this "functional paradigm" is contained in that essay, the second section of the General Introduction.

Requirements of Social Systems

We might anticipate it briefly here. Concrete social arrangements can be conceived as composed of several elements at once, as we know from simply examining our experience. There are various ways of labeling these elements. We can, as the introductory material of this Reader proposes, speak about roles, collectivities, norms, and values. That is, we can distinguish between the particular ways in which people expect one another to co-operate with each other in some enterprise that one or another has instituted. We can seek the ways in which they conceive of their mutual relation during the time it lasts. We can ask, then, to what extent they think of their encounter as something to be repeated or as a chance affair not likely to recur. We can ask about the kinds of expectations by which each feels surrounded, in the other's presence, with regard to the mode of interaction that is to take place. We can ask about those more basic and more general moral commitments that would make this occasion a particular one, spatially and temporally located. We can also dissect the order that two or more people in each other's presence, or in some less surveyable and larger collectivity, seem to sustain, by starting, not with individual experience as this proceeds within the course of interaction, but with the question: What at the least are the domains to which some attention must be paid if a smaller or larger number of people wish to maintain the possibility of being part of a social order that can in some measure be taken for granted? This is a most cumbersome question, making many assumptions.

The second introductory essay argues that one should remember at least four issues as necessary to the persistence of social arrangements. As issues, they are both matters demanding attention and matters which, as such, help comprise the very arrangements that constitute, in turn, a solution for them. One such issue concerns the mode of coherence among the members of a going arrangement. Social arrangements always involve the integration of the separate actions of its constituent actors. They must somehow solve the problems of coherence and of attachment. In addition to settling the mutual relation among its constituent actors, a social arrangement, since it does take place in time and space, is therefore faced with establishing relations to a surrounding world. These relations settle the problems of adaptation. The terminology is incidental. Adaptation and coherence arise, in turn, with respect to two further matters. Whether they be tangible or not, social arrangements are invested with purposes. People have wants. These may simply involve the company of others; they may take the form of wishing not so much to get as to give, or to express themselves. Besides, the wants with which people begin, or are forced into, social arrangement become compounded by the interaction among wants facilitated by the company in question. Yet in any case, social arrangements proceed under the aspect of some accomplishment. This involves the pursuit of goals.

This, then, is the third domain demanding attention. Goals, coherence, and adaptation, moreover, are pursued within the confines of shared moral commitments and private motives. Commitments and motives posit the patterns which make sense of the world and confront us with alternatives whose solution must constitute our aliveness. In the next essay, this domain will be called the issue of pattern-maintenance.

To repeat: the terminology can well be replaced. Yet by considering social arrangements this way, we can compare them. We can see them as more than unique constellations. We can make sense of the inner struggles and patterns of change characterizing them.

THE PERSONAL AND
THE IMPERSONAL

The Form of Sociological Questions

Question-and-answer involves a set of distinctions and ideas, which may be ordered chronologically. For the individual, we can remember the sequence of questions which appear to accompany (and so help constitute) growth and development. We know that a child has many whys and whats: manners, stars, names, things. By convention and logic, we have come to consider that which we confront, through the questions we can ask of it, as lying in different realms—e.g., the realms of the organic and the inorganic, the mechanical and the logical, the psychological and the meaningless. Though we may be annoyed by the distinctions, we cannot go *against* the fact that doing a Virginia reel or repairing a carburetor, spraying roses against insects, sorting mail, or flying in formation are occasions bringing into prominence different sorts of relations among things, bodies, and people. The picture is not, to the wall, what it is to the viewer—unless he wants it so. This particular set of discrepancies we have tentatively, yet stubbornly, let settle

into realms of knowledge. These realms share many properties, and their distinctions lie only partially in *what* they confront and, in much larger part, in *how* they do so. In a measure, physics and zoology are the same thing: we distinguish them by the questions they ask. The sequence of the child's questions does not occur in a vacuum. There are shared traditions to which he must order his questions, as he learns to accept answers that others give him. Indeed, questions presuppose previous answers. This is not the place to explore the significance of the fact that we can ask questions or inquire how it is possible to ask them at all. The chronological sequence of the child's question is not only pulled apart—and in different ways, in different circles and cultures—by an inescapable pattern of grouped distinctions; this pattern itself is subject to change. Physics preceded sociology. Knowledge, that is, has a history. It also is divisible into different forms. To know about the functioning of a person's heart and to know that same person's name or his sense of humor imply different kinds of knowledge. For logic and convenience, we have grouped these kinds of knowing into major classes, of which science is one and philosophy another. There are more than these. Their difference does not deny their mutual dependence. Nor will the matter rest there. Science can be further divided, into either its pure and applied forms, or its natural and social ones. The old quarrels and questions necessarily connected with such a classification need not concern us just yet. To be sure, one cannot go far in pursuing an effort at an orderly unravelling of one or the other puzzle in the ordering of human affairs without also having to ask, for instance: In what lies the difference between the "social" and the "natural"? Between the social and the natural sciences? In what lies the difference between literature and social science?

We shall have to compose some answers to these questions in these introductory essays and in our various Introductions, knowing full well that a later generation will raise the same issues again and, perhaps, come to different conclusions. In this instance, as in many others, discovery and presupposition go hand in hand. One must create some sociology before one can know what it is; and one must know, at least, what it might be, before one can help create it.

My claim has been that sociology must be characterized through an account of the questions it asks and the answers it accepts. Weber and Dickens both asked how one might give an account of a phenomenon called "bureaucracy." In one case, the answer takes the form of propositions that can be revised; in the other, the form of declarations that are accepted as fiction.

Revisable propositions must be clear—i.e., one must be able to consider them apart from their author. Yet their history is not irrelevant. One must be able to ask: How do you know, and how can I come to know this too? In sociology, as one form of confronting the world through science, the emphasis, as in the rest of science, is on the world, not on the observer. The concern is not with quoting one's self correctly—though this may be a necessary beginning—but with formulating claims by routes that others can travel and with traveling to places that others can show not to have been terminal. Such intentions lead to a familiar combination of slightly contradictory qualities that together constitute any and all science: propositions that can be disproved and shared, that are impersonal and public, that involve matters of fact and training in ways of establishing these facts.

The Substance of Sociological Questions

Such, in outline, is the form of at least the answers that questions in sociology must take. But what of their content? Any field of disciplined inquiry involves a provisional image of an order within a wider order that can be made to yield some regularities demonstrably more than personal impressions. In the case of sociology, the order "lies in between." Yet it also lies near at hand. These circumstances have helped to delay its cumulative apprehension. In the West, we manage what confronts us with the help of a number of ideas that seem to sort matters out. "Nature" is one of the most prominent of these; it is a collected and growing set of questions and answers, and the assumption that there is an impersonal givenness. Thus we can give accounts of it omitting some of the qualities that those who give the accounts claim for themselves—we can account for it without having to deal with the issues of choice, intention, or meaning. This, of course, we have to learn. The distinction between the personal and the impersonal is an achievement with an individual and a collective history. We tend, further, to see the natural universe as varyingly distant from the personal realm from which we view and move toward it. We tend to distinguish between inorganic and organic matters, between what is alive, what is dead, and what knows no life or death at all.

The personal moves into view as we succeed in distinguishing it from that which it is not. It is a most rewarding enterprise to see precisely how different categories of people, different cultures, or different members of the successive stages in the history of some society, have in fact thought about the world and thereby fashioned their own. Such an enterprise is possible only if one is willing to assume that some ideas are hospitable enough both to represent a consensus among different investigators, and to allow us to characterize the differences among ways of thinking without distorting these differences through the limitations which are part of any and all ideas. The see-saw between the personal and the impersonal is not a governing distinction among all adults; but it is one mode of dividing the world which has deeply affected the development of sociology.

The discrepancy between the personal and the impersonal is ambiguous. We can use it to distinguish ourselves from that which is not human, does not have a self. (Unfortunately, the word "distinguish" is also ambiguous. For some, it carries an implication of superiority—a connotation excluded here.) We can also use it to distinguish different kinds of relations among persons. This is endlessly cumulative, for we cannot escape reading into the world, as we see and build it, what is true of ourselves; and not reading into ourselves what we deem to be true about the impersonal surroundings helping to provide the contrasts by which we come to know what we are through determining what we are not. Yet the discrepancy is not enough for a conception of a social, as distinct from a personal or a natural, order. Society lies between individuals, and between the personal and the impersonal in the first sense of that distinction. As an expression referring to the unceasing exchange of events between people as members of different groupings, it stands for a way of apprehending the world that seems not to be equally distant from or close to rival *moral* perspectives. When we construct a triangle, in our sense of order, we see that, in addition to the nexus of personal happenings or of natural events, it is promising to conceive as well of a nexus of social exchanges and results. Then we find that we must combine a view of social orders, as involving moral calculations (and the guide lines by which these are performed), with the object of being free, in our questions, to distinguish between "what is" and "what ought to be."

If our own moral universe includes, among its prominent commitments or displeasures, potent notions of "individualism" or "freedom," then the intellectual claim that events in the world can be ordered to *several* comprehensible realms (which here we have provisionally called personal, impersonal, and social) always has its own moral consequences. These affect the search for a discovery of the regularities of the social order. Still, in human affairs, including building science through discovery and invention, it seems possible to imagine a resolution while we are still dogged by many logical and technical difficulties. From these considerations, it follows that, in the investigations of social affairs, one is always liable to some temptations.

One must necessarily begin within the realm of personal matters and see society as an elaboration of the different kinds of relations that people develop toward others. This yields the notion that we are dealing with an order involving me or you, *wanting* something concerning you or me. This can produce a whole set of questions about the ways social relations are constructed and the ways they differ from other sorts of relations, e.g., those of logic or mechanics. What is the difference between the way I am bound to another who has done me a favor, and the way rope is bound to a bushel of wheat?

But society is more than a multiplication of personal relations. The first temptation, in fashioning a guiding image helping to define a social order and its field of study, lies in *not going beyond a proper starting point*. The temptation not to see society beyond social relations is the stronger because the realm of social relations seems so very rich. This realm comprises individuals addressing one another —directly, within each other's hearing, sight, or full presence; or indirectly, through mediators, like, e.g., real estate salesmen and marriage brokers. Social relations are, of course, not confined to straight lines, triangles, or small circles. They are, as it were, not confined to themselves; they appear as webs.

The best example of this is kinship. But kinship is also a special case, growing by two processes alone: marriage and birth. It belongs to those social arrangements which combine a maximum of continuity with a minimum of legal formality. In contrast, many social arrangements proceed within the confines of different kinds of corporate groups. This fact has led to considering social organizations, factories, hospitals, schools, government offices. But neither the web of kinship nor the web of corporate organizations, jointly composed of formal and informal arrangements, exhausts the structure of society. The second temptation then, is to shy away from the multiplicity of comparable yet different arrangements and thus to confine one's self either to the inwardly understandable web of social relations or to explanations referring to social forces.

The image of social forces contains an important clue. It refers in one respect to the experience each of us has had of being surrounded by arrangements —of law, religion, economics, education, or whatever they be—that have preceded us and whose tradition will outlive us. To feel surrounded is one aspect of the fact that society usually contains more

people and more patterns than any one person, who is nevertheless a member of the society, can come to know. The society's structure, in addition to involving a division of labor, involves the unequal distribution of power and privilege. Organization and social relations thus fall within the variety of identifiable domains. Conventionally we distinguish between the economic, the religious, the political, the educational, and perhaps the social realms. This will be further discussed in the Introduction to the last two sections of Part One; and the differentiation of these realms is discussed in considerable detail in the Introduction to Part Two. In the case of any one society, the assessment of the actual balance of continuity and dissociation among these domains is one of the most delicate tasks for sociological analysis. As domains, they meet in different ways among circles that differ by virtue of the style of life that they share with one another.

The groups and corporate organizations distributed among the domains of society, and yielding styles of life that help deposit strata among the population of a society, still do not exhaust the major dimensions of a social order. This coherence involves a central value-system—a notion far more fully developed in the essays written by Talcott Parsons and Edward Shils. Central values help constitute such ideas as "individuality," "privacy," "sovereignty," "responsibility," or "rights." At some point, society involves its members in ultimate considerations, even if societies differ in the chances they hold out for different sectors of their populations to challenge, accept, or change these ultimate considerations. Their change, of course, is not a self-contained matter.

We do make distinctions between what people believe and what people do, between ideals and conditions. Often these are not happy distinctions, for people's acts involve beliefs, even though these beliefs may differ from the ones that the people assert. The discrepancy between ideal and practice is less a matter of the attenuation of ideals, more a matter of the fact that, in practice, people act under the aspect of what then become competing considerations. Moreover, as persons with shared ultimate commitments, they are often—especially in the market place—in the presence of what appear as impersonal forces. Social orders, as the history of economics as a discipline illustrates, can profitably be considered through the perspective of measurable regularities that would represent the social order, in turn, as a relatively determinate pattern of variables.

Economics, as later sections of this book will demonstrate, provides, perhaps more than any other sister discipline of sociology, valuable and

clear models for the steady study of social arrangements. It comes closest to precision about strategic
matters. But sociology's core concerns are considered peripheral in economics. In a measure, sociology grew by opposition to economics. Logically,
of course, the two disciplines are complementary;
but the conditions of growth of human enterprises
are not only a matter of logic. In any case, the sociological study of society, while being one of several
disciplines studying human arrangements, their
conditions, and their products, seems logically to
involve an extended awareness of impersonal and
personal patterns and of ultimate commitment.

Slowly, fragmentarily, and from various sources,
we have been combining views to bring a social
order into view. As one cumulative attempt to study
this order, sociology must approach its task on several planes. The order it studies lies not only "in
between" the felt coherence of things personal, or
the organization of processes called biological, or
the clearly impersonal nexus of the physical universe; it also has a severalness of its own. The
social implies a recognition of reciprocity sustained
by people who are themselves aware of at least part
of the reciprocity by which they interrelate. This
provides a focus, the focus of *social action*. The
next essay develops the central importance, as we
see it, of this idea and its particular use for seeing a
common theme in much diverse work carried out in
the name of the social sciences, and sociology in
particular.

Social action stands for creating or enacting a
course of self-engagement in the world, a course
that has a reference, in the agent's calculation, to
others considered as likewise capable of being
authors of acts toward one's self or others. Several
circles can be drawn around this focus.

People Face to Face

Some sociologists have concentrated on the realm
of immediate encounters, trying to learn how the
meetings of people run the courses they do. They
want to discover regularities among the happenings
between people in each other's presence. Who, they
ask, talks to whom, and how much? Or, what are the
ways by which conversations are begun, deflected,
or ended? What are the differences between a cocktail party and a committee meeting? To use a classical expression: How do people come to define different situations differently? Or, to put it yet
another way, what can we isolate as the recurring
elements together composing social situations,
which, by variation in their combination, also allow
us to characterize the differences among such situations?

Let us take the case of a man chasing a 'bus that
is about to pull away from its stop; there are other
people about, watching. At first, it seems most convenient to think of this example in theatrical terms
—as a scene involving actors, audience, time, and
stage. But who are the actors? The busdriver and
his potential, though late, passenger? One might
begin with these. Yet each is surrounded by further
actors. There are the passengers already in the bus,
and the onlookers on the street. Some are near the
situation; yet not all are *in* it, for only some have
noticed that someone is still trying to board the
'bus. Time can change this, through an onlooker's
drawing the driver's attention to the man. Thereby,
the distributed passengers on the bus can become a
mutually aware grouping watching "their" driver
and someone who might join them. The situation is
now enhanced, for it allows alternatives. The driver
may ignore the man and drive on. The latecomer
may see this and give up; or he may run faster, hoping still to be able to knock on the window. The people outside may look to see what will happen, or
look away to save embarrassment. The driver,
within himself, may balance notions of anger, kindliness, sticking to a schedule. He looks, and responds
to what he observes—a man rather than a woman, a
young person rather than an old one. His passengers
may say things to each other while he drives off.
One can see this as the end; it is certainly *an* end. A
wish has been thwarted. A man, slightly breathless,
has been left behind. Others may surround him
and, by watching, help re-define his experience as
defeat—showing him as a bad calculator or a bad
runner, as a symbol of the little man defeated by
impersonal timetables, or as a muddleheaded man
who misunderstands the logic of transportation systems. On the other hand, if the driver stops, a different logic may unfold. The driver can put someone in his debt, since he has the right to drive on.
The latecomer is now a passenger; while he has left
the onlookers on the street behind, he now may be
looked over by fellow travelers. He is likely to round
out his success not only by a "thank you," but also
by referring to the defeat of defeat with the expression, "Just made it." This acknowledges the contingency which hovers about the co-ordination of
human affairs.

Some readers may feel that all this is much ado
about nothing, another painful elaboration of the
obvious—or, at best, the trivial. That might be a
useful critique, if it led to a clear distinction between the trivial and the significant in social affairs.
Meanwhile, even this admittedly slight example is
demonstrably a sample of social reality and is,
therefore, one combination of recurrent elements.
Our description has been haphazard and personal,

but it has indicated some possibilities that social situations have beginnings and ends, that they unfold in time, and that, as such, they have "boundaries." Consequently, the course of social action creates distinctions between *insiders* and *outsiders*. *Participation* can assume different forms; it is, moreover, given through viewing others under some *selected aspect,* as passengers, drivers, onlookers, fellow passengers. That is, others must become *defined;* so must one's self, in *distinction* from them and in *similarity* to them. Actors and onlookers then come to sustain a *division of labor,* which implies some *agreement* on *ends* and *means,* some notion of *appropriateness.* Appropriateness is the recognition of possibility, of alternatives. We often refer to this by denying it. We talk about things "one just doesn't do." To the listener, this may be a reminder of all that one could do. One does not play hide-and-seek in church or treat *Macbeth* as a comedy; one does not laugh at the man as the 'bus drives off without him. Social situations, then, involve *judgments* and *sanctions.* Or, again, they involve *expectations* and *consequences.* This incomplete sample of communicable ideas suggests lines for a dissection and view of the social order as an order that has to be carried on.

The Larger Social Order

One can—and usually must—*start* with social situations as one thinks about the character of the social order and the possibility of studying it. Inevitably, one cannot end there; social situations are only samples of social reality. Their analysis necessitates previous ideas concerning the coherence and differentiation of this order and the processes whereby it is carried on. These volumes suggest one way that, especially during the last seventy-five years, sociological theories, in dissecting this order, can themselves be distributed about a sequence of questions. This sequence—and we must repeat that it is one of a *series* of possible sequences—is itself the collective product, as it were, of the growth of sociological theory, whose nature will concern us presently. For the present, we should continue the attempt to characterize its product. In ten years, this characterization may well be markedly out of date; one of the intentions of this Reader is that this should become the case.

Just as social situations, as the specific occasions for the enactment of social arrangements, are the place to "catch" society, so social acts and the give-and-take of interaction are the stuff of which society is made. The growth of sociological analysis has involved dissecting a given sequence of social acts, as well as comparing large-scale societies. This has led to attempts to distinguish the component spheres of societies. These "opposite" directions of growth are, of course, complementary; they yield a series of planes on which sociological questions are asked. In turn, the existence of such planes raises the question of their links.

There are times when the study of the coherence of men's arrangements seems to have no coherence itself. Sociological theory has analyzed immediate and intimate encounters, like meals and confessions; it has also become concerned with the mass. It might profitably ask, for instance, what social arrangements are necessary for the distribution of urban populations on public beaches on a hot summer weekend afternoon. A thorough answer would reveal much of history and society. This lively phenomenon—combining nature and commerce, leisure and potential danger, the sun-tan cult, the art of swimming, and the enjoyment of sundry pleasures—presupposes notions of private and public property, attitudes about the body, and distinctions of work and play. Concern with the mass can also comprehend an analysis of the distributed audience of a radio program or the gathered collection of a cathedral service. Behind the temporary convergence and dispersal of large and small groupings one can look for persistent structures: the bureaucracies of industry, government, and churches; the formal and informal patterns of procedure in hospitals, universities, and libraries. Then there are the orders of quantitative emergent fact: the rates of population increase and decline; the rates of incidence and prevalence of some countable attribute, like admission to a mental hospital, suicide, marriage, or divorce; or the direction and volume of a choice, like a vote or a car purchase. Sociological theorizing has gone farther: it has become concerned with a wide range of migrations—people moving from the country to the city, from one nation to another, from one religious or political persuasion to another, from one age to another, from one status to another. Such movement has several related aspects calling for distinction and for mutual ordering.

One can examine this ordering in terms of sheer quantity. Rates of migration and mobility, ratios of mobile and sedentary numbers in given congregations of people (be these cities, regions, or nations), or shifts in such rates—including the magnitudes of upward and downward social mobility characterizing comparable social structures—all these are significant in the comprehension of social systems. They become measurable, outward signs of inward and invisible facts. Concern with them is part of the inevitable attempt to make the society manageable, to bring it into steady view. Yet these magnitudes also remove society: they remind one of it as something that lies behind the intellectually comprehended figures of consumption, travel, births, deaths, or years of schooling completed. By the same token, they make society something lying beyond the experienced pattern of social connection that even the richest individual life brings into apprehended clarity, on subsequent reflection, to any of us.

In this connection, another theme of questioning (and charting of fact) has helped constitute the scope of sociology. The social "takes place"—in time and space. As an alive phenomenon—constituted by the succession of encounters, and their products, of persons in their capacity as members of a variety of groupings—any social arrangement has, in fact, a "boundary." (This idea is stated much more systematically in the second part of this Introduction.) A birthday party or a national election, a village or a concert, an army or a university, are diverse examples of social arrangements, all of which have beginnings and ends: they occur in time. One may realistically ask how long they last, when they began, or why they ended. In a sense, social arrangements, like melodies, are disclosed only over time; but usually they lack a directly apprehensible "thereness." Social arrangements are carried on and along by real individuals. Most of the time, in complex societies, they are carried on indoors: they occur inside walls that form patterns between and among themselves. The study of these patterns, ecology, is another dimension of sociological questioning, concerned with the ways in which people settle, stay, or move again, thereby building housing for many purposes. The arrangement of such housing into distinguishable kinds of aggregations—e.g., cities or villages, towns or hamlets, camps or air bases—can be observed and then comprehended as the places where social relations and institutions are begun or carried on, and as visible expressions of these invisible structures. Sociologists, and others, have studied cities, created a distinction between rural and urban sociology, and concerned themselves with a variety of smaller and larger communities. Such explorations are one form of the more general attempt to give even social subject matter some concrete place in which one can see it—to make it tangible, and yet to observe a segment of it large enough to seem to make some difference when one considers the wider realities of national societies. These have their territorial possession and limits; yet, until recently, they seemed to elude clear thought and precise, systematically gathered, documentation.

Face-to-face encounters have ramifications beyond themselves. They also come from elsewhere.

We come to them with expectations and carry these, confirmed or revised, away again. A sociology consistent with itself can, therefore, never be only a study of social situations. As it moves away from the latter (though it never really completely leaves them behind), its tasks divide on several planes. It becomes concerned with sorting out the kinds of possible social associations. For example, think of a beach or a ski hill: each places private groupings in public places; each reminds us of distinctions between families, crowds, queues; the sand and the snow become appropriated.

The range of sociological theory has become wide, the planes of sociological inquiry have been multiplied. One way or another we have distinguished at least six planes on which the structure of social arrangements may be dissected. Some scholars work on immediate encounters, or groupings of persons in each other's presence. Some, though not too many, deal with public gatherings, especially when these involve ritual transactions—e.g., a coronation or a parade. Other scholars are concerned with various collective audiences—in a cathedral, or of radio or TV shows. Others analyze the persistent systems, such as science considered as a social enterprise, the civil service, or different political systems; or, more social-psychologically, the specific roles of businessmen, lawyers, teachers, doctors, waitresses—their structure and their context. Still others study emergent facts, ecological distributions, rates of birth and death, the diverse consequences of specific social arrangements, and the conditions for further ones. Finally, some concern themselves with the ultimate grounds embodied in central values, in elites, and in the occasions recognized as great accomplishments.

MODES OF WORK[1]

The concern of this Introduction, as of the Reader itself, is always the further creation of better theory and research upon social phenomena. We know that men's actions and what they say are not the same. This is not just a matter of hypocrisy; in fact, hypocrisy is likely to play a small part in it. It is due to the coincidence of several stubborn and difficult facts.

A course of social action—taking a child for a swim in a lake; buying a watermelon; or walking

---

1. The bulk of the ideas in this section have been previously stated, in slightly different form, in my article: "Attachment and Alienation: Complementary Aspects of the Work of Durkheim and Simmel," *American Journal of Sociology*, LXIII, No. 6 (May, 1958).

down the gangway of an airplane, saying good-bye to the stewardess and looking for anyone who might have come to meet one—is too big for one participant to survey fully. What he surveys, knows, or experiences, furthermore, is greater than he can "say"—even if we include in that word the language of his body, his expressions, his hands. What he observes "at once," he must say in sequence. Besides, what is said, in the form of findings or related distinctions with which we are concerned in these volumes, must take a written, printed form.

Usually, a struggle intervenes between inner thoughts and written formulations. The latter, especially in science, must be expressed in such a way that they may be understood by others—in other words, the form of expression must transcend the purely personal. (Gertrude Stein, e.g., does not write science.) Scientific works are written under the additional constraint imposed by the logic of clarity or proof; they are concerned with confirming or disproving proposed regularities. Definite traditions and forms have developed for the steps of positive and negative confirmation. The ability to frame one's reasoning within these forms is a requisite for scientific writing. Yet the step by which one initially made one's discoveries may well have been quite different. In science, process and product almost necessarily diverge. Printed matter, moreover, has a kind of finality about it; once published, it is there to be read.

Nevertheless, reading almost requires reversing the process of writing. The concrete and meandering chain of reasoning connecting hunches or hypotheses with assembled data and subsequent interpretations is not, as a rule, fully stated by any scientific author. It cannot be fully stated. In addition, science involves abstraction. It must regard experience or contrived reality under the aspect of selecting distinctions. These become a part of a triangle constituted by those who produce science, the stream of products that they create together, and the persistence of the reality about which science—in the company of other forms of knowledge or assertion, like art or theology—has something, though not everything, to say.

The struggle of question and answer underlying any one of the excerpts in this Reader cannot easily be deciphered through merely reading it. For each author, this struggle takes its own characteristic form, which others are able to discern only reasonably accurately through considering his work as a whole. This is one of the many limitations, even dangers, of a venture like this. Only the original works, in their chronological sequence and in entirety, disclose an author—be he scientist or novelist—as a person at work. From one point of view,

such a picture is dispensable. Science, as a cumulative product, consists in work done: it consists in questions, methods for answering them, findings, interpretations, and continuous revision of these interpretations. How Adam Smith came to formulate his thoughts on the division of labor, or how Machiavelli arrived at his observations on the management of power, is irrelevant. Having been stated, their thoughts can now be examined, used for research, dismissed as outside the present scope of social scientific inquiry or theory, and the like.

Yet a systematic exploration of the social order is an accomplishment. It must be created; and the previous struggle of others can be a guide or a consolation. Examination of the patterns and conditions of creativity of the sociological theorists who preceded us can be instructive in several respects. The printed and irrevocable proposals—like those gathered in these volumes as examples of the resources available to any student of society—are fragments in more than one way. Each is part of larger works and of the completed work of one individual (usually, in this field, a man). Such completed work exhibits its own patterns, whether or not these are known to the author when he finally ends his efforts. Some men may be more productive if they do not think too much about the inner pattern of their productivity. Others are likely to learn useful things from observing how a Weber, a George Herbert Mead, or a Durkheim poses questions, and either moves from one area of questions to another or, staying within some sphere—as Piaget does—deepens or varies his concern. For example, one might—in a necessarily condensed manner—think of Durkheim and Simmel as representing contrasting, though complementary, modes of work.

At this distance, Durkheim's work seems well contained in a few themes; its distinct foci and boundaries give it a completeness. They also invite us, quite appropriately, to use his work as a model. The logic that arranged and interpreted the facts of suicide will serve equally well with the puzzles of alcoholism or cross-cousin marriage. In all three cases, we must distinguish between rates and individual histories; we need to search for types among a determinate, and hence apparently uniform, category of events; we need a commitment to explanations seeking to exploit the constituent elements of social relations and their organization as causes for the unequal distribution of phenomena—a distribution that is not solely a matter of meaningless nature.

The themes combine rejection and acceptance. Part of the assertion that the social is something *sui generis* consists of withdrawing from the image of a single, ultimate order—individual or physical—that alone is real and is thus the only context of all explanations. Instead, Durkheim dignifies society as a moral phenomenon standing stubbornly beside nature; that must be understood in its impersonal "thereness," much as though it were a collection of related things; and that must also be perceived for what it is and what it is not—a coherence of representations coercing individuals by virtue of their ability to fuse what is obligatory with what is desirable, a fusion analogous to the double face of the sacred. Sacred implies distance and the forbidden. Yet it stands for sought-after qualities, for an appropriation that traverses distance. Durkheim remains with his concern with society. He moves through a progression of empirical concerns: the coherence and differentiation of society; the supports and burdens that different kinds of social orders provide their numbers; the ways ultimate commitments and modes of thought are constituted in enduring demands, mediated and expressed through rituals which outlast individuals while, in principle, requiring them. The progression from *The Division of Labor*, via *Suicide,* to *The Elementary Forms of the Religious Life* will probably long remain a double model: as a fruitful trinity of researches into phenomena that one must apprehend as part of the very core of any and all social phenomena; and as an inspired continuity that is cumulative.

But his work comprises far more. There are the recurrent methodological examinations and revisions, initially driven on by the wish to keep sociology a positive science, by recognizing that social facts are moral, and by the ambiguous insistence that social facts be treated as things. In one of these works, a discussion of pragmatism,[2] his persistent concern with the relative difference and connection between ideas and acts is set out, as if under a microscope, in a condensed but decisive dissection of the forms and conditions of certainty.

Further, there are the discussions of socialism, individualism, and the position of intellectuals; of the place of elites in a democracy; of the character of the German mentality and the significance of World War I—pre-political diagnoses that do not keep Durkheim from a continuous reconsideration of the "spirit of discipline," which is "the essential condition of all common life."[3]

No wonder that the related structures of morality and education become at once the labels of his academic chair and, in various forms, the titles of several of his collected series of lectures. In one of these collections, the diverse and complementary bonds dividing and binding the several spheres of economic activity, political coherence, professional service, and familial life are characterized as much for their own sake as to demonstrate that the social is indeed the moral, while society cannot do without crime.[4] Crime and punishment, the normal and the pathological—these are never far from Durkheim's attention; they provide a circle of facts, in quantitative or statutory form, that he likes to use or explain.

Yet he also turns from homicides and suicides, from the formative categories of thought, or from the dominant modes of large-scale social coherence and their historic succession, to the more immediate sphere of the family, the origins of marriage, and the prohibition of incest. He discusses moral education and education and sociology. Very deliberately, he writes accounts of a few predecessors. He finds in Montesquieu two ideas necessary to social science: the lawfulness of society and the existence of discoverable types of society. To formulate such types is to look for generic characteristics of social structure and their alternative combinations. Durkheim is also explicitly interested in Saint-Simon, Comte, Rousseau, and Schaeffle. But it is to the twin issues of anomie and education that he returns again and again. "What," one might paraphrase his insistent query, "are the conditions under which a complex contemporary society can avoid loss of direction or meaning? How adequate, given our growing knowledge of society, are such solutions as the variant forms of socialism? Is it not true that the coherence necessary for a large society requires a deliberate and specialized division of labor, in which people balance a sense of the collectivity with a concentration on their own efforts?" Durkheim sees education as the agency by which society re-creates itself, an agency at once diverse and uniform. In North America during the last decade or so, education has received astonishingly little attention from sociologists; while right now it is singled out as the cause of Western society's failure to remain unequivocally pre-eminent in physical science and technology.

Neither Durkheim nor Simmel completed his work. Yet each left a distinct "whole," as well as a distinct style of question and answer.

Simmel seems almost the opposite of Durkheim—but then, as the French say, extremes meet. His writings are profuse. Happily, to revive attention in his work, in Germany, during his anniversary year of 1958, a selection of his writings—especially of earlier or less accessible pieces—has been pub-

2. E. Durkheim, *Pragmatisme et sociologie* (Paris: Librairie philosophique, 1955), pp. 199–202.
3. Durkheim, *The Rules of Sociological Method* (Chicago: University of Chicago Press, 1938), p. 124.
4. *Leçons de sociologie: physique des moeurs et du droit* (Paris: Presses universitaires de France, 1950).

lished, under the appropriate title, *Bridge and Door*.[5]

This collection is a partially representative sample of the range of specific topics that Simmel discussed: fate, life, and death as the co-ordinates of "experience"; the characters of history and of culture; religion as a mode of coherence of the self, and not primarily as a matter of specific beliefs; landscapes and faces as types of unity confronting a beholder; the moral alternatives proposed by Kant and Nietzsche; the different ways in which a man's work and his life can be connected, as exemplified by Goethe and Rodin. The collection also contains some lesser-known sociological pieces on individualism, on meals (their regularity, sequence, and style, their double meaning), on the role of certain aesthetic categories in social arrangements and in ideologies. With extraordinary ease, Simmel begins with any one of a multitude of obvious events or ideas, and ends by using them as appropriate illustrations of his basic theme.

Simmel's work is so diverse that one could easily be tempted to list at least the major issues with which he is concerned. Yet lists give the impression of being linear; and Simmel's writings do not form a single line of analyses successively emerging from each other. Rather, his work is connected but uncumulative. In the best sense, it is the work of an artist seeking to work the way he saw his model, Goethe, live: re-creating, through the paradoxical use of terms, the experienced relations and activities of our selves and of the varieties of confrontations through which we live. Simmel's work includes several spheres, but it does not fall into disciplines.

It is vain to classify him as primarily a philosopher or a sociologist. It is necessary to see his sociological analyses as an accompaniment to *all* his work: they are not confined to what he himself might have labeled sociology, any more than his work itself is confined to any one discipline. The very range of his reflection is an instructive accomplishment. He wrote about the character of knowledge; but he also discussed the nature of understanding others and historic events, as well as the processes which constitute our apprehension of the other when we see him "first." This last question is pursued in a study of Rembrandt. Simmel focused his thought on the work of a series of men—Dante, Goethe, Michelangelo, Moltke, Nietzsche, Schopenhauer, Kant, George. He considers each man, not as a person, but as the creator or exemplar of one or another alternative solution to a problem of life.

There are the recurrent essays on aesthetic matters: on ruins, mountains, landscapes, bridges, doors, vessels, and their handles. These become, in fact, the occasion for further juxtapositions of opposites: ruins allow one to experience as the work of nature what originally must have been the work of men; handles serve as links between an environment and what is nevertheless a self-contained object placed and seen within it. One can turn from this with mild amusement or annoyed indifference, feel tempted to dismiss it as a play on words, as utterly irrelevant to the serious study of social matters. But in Simmel's view, "the play's the thing": the serious is often best caught in its translated forms—in caricature, in small talk, in the unique event. His essay on adventures displays a parade of complementary notions concerning routine and disruption, accident and fate, periphery and center, repetition and irrevocability, beginning and end—all of which help constitute social situations. Simmel's explicit sociological scope is now known: like Durkheim, he sees in numbers a strategic starting point for accounting for certain differences between social arrangements and for the direction that change can take.

Durkheim fruitfully (yet questionably) proposes links among the complexity of social arrangements, moral density, and an increase in the numbers whose affairs must be co-ordinated; Simmel remains, in the main, among knowable groups of different size. True to his wish to explore an attitude; to ending anywhere, yet always beginning from the same place; to being concerned far more with the *terminus a quo* than with the *terminus ad quem*—Simmel took up other themes: poverty, intersecting group memberships, conflict, secrecy, strangers and nobility, gratitude, competition and exclusion, the social functions of eyes and ears.

Cutting across these studies are several contributions to a sociology of women, beginning with an essay on female psychology (written in 1890) and including considerations of the feminist movement, the relations of women to militarism, and three long pieces on coquetry, "feminine culture," and the reciprocities of male and female. Here Simmel again seeks to formulate facts through stating contradictions: male and female are merely an example of what we might now call the reciprocal differentiation of roles. As such, they imply one another. As a category, each also stands alone: the male represents our image of some coherent, impersonal, or demanding reality; the female represents aliveness that has not yet been complicated by an elaborate self-consciousness. Such formulations are no longer

5. Georg Simmel (Michael Landmann and Margaret Susman, eds.), *Bruecke und Tuer* (Stuttgart: K. F. Koehler, 1957).

likely to attract attention and research; but we can
convert them into an approach to the study of types
of moral commitment. We seem to balance a sense
of the *reciprocity* of our contributions or standards
with a belief in their ultimate "so-ness." Perhaps,
as adults, we combine two moralities. In different
ways, Durkheim and Simmel formulated the respective character of these moralities; while Piaget creates experiments to present them to us as stages in
the life cycle.[6]

Par excellence, Simmel is a sociologist of intimacy. Closeness and anonymity, faithfulness and
the faithlessness of fashion, private correspondence
and adornment—these always concern him. Wider
society, as the more impersonal middle between
specific selves and general ideas, is included in his
dissection more as background than as foreground.
However, general ideas, especially in the form of
governing webs of attitudes, also attract him—particularly the normative constellations, like optimism
and pessimism and love. Ultimately, he is moved
and caught by the spectacle of a cumulative conflict
between ourselves and the products of our selves.
To be humanly alive is to create objects as part of a
labor that divides the self into subject and object.
Objects can and do grow in number; they outgrow
us. To live, we must create the things that, by the
oppressive embarrassment of alien riches, destroy
us. Durkheim's anomie here finds a complementary
notion: *omnia habentes, nihil possidentes.* It should
be possible to translate this—into research—and
to ask how people see the discrepancies between
what they know and what they do not know, what
they have and what they do not have. When are their
relative deprivations less important than their sense
of not having enough inner room for all that is in
their grasp?

Simmel collected neither facts nor figures. He
sought to represent, through ideas, what he defined
as transcending them. This forced him into the device of paradox. He may have been hypnotized by
his own penchant.

He constantly represents life as a stream of
events which come to confront their authors. Together, events and authors are part of something
else. This "something else" and something further
compose life. All this involves the facts of distance
and exclusion. Life, like individuals and social arrangements, always goes farther (while it lasts) but
also involves limits. These limits can be crossed. It
is precisely the acts of crossing, of going farther, of
leaving something behind, that constitute the very
character of aliveness.

By the same logic, boundaries—the divisions be-

tween inside and outside, here and there, now and
then, I and You, We and They—constitute part of
the recurrent structure that the sociologist has appointed himself to explain. Ultimately, it is the
discrepancy between what one can say and what
one experiences that is the poignant puzzle for Simmel. He holds fast to a solution which would make
the discrepancy itself both a gap and a bridge between "life" and the forms or the products of it.

One book contains the theme on which his many
books are variations: *Lebensanschauung: Vier
metaphysische Kapitel* (1918). We can go back to
this source and rework it into a tentative scheme for
seeing how people actually see themselves related
to others: what do they mean by being "part of
something," or "surrounded," or "on the edge"? Or
we can ignore this and begin in the middle: for instance, we can concentrate on any one of a series of
fragmentary observations on the properties of human groups or on the shifts when one social constellation gives way to another. Or we can extend
some of the inquiries he began on topics like consolation or gratitude, secrecy or multiple group
membership. In any case, we are bound to fail if
we take him seriously by taking him literally.

Formal sociology is dead. It confounds description and explanation. Simmel used many reciprocal
distinctions to bring to mind our immediate and receding surroundings, in order that, eventually, their
structure could be explained. Formal sociology
simply distributes such distinctions over haphaz-
ardly apprehended facts. I shall return to this point
later. Three lessons, however, seem to lie between
the attempt to reformulate his philosophy of life
and the immediate use of selected proposals.[7] He
seems to urge us to look for the "duplicity" in social
arrangements, to determine the boundaries making
relations social, and to distinguish varieties of distance through which human acts can be sorted out.[8]

Admittedly, in the end, Simmel wishes to stay
with the self—at least, he never wants to leave it
for long. But his intentions need not imprison his
contributions. A meal, the settlement of a quarrel,
a conversation—in Simmel's perspective, these
samples of social arrangements exhibit a "severalness" of divergent characteristics which nevertheless cohere. Forgiveness after a quarrel, for instance, can reconstitute a former solidarity on a

---

6. Jean Piaget, *The Moral Judgement of the Child* (London: Kegan Paul, Trench, Trubner, 1932).

7. Besides the work of Theodore M. Mills, see, in par-
ticular, Robert K. Merton's provisional list of group-
properties which is, *inter alia,* explicitly indebted to Simmel:
"Continuities in the Theory of Reference Groups and Social
Structure," in *Social Theory and Social Structure,* (Glencoe,
Ill.: Free Press, 1957), pp. 310–26.

8. For a parallel formulation of Simmel's basic procedure, see the circumspect doctoral dissertation by D.
Levine on a comparison of Parsons and Simmel (University of Chicago, 1957; unpublished).

higher level—while exhibiting the reciprocities of acknowledging and "forgetting" injuries, of deliberate self-humiliation that runs the risk of rejection while seeking the reward of acceptance, and of a consensus on what is appropriate behavior after a violation of expectations. Simmel directs us to move social reality into focus with the help of a series of co-ordinates constituting a set of mutually contrary ideas. He moreover suggests that all social arrangements are in the first instance sustained, remembered, or rehearsed by selves, who thereby form social relations that can never fully include their parties. Even in excluding us, society has a place for us all. Yet social relations have boundaries; they are as much defined by what they are as by what they are not. Distance and proximity are, at the same time, names for distinguishing between others —related or not—and simultaneous attributes of all social relations. In addition, distance, being variable, stands for alternative possibilities of seeing the same phenomenon close at hand or far away. Sociology itself is a form of distance vis-à-vis the stream of recurrent confrontations of individuals in varying combinations of numbers.

The foregoing are, at best, reminders of the range and direction of the accomplishments of Simmel and Durkheim. A complementary and equally fragmentary comparison might still give the previous sections some coherence and lead to the last questions: What properties of social relations does each man bring to our attention? how differently must the single word "continuity" be applied to this double stream of proposals? and how incomplete would our view of society be if we used only Durkheim and Simmel as our guides?

For clarity and brevity, though at the cost of accuracy, either Durkheim or Simmel might be described as exhibiting what the other is without. Their similarities may then become plain. Durkheim confronts gathered facts, including numerical regularities. He is concerned with method. He has an end in view and wishes to reach it through the answers to successive questions. He moves from answer to question, from the signs of unhappiness to its distribution, from the apparent sameness of a phenomenon to its typical variant forms, from the apparent associations of specific ideas to some "eternal" attitudes. Often he seeks to establish his own position by the successive elimination of rival alternatives. His is a succession of analyses of the generic features of a few strategic elements of society: work, attachment to one's self and to others, religion, education, patterns of injunctions. He pays explicit attention to the succession of shifts within these. He is also concerned with the fact that society

moves into the future by educating all its young but dispersing them to different places. He remembers always that society is in transition, although phases —like his own era—he recognizes as "in-between times," jointly characterized by "moral mediocrity" and the possibilities of dispersing coherent images that can be shared. Yet he is not prepared to see the whole process as tragic. Discipline, a sense of the whole, occupational groupings, and meaningful occasions for remembering and so continuing the collective agreements that can distribute solemnity and direction—these seem almost sufficient resources for continuity.

In a series of cumulative monographs, Durkheim economically incloses a sequence of questions leading to the progressive differentiation of the primal concept of social relations as constituting phenomena in their own right. He, too, sees the severalness of person and social pattern; and he speaks about the non-contractual elements *in* contract, the impersonal elements *in* personality, the duality *of* the individual. Yet the methodological device of considering the social as a "thing" facilitates or expresses the substantive view of the social as in serious respects impersonal, as that which (eventually) confronts (and contains) the immediate self. This view leads Durkheim to write about solemnity. In Simmel's hands, when he writes on the inclined plane of tragedy, the "same" confrontation becomes a matter of alienation, of the strange, of proximity and distance—a theme which Durkheim also uses, to describe our encounters with taboos and with the sacred. Simmel, in heuristic contrast, *discloses* a very full world of transitory occasions representing the chronic duality of the self, which thus becomes a pre-eminently social condition and accomplishment. Potentially dramatic or apparently ordinary occasions and a huge panoply of confrontations with the specific accomplishments or completed lives of others, with the contrary features of lifeless objects in space and the meaningful but puzzling coherence of faces and landscapes, styles and money—all are considered, in unceasing succession, and analyzed alike. Subsequent analyses do not grow from previous ones. But all of them seek to catch the flow of temporal exchange between people. Simmel tells us what he sees. While he represents it, it is alive. He stays within the structure of vivid experience and at the same time enlarges it. But he never enlarges it to the point where he arrives at a concept of the social system.

Simmel states his claims via *contrary* notions that claim equal relevance to the *one* phenomenon under discussion. In this way, he manages to isolate and attract facts with one idea, and then attract them away again to another idea. This is more than a literary accomplishment. It proceeds expressly with the help of clear abstractions. Experience is translated into many proposals, each open to examination and revision. Yet this involves style rather than method. It cannot be directly continued. Ironically, for all its aliveness, it completely bypasses the strategic fact that society includes children. Otherwise, Simmel, perhaps more than anyone else, forces upon us the wealth of the surrounding world, the strangeness of the familiar. Now *we* must choose, but now we also *can* choose.

Still, they diverge in their roles as forefathers. Durkheim can be followed as a predecessor: rates, index formation, types of social acts and of social relations, the search for the functions of social patterns—all these persist as direct puzzles or resources. Simmel wants no immediate descendants; he expects only to provide resources that others can use for their own purposes. He does not expect his successors and debtors to remember him as the source of the ideas that, in fact, he originated.[9] One can confront certain of his specific propositions with further or actual facts, as Mills and Hawthorn have done[10] with promising results; or one can, like Merton, collect Simmel's suggestions as part of the continuing effort to set forth a coherent identification of the generic features of social groups. Similarly, Simmel's ideas could be much further exploited in the direction of a sociology of work. After all, the serious gap between producer and product and the playful coherence between host and guest are among Simmel's characteristic themes.

His thoughts, more than anyone else's, lead to the question: What is the significance of the difference between what we study and what we do not study within the boundaries of social phenomena? He had the courage to start with the visible, and the imagination to end nowhere. If we could, step by step, go to the limits of his work, we would, I think, find in it more resources than its "content" alone can yield. But this takes time.

Simmel and Durkheim are complementary within the gathering enterprise of sociology; they also converge. Both see social relations as involving a confrontation of several dimensions. To Durkheim, the emphasis is on the character of commitment; to Simmel, on involvement. The first, as we

know, speaks of constraint as the combination of duty and desire. The second sees social relations as typical balances of distance and proximity. Durkheim analyzes sanctions which define and greet offenders, who, through their offense, create gaps between the actual and the ideal. Simmel traces the functions of gratitude and faithfulness, since he sees, in these two enjoined dispositions, resources for continued coherence among persons. Both, then, are concerned with the conditions necessary if people are to act attached. Both distinguish varieties of attachment. Both are prepared to admit some generic features of attachment.

Simmel and Durkheim seem to come back to four reciprocal themes: coherence, differentiation, alienation, and involvement. These may, in turn, be considered as two pairs of opposites. Social relations are constituted in some mutual regulation that can be experienced simultaneously as both impersonal and relevant demands. They involve an agreement, and also a temporal succession of exchanges. They involve the taking and giving of turns, the creation of parties to the agreement. They raise the matter of commitment to the future and to the memory of the past. Even where nothing tangible is produced—as in friendship—the previous coherence and differentiation constitute something left behind, something raising the matter of appropriation and alienation. Given the impersonal component to all personal matters, any one person may in principle select "how much" or how seriously he "puts himself" into the very succession of events constituting his life, while always remaining less than the whole of it.

Both Simmel and Durkheim direct their discoveries toward the serious life and the serious in life. Simmel, unlike Durkheim, considers in some detail the realm between the ordinary and the solemn, or between the actual and the ideal. He analyzes coquetry, sociability, and acting. These can hold up mirrors to the "real" or the "serious." They enact the distinctions and discrepancies between such contrasts as trivial and important, actual and possible; as "play-forms" of society, they help reveal the nature of the dumb and considered calculations, private or shared, that help constitute social arrangements. Social arrangements necessarily both involve and deflect images of relative importance. In that way they yield economies of exchange in emotions, goods, or ideas. The large-scale coherence of such economies does not explicitly concern Simmel. Instead, he writes often about our chances of ordering events to a notion of periphery or core. Questioningly, he comes to the conclusion that "deeper" people can survive only through maintaining a measure of superficiality. Ultimately, what-

---

9. See both the Introduction to *Philosophische Kultur* (Potsdam: Gustav Kirpenheuer Verlag, 1923), and the introductory quotation in *Fragmente und Aufsätze* (Munich: Drei Masken Verlag, 1923).

10. For one example of Mills's work, see his essay "Some Hypotheses on Small Groups from Simmel," *American Journal of Sociology*, LXIII, 642–50. H. B. Hawthorn has examined some aspects of the proposals on secrecy in "A Test of Simmel on the Secret Society: The Doukhobors of British Columbia," *American Journal of Sociology*, LXII, 1–7.

ever their logical compatibility, the several lines of moral assessment by which we constitute ourselves in society must clash insanely in any member of society who really thinks these matters through. Here Simmel meets Weber, who is said to have responded, when asked why he studied sociology, "To see how much I can stand!" By contrast, Durkheim is concerned with the aliveness of the resources to which collectivities can remain committed. Where Simmel sees conflict and alienation, Durkheim sees emptiness and the uncommitted pursuit of rituals as the inclusive, disruptive forces given with the very constitution of society itself.

Neither Simmel nor Durkheim, however, is adequate, alone or with the other, as a guide to attempting to isolate the major features of societies. They do not communicate a vivid sense of the large and rivalrous political units that claim men's lives and loyalties. Neither Durkheim nor Simmel asks about the ways in which national boundaries create political and other differences, while at the same time being cut across by strategic similarities—especially in the sphere of occupational ranking and the judgments of importance that such ranking can imply. Admittedly, even the relative political indifference of Simmel does not make his work irrelevant to those who wish to examine those commitments and structures involving the co-ordination and representation of men in their capacity as members of civil society or as voters, legislators, and government officials. Of the two, Simmel is primarily the apolitical thinker. Durkheim, after all, concerned himself with elites and with socialism.

As two major creators of sociology, Simmel and Durkheim complement each other. One lays before us a range of phenomena with which we can now compare the actual range of issues that have become included in our efforts. His distinctions must still be translated into the language of research; but his scope, where it exceeds ours, can be used for an assessment of our intellectual patterns of inclusion and exclusion. Admittedly, we may have to subordinate his intent to state, on the plane of ideas, the great flux of inner and outer occurrences to our wish to explain only some of them—yet how should we choose best? By contrast, the other presents an economy of continuous questions rather than a discontinuity of phenomena shown to have a constant structure. He produced a monograph that is a model of procedure. Simmel, for all his wish to write about life, cannot show us how to proceed—perhaps, precisely because he himself succeeded so persistently. But he can tell us clearly how much there is about which to ask. Between them, Durkheim and Simmel represent at least two sides of the study of social relations: the effort to bring social reality into a per-

spective that can be shared; and the effort to select a sufficiently clear question, whose answer will explain some strategic regularity.

Weber, Mead, Freud, or Pareto would not fit this oversimple pattern. Indeed, the contrast just discussed in no way exhausts comparisons between pioneers. We should now attempt, at even greater length, similar descriptions for Pareto or Mead, Freud or Weber. A huge literature, of course, has accumulated about Freud, including Ernest Jones's impressive three-volume biography. The biography, as its title suggests, deals with both Freud's life and his work, and suggests very clearly the ways that a style of life and a mode of work are—as they always are—mutually related. The growth of sociological thought is not merely a matter of the history of ideas. It is an aspect of the inner struggle of variously gifted people confronting themselves with old and new puzzles. Freud translated, into economic and elegant language, a clear and invading view of the character and cure of men and women; Max Weber, his contemporary, wrestled with an ancient trinity—the issues of economics, politics, and religion.

Weber, of all the sociologists represented in these two volumes, probably took most seriously Aristotle's formulation of man as a political animal. Weber was born in 1864; he died in 1920. Biographies of him have been written by his wife, Karl Jaspers, and Gerth and Mills, among others. These biographies, together with his work, show what he was: one of the last universal scholars, as well as a man much engaged in public life—while often also consumed by an illness that affected his capacity to read, write, or talk, frequently for considerable periods of time. His formal academic career began with the study of law, but it soon included economics and economic history. Toward the end of his career, in April, 1918, he lectured on what today might be called the sociology of religion. His work seems like a succession of huge, rich, dense fragments, unwaveringly reaching the heart of a circle of topics that today are distributed among many kinds of experts. Besides a general economic history, he wrote a series of studies of the political economy in the Middle Ages, in eastern Germany, and in antiquity. For instance, in 1896 he published an essay on the social causes of the decline of classical culture, in which he analyzes the decline of an urban culture surrounded by a rising rural and feudal culture. He shows this to be related to the decline of slavery, the rise of kinship, and private property, within the mass of the otherwise underprivileged. The imagery alone of this essay justifies consulting it in the original; but it is one essay among many within the domain of social economic history and within that wider domain of social change about which Weber wrote. Characteristically, he wrote essays, not books. A series of his essays deal with methodological issues: the notion of understanding, the use of ideal types, the sense in which there can be a systematic study of both the structure and history of society that goes beyond economics and history.

For our purposes, two sequences of essays stand out. One, which in English one might call "Economy and Society," is at once an explication of various fundamental sociological categories and a set of observations on the generic properties of the strategic constituent phenomena of complicated societies. In this connection Weber proposes his famous analysis of authority and of bureaucracy. He writes about forms of social stratification and of ethnic association, about the market-place as well as about the city. The series includes lengthy analyses of the domains of law and of religion. It ends with an essay on music—which, had Weber lived longer, would presumably have been the first in another series of essays devoted to the social relations of art.

Even his most well known series, the essays on religious systems, is in fact incomplete. He was to have filled the gap between the end of the essay on ancient Judaism and the beginning of the essay on Luther and Calvin with a corresponding analysis of the early Christian church. If Weber did have one central intellectual concern, it was with the relations between the major domains within society, seen under the aspect of their change. This involved a concern with the alternative forms of economic life in relation to the alternative forms of moral commitment that have so far provided the structure of history, particularly in the West. He knew how to stay close to important distinctions. If he asked about the conditions necessary for the rise of capitalism, he also assumed that these prerequisites would not be necessary for its maintenance. Concerned with the motives of men, he also was aware that the actions which they impelled would produce unintended consequences. Deeply concerned with the possibilities of freedom within men's actions, he was also concerned with freeing himself from illusions about the conditionality of human actions and the relativity of the moral commitments guiding them. If he saw in the progressive rationalization—facilitated by the engine of bureaucracy—at least one consuming trend in the history of the West, he was not blind to the non- and irrational elements that also guide men.

He was concerned with education and the alternative educational ideals exhibited by the cultures of Greece, of China, of England, and of the contemporary industrialized West. He also saw that educational ideals and practices are discussed and implemented within a going society, whose course of change is always affected by the intended and unintended economic and associated social arrangements that give it shape.

In reading Weber, one can see him in many ways. He may be seen as a man struggling alike against the vague, even irresponsible, claims of the German idealistic and intuitionist tradition of his time, and against the too narrow perspective of a classical Marxian analysis. Or one can read him as a man truly imprisoned by a productive inner treadmill that seeks to declare the anatomy of capitalism and of the inward alternative meanings of Hindu or Confucian or Hebraic or Puritan thought. At the same time, he was engaged in politics; he went to Versailles in 1918; he engaged in political polemics. It is not surprising that the center of gravity of his explicit categorial system is action, and the ways of relating ends and means that are in fact open to the individual. If his work does not include an attempt at a systematic view of human character, Weber's particular greatness appears in its most distilled form in the chapter on the sociology of religion that forms part of his two-volume work on the economy and society. In the twelve sections of this chapter, he reduces the idiosyncratic profusion of a large range of history, and uses types and distinctions that make the systematic study of society feasible.

In the section on estates, classes, and religion, the mutual relations between styles of life, economic position, and forms of religious commitment are masterfully discussed. He shows, for example, how, within the circles of privileged groups, an idea of dignity is consonant with a certain antipathy to salvation religions; while less privileged people are inclined to complement their present deprivation by a concern with future amelioration. In Weber's view, the privileged man receives confirmation of his dignity from the state of things already surrounding him; by contrast, the under-privileged nourishes his sense of dignity on notions of "calling," "function," and "mission." In their intention, these concepts are transcendent.

But out of context, this description is too simple, and unfair to Weber. Yet the full context of Weber's writings is still available in English only unevenly, in a variety of different translations.[11]

Considering Weber, then, makes the previous contrast between Durkheim and Simmel become a more complicated triangle. Durkheim wanted to formulate relatively precise proposals concerning the relations between the structure of social rela-

---

11. This was written before the appearance of Reinhard Bendix's most helpful *Max Weber: An Intellectual Portrait* (New York: Doubleday, 1960).

tions and identifiable, preferably measurable, specific patterns of events; Weber stated a far-flung and wild profusion of connections between the understandable orientation of different circles in any one society and the characteristic features of the economic, legal, educational, and class characteristics of the same society. Simmel was continuously concerned with the structure of *relations* of two or more people and the paradoxical formulations necessary for their essential characterization; Weber seems more concerned with the conditions of individual action and their intended or unintended consequences, when these are observed within the context of variously distributed styles of life and forms of power. What Simmel enjoys as paradox, Weber suffers as antinomy. Weber confronts us with the conflict between traditional and rational consideration, between an ethic of intention and an ethic of responsibility, between the educational ideal of a specialized and technical expert and that of a cultivated gentleman. More than Simmel and Durkheim, Weber is a pessimist—but a pessimist who is also a stoic. He is free from self-pity.

The study of the perspective necessary for the analysis of society is not the same as the study of the personalities of those who helped create these perspectives. Yet it is equally certain that the theories proposed or the problems selected for analysis presuppose certain combinations of human qualities. In other words, people who are alienated or self-pitying, or resentful about the strivings and circumstances of others whom they wish to understand, are likely to propose different formulations from those proposed by others who are stoic, compassionate, or morally incensed. It is vitally important not to confuse a knowledge of the origins of a view with an assessment of its claim. Jealousy can generate insights which are no less valid for being the fruits of jealousy. Yet certain insights may grow only on the grounds of qualities like courage, compassion, or commitment. This problem must be left unsolved, though the study of society continually poses it.

The readers of this Reader should form their own image of the progression and coherence in the work of the above men and others. There is, after all, more than one way of regarding the direction and whole of their work.

ON THE TIMING OF THE BIRTH
OF SOCIOLOGY

Only living creatures are born in a single act of parturition; a scientific discipline, like sociology, has no clear single beginning. Inherently, it has no end. Still, before the nineteenth century, there was no sociology—at least, none in the sense in which this Reader and these Introductions use the term. Yet, since Comte first coined the expression "sociology," the sociological developments that have occurred would have been impossible without ideas, distinctions, and procedures that had taken many centuries to become settled possessions of the intellectuals, particularly in the Occident.

Sociology is a bastard term: it has a Latin beginning, a Greek ending, and many intervening and variable meanings. Comte conceived it as a positive science—as part of the great effort to master life and the world through the impersonal accomplishments of a human reason that had freed itself of what, in retrospect, would then become recognized as the less reliable and less true claims of religion or philosophy. He conceived it as a discipline yielding laws and providing statements of interpreted fact that had the authority of the formulations of physical science. He saw sociology as providing, eventually, means of predicting and of having power over social events. His explicit hopes, and the appropriateness and possibility of their implementation, have led to much argument. We are still debating the precise range of variation of ideas and procedures that the single expression "science" can accommodate, or the exact boundaries that separate it from other forms of knowledge, like literature. There is no simple consensus, either, on the minimal conditions that a discipline must meet before it may appropriately be called a science, or on the actual differences between the social, biological, and physical sciences. The logic of these matters is compounded by considerations of power and honor.

Scientific disciplines are not valued equally within a society. Their fortunes are uneven, and they are subject, among other forces, to destruction by unfavorable political climates. The history of sociology in Germany during the last sixty years fully illustrates this. Still, Comte asserted the systematic intelligibility of social phenomena—and gave this understanding a name that implied methods. These methods were to make the understanding a great scientific enterprise, which in turn would benefit a mankind growing reasonable through practicing the methods and benefiting from their results. The vision has been scattered—in various ways, the component elements of Comte's conceptions have become distributed over the work of his successors. The dependence of science, itself an organized and social pattern of efforts, on institutions, climates of opinion, and specially motivated and trained people, has become established beyond question. The controversy about the actual difference between social and natural science continues. Still, social phenomena—for all their intelligibility and their frequent, almost impersonal, yet constraining "there-ness"—have become irrevocably defined to include a recognition of the fact that they are sustained among persons; they involve previous notions of appropriateness and depend on some emotional involvement of variously placed participants. At some point, it is necessary to ask, in explaining a social phenomenon, with what meaning one or more persons began or continued a sequence of events. Such events are perceived as forming (or coming from) a pattern of regularities that no one person, or plurality of persons, intended. Wars, birth rates, cities, the uneven participation of a few people in a small gathering, the role conflicts of foremen, the volume of suicide and divorce, the class structure of a community—no one intends these, no one can, alone and directly, bring them about. Yet they presuppose persons, or persons intending to form others into persons, who can ask questions or keep quiet, expect others and themselves to do certain things and not do certain other things, draw lines between what makes (common) sense and what does not. Comte clearly argued that such lines are unreliable. Society involves people's ideas concerning it. Yet these ideas may, through being incomplete or mistaken, be quite erroneous. Our economy is apprehended, by a majority, with a mixture of ignorance and distortion; the extent of this mixture might be discovered by research.

Comte and Spencer, without so expressing it, intended to found a discipline that would confront the varied and subjective experience those who in fact constitute society have of it, with a body of reliable (i.e., objective) knowledge concerning the social order. We know that such knowledge must proceed with reference to the subjective experiences of people. The very order of these experiences, and their divergencies from facts collected by a differently placed observer, constitute, at least, in part, that which is to be explained. The vision of Comte and Spencer also included the desire to see the historical and geographic expanse of society, and its fragmentary appearance to individuals, as a valid whole. They were content to realize such desires through the help of ideas from biology and physics. History has demonstrated that the use of such analogies is both inevitable and precarious. Societies are not organisms; yet the idea of function implied in the biological usage of the term *organism* is a useful device for declaring the natural connection, often hidden, between a variety of recurrent events.

Unlike the growth of organisms, the growth of sociology as a field has occurred through its becoming smaller in its reach. Having become concerned with "making findings," it is no longer free from arranging social reality into technically manageable pieces or areas. This has led to a process of inner differentiation. Recently, it has posed problems of the coherence of such efforts. I shall return to these matters in another section of this set of observations on the development of sociological analysis.

To the question, "What explanation is available for the timing of the birth of sociology?" we can give no single or definite answer. We know that the thought of children has its timetable. One of the most productively single-minded and devoted students of the individual history of the categories and logic of adult thinking, Jean Piaget, has persuasively demonstrated the shifts by which we arrive, so far as we do, at the ability to think logically. It is probable that there are some parallels between individual and social development. In biology, this parallel is expressed in the famous dictum: ontogeny recapitulates phylogeny. Yet this mode of thought, unless great caution is exercised, is likely to repeat the errors of Comte and Spencer. The relation between groups and individuals is, after all, different from the relations between individuals and their species or phyla. Besides, the social sciences, as late arrivals, do not represent a mode of knowing and explaining that is "higher" or "more adult"— whatever these ambiguous yet inescapable terms may mean—than the forms of knowledge, be they physics, mathematics, or chemistry, that preceded them. At times, however, people seem inclined to see, in the precision and determinateness of the physical sciences, an unambiguous model for the straggling, late arrival of the social sciences. We cannot stop to wonder now whether many sociologists, with notable exceptions, have, at least until quite recently, had little working acquaintance with the inner struggles of physical science, historically and individually—whether they have exaggerated their precision and neatness, and have then applied models to their own work that are valid for no scientific work.

In reaction against this, some have suggested that social science is, after all, an art. In these terms, the debate seems fast becoming a matter of past misunderstandings and ambiguities. The genuine elements of the debate, as well as the fruitfulness of its very errors, must concern us presently; here, let it suffice to suggest that any explanation of the historic sequence of scientific disciplines must first free itself from those conceptions of a hierarchy (as distinct from a sequence) of the sciences that inspired Comte. This error may have been (psychologically, if not logically) necessary for his conception of sociology. Retrospectively, "correct" as well as "incorrect" ideas are fruitful in the arduous process of accumulating valid proposals about the character of social phenomena.

Our question about the birth of sociology has become complicated. Why was it founded at Comte's time? We also want to know why the sequence of scientific disciplines has taken the form it has. This leads to the question: Under what conditions, if any, could the history of science have been very different? Could Newton and Adam Smith have done their work in reverse chronological order? We shall be concerned with answers to these and other implied questions, to the extent to which they ultimately help define and reveal the structure and history of social arrangements. We shall assume that deliberately gathered knowledge grows only under some social conditions, that a line of intellectual effort continues to pose new tasks, and that science yields many consequences for social arrangements. The last may take the more obvious and massive forms of technology or of the practices of various professions, like medicine. They can occur as conflicts between various circles within a society or within persons. The history of sociology has included a part in the ostensible conflict between religion and science. One might even suggest that the development of the social sciences itself is an aspect of the rationalization and disenchantment of the world—to employ terms which some, notably Max Weber, have used to characterize broad historic tendencies and directions of the drift of social change by which we come to recognize some of the differences between the present and the past.

The social consequences of the sciences are huge and subtle. They include the creation of special institutional forms for the recruitment and training of people capable of sustaining scientific work. They also include the necessity for formal and informal arrangements whereby the continuous dialogue between common sense and divergent discovery may be absorbed by a society, both through a continuous and almost imperceptible process of revising ideas, and through concentrated crises. The debate about evolution and the resultant Scopes trial in the United States, the discussion of the Dead Sea Scrolls, book burning, or the commemoration of men defined as great—e.g., Freud, Durkheim, Simmel, Darwin—are illustrations of such crises or turning points. But they are not sufficient to account for the difference between, e.g., a Detroit automobile worker's conception of nature and society in the 1950's and the conceptions of a Greek slave, an Old Testament Israelite shepherd, a medieval tinsmith in Paris, and a nineteenth-century wall painter in Germany.

This drift is borne along by events within and outside it. By Comte's time, it had accomplished some remarkable combinations of qualities. Physics and chemistry were established. A growing technology and a growing romanticism helped shape the nineteenth century. Biology was about to extend radically our knowledge of organisms as a type of order, by stating regularities concerning the historical succession of organisms. In turn, this involves the *relations* among organisms and between them and the environment. The nineteenth century included the fast-growing establishment of industry and of technology in general, expressing both mastery—and potentially more leisure for more people—and some kind of victimization. Machines can be experienced as the source of boredom and as alien tools.

Marx had much to say on this score. He indicated the processes which he felt divided society increasingly into exploiters and exploited. He linked social diagnosis with political ideology, just as theology had earlier been linked with a view of man. But there was far more than that: the pessimism of Malthus; the Darwinian definition of existence as involving a struggle; the prudery of the Victorians; the increasing ugliness in the growing cities; Nietzsche's call for a certain inner honesty and strength; the discovery—through better communication—of the variedness and consequent relativity of beliefs and moral commitments; the contradictory clamor of romanticism and technological advance, socialist counter-ideologies and rising entrepreneurs; nationalist developments (particularly in Germany, Italy, and France); and, at the end of the century, the discovery through systematic thought, that a "true" image of man must allow far more room for his "irrationality."

In retrospect, it would seem that sociology could have developed only when a certain kind of puzzlement (and even practical urgency) coincided with a faith in inquiry and a disbelief in both "revealed" truths concerning the immediate character of man and his arrangements, and in "rational speculation." The relatively late development of the social sciences in the history of science—if one may put it that way—can be attributed in part to the character of society itself. Only after its complexity becomes compounded by industrialization and its many associated features do conditions arise requiring or facilitating the deliberate and impersonal analysis of personal and social phenomena. This assertion does not imply that the study of society is only as old as the term *sociology*—that would be a silly error. Everything has many forerunners. Here, we are concerned only with the relatively systematic study of social phenomena, carried on within es-

tablished institutions of the society under examination.

Sociology requires a variety of dissociations. It
thrives on the distinction between normative and
existential propositions. It must distinguish, almost
ruthlessly, a concern with "what is" from a concern
with "what ought to be," while also remembering
that the relative "openness" of the social order always makes it relevant to ask the further, yet equally
distinct, question: What can be? It must retain a
keen sense of these distinctions, precisely because
many of its facts are, in fact, constituted by the
moral judgments of persons in their capacities as
members, representatives, or detractors of the multitude of separate and overlapping social arrangements comprising a society.

Yet social arrangements themselves involve judgments and commitments of importance and of
appropriateness, as well as various bodies of knowledge or opinion concerning the nature of things—
including people. In reality, these judgments are
intermingled. Grammatically, they are often confused. The "self-evident truth" that men are born
equal is really a moral decision, to see, running
across men's uniqueness and their difference, an
equal right to certain kinds of opportunity. Only as
moral judgments within the same sphere of decision
become subject to varied controversy can a previous
fusion of moral commitments, opinions about the
world, and participation in society be dissolved. It
is only when such dissolution affects a number of
people and challenges them to share a like interest
in its examination that a discipline like sociology
can gain momentum. Once begun, such an examination necessarily means questioning any and all
social facts. Yet societies involve a measure of secrecy and sacredness, as part of the potent notions
of privacy and security; secrecy also inheres in the
use of power. Ironically enough, sociology began to
flourish just when *private* capitalist enterprise
gained great momentum and extended earlier traditions of individualism. Sociology owes much of
its impetus in this connection to Durkheim, who
demonstrated cogently that individualism itself is
a form of social arrangement, and that the disparate
goals of lonely strivers after wealth, salvation, happiness, or amusement are possible only as the other
side of a consensus that demands and allows this
very disparateness.

While Comte and Spencer were, in a sense, the
founders of sociology, one might also refer to them
as protosociologists and consider that sociology
really originated with Durkheim and Weber. Durkheim is the first to make the social order deliberately
problematic and, as such, an object of disinterested
inquiry. This involves a radical break with the past;
but, once this break has been made, sociologists'
efforts can be shown, as in this Reader, to exhibit
important continuities with the past. Ultimately,
the questions that sociologists ask today are con-
tinuations of the questions that Hobbes asked.

It has been the theme of this essay, though, that
the growth of sociology involves, as a necessary, not
as a sufficient, condition, an accomplishment of
dissociation. This must proceed on at least two
planes. The human order, with its gravitation toward questions of meaning and of value, must be
distinguished from the non-human order. Within
the human order, the distinction between personal
and impersonal patterns must be clear. Distinctions,
of course, do not deny continuities; properly used,
they warn against reductionism. When reductionism is avoided, one is free to see parallels in, e.g.,
biological and social evolution, and continuities
between the organic realm and the motives of
human personalities.

Perhaps, again, the dissociation of society into
ostensibly independent actors and seekers is a
precondition for the search for the anatomy of
society. This search, to return to the previous point,
can logically have no end. It cannot exclude the
secret or the sacred—both of which are necessary
features of *all* societies, as subsequent thought and
research has now clearly shown. Sociology cannot
proceed, therefore, until a radical measure of intellectual freedom is safe. This freedom is continuous
with the freedom requisite for the physical sciences,
but presents its own additional complications. The
social sciences benefited from the struggles that had
to be fought, against a variety of vested interests, so
that the theories of Newton or Galileo, the dissection of the body, and the teaching of evolution
could be sufficiently accepted as legitimate resources in the further development of valid
knowledge.

The only writer prominent in these two volumes
whose thought involved him in serious and continuing conflict with significant parts of his social
environment was Freud. If a dramatic struggle with
an opposing world is a necessary mark for greatness
of intellect, sociology has not produced many great
men so far. In any case, sociology depends on the
freedom to see the constraining and liberating
qualities of social arrangements, while looking beyond their "heaviness" and treating any one group
or institution as though it could also be otherwise.

In that sense, sociology is a curious mixture of
a most sober and secular effort to state the processes
through which society achieves its order, and standing beyond that order with a perspective that is
logically akin to utopianism but does not seek after
perfection. The growth of sociology requires dis-

tance; it demands participants who observe. It calls for small- and large-scale "accounting" of the measurable facts, just as economics depends for its growth on the availability of a variety of statistics concerning production, consumption, gross national products, etc. The nineteenth century saw the large-scale development of keeping national accounts of economic, demographic, and medical facts. The arrangement of such facts into rates further symbolizes the non-personal elements in personal affairs.

Many additional considerations must be brought into mutual relation and focus for a proper explanation of the timing of the rise of sociology. A child must learn that the world contains more than human motives; the history of science proceeded almost in the reverse direction.

CONCLUSION

During its hundred years or so of formal existence, sociological questioning has clarified its focus and widened its concern. Ultimately, the widely distributed efforts at comprehending birth rates and triangles, voting and trade unions, professional activities and the pursuit of leisure, circle about the chronic questions: What are the persistent properties of social relations and the arrangements they imply? What range of combinations do and can social relations assume, and how do these combinations come about, change, or cease? As argued above, these questions lead to efforts on more than one plane within the boundary of the social. Today, inevitably, they also lead to attempts to realign, into productive combinations, the social and cognate concerns with the psychological or the cultural components of life in society. Their proper distinction and combination, leading to a productive division of labor and coherence of effort, is a matter of continuous experiment and revision.

Such experiment and revision can take the form of concerted efforts, in a given and circumscribed area of empirical research, by people trained in different disciplines. Issues of culture and personality, mental illness, national character, the structure of small groups, etc., have become occasions for collaboration among anthropologists, social and clinical psychologists, sociologists, and psychiatrists. At present, sociology is also re-establishing a solid interest in phenomena traditionally labeled as "political" or "economic" and, as such, "reserved" for political scientists or economists.

Co-operation among sociologists committed to

seemingly very different theoretical perspectives has been far less frequent. Yet these volumes are likely to be read by a generation of younger sociologists who are taught, if not involved in, a *convergence* of theoretical positions. This convergence—for which there already exist diverse formulations—is accompanied by the growth of inner differentiation. Such growth involves various fashions and fads. It also leads to the founding of special, more or less formal, groupings devoted to a specific line of inquiry, such as research on public opinion, on medical institutions, on social problems, or on industrial organization.

The multitude of sociological endeavors that go on today bear a relation to the past. They also yield an emergent coherence, discussed by Edward Shils at the end of this Reader.

The past, from which we have selected, has here been ordered into an arrangement that is only one of several possible arrangements of these materials. It is, however, not an arbitrary arrangement. The general rationale behind it is discussed in the other introductory essay. These selections illustrate the several planes of sociological analysis. In one way, as stated, the most persistent concern has been with the generic properties of social relations themselves, about which one may well ask: What kind of an order is the social order? Various answers are represented in this Reader. Malthus and Marx, Hobbes and Machiavelli, Weber and Freud would, if they could discuss it together, weave quite an argument. Their logical differences would first be obscured by their different preferences for a starting point and for the respective features of social reality which each prefers to dissect. Their differences might be ordered with reference to a few further questions.

Eventually, they would have to contrast the social form of coherence to other forms of coherence, like those of nature, music, mathematics, or an individual. Various alternatives seem open. Society can be conceived as an entirely natural phenomenon, thus preventing it from escaping systematic inquiry and becoming an ideal or mystic, or even partly supernatural, phenomenon. One can insist that the "natural" is a relatively narrower category and that the "non-natural" comprises a variety of orders, some admitting of scientific exploration. One can leave ultimate questions of reality open, but insist on some provisional distinctions—such as the differences between mechanical, organic, and psychological processes—which in turn stand for the assumption that there is coherence in a working electric range and a bridge party, in a jumping frog and in a man's contemplation during a Quaker meeting. They are coherences that are *similar* and *different*. Their similarity consists in their being, at least in principle, equally open to scientific research; their difference consists in the fact that the distinctions necessary to explain their occurrence or operation would be seriously different.

The constitution of social coherence, in its contrasts or similarity to other coherences, including nature, is a basic theme with sociological theorists. This has been accompanied by three additional themes: Section C of Part One of the Reader introduces one of these, just as the first two sections of Part One introduce the theme of the constitution of social relations. Section C raises the questions: What kinds or forms of social coherence is it necessary or useful to distinguish? What sorts of social relations—and with the help of the combination of what recurrent variables—must be analytically separated? What types of society is it necessary to recognize?

To a degree, this is the theme of classification. Classification is not sufficient for scientific development; but it is assuredly necessary—logically as well as historically. The history of biology bears out this contention most unequivocally.

The growth of sociological theory has, then, included a persistent concern with alternative ways of defining the major elements of social relations—alternatively labeling them actions, norms, ends, means, roles, expectations, and so forth—and then finding ways of distinguishing kinds of them. Such effort has reached up and down; it has included attempts to formulate, e.g., types of society, types of authority, types of groups, types of kinship systems.

A third theme has been to distinguish more inclusive coherences, like communities or national societies, and to propose a steady way for designating their component "spheres." Part Two of the Reader takes up this theme. Together, these themes provide a framework for finding and stating regularities that then need explanation. They confront common sense with the possibilities of seeing connections where our experience might show none; and of proposing distinctions in areas where, impelled by the economy of having to act, we must as acting members of society, "lump things together" in order not to be paralyzed by a sense of complexity.

A further theme, then, has been to state the processes by which social arrangements cohere, endure, change, begin, or end. Less, perhaps, is said directly about this in this Reader than is said about the other themes. Nevertheless, the last three parts contain some relevant material. Theoretical developments that have taken place since our self-imposed time limits have made substantial contributions to this theme of the dynamic of social arrangements.

Two additional themes may now be identified. One concerns the link—and, therefore, the distinction—between social coherences (in the form of formal organizations or purely voluntaristic relations, like those of friendship) and personality, on the one hand, or culture, on the other. Or, more broadly: in what sense is the social a reality *sui generis*? What kind of autonomy does this imply? What kinds of dependence do social arrangements sustain to different kinds of other orders, be these systems of expression and meaning (like language), personalities, or various kinds of non-social conditions, like numbers of people, spatial possibilities, states of organic functioning?

The other theme is related to a matter of method. Lack of space prevented us from discussing the craft of research and developments of specific techniques as integral elements of the development of sociological theory. Yet the Reader as a whole is, in fact, a declaration of sociological questioning. Questions imply a method and demand techniques. Sociology, as a discipline—and, hence, a method—of inquiry deals with the facts of which history is made. In the name of experimentation, it can also create small passages of history. Yet it differs from history as a discipline. It is concerned with regularities. They can be studied only in time and place, but their formulation seeks to be more generally valid and to be applicable to the future. The twin face of sociology—its inevitable link to history, albeit often immediate history, and to the analytic enterprise of discovering regularities indifferent to the uniqueness of events—is best prevented from becoming a caricature by a deliberately comparative perspective.

Comparison can take several forms and proceed on several planes. Much of Max Weber's work has been included in this Reader. On the planes of world religions, national societies, and the interdependence of the spheres of the economy, the polity, and normative orientations, he has used historic comparison. Comparison is possible only when one combines a vivid sense of the variedness of social relations and the relativity of cultural facts with a steady sense of the recurrent features of social arrangements. It remains a difficult task to formulate these features in such a way that one is not unduly influenced by one rather than another pattern of culture and society. Much social reality is sufficiently "soft" that one can read into it interpretations which cannot be clearly corrected. Interpretations of social facts, moreover, become themselves the grounds for additional facts. Their occurrence is no proof of the correctness of one's original claims. Comparison—beyond the point where it inheres in the use of logical reasoning and proof as such—seems to mark the best sociological writing.

In this way, the simplicity and elusiveness of society moves properly into view. Much sociological writing seems suspended between two images. One of these conceives of society as the arrangements of sleepwalkers; and the other, as a play involving both actors and audience, a stage and a realm behind the scene. Obviously, both images are appropriate, and both are incomplete. Nor can sociologists seek after completeness: completeness is the privilege of art. Social action goes far beyond sleepwalking and play-acting. Rational planning and ritual, the deliberate creation of new communities and the destruction of old prerogatives, the serious life—all these are social facts. The excerpts assembled here will surely help in the progressive understanding and explanation of the characteristic ways in which social relations combine simplicity with complexity and unconscious resources with self-awareness.

II. *An Outline of the Social System*

BY TALCOTT PARSONS

THIS SECOND PART OF THE GENeral Introduction is designed to present an outline of the main conceptual resources of current sociological theory. It is necessarily incomplete in at least two ways. First, it is inevitably a personal statement, using components and the ways of organizing them that seem most strategic to the author. Any discerning reader will recognize that these materials come from many sources. But this is not meant to be a scholarly essay in the history of theory, attempting to document the immense diversity of sources and influences. It is, on the contrary, guided by a conviction of the enormous significance of the element of system in the theory of any scientific discipline. Because of this, great attention had to be given to the systematic fit of the different theoretical components, regarding both their selection and their empirical significance. At the present stage of theoretical development, any such systematic attempt must be tentative. Major changes are to be expected, as have indeed occurred within the course even of its relatively mature development.

Second, this outline is incomplete because, long as it is for an introduction, it is a mere fragment of what would be required to make the best possible case for systematic theory by outlining an adequate systematic theory; this would clearly require a major treatise.[1] Thus, the present essay is deficient in conceptual precision. It includes only a very fragmentary statement of the logical, methodological, and empirical grounds for selecting such concepts. Furthermore, the development it presents is incomplete, and the application to empirical materials is merely illustrative.

The principal gain, however, bought at the cost of these and doubtless other deficiencies, is the attempt to cover all the main problems that a systematic theory must face.

This attempt has been based on the conviction that there are two essential reference points for this type of systematic analysis: a classification of the functional requirements of a system and the arrangement of these with reference to processes of control in the cybernetic sense. More specifically, the theory of social systems belongs within the more general class of conceptual schemes seen in the frame of reference of *action*. Within that framework, the boundaries of social systems have been defined in terms of their relations, first to each other, then to the behavioral organism, to the personality of the individual, and to cultural systems. The relation to the physical environment is mediated through these others, and hence is not direct. Seen in this context, a social system is always "open," engaged in processes of interchange with environing systems.

It will further be held that most empirically significant sociological theory must be concerned with complex systems, that is, systems composed of many subsystems. Hence the primary empirical type-reference has been to the society, which, in the nature of the case, is highly complex.

The basic functional classification underlying the whole scheme involves the discrimination of four primary categories: pattern-maintenance, integration, goal-attainment, and adaptation, placed in that order in the series of control-relations. But, on another axis, it has been necessary to discriminate the structural components of such systems. These will always constitute patterns of institutionalized normative culture, differentiated both functionally and by levels of specification and of segmentation of units of the system. The structural classification is organized about the concepts of system values, institutionalized norms, collectivities, and roles.

It will also be necessary to categorize and classify

---

1. From the author's point of view this would take the form of a rather far-reaching revision of his earlier book, *The Social System* (1951). To be reasonably adequate, the result would have to be a longer book than that one was (about 550 pages).

the resources involved in the interchange processes, not only between a society and its environing systems, but between subsystems within the society. From these, finally, must be distinguished the regulatory mechanisms, like money, which are involved in dynamic process.

More generally, a fundamental distinction will be made between the morphological analysis of the structure of systems and the "dynamic" analysis of process. Neither has special priority over the other except that, at a particular level, stable structural reference points are necessary for determining generalizations about process. Furthermore, with respect to process, it is necessary to distinguish the "equilibrium" level of analysis, which assumes structure to be given, from the "structural change" level, which attempts to explain such processes of change. In the empirical analysis of complex systems, however, it is almost always necessary to assume some structural elements to be given while analyzing processes of change in others, particularly changes in the structure of subsystems of the more extensive system.

These seem to be the minimum of theoretical problems and components which must be taken into account in any sociological theory that lays claim to systematic generality. We think that all of them grow out of the work of the authors of the selections which follow. Considerable variations from their proposals here put forward would probably result if other contemporary theorists attempted such a task. But we think they would be primarily variations of emphasis, rather than departures from the basic theoretical structure with which we are concerned. Whether or not this is true, only critical reaction to this and other attempts, and to theoretical analysis of empirical data, can tell. Such reaction will be one of the most important tests of how far sociology can be said to be on the way to consolidation as a genuine theoretically codified field of science.

It may also help the reader's orientation to this introductory material if something is said about the stages by which it has developed in the author's own work. The most important sources are: for the central conception of the social system and the bases of its integration, the work of Durkheim; for the comparative analysis of social structure and for the analysis of the borderline between social systems and culture, that of Max Weber; and for the articulation between social systems and personality, that of Freud. The first main stage of thinking was documented, in terms of critical analysis of the work of several other theorists, in *The Structure of Social Action* (1937). A new phase of theoretical integration, particularly involving systematization of the general frame of reference of action and the articulation of social systems with those of culture and of personality, was documented in the two publications, *Toward a General Theory of Action*, in collaboration with Shils and others, and *The Social System* (both 1951). The scheme was further systematized and extended, particularly by consolidating the "pattern variables" into the scheme of the four fundamental functional problems of all systems of action, in *Working Papers in the Theory of Action*, with Bales and Shils (1953). The articulation between social systems and personality, with special reference to the process of socialization, was further explored in *Family, Socialization and Interaction Process*, with Bales and others (1955); finally, the present phase of the analysis of input-output relations and of the relations between a total social system and its subsystems was further developed in *Economy and Society*, with Smelser (1956).

Some Areas of Current Theoretical Consensus

Part I of this General Introduction has rightly stressed the indefiniteness of the boundaries of sociology and the ways in which these have tended to shift. The diversity of points of view from which important questions have been and may be asked, and of the frames of reference in which answers may be obtained, has also been discussed.

However, we believe that there is a substantial element of cumulative continuity, which becomes the more clearly visible when seen in temporal perspective. This element of continuity can be observed at different levels. In certain very general terms, something approaching consensus can be claimed among those who may be considered professionally competent. But, as the content of theory becomes more particularized, agreement tends to give way to a war of conflicting schools. Even here, however, the question of just how deep these differences are is a relevant one. It is our conviction that much explicit disagreement conceals implicit consensus.[2]

2. In my own case, this conviction was firmly established as a result of the work done in connection with *The Structure of Social Action,* referred to above. That study dealt primarily with four major figures in the theory of social systems of the generation from approximately 1890–1915: Alfred Marshall, Vilfredo Pareto, Emile Durkheim, and Max Weber. Judging by the secondary literature available at the time, they should be considered as diverse in points of view as any four thinkers one could have picked. It was possible, however, to demonstrate that their major conceptual schemes converged in terms of a common frame of reference and, at certain levels, a common substantive theoretical system. This common scheme was not confined to the work of these four men; with important further developments, it has been just as central to subsequent work.

Probably the greatest consensus exists regarding the applicability to our discipline of the general canons of scientific method. The battle about whether science is possible in the field of human social behavior may be said to be over in its main phase, however much may remain to be settled on many of the subtler points, particularly the borderline problems.

This agreement clearly includes the role of theory in science and the nature of the conceptual schemes which scientific theory employs; most scholars would accept the basic methodological premises formulated in the work of such writers as A. N. Whitehead, L. J. Henderson, and James B. Conant. Despite differences of emphasis and preference for personal types of work, the old battle of theory *versus* empiricism may be considered to be over. The same may be said regarding the merits of nomothetic *versus* ideographic modes of conceptualization. Logically, the situation seems to be entirely parallel to that of heredity and environment in the biological sciences, where the formulation in terms of "versus" is now largely obsolete. Since this Reader is concerned with the development of theory, consensus on this point is vital.

With regard to theory itself as a vital component of organized scientific knowledge, and to theoretical formulations as crucial tools of investigation, two somewhat more specific points may also be claimed as fundamental and generally accepted. The first of these is the role of analytical abstraction in all the more general theoretical schemes of science. Theoretical schemes are made up of concepts and logically interrelated propositions. To be capable of logical manipulation, such schemes must always be relatively simple and cannot possibly embrace everything empirically knowable about the concrete phenomena at hand. They must select, i.e., abstract, according to their own criteria of relevance to theoretical problems.

Finally, the concept of system is also vital to science. Besides empirical validity and conceptual precision, there are two other essential criteria of the scientific usefulness of sets of theoretical propositions, namely, their level of generality with reference to empirical phenomena and their logical integration with each other. The concept of system is essentially nothing but an application of the criterion of logical integration of generalized propositions. That is, theoretical propositions are scientifically useful in so far as they are general and are related in such ways that data accounted for by one proposition may, by logical inference, be shown to have implications for data that should fit into other propositions in the set. The difference between description and theoretical explanation is precisely that between the isolation of particular propositions and their integration with each other in such ways that logical inference is possible.

Logical integration, or systematization, is in this sense a matter of degree. The ideal, however, is a system of propositions so related that their logical *inter*dependence is complete, so that all the propositions in the system can be rigorously derived from a set of primary postulates and definitions. Few schemes of scientific theory have approached this goal, but it remains the ideal and provides essential critical canons. We do not claim, of course, that the scheme presented here possesses anything approaching complete logical integration.

Systematization of theory clearly implies the concept of *empirical* system as its counterpart; this follows from the point made about analytical abstraction. If theory is to be empirically relevant, it must present demonstrably verifiable patterns of interdependence among empirical phenomena. In order to do this, however, it must delineate and classify phenomena according to criteria of relevance and importance. An empirical system, then, is a body of presumptively interdependent phenomena to which a given abstract analytical scheme is presumptively relevant. It is impossible to study everything at once empirically. An empirical system is a theoretically defined field of relevant phenomena, with reference to which certain problem-statements have been abstracted.

So far, the points of agreement have concerned matters common to all the empirical sciences. Approaching our own field more closely, another crucial point should be made, namely, that the study of human social behavior necessarily involves a frame of reference here called "action." The term itself is not important. But the content it refers to is highly so. Essentially, it means a type of theoretical scheme incompatible with the form of "reductionism" characteristic of a great deal of our earlier scientific tradition. Action treats behavior as "goal-directed," as "adaptive," as "motivated," and as guided by symbolic processes. The concept of culture as developed in anthropology is crucial here. Another way of putting the matter is that neither the theory of mechanics in the older sense nor that of nineteenth-century physiology would be adequate if simply "applied" to the behavioral field.

A major focus of this problem was the "behaviorist" controversy of the 1920's. The behaviorist position was a major example of reductionism and tended to deny the scientific legitimacy of all "subjective" categories, of all concepts of "meaning." As in the battles over the status of science itself and over empiricism in this area, it can be said that the fight is over. Sociological theory today is clearly couched in terms of motives, goals, symbols, meanings, means and ends, and the like.

In short, I have suggested that general agreement exists regarding the relevance of the classical canons of scientific method; the significance of analytical theory within this method; the necessity of analytical abstraction for theory; the concept of system; and, finally, the "action" frame of reference. For purposes of defining the subject matter of sociology, one more point of agreement can be presumed, namely, that the empirical systems with which sociology is concerned involve the *inter-action* of pluralities of human[3] individuals. Clearly, the study of the analytically isolated "individual" is not a problem for sociology. In this empirical sense, the concern with "social systems" is one of the hallmarks of sociological interest. But when we remember that a theoretical scheme is based on analytical abstraction, merely pointing to an empirical field is not enough. In order to achieve any high level of theoretical specificity, it is necessary to take positions on a series of other general issues where consensus, even in the sense so far taken for granted, cannot yet be presumed.

It is at this point that the positions held by the editors must be considered. We have had to follow specific policies of selection from a literature far too large to be included through more than a small sample, and we have had to organize the selected material in a relatively definite and coherent way. We do not think that the present level of *explicit* consensus in the field of sociology is high enough to provide an automatic rationale for the policies of selection and organization which must be adopted in order to produce an intelligibly coherent anthology. We have, therefore, frankly and explicitly brought to bear our own views of the most useful and important organization of problems and concepts in the field.

The Concept of Social System

The function of this part of the General Introduction is to present an outline of our concept of social system, in order to make explicit the main considerations that have guided our policies of selection and organization.

Let us start with the issue just mentioned, that of the delineation of the place of social systems within the frame of reference of action. One aspect of the issue, that of the distinction between the

analytically defined "individual"[4] and the systems generated by the process of social interaction, can be taken for granted. But this is not enough for our purposes, primarily because it fails to make another analytically crucial distinction, namely, that between social systems and cultural systems. In the case of the individual-social distinction, the distinction itself is scarcely in question; the difficulties center about its analytical character and the ways of drawing the analytical lines. In the case of the social system-culture distinction, the clear need for such a distinction has only gradually been emerging in sociology and anthropology.[5]

Social and Cultural Systems. In the most important tradition of thought for the English-speaking countries, that growing out of utilitarianism and Darwinian biology, an independent position for the social sciences depended on the delineation of a field of interest which could not simply be subsumed under the rubric of general biology. It was, above all, the rubric of "social heredity" in Spencer's sense, of "culture" in Tylor's sense, which became the main focus of this delineation. Regarded in general biological terms, this field fell clearly in the realm of "environmental" rather than hereditary influence. The category of social interaction played a secondary role at this stage, although it was clearly implicit in Spencer's emphasis on social differentiation.

The common background of modern sociology and anthropology has emphasized a socio-cultural sphere. This sphere had the properties of creating and maintaining a patterned cultural tradition, shared in various ways between the members of living societies and transmitted from generation to generation through learning processes and not through biological inheritance. At the same time, it involved organized systems of structured or "institutionalized" interaction between large numbers of individuals.

In the United States, anthropologists have tended to emphasize the cultural aspect of this complex; sociologists, the interactive aspect. It seems to us important that the two, however empirically inter-

---

3. In the most general sense, sociology should be relevant to all living organisms in so far as they interact, but for present purposes it is not necessary to go beyond the human case.

4. The relevance of the term "analytical" is vital in this connection. All concrete behavior is the behavior of individuals, and no theory of interaction can avoid dealing with *components* of the behavior of individuals. But this is very different from what was referred to above as the "analytically isolated" individual. Some versions of empiricist methodology in psychology have tended to erase this vital distinction by treating psychology not as concerned with the analytically defined individual, or a subsystem of him, but as the "science of behavior." Such a conception clearly makes sociology one type of "applied psychology."

5. Cf. A. L. Kroeber and Talcott Parsons, "The Concepts of Culture and of Social System," *American Sociological Review*, October, 1958.

dependent they may be, should be kept analytically distinct. The social-system focus is on the conditions involved in the interaction of actual human individuals who constitute concrete collectivities with determinate membership. The cultural-system focus, on the other hand, is on "patterns" of meaning, e.g., of values, of norms, of organized knowledge and beliefs, of expressive "form." The basic concept for the integration and interpenetration of the two is *institutionalization,* which will be a subject of much attention in subsequent introductory discussions.

Thus, an essential part of our policy is to distinguish social systems from cultural systems and to treat the former as the primary focus of the analytical concerns of sociological theory. However, the relationships between the two are so intimate that we devote an entire part of our Reader (Part Four) to materials emphasizing and analyzing these relations—including, of course, many selections from the work of authors who themselves did not emphasize the distinction or who in many cases were not even aware of it.

As noted, insistence on an analytically independent socio-cultural realm was a major feature of the intellectual history most relevant to the background of contemporary sociological theory. Essential as this was, its proponents overshot the mark by tending to deny the relevance of social interaction to the subhuman levels of the biological world, as well as the relevance of the subhuman prototypes of human culture. But once the fundamental analytical lines have been established, it becomes easier to attempt to restore this type of balance, and we shall attempt to do so at relevant places in our more detailed introductory materials. The clearest single trend since then has been an increasing insistence on the importance of "motivated" social interaction throughout the biological evolutionary scale, especially in its higher reaches.

Social Systems and "the Individual." Another set of problems has emerged parallel to the basic distinction between the socio-cultural and the "individual" realms. Just as social and cultural systems were not clearly differentiated, the behavior of the "organism" has tended even more predominantly to be treated as a unitary object of scientific analysis by psychologists. At the same time, the problem of the role of learning has been at the center of psychological preoccupation. Correspondingly, there has recently appeared an analytical distinction parallel to that between social and cultural systems, one that discriminates between the "organism" taken as an analytical category, centering on its genetically given constitution so far as this is relevant to the analysis of behavior and, on the other hand, the "personality," the system constituted by the learned components of the *organization* of his behavior.[6]

In organizing our material in the Reader we have not taken explicit account of this distinction, but have put together, in Part Three, all the main materials bearing on the determinants of social behavior relevant to the analytically isolated "individual" and his interdependence with social systems. When we consider these materials in more detail in the introductions to that Part and to its subsections, we will keep this distinction in mind.

Society, Economy, and Polity. Quite clearly, the considerations regarding the principal areas of knowledge located on the boundaries of the theory of social systems concern the broad problem of defining the "jurisdictions" of the disciplines within the behavioral or action area. We do not propose to discuss this problem in detail here. There is, however, another set of problems internal to the social system which should be mentioned before proceeding, problems concerning the place of the subject matters of economics and political science. Clearly, both are disciplines dealing with phases of the functioning of large-scale and differentiated social systems.

Some consider the scope of sociology, in a relatively encyclopedic sense, to include all phases of the structure and functioning of social systems. By this definition, economics and political science would be branches of sociology. This is not, however, our conception. In very general terms, the kind of problem of boundaries which arises between social systems and other types of action systems arises again *within* the social system, becoming more salient as such systems become more highly differentiated. Our view is that the economy and the polity should be treated as functional subsystems within a society. The primary concern of sociology is not with the functioning of these subsystems, but with the other two primary functional subsystems: those concerned with the functions of integration and of "pattern-maintenance." Between the latter, on the one hand, and the economy and polity, on the other, there exists the same order of interdependence and interpenetration that exists between social systems as a whole and cultural and psychological (especially personality) systems.

The economic and political categories occupy prominent places in the organization of the selec-

6. This distinction between (analytically defined) organism and personality was not included in the general analysis of systems of action put forward by Parsons and Shils in *Toward a General Theory of Action* (1951). Emphasis on its importance is a matter of subsequent development. It has been most fully stated in Parsons' "An Approach to Psychological Theory in Terms of the Theory of Action," in Sigmund Koch (ed.), *Psychology: A Study of a Science,* Vol. III (New York: McGraw-Hill, 1959).

tions of Part Two. In dealing with them, however, our main concern will be with institutional structure rather than with the types of functional interconnection most important to the economist and the political scientist. We will select the aspects of economies and polities that are most directly relevant to sociological interest. The rationale of this selective procedure will be more fully explained in two places: later in the present General Introduction and in the Introduction to Part Two.

This rationale will become more evident as we proceed. Though it is true that, historically, the fields of economic and of political theory were defined before that of sociology, it does not follow that the conception of sociology with which we are here working is a residual one. In the first place, in connection with the problem of societal structure, we will deal with the hierarchy of the relations of control in a social system; we will argue that the economic and the political constitute two distinct and relatively well defined levels, the two lowest in the hierarchy from the technical viewpoint of social-system analysis.[7] The other two levels, those dealing with the functions of integration and of pattern-maintenance, are not systematically dealt with in either of the other two disciplines, nor are they, as functions in the social system, merely aspects of culture.

The second reason that sociology is not a residual science is a consequence of the first. The problems of social integration and of pattern-maintenance stand in a different relation to the motivation of the individual than do adaptation and goal-attainment. The latter two are concerned primarily with the mechanisms of "rational" orientation to the conditions of action, a conception most highly developed in economic theory. The former two, on the other hand, have to do with "nonrational" factors, that is, those involved in the operation of *internalized* values and norms. This process, as will be partly developed in this essay, and more extensively in later introductory materials (Introductions to Part One, Section C; to Part Three; and to Part Four), is the essential basis of the phenomenon of *institutionalization* as seen from the point of view of the relation of the individual to his society.

The Organization of Selections in the Reader. It should now be clear that Parts Three and Four are designed to deal with the two fundamental areas of "boundary" problems of social systems: those relating to the individual as a system, and those

relating to the cultural system. The main treatment of the social system, in a more strictly autonomous sense, will be found not only in the introductory materials of Part One but also in Parts Two and Five. These two Parts are broadly distinguished as follows: Part Two deals with the delineation of the structure of social systems, including the institutionalized mechanisms that regulate the processes within the structure; Part Five concentrates upon the problems connected with the structural changes of social systems, the processes by which a given system is transformed into one of a different character, whether it be through structural differentiation or through an alteration of type in a more fundamental sense.

Part One is composed of selections introductory to the main body of the Reader in three different respects. First, as explained in the Preface and elaborated in the preceding section of this General Introduction, we conceive the generation spanning the nineteenth and twentieth centuries as the one which established the main lines of sociological theory today. Before that time, the sociological element was much more diffused in a general tradition which had strong affiliations with the philosophy of history and with a general theory of behavior of the type exemplified by utilitarianism. Section A of Part One is devoted to selections from the literature *preceding* the decisive crystallizing phase of the newer sociological thinking. In this Section, as will be explained more fully in the Foreword devoted specifically to it, we have attempted to present selections embodying the most important conceptual materials utilized by later theorists.

The other two sections of Part One concern the two aspects of what we conceive to be the most central conceptual components underlying the development of a more technical analysis of social systems as such: systems of interaction between individuals. The first of these (Section B) concerns the ways in which the aspects of behavior directly involved in interaction are focused relative to more diffuse conceptions of the general behavior of individuals. These are the conceptual materials that have led to the basic structural concepts of role and collectivity; the two concepts will be more fully explained presently and illustrated in far more detail in the selections in Part Two.

Section C of Part One, finally, concerns the basic phenomenon of "institutionalization." This consists essentially in the integration of cultural-pattern elements at the levels of values and norms with elements of the motivational systems of individuals in such ways as to define and support structured systems of social interaction. The selections here are meant to illustrate some of the most general types

---

7. This view has been most fully developed in *Economy and Society*. With respect to the polity it is somewhat further spelled out in " 'Voting' and the Equilibrium of the American Political System," in E. Burdick and A. J. Brodbeck (eds.), *American Voting Behavior* (Glencoe, Ill.: The Free Press, 1959), especially in the Technical Note.

of insight and analysis underlying the more detailed developments illustrated in the later Parts of the work. The rationale of the selection and organization with respect to all three of these introductory themes will be discussed more fully in the relevant introductions.

A Paradigm for the Analysis of Social Systems

Let us now turn to a more detailed discussion of our conception of a social system. First, the concept of interpenetration implies that, however important *logical* closure may be as a theoretical ideal, *empirically* social systems are conceived as *open* systems, engaged in complicated processes of interchange with environing systems. The environing systems include, in this case, cultural and personality systems, the behavioral and other subsystems of the organism, and, through the organism, the physical environment. The same logic applies internally to social systems, conceived as differentiated and segmented into a plurality of subsystems, each of which must be treated analytically as an open system interchanging with environing subsystems of the larger system.

The concept of an open system interchanging with environing systems also implies *boundaries* and their maintenance. When a set of interdependent phenomena shows sufficiently definite patterning and stability over time, then we can say that it has a "structure" and that it is fruitful to treat it as a "system." A boundary means simply that a theoretically and empirically significant difference between structures and processes internal to the system and those external to it exists and tends to be maintained. In so far as boundaries in this sense do not exist, it is not possible to identify a set of interdependent phenomena as a system; it is merged in some other, more extensive system. It is thus important to distinguish a set of phenomena not meant to constitute a system in the theoretically relevant sense—e.g., a certain type of statistical sample of a population—from a true system.

Structural and Functional Modes of Analysis. Besides identifying a system in terms of its patterns and boundaries, a social system can and should be analyzed in terms of three logically independent— i.e., cross-cutting—but also interdependent, bases or axes of variability, or as they may be called, bases of selective abstraction.

The first of these is best defined in relation to the distinction between "structural" and "functional" references for analysis. However relative these two concepts may be, the distinction between them is highly important. The concept of structure focuses

on those elements of the patterning of the system which may be regarded as independent of the lower-amplitude and shorter time-range fluctuations in the relation of the system to its external situation. It thus designates the features of the system which can, in certain strategic respects, be treated as constants over certain ranges of variation in the behavior of other significant elements of the theoretical problem.

Thus, in a broad sense, the American Constitution has remained a stable reference point over a period of more than a century and a half. During this time, of course, the structure of American society has changed very greatly in certain respects; there have been changes in legal terms, through legislation, through legal interpretations, and through more informal processes. But the federal state, the division between legislative and executive branches of government, the independent judiciary, the separation of church and state, the basic rights of personal liberty, of assembly, and of property, and a variety of other features have for most purposes remained constant.

The functional reference, on the other hand, diverges from the structural in the "dynamic" direction. Its primary theoretical significance is integrative; functional considerations relate to the problem of *mediation* between two fundamental sets of exigencies: those imposed by the relative constancy or "givenness" of a structure, and those imposed by the givenness of the environing situation external to the system. Since only in a theoretically limiting case can these two be assumed to stand in a constant relation to each other, there will necessarily exist a system of dynamic processes and mechanisms.

Concepts like "structure" and "function" can be considered as either concrete or analytical. Our present concern is with their analytical meaning; we wish to state in a preliminary way a fundamental proposition about the structure of social systems that will be enlarged upon later—namely, that their structure as treated within the frame of reference of action *consists* in institutionalized patterns of normative culture. It consists in components of the organisms or personalities of the participating individuals only so far as these "interpenetrate" with the social and cultural systems, i.e., are "internalized" in the personality and organism of the individual. I shall presently discuss the problem of classifying the elements of normative culture that enter into the structure of social systems.

The functional categories of social systems concern, then, those features in terms of which systematically ordered modes of adjustment operate in the changing relations between a given set of patterns of institutionally established structure in the system and a given set of properties of the relevant environing systems. Historically, the most common model on which this relationship has been based is that of the behaving organism, as used in psychological thinking. From this point of view, the functional problem is that of analyzing the mechanisms which make orderly response to environmental conditions possible. When using this model in analyzing social systems, however, we treat not only the environment but the structure of the system as problematical and subject to change, in a sense which goes farther than the traditional behavior psychologist has been accustomed to go.[8]

In interpreting this position, one should remember that the immediately environing systems of a social system are not those of the physical environment. They are, rather, the other primary subsystems of the general system of action—i.e., the personalities of its individual members, the behaviorally organized aspects of the organisms underlying those personalities, and the relevant cultural systems in so far as they are not fully institutionalized in the social system but involve components other than "normative patterns of culture" that are institutionalized.[9]

"Dynamic" Modes of Analysis. The importance of the second basis or axis of empirical variability, and hence of theoretical problem formulation, follows directly. A fundamental distinction must be made between two orders of "dynamic" problems relative to a given system. The first of these concerns the processes which go on under the assumption that the structural patterns of institutionalized culture are given, i.e., are assumed to remain constant. This is the area of problems of *equilibrium* as that concept has been used by Pareto, Henderson, and others, and of homeostasis as used by Cannon. The significance of such problems is directly connected with both the concept of system and the ways in which we have defined the relation between structure and function.

The concept of equilibrium is a fundamental reference point for analyzing the processes by which a system either comes to terms with the exigencies imposed by a *changing* environment, without essential change in its own structure, or fails to come to terms and undergoes other processes, such as structural change, dissolution as a boundary-maintaining

system (analogous to biological death for the organism), or the consolidation of some impairment leading to the establishment of secondary structures of a "pathological" character. Theoretically, the concept of equilibrium has a normative reference in only one sense. Since the structure of social systems consists in institutionalized normative culture, the "maintenance" of these normative patterns is a basic reference point for analyzing the equilibrium of the system. However, whether this maintenance actually occurs or not, and in what measure, is entirely an empirical question. Furthermore, "disequilibrium" may lead to structural change which, from a higher-order normative point of view, is desirable.

The second set of dynamic problems concerns processes involving change in the structure of the system itself. This involves, above all, problems of interchange with the cultural system, however much these may in turn depend upon the internal state of the social system and its relations to other environing systems. Leaving distinctions within the category of internal adjustive processes aside for the moment, one can say that, with respect to its external interchanges, problems of equilibrium for the social system involve primarily its relations to its individual members as personalities and organisms, and, through these, to the physical environment. Problems of structural change, on the other hand, primarily involve its relations to the cultural systems affecting its patterns of institutionalized normative culture.

However fundamental the distinction between dynamic problems which do and do not involve structural change may be, the great importance of an intermediate or mixed case should be emphasized. This is the problem of change involving the structure of subsystems of the social system, but not the over-all structural pattern. The most important case in this category is that of processes of structural differentiation. Structural differentiation involves genuine *reorganization* of the system and, therefore, fundamental structural change of various subsystems and their relations to each other. Its analysis therefore presents problems of structural change for the relevant subsystems, but not in the same sense for the system as a whole. The problems involved concern the organization of the structural components of social systems, particularly the hierarchical order in which they are placed. Further discussion will have to await clarification of these problems.

The Hierarchy of Relations of Control. The third of the three essential axes of theoretical analysis may be defined as concerning a hierarchy of relations of control. The development of theory in the

8. In addition, of course, our analysis is couched explicitly in terms of action and not of the type of physiology which has so preoccupied many behavior psychologists.

9. It is too technical an issue to discuss here, but we would take the position that a social system in the *analytical* sense has *no* immediate and direct input-output interchange with the physical environment; all such interchange, which is of crucial importance empirically, *is* mediated through the "behavioral organism."

past generation in both the biological and the behavioral sciences has revealed the primary source of the difficulty underlying the prominent reductionism of so much earlier thought. This was the reductionist tendency to ignore the importance of the ways in which the organization of living systems involved structures and mechanisms that operated as agencies of control—in the cybernetic sense of control—of their metabolic and behavioral processes. The concept of the "behavioral organism" put forward above is that of a cybernetic system located mainly in the central nervous system, which operates through several intermediary mechanisms to control the metabolic processes of the organism and the behavioral use of its physical facilities, such as the motions of limbs.

The basic subsystems of the general system of action constitute a hierarchical series of such agencies of control of the behavior of individuals or organisms. The behavioral organism is the point of articulation of the system of action with the anatomical-physiological features of the physical organism and is its point of contact with the physical environment. The personality system is, in turn, a system of control over the behavioral organism; the social system, over the personalities of its participating members; and the cultural system, a system of control relative to social systems.

It may help if we illustrate the nature of this type of heirarchical relationship by discussing the sense in which the social system "controls" the personality. There are two main empirical points at which this control operates, though the principles involved are the same in both cases. First, the situation in which any given individual acts is, far more than any other set of factors, composed of *other* individuals, not discretely but in ordered sets of relationship to the individual in point. Hence, as the source of his principal facilities of action and of his principal rewards and deprivations, the concrete social system exercises a powerful control over the action of any concrete, adult individual. However, the *patterning* of the motivational system in terms of which he faces this situation also depends upon the social system, because his own personality *structure* has been shaped through the internalization of systems of social objects and of the patterns of institutionalized culture. This point, it should be made clear, is independent of the sense in which individuals are concretely autonomous or creative rather than "passive" or "conforming," for individuality and creativity are, to a considerable extent, phenomena of the institutionalization of expectations. The social system which controls the personality is here conceived analytically, not concretely.

This problem will be further discussed in the Introduction to Part Three.

Control Relations within the Social System. The same basic principle of cybernetic hierarchy that applies to the relations between general subsystems of action applies again *within* each of them, notably to social systems, which is of primary concern here. The principle of the order of cybernetic priority, combined with primacy of relevance to the different boundary-interchange exigencies of the system, will be used as the fundamental basis for classifying the components of social systems. The relevance of this hierarchy applies, of course, to all the components distinguished according to the first of our three ranges of variation, to structures, functions, mechanisms, and categories of input and output.

The most strategic starting point for explaining this basic set of classifications is the category of functions, the link between the structural and the dynamic aspects of the system. I have suggested that it is possible to reduce the essential functional imperatives of any system of action, and hence of any social system, to four, which I have called pattern-maintenance, integration, goal-attainment, and adaptation. These are listed in order of significance from the point of view of cybernetic control of action processes in the system type under consideration.

The Function of Pattern-Maintenance. The function of pattern-maintenance refers to the imperative of maintaining the stability of the patterns of institutionalized culture defining the structure of the system. There are two distinct aspects of this functional imperative. The first concerns the character of the normative pattern itself; the second concerns its state of "institutionalization." From the point of view of the individual participant in a social system, this may be called his motivational *commitment* to act in accordance with certain normative patterns; this, as we shall see, involves their "internalization" in the structure of his personality.

Accordingly, the focus of pattern-maintenance lies in the structural category of *values,* which will be discussed presently. In this connection, the essential function is maintenance, at the cultural level, of the stability of institutionalized values through the processes which articulate values with the belief system, namely, religious beliefs, ideology, and the like. Values, of course, are subject to change, but whether the empirical tendency be toward stability or not, the potentialities of disruption from this source are very great, and it is essential to look for mechanisms that tend to protect such order—even if it is orderliness in the process of change.

The second aspect of this control function concerns the motivational commitment of the individual—elsewhere called "tension-management." A very central problem is that of the mechanisms of socialization of the individual, i.e., of the processes by which the values of the society are internalized in his personality. But even when values have become internalized, the commitments involved are subject to different kinds of strain. Much insight has recently been gained about the ways in which such mechanisms as ritual, various types of expressive symbolism, the arts, and indeed recreation, operate in this connection. Durkheim's analysis of the functions of religious ritual may be said to constitute the main point of departure here.

Pattern-maintenance in this sense plays a part in the theory of social systems, as of other systems of action, comparable to that of the concept of inertia in mechanics. It serves as the most fundamental reference point to which the analysis of other, more variable factors can be related. Properly conceived and used, it does not imply the empirical predominance of stability over change. However, when we say that, because of this set of functional exigencies, social systems show a *tendency* to maintain their structural patterns, we say essentially two things. First, we provide a reference point for the orderly analysis of a whole range of problems of variation which can be treated as arising from sources *other* than processes of structural change in the system, including, in the latter concept, its dissolution. Second, we make it clear that when we do analyze structural change we are dealing with a different kind of theoretical problem than that involved in equilibration. Hence, there is a direct relation between the function of pattern-maintenance —as distinguished from the other three functional imperatives—and the distinction between problems of equilibrium analysis, on the one hand, and the analysis of structural change on the other. The distinction between these two types of problems comes to focus at this point in the paradigm.

The Function of Goal-Attainment. For purposes of exposition it seems best to abandon the order of control set forth above and to concentrate next upon the function of goal-attainment and its relation to adaptation. In contrast to the constancy of institutionalized cultural patterns, we have emphasized the variability of a system's relation to its situation. The functions of goal-attainment and adaptation concern the structures, mechanisms, and processes involved in this relation.

We have compared pattern-maintenance with inertia as used in the theory of mechanics. Goal-attainment then becomes a "problem" in so far as there arises some discrepancy between the inertial tendencies of the system and its "needs" resulting from interchange with the situation. Such needs necessarily arise because the internal system and the environing ones cannot be expected to follow immediately the changing patterns of process.[10] A goal is therefore defined in terms of equilibrium. It is a directional change that tends to reduce the discrepancy between the needs of the system, with respect to input-output interchange, and the conditions in the environing systems that bear upon the "fulfilment" of such needs. Goal-attainment or goal-orientation is thus, by contrast with pattern-maintenance, essentially tied to a specific situation.

A social system with only one goal, defined in relation to a generically crucial situational problem, is conceivable. Most often, however, the situation is complex, with many goals and problems. In such a case two further considerations must be taken into account. First, to protect the integrity of the system, the several goals must be arranged in some scale of relative urgency, a scale sufficiently flexible to allow for variations in the situation. For any complex system, therefore, it is necessary to speak of a system of goals rather than of a single unitary goal, a system, however, which must have some balance between integration as a system and flexible adjustment to changing pressures.

For the social system as such, the focus of its goal-orientation lies in its relation as a system to the personalities of the participating individuals. It concerns, therefore, not commitment to the values of the society, but motivation to contribute what is necessary for the functioning of the system; these "contributions" vary according to particular exigencies. For example, considering American society, one may suggest that, given the main system of values, there has been in the cold-war period a major problem of motivating large sectors of the population to the level of national effort required to sustain a position of world leadership in a very unstable and rapidly changing situation. I would interpret much of the sense of frustration expressed in isolationism and McCarthyism as manifestations of the strains resulting from this problem.[11]

The Function of Adaptation. The second consequence of plurality of goals, however, concerns the difference between the functions of goal-attain-

---

10. When we speak of the *pattern* of the system tending to remain constant, we mean this in an analytical sense. The outputs to environing systems need not remain constant in the same sense, and their variations may disturb the relationship to the environing system. Thus scientific investigation may be stably institutionalized in a structural sense but result in a continuing output of new knowledge, which is a dynamic factor in the system's interchanges with its situation.

11. Cf. the paper, Parsons, "McCarthyism and American Social Tension," *Yale Review*, Winter, 1955. Reprinted as Chap. 7, *Structure and Process in Modern Societies.*

ment and adaptation. When there is only one goal, the problem of evaluating the usefulness of facilities is narrowed down to their relevance to attaining this particular goal. With a plurality of goals, however, the problem of "cost" arises. That is, the same scarce facilities will have *alternative* uses within the system of goals, and hence their use for one purpose means sacrificing the gains that would have been derived from their use for another. It is on this basis that an analytical distinction must be made between the function of effective goal-attainment and that of providing disposable facilities independent of their relevance to any particular goal. The adaptive function is defined as the provision of such facilities.

Just as there is a pluralism of lower-order, more concrete goals, there is also a pluralism of relatively concrete facilities. Hence there is a parallel problem of the organization of such facilities in a system. The primary criterion is the provision of flexibility, so far as this is compatible with effectiveness; for the system, this means a maximum of generalized disposability in the processes of allocation between alternative uses. Within the complex type of social system, this disposability of facilities crystallizes about the institutionalization of money and markets. More generally, at the macroscopic social-system level, the function of goal-attainment is the focus of the political organization of societies, while that of adaptation is the focus of economic organization.[12]

The most important kinds of facilities involve control of physical objects, access to the services of human agents and certain cultural elements. For their mechanisms of control to be at all highly generalized, particular units of such resources must be "alienable," i.e., not bound to specific uses through ascription. The market system is thus a primary focus of the society's organization for

adaptation. Comparable features operate in less differentiated societies, and in more differentiated subsystems where markets do not penetrate, such as the family.[13]

Within a given system, goal-attainment is a more important control than adaptation. Facilities subserve the attainment of goals, not vice versa—though of course the provision or "production" of facilities may itself be a goal, with a place within the more general system of goals. There are, however, complications in the implications of this statement.

The Function of Integration. The last of the four functional imperatives of a system of action—in our case, a social system—is that of integration. In the control hierarchy, this stands between the functions of pattern-maintenance and goal-attainment. Our recognition of the significance of integration implies that all systems, except for a limiting case, are differentiated and segmented into relatively independent units, i.e., must be treated as boundary-maintaining systems within an environment of other systems, which in this case are other subsystems of the same, more inclusive system. The functional problem of integration concerns the mutual adjustments of these "units" or subsystems from the point of view of their "contributions" to the effective functioning of the system as a whole. This, in turn, concerns their relation to the pattern-maintenance problem, as well as to the external situation through processes of goal-attainment and adaptation.

In a highly differentiated society, the primary focus of the integrative function is found in its system of legal norms and the agencies associated with its management, notably the courts and the legal profession. Legal norms at this level, rather than that of a supreme constitution, govern the *allocation* of rights and obligations, of facilities and rewards, between different units of the complex system; such norms facilitate internal adjustments compatible with the stability of the value system or its orderly change, as well as with adaptation to the shifting demands of the external situation. The institutionalization of money and power are primarily integrative phenomena, like other mechanisms of social control in the narrower sense. These problems will be further discussed in later sections of this essay.

For any given type of system—here, the social— the integrative function is the focus of its most distinctive properties and processes. We contend,

12. It should be noted that the above formulation of the function of adaptation carefully avoids any implication that "passive" adjustment is the keynote of adaptation. Adaptation is relative to the values and goals of the system. "Good adaptation" may consist either in passive acceptance of conditions with a minimization of risk or in active mastery of conditions. The inclusion of active mastery in the concept of adaptation is one of the most important tendencies of recent developments in biological theory. An important relation between the two functional categories of goal-attainment and adaptation and the old categories of ends and means should be noted. The basic discrimination of ends and means may be said to be the special case, for the personality system, of the more general discrimination of the functions of goal-attainment and adaptation. In attempting to squeeze analysis of social behavior into this framework, utilitarian theory was guilty both of narrowing it to the personality case (above all, denying the independent analytical significance of social systems) and of overlooking the independent significance of the functions of pattern-maintenance and of integration of social systems themselves.

13. The importance of adaptive flexibility for the functioning of families as systems is well illustrated in the study of Robert Angell, *The Family Encounters the Depression* (New York: Chas. Scribner's Sons, 1936).

therefore, that the problems focusing about the integrative functions of social systems constitute the central core of the concerns of sociological theory. This point of view will guide our analyses in subsequent introductory discussions and will receive strong emphasis in selections presented at various points in the Reader. Until a broad structural outline of the social system has been presented, it seems best to defer further discussion of the ways in which the integrative function meshes more specifically with the others.

II. CATEGORIES OF SOCIAL STRUCTURE

Historically, the theoretical preoccupations of sociological theory have emerged from two main points of reference. One concerns the relations of social systems and culture and focuses on the problem of values and norms in the social system. The second concerns the individual as organism and personality and focuses on the individual's participation in social interaction. Generally, neither of these reference points may be considered more important than the other. However, since the foregoing discussion of functional imperatives has started with pattern-maintenance, which chiefly concerns the institutionalization of normative culture, it may help to balance the picture if we begin our detailed discussion of structure at the other end, with the problem of the interaction of individuals.

Social Interaction and Roles

For sociology, the essential concept here is that of *role*. I should like to treat this concept as the "bottom" term of a series of structural categories, of which the other terms, in ascending order, are *collectivity, norm,* and *value*. (It is interesting, and I think significant, that systematic introduction of the concept of role has been, perhaps, the most distinctively American contribution to the structural aspects of sociological theory.)

The essential starting point is the conception of two (or more) individuals interacting in such a way as to constitute an interdependent system. As personalities, each individual may be considered a system with its own values, goals, etc., facing the others as part of an "environment" that provides certain opportunities for goal-attainment as well as certain limitations and sources of frustration. Though interdependence can be taken into account at this level, this is not equivalent to treating the process of interaction as a social system. True, the

action of alter is an essential part of the conditions bearing on the attainment of ego's goals, but the vital sociological question concerns the nature and degree of the integration of the *system* of interaction as a social system. Here the question arises of the conditions under which the interaction process can be treated as stable—in the sense, at least, that it does not prove to be so mutually frustrating that dissolution of the system (i.e., for the individual, "leaving the field") seems more likely than its continuation.

The problem of stability introduces considerations of temporal continuity, which immediately brings us to the relevance of normative orientation. It can be shown that, within the action frame of reference, stable interaction implies that acts acquire "meanings" which are interpreted with reference to a common set of normative conceptions. The particularity of specific acts is transcended in terms of the generalization of the normative common culture as well as in the normative component of the expectations that get built into the guiding mechanisms of the process. This means that the response of Alter to an act of Ego may be interpreted as a sanction expressing an evaluation of the past act and serving as a guide to desirable future behavior.

The essentials of the interaction situation can be illustrated by any two-player game, such as chess. Each player is presumed to have some motivation to participate in the game, including a "desire to win." Hence, he has a goal, and, relative to this, some conception of effective "strategies." He may plan an opening gambit but he cannot carry advance planning too far, because the situation is not stable: it is contingent on the moves made both by himself and by his opponent as the game proceeds. The basic facilities at his command consist of his knowledge of the opportunities implicit in the changing situation; his command of these opportunities means performance of the adaptive function. Hence, at the goal-attainment and adaptive levels, goals are defined and facilities are provided, but *specific acts are not prescribed*. The facilities are generalized, and their allocation between the players depends upon each player's capacities to take advantage of opportunities.

In turn, the meaningfulness of the goals and the stability of the generalized pattern of facilities depend on the existence of a well defined set of rules, which forms the center of the integration of the system. The roles, in this case, are not differentiated on a permanent basis; rather, the rules define the consequences of any given move by one player for the situation in which the other must make his next choice. Without such rules the interactive process could not be stable, and the system of adaptive facilities would break down; neither player would know what was expected of him or what the consequences of a given set of moves would be. Finally, the differentiated and contingent rules must be grounded in a set of values which define the nature of a "good game" of this sort, including the value of equality of opportunity for both contestants and the meaningfulness of the goal of "winning."

A stable system of interaction, therefore, orients its participants in terms of mutual expectations, which have the dual significance of expressing normative evaluations and stating contingent predictions of overt behavior. This mutuality of expectations implies that the *evaluative* meanings of acts are shared by the interacting units in two ways: what a member does can be categorized in terms meaningful to both; also, they share criteria of behavior, so that there are common standards of evaluation for particular acts.

We can say that even such an elementary two-member system of social interaction has most of the structural essentials of a social system. The essential property is mutuality of orientation, defined in terms of shared patterns of normative culture. Such normative patterns are *values;* the normatively regulated complex of behavior of one of the participants is a *role;* and the system composed by the interaction of the two participants, so far as it shares a common normative culture and is distinguishable from others by the participation of these two and not others, is a *collectivity.*

One further condition, not present in our chess game example, is necessary in order to complete the roster of structural components, namely, differentiation between the roles of the participants. This is to say that, in most social systems, participants do not *do* the same things; their performances may be conceived as *complementary* contributions to the "functioning" of the interaction system. When there are two or more structurally distinct units which perform essentially *the same* function in the system (e.g., nuclear families in a community) we will speak of segmentation as distinguished from differentiation. When differentiation of roles is present, it becomes necessary to distinguish between two components of the normative culture of the system: that of values, which are shared by the members over and above their particular roles, and that of role-expectations, which are differentiated by role and therefore define rights and obligations applicable to one role but not to the other. I propose to use the term *values* for the shared normative component, and the term (differentiated) *norm* for the component that is specific to a given role or, in more complex systems, to other empirical units of the system, i.e., various collectivities such as families,

churches, business firms, governmental agencies, universities.

Where roles are differentiated, the sharing of values becomes an essential condition of integration of the system. Only on this assumption can the reactions of Alter to Ego's performances have the character of sanctions regulating Ego's action in the interests of the system. However, it should be clear that for Alter to be in a position to evaluate Ego's acts, the acts need not be such that Alter is, by virtue of his role, expected to perform. Thus, in marriage, one of the most important diadic relationships in all societies, the roles of the partners are differentiated by sex. The mutual evaluation of performance is an essential regulatory mechanism, but to be in a position to evaluate the partner's performance is not to assume his role.

The Concepts of Role and Collectivity. A role may now be defined as the structured, i.e., normatively regulated, participation of a person in a concrete process of social interaction with specified, concrete role-partners. The system of such interaction of a plurality of role-performers is, so far as it is normatively regulated in terms of common values and of norms sanctioned by these common values, a collectivity. Performing a role within a collectivity defines the category of *membership,* i.e., the assumption of obligations of performance in that concrete interaction system. Obligations correlatively imply rights.

Since the normal individual participates in many collectivities, it is a commonplace, though a crucial one, that only in a limiting case does a single role constitute the entire interactive behavior of a concrete individual. The role is rather a *sector* in his behavioral system, and hence of his personality. For most purposes, therefore, it is not the individual, or the person as such, that is a unit of social systems, but rather his role-participation at the boundary directly affecting his personality. It is largely when interpreted as this particular boundary-concept that the concept of role has an important theoretical significance for sociology.

So long as we restrict our illustrations to the diadic interaction system it may seem that the distinction of four analytical structural components—role, collectivity, norm, and value—is overelaborate. At this level it is still possible to identify values and the collectivity, norms and the role. In more complex social systems, however, there is not just one collectivity but many; and a differentiated norm does not define expectations for just one role but for a class of roles (and also for classes of collectivities). The social systems with which the sociologist normally deals are complex networks of many different types or categories of roles and collectivities on many different levels of organization. It therefore becomes essential to conceptualize values and norms independently of any particular collectivity or role.

Values and Norms

We now turn from the analysis of interaction to that of the more explicitly normative content of the structure of social systems, within which values and norms have been distinguished. We have already suggested that such values and norms must be involved in any stable process of interaction, however simple. In the attempt to analyze the structure of complex societies, however, the analytically distinct significance of these components becomes much more salient. The following sections will therefore be devoted to a more explicit analysis of them and of their relations to the segmentation of social structure, to the various levels of values and norms, and to the patterns of differentiation of structure, always taking account both of the problems of function and of the system's relation to its situation.

Throughout this analysis, our major concern will be to make clear the basic functional paradigm we have presented for the intricate relations involved in a complex society segmented and differentiated into many subsystems. A paramount underlying question will be, how is the integration of a system with a large population and high differentiation possible? Or, more theoretically, what kinds of statements have to be made, what concepts formulated, and what discriminations worked out in order to do justice to these empirical intricacies?

The concepts of universalism and particularism will be helpful in this connection. In any given system, the concepts of role and collectivity are particularistic. Though, of course, we must talk about classes and types of roles, a role is always the role of a particular concrete individual. Similarly, a collectivity always has a concrete membership of specific interacting role-incumbents. A norm, however, is always universalistically defined within the universe of its relevance, whether it be a universe of acts, of roles, or of collectivities. To be sure, the definition of a relevant universe involves a particularistic reference of a higher order; thus, a norm may apply only to citizens or residents of the United States, but it may cut across all concrete collectivity-membership differences within that universe. Values are also universalistically defined in terms of relevance. When a particular *type* of society is evaluated as good, the judgment is inherently applicable to more than one specific society.

The universalistic aspect of values implies that, at the relevant level of reference, they are neither situation-specific nor function-specific. In this connection, it should be remembered that the most crucial aspects of the situation of a social system consist in the personalities and the patterns of culture with which the system is in contact. When values are said not to be situation-specific, it is implied that their normative validity is not a function of the particular categories of personalities available for membership, nor, for example, of the particular levels of technological knowledge available for implementing these values. When situation-specificity is introduced, we speak analytically not of values, but of goals.

Similarly, values are independent of the internal differentiation of the systems in which they are institutionalized; they are relevant on a level of generality which "transcends" functional differentiation. The keynote of differentiation, however, is functional. Hence, norms, which by the above definition are differentiated with reference to function, must be function-specific. They are "legitimized" by values, but operate at a lower level of generality with respect to expected concrete collective and role performance. With respect to concrete roles in concrete collectivities, however, most norms are still not situation-specific—especially since they do not specify the particular roles but are generally formulated in classes and types of roles, and hence of persons and collectivities.

The relativity of the universalistic-particularistic distinction must again be emphasized. In general, the principle is that the universe relevant to the universalistic elements of normative culture is defined by the role and collectivity structure at the next higher level of system organization. It thus refers to a hierarchy of system-subsystem organization. The top of this hierarchy is the concept of society, which is the highest-order concrete system of interaction treated as theoretically relevant for the analytical purposes of sociology (including the possibility of an emergent "world society").

In line with the conception of the structure of social systems as consisting in the normative culture institutionalized in the system, we have so far presented a classification of its components organized with reference to the hierarchical order of the organization of the system. Structurally speaking, then, the role component is the normative component which governs the participation of individual persons in given collectivities. The collectivity component is the normative culture which defines the values, norms, goal-orientations, and ordering of roles for a concrete system of interaction of specifiable persons; the component of norms is the set of universalistic rules or norms which define expectations for the performance of classes of differentiated units within the system—collectivities, or roles, as the case may be; and values are the normative patterns defining, in universalistic terms, the pattern of desirable orientation for the system as a whole, independent of the specification of situation or of differentiated function within the system.

It should be made clear that roles are governed or controlled by the normative exigencies of the functioning of the collectivities within which they operate, if the collectivity itself is to be defined as a system. Therefore, in so far as a more inclusive social system comprises many collectivities as subsystems, the behavior of these collectivities is controlled by the institutionalized norms that specify how each type of collectivity must and may behave according to its place within the system. Finally, norms themselves are legitimized, and therefore, in a normative sense, controlled by the values institutionalized in the society. Subject to exigencies of situation and function, values define the direction of orientation that is desirable for the system as a whole.

The Structure of Complex Systems

Having outlined these essential structural components of a social system and their rank in the general hierarchy of control, we can now outline their main pattern of organization so as to constitute a relatively complex system. What is here presented is necessarily a schematic "ideal type," one that pretends merely to define and distinguish rather broad structural categories; we cannot take into account the immense richness of various concrete social structures. Something more concrete will be found in the Introduction to Part Two.

The main guiding line of the analysis is the concept that a complex social system consists of a network of interdependent and interpenetrating subsystems, each of which, seen at the appropriate level of reference, is a social system in its own right, subject to all the functional exigencies of any such system relative to *its* institutionalized culture and situation and possessing all the essential structural components, organized on the appropriate levels of differentiation and specification.

The Concept of a Society. The starting point must be the concept of a *society,* defined as a collectivity, i.e., a system of concrete interacting human individuals, which is the primary bearer of a distinctive institutionalized culture and which cannot be said to be a differentiated subsystem of a higher-order collectivity oriented to most of the functional exigencies of a social system. It will be noted that this conception is stated in terms that leave the question of the "openness" of a society in various directions

to be treated empirically. At the social-system level, however, rather than the cultural,[14] the main criterion is *relative* self-sufficiency.

To approach the structural analysis of the subsystem organization of a society, we must refer to the appropriate functional exigencies of both the societal system itself and its various subsystems. The primary, over-all principle is that of differentiation in relation to functional exigency; this is the master concept for the analysis of social structure. By itself, however, it is not adequate; it must be supplemented by the two principles of specification and segmentation. The first refers primarily to the institutionalized culture components of the structure, the second to the exigencies confronting the concrete behaving units, i.e., to collectivities and roles. It seems preferable to discuss the latter first.

We have noted that, in *one* (but only one) of its aspects, a society is a *single* collectivity with a specifiable, though naturally changing, membership of individuals. This fact is related to three fundamental imperatives. First, there must be, to some degree and on some level, a unitary system of institutionalized values, in this aspect a common culture. In so far as maintenance of a common value system requires the kinds of functions collectivities must perform, the society will have to constitute a single collectivity—what Durkheim called a "moral community." Second, however, since the system is differentiated, the implementation of these values for different units requires a relatively *consistent* system of norms that receive a unitary formulation and interpretation. In highly differentiated societies this system of norms takes the form of an integrated legal system administered by courts. The need for coordinated dealing with the external situation is also relevant, as will be brought out presently.

The Segmentation of Social Units. But if, for one set of reasons, a society must be a single collectivity, other reasons prevent its being only that. These reasons can be summed up in the generalized principles economists refer to as determining the "economies of scale." Beyond certain points, that is to say, "costs" increase as the size of the unit of organization increases, though what the points are varies

14. By this criterion a system such as the Catholic Church is not a society. It clearly transcends and interpenetrates with a number of different societies in which its values are more or less fully institutionalized and its subunits are constituent collectivities. But the Church, primarily a *culturally* oriented social system, is not itself capable of meeting very many of the functional exigencies of a society, especially the political and economic needs. Similarly, even a "world government," should anything approaching that conception come into being, need not itself constitute a "world-society," though its effectiveness would imply a level of normative integration which would make the degree of separateness we have traditionally attributed to "national societies" problematic.

greatly according to the specific factors involved. Thus, under modern industrial conditions the manufacture of such commodities as automobiles takes place in very large units indeed, whereas there seem to be important reasons which inhibit entrusting the early socialization of children primarily to units with membership much larger than the nuclear family.

Perhaps the most fundamental determinant underlying the segmentation of social systems is the indispensability of the human individual as an agency of performance. But there are essential limits, not only to what a given individual can do, but to the effectiveness with which individuals can co-operate. The problems of communication and other aspects of integration may thus multiply as a result of an increasing scale of organization; in certain respects, therefore, subcollectivities may acquire a distinctive organization, including a special integration or solidarity relative to the larger systems of which they are parts.

By the concept *segmentation* I refer, in discussing the formation of collectivities, to the development of subcollectivities, within a larger collectivity system, in which some of the members of the larger system participate more intimately than in others. In this sense, segmentation is a factor independent of the differentiation of function between the subcollectivities. Thus a large-scale society may comprise millions of nuclear families, all of which perform essentially similar functions in the socialization of children; here the structure is highly segmented but not highly differentiated.

The necessity of segmentation derives largely from the problems of integration resulting from the other exigencies to which units of the system are subject. At the same time, however, it gives rise to new problems of integration: the more units there are, the less likely they will be just "naturally" to co-ordinate their activities in ways compatible with the smooth functioning of the system as a whole. This tends, in more complex systems, to give rise to special mechanisms of integration, which will have to be discussed in due course.

The Specification of Normative Culture. As already noted, there is an important relation between the hierarchy of control and the levels of generality of the components of normative culture. Thus, values were defined as standing at the highest level of generality of "conceptions of the desirable," i.e., without specification of function or situation. In comparison to values, therefore, norms are differentiated on the basis of specification of function of the units or subunits to which they apply. Subcollectivities, in turn, involve further specification on the basis of situation. This is to say that, given its

function(s), a collectivity is identified in terms of specified memberships of concrete individuals acting in concrete situations. When the collectivity is treated as a differentiated system, there must be further specifications applicable to the roles of the participating members.

There is, therefore, a hierarchy of generality of the patterns of normative culture institutionalized in a social system, one that corresponds to the general hierarchical relations of its structural components. Each subunit of the society, as collectivity, will have its own institutionalized values, which should be conceived as specifications, at the appropriate level, of the more general values of the society. To cope with its own internal differentiation of function, then, each subunit will have a set of differentiated norms, which should be regarded as specifications both of the subcollectivity values and of the more general norms applicable both to it and to other types of subcollectivity. The principle of specification restricts the generality of the pattern of culture by introducing qualifications arising from specialization of function, on the one hand, and from specificity of situation, on the other.

The last of the three principles of organization of complex systems, functional differentiation, has already been discussed in general terms. In accord with this principle, structured units acquire specialized significance in the functioning of the system. The general scheme of functional categories that we have presented is very simple, being limited to four categories. In using it, however, one must do justice to the empirical complexity of the situation by taking acount of the many steps in segmentation and specification, and hence of the compounding of the patterns of differentiation by their repetition for subsystems at each level of segmentation.

Since our general approach has been in terms of the hierarchy of control observed in descending order, a brief account should now be given of the "anchorage" of social systems at the base. This anchorage is in the personalities and behavioral organisms of the individual members and, *through* these, in the lower-order subsystems of the organism and in the physical environment. Concretely, all social interaction is bound to the physical task performance of individuals in a physical environment; it is bound to spatial location in the physical sense. Following the usage of ecologically oriented theory, I have elsewhere referred to this spatial location as the "community" aspect of social structure.[15] It can be broken down most conveniently into four com-

15. Cf. Parsons, "The Principal Structures of Community" in C. J. Friedrich, Ed., *Community*, Nomos, Vol. II, Liberal Arts Press, 1959, and in Parsons, *Structure and Process in Modern Societies*, Free Press, 1959, Chap. 8

plexes: (1) residential location and the crystallization of social structure around that focus; (2) functional task-performance through occupation, and
the attendant locational problems; (3) jurisdictional
application of normative order through the specification of categories of persons, and the relevance of
this to the spatial locations of their interests and
activities; and (4) the physical exigencies of communication and of the movements of persons and
commodities. More generally, the category of technology—not only what is usually called "physical
production," but all task-performance involving the
physical organism in relation to its physical environment—belongs in this area of borderline problems. Technology relates to physical exigencies, but
it is also based on *cultural* resources in their significance as facilities for social action. Empirical
knowledge of the physical world is an instance of
such a cultural resource.

The Integration of Societies as Collectivities. Let
us now approach the problem of outlining the structure of a complex society as a social system. As we
have said, three different exigencies underlie the
fact that a society can always be regarded as a single
collectivity, namely, the maintenance of its patterns
of institutionalized culture at the value level, the
integration of its system of differentiated norms,
and the co-ordinated handling of external situations.

The prevalence of fundamental patterns of value
and the general commitment of units to common
values are so crucial that the problem of the relation
of the over-all collectivity to values is a universal
one. At the other end, however, the problems of
jurisdiction and enforcement with reference to
normative order are equally crucial; the over-all
collectivity structure cannot be divorced from
political organization, oriented to maintaining
commitments to this order and to the jurisdictional
functions associated with it, in relation both to its
own population and to other societies. This means
that the boundaries of a society tend to coincide
with the territorial jurisdiction of the highest-order
units of political organization.

The primary area in which the problems of value-
commitment are played out is that of religion; for
most societies, the paramount over-all collectivity
has been at the same time a religious collectivity
and a political collectivity, both a "church" and a
"state." Law, we may say, has tended to stand in the
middle, to be legitimized by religion and enforced
by political authority; often the function of interpreting it has been a serious bone of contention.

However, the formula of religio-political-legal
unity is not, by itself, adequate as a universal generalization. In the first place, within the over-all

collectivity these functions have tended to be differentiated with respect to personnel and subcollectivities. But, in a more radical sense, in the Western
world since the Christian era there has been a
process of fundamental differentiation of church
and state. In interpreting the sociological implications of this, one must consider this process in terms
of the relation between social and cultural systems.
Even before its Protestant phase, Western Christianity was characterized by a special type of religious
"individualism." In the present context, this means
that, except on the most general level of over-all
societal membership, the individual's religious and
social status did not necessarily coincide. The
church was an organization of the religious interests
and orientations of the population conceived as independent of (but not unrelated to) their secular or
temporal orientations, especially at the level of
societal value-commitment. It was a "Christian
society," but one in which the function of religion
was more specialized than in other pre- and non-
Christian types.

This I interpret to mean that, in societal as distinguished from cultural terms, the "moral community" aspect shifted from religious organization as
such to the area of interpenetration between the
religious and the secular. The paramount societal
collectivity became the "state," administered by
laymen—or when administered, in fact, by priests,
not in their special clerical capacity. This differentiation was never fully carried out in medieval
Europe—for instance, it was impossible to divest
bishops of secular functions that went beyond the
administration of ecclesiastical affairs—but it was,
nevertheless, the main pattern.

Since the Reformation, this process has gone
farther, particularly where the principle of the
separation, as distinguished from the differentiation,
of church and state has prevailed. As in the United
States today, the values are still clearly anchored in
theistic religion ("In God We Trust"), but on the
level of collectivity organization the "moral community" is clearly the "politically organized community." What has happened, essentially, is that
any agency whose orientation is primarily cultural
rather than societal has been deprived of legitimate
authority to prescribe values and enforce norms for
the society; in this sense the society has become
"secularized." The religious anchorage of the values
is still there, but religion is pluralistically and "privately" organized. Formally, the values are embodied in the Constitution and in the official interpretations of it, above all by judicial and legislative
agencies.

The universal association of the over-all collectivity structure with political organization is based

on another set of imperatives, involving the special significance of physical force as a sanction. The central point here is that, while there are many limitations on the efficacy of this sanction, control of sufficiently superior socially organized force is almost always a completely effective preventive of any undesired action. Therefore, without the control that includes "neutralization" of organized force, which is inherently territorial in its reference, the guarantee of the binding power of a normative order is not possible.

I conceive of political organization as functionally organized about the attainment of *collective* goals, i.e., the attainment or maintenance of states of interaction between the system and its environing situation that are relatively desirable from the point of view of the system. The maintenance of security against the adverse use of force is a crucial collective goal for every society. Considerations such as these underlaid the general tendency of the over-all collectivity to develop an effective monopoly of the internal organization of force through police and military agencies. Such statements are not meant to imply that the control of force is the paramount function of political organization. Force is not the only function that is primarily negative, i.e., "protective" in significance, and, in general, government is a central agency of positive societal goal-attainment. But force is so strategically significant that its control is an indispensable function, a necessary, but not sufficient, condition of social order. Accordingly, in a well-integrated society, most sub-collectivities except those specifically concerned with force are almost totally deprived of it.

Because of the problems involved in the use and control of force, the political organization must always be integrated with the legal system, which is concerned with administering the highest order of norms regulating the behavior of units within the society. No society can afford to permit any other normative order to take precedence over that sanctioned by "politically organized society." Indeed, the promulgation of any such alternative order is a revolutionary act, and the agencies responsible for it must assume the responsibility of political organization.

In this context it is of great significance that in a few societies, notably in the modern West, the organization of the legal system has attained a significant degree of independence in the judicial and, to some extent, in the legislative departments. There are two main aspects of this independent collectivity structure: the judiciary, with certain types of insulation from the pressures of "politics"; second, very notable, the development of a legal profession whose members occupy an interstitial status,

partly through membership in the bar, functioning as "officers of the court," and partly by dealing privately with clients—indeed, protected from even governmental intervention by such institutions as privileged communication.

Summing up, we may say that the highest overall collectivity in even a modern society is, to an important degree, necessarily "multifunctional," or functionally "diffuse." At the same time, under certain circumstances the diffuseness characteristic of the more "monolithic" religio-political structures—even of such high development as classical China or late Republican Rome—has tended to differentiate further. The most notable of these differentiations have been the "secularization" of political organization, which has gone through many stages and modes, and the institutionalization of a relatively independent legal function.[16]

The problem of the kind and degree of differentiation likely to occur at this highest level of societal collectivity organization may be described as a function of four primary sets of factors, all variable over considerable ranges. These are: (1) the *type* of societal values which are more or less fully institutionalized in the society (classified in terms of modes of categorizations of the society, at the highest level of generality, as an evaluated object—the appropriate categories seem to be pattern variables); (2) the degree and mode of their institutionalization, including its "security" relative particularly to the religious and cultural foundations of value-commitments in the society (long-range institutionalization of new values implies a relatively low level of such security); (3) the kind and level of structural differentiation of the society, with special reference to the severity and kinds of integrative problems they impose on the society; and (4) the kinds of situational exigencies to which the system is exposed.

Modes of Differentiation within Societies

Kinship and the Articulation with Personality. The question of the kind and level of functional

16. It may be noted that allowing the institutionalized values to be determined through agencies not fully controlled by the paramount political collectivity involves a certain risk to it. The relatively full institutionalization of anything like the separation of church and state is therefore probably an index of the completeness of institutionalization of values. Modern totalitarian regimes are partly understandable in terms of the insecurity of this institutionalization. Therefore totalitarian parties are functionally equivalent to "churches," though they may put their value focus at a nontranscendental level, which is, e.g., allegedly "economic," which attempts to establish the kind of relation to government typical of a less differentiated state of the paramount collectivity than has existed in the modern West.

diffuseness characterizing some social structures arises at an additional and particularly important point, besides that of the society as "moral community." This is the point of primary articulation with the personalities of the constituent members. Any system sociologically treated as a society is likely to include many such members—at least a thousand, and in many cases tens if not hundreds of millions. Because of the types of exigencies noted above, in this context societies tend to be relatively highly segmented. The types of units into which the segmentation occurs are, in the first instance, those known as "kinship units." *Kinship* is essentially the point of articulation, i.e., interpenetration, between the structure of social systems and the relations involved in the biological process of reproduction. Biologically, there are three crucial structural components: (1) the differentiation of human populations into two sex groups, each with different functions in the reproductive process, but both essential to it; (2) the sharp human differentiation between the mature and the immature organism, involving a relatively long period of gestation and then a prolonged period of relative "helplessness" which, though progressively decreasing, makes impossible the order of independence characteristic of the young of many other species; and (3) the fact that the sexual union of two specific individuals of opposite sex is necessary to, and likely to result in, pregnancy and reproduction. Thus, biologically all human populations are differentiated by sex and by generation, and are particularistically related to two ancestral lines through biological descent—the filial generation as the offspring of two specific biological parents and, through them, the descendants of remoter ancestors; the parental, through their common relation by parenthood to their offspring and to more remote descendants. The relation between sexual union and reproduction means that the former is never divested of an underlying relation to potential parenthood.

In social structure there are many variations, but a constant and fundamental point of reference is the nuclear family, the collectivity constituted by a conjugal pair and their biological offspring. In every known society, there is institutionalization of some continuing sexual relationship in relation to reproduction, and of some continuing responsibility for such offspring on the part (often backed up by wider groups) of at least one of the parents, though generally of both. Generally the nuclear family is, during the period of the children's dependency, at least included in the primary unit of residence—it is often, particularly in modern industrial societies, primarily constitutive of it.

Within this setting, the problem of functional diffuseness rests first on the fact that every human individual starts life as a helpless infant, whose development depends almost completely on his relations to the particular, very small circle of adults responsible for his physical care and his socialization. Biological parenthood is not essential to this crucial relation; but, particularly with respect to the mother, the cases where this does not play a strategic role are minor variations and do not anywhere constitute a major structural type.

A generally significant crucial fact is that the types of social structure which, in an evolutionary sense, can be clearly categorized as "primitive" display a special prominence of kinship as a basis of the categorization of memberships and eligibilities in important collectivities. There is also an important group of societies where no important collectivity exists that is independent of kinship, however complex the internal ramifications of the kinship system may be.

Kinship structures as such are clearly subject to important processes of functional differentiation. Economic and political functions are very widely institutionalized in kinship units, though these functions generally, in extension of membership and in time span, transcend the nuclear family. On the higher societal levels, however, integrative functions present a major obstacle to such institutionalization, because of the inherent particularism of kinship references. Hence, at certain stages in the structural development of societies, particularism on kinship bases presents one of the major obstacles to higher-level integration. At the primary levels of the function of socialization, pattern-maintenance is everywhere very closely bound to kinship units. But in terms of the imperative of societal value-stabilization, i.e., a higher level of pattern-maintenance, this necessarily centers at a low level in the specification series. Precisely because segmentation is so important in the kinship sphere, dependence solely on kinship units for pattern-maintenance is precarious. These statements should not, of course, imply that the connection cannot be maintained through differentiation in the statuses of different kinship units. The differentiation of royal and aristocratic kinship lineages from the "common" people is one mechanism by which, within certain limits, pattern-maintenance and integrative functions can be performed without sacrificing the kinship basis of organization.

In this sense, every structural unit carries some share in meeting every functional imperative of the society as a whole. But the effectiveness of allocating such responsibilities among highly segmented units tends to decrease as the functions go from a lower to a higher position in the hierarchy of control. There is, to be sure, a very important countervailing consideration concerning the firmness of institutionalization; as noted above, under certain circumstances a very important part of the pattern-maintenance function may be highly decentralized. Since kinship units, however, are by nature highly segmented beyond the performance of pattern-maintenance functions for their constituent personalities and integrative functions within the units themselves, the other least problematical function for these units is the economic. Indeed, it is striking in comparative sociology that only in the relatively very recent types of modern industrial societies (with minor exceptions, like slave-plantation economies) has more than a small fraction of the function of economic production become emancipated from diffuse "embeddedness" in kinship structures. This development has been closely associated with the fact that in all except truly primitive preindustrial societies, the major portion of productivity has come from agriculture. Despite important variations, there are certain common structural features of peasant societies where most of the population have been organized as kinship units, living from agricultural production in a subsystem operated predominantly by members of the kinship group working by virtue of their ascribed status in the unit. In such cases, the ascribed pattern has in general extended to institutionalization of generational succession in property-holding and productive function. In an important sense, the family firm, in the earlier stages of industrialism and before, has in nonagricultural fields extended the same basic organizational pattern; but except on a very small scale, this embeddedness has been confined to the higher "managerial" functions, and non-kin have worked in operative capacities. However, various types of patriarchal collectivities have assimilated non-kin employees in patterns of relationship similar to those of kinship. Again, economic function within this structural framework must be performed at a relatively low level of differentiation. It is closely connected with a rather elementary phase of the economic division of labor and the corresponding extensiveness of markets.

Any collectivity is also, functionally considered, a political unit of the society. A unit like the nuclear family is, however, so small that only by virtue of very special status can it perform important political functions at any but a low level of specification. This applies even to lineages, though, since they can institutionalize generational succession, they can be much more important than nuclear families—and, as in the case of royal families, they have been the paramount agencies of society-wide political responsibility. The kinship principle has then been extended to the political role of a complex of aristocratic lineages which stand in varying relations to royalty.

There are, however, severe functional difficulties in the institutionalization of nearly "pure" government by privileged kinship units. It has been most stable in certain small-scale societies, like the city-states of antiquity or the semi-independent city-states of late medieval and early modern Europe—where, incidentally, monarchy has been the exception rather than the rule.

It seems, after the above analysis, that integrative functions tend to become structurally differentiated near the top of the societal system of organization, most conspicuously in the case of the judiciary element of the legal system. Almost always a private legal profession has developed later, and is more exceptional.

The Differentiation of Political Structures

Because of the connection of paramount societal collectivity organization and political function outlined, the functional differentiation of political from other structures also tends to come near the top of the societal hierarchy. There are two preliminary steps. The first is the differentiation of kinship units carrying high political responsibility (and enjoying corresponding privileges)—royal and aristocratic lineages—from the common kinship units. The second is the differentiation of the political from the pattern-maintenance and integrative functions of such high-level units. Because of the imperatives discussed above, this occurs slowly and is never complete at the top; though, of course, as in most modern societies now, all these functions may be taken from the kinship units as such.

Lower down, however, an important process of differentiation involves the political function. The focal initial problem here concerns the restrictions on the mobility of resources imposed by the ascriptive aspect of kinship. One crucial process is the development of some kind of "bureaucracy." For understandable reasons, there are serious obstacles to the relinquishment of control, by the functionally diffuse "highest authorities," of the classical functions of government, in the "top policy-making" and later the legislative fields. It is thus in the "administrative" area of political function—the implementation of decisions through "technical" procedures—that this process of differentiation tends to center. Enfranchisement of political support is generally more difficult to institutionalize but sometimes has happened—e.g., in Greek democracy.

From this point of view, within certain limits, the primacy of the "policy decisions" must be taken as given. Within these limits, the crucial considerations are, first, the disposability of human and material resources, and, second, their quality relative to the need. In the latter context, the competence of personnel is salient. Clearly, kinship ascription imposes frustrating limits in both respects. Though the deficiency may be partly compensated through training ascribed personnel, there is no guarantee that the person ascribed for a function by kinship status is the most competent available; in any case, the very diffuseness of kinship relations severely limits disposability.

In this connection, one must consider the relativity of the functional categories being used here. Of course, the functions of a bureaucratic organization may, from a more general point of view, fall in any category. In particular, early bureaucracies very frequently have subserved "economic" functions for the society. A prominent example is the water-control function in river-valley civilizations, emphasized by Weber and Wittvogel. The essential points, however, are rather that the focus of collective responsibility for the bureaucratic organization is the "top control" of the over-all societal collectivity and that the process of differentiation proceeds from this focal point. This is the primary criterion of its subserving a political function, in that it subserves goals defined as essential to the society as a system (through the eyes, of course, of its "ruling groups"), and not to its subunits in their "private" capacities.

A parallel process of development may occur where a subunit of the society, originally organized on the basis of kinship, undergoes structural differentiation in the political functions relative to the more diffuse matrix of kinship. Perhaps the most familiar example is the evolution of the family firm into a bureaucratic organization. Similar phenomena may, however, be found in the military field and many others.

In this sense, we may say that there are two essential structural features of bureaucracy. The character of the organization unit, seen in relation to its environment, has the primary characteristic of "functional specificity" and thus of the relative emancipation of its subunits from structural amalgamation with structures subserving other functions. For the individual member units, on the other hand, the essential point is the definition of their roles in terms of occupation.

Functional specificity for the collectivity implies the collectivity's relative independence from structural involvements or "fusions" with structural units subserving other functions. As Weber made so clear, however, there must be a "non bureaucratic" element in control of such a collectivity,

giving it its primary functional orientations—indeed, there may be several layers of such non bureaucratic control. Also, in so far as its functions are specialized within the larger system, such an organization will, in addition to its internal arrangements, have to be relatively specifically organized in two fundamental respects. First, its own members will not be the primary "consumers" of its output, whether this output be governmental administrative services, economic production, education, or even the "cure of souls." There will, then, have to be some form of institutionalization of the terms on which the outputs are made available to or, in some cases, compulsorily imposed[17] upon, these "consumers." One particularly important line of differentiation here is that between organizations which do and which do not take their beneficiaries into some type of membership status. The ordinary business firm is of the kind which does not; a physical commodity, once sold, usually does not imply a continuing relation of solidarity between seller and purchaser. In such fields as education, however, the process of "selling," of disposal, cannot be completed in a single quick transaction, but implies both a long continuing relation between teacher and student, and a process of interaction impossible without common collectivity membership. Pupils or students are, thus, members of their school or college in a sense in which customers are not members of the firm from which they purchase.

The third basic set of relations of a functionally specific collectivity to its environment concern the processes of procurement of the resources necessary for the performance of its functions. These can be classified under two general headings, namely, physical facilities, including work premises, and human services. The terms of acquisition, utilization, and disposal of the former are institutionalized as property; those of the latter, as occupation. There is a fundamental asymmetry in the relations between these two essential categories of resources, in that physical facilities can be definitively separated from the agents of their production,[18] whereas human services are inseparable from the organism and personality of the individual agent—they require either his physical presence at a work location or control over his activities in some other location; and, most important, utilization of the individual's services is conditioned by his adjustment between

---

17. For example, the services of tax-collecting agencies are often unwelcome to their "consumers," the taxpayers, but are just as institutionally regulated as are the relations of sellers and buyers in an ordinary commercial market.

18. Land is a special limiting case, both because of its nonproductibility and because the location of a given area is irrevocably fixed.

the expectations in his work role and the other roles in which he is involved.

Given that all human personalities are anchored in the nexus of kinship, the most crucial of these role-adjustment problems is the one between the occupational and kinship roles of the same person. As noted, one very common case is the simple fusion of the two—the "work" a person does is performed in his kinship role as such. At the opposite extreme is full "chattel" slavery, where maximum disposability over services is obtained through complete denial of institutional legitimacy to any kinship roles at all—clearly, an exceptional and inherently unstable arrangement. The most important additional type is the modern one of occupational role characterized by structural segregation of work roles from kinship, but with the concomitant expectation that most normal workers will have kinship roles as well—though some, like celibate priesthoods and religious orders, are similar to slavery in denying kinship roles. The most important features of the modern occupational role are structural separation of the household and kinship group from control over work performance, and control of both performance and rewards by the functionally specific organization. This generally implies the separation of physical premises of work from the household, and separation of property rights in physical facilities and sources of remuneration from the personal property of the role-incumbent. It is important that these criteria have applied to a very small proportion of adult human beings, except in the modern industrial type of society.

The above discussion began with the problem of the structural differentiation of political function from the diffuse matrix involving pattern-maintenance and integrative functions. It also started with the over-all societal level of collectivity structure, i.e., the paramount collectivity which institutionalizes the underlying moral community. By logical progression, however, we arrived at the problem of structure and status in the society of specific-function collectivities generally. When we discussed the regulation of their "disposal" functions and their access to disposable resources, we inevitably touched on what is usually called the economic organization of a society. It is now necessary to discuss the latter somewhat more fully and to relate it to political organization.

The Structural Differentiation of the Economy from Other Subsystems. Political function is particularly intimately related to the collectivity component of social structure. It is essentially the facilitation of attaining collective goals and centers on the decisions about such goals and the mobiliza-

tion of societal resources relative to them, especially the integration of the relevant collectivities for these goals. Political function is, as noted, fundamental to the society as a whole. But analytically, the same considerations apply to all the society's subcollectivity units. It follows that what has been called the specific-function collectivity is defined precisely as a collectivity for which, in its *internal* organization, political function, i.e., effectiveness, has primacy over other functions. For subcollectivities, however, the goals are not in this structural sense set "internally," though they may or may not be set autonomously, and in reference to the more inclusive system their goal may or may not be political. Thus the function of a business firm is primarily economic; its goal is "production," but its internal organization must be analyzed first in political terms. The category *political* is, however, here conceived as analytical; hence, the relation between the political and the other aspects of the subsystem will be different in different types of specific-function collectivities. The respective organizations of a government administrative agency, of a university, and of a business firm naturally differ greatly. In spite of these variations, the relative prominence of specific-function collectivities in the structure of the society is the most important single index of the differentiation of the political from other structures. Societies differ, however, both in the degree of this differentiation and in its incidence. Compared to some European societies, American society, at least until recently, has had substantially less development of bureaucracy in government and more of it in the field of economic production.

Later, we will discuss specific mechanisms by which political function is differentially institutionalized. The most important categories may be defined as leadership, authority, and power.

Economic function, as distinguished from the political, involves the production and allocation of disposable resources. *Economic* function is exercised only when important available resources are means to alternative ends, and at some stage are not committed to a specific use. Analysis of small groups shows that this is always and necessarily true of social interaction. Thus approval as a sanction cannot effectively regulate action if it is committed in advance to one predicted act of one group member without reference to the availability of more highly valued alternatives. This would be equivalent to awarding prizes for success in a contest, without holding any competition.

In society, however, such units are structured as roles and collectivities, as exchangeable physical facilities, and in certain other categories—e.g., "packages" of communicable symbolic meaning.

Traditionally one main criterion of the value of economic resources is relative scarcity. The other most important one is general utility for different functions. Some physical commodities are extremely limited in adaptability, while others have considerable range. For example, land, its utility limited only by type of soil and climate, can be used for growing a wide variety of things. Another example is the automobile, a highly generalized facility of "private" transportation, whose usefulness, however, is entirely dependent on the system of roads.

The possibilities of generalizing about physical commodities and human services as resources are, however, inherently limited. The utilization of scarce resources is dependent on the institutionalization of mechanisms which, independent of possession of or advance commitment to any specific commodities, services, information, etc., make it possible to gain access to wide ranges of different facilities as need for them develops. In known societies, there are in particular two highly generalized mechanisms of this type, namely political power and money; the latter, of course, has primacy of economic function.

Both political power and money require the institutionalization of the disposability of facilities. Negatively, this means eliminating or drastically weakening the ascriptive rights to such facilities, which are always prominent in the more undifferentiated social structures. Positively, it involves institutionalizing adequate rights of control and disposal, in the form of rights of contract, property, and occupational use of human services. The prominence of ascription makes the right of disposal or "alienation" particularly important; especially with regard to human services, relative clarity of rights of control within the limits of occupational commitment are important. The modern institution of property, as applied to physical commodities rather than money, ties together various components which, in European feudal law, were distributed between different units all having rights in the same "thing"—land being of course, the most important single example. Property rights have become much more clearly differentiated from various other contractual rights, notably those involving services, and from political jurisdiction over land and over persons' acts on land. There are limits on the property owner's freedom; but modern ownership is an essential condition of generalized disposability of physical commodity resources, independent of political power. The same applies, of course, to the institutionalization of occupational roles including freedom to contract for services through employment.

Money is not a commodity, but is a very special mode of the institutionalization of expectations and commitments through communication. It is a generalized type of cybernetic mechanism which makes it possible for the unit to mobilize, subject to normative regulation, whatever resources it needs or wishes, within the limits of its "means," expressed in monetary terms. Money, in the social system in which it operates, depends on a balancing system of reciprocities, developing out of the kinds of more diffuse reciprocities which certain anthropologists like Malinowski and Lévy-Strauss have analyzed. Inflation and deflation are symptoms that this reciprocal system is somehow out of balance.

We noted that the usefulness of the automobile is dependent on a system of roads and, it may be added, on the implementation of adequate rules of traffic control. The usefulness of money as a much more generalized facility is dependent on a system of markets and adequate rules governing the continual flow of transactions through markets. A market is a defined social system in which there are institutionalized expectations of willingness to exchange disposable facilities for money and vice versa under a set of rules for settling terms and for the rights and obligations assumed and relinquished in the process. Generally, markets become more significant as access to them is not particularistically restricted, especially on an ascribed basis.[19] The institutions of contract and property, and the monetary mechanism itself, are the bases of the market as a system; and the basis of "labor market," the institution of occupational employment.

Money and Power. The concept of political power has been highly controversial in sociological literature, and there is not the consensus about it that there is among economists about money. I would, however, like to suggest a concept which builds directly on the parallel with money as a generalized mechanism for controlling the allocation of resources. The political function has been defined as that of facilitating the effective attainment of a collectivity's goals. Goal-attainment has been specifically related to the processes of change in the interrelations between a system and its environing situation. For those exercising political responsibility, this inevitably involves important elements of uncertainty. Effectiveness, therefore, necessitates the capacity to make decisions and to commit resources, *independently of specific conditions prescribed in advance* by ascription or by some kind of prior agreement or contract.

19. Very specialized markets where access is limited to special groups of "professionals," like the New York Stock Exchange, are not really exceptions to this generalization.

We may define power (in the analytical, political sense) as generalized capacity, independent of prior commitments on the relevant level of specification, to influence the allocation of resources for the goals of a collectivity through invoking the institutionalized obligations (i.e., loyalties) of member units, utilizing such sanctions as are legitimized through these obligations and institutionalized roles involved in the power system. Power should be conceived as a circulating medium and, for any unit, as a scarce resource. Power is unequally distributed in a society, a disproportionate share being held by units carrying political responsibility—just as a disproportionate share of the wealth of an economically developed society is controlled by the units specializing in economic production.[20] Like economic firms, units specializing in political function are dependent on the return of the power they have "spent" or "invested" through their decisions about the allocation of resources. This return, analogous to that from consumers' spending, takes the form of the constituency's satisfaction or dissatisfaction with these decisions, and it thus directly affects the leadership's capacity to make further commitments. The mechanisms of power are not nearly so sharply structured as is the monetary mechanism, though, in democratic societies and in various types of association within them, the vote has functions as a unit which are partly analogous to those of the monetary unit. It does not, however, cover anything like the proportion of the whole range of power phenomena that the monetary unit does.

There is a parallel between political enfranchisement, as the capacity to exercise political power independently of ascribed definitions of obligation or those imposed from above, and the development of consumers' markets where the consumer may select from the offerings available and have their preferences exercise a crucial influence on the process of production itself.

Just as money depends on the institutionalization of contract, property, and occupation, flexible political action is made possible by the institution-alization of power. The institutionalization of leadership is parallel to that of contract in the economic field. It is essentially the institutionalization of the right to make decisions committing the collectivity as a whole and thereby imposing obligations on its member units in their various capacities.

Authority, like *power,* is another highly ambiguous term. It designates the political institution which is parallel to property in economics. It is the complex of institutionalized rights over the contributory actions (in economic terminology, "services") of member units of a collectivity. That is, authority institutionalizes rights to make decisions binding in specific respects on the relevant categories of member units, e.g., paying taxes or having to enter military service. Authority comprises the general rules which govern the making of specific binding decisions. Power, on the other hand, is a mechanism regulating the process of making actual commitments. Specific rights of authority can be relinquished, just as specific rights of ownership can be. But "authority" is a non-circulating medium in the same sense that property is. It is the institutional matrix of the functioning of power.[21]

Some Limits of Political and Economic Specialization

As used here, political and economic categories are generalized functional categories that permeate the *entire* structure of the social system. Structures with either political or economic primacy are found at all four levels of institutionalized normative culture and interpenetrate in different ways. Thus, fully differentiated occupational role-performance is a role-category with relative economic primacy, no matter in what functional context it is eventually utilized, and the same is true regarding the command of other facilities, e.g., through ownership of physical commodities. This follows from the fact that the criterion of economic function is that it concerns a resource disposable through market channels. Hence, this resource, the "labor" of eco-

---

20. In both connections it is important not to confuse inequality, as applied to "consuming" units alone, with that for the society as a whole. Even a socialist society imposing absolute equality of income on all household units would give effective control of most of the economic resources of the society to its socialized agencies of production. Similarly, in a "perfect" democracy, all adult citizens might have equal power to influence the selection of leadership and certain highly generalized orientations of government. But, in the *operative* functioning of collective action, control of power would have to be relatively concentrated in organizations and leadership roles carrying special responsibility for political function. Otherwise, there would be no differentiated political function in the society.

21. These considerations show how voting is quite literally an exercise of power, resting on the institutionalization of the authority of the electorate. That is, after each voter has registered his own decision at the polls, the aggregate result of these many individual decisions is institutionally *binding* on the collectivity as a whole. This is most dramatic when an election turns out an incumbent administration. The incumbents are obligated to vacate their offices and permit the opposition to come in. In the light of the facilities of power commanded by a government, it is clear that this involves a very drastic renunciation, particularly when the incumbents are, as is often the case, convinced that the opposition are little short of scoundrels. The great difficulty with which this pattern has come to be institutionalized is understandable.

nomic theory, is economically differentiated if a developed labor market exists. Inevitably, however, there are various constraints in the structure of labor markets caused by the interpenetration of the economic and various non-economic factors. Even in the types of labor of maximum disposability—e.g., "operative" duties at relatively low levels of organizational responsibility or technical competence—there are basic limits imposed by the incumbent's membership in kinship and other non-economic collectivities. The kin case is, in a highly differentiated society, one of the impinging of pattern-maintenance functions on the economic. As we have seen, the same kinds of limits do not apply to physical commodities. Similarly, the executive role in specific-function collectivities, even in business firms, has special features, because the political component of the role is so prominent within the collectivity. This fact causes much of the persistent recruitment for such roles through channels other than a labor market—e.g., in the family firm—even when management has become almost fully "professionalized," certain constraints remain. One constraint is the "particularizing" of selection for employment—from outside the organization or by promotion. No system of selection entirely by competitive examination for particular posts has been successfully institutionalized, apparently because of the functional diffuseness of the role and the importance of relations between people at the top of an organization. In one sense, the selection of leadership of the nuclear family through marriage, through the "irrational" mechanism of romantic love rather than through rational assessment of suitability for parental roles, is parallel. Both top management and families are small groups whose members must associate very intimately with each other over long periods.

Another constraint on the labor market is employment for professional roles. Here the primary organizational goals belong to either integrative or pattern-maintenance functions. Two prominent structural deviations from the normal commercial market in this field are the "sliding scale" and tenure. They are associated with institutions, like privileged communication and academic freedom, that insulate the role-incumbent from some of the pressures from laymen that might impede the performance of complicated and delicate functions.

The differentiation of economic and political functions from each other and from the other two is found operating at the collectivity level. In the first place, at the entire society's functional level, there is differentiation of collectivities with primacy of one function or another. In the economic category, the business firm is a clear case; with it goes

monetary success, i.e., the monetary cost-earnings balance, as the primary criterion—whether or not it is linked with profit actually going to the organization's internal "proprietary" elements. The cost accounting of socialized enterprise is just as subject to this criterion as the profitability of private enterprise. In politics the clearest case, because of the element of inevitable functional diffuseness discussed above, is the administrative agency of government. The exclusiveness with which criteria of effectiveness govern the evaluation of collective performance is the main symptom of the degree of differentiation of political function. In other words, the amount of power generated by a collective unit—the power output relative to the cost of its acquisition, stated in terms of the loss or impairment of loyalties incurred in the process—is the main criterion of effectiveness. Whereas some collectivities in a differentiated society have political primacy in this sense, in all specific-function collectivities a political component centers in what we have called "management" or "administration." In all large-scale organizations, these functions become differentiated from the operative ones.

Just as constraints on the commercial or competitive structure of markets are imposed by impinging non-economic factors, so in many collectivities there are constraints on the political primacy of their organization and orientation to situations. In the business firm, the standard of monetary success incorporates one set of such criteria. In one direction, it limits devotion to "technical" perfection by applying criteria of monetary profit—a fact the importance of which technocrats cannot see—while also limiting the relevance and legitimacy of pursuing political power. In both directions, the limitations take the form of institutionalized mechanisms of control which establish rank orders of considerations which are legitimately taken into account in decision-making.

Another example of the interpenetration of politics and economics is the universality with which, in societies with a highly developed monetary economy, command of adequate monetary funds becomes an indispensable condition of effective operation—especially as the mechanism for mobilizing both physical facilities and necessary human services. The differences between types of functionally specific collectivities lie in the importance of the criterion of monetary success—whether all monetary costs are expected eventually to be balanced by proceeds derived from operation, or it is legitimate for the organization to incur deficits which must be made up by special measures like taxation or soliciting contributions. It is significant that, in the modern liberal type of society, the criterion of monetary independence applies above all to two classes of collectivities, business firms and households.

The leadership and authority-power structure of the modern university provide examples of the limitations on internal political primacy parallel to economic ones in non-business collectivities. The most important operative personnel are highly qualified technical specialists working in many different fields; the tightness of control by top management typical of firms engaged in physical production is impossible. That is, internal to the organization, power is much more decentralized in its distribution than it is in the business organization. The institution of tenure is important both as a modification of the structure of the labor market and as a limitation on administrative power within the organizations.

Functional Differentiation of Norms and Values.
The same basic order of functional differentiation we have been analyzing occurs at the level of differentiated norms. At the societal level, the legal institutional complex of contact, property, and occupational roles is primarily of economic significance. This complex includes the institutional norms governing money and its uses, involved in all three. Money is integrally involved in the institution of contract, because a large proportion of contracts involve monetary considerations, and because it is an institutionalized symbol—the paramount sanction of "restitutive law," as Durkheim called it. Money also is the apex of the property system; the monetary evaluation of other objects and the convertibility of "real" assets into money are vital features of any modern property system. The controversies about units of account in socialist economies show that money can be abolished only by inventing its functional equivalent; indeed, no socialist economy has seriously attempted to abolish it, however much its market system may differ from free-enterprise. Money is absent only in a primitive *Naturalwirtschaft*. Such a society has not reached a high level of differentiating economic function. Finally, money is involved with the institutionalization of occupation, by virtue of the institutionalization of the legitimacy of monetary remuneration for occupational performances.

Basic economic institutions are embodied in the formal legal system, as are the expected variations between contexts where they are involved, with or without primacy of economic function. Thus the directors of a business corporation are legally obliged, on penalty of liquidation, to operate to maintain financial solvency; governmental units are legally authorized to impose taxes to maintain their functions; and voluntary contributors to religious, charitable, and educational collectivities are legally privileged to deduct such contributions from taxable income.

Similar considerations apply to the normative system governing political functions, in governmental and other contexts. One example is the governmental constitution of the society, prescribing the norms defining the procedures for selecting governmental leadership, the nature and limits of their authority when in office, and the modes in which they may legitimately exercise power. The law involves a complex set of prescriptions for the norms governing leadership, authority, and power in private collectivities, including the definition of variations permissible by virtue of differences in their functions. An important example of this in American law is the doctrine of "public interest." Essentially, this draws a line between two broad categories of activities and, hence, between the collectivities carrying them on. In one case, their actions are their "private" concern, and the law is conceived as regulatory in the negative sense. Rules keeping the activities within bounds preventing them from injuring other parties or otherwise violating societal values and norms must be observed. If, on the other hand, an activity is affected with a public interest, those performing it both enjoy privileges—e.g., franchises to use rights of way—and assume obligations, like regulation of rates charged to the public, not otherwise applicable. Essentially, activities which affect the public interest are defined as involving a larger component of social political responsibility than those that do not. The obligations deriving from this responsibility must be fulfilled; those who undertake them will be given the special privileges, exemptions, and facilities necessary for their fulfilment. Under the law, whether it be formally written or not, every private collectivity has its "constitution" or set of norms governing the political functions necessary for its effective operation.

The type of differentiation under discussion also applies to values. Values cannot control action by mere "emanation." Their institutionalization involves their specification through a series of levels of function and situation. The values of a primary functional subsystem, of a society, like the economy or the polity, constitute the *first* level of specification relative to the general societal values. This specification, it is clear, is by function. For example, the concept of economic rationality has usually been interpreted as a psychological generalization. It also has a definitely normative aspect; and at the highest normative level it is the focus of the value system of the economy as a functional subsystem of the society.

No society can accept economic rationality as its most general societal value-orientation, though it can place the economic highest among its functional priorities. Empirically, economic rationality must be evaluated according to its place and limits in relation to the higher-level societal values, to the system's level of structural differentiation, and to the situation of the society. In so far, however, as units of the society at all three of the levels below that of values becomes structurally differentiated in terms of primacy of economic function, the hallmark of this differentiation is that, relative to *their* functions and situations within the system, units are governed by this economic standard. Thus, though collectivities need not be specifically oriented to economic function, there may still be, in the fields of contract, money, property, and occupation, complexes of institutional norms which are highly emancipated from non-economic considerations. For example, the institutionalization of land ownership makes land far more disposable as an economic resource than it would be, for instance, where rights of alienation were not institutionalized.

Similar considerations apply at the collectivity level. Economic values and norms apply in some degree to all collectivities in certain aspects of their functioning, whether this involves economic primacy or not; thus even a church, whose central function is far removed from economic primacy, must exercise some degree of financial prudence— i.e., subscribe, within a limited sphere, to economic values. It is, however, the institutionalization of the criterion of monetary success as the paramount measure of function which is the hallmark of a collectivity's economic primacy. This, however, is a functional value; and its implications are always subject to qualification in terms of institutional variability at higher levels and situational variability at lower ones. Thus a firm producing dangerous drugs or firearms is regulated to protect incompetent and innocent parties from misusing these products; such protection of third parties is one fundamental focus of the *institution* of contract. Correspondingly, a retail food firm will adapt to the whims (perhaps, "convenience") of its customers as the producer of power plants for large, fast ships will not, because of the overwhelming importance of technical standards of effective performance in the latter case. The classical economists were not wholly unrealistic in speaking of money as a measure of value. Even given the higher-level societal values and still higher-level cultural values, that of economic rationality is authentic and genuine.[22]

---

22. For the sociologist, the criterion of a "genuine" value cannot be its "absoluteness." In social and cultural systems, as we analyze them, there must be hierarchies of values, each of which must take a relative place. The system governed by a single, unitary, absolute value is the limiting case which is literally "out of this world."

The same considerations apply to occupational roles. Some of these roles are mainly economic in function. Marginal productivity is a primary standard of whether the service should be employed— which can roughly be equated, under economically ideal conditions, with that service's contribution to the monetary success of the organization employing it. Such roles institutionalize economic rationality as their primary value. In other roles, such as most professional ones, it is a subsidiary value. In choosing between employments, the professional, other things equal, legitimately prefers the financially more remunerative job; and the employing organization offers more to those who, from its point of view, are more desirable personnel. But it does not follow on either side that the greatest financial return or financial contribution is the first criterion of desirability for the collectivity.

What is true of economic rationality as a differentiated functional value-system is also true for the other functions. In the polity the value-system centers on collective or organizational effectiveness for the societal collectivity itself or for any legitimate goals of subcollectivities. Such effectiveness (or power, in a larger, e.g., "international" system) may be the paramount functional value of a whole society, though it as such cannot be a societal value-pattern—that would necessitate some higher basis for the legitimate pursuit of power. The range within which greater power is valued will, as in economics, depend on the societal value-system and on considerations of the society's structural differentiation and situation. Similarly, some subcollectivities will be guided within the system by values of political primacy, while in others this component is subordinated. Thus, while a governmental administrative bureau may be evaluated primarily in political terms, a university or a family cannot be. Values of political function will be institutionalized at each of the society's levels of structural hierarchy.

Specialized values for the integrative system are oriented, *within* the societal value system, to maximum internal harmony and mutual complementing among the units of the system. Such integrative values are expressed in various contexts. There is the general ethical one of doing one's duty to others; there is the political one, stressing the importance of collective loyalty and individual self-sacrifice; there is the legal interest in the equitable settlement of conflicts; and there is the medical concern for the patient's welfare. These different levels of expression share the explicit repudiation of the relevance of *unit*-effectiveness, or power, or of economic success as such, as valid criteria.

Differentiation between Pattern-Maintenance and Integrative Function

We have discussed at length both the relations between economic and political function, and social structure at all four levels, because in social science traditions these seem to have been more adequately analyzed and are better known. The same basic principles of the relations between structure and function, between segmentation, specification, and differentiation, apply to the pattern-maintenance and the integrative functions, to the relations of the relevant structures to each other and to the economic and political. We shall here confine the discussion to a very brief outline of the principal components of structural content involved in these other two functions.

There are two important considerations. First, societies will differ in so far as structures with clear primacy of these functions have come to be differentiated from those whose functions are more diffuse. Second, relevant structures will be located at different levels on the scales of segmentation and specification, and may thus not be directly comparable with each other.

Within the framework suggested by the distinction between the theoretical problems involved in equilibrium analysis and in analysis of structural change of social systems, the concept of *pattern-maintenance* as a functional category is not meant to have empirically static connotations. Analytically, specialization in both maintenance and change of values should be placed in this category.

Religion is one of the areas of concern which belong most directly here. Religious values as such should be located in the cultural and not in the social system. Societal values stand at a lower level in the general specification scale of value-patterns than do religious ones. But in some sense, all societal values are here conceived analytically as religiously grounded. However, the structural implications of this may vary greatly, as a function of the nature of both the religion and the social system.

It has been pointed out that sometimes the overall societal collectivity is also a religious collectivity —to quote Durkheim, a "moral community usually called a church."[23] Often, however, this is not the case—as in Western Christianity generally and, more particularly, in recent denominational pluralism as institutionalized in the United States. There are an indefinite plurality of churches, each of which is a voluntary association. The state is no longer a religious collectivity, and there is no established church which claims or is allowed to claim universal religious jurisdiction over the whole society. However, values derived from common religious orientations are still institutionalized. Moreover, an important part of the normative system of the society comprises rules governing behavior in this sphere—for example, the Constitutional provisions for the separation of church and state, and the institutionalization of religious freedom and tolerance. Thus pluralism—at the collectivity level of structure, and, even more, the role level, where every individual can within certain limits adhere to his own beliefs and practices—does not imply that there is *no* institutionalization of religious orientations at the norm and the value levels. This idea is a very common misinterpretation of the sense in which such a society as the American is described as "secularized."

As institutionalization of religious orientation has become a more specialized and differentiated function, it has been allocated to more diverse subcollectivities at lower levels in the social structure's scale of segmentation and specification than was the older type of universal church. But this process has coincided with the development of *higher* levels of generality in the religious requirements of normal societal membership. For example, the societal "common denominator" is considerably more general than was that of medieval Catholicism. It has, as it were, been proved that such a narrow and detailed religious consensus is not a necessary condition of stable value-consensus at the societal level.

A second primary component of the pattern-maintenance function is that usually called "socialization." Whereas the primary focus of religion is in the cultural system, that of socialization is in the personality system. The underlying conditions are the relative shortness of the individual's life-span in comparison to the duration of societies, and the resulting functional imperative for the society to assimilate a continuing stream of new members, primarily through birth and biological maturation. Within this framework, the most important imperatives are anchoring the process of socialization in the genetic sequence of the development of personality, essentially through successively internalizing increasingly complex and differentiated systems of social objects, and the corresponding internalization of increasingly generalized patterns of culture.

Universally, at least one kinship unit, always with the nuclear family's prominent participation, is the primary collective agent of early socialization; in most non-literate societies, the function remains embedded in diffuse kinship structures. In modern

23. E. Durkheim, *Elementary Forms of the Religious Life*. Introduction. London: Allen & Unwin, Ltd., 1926.

industrial societies, however, the nuclear family has become a far more differentiated, though still highly segmented, unit, adapted to the functions of socialization and "tension-management." In the process, its connections with the extended kinship nexus have been greatly attenuated; it has become structurally "isolated"; and most of the other functions of older kinship structures have passed to non-kinship units, notably those of economic production. Because, in this situation, its primary functions concern early, pre-school socialization, the family operates at very low levels of generality in the scale of specification of the value-patterns which are internalized in the process.

All more highly differentiated societies have developed non-kinship structures centering about the functions of formal education in which the higher-level patterns of normative culture and systems of objects are internalized in the personality. In a few societies, there have finally developed institutions of higher education in which a highly important fusion for sub-functions of pattern-maintenance occurs: the combination of the highest levels of training with, through scholarship and research, the functions of codifying and developing important parts of the cultural tradition itself.

This concern with the cultural tradition operates in the aspects having to do with value patterns, and in fields of existential belief systems—non-empirical, as in religious and philosophy, and empirical, as in science, technology, and ideology—and expressive symbolization, as in the arts. It constitutes another basic focus of the society's pattern-maintenance systems, which tends to become closely associated with the higher ranges of the socialization system. Expressive symbolization, which reaches its highest levels of "universal" significance in the sophisticated fine arts, including literature, at lower levels of specification involves the modes of taste constituting the framework within which expressive, i.e., otherwise non-functional, activities—including what is ordinarily called recreation—are carried out.

As these functions become less imbedded in functionally diffuse structures, the same basic imperatives outlined for structures with economic or political functional primacy apply. A school system, like a church or a government bureau, must have institutionalized leadership and patterns of authority; it must have access to mobile resources; and it must regulate the relations of its services to its consumers. This is true of a theatrical enterprise or an art institute, either requiring the appropriately specified values, norms legitimized by these values, collectivity organization, and institutionalization of different role types. In spite of the non-economic or non-political primacy of their functions, they cannot escape involvement in the functional imperatives in these areas—everywhere the conditions of successful institutionalization of any function.

Structures with Integrative Primacy. It has been suggested that the focus of the integrative subsystem is the legal system; in a modern Western type of society, particularly in the functioning of the appellate courts, and their relation to the more generalized aspects of legislation (much actual legislation is, considered functionally, more concerned with policy decisions than with establishing generalized norms). The establishment of a norm is not alone functionally adequate. The courts are concerned with fundamental problems: interpretation; determination of jurisdictional problems, i.e., in what circumstances a norm applies and to whom; and problems of sanctions or enforcement, i.e., determining the consequences to the actor of compliance or non-compliance. The central judicial function is interpretation, of which these other two are subcategories.

Norms, however, must be defined and interpreted, and also implemented. (We are not here concerned primarily with the executive function of enforcement, which is goal-attainment rather than integration.)

The first imperative of a system of norms is its internal consistency. This is a primary focus of the function of interpretation and, in highly differentiated systems, is primarily a judicial function, though sometimes codes are prepared and legislatively enacted. Second, however, there is the specification of the application of higher-order norms to levels where they can guide the action of the society's lower-level structural units by defining the situation for them. This particularly involves the collectivity and role levels of structure, and hence the institutionalization of the basic patterns governing these in political and economic respects.

Another major functional problem of a normative system concerns the adjustments occurring because a social system is always involved in processes of interchange with a changing environment—indeed, always is subject to endogenous sources of change as well. These naturally have repercussions on units' interrelationships, whose significance for the integration of the system is focussed in the bearing of these relations on the content of the system of norms, and on the degrees and motivation of conformity with norms.

There seem to be three basic types of processes of adjustment. One concerns keeping the regulatory norms at a sufficiently high level of generality so that much of the adjustment can be left to the spontaneous, i.e., unprescribed, action of the units themselves. A system of norms is analogous to a language, in that its rules as such do not "say" anything concrete, but provide a framework within which very many different things can be said and understood according to the occasion for saying them. In certain respects—not exclusively the economic sense—it is legitimate to refer to this as the area within which self-interest is permitted to operate. This "unit-individualism"—*unit* rather than *personal,* for much of it concerns collectivities—is not emancipation from all control through institutionalized norms. Rather, as Durkheim so clearly brought out, high levels of "responsible freedom" can be attained only through positive institutionalization, through systems of norms and sanctions imposing the *obligation* of accepting responsibility and utilizing freedom over wide areas. It may thus be referred to as "institutionalized individualism."

The second basic process of integrative adjustment is altering the content of normative patterns. The great integrative problem is to make such adjustments meet the varying functional needs without threatening the stability of the higher-level system of norms. The dangers of a system of norms are rigidity, or such flexibility that either adequate definition of the situation is lost or that what there is is functionally inappropriate. This operates at the higher levels through legislative, judicial, and administrative rulings and decisions, and, at lower and private collectivities, through functionally cognate mechanisms.

The third type of process operates, short of major structural change itself, in the areas where the other two are inadequate. The essential common feature of the first two is the expectation that the acting unit whose activities are to be controlled will, properly situated through definition of norms and sanctions, act as desired—operating through the situation, without attempting to change the internal structure of the unit, be it person-in-role or collectivity. The processes of social control, in the narrower sociological sense, operate upon the "internal" system of the unit; in the case of the individual-in-role, on his motivations or sentiments. They not only facilitate or hinder his getting what he wants, but they redefine what he wants. Behavior subject to control can be technically termed deviant only when seen this way.

A complex society has institutionalized a variety of processes of social control. We shall not attempt to list or classify them here. But certain aspects of religious ritual certainly fit—those particularly concerned with reinforcing value-commitment when deviance develops or threatens. For the over-all societal collectivity and the definition of its goals, certain aspects of political ideology and its involvement

in the definitions of political orientation have this type of significance. In implementing norms in relational systems, particularly those involving contract in the sociological sense, the private practice of law in the system of courts is such a mechanism of social control. Finally, when concern is focused on the individual's capacity for role-performance, the motivated aspect of illness and its therapy, i.e., in psychosomatic and mental illness, have a similar significance.

Stratification. A final aspect of social structure of primarily integrative significance is social stratification. That is, the ordering of units of the system in a scale of relative prestige which, to function in a positively integrative way, must be a genuine expression of the institutionalized system of values. In other words, prestige reflects functional contribution to the society's welfare. Perhaps the most important and necessary functional focus of positive institutionalization of stratification is the tendency of societal differentiation to lead to bases of polarization of conflicting interests. The two most obvious bases of polarization are political power and wealth, i.e., command of more or less generalized facilities. Here, the focus of institutionalized stratification is *legitimizing* differential power and wealth, and, more generally, access to valued objects and statuses.

"Social class" is the most common basis of stratification. This term includes the differential prestige-evaluation of various categories of *kinship* units, differentiated by their members' functions in the social system, by access to power and wealth, and by "styles of life," (i.e., patterns of expressive symbolism associated with their standards of living). Kinship is involved because the solidarity of the kinship unit, including as it does both sexes and all ages, is at some level a central functional imperative of every society, even though many partial social systems can operate without it. Therefore, certain differential advantages, like better living conditions and the younger generation's access to opportunity, must be shared by all members of the unit, regardless of the extent to which they have been "earned" by the individual. Thus the wife and children of a successful man will share the rewards of his performance whether or not they have contributed very much to it—the question of their contribution is irrelevant to the family's status as a unit. Though class mobility is possible in varying degrees, no society has over a long period operated without *any* differentiation in class status. Empirically, the extent to which such class differentiation involves class conflict is highly variable. The major function of the institutionalization of class status is to minimize class conflict; but often it is not very successful.

It is unnecessary to assume that there should always be a single unequivocal prestige-ranking scale of kinship units. As we will argue in the Introduction to Part Two, a highly generalized prestige and power differential between two principal classes is a common feature of early civilizations. In later, more highly differentiated societies, however, the multiplicity of groups with widely varying functional significance, and the corresponding differentiation of reward patterns, mean that only on a very broad and general basis is it possible to speak of a single scale; over considerable ranges, the "upper" groups in different functional categories are not directly comparable. In contemporary society, e.g., it is difficult to compare the prestiges held by leading business men, physicians, scientists, and politicians respectively. Money income is far from an exact measure. There is, however, no question that few families in the United States with incomes under five thousand dollars (at the principal income earner's full career maturity) could be described as in the higher prestige groups.

All these integrative functions are performed in structural settings which must be analyzed in the same general terms applied to the other three functional subsystems. They involve their subvalues at the requisite levels of specification, their own norms, collectivities specialized in this direction, and roles (except stratification, which cannot be specialized on a collectivity or role basis). They must meet their own economic, political, and pattern-maintenance prerequisites, etc. A wide range of structural variation in all these respects exist.

III. THE DYNAMICS OF SOCIAL EQUILIBRIUM

The foregoing discussion may serve as transition to the consideration of analyzing the dynamic processes and mechanisms of social systems, first, with reference to the problem of equilibrium within a given structural framework. Technical conceptualization in this field has developed more slowly than in structural morphology or in functional categorization. Since, therefore, it is less prominent in the literature of the period covered by these volumes, this Introduction will treat these problems less fully than others. It is, however, essential to give it some place, if only on the agenda of unfinished business of sociological theory—though more than that can be done.

The analysis of dynamic process at the equilibration level must center around two categories of the system's components. The first are the *resources* which, starting from outside the system, go through various phases as they pass through the system, and at certain points are utilized in system functioning, i.e., consumed, some "products" then being finally put out to other systems. The process can be conceived as one combining various resources to produce a new phase, and then recombining the results with still other factors to produce still other phases. The second category of component comprises the types of mechanisms which mediate these processes of generation and utilization of resources and regulate their rates of flow, direction of use, etc. Money and power, as discussed, are the prototypes of these mechanisms.

Societal Resources: Categories of Input and Output.[24] First, something about the resource problem. Fortunately for sociology, our sister-discipline, economics, has developed and refined a theoretical model of this process of factor-combination that is capable of generalization. This is the theory concerning the combination of the factors of production to produce commodities and shares of income. In the version important for our purposes, there are four factors of production, namely, land, labor, capital, and organization.

The factors of production occupy an intermediate place in the combinatorial flow, through the social system, from socially ultimate resources to socially ultimate outputs. They are the input-categories into the economy as one of the four primary functional subsystems of the society. There should, therefore, be cognate input-categories for each of the other three primary subsystems. It should also be possible to use the same pattern of classification and analysis at other levels, especially for the societal system as a whole and for units at lower levels of specification than the primary functional subsystem.

Let us attempt to outline this for the society as a system. None of the socially ultimate inputs consists in either actual physical objects or the physical behavior of organisms, nor can any of the ultimate outputs be placed in these categories. The social system is one of controlling behavior and the physical environment through behavior. Its ultimate resources are the factors in the system's capacity to attain such control, and ultimate outputs for aspects of the actual attainment and/or exercise of that capacity, including improvements in previous capacity. Where physical objects and physical behav-

24. For convenient reference, a schematic tabulation of the categories to be discussed in this section is included in the accompanying table.

Schematic Tabulation of
Societal Inputs and Outputs

Primary Social Subsystem	Input and Source	Output and Destination
Pattern-Maintenance	Given structure as institutionalized patterns of normative culture (no external source)	Maintenance of structure and specification of values (no external destination)
Integration	Plasticity (from behavioral organism)	Patterns for purposive response (to behavioral organism)
Goal-Attainment	Capacity for socialized motivational commitments (from personality)	Goal-gratification (to personality)
Adaptation	Codes for organization of information (from cultural system)	Validation of standards of competence (to cultural system)

ior are involved, as they always are, the rights or ways to control these entities, not the entities themselves, are the object of sociological analysis. Thus, in an economic exchange involving a physical commodity, what changes hands is not the commodity but property rights *in* the commodity. Analytically, physical transfer of possession is a "technological" process and not a social system process.

The ultimate resources of a society (and of other social systems on the appropriate level of specification) should comprise the ultimate outputs of the other subsystems of the general system of action as these impinge on the social system itself. It is critical, in the economic theory of the factors of production, that land is a special case relative to the other three. It has two special properties—it is neither consumed in the production process, nor produced; and in consequence, its total quantity in the system is not a function of its price, though, through the market mechanism, particular units of land may be allocated to particular uses and users. For the economy to function, land as a physical resource must be included in this category; so also must the institutionalized structure of the society, so far as this is treated as given for purposes of economic analysis and so far as it is differentially utilized in productive processes.

In the society as a system, the analogue of land is the institutionalized normative culture, i.e., the social structure, which for the system reference and time period under consideration is treated as given. At the highest normative level, this consists in the

system's values. Treating values as analogous to the quantity of land thus becomes another way of stating the general methodological postulate enunciated earlier: there is a set of theoretical problems concerning the dynamics of equilibrium analysis which should be distinguished from problems involved in the analysis of structural change. So far as analysis is confined to the equilibrium level, institutionalized normative culture is not consumed in the process but is assumed to remain given and stable. The ways these structural components are utilized in social process, however, are variable as a function of the operation of the same mechanisms affecting the utilization of the other resources.

What are these other resources? According to the logic of our paradigm, there should be three: inputs respectively from the personality, the behavioral organism, and the cultural system. Another interesting point is that the situation of the social system, i.e., its goal-attainment and adaptive boundaries taken together, comprises the personality and cultural systems,[25] which fall into these two categories respectively; whereas the integrative boundary, with certain special features, is, rather surprisingly, related to the behavioral organism.

Tentatively, we suggest that the category of pri-

25. It is not possible here to amplify this statement. The reader interested in following it may refer to Parsons and Smelser, *Economy and Society*, Free Press, 1956, especially Chapter II. In that publication, however, the analysis was not applied to the action system as a whole in terms of the interchanges of its four primary subsystems, but only to the primary subsystems of a society.

mary input from the personality system may be called "capacity to socialize motivational commitments," extending ultimately to role-performance. The input from the cultural system may be called codified "information," in that it provides the cultural basis of empirical societal problem-solution. When this input is specified and made relevant to motivational, evaluative, and integrative references in the system, it becomes utilizable knowledge. Knowledge, on the societal level, is the basic facility-category. Finally, the basic input from the organism is that plasticity which, through appropriate learning processes, can be built into patterns of purposive response. These, in turn, can be utilized in integrated social interaction. The patterning of the responses in systems, not the discrete units of response, is of crucial significance in this connection.[26]

What, then, are the ouput categories analogous to the income shares of economic theory? Generally, the output corresponding to the input of institutionalized normative culture is the *maintenance* of that structure intact. Only within limitations would an important process in a complex system operate for long without involving structural change at some lower levels of specification, segmentation, and differentiation in the system. In this case, the essential pattern-maintenance output is the *specification* of the higher-order value-system to the appropriate levels for the functional and situational exigencies of the subsystems involved in the secondary processes of structural change .

In interpreting the meaning of the other three output categories, one must remember that the locus of all the other three subsystems is in individual persons—except for the embodiment of culture in inanimate physical objects, notably written documents. Therefore, in one sense all three of these are of psychological significance.

The primary output to the personality system, analytically speaking, is goal-gratification (and, of course, its negative, deprivation). For the equilibrium of the personality as a system, this is the establishment of a stable relation to a structurally significant situational object or system of objects. Role-partners participate in social structure on an interactive basis through action in a role; the relevant object is social, a role-partner or a collectivity. This output thus matches the input of capacity for socialized motivational commitments. One might say that the promise of gratification is the ultimate

reward for accepting the disciplines of socialization.

The ouput to the cultural system that matches the input of information is the validation, by competent performance, of the cultural standard of competence. This is essentially the institutionalization of instrumentally significant culture (as distinguished from normative and expressive). This institutionalization in turn comprises operative units of the society—ultimately, individual persons in roles—hence its specification to the functions, situations, and tasks required by social system operation. This suggests that such institutionalization and specification, which are factors in restructuring the cultural tradition, are products, i.e., ouputs, of the social system. The process is that of adapting knowledge to social uses, and validating it by effective use.

The output to the behavioral organism that corresponds to the input of purposive response is the patterning of responses at the level of behavior, as distinguished from personality psychology. At least one of the meanings of pleasure is associated with this as a reward.[27] For the population, a primary function of the social system is to create optimum situations for patterned regulation of behavioral processes, through mechanisms like pleasure. This includes both giving pleasure and imposing the necessary controls on it, since evidence indicates that the pleasure mechanism, like money, easily gets out of hand. As regulator, it also requires regulation.[28]

Resource-Processing within the System. Let us proceed to a brief outline of the dynamics of "resource-processing" within the social system; that is, of what happens between ultimate input and ultimate output. The process may be divided into three major phases: (1) the generation of utilizable factors or internal resources; (2) the allocation of these resources; and (3) their utilization. The first and third may be subdivided. At each phase and significant subphase there is a combination of the categories of resources emerging from the preceding phase, resulting in a set of modifications preparing them for the next phase.

An Example: The Socialization of Motivational

---

26. This suggestion, which may seem strange to many readers, is not arbitrary. It has grown largely from discussions with Dr. James Olds about the application in the theory of action of his findings about the pleasure mechanism in regulating behavior, including this mechanism's base in the anatomical structure of the brain.

27. These suggestions—above all, that pleasure, as a generalized mechanism of control of behavior, not the specific input necessary for metabolic equilibrium (e.g., food), is the focus of the phenomena and significance of reward—are based primarily on the work of Dr. Olds. See Olds, "Self-Stimulation of the Brain," *Science*, Feb. 14, 1958.

28. I might remark, parenthetically, that the analytical distinction between goal gratification and pleasure or, more generally, reward, is a fundamental one which much psychology has tended to ignore. It underlies, in my opinion, the major axis of Freud's theory, the distinction between the "pleasure principle" and the "reality principle." See Parsons, "Social Structure and the Development of Personality," *Psychiatry*, November, 1958.

Capacity. Motivation as a resource provides a good illustration, as a fairly well analyzed case. At the societal level, motivation originates as an input from the personality system. The major phase of generation may be divided into three principal subphases. The first is the one known to psychoanalytic theory as the oral phase. In this, through identification with the primary agent of care (usually the mother), the individual builds up a system of "socialized" motivation whereby his maintaining the attachment to this agent becomes the paramount goal of the emerging personality system.

The next phase extends from the resolution of the oral attachment to that of the Oedipus complex. Then differentiation of the original internalized oral-maternal object occurs, yielding a personality system consisting of four primary motivational subsystems or need-dispositions—adequacy, security, conformity, and nurturance.[29] The balance among these differs in different personalities; in particular, one major factor of differential balance is established through sex-role identification, whose foundations are laid in this period. But the relevance of this broad structural pattern may be treated as a constant.

These processes of differentiation, and hence increasing capacity to cope with motivational problems, are clearly not a function simply of the unaided maturation of motivational capacity; the socialization of this capacity is dependent on the combination of original capacity with three other components, at the proper levels of specification. The first component is one of value-pattern internalized, by the time of the Oedipal resolution, to form the primary basis of the super-ego. The second is a component of socialized information which becomes the basis of the child's early cognitive development. The third is a component of properly measured and specified pleasure-rewards, to which the organism responds and which is especially important to motor skills. In relevance to socialization, the primary type, at least, are the rewards associated with pre-Oedipal eroticism, which Freud has made famous. The strength and, possibly, certain other qualitative variations of original motivation, and variations in corresponding inputs of value-pattern, of information, and of the pleasure-reward depri-

vation balance, explain variations in outcome for the post-Oedipal personality structure.

Even apart from variations in maturational quantitative factors, the motivational capacity of the immediately post-Oedipal child is not yet utilizable for role-performance in complex social systems, because it is too undifferentiated to perform the multiple roles required of the adult. The primary differentiation leading up to this order of capacity for multiple role-commitments occurs in the latent and adolescent periods. There are further inputs, from other subsystems, into the "socialization" subsystem of the society—value-components, information, and pleasure-rewards—but at *different* levels of specification and qualitative differentiation from the pre-Oedipal phases. It is striking that, in our type of society, the informational input is predominantly at the higher levels of generality required by a *literate* culture.

A personality structure results which, with varying emphases in each of the primary role categories, should be capable of playing *differentiated* roles simultaneously: in a family, procreation through marriage and parenthood; in a functionally specialized collectivity, through occupation; in a setting of community responsibility (especially in political terms); and in a setting concerned with the value-stability of the system, especially through religion.

The other three types of input undergo corresponding kinds of "processing." For values, the point of input is the value system's highest socially relevant level of generality; for information, it is the *culturally codified* body of knowledge available in the society; for the purposive response factor, it is the "plastic potentiality" of the constituent organisms. These four factors have an obverse relationship in the societal scale of specification. The value-pattern and the informational components are introduced at the highest level of generality so far as their relevance to social system function is concerned, whereas the motivational and purposive response components are the most specific in terms of social system function. In one sense, concerned with the system-reference of their sources, these factors also are introduced in highly generalized form, and must be redefined on the appropriate levels for their use in the social system. Thus only collectivity- and role-level values are operatively realizable, and only role-level information is "practical." Correspondingly, only role-level motivation is functional to the social system. The old question, "What use is a baby?" is relevant.

The Allocation of Resources to Operative Units. In temporal sequence, the generation of internal resources must precede their allocation. Allocation

---

29. These views are derived from Freud and H. A. Murray. My own treatment is stated most fully in *Family, Socialization and Interaction Process,* Free Press, 1955, Chapter II, and, with some modification and extension, in "Social Structure and the Development of Personality," *Psychiatry,* Nov., 1958. Though important empirical qualifications need to be made for variations in the social structures of different societies, the relevance of the general paradigm of three major phases, marked by the oral, Oedipal, and adolescent patterns is a constant which transcends cultural relativity.

is made to *operative units* of the system, to which resources are committed for use.

Economics again provides us with a prototype of the allocating mechanism, namely, the market. The output of the generation phase which the economist calls labor as a "factor of production" may be defined as capacity for functional performance in occupational roles. It is the product of the socialization process, in "developed" societies focusing, in its terminal phase, at the point of the individual's emergence from formal education. An important current concept of the supply of potential occupational services is that of the *labor force*. The economist treats this concept of supply as relevant; and it is parallel to the concept of "effective demand." Many persons with skills and other usable capacities are not in the labor force, because they are not accessible to offers of employment—perhaps the largest group comprises housewives. A member of the labor force is either employed or seeking employment—presumably with real chance of success.

The labor market is the mechanism by which employing organizations and persons seeking employment are brought together. At the market level, the primary directly operating factor is comparative monetary remuneration. The operation of the market mechanism makes possible a relatively "functional" allocation, without the need of centralized administrative decision.

It follows from the above account of the generation process of occupational capacity that not an undifferentiated stream, but a highly differentiated set of substreams, are fed into the labor market. There is not one completely integrated labor market, but many, partially integrated with each other. There are two main bases of differentiating these from each other. The first concerns level of capacity, from unskilled labor to the high qualifications required for specialized functions or responsibilities. The second concerns qualitative role—once one is committed to medicine or science, he is unlikely to seek a role in governmental administration. Above all, qualitative differentiation concerns different types of combination, in the phase of the socialization process called "training," of more generalized performance capacity with other factors contributing to trained capacity—functional values, information, and types of reward in the behavioral sense.[30]

The closest possible approach to the economist's "perfect market," where labor is the resource involved, is in the field of low-level relatively undifferentiated capacities, where the interchangeability of units is prominent. As capacities become more rare and more differentiated, other factors intervene to "skew" the classical market pattern—e.g., the market for professional services is substantially different from the competitive model.

Where societies are highly enough differentiated politically there are allocative processes, governed by the power mechanism, that are analogous to markets. Leadership capacity is the resource allocated through this type of channel—including the organizational patterning which makes it effective, if this is not ascriptively fixed. One of the best analyzed cases of leadership capacity is that of organization as a factor of production, which as a mobile resource has in particular been analyzed as "entrepreneurship" in Schumpeter's sense, or "organizational responsibility" in the sense Barnard employs.[31]

In executive roles in specific-function collectivities, personalized leadership capacity is acquired through a special type of labor market. In this connection, components of this internal resource are fused with the performance-capacity resource. In other connections, this is not the case. For example, in the allocation of political leadership through the electoral process, voting is an exercise of power through the agency of which those to assume actual operative responsibility are selected from a pool of aspirants to leadership. In the American governmental system, e.g., this operates both in the executive and the legislative branches, and at the federal, state, and local levels. Comparable processes operate in countless democratic associations.

In modern totalitarian regimes (and in some subassociations in democratic societies), effective enfranchisement is made impossible by the one-party system. Nevertheless, that party is ceaselessly concerned with legitimizing, through propaganda and agitation, its selection for leadership in the eyes of the public and, as recently in Hungary, when its claims are not validated a major crisis may develop.

The essential point is that leadership capacity is generated within the society, through the socialization of individuals and through the development of mobile and adaptable potentialities of organization. Then, where this resource is not ascribed to a particular use, there must be some mechanism for allocating it to operative units which can utilize it.

There are comparable processes of allocating the

---

30. Markets in the present sense appear only on certain levels of the general differentiation of social structure. On less differentiated levels, the functional equivalents of these allocative processes are embedded in functionally diffuse structures. The utilization of the resources is likely to be much less fluid, much more strictly ascribed to particular collective units.

31. Chester I. Barnard, *The Functions of the Executive,* Harvard University Press, Cambridge, Mass., 1938. J. A. Schumpeter, *The Theory of Economic Development.*

other categories of internal societal resource, one deriving from the value-system through processes of specification, and the other deriving from the integrative exigencies of the system: these are ultimately concerned with the relation of purposive response and reward. The former concerns allocating legitimation to new and altered collectivity structures and functions—an important process in a rapidly developing society. The latter concerns the social-control function, discussed above, and the problem of institutional commitment to conformity with generalized norms. This latter is "motivational," but it operates at a variety of levels. There is in this, as in the other cases, a variety of processes analogous to those of the market.

The Utilization of Resources. The stage in the natural history of a resource-unit that follows its allocation is utilization. Like generation, this may be subdivided into three phases. First, the usual immediate recipient of a resource-unit through societal allocation is a collectivity. Independent occupational roles, like those of the private professional practitioner or the independent artisan, should be treated as limiting cases, constituting the one-man collectivity. This becomes more significant as resources become more mobile and larger proportions of them are utilized in specific-function processes. Then there is a fundamental structural difference between the field of the allocative process, e.g., a market, and the agency of utilization, e.g., a firm. From one point of view, the difference is one of degree of stringency of control. In the allocative process, the utilization unit is in the position of bidding for resources which other units also want. Once allocated, however, the resource-unit is controlled by its recipient—sometimes to the point of complete consumption. Such complete consumption occurs most obviously with physical commodities—which are not, as such, units of social-system resource, but are facilities controlled in the interest of social-system process.

Utilization is essentially a process of successively more particularized decision-making; action-opportunities, facilities, and responsibilities are allocated more specifically at each step. The most broadly defined stages are the allocation to the collectivity, to the role, and to the task. The function of the collectivity is to define what is to be done; that of allocation to role, to define who is to do it; and that of the task level, how it is to be done.

As in the generation of resources, in the process of utilization, each step (including the substeps within it) involves combining the resource-units in question with other units. The organization employs labor units through the labor market. It supplies an organizational framework within which these units can function effectively.[32] It supplies facilities essential for this, such as physical facilities whose procurement was beyond the worker's control—e.g., office, laboratory, and library—though some of these may be determined by negotiation. The organization may supply funds which, within certain rules, he may use to procure equipment and employ service.

There is, in the operation of the social system, a *terminus ad quem* of the process, i.e., the ultimate accomplishment of tasks. This may be defined as the point at which no further commitment of societal resources is required as "reasonable" in that *particular* task-context. For example, maintaining an elderly person is an institutionalized social obligation. On his death, however, the obligation of maintenance is terminated and the tasks of relatives, health-care personnel, etc., involved are completed, except for the functions of funeral observance, settlement of a possible estate, etc.[33] The resources previously committed to this task are, if still unconsumed, freed for another.

The specific content of the economic paradigm used in this discussion as an analytical model cannot be generalized to apply to all essential social processes, but its *logical structure* can be so generalized. Differences arise from two sources. One is the level of specification of resources in their progress through the system; the most direct relevance of the economic paradigm is at the market level of most general allocation. The second is the qualitative differentiation of types of resources. The only resources which fit the economic paradigm very closely are monetary funds and instruments.[34] Finely divisible, not very perishable, and highly standardized commodities come next. Any form of labor service is a rather bad third; and organization as a factor is probably much farther away from the paradigm of the perfect market.

Value specification (legitimation), institutionalized permissiveness in processes of social control, and the like, cannot be bought, though in a sense they must be paid for. The solution of this apparent paradox lies in the independent yet interpenetrating subsystems of a social system in both dynamic and structural respects. Thus the decision to employ a

32. One example is the framework establishing the main relation to students of the college or university teacher. In a modern society, it would be difficult for the sociologist, for example, just to "hang out his shingle" and hope to attract (and make a living from) competent students and, in turn, to give them prospects of acceptable future employment as professionals.

33. Of course, this does not mean that the fact that the particular person has lived and died has no further social consequences.

34. See Parsons and Smelser, *op. cit.,* pp. 156 ff.

particular professional service involves employer and employee in a special kind of market which involves monetary transactions, among other things. But rights and obligations of privileged communication may be concomitants of the established relationship, and may not then be contracted away or waived—as, e.g., in the relationship between attorney and client. This is precisely what Durkheim meant by one of the "non-contractual elements of contract."[35] Within this sphere, the relationship is protected from both monetary and political intervention; the non-economic resource of permissiveness is utilized to solve the client's problems. A kind of contractual freedom exists: the client may choose what confidential information he reveals to his attorney; and the latter may choose how he reacts to these disclosures or to what he suspects the client of withholding. Hence the interchange, though structurally *analogous* to a market, is, in content and in functional signficance in the system, fundamentally different from *any* market.

Mechanisms Controlling Resource-Processing

For present purposes, this account of the processing of resources through the system will have to suffice, supplemented only by a brief discussion of the mechanisms most immediately controlling these processes. A somewhat fuller picture of the nature of dynamic process can be presented only by discussing the processes of resource-flow in relation to the controlling mechanisms.

Money. Again, the best-analyzed control mechanism is economic, namely, money. It has been noted that money is not a commodity, but is essentially a specialized mode of communication mediating in the circulation of expectations and binding commitments of certain types. As such, money has the characteristic two-level structure found in all languages; a system of categorizing meaning, and of operative utterances. In the language of the classical economists, money is simultaneously both a measure of value and a medium of exchange. In the former sense it provides the criteria of *economic* valuation by specification of the general value pattern to the level of economic function. It is the *economic* common denominator of many commodities and services considered as both products and factors of production; thus it serves further as a standard for economically rational allocation of resources. In this capacity, however, the use of

monetary standards does not imply that anything changes hands.

When money functions as a real medium of exchange, however—when real dollars and not units of account are involved—the spending unit is relinquishing, the receiving unit acquiring, something of value. But that something cannot be technologically utilized or consumed; it can be used only to *control* the allocating of what economists call "real" resources and products. The significant point is that possessing money involves a power or capacity to get things done, while *avoiding* specific commitments at the moment—i.e., about specific channels of expenditure in terms of object or of source of supply, about time of purchase, and about price. The combination of effectiveness (purchasing power) and freedom from commitment makes money such an important mechanism. Spending money is like speaking: the utterance, once made, has consequences; but the speaker who commands a language and has certain knowledge he can formulate in its terms retains his freedom to say what he likes until he is committed through acts of utterance.

As a medium of exchange, money can function in either of two generalized ways, namely, as a facility, or as a reward. As a facility, it is the generalized capacity to command more specific facilities; as a reward, it is a generalized measure of the value of a performance or of a variety of performances, and also the transmitting of something of value.[36]

Involving money, the paradigm of supply and demand, as a specification of the nature of market process, is important to all social system process. As the paradigm is used by economists, supply functions are always stated in terms of "real" assets, e.g., commodities, services, products, or factors of production; whereas demand functions are stated in monetary terms. This may validly be identified with the performance-sanction paradigm of the general analysis of action, in that supply-demand is a case of performance-sanction. The monetary mechanism, as a mechanism of control, stands higher on the generalization-specification scale than does the resource which it controls; this is generally true of the performance-sanction relationship.

Money is only one of several analogous mechanisms controlling resource combination and allocation in social systems; but the logical paradigm outlined for its case should be applicable to the others —e.g., to political power.

"Real Commitments." Economists have gener-

35. *Division of Labor in Society,* Free Press, Book I, Chap. VII.

36. Olds's work indicates that, in behavioral psychology, the relation of goal-gratification to pleasure is theoretically parallel to the relation between acquiring possession of a physical commodity and money. Pleasure and money, not food and commodities, are the primary reward categories.

ally spoken as if market trade were in physical commodities and services. This concept is elliptical; it does not refer to the factor of *rights of disposal* over goods and services that constitutes another mechanism of control over resources standing lower in the control and specification scale than money. The economist's "real" resources and income must not be directly identified with this level. In the case of services, the employment contract establishes certain mutual rights and obligations between employer (typically, an organization) and employee (typically, an individual assuming a role). But a series of decisions of specification must be made before ultimate utilization of the labor resource as a factor in production. Per se, the act of employment excludes units other than the employing one from encroaching on the rights of the employing unit; it also defines both the obligations assumed by the employee within the organization, and the obligations assumed by the employing organization for remuneration, type of work expected, times, etc.

Operative work is performed in a technical subsystem of the employing organization. Employment is neither the process of work nor specific commitment to it; it is crossing the boundary into membership in the employing organization. Particular steps may be compressed, but each must be analytically recognized. For physical facilities, the analogy to employment is the acquisition of property rights.

The institutions of occupation and property are thus structurally analogous to money. At the institutional level they are generalized norms governing the allocation and utilization of resources. But as "jobs" and possessive rights over physical objects, their character is analogous to that of money as a medium of exchange. Rights to jobs and to commodities thus change hands, just as money changes hands. A job commits its incumbent to a series of performances which are still relatively unspecified.

Moreover, markets and money are impossible while the allocation of economically significant resources is sufficiently embedded in ascriptive systems of rights and obligations. These structures' diffuseness is associated with the dispersal of property-rights and work-obligations. Their combination into ownership and occupation is the prerequisite of the resource-mobility necessary for extensive control of allocation through markets. This is a complex hierarchy. Money can control only certain steps in the process—i.e., the allocation of resources to units, but not their effective utilization within units.

The mechanism most closely analogous to money is the utilization of real commitments. These commitments operate by manipulating both property rights over physical possessions and occupational rights over employed persons in their organizational roles. In the latter case, the authority of the organization's management or administration over its personnel is analogous to property rights over physical objects. It is an institutionalized mechanism which, given the commitment to employment, enables management to make realistic further decisions of specification about utilizing the resource. At the time of commitment to employment, the content of these specifications need not be known by or agreed to by either party. Therefore, the same fundamental freedom from detailed advance commitments operates in the case of organizational authority as in that of property. Authority is thus a generalized medium underlying power in the same sense that property underlies money.

In economic parlance, these capacities for utilization, of which property and occupational role are prototypes, may be called real commitments, in the economist's sense of "real" as contrasted with monetary. The allocation of real commitments in this sense is controlled by the monetary mechanism, while these commitments constitute mechanisms governing the processes of further specification of the utilization of resources. At least one intermediate step is necessary to solve the problem of how specification of the physical operations of the behavioral process is brought about.

Power. Let us now consider the step above money in the hierarchy of mechanisms of control. This brings us back to the problem of power, whose most important points we will discuss in terms of their relevance to the present context. We may begin with the fact that in complex societies, structurally, there is a gap between the functional imperatives of co-ordinating collectivities relative to their collective goals and the structurally institutionalized obligation of units at the requisite levels of specification. This gap is comparable to the one created by the division of labor between markets for products and markets for labor services. If ascriptive obligations do not close the gap, then particularized "deals" may occur, between units with leadership responsibilities and units on whose co-operation they must depend, about the terms of this co-operation—these deals are analogous to economic barter. But flexible orientation to changing situations on this basis is extremely limited. Higher flexibility, and hence effectiveness, depends on the institutionalization of a generalized mechanism for structuring and legitimating expectations on both sides without too definite advance specification of detailed rights and obligations. In the analytically defined political field, such a mechanism is power. For the leadership function, it is the legitimized capacity to claim loyal co-operation, within institutionalized limits, *without prior specification of the content of the expected performances.* In the political field this takes the form of the rights to make binding decisions—rights which are institutionalized as leadership, authority, and regulation at the appropriate levels of specification.

For "followership," analytically considered, essentially the same considerations apply. Negatively, the institutionalization of power protects status positions against interference and, if interference is threatened, acts against the threat in such a way that those in authority must listen. One example is the institutionalization of civil rights, with access to the courts, to legislators, and to executive officials. Positively, it is the institutionalization of expectations that, within limits, the public's demands will be given a serious hearing—e.g., most formally in the electoral process.

A "power system" in this sense, as in the case of a market, is a mechanism for adjusting inevitably conflicting interests over considerable areas, where the power held on each side must be considered by the other, and where relatively stable "rules of the game" hold conflicts within bounds. The units involved may be identified with those many political scientists call "interest groups." From one point of view, the outcome is always some sort of "compromise." This situation is parallel to the market, where the seller by definition has a monetary interest in a higher price and the buyer in a lower one, so that an agreed price is a compromise (except at a limiting extreme).

The measure of value in the case of power is the concept of the public interest. Interest groups, including governmental incumbents, are never content to operate in terms of "naked power," but always attempt to legitimize their claims in terms of the public interest. However imperfect the integration achieved may be, this concept's weight is far from negligible in a moderately stable political system. At the level of medium, there is no institutionalized unit which is generally comparable to the monetary unit, though in one crucial sector of the power system the vote is a very precisely defined unit. The vote is the followership's instrument of the exchange process of power, though it does not stand alone; there are a variety of other means to exert political influence. Leadership must earn votes by establishing, among groups of voters, the expectation that in future contingencies the leaders will act in ways relatively acceptable to the group in question—but *not* in terms of specified commitments. This would reduce the system to political barter; an economic equivalent of frequent occur-

rence is the employer's specific contractual provision of family living quarters to employees.

Political power stands higher in the hierarchy of societal control mechanisms than money. They are interrelated, in that money funds can be a means of acquiring political power, while the holder of political power is in a favored position for acquiring money. But these relationships should not obscure the fundamental hierarchical order, as is shown by, e.g., the governmental control of the monetary *system* as a system—a control necessary because in a differentiated, yet integrated, society there can be only one paramount collectivity and system of legal norms. Another indication of their hierarchal discreteness is the fact that the functioning of a market system depends on basic normative conditions controlled more by a governmental system than by the various "private" interest groups involved in market transactions.

Integrative Communication. To complete the picture, a suggestion may be made about still another class of mechanisms, these at the top of the hierarchy of control. This class is integrative communication, and is related to the functions of social control in the narrow technical sense discussed above in a structural-functional connection. The operational focus of this type of mechanism is the motivational commitment of units of the system to the fulfilment of institutionalized expectations.

The hierarchy thus far reviewed may be summarized as follows: real commitments form the institutionalized basis for regulating the processes of fulfilling the contractual obligations assumed by units in the social system. They define generalized expectations within which, through authority (in the operative subsystem, not at the societal level), negotiation, etc., the specification of performance obligations, its rewards, etc., can be worked out. In the major allocative contexts, the operative collective unit typically acquires only the real commitments to the use of its essential resources, leaving further specification to be made as new situations develop.

The proximate mechanism of allocating real commitments is the monetary mechanism—qualified, as necessary when one generalizes sociologically about market processes. Operative control of the uses to which these commitments are to be put is not relevant to the monetary mechanism; their contractual availability for use, and the generalized conditions on which this works out—particularly in competition with other utilising units—are relevant to the monetary mechanism. We must still consider both the legitimation of the goals of operating units at the requisite level of specification, and a variety of questions about structuring the situation in which they may operate. The function of the political process is one fundamental level of this specification of goals and conditions. By structural fusion, political authority may, in certain fields, undertake specific allocation below the monetary level, or operation, or both. For example, this is universally the case for the functions of military defense; in a socialist society, it comprises a much broader field.

In all three of these types of process, the "interests" of the units in question can be taken for granted; given the situation, including normative prescriptions and the sanctions attached to them, units know what they want and can be expected to act in accord with their interests. At a still higher level of the problem of control, this assumption is suspended and the question arises of mechanisms for bringing the individual or collective unit to accept the institutionalized definition of the situation.[37] It is probable that applying direct negative sanction will reinforce deviant tendencies; if conformity is to be motivated one must go behind rational mechanisms and modify the underlying structure determining the unit's orientation. One typical case is the mechanism of therapy operating with reference to the motivated components of illness, when the object is the individual's personality. In other cases, however, the object may be a collectivity, like a delinquent gang; and, in others, a relational system not formally organized as a collectivity—as in the practice of civil law, where the typical system is defined as comprising two opposed parties, their attorneys, and the normative system represented through a court; whether or not there is actual resort to court, the presence of the courts is of fundamental significance. Some aspects of the functioning of partisan politics, of religious ritual, and of other phenomena also belong in this category.

The mechanisms of control in such cases must operate in situations insulated from the pressures of normal sanction systems. One such institution is privileged communication. Another example is found in religious ritual, where the situation is defined as exceptional—e.g., the treatment of bereaved persons, set apart as sacred. Permissiveness provides an opportunity for giving an order of support to which the unit would not otherwise be entitled, i.e., in spite of attitudes or conduct which otherwise would be "punished" with negative sanctions. Within this protected sphere, a special process of conditional sanctioning of behavior can operate until a pattern consistent with the general institutional expectations is so strongly established that the special permissiveness and support are unnecessary.

This set of mechanisms has the same formal structure as the others which have been reviewed. So far as the mechanisms operate effectively, permissiveness and support do not imply abandonment of the institutionalized expectations; they are justified by special circumstances making it difficult or impossible for the unit to fulfil those expectations—e.g., because an individual is sick, or a pair of conflicting units cannot know their legal obligations until these have been worked out with their attorneys or through court decision. Thus, the measure of value is very much involved. Facilities, in the form of information, e.g., as interpretations, and rewards, e.g., evaluative sanctions, especially approval, definitely circulate. Moreover, these are scarce media; any good psychiatrist or appellate judge knows that interpretations must not be too lavishly offered. Just "thinking out loud" without carefully considering the impact of what is said on the patient or on the pool of potential litigants would not be good therapy or jurisprudence.

This set of mechanisms ranks first in the hierarchy. Resort is made to them only when others have failed to operate; indeed, such failure is a direct criterion of the need for them. Thus the disability aspect of illness is the primary criterion of the need for therapeutic help. Furthermore, on theoretical grounds this category of mechanisms is at the top of the whole hierarchical series—going farther brings one to the problem of structural change as such, which has been defined as a different order of problem. It lifts the restriction that the structure of the system, i.e., the institutionalized normative culture, must be treated as given.

Summary of the Equilibrating Process. The equilibrium processes of a social system are intermeshing processes involving two sets of changeable factors, each defined in terms of the system's structure. The first set comprises the categories of resources which, at each stage of being processed through the system, are combined with the appropriate complementary resources. The progress of each resource through the system is a process of specification through decision-making about disposition through allocation and about proportions of combination. The second set of changeable factors comprises the mechanisms just discussed. Resources are differentiated from mechanisms in that resources, from the point of view of the system, are, at any given stage, consumed (with the exception of structure, e.g., land); whereas mechanisms, as media of con-

---

37. In cases falling under the present heading, deviant attitudes toward institutionalized expectations are ambivalent. That is, the problem of institutionalizing *new* expectations must be treated as analytically distinct from that of implementing expectations already institutionalized. See *The Social System,* Parsons, Free Press, 1951, Chapter VII.

trol, are, from the point of view of the *unit,* spent and acquired, while, from that of the *system,* they circulate from one unit to another but are not consumed. For instance, money cannot be consumed, but only transferred from one possessor to another. We have described how the same is true of real commitments, of power, and of integrative communication. The component of structure in which these changeables are based is neither consumed nor circulated.

The general significance of the hierarchical interrelations of these components indicates that the social system as a whole and its internal processes should, in regard to behavior, be considered as a complex set of cybernetic controlling mechanisms —not just one governor, but a complex series of them. In this broad sense, the problem of the dynamics of social systems is not so much a problem of the transformation of energy as of the processing of information.

The analysis of these processes is now in an elementary stage. Some fundamental definitions and classifications are now being formulated, as are some important sequences, such as specification of the broad combinations needed at each stage, and the broad quantitative differences made by grossly different proportions. Furthermore, in an interdependent system, every long sequence of process-stage, to be accurately analyzed, must specifically account for the effect of repercussions through the rest of the system and for the resulting feedback on the original points for analysis.

For all aspects of this problem, important points of reference—e.g., the combination processes of economic theory and their relation to the monetary mechanism; the socialization process in relation to social structure; certain salient aspects of power systems; recent work on decision-making in collectivities; and knowledge of therapeutics. But these are still fragments, at best partially woven into the fabric of a genuinely systematic analysis. The concept of system itself is the most important guide to developing such analysis.

The problem of systematizing the morphology of living—i.e., biological, psychological, social, and cultural—systems is intrinsically easier to solve than that of their dynamics in the present sense. This is the reason that the first major section of this essay is longer than the second and that, in the following selections, there is more documentation in the field of structural analysis than in analysis of dynamic process. Dynamic analysis must, in our theoretical scheme, be referred to morphological premises, or else be subject to complete loss of orientation. The statement that everything empirical is subject to change may be metaphysically correct; but this is often translated into the scientifically untenable doctrine condemning as invalid a heuristic assumption that any reference point is structurally given, on the grounds that such an assumption would commit the investigator to deny the fluidity of ultimate reality. Science is not a photographic reproduction of reality, but is a highly selective mode of organizing man's orientation to reality—however philosophers define the latter. The scientifically specific component of this organization depends on ability to establish reference-points structurally stable enough to justify the *simplification* of dynamic problems prerequisite to logically manageable analysis. Empirically, these reference-points are relative and may be expected to change as the science develops. The categorical assertion that any assumptions about structure are scientifically inadmissible, because in the last analysis everything is in flux, denies the legitimacy of science. In any science, and in sociology in particular, the concept of change is meaningful only in terms of a definable *something,* i.e., something which can be described in structural terms.

IV. THE PROBLEM OF STRUCTURAL CHANGE

According to the program laid out above, the last major problem area is the analysis of processes of structural change in social systems. The process of structural change may be considered the obverse of equilibrating process; the distinction is made in terms of boundary-maintenance. Boundary implies both that there is a difference of state between phenomena internal and external to the system; and that the type of process tending to maintain that difference of state is different from the type tending to break it down. In applying this concept to social systems, one must remember that their essential boundaries are those vis-à-vis personalities, organisms, and cultural systems, and not those directly vis-à-vis the physical environment.

A boundary is thus conceived as a kind of watershed. The control resources of the system are adequate for its maintenance up to a well-defined set of points in one direction: beyond that set of points, there is a tendency for a *cumulative* process of change to begin, producing states progressively farther from the institutionalized patterns. The metaphor of the watershed, however, fails to demonstrate the complexity of the series of control levels and, hence, of the boundaries of subsystems within larger systems. The mechanisms discussed earlier are involved in the dynamic aspects of such a hierarchical series of subboundaries; if a subboundary is broken, resources within the larger system counteract the implicit tendency to structural change. This is most dramatically shown in the capacity of social control mechanisms, in a narrow sense, to reverse cumulative processes of deviance. The conception of the nature of the difference between processes of equilibration and processes of structural change seems inherent in the conception of a social system as a cybernetic system of control over behavior.

As observed, structural change in subsystems is an inevitable part of equilibrating process in larger systems. The individual's life-span is so short that concrete role-units in any social system of societal scope must, through socialization, continually undergo structural change. Closely bound to this is a low-order collectivity like the nuclear family. Though the institutional norms defining "the family" in a society or a social sector may remain stable over long periods, *the family* is never a collectivity; and real families are continually being established by marriages, passing through the "family cycle," and, eventually, disappearing, with the parents' death and the children's dispersion. Similar considerations apply to other types of societal subsystems.

Within this frame of reference, the problem of structural change can be considered under three headings, as follows: (1) the sources of tendencies toward change; (2) the impact of these tendencies on the affected structural components, and the possible consequences; and (3) possible generalizations about trends and patterns of change.

The Sources of Structural Change

The potential sources of structural change are exogenous and endogenous—usually in combination. The foregoing discussion has stressed the instability of the relations between any system of action and its situation, because this is important for defining the concepts of goal and the political function. We were emphasizing *relation,* and a relation's internal sources of instability may derive from external tendencies to change.

Exogenous Sources of Change. The exogenous sources of social structural change consist in endogenous tendencies to change in the organisms, personalities, and cultural systems articulated with the social systems in question. Among such sources are those operating through genetic changes in the constituent human organisms and changes in the distribution of genetic components within populations, which have an impact on behavior as it affects social role-performance, including the social sys-

tem's capacities for socialization. Changes in the physical environment are mediated most directly either through the organism—e.g., through perception—or through appropriate aspects of the cultural system—e.g., technological knowledge.

One particularly important source of exogenous change is a change originating in other social systems. For the politically organized society, the most important are other politically organized societies. To consider change in this context, it is essential to treat the society of reference as a unit in a more inclusive social system. Even when the system's level of integration is relatively low and chronic conflicts between its subunits continually threaten to break into war, *some* element of more or less institutionalized order always governs their interrelations—otherwise, a concept like "diplomacy" would be meaningless. Of course, exogenous cultural borrowing and diffusion are mediated through interrelations among societies.

Endogenous Sources: "Strains." The most general, commonly used term for an endogenous tendency to change is "strain." *Strain* here refers to a condition in the *relation* between two or more structured units (i.e., subsystems of the system) that constitutes a tendency or pressure toward changing that relation to one incompatible with the equilibrium of the relevant part of the system. If the strain becomes great enough, the mechanisms of control will not be able to maintain that conformity to relevant normative expectations necessary to avoid the breakdown of the structure. A strain is a tendency to disequilibrium in the input-output balance between two or more units of the system.

Strains can be relieved in various ways. For the system's stability, the ideal way is resolution—i.e., restoring full conformity with normative expectations, as in complete recovery from motivated illness. A second relieving mechanism is arrestation or isolation—full conformity is not restored, but some accommodation is made by which less than normal performance by the deficient units is accepted, and other units carry the resulting burden. However, it may be extremely difficult to detect a unit's failure to attain full potentiality, as in the case of handicap contrasted with illness. Completely eliminating the unit from social function is the limiting case here.

Strain may also be relieved by change in the structure itself. Since we have emphasized strain in the *relations* of units (instability internal to the unit itself would be analyzed at the next lower level of system reference), structural change must be defined as alteration in the normative culture defining the expectations governing that relation—thus, at the systemic level, comprising all units standing in strained relations. The total empirical process may also involve change in the structure of typical units; but the essential reference is to *relational pattern.* For example, chronic instability in a typical kind of market might lead to a change in the norms governing that market; but if bargaining units change their tactics in the direction of conforming with the old norms, this would not constitute *structural* change of *this* system. In line with the general concepts of inertia and of the hierarchy of controls, we may say that endogenous change occurs only when the lower-order mechanisms of control fail to contain the factors of strain.

Factors in Change. In introducing our discussion of the factors in structural change, we must establish the essential point that the conception of a system of interdependent variables, on the one hand, and of units or parts, on the other, by its nature implies that there is no necessary order of teleological significance in the sources of change. This applies particularly to such old controversies as economic or interest explanations *versus* explanations in terms of ideas or values. This problem is logically parallel to the problem of the relations between heredity and environment. Of a set of "factors," *any or all may be sources of change,* whose nature will depend on the ways an initial impetus is propagated through the system by the types of dynamic process analyzed under subhead III, above.

To avoid implying a formless eclecticism we must add two other points. First, careful theoretical identifications must be made of the nature of the factors to which an impetus to structural change is imputed. Many factors prominent in the history of social thought are, according to the theory of social systems, exogenous—including factors of geographical environment and biological heredity, and outstanding personalities, as "great men," who are never conceived of simply as products of their societies. This category of exogenous factors also includes cultural explanations, as those in terms of religious ideas. Furthermore, these different exogenous sources are not alike in the nature of their impact on the social system.

Among these exogenous sources of change is the size of the population of any social system. Perhaps the most important relevant discussion of this was Durkheim's, in the *Division of Labor,* where he speaks of the relations between "material" and "dynamic" density. Populations are partially resultants of the processes of social systems, but their size is in turn a determinant.[38]

The second, related point concerns the implications of the hierarchy of control in social systems. It may be difficult to define magnitude of impact; however, given approximate equality of magnitude, the probability of producing structural change is greater in proportion to the position in the order of control at which the impact of its principal disturbing influence occurs. This principle is based on the assumption that stable systems have mechanisms which can absorb considerable internal strains, and thus endogenous or exogenous variabilities impinging at lower levels in the hierarchy of control may be neutralized before extending structural changes to higher levels. It follows that the crucial focus of the problem of change lies in the stability of the value system.

The analytical problems in this area are by no means simple. Difficulties arise because of the complex ways in which societies are composed of interpenetrating subsystems, and because of the ways in which the exogenous factors impinge somehow on every role, collectivity norm, and subvalue. Thus the collectivity component of social structure has been placed, in general analytical terms, only third in the general control hierarchy. Yet every society must be organized as a whole on the collectivity level, integrating goal-attainment, integrative, and pattern-maintenance functions. Hence an important change in the leadership composition of the over-all societal collectivity *may* have a far greater impact on the norms and values of the society generally than would a value change in lower-order subsystems. Hence a naïve use of the formula, the higher in the control hierarchy the greater the impact, is not recommended.

The Impact of the Forces of Change

Our approach to the problem of impact has already been foreshadowed. Disturbance may result from deficient or excessive input at a given point in the system. The generalization about the disturbing effects of excess is a direct corollary of the concept of equilibrium; it seems contrary often to common sense, but it has been clearly validated for many cases in social interaction. One of the best known cases is the Keynesian point about the relation between oversaving and unemployment; another is Durkheim's generalization about the positive relation between increasing economic prosperity and rates of suicide; a third would be the pathogenic effect of maternal overprotection on a developing child. The point is crucial for present purposes, because, in any important boundary relation of a society, the stability of both systems is a function of a *balancing* of rates of input and output

---

38. We have recently been reminded by Schnore of the importance of this aspect of Durkheim's analysis. See Leo Schnore, "Social Morphology and Human Ecology," *American Journal of Sociology,* May, 1958, pp. 620–34.

which go *both* ways. This consideration also clearly applies to both exogenous and endogenous sources of change.

Impact will vary as a function of at least five ranges of variation in the nature of the impinging process, as described below: (1) the magnitude of the disturbance—not an absolute quantity, but magnitude of *change* from previous customary input-output rates, which have become accommodated to the system's conditions of equilibrium. (2) The proportion of units in the system at the relevant levels that are affected. (3) The strategic character of the unit's functional contribution to the system —e.g., the sudden death of 50 per cent of the unskilled workers would not have the same impact as the death of 50 per cent of the highest 10 per cent of political leaders. (4) The incidence of the disturbance on analytically distinguishable components of the system's structure. Given the strategic significance of a structural unit, roles are most readily replaceable or reparable, subcollectivities less so, norms even less so, and value-commitments least. The reverse order holds for exposure to the impact of change; the conditions of individuals' role-performances are most exposed and therefore most likely to "give," whereas value-commitments are least exposed because they are neither function- nor situation-specific. Finally, (5) there is the degree of resistance by the relevant parts of the system to the impact of forces of change—i.e., the level of effectiveness of the mechanisms of control. A relatively large disturbance may not lead to major change in a very stable system; a much smaller disturbance may lead to drastic change in an unstable system. Stability is variable both quantitatively and qualitatively.

Empirically, forces making for change seldom operate neatly according to discrete analytical categories; their impact is diffused. Thus the Cold War's impact on American society operates primarily on two levels. One is by its effect on national security—primarily a political problem. Since the United States can no longer rely on a stable European power system for its security, as it did through the nineteenth century, the Cold War is the immediate cause for maintaining a large military establishment and attempting to foster the rapid development of military technology—with all the repercussions that this essentially new peacetime situation has throughout the society. The Cold War also has an important impact at the level of commitments to values and the most generalized level of norms. Without this "challenge of communism"— not just the challenge of a strong military power, but a challenge to the *legitimacy* of the "American

way"—the current situation would be far less disturbing.

These two components are empirically associated. But they are analytically distinguishable, and their proportionate importance may vary, in the same case over time as well as in different cases. A comparably serious military threat to national security, unaccompanied by the ideological factor, would be much less disturbing at present to the United States, because internal changes in American society have produced factors of instability at integrative levels that were not previously so acute. Our problem in really accepting our universalistic values, for example, is clearly shown in the present segregation-desegregation issue. A major development of societal political responsibility, as a function of both internal development and changed international position, is necessary. Without special sensitivities to the symbolic reverberations of "communism"—independent of "realistic" dangers—a phenomenon like McCarthyism would be incomprehensible.

Analytical discrimination of factors within the framework of empirical variation makes more precision about matters of impact possible. Thus technological processes concerning the physical environment have quite a different significance from problems of the motivational commitments of individuals and collective subunits to functional performance in the system. For example, in America there has allegedly been a major shift recently in this respect—in Riesman's terms, from "inner-directed" to "other-directed"; in Kluckhohn's, a "decline of the Protestant Ethic."[39] Both interpretations suggest a retreat from occupational contributions into the sphere of private preoccupations. Though discussions of such problems are often couched in the terminology of values, this problem belongs more at the level of motivation to functional contribution. Whether or not a change in the societal value-system underlies this at a higher level of control is an analytically distinguishable part of the empirical problems.[40]

By present definition, a change in the structure of a social system is a change in its normative culture. At the most general level, it is a change in the paramount value system. From this level through the

39. See David Riesman, *The Lonely Crowd;* Clyde Kluckhohn, "Have There Been Discernible Shifts in American Values during the Past Generation?" in Elting Morrison (ed.), *The American Style* (New York: Harper, 1958) pp. 145–217.

40. I have attempted to deal more fully with this problem in "The Link between Character and Society" (with Winston White), in Lipset and Lowenthal (eds.), *Culture and Social Character: The Work of David Riesman Reviewed* (Glencoe: The Free Press, 1961).

series of differentiation, segmentation, and specification, it involves changes in the normative culture of subsystems, of progressively lower order, that are increasingly specific with reference to function in the larger system and to situation. Through specification we arrive eventually at the *role* level and, with this, at the psychological motivation of the individual. It is my thesis that *any* major disturbance will occasion widespread disturbances in individuals' motivations at the role level, and under the requisite conditions will lead to structural changes at least there. But it does not follow either from the presence of widespread symptoms of disturbance, or from important structural changes in such motivational patterning, that the structure of the system at all levels—especially in the paramount value system—has changed.

In considering the general problem of impact, we must remember that every structurally distinguished subsystem of a society is both complex and never fully integrated. Moreover, the structural components are interlarded in all the different subsystems; yet even minimal integration requires some measure of consistency between values and norms both at the higher and lower levels of specification and across the lines of functional differentiation. Such considerations help account for the facts that many processes of change occur simultaneously at several levels, and that influences are propagated through the levels of control in the system from one to another.

An important example is presented by underdeveloped societies at the present time. If we take economic development, in the sense of industrialization, as the focal content of the process, the two primary foci of the impact of inputs are political and cultural, in the value-sense; they are not, in the usual analytical sense, economic. Both focus primarily on the relations of underdeveloped societies to economically advanced societies.

The great stirring which has been going on focuses first on national independence and power, as evidenced by the acute sensitivity to the negative symbol of "imperialism." This political preoccupation's effect then seems to be propagated in two directions: to economic development as *instrumental* to political power (and as a symbol of collective achievement); and to the *functional* value-systems associated with political power and economic productivity. The highest-level values will still be carefully *contrasted* with those of the societies serving as models of political and economic development. Another important symbolic expression of this is the common imputation of materialism to Western societies, whereas it is alleged that India, for example, can somehow have all the advantages of high

industrialization without being infected with the materialistic values of the Western world. Further —contrary to the explicit content of Marxian ideology—it is often alleged that communism, because collectivistic, is less materialistic than so-called "capitalism," though communist societies have been marked by a far more exclusive dedication to economic development than *any* capitalistic society. The essential point here is the tendency to maintain the highest-level values while permitting major changes in the next level of value-specification, i.e., that of the primary functional subsystem.[41]

It is difficult to see how, in the longer run, this can fail to engender major strains; however, there is a twofold proximate ideological defense, namely, the instrumental character of political and economic development, and the bridging of the implicit conflict by symbols like "socialism." The important point analytically is that, without at least two different orders of input beyond normal levels, impetus for major change is unlikely to occur. One order is the *real* political inferiority, symbolized as "colonial dependency," of the disturbed society. The other is the existence, in the social environment, of a *model* of instrumentally appropriate reorganization, whose partial functional values can be adopted, initially allegedly without disturbing the highest-level values of the system.[42]

Types of Process of Structural Change

Finally, we must attempt to determine whether any important generalizations can be made about the types of process of change found at the structural level. The phenomena of the institutionalization of normative culture imply internalization in the personality structures of constituent personalities, which in turn implies that institutionalization is embedded in the non-rational layers of motivational organization. It is not accessible to change simply through the presentation, to an actor, of rational advantages in the external definition of the situation.

In social structure, the relation of normative culture to personality is expressed by the fundamental

41. Further analysis of these problems is contained in the paper "Some Reflections on the Sociological Framework of Economic Development," *Structure and Process in Modern Societies* (Glencoe, Ill.: Free Press, 1959), Chapter III.
42. Naturally in the total picture, specifically economic factors of production are also necessary inputs, from other societies or from other "systems" operating in the territory of the society, like motivation, capital, etc. But because of the relation to the hierarchical structure of social systems, the inputs of political urgency and functional value-commitment are far more critical in what Rostow calls the "take-off" phenomenon than is the availability of adequate factors of production in the strictly economic sense.

distinction between two types of integrative mechanism in the social system—those allocative mechanisms, operating through media like money and power, that affect the balance of advantages and disadvantages in the situation of an acting unit; and those which, like integrative communication, operate through affecting the motivational state of the unit, concerning the definition of what he wants and not how he can get it.

Only when strain impinges on and involves this level of the system of behavioral control can structural change in the present sense become possible. Once it has occurred, the question is whether the impetus to change goes "over the watershed" or, under the countervailing impact of the mechanisms of social control, falls back again.

In either case, strain at this level is manifested by a series of symptoms of disturbance showing the psychological marks of irrationality. These will be organized along the major axes of hope and fear, of "wishful thinking" and "anxiety" showing unrealistic trends in *both* respects. Psychologically, this goes back to the ambivalent structure of motivation to deviance already mentioned.

The directions of this positive-negative polarization are defined in terms of the structural possibilities of deviance.[43] The most important variables are the polarizations between activity and passivity, between compulsive alienation and compulsive conformity, that yield the types of rebelliousness, withdrawal, "ritualism," and compulsive performance. In other words, there will be fantasies of utopian ideal future states, of idealized past states, of security in a status quo from which sources of disturbance could conveniently be banished, and of eliminating sources of disturbance directly within the framework of the old structure. There will be corresponding foci of anxiety.

These motivational components are common to all symptoms of disturbance in the institutionalization of social structures. The symbols to which they become attached will depend on the appropriate system references and situations. At the societal level, it is not difficult to detect the utopian element in "communism," in the sense of an alleged actual type of society; or, on the other side, a complete "free enterprise" system. The socially regressive idealization of an unrealistically conceived past appears in such symbols as the simple, unspoiled "Americanism" of the McCarthyites, or in the *Volksgemeinschaft* of German Romantics (particularly in its most extreme version, Naziism). Such symbols as "imperialism," "capitalism," and "communism" are foci of irrational anxiety and aggression.

Another symbolic content is found where the focus of disturbance is a different order of social system. "Authoritarianism" and "conformity" are good examples of anxiety-laden symbols widely current in our society. Some of the irrational symbols in this context have functions in social systems analogous to those of the personality's mechanisms of defense. The equivalents of displacement and projection are found in the imputation of the sources of disturbance to exogenous systems—particularly similar systems—when much of the motivation really arises from internal strain. Indeed, displacement and/or projection on *personalities* of the products of strain in social systems cause much of the attributing of ill-will to, e.g., "ruling circles."

Symptoms of disturbance, with the kind of structure just sketched, are common to processes which do and do not result in structural change. Whether or not the change occurs depends on the *balance* between the strength of the disturbing forces and the kinds of reception they meet—i.e., the balance between acts motivated by response to disturbance and the sanctions that they stimulate in both endogenous and exogenous agencies. This statement is not a tautology if these conceptions are given content through definition of the nature of the performances and sanctions, and of the strategic significance of content for the equilibrium of the system.

Structural change is possible only when a certain level of strain on institutionalized structure is reached. Such strain may be propagated from technological, economic, and political levels; but the fact that a system is faced with severe problems on those levels is never *by itself* a sufficient explanation of structural change. It is necessary to trace the repercussions of these strains on the higher levels of the control system.

Even when the institutional level is reached, severity of strain is never alone an adequate explanation of change. Structural change is only one possible outcome of strain. Other results are the resolution of the strain, through mechanisms of control, that leaves the old structure intact; and the isolation of disturbing forces, at the cost of some impairment of the system's functioning—and, of course, radical dissolution of the system.

Besides the generalized strength-weakness balance of the disturbances and controls respectively, the most important factors favoring structural change are the following: (1) Adequate mechanisms for overcoming the inevitable resistances of institutionalized structural patterns (vested interests) to abandonment. Overwhelming force or polit-

43. See Merton, "Social Structure and Anomie," *Social Theory and Social Structure*, revised and extended edition, Free Press, 1957; and Parsons, *The Social System*, Free Press, 1951, Chap. VII.

ical coercion may impose very severe strains, but, in the absence of such mechanisms, they lead only to active or passive resistance, even though the resistance is realistically hopeless.[44] Endogenously, the balance between positive and negative components in the symptoms of disturbance is the primary factor. For example, if the negative side outweighs the positive, anxiety and aggression will block new institutionalization. (2) Among the positive reactions, there must be combinations with adequate constructive possibilities. The component of alienation must be strong enough to motivate detachment from the older patterns, but not so closely connected with other negative components that it motivates only destructive behavior. On the other hand, too great passivity would motivate only withdrawal. (3) A model, from exogenous sources or endogenously produced, of the pattern to be newly institutionalized is necessary. In socializing the child, the parents, older peers, teachers, and others serve as "role-models" whose personalities and actions embody the patterns of value and norms which the child is expected to internalize; without such adequate models, the internalization would be impossible. (4) The pattern of sanctions evoked by behavior in the transitional phases must selectively reward action conforming with the new model (and must not reward action in terms of the old pattern), and must be sufficiently consistent over a period to bring about the coinciding of the values of units and their self-interest that is the hallmark of institutionalization.

The socialization of the child actually constitutes a process of structural change in one set of structural components of social systems, namely, the role-patterns of the individual—indeed, much of the foregoing paradigm has been derived from this source.[45] These considerations may then be extended to the next level: the corollary of the proposition that the child internalizes new roles in the process of socialization is that the social systems in which this process occurs, e.g., the mother-child system and the nuclear family, must undergo processes of structural change. Thus, the nuclear family with one infant is, structurally speaking, not the same system as that with two adolescent children and one latency-period child, though in another perspective it may still be the same family.

For a more general sociological analysis, however, it may be better to illustrate by two types of process of structural change close to the societal level, in one of which the "model" is predominantly endogenous to the system, in the other, exogenous. The first is the case usually referred to as "structural differentiation" affecting the level of primary functional subsystems; the second, the case involving change in the value-system at the societal level.

The Differentiation of Occupational from Kinship Roles. In the above discussion, reference has often been made to the relative "functional diffuseness" of many social structures. The process of functional differentiation is one of the fundamental types of social change, and has evolutionary aspects and implications. In its bearing on the type of system, it involves more than increasing complexity— e.g., the fact that flexible disposability of resources depends on such differentiation. This dependence requires higher-order mechanisms of integration, substituting the more specialized processes of control associated with markets, power systems, etc., for control through embeddedness in diffuse structures.

Perhaps the best example is the differentiation of occupational roles, in the ideal sense already discussed, from embeddedness in kinship structures which have enjoyed ascribed claims to the functional equivalents of such services. On the role-structure level, the change means that what has been one role of an individual in a single kinship collectivity (which may, however, be internally differentiated) becomes differentiated into two roles in two distinct collectivities, the kinship group and the employing organization.[46]

The first prerequisite of change is disengagement from the preceding pattern.[47] In other words, some order of relative deprivation becomes attached to following the old way. The impingement of the deprivation is on the individual and on the kinship collectivity. The impingement may take such forms as deterioration of previously assumed market conditions, or of the availability of new opportunities which cannot be utilized within the old structural framework. Such severe and prolonged relative deprivation would eventually give rise to symptoms of disturbance of the sort discussed.

---

44. In certain respects, the Hungarian crisis of 1956 seems to fit this pattern, so far as institutionalization of the new patterns of Stalinist communism is concerned. The social system equivalents of the therapeutic mechanisms centering on permissiveness and support seem particularly crucial in this connection.

45. This assumption is based largely on Freud's work. See Parsons and Olds, Chapter IV of Parsons and Bales, *Family, Socialization and Interaction Process,* Free Press, 1955 and Parsons, "Social Structure and the Development of Personality: Freud's Contribution to the Integration of Psychology and Sociology," *Psychiatry,* November, 1958.

46. The operation of this process at the "working class" level has, to my knowledge been most thoroughly analyzed in Neil J. Smelser, *Social Change or the Industrial Revolution,* U. of Chicago Press, 1959.

47. The general paradigm of the process of differentiation somewhat elliptically followed here was set forth in Parsons and Smelser, *Economy and Society,* Free Press, 1956, Chap. V, and much more extensively developed and applied in Smelser, *op. cit.*

In order to prevent the overwhelming consolidation of the negative components of the reactions to disturbance, there must be an adequate range of institutionalized permissiveness and support, in addition to the imposition of deprivations for following the old pattern. There should not be too great immediate pressure for abandoning the old ways precipitately and totally. In the Industrial Revolution in England, this institutionalized permissiveness, as Smelser shows, comprised considerable remaining realistic opportunity in the old domestic pattern of industrial organization, compromise organizational patterns whereby whole families were hired by the cotton mills as units, and considerable "romantic" ideological support for the value of the old ways.

A positive model for the new patterning of work contribution must be demonstrated, first on the immediately relevant organizational level—e.g., factories are organized and jobs made available which offer advantages, i.e., various components of reward, including but not confined to money wages, to the worker and his household. But one crucial problem concerns the ways in which this new model can be made legitimate in terms of the relevant values.

As Smelser shows, it was very important in the British case that the structural changes in the role-organization of the labor force of the late eighteenth century were preceded, and for some time accompanied, by a marked revival, in precisely the geographical section and population groups involved, of the Puritan religion. According to the famous Weber hypothesis, Puritanism has legitimized both profit-making and more broadly effective contribution to instrumental function in society. More immediately, the main justification of the factory system was its greater productive effectiveness. In the typical working-class household, there was promise of both realistic opportunity to organize work in a new way, and legitimation of that way in terms of a firmly institutionalized religious tradition. A steady pattern of sanctions operated to reinforce the change, whose most tangible aspect was the steady increase of real wages, largely derived from the productivity of the new industry.[48]

48. A tragic case of the misfiring of such a process of change, illustrating the importance of the balance of these factors, was the case of the hand-loom weavers. The original impetus for greatly increased productivity came in spinning. The resulting greatly increased supply of yarn put pressure on the weaving branch. But in the absence of usable inventions—which came later—and of other aspects of reorganization in this field, the main result was an enormous quantitative expansion of the weaving trade on the *old* basis of social structure. When the power loom took over, the unrestructured weaving trade was left high and dry. It is not surprising that this group was the main center of disturbance in North England in that period. Smelser, *op. cit.,* treats this case in some detail.

The outcome of the process was the incorporation of a very large new group of the working-class labor force into the factory system, in fully differentiated occupational roles, with the concomitant loss of most of the function of family economic production. Working in factory premises, for an individual wage and under factory rather than kinship discipline, was a main structural feature of the outcome. Smelser makes it clear that this was not a simple matter of attracting workers by better wages than could be offered elsewhere—it was only possible through a major restructuring of the institutional structure of the working-class kinship system.

For the larger system, the part played by the *endogenous* sources of the model components of the process was particularly important. It is not necessary to question the common belief that the immediate impetus came from mechanical inventions. Implementing this impetus at levels bearing on the structure of occupational roles, however, was mainly the work of entrepreneurs—some of whom, like Arkwright, were also the inventors. But the legitimation of the new opportunities could be derived by *specification,* in the light of the new opportunities, of an already firmly institutionalized value-system. The essential point is that enhanced economic productivity was defined as good, in a way justifying the major disturbances of institutional structures at lower levels necessary for taking advantage of the greater opportunities. The legitimation of profit-making is only part of a larger complex, whose focus is on the valuation of productivity.

The distinction between the process of structural differentiation and that involving the value-system of a society is relative. In complex societies, processes of differentiation are continually going on at relatively low levels of specification and high levels of structural segmentation. The differentiation of occupational roles from embeddedness in kinship should, however, be placed among the very important processes having repercussions in the society extending far beyond their immediate locations. It is clearly a function of great extension in the division of labor and, consequently, in the extent of markets. It makes salient a whole series of new problems with respect to the institution of contract and the conditions of employment—including the beginnings of large-scale union organization and collective bargaining, and various other questions about the status of the working classes. When a process occurs of the magnitude of the rise of the cotton textile industry until about 1840—*magnitude* not only absolutely but in terms of its place in the total economy of Great Britain—it constitutes a major change in the structure of the society. It is not surprising that the disturbances associated with it included much agitation in national politics and noticeable "effervescence" in religion. At the same time, the change did not involve introducing a new value system at the national level—i.e., the fundamentals of Puritan orientation and its place in British national values had been settled in the sixteenth and seventeenth centuries.

Change in the Societal Value System. At the highest normative level, two main types of structural change may be distinguished. The first, already described, is the one where the principal model component comes from outside the society. This has been true of the contemporary underdeveloped areas, as outlined. To some degree, it was true of all the post-British cases of industrialization, including the American.

The American case went farthest in accepting the British model of free enterprise, though with some important qualifications. This can be attributed first to the fact that the value system deriving mainly from the ethic of ascetic Protestantism had been strongly institutionalized in this country by the early nineteenth century; furthermore, the basic structural position of religion had been settled by the adoption of the Constitutional separation of church and state that paved the way for denominational pluralism. The British model, therefore, posed no serious problem of value-orientation; the American case was considerably closer to a pure culture of the ascetic branch of Protestantism most involved in industrialization than was the British. The problem in our case was primarily the process of structural differentiation. Many religious movements, especially revivalist ones, played an important part on the fringes of the spread of industrialization. These have been essentially similar to Methodism in the north of England in the later eighteenth century.

This is probably one of the major causes of the relatively small role of political agency in the American case, though political agency played a greater part in such fields as the subsidizing of railway-building in America than in Britain. Essentially, there was no very serious problem of gaining general acceptance of the functional values necessary for industrialization, as there was in underdeveloped areas or even in most Continental European countries. It is probably not entirely fortuitous that both Japan and the Soviet Union, although very different, became industrialized under very heavy governmental pressure; in both cases, the ideological justification of the requisite value-commitments played a particularly important part. In Japan, the nationalistic connotations of aspects of the Shinto

religious tradition were particularly important.[49] In the Soviet case, the revolutionary force of the Communist movement was grafted onto a Russian social structure that had always emphasized the priority of the state over private interests—far more strongly than in most Western countries. The Party functioned as the primary agency of ideological indoctrination which, under the utopian conception of communism, has inculcated the values necessary for high commitment to economic productivity—values which seem to have been relatively weak in pre-Revolutionary Russia.

The combination of practical urgency and the absence of the functional-level value commitment constitutes a major reason that, for the underdeveloped countries, governmental agency and the importance of the ideological symbol of "socialism" play such an important role in industrialization. Even the rigid authoritarianism of Communist organizational practices occasions far less resistance in these circumstances, since there is both the factor of urgency, to an extent which we do not feel, and, perhaps even more important, the necessity of counterbalancing, in the inevitable ambivalent structure, the profound resistance to value change.[50]

The second main type of societal value-change is that occurring when the cultural model cannot be supplied from a socially exogenous source, but must, so far as the social system reference is concerned, be evolved from within the society. This is the situation to which Max Weber's famous category of charismatic innovation applies. The focus of the change must be in the cultural system's religious aspects. It must concern alterations in the definition of the meaning of the life of the individual in society and of the character of the society itself.

In the process of development, a cultural change which could change values at a societal level would arise, through some complex process involving the interaction and interdependence of social and cultural systems. Considerations such as those reviewed by Weber in the selection on classes, status groups and religion (see end of Section B in

49. On the political primacy of Japanese society and its role in industrialization, as well as its relation to the religious background, see R. N. Bellah, *Tokugawa Religion* (Glencoe, Ill.: Free Press, 1957).

50. The most conspicuous example of a failure to overcome this resistance, very probably because of the failure to provide the necessary permissiveness and support to ease the process of relinquishment of old values, is probably the case of the Russian peasantry. Agriculture is clearly the main sore spot of Soviet productivity, and this seems to go back to the violently coercive procedures adopted in the collectivization program. See Bauer, Inkeles, and Kluckhohn, *How the Soviet System Works,* Harvard Press, 1957.

Part Four) would be highly relevant in so far as they concern society. The whole system of action, and the action-exogenous environment impinging upon it, is also relevant to this problem. The special role of the charismatic personality may involve problems specific to personality theory and not reducible either to sociological or cultural terms.

The obverse is the process of institutionalizing new religious values. The first question arising concerns the specification of the values from the cultural to the social system level, that is, defining of the implications of the cultural premises for the *kind of society* considered desirable. The second basic problem concerns the processes by which, once such a set of societal values is available, the strategically most important elements in the population may be motivationally committed to them. In other words, these elements must be socialized in the new definition of the situation if they are to exert the leverage necessary for extending the institutionalization of the values to all the important levels of specification and areas of differentiated function in the society.

A few points may be mentioned that are pertinent. The bearers of the new values must somehow become established in such a way that they cannot be reabsorbed in the older system. Religious or semi-religious movements, churches, etc., must be structurally independent of the paramount politically organized collectivity. Once consolidated, however, the institutionalization of new values in the secular society is possible only when these bearers can acquire a fundamental influence over the leadership elements of the paramount political system, through conversion of these elements, through infiltration, or through revolution. In early medieval Europe, the Church was the main locus of the values which later underlay the activism of modern Western society. The religious orders were the main locus of the values' growth and consolidation. If the Church and its orders had merely been a part of the political organization, this would not have occurred. In the great period from Gregory VII to Innocent III, the Church was able to impose much more of its values on a reluctant political laity than it otherwise could have. This did not happen without a good deal of direct interpenetration of political and religious leadership; but the basic principle of differentiation of church and state, though under considerable strain, was not abandoned.

A variety of other considerations about this process could be discussed, but perhaps these are enough to show the general nature of the process of change involved in the institutionalization of new values at the societal level.

V. CONCLUSION

Although it may seem long, relative to the task the above outline is obviously just a sketch, and a very tentative one. It is a statement of what seems to *one* particular author at *one* particular time to be the most useful way of organizing his view of the complex problems and materials which must somehow enter into the analysis of social systems. We have emphasized, throughout the introductory materials of this Anthology, that in our opinion sociology, as a theoretical as well as an empirical science, is in an early stage of development. We hold, therefore, that *any* statement made in our generation, even in outline, is in the nature of the case destined to be superseded, and relatively quickly. Any other view would contradict the established fact that science is an *inherently* evolving thing; if it should stop developing and become fixated on any particular set of "doctrines," it would *ipso facto* cease to be science.

This is the statement of our fundamental conviction. It does not imply, as is sometimes suggested, that, in the theory of sociology as in other sciences, there is an indefinite plurality of equally legitimate positions on all questions, an eclecticism which is the counterpart, for the sociology of science, of radical cultural relativism in a broader context. Such an implication would directly contradict our equally fundamental conviction that there has been a definite emerging structure of problems in our field, and a cumulative development of analytical thinking relative to them.

We have conscientiously tried to avoid the Scylla of dogmatism in presenting a theoretical view which is inevitably selective and incomplete, but is the best *we* can do at this time. We think it equally necessary to avoid the Charybdis of that formless eclecticism, common at least by implication in contemporary discussions, according to which in our field "anything goes," or "you pays your money and you takes your choice"; according to which there are alleged to be *no* serious professional criteria of theoretical excellence on any generalized level.[51]

51. It is perhaps pertinent to note (January, 1961) that this Introduction was written in the late summer and early fall of 1958. Sufficient developments have taken place in the interim so that had it been written two years later, it would have been somewhat different and we hope better. It was not, however, possible to undertake extensive revisions at that time. For the interested reader there are two places where some of the pertinent further theoretical developments are available, namely "Pattern Variables Revisited: A Response to Professor Dubin," *American Sociological Review*, August, 1960; and "The Point of View of the Author," the final chapter in Max Black (ed.), *The Social Theories of Talcott Parsons*, New York, Prentice-Hall, 1961.

PART ONE

Historical and Analytical Foundations

Section A

The Interpretation of Action in the History of Social Thought

Editorial Foreword, BY TALCOTT PARSONS   *85*

1. *On Hatreds and Dissensions in the Republic*, BY NICCOLO MACHIAVELLI   *98*
2. *Of the Natural Condition of Mankind*, BY THOMAS HOBBES   *99*
3. *Of the State of Nature*, BY JOHN LOCKE   *101*
4. *Of the Principle Which Gives Occasion to the Division of Labour*, BY ADAM SMITH   *104*
5. *Of Systems of Equality*, BY THOMAS R. MALTHUS   *106*
6. *The Civic Community*, BY GEORG W. F. HEGEL   *112*
7. *The Functions of Government in General*, BY JOHN STUART MILL   *117*
8. *On the Social Contract*, BY JEAN JACQUES ROUSSEAU   *119*
9. *Society and Government*, BY AUGUSTE COMTE   *125*
10. *The Material Forces and the Relations of Production*, BY KARL MARX *136*
11. *On Status and Contract*, BY SIR HENRY SUMNER MAINE   *138*
12. *The Nature of Society*, BY HERBERT SPENCER   *139*

The General Interpretation of Action

by Talcott Parsons

Sociological theory, as we understand it, has evolved, through a series of steps, from a more general matrix of thought about human action in society. In our opinion, the most decisive steps made, in the Western world, toward a differentiated conceptual scheme were taken by the 1890–1935 generation of writers. Selections from their writings compose the major part of this Reader. Prior to that period, however, a long series of writings had already dealt, in a variety of different ways and contexts, with the principal parts of the field, and had stated a considerable proportion of the conceptual components which have figured in the later work. These earlier writings were the main sources of the statements of problems from which the later authors evolved their own altered and refined statements, through a process of taking over elements from their predecessors and modifying and changing the conceptual structure they inherited.

The volume of early writings relevant here is, in proportion to the space available for them in the Reader, very large—far larger than is true for other areas represented in the Reader. Hence, in this area, the Reader can serve least as a substitute, either for reading the original works represented or others, or for reading the extensive secondary analyses done by historians of ideas. In this section, we can at most present a few samples representing the important currents of thought antecedent to our main period of concern. The object of the present Foreword is to present a rationale of this selection by outlining what we consider these main trends to be and which of their components have been important in later theoretical constructions. The first problem in making such selections is how far back in the historical sequence to go. It is generally agreed that the primary roots of Western culture

are in the Hebraic religious tradition and in Greek philosophy: hence one might include selections from the Old Testament and from the Greek philosophers. However, we are not historians; our concern is with the more immediate background of the structure of thought underlying contemporary thinking in our field. Our concern, therefore, should be temporally limited to the first appearance of frankly secular general thinking about human conduct in society in "modern" Western thought; and Machiavelli seems to be the first major figure who fits this criterion.

There were many predominantly secular writers in later antiquity; but within Christian Western Europe this phenomenon did not emerge again until the late Renaissance. Both in the Middle Ages and during the Reformation, most of the writing attempting general analysis of social phenomena consisted in statements and defenses of religious positions. In the sixteenth century, Machiavelli stands almost alone in lacking direct concern for the bearing of what he says on the problem of the moral justification of the conduct he describes. This is one principal reason for placing a selection from his writings first.

There is also a second reason for placing him first. The bearing of "normative" considerations on our problems has a complex—at least double—incidence. The primary significance of the secularization of social thought—of which Machiavelli is the first outstanding example—is that the capacity somehow to stand "above the battle" is an essential prerequisite for attaining a scientific attitude toward the phenomena studied. These phenomena are, on a generalized level, always close to the concerns of religion; and commitment to a specific religous position makes it very difficult to be an affectively neutral analyst of the phenomena in which such positions are implicated. Probably, the presence, in the intellectual milieu, of a plurality of religious positions differing fundamentally from each other—a condition first fulfilled in Europe during the Reformation—was one factor in the possibility of taking a secular point of view bound to none of these positions. There is another sense in which the normative is a crucial category for all social science of the kind concerning us. The observer must be able to achieve a certain "distance," to be uncommitted, in the immediate action sense, to a set of specific normative components; he must also be able to appreciate and analyze the normative components functioning as determinants of the actions of the individuals and groups which are objects of his study. This is the second reason for the selection we have made from Machiavelli's works as well as for selecting his work as contrasted with Luther's, Calvin's, or a Jesuit writer's. Machiavelli is best known for *The Prince,* an extremely pragmatic handbook of measures recommended for acquiring and retaining political power. Considerations of the normative sentiments and commitments of the people with whom the prince must deal are mentioned there. However, Machiavelli's acute awareness of these factors' importance in determining the social process is more clear in the selection we have chosen, where he is more concerned with reflection on the historical record than with action in an immediate situation. Machiavelli began directing attention to the problems, not of the moral rightness or wrongness of a particular religious position, but of the more generalized empirical importance of religious commitments and the sentiments associated with them—which might vary over a considerable range; first, in determining how people will act, and, more theoretically, in the possibility of their action's constituting a stable social organization.

Machiavelli thus exhibits, extraordinarily early, the combination of the attitude of scientific objectivity, of ability to see human action as an external phenomenon, and of awareness of the importance of the normative considerations which are critical *from the actor's point of view.* He was able to state many observations and insights worthy of attention today.

The considerably fuller flow of what would now be termed secular general social thought did not begin until the seventeenth century. When it had become established, sociologically the most relevant polarization there was was that between "individualistic" and "collectivistic" references. However, this is a complex matter; a number of important

discriminations must be made between various nuances of the problem.

Regarded historically, the individualistic strain in Christianity—the concern, on the religious level, with the fate of the individual soul—has underlain the problem of individualism in Western thought. Within the medieval tradition, however, it could be insulated from the problems of society, since all the individual's earthly relations to religion had to be mediated through the Church, as an organized collectivity which was held to be the sole trustee of his religious interests. With the Reformation, the significance of the church was fundamentally altered, for Protestants; and the individual, in his ultimate religious concern, was, as it were, immediately juxtaposed with the problems of society in both its religious and its secular aspects.

The very word "Protestant" indicates that, from a normative point of view, defending the individual's rights and freedoms against the claims of ecclesiastical and then also of political authority constituted a major focus of general, i.e., at least potentially theoretical, concern. It is not too large a step from defending the rights of an acting unit to asserting the substantive importance of that unit in the empirical determination of the course of events. There is, therefore, a relatively clear and direct line of descent from the individualistic religious implications of Protestantism, differently structured in its different branches, for the individual's role in society on this earth, to the type of generalization about action in society that claims that, in the last analysis, the actions and decisions of individuals determine social structure and process.

Opposed to this is the one major source of more "collectivistic" social theories that is relatively directly descended from the Catholic viewpoint, which sees a collectively organized church, and the other collectivities of a society infused with the collective Christian spirit, interposed between the essential individual and the system of interactive rights and obligations in which he is involved.

However correct this differentiation may be as the broadest generalization, there are various complications. Substantive or analytical individualism may raise, in an acute form, the "problem of order"—namely, of the conditions making a stable society possible—and one possible solution is to emphasize the importance of restraints on the freedom of individuals as a condition of such order. By this path, especially favored by Hobbes, analytical individualism may lead into normative collectivism. On the other hand, in both Protestant-inspired and secularized branches of Western social thought the church, as the main focus of collective trusteeship over the individual, may be replaced by secular collectivities—notably the paramount political organization, the state, but, under certain circumstances, others, such as "class" or "party"; a variety of possible collectivistic emphases may be derived from this source. It need not be a collectivity as such; certain elements of cultural tradition, like science, may form the primary points of reference. Finally, these two broad traditions may cross in various ways. Just as Hobbes, working from an analytically individualistic base, arrived at a normative collectivism, so Hegel, from a normatively individualistic base, a particular concept of "freedom," arrived at an analytical collectivism, asserting the predominance of the state over the individual.

As social scientists, we must find our primary points of reference in the analytical rather than the normative aspects of the individualism-collectivism axis. But the subtle relations outlined above between substantive and normative considerations make it impossible to ignore either side.

Within this frame of reference, the most important single tradition of thought lying in the background of our primary concern is that of analytical individualism; but the others are also crucially important. Modern sociological theory may be described as a result of a special type of "marriage" between the individualistic and the collectivistic strands. In terms of historical genesis, it is not understandable as one or the other. However, the individualistic strand is especially important in the attempts to formulate *scientifically* the determinants of social behavior. This importance provides the main justification for representing this tradition more than the collectivistic one in our selections.

Significantly, Hobbes, the first major "sociological" landmark after Machiavelli, was the first to pose cogently the problem of order deriving from his version of analytical individualism. Hobbes considered the "passions" of the individual to be the ultimate determinants of his action, and he specifically denied that there could be any "common measure" between the passions of different individuals. Perhaps more clearly than any subsequent writer, Hobbes stated the utilitarian postulate of the independence of any one individual's ends from those of any other. (Hobbes, though he did not carry the point so far as later writers did, implied that the individual himself was motivated by a "bundle" of more or less random wants.) Hobbes was principally concerned with the implications of this independence of one individual's passions from those of another. By adding the postulate of "equality of hope," and through the funda-

mental insight that other individuals are important as obstacles or aids to one individual in his gaining the ends dictated by his passions, Hobbes came to his famous proposition: each individual's unregulated attempts to gain his ends would, through individuals' mutual attempts to "subdue or destroy one another," result in the war of all against all. This is because, in such a situation, the most effective means of gaining any end through social interaction are force and fraud.

Hobbes's only solution of the resulting problem of order was for each individual to surrender his "natural rights" to use force and fraud to a sovereign who would forcibly constrain everyone to observe minimum rules, so that security would be achieved. From a sociological point of view, Hobbes's type of social contact was most unsatisfactory. Yet he posed the problem of order with a clarity which has never been surpassed, enabling it to enter directly into, e.g., the formulation of what was the major point of reference for Durkheim's quite different solution.

With Locke, the individualistic tradition changed in a way which can conveniently be described in terms of Locke's difference from Hobbes in the treatment of normative problems. Locke, through the implicit postulate which Halevy[1] has called the "natural identity of interests," simply pushed aside the problem of order as Hobbes posed it. Locke assumed that natural rights would be reciprocally respected, except by a minority of "bad men"; and that, on this basis of natural harmony, men could strive to improve their positions, to "appropriate the gifts of nature," and, rather than endeavoring to "subdue or destroy one another," to exchange goods and services to mutual advantage. Locke contributed almost nothing to analysis of the conditions under which such a harmony of interests would hold; he merely assumed that it would occur in the state of nature. But with respect to some societies and to some of their features, he was more nearly empirically correct than Hobbes. In fact, order does exist; and it is not merely a function of the coercive authority of a sovereign. Since he was empirically correct about this, Locke could analyze some of the things men did within the spheres of security and freedom thus enjoyed.

Hobbes is the theorist of the individualistic tradition who, through his formulation of problem of order, focused attention on the political aspects of the problem of institutional order in a society. He was interested in the control of force and fraud

1. Halevy, *Growth of Philosophical Radicalism*, Macmillan Co., N.Y., 1928. This is by far the best guide to the history of utilitarian thought.

and the problem of the functions of authority; but he was more concerned with the negative side— with the ways political organization could prevent degeneration into the war of all against all, rather than with the ways it could serve as an instrument implementing positive values and collective goals. Within the same tradition, Locke was the theorist of the economic aspects—of how, within an assumed natural order, the mutual advantages of association could be attained, especially through exchange and, eventually, the division of labor.

Locke is, if not the founder, at least the spiritual father of modern economics, which is both an essential constitutive part of the theory of social systems and a continual point of reference for the sociological part of the theory. Locke may be regarded as the principal discoverer of the possibility of mutual advantage in exchange and of the modern conceptions of property, prerequisite to such advantage. Above all, however unsatisfactorily he formulated it, he originated the concept of property as founded in the functional necessities of individualistic production as a societal function. In our selections, we have followed this theme one step farther by introducing Adam Smith's account of the advantages to be gained, not merely from exchanging independently held possessions, but also from introducing the division of labor into the process of production itself. These fundamentals, plus the understanding of the positive functions of capital—in which Smith was far more advanced than Locke—laid the main conceptual foundations of the classical economics.

From Locke through Smith and the later economists, the tradition has been to consider the individual, actuated by his own "self-interest," as exchanging with other individuals and thereby bringing about outcomes which redounded to the social advantage. Even in the use of capital, the relation between "capitalist" and "laborer" was considered mainly as an exchange relationship, one of capitalists "making advances to labor" to cover the time-interval before the products of labor could become consumable.

Hobbes initiated consideration of the senses in which an aggregate of discrete individuals could be combined into what we would now call a collectivity—an organized social system in which relations of leadership and authority figure prominently. Hobbes was concerned most with the absolute authority of the sovereign necessitated by the extreme precariousness of even a minimum of order. But the general theme was open to many other variations. One was the translation of Hobbes's concept of the central authority of a real political sovereign into a theory of legal sovereignty, as carried out by the jurist Austin. The most important part of Austin's theory is the conception of the normative integration of a legal system, one in which there could not be a plurality of independent decision-making units, each equally authorized to claim ultimate authoritativeness for its decisions. A second variation concerned the problem of participation in the process of collective decision-making itself. Here Bentham, one of the great forerunners of political democracy, is preeminent; but in our selections, this variation is represented by John Stuart Mill. The postulate, that each individual should be considered equal to every other, characterizing this trend of political utilitarianism, raised questions about social stratification, levels of competence and responsibility, etc., which were embarrassing in that tradition; but within it, no important solutions were contributed.

Generally speaking, the axis on which the statement of problems turned stretched from the Hobbesian pole, where authority was absolute and the sovereign's word not to be questioned, to the democratic pole, where each individual should have an equal voice. Both poles, and their many variants and compromises, implied a set of questions about whether (and how) the analytical individualism of the utilitarians constituted an adequate frame of reference for explaining either the tolerability of such authority as existed, or the elements of responsibility and the like in more egalitarian and democratic arrangements. Contemporaneous traditions of thought like those associated with Rousseau and Hegel would eventually formulate elements essential in this area of problems.

In so far as authority—along the whole range, but particularly toward the democratic pole—was not based on coercion, a crucial problem was that of the basis of consensus: of the coming together of ends, sentiments, values, or "wills" that could motivate acceptance of authority and the definition of collective as discriminated from individual interests and goals. Mill's formula of social utilitarianism may be regarded as the final attempt to deal with this problem within the classic utilitarian tradition.

By a subtle shift, a plausible formula was evolved solving this problem with a minimum of change in the conceptual framework. This was to assume that the variability of the wants or interests of individuals did not matter; but that, because of the uniformities of "human nature" and/or of the conditions in which people were placed, the individualistic competitive element would be eliminated, and social action would then consist mostly of "spontaneous co-operation." Deviations from this model could be explained by some specific obstacles to its realization, the most important of which would be ignorance. The general rationalist utopian strain of much thought of the French Enlightenment tended in this direction; in England, its principal spokesman was William Godwin.

Godwin's espousal of this position provided the principal stimulus to Malthus. For our present purposes, it is relevant that Malthus emphasized the importance of the biological urge—though this early version of such thinking apparently had an influence on Darwin. It is more centrally relevant that Malthus' views on the reproductive urge questioned Locke's version of spontaneous order as well as Godwin's. Malthus raised the Hobbesian problem again. In coping with this, Malthus gave new emphasis to three major themes which had been, in the utilitarian tradition, much less prominent, but that figure importantly in later development. The first theme took a long time to come to fruition; it was concern with the family as an institutionalized social organization—a concern which, to the modern sociologist, was conspicuously absent from the early traditions of thought. Malthus saw the family both as facilitating reproduction and, through enforcing parents' economic responsibility for offspring, as the principal mechanism of controlling the excesses of reproduction. At the same time, the pressure of population would put a high premium on efficient economic production, which would necessitate that production be carried on predominantly in organized units—where the capitalist was both a supporter of labor and an organizer of the productive process, and hence the "boss" exercising authority over his workers. The firm then became a small political organization in which the authority problem, with emphasis on its severe Hobbesian form, had a prominent place. Moreover, the fact that capitalist-employers and workers were of different status, both within the firm as an organization and in their incomes and styles of life, meant that this organizational differentiation became the basis of a "division of society into classes." Thus Malthus emphasized strongly two crucial structural components of an economy with advanced division of labor, managerial authority, and class differentiation—far more strongly than they were emphasized in the economic tradition of Locke, or in the political tradition of Bentham and Mill. The relevance of these themes to the later Marxian concept of the capitalistic economy is clear. Malthus' conception may be said, in these respects, to have resulted from a special synthesis of Hobbes's and Locke's versions of the utilitarian tradition—the organized business firm was pic-

tured as operating under a Hobbesian absolute sovereignty, whose acceptance by workers was motivated, not directly by the fear of force, but by the fear of starvation.

An important feature of early nineteenth-century utilitarian thought that contrasted with its previous phases was the attention given to levels of organization between the individual and the highest-order secular collectivity, the state. The emphasis on the fact that economic production and hence much exchange were not carried on by isolated individuals, but by some kind of organized collective units, was a relatively new one. This made the basis of their organization a problem.

We must mention two additional important ingredients which came into the field of sociological concern from the individualistic tradition; both figured prominently only after the middle of the nineteenth century. The first is the concept of treating the biological nature of the individual as a crucial set of independent factors which could not be modified by environmental influences. The second is the conception that societies undergo essential processes of change rather than remaining static. Darwin and Spencer are particularly important in this connection.

In connection with the biological nature of the individual, Malthus had already forceably introduced the instinctive basis of the reproductive urge as a major determinant of human societies, one whose control was difficult and could be achieved not by will power alone, but necessitated institutionalized situations making it overwhelmingly to individuals' interest to control it. Darwinism, by greatly generalizing biological thought relative to its previous levels, gave a general foundation to a type of theory supporting a more radical analytical individualism than that of the utilitarian tradition. In certain respects, even more broadly than Malthus, Darwin tipped balances in the Hobbesian direction, treating the competitive aspects of human relations as a special case of natural selection. It thereby checked the tendency to shift to a theory of spontaneous co-operation of the sort emphasized by Godwin. The peculiar balance between competition and order seen by Locke and the economists was theoretically precarious. Darwinism, by associating competition with natural selection, strengthened the competitive side of the dilemma—at the cost of undermining the normative element which had accounted for order through Locke's postulate of the identity of interests.

If competition was to be real, then the individual had to be motivated to enter into the competition, to be exposed to the forces of natural selection.

Since in utilitarian terms, it was difficult to see how this exposure could be in the individual's interest, he had to be endowed with inborn "propensities," like the reproductive urge, that would propel him into the fray. This shift would close the gap left yawning in utilitarian theory, which simply assumed that men had a variety of ends or goals as individuals, but did not locate their origin, nor give any clue as to their relative urgency that would enable an estimate to be made of the costs actors would be willing to pay to achieve them. This theoretical closure was, however, attained at the expense of certain degrees of theoretical freedom for development in the direction of special interest here. In other words, if the primary determinants of action are held to be (a) the inborn propensities or instincts of the individual, and (b) the struggle for survival dominated by the principle of natural selection, then there is no room for the normative factors which had been built into Locke's position by the route of implicit assumption, but which had never been given a satisfactory systematic status within it. This is, by and large, the path taken both by instinct theory in psychology and by "social Darwinism" in the latter part of the nineteenth century. It is an important reference point, both for a good deal of the psychological theory to be presented in Part Three, and in much of the discussion of social change to be represented in Part Five.

This is reductionism of social action to an essentially biological process—*biological* in terms of the biological theory dominant at the time.[2] Since then, it has become much more clear that the unit of the selective process is only partially the individual organism; various social aggregates of organisms—notably the species, but also subgroups within it—figure in this respect. Thus the social dimension whereby individual organisms are often, by behavioral mechanisms, sacrificed to the interests of larger systems, has become increasingly built into biological theory itself. Second, the concepts of adaptation and of natural selection have been greatly altered in emphasis. The older emphasis was on the passive aspect of adaptation: the environment presented certain inexorable conditions which had to be met, "or else." Since Darwin did not have the modern theory of genetics at his command, he had no principles of developing organization of biological systems on the genetic side; he tended to postulate a continual set of random variations that were the logical counterparts of the utilitarians' random ends. The more

recent trend of biological theory is to emphasize the evolution of progressively higher levels of organization which must be passively adapted to the exigencies of the environment, but which also achieve that adaptation by mechanisms enabling them to cope actively with the environment, rather than merely "submitting" to it. Locomotion is a primary example of evolutionary development; but even more important is the development of intelligence—capacity to react to changing environmental situations without being bound by rigid predetermined patterns of behavior. Natural selection, then, favors not only passively adapted organic types, but types with higher levels of organization—especially those possessing mechanisms enabling them to adopt varying and versatile behavior in reaction to varying environmental conditions. On the whole, however, this important shift in biological thinking, particularly as it became known to social scientists and influenced their theories, occurred only after a corresponding main trend within the social sciences themselves. The major early influence of biology was in the reductionist direction.

If not the prime source, biological theory was at least a major reference point for another critical idea which figured very prominently in the second half of the nineteenth century in the social field, namely, the idea of evolution. The utilitarian tradition, from Hobbes through Locke and later, was concerned less with problems of the change of societies over time, and more with the invariant conditions underlying the problem of social order and of gaining individuals' ends through economic production and exchange, and, peripherally, through political association. Conceptions of evolution had, however, already appeared, notably in the French Enlightenment in the case of Condorcet, who set a model which was important for Saint-Simon and Comte. They also appeared in the early nineteenth century in German Idealism, especially in Hegel's work, which will be briefly discussed presently. There were also overtones of evolution in writers like Malthus and Ricardo. The emergence of the Darwinian theory immediately focused primary attention on this area. We represent this mode of thinking by a selection from the writings of Herbert Spencer, because Spencer was the most prominent evolutionist in the social field, and also because he incorporated the idea with a minimum of modification of the older utilitarian framework. Spencer was not, strictly speaking, a Darwinian. He had worked with the idea of evolution before the publication of the *Origin of Species;* and he never abandoned the belief in the inheritance of acquired characters. In a sense, he never faced the

---

2. See T. H. Huxley's famous essay, "Evolution and Ethics," N.Y., D. Appleton and Co., 1905, which put natural selection and *all* normative considerations in radical conflict with each other.

problem of reduction that came to a head in later discussion of the relations between social science and biology.

Spencer did present an ingenious combination of components drawn from rationalism and from the Hobbesian and Lockean versions of utilitarianism. An important contribution by Spencer (as in the works of the founder of modern anthropology, E. B. Tylor) was focusing attention on the phenomena of religion, which had been grossly neglected in the traditions of thought we have been reviewing. In part, this attention reflected greater awareness of the customs of non-literate peoples, among whom religious phenomena figured very prominently. This prominence made it plausible for Spencer to see religious beliefs as derived from the relative ignorance of man in the early stages of his social and cultural development. The most clear example was the derivation of the idea of the soul from the experience of dreams. However much Spencer's ideas in this area have had to be modified, he—like Comte, in a different tradition—was among the first to bring a crucially important subject matter back as a focus of attention.

By relating religion to ignorance, Spencer relegated it, as a genuinely important social phenomenon, to the early phases of social evolution. He blended Hobbes and Locke in relation to two later phases, in his concepts of "militant" and "industrial" societies. He was thus able to conceive a formula which, instead of presenting two rigid, mutually exclusive alternatives, allowed both to be right in a sense, as formulating two different special cases derived from the application of the same principles to different conditions. In spite of the ingenuity of this solution, the basic problem of order which Hobbes had raised remained unsolved.

It was also within the evolution framework, with a comparative reference as well, that the concept of traditionalism and its relation to ascriptive immobility of resources entered modern sociological thinking. A selection from the *Ancient Law* of Sir Henry Sumner Maine represents this important conception. Intimate knowledge of a non-European society (in this case, India) as well as of Western legal history played a dominant part in Maine's thinking. His developmental formula of the process of shift from status (to which the modern sociologist would be inclined to add the adjective "ascribed"), to "contract," where rights and obligations could be voluntarily assumed, was a landmark in the analysis of social structures. It influenced much subsequent thinking, including Durkheim's. Another important version of very

similar ideas was presented by Walter Bagehot in *Physics and Politics*. This was the concept of the "cake of custom," which held social action in a rigid framework but, with development of such things as markets, tended to be broken up, giving the individual far more freedom.

After enjoying a tremendous vogue in both sociology and anthropology, the conception of social evolution underwent a dramatic eclipse shortly after the turn of the twentieth century. This eclipse was associated with the movement of theoretical thinking which is the primary concern of this Reader. One factor was the sheer accumulation of empirical knowledge that made many of the early generalizations, particularly so far as they involved a simple "unilineal" conception of the process, untenable. On another level, however, the new emphases, particularly on the normative components of culture and the structure of societies, simply did not fit with the ways in which the conception had been formulated, either in Spencer's modified but not basically changed utilitarian terms, or in Comte's special version of French rationalism, or in the Hegelian dialectic. The problem was not solved by these difficulties; and a very interesting symptom of a current shift to a new level of social science theory is a revival of interest in the problem of evolution.

Let us now turn to what is, in an analytical sense, the "collectivistic" side of the main traditions of modern social thought. There are two primary branches of this, going back to common roots in European intellectual history; they can be broadly distinguished as those of French rationalism and of German Idealism. In the former tradition, the most important people are Rousseau and Comte; in the latter, for our purposes, Hegel and, in one aspect of his thinking, Marx—though others like Dilthey and even Sombart, might be mentioned.

It might be questionable to classify Rousseau as a rationalist, since in many ways he was the fountainhead of Romanticism and similar movements. However, Rousseau, though on the whole he shared Locke's conception of the state of nature as one in which each individual had the right to pursue his interests in his own way, treated the problem of unifying such discrete individuals to form a political collectivity as a much more positive problem than did the economically oriented individualists in the utilitarian tradition. Rousseau broke through the Hobbes-Locke dilemma, postulating a factor very different from those they had considered, the famous *general will*. Its difference is made clear by Rousseau's insistence on the distinction between *volonté générale* and *volonté des tous*. *Volonté générale* is generated by a Hobbesian social contract to surrender control of natural rights to an absolute sovereign. The difference is also related to the fact that Rousseau's political theory was formulated in the interest of democracy—not, as in Hobbes's case, of monarchy.

Rousseau and his followers found insuperable difficulties in defining an acceptable relationship between his postulated general will and any concrete political institutions which could effect it without risking uncontrolled dictatorship by a self-appointed minority or a tyranny of the majority. The difficulties arose from the fact that Rousseau, like his utilitarian predecessors, did not consider a basis in societal values and institutionalized norms somehow independent of and underlying the state; he tried to elevate political theory into a general theory of social systems. At the same time, he did contend that there was a factor of the integration of the system that was not reducible to terms of the discrete individual rationally following his self-interest or his "passions," nor a matter of in-born instincts. It was an analytically independent set of factors which (to use Durkheim's term) must be postulated to account for solidarity.

In the French tradition of social thought, Rousseau's new note blended with one derived from the conservative thought of writers like De Bonald and de Maistre, who tended to challenge the tradition of the Revolution and to defend the record of the Old Regime. In this period, the most significant figure for the development of sociology—particularly for Durkheim's work—was Auguste Comte. In Comte's theory, the concept corresponding to, and certainly at least partially derived from, Rousseau's general will is that of *consensus* as the essential basis of the cohesion or integration of a society. Comte said very little about the ways in which a basis of consensus, once established, could be understood to be implicated in the complex differentiated subsystems of a society—how, in other words, a consensus which must, by the terms of his statement, be conceived at a very high level of generality, could effectively control the varieties of behavior of many different types of collective and individual units of a social structure in many different and varying situations. Serious progress toward solving these problems was not made until Durkheim's generation.

Comte undoubtedly was a certain type of rationalist, in that he conceived the consensus in terms of ideas or common cognitive orientations. (This focus on ideas was the basis of his famous law of the three stages, which will be discussed later, in relation to the problems of social change.) In making science the essential basis of consensus in his final positive stage,

Comte approached the position of Godwin and other utopian rationalists. The basis of a possible difference from this utopian position lies in the special sense in which society is simultaneously both an object of scientific study and a creation of the processes of human action. This theme is prominent in Comte, for whom sociology was both the science of society as an existing object, and the primary guide to building a different and better society. The structure of problems—including the very formidable difficulties Comte's positivism involved—leads directly into the later work of Durkheim. Comte's version of evolutionary theory, built directly on the predominance of ideas as a factor, was not immediately so fruitful for a theory of social change as was that of Marx, since Comte's did not even begin to present an acceptable account of the mechanisms by which the influence of ideas could operate. However, the pattern of the stages, from theological through metaphysical to positive, shows a process of "rationalization" affiliated with various contemporary and subsequent trends of thought, including Max Weber's.

From the present point of view, Comte's most important contribution was his injection, into a strategic point of the stream of sociological thinking, of the collectivistic element with respect to the problem of integration. Though Comte's accounts of the basis of integration and of its working within the society are not acceptable to the modern sociologist, he posed a problem which had proved essentially insoluble within the utilitarian tradition. In the history of ideas, posing a problem fruitfully is almost as important a contribution as its positive solution.

For the future development of sociology, Comte provided, more directly than Rousseau, a fruitful antithesis to the individualistic utilitarian tradition of thought. That it was a genuine antithesis is vividly shown in the relations between Comte and John Stuart Mill, which ended in a break in their personal friendship.[3] The problem of synthesizing these apparently antithetical elements in one very important way set the stage for the new phase of the development of sociology.

The second most important source of the collectivistic trend is German Idealism. This was greatly influenced by Rousseau, as well as by other sources which need not be discussed here. The relevant version of the idealistic movement is Hegel's—not least because of Hegel's influence on Marx. Relevant to our present interest, there are

3. See John Stuart Mill, *Auguste Comte and Positivism*, London: Kegan Paul, Trench Treubner & Co., Ltd., 4th ed., 1891.

three essential components in Hegel's thought. The first is the concept of the primacy of the "ideal" component (*Geist* is the almost untranslatable German term), or, as we would now be inclined to say, the component of cultural orientation. The second is the evolutionary conception—culture is not static, but is involved in an inherent "dynamism" of development from an initial to a terminal stage. The third is a conception of the nature of this process, which Hegel called "dialectic" in the famous formula that a thesis gives rise to its antithesis and then, when both are present, a synthesis can be formed.

Consideration of Comte's theories has shown that there is a natural line of reasoning from Rousseau's concept that consensus consists in some kind of unification of "wills" to the concept of a basis in common cultural orientations, in ideas or values. Comte's thinking went in this direction, ending with the concept of science as this basis, and sociology functioning, in this respect, as the queen of the sciences. In general, at the time of Hegel and Comte, clear discrimination between the normative and the existential aspects of systems of ideas was not easy to make; neither in Comte nor in Hegel does this distinction, so essential later to Max Weber, figure at all prominently.

This central problem is closely connected with the one mentioned in connection with Rousseau and Comte, namely, that of an intelligent account of the processes and mechanisms by which ideas, existential or normative, in fact influence the processes of action. Theories which have approached the philosophical idealistic pole have continually been forced into postulating a mysterious process of emanation which, like Locke's identity of interest, becomes a name for a problem rather than a solution of it. This is the case with the Hegelian version of idealism in relation to society. Nevertheless, however unsatisfactory the account of *how* common cultural orientations can become crucial determinants of social action is, sharp focusing of attention on the fact that they *are* centrally involved in the structure of societies can be a factor of the first importance in leading thought toward a solution.

The second virtue of the Hegelian tradition as a forerunner of the theoretical development in which we are interested is that it did not confine itself to asserting the importance of the cultural factor—in two different contexts, it introduced conceptual differentiation into its concept of the role of culture. The first context was the evolutionary, in which the recent stage of development of the *Weltgeist* was considered the culmination of a process of dialecti-

cal development from a primitive beginning. Condorcet had treated the evolutionary process as a very simple continuous process of the growth of "reason." Comte elaborated this by a concept of well-marked stages involving an element of qualitative difference from one another. The Hegelian concept, presented a little earlier than Comte's, added the dialectical principle of interconnection between the stages that raised, on a certain level, the question of the mechanisms of the transition from one stage to the next. Another noteworthy feature of Hegel's philosophy of history is that he began to pay serious attention to the significance of the development of civilizations in areas of the world other than the West.

The second context in which Hegel differentiated the application of his ideas was with reference to the structure of society contemporary to him. This aspect is especially emphasized in the selection from his *Philosophy of Law* below. Here he distinguished the levels of "incorporation" of the *Geist* in society—the state as the highest, the "bourgeois society" as next in line, and the common people (which, in his time, meant primarily the peasantry) as the lowest. This was a step toward a more differentiated treatment of the relation of culture to society than had, from a collectivistic starting point, been prominent either in Rousseau or in Comte. The concept of bourgeois society was a recognition of the possible soundness in the utilitarian conception of a market-oriented system of relationships; it was used as a point of reference for Marx's theory of class conflict. It represents a genuine convergence between idealist-collectivistic and utilitarian-individualistic patterns of thought—again, however unsatisfactory to the modern sociologist Hegel's specific formulations may be. It helped set the stage for a more scientific treatment of the problem of emanation—of the ways, given the existence of cultural ideas and ideals, these could be conceived as related to the other components of systems of social action.

The Hegelian pattern of idealistic evolutionism provided an important reference point for three subsequent developments, all sharing, in certain respects, its cultural-collectivistic orientation. These were German idealistic "historicism," Marxism, and the type of analysis of the involvement of ideas in action of which Max Weber was the most eminent exponent. The third is central to the material included in this Reader, but the other two should be discussed briefly for background.

One important consequence of the Hegelian method was the breaking of the evolutionary sequence into what were, to some extent, qualitatively distinct phases of the *Weltgeist's* development. It was natural for some, skeptical of the dialectic's sweeping generalizations, simply to cease worrying about the connections and to attempt to portray a cultural epoch in terms of its unique and independent *Geist*.[4] This tendency fitted well with the general emphasis on uniqueness and historical particularity that was prominent in the nineteenth century, particularly in Germany; it also fitted with the general idealistic tendency to see the key to understanding in the spirit or particular themes of a culture. This type of thinking permeated a whole range of historically oriented fields, concerning the arts, jurisprudence, and economics.

In German philosophy and methodology of science, it was associated with the Kantian dualism between the worlds of nature and of *Geist* or *Kultur*. The most important tenet was that, whereas nature was subject to understanding in terms of systems of generalized analytical concepts, culture could be "depicted" and "appreciated" only in terms of its specific uniqueness of configuration. Toward the end of the century, a moderate version of this view was presented by Windelband and Rickert, a more radical one by Dilthey. In something approaching sociology, perhaps its best-known exponents are Sombart and Spengler.

This approach is fundamentally at variance with the aims of generalized theory central to this Reader. It either eliminates generalized theory completely from the field of the social sciences, or it establishes an unbridgeable duality between the naturalistic and the cultural components. For this reason, Max Weber's fundamental critique of the methodology of *Historismus* is so important a reference point in relation to the question of the status of normative components in social action. Weber did not carry his position through to a logical conclusion; but his break with the tradition of historical uniqueness was a major turning-point.

The views Weber criticized have continued to be influential in many connections, as represented in this Reader in the work of Weber's brother Alfred and in that of a number of anthropologists particularly concerned with the configurational aspects of culture. These writers have made important contributions to a variety of more specific problems, but their methodological position cannot be considered to be in the primary line of development of social science theory as such.

In one sense, the use to which Marx put Hegel's ideas is diametrically opposed to that of the historical schools. Rather than accepting literally Marx's own statement that he "set Hegel on his head," we would be more accurate in saying that Hegelian idealism, like utilitarianism, was an inherently unstable conceptual scheme, and that it tended to break down in two antithetical directions, whose opposition, in the absence of a synthesis, was irreconcilable. In utilitarianism, the central point of reference was "economic." One half of the dichotomy was biological—instinctivism and social Darwinism—while the other was Hobbesian concept of a coercively unified collectivity-system where action was motivated by the "rational" hopes and fears of men. In the Hegelian case, one part of the duality was "pure" idealism, tending to taper into historicist emanationism of the Spenglerian variety. The other part was best represented by Marxism, which should be considered in a special sense as one particular variety of utilitarianism, with certain infusions from its idealistic antecedents.

Marx's central concept of human social action is inherited from Locke and the classical economists; it is that of individuals rationally pursuing their self-interest, in a system of the division of labor, through relations of exchange. In his more technical economic theory, Marx built directly on Ricardo, incorporating many of the now obsolete—if not erroneous—elements of Ricardian theory. At the same time, in his work there appear—far more accentuated than in the liberal and classical traditions—the two fundamental structural elements of a "capitalist" economy that had already appeared in Malthus, namely, the authority-structure of the productive unit, and the "division of society into classes."

In his sociological theory, Marx added two further essential components, both somehow derived from the Hegelian tradition. One of these was the conception of a dialectically structured evolutionary process, in the course of which there were well-marked, qualitatively different stages, and a "dynamic" built on the thesis-antithesis model of a conflict between two opposing elements. Here, however, what evolved was not a *Geist* but an empirical social system, a system of the "relations of production"; and the conflict was not a logical one, a contradiction, in the Hegelian sense; it was a conflict of the interests—in the last analysis, the economic and power interests—of social groups, the classes involved in the productive process.[5]

It is most important to note that utilitarian

4. Thus substituting the particular *Zeitgeist* for a phase of the more comprehensive *Weltgeist*.

5. It is, however, significant that Marxist language today speaks of "contradictions" as if there were no essential difference between logical incompatibility of ideas and conflicts of economic or social interests.

theory was, in a psychological sense, not "deterministic," rather "voluntaristic"; and this is true of Marxism. There were, however, essential deterministic elements in the *system* of social relations involved in the interlocking interests of many men. For the system of capitalism, Marx elevated these deterministic elements to a far higher degree of inevitability than his predecessors had. Within the general scheme of rational goal-oriented action, the effect of this was to emphasize the situational as opposed to the volitional element. Men acted as they did because, in the situation in which they were placed in the particular set of relations of production, they could not act otherwise: for the worker, the alternative to accepting capitalistic employment, and thus being exploited, was starvation; for the employer, the alternative to employing was, through the mechanism of competition, elimination from business, presumably reduction to the status of worker.

In the discussion of Comte, attention has been directed to the possibility of changing the whole basis of such a situation by concerted action. The environment of the individual is composed of the actions of others. Hence if interests can be structured in a given direction, the constraints of a particular set of the relations of production can be overcome. Then it is possible for an impetus toward change to become what Merton has called a "self-fulfilling prophecy." This possibility is inherent in any form of collectivist theory—including the idealistic branch, so long as it is not a pure form of "emanationism"; if it is, nothing like a mechanism of change is felt to be necessary. Marxism cannot be classified here, but it was caught in this aspect of its theoretical structure, in a dilemma of considerable interest in the present context.

The great shift is defined as the "leap into freedom," the *Sprung in die Freiheit*. The first inquiry is how this is to take place, and here, in turn, it is a question of how far the change is the consequence of the unplanned evolution of the forces of production, and how far it is to be furthered by a voluntaristic movement bringing about the revolution and engineering the transition. Here Marx was, as Schumpeter said, both a sociologist and a revolutionist. As revolutionist, he was committed to foster the possibility of aiding the forces of production and the "contradictions"—this has become the dominant note of recent Marxist thought. The emphasis has, particularly through Lenin's influence, become placed on maximally effective *organization* for revolutionary, i.e., political, action. Hence the conception of the centrally led and controlled party, introducing the dictatorship of the "proletariat"—in effect, of the leadership of the party.[6]

What happens, then, is that for the unplanned constraint of the capitalistic system, operating through the mechanisms of competition, are substituted the planned and coercively enforced constraint of the party, and the "building of socialism" under stringently dictatorial party control. The result is a very Hobbesian version of absolute sovereignty, serving, not a negative concept of security (except, of course—and a far from negligible exception—so far as the revolution is felt to be threatened), but a positive programming for building a new society. The new society is purported to be the most free in history, but the process of achieving it involves a drastic minimization of freedom. Hence the problem of when and under what circumstances the famous "withering away" of the state is to occur becomes cardinal for Marxism.

The other side of the dilemma lies in the extent to which Marx took over the elements of utopian rationalism, largely from the French Enlightenment. His statements about the state of communism itself are notably vague, but on the whole they are far more Godwinian than anything else. They seem to hold that only the special constraints of capitalism have been obstacles to spontaneous order and happiness for all; once these have been eliminated, there will be universal freedom without political coercion or institutions in any form. From the above discussion, it seems clear that Marx did not solve the Hobbesian problems of order, any more than did the utilitarians. In "setting Hegel on his head," he threw away the normative component which might have been built into a solution; and by projecting the problem into the vague future state of "communism," he in effect "swept it under the rug." For the intermediate period, however, he provided, through the concept of the dictatorship of the proletariat, a rationalization for a truly Hobbesian version of order through coercion.

However, this is not quite the whole story. The Communist parties have recognized that "educating" their followers through propaganda and "agitation" is a necessary factor in success. It could not rest on coercive measures alone. Essentially, this education has been directed to inculcating belief in the Marxist-Leninist system as an eschatological system, a quasi-religious set of answers to

---

6. The same difficulty of relating a concept of the basis of solidarity to the mechanism of implementation, which Rousseau could not solve, is present here. Thus the "general will" could justify Jacobin dictatorship. Similarly, the "proletariat" has become an abstraction used to justify Communist party dictatorship.

the problems of teleological meaning; and, at another level, inculcating loyalty to the party as such and to the governments established under its control. There is some question of just how this set of normative elements, as common value-orientations and loyalties, fits in the framework of Marxist theory; but there is no doubt of its practical importance to the revolutionary movement.

No American authors are included in this preliminary section of the Reader. This is because, in this preliminary period, there were no American works of importance comparable to the European ones on which we have drawn. It may be stated, however, that the general trend of American social thought was, as would be expected, far closer to the utilitarian individualistic trend than either of the versions of the collectivistic trend discussed above. In this trend, understandably, the version associated with Locke, economics, and the ideas of liberal political democracy were most prominent. The Hobbesian version, with its tendency to association with rigidly authoritarian collectivism, has been minimized.

As shown in Section B, and to some extent in Section C of Part One, the distinctively American contribution has been mainly in the area of "social psychology," which, in the frame of reference used in this Introduction, lies mostly in the borderline between the utilitarian version of individualistic "rationalism" and the more biologically oriented analysis of the factors involved in the individual's behavior. However, at least one branch of American thought was less concerned than its British counterpart with a set of postulates on whose basis the macroscopic functioning of the economy and the political system could be analyzed, and more concerned with the determinants of the individual's behavior and its relations to the more intimate contexts of interaction in which he was placed. It was in this area of greater flexibility that it became possible to take explicit account of the normative components of the determination of social interaction. The most important men in this area were Cooley, G. H. Mead, and, later, W. I. Thomas. The background of their role will be further discussed in the Foreword to Section B.

The trends of social thought reviewed in this Foreword were, with few exceptions, not based on empirical research in the present sense. Perhaps the most notable exception was Malthus' survey of the relation of kinship structure and property-holding in several European countries, reported in later editions of his *Principle of Population*. There was also some historical research, and, on the part of the economists, statistical investigation. Only in the most limited sense, however, could these works be considered as representing a science, which necessarily relates deliberately designed empirical research and theory. Most of it consists in "reflection on experience."

This reflection, however—including acute, though unsystematic, observations of empirical phenomena—is the stuff of which the *beginnings* of a science are made. What emerged from the complicated and often conflicting movements of these philosophical, semi-philosophical, ideological, and very partially scientifically oriented movements of thought was a relatively determinate *structure of problems* which, in a later generation, could be handled through more systematic empirical observation and a higher level of theoretical analysis.

The first of these great problems is that of order in Hobbes's sense—which, though stated and discussed as a problem of how to guarantee order in a practical sense, could also be treated as a scientific problem, namely, of how to specify the conditions on which the empirically observed levels of social order depended. While utilitarianism yielded rich returns in the intermediate sphere of economic analysis, the logic of the problem drove thinking in two directions, whose eventual convergence is very important in our universe of discourse. The first direction was the question of what normative components of the social system must be understood to operate, in order to explain social order without abandoning the whole voluntaristic and, in a sense, rationalistic concept of action which the utilitarians had assumed, by accepting the "reductionist" line of argument. In the "voluntarist" direction this problem led inevitably to convergence with the "collectivist" trend of thought. The one traced, through Rousseau and Comte, to Durkheim, was the one of major present significance.

On the other hand, demonstrating the empirical existence and the functional necessity of these normative components did not solve the problem of mechanisms, of how in fact such components entered into the determination of the individual's behavior. Hence the other end of the utilitarian problem-range: the problem of what scientifically analyzable phenomena underlay the early postulates of the "rational pursuit of self-interest" was necessarily thrown open to thorough reconsideration. Here a most notable convergence occurred— on the one hand, Durkheim, stating from the "collectivistic" end, was forced to consider the motivation of the individual, and eventually arrived at the concept of the internalization of normative culture. On the other hand, Freud, starting from what may be called the "medical" version of biological determinism, arrived, through his theory of the significance of "object-relations," at the complementary view—a view at which the Americans cited above, from a more "social" version of psychology, also arrived.

When problems are considered on this level of generality, it is easy to forget that a society, above all a modern society, is very complex and highly differentiated. Durkheim took an essential step to cover this difficulty by not, like Comte, speaking only of consensus in general; he dealt directly with the problem of solidarity in the type of differentiated system characterized by an advanced division of labor.

Once there was a clear focus on the importance of a "collective" normative component, the problem of its basis in human experience became progressively more salient. The tradition of French thought provided a basis for a far more explicit emphasis on its importance, but less for its further analysis. Rousseau went directly into the problems of practical politics, and Comte came to rest on science as such. In this connection, however, German Idealism was in a position to develop a more differentiated basis for analyzing "culture." For Western empiricism, this trend represented a distressing dissociation from the "realities" of economic and political interest—to say nothing of the biological level. But it presented the beginning of a more differentiated analysis of an essential set of components. Hegel is important specifically because his version is more differentiated than that of other "classical idealists" or of his "historicist" successors. From the sociological point of view, Marx worked out a premature synthesis between the two traditions; he ignored the problem of how the "realistic" elements of "economic interest" and the "idealistic" elements of the normative component of an ordered social system could belong together, unresolved, in a single system. One is forced to conclude that order is possible only in

the ferment of the transition from an inherently conflict-filled previous society to an undefined presumptive future society; the only Marxist order is the order of the revolutionary process. Weber's later excursion from the idealistic into the "realistic" realm seems far more successful than Marx's, from a scientific point of view. Its key question was how the normative component (in Weber's case, rooted in religious commitments) could operate through the motivation of individuals in both "revolutionary" and stable social situations—this completed the circle by converging with Durkheim and with Freud.

The bearing of the above summary on the organization of the materials in this Reader should be clear. After presenting the fundamentals in Part One, we proceed to presenting problems of the internal structure of social systems themselves in Part Two. This may be considered the area of primarily "Durkheimian" emphasis. We feel that the "institutionalization" of normative culture is, for sociology, the keynote of social structure. Second, however, a very important set of problems is concerned with the motivation of social action. This area leads us into the problems associated with the relation of the individual to the social system. Here Freud's work, and various other schools and trends of "individual" and "social" psychology, are paramount. "Normative Culture," as institutionalized in the values and norms of social systems, cannot be dissociated from a variety of other aspects of the development of culture, e.g., religious movements, science, art, etc. Part Four is devoted primarily to selections bearing on this range of problems. Weber is the theorist who contributed more in this area than anyone else. Part Five is devoted to the relatively few notable ideas which have emerged on the question of the patterns and processes of change which social systems, constituted as we think they are, may be thought to undergo.

1. On Hatreds and Dissensions in the Republic

BY NICCOLO MACHIAVELLI

IT WAS my intention when I first resolved upon writing the things done by the Florentine people, within and without their city, to begin my narrative with the year 1434 of the Christian era, at which time the family of the Medici, by the merits of Cosimo and his father Giovanni, exercised more authority in Florence than any one else. For I thought to myself that Messer Lionardo d'Arezzo and Messer Poggio, two excellent historians, had related all the events that had occurred previous to that time. But having afterwards diligently read their writings to see in what order and manner they had proceeded, so that by imitating them our history might be the more approved by the reader, I found that in their descriptions of the wars carried on by the Florentines with foreign princes and peoples they had been most diligent; but of their civil discords and internal dissensions, and of the effects resulting therefrom, they had in part been silent, and in part had described them very briefly, which to the reader could be neither useful nor agreeable. I believe they did so because these facts seemed to them so unimportant that they judged them unworthy of being recorded in history, or because they feared to offend the descendants of those who took part in them, and who by the narration of these facts might have deemed themselves calumniated. These two reasons (be it said with their leave) seemed to me wholly unworthy of such great men; because if anything delights or instructs in history, it is that which is described in detail; and if any lesson is useful to the citizens who govern republics, it is that which demonstrates the causes of the hatreds and dissensions in the republic, so that, having learned wisdom from the perils experienced by others, they may maintain themselves united. And if the divisions of any republic were ever noteworthy, those of Florence certainly are most so, because the greater part of the other republics of which we have any knowledge were content with one division, by which, according to chance, they either increased or ruined their city. But Florence, not content with one division, had

Reprinted from Niccolo Machiavelli, Preface to *The History of Florence*, in *The Historical, Political and Diplomatic Writings of Niccolo Machiavelli*, trans. Christian E. Detmold (Boston: James R. Osgood & Co., 1882), I, 7–9.

many. In Rome, as everybody knows, after the expulsion of the kings, a division arose between the nobles and the people, and with that she maintained herself until her downfall. So did Athens, and so all the republics that flourished in those times. But in Florence, the first division was amongst the nobles, afterwards between the nobles and the citizens, and finally between the citizens and the populace; and many times it happened that one of the parties that remained in power again divided in two. These divisions caused so many deaths, so many exiles, so much destruction of so many families, as never occurred in any other city of which we have any record. And truly no other circumstance so much illustrates the power of our city as that which resulted from these divisions, which would have been enough to destroy any other great and powerful republic.

Ours, nevertheless, seems always to have increased in power; such was the virtue of her citizens and the strength of their genius and courage to make themselves and their country great, that the many who remained untouched by so many evils could by their virtues exalt their city more than the malignity of those events that diminished her greatness could have oppressed her. And doubtless if Florence had had so much good fortune that, after having freed herself from the Empire, she could have adopted a form of government that would have kept her united, I know not what republic, modern or ancient, would have been her superior, such abundance of power of arms and industry would she in that case have possessed. For it will be seen that after she had expelled the Ghibellines in such numbers that Tuscany and Lombardy were full of them, the Guelfs, together with those who remained in Florence, drew from the city, and of her own citizens, twelve hundred mounted men and twelve thousand infantry for the war against Arezzo, one year before the battle of Campaldino.

Afterwards, in the war against Filippo Visconti, Duke of Milan, having to make trial of her own resources, but not of her own troops (for they had exhausted them at that time), it will be seen that she spent during the five years that this war lasted the sum of three and a half millions of florins; and after that war was finished they were not satisfied to remain at peace, but took the field against Lucca. I cannot see therefore what reasons there can be why these divisions should not be worthy of being particularly described. And if those most noble writers were withheld from doing so by fear of offending the memory of those of whom they would have to speak, they deceive themselves in that respect, and show that they little know the ambition of men, and the desire they have to perpetuate the names of their ancestors and their own. And they do not remember that many, not having had the opportunity of acquiring fame by any praiseworthy acts, have endeavored to acquire it by disgraceful ones. Nor have they considered how the actions that have inherent greatness, such as those of governments and states, however they may have originated, or whatever their object may

have been, always bring more honor than discredit to the actors. But I, having considered these things, have been induced thereby to change my purpose, and have resolved to begin my history from the origin of our city. And as it is not my intention to occupy the same ground as others, I shall describe particularly only those things up to the year 1434 that occurred within the city, and of the foreign relations I shall say no more than what may be necessary for a proper understanding of the internal affairs. From and after the year 1434, however, I shall fully describe both the one and the other. Beyond that, for the better understanding of each period, before I treat of Florence I shall relate by what means Italy came to be under the rule of those potentates who governed her at that time.

2. *Of the Natural Conditions of Mankind*

BY THOMAS HOBBES

NATURE hath made men so equall, in the faculties of body, and mind; as that though there bee found one man sometimes manifestly stronger in body, or of quicker mind then another; yet when all is reckoned together, the difference between man, and man, is not so considerable, as that one man can thereupon claim himselfe any benefit, to which another may not pretend, as well as he. For as to the strength of body, the weakest has strength enough to kill the strongest, either by secret machination, or by confederacy with others, that are in the same danger with himself.

And as to the faculties of the mind, (setting aside the arts grounded upon words, and especially that skill of proceeding upon generall, and infallible rules, called Science; which very few have, and but in few things; as being not a native faculty, born with us; nor attained, (as Prudence,) while we look after somewhat els,) I find yet a greater equality amongst men, than that of strength. For Prudence, is but Experience; which equall time, equally bestowes on all men, in those things they equally apply themselves unto. That which may perhaps make such equality incredible, is but a vain con-

ceipt of ones owne wisdome, which almost all men think they have in a greater degree, than the Vulgar; that is, than all men but themselves, and a few others, whom by Fame, or for concurring with themselves, they approve. For such is the nature of men, that howsoever they may acknowledge many others to be more witty, or more eloquent, or more learned; Yet they will hardly believe there be many so wise as themselves: For they see their own wit at hand, and other mens at a distance. But this proveth rather that men are in that point equall, than unequall. For there is not ordinarily a greater signe of the equall distribution of any thing, than that every man is contented with his share.

From this equality of ability, ariseth equality of hope in the attaining of our Ends. And therefore if any two men desire the same thing, which neverthelesse they cannot both enjoy, they become enemies; and in the way to their End, (which is principally their own conservation, and sometimes their delectation only,) endeavour to destroy, or subdue one an other. And from hence it comes to passe, that where an Invader hath no more to feare, than an other mans single power; if one plant, sow, build, or possesse a convenient Seat, others may

Reprinted from Thomas Hobbes, *Leviathan* (Oxford: James Thornton, 1881), chap. xiii, pp. 91–96.

probably be expected to come prepared with forces united, to dispossesse, and deprive him, not only of the fruit of his labour, but also of his life, or liberty. And the Invader again is in the like danger of another.

And from this diffidence of one another, there is no way for any man to secure himselfe, so reasonable, as Anticipation; that is, by force, or wiles, to master the persons of all men he can, so long, till he see no other power great enough to endanger him: And this is no more than his own conservation requireth, and is generally allowed. Also because there be some, that taking pleasure in contemplating their own power in the acts of conquest, which they pursue farther than their security requires; if others, that otherwise would be glad to be at ease within modest bounds, should not by invasion increase their power, they would not be able, long time, by standing only on their defence, to subsist. And by consequence, such augmentation of dominion over men, being necessary to a mans conservation, it ought to be allowed him.

Againe, men have no pleasure, (but on the contrary a great deale of griefe) in keeping company, where there is no power able to over-awe them all. For every man looketh that his companion should value him, at the same rate he sets upon himselfe: And upon all signes of contempt, or undervaluing, naturally endeavours, as far as he dares (which amongst them that have no common power to keep them in quiet, is far enough to make them destroy each other,) to extort a greater value from his contemners, by dommage; and from others, by this example.

So that in the nature of man, we find three principall causes of quarrell. First, Competition; Secondly, Diffidence, Thirdly, Glory.

The first, maketh men invade for Gain; the second, for Safety; and the third, for Reputation. The first use Violence, to make themselves Masters of other mens persons, wives, children, and cattell; the second, to defend them; the third, for trifles, as a word, a smile, a different opinion, and any other signe of undervalue, either direct in their Persons, or by reflexion in their Kindred, their Friends, their Nation, their Profession, or their Name.

Hereby it is manifest, that during the time men live without a common Power to keep them all in awe, they are in that condition which is called Warre; and such a warre, as is of every man, against every man. For WARRE, consisteth not in Battell onely, or the act of fighting; but in a tract of time, wherein the Will to contend by Battell is sufficiently known: and therefore the notion of *Time,* is to be considered in the nature of Warre; as it is in the nature of Weather. For as the nature of Foule weather, lyeth not in a showre or two of rain; but in an inclination thereto of many dayes together: So the nature of War, consisteth not in actuall fighting; but in the known disposition thereto, during all the time there is no assurance to the contrary. All other time is PEACE.

Whatsoever therefore is consequent to a time of Warre, where every man is Enemy to every man; the same is consequent to the time, wherein men live without other security, than what their own strength, and their own invention shall furnish them withall. In such condition, there is no place for Industry; because the fruit thereof is uncertain: and consequently no Culture of the Earth; no Navigation, nor use of the commodities that may be imported by Sea; no commodious Building; no Instruments of moving, and removing such things as require much force; no Knowledge of the face of the Earth; no account of Time; no Arts; no Letters; no Society; and which is worst of all, continuall feare, and danger of violent death; And the life of man, solitary, poore, nasty, brutish, and short.

It may seem strange to some man, that has not well weighed these things; that Nature should thus dissociate, and render men apt to invade, and destroy one another: and he may therefore, not trusting to his Inference, made from the Passions, desire perhaps to have the same confirmed by Experience. Let him therefore consider with himselfe, when taking a journey, he armes himselfe, and seeks to go well accompanied; when going to sleep, he locks his dores; when even in his house he lockes his chests; and this when he knowes there bee Lawes, and publike Officers, armed, to revenge all injuries shall bee done him; what opinion he has of his fellow subjects, when he rides armed; of his fellow Citizens, when he locks his dores; and of his children, and servants, when he locks his chests. Does he not there as much accuse mankind by his actions, as I do by my words? But neither of us accuse mans nature in it. The Desires, and other Passions of man, are in themselves no Sin. No more are the Actions, that proceed from those Passions, till they know a Law that forbids them: which till Lawes be made they cannot know: nor can any Law be made, till they have agreed upon the Person that shall make it.

It may peradventure be thought, there was never such a time, nor condition of warre as this; and I believe it was never generally so, over all the world: but there are many places, where they live so now. For the savage people in many places of *America,* except the government of small Families, the concord whereof dependeth on naturall lust, have no government at all; and live at this day in that brutish manner, as I said before. Howsoever, it may be perceived what manner of life there would be, where there were no common Power to feare; by the manner of life, which men that have formerly lived under a peaceful government, use to degenerate into, in a civil Warre.

But though there had never been any time, wherein particular men were in a condition of warre one against another; yet in all times, Kings, and Persons of Soveraigne authority, because of their Independency, are in continuall jealousies, and in the state and posture of Gladiators; having their weapons pointing, and their eyes fixed on one another; that is, their Forts, Garrisons, and Guns upon the Frontiers of their Kingdomes; and continuall Spyes upon their neighbours; which is a posture of War. But because they uphold thereby, the Industry of their Subjects; there does not follow from it, that misery, which accompanies the Liberty of particular men.

To this warre of every man against every man, this also is consequent; that nothing can be Unjust. The notions of Right and Wrong, Justice and Injustice have there no place. Where there is no common Power, there is no Law: where no Law, no Injustice. Force, and Fraud, are in warre the two Cardinall vertues. Justice, and Injustice are none of the Faculties neither of the Body, nor Mind. If they were, they might be in a man that were alone in the world, as well as his Senses, and Passions. They are Qualities, that relate to men in Society, not in Solitude. It is consequent also to the same condition, that there be no Propriety, no Dominion, no *Mine* and *Thine* distinct; but onely that to be every mans, that he can get; and for so long, as he can keep it. And thus much for the ill condition, which man by meer Nature is actually placed in; though with a possibility to come out of it, consisting partly in the Passions, partly in his Reason.

The Passions that encline men to Peace, are Feare of Death; Desire of such things as are necessary to commodious living; and a Hope by their Industry to obtain them. And Reason suggesteth convenient Articles of Peace, upon which men may be drawn to agreement. These Articles, are they, which otherwise are called the Lawes of Nature: whereof I shall speak more particularly, in the two following Chapters.

3. *Of the State of Nature*

BY JOHN LOCKE

TO UNDERSTAND political power right, and derive it from its original, we must consider, what state all men are naturally in, and that is, *a state of perfect freedom* to order their actions, and dispose of their possessions and persons, as they think fit, within the bounds of the law of nature, without asking leave, or depending upon the will of any other man.

A *state* also *of equality,* wherein all the power and jurisdiction is reciprocal, no one having more than another; there being nothing more evident, than that creatures of the same species and rank,

Reprinted from John Locke, *Second Treatise of Civil Government,* chap. ii, secs. 4, 6–8, 11–14, in *Two Treatises on Government* (London: Printed for R. Butler, Bruton-Street, Berkeley-Square; W. Reid, Charing-Cross; W. Sharpe, King-Street, Covent Garden; and John Bumpas, Holborn Bars, 1821), pp. 189–93, 195–99.

promiscuously born to all the same advantages of nature, and the use of the same faculties, should also be equal one amongst another without subordination or subjection, unless the lord and master of them all should, by any manifest declaration of his will, set one above another, and confer on him, by an evident and clear appointment, an undoubted right to dominion and sovereignty.

But though this be *a state of liberty,* yet *it is not a state of license:* though man in that state have an uncontroulable liberty to dispose of his person or possessions, yet he has not liberty to destroy himself, or so much as any creature in his possession, but where some nobler use than its bare preservation calls for it. The *state of nature* has a law of nature to govern it, which obliges every one: and reason, which is that law, teaches all mankind, who will but consult it, that being all *equal and independent,* no one ought to harm another in his life, health, liberty, or possessions: for men being all the workmanship of one omnipotent, and infinitely wise maker; all the servants of one sovereign master, sent into the world by his order, and about his business; they are his property, whose workmanship they are, made to last during his, not one another's pleasure: and being furnished with like faculties, sharing all in one community of nature, there cannot be supposed any such *subordination* among us, that may authorize us to destroy one another, as if we were made for one another's uses, as the inferior ranks of creatures are for ours. Every one, as he is *bound to preserve himself,* and not to quit his station wilfully, so by the like reason, when his own preservation comes not in competition, ought he, as much as he can, to *preserve the rest of mankind,* and may not, unless it be to do justice on an offender, take away, or impair the life, or what tends to the preservation of the life, the liberty, health, limb, or goods of another.

And that all men may be restrained from invading others rights, and from doing hurt to one another, and the law of nature be observed, which willeth the peace and *preservation of all mankind,* the *execution* of the law of nature is, in that state, put into every man's hands, whereby every one has a right to punish the transgressors of that law to such a degree, as may hinder its violation: for the *law of nature* would, as all other laws that concern men in this world, be in vain, if there were nobody that in the state of nature had a *power to execute* that law, and thereby preserve the innocent and restrain offenders. And if any one in the state of nature may punish another for any evil he has done, every one may do so: for in that *state of perfect equality* where naturally there is no superiority or jurisdiction of one over another, what any may do in prosecution of that law, every one must needs have a right to do.

And thus, in the state of nature, *one man comes by a power over another;* but yet no absolute or arbitrary power, to use a criminal, when he has got him in his hands, according to the passionate heats, or boundless extravagancy of his own will; but only to retribute to him, so far as calm reason and conscience dictate, what is proportionate to his transgression, which is so much as may serve for *reparation* and *restraint:* for these two are the only reasons, why one man may lawfully do harm to another, which is that we call *punishment.* In transgressing the law of nature, the offender declares himself to live by another rule than that of reason and common equity, which is that measure God has set to the actions of men, for their mutual security; and so he becomes dangerous to mankind, the tye, which is to secure them from injury and violence, being slighted and broken by him. Which being a trespass against the whole species, and the peace and safety of it, provided for by the law of nature, every man upon this score, by the right he hath to preserve mankind in general, may restrain, or where it is necessary, destroy things noxious to them, and so may bring such evil on any one, who hath transgressed that law, as may make him repent the doing of it, and thereby deter him, and by his example others, from doing the like mischief. And in this case, and upon this ground, *every man hath a right to punish the offender, and be executioner of the law of nature.*

*   *   *

From* these *two distinct rights,* the one of *punishing* the crime *for restraint,* and preventing the like offence, which right of punishing is in every body; the other of taking *reparation,* which belongs only to the injured party, comes it to pass that the magistrate, who by being magistrate hath the common right of punishing put into his hands, can often, where the public good demands not the execution of the law, *remit* the punishment of criminal offences by his own authority, but yet cannot *remit* the satisfaction due to any private man for the damage he has received. That, he who has suffered the damage has a right to demand in his own name, and he alone can remit: the damnified person has this power of appropriating to himself the goods or service of the offender, *by right of self-preservation,* as every man has a power to punish the crime, to prevent its being committed again, *by the right he has of preserving all mankind,* and doing all reasonable things he can in order to that end: and thus it is, that every man, in the state of nature, has a power to kill a murderer, both *to deter* others from doing the like injury, which no reparation can compensate, by the example of the punishment that attends it from every body, and also to secure men from the attempts of a criminal, who having renounced reason, the common rule and measure God hath given to mankind, hath, by the unjust violence and slaughter he hath committed upon one, declared war against all mankind, and therefore may be destroyed as a *lion* or a *tyger,* one of those wild savage beasts, with whom men can have no society nor security: and upon this is grounded that great law of nature, "Whoso sheddeth man's blood, by man shall his blood be shed." And Cain was so fully convinced, that every one had a right to destroy such a criminal, that after the murder of his

---

* This section reprinted from pp. 195–99.

brother, he cries out, *Every one that findeth me shall slay me;* so plain was it writ in the hearts of all mankind.

By the same reason may a man in the state of nature *punish the lesser breaches* of that law. It will perhaps be demanded, with death? I answer, each transgression may be *punished* to that *degree,* and with so much *severity,* as will suffice to make it an ill bargain to the offender, give him cause to repent, and terrify others from doing the like. Every offence, that can be committed in the state of nature, may in the state of nature be also punished equally, and as far forth as it may, in a commonwealth: for though it would be besides my present purpose, to enter here into the particulars of the law of nature, or its *measures of punishment;* yet, it is certain there is such a law, and that too, as intelligible and plain to a rational creature, and a studier of that law, as the positive laws of commonwealths: nay, possibly plainer; as much as reason is easier to be understood, than the fancies and intricate contrivances of men, following contrary and hidden interests put into words; for so truly are a great part of the *municipal* laws of countries, which are only so far right, as they are founded on the law of nature, by which they are to be regulated and interpreted.

To this strange doctrine, *viz.* That *in the state of nature every one has the executive power* of the law of nature, I doubt not but it will be objected, that it is unreasonable for men to be judges in their own cases, that self-love will make men partial to themselves and their friends: and on the other side, that ill-nature, passion and revenge will carry them too far in punishing others; and hence nothing but confusion and disorder will follow; and that therefore God hath certainly appointed government to restrain the partiality and violence of men. I easily grant, that *civil government* is the proper remedy for the inconveniences of the state of nature, which must certainly be great, where men may be judges in their own case, since it is easy to be imagined, that he who was so unjust as to do his brother an injury, will scarce be so just as to condemn himself for it; but I shall desire those who make this objection, to remember, that *absolute monarchs* are but men; and if government is to be the remedy of those evils, which necessarily follow from men's being judges in their own cases, and the state of nature is therefore not to be endured, I desire to know what kind of government that is, and how much better it is than the state of nature, where one man, commanding a multitude, has the liberty to be judge in his own case, and may do to all his subjects whatever he pleases, without the least liberty to any one to question or controul those who execute his pleasure? and in whatsoever he doth, whether led by reason, mistake or passion, must be submitted to? much better it is in the state of nature, wherein men are not bound to submit to the unjust will of another; and if he that judges, judges amiss in his own, or any other case, he is answerable for it to the rest of mankind.

It is often asked as a mighty objection, *where are,* or ever were there any *men in such a state of nature?* To which it may suffice as an answer at present, that since all princes and rulers of *independent* governments all through the world, are in a state of nature, it is plain the world never was, nor ever will be, without numbers of men in that state. I have named all governors of *independent communities,* whether they are, or are not, in league with others: for it is not every compact that puts an end to the state of nature between men, but only this one of agreeing together mutually to enter into one community, and make one body politic; other promises, and compacts, men may make one with another, and yet still be in the state of nature. The promises and bargains for truck, &c. between the two men in the desert island, mentioned by Garcilasso de la Vega, in his history of Peru; or between a Swiss and an Indian, in the woods of America, are binding to them, though they are perfectly in a state of nature, in reference to one another: for truth and keeping of faith belongs to men, as men, and not as members of society.

4. Of the Principle Which Gives Occasion to the Division of Labour

BY ADAM SMITH

THIS DIVISION of labour, from which so many advantages are derived, is not originally the effect of any human wisdom, which foresees and intends that general opulence to which it gives occasion. It is the necessary, though very slow and gradual, consequence of a certain propensity in human nature which has in view no such extensive utility; the propensity to truck, barter, and exchange one thing for another.

Whether this propensity be one of those original principles in human nature, of which no further account can be given; or whether, as seems more probable, it be the necessary consequence of the faculties of reason and speech, it belongs not to our present subject to enquire. It is common to all men, and to be found in no other race of animals, which seem to know neither this nor any other species of contracts. Two greyhounds, in running down the same hare, have sometimes the appearance of acting in some sort of concert. Each turns her towards his companion, or endeavours to intercept her when his companion turns her towards himself. This, however, is not the effect of any contract, but of the accidental concurrence of their passions in the same object at that particular time. Nobody ever saw a dog make a fair and deliberate exchange of one bone for another with another dog. Nobody ever saw one animal by its gestures and natural cries signify to another, this is mine, that yours; I am willing to give this for that. When an animal wants to obtain something either of a man, or of another animal, it has no other means of persuasion but to gain the favour of those whose service it requires. A puppy fawns upon its dam, and a spaniel endeavours by a thousand attractions to engage the attention of its master who is at dinner, when it wants to be fed by him. Man sometimes uses the same arts with his brethren, and when he has no other means of engaging them to act according to his inclinations, endeavours by every servile and fawning attention to obtain their good will. He has not time, however, to do this upon every occa-

sion. In civilized society he stands at all times in need of the co-operation and assistance of great multitudes, while his whole life is scarce sufficient to gain the friendship of a few persons. In almost every other race of animals, each individual, when it is grown up to maturity, is entirely independent, and in its natural state has occasion for the assistance of no other living creature. But man has almost constant occasion for the help of his brethren, and it is in vain for him to expect it from their benevolence only. He will be more likely to prevail if he can interest their self-love in his favour, and shew them that it is for their own advantage to do for him what he requires of them. Whoever offers to another a bargain of any kind, proposes to do this: Give me that which I want, and you shall have this which you want, is the meaning of every such offer; and it is in this manner that we obtain from one another the far greater part of those good offices which we stand in need of. It is not from the benevolence of the butcher, the brewer, or the baker, that we expect our dinner, but from their regard to their own interest. We address ourselves, not to their humanity but to their selflove, and never talk to them of our own necessities but of their advantages. Nobody but a beggar chuses to depend chiefly upon the benevolence of his fellow-citizens. Even a beggar does not depend upon it entirely. The charity of well-disposed people, indeed, supplies him with the whole fund of his subsistence. But though this principle ultimately provides him with all the necessaries of life which he has occasion for, it neither does nor can provide him with them as he has occasion for them. The greater part of his occasional wants are supplied in the same manner as those of other people, by treaty, by barter, and by purchase. With the money which one man gives him he purchases food. The old cloaths which another bestows upon him he exchanges for other old cloaths which suit him better, or for lodging, or for food, or for money, with which he can buy either food, cloaths, or lodging, as he has occasion.

As it is by treaty, by barter, and by purchase, that we obtain from one another the greater part of those mutual good offices which we stand in

Reprinted from Adam Smith, *An Inquiry into the Nature and Causes of the Wealth of Nations* (7th ed.; London, 1793), Book I, chap. ii, pp. 19–25.

need of, so it is this same trucking disposition which originally gives occasion to the division of labour. In a tribe of hunters or shepherds a particular person makes bows and arrows, for example, with more readiness and dexterity than any other. He frequently exchanges them for cattle or for venison with his companions; and he finds at last that he can in this manner get more cattle and venison, than if he himself went to the field to catch them. From a regard to his own interest, therefore, the making of bows and arrows grows to be his chief business, and he becomes a sort of armourer. Another excels in making the frames and covers of their little huts or moveable houses. He is accustomed to be of use in this way to his neighbours, who reward him in the same manner with cattle and with venison, till at last he finds it his interest to dedicate himself entirely to this employment, and to become a sort of house-carpenter. In the same manner a third becomes a smith or a brazier; a fourth a tanner or dresser of hides or skins, the principal part of the cloathing of savages. And thus the certainty of being able to exchange all that surplus part of the produce of his own labour, which is over and above his own consumption, for such parts of the produce of other men's labour as he may have occasion for, encourages every man to apply himself to a particular occupation, and to cultivate and bring to perfection whatever talent or genius he may possess for that particular species of business.

The difference of natural talents in different men is, in reality, much less than we are aware of; and the very different genius which appears to distinguish men of different professions, when grown up to maturity, is not upon many occasions so much the cause, as the effect of the division of labour. The difference between the most dissimilar characters, between a philosopher and a common street porter, for example, seems to arise not so much from nature, as from habit, custom, and education. When they came into the world, and for the first six or eight years of their existence, they were, perhaps, very much alike, and neither their parents nor playfellows could perceive any remarkable difference. About that age, or soon after, they come to be employed in very different occupations. The difference of talents comes then to be taken notice of, and widens by degrees, till at last the vanity of the philosopher is willing to acknowledge scarce any resemblance. But without the disposition to truck, barter, and exchange, every man must have procured to himself every necessary and conveniency of life which he wanted. All must have had the same duties to perform, and the same work to do, and there could have been no such difference of employment as could alone give occasion to any great difference of talents.

As it is this disposition which forms that difference of talents, so remarkable among men of different professions, so it is this same disposition which renders that difference useful. Many tribes of animals acknowledged to be all of the same species, derive from nature a much more remarkable distinction of genius, than what, antecedent to custom and education, appears to take place among men. By nature a philosopher is not in genius and disposition half so different from a street porter, as a mastiff is from a greyhound, or a greyhound from a spaniel, or this last from a shepherd's dog. Those different tribes of animals, however, though all of the same species, are of scarce any use to one another. The strength of the mastiff is not in the least supported either by the swiftness of the greyhound, or by the sagacity of the spaniel, or by the docility of the shepherd's dog. The effects of those different geniuses and talents, for want of the power or disposition to barter and exchange, cannot be brought into a common stock, and do not in the least contribute to the better accommodation and conveniency of the species. Each animal is still obliged to support and defend itself, separately and independently, and derives no sort of advantage from that variety of talents with which nature has distinguished its fellows. Among men, on the contrary, the most dissimilar geniuses are of use to one another; the different produces of their respective talents, by the general disposition to truck, barter, and exchange, being brought, as it were, into a common stock, where every man may purchase whatever part of the produce of other men's talents he has occasion for.

5. *Of Systems of Equality*

BY THOMAS R. MALTHUS

IN READING Mr. Godwin's ingenious and able work on political justice, it is impossible not to be struck with the spirit and energy of his style, the force and precision of some of his reasonings, the ardent tone of his thoughts, and particularly with that impressive earnestness of manner which gives an air of truth to the whole. At the same time, it must be confessed, that he has not proceeded in his enquiries with the caution that sound philosophy seems to require. His conclusions are often unwarranted by his premises. He fails sometimes in removing the objections which he himself brings forward. He relies too much on general and abstract propositions which will not admit of application. And his conjectures certainly far outstrip the modesty of nature.

The system of equality which Mr. Godwin proposes, is, without doubt, by far the most beautiful and engaging of any that has yet appeared. An amelioration of society to be produced merely by reason and conviction, wears much more the promise of permanence, than any change effected and maintained by force. The unlimited exercise of private judgment, is a doctrine inexpressibly grand and captivating, and has a vast superiority over those systems where every individual is in a manner the slave of the public. The substitution of benevolence as the master-spring, and moving principle of society, instead of self-love, is a consummation devoutly to be wished. In short, it is impossible to contemplate the whole of this fair structure, without emotions of delight and admiration, accompanied with ardent longing for the period of its accomplishment. But, alas! that moment can never arrive. The whole is little better than a dream, a beautiful phantom of the imagination. These "gorgeous palaces" of happiness and immortality, these "solemn temples" of truth and virtue will dissolve, "like the baseless fabric of a vision," when we awaken to real life, and contemplate the true and genuine situation of man on earth.

Mr. Godwin, at the conclusion of the third chapter of his eighth book, speaking of population, says, "There is a principle in human society, by which

population is perpetually kept down to the level of the means of subsistence. Thus among the wandering tribes of America and Asia, we never find through the lapse of ages that population has so increased as to render necessary the cultivation of the earth." This principle, which Mr. Godwin thus mentions as some mysterious and occult cause, and which he does not attempt to investigate, will be found to be the grinding law of necessity; misery, and the fear of misery.

The great error under which Mr. Godwin labours throughout his whole work, is, the attributing almost all the vices and misery that are seen in civil society to human institutions. Political regulations, and the established administration of property, are with him the fruitful sources of all evil, the hotbeds of all the crimes that degrade mankind. Were this really a true state of the case, it would not seem a hopeless task to remove evil completely from the world; and reason seems to be the proper and adequate instrument for effecting so great a purpose. But the truth is, that though human institutions appear to be the obvious and obstrusive causes of much mischief to mankind; yet, in reality, they are light and superficial, they are mere feathers that float on the surface, in comparison with those deeper seated causes of impurity that corrupt the springs, and render turbid the whole stream of human life.

Mr. Godwin, in his chapter on the benefits attendant on a system of equality, says, "The spirit of oppression, the spirit of servility, and the spirit of fraud, these are the immediate growth of the established administration of property. They are alike hostile to intellectual improvement. The other vices of envy, malice, and revenge, are their inseparable companions. In a state of society, where men lived in the midst of plenty, and where all shared alike the bounties of nature, these sentiments would inevitably expire. The narrow principle of selfishness would vanish. No man being obliged to guard his little store, or provide with anxiety and pain for his restless wants, each would lose his individual existence in the thought of the general good. No man would be an enemy to his neighbour, for they would have no subject of contention; and, of consequence, philanthropy would resume the empire which reason assigns her. Mind would be delivered

Reprinted from Thomas R. Malthus, *An Essay on the Principle of Population* (London: J. Johnson, 1798), chap. **x**, pp. 173–207; chap. xi, pp. 210–18.

from her perpetual anxiety about corporal support, and free to expatiate in the field of thought, which is congenial to her. Each would assist the enquiries of all."

This would, indeed, be a happy state. But that it is merely an imaginary picture, with scarcely a feature near the truth, the reader, I am afraid, is already too well convinced.

Man cannot live in the midst of plenty. All cannot share alike the bounties of nature. Were there no established administration of property, every man would be obliged to guard with force his little store. Selfishness would be triumphant. The subjects of contention would be perpetual. Every individual mind would be under a constant anxiety about corporal support; and not a single intellect would be left free to expatiate in the field of thought.

How little Mr. Godwin has turned the attention of his penetrating mind to the real state of man on earth, will sufficiently appear from the manner in which he endeavours to remove the difficulty of an overcharged population. He says, "The obvious answer to this objection, is, that to reason thus is to foresee difficulties at a great distance. Three fourths of the habitable globe is now uncultivated. The parts already cultivated are capable of immeasurable improvement. Myriads of centuries of still increasing population may pass away, and the earth be still found sufficient for the subsistence of its inhabitants."

I have already pointed out the error of supposing that no distress and difficulty would arise from an overcharged population before the earth absolutely refused to produce any more. But let us imagine for a moment Mr. Godwin's beautiful system of equality realized in its utmost purity, and see how soon this difficulty might be expected to press under so perfect a form of society. A theory that will not admit of application cannot possibly be just.

Let us suppose all the causes of misery and vice in this island removed. War and contention cease. Unwholesome trades and manufactories do not exist. Crowds no longer collect together in great and pestilent cities for purposes of court intrigue, of commerce, and vicious gratifications. Simple, healthy, and rational amusements take place of drinking, gaming and debauchery. There are no towns sufficiently large to have any prejudicial effects on the human constitution. The greater part of the happy inhabitants of this terrestrial paradise live in hamlets and farm-houses scattered over the face of the country. Every house is clean, airy, sufficiently roomy, and in a healthy situation. All men are equal. The labours of luxury are at end. And the necessary labours of agriculture are shared amicably among all. The number of persons, and the produce of the island, we suppose to be the same as at present. The spirit of benevolence, guided by impartial justice, will divide this produce among all the members of the society according to their wants. Though it would be impossible that they should all have animal food every day, yet vegetable food, with meat occasionally, would satisfy the desires of a frugal people, and would be sufficient to preserve them in health, strength, and spirits.

Mr. Godwin considers marriage as a fraud and a monopoly. Let us suppose the commerce of the sexes established upon principles of the most perfect freedom. Mr. Godwin does not think himself that this freedom would lead to a promiscuous intercourse; and in this I perfectly agree with him. The love of variety is a vicious, corrupt, and unnatural taste, and could not prevail in any great degree in a simple and virtuous state of society. Each man would probably select himself a partner, to whom he would adhere as long as that adherence continued to be the choice of both parties. It would be of little consequence, according to Mr. Godwin, how many children a woman had, or to whom they belonged. Provisions and assistance would spontaneously flow from the quarter in which they abounded, to the quarter that was deficient. And every man would be ready to furnish instruction to the rising generation according to his capacity.

I cannot conceive a form of society so favourable upon the whole to population. The irremediableness of marriage, as it is at present constituted, undoubtedly deters many from entering into that state. An unshackled intercourse on the contrary, would be a most powerful incitement to early attachments: and as we are supposing no anxiety about the future support of children to exist, I do not conceive that there would be one woman in a hundred, of twenty-three, without a family.

With these extraordinary encouragements to population, and every cause of depopulation, as we have supposed, removed, the numbers would necessarily increase faster than in any society that has ever yet been known. I have mentioned, on the authority of a pamphlet published by a Dr. Styles, and referred to by Dr. Price, that the inhabitants of the back settlements of America doubled their numbers in fifteen years. England is certainly a more healthy country than the back settlements of America; and as we have supposed every house in the island to be airy and wholesome, and the encouragements to have a family greater even than with the back settlers, no probable reason can be assigned, why the population should not double itself in less, if possible, than fifteen years. But to be quite sure that we do not go beyond the truth, we will only suppose the period of doubling to be twenty-five years, a ratio of increase, which is well known to have taken place throughout all the Northern States of America.

There can be little doubt, that the equalization of property which we have supposed, added to the circumstance of the labour of the whole community being directed chiefly to agriculture, would tend greatly to augment the produce of the country. But to answer the demands of a population increasing so rapidly, Mr. Godwin's calculation of half an hour a day for each man, would certainly not be sufficient. It is probable that the half of every man's time must be employed for this purpose. Yet with such, or much greater exertions, a person who is acquainted with the nature of the soil in this country, and who reflects on the fertility of the lands already in cultivation, and the barrenness of those that are not cultivated, will be very much disposed to doubt, whether the whole average produce could possibly be doubled in twenty-five years from the present period. The only chance of success would be the ploughing up all the grazing countries, and putting an end almost entirely to the use of animal food. Yet a part of this scheme might defeat itself. The soil of England will not produce much without dressing; and cattle seem to be necessary to make that species of manure, which best suits the land. In China, it is said, that the soil in some of the provinces is so fertile, as to produce two crops of rice in the year without dressing. None of the lands in England will answer to this description.

Difficult, however, as it might be, to double the average produce of the island in twenty-five years, let us suppose it effected. At the expiration of the first period therefore, the food, though almost entirely vegetable, would be sufficient to support in health, the doubled population of fourteen millions.

During the next period of doubling, where will the food be found to satisfy the importunate demands of the increasing numbers. Where is the fresh land to turn up? where is the dressing necessary to improve that which is already in cultivation? There is no person with the smallest knowledge of land, but would say, that it was impossible that the average produce of the country could be increased during the second twenty-five years by a quantity equal to what it at present yields. Yet we will suppose this increase, however improbable, to take place. The exuberant strength of the argument allows of almost any concession. Even with this concession, however, there would be seven millions at the expiration of the second term, unprovided for. A quantity of food equal to the frugal support of twenty-one millions, would be to be divided among twenty-eight millions.

Alas! what becomes of the picture where men lived in the midst of plenty: where no man was obliged to provide with anxiety and pain for his restless wants: where the narrow principle of selfishness did not exist: where Mind was delivered from her perpetual anxiety about corporal support, and free to expatiate in the field of thought which is congenial to her. This beautiful fabric of imagination vanishes at the severe touch of truth. The spirit of benevolence, cherished and invigorated by plenty, is repressed by the chilling breath of want. The hateful passions that had vanished, reappear. The mighty law of self-preservation, expels all the softer and more exalted emotions of the soul. The temptations to evil are too strong for human nature to resist. The corn is plucked before it is ripe, or secreted in unfair proportions; and the whole black train of vices that belong to falsehood are immediately generated. Provisions no longer flow in for the support of the mother with a large family. The children are sickly from insufficient food. The rosy flush of health gives place to the pallid cheek and hollow eye of misery. Benevolence yet lingering in a few bosoms, makes some faint expiring struggles, till at length self-love resumes his wonted empire, and lords it triumphant over the world.

No human institutions here existed, to the perverseness of which Mr. Godwin ascribes the original sin of the worst men. No opposition had been produced by them between public and private good. No monopoly had been created of those advantages which reason directs to be left in common. No man had been goaded to the breach of order by unjust laws. Benevolence had established her reign in all hearts: and yet in so short a period as within fifty years, violence, oppression, falsehood, misery, every hateful vice, and every form of distress, which degrade and sadden the present state of society, seem to have been generated by the most imperious circumstances, by laws inherent in the nature of man, and absolutely independent of all human regulations.

If we are not yet too well convinced of the reality of this melancholy picture, let us but look for a moment into the next period of twenty-five years; and we shall see twenty-eight millions of human beings without the means of support; and before the conclusion of the first century, the population would be one hundred and twelve millions, and the food only sufficient for thirty-five millions, leaving seventy-seven millions unprovided for. In these ages want would be indeed triumphant, and rapine and murder must reign at large: and yet all this time we are supposing the produce of the earth absolutely unlimited, and the yearly increase greater than the boldest speculator can imagine.

This is undoubtedly a very different view of the difficulty arising from population, from that which Mr. Godwin gives, when he says, "Myriads of centuries of still increasing population may pass away, and the earth be still found sufficient for the subsistence of its inhabitants."

I am sufficiently aware that the redundant twenty-eight millions, or seventy-seven millions, that I have mentioned, could never have existed. It is a perfectly just observation of Mr. Godwin, that, "There is a principle in human society, by which population is perpetually kept down to the level of the means of subsistence." The sole question is, what is this principle? Is it some obscure and occult cause? Is it some mysterious interference of heaven, which at a certain period, strikes the men with impotence, and the women with barrenness? Or is it a cause, open to our researches, within our view, a cause, which has constantly been observed to operate, though with varied force, in every state in which man has been placed? Is it not a degree of misery, the necessary and inevitable result of the laws of nature, which human institutions, so far from aggravating, have tended considerably to mitigate, though they never can remove?

It may be curious to observe, in the case that we have been supposing, how some of the laws which at present govern civilized society, would be successively dictated by the most imperious necessity. As man, according to Mr. Godwin, is the creature of the impressions to which he is subject, the goadings of want could not continue long, before some violations of public or private stock would necessarily take place. As these violations increased in number and extent, the more active and comprehensive intellects of the society would soon perceive, that while population was fast increasing, the yearly produce of the country would shortly begin to diminish. The urgency of the case would suggest the necessity of some immediate measures to be taken for the general safety. Some kind of convention would then be called, and the dangerous situation of the country stated in the strongest terms. It would be observed, that while they lived in the midst of plenty, it was of little consequence who laboured the least, or who possessed the least, as every man was perfectly willing and ready to supply the wants of his neigbour. But that the question was no longer, whether one man should give to another, that which he did not use himself; but whether he should give to his neighbour the food which was absolutely necessary to his own existence. It would be represented, that the number of those that were in want very greatly exceeded the number and means of those who should supply them: that these pressing wants, which from the state of the produce of the

country could not all be gratified, had occasioned some flagrant violations of justice: that these violations had already checked the increase of food, and would, if they were not by some means or other prevented, throw the whole community in confusion: that imperious necessity seemed to dictate that a yearly increase of produce should, if possible, be obtained at all events: that in order to effect this first, great, and indispensible purpose, it would be adviseable to make a more complete division of land, and to secure every man's stock against violation by the most powerful sanctions, even by death itself.

It might be urged perhaps by some objectors, that, as the fertility of the land increased, and various accidents occurred, the share of some men might be much more than sufficient for their support, and that when the reign of self-love was once established, they would not distribute their surplus produce without some compensation in return. It would be observed, in answer, that this was an inconvenience greatly to be lamented; but that it was an evil which bore no comparison to the black train of distresses, that would inevitably be occasioned by the insecurity of property: that the quantity of food which one man could consume, was necessarily limited by the narrow capacity of the human stomach: that it was not certainly probable that he should throw away the rest; but that even if he exchanged his surplus food for the labour of others, and made them in some degree dependent on him, this would still be better than that these others should absolutely starve.

It seems highly probable, therefore, that an administration of property, not very different from that which prevails in civilized States at present, would be established, as the best, though inadequate, remedy, for the evils which were pressing on the society.

The next subject that would come under discussion, intimately connected with the preceding, is, the commerce between the sexes. It would be urged by those who had turned their attention to the true cause of the difficulties under which the community laboured, that while every man felt secure that all his children would be well provided for by general benevolence, the powers of the earth would be absolutely inadequate to produce food for the population which would inevitably ensue: that even, if the whole attention and labour of the society were directed to this sole point, and if, by the most perfect security of property, and every other encouragement that could be thought of, the greatest possible increase of produce were yearly obtained; yet still, that the increase of food would by no means keep pace with the much more rapid increase of population: that some check to population therefore was imperiously called for: that the most natural and obvious check seemed to be, to make every man provide for his own children: that this would operate in some respect, as a measure and guide, in the increase of population; as it might be expected that no man would bring beings into the world, for whom he could not find the means of support: that where this notwithstanding was the case, it seemed necessary, for the example of others, that the disgrace and inconvenience attending such a conduct, should fall upon that individual, who had thus inconsiderately plunged himself and innocent children in misery and want.

The institution of marriage, or at least, of some express or implied obligation on every man to support his own children, seems to be the natural result of these reasonings in a community under the difficulties that we have supposed.

The view of these difficulties, presents us with a very natural origin of the superior disgrace which attends a breach of chastity in the woman, than in the man. It could not be expected that women should have resources sufficient to support their own children. When therefore a woman was connected with a man, who had entered into no compact to maintain her children; and aware of the inconveniences that he might bring upon himself, had deserted her, these children must necessarily fall for support upon the society, or starve. And to prevent the frequent recurrence of such an inconvenience, as it would be highly unjust to punish so natural a fault by personal restraint or infliction, the men might agree to punish it with disgrace. The offence is besides more obvious and conspicuous in the woman, and less liable to any mistake. The father of a child may not always be known, but the same uncertainty cannot easily exist with regard to the mother. Where the evidence of the offence was most complete, and the inconvenience to the society at the same time the greatest, there, it was agreed, that the largest share of blame should fall. The obligation on every man to maintain his children, the society would enforce, if there were occasion; and the greater degree of inconvenience or labour, to which a family would necessarily subject him, added to some portion of disgrace which every human being must incur, who leads another into unhappiness, might be considered as a sufficient punishment for the man.

That a woman should at present be almost driven from society, for an offence, which men commit nearly with impunity, seems to be undoubtedly a breach of natural justice. But the origin of the custom, as the most obvious and effectual method of preventing the frequent recurrence of a serious in-

convenience to a community, appears to be natural, though not perhaps perfectly justifiable. This origin, however, is now lost in the new train of ideas which the custom has since generated. What at first might be dictated by state necessity, is now supported by female delicacy; and operates with the greatest force on that part of society, where, if the original intention of the custom were preserved, there is the least real occasion for it.

When these two fundamental laws of society, the security of property, and the institution of marriage, were once established, inequality of conditions must necessarily follow. Those who were born after the division of property, would come into a world already possessed. If their parents, from having too large a family, could not give them sufficient for their support, what are they to do in a world where every thing is appropriated? We have seen the fatal effects that would result to a society, if every man had a valid claim to an equal share of the produce of the earth. The members of a family which was grown too large for the original division of land appropriated to it, could not then demand a part of the surplus produce of others, as a debt of justice. It has appeared, that from the inevitable laws of our nature, some human beings must suffer from want. These are the unhappy persons who, in the great lottery of life, have drawn a blank. The number of these claimants would soon exceed the ability of the surplus produce to supply. Moral merit is a very difficult distinguishing criterion, except in extreme cases. The owners of surplus produce would in general seek some more obvious mark of distinction. And it seems both natural and just, that except upon particular occasions, their choice should fall upon those, who were able, and professed themselves willing, to exert their strength in procuring a further surplus produce; and thus at once benefiting the community, and enabling these proprietors to afford assistance to greater numbers. All who were in want of food would be urged by imperious necessity to offer their labour in exchange for this article so absolutely essential to existence. The fund appropriated to the maintenance of labour, would be, the aggregate quantity of food possessed by the owners of land beyond their own consumption. When the demands upon this fund were great and numerous, it would naturally be divided in very small shares. Labour would be ill paid. Men would offer to work for a bare subsistence, and the rearing of families would be checked by sickness and misery. On the contrary, when this fund was increasing fast; when it was great in proportion to the number of claimants; it would be divided in much larger shares. No man would exchange his labour without receiving an ample quantity of food in return. Labourers would live in ease and comfort; and would consequently be able to rear a numerous and vigorous offspring.

On the state of this fund, the happiness, or the degree of misery, prevailing among the lower classes of people in every known State, at present chiefly depends. And on this happiness, or degree of misery, depends the increase, stationariness, or decrease of population.

And thus it appears, that a society constituted according to the most beautiful form that imagination can conceive, with benevolence for its moving principle, instead of self-love, and with every evil disposition in all its members corrected by reason and not force, would, from the inevitable laws of nature, and not from any original depravity of man, in a very short period, degenerate into a society, constructed upon a plan not essentially different from that which prevails in every known State at present; I mean, a society divided into a class of proprietors, and a class of labourers, and with self-love for the main-spring of the great machine.

*   *   *

We* have supposed Mr. Godwin's system of society once completely established. But it is supposing an impossibility. The same causes in nature which would destroy it so rapidly, were it once established, would prevent the possibility of its establishment. And upon what grounds we can presume a change in these natural causes, I am utterly at a loss to conjecture. No move towards the extinction of the passion between the sexes has taken place in the five or six thousand years that the world has existed. Men in the decline of life have, in all ages, declaimed against a passion which they have ceased to feel, but with as little reason as success. Those who from coldness of constitutional temperament have never felt what love is, will surely be allowed to be very incompetent judges, with regard to the power of this passion, to contribute to the sum of pleasurable sensations in life. Those who have spent their youth in criminal excesses, and have prepared for themselves, as the comforts of their age, corporal debility, and mental remorse, may well inveigh against such pleasures as vain and futile, and unproductive of lasting satisfaction. But the pleasures of pure love will bear the contemplation of the most improved reason, and the most exalted virtue. Perhaps there is scarcely a man who has once experienced the genuine delight of virtuous love, however great his intellectual pleasures may have been, that does not look back to the period, as the sunny spot in his whole life, where his imagination loves to bask, which he recollects and contemplates with

* This section reprinted from chap. xi, pp. 210–18.

the fondest regrets, and which he would most wish to live over again. The superiority of intellectual, to sensual pleasures, consists rather, in their filling up more time, in their having a larger range, and in their being less liable to satiety, than in their being more real and essential.

Intemperance in every enjoyment defeats its own purpose. A walk in the finest day, through the most beautiful country, if pursued too far, ends in pain and fatigue. The most wholesome and invigorating food, eaten with an unrestrained appetite, produces weakness, instead of strength. Even intellectual pleasures, though certainly less liable than others to satiety, pursued with too little intermission, debilitate the body, and impair the vigour of the mind. To argue against the reality of these pleasures from their abuse, seems to be hardly just. Morality, according to Mr. Godwin, is a calculation of consequences, or, as Archdeacon Paley very justly expresses it, the will of God, as collected from general expediency. According to either of these definitions, a sensual pleasure, not attended with the probability of unhappy consequences, does not offend against the laws of morality: and if it be pursued with such a degree of temperance, as to leave the most ample room for intellectual attainments, it must undoubtedly add to the sum of pleasurable sensations in life. Virtuous love, exalted by friendship, seems to be that sort of mixture of sensual and intellectual enjoyment particularly suited to the nature of man, and most powerfully calculated to awaken the sympathies of the soul, and produce the most exquisite gratifications.

Mr. Godwin says, in order to shew the evident inferiority of the pleasures of sense, "Strip the commerce of the sexes of all its attendant circumstances, and it would be generally despised." He might as well say to a man who admired trees; strip them of their spreading branches and lovely foliage, and what beauty can you see in a bare pole? But it was the tree with the branches and foliage, and not without them, that excited admiration. One feature of an object, may be as distinct, and excite as different emotions, from the aggregate, as any two things the most remote, as a beautiful woman, and a map of Madagascar. It is "the symmetry of person, the vivacity, the voluptuous softness of temper, the affectionate kindness of feelings, the imagination and the wit" of a woman that excite the passion of love, and not the mere distinction of her being a female. Urged by the passion of love, men have been driven into acts highly prejudicial to the general interests of society; but probably they would have found no difficulty in resisting the temptation, had it appeared in the form of a woman, with no other attractions whatever but her sex. To strip sensual pleasures of all their adjuncts, in order to prove their inferiority, is to deprive a magnet of some of its most essential causes of attraction, and then to say that it is weak and inefficient.

In the pursuit of every enjoyment, whether sensual or intellectual, Reason, that faculty which enables us to calculate consequences, is the proper corrective and guide. It is probable therefore that improved reason will always tend to prevent the abuse of sensual pleasures, though it by no means follows that it will extinguish them.

I have endeavoured to expose the fallacy of that argument which infers an unlimited progress from a partial improvement, the limits of which cannot be exactly ascertained. It has appeared, I think, that there are many instances in which a decided progress has been observed, where yet it would be a gross absurdity to suppose that progress indefinite. But towards the extinction of the passion between the sexes, no observable progress whatever has hitherto been made. To suppose such an extinction,

therefore, is merely to offer an unfounded conjecture, unsupported by any philosophical probabilities.

It is a truth, which history I am afraid makes too clear, that some men of the highest mental powers, have been addicted not only to a moderate, but even to an immoderate indulgence in the pleasures of sensual love. But allowing, as I should be inclined to do, notwithstanding numerous instances to the contrary, that great intellectual exertions tend to diminish the empire of this passion over man; it is evident that the mass of mankind must be improved more highly than the brightest ornaments of the species at present, before any difference can take place sufficient sensibly to affect population. I would by no means suppose that the mass of mankind has reached its term of improvement; but the principal argument of this essay tends to place in a strong point of view, the improbability, that the lower classes of people in any country, should ever be sufficiently free from want and labour, to attain any high degree of intellectual improvement.

6. *The Civic Community*

BY GEORG W. F. HEGEL

182. THE CONCRETE PERSON, who as particular is an end to himself, is a totality of wants and a mixture of necessity and caprice. As such he is one of the principles of the civic community. But the particular person is essentially connected with others. Hence each establishes and satisfies himself by means of others, and so must call in the assistance of the form of universality. This universality is the other principle of the civic community. . . .

*   *   *

183. The self-seeking end is conditioned in its realization by the universal. Hence is formed a system of mutual dependence, a system which interweaves the subsistence, happiness, and rights of the individual with the subsistence, happiness, and right of all. The general right and well-being

Reprinted from Georg W. F. Hegel, *The Philosophy of Right*, trans. S. W. Dyde (London: George Bell & Sons, 1896), secs. 182–83, 187–88, 190–93, 196–99, 201, 207, 209–10, 229–32, 235, 249, 252, 256–57, 259, with omissions.

form the basis of the individual's right and well-being, which only by this connection receives actuality and security. This system we may in the first instance call the external state, the state which satisfies one's needs, and meets the requirements of the understanding.

*   *   *

187. Individuals in the civic community are private persons, who pursue their own interests. As these interests are occasioned by the universal, which appears as a means, they can be obtained only in so far as individuals in their desire, will, and conduct, conform to the universal, and become a link in the chain of the whole. The interest of the idea as such does not, it is true, lie in the consciousness of the citizens; yet it is not wholly wanting. It is found in the process, by means of which the individual, through necessity of nature and the caprice of his wants, seeks to raise his individual natural existence into formal freedom and the formal universality of knowing and willing.

Thus, without departing from its particular nature, the individual's character is enlarged.

Note.—The view that civilization is an external degenerate form of life is allied to the idea that the natural condition of uncivilized peoples is one of unsophisticated innocence. So also the view that civilization is a mere means for the satisfaction of one's needs, and for the enjoyment and comfort of one's particular life, takes for granted that these selfish ends are absolute. Both theories manifest ignorance of the nature of spirit and the end of reason. Spirit is real only when by its own motion it divides itself, gives itself limit and finitude in the natural needs and the region of external necessity, and then, by moulding and shaping itself in them, overcomes them, and secures for itself an objective embodiment. The rational end, therefore, is neither the simplicity of nature nor the enjoyments resulting from civilization through the development of particularity. It rather works away from the condition of simple nature, in which there is either no self or a crude state of consciousness and will, and transcends the naïve individuality, in which spirit is submerged. Its externality thus in the first instance receives the rationality, of which it is capable, namely, the form of universality characteristic of the understanding. Only in this way is spirit at home and with itself in this externality as such. Hence in it the freedom of spirit is realized. Spirit, becoming actualized in an element, which of itself was foreign to its free character, has to do only with what is produced by itself and bears its own impress.—In this way the form of universality comes into independent existence in thought, a form which is the only worthy element for the existence of the idea.

Culture or education is, as we may thus conclude, in its ultimate sense a liberation, and that of a high kind. Its task is to make possible the infinitely subjective substantiality of the ethical life. In the process we pass upwards from the direct and natural existence to what is spiritual and has the form of the universal.—In the individual agent this liberation involves a struggle against mere subjectivity, immediate desire, subjective vanity, and capricious liking. The hardness of the task is in part the cause of the disfavor under which it falls. None the less is it through the labour of education that the subjective will itself wins possession of the objectivity, in which alone it is able and worthy to be the embodiment of the idea.— At the same time the form of universality, into which particularity has moulded itself and worked itself up, gives rise to that general principle of the understanding, in accordance with which the particular passes upward into the true, independent existence of the individual. And since the particular gives to the universal its adequate content and unconditioned self-direction, it even in the ethical sphere is infinitely independent and free subjectivity. Education is thus proved to be an inherent element of the absolute, and is shown to have infinite value. . . .

188. The civic community contains three elements:

A. The recasting of want, and the satisfaction of the individual through his work, through the work of all others, and through the satisfaction of their wants. This is a system of wants.

B. Actualization of the general freedom required for this, *i.e.,* the protection of property by the administration of justice.

C. Provision against possible mischances, and care for the particular interest as a common interest, by means of police and the corporation. . . .

WANT AND ITS SATISFACTION

190. The animal has a limited range of ways and means for satisfying his limited wants. Man in his dependence proves his universality and his ability to become independent, firstly, by multiplying his wants and means, and, secondly, by dissecting the concrete want into parts. The parts then become other wants, and through being specialized are more abstract than the first.

Note.—The object is in right a person, in morals a subject, in the family a member, in the city generally a burgher (*bourgeois*); and here, at the standpoint of want, he is the concrete product of picture-thought which we call man. Here, and properly only here, is it that we first speak of man in this sense. . . .

191. The means for satisfying the specialized wants are similarly divided and increased. These means become in their turn relative ends and abstract wants. Hence the multiplication expands into an infinite series of distinctions with regard to these phases, and of judgments concerning the suitability of the means to their ends. This is refinement. . . .

192. The satisfaction of want and the attainment of means thereto become a realized possibility for others, through whose wants and labour satisfaction is in turn conditioned. The abstraction, which becomes a quality of wants and means (§ 191), helps to determine the mutual relation of individuals. This general recognition of others is the element which makes the isolated abstract wants and means concrete and social. . . .

193. The social element is a special instrument both of the simple acquisition of the means, and

also of the reduplication of the ways by which want is satisfied. Further, it contains directly the claim of equality with others. Both the desire for equality, including the imitation of others, and also the desire of each person to be unique, become real sources of the multiplication and extension of wants.

*   *   *

LABOUR

196. The instrument for preparing and acquiring specialized means adequate to specialized wants is labour. By labour the material, directly handed over by nature for these numerous ends, is specialized in a variety of ways. This fashioning of the material gives to the means value and purpose, so that in consumption it is chiefly human products and human effort that are used up.

Addition.—The direct material, which requires no working up, is small. Even air must be acquired, since it has to be made warm. Perhaps water is the only thing which man can use, simply as it is. Human sweat and toil win for men the means for satisfying their wants.

197. Training on its theoretical side is developed by the great variety of objects and interests, and consists not only in numberless picture-thoughts and items of knowledge, but also in mobility and quickness of imagination, a mental alertness in passing from one image, or idea, to another, and in the apprehension of intricate general relations. This is the training of the understanding, with which goes the development of language. Practical training, or training by labour, consists in habituation to an employment, which satisfies a self-caused want. Its action is limited partly by the nature of the material, but chiefly by the caprice of others. It involves an habitual use of skill acquired by practice and implying objective conditions.

*   *   *

198. The universal and objective in work is to be found in the abstraction which, giving rise to the specialization of means and wants, causes the specialization also of production. This is the division of labour. By it the labour of the individual becomes more simple, his skill in his abstract work greater, and the amount he produces larger. The result of the abstraction of skill and means is that men's interdependence or mutual relation is completed. It becomes a thorough necessity. Moreover, the abstraction of production causes work to be continually more mechanical, until it is at last possible for man to step out and let the machine take his place.

WEALTH

199. Through the dependence and co-operation involved in labour, subjective self-seeking is converted into a contribution towards the satisfaction of the wants of all others. The universal so penetrates the particular by its dialectic movement, that the individual, while acquiring, producing, and enjoying for himself, at the same time produces and acquires for the enjoyment of others. This is a necessity, and in this necessity arising out of mutual dependence is contained the fact of a general and permanent wealth. In it each person may share by means of his education and skill. Each, too, is by it assured of subsistence, while the results of his labour preserve and increase the general wealth.

*   *   *

201. The infinitely varied means and their infinitely interlacing play of mutual production and exchange are gathered together by virtue of the universality inherent in their content, and become divided into general masses. The whole is thus formed into particular systems of wants, means, and labour, ways and methods of satisfaction, and theoretical and practical training. Amongst these systems the individuals are apportioned, and compose a cluster of classes or estates.

*   *   *

207. The particularity of the individual becomes definitely and actually realized, only by his limiting himself exclusively to one of the particular spheres of want. In this system the ethical sense is that of rectitude or class-honour. It involves the decision of the individual by means of his own native activity, diligence, and skill to make himself a member of one of these classes, preserve himself in it, and provide for himself only through the instrumentality of the universal. He should acknowledge this position, and also claim to have it recognized by others.—Morality has its peculiar place in this sphere, where the ruling factor is reflection upon one's action, or consideration of the end involved in particular wants and in well-being. Here also the element of chance in satisfying these ends makes random and individual assistance a duty.

Note.—Youth is specially apt to struggle against the proposal that it should decide upon a particular vocation, on the ground that any decision is a limitation of its universal scope and a mere external necessity. This aloofness is a product of the abstract thinking, which clings to the universal and unreal. It fails to recognize that the conception must experience a division into conception and its reality, if it is to have a definite and particular realization, and to win for itself reality and ethical objectivity.

Addition.—By the sentence that a man must be something we understand that he must belong to a definite class; for this something signifies a substantive reality. A human being without a vocation is a mere private person, who has no place in any real universal. Still, the individual in his exclusiveness may regard himself as the universal, and may fancy that when he takes a trade or profession, he is sinking to a lower plane. That is the false notion that a thing, when it attains the realization which properly belongs to it, limits itself and gives up its independence.

*   *   *

Administration of Justice

209. The relative principle of the mutual exchange of wants and labour for their satisfaction has in the first instance its return into itself in the infinite personality generally, *i.e.,* in abstract right. Yet it is the very sphere of the relative which in the form of education gives embodiment to right, by fixing it as something universally acknowledged, known, and willed. The relative also, through the interposition of knowledge and will, supplies right with validity and objective actuality.

Note.—It is the essence of education and of thought, which is the consciousness of the individual in universal form, that the I should be apprehended as a universal person, in whom all are identical. Man must be accounted a universal being, not because he is a Jew, Catholic, Protestant, German, or Italian, but because he is a man. This thinking or reflective consciousness, is of infinite importance. It is defective only when it plumes itself upon being cosmopolitan, in opposition to the concrete life of the citizen. . . .

210. The objective actuality of right consists partly in existing for consciousness, or more generally in its being known, and partly in having, and being generally recognized as having, the validity and force of a reality.

*   *   *

229. In the civic community the idea is lost in particularity, and dispersed by the separation of inner and outer. But in the administration of justice the community is brought back to the conception, that is, to the unity of the intrinsic universal with subjective particularity. But as subjective particularity is present only as one single case, and the universal only as abstract right, the unification is in the first instance relative. The realization of this relative unity over the whole range of particularity is the function of the police, and within a limited but concrete totality constitutes the corporation.

Addition.—In the civic community universality is only necessity. In the relation of wants, right as such is the only steadfast principle. But the sphere of this right is limited, and refers merely to the protection of what I have. To right as such, happiness is something external. Yet in the system of wants well-being is an essential element. The universal, which is at first only right, has to spread itself over the whole field of particularity. Justice, it is true, is a large factor in the civic community. The state will flourish, if it has good laws, of which free property is the fundamental condition. But since I am wholly environed by my particularity, I have a right to demand that in connecting myself with others I shall further my special happiness. Regard to my particular well-being is taken by the police and the corporation.

Police and Corporation

230. In the system of wants the subsistence and happiness of every individual is a possibility, whose realization is conditioned by the objective system of wants. By the administration of justice compensation is rendered for injury done to property or person. But the right, which is actualized in the particular individual, contains the two following factors. It asks firstly that person and property should be secured by the removal of all fortuitous hindrances, and secondly that the security of the individual's subsistence and happiness, his particular well-being should be regarded and actualized as a right.

POLICE

231. So far as the particular will is the principle of a purpose, the force by which the universal guarantees security is limited to the realm of mere accident, and is an external arrangement.

232. Crimes are in their nature contingent or casual, taking the form of capricious choice of evil, and must be prevented or brought to justice by the general force. Apart from them, however, arbitrary choice must be allowed a place in connection with acts in themselves lawful, such as the private use of property. Here it comes into external relation with other individuals, and also with public institutions for realizing a common end. In this way a private act is exposed to a haphazard play of circumstances, which take it beyond my control. It thus may or actually does effect an injury or wrong to others.

*   *   *

235. Although everyone relies on the untrammelled possibility of satisfying his daily wants, yet

when in the indefinite multiplication and limitation of them it is sought to procure or exchange the means and it is desired to expedite the transaction, there comes into sight a common interest, which makes the business of one subverse the interest of all. There appear, likewise, ways and means, which may be of public utility. To oversee and foster the ways and means calculated to promote the public welfare is the function of a public power.

*   *   *

249. The universal, which is contained in the particularity of the civic community, is realized and preserved by the external system of police supervision, whose purpose is simply to protect and secure the multitude of private ends and interests subsisting within it. It has also the higher function of caring for the interests which lead out beyond the civic community (§ 246). In accordance with the idea particularity itself makes the universal, which exists in its special interests, the end and object of its will and endeavour. The ethical principle thus comes back as a constituent element of the civic community. This is the corporation.

*   *   *

252. In keeping with this view, the corporation, under the oversight of the public authority, has the right to look after its own clearly-defined interests, according to the objective qualifications of skill and rectitude to adopt members, whose number is determined by the general system, to make provision for its adherents against fortuitous occurrences, and to foster the capacity necessary in any one desiring to become a member. In general it must stand to its members as a second family, a position which remains more indefinite than the family relation, because the general civic community is at a farther remove from individuals and their special needs.

Note.—The tradesman is different from the day-labourer, as well as from him who is ready for any casual employment. The trader, be he employer or employee, is a member of an association, not for mere accidental gain but for the whole circuit of gain, or the universal involved in his particular maintenance. The privileges, which are rights of a corporate branch of the civic community, are not the same as special privileges in the etymological sense of the term. Special privileges are haphazard exceptions to a general law, but the other privileges are legal phases of the particularity of an essential branch of the community. . . .

*   *   *

256. The limited and finite end of the corporation has its truth in the absolutely universal end and the absolute actuality of this end. This actualized end is also the truth of the division involved in

the external system of police, which is merely a relative identity of the divided elements. Thus, the sphere of the civic community passes into the state.

Note.—City and country are the two as yet ideal constituents, out of which the state proceeds. The city is the seat of the civic society, and of the reflection which goes into itself and causes separation. The country is the seat of the ethical, which rests upon nature. The one comprises the individuals, who gain their livelihood by virtue of their relation to other persons possessed of rights. The other comprises the family. The state is the true meaning and ground of both.

The development of simple ethical observance into the dismemberment marking the civic community, and then forward into the state, which is shown to be the true foundation of these more abstract phases, is the only scientific proof of the conception of the state.—Although in the course of the scientific exposition the state has the appearance of a result, it is in reality the true foundation and cause. This appearance and its process are provisional, and must now be replaced by the state in its direct existence. In actual fact the state is in general primary. Within it the family grows into the civic community, the idea of the state being that which sunders itself into these two elements. In the development of the civic community the ethical substance reaches its infinite form, which contains the following elements:—(1) infinite differentiation even to the point at which consciousness as it is in itself exists for itself, and (2) the form of universality, which in civilization is the form of thought, that form by which spirit is itself in its laws and institutions. They are its thought will, and it and they together become objective and real in an organic whole.

The State

257. The state is the realized ethical idea or ethical spirit. It is the will which manifests itself, makes itself clear and visible, substantiates itself. It is the will which thinks and knows itself, and carries out what it knows, and in so far as it knows. The state finds in ethical custom its direct and unreflected existence, and its indirect and reflected existence in the self-consciousness of the individual and in his knowledge and activity. Self-consciousness in the form of social disposition has its substantive freedom in the state, as the essence, purpose, and product of its activity.

Note.—The Penates are the inner and lower order of gods; the spirit of a nation, Athene, is the divinity which knows and wills itself. Piety is feeling, or ethical behaviour in the form of feeling;

political virtue is the willing of the thought-out end, which exists absolutely.

* * *

259. (*a*) The idea of the state has direct actuality in the individual state. It, as a self-referring organism, is the constitution or internal state-organization or polity.

(*b*) It passes over into a relation of the individual state to other states. This is its external organization or polity.

(*c*) As universal idea, or kind, or species, it has absolute authority over individual states. This is the spirit which gives itself reality in the process of world-history.

7. The Functions of Government in General

BY JOHN STUART MILL

IN ATTEMPTING to enumerate the necessary functions of government, we find them to be considerably more multifarious than most people are at first aware of, and not capable of being circumscribed by those very definite lines of demarcation, which, in the inconsiderateness of popular discussion, it is often attempted to draw round them. We sometimes, for example, hear it said that governments ought to confine themselves to affording protection against force and fraud: that, these two things apart, people should be free agents, able to take care of themselves, and that so long as a person practises no violence or deception, to the injury of others in person or property, legislatures and governments are in no way called on to concern themselves about him. But why should people be protected by their government, that is, by their own collective strength, against violence and fraud, and not against other evils, except that the expediency is more obvious? If nothing, but what people cannot possibly do for themselves, can be fit to be done for them by government, people might be required to protect themselves by their skill and courage even against force, or to beg or buy protection against it, as they actually do where the government is not capable of protecting them: and against fraud every one has the protection of his own wits. But without further anticipating the discussion of principles, it is sufficient on the present occasion to consider facts.

Under which of these heads, the repression of force or of fraud, are we to place the operation, for example, of the laws of inheritance? Some such laws

Reprinted from John Stuart Mill, *Principles of Political Economy* (London: Longman, Green, Longman, Robertson, Green, 1865), Book V, chap. i, sec. 2, pp. 480–82.

must exist in all societies. It may be said, perhaps, that in this matter government has merely to give effect to the disposition which an individual makes of his own property by will. This, however, is at least extremely disputable; there is probably no country by whose laws the power of testamentary disposition is perfectly absolute. And suppose the very common case of there being no will: does not the law, that is, the government, decide on principles of general expediency, who shall take the succession? and in case the successor is in any manner incompetent, does it not appoint persons, frequently officers of its own, to collect the property and apply it to his benefit? There are many other cases in which the government undertakes the administration of property, because the public interest, or perhaps only that of the particular persons concerned, is thought to require it. This is often done in cases of litigated property; and in cases of judicially declared insolvency. It has never been contended that in doing these things, a government exceeds its province.

Nor is the function of the law in defining property itself, so simple a thing as may be supposed. It may be imagined, perhaps, that the law has only to declare and protect the right of every one to what he has himself produced, or acquired by the voluntary consent, fairly obtained, of those who produced it. But is there nothing recognised as property except what has been produced? Is there not the earth itself, its forests and waters, and all other natural riches, above and below the surface? These are the inheritance of the human race, and there must be regulations for the common enjoyment of it. What rights, and under what conditions, a person shall be allowed to exercise over any portion of this common inheritance, cannot be left undecided. No function of government is less optional than the regulation of these things, or more completely involved in the idea of civilized society.

Again, the legitimacy is conceded of repressing violence or treachery; but under which of these heads are we to place the obligation imposed on people to perform their contracts? Non-performance does not necessarily imply fraud; the person who entered into the contract may have sincerely intended to fulfil it: and the term fraud, which can scarcely admit of being extended even to the case of voluntary breach of contract when no deception was practised, is certainly not applicable when the omission to perform is a case of negligence. Is it no part of the duty of governments to enforce contracts? Here the doctrine of non-interference would no doubt be stretched a little, and it would be said, that enforcing contracts is not regulating the affairs of individuals at the pleasure of government, but giving effect to their own expressed desire. Let us acquiesce in this enlargement of the restrictive theory, and take it for what it is worth. But governments do not limit their concern with contracts to a simple enforcement. They take upon themselves to determine what contracts are fit to be enforced. It is not enough that one person, not being either cheated or compelled, makes a promise to another. There are promises by which it is not for the public good that persons should have the power of binding themselves. To say nothing of engagements to do something contrary to law, there are engagements which the law refuses to enforce, for reasons connected with the interest of the promiser, or with the general policy of the state. A contract by which a person sells himself to another as a slave, would be declared void by the tribunals of this and of most other European countries. There are few nations whose laws enforce a contract for what is looked upon as prostitution, or any matrimonial engagement of which the conditions vary in any respect from those which the law has thought fit to prescribe. But when once it is admitted that there are any engagements which for reasons of expediency the law ought not to enforce, the same question is necessarily opened with respect to all engagements. Whether, for example, the law should enforce a contract to labour, when the wages are too low, or the hours of work too severe: whether it should enforce a contract by which a person binds himself to remain, for more than a very limited period, in the service of a given individual: whether a contract of marriage, entered into for life, should continue to be enforced against the deliberate will of the persons, or of either of the persons, who entered into it. Every question which

can possibly arise as to the policy of contracts, and of the relations which they establish among human beings, is a question for the legislator; and one which he cannot escape from considering, and in some way or other deciding.

Again, the prevention and suppression of force and fraud afford appropriate employment for soldiers, policemen, and criminal judges; but there are also civil tribunals. The punishment of wrong is one business of an administration of justice, but the decision of disputes is another. Innumerable disputes arise between persons, without *mala fides* on either side, through misconception of their legal rights, or from not being agreed about the facts, on the proof of which those rights are legally dependent. Is it not for the general interest that the State should appoint persons to clear up these uncertainties and terminate these disputes? It cannot be said to be a case of absolute necessity. People might appoint an arbitrator, and engage to submit to his decision; and they do so where there are no courts of justice, or where the courts are not trusted, or where their delays and expenses, or the irrationality of their rules of evidence, deter people from resorting to them. Still, it is universally thought right that the State should establish civil tribunals; and if their defects often drive people to have recourse to substitutes, even then the power held in reserve of carrying the case before a legally constituted court, gives to the substitutes their principal efficacy.

Not only does the State undertake to decide disputes, it takes precautions beforehand that disputes may not arise. The laws of most countries lay down rules for determining many things, not because it is of much consequence in what way they are determined, but in order that they may be determined somehow, and there may be no question on the subject. The law prescribes forms of words for many kinds of contract, in order that no dispute or misunderstanding may arise about their meaning: it makes provision that if a dispute does arise, evidence shall be procurable for deciding it, by requiring that the document be attested by witnesses and executed with certain formalities. The law preserves authentic evidence of facts to which legal consequences are attached, by keeping a registry of such facts; as of births, deaths, and marriages, of wills and contracts, and of judicial proceedings. In doing these things, it has never been alleged that government oversteps the proper limits of its functions.

Again, however wide a scope we may allow to the doctrine that individuals are the proper guardians of their own interests, and that government owes nothing to them but to save them from being interfered with by other people, the doctrine can never be applicable to any persons but those who are capable of acting in their own behalf. The individual may be an infant, or a lunatic, or fallen into imbecility. The law surely must look after the interests of such persons. It does not necessarily do this through officers of its own. It often devolves the trust upon some relative or connexion. But in doing so is its duty ended? Can it make over the interests of one person to the control of another, and be excused from supervision, or from holding the person thus trusted, responsible for the discharge of the trust?

There is a multitude of cases in which governments, with general approbation, assume powers and execute functions for which no reason can be assigned except the simple one, that they conduce to general convenience. We may take as an example, the function (which is a monopoly too) of coining money. This is assumed for no more recondite purpose than that of saving to individuals the trouble, delay, and expense of weighing and assaying. No one, however, even of those most jealous of state interference, has objected to this as an improper exercise of the powers of government. Prescribing a set of standard weights and measures is another instance. Paving, lighting, and cleansing the streets and thoroughfares, is another; whether done by the general government, or, as is more usual, and generally more advisable, by a municipal authority. Making or improving harbours, building light-houses, making surveys in order to have accurate maps and charts, raising dykes to keep the sea out, and embankments to keep rivers in, are cases in point.

Examples might be indefinitely multiplied without intruding on any disputed ground. But enough has been said to show that the admitted functions of government embrace a much wider field than can easily be included within the ring-fence of any restrictive definition, and that it is hardly possible to find any ground of justification common to them all, except the comprehensive one of general expediency; nor to limit the interference of government by any universal rule, save the simple and vague one that it should never be admitted but when the case of expediency is strong.

8. *On the Social Contract*

BY JEAN JACQUES ROUSSEAU

On the Necessity of Recurring Always to the Primitive Convention

ON THE SUPPOSITION, that I should grant to be true what I have hitherto disproved, the advocate for despotism would, however, profit but little. There will be always a great difference between subjecting a multitude, and governing a society. Let individuals, in any number whatever, become severally and successively subject to one man, they are all, in that case, nothing more than master and slaves; they are not a people governed by their chief; they are an Aggregate if you will, but do not form an association; there subsists among them neither commonwealth nor body politic. Such a superior, though he should become the master of half the world, would be still a private person, and

Reprinted from Jean Jacques Rousseau, *A Treatise on the Social Compact,* Book I, chaps. v–ix, and Book II, chaps. i–iii, in *The Miscellaneous Works of Mr. J. J. Rousseau* (London: T. Becket and P. A. DeHondt, 1767), pp. 16–37.

his interest, separate and distinct from that of his people, would be still no more than a private interest. When such a person dies, also the empire over which he presided is dissolved, and its component parts remain totally unconnected, just as an oak falls into a heap of ashes, when it is consumed by the fire.

A people, says Grotius, may voluntarily bestow themselves on a king: according to Grotius, therefore, a people are a people before they thus give themselves up to regal authority. Even this gift, however, is an act of society, and presupposes a public deliberation on the matter. Hence, before we examine into the act, by which a people make choice of a king, it is proper to examine into that by which a people became a people, for, on this, which is necessarily prior to the other, rests the true foundation of society.

For, if, in fact, there be no prior convention, whence arises (unless indeed the election was unanimous) the obligation of the smaller number to submit to the choice of the greater? and whence comes it, that an hundred persons, for instance, who might desire to have a master, had a right to vote for ten others who might desire to have none? The choice by a plurality of votes is itself an establishment of convention, and supposes, that unanimity must at least for once have subsisted among them.

On the Social Pact or Covenant

I suppose mankind arrived at that term, when the obstacles to their preservation, in a state of nature, prevail over the endeavours of individuals, to maintain themselves in such a state. At such a crisis this primitive state therefore could no longer subsist, and the human race must have perished, if they had not changed their manner of living.

Now as men cannot create new powers, but only compound and direct those which really exist, they have no other means of preservation, than that of forming, by their union, an accumulation of forces, sufficient to oppose the obstacles to their security, and of putting these in action by a first mover, capable of making them act in concert with each other.

This general accumulation of power cannot arise but from the concurrence of many particular forces; but the force and liberty of each individual being the principal instruments of his own preservation, how is he to engage them in the common interest, without hurting his own, and neglecting the obligations he lies under to himself? This difficulty, being applied to my present subject, may be expressed in the following terms:

"To find that form of association which shall protect and defend, with the whole force of the community, the person and property of each individual, and in which each person, by uniting himself to the rest, shall nevertheless be obedient only to himself, and remain as fully at liberty as before." Such is the fundamental problem, of which the social compact gives the solution.

The clauses of this compact are so precisely determined by the nature of the act, that the least restriction or modification renders them void and of no effect; in so much, that, although they may perhaps never have been formally promulgated, they are yet universally the same, and are every where tacitly acknowledged and received. When the social pact, however, is violated, individuals recover their natural liberty, and are re-invested with their original rights, by losing that conventional liberty for the sake of which they had renounced them.

Again; these clauses, well understood are all reducible to one, viz. the total alienation of every individual, with all his rights and privileges, to the whole community. For, in the first place, as every one gives himself up entirely and without reserve, all are in the same circumstances, so that no one can be interested in making their common connection burthensome to others.

Besides, as the alienation is made without reserve, the union is as perfect as possible, nor hath any particular associate any thing to reclaim; whereas, if they should severally retain any peculiar privileges, there being no common umpire to determine between them and the public, each being his own judge in some cases, would, in time, pretend to be so in all, the state of nature would still subsist, and their association would necessarily become tyrannical or void.

In fine, the individual, by giving himself up to all, gives himself to none; and, as he acquires the same right over every other person in the community, as he gives them over himself, he gains an equivalent for what he bestows, and still a greater power to preserve what he retains.

If, therefore, we take from the social compact every thing that is not essential to it, we shall find it reduced to the following terms: "We, the contracting parties, do jointly and severally submit our persons and abilities, to the supreme direction of the general will of all, and, in a collective body, receive each member into that body, as an indivisible part of the whole."

This act of association accordingly converts the several individual contracting parties into one moral collective body, composed of as many members as there are votes in the assembly, which receives also from the same act its unity and existence. This public personage, which is thus formed by the union of all its members, used formerly to be denominated a City,[1] and, at present, takes the name of a *repub-*

---

1. The true sense of this word is almost entirely perverted among the moderns; most people take a town for a city, and an house-keeper for a citizen. Such are ignorant, however, that, though houses may form a town, it is the citizens only that constitute a city. This same errour formerly cost the Carthaginians very dear. I do not remember, in the course of my reading, to have ever found the title of *Cives* given to the subjects of a prince, not even formerly to the Macedonians, nor, in our times, to the English, though more nearly bordering on liberty than any other nation. The French are the only people who familiarly take on themselves the name of *citizens,* because they have no just idea of its meaning, as may be seen in their dictionaries; for, were it otherwise, indeed, they would be guilty of high treason in assuming it. This term is with them rather expressive of a virtue than a privilege. Hence, when Bodin spoke of the citizens and inhabitants of Geneva, he committed a wretched blunder, in mistaking one for the other. Mr. d'Alembert indeed has avoided this mistake in the Encyclopoedia, where he has properly distinguished the four orders of people (and even five, reckoning mere strangers) that are found in our city, and of which two only compose the republic: No other French author that I know of hath ever comprehended the meaning of the word *citizen.*

lic, or *body politic*. It is also called, by its several members, a *state,* when it is passive; the *sovereign,* when it is active; and simply a *power,* when it is compared with other bodies of the same nature. With regard to the associates themselves, they take collectively the name of the *people,* and are separately called *citizens,* as partaking of the sovereign authority, and *subjects,* as subjected to the laws of the state. These terms, indeed, are frequently confounded, and mistaken one for the other; it is sufficient, however, to be able to distinguish them, when they are used with precision.

Of the Sovereign

It is plain from the above formula, that the act of association includes a reciprocal engagement between particulars and the public; and that each individual, in contracting, if I may so say, with himself, is laid under a twofold engagement, *viz.* as a member of the sovereignty toward particular persons, and as a member of the state toward the sovereign. That maxim of the civil law, however, is inapplicable here, which says, that no one is bound by the engagements he enters into with himself; for, there is a wide difference between entering into a personal obligation with one's self, and with a whole, of which one may constitute a part.

It is farther to be observed, that the public determination, which is obligatory on the subject, with regard to the sovereign, on account of the twofold relation by which each stands contracted, is not, for the contrary reason, obligatory on the supreme power towards itself: and that it is consequently inconsistent with the nature of the body politic, that such supreme power should impose a law, which it cannot break. For, as the sovereign stands only in a single relation, it is in the same case as that of an individual contracting with himself; whence it is plain, that there neither is, nor can be, any fundamental law obligatory on the whole body of a people, even the social compact itself not being such. By this, however, it is not meant, that such a body cannot enter into engagements with others, in matters that do not derogate from this contract; for, with respect to foreign objects, it is a simple and individual person.

But, as the body politic, or the sovereign, derives its very existence from this inviolable contract, it can enter into no lawful engagement, even with any similar body, derogatory from the tenour of this primitive act; such as that of alienating any part of itself, or of submitting itself intirely to a foreign sovereign. To violate the act whereby it exists would

be to annihilate itself, and from nothing can arise nothing.

No sooner are a multitude of individuals thus united in a body, than it becomes impossible to act offensively against any of the members, without attacking the whole, and still less to offend the whole body, without injuring the members. Hence both duty and interest equally oblige the two contracting parties to assist each other, and the same persons ought to endeavour to include, within this twofold relation, all the advantages which depend on it.

Now the sovereign, being formed only by the several individuals of which the state is composed, can have no interest contrary to theirs; of course the supreme power stands in no need of any guarantee toward the subjects, because it is impossible, that the body should be capable of hurting all its members; and we shall see hereafter, that it can as little tend to injure any of them in particular. Hence the sovereign is necessarily, and for the same reason that it exists, always such as it ought to be.

The case is different, however, as to the relation in which the subjects stand to the sovereign; as, notwithstanding their common interest, the latter can have no security that the former will discharge their engagements, unless means be found to engage their fidelity.

In fact, every individual may, as a man, entertain a particular will, either contradictory or dissimilar to his general will, as a citizen. His private interest may influence him, in a manner diametrically opposite to the common interest of the society. Reflecting on his own existence as positive and naturally independent, he may conceive what he owes to the common cause, to be a free and gratuitous contribution, the want of which will be less hurtful to others, than the discharge of it will be burthensome to himself; and, regarding the moral person of the state as an imaginary being, because it is not a man, he may be desirous of enjoying all the privileges of a citizen without fulfilling his engagement as a subject; an injustice, that, in its progress, must necessarily be the ruin of the body politic.

To the end, therefore, that the social compact should not prove an empty form, it tacitly includes this engagement, which only can enforce the rest, *viz.* that whosoever refuses to pay obedience to the general will, shall be liable to be compelled to it by the force of the whole body. And this is in effect nothing more, than that they may be compelled to be free; for such is the condition which, in uniting every citizen to the state, secured him from all personal dependence; a condition, which forms the whole artifice and play of the political machine: it is this alone that renders all social engagements just and equitable which, without it, would be absurd, tyrannical, and subject to the most enormous abuses.

Of Civil Society in General

The transition of man from a state of nature to a state of society is productive of a very remarkable change in his being, by substituting justice instead of instinct, as the rule of his conduct, and attaching that morality to his actions, of which they were before destitute. It is in immediate consequence of this change, when the voice of duty succeeds to physical impulse and the law of appetite, that man, who hitherto regarded only his own gratification, finds himself obliged to act on other principles, and to consult his reason, before he follows the dictates of his passions. Although, by entering into a state of society, he is deprived also of many advantages which depend on that of nature, he gains by it others so very considerable, his faculties exert and expand themselves, his ideas are enlarged, his sentiments ennobled, and his whole soul is elevated to so great a degree, that, if the abuses of this new state do not degrade him below the former, he ought incessantly to bless that happy moment in which he was rescued from it, and converted from a stupid and ignorant animal into an intelligent and wise Being.

To state the balance of what is lost and gained by this change, we shall reduce it to comparative terms. By entering into the social compact, man gives up his natural liberty, or unlimited right to every thing which he is desirous of, and can attain. In return for this, he gains social liberty, and an exclusive property in all those things of which he is possessed. To avoid any mistake, however, in the nature of these compensations, it is necessary to make a just distinction between natural liberty, which is limited by nothing but the inabilities of the individual, and social liberty, which is limited by the general will of the community; and also, between that possession, which is only effected by force, or follows the right of prior occupancy, and that property, which is founded only on a positive title.

To the preceding also may be added, as the acquisition of a social state, moral liberty, which only renders a man truly master of himself: for to be under the direction of appetite alone is to be in a state of slavery, while to pay obedience only to those laws which we prescribe to ourselves, is liberty. But I have said too much already on this subject, the philosophical meaning of the word Liberty, being, in this place, out of the question.

Of Real Demesnes

Each member of the community, in becoming such, devotes himself to the public from that moment, in such a state as he then is, with all his power and abilities, of which abilities his possessions make a part. Not that in consequence of this act the possession changes its nature, by changing hands, and becomes actual property in those of the sovereignty; but as the power of the community is incomparably greater than that of an individual, the public possession is in fact more fixed and irrevocable, without being more lawful, at least with regard to foreigners. For every state is, with respect to its members, master of all their possessions, by virtue of the social compact, which, in a state, serves as the basis of all other rights; but, with regard to other powers or states, it is master of them only, by the right of prior occupancy, which it derives from individuals.

The right of prior occupancy, although more real than that of the strongest, becomes not an equitable right, till after the establishment of property. Every man hath naturally a right to every thing which is necessary for his subsistence; but the positive act by which he is made the proprietor of a certain possession excludes him from the property of any other. His portion being assigned him, he ought to confine himself to that, and hath no longer any right to a community of possession. Hence it is that the right of prior occupancy, though but of little force in a state of nature, is so respectable in that of society. The point to which we are chiefly directed in the consideration of this right, is rather what belongs to another, than what does not belong to us.

To define the right of prior occupancy in general terms, it is founded on the following conditions. It is requisite, in the first place, that the lands in question should be unoccupied; secondly, that no greater quantity of it should be occupied than is necessary for the subsistence of the occupiers; and, in the third place, that possession should be taken of it, not by a vain ceremony, but by actual cultivation, the only mark of property, which, in defect of judicial titles, should be at all respected.

To allow the first occupier a right to as much territory as he may cultivate, and is necessary to his subsistence, is certainly carrying the matter as far as is reasonable. Otherwise we know not how to set bounds to this right. Is it sufficient for a man to set foot on an uninhabited territory, to pretend immediately an exclusive right to it? Is it sufficient for him to have power enough at one time to drive others from the spot, to deprive them for ever afterwards of the right of returning to it? How can a man, or even a whole people, possess themselves of an immense territory, and exclude from it the rest of mankind, without being guilty of an illegal usurpation, since, by so doing, they deprive the rest of mankind of an habitation, and those means of subsistence, which nature hath given in common to them all? When Nunez Balbao stood on the sea-shore, and, in the name of the crown of Castile, took possession of the Pacific Ocean, and of all South America, was this sufficient to dispossess all the inhabitants of that vast country, and exclude all the other sovereigns in the world? On such a supposition, the like idle ceremonies might have been ridiculously multiplied, and his Catholic Majesty would have had no more to do, than to have taken possession in his closet of all the countries in the world, and to have afterwards only deducted from his empire such as were before possessed by other princes.

It is easy to conceive, how the united and contiguous estates of individuals become the territory of the public, and in what manner the right of sovereignty, extending itself from the subjects to the lands they occupy, becomes at once both real and personal; a circumstance which lays the possessors under a state of the greatest dependence, and makes even their own abilities a security for their fidelity. This is an advantage which does not appear to have been duly attended to, by sovereigns among the ancients, who, by stiling themselves only kings of the Persians, the Scythians, the Macedonians, seemed to look on themselves only as chief of men, rather than as masters of a country. Modern princes more artfully stile themselves the kings of England, France, Spain, &c. and thus, by claiming the territory itself, are secure of the inhabitants.

What is very singular in this alienation is, that the community, in accepting the possessions of individuals, is so far from despoiling them thereof, that, on the contrary, it only confirms them in such possessions, by converting an usurpation into an actual right, and a bare possession into a real property. The possessors also being considered as the depositaries of the public wealth, while their rights are respected by all the members of the state, and maintained by all its force against any foreign power, they acquire, if I may so say, by a cession advantageous to the public, and still more so to themselves, every thing they ceded by it: a paradox which is easily explained by the distinction to be made between the rights which the sovereign and the proprietor have in the same fund, as will be seen hereafter.

It may also happen, that men may form themselves into a society, before they have any possessions; and that, acquiring a territory sufficient for all, they may possess it in common, or divide it among them, either equally, or in such different proportions as may be determined by the sovereign. Now, in whatsoever manner such acquisition may be made, the right which each individual has to his own estate, must be always subordinate to the right which the community hath over the possessions of all; for, without this, there would be nothing binding in the social tie, nor any real force in the exercise of the supreme power.

I shall end this book, with a remark, that ought to serve as the basis of the whole social system: and this is, that, instead of annihilating the natural equality among mankind, the fundamental compact substitutes, on the contrary, a moral and legal equality, to make up for that natural and physical difference which prevails among individuals, who, though unequal in personal strength and mental abilities, become thus all equal by convention and right.[2]

That the Sovereignty Is Unalienable

The first and most important consequence to be drawn from the principles already established, is, that the general *will* only can direct the forces of the state agreeable to the end of its original institution, which is the common good; for, though the opposition of private interests might make the establishment of societies necessary, it must have been through the coalition of those interests, that such establishment became possible. The bonds of society must have been formed out of something common to those several interests, for, if there had been no point to which they could have been reconciled, no society could possibly have subsisted. Now it is only on these points that the government of society should be founded.

I say, therefore, that the sovereignty, being only the exertion of the general will, cannot be alienated, and that the sovereign, which is only a collective being, cannot be represented but by itself: the power of a people may be transmitted or delegated, but not their will.

It may not be absolutely impossible, that the will of an individual should agree, in some particular point, with the general will of a whole people; it is, however, impossible, that such agreement should be constant and durable, for the will of particulars always tends to make distinctions of preference,

2. This equality, indeed, is under some governments merely apparent and delusive, serving only to keep the poor still in misery, and favour the oppression of the rich. And, in fact, the laws are always useful to persons of fortune, and hurtful to those who are destitute: whence it follows, that a state of society is advantageous to mankind in general, only when they all possess something, and none of them have anything too much.

and the general will to a perfect equality. It is further still more impossible, supposing such agreement might always subsist, to have any security that it would do so, as it could never be the effect of art, but of chance. The sovereign may say, My will is now agreeable to the will of such an individual, or at least to what he pretends to be his will; but it cannot pretend to say, I agree to whatever may be the will of such individual to morrow; as it is absurd for the will to lay itself under any restraint regarding the future, and as it is impossible for the will to consent to any thing contrary to the interest of the being whose will it is. Should a people therefore enter into the engagement of simply promising obedience, they would lose their quality, as a people, and be virtually dissolved by that very act. The moment there exists a master, there can be no longer a sovereign, the body politic being thereby destroyed.

I would not be understood to mean, that the orders of a chief may not pass for the dictates of the general will, when the sovereign, though at liberty to contradict, does not oppose it. In such a case, it is to be presumed, from the universal silence of the people, that they give their consent. This will be farther explained in the end.

That the Sovereignty Is Indivisible

For the same reason that the sovereignty is unalienable, it is also indivisible; for the will is general,[3] or it is not; it is that of the body of the people, or only that of a part. In the first case, this will, when declared, is an act of sovereignty, and becomes a law: in the second, it is only a particular will, or an act of the magistracy, and is at most a decree.

But our politicians, incapable of dividing the sovereignty in its first principles, divide it in its object; they distinguish it into power and will; into a legislative and executive power; into the prerogatives of taxation, of executing justice, and of making war; into departments of domestic and foreign administration. Sometimes they blend all these confusedly together, and, at others, consider them as distinct and separate, making out the sovereign to be a fantastic compound, just as if they should compose a man out of several bodies, of which one should have only eyes, another arms, a third feet, and nothing more. It is said of the jugglers in Japan, that they will take a child, and cut it into pieces in the presence of the spectators, then, throwing up its dismembered limbs one after

another into the air, they are united, and the child descends alive, and well as before. The legerdemain of our modern politicians greatly resembles this trick of the Japonese; for they, after having dismembered the body politic with equal dexterity, bring all its parts together by *hocus pocus* again, and represent it the same as before.

This error arises from their not having formed precise ideas of the sovereign authority, and from their mistaking the simple emanations of this authority, for parts of its essence. Thus, for instance, the acts of declaring war and making peace are usually regarded as acts of sovereignty, which they are not; for neither of these acts are laws, but consist only of the application of the law. Each is a particular act, determinate only of the meaning of the law in such case, as will be seen more clearly, when the idea attached to the word *law* shall be precisely settled.

By tracing, in like manner, their other divisions, we shall find, that we are constantly mistaken, whenever we think the sovereignty divided; and that the prerogatives, which are supposed to be parts of the sovereignty, are all subordinate to it, and always suppose the predetermination of a superior will, which those prerogatives only serve to put in execution.

It is impossible to say, in how much obscurity this want of precision hath involved the reasonings of authors, on the subject of political law, when they came to examine into the respective rights of kings and people, on the principles they had established. By turning to the third and fourth chapters of the first book of Grotius, the reader may see, how that learned author and his translator, Barbeyrac, bewildered and entangled themselves in their own sophisms, thro' fear of saying too much or too little for their purpose, and of making those interests clash, which it was their business to reconcile. Grotius being dissatisfied with his own countrymen, a refugee in France, and willing to pay his court to Lewis XIII. to whom his book is dedicated, spared no art nor pains to strip the people of their privileges, and to invest kings with prerogative. Barbeyrac also wrote with a similar view, dedicating his translation to George I. of England. But, unluckily, the expulsion of James II. which he calls an abdication, obliged him to be much on the reserve, to turn and wind about, as he saw occasion, in order not to make William III. an usurper. Had these two writers adopted true principles, all these difficulties would have vanished, and they would have written consistently; in such a case, however, they could only, in sober sadness, have told the truth, and would have paid their court only to the people. Now, to tell the

---

3. In order that this will should be general, it is not always necessary it should be unanimous: it is necessary, however, that every individual should be permitted to vote; every formal exclusion infringing the generality.

truth, is not the way to make a fortune; nor are ambassadors appointed, or places and pensions given away by the populace.

Whether the General Will
Can Be in the Wrong

It follows, from what has been said, that the general Will is always in the right, and constantly tends to the public good; it does not follow, however, that the deliberations of the people will always be attended with the same rectitude. We are ever desirous of our own good, but we do not always distinguish in what it consists. A whole people never can be corrupted, but they may be often mistaken, and it is in such a case only that they appear to seek their own disadvantage.

There is often a considerable difference between the will of all the members and the general will of the whole body; the latter regards only the common interest, the other respects the private interest of individuals, and is the aggregated sum of their particular wills; but, if we take from this sum those contradictory wills that mutually destroy each other,[4] the sum of the remaining differences is the general will.

4. *Each interest,* says the Marquis d'A. *has different principles. A coalition between two particular interests may be formed, out of opposition to that of a third.* He might have added, that a coalition of all is formed out of opposition to the interest of each. Were there no different and clashing interests, that of the whole would be hardly distinguishable, as it would meet with no obstacle. All things would go regularly on of their own accord, and civil policy would cease to be an art.

If a people, sufficiently informed of the nature of the subject under their consideration, should deliberate, without having any communication with each other, the general will would always result from the greater number of their little differences, and their deliberation would be such as it ought to be. But when they enter into cabals, and form partial associations, at the expence of the general one, the will of each of these associations becomes general, with regard to the particular members of each, and, in itself, particular, with regard to the state. In such a case, therefore, it may be said, there is no longer as many voters as individuals, but only as many voices as there are associations. The differences then become less numerous, and give a less general result. Again, should one of these partial associations be so great, as to influence all the rest, the result would no longer be the sum of many little differences, but that of one great one; in which case, a general will would no longer subsist.

It is requisite, therefore, in order that each resolution may be dictated by the general will, that no such partial societies should be formed in a state, and that each citizen should think for himself. Such was the sublime institution of the great Lycurgus. But, if such partial societies must and will exist, it is then expedient to multiply their number, and prevent their inequality, as was done by Solon, Numa, and Servius. These are the only salutary precautions that can be taken, in order that the general will may be properly informed, and the people not be mistaken as to their true interest.

9. *Society and Government*

by AUGUSTE COMTE

HAVING NOW ascertained the fundamental position of the problems of political philosophy, and thus obtained guidance as to the scientific aim to be attained, the next step is to exhibit the general spirit of Social Physics, whose conditions we have been deciding.

Reprinted from Auguste Comte, *The Positive Philosophy,* freely translated and condensed by Harriet Martineau (London: George Bell & Sons, 1896), Vol. II, Book VI, chap. iii, pp. 218–32, and chap. v, pp. 275, 280–81, 289–98.

SPIRIT OF SOCIAL SCIENCE.

The philosophical principle of the science being that social phenomena are subject to natural laws, admitting of rational prevision, we have to ascertain what is the precise subject, and what the peculiar character of those laws. The distinction between the Statical and Dynamical conditions of the subject must be extended to social science; and I shall treat of the conditions of social existence as, in biology, I treated of organization under the head of anatomy; and then of the laws of social movement, as in biology of those of life, under the head of physiology. This division, necessary for exploratory purposes, must not be stretched beyond that use: and, as we saw in Biology, that the distinction becomes weaker with the advance of science, so shall we see that when the science of social physics is fully constituted, this division will remain for analytical purposes, but not as a real separation of the science into two parts. The distinction is not between two classes of facts, but between two aspects of a theory. It corresponds with the double conception of order and progress: for order consists (in a positive sense) in a permanent harmony among the conditions of social existence; and progress consists in social development; and the conditions in the one case, and the laws of movement in the other, constitute the statics and dynamics of social physics.—And here we find again the constant relation between the science and the art,—the theory and the practice. A science which proposes a positive study of the laws of order and of progress cannot be charged with speculative rashness by practical men of any intelligence, since it offers the only rational basis for the practical means of satisfying the needs of society, as to order and progress; and the correspondence in this case will be found to be analogous to that which we have seen to exist between biological science and the arts which relate to it,—the medical art especially.—One view of the deepest interest in this connection is that the ideas of order and progress which are in perpetual conflict in existing society, occasioning infinite disturbance, are thus reconciled, and made necessary to each other, becoming as truly inseparable as the ideas of organization and life in the individual being. The further we go in the study of the conditions of human society, the more clearly will the organizing and progressive spirit of the positive philosophy become manifest.

The statistical study of sociology consists in the investigation of the laws of action and reaction of the different parts of the social system,—apart, for the occasion, from the fundamental movement which is always gradually modifying them. In this view, sociological prevision, founded upon the exact general knowledge of those relations, acts by judging by each other the various statical indications of each mode of social existence, in conformity with direct observation,—just as is done daily in the case of anatomy. This view condemns the existing philosophical practice of contemplating social elements separately, as if they had an independent existence; and it leads us to regard them as in mutual relation, and forming a whole

which compels us to treat them in combination. By this method, not only are we furnished with the only possible basis for the study of social movement, but we are put in possession of an important aid to direct observation; since many social elements which cannot be investigated by immediate observation may be estimated by their scientific relation to others already known. When we have a scientific knowledge of the interior relation of the parts of any science or art; and again, of the relations of the sciences to each other: and again, of the relations of arts to their respective sciences, the observation of certain portions of the scheme enables us to pronounce on the state of other portions, with a true philosophical security. The case is the same when, instead of studying the collective social phenomena of a single nation, we include in the study those of contemporary nations, whose reciprocal influence cannot be disputed, though it is much reduced in modern times, and, as in the instance of western Europe and eastern Asia, apparently almost effaced.

SOCIAL ORGANIZATION.

The only essential case in which this fundamental relation is misconceived or neglected is that which is the most important of all,—involving, as it does, social organization, properly so called. The theory of social organization is still conceived of as absolute and isolated, independent altogether of the general analysis of the corresponding civilization, of which it can, in fact, constitute only one of the principle elements. [This vice is chargeable in an almost equal degree upon the most opposite political schools, which agree in abstract discussions of political systems, without thinking of the coexisting state of civilization, and usually conclude with making their immutable political type coincide with an infantile state of human development.] If we ascend to the philosophical source of this error, we shall find it, I think, in the great theological dogma of the Fall of Man. This fundamental dogma, which reappears, in one form or another, in all religions, and which is supported in its intellectual influence by the natural propensity of men to admire the past, tends, directly and necessarily, to make the continuous deterioration of society coincide with the extension of civilization. We have noticed before how, when it passes from the theological into the metaphysical state, this dogma takes the form of the celebrated hypothesis of a chimerical state of nature, superior to the social state, and the more remote, the further we advance in civilization. We cannot fail to perceive the extreme seriousness, in a political as well as a philosophical sense, of an error so completely incorporated with existing doctrines, and so deeply influencing in an unconscious way, our collective social speculations,—the more disastrously perhaps for not being expressly maintained as a general principle.—If it were so presented, it must immediately give way before sound philosophical discussion; for it is in direct contradiction to many ideas in political philosophy which, without having attained any scientific consistency, are obtaining some intellectual ascendancy, through the natural course of events, or the expansion of the general mind. For instance, all enlightened political writers acknowledge more or less mutual relation between political institutions; and this is the first direct step towards the rational conception of the agreement of the special system of institutions with the total system of civilization. We now see the best thinkers admitting a constant mutual connection between the political and the civil power: which means, in scientific language, that preponderating social forces always end in assuming the direction of society. Such partial advances towards a right view,—such fortunate feeling after the right path, must not, however, induce us to relax in our requirements of a true philosophical conception of that general social agreement which can alone constitute organization. Desultory indications, more literary than scientific, can never supply the place of a strict philosophical doctrine, as we may see from the fact that, from Aristotle downwards, (and even from an earlier period,) the greater number of philosophers have constantly reproduced the famous aphorism of the necessary subordination of laws to manners, without this germ of sound philosophy having had any effect on the general habit of regarding institutions as independent of the coexisting state of civilization,—however strange it may seem that such a contradiction should live through twenty centuries. This is, however, the natural course with intellectual principles and philosophical opinions, as well as with social manners and political institutions. When once they have obtained possession of men's minds, they live on, notwithstanding their admitted impotence and inconvenience, giving occasion to more and more serious inconsistencies, till the expansion of human reason originates new principles, of equivalent generality and superior rationality. We must not therefore take for more than their worth the desultory attempts that we see made in the right direction, but must insist on the principle which lies at the heart of every scheme of social organization,—the necessary participation of the collective political *régime* in the universal consensus of the social body.

The scientific principle of the relation between the political and the social condition is simply this;—that there must always be a spontaneous harmony between the whole and the parts of the social system, the elements of which must inevitably be, sooner or later, combined in a mode entirely conformable to their nature. It is evident that not only must political institutions and social manners on the one hand, and manners and ideas on the other, be always mutually connected; but, further, that this consolidated whole must be always connected, by its nature, with the corresponding state of the integral development of humanity, considered in all its aspects, of intellectual, moral, and physical activity: and the only object of any political system whatever, temporal or spiritual, is to regulate the spontaneous expansion so as best to direct it towards its determinate end. Even during revolutionary periods, when the harmony appears furthest from being duly realized, it still exists: for without it there would be a total dissolution of the social organism. During those exceptional seasons, the political *régime* is still, in the long run, in conformity with the corresponding state of civilization, as the disturbances which are manifest in the one proceed from equivalent derangements in the other. It is observable that when the popular theory attributes to the legislator the permanent power of infringing the harmony we are speaking of, it supposes him to be armed with a sufficient authority. But every social power, whether called authority or anything else, is constituted by a corresponding assent, spontaneous or deliberate, explicit or implicit, of various individual wills, resolved, from certain preparatory convictions, to concur in a common action, of which this power is first the organ, and then the regulator. Thus, authority is derived from concurrence, and not concurrence from authority, (setting aside the necessary reaction:) so that no great power can arise otherwise than from the strongly prevalent disposition of the society in which it exists: and when there is no strong preponderance, such powers as exist are weak accordingly: and the more extensive the society, the more irresistible is the correspondence. On the other hand, there is no denying the influence which, by a necessary reaction, the political system, as a whole, exercises over the general system of civilization, and which is so often exhibited in the action, fortunate or disastrous, of institutions, measures, or purely political events, even upon the course of the sciences and arts, in all ages of society, and especially the earliest. We need not dwell on this; for no one denies it. The common error, indeed, is to exaggerate it, so as to place the reaction before the primary action. It is evident, considering their scientific relation to each other, that both concur in creating that fundamental agreement of the social organism which I propose to set forth in a brief manner, as the philosophical principle of statical sociology. We shall have to advert repeatedly to the subject of the general correspondence between the political *régime* and the contemporary state of civilization, in connection with the question of the necessary limits of political action, and in the chapter which I must devote to social statics: but I did not think fit to wait for these explanations before pointing out that the political system ought always to be regarded as relative. The relative point of view, substituted for the absolute tendency of the ordinary theories, certainly constitutes the chief scientific character of the positive philosophy in its political application. If, on the one hand, the conception of this connection between government and civilization presents all ideas of political good or evil as necessarily relative and variable (which is quite another thing than being arbitrary), on the other hand, it provides a rational basis for a positive theory of the spontaneous order of human society, already vaguely perceived, in regard to some minor relations, by that part of the metaphysical polity which we call political economy; for, if the value of any political system can consist in nothing but its harmony with the corresponding social state, it follows that in the natural course of events, and in the absence of intervention, such a harmony must necessarily be established.

INTERCONNECTION OF THE SOCIAL ORGANISM.

There are two principal considerations which induce me to insist on this elementary idea of the radical consensus proper to the social organism: first, the extreme philosophical importance of this master-thought of social statics, which must, from its nature, constitute the rational basis of any new political philosophy; and, secondly, in an accessory way, that dynamical considerations of sociology must prevail throughout the rest of this work, as being at present more interesting, and therefore better understood; and it is, on that account, the more necessary to characterize now the general spirit of social statics, which will henceforth be treated only in an indirect and implicit way. As all artificial and voluntary order is simply a prolongation of the natural and involuntary order to which all human society tends, every rational political institution must rest upon an exact preparatory analysis of corresponding spontaneous tendencies, which alone can furnish a sufficiently solid basis. In brief, it is our business to contemplate order, that we may perfect it; and not to create it; which would be impossible. In a scientific

view, this master-thought of universal social interconnection becomes the consequence and complement of a fundamental idea established, in our view of biology, as eminently proper to the study of living bodies. Not that this idea of interconnection is peculiar to that study: it is necessarily common to all phenomena; but amidst immense differences in intensity and variety, and therefore in philosophical importance. It is, in fact, true that wherever there is any system whatever, a certain interconnection must exist. The purely mechanical phenomena of astronomy offer the first suggestion of it; for the perturbations of one planet may sensibly affect another, through a modified gravitation. But the relation becomes closer and more marked in proportion to the complexity and diminished generality of the phenomena, and thus, it is in organic systems that we must look for the fullest mutual connection. Hitherto, it had been merely an accessory idea; but then it becomes the basis of positive conceptions; and it becomes more marked, the more compound are the organisms, and the more complex the phenomena in question, —the animal interconnection being more complete than the vegetable, and the human more than the brute; the nervous system being the chief seat of the biological interconnection. The idea must therefore be scientifically preponderant in social physics, even more than in biology, where it is so decisively recognized by the best order of students. But the existing political philosophy supposes the absence of any such interconnection among the aspects of society: and it is this which has rendered it necessary for me now to establish the point,— leaving the illustration of it to a future portion of the volume. Its consideration is, in fact, as indispensable in assigning its encyclopædic rank to social science as we before saw it to be in instituting Social Physics a science at all.

It follows from this attribute that there can be no scientific study of society, either in its conditions or its movements, if it is separated into portions, and its divisions are studied apart. I have already remarked upon this, in regard to what is called political economy. Materials may be furnished by the observation of different departments; and such observation may be necessary for that object: but it cannot be called science. The methodical division of studies which takes place in the simple inorganic sciences is thoroughly irrational in the recent and complex science of society, and can produce no results. The day may come when some sort of subdivision may be practicable and desirable; but it is impossible for us now to anticipate what the principle of distribution may be; for the principle itself must arise from the development of the science; and that development can take place no otherwise than by our formation of the science as a whole. The complete body will indicate for itself, at the right season, the particular points which need investigation; and then will be the time for such special study as may be required. By any other method of proceeding, we shall only find ourselves encumbered with special discussions, badly instituted, worse pursued, and accomplishing no other purpose than that of impeding the formation of real science. It is no easy matter to study social phenomena in the only right way,—viewing each element in the light of the whole system. It is no easy matter to exercise such vigilance as that no one of the number of contemporary aspects shall be lost sight of. But it is the right and the only way; and we may perceive in it a clear suggestion that this lofty study should be reserved for the highest order of scientific minds, better prepared than others, by wise educational discipline, for sustained speculative efforts, aided by an habitual subordination of the passions to the reason. There is no need to draw out any lengthened comparison between this state of things as it should be and that which is. And no existing degree of social disturbance can surprise us when we consider how intellectual anarchy is at the bottom of such disturbance, and see how anarchical our intellectual condition appears in the presence of the principle I have laid down.

ORDER OF STATICAL STUDY.

Before we go on to the subject of social dynamics, I will just remark that the prominent interconnection we have been considering prescribes a procedure in organic studies different from that which suits inorganic. The metaphysicians announce as an aphorism that we should always, in every kind of study, proceed from the simple to the compound: whereas, it appears most rational to suppose that we should follow that or the reverse method, as may best suit our subject. There can be no absolute merit in the method enjoined, apart from its suitableness. The rule should rather be (and there probably was a time when the two rules were one) that we must proceed from the more known to the less. Now, in the inorganic sciences, the elements are much better known to us than the whole which they constitute: so that in that case we must proceed from the simple to the compound. But the reverse method is necessary in the study of Man and of Society; Man and Society as a whole being better known to us, and more accessible subjects of study, than the parts which constitute them. In exploring the universe, it is as a whole that it is inaccessible to us; whereas, in

investigating Man or Society, our difficulty is in penetrating the details. We have seen, in our survey of biology, that the general idea of animal nature is more distinct to our minds than the simpler notion of vegetable nature; and that man is the biological unity; the idea of Man being at once the most compound, and the starting-point of speculation in regard to vital existence. Thus, if we compare the two halves of natural philosophy, we shall find that in the one case it is the last degree of composition, and, in the other, the last degree of simplicity, that is beyond the scope of our research. As for the rest, it may obviate some danger of idle discussion to say that the positive philosophy, subordinating all fancies to reality, excludes logical controversies about the absolute value of this or that method, apart from its scientific application. The only ground of preference being the superior adaptation of any means to the proposed end, this philosophy may, without any inconsistency, change its order of proceeding when the one first tried is found to be inferior to its converse:—a discovery of which there is no fear in regard to the question we have now been examining.

DYNAMICAL STUDY.

Passing on from statical to dynamical sociology, we will contemplate the philosophical conception which should govern our study of the movement of society. Part of this subject is already despatched, from the explanations made in connection with statics having simplified the chief difficulties of the case. And social dynamics will be so prominent throughout the rest of this work, that I may reduce within very small compass what I have to say now under that head.

Though the statical view of society is the basis of sociology, the dynamical view is not only the more interesting of the two, but the more marked in its philosophical character, from its being more distinguished from biology by the master-thought of continuous progress, or rather, of the gradual development of humanity. If I were writing a methodical treatise on political philosophy, it would be necessary to offer a preliminary analysis of the individual impulsions which make up the progressive force of the human race, by referring them to that instinct which results from the concurrence of all our natural tendencies, and which urges man to develop the whole of his life, physical, moral, and intellectual, as far as his circumstances allow. But this view is admitted by all enlightened philosophers; so that I must proceed at once to consider the continuous succession of human development, regarded in the whole race, as if humanity were one. For clearness, we may take advantage of Condorcet's device of supposing a single nation to which we may refer all the consecutive social modifications actually witnessed among distinct peoples. This rational fiction is nearer the reality than we are accustomed to suppose; for, in a political view, the true successors of such or such a people are certainly those who, taking up and carrying out their primitive endeavours, have prolonged their social progress, whatever may be the soil which they inhabit, or even the race from which they spring. In brief, it is political continuity which regulates sociological succession, though the having a common country must usually affect this continuity in a high degree. As a scientific artifice merely, however, I shall employ this hypothesis, and on the ground of its manifest utility.

SOCIAL CONTINUITY.

The true general spirit of social dynamics then consists in conceiving of each of these consecutive social states as the necessary result of the preceding, and the indispensable mover of the following, according to the axiom of Leibnitz,—*the present is big with the future*. In this view, the object of science is to discover the laws which govern this continuity, and the aggregate of which determines the course of human development. In short, social dynamics studies the laws of succession, while social statics inquires into those of co-existence; so that the use of the first is to furnish the true theory of progress to political practice, while the second performs the same service in regard to order; and this suitability to the needs of modern society is a strong confirmation of the philosophical character of such a combination.

PRODUCED BY NATURAL LAWS.

If the existence of sociological laws has been established in the more difficult and uncertain case of the statical condition, we may assume that they will not be questioned in the dynamical province. In all times and places, the ordinary course of even our brief individual life has disclosed certain remarkable modifications which have occurred, in various ways, in the social state; and all the most ancient representations of human life bear unconscious and most interesting testimony to this, apart from all systematic estimate of the fact. Now it is the slow, continuous accumulation of these successive changes which gradually constitutes the social movement, whose steps are ordinarily marked by generations, as the most appreciable elementary variations are wrought by the constant renewal of adults. At a time when the average

rapidity of this progression seems to all eyes to be remarkably accelerated, the reality of the movement cannot be disputed, even by those who most abhor it. The only question is about the constant subjection of these great dynamical phenomena to invariable natural laws, a proposition about which there is no question to any one who takes his stand on positive philosophy. It is easy however to establish, from any point of view, that the successive modifications of society have always taken place in a determinate order, the rational explanation of which is already possible in so many cases that we may confidently hope to recognize it ultimately in all the rest. So remarkable is the steadiness of this order, moreover, that it exhibits an exact parallelism of development among distinct and independent populations, as we shall see when we come to the historical portion of this volume. Since, then, the existence of the social movement is unquestionable, on the one hand, and, on the other, the succession of social states is never arbitrary, we cannot but regard this continuous phenomenon as subject to natural laws as positive as those which govern all other phenomena, though more complex. There is in fact no intellectual alternative; and thus it is evident that it is on the ground of social science that the great conflict must soon terminate which has gone on for three centuries between the positive and the theologico-metaphysical spirit. Banished for ever from all other classes of speculation, in principle at least, the old philosophies now prevail in social science alone; and it is from this domain that they have to be excluded, by the conception of the social movement being subject to invariable natural laws, instead of to any will whatever.

Though the fundamental laws of social interconnection are especially verified in this condition of movement, and though there is a necessary unity in this phenomenon, it may be usefully applied, for preparatory purposes, to the separate elementary aspects of human existence, physical, moral, intellectual and, finally, political,—their mutual relation being kept in view. Now, in whichever of these ways we regard, as a whole, the movement of humanity, from the earliest periods till now, we shall find that the various steps are connected in a determinate order; as we shall hereafter see, when we investigate the laws of this succession. I need refer here only to the intellectual evolution, which is the most distinct and unquestionable of all, as it has been the least impeded and most advanced of any, and has therefore been usually taken for guidance. The chief part of this evolution, and that which has most influenced the general progression, is no doubt the development of the scientific spirit, from the primitive labours of such philosophers as Thales and Pythagoras to those of men like Lagrange and Bichat. Now, no enlightened man can doubt that, in this long succession of efforts and discoveries, the human mind has pursued a determinate course, the exact preparatory knowledge of which might have allowed a cultivated reason to foresee the progress proper to each period. Though the historical considerations cited in my former volume were only incidental, any one may recognize in them numerous and indisputable examples of this necessary succession, more complex perhaps, but not more arbitrary than any natural law, whether in regard to the development of each separate science, or to the mutual influence of the different branches of natural philosophy. In accordance with the principles laid down at the beginning of this work, we have already seen in various signal instances, that the chief progress of each period, and even of each generation, was a necessary result of the immediately preceding state; so that the men of genius, to whom such progression has been too exclusively attributed, are essentially only the proper organs of a predetermined movement, which would, in their absence, have found other issues. We find a verification of this in history, which shows that various eminent men were ready to make the same great discovery at the same time, while the discovery required only one organ. All the parts of the human evolution admit of analogous observations, as we shall presently see, though they are more complex and less obvious than that which I have just cited. The natural progression of the arts of life is abundantly evident; and in our direct study of social dynamics we shall find an explanation of the apparent exception of the fine arts, which will be found to oppose no contradiction to the general course of human progression. As to that part of the movement which appears at present to be least reducible to natural laws, the political movement (still supposed to be governed by wills of adequate power), it is clear as in any other case that political systems have exhibited an historical succession, according to a traceable filiation, in a determinate order, which I am prepared to show to be even more inevitable than that of the different states of human intelligence.

The interconnection which we have examined and established in a statical view may aid us in developing the conception of the existence of positive laws in social dynamics. Unless the movement was determined by those laws, it would occasion the entire destruction of the social system. Now, that interconnection simplifies and strengthens the preparatory indications of dynamic order; for,

when it has once been shown in any relation, we are authorized to extend it to all others; and this unites all the partial proofs that we can successively obtain of the reality of this scientific conception. In the choice and the application of these verifications, we must remember that the laws of social dynamics are most recognizable when they relate to the largest societies, in which secondary disturbances have the smallest effect. Again, these fundamental laws become the more irresistible, and therefore the more appreciable, in proportion to the advancement of the civilization upon which they operate, because the social movement becomes more distinct and certain with every conquest over accidental influences. As for the philosophical co-ordination of these preparatory evidences, the combination of which is important to science, it is clear that the social evolution must be more inevitably subject to natural laws, the more compound are the phenomena, and the less perceptible therefore the irregularities which arise from individual influences. This shows how inconsistent it is, for instance, to suppose the scientific movement to be subject to positive laws, while the political movement is regarded as arbitrary; for the latter, being more composite, must overrule individual disturbances, and be therefore more evidently predetermined than the former, in which individual genius must have more power. Any paradoxical appearance which this statement may exhibit will disappear in the course of further examination.

* * *

THREE ASPECTS.

Every sociological analysis supposes three classes of considerations, each more complex than the preceding: viz., the conditions of social existence of the individual, the family, and society; the last comprehending, in a scientific sense, the whole of the human species, and chiefly, the whole of the white race. . . .

* * *

THE FAMILY.

As every system must be composed of elements of the same nature with itself, the scientific spirit forbids us to regard society as composed of individuals. The true social unit is certainly the family,—reduced, if necessary, to the elementary couple which forms its basis. This consideration implies more than the physiological truth that families become tribes, and tribes become nations: so that the whole human race might be conceived of as the gradual development of a single family, if local diversities did not forbid such a supposition. There is a political point of view from which also we must consider this elementary idea, inasmuch as the family presents the true germ of the various characteristics of the social· organism. Such a conception is intermediate between the idea of the individual and that of the species, or society. There would be as many scientific inconveniences in passing it over in a speculative sense as there are dangers in practice in pretending to treat of social life without the inevitable preparation of the domestic life. Whichever way we look at it, this necessary transition always presents itself, whether in regard to elementary notions of fundamental harmony, or for the spontaneous rise of social sentiment. It is by this avenue that Man comes forth from his mere personality, and learns to live in another, while obeying his most powerful instincts. . . .

*　　*　　*

SOCIETY.

The third head of our statical analysis brings us to the consideration of society, as composed of families and not of individuals, and from a point of view which commands all times and places.

The main cause of the superiority of the social to the individual organism is, according to an established law, the more marked speciality of the various functions fulfilled by organs more and more distinct, but interconnected; so that unity of aim is more and more combined with diversity of means. We cannot, of course, fully appreciate a phenomenon which is for ever proceeding before our eyes, and in which we bear a part; but if we withdraw ourselves in thought from the social system, and contemplate it as from afar, can we conceive of a more marvellous spectacle, in the whole range of natural phenomena, than the regular and constant convergence of an innumerable multitude of human beings, each possessing a distinct and, in a certain degree, independent existence, and yet incessantly disposed, amidst all their discordance of talent and character, to occur in many ways in the same general development, without concert, and even consciousness on the part of most of them, who believe that they are merely following their personal impulses? This is the scientific picture of the phenomenon: and no temporary disturbances can prevent its being, under all circumstances, essentially true. This reconciliation of the individuality of labour with co-operation of endeavours, which becomes more remarkable as society grows more complex and extended, constitutes the radical character of human operations

when we rise from the domestic to the social point of view. The degree of association that we observe among the superior animals has something voluntary in it, but there is no organization which can make it resemble the human: and the first individual specializing of common functions is seen in our simple domestic life, which is thus a type of the social organization. The division of labour can never, however, be very marked in the family, because the members are few; and yet more because such a division would soon show itself to be hostile to the spirit of the institution; for domestic training, being founded on imitation, must dispose the children to follow parental employments, instead of undertaking new ones: and again, any very marked separation in the employments of the members must impair the domestic unity which is the aim of the association. The more we look into the subject, the more we shall see that the appropriation of employments, which is the elementary principle of general society, cannot hold anything like so important a place in the family. In fact, the domestic relations do not constitute an association, but a *union,* in the full force of the term; and, on account of this close intimacy, the domestic connection is of a totally different nature from the social. Its character is essentially moral, and only incidentally intellectual; or, in anatomical language, it corresponds more to the middle than to the anterior part of the brain. Founded chiefly upon attachment and gratitude, the domestic union satisfies, by its mere existence, all our sympathetic instincts, quite apart from all idea of active and continuous co-operation towards any end, unless it be that of its own institution. Though more or less co-ordination of different employments must exist, it is so secondary an affair that when, unhappily, it remains the only principle of connection, the domestic union degenerates into mere association, and is even too likely to dissolve altogether. In society the elementary economy presents an inverse character, the sentiment of co-operation becoming preponderant, and the sympathetic instinct, without losing its steadiness, becoming secondary. No doubt there are a multitude of men well enough organized to love their fellow-labourers, however numerous or remote they may be, and however indirect may be their co-operation; but such a sentiment, arising from the reaction of the reason upon the social feelings, could never be strong enough to guide social life. Even under the best circumstances the intellectual mediocrity of the majority of men does not allow them to form any distinct idea of relations which are too extensive, too indirect, and too foreign to their own occupations to impart any sympathetic stimulus which could be of permanent use. It is only in domestic life that Man can habitually seek the full and free expansion of his social affections; and perhaps this is the chief reason why it is the last indispensable preparation for social life; for concentration is as necessary to the feelings as generalization to the thoughts. Even the most eminent men, who direct their sympathetic instincts upon their race at large or the society in which they live, are usually impelled to this by the moral disappointments of a domestic life which has failed in some of its conditions; and however genial the imperfect compensation may be to them, this abstract love of their species admits of nothing like that satisfaction of the affections which arises from a very limited, and especially an individual attachment. However this may be, such cases are besides too evidently exceptional to affect any inquiry into the social economy. Thus, though the sympathetic instinct exists wherever there is association, more or less, the principle of co-operation is that which must prevail, when we pass on from the consideration of the family to the general co-ordination of families. To attribute to it the formation of the social state, as it was the fashion of the last century to do, is a capital error; but, when the association has once begun, there is nothing like this principle of co-operation for giving consistency and character to the combination. In the lower stages of savage life we see families combining for a temporary purpose, and then returning, almost like the brutes, to their isolated independence, as soon as the expedition, which is usually one of war or the chase, is ended, though already some common opinions, expressed in a certain uniform language, are preparing them for permanent union in tribes, more or less numerous. It is upon the principle of co-operation, then, spontaneous or concerted, that we must found our analysis of the last division of social statics.

DISTRIBUTION OF DEVELOPMENTS.

We must include in our view of the division of employments something much more extensive than the material arrangements which the expression is usually understood to convey. We must include under it all human operations whatever, regarding not only individuals and classes, but also, in many ways, different nations, as participating in a special mode and degree, in a vast common work, the gradual development of which connects the fellow-labourers with the whole series of their predecessors, and even with their successors. This is what is meant when we speak of the race being bound up together by the very distribution of their occupations; and it is this distribution which causes

the extent and growing complexity of the social organism, which thus appears as comprising the whole of the human race. Man can hardly exist in a solitary state: the family can exist in isolation, because it can divide its employments and provide for its wants in a rough kind of way: a spontaneous approximation of families is incessantly exposed to temporary rupture, occasioned by the most trifling incidents. But when a regular division of employments has spread through any society, the social state begins to acquire a consistency and stability which place it out of danger from particular divergencies. The habit of partial co-operation convinces each family of its close dependence on the rest, and, at the same time, of its own importance, each one being then justified in regarding itself as fulfilling a real public function, more or less indispensable to the general economy, but inseparable from the system as a whole. In this view the social organization tends more and more to rest on an exact estimate of individual diversities, by so distributing employments as to appoint each one to the destination he is most fit for, from his own nature (which however is seldom very distinctly marked), from his education and his position, and, in short, from all his qualifications; so that all individual organizations, even the most vicious and imperfect (short of monstrosity), may be finally made use of for the general good. Such is, at least, the social type which we conceive of as the limit of the existing social order, and to which we may be for ever approximating, though without the hope of ever attaining it; and it is, in fact, a reproduction, with a large extension, of the domestic organism, with less power, in proportion to its extent, of appointing a due destination to every member; so that the social discipline must always be more artificial, and therefore more imperfect, than the domestic, which nature herself ordains and administers.

The necessities of this co-ordination and distribution of special offices, cause inconvenience which I am compelled to advert to; for it is in the investigation of these that we find the scientific germ of the relation between the idea of society and that of government.

INCONVENIENCES.

Some economists have pointed out, but in a very inadequate way, the evils of an exaggerated division of material labour; and I have indicated, in regard to the more important field of scientific labour, the mischievous intellectual consequences of the spirit of speciality which at present prevails. It is necessary to estimate directly the principle of such an influence, in order to understand the object of the spontaneous system of requisites for the continuous preservation of society. In decomposing, we always disperse; and the distribution of human labours must occasion individual divergencies, both intellectual and moral, which require a permanent discipline to keep them within bounds. If the separation of social functions develops a useful spirit of detail, on the one hand, it tends, on the other, to extinguish or to restrict what we may call the aggregate or general spirit. In the same way, in moral relations, while each individual is in close dependence on the mass, he is drawn away from it by the expansion of his special activity, constantly recalling him to his private interest, which he but very dimly perceives to be related to the public. On both grounds the inconveniences of the division of functions increase with its characteristic advantages, without their being in the same relation, throughout the spontaneous course of the social evolution. The growing speciality of habitual ideas and familiar relations must tend to restrict the understanding more and more, while sharpening it in a certain direction, and to sever more and more the private interest from a public interest which is for ever becoming more vague and indirect; while, at the same time, the social affections, gradually concentrated among individuals of the same profession, become more and more alienated from all other classes, for want of a sufficient analogy of ways and ideas. Thus it is that the principle by which alone general society could be developed and extended, threatens, in another view, to decompose it into a multitude of unconnected corporations, which almost seem not to belong to the same species; and hence it is that the gradual expansion of human ability seems destined to produce such minds as are very common among civilized peoples, and prodigiously admired by them,—minds which are very able in some one respect and monstrously incapable in all others. If we have been accustomed to deplore the spectacle, among the artisan class of a workman occupied during his whole life in nothing else but making knife-handles or pins' heads, we may find something quite as lamentable in the intellectual class, in the exclusive employment of a human brain in resolving some equations, or in classifying insects. The moral effect is, unhappily, analogous in the two cases. It occasions a miserable indifference about the general course of human affairs, as long as there are equations to resolve and pins to manufacture. This is an extreme case of human automatism; but the frequency, and the growing frequency, of the evil gives a real scientific importance to the case, as indicating the general tendency, and warning us to restrain it. Thus

it appears to me that the social destination of government is to guard against and restrain the fundamental dispersion of ideas, sentiments, and interests, which is the inevitable result of the very principle of human development, and which, if left to itself, would put a stop to social progression in all important respects.

BASIS OF THE TRUE THEORY OF GOVERNMENT.

Here we have, in my opinion, the basis of the elementary and abstract theory of government, regarded in its complete scientific extension; that is, as characterized by the universal necessary reaction,—first spontaneous and then regulated,—of the whole upon the parts. It is clear that the only way of preventing such a dispersion is by setting up this reaction as a new special function, which shall intervene in the performance of all the various functions of the social economy, to keep up the idea of the whole, and the feeling of the common interconnection: and the more energetically, the more individual activity tends to dissolve them. Not itself affecting any determinate social progress, it contributes to all that society can achieve, in any direction whatever, and which society could not achieve without its concentrating and protective care. The very nature of its action indicates that it cannot be merely material, but also, and much more, intellectual and moral; so as to show the double necessity of what has been called the temporal and spiritual government, the rational subordination of which was the best feature of the social organization that was happily effected in its day, under the influence of the prevalent Catholicism. Moreover, this ruling function must become more, instead of less necessary, as human development proceeds, because its essential principle is inseparable from that of the development itself.—Thus, it is the habitual predominance of the spirit of the whole which constitutes government, in whatever way it is regarded. The next consideration is, how such an action arises, independently of all systematic combination, in the natural course of the social economy.

ELEMENTARY SUBORDINATION.

If the dispersive tendency arising from the distribution of functions naturally propagates itself, it is clear that any influence capable of neutralizing it must also be constantly expanding. In fact, an elementary subordination must always be growing out of the distribution of human operations, which gives birth to government, in the bosom of society itself, as we could easily discover by analyzing any marked subdivision which has just taken place in any employment whatever. This subordination is not only material, but yet more intellectual and moral; that is, it requires, besides practical submission, a corresponding degree of real confidence in both the capacity and the probity of the special organs to whom a function, hitherto universal, is confided. Every one of us relies, even for life itself, on the aptitude and the morality of a multitude of almost unknown agents, whose folly or wickedness might affect the welfare of vast numbers of human beings. Such a condition belongs to all modes of social existence. If it is especially attributed to industrial societies, it is only because it must be most conspicuous where the division of labour goes furthest; and it is as certainly to be found in purely military societies; as the statical analysis of an army, a man-of-war, or any other active corporation shows in a moment.

This elementary subordination discloses its own law; which is, that the various operations in which individuals are engaged fall naturally under the direction of those which are next above them in generality. We may easily convince ourselves of this by analysing any special occupation at the moment when it assumes a separate character: because the task thus separated is necessarily more special than the function from which it proceeds, and to which its own fulfilment must be subordinated. This is not the occasion on which to expatiate on this law; but its political bearing concerns us here, —indicating as it does the germ of a true classification of social functions. We shall hereafter meet with a full verification of this law in regard to the industrial life of modern societies: the eminent regularity of military associations renders the law obvious at once; and when the law is once admitted, it discloses the spontaneous connection of this elementary social subordination with that political subordination, properly so called, which is the basis of government, and which presents itself as the last degree in the hierarchy formed by the subjection of the more special to the more general classes of phenomena. For, as the various particular functions of the social economy are naturally implicated in relations of greater generality, all must at length be subject to the direction of the most general function of all, which is characterized, as we have seen, by the constant action of the whole upon the parts. On the other hand, the organs of this direction must be much strengthened by the encouragement afforded to intellectual and moral inequality under a system of division of employments. It is clear that while men were obliged to do everything for themselves, they must have been confined to domestic life, devoting all their activity to supply the wants of the family; and there could be little expansion of individual ability and character. Though marked individuality must always have made itself felt, in every state of society, the division of labour, and the leisure which it brings, have been needful to the conspicuous development of that intellectual superiority on which all political ascendancy must mainly rest. We must observe, moreover, that there can be no such division of intellectual as of material labour; so that the intellectual functions must be less affected than the industrial by the dispersive tendencies of such a division. We are familiar with the effect of civilization in developing moral, and yet more, intellectual inequalities; but we must bear in mind that moral and intellectual forces do not admit, like the physical, of being accumulated and compounded: so that, eminently as they can occur, and clearly as they are the creators of social concurrence, they are much less adapted for direct cooperation. A sufficient coalition of the most insignificant individuals can easily carry any point of physical conflict, or of acquisition of wealth, against the highest superiority in an individual or a family; so that, for example, the most enormous private fortune cannot sustain any competition with the financial power of a nation, whose treasury is filled by a multitude of the smallest contributions. But, on the contrary, if the enterprise depends on a high intellectual power, as in the case of a great scientific or poetical conception, there can be no association of ordinary minds, however extensive, which can compete with a Descartes or a Shakspere. It is the same in the moral case; as, for instance, if society is in need of any great resource of devotedness, the want cannot be supplied by accumulating any amount of moderate zeal furnished by individuals. The only use of a multitude in such a case is that it improves the chance of finding the *unique* organ of the proposed function; and when that singular agent is once found, there is no degree of multitude which can weigh down its preponderance. It is through this privilege that intellectual and moral forces tend to an ever-increasing social authority, from the time when a due division of employments admits of their proper development.

TENDENCY OF SOCIETY TO GOVERNMENT.

Such is, then, the elementary tendency of all human society to a spontaneous government. This tendency accords with a corresponding system, inherent in us as individuals, of special dispositions towards command in some, and towards obedience in others. We must not, with regard to the first, confound the desire to rule with the fitness to do so; though the desire is one element of the fitness:

and, on the other hand, there is a much stronger inclination to obedience in the generality of men than it is customary in our day to suppose. If men were as rebellious as they are at present represented, it would be difficult to understand how they could ever have been disciplined: and it is certain that we are all more or less disposed to respect any superiority, especially any intellectual or moral elevation, in our neighbours, independently of any view to our own advantage: and this instinct of submission is, in truth, only too often lavished on deceptive appearances. However excessive the desire of command may be in our revolutionary day, there can be no one who, in his secret mind, has not often felt, more or less vividly, how sweet it is to obey when he can have the rare privilege of consigning the burdensome responsibility of his general self-conduct to wise and trustworthy guidance: and probably the sense of this is strongest in those who are best fitted for command. In the midst of political convulsion, when the spirit of revolutionary destruction is abroad, the mass of the people manifest a scrupulous obedience towards the intellectual and moral guides from whom they accept direction, and upon whom they may even press a temporary dictatorship, in their primary and urgent need of a preponderant authority. Thus do individual dispositions show themselves to be in harmony with the course of social relations as a whole, in teaching us that political subordination is as inevitable, generally speaking, as it is indispensable. And this completes the elementary delineation of Social Statics.

My sketch has perhaps been so abstract and condensed that the conceptions of this chapter may appear obscure at present; but light will fall upon them as we proceed. We may already see, however, the practical advantage which arises from the scientific evolution of human relations. The individual life, ruled by personal instincts; the domestic, by sympathetic instincts; and the social, by the special development of intellectual influences, prepare for the states of human existence which are to follow: and that which ensues is, first, personal morality, which subjects the preservation of the individual to a wise discipline; next, domestic morality, which subordinates selfishness to sympathy; and lastly, social morality, which directs all dividual tendencies by enlightened reason, always having the general economy in view, so as to bring into concurrence all the faculties of human nature, according to their appropriate laws.

10. The Material Forces and the Relations of Production

BY KARL MARX

THE SUBJECT of our discussion is first of all *material* production by individuals as determined by society, naturally constitutes the starting point. The individual and isolated hunter or fisher who forms the starting point with Smith and Ricardo, belongs to the insipid illusions of the eighteenth century. They are Robinsonades which do not by any means represent, as students of the history of civilization imagine, a reaction against over-refinement and a return to a misunderstood natural life. They are no more based on such a naturalism than is Rousseau's "contrat social," which makes naturally independent individuals come in contact and have mutual intercourse by contract. They are the fiction and only the æsthetic fiction of the small and great Robinsonades. They are, moreover, the anticipation of "bourgeois society," which had been in course of development since the sixteenth century and made gigantic strides towards maturity in the eighteenth. In this society of free competition the individual appears free from the bonds of nature, etc., which in former epochs of history made him a part of a definite, limited human conglomeration. To the prophets of the eighteenth century, on whose shoulders Smith and Ricardo are still standing, this eighteenth century individual, constituting the joint product of the dissolution of the feudal form of society and of the new forces of production which had developed since the sixteenth century, appears

Reprinted from Karl Marx, *A Contribution to the Critique of Political Economy*, Trans. N. I. Stone, from the 2d German ed. (New York: International Library Publishing Co., 1904), Appendix, secs. 1, 2, pp. 265–69, 291–92, Author's Preface, pp. 11–13.

as an ideal whose existence belongs to the past; not as a result of history, but as its starting point.

Since that individual appeared to be in conformity with nature and [corresponded] to their conception of human nature, [he was regarded] not as a product of history, but of nature. This illusion has been characteristic of every new epoch in the past. Steuart, who, as an aristocrat, stood more firmly on historical ground, contrary to the spirit of the eighteenth century, escaped this simplicity of view. The further back we go into history, the more the individual and, therefore, the producing individual seems to depend on and constitute a part of a larger whole: at first it is, quite naturally, the family and the clan, which is but an enlarged family; later on, it is the community growing up in its different forms out of the clash and the amalgamation of clans. It is but in the eighteenth century, in "bourgeois society," that the different forms of social union confront the individual as a mere means to his private ends, as an outward necessity. But the period in which this view of the isolated individual becomes prevalent, is the very one in which the inter-relations of society (general from this point of view) have reached the highest state of development. Man is in the most literal sense of the word a *zoon politikon* not only a social animal, but an animal which can develop into an individual only in society. Production by isolated individuals outside of society—something which might happen as an exception to a civilized man who by accident got into the wilderness and already dynamically possessed within himself the forces of society—is as great an absurdity as the idea of the development of language without individuals living together and talking to one another. We need not dwell on this any longer. It would not be necessary to touch upon this point at all, were not the vagary which had its justification and sense with the people of the eighteenth century transplanted in all earnest into the field of political economy by Bastiat, Carey, Proudhon and others. Proudhon and others naturally find it very pleasant, when they do not know the historical origin of a certain economic phenomenon, to give it a quasi historical-philosophical explanation by going into mythology. Adam or Prometheus hit upon the scheme cut and dried, whereupon it was adopted, etc. Nothing is more tediously dry than the dreaming *locus communis*.

Whenever we speak, therefore, of production, we always have in mind production at a certain stage of social development, or production by social individuals. Hence, it might seem that in order to speak of production at all, we must either trace the historical process of development through its various phases, or declare at the outset that we are dealing with a certain historical period, as, e.g., with modern capitalistic production which, as a matter of fact, constitutes the subject proper of this work. But all stages of production have certain landmarks in common, common purposes. *Production in general* is an abstraction, but it is a rational abstraction, in so far as it singles out and fixes the common features, thereby saving us repetition. Yet these general or common features discovered by comparison constitute something very complex, whose constituent elements have different destinations. Some of these elements belong to all epochs, others are common to a few. Some of them are common to the most modern as well as to the most ancient epochs. No production is conceivable without them; but while even the most completely developed languages have laws and conditions in common with the least developed ones, what is characteristic of their development are the points of departure from the general and common. The conditions which generally govern production must be differentiated in order that the essential points of difference be not lost sight of in view of the general uniformity which is due to the fact that the subject, mankind, and the object, nature, remain the same. The failure to remember this one fact is the source of all the wisdom of modern economists who are trying to prove the eternal nature and harmony of existing social conditions.

*   *   *

The result we arrive at is not that production, distribution, exchange, and consumption are identical, but that they are all members of one entity, different sides of one unit. Production predominates not only over production itself in the opposite sense of that term, but over the other elements as well. With it the process constantly starts over again. That exchange and consumption can not be the predominating elements is self evident. The same is true of distribution in the narrow sense of distribution of products; as for distribution in the sense of distribution of the agents of production, it is itself but a factor of production. A definite [form of] production thus determines the [forms of] consumption, distribution, exchange, and *also the mutual relations between these various elements*. Of course, production *in its one-sided form* is in its turn influenced by other elements; e.g. with the expansion of the market, i.e. of the sphere of exchange, production grows in volume and is subdivided to a greater extent.

With a change in distribution, production undergoes a change; as e.g. in the case of concentration of capital, of a change in the distribution of population in city and country, etc. Finally, the demands of consumption also influence production. A mutual interaction takes place between the various elements. Such is the case with every organic body.

*   *   *

In the social production which men carry on they enter into definite relations that are indispensable and independent of their will; these relations of production correspond to a definite stage of development of their material powers of production. The sum total of these relations of production constitutes the economic structure of society—the real foundation, on which rise legal and political superstructures and to which correspond definite forms of social consciousness. The mode of production in material life determines the general character of the social, political and spiritual processes of life. It is not the consciousness of men that determines their existence, but, on the contrary, their social existence determines their consciousness. At a certain stage of their development, the material forces of production in society come in conflict with the existing relations of production, or—what is but a legal expression for the same thing—with the property relations within which they had been at work before. From forms of development of the forces of production these relations turn into their fetters. Then comes the period of social revolution. With the change of the economic foundation the entire immense superstructure is more or less rapidly transformed. In considering such transformations the distinction should always be made between the material transformation of the economic conditions of production which can be determined with the precision of natural science, and the legal, political, religious, æsthetic or philosophic—in short ideological forms in which men become conscious of this conflict and fight it out. Just as our opinion of an individual is not based on what he thinks of himself, so can we not judge of such a period of transformation by its own consciousness: on the contrary, this consciousness must rather be explained from the contradictions of material life, from the existing conflict between the social forces of production and the relations of production. No social order ever disappears before all the productive forces, for which there is room in it, have been developed; and new higher relations of production never appear before the material conditions of their existence have matured in the womb of the old society. Therefore, mankind always takes up only such problems as it can solve; since, looking at the matter more closely, we will always find that the problem itself arises only when the material conditions necessary for its solution already exist or are at least in the process of formation. In broad outlines we can designate the Asiatic, the ancient, the feudal and the modern bourgeois methods of production as so many epochs in the progress of the economic formation of society. The bourgeois relations of production are the last antagonistic form of the social process of production—antagonistic not in the sense of individual antagonism, but of one arising from conditions surrounding the life of individuals in society; at the same time the productive forces developing in the womb of bourgeois society create the material conditions for the solution of that antagonism. This social formation constitutes, therefore, the closing chapter of the prehistoric stage of human society.

11. *On Status and Contract*

BY SIR HENRY SUMNER MAINE

THE MOVEMENT of the progressive societies has been uniform in one respect. Through all its course it has been distinguished by the gradual dissolution of family dependency and the growth of individual obligation in its place. The individual

Reprinted from Sir Henry Sumner Maine, *Ancient Law* (New York: H. Holt & Co., 1885; from the 5th London edition), chap. v, pp. 163–65.

is steadily substituted for the Family, as the unit of which civil laws take account. The advance has been accomplished at varying rates of celerity, and there are societies not absolutely stationary in which the collapse of the ancient organisation can only be perceived by careful study of the phenomena they present. But, whatever its pace, the change has not been subject to reaction or recoil, and apparent retardations will be found to have been occasioned through the absorption of archaic ideas and customs from some entirely foreign source. Nor is it difficult to see what is the tie between man and man which replaces by degrees those forms of reciprocity in rights and duties which have their origin in the Family. It is Contract. Starting, as from one terminus of history, from a condition of society in which all the relations of Persons are summed up in the relations of Family, we seem to have steadily moved towards a phase of social order in which all these relations arise from the free agreement of individuals. In Western Europe the progress achieved in this direction has been considerable. Thus the status of the Slave has disappeared—it has been superseded by the contractual relation of the servant to his master. The status of the Female under Tutelage, if the tutelage be understood of persons other than her husband, has also ceased to exist; from her coming of age to her marriage all the relations she may form are relations of contract. So too the status of the Son under Power has no true place in the law of modern European societies. If any civil obligation binds together the Parent and the child of full age, it is one to which only contract gives its legal validity. The apparent exceptions are exceptions of that stamp which illustrate the rule.

The child before years of discretion, the orphan under guardianship, the adjudged lunatic, have all their capacities and incapacities regulated by the Law of Persons. But why? The reason is differently expressed in the conventional language of different systems, but in substance it is stated to the same effect by all. The great majority of Jurists are constant to the principle that the classes of persons just mentioned are subject to extrinsic control on the single ground that they do not possess the faculty of forming a judgment on their own interests; in other words, that they are wanting in the first essential of an engagement by Contract.

The word Status may be usefully employed to construct a formula expressing the law of progress thus indicated, which, whatever be its value, seems to me to be sufficiently ascertained. All the forms of Status taken notice of in the Law of Persons were derived from, and to some extent are still coloured by, the powers and privileges anciently residing in the Family. If then we employ Status, agreeably with the usage of the best writers, to signify these personal conditions only, and avoid applying the term to such conditions as are the immediate or remote result of agreement, we may say that the movement of the progressive societies has hitherto been a movement *from Status to Contract*.

12. *The Nature of Society*

BY HERBERT SPENCER

212. THIS QUESTION has to be asked and answered at the outset. Until we have decided whether or not to regard a society as an entity; and until we have decided whether, if regarded as an entity, a society is to be classed as absolutely unlike all other entities or as like some others; our conception of the subject-matter before us remains vague.

It may be said that a society is but a collective name for a number of individuals. Carrying the controversy between nominalism and realism into another sphere, a nominalist might affirm that just as there exist only the members of a species, while

Reprinted from Herbert Spencer, *The Principles of Sociology* (New York: D. Appleton & Co., 1898), Vol. II, Book II, secs. 212–17, 223, 270–71, pp. 447–53, 456, 593–97.

the species considered apart from them has no existence; so the units of a society alone exist, while the existence of the society is but verbal. Instancing a lecturer's audience as an aggregate which by disappearing at the close of the lecture, proves itself to be not a thing but only a certain arrangement of persons, he might argue that the like holds of the citizens forming a nation.

But without disputing the other steps of his argument, the last step may be denied. The arrangement, temporary in the one case, is permanent in the other; and it is the permanence of the relations among component parts which constitutes the individuality of a whole as distinguished from the individualities of its parts. A mass broken into fragments ceases to be a thing; while, conversely, the stones, bricks, and wood, previously separate, become the thing called a house if connected in fixed ways.

Thus we consistently regard a society as an entity, because, though formed of discrete units, a certain concreteness in the aggregate of them is implied by the general persistence of the arrangements among them throughout the area occupied. And it is this trait which yields our idea of a society. For, withholding the name from an ever-changing cluster such as primitive men form, we apply it only where some constancy in the distribution of parts has resulted from settled life.

213. But now, regarding a society as a thing, what kind of thing must we call it? It seems totally unlike every object with which our senses acquaint us. Any likeness it may possibly have to other objects, cannot be manifest to perception, but can be discerned only by reason. If the constant relations among its parts make it an entity; the question arises whether these constant relations among its parts are akin to the constant relations among the parts of other entities. Between a society and anything else, the only conceivable resemblance must be one due to *parallelism of principle in the arrangement of components.*

There are two great classes of aggregates with which the social aggregate may be compared—the inorganic and the organic. Are the attributes of a society in any way like those of a not-living body? or are they in any way like those of a living body? or are they entirely unlike those of both?

The first of these questions needs only to be asked to be answered in the negative. A whole of which the parts are alive, cannot, in its general characters, be like lifeless wholes. The second question, not to be thus promptly answered, is to be answered in the affirmative. The reasons for asserting that the permanent relations among the parts of a society, are analogous to the permanent relations among the parts of a living body, we have now to consider.

A Society Is an Organism

214. When we say that growth is common to social aggregates and organic aggregates, we do not thus entirely exclude community with inorganic aggregates. Some of these, as crystals, grow in a visible manner; and all of them, on the hypothesis of evolution, have arisen by integration at some time or other. Nevertheless, compared with things we call inanimate, living bodies and societies so conspicuously exhibit augmentation of mass, that we may fairly regard this as characterizing them both. Many organisms grow throughout their lives;

and the rest grow throughout considerable parts of their lives. Social growth usually continues either up to times when the societies divide, or up to times when they are overwhelmed.

Here, then, is the first trait by which societies ally themselves with the organic world and substantially distinguish themselves from the inorganic world.

215. It is also a character of social bodies, as of living bodies, that while they increase in size they increase in structure. Like a low animal, the embryo of a high one has few distinguishable parts; but while it is acquiring greater mass, its parts multiply and differentiate. It is thus with a society. At first the unlikenesses among its groups of units are inconspicuous in number and degree; but as population augments, divisions and sub-divisions become more numerous and more decided. Further, in the social organism as in the individual organism, differentiations cease only with that completion of the type which marks maturity and precedes decay.

Though in inorganic aggregates also, as in the entire Solar System and in each of its members, structural differentiations accompany the integrations; yet these are so relatively slow, and so relatively simple, that they may be disregarded. The multiplication of contrasted parts in bodies politic and in living bodies, is so great that it substantially constitutes another common character which marks them off from inorganic bodies.

216. This community will be more fully appreciated on observing that progressive differentiation of structures is accompanied by progressive differentiation of functions.

The divisions, primary, secondary, and tertiary, which arise in a developing animal, do not assume their major and minor unlikenesses to no purpose. Along with diversities in their shapes and compositions go diversities in the actions they perform: they grow into unlike organs having unlike duties. Assuming the entire function of absorbing nutriment at the same time that it takes on its structural characters, the alimentary system becomes gradually marked off into contrasted portions; each of which has a special function forming part of the general function. A limb, instrumental to locomotion or prehension, acquires divisions and sub-divisions which perform their leading and their subsidiary shares in this office. So is it with the parts into which a society divides. A dominant class arising does not simply become unlike the rest, but assumes control over the rest; and when this class separates into the more and the less dominant, these, again, begin to discharge distinct parts of the entire control. With the classes whose actions are controlled it is the same. The various groups into which they fall have various occupations: each of such groups also, within itself, acquiring minor contrasts of parts along with minor contrasts of duties.

And here we see more clearly how the two classes of things we are comparing, distinguish themselves from things of other classes; for such differences of structure as slowly arise in inorganic aggregates, are not accompanied by what we can fairly call differences of function.

217. Why in a body politic and in a living body, these unlike actions of unlike parts are properly regarded by us as functions, while we cannot so regard the unlike actions of unlike parts in an inorganic body, we shall perceive on turning to the next and most distinctive common trait.

Evolution establishes in them both, not differences simply, but definitely-connected differences—differences such that each makes the others possible. The parts of an inorganic aggregate are so related that one may change greatly without appreciably affecting the rest. It is otherwise with the parts of an organic aggregate or of a social aggregate. In either of these, the changes in the parts are mutually determined, and the changed actions of the parts are mutually dependent. In both, too, this mutuality increases as the evolution advances. The lowest type of animal is all stomach, all respiratory surface, all limb. Development of a type having appendages by which to move about or lay hold of food, can take place only if these appendages, losing power to absorb nutriment directly from surrounding bodies, are supplied with nutriment by parts which retain the power of absorption. A respiratory surface to which the circulating fluids are brought to be aerated, can be formed only on condition that the concomitant loss of ability to supply itself with materials for repair and growth, is made good by the development of a structure bringing these materials. Similarly in a society. What we call with perfect propriety its organization, necessarily implies traits of the same kind. While rudimentary, a society is all warrior, all hunter, all hut-builder, all tool-maker: every part fulfils for itself all needs. Progress to a stage characterized by a permanent army, can go on only as there arise arrangements for supplying that army with food, clothes, and munitions of war by the rest. If here the population occupies itself solely with agriculture and there with mining—if these manufacture goods while those distribute them, it must be on condition that in exchange for a special kind of service rendered by each part to other parts, these other parts severally give due proportions of their services.

This division of labour, first dwelt on by political economists as a social phenomenon, and thereupon recognized by biologists as a phenomenon of living bodies, which they called the "physiological division of labour," is that which in the society, as in the animal, makes it a living whole. Scarcely can I emphasize enough the truth that in respect of this fundamental trait, a social organism and an individual organism are entirely alike. When we see that in a mammal, arresting the lungs quickly brings the heart to a stand; that if the stomach fails absolutely in its office all other parts by-and-by cease to act; that paralysis of its limbs entails on the body at large death from want of food, or inability to escape; that loss of even such small organs as the eyes, deprives the rest of a service essential to their preservation; we cannot but admit that mutual dependence of parts is an essential characteristic. And when, in a society, we see that the workers in iron stop if the miners do not supply materials; that makers of clothes cannot carry on their business in the absence of those who spin and weave textile fabrics; that the manufacturing community will cease to act unless the food-producing and food-distributing agencies are acting; that the controlling powers, governments, bureaux, judicial officers, police, must fail to keep order when the necessaries of life are not supplied to them by the parts kept in order; we are obliged to say that this mutual dependence of parts is similarly rigorous. Unlike as the two kinds of aggregates otherwise are, they are unlike in respect of this fundamental character, and the characters implied by it.

*   *   *

223. From this last consideration, which is a digression rather than a part of the argument, let us now return and sum up the reasons for regarding a society as an organism.

It undergoes continuous growth. As it grows, its parts become unlike: it exhibits increase of structure. The unlike parts simultaneously assume activities of unlike kinds. These activities are not simply different, but their differences are so related as to make one another possible. The reciprocal aid thus given causes mutual dependence of the parts. And the mutually-dependent parts, living by and for one another, form an aggregate constituted on the same general principle as is an individual organism. The analogy of a society to an organism becomes still clearer on learning that every organism of appreciable size is a society; and on further learning that in both, the lives of the units continue for some time if the life of the aggregate is suddenly arrested, while if the aggregate is not destroyed by violence, its life greatly exceeds in duration the lives of its units. Though the two are contrasted as respectively discrete and concrete, and though there results a difference in the ends subserved by the organization, there does not result a difference in the laws of the organization: the required mutual influences of the parts, not transmissible in a direct way, being, in a society, transmitted in an indirect way.

Having thus considered in their most general forms the reasons for regarding a society as an organism, we are prepared for following out the comparison in detail. . . .

*   *   *

270. But now let us drop this alleged parallelism between individual organizations and social organizations. I have used the analogies elaborated, but as a scaffolding to help in building up a coherent body of sociological inductions. Let us take away the scaffolding: the inductions will stand by themselves.

We saw that societies are aggregates which grow; that in the various types of them there are great varieties in the growths reached; that types of successively larger sizes result from the aggregation and re-aggregation of those of smaller sizes; and that this increase by coalescence, joined with interstitial increase, is the process through which have been formed the vast civilized nations.

Along with increase of size in societies goes increase of structure. Primitive hordes are without established distinction of parts. With growth of them into tribes habitually come some unlikenesses; both in the powers and occupations of their members. Unions of tribes are followed by more unlikenesses, governmental and industrial—social grades running through the whole mass, and contrasts between the differently-occupied parts in different localities. Such differentiations multiply as the compounding progresses. They proceed from the general to the special. First the broad division between ruling and ruled; then within the ruling part divisions into political, religious, military, and within the ruled part divisions into food producing classes and handi-craftsmen; then within each of these divisions minor ones, and so on.

Passing from the structural aspect to the functional aspect, we note that so long as all parts of a society have like natures and activities, there is hardly any mutual dependence, and the aggregate scarcely forms a vital whole. As its parts assume different functions they become dependent on one another, so that injury to one hurts others; until, in highly-evolved societies, general perturbation is caused by derangement of any portion. This contrast between undeveloped and developed societies, arises from the fact that with increasing specialization of functions comes increasing inability in each part to perform the functions of other parts.

The organization of every society begins with a contrast between the division which carries on relations, habitually hostile, with environing societies, and the division which is devoted to procuring necessaries of life; and during the earlier stages of development these two divisions constitute the whole. Eventually there arises an intermediate division serving to transfer products and influences from part to part. And in all subsequent stages, evolution of the two earlier systems of structures depends on evolution of this additional system.

While the society as a whole has the character of its sustaining system determined by the character of its environment, inorganic and organic, the respective parts of this system differentiate in adaptation to local circumstances; and, after primary industries have been thus localized and specialized, secondary industries dependent on them arise in conformity with the same principle. Further, as fast as societies become compounded and re-compounded, and the distributing system develops, the parts devoted to each kind of industry, originally scattered, aggregate in the most favourable localities; and the localized industrial structures, unlike the governmental structures, grow regardless of the original lines of division.

Increase of size, resulting from the massing of groups, necessitates means of communication; both for achieving combined offensive and defensive actions, and for exchange of products. Faint tracks, then paths, rude roads, finished roads, successively arise; and as fast as intercourse is thus facilitated, there is a transition from direct barter to trading carried on by a separate class; out of which evolves a complex mercantile agency of wholesale and retail distributors. The movement of commodities effected by this agency, beginning as a slow flux to and re-flux from certain places at long intervals, passes into rhythmical, regular, rapid currents; and materials for sustentation distributed hither and thither, from being few and crude become numerous and elaborated. Growing efficiency of transfer with greater variety of transferred products, increases the mutual dependence of parts at the same time that it enables each part to fulfil its function better.

Unlike the sustaining system, evolved by converse with the organic and inorganic environments, the regulating system is evolved by converse, offensive and defensive, with environing societies. In primitive headless groups temporary chieftainship results from temporary war; chronic hostilities generate permanent chieftainship; and gradually from the military control results the civil control. Habitual war, requiring prompt combination in the actions of parts, necessitates subordination. Societies in which there is little subordination disappear, and leave outstanding those in which subordination is great; and so there are produced, societies in which the habit fostered by war and surviving in peace, brings about permanent submission to a government. The centralized regulating thus evolved, is in early stages the sole regulating system. But in large societies which have become predominantly industrial, there is added a decentralized regulating system for the industrial structures; and this, at first subject in every way to the original system, acquires at length substantial independence. Finally there arises for the distributing structures also, an independent controlling agency.

Societies fall firstly into the classes of simple, compound, doubly-compound, trebly-compound; and from the lowest the transition to the highest is through these stages. Otherwise, though less definitely, societies may be grouped as militant and industrial; of which the one type in its developed form is organized on the principle of compulsory co-operation, while the other in its developed form is organized on the principle of voluntary co-operation. The one is characterized not only by a despotic central power, but also by unlimited political control of personal conduct; while the other is characterized not only by a democratic or representative central power, but also by limitation of political control over personal conduct.

Lastly we noted the corollary that change in the predominant social activities brings metamorphosis. If, where the militant type has not elaborated into so rigid a form as to prevent change, a considerable industrial system arises, there come mitigations of the coercive restraints characterizing the militant type, and weakening of its structures. Conversely, where an industrial system largely developed has established freer social forms, resumption of offensive and defensive activities causes reversion towards the militant type.

271. And now, summing up the results of this general survey, let us observe the extent to which we are prepared by it for further inquiries.

The many facts contemplated unite in proving that social evolution forms a part of evolution at large. Like evolving aggregates in general, societies show *integration,* both by simple increase of mass and by coalescence and re-coalescence of masses.

The change from *homogeneity* to *heterogeneity* is multitudinously exemplified; up from the simple tribe, alike in all its parts, to the civilized nation, full of structural and functional unlikenesses. With progressing integration and heterogeneity goes increasing *coherence.* We see the wandering group dispersing, dividing, held together by no bonds; the tribe with parts made more coherent by subordination to a dominant man; the cluster of tribes united in a political plexus under a chief with sub-chiefs; and so on up to the civilized nation, consolidated enough to hold together for a thousand years or more. Simultaneously comes increasing *definiteness.* Social organization is at first vague; advance brings settled arrangements which grow slowly more precise; customs pass into laws which, while gaining fixity, also become more specific in their applications to varieties of actions; and all institutions, at first confusedly intermingled, slowly separate, at the same time that each within itself marks off more distinctly its component structures. Thus in all respects is fulfilled the formula of evolution. There is progress towards greater size, coherence, multiformity, and definiteness.

Besides these general truths, a number of special truths have been disclosed by our survey. Comparisons of societies in their ascending grades, have made manifest certain cardinal facts respecting their growths, structures, and functions—facts respecting the systems of structures, sustaining, distributing, regulating, of which they are composed; respecting the relations of these structures to the surrounding conditions and the dominant forms of social activities entailed; and respecting the metamorphoses of types caused by changes in the activities. The inductions arrived at, thus constituting in rude outline an Empirical Sociology, show that in social phenomena there is a general order of co-existence and sequence; and that therefore social phenomena form the subject-matter of a science reducible, in some measure at least, to the deductive form.

Guided, then, by the law of evolution in general, and, in subordination to it, guided by the foregoing inductions, we are now prepared for following out the synthesis of social phenomena. We must begin with those simplest ones presented by the evolution of the family.

Section B

The Elements of Social Interaction: Roles and Collectivities

Editorial Foreword, BY KASPAR D. NAEGELE   *147*

1. *The Sociology of Sociability*, BY GEORG SIMMEL   *157*
2. *The I and the Me*, BY GEORGE H. MEAD   *163*
3. *Reciprocity*, BY MARCEL MAUSS   *168*
4. *Social Action and Its Types*, BY MAX WEBER   *173*

Interaction: Roles and Collectivities

by *Kaspar D. Naegele*

(i)

AMONG THEM, THE THREE sections of Part One of this Reader provide a view of the character of society. More than one such view is possible. For example, Emerson, the American transcendentalist, would see it as a form of mutual discovery. The Church fathers would see it as part of the sinful world. The medieval believer would see it in orders of rank ordained by God. Plato and Aristotle would combine a distinction between nature and convention with a fusion of social and political distinctions: they would see society fully embodied in the city-state.

The history of such views itself can be a part of the study of society. But the study of society is possible only with certain views of it. Our concern is with the possibility and growth of this study, entailing, we believe, efforts in *three* directions: (1) The continuous *distinction* between "normative" and "existential" questions, *so that* the *relation* between them can become evident. (2) The continuous revision of a *differentiated* view of society *both* as a reality *sui generis* and as an order involved with such other orders as those of *culture, personality* and the several realms of *nature* (from the weather to the organism). (3) The continuous balance between a view of differentiated society as *also* a *coherent* order (whatever the strategic elements of this coherence may be, such as conflict, ritual, consensus, and loyalty) *and* as an order *with a history*.

Parts Two and Three deal with many of the issues implied by the view that society is a differentiated phenomenon involving other *orders* of coherence. Part Four concerns some of the questions posed by the relation of social and other orders. All these questions cut across the Reader as a whole. They emerge from the materials that the first section of this part has just presented. Part One of this Reader is, however, primarily concerned with establishing the basic issues that confront and constitute efforts to make the study of social phenomena a scientific, and hence a cumulative enterprise. There are various kinds of cumulative enterprises. In a sense, technology is one, as are the Roman Catholic Church and language. We are concerned with the growth of explanation of facts defined as social facts. Such explanations—as distinct from wise and indispensable assertions or primarily reasoned proposals (in the realm of social phenomena)—have a shorter history than explanations in the realm of physical phenomena. We believe that the distinctions—between the questions of rightness and the questions of "so-ness" implied by the previous section—are necessary for a cumulative study of society; moreover, they probably could not have arisen until social arrangements themselves presented a certain division and rivalry of fundamental positions. We want to avoid the old fallacy, *post hoc, ergo propter hoc*. Neither the Greeks nor the Church fathers, neither the thirteenth century nor the seventeenth, really embarked on the empirical study of social phenomena. As the previous section has shown, it took the criss-cross of alternative and yet convergent positions—like those of Machiavelli and Hobbes, Smith and Malthus, Hegel and Comte, Locke and Marx, Maine and Spencer—to set the stage for work that could confront the tasks of empirical research.

It is sometimes difficult to remember this remarkable dialogue in a form helpful in solving questions we want to pose now. The Foreword to the foregoing section stressed several themes; among them, that to study social phenomena is to study, among other things, what men believe. What men believe includes their commitments to ideals. It includes, as will be discussed, a whole range of understandings and preferences concerning *appropriateness*.

Sociologists want to see what men consider appropriate, why they draw the lines of appropriateness and inappropriateness as they do, and what the consequences are of these facts. They want to see into the character of the various corporate bodies of which individuals come to see themselves as members. They want to help explain the nature of the relation that individuals have to the *public life*. This life—with its involvement in such phenomena as "the state," "the church," "society," "rights," "the community"—is constituted through invisible matters. These, however, become *represented:* in royal courts and courts of law, church buildings and banks, the stock exchange and legal documents. The first section of this Reader has presented some rival proposals for the analysis of the nature of the public life. It has dealt with some possible questions about it. It has shown how, within the same domain of questions, different thinkers, in order to raise questions at all, must assume that other matters have been provisionally answered. None of the contributors of this section, for instance, seeks to dissect "human nature": instead, they all make assumptions about it. Their view, in the main, is "outward" into the realm of the political economy, of law, of the wide divisions—like social class—of the division of labor and of authority. At the same time, they keep "the individual" in mind. They have a sense of history. We may not be able to agree with their formulations nor even understand these formulations in their authors' terms. But their formulations, somehow surrounded by the tranquility that the distance of time seems to bestow, help to give direction and root to our immediate labors, even if these must—to lead farther—assume the risks of departure. As Whitehead reminds us, "A science which hesitates to forget its founders is lost."

Still, among them, the thirteen men—and it is interesting to speculate about how equally endowed women would have formulated these matters, if in those times they had been free to do so—represent, in the medium of abstractions, a sense of the *order* and its development that *surrounds* us. In one respect, they are all *political* thinkers. Yet they recognize this surrounding order as, at least in some ways, *distinct* from the mechanical coherence of the utterly impersonal world. Though the state may be a matter of fate or of history, it is never consistently and responsibly considered as though it were in no important respects different from the weather. Similarly, yet quite unequally, there is implied in these previous selections a view of public order as an *organization:* as a coherence that comprehends such diverse matters as rulers and ruled, private interests and covenants, rival classes and alternative ways of settling economic transactions.

(ii)

Sociological analysis proceeded by applying, again and again, the distinction between concrete and analytic uses of the same term, such as "individualism" and "collectivism," to what then become recognizable as the spheres and groupings of society. A society thus becomes the matrix of kinship and religion, stratification and government, of an economy and an educational system. When seen as a historic phenomenon within the wider context of nature, it becomes the ground and resultant of the processes of work and play carried on by people who can both learn and contribute in relation to others who learn and contribute before and after them. Words like "political" and "economic" come to refer alike to the *spheres* of (national) societies with their representative institutions, electoral bodies, civil service, corporations, free or regulated enterprise, etc., *and* to the component features of the *relations* between individuals. Historically, the study of society involved a *separation* of politics, economics, and law, considered as disciplines, from the disciplined study of social relations.

This history helps to give the word "social" an ambiguity that exceeds the ambiguity of terms like "legal," "political," "economic," or "psychological." "Social" stands for those spheres of human life which are neither biological nor among these latter four. To the extent to which the first three classifications deal with specific institutions and the processes associated with them, the social then deals with the institutions "left over," e.g., voluntary associations, the kinship system, religious organizations. It soon becomes clear, however, that *any* institution has economic and political and legal features. These are understood as matters dealing with the production and distribution of resources, of power, and of legal justice respectively. Indeed, the term *social institution* thus becomes redundant, in the sense that there are no non-social institutions. This adds a further meaning to "social." It becomes a matter of two opposing concerns: with *organization* and *consensus;* and with *conduct* in the *presence* (imagined or actual) of *another* person who can (now or later) similarly act with reference to another person. In either case, "social" includes a temporal dimension which combines two features: repetition and innovation. This dimension of social facts and social arrangements will be discussed in later sections of this Reader, particularly in Part Five. Yet the historic character of all social facts, whether it be acknowledged or not, is, for the editors at least, part of the settled matter of social scientific analysis. Meanwhile, we must turn directly to the developing meaning of the term "social" itself, in order to link the analyses of public matters with the more immediately "personal" analyses provided, especially by the first two selections of this section.

Already we have distinguished four "layers" to the term "social": most generally conceived, it refers to the problem of *order* as such, as this arises through *two* facts: the mutual dependence of human beings on one another, made possible by their relative freedom from a pattern of specific instincts; and the capacity, however differently and unequally developed, to think of one's self as different from others. George Herbert Mead makes much of these facts. As facts, they raise additional questions of the mutual relations among common values, different roles, similar conduct, and consensus. As we saw in Section A, these apparently private facts of dependence and difference were seen in their public and political form by those who provided the first great impetus for the growth of knowledge concerning phenomena considered under the aspect of their social structure and development. "Social" means an inclusive order in or against which any individual acts—but without which he cannot act at all. The *forms* this order takes (*Gemeinschaft* versus *Gezelschaft*, etc.), the differentiations which can occur within it (modes of political and economic patterns, their mutual relation, etc.), and the alternate ways in which individuals can be seen to be *related* to it (under the aspect of their dependence on it, autonomy from it, contribution to it, or victimization by it) thus become chronic issues that are dealt with in every page of this Reader. In that form, "social" refers to the *coherence*—individually experienced as common membership in a historic enterprise—that can be discovered among the arrangements by which people live out their lives; and to the *severalness* of spheres and groupings that marks all but the most primitive self-sufficient groupings that can contain, in principle, the whole of the life spans of all of their members. This coherence, however, is a matter of function and of meaning. Even in its most inclusive sense, the term "social" is not free from ambiguity: it refers alike to the discoverable interconnections among arrangements, like politics and stratification, even when these connections are not perceived by those whom they affect or from whose intentions they are in fact created; *and* to the agreements marking or underlying the enterprises by which people carry on, be it in the market place or at home, in a factory or at a pub. Curiously, the social as the province of sociology required, for its systematic dissection, the *addition* of another discipline to the company of economics, political science, psychology, and anthropology. The subject matter of this discipline is old. The new material, particularly through the works of Weber and of Durkheim, was the dissection of the special character of social relations and institutions with reference to the question: What existential ideas are most necessary and suitable to analyze—and, eventually, explain—the alternative ways in which human beings organize themselves into such corporate enterprises as societies, religious groups, political parties, occupational associations, and the like?

The "additional" and "residual" characters of the social dimension—elegantly reversed by Durkheim's famous dictum that society is a reality *sui generis*—had, as we already saw, two consequences: it made of the social something that lies behind (or "in," as it might be better put today) *all* human enterprises, including those that appear to be analyzable apart from it (e.g., economic systems, political arrangements, or religious institutions); and it made accessible for respectable study those features of immediate and contemporary life which were less formal than economic, political, or legal arrangements and yet on a plane other than psychological processes of individuals.

This ambiguity of "social" suggests the second level of its meaning—its reference to the *membership* aspect of human phenomena; its reference, in other words, to the phenomenon of organization. On the first level, the experiential counterpart to the abstract notion of social was, as we have seen, the *sense of consensus* or of common commitment. On the second level, we find the sense of belonging. The first deals with a wide mold of agreements, including the agreements about "rights" to disagree. Given a variety of historic circumstance, the social on this plane may appear in the first instance as an "antithetical" matter; society as constraint ranged against the individual and his freedom. The character of the tensions between individual and collectivity have been traced in the Foreword to Section A. It was shown there that there are two different uses of this distinction; one is analytic and the other concrete. Both usages affect the progress of the study of society, even if sociology can itself grow only to the extent to which it is neutral in the moral debate about the "proper" balance among the rival claims for the enhancement and limitation of different kinds of freedom and obligations. Under the aspect of inclusive commitment, the social appears, however, as the condition of corporate or individual freedom. In this sense, analysis and experience often part company. This inclusive sense of the social is generally a matter of *a* (national) society—of a politically more or less autonomous unit in which membership is a matter of citizenship. Still, separating the terms "political" and "social," "state" and "society," was indispensable for studying society. This separation poses the fruitful problem of the alternative relations between different political and social patterns. In that case, "political" refers primarily to the distribution of "public" power, and "social," to the *range* of *different* webs of relationships (and their mutual traversibility by any one person) found within any one society. Politics constitutes a *sphere* of action within a society, while all actions within it are social. Similarly, all actions are accessible to political analysis. The political is thus gathered into a separate sphere (in one aspect called government) in a way in which the social is not—with the possible exception of sociability, about which Simmel speaks in the first selection below, which will be discussed later.

The foregoing was intended to show a link between the levels of commitment and of organization, as these terms have been used here. The terms themselves are not important. On this second plane, social refers to the "corporateness" of much human enterprise. Two variable facts immediately occur in that connection: their formality, and their size. The multiplicity of definite corporate enterprises within modern human society is an obvious fact. Most of us work in an organizational context, be it corporations, small businesses, hospitals, or educational institutions. Most of us spend some time in one or more voluntary organizations: trade unions, professional bodies, political parties, religious groupings. We can immediately think of a whole host of characteristics of these structures—among them, the fact that they can be experienced or described as structures, since in some measure they are arranged in a recurrent way. This makes the social dimension of human enterprise a chronically second fact. The first fact about such enterprises seems to be the ends they are to accomplish: the provision of work, salvation, profits, entertainment, edification, security. Their pursuit usually involves some order of *concerted* activity, which constitutes the social character of human enterprise. It always involves coherence and differentiation. One aspect of the latter is the establishment of a boundary, however permeable, between being part of a social system and being outside it. Another aspect is the phenomenon of the division of labor, responsibility, and power that is part of any organization.

These issues will be more systematically treated elsewhere in this Reader. At present, we are concerned only with seeing the emergent aspect of the social dimension of phenomena. While pursuing their ends, men establish relations with one an-

other that confront them with further issues. These issues bear no simple relations to the ends whose pursuit brought them into prominence. They arise out of an irreducible set of exigencies created when two or more persons want to *sustain* (or impose), on themselves or others, an arrangement affecting conduct. In that respect, the social aspect of phenomena involves the settlement of a variety of issues, including how the ends and the rules governing the means necessary to implement such ends should be related. Ends can be various—e.g., the attainment of salvation, maximization of profit, insurance against premature death, accomplishment of national independence. Should they be committed to paper (in the form of written constitutions, contracts, etc.)? Should they be "left" to general consensus? Or, in other words: organizations become comprehensible only to the extent they are perceived as historic arrangements involved in pursuing ends that necessarily exceed the ends that they set themselves. In that respect, ostensibly dissimilar social systems, such as the Roman Catholic Church and General Motors, are necessarily involved in solving quite similar issues. Social organizations may be compared to musical compositions: the elements of their composition are few; their alternative combinations are many.

We have made a double shift. We began with the notion of the social applicable to that order in which one participates as a citizen. In one respect, it is this order to which the first selections were ultimately addressed. It is the order in which the political and social meet most completely. Yet for all their generality and invisibility and consequent reliance on mediation through various symbols—from flags to anthems to votes—subsequent thought has tended to consider national societies as a particular instance of a more general and more "analytic" usage of "social." Sociology, after all, began in a complex society. Persistent coherences involving the notion of membership—sometimes referred to as social systems—thus become the major illustrative phenomena through which the term "social" received its distinct meaning. Social systems are less inclusive than societies, concretely speaking, and more inclusive, logically speaking. All societies are examples of social systems; but the reverse does not hold. Social systems, moreover, are obviously not of a piece, as Part Two of the Reader shows. Quite apart from their ends, groups vary in their corporateness and their size, and also in the coincidence or limitation of grounds on which they establish their inclusiveness or their exclusiveness. Circles of friends, cabals, secret societies, sects, seminars—all these are forms of social groupings, which are also sometimes parts of more encompassing and more formal organizations.

It is time to move to the third plane on this framework. If our readings had begun with the Greeks, we would have seen that they confined "social" to the realm of private and "natural" bonds, and that there was thus a contrast between the social and political realms. In time, a horizontal distinction has become a vertical one.[1] The distinctions between private and public, social and political, have had to be rearranged. The status of the terms of these distinctions has become complicated by the difference, applicable to them all, between their "analytic" and "concrete" uses. By this logic, each of these terms refers alike to *realms of* activities and to *elements in* the relations among men. Other distinctions have been added—e.g., those between formal and informal, communal and associational. Yet ultimately, "social" always stands for a nexus. This Reader begins with writers who have contributed to a tradition of thought which would claim this nexus to be fully intelligible in its own right. Unless properly qualified, this statement may easily claim too much. The "social," as that which is given by the fact that human beings sustain relations to one another regardless of what these relations are about, obviously *involves* the psychological dispositions of the parties to such relations. The nature of this involvement is taken up in Part Three. The Introduction to that part will also discuss whether "social" considerations can be reduced to "psychological" ones. Similarly, Part Four will show that social relations involve commitments to normative and existential ideas. These always involve some form of "ultimacy" and hence of belief, including religious positions. Yet it is inherent, in the distinctions and proposals that make up this Reader, that the relations among men and the connections arising from them are comprehensible without commitments to specific religious (non-empirical) positions—even if such commitments are themselves to be taken seriously in any attempt at accounting for the genesis, maintenance, and change characterizing these relations. Furthermore, though the social is constituted by relatedness, relatedness obviously takes more than a social form. It can be logical, meaningful, stylistic, mechanical, spacial, temporal, and so forth. Watches sustain no social relations to arms, nor do wheels to carts.

A nexus is social, then, to the degree to which it involves the possibilities and facts of *mutual* orientation by two or more people. Such mutual orientation is always "about something": employment, love, common beliefs, feuds. Like any bonds, these require their appropriate occasions: conversation, exchange of goods and money, obedience to orders, formulation of policy, declaration of love. They require enactment, occurring within the confines of time and space, within some created situation, recurrent or new. Yet social relations are less confined than social situations: they have a past and a future. Social situations are the necessary *samples* of the (changing) character of someone's relation to his brother or his boss or his father or his son. These relations, while created only in the occasions without which we cannot act, are not a matter only of these occasions. Their qualities of love and hate, inclusiveness and limitation, intensity or peripheralness, exceed the possibilities of any one occasion and require a succession of occasions. The character of this succession requires resources that are not fully contained in any one social occasion. Respect for an expert and affection for a father, dependence on an employer and love for a woman—these are examples of *social* relations. They are *known,* to their parties or their observers, only within the disclosures contained by particular occasions. Yet they are *constituted* by acts and memories, commitments and expectations, ideas and feelings, which do not disappear with the situation in which they are displayed and are not always displayed on every occasion. On this plane, moreover, the "social" appears as the generic feature of *all* human relations. The latter involve some reciprocity of two or more people whose *difference*, as individuals, is in some measure also an aspect of their mutual involvement. In that sense the "social" is a very open concept: it includes relations of conflict and of cooperation; arrangements that are exclusive—like emotions; and arrangements of coherence that are, in principle, indefinitely inclusive, as, e.g., recognizing another as a human being.

The fourth plane of "social" is now apparent. Social relations are constituted through social acts. To act is to make a difference; to act socially is to make this difference with some intended reference to another person or category or collectivity about whom one believes (or knows) that now or later (if not previously) he too can act socially.

The wider detour is now complete. It was necessary in order to remember the drastic difference between the characters of the dissections of social and individual life demonstrated in the works of most of the authors from whose writings the rest of the Reader has been selected and the work which constitutes the first section. The distinction is not invidious. It concerns merely the relative emphasis, beginning primarily with Weber and Durkheim, on

---

1. For many illuminating observations on this and diverse related matters, see, in particular, Hannah Arendt's beautiful book, *The Human Condition* (Chicago: University of Chicago Press, 1958).

a pattern of concepts which can guide specific efforts of research. Ideally, such research would *explain* discoverable relations within or among the several planes of socialness that the previous discussion has suggested.

The difference is not absolute. It is accompanied by important, though easily forgotten *continuities* between the more autonomous and self-contained claims and interpretations of the thinkers of the nineteenth, eighteenth, and seventeenth centuries, and those of the twentieth. The continuities lie in the plane of the questions asked and the distinctions proposed to enable someone to find an answer. To ask about government and its functions, about the structure of status or contract, or about the significance of sovereignty, is, after all, to have a phenomenon already in view. Questions presuppose answers to previous questions.

Three of the selections in this section are concerned with the two last planes of the social—relatedness, and action. They almost constitute a triangle, with Mead's account and Weber's definition as the two corners of the base. Simmel's dissection of one type of occasion is a more concrete exercise in analyzing the mutual involvement of concepts dealing with social relations, roles, acts, and actors. In the following section we move toward and on the two other planes, social organization and society. The discussion continues thus, being at the same time much involved in the further dissection of the structure of social relations. Chronology, from now on, is likely to be in reverse order. Contributions are grouped around themes and arranged in some succession of logical priority. In the main, our ordering is intended to be continuous with the more general proposals of the two introductory essays at the beginning of the Reader.

(iii)

Simmel asked about society what Kant asked about knowledge: how is it possible? Hidden in such a question, even though it may be an attempt to leave it behind, is usually the additional question:*What* is society like? Spencer has already provided one explicit answer to this question. Simmel has been discussed at perhaps too great length in one of the introductory essays. The selection used here is one attempt to state the generic character of the "social." To do so, it makes use of a most important group of distinctions, those inherent in the fact that, in relating to one another for any reason, we must make use, simultaneously, of both ideas and feelings. These create contrasts, as well as themselves being part of the contrast between

two or more persons that the notion of social relation implies.

In Western tradition, contrasts are usually expressed as dichotomies: essence and accident, body and mind, environment and heredity, true and false, absolute and relative. This tendency toward dualism provides much opportunity for efforts to dissolve these as mere artifacts of language. There is, for instance, no heredity without an environment, and vice versa. For many people, willing to grant the *difference* between ideas and matter, this is again a contrast which at least, from the point of view of ideas, depends on the existence of the other side. An extraordinary amount has been written about these issues. Yet all known societies —however differently they might view them—recognize many contrasts, such as those of day and night, old and young, male and female. They may think of them as matters of degree, as variations on a few themes. They may consider them as embodied, as the previous contrasts are, in diurnal, anatomic, and physiological differentiation of nature itself. Embodiment, however, is an ambiguous term; it leaves undistinguished, e.g., the extent to which the contrast between male and female is given by the fact that human bodies "come" in two forms or by the fact that as a contrast, it is socially elaborated within the limits of these forms but not in a uniform manner. One may also think of contrasts in a number of spheres: landscapes, cities, culture, lines of work, periods in a lifetime. One may think of them as alternatives or as complements.

Male and female are not alternatives for individuals. They are stubborn contrasts. As "roles," with certain exceptions, they are virtually social absolutes, paralleling in their immutability within any one society the more general immutability of anatomy and biological function.

Simmel addresses himself to a different order of contrast: that between art or play, and "reality" (real life). To a degree, this is an exercise in applying a distinction which plays a cardinal role in all his work: the distinction between form and content. In some ways this is not too fortunate a distinction; or, at least, it is not too fortunate a definition of it, especially since we think of form as "empty" or as "outside," much as we think of the bowl containing the rising dough. This is not what is meant. Forms, like play, conflict, or subordination, are both modes of association among people and elements within any association. In the second capacity, they vary in their importance in relation to the other elements with which they help constitute any specific social constellation, be it a specific occasion or some durable organization.

Simmel is neither consistent nor systematic in this regard. Yet he introduces a far-reaching reminder of a chronic contrast in social affairs: the contrast between the concatenated events of real and every-day life and the more isolated occasions of play, as these parallel the contrast between daily actions of work and sleep and the phenomena of art. The selection will speak for itself. The contrast on which it depends is certainly an ambiguous one, for it involves the relations and differences between such terms as serious, real, and consequential, and playful, fictitious, and isolated. One specific form of this contrast—the divergence between the round of life and drama, as one representation of life—has been most influential in a great deal of sociological analysis. The next selection from Mead's work also shows this. The weakness of contrasting play and life or art and life is in the first instance a logical one, since life presumably includes what is said to differ from it. Substantively, however, the essay (originally a lecture) brings to the fore a variety of questions and themes that, from now on, will in different fashion be part of most of the other selections of this Reader.

Schematically described, these questions and themes include the following:

The differentiation of society. The selection suggests that the occasion of sociability differs from other occasions. This is self-evident. Yet through Simmel's eyes, and thence through the compounded interpretations that can extend farther what he saw with them, this difference can become fruitfully problematic. It is a difference among the differences of social occasions. These, as already suggested, are samples of social arrangements: necessary and particular encounters in definite places and at definite times, which include, in their meaning both to those included and, potentially, to many then excluded, commitments and consequences that transcend them. The differentiation of occasions within society proceeds along a variety of axes. Simmel, in the present instance, is concerned with the relative prominence of the motive of association for its own sake. Occasions differ, in other words, precisely in the manner in which their social encounters are means or ends. They differ, further, in either sphere. They can be means to the ends of bargaining or cure, learning or eating. Their ends can involve play or ritual. The chances are that any occasion contains *all* the basic themes—but in a typical combination. The differentiation of occasions, moreover, requires certain conditions. In the case of sociability, it requires notions of guest and host. These are terms for social roles; individuals are differentiated—reciprocally, to some extent, to social arrangements—by a set or repertoire of roles. This is a plausible observation, but one which theoretically has turned out to be as fruitful as it is equivocal. The same individual, on different occasions, can be host or guest. Yet the occasions of sociability require the difference between guest and host. The selection suggests, therefore, that in the term "role," whatever difficulty there may be in reaching consensus and clarity about its definition, we may have a way to spring the trap of the long dialogue concerning the relation between individuals and their circles, groups, and institutional contexts.

Simmel introduces another aspect of differentiation, that between form and motive—how one behaves at a party is one question; why one goes is another. The same occasion can include a variety of motives, yet it imposes limits on their expression—while also, conceivably, producing or liberating motives which were not wittingly, at least, part of one's reasons for coming.

Simmel emphasizes the "isolation" of sociability from all other spheres of activity. He conceives this isolation to be part of its meaning to its participants. Without taking pains to make the distinction persistent, he combines, in his analysis, an attempt to represent the concrete meanings the social occasion of sociability has for its participants with the question of what analytic distinctions are needed by me as an observer, to observe and state the character of social interaction between people at a party which allow me to describe what goes on and to account for what does not go on. In another essay (not included in this Reader), he complements his present emphasis by an analysis of the meal. We all must eat, but how and with whom and when and what we eat are social questions. Their answers help the process of differentiating the social from a natural order.

There are several planes to the concern with differentiation: it applies to the differences *between* social and non-social facts; the differences (in occasions, roles, and, as we shall see, institutional patterns) *within and among* social systems; and to the differences between the patterns of distinctions which as persons and citizens we *need* or *create* as we *live* and act within societies, and the pattern of distinctions we require in order to *account* for social facts. Having to do with *inter*-action or with mutual expectation, social facts ultimately always involve a severalness that points to a relation, but a relation with an "inwardness." Yet the complementary or parallel inwardness of guests and host are addressed to conversation or to games—to activities seriously limiting the simultaneous pursuit of other kinds of activities, except eating, dancing, or singing. More than that, Simmel attributes to this particular occasion an element of *fictitiousness.*

The representational character of society. Fictitiousness is one aspect of the phenomenon of symbolism. Mead, in the next selection, will return to the question of gestures and symbols, just as Durkheim in another selection writes about representations. Play and art are other cognate phenomena. Societies are deeply affected by the stubborn realities of the material, including the organic, world. The facts that we have only two eyes, that we walk upright, that we have to eat, that we must die, that we are not, as a rule, born in litters, etc., are deep in the arrangements by which we carry on. Our carrying on also involves ideas and beliefs, agreements and disagreements. Our experience implies awareness, which necessarily involves a recognition of what is so and of what could be so. Recognition of the possible carries the implication of fiction, which is facilitated by the paradox that our relations to one another involve our differences. Differences among people involve the recognition of varieties of experience—and these varieties, in becoming known, form the other side of our recognition of the difference between an inwardness and an outwardness. It is one of several kinds of discrepancies related to one another. We do not or cannot always say what we mean, do what we intend, or want what we have. Besides, what binds us in our differences has to transcend these, as symbols and art do. Through them, we express and elaborate the contrast between word and thing, actual and possible, or real and fictitious. Since symbols and art are part of the real world—in that people cannot move in that world without them—it follows that what we call social intercourse requires the use of metaphor and analogy. The social and the use of expression become mutually implicated. But self-expression—just talking to another, reading a story, etc.—a form of social action, as we shall discuss presently, is also an element, in another sense, of all actions. In this way, the social and the self-expressive introduce a contrast. Further, social occasions differ from one another by virtue of the order of contrast each assumes toward all other occasions.

The coherence of society. Simmel's analysis of sociability also indicates the role in social occasions of what others have called the common definition of the situation. This combines host and guests, though their respective roles differ. Simmel does not use the word "role," but he describes its phenomena. Any one role always implies at least one other with which it somehow becomes reciprocal. There can be no host without guests. Such differentiation also relates them. Simmel sees the differentiation of roles as a way by which occasions hang together; he also indicates, in this selection, the importance of agreed standards. Though he says little about them, such standards include the notion of invitation. The occasion coheres by virtue of the absence of the uninvited.

Simmel treats sociability as an occasion to be analyzed in its own right. He could have asked questions about the contribution of such occasions to other social arrangements, or he could have asked about the history of sociability and the shifts within it in some given society. In the West, at least, this is one occasion in which one combines the fictions that Simmel indicates with being absorbed by the occasion. It may be true that sociability demands that its guests and hosts be deliberately restricted in their involvement: "doing business," "talking shop," displaying one's personal problems—potentially any of these may be inappropriate. Yet, by its freedom from the serious and consequential life, sociability also constitutes a form of freedom. Since it is an occasion addressed to mutual conversation, the freedom generated within it—however stylized its expression—would become expressive of one's personality. It is not fortuitous that the man who wrote about sociability also wrote about letter writing. For the reasons above, the study of sociable occasions by participant observers would seem doubly inappropriate. Simmel's analysis is a speculative conspectus. It provides perspective; it moves into manageable focus the contrasts of serious and playful, and real and fictitious, without which the study of society may easily become trivial and false. It establishes links between the work of the artist and the scientist, without confusing them.

The selection from George Herbert Mead deals with an old problem: the phenomenon of the self. Nietzsche spoke of it as a grammatical illusion. As it stands, the sense of the self, with its inevitable indication of a cognate sense of being different from others, would appear to limit sociological analysis as such. Mead meets the problem directly, by conceiving the self as itself a social phenomenon. There are various ways of understanding his analysis. As we read it today, fortified by Freud and others, we may find it impossible to assess the full import of Mead's analysis. It is deeply influenced by the cardinal importance of communication, particularly of language. The concern with communication in this sense is a peculiarly modern one, though the study of language is certainly old. Mead seeks to cope with the experienced contrast of self and group, or self and others, by starting with the very character of this contrast and considering it as comprehending what, from the point of view of any one person, appear as gaps and divergences.

In previous selections, the divergence between self and organization, self and society, or self and state was primarily considered as one aspect of the question of order. It thus is, in this case, a moral problem. In Mead's case, it is primarily considered as a cognitive matter. He wants to know how it occurs that I think of myself *as* myself. He takes seriously the observation that I can, in fact, think of myself. I can make myself my own object. In that respect, I am a duality. The duality of I and Other has its emergent counterpart in the duality of I and Me, about which the selection speaks in detail. From that point of view, the self as the seat of one's aloneness, of one's irreducible sense of difference from all others, is indeed a social emergent. We think of ourselves precisely because, in the company of others, we have learned to think of ourselves as they think of us. They think of us as they have learned to think of themselves, namely, as persons each of whom has a self. As we internalize their view of us, we become linked to them in a web of relations, and aware that we are different from them. Our very sense of difference is, then, a social product.

Today, this account has ramifications in several directions. It may be associated with some of the observations on the patterns of inner striving and equilibrium that Freud and others have indicated. It might also be suggested that we do not think of ourselves as others think of us, but as we *think* others think of us. Still, Mead's questions and proposals belong to the chronic and ultimate issues that are revealed by any persistent thought about the possibilities of studying society.

The *self* may be one of those concepts about which there cannot be any clear consensus and without which much social research cannot proceed. Mead certainly addressed himself to some very fundamental and very immediate issues when he inquired about the self. He asked, as suggested, because he was very much impressed by the pervasive importance of social phenomena, which he felt were the necessary matrix for *any* thought. He began to think about not only the self, but also about symbolism as one aspect of the wider phenomenon of communication. A concern with gestures as well as with language became central for him. The fertile puzzle of conversations as accomplished facts was his working grounds.

Mead had predecessors—Baldwin and Cooley, especially, in the sociological tradition. (If not for the space limitations in this Reader, it would have included more writings from these authors.) Their important contributions were, logically at least, incorporated in Mead's analysis of the self and its emergent character. This emergence provided incisive commentaries about the distinction between play and games. When Simmel, in the earlier selection, discusses sociability as a play form of society, he means what Mead, in the present selection, would discuss as the *game*. The game is play with shared rules. Thus, again and again, perceptions of similar phenomena by two different people become mutually disconnected through the use of different terms.

Mead, unlike Simmel, goes into detail about the concept of role. The self is constituted in the act of adopting attitudes of others. I assume them, I perceive as they perceive. In a measure, to perceive as they do is to be them. To be another is to play his role—play, for they take it seriously that we are not them. For Mead, it follows from all this that there is no human nature outside society. The mind and the self "are without residue social emergents." This is made possible by language, in the broadest sense of that term. Language mediates. Language, as Mead says, is a principle of social organization making the distinctively human society possible. Mead links this possibility closely with the facts of the organism, including, in the human case, the dependence of the organism on other organisms and on an environing context in which organisms are sustained. One might conceivably call Mead a biosocial theorist.

Mead's formulations provide as many solutions as they do problems. The I and the Me are perceived as engaged in an inner dialogue to which the I contributes an unpredictable and creative element. The Me is an ambiguous concept, compounded of the I as object, and of the incorporated social attitudes. The "generalized other," as a term, opens many vistas for the way in which we structure our social world, though it obscures some distinctions made by other thinkers. We would distinguish between persons and patterns within the social world; or between a meaningful world, to which we can respond because it responds to us, and a wider environment, which we must treat as though it were not human.

Mead's belief in the "normalcy of multiple personality" may parallel in importance Durkheim's concept of the normalcy of crime. In any case, this selection represents part of the thought of a man who, perhaps more than any other, has helped define the opportunities of social psychology. He proposes the dimensions that help constitute the facts of someone's action when he is in the presence of others.

The selection by Max Weber begins with the concept of social act. Weber clarifies and begins to classify the concept of social action, which is logically part of any sociological analysis. As such, the phenomenon of social action has really not been subject to much direct research, possibly because actions are both the immediate events of social arrangements and the ultimate facts to which one can refer them.

As events, social actions are a particular class. Max Weber proposes a way of describing the anatomy of this class as well as the forms that social actions can take. Judged by their languages, all known human societies recognize action. From a sociological perspective, actions become relevant when they occur with reference to another person. Social acts are more easily analyzed and classified than circumscribed. They imply an agent whose presence makes some difference to another agent with whom he shares the particular occasion, or else whose conduct within an occasion he considers to be affected by the presence of that other agent. Such presence may be imaginary. Without agents there are no acts, but acting is only one kind of accomplishment of a particular actor, an accomplishment involving some order of intent. The nature of the relation between agents and their acts is far from simple. Today we would speak of unconscious and conscious acts, of acts involving responsibility and of acts not involving it. The concept *agent* has ceased to be simple. Agents are perceived as subject to influence, just as acts, in Weber's discussion, are seen to be unequally related to matters of tradition, impulse, interest, custom, etc. In line with Mead's reasoning, acts may be considered as both outward and inward phenomena—then the distinction between contemplation and action is one of a classification of actions as such. Similarly, in their structure, actions involve some distinction between ends and means; yet acts differ in the relation between means and ends. The distinction may well be applicable to all acts; but we would recognize a difference between shaking someone's hand, and putting money into his hand because we define him as a salesman in a department store. From one point of view, both actions are means; but they stand for quite different relations between the two persons in the two cases. In the first instance, we may, as Simmel did in the first selection, speak about an association for its own sake. In its context, the handshake is a gesture of recognizing this association. In the second case, we can speak about an economic transaction: it involves one person's relation to another as primarily a means. The consideration of social actions thus raises virtually the whole range of questions which link the variety of selections within this bulky Reader. Moreover, it is not clear, except to the extent to which we do not think

about it pedantically, where actions begin and stop. Nor is it clear what we mean by the difference between who one is and what one does, once actions are perceived as the accomplishments of agents. Still, as Linton and others indicate in the next section, for social arrangements, the distinction between person and actor is strategic.

These selections, then, share a concern with those phenomena which appear when one considers immediate encounters between two or more persons. Each represents a group of explicit proposals surrounded by tacit assumptions and recognitions. Mead suggests that social phenomena are facilitated by language, the instrument of meaning *par excellence. Social* phenomena imply the issues of meaning. Weber and Simmel point, in particular, to the normative aspects of meaning with regard to their strategic significance for the possibilities of social interaction. The normative, as the dimension of appropriateness and inappropriateness, is the ground for characterizing the differences between occasions, between roles, or between one social system and another. Appropriateness includes not only the matter of the ends that people seek or with which they begin their seeking (whatever new ends may then appear to them). It refers also to the question of means by which, within given occasions, they hope to accomplish some end. Democracy as a pattern of equality becomes the means for the apparent purity of association within occasions of sociability.

The obviousness of a handshake, of a cocktail party, of a conversation among two or three people —these would seem, at first thought, to be ill served by such abstraction. Yet the questions of how these occasions are possible, what kinds of occasions one can possibly distinguish, and how one can account for their occurrence and their sequences, require this detour to the platform of more general ideas, from which one can then return to the occasions of social life.

The third selection, from Marcel Mauss's essay on *The Gift,* deals with social reciprocity as it transcends particular encounters among individuals in each other's presence. Mauss sees society contained by the obligations of giving and receiving. We may think of receiving—in contrast to giving— as a privilege; yet as we know from our experience of unwelcome invitations or presents, they too must be "received." Reciprocity, then, proceeds with reference to three obligations: to give, to receive, and to repay.

Mauss makes two further points. Gifts seem to stand in sharp, even moral, contrast to self-interested and calculating acts. Unlike the latter, they seem to represent spontaneous and disinterested concerns. This contrast raises the old and persistent question of self-interest. Mauss argues that if by economically self-interested activities we refer to utilitarian and rational calculations, then the previous contrast is by no means simple. Gifts are not just spontaneous. They represent the recognition, at least, of ultimate obligations and sanctions. Further, gifts typically take a material form. They are part of an on-going process of exchange. The medium of exchange may be concrete and calculable. The meaning of exchange, however, involves personal intentions and social agreements. Thus, economic

acts have kinship with gifts, and gifts contain economic elements.

In other words, a society must traffic in things: "everything is stuff to be given away and repaid." But this exchange issues from persons; and these persons are not simply individuals in their own right —they are also representatives and members of various corporate groupings whose character further affects the process of exchange. By linking material and nonmaterial, spontaneous and obligatory, immediately reciprocal and enduringly consequential *aspects* of social interaction, Mauss fittingly rounds out this Section of the Reader.

1. The Sociology of Sociability

BY GEORG SIMMEL

THERE IS an old conflict over the nature of society. One side mystically exaggerates its significance, contending that only through society is human life endowed with reality. The other regards it as a mere abstract concept by means of which the observer draws the realities, which are individual human beings, into a whole, as one calls trees and brooks, houses and meadows, a "landscape." However one decides this conflict, he must allow society to be a reality in a double sense. On the one hand are the individuals in their directly perceptible existence, the bearers of the processes of association, who are united by these processes into the higher unity which one calls "society"; on the other hand, the interests which, living in the individuals, motivate such union: economic and ideal interests, warlike and erotic, religious and charitable. To satisfy such urges and to attain such purposes, arise the innumerable forms of social life, all the with-one-another, for-one-another, in-one-another, against-one-another, and through-

one-another, in state and commune, in church and economic associations, in family and clubs. The energy effects of atoms upon each other bring matter into the innumerable forms which we see as "things." Just so the impulses and interests, which a man experiences in himself and which push him out toward other men, bring about all the forms of association by which a mere sum of separate individuals are made into a "society."

Within this constellation, called society, or out of it, there develops a special sociological structure corresponding to those of art and play, which draw their form from these realities but nevertheless leave their reality behind them. It may be an open question whether the concept of a play impulse or an artistic impulse possesses explanatory value; at least it directs attention to the fact that in every play or artistic activity there is contained a common element not affected by their differences of content. Some residue of satisfaction lies in gymnastics, as in card-playing, in music, and in plastic, something which has nothing to do with the peculiarities of music or plastic as such but only with the fact that both of the latter are art and both of the former are play. A common element, a likeness of psychological reaction and need, is found in all these various things—something easily distinguishable from the special interest which gives each its distinction. In the same

Reprinted from Georg Simmel, "The Sociology of Sociability," trans. Everett C. Hughes, *American Journal of Sociology*, LV, No. 3 (November, 1949), 254–61, by permission of the University of Chicago Press. Copyright 1949 by the University of Chicago. A translation of "Soziologie der Geselligkeit," the opening speech at the first meeting of the German Sociological Society (*Verhandlungen des Ersten Deutschen Soziologentages vom 19–20 Oktober, 1910, in Frankfurt A.M.* [Tübingen: J. C. B. Mohr, 1911], pp. 1–16) sense one may speak of an impulse to sociability in man. To be sure, it is for the sake of special needs and interests that men unite in economic associations or blood fraternities, in cult societies or robber bands. But, above and beyond their special content, all these associations are accompanied by a feeling for, by a satisfaction in, the very fact that one is associated with others and that the solitariness of the individual is resolved into togetherness, a union with others. Of course, this feeling can, in individual cases, be nullified by contrary psychological factors; association can be felt as a mere burden, endured for the sake of our objective aims. But typically there is involved in all effective motives for association a feeling of the worth of association as such, a drive which presses toward this form of existence and often only later calls forth that objective content which carries the particular association along. And as that which I have called artistic impulse draws its form from the complexes of perceivable things and builds this form into a special structure corresponding to the artistic impulse, so also the impulse to sociability distils, as it were, out of the realities of social life the pure essence of association, of the associative process as a value and a satisfaction. It thereby constitutes what we call sociability in the narrower sense. It is no mere accident of language that all sociability, even the purely spontaneous, if it is to have meaning and stability, lays such great value on form, on good form. For "good form" is mutual self-definition, interaction of the elements, through which a unity is made; and since in sociability the concrete motives bound up with life-goals fall away, so must the pure form, the free-playing, interacting interdependence of individuals stand out so much the more strongly and operate with so much the greater effect.

And what joins art with play now appears in the likeness of both to sociability. From the realities of life play draws its great, essential themes: the chase and cunning; the proving of physical and mental powers, the contest and reliance on chance and the favor of forces which one cannot influence. Freed of substance, through which these activities make up the seriousness of life, play gets its cheerfulness but also that symbolic significance which distinguishes it from pure pastime. And just this will show itself more and more as the essence of sociability; that it makes up its substance from numerous fundamental forms of serious relationships among men, a substance, however, spared the frictional relations of real life; but out of its formal relations to real life, sociability (and the more so as it approaches pure sociability) takes on a symbolically playing fulness of life and a sig-

nificance which a superficial rationalism always seeks only in the content. Rationalism, finding no content there, seeks to do away with sociability as empty idleness, as did the savant who asked concerning a work of art, "What does that prove?" It is nevertheless not without significance that in many, perhaps in all, European languages, the word "society" (Gesellschaft) indicates literally "togetherness." The political, economic, the society held together by some purpose is, nevertheless, always "society." But only the sociable is a "society" without qualifying adjective, because it alone presents the pure, abstract play of form, all the specific contents of the one-sided and qualified societies being dissolved away.

Sociability is, then, the play-form of association and is related to the content-determined concreteness of association as art is related to reality. Now the great problem of association comes to a solution possible only in sociability. The problem is that of the measure of significance and accent which belongs to the individual as such in and as against the social milieu. Since sociability in its pure form has no ulterior end, no content, and no result outside itself, it is oriented completely about personalities. Since nothing but the satisfaction of the impulse to sociability—although with a resonance left over—is to be gained, the process remains, in its conditions as in its results, strictly limited to its personal bearers; the personal traits of amiability, breeding, cordiality, and attractiveness of all kinds determine the character of purely sociable association. But precisely because all is oriented about them, the personalities must not emphasize themselves too individually. Where real interests, cooperating or clashing, determine the social form, they provide of themselves that the individual shall not present his peculiarities and individuality with too much abandon and aggressiveness. But where this restraint is wanting, if association is to be possible at all, there must prevail another restriction of personal pushing, a restriction springing solely out of the form of the association. It is for this reason that the sense of tact is of such special significance in society, for it guides the self-regulation of the individual in his personal relations to others where no outer or directly egoistic interests provide regulation. And perhaps it is the specific function of tact to mark out for individual impulsiveness, for the ego and for outward demands, those limits which the rights of others require. A very remarkable sociological structure appears at this point. In sociability, whatever the personality has of objective importance, of features which have their orientation toward something outside the circle, must not interfere. Riches and social position, learning and fame, exceptional capacities and merits of the individual have no role in sociability or, at most, as a slight nuance of that immateriality with which alone reality dares penetrate into the artificial structure of sociability. As these objective qualities which gather about the personality, so also must the most purely and deeply personal qualities be excluded from sociability. The most personal things—character, mood, and fate—have thus no place in it. It is tactless to bring in personal humor, good or ill, excitement and depression, the light and shadow of one's inner life. Where a connection, begun on the sociable level— and not necessarily a superficial or conventional one —finally comes to center about personal values, it loses the essential quality of sociability and becomes an association determined by a content—not unlike a business or religious relation, for which contact, exchange, and speech are but instruments for ulterior ends, while for sociability they are the whole meaning and content of the social processes. This exclusion of the personal reaches into even the most external matters; a lady would not want to appear in such extreme *décolletage* in a really personal, intimately friendly situation with one or two men as she would in a large company without any embarrassment. In the latter she would not feel herself personally involved in the same measure and could therefore abandon herself to the impersonal freedom of the mask. For she is, in the larger company, herself, to be sure, but not quite completely herself, since she is only an element in a formally constituted gathering.

A man, taken as a whole, is, so to speak, a somewhat unformed complex of contents, powers, potentialities; only according to the motivations and relationships of a changing existence is he articulated into a differentiated, defined structure. As an economic and political agent, as a member of a family or of a profession, he is, so to speak, an *ad hoc* construction; his life-material is ever determined by a special idea, poured into a special mold, whose relatively independent life is, to be sure, nourished from the common but somewhat undefinable source of energy, the ego. In this sense, the man, as a social creature, is also a unique structure, occurring in no other connection. On the one hand, he has removed all the objective qualities of the personality and entered into the structure of sociability with nothing but the capacities, attractions, and interests of his pure humanity. On the other hand, this structure stops short of the purely subjective and inward parts of his personality. That discretion which is one's first demand upon others in sociability is also required of one's own ego, because a breach of it in either

direction causes the sociological artifact of sociability to break down into a sociological naturalism. One can therefore speak of an upper and a lower sociability threshold for the individual. At the moment when people direct their association toward objective content and purpose, as well as at the moment when the absolutely personal and subjective matters of the individual enter freely into the phenomenon, sociability is no longer the central and controlling principle but at most a formalistic and outwardly instrumental principle.

From this negative definition of the nature of sociability through boundaries and thresholds, however, one can perhaps find the positive motif. Kant set it up as the principle of law that everyone should have that measure of freedom which could exist along with the freedom of every other person. If one stands by the sociability impulse as the source or also as the substance of sociability, the following is the principle according to which it is constituted: everyone should have as much satisfaction of this impulse as is consonant with the satisfaction of the impulse for all others. If one expresses this not in terms of the impulse but rather in terms of success, the principle of sociability may be formulated thus: everyone should guarantee to the other that maximum of sociable values (joy, relief, vivacity) which is consonant with the maximum of values he himself receives. As justice upon the Kantian basis is thoroughly democratic, so likewise this principle shows the democratic structure of all sociability, which to be sure every social stratum can realize only within itself, and which so often makes sociability between members of different social classes burdensome and painful. But even among social equals the democracy of their sociability is a play. Sociability creates, if one will, an ideal sociological world, for in it—so say the enunciated principles— the pleasure of the individual is always contingent upon the joy of others; here, by definition, no one can have his satisfaction at the cost of contrary experiences on the part of others. In other forms of association such lack of reciprocity is excluded only by the ethical imperative which govern them but not by their own immanent nature. This world of sociability, the only one in which a democracy of equals is possible without friction, is an *artificial* world, made up of beings who have renounced both the objective and the purely personal features of the intensity and extensiveness of life in order to bring about among themselves a pure interaction, free of any disturbing material accent. If we now have the conception that we enter into sociability purely as "human beings," as that which we really are, lacking all the burdens, the agitations, the inequalities with which real life disturbs the purity of our picture, it is because modern life is overburdened with objective content and material demands. Ridding ourselves of this burden in sociable circles, we believe we return to our natural-personal being and overlook the fact that this personal aspect also does not consist in its full uniqueness and natural completeness, but only in a certain reserve and stylizing of the sociable man. In earlier epochs, when a man did not depend so much upon the purposive, objective content of his associations, his "formal personality" stood out more clearly against his personal existence: hence personal bearing in the society of earlier times was much more ceremonially rigidly and impersonally regulated than now. This reduction of the personal periphery of the measure of significance which homogeneous interaction with others allowed the individual has been followed by a swing to the opposite extreme; a specific attitude in society is that courtesy by which the strong, outstanding person not only places himself on a level with the weaker but goes so far as to assume the attitude that the weaker is the more worthy and superior. If association is interaction at all, it appears in its purest and most stylized form when it goes on among equals, just as symmetry and balance are the most outstanding forms of artistic stylizing of visible elements. Inasmuch as sociability is the abstraction of association—an abstraction of the character of art or of play—it demands the purest, most transparent, most engaging kind of interaction—that among *equals*. It must, because of its very nature, posit beings who give up so much of their objective content, who are so modified in both their outward and their inner significance, that they are sociably equal, and every one of them can win sociability values for himself only under the condition that the others, interacting with him, can also win them. It is a game in which one "acts" as though all were equal, as though he especially esteemed everyone. This is just as far from being a lie as is play or art in all their departures from reality. But the instant the intentions and events of practical reality enter into the speech and behavior of sociability, it does become a lie—just as a painting does when it attempts, panorama fashion, to be taken for reality. That which is right and proper within the self-contained life of sociability, concerned only with the immediate play of its forms, becomes a lie when this is mere pretense, which in reality is guided by purposes of quite another sort than the sociable or is used to conceal such purposes—and indeed sociability may easily get entangled with real life.

It is an obvious corollary that everything may be subsumed under sociability which one can call sociological play-form; above all, play itself, which assumes a large place in the sociability of all epochs. The expression "social game" is significant in the deeper sense which I have indicated. The entire interactional or associational complex among men: the desire to gain advantage, trade, formation of parties and the desire to win from another, the movement between opposition and co-operation, outwitting and revenge—all this, fraught with purposive content in the serious affairs of reality, in play leads a life carried along only and completely by the stimulus of these functions. For even when play turns about a money prize, it is not the prize, which indeed could be won in many other ways, which is the specific point of the play; but the attraction for the true sportsman lies in the dynamics and in the chances of that sociologically significant form of activity itself. The social game has a deeper double meaning—that it is played not only *in* a society as its outward bearer but that *with* the society actually "society" is played. Further, in the sociology of the sexes, eroticism has elaborated a form of play: coquetry, which finds in sociability its lightest, most playful, and yet its widest realization. If the erotic question between the sexes turns about consent or denial (whose objects are naturally of endless variety and degree and by no means only of strictly physiological nature), so is it the essence of feminine coquetry to play hinted consent and hinted denial against each other to draw the man on without letting matters come to a decision, to rebuff him without making him lose all hope. The coquette brings her attractiveness to its climax by letting the man hang on the verge of getting what he wants without letting it become too serious for herself; her conduct swings between yes and no, without stopping at one or the other. She thus playfully shows the simple and pure form of erotic decision and can bring its polar opposites together in a quite integrated behavior, since the decisive and fateful content, which would bring it to one of the two decisions, by definition does not enter into coquetry. And this freedom from all the weight of firm content and residual reality gives coquetry that character of vacillation, of distance, of the ideal, which allows one to speak with some right of the "art"—not of the "arts"—of coquetry. In order, however, for coquetry to spread as so natural a growth on the soil of sociability, as experience shows it to be, it must be countered by a special attitude on the part of men. So long as the man denies himself the stimulation of coquetry, or so long as he is—on the contrary—merely a victim who is involuntarily carried along by her vacillations from a half-yes to a half-no—so long does coquetry lack the adequate structure of sociability. It lacks that free interaction and equivalence of the elements which is the fundamental condition of sociability. The latter appears only when the man desires nothing more than this free moving play, in which something definitively erotic lurks only as a remote symbol, and when he does not get his pleasure in these gestures and preliminaries from erotic desire or fear of it. Coquetry, as it unfolds its grace on the heights of sociable cultivation, has left behind the reality of erotic desire, of consent or denial, and becomes a play of shadow pictures of these serious matters. Where the latter enter or lurk, the whole process becomes a private affair of the two persons, played out on the level of reality; under the sociological sign of sociability, however, in which the essential orientation of the person to the fulness of life does not enter, coquetry is the teasing or even ironic play with which eroticism has distilled the pure essence of its interaction out from its substantive or individual content. As sociability plays at the forms of society, so coquetry plays out the forms of eroticism.

In what measure sociability realizes to the full the abstraction of the forms of sociological interaction otherwise significant because of their content and gives them—now turning about themselves, so to speak—a shadow body is revealed finally in that most extensive instrument of all human common life, conversation. The decisive point is expressed in the quite banal experience that in the serious affairs of life men talk for the sake of the content which they wish to impart or about which they want to come to an understanding—in sociability talking is an end in itself; in purely sociable conversation the content is merely the indispensable carrier of the stimulation, which the lively exchange of talk as such unfolds. All the forms with which this exchange develops: argument and the appeals to the norms recognized by both parties; the conclusion of peace through compromise and the discovery of common convictions; the thankful acceptance of the new and the parrying-off of that on which no understanding is to be hoped for—all these forms of conversational interaction, otherwise in the service of innumerable contents and purposes of human intercourse, here have their meaning in themselves; that is to say, in the excitement of the play of relations which they establish between individuals, binding and loosening, conquering and being vanquished, giv-

ing and taking. In order that this play may retain its self-sufficiency at the level of pure form, the content must receive no weight on its own account; as soon as the discussion gets business-like, it is no longer sociable; it turns its compass point around as soon as the verification of a truth becomes its purpose. Its character as sociable converse is disturbed just as when it turns into a serious argument. The form of the common search of the truth, the form of the argument, may occur; but it must not permit the seriousness of the momentary content to become its substance any more than one may put a piece of three-dimensional reality into the perspective of a painting. Not that the content of sociable conversation is a matter of indifference; it must be interesting, gripping, even significant—only it is not the purpose of the conversation that these qualities should square with objective results, which stand by definition outside the conversation. Outwardly, therefore, two conversations may run a similar course, but only that one of them is sociable in which the subject matter, with all its value and stimulation, finds its justification, its place, and its purpose only in the functional play of conversation as such, in the form of repartee with its special unique significance. It therefore inheres in the nature of sociable conversation that its object matter can change lightly and quickly; for, since the matter is only the means, it has an entirely interchangeable and accidental character which inheres in means as against fixed purposes. Thus sociability offers, as was said, perhaps the only case in which talk is a legitimate end in itself. For by the fact that it is two-sided—indeed with the possible exception of looking-each-other-over the purest and most sublimated form of mutuality among all sociological phenomena—it becomes the most adequate fulfilment of a relation, which is, so to speak, nothing but relationship, in which even that which is otherwise pure form of interaction is its own self-sufficient content. It results from this whole complex that also the telling of tales, witticisms, anecdotes, although often a stopgap and evidence of conversational poverty, still can show a fine tact in which all the motives of sociability are apparent. For, in the first place, the conversation is by this means kept above all individual intimacy, beyond everything purely personal which would not fit into the categories of sociability. This objective element is brought in not for the sake of its content but in the interest of sociability; that something is said and accepted is not an end in itself but a mere means to maintain the liveliness, the mutual understanding, the common consciousness of the group. Not only thereby is it given a content which all can share but it is a gift of the individual to the whole, behind which the giver can remain invisible; the finest sociably told story is that in which the narrator allows his own person to remain completely in the background; the most effective story holds itself in the happy balance of the sociable ethic, in which the subjectively individual as well as the objectively substantive have dissolved themselves completely in the service of pure sociability.

It is hereby indicated that sociability is the play-form also for the ethical forces of concrete society. The great problems placed before these forces are that the individual has to fit himself into a whole system and live for it: that, however, out of this system values and enhancement must flow back to him, that the life of the individual is but a means for the ends of the whole, the life of the whole but an instrument for the purposes of the individual. Sociability carries the seriousness, indeed the frequent tragedy of these requirements, over into its shadow world, in which there is no friction, because shadows cannot impinge upon one another. If it is, further, the ethical task of association to make the coming-together and the separation of its elements an exact and just expression of their inner relations, determined by the wholeness of their lives, so within sociability this freedom and adequacy are freed of their concrete and substantively deeper limitations; the manner in which in a "society" groups form and break up, conversation spins itself out, deepens, loosens, cuts itself off purely according to impulse and opportunity, that is a miniature picture of the social ideal that man might call the freedom of bondage.

If all association and separation shall be the strictly appropriate representation of inner realities, so are the latter here fallen by the way, and only the former phenomenon is left, whose play, obedient to its own laws, whose closed charm, represents *aesthetically* that moderation which the seriousness of realities otherwise demands of its ethical decisions.

This total interpretation of sociability is evidently realized by certain historical developments. In the earlier German Middle Ages we find knightly fraternities which were founded by friendly patrician families. The religious and practical ends of these unions seem to have been lost rather early, and in the fourteenth century the chivalrous interests and conduct remain their only specific content. Soon after, this also disappears, and there remain only purely sociable unions of aristocratic strata. Here the sociability apparently

develops as the residuum of a society determined by a content—as the residuum which, because the content has been lost, can exist only in form and in the forms of with-one-another and for-one-another. That the essential existence of these forms can have only the inner nature of play or, reaching deeper, of art appears even more clearly in the court society of the *ancien régime*. Here by the falling-off of the concrete life-content, which was sucked away from the French aristocracy in some measure by the monarchy, there developed free-moving forms, toward which the consciousness of this class was crystallized—forms whose force, definitions, and relations were purely sociable and in no way symbols or functions of the real meanings and intensities of persons and institutions. The etiquette of court society became an end in itself; it "etiquetted" no content any longer but had elaborated immanent laws, comparable to those of art, which have validity only from the viewpoint of art and do not at all have the purpose of imitating faithfully and strikingly the reality of the model, that is, of things outside art.

With this phenomenon, sociability attains its most sovereign expression but at the same time verges on caricature. To be sure, it is its nature to shut out realities from the interactive relations of men and to build its castle in air according to the formal laws of these relations which move within themselves and recognize no purpose outside themselves. But the deep-running source, from which this empire takes its energies, is nonetheless to be sought not in these self-regulating forms but only in the vitality of real individuals, in their sensitivities and attractions, in the fulness of their impulses and convictions. All sociability is but a symbol of life, as it shows itself in the flow of a lightly amusing play; but, even so, a symbol of *life*, whose likeness it only so far alters as is required by the distance from it gained in the play, exactly as also the freest and most fantastic art, the furthest from all reality, nourishes itself from a deep and true relation to reality, if it is not to be empty and lying. If sociability cuts off completely the threads which bind it to real life and out of which it spins its admittedly stylized web, it turns from play to empty farce, to a lifeless schematization proud of its woodenness.

From this context it becomes apparent that men can complain both justly and unjustly of the superficiality of social intercourse. It is one of the most pregnant facts of mental life that, if we weld certain elements taken from the whole of being into a realm of their own, which is governed by its own laws and not by those of the whole, this realm, if completely cut off from the life of the whole, can display in its inner realization an empty nature suspended in the air; but then, often altered only by imponderables, precisely in this state of removal from all immediate reality, its deeper nature can appear more completely, more integrated and meaningful, than any attempt to comprehend it realistically and without taking distance. Accordingly as the former or the latter experience predominates, will one's own life, running its own course according to its own norms, be a formal, meaningless dead thing—or a symbolic play, in whose aesthetic charm all the finest and most highly sublimated dynamics of social existence and its riches are gathered. In all art, in all the symbolism of the religious life, in great measure even in the complex formulations of science, we are thrown back upon this belief, upon this feeling, that autonomies of mere parts of observed reality, that the combinations of certain superficial elements possess a relation to the depth and wholeness of life, which, although often not easy to formulate, makes such a part the bearer and the representative of the fundamental reality. From this we may understand the saving grace and blessing effect of these realms built out of the pure forms of existence, for in them we are released from life but have it still. The sight of the sea frees us inwardly, not in spite of but because of the fact that in its rushing up only to recede, its receding only to rise again, in the play and counter-play of its waves, the whole of life is stylized to the simplest expression of its dynamic, quite free from all reality which one may experience and from all the baggage of individual fate, whose final meaning seems nevertheless to flow into this stark picture. Just so art perhaps reveals the secret of life; that we save ourselves not by simply looking away from it but precisely in that in the apparently self-governing play of its forms we construct and experience the meaning and the forces of its deepest reality but without the reality itself. Sociability would not hold for so many thoughtful men who feel in every moment the pressure of life, this emancipating and saving exhilaration if it were only a flight from life, the mere momentary lifting of its seriousness. It can often enough be only this negative thing, a conventionalism and inwardly lifeless exchange of formulas; so perhaps in the *ancien régime*, where gloomy anxiety over a threatening reality drove men into pure escape, into severance from the powers of actual life. The freeing and lightening, however, that precisely the more thoughtful man finds in sociability is this; that association and exchange of stimulus, in which all the tasks and the whole weight of life are realized, here is consumed in an artistic play, in that simultaneous sublimation and dilution, in which the heavily freighted forces of reality are felt only as from a distance, their weight fleeting in a charm.

2. *The I and the Me*

BY GEORGE H. MEAD

WE WERE SPEAKING of the social conditions under which the self arises as an object. In addition to language we found two illustrations, one in play and the other in the game, and I wish to summarize and expand my account on these points. I have spoken of these from the point of view of children. We can, of course, refer also to the attitudes of more primitive people out of which our civilization has arisen. A striking illustration of play as distinct from the game is found in the myths and various of the plays which primitive people carry out, especially in religious pageants. The pure play attitude which we find in the case of little children may not be found here, since the participants are adults, and undoubtedly the relationship of these play processes to that which they interpret is more or less in the minds of even the most primitive people. In the process of interpretation of such

Reprinted from George H. Mead, in *Mind, Self, and Society*, ed. Charles Morris (Chicago: University of Chicago Press, 1934), Part III, sec. 20, pp. 152–64, with the permission of the University of Chicago Press. Copyright 1934 by the University of Chicago.

rituals, there is an organization of play which perhaps might be compared to that which is taking place in the kindergarten in dealing with the plays of little children, where these are made into a set that will have a definite structure or relationship. At least something of the same sort is found in the play of primitive people. This type of activity belongs, of course, not to the everyday life of the people in their dealing with the objects about them—there we have a more or less definitely developed self-consciousness—but in their attitudes toward the forces about them, the nature upon which they depend; in their attitude toward this nature which is vague and uncertain, there we have a much more primitive response; and that response finds its expression in taking the role of the other, playing at the expression of their gods and their heroes, going through certain rites which are the representation of what these individuals are supposed to be doing. The process is one which develops, to be sure, into a more or less definite technique and is controlled; and yet we can say that it has arisen out of situations similar to those in which little children play at being a parent, at being a teacher—vague personalities that are about them and which affect them and on which they depend. These are personalities which they take, roles they play, and in so far control the development of their own personality. This outcome is just what the kindergarten works toward. It takes the characters of these various vague beings and gets them into such an organized social relationship to each other that they build up the character of the little child. The very introduction of organization from outside supposes a lack of organization at this period in the child's experience. Over against such a situation of the little child and primitive people, we have the game as such.

The fundamental difference between the game and play is that in the latter the child must have the attitude of all the others involved in that game. The attitudes of the other players which the participant assumes organize into a sort of unit, and it is that organization which controls the response of the individual. The illustration used was of a person playing baseball. Each one of his own acts is determined by his assumption of the action of the others who are playing the game. What he does is controlled by his being everyone else on that team, at least in so far as those attitudes affect his own particular response. We get then an "other" which is an organization of the attitudes of those involved in the same process.

The organized community or social group which gives to the individual his unity of self may be called "the generalized other." The attitude of the generalized other is the attitude of the whole community.[1] Thus, for example, in the case of such a social group as a ball team, the team is the generalized other in so far as it enters—as an organized process or social activity—into the experience of any one of the individual members of it.

If the given human individual is to develop a self in the fullest sense, it is not sufficient for him merely to take the attitudes of other human individuals toward himself and toward one another within the human social process, and to bring that social process as a whole into his individual experience merely in these terms: he must also, in the same way that he takes the attitudes of other individuals toward himself and toward one another, take their attitudes toward the various phases or aspects of the common social activity or set of social undertakings in which, as members of an organized society or social group, they are all engaged; and he must then, by generalizing these individual attitudes of that organized society or social group itself, as a whole, act toward different social projects which at any given time it is carrying out, or toward the various larger phases of the general social process which constitutes its life and of which these projects are specific manifestations. This getting of the broad activities of any given social whole or organized society as such within the experiential field of any one of the individuals involved or included in that whole is, in other words, the essential basis and prerequisite of the fullest development of that individual's self: only in so far as he takes the attitudes of the organized social group to which he belongs toward the organized, co-operative social activity or set of such activities in which that group as such is engaged, does he develop a complete self or possess the sort of complete self he has developed. And on the other hand, the complex co-operative processes and activities and institutional functionings of or-

---

1. It is possible for inanimate objects, no less than for other human organisms, to form parts of the generalized and organized—the completely socialized—other for any given human individual, in so far as he responds to such objects socially or in a social fashion (by means of the mechanism of thought, the internalized conversation of gestures). Any thing—any object or set of objects, whether animate or inanimate, human or animal, or merely physical—toward which he acts, or to which he responds, socially, is an element in what for him is the generalized other; by taking the attitudes of which toward himself he becomes conscious of himself as an object or individual, and thus develops a self or personality. Thus, for example, the cult, in its primitive form, is merely the social embodiment of the relation between the given social group or community and its physical environment—an organized social means, adopted by the individual members of that group or community, of entering into social relations with that environment, or (in a sense) of carrying on conversations with it; and in this way that environment becomes part of the total generalized other for each of the individual members of the given social group or community.

ganized human society are also possible only in so far as every individual involved in them or belonging to that society can take the general attitudes of all other such individuals with reference to these processes and activities and institutional functionings, and to the organized social whole of experiential relations and interactions thereby constituted—and can direct his own behavior accordingly.

It is in the form of the generalized other that the social process influences the behavior of the individuals involved in it and carrying it on, i.e., that the community exercises control over the conduct of its individual members; for it is in this form that the social process or community enters as a determining factor into the individual's thinking. In abstract thought the individual takes the attitude of the generalized other[2] toward himself, without reference to its expression in any particular other individuals; and in concrete thought he takes that attitude in so far as it is expressed in the attitudes toward his behavior of those other individuals with whom he is involved in the given social situation or act. But only by taking the attitude of the generalized other toward himself, in one or another of these ways, can he think at all; for only thus can thinking—or the internalized conversation of gestures which constitutes thinking—occur. And only through the taking by individuals of the attitude or attitudes of the generalized other toward themselves is the existence of a universe of discourse, as that system of common or social meanings which thinking presupposes at its context, rendered possible.

The self-conscious human individual, then, takes or assumes the organized social attitudes of the given social group or community (or of some one section thereof) to which he belongs, toward the social problems of various kinds which confront that group or community at any given time, and which arise in connection with the correspondingly different social projects or organized co-operative

enterprises in which that group or community as such is engaged; and as an individual participant in these social projects or co-operative enterprises, he governs his own conduct accordingly. In politics, for example, the individual identifies himself with an entire political party and takes the organized attitudes of that entire party toward the rest of the given social community and toward the problems which confront the party within the given social situation; and he consequently reacts or responds in terms of the organized attitudes of the party as a whole. He thus enters into a special set of social relations with all the other individuals who belong to that political party; and in the same way he enters into various other special sets of social relations, with various other classes of individuals respectively, the individuals of each of these classes being the other members of some one of the particular organized subgroups (determined in socially functional terms) of which he himself is a member within the entire given society or social community. In the most highly developed, organized, and complicated human social communities—those evolved by civilized man—these various socially functional classes or subgroups of individuals to which any given individual belongs (and with the other individual members of which he thus enters into a special set of social relations) are of two kinds. Some of them are concrete social classes or subgroups, such as political parties, clubs, corporations, which are all actually functional social units, in terms of which their individual members are directly related to one another. The others are abstract social classes or subgroups, such as the class of debtors and the class of creditors, in terms of which their individual members are related to one another only more or less indirectly, and which only more or less indirectly function as social units, but which afford or represent unlimited possibilities for the widening and ramifying and enriching of the social relations among all the individual members of the given society as an organized and unified whole. The given individual's membership in several of these abstract social classes or subgroups makes possible his entrance into definite social relations (however indirect) with an almost infinite number of other individuals who also belong to or are included within one or another of these abstract social classes or subgroups cutting across functional lines of demarcation which divide different human social communities from one another, and including individual members form several (in some cases from all) such communities. Of these abstract social classes or subgroups of human individuals the one which is most inclusive and extensive is, of course, the one defined by the logical universe of discourse (or sys-

2. We have said that the internal conversation of the individual with himself in terms of words or significant gestures—the conversation which constitutes the process or activity of thinking—is carried on by the individual from the standpoint of the "generalized other." And the more abstract that conversation is, the more abstract thinking happens to be, the further removed is the generalized other from any connection with particular individuals. It is especially in abstract thinking, that is to say, that the conversation involved is carried on by the individual with the generalized other, rather than with any particular individuals. Thus it is, for example, that abstract concepts are concepts stated in terms of the attitudes of the entire social group or community; they are stated on the basis of the individual's consciousness of the attitudes of the generalized other toward them, as a result of his taking these attitudes of the generalized other and then responding to them. And thus it is also that abstract propositions are stated in a form which anyone—any other intelligent individual—will accept.

tem of universally significant symbols) determined by the participation and communicative interaction of individuals; for of all such classes or subgroups, it is the one which claims the largest number of individual members, and which enables the largest conceivable number of human individuals to enter into some sort of social relation, however, indirect or abstract it may be, with one another—a relation arising from the universal functioning of gestures as significant symbols in the general human social process of communication.

I have pointed out, then, that there are two general stages in the full development of the self. At the first of these stages, the individual's self is constituted simply by an organization of the particular attitudes of other individuals toward himself and toward one another in the specific social acts in which he participates with them. But at the second stage in the full development of the individual's self that self is constituted not only by an organization of these particular individual attitudes, but also by an organization of the social attitudes of the generalized other or the social group as a whole to which he belongs. These social or group attitudes are brought within the individual's field of direct experience, and are included as elements in the structure or constitution of his self, in the same way that the attitudes of particular other individuals are; and the individual arrives at them, or succeeds in taking them, by means of further organizing, and then generalizing, the attitudes of particular other individuals in terms of their organized social bearings and implications. So the self reaches its full development by organizing these individual attitudes of others into the organized social or group attitudes, and by thus becoming an individual reflection of the general systematic pattern of social or group behavior in which it and the others are all involved—a pattern which enters as a whole into the individual's experience in terms of these organized group attitudes which, through the mechanism of his central nervous system, he takes toward himself, just as he takes the individual attitudes of others.

The game has a logic, so that such an organization of the self is rendered possible: there is a definite end to be obtained; the actions of the different individuals are all related to each other with reference to that end so that they do not conflict; one is not in conflict with himself in the attitude of another man on the team. If one has the attitude of the person throwing the ball he can also have the response of catching the ball. The two are related so that they further the purpose of the game itself. They are interrelated in a unitary, organic fashion. There is a definite unity, then, which is introduced into the

organization of other selves when we reach such a stage as that of the game, as over against the situation of play where there is a simple succession of one role after another, a situation which is, of course, characteristic of the child's own personality. The child is one thing at one time and another at another, and what he is at one moment does not determine what he is at another. That is both the charm of childhood as well as its inadequacy. You cannot count on the child; you cannot assume that all the things he does are going to determine what he will do at any moment. He is not organized into a whole. The child has no definite character, no definite personality.

The game is then an illustration of the situation out of which an organized personality arises. In so far as the child does take the attitude of the other and allows that attitude of the other to determine the thing he is going to do with reference to a common end, he is becoming an organic member of society. He is taking over the morale of that society and is becoming an essential member of it. He belongs to it in so far as he does allow the attitude of the other that he takes to control his own immediate expression. What is involved here is some sort of an organized process. That which is expressed in terms of the game is, of course, being continually expressed in the social life of the child, but this wider process goes beyond the immediate experience of the child himself. The importance of the game is that it lies entirely inside of the child's own experience, and the importance of our modern type of education is that it is brought as far as possible within this realm. The different attitudes that a child assumes are so organized that they exercise a definite control over his response, as the attitudes in a game control his own immediate response. In the game we get an organized other, a generalized other, which is found in the nature of the child itself, and finds its expression in the immediate experience of the child. And it is that organized activity in the child's own nature controlling the particular response which gives unity, and which builds up his own self.

What goes on in the game goes on in the life of the child all the time. He is continually taking the attitudes of those about him, especially the roles of those who in some sense control him and on whom he depends. He gets the function of the process in an abstract sort of a way at first. It goes over from the play into the game in a real sense. He has to play the game. The morale of the game takes hold of the child more than the larger morale of the whole community. The child passes into the game and the game expresses a social situation in which he can completely enter; its morale may have a greater hold on him than that of the family to which he belongs or the community in which he lives. There are all sorts of social organizations, some of which are fairly lasting, some temporary, into which the child is entering, and he is playing a sort of social game in them. It is a period in which he likes "to belong," and he gets into organizations which come into existence and pass out of existence. He becomes a something which can function in the organized whole, and thus tends to determine himself in his relationship with the group to which he belongs. That process is one which is a striking stage in the development of the child's morale. It constitutes him a self-conscious member of the community to which he belongs.

Such is the process by which a personality arises. I have spoken of this as a process in which a child takes the role of the other, and said that it takes place essentially through the use of language. Language is predominantly based on the vocal gesture by means of which co-operative activities in a community are carried out. Language in its significant sense is that vocal gesture which tends to arouse in the individual the attitude which it arouses in others, and it is this perfecting of the self by the gesture which mediates the social activities that gives rise to the process of taking the role of the other. The latter phrase is a little unfortunate because it suggests an actor's attitude which is actually more sophisticated than that which is involved in our own experience. To this degree it does not correctly describe that which I have in mind. We see the process most definitely in a primitive form in those situations where the child's play takes different roles. Here the very fact that he is ready to pay out money, for instance, arouses the attitude of the person who receives money; the very process is calling out in him the corresponding activities of the other person involved. The individual stimulates himself to the response which he is calling out in the other person, and then acts in some degree in response to that situation. In play the child does definitely act out the role which he himself has aroused in himself. It is that which gives, as I have said, a definite content in the individual which answers to the stimulus that affects him as it affects somebody else. The content of the other that enters into one personality is the response in the individual which his gesture calls out in the other.

We may illustrate our basic concept by a reference to the notion of property. If we say "This is my property, I shall control it," that affirmation calls out a certain set of responses which must be the same in any community in which property exists.

It involves an organized attitude with reference to property which is common to all the members of the community. One must have a definite attitude of control of his own property and respect for the property of others. Those attitudes (as organized sets of responses) must be there on the part of all, so that when one says such a thing he calls out in himself the response of the others. He is calling out the response of what I have called a generalized other. That which makes society possible is such common responses, such organized attitudes, with reference to what we term property, the cults of religion, the process of education, and the relations of the family. Of course, the wider the society the more definitely universal these objects must be. In any case there must be a definite set of responses, which we may speak of as abstract, and which can belong to a very large group. Property is in itself a very abstract concept. It is that which the individual can control himself and nobody else can control. The attitude is different from that of a dog toward a bone. A dog will fight any other dog trying to take the bone. The dog is not taking the attitude of the other dog. A man who says "This is my property" is taking an attitude of the other person. The man is appealing to his rights because he is able to take the attitude which everybody else in the group has with reference to property, thus arousing in himself the attitude of others.

What goes to make up the organized self is the organization of the attitudes which are common to the group. A person is a personality because he belongs to a community, because he takes over the institutions of that community into his own conduct. He takes its language as a medium by which he gets his personality, and then through a process of taking the different roles that all the others furnish he comes to get the attitude of the members of the community. Such, in a certain sense, is the structure of a man's personality. There are certain common responses which each individual has toward certain common things, and in so far as those common responses are awakened in the individual when he is affecting other persons he arouses his own self. The structure, then, on which the self is built is this response which is common to all, for one has to be a member of a community to be a self. Such responses are abstract attitudes, but they constitute just what we term a man's character. They give him what we term his principles, the acknowledged attitudes of all members of the community toward what are the values of that community. He is putting himself in the place of the generalized other, which represents the organized responses of all the members of the group. It is that which guides conduct controlled by principles, and a person who has such an organized group of responses is a man whom we say has character, in the moral sense.

It is a structure of attitudes, then, which goes to make up a self, as distinct from a group of habits. We all of us have, for example, certain groups of habits, such as the particular intonations which a person uses in his speech. This is a set of habits of vocal expression which one has but which one does not know about. The sets of habits which we have of that sort mean nothing to us; we do not hear the intonations of our speech that others hear unless we are paying particular attention to them. The habits of emotional expression which belong to our speech are of the same sort. We may know that we have expressed ourselves in a joyous fashion but the detailed process is one which does not come back to our conscious selves. There are whole bundles of such habits which do not enter into a conscious self, but which help to make up what is termed the unconscious self.

After all, what we mean by self-consciousness is an awakening in ourselves of the group of attitudes which we are arousing in others, especially when it is an important set of responses which go to make up the members of the community. It is unfortunate to fuse or mix up consciousness, as we ordinarily use that term, and self-consciousness. Consciousness, as frequently used, simply has reference to the field of experience, but self-consciousness refers to the ability to call out in ourselves a set of definite re-sponses which belong to the others of the group. Consciousness and self-consciousness are not on the same level. A man alone has, fortunately or un-fortunately, access to his own toothache, but that is not what we mean by self-consciousness.

I have so far emphasized what I have called the structures upon which the self is constructed, the framework of the self, as it were. Of course we are not only what is common to all: each one of the selves is different from everyone else; but there has to be such a common structure as I have sketched in order that we may be members of a community at all. We cannot be ourselves unless we are also members in whom there is a community of attitudes which control the attitudes of all. We cannot have rights unless we have common attitudes. That which we have acquired as self-conscious persons makes us such members of society and gives us selves. Selves can only exist in definite relationships to other selves. No hard-and-fast line can be drawn between our own selves and the selves of others, since our own selves exist and enter as such into our experience only in so far as the selves of others exist and enter as such into our experience also. The individual possesses a self only in relation to the selves of the other members of his social group; and the structure of his self expresses or reflects the gen-eral behavior pattern of this social group to which he belongs, just as does the structure of the self of every other individual belonging to this social group.

3. *Reciprocity*

BY MARCEL MAUSS

WE INTEND in this book to isolate one important set of phenomena: namely, prestations which are in theory voluntary, disinterested and spontaneous, but are in fact obligatory and inter-ested. The form usually taken is that of the gift generously offered; but the accompanying be-haviour is formal pretence and social deception, while the transaction itself is based on obligation and economic self-interest. We shall note the various principles behind this necessary form of exchange (which is nothing less than the division of labour itself), but we shall confine our detailed study to the enquiry: *In primitive or archaic types of society what is the principle whereby the gift re-ceived has to be repaid? What force is there in the thing given which compels the recipient to make a return?* We hope, by presenting enough data, to be able to answer this question precisely, and also to indicate the direction in which answers to cognate questions might be sought. We shall also pose new problems. Of these, some concern the morality of

Reprinted from Marcel Mauss, *The Gift,* trans. Ian Cunnison (Glencoe, Ill.: The Free Press, 1954), pp. 1–2, 3, 10–12, 69–77, with the permission of The Free Press.

the contract: for instance, the manner in which to-day the law of things remains bound up with the law of persons; and some refer to the forms and ideas which have always been present in exchange and which even now are to be seen in the idea of individual interest.

* * *

In the systems of the past we do not find simple exchange of goods, wealth and produce through markets established among individuals. For it is groups, and not individuals, which carry on exchange, make contracts, and are bound by obligations; the persons represented in the contracts are moral persons—clans, tribes, and families; the groups, or the chiefs as intermediaries for the groups, confront and oppose each other. Further, what they exchange is not exclusively goods and wealth, real and personal property, and things of economic value. They exchange rather courtesies, entertainments, ritual, military assistance, women, children, dances, and feasts; and fairs in which the market is but one element and the circulation of wealth but one part of a wide and enduring contract. Finally, although the prestations and counter-prestations take place under a voluntary guise they are in essence strictly obligatory, and their sanction is private or open warfare. We propose to call this the system of *total prestations*.

* * *

The Obligation to Give and the Obligation to Receive

To appreciate fully the institutions of total prestation and the potlatch we must seek to explain two complementary factors. Total prestation not only carries with it the obligation to repay gifts received, but it implies two others equally important: the obligation to give presents and the obligation to receive them. A complete theory of the three obligations would include a satisfactory fundamental explanation of this form of contract among Polynesian clans. For the moment we simply indicate the manner in which the subject might be treated.

It is easy to find a large number of facts on the obligation to receive. A clan, household, association or guest is constrained to demand hospitality, to receive presents, to barter or to make blood and marriage alliances. The Dayaks have even developed a whole set of customs based on the obligation to partake of any meal at which one is present or which one has seen in preparation.

The obligation to give is no less important. If we understood this, we should also know how men came to exchange things with each other. We merely point out a few facts. To refuse to give, or to fail to invite, is—like refusing to accept—the equivalent of a declaration of war; it is a refusal of friendship and intercourse. Again, one gives because one is forced to do so, because the recipient has a sort of proprietary right over everything which belongs to the donor. This right is expressed and conceived as a sort of spiritual bond. Thus in Australia the man who owes all the game he kills to his father- and mother-in-law may eat nothing in their presence for fear that their very breath should poison his food. We have seen above that the *taonga* sister's son has customs of this kind in Samoa, which are comparable with those of the sister's son (*vasu*) in Fiji.

In all these instances there is a series of rights and duties about consuming and repaying existing side by side with rights and duties about giving and receiving. The pattern of symmetrical and reciprocal rights is not difficult to understand if we realize that it is first and foremost a pattern of spiritual bonds between things which are to some extent parts of persons, and persons and groups that behave in some measure as if they were things.

All these institutions reveal the same kind of social and psychological pattern. Food, women, children, possessions, charms, land, labour, services, religious offices, rank—everything is stuff to be given away and repaid. In perpetual interchange of what we may call spiritual matter, comprising men and things, these elements pass and repass between clans and individuals, ranks, sexes and generations.

* * *

Political and Economic Conclusions

Our facts do more than illumine our morality and point out our ideal; for they help us to analyse economic facts of a more general nature, and our analysis might suggest the way to better administrative procedures for our societies.

We have repeatedly pointed out how this economy of gift-exchange fails to conform to the principles of so-called natural economy or utilitarianism. The phenomena in the economic life of the people we have studied (and they are good representatives of the great neolithic stage of civilization) and the survivals of these traditions in societies closer to ours and even in our own custom, are disregarded in the schemes adopted by the few economists who have tried to compare the various forms of economic life. We add our own observations to those of Malinowski who devoted a whole work to ousting the prevalent doctrines on primitive economics.

Here is a chain of undoubted fact. The notion of value exists in these societies. Very great surpluses, even by European standards, are amassed; they are expended often at pure loss with tremendous extravagance and without a trace of mercenariness; among things exchanged are tokens of wealth, a kind of money. All this very rich economy is nevertheless imbued with religious elements; money still has its magical power and is linked to clan and individual. Diverse economic activities—for example, the market—are impregnated with ritual and myth; they retain a ceremonial character, obligatory and efficacious; they have their own ritual and etiquette. Here is the answer to the question already posed by Durkheim about the religious origin of the notion of economic value. The facts also supply answers to a string of problems about the forms and origins of what is so badly termed exchange—the barter or *permutatio* of useful articles. In the view of cautious Latin authors in the Aristotelian tradition and their *a priori* economic history, this is the origin of the division of labour. On the contrary, it is something other than utility which makes goods circulate in these multifarious and fairly enlightened societies. Clans, age groups and sexes, in view of the many relationships ensuing from contacts between them, are in a state of perpetual economic effervescence which has little about it that is materialistic; it is much less prosaic than our sale and purchase, hire of services and speculations.

We may go farther than this and break down, reconsider and redefine the principal notions of which we have already made use. Our terms 'present' and 'gift' do not have precise meanings, but we could find no others. Concepts which we like to put in opposition—freedom and obligation; generosity, liberality, luxury on the one hand and saving, interest, austerity on the other—are not exact and it would be well to put them to the test. We cannot deal very fully with this; but let us take an example from the Trobriands. It is a complex notion that inspires the economic actions we have described, a notion neither of purely free and gratuitous prestations, nor of purely interested and utilitarian production and exchange; it is a kind of hybrid.

Malinowski made a serious effort to classify all the transactions he witnessed in the Trobriands according to the interest or disinterestedness present in them. He ranges them from pure gift to barter with bargaining, but this classification is untenable. Thus according to Malinowski the typical 'pure gift' is that between spouses. Now in our view one of the most important acts noted by the author, and one which throws a strong light on sexual rela-

tionships, is the *mapula,* the sequence of payments by a husband to his wife as a kind of salary for sexual services. Likewise the payments to chiefs are tribute; the distributions of food (*sagali*) are payments for labour or ritual accomplished, such as work done on the eve of a funeral. Thus basically as these gifts are not spontaneous so also they are not really disinterested. They are for the most part counter-prestations made not solely in order to pay for goods or services, but also to maintain a profitable alliance which it would be unwise to reject, as for instance partnership between fishing tribes and tribes of hunters and potters. Now this fact is widespread—we have met it with the Maori, Tsimshian and others. Thus it is clear wherein this mystical and practical force resides, which at once binds clans together and keeps them separate, which divides their labour and constrains them to exchange. Even in these societies the individuals and the groups, or rather the sub-groups, have always felt the sovereign right to refuse a contract, and it is this which lends an appearance of generosity to the circulation of goods. On the other hand, normally they had neither the right of, nor interest in, such a refusal; and it is that which makes these distant societies seem akin to ours.

The use of money suggests other considerations. The Trobriand *vaygu'a,* armshells and necklaces, like the North-West American coppers and Iroquois *wampum,* are at once wealth, tokens of wealth, means of exchange and payment, and things to be given away or destroyed. In addition they are pledges, linked to the persons who use them and who in turn are bound by them. Since, however, at other times they serve as tokens of money, there is interest in giving them away, for if they are transformed into services or merchandise that yield money then one is better off in the end. We may truly say that the Trobriand or Tsimshian chief behaves somewhat like the capitalist who knows how to spend his money at the right time only to build his capital up again. Interest and disinterestedness taken together explain this form of the circulation of wealth and of the circulation of tokens of wealth that follows upon it.

Even the destruction of wealth does not correspond to the complete disinterestedness which one might expect. These great acts of generosity are not free from self-interest. The extravagant consumption of wealth, particularly in the potlatch, always exaggerated and often purely destructive, in which goods long stored are all at once given away or destroyed, lends to these institutions the appearance of wasteful expenditure and child-like prodigality. Not only are valuable goods thrown away and foodstuffs consumed to excess but there is destruction for its own sake—coppers are thrown into the sea or broken. But the motives of such excessive gifts and reckless consumption, such mad losses and destruction of wealth, especially in these potlatch societies, are in no way disinterested. Between vassals and chiefs, between vassals and their henchmen, the hierarchy is established by means of these gifts. To give is to show one's superiority, to show that one is something more and higher, that one is *magister*. To accept without returning or repaying more is to face subordination, to become a client and subservient, to become *minister*.

The magic ritual in the *kula* known as *mwasila* contains spells and symbols which show that the man who wants to enter into a contract seeks above all profit in the form of social—one might almost say animal—superiority. Thus he charms the betel-nut to be used with his partners, casts a spell over the chief and his fellows, then over his own pigs, his necklaces, his head and mouth, the opening gifts and whatever else he carries; then he chants, not without exaggeration: 'I shall kick the mountain, the mountain moves . . . the mountain falls down. . . . My spell shall go to the top of Dobu Mountain. . . . My canoe will sink. . . . My fame is like thunder, my treading is like the roar of flying witches. . . . Tudududu.' The aim is to be the first, the finest, luckiest, strongest and richest and that is how to set about it. Later the chief confirms his *mana* when he redistributes to his vassals and relatives what he has just received; he maintains his rank among the chiefs by exchanging armshells for necklaces, hospitality for visits, and so on. In this case wealth is, in every aspect, as much a thing of prestige as a thing of utility. But are we certain that our own position is different and that wealth with us is not first and foremost a means of controlling others?

Let us test now the notion to which we have opposed the ideas of the gift and disinterestedness: that of interest and the individual pursuit of utility. This agrees no better with previous theories. If similar motives animate Trobriand and American chiefs and Andaman clans and once animated generous Hindu or Germanic noblemen in their giving and spending, they are not to be found in the cold reasoning of the business man, banker or capitalist. In those earlier civilizations one had interests but they differed from those of our time. There, if one hoards, it is only to spend later on, to put people under obligations and to win followers. Exchanges are made as well, but only of luxury objects like clothing and ornaments, or feasts and other things that are consumed at once. Return is made with interest, but that is done in order to humiliate the original donor or exchange partner and not merely

to recompense him for the loss that the lapse of time causes him. He has an interest but it is only analogous to the one which we say is our guiding principle.

Ranged between the relatively amorphous and disinterested economy within the sub-groups of Australian and North American (Eastern and Prairie) clans, and the individualistic economy of pure interest which our societies have had to some extent ever since their discovery by Greeks and Semites, there is a great series of institutions and economic events not governed by the rationalism which past theory so readily took for granted.

The word 'interest' is recent in origin and can be traced back to the Latin *interest* written on account books opposite rents to be recovered. In the most epicurean of these philosophies pleasure and the good were pursued and not material utility. The victory of rationalism and mercantilism was required before the notions of profit and the individual were given currency and raised to the level of principles. One can date roughly—after Mandeville and his *Fable des Abeilles*—the triumph of the notion of individual interest. It is only by awkward paraphrasing that one can render the phrase 'individual interest' in Latin, Greek or Arabic. Even the men who wrote in classical Sanskrit and used the word *artha,* which is fairly close to our idea of interest, turned it, as they did with other categories of action, into an idea different from ours. The sacred books of ancient India divide human actions into the categories of law (*dharma*), interest (*artha*) the desire (*kama*). But *artha* refers particularly to the political interest of king, Brahmins and ministers, or royalty and the various castes. The considerable literature of the *Niticastra* is not economic in tone.

It is only our Western societies that quite recently turned man into an economic animal. But we are not yet all animals of the same species. In both lower and upper classes pure irrational expenditure is in current practice: it is still characteristic of some French noble houses. *Homo oeconomicus* is not behind us, but before, like the moral man, the man of duty, the scientific man and the reasonable man. For a long time man was something quite different; and it is not so long now since be became a machine —a calculating machine.

In other respects we are still far from frigid utilitarian calculation. Make a thorough statistical analysis, as Halbwachs did for the working classes, of the consumption and expenditure of our middle classes and how many needs are found satisfied? How many desires are fulfilled that have utility as their end? Does not the rich man's expenditure on luxury, art, servants and extravagances recall the expenditure of the nobleman of former times or the savage chiefs whose customs we have been describing?

It is another question to ask if it is good that this should be so. It is a good thing possibly that there exist means of expenditure and exchange other than economic ones. However, we contend that the best economic procedure is not to be found in the calculation of individual needs. I believe that we must become, in proportion as we would develop our wealth, something more than better financiers, accountants and administrators. The mere pursuit of individual ends is harmful to the ends and peace of the whole, to the rhythm of its work and pleasures, and hence in the end to the individual.

We have just seen how important sections and groups of our capital industries are seeking to attach groups of their employees to them. Again all the syndicalist groups, employers' as much as wage-earners', claim that they are defending and representing the general interest with a fervour equal to that of the particular interests of their members, or of the interests of the groups themselves. Their speeches are burnished with many fine metaphors. Nevertheless, one has to admit that not only ethics and philosophy, but also economic opinion and practice, are starting to rise to this 'social' level. The feeling is that there is no better way of making men work than by reassuring them of being paid loyally all their lives for labour which they give loyally not only for their own sakes but for that of others. The producer-exchanger feels now as he has always felt—but this time he feels it more acutely—that he is giving something of himself, his time and his life. Thus he wants recompense, however modest, for this gift. And to refuse him this recompense is to incite him to laziness and lower production.

We draw now a conclusion both sociological and practical. The famous Sura LXIV, 'Mutual Deception,' given at Mecca to Mohammed, says:

15. Your possessions and your children are only a trial and Allah it is with whom is a great reward.
16. Therefore be careful [of your duty to] Allah as much as you can, and hear and obey and spend (*sadaqa*), it is better for your souls; and whoever is saved from the greediness of his soul, these it is that are the successful.
17. If you set apart from Allah a goodly portion, He will double it for you and forgive you; and Allah is the multiplier of rewards, forebearing.
18. The knower of the unseen and the seen, the mighty, the wise.

Replace the name of Allah by that of the society or professional group, or unite all three; replace the concept of alms by that of co-operation, of a prestation altruistically made; you will have a fair idea of the practice which is now coming into being. It can be seen at work already in certain economic groups and in the hearts of the masses who often enough know their own interest and the common interest better than their leaders do.

Sociological and Ethical Conclusions

We may be permitted another note about the method we have used. We do not set this work up as a model; it simply proffers one or two suggestions. It is incomplete: the analysis could be pushed farther. We are really posing questions for historians and anthropologists and offering possible lines of research for them rather than resolving a problem and laying down definite answers. It is enough for us to be sure for the moment that we have given sufficient data for such an end.

This being the case, we would point out that there is a heuristic element in our manner of treatment. The facts we have studied are all 'total' social phenomena. The word 'general' may be preferred although we like it less. Some of the facts presented concern the whole of society and its institutions (as with potlatch, opposing clans, tribes on visit, etc.); others, in which exchanges and contracts are the concern of individuals, embrace a large number of institutions.

These phenomena are at once legal, economic, religious, æsthetic, morphological and so on. They are legal in that they concern individual and collective rights, organized and diffuse morality; they may be entirely obligatory, or subject simply to praise or disapproval. They are at once political and domestic, being of interest both to classes and to clans and families. They are religious; they concern true religion, animism, magic and diffuse religious mentality. They are economic, for the notions of value, utility, interest, luxury, wealth, acquisition, accumulation, consumption and liberal and sumptuous expenditure are all present, although not perhaps in their modern senses. Moreover, these institutions have an important æsthetic side which we have left unstudied; but the dances performed, the songs and shows, the dramatic representations given between camps or partners, the objects made, used, decorated, polished, amassed and transmitted with affection, received with joy, given away in triumph, the feasts in which everyone participates—all these, the food, objects and services, are the source of æsthetic emotions as well as emotions aroused by interest. This is true not only of Melanesia but also, and particularly, of the potlatch of North-West America and still more true of the market-festival of the Indo-European world. Lastly, our phenomena are clearly morphological. Everything that happens in the course of gatherings, fairs and markets or in the feasts that replace them, presupposes groups whose duration exceeds the season of social concentration, like the winter potlatch of the Kwakiutl or the few weeks of the Melanesian mari-

time expeditions. Moreover, in order that these meetings may be carried out in peace, there must be roads or water for transport and tribal, inter-tribal or international alliances—*commercium* and *connubium*.

4. *Social Action and Its Types*

BY MAX WEBER

The Definition of Sociology and of Social Action

1. SOCIOLOGY (in the sense in which this highly ambiguous word is used here) is a science which attempts the interpretive understanding of social action in order thereby to arrive at a causal explanation of its course and effects. In "action" is included all human behaviour when and in so far as the acting individual attaches a subjective meaning to it. Action in this sense may be either overt or purely inward or subjective; it may consist of positive intervention in a situation, or of deliberately refraining from such intervention or passively acquiescing in the situation. Action is social in so far as, by virtue of the subjective meaning attached to it by the acting individual (or individuals), it takes account of the behaviour of others and is thereby oriented in its course.[1] . . .

THE CONCEPT OF SOCIAL ACTION

1. Social action, which includes both failure to

act and passive acquiescence, may be oriented to the past, present, or expected future behaviour of others. Thus it may be motivated by revenge for a past attack, defence against present, or measures of defence against future aggression. The "others" may be individual persons, and may be known to the actor as such, or may constitute an indefinite plurality and may be entirely unknown as individuals. Thus "money" is a means of exchange which the actor accepts in payment because he orients his action to the expectation that a large but unknown number of individuals he is personally unacquainted with will be ready to accept it in exchange on some future occasion.

2. Not every kind of action, even of overt action, is "social" in the sense of the present discussion. Overt action is non-social if it is oriented solely to the behaviour of inanimate objects. Subjective attitudes constitute social action only so far as they are oriented to the behaviour of others. For example, religious behaviour is not social if it is simply a matter of contemplation or of solitary prayer. The economic activity of an individual is

Reprinted from Max Weber, *The Theory of Social and Economic Organization*, trans. A. M. Henderson and Talcott Parsons, ed. Talcott Parsons (Glencoe, Ill.: The Free Press, 1947), Part I, secs. 1–4, pp. 88, 112–23. Copyright 1947 by Oxford University Press.

1. In this series of definitions Weber employs several important terms which need discussion. In addition to *Verstehen,* which has already been commented upon, there are four important ones: *Deuten, Sinn, Handeln,* and *Verhalten. Deuten* has generally been translated as "interpret." As used by Weber in this context it refers to the interpretation of subjective states of mind and the meanings which can be imputed as intended by an actor. Any other meaning of the word "interpretation" is irrelevant to Weber's discussion. The term *Sinn* has generally been translated as "meaning"; and its variations, particularly the corresponding adjectives, *sinnhaft, sinnvoll, sinnfremd,* have been dealt with by appropriately modifying the term meaning. The reference here again is always to features

of the content of subjective states of mind or of symbolic systems which are ultimately referable to such states of mind.

The terms *Handeln* and *Verhalten* are directly related. *Verhalten* is the broader term referring to any mode of behaviour of human individuals, regardless of the frame of reference in terms of which it is analysed. "Behaviour" has seemed to be the most appropriate English equivalent. *Handeln,* on the other hand, refers to the concrete phenomenon of human behaviour only in so far as it is capable of "understanding," in Weber's technical sense, in terms of subjective categories. The most appropriate English equivalent has seemed to be "action." This corresponds to the editor's usage in *The Structure of Social Action* and would seem to be fairly well established. "Conduct" is also closely similar and has sometimes been used. *Deuten, Verstehen,* and *Sinn* are thus applicable to human behaviour only in so far as it constitutes action or conduct in this specific sense.—ED.

only social if, and then only in so far as, it takes account of the behaviour of someone else. Thus very generally in formal terms it becomes social in so far as the actor's actual control over economic goods is respected by others. Concretely it is social, for instance, if in relation to the actor's own consumption the future wants of others are taken into account and this becomes one consideration affecting the actor's own saving. Or, in another connexion, production may be oriented to the future wants of other people.

3. Not every type of contact of human beings has a social character; this is rather confined to cases where the actor's behaviour is meaningfully oriented to that of others. For example, a mere collision of two cyclists may be compared to a natural event. On the other hand, their attempt to avoid hitting each other, or whatever insults, blows, or friendly discussion might follow the collision, would constitute "social action."

4. Social action is not identical either with the similar actions of many persons or with action influenced by other persons. Thus, if at the beginning of a shower a number of people on the street put up their umbrellas at the same time, this would not ordinarily be a case of action mutually oriented to that of each other, but rather of all reacting in the same way to the like need of protection from the rain. It is well known that the actions of the individual are strongly influenced by the mere fact that he is a member of a crowd confined within a limited space. Thus, the subject matter of studies of "crowd psychology," such as those of Le Bon, will be called "action conditioned by crowds." It is also possible for large numbers, though dispersed, to be influenced simultaneously or successively by a source of influence operating similarly on all the individuals, as by means of the press. Here also the behaviour of an individual is influenced by his membership in the crowd and by the fact that he is aware of being a member. Some types of reaction are only made possible by the mere fact that the individual acts as part of a crowd. Others become more difficult under these conditions. Hence it is possible that a particular event or mode of human behaviour can give rise to the most diverse kinds of feeling—gaiety, anger, enthusiasm, despair, and passions of all sorts—in a crowd situation which would not occur at all or not nearly so readily if the individual were alone. But for this to happen there need not, at least in many cases, be any meaningful relation between the behaviour of the individual and the fact that he is a member of a crowd. It is not proposed in the present sense to call action "social" when it is merely a result of the effect on the individual of the existence of a crowd as such and the action

is not oriented to that fact on the level of meaning. At the same time the borderline is naturally highly indefinite. In such cases as that of the influence of the demagogue, there may be a wide variation in the extent to which his mass clientele is affected by a meaningful reaction to the fact of its large numbers; and whatever this relation may be, it is open to varying interpretations.

But furthermore, mere "imitation" of the action of others, such as that on which Tarde has rightly laid emphasis, will not be considered a case of specifically social action if it is purely reactive so that there is no meaningful orientation to the actor imitated. The borderline is, however, so indefinite that it is often hardly possible to discriminate. The mere fact that a person is found to employ some apparently useful procedure which he learned from someone else does not, however, constitute, in the present sense, social action. Action such as this is not oriented to the action of the other person, but the actor has, through observing the other, become acquainted with certain objective facts; and it is these to which his action is oriented. His action is then *causally* determined by the action of others, but not meaningfully. On the other hand, if the action of others is imitated because it is "fashionable" or traditional or exemplary, or lends social distinction, or on similar grounds, it is meaningfully oriented either to the behaviour of the source of imitation or of third persons or of both. There are of course all manner of transitional cases between the two types of imitation. Both the phenomena discussed above, the behaviour of crowds and imitation, stand on the indefinite borderline of social action. The same is true, as will often appear, of traditionalism and charisma. The reason for the indefiniteness of the line in these and other cases lies in the fact that both the orientation to the behaviour of others and the meaning which can be imputed to the actor himself, are by no means always capable of clear determination and are often altogether unconscious and seldom fully self-conscious. Mere "influence" and meaningful orientation cannot therefore always be clearly differentiated on the empirical level. But conceptually it is essential to distinguish them, even though merely "reactive" imitation may well have a degree of sociological importance at least equal to that of the type which can be called social action in the strict sense. Sociology, it goes without saying, is by no means confined to the study of "social action"; this is only, at least for the kind of sociology being developed here, its central subject matter, that which may be said to be decisive for its status as a science. But this does not imply any judgment on the comparative importance of this and other factors.

The Types of Social Action

Social action, like other forms of action, may be classified in the following four types according to its mode of orientation: (1) in terms of rational orientation to a system of discrete individual ends (*zweckrational*), that is, through expectations as to the behaviour of objects in the external situation and of other human individuals, making use of these expectations as "conditions" or "means" for the successful attainment of the actor's own rationally chosen ends; (2) in terms of rational orientation to an absolute value (*wertrational*); involving a conscious belief in the absolute value of some ethical, aesthetic, religious, or other form of behaviour, entirely for its own sake and independently of any prospects of external success; (3) in terms of affectual orientation, especially emotional, determined by the specific affects and states of feeling of the actor; (4) traditionally oriented, through the habituation of long practice.[2]

1. Strictly traditional behaviour, like the reactive

2. The two terms *zweckrational* and *wertrational* are of central significance to Weber's theory, but at the same time present one of the most difficult problems to the translator. Perhaps the keynote of the distinction lies in the absoluteness with which the values involved in *Wertrationalität* are held. The sole important consideration to the actor becomes the realization of the value. In so far as it involves ends, rational considerations, such as those of efficiency, are involved in the choice of means. But there is no question either of rational weighing of this end against others, nor is there a question of 'counting the cost' in the sense of taking account of possible results other than the attainment of the absolute end. In the case of *Zweckrationalität,* on the other hand, Weber conceives action as motivated by a plurality of relatively independent ends, none of which is absolute. Hence, rationality involves on the one hand the weighing of the relative importance of their realization, on the other hand, consideration of whether undesirable consequences would outweigh the benefits to be derived from the projected course of action. It has not seemed possible to find English terms which would express this distinction succinctly. Hence the attempt has been made to express the ideas as clearly as possible without specific terms.

It should also be pointed out that, as Weber's analysis proceeds, there is a tendency of the meaning of these terms to shift, so that *Wertrationalität* comes to refer to a system of ultimate ends, regardless of the degree of their absoluteness, while *Zweckrationalität* refers primarily to considerations respecting the choice of means and ends which are in turn means to further ends, such as money. What seems to have happened is that Weber shifted from a classification of ideal types of action to one of elements in the structure of action. In the latter context "expediency" is often an adequate rendering of *Zweckrationalität.* This process has been analysed in the editor's *Structure of Social Action,* chap. xvi.

The other two terms *affektuell* and *traditional* do not present any difficulty of translation. The term affectual has come into English psychological usage from the German largely through the influence of psychoanalysis.

type of imitation discussed above, lies very close to the borderline of what can justifiably be called meaningfully oriented action, and indeed often on the other side. For it is very often a matter of almost automatic reaction to habitual stimuli which guide behaviour in a course which has been repeatedly followed. The great bulk of all everyday action to which people have become habitually accustomed approaches this type. Hence, its place in a systematic classification is not merely that of a limiting case because, as will be shown later, attachment to habitual forms can be upheld with varying degrees of self-consciousness and in a variety of senses. In this case the type may shade over into number two (*Wertrationalität*).

2. Purely affectual behaviour also stands on the borderline of what can be considered "meaningfully" oriented, and often it, too, goes over the line. It may, for instance, consist in an uncontrolled reaction to some exceptional stimulus. It is a case of sublimation when affectually determined action occurs in the form of conscious release of emotional tension. When this happens it is usually, though not always, well on the road to rationalization in one or the other or both of the above senses.

3. The orientation of action in terms of absolute value is distinguished from the affectual type by its clearly self-conscious formulation of the ultimate values governing the action and the consistently planned orientation of its detailed course to these values. At the same time the two types have a common element, namely that the meaning of the action does not lie in the achievement of a result ulterior to it, but in carrying out the specific type of action for its own sake. Examples of affectual action are the satisfaction of a direct impulse to revenge, to sensual gratification, to devote oneself to a person or ideal, to contemplative bliss, or, finally, toward the working off of emotional tensions. Such impulses belong in this category regardless of how sordid or sublime they may be.

Examples of pure rational orientation to absolute values would be the action of persons who, regardless of possible cost to themselves, act to put into practice their convictions of what seems to them to be required by duty, honour, the pursuit of beauty, a religious call, personal loyalty, or the importance of some "cause" no matter in what it consists. For the purposes of this discussion, when action is oriented to absolute values, it always involves "commands" or "demands" to the fulfilment of which the actor feels obligated. It is only in cases where human action is motivated by the fulfilment of such unconditional demands that it will be described as oriented to absolute values. This is empirically the case in widely varying degrees, but for the most part only to a relatively slight extent. Nevertheless, it will be shown that the occurrence of this mode of action is important enough to justify its formulation as a distinct type; though it may be remarked that there is no intention here of attempting to formulate in any sense an exhaustive classification of types of action.

4. Action is rationally oriented to a system of discrete individual ends (*zweckrational*) when the end, the means, and the secondary results are all rationally taken into account and weighed. This involves rational consideration of alternative means to the end, of the relations of the end to other prospective results of employment of any given means, and finally of the relative importance of different possible ends. Determination of action, either in affectual or in traditional terms, is thus incompatible with this type. Choice between alternative and conflicting ends and results may well be determined by considerations of absolute value. In that case, action is rationally oriented to a system of discrete individual ends only in respect to the choice of means. On the other hand, the actor may, instead of deciding between alternative and conflicting ends in terms of a rational orientation to a system of values, simply take them as given subjective wants and arrange them in a scale of consciously assessed relative urgency. He may then orient his action to this scale in such a way that they are satisfied as far as possible in order of urgency, as formulated in the principle of "marginal utility." The orientation of action to absolute values may thus have various different modes of relation to the other type of rational action, in terms of a system of discrete individual ends. From the latter point of view, however, absolute values are always irrational. Indeed, the more the value to which action is oriented is elevated to the status of an absolute value, the more "irrational" in this sense the corresponding action is. For, the more unconditionally the actor devotes himself to this value for its own sake, to pure sentiment or beauty, to absolute goodness or devotion to duty, the less is he influenced by considerations of the consequences of his action. The orientation of action wholly to the rational achievement of ends without relation to fundamental values is, to be sure, essentially only a limiting case.

5. It would be very unusual to find concrete cases of action, especially of social action, which were oriented *only* in one or another of these ways. Furthermore, this classification of the modes of orientation of action is in no sense meant to exhaust the possibilities of the field, but only to formulate in conceptually pure form certain sociologically important types, to which actual action is more or less

closely approximated or, in much the more common case, which constitute the elements combining to make it up. The usefulness of the classification for the purposes of this investigation can only be judged in terms of its results.

The Concept of Social Relationship

The term "social relationship" will be used to denote the behaviour of a plurality of actors in so far as, in its meaningful content, the action of each takes account of that of the others and is oriented in these terms. The social relationship thus *consists* entirely and exclusively in the existence of a *probability* that there will be, in some meaningfully understandable sense, a course of social action. For purposes of definition there is no attempt to specify the basis of this probability.

1. Thus, as a defining criterion, it is essential that there should be at least a minimum of mutual orientation of the action of each to that of the others. Its content may be of the most varied nature; conflict, hostility, sexual attraction, friendship, loyalty, or economic exchange. It may involve the fulfilment, the evasion, or the denunciation of the terms of an agreement; economic, erotic, or some other form of "competition"; common membership in national or class groups or those sharing a common tradition of status. In the latter cases mere group membership may or may not extend to include social action; this will be discussed later. The definition, furthermore, does not specify whether the relation of the actors is "solidary" or the opposite.

2. The "meaning" relevant in this context is always a case of the meaning imputed to the parties in a given concrete case, on the average or in a theoretically formulated pure type—it is never a normatively "correct" or a metaphysically "true" meaning. Even in cases of such forms of social organization as a state, church, association, or marriage, the social relationship consists exclusively in the fact that there has existed, exists, or will exist a probability of action in some definite way appropriate to this meaning. It is vital to be continually clear about this in order to avoid the "reification" of these concepts. A "state," for example, ceases to exist in a sociologically relevant sense whenever there is no longer a probability that certain kinds of meaningfully oriented social action will take place. This probability may be very high or it may be negligibly low. But in any case it is only in the sense and degree in which it does exist or can be estimated that the corresponding social relationship exists. It is impossible to find any other clear meaning for the statement that, for instance, a given "state" exists or has ceased to exist.

3. The subjective meaning need not necessarily be the same for all the parties who are mutually oriented in a given social relationship; there need not in this sense be "reciprocity." "Friendship," "love," "loyalty," "fidelity to contracts," "patriotism," on one side, may well be faced with an entirely different attitude on the other. In such cases the parties associate different meanings with their actions and the social relationship is in so far objectively "asymmetrical" from the points of view of the two parties. It may nevertheless be a case of mutual orientation in so far as, even though partly or wholly erroneously, one party presumes a particular attitude toward him on the part of the other and orients his action to this expectation. This can, and usually will, have consequences for the course of action and the form of the relationship. A relationship is objectively symmetrical only as, according to the typical expectations of the parties, the meaning for one party is the same as that for the other. Thus the actual attitude of a child to its father may be at least approximately that which the father, in the individual case, on the average or typically, has come to expect. A social relationship in which the attitudes are completely and fully corresponding is in reality a limiting case. But the absence of reciprocity will, for terminological purposes, be held to exclude the existence of a social relationship only if it actually results in the absence of a mutual orientation of the action of the parties. Here as elsewhere all sorts of transitional cases are the rule rather than the exception.

4. A social relationship can be of a temporary character or of varying degrees of permanence. That is, it can be of such a kind that there is a probability of the repeated recurrence of the behaviour which corresponds to its subjective meaning, behaviour which is an understandable consequence of the meaning and hence is expected. In order to avoid fallacious impressions, let it be repeated and continually kept in mind, that it is *only* the existence of the probability that, corresponding to a given subjective meaning complex, a certain type of action will take place, which constitutes the "existence" of the social relationship. Thus that a "friendship" or a "state" exists or has existed means this and only this: that we, the observers, judge that there is or has been a probability that on the basis of certain kinds of known subjective attitude of certain individuals there will result in the average sense a certain specific type of action. For the purposes of legal reasoning it is essential to be able to decide whether a rule of law does or does not carry legal authority, hence whether a legal relationship does or does not "exist." This type of question is not, however, relevant to sociological problems.

5. The subjective meaning of a social relationship may change, thus a political relationship, once based on solidarity, may develop into a conflict of interests. In that case it is only a matter of terminological convenience and of the degree of continuity of the change whether we say that a new relationship has come into existence or that the old one continues but has acquired a new meaning. It is also possible for the meaning to be partly constant, partly changing.

6. The meaningful content which remains relatively constant in a social relationship is capable of formulation in terms of maxims which the parties concerned expect to be adhered to by their partners, on the average and approximately. The more rational in relation to values or to given ends the action is, the more is this likely to be the case. There is far less possibility of a rational formulation of subjective meaning in the case of a relation of erotic attraction or of personal loyalty or any other affectual type than, for example, in the case of a business contract.

7. The meaning of a social relationship may be agreed upon by mutual consent. This implies that the parties make promises covering their future behaviour, whether toward each other or toward third persons. In such cases each party then normally counts, so far as he acts rationally, in some degree on the fact that the other will orient his action to the meaning of the agreement as he (the first actor) understands it. In part, they orient their action rationally to these expectations as given facts with, to be sure, varying degrees of subjectively "loyal" intention of doing their part. But in part also they are motivated each by the value to him of his "duty" to adhere to the agreement in the sense in which he understands it. This much may be anticipated.

Modes of Orientation of Social Action

It is possible in the field of social action to observe certain empirical uniformities. Certain types, that is, of action which correspond to a typically appropriate subjective meaning attributable to the same actors, are found to be wide-spread, being frequently repeated by the same individual or simultaneously performed by many different ones. Sociological investigation is concerned with these typical modes of action. Thereby it differs from history, the subject of which is rather the causal explanation of important individual events; important, that is, in having an influence on human destiny.

An actually existent probability of a uniformity in the orientation of social action will be called "usage" (*Brauch*), if and in so far as the probability of its maintenance among a group of persons is determined entirely by its actual practice. Usage will be called "custom" (*Sitte*) if the actual performance rests on long familiarity. On the other hand, a uniformity of action may be said to be "determined by the exploitation of the opportunities of his situation in the self-interest of the actor." This type of uniformity exists in so far as the probability of its empirical performance is determined by the purely rational (*zweckrational*) orientation of the actors to similar ulterior expectations.[3]

1. Usage also includes "fashion" (*Mode*). As distinguished from custom and in direct contrast to it, usage will be called fashion so far as the mere fact of the novelty of the corresponding behaviour is the basis of the orientation of action. Its place is closely related to that of "convention,"[4] since both of them usually spring from a desire for social prestige. It will not, however, be further discussed here.

2. As distinguished from both "convention" and "law," "custom" refers to rules devoid of any external sanction. The actor conforms with them of his own free will, whether his motivation lies in the fact that he merely fails to think about it, that it is more comfortable to conform, or whatever else the reason may be. But always it is a justified expectation on the part of the members of the group that a customary rule will be adhered to. Thus custom is not "valid"[5] in anything like the legal sense; conformity with it is not "demanded" by anybody. Naturally, the transition from this to validly enforced convention and to law is gradual. Everywhere what has been traditionally handed down has been an important source of what has come to be enforced. To-day it is customary every morning to eat a breakfast which, within limits, conforms to a certain pattern. But there is no obligation to do so, except possibly for hotel guests ("American plan"), and it has not always been customary. On the other hand, the current mode of dress, even though it has partly originated in custom, is to-day very largely no longer customary alone, but conventional.

3. Many of the especially notable uniformities in the course of social action are not determined by orientation to any sort of norm which is held to be valid, nor do they rest on custom, but entirely on the fact that the corresponding type of social action is in the nature of the case best adapted to the normal interests of the actors as they themselves are aware of them. This is above all true of economic action, for example, the uniformities of price determination in a "free" market, but is by no means confined to such cases. The dealers in a market thus treat their own actions as means for obtaining the satisfaction of the ends defined by what they realize to be their own typical economic interests, and similarly treat as conditions the corresponding typical expectations as to the prospective behaviour of others. The more strictly rational their action is, the more will they tend to react similarly to the same situation. In this way there arise similarities, uniformities, and continuities in their attitudes and actions which are often far more stable than they would be if action were oriented to a system of norms and duties which were considered binding on the members of a group. This phenomenon—the fact that orientation to the situation in terms of the pure self-interest of the individual and of the others to whom he is related can bring about results which are very similar to those which an authoritarian agency, very often in vain, has attempted to obtain by coercion—has aroused a lively interest, especially in economic affairs. Observation of this has, in fact, been one of the important sources of economics as a science. But it is true in all other spheres of action as well. This type, with its clarity of self-consciousness and freedom from subjective scruples, is the polar antithesis of every sort of unthinking acquiescence in customary ways, as well as, on the other hand, of devotion to norms consciously accepted as absolute values. One of the most important aspects of the process of "rationalization" of action is the substitution for the unthinking acceptance of ancient custom, of deliberate adaptation to situations

---

3. In the above classification as well as in some of those which follow, the terminology is not standardized either in German or in English. Hence, just as there is a certain arbitrariness in Weber's definitions, the same is true of any corresponding set of definitions in English. It should be kept in mind that all of them are modes of orientation of action to patterns which contain a normative element. "Usage" has seemed to be the most appropriate translation of *Brauch* since, according to Weber's own definition, the principal criterion is that "it is done to conform with the pattern." There would also seem to be good precedent for the translation of *Sitte* by "custom." The contrast with fashion, which Weber takes up in his first comment, is essentially the same in both languages. The term *Interessenlage* presents greater difficulty. It involves two components: the motivation in terms of self-interest and orientation to the opportunities presented by the situation. It has not seemed possible to use any single term to convey this meaning in English and hence, a more roundabout expression has had to be resorted to.—ED.

4. The term "convention" in Weber's usage is narrower than *Brauch*. The difference consists in the fact that a normative pattern to which action is oriented is conventional only in so far as it is regarded as part of a legitimate order, whereas the question of moral obligation to conformity which legitimacy implies is not involved in "usage." The distinction is closely related to that of W. G. Sumner between "mores" and "folkways." It has seemed best to retain the English term closest to Weber's own. —ED.

5. The German term which has been translated as "validity" is *Geltung*. The primary use of this term is in a legal context and hence the validity in question is not empirical or logical validity, but legal. A legal rule is "valid" in so far as it is judged binding upon those who recognize the legitimacy of the legal order.—ED.

in terms of self-interest. To be sure, this process by no means exhausts the concept of rationalization of action. For in addition this can proceed in a variety of other directions; positively in that of a conscious rationalization of ultimate values; or negatively, at the expense not only of custom, but of emotional values; and, finally, in favour of a morally sceptical type of rationality, at the expense of any belief in absolute values. The many possible meanings of the

6. It is, in a sense, the empirical reference of this statement which constitutes the central theme of Weber's series of studies in the Sociology of Religion. In so far as he finds it possible to attribute importance to "ideas" in the determination of action, the most important differences between systems of ideas are not so much those in the degree of rationalization as in the direction which the process of rationalization in each case has taken. This series of studies was left uncompleted at his death, but all the material which was in a condition fit for publication has been assembled in the three volumes of the *Gesammelte Aufsätze zur Religionssoziologie.*—ED.

concept of rationalization will often enter into the discussion.[6] Further remarks on the analytical problem will be found below.[7]

4. The stability of merely customary action rests essentially on the fact that the person who does not adapt himself to it is subjected to both petty and major inconveniences and annoyances as long as the majority of the people he comes in contact with continue to uphold the custom and conform with it.

Similarly, the stability of action in terms of self-interest rests on the fact that the person who does not orient his action to the interests of others, does not "take account" of them, arouses their antagonism or may end up in a situation different from that which he had foreseen or wished to bring about. He thus runs the risk of damaging his own interests.

7. It has not been possible to identify this reference of Weber's. It refers most probably to a projected conclusion of the whole work which was never written.—ED.

Section C

The Modes of the Institutionalization of Action

Editorial Foreword, BY KASPAR D. NAEGELE   *183*

1. *Gemeinschaft and Gesellschaft,* BY FERDINAND TOENNIES   *191*
2. *Status and Role,* BY RALPH LINTON   *202*
3. *On Mechanical and Organic Solidarity,* BY EMILE DURKHEIM   *208*
4. *Types of Suicide,* BY EMILE DURKHEIM   *213*
5. *Types of Social Organization,* BY MAX WEBER   *218*
6. *Legitimate Order and Types of Authority,* BY MAX WEBER   *229*

The Institutionalization of Action

by Kaspar D. Naegele

T HE FOLLOWING SECTION AP-
propriately concludes Part One of this Reader. It
returns to some themes underlying the selections
in Section A. More particularly, it concentrates
on a question prominent for Hobbes, Marx, and
Maine: What *kinds* of social relations is it necessary to distinguish? It asks: how can we describe
the important differences in the relations between
individuals in such a way that we can state as
clearly as possible what we experience as recurrent
contrasts? These contrasts can be contained within
one society at one time. They can refer, e.g., to the
differences that we recognize in our dealings with
the milkman and our dealings with our brothers.
Or, more generally, they can refer to the contrasts
between spheres of social life, such as kinship,
economic activities, or religion. Often we see these
as actually separate matters. To describe these contrasts even more generally—they can as well be
those which we recognize between contemporary
times and a previous period, like the Middle Ages.

The foregoing section has linked a concern with
social relations with the logically necessarily related
interests in both social acts, and social systems
and societies. In addition, the Introduction to Section A has emphasized the difference between concrete and analytic distinctions—a difference that
the analysis of social phenomena requires as much
as it makes it difficult. One major source of this
difficulty has also been suggested: social phenomena
are themselves partially constituted by the distinctions people make. If we then contrast a business
relation between two men with a friendship relation or, what may be the same thing, try to understand what is meant by the maxim that we should
not do business with our friends, we are asking
quite a number of questions. (1) How can we describe the norms that govern these two relations?

(2) In what ways might *one* set of distinctions
state the differences between these relations? and
(3) Of what import is it to be able to distinguish
friendship from business?

This all sounds descriptive and classifying. It also
sounds mundane. Yet progressive refinement within
a persistent effort at characterizing the "essential"
and "typical" differences among the governing features of social relations has been a durable part of
virtually all sociological analysis, and has provided
the opportunity for the convergence of ideas partially documented in this section. It has provided,
because of this and additional reasons still to be
discussed, an encouraging impetus to keep sociology comparative. Often the wish to compare,
among societies or among periods or sectors of the
same society, has been relegated to background,
or dropped. It is, nevertheless, a stubborn wish.

Four authors have been chosen to show solutions available for the analytical sorting out of
social relations. Among them, the six selections of
the section provide the essential dimensions of the
issue which more recent analysis has found necessary.

The sequence of the selections reflects the fact
that the classification of social relations, in starting in "the middle" as it were, is both a matter of
characterizing the very coherence of different societies—of contrasting sections of it, if such there
be—and of specifying roles available to specific
individuals. Ultimately, such an enterprise leads
back to the logically prior question: what "elements" of social relations can be used for a classification? We have ended the section with material
from Max Weber's fundamental proposals concerning the categories necessary for sociological analysis, that discusses this last question.

We have begun with Toennies. In the history

of sociological analysis, he probably provides the clearest beginning of an extended analysis of "paired comparison." His distinction of *Gemeinschaft* and *Gesellschaft* has become famous and productive. It brings into view, if only as a reminder, the contrasts between industrial and feudal society, city and village, business and friendship, impersonal market and kinship, complex and simple divisions of labor, impersonal and personal encounters with other people. How are these paired contrasts related? In mentioning one side of a contrast—e.g., distant, impersonal, instrumental—what becomes of the other side? Is it a "residual" category and as such less clear and more heterogeneous than what is now its opposite? Are close, personal, and expressive just other terms for not distant, not impersonal, not instrumental?

For all their difficulties, dichotomous contrasts of this kind are made easy for us by experience and language. True and false, male and female, old and young, past and future, in and out—these are among the fundamental categories by which we order the world. Toennies was not the first to propose a dichotomous way of ordering the multiplicity and succession of inclusive social arrangements and of cultures. We have seen cognate contrasts drawn by Spencer, Maine, and, in a sense, by Marx, in Section A above. Again, Toennies' proposals are parallel, in some respects, to those of Durkheim, who wrote after him. *Gemeinschaft* and mechanical solidarity differ respectively from *Gesellschaft* and organic solidarity. Unfortunately, Toennies' description of *Gemeinschaft*, of a personal nexus in which persons appear to one another more as ends and less as means, is close to what might be, for other reasons, spontaneously described as an "organic" state of affairs. Once this terminological "crossing" is recognized, it can be dismissed again.

Toennies used the facts of industrial society as his point of departure. He saw them embedded in a conflicting heterogeneity of values, that easily obscures the extent of consensus also marking and binding this society. He wrote in the Germany of the 1880's. He wrote his famous book as a young man. He died in 1936.

His starting point is the individual involved in the "rational pursuit of his self interest." This is "society," as different from "community." It is a positive form of social relation, characterized by the coincidence of a number of facts. As a social relation, it is typically sustained as a means to the ends of otherwise separate individuals. Each needs the other, as, e.g., a man making a person-to-person long-distance call still needs an operator. The relation is limited to the facilitation of interest, and

excludes the personalities of the involved parties. Characteristically, it can be studied when people are involved in economic exchange or in forming associations—*Vereine*—to establish some rather specific purpose.

According to Toennies, relations divide into those of equality and those of authority. This division cuts across the previous distinctions. Still, *Gesellschaft* is characterized by *Kuerwille:* deliberate choice, planning, voluntary association, segmental encounters. *Gemeinschaft* involves *Wesenswille:* the acting out of consensus and tradition—by contrast, it allows for much less individual scope. Relations of the *Gemeinschaft* type are more inclusive: persons confront each other as ends; they cohere more durably. They thus constitute a more "organic" nexus. Their coherence in the other case is, instead, a matter of compromising between divergent, if not conflicting, interests. Such compromises are adjudicated by a variety of standards and rules defining obligations. In *Gemeinschaft*, one shares a common fate: men then are not islands unto themselves. In *Gesellschaft*, their mutual regard is circumscribed by a sense of specific, if not formal, obligation. They are bound, in the extreme case, by contract, by agreements which set up relatively clear boundaries of obligation. *Gemeinschaft* nexi cannot be so clearly specified. Obligations ramify. Coherence itself becomes a valued matter. Specific acts—unlike the specific acts of buying and selling—are simultaneously both *means,* in relation to the daily or physical exigencies of some given solidarity, and *expressions* of past intentions and future attitudes. Friendship and parenthood, examples of relations of *Gemeinschaft,* are constituted by expectations of respect, reliability, generosity, wisdom, or whatever—in any case, they involve qualities cutting across specific acts. Specific acts express them. Social acts, especially in this context, require their wider setting. This is also true within the context of *Gesellschaft*. But the relations between specific acts and their contexts differ. In the *Gesellschaft* case, e.g., a transaction requires rules; a contract implies promises and sanctions. Yet the transaction can occur without any other encounters, leaving both parties virtually anonymous. In the *Gemeinschaft* case, specific acts tend to be consequential for a state of social relatedness between specific persons. *Gemeinschaft* militates against anonymity.

These reminders of some, and by no means of all, of Toennies' classifying accomplishment should suffice to show its importance. This importance is not diminished by its difficulties, or the necessary revisions others have introduced into it. Besides, classification, as a form of description, is not yet explanation—even if, as is sometimes true, certain kinds of explanations first require classification.

The associated elements of Toennies' dichotomy are a compound of logic and observation, of definition and interpretation. Some of the contrasts clearly intersect, rather than oppose, each other. The coercive quality of *Gemeinschaft,* for instance, is questionable when one considers marriage in our society. Presumably, no one *must* get married. The fact that marriage is normatively conditional for certain privileges and accomplishments, given additional regulations of sexuality and parenthood, is a different matter.

It is not fortuitous that Toennies' distinction between *Gemeinschaft* and *Gesellschaft* has persisted. It is concerned alike with the major distinctions among social relations, the components of social relations, and the history of society. Subsequent developments, as the Epilogue to this Reader will show, have involved far-reaching revisions and criticism of this dichotomy; but they have not discredited it as such. The nature of social bonds, and hence the question of their kinds, remains a perennial issue. Toennies' distinctions, as they stand, are not sufficient for an adequate distinction between the coherences represented by such pairs as mothers and daughters, businessmen and buyers, doctors and patients, priests and confessors, employers and employees, teachers and pupils. Yet any attempt to state the differences between the members of these pairs, with reference to the least number of elements necessary for their distinction, usually involves recourse to the contrast between the personal and the impersonal as modes of relatedness among persons.

Toennies' contribution also raises the question of the ultimate unit of sociological analysis. This implies a number of things. Genes and morphemes, phonemes and particles of matter—these are examples of some ultimate units in other universes. In sociology, there has as yet been no stability in this regard. Still, it is possible to demonstrate that a concept of the social act generally runs through most sociological analysis of the kind represented in this Reader. One can also begin, as Toennies did, with the notion of social relation. In that case, acts themselves become different by virtue of their relation to social relations; and relations, in turn, can be contrasted precisely through the manner in which specific acts come to represent them.

Social relations have an inner structure, composed of mutually related elements—this is also true of genes. One possible mark of an ultimate unit could be that it both ends and begins analysis. In the case of social phenomena and social facts, we are also often searching for an illustrative,

simple, yet significant model which would characterize the nature of social coherence. A chess game or a conversation, an economic transaction or a religious ritual—as occasions, these cut across the distinction of personal and impersonal nexus; though each involves the simultaneous presences of actors. Yet the social goes beyond this. It often involves mediated coherence—in contrast to which, as we shall see in the subsequent section, we begin to think of primary or small groups.

Durkheim returns to these themes in the two important selections that continue this section. Another author, however, intervenes between selections from Toennies and Durkheim. Ralph Linton's discussion of the difference between ascription and achievement, as principles for the distribution of social privilege or social opportunity, concerns, on the level of role, one of the several ideas included in Toennies' distinction. Linton's discussion suggests a further contrast that has become indispensable to all subsequent analysis. This may be described crudely as the contrast between inheritance and accomplishment, both considered within the context of social orders. In our society, to be someone's son is an ascribed fact; to be someone else's doctor is an accomplishment. This distinction leads to the distinction between open and closed, a contrast used by Weber in his discussion of social relations. The contrast between open and closed can be applied on a variety of planes, including that of large societies. As a dimension, it refers to the extent to which any one acknowledged status in a specific social arrangement is or is not available to a variety of others who were not born into this status.

As suggested, the distinction between inheritance and accomplishment has the merits of being applicable on a variety of planes. Within the sphere of kinship, for instance, at least in our society, the roles of son and daughter may be ascribed; the role of husband, and in a sense the role of father and the comparable roles of wife and mother, are achieved. Yet their achievement differs from that of the roles of banker, fireman, barber, or politician. The sphere of kinship and the sphere of the occupational world seem to involve a contrast of ascription and achievement. Our system of stratification, by contrast to the classical Indian caste system, appears to involve differences in proportion within each of the ascribed and the achieved positions and possibilities. Ascribed social status involves the act of bestowal. This leads to the very heart of social orders. Since society involves a membership, however unequal or differentiated it may be in any one case, it is an order which must find a place for all those born to it. In the case of national, contemporary, industrialized societies, this problem has been solved by the concept of citizenship, which involves various combinations of the social interpretation of place and of parenthood. Typically, the kinship system is one way of distributing social positions to the newborn. We make this legitimate or illegitimate through the institutions of marriage. In addition, we simultaneously bestow upon the infant both a position within society and a position within a family—as though we balanced the absence of any choice about being born with the automatic privilege of thereby being part of a relational nexus.

The principle of ascription means the enhancement of those considerations which would have us think of others by virtue of their embeddedness in a variety of social connections. From this point of view, the British monarchy is a matter of hereditary ascription. It is not open to achievement. The same is true of the Norwegian monarchy, though the descendants of Haakon V are descendants of a king who demanded a popular election, and who wanted to combine bestowal with the possibility of accomplishment. Bestowal of privilege and obligation involves also its opposites— possible exclusion and rejection. Bestowal and exclusion need not be confined to relational matters. The notion of second-class citizenship, for instance, is often a matter of the invidious comparison of classifications, through membership in what is socially defined as a different category of person.

The distinction between achievement and ascription intersects, therefore, the important additional distinction underlying the way in which we think about other persons. This involves the contrast between thinking of them by virtue of their social connectedness, or the lack thereof, to others, or by virtue of their membership in a logically defined class. One can think of another person as someone's son, or someone's plumber, as tall, or as someone's sister or brother. Ascribed statuses are those which make use of relational or classifying attributes that, as such, involve bestowal rather than individual or collective efforts. It is quite a different matter that such efforts, which then lead to achieved statuses, may in some ultimate sense involve previously ascribed positions whence a person starts. In other words, no society can be wholly free of either of these principles. Societies differ in the proportion between them and in the relative prominence of either in the different spheres together constituting that society.

Ascribed statuses cannot be sought; but they can, in a sense, be lost. They share a certain conditionality. The latter differs from the more extensive conditionality of effort that characterizes achieved

statuses. The son can become wicked and be disowned. Yet the ascribed statuses within the sphere of kinship particularly belong to a kind of irrevocable social position that is characteristically absent from the achieved social positions within the sphere of economic success or social mobility. These achieved positions are contingent on effort; they presuppose, therefore, freedom to make the effort. Achievement also demands that positions be occupied primarily by virtue of characteristics which can be acquired. In these terms, the position of guest that Simmel discussed in a previous selection occupies an interesting intermediary position. One can manipulate social affairs to become part of certain social occasions. Yet the guest's role is still contingent upon an invitation. Invitations are one form of social bestowal.

As a principle, ascription makes prominent relational qualities in the occupation of social positions and the performance of their implied roles. By contrast, achievement emphasizes individual or collective striving, and the deliberate acquisition of skills, resources, or other attributes deemed necessary for a certain position. The term obscures, for other than logical reasons, the fact that social arrangements emphasizing achievement imply agreed freedoms as well as recognizing successful striving. The doctor, as an achieved role, implies both validation and acknowledgment. It implies judges, in the form of patients and colleagues, who are willing to attribute competence. If the counterpart to ascription is rejection, the counterpart to achievement is failure.

All these elaborations of Linton's distinction, many of them contained in his own discussion, are intended to illustrate the cardinal importance of this particular distinction when it is used as a starting point for restating the characteristic issues that social orders create and solve.

The two selections from Durkheim constitute a classic illustration of a sequence of conceptual analysis and specific empirical research, both carried forward by a persistent theoretic concern with the character of social facts. The first selection starts with a vague contrast of present (i.e., the nineteenth- and early twentieth-century French milieu) and past society. Within this, he proposes a keen, sharp distinction between mechanical and organic solidarity—a distinction that closely parallels Toennies' distinction between *Gemeinschaft* and *Gesellschaft;* it complements Toennies' in many respects, some of which are "extra-scientific," though they have a bearing on the pursuit of sociological analysis per se. Toennies' distinction between *Gemeinschaft* and *Gesellschaft* is often more than disinterested and conceptual. It can easily become transformed into a moral preference—if it does not actually originate in one. The personalness of *Gemeinschaft* is often favorably contrasted with the impersonalness of society. Sociological theorizing—as an attempt to make explicit the elements from which social arrangements, including cherished examples of it, are built—must tend toward a criticism of the analyzed phenomena. Self-consciousness and questioning about arrangements by which people historically have wished to live are almost automatically an order of critique. In addition, the questioning necessary for understanding and explaining social facts is likely to be facilitated in minds feeling themselves somehow out of tune. Besides facilitating that analysis, such distance also often distorts it.

In any case, the *Gemeinschaft-Gesellschaft* distinction is not always easily disentangled from a critique of the competitive, impersonal individualism of capitalist, industrialized, contemporary society. A logical irony which has not impeded such criticism is that people who extol the virtues of *Gemeinschaft* often also jealously argue for the preservation of individuality and private freedoms.

Durkheim goes beyond such controversy, by adding a concern with individuality and individual happiness to a concern for the available alternatives of social orders. He is interested in "peace of mind," as he calls it in lectures on professional ethics and civic morality. Yet he is equally interested in the systematic analysis of social facts considered as real and intelligible regularities open to the same order of systematic inquiry possible within the realm of natural phenomena. Like Toennies, he distinguishes two forms of solidarity, forms that represent a historic succession as well as a formulation of elements constituting social relations or larger social units. In other words, both Toennies and Durkheim address themselves to the tasks of characterizing actual relations and of proposing distinctions necessary for the analytical separation of simultaneous relations in which any one person may be involved.

Durkheim's contrast between mechanical and organic solidarity involves him simultaneously in elaborating indices of social orders, and in proposing the mutual relations between numbers, individuality, division of labor, and the role of common moral values. For all his belief in the hard and "tangible" character of social phenomena— a belief that, at least in his earlier writing, he finds necessary for the scientific study of society—he is never blind to their essential invisibility. As the Book of Common Prayer would say, he is in search of outward and visible signs for these inward and invisible matters. Consistent with his concern with

the peculiar character of social facts, Durkheim regards law as one of the main indicators of social arrangement. Law, as one form of norm and sanction, reveals, together with other sanctions, the peculiar character of social phenomena—their moral constitution. Mechanical and organic solidarity—as two forms of social, i.e., moral orders— differ by virtue of the relative role of repressive and restitute law, the amount of division of labor, the degree of individuality, possible within them, and the immediate conspicuousness of a binding social consensus constraining the members of this order. Moral consensus under conditions of organic solidarity is less conspicuous. Durkheim insists that conspicuousness and importance must not be confused. Population growth is the engine of change which would have organic solidarity grow out of mechanical solidarity and which in fact presupposes the latter. Such growth makes for differentiation, which leads to specialization and enhancement of individual variety, but also to misunderstanding of the moral consensus on which such individuality in fact depends. Sociology, then, becomes the study of complex social arrangements involved in a poignant dilemma of combining a consensus necessary for the development of individuality with enhancing such individuality.

In other words, Durkheim considers the problem of order that has accompanied the writing of the men who open Section A above. His concern with moral issues, however, is carried forward by questions opening these issues to systematic exploration. In one respect, these questions fall into two main classes. Durkheim wants to know both about the history of social arrangements and about the function of any one of them within the context of a given society. He combines what have often since then become arraigned as rival perspectives. He shows, furthermore, how the division of labor —with its concomitant mutual distance between individuals and the specialization and intensification of their faculties—provides a cohesive function. It makes for mediated interdependence. Today, we would add that those who tend to depend on it are likely to take such interdependence for granted, and that it is clearly noticed only in the face of crises, like strikes or unemployment, when the mutual relations among the disparate spheres of society become painfully visible.

In his work on suicide, Durkheim considers in greater detail the relative advantages and costs of different forms of social solidarity. He is interested in the questions of both social and personal stability. Perhaps for the first time in history, Durkheim, in his classic monograph on suicide, provides a model for sociological research involving the deliberate gathering or interpretation of quantitative facts outside the realm of economic transaction or of demographic development. The importance of his monograph on suicide is manifold. It continues the discussion of the elements of solidarity. It calls for the distinction between the analysis of rates and the analysis of the individual case, while showing that such interests are related, and that their proper relation depends on their proper distinction. It begins with the unequivocal fact of self-inflicted death, and immediately asks two questions: What is the relative distribution of this phenomenon among persons differing in their typical relation to others? And, in what sense is this simple fact a single fact?

He answers the first question by taking religious membership as an index of typical differences among possible relations between a person and a surrounding social circle, organization, or group. After eliminating explanations preceding his own, he looks to these dimensions as resources for explanations in the given variation of suicides within a given population.

With regard to the second question, Durkheim suggests that the single fact of suicide must be understood with relation to the social evaluation of suicide as such. He remembers that, as an event, it can be permitted or forbidden. Obviously, he does not suggest that it does not occur where it is forbidden. On the contrary—he is struck by the fact that while Catholics, Protestants, and Jews agree in disapproving of suicide, they differ in the frequency with which their members engage in it. He relates this difference to his earlier distinction between mechanical and organic solidarity. The notion of mechanical solidarity helps him formulate the concept of altruistic suicide. Under conditions of mechanical solidarity, individual, private interests are subordinate to collective concerns. In this connection, Durkheim recognizes the fact that in the army, e.g., officers have a higher rate of suicide than enlisted men. In other words, attachment to an order in which individual survival is subordinated to honor enhances one's inclination to suicide when faced with some loss of esteem. In this sense, altruistic suicide differs from two other forms: egoistic and anomic. Durkheim suggests a fourth form, fatalistic, but does not develop it. If one can end one's life because of one's involvement in an organization whose honor is compromised by one's own survival, one can similarly add to one's chances of suicide by being part of a social circle which values the enhancement of personal responsibility. Such circles are likely to differ in their chances of generating suicide to the

extent to which they do not provide social support in the face of guilt and failure.

From this point of view, the terms Catholic, Protestant, and Jewish are indices for alternative solutions (or lack thereof) of the question of social support in the face of failure. The Protestant, more than the Catholic and the Jew, is burdened by an order of unsupported responsibility which facilitates his managing failure by death. Today, psychodynamic considerations would be added to Durkheim's description of the typical relations between Protestants, Catholics, and Jews, and their co-believers. This would provide additional links between the private and the public spheres; it would not undo Durkheim's analysis. In any case, in Durkheim's analysis, the higher rate of Protestant suicides is a reflection of a relative lack of social support in the face of the burdens and strivings that are the result of social membership. This is one possible cost of organic solidarity, with its emphasis on enhancing individual personality. Organic solidarity, as discussed above, is characterized by the greater generality of its binding consensus. Such generality is necessary when individual difference and variation become valued accomplishments.

Both altruistic and egoistic suicides occur under conditions of clear rules. Whatever despair either may involve, it is not the despair of uncertainty; it is, if anything, the despair of a disproportion between the desirable and the actual. Typically organic solidarity, however, contains another possibility. The ends which people seek within its confines and the norms governing their pursuit can become elusive. Within the fluctuations of its economic change, organic solidarity can give rise to the possibilities of other forms of social discontinuities, including social mobility. It can lead to a moral vacuum. Durkheim uses the word *anomie* to describe this state of affairs. The term is ambiguous, since it seems sometimes to refer to a conflict in the ends that men seek, and sometimes to the absence of a clear view of any end that they might wish to attain.

In any case, Durkheim faces the fact that economic depression, as well as sudden economic prosperity, is often accompanied by an increase in suicide. Later research may have shown his statistics to be faulty; but his ideas have remained productive. Both situations are cases of a more general phenomenon. Both demonstrate that people's actions and stability are contingent on commitments to standards and beliefs making life meaningful and providing bases of choice among alternative courses of conduct. Sudden change in any direction—enhancing or undermining one's fortune—is in fact constituted by new conditions, in which one often lacks the requisite guides for necessary action. Whether, by *anomie,* one means the attrition of a landscape of ends toward which one wishes to proceed, or of standards by which one can choose when one comes to road-forks, it constitutes an individual or collective situation making action difficult. Yet Durkheim's analysis, particularly of suicide, assumes that the pursuit of ends is a constitutive element of personality itself. This position provides a restatement of the question of the relation between individuals and social arrangements.

In Durkheim's analysis, in spite of its ambiguity and shift over time, the social becomes simultaneously an order of external constraint and support, and part of the necessary inner resources constituting personality as such. Anomic suicide is, so to speak, the empirical answer to the logical fallacy of an original human nature. Isolated from ends, human nature could not have arisen; and in facing the attrition of ends, it is once more helped toward decay.

These comments are intended to provide some continuity among the necessarily select and disparate passages in this Reader. Our purpose throughout is to let the passages speak for themselves, while we justify our having selected them.

This section is logically concluded by Max Weber's dissection of the elements of social action, social relations, social organization, and legitimate order. Like Durkheim, Weber began by facing concrete historic circumstances and wishing to impose some approximate first order on them. Linton developed one strand of distinction. Max Weber, in this section, is more concerned with the logically complementary question of what conceptual distinctions must be made in order to be just to the known and experienced complexity of social orders and their historic succession. He is concerned, in this context, with the clarification of categories. In his case, this accompanied a huge enterprise of historic analysis, with particular reference to the mutual relations between religiosity and economic systems. About Durkheim's selection preceding the two by Max Weber, one may ask what validity the proposed explanations have, and to what other regularities Durkheim's proposals about suicide could be applied. Of Weber's specific contributions it is necessary to inquire how clear the distinctions he proposes are, what alternative distinctions could have been made, and what kind of research such distinctions facilitate. This Reader is not directly concerned with providing answers, but with raising questions; it cannot be reiterated too often that the assembling of

materials for it has primarily been guided by the aim of documenting and suitably arranging the resources available for sociological analysis, so that the continuity among sociologists' works can be enhanced.

Max Weber suspends a huge panoply of distinctions between the two poles of social action and social order. This panoply is intended to make social change and stability intelligible. It proceeds from the assumption that the systematic (scientific) inquiry into social phenomena, which are also historic phenomena, is always a matter of both stability and change. Like Durkheim's simultaneous interest in history and function, Weber's simultaneous interest in stability and change has often become a matter of rival perspective, as will be discussed again in the introductory material to the last part of this Reader.

The selections from Max Weber rounding out this section follow directly from the Weber selection that completed Section B above. While elaborating his monumental gridwork of distinctions, Max Weber interrupts a discussion of the difference between open and closed social relations with the comment that this laborious effort at defining everyday facts may well appear to be a dry and useless enterprise. On the other hand, the enterprise demonstrates that what we take as self-evident is least likely to be thought through. The present section represents part of this rich thinking process. It leads to a variety of cardinal ideas which help constitute the universe of sociological analysis. Readers of this Reader will come to different conclusions about the worth and importance of such an enterprise; about the relations, in Max Weber's case, between his theoretic distinctions and the history of his own more specific empirical work.

One of the admitted shortcomings of this or any anthology should once more become apparent: Even though we have often quoted from Max Weber throughout these volumes and even if all his selections were seen only in their mutual relation, this would still not provide an adequate representation of his total work. The same is true for all the other authors from whom we have taken selections. In Max Weber's case, it is particularly serious. His is one of the few cases in which the work of one man comes to assume a fragmentary hugeness which is visible only when one sees it as a whole. Freud, Durkheim, and Simmel, from this point of view, represent quite different configurations of accomplishment. In any event, the two selections dealing with the constitutive elements of social organization and legitimate orders can be read as a circumspect, tough, and discriminating effort to propose a latticework of distinctions which are as much a summary of a man's knowledge as they are a statement of his intentions. Durkheim returned again and again to the moral quality of social facts; Weber was equally insistent on their meaningful character. His category is perhaps the wider one; his efforts are more those of a universal historian. Durkheim preferred, as a method of analysis, the progressive elimination of alternative perspectives in relation to a specified and delimited phenomenon, like suicide, religious ritual, or division of labor; Max Weber, like him, also has a guiding and single focus—the rationalization of the world.

He also wishes to formulate a categorical arsenal for coming to terms with the properties of social phenomena on four levels: social action, social relations, regularities of choice, and legitimate orders. He tries to outline the generic features of social acts or of social relations, of such regularities as convention and fashion, or of legitimate orders. He also seeks to distinguish *kinds* of each of these coherences. If a social act is an act involving mutual orientation, he distinguishes four forms of such orientation: those concerned with the implementation of specific ends or consequences; those concerned with the expression of moral positions; those issuing from affective dispositions; and those arising from tradition. One may be quite critical of such a classification, as it seems to lack an explicit principle of differentiation. Still, the proposal reminds one of the constituted dimensions of social interaction, and releases one from imprisonment by the immediately experienced. Similarly, on the plane of social relations, Weber proposes both variables of their inner structure, and a classification of their concrete forms. For example, he distinguishes the mutability of a relation, or its durability, from its definability, or its definability from its degree of formality. He separates open and closed relations on the basis of their accessibility, or lack of it, to others also interested in the intended meaning of a given social relation. He uses this distinction to cut across the previous differentiation between conflict, communal and associational relations. Again, we may be critical and wonder whether concrete and analytical matters

have been properly separated. Too, we are reminded of a continuity among Toennies, Durkheim, and Weber. Considering action, Weber distinguishes between usage, interest, and legitimate order. He then inquires seriously how the legitimacy of action can be guaranteed and how legitimacy is attributed to it. This leads him to distinguish kinds of sanctions. He proposes terms like "convention" and "legal order," to bring into line the experienced difference between disapproval and legal coercion. Such distinctions become related to his analysis of authority and power. Max Weber's primary concern is with the bases on which power—i.e., the chances of imposing one's will successfully—becomes justified or justifiable. Weber distinguishes between power and authority, for he considers power to be sociologically amorphous. By contrast, in his work, authority becomes more precise: it refers to the chances that an order meets obedience among specifiable persons.

Weber acknowledges the continuity between his efforts and the accomplishments of the past. He wishes to enhance self-consciousness in using the ideas necessary for an account of the structure and history of social arrangements. Given the serious center of meaning, the co-ordinates of his analysis typically involve the contrasts of reason and tradition, emotion and interest, felt coherence and calculating association, legal requirement and charismatic demand. Distributed over the several planes of social action, social relation, social regularity, and legitimate order, such contrasts soon return him to a concern with the social constellations that indicate law as a form of obligatory order —distinct from convention, which leads to disapproval. Law requires a bureaucratic staff.

Max Weber extends his ordering of social constellations by sorting out kinds of corporate groups. This sorting is facilitated by his concern with authority, power, and representation.

In summary: like Toennies, Linton, and Durkheim, Max Weber in the following selections is concerned with consensus, and with the regulative principles through which a variety of disparate persons come to produce the regularities among their acts that are not explicable on the basis either of their biological constitutions or of purely economic considerations.

1. Gemeinschaft and Gesellschaft

BY FERDINAND TOENNIES

Subject

RELATIONS BETWEEN HUMAN WILLS—
GEMEINSCHAFT (COMMUNITY) AND
GESELLSCHAFT (SOCIETY) FROM A
LINGUISTIC POINT OF VIEW[1]

HUMAN WILLS stand in manifold relations to one another. Every such relationship is a mutual action, inasmuch as one party is active or gives while the other party is passive or receives. These actions are of such a nature that they tend either towards preservation or towards destruction of the other will or life; that is, they are either positive or negative. This study will consider as its subject of investigation only the relationships of mutual affirmation. Every such relationship represents unity in plurality or plurality in unity. It consists of assistance, relief, services, which are transmitted back and forth from one party to another and are to be considered as expressions of wills and their forces. The group which is formed through this positive type of relationship is called an association (*Verbindung*) when conceived of as a thing of being which acts as a unit inwardly and outwardly. The relationship itself, and also the resulting association, is conceived of either as real and organic life—this is the essential characteristic of the *Gemeinschaft* (community),—or as imaginary and mechanical structure—this is the concept of *Gesellschaft* (society).

Through the application of these two terms we shall see that the chosen expressions are rooted in their synonymic use in the German language. But to date in scientific terminology they have been customarily confused and used at random without any distinction. For this reason, a few introductory re-

marks may explain the inherent contrast between these two concepts. All intimate, private, and exclusive living together, so we discover, is understood as life in Gemeinschaft (community). Gesellschaft (society) is public life—it is the world itself. In Gemeinschaft (community) with one's family, one lives from birth on bound to it in weal and woe. One goes into Gesellschaft (society) as one goes into a strange country. A young man is warned against bad Gesellschaft (society), but the expression bad Gemeinschaft (community) violates the meaning of the word. Lawyers may speak of domestic (*häusliche*) Gesellschaft (society) thinking only of the legalistic concept of a social association, but the domestic Gemeinschaft (community) or home life with its immeasurable influence upon the human soul has been felt by everyone who ever shared it. Likewise, each member of a bridal couple knows that he or she goes into marriage as a complete Gemeinschaft (community) of life (*communio totius vitae*). A Gesellschaft (society) of life would be a contradiction in and of itself. One keeps or enjoys another's Gesellschaft (society or company) but not his Gemeinschaft (community) in this sense. One becomes a part of a religious Gemeinschaft (community); religious Gesellschaften (associations, or societies) like any other groups formed for given purposes, exist only in so far as they, viewed from without, take their places among the institutions of a political body or as they represent conceptual elements of a theory; they do not touch upon the religious Gemeinschaft as such. There exists a Gemeinschaft (community) of language, of folkways, or mores, or of beliefs; but, by way of contrast, Gesellschaft (society or company) exists in the realm of business, travel, or sciences. So of special importance are the commercial Gesellschaften (societies or companies), whereas, even though a certain familiarity and Gemeinschaft (community) may exist among business partners, one could indeed hardly speak of commercial Gemeinschaft (community). To make the word combination, "joint-stock Gemeinschaft," would be abominable. On the other hand, there exists a Gemeinschaft (community) of ownership in fields, forest, and pasture. The Gemeinschaft (community) of property between man and wife cannot be called Gesellschaft

Reprinted from Ferdinand Toennies, *Community and Society* (*Gemeinschaft und Gesellschaft*, trans. and introduced by Charles P. Loomis (East Lansing, Mich.: Michigan State University Press, 1957) Book I, secs. 1, 2, pp. 33–40, 42–44, 46–48, 64–69, 75–78, with the permission of Michigan State University Press.

1. The parenthetical English renditions of the words *Gemeinschaft* and *Gesellschaft* found in this section indicate the difficulty which would be encountered if one attempted their translation by any one pair of terms. Elsewhere in the text these two substantives and their adjective forms are not translated when they are used in the ideal typological sense.

(society) of property. Thus many differences become apparent.

In the most general way, one could speak of a Gemeinschaft (community) comprising the whole of mankind, such as the church wishes to be regarded. But human Gesellschaft (society) is conceived as mere coexistence of people independent of each other. Recently, the concept of Gesellschaft as opposed to and distinct from the state has been developed. This term will also be used in this treatise, but can only derive its adequate explanation from the underlying contrast to the Gemeinschaft of the people.

Gemeinschaft (community) is old; Gesellschaft (society) is new as a name as well as a phenomenon. This has been recognized by an author who otherwise taught political science in all its aspects without penetrating to its fundamentals. "The entire concept of Gesellschaft (society) in a social and political sense," says Bluntschli (*Staatswörterbuch* IV), "finds its natural foundation in the folkways, mores, and ideas of the third estate. It is not really the concept of a people (*Volks-Begriff*) but the concept of the third estate . . . Its Gesellschaft has become the origin and expression of common opinions and tendencies . . . Wherever urban culture blossoms and bears fruits, Gesellschaft appears as its indispensable organ. The rural people know little of it." On the other hand, all praise of rural life has pointed out that the Gemeinschaft (community) among people is stronger there and more alive; it is the lasting and genuine form of living together. In contrast to Gemeinschaft, Gesellschaft (society) is transitory and superficial. Accordingly, Gemeinschaft (community) should be understood as a living organism, Gesellschaft (society) as a mechanical aggregate and artifact.

ORGANIC AND MECHANICAL FORMATIONS

Everything real is organic in so far as it can be conceived only as something related to the totality of reality and defined in its nature and movements by this totality. Thus attraction in its manifold forms makes the universe, in so far as it is accessible to our knowledge, into a totality, the action of which expresses itself in the movements by which any two bodies change their mutually held positions. But for observation and scientific theory based thereupon, a totality must be limited to be effective, and each such totality will consist of smaller totalities which have a certain direction and speed in relation to each other. Attraction itself remains either unexplained (as force in space) or is understood as mechanical force (by exterior contact) making itself effective, perhaps in some unknown manner.

Thus the masses of matter may be divided into homogeneous molecules which attract each other with more or less energy and which in their aggregate state appear as bodies. The molecules are divided into dissimilar (chemical) atoms, the dissimilarity of which remains to be explained by further analysis of the different arrangement which similar atom constituents take within the atom. Pure theoretical mechanics, however, presupposes the existence of centers of force without dimension as sources of real actions and reactions. The concept of these centers is very close to the concept of metaphysical atoms and it excludes from the calculation all influence of the movements, or tendencies thereto, of the parts. For all practical applications the physical molecules, when thought of in relation to the same body as their systems, can be considered equally well as carriers of energy, as substance itself, since these molecules are equal in size and no attention is given to their possible subdivision. All real masses may be compared by weight and expressed as quantities of a similar definite substance when their parts are conceived as being in a perfectly solid state of aggregation.

In every case the unit, which is assumed as the subject of a movement or as an integral part of a totality (a higher unit), is the product of a fiction necessary for scientific analysis. Strictly speaking, only the ultimate units, metaphysical atoms, could be accepted as their adequate representatives: somethings which are nothings or nothings which are somethings (*Etwasse, welche Nichtse, oder Nichtse, welche Etwasse sind*). But in so reasoning, the relative meaning of all concepts of size must be kept in mind.

In reality, however, even if they may be anomalies in the mechanical concept, there exist bodies other than these combinable and combining particles of matter conceived of as dead. Such bodies appear to be natural totalities which, as totalities, have movement and action in relation to their parts. These are the organic bodies. To these we human beings, who strive for knowledge and understanding, ourselves belong. Each of us has, in addition to imparted knowledge of all possible bodies, an immediate knowledge of his own. We are driven to the conclusion that psychic life is connected with every living body, existing as an entity in the same way as we know ourselves to exist. But objective observation teaches not less clearly that in the case of a living body we deal each time with a totality which is not a mere aggregation of its parts but one which is made up of these parts in such a manner that they are dependent upon and conditioned by the totality, and that such a body as a totality and hence as a form possesses reality and substance.

As human beings we are able to produce only

inorganic things from organic materials, dividing and recombining them. In the same way things are also made into a unity through scientific manipulation and are a unity in our concepts. Naïve interpretation or attitudes and artistic imagination, folk belief, and inspired poetry lend life to the phenomena. This creative element is also apparent in the fictions of science. But science also reduces the living to the dead in order to grasp its relations and conditions. It transforms all conditions and forces into movements and interprets all movements as quantities of labor performed, i.e., expended energy, in order to comprehend processes as similar and commensurable. This last is true to the same extent that the assumed units are realities, and the possibility for thought is unlimited. Thus understanding, as an end, is attained, and therewith other objectives.

However, the tendencies and inevitableness of organic growth and decay cannot be understood through mechanical means. In the organic world the concept itself is a living reality, changing and developing as does the idea of the individual being. When science enters this realm it changes its own nature and develops from a logical and rational to an intuitive and dialectic interpretation; it becomes philosophy. However, the present study does not deal with genus and species, i.e., in regard to human beings it is not concerned with race, people, or tribe as biological units. Instead, we have in mind their sociological interpretation, which sees human relationships and associations as living organisms or, in contrast, mechanical constructions. This has its counterpart and analogy in the theory of individual will, and in this sense to present the psychological problem will be the text of the second book of this treatise.

Theory of Gemeinschaft

EMBRYO OR EMERGENT FORMS

In accordance with the preliminary explanations, the theory of Gemeinschaft starts from the assumption of perfect unity of human wills as an original or natural condition which is preserved in spite of actual separation. This natural condition is found in manifold forms because of dependence on the nature of the relationship between individuals who are differently conditioned. The common root of this natural condition is the coherence of vegetative life through birth and the fact that the human wills, in so far as each one of these wills is related to a definite physical body, are and remain linked to each other by parental descent and by sex, or by necessity become so linked. This close interrelation

as a direct and mutual affirmation is represented in its most intense form by three types of relationships, namely: (1) the relation between a mother and her child; (2) the relation between husband and wife in its natural or general biological meaning; (3) the relation among brothers and sisters, that is, at least among those who know each other as being the offspring of the same mother. If in the relations of kindred individuals one may assume the embryo of Gemeinschaft or the tendency and force thereto, rooted in the individual wills, specific significance must be attributed to the three above-mentioned relationships, which are the strongest and most capable of development. Each, however, is important in a special way:

(A) The relation between mother and child is most deeply rooted in liking or in pure instinct. Also, in this case the transition from an existing physical to a purely psychic bond is evident. But the physical element is the more apparent the closer the relation remains to its origin (birth). The relationship implies long duration as the mother has to feed, protect, and educate the child until it becomes capable of doing this alone. With this development the relation loses in essentiality, and separation of mother and child becomes more probable. This tendency toward separation, however, can be counterbalanced, or at least restrained, by other tendencies, namely, through the mother and child becoming accustomed to one another and through remembrance of the pleasures which they have given each other, especially the gratitude of the child for the care and painstaking attention of the mother. To these direct mutual relations other common and indirectly binding relations involving other things are added: pleasure, habit, remembrance of objects in the environments which were, or have become, pleasant. The same holds also of shared remembrances of intimate, helpful, beloved persons such as the father, if he lives with the mother, or the brothers and sisters of the mother or child, etc.

(B) The sexual instinct does not in any way necessitate a permanent living together. Moreover, in the beginning it does not lead so much to a fixed mutual relationship as to one-sided subjugation of the woman, who, weaker by nature, can be reduced to an object of mere possession or to servitude. For this reason the relationship between man and wife, if considered independent from kinship and from all social forces based thereupon, has to be supported mainly by habituation to one another in order that the relationship may shape itself into one of mutual affirmation. Besides this, there are, as will be readily understood, the other previously mentioned factors which assist in strengthening the bond. Especially in this connection may be mentioned the relationship to the children as common possession, and, further, the common possessions and household.

(C) Among brothers and sisters there is no such innate and instinctive affection and natural liking or preference as between mother and children or between husband and wife. This is true even though the husband-wife relationship may resemble that among brothers and sisters, and there are many reasons to believe that this has frequently been the case with some tribes in an earlier period in the history of man. It must be remembered, however, that among such tribes, as long as descent was reckoned only from the mother, the relationship between brothers and sisters was extended in name, as well as in its emotional aspects, to the corresponding generations of cousins. This practice was so general that the more limited meaning of the concept was, as in many other cases, developed only in a later period. It was through a similar development in the most important ethnic groups that marriage between brothers and sisters came to be regarded as illicit, and where exogamy prevailed, marriage and clan membership (but not kinship) also became mutually exclusive. Therefore, one is justified in considering love between brother and sister, although essentially based upon blood kinship, as the most "human" relationship between human beings. The intellectual quality of this relationship as compared to the two others discussed above is also apparent from the fact that while instinct plays only a small part, the intellectual force of memory is the foremost in creating, conserving, and consolidating this bond of hearts. For where children of the same mother, in living with her, are also living together with each other, the reminiscences of each of them about pleasant impressions and experiences will necessarily include the person and the activities of the other one. This all the more so, the more closely the group is tied together, especially where, endangered from the outside, it is compelled to strive and act in unison. Thus habit makes such life easier and dearer. At the same time the greatest possible *similarity* of nature and equality of strength may be expected among brothers even though the differences in intelligence and experience, as a purely human or mental element, may easily be perceived.

THEIR UNITY

Many other less intimate relationships are linked to those most fundamental and familiar types. They find their unity and perfection in the relationships between father and children. The existence of an organic basis which keeps the intelligent being connected with the offspring of his body makes this relationship in the most important aspect similar to the first one mentioned (A), from which it differs in that the instinctive part of it is so much weaker. Thus it resembles more closely the husband-wife relationship and is, therefore, more readily conceived as merely coercive. But while the affection of the husband, as to duration more than as to intensity, is inferior to that of the mother, the love of a father differs from the love of a mother in the opposite direction. If present to any considerable degree, therefore, it is similar through its spiritual nature to the affection among brothers and sisters, but, in contrast to the latter, it is defined by an inequality of nature, especially that of age and intellectual power.

Thus the idea of authority is, within the Gemeinschaft, most adequately represented by fatherhood or paternity. However, authority, in this sense, does not imply possession and use in the interest of the master; it means education and instruction as the fulfilment of procreation, i.e., sharing the fullness of one's own life and experiences with the children who will grow gradually to reciprocate these gifts and thus to establish a truly mutual relationship. In this regard the first-born son has a natural preference—he is the closest to the father and will occupy the place which the aging father leaves. The full authority of the father is, therefore, at least implicitly, passed on to the first-born son at his very birth. Thus the idea of an ever-renewed vital force finds its expression in the continuous succession of fathers and sons. We know that this rule of inheritance is not the original one. Apparently the patriarchate has been preceded by the matriarchate and the rule of the brother on the mother's side, and even if collateral succession (the system of tanistry) has precedence over primogeniture, this precedence is based only on the relation to a former generation: the succeeding brother does not derive his right from the brother but from the common father.

*   *   *

GEMEINSCHAFT BY BLOOD—OF PLACE—OF MIND. KINSHIP—NEIGHBORHOOD—FRIENDSHIP

The Gemeinschaft by blood, denoting unity of being, is developed and differentiated into Gemeinschaft of locality, which is based on a common habitat. A further differentiation leads to the Gemeinschaft of mind which implies only co-operation and co-ordinated action for a common goal. Gemeinschaft of locality may be conceived as a community of physical life, just as Gemeinschaft of mind expresses the community of mental life. In conjunction with the others, this last type of Gemeinschaft represents the truly human and supreme form of community. The first or kinship Gemeinschaft signifies a common relation to, and share in, human beings themselves, while in the second one such a common relation is established through collective ownership of land, and in the third the common bond is represented by sacred places and worshiped deities. All three types of Gemeinschaft are closely interrelated in space as well as in time. They are, therefore, also related in all such single phenomena and in their development as well as in general human culture and its history. Wherever human beings are related through their wills in an organic manner and affirm each other, we find Gemeinschaft of one or another of the three types. Either the earlier type involves the later one, or the later type has developed to relative independence from some earlier one. It is, therefore, possible to deal with (1) kinship, (2) neighborhood, and (3) friendship as definite and meaningful derivations of these original categories.

The house constitutes the realm and, as it were, the body of kinship. Here people live together under one protecting roof, here they share their possessions and their pleasures; they feed from the same supply, they sit at the same table. As invisible spirits the dead are venerated here, as if they were still powerful and held a protecting hand over their family. Thus common fear and common honor ensure with greater certainty peaceful living and co-operation. The will and spirit of kinship is not confined within the walls of the house nor bound up with physical proximity; but where it is strong and alive in the closest and most intimate relationship, it can live on itself, thrive on memory alone, and overcome any distance by its feeling and its imagination of nearness and common activity. But, nevertheless, it seeks all the more for physical proximity and is loath to give it up, because such nearness alone will fulfill the desire for love. The ordinary human being, therefore—in the long run and for the average of cases—feels best and most cheerful if he is surrounded by his family and relatives. He is among his own (*chez soi*).

Neighborhood describes the general character of living together in the rural village. The proximity of dwellings, the communal fields, and even the mere contiguity of holdings necessitate many contacts of human beings and cause inurement to and intimate knowledge of one another. They also necessitate co-operation in labor, order, and management, and lead to common supplication for grace and mercy to the gods and spirits of land and water who bring blessing or menace with disaster. Although essentially based upon proximity of habitation, this neighborhood type of Gemeinschaft can nevertheless persist during separation from the locality, but it then needs to be supported still more than before

by well-defined habits of reunion and sacred customs.

Friendship is independent of kinship and neighborhood, being conditioned by and resulting from similarity of work and intellectual attitude. It comes most easily into existence when callings or crafts are the same or of similar character. Such a tie, however, must be made and maintained through easy and frequent meetings, which are most likely to take place in a town. A worshiped deity, created out of a common mentality, has an immediate significance for the preservation of such a bond, since only, or at least mainly, this deity is able to give it living and lasting form. Such good spirit, therefore, is not bound to any place but lives in the conscience of its worshipers and accompanies them on their travels into foreign countries. Thus, those who are brethren of such a common faith feel, like members of the same craft or rank, everywhere united by a spiritual bond and the co-operation in a common task. Urban community of life may be classified as neighborhood, as is also the case with a community of domestic life in which nonrelated members or servants participate. In contradistinction, spiritual friendship forms a kind of invisible scene or meeting which has to be kept alive by artistic intuition and creative will. The relations between human beings themselves as friends and comrades have the least organic and intrinsically necessary character. They are the least instinctive and they are based less upon habit of neighborhood. They are of a mental nature and seem to be founded, therefore, as compared with the earlier relationships, upon chance or free choice.

* * *

AUTHORITY AND SERVICE—INEQUALITY AND ITS LIMITS

All authority is characterized by particular and enhanced freedom and honor, and thus represents a specific sphere of will. As such it must be derived from the general and equal share of will of the Gemeinschaft. It finds its corollary in service as a particular and diminished freedom and honor. Each authority can be regarded as service and each service as authority, provided the particularity involved is taken into consideration. The realm of will and therefore the will of the Gemeinschaft is a mass of determined force, power, or right. And right is, in essence, will as being able or being allowed and will as obligation or duty. This is the nature of all derived realms of will in which rights and duties are the two corresponding aspects of the same thing, or nothing but the subjective modalities of the same objective substance of right or force. In this way, through increased and diminished duties and rights, real inequalities exist and develop within the Gemeinschaft through its will. These inequalities can be increased only to a certain limit, however, because beyond this limit the essence of the Gemeinschaft as the unity of unequal beings would be dissolved: In case the superiors' legal power would become too great, their relation to the common sphere of right would become indifferent and without value and the inferiors' legal power would become too small and their relationship thereto unreal and insignificant.

The less human beings who remain or come into contact with each other are bound together in relation to the same Gemeinschaft, the more they stand opposite each other as free agents of their wills and abilities. The less this freedom is dependent upon a preconditioned will of the individual himself, which is to say the less this will is dependent upon or influenced by a common will, the greater is the freedom. For, besides the inherited forces and instincts, the influence of a community as an educating and guiding will is the most important factor determining the condition and formation of every individual habit and disposition. Especially is the family spirit (*Familiengeist*) important, but so also is every spirit (*Geist*) which is similar to it and has the same effects.

●

COMMON WILL—UNDERSTANDING—NATURAL LAW
—LANGUAGE—MOTHER TONGUE—CONCORD

Reciprocal, binding sentiment as a peculiar will of a Gemeinshaft we shall call understanding (*consensus*).[2] It represents the special social force and sympathy which keeps human beings together as members of a totality. As everything instinctive in the man is related to reasons and requires the capacity of speech, this mentality can be regarded also as the reason and significance of such a relationship. This mentality exists, for instance, between the parent and the child only to the degree in which the child is conceived as possessing speech, intellect, and reason. In the same way it can be said that everything that conforms to the conception of a Gemeinschaft relationship and what in and for this situation has meaning, forms its laws. Everything that conforms to the conception of this Gemeinschaft relationship is to be considered as the proper and real will of those bound together. In so far as enjoyment and labor are differentiated according to the very nature and capability of individuals, es-

pecially in such a manner that one part is entitled to guidance, the other bound to obedience, this constitutes a natural law as an order of group life, which assigns a sphere and function, incorporating duties and privileges, to every will. Understanding is based upon intimate knowledge of each other in so far as this is conditioned and advanced by direct interest of one being in the life of the other, and readiness to take part in his joy and sorrow. For that reason understanding is the more probable, the more alike the constitution and experience or the more the natural disposition, character, and intellectual attitude are similar or harmonize.

The real organ of understanding, through which it develops and improves, is language. Language given by means of gestures and sounds enables expressions of pain and pleasure, fear and desire, and all other feelings and emotions to be imparted and understood. Language has—as we all know—not been invented and, as it were, agreed upon as a means and tool by which one makes oneself understood. It is itself the living understanding both in its content and in its form. Similar to all other conscious activities of expression, the manifestation of language is the involuntary outcome of deep feelings and prevailing thoughts. It is not merely an artificial means of overcoming a natural lack of understanding, nor does it serve merely the purpose of enabling one to make oneself understood. Language can be used, however, among those who do understand each other, as a mere system of symbols, the same as other symbols which have been agreed upon. All these manifestations can be expressions of hostile as well as friendly passions. This justifies the general statement that friendly and hostile moods and passions underlie the same or very similar conditions. We must, however, distinguish between the hostility which springs from the rupture or loosening of natural and existing ties and the other type of hostility which is based upon strangeness, misunderstanding, and distrust. Both are instinctive, but the first one is anger, hatred, displeasure; the second one is fear, abhorrence, dislike. The first one is acute, the second one chronic. Of course language, like any other means of communication between minds, did not spring from either of these two kinds of hostility—which is only an unnatural and diseased state—but from intimacy, fondness, and affection. Especially from the deep understanding between mother and child, mother tongue should develop most easily and vigorously. Underlying the open hostility associated with an intimate understanding, on the contrary, we can always think of a certain friendship and unity.

The real foundation of unity, and consequently the possibility of Gemeinschaft, is in the first place

---

2. *Verständnis* is translated "understanding." The concept as here used should also carry the meaning of mutual understanding and possession of similar sentiments, hopes, aspirations, desires, attitudes, emotions, and beliefs.

closeness of blood relationship and mixture of blood, secondly physical proximity, and finally—for human beings—intellectual proximity. In this gradation are, therefore, to be found the sources of all kinds of understanding.

We may now establish the great main laws of Gemeinschaft. (1) Relatives and married couples love each other or easily adjust themselves to each other. They speak together and think along similar lines. Likewise do neighbors and other friends. (2) Between people who love each other there is understanding. (3) Those who love and understand each other remain and dwell together and organize their common life. A mixed or complex form of common determinative will, which has become as natural as language itself and which consists of a multitude of feelings of understanding which are measured by its norm, we call concord (*Eintracht*) or family spirit (*concordia* as a cordial allegiance and unity). Understanding and concord are one and the same thing; namely, will of the Gemeinschaft in its most elementary forms, including understanding in their separate relations and actions and concord in their total force and nature.

*   *   *

Theory of Gesellschaft

THE FUNDAMENTAL CHARACTERISTIC OF THE GESELLSCHAFT, A NEGATION—EQUALITY OF VALUE—THE OBJECTIVE JUDGMENT

The theory of the Gesellschaft deals with the artificial construction of an aggregate of human beings which superficially resembles the Gemeinschaft in so far as the individuals peacefully live and dwell together. However, in the Gemeinshaft they remain essentially united in spite of all separating factors, whereas in the Gesellschaft they are essentially separated in spite of all uniting factors. In the Gesellschaft, as contrasted with the Gemeinschaft, we find no actions that can be derived from an a priori and necessarily existing unity; no actions, therefore, which manifest the will and the spirit of the unity even if performed by the individual; no actions which, in so far as they are performed by the individual, take place on behalf of those united with him. In the Gesellschaft such actions do not exist. On the contrary, here everybody is by himself and isolated, and there exists a condition of tension against all others. Their spheres of activity and power are sharply separated, so that everybody refuses to everyone else contacts with and admittance to his sphere; i.e., intrusions are regarded as hostile acts. Such a negative atti-

tude towards one another becomes the normal and always underlying relation of these power-endowed individuals, and it characterizes the Gesellschaft in the condition of rest; nobody wants to grant and produce anything for another individual, nor will he be inclined to give ungrudgingly to another individual, if it be not in exchange for a gift or labor equivalent that he considers at least equal to what he has given. It is even necessary that it be more desirable to him than what he coud have kept himself; because only for the sake of receiving something that seems better to him will he be moved to give away a good. Inasmuch as each and every one is possessed of such will it is self-evident that for the individual "B" the object "a" may possibly be better than the object "b," and correspondingly, for the individual "A" the object "b" better than the object "a"; it is, however, only with reference to these relations that "a" is better than "b" and at the same time "b" is better than "a." This leads us to the question, With what meaning may one speak of the worth or of the value of things, independently of such relationships?

The answer runs as follows: In the concept presented here, all goods are conceived to be separate, as are also their owners. What somebody has and enjoys, he has and enjoys to the exclusion of all others. So, in reality, something that has a common value does not exist. Its existence may, however, be brought about through fiction on the part of the individuals, which means that they have to invent a common personality and his will, to whom this common value has to bear reference. Now, a manipulation of this kind must be warranted by a sufficient occasion. Such an occasion is given when we consider the simple action of the delivery of an object by one individual and its acceptance by another one. For there a contact takes place and there is brought into existence a common sphere which is desired by both individuals and lasts through the same length of time as does the "transaction." This period of time may be so small as to be negligible, but, on the other hand, it may also be extended indefinitely. At any rate, during this period the piece which is getting separated from the sphere of, for example, the individual "A" has ceased to be under the exclusive dominion of "A" and has not yet begun to be entirely under the dominion of "B": it is still under the partial dominion of "A" and already under the partial dominion of "B." It is still dependent upon both individuals, provided that their wills with reference to it are in accord. This is, however, the case as long as the act of giving and receiving continues. During this time it is a common good and represents a social value. Now the will that is directed to this common good is combined and mutual and *can* also be regarded as homogeneous in that it keeps demanding from either individual the execution of the twofold act until it is entirely completed. This will *must* however, be regarded as a unity inasmuch as it is conceived as a personality or inasmuch as a personality is assigned to it; for to conceive something as existing or as a thing is the same as conceiving it as a unity. There, however, we must be careful to discern whether and to what extent such an *ens fictivum* (artificial being) exists only in the theory, i.e., in scientific thinking, or whether and under which conditions it is also implanted in the thinking of the individuals who are its thinking agents. This last-mentioned possibility presupposes, of course, that the individuals are already capable of common willing and acting. For, again, it is quite a different proposition if they are imagined to be only participants in the authorship of something that is conceived as objective in the scientific sense because it is that which under given conditions "each and every one" is compelled to think.

Now, it is to be admitted that each act of giving and receiving implicitly includes a social will, in the way just indicated. These acts are, furthermore, not conceivable except in connection with their purpose or end, i.e., the receipt of the compensating gift. As, however, this latter act is conditioned in like manner, neither act can precede the other; they must concur. Or, expressing the same thought in other words, the acceptance equals the delivery of an accepted compensation. Thus, the exchange itself, considered as a united and single act, represents the content of the assumed social will. With regard to this will the exchanged goods are of equal value. This equality is the judgment of the will and is valid for both individuals, since they have passed it when their wills were in concord; hence it is binding only for the moment in which the act of exchange takes place or for the space of time during which it continues. In order that the judgment may even with this qualification become objective and universally valid, it must appear as a judgment passed by "each and every one." Hence, each and every one must have this single will; in other words, the will of the exchange becomes universal; i.e., each and every one becomes a participant in the single act and he confirms it; thus it becomes an absolute and public act. On the contrary, the Gesellschaft may deny this act and declare "a" is not equal to "b," but smaller than "b" or greater than "b," i.e., the objects are not being exchanged according to their true values. The true value is explained as that value which each and every one attributes to a thing that we thus regard as a general Gesellschaft-conditioned

good. Hence, the true value is ascertained if there is nobody who estimates either object as higher or lower in terms of the other. Now, a general consensus of each and every one that is not accidental, but necessary, will be effected only with reference to what is sensible, right, and true. Since all individuals are thus of one mind we may imagine them as concentrated in the person of a measuring, weighing, and knowing judge who passes the objective judgment. The judgment must be recognizable by each and every one, and each and every one must conform to it inasmuch as they themselves are endowed with judgment and objective thinking, or, figuratively speaking, as they use the same yardstick or weigh with the same scales.

VALUE AS AN OBJECTIVE QUALITY—QUANTITIES OF NECESSARY LABOR

We are now confronted with the following question: What shall we consider to be the yardstick or balances in this procedure of deliberative comparing? We know the "quality" which is to be determined quantitatively by means of this constant tester, and we call it "value." Value must not, however, be identified with "worth," since worth is a quality which is perceived by the real individual. Moreover, the very difference of worth as it is sensed by real individuals, in relation to the same object, is the basis of a reasonable exchange. We, however, are concerned to find equality of value in objective judgment of different objects. In natural and naïve evaluation one takes things of the same category in order to compare them. The evaluation takes the form of a question, the answer to which consists of an affirmation or negation, in a stronger or lesser degree, according as the objects submit to the idea of such a comparison. In this sense we may establish a general category of serviceable (or useful) things. Some may be considered as necessary, some as superfluous, some may be given prominence as very useful, and others rejected as very harmful. In this connection humanity would have to be pictured as a whole, or at least as a Gemeinschaft of human beings which —like the real individual—lives and therefore has needs; it has to be regarded as uniform in its will, so that it shares profit and loss (since the judgment is at the same time considered as a subjective one).

Now, if one asserts the equality of value of two exchanged objects, this does not at all mean that they are equally useful and necessary for an aggregate being. Otherwise the possibility of someone buying absolutely harmful things would have to be set up. But that would be monstrous and utopian. One may assert on good grounds that a judgment is wrong when conditioned by desire, so that many a one acquires through exchange an object that is harmful to himself. But it is self-evident that the same liquor which is harmful to the workman is positively useful to the owner of the distillery, since he does not drink it but sells it. In order that a thing may be at all of value in the Gesellschaft, it is only necessary that it be possessed by one party to the exclusion of another and be desired by one or another individual of this latter party. Apart from this requirement all its other characteristics are insignificant. Saying that a thing has a certain value does not mean that it is endowed with an equal amount of usefulness. Value is an objective quality; as length is an objective quality for the senses of vision and of touch, and as weight for the muscular sense and the sense of touch, so value is an objective quality for the understanding that examines and comprehends social facts. This understanding takes note of and examines the objects as to whether they can be manufactured quickly, or whether they require much time; as to whether they can be easily provided, or whether they require toil and drudgery. In other words, the understanding analyzes the actuality of the objects by examining the possibility of their existence, and it then determines their probability. For determining value the probability of existence is the only test, being subjective in regard to the sensible exchanging individual, and objective in regard to the Gesellschaft. This dictum in the first place carries only the following purport: if a sensible individual is confronted with objects being offered for sale, the thought comes (must come) to him that those objects naturally have a cost in order to be there at all, and particularly to be at that special place at that special time, be this cost represented by other objects against which they have been exchanged, or by labor, or by both items. However, the Gesellschaft, as it is an *ens fictivum* (artificial being) does not exchange anything, unless it be conceived of as an individual person, which here is quite out of the question. Therefore, since the exchange takes place only between human individuals, there is no being that could confront the Gesellschaft. From the viewpoint of the Gesellschaft the cost of the objects is, therefore, represented only by toil and labor. Robbery, as well as exchange, when considered as a means of acquiring objects, is based upon the assumption that goods already exist. Only producing, nurturing, creating, and fashioning labor is to be considered in this connection as the cause of the existence of things at a particular time. To this inherent labor can be added the extraneous labor of movement in space, as the cause of the existence of a given good at a particular place.

Things are considered as equal in so far as each object or each quantity of objects stands merely for a certain quantity of necessary labor. Thus the Gesellschaft disregards the fact that some producers work faster or with better yield (more productively) than others, so that with greater skill or better tools the same objects can be produced with less labor. All such individual differences can be reduced to a common denominator. This process becomes all the more complete in the degree that the exchange of commodities becomes general or Gesellschaft-like. That is to say: each individual offers his commodity to everyone else, and all are capable of producing the same commodities, but everyone, through his own insight and free choice, confines himself to that commodity which presents the least difficulties to him. Thus we exclude here the case of a work which is essentially Gemeinschaft-like but which is divided or divides itself up so that special arts are developed, inherited, and taught. But here we rather have in mind that each individual takes that piece of work which most closely approaches the price that the Gesellschaft attributes to it; that is to say, a piece of work which requires as little extra labor as possible. Thus the Gesellschaft can be imagined to be in reality composed of such separate individuals all of whom are busy for the general Gesellschaft inasmuch as they seem to be active in their own interests and who are working for their own interests while they seem to be working for the Gesellschaft. As a consequence of repeated dividing (of labors) and of indefinite exercise of free choice, there finally falls to each individual an actually equal and simple or elementary labor, representing an atom that he contributes and which forms an integrating part of the total labor of the Gesellschaft. By means of exchange each individual disposes of value not useful to him in order to acquire an equal value that he can use. The present investigation will show what relationship the real structure of the Gesellschaft bears to the concept presented here.

* * *

ACTIVITY AS OBJECT OF A PROMISE—POWER TO ENFORCE IT—RELATION—NATURAL LAW—CONVENTION

In every exchange the place of a perceivable object can be taken by an activity. The activity itself is given and received. It must be useful or agreeable to the receiver as a commodity. This activity is thought of as a commodity the production and consumption of which coincide in time.

Although the performance which is not given but only promised may be contrasted with the thing which is not given and only promised, the result in both cases is similar. It belongs to the receiver legally; after the term expires he can force the promising party legally to perform the activity promised, just as he could legally force the debtor to give that which is owed or have it taken with force. A performance which is owed can be acquired only by force. The promise of a performance can as well be mutual as one-sided; therefore, resulting rights to coercion can also be mutual or one-sided as the case may be. In this respect several people can bind themselves for a certain equal activity in such a manner that everyone uses the performance of the other as an aid to himself. Finally, several people can agree to regard their association as an existing and independent being of the same individual nature as they are themselves, and to grant this fictitious person a special will and the capacity to act and therefore to make contracts and to incur obligations. Like all other things related to contracts, this so-called person is to be conceived as objective and real only in so far as the Gesellschaft seems to co-operate with it and to confirm its existence. Only in this way is this so-called person a thinking agent of the legal order of the Gesellschaft, and it is called a society, an association or special-interest group, a corporation, or any such name. The natural content of such an order can be comprised in the one formula: *"Pacta esse observanda"*—contracts must be executed. This includes the presupposition of a condition of separate realms or spheres of will so that an accepted and consequently legal change of each sphere can take place by contract in favor or in disfavor of spheres which are outside the system, or within the system. This means that the agreement of all is involved. Such concurrence of wills is according to its nature momentarily punctual so that the change, as creation of a new situation, does not have to have a duration in time. This necessitates no modification of the most important rule, that everyone can do legally within his realm that which he wishes, but nothing outside. If, however, a common realm originates, as might be the case in a lasting obligation and in an organization, freedom itself, as the total of rights to act freely, must be divided and altered or a new artificial or fictitious form of freedom created. The simple form of the general will of the Gesellschaft, in so far as it postulates this law of nature, I call *convention*. Positive definitions and regulations of all kinds, which according to their origin are of a very different style, can be recognized as conventional, so that convention is often under-

stood as a synonym for tradition and custom. But what springs from tradition and custom or the folkways and mores is conventional only in so far as it is wanted and maintained for its general use, and in so far as the general use is maintained by the individual for his use. Convention is not, as in the case of tradition, kept as sacred inheritance of the ancestors. Consequently, the words tradition, customs, or folkways and mores, are not adequate to convey the meaning of convention.

BOURGEOIS SOCIETY (*bürgerliche Gesellschaft*)—EVERYONE A MERCHANT—UNIVERSAL COMPETITION—GESELLSCHAFT IN A MORAL SENSE

Gesellschaft, an aggregate by convention and law of nature, is to be understood as a multitude of natural and artificial individuals, the wills and spheres of whom are in many relations with and to one another, and remain nevertheless independent of one another and devoid of mutual familiar relationships. This gives us the general description of "bourgeois society" or "exchange Gesellschaft," the nature and movements of which legislative economy attempts to understand; a condition in which, according to the expression of Adam Smith, "Every man . . . becomes in some measure a merchant, . . ." Where merchants, companies, or firms or associations deal with one another in international or national markets and exchanges, the nature of the Gesellschaft is erected as in a concave mirror or as in an extract.

The generality of this situation is by no means, as the famous Scotchman imagined, the immediate or even probable result of the innovation that labor is divided and products exchanged. It is more a remote goal with respect to which the development of the Gesellschaft must be understood. To the extent that this goal is realized, the existence of a Gesellschaft in the sense that it is used here is real at a given time. It is something in the process of becoming, something which should be conceived here as personality of the general will or the general reason, and at the same time (as we know) it is fictitious and nominal. It is like an emanation, as if it had emerged from the heads of the persons in whom it rests, who join hands eagerly to exchange across all distances, limits, and scruples, and establish this speculative Utopia as the only country, the only city, in which all fortune seekers and all merchant adventurers have a really common interest. As the fiction of money is represented by metal or paper, it is represented by the entire globe, or by a circumscribed territory.

In the conception of Gesellschaft the original or natural relations of human beings to each other must be excluded. The possibility of a relation in the Gesellschaft assumes no more than a multitude of mere persons who are capable of delivering something and consequently of promising something. Gesellschaft as a totality to which a system of conventional rules applies is limitless; it breaks through its chance and real boundaries constantly. In Gesellschaft every person strives for that which is to his own advantage and affirms the actions of others only in so far as and as long as they can further his interest. Before and outside of convention and also before and outside of each special contract, the relation of all to all may therefore be conceived as potential hostility or latent war. Against this condition all agreements of the will stand out as so many treaties and peace pacts. This conception is the only one which does justice to all facts of business and trade where all rights and duties can be reduced to mere value and definitions of ability to deliver. Every theory of pure private law or law of nature understood as pertaining to the Gesellschaft has to be considered as being based upon this conception. Buyer and seller in their manifold types stand in relation one to the other in such a manner that each one, for as little of his own wealth as possible, desires and attempts to obtain as much of the wealth of others as possible. The real commercial and business people race with each other on many sprinting tracks, as it were, trying each to get the better of the other and to be the first to reach the goal: the sale of their goods and of as large a quantity as possible. Thus they are forced to crowd each other out or to trip each other up. The loss of one is the profit of the other, and this is the case in every individual exchange, unless owners exchange goods of actually equal value. This constitutes general competition which takes place in so many other spheres, but is nowhere so evident and so much in the consciousness of people as in trade, to which, consequently, the conception is limited in its common use. Competition has been described by many pessimists as an illustration of the war of all against all, which a famous thinker has conceived as the natural state of mankind.

However, even competition carries within it, as do all forms of such war, the possibility of being ended. Even enemies like these—although among these it may be the least likely—recognize that under certain conditions it is to their advantage to agree and to spare each other. They may even unite themselves together for a common purpose (or also—and this is the most likely—against a common enemy). Thus competition is limited and abolished by coalition.

In analogy to this situation, based upon the exchange of material goods, all conventional society life, in the narrower sense of the word, can be understood. Its supreme rule is politeness. It consists of an exchange of words and courtesies in which everyone seems to be present for the good of everyone else and everyone seems to consider everyone else as his equal, whereas in reality everyone is thinking of himself and trying to bring to the fore his importance and advantages in competition with the others. For everything pleasant which someone does for someone else, he expects, even demands, at least an equivalent. He weighs exactly his services, flatteries, presents, and so on, to determine whether they will bring about the desired result. Formless contracts are made continuously, as it were, and constantly many are pushed aside in the race by the few fortunate and powerful ones.

Since all relations in the Gesellschaft are based upon comparison of possible and offered services, it is evident that the relations with visible, material matters have preference, and that mere activities and words form the foundation for such relationships only in an unreal way. In contrast to this, Gemeinschaft as a bond of "blood" is in the first place a physical relation, therefore expressing itself in deeds and words. Here the common relation to the material objects is of a secondary nature and such objects are not exchanged as often as they are used and possessed in common.

2. *Status and Role*

BY RALPH LINTON

IN THE PRECEDING CHAPTER we discussed the nature of society and pointed out that the functioning of societies depends upon the presence of patterns for reciprocal behavior between individuals or groups of individuals. The polar positions in such patterns of reciprocal behavior are technically known as *statuses.* The term *status,* like the term *culture,* has come to be used with a double significance. *A status,* in the abstract, is a position in a particular pattern. It is thus quite correct to speak of each individual as having many statuses, since each individual participates in the expression of a number of patterns. However, unless the term is qualified in some way, *the status* of any individual means the sum total of all the statuses which he occupies. It represents his position with relation to the total society. Thus the status of Mr. Jones as a member of his community derives from a combination of all the statuses which he holds as a citizen, as an attorney, as a Mason, as a Methodist, as Mrs. Jones's husband, and so on.

A status, as distinct from the individual who may occupy it, is simply a collection of rights and duties. Since these rights and duties can find expression only through the medium of individuals, it is extremely hard for us to maintain a distinction in our thinking between statuses and the people who hold them and exercise the rights and duties which constitute them. The relation between any individual and any status he holds is somewhat like that between the driver of an automobile and the driver's place in the machine. The driver's seat with its steering wheel, accelerator, and other controls is a constant with ever-present potentialities for action and control, while the driver may be any member of the family and may exercise these potentialities very well or very badly.

A *role* represents the dynamic aspect of a status. The individual is socially assigned to a status and occupies it with relation to other statuses. When he puts the rights and duties which constitute the status into effect, he is performing a role. Role and status are quite inseparable, and the distinction

between them is of only academic interest. There are no roles without statuses or statuses without roles. Just as in the case of *status,* the term *role* is used with a double significance. Every individual has a series of roles deriving from the various patterns in which he participates and at the same time *a role,* general, which represents the sum total of these roles and determines what he does for his society and what he can expect from it.

Although all statuses and roles derive from social patterns and are integral parts of patterns, they have an independent function with relation to the individuals who occupy particular statuses and exercise their roles. To such individuals the combined status and role represent the minimum of attitudes and behavior which he must assume if he is to participate in the overt expression of the pattern. Status and role serve to reduce the ideal patterns for social life to individual terms. They become models for organizing the attitudes and behavior of the individual so that these will be congruous with those of the other individuals participating in the expression of the pattern. Thus if we are studying football teams in the abstract, the position of quarter-back is meaningless except in relation to the other positions. From the point of view of the quarter-back himself it is a distinct and important entity. It determines where he shall take his place in the line-up and what he shall do in various plays. His assignment to this position at once limits and defines his activities and establishes a minimum of things which he must learn. Similarly, in a social pattern such as that for the employer-employee relationship the statuses of employer and employee define what each has to know and do to put the pattern into operation. The employer does not need to know the techniques involved in the employee's labor, and the employee does not need to know the techniques for marketing or accounting.

It is obvious that, as long as there is no interference from external sources, the more perfectly the members of any society are adjusted to their statuses and roles the more smoothly the society will function. In its attempts to bring about such adjustments every society finds itself caught on the horns of a dilemma. The individual's formation of

From *The Study of Man* by Ralph Linton. Copyright 1936 by D. Appleton-Century Co., Inc. By permission of Appleton-Century-Crofts, Inc.

habits and attitudes begins at birth, and, other things being equal, the earlier his training for a status can begin the more successful it is likely to be. At the same time, no two individuals are alike, and a status which will be congenial to one may be quite uncongenial to another. Also, there are in all social systems certain roles which require more than training for their successful performance. Perfect technique does not make a great violinist, nor a thorough book knowledge of tactics an efficient general. The utilization of the special gifts of individuals may be highly important to society, as in the case of the general, yet these gifts usually show themselves rather late, and to wait upon their manifestation for the assignment of statuses would be to forfeit the advantages to be derived from commencing training early.

Fortunately, human beings are so mutable that almost any normal individual can be trained to the adequate performance of almost any role. Most of the business of living can be conducted on a basis of habit, with little need for intelligence and none for special gifts. Societies have met the dilemma by developing two types of statuses, the *ascribed* and the *achieved*. *Ascribed* statuses are those which are assigned to individuals without reference to their innate differences or abilities. They can be predicted and trained for from the moment of birth. The *achieved* statuses are, as a minimum, those requiring special qualities, although they are not necessarily limited to these. They are not assigned to individuals from birth but are left open to be filled through competition and individual effort. The majority of the statuses in all social systems are of the ascribed type and those which take care of the ordinary day-to-day business of living are practically always of this type.

In all societies certain things are selected as reference points for the ascription of status. The things chosen for this purpose are always of such a nature that they are ascertainable at birth, making it possible to begin the training of the individual for his potential statuses and roles at once. The simplest and most universally used of these reference points is sex. Age is used with nearly equal frequency, since all individuals pass through the same cycle of growth, maturity, and decline, and the statuses whose occupation will be determined by age can be forecast and trained for with accuracy. Family relationships, the simplest and most obvious being that of the child to its mother, are also used in all societies as reference points for the establishment of a whole series of statuses. Lastly, there is the matter of birth into a particular socially established group, such as a class or caste. The use

of this type of reference is common but not universal. In all societies the actual ascription of statuses to the individual is controlled by a series of these reference points which together serve to delimit the field of his future participation in the life of the group.

The division and ascription of statuses with relation to sex seems to be basic in all social systems. All societies prescribe different attitudes and activities to men and to women. Most of them try to rationalize these prescriptions in terms of the physiological differences between the sexes or their different roles in reproduction. However, a comparative study of the statuses ascribed to women and men in different cultures seems to show that while such factors may have served as a starting point for the development of a division the actual ascriptions are almost entirely determined by culture. Even the psychological characteristics ascribed to men and women in different societies vary so much that they can have little physiological basis. Our own idea of women as ministering angels contrasts sharply with the ingenuity of women as torturers among the Iroquois and the sadistic delight they took in the process. Even the last two generations have seen a sharp change in the psychological patterns for women in our own society. The delicate, fainting lady of the middle eighteen-hundreds is as extinct as the dodo.

When it comes to the ascription of occupations, which is after all an integral part of status, we find the differences in various societies even more marked. Arapesh women regularly carry heavier loads than men "because their heads are so much harder and stronger." In some societies women do most of the manual labor; in others, as in the Marquesas, even cooking, housekeeping, and baby-tending are proper male occupations, and women spend most of their time primping. Even the general rule that women's handicap through pregnancy and nursing indicates the more active occupations as male and the less active ones as female has many exceptions. Thus among the Tasmanians seal-hunting was women's work. They swam out to the seal rocks, stalked the animals, and clubbed them. Tasmanian women also hunted opossums, which required the climbing of large trees.

Although the actual ascription of occupations along sex lines is highly variable, the pattern of sex division is constant. There are very few societies in which every important activity has not been definitely assigned to men or to women. Even when the two sexes coöperate in a particular occupation, the field of each is usually clearly limited. Thus in Madagascar rice culture the men make the seed beds and terraces and prepare the fields for transplanting. The women do the work of transplanting, which is hard and back-breaking. The women weed the crop, but the men harvest it. The women then carry it to the threshing floors, where the men thresh it while the women winnow it. Lastly, the women pound the grain in mortars and cook it.

When a society takes over a new industry, there is often a period of uncertainty during which the work may be done by either sex, but it soon falls into the province of one or the other. In Madagascar, pottery is made by men in some tribes and by women in others. The only tribe in which it is made by both men and women is one into which the art has been introduced within the last sixty years. I was told that during the fifteen years preceding my visit there had been a marked decrease in the number of male potters, many men who had once practised the art having given it up. The factor of lowered wages, usually advanced as the reason for men leaving one of our own occupations when women enter it in force, certainly was not operative here. The field was not overcrowded, and the prices for men's and women's products were the same. Most of the men who had given up the trade were vague as to their reasons, but a few said frankly that they did not like to compete with women. Apparently the entry of women into the occupation had robbed it of a certain amount of prestige. It was no longer quite the thing for a man to be a potter, even though he was a very good one.

The use of age as a reference point for establishing status is as universal as the use of sex. All societies recognize three age groupings as a minimum: child, adult, and old. Certain societies have emphasized age as a basis for assigning status and have greatly amplified the divisions. Thus in certain African tribes the whole male population is divided into units composed of those born in the same years or within two- or three-year intervals. However, such extreme attention to age is unusual, and we need not discuss it here.

The physical differences between child and adult are easily recognizable, and the passage from childhood to maturity is marked by physiological events which make it possible to date it exactly for girls and within a few weeks or months for boys. However, the physical passage from childhood to maturity does not necessarily coincide with the social transfer of the individual from one category to the other. Thus in our own society both men and women remain legally children until long after they are physically adult. In most societies this difference between the physical and social transfer is more clearly marked than in our own. The child becomes a man not when he is physically mature but when he is formally recognized as a man by his society. This recognition is almost always given ceremonial expression in what are technically known as puberty rites. The most important element in these rites is not the determination of physical maturity but that of social maturity. Whether a boy is able to breed is less vital to his society than whether he is able to do a man's work and has a man's knowledge. Actually, most puberty ceremonies include tests of the boy's learning and fortitude, and if the aspirants are unable to pass these they are left in the child status until they can. For those who pass the tests, the ceremonies usually culminate in the transfer to them of certain secrets which the men guard from women and children.

The passage of individuals from adult to aged is harder to perceive. There is no clear physiological line for men, while even women may retain their full physical vigor and their ability to carry on all the activities of the adult status for several years after the menopause. The social transfer of men from the adult to the aged group is given ceremonial recognition in a few cultures, as when a father formally surrenders his official position and titles to his son, but such recognition is rare. As for women, there appears to be no society in which the menopause is given ceremonial recognition, although there are a few societies in which it does alter the individual's status. Thus Comanche women, after the menopause, were released from their disabilities with regard to the supernatural. They could handle sacred objects, obtain power through dreams and practise as shamans, all things forbidden to women of bearing age.

The general tendency for societies to emphasize the individual's first change in age status and largely ignore the second is no doubt due in part to the difficulty of determining the onset of old age. However, there are also psychological factors involved. The boy or girl is usually anxious to grow up, and this eagerness is heightened by the exclusion of children from certain activities and knowledge. Also, society welcomes new additions to the most active division of the group, that which contributes most to its perpetuation and well-being. Conversely, the individual who enjoys the thought of growing old is atypical in all societies. Even when age brings respect and a new measure of influence, it means the relinquishment of much that is pleasant. We can see among ourselves that the aging usually refuse to recognize the change until long after it has happened.

In the case of age, as in that of sex, the biological factors involved appear to be secondary to the cultural ones in determining the content of status. There are certain activities which cannot be ascribed to children because children either lack the necessary strength or have not had time to acquire the necessary technical skills. However, the attitudes between parent and child and the importance given to the child in the family structure vary enormously from one culture to another. The status of the child among our Puritan ancestors, where he was seen and not heard and ate at the second table, represents one extreme. At the other might be placed the status of the eldest son of a Polynesian chief. All the *mana* (supernatural power) of the royal line converged upon such a child. He was socially superior to his own father and mother, and any attempt to discipline him would have been little short of sacrilege. I once visited the hereditary chief of a Marquesan tribe and found the whole family camping uncomfortably in their own front yard, although they had a good house built on European lines. The eldest son, aged nine, had had a dispute with his father a few days before and had tabooed the house by naming it after his head. The family had thus been compelled to move out and could not use it again until he relented and lifted the taboo. As he could use the house himself and eat anywhere in the village, he was getting along quite well and seemed to enjoy the situation thoroughly.

The statuses ascribed to the old in various societies vary even more than those ascribed to children. In some cases they are relieved of all heavy labor and can settle back comfortably to live off their children. In others they perform most of the hard and monotonous tasks which do not require great physical strength, such as the gathering of firewood. In many societies the old women, in particular, take over most of the care of the younger children, leaving the younger women free to enjoy themselves. In some places the old are treated with consideration and respect; in others they are considered a useless incumbrance and removed as soon as they are incapable of heavy labor. In most societies their advice is sought even when little attention is paid to their wishes. This custom has a sound practical basis, for the individual who contrives to live to old age in an uncivilized group has usually been a person of ability and his memory constitutes a sort of reference library to which one can turn for help under all sorts of circumstances.

In certain societies the change from the adult to the old status is made more difficult for the individual by the fact that the patterns for these statuses ascribe different types of personality to each. This was the case among the Comanche, as

it seems to have been among most of the Plains tribes. The adult male was a warrior, vigorous, self-reliant, and pushing. Most of his social relationships were phrased in terms of competition. He took what he could get and held what he had without regard to any abstract rights of those weaker than himself. Any willingness to arbitrate differences or to ignore slights was a sign of weakness resulting in loss of prestige. The old man, on the other hand, was expected to be wise and gentle, willing to overlook slights and, if need be, to endure abuse. It was his task to work for the welfare of the tribe, giving sound advice, settling feuds between the warriors, and even preventing his tribe from making new enemies. Young men strove for war and honor, old men strove for peace and tranquillity. There is abundant evidence that among the Comanche the transition was often a difficult one for the individual. Warriors did not prepare for old age, thinking it a better fate to be killed in action. When waning physical powers forced them to assume the new role, many of them did so grudgingly, and those who had strong magic would go on trying to enforce the rights which belonged to the younger status. Such bad old men were a peril to young ones beginning their careers, for they were jealous of them simply because they were young and strong and admired by the women. The medicine power of these young men was still weak, and the old men could and did kill them by malevolent magic. It is significant that although benevolent medicine men might be of any age in Comanche folklore, malevolent ones were always old.

Before passing on, it might be well to mention still another social status which is closely related to the foregoing. This is the status of the dead. We do not think of the dead as still members of the community, and many societies follow us in this, but there are others in which death is simply another transfer, comparable to that from child to adult. When a man dies, he does not leave his society; he merely surrenders one set of rights and duties and assumes another. Thus a Tanala clan has two sections which are equally real to its members, the living and the dead. In spite of rather half-hearted attempts by the living to explain to the dead that they are dead and to discourage their return, they remain an integral part of the clan. They must be informed of all important events, invited to all clan ceremonies, and remembered at every meal. In return they allow themselves to be consulted, take an active and helpful interest in the affairs of the community, and act as highly efficient guardians of the group's mores. They carry over into their new status the conservatism characteristic of the aged, and their invisible presence and constant watchfulness does more than anything else to ensure the good behavior of the living and to discourage innovations. In a neighboring tribe there are even individual statuses among the dead which are open to achievement. Old Betsileo men and women will often promise that, after their deaths, they will give the living specific forms of help in return for specified offerings. After the death of one of these individuals, a monument will be erected and people will come to pray and make offerings there. If the new ghost performs his functions successfully, his worship may grow into a cult and may even have a priest. If he fails in their performance, he is soon forgotten.

Biological relationships are used to determine some statuses in all societies. The mere fact of birth immediately brings the individual within the scope of a whole series of social patterns which relate him to his parents, either real or ascribed, his brothers and sisters, and his parents' relatives. The biological basis for the ascription of these family statuses is likely to blind us to the fact that the physiological factors which may influence their content are almost exactly the same as those affecting the content of sex and age statuses. While there is a special relationship between the young child and its mother, based on the child's dependence on nursing, even this is soon broken off. After the second year any adult woman can do anything for the child that its mother can do, while any adult male can assume the complete role of the father at any time after the child is conceived. Similarly, the physiological factors which might affect the statuses of uncle and nephew, uncle and niece, or brother and sister are identical with those affecting the relations of persons in different age or sex groupings. This lack of physiological determinants may be responsible in part for the extraordinarily wide range of variation in the contents of the statuses ascribed on the basis of biological relationships in various societies.

*   *   *

The bulk of the ascribed statuses in all social systems are parceled out to individuals on the basis of sex, age, and family relationships. However, there are many societies in which purely social factors are also used as a basis of ascription. There seems to be a general tendency for societies to divide their component individuals into a series of groups or categories and to ascribe to such categories differing degrees of social importance. Such divisions may originate in many different ways. They may grow out of individual differences in technical skill or other abilities, as in the case of craft groups or the aristocracies of certain Indian tribes, membership

in which was determined by the individual's war record. They may also originate through the conscious formation of some social unit, such as the first college fraternity or the first business men's club, which is usually followed by the formation of a series of similar units organized upon nearly the same lines. Lastly, such divisions may originate through the subjugation of one society by another society, with the subsequent fusion of both into a single functional unit, as in the case of Old World aristocracies deriving from conquest. Even when the social divisions originate in individual differences of ability, there seems to be a strong tendency for such divisions to become hereditary. The members of a socially favored division try to transmit the advantages they have gained to their offspring and at the same time to prevent the entry into the division of individuals from lower divisions. In many cases these tendencies result in the organization of the society into a series of hereditary classes or castes. Such hereditary units are always used as reference points for the ascription of status.

The factor of social class or caste rarely if ever replaces the factors of sex, age, and biological relationship in the determination of status. Rather, it supplements these, defining the roles of individuals still more clearly. Where the class system is strong, each class becomes almost a society in itself. It will have a series of sex, age, and relationship statuses which are peculiar to its members. These will differ from the statuses of other classes even when both are determined by the same biological factors. Not only is the commoner debarred from the occupation of aristocratic statuses, but the aristocrat is similarly debarred from the occupation of common statuses. It may be mentioned in passing that this arrangement is not always entirely to the advantage of the members of the upper class. During the nineteenth century the aristocratic prohibition against engaging in trade condemned many aristocrats to genteel poverty.

Feudal Europe offers an excellent example of the ascription of statuses on the basis of social class. A man born into the noble class could look forward to being a bachelor, in the technical sense of a boy beginning his training for knighthood, a squire, and lastly a knight and lord of a manor. The performance of the roles connected with the final status required a long and arduous training both in the use of arms and in administration. The woman born into the same class could also look forward to being lady of a manor, a task which entailed special knowledge and administrative ability fully on a par with that of her husband. A man born into the peasant class could look forward only to becoming a tiller of the soil. He would pass through no statuses corresponding to those of bachelor or squire, and although he might be trained to the use of weapons, these would be different weapons from those used by the knight. The woman born in this class could only look forward to becoming a simple housewife, and her necessary training for this status was limited to a knowledge of housekeeping and baby-tending. The third class in medieval society, the burghers, also had its own series of statuses, the boy looking forward to becoming first an apprentice and then a master training apprentices in turn. All these divergent, class-determined statuses were mutually interdependent, and all contributed to the successful functioning of medieval society. The noble provided protection and direction, the peasant provided food, and the burgher took care of trade and manufactures.

Ascribed statuses, whether assigned according to biological or to social factors, compose the bulk of all social systems. However, all these systems also include a varying number of statuses which are open to individual achievement. It seems as though many statuses of this type were primarily designed to serve as baits for socially acceptable behavior or as escapes for the individual. All societies rely mainly on their ascribed statuses to take care of the ordinary business of living. Most of the statuses which are thrown open to achievement do not touch this business very deeply. The honored ones are extremely satisfying to the individuals who achieve them, but many of them are no more vital to the ordinary functioning of the society than are honorary degrees or inclusions in "Who's Who" among ourselves.

Most societies make only a grudging admission of the fact that a limited number of statuses do require special gifts for their successful performance. Since such gifts rarely manifest themselves in early childhood, these statuses are, of necessity, thrown open to competition. At the same time, the pattern of ascribing all vital statuses is so strong that all societies limit this competition with reference to sex, age, and social affiliations. Even in our own society, where the field open to individual achievement is theoretically unlimited, it is strictly limited in fact. No woman can become President of the United States. Neither could a Negro nor an Indian, although there is no formal rule on this point, while a Jew or even a Catholic entering the presidential race would be very seriously handicapped from the outset. Even with regard to achievable statuses which are much less social importance and which, perhaps, require more specific gifts, the same sort of limited competition is evident. It would be nearly if not quite impossible for either a woman or a Negro to become conductor of our best symphony orchestra, even if better able to perform the duties involved than anyone else in America. At the same time, no man could become president of the D.A.R., and it is doubtful whether any man, unless he adopted a feminine *nom de plume,* could even conduct a syndicated column on advice to the lovelorn, a field in which our society assumes, *a priori,* that women have greater skill.

These limitations upon the competition for achieved statuses no doubt entail a certain loss to society. Persons with special talents appear to be mutants and as such are likely to appear in either sex and in any social class. At the same time, the actual loss to societies through this failure to use their members' gifts to the full is probably a good deal less than persons reared in the American tradition would like to believe. Individual talent is too sporadic and too unpredictable to be allowed any important part in the organization of society. Social systems have to be built upon the potentialities of the average individual, the person who has no special gifts or disabilities. Such individuals can be trained to occupy almost any status and to perform the associated role adequately if not brilliantly. The social ascription of a particular status, with the intensive training that such ascription makes possible, is a guarantee that the role will be performed even if the performance is mediocre. If a society waited to have its statuses filled by individuals with special gifts, certain statuses might not be filled at all. The ascription of status sacrifices the possibility of having certain roles performed superlatively well to the certainty of having them performed passably well.

When a social system has achieved a good adjustment to the other sectors of the group's culture and, through these, to the group's environment, it can get along very well without utilizing special gifts. However, as soon as changes within the culture or in the external environment produce maladjustments, it has to recognize and utilize these gifts. The development of new social patterns calls for the individual qualities of thought and initiative, and the freer the rein given to these the more quickly new adjustments can be arrived at. For this reason, societies living under new or changing conditions are usually characterized by a wealth of achievable statuses and by very broad delimitations of the competition for them. Our own now extinct frontier offered an excellent example of this. Here the class lines of the European societies from which the frontier population had been drawn were completely discarded and individuals were given an unprecedented opportunity to find their place in the new society by their own abilities.

As social systems achieve adjustment to their settings, the social value of individual thought and initiative decreases. Thorough training of the component individuals becomes more necessary to the survival and successful functioning of society than the free expression of their individual abilities. Even leadership, which calls for marked ability under conditions of change, becomes largely a matter of routine activities. To ensure successful training, more and more statuses are transferred from the achieved to the ascribed group, and the competition for those which remain is more and more rigidly delimited. To put the same thing in different terms, individual opportunities decrease. There is not an absolute correlation between the degree of adjustment of a social system to its setting and the limitation of individual opportunity. Thus if the group attaches a high value to individual initiative and individual rights, certain statuses may be left open to competition when their ascription would result in greater social efficiency. However, well-adjusted societies are, in general, characterized by a high preponderance of ascribed over achieved statuses, and increasing perfection of adjustment usually goes hand in hand with increasing rigidity of the social system.

3. On Mechanical and Organic Solidarity

BY EMILE DURKHEIM

THIS WORK had its origins in the question of the relations of the individual to social solidarity. Why does the individual, while becoming more autonomous, depend more upon society? How can he be at once more individual and more solidary? Certainly, these two movements, contradictory as they appear, develop in parallel fashion. This is the problem we are raising. It appeared to us that what resolves this apparent antinomy is a transformation of social solidarity due to the steadily growing development of the division of labor. That is how we have been led to make this the object of our study.

*   *   *

The social relations to which the division of labor gives birth have often been considered only in terms of exchange, but this misinterprets what such exchange implies and what results from it. It suggests two beings mutually dependent because they are each incomplete, and translates this mutual dependence outwardly. It is, then, only the superficial expression of an internal and very deep state. Precisely because this state is constant, it calls up a whole mechanism of images which function with a continuity that exchange does not possess. The image of the one who completes us becomes inseparable from ours, not only because it is frequently associated with ours, but particularly because it is the natural complement of it. It thus becomes an integral and permanent part of our conscience, to such a point that we can no longer separate ourselves from it and seek to increase its force. That is why we enjoy the society of the one it represents, since the presence of the object that it expresses, by making us actually perceive it, sets it off more. On the other hand, we will suffer from all circumstances which, like absence or death, may have as effect the barring of its return or the diminishing of its vivacity.

As short as this analysis is, it suffices to show that this mechanism is not identical with that which serves as a basis for sentiments of sympathy whose source is resemblance. Surely there can be no solidarity between others and us unless the image of others unites itself with ours. But when the union results from the resemblance of two images, it consists in an agglutination. The two representations become solidary because, being indistinct, totally or in part, they confound each other, and become no more than one, and they are solidary only in the measure which they confound themselves. On the contrary, in the case of the division of labor, they are outside each other and are linked only because they are distinct. Neither the sentiments nor the social relations which derive from these sentiments are the same in the two cases.

We are thus led to ask if the division of labor would not play the same role in more extensive

Reprinted from Emile Durkheim, *The Division of Labor in Society*, trans. George Simpson (Glencoe, Ill.: The Free Press, 1949), Preface, pp. 37–38; Book I, chap. i, 61–62, 64–65, 68–69; chap. ii, pp. 109–10; chap. iii, pp. 111–15, 127–31, with the permission of The Free Press.

groups, if, in contemporary societies where it has developed as we know, it would not have as its function the integration of the social body to assure unity. It is quite legitimate to suppose that the facts which we have just observed reproduce themselves here, but with greater amplitude, that great political societies can maintain themselves in equilibrium only thanks to the specialization of tasks, that the division of labor is the source, if not unique, at least principal, of social solidarity.

*   *   *

But social solidarity is a completely moral phenomenon which, taken by itself, does not lend itself to exact observation nor indeed to measurement. To proceed to this classification and this comparison, we must substitute for this internal fact which escapes us an external index which symbolizes it and study the former in the light of the latter.

This visible symbol is law. In effect, despite its immaterial character, wherever social solidarity exists, it resides not in a state of pure potentiality, but manifests its presence by sensible indices. Where it is strong, it leads men strongly to one another, frequently puts them in contact, multiplies the occasions when they find themselves related. To speak correctly, considering the point our investigation has reached, it is not easy to say whether social solidarity produces these phenomena, or whether it is a result of them, whether men relate themselves because it is a driving force, or whether it is a driving force because they relate themselves. However, it is not, at the moment, necessary to decide this question; it suffices to state that the two orders of fact are linked and vary at the same time and in the same sense. The more solidary the members of a society are, the more they sustain diverse relations, one with another, or with the group taken collectively, for, if their meetings were rare, they would depend upon one another only at rare intervals, and then tenuously. Moreover, the number of these relations is necessarily proportional to that of the juridical rules which determine them. Indeed, social life, especially where it exists durably, tends inevitably to assume a definite form and to organize itself, and law is nothing else than this very organization in so far as it has greater stability and precision. The general life of society cannot extend its sway without juridical life extending its sway at the same time and in direct relation. We can thus be certain of finding reflected in law all the essential varieties of social solidarity.

*   *   *

To proceed scientifically, we must find some characteristic which, while being essential to juridical phenomena, varies as they vary. Every precept of law can be defined as a rule of sanctioned conduct. Moreover, it is evident that sanctions change with the gravity attributed to precepts, the place they hold in the public conscience, the role they play in society. It is right, then, to classify juridical rules according to the different sanctions which are attached to them.

They are of two kinds. Some consist essentially in suffering, or at least a loss, inflicted on the agent. They make demands on his fortune, or on his honor, or on his life, or on his liberty, and deprive him of something he enjoys. We call them repressive. They constitute penal law. It is true that those which are attached to rules which are purely moral have the same character, only they are distributed in a diffuse manner, by everybody indiscriminately, whereas those in penal law are applied through the intermediary of a definite organ; they are organized. As for the other type, it does not necessarily imply suffering for the agent, but consists only of *the return of things as they were,* in the reestablishment of troubled relations to their normal state, whether the incriminated act is restored by force to the type whence it deviated, or is annulled, that is, deprived of all social value. We must then separate juridical rules into two great classes, accordingly as they have organized repressive sanctions or only restitutive sanctions. The first comprise all penal law; the second, civil law, commercial law, procedural law, administrative and constitutional law, after abstraction of the penal rules which may be found there.

*   *   *

There exists a social solidarity which comes from a certain number of states of conscience which are common to all the members of the same society. This is what repressive law materially represents, at least in so far as it is essential. The part that it plays in the general integration of society evidently depends upon the greater or lesser extent of the social life which the common conscience embraces and regulates. The greater the diversity of relations wherein the latter makes its action felt, the more also it creates links which attach the individual to the group; the more, consequently, social cohesion derives completely from this source and bears its mark. But the number of these relations is itself proportional to that of the repressive rules. In determining what fraction of the juridical system penal law represents, we, at the same time, measure the relative importance of this solidarity. It is true that in such a procedure we do not take into account certain elements of the collective conscience which, because of their smaller power or their indeterminateness, remain foreign to repressive law while contributing to the assurance of social harmony.

These are the ones protected by punishments which are merely diffuse. But the same is the case with other parts of law. There is not one of them which is not complemented by custom, and as there is no reason for supposing that the relation of law and custom is not the same in these different spheres, this elimination is not made at the risk of having to alter the results of our comparison.

Organic Solidarity Due to the Division of Labor

The very nature of the restitutive sanction suffices to show that the social solidarity to which this type of law corresponds is of a totally different kind.

What distinguishes this sanction is that it is not expiatory, but consists of a simple *return in state*. Sufferance proportionate to the misdeed is not inflicted on the one who has violated the law or who disregards it; he is simply sentenced to comply with it. If certain things were done, the judge reinstates them as they would have been. He speaks of law; he says nothing of punishment. Damage-interests have no penal character; they are only a means of reviewing the past in order to reinstate it, as far as possible, to its normal form. Tarde, it is true, has tried to find a sort of civil penality in the payment of costs by the defeated party. But, taken in this sense, the word has only a metaphorical value. For punishment to obtain, there would at least have to be some relation between the punishment and the misdeed, and for that it would be necessary for the degree of gravity of the misdeed to be firmly established. In fact, however, he who loses the litigation pays the damages even when his intentions were pure, even when his ignorance alone was his culpability. The reasons for this rule are different from those offered by Tarde: given the fact that justice is not rendered gratuitously, it appears equitable for the damages to be paid by the one who brought them into being. Moreover, it is possible that the prospect of such costs may stop the rash pleader, but that is not sufficient to constitute punishment. The fear of ruin which ordinarily follows indolence or negligence may keep the negotiant active and awake, though ruin is not, in the proper sense of the word, the penal sanction for his misdeeds.

Neglect of these rules is not even punished diffusely. The pleader who has lost in litigation is not disgraced, his honor is not put in question. We can even imagine these rules being other than they are without feeling any repugnance. The idea of tolerating murder arouses us, but we quite easily accept modification of the right of succession, and can even conceive of its possible abolition. It is at least a question which we do not refuse to discuss. Indeed, we admit with impunity that the law of servitudes or that of usufructs may be otherwise organized, that the obligations of vendor and purchaser may be determined in some other manner, that administrative functions may be distributed according to different principles. As these prescriptions do not correspond to any sentiment in us, and as we generally do not scientifically know the reasons for their existence, since this science is not definite, they have no roots in the majority of us. Of course, there are exceptions. We do not tolerate the idea that an engagement contrary to custom or obtained either through violence or fraud can bind the contracting parties. Thus, when public opinion finds itself in the presence of such a case, it shows itself less indifferent than we have just now said, and it increases the legal sanction by its censure. The different domains of the moral life are not radically separated one from another; they are, rather, continuous, and, accordingly, there are among them marginal regions where different characters are found at the same time. However, the preceding proposition remains true in the great majority of cases. It is proof that the rules with a restitutive sanction either do not totally derive from the collective conscience, or are only feeble states of it. Repressive law corresponds to the heart, the centre of the common conscience; laws purely moral are a part less central; finally, restitutive law is born in very ex-centric regions whence it spreads further. The more it becomes truly itself, the more removed it is.

This characteristic is, indeed, made manifest by the manner of its functioning. While repressive law tends to remain diffuse within society, restitutive law creates organs which are more and more specialized: consular tribunals, councils of arbitration, administrative tribunals of every sort. Even in its most general part, that which pertains to civil law, it is exercised only through particular functionaries: magistrates, lawyers, etc., who have become apt in this role because of very special training.

But, although these rules are more or less outside the collective conscience, they are not interested solely in individuals. If this were so, restitutive law would have nothing in common with social solidarity, for the relations that it regulates would bind individuals to one another without binding them to society. They would simply be happenings in private life, as friendly relations are. But society is far from having no hand in this sphere of juridical life. It is true that, generally, it does not intervene of itself and through its own movements; it must be solicited by the interested parties. But, in being called forth, its intervention is none the less the essential cog in the machine, since it alone makes it function. It propounds the law through the organ of its representatives.

It has been contended, however, that this role has nothing properly social about it, but reduces itself to that of a conciliator of private interests; that, consequently, any individual can fill it, and that, if society is in charge of it, it is only for commodious reasons. But nothing is more incorrect than considering society as a sort of third-party arbitrator. When it is led to intervene, it is not to put to rights some individual interests. It does not seek to discover what may be the most advantageous solution for the adversaries and does not propose a compromise for them. Rather, it applies to the particular case which is submitted to it general and traditional rules of law. But law is, above all, a social thing and has a totally different object than the interest of the pleaders. The judge who examines a request for divorce is not concerned with knowing whether this separation is truly desirable for the married parties, but rather whether the causes which are adduced come under one of the categories foreseen by the law.

But better to appreciate the importance of social action, we must observe it, not only at the moment when the sanction is applied, when the troubled relation is adjudicated, but also when it is instituted.

It is, in effect, necessary either to establish or to modify a number of juridical relations which this law takes care of and which the consent of the interested parties suffices neither to create nor to change. Such are those, notably, which concern the state of the persons. Although marriage is a contract, the married persons can neither form it nor break it at their pleasure. It is the same with all the other domestic relations and, with stronger reason, with all those which administrative law regulates. It is true that obligations properly contractual can be entered into and abrogated solely through the efforts of those desiring them. But it must not be forgotten that, if the contract has the power to bind, it is society which gives this power to it. Suppose that society did not sanction the obligations contracted for. They become simply promises which have no more than moral authority.[1] Every contract thus supposes that behind the parties implicated in it there is society very ready to intervene in order to gain respect for the engagements which have been made. Moreover, it lends this obligatory force only to contracts which have in themselves a social value, which is to say, those which conform to the rules of law. We shall see that its intervention is sometimes even more positive. It is present in all relations which restitutive law determines, even in those which appear most completely private, and its presence, though not felt, at least in normal circumstances, is none the less essential.[2]

Since rules with restitutive sanctions are strangers to the common conscience, the relations that they determine are not those which attach themselves indistinctly everywhere. That is to say, they are established immediately, not between the individual and society, but between restricted, special parties in society whom they bind. But, since society is not absent, it must be more or less directly interested, it must feel the repercussions. Thus, according to the force with which society feels them, it intervenes more or less concomitantly and more or less actively, through the intermediary of special organs charged with representing it. These relations are, then, quite different from those which repressive law regulates, for the latter attach the particular conscience to the collective conscience directly and without mediation; that is, the individual to society.

* * *

To sum up: the relations governed by co-operative law with restitutive sanctions and the solidarity which they express, result from the division of social labor. We have explained, moreover, that, in general, co-operative relations do not convey other sanctions. In fact, it is in the nature of special tasks to escape the action of the collective conscience, for, in order for a thing to be the object of common sentiments, the first condition is that it be common, that is to say, that it be present in all consciences and that all can represent it in one and the same manner. To be sure, in so far as functions have a certain generality, everybody can have some idea of them. But the more specialized they are, the more circumscribed the number of those cognizant of each of them. Consequently, the more marginal they are to the common conscience. The rules which determine them cannot have the superior force, the transcendent authority which, when offended, demands expiation. It is also from opinion that their authority comes, as is the case with penal rules, but from an opinion localized in restricted regions of society.

Moreover, even in the special circles where they apply and where, consequently, they are represented in people, they do not correspond to very active sentiments, nor even very often to any type of emotional state. For, as they fix the manner in which the different functions ought to concur in diverse combinations of circumstances which can arise, the objects to which they relate themselves are not always present to consciences. We do not always have

---

1. And even this moral authority comes from custom, which is to say, from society.

2. We must restrict ourselves to general indications, common to all the norms of restitutive law.

to administer guardianship, trusteeship,[3] or exercise the rights of creditor or buyer, etc., or even exercise them in such and such a condition. But the states of conscience are strong only in so far as they are permanent. The violation of these rules reaches neither the common soul of society in its living parts, nor even, at least not generally, that of special groups, and, consequently, it can determine only a very moderate reaction. All that is necessary is that the functions concur in a regular manner. If this regularity is disrupted, it behooves us to re-establish it. Assuredly, that is not to say that the development of the division of labor cannot be affective of penal law. There are, as we already know, administrative and governmental functions in which certain relations are regulated by repressive law, because of the particular character which the organ of common conscience and everything that relates to it has. In still other cases, the links of solidarity which unite certain social functions can be such that from their break quite general repercussions result invoking a penal sanction. But, for the reason we have given, these counter-blows are exceptional.

This law definitely plays a role in society analogous to that played by the nervous system in the organism. The latter has as its task, in effect, the regulation of the different functions of the body in such a way as to make them harmonize. It thus very naturally expresses the state of concentration at which the organism has arrived, in accordance with the division of physiological labor. Thus, on different levels of the animal scale, we can measure the degree of this concentration according to the development of the nervous system. Which is to say that we can equally measure the degree of concentration at which a society has arrived in accordance with the division of social labor according to the development of co-operative law with restitutive sanctions. We can foresee the great services that this criterion will render us.

Since negative solidarity does not produce any integration by itself, and since, moreover, there is nothing specific about it, we shall recognize only two kinds of positive solidarity which are distinguishable by the following qualities:

1. The first binds the individual directly to society without any intermediary. In the second, he depends upon society, because he depends upon the parts of which it is composed.

2. Society is not seen in the same aspect in the two cases. In the first, what we call society is a more or less organized totality of beliefs and sentiments common to all the members of the group: this is the collective type. On the other hand, the society in which we are solidary in the second instance is a system of different, special functions which definite relations unite. These two societies really make up only one. They are two aspects of one and the same reality, but none the less they must be distinguished.

3. From this second difference there arises another which helps us to characterize and name the two kinds of solidarity.

The first can be strong only if the ideas and tendencies common to all the members of the society are greater in number and intensity than those which pertain personally to each member. It is as much stronger as the excess is more considerable. But what makes our personality is how much of our own individual qualities we have, what distinguishes us from others. This solidarity can grow only in inverse ratio to personality. There are in each of us, as we have said, two consciences: one which is common to our group in its entirety, which, consequently, is not ourself, but society living and acting within us; the other, on the contrary, represents that in us which is personal and distinct, that which makes us an individual.[4] Solidarity which comes from likenesses is at its maximum when the collective conscience completely envelops our whole conscience and coincides in all points with it. But, at that moment, our individuality is nil. It can be born only if the community takes smaller toll of us. There are, here, two contrary forces, one centripetal, the other centrifugal, which cannot flourish at the same time. We cannot, at one and the same time, develop ourselves in two opposite senses. If we have a lively desire to think and act for ourselves, we cannot be strongly inclined to think and act as others do. If our ideal is to present a singular and personal appearance, we do not want to resemble everybody else. Moreover, at the moment when this solidarity exercises its force, our personality vanishes, as our definition permits us to say, for we are no longer ourselves, but the collective life.

The social molecules which can be coherent in this way can act together only in the measure that they have no actions of their own, as the molecules of inorganic bodies. That is why we propose to call this type of solidarity mechanical. The term does not signify that it is produced by mechanical and artificial means. We call it that only by analogy to the cohesion which unites the elements of an inanimate body, as opposed to that which makes a unity out of the elements of a living body. What justifies

3. That is why the law which governs the relations of domestic functions is not penal, although these functions are very general.

4. However, these two consciences are not in regions geographically distinct from us, but penetrate from all sides.

this term is that the link which thus unites the individual to society is wholly analogous to that which attaches a thing to a person. The individual conscience, considered in this light, is a simple dependent upon the collective type and follows all of its movements, as the possessed object follows those of its owner. In societies where this type of solidarity is highly developed, the individual does not appear, as we shall see later. Individuality is something which the society possesses. Thus, in these social types, personal rights are not yet distinguished from real rights.

It is quite otherwise with the solidarity which the division of labor produces. Whereas the previous type implies that individuals resemble each other, this type presumes their difference. The first is possible only in so far as the individual personality is absorbed into the collective personality; the second is possible only if each one has a sphere of action which is peculiar to him; that is, a personality. It is necessary, then, that the collective conscience leave open a part of the individual conscience in order that special functions may be established there, functions which it cannot regulate. The more this region is extended, the stronger is the cohesion which results from this solidarity. In effect, on the one hand, each one depends as much more strictly on society as labor is more divided; and, on the other, the activity of each is as much more personal as it is more specialized. Doubtless, as circumscribed as it is, it is never completely original. Even in the exercise of our occupation, we conform to usages, to practices which are common to our whole professional brotherhood. But, even in this instance, the yoke that we submit to is much less heavy than when society completely controls us, and it leaves much more place open for the free play of our initiative. Here, then, the individuality of all grows at the same time as that of its parts. Society becomes more capable of collective movement, at the same time that each of its elements has more freedom of movement. This solidarity resembles that which we observe among the higher animals. Each organ, in effect, has its special physiognomy, its autonomy. And, moreover, the unity of the organism is as great as the individuation of the parts is more marked. Because of this analogy, we propose to call the solidarity which is due to the division of labor, organic.

4. Types of Suicide

BY EMILE DURKHEIM

WE HAVE thus successively set up the three following propositions:

> *Suicide varies inversely with the degree of integration of religious society.*
> *Suicide varies inversely with the degree of integration of domestic society.*
> *Suicide varies inversely with the degree of integration of political society.*

This grouping shows that whereas these different societies have a moderating influence upon suicide, this is due not to special characteristics of each but to a characteristic common to all. Religion does not owe its efficacy to the special nature of religious sentiments, since domestic and political societies both produce the same effects when strongly integrated. This, moreover, we have already proved when studying directly the manner of action of different religions upon suicide. Inversely, it is not the specific nature of the domestic or political tie which can explain the immunity they confer, since religious society has the same advantage. The cause can only be found in a single quality possessed by all these social groups, though perhaps to varying degrees. The only quality satisfying this condition is that they are all strongly integrated social groups. So we reach the general conclusion: suicide varies inversely with the degree of integration of the social groups of which the individual forms a part.

But society cannot disintegrate without the individual simultaneously detaching himself from social life, without his own goals becoming preponderant over those of the community, in a word without his personality tending to surmount the collective personality. The more weakened the groups to which he belongs, the less he depends

Reprinted from Emile Durkheim, *Suicide,* trans. John A. Spaulding and George Simpson (Glencoe, Ill.: The Free Press, 1951), Book II, chap. iii, pp. 208–16; chap. iv, p. 217, 221–22, 227–28, 239–40.

on them, the more he consequently depends only on himself and recognizes no other rules of conduct than what are founded on his private interests. If we agree to call this state egoism, in which the individual ego asserts itself to excess in the face of the social ego and at its expense, we may call egoistic the special type of suicide springing from excessive individualism.

But how can suicide have such an origin?

First of all, it can be said that, as collective force is one of the obstacles best calculated to restrain suicide, its weakening involves a development of suicide. When society is strongly integrated, it holds individuals under its control, considers them at its service and thus forbids them to dispose wilfully of themselves. Accordingly it opposes their evading their duties to it through death. But how could society impose its supremacy upon them when they refuse to accept this subordination as legitimate? It no longer then possesses the requisite authority to retain them in their duty if they wish to desert; and conscious of its own weakness, it even recognizes their right to do freely what it can no longer prevent. So far as they are the admitted masters of their destinies, it is their privilege to end their lives. They, on their part, have no reason to endure life's sufferings patiently. For they cling to life more resolutely when belonging to a group they love, so as not to betray interests they put before their own. The bond that unites them with the common cause attaches them to life and the lofty goal they envisage prevents their feeling personal troubles so deeply. There is, in short, in a cohesive and animated society a constant interchange of ideas and feelings from all to each and each to all, something like a mutual moral support, which instead of throwing the individual on his own resources, leads him to share in the collective energy and supports his own when exhausted.

But these reasons are purely secondary. Excessive individualism not only results in favoring the action of suicidogenic causes, but it is itself such a cause. It not only frees man's inclination to do away with himself from a protective obstacle, but creates this inclination out of whole cloth and thus gives birth to a special suicide which bears its mark. This must be clearly understood for this is what constitutes the special character of the type of suicide just distinguished and justifies the name we have given it. What is there then in individualism that explains this result?

It has been sometimes said that because of his psychological constitution, man cannot live without attachment to some object which transcends and survives him, and that the reason for this necessity is a need we must have not to perish entirely. Life

is said to be intolerable unless some reason for existing is involved, some purpose justifying life's trials. The individual alone is not a sufficient end for his activity. He is too little. He is not only hemmed in spatially; he is also strictly limited temporally. When, therefore, we have no other object than ourselves we cannot avoid the thought that our efforts will finally end in nothingness, since we ourselves disappear. But annihilation terrifies us. Under these conditions one would lose courage to live, that is, to act and struggle, since nothing will remain of our exertions. The state of egoism, in other words, is supposed to be contradictory to human nature and, consequently, too uncertain to have chances of permanence.

In this absolute formulation the proposition is vulnerable. If the thought of the end of our personality were really so hateful, we could consent to live only by blinding ourselves voluntarily as to life's value. For if we may in a measure avoid the prospect of annihilation we cannot extirpate it; it is inevitable, whatever we do. We may push back the frontier for some generations, force our name to endure for some years or centuries longer than our body; a moment, too soon for most men, always comes when it will be nothing. For the groups we join in order to prolong our existence by their means are themselves mortal; they too must dissolve, carrying with them all our deposit of ourselves. Those are few whose memories are closely enough bound to the very history of humanity to be assured of living until its death. So, if we really thus thirsted after immortality, no such brief perspectives could ever appease us. Besides, what of us is it that lives? A word, a sound, an imperceptible trace, most often anonymous,[1] therefore nothing comparable to the violence of our efforts or able to justify them to us. In actuality, though a child is naturally an egoist who feels not the slightest craving to survive himself, and the old man is very often a child in this and so many other respects, neither ceases to cling to life as much or more than the adult; indeed we have seen that suicide is very rare for the first fifteen years and tends to decrease at the other extreme of life. Such too is the case with animals, whose psychological constitution differs from that of men only in degree. It is therefore untrue that life is only possible by its possessing its rationale outside of itself.

Indeed, a whole range of functions concern only the individual; these are the ones indispensable for

---

1. We say nothing of the ideal protraction of life involved in the belief in immortality of the soul, for (1) this cannot explain why the family or attachment to political society preserves us from suicide; and (2) it is not even this belief which forms religion's prophylactic influence, as we have shown above.

physical life. Since they are made for this purpose only, they are perfected by its attainment. In everything concerning them, therefore, man can act reasonably without thought of transcendental purposes. These functions serve by merely serving him. In so far as he has no other needs, he is therefore self-sufficient and can live happily with no other objective than living. This is not the case, however, with the civilized adult. He has many ideas, feelings and practices unrelated to organic needs. The roles of art, morality, religion, political faith, science itself are not to repair organic exhaustion nor to provide sound functioning of the organs. All this supra-physical life is built and expanded not because of the demands of the cosmic environment but because of the demands of the social environment. The influence of society is what has aroused in us the sentiments of sympathy and solidarity drawing us toward others; it is society which, fashioning us in its image, fills us with religious, political and moral beliefs that control our actions. To play our social role we have striven to extend our intelligence and it is still society that has supplied us with tools for this development by transmitting to us its trust fund of knowledge.

Through the very fact that these superior forms of human activity have a collective origin, they have a collective purpose. As they derive from society they have reference to it; rather they are society itself incarnated and individualized in each one of us. But for them to have a raison d'etre in our eyes, the purpose they envisage must be one not indifferent to us. We can cling to these forms of human activity only to the degree that we cling to society itself. Contrariwise, in the same measure as we feel detached from society we become detached from that life whose source and aim is society. For what purpose do these rules of morality, these precepts of law binding us to all sorts of sacrifices, these restrictive dogmas exist, if there is no being outside us whom they serve and in whom we participate? What is the purpose of science itself? If its only use is to increase our chances for survival, it does not deserve the trouble it entails. Instinct acquits itself better of this role; animals prove this. Why substitute for it a more hesitant and uncertain reflection? What is the end of suffering, above all? If the value of things can only be estimated by their relation to this positive evil for the individual, it is without reward and incomprehensible. This problem does not exist for the believer firm in his faith or the man strongly bound by ties of domestic or political society. Instinctively and unreflectively they ascribe all that they are and do, the one to his Church or his God, the living symbol of the Church, the other to his family, the

third to his country or party. Even in their sufferings they see only a means of glorifying the group to which they belong and thus do homage to it. So, the Christian ultimately desires and seeks suffering to testify more fully to his contempt for the flesh and more fully resemble his divine model. But the more the believer doubts, that is, the less he feels himself a real participant in the religious faith to which he belongs, and from which he is freeing himself; the more the family and community become foreign to the individual, so much the more does he become a mystery to himself, unable to escape the exasperating and agonizing question: to what purpose?

If, in other words, as has often been said, man is double, that is because social man superimposes himself upon physical man. Social man necessarily presupposes a society which he expresses and serves. If this dissolves, if we no longer feel it in existence and action about and above us, whatever is social in us is deprived of all objective foundation. All that remains is an artificial combination of illusory images, a phantasmagoria vanishing at the least reflection; that is, nothing which can be a goal for our action. Yet this social man is the essence of civilized man; he is the masterpiece of existence. Thus we are bereft of reasons for existence; for the only life to which we could cling no longer corresponds to anything actual; the only existence still based upon reality no longer meets our needs. Because we have been initiated into a higher existence, the one which satisfies an animal or a child can satisfy us no more and the other itself fades and leaves us helpless. So there is nothing more for our efforts to lay hold of, and we feel them lose themselves in emptiness. In this sense it is true to say that our activity needs an object transcending it. We do not need it to maintain ourselves in the illusion of an impossible immortality; it is implicit in our moral constitution and cannot be even partially lost without this losing its raison d'etre in the same degree. No proof is needed that in such a state of confusion the least cause of discouragement may easily give birth to desperate resolutions. If life is not worth the trouble of being lived, everything becomes a pretext to rid ourselves of it.

But this is not all. This detachment occurs not only in single individuals. One of the constitutive elements of every national temperament consists of a certain way of estimating the value of existence. There is a collective as well as an individual humor inclining peoples to sadness or cheerfulness, making them see things in bright or sombre lights. In fact, only society can pass a collective opinion on the value of human life; for this the individual is incompetent. The latter knows nothing but himself and his own little horizon; thus his experience is too limited to serve as a basis for a general appraisal. He may indeed consider his own life to be aimless; he can say nothing applicable to others. On the contrary, without sophistry, society may generalize its own feeling as to itself, its state of health or lack of health. For individuals share too deeply in the life of society for it to be diseased without their suffering infection. What it suffers they necessarily suffer. Because it is the whole, its ills are communicated to its paths. Hence it cannot disintegrate without awareness that the regular conditions of general existence are equally disturbed. Because society is the end on which our better selves depend, it cannot feel us escaping it without a simultaneous realization that our activity is purposeless. Since we are its handiwork, society cannot be conscious of its own decadence without the feeling that henceforth this work is of no value. Thence are formed currents of depression and disillusionment emanating from no particular individual but expressing society's state of disintegration. They reflect the relaxation of social bonds, a sort of collective asthenia, or social malaise, just as individual sadness, when chronic, in its way reflects the poor organic state of the individual. Then metaphysical and religious systems spring up which, by reducing these obscure sentiments to formulae, attempt to prove to men the senselessness of life and that it is self-deception to believe that it has purpose. Then new moralities originate which, by elevating facts to ethics, commend suicide or at least tend in that direction by suggesting a minimal existence. On their appearance they seem to have been created out of whole cloth by their makers who are sometimes blamed for the pessimism of their doctrines. In reality they are an effect rather than a cause; they merely symbolize in abstract language and systematic form the physiological distress of the body social.[2] As these currents are collective, they have, by virtue of their origin, an authority which they impose upon the individual and they drive him more vigorously on the way to which he is already inclined by the state of moral distress directly aroused in him by the disintegration of society. Thus, at the very moment that, with excessive zeal, he frees himself from the social environment, he still submits to its influence. However individualized a man may be, there is always something collective remaining—the very depression and melancholy resulting from this same exaggerated individualism. He effects communion through sadness when he no longer has anything else with which to achieve it.

Hence this type of suicide well deserves the name we have given it. Egoism is not merely a contributing factor in it; it is its generating cause. In this case the bond attaching man to life relaxes because that attaching him to society is itself slack. The incidents of private life which seem the direct inspiration of suicide and are considered its determining causes are in reality only incidental causes. The individual yields to the slightest shock of circumstance because the state of society has made him a ready prey to suicide.

Several facts confirm this explanation. Suicide is known to be rare among children and to diminish among the aged at the last confines of life; physical man, in both, tends to become the whole of man. Society is still lacking in the former, for it has not had the time to form him in its image; it begins to retreat from the latter or, what amounts to the same thing, he retreats from it. Thus both are more self-sufficient. Feeling a lesser need for self-completion through something not themselves, they are also less exposed to feel the lack of what is necessary for living. The immunity of an animal has the same causes. We shall likewise see in the next chapter that, though lower societies practice a form of suicide of their own, the one we have just discussed is almost unknown to them. Since their social life is very simple, the social inclinations of individuals are simple also and thus they need little for satisfaction. They readily find external objectives to which they become attached. If he can carry with him his gods and his family, primitive man, everywhere that he goes, has all that his social nature demands.

This is also why woman can endure life in isolation more easily than man. When a widow is seen to endure her condition much better than a widower and desires marriage less passionately, one is led to consider this ease in dispensing with the family a mark of superiority; it is said that woman's affective faculties, being very intense, are easily employed outside the domestic circle, while her devotion is indispensable to man to help him endure life. Actually, if this is her privilege it is because her sensibility is rudimentary rather than highly developed. As she lives outside of community existence more than man, she is less penetrated by it; society is less necessary to her because she is less impregnated with sociability. She has few needs in this direction and satisfies them easily. With a few devotional practices and some animals to care for, the old unmarried woman's life is full. If she remains faithfully attached to religious traditions and thus finds ready protection against sui-

---

2. This is why it is unjust to accuse these theorists of sadness of generalizing personal impressions. They are the echo of a general condition.

cide, it is because these very simple social forms satisfy all her needs. Man, on the contrary, is hard beset in this respect. As his thought and activity develop, they increasingly overflow these antiquated forms. But then he needs others. Because he is a more complex social being, he can maintain his equilibrium only by finding more points of support outside himself, and it is because his moral balance depends on a larger number of conditions that it is more easily disturbed.

Altruistic Suicide

In the order of existence, no good is measureless. A biological quality can only fulfill the purposes it is meant to serve on condition that it does not transgress certain limits. So with social phenomena. If, as we have just seen, excessive individuation leads to suicide, insufficient individuation has the same effects. When man has become detached from society, he encounters less resistance to suicide in himself, and he does so likewise when social integration is too strong.

*   *   *

We thus confront a type of suicide differing by incisive qualities from the preceding one. Whereas the latter is due to excessive individuation, the former is caused by too rudimentary individuation. One occurs because society allows the individual to escape it, being insufficiently aggregated in some parts or even in the whole; the other, because society holds him in too strict tutelage. Having given the name of *egoism* to the state of the ego living its own life and obeying itself alone, that of *altruism* adequately expresses the opposite state, where the ego is not its own property, where it is blended with something not itself, where the goal of conduct is exterior to itself, that is, in one of the groups in which it participates. So we call the suicide caused by intense altruism *altruistic suicide*. But since it is characteristically performed as a duty, the terminology adopted should express this fact. So we will call such a type *obligatory altruistic suicide*.

The combination of these two adjectives is required to define it; for not every altruistic suicide is necessarily obligatory. Some are not so expressly imposed by society, having a more optional character. In other words, altruistic suicide is a species with several varieties.

*   *   *

We have thus constituted a second type of suicide, itself consisting of three varieties: obligatory altruistic suicide, optional altruistic suicide, and acute altruistic suicide, the perfect pattern of which

is mystical suicide. In these different forms, it contrasts most strikingly with egoistic suicide. One is related to the crude morality which disregards everything relating solely to the individual; the other is closely associated with the refined ethics which sets human personality on so high a pedestal that it can no longer be subordinated to anything. Between the two there is, therefore, all the difference between primitive peoples and the most civilized nations.

However, if lower societies are the theatre par excellence of altruistic suicide, it is also found in more recent civilizations. Under this head may notably be classified the death of some of the Christian martyrs. All those neophytes who without killing themselves, voluntarily allowed their own slaughter, are really suicides. Though they did not kill themselves, they sought death with all their power and behaved so as to make it inevitable. To be suicide, the act from which death must necessarily result need only have been performed by the victim with full knowledge of the facts. Besides, the passionate enthusiasm with which the believers in the new religion faced final torture shows that at this moment they had completely discarded their personalities for the idea of which they had become the servants. Probably the epidemics of suicide which devastated the monasteries on several occasions during the Middle Ages, apparently caused by excesses of religious fervor, were of this nature.

In our contemporary societies, as individual personality becomes increasingly free from the collective personality, such suicides could not be widespread. Some may doubtless be said to have yielded to altruistic motives, such as soldiers who preferred death to the humiliation of defeat, like Commandant Beaurepaire and Admiral Villeneuve, or unhappy persons who kill themselves to prevent disgrace befalling their family. For when such persons renounce life, it is for something they love better than themselves. But they are isolated and exceptional cases. Yet even today there exists among us a special environment where altruistic suicide is chronic: namely, the army.

*   *   *

It may now be better understood why we insisted on giving an objective definition of suicide and on sticking to it.

Because altruistic suicide, though showing the familiar suicidal traits, resembles especially in its most vivid manifestations some categories of action which we are used to honoring with our respect and even admiration, people have often refused to consider it as self-destruction. It is to be remembered that the deaths of Cato and of the

Girondins were not suicides for Esquirol and Falret. But if suicides with the spirit of renunciation and abnegation as their immediate and visible cause do not deserve the name, it can be no more appropriate for those springing from the same moral disposition, though less apparently; for the second differ by only a few shades from the first. If the inhabitant of the Canary Islands who throws himself into an abyss to do honor to his god is not a suicide, how give this name to a Jain sectary who kills himself to obtain entry to oblivion; to the primitive who, under the influence of the same mental state, renounces life for a slight insult done him or merely to express his contempt for existence; to the bankrupt who prefers not to survive his disgrace; and finally to the many soldiers who every year increase the numbers of voluntary deaths? All these cases have for their root the same state of altruism which is equally the cause of what might be called heroic suicide. Shall they alone be placed among the ranks of suicides and only those excluded whose motive is particularly pure? But first, according to what standard will the division be made? When does a motive cease to be sufficiently praiseworthy for the act it determines to be called suicide? Moreover, by separating these two classes of facts radically from each other, we inevitably misjudge their nature. For the essential characteristics of the type are clearest in obligatory altruistic suicide. Other varieties are only derivative forms. Either a considerable number of in-

structive phenomena will be eliminated or, if not all are eliminated, not only will a purely arbitrary choice be the only one possible among them, but it will be impossible to detect the common stock to which those that are retained belong. Such is the risk we incur in making the definition of suicide depend on the subjective feelings it inspires.

Besides, not even the reasons for the sentiment thought to justify this exclusion are well founded. The fact is stressed that the motives of certain altruistic suicides reappear in slightly different forms as the basis of actions regarded by everyone as moral. But is egoistic suicide any different? Has not the sentiment of individual autonomy its own morality as well as the opposite sentiment? If the latter serves as foundation to a kind of courage, strengthening and even hardening the heart, the other softens and moves it to pity. Where altruistic suicide is prevalent, man is always ready to give his life; however, at the same time, he sets no more value on that of another. On the contrary, when he rates individual personality above all other ends, he respects it in others. His cult for it makes him suffer from all that minimizes it even among his fellows. A broader sympathy for human suffering succeeds the fanatical devotions of primitive times. Every sort of suicide is then merely the exaggerated or deflected form of a virtue. In that case, however, the way they affect the moral conscience does not sufficiently differentiate them to justify their being separated into different types.

5. Types of Social Organization

BY MAX WEBER

Types of Solidary Social Relationships

A SOCIAL RELATIONSHIP will be called "communal"[1] if and so far as the orientation of

social action—whether in the individual case, on the average, or in the pure type—is based on a subjective feeling of the parties, whether affectual

Reprinted from Max Weber, *The Theory of Social and Economic Organization,* trans. A. H. Henderson and Talcott Parsons, ed. Talcott Parsons (Glencoe, Ill.: The Free Press, 1947), Chap. i, secs. 9–17, pp. 136–57, with the permission of The Free Press. Copyright 1947 by Oxford University Press.

1. The two types of relationship which Weber distinguishes in this section he himself calls *Vergemeinschaftung* and *Vergesellschaftung.* His own usage here is an adaptation of the well-known terms of Toennies, *Gemein-*

schaft and *Gesellschaft,* and has been directly influenced by Toennies' work. Though there has been much discussion of them in English, it is safe to say that no satisfactory equivalent of Toennies' terms have been found. In particular, "community" and either "society" or "association" are unsatisfactory, since these terms have quite different connotations in English. In the context, however, in which Weber uses his slightly altered terms, that of action within a social relationship, the adjective forms "communal" and "associative" do not seem to be objectionable. Their exact meanings should become clear from Weber's definitions and comments.—ED.

or traditional, that they belong together. A social relationship will, on the other hand, be called "associative" if and in so far as the orientation of social action within it rests on a rationally motivated adjustment of interests or a similarly motivated agreement, whether the basis of rational judgment be absolute values or reasons of expediency. It is especially common, though by no means inevitable, for the associative type of relationship to rest on a rational agreement by mutual consent. In that case the corresponding action is, at the pole of rationality, oriented either to a rational belief in the binding validity of the obligation to adhere to it, or to a rational expectation that the other party will live up to it.[2]

1. The purest cases of associative relationships are: (a) rational free market exchange, which constitutes a compromise of opposed but complementary interests; (b) the pure voluntary association based on self-interest,[3] a case of agreement as to a long-run course of action oriented purely to the promotion of specific ulterior interests, economic or other, of its members; (c) the voluntary association of individuals motivated by an adherence to a set of common absolute values,[4] for example, the rational sect, in so far as it does not cultivate emotional and affective interests, but seeks only to serve a "cause." This last case, to be sure, seldom occurs in anything approaching the pure type.

2. Communal relationships may rest on various types of affectual, emotional, or traditional bases. Examples are a religious brotherhood, an erotic relationship, a relation of personal loyalty, a national community, the *esprit de corps* of a military unit. The type case most conveniently illustrated by the family. But the great majority of social relationships has this characteristic to some degree, while it is at the same time to some degree determined by associative factors. No matter how calculating and hard-headed the ruling considerations in such a social relationship—as that of a merchant to his customers—may be, it is quite possible for it to involve emotional values which transcend its utilitarian significance. Every social relationship which goes beyond the pursuit of immediate common ends, which hence lasts for long periods, involves relatively permanent social relationships between the same persons, and these cannot be exclusively confined to the technically

necessary activities. Hence in such cases as association in the same military unit, in the same school class, in the same workshop or office, there is always some tendency in this direction, although the degree, to be sure, varies enormously.[5] Conversely, a social relationship which is normally considered primarily communal may involve action on the part of some or even all of the participants, which is to an important degree oriented to considerations of expediency. There is, for instance, a wide variation in the extent to which the members of a family group feel a genuine community of interests or, on the other hand, exploit the relationship for their own ends. The concept of communal relationship has been intentionally defined in very general terms and hence includes a very heterogeneous group of phenomena.

3. The communal type of relationship is, according to the usual interpretation of its subjective meaning, the most radical antithesis of conflict. This should not, however, be allowed to obscure the fact that coercion of all sorts is a very common thing in even the most intimate of such communal relationships if one party is weaker in character than the other. Furthermore, a process of the selection of types leading to differences in opportunity and survival, goes on within these relationships just the same as anywhere else. Associative relationships, on the other hand, very often consist only in compromises between rival interests, where only a part of the occasion or means of conflict has been eliminated, or even an attempt has been made to do so. Hence, outside the area of compromise, the conflict of interests, with its attendant competition for supremacy, remains unchanged. Conflict and communal relationships are relative concepts. Conflict varies enormously according to the means employed, especially whether they are violent or peaceful, and to the ruthlessness with which they are used. It has already been pointed out that any type of order governing social action in some way leaves room for a process of selection among various rival human types.

4. It is by no means true that the existence of common qualities, a common situation, or common modes of behaviour imply the existence of a communal social relationship. Thus, for instance, the possession of a common biological inheritance by virtue of which persons are classified as belonging to the same "race," naturally implies no sort of

---

2. This terminology is similar to the distinction made by Ferdinand Toennies in his pioneering work, *Gemeinschaft und Gesellschaft;* but for his purposes, Toennies has given this distinction a rather more specific meaning than would be convenient for purposes of the present discussion.

3. *Zweckverein.*

4. *Gesinnungsverein.*

5. Weber's emphasis on the importance of these communal elements even within functionally specific formal organizations like industrial plants has been strongly confirmed by the findings of research since this was written. One important study which shows the importance of informal organization on this level among the workers of an industrial plant is reported in Roethlisberger and Dickson, *Management and the Worker.*—Ed.

communal social relationship between them. By restrictions on social intercourse and on marriage persons may find themselves in a similar situation, a situation of isolation from the environment which imposes these distinctions. But even if they all react to this situation in the same way, this does not constitute a communal relationship. The latter does not even exist if they have a common "feeling" about this situation and its consequences. It is only when this feeling leads to a mutual orientation of their behaviour to each other that a social relationship arises between them, a social relationship to each other and not only to persons in the environment. Furthermore, it is only so far as this relationship involves feelings of belonging together that it is a "communal" relationship. In the case of the Jews, for instance, except for Zionist circles and the action of certain associations promoting specifically Jewish interests, there thus exist communal relationships only to a relatively small extent; indeed, Jews often repudiate the existence of a Jewish "community."

Community of language, which arises from a similarity of tradition through the family and the surrounding social environment, facilitates mutual understanding, and thus the formation of all types of social relationships, in the highest degree. But taken by itself it is not sufficient to constitute a communal relationship, but only for the facilitation of intercourse within the groups concerned, thus for the development of associative relationships. In the first place, this takes place between *individuals,* not because they speak the same language, but because they have other types of interests. Orientation to the rules of a common language is thus primarily important as a means of communication, not as the content of a social relationship. It is only with the emergence of a consciousness of difference from third persons who speak a different language that the fact that two persons speak the same language, and in that respect share a common situation, can lead them to a feeling of community and to modes of social organization consciously based on the sharing of the common language.

Participation in a "market" is still another kind. It encourages association between the individual parties to specific acts of exchange and a social relationship, above all that of competition, between the individual participants who must mutually orient their action to each other. But no further modes of association develop except in cases where certain participants enter into agreements in order to better their competitive situations, or where they all agree on rules for the purpose of regulating transactions and of securing favourable general conditions for

all. It may further be remarked that the market and the competitive economy resting on it form the most important type of the reciprocal determination of action in terms of pure self-interest, a type which is characteristic of modern economic life.

Open and Closed Relationships

A social relationship, regardless of whether it is communal or associative in character, will be spoken of as "open" to outsiders if and in so far as participation in the mutually oriented social action relevant to its subjective meaning is, according to its system of order, not denied to anyone who wishes to participate and who is actually in a position to do so. A relationship will, on the other hand, be called "closed" against outsiders so far as, according to its subjective meaning and the binding rules of its order, participation of certain persons is excluded, limited, or subjected to conditions. Whether a relationship is open or closed may be determined traditionally, affectually, or rationally in terms of values or of expediency. It is especially likely to be closed, for rational reasons, in the following type of situation: a social relationship may provide the parties to it with opportunities for the satisfaction of various interests, whether the satisfactions be spiritual or material, whether the interest be in the end of the relationship as such or in some ulterior consequence of participation, or whether it is achieved through co-operative action or by a compromise of interests. If the participants expect that the admission of others will lead to an improvement of their situation, an improvement in degree, in kind, in the security or the value of the satisfaction, their interest will be in keeping the relationship open. If, on the other hand, their expectations are of improving their position by monopolistic tactics, their interest is in a closed relationship.

There are various ways in which it is possible for a closed social relationship to guarantee its monopolized advantages to the parties. Such advantages may be left free to competitive struggle within the group; they may be regulated or rationed in amount and kind, or they may be appropriated by individuals or sub-groups on a permanent basis and become more or less inalienable. The last is a case of closure within, as well as against, outsiders. Appropriated advantages will be called "rights." As determined by the relevant order, appropriation may be for the benefit of the members of particular communal or associative groups (for instance, household groups), or for the benefit of individuals. In the latter case, the individual may enjoy his rights on a purely personal basis or in such a way that in case of his death one or more other persons related to the holder of the right by birth (kinship), or by some other social relationship, may inherit the rights in question. Or the rights may pass to one or more individuals specifically designated by the holder. Finally, it may be that the holder is more or less fully empowered to alienate his rights by voluntary agreement, either to other specific persons or to anyone he chooses. This is "alienable" appropriation. A party to a closed social relationship will be called a "member";[6] in case his participation is regulated in such a way as to guarantee him appropriated advantages, a "privileged" member. Appropriated rights which are enjoyed by individuals through inheritance or by hereditary groups, whether communal or associative, will be called the "property" of the individual or of groups in question; and, in so far as they are alienable, "free" property.

The apparently gratuitous tediousness involved in the elaborate definition of the above concepts is an example of the fact that we often neglect to think out clearly what seems to be "obvious," because it is intuitively familiar.

1. (a) Examples of communal relationships, which tend to be closed on a traditional basis, are those membership in which is determined by family relationship.

(b) Personal emotional relationships are usually affectually closed. Examples are erotic relationships and, very commonly, relations of personal loyalty.

(c) Closure on the basis of rational commitment to values is usual in groups sharing a common system of explicit religious belief.

(d) Typical cases of rational closure on grounds of expediency are economic associations of a monopolistic or a plutocratic character.

A few examples may be taken at random. Whether a group of people engaged in conversation is open or closed depends on its content. General conversation is apt to be open, as contrasted with intimate conversation or the imparting of official information. Market relationships are in most, or at least in many, cases essentially open. In the case of many relationships, both communal and associative, there is a tendency to shift from a phase of expansion to one of exclusiveness. Examples are the guilds and the democratic city-states of Antiquity and the Middle Ages. At times these groups sought to increase their membership in the interest of improving the security of their position of power by adequate numbers. At other times they restricted their membership to protect the value of their monopolistic position. The same

phenomenon is not uncommon in monastic orders and religious sects which have passed from a stage of religious proselytizing to one of restriction in the interest of the maintenance of an ethical standard or for the protection of material interests. There is a similar close relationship between the extension of market relationships in the interest of increased turnover on the one hand, their monopolistic restriction on the other. The promotion of linguistic uniformity is to-day a natural result of the interests of publishers and writers, as opposed to the earlier, not uncommon, tendency for class groups to maintain linguistic peculiarities or even for secret languages to be built up.

2. Both the extent and the methods of regulation and exclusion in relation to outsiders may vary widely, so that the transition from a state of openness to one of regulation and closure is gradual. Various conditions of participation may be laid down; qualifying tests, a period of probation, requirement of possession of a share which can be purchased under certain conditions, election of new members by ballot, membership or eligibility by birth or by virtue of achievements open to anyone. Finally, in case of closure and the appropriation of rights within the group, status may be dependent on the acquisition of an appropriated right. There is a wide variety of different degrees of closure and of conditions of participation. Thus regulation and closure are relative concepts. There are all manner of gradual shadings as between an exclusive club, a theatrical audience the members of which have purchased tickets, and a party rally to which the largest possible number has been urged to come; similarly, from a church service open to the general public through the rituals of a limited sect to the mysteries of a secret cult.

3. Similarly, closure within the group as between the members themselves and in their relations with each other may also assume the most varied forms. Thus a caste, a guild, or a group of stock exchange brokers, which is closed to outsiders, may allow to its members a perfectly free competition for all the advantages which the group as a whole monopolizes for itself. Or it may assign every member strictly to the enjoyment of certain advantages, such as claims over customers or particular business opportunities, for life or even on a hereditary basis. This is particularly characteristic of India. Similarly a closed group of settlers may allow its members free use of the resources of its area or may restrict them rigidly to a plot assigned to each individual household. A closed group of colonists may allow free use of the land or sanction and guarantee permanent appropriation of separate holdings. In such cases all conceivable transitional and intermediate

---

6. *Rechtsgenosse.*

forms can be found. Historically, the closure of eligibility to fiefs, benefices, and offices within the group, and the appropriation on the part of those enjoying them, have occurred in the most varied forms. Similarly, the establishment of rights to and possession of particular jobs on the part of workers may develop all the way from the "closed shop" to a right to a particular job. The first step in this development may be to prohibit the dismissal of a worker without the consent of the workers' representatives. The development of the "works councils" in Germany after 1918 might be a first step in this direction, though it need not be.[7]

All the details must be reserved to particular studies. The most extreme form of permanent appropriation is found in cases where particular rights are guaranteed to an individual or to certain groups of them, such as households, clans, families, in such a way that it is specified in the order either that, in case of death, the rights descend to specific heirs, or that the possessor is free to transfer them to any other person at will. Such a person thereby becomes a party to the social relationship so that, when appropriation has reached this extreme within the group, it becomes to that extent an open group in relation to outsiders. This is true so long as acquisition of membership is not subject to the ratification of the other, prior members.

4. The principal motives for closure of a relationship are: (a) The maintenance of quality, which is often combined with the interest in prestige and the consequent opportunities to enjoy honour, and even profit. Examples are communities of ascetics, monastic orders, especially, for instance, the Indian mendicant orders, religious sects like the Puritans, organized groups of warriors, of retainers (*Ministerialen*) and other functionaries, organized citizen bodies as in the Greek states, craft guilds; (b) orientation to the scarcity of advantages in their bearing on consumption needs (*Nahrungsspielraum*).[8] Examples are monopolies of consumption, the most developed form of which is a self-subsistent village community; (c) orientation to the scarcity of oppor-

tunities for acquisition (*Erwerbsspielraum*). This is found in trade monopolies such as the guilds, the ancient monopolies of fishing rights, and so on. Usually motive (a) is combined with (b) or (c).

Representation and Responsibility

The order which governs a social relationship by tradition or by virtue of its legal establishment, may determine that certain types of action of some of the parties to the relationship will have consequences which affect the others. It may be that all are held responsible for the action of *any* one. In that case they will be spoken of as "solidary" members. Or, on the other hand, the action of certain members, the "representatives," may be binding upon the others. That is, the resulting advantages will go to them, they will enjoy the benefits, or conversely bear the resulting losses.

Representative authority (*Vertretungsgewalt*) may be conferred in accordance with the binding order in such a way (a) that it is completely appropriated in all its forms—the case of "independent" authority; or (b) it may be conferred in accordance with particular criteria, permanently or for a limited term; or (c) it may be conferred by specific acts of the members or of outside persons, again permanently or for a limited term—the case of appointment. There are many different conditions which determine the ways in which social relationships, communal or associative, develop relations of solidarity, or of representation. In general terms, it is possible only to say that one of the most decisive is the extent to which the action of the group is oriented to violent conflict or to peaceful exchange as its end. Besides these, many special circumstances, which can only be discussed in a detailed analysis, may be of crucial importance. It is not surprising that this development is least conspicuous in groups which pursue purely ideal ends by peaceful means. Often the degree of closure against outsiders is closely related to the development of solidarity or of representation. But this is by no means always the case.

1. This "imputation" of responsibility may in practice involve both active and passive solidarity. All the participants may be held responsible for the action of any one just as he himself is, and similarly may be entitled to enjoy any benefits resulting from his action. This responsibility may be owed to spirits or gods, that is, involve a religious orientation. Or, on the other hand, it may be responsibility to other human beings, as regulated by convention or by law. Examples of regulation by convention are

---

7. This is a reference to the *Betriebsräte* which were formed in German industrial plants during the Revolution of 1918–19 and were organized in the Weimar Constitution as entitled to representation in the Federal Economic Council.—Ed.

8. Weber here refers to *Nahrungsspielraum*. The concept refers to the scope of economic resources and opportunities on which the standard of living of an individual or a group is dependent. By contrast with this, *Erwerbsspielraum* is a similar scope of resources and economic opportunities seen from the point of view of their possible role as sources of profit. The basic distinction implied in this contrast is of central importance to Weber's analysis later on.—Ed.

blood revenge carried out against or with the help of members of the kin-groups, reprisals against the inhabitants of the town or the country of the offender; of the legal type, formal punishment of relatives, members of the household or fellow-members of a communal group, instead of, or in addition to, the actual offender, and personal liability of members of a household or of a commercial partnership for each other's debts. Solidarity in relation to gods has also had very significant historical results. For instance, in the covenant of Israel with Jahveh, in early Christianity, and in the early Puritan community.

On the other hand, the imputation of solidarity may mean no more than that the participants in a closed social relationship, by virtue of the traditional or legal order, are held legally entitled to enjoy some kind of access to advantages and benefits, especially economic, which a representative has procured. Examples are the control over the powers exercised by the "executive committee" of a club or association, or by the responsible agent of a political or economic association over resources which, as specified in the order, are meant to serve the corporate purpose of the group.

2. Solidarity is typically found in the following cases: (a) In traditional, communal groups based on birth or the sharing of a common life; for example, the household and the kinship unit; (b) in closed relationships which maintain a monopolized position, and control over the corresponding benefits by their own power. The typical case is corporate political groups, especially in the past. But the same situation exists to-day to a high degree, most strikingly in time of war; (c) in profit-making organizations where the participants personally conduct the business. The type case is the business partnership; (d) in some cases, in labour organizations. An example is the Artel. Representation is most frequently found in associations devoted to specific purposes and in legally organized groups, especially when funds have been collected and must be administered in the interests of the group. This will be further discussed in the Sociology of Law.

3. Representative authority is conferred according to "criteria" (see above) in such cases as when it goes by seniority or some other such rule.

4. It is not possible to carry the analysis of this subject further in general terms. Its elaboration must be reserved to detailed investigation of particular fields. The most ancient and most universal phenomenon in this field is that of reprisal, meant either as revenge or as a means of gaining control of hostages, or some other kind of security against future injury.

The Concept of "Corporate Group" and Its Types

A social relationship which is either closed or limits the admission of outsiders by rules, will be called a "corporate group" (*Verband*)[9] so far as its order is enforced by the action of specific individuals whose regular function this is, of a chief or "head" (*Leiter*) and usually also an administrative staff. These functionaries will normally also have representative authority. The incumbency of a directing position or participation in the functions of the administrative staff constitute "governing authority" (*Regierungsgewalt*). This may be appropriated, or it may be assigned in accordance with the binding rules of the association according to specific criteria or procedures. It may be assigned permanently, for a term, or for dealing with a specific situation. "Corporate action" is either the action of the administrative staff, which by virtue of its governing or representative authority is oriented to carrying out the terms of its order, or it is the action of the members as directed by the administrative staff.

1. It is indifferent, so far as the concept is concerned, whether the relationship is of a communal or associative character. It is sufficient for there to be a person or persons in authority—the head of a family, the executive committee of an association, a managing director, a prince, a president, the head of a church—whose action is concerned with carrying into effect the order governing the corporate group. This criterion is decisive because it is not merely a matter of action which is *oriented* to an order, but which is specifically directed to its *enforcement*. Sociologically this adds to the concept of a closed social relationship, a further element, which is of far-reaching empirical importance. For by no means every closed communal or associative relationship is a corporate group. For instance, this is not true of an erotic relationship or of a kinship group without a formalized system of authority.

2. Whether or not a corporate group exists is entirely a matter of the presence of a person in authority, with or without an administrative staff. More precisely, it exists so far as there is a proba-

9. The term *Verband,* which is one of the most important in Weber's scheme, has, in the technical sense defined in this paragraph, been translated as "corporate group." "Association" has not been used because it does not imply the formal differentiation between a head or chief and ordinary members. A "corporation" is, from this point of view, one specific kind of corporate group. The term *Leiter* is not readily translatable. "Chief" has most frequently been used because it seems to have less objectionable connotations than any alternative. Thus we speak of the "chief" of the medical staff of a hospital and use the term in other similar connexions.

bility that certain persons will act in such a way as to tend to carry out the order governing the group; that is, that persons are present who can be counted on to act in this way whenever the occasion arises. For purposes of definition, it is indifferent what is the basis of the relevant expectation, whether it is a case of traditional or affectual devotion to duty, or a case of devotion by virtue of rational values, any of which may be involved in feudal fealty, loyalty to an office or to a service. It may, on the other hand, be a matter of expediency, as, for instance, a pecuniary interest in the attached salary. Thus for purposes of the terminology of this discussion, the corporate group does not "exist" apart from the probability that a course of action oriented in this way will take place. If there is no probability of this type of action on the part of a particular group of persons or of a given individual, there is in these terms a social relationship, but no corporate group. On the other hand, so long as there is a probability of such action, the corporate group, as a sociological phenomenon, continues to exist, in spite of the fact that the specific individuals whose action is oriented to the order in question, may have been completely changed. The concept has been defined intentionally to include precisely this phenomenon.

3. It is possible (a) that, in addition to the action of the administrative staff itself or that which takes place under its direction, there may be other cases where action of the members is intended to uphold the authority of the order; for instance, contributions or "liturgies"[10] and certain types of personal services, such as jury service or military service. It is also possible (b) for the binding order to include norms to which it is expected that the action of the members of a corporate group will be oriented in respects other than those pertaining to the affairs of the corporate group as a unit. For instance, the law of the state includes rules governing private economic relations which are not concerned with the enforcement of the state's legal order as such, but with action in the service of private interests. This is true of most of the "civil" law. In the first case (a) one may speak of action "oriented to corporate affairs" (*Verbandsbezogenes Handeln*); in the second (b) of action "subject to corporate regulation" (*Verbandsgeregeltes Handeln*). It is only in the cases of the action of the administrative staff itself and

of that deliberately directed by it that the term "corporate action" (*Verbandshandeln*) will be used. Examples of corporate action would be participation in any capacity in a war fought by a state, or a contribution paid in accordance with a levy authorized by the executive committee of an association, or a contract entered into by the person in authority, the validity of which is recognized by the members and its consequences carried out by them. Further, all administration of justice and administrative procedure belongs in this category.

A corporate group may be either autonomous or heteronomous, either autocephalous or heterocephalous. Autonomy means that the order governing the group has been established by its own members on their own authority, regardless of how this has taken place in other respects. In the case of heteronomy, it has been imposed by an outside agency. Autocephaly means that the chief and his staff act by the authority of the autonomous order of the corporate group itself, not, as in the case of heterocephaly, that they are under the authority of outsiders. Again, this is regardless of any other aspects of the relationship.

A case of heterocephaly is the appointment of the governors of the Canadian provinces by the central government of the Dominion. It is possible for a heterocephalous group to be autonomous and an autocephalous group to be heteronomous. It is also possible in both respects for a corporate group to have both characters at the same time in different spheres. The member-states of the German Empire, a federal state, were autocephalous. But in spite of this, within the sphere of authority of the Reich, they were heteronomous; whereas, within their own sphere, in such matters as religion and education, they were autonomous. Alsace-Lorraine was, under German jurisdiction, in a limited degree autonomous, but at the same time heterocephalous in that the governor was appointed by the Kaiser. All these elements may be present in the same situation to some degree. A corporate group, which is at the same time completely heteronomous and completely heterocephalous, is usually best treated as a "part" of the more extensive group, as would ordinarily be done with a "regiment" as part of an army. But whether this is the case depends on the actual extent of independence in the orientation of action in the particular case. For terminological purposes, it is entirely a question of convenience.

Types of Order in Corporate Groups

The legally-established order of an associative relationship may originate in one of two ways: by voluntary agreement, or by being imposed (*oktroyi-*

---

10. Weber here uses the term "liturgies" not in the current religious sense but in that of the institution characteristic of the classical Greek city state. This consisted in the provision of entertainments or services for the public ostensibly as a voluntary gift of an individual, but which were in fact obligatory on persons occupying a given status or office. Weber later uses this term in a technical sense which is defined in chapter ii, sec. 12.—ED.

ert) and acquiesced in. The governing authority of a corporate group may claim a legitimate right to impose new rules. The "constitution" (*Verfassung*) of a corporate group is the empirically existing probability, varying in extent, kind, and conditions, that rules imposed by the governing authority will be acceded to. The system of order may, among these conditions, in particular specify that certain groups or sections of the members must consent, or at least have been heard. Besides this, there may be any number of other conditions.

The system of order of a corporate group may be imposed, not only on its members, but also on non-members who conform to certain criteria. This is especially likely to be true in so far as people are related to a given territorial area, by virtue of residence, birth, or the performance of certain actions within the area. An order which controls by virtue of these criteria possesses "territorial validity" (*Gebietsgeltung*). A corporate group, the governing order of which is in principle concerned with territorial validity, will be called a "territorial corporate group" (*Gebietsverband*). This usage will be employed regardless of how far the claim to the authority of its order over its own members is confined to matters pertaining to the area. Such limitation is possible[11] and certainly occurs to some extent.

1. For purposes of this investigation, an order is always "imposed" to the extent that it does not originate from a voluntary personal agreement of all the individuals concerned. The concept of imposition hence includes "majority rule," in that the minority must submit. For that reason there have been long periods when the legitimacy of majority rule has either not been recognized at all, or been held doubtful. This was true in the case of the estates of the Middle Ages, and in very recent times, in the Russian *Obschtschina*. This will be further discussed in the Sociology of Law and of Authority.

2. Even in cases where there is formally "voluntary" agreement, it is very common, as is generally known, for there to be a large measure of imposition. This is true of the *Obschtschina*. In that case, it is the actual state of affairs which is decisive for sociological purposes.

3. The concept of constitution made use of here is that also used by Lassalle. It is not the same as

what is meant by a "written" constitution, or indeed by "constitution" in any sort of legal meaning. The only relevant question for sociological purposes is when, for what purposes, and *within what limits*, or possibly under what special conditions (such as the approval of gods or priests or the consent of electors), the members of the corporate group will submit to the governing authority. Furthermore, under what circumstances in these respects the administrative staff and the corporate action of the group will be at the disposal of the supreme authority when it issues orders, or, in particular, imposes new rules.

4. The best cases of the imposition of an order within a territory are the precepts of criminal law and various other legal rules. In such cases political corporate groups use the criteria of whether the actor was resident, born, performed or completed the action, within the area controlled by the corporate group, to decide on the applicability of the rules.

Types of Order Governing Action in Corporate Groups

A system of order which governs corporate action as such, will be called an "administrative" order (*Verwaltungsordnung*). A system of order which governs other kinds of social action and thereby protects the actors in enjoyment of the benefits derived from their relation to the order, will be called a "regulative" order (*Regulierungsordnung*). So far as a corporate group is solely oriented to the first type of order, it will be called an "administrative" group (*Verwaltungsverband*). So far as it is oriented to the second type, a "regulative" group.

1. It goes without saying that the majority of actual corporate groups partake of both characteristics. The type of state, which was the ideal of the theory of absolute laissez faire, would be an example of a purely regulative corporate group. This would, however, assume that the control of the monetary system was left entirely to private enterprise.

2. On the concept of "corporate action," see above, sec. 12, para. 3. Under the concept of administrative order would be included all the rules which govern, not only the action of the administrative staff, but also that of the members in their direct relations to the corporate group. This latter type consists in action in the service of ends, the attainment of which is made mandatory in the system of order governing the group, and for which a positive course of action has deliberately been laid down in advance with directions for its execution by the

11. The concept "objective possibility" (*objektive Möglichkeit*) plays an important technical role in Weber's methodological studies. According to his usage, a thing is "objectively possible" if it "makes sense" to conceive it as an empirically existing entity. It is a question of conforming with the formal, logical conditions. The question whether a phenomenon which is in this sense "objectively possible" will actually be found with any significant degree of probability or approximation, is a logically distinct question.—ED.

administrative staff and by the members. In a completely communistic economic system, a situation would be approximated where all social action was of this character. In a laissez-faire state, on the other hand, it would include only the functions of judges, police authorities, jurors, soldiers, legislators, and of the general public in the capacity of voters. The distinction between administrative and regulative order coincides in its broad lines, though not always in detail, with the distinction of political theory between public and private law. All further details are treated in the Sociology of Law.

Types of Organization and of Corporate Groups

An "organization" (*Betrieb*) is a system of continuous purposive activity of a specified kind. A "corporate organization" (*Betriebsverband*) is an associative social relationship characterized by an administrative staff devoted to such continuous purposive activity.

A "voluntary association" (*Verein*) is a corporate group originating in a voluntary agreement and in which the established order claims authority over the members only by virtue of a personal act of adherence.

A "compulsory association" (*Anstalt*) is a corporate group the established order of which has, within a given specific sphere of activity, been successfully imposed on every individual who conforms with certain specific criteria.[12]

1. The administration of political and ecclesiastical affairs and of the business of associations is included in the concept of "organization" so far as it conforms to the criterion of continuity.

2. Voluntary and compulsory associations are both types of corporate groups where action is subject to a rationally established order. Or, more accurately, so far as a corporate group has a rationally established order, it will be called a voluntary or compulsory association. The type case of a compulsory association is the state, along with all its subsidiary heterocephalous groups. But, so far as its order

is rationally established, the church[13] is also included. The order governing a compulsory association claims to be binding on all persons to whom the particular relevant criteria apply—such as birth, residence, or the use of certain facilities. It makes no difference whether the individual has, as in the case of a voluntary association, personally assumed the obligation; nor does it matter whether he has taken any part in establishing the order. It is thus a case of imposed order in the most definite sense. One of the most important fields of the compulsory association is the control of territorial areas.

3. The distinction between voluntary and compulsory associations is relative in its empirical application. The rules of a voluntary association may affect the interests of non-members, and recognition of the validity of these rules may be imposed upon them by usurpation or by the exercise of the naked power of the association, as well as by processes of legal promulgation, as in the case of the law governing corporate securities.

4. It is hardly necessary to emphasize that the concepts of voluntary and compulsory associations are by no means exhaustive of all conceivable types of corporate groups. Furthermore, they are to be thought of only as "polar" antitheses. In the religious sphere, the corresponding types are "sect" and "church."

Power, Authority, and Imperative Control

"Power" (*Macht*) is the probability that one actor within a social relationship will be in a position to carry out his own will despite resistance, regardless of the basis on which this probability rests.

"Imperative control" (*Herrschaft*)[14] is the probability that a command with a given specific content will be obeyed by a given group of persons. "Discipline" is the probability that by virtue of habituation a command will receive prompt and automatic obedience in stereotyped forms, on the part of a given group of persons.

---

12. *Betrieb* is a word which in German has a number of different meanings in different contexts. It is only in the present technical use that it will be translated by "organization." It should, however, be recognized that the term "organization" is here also used in a technical sense which conforms with Weber's explicit definition. The distinction of *Verein* and *Anstalt* is one of far-reaching sociological importance, which has not become established in English usage. The terms "voluntary" and "compulsory" association seem to be as adequate as any available terms. They should, however, not be interpreted on a common-sense basis but referred to Weber's explicit definitions.—ED.

13. "Church" (*Kirche*) also is here used in a technical sense. We speak of the "Baptist Church," but in Weber's technical terms this is not a church but a sect. The Roman Catholic Church, on the other hand, since it claims jurisdiction over all children of Catholic parents, *is* a church in the technical sense.—ED.

14. As has already been noted, the term *Herrschaft* has no satisfactory English equivalent. The term "imperative control," however, as used by N. S. Timasheff in his *Introduction to the Sociology of Law* is close to Weber's meaning and has been borrowed for the most general purposes. In a majority of instances, however, Weber is concerned with *legitimate Herrschaft*, and in these cases "authority" is both an accurate and a far less awkward translation. *Macht*, as Weber uses it, seems to be quite adequately rendered by "power."—ED.

1. The concept of power is highly comprehensive from the point of view of sociology. All conceivable qualities of a person and all conceivable combinations of circumstances may put him in a position to impose his will in a given situation. The sociological concept of imperative control must hence be more precise and can only mean the probability that a *command* will be obeyed.

2. The concept of "discipline" includes the "habituation" characteristic of uncritical and unresisting mass obedience.

The existence of imperative control turns only on the actual presence of one person successfully issuing orders to others; it does not necessarily imply either the existence of an administrative staff, or, for that matter, of a corporate group. It is, however, uncommon to find it not associated with at least one of these. A corporate group, the members of which are by virtue of their membership subjected to the legitimate exercise of imperative control, that is to "authority," will be called an "imperatively coordinated" group[15] (*Herrschaftsverband*).

1. The head of a household exercises authority without an administrative staff. A Beduin chief, who levies contributions from the caravans, persons, and shipments of goods which pass his stronghold, exercises imperative control over the total group of changing and indeterminate individuals who, though they are not members of any corporate group as such, have gotten themselves into a particular common situation. But to do this, he needs a following which, on the appropriate occasions, serves as his administrative staff in exercising the necessary compulsion. This type of imperative control is, however, conceivable as carried out by a single individual without the help of any administrative staff.

2. If it possesses an administrative staff, a corporate group is always, by virtue of this fact, to some degree imperatively co-ordinated. But the concept is relative. The usual imperatively co-ordinated group is at the same time an administrative organization. The character of the corporate group is determined by a variety of factors: the mode in which the administration is carried out, the character of the personnel, the objects over which it exercises control, and the extent of effective jurisdiction of its authority. The first two factors in particular are dependent in the highest degree on the way in which the authority is legitimized.

Political and Religious Corporate Groups

An imperatively co-ordinated corporate group will be called "political" if and in so far as the enforcement of its order is carried out continually within a given *territorial* area by the application and threat of physical force on the part of the administrative staff. A compulsory political association with continuous organization (*politischer Anstaltsbetrieb*) will be called a "state" if and in so far as its administrative staff successfully upholds a claim to the *monopoly* of the *legitimate* use of physical force in the enforcement of its order. A system of social action, especially that of a corporate group, will be spoken of as "politically oriented" if and in so far as it aims at exerting influence on the directing authorities of a corporate political group; especially at the appropriation, expropriation, redistribution or allocation of the powers of government.

An imperatively co-ordinated corporate group will be called a "hierocratic" group (*hierokratischer Verband*) if and in so far as for the enforcement of its order it employs "psychic" coercion through the distribution or denial of religious benefits ("hierocratic coercion"). A compulsory hierocratic association with continuous organization will be called a "church" if and in so far as its administrative staff claims a monopoly of the legitimate use of hierocratic coercion.

1. It goes without saying that the use of physical force is neither the sole, nor even the most usual, method of administration of political corporate groups. On the contrary, their heads have employed all conceivable means to bring about their ends. But, at the same time, the threat of force, and in case of need its actual use, is the method which is specific to political association and is always the last resort when others have failed. Conversely, physical force is by no means limited to political groups even as a legitimate method of enforcement. It has been freely used by kinship groups, household groups, the medieval guilds under certain circumstances, and everywhere by all those entitled to bear arms. In addition to the fact that it uses, among other means, physical force to enforce its system of order, the political group is further characterized by the fact that the authority of its administrative staff is claimed as binding within a territorial area and this claim is upheld by force. Whenever corporate groups which make use of force are also characterized by the claim to territorial jurisdiction, such as village communities or even some household groups, federations of guilds

---

15. In this case imperative control is confined to the legitimate type, but it is not possible in English to speak here of an "authoritarian" group. The citizens of any state, no matter how "democratic," are "imperatively controlled" because they are subject to law.—Ed.

or of trade unions, they are by definition to that extent political groups.

2. It is not possible to define a political corporate group, including the state, in terms of the end to which its corporate action is devoted. All the way from provision for subsistence to the patronage of art, there is no conceivable end which *some* political corporation has not at some time pursued. And from the protection of personal security to the administration of justice, there is none which *all* have recognized. Thus it is possible to define the "political" character of a corporate group only in terms of the *means* peculiar to it, the use of force. This means is, however, in the above sense specific, and is indispensable to its character. It is even, under certain circumstances, elevated into an end in itself.

This usage does not exactly conform to everyday speech. But the latter is too consistent to be used for technical purposes. We speak of the "open market" policy[16] of a central bank, of the "financial" policy of an association, of the "educational" policy of a local authority, and mean the systematic treatment and control of a particular problem. It comes considerably closer to the present meaning when we distinguish the "political" aspect or implication of a question. Thus there is the "political" official, the "political" newspaper, the "political" revolution, the "political" club, the "political" party, and the "political" consequences of an action, as distinguished from others such as the economic, cultural, or religious aspect of the persons, affairs or processes in question. In this usage we generally mean by "political," things that have to do with relations of authority within what is, in the present terminology, a political organization, the state. The reference is to things which are likely to uphold, to change or overthrow, to hinder or promote, the interests of the state, as distinguished from persons, things, and processes which have nothing to do with it. This usage thus seeks to bring out the common features of the various *means* of exercising authority which are used within the state in enforcing its order, abstracting them from the ends they serve. Hence it is legitimate to claim that the definition put forward here is only a more precise formulation of what is meant in everyday usage in that it gives sharp emphasis to what is the most characteristic of these means, the actual or threatened use of force. It is, of course, true that everyday usage applies the

term "political," not only to groups which are the direct agents of the legitimate use of force itself, but also to other, often wholly peaceful groups, which attempt to influence politically corporate action. It seems best for present purposes to distinguish this type of social action, "politically oriented" action, from political action as such, the actual *corporate* action of political groups.

3. Since the concept of the state has only in modern times reached its full development, it is best to define it in terms appropriate to the modern type of state, but at the same time, in terms which abstract from the values of the present day, since these are particularly subject to change. The primary formal characteristics of the modern state are as follows: It possesses an administrative and legal order subject to change by legislation, to which the organized corporate activity of the administrative staff, which is also regulated by legislation, is oriented. This system of order claims binding authority, not only over the members of the state, the citizens, most of whom have obtained membership by birth, but also to a very large extent, over all action taking place in the area of its jurisdiction. It is thus a compulsory association with a territorial basis. Furthermore, to-day, the use of force is regarded as legitimate only so far as it is either permitted by the state or prescribed by it. Thus the right of a father to discipline his children is recognized—a survival of the former independent authority of the head of a household, which in the right to use force has sometimes extended to a power of life and death over children and slaves. The claim of the modern state to monopolize the use of force is as essential to it as its character of compulsory jurisdiction and of continuous organization.

4. In formulating the concept of a hierocratic corporate group, it is not possible to use the character of the religious sanctions it commands, whether worldly or other-worldly, material or spiritual, as the decisive criterion. What is important is rather the fact that its control over these sanctions can form the basis of a system of spiritual imperative control over human beings. What is most characteristic of the church, even in the common usage of the term, is the fact that it is a rational, compulsory association with continuous organization and that it claims a monopolistic authority. It is normal for a church to strive for complete imperative control on a territorial basis and to attempt to set up the corresponding territorial or parochial organization. So far as this takes place, the means by which this claim to monopoly is upheld, will vary from case to case. But historically, its control over terri-

---

16. The German is *Devisenpolitik*. Translation in this context is made more difficult by the fact that the German language does not distinguish between "politics" and "policy," *Politik* having both meanings. The remarks which Weber makes about various kinds of policy would have been unnecessary, had he written originally in English.—ED.

torial areas has not been nearly so essential to the church as to political corporations; and this is particularly true to-day. It is its character as a compulsory association, particularly the fact that one becomes a member of the church by birth, which distinguishes a church from a "sect." It is characteristic of the latter that it is a voluntary association and admits only persons with specific religious qualifications. This subject will be further discussed in the Sociology of Religion.[17]

17. This reference is presumably to the section entitled *Religionssoziologie* which is published as part ii, chap. iv of *Wirtschaft und Gesellschaft,* but is not included in the present translation. In it Weber attempted a systematic typological analysis of the social aspects of religious phenomena. This chapter should not be confused with the three volumes of the *Gesammelte Aufsätze zur Religions-* *soziologie* which consist of a series of comparative empirical studies of particular religious systems in terms of their bearing on the development of modern capitalism. In the section of *Wirtschaft und Gesellschaft* to which he refers, Weber has attempted a more connected and complete typological analysis than is to be found in the comparative study.—ED.

6. *Legitimate Order and Types of Authority*

BY MAX WEBER

The Concept of Legitimate Order

ACTION, especially social action which involves social relationships, may be oriented by the actors to a *belief* (*Vorstellung*) in the existence of a "legitimate order." The probability that action will actually empirically be so oriented will be called the "validity" (*Geltung*) of the order in question.[1]

1. Thus, orientation to the validity of an *order* (*Ordnung*) means more than the mere existence of a uniformity of social action determined by custom or self-interest. If furniture movers regularly advertise at times of the large-scale expiration of leases, this uniformity is determined by self-interest in the exploitation of opportunities. If a salesman visits certain customers on particular days of the month or the week, it is either a case of customary behaviour or a product of some kind of self-interested orientation. But when, on the other hand, a civil servant appears in his office daily at a fixed time, it may involve these elements, but is not determined by custom or self-interest alone, for with these he is at liberty to conform or not as he pleases. As a rule such action in addition is determined by his subjection to an order, the rules governing the department which impose obligations on him, which he is usually careful to fulfil, partly because disobedience would carry disadvantageous consequences to him, but usually also in part because it would be abhorrent to the sense of duty, which, to a greater or lesser extent, is an absolute value to him.

2. The subjective meaning of a social relationship will be called an "order" only if action is approximately or on the average oriented to certain determinate "maxims" or rules. Furthermore, such an order will only be called "valid" if the orientation to such maxims includes, no matter to what actual extent, the recognition that they are binding on the actor or the corresponding action constitutes a desirable model for him to imitate. Naturally, in concrete cases, the orientation of action to an order involves a wide variety of motives. But the circumstance that along with the other sources of conformity the order is also held by at least part of the actors to define a model or to be binding, naturally increases the probability that action will in fact conform to it, often to a very considerable degree. An order which is adhered to from motives of pure expediency is generally much less stable than one upheld on a purely customary basis through the fact that the corresponding behaviour has become habitual. The latter is much the most common type of subjective attitude. But even this type of order is in turn much less stable than an order which enjoys the

Reprinted from Max Weber, *The Theory of Social and Economic Organization,* trans. A. M. Henderson and Talcott Parsons, ed. Talcott Parsons (Glencoe, Ill.: The Free Press, 1947), chap. i, secs. 5–8, pp. 124–35; chap. iii, secs. 1–2, pp. 328–29. Copyright 1947 by Oxford University Press.

1. The term *Gelten* has already been dealt with. From the very use of the term in this context it is clear that by "order" (*Ordnung*) Weber here means a *normative* system. The pattern for the concept of "order" is not, as in the law of gravitation, the "order of nature," but the order involved in a system of law.

prestige of being considered binding, or, as it may be expressed, of "legitimacy." The transitions between orientation to an order from motives of tradition or of expediency on the one hand to the case where on the other a belief in its legitimacy is involved, are naturally empirically gradual.

3. It is possible for action to be oriented to an order in other ways than through conformity with its prescriptions, as they are generally understood by the actors. Even in the cases of evasion of or deliberate disobedience to these prescriptions, the probability of its being recognized as a valid norm may have an effect on action. This may, in the first place, be true from the point of view of sheer expediency. A thief orients his action to the validity of the criminal law in that he acts surreptitiously. The fact that the order is recognized as valid in his society is made evident by the fact that he cannot violate it openly without punishment. But apart from this limiting case, it is very common for violation of an order to be confined to more or less numerous partial deviations from it, or for the attempt to be made, with varying degrees of good faith, to justify the deviation as legitimate. Furthermore, there may exist at the same time different interpretations of the meaning of the order. In such cases, for sociological purposes, each can be said to be valid in so far as it actually determines the course of action. The fact that, in the same social group, a plurality of contradictory systems of order may all be recognized as valid, is not a source of difficulty for the sociological approach. Indeed, it is even possible for the same individual to orient his action to contradictory systems of order. This can take place not only at different times, as is an everyday occurrence, but even in the case of the same concrete act. A person who fights a duel orients his action to the code of honour; but at the same time, in so far as he either keeps it secret or conversely gives himself up to the police, he takes account of the criminal law.[2] To be sure, when evasion or contravention of the generally understood meaning of an order has become the rule, the order can be said to be "valid" only in a limited degree and, in the extreme case, not at all. Thus for sociological purposes there does not exist, as there does for the law, a rigid alternative between the validity and lack of validity of a given order. On the contrary, there is a gradual transition between the two extremes; and also it is possible, as it has been pointed out, for contradic-

tory systems of order to exist at the same time. In that case each is "valid" precisely to the extent that there is a probability that action will in fact be oriented to it.[3]

The Types of Legitimate Order

The legitimacy of an order may be guaranteed or upheld in two principal ways:[4] (1) from purely

---

3. Those familiar with the literature of this subject will recall the part played by the concept of "order" in the brilliant book of Rudolf Stammler, which was cited in the prefatory note, a book which, though like all his works it is very able, is nevertheless fundamentally misleading and confuses the issues in a catastrophic fashion. The reader may compare the author's critical discussion of it, which was also cited in the same place, a discussion which, because of the author's annoyance at Stammler's confusion, was unfortunately written in somewhat too acrimonious a tone.

Stammler fails to distinguish the normative meaning of "validity" from the empirical. He further fails to recognize that social action is oriented to other things beside systems of order. Above all, however, in a way which is wholly indefensible from a logical point of view, he treats order as a "form" of social action and then attempts to bring it into a type of relation to "content," which is analogous to that of form and content in the theory of knowledge. Other errors in his argument will be left aside. But actually, action which is, for instance, primarily economic, is oriented to knowledge of the relative scarcity of certain available means to want satisfaction, in relation to the actor's state of needs and to the present and probable action of others, in so far as the latter affects the same resources. But at the same time, of course, the actor in his choice of economic procedures naturally orients himself *in addition* to the conventional and legal rules which he recognizes as valid, or of which he knows that a violation on his part would call forth a given reaction of other persons. Stammler succeeds in introducing a state of hopeless confusion into this very simple empirical situation, particularly in that he maintains that a causal relationship between an order and actual empirical action involves a contradiction in terms. It is true, of course, that there is no causal relationship between the *normative* validity of an order in the legal sense and any empirical process. In that context there is only the question of whether the order as correctly interpreted in the legal sense "applies" to the empirical situation. The question is whether in a *normative* sense it *should* be treated as valid and, if so, what the content of its normative prescriptions for this situation should be. But for sociological purposes, as distinguished from legal, it is only the probability of orientation to the subjective *belief* in the validity of an order which constitutes the valid order itself. It is undeniable that, in the ordinary sense of the word "causal," there is a causal relationship between this probability and the relevant course of economic action.

4. The reader may readily become confused as to the basis of the following classification, as compared with that presented in the next section. The first classification is one of motives for maintaining a legitimate order in force, whereas the second is one of motives for attributing legitimacy to the order. This explains the inclusion of self-interested motives in the first classification, but not in the second. It is quite possible, for instance, for irreligious persons to support the doctrine of the divine right of kings, because they feel that the breakdown of an order which depends on this would have undesirable consequences. This is not, however, a possible motive on which to base a direct sense of personal moral obligation to conform with the order.—ED.

---

2. When this was written (probably about 1913), duelling was still a relatively common practice in Germany and, in certain circles, was regarded as a definite obligation of honour in the face of some kinds of provocation. It was, however, at the same time an explicitly punishable offence under the criminal law.—ED.

disinterested motives, which may in turn be (a) purely affectual, consisting in an emotionally determined loyalty; or (b) may derive from a rational belief in the absolute validity of the order as an expression of ultimate values,[5] (*Wertrational*) whether they be moral, esthetic or of any other type; or (c) may originate in religious attitudes, through the belief in the dependence of some condition of religious salvation on conformity with the order; (2) also or entirely by self-interest, that is, through expectations of specific ulterior consequences, but consequences which are, to be sure, of a particular kind.

A system of order will be called *convention* so far as its validity is externally guaranteed by the probability that deviation from it within a given social group will result in a relatively general and practically significant reaction of disapproval. Such an order will be called *law* when conformity with it is upheld by the probability that deviant action will be met by physical or psychic sanctions aimed to compel conformity or to punish disobedience, and applied by a group of men especially empowered to carry out this function.

1. The term convention will be employed to designate that part of the custom followed within a given social group which is recognized as "binding" and protected against violation by sanctions of disapproval. As distinguished from "law" in the sense of the present discussion, it is not enforced by a functionally specialized agency. Stammler distinguishes convention from law in terms of the entirely voluntary character of conformity. This is not, however, in accord with everyday usage and does not even fit the examples he gives. Conformity with convention in such matters as the usual forms of greeting, the mode of dress recognized as appropriate or respectable, and various of the rules governing the restrictions on social intercourse, both in form and content, is very definitely expected of the individual and regarded as binding on him. It is not, as in the case of certain ways of preparing food, a mere usage, which he is free to conform to or not as he sees fit. A violation of conventional rules—such as standards of "respectability"—often leads to the extremely severe and effective sanction of an informal boycott on the part of members of one's group. This may actually be a more severe punishment than any legal penalty. The only thing lacking is the group of men with the specialized function of maintaining enforcement of the order, such as judges, prosecuting attorneys, and administrative officials. The transition, however, is gradual. The case of conventional guarantee of an order which most closely approaches the legal, is the application of a formally threatened and organized boycott. For terminological purposes, this is best considered a form of legal compulsion. Conventional rules may, in addition to mere disapproval, also be upheld by other means; thus domestic authority may be employed to deal with behaviour in defiance of convention. This fact is not, however, important in the present context. The decisive point is that the individual, by virtue of the existence of conventional disapproval, applies these sanctions, however drastic, on his own authority, not as a member of an organized group endowed with a specific authority for this purpose.

2. For the purposes of this discussion the concept "law" will be made to turn on the presence of a group of men engaged in enforcement, however useful it might be to define it differently for other purposes. The character of this agency naturally need not be at all similar to what is at present familiar. In particular it is not necessary that there should be any specifically "judicial" authority. The clan, as an agency of blood revenge and of the prosecution of feuds, is such an enforcing agency if there exist any sort of rules which governs its behaviour in such situations. But this is on the extreme borderline of what can be called legal enforcement. As is well known it has often been denied that international law could be called law, precisely because there is no legal authority above the state capable of enforcing it. In terms of the present terminology this would be correct, for a system of order the sanctions of which consisted wholly in expectations of disapproval and of the reprisals of injured parties, which is thus guaranteed entirely by convention and self-interest without the help of a specialized enforcement agency, is not a case of legal order. But for purposes of legal terminology exactly the opposite usage might well be acceptable.

In any case the means of coercion are irrelevant. Even a "friendly admonition," such as has been used in various religious sects as a form of gentle pressure on sinners, is to be included if it is carried out according to rules by a specially designated group. Another case is the use of the censure as a means of enforcing norms of moral conduct. Psychic coercion has indeed become the specific disciplinary technique of the church. It is thus

---

5. The antithesis *innerlich-äusserlich* as applied to elements of motivation does not have any direct English counterpart. The aspect of *innerlich,* however, which is most important in the present context seems to be adequately expressed by the term "disinterested." The essential point is that the object of such motivation is valued for its own sake or as a direct expression of ultimate values rather than as a means to some "ulterior" end.—Ed.

naturally just as much a case of "law" whether an order is upheld by ecclesiastical or by a political organization, whether in conformity with the rules of an association or by the authority of the head of a household. Even the rules contained in a commentary may be regarded, for this terminology, as law. Article 888, sec. 2, of the German Code of Civil Procedure (*Reichs-Zivil-Prozess-Ordnung*) dealing with unenforceable rights, is a case in point. The *leges imperfectae,* and the category of "natural obligations," are forms of legal terminology which express indirectly limits of conditions of the application of compulsion. In the same sense a trade practice which is compulsorily enforced is also law.[6]

3. It is not necessary for a valid order to be of a general and abstract character. The distinction between a legal precept and the decision in a concrete case, for instance, has not always and everywhere been as clearly made as we have to-day come to expect. An "order" may thus occur simply as the order governing a single concrete situation. The details of this subject belong in the sociology of law.[7] But for present purposes, unless otherwise specified, the modern distinction between a precept and a specific decision will be taken for granted.

4. A system of order which is guaranteed by external sanctions may at the same time be guaranteed by disinterested subjective attitudes. The relations of law, convention, and "ethics" do not constitute a problem for sociology. From a sociological point of view an "ethical" standard is one to which men attribute a certain type of value and which, by virtue of this belief, they treat as a valid norm governing their action. In this sense it can be spoken of as defining what is ethically good in the same way that action which is called beautiful is measured by aesthetic standards. It is possible for ethically normative beliefs of this kind to have a profound influence on action in the absence of any sort of external guarantee. This is often the case when the interests of others would be little affected by their violation.

Such ethical beliefs are also often guaranteed by religious motives, but they may at the same time in the present terminology be upheld to an important extent by disapproval of violations and

the consequent boycott, or even legally with the corresponding sanctions of the criminal law, police measures, or civil penalties. Every system of ethics which has in a sociological sense become validly established is likely to be upheld to a large extent by the probability that disapproval will result from its violation, that is, by convention. On the other hand, it is by no means necessary that all conventionally or legally guaranteed forms of order should claim the authority of ethical norms. Legal rules, much more often than conventional, may have been established entirely on grounds of expediency. Whether a belief in the validity of an order as such, which is current in a social group, is to be regarded as belonging to the realm of "ethics" or is a mere convention or a mere legal norm, cannot, for sociological purposes, be decided in general terms. It must be treated as relative to the conception of what values are treated as "ethical" in the social group in question. What these are is, in the relevant respect, not subject to generalization.

The Bases of Legitimacy of an Order

Legitimacy may be ascribed to an order by those acting subject to it in the following ways:—

(a) By tradition; a belief in the legitimacy of what has always existed; (b) by virtue of affectual attitudes, especially emotional, legitimizing the validity of what is newly revealed or a model to imitate; (c) by virtue of a rational belief in its absolute value (*Wertrational*), thus lending it the validity of an absolute and final commitment; (d) because it has been established in a manner which is recognized to be *legal.* This legality may be treated as legitimate in either of two ways: on the one hand, it may derive from a voluntary agreement of the interested parties on the relevant terms. On the other hand, it may be imposed on the basis of what is held to be a legitimate authority over the relevant persons and a corresponding claim to their obedience.

All further details, except for a few other concepts to be defined below, belong in the sociology of law and the sociology of authority. For the present, only a few remarks are necessary.

1. The derivation of the legitimacy of an order from a belief in the sanctity of tradition is the most universal and most primitive case. The fear of magical penalties confirms the general psychological inhibitions against any sort of change in customary modes of action. At the same time the multifarious vested interests which tend to become attached to upholding conformity with an order,

---

6. See secs. 157 and 242 of the German Civil Code. *Bürgerliches Gesetz-Buch* on the concept of "common law obligations," that is, obligations arising out of community standards of acceptable behaviour which come to be sanctioned by law. See the paper of Max Rümelin in *Schwäbische Heimatsgabe für Theodor Häring.*

7. An extended discussion of this subject is included in the German edition of *Wirtschaft und Gesellschaft,* part ii, chap. vii, pp. 386–512. It is not, however, included in the present translation.—Ed.

once it has become established, have worked in the same direction.[8]

2. Conscious departures from tradition in the establishment of a new order have originally been due almost entirely to prophetic oracles or at least to pronouncements which have been sanctioned as prophetic. This was true as late as the statutes of the Greek Aisymnetes. Conformity has then depended on belief in the legitimacy of the prophet. In times of strict traditionalism a new order, that is one which was *regarded* as new, could, without being revealed in this way, only become legitimized by the claim that it had actually always been valid though not yet rightly known, or that it had been obscured for a time and was now being restored to its rightful place.

3. The type case of legitimacy by virtue of rational belief in an absolute value is that of "Natural Law." However limited its actual effect, as compared with its ideal claims, it cannot be denied that its logically developed reasoning has had an influence on actual action which is far from negligible. This mode of influence should be clearly distinguished from that of a revealed law, of one imposed by authority, or of one which is merely traditional.

4. To-day the most usual basis of legitimacy is the belief in legality, the readiness to conform with rules which are formally correct and have been imposed by accepted procedure. The distinction between an order derived from voluntary agreement and one which has been imposed is only relative. For so far as the agreement underlying the order is not unanimous, as in the past has often been held necessary for complete legitimacy, its functioning within a social group will be dependent on the willingness of individuals with deviant wishes to give way to the majority. This is very frequently the case and actually means that the order is imposed on the minority. At the same time, it is very common for minorities, by force or by the use of more ruthless and far-sighted methods, to impose an order which in the course of time comes to be regarded as legitimate by those who originally resisted it. In so far as the ballot is used as a legal means of altering an order, it is very

common for the will of a minority to attain a formal majority and for the majority to submit. In this case majority rule is a mere illusion. The belief in the legality of an order as established by voluntary agreement is relatively ancient and is occasionally found among so-called primitive peoples; but in these cases it is almost always supplemented by the authority of oracles.

5. So far as it is not derived merely from fear or from motives of expediency, a willingness to submit to an order imposed by one man or a small group, always in some sense implies a belief in the legitimate *authority* of the source imposing it.

6. Submission to an order is almost always determined by a variety of motives; by a wide variety of interests and by a mixture of adherence to tradition and belief in legality, unless it is a case of entirely new regulations. In a very large proportion of cases, the actors subject to the order are of course not even aware how far it is a matter of custom, of convention, or of law. In such cases the sociologist must attempt to formulate the typical basis of validity.

The Concept of Conflict

A social relationship will be referred to as "conflict" (*Kampf*) in so far as action within it is oriented intentionally to carrying out the actor's own will against the resistance of the other party or parties. The term "peaceful" conflict will be applied to cases in which actual physical violence is not employed. A peaceful conflict is "competition" in so far as it consists in a formally peaceful attempt to attain control over opportunities and advantages[9] which are also desired by others. A competitive process is "regulated" competition to the extent that its ends and means are oriented to an order. The struggle, often latent, which takes place between human individuals or types of social status, for advantages and for survival, but without a meaningful mutual orientation in terms of conflict, will be called "selection." In so far as it is a matter of the relative opportunities of individuals during their own lifetime, it is "social selection"; in so far as it concerns differential chances for the survival of inherited characteristics, "biological selection."

1. There are all manner of continuous transitions ranging from the bloody type of conflict which, setting aside all rules, aims at the destruction of the adversary, to the case of the battles of medieval chivalry, bound as they were to the

8. The term "authority" is used to translate *Herrschaft*. It is not adequate for all purposes, but a discussion of the difficulties will be deferred to the point at which the concept becomes of primary importance. See below, sec. 16, p. 152. Weber dealt with this range of problems systematically in two different places, one of which is chapter iii of the present volume. The material of that chapter, however, is expanded and copiously illustrated in part iii of the German edition of *Wirtschaft und Gesellschaft* which is not included in the present translation. This part, like many other parts of the work, was left uncompleted at Weber's death.—ED.

9. *Chancen.* This usage of the term is to be distinguished from that translated as probability or likelihood. —ED.

strictest conventions, and to the strict regulations imposed on sport by the rules of the game. A classic example of conventional regulation even in war is the herald's call before the battle of Fontenoy: "Messieurs les Anglais, tirez les premiers." There are transitions such as that from unregulated competition of, let us say, suitors for the favour of a woman to the competition for economic advantages in exchange relationships, bound as that is by the order governing the market, or to strictly regulated competitions for artistic awards or, finally, to the struggle for victory in election campaigns. The treatment of conflict involving the use of physical violence as a separate type is justified by the special characteristics of the employment of this means and the corresponding peculiarities of the sociological consequences of its use.

2. All typical struggles and modes of competition which take place on a large scale will lead, in the long run, despite the decisive importance in many individual cases of accidental factors and luck, to a selection of those who have in the higher degree, on the average, possessed the personal qualities important to success. What qualities are important depends on the conditions in which the conflict or competition takes place. It may be a matter of physical strength or of unscrupulous cunning, of the level of mental ability or mere lung power and skill in the technique of demagoguery, of loyalty to superiors or of ability to flatter the masses, of creative originality, or of adaptability, of qualities which are unusual, or of those which are possessed by the mediocre majority. *Among the decisive conditions*, it must not be forgotten, belong the systems of order to which the behaviour of the parties is oriented, whether traditionally, as a matter of rationally disinterested loyalty, or of expediency. Each type of order influences opportunities in the process of social selection differently.

Not every process of social selection is, in the present sense, a case of conflict. Social selection, on the contrary, means only in the first instance that certain types of behaviour, and hence of the corresponding personal qualities, are more favourable than others in procuring differential advantages in attaining to certain social relationships, as in the role of "lover," "husband," "member of parliament," "official," "contractor," "managing director," "successful business man," and so on. But the concept does not specify whether this differential advantage in selection for social success is brought to bear through conflict or not, neither does it specify whether the biological chances of survival of the type are affected one way or the other. It is only where there is a genuine com-

petitive process that the term conflict will be used.

It is only in the sense of "selection" that it seems, according to our experience, that conflict is empirically inevitable, and it is furthermore only in the sense of *biological* selection that it is inevitable in principle. Selection is inevitable because apparently no way can be worked out of eliminating it completely. It is possible even for the most strictly pacific order to eliminate means of conflict and the objects of and impulses to conflict only in that it deals with each type individually. But this means that other modes of conflict would come to the fore, possibly in processes of open competition. But even on the utopian assumption that all competition were completely eliminated, conditions would still lead to a latent process of selection, biological or social, which would favour the types best adapted to the conditions, whether their relevant qualities were mainly determined by heredity or by environment. On an empirical level the elimination of conflict cannot go beyond a point which leaves room for some social selection, and in principle a process of biological selection necessarily remains.

3. From the struggle of individuals for personal advantages and survival, it is naturally necessary to distinguish the "conflict" and the "selection" of social relationships. It is only in a metaphorical sense that these concepts can be applied to the latter. For relationships exist only as systems of human action with particular subjective meanings. Thus a process of selection or a conflict between them means only that one type of action has in the course of time been displaced by another, whether it is action by the same persons or by others. This may occur in various ways. Human action may in the first place be consciously aimed to alter certain social relationships—that is, to alter the corresponding action—or it may be directed to the prevention of their development or continuance. Thus a "state" may be destroyed by war or revolution, or a conspiracy may be broken up by savage suppression; prostitution may be suppressed by police action; "shady" business practices, by denial of legal protection or by penalties. Furthermore, social relationships may be influenced by the creation of differential advantages which favour one type over another. It is possible either for individuals or for organized groups to pursue such ends. Secondly, it may, in various ways, be an unanticipated consequence of a course of social action and its relevant conditions that certain types of social relationships (meaning, of course, the corresponding actions) will be adversely affected in their opportunities to maintain themselves or to

arise. All changes of natural and social conditions have some sort of effect on the differential probabilities of survival of social relationships. Anyone is at liberty to speak in such cases of a process of "selection" of social relationships. For instance, he may say that among several states the "strongest," in the sense of the best "adapted," is victorious. It must, however, be kept in mind that this so-called "selection" has nothing to do with the selection of types of human individuals in either the social or the biological sense. In every case it is necessary to inquire into the reasons which have led to a change in the chances of survival of one or another form of social action or social relationship, which has broken up a social relationship or which has permitted it to continue at the expense of other competing forms. The explanation of these processes involves so many factors that it does not seem expedient to employ a single term for them. When this is done, there is always a danger of introducing uncritical value-judgments into empirical investigation. There is, above all, a danger of being primarily concerned with justifying the success of an individual case. Since individual cases are often dependent on highly exceptional circumstances, they may be in a certain sense "fortuitous." In recent years there has been more than enough of this kind of argument. The fact that a given specific social relationship has been eliminated for reasons peculiar to a particular situation, proves nothing whatever about its "fitness to survive" in general terms.

There are three pure types of legitimate authority. The validity of their claims to legitimacy may be based on:

1. Rational grounds—resting on a belief in the "legality" of patterns of normative rules and the right of those elevated to authority under such rules to issue commands (legal authority).

2. Traditional grounds—resting on an established belief in the sanctity of immemorial traditions and the legitimacy of the status of those exercising authority under them (traditional authority); or finally,

3. Charismatic grounds—resting on devotion to the specific and exceptional sanctity, heroism or exemplary character of an individual person, and of the normative patterns or order revealed or ordained by him (charismatic authority).

In the case of legal authority, obedience is owed to the legally established impersonal order. It extends to the persons exercising the authority of office under it only by virtue of the formal legality of their commands and only within the scope of authority of the office. In the case of traditional authority, obedience is owed to the *person* of the chief who occupies the traditionally sanctioned position of authority and who is (within its sphere) bound by tradition. But here the obligation of obedience is not based on the impersonal order, but is a matter of personal loyalty within the area of accustomed obligations. In the case of charismatic authority, it is the charismatically qualified leader as such who is obeyed by virtue of personal trust in him and his revelation, his heroism or his exemplary qualities so far as they fall within the scope of the individual's belief in his charisma.

1. The usefulness of the above classification can only be judged by its results in promoting systematic analysis. The concept of "charisma" ("the gift of grace") is taken from the vocabulary of early Christianity. For the Christian religious organization Rudolf Sohm, in his *Kirchenrecht*, was the first to clarify the substance of the concept, even though he did not use the same terminology. Others (for instance, Hollin, *Enthusiasmus und Bussgewalt*) have clarified certain important consequences of it. It is thus nothing new.

2. The fact that none of these three ideal types, the elucidation of which will occupy the following pages, is usually to be found in historical cases in "pure" form, is naturally not a valid objection to attempting their conceptual formulation in the sharpest possible form. In this respect the present case is no different from many others. Later on the transformation of pure charisma by the process of routinization will be discussed and thereby the relevance of the concept to the understanding of empirical systems of authority considerably increased. But even so it may be said of every empirically historical phenomenon of authority that it is not likely to be "as an open book." Analysis in terms of sociological types has, after all, as compared with purely empirical historical investigation, certain advantages which should not be minimized. That is, it can in the particular case of a concrete form of authority determine what conforms to or approximates such types as "charisma," "hereditary charisma," "the charisma of office," "patriarchy," "bureaucracy," the authority of status groups, and in doing so it can work with relatively unambiguous concepts. But the idea that the whole of concrete historical reality can be exhausted in the conceptual scheme about to be developed is as far from the author's thoughts as anything could be.

PART TWO

Differentiation and Variation in Social Structures

Introduction

BY TALCOTT PARSONS

Part two deals with the ma-
terial that, for the generation with which we are concerned, was probably the core subject-matter of sociology—and which will probably continue to be so
for some time. Broadly speaking, this is the
structural morphology of social systems. In the first
instance, it is the kinds of groupings of persons in
roles that, combined with their complex interlacings
and criss-crossings, constitute the structure of societies. When dealing with the larger patterns of
form and bases of differentiation of social systems,
it becomes necessary to consider, in addition to the
morphology of collectivities and roles, general
systems of institutionalized values and complex
systems of norms, of the types outlined in the
General Introduction.

The material dealing with structure has been
placed first in the arrangement of selections. This
is because we believe, first, that this material had
reached a higher level of maturity at an earlier
stage of the development of thought than had
those parts of the theoretical structure devoted
primarily to problems of dynamics and change.
In this, as in other respects, we think that the
development of the social sciences is analogous
to that of the biological. It is easier to observe
morphological patterns than the phenomena of
process; and such observations can be more readily
codified into an intelligible set of patterns.

Second, we believe that the properties most
distinctive of social systems as distinguished from
the other subsystems of action, notably culture and
personalities, can be identified and characterized in
the area of structure. The treatment of social
structure has been the most important means of
separating the analytical independence of the
social system from the complex matrix of the
phenomena of action in general, particularly culture. Dynamic processes, particularly those involving change in the structure of social systems, involve intimately the interdependence of social and
cultural factors, and of social and psychological
and organic factors. Since we believe that the
analytical separation of these subsystems of action
is a very important theoretical task, we feel that
the analysis of social structure has been perhaps
the most important single "sieve" through which
this sifting has been possible and fruitful.

THE FRAME OF REFERENCE OF STRUCTURAL MORPHOLOGY

The frame of reference within which we have
organized the selections in Part Two is both comparative and evolutionary. Our emphasis on the
comparative needs little justification. Every segment of knowledge about the range of variation of
structural types in the social field helps clarify the
formulation of the problems which dynamic theory
faces. This knowledge of range is of little theoretical significance unless the data can be codified in
terms of relatively definite classifications. Such
classifications are the first-order statements of the
existence and nature of systematic relations of
interdependence between the factors and variables
involved in the processes of social interaction. As
such, they are the indispensable preliminaries to
attempting deeper penetration.

A good example is the incest taboo, i.e., the
series of prohibitions of marriage and sexual
relations between persons related by kinship. Before the development of modern anthropology, it
was generally simply taken for granted that people
did not marry close relatives—though there was
very little awareness of the reasons for this; it was
considered a matter of "nature" or divine decree.
Increasing knowledge of non-literate societies,

however, showed that, in many such societies, the prohibitions were extended to lengths that seemed extreme to Western eyes—so that as many as three-fourths of the members of the opposite sex in the society might be included in the prohibition. On the other hand, sometimes the prohibition of marriage to distant relatives—so distant that in our society their relationship would not be recognized at all—was accompanied by mandatory cross-cousin marriage well within what, in most Western tradition, have been prohibited degrees of relationship. Development of considerable sophistication in the structural analysis of kinship systems was necessary before these accumulating data made sense—particularly when they showed such phenomena as the mandatory Egyptian and Inca brother-sister marriages in royal and aristocratic subgroups.

Only within our own generation has the emphasis on the special importance of certain types of solidarity of kinship units—a solidarity structurally variable over a wide range—been identified as a major aspect of the problem. In this context, the nuclear family has gradually been perceived to be a very special case because, though there are certain secondary variations, it comes nearer than any other unit of kinship structure to having universal structural significance. Eventually, from an ostensible chaos of evidence—that produced, e.g., the fantastic "primitive promiscuity" hypothesis—a certain amount of order has begun to emerge. The order is greatly strengthened by psychological considerations whose appreciation goes back to Freud far more than to any other source. These considerations concern particularly the role of infantile eroticism in the process of socializing the child, and the necessity of overcoming the attachments the child originally forms within his own family of orientation—overcoming them is necessary if he is to be motivated to the higher-order role-performance of the adult. In this connection, the incest taboo within the nuclear family has become perceived—in spite of certain peripheral exceptions—as a principal universal of human social organization and as very deeply involved in the motivational processes by which social systems are maintained. The clarification which we feel is progressing could not occur without the morphological evidence that comparative research—in this case mostly in anthropology—has accumulated and systematized.

This same example has special relevance to the other dimension of our treatment of structural morphology, namely, the evolutionary dimension. In the Introduction to Section A of Part One, we discussed the importance of the concept of social evolution in the generations immediately preceding the one concerning this Reader. During the period of our attention, there was a strong reaction against the oversimplified aspects of the concept, in the versions put forward in the name of sociology by Comte and Spencer especially, but also by a number of other writers usually classified as anthropologists. Then, particularly in anthropology, radically anti-evolutionist views emerged, taking either the form of the extreme "diffusionism" of discrete cultural traits, or the form of cultural relativity, regarding the socio-cultural world as composed of an indefinite plurality of discrete total cultures, each with its own special individuality without genetic or systematic interrelations. In their more extreme forms, both doctrines seem to negate the possibility of comparative study, through insisting on the uniqueness of the unit of analysis.

The connection between this anti-evolutionist trend and the methodological positions deriving from German Idealist "historicism" is clear.[1] In American sociology, however, interest in evolutionary ideas faded away rather than becoming involved in a dramatic clash of fundamental views. Ward and Sumner failed to hold the central attention of the major figures in the profession during the earlier part of the present century. This was associated with the writings of, e.g., Cooley, Mead, Thomas, and Park, focusing primary attention on smaller-scale structures and processes within the society. For the most part, the "historical" status of American society was not problematical to the last generation of American sociologists.

The most eminent European figures at the turn of the century were, however, much concerned with the problem of social evolution. Though they introduced very important modifications into the earlier versions, they were all fundamentally evolutionists. This statement applies least directly to Pareto, who evinced relatively little concern with any problems of structural morphology—this is one reason that his influence has not been greater. However, he had a strong historical interest concerning Western society and its relations to classical antiquity, as demonstrated in the two final chapters (the entire Volume IV in the English translation) of his *Treatise*.

Though Freud was far more important to our field as a psychologist than as a sociologist, his serious concern with evolutionary problems on the social level is significant. Many of his ideas must

---

1. Probably the most important connecting link between German thought and American anthropology was Franz Boas, himself of German origin.

be drastically revised. But they contained elements of striking insight; and Freud was clearly aware that a coherent theory in this field was a necessary component of the general theory of human behavior to which he contributed so much. Durkheim was one of the most cogent critics, in the relevant respects, of Comte and Spencer. But Durkheim never suggested abandoning the general evolutionary frame of reference, and his last major work, the *Elementary Forms,* was explicitly oriented to this problem. He never attempted to trace main lines of development or to delineate the main pattern of branches of the tree of social evolution; but the problem was always dominant in his thought.[2]

Max Weber was, however, the most striking figure in this connection. In one sense, Weber's primary emphasis could be described as comparative. In his later work, his central program of research was concerned with the relation of the great religious movements to the characters of the societies which developed under their influence. He analyzed the orientations and values of the religious movements themselves, and developed an elaborate system of ideal types—dealing with many phases of social structure, especially the economic and political—that, taken as a whole, is by far the most highly developed framework for comparative analysis yet available in the field. Only very recently have equally serious attempts again been made.

Seen in its larger context, Weber's scheme is evolutionary as well as comparative. He was deeply concerned with the stages by which the various principal civilizations developed from the periods in which their major religious orientations first crystallized. He was also concerned with a total picture of world history, however far he was from having worked out a complete or generally satisfactory morphological account of it. In a sense, the present task of comparative and evolutionary sociology is to resume the problem where Weber left it.

The comparative and the evolutionary perspectives are vital to sociology, and they are inseparable from each other. In the social world, as in the organic, there is a general direction, so that societies are more or less advanced in the scientifically objective and not merely the ethical senses. There is differentiation, both between types of

society, and in the internal structure of each. This does not imply that the evolution of social structure is unilinear in the traditional sense: the "branching tree" model that has become generally accepted in biology seems much closer to the facts.

There is both a direct empirical continuity and a basic similarity of pattern between biological, social, and cultural evolution. The world of action is one primary aspect of the larger world of life phenomena; and the whole is subject to common principles of organization and process. However, some aspects of systems of action are not salient or not present in other parts of the life process, and these become increasingly prominent in human social and cultural evolution. Hence, the theory of social evolution is not simply a matter of applied biology in the most general sense, as some of the early social evolutionists thought. Sociology, in particular, must develop its own autonomous analysis and classifications from its own frame of reference. In this respect, we agree with the objections so frequently raised against the use of organic analogies by various earlier writers (e.g., Spencer)—society certainly is not, in the naïve sense, "an organism."

One very important feature of the evolution of human societies derives from culture's special role in them. In this case, there is some truth in the diffusionist theories of the last generation—structural components can, under certain conditions, be transferred from one social system to others which are genetically (in the historical sense) unrelated to it. The different kinds of this type of transmission and the circumstances under which it can occur constitute a crucial problem area for the sociologist. We shall return to this problem in the Introduction to Part Four, when discussing the general relations of society and culture, and in the Introduction to Part Five, which deals with social change.

The Classification of Structural Materials

From the above considerations, it follows that a theoretically adequate scheme of structural morphology should be capable of systematizing data in three different reference contexts: comparison of different types of society at any given time; delineation of the genetic sequences by which one type becomes transformed into another; and delineation of the differentiated subsystems which, in relation to each other, constitute the structure internal to any given society. Ideally, all three aspects of structural morphology must be integrated in one conceptual scheme. Since all these aspects are ultimately based in the same set of premises, the choice of one among them to serve as the primary point of reference is arbitrary.

2. This aspect of Durkheim's thought has recently been thoroughly reviewed by Robert N. Bellah, "Durkheim and History" *American Sociological Review,* Vol. 24, p. 447, 1959. Dr. Bellah's paper brings out this aspect so strongly that it can probably never again be seriously claimed that Durkheim's main tendency was to "static," ahistorical analysis.

We have given primacy to the third aspect, since work within it has been most highly developed. Most of the material bearing on genetic sequences is included in Part Five rather than Part Two; and what is available is distressingly fragmentary. In Part Two, we have deliberately included a good deal of comparative material.

If the internal structure of a given society is the primary point of reference, the problem of classifying structural components is difficult and troublesome. Theory in this field has not yet reached a satisfactory state—especially in any sense which could be the common property of the professional groups concerned with the field.[3] For this reason, and because of this problem's involvement with those of the relation of social systems to culture and to the individual, arranging the selections in Part Two and dividing it from Parts Three and Four posed a difficult problem.

The best procedure might have been to use the available classification with the most general theoretical merit—e.g., along the lines outlined in the second essay in the General Introduction above. However, there is one serious objection to this procedure. In the period from which the selections have been taken, thinking in terms of this kind of classification did not occur—Weber's work comes closest to our own conceptions, but is still considerably removed. Inevitably, we had to use a compromise, constituting a relative approximation to what we considered an adequate basis for ordering this type of materials.

Let us try to develop the rationale for our classification in its relations both to our own preferred scheme and to the nature of the materials we are presenting. First, the most general principle of organization is, in a modified form, that hierarchy of control relations outlined in the General Introduction—from the lowest level to the highest in that hierarchy. Since this principle must be intersected by others, we have applied it in a broad way.

The two other principal bases of our classification are the categories of economic and political structures. These categories are the least ambiguous of the conventional list of "institutions"; we will discuss later certain ambiguities which should be remembered in orienting to such materials.

"Ascriptive solidarities" are at the bottom of the classification, and "religion," in its structural aspect

for society, is at the top.[4] In the middle, between the economic and the political categories, we have placed social stratification; it is, perhaps, the central focus of internal social conflict in sociological thinking, and hence is the most crucial single point at which existing integrative mechanisms can be expected to focus.

As noted, the fundamental point of reference for this classification is the relation to the hierarchy of control; but, because of the inherent multidimensional character of social systems, this relation alone cannot be adequate. For further analysis of these cross-cutting relations, the evolutionary concept is the most convenient point of reference.

Ascriptive Solidarity as a Point of Departure

Kinship. In the structure of primitive or relatively undifferentiated societies, ascriptive components are overwhelmingly predominant. The first focus of the ascriptive structure is generally kinship. But kinship is not, as such, a factor or a causal category —except in the special methodological sense in which any structure can be treated as such. Kinship is structurally (in the sense of defining the patterning of social relationships) the most salient and tangible aspect of a functionally diffuse, i.e., relatively undifferentiated, system. Though the kinship system is itself relatively complex—a result in part of the incest taboo—the situation approximates one in which the total status of the individual in the society is determined by his kinship statuses. But structurally and functionally, this includes far more than is involved in kinship in a modern society. As recent anthropological work has shown, it involves the whole complex of territorial references involved in status—residence;[5] the territorial relational context in which "work" is done, i.e., the prototype of later occupational functions; the jurisdictional focus of organization in its legal and political aspects; and the modes of communicative interrelationship which can exist, including messages and the movements of persons and commodities.

The kinship system is, thus, the focus of what in more differentiated contexts would be called the economic and technological aspects of social function. In other words, roles in these functional connections are performed by given persons in given ways by virtue of their places in the ascribed net-

3. The author of this Introduction is now struggling with the problem in connection with an attempt to analyze American society as a total social system. The currently preferred classifications, such as are found in even the best general textbooks, seem seriously unsatisfactory for the purpose. I therefore expect to use a rather radically revised one, which is partly foreshadowed above in Part Two of the General Introduction.

4. We will deal with the other principal aspect of religion in Part Four.
5. See G. P. Murdock, *Social Structure*, N. Y., Macmillan Co., 1949, for an illuminating analysis of the complex interrelations of kinship status, in the sense of biological-affinal relatedness, and residential location.

work of kinship relations. The same applies to the more central functions on behalf of societies as systems. Its most tangible focus is the organization of political authority. Such institutions as clan eldership, chieftainship, etc., are universally associated with kinship status. Whatever primitive equivalent of law there is in such a society is clearly organized at the kinship and religious levels. This last is also generally associated with the same functionally diffuse matrix. The classic analysis based on this general supposition is Durkheim's study of the Australian society (in the *Elementary Forms*).

Whatever differentiations on other levels may underlie the structure of a primitive, kinship-centered society—in the patterns of differentiation which become of primary significance to the comparative study of social structures at more advanced levels—there is a common base, the ascriptive embeddedness in a kinship nexus of all major societal functions.

For this reason, our first major category of structural components of societies has a dual significance. First, it is meant to present some particularly important examples of the description and analysis of types of general social organization in which this ascriptive component clearly dominates all others. Second, it concerns this component's continuing significance, through all the various vicissitudes of the modes of structural differentiation that have occurred from the base line of ascriptive embeddedness. If our concern were only with the primitive base line, we could have confined our selections to the first subsection.[6] It was necessary to add three other rubrics, because, in the further process of differentiation, aspects of the more general ascriptive complex become differentiated both from each other and from non-ascriptive components.

In more general theoretical terms, the category of ascriptive solidarity is the primary, though not the exclusive, base point of the interrelations between the social system and the individual. There are two primary foci of this relationship. The first is the basic connection between sexual reproduction as a biological mechanism, and the family as the primary agency of the process of socialization. The family is primary in that it is the first social agency powerfully to affect the child; it hence lays the foun-

dation of personality structure. Although many imposing social structures are independent of the specificities of the kinship base, there is no tendency to eliminate this base. In social evolution, the principal trend has been toward enhancing the generality of the foundations thereby laid down, not toward eliminating their necessity or even the most general location of the mechanisms of their construction. There is, here, a close analogy with the role of genetic factors in the determination of behavior. The plasticity of the human organism is not an example of the elimination of the relevance of genetic factors; it is an example of a special type of organization of such factors.

Ethnic Solidarity. Kinship, with special reference to the nuclear family, is the continuing base for the socialization of the individual's personality. Two other subcategories in our classification of components of ascriptive solidarity may be considered as extensions, in different directions, from this point of reference. One concerns ethnic solidarity. In the more undifferentiated situation, ethnic solidarity is simply taken for granted. It is the unity of a collectivity whose members are bound together by kinship ties—that is, where the member acquires ascriptively, by birth, his membership in the relevant collectivities. Our concern here, however, is the operation of the same principle within a larger structural context involving more than one ethnic group. This pluralism constitutes a fundamental difference from the primitive situation. On the general evolutionary scale, one major reference point is the necessity of juxtaposing those groups who differ in allegiance at this level within another setting of imperatives.

In Western history, the Jews provide the most salient example of this—the problem of the status of the diaspora groups within the wider societies of which they have become parts. If Jewishness had been, in the sectarian sense, a special religious adherence, the problem would have been different. But the Jewish pattern was one of religio-social community, in which membership was by hereditary ascription and to which loyalties were diffuse. By extending the pattern of kinship ascription to a sub-community within a larger one, a special pattern of differentiated social organization was evolved. The Jews in medieval and early modern Europe were a special and rather extreme case, but they illustrate the principle vividly. The ethnic group and the social class, as bases of organization, share some important common elements, which will be discussed later.

The Primary Group. The other extension from kinship ascription as such is the primary group. This is not a direct application of the principle of kin-

6. It might be debated whether concern with the very important types of difference and ranges of variation *within* this base line category of "primitive" society was primarily a function of sociology, or of the anthropologists, who have made vitally important contributions to it. Apart from this jurisdictional question between disciplines, the problems of differentiation beyond this base line are sufficiently formidable, and have played a sufficient part in the preoccupations of the main figures of sociological theory, so that we are justified in concentrating our attention on them.

ship ascription, but is classified with it because they have the common factor of functionally diffuse involvement of the personality. The nuclear family is the prototype of all primary groups. The principle of solidarity based on relatively particularized "personal" loyalty can, however, be extended to types of relation which are more specialized in their functions for the wider society, even up to the case of occupational groups. The relations between these levels, exemplified in the selections of Section A-III will be discussed further in the introduction to that section.

Territorial Groupings. The second of the two primary foci of the individual's anchorage in social processes is the territorial location of activities and, with that, the territorial incidence of the jurisdictional application of systems of normative order. As already noted, the more primitive focus of this is the mutual involvement of kinship structure and residential location. With further differentiation, the locations of many activities become progressively more separated from place of residence, and responsibility for both jurisdiction and communication becomes segregated from kinship grouping as such. Just as in the case of biological relatedness, the complex concerned with territorial location, though progressively differentiating, is an indispensable foundation for structuring the basis of the individual's participation in social relationships—including the control of such participation. Like kinship, it can be superseded only in that it may become more "plastic"—a more generalized base permitting wider and more flexible ranges of variation for the individual. Territorial mobility of populations is largely a main trend of general social development, however prominent the exceptions may be.

Primary Differentiation from the Ascription Nexus

Partly because of the importance of this set of exigencies of the individual's foundation in the social system, a complementary set of imperatives concerned with the integration of these many persons in a larger social system always exists at the same time. On the lowest evolutionary levels, this is closely associated with, or embedded in, the general kinship structure itself. The imperative is demonstrated by the incest taboo and, relative to the nuclear family, by the cross-cutting nexus of extended kin groupings. Such groupings are, as noted, agencies defining and enforcing territorially extended systems of normative order, and regulating systems of communication and movement. In other connections, they are the focus of defining and symboliz-

ing values, and of whatever societal goal-orientation occurs.

The most frequent and important differentiation proceeding immediately from this base is that between the diffuse matrix and the structural elements organized about higher-order, more nearly society-wide functional exigencies. The diffuse matrix remains more directly concerned with maintaining the masses of the population, and their reproduction, economic provision, etc.

The most salient of these society-wide exigencies are either religious or political. The religious are concerned primarily with maintaining the basic cultural tradition, with special reference to its value content—i.e., values for the society as a system. The political have primary reference to maintaining cohesion and conformity with the traditionally defined institutionalized order. The paramount political exigencies are those associated with quite specific goals affecting the whole society, like defense, certain society-wide problems of economic production (e.g., the famous irrigation system), and the maintenance of internal loyalty to the institutionalized order. In general, law forms a bridge between these two major components of differentiated societal responsibility.

As a general rule, however much the emphasis on the religious and the political functions may vary, the agencies responsible for them do not, in early stages and at the higher levels, readily become structurally differentiated from each other. Aristocracies and royal lineages are usually *both* political and religious elites; and responsibility for law as general normative prescription, whether it emphasizes the political or the religious more, is vested in the same groups. Usually, these upper groups are differentiated from the lower as ascriptively hereditary kinship groups. Therefore the tendency to differentiate a functionally diffuse leadership element from the diffuse kinship nexus also tends to become the basis of a generalized pattern of social stratification which *includes* a kinship component.

Though complicated, this broad basis of earlier structural differentiation corresponds roughly to the main axis of our organization of materials. Kinship per se cannot be the major basis of this type of differentiation, nor can the other components of the ascriptive complex. Only as kinship groups—or, more rarely, ethnic groups—become specialized with reference to responsibility for societal functions of this order, can they become systematically distinguished from the general run of such groups. The central focus of stratification lies in differentiation for society-wide function. The degree to which this differentiation is institutionalized is variable.

In general, clear differentiation of economic production from a functionally diffuse matrix is a late development in structural evolution. With certain exceptions, some one kinship unit or combination of kinship units remains the principal agency of the productive process. Differentiation in terms of the political and religious functions discussed above, however, requires a higher order of consumption than the production of the kinship units to which the incumbents belong can provide. In transitional cases, like the polygyny of the Trobriand chief described by Malinowski, a predominant position within a particularly wide nexus of kinship relations can provide for this. But usually, more specialized bases of insuring an income to the higher groups of the society develop. There are two alternative emphases. The far commoner is to leave most of the organization of production itself to lower-order units, but to institutionalize, for various types of higher groups, rights to some fraction of the proceeds. Perhaps the commonest example of this is the institutionalization of some sort of rent rights— i.e., to a share of the produce of the land for "owning" groups, as distinct from the cultivators themselves. The second alternative is to put the productive process itself directly under the control of the ruling elements. Various versions of the *oikos* pattern of organization belong in this category, as do the *latifundia* of the Roman upper class. Cases like this should not, however, be considered "economic enterprises" in the usual sense. They do not typically constitute production for an indefinite market; they are modes of providing for the *specific* economic needs of units of the upper groups, that, as such, have a status of diffuse political and religious superiority.

Thus, though in one aspect, this relation between elite and non-elite elements, however one-sided, may be treated as "economic exchange," under these conditions it is never closely analogous to such exchange in a "free market" economy—the economic element is still embedded in a more diffuse matrix whose other elements are primarily non-economic.[7] Similar statements may be made about the factors of political power and support as they operate in such relationships. Because the political component stands at a higher level than the economic in the hierarchy of control relations, within the type of diffuse matrix under consideration, in general, political rather than economic superiority is paramount, in a more analytical sense. On this type of broad two-class basis, those groups enjoying positions of marked economic superiority are very

directly integrated in the upper political structure of the society.

The more directly political functions concern the capacity to mobilize societal resources through mechanisms which are not a simple function of the institutionalized obligations of a seamless web of kinship relations as such. Understandably, military service is important in this respect, as is providing economic income for maintaining the upper groups' style of life. In general, this style of life includes a variety of components which have direct symbolic significance for the integration of the society and the expression of its values. It also includes provision for the primary centralized religious functions of the society, and the obligation to enforce internal order in relation to some sort of normative system.

These political components are typically embedded in a diffuse matrix of integrative and pattern-maintenance functions. In this context, the pattern-maintenance functions appear most conspicuously in the religious status of the upper groups, which are nearly universally accorded some special prerogatives—though special subgroups often have more differentiated religious functions. The most conspicuous manifestation of the integrative component is kinship's involvement in the general differentiation. In other words, membership in the upper groups is almost universally mostly hereditary; their lineages become differentiated from those of the lower ranks—even though certain types of mobility may be possible, e.g., through military channels. Political and economic superiority would not be viable without the legitimation provided by integrating a religious tradition with its institutional forms, and without institutionalizing the superiority of the relevant kinship units as such as a superior class or caste. When we speak of a "ruling class," we refer to a differentiated group which enjoys superiority in *all* of these functional respects—though there may be different emphases in subgroups within it, and the characteristics of ruling classes may differ in different societies.

One important case in this area is that where the upper group is ethnically distinct from the lower. Some sociologists, like Franz Oppenheimer, have gone so far as to contend that differentiated political authority and landlordism can arise only through conquest. This seems contrary to the facts; but foreign rule has been a common phenomenon.

In its essentials, this case need not differ much from one whose stratification arises by a process of internal differentiation. The primacy of the political factor over the economic is more marked; economic superiority is achieved and maintained largely through the use of political power. It is a somewhat more subtle point that the needs for legitimation

7. Karl Polanyi, Conrad Arensberg, and Harry Pearson, *Trade and Market in the Early Empires* (Glencoe, Ill.: Free Press, 1957).

and integration are even more acute in this type of case than in the other—as Max Weber made particularly clear. An alliance between foreign political elites and indigenous religious groups is not uncommon—with the latter performing the function, in particular, of "domestication." If such a regime is stable over a long period, a general process of amalgamation is likely to occur, to a point where the ethnic basis of difference disappears. Thus, in England, the uniqueness of the Norman French element was gradually attenuated, so that eventually the use of French and other signs of the ethnic distinction vanished—though they left important residues, like the large French component in the modern English vocabulary.

In medieval English society, this problem of integration was an important focus of the processes by which the Common Law developed and eventually became a highly distinctive system. The fact that the Norman regime was foreign and established by conquest was involved in the early centralization of the English monarchy. But in the conditions of feudalism, the Common Law developed above all in the area of the relations between lord and tenant. In the upper strata of the system, both parties to any conflict were usually French; but lower on the social scale, relations between French and Anglo-Saxon were involved. Probably the ethnic line was the most important single focus of conflict in the system. The Common Law, spreading under royal sponsorship, introduced mechanisms for regulating such conflicts, especially through its procedural emphases. In strict feudal law, a tenant had no rights that could be enforced in the King's courts against his lord. The celebrated rights of Englishmen became institutionalized by a process of encroaching on this privileged relationship. The law increasingly protected the individual from arbitrary action by the lord, usually in the local area. Also, the lords' rights were increasingly freed from the more or less personal basis of feudal tenancy, and institutionalized as rights of property and of local jurisdiction. The general tendency was toward stabilizing the system, and also toward allowing certain types of mobility not possible in a strictly feudal society.

The keynote of the above discussion has been that political and economic functions, in the earlier stages of structural social evolution, are embedded in the three-fold matrix of ascriptive solidarities (notably of kinship and ethnic group, but also of relative territorial fixity), of religion, and of stratification with its introduction of hierarchically differentiated ascriptions. The political functions tend to be more specialized in upper groups and more closely associated with society-wide religious leadership; and economic functions tend to be more segmented and distributed among the masses of the population organized in largely ascriptive units.

POLITICAL FOCI OF FURTHER DIFFERENTIATION

Bureaucracy. In general, two types of sources provide the impetus to further differentiation. The more obvious and more frequently considered centers in the political sphere and is primarily concerned (with respect to one main subtype) with the extension of various types of bureaucratic organization, both military and civil. The second is the development of modes of religious organization and orientation that are autonomous in relation to the more general social structure, particularly its upper echelons.

The essential point about bureaucratization is that it frees the necessary resources from ascriptive ties, which would prevent their disposability, for collective goals according to the exigencies which arise. The most obvious of these ascriptive ties are extended kinship and the kinds of decentralized territorial jurisdiction associated, for example, with feudal systems. The crucial resource in this case is the services of persons, organized in such a way that their loyalty to the implementing political organization takes precedence over other loyalties.

Though top political authority usually remains embedded in the lineage structures of kinship, in and below ministerial and high command levels there may be more or less free disposability of personnel for the goals of higher authority. This process is, however, subject to a series of complex exigencies. The most important such contingency is probably the "internal" problem of the patterning of the organizational structure itself. Others are the problems of economic provision; of integration with other structures, with special reference to the bases on which personnel in the bureaucratic structure are given "security" in relation to conflicting claims on their loyalty; and of the basis of making legitimate such extensive claims on the societal resources.

Different sorts of organizational tasks vary widely. The military looms large in many societies, and usually the line between defense and offense is a thin one. But the great, economically significant public works of earlier eras belong mainly in this category—e.g., the irrigation and canal works of the river valley civilizations. Such projects may also be oriented to goals concerned with religion and/or integrative symbolization. Two cases of this are the enormous mobilization of resources for building temples and other religio-political monuments, like the pyramids of Egypt; and building palaces, which are both utilitarian facilities and symbols of the regimes' greatness and contributions to the society.

Necessarily qualified, Weber's dictum that bureaucracy is the most effective administrative instrument ever developed may be adopted as our point of reference. Internally, bureaucracy's principal characteristics as an ideal type consist in an adequate balance between competence and responsibility on the part of its various units. The requisite standards of competence vary with the nature of the task, and are connected with the related evolution of culture in the instrumental fields, the various technologies, etc. It is only very late that full-fledged science becomes an important component of competence. Responsibility concerns primarily the effectiveness with which units can be co-ordinated in the service of any organization task. Responsibility is associated especially with the nature of the authority and leadership operating within the organization. The fundamental problem is balancing the two essentially independent elements of competence and authority.

The effectiveness of internal organization is dependent on the external relations of a bureaucratic organization, in proportion to the large-scale and formidable character of the task. The factors of economic provision and security come to a head in the problem of the degrees of approximation to the institutionalization of occupational roles. The crucial problem is that of the ways in which and the degrees to which the performance of service can be made independent of involvement in relational contexts external to the organization, when organizational interests conflict potentially with the external interest. As Weber has made clear, the optimum arrangement is full money remuneration, so that neither the operative organization nor any of its subunits need have any claim or stake in the *sources* of economic provision; conversely, the structures constituting these sources need not have control over the organization's operation. This involves complex conditions, two of the most important being the extent of market systems and the feasibility of money taxation. Anything approximating a full system of money remuneration for a large-scale bureaucratic apparatus is found only in a few historical cases. Anything less than a full system, however, imposes severe constraints on the independence of the bureaucratic organization; even more important, where subunits are independently provided for through fiefs, benefices, etc., a powerful centrifugal force tends to arise that easily

threatens the internal authority structure of the organization.

The problem of security is closely related to this. The fortunes of the organization may be subject to severe and unexpected vicissitudes; and the status of the individual or subunit within the organization may be seriously insecure. The specialization of bureaucratic roles *ipso facto* means that other, more particularistic bases of security must be sacrificed; because, in general, these involve a diffuse fusion with non-bureaucratic bases of status. Only through the very wide extension of occupational organization through the society as a whole can a close and stable approximation to Weber's ideal type of bureaucracy be achieved.

The famous Chinese Mandarin bureaucracy is an illuminating example of a "compromise" formation. In the society as a whole, this stood virtually alone. The individual had no alternative "occupational" career. Yet there was considerable risk in the process of qualification for office through the examination system, in part as a direct consequence of its universalistic rigor. Furthermore, once qualified, the individual's career chances were still uncertain. This situation influenced strongly the co-existence, over so many centuries, of the bureaucratic system and the social predominance of a landed gentry with full political control at the local levels. The gentry lineage was the security base from which it was possible to take the risks of an official career, and to which were fed back the proceeds of success. This was a mutually profitable symbiosis; but the functional necessity of the security base was a fundamental barrier to the further rationalization of Chinese bureaucracy.

Extreme predominance of the security base over organizational obligations is demonstrated in the military organization of Western feudalism. The leadership of military contingents was so strongly based in their own local feudal nexus that a central command could be sure of commanding their loyalty only within very narrow limits. A truly national level of military organization was not possible without structurally segregating military roles from the feudal network.

For present purposes, the most significant aspect of the problem of the legitimation of bureaucratic organizations and their operations is the relation of bureaucratic organization to any generalized system of law existing in the society. In other words, under certain circumstances groups who are somehow recognized as authorities on what is "normatively correct" in the society tend to become dominant in directing and operating bureaucracies. Another aspect of the Chinese case demonstrates this: the famous Confucian literati were essentially "lawyers";

they were trained in the "proprieties"; they knew what conduct was right and proper for the superior man. Their expert status took in this respect precedence over any standards of technical competence or even organizational effectiveness, thus providing another very severe set of limitations on the rationalization of the bureaucracy.

Another example is the prominent role played by legally trained personnel in the civil bureaucracies of Continental Europe in modern times, particularly in Germany. In general, emancipation from the restrictive aspects of "legalism" while not yet having attained adequate legitimation presents a serious set of problems. Often, the alternative to such legalistic restriction has been a Machiavellian power-orientation by the bureaucracy that has led to severe problems of integration in another direction.[8]

Political Democracy. There is a second mode of differentiating the political components of social structure from their diffuse matrices. Bureaucratic organization concerns the *implementation* of goal-oriented decisions and leadership. The other case concerns the mechanisms for arriving at such decisions and for structuring the support for leadership. The development of "political democracy" in classical antiquity is the great example of emancipation from ascription. In the bureaucratic empires, political allegiance remained, as in primitive societies, in virtually all respects ascribed to the "legitimate" authority structure—generally including a generous component of prescription by force. But in Greece and Rome, the institutionalization of the role of citizenship, though restricted to privileged minorities of the total population, included the right to participate in collective decision- and policy-making, and hence the right to allocate support between alternative leadership elements rather than restriction to the one legitimate authority. It is obvious that the stability of such a system would be precarious; it is not surprising that this pattern appeared only under special circumstances and in small-scale units. However, its importance as the basic model for modern political enfranchisement is clear.

It is important that the differentiation of the po-

litical from other elements was still incomplete in classical Greece and Rome. In the Greek *polis* and the Roman *urbs,* no clear differentiation between political and religious functions developed. The *polis* was both church and state, though, through certain types of secularization, its political aspect tended to become predominant. For present purposes, the essential point that a considerable proportion of the population were enfranchised, that is, they were freed from specific ascriptive allegiances *within* (not *to*) the *polis.* It is significant that this development did not occur originally in societies which developed complex bureaucratic structures, and that, in Rome, as the *urbs* increased in scale, the incidence of the development became greatly attenuated. This set of circumstances, because of Rome's historical background as a city-state, probably played an important part in the acuteness of the problem of legitimacy in later Rome.

Law. The same general social complex—classical antiquity—is the most important source of development of an *independent* system of law. As noted, the legal element was central in the Chinese development; but it took a form which did not readily become differentiated from either the political or the religious—on the contrary, it formed the focus of a special kind of codification of the religio-political fusion. There was thus essentially no pattern of institutionalization of legal rights *against* the state or religion.

The Greek legal system was similar, except that the all-important democratic element institutionalized rights, within the state, to participate in decision-making. In Greece, the legal system did not become generalized on an independent basis. In Rome, whose political dominion grew while internally the democratic element declined in importance, relations to the populations of the Empire became structured in dual form: the extension of the privileges of Roman citizenship to larger and larger circles throughout the Empire; and the development of the *jus gentium* as a legal system applicable to all under Roman jurisdiction. Though administered by political authority and backed by religious sanctions, the system of Roman Law became an independent entity in a unique sense. Roman Law, in addition to classical culture, was clearly one of the most important legacies from antiquity to the modern Western world.

This aspect of law should be distinguished from the types of religious law, to be discussed briefly below, institutionalized in Judaism and Islam. The most important achievement of Roman Law was its type of differentiation of law from religion and from political leadership. In Judaism and Islam, religious sanction was lent to detailed prescriptions of con-

---

8. The same essential sociological principles apply to the cases of economic and of political bureaucracy; the firm, though oriented to economic production, has a prominent "political" (in the analytical sense) component in its organization. In this context, the association of the family firm with a kinship lineage has had functions similar to those of the gentry lineages in Chinese bureaucracy. The market is, like the official career, a field of serious risk-taking; and family property and the continuity of kinship status in the community have provided an important cushion underlying the risk. Only with the development of a very extensive occupational system in recent times could stable economic and political bureaucracy exist without some such cushion.

duct—this made the Roman type of differentiation impossible. To this day, this is a central problem in Islamic societies.

TYPES OF RELIGIOUS AUTONOMY

The other massive basis of a further process of structural differentiation toward the upper end of the control hierarchy is the development of religious collectivities and movements which can be considered "autonomous" relative to the main structure of the social system. Our previous generalization that various functional performances are embedded in ascribed matrices, characteristically in primitive societies, especially those organized around kinship, applies to religion as much as to any other principal aspect of the social system. Religious beliefs are typically shared throughout the society, and rituals are symbolically integrated in the social system itself. There is no religious point of view which opposes the point of view assumed to be institutionalized; the only behavior condemned in the name of religion is what is socially deviant, in a general sense. Though there are individual classes of specialists in religious (including magical) matters, no religiously specialized collectivity is structurally distinct from others.

As noted, this fusion tends strongly to be maintained when a marked hierarchical differentiation takes place. Elites are usually both political and religious at the same time.[9]

Religion's position high on the hierarchy of control in the social system implies that it should provide, under favorable conditions, the most powerful source of leverage for structural change in societies. Cases where this leverage has operated fairly autonomously seem rather rare historically and difficult to identify or analyze. Tendencies to religious innovation seem to be generally kept under tighter controls than is the case with other components of the social system.[10]

Interstitial Autonomy. In general, the earliest types of religious orientation that are significantly autonomous in relation to the main structure of societies are found in situations interstitial to societies. A typical example is the "holy place." In early Semitic religion, as analyzed by Robertson Smith, the society was largely nomadic. However, it maintained some kind of permanent installation at a holy place—usually an oasis—and a socially separate group, functioning as its custodians, readily developing into a kind of priesthood. This group was an interstitial subsociety, enjoying but dependent upon the tolerance and protection of the major societal powers in the region. These priesthoods of holy places are thought to have played an important part in developing the patterns of religious autonomy that came to fruition in Judaism and later in Islam. A different but related example is the special status of the Oracles in the Hellenic world, situated outside the structure of the *polis.*

Other movements, like early Buddhism in India and Taoism in China, could develop within the structure of a society; but they quickly became isolated as internally interstitial elements, taking the form of special religious subcommunities deprived of any major status in the central social structure. This trend was easiest when the religious movement itself was built on the devaluation of worldly concerns. The early Christian communities within the society of the Eastern part of the Roman Empire show this. "Rendering unto Caesar the things that are Caesar's" meant, in these circumstances, accepting the position of not belonging in the secular society, of being "in it but not of it," hence expecting only to be tolerated within it. The connection of this orientation with the eschatological hopes of early Christianity is clear.

Movements like this, which started out in an internally interstitial position within the society, might ultimately, if they spread far enough, have profound consequences for the society's main course of development. This was particularly true of Christianity.

Monastic Orders and Sects. There is an important range of transition from this kind of internally interstitial religious autonomy to that involving rather direct influence over the character of the society itself. One of the most common patterns in which the interstitial type could find relative stability is that of religious orders, usually consisting of adults of one sex living in segregation from the secular society. This pattern was particularly prominent in Buddhism and Taoism in the Orient, where such groups never become wholly independent of the surrounding society. They are dependent on other sources for recruitment, for political protection, and generally for economic subsistence. Moreover,

---

9. It is notable that the two most important sociologists of religion of our central generation, Durkheim and Weber, both postulated the generality of an embedded type of primitive religion from which more differentiated types might evolve.

10. Religion is placed primarily in the cultural, rather than the social, system. Because, however, of its special relation to the problem of values and the stabilization of value-orientations, it is crucial to the highest level of social structure. The general relation is interpenetration. Generally speaking, the less differentiated both the social and the cultural systems, the more comprehensive the range of interpretation, and hence the more important the more direct forms of social control over religion, and vice versa.

they are rarely content to be completely isolated. They generally wish somehow to take their religious message to the outside world, to share their religious good fortunes with others. Their withdrawal in the name of religion is, with wide variations, always to some extent a withdrawal with intent to return.

An important difference occurs when the group organized about an autonomous religious orientation is composed primarily of families, i.e., of both sexes and all ages living in household units. This is the "sect," in Weber's and Troeltsch's sense; the early Christian communities were of this type. It should be distinguished from a discipleship or "brotherhood," which leads into the monastic order type. The sect is characterized by commitment to make its religion the unequivocally dominant consideration in its members' lives. It therefore involves strong pressure to establish real communities consisting exclusively of believers attempting to lead a religiously ideal life. Two outstanding examples of this are the Anabaptists in the Reformation period in Europe, and the Mormons in nineteenth-century America. Since the religiously ideal pattern of social life is likely to be very different from that of the surrounding general society, the problem of the relation between the two is likely to be acute. Sects thus form the most persistent foci of phenomena of religious persecution, because a genuinely serious conflict at the level of societal values is likely. Many compromises are possible and found in actuality; one important line of accommodation, which will be discussed presently, is that leading from sect to denomination in the modern sense.

Religious Control of a Total Society. The importance of the type of social system in which religious and political components were essentially fused has been stressed. It is possible for a movement that is functionally classified as "religiously autonomous" to capture control of such a structure without establishing a structurally differentiated organization of religion. Then the socio-religious structure, especially its elite elements, will tend to give primacy to religious considerations in their general and diffuse functioning.

The Semitic world provides examples of this, in both Judaism and Islam. In Judaism, it apparently occurred in two distinct phases. The first is the one culminating in the Mosaic pattern, in which the Israelites, as Jahweh's chosen people, embarked on the conquest of the Promised Land and the establishment of a society which was conceived as directly governed by Divine Law. The second phase was the Prophetic, during which, under the direct and terrible threat of political disaster, the total Jewish community was enjoined to continue being loyal to religious commitments, even at the sacrifice of political independence. Here, the religion was a kind of lever controlling the development of the whole real society. The Islamic case is, in this respect, very similar. Mohammed, as the Prophet of God, became the religio-political leader of the Arab community; and from then on the community as a whole was conceived as an instrument of the Divine Will, to be guided exclusively by God's law as formulated in the Koran.

The Differentiation of Religious and Political Structures. The second possibility for religion is exemplified by Christianity's evolution beyond the sect, namely, to the "church" in the Weber-Troeltsch sense. The values of the religion, specifically as formulated by and institutionalized in the autonomous religious collectivity, the church, are assumed to be binding both on and in the secular society of which the church is a part. However, there is a structural differentiation between religious and secular collectivities that does not exist in Judaism and Islam. "Church" and "state" are no longer one, but "politically organized society" —the "state," in the medieval sense—is, though unequivocally Christian, still autonomous from the Church as a collectivity organization. Pope Innocent III's claim, that the Emperor was a feudal vassal of the Pope was short-lived. In religious terms, the "temporal arm" was conceived as ordained directly by God and responsible directly to God, and not requiring mediation through the Church. Coronation by a religious authority was a recognition of common Christianity, not of Papal suzerainty.

For present purposes, the most significant aspect of this development was its institutionalization of a primary differentiation between these two crucial aspects of the cultural system, and the social. The common Christianity of Church and state designated an area of interpenetration. A certain rigidity involved in their fusion, in collectivity structure, could be broken down on this basis, with far-reaching consequences for wide ranges of social and of cultural freedom and mobility.

Western Christianity gave rise to a series of sect movements, both before and after the Reformation, and to the development of at least two major new church types, the Lutheran and the Calvinistic. These Reformation churches, however, shared, with the Catholic, the concept of the established church—which, ideally, meant that membership in and hence subjection to the normative jurisdiction of both political state and church were coextensive.

In other areas, and particularly in the United States, a somewhat different type of church has emerged within Protestantism; this is the "denomination." It shares with the sect type the purely voluntary basis of membership and the expectation that its members will be responsible for its own affairs, including financial support. It shares, with the church type, however, the status and expectation of being not only in but of the society. That is, it recognizes legitimacy of a secular sphere which is not, in the collectivity sense, under religious control; and it assumes that its members will, on the whole, participate normally in this secular life. Membership in the religious collectivity is only one role, genuinely differentiated from the other roles in which the same individuals are involved. In America, there is the important feature of a plurality of denominational groups which are recognized as legitimate, not only by secular authority, but by each other mutually on the religious plane. The distinction has been made between a generally legitimate religious orientation, and the particularities of a specific denominational position. To be authentically religious, it is no longer necessary to subscribe to one religious group's credally or traditionally specific beliefs and practices.

The great difference of the denomination from the sect and from the interstitial movement lies in its recognition of the secular society's *legitimacy*. It is not set against a "world" defined as inherently evil if not incorporated into the system of explicitly religious control; but it is differentiated *from* the secular world, thus remaining part of the same more generally legitimate system.[11]

Religion has been included, in Part Two of the Reader, as one of our five main major categories of social structure because, seen in the broadest comparative and evolutionary perspective, it is the focal point of articulation between social and cultural systems—notably, that at which the role of value components is most directly involved. Here, only the relation of religion as a focus of values to the structure of the society is primarily at issue. Religion will, however, appear again—both in the general treatment of the relations of society and culture in Part Four, and in the treatment of social change in Part Five.

Other components of culture, which will be discussed in more detail in the Introduction to Part Four, are of great empirical significance. The "secular intellectual culture," whose two principal forms are philosophy and science, but that also involves ideology and technology, is paramount. In this area, there have been problems of relative

autonomy vis-à-vis both religion and various sectors of the secular structure, notably the political. Autonomous intellectual culture is one of the most striking features of Western society; the conditions underlying this are necessarily of particular importance in any general sociological analysis of this great complex of societies.

THE BASES OF ECONOMIC AUTONOMY

In our dialectical progression among the complexities of the five categories of social structure, let us now consider the economic, seen in the context of its relations to the political and religious, and to the ascriptive solidarities.

As emphasized, any large-scale differentiation of the primary functions of economic production from the matrix of ascriptive solidarity occurs later in the general pattern of societal evolution, and it depends on rather specific conditions. In general, first "consumption" and then exchange become economically specialized, before the impetus reaches back to the productive levels. The two major trends noted above, in the economic relations between an upper politico-religious elite class and the mass of the population, may be regarded in this framework. One basis of the more general differentiation is the lower groups' specialization for economically providing for the needs of the larger collectivity and/or of the upper groups. This usually takes the form of continuing the productive process within the framework of a system of ascriptive solidarities, especially of kinship and of the village community. The upper groups—landlords, etc.—receive an important share of the product. The alternative would be to move an important share of economic production into the framework of collective organization somehow directly controlled by the upper groups themselves.

In the latter type of case, the result is not differentiated economic enterprise, except in a highly qualified sense. Religio-political collectivities control the process, though these collectivities may have branches whose primary concern is with economic production. Such branches may be landed estates raising food-stuffs, or they may be workshops producing luxury goods or armaments. They may also involve requisitioning labor for various kinds of public works. Also, a very substantial economic factor is involved in the direct provision of more or less personalized service in the complex households of various types of magnates.

As Durkheim showed, the more specifically eco-

---

11. I have the impression that, different as the general situation has been from the West, many of the Shinto and Buddhist sects of Japan, at least from the Tokugawa period on, approach the status of being denominations in this sense.

nomic aspect of functional specialization is deeply involved with the development of the division of labor; this may be considered its focal point of development. The division of labor, however, directly implies the necessity of developing and institutionalizing relationships between the consequent differentiated functional units—in the first instance, between producing and consuming units.

In all primitive societies where division of labor exists, the exchange relationship is always embedded in a network of diffuse ascriptive solidarity, one part of which is usually some mutuality of obligations involving terms which could be called "economic." Under these circumstances, this is the fundamental basis of the "traditionalization" of economic relations. The same general pattern is likely to obtain when the first major step in structural differentiation, separating the religio-political upper classes from the general population, has occurred. The producing elements usually have diffuse relations of dependency, involving especially political protection to the recipients of their surplus production.

A familiar example is the relation between land ownership, hence "rent"-paying, and paternalistic solidarity, in the manorial communities of Western feudalism. The landlord was much more than a property holder; he was a political suzerain and the general protector of his community. This was the meaning of the legal formula that a tenant had no rights against his lord—no outside agency could legitimately intervene in this diffuse solidary relationship.

The Emergence of Money and Markets: Contract. There is a vital connection between the breakdown of this kind of relation of diffuse solidarity through differentiation, and the emergence of money and markets. This exists because very severe limitations on differentiation are imposed by the directness of the relations between producer and consumer, that are necessitated by patterns of organization unmediated by any generalized medium of exchange and measure of value.

Differentiating exchange relationships from the diffuse ascribed matrix requires first the institutionalization of patterns governing the field of contract (in the broad sociological sense of the term). To a point, this can proceed independently of money, as a set of expectations of the conditions under which ad hoc agreements can be made. The extent of a contractual system is, however, greatly dependent on the development and acceptance of the medium itself; hence they can be discussed together. Money, as an institutional phenomenon, may be regarded as a special case of the institutionalization of contract.

As noted, the institution of contract consists in a complex of norms independent of the ad hoc content of any particular agreements. The complex is based on some concept of the societal interest in the kinds of contractual agreements that are and can be made, including the kinds that must be prohibited—such as, in our society, any contract infringing the personal freedoms of any individuals, including the contracting parties themselves. From this central focus, rules are defined about the content of permitted and prohibited contracts, with the means for securing the other party's assent either sanctioned or prohibited—i.e., the prohibition of fraud and coercion—and for unforeseen consequences, since the essence of the contractual relation is that rights and obligations must extend over a period of time.

From this point of view, money is a special kind of generalization of such a system of expectations. It advances one step beyond institutionalizing barter, by setting up a system of rules saying that, independent of any specific commitments from any specific contracting parties, the expectations of an as yet undefined set of contractural relations can be formulated, concerned with the expectation that suppliers of potentially wanted goods or services will, over a range of suppliers of the same object and also of types of object, be ready to purvey them in exchange for money. Furthermore, the expectation is that this probability is not specifically limited to any particular time or to any particular terms of exchange.

Two primary sets of problems are concerned with the institutionalization of contract and money. One of these involves regulating the basis for settling terms in cases where there is no ascribed basis on which it is understood that this must occur. The other set concerns the "prior" questions of the terms on which exchangeables will be available for disposal on any terms, or of various sorts of ad hoc arrangement.

The earliest development of markets is, understandably, limited to tangible physical goods. The simplest case is one where the goods "just happen" to be available; that is, where the process of their exchange is not associated with any specific orientation of production to the prospect of exchange. Possibilities under these assumptions are severely limited, and the really important cases are associated with production for the market, i.e., in the expectation of exchanging products for money. Such a situation implies a ramified *system* of markets, since accepting money in exchange for products is meaningful only if it can be spent advantageously in markets other than the one in which it was received.

The more mobile the physical object is, the more readily it can become an object of market exchange. Limiting cases in this respect are land, and permanent fixtures, like buildings and other improvements, which are physically inseparable from land. The fixed position of land and buildings means, in general, that they are involved in a diffuse matrix of relationships making their segregation for purposes of exchange difficult. Alienability of land is likely to be a late development in economic evolution; various kinds of tenancy arrangements are common much earlier. They must fit into a variety of patterns of more or less diffuse solidarity; in many respects, they are thus parallel to relations of employment. The modern type of tenancy, almost purely an arrangement to permit utilization of land and permanent fixtures without other involvements, is nearly as late a development as alienability of land itself.

Property and Money. The general problem of the conditions under which physical objects are available for market transactions is very closely associated with that of the institutionalization of property. Probably no society is almost completely lacking in institutionalized rights of individual property in "personal possessions," such as clothing, trinkets, some tools, weapons, ritual objects, etc. These and the most immediate products of the individual's own labor are presumably the most easily marketable commodities. There is, however, a range, from these objects in the direction of those of greater general importance or of greater fixity. Land is at the extreme in the latter respect; and "private" property in land—by whose virtue its uses and tenancy may be prescribed and its ownership may be freely alienated (and bequeathed)—is generally a product of late stages of development. The final result of this general process of differentiating property rights from the diffuse matrix is the institution of ownership, in which the rights of use, control, and disposal or alienation are brought together in the same hands, thereby maximizing the disposability of the physical object and its uses as a mobile resource.[12]

Two other special cases besides land should be discussed briefly. First, the human individual is in one major aspect a physical object, and rights in him may, to a greater or lesser extent, be assimilated to the general pattern of ownership of physical objects. The extreme of this institution is chattel slavery. It has played an important part in certain phases of economic development, especially in classical antiquity and in the relations of the early modern West with colonial areas. It implies a particularly strong accentuation of the bureaucratic type of authority over individuals; and it is an inherently unstable type, because it conflicts with the complex dealing with the importance of the individual's motivational commitment to autonomous role-performance. Weber was right in emphasizing the importance of the institutionalization of "formally free" labor as the paramount "human" factor of production.

The second special case is money. The essential point here is the relation of money to the general category of commodities. Until recently, most economists have considered that money should be treated as a special class of commodity. Today this is an unrealistic view; money is essentially a mechanism of a specialized type of communication, with respect to which the "medium" is relatively indifferent. This situation is the result of a long and complex evolution. The monetary metals have, historically, been valued in their own right as well as in their capacities as media of exchange—significantly, an important part of this valuation has had a "ritual" basis. As the myth of Midas shows, gold cannot be eaten—and, though it can be worn, this is more as a decoration than a matter of "utility." The monetary metals have, as commodities, been prestige symbols much more than utilitarian objects.

The very human aspect of the monetary problem is the concrete variability of pieces of money as physical objects: the problems of standardizing alloy content and weights of individual coins, the problem of clipping, and the like. It was difficult to arrive at the point where the unit of money unequivocally became a symbolic abstraction, whose most adequate expression was a set of notations on a piece of paper—and the still later form, the entry in an account book. Only when this point is reached is the differentiation of money from the general run of commodities complete. And only after the completion of this differentiation can money assume its place as the central controlling apex of the general system of property—the abstract unit which is the equivalent of a unit of economic valuation of *any* commodity or service.

The Alienability of Human Services. The above discussion has deliberately concentrated on physi-

---

12. This statement, like many others in this essay, should not be taken without qualification. Thus, with special reference to land, it seems probable, as indicated in the selection from Pollock and Maitland below, that English law was more favorable to economic development than was Continental law at the time, in spite of the fact that Continental law had adopted more fully the Roman institution of ownership, particularly in land. There seems, however, to be little doubt that in the long run the single ownership is the most favorable to high mobility of productive facilities, which is the central point at issue here.

cal objects as the negotiables of market exchange. There is, however, a second major category, namely, the services of human beings. The problem of institutionalizing the marketing of human services has involved far greater difficulties than the marketing of physical objects, because of considerations of time and context. The sale and purchase of a commodity can be completed in a single transaction, leaving no continuing concern. A "contract of employment," on the other hand, establishes a continuing relationship, between employer and employee, at least until the service contracted for is completed. This relationship is necessarily part of a larger social system and cannot be isolated in the same sense that the usual commodity transaction is isolated. (The case of land as physical object approaches closest to service, because the plot of land remains an object of human evaluation almost indefinitely and cannot be abstracted from a larger context.)

To a limited extent, human services can be purveyed in a labor market on a relatively ad hoc basis. To a somewhat greater extent, they can be specifically oriented to such a market without disturbing the context of solidary relations within which the individual worker is embedded—notably, his household. But in a larger sense, although ownership of a particular commodity can be merely transferred from one subsystem of the society to another, in the case of employment the worker must maintain a *continuing* balanced set of involvements both in the collectivities which "produce" him, *and* in the one (or more) which utilizes his services. Typically, human services establish a *solidary* relation between provider and consumer of the service—whether the latter be an individual, as in fee-for-service professional practice, or a collectivity, as in the more usual category of the contract of employment. The "alienation" of labor presents a quite different order of functional problem in social systems than does the alienation of commodities. The alienation of land is, as noted, in some respects an intermediate case.

Mobility of the Factors of Production. Related to the above line of analysis, though not identical with it, is the distinction between access, through the market mechanism, to "consumables," whether they be commodities or services, and to the factors of production. This is much involved with the problem of the extent to which the *producing* unit can become differentiated in its orientation to economic considerations.

This essential process has two aspects. Negatively, it is the process of differentiation—of re-

sources as factors of production becoming sufficiently emancipated from the diffuse nexus to be mobilized through the market mechanism. For commodities as physical objects, this concerns extending what, in the technical economic sense, has been called the "capitalistic" method of production, i.e., the production of many goods which then become instruments of further production. Raw materials thus are produced by special enterprises for the markets on which they are bought—perhaps through a series of intermediaries—by manufacturers. Producing plant and equipment become specialized industries.

The more serious problems concern the element of human service, on both an individual level and an organizational one. The general pattern of the process of differentiation from the bottom is that of the specialization of *collective* segmental units of the social structure in one or another field of economic production. That is, *kinship units* become the units of production for the market; as such, they become mobile factors of production. One of the most familiar examples is that of peasant agriculture. There, the combination of subsistence-orientation and manorial payments in kind and service, in a local setting of diffuse solidarity, gives way to production for a more impersonal market, initially very often in a nearby urban community, then possibly spreading to more distant markets requiring merchant mediation.

It is highly important that the main framework of organization tends to remain embedded in the kinship nexus for so long. This is exemplified in the family firm, the dominant type of organization for economic production in "classical" capitalism. It involves re-directing the whole kinship unit, generally in terms emphasizing continuity over an indefinite series of generations, in the direction of economic function. Family property and firm property are not differentiated, and positions of leadership and authority in the producing organization are ascribed on a kinship basis. From this point of view, the classical entrepreneur may be regarded mostly as the founder of a family enterprise who expects it to be continued under the direction of his heirs. Only in a highly qualified sense is this an "individual" occupational role.

In this general process of development, the early approaches to the occupational type tend to come at or near the bottom of the hierarchy. Labor roles, not technical or managerial roles, are first institutionalized on this basis, involving the differentiation of the organizational setting of work, regulated through the contract of employment, from the household and its various concerns, including premises, property interests, etc.[13] As the scale of organization and the involvement of higher levels of technical competence increase, the occupational role type spreads upward. In the Western world, it has only in the past fifty years reached the managerial levels on a large scale.[14] It has been dependent on a sufficiently extensive occupational system so that failure in business did not necessarily mean a loss of fundamental social status.

The above are the barest essentials of the process by which differentiated economic organization, oriented to the market, may be considered to develop from a diffuse nexus independently of political organization. A concomitant process is the differentiation of types of productive unit by industries—a matter of more interest to the economist and economic historian than to the sociologist. One major aspect of this differentiation concerns the stages in the productive process as it becomes more elaborate and more "capitalistic." Such differentiation necessitates more transportation, more specialization in marketing functions, etc. Thus shipping, canals, railways, etc., become very important.

Another fundamental basis of differentiation is functional in the more purely economic sense. The complex of arrangements concerned with financing assume a central place. The extension of time periods involved, and the lack of direct contact between producers at various stages and the ultimate consumers, necessitate such arrangements. Specialized financial agencies develop, especially in insurance and banking, and the fundamental phenomenon of credit emerges. It is particularly important that banking becomes involved with the constitution of the monetary system itself. Banking and credit constitute the principal paths for emancipating money from its origins in the category of commodities.

It is thus probably more than a quaint historical accident that English banking seems to have originated, at least partially, in the activities of the Lon-don goldsmiths. Gold was a semi-sacred symbol of high status, as manifested by, e.g., the requirement that a royal crown be made of gold. It was very difficult to substitute "worthless" promises for this crucial commodity as a circulating medium. The function of the goldsmiths as custodians of gold for safekeeping seems to have been a particularly important step in the process—after all, the gold was not being abandoned as the "real" money; it was being protected against risk of loss. It was not a very great additional step for the goldsmiths to lend on the security of gold holdings, thus issuing credit against which a reserve was held. Even so, Schumpeter was fond of suggesting that banking originated in "crime"—in making available to borrowers what in fact did not "belong" to the lender.

In any case, the invention of credit was a fundamental step in the evolution of economic institutions; it meant the definitive emancipation of the allocation of fluid resources that could operate through the communication of mutual expectations alone. Money became more than the medium of exchange of classic theory; it was, in the form of expandable credit, the primary mechanism for facilitating investment, that is, of autonomous development of economic production.

Finally, the processes of mobilizing the factor of organization within the collective unit—in this case, the firm—through making its managerial functions occupational, must be articulated with processes in the structuring of the organizational environment in which these units operate. Since, in the context presently relevant, these are "independent" units and are not incorporated in larger collectivities, the most essential part of this environment consists in the institutionalized norms to which their operations are subject. This returns us to the institutions of contract, property, and occupation or employment discussed at the beginning of our treatment of the division of labor and economic production. In the structure of the society, the focus of these norms is found in the legal system.

Law and Economic Autonomy

The civilizations in which ramified differentiation of economic function has developed on the basis of private enterprise have been those in which relatively firm and specialized legal systems have also existed. Commercial development reached a relatively high point in Roman society in the late Republic and the Empire. This was made possible largely by the systematization of Roman Law, especially the *jus gentium* mediating the relations of ethnically distinct groups. Then, with the European

13. A very illuminating analysis of the stages and process by which this differentiation can take place, from "domestic" or "putting-out" forms of organization, has been given by Neil J. Smelser, in *Social Change in the Industrial Revolution, 1780–1840* (Chicago: University of Chicago Press, 1959).

14. It is important to note that the Marxian picture of the structure of capitalism is asymmetrical in this respect. Against the occupationally "alienated" labor class, it sets the bourgeoisie, composed of owning-managing kinship groups. The generalization of the occupational role-type to the whole structure (economic "bureaucracy," in Weber's sense) and the virtual disappearance of kinship as a basis of control of the larger business firms, has occurred in the "capitalistic" world without the revolution postulated as necessary by Marx. A rather sketchy analysis of the process of differentiation at the top, with special reference to American industry, is given in Parsons and Smelser, *Economy and Society,* Chapter V.

economic revival that followed the Middle Ages, economic development coincided broadly with the revival of Roman Law and, in England, the development of the Common Law. Private enterprise could develop only within a framework of legal order which above all could protect enterprise against ad hoc political interventions.[15]

It is highly important that the development of these legal systems was by no means a simple function of the business groups' economic interests. One important aspect of their development was the role of relatively autonomous legal professions which were, to a significant degree, independent of *both* political authority and business interest.

The above discussion has been concerned with the process of differentiation "from the bottom up," i.e., essentially independent of the main political-religious leading elements and the more tightly organized collectivity structures under their control. There has also been a process of differentiation from the top down. Probably the most important has been utilizing political bureaucracy, as discussed above, for public works of considerable economic significance for the society as a whole, like irrigation systems, canals, etc. Using the Roman Legions to build the famous Roman roads is another important example. Where political organization itself has been decentralized, as in more or less feudal types of society the same kind of phenomena could occur in smaller-scale, local units of government. On occasion, such enterprises could be oriented to market systems—as when members of the landed nobility in late medieval or early modern Europe engaged in mining.

These developments have been very important in furthering the mobility of resources—particularly human services, through occupational types of role; but, perhaps even more frequently, in some form of requisitioning or serfdom. However, a central difficulty has generally prevented the process of differentiation starting from this point from going through to a full conclusion. This difficulty involves the differentiation of the economic component from the controlling political structure itself. This, in turn, is concerned with the controlling effects of the power interests of political groups, which cause predisposition to shorter-run interests.

For reasons associated with these considerations, the greatest economic "break-through" of all, the Industrial Revolution, did not occur in one of the highly "bureaucratized" early empires like China, Egypt, or Assyria-Babylonia. It is probably significant that the Industrial Revolution did not occur

even in the mercantilist France of Louis XIV, which in certain respects was considerably more "advanced" than England; it occurred in England, which, by Continental standards, had a much more rudimentary governmental administrative system. But crucial sectors of England's population had the ethic of ascetic Protestantism; and England had a particularly favorable system of law, as well as a sea-faring tradition and hence access to distant markets and sources of material.

(Parenthetically, it may be remarked that innovation of the most radical kind of economic development is probably independent of the guidance of collective authority—indeed, flourishes best when institutionally protected against such authority. This probably applies just as much to radical cultural developments, particularly to science. This will be discussed more fully in the Introduction to Part Four.)

Though the initial development of industrialization is most favored in a setting of "free enterprise" within a legal order, it does not follow that, once the model is in existence, the same is true of its diffusion to other societies. The process by which the pattern of industrialization has spread from its British point of origin shows a substantially larger participation of political authority in the cases of "imitation." This was true both of Continental Europe and of the United States, and even more, outside this area, for Japan and still more the Soviet Union. A large component of political participation seems very much the rule in this process in the underdeveloped areas today.[16]

SOCIAL STRATIFICATION

The final topic to be discussed here is the one placed in the middle of our classification series, that of social stratification with special reference to its relation to the problems of the integration of societies. In our initial discussion of the classification we noted that a good deal of social theory has held that this was the primary focus of integrative strain in societies. We do not believe that matters

---

15. A vivid example of the economic consequences of such intervention is pre-communist China, where no enterprise could survive without specific political "protection."

16. Further discussion of these problems is found in "Some Reflections on the Institutional Framework of Economic Development," *The Challenge of Development* (Jerusalem: Hebrew University, 1958), and "The Principal Characteristics of Industrial Societies," in *The Transformation of Russian Society Since 1861* (ed., C. E. Black; Cambridge: Harvard University Press, 1960). Both are reprinted in Parsons, *Structure and Process in Modern Society* (Glencoe, Ill.: Free Press, 1959). I am also greatly indebted to Professor David S. Landes, of the University of California (Berkeley), for much stimulating insight in this field.

are quite so simple; but this idea is a convenient point of departure.

First, in systems of social interaction tendencies toward polarization are definitely present, on a very general basis. Almost any source of conflict can become a focus around which opposing parties choose sides and draw less directly involved elements into the conflict. Then the premium on effectiveness presents an incentive to resort to progressively more drastic means of promoting one's own interest—the resort to the use of physical force is the ultimate result of this vicious circle.

Second, a strong tendency exists, particularly in the early stages of structural differentiation, toward developing polarization internally along a hierarchical axis. As noted, this focuses most on two problems: the problem of political leadership, and the problem of legitimation in the society with reference to its religion-based values. In general, these two functional references are fused together in the establishment of a politico-religious elite which is set up over the "masses" of the society. When such a process of differentiation (possibly originating in conquest) has begun, it is extremely likely that it will result in (or originate in) the bifurcation of the structure of ascriptive solidarity in the society, in that the elite groups will consist in kinship units, and not in "individuals"—the individual's status remains primarily ascribed. Furthermore, the economic organization is likely to be one where the great bulk of economic production is dispersed in highly segmented ascribed units of the peasant agriculture variety. In this case, the elite groups are usually in a position to claim an important share of the proceeds, both because of the general high prestige of their station, reinforced by legitimation, and because of political power. Hence, in terms of consumption, they are usually far wealthier than the masses. Political centralization, however, usually results in various types of bureaucratically organized enterprises and public works; the relatively centralized political authority controls a disproportionate share of the factors of production.

We are outlining a polarized society whose hierarchical dimension of stratification involves all the other four major bases or organization of social structure. The superior groups are superior on every count—legitimized prestige; political power; control of economic resources; and the prestige of the ascribed solidarities themselves, especially kinship, but sometimes generalized on an ethnic basis. It follows that there are approximations to this pattern on many different levels of structural development. In spite of considerably complicating factors, this was true of the peasantry-gentry structure of classical Chinese society; of the upper- and lower-class differentiation that appeared, in a number of different forms, in classical antiquity; and of eighteenth- and nineteenth-century Western Europe, where the rising bourgeoisie tended to ally and partially amalgamate themselves with the older hereditary aristocracies while, lower down, the humbler rural groups (generally, the "peasants,") tended to become allied with the urban and industrial "working classes."

Perhaps the most pervasive common factor in these tendencies to polarization is the involvement of kinship units as such; upper- or lower-class status is then the status of kinship units involving both sexes and all ages—though considerable mobility between the classes may be possible. However, it must be remembered that the kinship structure itself is not a constant. There has been a historic trend to whittle down the size of kinship units, in the general direction of isolating the nuclear family. In general, in cases where the dichotomy of the class structure is more advanced, the significant units have been lineages which spanned several generations, and not "families" in the modern sense.

Polarization vs. *Differentiation.* These considerations suggest, however, that there are tendencies toward invalidating the concept of a simple one-dimensional scale of stratification that could be polarized into a dichotomous antagonism or "class struggle" at a convenient "cutting point." We have already mentioned the most important points of departure for such processes of differentiation.

Religious Autonomy and Stratification: Four Cases. Let us consider the principal types already reviewed from this point of view: first, the differentiation, focusing at or near the top of the power structure, of political from religious bases of autonomous organization. Regarded from the religious side first, the most important consideration concerns ways by which religious developments have occurred that would establish bases of high valuation of strata independent of the politico-religious fusion; and would also shake up some of religion's traditionist stereotyping influence on the higher-status structure, thus facilitating political innovation.

Without leading to a major differentiation between "church" and "state" at the collectivity level, this has occurred to an important degree in a number of historical cases, most clearly in those associated with the developments underlying the "world religions." The problem of the nature and type of law as a generalized normative system is intimately involved in them.

In China, the general religious ferment—of

which Taoism and Confucianism were the nearly contemporary outcomes—was a source of a major loosening of the Chou pattern of social structure. By this structure, a kind of religio-political feudalism, tempered with a limited "patrimonial" level of bureaucracy, had become established on a river-valley basis. The Taoist wing of the religious movement led away from the institutionalization of any form of social responsibility; its only direct structural outcome was the establishment of rather unstable types of monastic collectivities and temple priesthoods. It must, however, have had a very important influence in freeing important higher-level population groups from unquestioned allegiance to the older order.

The Confucian wing of the religious movement became the positive source of a pattern of restructuring the society. The Confucians' general integrative doctrine began to set the tone for the society as a whole; they made an orderly polity under a morally responsible dynasty legitimate—with the Confucian priests, as Mandarin officials, assuming the main governing responsibility. On this basis, there was a tendency toward a consolidation of the special Chinese version of the two-class system, since under the Confucian definition of the system there was only one basic type of "superiority," that embodied in the socially responsible scholar-official. To state an apparent paradox: it was an extraordinary case of the "rationalization of traditionalism."

In India, religious autonomy reinforced traditionalism much more radically. Buddhism, at least in its earlier versions, was in this respect like Taoism, though it seems to have been more radical. Salvation lay in complete rejection of all worldly interests—including any kind of social responsibility. The only possible positive social organization sanctioned by Buddhism was the monastic community, composed of fellow-seekers of salvation. In relation to the general society, Buddhism's effect was mostly negative, since it tended to withdraw religious sanction from *any* sort of temporal social organization, including caste.

This problem probably underlay the bifurcation of the major Indian religious tradition into its Hindu and Buddhist streams, and led eventually to the virtual elimination of Buddhism from India. Hinduism took another path, sanctioning the traditional society as the base of departure for the quest for individual salvation. The Brahman priesthood, as the custodians of the historic religious tradition and of the main basis of legitimation of the social order, functioned to uphold consistently a traditional social order, in the most conservative sense. He who felt qualified might, with the Brah-

mans' positive encouragement, embark on the radical search for personal salvation—but only in the Buddhist manner, by renouncing all worldly responsibilities and interests.

The compromise between the two essential components of the Hindu tradition is expressed in the doctrine of the stages of life. According to this, the individual should spend part of his life fulfilling the traditional obligations of his social status. But later, typically when he has a mature son to take over these obligations, he should renounce the world and seek salvation. In a sense far more radical than that applying to Confucianism, Hinduism renounced any interest in exerting leverage over society on the basis of religious values. Thus the Indian conception of salvation was far more radical than China's—but its extreme otherworldliness meant, in one crucial context, a more drastic positive sanctioning of traditionalism.

In the ancient Greek and Semitic worlds, things were very different. The Greek movement developed in terms of a pattern of rationalization of the immanent order of the world, including the social world. In general, it did not break the fusion of religious and political components; but it made several new processes of differentiation possible. Culturally it laid the foundations of all subsequent Western philosophy and science—the foundations of what eventually became a main framework of secular culture. On a more direct social level it was, as noted, the major source of political democracy, and, in its Roman extension, of an independent, largely secularized legal system.

The keynote of the Greek contribution was a mode of rationalization very different from the Chinese, which could develop a dynamism independent of the structure of the given society. Under the conditions of antiquity, the spread of political democracy seemed inherently limited. But Greek secular culture and the Roman politico-legal system eventually permeated what for that time was an immense population, with an immense diversity of ethnic origins and character, and welded these into a relatively stable society. This society still retained the broad two-class pattern of stratification, but had an immensely greater range of diversification of components with varying characteristics. In religion, it was a "free" society in a sense that had not applied to any other historical case, and would not again be applicable until very modern times. One of its important features was its provisions of a ground in which a movement like Christianity could spread; it also contributed essential ingredients to it.

In the Semitic world, the most extreme source of religious leverage over social development originated—transcendental monotheism as institutionalized in Judaism, Christianity, and Islam. Christianity was to be the sole independent source of a very fundamental pattern of structural differentiation, the differentiation of church and state, that came to its first fruition within the framework of a generally Christian society only in the European Middle Ages and has undergone a series of complex developments since then.

Though this process of differentiation did not occur independently in either Judaism or Islam, in both movements the special emphasis on religion, and its character as stressing the commandments of a transcendental God, caused the high status and high sophistication of a class of experts in religious law. This is certainly one of the most important sources of a specialized commitment to intellectual values in the history of culture, besides the Indian religious intellectualism and the intellectualism originating in Greece.

Secular Elite Groups. In Christianity, perhaps the most important consequence of the differentiation of church and state was that it allowed the development of secular elite groups who did not have to, or could not, base the legitimation of their status on religious qualifications. Legitimation in relation to religious *values* was necessary; but this is very different from qualification for the performance of religious functions as such. This development, combined with the dynamism inherent in the Semitic type of religious transcendentalism, constituted a major impetus to the dynamic development of secular society independent of the traditionalizing influence which, in the long run, seems inherent in the fusion of religious and secular leadership.

Initially, the secular elite would necessarily be political, in a diffuse sense. But with the further development of secular society, other foci of differentiation could assume a prominent position—the foci based on legal as distinct from political competence and functions, on secular intellectual competence, and on functions in economic production.

Legal Professionalism. As noted above, legal experts emerged as a specialized elite group in the later history of Rome—for the first time in history, on a clearly secular basis. This model was fundamental to the re-emergence of Roman Law in postmedieval Europe. On the Continent, two important developments of partial differentiation occurred. The Catholic Church itself became an elaborately differentiated and rationalized system, whose most important aspects included the technical development of the Canon Law, heavily influenced by Roman Law. Within the Church, there were specialists in Canon Law. Though religiously committed,

these specialists were in a very different category from the ordinary priest, whose primary functions were sacramental and pastoral, or the Bishop, with his directly administrative functions. In the secular world, however, the legally trained expert civil servant eventually occupied a special place in the structure of the emerging territorial state. There was a virtual fusion of the higher administrative bureaucracy and one main branch of the legal profession. The revival of Roman Law in a secular context, in the Italian universities first, established a crucial connection between a branch of secular learning, the legal system, and the structure of governmental organization.

Law's independence from government, became most fully developed in England, which established patterns for the English-speaking world and beyond. The Continental type of civil service developed late in England, and when developed, it was largely dissociated from legal professionalism. The legal profession became established as an independent entity much earlier in England than on the Continent, and has a firm monopoly of access to judicial office, and its own corporate control of the bar through the Inns of Court. In contrast with this development on the Continent, in England it occurred essentially independently of the universities. In Europe generally, and particularly in England, the legal profession thus became a secular element of great consequence in social affairs—it was not a simple branch or organ of central political authority.

Bureaucratic Elites. Of the two more specifically political components of differentiation and hence of potential elite status, the bureaucratic is usually the first to develop a relative independence; it then divides into two branches, military and civil. In these terms, it is extremely difficult to establish and institutionalize a basis of independent elite status—independent above all of the central basis of political organization at the top level. The primary limitation here rests on what Weber called the problem of legitimation in a system of rational-legal authority.

The military is probably more problematical than the civil. This is concerned with the facts that (1) the use of physical force is itself in general ethically problematical; and (2) in most societies, war cannot be presumed a normal state of affairs, and therefore a military force necessarily spends a large part of the time not doing what it is trained to do. In many societies, activation of military forces is widely interpreted as a disastrous breakdown of normal order.

There is, perhaps, no major component of social structure that has such an ambiguous status. Societies often depend greatly on their military organization; and this dependence is peculiarly dramatic because of the emergency character and high immediate stakes of war. Command of organized force is often a crucial factor in the internal balance of a society, the more so the more unstable the society's balance is in other respects. Therefore, the military components tend to occupy a prominent, if not a dominant, place in political elites. On the other hand, there are problems: first, a particularly acute problem of legitimation; and second, the severe limitations of functional orientation to other problems in the society. As Weber indicated, from many points of view, notably the economic, war is specifically "irrational." These reasons probably cause the rarity of fully "professional" military forces in history, even at the officer level; and they probably underlie the strong tendency for military status to fuse with general hereditary upper-class status. This fusion has been prominent in medieval and post-medieval European history, where a military role was often a generally ascribed role of the male aristocrat. The connection has lasted, until very recent times, in the concept that an officer was a "gentleman" in the specific aristocratic sense.

In certain circumstances, this fusion could give the whole upper class a strongly militaristic cast. Japan, through a good deal of its history, and Prussia provide prominent examples of this. However, the fusion can also act as a strong brake on the militarization of the state. Early modern England, favored by her insular position, provides a good example of this. In the non-militaristic direction, the most important alternative to military professionalization has been treating the military role on an "amateur" basis, as a simple aspect of citizenship. A classic instance of this is the military organization of the Greek *polis;* in this case Sparta could become, as a political organization, virtually a professional army—but a very special kind of one. This militia pattern was also important in the American colonies.

Making high civil bureaucracies legitimate has posed a somewhat parallel problem. The moral problems are not so acute; but civil bureaucracy does not possess the dramatic possibilities of the military, nor can it seize control in emergency situations. These weaknesses are rooted in its primarily instrumental character, as symbolized by the concept of the civil "servant." Hence the articulation of civil bureaucracy with the top level of political structure has always been highly problematical. In general it has, therefore, been associated with "fusions," such as that of the Chinese Mandarins with gentry status, or the English

method of honoring the highest civil servants with knighthoods and other titles, in some sense and to some degree thus assimilating them to the aristocracy. If the civil servant were not originally a "gentleman," by being sufficiently successful he could eventually become one. Civil service's connection with legal training on the Continent was another example of this fusion. In general, an extensive civil service built up on a relatively strict "occupational" basis can be a major stable component of the upper political structure only when it is part of a much more extensive occupational system. This condition has been fulfilled only in the modern West, in very recent times.

Politicians. Politically elite elements based mainly on leadership in the democratic type of politics have emerged into prominence only in the modern West. This phenomenon appeared on a very small scale in Greece and Rome, but it was never very fully dissociated from ascribed class status, and it still proved unstable. To some degree, it re-emerged in the Italian city-states and in northern Europe during the Renaissance; but its big development occurred only in the late eighteenth and the nineteenth centuries in the West. Here the problem of legitimation is severe, because it is inseparable from the concept of "party," and hence contributes to *division* within the political community while purporting to serve it and its integration. The most successful examples seem to be the British (including the Dominions), the Scandinavian-Dutch, and the American. The first two have solved the dilemma by differentiating between an institutionalized sovereign who is above party, and a politically responsible government dependent on party backing. In America, the place of the sovereign is occupied by the written Constitution, which is held in equal sanctity.

Modern political democracy, especially in reference to its leadership component, is precarious and cannot be expected to operate without favoring conditions. In the British and Scandinavian cases, these conditions include the civil service's partial fusion with the aristocracy, along with the British custom of elevating prominent politicians to the Peerage, whatever their party affiliation or social origin. In America, the most important condition is probably the vast extension of the upper occupational system and the associated cushion of private wealth, which mean that any prominent politician usually can, in case of political difficulty, find "jobs" of acceptable status. In both systems, the legal profession is a special case. A large number of politicians—particularly members of Parliament, of Congress, and of state legislatures—are lawyers. This is caused by the lawyer's special "expertness" in politics, and by the fact that a legal practice can be conducted relatively easily on a part-time basis—an individual can neglect it and then resume it, leaving its conducting to his partners while he is otherwise engaged. This is a functional equivalent of the *Honoratiorenherrschaft*, which Weber considered important and which is by no means dead today.

The "breakdown," or reversion, of modern political democracy in the totalitarian (as distinguished from the "legitimist") direction seems related to the strains of differentiating a "politician" elite from other elite components. This eases the strains involved in openly institutionalized division and factionalism, but does so at the expense of driving the conflicts of interest, and their underlying orientation, underground. In this situation, the totalitarian party, because of the urgency of its problem of legitimation, tends to assume at least a quasi-religious status. Relative to the general process of differentiation under analysis, it represents at least a partial "de-differentiation."

Secular Cultural Elites. Another important kind of differentiation focusing near the top of the status hierarchy is the one centering about the role of secular intellectual and aesthetic culture. In an important sense, in the Western world the element of rational theology, derived largely from Greece, contains at least the seeds of this differentiation. Thus in the medieval Church, theology and Scholastic philosophy, originally almost indistinguishable from each other, each became the basis of a specialized professional group, distinct from the Church hierarchy's sacramental and administrative functions. To a certain degree, the same was applicable to the semi-independence of Canon Law within the Church.

The origins of the Western university are associated with the relative secularization of philosophy and letters, oriented particularly to the classical heritage, and with secular law. In general, the universities included theology, but in a separate faculty. Then they added medicine; and as the natural sciences emerged, they could find a place. The problems of the independence of universities, and of various types of private scholars and artists, have been subtle and difficult, with the patterning taking many forms. In certain cases, emancipation from Church control meant only falling under the control of political authority. Another important pattern is patronage by noblemen. But by and large, whatever the source of economic support, the general trend has been toward establishing a complex of mostly autonomous professional groups definitely belonging to the upper social strata, though usually not to the hereditary aristoc-

racy. After about 1850, with the development of science to a position of major social importance, this has become one of the few major points of reference for the organization of the general system of social stratification.

There has always been an important connection between some order of formal education and the conduct of the leadership functions in the society as a whole. In earlier phases, the main foci of learning have been in groups of religious specialists—even the Confucian literati can be counted in this category, if one recognizes that they were also a political elite. The classical intellectual traditions disseminated literary culture to an extent unattained by any prior civilization; and its revival in the Renaissance established one major cultural foundation of Western society. But in the nineteenth century, with the advent of social and political democracy and the development of science, for the first time in history general literacy and increasingly higher levels of mass education appeared. The university system constitutes the main institutionalized focus of trusteeship of this great development of secular knowledge and learning. It is perhaps the most important structural component of modern societies that had no direct counterpart in earlier types of society.

The institutionalization of intellectual culture includes both "pure" scholars and scientists, and also the applied professions. The oldest of these are theology and law; medicine emerges quite early, in spite of the deficiencies in its scientific base. In the earlier stages even of the Industrial Revolution, most technological innovation—to say nothing of routine administration of processes—was in the hands of "inventors" who were not scientifically, often not even academically, trained. During the last two generations, however, these modes of competence have converged; and with this convergence has come the enormously increased practical importance of personnel with high intellectual training, especially in the sciences. Recently, in an unmistakably significant way, this has begun to be extended to the disciplines dealing scientifically with human behavior and social relationships.

The Business Class: Entrepreneurship and Management. The last of the primary bases of differentiation that enters importantly into the structure of stratification systems is the economic. As noted, the economic base, as an independent focus, on a large scale, has been a late development, and it has come mainly from "below." Its operation as a mass phenomenon forming a major independent focus of the social structure is confined to the modern West. In terms of economic structure as such, the crucial focus is the extension of "private

enterprise" into the field of manufacturing, as
distinguished both from commerce and from primary or "extractive" production.

It is essential to distinguish two main phases of
the process, each having quite different consequences for stratification. The first phase is the
emergence in manufacturing of "family firm"
capitalism—where, though the main "labor force"
was composed of "employees" standing in widely
varying modes of relation to their employers, the
ownership and managerial functions were fused in
a kinship unit, in which status was, once the firm
had been "founded," definitely ascriptive. It was
a kind of petty monarchy, flanked by a hereditary
aristocracy, within its own little sphere. Because of
the common organization in lineage terms, members of the bourgeois class fitted, in this area, into
a pattern which was structurally isomorphic with
that of the aristocracies already occupying the top
positions of prestige in their own societies. Consequently, there was powerful ambition to secure
acceptance as aristocratic lineages; and through
much of Europe, a good deal of actual fusion of
these two population elements did occur. This was
probably most successful in England, but the
strong focus on it was most persistent in France.[17]
This structural pattern obviously bears on the
plausibility of treating the Western class system
after the Industrial Revolution on a polarized
basis.

This situation has been fundamentally changed
by the "occupationalizing" of the management of
economic production. As noted, managerial functions have been dissociated from the property
interests of owning groups—particularly tightly
held property complexes. Concomitantly, a managerial class has developed whose status is not
dependent on a personal property stake in the
enterprise nor on an ascribed position in an owning
lineage. Business administration has become a
career line, comparable to civil service or a profession. In close association with this development,
a much larger contingent of professional experts
occupying more strategic positions than ever before have become involved in industrial and governmental bureaucracies. The role of lawyers is
relatively old in both connections, though its importance has increased. The roles of engineers, and
more lately of research scientists, on any com-

parable scale, are a relatively recent development.
In the United States, and increasingly in Western
Europe, the main control of productive wealth
through kinship lineage, which was a continuation from the feudal background of the Western
class system, has, for practical purposes, been
broken for the pace-setting large business element
of the economy.

In terms of social stratification, this has meant
a shift from an upper group, primarily organized
about the prestige of kinship lineages, to one primarily organized about occupational status. Since
the family remains the primary unit of class structure, continuity of status between adjacent generations is a very important factor. But the link to
the *particular* organizational unit of production
has largely been broken; and, especially if there is
general expansion, and hence considerable upward
mobility. The system of formal education has been
becoming increasingly significant as the major
channel of this mobility.

Occupational Differentiation and Stratification.
For the higher-level structures of the stratification
system, the fact that the occupational system itself
has become so highly differentiated in its upper
levels is most important. A complex network of
upper "groups" (which it is somewhat dangerous
to reify) has developed. There are the great organizations—in civil and military government; in
business with many different branches; in education, science, and research; in health care; and in
religion. In addition, *cross-cutting* the differentiation of organizations, there is occupational differentiation between executives and administrators,
the various types of professional people at levels
dealing with science and learning as such and with
many different applied fields. There are politicians
and promoters of many kinds of causes, including
organizers of associations. It is certainly a stratified society; but it no longer has anything like a
unitary elite based on lineages, on wealth, on
political power, or on monopoly of religious
legitimation.

A crucial development has also occurred in the
lower levels of the stratification system—the great
historic dichotomy between urban lower classes and
peasantry has been virtually eliminated. Only 10 per
cent of the labor force is engaged in agriculture now
in the United States—one of the greatest of all agricultural societies. Furthermore, agriculture itself
has become much more assimiliated to the rest of
economic production; it is no longer anything approaching a "peasant" type of production. The
whole lower range of the social structure has become urbanized and, in a very broad sense,
"industrialized"—but definitely *not,* in the Marx-

17. The concept that the driving motive of the entrepreneur was to establish a "family dynasty" has been
perhaps most forcefully put forward by Schumpeter in
Capitalism, Socialism and Democracy, N.Y. & London:
Harper & Bros., 1942. For an illuminating analysis of an
earlier phase see Elinor Barber, *The Bourgeoisie in
Eighteenth-Century France,* Princeton Univ. Press, 1955,
also Jesse R. Pitts, "The Bourgeois Family and French
Economic Retardation," Ph.D thesis, Harvard Univ., 1958.

ian sense, "proletarianized." The proportion of the population engaged in industrial labor (narrowly defined) has declined; and there has been an enormous development of the "tertiary" sector of the economy. Even more important, the lower fringe of the early industrial labor role has been almost eliminated by the general upgrading process, in which mechanization and education have played primary parts.

Modern industrial society has, probably for the first time in the history of complex societies, developed a situation making simple polarization of the social structure in terms of the opposing interests of generalized upper and lower groups impossible. Ironically, the most modern version of a theory of radical two-class conflict became prominent just at the time when a social structure to which this theory was drastically inapplicable began to develop. The appeal of radical Marxism has been in roughly inverse proportion to the level of industrialization of the society in question—exactly the contrary of Marx's own prediction.

The irony can be carried a step farther. Various observers have noted that, in certain structural respects, there were a series of characteristics common to all industrial societies—both the capitalist or free enterprise type of the West, and the socialist type of the Soviet Union. These characteristics especially concern the occupational structure, in the sense just outlined, and particularly the development of an occupational managerial class and of a class of professional technical experts in many different fields. The important difference between the two types of society concerns the relation of the economy to the political structure, and the latter's character. In the West the problems are the stability of political democracy, and the legal and normative maintenance of the relative independence of economic organization from government. Both these structural patterns are deeply rooted in the long-run evolutionary trends of social development.

In the U.S.S.R., the primary problem concerns the long-run status of the Communist Party—can this quasi-religious structure remain differentiated from the "state" and still maintain a very tight control over it? This question involves both the status of religion (in the more analytical sense), and the possibilities of relaxing control in the direction of political democratization. The major problem is closely linked to the latter—it is the question of bases of genuine autonomy, relative to both party and state, of non-political spheres of organization; notably both of the economy, and of the professions and the services in which they are involved. At present, the most acute focus of tendencies to

seek this type of autonomy is the "intellectuals"—in what sense may science and the arts be treated as the simple handmaidens of the Party?

In the long run (though perhaps not in the near future), we feel that the pressures to genuine structural differentiation in the upper levels may well be irresistible—though it is difficult to anticipate the exact ways this differentiation can occur. In any case, in the present, Western "capitalism" cannot be described in Marxian terms as a two-class society; nor can Soviet society be described as a one-class society, least of all if that one class is claimed to be the "proletariat." Each society has been becoming progressively more highly differentiated, in two ways: in terms of the number of levels in a scale of stratification; and, more important, in terms of a cross-cutting web of relations of the *qualitative* differentiation of collectivities and role-types that must be integrated with each other by mechanisms other than the simple maintenance of hierarchical control. This differentiation is most important in the higher strata. Concepts like hierarchical polarization, and the differentiation of the "masses" from "power-elites" and from controllers of capital are not adequate for analyzing the integration of such a society.

CONCLUSION

The above outline of comparative social structure has been sketched from a frankly evolutionary frame of reference. We have taken the concept of ascriptive solidarities as not merely designating one structural type, but as a broad evolutionary base line. In the process, old ascriptive solidarities are "whittled away," and in a wide variety of ways, new ones are created—e.g., those of feudalism, which are certainly not primitive, and of such structures as the Communist party. However, the *relative* importance of ascriptive solidarity tends to decline, though the process is uneven and reversions are common—the fall of the Roman Empire was such a reversion, and on the largest scale.

Within this framework, there are two keynotes of the evolutionary process. One is the very broad leadership role of innovation in the field of cultural orientation. In earlier stages of innovation, this leadership is usually carried by a diffuse religio-political elite. But a critically important phenomenon is the emergence of the type of autonomous religious orientation which is in a position to exert generalized leverage on the development of a society or complex of societies. The

Semitic religious complex provides the grandest-scale example of this.

A very important innovating role can be played by other types of structural component—especially by the political, as it is differentiated from the religious, the legal, the non-religious aspects of culture (notably science), and the economic. Our broad conviction, however, is that the primary significance of these latter components lies in the context of differentiation, rather than in the context of the broadest leadership of structural innovation, i.e., at the level of values.

We are concerned with differentiation in the structure of the society as a system. We presume a multiple origin of human societies, or at least great dispersion of small units which became socially, culturally, and biologically segmented or differentiated from one another. Partly because of independent origins, partly because of fissions and amalgamations, a variety of societies have existed in the world at any one time, in widely varying degrees and modes of contact with each other. But there has been a process of differentiation within societies as well as among them. We have attempted to outline the place of the principal elements in each of the five main categories of our classification of selections in terms of their relation to various aspects and phases of that process.

In outlining these relations, we have tried to work on intermediate ground. With a great deal more work than has gone into this introductory essay, it might have been possible to attempt a far more strictly systematic morphological analysis than that presented here. Such an analysis would have started from the broad conceptual scheme of the social system presented in the second essay of the General Introduction, and then attempted to work it through in the relevant contexts. But this would have been a very onerous task; and it would have involved departing much farther from the level of the selections which follow, and would have made their mutual relevance difficult for the reader to see.

On the other hand, the selections themselves do not contain any single consistent morphological scheme. Such a scheme did not exist in the generation when these selections were written—though Weber had made great advances toward one. Hence it has seemed advisable to attempt to be as systematic and consistent as possible without attempting to be rigorously formal. Our purpose is to present, as a guide to the interpretation of the selections, a general picture consistent both with the best theory we have and with the present level of empirical knowledge, but to do so without the complex paraphernalia of a highly technical and detailed analytical procedure.

There will be a very brief Foreword to each of the five sections of selections below. These are meant to give the reader a general guide to the nature of the selections, and to explain why they were chosen and organized as they are.

Section A

Ascriptive Solidarities

Editorial Foreword, BY TALCOTT PARSONS   *267*

I–KINSHIP

1. *Systems of Consanguinity,* BY LEWIS H. MORGAN   *269*
2. *Classificatory Systems of Relationship,* BY ALFRED L. KROEBER   *271*
3. *The Complex of Mother-Right,* BY BRONISLAW MALINOWSKI   *276*
4. *The Study of Kinship Systems,* BY A. R. RADCLIFFE-BROWN   *278*
5. *The Household Community,* BY MAX WEBER   *296*

II–ETHNIC SOLIDARITIES

1. *Ethnic Groups,* BY MAX WEBER   *305*
2. *The Problem of Minority Groups,* BY LOUIS WIRTH   *309*

III–PRIMARY GROUPS

1. *Primary Groups,* BY CHARLES H. COOLEY   *315*
2. *Secrecy and Group Communication,* BY GEORG SIMMEL   *318*
3. *The Sociological Category of Communion,* BY HERMAN SCHMALENBACH   *331*
4. *The Organization of the Primary Working Group,* BY F. J. ROETHLIS-
   BERGER AND WILLIAM J. DICKSON   *348*
5. *The Solidarity of Occupational Groups,* BY EMILE DURKHEIM   *356*

IV–TERRITORIAL COMMUNITY

1. *On the Origins of the State,* BY ROBERT H. LOWIE   *364*
2. *The Village Community,* BY SIR HENRY SUMNER MAINE   *370*
3. *The Urban Community,* BY MAX WEBER   *380*
4. *European Feudalism,* BY MARC BLOCH   *385*
5. *Nationality,* BY LORD ACTON   *392*

Ascriptive Solidarities

by Talcott Parsons

As observed in the intro-duction to this Part of the Reader, the analysis of ascriptive solidarities is the point of departure for the treatment of the structure of social systems with which we are concerned. The importance of these reference points has always been known and appre-ciated. Until the generation with which we are concerned, however, they had received very little of the kind of attention which can be a source of genuinely technical analysis—though we are in-cluding selections from two authors of an earlier period, Morgan and Maine, who laid important foundations for such analysis.

The two major foci of the problem are biological relatedness as the ascriptive basis of kinship struc-ture, and the territorial location of persons and their activities. These foci converge at the concept of residence. Because of limitations on the tech-nology of communication and transportation, the earlier the society's stage of evolution, the more closely its territorial organization is bound to the residential locations and distribution of popula-tions.

The most important development of the struc-tural analysis of kinship occurred after the period most represented in these volumes. The leaders were the group of British social anthropologists, and a few others, like Levy-Strauss in France. We have included only a few samples of the most im-portant contributions to initiating this develop-ment. Morgan may be regarded as the founder of the technical analysis of kinship. He was the first to consider seriously the problems presented by the existence of kinship systems differing radically from those taken for granted in the intellectual traditions of the Western world. These differing systems were presented to him in material on American Indians but were also becoming recog-nized as widely distributed among non-literate societies in many parts of the world.

Kroeber's famous paper on classificatory systems brought Morgan up to date by purging him of many associations with now untenable evolution-ary ideas, and relating the problem to the growing body of research, in which Kroeber himself played a prominent part. Certainly, in American anthro-pology Kroeber's paper was the major starting point of truly modern analysis of kinship.

Malinowski's paper is selected partly because of Malinowski's general importance in this field.[1] But it is included particularly because of his contribu-tion to recognizing the importance of the broadest type of pattern of descent, apart from "classifica-tory" components as such, contrasting violently with the common sense of Western social studies, namely, matrilineal descent. By the latter part of the generation concerned, this problem had become a central preoccupation of the analysis of kinship systems in general.

That generation's contribution in this field cul-minated in the work of Radcliffe-Brown. Though it was written after our terminal point, we would have liked to include his classic Introduction to the volume *African Systems of Kinship and Marriage* (London: Oxford University Press, 1950). Because of its length and the impossibility of making a meaningful selection from it, we have reluctantly included instead an earlier statement, taken from *Structure and Function in Primitive Society*. No other writer of the period reached a level of general analysis in the kinship field comparable with Radcliffe-Brown's.

---

1. See Meyer Fortes, "Malinowski and the Study of Kinship," in Raymond Firth (ed.), *Man and Culture* (London: Routledge, Kegan & Paul, 1957).

Max Weber was not an expert in the analysis of kinship. His major interests were in a different set of aspects of the structure of social systems. In spite of this, however, he was unusually sensitive to the importance of kinship problems. A brief selection from his work is included here, for this reason, and also because it is one of the best works written in that generation on the significance of the household as a residential unit, linking kinship with territorial location. This is a theme of great importance, which Murdock has probably most fully developed so far. It should receive increasing attention in the future.

We have treated ethnic solidarity as an extension of the reference point of kinship. Though it is a very important theme in social analyses, there have been few attempts to treat it in really general terms. We have selected, from a very large and diffuse literature bearing on the subject, only two samples—a brief selection from Weber that belongs in a very general comparative setting, and one from the late Louis Wirth that deals with the problem in recent phases of development of American society. Because the available space here is so limited, only a token recognition of the importance of the problem was possible.

The subject of primary groups is included here, not because they are in the strict sense ascriptive in structural focus, but because of the direct psychological continuity between kinship and all other primary group structures. The keynote is the base in social structure for the individual's psychological security. In all societies, this security is rooted in the kinship system, especially the nuclear family— first of orientation, then of procreation. In the process of social differentiation, however, it can be generalized from this base to non-kin groups.

The selections relevant in this area illustrate a variety of this type of possibilities. Cooley's famous general statement that introduced the concept of the primary group into sociology is the inevitable starting point. Simmel's essay on secrecy indicates the importance of the ways in which primary groups erect barriers to communication with outsiders and thereby protect their internal solidarity. For Simmel, secrecy shades into important problems of privileged communication and privacy. Schmalenbach was one of the first to analyze the importance of "fraternal" groupings, e.g., "brotherhoods" of various kinds and the one-sex peer group. In certain respects, they may be described as deriving, by affective generalization, from the sibling relationship.

Later research has been particularly concerned with the importance of these types of relation in the area ordinarily associated with Toennies' *Gesellschaft.* The Western Electric studies made at the very end of that generation present a classic instance of the development of primary groups within modern occupational contexts under the heading of "informal organization." Durkheim's famous Introduction to the second edition of his *Division of Labor* proposes that principles somehow related to this context may be extended to larger units of social solidarity. The more general theoretical problems associated with personal security and its relation to the personality's regressive substructures will be discussed more fully in Part Three; and the way they fit the analysis of social structure will be discussed in the Introductions to that and its subsections.

The last subsection of Section A concerns the territorial reference point of ascriptive solidarity. Its relation to the residence of the household unit of kinship was recognized in Section A, Subsection I, fifth selection—Weber's statement. This is taken for granted. The importance of a wider territorial principle in primitive societies has, however, been widely neglected. Lowie, in the *Origin of the State,* was one of the first to indicate clearly the importance of this principle—even in that prototype of primitiveness, the Australian society. Then Sir Henry Maine, through his studies in India, was one of the first to emphasize the village community's importance as a general pattern of social organization oriented to a territorial base. Weber, far more than any other writer, has helped to clarify the problems of the nature of urban communities on a comparative basis. The two last selections deal with the higher-order integration of populations in politically organized societies with reference to territoriality—these selections are Marc Bloch's classic delineation of this aspect of European feudalism, and Lord Acton's famous discussion of the nationality principle.

The connection between the territorial principle and the general field of political organization and jurisdiction is of paramouut importance. The last subsection of Section A should be regarded as leading into the materials of Section D, on Political Organization and Authority. Their connection will be discussed again in the Introduction to Section D.

I–KINSHIP

1. Systems of Consanguinity

BY LEWIS H. MORGAN

IN CONSIDERING the elements of a system of consanguinity the existence of marriage between single pairs must be assumed. Marriage forms the basis of relationships. In the progress of the inquiry it may become necessary to consider a system with this basis fluctuating, and, perhaps, altogether wanting. The alternative assumption of each may be essential to include all the elements of the subject in its practical relations. The natural and necessary connection of *consanguinei* with each other would be the same in both cases; but with this difference, that in the former the lines of descent from parent to child would be known, while in the latter they would, to a greater or less extent, be incapable of ascertainment. These considerations might affect the form of the system of consanguinity.

The family relationships are as ancient as the *family*. They exist in virtue of the law of derivation, which is expressed by the perpetuation of the species through the marriage relation. A system of consanguinity, which is founded upon a community of blood, is but the formal expression and recognition of these relationships. Around every person there is a circle or group of kindred of which such person is the centre, the *Ego,* from whom the degree of the relationship is reckoned, and to whom the relationship itself returns. Above him are his father and his mother and their ascendants, below him are his children and their descendants; while upon either side are his brothers and sisters and their descendants, and the brothers and sisters of his father and of his mother and their descendants, as well as a much greater number of collateral relatives descended from common ancestors still more remote. To him they are nearer in degree than other individuals of the nation at large. A formal arrangement of the more imme-

diate blood kindred into lines of descent, with the adoption of some method to distinguish one relative from another, and to express the value of the relationship, would be one of the earliest acts of human intelligence.

Should the inquiry be made how far nature suggests a uniform method or plan for the discrimination of the several relationships, and for the arrangement of kindred into distinct lines of descent, the answer would be difficult, unless it was first assumed that marriage between single pairs had always existed, thus rendering definite the lines of parentage. With this point established, or assumed, a natural system, numerical in its character, will be found underlying any form which man may contrive; and which, resting upon an ordinance of nature, is both universal and unchangeable. All of the descendants of an original pair, through intermediate pairs, stand to each other in fixed degrees of proximity, the nearness or remoteness of which is a mere matter of computation. If we ascend from ancestor to ancestor in the lineal line, and again descend through the several collateral lines until the widening circle of kindred circumscribes millions of the living and the dead, all of these individuals, in virtue of their descent from common ancestors, are bound to the "*Ego*" by the chain of consanguinity.

The blood relationships, to which specific terms have been assigned, under the system of the Aryan family, are few in number. They are grandfather and grandmother, father and mother, brother and sister, son and daughter, grandson and granddaughter, uncle and aunt, nephew and niece, and cousin. Those more remote in degree are described either by an augmentation or by a combination of these terms. After these are the affineal or marriage relationships, which are husband and wife, father-in-law and mother-in-law, son-in-law and daughter-in-law, brother-in-law and sister-in-law, step-father and step-mother, step-son and step-daughter, and step-brother and step-sister; together

Reprinted from Lewis H. Morgan, *Systems of Consanguinity and Affinity* ("Smithsonian Contributions to Knowledge," Vol. XVII [Washington, D.C.: Smithsonian Institute, 1870]), Part I, chap. ii, pp. 10–11; Part III, chap. vi, pp. 470–72.

with such of the husbands and wives of blood relatives as receive the corresponding designation by courtesy. These terms are barely sufficient to indicate specifically the nearest relationships, leaving much the largest number to be described by a combination of terms.

So familiar are these ancient household words, and the relationships which they indicate, that a classification of kindred by means of them, according to their degrees of nearness, would seem to be not only a simple undertaking, but, when completed, to contain nothing of interest beyond its adaptation to answer a necessary want. But, since these specific terms are entirely inadequate to designate a person's kindred, they contain in themselves only the minor part of the system. An arrangement into lines, with descriptive phrases to designate such relatives as fall without the specific terms, becomes necessary to its completion. In the mode of arrangement and of description diversities may exist. Every system of consanguinity must be able to ascend and descend in the lineal line through several degrees from any given person, and to specify the relationship of each to *Ego;* and also from the lineal, to enter the several collateral lines and follow and describe the collateral relatives through several generations. When spread out in detail and examined, every scheme of consanguinity and affinity will be found to rest upon definite ideas, and to be framed, so far as it contains any plan, with reference to particular ends. In fine, a system of relationship, originating in necessity, is a domestic institution, which serves to organize a family by the bond of consanguinity. As such it possesses a degree of vitality and a power of self-perpetuation commensurate with its nearness to the primary wants of man.

*   *   *

Do these systems of relationship rest upon and embody clearly defined ideas and principles; and do they contain the essential requisites of a domestic institution?

Some method of distinguishing the different degrees of consanguinity is an absolute necessity for the daily purposes of life. The invention of terms to express the primary relationships, namely, those for father and mother, brother and sister, son and daughter, and husband and wife, would probably be one of the earliest acts of human speech. With these terms all of the remaining relatives, both by blood and marriage, may be described by using the possessive case of the several terms. The Erse and Gaelic systems were never carried beyond this stage. After a descriptive system was adopted it would have a form, a method of distinguishing relatives one from another, and, as a consequence, an arrangement of kindred into lines of descent. The application of this method involves a series of conceptions which become, at the same time, clothed with definite forms. If this simple plan of consanguinity became permanently introduced into practical use, its transmission, through a few generations, would convert it into an indurated system capable of resisting radical innovations. The Erse and Gaelic are illustrations in point. The ideas embodied are few in number, but their association in fixed relations creates a system, as well as organizes a family. In its connection with the family, and in its structure as a system, its power of self-perpetuation resides. By these considerations it is raised to the rank of a domestic institution.

The invention of terms for collateral relationships must of necessity have been extremely difficult under the descriptive system. This is shown by the present condition of these forms in the several Aryan and Semitic nations, none of which developed their system far beyond the Erse. In process of time the relationship of paternal and maternal *uncle* and *aunt* might be turned from the descriptive into the concrete form by the invention of special terms, making each of the four distinct. This is the extent of the advance made in the Arabic and Hebraic forms. The discrimination of the relationships of *nephew* and *niece* in the concrete would be still more difficult, since it involves a generalization of the children of an individual's brothers and sisters into one class, and the turning of two descriptive phrases into a single concrete term with a masculine and feminine form. These relationships, as now used, were reached among such of the Aryan nations as possess them within the modern period. That of *cousin* was still more difficult of attainment, as it involved a generalization of four different classes of persons into a single class, and the invention of a term to express it in the concrete. Amongst the nations of the Aryan family the Roman and the German alone reached this, the ultimate stage of the system. Such of the remaining nations as possess this relationship borrowed it, with the term, from the Roman source; and it is probable that the Germans derived the conception from the same quarter, although their term was indigenous in the German speech. These terms were designed to relieve the inconvenience of the descriptive method as far as they applied. In so far as they were founded upon generalizations they failed, with some exceptions, to indicate with accuracy the manner of the relationships; whence it became necessary to resort to explanatory words, or to the descriptive method, to be specific. These considerations tend still further to show the stability of the system as a domestic institution, although the ideas which it embodies are limited in number.

In marked contrast with the *descriptive* is the *classificatory* system, which is complex in its structure, elaborate in its discriminations, and opulent in its nomenclature. A very different and more striking series of ideas and principles here present themselves, without any existing causes adequate for their interpretation or explanation. With marriage between single pairs, with the family in a modified sense, with the tribal organization still unimpaired in certain nations and abandoned in others, with polygamy, polyandria and the Hawaiian custom either unknown or of limited practice, and with promiscuous intercourse substantially eradicated, the classificatory system of relationship still exists in full vigor in a large portion of the human family, ages upon ages after the sequence of customs and institutions in which it apparently originated have ceased to exercise any influence upon its form or upon its preservation. This system as it now stands is seen to magnify the bond of consanguinity into stupendous proportions, and to use it as an organic instrument for the formation of a communal family upon the broadest scale of numbers. Differences in the degree of nearness are made to yield to the overmastering strength of the kindred tie. Its generalizations traverse the natural lines of descent, as they now exist through the marriage of single pairs, disregard equalities in the degree of nearness of related persons, and create relationships in contravention of those actually existing. There are upwards of twenty of these particulars, each of which develops a distinct idea, all uniting in the formation of a coherent intelligible and systematic plan of consanguinity. From the excessive and intricate specializations embodied in the system it might be considered difficult of practical use; but it is not the least singular of its characteristics that it is complicated without obscurity, diversified without confusion, and understood and applied with the utmost facility. With such a number of distinct ideas associated together in definite relations, a system has been created which must be regarded as a domestic institution in the highest sense of this expression. No other can properly characterize a structure the framework of which is so complete, and the details of which are so rigorously adjusted.

2. *Classificatory Systems of Relationship*

BY ALFRED L. KROEBER

THE DISTINCTION between classificatory and descriptive systems of relationship has been widely accepted, and has found its way into handbooks and general literature. According to the prevalent belief the systems of certain nations or languages group together distinct relationships and call them by one name, and are therefore classifying. Other systems of consanguinity are said to indicate secondary differences of relationship by descriptive epithets added to their primary terms and to be therefore descriptive.

Nothing can be more fallacious than this common view. A moment's reflection is sufficient to show that every language groups together under single designations many distinct degrees and kinds

Reprinted from Alfred L. Kroeber, *The Nature of Culture* (Chicago: University of Chicago Press, 1952), sec. 19, pp. 175–81, with the permission of the University of Chicago Press. Copyright 1952 by the University of Chicago.

of relationship. Our word brother includes both the older and the younger brother and the brother of a man and of a woman. It therefore embraces or classifies four relationships. The English word cousin denotes both men and women cousins; cousins on the father's or on the mother's side; cousins descended from the parent's brother or the parent's sister; cousins respectively older or younger than one's self, or whose parents are respectively older or younger than the speaker's parents; and cousins of men or women. Thirty-two different relationships are therefore denoted by this one English word. If the term is not strictly limited to the significance of first cousin, the number of distinct ideas that it is capable of expressing is many times thirty-two. Since then it is not only primitive people that classify or fail to distinguish relationships, the suspicion is justified that the current distinction between the two classes or systems of indicating relationship is subjective, and has its origin in the point of view of investigators, who, on approaching foreign languages, have been impressed with their failure to discriminate certain relationships between which the languages of civilized Europe distinguish, and who, in the enthusiasm of formulating general theories from such facts, have forgotten that their own languages are filled with entirely analogous groupings or classifications which custom has made so familiar and natural that they are not felt as such.

The total number of different relationships which can be distinguished is very large, and reaches at least many hundred. No language possesses different terms for all of these or even for any considerable proportion of them. In one sense it is obvious that a language must be more classificatory as the number of its terms of relationship is smaller. The number of theoretically possible relationships remaining constant, there must be more ideas grouped under one term in proportion as the number of terms is less. Following the accepted understanding of what constitutes classificatory consanguinity, English, with its twenty terms of relationship, must be not less but more classificatory than the languages of all primitive people who happen to possess twenty-five, thirty, or more terms.

It is clear that if the phrase classificatory consanguinity is to have any meaning it must be sought in some more discriminating way. The single fact that another people group together various relationships which our language distinguishes does not make their system classificatory. If there is a general and fundamental difference between the systems of relationship of civilized and uncivilized people, its basis must be looked for in something more exact than the rough-and-ready expressions of subjective point of view that have been customary.

It is apparent that what we should try to deal with is not the hundreds or thousands of slightly varying relationships that are expressed or can be expressed by the various languages of man, but the principles or categories of relationship which underlie these. Eight such categories are discernible.

1. *The Difference between Persons of the Same and of Separate Generations.*—The distinctions between father and grandfather, between uncle and cousin, and between a person and his father, involve the recognition of this category.

2. *The Difference between Lineal and Collateral Relationship.*—When the father and the father's brother are distinguished, this category is operative. When only one term is employed for brother and cousin, it is inoperative.

3. *Difference of Age within One Generation.*—The frequent distinction between the older and the younger brother is an instance. In English this category is not operative.

4. *The Sex of the Relative.*—This distinction is carried out so consistently by English, the one exception being the foreign word cousin, that the discrimination is likely to appear self-evident. By many people, however, many relationships are not distinguished for sex. Grandfather and grandmother, brother-in-law and sister-in-law, father-in-law and mother-in-law, and even such close relationships as son and daughter, are expressed respectively by single words.

5. *The Sex of the Speaker.*—Unrepresented in English and most European languages, this category is well known to be of importance in many other languages. The father, mother, brother, sister, and more distant relatives may receive one designation from a man and another from his sister.

6. *The Sex of the Person through Whom Relationship Exists.*—English does not express this category. In consequence we frequently find it necessary to explain whether an uncle is a father's or a mother's brother, and whether a grandmother is paternal or maternal.

7. *The Distinction of Blood Relatives from Connections by Marriage.*—While this distinction is commonly expressed by most languages, there are occasional lapses; just as in familiar English speech the father-in-law is often spoken of as father. Not strictly within the domain of relationship, but analogous to the occasional failure to express this category, is the frequent ignoring on the part of primitive people of the difference between actual relatives and fictitious clan or tribal relatives.

8. *The Condition of Life of the Person through Whom Relationship Exists.*—The relationship may be either of blood or by marriage; the person serving as the bond of relationship may be alive or dead, married or no longer married. Many North American Indians refrain from using such terms as "father-in-law" and "mother-in-law" after the wife's death or separation. Some go so far as to possess terms restricted to such severed relationship. It is natural that the uncle's relation to his orphaned nephew should tend to be somewhat different from his relation to the same boy while his natural protector, his father, was living. Distinct terms are therefore sometimes found for relatives of the uncle and aunt group after the death of a parent.

The adjoined table indicates the representation of the eight categories, and the degree to which they find expression, respectively in English and in several of the Indian languages of North America.

It appears that English gives expression to only four categories. With the exception, however, of the one and foreign word cousin, every term in Eng-

	ENG-LISH	N.A. INDIAN					CALIFORNIA INDIAN						
		Arap-aho	Da-kota	Paw-nee	Skoko-mish	Chi-nook	Yuki	Pomo	Washo	Mi-wok	Yo-kuts	Lui-seño	Mo-have
No. of terms	21*	20	31	19	18	28	24	27	28	24	28	34	35
Generation	21	20	31	11	13	23	24	21	27	24	22	30	26
Blood or marriage	21	19	31	17	18	26	24	27	28	24	28	32	34
Lineal or collateral	21	10	20	5	11	25	24	21	28	18	26	34	28
Sex of relative	20	18	29	17	2	12	16	21	20	20	17	18	22
Sex of connecting relative	0	6	6	2	0	20	13	13	14	10	14	19	21
Sex of speaker	0	3	18	4	0	15	3	3	10	2	12	10	14
Age in generation	0	3	7	2	2	2	3	4	4	4	4	12	8
Condition of connecting relative	0	0	0	0	8	1	0	0	0	0	†	0	1

* All terms are omitted, such as great-grandfather, great-uncle, and second cousin, which are not generally used in ordinary speech and exist principally as a reserve available for specific discrimination on occasion.

† Terms denoting relatives by marriage undergo a vocalic change to indicate the death of the connecting relative.

lish involves the recognition of each of these four categories. All the Indian languages express from six to eight categories. Almost all of them recognize seven. But in all the Indian languages the majority of the categories occurring are expressed in only part of the terms of relationship found in the language. There are even Indian languages, such as Pawnee and Mohave, in which not a single one of the seven or eight categories finds expression in every term. While in English the degree of recognition which is accorded the represented categories is indicable by a percentage of 100 in all cases but one, when it is 95, in Pawnee corresponding percentages range variously from about 10 to 90, and in Mohave from 5 to 95. All the other Indian languages, as compared with English, closely approach the condition of Pawnee and Mohave.

It is clear that this difference is real and fundamental. English is simple, consistent, and so far as it goes, complete. The Indian systems of relationship all start from a more elaborate basis but carry out their scheme less completely. This is inevitable from the fact that the total number of terms of relationship employed by them is approximately the same as in English. The addition of only one category to those found in English normally doubles the number of terms required to give full expression to the system; and the presence of three additional categories multiplies the possible total by about eight. As the number of terms occurring in any of the Indian languages under consideration is not much more than half greater than in English, and sometimes is not greater at all, it is clear that at least some of their categories must find only very partial expression.

In short, as far as the expression of possible categories is concerned, English is less complete than any of the Indian languages; but as regards the giving of expression to the categories which it recognizes, English is more complete. In potentiality, the English scheme is poorer and simpler; but from its own point of view it is both more complete and more consistent. As English may evidently be taken as representative of European languages, it is in this point that the real difference is to be found between the systems that have been called classificatory and those that have been called descriptive.

The so-called descriptive systems express a small number of categories of relationship completely; the wrongly-named classificatory systems express a larger number of categories with less regularity. Judged from its own point of view, English is the less classificatory; looked at from the Indian point of view it is the more classificatory, inasmuch as in every one of its terms it fails to recognize certain distinctions often made in other languages; regarded from a general and comparative point of view, neither system is more or less classificatory.

In short, the prevalent idea of the classificatory system breaks down entirely under analysis. And in so far as there is a fundamental difference between the languages of European and of less civilized peoples in the method of denoting relationship, the difference can be determined only on the basis of the categories described and can be best expressed in terms of the categories.

A tendency toward reciprocal expression is sometimes of importance and may influence the degree to which categories are given expression. Reciprocal terms are such that all the persons included in the relationship expressed by one term call by one name all the persons who apply this term to them. In the most extreme form of reciprocity the two groups of relatives use the same term. The paternal grandparents call their sons' children, whether boys or girls, by the same term which these children, both boys and girls, apply to their fathers' parents. Nevertheless, the reciprocal relation is just as clear, though less strikingly expressed, when each of the groups uses a different term for the other. Our English words father and child, or brother and sister, are not reciprocal, for the term child is employed also by the mother, and brother is used by the brother as well as by the sister. In fact the only reciprocal term in English is cousin. The tendency toward reciprocal expression is developed in many Indian languages. It is particularly strong in California. In some languages this tendency has brought it about that different categories are involved in the terms applied to a pair of mutual relationships. The term father's sister indicates the sex of the relative but not of the speaker. The exact reciprocal of father's sister is woman's brother's child. This term, however, does not recognize the sex of the relative indicated, but does imply the sex of the speaker. The two reciprocal terms therefore each involve a category which the other does not express. If the same categories were represented in the two terms, brother's daughter would correspond to father's sister and exact reciprocity would be impossible. When, therefore, the terms found are father's sister and woman's brother's child, it is clear that the tendency toward the establishment of exactly reciprocal terms has been stronger than the feeling favoring the consistent use or neglect of certain categories; in other words, the extent to which certain categories are expressed has been determined by the vigor of the reciprocal tendency.

The categories serve also to indicate the leading characteristics of systems of the same general order. It is obvious, for instance, that the most important difference between Dakota and Arapaho is the strong tendency of the former to recognize the sex of the speaker. Chinook is notable for laying more stress on the sex of the speaker and of the connecting relation than on the sex of the relative—no doubt owing to the fact that the sex of the relative is indicable by purely grammatical means. General differences such as naturally occur between the languages of one region and of another can also be expressed in terms of the categories. All the California systems, for instance, lay much more stress upon the sex of the connecting relative than do any of the Plains languages examined. The Plains systems are conspicuous for their weak development of the distinction between lineal and collateral relationship, this finding expression in two-thirds of all cases in Dakota, half in Arapaho, one-fourth in Pawnee. In seven California languages the corresponding values lie between three-fourths and com-

plete expression. The method can be applied successfully even in the case of smaller and contiguous geographical areas. Of the seven California languages Luiseño and Mohave are spoken in southern California. Their systems show a unity as compared with the systems of the five languages from northern and central California. Both the southern California languages have a greater number of terms; both are stronger in the expression of the categories of the sex of the connecting relative and of age within the same generation; and both are weaker in the category of sex of the relative, than the others. Again, Chinook and Skokomish, both of the North Pacific Coast, are alike in indicating the condition of the connecting relative and in failing, on account of the possession of grammatical sex gender, to distinguish the sex of relatives themselves in many terms of relationship. There is a very deep-going difference between them, however, in the fact that Skokomish is as free as English from recognizing the sex of the speaker and of connecting relatives, while Chinook generally expresses both categories. In short, the categories present a means of comparing systems of terms of relationship along the basic lines of their structure and of expressing their similarities and differences without reference to individual terms or details.

The reason why the vague and unsatisfactory idea of a classificatory system of consanguinity has found such wide acceptance is not to be sought in any primary interest in designations of relationship as such, but in the fact that terms of relationship have usually been regarded principally as material from which conclusions as to the organization of society and conditions of marriage could be inferred. If it had been more clearly recognized that terms of relationship are determined primarily by linguistic factors, and are only occasionally, and then indirectly, affected by social circumstances, it would probably long ago have been generally realized that the difference between descriptive and classificatory systems is subjective and superficial. Nothing is more precarious than the common method of deducing the recent existence of social or marital institutions from a designation of relationship. Even when the social condition agrees perfectly with expressions of relationship, it is unsafe to conclude without corroborative evidence that these expressions are a direct reflection or result of the condition.

In the Dakota language, according to Riggs, there is only one word for grandfather and father-in-law. Following the mode of reasoning sometimes employed, it might be deduced from this that these two relationships were once identical. Worked out to its implications, the absurd conclusion would be that marriage with the mother was once customary among the Sioux.

In the same language the words for woman's male cousin and for woman's brother-in-law have the same radical, differing only in a suffix. Similar reasoning would induce in this case that marriage of cousins was or had been the rule among the Sioux, a social condition utterly opposed to the basic principles of almost all Indian society.

The use of such identical or similar terms for distinct relationships is due to a considerable similarity between the relationships. A woman's male cousin and her brother-in-law are alike in sex, are both of opposite sex from the speaker, are of the same generation as herself, and are both collateral, so that they are similar under four categories. In view of the comparative paucity of terms as compared with possible relationships, it is entirely natural that the same word, or the same stem, should at times be used to denote two relationships having as much in common as these two.

No one would assume that the colloquial habit in modern English of speaking of the brother-in-law as brother implies anything as to form of marriage, for logically the use of the term could only be an indication of sister marriage. It is easily conceivable that in the future development of English the more cumbersome of these two terms might come into complete disuse in daily life and the shorter take its place, without the least change in social or marital conditions.

The causes which determine the formation, choice, and similarities of terms of relationship are primarily linguistic. Whenever it is desired to regard terms of relationship as due to sociological causes and as indicative of social conditions, the burden of proof must be entirely with the propounder of such views.

Even the circumstances that the father's brother is frequently called father is not necessarily due to or connected with the custom of the levirate; nor can group marriage be inferred from the circumstance that there is frequently no other term for mother's sister than mother. A woman and her sister are more alike than a woman and her brother, but the difference is conceptual, in other words linguistic, as well as sociological. It is true that a woman's sister can take her place in innumerable functions and relations in which a brother cannot; and yet a woman and her sister, being of the same sex, agree in one more category of relationship than the same woman and her brother, and are therefore more similar in relationship and more naturally

denoted by the same term. There are so many cases where the expression of relationship cannot have been determined by sociological factors and must be purely psychological, as in the instances just discussed, that it is fair to require that the preference be given to the psychological cause, or that this be admitted as of at least equal probability, even in cases where either explanation is theoretically possible and supporting evidence is absent.

On the whole it is inherently very unlikely in any particular case that the use of identical terms for similar relationships can ever be connected with such special customs as the levirate or group marriage. It is a much more conservative view to hold that such forms of linguistic expression and such conditions are both the outcome of the unalterable fact that certain relationships are more similar to one another than others. On the one hand this fact has led to certain sociological institutions; on the other hand, to psychological recognitions and their expression in language. To connect the institutions and the terms causally can rarely be anything but hazardous. It has been an unfortunate characteristic of the anthropology of recent years to seek in a great measure specific causes for specific events, connection between which can be established only through evidence that is subjectively selected. On wider knowledge and freedom from motive it is becoming increasingly apparent that causal explanations of detached anthropological phenomena can be but rarely found in other detached phenomena, and that it is even difficult to specify the most general tendencies that actuate the forms taken by culture as the immediate causes of particular phenomena.

The following conclusions may be drawn:

1. The generally accepted distinction between descriptive and classificatory systems of terms of relationship cannot be supported.

2. Systems of terms of relationship can be properly compared through an examination of the categories of relationship which they involve and of the degree to which they give expression to these categories.

3. The fundamental difference between systems of terms of relationship of Europeans and of American Indians is that the former express a smaller number of categories of relationship than the latter and express them more completely.

4. Terms of relationship reflect psychology, not sociology. They are determined primarily by language and can be utilized for sociological inferences only with extreme caution.

3. The Complex of Mother-Right

BY BRONISLAW MALINOWSKI

WE HAVE BEEN comparing the two civilizations, the European and the Melanesian, and we have seen that there exist deep differences, some of the forces by which society moulds man's biological nature being essentially dissimilar. Though in each there is a certain latitude given to sexual freedom, and a certain amount of interference with and regulation of the sex instinct, yet in each the incidence of the taboo and the play of sexual liberty within its prescribed bounds are entirely different. There is also a quite dissimilar distribution of authority within the family, and correlated with it a different mode of counting kinship. We have followed in both societies the growth of the average boy or girl under these divergent tribal laws and customs. We have found that at almost every step there are great differences due to the interplay between biological impulse and social rule which sometimes harmonize, sometimes conflict, sometimes lead to a short bliss, sometimes to an inequilibrium fraught, however, with possibilities for a future development. At the final stage of the child's life-history, after it has reached maturity, we have seen its feelings crystallize into a system of sentiments towards the mother, father, brother, sister, and in the Trobriands, the maternal uncle, a system which is typical of each society, and which, in order to adapt ourselves to psycho-analytic terminology, we called the "Family Complex" or the "nuclear complex."

Now allow me to restate briefly the main features of these two "complexes." The Oedipus complex, the system of attitudes typical of our patriarchal society, is formed in early infancy, partly during the transition between the first and second stages of childhood, partly in the course of the latter. So that, towards its end, when the boy is about five or six years old, his attitudes are well formed, though perhaps not finally settled. And these attitudes comprise already a number of elements of hate and suppressed desire. In this, I think, our results do not differ to any extent from those of psycho-analysis.

Reprinted from Bronislaw Malinowski, *Sex and Repression in Savage Society* (New York: Harcourt, Brace & Co.; and London: Kegan Paul, Trench, Trubner & Co., 1927), chap. iv, pp. 74–82, with the permission of Humanities Press, Inc., and Kegan Paul, Trench, Trubner & Co.

[I have come to realize since the above was written that no orthodox or semi-orthodox psycho-analyst would accept my statement of the "complex," or of any aspect of the doctrine.]

In the matrilineal society at that stage, though the child has developed very definite sentiments towards its father and mother, nothing suppressed, nothing negative, no frustrated desire forms a part of them. Whence arises this difference? As we saw, the social arrangements of the Trobriand matriliny are in almost complete harmony with the biological course of development, while the institution of father-right found in our society crosses and represses a number of natural impulses and inclinations. To trace it more in detail, there is the passionate attachment to the mother, the bodily desire to cling close to her, which in patriarchal institutions is in one way or another broken or interfered with; the influence of our morality, which condemns sexuality in children; the brutality of the father, especially in the lower strata, the atmosphere of his exclusive right to mother and child acting subtly but strongly in the higher strata, the fear felt by the wife of displeasing her husband—all these influences force apart parents and children. Even where the rivalry between father and child for the mother's personal attention is reduced to a minimum, or to naught, there comes, in the second period, a distinct clash of social interests between father and child. The child is an encumbrance and an obstacle to the parental freedom, a reminder of age and decline and, if it is a son, often the menace of a future social rivalry. Thus, over and above the clash of sensuality, there is ample room for social friction between father and child. I say advisedly "child" and not "boy," for, according to our results, the sex difference between the children does not play any great part at this stage, nor has a closer relation between father and daughter as yet made its appearance.

All these forces and influences are absent from the matrilineal society of the Trobriands. First of all—and that has, *bien entendu,* nothing to do with matriliny—there is no condemnation of sex or of sensuality as such, above all, no moral horror at the idea of infantile sexuality. The sensuous clinging of the child to his mother is allowed to take its natural course till it plays itself out and is diverted by other bodily interests. The attitude of the father to the child during these two early periods is that of a near friend and helper. At the time when our father makes himself pleasant at best by his entire absence from the nursery, the Trobriand father is first a nurse and then a companion.

The development of pre-sexual life at this stage also differs in Europe and Melanesia; the repressions of the nursery among us, especially in the higher classes, develop a tendency towards clandestine inquisitions into indecent things, especially excretory functions and organs. Among the savages we find no such period. Now this infantile pregenital indecency establishes distinctions between the decent-indecent, the pure-impure, and the indecent, parent-proof compartment reinforces and gives additional depth to the taboo which is suddenly cast over certain relations to the mother, that is to the premature banishment from her bed and bodily embraces.

So that here also the complications of our society are not shared by the children in the Trobriands. At the next stage of sexuality we find a no less relevant difference. In Europe there is a latency period more or less pronounced, which implies a breach of continuity in the sexual development and, according to Freud, serves to reinforce many of our repressions and the general amnesia, and to create many dangers in the normal development of sex. On the other hand, it also represents the triumph of other cultural and social interests over sexuality. Among the savages at this stage, sex in an early genital form—a form almost unknown among ourselves—establishes itself foremost among the child's interests, never to be dislodged again. This, while in many respects it is culturally destructive, helps the gradual and harmonious weaning of the child from the family influences.

With this we have entered already into the second half of the child's development, for the period of sexual latency in our society belongs to this part. When we consider these two later stages which form the second half of the development, we find another profound difference. With us during this early period of puberty, the Oedipus complex, the attitudes of the boy towards his parents, only solidify and crystallize. In Melanesia, on the other hand, it is mainly during this second epoch, in fact almost exclusively then, that any complex is formed. For only at this period is the child submitted to the system of repressions and taboos which begin to mould his nature. To these forces, he responds, partly by adaptation, partly by developing more or less repressed antagonisms and desires, for human nature is not only malleable but also elastic.

The repressing and moulding forces in Melanesia are twofold—the submission to matriarchal tribal law, and the prohibitions of exogamy. The first is brought about by the influence of the mother's brother, who, in appealing to the child's sense of honour, pride and ambition, comes to stand to him in a relation in many respects analogous to that of the father among us. On the other hand, both the efforts which he demands and the rivalry between successor and succeeded introduce the negative elements of jealousy and resentment. Thus an "ambivalent" attitude is formed in which veneration assumes the acknowledged dominant place, while a repressed hatred manifests itself only indirectly.

The second taboo, the prohibition of incest, surrounds the sister, and to a lesser degree other female relatives on the maternal side, as well as clanswomen, with a veil of sexual mystery. Of all this class of women, the sister is the representative to whom the taboo applies most stringently. We noted that this severing taboo, entering the boy's life in infancy, cuts short the incipient tenderness towards his sister which is the natural impulse of a child. This taboo also, since it makes even an accidental contact in sexual matters a crime, causes the thought of the sister to be always present, as well as consistently repressed.

Comparing the two systems of family attitudes briefly, we see that in a patriarchal society, the infantile rivalries and the later social functions introduce into the attitude of father and son, besides mutual attachment, also a certain amount of resentment and dislike. Between mother and son, on the other hand, the premature separation in infancy leaves a deep, unsatisfied craving which, later on, when sexual interests come in, is mixed up in memory with the new bodily longings, and assumes often an erotic character which comes up in dreams and other fantasies. In the Trobriands there is no friction between father and son, and all the infantile craving of the child for its mother is allowed gradually to spend itself in a natural, spontaneous manner. The ambivalent attitude of veneration and dislike is felt between a man and his mother's brother, while the repressed sexual attitude of incestuous temptation can be formed only towards his sister. Applying to each society a terse, though somewhat crude formula, we might say that in the Oedipus complex there is the repressed desire to kill the father and marry the mother, while in the matrilineal society of the Trobriands the wish is to marry the sister and to kill the maternal uncle.

With this, we have summarized the results of our detailed inquiry, and given an answer to the first problem set out at the beginning, that is, we have studied the variation of the nuclear complex with the constitution of the family, and we have shown in what manner the complex depends upon some of the features of family life and sexual morals.

We are indebted to psycho-analysis for the discovery that there exists a typical configuration of sentiments in our society, and for a partial explanation, mainly concerned with sex, as to why such a complex must exist. In the foregoing pages we were able to give an outline of the nuclear complex of another society, a matrilineal one, where it has never been studied before. We found that this complex differs essentially from the patriarchal one, and we have shown why it must differ and what social forces bring it about. We have drawn our comparison on the broadest basis, and, without neglecting sexual factors, we have also systematically drawn in the other elements. The result is important, for, so far, it has never been suspected that another

type of nuclear complex might be in existence. By my analysis, I have established that Freud's theories not only roughly correspond to human psychology, but that they follow closely the modification in human nature brought about by various constitutions of society. In other words, I have established a deep correlation between the type of society and the nuclear complex found there. While this is in a sense a confirmation of the main tenet of Freudian psychology, it might compel us to modify certain of its features, or rather to make some of its formulae more elastic. To put it concretely, it appears necessary to draw in more systematically the correlation between biological and social influences; not to assume the universal existence of the Oedipus complex, but in studying every type of civilization, to establish the special complex which pertains to it.

4. The Study of Kinship Systems

BY A. R. RADCLIFFE-BROWN

I

FOR SEVENTY-FIVE YEARS the subject of kinship has occupied a special and important position in social anthropology. I propose in this address to consider the methods that have been and are being used in that branch of our studies and the kinds of results that we may reasonably expect to arrive at by those methods. I shall consider and compare two methods which I shall speak of as that of conjectural history and that of structural or sociological analysis.

One of these methods was first applied to some social institutions by French and British (mostly Scots) writers of the eighteenth century. It was of this method that Dugald Stewart wrote in 1795: "To this species of philosophical investigation, which has no appropriated name in our language, I shall take the liberty of giving the title of *Theoretical* or *Conjectural History;* an expression which coincides pretty nearly in its meaning with that of *Natural History,* as employed by Mr. Hume (see his *Natural History of Religion*), and with what some

French writers have called *Histoire Raisonnée.*" I shall accept Dugald Stewart's suggestion and shall use the name "conjectural history."

The method of conjectural history is used in a number of different ways. One is to attempt to base on general considerations, on what Dugald Stewart calls "known principles of human nature," conjectures as to first beginnings—of political society (Hobbes), of language (Adam Smith), of religion (Tylor), of the family (Westermarck), and so on. Sometimes an attempt is made to deal with the whole course of development of human society, as in the works of Morgan, Father Schmidt and Elliot Smith. Sometimes we are offered a conjectural history of the development of a particular institution, as in Robertson Smith's treatment of sacrifice. The special form of the method with which we shall be concerned in what follows is the attempt to explain a particular feature of one or more social systems by a hypothesis as to how it came into existence.

An early example of the method of conjectural history applied to kinship is to be found in the essay on *Primitive Marriage* published by John F. M'Lennan in 1865. You will remember the two principal theses put forward in that book: the origin of the custom of exogamy from marriage by capture, and

Reprinted from A. R. Radcliffe-Brown, *Structure and Function in Primitive Society* (Gencoe, Ill.: The Free Press, 1952), chap. iii, pp. 49–89, with the permission of The Free Press.

the proposition that "the most ancient system in which the idea of blood relationship was embodied was a system of kinship through females only." Six years later there appeared *The Systems of Consanguinity and Affinity* of Lewis Morgan, a monument of scholarly, patient research in the collection of data, to be followed in 1877 by his *Ancient Society,* in which he offered a conjectural outline history of the whole course of social development. These works of M'Lennan and Morgan were followed by a considerable mass of literature, which has continued to be produced down to the present day, in which the method of conjectural history has been applied in different forms to various features of kinship organisation.

As I think you know, I regard the pursuit of this method as one of the chief obstacles to the development of a scientific theory of human society. But my position has often been misunderstood. My objection to conjectural history is not that it is historical, but that it is conjectural. History shows us how certain events or changes in the past have led to certain other events or conditions, and thus reveals human life in a particular region of the world as a chain of connected happenings. But it can do this only when there is direct evidence for both the preceding and succeeding events or conditions and also some actual evidence of their interconnection. In conjectural history we have direct knowledge about a state of affairs existing at a certain time and place, without any adequate knowledge of the preceding conditions and events, about which we are therefore reduced to making conjectures. To establish any probability for such conjectures we should need to have a knowledge of laws of social development which we certainly do not possess and to which I do not think we shall ever attain.

My own study of kinship began in 1904 under Rivers, when I was his first and at that time his only student in social anthropology, having for three years previously studied psychology under him. I owe a great deal to that contact with Rivers, and more rather than less because from the outset it appeared that we disagreed on the subject of method. For Rivers followed the method of conjectural history, at first under the influence of Morgan, and later in the form of what he called ethnological analysis, as exemplified in his *History of Melanesian Society* (1914a). But in his field work Rivers had discovered and revealed to others the importance of the investigation of the behaviour of relatives to one another as a means of understanding a system of kinship. In what follows I shall be criticising one side of Rivers' work, but the position I now hold is the one I held in my friendly discussions with him during a period of ten years, ending in an agreement

to go on disagreeing. My esteem for Rivers as man, as teacher, and as scientist, is in no way diminished by the fact that I find myself obliged to criticise adversely his use of the method of conjectural history.

At the outset it is necessary to give a definition. I shall use the term "kinship system" as short for a system of kinship and marriage or kinship and affinity. It is a pity that there is no inclusive term in English for all relationships which result from the existence of the family and marriage. It would be very tiresome to speak all the time of a system of kinship and affinity. I hope, therefore, that my use of the term will be accepted. It need not lead to ambiguity.

The unit of structure from which a kinship system is built up is the group which I call an "elementary family," consisting of a man and his wife and their child or children, whether they are living together or not. A childless married couple does not constitute a family in this sense. Children may be acquired, and thus made members of an elementary family, by adoption as well as by birth. We must also recognise the existence of compound families. In a polygynous family there is only one husband with two or more wives and their respective children. Another form of compound family is produced in monogamous societies by a second marriage, giving rise to what we call step-relationships and such relationships as that of half-brothers. Compound families can be regarded as formed of elementary families with a common member.

The existence of the elementary family creates three special kinds of social relationship, that between parent and child, that between children of the same parents (siblings), and that between husband and wife as parents of the same child or children. A person is born or adopted into a family in which he or she is son or daughter and brother or sister. When a man marries and has children he now belongs to a second elementary family, in which he is husband and father. This interlocking of elementary families creates a network of what I shall call, for lack of any better term, genealogical relations, spreading out indefinitely.

The three relationships that exist within the elementary family constitute what I call the first order. Relationships of the second order are those which depend on the connection of two elementary families through a common member, and are such as father's father, mother's brother, wife's sister, and so on. In the third order are such as father's brother's son and mother's brother's wife. Thus we can trace, if we have genealogical information, relationships of the fourth, fifth or *n*th order. In any given society a certain number of these relationships are recognised for social purposes, i.e. they have attached to them certain rights and duties, or certain distinctive modes of behaviour. It is the relations that are recognised in this way that constitute what I am calling a kinship system, or, in full, a system of kinship and affinity.

A most important character of a kinship system is its range. In a narrow range system, such as the English system of the present day, only a limited number of relatives are recognised as such in any way that entails any special behaviour or any specific right and duties. In ancient times in England the range was wider, since a fifth cousin had a claim to a share of the *wergild* when a man was killed. In systems of very wide range, such as are found in some non-European societies, a man may recognise many hundreds of relatives, towards each of whom his behaviour is qualified by the existence of the relationship.

It must be noted also that in some societies persons are regarded as being connected by relationships of the same kind although no actual genealogical tie is known. Thus the members of a clan are regarded as being kinsmen, although for some of them it may not be possible to show their descent from a common ancestor. It is this that distinguishes what will here be called a clan from a lineage.

Thus a kinship system, as I am using the term, or a system of kinship and affinity if you prefer so to call it, is in the first place a system of dyadic relations between person and person in a community, the behaviour of any two persons in any of these relations being regulated in some way, and to a greater or less extent, by social usage.

A kinship system also includes the existence of definite social groups. The first of these is the domestic family, which is a group of persons who at a particular time are living together in one dwelling, or collection of dwellings, with some sort of economic arrangement that we may call joint housekeeping. There are many varieties of the domestic family, varying in their form, their size, and the manner of their common life. A domestic family may consist of a single elementary family, or it may be a group including a hundred or more persons, such as the *zadruga* of the Southern Slavs or the *taravad* of the Nayar. Important in some societies is what may be called a local cluster of domestic families. In many kinship systems unilinear groups of kindred—lineage groups, clans and moieties—play an important part.

By a kinship system, then, I mean a network of social relations of the kind just defined, which thus constitutes part of that total network of social relations that I call social structure. The rights and duties of relatives to one another and the social usages that they observe in their social contacts, since it is by these that the relations are described, are part

of the system. I regard ancestor-worship, where it exists, as in a real sense part of the kinship system, constituted as it is by the relations of living persons to their deceased kindred, and affecting as it does the relations of living persons to one another. The terms used in a society in addressing or referring to relatives are a part of the system, and so are the ideas that the people themselves have about kinship.

You will perceive that by using the word "system" I have made an assumption, an important and far-reaching assumption; for that word implies that whatever it is applied to is a complex unity, an organised whole. My explicit hypothesis is that between the various features of a particular kinship system there is a complex relation of interdependence. The formulation of this working hypothesis leads immediately to the method of sociological analysis, by which we seek to discover the nature of kinship systems as systems, if they be really such. For this purpose we need to make a systematic comparison of a sufficient number of sufficiently diverse systems. We must compare them, not in reference to single, superficial, and therefore immediately observable characters, but as wholes, as systems, and in reference, therefore, to general characters which are only discovered in the process of comparison. Our purpose is to arrive at valid abstractions or general ideas in terms of which the phenomena can be described and classified.

I propose to illustrate the two methods, that of conjectural history and that of system analysis, by means of a particular example, and for this purpose I select a peculiar feature of the kinship terminology of a number of scattered tribes. When Morgan made his study of the terminology of kinship in North American tribes, he noted certain peculiarities in the terms for cousins. In the Choctaw tribe he found that a man calls his father's sister's son by the same term of relationship that he applies to his own father and his father's brother. We may say that the father's sister's son is thus treated in the terminology as though he were a younger brother of the father. Reciprocally a man calls his mother's brother's son by the term for "son." Consistently with this he applies one term of relationship to his father's sister and her daughter, and speaks of his mother's brother's daughter as a "daughter." In the Omaha tribe, on the other hand, Morgan found that a man calls his mother's brother's son "uncle," i.e. mother's brother, and calls his mother's brother's daughter "mother," so that reciprocally he speaks of his father's sister's son by the term that he uses for his sister's son, and a woman uses a single term for her own son, her sister's son and her father's sister's

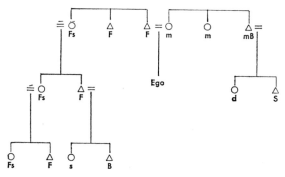

Fig. 1—Choctaw

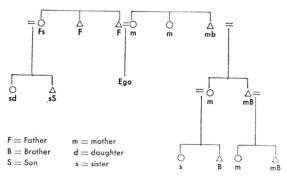

F = Father   m = mother
B = Brother   d = daughter
S = Son   s = sister

Fig. 2—Omaha

son. Figs. 1 and 2 will help to make these terminologies clear.

Terminologies similar to the Omaha are found in a number of regions: (1) in the Siouan tribes related to the Omaha, such as the Osage, Winnebago, etc.; (2) in certain Algonquian tribes, of which we may take the Fox Indians as an example; (3) in an area of California which includes the Miwok; (4) in some tribes of East Africa, both Bantu and non-Bantu, including the Nandi and the BaThonga; (5) amongst the Lhota Nagas of Assam; and (6) in some New Guinea tribes. Terminologies similar to the Choctaw are found: (1) in other south-eastern tribes of the United States, including the Cherokee; (2) in the Crow and Hidatsa tribes of the Plains area; (3) amongst the Hopi and some other Pueblo Indians; (4) in the Tlingit and Haida of the north-west coast of America; (5) in the Banks Islands in Melanesia; and (6) in one Twi-speaking community of West Africa.

There are some who would regard this kind of terminology as "contrary to common sense," but that means no more than that it is not in accordance with our modern European ideas of kinship and its terminology. It ought to be easy for any anthropolo-

gist to recognise that what is common sense in one society may be the opposite of common sense in another. The Choctaw and Omaha terminologies do call for some explanation; but so does the English terminology, in which we use the word "cousin" for all children of both brothers and sisters of both mother and father—a procedure which would probably seem to some non-Europeans to be contrary not only to common sense but also to morals. What I wish to attempt, therefore, is to show you that the Choctaw and Omaha terminologies are just as reasonable and fitting in the social systems in which they occur as our own terminology is in our own social system.

I would point out that the Choctaw system and the Omaha system exhibit a single structural principle applied in different ways, in what we may perhaps call opposite directions. We shall therefore consider them together, as varieties of a single species.

Attempts have been made to explain these terminologies by the method of conjectural history. The first was that of Kohler in 1897, in his essay "Zur Urgeschichte der Ehe." Kohler set out to defend Morgan's theory of group-marriage, and used the Choctaw and Omaha systems for his argument. He explained the Choctaw terminology as the result of marriage with the mother's brother's wife, and the Omaha system as the result of a custom of marriage with the wife's brother's daughter. Kohler's essay was reviewed by Durkheim (1898) in what was an important, if brief, contribution to the theory of kinship. He rejected Kohler's hypotheses, and pointed out the connection of the Choctaw and Omaha systems with matrilineal and patrilineal descent respectively.

The subject was considered again by Rivers in reference to the Banks Islands, and, without bringing in, as Kohler had done, the question of group-marriage, he explained the Banks Islands terminology as resulting from a custom of marriage with the mother's brother's widow. Gifford (1916), having found the characteristic feature of the Omaha system in the Miwok of California, followed the lead of Kohler and Rivers, and explained it as the result of the custom of marriage with the wife's brother's daughter. About the same time, and independently, Mrs. Seligman (1917) offered the same explanation of the Omaha feature as it occurs in the Nandi and other tribes of Africa.

Let me summarise the argument with reference to the Omaha type. The hypothesis is that in certain societies, mostly having a definite patrilineal organisation, a custom was for some reason adopted of permitting a man to marry his wife's brother's daughter. Referring to Fig. 3, this means that D

Fig. 3

Note—A and c are brother and sister

would be allowed to marry f. When such a marriage occurred, then for G and h, f, who is their mother's brother's daughter, would become their step-mother, and E, their mother's brother's son, would become the brother of their step-mother. The hypothesis then assumes that the kinship terminology was so modified as to anticipate this form of marriage wherever it might occur. G and h will call f, their mother's brother's daughter and therefore their possible future step-mother, "mother," and her brother E they will call "mother's brother." Reciprocally f will call G "son" and E will call him "sister's son." There is an exactly parallel argument for the Choctaw system. A custom arises by which a man may occasionally marry the widow of his mother's brother. In the figure, G would marry b, the wife of his mother's brother A. Thus E and f would become his step-children. If this marriage is anticipated in the terminology, then E and f will call G "father" and h "father's sister."

Let us note that in the Omaha tribe and in some others having a similar terminology it is regarded as permissible for a man to marry his wife's brother's daughter. Marriage with the mother's brother's widow does not seem to occur regularly with the Choctaw terminology, and does certainly occur without it, even in tribes with an Omaha terminology such as the BaThonga.

The basis of what we may call the Kohler hypothesis is the obvious fact that in each of the two varieties the terminology and the special form of marriage are consistent; the two things fit together in what may be called a logical way. This, I think, anyone can see by inspection of the data. But the hypothesis goes far beyond this. It supposes that there is some sort of causal connection such that the marriage custom can be said to have caused, produced, or resulted in, the special terminology. No evidence is adduced that this is actually the way in which things happened. The argument is entirely *a priori*. It is the essential weakness of conjectural history that its hypotheses cannot be verified. Thus this hypothesis cannot be considered as anything more than a speculation or conjecture as to how things might have happened.

Now it would be equally plausible to suggest that the special form of marriage is the result of the terminology. If, as in the terminology of the Omaha type, I treat my wife's brother's daughter as being the younger sister of my wife, and, by the custom of the sororate, it is considered proper for me to marry my wife's younger sister, then I might well be permitted to marry the woman who, in the terminological system, is treated as such, namely her brother's daughter. This hypothesis is, of course, equally lacking in proof. If we adopt the Kohler hypothesis the terminology is conceived to be in some sense explained, but there is no explanation of the marriage custom. By the alternative hypothesis the marriage custom is explained, but the terminology is not. I do not see how there can be any ground for a choice of one of these two hypotheses in preference to the other except purely personal predilection.

However, while we could conceive of the marriage custom as being the immediate result of the terminology in a society which already has sororal polygyny, the terminology cannot be the immediate result of the marriage custom without the concomitant action of some other undetermined factor. We have examples of societies in which a man sometimes marries the widow of his mother's brother, but only uses the terminology which this marriage makes appropriate after the marriage has taken place. Although we have no recorded instance of this procedure in marriage with the wife's brother's daughter it is at least conceivable that it might occur. What is lacking in the hypothesis we are examining is some reason why the whole terminology should be adjusted so as to fit a particular form of marriage which only occasionally occurs.

Let us now leave the hypothesis and examine the structural principles of those kinship systems in which this terminology occurs, whether in the Choctaw or the Omaha form. It is necessary, however, to say something on the subject of kinship terminologies, about which there has been a great deal of controversy. Morgan's first interest in the subject was as an ethnologist, i.e. one seeking to discover the historical relations of the peoples of the earth. He thought that by collecting a sufficient sample of terminologies and comparing them he could reveal the historical relation of the American Indians (the Ganowanian peoples as he called them) to the peoples of Asia. In the course of his work, however, he decided that these terminologies could be used to infer the former existence of forms of social organisation. He supposed that the classificatory terminology which he found in North American tribes such as the Iroquois was inconsistent with the form of social organisation with which it is actually found, and therefore could not have arisen in a society so organised, but must be a "survival" from some different kind of social system.

This was, of course, pure assumption, but it is the kind of assumption that the method of conjectural history encourages us to make, often unconsciously or implicitly. Morgan was thus led to a hypothesis that is one of the most fantastic in a subject that is full of fantastic hypotheses. The truth is that he had quite failed to understand the nature and function of the classificatory terminology. There is nothing that so effectively prevents the perception and understanding of things as they are as hypotheses of conjectural history, or the desire to invent such hypotheses.

One of Morgan's early critics, Starcke (1889), was, I believe, the first to maintain the position which has always been my own. He held that in general a kinship nomenclature is "the faithful reflection of the juridical relations which arise between the nearest kinsfolk in each tribe." He condemned as unsound the attempt to use such nomenclatures to make historical reconstructions of past societies. It would be interesting to consider why it is that Starcke has had so few followers and Morgan so many, but that I cannot here undertake.

In 1909 Kroeber published in our *Journal* a paper on "Classificatory Systems of Relationship." To the contentions of that paper Rivers made a reply in his lectures on *Kinship and Social Organisation* (1914b), and Kroeber answered the criticisms of Rivers in his *California Kinship Systems* (1917).

I discussed Kroeber's paper with Rivers when it appeared and found myself in the position of disagreeing with both sides of the controversy. Kroeber wrote: "Nothing is more precarious than the common method of deducing the recent existence of social or marital institutions from a designation of relationship." This is a restatement of Starcke's contention of 1889, and with it I was, and still am, in complete agreement, thereby disagreeing with Rivers. Kroeber also wrote: "It has been an unfortunate characteristic of the anthropology of recent years to seek in a great measure specific causes for specific events, connection between which can be established only through evidence that is subjectively selected. On wider knowledge and freedom from motive it is becoming increasingly apparent that causal explanations of detached anthropological phenomena can be but rarely found in other detached phenomena." With this statement I am in agreement.

But both Kroeber and Rivers seemed to agree that causal explanations are necessary for the con-

stitution of what Kroeber calls "true science." For Rivers anthropology is a true science because, or to the extent that, it can show causal connections; for Kroeber it is not a true science. Here I disagree with both Kroeber and Rivers, holding that a pure theoretical science (whether physical, biological or social) is not concerned with causal relations in this sense. The concept of cause and effect belongs properly to applied science, to practical life and its arts and techniques and to history.

This brings us to the crux of the Rivers-Kroeber debate. Rivers held that the characteristics of a kinship nomenclature are determined by social or sociological factors, that particular features of terminology result from particular features of social organisation. Against this Kroeber held that the features of a system of terminology "are determined primarily by language" and "reflect psychology not sociology." "Terms of relationship," he wrote, "are determined primarily by linguistic factors and are only occasionally, and then indirectly, affected by social circumstances." But in his later paper Kroeber explains that what he calls psychological factors "are social or cultural phenomena as thoroughly and completely as institutions, beliefs or industries are social phenomena." His thesis is therefore concerned with a distinction between two kinds of social phenomena. One of these he calls institutional, defined as "practices connected with marriage, descent, personal relations, and the like." These are what he called in his first paper "social factors." The other kind he speaks of as the "psyche" of a culture, "that is, the ways of thinking and feeling characteristic of the culture." These constitute what he calls the psychological factors.

Thus Kroeber's thesis, on its positive side, is that similarities and differences of kinship nomenclature are to be interpreted or understood by reference to similarities and differences of kinship nomenclature of thought." On its negative side, and it is with this that we are concerned, Kroeber's thesis is that there is no regular close connection between similarities and differences of kinship nomenclature and similarities and differences of "institutions," i.e. practices connected with marriage, descent and personal relations. He admits, in 1917, the existence of "undoubted correspondence of terminology and social practice in certain parts of Australia and Oceania," but denies that such are to be found in California. It may be pointed out that in Australia and Oceania they have been deliberately looked for, in California they have not. It may well be that in the remnants of Californian tribes it is now too late to look for them.

In opposition to Kroeber, and in a certain sense in agreement with Rivers, I hold that all over the world there are important correspondences between kinship nomenclature and social practices. Such correspondences are not to be simply assumed; they must be demonstrated by field work and comparative analysis. But their absence may not be assumed either; and Kroeber's arguments from their alleged absence in California remain, I think, entirely unconvincing.

For Kroeber the kinship nomenclature of a people represents their general manner of thought as it is applied to kinship. But the institutions of a people also represent their general manner of thought about kinship and marriage. Are we to suppose that in Californian tribes the way of thinking about kinship as it appears on the one hand in the terminology and on the other hand in social customs are not merely different but are not connected? This seems to be in effect what Kroeber is proposing.

Kroeber pointed out in 1917 that his original paper represented "a genuine attempt to understand kinship systems as kinship systems." But by "kinship system" Kroeber means only a system of nomenclature. Moreover, Kroeber is an ethnologist, not a social anthropologist. His chief, if not his sole, interest in the subject is in the possibility of discovering and defining the historical relations of peoples by comparison of their systems of nomenclature.

My own conception is that the nomenclature of kinship is an intrinsic part of a kinship system, just as it is also, of course, an intrinsic part of a language. The relations between the nomenclature and the rest of the system are relations within an ordered whole. My concern, both in field work in various parts of the world and in comparative studies, has been to discover the nature of these relations.

In the actual study of a kinship system the nomenclature is of the utmost importance. It affords the best possible approach to the investigation and analysis of the kinship system as a whole. This, of course, it could not do if there were no real relations of interdependence between the terminology and the rest of the system. That there are such relations I can affirm from my own field work in more than one region. It will be borne out, I believe, by any anthropologist who has made a thorough field study of a kinship system.

I have dealt with the controversy between Kroeber and Rivers because, as both the controversialists point out, the real issue is not simply one concerning kinship terms, but is a very important question of the general method of anthropological studies. It seemed to me that I could best make clear my own position by showing you how it differs from that of Rivers on the one side and that of Kroeber on the other.

Kinship systems are made and re-made by man, in the same sense that languages are made and re-made, which does not mean that they are normally constructed or changed by a process of deliberation and under control of conscious purpose. A language has to work, i.e. it has to provide a more or less adequate instrument for communication, and in order that it may work it has to conform to certain general necessary conditions. A morphological comparison of languages shows us the different ways in which these conditions have been compiled with by using different morphological principles such as inflection, agglutination, word order, internal modification or the use of tone or stress. A kinship system also has to work if it is to exist or persist. It has to provide an orderly and workable system of social relations defined by social usage. A comparison of different systems shows us how workable kinship systems have been created by utilising certain structural principles and certain mechanisms.

One common feature of kinship systems is the recognition of certain categories or kinds into which the various relatives of a single person can be grouped. The actual social relation between a person and his relative, as defined by rights and duties or socially approved attitudes and modes of behaviour, is then to a greater or less extent fixed by the category to which the relative belongs. The nomenclature of kinship is commonly used as a means of establishing and recognising these categories. A single term may be used to refer to a category of relatives and different categories will be distinguished by different terms.

Let us consider a simple example from our own system. We do what is rather unusual in the general run of kinship systems: we regard the father's brother and the mother's brother as relatives of the same kind of category. We apply a single term originally denoting the mother's brother (from the Latin *avunculus*) to both of them. The legal relationship in English law, except for entailed estates and titles of nobility, is the same for a nephew and either of his uncles; for example, the nephew has the same rights of inheritance in case of intestacy over the estate of either. In what may be called the socially standardised behaviour of England it is not possible to note any regular distinction made between the maternal and the paternal uncle. Reciprocally the relation of a man to his different kinds of nephews is in general the same. By extension, no significant difference is made between the son of one's mother's brother and the son of one's father's brother.

In Montenegro, on the contrary, to take another European system, the father's brothers constitute one category and the mother's brothers another. These relatives are distinguished by different terms, and so are their respective wives, and the social relations in which a man stands to his two kinds of uncles show marked differences.

There is nothing "natural" about the English attitude towards uncles. Indeed many peoples in many parts of the world would regard this failure to distinguish between relatives on the father's side and those on the mother's side as unnatural and even improper. But the terminology is consistent with our whole kinship system.

The kinship systems with which we shall be concerned here all have certain forms of what Morgan called the "classificatory" terminology. What Morgan meant by this term is quite clear from his writings, but his definition is often ignored, perhaps because people do not bother to read him. A nomenclature is classificatory when it uses terms which primarily apply to lineal relatives, such as "father," to refer also to collateral relatives. Thus, by Morgan's definition, the English word "uncle" is not a classificatory term, but the very opposite, since it is used only for collateral relatives. Kroeber (1909) criticises Morgan and rejects his conception of classificatory terminologies, and then proceeds to make use of the same distinction by taking as one of the important features of terminologies the extent to which they separate or distinguish lineal from collateral relatives. It seems to be merely the word "classificatory" that Kroeber does not like. Doubtless it is not the ideal word; but it has long been in use and no better one has been suggested, though others have been put forward.

I do not propose to deal with all systems in which the classificatory principle is applied in the terminology, but only with a certain widespread type. In these systems the distinction between lineal and collateral relatives is clearly recognised and is of great importance in social life, but it is in certain respects subordinated to another structural principle, which can be spoken of as the principle of the solidarity of the sibling group. A group of siblings is constituted by the sons and daughters of a man and his wife in monogamous societies, or of a man and his wives where there is polygyny, or of a woman and her husbands in polyandrous communities. The bond uniting brothers and sisters together into a social group is everywhere regarded as important, but it is more emphasised in some societies than in others. The solidarity of the sibling group is shown in the first instance in the social relations between its members.

From this principle there is derived a further principle which I shall speak of as that of the unity of the sibling group. This refers not to the internal unity of the group as exhibited in the behaviour of members to one another, but to its unity in relation

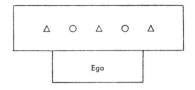

Fig. 4

to a person outside it and connected with it by a specific relation to one of its members.

A diagram may help the discussion. Fig. 4 represents a sibling group of three brothers and two sisters, to which Ego is related by the fact that he is the son of one of the three men. In the kinship systems with which I am now dealing, Ego regards himself as standing in the same general kind of relation to all the members of the group. For him it constitutes a unity. His relation to the brothers and sisters of his father is conceived as being of the same general kind as his relation to his father. Within the group, however, there are two principles of differentiation, sex and seniority, which have to be taken into account. In systems in which seniority is not emphasised a man treats his father's brothers, both older and younger, as being like his father. He refers to them or addresses them by the same term of kinship that he applies to his own father, and in certain important respects his behaviour towards them is similar to his behaviour towards his own father. What defines this behaviour is, of course, different in different systems. Where seniority is strongly emphasised, a man may distinguish between the senior brother and the junior brother either in behaviour alone or both in behavior and terminology, but there still remains a common element in the pattern of behaviour towards all "fathers."

The difference of sex is more important than the difference of seniority, and in this matter there is considerable variation in the systems we are considering. But in quite a considerable number of systems, in different parts of the world, there are certain features of a man's relationship to his father's sister which can be correctly described by saying that he regards her as a sort of female father. In some of these systems he actually calls her "female father," or some modification of the term for father. If it seems to you impossible that a man should regard his father's sister as a relative of the same kind as his own father, this is because you are thinking, not about social relationships as defined by modes of behaviour, with which we are here concerned, but about the physiological relationship, which is irrelevant.

The same kind of thing happens with the sibling group of the mother. The mother's sisters are treated as relatives of the same kind as the mother, both in terminology and in certain principles of behaviour or attitude. In a number of systems the mother's brother is also treated as a relative of the same kind as the mother. He may be called "male mother," as in Bantu tribes of Africa and in Tonga in the Pacific. If the principle of seniority is stressed, the mother's brothers may be distinguished according as they are older or younger than the mother.

Those of you who have never had any direct contact with systems of this kind find it difficult to comprehend how a father's sister can be regarded as a female father or a mother's brother as a male mother. This is due to the difficulty of dissociating the terms "father" and "mother" from the connotations they have in our own social system. It is absolutely essential to do this if the kinship systems of other societies are ever to be understood. Perhaps it will help somewhat if I refer to another terminology which seems to us peculiar. Most of the systems with which I am now dealing have a word for "child," or words for "son" and "daughter," which a man applies to his own children and his brother's children, and a woman applies to her own children and her sister's children. But in some Australian tribes there are two different words for "child." One is used by a man for his own child (or his brother's child) and by a woman for her brother's child; the other is used by a woman for her own or her sister's child, and by a man for his sister's child. I think you will see that this is another way of expressing in the terminology the unity that links brother and sister in relation to the child of either of them. I am called by one term by my father and his brothers and sisters; and by another term by my mother and her sisters and brothers.

The same principle, that of the unity of the sibling group, is applied to other sibling groups. Thus the father's father's brother is regarded as belonging to the same category as the father's father, with the result that his son is a somewhat more distant relative of the same kind as the father and his brothers. By means of such extension of the basic principle, a very large number of collateral relatives of different degrees of distance can be brought under a limited number of categories. A man may have many, even hundreds, of relatives whom he thus classifies as "fathers," "brothers," "mother's brothers" and so on. But there are different ways in which this extension of the basic classificatory principle can be applied, so that there result systems of different types. What is common to them all is that they make some use of this structural principle which I have briefly illustrated.

What I am trying to show you is that the classificatory terminology is a method of providing a wide-range kinship organisation, by making use of the unity of the sibling group in order to establish a few categories of relationship under which a very large number of near and distant relatives can be included. For all the relatives who are denoted by one term, there is normally some element of attitude or behaviour that is regarded as appropriate to them and not to others. But within a category there may be and always are important distinctions. There is, first, the very important distinction between one's own father and his brother. There are distinctions within the category between nearer and more distant relatives. There is sometimes an important distinction between relatives of a certain category who belong to other clans. There are other distinctions that are made in different particular systems. Thus the categories represented by the terminology never give us anything more than the skeleton of the real ordering of relatives in the social life. But in every system that I have been able to study they do give us this skeleton.

If this thesis is true, if this is what the classificatory terminology actually is in the tribes in which it exists, it is obvious that Morgan's whole theory is entirely ungrounded. The classificatory system, as thus interpreted, depends upon the recognition of the strong social ties that unite brothers and sisters of the same elementary family, and the utilisation of this tie to build up a complex orderly arrangement of social relations amongst kin. It could not come into existence except in a society based on the elementary family. Nowhere in the world are the ties between a man and his own children or between children of one father stronger than in Australian tribes, which, as you know, present an extreme example of the classificatory terminology.

The internal solidarity of the sibling group, and its unity in relation to persons connected with it, appear in a great number of different forms in different societies. I cannot make any attempt to deal with these, but for the sake of the later argument I will point out that it is in the light of this structural principle that we must interpret the customs of sororal polygyny (marriage with two or more sisters), the sororate (marriage with the deceased wife's sister), adelphic polyandry (marriage of a woman with two or more brothers, by far the commonest form of polyandry), and the levirate (marriage with the brother's widow). Sapir, using the method of conjectural history, has suggested that the classificatory terminology may be the result of the customs of the levirate and sororate. That the two things are connected is, I think, clear, but for the supposed causal connection there is no evidence whatever. Their real connection is that they are different ways of applying or using the principle of the unity of the sibling group, and they may therefore exist together or separately.

An organisation into clans or moieties is also based on the principle of the solidarity and unity of the sibling group in combination with other principles. Tylor suggested a connection between exogamous clans and the classificatory terminology. Rivers put this in terms of conjectural history, and argued that the classificatory terminology must have had its origin in the organisation of society into exogamous moieties.

II

It is necessary, for our analysis, to consider briefly another aspect of the structure of kinship systems, namely the division into generations. The distinction of generation has its basis in the elementary family, in the relation of parents and children. A certain generalising tendency is discoverable in many kinship systems in the behaviour of relatives of different generations. Thus we find very frequently that a person is expected to adopt an attitude of more or less marked respect towards all his relatives of the first ascending generation. There are restraints on behaviour which maintain a certain distance or prevent too close an intimacy. There is, in fact, a generalised relation of ascendancy and subordination between the two generations. This is usually accompanied by a relation of friendly equality between a person and his relatives of the second ascending generation. The nomenclature for grandparents and grandchildren is of significance in this connection. In some classificatory systems, such as those of Australian tribes, the grandparents on the father's side are distinguished, in terminology and in behaviour, from those on the mother's side. But in many classificatory systems the generalising tendency results in all relatives of the generation being classed together as "grandfathers" and "grandmothers."

We may note in passing that in classificatory terminologies of what Morgan called the Malayan type and Rivers the Hawaiian type, this generalising process is applied to other generations, so that all relatives of the parents' generation may be called "father" and "mother" and all those of one's own generation may be called "brother" and "sister."

There are many kinship systems in various parts of the world that exhibit a structural principle which I shall speak of as the combination of alternate generations. This means that relatives of the grandfather's generation are thought of as combined with those of one's own generation over against the relatives of the parents' generation. The extreme development of this principle is to be seen in Australian tribes. I shall refer to this later.

While some systems emphasise the distinction of generations in their terminology or in their social structure, there are also systems in which relatives of two or more generations are included in a single category. So far as I have been able to make a comparative study, the various instances of this seem to fall into four classes.

In one class of instances the term of relationship does not carry a connotation referring to any particular generation and is used to mark off a sort of marginal region between non-relatives and those close relatives towards whom specific duties and over whom specific rights are recognised. The application of the term generally only implies that since the other person is recognised as a relative he or she must be treated with a certain general attitude of friendliness and not as a stranger. A good example is provided by the terms *ol-le-sotwa* and *en-e-sotwa* in Masai. I would include the English word "cousin" in this class.

A second class of instances includes those in which there is conflict or inconsistency between the required attitude towards a particular relative and the required general attitude towards the generation to which he belongs. Thus in some tribes in South-East Africa there is conflict between the general rule that relatives of the first ascending generation are to be treated with marked respect and the custom of privileged disrespect towards the mother's brother. This is resolved by placing the mother's brother in the second ascending generation and calling him "grandfather." An opposite example is found in the Masai. A man is on terms of familiarity with all his relatives of the second descending generation, who are his "grandchildren." But it is felt that the relation between a man and the wife of his son's son should be one not of familiarity but of marked reserve. The inconsistency is resolved by a sort of legal fiction by which she is moved out of her generation and is called "son's wife."

A third class of instances are those resulting from the structural principle, already mentioned, whereby alternate generations are combined. Thus the father's father may be called "older brother" and treated as such, and the son's son may be called "younger brother." Or a man and his son's son may be both included in a single category of relationship. There are many illustrations of this in Australian tribes and some elsewhere. An example from the Hopi will be given later.

The fourth class of instances includes the systems of Choctaw and Omaha type and also certain others, and in these the distinction between generations is set aside in favour of another principle, that of the unity of the lineage group.

Since the word lineage is often loosely used, I must explain what I mean by it. A patrilineal or agnatic lineage consists of a man and all his descendants through males for a determinate number of generations. Thus a minimal lineage includes three generations, and we can have lineages of four, five or *n* generations. A matrilineal lineage consists of a woman and all her descendants through females for a determinate number of generations. A lineage group consists of all the members of a lineage who are alive at a particular time. A clan, as I shall use the term here, is a group which, though not actually or demonstrably (by genealogies) a lineage, is regarded as being in some ways similar to a lineage. It normally consists of a number of actual lineages. Lineages, both patrilineal and matrilineal, exist implicitly in any kinship system, but it is only in some systems that the solidarity of the lineage group is an important feature in the social structure.

Where lineage groups are important we can speak of the solidarity of the group, which shows itself in the first instance in the internal relations between the members. By the principle of the unity of the lineage group I mean that for a person who does not belong to the lineage but is connected with it through some important bond of kinship or by marriage, its members constitute a single category, with a distinction within the category between males and females, and possibly other distinctions also. When this principle is applied in the terminology a person connected with a lineage from outside applies to its members, of one sex, through at least three generations, the same term of relationship. In its extreme development, as applied to the clan, a person connected with a clan in a certain way applies a single term of relationship to all members of the clan. An example will be given later.

The Omaha type of terminology may be illustrated by the system of the Fox Indians, which has been carefully studied by Dr. Sol Tax (1937). The features of the system that are relevant to the argument are illustrated in the accompanying diagrams (Figs. 5–9).*

---

* In these diagrams △ represents a male person and ○ a female. The sign = connects a man and his wife and the lines descending from it indicate their children. The letters (capitals for males and lower case for females) stand for the kinship terms of a classificatory system, in which the same term is applied to a number of relatives. GF stands for the term used in referring to a grandfather, and similarly gm for grandmother; the others are F, father, m. mother, ms, mother's sister, fs, father's sister, MB, mother's brother, FL, father-in-law, ml, mother-in-law, B, brother, sis ,sister, BL, brother-in-law, sl, sister-in-law, S, son, d, daughter, N, nephew (strictly speaking sister's son) n, niece (sister's daughter of a male) GC or gc, grandchild.

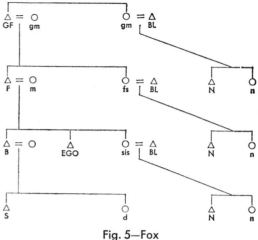

Fig. 5—Fox

Father's Lineage

In his own patrilineal lineage a man distinguishes his relatives according to generation as "grandfather" (GF), "father" (F), "older or younger brother" (B), "son" (S), "grandmother" (gm), "father's sister" (fs), "sister" (sis) and "daughter" (d). I would draw your attention to the fact that he applies a single term, "brother-in-law" (BL), irrespective of generation, to the husbands of the women of the lineage through three generations (his own and the two ascending generations), and that he calls the children of all these women by the same terms, "nephew" (N) and "niece" (n). Thus the women of Ego's own lineage of these generations constitute a sort of group, and Ego regards himself as standing in the same relationship to the children and hus-

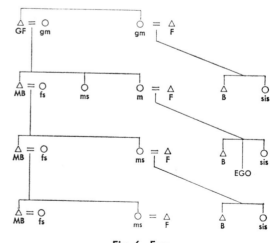

Fig. 6—Fox

Mother's Lineage

bands of all of them, although these persons belong to a number of different lineages.

Turning to the mother's patrilineal lineage, it can be seen that a man calls his mother's father "grandfather," but calls all the males of the lineage in the three succeeding generations "mother's brother" (MB). Similarly he calls the women of these three generations, except his own mother, by a term translated as "mother's sister" (ms). He applies the term "father" (F) to the husbands of all the women of the lineage through four generations (including the husband of the mother's father's sister) and the children of all these women are his "brothers" and "sisters." He is the son of one particular woman of a unified group, and the sons of the other women of the group are therefore his "brothers."

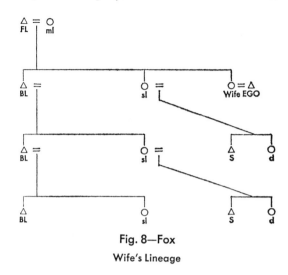

Fig. 8—Fox

Wife's Lineage

the men and women of a lineage through three generations. The children of all these "sisters-in-law" are "sons" and "daughters."

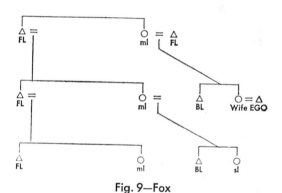

Fig. 9—Fox

Wife's Mother's Lineage

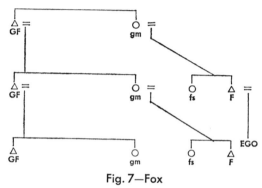

Fig. 7—Fox

Father's Mother's Lineage

In his father's mother's lineage Ego calls all the men and women throughout three generations "grandfather" and "grandmother." The children of these "grandmothers" are all his "fathers" and "father's sisters," irrespective of generation. In his mother's mother's lineage he also calls all the males "grandfather" and the females "grandmother," but I have not thought it necessary to include a figure to show this.

In his wife's lineage a man calls his wife's father by a term which we will translate "father-in-law" (FL). It is a modification of the word for "grandfather."* The sons and brother's sons of the "fathers-in-law" are "brothers-in-law" (BL), and the daughters are "sisters-in-law" (sl). The children of a "brother-in-law" are again "brother-in-law" and "sister-in-law." Thus these two terms are applied to

Fig. 9 shows the lineage of the wife's mother. In this lineage, through three generations, all the men are called "father-in-law" and all the women "mother-in-law."

Is the classification of relatives in the Fox terminology simply a matter of language, as some would have us believe? Dr. Tax's observations (1937) enable us to affirm that it is not. He writes:

The kinship terminology is applied to all known relatives (even in some cases where the genealogical relationship is not traceable) so that the entire tribe is divided into a small number of types of relationship pairs. Each of these types carries with it a more or less distinct traditional pattern of behaviour. Generally speaking, the behaviour of close relatives follows the pattern in its greatest intensity, that of farther relatives

---

* The Fox terms for father-in-law and mother-in-law are modifications of the terms for grandfather and grandmother. In the Omaha tribe the terms for grandparents, without modification, are appled to the parents-in-law and to those who are called "father-in-law" and "mother-in-law" in the Fox tribe.

in lesser degree; but there are numerous cases where, for some reason, a pair of close relatives "do not behave towards each other at all as they should."

Dr. Tax goes on to define the patterns of behaviour for the various types of relationship. Thus the classification of relatives into categories, carried out by means of the nomenclature, or therein expressed, appears also in the regulation of social behaviour. There is good evidence that this is true of other systems of Omaha type, and, contrary to Kroeber's thesis, we may justifiably accept the hypothesis that it is probably true of all.

Charts similar to those given here for the Fox Indians can be made for other systems of the Omaha type. I think that a careful examination and comparison of the various systems shows that, while there are variations, there is a single structural principle underlying both the terminology and the associated social structure. A lineage of three (or sometimes more) generations is regarded as a unity. A person is related to certain lineages at particular points: in the Fox tribe to the lineages of his mother, his father's mother, his mother's mother, his wife, and his wife's mother. In each instance he regards himself as related to the succeeding generations of the lineage in the same way as he is related to the generation with which he is actually connected. Thus all the men of his mother's lineage are his "mother's brothers," those of his grandmother's lineage his "grandfathers," and those of his wife's lineage are his "brothers-in-law."

This structural principle of the unity of the patrilineal lineage is not a hypothetical cause of the terminology. It is a principle that is directly discoverable by comparative analysis of systems of this type; or, in other words, it is an immediate abstraction from observed facts.

Let us now examine a society in which the principle of the unity of the lineage group is applied to matrilineal lineages. For this I select the system of the Hopi Indians, which has been analysed in a masterly manner by Dr. Fred Eggan (1950). The most significant features of the system are illustrated in the accompanying figures.

A man's own lineage is, of course, that of his mother. He distinguishes the women of his lineage by generation as "grandmother" (gm), "mother" (m), "sister" (sis), "niece" (n), and "grandchild" (gc). Amongst the men of his lineage he distinguishes his "mother's brothers" (MB), "brothers" (B) and "nephews" (N). But he includes his mother's mother's brother and his sister's daughter's son in the same category as his brothers. The structural principle exhibited here is that already referred to as the combination of alternative generations. It should be noted that a man includes the children of

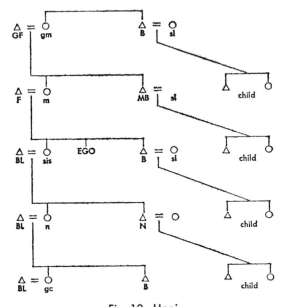

Fig. 10—Hopi

Mother's Lineage

all men of his own lineage, irrespective of generation, in the same category as his own children. Fig. 10 should be carefully compared with Fig. 5, for the Fox Indians, as the comparison is illuminating.

In his father's lineage a man calls all the male

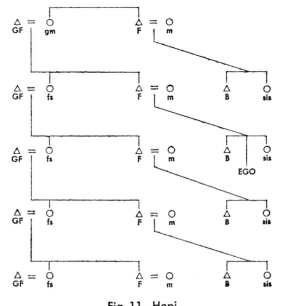

Fig. 11—Hopi

Father's Lineage

members through five generations "father" and, with the exception of his father's mother (his "grandmother"), he calls all the women "father's sister." The husband of any woman of the lineage is a "grandfather," and the wife of any man of the lineage is a "mother." The children of his "fathers" are "brothers" and "sisters." Fig. 11 should be carefully compared with Fig. 6.

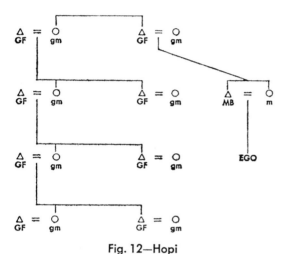

Fig. 12—Hopi
Mother's Father's Lineage

In his mother's father's lineage a man calls all the men and women through four generations "grandfather" and "grandmother."

The Hopi do not regard a man as related to his father's father's lineage as a whole, and the principle is therefore not applied to it. He does call his own father's father "grandfather."

Dr. Eggan has shown that for the Hopi this classification of relatives into categories is not simply a matter of terminology or language, but is the basis of much of the regulation of social life.

What is, I think, clearly brought out by a comparison of the Fox and Hopi systems is their fundamental similarity. By the theories of conjectural history this similarity is the accidental result of different historical processes. By my theory it is the result of the systematic application of the same structural principle, in one instance to patrilineal and in the other to matrilineal lineages.

I cannot, of course, discuss all the various systems of Choctaw and Omaha type. The variations that they show in certain features are very interesting and important. If you wish to test my theory you will examine them, or some of them, for yourselves, and the easiest way to analyse any system is to reduce it to a set of lineage charts similar to those

given here for the Fox and the Hopi. For any system such a set of charts will reveal the exact way in which the general principle of the unity of the lineage is applied. The manner of application varies somewhat, but the principle appears in each system of the type.

You will doubtless already have noticed that in these systems there are an extraordinary number of relatives of all ages to whom a man applies the terms "grandfather" and "grandmother." There is, I believe, a good reason for this, which should be briefly indicated. It is a general rule in societies having a classificatory terminology that for all the various relatives included under a single term there is some more or less definite pattern of behaviour which is regarded as normal or appropriate. But there are important differences in this matter. In certain instances the pattern can be defined by reference to specific rights and duties, or by specific modes of behaviour. For example, in the Kariera tribe of Australia a man must practice the most careful avoidance of all women who are included in the category of "father's sister," of whom there are very many and of whom his wife's mother is one. But in other instances all that the application of a term implies is a certain general attitude rather than any more specific relation. Within such a category there may be a specific jural or personal relation to a particular individual. In many classificatory systems the terms for grandfather and grandmother are used in this way, as implying a general attitude of friendliness, relatively free from restraint, towards all persons to whom they are applied. Grandparents and grandchildren are persons with whom one can be on free and easy terms. This is connected with an extremely widespread, indeed almost universal, way of organising the relation of alternate generations to one another.

In the Fox and Hopi systems all the members of the lineage of a grandparent are included in one category with the grandparents and the attitude that is appropriate towards a grandparent is extended to them. This does not imply any definite set of rights and duties, but only a certain general type of behaviour, of a kind that is regarded as appropriate towards relatives of the second ascending generation in a great many societies not belonging to the Choctaw and Omaha type.

I should have liked to discuss this further and to have dealt with those varieties of the Omaha type (such as the VaNdau) in which the mother's brother and the mother's brother's son are called "grandfather." But I have only time to draw your attention to a special variety of the Choctaw type which is of great interest in this connection. The Cherokee were divided into seven martrilineal clans. In the father's clan a man called all the men and women of his father's and all succeeding generations "father" and "father's sister," and this clan and all its individual members had to be treated with great respect. A man could not marry a woman of his father's clan, and of course he could not marry into his own clan. In the clan of his father's father and that of his mother's father a man calls all the women of all generations "grandmother." He thus treats, not the lineage, but the whole clan as a unity, although a clan must have numbered many hundreds of persons. With any woman whom he calls "grandmother" a man is allowed to be on free and easy terms. It was regarded as particularly appropriate that a man should marry a "grandmother," i.e. a woman of his mother's father's or father's father's clan.

Let us now return to a brief consideration of the special customs of marriage that have been proposed as causes of the Choctaw and Omaha terminologies respectively. Marriage with the wife's brother's daughter is theoretically possible and does perhaps actually, though only occasionally, occur in some of the tribes having a system of Omaha type. Though there has been no marriage of this kind in the Fox tribe in recent times it is spoken of as a custom that formerly existed. We have seen that the marriage custom and the terminology fit consistently. The reason for this should now be easy to understand, for a little consideration will show that this particular marriage is an application of the principle of the unity of the lineage combined with the custom of the sororate or sororal polygyny. In the usual form of these customs we are concerned only with the principle of the unity of the sibling group. A man marries one woman of a particular sibling group and thereby establishes a particular relation to that group as a unity. The men are now permanently his brothers-in-law. Towards one of the women he stands in a marital relationship, and therefore towards the others he is conceived as standing in a similar relationship which may be called a quasi-marital relationship. For instance, they will regard his children as being their "children." Thus it is appropriate that when he takes a second wife, whether before or after the death of his first, he should marry his wife's sister.

I am quite aware that sororal polygyny can be attributed to the fact that co-wives who are sisters are less likely to quarrel seriously than two who are not so related, and that the sororate may similarly be justified by the fact that a stepmother is more likely to have proper affection for her stepchildren if they are the children of her own sister. These propositions do not conflict with my explanation but support it, for the principle of the unity of the sibling group as a structural principle is based on the solidarity of brothers and sisters within one family.

When we turn to systems of the Omaha type, we see that in place of the unity of the sibling group we now have a unity of the larger group, the lineage group of three generations. When a man marries one woman of this group he enters into a relation with the group as a unity, so that all the men are now his brothers-in-law, and he at the same time enters into what I have called a quasi-marital relationship with all the women, including not only his wife's sisters but also his wife's brother's daughters, and in some systems his wife's father's sisters. The group within which, by the principle of the sororate, he may take a second wife without entering into any new social bonds is thus extended to include his wife's brother's daughter; and the custom of marriage with this relative is simply the result of the application of the principle of the unity of the lineage in a system of patrilineal lineages. The special form of marriage and the special system of terminology, where they occur together, are directly connected by the fact that they are both applications of the one structural principle. There is no ground whatever for supposing that one is the historical cause of the other.

The matter is much more complex when we come to the custom of marriage with the mother's brother's widow. This form of marriage is found associated with terminology of the Choctaw type in the Banks Islands, in the tribes of North-West America and in the Twi-speaking Akim Abuakwa. But it is also found in many other places where that type of terminology does not exist. Nor is it correlated with matrilineal descent, for it is to be found in African societies that are markedly patrilineal in their institutions. There does not seem to be any theoretical explanation that will apply to all the known instances of this custom. There is no time on this occasion to discuss this subject by an analysis of instances.

I must briefly refer to another theory, which goes back to Durkheim's review (1898) of Kohler, and by which the Choctaw and Omaha terminologies are explained as being the direct result of emphasis on matrilineal and patrilineal descent respectively. We have, fortunately, a crucial instance to which we can refer in this connection, in the system of the Manus of the Admiralty Islands, of which we have an excellent analysis by Dr. Margaret Mead (1934). The most important feature of the Manus system is the existence of patrilineal clans (called by Dr. Mead "gentes") and the major emphasis is on patrilineal descent. The solidarity of the patrilineal lineage is exhibited in many features of the system, but not in the terminology. However this emphasis on patrilineal descent is to a certain extent counterbalanced by the recognition of matrilineal lineages, and this does appear in the terminology in features that make it similar to the Choctaw type. Thus a single term, *pinpapu*, is applied to the father's father's sister and to all her female descendants in the female line, and a single term, *patieye*, is applied to the father's sister and all her descendants in the female line. The unity of the matrilineal lineage is exhibited not only in the use of these terms, but also in the general social relation in which a person stands to the members of it, and is an important feature of the total complex kinship structure.

One of the strange ideas that has been, and I fear still is, current is that if a society recognises lineage at all it can only recognize either patrilineal or matrilineal lineage. I believe the origin of this absurd notion, and its persistence in the face of known facts, are the result of that early hypothesis of conjectural history that matrilineal descent is more primitive, i.e. historically earlier, than patrilineal descent. From the beginning of this century we have been acquainted with societies, such as the Herero, in which both matrilineal and patrilineal lineages are recognised; but these were dismissed as being "transitional" forms. This is another example of the way in which attachment to the method and hypotheses of conjectural history prevents us from seeing things as they are. It was this, I think, that was responsible for Rivers' failing to discover that the Toda system recognises matrilineal lineage as well as patrilineal, and that the islands of the New Hebrides have a system of patrilineal groups in addition to their matrilineal moieties. Apart from the presuppositions of the method of conjectural history, there is no reason why a society should not build its kinship system on the basis of both patrilineal and matrilineal lineage, and we know that there are many societies that do exactly this.

In my criticism of the method of conjectural history I have insisted on the need for demonstration in anthropology. How then am I to demonstrate that my interpretation of the Choctaw-Omaha terminologies is the valid one? There are a number of possible arguments, but I have time for only one, which I hope may be considered sufficient. This is drawn from the existence of terminologies in which the unity of lineage or clan is exhibited, but which do not belong to either the Choctaw or the Omaha type; and I will mention one example, that of the Yaralde tribe of South Australia.

The Yaralde are divided into local patrilineal totemic clans. A man belongs to his father's clan, and we will consider his relation to three other clans: those of his mother, his father's mother and his mother's mother. The Yaralde, like many other Australian tribes, such as the Aranda, have four terms for grandparents, each of which is applied to both men and women. The term *maiya* is applied to the father's father and his brothers and sisters and to all members of a man's own clan of the second ascending generation. A second term, *naitja*, is applied to the mother's father and his brothers and sisters, i.e. to persons of the mother's clan of the appropriate generation. The third term, *mutsa*, is applied not only to the father's mother and her brothers and sisters, but to all persons belonging to the same clan, of all generations and of both sexes. The clan is spoken of collectively as a man's *mutsaurui*. Similarly the term *baka* is applied to the mother's mother and her brothers and sisters and to all members of her clan of all generations, the clan being spoken of as a man's *bakaurui*. The structural principle here is that for the outside related person the clan constitutes a unity within which distinctions of generation are obliterated. Compare this with the treatment of lineages or clans of grandparents in the Fox, Hopi and Cherokee systems.

The Yaralde terminology for relatives in the mother's clan is shown in Fig. 13. It will be noted that the mother's brother's son and daughter are not called mother's brother (*wano*) and mother (*nenko*) as in Omaha systems. But the son's son and daughter of the mother's brother are called "mother's brother" and "mother." If we wish to explain this by a special form of marriage it would have to be

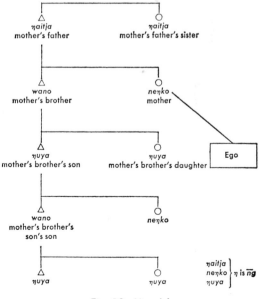

Fig. 13—Yaralde

Mother's Lineage

marriage with the wife's brother's son's daughter. I am not certain that such a marriage would be prohibited by the Yaralde system, but I am quite sure that it is not a custom so regular as to be regarded as an effective cause in producing the Yaralde terminology, and it would afford no explanation whatever for the terminological unification of the clans of the father's mother and the mother's mother. The structural principle involved is obviously that of the merging of alternate generations, which is of such great importance in Australia, and which we have also seen in the Hopi system. A system very similar to the Yaralde is found in the Ungarinyin tribe of North-West Australia, but I will not do more than refer to it.

Earlier in this address I said that I would try to show you that the Omaha type of terminology is just as reasonable and fitting in those social systems in which it is found as our own terminology is in our system. I hope I have succeeded in doing this. On the basis of the elementary family and the genealogical relationships resulting therefrom, we English have constructed for ourselves a certain kinship system which meets the necessities of an ordered social life and is fairly self-consistent. The Fox or the Hopi have on the same basis constructed a relatively self-consistent system of a different type which provides for the needs of social cohesion in a different way and over a wider range. We understand the terminology in each instance as soon as we see it as part of an ordered system. The obvious connection of the Omaha terminology with the custom of marriage with the wife's brother's daughter is seen as a relation between two parts of a self-consistent working system, not as a relation of cause and effect.

If you ask the question, "How is it that the Omaha (or any other of the tribes we have considered) have the system that they do?" then it is obvious that the method of structural analysis does not afford an answer. But neither does conjectural history. The proffered but purely hypothetical explanation of the Omaha terminology is that it resulted from the adoption of a certain unusual custom of marriage. This obviously gives us no explanation until we know why the Omaha and other tribes came to adopt this custom. The only possible way of answering the question why a particular society has the social system that it does have is by a detailed study of its history over a sufficient period, generally several centuries. For the tribes with which we are here concerned the materials for such a history are entirely lacking. This is, of course, very regrettable, but there is nothing that we can do about it. If you want to know how England comes to have its present system of constitutional monarchy and par-

liamentary government, you will go to the history books, which will give you the details of the growth of the system. If there were no records at all of this historical development, would the anthropologists think it worth while to spend their time in making conjectures as to what it might have been?

Even when there are historical records, they only enable us to discover how a particular system has grown out of a somewhat different particular system. Thus it would be possible to write a historical account of the changes of the kinship system of England during the past ten centuries. This would take us back to the Teutonic bilateral sib system, as exhibited in the institution of *wergild*. But we still should not know why the Teutonic peoples had this kind of system, while the Romans had a different system of agnatic lineages. The great value of history for a science of society is that it gives us materials for the study of how social systems change. In this respect conjectural history is absolutely worthless.

But if you ask, not how the English kinship system or the English political system came into existence, but how it works at the present time, that is a question that can be answered by research of the same kind as anthropological field-work, and historical considerations are relatively, if not absolutely, unimportant. Such knowledge of how social systems work is of great value for any understanding of human life. It often has been and still is neglected by anthropologists who consider it their principal task to write the history of peoples or institutions that have no history.

If you accept the analysis that I have given, but still wish to apply the method of conjectural history, what you have to conjecture is why all the tribes that have been enumerated elected to construct their kinship systems on the basis of the unity of the lineage.

What kind of results can we expect to obtain from the method of sociological analysis? Nothing, of course, that will be acceptable as significant by those who demand that any explanation of a social phenomenon must be a historical explanation, or by those who demand what is called psychological explanation, i.e. explanation in terms of the individual and his motives. I suggest that the results that we may reasonably expect are as follows:

1. It will enable us to make a systematic classification of kinship systems. Systematic classification is an essential in any scientific treatment of any class of phenomena, and such classification must be in terms of general properties.

2. It enables us to understand particular features of particular systems. It does this in two ways: (*a*) by revealing the particular feature as a part of an

organised whole; (*b*) by showing that it is a special example of a recognisable class of phenomena. Thus I have tried to show that the Choctaw and Omaha terminologies belong to a class which also includes the Yaralde terminology, and that these are all special applications of the general principle of the solidarity and continuity of the lineage, which appears in many other forms in a great number of different societies.

3. It is the only method by which we can hope ultimately to arrive at valid generalisations about the nature of human society, i.e. about the universal characteristics of all societies, past, present, and future. It is, of course, such generalisations that are meant when we speak of sociological laws.

In the method of conjectural history single problems are usually considered in isolation. On the other hand, the method of structural analysis aims at a general theory, and a great many different facts and problems are, therefore, considered together and in relation to one another. It is obvious that in this address, inordinately long as it has been, I have only been able to touch on a few points in the general theory of kinship structure. I have dealt briefly with one or two other points in earlier publications. That particular part of the general theory which has occupied us today may be said to be the theory of the establishment of type relationships. I have mentioned the tendency present in many societies to set up a type relationship between a person and all his relatives of the parents' generation, and the even more marked tendency to establish a type relationship, usually one of free and easy behaviour, towards the relatives of the grandparents' generation. I have not tried to deal with this except incidentally. The major part of the exposition has been concerned with two structural principles which are themselves examples of a more general structural principle or class of principles. By the principle of the unity of the sibling group a type relationship is set up between a given person and all the members of a sibling group to which he is related in a certain way. It is by reference to this principle, I hold, that we must interpret the classificatory terminology and such customs as the sororate and levirate. By the principle of the unity of the lineage group a type relationship is set up between a given person and all the members of a lineage group to which he is related in a certain way. It is by reference to this principle, I hold, that we must interpret the terminologies of the Fox, the Hopi and the Yaralde, and other similar systems in many scattered parts of the world.

If you will take the time to study two or three hundred kinship systems from all parts of the world you will be impressed, I think, by the great diversity that they exhibit. But you will also be impressed by

the way in which some particular feature, such as an Omaha type of terminology, reappears in scattered and widely spread regions. To reduce this diversity to some sort of order is the task of analysis, and by its means we can, I believe, find, beneath the diversities, a limited number of general principles applied and combined in various ways. Lineage solidarity in one form or another is found in a majority of kinship systems. There is nothing at all surprising in the fact that terminologies of the Choctaw and Omaha type, in which it finds what may be called an extreme development, should be encountered in separated regions of America, Africa, Asia and Oceania, in many different families of languages, and in association with many different types of "culture."

Last year I explained in general terms how I conceive the study of social structure (Radcliffe-Brown, 1940*b*). In this address, by means of a particular example, I have tried to show you something of the nature of a certain method of investigation. But do not think that this method can be applied only to the study of kinship. It is applicable in one way or another to all social phenomena, for it is simply the method of abstractive generalisation by the comparison of instances, which is the characteristic method of the inductive sciences.

"Why all this fuss about method?" some of you may perhaps ask. We cannot reach agreement as to the validity or the value of results unless we first reach some agreement as to objectives and the proper methods of attaining them. In the other natural sciences there is such agreement; in social anthropology there is not. Where we disagree, it should be the first purpose of discussion to define as precisely as possible the ground of difference. I have put my case before you, without, I hope, any unfairness towards those with whom I disagree. It is for you to judge which of the two methods that I have compared is most likely to provide that kind of scientific understanding of the nature of human society which it is the accepted task of the social anthropologist to provide for the guidance of mankind.

References

Durkheim, E. (1898). "Zur Urgeschichte der Ehe. Prof. J. Kohler," Analysis III, La Famille, *Année Sociologique*, Vol. I, pp. 306–319.

Eggan, F. (1950). *Social Organisation of the Western Pueblos*. Chicago University Press.

Gifford, E. W. (1916). "Miwok Moieties," *Arch and Ethn. Publ., Univ. California*, Vol. XII, No. 4.

Gilbert, William H., Jr. (1937). "Eastern Cherokee Social Organisation," in *Social Anthropology of North American Tribes* (ed. Fred Eggan). Chicago University Press, pp. 283–338.

Kohler, J. (1897). "Zur Urgeschichte der Ehe," *Zeitschrift für Vergleichende Rechtswissenschaft* (Stuttgart), Bd. 11.

Kroeber, A. L. (1909). "Classificatory Systems of Relationship," *F. R. Anthrop. Inst.*, Vol XXXIX, pp. 77–84.

———, (1917). "California Kinship Systems," *Arch. and Ethn. Publ. Univ. California*, Vol. XII, No. 9.

Mead, Margaret (1934). "Kinship in the Admiralty Islands," *Anthrop. Papers Amer. Mus. Nat. History*, Vol. XXXIV, Pt. II, pp. 181–358.

M'Lennan, John F. (1865). *Primitive Marriage.* Edinburgh: Adam & Charles Black.

Morgan, Lewis H. (1871). "The Systems of Consanguinity and Affinity," *Smithsonian Institution Contributions to Knowledge,* Vol. XVII.

———, (1877). *Ancient Society or Researches in the Lines of Human Progress from Savagery to Civilisation.* London: Macmillan; New York: Henry Holt.

Opler, M. E., (1937a). "Chiricahau Apache Social Organisation," in *Social Anthropology of North American Tribes.* (ed. Fred Eggan), Chicago University Press.

———, (1937b). "Apache Data Concerning the Relation of Kinship Terminology to Social Classification," *Amer. Anthrop.*, Vol. XXXIX, pp. 201–212.

Radcliffe-Brown, A. R. (1918). "Notes on the Social Organisation of Australian Tribes," Pt. I, *F. R. Anthrop. Inst.*, Vol. XLVIII, pp. 222–253.

———, (1924). "The Mother's Brother in South Africa," *South African F. Science*, Vol. XXI.

———, (1930–31). "The Social Organisation of Australian Tribes," Pts. I–III, *Oceania*, Vol. I, pp. 34–63, 206–246, 322–341, 426–456.

———, (1935). "Patrilineal and Matrilineal Succession," *Iowa Law Review,* Vol. XX, No. 2.

———, (1940a). "On Joking Relationships," *Africa*, Vol XIII, No. 3, pp. 195–210.

———, (1940b). "On Social Structure," *F. R. Anthrop. Inst.*, Vol. LXX, pp. 1–12.

Rivers, W. H. R. (1907). "On the Origin of the Classificatory System of Relationship," in *Anthropological Essays Presented to Edward Burnett Tyler.* Oxford: Clarendon Press. (Reprinted in *Social Organisation.* London: Kegan Paul, 1924, App. 1, pp. 175–192.)

———, (1914a). *History of Melanesian Society.* Cambridge University Press.

———, (1941b). *Kinship and Social Organisation.* London: London School of Economics.

Seligman, Brenda Z. (1917). "The Relationship Systems of the Nandi Masai and Thonga," *Man,* Vol. XVII, 46.

Starcke, C. N. (1889). *The Primitive Family* (The International Scientific Series, Vol. LXVI). London: Kegan Paul.

Stewart, Dugald (1795). Introduction to *Essays of Adam Smith.*

Tax, Sol (1937). "The Social Organisation of the Fox Indians," in *Social Anthropology of North American Tribes* (ed. Fred Eggan). Chicago University Press, pp. 241–282.

5. *The Household Community*

BY MAX WEBER

THE EXAMINATION of the specific, often highly complex effects of the ways in which human communities satisfy their economic requirements will not be undertaken in the following general review, and concrete individual instances will be considered merely as examples.

While abandoning any attempt to systematically classify community types according to their structure, content, and means of communal action—a task which belongs to general sociology—we turn to a brief elucidation of those types of community which are of the greatest importance for our argument. Only the relationship of the economy to society in general—that is to say, the general structural forms of human communities—will be discussed here and not the relationship between the economic sphere and specific areas of culture—literature, art, science, etc. Contents and directions of communal action are discussed only in so far as they give rise to specifically patterned forms of communal action that are also economically relevant. The resulting boundary is no doubt quite fluid. At any rate, we shall be concerned only with certain universal types of communities. What follows next is only a general characterization. Concrete historical forms of these types of communities will be discussed in greater detail in a later part of this work, devoted to authority.

The relationships between father, mother, and children, established by a stable sexual grouping [*sexuelle Dauergemeinschaft*], appear to us today as

Translated by Ferdinand Kolegar, from Max Weber, "Die Hausgemeinschaft," "Die sexuellen Beziehungen in der Hausgemeinschaft," "Die Entwicklung zum 'Oikos,'" "Die Aufloesung der Hausgemeinschaft: Aenderungen ihrer funktionellen Stellung und zunehmende 'Rechenhaftigkeit.' Entstehung der modernen Handelsgesellschaften," in *Wirtschaft und Gesellschaft* (Tübingen: J. C. B. Mohr [Paul Siebeck], 1947), I, 212–15, 218–19, 230–34, 226–30, with the permission of J. C. B. Mohr.

particularly fundamental relationships. However, separated from the extended kinship household as a producing unit, the sexually based relationship between husband and wife, and the physiologically determined relationships between father and children are wholly unstable and tenuous. The father relationship cannot exist without a producing household unit of father and mother; even where there is such a unit the father relationship may not always be of great import. Of all the communal relationships arising on the basis of sexual intercourse, only the mother-child relationship is fundamental, because it is a household unit whose biologically based stability is sufficient to cover the period until the child is able to search for means of subsistence on his own. Thereupon comes the community of experience of siblings brought up together. In this connection, it may be noted that the Greeks spoke of *homogalaktes* (literally: persons suckled with the same milk; hence, foster brothers or sisters) to denote the closest kin. Here, too, the decisive thing is not the fact of the common mother, but the existence of the extended kinship household as a producing unit. Criss-crossing of communal, sexual, and physiological relationships occurs particularly in the family as a specific social institution. Historically, the concept of the family had several meanings and it is useful only if its particular meaning is always clearly defined. More will be said later on about this.

Although the maternal grouping, i.e., the subgroup within the nuclear family formed by mother and children, must be regarded as (in the present sense) the most primitive community of familial character, it does not mean—indeed, it is unimaginable—that there ever were human forms of existence in which maternal groupings were the only communities. As far as it is known, wherever the maternal grouping prevails as a family type, communal relationships, economic and military, exist among men as well, and so do those of men with women (relationships of both sexual and economic nature). The pure maternal grouping as a normal, but obviously secondary, form of community is often found precisely where men's everyday life is confined to the stable community of a "men's house," at first for military purposes, later on for other reasons. Men's houses [*Männerhäuser*] can be found in various countries as a specific concomitant and a resultant of militaristic development.

One cannot think of marriage as a mere combination of the sexual community and the community of experience of father, mother, and children. The concept of marriage can be defined only with reference to other communities and relationships besides these. Marriage as a social institution comes into existence everywhere only as an antithesis to sexual relationships which are *not* regarded as marriage. The existence of a marriage means that (1) a relationship formed against the will of the wife's or the husband's kin will not be tolerated and may even be avenged by a corporate group, such as in olden times the kinsmen of the husband or of the wife or both. (2) It means especially that only children born of stable sexual relationships within a more inclusive economic, political, religious, or other community to which one or both parents belong will be treated, by virtue of their descent, as equal members of a corporate group—house, village, kin, political group, status group, religious group; while descendants who are a product of other sexual relationships will not be treated in such a manner. It should be noted that this is the meaning of the distinction between birth in wedlock and out of wedlock. The prerequisites of a legitimate marriage, the classes of persons not allowed to enter into stable relationships with each other, the kinds of permission and kinds of kinship or other corporate connections required for their validity, the usages which must be observed—all these matters are regulated by "sacred" traditions and orders of those corporate groups. Thus, it is the regulations of communal groups other than mere sexual groupings and sibling communities of experience which endow the marriage with its specific quality. We do not intend to expound here the anthropologically very significant development of these regulations, since it is only their most important economic aspects which concern us.

Sexual relationships and the relationships between children based on the fact of their common parent or parents can engender communal action only by becoming the normal, though not the only, bases of a specific economic corporate group: the household community.

The household community cannot be regarded as simply a primitive institution. Its prerequisite is not a "household" in the present-day sense of the word, but rather a certain degree of organized cultivation of soil. The household community does not seem to have existed in a primitive economy of hunters and nomads. However, even under the conditions of a technically well-advanced agriculture, the household community is often secondary with respect to a preceding state which accorded more power to the inclusive communal groups of kinship and neighborhood on the one hand, and more freedom to the individual vis-à-vis the community of parents, children, grandchildren, and siblings on the other hand. The almost complete separation of the husband's and wife's means and belongings, which was very frequent especially where social differentiation was low, seems to point in this direction, as does the occasional custom according to which man and wife were seated back to back during their meals or even took their meals separately, and the fact that even within the political corporate group there existed independent organizations of women with female chieftains alongside the men's organizations. However, one should not infer from such facts the existence of an individualistic primitive condition.

Conditions that are due to a certain type of military organization, such as the man's absence from the house for his military service, lead to a "manless" household management by the wives and mothers. Such conditions were in part preserved in the family structure of the Spartans, which was based on man's absence from home and separation of belongings. The size and inclusiveness of the household community varies. But it is the most widespread economic group [Wirtschaftsgemeinschaft] and involves a continuous and intensive communal action. It is the fundamental basis of loyalty and authority, which in turn is the basis of many other human communal groups. This "authority" is of two kinds: (1) the authority derived from superior strength; and (2) the authority derived from practical knowledge and experience. It is, thus, the authority of men as against women and children; of the able-bodied and brave as against those of lesser capability; of the adult as against the child; of the old as against the young. The "loyalty" again unites those who are subjected to an authority against those who yield authority, but it also binds one to the other. As reverence for ancestors, it finds its way into religion; as a loyalty of the patrimonial official, retainer, or vassal, it becomes a part of the relationships originally having a domestic character.

In terms of economic and personal relationships, the household community in its "pure," though not necessarily primitive, form implies solidarity in dealing with the outside and communism of property and consumption of everyday goods (household communism) within the household. The principle of solidarity in facing the outside world was still found in its pure form in the periodically contractually regulated household communities as enterpreneurial units in the medieval cities of northern and central Italy, especially those most advanced in capitalist economy. All members of the household, including at times even the clerks and apprentices who were by contract members of the community, were jointly responsible to the creditors. This is the historic source of the joint liability of the owners of a private company for the debts incurred by the firm. This concept of joint liability was of great importance in the subsequent development of the legal forms of modern capitalism.

There was nothing corresponding to our law of inheritance in the old household communism. In its place there was, rather, the simple idea that the household community is "immortal." If one of its members dies, or is expelled (after committing an inexpiable ill deed), or is permitted to join another household community (by adoption), or is dismissed (emancipatio), or leaves out of his own accord (where this is permitted), he cannot possibly lay claim to his "share." By leaving the household community he has relinquished his share. If a member of the household dies, the communal economy of the survivors simply goes on. The Swiss communes [Gemeinderschaft] operate in such a way to the present day.

The principle of household communism, according to which everybody contributes what he can and takes what he needs (as far as the supply of goods suffices), constitutes even today the essential feature of our family household, but is limited in the main to household consumption.

Common residence is an essential attribute of the pure type of household community. Increase in size brings about a division and creation of separate household communities. In order to keep the property and the labor force intact, a compromise based on local dencentralization without partition could be adopted. Granting some special privileges to the individual household is an inevitable consequence of such a solution. Such a partition can be carried to a complete legal separation and independence in the control of the business, yet a surprisingly large measure of household communism can still be preserved. It often happens in Europe, particularly in the Alps (cf. Swiss hotel-keepers' families), and also in the large family firms of international trade that, while the household community and household authority have outwardly completely disappeared, a communism of risk and profit, i.e., sharing of profit and loss of otherwise altogether independent business managements, continues to exist.

I have been told about conditions in international houses with earnings amounting to millions, whose capital belongs for the most part, but not exclusively, to relatives of varying degree and whose management is predominantly, but not solely, in the hands of the members of the family. The individual establishments operate in very diverse and everchanging lines of business; they possess highly variable amounts of capital and labor force; and they achieve widely variable profits. In spite of this, after the deduction of the usual interest on capital, the annual returns of all the branches are simply thrown into one hopper, divided into equal portions, and allotted according to an amazingly simple formula (often by the number of heads). The household communism on this level is being preserved for the sake of mutual economic support, which guarantees a compensation of capital requirements and capital surplus between the business establishments and spares them from having to solicit credit from outsiders. The calculating of gain ceases once the point of balance of assets and liabilities is reached. This calculability is practiced only within the establishment which makes the profit. But there it is applied without exception: even a close relative without capital and working as an employee will not be paid more than any other employee, because calculated costs of operation cannot be arbitrarily altered in favor of one individual without creating dissatisfaction in others.

Sexual Relationships in the Household Community

We now return to the household community as the most fundamental type of communal action that is "closed against outsiders." The typical course of development from the old full-fledged household communism is the exact opposite of the previously discussed development, in which the productive unit is preserved in spite of the outward separation of the households, namely internal relaxation of communism and progressive "closure" of the community within, while the outward unity of the household is preserved.

The earliest decline of the continuous household authority evidently does not stem directly from economic motives but from the development of exclusive sexual claims of the household partners on the women who are subject to the common household jurisdiction. This has led to an often highly casuistic regulation of sexual relationships, but, considering the low degree of rationalization of the communal action, these regulations were very strictly observed. Sometimes there exist "communistic" (polyandric) sexual rights. But these polyandrically shared rights, as far as it is known, invariably represent only a relative communism, i.e., a joint possession of a woman by a circumscribed group of persons (brothers or inmates of a "men's house"), from which all outsiders are excluded.

Nowhere, not even where sexual relationships among siblings are institutionalized, does one find complete sexual promiscuity within the household. At least not as a norm. On the contrary, a communistic freedom of sexual intercourse is banished from those households which practice communism in the possession of goods. This was made possible and customary by the attenuation of sexual excitation brought about by living together from childhood on. The "normalization" of this state was obviously in the interest of securing the house solidarity and freedom from rivalry in the household. Wherever the household inmates were assigned to different clans through "clan exogamy," and when the principles of clan exogamy thus made sexual intercourse within the household permissible, certain members of the household had to avoid each other. Household exogamy is an older institution than clan exogamy and continues to exist along with it. Household exogamy, brought about by "associations for the exchange of women" [*Frauentauschkartelle*], of household and kinship communities may be regarded as the beginning of regulated exogamy. At any rate, the conventional disapproval of sexual intercourse applies also to those close relatives who are not excluded from it by the clan's kinship code, e.g., very close paternal relatives in case of exclusive matrilineal succession in kinship exogamy. The institution of marriage among siblings and relatives, on the other hand, is usually confined to socially prominent families, especially royal families. Here it is instrumental to maintaining the household's economic means of power, as well as eliminating political struggles among pretenders, and preserving purity of blood.

Normally, when a man brings a wife into his household community or when, lacking the necessary means, he moves into her own household community, he acquires exclusive sexual rights to that woman. In reality, these exclusive rights are quite often precarious when compared with those enjoyed by an autocratic possessor of household power. For instance, the privileges enjoyed by the father-in-law within the extended family in Russia until modern times are notorious.

However, the household community becomes, as a rule, subdivided into stable sexual groupings, composed of a man, his wife, and their children. The community of parents with their children, their domestics, and unmarried relatives is the normal size of the household community in our society. The household communities of the earlier epochs were not always very large structures. On the contrary, they were often rather small units, especially when the way of earning a livelihood made dispersion necessary. In the past, there were large household communities which, while rooted in the parent and children relationship, extended far beyond it, including grandsons, brothers, cousins, and sometimes also non-kin, to a degree which is very rare among civilized peoples today (*viz.*, extended family). Extensive kinship households prevail where mass labor is employed, e.g., in intensive agricultural economies, but also in aristocratic and pluto-cratic strata, where, in order to preserve social and economic power positions, it is necessary to keep the property intact.

Apart from the early prohibition of sexual intercourse within the household community, the sexual sphere in an otherwise undeveloped culture is very often curbed by social structures that cut across the household authority in such a fashion that one can say that the first decisive break of the limitless household authority occurs in this area. With increasing attention paid to "blood relationship," the concept of incest extends beyond the household to wider circles of blood relatives living away from the household and becomes subject to clan regulation.

The Development to "Oikos"

In this section we are not particularly concerned with those forms of economic enterprise that became separated from the household community, and which represent the foundation of capitalistic enterprise. Rather, we are interested in the evolution of the household community that took an opposite course. We can distinguish between two lines of development. On the one hand, there is the internal dissolution of household authority and household community by means of "exchange with the outside world" (in the broadest sense of the term), and the consequences of this exchange up until the birth of capitalistic enterprise. On the other hand, there is the development in the opposite direction: the internal differentiation of the household community, its development to *oikos,* to use the term of Rodbertus. *Oikos* in the technical sense is not simply any extended household community or any group which produces on its own various products, industrial or agricultural. Rather, *oikos* refers to the authoritatively governed, expanded household of a prince, great landowner, or a patrician, the principle of which is not to earn money but to produce enough to satisfy the needs of the master through income received in kind. To this end, the master may use any means, including exchange. That the formative principle for him is the utilization of property for consumption needs and not as capital assets is of crucial importance. The essence of *oikos* is in the systematic satisfying of needs rather than in working for profit, even though individual industrial establishments oriented to profit-making may be attached to an *oikos.*

Between these two principles there is, of course, a whole range of gradual transitions and a frequent overlapping between the two. Actually, *oikos* in the

sense of a pure collective economy is seldom necessary once material culture reaches some appreciable degree of development. The *oikos* in its pure form, i.e., with the exclusion of exchange for profit, is possible only in "autarkic" economy, i.e., as an independent economic unit with a minimum of exchange. A staff of workers dependent on the household, often with highly specialized skills, is engaged in providing the master's economic, military, and sacramental goods and services. His own fields provide the master with all the necessary raw materials; his workshops and workers produce all the required goods; his own domestic servants, clerks, house priests, and warriors provide the rest. The only purpose of exchange, then, is to get rid of occasional surpluses and secure what the household itself cannot produce. This state of affairs is closely approximated by the royal economies of the Orient, especially of Egypt, and, to a lesser degree, by the economy of the noblemen and princes of the Homeric type. The royal households of the Persian and Franconian kings are closely related to it. The development of the landed proprietorships of the Roman Empire took this direction as their size and the bureaucratic and liturgical restrictions upon capitalistic acquisition increased and the influx of slaves decreased. The opposite tendency took place in the Middle Ages, with the growing importance of transportation of goods, cities, and money economy.

Oikos was never entirely autarkic in either of these types. The pharaohs and most of the kings and noblemen of the Mediterranean area, especially the primitive ones, were engaged in foreign trade; their treasures depended to a considerable extent on the revenues from this trade. The revenues of the landlords, as early as the Franconian Empire, included a large amount of money or valuable stock and incomes of all sorts. The capitularies of the Franconian law presuppose as a common occurrence the sale of the surpluses of the royal *fisci* not needed by the court and the army.

The unfree laborers of the large land- and slave-holders were usually only partly integrated into the economic organization controlled by the landlord. In the strict sense, this is true for personal servants and for those workers engaged in the economy satisfying the needs of the lord and who were fully taken care of by him ("autarkic units"). Yet, it is also true for those unfree laborers who worked for the master in his own enterprise for the market, in the same manner as the slaves of the landlords of Carthage, Sicily, and Rome worked on their plantations; or the slaves of Demosthenes' father worked in his two *ergasteria;* or, in modern times, Russian peasants worked in their landlords' factories ("market-oriented economy").

A large proportion of these slaves on plantations and in *ergasteria* were purchased in the market and were not "home-grown." Unfree laborers born in a household presuppose the existence of unfree families, i.e., a decentralization of the dependence on the household and usually a partial relinquishment by the lord of his total exploitation of the labor power.

The overwhelming majority of hereditarily unfree laborers is not used in centralized enterprises, and only a part of their productive power is at the disposal of the lord. These laborers pay him taxes, in kind or in money, fixed at a more or less arbitrary or traditional level. The question of how to use this labor force most profitably determines whether the lord will prefer to use the unfree labor as a working force or as a source of rent. In order to have a supplementary labor force of slaves without families lodged in barracks [*familienlose Kasernensklaven*], a cheap and continuous supply of slaves is necessary. Presuppositions of this are wars of slavery [*Menschenraubkriege*] and the availability of cheap food for the slaves, in other words, a southern climate.

Peasants in hereditary dependence can pay feudal dues in money only when they can bring their produce to an accessible—which means, generally, local—market, and when the towns of the area are sufficiently developed. Where cities are insufficiently developed and where crops can be sold only through export, the employment of peasants by way of *corvée* on the landlord's own estate was often the only way of using their labor force with profit. This was the case in eastern Germany and eastern Europe, in contrast to western Europe, in the beginning of the modern era, and in the Russian "black earth" area in the nineteenth century.

These conditions gave rise to the development of a large-scale agricultural enterprise within the *oikos*. The creation of large-scale industrial enterprises with unfree labor, or with the aid or exclusive use of hired free or unfree labor in his own or rented *ergasteria*, can make the manager of an *oikos* very much like a capitalistic entrepreneur, or can change him into one. This is exactly what happened, for instance, with the founders of the industrial system of the *starostas** in Silesia.

Utilizing the existing property so as to produce income is characteristic of the *oikos*. This, from the managerial point of view, can be actually indistinguishable from, and can finally become identical with, the enterpriser's own capital. Certain features of the *starostas* industry, as are to be found in Silesia, remind one of manorial economy. One such is

the combination of various enterprises, as, for instance, huge forestries with brick-yards, distilleries, sugar factories, and coal mines. These works are not linked with one another in the same way as a cluster of enterprises is united in a single modern enterprise ("combined" or "mixed"), by virtue of the fact that they represent different stages in the manufacture of certain raw material (including utilization of by-products and waste) or because they are connected by market conditions. The landlord who affiliates a foundry and perhaps even a steel mill with his coal mines, or who attaches sawmills and cellulose factory to his forestry, can achieve practically the same result; the difference then lies only in the point of departure, not in the outcome.

The beginnings of combinations of workshops based on the possession of a certain raw material can be found as early as the *ergasteria* of antiquity. The father of Demosthenes, coming from an Attic merchant family, was an importer and salesman (τῷ βουλομένῳ) of ivory, which could be used as an inlay in both knife handles and in furniture. Having already begun to let his own trained slaves manufacture knives in his workshop, he had to take over the *ergasterion* of an insolvent cabinet-maker, including the slaves working in that *ergasterion*. He owned then a cutler's and a cabinet-maker's *ergasterion*.

The development of *ergasteria* progressed in the Hellenistic, especially Alexandrine, and old-Islamic civilizations. Utilizing unfree industrial labor as a source of income was quite common in oriental and classic antiquity, in the early Middle Ages, and in Russia before the abolition of serfdom. The master used to lease his slaves as labor force. Nikias did so on a large scale, hiring out his untrained slaves to the mine-owners. Ultimately, he had the slaves taught some craft in order to utilize them more efficiently. We find this situation through all antiquity, beginning with a contract naming prince Cambyses an owner of a tutor up until the Pandects. The same phenomenon existed in Russia in the eighteenth and nineteenth centuries. After having them trained, the master may leave it up to the slaves to work as craftsmen on their own. Should they do so, they were obliged to pay him rent (in Greek, *apophora*; in Babylonian, *mandaku*; in German, *Halssteuer*; in Russian, *obrok*). The master may also provide a workshop for them and supply them with machinery (*peculium*) and capital (*merx peculiaris*). In the master's enterprise, there is a wide variety of all conceivable gradations that are historically documented, from almost complete freedom of movement to a complete caserne-like regimentation. The economic details and peculiarities of the "enterprises" that arose on the basis of the *oikos*, managed

* *Starosta* (in Poland) is a nobleman holding an estate of the Crown, with or without jurisdiction. Translator's note.

either by the lord or by his subordinates, belong within another context. The development and transformation of the *oikos* into patrimonial authority will be examined later, in connection with our analysis of the types of authority.

The Dissolution of the Household Community; Its Changing Function and Increasing "Calculability": The Origin of Modern Trading Companies

In the course of cultural development, the internal and external determinants of the weakening of household authority gain ascendancy. Operating from within, and correlated with the quantitative growth of economic means and resources, is the development and differentiation of abilities and wants. With the improvement and multiplication of life chances and opportunities, the individual becomes less and less content with being bound to rigid and undifferentiated forms of life prescribed by the community. Increasingly he desires to shape his life as an individual and to enjoy the fruits of his own abilities and labor as he himself wishes.

The dissolution of the household authority is furthered by a number of outside factors. One of them is the fiscal interest in a more intensive exploitation of the individual tax-paying capacity. While this is in favor of fitness for military service, it may work contrary to the interests in keeping one's property intact.

The usual consequence of these disintegrative tendencies is, in the first place, the increasing likelihood of division of household communities in case of inheritance or marriage of children. In the early times of relatively primitive agriculture without tools, employment of mass labor was the only means of increasing productivity. As a result, the household communities grew in size. The historical development and the concomitant development of individualized production brought about a decrease in the size of household communities, which continued until the family unit of parents and children reached its normal size today.

The function of the household community has changed so much that it is becoming increasingly inopportune for an individual to join a large communistic household. An individual no longer gets protection from the household and kinship groups but rather from the corporate political authority, which exercises compulsory jurisdiction. Furthermore, household and occupation became ecologically separated, and the household is no longer a unit of common production but a unit of common consumption. Moreover, the individual receives his entire education increasingly from agencies outside his home and by means which are supplied not by his home but by various institutions of the larger society: schools, bookstores, theaters, concert halls, clubs, public lectures, meetings, etc. He cannot thus regard the household community as the bearer of those cultural values in whose service he places himself.

This decrease in the size of household communities is not due to a growing "subjectivism" but to the objective determinants of its growth. It should not be overlooked that there exist also hindrances to this development, particularly on the highest levels of the economic scale. In agriculture, the possibility of unrestricted splitting up of landed estates is tied in with certain technological conditions. An estate of circular shape, even a large one, with valuable buildings on it, can be partitioned only at a loss. The division is technically facilitated by a sort of common farming, in which the various holdings lie side by side in strips, and by village settlement. Isolated location makes such a partition difficult. Separate farms and large estates, operated with an intensive expenditure of capital, therefore tend to be inherited by one individual. A small farm, operated with intensive expenditure of labor and whose holdings lie side by side without footpaths, so that a particular holding can only be reached by crossing that of a neighbor, has a tendency to continuous splintering. In addition, the separate farm and large estate are much more suitable objects from which to extract tributary taxes on movable property in the form of long-term mortgages and pawns, and they are thus kept intact for the benefit of the creditors.

Large property-holding, being a determinant of position and prestige, is conducive to the desire to keep it intact in the family. A small farm, on the other hand, is merely a place where work is done. There is an appositeness between the seigniorial standard of life, with its fixed conventions, and the large household communities. Given the spaciousness of, say, a castle and the almost inevitable "inner distance" even between the closest members, these large household communities do not restrain the freedom that the individual demands to such an extent as does the middle-class household, which may consist of an equally large number of persons but occupies a smaller space and lacks the aristocratic sense of distance. Today, the large household community provides an appropriate way of life, aside from the seigniorial one, only for an intense ideological community of a religious sect, or a social-ethical sect, or an artistic coterie—corresponding to the monasteries and cloister-like communities of the past.

Even where the household unit remains outwardly intact, the process of internal dissolution of household communism goes on irresistibly along with the growing "calculability." We shall now examine the consequences of this factor in somewhat greater detail.

In the large capitalistic household communities of medieval cities—for example, in Florence—every person has his own account. He has pocket money (*danari borsinghi*) at his free disposal. Specific upper limits are set for certain expenditures—for example, visitors staying at the house upon invitation. He has to settle his account in the same way as do partners in any modern trading company. He has capital shares "within" the community, and he has property (*fuori della compagnia*) deposited with the community, on which he draws interest but which is not regarded as capital and therefore does not share in the profit. Participation in the communal action of the household, with its advantages and obligations, which one is "born into" has thus been replaced by a rational consociation [*Vergesellschaftung*]. The individual is "born into" the household community, but even as a child he is already a potential commercial clerk and business partner of the rationally ordered business enterprise. It is evident that such conduct became possible only within the framework of a money economy; the development of the money economy therefore plays a crucial role in the internal dissolution of the household community. The money economy makes possible an objective calculation both of the productive performances and of the consumption of the individuals, and it makes it possible for them to satisfy their individual wants by "indirect exchange," through the medium of money.

The parallelism of the money economy and the attenuation of household authority is, of course, far from complete. Household authority and household community are economically "irrational" institutions independent of economic conditions of a particular period. In fact, their historical structure exercises considerable influence on the economic relationships. The socio-economic, political, and religious factors—such as the interest in keeping the property of a noble house intact; the military organization according to kinship and presumably household groups; the father's position as a house-priest—determined the origin of the *patria potestas* wielded by the Roman head of the family all his life. But it has persisted throughout the most diverse stages of economic development, until it attenuated in the period of Roman Empire.

A similar situation has been brought about in China by the principle of filial piety, reinforced by the code of duties and bolstered by the state authority and the Confucian bureaucratic ethic, for the purpose of maintaining political control over the subjects—among other things. This principle of filial piety in practice led to a number of undesirable consequences, both economically and politically. Regulations concerning mourning were one case in point. For example, frequent vacancies of offices occurred, because piety to the deceased head of the household—originally fear of the dead man's envy—forbade the use of his property and the occupation of his office. The economic factors originally determine whether a property is inherited by one person or principal heir or whether it is divided. This practice varies with economic influences, but it cannot be explained solely by economic factors, and especially not by contemporary economic conditions. This was demonstrated particularly in the recent studies of Sering. Under identical conditions and in contiguous areas, there exist often quite disparate systems, affected especially by different ethnic composition, e.g., Poles and Germans. The far reaching economic consequences of these differing structures were caused by factors that could be regarded as "irrational" from the economic point of view at the very beginning, or that became irrational as a consequence of changes in economic conditions.

In spite of all, the economic realities intervene in a compelling manner. First, there are characteristic differences depending on whether economic gain is attributed to common work or to common property. If the former situation obtains, the household authority is usually basically unstable, no matter how autocratic it may be. Mere separation from the parental household and the establishment of an independent household is sufficient for a person to be set free from the household authority. This is mostly the case in the large household communities of primitive agricultural peoples. The *emancipatio legis Saxonicae* of the German law clearly has its economic foundation in the recognition of the importance of personal work performance, which antedated the formulation of this law.

On the other hand, the household authority is typically stable wherever ownership of livestock, and property in general, forms the prime basis of existence. This is particularly true when land ceases to be abundant and becomes a scarce commodity. For reasons already alluded to, family and lineage cohesion is generally an attribute of the landed aristocracy. The man without any landed property or with only little of it is also without the corporate lineage group.

The same difference is to be found in the capitalistic stage of development. The large household communities of Florence and other parts of northern Italy practiced the principle of joint responsibility and of maintaining the property intact. In the trading places of the Mediterranean, especially in Sicily and southern Italy, the exact opposite was the case: each adult member of the household could at any time request the apportionment and his share while the legator was still alive. Nor did joint personal liability to the outsiders exist. In the family enterprises of northern Italy, the inherited capital represented the basis of economic power position to a greater degree than did the personal business activities of the partners. The opposite was true in southern Italy, where common property was treated as a product of common work. With the increasing importance of capital, the former practice gained ascendancy.

In terms of a hypothetical sequence of developmental stages starting with the continuous communal action, the "later" stage, i.e., capitalistic type of economy, determines a theoretically "earlier" structure, in which the members of the household are more tightly bound to the household and subjected to the household authority.

A far more significant transformation of household authority and household community, one which is characteristic of the Occident, took place in the household communities oriented to capitalistic enterprise, in Florence and other cities. The entire economic life of such a large household community was periodically regulated by contracts. Whereas, originally, the personal funds and the business organization were regulated by the same set of rules, the situation gradually changed. The conduct of continuous capitalistic enterprise became a special occupation, performed in a special undertaking [Betrieb], which became increasingly separated from the activity of the household community, in such a way that the old identity of household, workshop, and office fell apart. The household community ceased to exist as a necessary basis of rational consociation or associative relationship in business. Henceforth, the business partner is not necessarily—or typically—an inmate of the household. Consequently, it was mandatory to separate the business assets from the private property of the partners. Similarly, distinction began to be made between the employees of the business and the personal domestic servants. Above all, distinction had to be made between the debts of the commercial house and the private household debts of the individual partners. The joint responsibility of the partners was limited to the debts of the company, which were identified as such by being transacted under the "firm." i.e., under the name of the business company. This whole development is obviously a precise parallel to the separation of the bureaucratic

office as occupation from the private life; the separation of the "bureau" from the private household of the official; the separation of assets and liabilities of the office from the official's private property; and of the official dealings from private dealings. The capitalistic business organization, whose seeds are within the household community, is thus already related to the "bureau," and thus also to the now obvious bureaucratization of the private economic life.

But the factor of decisive importance in this development is not the spatial differentiation or separation of the household from the workshop and the store. This is rather typical of the bazaar system of the Islamic cities in the Orient, which rests throughout on the separation of the borough (Kasbeh), bazaar (suk), and residence. What is crucial is the separation of household and business for accounting and legal purposes; and the development of a suitable body of laws, such as the commercial register, elimination of dependence of the association and the firm upon the family, and the creation of appropriate laws on bankruptcy. This fundamental development is the characteristic feature of the Occident, and it is worthy of note that the legal forms of our present commercial law were almost all developed as early as the Middle Ages—whereas they were almost entirely foreign to the law of antiquity with its capitalism which was quantitatively sometimes much more developed. This is one of the many phenomena characterizing most clearly the qualitative uniqueness of the development of modern capitalism, since both the concentration of the family property for the purpose of mutual economic support and the development of a "firm" from a family name existed, for example, in China as well. There, too, the joint liability of the family stands behind the debts of the individual. The name used by a company in commercial transactions does not provide information about the actual proprietor: there, too, the "firm" is related to the business organization and not to the household. But the laws on private property and bankruptcy as they were developed in Europe seem to be absent in China. Two things are of special relevance: Association and credit, until the modern era, were to a large degree dependent on the kinship group. Likewise, the keeping of the property intact in the well-to-do kinship groups and the mutual granting of credit within the kinship groups served different purposes. They were concerned not with capitalistic profit but with raising money to cover the costs of family members' preparation for the examinations and afterwards for the purchase of an office. The incumbency of the office then offered the relatives an opportunity to recover their expenses with a profit from the legal and illegal revenues that the office afforded. Furthermore, these relatives could benefit from the protection of the office-holder. It was the chances of the politically rather than economically determined gain that were conducive to the "capitalistic" cohesion of the family, especially one that was well-off economically.

The capitalistic type of association, which corresponds to our joint-stock company and is completely detached, at least formally, from kinship and personal ties, has its antecedents in antiquity only in the area of politically oriented capitalism, i.e., in companies of tax farmers. In the Middle Ages, these were the companies organized partly for colonizing ventures—such as the big branches of the Maone in Genoa—and partly for state credit —such as the Genoese association of creditors, which actually managed the municipal finances. In the area of private enterprise, the strictly commercial and capitalistic association is at first developed merely as an *ad hoc* company (*commenda*) for distant trading, in the manner of occasional business according to varying circumstances, which existed already in the old Babylonian empire. An investor gave money to a traveling salesman for a specific trip, and they both then shared profit and loss. Enterprises that were endowed with monopolistic privilege by the state, especially joint-stock-company-type of colonial enterprises, formed then the transition to the application of these kinds of enterprises in private business.

II—ETHNIC SOLIDARITIES

1. Ethnic Groups

BY MAX WEBER

THE QUESTION of whether conspicuous "racial" differences are based on biological heredity or on social and cultural tradition is usually of no importance as far as their effect on mutual attraction or repulsion is concerned. This is true of the development of endogamous conjugal groups, and even more so of attraction and repulsion in other kinds of social intercourse, i.e., of whether all sorts of friendly, companionable, or economic relationships between such groups are established easily and on the footing of mutual trust and respect, or whether such relationships are established with difficulty and with precautions that betray mistrust.

Groups within which easy social intercourse is possible may have their source and beginning in the most superficial differences of outward habits of life, which were formed due to some historical accident, just as well as in inherited racial characteristics. That the deviant custom is not understood in its subjective meaning since the key to it is lacking, is almost as decisive as the peculiarity of the deviant customs as such. But, as we shall soon see, not all repulsion is attributable to the absence of mutual understanding. Differences in the style of beard and hairdo, clothes, food and eating habits, division of labor between the sexes, and all kinds of visible differences can, in some cases, give rise to repulsion and contempt for the bearers of these strangely different ways. In their effect on the feeling of attraction or repulsion, there are as few distinctions between the importance or unimportance of the above-mentioned differences as in the primitive travel descriptions, or in the Histories of Herodotus, or in the old prescientific ethnography. Seen from their positive aspect, however, these differences may give rise to a consciousness of kind. This consciousness of kind may then become the bearer of communal social relationships. Likewise, every type of community, from a household group or neighborhood group to a political or religious community, typically becomes a bearer of shared customs. All differences of custom can sustain a specific sense of

Translated by Ferdinand Kolegar, from Max Weber, "Entstehung ethnischen Gemeinsamkeitsglaubens. Sprach- und Kultgemeinschaft," in *Wirtschaft und Gesellschaft* (Tübingen: J. C. B. Mohr [Paul Siebeck], 1947), I, 234– 40, with the permission of J. C. B. Mohr.

"honor" or "dignity" in their practitioners. The original motives or reasons for the inception of different habits of life are forgotten and the contrasts are then perpetuated as conventions.

Any community can create customs, and it can also effect, in certain circumstances very decisively, the selection of anthropological types. This it can do by breeding, by providing favorable chances of life, survival, and reproduction for certain hereditary qualities and traits. This holds both for internal assimilation and for external differentiation.

Any aspect or cultural trait, no matter how superficial, can serve as a starting point for the familiar tendency to monopolistic closure. The universal force of imitation has the general effect of only gradually changing both the anthropological types through racial mixing and the traditional customs and usages. Sharp boundaries between areas of externally observable styles of life often arose by conscious monopolistic closure. This started from small differences, which were then purposely cultivated and intensified. Or they arose when, as a result of either peaceful or warlike migrations, communities that had previously lived far from each other and had accommodated themselves to their heterogeneous conditions of existence now came to live side by side. Similarly, sharply different racial types, which came into being by breeding in isolation, may come into close mutual contact either because of monopolistic closure or because of migration.

Similarity and contrast of physical type and of custom have the same effect on formation of a community and are subject in their origin and change to identical conditions of communal life, regardless of whether they are biologically inherited or culturally transmitted. The difference lies partly in their differential instability, depending on whether they are biologically inherited or transmitted by tradition, partly in the fixed (though often unknown) limit to engendering new hereditary qualities. Compared to this, the scope for assimilation of new customs is incomparably greater, although there are considerable variations in the transmissibility of traditions.

Almost any kind of similarity or contrast of physical type and of habits can induce the belief that a tribal affinity or disaffinity exists between groups that attract or repel each other. Not every belief in tribal affinity, however, is founded on the resemblance of customs or of physical type. But, in spite of great variations in this area, such a belief can exist and can develop community-forming powers when it is buttressed by a memory of an actual migration, be it colonization or individual migration. The persistent effect of the old and traditional ways

and of childhood reminiscences can be a source of a homeland or native-country sentiment [*Heimatsgefuehl*] among emigrants, even when they have become so thoroughly adjusted to the new country that return to their homeland would be intolerable (this being the case of most German-Americans, for example).

In colonies, the attachment to the colonists' homeland survives despite considerable mixing with the inhabitants of the colonial land and despite profound changes in tradition and hereditary type as well. In case of political colonization, the decisive factor is the need of political support. In general, the continuation of relationships created by marriage is important, and so are the market relationships, provided that the "customs" remained unchanged. These market relationships between the homeland and the colony may be very close, especially when colonies are in an almost absolutely alien environment and within an alien political territory.

The belief in tribal kinship, regardless of whether it has any objective foundation, can have important consequences especially for the formation of a political community. Those human groups that entertain a subjective belief in their common descent —because of similarities of physical type or of customs or both, or because of memories of colonization and migration—in such a way that this belief is important for the continuation of non-kinship communal relationship, we shall call "ethnic" groups, regardless of whether an objective blood relationship exists or not. The ethnic group differs from the kinship community precisely in being a group (which believes in its common descent) but not a community, unlike the kinship group which is characterized by actual communal action. In our present sense, the ethnic community itself is not a community; it only facilitates communal relationships. It facilitates and promotes all types of communal relationships, particularly in the political sphere. On the other hand, it is primarily the political community, no matter how artificial, that inspires the belief in common ethnicity. This belief tends to persist even after the disintegration of the political community, unless drastic differences in the custom, physical type, or, above all, language exist among its members.

This artificial origin of the belief in common ethnicity is in full accord with the already described schema of transmutation of rational associative relationships into personalized communal relationships. In the relative absence of rational associative action, almost any, even a purely rational, consociation can attract communal consciousness in the form of personal confraternity based on the belief in common ethnicity. The Greeks still viewed even the arbitrary divisions of the *polis* in terms of personal "corporate groups," with a distinct community of cult and claiming a common artificial ancestor. The twelve tribes of Israel were subdivisions of a political community, and they alternated in performing certain functions on a monthly basis. The same holds for the Greek tribes (*phyle*) and their subdivisions. But even the latter are regarded as units of common ethnic descent. The original division may have been induced by political or actual ethnic differences. The effect, however, was the same, even where such a division was made quite purposely and on the basis of rational considerations, after the break-up of old corporate groups and relinquishment of local cohesion, as it was done by Cleisthenes. This does not mean that, as a rule, the Greek *polis* was actually or originally a tribal or dynastic state. But it is, in general, a sign of the rather low degree of rationalization of Greek communal [political] life. Conversely, it is a symptom of the greater rationalization of the Roman political community that its old schematic subdivisions (*curiae*) took on religious importance with a pretense to ethnic origin to only a small degree.

The belief in common ethnicity is very often, though not always, an obstacle to the existence of groups where easy social intercourse [*soziale Verkehrsgemeinschaften*] is possible. Such groups are not identical with the endogamous conjugal groups, since both of them can be of varying scope and range. But they both rest on a similar basis, which is the belief in a specific "honor" of their members, not shared by the outsiders, i.e., the sense of ethnic honor. Later on we shall discuss how it is related to the sense of honor of a distinctive social group [*staendische Ehre*]. At this point a few remarks will suffice. A rigorous sociological investigation would have to make a much finer distinction between these concepts than we have done for our limited purpose here.

Communities can engender sentiments of community [*Gemeinsamkeitsgefuehle*], which will persist even after the community itself has disappeared and which will have an "ethnic" connotation. The political community in particular can produce such an effect. This is especially so in the case of that type of a community which is the bearer of a specific "culture value of the masses" [*Massenkulturgut*] and which makes mutual understanding possible or easier, namely, the community of language.

Wherever the memory of the origin of an *émigré* community by peaceful secession or emigration ("colony," *ver sacrum,* and the like) from a mother community remains for some reason continually alive, there undoubtedly exists a very specific and often extremely powerful sense of ethnic community. This sense of ethnic community is determined by several factors: by the shared political "memory" or, even more importantly in the earlier times, by the existence of ties with the old cult-communities; and by unceasing strengthening of the kinship groups and other communal relationships by means of pervasive and ever felt relations between the old and the new community. Where these relationships are lacking, or once they cease to exist, the sense of ethnic community is absent, regardless of how close the kinship may be.

Apart from the community of language, which may or may not coincide with objective or subjectively believed consanguinity, and apart from common religious belief, which is also independent of consanguinity, and apart from the effect of common political fortunes and the memories thereof, which at least objectively have nothing to do with consanguinity, the ethnic differences that remain are, on the one hand, aesthetically conspicuous differences of the external physical appearance and, on the other hand and of equal weight, the perceptible differences in the conduct of everyday life. Of special importance are precisely those items which may otherwise seem to be of small social relevance, since when ethnic differentiation is concerned it is always the outward conspicuous differences that come into play.

The community of language and, along with it, the identity of the "ritual regimentation of life," as determined by shared religious beliefs, obviously are universal elements of feelings of ethnic affinity [*ethnische Verwandtschaftsgefuehle*], especially since the meaningful "intelligibility" [*sinnhafte Verstaendlichkeit*] of the behavior of others is the most fundamental presupposition of communal relationship. But since we shall not consider these two elements in the present context, we ask: what is it that remains? It must be admitted that palpable differences in dialect and differences of religion in themselves do not exclude sentiments of common ethnicity.

Next to pronounced differences in the style of economic life, the belief in ethnic affinity has at all times been affected by outward differences in clothes, in the style of housing, food and eating habits, the division of labor between the sexes, and between the free and the unfree. That is to say, these things concern one's conception of what is correct and proper and, above all, of what affects the individual's sense of honor and dignity. All those things we shall find later on as objects of specific differences between "status" groups. The conviction of the excellence of one's own customs and the inferiority of alien ones, a conviction which sustains the sense of ethnic honor, is actually quite analogous to the sense of honor of distinctive status groups.

The sense of ethnic honor is a specific honor of the masses [*Massenehre*], for it is accessible to anybody who belongs to the subjectively believed community of descent. The "poor white trash," i.e., the propertyless and, in the absence of free work opportunities, very often destitute white inhabitants of the southern states of the United States of America in the period of slavery, were the actual bearers of racial antipathy, which was quite foreign to the planters. This was so because the social honor of the "poor whites" was dependent upon the social *déclassement* of the Negroes.

And behind all ethnic diversities there is somehow naturally the notion of the "chosen people," which is nothing else but a counterpart of status differentiation translated into the plane of horizontal coexistence. The idea of a chosen people derives its popularity from the fact that it can be claimed to an equal degree by any and every member of the mutually despising groups, in contrast to status differentiation which always rests on subordination. Consequently, ethnic repulsion may take hold of all conceivable differences between the notions of propriety and transforms them into "ethnic conventions."

Besides the previously mentioned elements, which were still more or less closely related to the economic order, conventionalization (a term to be expounded later) may take hold of such things as a hairdo or style of beard and the like. The differences thereof have an "ethnically" repulsive effect, because they are thought of as symbols of ethnic membership. The repulsion naturally is not based merely on the "symbolic" character of the distinguishing traits. The fact that the Scythian women oiled their hair with butter, which then gave off a rancid odor, while Greek women used perfumed oil to achieve the same purpose, thwarted—according to an ancient report—all attempts at social intercourse between the aristocratic ladies of these two groups. The smell of butter certainly had a more compelling effect than even the most prominent racial differences, or than—as far as I could see—the "odor of Negroes," of which so many fables are told. In general, racial qualities are effective as limiting factors in giving rise to the belief in common ethnicity, such as in case of an excessively heterogeneous and aesthetically unaccepted physical type; they are not positively "community-forming."

Pronounced differences of custom, which play a role equal to that of inherited physical type in the creation of feelings of common ethnicity and ideas of kinship, are usually caused, in addition to linguistic and religious differences, by the diverse economic and political conditions of various human social groups. If we ignore clear-cut linguistic boundaries and sharply demarcated political or religious communities as a basis of differences of custom—and these in fact are lacking in wide areas of the African and South American continents—then there are only gradual transitions of custom and no immutable ethnic frontiers, except those due to gross geographical differences. The sharp demarcation of areas wherein ethnically relevant customs predominate, which were not conditioned either by political or economic or religious factors, usually came into existence by way of migration or expansion, when groups of people that had previously lived in complete or partial isolation from each other and became accommodated to heterogeneous conditions of existence came to live side by side. As a result, the obvious contrast usually evokes, on both sides, the idea of blood disaffinity or "foreignness" [*Blutsfremdheit*], regardless of the objective state of affairs.

It is understandably difficult to determine in general—and it is of questionable importance even in a concrete individual case—what influence specific ethnic factors (i.e., the belief in a blood relationship, or its opposite, which rests on similarities, or differences, of a person's physical appearance and style of life) have on the formation of a community.

There is no difference between the ethnically relevant customs and customs in general, as far as their effect is concerned. The belief in affiliation of descent [*Abstammungsverwandtschaft*], in combination with a similarity of customs, is likely to promote the diffusion of communal action among those allied by ethnic ties, because "imitation" is generally encouraged by the consciousness of community. This is especially true of the propaganda of religious communities. But these are all-too-vague statements. The content of communal action that is possible on an ethnic basis remains indefinite. There is a corresponding ambiguity of concepts denoting ethnically determined communal action, i.e., determined by the belief in blood relationship. Such concepts are "clan," "tribe," "nation," each of which is ordinarily used in the sense of an ethnic subdivision of the following one (although the first two may be used in reversed order). Using such terms, one usually tacitly assumed either the existence of a contemporary political community, be it even a loose one; or memories of an extinct political community, such as they are preserved in epic tales and legends; or the existence of a linguistic community; or, finally, of a religious community.

Certain religious communities especially were the typical concomitants of a tribal or national consciousness based on a belief in blood relationship. But in the absence of the political community, present or past, the external delimitation of such a community was usually rather indistinct. The religious communities of Germanic tribes, as late as the late Burgundian period, were rudiments of political communities and therefore apparently firmly delimited. The Delphian oracle was an undoubted cultic sign of the national identity of the Greek world. But God revealed information even to the barbarians and accepted their adulation, too, and only few segments of Greeks, and none of their

most powerful communities, took part in the "societalized" administration of this cult. The community of cult as an index of "tribalism" is thus generally either a remnant of a largely political type of community, which once existed but was destroyed by disunion and colonization, or it is—as in the case of Delphian Apollo—a product of a "culture-community" brought about by other than purely ethnic conditions, and which in its turn gives rise to the belief in blood relationship. All history shows how easily political communal action can give rise to the idea of blood relationship, unless gross differences of anthropological type are there to impede it.

2. *The Problem of Minority Groups*

BY LOUIS WIRTH

WE MAY DEFINE a minority as a group of people who, because of their physical or cultural characteristics, are singled out from the others in the society in which they live for differential and unequal treatment, and who therefore regard themselves as objects of collective discrimination. The existence of a minority in a society implies the existence of a corresponding dominant group enjoying higher social status and greater privileges. Minority status carries with it the exclusion from full participation in the life of the society. Though not necessarily an alien group, the minority is treated and regards itself as a people apart.

To understand the nature and significance of minorities it is necessary to take account of their objective as well as their subjective position. A minority must be distinguishable from the dominant group by physical or cultural marks. In the absence of such identifying characteristics it blends into the rest of the population in the course of time. Minorities objectively occupy a disadvantageous position in society. As contrasted with the dominant group they are debarred from certain opportunities—economic, social and political. These deprivations circumscribe the individual's freedom of

choice and self-development. The members of minority groups are held in lower esteem and may even be objects of contempt, hatred, ridicule, and violence. They are generally socially isolated and frequently spatially segregated. Their subordinate position becomes manifest in their unequal access to educational opportunities and in their restricted scope of occupational and professional advancement. They are not as free as other members of society to join the voluntary associations that express their interests. They suffer from more than the ordinary amount of social and economic insecurity. Even as concerns public policy they are frequently singled out for special treatment; their property rights may be restricted; they may not enjoy the equal protection of the laws; they may be deprived of the right of suffrage and may be excluded from public office.

Aside from these objective characteristics by which they are distinguished from the dominant group and in large measure as a result of them, minorities tend to develop a set of attitudes, forms of behavior, and other subjective characteristics which tend further to set them apart. One cannot long discriminate against people without generating in them a sense of isolation and of persecution and without giving them a conception of themselves as more different from others than in fact they are. Whether, as a result of this differential treatment, the minority

Reprinted from Louis Wirth, "The Problem of Minority Groups," in Ralph Linton (ed.), *The Science of Man in the World Crisis* (New York: Columbia University Press, 1945), pp. 347–52, 354–56, 358–60, 361–64, with the permission of Columbia University Press.

comes to suffer from a sense of its own inferiority or develops a feeling that it is unjustly treated—which may lead to a rebellious attitude—depends in part upon the length of time that its status has existed and in part upon the total social setting in which the differential treatment operates. Where a caste system has existed over many generations and is sanctioned by religious and other sentiments, the attitude of resignation is likely to be dominant over the spirit of rebellion. But in a secular society where class rather than caste pervades the stratification of people, and where the tradition of minority status is of recent origin, minorities, driven by a sense of frustration and unjustified subordination, are likely to refuse to accept their status and their deprivation without some effort to improve their lot.

When the sentiments and attitude of such a disadvantaged group become articulate, and when the members become conscious of their deprivations and conceive of themselves as persons having rights, and when they clamor for emancipation and equality, a minority becomes a political force to be reckoned with. To the individual members of such a group the most onerous circumstance under which they have to labor is that they are treated as members of a category, irrespective of their individual merits. Hence, it is important to recognize that membership in a minority is involuntary; our own behavior is irrelevant. Many of us are identified with political, social, and intellectual groups which do not enjoy the favor of the dominant group in society, but as long as we are free to join and to leave such groups at will we do not by virtue of our membership in them belong to a minority. Since the racial stock from which we are descended is something over which we have perhaps least control and since racial marks are the most visible and permanent marks with which we are afflicted, racial minorities tend to be the most enduring minorities of all.

It should be noted further that a minority is not necessarily an alien group. Indeed, in many parts of the world it is the native peoples who constitute the minority, whereas the invaders, the conquerors, or the newcomers occupy the status of dominant groups. In the United States the indigenous Indians occupy the position of a minority. In Canada the earlier French settlers are a minority in relation to the more recent English migrants. In almost all colonial countries it is the "foreigners" who are dominant and the indigenous populations who are subordinate.

Nor should it be assumed that the concept is a statistical one. Although the size of the group may have some effect upon its status and upon its relationship to the dominant group, minorities are not to be judged in terms of numbers. The people whom we regard as a minority may actually, from a numerical standpoint, be a majority. Thus, there are many parts of the South in the United States where the Negroes are the overwhelming majority of the inhabitants but, nevertheless, are an unmistakable minority in the sense that they are socially, politically, and economically subordinate.

It may even be true that a people may attain the status of a minority even though it does not become the object of disesteem, discrimination, and persecution. If it considers itself the object of such inferior treatment, an oppression psychosis may develop. If a group sets itself apart from others by a distinctive culture and perpetuates itself in this isolated condition long enough, the social distances between itself and others may grow so great as to lead to the accumulation of suspicion and non-intercourse which will make it virtually impossible for members of these groups to carry on a truly collective life. Lack of intimate knowledge of and contact with others may in the course of time generate an incapacity for mutual understanding and appreciation which allows mental stereotypes to arise which the individual cannot escape. What matters, then, about minorities is not merely their objective position but the corresponding patterns of behavior they develop and the pictures they carry around in their heads of themselves and of others. While minorities more often than not stand in a relationship of conflict with the dominant group, it is their nonparticipation in the life of the larger society, or in certain aspects thereof, that more particularly marks them as a minority people and perpetuates their status as such.

It is easy enough to catalog the minority peoples in various parts of the world in accordance with a set of criteria such as race, national origin, language, religion, or other distinctive cultural traits. Thus it is possible to define the areas of the world where one or another racial, ethnic, linguistic, or religious group occupies a subordinate status with reference to some other group. In different parts of the world different groups are consigned to minority status. A given racial, ethnic, linguistic, or religious group may be dominant in one area and be the minority in another. Similar variations are found throughout history. Groups which in one epoch were dominant may in another be reduced to subordinate status. Because of the colonizing enterprises of some of the nation-states of Western Europe a large part of the rest of the world has been subordinated to their political rule, their economic control, and the technology and culture which the European settlers managed to superimpose upon the peoples and areas which they brought under their domain. On a world scale, therefore, there is an extraordinarily close association between the white Western Europeans as colonizers and conquerors and their status as dominant groups. Correspondingly, there is a close association between the nonwhite peoples of the world as the conquered and enslaved peoples and their status as minority groups. There are notable exceptions, however, both in time and in space. In an earlier period of European history the yellow peoples of the East overran vast stretches of the European continent and for a time at least reduced the natives to inferior status. There had been similar, though temporary, invasions of Europe from Africa in the course of which Negroid groups became dominant over the white Europeans. Similarly, the enterprise and military prowess of the Japanese has led to the subjugation of vast stretches of the Orient beyond their island empire which contain many areas and great populations of non-Japanese stock, including European whites. On the whole, however, the expansion of European civilization to the ends of the earth has been so irresistible that from a racial standpoint, virtually the world over, the whites constitute the dominant group and the colored peoples the minorities.

We are less concerned, however, in this analysis, with racial minorities than with ethnic minorities, and hence it will be well to examine in some detail the linguistic, religious, and national minorities within the white group in Europe and in America. The existence of such groups in virtually every European and American country calls attention to the fact that the modern nation-states into which we are accustomed to divide the world and to which we are wont to ascribe a high degree of ethnic homogeneity are far from being as closely knit by intermarriage, in-breeding, social intercourse, and freedom of opportunity for everyone as the stereotypes of national cultures appear to indicate.

In Europe and in America there are today vast differences between the status of different ethnic groups from country to country and from region to region. In pre-war Poland under the Czarist regime the Poles were a distinct ethnic minority. When they gained their independence at the end of the first World War, they lost their minority status but reduced their Jewish fellow Poles to the status of a minority. As immigrants to the United States the Poles again became themselves a minority. During the brief period of Nazi domination the Sudeten Germans of Czechoslovakia reveled in their position of dominance over the Czechs among whom they had only recently been a minority. The European immigrants to the United States from such dominantly Catholic countries as Italy and Poland, for instance, find themselves reduced from a dominant

to a minority group in the course of their immigration. It is not the specific characteristics, therefore, whether racial or ethnic, that mark a people as a minority but the relationship of their group to some other group in the society in which they live. The same characteristics may at one time and under one set of circumstances serve as marks of dominant status and at another time and under another set of circumstances symbolize identification with a minority.

It is much more important, therefore, to understand the nature and the genesis of the relationship between dominant group and minority group than it is to know the marks by the possession of which people are identified as members of either. Once we know that almost any distinctive characteristics, whether it be the physical marks of race, or language, religion, and culture, can serve as criteria of membership in a minority we will not be inclined to construct a typology of minorities upon the marks by which they are identified. A fruitful typology must rather be useful in delineating the kinds of relationships between minorities and dominant groups and on the kinds of behavior characteristically associated with these types of relationships.

An adequate typology of minorities must, therefore, take account of the general types of situations in which minorities find themselves and must seek to comprehend the *modus vivendi* that has grown up between the segments of those societies in which minority problems exist. There are a number of axes alongside of which the problems of minorities range themselves. Among these are: (1) the number and size of distinct minorities in the society in question; (2) the degree to which minority status involves friction with the dominant group or exclusion from participation in the common life of the society; (3) the nature of the social arrangement governing the relationship between minority and dominant group; and, (4) the goals toward which the minority and dominant groups are striving in quest of a new and more satisfactory equilibrium. A survey of historical and contemporary minority problems along these lines will probably not cover the whole range of minority problems and to that extent the typology will be partial. At the same time it should be understood that as long as the relations between minority and dominant group are fluid—and wherever they do not rest upon long-accepted and settled premises—any rigid typology will prove unsatisfactory. Conversely where the minority's relationship to the dominant group is definitely structuralized and embedded in the mores, laws, and institutions a typological approach may be highly rewarding.

*　　*　　*

While the above criteria might give us a basis for the classification of minorities, they do not come as close to the actual minority problems that plague the modern world as we can come by analyzing the major goals toward which the ideas, the sentiments, and the actions of minority groups are directed. Viewed in this way minorities may conveniently be typed into: (1) pluralistic; (2) assimilationist; (3) secessionist; and (4) militant.

A pluralistic minority is one which seeks toleration for its differences on the part of the dominant group. Implicit in the quest for toleration of one's group differences is the conception that variant cultures can flourish peacefully side by side in the same society. Indeed, cultural pluralism has been held out as one of the necessary preconditions of a rich and dynamic civilization under conditions of freedom. It has been said in jest that "tolerance is the suspicion that the other fellow might be right."

Toleration requires that the dominant group shall feel sufficiently secure in its position to allow dissenters a certain leeway. Those in control must be convinced either that the issues at stake are not too vital, or else they must be so thoroughly imbued with the ideal of freedom that they do not wish to deny to others some of the liberties which they themselves enjoy. If there is a great gulf between their own status and that of the minority group, if there is a wide difference between the two groups in race or origin, the toleration of minorities may go as far as virtually to perpetuate several subsocieties within the larger society.

Even in the "sacred" society of medieval Europe dominated by the Church, there were long periods when heretics were tolerated, although at other times they faced the alternatives of conformity or extermination. The history of the Jews in medieval Europe offers ample evidence of the ability of a minority to survive even under minimum conditions of toleration. It should be noted, however, that at times the margin of safety was very narrow and that their ultimate survival was facilitated by the fact that they formed an alien cultural island within the larger Christian world and performed useful functions such as trade and commerce in which the creed of the dominant group would not allow its own members to engage. The coexistence of the Jews and Christians in the same countries often did not transcend the degree of mutuality characteristic of the symbiotic relations existing between different species of plants and animals occupying the same habitat but which are forced by their differential structure to live off one another. It involved a minimum of consensus.

The range of toleration which a pluralistic minority seeks may at first be quite narrow. As in the case of the Jews in medieval Europe, or the Protestants in dominantly Catholic countries, it may be confined to freedom to practice a dissenting religion. Or, as in the case of the ethnic minorities of Czarist Russia and the Austro-Hungarian empire of the Hapsburgs, it may take the form of the demand for the recognition of a language as the official medium of expression for the minority and the right to have it taught in their schools. While on the one hand the pluralistic minority craves the toleration of one or more of its cultural idiosyncrasies, on the other hand it resents and seeks protection against coerced absorption by the dominant group. Above all it wishes to maintain its cultural identity.

The nationalities of Europe, which in the nineteenth and early twentieth centuries embarked upon a course of achieving national independence, began their careers as pluralistic minorities bent merely upon attaining cultural autonomy. Some of these minorities had enjoyed national independence at an earlier period and merely wished to recover and preserve their cultural heritage. This was the case in Poland, for instance, which sought to recover from Czarist Russia a measure of religious and linguistic autonomy. Czech and Irish nationalism was initiated under similar historic circumstances.

It would be an error, however, to infer that the claims for cultural autonomy are generally pursued independently of other interests. Coupled with the demand, and often precedent to it there proceeds the struggle for economic and political equality or at least equalization of opportunity. Although the pluralistic minority does not wish to merge its total life with the larger society, it does demand for its members a greater measure of economic and political freedom if not outright civic equality. Ever since the revolutionary epoch of the late eighteenth century the economic and political enfranchisement of minorities has been regarded not merely as inherent in the "rights of man" but as the necessary instrument in the struggle for cultural emancipation. Freedom of choice in occupations, rights of land-ownership, entry into the civil service, access to the universities and the professions, freedom of speech, assembly, and publication, access to the ballot with a view to representation of minority voices in parliament and government—these and other full privileges of citizenship are the foundation upon which cultural freedom rests and the instruments through which it must be achieved and secured.

*   *   *

Whereas a pluralistic minority, in order to maintain its group integrity, will generally discourage intermarriage and intimate social intercourse with the dominant group, the assimilationist minority puts no such obstacles in the path of its members but looks upon the crossing of stocks as well as the blending of cultures as wholesome end products. Since assimilation is a two-way process, however, in which there is give and take, the mergence of an assimilationist minority rests upon a willingness of the dominant group to absorb and of the minority group to be absorbed. The ethnic differences that exist between the minority and the dominant group are not necessarily an obstacle to assimilation as long as the cultural traits of each group are not regarded as incompatible with those of the other and as long as their blending is desired by both. The "melting pot" philosophy in the United States which applied to the ethnic minorities but excluded the racial minorities, notably the Negro, in so far as it was actually followed, tended to develop both among immigrants and natives an atmosphere conducive to the emergence of a crescive American culture to which both the dominant and minority groups contributed their share. This new culture, which is still in the process of formation, comprises cultural elements derived from all the ethnic groups constituting the American people, but integrates them into a new blend.

The success with which such an experiment proceeds depends in part upon the relative numbers involved and the period of time over which the process extends. Although since the beginning of the nineteenth century the United States absorbed some 38 million immigrants from abroad, the influx was relatively gradual and the vast spaces and resources of the continent facilitated the settlement and absorption of the newcomers. America was a relatively young country, dominated by the spirit of the frontier and by a set of laws and social ideals strongly influenced by the humanistic, liberalistic doctrines of religious toleration and the rights of man. This, together with the great need for labor to exploit the vast resources of the continent, contributed to keeping American culture fluid and its people hospitable to the newcomers and the heritages they brought with them. No one group in the United States had so much power and pride of ancestry as to be able to assert itself as superior to all others.

Nevertheless as the immigrants came in great waves, and as the wide margin of economic opportunity shrank periodically, outbursts of intolerant and sometimes violent nativism and antialien feeling became manifest here too. As newer immigrant groups followed older waves the latest comers increasingly became the objects of prejudice and discrimination on the part of natives and older immigrants alike. Moreover, as the various ethnic groups concentrated in specific areas and in large urban colonies and thus conspicuously unfolded their old world cultural heritages, their life became virtually

autonomous and hence, by isolating themselves, their contact with the broad stream of American culture was retarded. In addition, their very success in competing with native and older settlers in occupations, professions, and business provoked antipathies which found expression in intolerance movements and in the imposition of official and unofficial restrictions and handicaps.

Although the ethnic minorities in the United States suffer mainly from private prejudices rather than restrictive public policies, their path of assimilation is not without its serious obstacles. The distinctive cultures of the various ethnic groups are not merely assemblages of separable traits but historically welded wholes. Each immigrant group not only has its own language or dialect which serves as a barrier to intergroup communication and to the sharing of common ideas and ideals, but also its own religious, social, and even political institutions which tend to perpetuate group solidarity and to inhibit social intercourse with members of the "out" group. Moreover, each ethnic group in the United States, especially in the early period after its arrival, tends to occupy a characteristic niche in the economy which generates certain definite similarities among its members in occupation, standard of living, place of residence, and mode of life. On the basis of such likenesses within the group and differences without, stereotypes are built up and fixed attitudes arise which inhibit contact and develop social distances and prejudices. Overanxiety about being accepted sometimes results in a pattern of conduct among minorities that provokes a defense reaction on the part of the dominant group; these defense reactions may take the form of rebuffs which are likely to accentuate minority consciousness and thus retard assimilation.

No ethnic group is ever unanimous in all of its attitudes and actions, and minority groups are no exception. They, too, have their internal differentiations, their factions and ideological currents and movements. It should be understood, therefore, that the difference between a pluralistic and an assimilationist minority must be sought in the characteristic orientation and directing social movement of these groups. The Jews furnish an excellent illustration of a minority which especially in modern times has vacillated between these two types. When the "out" group was favorably disposed toward the Jews, assimilation proceeded apace, even in the face of occasional rebuffs and persistent discrimination. When the dominant group made entry of the Jews difficult, when intolerance movements became powerful and widespread, and when persecution came to be the order of the day, the Jews as a minority group generally withdrew into themselves and by virtue of being excluded became clannish. The most conspicuous example of this transformation is to be found in the shift in the attitude of the German Jews who—before the anti-Semitic wave climaxed by the Hitler epic—could have been correctly characterized as an assimilationist minority and whose optimum longing upon the advent of Hitler was for even a modicum of toleration. Among Jews in this country a similar differentiation is contemporaneously found. The older settlers and those who have climbed the economic and social scale seek on the whole full incorporation into the larger society and may truly be regarded as an assimilationist minority; but the later comers and those whose hopes have been frustrated by prejudice, those who through generations of persecution in the Old World retain a more orthodox ritual and a more isolated and self-sufficient community life, generally do not seek full cultural identification with American society at large. To be sure they aspire to full social and economic equality with the rest of the population, but they seek to retain a degree of cultural autonomy.

*   *   *

The principal and ultimate objective of such a minority is to achieve political as well as cultural independence from the dominant group. If such a group has had statehood at an earlier period in its career, the demand for recognition of its national sovereignty may be based upon the cultivation among its members of the romantic sentiments associated—even if only in the imagination—with its former freedom, power, and glory. In such a case the minority's cultural monuments and survivals, its language, lore, literature, and ceremonial institutions, no matter how archaic or reminiscent of the epoch of the group's independence, are revivified and built up into moving symbols of national grandeur.

In this task the intellectuals among the minority group play a crucial role. They can find expression for their talents by recovering, disseminating, and inspiring pride in the group's history and civilization and by pleading its case before world public opinion. Having been rejected by the dominant group for higher positions of leadership, and often having been denied equal opportunity and full participation in the intellectual, social, economic and political life of the larger society, the intellectuals of such minorities tend to be particularly susceptible to a psychic malady bordering on an oppression psychosis. They find their compensation by plunging into the life of the smaller but more hospitable world of their minority.

The Irish, Czech, Polish, Lithuanian, Esthonian, Latvian and Finnish nationalistic movements cul-

minating in the achievement of independent statehood at the end of the first World War were examples of secessionist minority groups. The case of the Jews may also be used to illustrate this type of minority. Zionism in its political, as distinguished from its cultural variety, has acquired considerable support as a result of the resurgence of organized anti-Semitic movements. The forced wholesale migration out of the countries practicing violent persecution and extermination has changed the conception of Palestine from a haven of refuge in which Jews are tolerated to a homeland to which Jews lay official claim.

The protest against the dominant group, however, does not always take the form of separatism and secessionism. It may, under certain circumstances express itself in movements to get out from under the yoke of a dominant group in order to join a group with whom there exists a closer historical and cultural affinity. This is particularly true of minorities located near national frontiers. Wars, and the accompanying repeated redefinitions of international boundaries rarely fail to do violence to the traditions and wishes of some of the populations of border territories. It is generally true that these marginal ethnic groups exhibit more fervid nationalistic feelings than those who have not been buffeted about by treaty-makers.

Secessionist minorities occupying border positions, moreover, generally can count upon the country with which they seek reunion for stimulation of minority consciousness. When France lost Alsace and Lorraine at the end of the Franco-Prussian war in 1871, the French culture of these "lost provinces" became the object of special interest on the part of Frenchmen in and out of these territories. And when these same provinces were lost to Germany at the end of the first World War, a similar propaganda wave on the German side was set in motion. When the Nazis came to power and embarked upon their imperialistic adventures they made the "reunion with the Fatherland" of such territories as the Saar, Alsace, Lorraine, Eupen-et-Malmédy; Sudetenland and the Danzig Corridor an object of frenzied agitation. By every means at their command they revived the flagging or dormant secessionist spirit among these ethnic groups. The created incidents wherever the slightest pretext existed to provoke violent outbreaks so as to elicit from the neighboring governments countermeasures that could be exploited for the purpose of creating a world opinion that the German minorities in these territories were suffering from extreme persecution and were anxiously waiting to be rescued by the armed might of the Fatherland.

The solidarity of modern states is always subject to the danger of the undermining influence of secessionist minorities, but it becomes particularly vulnerable if the minorities are allied with neighboring states which claim them as their own. Out of such situations have arisen many of the tensions which have provoked numerous wars in recent times.

There is a fourth type of minority which may be designated as militant. Its goal reaches far beyond toleration, assimilation, and even cultural and political autonomy. The militant minority has set domination over others as its goal. Far from suffering from feelings of inferiority, it is convinced of its own superiority and inspired by the lust for conquest. While the initial claims of minority movements are generally modest, like all accessions of power, they feed upon their own success and often culminate in delusions of grandeur.

Thus, for instance, the Sudeten Germans, aided and abetted by the Nazi propaganda, diplomatic, and military machine, made claims on the Czecho-Slovak republic which, if granted, would have reduced the Czechs to a minority in their own country. The story, let us hope it is legendary, of the slave who upon his emancipation immediately proceeded to buy himself a slave, suggests a perverse human tendency which applies to minorities as well. No imperialism is as ruthless as that of a relatively small upstart nation. Scarcely had Italy escaped the humiliation of utter defeat in the first World War when she embarked upon the acquisition of *Italia Irredenta* far beyond her own borders across the Adriatic. In recent times, the rise of the relatively obscure Prussian state to a position of

dominance in Central Europe is illustrative of the dynamics of a militant minority in quest not merely of a secure basis of national existence but of empire. The none too generous treatment accorded by the newly emancipated Poles between the two World Wars to the Ukrainian, White Russian, Lithuanian, Jewish, and other minorities allotted to the Polish state offers another case of the lack of moderation characteristic of militant minorities once they arrive at a position of power.

The problem of finding a suitable formula for self-government in India would probably have been solved long ago if the Hindu "majority," which considers itself a minority in relation to British imperial rule, could have been satisfied with an arrangement which stopped short of Hindu domination over Moslems. Similarly the problem of Palestine could be brought much nearer a sensible solution if certain elements among Jewish and Arab groups were less militant and did not threaten, in case either were given the opportunity, to reduce the other to the status of a minority.

The justification for singling out the four types of minorities described above for special delineation lies in the fact that each of them exhibits a characteristic set of collective goals among historical and contemporary minority groups and a corresponding set of motives activating the conduct of its members. These four types point to significant differences between actual minority movements. They may also be regarded as marking crucial successive stages in the life cycle of minorities generally.

III—PRIMARY GROUPS

1. *Primary Groups*

BY CHARLES H. COOLEY

MEANING OF PRIMARY GROUPS—FAMILY, PLAYGROUND, AND NEIGHBORHOOD—HOW FAR INFLUENCED BY LARGER SOCIETY—MEANING AND PERMANENCE OF "HUMAN NATURE"—PRIMARY GROUPS, THE NURSERY OF HUMAN NATURE

BY *primary groups* I mean *those characterized by intimate face-to-face associations and cooperation.* They are primary in several senses, but

chiefly in that they are fundamental in forming the social nature and ideals of the individual. The result of intimate association, psychologically, is a certain fusion of individualities in a common whole, so that one's very self, for many purposes at least, is the common life and purpose of the group. Perhaps the simplest way of describing this wholeness is by

Reprinted from Charles H. Cooley, *Social Organization* (Glencoe, Ill.: The Free Press, 1956), chap. iii, pp. 23–31, with the permission of The Free Press.

saying that it is a "we"; it *involves the sort of sympathy and mutual identification for which "we" is the natural expression.* One lives in the feeling of the whole and finds the chief aims of his will in that feeling.

It is not to be supposed that the unity of the primary group is one of mere harmony and love. It is always a differentiated and usually a competitive unity, admitting of self-assertion and various appropriative passions; but these passions are socialized by sympathy, and come, or tend to come, under the discipline of a common spirit. *The individual will be ambitious, but the chief object of his ambition will be some desired place in the thought of the others, and he will feel allegiance to common standards of service and fair play.* So the boy will dispute with his fellows a place on the *team,* but above such disputes will place the common glory of his class and school.

The most important spheres of this intimate association and cooperation—though by no means the only ones—are the *family, the play-group of children, and the neighborhood or community group of elders.* These are practically universal, belonging to all times and all stages of development; and are accordingly a chief basis of what is universal in human nature and human ideals. The best comparative studies of the family, such as those of Westermarck[1] or Howard,[2] show it to us as not only a universal institution, but as more alike the world over than the exaggeration of exceptional customs by an earlier school had led us to suppose. Nor can any one doubt the general prevalence of play-groups among children or of informal assemblies of various kinds among their elders. Such association is clearly the nursery of human nature in the world about us, and there is no apparent reason to suppose that the case has anywhere or at any time been essentially different.

As regards play, I might, were it not a matter of common observation, multiply illustrations of the universality and spontaneity of the group discussion and cooperation to which it gives rise. The general fact is that children, especially boys after about their twelfth year, live in fellowships in which their sympathy, ambition, and honor are engaged even more, often, than they are in the family. Most of us can recall examples of the endurance by boys of injustice and even cruelty, rather than appeal from their fellows to parents or teachers—as, for instance, in the hazing so prevalent at schools, and so difficult, for this very reason, to repress. And how elaborate the discussion, how cogent the public opinion, how hot the ambitions in these fellowships.

Nor is this facility of juvenile association, as is sometimes supposed, a trait peculiar to English and American boys; since experience among our immigrant population seems to show that the offspring of the more restrictive civilizations of the continent of Europe form self-governing play-groups with almost equal readiness. Thus, Miss Jane Addams, after pointing out that the "gang" is almost universal, speaks of the interminable discussion which every detail of the gang's activity receives, remarking that "in these social folk-motes, so to speak, the young citizen learns to act upon his own determination."[3]

Of the neighborhood group it may be said, in general, that from the time men formed permanent settlements upon the land, down, at least, to the rise of modern industrial cities, it has played a main part in the primary, heart-to-heart life of the people. Among our Teutonic forefathers the village community was apparently the chief sphere of sympathy and mutual aid for the commons all through the "dark" and Middle Ages, and for many purposes it remains so in rural districts at the present day. In some countries we still find it with its ancient vitality, notably in Russia, where the *mir,* or self-governing village group, is the main theatre of life, along with the family, for perhaps fifty millions of peasants.

In our own life the intimacy of the neighborhood has been broken up by the growth of an intricate mesh of wider contacts which leaves us strangers to people who live in the same house. And even in the country the same principle is at work, though less obviously, diminishing our economic and spiritual community with our neighbors. How far this change is a healthy development, and how far a disease, is perhaps still uncertain.

Besides these almost universal kinds of primary association, there are many others whose form depends upon the particular state of civilization; the only essential thing, as I have said, *being a certain intimacy and fusion of personalities. In our own society, being little bound by place, people easily form clubs, fraternal societies, and the like, based on congeniality, which may give rise to real intimacy.* Many such relations are formed at school and college, and among men and women brought together in the first instance by their occupations—as workmen in the same trade, or the like. Where there is a little common interest and activity, kindness grows like weeds by the roadside.

But the fact that the family and neighborhood

---

1. *The History of Human Marriage.*
2. *A History of Matrimonial Institutions.*

3. *Newer Ideals of Peace,* p. 177.

groups are ascendant in the open and plastic time of childhood makes them even now incomparably more influential than all the rest.

Primary groups are primary in the sense that they give the individual his earliest and most complete experience of social unity, and also in the sense that they do not change in the same degree as more elaborate relations, but form a comparatively permanent source out of which the latter are ever springing. Of course they are not independent of the larger society, but to some extent reflect its spirit; as the German family and the German school bear somewhat distinctly the print of German militarism. But this, after all, is like the tide setting back into creeks, and does not commonly go very far. Among the German, and still more among the Russian, peasantry are found habits of free cooperation and discussion almost uninfluenced by the character of the state; and it is a familiar and well-supported view that the village commune, self-governing as regards local affairs and habituated to discussion, is a very widespread institution in settled communities, and the continuator of a similar autonomy previously existing in the clan. "It is man who makes monarchies and establishes republics, but the commune seems to come directly from the hand of God."[4]

In our own cities the crowded tenements and the general economic and social confusion have sorely wounded the family and the neighborhood, but it is remarkable, in view of these conditions, what vitality they show; and there is nothing upon which the conscience of the time is more determined than upon restoring them to health.

These groups, then, are springs of life, not only for the individual but for social institutions. They are only in part moulded by special traditions, and, in larger degree, express a universal nature. The religion or government of other civilizations may seem alien to us, but the children or the family group wear the common life, and with them we can always make ourselves at home.

By human nature, I suppose, we may understand those sentiments and impulses that are human in being superior to those of lower animals, and also in the sense that they belong to mankind at large, and not to any particular race or time. It means, particularly, sympathy and the innumerable sentiments into which sympathy enters, such as love, resentment, ambition, vanity, hero-worship, and the feeling of social right and wrong.[5]

Human nature in this sense is justly regarded as a comparatively permanent element in society. Always and everywhere men seek honor and dread ridicule, defer to public opinion, cherish their goods and their children, and admire courage, generosity, and success. It is always safe to assume that people are and have been human.

It is true, no doubt, that there are differences of race capacity, so great that a large part of mankind are possibly incapable of any high kind of social organization. But these differences, like those among individuals of the same race, are subtle, depending upon some obscure intellectual deficiency, some want of vigor, or slackness of moral fibre, and do not involve unlikeness in the generic impulses of human nature. In these, all races are very much alike. The more insight one gets into the life of savages, even those that are reckoned the lowest, the more human, the more like ourselves, they appear. Take for instance the natives of central Australia, as described by Spencer and Gillen,[6] tribes having no definite government or worship and scarcely able to count to five. They are generous to one another, emulous of virtue as they understand it, kind to their children and to the aged, and by no means harsh to women. Their faces as shown in the photographs are wholly human and many of them attractive.

And when we come to a comparison between different stages in the development of the same race, between ourselves, for instance, and the Teutonic tribes of the time of Caesar, the difference is neither in human nature nor in capacity, but in organization, in the range and complexity of relations, in the diverse expression of powers and passions essentially much the same.

There is no better proof of this generic likeness of human nature than in the ease and joy with which the modern man makes himself at home in literature depicting the most remote and varied phases of life—in Homer, in the Nibelung tales, in the Hebrew Scriptures, in the legends of the American Indians, in stories of frontier life, of soldiers and sailors, of criminals and tramps, and so on. The more penetratingly any phase of human life is studied, the more an essential likeness to ourselves is revealed.

To return to primary groups: the view here maintained is that human nature is not something existing separately in the individual, but a *group-nature or primary phase of society,* a relatively

4. De Tocqueville, *Democracy in America,* Vol. I, chap. v.

5. These matters are expounded at some length in the writer's *Human Nature and the Social Order.*

6. *The Native Tribes of Central Australia.* Compare also Darwin's views and examples given in chap. vii of his *Descent of Man.*

simple and general condition of the social mind. It is something more, on the one hand, than the mere instinct that is born in us—though that enters into it—and something less, on the other, than the more elaborate development of ideas and sentiments that makes up institutions. It is the nature which is developed and expressed in those simple, face-to-face groups that are somewhat alike in all societies; groups of the family, the playground, and the neighborhood. In the essential similarity of these is to be found the basis, in experience, for similar ideas and sentiments in the human mind. In these, everywhere, human nature comes into existence. Man does not have it at birth; he cannot acquire it except through fellowship, and it decays in isolation.

If this view does not recommend itself to common sense I do not know that elaboration will be of much avail. It simply means the application at this point of the idea that society and individuals are inseparable phases of a common whole, so that wherever we find an individual fact we may look for a social fact to go with it. If there is a universal nature in persons there must be something universal in association to correspond to it.

What else can human nature be than a trait of primary groups? Surely not an attribute of the separate individual—supposing there were any such thing—since its typical characteristics, such as affection, ambition, vanity, and resentment, are inconceivable apart from society. If it belongs, then, to man in association, what kind or degree of association is required to develop it? Evidently nothing elaborate, because elaborate phases of society are transient and diverse, while human nature is comparatively stable and universal. In short, the family and neighborhood life is essential to its genesis and nothing more is.

Here, as everywhere in the study of society, we must learn to see mankind in psychical wholes, rather than in artificial separation. We must see and feel the communal life of family and local groups as immediate facts, not as combinations of something else. And perhaps we shall do this best by recalling our own experience and extending it through sympathetic observation. What, in our life, is the family and the fellowship; what do we know of the we-feeling? Thought of this kind may help us to get a concrete perception of that primary group-nature of which everything social is the outgrowth.

2. *Secrecy and Group Communication*

BY GEORG SIMMEL

BEFORE COMING to the secret in the sense of a consciously desired concealment, one must note the different degrees to which various relationships leave the reciprocal knowledge of the total personalities of their members outside their province.

INTEREST GROUPS

Among the various groups still involving direct interaction, the most important is the association based on some particular interest [*Zweckverband*], more especially that which involves completely objective member contributions, determined by mere

Reprinted from *The Sociology of Georg Simmel*, trans. and ed. Kurt H. Wolff (Glencoe, Ill.: The Free Press, 1950), pp. 317–29, 361–76, with the permission of The Free Press.

membership. The purest form here is monetary contribution. In this case, interaction, solidarity, and the pursuit of common purposes do not depend on everybody's psychological knowledge of everybody else. As a group member, the individual is only the executor of a certain function. Questions concerning those individual motives which determine this performance, or the sort of total personality in which his conduct is imbedded, are completely irrelevant. The association based on some particular interest is the discreet sociological form *par excellence*. Its members are psychologically anonymous. In order to form the association, all they have to know of one another is precisely this fact—that they form it. The increasing objectification of our culture, whose phenomena consist more and more of impersonal elements and less and less absorb the subjective totality of the individual (most simply shown by the contrast between handicraft and factory work), also involves sociological structures. Therefore, groups into which earlier man entered in his totality and individuality and which, for this reason, required reciprocal knowledge far beyond the immediate, objective content of the relationship —these groups are now based exclusively on this objective content, which is neatly factored out of the whole relation.

CONFIDENCE UNDER MORE AND LESS COMPLEX CONDITIONS

This development also gives a peculiar evolution to an antecedent or subsequent form of knowledge about a human being, namely, confidence in him. Confidence, evidently, is one of the most important synthetic forces within society. As a hypothesis regarding future behavior, a hypothesis certain enough to serve as a basis for practical conduct, confidence is intermediate between knowledge and ignorance about a man. The person who knows completely need not trust; while the person who knows nothing can, on no rational grounds, afford even confidence.[1] Epochs, fields of interest, and individuals differ, characteristically, by the measures of knowledge and ignorance which must mix in order that the single, practical decision based on confidence arise.

The objectification of culture has decisively differentiated the quanta of knowledge and ignorance necessary for confidence. The modern merchant who enters business with another; the scholar who together with another embarks upon an investiga-

tion; the leader of a political party who makes an agreement with the leader of another party concerning matters of election or the treatment of pending bills; all these know (if we overlook exceptions and imperfections) only exactly *that* and no more about their partner which they *have* to know for the sake of the relationship they wish to enter. The traditions and institutions, the power of public opinion and the definition of the position which inescapably stamps the individual, have become so solid and reliable that one has to know only certain external facts about the other person in order to have the confidence required for the common action. The question is no longer some foundation of personal qualities on which (at least in principle) a modification of behavior within the relation might be based: motivation and regulation of this behavior have become so objectified that confidence no longer needs any properly personal knowledge. Under more primitive, less differentiated conditions, the individual knows much more about his partner in regard to personal matters, and much less in regard to his purely objective competence. The two belong together: in order to produce the necessary confidence despite a lack of knowledge in objective matters, a much higher degree of knowledge in personal matters is necessary.

The purely general knowledge, which extends only to the objective elements of the person and leaves its secret—the personal-individual area—untouched, must be supplemented considerably by the knowledge of this very area, whenever the interest group is of essential significance to the total existence of its members. The mercant who sells grain or oil needs to know only whether his correspondent is good for the price. But if he takes him as his associate, he must not only know his financial standing and certain of his very general qualities, but he must have thorough insight into him as a personality; he must know whether he is decent, compatible, and whether he has a daring or hesitant temperament. Upon such reciprocal knowledge rest not only the beginning of the relationship, but also its whole development, the daily common actions, and the division of functions between the partners. Today the secret of the personality is sociologically more limited. In view of the large extent to which the interest in the common pursuit is borne by personal qualities, the personal element can no longer be so autonomous.

"ACQUAINTANCE"

Aside from interest groups but aside, equally, from relationships rooted in the total personality, there is the sociologically highly peculiar relation which, in our times, among educated strata, is desig-

---

1. There is, to be sure, also another type of confidence. But since it stands outside the categories of knowledge and ignorance, it touches the present discussion only indirectly. This type is called the *faith* of one man in another. It belongs in the category of religious faith. Just as nobody has ever believed in God on the basis of any "proof of the existence of God," since, on the contrary, these proofs are *post-festum* justifications or intellectual mirrors of a completely immediate, affective attitude, so one "believes" in a particular man without justifying this faith by proofs of his worthiness, and often even in spite of proofs to the contrary. This confidence, this inner unreservedness in regard to another individual, is mediated neither by experiences nor by hypotheses; it is a primary, fundamental attitude toward the other. In an entirely pure form, detached from any empirical consideration, this state of faith probably exists only within religion. In regard to men, it always, presumably, needs some stimulation or confirmation by the knowledge or expectation mentioned above. On the other hand, even in the social forms of confidence, no matter how exactly and intellectually grounded they may appear to be, there may yet be some additional affective, even mystical, "faith" of man in man. Perhaps what has been characterized here is a fundamental category of human conduct, which goes back to the metaphysical sense of our relationships and which is realized in a merely empirical, accidental, fragmentary manner by the conscious and particular reasons for confidence.

nated simply as "acquaintance." Mutual "acquaintance" by no means is *knowledge* of one another; it involves no actual insight into the individual nature of the personality. It only means that one has taken notice of the other's existence, as it were. It is characteristic that the idea of acquaintance is suggested by the mere mentioning of one's name, by "introducing oneself": "acquaintance" depends upon the knowledge of the *that* of the personality, not of its *what*. After all, by saying that one is acquainted, even well acquainted, with a particular person, one characterizes quite clearly the lack of really intimate relations. Under the rubric of acquaintance, one knows of the other only what he is toward the outside, either in the purely social-representative sense, or in the sense of that which he shows us. The degree of knowledge covered by "being well acquainted with one another," refers not to the other *per se;* not to what is essential in him, intrinsically, but only to what is significant for that aspect of him which is turned toward others and the world.

DISCRETION

Acquaintance in this social sense is, therefore, the proper seat of "discretion." For, discretion consists by no means only in the respect for the secret of the other, for his specific will to conceal this or that from us, but in staying away from the knowledge of all that the other does not expressly reveal to us. It does not refer to anything particular which we are not permitted to know, but to a quite general reserve in regard to the total personality. Discretion is a special form of the typical contrast between the imperatives, "what is not prohibited is allowed," and "what is not allowed is prohibited." Relations among men are thus distinguished according to the question of mutual knowledge—of either "what is not concealed may be known," or "what is not revealed must not be known."

To act upon the second of these decisions corresponds to the feeling (which also operates elsewhere) that an ideal sphere lies around every human being. Although differing in size in various directions and differing according to the person with whom one entertains relations, this sphere cannot be penetrated, unless the personality value of the individual is thereby destroyed. A sphere of this sort is placed around man by his "honor." Language very poignantly designates an insult to one's honor as "coming too close": the radius of this sphere marks, as it were, the distance whose trespassing by another person insults one's honor.

Another sphere of the same form corresponds to what is called the "significance" of a personality. In regard to the "significant" ["great"] man, there is

an inner compulsion which tells one to keep at a distance and which does not disappear even in intimate relations with him. The only type for whom such distance does not exist is the individual who has no organ for perceiving significance. For this reason, the "valet" knows no such sphere of distance; for him there is no "hero"; but this is due, not to the *hero*, but to the valet. For the same reason, all importunity is associated with a striking lack of feeling for differences in the significance of men. The individual who fails to keep his distance from a great person does not esteem him highly, much less too highly (as might superficially appear to be the case); but, on the contrary, his importune behavior reveals lack of proper respect. The painter often emphasizes the significance of a figure in a picture that contains many figures by arranging the others in a considerable distance from it. In an analogous fashion, the sociological simile of significance is the distance which keeps the individual outside a certain sphere that is occupied by the power, will, and greatness of a person.

The same sort of circle which surrounds man—although it is value-accentuated in a very different sense—is filled out by his affairs and by his characteristics. To penetrate this circle by taking notice, constitutes a violation of his personality. Just as material property is, so to speak, an extension of the ego,[2] and any interference with our property is, for this reason, felt to be a violation of the person, there also is an intellectual private-property, whose violation effects a lesion of the ego in its very center. Discretion is nothing but the feeling that there exists a right in regard to the sphere of the immediate life contents. Discretion, of course, differs in its extension with different personalities, just as the positions of honor and of property have different radii with respect to "close" individuals and to strangers and indifferent persons. In the case of the above-mentioned, more properly "social" relations, which are most conveniently designated as "acquaintances," the point to which discretion extends is, above all, a very typical boundary: beyond it, perhaps there *are* not even any jealously guarded secrets; but conventionally and discreetly, the other individual, nevertheless, does not trespass it by questions or other invasions.

The question where this boundary lies cannot be answered in terms of a simple principle; it leads into the finest ramifications of societal formation. For, in an absolute sense, the right to intellectual private-property can be affirmed as little as can the

---

2. Property is that which obeys the will of the owner, as, for instance (with a difference of degree only), our body which is our first "property."

right to material property. We know that, in higher civilizations, material private-property in its essential three dimensions—acquisition, insurance, increase—is never based on the individual's own forces alone. It always requires the conditions and forces of the social milieu. From the beginning, therefore, it is limited by the right of the whole, whether through taxation or through certain checks on acquisition. But this right is grounded more deeply than just in the principle of service and counter-service between society and individual: it is grounded in the much more elementary principle, that the part must sustain as great a restriction upon its autonomous existence and possessiveness as the maintenance and the purposes of the whole require.

This also applies to the inner sphere of man. In the interest of interaction and social cohesion, the individual *must* know certain things about the other person. Nor does the other have the right to oppose this knowledge from a moral standpoint, by demanding the discretion of the first: he cannot claim the entirely undisturbed possession of his own being and consciousness, since this discretion might harm the interests of his society. The businessman who contracts long-range obligations with another; the master who employs a servant (but also the servant before entering the service); the superior who advances a subordinate; the housewife who accepts a new member into her social circle: all these must have the right to learn or infer those aspects of the other's past and present, temperament, and moral quality on the basis of which they can act rationally in regard to him, or reject him. These are very crude instances of the case where the duty of discretion—to renounce the knowledge of all that the other does not voluntarily show us—recedes before practical requirements. But even in subtler and less unambiguous forms, in fragmentary beginnings and unexpressed notions, all of human intercourse rests on the fact that everybody knows somewhat more about the other than the other voluntarily reveals to him; and those things he knows are frequently matters whose knowledge the other person (were he aware of it) would find undesirable.

All this may be considered indiscretion in the individual sense: in the social sense, it is a condition necessary for the concrete density and vitality of interaction. Nevertheless, it is extremely difficult to trace the legal limit of this trespass into intellectual private-property. In general, man arrogates to himself the right to know all he can find out through mere observation and reflection, without applying externally illegitimate means. As a matter of fact,

however, indiscretion practiced in this fashion can be just as violent and morally inadmissible as listening behind closed doors and leering at a stranger's letters. To the man with the psychologically fine ear, people innumerable times betray their most secret thoughts and qualities, not only *although,* but often *because,* they anxiously try to guard them. The avid, spying grasp of every inconsiderate word, the boring reflection on what this or that tone of voice might mean, how such and such utterances might be combined, what blushing on mentioning a certain name might betray—none of this transcends the limits of external discretion; it is entirely the work of one's own intellect and, for this reason, one's apparently indisputable right. And all the more so, since such an abuse of psychological superiority often occurs quite involuntarily: often we simply cannot check our interpretation of the other, our construction of his inner nature. No matter how much every decent person tells himself that he must not muse on what the other hides, that he must not exploit the slips and helplessnesses of the other; knowledge, nevertheless, occurs often so automatically, and its result confronts us with such striking suddenness, that mere good will has no power over it. Where the doubtlessly impermissible can yet be so inevitable, the boundary between what is allowed and what is not, is all the more blurred. How far discretion must refrain from touching even intellectually "all that is his"; how far, on the other hand, the interests of interaction and the interdependence of the members of society limit this duty—this is a question for whose answer neither moral tact nor knowledge of objective conditions and their requirements alone is sufficient, since *both* are needed. The subtlety and complexity of this question relegate it to the individual decision which cannot be prejudiced by any general norm—to a much higher degree than does the question of private property in the material sense.

FRIENDSHIP AND LOVE

In this pre-form or complementation of the secret, the point is not the behavior of the individual who keeps a secret, but the behavior of another individual: within the mixture of reciprocal knowledge of ignorance, the accent is more on the degree of knowledge than of ignorance. We now come to a totally different configuration. It is found in those relationships which, in contrast to the ones discussed, do not center around clearly circumscribed interests that must be fixed objectively if only because of their "superficiality." Instead, they are built, at least in their idea, upon the person in its totality. The principal types here are friendship and marriage.

To the extent that the ideal of friendship was received from antiquity and (peculiarly enough) was developed in a romantic spirit, it aims at an absolute psychological intimacy, and is accompanied by the notion that even material property should be common to friends. This entering of the whole undivided ego into the relationship may be more plausible in friendship than in love for the reason that friendship lacks the specific concentration upon one element which love derives from its sensuousness. To be sure, by virtue of the fact that *one* among the total range of possible reasons for a relation takes the lead, these reasons attain a certain organization, as a group does through leadership. A particularly strong relational factor often blazes the trail on which the rest follow it, when they would otherwise remain latent; and undoubtedly, for most people, sexual love opens the doors of the total personality more widely than does anything else. For not a few, in fact, love is the only form in which they can give their ego in its totality, just as to the artist the form of his art offers the only possibility for revealing his whole inner life. Probably, this observation can be made especially often of women (although the very differently understood "Christian love" is also designed to achieve the same result). Not only because they love do women unreservedly offer the total remainder of their being and having; but all of this, so to speak, is chemically dissolved in love, and overflows to the other being exclusively and entirely in the color, form, and temperament of love. Yet, where the feeling of love is not sufficiently expansive, and the remaining psychological contents of the relationship are not sufficiently malleable, the preponderance of the erotic bond may suppress, as I have already suggested, the other contacts (practical-moral, intellectual), as well as the opening-up of those reservoirs of the personality that lie outside the erotic sphere.

Friendship lacks this vehemence, but also the frequent unevenness, of this abandon. It may be, therefore, more apt than love to connect a whole person with another person in its entirety; it may melt reserves more easily than love does—if not as stormily, yet on a larger scale and in a more enduring sequence. Yet such complete intimacy becomes probably more and more difficult as differentiation among men increases. Modern man, possibly, has too much to hide to sustain a friendship in the ancient sense. Besides, except for their earliest years, personalities are perhaps too uniquely individualized to allow full reciprocity of understanding and receptivity, which always, after all, requires much creative imagination and much

divination which is oriented only toward the other. It would seem that, for all these reasons, the modern way of feeling tends more heavily toward differentiated friendships, which cover only one side of the personality, without playing into other aspects of it.

Thus a very special type of friendship emerges, which is of the greatest significance for our problem (the degrees of invasion and reserve within the friendship relation). These differentiated friendships which connect us with one individual in terms of affection, with another, in terms of common intellectual aspects, with a third, in terms of religious impulses, and with a fourth, in terms of common experiences—all these friendships present a very peculiar synthesis in regard to the question of discretion, of reciprocal revelation and concealment. They require that the friends do not look into those mutual spheres of interest and feeling which, after all, are not included in the relation and which, if touched upon, would make them feel painfully the limits of their mutual understanding. But the relation which is thus restricted and surrounded by discretions, may yet stem from the center of the total personality. It may yet be reached by the sap of the ultimate roots of the personality, even though it feeds only part of the person's periphery. In its idea, it involves the same affective depth and the same readiness for sacrifice, which less differentiated epochs and persons connect only with a common *total* sphere of life, for which reservations and discretions constitute no problem.

MARRIAGE

The measures of self-revelation and self-restraint, with their complements of trespass and discretion, are much more difficult to determine in the case of marriage. Their ratio here belongs in a very general problem area of extreme importance to the sociology of intimate relations. This problem area centers around the question whether the maximum of common values can be attained under the condition that the personalities reciprocally relinquish their autonomies altogether, or under the condition of reserve: the question whether, perhaps, they do not belong *more* to one another qualitatively if, quantitatively, they do so less. This question can be answered, of course, only along with the other question as to how, within the total communicability of man, one can draw the line where restraint and respect of the other begin. The advantage of modern marriage—which, certainly, can answer both questions only from case to case—is that this line is not fixed from the beginning, as it is in other and earlier civilizations. In earlier cultures particularly, marriage is not an erotic but, in principle, only a social and economic institution. The satisfaction of the desire for love is only accidentally connected with it; it is contracted (with exceptions, of course), not only on the basis of individual attraction, but on the ground of family connections, working conditions, and descendants. In this respect, the Greeks achieved a particularly clear differentiation—according to Demosthenes: "We have hetaerae for pleasure; concubines for our daily needs; and wives to give us legitimate children and take care of the interior of the house." In such a mechanical relationship, the psychic center is obviously put out of function. Nevertheless (incidentally), this kind of marriage is constantly illustrated, though with certain modifications, by history and by the observation of actual contemporary marriages. There probably exists in it neither the need for any intimate, reciprocal self-revelation, nor the possibility of it. On the other hand, there is probably an absence of certain reserves of delicacy and chastity which, in spite of their seemingly negative character, are yet the flower of a fully internalized and personal, intimate relation.

The same tendency to exclude, *a priori* and by super-individual decree, certain life-contents from the common features of marriage lies in the variety of marriage forms which may coexist among the same people. Prior to entering marriage, the prospective spouses must choose among these forms, which variously distinguish economic, religious, and domestic-legal interests in their bearing upon matrimony. We find this among many nature peoples, as well as among the Hindus and Romans. Nobody will deny, of course, that even in modern life, marriage is probably contracted overwhelmingly from conventional or material motives. Yet no matter how often it is actualized, the sociological *idea* of modern marriage is the commonness of all life-contents, insofar as they determine the value and fate of the personality, immediately or through their effects. Nor is the nature of this ideal requirement without results: often enough it allows, or even stimulates, an initially quite imperfect union to develop into an ever more comprehensive one. But, whereas the very interminability of this process is the instrument of the happiness and inner vitality of the relationship, its reversal usually entails grave disappointments—namely, when absolute unity is anticipated from the beginning, when neither demand nor revelation knows restraint, not even the restraint which, for all finer and deeper natures, remains locked in the obscurity of the soul even where it seems to pour itself out before the other entirely.

During the first stages of the relationship there is a great temptation, both in marriage and in marriage-like free love, to let oneself be completely absorbed by the other, to send the last reserves of the soul after those of the body, to lose oneself to the other without reservation. Yet, in most cases, this abandon probably threatens the future of the relationship seriously. Only those individuals can give themselves *wholly* without danger who *cannot* wholly give themselves, because their wealth consists in a continuous development in which every abandon is at once followed by new treasures. Such individuals have an inexhaustible reservoir of latent psychological possessions, and hence can no more reveal and give them away at one stroke than a tree can give away next year's fruits with those of the season. But other individuals are different. With every flight of feeling, with every unconditional abandonment, with every revelation of their inner life, they make inroads (as it were) into their capital, because they lack the mainspring of ever renewed psychic affluence which can neither be exhaustively revealed nor be separated from the ego. In these cases, the spouses have a good chance of coming to face one another with empty hands; and the Dionysian bliss of giving may leave behind it an impoverishment which, unjustly, but no less bitterly for that, belies in retrospect even past abandons and their happiness.

We are, after all, made in such a way that we need not only a certain proportion of truth and error as the basis of our lives (as was pointed out earlier), but also a certain proportion of distinctness and indistinctness in the image of our life-elements. The other individual must give us not only gifts we may accept, but the possibility of our giving *him*—hopes, idealizations, hidden beauties, attractions of which not even *he* is conscious. But the place where we deposit all this, which *we* produce, but produce for *him*, is the indistinct horizon of his personality, the interstitial realm, in which faith replaces knowledge. But it must be strongly emphasized that this is, by no means, only a matter of illusions and optimistic or amorous self-deceptions, but that portions even of the persons closest to us must be offered us in the form of indistinctness and unclarity, in order for their attractiveness to keep on the same high level.

It is in this way that the majority of people replace the attraction values, which the minority possess in the inexhaustibility of their inner life and growth. The mere fact of absolute knowledge, of a psychological having-exhausted, sobers us up, even without prior drunkenness; it paralyzes the vitality of relations and lets their continuation really appear pointless. This is the danger of complete and (in more than an external sense) shameless abandon, to which the unlimited possibilities of intimate relations tempt us. These possibilities, in fact, are easily felt as a kind of duty—particularly where there exists no absolute certainty of one's own feeling; and the fear of not giving the other enough leads to giving him too much. It is highly probable that many marriages founder on this lack of reciprocal discretion—discretion both in taking and in giving. They lapse into a trivial habituation without charm, into a matter-of-factness which has no longer any room for surprises. The fertile depth of relations suspects and honors something even more ultimate behind every ultimateness revealed; it daily challenges us to reconquer even secure possessions. But this depth is only the reward for that tenderness and self-discipline which, even in the most intimate relation that comprises the total individual, respects his inner private property, and allows the right to question to be limited by the right to secrecy.

*   *   *

The essence of the secret society, as such, is autonomy. But this autonomy approaches anarchy: the consequences of leaving the general normative order easily are rootlessness and the absence of a stable life-feeling and of a norm-giving basis. The fixed and minute character and the ritual helps to overcome this lack. In this, we see once more how much man needs a certain ratio between freedom and law; and how, when he does not receive it from *one* source, he seeks to supplement what he obtains of the one by the missing quantity of the other, no matter from what additional source, until he has the ratio he needs. In ritual, the secret society voluntarily imposes upon itself a formal coercion, a complement required by its material separateness and autonomy. It is characteristic that, among the Freemasons, precisely those who enjoy the greatest political freedom, namely, the Americans, request of all their lodges the most rigorous uniformity of work procedure and ritual, whereas in Germany the practice involves a greater autonomy of the individual lodge: here, Freemasonry is so integrated with the general society that it does not demand such freedoms as would easily lead to the counterclaim of their being curtailed. In short, in the secret society the nature of ritual—objectively often quite senseless and schematically coercive—is by no means inconsistent with that group freedom which resembles anarchy, with severance from the norms of the inclusive society. On the contrary: just as the widespread diffusion of secret societies is usually a proof of public un-freedom, of a tendency toward police

regimentation, and of political oppression, in short, just as it is a reaction stemming from the need for freedom—so, conversely, the internal, ritual regimentation of secret societies reflects a measure of freedom and severance from society at large which entails the counter-norm of this very schematism, in order to restore the equilibrium of human nature.

FEATURES OF THE SECRET SOCIETY AS QUANTITATIVE MODIFICATIONS OF GENERAL GROUP FEATURES

These last considerations suggest the methodological principle on the basis of which I wish to analyze those traits of the secret society which have not yet been discussed. The question is, to what extent can they be shown to be essentially quantitative modifications of the typical features of sociation in general? The justification of this conception of the secret society leads once more to a consideration of its position in the whole complex of sociological forms.

The secret element in societies is a primary sociological fact, a particular kind and shading of togetherness, a formal quality of relationship. In direct or indirect interaction with other such qualities, it determines the shape of the group member or of the group itself. Yet, from a historical standpoint, the secret society is a secondary phenomenon; that is, it always develops only within a society already complete in itself. To put it differently: the secret society is characterized by its secrecy in the same way in which other societies (or even secret societies themselves) are characterized by their superordination and subordination, or by their aggressive purposes, or by their imitative character; but, that it can develop with these characteristics is possible only on the condition that a society already exists. Within this larger circle, it opposes it as a narrower one; whatever the purpose of the society, this opposition has, at any rate, the sense of exclusion. Even the altruistic secret society, which merely wants to render a certain service to the total group and intends to disband after achieving it, evidently considers temporary separation from this total group a technique unavoidable in view of its purpose.

Separateness,   Formality,   Consciousness.—Among the many smaller groups which are included in larger ones, there is none whose sociological constellation forces it to emphasize its formal self-sufficiency to the same extent as it does the secret society. Its secret surrounds it like a boundary outside of which there is nothing but materially, or at least formally, opposite matter, a boundary which therefore fuses, within itself, the secret society into a perfect unity. In groups of every other sort, the *content* of group life, the actions of the members in terms of rights and duties, can so occupy the members' consciousness that, normally, the formal fact of sociation plays scarcely any role at all. The secret society, on the other hand, cannot allow its members to forget the distinct and emphatic consciousness that they form a *society*. In comparison with other associations, it here is the passion of secrecy —always felt and always to be preserved—which gives the group-form, depending on it, a significance that is far superior to the significance of content. The secret society completely lacks organic growth, instinctive expansions, and, on the part of its members, all naïve, matter-of-fact feeling of belonging together and forming a unit. However irrational, mystical, or emotional its contents may be, the way in which it is formed is thoroughly conscious and intentional. In its *consciousness* of being a society— a consciousness which is constantly emphasized during its formative period and throughout its lifetime—it is the opposite of all spontaneous groups, in which the joining is only the expression, more or less, of elements which have grown together like roots. Its social-psychological form clearly is that of the interest group [*Zweckverband*]. This constellation makes it understandable why the formal characteristics of group formation in general are specifically pointed up in the secret society, and why some of its essential sociological traits develop as mere quantitative intensifications of very general types of relationship.

Seclusion: Signs of Recognition.—One of these has already been indicated, namely, the characterization as well as the cohesion of the secret society by means of seclusion against the social environment. This is the function of the often complicated signs of recognition through which the individual legitimates himself as a member. It should be noted that, prior to the more general diffusion of writing, these signs were more indispensable than later, when their other sociological uses became more important than those of mere legitimation. As long as there were no credentials of acceptance, notifications, or written descriptions of persons, an association with branches in several different places, had nothing but such signs for excluding unauthorized persons, and for having only individuals entitled to them receive its benefits or communications. These signs were revealed only to the legitimate members who, by means of them, were able to legitimate themselves wherever the group existed, and who had the duty to keep them secret.

The *purpose of seclusion* is clearly illuminated by the development of certain secret orders among nature peoples, especially in Africa and among the Indians. These orders are composed only of men.

Their essential purpose is to emphasize the differentiation of men from women. Whenever their members act in this capacity, they appear in masks, and women are usually forbidden on severe penalty to approach them. Yet sometimes women succeed in discovering the secret that the horrible apparitions are not ghosts but their husbands. When this happens, the orders often lose their whole significance and become harmless mummeries. The man of nature with his undifferentiated, sensuous conception, cannot imagine a more perfect separateness, such as he wants to emphasize, than for those who wish it and are entitled to it to *hide* themselves, to make themselves invisible. This is the crudest and, externally, most radical manner of concealment; not only a particular act of man, but all of man at once, is concealed—the group does not do something secret, but the totality of its members makes *itself* into a secret. This form of the secret society is perfectly in line with that primitive stage of mind in which the whole personality is still absorbed in every particular activity, and in which the activity is not yet sufficiently objectified to have any character that the whole personality does not automatically share. It is also understandable, therefore, why the whole separateness becomes invalid once the secret of the mask is broken, and why, then, the secret society loses its inner significance along with its means and its expression.

The Aristocratic Motive; Aristocracy.—The separateness of the secret society expresses a value: people separate from others because they do not want to make common cause with them, because they wish to let them feel their superiority. This motive leads everywhere to group formations, which evidently are very different from those undertaken for objective purposes. By joining one another, those who want to distinguish themselves give rise to the development of an aristocracy, which strengthens and (so to speak) enlarges their position and self-consciousness by the weight of their own sum. Separation and group formation are thus connected through the aristocratizing motive. In many cases, this connection gives separation itself the stamp of something "special," in an honorific sense. Even in school classes, it can be observed how small, closely integrated cliques of classmates think of themselves as the elite over against the others who are not organized—merely because of the formal fact of constituting a special group; and the others, through their hostility and envy, involuntarily acknowledge this higher value. In these cases, secrecy and mystification amount to heightening the wall toward the outside, and hence to strengthening the aristocratic character of the group.

This significance of the secret society as the intensification of sociological exclusiveness in general, is strikingly shown in political aristocracies. Secrecy has always been among the requisites of their regime. In the first place, by trying to conceal the numerical insignificance of the ruling class, aristocracies exploit the psychological fact that the unknown itself appears to be fearsome, mighty, threatening. In Sparta, the number of warriors was kept secret as much as possible. In Venice, the same end was intended by the decree that all *nobili* [noblemen] had to wear a simple black costume: no striking dress was to call the small number of men in power to the attention of the people. This was even carried to the point where the group of the highest elite was concealed completely: the names of the three state inquisitors were unknown to everybody except the council of ten who elected them. In some Swiss aristocracies, one of the most important authorities was simply called "the Secret Ones"; and in Freiburg, the aristocratic families were known as "the secret lineages" [*die heimlichen Geschlechter*]. The democratic principle, on the contrary, is associated with the principle of publicity and, in the same sense, with the tendency toward general and basic laws. For, these laws apply to an unlimited number of subjects and are, therefore, public in their very essence. Conversely, the use of secrecy by aristocratic regimes is only the extreme intensification of the social exclusiveness and exemption which, ordinarily, make aristocracies opposed to general, fundamentally fixed legislations.

Where the aristocratic idea does not characterize the policies of a group but the disposition of an individual, the relation between exclusiveness and secrecy manifests itself on a very different plane. The morally and intellectually distinguished person despises all concealment, because his inner certainty makes him indifferent to what others know or do not know of him, and to the question whether he is appraised correctly or falsely by them, or held in high or low esteem. For him, secrecy is a concession to outsiders; secrecy is dependence of conduct upon regard for others. For this reason, the "mask" which many consider sign and proof of an aristocratic personality that is turned away from the multitude, on the contrary proves the importance of the multitude to the wearer of the mask. The "mask" of the truly noble person is that even when he shows himself without disguise, the many do not understand him, do not even see him, so to speak.

Degrees of Initiation: Formal and Material Separation from the Outside.—This exclusion of everything outside the group is a general formal-sociological fact, which merely uses secrecy as a more

pointed technique. It attains a particular nuance in the plurality of degrees in which it is customary for initiation into the secret society, down to its last mysteries, to take place. The existence of such degrees threw light earlier upon another sociological feature of the secret society. As a rule, before he is even accepted into the first degree, the novice must give a solemn promise of secrecy concerning everything he may experience, whereby the absolute, *formal* separation, achievable by secrecy, is effected. Yet, inasmuch as the actual content or purpose of the society becomes accessible to the neophyte only gradually—whether this purpose is the perfect purification and sanctification of the soul through the consecration of the mysteries, or the absolute suspension of every moral barrier, as among the Assassins and other criminal societies—the *material* separation is achieved differently, in a more continuous, relative manner. In this material respect, the neophyte is still closer to the status of non-participant, from which testing and education eventually lead him to grasp the totality or core of the association. This core, evidently, thus gains a protection and isolation from the outside far beyond those by means of the oath upon entrance. It is seen to (as has already been shown in the example of the Druids) that the still untried neophyte does not have much he could betray: within the general secrecy that encompasses the group as a whole, the graduated secrecy produces an elastic sphere of protection (as it were) around its innermost essence.

The contrast between exoteric and esoteric members, such as is attributed to the Pythagorean order, is the most poignant form of this protective measure. The circle composed of those only partially initiated formed a sort of buffer region against the non-initiates. It is everywhere the dual function of the "middler" to connect and to separate, or, actually, rather to play only one role which, according to our perceptual categories and our viewpoint, we designate as connecting or as separating. In the same way, the real unity of superficially contradictory activities is here seen in its clearest light: precisely because the lower grades of the order mediate the transition to the center of the secret, they create a gradual densification of the sphere of repulsion which surrounds this center and which protects it more securely than could any abrupt and radical alternative between total inclusion and total exclusion.

Group Egoism.—In practice, sociological autonomy presents itself as group egoism: the group pursues its own purposes with the same inconsiderateness for all purposes outside itself which, in the case of the individual, is precisely called egoism. Usually, to be sure, this inconsiderateness is morally justified in the consciousness of the individual members by the fact that the group purposes themselves have a super-individual, objective character; that it is often impossible to name any particular individual who profits from the group's egoistic behavior; and that, as a matter of fact, this behavior often requires the group members' selflessness and sacrifice. But the point here is not to make any ethical valuation, but only to stress the group's separation from its environment, which is brought about or characterized by the egoism of the group. However, in the case of a small circle, which intends to preserve and develop itself within a larger one, this egoism has certain limits as long as it exists publicly. An open association, no matter how violently it fights against other associations within the same larger society, or against the general foundations of this society itself, must always maintain that the realization of its own ultimate purposes is to the advantage of the whole; and the necessity of this outward assertion somewhat restricts the actual egoism of its actions. This necessity does not exist in the case of secret societies, which always therefore, at least potentially, can afford to be hostile to other groups or to the whole. Non-secret groups cannot admit such a hostility, and, therefore, cannot unconditionally practice it. Nothing symbolizes, or possibly promotes, the separation of the secret society from its social environment as decisively as the elimination of the hypocrisy, or of the actual condescension, by means of which the non-secret society is inevitably integrated with the teleology of its environment.

Inclusiveness and Exclusiveness as Group Principles.—In spite of the actual quantitative delimitation of every true community, there exists a considerable number of groups whose inner tendency is to include all those who are not explicitly excluded. Within certain political, religious, and status limits, everybody is considered immediately as "belonging" so long as he satisfies certain external conditions, which are usually not a matter of his will, but are given with his existence itself. All people, for instance, who are born within the territory of a given state, are members, unless particular circumstances make exceptions of them, of the (often very complex) civic society. The member of a given social class is included, as a matter of course, in the social conventions and forms of connection of this class, unless he becomes a voluntary or involuntary outsider. The extreme case is the claim of a church that it includes all mankind; and that, if any individuals are excluded from the religious association, which, ideally, is valid also for them, it is only through historical accident, sinful stubbornness, or God's special intention.

We note here the distinction of two principles, which clearly indicate a basic differentiation of the sociological significance of groups generally, no matter how much practice may mix them and make the difference lose some of its sharpness. On the one hand, there is the principle of including everybody who is not explicitly excluded; and, on the other, there is the principle of excluding everybody who is not explicitly included. The second type is represented in greatest purity by the secret society. The unconditional character of its separation, which is borne by the consciousness of it at every step of the group's development, causes, and is caused by, the fact that those who are not explicitly accepted, are for this simple reason explicitly excluded. The Masonic order could no better have supported its recent emphatic assertion that it is not a "secret order," properly speaking, than by simultaneously professing its ideal of including *all* men, of representing humanity.

Seclusion Against the Outside and Internal Cohesion.—Here, as everywhere else, the intensified seclusion against the outside is associated with the intensification of cohesion internally: we have here two sides, or external forms, of the same sociological attitude. A purpose which occasions an individual to enter into secret association with others, excludes almost always such an overwhelming part of his general social circle from participation, that the potential and real participants gain rarity value. He must keep on good terms with them because it is much more difficult to replace them here than (other things being equal) in a legitimate association. Furthermore, every discord inside the secret society brings danger of betrayal, which usually both the self-preservation of the individual and that of the group are interested in avoiding.

Finally, the isolation of the secret society from the surrounding social syntheses removes a number of occasions for conflict. Among all the bonds of the individual, the bond of secret sociation always has an exceptional position. In comparison with it, the official bonds—familial, civic, religious, economic, through rank and friendship—no matter how varied their contents, touch contact surfaces of a very different kind and measure. Only the contrast with the secret societies makes it clear that their claims criss-cross one another, because they lie (so to speak) in the same plane. Since these claims openly compete for the individual's strength and interests, individuals collide within any one of these circles: each individual is simultaneously claimed by the interests of other groups.

The sociological isolation of the secret society greatly limits such collisions. In accordance with its purpose and operation, competing interests of open-society origin are shut out. Every secret society—if only because it usually fills its own sphere alone (the same individual hardly ever belongs to more than one secret society)—exercises over its members a sort of absolute dominion, which gives them little opportunity to engage in conflicts such as result from the coordination of the plurality of spheres that represent open groups. The "king's peace," which really ought to reign within every association, is promoted in a formally unsurpassable manner, by the peculiar and exceptional conditions of the secret society. In fact, it seems as if, aside from the more realistic reason in favor of the "king's peace," the mere form of secrecy itself kept the members freer from other influences and disturbances, and thus facilitated their accord. A certain English politician found the basis for the strength of the English cabinet in the secrecy which surrounds it: everybody who has ever been active in public life, he suggested, knows that a small number of people can be brought to agree the more easily, the more secret are its negotiations.

Centralization.—Corresponding to the outstanding degree of cohesion within the secret society is the thoroughness of its centralization. The secret society offers examples of unconditional and blind obedience to leaders who—although, naturally, they may also be found elsewhere—are yet particularly remarkable in view of the frequent anarchic character of the secret society that negates all other law. The more criminal its purposes, the more unlimited, usually, is the power of the leaders and the cruelty of its exercise. The Assassins in Arabia; the Chauffeurs, a predatory band with a widely ramified organization which raged, particularly, in eighteenth-century France; the Gardunas in Spain, a criminal society that had relations with the Inquisition from the seventeenth to the beginning of the nineteenth century—all these, whose very nature was lawlessness and rebellion, unconditionally and without any criticism submitted to chiefs whom they themselves (as least in part) appointed.

The interrelation between the needs for freedom and for a bond operates here; it appears in the rigor of ritual, which combines the extremes of both: for the sake of a balanced life-feeling, the excess of freedom from all otherwise valid norms must be brought into equilibrium by a similarly excessive submission and renunciation of the will. Yet more essential, probably, is the necessity of centralization, which is the life condition of the secret society. It is especially important for that type—for instance, the criminal band—which lives off surrounding groups, interferes with them through all kinds of radiations and actions, and thus is gravely threatened by treason and the distraction of interests, once it is no longer governed by the most intransigent cohesion with its point of origin in its own center.

Secret societies which, for whatever reasons, fail to develop a tightly solidifying authority are, therefore, typically exposed to very grave dangers. Originally, the Waldenses were not a secret society; they became one in the thirteenth century, only because of external pressure to keep themselves hidden. This made it impossible for them to meet regularly, which in turn deprived their doctrine of its unity. A number of branches arose, which lived and developed separately, and were often hostile to one another. The order declined because it lacked the necessary complement of the secret society: uninterruptedly effective centralization. Freemasonry, probably, owes the evident lag in its power behind its diffusion and means, to the considerable autonomy of its parts, which have neither a unified organization nor a central authority. Their common features merely cover principles and signs of recognition, and thus are traits of equality and of relations between person and person only, not of centralization, which holds the energies of the members together and is the complement of separation.

It is merely an exaggeration of this formal motive of centralization that secret societies are often directed by *unknown* leaders: the lower echelons are not to know whom they obey. To be sure, this occurs, above all, for the sake of preserving the secret. With this intention, it was developed to an extraordinary degree in the organization of an early nineteenth-century Italian secret society, the Welfic Knights, which worked for the liberation and unification of Italy. At each of their various branches, the Knights had a highest council of six persons, who did not know one another and communicated only by means of an intermediary, called "The Visible One." But the preservation of secrecy is by no means the only purpose of unknown leaders. Instead, they exemplify the most extreme and abstract sublimation of dependence upon a center: the tension between dependent and leader reaches the highest degree when the leader becomes invisible. All that remains then, is the pure fact of obedience—merciless, as it were, and unmodified by any personal nuances—out of which the superordinate as a subject has vanished. If obedience to impersonal authority, to mere office, to the executor of an objective law, has the character of invincible strength, it is intensified to the point of an uncanny absoluteness when the ruling personality remains, in principle, hidden. For if, with the visibility and familiarity of the ruler, the individual suggestion and the power of personality are removed from the relationship or domination, domination also loses all attenuations, all relative and "human" elements inherent in the empirical, unique personality. Obedience is thus colored by the feeling of subjection to an intangible power, whose limits cannot be traced, and which can nowhere be seen, but must, for this reason, be suspected everywhere. In the secret society with an unknown leader, the general sociological cohesion of a group through the unity of its ruling authority is transferred, as it were, into an imaginary focus, and thus attains its purest, most intense form.

De-individualization.—De-individualization is the sociological character which, in the individual member, corresponds to this centralistic subordination. Where the immediate concern of the society is not the interests of its elements; where the society rather transcends itself (as it were) by using its members as means for purposes and actions extraneous to them—the secret society shows, once more, a heightened measure of leveling of the individuality, of "de-selfing" [*Entselbstung*]. *Some* measure of this is characteristic of everything social, generally. But the secret *society* uses de-individualization to compensate for the above-mentioned individualizing and differentiating character of the *secret*. This begins with the secret orders of nature peoples, whose appearance and activities are accompanied almost everywhere by the wearing of masks—so that an outstanding expert suggested that the presence of masks among a nature people should at once make one suspect the existence of secret societies. It is, of course, in the nature of the secret order for its members to conceal themselves. But, when a particular individual appears and acts unambiguously as a member of a secret order, and merely does not show what individuality (which is normally well known) is associated with him, the disappearance of personality behind its role is most strongly emphasized. In the Irish conspiracy which was organized under the name of Clan-na-gael in America in 1870, the individual members were never designated by their names, but only by numbers. This, too, of course, was done for the practical purpose of secrecy; but, at the same time, it proves how much this purpose suppresses individuality. Leadership can proceed with much greater inconsiderateness and indifference to individual wishes and capacities of persons who appear only as numbers and who may not be known by their personal names even to the other members (which at least occurred in groups similar to the Clan-na-gael), than it can if the group includes each member as a personal entity. No less effective,

toward the same end, is the comprehensive role and strength of ritual, which always indicates the fact that the objective organization has overcome the personal element in the members' activities and contributions to the group. The hierarchical order admits the individual only as the discharger of a predetermined role; for each member, it holds ready a stylized garb in which his personal outlines disappear.

Equality of Members.—It is merely another name for this elimination of the differentiated personality if secret societies practice great relative equality among their members. This does not contradict the despotic character of their organization: in all kinds of other groups, too, despotism is correlated with the leveling of the ruled. Within the secret society, there often is a brotherly equality among the members, which constitutes a sharp and tendentious contrast to their differences in their other life situations. Characteristically, this is most noticeable in secret societies of a religio-ethical nature—which strongly accentuate brotherhood—and, on the other hand, in those of an illegal character. In his memoirs, Bismarck writes of a pederastic organization, wide-spread in Berlin, with which he became acquainted as a young justiciary; he stresses "the *equalizing* effect throughout all strata of the collective practice of the forbidden."

This de-personalization, wherein the secret group exaggerates in a one-sided manner a typical relationship between individual and society, appears, finally, as characteristic *irresponsibility*. Here, too, the mask is the most primitive phenomenon. Most African secret orders are represented by a man disguised as a spirit of the woods, who commits all violations, including robbery and murder, against anyone he happens to meet. He is not held responsible for his crimes—obviously, only because of his mask. The mask is the somewhat clumsy form in which these groups let the personalities of their members disappear, and without which the members would undoubtedly be overtaken by revenge and punishment. But responsibility is so immediately connected with the ego (philosophically, too, the whole problem of responsibility belongs in the problem of the ego), that, for such naïve feeling, the disguise of the person suspends all responsibility.

This connection is used no less in political finesse. In the North American House of Representatives, actual decisions are made in the standing committees, with which the House is almost always in agreement. But the transactions of these committees are secret; thus, the most important part of legislative activity is hidden from the public. In large measure, this seems to extinguish the political responsibility of the delegates, since nobody can be held responsible for uncontrollable procedures. Inasmuch as individual contributions toward a particular decision remain hidden, the decision appears to be made by some super-individual authority. Here, too, irresponsibility is the consequence or the symbol of the intensified sociological de-individualization, which corresponds to the secrecy of group action. This also hold for all directorates, faculties, committees, administrations, etc., whose transactions are secret: the individual, as a person, disappears as the quasi-nameless group member, and with his disappearance as a person disappears the responsibility that cannot be imagined to inhere in a being whose concrete activities are intangible.

The Secret Society and the General Government. —This one-sided intensification of general sociological features is confirmed, finally, by the danger with which society at large believes, rightly or wrongly, secret societies threaten it. Where the over-all aim of the general society is strong (particularly political) centralization, it is antagonistic to all special associations, quite irrespective of their contents and purposes. Simply by being units, these groups compete with the principle of centralization which alone wishes to have the prerogative of fusing individuals into a unitary form. The preoccupation of the central power with "special associations" runs through all of political history—a point which is relevant in many respects to the present investigations and has already been stressed. A characteristic type of this preoccupation is suggested, for instance, by the Swiss Convention of 1481, according to which no separate alliances were permitted between any of the ten confederated states. Another example is the persecution of apprentices' associations by the despotism of the seventeenth and eighteenth centuries. A third is the tendency to disenfranchise local political communities which is so often demonstrated by the modern state.

The secret society greatly increases this danger which the special association presents to the surrounding totality. Man has rarely a calm and rational attitude toward what he knows only little or vaguely. Instead, his attitude consists in part in levity, which treats the unknown as if it did not exist, and in part in anxious fantasy, which, on the contrary, inflates it into immense dangers and terrors. The secret society, therefore, appears dangerous by virtue of its mere secrecy. It is impossible to know whether a special association might not one day use its energies for undesirable purposes, although they were gathered for legitimate ones: this fear is the main source of the basic suspicion which central powers have of all associations among their subjects.

In regard to groups which make it their principle to conceal themselves, the suspicion that their secrecy hides dangers is all the more readily suggested. The Orange Societies which were organized in England, in the beginning of the nineteenth century, for the suppression of Catholicism, avoided all public discussion, working only in secret, through personal connections and correspondence. But this very secrecy let them appear as a public danger: the suspicion arose "that men, who shrank from appealing to public opinion, mediated a resort to force." Purely on the grounds of its secrecy, the secret order thus appears dangerously close to a conspiracy against the reigning powers. How much this is only an intensification of the general political questionability of special associations is clearly shown in a case like the following. The oldest German guilds offered their members effective legal protection, and thus replaced the protection of the state. For this reason, the Danish kings promoted them, since they saw in them a support of the public order. But, on the other hand, for the very same reason, the guilds also were considered to be *competitors* of the state: they were condemned in this capacity by the Frankish capitularies—more particularly, because they were designated as *conspiracies*. The secret society is so much considered an enemy of the central power that, even conversely, every group that is politically rejected, is called a secret society.

3. The Sociological Category of Communion

BY HERMAN SCHMALENBACH

FOR Ferdinand Toennies, the family, particularly the peasant and small-town family, is the prime example of a human community. The basis of family bonds is a natural and physical coherence. Such coherence is generated by proximity and consanguinity. Like other natural phenomena, families are situated in time and space. They can be located. Yet, social relations are more than physical. They are "psychical" phenomena as well. The natural features of the family are, it would seem, merely external: They only establish the possibilities for the emergence of community. Even consanguinity does not generate social relations unless a commonality is recognized "by the persons concerned." Community, then, can be characterized as that order of social coherence which develops on the basis of natural interdependence.

This is often misunderstood. We speak of "beginning life in earnest," as in the case of youth, but

Translated by Kaspar D. Naegele and Gregory P. Stone, from Herman Schmalenbach, *Die Dioskuren* ("Die Soziologische Kategorie des Bundes," Vol. I).

This is a free translation. Besides the usual complicated German sentence structure, the original contains passages from the poetry of Stefan George. These have been omitted, as have the extensive footnotes and references, which are often not essential to the main argument. References to Max Weber at the end of the essay are, for the most part, to the first chapter of his *Wirtschaft und Gesellschaft*, now available in translation. Because the references are so well known to sociologists, they have not been documented. We have attempted to restrict our translation only to those portions of the original which carry forward the author's plea for supplementing Toennies' familiar distinction between *Gemeinschaft* and *Gesellschaft* with the concept, *Bund*, so that the objective relations of *Gemeinschaft* will not be confused with relations built on sentiment and affect.

There is no ready English equivalent for Schmalenbach's concept or for Toennies' concepts. For the latter, we have employed "community" and "society," and we ask the reader always to interpret the translations in the particular usage of Toennies. Both terms have a multiplicity of referents in sociology, any of which could confuse the main issues of the essay. *Bund* refers to those social relations in which persons are characteristically *en rapport*. It carries with it the notion of a sympathetic comradeship—a camaraderie. Yet such relations are not always sustained by positive emotions. Persons may be caught up with one another as they share in any and all manner of sentiment— love and hate, joy and despair. Thus, the term reminds us of Cooley's early effort to propose the communion as a general mode of human association. We have selected Cooley's term to translate the concept, *Bund*, in the somewhat arbitrary and forced effort to establish some continuity beween American and German thinking on these matters.

we actually refer to several matters: separation from one's home and the style of life of one's parents, the impulsive entry into a free and open world, and joining with others in association and friendship. Such associations are nowadays referred to as communities. But is this appropriate? Are such "communities" constituted by natural bonds? Are not the original and natural bonds that joined child to family rent asunder?

Perhaps our version of the concept of community represents an illegitimate narrowing of that term. Surely, there are conflicts between community and community, between peer group and family. The real problem is whether such conflicts represent special peculiarities of unique relations or general characteristics of social relations. We do not have to prove here that the wish to separate oneself from one's home and to wander far afield is independent of specific features of one's family of origin. Neither is it solely a matter of desiring to repudiate such origins, although it may be manifest in that form. Nor are such wishes merely symptomatic of specific periods when the generations as such appear to be in sharp conflict. Again, these wishes are not exclusively confined to those sectors of the population that are relatively emancipated from the demands of tradition. Apprentices of every calling have always had their time of travel. Admittedly there are times and circles that value the settled life more than others. Yet the desire for travel arises in any young person about the time he is twenty. Such desire need not necessarily be confined to the short and temporarily impulsive period of romantic youth. Associations and friendships formed as part of this process can be anything but transitory. When they are taken seriously, such friendships even exhibit an affinity to religious phenomena. At any rate, religious associations seem originally always to have been communions.

Innumerable friendships develop among people in their youth. As such, they may be quite free from any religious motives, while betraying, at the same time, the general religious affinity just described. Such an affinity is especially characteristic of all associations that are taken very seriously by their members. In any case, the general yearning, found all through the world these days, for some human community clearly seems to be associated with religious yearning as well. One can see this in the cult of friendship as practiced by the Romantics. Even where all this is not manifestly the case, an element of religiosity (which I hesitate to call "religious") seems to bind deeply some social relations and impart to them a profoundly sacred character. You can observe this in the collective enthusiasm of youth for high ideals, in their national loyalties, in the patriotic concern with national symbols on the part of the youth of a country, or in the mutual devotion of Communist young people. But, just as such communions present the aspect of religiosity, so do religious groupings present the aspect of communion at their inception.

All natural bonds may be torn asunder by the formation of associations, brotherhoods, fraternities, and the like. In line with this, Max Weber and, following him, Ernest Troeltsch formulated the important distinction between church and sect. The church is a community, and may become a society. Sect is a pure communion. Max Weber did not exploit his discovery to transform the basic categories of sociology from the dichotomy presented by Toennies into a necessary trichotomy. Still he came close to it. He distinguished, within community, between traditional and affective or emotional bonds. It is indeed the case that communions are borne along by waves of emotion, reaching ecstatic heights of collective enthusiasm, rising from the depths of love or hate. This raises the question: are such communions merely a subform of community or an alternative social form altogether, differing both from community and from society?

Community and Communion

It may be too narrow to characterize community as an association based on the natural coherence of its members. Even Toennies admitted that habit and memory can constitute communal ties in the absence of blood ties, although communal ties are strengthened by blood bonds. Max Weber suggested that the basis of communal ties frequently lies in tradition. Yet, ties of blood and matters of tradition are surely separate issues. Presumably ties of blood can establish communities in the absence of habits and common memories among the individuals concerned, but this presupposes cultural traditions and, at some point, a knowledge of "common ancestry." The father comes immediately to stand in a characteristic relation to his son when he returns after a decade or more from foreign parts and, for the first time, meets a son born during his absence. Such an encounter need not involve floods of emotion. It is not necessarily influenced by the attitudes of the mother (who may already be dead), nor does it require memories of

a mother even though this may be part of the whole matter. Even love seems to be dispensable. Any creature that recognizes "ties of blood" will be responsive accordingly when it becomes aware of them, or first senses or suspects them. It will respond with a kind of communal consciousness.

This is a precarious term. Still, I must admit that it belongs to the natural features of community. We often refer to a village, a province, or a country as handing down patterns of values. The natural, then, includes all those attributes that one has inherited collectively, into which one has grown and been born, and through which one has grown together with others. It happens that what appear to be bonds of blood are also a matter of common usage, a matter of custom and of shared modes of thought or expression, all of which have no other sanction than tradition.

Even the purely local neighborhood seems, in the past at least, to have had features in common with a kinship system. This does not mean that there have to be memories stretching far back. Still, where this is the case, the natural coherence of the neighborhood becomes much more firmly established. Less intense forms of neighborly community can become established by the sheer fact that individuals have lived the adult portion of their life in one place. Indeed, there are forms of community that can be sustained between the salesman and the customer in shops that one frequents with some regularity. One can sustain a kind of community even with the silent passerby whom one sees frequently on the street. In general, even the shortest of encounters can, as a limiting case, become the basis of subsequent community, if a trace of those contacts is impressed on the mind. Such encounters leave a latent remnant, which later can re-emerge. It is essential in this connection simply to admit the assertion that social phenomena are based on natural conditions. But, as soon as other than natural facts provide the social ferment, human associations take on a noncommunal character.

Included in the natural realm are not only matters of locality or space but also matters of time. Time and space, after all, lack qualitative features only on the plane of abstract thought. The precondition for the formation of human community consists only in the chance that the qualitative features of time and place operate not as such, but exclusively as a consequence of their translation into a socially spatial and temporal contiguity.

Spatial and temporal contiguity, then, seem to be an essential basis of that order of coalescence which we call community. If one were to attempt to specify this more closely, one would have to enumerate all "the basic conditions of life." Yet this could never suffice, for only socially consequential conditions can lead to community. It is as though the conditions of community are independent of us, while we are dependent on them; as though, in fact, we cannot purposely act to create community.

At best this is a tentative way of speaking about the matter. It is not quite true that one cannot deliberately act to bring about community. One can, inadvertently or intentionally, do something toward the formation of community by pursuing any course of action. One may produce, as an intentional by-product, a state of community, or at least a basis for it, in the hope or anticipation that a community has been initiated. Such action, to be sure, is often indirect. Still, in some respects, the conditions of community are dependent on what individuals do. In contrast and for opposite reasons, the conditions of communion may be so completely independent of us that we cannot intervene and must adapt ourselves to them as given. In that case, the distinguishing characteristics of community are simply the natural qualities of its basis and the fact that only communities have such natural bases. But even these must be qualified so that they include tradition, custom, etc. By contrast, communions are likely to take such categories of nature, give them metaphysical and other forms of exaggerated interpretations, and in turn claim them for themselves in the name of a concept of "true" nature.

One additional consideration is essential for the proper characterization of community. It is in this connection that I have decided to regard ties of blood as an archetype of community, as it were. In this respect my argument begins at the same point as Toennies', but we end in opposite places. I have already skirted the issue: how do primarily natural occasions become transformed into social relations, given the fact that, after all, social phenomena are psychic? I have argued that ties of blood have to become recognized as such. Their sheer existence is not sufficient to establish those social phenomena that, nevertheless, depend on them. However, this might lead one to consider all forms of mutual attraction—which, in turn, one might see as part of the nature of things—as the equivalent of sympathy and then consider sympathy as the basis of community. After all, do we not *feel* close or related, consider ourselves bound to others through some secret bond? If that is the case, does not the distinction between community and communion become rather ambiguous? Yet communal bonds, even in the unconscious, are psychic phenomena. The bases of community are psychic whether they be un-

conscious or not. More important, unconscious processes, too, are psychic and can, as such, be part of the basic community. Objective knowledge about ties of blood is indeed not sufficient. The recognition of such bonds must be accompanied by a simultaneous sense of inner or psychic coherence.

Such a sense of coherence may have an unconscious component. One may know of it and about it, but, even in that case, the knowledge takes the form of an inner glow in a clouded stream which shimmers below and is neither comprehensive nor totally elucidating. The murkiness is never fully dispelled. The "unconscious" is not directly comparable to the "conscious," but to another idea—the "condition of consciousness"—the same content in a different form (I refer to Eduard von Hartmann, and also to Fechner). This is extremely important, because it follows that the unconscious may be known but never entirely revealed. The unconscious remains "generically there," or better "existentially there." (Although it can be detected, analyzed, and perhaps confirmed consciously, certainly the total unconscious can not be lifted into consciousness and remain the same.)[1]

---

1. The conscious and unconscious are not construed here as opposites. Actually there are two conceptions of the condition of consciousness. Actual "knowing," as knowledge *of* something, is always only knowledge of circumstances (I know that . . .). The circumstances are "there" (phenomenologically) and the conditions of existence in which they occur are independent of "knowing." Only "then," in such a way, can they be known, and they cannot be disclosed otherwise. Thus, there is an unmediated directly perceived apprehension of the conditions of existence itself and, beyond those objective circumstances, lies the question of the relation of knowledge to them in so far as the existence of knowledge as a phenomenon of its own kind has not been considered. Knowledge may or may not affect the "unconscious." It remains "the unconscious." As long as we "know" it is real, it remains real. The matter of "consciousness," then, is raised along with "the unconscious." Understandably this too can become an object of knowing—in spite of its usefulness the expression is certainly awkward. However, this is not essential: the expression "unconscious consciousness"—or better "unknown consciousness"—is not nonsense. One can live predominantly in "the bright light of awareness" without ever being aware, for example, of that fact. Moreover, someone else may be very much aware of the many peculiarities of such a person's "unconscious." For the most part "ignorance" belongs to the "unknown consciousness," as do those things that have readily disappeared from consciousness while being preserved in the "unconscious," or, in any case, functioning there, even if they are then quite something else. On the whole, the conscious is more closely related to the process of knowing than is the "unconscious." Knowing is a function of the conscious, although occasionally knowing may affect the unconscious. (Only as a function of consciousness can knowing destroy the unconscious. The impact of the unconscious upon knowing and upon the conscious is highly problematical and complicated in any case.) I believe that these allusions are needed here. Perhaps I should also have emphasized that the unconscious, if you will, is a phenomenon of consciousness or, better, something directly known as well as something that may be revealed.

The formative conditions of community ordinarily are unconscious and are not exclusively in the province of the external and the physical (consequently they become primarily social). Not only common blood ties—which are advanced here as the prototype—but also common ancestry of all other kinds, and the acquisitions of one's personal and more or less "waking" life may be activated as the formative conditions of community upon a relatively brief spatial and temporal contact. I suggest that these things leave behind them a "trace" in the "unconscious." To be sure, we may "know" about these things, but, apart from the fact that expressed knowledge is by no means an irrelevant matter here, the formulation upon which community rests is not recognition, but a modification that the "unconscious" has established as part of our psychic make-up. Moreover, we may even consciously resist acknowledging community by interpreting it as fortuitous, unreal, and consequently incredible. This, too, may have consequences.

Principally, we have, as it were, surrendered ourselves to our unconscious; we have surrendered without resistance. The consideration of the psychic "substance" on which community is based establishes, in a profound sense, the manner in which the foundations for such a relationship are actually constituted by conditions and states of which "we" are "independent" but upon which "we" "depend." The "unconscious" suggests a matter far different from the fact that natural and innate conditions are antithetical to psychic conditions, because it affects the "psyche" in somewhat the same way as the natural and innate does—similar to the way nature affects plants or unthinking vegetables.

Speaking experimentally, this is what differentiates community from communion: community implies the recognition of something taken for granted and the assertion of the self-evident. Generally speaking, one will not expressly sanction or condemn those communities to which one belongs. One is usually not fully aware of them. They are given. They simply exist. As a rule we are not likely to take much notice of our membership in them, even when it is a question of our membership in far-flung communities—such as commonalities of language, of ethnicity, or of the fact of a common humanity. The communal circles of which we are part reach into imponderable distances and cover connections of all kinds. One cannot be aware of all of them. Yet, as persons, we are always affected by them. Our own unconscious is directly or indirectly constituted in and through them. Only through contrasts and disturbances does a community become an object of attention for its members.

Often this merely takes the form of coming to their notice. At least this is so when fate strikes, provided it strikes not wholly unexpectedly, and without radically contravening a legitimate order.

In the event of death of the next of kin, especially when the person concerned is already old or has been ill for a long time, a peasant does not undergo especially disturbing experiences, at least not consciously. Rather, he turns to the task to be done. In other respects, however, communal disturbances can give rise to strong emotions, particularly when daily routines are suddenly and profoundly disturbed. This is particularly the case when one faces a threat, especially an avoidable one. When the threat is absolutely inescapable, then people, very much bound to their communal existence, accept their fate. Their thought is blanketed by sentiment. Where there is a choice, emotions seethe, and sometimes considerable violence ensues. As a rule, the disturbance itself becomes the object of these emotions. In that case, they take on a negative character. Such emotions, indeed, take the shape of rage, anger, hatred and, in the case of success, of triumph. In the case of failure, there arise spite, bitterness. resentment. and, eventually perhaps, sorrow, regret, and pain. Positive feelings oriented toward community are much rarer. They too constitute reactions to disturbances, particularly successfully managed disturbances, or, at least, disturbances limited in their import. They also arise in the presence of outsiders.

However, disturbances can also come from within. A young person, for instance, may demand to leave home. Should this be considered unwarranted, a father might respond to it with the words, "Here you are, and here you will remain, for you belong here." All the person knows then is that he belongs; there is little in the way of positive communal emotion. Filial devotion, parental love, or the love of siblings—these are for the most part simply forms of speech or perhaps expressions that derive their meaning more from the spirit of communion. In the case of a community, one just belongs and generally irrevocably so. One *is* mutually related; one need never feel or think it so. Children of two families simply know that one belongs to one family and the other to the other family. That is all that they know about families as such. None of these experiences are attended by any specific emotions. Nowadays, however, one is inclined to consider a consciousness of kind or of community as a matter of feeling. It must be remembered that the feeling of communal belonging always presupposes a conscious recognition of community.

To belong together and to be tied to one another,

perhaps irrevocably, is the essential matter. One need not feel anything in particular. Still, sense of community might lead to experiences of tenderness, happiness, or pride. Nevertheless, it is characteristic of the peasant, who is after all the best example of a person typically bound to the community, to become uncomfortable when emotions are displayed. They seem alien to him. Similarly, cosmopolitan people, but for opposite reasons, shy away from emotionality. It seems irrational to them. To the peasant, emotionality is to be avoided because it gives psychic processes too much autonomy. Often a peasant is considered sparse and dour in his emotional expressions. He is even said to lack feeling for nature. On the other hand, people argue that he not so much lacks feeling as words for its expression. Actually, peasants probably do "have" extraordinarily few of these feelings by way of conscious experience. This is not because they do not have them at all, but because, being unconsciously tied both to community and to nature, emotional experiences do not articulate a peasant's relations to the world around him.

It is really strange that, given these facts, one should think of community as something both represented among peasants and based on feeling. This simply constitutes a sentimentalizing of peasantry. Urban people are prone to such distortions. They reflect the rootlessness of the person who lives his life in urban society. Actually they are an expression of a desire for communion. Such a desire tends to combine a wish for belongingness with a high valuation of peasantry, of community, and of nature. In itself it does not, of course, constitute community, nor does it lead to a proper understanding of community. Instead, it confuses community with communion.

There are many instances of such sentimental proclivities. A contemporary yearning for community, which is genuine, though romantic, is one form of this attitude. Even Toennies exhibited it in some measure. He emphasized community so much that he must bear the responsibility for the confusion. Toennies (and everyone else) knows that rural neighbors may become mortal enemies when, for example, a boundary is disputed, just as brothers may become enemies when an inheritance is challenged. Despite this, neighbors and brothers always remain neighbors and brothers. Neighborliness and brotherhood persist psychically. There is probably no better example anywhere to demonstrate how minor a role "feelings" play as a basis of community.

Often feelings are construed as the basis of community relations, because they are erroneously thought to be "deeper," or "nearer" the uncon-

scious, than rational thought. However, all mental activity, including thought, has an unconscious component. Now, it is precisely in this context that the fundamental difference between community and communion may be established. The reality and basis of community do not consist in feeling. Nevertheless, a community does exhibit quite specific emotions, some of them directed toward itself, even if the community does not owe its reality or its basis to these feelings. Such sentiments include the sense of tenderness for the other members of the community, or for the community as such, the feeling of happiness in knowing of one's belonging, or even a sense of pride. The essence of community is association constituted in the unconscious. Community, as an organic and natural coalescence, precedes emotional recognition of it by its members. Feelings are simply subsequent forms of experience at the level of consciousness. They are *products* of community. To speak this way is not simply to speak in the language of interpretative psychology, but to proceed phenomenologically. Our very feelings tell us these things.

As you examine general feelings of community you generally discover an element of gratitude. Gratitude necessarily presupposes a relationship that already exists, and it arises as mutual concessions and generosity are recognized, just as tenderness, happiness, or pride also develop in response to extant social relations. In all of its forms, feelings associated with community or directed toward it, be they positive or negative, presuppose something that already exists. They are addressed to a world that is considered to precede them. Even if someone insisted stubbornly that the reality of community is positivistically equated with the feltness of it, he would find, in examining such feelings, that they always point to something that pre-existed.

In the case of human communion this is radically different. Emotional experiences are the very stuff of the relationship. They are, in fact, their basis. Jubilant followers who swarm around a leader chosen in an inspired flood of passion do not intend (at least their "feelings" do not intend) to be bound up with him and with one another on the basis of characteristics they naturally have in common. They are bound together by the feeling actually experienced. Indeed, each one is *en rapport*. Admittedly, feelings are conditioned for us all by our character and our disposition, of whatever kind these may be, and character and disposition lie in the unconscious. Still, though the unconscious is, as it were, the precondition of all emotionality, it does not as yet contain human communion. The unconscious contains potential emotions and as such enables the individuals to enter into communion. Yet, that communion is founded beyond the unconscious. The stuff of which it is made—the basis of its sustenance—is actually the cognitive recognition of feeling.

It may seem questionable that feelings are in fact constitutive of communions. Some may argue that a religious congregation, for instance, is kept together not so much by the several feelings of its individual members as by the deity to whom they pray. No doubt the primary objects of religious feelings are not so much the social structure of the religious community or some combination of parts of that structure, but the noumenal objects of their religious orientation. And yet the noumenal must be felt, if religious and established social phenomena are to appear. At least it must be received with some kind of religious feeling. Then the religious congregation becomes in fact a communion. It is feelings that hold it together. To put it another way, it is their deity as a felt object that gives the religious group its coherence. This does not mean that religion is completely reduced to subjective dispositions.

Conventionally, feelings are regarded as only subjective phenomena. This is an error. Feelings can be intentional and, as such, oriented toward objects. This leaves open the question whether such objects in fact exist or not. Primary religious feelings are in this sense intentional, for religion surely arises only when a religion has established patterns of the noumenal and the human world that can be experienced. Feelings are the psychic organs for such experience. But feelings, as we have argued, embrace the objects to which they are directed. Admittedly, to the religious person, it is less his feelings and more the phenomena he experiences that are all important. In that connection, there seems to be a general aversion toward even the term "experience" because, plausibly enough, it suggests subjectivity, as does the term "emotion."

For sociologists, quite apart from psychologists, it is, however, psychic events that constitute primary data. They too would err if, in their analysis of religious objects, they were not to take into account the feelings directed to such objects. Only such psychic matters can constitute the basis of communion. Sociologically speaking, however, psychic reality in the case of religion is not a deity, but the believer. This is not to deny that a deity may not, in turn, be considered as a formal psychic reality; but, in that case, it constitutes an objective psychic reality, while the sociologist is primarily concerned with the subjective psychic existence of deities from the standpoint of those who accept them. The study of primary religious feelings in terms of their "cognitive recognition" has much to teach a sociologist concerned with communion. In the primary central religious experience, the soul is absolutely alone with its god. The individual returns from this encounter with a strange and new perspective. He then enters a new set of social relations. Through these, his religious experiences are reaffirmed in a spirit of closeness and compassion. A communion is established. Originally this is the case even in the extreme instances of Calvinistic and Jesuitic religious experience.

The social transformation of religious events need not always take this form. Despite the oneness of the soul in its absolute dedication to a god, it frequently senses simultaneously the presence of others. It is as though religious attention were encircled by a recognition of one's relatedness to others, much as light is encircled by a halo. And yet, in that case, the social is logically secondary to the center of original religiosity. Still, to the extent to which the social plays a role at all, it does so through feelings. These found and help constitute a communion.

Actually the feelings founding a communion need not, in the first instance, refer to specific other members of such a communion. Youths, collectively enthused by some high ideal, coalesce into one organization, even if they do not specifically concern themselves one with the other. Still, the awareness of one's emotions is likely, if coherently, to be accompanied by a felt connectedness. More frequently, however, friends, like like-minded religious persons, are prone to develop a kind of enthusiastic solidarity with one another.

Now it would seem that in the case of religious communion, as well as community, feelings point to a condition previously established. In the case of religious groupings, the precondition is a deity. The succession of the two events (of the recognition of the noumenal and the development of the social) once more suggests the pre-existence of objects toward which feelings can be developed. But if the precondition is not psychic, or, at any rate, is not social, then what is given beforehand is a deity. The deity, admittedly, to the extent that it is recognized as such, must be a felt deity. In that case feeling and object go together. The psychic fact also pre-exists. Thus, the original givenness is still not social, as we ordinarily use the term. In the experience of a deity, it can be assumed that those who have this experience have it as separate individuals whose individual religious feelings have not yet forged a felt community. Their solidarity develops only as these individuals, with their several religious experiences, encounter one another, recognize the general and similar direction of their feelings, and, on the basis of this recognition, kindle still further enthusiasm in one another. This, in turn, creates a new dimension of feeling. Only this dimension includes a social component and can be characterized as the emotion of communion.

In contrast, a community pre-exists as such and is experienced as pre-existing. Subsequent communal emotions may, nevertheless, arise. In that case one finds not only the conditions for a conscious "coming together," but also sees the community itself as already existing, whereas communion arises only through the actual and experienced recognition of a mutual sense of belonging. On the other hand, one has to admit that the similarity of direction in religious feelings that characterizes individuals who otherwise stand in no mutual relation with each other constitutes more than a mere coincidence of parallel sentiments. It involves an element of the social. In that event the social too is part of the givenness of things. It will be discovered by those who meet after having previously succumbed to religious experience in similar ways. Then they will recognize their solidarity. In that case the so-called social element appears not as communion, but as community.

This is true in other instances as well. There are a variety of structures within the context of community that allow no unequivocal classification into community or communion. In their case too one might think that the original state of coherence consists in consensus, and that the recognition of such a consensus, in turn, helps constitute community. In fact, recognition only means that community becomes visible. In other words, community makes its appearance in this fashion, but does not derive its existence thereby.

Nationals meeting each other abroad, for instance, do not first have to enter into communion. They acknowledge each other as members of one circle to which they belong. The same can be the case with coreligionists, although this is likely to occur only in the case of well-established religions. When one deals with ecstatic or orgiastic notions of features of fundamentalist religions, the encounters of previously unacquainted coreligionists are different. They become aware of their preexisting ties. These have, in fact, the form of community. On the basis of such coherence they establish a deliberate communion that differs radically from the natural coherence provided by the sheer existence of those religions as communities.

It is self-evident that one can be a member of a community and in addition sustain special relations of a different kind with selected members of that community or, in fact, the community as a whole. Such relations constitute communions. In that sense, brothers can be close friends. This, however, can lead to difficulties: the essential features of such social relations as kinship and friendship are in potential conflict.

When the sense of belonging together characteristic of community is not so deeply rooted, as in newly established religions, the opportunities for establishing communions are increased. It is quite possible to imagine a group of established and mature men meeting one another as adherents of the same still-young religion. Under these circumstances their community becomes apparent; their conduct is now oriented toward their mutual coherence. A communion may not arise at all. Conduct in this case may well be consciously a matter of community behavior. The odds are, though, that their conduct will more often issue from unconscious dispositions, even if the first cause of such conduct lies in a recognition of their membership in the same religious community. It is an unconscious response leading simply to a sense of belonging. The unconscious, in other words, is modified by the conditions of community; in turn, community becomes incorporated in the unconsciousness. There, it is considered virtually a matter of nature. Communal facts both penetrate the unconscious and modify it. This is surely the case with great experiences, such as religious ones. Nevertheless, it is more likely that such encounters will rekindle original and primary religious sentiments. In that case, a communion may arise, for communion is formed by an actual experience of common feeling. At the same time, every experience of communion has the effect of establishing communal bonds. Communion, after all, is constituted by a complex of emotions, the central objects of which need not be other people. The objects can also be external manifestations, including a deity. That might lead one to think that the communion is, as it were, only a secondary by-product whose valence is less than the valence of the objects toward which feelings are primarily directed. This would be erroneous. Such feelings are consciously experienced, but they are somewhat removed from the center of one's awareness.

In this connection, too, the absolute difference between community and communion once more appears. It may be quite easy for enthusiastic apologists of one kind of communion to claim that members passionately devoted to some solidarity such as a religious sect must, for that reason, belong with the whole of their beings, with all of what they are, so to speak, including their unconscious dispositions. Actually a superficial kind of emotionality, indeed, leads only to a superficial sort of communion. Still, it does lead to a communion.

This superficiality can have a variety of sources. It may come from the fact that the feelings in question are in fact not deeply rooted in the unconscious regions of the persons concerned, or that their consequences exert less influence on the unconscious. After all, it is part of the question of the depth of a feeling—whence it comes, and where it leads. Truly, a communion will be all the more tightly knit, the more the feelings that are constituted in it mobilize the unconscious dispositions of the members in question. In any case, conscious experiences of emotion are still wholly involved. Only such experiences can inflame unconscious dispositions when, in an ultimate sense, the very condition of experience in turn is rooted in the unconscious. But, to repeat, only feelings establish communions. The consequences of these feelings include not only the formation of the communion, but also that of a community.

It does not follow from this, however, that a more deeply established communion must for that very reason constitute a community. Such a communion indeed may lead to community and will, in fact, do so, but only to the extent to which the communion is then left behind. This possibility is, however, limited. We must distinguish between, as it were, the inclination of unconscious attitudes and the establishment, within the unconscious, of social relations. Where we have the former, feelings are likely to appear and reappear. Only where periodic excitement calms down once more—perhaps even dies out—and is then replaced by a kind of coalescence between emotion and unconscious disposition, can one speak of community. It is for this reason that, in the case of younger religions, the meetings of similarly excited persons are more likely to lead to communion than to community.

Perhaps I might add here, too, that the apologists for communion should remember that community is typically marked by a certain settled quietness and persistence. It is a structure taken for granted. The qualities tend not to be overly appreciated by the apologists of communion. I should also add, however, that the feelings constitutive of communion, while not necessarily focused on other persons, but rather on a variety of impersonal or other sorts of objects, may nevertheless be directly concerned with persons. Where one analyzes feelings oriented toward community, both these concerns are simultaneously present. It is quite possible to become related to a community in a double sense, as a community and as a communion. There are certain strains and antinomies involved in such a relation. A deep conflict between community and communion remains. It is the hidden reason why those who are very much part of a community distrust those others whose relations include the elements of communion. It is also noteworthy that those social relations within a community that suggest communion are the ones preferred by people who are not in fact members of a community. Much of the present-day yearning for communal coherence assumes this character. Such yearning is usually less directed toward a specific community than toward coherence as such.

In all this there occurs a frequent misuse of the word community. Even though the character of community is properly understood, those yearning for it would probably not be able to live within it. They are, after all, often people of developed sensitivities and differentiated emotions who, as such, are not likely to be capable of complete immersion in a communal relationship.

There is another matter that also obscures the boundary between community and communion. We feel attracted to someone, feel close or related to someone, feel tied to him by some secret or silent bond. Is this any different from feeling a social relation involving ties of blood? Are we dealing here only with a matter of degree? In any case, it would appear not to be a matter of community but of communion. When one feels sympathy, this is distinctly a matter of communion. Similarly, when one recognizes ties of blood or feels them, the extent to which genuine emotions are indeed involved raises a question not only of community but also of communion. Feelings emanating from a sense of kin provide one also with a sense of the organic, genetic, and pre-existing character of community. In that case, community dominates; one's feelings are relatively insignificant. True, someone who feels attracted to someone else similarly feels a givenness, and hence a communal bond. Yet this only constitutes an invitation for the development of communion. The main thing is not so much a pre-existing community as a yet-to-be-founded communion. Still, there are limiting cases. One may speak about communities of sympathy that are constituted only in manifest behavior. They differ in degree from proper ties of blood.

These things should not, however, obscure the fundamental difference between the types of social relations we have been trying to analyze. Admittedly, in our experience of the real world, conceptual distinctions always become blurred. Artificial differentiations are not to be developed to the point where one is no longer able to see their mutual relations. We do not wish to provide a perspective that apprehends the world as an either-or proposition and becomes an inappropriate and scholastic confusion of concepts and reality.

This line of analysis may appear rather forced.

Some may raise objections to any claim of absolute difference between community and communion, since it is not a difference to be found as such in social life, itself. Others may agree that there are differences of direction among social groupings, that these go deep, and that it becomes important to distinguish them conceptually. But—so the counterargument may continue—this is simply a matter of conceptual distinctions, the justification for which lies in their usefulness. I can only say by way of general rebuttal to this argument that part of the great importance of more recent philosophy, especially as found in the work of Edmund Husserl, lies in the rediscovery of the Platonic idea (eidos). The whole notion of "species," for instance, is not just a more-or-less adequate crutch for the reconstruction of a more-or-less adequate notion of the order of things. The term species is not deduced from experience. The latter would indeed deny its validity. Rather, within the realm of ideas itself, various fundamental lines of cleavage appear. Reality has no choice but to "follow" the same lines. Still it may be quite true that within reality it is often not at all easy to see the lines of distinction that our concepts in fact draw. One can speak about intermediate cases only where such cases are themselves posited by our conceptual schemes. Perhaps my argument will become clearer and more plausible, if I now add a third term—the notion of society—to the previous distinction between community and communion.

Community, Communion, and Society

The respective differences among these three terms should make exposition of this last term less difficult. The essential character of society, in contrast to community, lies in the priority of individual over social existence. Society refers to those relations that are entered into by previously unrelated individuals. In the case of community, its parts are bound from the very beginning as are the parts of an organic whole. One has, of course, to admit that the autonomy of independent individuals whence society develops simply does not exist in isolation and cannot ever exist in that way. Society is a form of relatedness that presupposes the essential separateness of individuals, although it may well be that their very individuality presupposes membership in a variety of other social relations. The old antithesis of the priority of the whole over its parts, or of the parts over its whole, is repeated in the contrast between society and community. Yet, even this contrast needs to be complemented by the reminder that the essential separateness of the individual in the case of society remains intact

within society. Though individuals may have to or may want to bind themselves in a variety of societies, they remain separable and separate individuals even after they have accomplished this. They continue to sustain a mutual distance. They bridge this mutual distance with various connections. These connections, however, remain visible and hence rational, just as the totality of societal relations is only indeed a relational matter. The spirit of society is inspired by the ethos of a cool reserve.

The members of community, then, are originally interdependent. The parts of a society are originally apart. The comrades of a communion have, in the first instance, no joint interest. Communions develop only as members meet or when a community is already formed. The experiences leading to their creation are individual experiences. It follows in this regard that communion and society are more like each other, because the interpersonal basis of communion is so narrow and specified.

A friend is an alter ego. We feel his pain and pleasure as our own pain and pleasure. The waning of such a relation hurts. While we may speak about coalescence in this regard—as we have used the term in connection with community—one may speak about a perhaps more intensive mutual fusion. Such a fusion can, of course, take on a variety of forms and degrees, but it emphasizes the principle of "separateness." From this point of view, community and society form a straight line. Communion lies between them. But, in another respect, community and society are alike and differ from communion. Or, to put it yet another way: one can think of a series starting with society, leading to community, and hence to communion; or of one starting with community, continuing with society, and ending with communion.

Society is characterized by the fact that its constitutive relations involve reciprocity: every action as a rule takes place on behalf of some counter action and in the expectation of it. Contract is representative of society, it is alien to community. The members of a family cannot be bound to one another merely by the instrument of contract. In that situation contract plays only a subordinate role. It arises in connection with specific matters. In the case of the thought-ways of peasants one finds a perspective different from the type of mentality that calculates. Communion, on the other hand, cherishes and perhaps even demands unreserved devotion, complete sacrifice and unreserved giving not only of material things, but also of one's self. At least this would be the extreme case. The other cases are simply deviations in degree from this ideal.

Society, then, is characterized by the relation of parts or members to the whole and by the role of exchange. Communal bonds, in contrast, are by their very nature enduring. They might become loosened over time, but their original tendency is to endure. Even the simplest and most peripheral of memories suffices for the resurrection of any community including one that seems to have died. On the other hand, societal relations are oriented toward momentary, definite, perhaps even unique occurrences. In their case, when the business is settled, individuals go their separate ways. Yet the "business" with respect to which people convene and disperse in this way recurs, unless there are some definite obstacles. People often wish to resume once more those relations that have brought satisfaction in the past. Even society, then, appears to be molded by a seeming quality of duration, but the connectedness of society is constituted, in fact, only by a sequence of single and repeated acts.

Communion, on the other hand, is a precarious or unstable structure by its very nature. As long as it persists, it persists in single and discrete acts, never outside those acts. Thus, we have spoken of fusion rather than coalescence. After all, the character of human communion requires fairly intense mutual involvement, and the emotional ecstasy on which communions depend is a fleeting thing. The emotions come and go like tides of the sea. Their power may be great. They can shake us to the very root, destroy us, or even drive us to distraction or madness, but they do not endure. In excitement or drunkenness, emotions may engender much, but they also are displaced once more by soberness. The affective qualities of one's awareness decline or are replaced by other matters. These contrasts of the three structures flow directly from their respective essential differences.

It is equally evident that communions always tend to become transformed into societal or communal structures. The main reason for this is their previously mentioned lability. One instance of this lability is provided by "the vow of eternal love." It has provided subject matter for humor even in ancient times. It reflects the inner contradiction of communion as well as the remedy used to resolve the contradiction. The vow, after all, contains the seeds of societal organization. Still, with its intention to create an enduring arrangement, it also is a step toward community. In this way, through these two links, in turn, communion contradicts itself.

More generally stated, it is the ethos of loyalty by means of which communions try to overcome their inherent precariousness. In doing this, communions are subject to partly societal, partly communal tendencies. Today we consider marriage as one of the most important communions. Every marriage begins with a sacred promise of mutual faithfulness and loyalty. This institution, involving monogamous and patrimonial arrangements, could probably only become established historically by transforming obligations of mutual loyalty into definitely binding expectations. We find similar situations among religions. They demand that children who begin their religious life as members of a community into which they are born (baptism) should voluntarily swear loyalty to their church (confirmation) at a time when they reach the age when their social relations are frequently characterized by the impulse toward communion. Religious ties are, then, ties of communion and are exposed to all the risks of communion.

Faithfulness, when more precisely analyzed—as Simmel noted—is a "substitution for love." As long as one loves, one need not be concerned about faithfulness. Love is its own guarantee. Yet, through loyalty and the pledge of loyalty, bonds of love, originally constituted as a communion, are transformed in part into a communal arrangement and in part into a societal one. Society, too, requires faithfulness. Virtue in the case of society is tantamount to honoring one's contracts. Contracts made for long periods of time require some assurance that the parties involved cannot withdraw from their mutual obligations. Such obligations were voluntarily undertaken in the first instance but subsequently constitute a constraint on the freedom of the parties concerned. A promise is the seed of contract. Promises as such, or promises taken in the abstract, are in fact pledges of loyalty. In a sense every promise promises faithfulness toward those who have been promised. To promise loyalty is simply a promise in principle, specifying nothing in particular. This, certainly, represents an attitude characteristic of communion. But only persons who are in fact free, unconstrained, and not hampered by irrational ties can make promises or sign contracts. Otherwise they would be subject to quite unpredictable conflicts. Only a man autonomous in his decision, free from all irrational bonds, can be expected not to promise or to make commitments he cannot keep. To be in this position requires that one is at all times thoroughly cognizant of one's various obligations. Similarly, only people who *remain* free and do not become the victims of irrational forces or superior powers at some later date can, in fact, sustain promises or sign agreements. Contract requires a persistent comprehensibility of social affairs. Contract, therefore, proceeds within a relational context. Faithfulness, thus, is a societal phenomenon. Only where faithfulness is taken for granted, is it possible for arrangements as a whole to be, in fact, societal. Indeed, it is only then that one can speak about society and yet there are traces of societal arrangements on all planes of culture.

It appears that, whenever one deals with economic or juridical arrangement, in fact where one deals with any arrangements that demand some frame of reference and some durability, elements of society are present. Sometimes, such arrangements have not become differentiated and autonomous; they may still have the aspect of community or communion. However, in these cases, for societal features to emerge, they require particular guarantees against the irrational factors that might otherwise prevent individuals from meeting the impersonal demands of societal arrangements. Similarly, it is necessary that freedom from irrational demands not merely be achieved for the moment, but become an established fact, so that contract obligations can, in effect, be entered into. It is for these reasons that ceremony and ritual accompanied juridical and even economic arrangements in earlier times. Yet, at this very point, societal demands become converted into communal ones, for, in this instance, people have not yet reached the point where they can take societal kinds of expectations for granted. They are not yet free. They do not face irrational forces in an autonomous fashion. Accordingly, we surround juridical and economic proceedings with an appropriate dignity. In this way, such arrangements become memorable and remembered, and, as such, they also become part of a communal routine of life. Even communions, then, can become transformed alike into societal and communal structures through various kinds of votes and oaths on the basis of which members promise mutual loyalty.

Other forms of the expression of mutual loyalty are even more illustrative of these processes. The founding of blood bonds by drinking a few drops of one another's blood constitutes an attempt to found a communion of such intense loyalty that it has, in fact, all the features of community as such. In that connection one should mention, too, that the term "brother" is often transferred to people jointly belonging to the same communal communion. However, wherever communions persist or are intended to persist, they come to assume characteristics of both community and society. This is partly intentional; partly it is a matter of automatic unintended development. This is particularly true of religious associations. The history of Christianity furnishes one outstanding example in this regard. Christianity had to take on the features of statutory coherence in order, in fact, to become an enduring phenomenon. Every enduring communion needs some kind of formal agreement that permits little or no deviation and that requires further agreement for its abrogation. Only momentary social arrangements, like leaving for a day's outing, can dispense with some kind of formal agreement.

To be sure, religious institutions are primarily of religious significance. Still, in their social consequence they lead to the creation of societal structures. This, in turn, brings with it the danger of spiritless rigidity. In the case of the Roman Catholic Church, the quasi-military establishment of the ancient Romans played its role. This process, with its orientation toward durable and taken-for-granted features, leads to a further transformation into communal forms. For later generations, previous associations are givens: they are forms incorporated in their unconscious. The most eminent symbol of the transformation of a religious communion into a religious community is provided by infant baptism. Yet religious movements take periodical cognizance of the fact that the essence of their religious attitude is most appropriately expressed through the social relations of communion and not through those of a community or a society.

Christianity, for instance, calls its adherents back again and again to consider the demands of love. It asks them to replace the processes of calculation and other forms of societal conduct with love for their neighbors. At least periodical attempts are made to persuade genuine believers not to become immersed in the distracting obligations imposed by community affiliations. This is the social meaning of celibacy among priests or priestesses (or, as in the case of the Roman Catholic Church, among monks). In the context of Christianity we again see very clearly that the character of communion conflicts fundamentally with the respective characteristics of community and society.

It is at this point also that the essential sociological differences between church and sect appear. With the help of sects the source of communion in individual religious experience can become enlivened again. Sects displace the inarticulate givenness of community and the calculating coolness of society. The marks of such processes of rejuvenation are provided by an emphasis on a communistic ethic of love and by adult baptism. Socially speaking then, religion is originally a matter of communions. Hence, religious renewal requires sectarian movements. Yet, in the course of their establishment they incorporate societal elements, while they persist only in the form of community structures. (Incidentally, the question of original and genuine religiosity is not for debate at this point. The two terms are certainly not to be equated.

This discussion seeks to by-pass judgments of value.)

Even with regard to loyalty, communions become mindful of their actual character. Loyalty easily becomes "sheer loyalty" or "cold faithfulness." In fact, communions might counter the threat of a transformation into communal or societal structures with a positive emphasis on the complementary threat to their lability. At any rate, lability may be deliberately valued. Some people, deeply attached to the characteristic qualities of communions, go so far as to keep themselves open to ever-new communions. Artists, for instance, sometimes develop a distinct distaste for small town Philistinism and urban heartlessness. Such distaste is the other side of a positive attachment to communions. For them, community has a negative ring. It appears stale, superficial, and narrow. To remain confined by it seems hypocritical. At the same time, society is experienced primarily as a kind of calculating and mechanized state of affairs. Under these circumstances, the uncertain, transitory, and discontinuous features of communion become positively valued. Such people see in various parts of the world a reservoir of new and beckoning adventurous possibilities. They look for new enthusiasms and happenings, for the see-saw of new friendships or love affairs.

For the systematic development of sociology, then, the categories of community, society, and communion are of basic importance. They are general and modal categories. They do not constitute species of concrete structures, such as are represented by the terms, "peasantry," "bourgeoisie," "nobility," or even by such expressions as "family," "clan," and the like. Rather, they are forms of being that may or may not be assumed by such concrete structures.

All this, however, has to be further limited and specified. Certain specific social structures have a particular affinity for one or the other of these three modes of social organization. We have already discussed this in connection with religious organizations. We have argued, too, that economic and judicial relations are essentially of a societal character. They cannot be fully developed among peasants, among villagers, or among friends, lovers, or coreligionists. They are prevented from full development there by the work of counterforces that precede economic and juridical matters while, of course, being related to them as well.

Contrariwise, the family is by its very nature a community. Families that present themselves as communions appear affected and artificial, at least to families with obvious roots in a common past. Where the members of a family regard each other with the distance characteristic of society, the coherence typical of kinship seems to have been lost. When conflicts arise concerning inheritance, it is considered a sign of family breakdown to go to a court of law for a decision, even if this might be the most expeditious procedure. Such a decision, nevertheless, would seem worse than a feud. Similarly, the peasantry and even villagers are, like a family, preferably linked by communal ties.

In addition to showing a special affinity between new religious structures and communions as such, I might have also referred to the camaraderie of the military. The clearest models, however, in each case are as follows: For society, judicial and economic relations; for community, the family; for communion, friendship. Admittedly, there are friendships of all kinds. One can find friendship in the realm of business as well as in the sphere of politics. Such relations may indeed involve elements of perfection and mutual good will. Yet their bases remain economic and political. It seems almost like a misuse of the term to apply the notion of friendship in this connection. It is true that genuine friendships become communities through enduring and frequent encounters. But this can also be a matter of embarrassment. Often it is wise for friends to sustain some temporary separation, particularly if the suspicion arises that the relation is a communal one rather than a true communion. If upon meeting again they find that a community has, in fact, replaced friendship, there is bound to be some disappointment.

All these examples show that actual, concrete social structures are, up to a point, indifferent to the modes of organization that we have distinguished. At the same time, they show selective affinities for one or the other of these basic categories. The categories, in turn, are mutually independent. This is true not only on the plane of ideas, but points to a more essential analytic independence, which can be implemented to explain the mixtures and transitions of concrete social relations.

Society does not develop in a simple or straight line from community. A specific ethos underlies it, and that some ethos, particularly when it first appears, may be consolidated by communion. The rise of capitalism and the modern state had its age of heroes. Predatory warfare, patriotism, and religious enthusiasm have culminated in the birth of "society." Actually society was possible only as people slowly realized—and this in anything but a continuous fashion—that their ethos, as ethos, conflicted with its content. Even today a great deal of entrepreneurial activity is accomplished in the spirit of communion.

The family, too, provides an instance of community developing for communion, for the family consists, in the first instance, in marriage. Young marriages are perhaps not yet real marriages or, at any rate, not yet families. Permanently childless marriages seem incomplete. It is only through children that spouses are really brought together. Still, the family necessarily begins with marriage. Matriarchal arrangements are no exceptions. Now, at the time of its consummation, marriage can have a strong community character, and it is always undertaken as a community. Spouses find each other as members of circles that have similar values, mores, or styles of life. Admittedly, in the case of certain individuals or even in the case of certain circles or status groupings, one finds a preference for selecting mates from the widest possible sphere so as to provide distance and unfamiliarity. At the other extreme, there are courtship arrangements that completely determine the selection of spouses. Marital selection seems to involve the demand for some kind of status endogamy, while involving economic calculations as well. For the most part these demands are simply external manifestations of community relations. Finally, one can find virtually all kinds of "societal" marital arrangements, including the use of professional marriage brokers, newspapers, advertisements, and the like. Yet, even here, spouses concerned with becoming genuinely married or founding families must develop community bonds. As a rule such "societally contracted" marriages tend to keep their origins a secret, since impersonal selection procedures are felt to be poignantly incongruous with the communal character of kinship arrangements. Such incongruity would also be felt, were marriages to derive exclusively from considerations of community.

In all times the ideal of marriage has been the marriage of love, an idea that has been realized to some extent, anyway. Perhaps this reflects a misunderstanding deriving from the extension of those attitudes appropriate for communion into fields where they are actually inappropriate. Young people sometimes consider marriage a profane affair and contrast it rather prosaically with love and the bonds of love. In fact, a fair amount of experience seems to teach that love, in the specific sense of actual feelings, dies in marriage. Love finds this painful and rejects the transformation of itself into a community arrangement. Marriages of love are not always happy in the face of daily and enduring routine. Marriages and, even more so, families must of necessity become what in fact they naturally are: communities. This is so much the case that spouses often take one another for granted. This taking-things-for-granted, this everydayness, is disliked by persons who are brought together in the spirit of communion. Yet, what they respond to negatively has positive value for a community. From the point of view of community, a taken-for-granted establishment of social arrangements symbolizes its fullness and maturity. Still, we tend at times to value social relations based on spontaneous love more than arrangements that exhibit qualities of endurance or reliability that love, in this sense, does not necessarily imply. In the reverse direction, community and societal structures exert pressures at least on some people that, in turn, give rise to a desire for communion.

Community becomes transformed into society. Society coalesces into a community. In a sense the three modes of organization sustain a mutual dependence. Further, the very relations of society and communion require for their existence the elements of community such as language, shared values, similarity of age, or other commonalties that are, as it were, given by nature. And, by the same logic, communion and community cannot persist in the absence of societal forces. To complete the chain, community and society arise out of the conditions of communion. I would call juridical and economic relations the earliest elements of society that can be discovered in the contexts of the community and the communion. I have supposed too that these societal beginnings are originally thoroughly embedded in the context of community. There is also an aspect of communion and sentiment provided by the dignified atmosphere of ceremony. These, in turn, imbue the social relation with enhanced status. Yet even where society, as a form, predominates, it has been preceded by communion. At any rate, the three modal forms are qualified reciprocally from the first.

Implications for Max Weber's Types of Social Action

Toennies' distinction between community and society treated communion as a sublimation, so to speak, of community. The problem of communion was also not differentiated in Toennies' psychology. He treated the phenomenon of community simultaneously in a naturalistic organic—namely, an unconscious—setting and in the context of pure instinct or pleasure. Thus, mother and child were construed to be in communion, because they constituted a community.

Yet, empirical observation has already led to the more precise analyses of Max Weber, setting "traditional" bonds apart from the "affective," particularly the emotional bonds that are sometimes found in communities. That Max Weber, in this case, reached an impasse is explained by his biased perspective. First, he located the subject matter of sociology in "social action," that is, in the "ideal-typical constructions" of social life rather than in social life itself. Second, he restricted "understanding" to such an extent that only acts of "consciousness" were included.

To me "understanding" implies a *Geisteswissenschaftliche sociology*," rather than a "*Verstehende sociology*." This is the sense in which Dilthey constructed the meaning of the term, "understanding." Weber, on the other hand, referred to Jaspers and then to Simmel and Rickert. Thus, he erred, in that only "subjectively intended meaning" in the sense of the "conscious import of social action" is interpreted as capable of study. A misunderstanding of Husserl has probably produced the confusion, as we shall see. The consequence is, as Weber put it, that "a very significant part of sociologically relevant conduct, especially purely traditional action, is treated as being on the margin" of incomprehensibility. This is an absurdity of Max Weber's epistomological asceticism. Although he strained for methodological precision, his methodology was not always profound. The implication is that the pure and genuine community should, in the strict sense, be interpreted as unanalyzable, in spite of its sociological relevance as well as the wealth of knowledge that Max Weber himself had of that social form. Only that aspect of community manifested explicitly in consciousness can be studied. Now this is often a "consciousness of feeling." Yet, for sociological study, "comprehensible meaning" must be abstracted from feeling, in Weber's sense, and then the distinctions between "traditional" action—in so far as it is still "comprehensible"—and "affective-emotional" action, between community and communion, become fluid and intermingle.

We can see this difficulty clearly in Weber's own writing:

Predominantly traditional conduct—just as that which is merely mimetic response—stands wholly and absolutely on the borderline of and often beyond that which can be called a "meaningfully" oriented action, because it is very frequently only a hollow response in the direction of a long and firmly established attitude or resigned reaction to a customary stimulus. The bulk of all long established daily routine approaches this type, which belongs in the theoretical system not only as a marginal case, . . . but also, therefore, because the tie to customary ways of doing things can be preserved in different degrees and senses.

In this case, the type approaches that of affective conduct. Therefore, there is really a transition be-

tween these things, because Max Weber's position on consciousness takes community into consideration only at that point where there is an interpreted meaning that is "comprehensible" for him—the point where community merges over into communion. Indeed, Weber knows that even the "meaning of social action," in his sense, as well as "comprehensible meaning," often and frequently lie, for the most part, in the unconscious:

Evident "motives" and "repressions" often directly disguise . . . actions and even the real context of the performance of action. . . . In this case sociology is confronted with the task of defining, explaining, and confirming the context, whether or not it has entirely or in part been raised into consciousness or concretely "intended."

As a matter of fact, the entire methodology of Max Weber breaks down at this "marginal instance of meaningful interpretation." And it leads at the same time to a point where central social phenomena are excluded from possible observation: "All traditional actions and broad categories of charisma, almost but not quite," are comprised "by fragments of comprehensibility." Max Weber himself was not entirely satisfied with the matter; and he revealed the premises that led to the difficulty; yet this does not permit any alternative judgment about the matter. He writes:

Actual conduct is carried on, in the large part of its manifestation, in semiconsciousness or unconsciousness of its "intended meaning." Action carried on instinctually or habitually "feels" more uncertain in the majority of cases than that which is cognitive or has "made itself clear." In the case of most such conduct, only rarely and often only in individual instances, will a meaning (whether rational or irrational) of an act emerge into consciousness. Genuinely effective, that is wholly and clearly apprehended, meaningful action is in reality always only a marginal case. Every historical and sociological observation will always have to take these considerations into account in analyzing reality. However, that should not preclude the fact that sociology forms its concepts through the classification of objectively possible intended meaning, *all the more so, whether or not conscious conduct is carried on in a meaningfully oriented manner.*

This last (italicized) suggestion (which I oppose) permits the speculation that its consequences are already suspect to Weber himself. Surely, sociological concepts must have the breadth to comprehend all objectively possible reality. An ideal-type ought never to establish "exceptions," but always only "deviations."

Max Weber did not heed his own proscription at all, at least not completely: concepts like "affective," "emotional" are not at all "derived from the classification of intended meaning," but are types of psychic *acts* (they are acts in themselves, not in their "intent")! The phrase, "intended meaning," is the place, in principle, where the misunderstanding of Husserl has produced confusion.

I am so close to the perspective of Weber's "*Verstehende* sociology" that I deplore the fact that I cannot agree with it completely. The concept, "intended meaning," is exceedingly ambiguous. Max Weber's "intent of consciousness" concerns him only slightly if at all. It doesn't belong in sociology where Weber has put it. But, how sociological he is in his actions! Weber tries at last to exclude the most fundamental social phenomena from the concept of "social action."

Finally, it follows that Max Weber's "*Verstehende* sociology"—*nolens volens*—is rationalistic! Weber has various misgivings about "irrational understandings" and "irrational meaning." For example, he writes:

Predominantly affective behavior belongs also [like "traditional"] on the border of and often beyond that which is meaningfully oriented; it can be an impulsive response to an unusual stimulus. It is a sublimation when affectively conditioned behavior erupts as a conscious discharge of a feeling-state. For then it is already on the way (not always) to rationalization.

In fact an "intended meaning," in the sense employed by Weber, precludes the irrational from "conscious-import" in the case of "affective behavior." An inquiry in terms of "intended meaning" is always obliged either to fall short of its purpose or to rationalize its operation after the fact in an artificial manner.

Therefore, there is, in any case, no final solution. Weber's examples are entirely rational *and* entirely irrational in their basic motive. What can be more *rational* than to counteract irritability by chopping wood! What is more *irrational* than striving for relaxation! What Weber really has in mind is the "meaning of the act" and the "intent of the act." "Consciousness" is completely irrelevant to these things. His entire position is altered by this observation. Moreover, it has ramifications in completely different directions. Rationalism impressed Weber conclusively and in a completely positive way. He meant perhaps that "all irrational, affectively conditioned, meaningful contexts of conduct are most clearly represented and studied as 'deviations' from a constructed purely rational purposeful course"! Even if reality is preponderantly irrational, the method of "*Verstehende* sociology" must be "rationalistic" in the construction of concepts!

Of course, there is, by virtue of another theory of Max Weber, a dichotomy of "social action" within the "rational society." In that case, it is still dubious

whether what he calls "value-rational" and "rational-purposeful" activity may not legitimately provide a nice parallel dichotomy within community—a dichotomy within a dichotomy.

"Value" and "purpose" are closely related. This may be presumed wherever there is ultimate purpose or self-interest (which may freely convert into one another). At least in the case of ultimate purpose, "irrationality" and "value" both enter into the "rational-purposeful" act. Accordingly, Weber has necessarily indicated that "rational-purposeful action" is always dependent upon purposes that lie beyond the act itself and refer to external matters. As opposed to this, "value-rational action" should be characterized in such a way that—seen in the perspective of "purpose," which is dissipated in the act—it is self-contained. Then "purpose" is truly tied to "value," but "value" is not truly tied to "purpose." Here, consequently, Weber's terminology is vindicated. "Rational-purposeful" refers, first of all, to purpose; "value-rational," to unmediated value, but the latter is always valued and, therefore, irrational.

If a thing has value in itself, then it may be asked whether this distinction constitutes anything more than a difference in degree. "Irrational" and "externally given," "proffered," "demanded" value is in any case indispensable, whether it is affixed only to the "purpose" and consequently to results, or whether to the "intrinsic value" of the action irrespective of the consequences. Beyond this, however, as has been uniquely demonstrated by Weber himself, that action which he calls "rational-purposeful" likewise has its own distinctive and irrational value, and in this case is pervaded by it, not only from the standpoint of "purpose," but also in the action itself. To be sure, this is the case, not only for the contents of the act, which are only indirectly significant here, since they are "value-rational," but also for "rationality"—rationality as such. Moreover, in the case of "rational-purposeful activities," the "purpose" is neither the basic nor the only source of "value," and, in such a case, the "purpose" as well as the results can even be highly irrelevant.

This can be seen by assessing the "good intentions" in so many theoretical as well as practical moral systems of "rational-purposeful" modes of thought. Those whose "intentions" were "good" are not censured. Their failure results only in chagrin. Even a rational painstaking attempt to achieve a "purpose" whose "value" seems imprudent or unintelligible to a "rational-purposeful" critic is rejected as odd or foolish or droll or ultimately as mad, whereas an act not really "rational" meets up with ethical aversion. In all of these cases there is certainly a difference between "value-rational" and "rational-purposeful" activity. The "rational-purposeful" act is that which I have elsewhere called "autarchic rationality." One can even call the difference absolute. However, the contrary case of "nonautarchic rationality" means precisely that which is not totally uninhibited, whether it is found in community or in communion. And, instead of a category, there is a mixed type.

Nowhere may "rational-purposeful" and "value-rational" acts be separated conceptually. Only in one respect is a basic difference established, if not conceived conceptually. It is established within the category "society." This is accomplished by virtue of the fact that the "irrational," the rationality of which is always necessarily required, can be given and legitimated "emotionally-affectively" or "traditionally"—better "naturally" (comprehending the "traditional" act). With only an imperceptible nuance, Weber's terms (though to be sure he is difficult to understand) may be applied to the actual difference. "Purposes," therefore, lie within "value-rational" activities, and these, above all, are irrationally rational or "emotional-affective." Thus, they appear in collective experience as "values" of "action." In "rational-purposeful" activities, they are more precisely "purposes." Still the "claims" and "precepts" of "rationality" are "traditional" and "natural." Consequently, they are taken for granted and remain unemphasized.

There is no gainsaying the fact that Max Weber's exposition did not specify this distinction but rather the distinction discussed earlier. However, it appears that his discussion ultimately leads to the present distinction. In this view, "rational-purposeful" and "value-rational" acts, as far as their distinction can have lasting significance, are both merely agencies by which society is transformed in one instance into community, in the other into communion. They are not merely different categories of action that are incidentally there, but agencies of transformation. Thence it follows that, if we confront the distinction between community and communion and the vastly different dichotomy of "rational" action with the contrast provided by rational and irrational domains, we arrive at a fourfold over-all classification. In actuality "rational" and "irrational" action do not exhaust the possibilities, but, when considered along with "emotional" action and the "unconscious," they form a trichotomy in which both areas of consciousness as well perhaps as both areas of irrational action are included.

Moreover, this exhibits again, by its very resistance to manipulation, a weighty justification for the

analytical separation of community and communion.

Weber's strangely terse statements about "value-rational" and "rational-purposeful" action may be clear to him. They are not completely clear to us. However, he saw at least that the irrational in its relationship to purpose does permeate "rational-purposeful" action: "action, therefore, is rational-purposeful only in the means employed." To be sure, there are purposes "simply as given subjectively regnant necessities." Weber appeared to regard these as admittedly not rational, but neither did he regard them as irrational. He never made up his mind. Yet, in the end, he did say that "absolute rational-purposeful action" is "only in reality one constructed marginal case." Actually, it is not even that. As opposed to "value-rational" action, one might think that such action must be manifested as rational only in the attitude adopted to the consideration of means for accomplishing purposes. In any case, that is the impression conveyed by all the examples of the type proffered by Weber. However, "value-rational" action can often be included with action that is "rational-purposeful only in its means," and consequently "rational-purposeful" action may be included with it!

With respect to that which Weber *abstractly* asserts to be the essence of "value-rational" action, one is certanly not led, in the first instance at least, to consider the attainment of ends in trying to assess the value of such action. Furthermore, it is not necessary to take ends into account in assessing the rationality of an act. When one meets a specified number of obligations, one acts in a "value-rational" but *purpose*less way. Ideally, the obligations are never weighed, nor are affirmations sought from others; only spontaneous gratitude may arise. Whether there can be complete freedom from "purpose" in "autarchical rationality," or in rational-purposeful action, to use Weber's term, remains an open question. There are certainly instances of "autarchical rationality" where the end in view has no relevance. Examples are bureaucratic memoranda, filing and tabulation, classification of all kinds, military exercises, and the academic mania for filing data. Stamp collecting is another example of "autarchical rationality devoid of purpose." Many children's games belong here, as do most forms of play. In the case of "dedicated" rational-purposeful action, then, it is not necessary to place a "value" upon the end in view or to consider its accomplishment.

In other respects, one might well speak of "autarchical rationality" as a "constructed marginal case." Nevertheless, we are dealing with analytic, not substantive, distinctions. Weber's distinction is, again, different. Concerning an "action that is only rational-purposeful in its choice of means," he contrasts value-rationally given ends with long established ends that are "given simply as regnant subjective necessities." These latter obviously do not appear "more rational" to him, but "more commensurate with rationality" (thus, superficial considerations lead him to a logical impossibility).

This really adds nothing to the matter, although it may appear to do so. It introduces the notion of "self-evident" ends. Yet, Weber must certainly realize that "self-evidence" is something very subjective. It means one thing for a person in one culture and something else for another person in another culture! "Self-evidence" is always only evidence to which we have become accustomed. Rational-purposeful action is, therefore, only an aspect of rationality transformed by community. However, if there were universal self-evidence of a natural kind, then it is fitting to allude to Weber's "regnant subjective necessities" as a part of nature, otherwise they would be included by him in the narrower sense of natural as always preferably "traditional." Economic efficiency, which Weber cites most frequently to illustrate a purely "rational-purposeful" end, has certainly been shown earlier by Weber to be in no way "self-evident" at all times or in all places. Economics is, as I have pointed out, only coincident with rationalism. Rational action as such, however, was not always self-evident: it had its heroes and age of communions; only then did it become "self-evident." For Weber himself, the affairs of Puritanism—already characterized by "autarchical rationality"!—are justly regarded as a prime example of "value-rational" activity.

Be that as it may, some qualification is needed here. In a later part of his systematic treatise, where the obstacles of a distorted methodology and the related distorted conceptualization have become less imposing, Max Weber deals with a special, yet very important, social phenomenon. He apprehended precisely the trichotomy of fundamental sociological categories we have proposed. I speak of his types of authority:

There are three pure types of legitimate authority. Their legitimate value is, so to speak, primarily: (1) rational in character . . . , (2) traditional in character . . . , (3) charismatic in character: on the basis of unusual devotion to the sacredness, the heroic power, or the mimesis of a person and the order revealed or created by him.

With reference to charismatic authority Weber emphasized above all its *unusual* character. This allows him to show, in a fundamental and excellent manner, the abrupt contrasts between charismatic and "rational" authority on the one hand and "traditional" authority on the other ("both are specifically everyday forms of authority"). Weber realized that charismatic authority manifests above all "an emotional tendency toward community." Beyond its unusual character, he notes further that charismatic authority is intrinsically transitory. To overcome this fact, "charismatic authority which, so to speak, occurs in its ideal-typical form only *in statu nascendi* must alter its essential character: it is traditionalized or rationalized." Thus, like the forms of social relations I have proposed, the three types of authority merge into and give rise to one another.

[*Translators' Postscript:* The original essay is much longer than this extract. It concludes with an attempt to link the three modalities to history. Our present situation, as a kind of world-wide economy and communication system, is seen as the logical extension of the notion of society. At the same time, Schmalenbach argues that the extension of society provokes new enthusiasms for the founding of all the more intimate communions. He sees contemporary society as a kind of syncretistic mixture of a variety of quite extreme contrasts. From this mixture he promises himself some fertile new developments.]

4. The Organization of the Primary Working Group

BY F. J. ROETHLISBERGER AND WILLIAM J. DICKSON

THE PROBLEM of analyzing the data usually proves to be more difficult than obtaining it. The questions our investigators were asking of their data, more particularly of the observation material, can be stated as follows: Do we have here just so many "individuals," or are they related to one another in such a way that they form a group or configuration? If they do form a configuration, how are they differentiated from or integrated with other groups? In short, do we have here evidences of social organization? Clearly, the method of analyzing the data had to be designed to bring out whatever evidences of social organization there might be. The procedure may be summarized briefly.

First, each person entering into the study, whether operator, inspector, or supervisor, was considered separately. The observation material and interview material were examined carefully and every entry in which a particular person was mentioned or referred to was lifted out and listed under his name. Through this method of classification, the degree and kind of social participation of each individual in the Bank Wiring Observation Room became apparent.

Secondly, the material thus listed for each person was examined for evidence of the extent of his participation. Two questions were asked: (1) To whom do this person's relations extend? Does he associate with everyone in the group, or are his social activities restricted to a few? (2) Does he enter a great deal or relatively little into social relations with the people with whom he associates? In other words, if S_1 converses and associates with the men in his soldering unit to the exclusion of everyone else, does he do so frequently or infrequently?

Thirdly, an attempt was made to determine the kind of participation manifested by each person. Such questions as the following were considered: Does he assume a superordinate or subordinate role? Does he strive for leadership? If so, is he permitted to do so, or are his attempts in that direction opposed by others? Are most of his social contacts related to his job, or are they in the nature of arguments, conversations, or games which have no immediate relation to his work?

Fourthly, each occurrence in which a person entered into association with another person was examined to see whether the relation thus manifested expressed an antagonism, a friendship, or was merely neutral. Each incident, of course, had to be related to its social context before its significance could be determined. Take, for example, the following entry: "S_4 spent most of his spare time today drawing pictures. He drew an elaborate picture of a ship which he called 'Old Ironsides.'" A conclusion which might be drawn from this statement as it stands is that S_4 apparently preferred to spend his time in drawing pictures rather than in mingling with the other operators. This, then, might be construed to reflect a negative relation between S_4 and the group, that is, that he preferred his own company to theirs. But when considered in connection with other factors in the situation, this interpretation is seen to be the opposite of that finally assigned to it by the investigators. S_4 at the time was a newcomer, having just replaced S_3. He was not well acquainted with anyone in the group. Furthermore, after he had been in the room a week and had become better acquainted, he no longer spent his spare time drawing pictures. The investigators concluded, therefore, that drawing pictures was a means by which S_4 attracted attention to himself, excited comment, and thus tended to integrate himself with the group. It was a way of approach rather than of avoidance.

In the two preceding chapters the results obtained from analyzing the material according to this procedure have been given. The participation of each individual in the social activities of the group has been described. After having analyzed the data in this manner, however, the question arises: Are there any similarities in the participation of certain individuals? For example, does W_1 almost always associate with W_2 and W_3 to the exclusion of W_7, W_8, and W_9, and, likewise, do W_2 and W_3 both associate with W_1 to the exclusion of W_7, W_8, and W_9? Do the members of one occupational group look up to or down upon the members of another? Do the employees arrange themselves in any social

Reprinted by permission of the publishers from Fritz Jules Roethlisberger and W. J. Dickson, *Management and the Worker* (Cambridge, Mass.: Harvard University Press, 1939), chap. xxi, pp. 493–510. Copyright, 1939, by the President and Fellows of Harvard College.

order with regard to games, job trading, controversies over windows, and other matters? In this chapter these and similar questions will be considered.

Relations between Nonsupervisory Occupational Groups

The first question the investigators asked was this: There are four occupational groups in the department: wiremen, soldermen, inspectors, and trucker. From a purely technical standpoint the members of these groups are all "operators," that is, they are of nonsupervisory rank. Are they differentiated only from the standpoint of the jobs they perform, or have these technical divisions of labor become the basis of a social stratification? Do workmen in one group look upon themselves as superior or inferior to workmen in another group and, if so, how is this social distinction manifested? In order to answer this question, similarities in the behavior of different people in each occupational group, which could be said to be independent of the personalities involved, were noted. Wiremen as a group were considered in relation to soldermen as a group, and so on.

CONNECTOR WIREMEN IN RELATION TO SELECTOR WIREMEN

The wiremen in the department worked upon two types of equipment, one type called "connectors," the other "selectors." The technique of wiring was exactly the same for both types. The only differences, apart from the names, were (1) that a connector equipment might be and usually was eleven banks long, whereas a selector equipment was never more than ten, and (2) that a connector fixture weighed only about half as much as a selector fixture. In the observation room W_7, W_8, and W_9 ordinarily worked on selectors, and the other operators worked on connectors.

Some of the wiremen interviewed in the regular department expressed a preference for connector wiring. The reasons given usually related to the lightness of the fixture. In reality, however, the weight of the fixture was inconsequential. The fixtures were easily lifted, and only two of them had to be carried during an average day. The effort required was scarcely great enough to be felt by healthy young men who frequently engaged in strenuous sports after work. This explanation, therefore, could hardly be taken as the reason for their preference. Further study revealed the real significance of the preference for connector wiring.

In the department the connector wiremen were all placed together toward the front of the room, the direction the men faced while working, and the selector wiremen were located back of them. They were, therefore, spatially arranged in such a way as to suggest that the connector wiremen, since they were in front, were somewhat superior to those to whom their backs were turned. From talking to the supervisors and some of the wiremen the investigators learned that the newer members of the wiring group and some of the slower ones were located "in back." As these men "in back" acquired proficiency and new men were added, they were moved forward. Inasmuch as increases in efficiency were usually rewarded by increases in hourly rates, this meant that the people who were moving forward spatially were also moving upward socially. An individual's location roughly reflected his relative standing in efficiency, earnings, and the esteem of his supervisors. The connector wiremen represented the elite. Indeed, some of the wiremen looked upon "going on connectors" as a promotion even if their hourly rates were not changed. Conversely, some of the connector wiremen felt injured if they were "put back on selectors" and regarded such a change as a demotion even though their hourly rates were not changed. Here, then, a minor technical distinction had become so elaborated that it provided a basis upon which the wiremen were in some measure socially differentiated.

WIREMEN IN RELATION TO SOLDERMEN

The position of wireman was regarded in the department as somewhat superior to that of solderman. Beginners were usually started as soldermen, and from soldering they passed on to wiring. The change in job was usually accompanied by an increase in hourly rate. This, together with the fact that the wireman's job required more specialized abilities than that of the solderman, gave the wiremen a slightly higher status in the department, which was expressed in numerous ways, some of which will be described below.

One of the most frequent ways in which the wiremen demonstrated their superior standing was in job trading. Theoretically, there was supposed to be no job trading. Wiremen were supposed to wire and soldermen were supposed to solder. The purpose of this rule was, of course, to promote efficiency through specialization. In spite of the rule, however, the men did trade jobs. The important point here is that in practically every case the request for trading originated with a wireman and the soldermen almost always traded without protest. Sometimes the wiremen presented their requests to trade to the group chief but more frequently they did not. Though occasionally the soldermen protested over trading, they usually gave in. In other words, the wiremen ordered and the soldermen obeyed.

In the task of getting lunches for the group the difference of status between wiremen and soldermen was apparent. It was common practice in the department for one of the men to go out to one of the near-by lunch counters and get lunches for those in the department who wanted them. This practice prevented congestion at the lunch counters, and it saved the people in the department a great deal of trouble. The person who got the lunches was called the "lunch boy," even though he was a grown man and was not assigned the duties of an office boy. When the men were moved to the observation room, they continued with this practice until the regular "lunch boy" was transferred. The group chief, after announcing the transfer, asked if anyone in the group wanted to take over the job. After some discussion S_1 said that he would. On the first day the group chief went with S_1 to assist him. On the second day, however, the group chief refused to go, saying that there was no use in wasting two men's time. As long as the group chief lent his prestige to the task the group said nothing, but as soon as the solderman had to go alone they started "kidding" him. S_1 kept on getting the lunches for about a week, and then S_4 started getting them as a regular part of his job. Toward the end of the study, when S_4 was moved out to the department, the job reverted to S_1. He kept the job until the group chief himself took it over. The group chief, however, was careful to explain to the observer that he was not actually getting the lunches but merely taking the orders and giving them to a man in the department. He apparently felt that the job was a bit below his dignity. In the observer's record there was no instance of a wireman's getting the lunches. One day W_1 went around and took the orders for lunches and collected the money, but when he had done so he turned the orders over to S_1. As soon as W_1 started taking the orders, I_1 shouted, "Look who's getting the lunches today," which may be taken as an indication that it was an unusual thing for a wireman to do. W_1 continued taking the orders for some time, but S_1 always bought the food and brought it back to the room.

The following illustration also serves to show that the wiremen felt themselves a little superior.

The section chief came in and found S_1 soldering without goggles. He told S_1 to stop until he put them on. S_1 had mislaid them and spent about five minutes looking for them. He grumbled about having to wear goggles as he looked for them.

S_1: "I don't know where the hell those glasses are. I suppose one of you guys hid them. There ain't no sense to wearing them anyway. I soldered for four years before they ever thought of glasses. Now you've gotta keep them on. There ain't no solder gonna splash in a fellow's eye. That's just the damn fool notion somebody's got. I've gotta go around here all day in a fog just because some damn fool wants us to wear goggles."

SC: "Never mind why you've got to wear them, just get them and put them on."

W_2: "I worked on a job for three years where I had to wear goggles and it didn't kill me."

S_1: "Yes, and I suppose you wore them all the time."

W_2: "Well maybe I didn't, but it didn't hurt me to wear them when I had to. There's one thing you have to remember, S_1. Do you hear? Don't do as I do—do as I say. Get that?"

S_1: "Why don't you guys wear glasses when you fix repairs?"

W_3: "We don't have to put them on for that little bit of soldering, but you're a solderman. You've got to wear them."

S_1: "Aw, you guys are all a bunch of damn fools."

WIREMEN AND SOLDERMEN IN RELATION TO THE TRUCKER

The trucker's job was to keep the group supplied with piece parts and to remove completed equipments from the room. Before loading the completed units on his truck, which was pushed by hand, he stamped each one with an identification number, the purpose of which was to enable the Inspection Branch to trace the work back to the inspector who had passed upon it.

During the first few weeks nothing happened to indicate the relation the trucker had with the group. However, when the men felt more at ease in the presence of the observer, certain events began to occur which seemed to reflect the trucker-operator relation. For example, the group started referring to the trucker as a gigolo and as "Goofy." They annoyed him in numerous small ways: by spitting on the place where the identification number was supposed to be stamped, by jogging his arm just as he was about to affix the stamp, by holding the truck when he tried to push it out of the room, or by tickling him in the ribs while he was lifting an equipment onto the truck. That these incidents reflected a relation between occupational groups and not special personal relations is attested to by the fact that most of the wiremen and soldermen behaved in the same way toward the trucker, and by the fact that they displayed the same attitude toward a second trucker who replaced the first one about the middle of the study. Their general attitude was independent of the personalities involved.

WIREMEN AND SOLDERMEN IN RELATION TO THE INSPECTORS

The inspectors belonged to an outside organization, the Inspection Branch. They reported to a different set of supervisors, were paid on an hourly basis, and on the whole had more education than the men whose work they inspected. Their function as inspectors gave them a superordinate position to the operators. This was manifested in many ways. For example, when the wiremen and soldermen came to be interviewed they invariably appeared in their shirt sleeves, or, if it were chilly, in sweaters. The inspectors, however, always came dressed in coats and vests. The significance of this cannot be understood without knowing something about the subtle distinctions in dress in the Operating Branch. The foreman and his assistant usually wore ordinary business suits with coats and vests, the vest being optional. The section chiefs and group chiefs usually wore vests but not coats. Their shirts were usually white, and they wore neckties. Operators as a rule wore neither coats nor vests. They might wear white shirts and a necktie, but ordinarily left their shirts open at the throat, or if they wore a tie, the knot was not pulled up tightly around the neck and the collar button was usually left unfastened. This was the general pattern. There were many exceptions and deviations from it, but the fact remains that dress did have some social significance. Thus, the fact that the inspectors wore coats and vests when they came to be interviewed might be taken as a reflection of their social status in the company.

The inspectors were considered outsiders, and this was indicated in many ways other than by the fact that they did not report to the Operating Branch supervisors. That they did not trade jobs or go for lunches was evidence of this relation between the operators and the inspectors, but perhaps the best demonstration of it was in the matter of control over the windows. The wiremen who were situated on the side of the room facing the court took a proprietary interest in the windows opposite their workbenches. If W_6, for example, wanted the window open, he opened it even though other people protested. The people who were farthest removed from the windows protested a great deal because the draft was thrown on their side of the room. Endless controversy resulted. The point to be brought out here is that an inspector entered into one of these controversies only on one occasion, and it was this one occasion which

demonstrated clearly the relation between operators and inspectors. The inspector involved was a man who was substituting for I_3. He complained that the room was cold. Someone had turned the heat off and one of the windows was open. Since his complaint went unheeded, he walked over to close the window. As he was about to release the chain which held it open, W_9 ordered him to leave it open and seized the chain. The inspector then tried to turn on the heat, but W_9 scuffled with him and finally took the handle off the valve. During all this the other men lent W_9 their verbal support. Finally, after the operators had convinced the inspector that he had no jurisdiction over the window and he had given up, one of the soldermen walked over and closed the window. The inspector thanked him, and the controversy ended. Wiremen and soldermen might fix the windows if they pleased, but the inspectors could not do so without getting into trouble. The other inspectors probably sensed the situation and never attempted to overstep.

SOCIAL STRATIFICATION IN THE OBSERVATION GROUP

The foregoing analysis of the relations among the occupational groups in the observation room shows that social significance did attach to the occupations the several groups performed. An ordering process had taken place in the organization of the human element in the department, and social significance had become attached to the various tasks. From an informal standpoint, then, the observation group was differentiated into five gradations, ranging from highest to lowest in the following order: inspectors, connector wiremen, selector wiremen, soldermen, and trucker.

The Informal Organization of the Observation Group

The first question the investigators asked of their data was answered in the affirmative: the workmen were socially differentiated along occupational lines. But did this mean that only the people within each occupational group tended to associate together? Did the workmen tend to form occupational cliques, or were they organized on some other basis? If occupation was not the basis of their integration, just how were they organized? The answer to this question, it was thought, could be obtained by observing how the members of the group were differentiated in terms of such informal social activities as games, controversies over the windows, job trading, and helping one another.

GAMES

From the beginning of the study the observer noted and recorded a variety of activities which may be subsumed under this heading. For the most part, these were games of chance which included the following: matching coins, lagging coins, shooting craps, card games, bets on combination of digits in the serial numbers on their weekly pay checks, pools on horse racing, baseball, and quality records, chipping in to purchase candy, and "binging." The men usually engaged in these games during brief respites from work or during lulls in activity resulting from interruptions in the flow of work. The games were extremely varied and were seemingly elaborated spontaneously with reference to anything into which the element of chance entered. Financial gain was not the main inducement, for most of the wagers were small, ranging from one to ten cents. However, those who participated in the betting on the horse races usually did so seriously. They dubbed their favorite the "Test Room Horse" and bet on him fairly consistently.

Figure 1 shows the people who joined in these games and the people with whom each person participated. The symbols indicating the different operators are enclosed in small circles. The operators are arranged roughly by soldering units, which are indicated by the spacing of the wiremen. Thus, W_1, W_2, W_3, and S_1 constitute soldering unit A; W_4, W_5, W_6, and S_2 constitute soldering unit B; and W_7, W_8, W_9, and S_4 constitute soldering unit C. The inspectors are placed above the groups for which they inspected. The arrows connecting the different circles indicate that the people thus connected participated in one or more games either as pairs or as members of a larger group.

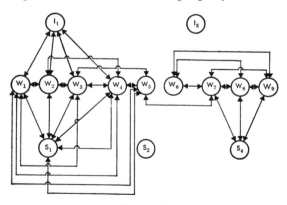

Figure 1

Participation in Games

BANK WIRING OBSERVATION ROOM

The significant point brought out in Figure 1 is that participation in games was confined to two groups and, furthermore, that each group participated to the exclusion of the other. One group, which for convenience will be referred to as group A, comprised W_1, W_2, W_3, W_4, W_5, S_1, and I_1. These people were in adjacent work positions and were all located toward the front of the room. The other group, referred to as group B, was composed of W_6, W_7, W_8, W_9, and S_4. These people were also in adjacent work positions and were located toward the rear of the room. Two people, S_2 and I_3, never took part in these activities. Although the frequency with which each person participated in games is not shown in this diagram, it should be stated that W_5 participated in only one game with the people in group A, whereas all the others in group A took part in a variety of games. It should also be noted that W_5 on one occasion took part with W_7. He was the only person in group A who participated with a member of group B.

Participation in games, then, was not at random. It was confined to two groups, which suggests that in this way the interpersonal relations among the people in the observation room were finding expression. This suggestion is strengthened by the fact that the kinds of games in which the two groups participated also tended to differentiate them. For example, all the gambling games occurred in group A, and all the "binging" occurred in group B. Both groups purchased candy from the Club store, but the purchases were made separately, and neither group shared with the other.

CONTROVERSIES ABOUT WINDOWS

It has already been mentioned that the wiremen who were stationed nearest the windows took a proprietary interest in them and that a great deal of controversy resulted over whether the windows should be open or closed. That this activity also expressed the interpersonal relations in the group is apparent from the following excerpt from the observer's record:

W_6 had his window open and W_5 closed it.
W_6: "You leave that window open. I want some fresh air in here."
W_5: "It's too cold. I want it closed."
W_6: "You take care of your own window. This one is mine and if I open it, it's going to stay open."

They opened and closed the window several times and had a heated argument over it. W_6 told W_5 that if he closed it again he would punch him in the nose.
S_1: (From the side lines) "That's right, W_6, stick up for your rights. If he closes it again, hang one on him. We've got to have a good fight in here before long."

W₅ left the window alone. This disappointed S₁, so he implied that W₅ was yellow.

S_1: "I'll tell you what you had better do if he closes that window again, W₆, sue him. He won't fight, so the only way you can do anything with him is to sue him."

The group had a lot of fun over this. W₅ and W₆ did not speak to each other during the rest of the morning.

This quarrel between W_5 and W_6 not only expressed their mutual antagonism but also gave S_1 an opportunity to express his antagonism toward W_5.

Figure 2 shows the men who joined in these controversies and those with whom they participated. This diagram is to be interpreted in the

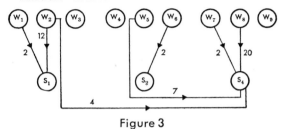

INITIATOR►─ACCEPTOR

Figure 3

Participation in Job Trading

BANK WIRING OBSERVATION ROOM

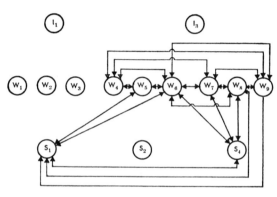

Figure 2

Participation in Controversies about Windows

BANK WIRING OBSERVATION ROOM

same way as that for games. A person was judged to be involved in these disputes even though he participated only verbally. The chief point brought out in this diagram is that most of the controversies over windows centered in group B (W₆, W₇, W₈, W₉, and S₄). The quarrels among the members of this group and between this group and other people in the observation room accounted for 90 per cent of the controversies. Their quarrels with people outside of their group were with S₁, W₄, and W₅. There was very little controversy over the windows among the members of group A, and what little there was occurred between W₄ and W₅ and between S₁ and W₅.

JOB TRADING

Job trading has already been mentioned in connection with the relation between wiremen and

soldermen. Accurate records of this activity were kept throughout the study and are summarized graphically in Figure 3.[1] The inspectors are omitted from this diagram because they did not participate. The arrows point from the person who initiated the request to trade to the person who accepted the request. The numbers alongside the arrows show the number of times the people so designated traded.

Perhaps the most interesting point brought out in this diagram is that most of the trading was requested of S₄, the solderman for the three selector wiremen. Thirty-three of the forty-nine times job trading occurred were with S₄. Furthermore, it will be noted that, whereas connector wiremen from soldering units A and B traded with S₄, none of the selector wiremen (W₇, W₈, and W₉) ever traded outside of their own soldering unit. In other words, the connector wiremen apparently felt free to change jobs either with their own soldermen or with the soldermen for the selector wiremen, but the latter did not feel free to trade outside of their own unit.

HELPING ONE ANOTHER

While there was no written rule to this effect, helping one another, like job trading, was in practice forbidden.[2] In spite of this rule, however, it

1. For the sake of simplicity, trading between wiremen and S₃, who was in the observation room only a short time, and trading between wiremen while one of them was soldering have been omitted from this figure. These omissions do not alter in any way the conclusions to be drawn from this figure.

2. The operators were permitted to help one another only when for observable technical reasons, such as a shortage of parts, they were prevented from working on their own equipments. The reason for this rule was that a wireman should be able to work faster when unmolested by another wireman's presence. In practice there were very few occasions when helping one another was technically justified and for this reason the greater part of this activity was against the rules.

was done a good deal when technically there was no justification for it. The wiremen said that it made them feel good to be helped. Their attitude is best expressed in the following excerpt from an interview with W_4. W_4 had just said that he liked working in the observation room because he felt more free to move around than in the regular department.

Int: "You do move around quite a bit, do you? Then you don't always work on your own equipment?"

W_4: "Oh no, not always, but most of the time. That is, once in a while if a fellow gets behind someone will go over and help him out."

Int: "Do they do that for anyone who is behind?"

W_4: "No. You know, it's a funny thing about that gang. It seems like if a fellow is loafing and gets behind, nobody will help him out, but if he is making an honest effort he will be helped. I've seen that happen time and again. Somebody who has been working along hard all day and has had a lot of tough luck will be helped out."

Int: "Do you find that certain people help certain other people all the time, or do they change around quite a bit?"

W_4: "Well, some people are friendlier than others, you know, and where that's the case you will find them helping each other out. Once in a while a fellow will get behind who ordinarily is a good worker. That sometimes happens to anyone. I know one fellow down there who did that and two other fellows went over and started helping him out. That was around a quarter to four. They had their job done and thought they would give him a hand. He didn't say anything, he let them go ahead and help him out, but you know he never helps anyone else out. Since then he has never given a hand to anybody. Do you think they would help him out again? No sir! They're off of him. They don't like a guy that does that. I think it's a good idea to help a fellow out once in a while. I know I appreciate it. It makes all the difference in the world. It's a funny thing, I'll be working along and be behind, and I'. feel all fagged out. Then somebody con.es over and starts in wiring on my equipment with me, and you know I perk up to beat the band. I don't know; it just seems to put new life in you, no matter if he only helps you for a couple of levels. I can pick up and work like the deuce then, up till quitting time."

Int: "I wonder why."

W_4: "I don't know why it is. You have a feeling when you're behind that you've got so much work behind it's going to be impossible to get it done, anyway. Then when somebody helps you out it gives you a fresh start, sort of."

HELPER→HELPED

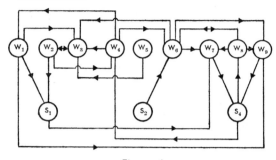

Figure 4

Participation in Helping

BANK WIRING OBSERVATION ROOM

Records were kept of this activity and are summarized graphically in Figure 4. The inspectors are again omitted because they did not participate. The arrows in the diagram point from helper to the person helped. The chief points brought out are, first, that everyone participated in helping and, secondly, that it was not confined within work groups. In these two respects this activity differed from the others thus far described. It seemed to integrate the whole group rather than parts of it.

The frequency with which different people helped one another is not shown in Figure 4 because only two people stood out from the group in this respect. They were W_3 and W_6. W_3 was helped out more than anyone else in the observation room, even though he did not need it. W_1, W_2, W_4, W_5, and W_6 helped him at one time or another. They liked to work with him. W_6, on the other hand, gave more help than anyone else in the room. His help was always accepted but it was rarely reciprocated. Two people, W_5 and S_2, gave help a few times, but on no occasion did they receive help.

FRIENDSHIPS AND ANTAGONISMS

To summarize the friendships and antagonisms which existed in this group, Figures 5 and 6 have been prepared. Figure 5 shows friendships; Figure 6 shows antagonisms. The three soldering units are arranged as in the previous diagrams.

Looking first at Figure 5, representing friendships, it will be seen that they tend to cluster in two groups. One group includes five people who were in the front of the room, W_1, W_3, W_4, S_1, and I_1. The other group comprises the members of soldering unit C, the four people in the rear of the room. Outside of these two groups the only strong friendship was that between S_1 and W_7. Five people, W_2,

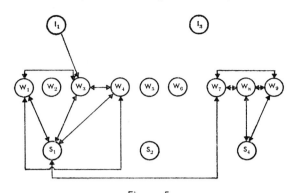

Figure 5

Friendships

BANK WIRING OBSERVATION ROOM

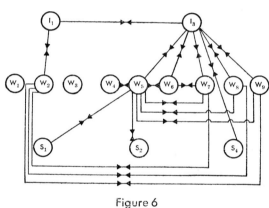

Figure 6

Antagonisms

BANK WIRING OBSERVATION ROOM

W_5, W_6, S_2, and I_3, were not bound by any strong friendships.

Looking next at the diagram representing antagonisms, Figure 6, it will be seen that they originated chiefly from the wiremen in soldering unit C and were directed by these people as a group toward W_2, W_5, and I_3, three of the people who were not bound by any strong friendships. Antagonisms arising outside of soldering unit C were directed chiefly toward W_5 and I_3, the two people who aroused more antagonism than anyone else in the group. It is also apparent that there were no antagonisms between the people in the front of the room who were bound together by friendships and people with whom they were not especially friendly. I_1 was antagonistic toward I_3 and W_2, S_1 toward W_5, and W_4 toward W_5, but there were no

antagonisms directed from W_1, W_3, W_4, S_1, and I_1 as a group toward anyone. In this respect the wiremen in soldering unit C were unique: they possessed an internal solidarity, a certain cohesion among themselves, and strong external antagonism or opposition to certain persons outside of their group.

The Two Cliques

On the basis of the material just reviewed some conclusion can now be drawn as to the informal organization of this group of workmen. In the first place, it is quite apparent that the question raised at the beginning of the preceding section must be answered in the negative: these people were not integrated on the basis of occupation; they did not form occupational cliques. In the second place, it is equally apparent that there did exist certain configurations of relations in this group. With one exception, every record examined seemed to be telling something about these configurations. Whether the investigators looked at games, job trading, quarrels over the windows, or friendships and antagonisms, two groups seemed to stand out. One of these groups was located toward the front of the room, the other toward the back. "The group in front" and "the group in back" were common terms of designation among the workmen themselves. The first of these groups will be referred to as clique A, the second, the group toward the rear of the room, as clique B.

What was the membership of these two cliques? This question can be answered only approximately. Clique A included W_1, W_3, W_4, S_1, and I_1, and clique B included W_7, W_8, W_9, and S_4. W_5, S_2, and I_3 were outside either clique. With W_2 and W_6, however, the situation was not so clear. W_2 participated in the games of clique A, but beyond this the similarity of his behavior to theirs ceased. He entered very little into their conversations and tended to isolate himself from them. Much of his behavior suggested that he did not feel his position in the group to be secure. He was the only wireman in soldering unit A who traded jobs with S_4, the solderman in clique B, and he traded jobs with his own solderman more than anyone else did. In so far as the social function of job trading was to differentiate wiremen from soldermen, this could be interpreted as meaning that W_2 felt rather keenly the necessity of constantly emphasizing his position by subordinating the soldermen. Taking all the evidence into consideration, then, it may be concluded that W_2 was not a bona fide member of clique A. W_6 tended to participate in clique B. He was continually "horsing around" with the selector wiremen and had relatively little to do with the members of clique A.

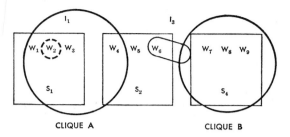

Figure 7

The Internal Organization of the Group

BANK WIRING OBSERVATION ROOM

That he was not entirely accepted in clique B was shown in many ways, chief of which was the way in which clique B co-operated in resisting his attempts to dominate anyone in their group. Yet he participated in clique B much more than W_2 did in clique A. It may be concluded that although W_6 tended to participate in clique B, he was still in many ways an outsider.

As a means of summarizing the results of this inquiry, Figure 7 has been prepared to represent diagrammatically the internal organization of the observation group. The soldering units into which the members of the group were divided are shown by the three rectangles. The two large circles demarcate the two cliques, A and B. There were three individuals, I_3, W_5, and S_2, who were clearly outside either clique.[3] The line around W_6 has been made to intersect that of clique B to indicate his partial participation in it. The instability of W_2's position is indicated by the broken circle around his number.

That the members of clique A regarded themselves as superior to clique B was indicated in many ways. Clique A did or refrained from doing certain things which were done by clique B. They did not trade jobs nearly so much, and on the whole they did not enter into the controversies about the windows. Clique A engaged in games of chance, whereas clique B engaged more often in "binging." Both groups purchased candy from the Club store, but purchases were made separately and neither clique shared with the other. Clique A bought chocolate candy in small quantities, whereas clique B bought a less expensive kind in such large quantities that W_9 one time became ill from eating too much. Clique A argued more and indulged in less noise and horseplay than clique B. The members of clique A felt that their conversations were on a higher plane than those which went on in clique B; as W_4 said, "We talk about things of some importance."

3. Perhaps a word of caution is necessary here. When it is said that this group was divided into two cliques and that certain people were outside either clique, it does not mean that there was no solidarity between the two cliques or between the cliques and the outsiders. There is always the danger, in examining small groups intensively, of over-emphasizing differentiating factors. Internal solidarity thus appears to be lacking. That this group, as a whole, did have very strong sentiments in common has already been shown in discussing their attitudes toward output and will be brought out more clearly in the next chapters. It should also be said that position in the group is not so static as one might assume from this diagram. Had the study continued longer, membership in the cliques might have shifted. Also, if the group had been larger, or if the group had been allowed to remain in the regular department, it is quite probable that the people who appear to be outsiders here would have formed cliques with others who had similar sentiments.

5. The Solidarity of Occupational Groups

by EMILE DURKHEIM

IF ALL CORPORATIVE ORGANIZA-tion is not necessarily an historical anachronism, is there any reason for believing that it may play, in contemporary societies, the great role we have

Reprinted from Emile Durkheim, *The Division of Labor in Society*, trans. George Simpson (Glencoe, Ill.: The Free Press, 1947), pp. 10–18, 22–31, with the permission of The Free Press.

attributed to it? For, if it be indispensable, it is not because of the economic services it can render, but because of the moral influence it can have. What we especially see in the occupational group is a moral power capable of containing individual egos, of maintaining a spirited sentiment of common solidarity in the consciousness of all the workers, of preventing the law of the strongest from being brutally applied to industrial and commercial relations. It is now thought to be unsuitable for such a role. Because it had its origin in short-lived interests, it appears that it can be used only for utilitarian ends, and the mementos left by corporations of the old regime seem only to confirm this impression. They are gratuitously represented in the future as they were during the last days of their existence, particularly busy in maintaining or increasing their privileges and their monopolies; and it cannot be seen how interests so narrowly occupational can have a favorable effect on the ethics of the body or its members.

But what has been true of certain corporations for a very short space of their development cannot be applied to all the corporative regime. Far from having acquired a sort of moral infirmity from its constitution, it has especially played a moral role during the major part of its history. This is particularly evident in the Roman corporations. "The corporations of workers," says Waltzing, "were, with the Romans, far from having an occupational character as pronounced as in the Middle Ages; we find there neither regulation of methods, nor imposed apprenticeship, nor monopoly; nor was their end to unite the necessary elements to exploit an industry."[1] To be sure, the association gave them more force in time of need for safeguarding their common interests. But that was only one of the useful consequences produced by the institution; that was not its *raison d'être*, its principal function. Above all, the corporation was a religious organization. Each one had its particular god whose cult was celebrated in a special temple when the means were available. In the same way as each family had its *Lar familiaris;* each city its *Genius publicus*, each organization had its protecting god, *Genius collegii.* Naturally, this occupational cult did not dispense with celebrations, with sacrifices and banquets in common. All sorts of circumstances were used as reasons for these joyful gatherings. Moreover, distribution of food-stuffs and money often took place at the community's expense. There have been questions as to whether the corporation had a sick-fund; if it regularly helped those members who were in need. Opinions on this point are divergent.[2] But what lends interest and import to this discussion is that these common banquets, more or less periodic, and the distribution accompanying them, often took the place of help, and formed a bureau of indirect assistance. Thus, the unfortunate knew they could count on this disguised aid. As corollary to this

religious character, the organization of workmen was, at the same time, a burial society. United in a cult during their lives, like the *Gentiles,* the members of these corporations also wished to rest together after death. All the fairly rich corporations had a collective *columbarium* where, when the organization had not the funds to buy a burial plot, there was at least the certainty that its members would have honorable burial at the expense of the common fund.

A common cult, common banquets, a common cemetery, all united together—are these not all the distinctive characteristics of the domestic organization at the time of the Romans? Thus, it has been said that the Roman corporation was a "great family." "No word," says Waltzing, "better indicates the nature of the relations uniting the brotherhood, and a great many indications prove a great fraternity reigned in their midst."[3] The community of interests took the place of the community of blood. "The members looked upon themselves as brothers, even to the extent of calling themselves by that name." The most ordinary expression, as a matter of fact, was that of *sodales*, but even that word expresses a spiritual relationship implying a narrow fraternity. The protectors of the organization often took the names of father and mother. "A proof of the devotion the brothers had for their organization lies in the bequests and donations they made. There are also funereal monuments upon which are found: *Pius in collegio,* he was faithful towards his organization, as if one said, *Pius in suos.*"[4] This familial life was so developed that Boissier makes it the principal aim of all the Roman corporations. "Even in the workers' corporations," he says, "there was association principally for the pleasure of living together, for finding outside oneself distractions from fatigue and boredom, to create an intimacy less restrained than the family, and less extensive than the city, and thus to make life easier and more agreeable."[5]

As Christian societies belong to a social type very different from the city-state, the corporations of the Middle Ages do not exactly resemble the Roman corporations. But they also constitute a moral environment for their members. "The corporation," says Levasseur, "united people of the same occupation by strong bonds. Rather often they were established in the parish house, or in a particular chapel and put themselves under the invocation of a saint who became the patron saint of all the community. . . . There they gathered, attended with great ceremony the solemn masses; after which the

1. *Etude historique sur les corporations professionelles chez les Romains,* I, p. 194.
2. The majority of historians believe that certain organizations, at least, were mutual-aid societies.

3. *Op. cit.,* I, p. 330.
4. *Op. cit.,* I, p. 331.
5. *La Religion romaine,* II, pp. 287–288.

members of the brotherhood went, all together, to end their day in joyous feasting. In this way the corporations of the Middle Ages closely resembled those of Roman times."[6] The corporation, moreover, often used part of its budgetary funds for charity.

Moreover, precise rules fixed the respective duties of employers and workmen, as well as the duties of employers toward each other, for each occupation. There are, to be sure, regulations not in accord with our present ideas, but judgment must be made according to the ethics of the time, since that is what the rules express. What is indisputable is that they are all inspired by zeal, not for individuals, but for corporative interest, whether poorly or well understood. Now the subordination of private utility to common utility, whatever it may be, always has a moral character, for it necessarily implies sacrifice and abnegation. In addition, a great many of these rules proceeded from moral sentiments still ours today.[7] The valet was protected from the caprices of his master who could not dismiss him at will. It is true that the obligation was reciprocal; but besides this reciprocity being just in itself, it is still more justified by reason of the important privileges the worker enjoyed then. Thus, masters were forbidden to negate his *right to work,* which allowed him to seek assistance from his neighbors, or even their wives. In short, as Levasseur says, "these regulations concerning the apprentices and workmen are worthy of consideration by historian and economist. They are the work of a barbarous century. They carry the mark of worth-while minds and good, common sense, worthy of observation."[8] Finally, a system of rules was designed to guarantee occupational honesty. All sorts of precautions were taken to prevent the merchant or workman from deceiving the buyer, to compel him "to perform good, loyal work."[9] To be sure, a time came when the rules became uselessly complicated, when the masters were a great deal busier safeguarding their privileges than caring about the good name of the occupation and the honesty of their members. But there is no institution which, at some given moment, does not degenerate, either because it does not know how to change and mobilize anew, or because it develops unilaterally, overdoing some of its activities. This makes it unsuited to furnish the services with which it is charged. That is reason to seek its re-

formation, not to declare it forever useless, nor to destroy it.

Whatever it may be from this standpoint, the preceding facts sufficiently prove that the occupational group is not incapable of exerting moral action. . . . The considerable place that religion took in life, in Rome as well as in the Middle Ages, makes particularly evident the true nature of its functions, for all religious community then constituted a moral milieu, in the same way as all moral discipline tended forcibly to take a religious form. And besides, this character of corporative organization comes from very general causes that can be seen acting in other circumstances. When a certain number of individuals in the midst of a political society are found to have ideas, interests, sentiments, and occupations not shared by the rest of the population, it is inevitable that they will be attracted toward each other under the influence of these likenesses. They will seek each other out, enter into relations, associate, and thus, little by little, a restricted group, having its special characteristics, will be formed in the midst of the general society. But once the group is formed, a moral life appears naturally carrying the mark of the particular conditions in which it has developed. For it is impossible for men to live together, associating in industry, without acquiring a sentiment of the whole formed by their union, without attaching themselves to that whole, preoccupying themselves with its interests, and taking account of it in their conduct. This attachment has in it something surpassing the individual. This subordination of particular interests to the general interest is, indeed, the source of all moral activity. As this sentiment grows more precise and determined, applying itself to the most ordinary and the most important circumstances of life, it is translated into definitive formulae, and thus a body of moral rules is in process of establishment.

At the same time that this result is produced of itself and by the force of circumstances, it is useful and the feeling of its utility lends confirmation to it. Society is not alone in its interest in the formation of special groups to regulate their own activity, developing within them what otherwise would become anarchic; but the individual, on his part, finds joy in it, for anarchy is painful to him. He also suffers from pain and disorder produced whenever interindividual relations are not submitted to some regulatory influence. It is not good for man to live with the threat of war in the midst of his immediate companions. This sensation of general hostility, the mutual defiance resulting from it, the tension it necessitates, are difficult states when they are chronic. If we love war, we also love the joys of

6. *Les classes ouvrières en France jusqu'a la Révolution,* I, pp. 217–218.
7. *Op. cit.,* I, p. 221.—See, on the same moral character of the corporation in Germany, Gierke, *Das Deutsche Genossenschaftswesen,* I, p. 384; for England, Ashley, *An Introduction to English Economic History and Theory.*
8. *Op. cit.,* p. 238.
9. *Op. cit.,* pp. 240–261.

peace, and the latter are of more worth as men are more profoundly socialized, which is to say (for the two words are synonymous) more profoundly civilized. Common life is attractive as well as coercive. Doubtless, constraint is necessary to lead man to surpass himself, to add to his physical nature another; but as he learns the charm of this new life, he contracts the need for it, and there is no order of activity in which he does not seek it passionately. That is why when individuals who are found to have common interests associate, it is not only to defend these interests, it is to associate, that is, not to feel lost among adversaries, to have the pleasure of communing, to make one out of many, which is to say, finally, to lead the same moral life together.

Domestic morality is not otherwise formed. Because of the prestige the family has in our eyes, it seems to us that if it has been, and if it is always, a school of devotion, of abnegation, the place *par excellence* of morality, it is because of quite particular, intrinsic characteristics found nowhere else. It is believed that consanguinity is an exceptionally powerful cause of moral relationship. But we have often had the occasion for showing[10] that consanguinity has not the extraordinary efficacy attributed to it. The proof is that in many societies the non-blood relations are found in numbers in the centre of the family; the so-called relationship is then contracted with great facility, and it has all the effects of a blood-tie. Inversely, it often happens that very near blood relations are, morally or juridically, strangers to each other; for example, the case of cognates in the Roman family. The family does not then owe its virtues to the unity of descent; it is quite simply a group of individuals who find themselves related to one another in the midst of political society by a particularly strong community of ideas, of sentiments and interests. Consanguinity facilitates this concentration, for it causes mutual adaptation of consciences. But a great many other factors come into play: material neighborhood, solidarity of interests, the need of uniting against a common danger, or simply to unite, are other powerful causes of relationship.

Now, they are not special to the family, but they are found, although in different forms, in the corporation. If, then, the first of these groups has played so considerable a role in the moral history of humanity, why should the second be incapable of doing the same? To be sure, there is always this difference between them, that members of a family live their lives together, while members of a corporation live only their occupational lives together. The family is a sort of complete society whose action controls our economic activity as well as our

religious, political, scientific activities. Anything significant we do, even outside the house, acts upon it, and provokes appropriate reactions. The sphere of influence of a corporation is, in a sense, more restricted. Still, we must not lose sight of the increasingly important position the occupation takes in life as work becomes more specialized, for the field of each individual activity tends steadily to become delimited by the functions with which the individual is particularly charged. Moreover, if familial action extends everywhere, it can only be general; detail escapes it. Finally, the family, in losing the unity and indivisibility of former times, has lost with one stroke a great part of its efficacy. As it is today broken up with each generation, man passes a notable part of his existence far from all domestic influence. The corporation has none of these disturbances; it is as continuous as life. The inferiority that it presents, in comparison with the family, has its compensation.

If we find it necessary thus to bring together the family and the corporation, it is not simply to establish an instructive parallel between them, but because the two institutions are closely connected. This is observable in the history of Roman corporations. We have seen, indeed, that they were formed on the model of domestic society, of which they were at first only a new and enlarged form. But, the occupational group would not, at this point, recall the familial group, if there were not some bond of relation between them. And, indeed, the corporation has been, in a sense, the heir of the family. As long as industry is exclusively agricultural, it has, in the family and in the village, which is itself only a sort of great family, its immediate organ, and it needs no other. As exchange is not, or is very little, developed, the farmer's life does not extend outside the familial circle. Economic activity, having no consequences outside the family, is sufficiently regulated by the family, and the family itself thus serves as occupational group. But the case is no longer the same once trades exist. For to live by trade, customers are necessary, and going outside the house to find them is necessary, as is having relations with competitors, fighting against them, coming to an understanding with them. In addition, trades demand cities, and cities have always been formed and recruited principally from the ranks of immigrants, individuals who have left their native homes. A new form of activity was thus constituted which burst from the old familial form. In order not to remain in an unorganized state, it was necessary to create a new form, which would be fitting to it; or otherwise said, it was necessary for a secondary group of a new kind to be formed. This is the origin of the corporation; it was substituted for

---

10. See especially *Année sociologique*, I, pp. 313 ff.

the family in the exercise of a function which had been domestic, but which could no longer keep this character. Such an origin does not allow us to attribute to it that sort of constitutional amorality which is generally gratuitously bestowed upon it. Just as the family has elaborated domestic ethics and law, the corporation is now the source of occupational ethics and law.

*   *   *

But there is more knowledge to be gathered from the summary we have just made.

First of all, it shows us how the corporation has fallen into discredit for about two centuries, and, consequently, what it must become in order to take its place again among our public institutions. We have just seen, indeed, that in the form it had in the Middle Ages it was narrowly bound to the organization of the commune. This solidarity was without inconvenience as long as the trades themselves had a communal character. While, as originally, merchants and workers had only the inhabitants of the city or its immediate environs for customers, which means as long as the market was principally local, the bodies of trades, with their municipal organization, answered all needs. But it was no longer the same once great industry was born. As it had nothing especially urban about it, it could not adapt itself to a system which had not been made for it. First, it does not necessarily have its centre in a city; it can even be established outside all pre-existing rural or urban agglomerations. It looks for that territory where it can best maintain itself and thrive. Thus, its field of action is limited to no determined region; its clientele is recruited everywhere. An institution so entirely wrapped up in the commune as was the old corporation could not then be used to encompass and regulate a form of collective activity which was so completely foreign to the communal life.

And, indeed, as soon as great industry appeared, it was found to be outside the corporative regime, and that was what caused the bodies of trades to do all in their power to prevent industry's progress. Nevertheless, it was certainly not freed of all regulation; in the beginning the State played a role analogous to that which the corporations played for small-scale commerce and urban trades. At the same time as the royal power accorded the manufacturers certain privileges, in return it submitted them to its control. That is indicated in the title of royal manufacturers. But as it is well known how unsuited the State is for this function, this direct control could not fail to become oppressive. It was almost impossible from the time great industry reached a certain degree of development and diversity; that is why classical economists demanded

its suppression, and with good cause. But if the corporation, as it then existed, could not be adapted to this new form of industry, and if the State could not replace the old corporative discipline, it does not follow that all discipline would be useless thenceforward. It simply meant that the old corporation had to be transformed to continue to fill its role in the new conditions of economic life. Unfortunately, it had not enough suppleness to be reformed in time; that is why it was discarded. Because it did not know how to assimilate itself to the new life which was evolving, it was divorced from that life, and, in this way, it became what it was upon the eve of the Revolution, a sort of dead substance, a strange body which could maintain itself in the social organism only through inertia. It is then not surprising that a moment came when it was violently expelled. But to destroy it was not a means of giving satisfaction to the needs it had not satisfied. And that is the reason the question still remains with us, and has become still more acute after a century of groping and fruitless experience.

The work of the sociologist is not that of the statesman. We do not have to present in detail what this reform should be. It will be sufficient to indicate the general principles as they appear from the preceding facts.

What the experience of the past proves, above all, is that the framework of the occupational group must always have relations with the framework of economic life. It is because of this lack of relationship that the corporative regime disappeared. Since the market, formerly municipal, has become national and international, the corporations must assume the same extension. Instead of being limited only to the workers of a city, it must enlarge in such a way as to include all the members of the occupation scattered over the territory,[11] for in whatever region they are found, whether they live in the city or the country, they are all solidary, and participate in a common life. Since this common life is, in certain respects, independent of all territorial determinations, the appropriate organ must be created that expresses and regularizes its function. Because of these dimensions, such an organ would necessarily be in direct contact with the central organ of the collective life, for the rather important events which interest a whole category of industrial enterprises

---

11. We do not have to speak of international organization which, in consequence of the international character of the market, would necessarily develop above this national organization, for the latter alone can actually constitute a juridical institution. The first, under present European law, can result only in freely concluded arrangements between national corporations.

in a country necessarily have very general repercussions of which the State cannot fail to take cognizance; hence it intervenes. Thus, it is not without reason that royal power tended instinctively not to allow great industry outside its control when it did appear. It was impossible for it not to be interested in a form of activity which, by its very nature, can always affect all society. But this regulatory action, if it is necessary, must not degenerate into narrow subordination, as happened in the seventeenth and eighteenth centuries. The two related organs must remain distinct and autonomous; each of them has its function, which it alone can take care of. If the functioning of making general principles of industrial legislation belongs to the governmental assemblies, they are incapable of diversifying them according to the different industries. It is this diversification which constitutes the proper task of the corporation[12] This unitarian organization for a whole country in no way excludes the formation of secondary organs, comprising workers of the same region, or of the same locality, whose role would be to specialize still more the occupational regulation according to the local or regional necessities. Economic life would thus be regulated and determined without losing any of its diversity.

For that very reason, the corporative regime would be protected against that tendency towards immobility that it has often been charged with in the past, for it is a fault which is rooted in the narrowly communal character of the corporation. As long as it was limited to the city, it was inevitable for it to become a prisoner of tradition as the city itself. As, in a group so restricted, the conditions of life are almost invariable, habit exercises a terrific effect upon people, and even innovations are dreaded. The traditionalism of the corporations was thus only an aspect of the communal traditionalism, and had the same qualities. Then, once it was ingrained in the mores, it survived the causes which had produced and originally justified it. That is why,

when the material and moral concentration of the country, and great industry which is its consequence, had opened minds to new desires, awakened new needs, introduced into the tastes and fashions a mobility heretofore unknown, the corporation, which was obstinately attached to its old customs, was unable to satisfy these new exigencies. But national corporations, by virtue of their dimension and complexity, would not be exposed to this danger. Too many diverse minds would be in action for stationary uniformity to be established. In a group formed of numerous and varied elements, new combinations are always being produced. There would then be nothing rigid about such an organization, and it would consequently find itself in harmony with the mobile equilibrium of needs and ideas.

Besides, it must not be thought that the entire function of the corporation is to make rules and apply them. To be sure, where a group is formed, a moral discipline is formed too. But the institution of this discipline is only one of the many ways through which collective activity is manifested. A group is not only a moral authority which dominates the life of its members; it is also a source of life *sui generis*. From it comes a warmth which animates its members, making them intensely human, destroying their egotisms. Thus, in the past, the family was the legislator of law and ethics whose severity went to extremes of violence, at the same time that it was the place where one first learned to enjoy the effusions of sentiment. We have also seen how the corporation, in Rome and in the Middle Ages, awakened these same needs and sought to satisfy them. The corporations of the future will have a complexity of attributes still greater, by reason of their increased growth. Around their proper occupational functions others which come from the communes or private societies will be grouping themselves. The functions of assistance are such that, to be well filled, they demand feelings of solidarity between assistants and assisted, a certain intellectual and moral homogeneity such as the same occupation produces. A great many educational institutions (technical schools, adult education, etc.) equally seem to have to find their natural environment in the corporation. It is the same for aesthetic life, for it appears in the nature of things that this noble form of sport and recreation develops side by side with the serious life which it serves to balance and relieve. In fact, there are even now syndicates which are at the same time societies of mutual aid; others found common houses where there are organized courses, concerts, and dramatic presentations. The corporative activity can thus assume the most varied forms.

---

12. This specialization could be made only with the aid of selected assemblies charged to represent the corporation. In the present state of industry, these assemblies, in the same way as tribunals charged with applying the occupational regulations, should evidently be comprised of representatives of employees and representatives of employers, as is already the case in the tribunals of skilled trades; and that, in proportions corresponding to the respective importance attributed by opinion to these two factors in production. But if it is necessary that both meet in the directing councils of the corporations, it is no less important that at the base of the corporative organization they form distinct and independent groups, for their interests are too often rival and antagonistic. To be able to go about their ways freely, they must go about their ways separately. The two groups thus constituted would then be able to appoint their representatives to the common assemblies.

There is even reason to suppose that the corporation will become the foundation or one of the essential bases of our political organization. We have seen, indeed, that if it first begins by being outside the social system, it tends to fix itself in it in proportion to the development of economic life. It is, therefore, just to say that if progress continues to be made in this direction, it will have to take a more prominent and more predominant place in society. It was formerly the elementary division of communal organization. Now that the commune, heretofore an autonomous organism, has lost its place in the State, as the municipal market did in the national market, is it not fair to suppose that the corporation also will have to experience a corresponding transformation, becoming the elementary division of the State, the fundamental political unity? Society, instead of remaining what it is today, an aggregate of juxtaposed territorial districts, would become a vast system of national corporations. From various quarters it is asked that elective assemblies be formed by occupations, and not by territorial divisions; and certainly, in this way, political assemblies would more exactly express the diversity of social interests and their relations. They would be a more faithful picture of social life in its entirety. But to say that the nation, in becoming aware of itself, must be grouped into occupations, —does not this mean that the organized occupation or corporation should be the essential organ of public life?

Thus the great gap in the structure of European societies we elsewhere point to would be filled. It will be seen, indeed, how, as advances are made in history, the organization which has territorial groups as its base (village or city, district, province, etc.) steadily becomes effaced. To be sure, each of us belongs to a commune, or a department, but the bonds attaching us there became daily more fragile and more slack. These geographical divisions are, for the most part, artificial and no longer awaken in us profound sentiments. The provincial spirit has disappeared never to return; the patriotism of the parish has become an archaism that cannot be restored at will. The municipal or departmental affairs affect and agitate us in proportion to their coincidence with our occupational affairs. Our activity is extended quite beyond these groups which are too narrow for it, and, moreover, a good deal of what happens there leaves us indifferent. There is thus produced a spontaneous weakening of the old social structure. Now, it is impossible for this organization to disappear without something replacing it. A society composed of an infinite number of unorganized individuals, that

a hypertrophied State is forced to oppress and contain, constitutes a veritable sociological monstrosity. For collective activity is always too complex to be able to be expressed through the single and unique organ of the State. Moreover, the State is too remote from individuals; its relations with them too external and intermittent to penetrate deeply into individual consciences and socialize them within. Where the State is the only environment in which men can live communal lives, they inevitably lose contact, become detached, and thus society disintegrates. A nation can be maintained only if, between the State and the individual, there is intercalated a whole series of secondary groups near enough to the individuals to attract them strongly in their sphere of action and drag them, in this way, into the general torrent of social life. We have just shown how occupational groups are suited to fill this role, and that is their destiny. One thus conceives how important it is, especially in the economic order, for them to emerge from that state of inconsistency and disorganization in which they have remained for a century, since these occupations today absorb the major part of our collective forces.[13]

Perhaps now we shall be better able to explain the conclusions we reached at the end of our book, *Suicide*.[14] We were already proposing there a strong corporative organization as a means of remedying the misfortune which the increase in suicides, together with many other symptoms, evinces. Certain critics have found that the remedy was not proportionate to the extent of the evil, but that is because they have undervalued the true nature of the corporation, and the place to which it is destined in social life, as well as the grave anomaly resulting from its disappearance. They have seen only an utilitarian association whose effect would at best bring order to economic interests, whereas it must really be the essential element of our social

13. We do not mean that the territorial divisions are destined to disappear entirely, but only that they will become of less importance. The old institutions never vanish before the new without leaving any traces of themselves. They persist, not only through sheer force of survival, but because there still persists something of the needs they once answered. The material neighborhood will always constitute a bond between men; consequently, political and social organization with a territorial base will certainly exist. Only, they will not have their present predominance, precisely because this bond has lost its force. Moreover, we have shown above, that even at the base of the corporation, there will always be found geographical divisions. Furthermore, between the diverse corporations of the same locality or region there will necessarily be special relations of solidarity which will, at all times, demand appropriate organization.
14. *Suicide*, trans. John A. Spaulding and George Simpson; ed. George Simpson (Glencoe, Ill.: The Free Press, 1951).

structure. The absence of all corporative institution creates, then, in the organization of a people like ours, a void whose importance it is difficult to exaggerate. It is a whole system of organs necessary in the normal functioning of the common life which is wanting. Such a constitutive lack is evidently not a local evil, limited to a region of society; it is a malady *totius substantiae,* affecting all the organism. Consequently, the attempt to put an end to it cannot fail to produce the most far reaching consequences. It is the general health of the social body which is here at stake.

That does not mean, however, that the corporation is a sort of panacea for everything. The crisis through which we are passing is not rooted in a single and unique cause. To put an end to it, it is not sufficient to regulate it where necessary. Justice must prevail. Now, as we shall say further on, "as long as there are rich and poor at birth, there cannot be just contract," nor a just distribution of social goods. But if the corporative reform does not dispense with the others, it is the first condition for their efficacy. Let us imagine that the primordial condition of ideal justice may be realized; let us suppose that men enter life in a state of perfect economic equality, which is to say, that riches have entirely ceased being hereditary. The problems in the environment with which we were struggling would not be solved by that. Indeed, there will always be an economic apparatus, and various agents collaborating in its functioning. It will then be necessary to determine their rights and duties, and that, for each form of industry. It will be necessary that in each occupation a body of laws be made fixing the quantity of work, the just remuneration of the different officials, their duties toward each other, and toward the community, etc. Life will be just as complex as ever. Because riches will not be transmitted any longer as they are today will not mean that the state of anarchy has disappeared, for it is not a question as to the ownership of riches, but as to the regulation of the activity to which these riches give rise. It will not regulate itself by magic, as soon as it is useful, if the necessary forces for the institution of this regulation have not been aroused and organized.

Moreover, new difficulties will arise which will remain insoluble without a corporative organization. Up to now, it was the family which, either through collective property or descendence, assured the continuity of economic life, by the possession and exploitation of goods held intact, or, from the time the old familial communism fell away, the nearest relatives received the goods of the deceased.[15] In the case of collective property, neither death nor a new generation changed the relations of things to persons; in the case of descent, the change was made automatically, and the goods, at no time, remained unowned and unused. But if domestic society cannot play this role any longer, there must be another social organ to replace its exercise of this necessary function. For there is only one way of preventing the periodic suspension of any activity: a group, perpetual as the family, must possess goods and exploit them itself, or, at the death of the owner, receive them and send them to some other individual holder to improve them. But as we have shown, the State is poorly equipped to supervise these very specialized economic tasks. There is, then, only the occupational group which can capably look after them. It answers, indeed, two necessary conditions; it is so closely connected with the economic life that it feels its needs, at the same time having a perpetuity at least equal to the family. But to fill this role, it must exist and be mature enough to take care of the new and complex role which devolves upon it.

If the problem of the corporation is not the only one demanding public attention, there is certainly none more urgent, for the others can be considered only when this has been solved. No modification, no matter how small, can be introduced into the juridical order, if one does not begin by creating the necessary organ for the institution of the new law. That is why it is vain to delay by seeking precisely what this law must be, for in the present state of knowledge, our approximation will be clumsy and always open to doubt. How much more important it is to put ourselves at once to work establishing the moral forces which alone can determine its realization!

15. It is true that where a will is permitted the proprietor can determine the transmission of his property. But a will only gives the right to act contrary to the law of succession. This law is the norm according to which the transfers are made. These cases are very generally limited and are always exceptional.

IV–TERRITORIAL COMMUNITY

1. On the Origins of the State

BY ROBERT H. LOWIE

IN 1861, Sir Henry Sumner Maine, the father of comparative jurisprudence, sharply separated two principles of uniting individuals for governmental purposes,—the blood tie and the territorial tie. He further combined this conceptual distinction with an historical theory, to wit, that in less advanced or earlier societies "kinship in blood is the sole possible ground of community in political functions." No revolution, he argued, could be "so startling and so complete as the change which is accomplished when some other principle—such as that, for instance, of local contiguity—establishes itself for the first time as the basis of common political action." And, again, he writes: ". . . the idea that a number of persons should exercise political rights in common simply because they happened to live within the same topographical limits was utterly strange and monstrous to primitive antiquity." Where members of alien lineage were taken into the fold it was at least on the basis of a legal fiction that they were "descended from the same stock as the people on whom they were engrafted."[1]

When Lewis H. Morgan developed his own scheme of "Ancient Society" (1877), he not only adopted Maine's basic distinction but also gave greater definiteness to the views of his predecessor, especially in point of chronology. All forms of government, he argued, belonged to one of two categories,—they were either founded on persons and personal relations or on territory and property. Ranged on one side were such units as the gens (clan, sib) and phratry; on the other, the series comprising the ward, township, county, province, and national domain. Political, that is, territorial organization was declared to have been unknown prior to classical antiquity. It was in 594 B.C. that Solon took the initial step of breaking up the patrilineal gentes (clans, sibs) of the Athenians by a property classification, and in 507 B.C. Cleisthenes completed the advance by substituting for the traditional gentile organization purely local lines of division, by cutting up the old noble lineages and assigning the fragments to different local groups. Henceforth every citizen was registered, taxed, and given a vote as a member not of a clan but of a township, that is, of a territorial unit.

This classical distinction between "social" or "tribal," and "political" or "territorial," organization is significant and unexceptionable. That is to say, there is a fundamental difference between the two principles discriminated, and of both the history of human society provides abundant examples. It is not the logical but the historical aspect of the theory that evokes doubt. Why should the peoples of the world, after contentedly living for millennia under a government based on the blood tie, engage in that startling revolution described by Maine, of substituting the totally novel alignment of persons by locality? Neither author provides an adequate solution. Must we here break with the notion of continuous evolution? That certainly grates on the sensibilities of latter-day historical-mindedness. In the presence of overwhelming positive evidence we should be willing to cast Continuity on the rubbish heap of exploded fictions, but without such rigorous demonstration we shall do well to cling to it and seek an alternative interpretation. Nor is it difficult to outline the avenue of approach. If 507 or 594 B.C. does *not* mark an abrupt departure from past tradition, then older and simpler communities must have displayed the local bond along with the consanguineal tie. The two principles, in other words, however antithetical, are not of necessity mutually exclusive. It is then possible to satisfy the postulate of Continuity. We are no longer face to face with the miracle of a spontaneous generation but with the scientific problem of how an originally weak but

1. *Ancient Law*, Chapter V, 124–126.

perceptible territorial sentiment, at first subordinate to the blood tie, was intensified to the point of assuming the dominant role.

Whether this interpretation is warranted, is of course a question to be determined by empirical facts.

In fairness we must, first of all, concede that these yield considerable justification for the position maintained by Maine and Morgan. Again and again, in going over the descriptive literature of social anthropology, the reader must be struck by the prominence of personal relationship in governmental affairs, such as the administration of justice. What, for instance, is the significance of the blood feud, which outside of Africa is such a common mode of adjusting misunderstandings? From the present angle it is simply a negation of the state: it implies the doctrine that persons living in the same village or country are not by such juxtaposition jointly subordinate to some transcendent local authority but have claims upon and obligations to their kin only, each lineage standing towards any other in the same relationship as, say, the United States to France or England,—perhaps actually at amity, yet at any time potentially shifting into a state of avowed hostility.

The condition thus abstractly defined is best illustrated by a series of examples taken from different parts of the primitive world.

Let us begin with the Yurok of northwestern California. We have already commented on the smallness of their political units; at present we are concerned with their composition. Examining one of the typical hamlets, such as Weitspus on the Klamath River, we find an aggregation of less than 200 souls, the male population comprising mainly or exclusively blood kindred. The women generally come from other settlements; apart from this tendency to "local exogamy," the village is a self-contained, independent center of population lacking a sense of attachment to any equivalent units, or of subordination to a major whole, and to that extent comparable with an Andamanese camp. Of adjacent settlements in a group, one "was sometimes involved in a feud while another directly across the river looked on." Indeed, even within the hamlet itself a communal sense is lacking: the individual Weitspus recognizes no duty to his fellow-townsfolk, no executive or judicial authority; his obligations are to his kin and his kin only, so that "all so-called wars were only feuds that happened to involve large groups of kinsmen, several such groups, or unrelated fellow townsmen of the original participants." Notwithstanding the complete absence of administrative and legal officials, the Yurok have a definite code of customary laws;

yet all "rights, claims, possessions, and privileges are individual and personal, and all wrongs are against individuals. There is no offense against the community, no duty owing it, no right or power of any sort inhering in it." And, as a corollary to this proposition, punishment of a public character is likewise wanting. "Each side to an issue presses and resists vigorously, exacts all it can, yields when it has to, continues the controversy when continuance promises to be profitable or settlement is clearly suicidal, and usually ends in compromising more or less."[2]

This description is, *mutatis mutandis,* wholly applicable to the Angami Naga, who occupy the hills between Assam and Burma. Though living in a village, the Angami looks upon the sib (clan) as the real unit of organization. "So distinct is the clan from the village that it forms almost a village in itself, often fortified within the village inside in its own boundaries and not infrequently at variance almost amounting to war with other clans in the same village. Under normal circumstances there are sporadic riots due to the internal dissensions between the kin groups since in most disputes between two men of different clans the clansmen on each side appear as partisans and foment the discord." Even in times of war clan jealousies prove a disruptive force.[3]

Perhaps a still more striking illustration is supplied by the Ifugao of northern Luzon, precisely because these Philippine Islanders exemplify the paradox of an exceedingly complicated body of customary law coupled with a condition of virtual anarchy. Our principal source, Dr. R. F. Barton,[4] is quite clear-cut on the subject. He represents the natives as acting with complete disregard of any considerations outside of relationship. An individual owes support to his kindred against all other kin groups, and in proportion to the proximity of his relationship, while he is free from any obligations to the remainder of the local group. This group has no authorized official to arrange disputes between distinct bodies of kindred; there is merely a go-between with purely advisory functions. According to the author's explicit interpretation the political life of the Ifugao rests on consanguinity, and on consanguinity only.

The three examples cited in some measure justify the views of Maine and Morgan. Here are three peoples remote from one another and described by as many independent witnesses, whose testimony

2. Kroeber, *Handbook of the Indians of California* (1925), 3, 8–15, 20, 49.
3. J. H. Hutton, *The Angami Nagas* (1921), 109.
4. *Ifugao Law,* in *Univ. of Cal. Pub. in Amer. Arch. and Ethnol.* (1919), XV: 1–127.

agrees as to the point at issue. Nevertheless, a closer scrutiny of the evidence reveals in each and every one of these instances that while the blood tie is the conspicuous one the local bond is by no means wholly in abeyance.

Let us begin by examining the Ifugao, on whom the descriptive material is most abundant. We find, first of all, that throughout Ifugao territory there is substantial agreement as to customary law. The principles on which a go-between intermediating between warring families renders his decision enjoy general acceptance, even though they may be warped in particular applications. In cases of adultery a fine is imposed on the offender, the amount varying with the relative status in society of the aggrieved and the guilty party. That *some* penalty should be inflicted, is acknowledged even by the offender and his relatives; they are merely leagued together to shield him from bodily harm and beat down exorbitant demands for indemnity. Even if the adulterer is a prominent man supported by a host of henchmen he does not seek wholly to evade punishment but only to reduce it to a minimum. In short, there *is* definite recognition of some obligations to *un*related members of the same community. This rudimentary sense of duty toward the local group stands forth most clearly in the treatment of thieves. If Barton's picture of Ifugao society were to be taken literally, we should expect the same punishment to be meted out to *any* person outside the aggrieved party's kindred. But this inference does not tally with the facts reported. Theft committed by a fellow villager is mulcted by a traditional fine; a marauding outsider, however, is almost certain to be slain forthwith. Similarly, the principle of collective responsibility is extended beyond the circle of consanguinity so as to embrace the neighborhood group. If a creditor remains unsatisfied, he may on occasion appropriate buffalo belonging not only to his tardy debtor or his kin but those of any person inhabiting the same village.

Finally, there is a tacit understanding among different kin groups that internecine strife should be discountenanced lest the *territorial* unit be unduly weakened as compared with corresponding units; and the individual Ifugao is expected to comport himself in such fashion as not to entangle his neighbors in hostilities with other *local* groups. In short, the apparently exclusive potency of blood relationship is seen to be appreciably limited by the recognition of local contiguity as a basis for political action and sentiment.

What is true of the Ifugao, holds likewise for the equally "anarchic" Yurok. Professor Kroeber successfully disproves the existence of any *national* sentiment among them in his account of their so-called wars, which would fail to unite more than one tenth of the whole "tribe" against, say, the Hupa. But the same narratives also show that local affiliations of lesser scope were operative: "under threat of attack from a remote and consolidated alien foe, village might adhere to village in joint war, just as, in lesser feuds, town mates, impelled by bonds of association or imperiled by their common residence, would sometimes unite with the group of individuals with whom the feud originated." Our author adds that "these are occasions such as draw neighbors together the world over, be they individuals, districts, or nations." But that is precisely my contention, to wit, that even in extreme cases of separatism the neighborhood tie becomes a significant element in governmental activity, not perhaps in itself adequate for the institution of what we call "political" organization but providing the germ from which such an organization may develop.

This factor is strengthened by two features. For one thing, the men of a settlement are united by the institution of the sudatory, where they both sweat and sleep together throughout the winter and often in the summer, "passing the evenings in talk and smoking." The type of social unit thus created will be discussed more fully in the following chapter. Secondly, the local tie clearly appears in ritualistic activity. Not only is each ceremony riveted to a particular spot but, what is far more important in the present context, the association with localities serves to knit people together. Every main performance is conducted by competing parties representing as many villages. "These match and outdo one another, as the rich man of each village gradually hands over more and more of his own and his followers' and friends' valuables to the dancers to display." Moreover, it may be said that the very fact of such amicable rivalry in some manner counteracts the excessive particularism described above. It might have paved the way, though apparently among the Yurok it never did, for a more extensive union of local bodies.[5]

Angami conditions are amazingly like those reported for the Yurok and the Ifugao. On the one hand, the same centrifugal tendency is expressed in exaggeratedly tangible form, so that one clan in the village may be separated from the rest by a wall twelve feet in thickness. Murder leads to a vendetta waged by the clans concerned rather than to the expulsion of the criminal by a judicial authority, and in cases of misunderstanding between persons of different villages the blood feud might be restricted to the kindred of the two parties "and it would be quite possible for all the

5. Kroeber, *op. cit.,* 15, 50, 55, 81.

other clans in both villages to be friendly, while the clans of the respective parties to the vendetta were on head-taking terms." Nevertheless, when a serious breach of the social code occurs "the clans in almost any village would be found agreed"; military operations are certainly carried on by villagers as such; and many important magico-religious observances are communal in character.[6]

The Yurok, Ifugao and Angami are *a fortiori* instances: they represent the maximum conceivable lack of governmental coördination of the kin groups occupying the same habitat. If even here the traditional theory of the exclusiveness of the blood tie breaks down, the presence of the local bond will have to be admitted for less extreme cases. However, it is possible to go further and to turn the tables on Maine and Morgan. Not only do local ties coexist with those of blood kinship, but it may be contended that the bond of relationship when defined in sociological rather than biological terms is itself in no small part a *derivative* of local contiguity. This view is so contrary to accepted notions that some evidence must be adduced in its defense.

Let us once more turn to the Angami Naga. Like many of the ruder peoples, they are divided into moieties, each child being reckoned from birth either a Pezoma or a Pepfüma according to his father's half of the tribe. This dual organization is traced to two legendary brothers, whose respective descendants the members of the two subdivisions are believed to be. But unlike such lineages elsewhere, the Angami moieties are not exogamous at the present time: often the population of a village is composed wholly of persons of one moiety and no objection is voiced against the marriage of fellow members. It is credibly stated by Mr. Hutton's informants that the customary taboo once held sway, but in course of time there seems to have been a constant shift of the marriage regulating function to lesser and lesser fragments of the moiety. Thus, the village of Kohima is inhabited exclusively by Pepfüma people, who freely intermarry so far as they belong to distinct sibs. Of these, at one time within native tradition, there were only two, *viz.*, the Cherama and the Pferonoma. These, accordingly, were at that time to all intents and purposes exogamous moieties on the familiar pattern, as Pezoma and Pepfüma are reputed to have once been. But while Cherama persisted unsegmented, its mate was broken up into six sections, making (with Cherama) seven sibs in all at the present time. The exogamous unit of Kohima has thus been repeatedly redefined: at first it was presumably the archaic Pepfüma

moiety, whose members were forced to seek spouses outside their own village; subsequently fellow-Pepfüma might marry, provided the union was that of a Cherama with a Pferonoma; and finally, a Pferonoma of sib *a* might marry either a Cherama or a Pferonoma of sibs *b, c, d, e, f*.

Nevertheless, so far there is no deviation from the widespread principle that marriage is regulated by *some* sort of kinship body, though the incest group, to use a convenient term, has materially shrunk in course of time. When, however, we scrutinize the data of Mr. Hutton's genealogical tables and his accompanying text, a new fact of the utmost importance emerges. *Permissible intermarriage is a function of locality no less than of consanguinity.* That is to say, the more inclusive kinship taboo is relaxed only in so far as the individuals concerned are not coresidents in the same community. To quote some striking sentences from our author's report:

"The marriage in the present generation is Pezoma-Pezoma, but *between different villages*."

"Here there is a Pezoma-Pezoma marriage in the last generation and a Pepfüma-Pepfüma marriage in the generation before, but in the latter case *between persons of different villages*."

The Cherhechima division "may not intermarry within itself *in the same village*."[7]

The kin group, in short, is not a marriage regulating group simply because it is a kin group but partly, at least, because it is a local group.

This interpretation, however, may be challenged on the ground that the territorial factor came to be stressed at a relatively late stage, while in the earlier periods the patrilineal kin group was the sole principle regulating sex relations. It might also be contended that even today the intrusion of the local factor is incidental or derivative: exogamy is local only because within the settlement there is certainty as to blood kinship while people living elsewhere are either not known to be related or known to be only remotely related. This argument is plausible enough, and in order to meet it we must proceed to a critique of the kinship concept itself.

While kinship is universally recognized between a child and both his parents, this resulting "bilateral" kin group corresponding to our own family is frequently supplemented among the simpler peoples of the globe by the familiar "unilateral" kin. That is to say, the child is linked either with the father *or* the mother, the Angami illustrating the patrilineal, the Hopi of Arizona the matrilineal variety of unilateral reckoning. Since the bilateral

---

6. Hutton, *op. cit.* 45, 109, 150 *seq.*, 193.

7. Hutton, *op. cit.*, 110 *seq.*, 125–132, 418 *seq.* The italics are mine.

family is omnipresent, this may seem to involve a contradiction, which, nevertheless, is more apparent than real. The bilateral family may, for instance, center in certain economic duties and sentimental attachments, while political functions —say, the blood feud—are connected solely with the patrilineal group.

Now, my contention is that both the bilateral (family) and the unilateral (clan, sib, moiety) unit are rooted in a local as well as a consanguine factor. Let us begin by considering the unilateral kin group, which in some quarters is still regarded as a distinguishing badge of primitive society generally.

Among the unilaterally organized tribes there are some in which the kin and the territorial group coincide. This is true of large sections of California. Mr. Gifford has recently shown that the Miwok, who live near the center of the state, were formerly split up into minute paternal lineages, each politically autonomous, each bearing a local name and owning a definite tract of land. Closely conforming to this model, the South Californian Diegueño were organized into patrilineal groups controlling areas so definitely circumscribed that it has been possible to plot their respective holdings. Similarly, in West Australia the local group embraces a body of blood relatives related through their fathers, and it is this small group, simultaneously consanguine and territorial, that acts as a miniature state, for example, by waging war.[8]

Now, what makes a group of this type cohere? It is easy to say that the sense of blood relationship is primary, but very difficult to prove; for what we observe is not such priority but the inextricable union of the consanguine and the local bond. Each unit in West Australia feels itself indissolubly linked with a definite locality by mystical ties. Why? Because of the reverence felt for the paternal ancestry settled there? But why *should* the paternal ancestry be singled out for reverential treatment? Is it not possible to invert the cheap and obvious explanation? It may be that the aborigines do not view a locality reverently because it is connected with their paternal ancestors but that they esteem their ancestors in so far as they are linked with a certain locality.

This leads us directly to the core of the clan problem. Why, we ask, do people ever feel a more special affiliation with one side of the family than with the other? It cannot be the kinship factor that accounts for the differential relationship, for that

factor would operate equally for the paternal and the maternal kindred. The clue to the solution was long ago supplied by E. B. Tylor.[9] Let us assume the rule of marriage that obtains among the Hopi of Arizona,—matrilocal residence. By this the bridegroom takes up his abode with his wife's parents, that is to say, since there is female house ownership, with his mother-in-law, to whom her other daughters likewise bring their several husbands. This explains forthwith why kinsfolk biologically on a par are discriminated sociologically. Between the mother's brother, who sees his sisters' children grow up under his own mother's roof, and his nephews and nieces there naturally develops a sentiment of attachment that cannot possibly obtain between them and the father's brother. Similarly, the mother's sister becomes a closer relation than the paternal aunt, who cannot possibly be a co-resident. It is equally clear why there is a discrimination between different types of cousin. A Hopi grows up with the children of his mother's sister, while the children of his *father's* sister are reared in another house. In corresponding fashion the scales are weighted in favor of the *paternal* kin wherever patrilocal residence takes the place of matrilocalism. In short, spatial segregation accounts to a large extent for the alignment of relatives found in a tribe organized into clans.

It is true that residence after marriage is not always rigidly or permanently fixed, and in such cases supplementary factors must be invoked. For instance, a paternal lineage may be lined, as in northeastern North America, by common utilization of a hunting territory. Again, as in sections of Australia, a maternal kin group may cohere through exploitation of the same seed gathering tract; or, as among the Hidatsa, by the joint cultivation of a plot by a mother, her daughters, and her daughters' daughters. But in each of these instances, the ultimate determinant of cohesion is evidently not mere kinship but kinship enforced by propinquity.

So far I have considered the blood bond only with reference to the unilateral kinship group which looms so large in the discussions of ancient law. At present, however, it is recognized by all ethnologists open to argument that the unilateral principle is not a primeval one but was superimposed at a relatively late period upon the bilateral principle, which invariably accompanies it. The evidence from nearly all the unequivocally simplest tribes of the globe, such as the Shoshoneans of Utah and Nevada, the Yahgan of Tierra del Fuego, the Andamanese of the Bay of Bengal,

8. E. W. Gifford, *Miwok Lineages and the Political Unit in Aboriginal California,* in *American Anthropologist* (1926), 389–401. L. Spier, *Southern Diegueño Customs,* in *Univ. Cal. Publs. Amer. Arch. and Ethnol.,* (1923), XX: 296–308. R. H. Lowie, *Primitive Society* (1920), 393.

9. *The Matriarchal Family System,* in *Nineteenth Century* (1896), 91–96.

and the Chukchi of northeastern Siberia seems to dispose of the hoary dogma that the clan is a truly archaic institution.[10] If, then, the basic importance of the local element is to be established, it must be demonstrated not only in association with the unilateral clan but with the bilateral family.

The very attempt to do this may seem fantastic; for how can anything claim equal rank with those fundamental blood ties upon which our very existence depends? Here, however, we must stress a point of the utmost importance, which has been recently expressed by Dr. Malinowski. Biological and sociological kinship are two distinct concepts. The one is based on instinctive response in accordance with biological utility; the other, however dependent for its origin on the former, is never wholly derived from it and may diverge from it very appreciably. As Malinowski insists, the maternal *instinct* ceases with the discharge of its biological functions; it becomes a *sociologically* creative force only when it has ripened into a specifically human "sentiment" in Shand's sense of the term. But what is it, I should ask, that fosters the sentiment unless it is the constant association during childhood,—prolonged in primitive communities by the generally extended period of lactation? Eliminate the element of contiguity, and the family as a *social* unit tends to disappear. Borgoras's graphic picture of Chukchi life introduces us to lone boys wandering away from home never to return. In what sense do they remain members of their families? Evidently only in a biological sense; sociologically the tie snaps when it fails to be reënforced by spatial proximity.

As for the bond between father and child, we have that whole range of usages which obscure biological paternity while in no way affecting the social or legal kinship. The case of the Bánaro, who live along the Potter's River in New Guinea, has been thoroughly elucidated by Dr. Thurnwald and may serve for purposes of illustration.[11] A Bánaro bride is not initiated into the mysteries of sex life by her husband, but by a friend of her husband's father and, subsequently, by her father-in-law. These activities take place in the so-called spirit hall of the village, and the men themselves are said to impersonate a spirit. As for the groom, he is not permitted access to his wife until after the birth of a child, which is designated as a "spirit's child" (*Geisterkind*) but is adopted by his mother's husband. Owing to the ceremonial laxity of sex relations during great tribal festivals, the husband cannot even be certain of his paternity in the case of subsequent

issue. But, as our authority again and again assures us, this is a matter of complete indifference to the natives: "*Ob der Gatte der wirkliche Vater der Kinder ist, kommt bei diesem System nicht in Betracht.*" The concept of fatherhood is linked with that not of procreator but of educator, provider and protector. It is the husband's cohabitation with the mother—in the etymological no less than in the customary sense of the term—that stamps him sociologically as a parent and makes the children members of *his* clan. Kinship is not kinship in its own right, but as a derivative of a local factor. As Dr. Malinowski has put it, there seems to be a "tendency in the human species, on the part of the male to feel attached to the children born by a woman with whom he has mated, has been living permanently and has kept watch over during her pregnancy."[12]

Dr. Thurnwald's Papuan case is but a special sample of the wider category of adoption,—that legal fiction by which children who need not even be related may become, for all social purposes, as their adoptive parents' real offspring. Whatever may be the motive in different areas, which presumably varies considerably, the psychological concomitant is usually a sentimental relationship that approximates, if it does not attain, the natural emotions. The data from other areas seem to me to corroborate my personal impression among the Crow Indians, that there is a generic love of children—no matter whose—which merely requires to be particularized in a definite instance by constant association in order to develop into a full-fledged parental sentiment.

To sum up our argument. The traditional distinction established by Maine and Morgan retains its validity in so far as conceptually a union of neighbors is different from a union of kinsmen. It must even be conceded that the blood tie is frequently the overshadowing element in the governmental activities of primitive peoples. Yet, though it often dwarfs the territorial factor, it never succeeds in eliminating it. Nay, if we inquire into the bond of consanguinity itself, we find lurking in the background a spatial determinant of the sentiments underlying it. Abstractly separated by a chasm, the two types of union are in reality intertwined. The basic problem of the state is thus not that of explaining the somersault by which ancient peoples achieved the step from a government by personal relations to one by territorial contiguity only. The question is rather to show what processes strengthened the local tie which must be recognized as not less ancient than the rival principle.

10. R. H. Lowie, *Primitive Society* (1920), 150 *seq.* W. Schmidt, *Völker und Kulturen* (1924), 79 *seq.*

11. Thurnwald, *Die Gemeinde der Bánaro* (Stuttgart, 1921), pp. 21 *seq.*, 37 *f.*, 99 *seq.*

12. B. Malinowski, *Crime and Custom in Savage Society* (1926), 107.

2. The Village Community

by SIR HENRY SUMNER MAINE

THE STUDENT of legal antiquities who has once convinced himself that the soil of the greatest part of Europe was formerly owned and tilled by proprietary groups, of substantially the same character and composition as those which are still found in the only parts of Asia which are open to sustained and careful observation, has his interest immediately drawn to what, in truth, is the great problem of legal history. This is the question of the process by which the primitive mode of enjoyment was converted into the agrarian system, out of which immediately grew the land-law prevailing in all Western Continental Europe before the first French Revolution, and from which is demonstrably descended our own existing real-property law. For this newer system no name has come into general use except Feudalism, a word which has the defect of calling attention to one set only of its characteristic incidents. We cannot reasonably doubt that one partial explanation of its origin is, so far as it goes, correct. It arose from or was greatly influenced by the Benefices, grants of Roman provincial land by the chieftains of the tribes which overran the Roman Empire; such grants being conferred on their associates upon certain conditions, of which the commonest was military service. There is also tolerably universal agreement that somewhere in Roman law (though *where,* all are not agreed) are to be found the rules which determined the nature of these beneficiary holdings. This may be called the theory of the official origin of feudalism, the enjoyment of land being coupled with the discharge of certain definite duties; and there are some who complete the theory by asserting that among the Teutonic races, at all events, there was an ineradicable tendency in all offices to become hereditary, and that thus the Benefices, which at first were held for life, became at last descendible from father to son.

There is no question, as I said, that this account is more than probable, and that the Benefices either began or hastened the changes which led ultimately to feudalism. Yet I think that nobody whose mind has dwelt on the explanation, has brought himself to regard it as complete. It does not tell us how the Benefices came to have so extraordinary a historical fortune. It does not account for the early, if partial, feudalisation of countries like Germany and England, where the cultivated soil was in the hands of free and fully organised communities, and was not, like the land of Italy or Gaul, at the disposal of a conquering king—where the royal or national grants which resembled the Benefices were probably made out of waste land—and where the influence of Roman law was feebly felt or not at all.

The feudalisation of any one country in Europe must be conceived as a process including a long series of political, administrative, and judicial changes; and there is some difficulty in confining our discussion of it to changes in the condition of property which belong more properly to this department of study. But I think we may limit our consideration of the subject by looking at it in this way. If we begin with modern English real-property law, and, by the help of its records and of the statutes affecting it, trace its history backwards, we come upon a period at which the soil of England was occupied and tilled by separate proprietary societies. Each of these societies is, or bears the marks of having been, a compact and organically complete assemblage of men, occupying a definite area of land. Thus far it resembles the old cultivating communities, but it differs from them in being held together by a variety of subordinate relations to a feudal chief, single or corporate, the Lord. I will call the new group the Manorial group, and though my words must not be taken as strictly correct, I will say that a group of tenants, autocratically organised and governed, has succeeded a group of households of which the organisation and government were democratic. The new group, as known to our law, is often in a state of dissolution, but, where it is perfect, it consists of a number of persons holding land of the Lord by free tenures, and of a number of persons holding land of the Lord by tenures capable of being shown to have been, in their origin, servile—the authority of the Lord being exercised over both classes, although in different ways, through the agency of a peculiar tribunal, the Court Baron. The lands held by the first description of tenants are technically known as the Tene-

Reprinted from Sir Henry Sumner Maine, *Village Communities in the East and West* (New York: Henry Holt & Co., 1889), Lect. IV, pp. 131–71.

mental lands; those held by the second class constitute the Lord's Domain. Both kinds of land are essential to the completeness of the Manorial group. If there are not Tenemental lands to supply a certain minimum number of free tenants to attend the Court Baron, and, according to the legal theory, to sit with the lord as its judges, the Court Baron can no longer in strictness be held; if it be continued under such circumstances, as it often was in practice, it can only be upheld as a Customary Manorial Court, sitting for the assessment and receipt of customary dues from the tenants of the Domain. On the other hand, if there be no Domain, or if it be parted with, the authority of the Lord over the free tenants is no longer Manorial; it becomes a Seignory in gross, or mere Lordship.

Since much of the public waste land of our country is known to have passed by national or royal grant to individuals or corporations, who, in all probability, brought it extensively under cultivation from the first by servile labour, it cannot be supposed that each of the new Manorial groups takes the place of a Village group which at some time or other consisted of free allodial proprietors. Still, we may accept the belief of the best authorities that over a great part of England there has been a true succession of one group to the other. Comparing, then, the two, let us ask what are the specific changes which have taken place? The first, and far the most important of all, is that, in England as everywhere in Western Europe, the waste or common-land of the community has become the lord's waste. It is still ancillary to the Tenemental lands; the free tenants of the lord, whom we may provisionally take to represent the freemen of the village-community, retain all their ascertained rights of pasture and gathering firewood, and in some cases similar rights have been acquired by other classes; but, subject to all ascertained rights, the waste belongs, actually or potentially, to the lord's domain. The lord's "right of approvement," affirmed by the Statute of Merton, and extended and confirmed by subsequent statutes, permits him to enclose and appropriate so much of the waste as is not wanted to satisfy other existing rights; nor can it be doubted that he largely exercises this right, reclaiming part of the waste for himself by his personal dependents and adding it to whatever share may have belonged to him from the first in the cultivated land of the community, and colonising other portions of it with settlements of his villeins who are on their way to become copyholders. The legal theory has altogether departed from the primitive view; the waste is now the lord's waste; the commoners are for the most part assumed to have acquired their rights by sufferance of the lord, and

there is a visible tendency in courts and text-writers to speak of the lord's rights, not only as superior to those of the commoners, but as being in fact of greater antiquity.

When we pass from the waste to the grass lands which were intermediate between the common land and the cultivated area, we find many varieties in the degree of authority acquired by the lord. The customs of manors differ greatly on the point. Sometimes, the lord encloses for his own benefit from Candlemas to Midsummer or Lammas, and the common right belongs during the rest of the year to a class of burgesses, or to the householders of a village, or to the persons inhabiting certain ancient tenements. Sometimes, the lord only regulates the inclosure, and determines the time of setting up and removing the fences. Sometimes, other persons enclose, and the lord has the grass when the several enjoyment comes to an end. Sometimes, his right of pasture extends to the baulks of turf which separate the common arable fields; and probably there is no manorial right which in later times has been more bitterly resented than this, since it is practically fatal to the cultivation of green crops in the arable soil.

Leaving the meadows and turning to the lands under regular tillage, we cannot doubt that the free holders of the Tenemental lands correspond in the main to the free heads of households composing the old village-community. The assumption has often been made, and it appears to be borne out by the facts which can be established as to the common fields still open or comparatively lately enclosed. The tenure of a certain number of these fields is freehold; they are parcelled out, or may be shown to have been in the last century parcelled out, among many different owners; they are nearly always distributed into three strips, and some of them are even at this hour cultivated according to methods of tillage which are stamped by their very rudeness as coming down from a remote antiquity. They appear to be the lands of a class which has never ceased to be free, and they are divided and cultivated exactly as the arable mark of a Teutonic township can be inferred by a large induction, to have been divided and tilled. But, on the other hand, many large tracts of intermixed land are still, or were till their recent enfranchisement, copyhold of particular manors, and some of them are held by the intermediate tenure, known as customary freehold, which is confined by the legal theory to lands which once formed part of the King's Domain. I have not been able to ascertain the proportion of common lands held by these base tenures to freehold lands of the same kind, but there is no doubt that much commonable or intermixed land is found, which is not freehold. Since the descent of copyhold and customary freehold tenures from the holdings of servile classes appears to be well established, the frequent occurrence of intermixed lands of this nature seems to bear out the inference suggested by Sir H. Ellis's enumeration of the conditions of men referred to in Domesday Book, that, during the long process of feudalism, some of the free villagers sank to the status, almost certainly not a uniform status, which was implied in villenage. (See also Mr. Freeman's remark, "Hist. Norm. Conq." i. 97.) But evidence, supplied from quarters so wide apart as British India and the English settlements in North America, leads me to think that, at a time when a system of customary tillage widely prevailed, assemblages of people planted on waste land would be likely to copy the system literally; and I conjecture that parts of the great wastes undoubtedly reclaimed by the exercise of the right afterwards called the lord's "right of approvement" were settled by servile colonies modelled on the ancient Teutonic township.

The bond which kept the Manorial group together was evidently the Manorial Court, presided over by the lord or his representative. Under the name of Manorial Court three courts are usually included, which legal theory keeps apart, the Court Leet, the Court Baron, and the Customary Court of the Manor. I think there cannot be reasonable doubt of the legitimate descent of all three from the assembly of the Township. Besides the wide criminal and civil jurisdiction which belonged to them, and which, though it has been partly abolished, has chiefly lost its importance through insensible decay, they long continued in the exercise of administrative or regulative powers which are scarcely distinguishable from legislation. Other vestiges of powers exerted by the collective body of free owners at a time when the conceptions of legislative and judicial authority had not yet been separated, remained in the functions of the Leet Jury; in the right asserted for the free tenants of sitting as Judges in the Court Baron; and in the election of various petty officers. It is true that, as regards one of these Courts, the legal theory of its character is to a certain extent inconsistent with the pedigree I have claimed for it. The lawyers have always contended that the Court Leet only existed through the King's grant, express or implied; and in pursuance of the same doctrine they have laid down that, whereas the lord might himself sit in the Court Baron, he must have a person of competent legal learning to represent him in the Court Leet. But this only proves that the Court Leet, which was entrusted with the examination of the Frankpledge, had more public importance than the other Manorial Courts, and

was therefore more distinctly brought under the assumption which had been gradually forming itself, that royal authority is the fountain of all justice. Even in the last extremity of decline, the Manorial Courts have not wholly ceased to be regarded as the tie which connects the common interests of a definite group of persons engaged in the cultivation of the soil. Marshall ("Rural Economy of Yorkshire," i. 27) mentions the remarkable fact that these Courts were sometimes kept up at the beginning of the century by the voluntary consent of the neighbourhood in certain districts where, from the disappearance of the servile tenures which had enabled the Customary Courts to be continued, the right to hold them had been forfeited. The manorial group still sufficiently cohered for it to be felt that some common authority was required to regulate such matters as the repair of minor roads, the cleansing of rivulets, the ascertainment of the sufficiency of ring-fences, the assessment of the damages of impounded cattle, the removal of nuisances, and the stocking of commons.

On the whole, the comparison of the Village group with the English group which I have called Manorial rather than Feudal, suggests the following general observations. Wherever that collective ownership of land which was a universal phenomenon in primitive societies has dissolved, or gone far to dissolve, into individual property, the individual rights thus formed have been but slightly affected by the process of feudalisation. If there are reasons for thinking that some free village societies fell during the process into the predial condition of villenage—whatever that condition may really have implied—a compensating process began at some unknown date, under which the base tenant made a steady approach to the level of the freeholder. Even rights which savoured of the collective stage of property were maintained comparatively intact, provided that they were ascertained: such as rights of pasture on the waste and rights of several or of common enjoyment (as the case might be) in the grass land. The encroachments of the lord were in proportion to the want of certainty in the rights of the community. Into the grass land he intruded more than into the arable land; into the waste much more than into either. The conclusion suggested to my mind is that, in succeeding to the legislative power of the old community, he was enabled to appropriate to himself such of its rights as were not immediately valuable, and which, in the event of their becoming valuable, required legislative adjustment to settle the mode of enjoying them. Let me add that the general truth of my description of the character of the change which somehow took place, is perhaps rendered antecedently more probable by the comparison of a mature, but non-feudal, body of jurisprudence, like the Roman law, with any deeply feudalised legal system. You will remember the class of enjoyable objects which the Roman lawyers call *res nullius, res publici usûs, res omnium* or *universorum;* these it reserves to the entire community, or confers on the first taker. But, under feudalised law, nearly all these objects which are capable of several enjoyment belong to the lord of the manor, or to the king. Even Prize of War, the most significant of the class, belongs theoretically to the sovereign in the first instance. By a very singular anomaly, which has had important practical results, Game is not strictly private property under English law; but the doctrine on the subject is traceable to the later influence of the Roman law.

There must be a considerable element of conjecture in any account which may be given of a series of changes which took place for the most part in remote antiquity, and which probably were far from uniform either in character or in rate of advance. It happens, however, that the vestiges of the earlier stages of the process of feudalisation are more discernible in Germany than elsewhere, both in documentary records and on the face of the land; owing in part no doubt to the comparatively feeble action of that superior and central authority which has obliterated or obscured so much in our own country. A whole school of writers, among whom Von Maurer has the first place, has employed itself in restoring and interpreting these traces of the Past. How did the Manor rise out of the Mark?—this is their way of stating the problem. What were the causes of indigenous growth which, independently of grants of land by royal or national authority, were leading to a suzerainty or superiority of one cultivating community over another, or of one family over the rest of the families composing the village-community? The great cause in the view of these writers was the exceeding quarrelsomeness of these little societies, and the consequent frequency of intertribal war. One community conquers another, and the spoil of war is generally the common mark or waste of the worsted community. Either the conquerors appropriate and colonise part of the waste so taken, or they take the whole domain and restore it to be held in dependence on the victor-society. The change from one of these systems to another occurred, you will remember, in Roman history, and constitutes an epoch in the development of the Roman Law of Property. The effect of the first system on the Teutonic communities was inequality of property; since the common land appropriated and occupied does not seem to have been

equally divided, but a certain preference was given to the members of the successful community who had most effectually contributed to the victory. Under the second system, when its land was restored to the conquered society, the superiority over it which remained to the victor, bore the strongest analogy to a suzerainty or lordship. Such a suzerainty was not, however, exclusively created by success in war. Sometimes a community possessed of common land exceptionally extensive or exceptionally fertile would send colonies of families to parts of it. Each of these new communities would receive a new arable mark, but such of the land as remained unappropriated would still be the common land of all the townships. At the head of this sort of confederacy there would, however, be the original mother community from which the colonists proceeded, and there seems no doubt that in such a state of things she claimed a superiority or suzerainty over all the younger townships.

But, even if we had the fullest evidence of the growth of suzerainties in this inchoate shape, we should still have advanced a very little way in tracing the transmutation of the village system into the manorial system, if it were not for another phenomenon to which Landau has more particularly called attention. The Teutonic communities, though their organisation (if modern language must be employed) can only be described as democratic, appear nevertheless to have generally had an abiding tradition that in some one family, or in some families, the blood which ran in the veins of all the freemen was purest; probably because the direct descent of such family or families from a common ancestor was remembered or believed in. From the members of these families, the leader for a military expedition would as a rule be chosen; but as in this stage of thought the different varieties of power were not distinguished from one another, the power acquired by the chieftain would be a combination of political, military, and judicial power. The choice of the leader would in great emergencies be a true election, but on less serious occasions would tend to become an acquiesence in the direction of the eldest male agnate of the family which had the primacy of the township. Similarly, the power which had at first been more military than anything else, would in more peaceful times tend rather to assume a political and judicial form. The leader thus taken from the privileged family would have the largest share of the lands appropriated from conquered village-societies; and there is ground for supposing that he was sometimes rewarded by an exceptionally large share of the common land belonging to the society which he had headed. Everything in fact which disturbed the peaceful order of the village system led to the aggrandisement of the leading family and of its chief. Among the privileges which he obtained was one of which the importance did not show itself till much later. He became powerful enough in his own township to sever his own plot of land from the rest, and, if he thought fit, to enclose it; and thus to break up or enfeeble that system of common cultivation under rules of obligatory custom which depended mainly on the concurrence of all the villagers.

There were therefore, in the cultivating communities of the German and Scandinavian races, causes at work which were leading to inequality of property in land. There were causes at work which were leading to the establishment of superiorities or suzerainties of one township over another. There were causes at work which tended to place the benefits of an unequal proprietary system and the enjoyment of these suzerainties in the hands of particular families, and consequently of their chiefs for the time being. Here you have all the elements of the system we are compelled to call feudal. But the system in its ultimate development was the result of a double set of influences. One set, which I have been describing, were of primitive growth. Another showed themselves when powerful Teutonic monarchies began to be formed, and consisted in grants of national waste land or of the soil of conquered provinces. Doubtless some of the grantees were chiefs of families already risen to power under indigenous Teutonic conditions; but in any case a Beneficiary would be a chieftain of a peculiarly powerful class. The cultivators of his land would either be persons settled on it by himself, or they would be vanquished provincials who had no rights which he did not choose to recognise or concede. It is not, therefore, surprising that there should have been a completer constitution of feudalism in the countries which at the time of conquest were filled with Romanised populations. The mould would be Teutonic, but the materials would be unusually plastic, and here would more especially come into play the influence of Roman law, giving precision to relations which under purely Teutonic social conditions may have been in a high degree vague and indefinite. It is well known that this systematic feudalism reacted upon the more purely Teutonic societies and gave an impulse to changes which were elsewhere proceeding at a slower pace.

I have very briefly summarised the results of a very long and laborious enquiry, and only so far as is necessary for my immediate purpose. Merely remarking that I can see little or nothing in the conclusions of these eminent German writers which is out of harmony with the account given by English scholars of the parallel phenomena of change manifested in England before the Conquest, I proceed to ask, following the scheme of these Lectures, whether the experience of Englishmen in India throws any light or has any bearing upon the questions which have been occupying us? It is not too much to say that the phenomena observed in the East, and those established in the West by historical research, illustrate one another at every point. In India these dry bones live. Not only, as I have told you, is the Village-Community the basis of British administration in those provinces in which the art of government has to be practised with skill and caution, but a number of controversies turning on the mode of transition from the village system to what I have called the manorial system are as earnestly, and sometimes even as violently, debated by our countrymen in the East as are the great aspects of politics among ourselves. All Indian disputes take, I should explain, a historical or antiquarian shape. The assumption universally made is that the country must be governed in harmony with the established usages of the natives, and each administrative school has therefore to justify its opinions by showing that the principles to which it adheres are found in some sense or other to underlie the known customary law of India. The extravagance of partisanship which here shows itself in unqualified assertion of the universal applicability of general propositions has its Indian counterpart in unqualified assertion of the universal existence of particular customs. The Indian controversy is, however, a controversy about facts which, though they are more complex than the disputants suppose, are nevertheless much simpler than the material of English political controversy; and the results are therefore proportionately more instructive to the bystander who has entire sympathy with neither party.

Let us suppose a province annexed for the first time to the British Indian Empire. The first civil act of the new government is always to effect a settlement of the land revenue; that is, to determine the amount of that relatively large share of the produce of the soil, or of its value, which is demanded by the sovereign in all Oriental States, and out of which all the main expenses of government are defrayed. Among the many questions upon which a decision must be had, the one of most practical importance is, "Who shall be settled with?" —with whom shall the settlement be made? What persons, what bodies, what groups, shall be held responsible to the British Government for its land revenue? What practically has to be determined is the unit of society for agrarian purposes; and you find that, in determining it, you determine everything, and give its character finally to the entire political and social constitution of the province. You are at once compelled to confer on the selected class powers co-extensive with its duties to the sovereign. Not that the assumption is ever made that new proprietary powers are conferred on it, but what are supposed to be its rights in relation to all other classes are defined; and in the vague and floating order of primitive societies, the mere definition of a right immensely increases its strength. As a matter of fact, it is found that all agrarian rights, whether superior or subordinate to those of the person held responsible to Government, have a steady tendency to decay. I will not ask you to remember the technical names of the various classes of persons "settled with" in different parts of India—Zemindars, Talukdars, Lumberdars—names which doubtless sound uncouth, and which, in fact, have not an identical meaning throughout the country—but I dwell on the fact that the various interests in the soil which these names symbolise are seen to grow at the expense of all others. Do you, on entering on the settlement of a new province, find that a peasant proprietary has been displaced by an oligarchy of vigorous usurpers, and do you think it expedient to take the government dues from the once oppressed yeomen? The result is the immediate decline, and consequently bitter discontent, of the class above them, who find themselves sinking to the footing of mere annuitants on the land. Such was the land settlement of Oudh, which was shattered to pieces by the Sepoy mutiny of 1857, and which greatly affected its course. Do you, reversing this policy, arrange that the superior holder shall be answerable to Government? You find that you have created a landed aristocracy which has no parallel in wealth or power except the proprietors of English soil. Of this nature is the more modern settlement of the province of Oudh, only recently consummated; and such will ultimately be the position of the Talukdars, or Barons, among whom its soil has been divided. Do you adopt a policy different from either of those which I have indicated and make your arrangements with the representative of the village-community? You find that you have arrested a process of change which was steadily proceeding. You have given to this peculiar proprietary group a vitality which it was losing, and a stiffness to the relations of the various classes composing it which they never had before.

It would be a mere conceit to try to establish any close analogy between the Teutonic Kings and the British government of India. Yet, so much as this is true and instructive. The only owner of the soil of India with whom the English Government has any relations, is, in its eyes, a mere functionary. It chooses him where it pleases, and extracts from him

services, chiefly pecuniary, but to a certain small extent personal. It is found, however, that when an official appointed by a powerful government acts upon the loose constitution of a primitive society he crushes down all other classes and exalts that to which he himself belongs. But for recent legislation this process would have gone to any length in India, and would have assuredly affected many other provinces than those which were its immediate theatre. It may, at least, be said that by observing it we gain a clearer conception of the effect of beneficiary gifts on the general tenure of land, and that we better understand the enormous power acquired by the chieftains who rendered immediate services to the Teutonic kings.

The English in India appear to have started with the assumption of the Mahometans that the sovereign might lawfully select anybody he pleased as the collector of his revenue; but they soon accepted the principle that the class to be "settled with" was the class best entitled to be regarded as having rights of property in the soil. At a later date they discovered that, even when this class was determined, they had to decide what it was that proprietary rights over Indian land implied, and what powers they carried with them. No questions fuller of inherent difficulties were ever proposed for solution. As regards the first of them, the functionaries administering India might, with some eminent exceptions, but still not unfairly, be distributed into two great schools—the partisans of the theory that the soil belongs to the peasantry either as individuals or as organised in groups; and the partisans of the theory that ownership of the soil ought to be, and but for British influence would be, everywhere in India vested in some sort of native aristocracy. As regards the second question, the Indian officials are much more exactly divided into those who contend that the highest right of property acknowledged to exist over the soil carries with it the same powers which attach to an English owner in fee-simple of the present day, and into those who are of opinion that, if these powers are to square with native idea and custom, they must be more or less limited and controlled. The controversies on these two points are the most vehemently debated of Indian disputes; and none ever presented greater difficulties to the person who tries to form an opinion on their merits, not from his own knowledge but upon the evidence supplied to him by others. He finds men of the utmost experience, of trained power of observation, and of the most unquestionable good faith, stating precisely opposite conclusions with precisely equal positiveness. But if he avail himself of the advantage given him by the parallel facts of European tenure, he will, perhaps, venture to have an opinion, and to think that in these, as in many other fierce disputes, both sides are right and both sides are wrong.

There is no doubt that the first point at issue was much obscured, and attention diverted to irrelevant matter, by the unlucky experiment tried at the end of the last century by Lord Cornwallis. A province, like Bengal Proper, where the village system had fallen to pieces of itself, was the proper field for the creation of a peasant proprietary; but Lord Cornwallis turned it into a country of great estates, and was compelled to take his landlords from the tax-gatherers of his worthless predecessors. The political valuelessness of the proprietary thus created, its failure to obtain any wholesome influence over the peasantry, and its oppression of all inferior holders, led not only to distrust of the economical principles implied in its establishment, but to a sort of reluctance to believe in the existence of any naturally privileged class in the provinces subsequently acquired and examined. The most distinguished public servants of that day have left much on record which implies an opinion that no ownership of Indian land was discoverable, except that of the village-communities, subject to the dominion of the State.

But in fact it appears that, of all the landmarks on the line of movement traced by German and English scholars from the Village group to the Manorial group, there is not one which may not be met with in India, saving always the extreme points at either end. I have not had described to me any village-community under the unmodified collective government of the heads of households, but there are those who think they find the vestiges of the original constitution in a sort of democratic spirit and habit of free criticism which prevail even when the government has passed to an hereditary officer. If any thoroughly authenticated example could be produced of a community exercising absolute liberty of choice in electing its Headman, it would point still more significantly to an unmodified original equality; but the preference alleged to be invariably shown to the members of particular families appears to show that these elections belong really to the phenomena of hereditary succession. It is not, however, disputed that villages are found in great numbers in which the government is lodged with a council, neither claiming to be nor regarded as being anything more than a representation of the entire cultivating body. The instances, however, in which the authority has passed to some particular family or families are extremely numerous. Sometimes the office of Headman belongs absolutely to the head of a particular family; sometimes it belongs to him primarily, but he may be set aside for in-

capacity or physical blemish; sometimes there is a power of choosing him limited to an election between the members of one or more privileged households. The powers which he enjoys—or which it perhaps should be said, he would enjoy under native conditions of society—are also very various. But the judicial power of mediating in disputes and of interpreting customs appears to be certainly vested in him, together with the duty of keeping order; and, independently of the functions which he discharges with the consent of his neighbours, the British Government often expressly confides to him a certain amount of regular jurisdiction and of regular authority in matters of police.

There is no question that many of the families whom the English have recognised as owners of villages were privileged families enjoying the primacy of the township; but the widest difference of opinion has prevailed as to the nature and origin of the rights claimed by certain families for their chiefs over whole tracts of country, embracing the domain of several village-communities. It has been strongly contended on one side that these great proprietors are nothing but the descendants of farmers of the revenue under Native Governments; on the other it is asserted that in some cases at all events they were Chieftains of Clans who were selected by preference to represent the Royal or Imperial native government in districts in which they had an hereditary influence. There appears to me reasonable evidence that this last theory is true of certain localities in India. Clan society is also in Europe the Celtic form of the family organisation of society; and, for myself, I have great difficulty in conceiving the origin of customary law otherwise than by assuming the former existence of larger groups, under patriarchal chieftains, which at a later date dissolved into the independent collections of families forming the cultivating communities of the Teutonic (including the Scandinavian) races and of the Hindoos.

If it be taken for granted that the English in India were bound to recognise rights of property somewhere, their selection of the persons in whom these rights should vest does not seem to have been as absurd as the adherents of one Indian school are in the habit of hinting, if not of asserting. Claims to some sort of superior right over land in fact existed which corresponded to every single stage through which the conception of proprietorship has passed in the Western world, excepting only the later stages. The variety of these claims was practically infinite, and not only did not diminish, but greatly increased, as native customs and ideas were more accurately examined. Even when the village-communities were allowed to be in some sense the proprietors of the land which they tilled, they proved on careful inspection not to be simple groups, but highly composite bodies, composed of several sections with conflicting and occasionally with irreconcilable claims. The English officials solved a problem of almost hopeless perplexity by registering all the owners of superior rights as landowners, their conception of ownership being roughly taken from their own country; but the fundamental question very soon revived under another form in the shape of the second issue disputed between the Indian administrative schools, which is, whether proprietorship in India is to be taken to be the same assemblage of powers which constitutes the modern English ownership of land in fee-simple.

It seems to me that the error of the school which asserts the existence of strong proprietary rights in India lies much less in merely making this assertion than in assuming the existence of a perfect analogy between rights of property as understood in India and as understood in this country. The presumption is strongly against the reality of any such correspondence. The rights of property are, in the eye of the jurist, a bundle of powers, capable of being mentally contemplated apart from one another and capable of being separately enjoyed. The historical enquirer can also, whenever there are materials for a history of the past, trace the gradual growth of the conception of absolute property in land. That conception appears to me, for reasons which I shall afterwards assign, to have grown out of the ownership of the lord in that portion of his domain which he cultivated by his immediate personal dependants, and therefore to be a late and gradually matured fruit of the feudalisation of Europe. A process closely resembling feudalisation was undoubtedly once at work in India; there are Indian phenomena answering to the phenomena of nascent absolute ownership in England and Europe; but then these Indian phenomena, instead of succeeding one another, are all found existing together at the present moment. The feudalisation of India, if so it may be called, was never in fact completed. The characteristic signs of its consummation are wanting. It may be doubted whether in any single instance the whole power of regulating the affairs of the village-community has passed to an hereditary official when the English entered the country; on the other hand, in the enormous majority of examples there are peculiarities of organisation which show conclusively that the village-group is either unmodified or has not yet nearly passed into the manorial group. Even, however, were we at liberty to believe that India has been completely feudalised, we should still be as far as possible from being entitled to assume that the highest Indian form of ownership corresponds to the absolute ownership of the English holder in fee-simple. It has been said that many persons talk and write as if all the Englishmen who lived between the Norman Conquest and the Reformation lived at exactly the same time; but this Indian assumption implies that there has been no change in our conception of landed property between the epoch at which England became completely feudal and the epoch (let us say) at which the Corn-laws were repealed. Yet during all these centuries England has been legislatively and to a great extent judicially centralised, and has been acted on by economical influences of very great uniformity. India, from the earliest ages till the British entered it, was under the dominion of comparatively powerful kings, who swept away the produce of the labour of the village-communities and carried off the young men to serve in their wars, but did not otherwise meddle with the cultivating societies. This was doubtless the great cause of their irregular development. Intertribal wars soon gave way to the wars of great kings leading mercenary armies, but these monarchs, with few and doubtful exceptions, neither legislated nor centralised. The village-communities were left to modify themselves separately in their own way.

This subject is one of much practical importance, and I propose to treat of the more difficult problems which it raises in the next Lecture; at present I will content myself with repeating that there seems to me the heaviest presumption against the existence in any part of India of a form of ownership conferring the exact rights on the proprietor which are given by the present English ownership in fee-simple. There are now, however, a vast number of vested rights in the country, fully recognised by the English Government, which assume the identity of Indian and English proprietorship, and neither justice nor policy permits them to be disturbed. Moreover it is abstractedly possible that further observation of particular localities by accurate observers may, so far as regards those localities, rebut the presumption of which I have spoken, provided that the enquirer be acquainted with the parallel phenomena which belong to European legal history, and provided that he possess the faculty, not very common among us, of distinguishing the rudimentary stages of legal thought from its maturity. The way in which, among the unlettered members of a primitive society, law and morality run into one another ought especially to be studied. The subordinate holder who in India states that the superior holder has the power to do a certain act, but that he ought not to do it, does not make an admission; he raises a question of the utmost difficulty.

It has been usual to speak of the feudalisation of Western Europe as if it had been an unmixed evil, and there is but too much reason to believe that it was accompanied in its course by a great amount of human suffering. But there are some facts of Indian experience which may lead us to think that the advantage of some of the economical and juridical results which it produced has been underrated. If the process indeed had really consisted, as some of the enthusiasts for its repetition in India appear to suppose that it did, merely in the superposition of the lord over the free owners of land, with power to demand such services or dues as he pleased and to vary his demands at pleasure, very little indeed could be said for it. But this picture of it is certainly untrue of our own country. We are not at liberty to assume that the obligations incurred by the free owner of land who *commended* himself to a lord were other than, within certain limits, fixed and definite services; and the one distinguishing characteristic which the English feudists discover in that free Socage tenure for which the English villagers most probably exchanged their allodial ownership is certainty, regularity and permanence of service. The great novelties which the transition from one form of property to another produced were, the new authority over the waste which the lord acquired (and which was connected with the transfer to him of the half judicial, half legislative, powers of the collective community) and the emancipation of the lord within his own domains from the fetters of obligatory agricultural custom. Now Europe was then full of great wastes, and the urgent business in hand was to reclaim them. Large forests were to be felled, and wide tracts of untilled land had to be brought under cultivation. In England, inexorably confined within natural boundaries, there pressed with increasing force the necessity for adopting the methods of agriculture which were fitted to augment the total supply of food for a growing population. But for this work society organised in village-communities is but little adapted. The Indian administrators who regard the cultivating groups with most favour, contend that they secure a large amount of comfort and happiness for the families included within them, that their industry is generally, and that their skill is occasionally, meritorious. But their admirers certainly do not claim for them that they readily adopt new crops and new modes of tillage, and it is often admitted that they are grudging and improvident owners of their waste-land. The British Government, as I before stated, has applied a remedy to this last defect by acting on the right to curtail excessive wastes which it inherited from its predecessors; and of late years it has done its utmost to extend and improve the cultivation of one great staple, Cotton—amid difficulties which seem to be very imperfectly understood by those who suppose that in order to obtain the sowing of a new crop, or the sowing of an old crop in a new way, from a peasant in bondage to hereditary custom, it is enough to prove to him that it is very likely to be profitable. There is Indian evidence that the forms of property imitated from modern English examples have a value of their own, when reclamation has to be conducted on a large scale, or novelties in agriculture have to be introduced. The Zemindars of Lower Bengal, the landed proprietary established by Lord Cornwallis, have the worst reputation as landlords, and appear to have frequently deserved it; but the grants of land originally made to them included great uncultivated tracts, and at the time when their power over subordinate holders was least limited they brought large areas of waste-land under tillage by the colonies of peasants which they planted there. The proprietorship conferred on them has also much to do with the introduction into Lower Bengal, nearly alone among Indian provinces, of new and vast agricultural industries, which, if they had been placed under timely regulation (which unfortunately they were not) would have added as much to the comfort of the people as they have added to the wealth of the country.

It appears therefore to me to be highly probable that the autocratically governed manorial group is better suited than the village group for bringing under cultivation a country in which waste-lands are extensive. So also does it seem to me likely to have been at all times more tolerant of agricultural novelties. It is a serious error to suppose that the non-feudal forms of property which characterised the cultivating communities had any real resemblance to the absolute property of our own day. The land was free only in the sense of being free from feudal services, but it was enslaved to custom. An intricate net of usage bound down the allodial owner, as it now binds the Indian peasant, to a fixed routine of cultivation. It can hardly be said that in England or Germany these usages had ceased to exercise a deadening influence even within living memory, since very recent writers in both countries complain of the bad agriculture, perpetuated by custom in the open common fields. The famous movement against Inclosures under the Tudor reigns was certainly in part provoked by inclosures of plots in the three common fields made with the intention of breaking the custom and extending the systematic cultivation of grasses; and it is curious to find the witnesses examined before the Select Committee of 1844 using precisely the same language which was employed by the writers who in the sixteenth century took the unpopular side, and declaring that the value and produce of the intermixed lands might be very greatly increased if the owner, instead of having one plot in each field, had three plots thrown together in one field and dealt with them as he pleased. As I said before, it seems to me a plausible conjecture that our absolute form of property is really descended from the proprietorship of the lord in the domain which—besides planting it with the settlements of "unfree" families—he tilled, when it was close to his castle or manor-house, by his own dependants under his own eye. He was free from the agricultural customs which shackled those below him, and the services exacted from above were not of a kind to affect his management of the land which he kept in his hands. The English settlers on the New England coast did not, as I shall point out, at first adopt this form of property, but they did so very shortly, and we unquestionably owe to it such an achievement as the cultivation of the soil of North America.

If, however, a society organised in groups on the primitive model is ineffective for Production, so also if left to develop itself solely under primitive influences it fails to secure any considerable improvement in Distribution. Although it is hardly possible to avoid speaking of the Western village groups as in one stage democratically governed, they were really oligarchies, as the Eastern communities always tend to become. These little societies had doubtless anciently a power of absorption, when men were of more value than land. But this they lose in time. There is plenty of evidence that, when Western Europe was undergoing feudalisation, it was full of enthralled classes; and I imagine that the authority acquired by the feudal chief over the waste was much more of an advantage than the contrary to these classes, whom he planted largely there in colonies which have probably been sometimes mistaken for assemblages of originally free villagers. The status of the slave is always deplorable; the status of the predial slave is often worse than that of the personal or household slave; but the lowest depth of miserable subjection is reached when the person enthralled to the land is at the mercy of peasants, whether they exercise their powers singly or in communities.

Whether the Indian village-communities had wholly lost their capacity for the absorption of strangers when the British dominion began, is a point on which I have heard several contradictory opinions; but it is beyond doubt that the influence of the British Government, which in this respect is nothing more than the ordinary influence of settled authority, has tended steadily to turn the communities into close corporations. The definition of rights which it has effected through its various judicial agencies—the process of law by which it punishes violations of right—above all the money value which it has given to all rights by the security which it has established from one end of India to another—have helped to make the classes in possession of vested rights cling to them with daily increasing tenacity. To a certain small extent this indirect and unintended process of shutting the door to the acquisition of new communal rights has been counteracted by a rough rule introduced by the English, and lately engrafted on the written law, under which the cultivator of the soil who has been in possession of it for a period of years is in some parts of India protected against a few of the extreme powers which attach to ownership of the modern English type. But the rule is now in some discredit, and the sphere of its operation has of late been much curtailed. And my own opinion (which I shall state more at length in the next Lecture) is, that even if the utmost effect were given to it, it would not make up for some of the inequalities of distribution between classes actually included in the village group which have made their way into it through the influence of economical ideas originating in the West. On the whole the conclusion which I have arrived at concerning the village-communities is that, during the primitive struggle for existence they were expansive and elastic bodies, and these properties may be perpetuated in them for any time by bad government. But tolerably good government takes away their absorptive power by its indirect effects, and can only restore it by direct interposition.

It was part of my design to append to these Lectures an epitome of the work in which Professor Nasse has attempted to connect the actual condition of landed property in much of England at the end of the last century as shown in the various publications of Marshall, with the early English forms of tenure and cultivation as known to us through the labours of English and German scholars. But I have abandoned my intention on learning that Nasse's book is likely to be made generally accessible through an English translation. The undertaking is one which presents considerable difficulties. Nasse complains of the unusual scarcity of English records bearing on tenure and agricultural custom, but in this place we may note another class of difficulties having its source in those abundant technicalities of English real-property law which are so hard to read by anybody except the professional lawyer; and yet another in the historical theory of their land law which almost all English lawyers have adopted, and which colours all English treatises and all the decisions of English Courts—a theory which, it is not unjust to say, practically regards the manorial system as having no ascertainable antecedents, and all rights *primâ facie* inconsistent with it as having established themselves through prescription and by the sufferance of the lord. I may be allowed to say that the book in which Nasse has knotted together the two ends of the historical thread is a very extraordinary one to be written by a foreigner. Much of it deals with matter which can only be discussed appropriately in other departments of study; but I may notice in this place one set of causes, of a purely juridical nature, which, besides those assigned by Nasse, tended in later times to throw small or yeoman properties into the hands of large landowners. The popular opinion much exaggerates the extent to which this accumulation of landed properties had proceeded before the great inclosures of the last century, but still it had gone some length, and undoubtedly one cause was the influence, not at first strongly felt, of the Statute of Devises. Each landed proprietor ultimately acquired the power—within limits certainly, but very wide ones—to create a private law for his own estate. The efforts of English judges to introduce order into this chaos made it rather worse; for the expedient which they adopted for the purpose was to give a forced technical meaning to the popular language of testators. One large and complex branch of English law is still concerned with the rules for construing in a technical sense the loose popular expressions found in wills. Every estate, willed away by a testator technically unlearned, was in danger of being burdened with a mass of conflicting rights and interests, for the most part never contemplated by the testator himself.

There was only one way of insuring oneself against this consequence, and that was the employment of an expert to make the will; but there is reason to believe that the wholesale employment of legal experts which is now one of the singularities of this country is of comparatively modern date, since it is one of the traditions of the English Bar, derived from the last generation of lawyers, that among the great sources of litigation were at one time wills made by village schoolmasters. Estates thus burdened could only be held by very rich men; as they alone could provide and insure against the technical traps which abounded in the private law under which the land was held, or could render them innocuous by continued possession ending in a prescriptive title. It is impossible not to see that the practice of unshackled devise tended to bring small estates into the market as unprofitable to the holders through the complication of interests in them, and at the same time tended to make them purchaseable by rich men only.

The simple truth is that, if a system of small or peasant holdings is to continue, the power of testators must be severely restrained in order to produce simplicity in the law of the estate. It does not at all follow that the restrictions must be those of the Code Napoleon; but restrictions there must be, and I venture to think that a not unsatisfactory solution of the problem is to be found in the law by which the Indian Government has recently sought to control the power of will-making, which the early English judges either introduced into India or invested with proportions which had never belonged to it before.

3. *The Urban Community*

BY MAX WEBER

Economic Character of the City: Market Settlement

THE MANY definitions of the city have only one element in common: namely that the city

Reprinted from Max Weber, *The City*, trans. and ed. Don Martindale and Gertrud Neuwirth (Glencoe, Ill.: The Free Press, 1958), chap. i, pp. 65–75, with the permission of The Free Press.

consists simply of a collection of one or more separate dwellings but is a relatively closed settlement. Customarily, though not exclusively, in cities the houses are built closely to each other, often, today, wall to wall. This massing of elements interpenetrates the everyday concept of the "city" which is thought of quantitatively as a large locality. In itself this is not imprecise for the city often represents a locality and dense settlement of dwellings forming a colony so extensive that personal reciprocal acquaintance of the inhabitants is lacking. However, if interpreted in this way only very large localities could qualify as cities; moreover it would be ambiguous, for various cultural factors determine the size at which "impersonality" tends to appear. Precisely this impersonality was absent in many historical localities possessing the legal character of cities. Even in contemporary Russia there are villages comprising many thousands of inhabitants which are, thus, larger than many old "cities" (for example, in the Polish colonial area of the German East) which had only a few hundred inhabitants. Both in terms of what it would include and what it would exclude size alone can hardly be sufficient to define the city.

Economically defined, the city is a settlement the inhabitants of which live primarily off trade and commerce rather than agriculture. However, it is not altogether proper to call all localities "cities" which are dominated by trade and commerce. This would include in the concept "city" colonies made up of family members and maintaining a single, practically hereditary trade establishment such as the "trade villages" of Asia and Russia. It is necessary to add a certain "versatility" of practiced trades to the characteristics of the city. However, this in itself does not appear suitable as the single distinguishing characteristic of the city either.

Economic versatility can be established in at least two ways: by the presence of a feudal estate or a market. The economic and political needs of a feudal or princely estate can encourage specialization in trade products in providing a demand for which work is performed and goods are bartered. However, even though the *oikos* of a lord or prince is as large as a city, a colony of artisans and small merchants bound to villein services is not customarily called a "city" even though historically a large proportion of important "cities" originated in such settlements. In cities of such origin the products for a prince's court often remained a highly important, even chief, source of income for the settlers.

The other method of establishing economic versatility is more generally important for the "city"; this is the existence in the place of settlement of a regular rather than an occasional exchange of goods. The market becomes an essential component in the livelihood of the settlers. To be sure, not every "market" converted the locality in which it was found into a city. The periodic fairs and yearly foreign-trade markets at which traveling merchants met at fixed times to sell their goods in wholesale or retail lots to each other or to consumers often occurred in places which we would call "villages."

Thus, we wish to speak of a "city" only in cases where the local inhabitants satisfy an economically substantial part of their daily wants in the local market, and to an essential extent by products which the local population and that of the immediate hinterland produced for sale in the market or acquired in other ways. In the meaning employed here the "city" is a market place. The local market forms the economic center of the colony in which, due to the specialization in economic products, both the non-urban population and urbanites satisfy their wants for articles of trade and commerce. Wherever it appeared as a configuration different from the country it was normal for the city to be both a lordly or princely residence as well as a market place. It simultaneously possessed centers of both kinds, *oikos* and market and frequently in addition to the regular market it also served as periodic foreign markets of traveling merchants. In the meaning of the word here, the city is a "market settlement."

Often the existence of a market rests upon the concessions and guarantees of protection by a lord or prince. They were often interested in such things as a regular supply of foreign commercial articles and trade products, in tolls, in moneys for escorts and other protection fees, in market tariffs and taxes from law suits. However, the lord or prince might also hope to profit from the local settlement of tradesmen and merchants capable of paying taxes and, as soon as the market settlement arose around the market, from land rents arising therefrom. Such opportunities were of especial importance to the lord or prince since they represented chances for monetary revenues and the increase in his treasure of precious metal.

However, the city could lack any attachment, physical or otherwise, to a lordly or princely residence. This was the case when it originated as a pure market settlement at a suitable intersection point (*Umschlageplatz*) where the means of transportation were changed by virtue of concession to nonresident lords or princes or usurpation by the interested parties themselves. This could assume the form of concessions to entrepreneurs—permitting them to lay out a market and recruit settlers for it. Such capitalistic establishment of cities was especially frequent in medieval frontier areas, particularly in East, North, and Central Europe. Historically, though not as a rule, the practice has appeared throughout the world.

Without any attachment to the court of a prince or without princely concessions, the city could arise through the association of foreign invaders, naval warriors, or commercial settlers or, finally, native parties interested in the carrying trade. This occurred frequently in the early Middle Ages. The resultant city could be a pure market place. However, it is more usual to find large princely or patrimonial households and a market conjoined. In this case the eminent household as one contact point of the city could satisfy its wants either primarily by means of a natural economy (that is by villein service or natural service or taxes placed upon the artisans and merchants dependent on it) or it could supply itself more or less secondarily by barter in the local market as that market's most important buyer. The more pronounced the latter relation the more distinct the market foundation of the city looms and the city ceases by degrees to be a mere appendaged market settlement alongside the *oikos*. Despite attachment to the large household it then became a market city. As a rule the quantitative expansion of the original princely city and its economic importance go hand in hand with an increase in the satisfaction of wants in the market by the princely household and other large urban households attached to that of the prince as courts of vassals or major officials.

Types of Consumer and Producer City

Similar to the city of the prince, the inhabitants of which are economically dependent upon the purchasing power of noble households are cities in which the purchasing power of other larger consumers, such as rentiers, determines the economic opportunities of resident tradesmen and merchants. In terms of the kind and source of their incomes such larger consumers may be of quite varied types. They may be officials who spend their legal and illegal income in the city or lords or other political power holders who spend their non-urban land rents or politically determined incomes there. In either of these cases the city closely approximates the princely city for it depends upon patrimonial and political incomes which supply the purchasing power of large consumers. Peking was a city of officials; Moscow, before suspension of serfdom, was a land-rent city.

Different in principle are the superficially similar cities in which urban land-rents are determined by traffic monopolies of landed property. Such cities originate in the trade and commerce consolidated in the hands of an urban aristocracy. This type of development has always been widespread: it appeared in Antiquity; in the Near East until the Byzantine Empire; and in the Middle Ages. The city that emerges is not economically of a rentier type but is, rather, a merchant or trade city the rents of which represent a tribute of acquisitors to the owners of houses. The conceptual differentiation of this case from the one in which rents are not deter-

mined by tributary obligations to monopolists but by non-urban sources, should not obscure the interrelation in the past of both forms. The large consumers can be rentiers spending their business incomes (today mainly interest on bonds, dividends or shares) in the city. Whereupon purchasing power rests on capitalistically conditioned monetary rentier sources as in the city of Arnheim. Or purchasing power can depend upon state pensions or other state rents as appears in a "pensionopolis" like Wiesbaden. In all similar cases one may describe the urban form as a consumer city, for the presence in residence of large consumers of special economic character is of decisive economic importance for the local tradesmen and merchants.

A contrasting form is presented by the producer city. The increase in population and purchasing power in the city may be due, as for example in Essen or Bochum, to the location there of factories, manufactures, or home-work industries supplying outside territories—thus representing the modern type. Or, again, the crafts and trades of the locality may ship their goods away as in cities of Asiatic, Ancient, and Medieval types. In either case the consumers for the local market are made up of large consumers if they are residents and/or entrepreneurs, workers and craftsmen who form the great mass, and merchants and benefactors of land-rent supported indirectly by the workers and craftsmen.

The trade city and merchant city are confronted by the consumer city in which the purchasing power of its larger consumers rests on the retail for profit of foreign products on the local market (for example, the woolen drapers in the Middle Ages), the foreign sale for profit of local products or goods obtained by native producers (for example, the herring of the Hansa) or the purchase of foreign products and their sale with or without storage at the place to the outside (intermediate commercial cities). Very frequently a combination of all these economic activities occurred: the *commenda* and *societas maris* implied that a *tractator* (travelling merchant) journied to Levantine markets with products purchased with capital entrusted to him by resident capitalists. Often the *tractator* traveled entirely in ballast. He sold these products in the East and with the proceeds he purchased oriental articles brought back for sale in the local market. The profits of the undertaking were then divided between *tractator* and capitalist according to prearranged formulas.

The purchasing power and tax ability of the commercial city rested on the local economic establishment as was also the case for the producers' city in contrast to the consumers' city. The economic opportunities of the shipping and transport trade and of numerous secondary wholesale and retail activities were at the disposal of the merchants. However the economic activity of these establishments was not entirely executed for the local retail trade but in substantial measure for external trade. In principle, this state of affairs was similar to that of the modern city, which is the location of national and international financiers or large banks (London, Paris, Berlin) or of joint stock companies or cartels (Dusseldorf). It follows that today more than ever a predominant part of the earnings of firms flow to localities other than the place of earning. Moreover, a growing part of business proceeds are not consumed by their rightful receivers at the metropolitan location of the business but in suburban villas, rural resorts or international hotels. Parallel with these developments "city-towns" or city-districts consisting almost exclusively of business establishments are arising.

There is no intention here of advancing the further casuistic distinctions required by a purely economic theory of the city. Moreover, it hardly needs to be mentioned that actual cities nearly always represent mixed types. Thus, if cities are to be economically classified at all, it must be in terms of their prevailing economic component.

Relation of the City to Agriculture

The relation of the city to agriculture has not been clear cut. There were and are "semi-rural cities" (*Ackerburgerstaedte*) localities which while serving as places of market traffic and centers of typically urban trade, are sharply separated from the average city by the presence of a broad stratum of resident burghers satisfying a large part of their food needs through cultivation and even producing food for sale. Normally the larger the city the less the opportunity for urban residents to dispose of acreage in relation to their food needs at the same time without controlling a self-sufficient pasture and wood lot in the manner of the village. Cologne, the largest German city in the Middle Ages, almost completely lacked the *Allmende* (commons) from the beginning though the commons was not absent from any normal village of the time. Other German and foreign medieval cities at least placed considerable pastures and woods at the disposal of their burghers.

The presence of large acreages accessible to the urbanite is found more frequently as one turns attention to the south or back toward antiquity. While today we justly regard the typical "urbanite" as a man who does not supply his own food need on his own land, originally the contrary was the case for the majority of typical ancient cities. In contrast to the medieval situation, the ancient urbanite was quite legitimately characterized by the fact that a *kleros, fundus* (In Israel: *chelek*) which he called his own, was a parcel of land which fed him. The full urbanite of antiquity was a semi-peasant.

In the Medieval period, as in Antiquity, agricultural property was retained in the hands of merchant strata. This was more frequently the case in the south than in the north of Europe. In both medieval and ancient city states agricultural properties, occasionally of quite exorbitant size, were found widely scattered, either being politically dominated by municipal authorities of powerful cities or in the possession of eminent individual citizen landlords. Examples are supplied by the Cheronesic domination of the Miltiades or the political or lordly estates of medieval aristocratic families, such as the Genoese Grimaldi, in the provinces or overseas.

As a general rule inter-local estates and the sovereign rights of individual citizens were not the objects of an urban economic policy. However, mixed conditions at times arose such that according to the circumstances estates were guaranteed to individuals by the city. In the nature of the case this only occurred when the individuals whose estates were guaranteed by the city belonged to the most powerful patricians. In such cases the estate was acquired and maintained through indirect help of civic power which in turn might share in its economic and political usufruct. This was frequently the case in the past.

The relation of the city as agent of trade and commerce to the land as producer of food comprises one aspect of the "urban economy" and forms a special "economic stage" between the "household economy" on the one hand and the "national economy" on the other. When the city is visualized in this manner, however, politico-economic aspects are conceptually fused with pure economic aspects and conceived as forming one whole. The mere fact that merchants and tradesmen live crowded together carrying on a regular satisfaction of daily needs in the market does not exhaust the concept of the "city." Where only the satisfaction of agricultural needs occurs within closed settlements and where—what is not identical with it— agricultural production appears in relation to nonagricultural acquisition, and when the presence or absence of markets constitutes the difference, we speak of trade and commercial localities and of small market-towns, but not of cities. There were, thus, hidden non-economic dimensions in the phenomena brought under review in the previous sections. It is time to expand the concept of the "city" to include extra-economic factors.

The Politico-Administrative Concept
of the City

Beside possessing an accumulation of abodes the city also has an economic association with its own landed property and a budget of receipts and expenditure. Such an economic association may also appear in the village no matter how great the quantitative differences. Moreover, it was not peculiar to the city alone, at least in the past, that it was both an economic and a regulatory association. Trespass restrictions, pasture regulations, the prohibition of the export of wood and straw, and similar regulations are known to the village, constituting an economic policy of the association as such.

The cities of the past were differentiated only by the kinds of regulations which appeared. Only the objects of political economic regulation on behalf of the association and the range of characteristic measures embraced by them were peculiar. It goes without saying that measures of the "urban economic policy" took substantial account of the fact that under the transportation conditions of the time the majority of all inland cities were dependent upon the agricultural resources of the immediate hinterland. As shown by the grain policies of Athens and Rome this was true for maritime cities. In a majority, not all, of urban trades areas, opportunity was provided for the natural "play of the market." The urban market supplied the normal, not the sole, place for the exchange of products, especially food.

Account also must be taken of the fact that production for trade was predominantly in the form of artisan technology organized in specialized small establishments. Such production operated without or with little capital and with strictly limited numbers of journeymen who were trained in long apprenticeships. Such production was economically in the form of wage worker as price work for customers. Sale to the local retailers was largely a sale to customers.

The market conditions of the time were the kind that would naturally emerge, given the above facts. The so-called "urban economic policy" was basically characterized by its attempt to stabilize the conditions of the local urban economy by means of economic regulations in the interest of permanently and cheaply feeding the masses and standardizing the economic opportunities of tradesmen and merchants. However, as we shall see, economic regulation was not the sole object of the urban economic policy nor, when it historically appears, was it fully developed. It emerges only under the political regime of the guild. Finally it can not be proved to be simply a transitional stage in the development of all

cities. In any case, the urban economic policy does not represent a universal stage in economic evolution.

On the basis of customer relations and specialized small establishments operating without capital, the local urban market with its exchange between agricultural and non-agricultural producers and resident merchants, represents a kind of economic counterpart to barter as against systematically divided performances in terms of work and taxes of a specialized dependent economy in connection with the *oikos,* having its basis in the accumulation and integration of work in the manner, without exchange occurring inside. Following out the parallel: the *regulation* (urban economic policy) of the exchange and production conditions in the city represent the counterpart to the *organization* (traditional and feudal-contractual) of activities united in the economy of the *oikos.*

The very fact that in drawing these distinctions we are led to use the concepts of an "urban economic area" and "urban area," and "urban authority," already indicates that the concept of the "city" can and must be examined in terms of a series of concepts other than the purely economic categories so far employed.

The additional concepts required for analysis of the city are political. This already appears in the fact that the urban economic policy itself may be the work of a prince to whom political dominion of the city with its inhabitants belongs. In this case when there is an urban economic policy it is determined *for* the inhabitants of the city not *by* them. However even when this is the case the city must still be considered to be a partially autonomous association, a "community" with special political and administrative arrangements.

The economic concept previously discussed must be entirely separated from the political-administrative concept of the city. Only in the latter sense may a special *area* belong to the city. A locale can be held to be a city in a political-administrative sense though it would not qualify as a city economically. In the Middle Ages there were areas legally defined as "cities" in which the inhabitants derived ninety percent or more of their livelihood from agriculture, representing a far larger fraction of their income than that of the inhabitants of many localities legally defined as "villages."

Naturally, the transition from such semi-rural cities to consumers', producers' or commercial cities is quite fluid. In those settlements which differ administratively from the village and are thus dealt with as cities only one thing, namely, the kind of regulations of land-owning, is customarily different from rural land-owning forms. Economically such cities are differentiated by a special kind of rent situation presented in urban real estate which consists in house ownership to which land ownership is accessory. The position of urban real estate is connected administratively with special taxation principles. It is bound even more closely to a further element decisive for the political-administrative concept of the city and standing entirely outside the purely economic analysis, namely, the fortress.

Fortress and Garrison

It is very significant that the city in the past, in Antiquity and the Middle Ages, outside as well as within Europe, was also a special fortress or garrison. At present this property of the city has been entirely lost, but it was not universal even in the past. In Japan, for example, it was not the rule. Administratively one may, with Rathgen, doubt the existence of cities at all. In contrast to Japan, in China every city was surrounded with a gigantic ring of walls. However, it is also true that many economically rural localities which were not cities in the administrative sense, possessed walls at all times. In China such places were not the seat of state authorities.

In many Mediterranean areas such as Sicily a man living outside the urban walls as a rural worker and country resident is almost unknown. This is a product of century-long insecurity. By contrast in old Hellas the Spartan polis sparkled by the absence of walls, yet the property of being a "garrison-town" was met. Sparta despised walls for the very reason that it was a permanent open military camp.

Though there is still dispute as to how long Athens was without walls, like all Hellenic cities except Sparta it contained in the Acropolis a castle built on rock in the same manner as Ekbantama and Persepolis which were royal castles with surrounding settlements. The castle or wall belonged normally to Oriental as well as to ancient Mediterranean and ordinary medieval cities.

4. European Feudalism

BY MARC BLOCH

THE ADJECTIVE *feodalis* (relating to the fief) and the French substantive *féodalité,* used in the restricted sense of a quality peculiar to a fief, date the first from the Middle Ages, the second probably from the sixteenth century. But it was not before the eighteenth century that the custom arose of using for the designation of a whole system of social organization either compound expressions like feudal regime, government or system or, a little later, abstract substantives such as *féodalité* or feudalism. German historians in general have adopted *Lehnwesen* from *Lehn,* the German equivalent of fief. The extension of the use of a word derived from a particular institution, the fief, which can scarcely be considered the central and only significant institution of feudalism, to characterize the social regime prevailing widely during the Middle Ages, and more particularly from the tenth to the thirteenth centuries, in the greater part of western and central Europe is mainly attributable to the influence of Montesquieu. Although Montesquieu considered the establishment in Europe of "feudal laws" a phenomenon *sui generis,* "an event occurring once in the world and destined perhaps never to occur again," modern sociologists and comparative historians have detected in other civilizations the existence of institutions analogous to those of the Middle Ages. Consequently the term feudalism has come to be applied to a mode of social organization that may recur in divers forms in differing periods and environments. Mediaeval European feudalism nevertheless remains the model of all feudal systems as well as the best known.

The origins of the European feudal regime have too frequently been discussed under the form of an ethnic dilemma: are they Roman or Germanic? As a matter of fact the social type that is called feudalism was born in Europe of conditions peculiar to the society from which it sprang. Since feudal society did not stamp itself upon a clean slate, but

Reprinted from Marc Bloch, "European Feudalism," in *Encyclopaedia of the Social Sciences* (New York: Macmillan Co., 1931), VI, 203–10, with the permission of the Macmillan Co.

evolved little by little through the slow adaptation and modification of older usages, it is not difficult to discover in it traces of earlier systems of organization. But these elements were borrowed from very diverse environments. The feudal vocabulary itself, which combines Roman elements—one of them, the term vassal, taken by the Romans from the Celts —with Germanic elements by its very medley represents the singularly mixed character of the society in which feudalism took its rise.

The most remarkable characteristic of the western world at the beginning of the Middle Ages was the fact that it had been constituted by the encounter and fusion of civilizations existing at very unequal stages of evolution. On the one hand, there was the Roman or Romano-Hellenic world, itself hardly a unit in its foundations. For under the apparent uniformity of the imperial façade many local usages persisted which imposed conditions of life at times quite dissimilar upon the various social groups. On the other hand, there was the still comparatively primitive civilization of the peoples of ancient Germany, who had invaded the Roman domains and carved kingdoms out of it.

The bankruptcy of the state represents the most potent fact during this period. Whatever care the kingdoms of the barbarians may have taken to turn to their profit the formidable administrative system of ancient Rome—already, moreover, far advanced in decay at the time of the great invasions—however remarkable an effort at rehabilitation the monarchy of the first Carolingians may have represented after a century of extreme disorder, the powerlessness of the central government to exercise an effective control over a territory much too extensive for the forces at its disposal betrayed itself more and more glaringly, and for a long period after the middle of the ninth century, in a manner truly irremediable. Undoubtedly the reenforcement accruing from the Germanic traditions was not in this regard entirely negligible; the conception of royalty as the appanage of a sacred family, which derived from the most primitive notions of ancient Germany, resulted in a dynastic perpetuity better established than any that the Roman Empire had ever known. The idea of the state—or, more accurately, the idea of royalty—never entirely vanished. Likewise the institutions codified by the Carolingians long continued, more or less deformed, to exercise an influence. Men, however, lost the habit of expecting protection from a too distant sovereign. They sought it elsewhere and supplanted their obedience to the more remote ruler by other ties of dependence. The state tax ceased to be collected and the administration of justice was parceled out among a crowd of local authorities that had little or no connection with a central organism.

Less apparent but not less grave was the disturbance among social groups founded but lately upon a kinship more or less remote and fictitious, such as clan or tribe. It is impossible to ascertain to what degree the tradition of the old clannish relations had been able to survive in Roman Gaul and Italy, although in Great Britain the history of the imperfectly Romanized Celtic lands at the beginning of the Middle Ages shows them still very strong. On the other hand, it cannot be doubted that this kind of social group was of great importance among the German peoples during the period immediately preceding that of the invasions. But the great turmoil of the conquest, together, no doubt, with certain tendencies from within, weakened these ties. Not that kinship relations ceased during the entire Middle Ages to be a human bond of immense strength. The numerous family feuds which jeopardized the active and passive solidarity of groups in all grades of the social hierarchy bear witness to the strength of these ties. So do various institutions juridical and economic. But these ties came to apply only to a comparatively restricted group whose common descent was easy to establish, namely, the family in the strict sense of the word and no longer the clan or the tribe. This group, which made room for paternal as well as maternal kinship, was not very clearly defined and most of the obligations or modes of living imposed upon its members resulted rather from habits and feelings than from legally defined constraints. The ties of kinship continued to exist very powerfully in the feudal society but they took their place beside new ties after which they tended to pattern themselves and to which they were at times considered inferior.

The social environment in which the feudal relations developed was characterized by an economic system in which exchange although not entirely absent was comparatively rare and in which the not very abundant specie played but a restricted role. It has sometimes been said that at that time land was the only form of wealth. This statement needs explanation and qualification. It cannot be denied that the paucity of commercial relations caused the very existence of every man to depend narrowly upon his possibility of disposing in some way of the resources furnished by a portion of the soil placed under his control. But an important fraction of the population drew its revenue from the land only indirectly under the form of personal service in money or in kind for the use of the land. Moreover, the possession of superior rights to the land was for the possessor in many respects but a means of exercising an effective power of command over the men to whom he conceded or permitted the direct enjoyment of the fields. One of the essential characteristics of feudalism is that prestige and social worth sprang less from the free disposal of property than from the free disposal of human forces. But the difficulty of commercial exchange had a considerable effect upon the structure of society. The absence of an easy flow of sales and purchases such as exists in present day societies prevented the formation of agricultural or industrial salaried classes and of any body of functionaries remunerated periodically in money.

In the absence then of a strong state, of blood ties capable of dominating the whole life and of an economic system founded upon money payments there grew up in Carolingian and post-Carolingian society relations of man to man of a peculiar type. The superior individual granted his protection and divers material advantages that assured a subsistence to the dependent directly or indirectly; the inferior pledged various prestations or various services and was under a general obligation to render aid. These relations were not always freely assumed nor did they imply a universally satisfactory equilibrium between the two parties. Built upon authority, the feudal regime never ceased to contain a great number of constraints, violences and abuses. However, this idea of the personal bond, hierarchic and synallagmatic in character, dominated European feudalism.

Societies before the rise of feudalism already contained examples of relations of this sort. These did not, however, play the preponderant role that they were to assume later. Rural lordship existed in the Roman world and also at least in germ in the Germanic world. Roman society never ceased to give a large place to patron and client relationship. Around the powerful surged a great crowd of persons—at times themselves of high rank—who commended themselves to them. In addition these clienteles included as a general rule numerous former slaves freed by their masters in exchange for certain obligations of an economic nature and a general duty of fidelity (*obsequium*). Celtic society before the conquest also contained similar groups. In Germany alongside the normal relations that united the freeman to his family, his clan and his people others more transitory had grown up in the form of bands of faithful men of every origin gathered around a chief. Nourished in his dwelling, receiving from him horses and armor, they accompanied him to battle and constituted his strength and prestige. In this way people became accustomed to a certain conception of social bonds which developing in a favorable environment were to give rise to feudalism proper.

The leading features of feudalism in its fully developed form are the system of vassalage and the institution of the fief. As early as the Frankish and Lombard periods a great number of freemen of all ranks felt the need of seeking the protection of someone more powerful than themselves or of securing a decent livelihood by offering their military services to a superior. The poorest became slaves or simply tenants. But all who could clung to their dignity as men legally free and preferred not to lower themselves to the less honorable services which burdened the tenant liable to the corvée. They "commended" themselves *ingenuili ordine*. Exalted persons, on the other hand, sought to surround themselves with loyal people who should be attached to them by solid bonds. Thus arose the contract of dependence most characteristic of the feudal system.

In Frankish law, at least, the relations of vassalage were established by means of a formal act to which a little later the name homage was applied (in German *Mannschaft* or *Hulde*). The future vassal placed his hands in the lord's joined hands while repeating a few words promising loyalty, after which lord and vassal kissed each other on the mouth. As this ceremony, probably borrowed from old German traditions, gave no place to any religious elements, the custom early arose of following it up with an oath of fealty taken by the vassal on the Gospel or on relics.

The obligations created by homage and fealty held as long as both contracting parties were alive. They were extinguished upon the death of either. When heredity later came into play it undermined the whole system of vassalage. But heredity itself, as applying to the vassalic bonds, always remained rather a matter of practise than of law. In case of the death of lord or vassal a new offer of homage was in every case considered necessary to revive the tie. Being attached to concrete forms the vassalic right held bound only the two persons whom the ceremony brought face to face.

The reciprocal obligations of lord and vassal rested upon general simple principles susceptible in their details of infinite modifications and regulated with an increasing precision by local custom. The vassal owed the lord fidelity, obedience in the face of the whole world and aid in all circumstances in which the lord might need it. He supported him with his counsel, assisted him on occasion in his judicial functions and opened his purse to him in case of necessity. Little by little the cases in which this pecuniary aid—also called tallage—was legitimately exactable tended to become more defined and restricted to such occasions as the celebration of the knighthood of the lord's eldest son and of the marriage of his eldest daughter, ransom and so on. Above all the vassal owed the lord military service. This form of aid gradually came to predominate over all others.

In return the lord owed his man his protection; he assumed his defense before the tribunals, when there still were state tribunals; he avenged his wrongs and cared for his orphans until they became of age. Besides he assured him a livelihood in various ways and especially in the form of an economic grant generally known as a fief.

In the absence of a salary system there existed but two means of remunerating services. The master could receive his dependents in his own house, assure them food and shelter (*provende*), even clothe them; or he could assign them a piece of land upon which they might support themselves either directly or through returns received from those allowed to work it.

Of "provided" vassals nurtured in the lord's dwelling there were certainly a great number in the ninth and tenth centuries. They were still to be met with in the France of Philip Augustus. But vassals and lords early agreed in preferring the system of allotments of land, which provided the former with a greater independence and relieved the latter from the responsibility of looking after the support—particularly difficult under a rudimentary economic regime—of numerous and at times turbulent bands. Gradually most of the vassals found themselves "housed" (*chasés, casati*). The land assigned to them derived its peculiar features from the fact that it carried with it certain clearly defined services that were to be performed for the grantor. The property thus granted was at first called *beneficium*. Then little by little in the countries of Romanic speech which had adopted Frankish customs this term was supplanted (to such an extent that it has left not a trace in the Gallo-Roman dialects) by a term of Germanic origin: fief (*fevum* or *feodum*). The possession of land without obligation to any superior was, after the Frankish period, called alodial tenure. When a freeholder of this kind felt the need of commending himself he was in most cases forced to turn over his holding to the lord and receive it back as a fief. With the more complete feudalization of society these alodia decreased in number.

As the tenure service was a general institution of the economy of the period, there always existed a very great number of fiefs whose holders were not vassals: fiefs of artisans attached to the lord, such as painters and carpenters; of servants, such as cooks and doorkeepers; of officials charged with the administration of the manors, such as mayors and provosts. But any land granted to a

vassal could be only a fief. Little by little, in proportion as the class of vassals tended to be transformed into nobility their fiefs appeared of a superior condition to those that were encumbered with humbler services, and eventually the jurists inclined to regard them as the only true fiefs. The institution of the fief, like that of homage, retained its personal character and was effective only for the lifetime of the contracting parties. Whenever either of them died the concession had to be renewed in the form of the symbolic tradition of investiture. With the establishment of the hereditary principle this ceremony became the means whereby the lord collected a sum of money (relief) as the price for the renewal of the fief.

On the other hand, it frequently happened that the vassal himself disposed of the very fiefs he held from a superior lord as fiefs for his own men. This subinfeudation, in principle, presumed the assent of the grantor of the original fief, but social necessities made it more and more customary to dispense with this. Thus alongside of and to a large extent parallel to the chains of personal dependence there arose chains of landed dependence. Mediaeval law in contrast with the Roman and modern notions of landed property conceived the soil as being subject to a great number of real rights differing among themselves and superimposed. Each of them had the value of a possession protected by custom (*saisine*, seisin, *Gewehr*) and none was clothed with that absolute character which the word property carries with it.

The seigniory, or manor, was the fundamental unit of the feudal regime. Under the name of villa it was very widespread in Gaul and in Roman Italy and in both cases doubtless went back to very old traditions such as those of village or clan chieftains. The seigniory usually consisted of several small farms. The cultivators were not the owners of the land but owed various duties and services to a lord who exercised over them a general power of command and from whom they held their lands on condition of a renewal of the investiture and the payment of a certain sum with every mutation. Generally in the Frankish period the lord also possessed a vast farm, the demesne, whose cultivation was assured in large part by the corvées due from the tenants. After the twelfth century these demesnes, chopped up into small farms, decreased in importance, first in France and Italy, more slowly in Germany, and the lord tended to become a mere receiver of land rents.

In gathering round the seigniory humble folk obeyed the same need of protection that men of a higher rank sought to satisfy in vassalage. The small peasant handed over his alodium to the lord and received it back under the form of a tenure with dues and corvées attached. Often he pledged his person and that of his descendants by the same act, thus entering into personal service. The life of the seigniory was regulated by custom. As the lords had every interest in keeping their lands peopled, the habit speedily arose of considering the peasant tenures, even the servile ones, as hereditary. Again, the seigniory fortified itself in the feudal period by appropriating a great number of state functions and by assuring the remuneration of the military class, which tended to rise above the others.

The churches figured among the principal possessors of seigniories. Some of them from the end of the Roman Empire obtained the right to retain the taxes levied upon their subjects. These privileges, confirmed and extended to churches more and more by the Frankish sovereigns, were the first form of immunity. This soon carried with it another advantage: the prohibition of representatives of the law—exacting and prone to be tyrannical—from trespassing upon immunized land to exercise their functions, notably their judicial powers. Analogous immunities were early obtained by lay lords.

In theory the men who lived upon a seigniory thus privileged remained answerable to the royal courts; their lord was responsible for their appearance. In reality the lord more and more tended to become a judge; he always had been so for his slaves, who at least in their relations to one another and to their master were answerable by the nature of things only to him. On the other hand, his role as protector seemed to confer upon him the right to maintain good order among his free tenants and his vassals. Under Charlemagne the state itself considered his intervention a guaranty of good order. After the fall of the Carolingian state the judicial power of the lord found a new lease of life in the usurpation of public functions, itself the consequence of the utilization of vassalage by the sovereigns.

In the Frankish period all freemen were liable to military service. But more and more the strength of armies seemed to center in horsemen equipped with complete armor and serving as leaders for little bands of other horsemen and of footmen. To remunerate the services of these knights, who accompanied them to the royal army or aided them in their blood feuds, the noblemen had acquired the habit of distributing fiefs among them; and, to make sure of their fidelity, of requesting homage. The sovereigns soon did the same. Notably Charles Martel, engrossed in his struggle against the Arabs and domestic enemies, created numerous military fiefs, carved largely from the domains of the

churches which he usurped. Commendation, which had in the beginning been a sure means for men of every class to find a protector, tended thus to become a social tie peculiar to a class of military vassals (of the king or the nobles), who were at the same time possessors of seigniories. By a parallel tendency the old ceremony of the delivery of arms, a heritage from Germanic traditions originally distinguishing the majority of all freemen, now applied only to specialized warriors. This was the "dubbing"; whoever had received it could give it in his turn and thereby make knights. This class, until the twelfth century still open to adventurers of every origin, had an ethics of its own, a code of honor and fidelity tinged more and more with religious ideas, and felt itself to be virtually an order.

On the other hand, to reward their representatives throughout the country, in particular the counts, the kings, not being able to put them on salary, distributed fiefs among them consisting either of lands or of a share of the royal revenues in the provinces. To bind them by a tie that had some strength they chose them from among their vassals or exacted homage of them. The royal vassals in their turn and the churches surrounded themselves with their own vassals and confided to them a part of their functions and the administration of a part of their property.

Social and economic conditions thus made for decentralization and produced a veritable parceling out of all the powers of the state, such as justice, the right to coin money, tolls and the like. The profits accruing from these powers fell not only to the former direct representatives of the state, such as the counts, or to the immunized churches, but also by a sort of secondary appropriation to the representatives of these first usurpers.

The introduction of the principle of heredity into the feudal system was of paramount importance. The lord, who had need of men, sought to retain the services of the dead vassal's sons. The vassal's son was usually quite willing to do homage to his father's lord, in whom he found a natural protector. Above all it was at this price alone that he could keep the ancestral fief. In fact heredity was adopted little by little as a rule of conduct demanded first by public opinion, then by custom, and the lord who demurred ran the risk of offending his men. Charles the Bald considered it to be normal. In Italy the emperor Conrad II established it as law for fiefs below those of a count. Neither in France nor in Germany was it ever the subject of any legislation. In France it was early made general with but few exceptions and in Germany it was adopted more quickly for fiefs of a lower order and more slowly for fiefs of greater importance.

At the same time that they became hereditary the fiefs tended to become alienable. Of course the lord's assent would always be necessary for alienation. But it became less and less admissible to refuse it. The fiefs, together with the authority attaching to them and with the fragments of state functions that often went along with them, became hereditary, resulting in a confusion of powers over men and things. Heredity, however, while it put a seal on the feudal system certainly compromised its very foundations.

In all consistency the vassal system would have required each vassal to have but one lord. That was the very condition of the entire devotion which was the first of his duties, and the Caroligian legislation had so decided. But it was a great temptation to take fiefs wherever one could get them; when the fiefs had become patrimonial it sometimes happened that a vassal received by inheritance or purchase a fief that was held from some lord other than the one to whom he had first done homage. Cases of vassals of two or more lords are found from the tenth century and they become more numerous in the later period. How was one to apportion obligations to the various masters? In France in the eleventh century the custom arose of choosing one of these allegiances as more binding than the others. This was called liege (pure) homage. But in the thirteenth century this system, in its turn, was rendered ineffectual by the very multiplication of the liege homages offered by the same vassal to different lords. One was then reduced to consider, among the liege homages, which always took the first place, and, among the simple ones, the first homage in date, or sometimes the one attached to the greater fief as the strongest. In Germany and Italy, where the liege homage never took root, these classifications by dates or according to the importance of the fiefs had always been in vogue. But such multifarious allegiances could no longer count for much.

An essential characteristic of the feudal contract was the theory that if one of the two contracting parties broke his pledges he thereby freed the other party from all obligations. But precise definition as to the circumstances under which non-fulfilment of the contract, whether on the part of the lord or of the vassal, justified the rupture was completely wanting. In spite of the efforts of Carolingian legislation this salient point remained vague. The absence of all recognized superior authority left it to the interested parties to arbitrate the particular case. This uncertainty, the unforeseen consequence of the synallagmatic character of the bond, smoothed the way for all kinds of felony.

Although the salient features of the feudal regime were very nearly the same in all countries of western Europe there were, nevertheless, certain national differences and peculiarities. Thus in France the parceling out of the powers of the state, notably the appropriation of justice, was carried farthest. There too the military class became most solidly constituted and developed its chivalrous code, which from there spread over all Europe. In Germany feudal conceptions did not pervade the judicial life so profoundly, and two codes of customary law developed side by side, the general laws of the different countries (*Landrecht*) and the laws of fiefs (*Lehnrecht*). The alodia there, as in Italy and the south of France, persisted in greater numbers than elsewhere. The exclusive right to invest the superior judges who dealt with criminal cases involving the death penalty remained in the hands of the royal power. The emperors also maintained a long and effective struggle against the inheritance of the great fiefs. But they had to accept the obligation to enfeoff again the fiefs having the powers of earldoms when they were left without heirs or had been confiscated. This, unlike the case of France, prevented the increase of the royal domain itself. In Italy the previous importance of the cities and the urban habits of a great part of the knights themselves early created a formidable rivalry to the powers of the landed lords.

In Russia a real feudal regime was in full process of development up to the moment when it was stifled by the power of the Muscovite state. As in the west, the vassalage of the boyars became transformed into a state nobility. They were, however, more strictly subject to the czar since the synallagmatic character of the contract of service had always been less marked than in the west. The seigniory, vigorously constituted, survived for a long time. In the Byzantine state of the first centuries there existed tenures burdened with military service for the state but these were tenures of peasant soldiers. The emperors viewed these free peasants as constituting the strength of the army and struggled against their being crushed by the seigniories. From the eleventh century their resistance weakened and finally the seigniory, favored with immunities and obliged by way of compensation to furnish soldiers to the state, became the keystone of the military organization. But these seigniories were not themselves subdivided in hierarchical form by bonds of fiefs and vassalage; so that one of the essential characteristics of feudalism—that gradation of obligations which in Europe preserved the homogeneity of the political organization—was always lacking in Byzantium. The Scandinavian peninsula offers a clear case of a country in which for want of one of the primary elements of feudal organization, that of seigniorial economy, a real feudalism failed to arise.

Much more significant is the distinction between countries in which feudalism had grown up spontaneously and those in which it had been planted by conquest. In the former the feudal regime was never able to attain that systematic character that hardly belongs to any but institutions formed fully accoutered and thereby unembarrassed with survivals. It appears, on the contrary, as a much more symmetrical edifice in the countries in which it was planted by conquest, such as the Latin states of the Holy Land, the Norman kingdom of southern Italy and especially England.

The social condition of England at the time of the conquest was in many respects analogous to that of Frankish Gaul at the time when the feudal system began to take shape. Both were marked by a slow absorption of the free peasants in the framework of a seigniory whose dependents still obeyed juridical statutes of extreme variety, by a tendency toward the generalization of dependent relations, by the appropriation of justice by the powerful, by the existence of tenures burdened with military service and called as in Germany *Laen,* and by the importance of the thanes, a class fairly similar to that of the Frankish royal vassals. But all that was poorly coordinated and the fusion of the relations of fief and vassalage had not been effected. The Norman kings imposed upon the country a feudal system conceived to their advantage. The boundaries of the seigniories (called manors) were definitely fixed; a sort of serfdom was introduced which, however, was in the course of time to evolve in a very different direction from the French; in spite of the much greater power of royal justice than in France the English lords were considered the exclusive judges of their tenants in their relations with them, which was finally to prevent the inheritance of tenures. Above all, the kings divided the whole country into military fiefs according to a system brought over from their Norman duchy. The tenants in chief were each to furnish the king with a certain number of knights. To be able to do so they distributed fiefs in their return. But these chains of dependence soon becoming practically hereditary all led back to the king, from whom in the last analysis all land was held, even that of the church (under the form of the "free alms"). The alodium, a foreign body in the feudal world of the continent, did not exist at all in England. Finally, the king could demand the oath of fealty of his vassals' vassals.

At the end of the twelfth century a profound change took place in European society characterized by the formation of classes, economic transformations and the development of the state. In the tenth or eleventh century society consisted primarily of groups of dependents. As the sense of personal ties wore away, the human mass tended to organize itself in large classes arranged in a hierarchy. Knighthood became hereditary and changed into nobility. In England indeed the noble never had precise lawful privileges clearly separating him from the freeman. In Italy, habituated to a kind of life increasingly urban, he was hardly to be distinguished from the rich burgher. In France, on the contrary, the nobility made of itself a single closed class to which only the king could introduce new members. In Germany a whole hierarchy established itself within the nobility, and according to the theory of the *Heerschild* no member of one of these subclasses could without derogation accept a fief from a man occupying a lower grade.

Beginning in the twelfth century economic exchange became more active. The cities developed and relations quite foreign to the feudal type came to light. Bound to his fellow townsmen by an oath of mutual aid, which unlike the vassal oath united equals, the townsman needed no other protector than the community to which he belonged. His social code too was quite different from that of the military vassal. Moreover, the advent of a new economic regime founded upon exchange and money payment permitted the extension of the salaried class and at every step of the social scale took away from the fief and the enfeoffment any *raison d'être* for their functions.

This economic transformation in turn contributed to the rebirth of the state. Hired troops took the place of the vassals, who nearly everwhere had greatly succeeded in limiting their obligations. Corps of salaried officials subject to dismissal were formed. Such concentration of power did not redound solely to the advantage of the kings. In France and Germany certain royal vassals had brought under their control a great number of earldoms and multiform seigniorial rights and exalted their power above the crowd of lesser seigniories. While in France the great principalities thus formed were at last absorbed by the royal power, in Germany they well nigh annihilated it. In Italy the states formed around and by leading cities chiefly benefited from this movement. Everywhere the state, whatever its nature, was henceforth a master and protector. He who now depended only on it without "commending" himself to anyone no longer felt isolated.

The rural seigniory lasted much longer. Being adapted to the needs of the capitalistic era it still continued to flourish throughout the sixteenth, seventeenth and eighteenth centuries; it was transplanted by Europeans into various colonies, notably French Canada. It was not abolished in France until the revolution; it disappeared definitely from Germany—aside from a few survivals—in 1848; in England it disappeared but very slowly from the statute book and left behind a very strong imprint on the constitution of rural society.

The same needs from which vassalage took its rise long continued to make themselves felt, at least intermittently in troubled periods. The homage, now but an empty rite, had its substitutes. The English liverymen in the time of the Wars of the Roses are reminiscent of the mesne tenants of the early Middle Ages. In the France of the seventeenth century to belong to a great lord afforded the gentry the best means of getting on. The orders of knighthood were invented by the princes at the close of the Middle Ages to insure the fidelity of those admitted to them; Napoleon himself in establishing the Legion of Honor had much the same idea. But those orders that have survived, as well as their contemporary imitations, have lost every role but that of honorific distinction.

In the last centuries of the Middle Ages the states had sought to turn to account the old feudal organization, requiring of vassals if not an active military service at least a compensatory tax. But these attempts had little success. In England a law of the Commonwealth in 1656, confirmed by the Restoration in 1660, abolished all distinction between the fiefs of knights and the free tenures (socages). The fiction that all land is held from the crown, the use of the word fee to designate the highest form of landed rights, are relics of the systematic organization introduced by the Norman kings; primogeniture applied in the absence of a will to all succession in real estate is a legacy of the law of fiefs. In certain German states, such as Prussia under Frederick William I, the fiefs were transformed into alodia in the eighteenth century by legislative action. France waited until the revolution of 1789 to abolish fiefs and vassalage, which had ceased to bring any considerable revenue to the coffers of lords and king. In the nineteenth century these antiquated institutions finally disappeared in Europe. The class of military vassals had given birth to the nobility. In France the latter saw its privileges completely abolished along with the feudal organization itself, and by the same act its social role was doomed to extinction. But in some other countries it has long outlived the fiefs both in fact and in law.

The clearest legacy of feudalism to modern societies is the emphasis placed upon the notion of the political contract. The reciprocity of obligations which united lord and vassal and caused with every grave dereliction by the superior the release of the inferior in the eyes of the law was transferred in the thirteenth century to the state. Practically everywhere, but with peculiar clearness in England and Aragon, the idea was expressed that the subject is bound to the king only so long as the latter remains a loyal protector. This sentiment counterbalanced the tradition of royal sanctity and finally triumphed over it.

5. *Nationality*

BY LORD ACTON

WHENEVER GREAT INTELLECTUAL cultivation has been combined with that suffering which is inseparable from extensive changes in the condition of the people, men of speculative or imaginative genius have sought in the contemplation of an ideal society a remedy, or at least a consolation, for evils which they were practically unable to remove. Poetry has always preserved the idea, that at some distant time or place, in the Western islands or the Arcadian region, an innocent and contented people, free from the corruption and restraint of civilised life, have realised the legends of the golden age. The office of the poets is always nearly the

Reprinted from Lord Acton, *Essays on Freedom and Power* (Glencoe, Ill.: The Free Press, 1949), chap. vi, pp. 166–95, with the permission of The Free Press.

same, and there is little variation in the features of their ideal world; but when philosophers attempt to admonish or reform mankind by devising an imaginary state, their motive is more definite and immediate, and their commonwealth is a satire as well as a model. Plato and Plotinus. More and Campanella, constructed their fanciful societies with those materials which were omitted from the fabric of the actual communities, by the defects of which they were inspired. The Republic, the Utopia, and the City of the Sun were protests against a state of things which the experience of their authors taught them to condemn, and from the faults of which they took refuge in the opposite extremes. They remained without influence, and have never passed from literary into political history, because something more than discontent and speculative ingenuity is needed in order to invest a political idea with power over the masses of mankind. The scheme of a philosopher can command the practical allegiance of fanatics only, not of nations; and though oppression may give rise to violent and repeated outbreaks, like the convulsions of a man in pain, it cannot mature a settled purpose and plan of regeneration, unless a new notion of happiness is joined to the sense of present evil.

The history of religion furnishes a complete illustration. Between the later mediæval sects and Protestantism there is an essential difference, that outweighs the points of analogy found in those systems which are regarded as heralds of the Reformation, and is enough to explain the vitality of the last in comparison with the others. Whilst Wycliffe and Hus contradicted certain particulars of the Catholic teaching, Luther rejected the authority of the Church, and gave to the individual conscience an independence which was sure to lead to an incessant resistance. There is a similar difference between the Revolt of the Netherlands, the Great Rebellion, the War of Independence, or the rising of Brabant, on the one hand, and the French Revolution on the other. Before 1789, insurrections were provoked by particular wrongs, and were justified by definite complaints and by an appeal to principles which all men acknowledged. New theories were sometimes advanced in the cause of controversy, but they were accidental, and the great argument against tyranny was fidelity to the ancient laws. Since the change produced by the French Revolution, those aspirations which are awakened by the evils and defects of the social state have come to act as permanent and energetic forces throughout the civilised world. They are spontaneous and aggressive, needing no prophet to proclaim, no champion to defend them, but popular, unreasoning, and almost irresistible. The Revolution effected this change, partly by its

doctrines, partly by the indirect influence of events. It taught the people to regard their wishes and wants as the supreme criterion of right. The rapid vicissitudes of power, in which each party successively appealed to the favour of the masses as the arbiter of success, accustomed the masses to be arbitrary as well as insubordinate. The fall of many governments, and the frequent redistribution of territory, deprived all settlements of the dignity of permanence. Tradition and prescription ceased to be guardians of authority; and the arrangements which proceeded from revolutions, from the triumphs of war, and from treaties of peace, were equally regardless of established rights. Duty cannot be dissociated from right, and nations refuse to be controlled by laws which are no protection.

In this condition of the world, theory and action follow close upon each other, and practical evils easily give birth to opposite systems. In the realms of free-will, the regularity of natural progress is preserved by the conflict of extremes. The impulse of the reaction carries men from one extremity towards another. The pursuit of a remote and ideal object, which captivates the imagination by its splendour and the reason by its simplicity, evokes an energy which would not be inspired by a rational, possible end, limited by many antagonistic claims, and confined to what is reasonable, practicable, and just. One excess or exaggeration is the corrective of the other, and error promotes truth, where the masses are concerned, by counterbalancing a contrary error. The few have not strength to achieve great changes unaided; the many have not wisdom to be moved by truth unmixed. Where the disease is various, no particular definite remedy can meet the wants of all. Only the attraction of an abstract idea, or of an ideal state, can unite in a common action multitudes who seek a universal cure for many special evils, and a common restorative applicable to many different conditions. And hence false principles, which correspond with the bad as well as with the just aspirations of mankind, are a normal and necessary element in the social life of nations.

Theories of this kind are just, inasmuch as they are provoked by definite ascertained evils, and undertake their removal. They are useful in opposition, as a warning or a threat, to modify existing things, and keep awake the consciousness of wrong. They cannot serve as a basis for the reconstruction of civil society, as medicine cannot serve for food; but they may influence it with advantage, because they point out the direction, though not the measure, in which reform is needed. They oppose an order of things which is the result of a selfish and violent abuse of power by the ruling classes, and of artificial restriction on the natural progress of the

world, destitute of an ideal element or a moral purpose. Practical extremes differ from the theoretical
extremes they provoke, because the first are both
arbitrary and violent, whilst the last, though also
revolutionary, are at the same time remedial. In one
case the wrong is voluntary, in the other it is inevitable. This is the general character of the contest
between the existing order and the subversive theories that deny its legitimacy. There are three principal theories of this kind, impugning the present
distribution of power, of property, and of territory,
and attacking respectively the aristocracy, the middle class, and the sovereignty. They are the theories
of equality, communism, and nationality. Though
sprung from a common origin, opposing cognate
evils, and connected by many links, they did not
appear simultaneously. Rousseau proclaimed the
first, Babœuf the second, Mazzini the third; and
the third is the most recent in its appearance, the
most attractive at the present time, and the richest
in promise of future power.

In the old European system, the rights of nationalities were neither recognised by governments nor
asserted by the people. The interest of the reigning
families, not those of the nations, regulated the frontiers; and the administration was conducted generally without any reference to popular desires.
Where all liberties were suppressed, the claims of
national independence were necessarily ignored,
and a princess, in the words of Fénelon, carried a
monarchy in her wedding portion. The eighteenth
century acquiesced in this oblivion of corporate
rights on the Continent, for the absolutists cared
only for the State, and the liberals only for the individual. The Church, the nobles, and the nation
had no place in the popular theories of the age; and
they devised none in their own defence, for they
were not openly attacked. The aristocracy retained
its privileges, and the Church her property; and the
dynastic interest, which overruled the natural inclination of the nations, and destroyed their independence, nevertheless maintained their integrity.
The national sentiment was not wounded in its most
sensitive part. To dispossess a sovereign of his hereditary crown, and to annex his dominions, would
have been held to inflict an injury upon all monarchies, and to furnish their subjects with a dangerous example, by depriving royalty of its inviolable
character. In time of war, as there was no national
cause at stake, there was no attempt to rouse national feeling. The courtesy of the rulers towards
each other was proportionate to the contempt for
the lower orders. Compliments passed between the
commanders of hostile armies; there was no bitterness, and no excitement; battles were fought with
the pomp and pride of a parade. The art of war be-

came a slow and learned game. The monarchies
were united not only by a natural community of interests, but by family alliances. A marriage contract
sometimes became the signal for an interminable
war, whilst family connections often set a barrier
to ambition. After the wars of religion came to an
end in 1648, the only wars were those which were
waged for an inheritance or a dependency, or
against countries whose system of government ex-
empted them from the common law of dynastic
States, and made them not only unprotected but
obnoxious. These countries were England and
Holland, until Holland ceased to be a republic, and
until, in England, the defeat of the Jacobites in the
forty-five terminated the struggle for the Crown.
There was one country, however, which still continued to be an exception; one monarch whose place
was not admitted in the comity of kings.

Poland did not possess those securities for stability which were supplied by dynastic connections and
the theory of legitimacy, wherever a crown could
be obtained by marriage or inheritance. A monarch
without royal blood, a crown bestowed by the nation, were an anomaly and an outrage in that age
of dynastic absolutism. The country was excluded
from the European system by the nature of its institutions. It excited a cupidity which could not be
satisfied. It gave the reigning families of Europe no
hope of permanently strengthening themselves by
intermarriage with its rulers, or of obtaining it by
request or by inheritance. The Hapsburgs had contested the possession of Spain and the Indies with
the French Bourbons, of Italy with the Spanish
Bourbons, of the empire with the house of Wittels-
bach, of Silesia with the house of Hohenzollern.
There had been wars between rival houses for half
the territories of Italy and Germany. But none
could hope to redeem their losses or increase their
power in a country to which marriage and descent
gave no claim. Where they could not permanently
inherit they endeavoured, by intrigues, to prevail at
each election, and after contending in support of
candidates who were their partisans, the neighbours
at last appointed an instrument for the final demoli-
tion of the Polish State. Till then no nation had been
deprived of its political existence by the Christian
Powers, and whatever disregard had been shown
for national interests and sympathies, some care had
been taken to conceal the wrong by a hypocritical
perversion of law. But the partition of Poland was
an act of wanton violence, committed in open defiance not only of popular feeling but of public law.
For the first time in modern history a great State
was suppressed, and a whole nation divided among
its enemies.

The famous measure, the most revolutionary act

of the old absolutism, awakened the theory of nationality in Europe, converting a dormant right into an aspiration, and a sentiment into a political claim. "No wise or honest man," wrote Edmund Burke, "can approve of that partition, or can contemplate it without prognosticating great mischief from it to all countries at some future time."[1] Thenceforward there was a nation demanding to be united in a State,—a soul, as it were, wandering in search of a body in which to begin life over again; and, for the first time, a cry was heard that the arrangement of States was unjust—that their limits were unnatural, and that a whole people was deprived of its right to constitute an independent community. Before that claim could be efficiently asserted against the overwhelming power of its opponents,—before it gained energy, after the last partition, to overcome the influence of long habits of submission, and of the contempt which previous disorders had brought upon Poland,—the ancient European system was in ruins, and a new world was rising in its place.

The old despotic policy which made the Poles its prey had two adversaries,—the spirit of English liberty, and the doctrines of that revolution which destroyed the French monarchy with its own weapons; and these two contradicted in contrary ways the theory that nations have no collective rights. At the present day, the theory of nationality is not only the most powerful auxiliary of revolution, but its actual substance in the movements of the last three years. This, however, is a recent alliance, unknown to the first French Revolution. The modern theory of nationality arose partly as a legitimate consequence, partly as a reaction against it. As the system which overlooked national division was opposed by liberalism in two forms, the French and the English, so the system which insists upon them proceeds from two distinct sources, and exhibits the character either of 1688 or of 1789. When the French people abolished the authorities under which it lived, and became its own master, France was in danger of dissolution: for the common will is difficult to ascertain, and does not readily agree. "The laws," said Vergniaud, in the debate on the sentence of the king, "are obligatory only as the presumptive will of the people, which retains the right of approving or condemning them. The instant it manifests its wish the work of the national representation, the law, must disappear." This doctrine resolved society into its natural elements, and threatened to break up the country into as many republics as there were communes. For true republicanism is the principle of self-government in the whole and in all the parts. In an extensive country, it can prevail only by the

1. "Observations on the Conduct of the Minority," *Works,* V, 112.

union of several independent communities in a single confederacy, as in Greece, in Switzerland, in the Netherlands, and in America; so that a large republic not founded on the federal principle must result in the government of a single city, like Rome and Paris, and in a less degree, Athens, Berne, and Amsterdam; or, in other words, a great democracy must either sacrifice self-government to unity, or preserve it by federalism.

The France of history fell together with the French State, which was the growth of centuries. The old sovereignty was destroyed. The local authorities were looked upon with aversion and alarm. The new central authority needed to be established on a new principle of unity. The state of nature, which was the ideal of society, was made the basis of the nation; descent was put in the place of tradition, and the French people was regarded as a physical product: an ethnological, not historic, unit. It was assumed that a unity existed separate from the representation and the government, wholly independent of the past, and capable at any moment of expressing or of changing its mind. In the words of Siéyès, it was no longer France, but some unknown country to which the nation was transported. The central power possessed authority, inasmuch as it obeyed the whole, and no divergence was permitted from the universal sentiment. This power, endowed with volition, was personified in the Republic One and Indivisible. The title signified that a part could not speak or act for the whole,—that there was a power supreme over the State, distinct from, and independent of, its members; and it expressed, for the first time in history, the notion of an abstract nationality. In this manner the idea of the sovereignty of the people, uncontrolled by the past, gave birth to the idea of nationality independent of the political influence of history. It sprang from the rejection of the two authorities,—of the State and of the past. The kingdom of France was, geographically as well as politically, the product of a long series of events, and the same influences which built up the State formed the territory. The Revolution repudiated alike the agencies to which France owed her boundaries and those to which she owed her government. Every effaceable trace and relic of national history was carefully wiped away,—the system of administration, the physical divisions of the country, the classes of society, the corporations, the weights and measures, the calendar. France was no longer bounded by the limits she had received from the condemned influence of her history; she could recognise only those which were set by nature. The definition of the nation was borrowed from the material world, and, in order to avoid a loss of territory, it became not only an abstraction but a fiction.

There was a principle of nationality in the ethnological character of the movement, which is the source of the common observation that revolution is more frequent in Catholic than in Protestant countries. It is, in fact, more frequent in the Latin than in the Teutonic world, because it depends partly on a national impulse, which is only awakened where there is an alien element, the vestige of a foreign dominion, to expel. Western Europe has undergone two conquests—one by the Romans and one by the Germans, and twice received laws from the invaders. Each time it rose again against the victorious race; and the two great reactions, while they differ according to the different characters of the two conquests, have the phenomenon of imperialism in common. The Roman republic laboured to crush the subjugated nations into a homogeneous and obedient mass; but the increase which the proconsular authority obtained in the process subverted the republican government, and the reaction of the provinces against Rome assisted in establishing the empire. The Cæsarean system gave an unprecedented freedom to the dependencies, and raised them to a civil equality which put an end to the dominion of race over race and of class over class. The monarchy was hailed as a refuge from the pride and cupidity of the Roman people; and the love of equality, the hatred of nobility, and the tolerance of despotism implanted by Rome became, at least in Gaul, the chief feature of the national character. But among the nations whose vitality had been broken down by the stern republic, not one retained the materials necessary to enjoy independence, or to develop a new history. The political faculty which organises states and finds society in a moral order was exhausted, and the Christian doctors looked in vain over the waste of ruins for a people by whose aid the Church might survive the decay of Rome. A new element of national life was brought to that declining world by the enemies who destroyed it. The flood of barbarians settled over it for a season, and then subsided; and when the landmarks of civilisation appeared once more, it was found that the soil had been impregnated with a fertilising and regenerating influence, and that the inundation had laid the germs of future states and of a new society. The political sense and energy came with the new blood, and was exhibited in the power exercised by the younger race upon the old, and in the establishment of a graduated freedom. Instead of universal equal rights, the actual enjoyment of which is necessarily contingent on, and commensurate with, power, the rights of the people were made dependent on a variety of conditions, the first of which was the distribution of property. Civil society became a classified organism instead of a formless combination of atoms, and the feudal system gradually arose.

Roman Gaul had so thoroughly adopted the ideas of absolute authority and undistinguished equality during the five centuries between Cæsar and Clovis, that the people could never be reconciled to the new system. Feudalism remained a foreign importation, and the feudal aristocracy an alien race, and the common people of France sought protection against both in the Roman jurisprudence and the power of the crown. The development of absolute monarchy by the help of democracy is the one constant character of French history. The royal power, feudal at first, and limited by the immunities and the great vassals, became more popular as it grew more absolute; while the suppression of aristocracy, the removal of the intermediate authorities, was so particularly the object of the nation, that it was more energetically accomplished after the fall of the throne. The monarchy which had been engaged from the thirteenth century in curbing the nobles, was at last thrust aside by the democracy, because it was too dilatory in the work, and was unable to deny its own origin and effectually ruin the class from which it sprang. All those things which constitute the peculiar character of the French Revolution,—the demand for equality, the hatred of nobility and feudalism, and of the Church which was connected with them, the constant reference to pagan examples, the suppression of monarchy, the new code of law, the breach with tradition, and the substitution of an ideal system for everything that had proceeded from the mixture and mutual action of the races,—all these exhibit the common type of a reaction against the effects of the Frankish invasion. The hatred of royalty was less than the hatred of aristocracy: privileges were more detested than tyranny; and the king perished because of the origin of his authority rather than because of its abuse. Monarchy unconnected with aristocracy became popular in France, even when most uncontrolled; whilst the attempt to reconstitute the throne, and to limit and fence it with its peers, broke down, because the old Teutonic elements on which it relied—hereditary nobility, primogeniture, and privilege—were no longer tolerated. The substance of the ideas of 1789 is not the limitation of the sovereign power, but the abrogation of intermediate powers. These powers, and the classes which enjoyed them, come in Latin Europe from a barbarian origin; and the movement which calls itself liberal is essentially national. If liberty were its object, its means would be the establishment of great independent authorities not derived from the State, and its model would be England. But its object is equality; and it seeks, like France in 1789, to cast out the elements of inequality which were introduced by the Teutonic race. This is the object which Italy and Spain have had in common with France, and herein consists the natural league of the Latin nations.

This national element in the movement was not understood by the revolutionary leaders. At first, their doctrine appeared entirely contrary to the idea of nationality. They taught that certain general principles of government were absolutely right in all States; and they asserted in theory the unrestricted freedom of the individual, and the supremacy of the will over every external necessity or obligation. This is in apparent contradiction to the national theory, that certain natural forces ought to determine the character, the form, and the policy of the State, by which a kind of fate is put in the place of freedom. Accordingly the national sentiment was not developed directly out of the revolution in which it was involved, but was exhibited first in resistance to it, when the attempt to emancipate had been absorbed in the desire to subjugate, and the republic had been succeeded by the empire. Napoleon called a new power into existence by attacking nationality in Russia, by delivering it in Italy, by governing in defiance of it in Germany and Spain. The sovereigns of these countries were deposed or degraded; and a system of administration was introduced which was French in its origin, its spirit, and its instruments. The people resisted the change. The movement against it was popular and spontaneous, because the rulers were absent or helpless; and it was national, because it was directed against foreign institutions. In Tyrol, in Spain, and afterwards in Prussia, the people did not receive the impulse from the government, but undertook of their own accord to cast out the armies and the ideas of revolutionised France. Men were made conscious of the national element of the revolution by its conquests, not in its rise. The three things which the Empire most openly oppressed—religion, national independence, and political liberty —united in a short-lived league to animate the great uprising by which Napoleon fell. Under the influence of that memorable alliance a political spirit was called forth on the Continent, which clung to freedom and abhorred revolution, and sought to restore, to develop, and to reform the decayed national institutions. The men who proclaimed these ideas, Stein and Görres, Humboldt,

Müller, and De Maistre,[2] were as hostile to Bonapartism as to the absolutism of the old governments, and insisted on the national rights, which had been invaded equally by both, and which they hoped to restore by the destruction of the French supremacy. With the cause that triumphed at Waterloo the friends of the Revolution had no sympathy, for they had learned to identify their doctrine with the cause of France. The Holland House Whigs in England, the Afrancesados in Spain, the Muratists in Italy, and the partisans of the Confederation of the Rhine, merging patriotism in their revolutionary affections, regretted the fall of the French power, and looked with alarm at those new and unknown forces which the War of Deliverance had evoked, and which were as menacing to French liberalism as to French supremacy.

But the new aspirations for national and popular rights were crushed at the restoration. The liberals of those days cared for freedom, not in the shape of national independence, but of French institutions; and they combined against the nations with the ambition of the governments. They were as ready to sacrifice nationality to their ideal as the Holy Alliance was to the interests of absolutism. Talleyrand indeed declared at Vienna that the Polish question ought to have precedence over all other questions, because the partition of Poland had been one of the first and greatest causes of the evils which Europe had suffered; but dynastic interests prevailed. All the sovereigns represented at Vienna recovered their dominions, except the King of Saxony, who was punished for his fidelity to Napoleon; but the States that were unrepresented in the reigning families—Poland, Venice, and

---

2. There are some remarkable thoughts on nationality in the State Papers of the Count de Maistre: "En premier lieu les nations sont quelque chose dans le monde, il n'est pas permis de les compter pour rien, de les affliger dans leurs convenances, dans leurs affections, dans leurs intérêts les plus chers. . . . Or le traité du 30 mai anéantit complétement la Savoie; il divise l'indivisible; il partage en trois portions une malheureuse nation de 400,000 hommes, une par la langue, une par la religion, une par le caractère, une par l'habitude invétérée, une enfin par les limites naturelles. . . . L'union des nations ne souffre pas de difficultés sur la carte géographique; mais dans la réalité, c'est autre chose; il y a des nations *immiscibles*. . . . Je lui parlai par occasion de l'esprit italien qui s'agite dans ce moment; il (Count Nesselrode) me répondit: 'Oui, Monsieur; mais cet esprit est un grand mal, car il peut gêner les arrangements de l'Italie.' "—*Correspondance Diplomatique de J. de Maistre*, II, 7, 8, 21, 25. In the same year, 1815, Görres wrote: "In Italien wie allerwarts ist das Volk gewecht; es will etwas grossartiges, es will Ideen haben, die, wenn es sie auch nicht ganz begreift, doch einen freien unendlichen Gesichtskreis seiner Einbildung eröffnen. . . . Es ist reiner Naturtrieb, dass ein Volk, also scharf und deutlich in seine natürlichen Gränzen eingeschlossen, aus der Zerstreuung in die Einheit sich zu sammeln sucht."—*Werke*, II, 20.

Genoa—were not revived, and even the Pope had great difficulty in recovering the Legations from the grasp of Austria. Nationality, which the old *régime* had ignored, which had been outraged by the revolution and the empire, received, after its first open demonstration, the hardest blow at the Congress of Vienna. The principle which the first partition had generated, to which the revolution had given a basis of theory, which had been lashed by the empire into a momentary convulsive effort, was matured by the long error of the restoration into a consistent doctrine, nourished and justified by the situation of Europe.

The governments of the Holy Alliance devoted themselves to suppress with equal care the revolutionary spirit by which they had been threatened, and the national spirit by which they had been restored. Austria, which owed nothing to the national movement, and had prevented its revival after 1809, naturally took the lead in repressing it. Every disturbance of the final settlements of 1815, every aspiration for changes or reforms, was condemned as sedition. This system repressed the good with the evil tendencies of the age; and the resistance which it provoked, during the generation that passed away from the restoration to the fall of Metternich, and again under the reaction which commenced with Schwarzenberg and ended with the administrations of Bach and Manteuffel, proceeded from various combinations of the opposite forms of liberalism. In the successive phases of that struggle, the idea that national claims are above all other rights gradually rose to the supremacy which it now possesses among the revolutionary agencies.

The first liberal movement, that of the Carbonari in the south of Europe, had no specific national character, but was supported by the Bonapartists both in Spain and Italy. In the following years the opposite ideas of 1813 came to the front, and a revolutionary movement, in many respects hostile to the principles of revolution, began in defence of liberty, religion, and nationality. All these causes were united in the Irish agitation, and in the Greek, Belgian, and Polish revolutionists. Those sentiments which had been insulted by Napoleon, and had risen against him, rose against the governments of the restoration. They had been oppressed by the sword, and then by the treaties. The national principle added force, but not justice, to this movement, which, in every case but Poland, was successful. A period followed in which it degenerated into a purely national idea, as the agitation for repeal succeeded emancipation, and Panslavism and Panhellenism arose under the auspices of the Eastern Church. This was the third phase of the resistance

to the settlement of Vienna, which was weak, because it failed to satisfy national or constitutional aspirations, either of which would have been a safeguard against the other, by a moral if not by a popular justification. At first, in 1813, the people rose against their conquerors, in defence of their legitimate rulers. They refused to be governed by usurpers. In the period between 1825 and 1831, they resolved that they would not be misgoverned by strangers. The French administration was often better than that which it displaced, but there were prior claimants for the authority exercised by the French, and at first the national contest was a contest for legitimacy. In the second period this element was wanting. No dispossessed princes led the Greeks, the Belgians, or the Poles. The Turks, the Dutch, and the Russians were attacked, not as usurpers, but as oppressors,—because they misgoverned, not because they were of a different race. Then began a time when the text simply was, that nations would not be governed by foreigners. Power legitimately obtained, and exercised with moderation, was declared invalid. National rights, like religion, had borne part in the previous combinations, and had been auxiliaries in the struggles for freedom, but now nationality became a paramount claim, which was to assert itself alone, which might put forward as pretexts the rights of rulers, the liberties of the people, the safety of religion, but which, if no such union could be formed, was to prevail at the expense of every other cause for which nations make sacrifices.

Metternich is, next to Napoleon, the chief promoter of this theory; for the anti-national character of the restoration was most distinct in Austria, and it is in opposition to the Austrian Government that nationality grew into a system. Napoleon, who, trusting to his armies, despised moral forces in politics, was overthrown by their rising. Austria committed the same fault in the government of her Italian provinces. The kingdom of Italy had united all the northern part of the Peninsula in a single State; and the national feelings, which the French repressed elsewhere, were encouraged as a safeguard of their power in Italy and in Poland. When the tide of victory turned, Austria invoked against the French the aid of the new sentiment they had fostered. Nugent announced, in his proclamation to the Italians, that they should become an independent nation. The same spirit served different masters, and contributed first to the destruction of the old States, then to the expulsion of the French, and again, under Charles Albert, to a new revolution. It was appealed to in the name of the most contradictory principles of government, and served all parties in succession, because it was one in which all could unite. Beginning by a protest against the dominion of race over race, its mildest and least-developed form, it grew into a condemnation of every State that included different races, and finally became the complete and consistent theory, that the State and the nation must be co-extensive. "It is," says Mr. Mill, "in general a necessary condition of free institutions, that the boundaries of governments should coincide in the main with those of nationalities."[3]

The outward historical progress of this idea from an indefinite aspiration to be the keystone of a political system, may be traced in the life of the man who gave to it the element in which its strength resides,—Giuseppe Mazzini. He found Carbonarism impotent against the measures of the governments, and resolved to give new life to the liberal movement by transferring it to the ground of nationality. Exile is the nursery of nationality, as oppression is the school of liberalism; and Mazzini conceived the idea of Young Italy when he was a refugee at Marseilles. In the same way, the Polish exiles are the champions of every national movement; for to them all political rights are absorbed in the idea of independence, which, however they may differ with each other, is the one aspiration common to them all. Towards the year 1830 literature also contributed to the national idea. "It was the time," says Mazzini, "of the great conflict between the romantic and the classical school, which might with equal truth be called a conflict between the partisans of freedom and of authority." The romantic school was infidel in Italy, and Catholic in Germany; but in both it had the common effect of encouraging national history and literature, and Dante was as great an authority with the Italian democrats as with the leaders of the mediæval revival at Vienna, Munich, and Berlin. But neither the influence of the exiles, nor that of the poets and critics of the new party, extended over the masses. It was a sect without popular sympathy or encouragement, a conspiracy founded not on a grievance, but on a doctrine; and when the attempt to rise was made in Savoy, in 1834, under a banner with the motto "Unity, Independence, God and Humanity," the people were puzzled at its object, and indifferent to its failure. But Mazzini continued his propaganda, developed his *Giovine Italia* into a *Giovine Europa*, and established in 1847 the international league of nations. "The people," he said, in his opening address, "is penetrated with only one idea, that of unity and nationality. . . . There is no interna-

tional question as to forms of government, but only a national question."

The revolution of 1848, unsuccessful in its national purpose, prepared the subsequent victories of nationality in two ways. The first of these was the restoration of the Austrian power in Italy, with a new and more energetic centralisation, which gave no promise of freedom. Whilst that system prevailed, the right was on the side of the national aspirations, and they were revived in a more complete and cultivated form by Manin. The policy of the Austrian Government, which failed during the ten years of the reaction to convert the tenure by force into a tenure by right, and to establish with free institutions the condition of allegiance, gave a negative encouragement to the theory. It deprived Francis Joseph of all active support and sympathy in 1859, for he was more clearly wrong in his conduct than his enemies in their doctrines. The real cause of the energy which the national theory has acquired is, however, the triumph of the democratic principle in France, and its recognition by the European Powers. The theory of nationality is involved in the democratic theory of the sovereignty of the general will. "One hardly knows what any division of the human race should be free to do, if not to determine with which of the various collective bodies of human beings they choose to associate themselves."[4] It is by this act that a nation constitutes itself. To have a collective will, unity is necessary, and independence is requisite in order to assert it. Unity and nationality are still more essential to the notion of the sovereignty of the people than the cashiering of monarchs, or the revocation of laws. Arbitrary acts of this kind may be prevented by the happiness of the people or the popularity of the king, but a nation inspired by the democratic idea cannot with consistency allow a part of itself to belong to a foreign State, or the whole to be divided into several native States. The theory of nationality therefore proceeds from both the principles which divide the political world,—from legitimacy, which ignores its claims, and from the revolution, which assumes them; and for the same reason it is the chief weapon of the last against the first.

In pursuing the outward and visible growth of the national theory we are prepared for an examination of its political character and value. The absolutism which has created it denies equally that absolute right of national unity which is a product of democracy, and that claim of national liberty which belongs to the theory of freedom. These two views of nationality, corresponding to the French and to the English systems, are connected in name

---

3 Mill's *Considerations on Representative Government*, p. 298.

4. Mill's *Considerations*, p. 296.

only, and are in reality the opposite extremes of political thought. In one case, nationality is founded on the perpetual supremacy of the collective will, of which the unity of the nation is the necessary condition, to which every other influence must defer, and against which no obligation enjoys authority, and all resistance is tyrannical. The nation is here an ideal unit founded on the race, in defiance of the modifying action of external causes, of tradition, and of existing rights. It overrules the rights and wishes of the inhabitants, absorbing their divergent interests in a fictitious unity; sacrifices their several inclinations and duties to the higher claim of nationality, and crushes all natural rights and all established liberties for the purpose of vindicating itself.[5] Whenever a single definite object is made the supreme end of the State, be it the advantage of a class, the safety or the power of the country, the greatest happiness of the greatest number, or the support of any speculative idea, the State becomes for the time inevitably absolute. Liberty alone demands for its realisation the limitation of the public authority, for liberty is the only object which benefits all alike, and provokes no sincere opposition. In supporting the claims of national unity, governments must be subverted in whose title there is no flaw, and whose policy is beneficent and equitable, and subjects must be compelled to transfer their allegiance to an authority for which they have no attachment, and which may be practically a foreign domination. Connected with this theory in nothing except in the common enmity of the absolute state, is the theory which represents nationality as an essential, but not a supreme element in determining the forms of the State. It is distinguished from the other, because it tends to diversity and not to uniformity, to harmony and not to unity; because it aims not at an arbitrary change, but at careful respect for the existing conditions of political life, and because it obeys the laws and results of history, not the aspirations of an ideal future. While the theory of unity makes the nation a source of despotism and revolution, the theory of liberty regards it as the bulwark of self-government, and the foremost limit to the excessive power of the State. Private rights, which are sacrificed to the unity, are preserved by the union of nations. No power can so efficiently resist the tendencies of centralisation, of corrup-

tion, and of absolutism, as that community which is the vastest that can be included in a State, which imposes on its members a consistent similarity of character, interest, and opinion, and which arrests the action of the sovereign by the influence of a divided patriotism. The presence of different nations under the same sovereignty is similar in its effect to the independence of the Church in the State. It provides against the servility which flourishes under the shadow of a single authority, by balancing interests, multiplying associations, and giving to the subject the restraint and support of a combined opinion. In the same way it promotes independence by forming definite groups of public opinion, and by affording a great source and centre of political sentiments, and of notions of duty not derived from the sovereign will. Liberty provokes diversity, and diversity preserves liberty by supplying the means of organisation. All those portions of law which govern the relations of men with each other, and regulate social life, are the varying result of national custom and the creation of private society. In these things, therefore, the several nations will differ from each other; for they themselves have produced them, and they do not owe them to the State which rules them all. This diversity in the same State is a firm barrier against the intrusion of the government beyond the political sphere which is common to all into the social department which escapes legislation and is ruled by spontaneous laws. This sort of interference is characteristic of an absolute government, and is sure to provoke a reaction, and finally a remedy. That intolerance of social freedom which is natural to absolutism is sure to find a corrective in the national diversities, which no other force could so efficiently provide. The co-existence of several nations under the same State is a test, as well as the best security of its freedom. It is also one of the chief instruments of civilisation; and, as such, it is in the natural and providential order, and indicates a state of greater advancement than the national unity which is the ideal of modern liberalism.

The combination of different nations in one State is as necessary a condition of civilised life as the combination of men in society. Inferior races are raised by living in political unions with races intellectually superior. Exhausted and decaying nations are revived by the contact of a younger vitality. Nations in which the elements of organisation and the capacity for government have been lost, either through the demoralising influence of despotism, or the disintegrating action of democracy, are restored and educated anew under the discipline of a stronger and less corrupted race.

---

5. "Le sentiment d'indépendance nationale est encore plus général et plus profondément gravé dans le cœur des peuples que l'amour d'une liberté constitutionnelle. Les nations les plus soumises au despotisme éprouvent ce sentiment avec autant de vivacité que les nations libres; les peuples les plus barbares le sentent même encore plus vivement que les nations policées."—*L'Italie au Dixneuvième Siècle*, p. 148, Paris, 1821.

This fertilising and regenerating process can only be obtained by living under one government. It is in the cauldron of the State that the fusion takes place by which the vigour, the knowledge, and the capacity of one portion of mankind may be communicated to another. Where political and national boundaries coincide, society ceases to advance, and nations relapse into a condition corresponding to that of men who renounce intercourse with their fellow-men. The difference between the two unites mankind not only by the benefits it confers on those who live together, but because it connects society either by a political or a national bond, gives to every people an interest in its neighbours, either because they are under the same government or because they are of the same race, and thus promotes the interests of humanity, of civilisation, and of religion.

Christianity rejoices at the mixture of races, as paganism identifies itself with their differences, because truth is universal, and errors various and particular. In the ancient world idolatry and nationality went together, and the same term is applied in Scripture to both. It was the mission of the Church to overcome national differences. The period of her undisputed supremacy was that in which all Western Europe obeyed the same laws, all literature was contained in one language, and the political unit of Christendom was personified in a single potentate, while its intellectual unity was represented in one university. As the ancient Romans concluded their conquests by carrying away the gods of the conquered people, Charlemagne overcame the national resistance of the Saxons only by the forcible destruction of their pagan rites. Out of the mediæval period, and the combined action of the German race and the Church, came forth a new system of nations and a new conception of nationality. Nature was overcome in the nation as well as in the individual. In pagan and uncultivated times, nations were distinguished from each other by the widest diversity, not only in religion, but in customs, language, and character. Under the new law they had many things in common; the old barriers which separated them were removed, and the new principle of self-government, which Christianity imposed, enabled them to live together under the same authority, without necessarily losing their cherished habits, their customs, or their laws. The new idea of freedom made room for different races in one State. A nation was no longer what it had been to the ancient world,—the progeny of a common ancestor, or the aboriginal product of a particular region,—a result of merely physical and material causes,—but a moral and political being; not the creation of geographical or physiological unity, but developed in the course of history by the action of the State. It is derived from the State, not supreme over it. A State may in course of time produce a nationality; but that a nationality should constitute a State is contrary to the nature of modern civilisation. The nation derives its rights and its power from the memory of a former independence.

The Church has agreed in this respect with the tendency of political progress, and discouraged wherever she could the isolation of nations, admonishing them of their duties to each other, and regarding conquest and feudal investiture as the natural means of raising barbarous or sunken nations to a higher level. But though she has never attributed to national independence an immunity from the accidental consequences of feudal law, of hereditary claims, or of testamentary arrangements, she defends national liberty against uniformity and centralisation with an energy inspired by perfect community of interests. For the same enemy threatens both; and the State which is reluctant to tolerate differences, and to do justice to the peculiar character of various races, must from the same cause interfere in the internal government of religion. The connection of religious liberty with the emancipation of Poland or Ireland is not merely the accidental result of local causes; and the failure of the Concordat to unite the subjects of Austria is the natural consequence of a policy which did not desire to protect the provinces in their diversity and autonomy, and sought to bribe the Church by favours instead of strengthening her by independence. From this influence of religion in modern history has proceeded a new definition of patriotism.

The difference between nationality and the State is exhibited in the nature of patriotic attachment. Our connection with the race is merely natural or physical, whilst our duties to the political nation are ethical. One is a community of affections and instincts infinitely important and powerful in savage life, but pertaining more to the animal than to the civilised man; the other is an authority governing by laws, imposing obligations, and giving a moral sanction and character to the natural relations of society. Patriotism is in political life what faith is in religion, and it stands to the domestic feelings and to homesickness as faith to fanaticism and to superstition. It has one aspect derived from private life and nature, for it is an extension of the family affections, as the tribe is an extension of the family. But in its real political character, patriotism consists in the development of the instinct of self-preservation into a moral duty which may involve self-sacrifice. Self-preservation is both an instinct and a duty, natural and involuntary in one respect, and at the same time a moral obligation. By the first it produces the family; by the last the State. If the nation could exist without the State, subject only to the instinct of self-preservation, it would be incapable of denying, controlling, or sacrificing itself; it would be an end and a rule to itself. But in the political order moral purposes are realised and public ends are pursued to which private interests and even existence must be sacrificed. The great sign of true patriotism, the development of selfishness into sacrifice, is the product of political life. That sense of duty which is supplied by race is not entirely separated from its selfish and instinctive basis; and the love of country, like married love, stands at the same time on a material and a moral foundation. The patriot must distinguish between the two causes or objects of his devotion. The attachment which is given only to the country is like obedience given only to the State—a submission to physical influences. The man who prefers his country before every other duty shows the same spirit as the man who surrenders every right to the State. They both deny that right is superior to authority.

There is a moral and political country, in the language of Burke, distinct from the geographical, which may be possibly in collision with it. The Frenchmen who bore arms against the Convention were as patriotic as the Englishmen who bore arms against King Charles, for they recognised a higher duty than that of obedience to the actual sovereign. "In an address to France," said Burke, "in an attempt to treat with it, or in considering any scheme at all relative to it, it is impossible we should mean the geographical, we must always mean the moral and political, country. . . . The truth is, that France is out of itself—the moral France is separated from the geographical. The master of the house is expelled, and the robbers are in possession. If we look for the corporate people of France, existing as corporate in the eye and intention of public law (that corporate people, I mean, who are free to deliberate and to decide, and who have a capacity to treat and conclude), they are in Flanders and Germany, in Switzerland, Spain, Italy, and England. There are all the princes of the blood, there are all the orders of the State, there are all the parliaments of the kingdom. . . . I am sure that if half that number of the same description were taken out of this country, it would leave hardly anything that I should call the people of England."[6] Rousseau draws nearly the same distinction between the country to which we happen

to belong and that which fulfils towards **us the** political functions of the State. In the *Emile* he has a sentence of which it is not easy in a translation to convey the point: "Qui n'a pas une patrie a du moins un pays." And in his tract on Political Economy he writes: "How shall men love their country if it is nothing more for them than for strangers, and bestows on them only that which it can refuse to none?" It is in the same sense he says, further on, "La patrie ne peut subsister sans la liberté."[7]

The nationality formed by the State, then, is the only one to which we owe political duties, and it is, therefore, the only one which has political rights. The Swiss are ethnologically either French, Italian, or German; but no nationality has the slightest claim upon them, except the purely political nationality of Switzerland. The Tuscan or the Neapolitan State has formed a nationality, but the citizens of Florence and of Naples have no political community with each other. There are other States which have neither succeeded in absorbing distinct races in a political nationality, nor in separating a particular district from a larger nation. Austria and Mexico are instances on the one hand, Parma and Baden on the other. The progress of civilisation deals hardly with the last description of States. In order to maintain their integrity they must attach themselves by confederations, or family alliances, to greater Powers, and thus lose something of their independence. Their tendency is to isolate and shut off their inhabitants, to narrow the horizon of their views, and to dwarf in some degree the proportions of their ideas. Public opinion cannot maintain its liberty and purity in such small dimensions, and the currents that come from larger communities sweep over a contracted territory. In a small and homogeneous population there is hardly room for a natural classification of society, or for inner groups of interests that set bounds to sovereign power. The government and the subjects contend with borrowed weapons. The resources of the one and the aspirations of the other are derived from some external source, and the consequence is that the country becomes the instrument and the scene of contests in which it is not interested. These States, like the minuter communities of the Middle Ages, serve a purpose, by constituting partitions and securities of self-government in the larger States;

---

6. Burke's "Remarks on the Policy of the Allies," *Works*, V. 26, 29, 30.

7. *Œuvres*, I, 593, 595; 11, 717. Bossuet, in a passage of great beauty on the love of country, does not attain to the political definition of the word: "La société humaine demande qu'on aime la terre où l'on habite ensemble, ou la regarde comme une mère et une nourrice commune. . . . Les hommes en effet se sentent liés par quelque chose de fort, lorsqu'ils songent, que le même terre qui les a portés et nourris étant vivants, les recevra dans son sein quand ils seront morts." "Politique tirée de l'Ecriture Sainte," *Œuvres*, X, 317.

but they are impediments to the progress of society, which depends on the mixture of races under the same governments.

The vanity and peril of national claims founded on no political tradition, but on race alone, appear in Mexico. There the races are divided by blood, without being grouped together in different regions. It is, therefore, neither possible to unite them nor to convert them into the elements of an organised State. They are fluid, shapeless, and unconnected, and cannot be precipitated, or formed into the basis of political institutions. As they cannot be used by the State, they cannot be recognised by it; and their peculiar qualities, capabilities, passions, and attachments are of no service, and therefore obtain no regard. They are necessarily ignored, and are therefore perpetually outraged. From this difficulty of races with political pretensions, but without political position, the Eastern world escaped by the institution of castes. Where there are only two races there is the resource of slavery; but when different races inhabit the different territories of one Empire composed of several smaller States, it is of all possible combinations the most favourable to the establishment of a highly developed system of freedom. In Austria there are two circumstances which add to the difficulty of the problem, but also increase its importance. The several nationalities are at very unequal degrees of advancement, and there is no single nation which is so predominant as to overwhelm or absorb the others. These are the conditions necessary for the very highest degree of organisation which government is capable of receiving. They supply the greatest variety of intellectual resource; the perpetual incentive to progress which is afforded not merely by competition, but by the spectacle of a more advanced people; the most abundant elements of self-government, combined with the impossibility for the State to rule all by its own will; and the fullest security for the preservation of local customs and ancient rights. In such a country as this, liberty would achieve its most glorious results, while centralisation and absolutism would be destruction.

The problem presented to the government of Austria is higher than that which is solved in England, because of the necessity of admitting the national claims. The parliamentary system fails to provide for them, as it presupposes the unity of the people. Hence in those countries in which different races dwell together, it has not satisfied their desires, and is regarded as an imperfect form of freedom. It brings out more clearly than before the differences it does not recognise, and thus continues the work of the old absolutism, and appears as a new phase of centralisation. In those countries, therefore, the power of the imperial parliament must be limited as jealously as the power of the crown, and many of its functions must be discharged by provincial diets, and a descending series of local authorities.

The great importance of nationality in the State consists in the fact that it is the basis of political capacity. The character of a nation determines in great measure the form and vitality of the State. Certain political habits and ideas belong to particular nations, and they vary with the course of the national history. A people just emerging from barbarism, a people effete from the excesses of a luxurious civilisation, cannot possess the means of governing itself; a people devoted to equality, or to absolute monarchy, is incapable of producing an aristocracy; a people averse to the institution of private property is without the first element of freedom. Each of these can be converted into efficient members of a free community only by the contact of a superior race, in whose power will lie the future prospects of the State. A system which ignores these things, and does not rely for its support on the character and aptitude of the people, does not intend that they should administer their own affairs, but that they should simply be obedient to the supreme command. The denial of nationality, therefore, implies the denial of political liberty.

The greatest adversary of the rights of nationality is the modern theory of nationality. By making the State and the nation commensurate with each other in theory, it reduces practically to a subject condition all other nationalities that may be within the boundary. It cannot admit them to an equality with the ruling nation which constitutes the State, because the State would then cease to be national, which would be a contradiction of the principle of its existence. According, therefore, to the degree of humanity and civilisation in that dominant body which claims all the rights of the community, the inferior races are exterminated, or reduced to servitude, or outlawed, or put in a condition of dependence.

If we take the establishment of liberty for the realisation of moral duties to be the end of civil society, we must conclude that those states are substantially the most perfect which, like the British and Austrian Empires, include various distinct nationalities without oppressing them. Those in which no mixture of races has occurred are imperfect; and those in which its effects have disappeared are decrepit. A State which is incompetent to satisfy different races condemns itself; a State which labours to neutralise, to absorb, or to expel them, destroys its own vitality; a State which does not include them is destitute of the chief basis of self-government. The theory of nationality, therefore, is a retrograde step in history. It is the most advanced form of the revolution, and must retain its power to the end of the revolutionary period, of which it announces the approach. Its great historical importance depends on two chief causes.

First, it is a chimera. The settlement at which it aims is impossible. As it can never be satisfied and exhausted, and always continues to assert itself, it prevents the government from ever relapsing into the condition which provoked its rise. The danger is too threatening, and the power over men's minds too great, to allow any system to endure which justifies the resistance of nationality. It must contribute, therefore, to obtain that which in theory it condemns,—the liberty of different nationalities as members of one sovereign community. This is a service which no other force could accomplish; for it is a corrective alike of absolute monarchy, of democracy, and of constitutionalism, as well as of the centralisation which is common to all three. Neither the monarchical nor the revolutionary, nor the parliamentary system can do this; and all the ideas which have excited enthusiasm in past times are impotent for the purpose except nationality alone.

And secondly, the national theory marks the end of the revolutionary doctrine and its logical exhaustion. In proclaiming the supremacy of the rights of nationality, the system of democratic equality goes beyond its own extreme boundary, and falls into contradiction with itself. Between the democratic and the national phase of the revolution, socialism had intervened, and had already carried the consequences of the principle to an absurdity. But that phase was passed. The revolution survived its offspring, and produced another further result. Nationality is more advanced than socialism, because it is a more arbitrary system. The social theory endeavours to provide for the existence of the individual beneath the terrible burdens which modern society heaps upon labour. It is not merely a development of the notion of equality, but a refuge from real misery and starvation. However false the solution, it was a reasonable demand that the poor should be saved from destruction; and if the freedom of the State was sacrificed to the safety of the individual, the more immediate object was, at least in theory, attained. But nationality does not aim either at liberty or prosperity, both of which it sacrifices to the imperative necessity of making the nation the mould and measure of the State. Its course will be marked with material as well as mortal ruin, in order that a new invention may prevail over the works of God and the interests of mankind. There is no principle of change, no phase of political speculation conceivable, more comprehensive, more subversive, or more arbitrary than this. It is a confutation of democracy, because it sets limits to the exercise of the popular will, and substitutes for it a higher principle. It prevents not only the division, but the extension of the State, and forbids to terminate war by conquest, and to obtain a security for peace. Thus, after surrendering the individual to the collective will, the revolutionary system makes the collective will subject to conditions which are independent of it, and rejects all law, only to be controlled by an accident.

Although, therefore, the theory of nationality is more absurd and more criminal than the theory of socialism, it has an important mission in the world, and marks the final conflict, and therefore the end, of two forces which are the worst enemies of civil freedom,—the absolute monarchy and the revolution.

Section B

Occupation and Economy

Editorial Foreword, BY TALCOTT PARSONS   *407*

I–GENERAL CONSIDERATIONS
Wants in Relation to Activities, BY ALFRED MARSHALL   *409*

II–ECONOMIC INSTITUTIONS
1. *Capitalists and Laborers*, BY ADAM SMITH   *411*
2. *The Division of Society into Classes*, BY THOMAS R. MALTHUS   *415*
3. *Types of Division of Labor*, BY MAX WEBER   *418*
4. *Ownership and Possession*, BY SIR FREDERICK POLLACK
   AND FREDERICK W. MAITLAND   *422*
5. *On Contract*, BY SIR HENRY SUMNER MAINE   *429*
6. *Organic Solidarity and Contract*, BY EMILE DURKHEIM   *436*

III–ORGANIZATION OF THE ECONOMY
1. *The Market*, BY MAX WEBER   *443*
2. *The Principal Modes of Capitalistic Orientation*, BY MAX WEBER   *446*
3. *The Essential Properties of Interest and Money*,
   BY JOHN MAYNARD KEYNES   *447*
4. *The Economic Organization*, BY FRANK H. KNIGHT   *454*

IV–UNITS OF THE ECONOMY
1. *Household Economy*, BY FRÉDÉRIC LE PLAY   *457*
2. *The Social Organization of Production*, BY MAX WEBER   *460*
3. *Budgetary Management and Profit-Making*, BY MAX WEBER   *470*
4. *Industrial Organization*, BY ALFRED MARSHALL   *478*

V–ECONOMIC DEVELOPMENT
1. *A Historical Survey of Industrial Systems*, BY KARL BÜCHER   *493*
2. *The Fundamentals of Economic Development*,
   BY JOSEPH A. SCHUMPETER   *505*

Occupation and Economy

by Talcott Parsons

Tʜe selections in this section deal with the economic aspect of the structure of societies in connection with the theme of occupational roles—the most important focus of the entrance of the services of human individuals in roles into the economic process. We are essentially concerned with analyzing the ways in which this economic aspect of social structure has become differentiated from other aspects. Here, at least as much as anywhere else, we have had to make a few selections from a very large literature. Our two principal criteria were the "classic" character of the statement, and its specific relevance to the sociological, as distinguished from the economic, aspects of the concrete problem areas.

We have classified the materials according to this criterion of sociological relevance. The first subsection is simply a statement of the economist's major frame of reference. The one selection in this subsection is from Alfred Marshall's *Principles,* which was certainly that generation's most influential general treatment of economic theory. The second subsection deals with the institutional framework of a more or less differentiated economy, as that concept was established in the General Introduction to the Reader, and also elaborated in the Introduction to Part Two. The crucial concepts in this area are the division of labor, contractual relations, property, and their relations to the problem of solidarity or integration of the social system. The third subsection deals with the ways in which an economy's structurally differentiated units can be related to each other, so far as the mechanisms are primarily economic. The fourth subsection returns to materials concerning the character of the units themselves. The fifth subsection includes two classic statements concerning problems of change in economic structure.

We have utilized a few sources written earlier than our main period because, in the present subject matter, they set a tone which has been seriously superseded in only a few respects. Adam Smith's famous statement about the division of labor was included in Part One, as one of the critical documents of utilitarian social thought. The second subsection begins with another selection from Smith. It deals with a crucial theme of the institutional setting of classical economic analysis: what the utilitarians considered the primary functional axis of differentiation in the economy—that between "capital," in their specific theoretical sense, and "labor." The problem of organizing the firm as a productive unit was not salient at that time; the primary concern was with financing production, with capital conceived as "making advances to labor." Smith's statement of this theme is followed by a classic statement by Malthus, in certain respects generalizing it into a pattern of differentiating the whole society into classes, on the basis of economic function. This theme leads directly into that of social stratification, particularly through the type of influence exerted on Marx by the classical economists.

The morphology of economic differentiation as such—of the forms taken by the division of labor —is an aspect of comparative social structure that has not been much considered. Here, as in so many areas, Weber's work stands almost alone in its analytical elaboration and comprehensiveness. As an example of the greater complication of the problems and the advance made over the simple classical framework, we present a selection from Weber's economic sociology[1] on types of the divi-

---

1. By the term "Weber's economic sociology," we refer to Chapter II of *The Theory of Social and Economic Organization.*

sion of labor. This provides many starting points for the structural analysis of occupational roles.

Sociologists have neglected the institution of property. Economic historians have paid some attention to it, but on the whole the best treatments are found in the works of legal historians. From the extensive literature, we have chosen a selection from Pollock and Maitland's *History of English Law* that deals with the earlier phases of the legal development which led eventually to the modern institution of ownership in land. This selection is obviously a very fragmentary representation of a large and important subject.

As noted in the two more general Introductions above, contract is the master institution in the economic field. Sir Henry Maine, as a legal historian with an evolutionary perspective, was probably most important in putting the problem into the center of social thinking.[2] He regarded contract as a positive institution, and not simply in the more negative terms common in the utilitarian tradition. However, Durkheim, above all, placed contract in a central position in the theoretical analysis of modern society, as well as in the structure of theory as such. The last selection in the second subsection (chapter 7 of Book I of his *Division of Labor*) is a classic of sociological theory. Polemically oriented to Spencer's concept of contractual relations, it is the definitive critique of utilitarianism from the point of view of the problem of order or social integration; and he built his own theory of organic solidarity on this foundation.

There is a direct transition from the institutional structure of contract to the organization of the more specifically economic modes of contractual relations in markets. Sociologists have also seriously neglected the market, tending to regard it as the subject matter of the economist; however, the latter has tended to neglect the market's sociological aspects. In the period under consideration, Weber's brief statement on the nature and types of markets is the most penetrating and comprehensive in the literature.

The subject of markets leads directly to the subject of the different modes of orientation to the problem of monetary proceeds—the more or less direct analytical sense in which we can speak of "capitalism." Again, Weber, in a brief selection from his economic sociology, presents the most penetrating discussion of this.

The Introduction to Part Two is concerned with the nature of money itself, as an institutionalized mechanism performing the two functions defined by the classical economists as constituting a "measure of value" and as constituting a "medium of exchange." However, it is difficult to find a more general analysis of the nature of money that links its economic characteristics with its institutional foundations. In this area, at the end of the period, a new level was reached in Keynes's famous *General Theory*. We have included the chapter from it that summarizes the principal characteristics of and presuppositions about money.

Finally, we have included Frank Knight's paper, though it verges on being too recent, as a general statement of the nature of a "free enterprise" economy. Though Professor Knight was not, in this Reader's terms, considering the economy as a subsystem of the total society, his delineation of it fits very well with this concept.

The fourth subsection returns to the consideration of structural units in the society. Rather earlier than most of our authors, Le Play made a classic study of European workers' households that provides a general account of the setting of the development of the recruitment of the "worker" level of the labor force in the course of the industrial revolution. This selection is followed by two selections from Weber's economic sociology. The first deals with the theme of "economic bureaucracy"—i.e., with the firm as a social organization, as distinguished from a "combinatorial mechanism" for the factors of production. For Weber, harnessing the mechanisms of bureaucracy to privately controlled economic production was the principal characteristic, structurally speaking, of "rational bourgeois capitalism," as distinguished from the other types described in the second selection in the third subsection. Weber in part directly analyzed and in part foresaw the trend of "occupationalizing" the process of production. The second Weber selection here deals with what he considered the two crucial types of orientation of such units to the market—orientation to profit, and orientation to "budgetary management." Structurally speaking, this is the line dividing orientation toward self-interest and orientation toward collective interest—alternatives often erroneously considered "psychological." Weber correctly treats this as a structural feature of organizational units involved in the economy, and not as a question of individuals' motivations.

A selection from Alfred Marshall on the problem of organization in industry completes this subsection. More than any other economic theorist, Marshall introduced organization, as a fourth factor of production, into the threefold classical

---

2. In relatively direct relation, that is, to sociological interests. The immense literature on the "social contract" preceding this belongs rather to political theory. See the Introduction to Part One, Section A.

scheme of land, labor, and capital. Marshall supported this important theoretical decision with a very shrewd survey of relatively empirical aspects of economic organization. The sociological relevance of this problem is evident; through the organizational factor, one of the major aspects of the society's institutional structure impinges on the economic process as such.

The final subsection essentially consists of a recognition of the problems of structural evolution and change in the economic field. It comprises two selections. The first, written by the Austrian economic historian Karl Bücher, served for long as the classic typology of modes of organization of production in the industrial field. The other is Joseph Schumpeter's famous concept of entrepreneurship, which has had a profound influence on studies of economic development, and is clearly as much sociological as economic in its theoretical orientation.

I–GENERAL CONSIDERATIONS

Wants in Relation to Activities

BY ALFRED MARSHALL

HUMAN WANTS AND DESIRES are countless in number and very various in kind. The uncivilized man indeed has not many more than the brute animal; but every step in his progress upwards increases the variety of his needs together with the variety in his methods of satisfying them. Thus though the brute and the savage alike have their preferences for chioce morsels, neither of them cares much for variety for its own sake. As, however, man rises in civilization, as his mind becomes developed, and even his animal passions begin to associate themselves with mental activities, his wants become rapidly more subtle and more various; and in the minor details of life he begins to desire change for the sake of change, long before he has consciously escaped from the yoke of custom. The first great step in this direction comes with the art of making a fire: gradually he gets to accustom himself to many different kinds of food and drink cooked in many different ways; and before long monotony begins to become irksome to him, and he finds it a great hardship when accident compels him to live for a long time exclusively on one or two kinds of food.

As a man's riches increase his food and drink becomes more various and costly, but his appetite is limited by nature, and when his expenditure on food is extravagant it is more often to gratify the desires of hospitality and display than to indulge his own senses.

This brings us to remark with Senior that "Strong as is the desire for variety, it is weak compared with the desire for distinction: a feeling which if we consider its universality, and its constancy, that it affects all men and at all times, that it comes with us from the cradle and never leaves us till we go into the grave, may be pronounced to be the most powerful of human passions." This great half-truth is well illustrated by a comparison of the desire for choice and various food with that for choice and various dress.

That need for dress which is the result of natural causes varies with the climate and the season of year, and a little with the nature of a person's occupations. But in dress conventional wants overshadow those which are natural. Thus in many of the earlier stages of civilization the sumptuary mandates of Law and Custom have rigidly prescribed to the members of each caste or industrial grade, the style and the standard of expense up to which their dress must reach and beyond which they may not go; and part of the substance of these mandates remains now, though subject to rapid change. In Scotland, for instance, in Adam Smith's time many persons were allowed by custom to go abroad without shoes and stockings who may not do so now; and many may still do it in Scotland who

Reprinted from Alfred Marshall, *Principles of Economics* (2d ed.; London: Macmillan and Co., 1891), chap. ii, pp. 144–48.

might not in England. Again, in England now a well-to-do labourer is expected to appear on Sunday in a black coat and, in some places, in a silk hat; though these would have subjected him to ridicule but a short time ago. In all the lower ranks of life there is a constant increase both in that variety and expensiveness which custom requires as a minimum, and in that which it tolerates as a maximum; and the efforts to obtain distinction by dress are extending themselves throughout the lower grades of English society.

But in the upper grades, though the dress of women is still various and costly, that of men is simple and inexpensive as compared with what it was in Europe not long ago, and is to-day in the East. For those men who are most truly distinguished on their own account, have a natural dislike to seem to claim attention by their dress; and they have set the fashion.[1]

House room satisfies the imperative need for shelter from the weather: but that need plays very little part in the effective demand for house room. For though a small but well-built cabin gives excellent shelter, its stifling atmosphere, its necessary uncleanliness, and its want of the decencies and the quiet of life are great evils. It is not so much that they cause physical discomfort as that they tend to stunt the faculties, and limit people's higher activities. With every increase in these activities the demand for larger house room becomes more urgent.[2]

And therefore relatively large and well appointed house room is, even in the lowest social ranks, at once a "necessary for efficiency," and the most convenient and obvious way of advancing a material claim to social distinction. And even in those grades in which everyone has house room sufficient for the higher activities of himself and his family, a yet further and almost unlimited increase is de-

sired as a requisite for the exercise of many of the higher social activities.

It is again the desire for the exercise and development of activities, spreading through every rank of society, which leads not only to the pursuit of science, literature and art for their own sake, but to the rapidly increasing demand for the work of those who pursue them as professions. This is one of the most marked characteristics of our age; and the same may be said of the growing desire for those amusements, such as athletic games and travelling, which develop activities, rather than indulge any sensuous craving.[3]

For indeed the desire for excellence for its own sake, is almost as wide in its range as the lower desire for distinction. As that graduates down from the ambition of those who may hope that their names will be in men's mouths in distant lands and in distant times, to the hope of the country lass that the new ribbon she puts on for Easter may not pass unnoticed by her neighbours; so the desire for excellence for its own sake graduates down from that of a Newton, or a Stradivarius, to that of the fisherman who, even when no one is looking and he is not in a hurry, delights in handling his craft well, and in the fact that she is well built and responds promptly to his guidance. Desires of this kind exert a great influence on the Supply of the highest faculties and the greatest inventions; and they are not unimportant on the side of Demand. For a large part of the demand for the most highly skilled professional services and the best work of the mechanical artisan, arises from the delight that people have in the training of their own faculties, and in exercising them by aid of the most delicately adjusted and responsive implements.

Speaking broadly therefore, although it is man's wants in the earliest stages of his development that give rise to his activities, yet afterwards each new step upwards is to be regarded rather as the development of new activities giving rise to new wants, than that of new wants giving rise to new activities.

We see this clearly if we look away from healthy conditions of life, where new activities are constantly being developed; and watch the West Indian negro, using his new freedom and wealth not to get the means of satisfying new wants, but in idle stagnation that is not rest; or again look at that rapidly lessening part of the English working classes, who have no ambition and no pride or delight in the growth of their faculties and activities,

---

1. A woman may display wealth, but she may not display only her wealth, by her dress; or else she defeats her ends. She must also suggest some distinction of character as well as of wealth: for though her dress may owe more to her dressmaker than to herself, yet there is a traditional assumption that, being less busy than man with external affairs, she can give more time to taking thought as to her dress. Even under the sway of modern fashions, to be "well dressed"—not "expensively dressed"—is a reasonable minor aim for those who desire to be distinguished for their faculties and abilities; and this will be still more the case if the evil dominion of the wanton vagaries of fashion should pass away. For to arrange costumes beautiful in themselves, various and well-adapted to their purposes is an object worthy of high endeavour; it belongs to the same class, though not to the same rank in that class, as the painting of a good picture.

2. It is true that many active minded working men prefer cramped lodgings in a town to a roomy cottage in the country; but that is because they have a strong taste for those activities for which a country life offers little scope.

3. As a minor point it may be noticed that those drinks which stimulate the mental activities are largely displacing those which merely gratify the senses. The consumption of tea is increasing very fast while that of alcohol is stationary; and there is in all ranks of society a diminishing demand for the grosser and more immediately stupefying form of alcohol.

and spend on drink whatever surplus their wages afford over the bare necessities of a squalid life.

It is not true therefore that "the Theory of Consumption is the scientific basis of economics." For much that is of chief interest in the Science of Wants, is borrowed from the Science of Efforts and Activities. These two supplement one another; either is incomplete without the other. But if either, more than the other, may claim to be the interpreter of the history of man, whether on the economic side or any other, it is the Science of Activities and not that of Wants; and McCulloch indicated their true relations when, discussing "the Progressive Nature of Man," he said:—"The grati-

fication of a want or a desire is merely a step to some new pursuit. In every stage of his progress he is destined to contrive and invent, to engage in new undertakings; and, when these are accomplished to enter with fresh energy upon others."

From this it follows that such a discussion of Demand as is possible at this stage of our work, must be confined to an elementary analysis of an almost purely formal kind. The higher study of Consumption must come after, and not before, the main body of economic analysis; and, though it may have its beginning within the proper domain of economics, it cannot find its conclusions there, but must extend far beyond.

II–ECONOMIC INSTITUTIONS

---

1. *Capitalists and Laborers*

BY ADAM SMITH

THE PRODUCE of labour constitutes the natural recompence or wages of labour.

In that original state of things, which precedes both the appropriation of land and the accumulation of stock, the whole produce of labour belongs to the labourer. He has neither landlord nor master to share with him.

Had this state continued, the wages of labour would have augmented with all those improvements in its productive powers, to which the division of labour gives occasion. All things would gradually have become cheaper. They would have been produced by a smaller quantity of labour; and as the commodities produced by equal quantities of labour would naturally in this state of things be exchanged for one another, they would have been purchased likewise with the produce of a smaller quantity.

But though all things would have become cheaper in reality, in appearance many things might have become dearer than before, or have been exchanged for a greater quantity of other goods. Let us sup-

pose, for example, that in the greater part of employments the productive powers of labour had been improved to tenfold, or that a day's labour could produce ten times the quantity of work which it had done originally; but that in a particular employment they had been improved only to double, or that a day's labour could produce only twice the quantity of work which it had done before. In exchanging the produce of a day's labour in the greater part of employments, for that of a day's labour in this particular one, ten times the original quality of work in them would purchase only twice the original quantity in it. Any particular quantity in it, therefore, a pound weight, for example, would appear to be five times dearer than before. In reality, however, it would be twice as cheap. Though it required five times the quantity of other goods to purchase it, it would require only half the quantity of labour either to purchase or to produce it. The acquisition, therefore, would be twice as easy as before.

But this original state of things, in which the labourer enjoyed the whole produce of his own labour, could not last beyond the first introduction of the appropriation of land and the accumulation of stock. It was at an end, therefore, long before the

Reprinted from Adam Smith, *An Inquiry into the Nature and Causes of the Wealth of Nations* (7th ed.; London: A. Strahan & T. Cadell, 1793), chap. viii, pp. 96–111.

most considerable improvements were made in the productive powers of labour, and it would be to no purpose to trace further what might have been its effects upon the recompence or wages of labour.

As soon as land becomes private property, the landlord demands a share of almost all the produce which the labourer can either raise, or collect from it. His rent makes the first deduction from the produce of the labour which is employed upon land.

It seldom happens that the person who tills the ground has wherewithal to maintain himself till he reaps the harvest. His maintenance is generally advanced to him from the stock of a master, the farmer who employs him, and who would have no interest to employ him, unless he was to share in the produce of his labour, or unless his stock was to be replaced to him with a profit. This profit makes a second deduction from the produce of the labour which is employed upon land.

The produce of almost all other labour is liable to the like deduction of profit. In all arts and manufactures the greater part of the workmen stand in need of a master to advance them the materials of their work, and their wages and maintenance till it be completed. He shares in the produce of their labour, or in the value which it adds to the materials upon which it is bestowed; and in this share consists his profit.

It sometimes happens, indeed, that a single independent workman has stock sufficient both to purchase the materials of his work, and to maintain himself till it be completed. He is both master and workman, and enjoys the whole produce of his own labour, or the whole value which it adds to the materials upon which it is bestowed. It includes what are usually two distinct revenues, belonging to two distinct persons, the profits of stock, and the wages of labour.

Such cases, however, are not very frequent, and in every part of Europe, twenty workmen serve under a master for one that is independent; and the wages of labour are every where understood to be, what they usually are, when the labourer is one person, and the owner of the stock which employs him another.

What are the common wages of labour, depends every where upon the contract usually made between those two parties, whose interests are by no means the same. The workmen desire to get as much, the masters to give as little as possible. The former are disposed to combine in order to raise, the latter in order to lower the wages of labour.

It is not, however, difficult to foresee which of the two parties must, upon all ordinary occasions, have the advantage in the dispute, and force the other into a compliance with their terms. The masters, being fewer in number, can combine much more easily; and the law, besides, authorises, or at least does not prohibit their combinations, while it prohibits those of the workmen. We have no acts of parliament against combining to lower the price of work; but many against combining to raise it. In all such disputes the masters can hold out much longer. A landlord, a farmer, a master manufacturer, or merchant, though they did not employ a single workman, could generally live a year or two upon the stocks which they have already acquired. Many workmen could not subsist a week, few could subsist a month, and scarce any a year without employment. In the long-run the workman may be as necessary to his master as his master is to him; but the necessity is not so immediate.

We rarely hear, it has been said, of the combinations of masters, though frequently of those of workmen. But whoever imagines, upon this account, that masters rarely combine, is as ignorant of the world as of the subject. Masters are always and every where in a sort of tacit, but constant and uniform, combination, not to raise the wages of labour above their actual rate. To violate this combination is every where a most unpopular action, and a sort of reproach to a master among his neighbors and equals. We seldom, indeed, hear of this combination, because it is the usual, and one may say, the natural state of things which nobody ever hears of. Masters too sometimes enter into particular combinations to sink the wages of labour even below this rate. These are always conducted with the utmost silence and secrecy, till the moment of execution, and when the workmen yield, as they sometimes do, without resistance, though severely felt by them, they are never heard of by other people. Such combinations, however, are frequently resisted by a contrary defensive combination of the workmen; who sometimes too, without any provocation of this kind, combine of their own accord to raise the price of their labour. Their usual pretenses are, sometimes the high price of provisions; sometimes the great profit which their masters make by their work. But whether their combinations be offensive or defensive, they are always abundantly heard of. In order to bring the point to a speedy decision, they have always recourse to the loudest clamour, and sometimes to the most shocking violence and outrage. They are desperate, and act with the folly and extravagance of desperate men, who must either starve, or frighten their masters into an immediate compliance with their demands. The masters upon these occasions are just as clamorous upon the other side, and never cease to call aloud for the assistance of the civil magistrate, and the rigorous execution of those laws which have been enacted with so much severity against the combinations of servants, labourers, and journeymen. The workmen, accordingly, very seldom derive any advantage from the violence of those tumultuous combinations, which, partly from the interposition of the civil magistrate, partly from the superior steadiness of the masters, partly from the necessity which the greater part of the workmen are under of submitting for the sake of present subsistence, generally end in nothing, but the punishment or ruin of the ringleaders.

But though in disputes with their workmen, masters must generally have the advantage, there is however a certain rate, below which it seems impossible to reduce, for any considerable time, the ordinary wages even of the lowest species of labour.

A man must always live by his work, and his wages must at least be sufficient to maintain him. They must even upon most occasions be somewhat more; otherwise it would be impossible for him to bring up a family, and the race of such workmen could not last beyond the first generation. Mr. Cantillon seems, upon this account, to suppose that the lowest species of common labourers must every where earn at least double their own maintenance, in order that one with another they may be enabled to bring up two children; the labour of the wife, on account of her necessary attendance on the children, being supposed no more than sufficient to provide for herself. But one half the children born, it is computed, die before the age of manhood. The poorest labourers, therefore, according to this account, must, one with another, attempt to rear at least four children, in order that two may have an equal chance of living to that age. But the necessary maintenance of four children, it is supposed, may be nearly equal to that of one man. The labour of an able-bodied slave, the same author adds, is computed to be worth double his maintenance; and that of the meanest labourer, he thinks, cannot be worth less than that of an able-bodied slave. Thus far at least seems certain, that, in order to bring up a family, the labour of the husband and wife together must, even in the lowest species of common labour, be able to earn something more than what is precisely necessary for their own maintenance; but in what proportion, whether in that above mentioned, or in any other, I shall not take upon me to determine.

There are certain circumstances, however, which sometimes give the labourers an advantage, and enable them to raise their wages considerably above this rate; evidently the lowest which is consistent with common humanity.

When in any country the demand for those who live by wages, labourers, journeymen, servants of every kind, is continually increasing; when every year furnishes employment for a greater number than had been employed the year before, the workmen have no occasion to combine in order to raise their wages. The scarcity of hands occasions a competition among masters, who bid against one another, in order to get workmen, and thus voluntarily break through the natural combination of masters not to raise wages.

The demand for those who live by wages, it is evident, cannot increase but in proportion to the increase of the funds which are destined to the payment of wages. These funds are of two kinds: first, the revenue which is over and above what is necessary for the maintenance; and, secondly, the stock which is over and above what is necessary for the employment of their masters.

When the landlord, annuitant, or monied man, has a greater revenue than what he judges sufficient to maintain his own family, he employs either the whole or a part of the surplus in maintaining one or more menial servants. Increase this surplus, and he will naturally increase the number of those servants.

When an independent workman, such as a weaver or shoemaker, has got more stock than what is sufficient to purchase the materials of his own work, and to maintain himself till he can dispose of it, he naturally employs one or more journeymen with the surplus, in order to make a profit by their work. Increase this surplus, and he will naturally increase the number of his journeymen.

The demand for those who live by wages, therefore, necessarily increases with the increase of the revenue and stock of every country, and cannot possibly increase without it. The increase of revenue and stock is the increase of national wealth. The demand for those who live by wages, therefore, naturally increases with the increase of national wealth, and cannot possibly increase without it.

It is not the actual greatness of national wealth, but its continual increase, which occasions a rise in the wages of labour. It is not, accordingly, in the richest countries, but in the most thriving, or in those which are growing rich the fastest, that the wages of labour are highest. England is certainly, in the present times, a much richer country than any part of North America. The wages of labour, however, are much higher in North America than in any part of England. In the province of New York, common labourers earn* three shillings and sixpence currency, equal to two shillings

---

* This was written in 1773, before the commencement of the late disturbances.

sterling, a day; ship carpenters, ten shillings and sixpence currency, with a pint of rum worth sixpence sterling, equal in all to six shillings and sixpence sterling; house carpenters and bricklayers, eight shillings currency, equal to four shillings and sixpence sterling; journeymen taylors, five shillings currency, equal to about two shillings and ten pence sterling. These prices are all above the London price; and wages are said to be as high in the other colonies as in New York. The price of provisions is every where in North America much lower than in England. A dearth has never been known there. In the worst seasons, they have always had a sufficiency for themselves, though less for exportation. If the money price of labour, therefore, be higher than it is any where in the mother country, its real price, the real command of the necessaries and conveniences of life which it conveys to the labourer, must be higher in a still greater proportion.

But though North America is not yet so rich as England, it is much more thriving, and advancing with much greater rapidity to the further acquisition of riches. The most decisive mark of the prosperity of any country is the increase of the number of its inhabitants. In Great Britain, and most other European countries, they are not supposed to double in less than five hundred years. In the British colonies in North America, it has been found, that they double in twenty or five-and-twenty years. Nor in the present times is this increase principally owing to the continual importation of new inhabitants, but to the great multiplication of the species. Those who live to old age; it is said, frequently see there from fifty to a hundred, and sometimes many more, descendants from their own body. Labour is there so well rewarded, that a numerous family of children, instead of being a burthen, is a source of opulence and prosperity to the parents. The labour of each child, before it can leave their house, is computed to be worth a hundred pounds clear gain to them. A young widow with four or five young children, who, among the middling or inferior ranks of people in Europe, would have so little chance for a second husband, is there frequently courted as a sort of fortune. The value of children is the greatest of all encouragements to marriage. We cannot, therefore, wonder that the people in North America should generally marry very young. Notwithstanding the great increase occasioned by such early marriages, there is a continual complaint of the scarcity of hands in North America. The demand for labourers, the funds destined for maintaining them, increase, it seems, still faster than they can find labourers to employ.

Though the wealth of a country should be very great, yet if it has been long stationary, we must not expect to find the wages of labour very high in it. The funds destined for the payment of wages, the revenue and stock of its inhabitants, may be of the greatest extent; but if they have continued for several centuries of the same, or very nearly of the same extent, the number of labourers employed every year could easily supply, and even more than supply, the number wanted the following year. There could seldom be any scarcity of hands, nor could the masters be obliged to bid against one another in order to get them. The hands, on the contrary, would, in this case, naturally multiply beyond their employment. There would be a constant scarcity of employment, and the labourers would be obliged to bid against one another in order to get it. If in such a country the wages of labour had ever been more than sufficient to maintain the labourer, and to enable him to bring up a family, the competition of the labourers and the interest of the masters would soon reduce them to this lowest rate which is consistent with common humanity. China has been long one of the richest, that is, one of the most fertile, best cultivated, most industrious, and most populous countries in the world. It seems, however, to have been long stationary. Marco Polo, who visited it more than five hundred years ago, describes its cultivation, industry, and populousness, almost in the same terms in which they are described by travellers in the present times. It had, perhaps, even long before his time, acquired that full complement of riches which the nature of its laws and institutions permits it to acquire. The accounts of all travellers, inconsistent in many other respects, agree in the low wages of labour, and in the difficulty which a labourer finds in bringing up a family in China. If by digging the ground a whole day he can get what will purchase a small qauntity of rice in the evening, he is contented. The condition of artificers is, if possible, still worse. Instead of waiting idolently in their work-houses, for the calls of their customers, as in Europe, they are continually running about the streets, with the tools of their respective trades, offering their service, and as it were begging employment. The poverty of the lower ranks of people in China far surpasses that of the most beggarly nations in Europe. In the neighbourhood of Canton many hundred, it is commonly said, many thousand families have no habitation on the land, but live constantly in little fishing boats upon the rivers and canals. The subsistence which they find there is so scanty that they are eager to fish up the nastiest garbage thrown overboard from any European ship. Any carrion, the carcase of a dead dog or cat, for example, though half putrid and stinking, is as welcome to them as the most wholesome food to the people of other countries. Marriage is encouraged in China, not by the profitableness of children, but by the liberty of destroying them. In all great towns several are every night exposed in the street, or drowned like puppies in the water. The performance of this horrid office is even said to be the avowed business by which some people earn their subsistence.

China, however, though it may perhaps stand still, does not seem to go backwards. Its towns are no where deserted by their inhabitants. The lands which had once been cultivated, are nowhere neglected. The same, or very nearly the same, annual labour must therefore continue to be performed, and the funds destined for maintaining it must not, consequently, be sensibly diminished. The lowest class of labourers, therefore, notwithstanding their scanty subsistence, must some way or another make shift to continue their race so far as to keep up their usual numbers.

But it would be otherwise in a country where the funds destined for the maintenance of labour were sensibly decaying. Every year the demand for servants and labourers would, in all the different classes of employments, be less than it had been the year before. Many who had been bred in the superior classes, not being able to find employment in their own business, would be glad to seek it in the lowest. The lowest class being not only overstocked with its own workmen, but with the overflowings of all the other classes, the competition for employment would be so great in it, as to reduce the wages of labour to the most miserable and scanty subsistence of the labourer. Many would not be able to find employment even upon these hard terms, but would either starve, or be driven to seek a subsistence either by begging, or by the perpetration perhaps of the greatest enormities. Want, famine, and mortality, would immediately prevail in that class, and from thence extend themselves to all the superior classes, till the number of inhabitants in the country was reduced to what could easily be maintained by the revenue and stock which remained in it, and which had escaped either the tyranny or calamity which had destroyed the rest. This perhaps is nearly the present state of Bengal, and of some other of the English settlements in the East Indies. In a fertile country which had before been much depopulated, where subsistence, consequently, should not be very difficult, and where, notwithstanding, three or four hundred thousand people die of hunger in one year, we may be assured that the funds destined for the maintenance of the labouring poor are fast decaying. The difference between the genius of the British constitution which protects and governs North America, and that of the mercantile company which oppresses and domineers in the East Indies, cannot perhaps be better illustrated than by the different state of those countries.

The liberal reward of labour, therefore, as it is the necessary effect, so it is the natural symptom of increasing national wealth. The scanty maintenance of the labouring poor, on the other hand, is the natural symptom that things are at a stand, and their starving condition that they are going fast backwards.

2. *The Division of Society into Classes*

BY THOMAS R. MALTHUS

DR. ADAM SMITH has very justly observed, that nations, as well as individuals, grow rich by parsimony, and poor by profusion; and that, therefore, every frugal man was a friend, and every spendthrift an enemy to his country. The reason he

Reprinted from Thomas R. Malthus, *First Essay on Population* (1798), reprinted for the Royal Economic Society (London: Macmillan Co., 1926), pp. 282–301, with the permission of the Macmillan Co.

gives is, that what is saved from revenue is always added to stock, and is therefore taken from the maintenance of labour that is generally unproductive, and employed in the maintenance of labour that realizes itself in valuable commodities. No observation can be more evidently just. The subject of Mr. Godwin's essay is a little similar in its first appearance, but in essence is as distinct as possible. He considers the mischief of profusion, as an acknowledged truth; and therefore makes his comparison between the avaricious man, and the man who spends his income. But the avaricious man of Mr. Godwin, is totally a distinct character, at least with regard to his effect upon the prosperity of the state, from the frugal man of Dr. Adam Smith. The frugal man in order to make more money, saves from his income, and adds to his capital; and this capital he either employs himself in the maintenance of productive labour, or he lends it to some other person, who will probably employ it in this way. He benefits the state, because he adds to its general capital; and because wealth employed as capital, not only sets in motion more labour, than when spent as income, but the labour is besides of a more valuable kind. But the avaricious man of Mr. Godwin locks up his wealth in a chest, and sets in motion no labour of any kind, either productive or unproductive. This is so essential a difference, that Mr. Godwin's decision in his essay, appears at once as evidently true. It could not, indeed, but occur to Mr. Godwin, that some present inconvenience might arise to the poor, from thus locking up the funds destined for the maintenance of labour. The only way, therefore, he had of weakening this objection, was to compare the two characters chiefly with regard to their tendency to accelerate the approach of that happy state of cultivated equality, on which he says we ought always to fix our eyes as our polar star.

I think it has been proved in the former parts of this essay, that such a state of society is absolutely impracticable. What consequences then are we to expect from looking to such a point, as our guide and polar star, in the great sea of political discovery? Reason would teach us to expect no other, than winds perpetually adverse, constant but fruitless toil, frequent shipwreck, and certain misery. We shall not only fail in making the smallest real approach towards such a perfect form of society; but by wasting our strength of mind and body, in a direction in which it is impossible to proceed, and by the frequent distress which we must necessarily occasion by our repeated failures, we shall evidently impede that degree of improvement in society, which is really attainable.

It has appeared that a society constituted according to Mr. Godwin's system, must, from the inevitable laws of our nature, degenerate into a class of proprietors, and a class of labourers; and that the substitution of benevolence, for self-love, as the moving principle of society, instead of producing the happy effects that might be expected from so fair a name, would cause the same pressure of want to be felt by the whole of society, which is now felt only by a part. It is to the established administration of property, and to the apparently narrow principle of self-love, that we are indebted for all the noblest exertions of human genius, all the finer and more delicate emotions of the soul, for every thing, indeed, that distinguishes the civilized, from the savage state; and no sufficient change, has as yet taken place in the nature of civilized man, to enable us to say, that he either is, or ever will be, in a state, when he may safely throw down the ladder by which he has risen to this eminence.

If in every society that has advanced beyond the savage state, a class of proprietors, and a class of labourers,[1] must necessarily exist, it is evident, that, as labour is the only property of the class of labourers, every thing that tends to diminish the value of this property, must tend to diminish the possessions of this part of society. The only way that a poor man has of supporting himself in independence, is by the exertion of his bodily strength. This is the only commodity he has to give in exchange for the necessaries of life. It would hardly appear then that you benefit him, by narrowing the market for this commodity, by decreasing the demand for labour, and lessening the value of the only property that he possesses.

Mr. Godwin would perhaps say, that the whole system of barter and exchange, is a vile and iniquitous traffic. If you would essentially relieve the poor man, you should take a part of his labour upon yourself, or give him your money, without exacting so severe a return for it. In answer to the first method proposed, it may be observed, that even if the rich could be persuaded to assist the poor in this way, the value of the assistance would be comparatively trifling. The rich, though they think themselves of great importance, bear but a small proportion in point of numbers to the poor, and would, therefore, relieve them but of a small part of their burdens by taking a share. Were all those that are employed in the labours of luxuries, added to the number of those employed in producing necessaries; and could these necessary labours be amicably divided among all, each man's share might indeed be comparatively light; but desireable as such an amicable division would undoubtedly be, I can-

---

1. It should be observed, that the principal argument of this essay, only goes to prove the necessity of a class of proprietors, and a class of labourers, but by no means infers, that the present great inequality of property, is either necessary or useful to society. On the contrary, it must certainly be considered as an evil, and every institution that promotes it, is essentially bad and impolitic. But whether a government could with advantage to society actively interfere to repress inequality of fortunes, may be a matter of doubt. Perhaps the generous system of perfect liberty, adopted by Dr. Adam Smith, and the French œconomists, would be ill exchanged for any system of restraint.

not conceive any practical principle[2] according to which it could take place. It has been shewn, that the spirit of benevolence, guided by the strict impartial justice that Mr. Godwin describes, would, if vigorously acted upon, depress in want and misery the whole human race. Let us examine what would be the consequence, if the proprietor were to retain a decent share for himself; but to give the rest away to the poor, without exacting a task from them in return. Not to mention the idleness and the vice that such a proceeding, if general, would probably create in the present state of society, and the great risk there would be, of diminishing the produce of land, as well as the labours of luxury, another objection yet remains.

It has appeared that from the principle of population, more will always be in want than can be adequately supplied. The surplus of the rich man might be sufficient for three, but four will be desirous to obtain it. He cannot make this selection of three out of the four, without conferring a great favour on those that are the objects of his choice. These persons must consider themselves as under a great obligation to him, and as dependent upon him for their support. The rich man would feel his power, and the poor man his dependence; and the evil effects of these two impressions on the human heart are well known. Though I perfectly agree with Mr. Godwin therefore in the evil of hard labour; yet I still think it a less evil, and less calculated to debase the human mind, than dependence; and every history of man that we have ever read, places in a strong point of view, the danger to which that mind is exposed, which is intrusted with constant power.

In the present state of things, and particularly when labour is in request, the man who does a days work for me, confers full as great an obligation upon me, as I do upon him. I possess what he wants; he possesses what I want. We make an amicable exchange. The poor man walks erect in conscious independence; and the mind of his employer is not vitiated by a sense of power.

Three or four hundred years ago, there was undoubtedly much less labour in England, in proportion to the population, than at present; but there was much more dependence: and we probably should not now enjoy our present degree of civil liberty, if the poor, by the introduction of manufac-

tures, had not been enabled to give something in exchange for the provisions of the great Lords, instead of being dependent upon their bounty. Even the greatest enemies of trade and manufactures, and I do not reckon myself a very determined friend to them, must allow, that when they were introduced into England, liberty came in their train.

Nothing that has been said, tends in the most remote degree to undervalue the principle of benevolence. It is one of the noblest and most godlike qualities of the human heart, generated perhaps, slowly and gradually from self-love; and afterwards intended to act as a general law, whose kind office it should be, to soften the partial deformities, to correct the asperities, and to smooth the wrinkles of its parent: and this seems to be the analogy of all nature. Perhaps there is no one general law of nature that will not appear, to us at least, to produce partial evil; and we frequently observe at the same time, some bountiful provision, which acting as another general law, corrects the inequalities of the first.

The proper office of benevolence is to soften the partial evils arising from self-love, but it can never be substituted in its place. If no man were to allow himself to act, till he had completely determined, that the action he was about to perform, was more conducive than any other to the general good, the most enlightened minds would hesitate in perplexity and amazement; and the unenlightened, would be continually committing the grossest mistakes.

As Mr. Godwin, therefore, has not laid down any practical principle, according to which the necessary labours of agriculture might be amicably shared among the whole class of labourers; by general invectives against employing the poor, he appears to pursue an unattainable good through much present evil. For if every man who employs the poor, ought to be considered as their enemy, and as adding to the weight of their oppressions; and if the miser is, for this reason, to be preferred to the man who spends his income, it follows, that any number of men who now spend their incomes, might, to the advantage of society, be converted into misers. Suppose then, that a hundred thousand persons who now employ ten men each, were to lock up their wealth from general use, it is evident, that a million of working men of different kinds would be completely thrown out of all employment. The extensive misery that such an event would produce in the present state of society, Mr. Godwin himself could hardly refuse to acknowledge; and I question whether he might not find some difficulty in proving, that a conduct of this kind tended more than the conduct of those who spend their incomes to

---

2. Mr. Godwin seems to have but little respect for practical principles; but I own it appears to me, that he is a much greater benefactor to mankind, who points out how inferior good may be attained, than he who merely expiates on the deformity of the present state of society, and the beauty of a different state, without pointing out a practical method, that might be immediately applied, of accelerating our advances from the one, to the other.

"place human beings in the condition in which they ought to be placed."

But Mr. Godwin says, that the miser really locks up nothing; that the point has not been rightly understood; and that the true development and definition of the nature of wealth have not been applied to illustrate it. Having defined therefore wealth, very justly, to be the commodities raised and fostered by human labour, he observes, that the miser locks up neither corn, nor oxen, nor clothes, nor houses. Undoubtedly he does not really lock up these articles, but he locks up the power of producing them, which is virtually the same. These things are certainly used and consumed by his contemporaries, as truly, and to as great an extent, as if he were a beggar; but not to as great an extent, as if he had employed his wealth, in turning up more land, in breeding more oxen, in employing more taylors, and in building more houses. But supposing, for a moment, that the conduct of the miser did not tend to check any really useful produce, how are all those, who are thrown out of employment, to obtain patents which they may shew in order to be awarded a proper share of the food and raiment produced by the society? This is the unconquerable difficulty.

I am perfectly willing to concede to Mr. Godwin that there is much more labour in the world than is really necessary; and that, if the lower classes of society could agree among themselves never to work more than six or seven hours in the day, the commodities essential to human happiness might still be produced in as great abundance as at present. But it is almost impossible to conceive that such an agreement could be adhered to. From the principle of population, some would necessarily be more in want than others. Those that had large families, would naturally be desirous of exchanging two hours more of their labour for an ampler quantity of subsistence. How are they to be prevented from making this exchange? It would be a violation of the first and most sacred property that a man possesses, to attempt, by positive institutions, to interfere with his command over his own labour.

Till Mr. Godwin, therefore, can point out some practical plan according to which the necessary labour in a society might be equitably divided; his invectives against labour, if they were attended to, would certainly produce much present evil, without approximating us to that state of cultivated equality to which he looks forward as his polar star; and which, he seems to think, should at present be our guide in determining the nature and tendency of human actions. A mariner guided by such a polar star is in danger of shipwreck.

Perhaps there is no possible way in which wealth could, in general, be employed so beneficially to a state, and particularly to the lower orders of it, as by improving and rendering productive that land, which to a farmer would not answer the expence of cultivation. Had Mr. Godwin exerted his energetic eloquence in painting the superior worth and usefulness of the character who employed the poor in this way, to him who employed them in narrow luxuries, every enlightened man must have applauded his efforts. The increasing demand for agricultural labour must always tend to better the condition of the poor; and if the accession of work be of this kind, so far is it from being true, that the poor would be obliged to work ten hours, for the same price, that they before worked eight, that the very reverse would be the fact; and a labourer might then support his wife and family as well by the labour of six hours, as he could before by the labour of eight.

3. *Types of Division of Labor*

BY MAX WEBER

EVERY TYPE of social action in a group which is oriented to economic considerations and every associative relationship of economic signifi-

Reprinted from Max Weber, *The Theory of Social and Economic Organization*, trans. A. M. Henderson and Talcott Parsons, ed. Talcott Parsons (Glencoe, Ill.: The Free Press, 1947), pp. 218–24. Copyright 1947 by Oxford University Press.

cance involves to some degree a particular mode of division and organization of human services in the interest of production. A mere glance at the facts of economic action reveals that different persons perform different types of work and that these are combined in the service of common ends, with each other and with the non-human means of production, in the most varied ways. The complexity of these phenomena is extreme, but yet it is possible to distinguish a few types.

Human services for economic purposes may be distinguished as (a) "managerial," or (b) oriented to the instructions of a managerial agency. The latter type will be called "labour" for purposes of the following discussion.

It goes without saying that managerial activity constitutes "labour" in the most definite sense if labour is taken to mean the expenditure of time and effort as such. The use of the term labour in contradistinction to managerial activity has, however, come to be generally accepted for social reasons and this usage will be followed in the present discussion. For more general purposes, the terms "services" or "work" will be used.

Within a social group the ways in which labour or other work may be carried on typically may be classified in the following way: (1) technically, according to the way in which the services of a plurality of co-operating individuals are divided up and combined, with each other and with the non-human means of production, to carry out the technical procedures of production; (2) socially. In the first place, forms of labour may vary according to whether particular services do or do not fall within the jurisdiction of autocephalous and autonomous economic units, and according to the economic character of these units. Closely connected with this is variation according to the modes and extent to which the various services, the non-human means of production, and opportunities for economic profit, used as sources of profit or as means of acquisition, are or are not appropriated. These factors determine the mode of occupational differentiation, a social phenomenon, and the organization of the market, an economic phenomenon; (3) finally, in every case of combination of services with each other and with non-human means of production, it is important, in determining their division among economic units and the modes of appropriation, to know whether they are used in a context of budgetary administration or of profit-making enterprise.

1. It should be emphatically stated that the present discussion is concerned only with a brief summary of the sociological aspects of these phenomena, so far as they are relevant to its context. The economic aspect is included only in so far as it is expressed in what are formally sociological categories. In a substantive sense, the discussion would be economic only if the conditions of price determination and market relationships, which have heretofore been dealt with only on a theoretical level, were introduced into it. It would, however, be possible to treat such substantive aspects of the

problem in such a general introduction to the field only in terms which would involve a very unfortunate kind of one-sidedness. Furthermore, attempts to explain these things in *purely* economic terms are both misleading and open to question. To take an example: The Dark Ages in the tenth to the twelfth centuries have been held to be the decisive period for the development of that type of Medieval labour which, though subject to corporate regulations, was in a sense free labour. In particular, it is held that the lords were in a situation of having to compete for the fees and income arising from the control over land, personal status, and jurisdiction; and that this situation permitted peasants, miners, and artisans to profit from the competition of the lords. It is further held that the decisive period for the development of capitalism was that of the great long-drawn-out price revolution of the sixteenth century. This led both to an absolute and a relative increase in the prices of almost all products of the land in the Western World. It is only necessary to apply well-known principles of agricultural economics to see that this both made possible and stimulated the development of enterprises which sold products on the market. This in turn led to the development of large-scale production, in part, as in England, of the capitalistic type; in part, as between the Elbe and Russia, more on the basis of patriarchal estates. Furthermore, it meant, in most cases, an absolute rise of prices, but, relatively in the normal case, a fall in the price of important industrial products. Then, so far as the necessary forms of organization and other conditions, both external and subjective, were given, there would be a stimulus to the development of market enterprises related in a competitive system. These were, to be sure, not present in Germany, but this fact is held to account for the economic decline which started there about that time. The consequence of all this is the development of capitalistic enterprises in the industrial field. Its necessary prerequisite was the development of extensive markets. An indication that this was actually happening is seen in certain changes of English commercial policy, to say nothing of other phenomena.

In order to verify theoretical reasoning about the substantive economic conditions of the development of economic structures, it would be necessary to employ theses, such as these and similar ones. This cannot, however, be attempted in the present discussion. These and numerous other equally controversial theories, even so far as they could be proved not to be wholly erroneous, cannot be incorporated into the present scheme which is intentionally limited to sociological *concepts*. In that the present discussion renounces any attempt to take account of this type of data, however, the following exposition in this chapter explicitly repudiates any claim to concrete "explanation" and restricts itself to working out a sociological typology. The same is true of the previous discussion in that it consciously omitted to develop a theory of money and price determination. This must be strongly emphasized. For the facts of the economic situation provide the flesh and blood for a genuine explanation of the process by which even a sociologically relevant development takes place. What can be done here is only to provide a scaffolding which is adequate to enable the analysis to work with relatively clear and definite concepts.

It is obvious, not only that no attempt is here made to do justice to the empirical historical aspect of economic development, but even the typology of the genetic order of possible forms is neglected. The present aim is only to develop a systematic scheme of classification.

2. A common and correct objection to the usual terminology of economics, is that it fails to make a distinction between the "organization" and the "enterprise."[1] In the field of economically oriented action, "organization" is a technical category which designates the ways in which various types of services are continuously combined with each other and with non-human means of production. Its antithesis is one of two things: either intermittent activity or that which is discontinuous from the technical point of view, as is true empirically of every household. The antithesis of enterprise, denoting as it does a type of economic orientation, namely, profit-making, is the budgetary unit which is oriented to provision for needs. Classification of types of economic orientation in terms of profit-making enterprise and budgetary units is not, however, exhaustive. There are actions oriented to acquisition which are not covered by the concept of enterprise. All cases of seeking earnings from work, like the work of the author, the artist, the official, are neither one nor the other. The receipt and uses of incomes from investment is a clear case of budgetary administration.

Despite the mixture of categories, a profit-making organization (*Erwerbsbetrieb*)[2] is spoken of wherever there is continuous permanent co-ordinated action on the part of an entrepreneur. Such action is in fact unthinkable without an "organization," though, in the limiting case, it may be merely the organization of his own activity, without any help from others. Here it is a matter primarily of distinguishing the budgetary unit from the enterprise and its attendant organization. The term "profit-making organization," instead of a continuous profit-making enterprise is, it may now be noted, to be accepted, because there it is unambiguous, only for the simplest case where the unit of technical organization coincides with the unit of enterprise. But in a market economy, it is possible for a number of technically separate organizations or "plants" to be combined in a single enterprise. The latter receives its unity by no means alone through the personal relationship of the various units to the same entrepreneur, but by virtue of the fact that they are all controlled in terms of some kind of consistent plan in their exploitation for purposes of profit. It is hence possible that there should be transitional forms. Where the term "organization" or "plant" is used by itself, it will always refer to the technically distinct unit consisting in buildings, equipment, labour forces, and technical management. The latter is possibly heterocephalous and heteronomous. This state of affairs would still exist, as even ordinary usage recognizes, in a communistic economy. The term "profit-making organization" will be used from now on only in cases where the technical and the economic unit, the enterprise, coincide.[3]

The relation between organization and enterprise raises particularly difficult terminological questions in the case of such categories as "factory" and "puting-out industry."[4] The latter is clearly a category of enterprise. From the point of view of organization, there are two types of units: The commercial organization and those which are parts of the workers' households without any centralized workshop except in certain cases where a master craftsman organizes one on his own initiative. The organizations in the worker's household perform certain specified functions for the commercial organization, and vice versa. The process is thus not understandable in terms of technical organization alone. It is necessary in addition to employ the categories of market, profit-making enterprise, household (of the individual worker), and exploitation of contracted services for profit.

---

1. *Betrieb* and *Unternehmung*. In a good deal of his discussion, Weber uses the term *Betrieb* in a context where this distinction is not important. Thus he speaks of an *Erwerbsbetrieb;* hence *Betrieb* has often been translated as "enterprise." But where the distinction is important in the context, "organization" is used.—ED.

2. See above note. In most cases it has seemed best to translate *Erwerbsbetrieb* with "enterprise," as to speak of a profit-making organization as distinguished from an enterprise would unduly complicate the terminology without bringing out sufficiently important empirical distinctions. —ED.

3. As has already been noted, it does not seem necessary to introduce this terminological complication into the translation.—ED.

4. *Hausindustrie.* This is often translated as "domestic industry." As Weber points out, however, this term designates the unit of technical organization, namely the household, and not of business enterprise. For this reason such authorities as Professor E. F. Gay prefer the term "putting out industry."—ED.

The concept of "factory" could, as has often been proposed, be defined in entirely non-economic terms as a mode of technical organization, leaving aside consideration of the status of the workers, whether free or unfree, the mode of division of labour, involving the extent of internal technical specialization, and the type of means of production, whether machines or tools. This would make it equivalent to an organized workshop. But besides this, it is neccessary to include in the definition the mode of appropriation in the hands of an owner of the premises and the means of production. Otherwise, the concept becomes confused with that of an "ergasterion."[5] If this distinction is made, it seems more appropriate to define both factory and "putting-out system" as strictly economic categories of capitalistic enterprise. Then, in a strictly socialistic economy, there would neither be factories nor "putting-out" enterprises, but only workshops, buildings, machines, tools, and various types of labour in the shop or at home.

3. The question of stages of economic development will be considered only in so far as it is absolutely necessary, and then only incidentally. The following points will suffice for the present.

It has fortunately become more common lately to distinguish types of economic system from types of economic policy. The stages which Schönberg first suggested, and, which in a somewhat altered form, have become identified with Schmoller's name, "domestic economy," "village economy," the economy of landed estates and royal households, "town economy," "territorial economy," and "national economy,"[6] have been formulated according to the type of corporate group regulating economic activity. But there is no implication of any specific mode of variation even in the type of regulation to which economic activity has been subjected by the different corporate groups thus classified in terms of the extent of their jurisdiction. Thus the territorial economic policies of the German states consisted to a large extent simply in taking over the measures developed in the town economy. Furthermore, their innovations were not greatly different from the "mercantilistic" policies, which were typical of those of the patrimonial states which had already achieved a relatively high level of rationality. They were thus similar to "national economic policies," to use the common term, which is, however, not very appropriate. This classification, futher, clearly does not imply that the inner structure of the economic system, the modes in which work roles were assigned, differentiated and combined, the ways in which these different functions were divided between independent economic units, and the modes of appropriation of control over labour, means of production, and opportunities for profit, in any way ran parallel to the extent of jurisdiction of the corporate group, which might be responsible for economic policy. Above all, it does not imply that this structure was a simple function of the extent of corporate jurisdiction. To demonstrate the untenability of this view, it is only necessary to compare the Western World with Asia and the situation in modern Europe with that of Antiquity. At the same time, in considering economic structure, it is by no means legitimate to ignore the existence or absence of corporate groups with substantive powers of regulation of economic activity, nor to ignore the essential purposes of their regulation. The modes of profit-making activity are strongly influenced by such regulation, but it is by no means only political corporations which are important in this respect.

4. In this connexion, as well as others, the purpose of the discussion has been to determine the optimum conditions for the formal rationality of economic activity and its relation to the various types of substantive demands which may be made on the economic system.

---

5. Weber himself takes over the Greek word, and since the closest English equivalent, "workshop," is too indefinite, it seems best to retain his own term.—ED.

6. The corresponding German terms are: *Hauswirtschaft, Dorfwirtschaft, Stadtwirtschaft, Territorialwirtschaft,* and *Volkswirtschaft.*—ED.

4. Ownership and Possession

BY SIR FREDERICK POLLACK AND FREDERICK W. MAITLAND

Seisin

IN THE HISTORY of our law there is no idea more cardinal than that of seisin. Even in the law of the present day it plays a part which must be studied by every lawyer; but in the past it was so important that we may almost say that the whole system of our land law was law about seisin and its consequences.

Seisin is possession. A few, but only a few words about etymology may be ventured. The inference has been too hastily drawn that this word speaks to us of a time of violence, when he who seized land was seised of it, when seizing land was the normal mode of acquiring possession. Now doubtless there is an etymological connexion between "seizing" and being "seised," but the nature of that connexion is not very certain. If on the one hand "seisin" is connected with "to seize," on the other hand it is connected with "to sit" and "to set":—the man who is seised is the man who is sitting on land; when he was put in seisin he was set there and made to sit there. Thus seisin seems to have the same root as the German *Besitz* and the Latin *possessio*. To our medieval lawyers the word *seisina* suggested the very opposite of violence; it suggested peace and quiet. It did so to Coke.

*   *   *

Now in the course of time *seisin* becomes a highly technical word; but we must not think of it having been so always. Few, if any, of the terms in our legal vocabulary have always been technical terms. The licence that the man of science can allow himself of coining new words is one which by the nature of the case is denied to lawyers. They have to take their terms out of the popular speech; gradually the words so taken are defined; sometimes a word continues to have both a technical meaning for lawyers and a different and vaguer meaning for laymen; sometimes the word that lawyers have adopted is abandoned by the laity. Such for a long time past has been the fate of *seisin*.

The process by which words are specified, by

Reprinted from Sir Frederick Pollack and Frederick W. Maitland, *The History of English Law* (2d ed.; London: Cambridge University Press, 1898), II, 29–30, 31–39, 40–44, 74–79.

which their technical meaning is determined, is to a first glance a curious, illogical process. Legal reasoning seems circular:—for example, it is argued in one case that a man has an action of trespass because he has possession, in the next case that he has possession because he has an action of trespass; and so we seem to be running round from right to remedy and then from remedy to right. All the while, however, our law of possession and trespass is being more perfectly defined. Its course is not circular but spiral; it never comes back to quite the same point as that from which it started. This play of reasoning between right and remedy fixes the use of words. A remedy, called an assize, is given to any one who is disseised of his free tenement:—in a few years lawyers will be arguing that X has been "disseised of his free tenement," because it is an established point that a person in his position can bring an assize. The word *seisin* becomes specified by its relation to certain particular remedies.

What those remedies were it will be our duty to consider. But first we may satisfy ourselves that, to begin with, seisin simply meant possession. Of this we may be convinced by two observations. In the first place, it would seem that for at least three centuries after the Norman Conquest our lawyers had no other word whereby to describe possession. In their theoretical discussions, they, or such of them as looked to the Roman books as models of jurisprudence, could use the words *possessio* and *possidere;* but these words are rarely employed in the formal records of litigation, save in one particular context. The parson of a church is "in possession" of the church:—but then this is no matter for our English law or our temporal courts; it is matter for the canon law and the courts Christian; and it is all the more expedient to find some other term than "seised" for the parson, since it may be necessary to contrast the rights of the parson who is possessed of the church with those of the patron who is seised of the advowson.

In the second place, this word "seisin" was used of all manner of things and all manner of permanent rights that could be regarded as things. At a later date to speak of a person as being seised, or in seisin of, a chattel would have been a gross solecism. But throughout the thirteenth century and in the most technical documents men are seised of chattels and in seisin of them, of a fleece of wool, of a gammon of bacon, of a penny. People were possessed of these things; law had to recognize and protect their possession; it had no other word than "seisin" and therefore used it freely. It may well be, as some think, that the ideas of seisin and possession are first developed in relation to land; one sits, settles, squats on land, and in early ages, preeminently during the feudal time, the seisin of chattels was commonly interwoven with the seisin of land. Flocks and herds were the valuable chattels; "chattel" and "cattle" are the same word; and normally cattle are possessed by him who possesses the land on which they are levant and couchant. Still when the possession of chattels was severed from the possession of land, when the oxen were stolen or were sold to a chapman, there was no word to describe the possession of this new possessor, this thief or purchaser, save seisin. Sometimes we meet with the phrase "vested and seised," which was common in France; this however seems to mean no more than "seised," and though we may now and then read of "investiture," chiefly in relation to ecclesiastical offices, this does not become one of the technical terms of the common law.

When we say that seisin is possession, we use the latter term in the sense in which lawyers use it, a sense in which possession is quite distinct from, and may be sharply opposed to, proprietary right. In common talk we constantly speak as though possession were much the same as ownership. When a man says "I possess a watch," he generally means "I own a watch." Suppose that he has left his watch with a watchmaker for repair, and is asked whether he still possesses a watch, whether the watch is not in the watchmaker's possession and if so whether both he and the watchmaker have possession of the same watch at the same time, he is perhaps a little puzzled and resents our questions as lawyers' impertinences. Even if the watch has been stolen, he is not very willing to admit that he no longer possesses a watch. This is instructive:—in our non-professional moments *possession* seems much nearer to our lips than *ownership*. Often however we slur over the gulf by means of the conveniently ambiguous verbs "have" and "have got"—I have a watch, the watchmaker has it—I have a watch, but some one else has got it. But so soon as there is any law worthy of the name, right and possession must emerge and be contrasted:—so soon as any one has said "You have got what belongs to me," the germs of these two notions have appeared and can be opposed to each other. Bracton is never tired of emphasizing the contrast. In so doing he constantly makes use of the

Roman terms *possessio* on the one hand, *proprietas* or *dominium* on the other. These are not the technical terms of English law; but it has terms which answer a like purpose, *seisina* on the one hand, *ius* on the other. The person who has right may not be seised, the person who is seised may not be seised of right.

The idea of seisin seems to be closely connected in our ancestors' minds with the idea of enjoyment. A man is in seisin of land when he is enjoying it or in a position to enjoy it; he is seised of an advowson (for of "incorporeal things" there may be seisin) when he presents a parson who is admitted to the church; he is seised of freedom from toll when he successfully resists a demand for payment. This connexion is brought out by the interesting word *esplees* (*expleta*). In a proprietary action for land the demandant will assert that he, or some ancestor of his, was "seised of the land in his demesne as of fee and of right, by taking thence esplees to the value of five shillings, as in corn and other issues of the land." The man who takes and enjoys the fruits of the earth thereby "exploits" his seisin, that is to say, he makes his seisin "explicit," visible to the eyes of his neighbours. In order that a seisin may have all its legal effects it must be thus exploited. Still a man must have seisin before he can exploit it, and therefore in a possessory action it is unnecessary for the plaintiff to allege this taking of esplees. The moment at which he acquires his seisin may not be the right moment for mowing hay or reaping corn. Seisin of land therefore is not the enjoyment of the fruits of the earth; it is rather that state of things which in due time will render such an enjoyment possible.

Law must define this vague idea, and it can not find the whole essence of possession in visible facts. It is so now-a-days. We see a man in the street carrying an umbrella; we can not at once tell whether or no he possesses it. Is he its owner, is he a thief, is he a borrower, a hirer, is he the owner's servant? If he is the owner, he possesses it; if he is a thief, he possesses it. If he is the owner's servant, we shall probably deny his possession. If he is a borrower, we may have our doubts; the language of every-day life may hesitate about the matter; law must make up its mind. Before we attribute possession to a man, we must apparently know something about the intentions that he has in regard to the thing, or rather about the intentions that he must be supposed to have when the manner in which he came by the thing has been taken into consideration. Probably the better way of stating the matter is not to speak of his real intentions, which are often beside the mark, nor of the intentions that he must be supposed to have, which are fictions, but to say at once that we require to know how he came by the thing.[1] This being known, problems await us. If the carrier of the umbrella is its owner, he possesses it; if he is a thief making off with a stolen chattel, he possesses it; if he has by mistake taken what he believes to be his own, he probably possesses it; if he has borrowed it or hired it, the case is not so plain; law must decide—and various systems of law will decide differently—whether possession shall be attributed to the borrower or to the lender, to the letter or the hirer.

When deciding to whom it would attribute a seisin, our medieval law had to contemplate a complex mass of facts and rights. In the first place, the actual occupant of the soil, who was cultivating it and taking its fruits, might be so doing in exercise, or professed exercise, of any one of many different rights. He might be there as tenant at will, tenant for term of years, tenant in villeinage, tenant for life, tenant in dower, tenant by the curtesy, tenant in fee simple, guardian of an infant, and so forth. But further, at the same moment many persons might have and be actually enjoying rights of a proprietary kind in the same plot of ground. Giles would be holding in villeinage of Ralph, who held in free socage of the abbot, who held in frankalmoin of the earl, who held by knight's service of the king. There would be the case of the reversioner to be considered and the case of the remainderman.

In the thirteenth century certain lines have been firmly drawn. The royal remedies for the protection of seisin given by Henry II. were given only to those who were seised "of a free tenement": the novel disseisin lies when a man has been disseised *de libero tenemento suo*. Doubtless these words were intended to exclude those who held in villeinage. This is well brought out by a change in the language of Magna Carta. The original charter of 1215 by its most famous clause declares that no free man is to be disseised, unless it be by the lawful judgment of his peers or the law of the land. The charter of 1217 inserts the words "de libero tenemento suo vel libertatibus vel liberis consuetudinibus suis." It is not intended, it would not be suffered, that a man holding in villeinage, even though personally *liber homo*, should have a possession protected by the king's court. Such a tenant is not seised of free tenement, and, as royal justice is now beginning to supplant all other justice, it is said that he has no seisin recognized by the common law. The lord of whom he holds is the person protected by the common law,

and is seised *de libero tenemento;* if you eject the villein tenant, you disseise the lord. But within the sphere of manorial justice this tenant is seised—seisin has been delivered to him by the rod according to the custom of the manor—and when he pleads in the manorial court he will say that he is seised according to the custom of the manor. Here then already we have a dual seisin:—the lord seised *quoad* the king's courts and the common law, the tenant seised *quoad* the lord's court and the manorial custom.

In the past the tenant for term of years, though he was in occupation of the soil, had not been considered to be seised of it. In the days of Henry II. when the great possessory remedy, the assize of novel disseisin, was being invented, tenancies for terms of years seem to have been novelties, and the lawyers were endeavouring to treat the "termor"—this is a conveniently brief name for the tenant for term of years—as one who had no right in the land, but merely the benefit of a contract. His lessor was seised; eject the lessee, and you disseise the lessor. Already in Bracton's day, however, this doctrine was losing its foundation; the termor was acquiring a remedy against ejectors. But this remedy was a new action and one which in no wise affected the old assize of novel disseisin. For a while men had to content themselves with ascribing a seisin of a certain sort to both the termor and his lessor. Eject the termor, you lay yourself open to two actions, a *Quare eiecit infra terminum* brought by him, an assize of novel disseisin brought by his lessor. The lessor still has the assize; despite the termor's occupation, he is seised, and seised in demesne, of the land; and he is seised, while the termor is not seised, "of a free tenement"—this is proved by his having the assize. Thus the term "free tenement" is getting a new edge; the termor has no free tenement, no freehold, no seisin of the freehold. At a later date lawyers will meet this difficulty by the introduction of "possession" as a new technical term; they will deny "seisin" of any sort or kind to the termor, and, on the other hand, will allow him possession. But of tenancies for years we shall have more to say hereafter.

An infant's guardian, though the wardship was a profitable, vendible right, was not seised of the infant's land; his occupation of the land was the infant's seisin. It is true that about this matter language might hesitate and fluctuate. It is, for example, common enough to speak of the lord and guardian putting the ward into seisin of the land when he has attained his majority; but for the main purposes of the law the guardian's own right, the *custodia,* is converted into an incorporeal thing, an incorporeal chattel, of which there may be a seisin or possession,

---

1. A servant who is carrying his master's goods can not become a possessor of them by merely forming the intent to appropriate them. If we say that he must be supposed to have an honest intent until by some act he shows the contrary, we are introducing a fiction.

and for the protection of such a seisin there is a special possessory action. If a person who is in occupation of the land as guardian is ejected from the land, and wishes to make good his own rights, he will complain, not of having been disseised of the land, but of having been ejected from the wardship.

As to the tenant for life—including under that term tenant in dower and tenant by the curtesy—our law seems never to have had any doubt. The tenant for life, if he is in occupation of the land by himself, his servants, his villein tenants or his termors, is seised, seised of the land, seised in demesne, seised of a free tenement. If ejected, he will bring exactly the same possessory action that he would have brought had he been a tenant in fee.

Then we must consider the ascending series of lords and tenants. Let us suppose that Ralph holds in fee and in free socage of the earl, who holds in fee by knight's service of the king. If all is as it should be, then both Ralph and the earl may be said to be seised of the land. Ralph, who is occupying the land by himself, his servants, his villein tenants or his termors, is seised in demesne. The earl, to whom Ralph is paying rent, also is seised; he is seised of the land, not in demesne but in service. We have here to remember that if the feudal idea of seignoral justice has been permitted to develop itself freely, this ascending series of seisins would have had as its counterpart an ascending series of courts. The king's court would have known of no seisin save that of the earl, the tenant in chief. The seisin of Ralph, the earl's immediate tenant, would have found protection—at least in the first instance—only in the earl's court; and so downwards, each seisin being protected by a different court. The seisin of the tenant in villeinage protected only in the manorial court is an illustration of this principle. But then Henry II. had restrained and crippled this principle; he had given a remedy in his own court to every one who could say that he had been disseised of a free tenement. The result of this is for a while a perplexing use of terms. Ralph, the tenant in demesne, he who has no freeholder below him, is indubitably seised of the land, however distant he may be in the feudal scale from the king. Eject him, and he will bring against you the assize of novel disseisin; indeed if his lord, the earl, ejects him or even distrains him outrageously, he will bring the assize against his lord, thus showing that as between him and his lord the seisin of the land is with him. It is possible that at one time by ejecting Ralph, a stranger would have disseised both Ralph and his lord and exposed himself to two actions; but this does not seem to have been the law of Bracton's day. The lord was ceasing to have any interest in what we may call the personality of his tenant. If Ralph is ejected by Roger, the earl can not complain of this; he is in no way bound to accept Roger as a tenant; he can distrain the tenement for the services due to him from Ralph; he is entitled to those services but to nothing else. More and more an incorporeal thing or group of incorporeal things supplants the land as the subject matter of the lord's right and the lord's seisin. He is entitled to and seised of, not the land itself, but a seignory, the services, fealty, homage of a tenant.

*   *   *

On the whole we may say that the possession of land which the law protects under the name of a "seisin of freehold," is the occupation of land by one who has come to it otherwise than as tenant in villeinage, tenant at will, tenant for term of years or guardian, that occupation being exercised by himself, his servants, guardians, tenants in villeinage, tenants at will or tenants for term of years. This seems the best statement of the matter:—occupation of land is seisin of free tenement unless it has been obtained in one of certain particular ways. If, however, we prefer to look at the other side of the principle, we may say that the *animus* required of the person who is "seised of free tenement" is the intent to hold that land as though he were tenant for life or tenant in fee holding by some free tenure.

More remains to be said of the nature of seisin, especially of that element in it which we have spoken of as occupation; but this can best be said if we turn to speak of the effects of seisin, its protection by law, its relation to proprietary rights.

We may make our task the lighter if for one moment we glance at controversies which have divided the legal theorists of our own day. Why does our law protect possession? Several different answers have been, or may be, given to this question. There is something in it that attracts the speculative lawyer, for there is something that can be made to look like a paradox. Why should law, when it has on its hands the difficult work of protecting ownership and other rights in things, prepare puzzles for itself by undertaking to protect something that is not ownership, something that will from time to time come into sharp collision with ownership? Is it not a main object of law that every one should enjoy what is his own *de iure,* and if so why are we to consecrate that *de facto* enjoyment which is signified by the term *possession,* and why, above all, are we to protect the possessor even against the owner?

It is chiefly, though not solely, in relation to the classical Roman law that these questions have been discussed, and, if any profitable discussion of them is to be had, it seems essential that some definite body of law should be examined with an accurate heed of dates and successive stages of development. If, scorning all relations of space and time, we ask why law protects possession, the only true answer that we are likely to get is that the law of different peoples at different times has protected possession for many different reasons. Nor can we utterly leave out of account motives and aims of which an abstract jurisprudence knows nothing. That simple justice may be done between man and man has seldom been the sole object of legislators; political have interfered with juristic interests. An illustration may make this plainer. We may well believe that Henry II. when he instituted the possessory assizes was not without thought of the additional strength that would accrue to him and his successors, could he make his subjects feel that they owed the beatitude of possession to his ordinance and the action of his court. Still, whatever may be the legislator's motive, judges must find some rational principle which shall guide them in the administration of possessory remedies; and they have a choice between different principles. These may perhaps be reduced in number to four, or may be said to cluster round four types.

In the first place, the protection given to possession may be merely a provision for the better maintenance of peace and quiet. It is a prohibition of self-help in the interest of public order. The possessor is protected, not on account of any merits of his, but because the peace must be kept; to allow men to make forcible entries on land or to seize goods without form of law, is to invite violence. Just so the murderer, whose life is forfeited to law, may not be slain, save in due form of law; in a civilized state he is protected against irregular vengeance, not because he deserves to live, for he deserves to die, but because the permission of revenge would certainly do more harm than good to the community. Were this then the only principle at work, we should naturally expect to find the protection of possession in some chapter of the criminal law dealing with offences against public order, riots, affrays, and the like.

Others would look for it, not in the law of crimes, but in the law of torts or civil injuries. The possessor's possession is protected, not indeed because he has any sort of right in the thing, but because in general one can not disturb his possession without being guilty, or almost guilty, of some injury to his person, some act which, if it does not amount to an assault, still comes so dangerously near to an assault that it can be regarded as an invasion of that sphere of peace and quiet which the law should guarantee to every one of its subjects. This doctrine which found expression in Savigny's famous essay has before now raised an echo in an English court:—"These rights of action are given in respect of the immediate and present violation of possession, independently of rights of property. They are an extension of that protection which the law throws around the person.[2]

A very different theory, that of the great Ihering, has gained ground in our own time. In order to give an adequate protection to ownership, it has been found necessary to protect possession. To prove ownership is difficult, to prove possession comparatively easy. Suppose a land-owner ejected from possession; to require of him to prove his ownership before he can be reinstated, is to require too much; thieves and land-grabbers will presume upon the difficulty that a rightful owner will have in making out a flawless title. It must be enough then that the ejected owner should prove that he was in possession and was ejected; the ejector must be precluded from pleading that the possession which he disturbed was not possession under good title. Possession then is an outwork of property. But though the object of the law in protecting possession is to protect the possession of those who have a right to possess, that object can only be obtained by protecting every possessor. Once allow any question about property to be raised, and the whole plan of affording easy remedies to ousted owners will break down. In order that right may be triumphant, the possessory action must be open to the evil and to the good, it must draw no distinction between the just and the unjust possessor. The protection of wrongful possessors is an unfortunate but unavoidable consequence of the attempt to protect rightful possessors. This theory would make us look for the law of possession, not in the law of crimes, nor in the law of torts, but in very close connexion with the law of property.

There is yet another opinion, which differs from the last, though both make a close connexion between possession and proprietary rights. Possession as such deserves protection, and really there is little more to be said, at least by the lawyer. He who possesses has by the mere fact of his possession more right in the thing than the non-possessor has; he of all men has most right in the thing until someone has asserted and proved a greater right. When a thing belongs to no one and is capable of appropriation, the mere act of taking possession of it gives right against all the world; when a thing belongs to A, the mere fact that B takes possession of it still gives B a right which is good against all who have no better.

---

2. *Rogers* v. *Spence*, 13 Meeson and Welsby, 581.

An attempt might be made, and it would be in harmony with our English modes of thought, to evade any choice between these various "abstract principles" by a frank profession of the utilitarian character of law. But the success which awaits such an attempt seems very doubtful; for, granted that in some way or another the protection of possession promotes the welfare of the community, the question still arises, why and in what measure this is so. Under what sub-head of "utility" shall we bring this protection? Shall we lay stress on the public disorder which would be occasioned by unrestricted "self-help," on the probability that personal injuries will be done to individuals, on the necessity of providing ready remedies for ousted owners, on the natural expectation that what a man possesses he will be allowed to possess until some one has proved a better title? This is no idle question, for on the answer to it must depend the extent to which and the mode in which possession ought to be consecrated. Measures, which would be quite adequate to prevent any serious danger of general disorder, would be quite inadequate to give the ejected owner an easy action for recovering what is his. If all that we want is peace and quiet, it may be enough to punish ejectors by fine or imprisonment; but this does nothing for ejected possessors, gives them no recovery of the possession that they have lost. Again, let us grant that the ejected possessor should be able to recover the land from the ejector if the latter is still in possession; but suppose that the land has already passed into a third hand; shall the ejected possessor be able to recover it from him to whom the ejector has given or sold it? If to this question we say Yes, we shall hardly be able to justify our answer by any theory which regards injury to the person, or something very like injury to the person, as the gist of the possessory action for here we shall be taking possession away from one who has come to it without violence.

Now we ought—so it seems to us—to see that there well may be a certain truth in all these theories. That the German jurists in their attempts to pin the Roman lawyers down to some one neat doctrine of possession and of the reasons for protecting it, may have been engaged on an impossible task, it is not for us to suggest in this place; but so far as concerns our own English law we make no doubt that at different times and in different measures every conceivable reason for protecting possession has been felt as a weighty argument and has had its influence on rights and remedies. At first we find the several principles working together in harmonious concert; they will work together because as yet they are not sharply defined. Gradually their outlines become clearer; discrepancies between them begin to appear; and, as the result of long continued conflict, some of them are victorious at the expense of others.

*   *   *

A graduated hierarchy of actions has been established. "Possessoriness" has become a matter of degree. At the bottom stands the novel disseisin, possessory in every sense, summary and punitive. Above it rises the mort d'ancestor, summary but not so summary, going back to the seisin of one who is already dead. Above this again are writs of entry, writs which have strong affinities with the writ of right, so strong that in Bracton's day an action begun by writ of entry may by the pleadings be turned into a final, proprietary action. The writs of entry are not so summary as are the assizes, but they are rapid when compared with the writ of right; the most dilatory of the essoins is precluded; there can be no battle or grand assize. Ultimately we ascend to the writ of right. Actions are higher or lower, some lie "more in the right" than others. You may try one after another; begin with the novel disseisin, go on to the mort d'ancestor, then see whether a writ of entry will serve your turn and, having failed, fall back upon the writ of right.

Now we can not consent to dismiss these rules about writs of entry as though they were matters of mere procedure. They seem to be the outward manifestation of a great rule of substantive law, for this graduated hierarchy of actions corresponds to a graduated hierarchy of seisins and of proprietary rights. The rule of substantive law we take to be this:—Seisin generates a proprietary right—an ownership, we may even say—which is good against all who have no better, because they have no older, right. We have gone far beyond the protection of seisin against violence. The man who obtains seisin obtains thereby a proprietary right that is good against all who have no older seisin to rely upon, a right that he can pass to others by those means by which proprietary rights are conveyed, a right that is protected at every point by the possessory assizes and the writs of entry. At one and the same moment there may be many persons each of whom is in some sort entitled in fee simple to this piece of land: —*C*'s title is good against all but *B* and *A*; *B*'s title is good against all but *A*; *A*'s title is absolute.

But is even *A*'s title absolute? Our law has an action which it says is proprietary—the writ of right. As between the parties to it, this action is conclusive. The vanquished party and his heirs are "abjudged" from the land for ever. In the strongest language that our law knows the demandant has to assert ownership of the land. He says that he, or his ancestor, has been seised of the land as of fee "and of right" and, if he relies on the seisin of an ancestor, he must trace the descent of "the right" from heir to heir into his own person. For all this, we may doubt whether he is supposed to prove a right that is good against all the world. The tenant puts himself upon the grand assize. What, we must ask, will be the question submitted to the recognitors? It will not be this, whether the demandant is owner of the land. It will be this, whether the demandant or the tenant has the greater right to the land. Of absolute right nothing is said; greater right is right enough. Next we must observe that the judgment in this action will not preclude a third person from claiming the land. The judgment if it is followed by inaction on his part for some brief period—ultimately year and day was the time allowed to him—may preclude him, should he be in this country and under no disability; but the judgment itself is no bar. But lastly, as we understand the matter, even in the writ of right the tenant has no means of protecting himself by an assertion that the ownership of the land belongs neither to him nor to the demandant but to some third person. This needs some explanation, for appearances may be against what we have here said.

Clement brings a writ of right against William. He pleads that his grandfather Adam was seised in fee and of right, that from Adam the right descended to Bernard as son and heir, and from Bernard to Clement as son and heir. William may put himself upon battle or upon the grand assize; in the latter case a verdict will decide whether Clement or William has the greater right. But a third course is open. William may endeavour to plead specially and to bring some one question of fact before a jury. In this way he may attack the pedigree that Clement has pleaded at any point; he may, for example, assert that Bernard was not Adam's son or was a bastard. In so doing he may seem at times to be setting up *ius tertii,* to be urging by way of defence for himself the right of a stranger. But really he is not doing this. He is proving that Clement's right is not better than his own. For example, he says: "Bernard was not Adam's heir, for Adam left an elder son, Baldwin by name, who is alive." Now if this be so, Clement has no right in the land whatever; Clement does not allege that he himself has been seised and he is not the heir of any one who has been seised. But what, as we think, William can not do is this, he can not shield himself by the right of a stranger to the action whose title is inconsistent with the statement that Adam was seised in fee and of right. He can not, for example, say, "Adam your ancestor got his seisin by disseising Odo, or by tak-

ing a feoffment from Odo's guardian, and Odo, or Odo's heir, has a better right than either of us."[3]

Thus our law of the thirteenth century seems to recognize in its practical working the relativity of ownership. One story is good until another is told. One ownership is valid until an older is proved. No one is ever called upon to demonstrate an ownership good against all men; he does enough even in a proprietary action if he proves an older right than that of the person whom he attacks. In other words, even under a writ of right the common law does not provide for any kind of judgment *in rem.*

The question whether this idea—"the relativity of proprietary right"—should be called archaic, is difficult. A discussion of it might lead us into controversies which are better left to those who have more copious materials for the history of very remote ages than England can produce. For our own part we shall be willing to allow that the evolution of the writs of entry, a process to be explained rather by politics than by jurisprudence, has given to this idea in England a preternatural sharpness. The proprietary action by writ of right is cumbrous and is irrational, for it permits trial by battle. Open attacks upon it can not be made, for it brings some profit to the lords and is supported by a popular sentiment which would gladly refer a solemn question of right to the judgment of the Omniscient. But covert attacks can be made, and they take the form of actions which protect the title begotten by seisin, actions in which artificial limits are set to the right of defence. On the other hand, we can not but think that this idea of relatively good proprietary right came very naturally to Englishmen. It developed itself in spite of cosmopolitan jurisprudence and a romanized terminology. The lawyers themselves believe that there is a wide gulf between possessory and proprietory actions; but they are not certain of its whereabouts. They believe that somewhere or another there must be an absolute ownership. This they call *dreyt dreyt,* mere right, *ius merum.* Apparently they have mistaken the meaning of their own phrases; their *ius merum* is but that *mere dreit* or *ius maius* which the demandant asserts in a writ

---

3. It is very difficult to offer any direct proof of this doctrine, more especially as Bracton never finished his account of the writ of right. But see the remarkable passage on f. 434b, 435, which culminates in "plura possunt esse iura proprietatis et plures possunt habere maius ius aliis, secundum quod fuerint priores vel posteriores." After reading the numerous cases of writs of right in the Note Book and many others as well, we can only say that we know no case in which the tenant by special plea gets behind the seisin of the demandant's ancestor. As to later times there can be no doubt. See *e.g.* Littleton, sec. 478, quoted below, p. 78. See also Lightwood, Possession of Land, 74.

of right.[4] Bracton more than once protests with Ulpian that possession has nothing in common with property, and yet has to explain how successive possessions beget successive ownerships which all live on together, the younger being invalid against the older. The land law of the later middle ages is permeated by this idea of relativity, and he would be very bold who said that it does not govern us in England at the present day, though the "forms of action" are things of the past and we have now no action for the recovery of land in which a defendant is precluded from relying on whatever right he may have.[5]

We can now say our last word about that curious term "estate." We have seen that the word *status,* which when it falls from Bracton's pen generally means personal condition, is soon afterwards set apart to signify a proprietary right in land or in some other tenement:—John atte Style has an estate of fee simple in Blackacre. We seem to catch the word in the very act of appropriating a new meaning when Bracton says that the estate of an infant whether in corporeal or in incorporeal things must not be changed during his minority. A person already has a status in things; that status may be

the status of tenant for life or the status of tenant in fee. It is of course characteristic of this age that a man's status—his general position in the legal scheme—is closely connected with his proprietary rights. The various "estates of men," the various "estates of the realm," are supposed to be variously endowed with land; the baron, for example, ought in theory to be the holder of a barony; he has the status of a baron because he has the estate of a baron. But a peculiar definiteness is given to the term by that theory of possession which we have been examining. Seisin generates title. At one and the same time there may be many titles to one and the same piece of land, titles which have various degrees of validity. It is quite possible that two of these titles should meet in one man and yet maintain an independent existence. If a man demands to be put into the possession of land, he must not vaguely claim a certain piece of land, he must point out some particular title on which he relies, and if he has more than one, he must make his choice between them. For example, he must claim that "status" in the land which his grandfather had and which has descended to him. It becomes possible to raise the question whether a certain possessor of the land was on the land "as of" one status, or "as of" another status; he may have had an ancient title to that land and also a new title acquired by disseisin. What was his status; "as of" which estate was he seised? One status may be heritable, another not heritable; the heritability of a third may have been restricted by the *forma doni.* And so we pass to a classification of estates; some are estates in fee, some are estates for life; some estates in fee are estates in fee simple, others are estates in fee conditional; and so forth. We have come by a word, an idea, in which the elements of our proprietary calculus can find utterance.

4. It is probable that the Latin *ius merum* is a mistaken translation of the Anglo-French *mere dreit,* or as it would stand in Modern French *majeur (*maire) droit.* We have Dr. Murray's authority for this note.

5. Holmes, Common Law, p. 215; Pollock and Wright, Possession, 93–100; Lightwood, Possession of Land, 104–127. One of the most striking statements of this doctrine is in Littleton, sec. 478. "Also if a man be disseised by an infant, who alien in fee, and the alienee dieth seised and his heir entreth, the disseisor being within age, now it is in the election of the disseisor to have a writ of entry *dum fuit infa aetatem* or a writ of right against the heir of the alienee, and, which writ of them he shall choose, he ought to recover by law." In other words, a proprietary action is open to the most violent and most fraudulent of land-grabbers as against one whose title is younger than his own; "and he ought to recover by law."

5. On Contract

BY SIR HENRY SUMNER MAINE

SOCIAL INQUIRIES, so far as they depend on the consideration of legal phenomena, are

Reprinted from Sir Henry Sumner Maine, *Ancient Law* (New York: Henry Holt Co., 1885, from the 5th London ed.), chap. ix, pp. 297–98, 301–23.

in so backward a condition that we need not be surprised at not finding these truths recognised in the commonplaces which pass current concerning the progress of society. These commonplaces answer much more to our prejudices than to our convictions. The strong disinclination of most men to regard morality as advancing seems to be especially powerful when the virtues on which Contract depends are in question, and many of us have an almost instinctive reluctance to admitting that good faith and trust in our fellows are more widely diffused than of old, or that there is anything in contemporary manners which parallels the loyalty of the antique world. From time to time, these prepossessions are greatly strengthened by the spectacle of frauds, unheard of before the period at which they were observed, and astonishing from their complication as well shocking from criminality. But the very character of these frauds shows clearly that, before they became possible, the moral obligations of which they are the breach must have been more than proportionately developed. It is the confidence reposed and deserved by the many which affords facilities for the bad faith of the few, so that, if colossal examples of dishonesty occur, there is no surer conclusion than that scrupulous honesty is displayed in the average of the transactions which, in the particular case, have supplied the delinquent with his opportunity. If we insist on reading the history of morality as reflected in jurisprudence, by turning our eyes not on the law of Contract but on the law of Crime, we must be careful that we read it aright. The only form of dishonesty treated of in the most ancient Roman law is Theft. At the moment at which I write, the newest chapter in the English criminal law is one which attempts to prescribe punishment for the frauds of Trustees. The proper inference from this contrast is not that the primitive Romans practised a higher morality than ourselves. We should rather say that, in the interval between their day and ours, morality had advanced from a very rude to a highly refined conception—from viewing the rights of property as exclusively sacred, to looking upon the rights growing out of the mere unilateral reposal of confidence as entitled to the protection of the penal law.

*   *   *

The favorite occupation of active minds at the present moment, and the one which answers to the speculations of our forefathers on the origin of the social state, is the analysis of society as it exists and moves before our eyes; but, through omitting to call in the assistance of history, this analysis too often degenerates into an idle exercise of curiosity, and is especially apt to incapacitate the inquirer for comprehending states of society which differ considerably from that to which he is accustomed. The mistake of judging the men of other periods by the morality of our own day has its parallel in the mistake of supposing that every wheel or bolt in the modern social machine had its counterpart in more rudimentary societies. Such impressions ramify very widely, and masque themselves very subtly, in historical works written in the modern fashion; but I find the trace of their presence in the domain of jurisprudence in the praise which is frequently bestowed on the little apologue of Montesquieu concerning the Troglodytes, inserted in the *Lettres Persanes*. The Troglodytes were a people who systematically violated their Contracts, and so perished utterly. If the story bears the moral which its author intended, and is employed to expose an anti-social heresy by which this century and the last have been threatened, it is most unexceptionable; but if the inference be obtained from it that society could not possibly hold together without attaching a sacredness to promises and agreements which should be on something like a par with the respect that is paid to them by a mature civilisation, it involves an error so grave as to be fatal to all sound understanding of legal history. The fact is that the Troglodytes have flourished and founded powerful states with very small attention to the obligations of Contract. The point which before all others has to be apprehended in the constitution of primitive societies is that the individual creates for himself few or no rights, and few or no duties. The rules which he obeys are derived first from the station into which he is born, and next from the imperative commands addressed to him by the chief of the household of which he forms a part. Such a system leaves the very smallest room for Contract. The members of the same family (for so we may interpret the evidence) are wholly incapable of contracting with each other, and the family is entitled to disregard the engagements by which any one of its subordinate members has attempted to bind it. Family, it is true, may contract with family, and chieftain with chieftain, but the transaction is one of the same nature, and encumbered by as many formalities, as the alienation of property, and the disregard of one iota of the performance is fatal to the obligation. The positive duty resulting from one man's reliance on the word of another is among the slowest conquests of advancing civilisation.

Neither Ancient Law nor any other source of evidence discloses to us society entirely destitute of the conception of Contract. But the conception, when it first shows itself, is obviously rudimentary. No trustworthy primitive record can be read without perceiving that the habit of mind which induces us to make good a promise is as yet imperfectly developed, and that acts of flagrant perfidy are often mentioned without blame and sometimes described with approbation. In the Homeric literature, for instance, the deceitful cunning of

Ulysses appears as a virtue of the same rank with the prudence of Nestor, the constancy of Hector, and the gallantry of Achilles. Ancient law is still more suggestive of the distance which separates the crude form of Contract from its maturity. At first, nothing is seen like the interposition of law to compel the performance of a promise. That which the law arms with its sanctions is not a promise, but a promise accompanied with a solemn ceremonial. Not only are the formalities of equal importance with the promise itself, but they are, if anything, of greater importance; for that delicate analysis which mature jurisprudence applies to the conditions of mind under which a particular verbal assent is given appears, in ancient law, to be transferred to the words and gestures of the accompanying performance. No pledge is enforced if a single form be omitted or misplaced, but, on the other hand, if the forms can be shown to have been accurately proceeded with, it is of no avail to plead that the promise was made under duress or deception. The transmutation of this ancient view into the familiar notion of a Contract is plainly seen in the history of jurisprudence. First one or two steps in the ceremonial are dispensed with; then the others are simplified or permitted to be neglected on certain conditions; lastly, a few specific contracts are separated from the rest and allowed to be entered into without form, the selected contracts being those on which the activity and energy of social intercourse depend. Slowly, but most distinctly, the mental engagement isolates itself amid the technicalities, and gradually becomes the sole ingredient on which the interest of the jurisconsult is concentrated. Such a mental engagement, signified through external acts, the Romans called a Pact or Convention; and when the Convention has once been conceived as the nucleus of a Contract, it soon becomes the tendency of advancing jurisprudence to break away the external shell of form and ceremony. Forms are thenceforward only retained so far as they are guarantees of authenticity, and securities for caution and deliberation. The idea of a Contract is fully developed, or, to employ the Roman phrase, Contracts are absorbed in Pacts.

The history of this course of change in Roman law is exceedingly instructive. At the earliest dawn of the jurisprudence, the term in use for a Contract was one which is very familiar to the students of historical Latinity. It was *nexum,* and the parties to the contract were said to be *nexi,* expressions which must be carefully attended to on account of the singular durableness of the metaphor on which they are founded. The notion that persons under a contractural engagement are connected together by a strong *bond* or *chain,* continued till the last to influence the Roman jurisprudence of Contract; and flowing thence it has mixed itself with modern ideas. What then was involved in this nexum or bond? A definition which has descended to us from one of the Latin antiquarians describes *nexum* as *omne quod geritur per æs et libram,* "every transaction with the copper and the balance," and these words have occasioned a good deal of perplexity. The copper and the balance are the well-known accomplishments of the Mancipation, the ancient solemnity described in a former chapter, by which the right of ownership in the highest form of Roman Property was transferred from one person to another. Mancipation was a *conveyance,* and hence has arisen the difficulty, for the definition thus cited appears to confound Contracts and Conveyances, which in the philosophy of jurisprudence are not simply kept apart, but are actually opposed to each other. The *jus in re,* right *in rem,* right "availing against all the world," or Proprietary Right, is sharply distinguished by the analyst of mature jurisprudence from the *jus ad rem,* right in *personam,* right "availing against a single individual or group," or Obligation. Now Conveyances transfer Proprietary Rights, Contracts create Obligations—how then can the two be included under the same name or same general conception? This, like many similar embarrassments, has been occasioned by the error of ascribing to the mental condition of an unformed society a faculty which pre-eminently belongs to an advanced stage of intellectual development, the faculty of distinguishing in speculation ideas which are blended in practice. We have indications not to be mistaken of a state of social affairs in which Conveyances and Contracts were practically confounded; nor did the discrepance of the conceptions become perceptible till men had begun to adopt a distinct practice in contracting and conveying.

It may here be observed that we know enough of ancient Roman law to give some idea of the mode of transformation followed by legal conceptions and by legal phraseology in the infancy of Jurisprudence. The change which they undergo appears to be a change from general to special; or, as we might otherwise express it, the ancient conceptions and the ancient terms are subjected to a process of gradual specialisation. An ancient legal conception corresponds not to one but to several modern conceptions. An ancient technical expression serves to indicate a variety of things which in modern law have separate names allotted to them. If, however, we take up the history of Jurisprudence at the next stage, we find that the subordinate conceptions have gradually disengaged themselves, and that the old general names are giving way to special appellations. The old general conception is not obliterated, but it has ceased to cover more than one or a few of the notions which it first included. So too the old technical name remains, but it discharges only one of the functions which it once performed. We may exemplify this phenomenon in various ways. Patriarchal Power of all sorts appears, for instance, to have been once conceived as identical in character, and it was doubtless distinguished by one name. The Power exercised by the ancestor was the same whether it was exercised over the family or the material property—over flocks, herds, slaves, children, or wife. We cannot be absolutely certain of its old Roman name, but there is very strong reason for believing, from the number of expressions indicating shades of the notion of *power* into which the word *manus* enters, that the ancient general term was *manus*. But, when Roman law has advanced a little, both the name and the idea have become specialised. Power is discriminated, both in word and in conception, according to the object over which it is exerted. Exercised over material commodities or slaves, it has become *dominium*—over children it is *Protestas*—over free persons whose services have been made away to another by their own ancestor, it is *mancipium*—over a wife, it is still *manus*. The old word, it will be perceived, has not altogether fallen into desuetude, but is confined to one very special exercise of the authority it had formerly denoted. This example will enable us to comprehend the nature of the historical alliance between Contracts and Conveyances. There seems to have been one solemn ceremonial at first for all solemn transactions, and its name at Rome appears to have been *nexum*. Precisely the same forms which were in use when a conveyance of property was effected seem to have been employed in the making of a contract. But we have not very far to move onwards before we came to a period at which the notion of a Contract has disengaged itself from the notion of a Conveyance. A double change has thus taken place. The transaction "with the copper and the balance," when intended to have for its office the transfer of property, is known by the new and special name of Mancipation. The ancient Nexum still designates the same ceremony, but only when it is employed for the special purpose of solemnising a contract.

When two or three legal conceptions are spoken of as anciently blended in one, it is not intended to imply that some one of the included notions may not be older than the others, or, when those others have been formed, may not greatly predominate over and take precedence over them. The reason why one legal conception continues so long to cover

several conceptions, and one technical phrase to do instead of several, is doubtless that practical changes are accomplished in the law of primitive societies long before men see occasion to notice or name them. Though I have said that the Patriarchal Power was not at first distinguished according to the objects over which it was exercised. I feel sure that Power over Children was the root of the old conception of Power; and I cannot doubt that the earliest use of the Nexum, and the one primarily regarded by those who resorted to it, was to give proper solemnity to the alienation of property. It is likely that a very slight perversion of the Nexum from its original functions first gave rise to its employment in Contracts, and that the very slightness of the change long prevented its being appreciated or noticed. The old name remained because men had not become conscious that they wanted a new one; the old notion clung to the mind because nobody had seen reason to be at the pains of examining it. We have had the process clearly exemplified in the history of Testaments. A Will was at first a simple conveyance of Property. It was only the enormous practical difference that gradually showed itself between this particular conveyance and all others which caused it to be regarded separately, and even as it was, centuries elapsed before the ameliorators of law cleared away the useless encumbrance of the nominal mancipation, and consented to care for nothing in the Will but the expressed intentions of the Testator. It is unfortunate that we cannot track the early history of Contracts with the same absolute confidence as the early history of Wills, but we are not quite without hints that contracts first showed themselves through the *nexum* being put to a new use and afterwards obtained recognition as distinct transactions through the important practical consequences of the experiment. There is some, but not very violent, conjecture in the following delineation of the process. Let us conceive a sale for ready money as the normal type of the Nexum. The seller brought the property of which he intended to dispose—a slave, for example—the purchaser attended with the rough ingots of copper which served for money—and an indispensable assistant, the *libripens*, presented himself with a pair of scales. The slave with certain fixed formalities was handed over to the vendee—the copper was weighed by the *libripens* and passed to the vendor. So long as the business lasted it was a *nexum,* and the parties were *nexi;* but the moment it was completed, the *nexum* ended, and the vendor and purchaser ceased to bear the name derived from their momentary relation. But now, let us move a step onward in commercial history. Suppose the slave transferred, but the money was not paid. In *that* case the *nexum* is finished, so far as the seller is concerned, and when he has once handed over his property he is no longer *nexus;* but, in regard to the purchaser, the *nexum* continues. The transaction, as to his part of it, is incomplete, and he is still considered to be *nexus.* It follows, therefore, that the same term described the conveyance by which the right of property was transmitted, and the personal obligation of the debtor for the unpaid purchase-money. We may still go forward, and picture to ourselves a proceeding wholly formal, in which *nothing* is handed over and *nothing* paid; we are brought at once to a transaction indicative of much higher commercial activity, an *executory Contract of Sale.*

If it be true that, both in the popular and in the professional view, a *Contract* was long regarded as an *incomplete Conveyance,* the truth has importance for many reasons. The speculations of the last century concerning mankind in a state of nature, are not unfairly summed up in the doctrine that "in the primitive society property was nothing, and obligation everything"; and it will now be seen that, if the proposition were reversed, it would be nearer the reality. On the other hand, considered historically, the primitive association of Conveyances and Contracts explains something which often strikes the scholar and jurist as singularly enigmatical, I mean the extraordinary and uniform severity of very ancient systems of law to *debtors,* and the extravagant powers which they lodge with *creditors.* When once we understand that the *nexum* was artificially prolonged to give time to the debtor, we can better comprehend his position in the eye of the public and of the law. His indebtedness was doubtless regarded as an anomaly, and suspense of payment in general as an artifice and a distortion of strict rule. The person who had duly consummated his part in the transaction must, on the contrary, have stood in peculiar favour; and nothing would seem more natural than to arm him with stringent facilities for enforcing the completion of a proceeding which, of strict right, ought never to have been extended or deferred.

Nexum, therefore, which originally signified a Conveyance of property, came insensibly to denote a Contract also, and ultimately so constant became the association between this word and the notion of a Contract, that a special term, Mancipium or Mancipatio, had to be used for the purpose of designating the true nexum or transaction in which the property was really transferred. Contracts are therefore now severed from Conveyances, and the first stage in their history is accomplished, but still they are far enough from that epoch of their de-

velopment when the promise of the contractor has a higher sacredness than the formalities with which it is coupled. In attempting to indicate the character of the changes passed through in this interval, it is necessary to trespass a little on a subject which lies properly beyond the range of these pages, the analysis of Agreement effected by the Roman jurisconsults. Of this analysis, the most beautiful monument of their sagacity, I need not say more than that it is based on the theoretical separation of the Obligation from the Convention or Pact. Bentham and Mr. Austin have laid down that the "two main essentials of a contract are these: first, a signification by the promising party of his *intention* to do the acts or to observe the forbearances which he promises to do or to observe. Secondly, a signification by the promisee that he *expects* the promising party will fulfil the proferred promise." This is virtually identical with the doctrine of the Roman lawyers, but then, in their view, the result of these "significations" was not a Contract, but a Convention or Pact. A Pact was the utmost product of the engagements of individuals agreeing among themselves, and it distinctly fell short of a Contract. Whether it ultimately became a Contract depended on the question whether the law annexed an Obligation to it. A Contract was a Pact (or Convention) *plus* an Obligation. So long as the Pact remained unclothed with the Obligation, it was called *nude* or *naked.*

What was an Obligation? It is defined by the Roman lawyers as "Juris vinculum, quo necessitate adstringimur alicujus solvendæ rei." This definition connects the Obligation with the Nexum through the common metaphor on which they are founded, and shows us with much clearness the pedigree of a peculiar conception. The obligation is the "bond" or "chain," with which the law joins together persons or groups of persons, in consequence of certain voluntary acts. The acts which have the effect of attracting an Obligation are chiefly those classed under the heads of Contract and Delict, of Agreement and Wrong; but a variety of other acts have a similar consequence which are not capable of being comprised in an exact classification. It is to be remarked, however, that the Pact does not draw to itself the Obligation in consequence of any moral necessity; it is the law which annexes it in the plenitude of its power, a point the more necessary to be noted, because a different doctrine has sometimes been propounded by modern interpreters of the Civil Law who had moral or metaphysical theories of their own to support. The image of a *vinculum juris* colours and pervades every part of the Roman law of Contract and Delict. The law bound the parties together, and the *chain* could only be undone by the process called *solutio,* an expression still figurative, to which our word "payment" is only occasionally and incidentally equivalent. The consistency with which the figurative image was allowed to present itself, explains an otherwise puzzling peculiarity of Roman legal phraseology, the fact that "Obligation" signifies rights as well as duties, the right, for example, to have a debt paid as well as the duty of paying it. The Romans kept, in fact, the entire picture of the "legal chain" before their eyes, and regarded one end of it no more and no less than the other.

In the developed Roman law, the Convention, as soon as it was completed, was, in almost all cases, at once crowned with the Obligation, and so became a Contract; and this was the result to which contract-law was surely tending. But for the purpose of this inquiry, we must attend particularly to the intermediate stage—that in which something more than a perfect agreement was required to attract the Obligation. This epoch is synchronous with the period at which the famous Roman classification of Contracts into four sorts—the Verbal, the Literal, the Real, and the Consensual—had come into use, and during which these four orders of Contract constituted the only descriptions of engagement which the law would enforce. The meaning of the fourfold distribution is readily understood as soon as we apprehend the theory which severed the Obligation from the Convention. Each class of contracts was in fact named from certain formalities which were required over and above the mere agreement of the contracting parties. In the Verbal Contract, as soon as the Convention was effected, a form of words had to be gone through before the vinculum juris was attached to it. In the Literal Contract, an entry in a ledger or table-book had the effect of clothing the Convention with the Obligation, and the same result followed, in the case of the Real Contract, from the delivery of the Res or Thing which was the subject of the preliminary engagement. The Contracting parties came, in short, to an understanding in each case; but, if they went no further, they were not *obliged* to one another, and could not compel performance or ask redress for a breach of faith. But let them comply with certain prescribed formalities, and the Contract was immediately complete, taking its name from the particular form which it has suited them to adopt. The exceptions to this practice will be noticed presently.

I have enumerated the four Contracts in their historical order, which order, however, the Roman Institutional writers did not invariably follow.

There can be no doubt that the Verbal Contract was the most ancient of the four, and that it is the eldest known descendant of the primitive Nexum. Several species of Verbal Contract were anciently in use, but the most important of all, and the only one treated of by our authorities, was effected by means of a *stipulation,* that is, a Question and Answer; a question addressed by the person who exacted the promise, and an answer given by the person who made it. This question and answer constituted the additional ingredient which, as I have just explained, was demanded by the primitive notion over and above the mere agreement of the persons interested. They formed the agency by which the Obligation was annexed. The old Nexum has now bequeathed to maturer jurisprudence first of all the conception of a chain uniting the contracting parties, and this has become the Obligation. It has further transmitted the notion of a ceremonial accompanying and consecrating the engagement, and this ceremonial has been transmuted into the Stipulation. The conversion of the solemn conveyance, which was the prominent feature of the original Nexum, into a mere question and answer, would be more of a mystery than it is if we had not the analogous history of Roman Testaments to enlighten us. Looking at that history, we can understand how the formal conveyance was first separated from the part of the proceeding which had immediate reference to the business in hand, and how afterwards it was omitted altogether. As then the question and answer of the Stipulation were unquestionably the Nexum in a simplified shape, we are prepared to find that they long partook of the nature of a technical term. It would be a mistake to consider them exclusively recommending themselves to the older Roman lawyers through their usefulness in furnishing persons mediating an agreement with an opportunity for consideration and reflection. It is not to be disputed that they had a value of this kind, which was gradually recognised; but there is proof that their function in respect to Contracts was at first formal and ceremonial in the statement of authorities, that not every question and answer was of old sufficient to constitute a Stipulation, but only a question and answer couched in technical phraseology specially appropriated to the particular occasion.

But although it is essential for the proper appreciation of the history of contract-law that the Stipulation should be understood to have been looked upon as a solemn form before it was recognised as a useful security, it would be wrong on the other hand to shut our eyes to its real usefulness. The Verbal Contract, though it had lost much of its ancient importance, survived to the latest period of Roman jurisprudence; and we may take it for granted that no institution of Roman law had so extended a longevity unless it served some practical advantage. I observe in an English writer some expressions of surprise that the Romans even of the earliest times were content with so meagre a protection against haste and irreflection. But on examining the Stipulation closely, and remembering that we have to do with a state of society in which written evidence was not easily procurable, I think we must admit that this Question and Answer, had it been expressly devised to answer the purpose which it served, would have been justly designated a highly ingenious expedient. It was the *promisee* who, in the character of stipulator, put all the terms of the contract into the form of a question, and the answer was given by the *promisor*. "Do you promise that you will deliver me such and such a slave, at such and such a place, on such and such a day?" "I do promise." Now, if we reflect for a moment, we shall see that this obligation to put the promise interrogatively inverts the natural position of the parties, and, by effectually breaking the tenor of the conversation, prevents the attention from gliding over a dangerous pledge. With us, a verbal promise is, generally speaking, to be gathered exclusively from the words of the promisor. In old Roman law, another step was absolutely required; it was necessary for the promise, after the agreement had been made, to sum up all its terms in a solemn interrogation; and it was of this interrogation, of course, and of the assent to it, that proof had to be given at the trial —*not* of the promise, which was not in itself binding. How great a difference this seemingly insignificant peculiarity may make in the phraseology of contract-law is speedily realised by the beginner in Roman jurisprudence, one of whose first stumbling-blocks is almost universally created by it. When we in English have occasion, in mentioning a contract, to connect it for convenience' sake with one of the parties,—for example, if we wished to speak generally of a contractor,—it is always the promis*or* at whom our words are pointing. But the general language of Roman law takes a different turn; it always regards the contract, if we may so speak, from the point of view of the promis*ee;* in speaking of a party to a contract, it is always the Stipulator, the person who asks the question, who is primarily alluded to. But the serviceableness of the stipulation is most vividly illustrated by referring to the actual examples in the pages of the Latin comic dramatists. If the entire scenes are read down in which these passages occur (ex. gra. Plautus, *Pseudolus,* Act I. sc. 1;

Act IV. sc. 6; *Trinummus,* Act V. sc. 2), it will be perceived how effectually the attention of the person meditating the promise must have been arrested by the question, and how ample was the opportunity for withdrawal from an improvident undertaking.

In the Literal or Written Contract, the formal act by which an Obligation was superinduced on the Convention, was an entry of the sum due, where it could be specifically ascertained, on the debit side of a ledger. The explanation of this contract turns on a point of Roman domestic manners, the systematic character and exceeding regularity of bookkeeping in ancient times. There are several minor difficulties of old Roman law, for example, the nature of the Slave's Peculium, which are only cleared up when we recollect that a Roman household consisted of a number of persons strictly accountable to its head, and that every single item of domestic receipt and expenditure, after being entered in waste books, was transferred at stated periods to a general household ledger. There are some obscurities, however, in the descriptions we have received of the Literal Contract, the fact being that the habit of keeping books ceased to be universal in later times, and the expression "Literal Contract," came to signify a form of engagement entirely different from that originally understood. We are not, therefore, in a position to say, with respect to the primitive Literal Contract, whether the obligation was created by a simple entry on the part of the creditor, or whether the consent of the debtor or a correspondent entry in his own books was necessary to give it legal effect. The essential point is however established, that, in the case of this Contract, all formalities were dispensed with on a condition being complied with. This is another step downwards in the history of contract-law.

The Contract which stands next in historical succession, the Real Contract, shows a great advance in ethical conceptions. Whenever any agreement had for its object the delivery of a specific thing—and this is the case with the large majority of simple engagements—the Obligation was drawn down as soon as the delivery had actually taken place. Such a result must have involved a serious innovation on the oldest ideas of Contract; for doubtless, in the primitive times, when a contracting party had neglected to clothe his agreement in a stipulation, nothing done in pursuance of the agreement would be recognised by the law. A person who had paid over money on loan would be unable to sue for its repayment unless he had formally *stipulated* for it. But, in the Real Contract, performance on one side is allowed to impose a legal duty on the other—evidently on ethical

ounds. For the first time then moral considera-
ns appear as an ingredient in Contract-law, and
the Real Contract differs from its two predecessors
in being founded on these, rather than on respect
for technical forms or on deference to Roman
domestic habits.

We now reach the fourth class, or Consensual
Contracts, the most interesting and important of
all. Four specified Contracts were distinguished by
this name: Mandatum, *i.e.* Commission or Agency;
Societas or Partnership; Emtio Venditio or Sale;
and Locatio Conductio or Letting and Hiring. A
few pages back, after stating that a Contract consisted of a Pact or Convention to which an Obligation had been superadded, I spoke of certain acts
or formalities by which the law permitted the
Obligation to be attracted to the Pact. I used this
language on account of the advantage of a general
expression, but it is not strictly correct unless it be
understood to include the negative as well as the
positive. For, in truth, the peculiarity of these Consensual Contracts is that *no* formalities are required
to create them of the Pact. Much that is indefensible, and much more that is obscure, has been
written about the Consensual Contracts, and it has
even been asserted that in them the *consent* of the
Parties is more emphatically given than in any
other species of agreement. But the term Consensual merely indicates that the Obligation is here

annexed at once to the *Consensus*. The Consensus,
or mutual assent of the parties, is the final and
crowning ingredient in the Convention, and it is
the special characteristic of agreements falling under one of the four heads of Sale, Partnership,
Agency, and Hiring, that, as soon as the assent of
the parties has supplied this ingredient, there is
at once a Contract. The Consensus draws with it
the Obligation, performing, in transactions of the
sort specified, the exact functions which are discharged, in the other contracts, by the *Res* or
Thing, by the *Verba* stipulationis, and by the
Literæ or written entry in a ledger. Consensual is
therefore a term which does not involve the
slightest anomaly, but is exactly analogous to Real,
Verbal, and Literal.

In the intercourse of life the commonest and
most important of all the contracts are unquestionably the four stlyed Consensual. The larger part
of the collective existence of every community is
consumed in transactions of buying and selling,
of letting and hiring, of alliances between men for
purposes of business, or delegation of business
from one man to another; and this is no doubt the
consideration which led the Romans, as it has led
most societies, to relieve these transactions from
technical incumbrance, to abstain as much as possible from clogging the most efficient springs of
social movement.

6. *Organic Solidarity and Contract*

BY EMILE DURKHEIM

I

IF HIGHER societies do not rest upon a
fundamental contract which sets forth the general
principles of political life, they would have, or
would be considered to have, according to Spencer,
the vast system of particular contracts which link
individuals as a unique basis. They would depend
upon the group only in proportion to their dependence upon one another, and they would depend upon one another only in proportion to conventions

Reprinted from Emile Durkheim, *The Division of Labor
in Society,* trans. George Simpson (Glencoe, Ill.: The
Free Press, 1947), pp. 203–17, 226–29, with the permission of The Free Press.

privately entered into and freely concluded. Social
solidarity would then be nothing else than the
spontaneous accord of individual interests, an accord of which contracts are the natural expression.
The typical social relation would be the economic,
stripped of all regulation and resulting from the
entirely free initiative of the parties. In short,
society would be solely the stage where individuals
exchanged the products of their labor, without any
action properly social coming to regulate this
exchange.

Is this the character of societies whose unity is
produced by the division of labor? If this were so,
we could with justice doubt their stability. For if
interest relates men, it is never for more than some

few moments. It can create only an external link between them. In the fact of exchange, the various agents remain outside of each other, and when the business has been completed, each one retires and is left entirely on his own. Consciences are only superficially in contact; they neither penetrate each other, nor do they adhere. If we look further into the matter, we shall see that this total harmony of interests conceals a latent or deferred conflict. For where interest is the only ruling force each individual finds himself in a state of war with every other since nothing comes to mollify the egos, and any truce in this eternal antagonism would not be of long duration. There is nothing less constant than interest. Today, it unites me to you; tomorrow, it will make me your enemy. Such a cause can only give rise to transient relations and passing associations. We now understand how necessary it is to see if this is really the nature of organic solidarity.

In no respect, according to Spencer, does industrial society exist in a pure state. It is a partially ideal type which slowly disengages itself in the evolutionary process, but it has not yet been completely realized. Consequently, to rightly attribute to it the qualities we have just been discussing, we would have to establish systematically that societies appear in a fashion as complete as they are elevated, discounting cases of regression.

It is first affirmed that the sphere of social activity grows smaller and smaller, to the great advantage of the individual. But to prove this proposition by real instances, it is not enough to cite, as Spencer does, some cases where the individual has been effectively emancipated from collective influence. These examples, numerous as they may be, can serve only as illustrations, and are, by themselves, devoid of any demonstrative force. It is very possible that, in this respect, socal action has regressed, but that, in other respects, it has been extended, and that, ultimately, we are mistaking a transformation for a disappearance. The only way of giving objective proof is not to cite some facts taken at random, but to follow historically, from its origins until recent times, the way in which social action has essentially manifested itself, and to see whether, in time, it has added or lost volume. We know that this is law. The obligations that society imposes upon its members, as inconsequential and unenduring as they may be, take on a juridicial form. Consequently, the relative dimensions of this system permit us to measure with exactitude the relative extent of social action.

But is is very evident that, far from diminishing, it grows greater and greater and becomes more and more complex. The more primitive a code is, the smaller its volume. On the contrary, it is as large as it is more recent. There can be no doubt about this. To be sure, it does not result in making the sphere of individual activity smaller. We must not forget that if there is more regulation in life, there is more life in general. This is sufficient proof that social discipline has not been relaxing. One of its forms tends, it is true, to regress, as we have already seen, but others, much richer and much more complex, develop in its place. If repressive law loses ground, restitutive law, which originally did not exist at all, keeps growing. If society no longer imposes upon everybody certain uniform practices, it takes greater care to define and regulate the special relations between different social functions, and this activity is not smaller because it is different.

Spencer would reply that he had not insisted upon the dimunition of every kind of control, but only of positive control. Let us admit this distinction. Whether it be positive or negative, the control is none the less social, and the principal question is to understand whether it has extended itself or contracted. Whether it be to command or to deny, to say *Do this* or *Do not do that,* if society intervenes more, we have not the right to say that individual spontaneity suffices more and more in all spheres. If the rules determining conduct have multiplied, whether they be imperative or prohibitive, it is not true that it depends more and more completely on private initiative.

But has this distinction itself any foundation? By positive control, Spencer means that which commands action, while negative control commands only abstention. As he says: A man has a piece of land; I cultivate it for him either wholly or in part, or else I impose upon him either wholly or in part the way in which he should cultivate it. This is a positive control. On the other hand, I give him neither aid nor advice about its cultivation; I simply do not molest my neighbor's crop, or trespass upon my neighbor's land, or put rubbish on his clearing. This is a negative control. The difference is very marked between ordering him to follow, as a citizen, a certain course, or suggesting means for the citizen to employ, and, on the other hand, not disturbing the course which some citizen is pursuing. If such is the meaning of these terms, then positive control is not disappearing.

We know, of course, that restitutive law is growing. But, in the large majority of cases, it either points out to a citizen the course he ought to pursue, or it interests itself in the means that this citizen is employing to attain his end. It answers the two following questions for each juridical relation: (1) Under what conditions and in what form does it normally exist? (2) What are the obligations it entails? The determination of the form and the conditions is essentially positive, since it forces the individual to follow a certain procedure in order to attain his end. As for the obligations, if they only forbid, in principle, our troubling another person in the exercise of his functions, Spencer's thesis would be true, at least in part. But they consist most often in the statement of services of a positive nature.

On this point we must go into some detail.

II

It is quite true that contractual relations, which originally were rare or completely absent, multiply as social labor becomes divided. But what Spencer seems to have failed to see is that non-contractual relations develop at the same time.

First, let us examine that part of law which is improperly termed private, and which, in reality, regulates diffuse social functions, or what may be called the visceral life of the social organism.

In the first place, we know that domestic law, as simple as it was in the beginning, has become more and more complex. That is to say, that the different species of juridical relations to which family life gives rise are much more numerous than heretofore. But the obligations which result from this are of an eminently positive nature; they constitute a reciprocity of rights and duties. Moreover, they are not contractual, at least in their typical form. The conditions upon which they are dependent are related to our personal status which, in turn, depends upon birth, on our consanguineous relations, and, consequently, upon facts which are beyond volition.

Marriage and adoption, however, are sources of domestic relations, and they are contracts. But it rightly happens that the closer we get to the most elevated social types, the more also do these two juridical operations lose their properly contractual character.

Not only in lower societies, but in Rome itself until the end of the Empire, marriage remains an entirely private affair. It generally is a sale, real among primitive people, later fictive, but valid only through the consent of the parties duly attested. Neither solemn formalities of any kind nor intervention by some authority were then necessary. It is only with Christianity that marriage took on another character. The Christians early got into the habit of having their union consecrated by a priest. An act of the emperor Leo the Philosopher converted this usage into a law for the East. The Council of Trent sanctioned it likewise for the West. From then on, marriage ceased to be freely contracted, and was concluded through the intermediary of a public power, the Church, and the role that the Church played was not only that of a witness, but it was she and she alone who created the juridical tie which until then the wills of the participants sufficed to establish. We know how, later, the civil authority was substituted in this function for the religious authority, and how at the same time the part played by society and its necessary formalities was extended.*

The history of the contract of adoption is still more instructive.

We have already seen with what facility and on what a large scale adoption was practiced among the Indian tribes of North America. It could give rise to all the forms of kinship. If the adopted was of the same age as the adopting, they became brothers and sisters; if the adopted was already a mother, she became the mother of the one who adopted her.

Among the Arabs, before Mohammed, adoption often served to establish real families. It frequently happened that several persons would mutually adopt one another. They then became brothers and sisters, and the kinship which united them was just as strong as if they had been descended from a common origin. We find the same type of adoption among the Slavs. Very often, the members of different families became brothers and sisters and formed was is called a confraternity (*probatinstvo*). These societies were contracted for freely and without formality; agreement was enough to establish them. Moreover, the tie which binds these elective brothers is even stronger than that which results from natural fraternity.

Among the Germans, adoption was probably quite as easy and frequent. Very simple ceremonies were enough to establish it. But in India, Greece, and Rome, it was already subordinated to determined conditions. The one adopting had to be of a certain age, could not stand in such relation to the age of the adopted that it would be impossible to be his natural father. Ultimately, this change of family became a highly complex juridical operation which necessitated the intervention of a magistrate. At the same time, the number of those who could enjoy the right of adoption became more restricted. Only the father of a family or a bachelor *sui juris* could adopt, and the first could, only if he had no legitimate children.

In our current law the restrictive conditions have been even more multiplied. The adopted must be of age, the adopting must be more than fifty years of age, and have long treated the adopted as his

---

* Of course, the case is the same for the dissolution of the conjugal bond.

child. We must notice that, thus limited, it has become a very rare event. Before the appearance of the French Code, the whole procedure had almost completely fallen into disuse, and today it is, in certain countries such as Holland and lower Canada, not permitted at all.

At the same time that it became more rare, adoption lost its efficacy. In the beginning, adoptive kinship was in all respects similar to natural kinship. In Rome, the similarity was still very great. It was no longer, however, a perfect identity. In the sixteenth century, the adopted no longer has the right of succession if the adoptive father dies intestate. The French Code has re-established this right, but the kinship to which the adoption gives rise does not extend beyond the adopting and the adopted.

We see how insufficient the traditional explanation is, which attributes this custom of adoption among ancient societies to the need of assuring the perpetuity of the ancestral cult. The peoples who have practiced it in the greatest and freest manner, as the Indians of America, the Arabs, the Slavs, had no such cult, and, furthermore, at Rome and Athens, where domestic religion was at its height, this law is for the first time submitted to control and restrictions. If it was able to satisfy these needs, it was not established to satisfy them, and, inversely, if it tends to disappear, it is not because we have less desire to perpetuate our name and our race. It is in the structure of actual societies and in the place which the family occupies that we must seek the determining cause for this change.

Another proof of the truth of this is that it has become even more impossible to leave a family by an act of private authority than to enter into it. As the kinship-tie does not result from a contract, it cannot be broken as a contract can. Among the Iroquois, we sometimes see a part of a clan leave to go to join a neighboring clan. Among the Slavs, a member of the Zadruga who is tired of the common life can separate himself from the rest of the family and become a juridical stranger to it, even as he can be excluded by it. Among the Germans, a ceremony of some slight complexity permitted every Frank who so desired to completely drop off all kinship-obligations. In Rome, the son could not leave the family of his own will, and by this sign we recognize a more elevated social type. But the tie that the son could not break could be broken by the father. Thus was emancipation possible. Today neither the father nor the son can alter the natural state of domestic relations. They remain as birth determines them.

In short, at the same time that domestic obligations become more numerous, they take on, as is said, a public character. Not only in early times do they not have a contractural origin, but the role which contract plays in them becomes ever smaller. On the contrary, social control over the manner in which they form, break down, and are modified, becomes greater. The reason lies in the progressive effacement of segmental organization. The family, in truth, is for a long time a veritable social segment. In origin, it confounds itself with the clan. If, later, it becomes distinguished from the clan, it is as a part of the whole. It is a product of a secondary segmentation of the clan, identical with that which has given birth to the clan itself, and when the latter has disappeared, it still keeps the same quality. But everything segmental tends to be more and more reabsorbed into the social mass. That is why the family is forced to transform itself. Instead of remaining an autonomous society along side of the great society, it becomes more and more involved in the system of social organs. It even becomes one of the organs, charged with special functions, and, accordingly, everything that happens within it is capable of general repercussions. That is what brings it about that the regulative organs of society are forced to intervene in order to exercise a moderating influence over the functioning of the family, or even, in certain cases, a positively arousing influence.

But it is not only outside of contractual relations, it is in the play of these relations themselves that social action makes itself felt. For everything in the contract is not contractual. The only engagements which deserve this name are those which have been desired by the individuals and which have no other origin except in this manifestation of free will. Inversely, every obligation which has not been mutually consented to has nothing contractual about it. But wherever a contract exists, it is submitted to regulation which is the work of society and not that of individuals, and which becomes ever more voluminous and more complicated.

It is true that the contracting parties can, in certain respects, arrange to act contrary to the dispositions of the law. But, of course, their rights in this regard are not unlimited. For example, the agreement of the parties cannot make a contract valid if it does not satisfy the conditions of validity required by law. To be sure, in the great majority of cases, a contract is no longer restricted to determined forms. Still it must not be forgotten that there are in our Codes solemn contracts. But if law no longer has the formal exigencies of yesterday, it subjects contracts to engagements of a different sort. It refuses all obligatory force to engagements contracted by an incompetent, or without object, or with illicit purpose, or made by a person who cannot sell, or transact over an article which cannot be sold. Among the obligations which it attaches to various contracts, there are some which cannot be changed by any stipulation. Thus, a vendor cannot fail in his obligation to guarantee the purchaser against any eviction which results from something personal to the vendor (art. 1628); he cannot fail to repay the purchase-price in case of eviction, whatever its origin, provided that the buyer has not known of the danger (art. 1629), nor to set forth clearly what is being contracted for (art. 1602). Indeed, in a certain measure, he cannot be exempt from guaranteeing against hidden defects (arts. 1641 and 1643), particularly when known. If it is a question of fixtures, it is the buyer who must not profit from the situation by imposing a price too obviously below the real value of the thing (art. 1674), etc. Moreover, everything that relates to proof, the nature of the actions to which the contract gives a right, the time in which they must be begun, is absolutely independent of individual transactions.

In other cases social action does not manifest itself only by the refusal to recognize a contract formed in violation of the law, but by a positive intervention. Thus, the judge can, whatever the terms of the agreement, grant a delay to a debtor (arts. 1184, 1244, 1655, 1900), or even oblige the borrower to restore the article to the lender before the term agreed upon, if the latter has pressing need of it (art. 1189). But what shows better than anything else that contracts give rise to obligations which have not been contracted for is that they "make obligatory not only what there is expressed in them, but also all consequences which equity, usage, or the law imputes from the nature of the obligation" (art. 1135). In virtue of this principle, there must be supplied in the contract "clauses pertaining to usage, although they may not be expressed therein" (art. 1160).

But even if social action should not express itself in this way, it would not cease to be real. The possibility of derogating the law, which seems to reduce the contractual right to the role of eventual substitute for contracts properly called, is, in the very great majority of cases, purely theoretical. We can convince ourselves of this by showing what it consists in.

To be sure, when men unite in a contract, it is because, through the division of labor, either simple or complex, they need each other. But in order for them to co-operate harmoniously, it is not enough that they enter into a relationship, nor even that they feel the state of mutual dependence in which they find themselves. It is still necessary that the conditions of this co-operation be fixed for the

duration of their relations. The rights and duties of each must be defined, not only in view of the situation such as it presents itself at the moment when the contract is made, but with foresight for the circumstances which may arise to modify it. Otherwise, at every instant, there would be conflicts and endless difficulties. We must not forget that, if the division of labor makes interests solidary, it does not confound them; it keeps them distinct and opposite. Even as in the internal workings of the individual organism each organ is in conflict with others while co-operating with them, each of the contractants, while needing the other, seeks to obtain what he needs at the least expense; that is to say, to acquire as many rights as possible in exchange for the smallest possible obligations.

It is necessary therefore to pre-determine the share of each, but this cannot be done according to a preconceived plan. There is nothing in the nature of things from which one can deduce what the obligations of one or the other ought to be until a certain limit is reached. Every determination of this kind can only result in compromise. It is a compromise between the rivalry of interests present and their solidarity. It is a position of equilibrium which can be found only after more or less laborious experiments. But it is quite evident that we can neither begin these experiments over again nor restore this equilibrium at fresh expense every time that we engage in some contractual relation. We lack all ability to do that. It is not at the moment when difficulties surge upon us that we must resolve them, and, moreover, we can neither foresee the variety of possible circumstances in which our contract will involve itself, nor fix in advance with the aid of simple mental calculus what will be in each case the rights and duties of each, save in matters in which we have a very definite experience. Moreover, the material conditions of life oppose themselves to the repetition of such operations. For, at each instant, and often at the most inopportune, we find ourselves contracting, either for something we have bought, or sold, somewhere we are traveling, our hiring of one's services, some acceptance of hostelry, etc. The greater part of our relations with others is of a contractual nature. If, then, it were necessary each time to begin the struggles anew, to again go through the conferences necessary to establish firmly all the conditions of agreement for the present and the future, we would be put to rout. For all these reasons, if we were linked only by the terms of our contracts, as they are agreed upon, only a precarious solidarity would result.

But contract-law is that which determines the juridical consequences of our acts that we have not determined. It expresses the normal conditions of equilibrium, as they arise from themselves or from the average. A résumé of numerous, varied experiences, what we cannot foresee individually is there provided for, what we cannot regulate is there regulated, and this regulation imposes itself upon us, although it may not be our handiwork, but that of society and tradition. It forces us to assume obligations that we have not contracted for, in the exact sense of the word, since we have not deliberated upon them, nor even, occasionally, had any knowledge about them in advance. Of course, the initial acts is always contractual, but there are consequences, sometimes immediate, which run over the limits of the contract. We co-operate because we wish to, but our voluntary co-operation creates duties for us that we did not desire.

From this point of view, the law of contracts appears in an entirely different light. It is no longer simply a useful complement of individual conventions; it is their fundamental norm. Imposing itself upon us with the authority of traditional experience, it constitutes the foundation of our contractual relations. We cannot evade it, except partially and accidentally. The law confers its rights upon us and subjects us to duties deriving from such acts of our will. We can, in certain cases, abandon them or change them for others. But both are none the less the normal type of rights and duties which circumstance lays upon us, and an express act is necessary for their modification. Thus, modifications are relatively rare. In principle, the rule applies; innovations are exceptional. The law of contracts exercises over us a regulative force of the greatest importance, since it determines what we ought to do and what we can require. It is a law which can be changed only by the consent of the parties, but so long as it is not abrogated or replaced, it guards its authority, and, moreover, a legislative act can be passed only in rare cases. There is, then, only a difference of degree between the law which regulates the obligations which that contract engenders and those which fix the other duties of citizens.

Finally, besides this organized, defined pressure which law exercises, there is one which comes from custom. In the way in which we make our contracts and in which we execute them, we are held to conform to rules which, though not sanctioned either directly or indirectly by any code, are none the less imperative. There are professional obligations, purely moral, which are, however, very strict. They are particularly apparent in the so-called liberal professions, and if they are perhaps less numerous in others, there is place for demanding them, as we shall see, if such demand is not the result of a morbid condition. But if this action is more diffuse than

the preceding, it is just as social. Moreover, it is necessarily as much more extended as the contractual relations are more developed, for it is diversified like contracts.

In sum, a contract is not sufficient unto itself, but is possible only thanks to a regulation of the contract which is originally social. It is implied, first, because it has for its function much less the creation of new rules than the diversification in particular cases of pre-established rules; then, because it has and can have the power to bind only under certain conditions which it is necessary to define. If, in principle, society lends it an obligatory force, it is because, in general, the accord of particular wills suffices to assure, with the preceding reservations, the harmonious coming together of diffuse social functions. But if it conflicts with social purposes, if it tends to trouble the regular operation of organs, if, as is said, it is not just, it is necessary, while depriving it of all social value, to strip it of all authority as well. The role of society is not, then, in any case, simply to see passively that contracts are carried out. It is also to determine under what conditions they are executable, and if it is necessary, to restore them to their normal form. The agreement of parties cannot render a clause just which by itself is unjust, and there are rules of justice whose violation social justice prevents, even if it has been consented to by the interested parties.

A regulation whose extent cannot be limited in advance is thus necessary. A contract, says Spencer, has for its object assuring the worker the equivalent of the expense which his work has cost him. If such is truly the role of a contract, it will never be able to fulfill it unless it is more minutely regulated than it is today, for it surely would be a miracle if it succeeded in bringing about this equivalence. In fact, it is as much the gain which exceeds the expense, as the expense which exceeds the gain, and the disproportion is often striking. But, replies a whole school, if the gains are too small, the function will be abandoned for others. If they are too high, they will be sought after and this will diminish the profits. It is forgotten that one whole part of the population cannot thus quit its task, because no other is accessible to it. The very ones who have more liberty of movement cannot replace it in an instant. Such revolutions always take long to accomplish. While waiting, unjust contracts, unsocial by definition, have been executed with the agreement of society, and when the equilibrium in this respect has been reestablished, there is no reason for not breaking it for another.

There is no need for showing that this intervention, under its different forms, is of an eminently positive nature, since it has for its purpose the determination of the way in which we ought to co-operate. It is not it, it is true, which gives the impulse to the functions concurring, but once the concourse has begun, it rules it. As soon as we have made the first step towards cooperation, we are involved in the regulative action which society exercises over us. If Spencer qualified this as negative, it is because, for him, contract consists only in exchange. But, even from this point of view, the expression he employs is not exact. No doubt, when, after having an object delivered, or profiting from a service, I refuse to furnish a suitable equivalent, I take from another what belongs to him, and we can say that society, by obliging me to keep my promise, is only preventing an injury, an indirect aggression. But if I have simply promised a service without having previously received remuneration, I am not less held to keep my engagement. In this case, however, I do not enrich myself at the expense of another; I only refuse to be useful to him. Moreover, exchange, as we have seen, is not all there is to a contract. There is also the proper harmony of functions concurring. They are not only in contact for the short time during which things pass from one hand to another; but more extensive relations necessarily result from them, in the course of which it is important that their solidarity be not troubled.

*   *   *

IV

The following propositions sum up the first part of our work.

Social life comes from a double source, the likeness of consciences and the division of social labor. The individual is socialized in the first case, because, not having any real individuality, he becomes, with those whom he resembles, part of the same collective type; in the second case, because, while having a physiognomy and a personal activity which distinguishes him from others, he depends upon them in the same measure that he is distinguished from them, and consequently upon the society which results from their union.

The similitude of consciences gives rise to juridical rules which, with the threat of repressive measures, impose uniform beliefs and practices upon all. The more pronounced this is, the more completely is social life confounded with religious life, and the nearer to communism are economic institutions.

The division of labor gives rise to juridical rules which determine the nature and the relations of divided functions, but whose violation calls forth

only restitutive measures without any expiatory character.

Each of these bodies of juridical rules is, moreover, accompanied by a body of purely moral rules. Where penal law is very voluminous, common morality is very extensive; that is to say, there is a multitude of collective practices placed under the protection of public opinion. Where restitutive law is highly developed, there is an occupational morality for each profession. In the interior of the same group of workers, there exists an opinion, diffuse in the entire extent of this circumscribed aggregate, which, without being furnished with legal sanctions, is rendered obedience. These are usages and customs common to the same order of functionaries which no one of them can break without incurring the censure of the corporation.* This morality is distinguished from the preceding by differences analogous to those which separate the two corresponding types of law. It is localized in a limited region of society. Moreover, the repressive character of the sanctions attaching to it is much less accentuated. Professional misdeeds call forth reprobation much more feeble than attacks against public morality.

The rules of occupational morality and justice, however, are as imperative as the others. They force the individual to act in view of ends which are not strictly his own, to make concessions, to consent to compromises, to take into account interests higher than his own. Consequently, even where society relies most completely upon the division of labor, it does not become a jumble of juxtaposed atoms, between which it can establish only external, transient contacts. Rather the members are united by ties which extend deeper and far beyond the short moments during which the exchange is made. Each of the functions that they exercise is, in a fixed way, dependent upon others, and with them forms a solidary system. Accordingly, from the nature of the chosen task permanent duties arise. Because we fill some certain domestic or social function, we are involved in a complex of obligations from which we have no right to free ourselves. There is, above all, an organ upon which we are tending to depend more and more; this is the State. The points at which we are in contact with it multiply as do the occasions when it is entrusted with the duty of reminding us of the sentiment of common solidarity.

Thus, altruism is not destined to become, as Spencer desires, a sort of agreeable ornament to social life, but it will forever be its fundamental basis. How can we ever really dispense with it? Men cannot live together without acknowledging, and,

---

* This censure, moreover, just as all moral punishment, is translated into external movements (discipline, dismissal of employees, loss of relations, etc.).

consequently, making mutual sacrifices, without tying themselves to one another with strong, durable bonds. Every society is a moral society. In certain respects, this character is even more pronounced in organized societies. Because the individual is not sufficient unto himself, it is from society that he receives everything necessary to him, as it is for society that he works. Thus is formed a very strong sentiment of the state of dependence in which he finds himself. He becomes accustomed to estimating it as its just value, that is to say, in regarding himself as part of a whole, the organ of an organism. Such sentiments naturally inspire not only mundane sacrifices which assure the regular development of daily social life, but even, on occasion, acts of complete self-renunciation and wholesale abnegation. On its side, society learns to regard its members no longer as things over which it has rights, but as co-operators whom it cannot neglect and towards whom it owes duties. Thus, it is wrong to oppose a society which comes from a community of beliefs to one which has a co-operative basis, according only to the first a moral character, and seeing in the latter only an economic grouping. In reality, co-operation also has its intrinsic morality. There is, however, reason to believe, as we shall see later, that in contemporary societies this morality has not yet reached the high development which would now seem necessary to it.

But it is not of the same nature as the other. The other is strong only if the individual is not. Made up of rules which are practiced by all indis-

tinctly, it receives from this universal, uniform practice an authority which bestows something super-human upon it, and which puts it beyond the pale of discussion. The co-operative society, on the contrary, develops in the measure that individual personality becomes stronger. As regulated as a function may be, there is a large place always left for personal initiative. A great many of the obligations thus sanctioned have their origin in a choice of the will. It is we who choose our professions, and even certain of our domestic functions. Of course, once our resolution has ceased to be internal and has been externally translated by social consequences, we are tied down. Duties are imposed upon us that we have not expressly desired. It is, however, through a voluntary act that this has taken place. Finally, because these rules of conduct relate, not to the conditions of common life, but to the different forms of professional activity, they have a more temporal character, which, while lessening their obligatory force, renders them more accessible to the action of men.

There are, then, two great currents of social life to which two types of structure, not less different, correspond.

Of these currents, that which has its origin in social similitudes first runs on alone and without a rival. At this moment, it confounds itself with the very life of society; then, little by little, it canalizes, rarefies, while the second is always growing. Indeed, the segmental structure is more and more covered over by the other, but without ever completely disappearing.

III—ORGANIZATION OF THE ECONOMY

---

1. *The Market*

by MAX WEBER

BY THE "market situation" (*Marktage*) for any object of exchange is meant all the opportunities of exchanging it for money which are

Reprinted from Max Weber, *The Theory of Social and Economic Organization*, trans. A. M. Henderson and Talcott Parsons, ed. Talcott Parsons (2d ed.; Glencoe, Ill.: The Free Press, 1956), pp. 181–86. Copyright 1947 by Oxford University Press.

known by the participants in the market situation to be available to them and relevant in orienting their attitudes to prices and to competition.

"Marketability" (*Marktgängigkeit*) is the degree of regularity with which an object tends to be an object of exchange on the market.

"Market freedom" is the degree of autonomy enjoyed by the parties to market relationships in price determination and in competition.

"Regulation of the market," on the contrary, is the state of affairs where there is a substantive restriction, effectively enforced by the provisions of an order, on the marketability of certain potential objects of exchange or on the market freedom of certain participants. Regulation of the market may be determined (1) traditionally, by the actors' becoming accustomed to traditionally accepted limitations on exchange or to traditional conditions. (2) By convention, through social disapproval of treating certain utilities as marketable or of subjecting certain objects of exchange to free competition and free price determination, in general or when undertaken by certain groups of persons. (3) By law, through legal restrictions on exchange or on the freedom of competition, in general or for particular groups of persons or for particular objects of exchange. Legal regulation may take the form of influencing the market situation of objects of exchange by price regulation or of limiting the possession, acquisition, or exchange of rights of control and disposal over certain goods to certain specific groups of persons. In the latter case it is a legally-guaranteed monopoly or a legal limitation of economic freedom. (4) By voluntary action arising from the play of interests. In this case there is substantive regulation of the market, though the market remains formally free. This type of regulation tends to develop when certain participants in the market are, by virtue of their totally or approximately exclusive control of the possession of or opportunities to acquire certain utilities—that is, of their monopolistic powers—in a position to influence the market situation in such a way as actually to abolish the market freedom of others. In particular, they may make agreements with each other and with typical exchange partners for regulating market conditions. Typical examples are market quota agreements and price cartels.

1. It is convenient, though not necessary, to confine the term "market situation" to cases of exchange for money because it is only then that uniform numerical statements of relationships become possible. Opportunities for exchange *in kind* are best described simply as exchange opportunities. Different kinds of goods are and have been marketable in widely different and variable degrees, even where a money economy was well developed. The details cannot be gone into here. In general, articles produced in standardized form in large quantities and widely consumed have been the most marketable; unusual goods, only occasionally in demand, the least. Durable consumption goods which can be made use of over long periods and means of pro-

duction with a long or indefinite life, above all, agricultural and forest land, have been marketable to a much less degree than finished goods of everyday use or means of production which are quickly used up, which can be used only once, or which give quick returns.

2. The regulation of markets, as an economically rational policy, has been historically associated with the growth of formal market freedom and the extension of marketability of goods. The original modes of market regulation have been various, partly traditional and magical, partly dictated by kinship relations, by class privileges, by military needs, by welfare policies, and not least by the interests and requirements of the governing authorities of corporate groups. But in each of these cases the dominant interests have not been primarily concerned with maximizing the opportunities of acquisition and economic provision of the participants in the market themselves; have, indeed, often been in conflict with them. (1) Sometimes the effect has been to exclude certain objects from market dealings, either permanently or for a time. This has happened in the magical case, by taboo; in that of kinship, by the hereditary appropriation of property; on the basis of social status, with fiefs. In times of famine the sale of grain has been temporarily prohibited. In other cases permission to sell has been made conditional on a prior offer to certain persons, such as kinsmen, co-members of class groups, and of guilds, or fellow-citizens of a town; or the sale has been limited by maximum prices, as is common in war time, or by minimum prices. Thus in the interests of the dignity of magicians, lawyers, physicians, they have not been allowed to accept fees below a certain minimum. (2) Sometimes certain categories of persons, such as members of the nobility, peasants, or sometimes even artisans, have been excluded from market trade in general or with respect to certain commodities. (3) Sometimes the market freedom of consumers has been restricted by regulations, as in regulations specifying consumption for different classes, rationing in case of war or of famine. (4) Another type is the restriction of the market freedom of potential competitors in the interest of the market position of certain groups, such as the professions or the guilds. Finally, (5) certain economic privileges, such as royal monopolies, have been reserved to the political authorities or to those holding a charter from such authorities. This was typical for the early capitalistic monopolies.

Of all these, the fifth type of market regulation has been the most highly rational in terms of the interests of market participants; the first type, the least. By "rational" in this sense is meant promoting the interests of the various groups whose action is oriented to the market situations as a means to the advantageous purchase and sale of goods, with consideration for the interests of other groups not thus oriented proportionally minimized. The groups which, relative to these forms of regulation have been most interested in the freedom of the market, have been those whose interests lay in the greatest possible extension of the marketability of goods, whether from the point of view of availability for consumption, or of ready opportunities for sale. Voluntary market regulation has not appeared extensively and permanently except where there have been highly developed profit-making interests. With a view to the securing of monopolistic advantages, this could take several forms: (1) the pure regulation of opportunities for purchase and sale, which is typical of the widespread phenomena of trading monopolies; (2) the monopolization of transportation facilities, as in shipping and railways; (3) the monopolization of the production of goods; and (4) that of the extension of credit and of financing. The last two types generally are accompanied by an increase in the regulation of economic activity by corporate groups other than the immediate participants in the market relationships. But unlike the primitive, irrational forms of regulation, this is apt to be deliberately oriented to the market situation. The starting point of voluntary market regulation has naturally in general been the fact that certain groups with a far-reaching degree of actual control over economic resources have been in a position to take advantage of the formal freedom of the market to establish monopolies. Voluntary associations of consumers, such as consumers' co-operative societies, have, on the other hand, tended to originate among those who were in an economically weak position. They have hence often been able to accomplish savings for their members, but only occasionally and in particular localities have they been able to establish an effective system of market regulation.

The Formal and Substantive Rationality of Economic Action

The term "formal rationality of economic action" will be used to designate the extent of quantitative calculation or accounting which is technically possible and which is actually applied. The "substantive rationality," on the other hand, is the degree in which a given group of persons, no matter how it is delimited, is or could be adequately provided with goods by means of an economically oriented course of social action. This course of action will be interpreted in terms of a given set of ultimate values no matter what they may be. There is a variety of different possibilities.

1. The terminology suggested above is thought of merely as a means of securing greater consistency in the use of the word "rational" in this field. It is actually only a more precise form of the meanings which are continually recurring in the discussion of "socialization" and of evaluation in money and in kind.

2. A system of economic activity will be called "formally" rational according to the degree in which the provision for needs, which is essential to every rational economy, is capable of being expressed in numerical, calculable terms, and is so expressed. In the first instance, it is quite independent of the technical form these calculations take, particularly whether estimates are expressed in money or in kind. The concept is thus unambiguous, at least in the sense that expression in money terms yields the highest degree of formal calculability. Naturally, even this is true only relatively, so long as other things are equal.

3. On the other hand, the concept of substantive rationality is full of difficulties. It conveys only one element common to all the possible empirical situations; namely, that it is not sufficient to consider only the purely formal fact that calculations are being made on grounds of expediency by the methods which are, among those available, technically the most nearly adequate. In addition, it is necessary to take account of the fact that economic activity is oriented to ultimate ends (*Forderungen*) of some kind, whether they be ethical, political, utilitarian, hedonistic, the attainment of social equality, or of anything else. Substantive rationality cannot be measured in terms of formal calculation alone, but also involves a relation to the absolute values or to the content of the particular given ends to which it is oriented. In principle, there is an indefinite number of possible standards of value which are "rational" in this sense. Socialistic and communistic standards which, though by no means unambiguous in themselves, always involve elements of social justice and equality, form only one group among the indefinite plurality of possible points of view. Others are action in the interest of a hierarchy of class distinctions or in furtherance of the power of a political unit, particularly by war. All these and many others are of potential "substantive" significance. These points of view are, however, significant only as bases from which to judge the outcome of economic action. In addition, it is possible to criticize the attitude toward the economic activity itself

or toward the means used, from ethical, ascetic, or aesthetic points of view. Of all of these, the merely formal calculation in money terms may seem either of quite secondary importance or even as fundamentally evil in itself, quite apart from the consequences of the modern methods of calculation.

There is no question in this discussion of attempting value judgments in this field, but only of determining and delimiting what is to be called "formal." In this context the concept of "substantive" is itself in a certain sense "formal"; that is, it is an abstract, generic concept.

2. *The Principal Modes of Capitalistic Orientation*

BY MAX WEBER

THERE ARE a number of qualitatively different modes in which it is possible for the orientation to profit to be determined in a capitalistic manner; that is, in proportion to its rationality in terms of capital accounting.

1. Profit-making activity may be oriented to the exploitation of market advantages in a continuous process of purchase and sale on the market where exchange is free; that is, formally not subject to compulsion and materially, at least relatively, free. Or it may be oriented to the maximization of profit in continuous productive enterprises which make use of capital accounting.

2. It may be oriented to opportunities for profit by trade and speculation in money, taking over debts of all sorts, and creating means of payment. A closely related type is the professional extension of credit, either for consumption or for profit-making purposes.

3. It may be oriented to opportunities for acquiring "booty" from corporate political groups or persons connected with politics. This includes the financing of wars or revolutions and the financing of party leaders by loans and supplies.

4. It may be oriented to opportunities for continuous profit by virtue of domination by force or of a position of power guaranteed by the political authority. There are two main sub-types: colonial capitalism operated through plantations with compulsory payments or compulsory labour and by monopolistic and compulsory trade. On the other hand there is the fiscal type, profit making by farm-

ing of taxes and of offices, whether in the home area or in colonies.

5. The orientation to opportunities for profit opened up by unusual transactions with political bodies.

6. The orientation to opportunities for profit of the following types: (a) To purely speculative transactions in standardized commodities or in the securities of an enterprise; (b) by carrying out the continuous financial operations of political bodies; (c) by the promotional financing of new enterprises in the form of sale of securities to investors; (d) by the speculative financing of capitalistic enterprises and of various other types of economic organization with the purpose of a profitable regulation of market situations or of attaining power.

Types (1) and (6) are to a large extent peculiar to the modern Western World. The other types have been common all over the world for thousands of years where the possibilities of exchange, money economy, and money financing have been present. In the Western World they have not had such a dominant importance as modes of profit-making as they had in Antiquity, except in restricted areas and for relatively brief periods, particularly in times of war. Where large areas have been pacified for a long period, as in the Chinese and later Roman Empires, these have tended to decline, leaving only commerce, money changing and lending, as forms of capitalistic acquisition. The capitalistic financing of political activities has always depended on two conditions: a competition of states with one another for power and the corresponding competition for control of capital which was free as between them. All this has ended only with the establishment of large-scale, unified states.

Reprinted from Max Weber, *The Theory of Social and Economic Organization,* trans. A. M. Henderson and Talcott Parsons, ed. Talcott Parsons (2d ed.; Glencoe, Ill.: The Free Press, 1956), pp. 279–80. Copyright 1947 by Oxford University Press.

It is only in the modern Western World that rational capitalistic enterprises with fixed capital, free labour, the rational specialization and combination of functions, and the allocation of productive functions on the basis of capitalistic enterprises, bound together in a market economy, are to be found. This involves the capitalistic type of organization of labour, which in formal times is purely voluntary, as the typical and dominant mode of providing for the wants of the masses of the population, with expropriation of the workers from the means of production and appropriation of the enterprises by security owners. It is also only here that we find public credit in the form of issues of government securities, the legal form of the business corporation, the issue of securities, and financing carried on as the business of rational enterprises, trade in commodities and securities or organized exchanges, money and capital markets, monopolistic associations as a type of economically rational organization of the production of goods by profit-making enterprises as opposed to the mere trade in them.

This difference calls for an explanation and the explanation cannot be given on economic grounds alone. Types (3) to (5) inclusive will be treated here together as "politically oriented capitalism." The whole of the later discussion will be devoted particularly, though not alone, to the problem of explaining the difference. In general terms, it is possible only to make the following statement:—

1. It is clear from the very beginning that the types of political events and processes which open up the kind of opportunities for profit which are exploited by political capitalism are, seen in economic terms—that is, from the point of view either of orientation to market advantages or of the consumption needs of budgetary units—irrational.

2. It is further clear that purely speculative opportunities for profit and pure consumption credit are, from the point of view both of want satisfaction and of the production of goods, irrational because they are determined by the fortuitous distribution of ownership and of market advantages. The same may also be true of opportunities for promotion and financing, under certain circumstances; but this is by no means necessarily always the case.

Apart from the rational capitalistic enterprise, the modern economic order is unique in its mode of regulation of the monetary system and in the commercialization of bills of exchange and securities.

3. The Essential Properties of Interest and Money

BY JOHN MAYNARD KEYNES

I

IT SEEMS, then, that the *rate of interest on money* plays a peculiar part in setting a limit to the level of employment, since it sets a standard to which the marginal efficiency of a capital-asset must attain if it is to be newly produced. That this should be so, is, at first sight, most perplexing. It is natural to enquire wherein the peculiarity of money lies as distinct from other assets, whether it is only money which has a rate of interest, and what would happen in a non-monetary economy. Until we have answered these questions, the full significance of our theory will not be clear.

The money-rate of interest—we may remind the reader—is nothing more than the percentage excess of a sum of money contracted for forward delivery, *e.g.* a year hence, over what we may call the "spot" or cash price of the sum thus contracted for forward delivery. It would seem, therefore, that for every kind of capital-asset there must be an analogue of the rate of interest on money. For there is a definite quantity of (*e.g.*) wheat to be delivered a year hence which has the same exchange value to-day as 100 quarters of wheat for "spot" delivery. If the former quantity is 105 quarters, we may say that the wheat-rate of interest is 5 per cent. per annum; and if it is 95 quarters, that it is *minus* 5 per cent. per annum. Thus for every durable commodity we have a rate

Reprinted from John Maynard Keynes, *The General Theory of Employment, Interest, and Money* (New York: Harcourt, Brace & Co., 1936), pp. 222–27, 229–42, with the permission of Harcourt, Brace & Co., Professor R. F. Kelin, and Macmillan & Co., London.

of interest in terms of itself,—a wheat-rate of interest, a copper-rate of interest, a house-rate of interest, even a steel-plant-rate of interest.

The difference between the "future" and "spot" contracts for a commodity, such as wheat, which are quoted in the market, bears a definite relation to the wheat-rate of interest, but, since the future contract is quoted in terms of money for forward delivery and not in terms of wheat for spot delivery, it also brings in the money-rate of interest. The exact relationship is as follows:

Let us suppose that the spot price of wheat is £100 per 100 quarters, that the price of the "future" contract for wheat for delivery a year hence is £107 per 100 quarters, and that the money-rate of interest is 5 per cent.; what is the wheat-rate of interest? £100 spot will buy £105 for forward delivery, and £105 for forward delivery will buy $105/_{107}$. 100 (=98) quarters for forward delivery. Alternatively £100 spot will buy 100 quarters of wheat for spot delivery. Thus 100 quarters of wheat for spot delivery will buy 98 quarters for forward delivery. It follows that the wheat-rate of interest is *minus* 2 per cent per annum.

It follows from this that there is no reason why their rates of interest should be the same for different commodities,—why the wheat-rate of interest should be equal to the copper-rate of interest. For the relation between the "spot" and "future" contracts, as quoted in the market, is notoriously different for different commodities. This, we shall find, will lead us to the clue we are seeking. For it may be that it is the *greatest* of the own-rates of interest (as we may call them) which rules the roost (because it is the greatest of these rates that the marginal efficiency of a capital-asset must attain if it is to be newly produced); and that there are reasons why it is the money-rate of interest which is often the greatest (because, as we shall find, certain forces, which operate to reduce the own-rates of interest of other assets, do not operate in the case of money).

It may be added that, just as there are differing commodity-rates of interest at any time, so also exchange dealers are familiar with the fact that the rate of interest is not even the same in terms of two different moneys, *e.g.* sterling and dollars. For here also the difference between the "spot" and "future" contracts for a foreign money in terms of sterling are not, as a rule, the same for different foreign moneys.

Now each of these commodity standards offers us the same facility as money for measuring the marginal efficiency of capital. For we can take any commodity we choose, *e.g.* wheat; calculate the wheat-value of the prospective yields of any capital asset; and the rate of discount which makes the present value of this series of wheat annuities equal to the present supply price of the asset in terms of wheat gives us the marginal efficiency of the asset in terms of wheat. If no change is expected in the relative value of two alternative standards, then the marginal efficiency of a capital-asset will be the same in whichever of the two standards it is measured, since the numerator and denominator of the fraction which leads up to the marginal efficiency will be changed in the same proportion. If, however, one of the alternative standards is expected to change in value in terms of the other, the marginal efficiencies of capital-assets will be changed by the same percentage, according to which standard they are measured in. To illustrate this let us take the simplest case where wheat, one of the alternative standards, is expected to appreciate at a steady rate of a per cent per annum in terms of money; the marginal efficiency of an asset, which is x per cent in terms of money, will then be $x-a$ per cent in terms of wheat. Since the marginal efficiencies of all capital-assets will be altered by the same amount, it follows that their order of magnitude will be the same irrespective of the standard which is selected.

If there were some composite commodity which could be regarded strictly speaking as representative, we could regard the rate of interest and the marginal efficiency of capital in terms of this commodity as being, in a sense, uniquely *the* rate of interest and *the* marginal efficiency of capital. But there are, of course, the same obstacles in the way of this as there are to setting up a unique standard of value.

So far, therefore, the money-rate of interest has no uniqueness compared with other rates of interest, but is on precisely the same footing. Wherein, then, lies the peculiarity of the money-rate of interest which gives it the predominating practical importance attributed to it in the preceding chapters? Why should the volume of output and employment be more intimately bound up with the money-rate of interest than with the wheat-rate of interest or the house-rate of interest?

II

Let us consider what the various commodity-rates of interest over a period of (say) a year are likely to be for different types of assets. Since we are taking each commodity in turn as the standard, the returns on each commodity must be reckoned in this context as being measured in terms of itself.

There are three attributes which different types of assets possess in different degrees; namely, as follows:

(i) Some assets produce a yield or output q, measured in terms of themselves, by assisting some process of production or supplying services to a consumer.

(ii) Most assets, except money, suffer some wastage or involve some cost through the mere passage of time (apart from any change in their relative value), irrespective of their being used to produce a yield; *i.e.* they involve a carrying cost c measured in terms of themselves. It does not matter for our present purpose exactly where we draw the line between the costs which we deduct before calculating q and those which we include in c, since in what follows we shall be exclusively concerned with $q - c$.

(iii) Finally, the power of disposal over an asset during a period may offer a potential convenience or security, which is not equal for assets of different kinds, though the assets themselves are of equal initial value. There is, so to speak, nothing to show for this at the end of the period in the shape of output; yet it is something for which people are ready to pay something. The amount (measured in terms of itself) which they are willing to pay for the potential convenience or security given by this power of disposal (exclusive of yield or carrying cost attaching to the asset), we shall call its liquidity-premium l.

It follows that the total return expected from the ownership of an asset over a period is equal to its yield *minus* its carrying cost *plus* its liquidity-premium, *i.e.* to $q - c + l$. That is to say, $q - c + l$ is the own-rate of interest of any commodity, where q, c and l are measured in terms of itself as the standard.

It is characteristic of instrumental capital (*e.g.* a machine) or of consumption capital (*e.g.* a house) which is in use, that its yield should normally exceed its carrying cost, whilst its liquidity-premium is probably negligible; of a stock of liquid goods or of surplus laid-up instrumental or consumption capital that it should incur a carrying cost in terms of itself without any yield to set off against it, the liquidity-premium in this case also being usually negligible as soon as stocks exceed a moderate level, though capable of being significant in special circumstances; and of money that its yield is *nil*, and its carrying cost negligible, but its liquidity-premium substantial. Different commodities may, indeed, have differing degrees of liquidity-premium amongst themselves, and money may incur some degree of carrying costs, *e.g.* for safe custody. But it is an essential difference between money and all (or most) other assets that in the case of money its liquidity-premium much exceeds its carrying cost, whereas in the case of other assets their carrying cost much exceeds their liquidity-premium.

* * *

III

In attributing, therefore, a peculiar significance to the money-rate of interest, we have been tacitly assuming that the kind of money to which we are accustomed has some special characteristics which lead to its own-rate of interest in terms of itself as standard being more reluctant to fall as output increases than the own-rates of interest of any other assets in terms of themselves. Is this assumption justified? Reflection shows, I think, that the following peculiarities, which commonly characterise money as we know it, are capable of justifying it. To the extent that the established standard of value has these peculiarities, the summary statement, that it is the money-rate of interest which is the significant rate of interest, will hold good.

(i) The first characteristic which tends towards the above conclusion is the fact that money has, both in the long and in the short period, a zero, or at any rate a very small, elasticity of production, so far as the power of private enterprise is concerned, as distinct from the monetary authority;—elasticity of production meaning, in this context, the response of the quantity of labour applied to producing it to a rise in the quantity of labour which a unit of it will command. Money, that is to say, cannot be readily produced;—labour cannot be turned on at will by entrepreneurs to produce money in increasing quantities as its price rises in terms of the wage-unit. In the case of an inconvertible managed currency this condition is strictly satisfied. But in the case of a gold-standard currency it is also approximately so, in the sense that the maximum proportional addition to the quantity of labour which can be thus employed is very small, except indeed in a country of which gold-mining is the major industry.

Now, in the case of assets having an elasticity of production, the reason why we assumed their own-rate of interest to decline was because we assumed the stock of them to increase as the result of a higher rate of output. In the case of money, however—postponing, for the moment, our consideration of the effects of reducing the wage-unit or of a deliberate increase in its supply by the monetary authority—the supply is fixed. Thus the characteristic that money cannot be readily produced by labour gives at once some *prima facie* presumption for the view that its own-rate of interest will be relatively reluctant to fall; whereas if money could be grown like a crop or manufactured like a motor-car, depressions would be avoided or mitigated because, if the price of other assets was tending to fall in terms of money, more labour would be diverted into the production of money;—as we see to be the case in gold-mining countries, though for the world as a whole the maximum diversion in this way is almost negligible.

(ii) Obviously, however, the above condition is satisfied, not only by money, but by all pure rent-factors, the production of which is completely inelastic. A second condition, therefore, is required to distinguish money from other rent elements.

The second *differentia* of money is that it has an elasticity of substitution equal, or nearly equal, to zero; which means that as the exchange value of money rises there is no tendency to substitute some other factor for it;—except, perhaps, to some trifling extent, where the money-commodity is also used in manufacture or the arts. This follows from the peculiarity of money that its utility is solely derived from its exchange-value, so that the two rise and fall *pari passu,* with the result that as the exchange value of money rises there is no motive or tendency, as in the case of rent-factors, to substitute some other factor for it.

Thus, not only is it impossible to turn more labour on to producing money when its labour-price rises, but money is a bottomless sink for purchasing power, when the demand for it increases, since there is no value for it at which demand is diverted—as in the case of other rent-factors—so as to slop over into a demand for other things.

The only qualification to this arises when the rise in the value of money leads to uncertainty as to the future maintenance of this rise; in which event, a_1 and a_2 are increased, which is tantamount to an increase in the commodity-rates of money-interest and is, therefore, stimulating to the output of other assets.

(iii) Thirdly, we must consider whether these conclusions are upset by the fact that, even though the quantity of money cannot be increased by diverting labour into producing it, nevertheless an assumption that its effective supply is rigidly fixed would be inaccurate. In particular, a reduction of the wage-unit will release cash from its other uses for the satisfaction of the liquidity-motive; whilst, in addition to this, as money-values fall, the stock of money will bear a higher proportion to the total wealth of the community.

It is not possible to dispute on purely theoretical grounds that this reaction might be capable of allowing an adequate decline in the money-rate of interest. There are, however, several reasons, which taken in combination are of compelling force, why in an economy of the type to which we are accustomed it is very probable that the money-rate of interest will often prove reluctant to decline adequately:

(*a*) We have to allow, first of all, for the reactions of a fall in the wage-unit on the marginal efficiencies of other assets in terms of money;—for it is the *difference* between these and the money-rate of interest with which we are concerned. If the effect of the fall in the wage-unit is to produce an expectation that it will subsequently rise again, the result will be wholly favourable. If, on the contrary, the effect is to produce an expectation of a further fall, the reaction on the marginal efficiency of capital may offset the decline in the rate of interest.

(*b*) The fact that wages tend to be sticky in terms of money, the money-wage being more stable than the real wage, tends to limit the readiness of the wage-unit to fall in terms of money. Moreover, if this were not so, the position might be worse rather than better; because, if money-wages were to fall easily, this might often tend to create an expectation of a further fall with unfavourable reactions on the marginal efficiency of capital. Furthermore, if wages were to be fixed in terms of some other commodity, *e.g.* wheat, it is improbable that they would continue to be sticky. It is because of money's other characteristics—those, especially, which make it *liquid*—that wages, when fixed in terms of it, tend to be sticky.[1]

(*c*) Thirdly, we come to what is the most fundamental consideration in this context, namely, the characteristics of money which satisfy liquidity-preference. For, in certain circumstances such as will often occur, these will cause the rate of interest to be insensitive, particularly below a certain figure, even to a substantial increase in the quantity of money in proportion to other forms of wealth. In other words, beyond a certain point money's yield from liquidity does not fall in response to an increase in its quantity to anything approaching the extent to which the yield from other types of assets falls when their quantity is comparably increased.

In this connection the low (or negligible) carrying-costs of money play an essential part. For if its carrying-costs were material, they would offset the effect of expectations as to the prospective value of money at future dates. The readiness of the public to increase their stock of money in response to a comparatively small stimulus is due to the advantages of liquidity (real or supposed) having no offset to contend with in the shape of carrying-costs mounting steeply with the lapse of time. In the case of a commodity other than money a modest stock of it may offer some convenience to users of the commodity. But even though a larger stock might have some attractions as representing a store of wealth of stable value, this would be offset by its carrying-costs in the shape of storage, wastage, etc. Hence,

---

1. If wages (and contracts) were fixed in terms of wheat, it might be that wheat would acquire some of money's liquidity-premium.

after a certain point is reached, there is necessarily a loss in holding a greater stock.

In the case of money, however, this, as we have seen, is not so,—and for a variety of reasons, namely, those which constitute money as being, in the estimation of the public, *par excellence* "liquid." Thus those reformers, who look for a remedy by creating artificial carrying-costs for money through the device of requiring legal-tender currency to be periodically stamped at a prescribed cost in order to retain its quality as money, or in analogous ways, have been on the right track; and the practical value of their proposals deserves consideration.

The significance of the money-rate of interest arises, therefore, out of the combination of the characteristics that, through the working of the liquidity-motive, this rate of interest may be somewhat unresponsive to a change in the proportion which the quantity of money bears to other forms of wealth measured in money, and that money has (or may have) zero (or negligible) elasticities both of production and of substitution. The first condition means that demand may be predominantly directed to money, the second that when this occurs labour cannot be employed in producing more money, and the third that there is no mitigation at any point through some other factor being capable, if it is sufficiently cheap, of doing money's duty equally well. The only relief—apart from changes in the marginal efficiency of capital—can come (so long as the propensity towards liquidity is unchanged) from an increase in the quantity of money, or—which is formally the same thing—a rise in the value of money which enables a given quantity to provide increased money-services.

Thus a rise in the money-rate of interest retards the output of all the objects of which the production is elastic without being capable of stimulating the output of money (the production of which is, by hypothesis, perfectly inelastic). The money-rate of interest, by setting the pace for all the other commodity-rates of interest, holds back investment in the production of these other commodities without being capable of stimulating investment for the production of money, which by hypothesis cannot be produced. Moreover, owing to the elasticity of demand for liquid cash in terms of debts, a small change in the conditions governing this demand may not much alter the money-rate of interest, whilst (apart from official action) it is also impracticable, owing to the inelasticity of the production of money, for natural forces to bring the money-rate of interest down by affecting the supply side. In the case of an ordinary commodity, the inelasticity of the demand for liquid stocks of it would enable

small changes on the demand side to bring its rate of interest up or down with a rush, whilst the elasticity of its supply would also tend to prevent a high premium on spot over forward delivery. Thus with other commodities left to themselves, "natural forces," *i.e.* the ordinary forces of the market, would tend to bring their rate of interest down until the emergence of full employment had brought about for commodities generally the inelasticity of supply which we have postulated as a normal characteristic of money. Thus in the absence of money and in the absence—we must, of course, also suppose—of any other commodity with the assumed characteristics of money, the rates of interest would only reach equilibrium when there is full employment.

Unemployment develops, that is to say, because people want the moon;—men cannot be employed when the object of desire (*i.e.* money) is something which cannot be produced and the demand for which cannot be readily choked off. There is no remedy but to persuade the public that green cheese is practically the same thing and to have a green cheese factory (*i.e.* a central bank) under public control.

It is interesting to notice that the characteristic which has been traditionally supposed to render gold especially suitable for use as the standard of value, namely, its inelasticity of supply, turns out to be precisely the characteristic which is at the bottom of the trouble.

Our conclusion can be stated in the most general form (taking the propensity to consume as given) as follows. No further increase in the rate of investment is possible when the greatest amongst the own-rates of own-interest of all available assets is equal to the greatest amongst the marginal efficiencies of all assets, measured in terms of the asset whose own-rate of own-interest is greatest.

In a position of full employment this condition is necessarily satisfied. But it may also be satisfied before full employment is reached, if there exists some asset, having zero (or relatively small) elasticities of production and substitution,[2] whose rate of interest declines more slowly, as output increases, than the marginal efficiencies of capital-assets measured in the terms of it.

IV

We have shown above that for a commodity to be the standard of value is not a sufficient condition for that commodity's rate of interest to be the signif-

---

2. A *zero* elasticity is a more stringent condition than is necessarily required.

icant rate of interest. It is, however, interesting to consider how far those characteristics of money as we know it, which make the money-rate of interest the significant rate, are bound up with money being the standard in which debts and wages are usually fixed. The matter requires consideration under two aspects.

In the first place, the fact that contracts are fixed, and wages are usually somewhat stable, in terms of money unquestionably plays a large part in attracting to money so high a liquidity-premium. The convenience of holding assets in the same standard as that in which future liabilities may fall due and in a standard in terms of which the future cost of living is expected to be relatively stable, is obvious. At the same time the expectation of relative stability in the future money-cost of output might not be entertained with much confidence if the standard of value were a commodity with a high elasticity of production. Moreover, the low carrying costs of money as we know it play quite as large a part as a high liquidity-premium in making the money-rate of interest the significant rate. For what matters is the *difference* between the liquidity-premium and the carrying-costs; and in the case of most commodities, other than such assets as gold and silver and bank-notes, the carrying-costs are at least as high as the liquidity-premium ordinarily attaching to the standard in which contracts and wages are fixed, so that, even if the liquidity-premium now attaching to (*e.g.*) sterling-money were to be transferred to (*e.g.*) wheat, the wheat-rate of interest would still be unlikely to rise above zero. It remains the case, therefore, that, whilst the fact of contracts and wages being fixed in terms of money considerably enhances the significance of the money-rate of interest, this circumstance is, nevertheless, probably insufficient by itself to produce the observed characteristics of the money-rate of interest.

The second point to be considered is more subtle. The normal expectation that the value of output will be more stable in terms of money than in terms of any other commodity, depends of course, not on wages being arranged in terms of money, but on wages being relatively *sticky* in terms of money. What, then, would the position be if wages were expected to be more sticky (*i.e.* more stable) in terms of some one or more commodities other than money, than in terms of money itself? Such an expectation requires, not only that the costs of the commodity in question are expected to be relatively constant in terms of the wage-unit for a greater or smaller scale of output both in the short and in the long period, but also that any surplus over the current demand at cost-price can be taken into stock without cost, *i.e.* that its liquidity-premium exceeds its carrying-costs (for, otherwise, since there is no hope of profit from a higher price, the carrying of a stock must necessarily involve a loss). If a commodity can be found to satisfy these conditions, then, assuredly, it might be set up as a rival to money. Thus it is not logically impossible that there should be a commodity in terms of which the value of output is expected to be more stable than in terms of money. But it does not seem probable that any such commodity exists.

I conclude, therefore, that the commodity, in terms of which wages are expected to be most sticky, cannot be one whose elasticity of production is not least, and for which the excess of carrying-costs over liquidity-premium is not least. In other words, the expectation of a relative stickiness of wages in terms of money is a corollary of the excess of liquidity-premium over carrying-costs being greater for money than for any other asset.

Thus we see that the various characteristics, which combine to make the money-rate of interest significant, interact with one another in a cumulative fashion. The fact that money has low elasticities of production and substitution and low carrying-costs tends to raise the expectation that money-wages will be relatively stable; and this expectation enhances money's liquidity-premium and prevents the exceptional correlation between the money-rate of interest and the marginal efficiencies of other assets which might, if it could exist, rob the money-rate of interest of its sting.

Professor Pigou (with others) has been accustomed to assume that there is a presumption in favour of real wages being more stable than money-wages. But this could only be the case if there were a presumption in favour of stability of employment. Moreover, there is also the difficulty that wage-goods have a high carrying-cost. If, indeed, some attempt were made to stabilise real wages by fixing wages in terms of wage-goods, the effect could only be to cause a violent oscillation of money-prices. For every small fluctuation in the propensity to consume and the inducement to invest would cause money-prices to rush violently between zero and infinity. That money-wages should be more stable than real wages is a condition of the system possessing inherent stability.

Thus the attribution of relative stability to real wages is not merely a mistake in fact and experience. It is also a mistake in logic, if we are supposing that the system in view is stable, in the sense that small changes in the propensity to consume and the inducement to invest do not produce violent effects on prices.

V

As a footnote to the above, it may be worth emphasising what has been already stated above, namely, that "liquidity" and "carrying-costs" are both a matter of degree; and that it is only in having the former high relatively to the latter that the peculiarity of "money" consists.

Consider, for example, an economy in which there is no asset for which the liquidity-premium is always in excess of the carrying-costs; which is the best definition I can give of a so-called "non-monetary" economy. There exists nothing, that is to say, but particular consumables and particular capital equipments more or less differentiated according to the character of the consumables which they can yield up, or assist to yield up, over a greater or a shorter period of time; all of which, unlike cash, deteriorate or involve expense, if they are kept in stock, to a value in excess of any liquidity-premium which may attach to them.

In such an economy capital equipments will differ from one another (a) in the variety of the consumables in the production of which they are capable of assisting, (b) in the stability of value of their output (in the sense in which the value of bread is more stable through time than the value of fashionable novelties), and (c) in the rapidity with which the wealth embodied in them can become "liquid," in the sense of producing output, the proceeds of which can be re-embodied if desired in quite a different form.

The owners of wealth will then weigh the lack of "liquidity" of different capital equipments in the above sense as a medium in which to hold wealth against the best available actuarial estimate of their prospective yields after allowing for risk. The liquidity-premium, it will be observed, is partly similar to the risk-premium, but partly different;—the difference corresponding to the difference between the best estimates we can make of probabilities and the confidence with which we make them. When we were dealing, in earlier chapters, with the estimation of prospective yield, we did not enter into detail as to how the estimation is made: and to avoid complicating the argument, we did not distinguish differences in liquidity from differences in risk proper. It is evident, however, that in calculating the own-rate of interest we must allow for both.

There is, clearly, no absolute standard of "liquidity" but merely a scale of liquidity—a varying premium of which account has to be taken, in addition to the yield of use and the carrying-costs, in estimating the comparative attractions of holding different forms of wealth. The conception of what contributes to "liquidity" is a partly vague one, changing from time to time and depending on social practices and institutions. The order of preference in the minds of owners of wealth in which at any given time they express their feelings about liquidity is, however, definite and is all we require for our analysis of the behaviour of the economic system.

It may be that in certain historic environments the possession of land has been characterised by a high liquidity-premium in the minds of owners of wealth; and since land resembles money in that its elasticities of production and substitution may be very low,[3] it is conceivable that there have been occasions in history in which the desire to hold land has played the same rôle in keeping up the rate of interest at too high a level which money has played in recent times. It is difficult to trace this influence quantitatively owing to the absence of a forward price for land in terms of itself which is strictly comparable with the rate of interest on a money debt. We have, however, something which has, at times, been closely analogous, in the shape of high rates of interest on mortgages.[4] The high rates of interest from mortgages on land, often exceeding the probable net yield from cultivating the land, have been a familiar feature of many agricultural economies. Usury laws have been directed primarily against encumbrances of this character. And rightly so. For in earlier social organisations where long-term bonds in the modern sense were non-existent, the competition of a high interest-rate on mortgages may well have had the same effect in retarding the growth of wealth from current investment in newly produced capital-assets, as high interest rates on long-term debts have had in more recent times.

That the world after several millennia of steady individual saving, is so poor as it is in accumulated capital-assets, is to be explained, in my opinion, neither by the improvident propensities of mankind, nor even by the destruction of war, but by the high liquidity-premiums formerly attaching to the ownership of land and now attaching to money. I differ

---

3. The attribute of "liquidity" is by no means independent of the presence of these two characteristics. For it is unlikely that an asset, of which the supply can be easily increased or the desire for which can be easily diverted by a change in relative price, will possess the attribute of "liquidity" in the minds of owners of wealth. Money itself rapidly loses the attribute of "liquidity" if its future supply is expected to undergo sharp changes.

4. A mortgage and the interest thereon are, indeed, fixed in terms of money. But the fact that the mortgagor has the option to deliver the land itself in discharge of the debt—and must so deliver it if he cannot find the money on demand—has sometimes made the mortgage system approximate to a contract of land for future delivery against land for spot delivery. There have been sales of lands to tenants against mortgages effected by them, which, in fact, came very near to being transactions of this character.

in this from the older view as expressed by Marshall with an unusual dogmatic force in his *Principles of Economics*, p. 581:—

Everyone is aware that the accumulation of

wealth is held in check, and the rate of interest so far sustained, by the preference which the great mass of humanity have for present over deferred gratifications, or, in other words, by their unwillingness to "wait."

4. *The Economic Organization*

BY FRANK H. KNIGHT

THE PROBLEM of organization, which sets the problem of economic science, deals with the concrete means or mechanism for dividing the general function of making a living for the people into parts and bringing about the performance of these parts in due proportion and harmony.

More specifically, it is a problem of the social machinery for accomplishing *five fairly distinct functions*. Every system of organization must perform these tasks, and it is its success or failure in discharging these functions which determines its value as a system. Back of the study of economics is the practical need of making the organization better, and we can hope for success in this task only if we proceed to it intelligently, which is to say on the basis of an understanding of the nature of the work which a system of organization has to perform, and of the alternatives open in the way of possible types of organization machinery.

The Five Main Functions of an Economic System

The general task of organizing the economic activity of society may be divided into a number of fundamental functions. These are in fact very much inter-connected and overlapping, but the distinction is useful as an aid to discussing the existing economic order both descriptively and critically, its structure as well as its workings. These functions fall into a more or less logical sequence. The first is to decide what is to be done, that is, what goods and services are to be produced, and in what proportions. It is the function of setting standards, of establishing a social scale of values, or the function

Reprinted from Frank H. Knight, *The Economic Organization* (New York: Augustus M. Kelley, 1951), pp. 7–15, with permission of Augustus M. Kelley.

of social choice; the second is the function of organizing production, in the narrow sense, of getting done the things settled upon as most worth doing; third is distribution, the apportioning of the product among the members of society; the fourth is really a group of functions having to do with maintaining and improving the social structure, or promoting social progress.

1. THE FUNCTION OF FIXING STANDARDS; THE NOTION OF EFFICIENCY

In a world where organizations were absent, where each individual carried on his life activities in isolation and independence of all others, the matter of standards would be simply a matter of individual choice. But when the production of wealth is socialized, there has to be a *social* decision as to the relative importance or different uses of productive power, as to which wants are to be satisfied and which left unsatisfied or to what extent any one is to be satisfied at the expense of any other. In the case of an individual, choice need be made only among his own wants; but in a social system, the wants of different individuals also come into conflict. As far as this is a quantitative question merely, of how far the wants of one are to be gratified at the expense of the wants of another, or left ungratified in favor of another, the problem is one of *distribution*, and will be noticed under another heading (the third function). But to a large and increasing extent, society finds it necessary or advisable further to regulate the individual's regulation of his own want-satisfaction, to enforce a community standard of living. As a matter of fact, these two problems are closely interlaced, the question of *whose* wants and that of *which* wants are to be given preference, and in what measure. It is important to observe that they are largely the same question. The difference in the "amount" consumed by different persons is not mainly a difference in the amounts of the same commodities; different persons consume different things, which are quantitatively compared only through the agency of the value scale itself. Nevertheless there seems to be ample justification for a logical separation of the questions of what is to be produced from that of who is to get the product, and for discussing separately the relations between the two phases of organization.

A point of fundamental importance in connection with the question of standards is that of the origin or ultimate source of wants. The system of social organization does more than reduce individual values to a common denominator or scale of equivalence. In large part the individual wants themselves are *created* by social intercourse, and their character is also largely dependent upon the form of organization of the economic system upon which they are dependent for their gratification. The workings of the economic organization in this connection form a problem too large and complex to be discussed at any length in a small book like this one. Indeed, the subject of wants is not only vast in scope but apparently cannot be reduced to scientific terms, except within rather narrow limits, falling rather in the field of art. The scientific discussion of economics has to be restricted in the main to the analysis of the organization of want-satisfaction. In the science of economics the wants are largely taken for granted as facts of the time and place, and the discussion of their origin and formation is left for the most part to the distinct studies of social psychology and cultural anthropology. The deliberate creation or changing of wants for specific commodities as by advertising, is to some extent an exception, but in the main such activities must be regarded as creating a *knowledge* of certain *means* of satisfying wants rather than as changing ultimate *wants*.

The problem of standards or values occupies a key position in Economics. The practical objective of economics, it must be kept in mind, is that of improving the social organization and increasing its efficiency. There is a common misconception that it is possible to measure or discuss efficiency in purely physical terms. The first principles of physics or engineering science teach that this is not true, that the term efficiency involves the idea of value, and some measure of value as well. It is perhaps the most important principle of physical science that neither matter nor energy can be created or destroyed, that whatever goes into any process must come out in some form, and hence as a mere matter of physical quantity, the efficiency of all operations

would equal one hundred per cent. The correct definition of efficiency is the ratio, not between "output" and "input" but between *useful* output and total output or input. Hence efficiency, even in the simplest energy transformation, is meaningless without a measure of usefulness or value. In any attempt to understand economic efficiency, the notion of value is more obviously crucial since most economic problems are concerned with a number of kinds both of outlay and of return, and there is no conceivable way of making comparisons without first reducing all the factors to terms of a common measure. It will appear in due course that the science of economics is largely taken up with description and analysis of the process by which this common denominator of things consumed and produced by the economic system is arrived at, that is, with the *problem of measuring values*.

2. THE FUNCTION OF ORGANIZING PRODUCTION

The second step, logically speaking, after the ranking and grading of the uses to which productive power may be put, is that of actually putting them to use in accordance with the scale of values thus established. From a social point of view, this process may be viewed under two aspects, (a) the assignment or *allocation* of the available productive forces and materials among the various lines of industry, and (b) the effective *coordination* of the various means of production in each industry into such groupings as will produce the greatest result. The second of these tasks properly belongs to technological rather than to economic science, and is treated in economics only with reference to the interrelations between the organization of society as a whole and the internal organization of the industries.

3. THE FUNCTION OF DISTRIBUTION

This third function would not exist at all in an unorganized world. Each individual, acting independently of all others, would simply consume what he produced. But where production is socialized, the separate productive contribution of one participant in the process cannot be directly identified or separated. It is apparent that a modern factory operative, say one who spends all his time putting buttons on shoes or nailing the covers on packing cases, cannot live on his own product, physically interpreted. When we further consider that different individuals contribute to production in fundamentally different ways, many by furnishing land or other "natural resources" or material equipment or money or managerial or supervisory services, or by selling goods, and in other ways which make no identifiable physical change in any product, it is manifest that if everyone is to get a living out of the process some *social mechanism* of distribution is called for.

In this connection should be recalled the close relation between distribution and the control of production. The decision as to what to produce is closely bound up with the decision for whom to produce. There is also a close relation between the third function and the second. In our social system distribution is the chief agency relied upon to control production and stimulate efficiency. Ours is a system of "private property," "free competition" and "contract." This means that every productive resource or agent, including labor power, typically "belongs" to some person who is free within the legal conditions of marketing, to get what he can out of its use. It is assumed, and the course of the argument will show at length why it is true, that there is in some effective sense a real positive connection between the productive contribution made by any productive agent and the remuneration which its "owner" can secure for its use. Hence this remuneration (a distributive share) and the wish to make it as large as possible, constitute the chief reliance of society for an incentive to place the agency into use in the general productive system in such a way as to make it as productive as possible. The strongest argument in favor of such a system as ours is the contention that this direct, selfish motive is the only dependable method, or at least the best method, for guaranteeing that productive forces will be organized and worked efficiently. The argument assumes that in spite of the difficulty above referred to of identifying the particular contribution to the social product made by any person or piece of property, it is possible to separate it out, and measure it, in terms of value and that the distributive system does this with accuracy enough to make remunerations vary in accord with product. If this were not true in the main, remuneration could not really afford an incentive to productive efficiency, and an economic order based on individualism would not function.

4. ECONOMIC MAINTENANCE AND PROGRESS

There is no moral connotation in the term progress; it refers to any persistent cumulative change, whether regarded as good or bad. The principal forms of economic progress include, (1) growth of population and any cumulative change in its composition or education which affects either its productive powers or its wants; (2) the accumulation of material aids to production or "capital" of all kinds, including such permanent sources of satisfaction as newly discovered natural resources and also works of art (destruction and exhaustion of resources not replaced is also a progressive change); (3) improvements in technical processes or changes in the form of business organization. It is to be noted especially that progress has two sorts of significance for the economic organization. First, it is one of the products or values created by the latter, at a cost; i.e., it involves using productive power for this purpose and sacrificing its use for other purposes; and second, it affects and changes the character of the economic system itself and the conditions under which the system works.

This fourth function of organization, especially the provision for progress, cuts across all the other three. It is a matter of standards or values to decide how much progress society can afford or cares to have at the cost of sacrificing present values, and what forms it shall take; it is a matter of productive organization to utilize the determined share of available productive power to bring about progress in the amount and of the kinds decided upon, and it is a problem of distribution to apportion the burdens and benefits of progress among the members of society. We may be reminded also that it is true of progress as of all other lines of human action that it comes within the field of economics just in so far as it is related to the organized system of producing and distributing the means of want-satisfaction.

The first three of these functions (or four, since No. 2 is really double, involving two aspects) are relatively "short-time" in character. They are all aspects of the general problem of an economic society working under "given conditions," in contrast with the fourth function which relates to the problem of improving the given conditions through the course of time. The first three therefore make up the problems of what may be called the "stationary economy." If society either could not or did not try to grow and progress and make improvements, its economic problem would be entirely within this field. But since economic societies do in fact face problems of growth and improvement, and make some effort to solve them intelligently, we have to add the fourth function, or group of functions. Such problems are frequently referred to under the head of "dynamic" economics; for reasons which cannot be given in detail here, this is a seriously misleading use of language, and they should be called simply problems of progress or historical problems.

The "given conditions" of the stationary economy are included under the three heads of *resources*, *wants*, and *technology*, which may be subdivided and classified in more elaborate ways. The separation is based on the plain and simple fact that with reference to social calculations and plans which look ahead only a few years, these factors, resources, wants and the technological system will not change enough to affect the argument or plans seriously. But looking ahead over historical time they do change, to an indefinite extent, and the production and guidance of changes in them becomes the dominant character of the social economic problem. In the "short-run" (of a few years), the problem is to utilize in the best way the existing resources and technology in the satisfaction of existing wants.

A FIFTH FUNCTION: TO ADJUST CONSUMPTION TO PRODUCTION WITHIN VERY SHORT PERIODS

For completeness, this survey of functions should point out that within *very short* periods society faces still another set of "given conditions," hence still another type of problem, and in consequence its economic organization has still another task or function to perform, though this fifth function is rarely distinguished sharply from those of the "stationary economy" point of view. From this latter point of view, the problem is to adjust production to consumption under the given conditions. But in many cases, production cannot be adjusted quickly, while demand conditions do change rapidly; and in addition, production in many fields is subject to fluctuations from causes beyond control. In consequence, the supply of many commodities is fixed for considerable periods of time, on a level more or less divergent from the best possible adjustment to existing conditions of demand. The supply on hand is of course the result of productive operations in the past, and has to suffice until it can be changed. In agriculture this is conspicuously true. The crop of a given year has to last until the next year's crop is produced (except in so far as other parts of the world having different crop seasons can be drawn upon). In the case of manufactured goods, production is not definitely periodic, but it is still true that the rate of production frequently cannot be changed in a short time, to meet changes in demand, at least not without enormous cost.

It follows that over short periods consumption has to be controlled and distributed with reference to an existing supply or current rate of production, at the same time that adjustment of production to consumption requirements is being made as rapidly as practicable. The existing supply of wheat or potatoes, for example, must be distributed (a) over the season for which it has to suffice and (b) among the different consumers and their different needs. Thus there is a fifth function or organization, the opposite in a sense, of number two in the four above discussed, namely the short-run adjustment of consumption to past or current production.

IV–UNITS OF THE ECONOMY

---

1. *Household Economy*

BY FRÉDÉRIC LE PLAY

The Means of Subsistence of Workers and the Account of Receipts, with the Main Items of This Account

THE FOUR SOURCES OF RECEIPTS: PROPERTIES, SUBSIDIES, CONSTRUCTION-TYPE WORK, AND COTTAGE INDUSTRIES

Translated by Jesse Pitts, from Frédéric le Play, *Les ouvriers européens* (2nd ed.; Tours: Mame, 1879), chap. x, pp. 240–47.

THOSE who have observed the living conditions of workers only in the large cities of the West cannot imagine how varied their resources may be in other areas; hence, they do not suspect how important the budgeting of a family's resources must be in a general scheme of observation. The diversity of these resources has two main sources: First, those who hire workers remunerate their services in many ways. They pay for the worker's time or his production, sometimes according to the needs of his family, sometimes according to the work performed. Second, the workers' statuses differ depending upon tradition, occupation, and geographic location. Sometimes they discharge only the lowest functions in society; sometimes, on the contrary, they constitute the very body of the society. Often, they add to their main occupation the roles of property owners, tenants, or master craftsmen, thus supplementing their remuneration from their regular occupation with various sorts of incomes and fees.

Only the accounts of a retainer can be reduced to a few entries. In most cases, these would be merely: the yearly allocation of room and board, plus clothing given to a bachelor, and the yearly salary allowance. Nevertheless, even under these conditions, the study of a remuneration system commensurate to needs is not without complications. Furthermore, certain particular circumstances, closely tied to local tradition, may introduce some variety into the budget of household workers. This happens, for instance, in the case of the Pen-Ty, or retainer of lower Britanny. At first, as merely general helper on the employer's farmstead, he is authorized by local custom to own two cows, which he raises and exploits for his benefit. According to this custom, the employer is obligated to feed, without recompense, the cows of his retainer with his own cattle. These animals and their produce constitute important items in the budget of the retainer and help him to establish himself later as Pen-Ty or tenant chief of his own household.

We see no such complexity in the case of the Carinthian charcoaler; and his budget represents the extreme example, in the Western world, of simplicity in the condition of the unmarried retainer. In the North and East, on the contrary, and in general in countries where the traditional structures of early times—as well as old customs—have been preserved, retainers have a more complex existence. This complication is generally due to two main causes: retainers who marry are allowed to remain in the vicinity of the employer's household; furthermore, through their sideline occupations, they belong, more or less, to the category of tenants or master craftsmen. For example, the retainers in Scandinavia, Russia, and Turkey often undertake on their own account with tools furnished by their employer, a little farming, a little husbandry, the making of cloth or clothing, as well as hunting and fishing and related activities. They may even do some transporting, trading, and speculation. However, since, after all, retainers must give the major part of their time to the service of their employer, they can never give much scope to these undertakings, however varied they may be. This obligation gives to their receipts a simplicity clearly evidenced by the method, and which differentiates at a glance these workers from the other five types. It is enough to peruse the various monographs to appreciate the differences in budget existing between that of the household worker cited above and the ordinary wage-worker. The difference is even more striking when one compares him with a worker-tenant, a master craftsman, or a land owner.

The simplest case in the category of workers who are heads of households would be that in which an entire family lives exclusively on the wage earned by the family head for a simple type of labor, proportional to the days worked. The account of receipts would have only one entry. In order to establish it, it would be enough to know, on the one hand, the quantity of work, that is, the number of days worked, and, on the other hand, the remuneration rates for each day. Several authors who have dealt with the question of wages seem to have taken for granted that European populations were made up of families of this type. This led them to many grievous errors. Such a family type is very rare, if it exists; as far as my own experience is concerned, I have never discovered a single case.

Usually, other members of the family—the wife, the children, and the grandparents who live in the household—are gainfully occupied and draw remunerations that contribute to the family welfare. Furthermore, the most active members—the father, the mother, and the adolescents—commonly undertake several sorts of gainful activities, besides their regular occupations. For instance, for some of the families described in the *Ouvriers européens*, one may count as many as ten such additional activities. It is obvious that the itemization of the revenues derived from these activities introduces into the accounting of receipts a fair amount of complexity.

On the other hand, I have rarely observed in Europe families living exclusively on the wages earned by their members. One may even consider as exceptional the cases in which a family does not add to its regular wages resources derived from three other types of receipts that may be recognized in the budget of European workers: income from properties, subsidies, and the profits of cottage industries. These latter receipts often become the main source of the family's financial security. In the Orient, there exist laboring classes whose vernacular has no word for the type of remuneration described in the West by the word "wage."

The institution of wage payments, i.e., of remuneration proportional to the work done, can develop only in the modern system of temporary work commitments. Whether freely entered into or not, as long as the commitment between master and workman is irrevocable, it is necessary that the latter's daily bread be guaranteed. Whether the worker is free or unfree, remuneration, whatever its nature, is necessarily proportional to the needs of the entire family. Thus is explained the feelings of serenity and the stability that characterized traditional Europe. The same obligation is no longer recognized in the modern world; hence, social peace is endangered. Furthermore, the common people are not sufficiently endowed in intelligence and morality to be self-sufficient. All the Oriental languages, and precisely those that are devoid of a word for wages, describe a remuneration proportional to the family's needs by a special expression that has disappeared from the modern languages of the Western world.

In each rural or industrial collectivity, custom determines once and for all the quantity of goods that enters into the daily consumption pattern of a family. On the other hand, the price of these commodities often fluctuates from year to year and season to season. It is obvious that remuneration in kind gives more security to a family than remuneration in money. No wonder, then, that money wages, common in the West, give rise to dissension; this is rare in the case of remuneration in kind, which is more common in the Orient or the North. The French language, to my knowledge, no longer has an expression covering the various types of remuneration in kind. Hence, I shall use for that purpose the word "subsidy," which includes among its accepted meanings the special meaning I have used in this book. Under this term, I shall henceforth describe all the payments in kind that, not being proportional to the work done, cannot be considered as wages.

The subsidy is usually established on the basis of the family's needs. It is granted regularly each year or only when special needs become manifest. Generally, it is not terminated when work is suspended or slackens, in response to market fluctuations, illness, the early onset of infirmities—which often afflict the working man—or any other cause independent of the latter's will. Often, the benefit of subsidies is extended to the wife, the children, or the grandparents, even when the head of the family shows willful neglect or misconduct.

The wage-earners—heads of working-class families of various categories—especially those who by their application to work and sobriety begin to be identified with the class of proprietors, rarely limit their activity to the work they accomplish for their employer's account: they commonly undertake for their own account some of the cottage industries described above as occasional resources for the retainer. These handicrafts are nearly always practiced with the help of the entire family. Their importance, in the economy of the country, resides precisely in their creating work opportunities for the wife, the children, and the grandparents. Sometimes, when the worker and family head, out of self-interest or necessity, is compelled to give all his time to his regular occupation, these industries will be the exclusive domain of the rest of the family. The cottage industries that families will undertake in these conditions present a variety that cannot be imagined without having thoroughly studied the lives of working men in the various regions of Europe. These industries often absorb considerable time, especially from the higher categories of workers; they always lead, even for the lower categories, to many entries of money and goods. The accounting would become very complicated if we were to include in it all the receipts and expenditures that these industries involve.

The workers who are heads of families are not limited to becoming wage-earners or master craftsmen: they often rise to the status of proprietors. They draw from the ownership of real estate several kinds of income, which should not be confused with the three other types of receipts previously described. Other workers, who as yet do not own real estate, own sums of money or other movable equities which, after having given some additional interest, will serve to acquire the former type of property. Finally, other workers who will not succeed in rising to the status of proprietors—because of their moral weaknesses, local customs, or any other cause—nevertheless own goods other than those serving the specific consumption needs of individuals. The family finds a source of income in these goods, by renting them or by using them in the execution of special construction work, or as resources for cottage industries. Among the movable goods of this sort that workers may ordinarily possess, one must give special mention to domestic animals, tools, and, in general, the specific raw materials of the construction trades and cottage industries. The possession of these goods, like that of real estate, by the fact that it insures an income independent of manual labor, is of great social importance. It links, by a subtle transition, the mores of the workers to those of the upper classes of the society. Hence, it was useful to establish in the account of receipts this subdivision for the income derived from properties.

2. The Social Organization of Production

BY MAX WEBER

Social Aspects of the Division of Labour

FROM the social point of view, types of the division of labour may be classified in the following way: In the first place, there is the question of the ways in which qualitatively different, especially complementary functions, are divided between more or less autocephalous and autonomous economic units, which may further be distinguished economically according to whether they are budgetary units or profit-making enterprises. There are two polar possibilities:

(1) A "unitary" economy (*Einheitswirtschaft*) where the specialization of functions is wholly internal, completely heterocephalous and heteronomous and carried out on a purely technical basis. The same would be true of the co-ordination of function. A unitary economy may, from an economic point of view, be either a budgetary unit or a profit-making enterprise.

On the largest possible scale a communistic organization of a national economy would be a unitary budgetary economy. On the smallest scale an example is the primitive family unit, which included all or the great majority of productive functions—a closed household economy. The type case of a profit-making enterprise with a high degree of internal specialization and co-ordination of functions is naturally the great vertical combination[1] which treats with outsiders only as an integrated unit. These two distinctions will suffice for for the moment as a treatment of the development of autonomous economic units; (2) the differentiation of functions may, on the other hand, exist as between autocephalous economic units. (a) It may consist in the specialization or specification of functions between units which are heteronomous,

but are autocephalous, which are thus oriented to an order established by agreement or imposed. The order, in turn, may be substantively oriented in a variety of ways. Its main concern may be to provide for the needs of a superior economic unit, which may be the budgetary unit of a lord, an *oikos*, or a profit-making enterprise controlled by a political body. The order may, on the other hand, be concerned with providing for the needs of the members of some organized group. From an economic point of view, this may be accomplished by the organization of subsidiary budgetary units, or of profit-making enterprises. The corporate group in question may exercise any one of a large number of functions. It may be confined to the regulation of economic activity or may, at the same time, be engaged in economic action on its own account. (b) The other main type is the specialization of autocephalous and autonomous units in a market economy, which are oriented on the one hand substantively only to their own self-interest, formally only to the order of a corporate group, such as the laissez-faire state, which enforces only formal, rather than substantive rules.

1. A typical example of the corporate group which, limiting its function to the regulation of economic activity, takes the form of a budgetary unit administered by an association of the members, is the organization of village handicrafts in India. Corporate groups, which are themselves engaged in economic activity, like the household of a great noble, are illustrated by the organizations which provide for the wants of great landlords or slaveowners by means of contributions from the individual holdings of subjects, dependents, serfs, slaves, cottars, or sometimes village craftsmen. These phenomena have been found spontaneously developed in every part of the world. Cases of production of compulsory payments in kind to a landlord or to a town corporation, have, in so far as they have not served substantive, but as has often been the case, only fiscal ends, constituted only the regulation of economic activity. This type of control has served profit-making ends in cases where the services of household industries have been exploited for the benefit of the controlling unit.

The types where there is specialization and spe-

Reprinted from Max Weber, *The Theory of Social and Economic Organization,* trans. A. M. Henderson and Talcott Parsons, ed. Talcott Parsons (Glencoe, Ill.: The Free Press, 1947), pp. 228–50. Copyright 1947 by Oxford University Press.

1. What Weber apparently has in mind is the type of "trust" which controls all stages of the process of production from raw material to the finished product. Thus many of our steel enterprises have not only blast furnaces and rolling mills, but coal mines, coke ovens, railways and ships, and iron ore mines. The most notable example in Germany in Weber's time was the Stinnes combine.—ED.

cification of function, as between heteronomous units, are all cases of the imposition of specialized functions. They have been common in many very old small-scale industries. The Solingen metal trade was originally organized in terms of a voluntary association determining the division of labour by agreement. It was only later that it became organized in terms of imperative co-ordination—that is, became a "putting-out industry." The type where the autocephalous economic units are subject only to regulation by a corporate group is illustrated by innumerable cases of the rules established by village communities and town corporations for the regulation of trade, so far at least as these have a substantive influence on the processes of production.

The case of specialization as between units in a market economy is best illustrated by the modern economic order.

2. A few further details may be added. The rules of those corporate groups which attempt to provide for the wants of their members on a budgetary basis, are related to the component budgetary units in a particular way—that is, they are oriented to the prospective needs of the individual members, not of the organized group, such as a village, itself. Specified services of this kind will be called demiurgic liturgies;[2] and this type of provision for needs, correspondingly, demiurgic. It is always a question of corporate regulation governing the division of labour and, in some cases, the ways in which specialized functions are co-ordinated.

This term will not, on the other hand, be applied to a corporate group, whether it is imperatively co-ordinated or based on voluntary co-operation, if it carries on economic activity on its own account, contributions to which are assigned on a specialized basis. The type cases of this category are the specialized and specified contributions in kind of feudal manors, landed estates, and other types of large household units. But assigned obligations are also common in various types of corporate groups which are not primarily oriented to economic ends, such as the households of princes, political groups and the budgetary administration of local communities. These contributions are generally for the benefit of the budgetary needs of the governing authority or for corporate purposes. This way of providing for the needs of a budgetary unit by means of qualitatively specified liturgies and payments in kind on the part of peasants, craftsmen, and merchants, will, when they are owed to a

personal superior, be called the *oikos*[3] type of organization. Where they are received by the corporate budgetary unit as such, they will be called "corporate liturgies in kind." The principle governing this mode of provision for the budgetary needs of a corporate group engaged in economic action, is "liturgical" provision. This mode of organization has played an exceedingly important historical role and will have to be discussed frequently. In many political corporations, it has taken the place of modern taxation and, in economic groups, it has made possible a decentralization of the central organization by providing for its needs through agencies which were not included in the single common unit. On the contrary, each unit has managed its own affairs, but has assumed the obligation to fulfil certain functions for the central unit and to that extent has been dependent on it. Examples are peasants and serfs, subject to various kinds of labour services and payments in kind; craftsmen attached to an estate; and a large number of other types. Rodbertus was the first to apply the term *"oikos"* to the large-scale household economies of Antiquity. He used as the principal criterion the tendency to self-sufficiency in provision for needs by using the services of members of the household unit itself or of others dependent on it. In all these cases, the non-human means of production were made available without relation to the market. It is a fact that the landed estates, and still more the royal households of antiquity, especially in the New Kingdom in Egypt, were cases where the greater part of the needs of the unit were provided by services and payments in kind, which were obligations of dependent household units. At the same time, the degree of approach to the pure type varies widely. The same phenomena are to be found at times in China and India, and to a less extent in our own Middle Ages, beginning with the *capitulare de villis*. It is true that exchange with the outside world has generally not been entirely lacking, but has tended to have the character of budgetary exchange. Obligations to money payment have also not been uncommon, but have generally played a subsidiary part in the main provision for needs and have tended to be traditionally fixed. It has also not been uncommon for the economic units subject to liturgical obligations to be involved in exchange relations. The decisive point, however, is that the main emphasis lay on the fact that the subsistence of the members was regarded as a return for the services of the land and equipment the members were privileged

---

2. The term "demiurgic" is taken over directly from Weber, who introduced it in this technical sense. It is not, apparently, current in the German literature.—Ed.

3. The term *"oikos"* is, of course, taken over from the Greek. As Weber notes below, however, it was introduced into economic discussion by Rodbertus and has been used in the German literature ever since.—Ed.

to use. There are, of course, many transitional forms. But in each case there is some kind of regulation of functions by a corporate group which is concerned with the mode of division of labour and of its co-ordination.

3. The cases where a corporate group regulating economic activity is oriented to considerations of economic profit, are well illustrated by the economic regulations of the communes of Medieval Europe and by the guilds and castes of China and India. The regulations governed the number of master craftsmen and their functions and also the technique of the craft, thus the way in which labour was oriented in the handicrafts. They belonged to this type so far as the rules were intended not primarily to secure provision for a given standard of living of the craftsmen, but, as was often though not always the case, to secure their market position by maintaining the quality of performance and by dividing up the market. Like every other type of economic regulation, that of the guilds, of course, involved limitations on market freedom and hence on fully autonomous orientation of craftsmen to the maximization of their profits. It was unquestionably intended to maintain the income standards of the existing craft shops and to that extent, in spite of its formal resemblance to profit-making enterprise, still involved a budgetary mode of orientation.

4. The cases where the corporate group carrying on economic activity has been concerned with profit making, are illustrated, apart from the cases of putting-out industry already discussed, by the agricultural estates of north-eastern Germany. These have been carried out by semi-independent tenants bound by a common system of rules. In the north-west it has taken the form of the part-time labour by individuals with small independent holdings (*Heuerlingswirtschaft*). These estates, like the putting-out industries, have been profit-making enterprises of the landlord as were those of the "putter-out." The economic activities of the tenants and of the domestic workers are oriented primarily to the obligations which have been imposed upon them both in the division of functions and in their co-ordination. These obligations determine the organization of labour on the estate as they determine the mode of dependency of the domestic worker. Apart from this, they are budgetary units. Their contribution to the profit-making activity is not autonomous, but is a heteronomous function on behalf of the enterprise of the landlord or the putter-out. According to the degree in which this orientation is substantively standardized, the technical aspects of the division of labour within a

single organization may approach the kind which is typical of the factory.

Social Aspects of the Division of Labour— (*Continued*)

From a social point of view, the modes of the division of labour may be further classified according to the mode in which the economic advantages, which are regarded as returns for the different functions, are appropriated. The objects of appropriation may be opportunities for realizing returns on work, non-human means of production, or opportunities for profit from the exercise of managerial functions.

When the returns from labour services are appropriated, the service may be owed to a particular recipient, such as a lord, or a particular corporate group; or it may be disposed of on the market. In either case, there may be any one of four radically different possibilities: (a) Monopolistic appropriation of opportunities for return by the individual worker—the case of "free guild labour." This may be hereditary but alienable, as for the Indian village craftsman; or personal and inalienable, as for the Medieval craftsman, who in addition disposed of his services on the market. Rights of eligibility for office are personal and inalienable, but not marketable. Or finally, they may be hereditary, but inalienable, as was the case with certain of the rights attached to the Medieval handicrafts, but above all, the Indian handicrafts and various types of Medieval offices. In all these cases the appropriation may be unconditional or subject to various substantive conditions; (b) The second possibility is that the return for labour services should be appropriated by an "owner" of the worker—the case of "unfree labour." There may be free appropriation which is both hereditary and alienable—the case of slavery proper. Or, though it is hereditary and alienable—the case of slavery proper. Or, though it is hereditary, it may not be freely alienable, but may, for instance, be bound to the non-human means of production, particularly the land. This includes serfdom and hereditary dependency (*Erbuntertänigkeit*).

The appropriation of the use of labour by a lord may be limited by substantive conditions, as in serfdom. The worker cannot leave his status of his own free will, but neither can it arbitrarily be taken from him.

The appropriation of returns of labour may be used by the owner for purposes of budgetary administration, as a source of income in kind or in money, or as a source of labour service in the unit, as in the case of domestic slaves or serfs. Or it may be used as a means of profit. In that case the dependent may be obligated to contribute goods or to work on raw materials provided by the owner. The owner will then sell the product. This is unfree domestic industry. He may, finally, be used as a labourer in an organized shop—a slave or serf workshop.

The person herein designated as the "owner" is very generally involved in the work process himself in a managerial capacity or even in part as a worker, but this need not be true. It may be that his position as owner, *ipso facto,* makes him the managing agent. But this is by no means necessary and is very generally not the case.

The use of slaves and serfs, the latter including various types of dependents, as part of a process of budgetary administration and not as workers in a profit-making enterprise, was typical of Antiquity and of the early Middle Ages. There are, for instance, inscriptions which mentioned slaves "of a Persian prince who were bound out as apprentices on the understanding that they might be used for labour services in the household, but might also be allowed, in return for a payment to the owner,[4] to work independently for customers." Though by no means without exception, this tended to be the rule for Greek slaves; and in Rome this type of independent economic activity became a legal institution which involved providing the slave with a *peculium* or *merx peculiaris.* He was naturally obligated to make payments to his owner. In the Middle Ages, body serfdom frequently involved merely a right to claim payments. This was usual in western and southern Germany. In Russia, also, an actual limitation to the receipt of these payments (*obrok*) from an otherwise free serf was, though not universal, very common. Its legal status was, however, precarious.

The use of unfree labour for profit-making purposes has taken the following principal forms, particularly in the domestic industries on the estates of landlords, including various royal estates, among them probably those of the Pharaohs: (1) Unfree obligation to payments in kind—the delivery of goods in kind, the raw material for which was produced by the workers themselves as well as worked on by them. Flax is an example; (2) unfree domestic industry—work on material provided by the lord. The product could be sold at least in part for money by the lord. But in many cases, as in Antiquity, the tendency was to confine market sale to occasional instances. In early modern times, however, particularly in the border regions between the Germans and the Slavs, this was not the case,

particularly, though not alone, where domestic industries have developed on the estates of landlords. The use of unfree labour in a continuous organization could take the form of unfree domestic labour or of labour in a workshop. Both forms are common. The latter was one of the various forms of the *Ergasterion* of Antiquity. It also was found on the estates of the Pharaohs, in temple workshops, and from the testimony of the frescoes on tombs, on the estates of private owners or lords. It also existed in the Orient, in Greece (Demosthenes' shop in Athens) in the Roman estate workshops, in Byzantium, in the Carolingian "genitium," and in modern times, for example, in Russian factories operated with serf labour; (c) the third possibility is the absence of every sort of appropriation—in this sense, formally free labour. The services of labour are treated as the subject of a contractual relationship which is formally free on both sides. The contract may, however, be substantively regulated in various ways through a conventional or legal order governing the conditions of labour.

Freely contracted labour may be used in various ways. In the first place, in a budgetary unit, as occasional labour, either in the household of the employer (*stör*) or in that of the worker himself. Or it may be permanent, again performed in the household of the employer, as in the case of domestic service, or in that of the worker, as typical of the colonate. It may, on the other hand, be used for profit, again on an occasional or a permanent basis; and in both cases either in the worker's own home or on premises provided by the employer. The latter is true of workers on an estate or in a workshop, but especially of the factory.

Where the worker is employed in a budgetary unit, he is directly in the service of a consumer who supervises his labour. Otherwise, he is in the service of a profit-making entrepreneur. Though the form is often legally identical, economically the difference is fundamental. Coloni may be in either status; but it is more typical for them to be workers in an *oikos;* (d) the fourth possibility is that opportunities for return for labour services may be appropriated by an association of workers, either without any appropriation by the individual worker or with important limitations on such appropriation. This may involve absolute or relative closure against outsiders and also prohibition of the dismissal of workers from employment by management without consent of the workers, or at least some kind of limitations on power of dismissal.

Examples of the type of appropriation involving closure of the group are castes of workers, the type of miners' association found in the Medieval

---

4. In Greek, "ἀποφορά"; Russian, "*obrok*"; German, "*Hals*" or "*Leibzips.*"

mining industry, the organized groups or retainers sometimes found at courts, or the threshers on a landed estate. This type of appropriation is found throughout the social history of all parts of the world in an endless variety of forms. The second type involving limitations on powers of dismissal, which is also very widespread, plays an important part in the modern situation in the "closed shop" of trade unions and especially in the "works councils."

Every form of appropriation of jobs by workers in profit-making enterprises, like the converse case of appropriation of the services of workers by owners, involves limitations on the free recruitment of the labour force. This means that workers cannot be selected solely on grounds of their technical efficiency, and to this extent there is a limitation on the formal rationalization of economic activity. These circumstances further impose substantive limitations on technical rationality in so far as: (1) The exploitation of the products of labour is appropriated by an owner. This may occur through the tendency to arbitrary restriction of the production of labour by tradition, by convention, or by contract. Or it may occur by the reduction or complete disappearance of the worker's own interest in maximizing the production. The latter occurs when, as in slavery, the worker is freely appropriated by an owner; (2) limitations on technical rationalization may also result from appropriation on the part of the worker. There may be a conflict of the self-interest of the worker, which lies in the maintenance of his traditional mode of life, with the attempts of his employer to get him to produce at the optimum technical level or to use other modes of production in place of his labour. For employers, there is always the possibility of transforming their exploitation of labour into a mere source of income. The tendency for the exploitation of the products to be appropriated by the workers thus under favourable circumstances generally leads to a more or less complete exclusion of the owner from management. But it also regularly tends to place workers in a state of dependence on people with whom they deal who enjoy a more favourable market position. These, such as putting-out entrepreneurs, then tend to assume a managerial position.

1. The tendency of appropriation of jobs by workers and that of workers by owners are formally antithetical. But in practice they have very similar results. This should not be surprising. In the first place, the two tendencies are very generally formally related. This is true when appropriation of the workers by an owner coincides with appropriation of opportunities for jobs by a closed corporate group of workers, as has happened in feudal courts. In such cases it is natural that exploitation of services should, to a large extent, be stereotyped; hence that production should be restricted and the worker have little interest in maximizing it. The result is generally a successful resistance of workers against any sort of technical innovation. But even where this does not occur, the fact that workers are appropriated by an owner means in practice that he is obliged to make use of this particular labour force. He is not in a position like that of the modern factory manager to select according to technical needs, but must utilize those he has without selection. This is particularly true of slave labour. Any attempt to exact performance from appropriated workers beyond that which has become traditionally established, encounters traditionalistic obstacles. These could only be overcome by the most ruthless methods, which are not without their danger from the point of view of the employer's own self-interest, since they might undermine the traditionalistic bases of his authority. Hence almost universally the production of appropriated workers has shown a tendency to restriction. Even where, as was particularly true of eastern Europe in early modern times, this has been broken up by the power of the propertied classes, the development of much higher technical levels of production has still been impeded by the absence of the selective process and by the absence of any element of self-interest or independent risk on the part of the appropriated workers. When jobs have been formally appropriated by workers, the same result has come about even more rapidly.

2. Appropriation by workers was particularly common in the development of the early Middle Ages, from the tenth to the thirteenth centuries. The Carolingian "beunden" and all the other beginnings of large-scale agricultural enterprise declined and disappeared. The income of feudal lords and landed proprietors became stereotyped at a very low level; and an increasing proportion of the products in kind, in agriculture and mining, and of the money proceeds from the handicrafts, went to the workers. In just this form this development was peculiar to the Western World. The principal circumstances which favoured it were as follows: (a) The fact that the propertied classes were heavily involved in political and military activity; (b) the absence of a suitable administrative staff. These two circumstances made it impossible to treat these workers in any other way than as a source of stereotyped income; (c) the fact that the freedom of movement of workers as between the potential employers competing for their services could not easily be

restricted; (d) the numerous opportunities of opening up new land, new mines, and new local markets; (e) the primitive level of the technical tradition. The more the appropriation of opportunities for profit by the workers took the place of the appropriation of workers by owners, the more the owners became merely recipients of income. Classical examples are the mining industry and the English guilds. But this, even at an early period, tended to go further to the point of repudiation of payments to a lord altogether, as exemplified in the saying, "A townsman is a freeman." Almost immediately all this led to a broadening of opportunities of making profit by market transactions, arising either from within the group of workers themselves or from without through the development of trade.

Social Aspects of the Division of Labour— (Continued)

THE APPROPRIATION OF THE NON-HUMAN MEANS OF PRODUCTION

The non-human means of production may be appropriated by workers as individuals or as corporate groups, by owners, or by regulating groups consisting of third parties.

When appropriated by workers, it may be by the individual worker who then becomes the "owner" of the non-human means of production; or the appropriation may be carried out by a more or less completely closed group of workers so that, though the individual worker is not the owner, the corporate group is. Such a corporate group may carry out its functions as a unitary economy as on a "communistic" basis, or with appropriation of shares (*Genossenschaftlich*). In all these cases, appropriation may be used for the purposes of budgetary administration or for profit making.

Appropriation by individual workers may exist in a system of completely free market relations, as between small peasants, artisans, boatmen, or taxi-drivers, each owning his own means of production. Where it is not the individual but a corporate group which is the agent of appropriation, there is a wide variety of possibilities, varying particularly with the extent to which the system is of a budgetary or a profit-making character. The household economy, which is in principle neither necessarily primitive nor in fact communistic, may be oriented wholly to provision for its own needs. Or it may, perhaps only occasionally, dispose of surpluses of certain types of raw material accumulated by virtue of a favourable location, or of products derived from some particular technical skill, as a means to better provision. This occasional sale may then develop into a regular system of profit-making exchange. In such cases it is common for "tribal" crafts to develop with an interethnic specialization of function and exchange. Generally speaking, marketability depends on maintaining a monopoly, which in turn is usually secured by inherited secrets. These may develop into wandering craft groups or possibly pariah[5] crafts. It is also possible, as in India, where these groups are united in a political structure and where there are ritual barriers between the ethnic elements, for them to develop into castes.

The case where members of the group possess appropriated shares is that of "producers' co-operation."[6] Household economies may, with the development of money accounting, approach this type. Otherwise, it is only occasionally found, as an organization of workmen. There is, however, one important case closely approaching this type—the mining industry of the early Middle Ages.

Since appropriation by organized groups of workers has already been discussed, appropriation by "owners" or organized groups of them can mean only the expropriation of the workers from the means of production, not merely as individuals, but as a whole. An owner may in this connexion appropriate one or more of the following items: land, including water; subterranean wealth; sources of power; work premises; labour equipment, such as tools, apparatus and machinery; and raw materials. In any given case all these may be concentrated in a single ownership or they may be appropriated by different owners. The owners may employ the means of production they appropriate in a context of budgetary administration, as means to provide for their own needs, or as sources of income by loans. In the latter case, the loans may in turn be used for budgetary purposes or as means for earning a profit, in which case they may be used in a profit-making enterprise without capital accounting, as capital goods in another's enterprise or as capital goods in the owner's own enterprise.

The appropriating agency may be a corporate group engaged in economic activity. In this case, all the alternatives just outlined are open to it. It is, however, also possible that the means of production should be appropriated by a corporate group which only *regulates* economic activity. In

---

5. The term *Paria* is used by Weber in a technical sense to designate a group occupying the same territorial area as others, but separated from them by ritual barriers which severely limit social intercourse between the groups. It has been common for such groups to have specialized occupations, particularly occupations which are despised in the larger society.—ED.

6. What is ordinarily called a "producers' co-operative association" would be included in this type, but Weber conceives the type itself more broadly. In certain respects, for instance, the medieval manor and other types of village community could be considered as examples.—ED.

this case, they are neither used as capital goods nor as a source of income, but are placed at the disposal of the members.

1. When land is appropriated by isolated economic units, it is usually for the period of actual cultivation until the harvest or, so far as, by virtue of clearing or irrigation, land is itself an artifact, for the period of continuous cultivation.

It is only when scarcity of land has become noticeable that it is common for rights of cultivation, pasturage and use of timber to be reserved to the members of a settlement group, and for the extent of their use to be limited: (1) When that happens, appropriation may be carried out by a corporate group. This may be of differing sizes, according to the mode of use to which the land is put—for gardens, meadows, arable land, pastures, or woodland. These have been appropriated by progressively larger groups from the individual household to the whole tribe. Typical cases are the appropriation of arable land, meadows, and pastures by a kinship group or a local community, usually a village. It has been usual for woodland to be appropriated by broader territorial groups, differing greatly in character and extent. The individual household has typically appropriated garden land and the area around the house and has had shares in arable fields and meadows. The assignment of these shares may take various forms. Where a wandering agricultural people takes over new areas, it may involve rigid equality. In a sedentary agricultural regime, there may be a rationally systematic redistribution. This usually occurs only as a consequence of fiscal claims when villagers are collectively responsible for taxes, or of claims of the members to political equality. The unit of technical organization has normally been the household group; (2) the subject of appropriation may be a landlord. This status may, as will be discussed later, be based primarily on the individual's position of authority in a kinship group or as political chieftain with claims to exact labour services, or on fiscal or military authority, or on some form of organization for the systematic exploitation of new land or an irrigation project.

Proprietorship over land may be made a source of utilities by the employment of the unfree labour of slaves or serfs. This, in turn, may be administered as part of a budgetary unit, through deliveries in kind or labour services, as as a means of profit, as a "plantation." On the other hand, it may be exploited with free labour. Here again it may be treated in budgetary terms, drawing income from the land in the form of payments in kind or from sharecropping by tenants or of money rents from tenants. In both cases the equipment used may be provided by the tenant himself or may be loaned to him by the landlord. A landlord may also exploit his holdings as a source of profit in the form of a large-scale rational enterprise.

Where the land is used as part of a budgetary economy with unfree labour, the landlord is apt to be bound traditionally in his exploitation of it, both with respect to his labour personnel, which is not subject to selection, and to their functions. The use of unfree labour in a profit-making organization, the "plantation," has only occurred in a few cases, notably in Antiquity in Carthage and in Rome, and in modern times in the plantations of colonial areas and in the Southern States of North America. Its use in large-scale profit-making enterprises with free labour has occurred only in the modern Western World. It is the mode of development of land proprietorship, in particular the way in which it was broken up, which has been most decisive in determining the modern forms of land appropriation. To-day, only the following pure types are found: the owner of land, the capitalistic tenant, and the propertyless agricultural labourer. The latter type is exceptional, found principally in England.

Sources of wealth adapted to exploitation by mining may be appropriated in the following ways: (a) By the owner of the land, who in the past has usually been a *landlord;* (b) by a political overlord or authority; (c) by any person discovering deposits worthy of mining; (d) by a corporate group of workers and (e) by a profit-making enterprise.

Landlords and political authorities may administer their holdings themselves, as they did occasionally in the early Middle Ages; or they may use them as a source of income, by leasing them to an organized group of workers or to any discoverer whatever or anyone who was a member of a given group. This was the case with the "free mines" of the Middle Ages and was the origin of the institution of "mining freedom" (*Bergbaufreiheit*).

In the Middle Ages, the groups of organized mine workers were typically sharing co-operatives where each member was under obligation either to the owner or to the other solidary members to work in the mine. This obligation was balanced by a right to a share in the products. There was also the type of association of owners which distributed shares of the proceeds and each of whom had to make contributions. The tendency was for the owners to be progressively expropriated in favour of the workers; but these, in turn, as their need for equipment increased, became more and more dependent on groups with command over capital goods. Thus in the end, the appropriation took the form of a capitalistic enterprise, a limited liability company.

2. Means of production which are bound to a fixed position, such as sources of power, particularly water power, "mills" for various different purposes, and workshops, sometimes including the apparatus in them, have in the past, particularly in the Middle Ages, generally been appropriated in one of the following ways: (a) by princes or landlords; (b) by towns (c) by associations of workers, such as guilds, without the development, in any of them, of a unified productive organization.

In the first two cases, they are usually exploited as a source of income, a charge being made for their use. This has often been combined with monopoly position and the compulsory use of the facilities. Each productive unit would make use of the facilities in turn, according to need or, under certain circumstances, it was made the monopoly of a closed, regulative group. Baking ovens, various kinds of grinding mills for grain or oil, fulling mills, polishing equipment, slaughter-houses, dye works, bleaching equipment, forges—which were usually, to be sure, leased—breweries, distilleries, other equipment including particularly shipyards in the possession of the Hanseatic towns, and all kinds of market booths have been appropriated in this way. Under pre-capitalistic conditions, these have all tended to be exploited by allowing workers to use them in return for a payment; thus as part of the budgetary resources of the owner, rather than as capital, whether the owner were an individual or a corporate group, including town corporations. This type of production and budgetary exploitation as a source of investment income for the owning individual or group, or possibly production by a producers' co-operative group, has preceded their transformation into the "fixed capital" of individual business units. Those using such equipment have tended to treat them in part as means of meeting their own needs, especially in the case of baking ovens, but also of equipment for brewing and distilling. In part they have used them in profit-making operations.

3. For maritime commerce the typical arrangement in past times has been the appropriation of the ship by a plurality of owners who have tended to become more and more sharply differentiated from the workers on ships. The organization of maritime enterprise has tended then to develop into a system of sharing risks with shippers in which ship owners, officers, and even the crew, were associated. This did not however, produce any fundamentally new forms of appropriation, but affected only the forms of calculation and hence the distribution of profit and loss.

4. To-day, it is usual for all kinds of equipment and tools to be appropriated under one controlling agency, as is essential to the modern factory; but in earlier times, this has been exceptional. In particular, the economic character of the Greek and Byzantine "ergasterion" and the corresponding Roman "ergastulum" has been highly equivocal, a fact which historians have persistently ignored. It was a "workshop" which might, on the one hand, be a part of a household unit in which slaves might carry out production for the owner's own needs, as on a landed estate. Or it might be a place where slaves carried out some subsidiary process of production of goods for sale. But, on the other hand, the workshop might be used as a source of profit in the ownership of a private individual or of a corporate group, which latter might be a town, as was true of the workshops of the Piraeus. A property would then be leased to individuals or to organized groups of workers in return for payment. Thus when it is stated that people worked in an ergasterion, especially in a town, it is always necessary to inquire further to whom it belonged and who was the owner of the other means of production necessary for the work process. Did it employ free labour? Did they work for their own profit? Or did it employ slaves, in which case it is necessary to know who their owners were and whether they were working on their own account, though making a ἀποφορά payment to their master, or directly for their master. According to the ways in which these questions are answered, the structure would be radically different from an economic point of view. In the great majority of cases, even as late as the Byzantine and Mohammedan types, the ergasterion seems to have been primarily a source of budgetary income and was hence fundamentally different from the modern factory and should not be treated as an early stage of its development. From an economic point of view, this category is, in lack of definiteness, most closely comparable to the various types of mills, found in the Middle Ages.

5. Even in cases where the workshop and the means of production are appropriated by an individual owner who hires labour, the situation is not, from an economic point of view, necessarily what would usually be called a factory to-day. It is necessary in addition to have the use of mechanical power, of machinery, and of an elaborate internal differentiation and combination of functions. The factory to-day is a category of the capitalistic economy. Hence in the present discussion, the concept will be confined to a type of organization which is at least potentially under the control of a profit-making enterprise with fixed capital. It thus takes the form of an organized workshop with internal differentiation of function, with the appro-

priation of all the non-human means of production and with a high degree of mechanization of the work process by the use of mechanical power and machinery. The great workshop of Jack of Newbury, which was famous among its sixteenth-century contemporaries, did not have any of these features. It is alleged to have contained hundreds of hand looms which were his property, and the entrepreneur bought the raw material for the workers, and maintained all manner of welfare arrangements for them. But each worker worked independently as if he were at home. It was possible for an internal differentiation and combination of functions to exist in an ergasterion in which a master employed unfree labourers in Egypt, Greece, Byzantium, and in the Mohammedan world. There is no doubt that such cases have existed. But the Greek texts show clearly that even in such cases it was common for the master to be content with the payment of an ἀποφορά from each worker though perhaps a higher one from persons in a supervisory position. This alone is sufficient to warn us not to consider such a structure economically equivalent to a factory or even to a workshop like that of Jack of Newbury. The closest approximation to the factory in the usual sense is found in royal manufactures, like the imperial Chinese porcelain manufactures and the European manufactures of court luxuries which were modelled on it. The best case of all is the manufacture of military equipment. No one can be prevented from calling these "factories." The Russian workshops operating with serf labour seem at first sight to stand even closer to the modern factory. Here the appropriation of the workers themselves is added to that of the means of production. But for present purposes the concept "factory" will, for the reasons stated, be limited to organized workshops where the non-human means of production are fully appropriated by an owner, but the workers are not; where there is internal specialization of functions, and where mechanical power and machines which must be "tended" are used. All other types of organized workshops will be designated as such with the appropriate additional description.

Social Aspects of the Division of Labour— (Concluded)

THE APPROPRIATION OF MANAGERIAL FUNCTIONS

In all cases of the management of traditional budgetary units, it is typical for the appropriation of managerial functions to take place either by the titular head himself, such as the head of the family or the kinship group, or by members of an administrative staff appointed for the management of the unit, such as household servants or officials.

In the case of profit-making enterprises, it occurs in the following situations: (a) When management and ordinary labour are entirely or very nearly identical. In this case there is usually also appropriation of the non-human means of production by the worker. This type of appropriation may be unlimited, that is, hereditary and alienable on the part of the individual, with or without a guaranteed market. It may, on the other hand, be appropriated by an organized group, with appropriation of the function by the individual restricted to personal tenure (that is, without rights of inheritance or alienation) or subject to substantive regulation, thus limited and dependent on various conditions. Again, a market may or may not be guaranteed; (b) where management and ordinary work are differentiated, there may be a monopolistic appropriation of entrepreneurial functions in various possible forms, notably by co-operative groups, such as guilds, or monopolies granted by the political authority.

In cases where managerial functions are, from a formal point of view, wholly unappropriated, the appropriation of the means of production or of the credit necessary for securing control over them is, in practice, in a capitalistic form of organization, identical with appropriation of control of management by the owners of the means of production. Owners can, in such cases, exercise their control by personally managing the business or by appointment of the actual managers. Where there is a plurality of owners, they will co-operate in the selection.

Wherever there is appropriation of technically complementary means of production, it generally means, in practice, at least some degree of effective voice in the selection of management and, to a relative extent at least, the expropriation of the workers from management. The expropriation of individual workers does not necessarily imply the expropriation of workers in general. Though they are formally expropriated, it is possible for an association of workers to be in fact in a position to play an effective part in management or in the selection of managing personnel.

The Expropriation of Workers from the Means of Production

The expropriation of the individual worker from ownership of the means of production is in part determined by the following purely technical factors: (a) The fact that sometimes the means of production require the services of many workers, at the same time or successively; (b) the fact that sometimes sources of power can only be rationally exploited by using them simultaneously for many similar types of work under a unified control; (c) the fact that often a technically rational organization of the work process is possible only by combining many complementary processes under continuous common supervision; (d) the fact that sometimes special technical training is needed for the management of co-ordinated processes of labour which, in turn, can only be exploited rationally on a large scale; (e) the fact that, if the means of production and raw materials are under unified control, there is the possibility of subjecting labour to a stringent discipline and thereby controlling both the speed of work and standardization and quality of products.

These factors, however, do not exclude the possibility of appropriation by an organized group of workers, a producers' co-operative. They necessitate only the separation of the *individual* worker from the means of production.

The expropriation of workers in general, including clerical personnel and technically trained persons, from possession of the means of production depends on the following principal economic factors: (a) The fact that, other things being equal, it is generally possible to achieve a higher level of technical efficiency if the management has extensive control over the selection and the modes of use of workers, as compared with the situation created by the appropriation of jobs or the existence of rights to participate in management. These latter conditions produce technically, as well as economically, irrational obstacles to efficiency. In particular, considerations appropriate to small-scale budgetary administration and the immediate interests of consumers are often in conflict with the efficiency of the organization; (b) in a market economy a management which is not hampered by any established rights of the workers, and which enjoys unrestricted control over the goods and equipment which underlie its borrowings, is in a superior credit position. This is particularly true if the management consists in individuals experienced in business affairs and with a good reputation for "safety" derived from their continuous conduct of business; (c) from a historical point of view, the expropriation of labour has developed since the sixteenth century in an economy characterized by a progressive development of the market system, both extensively and intensively, by the sheer technical superiority and actual indispensability of a type of autocratic management oriented to the particular market situations, and by the structure of power relationships in the society.

In addition to these general conditions, the effect

of the fact that enterprise has been oriented to the exploitation of market advantages has been to favour such expropriation: (a) As compared with every type of economic attitude which, from the point of view of calculation is less rational, it has favoured the maximum of technical rationality in capital accounting. This, however, has been a function of the complete appropriation of economic resources by owners; (b) it has favoured commercial abilities in management as opposed to the technical. It has also favoured the maintenance of technical and commercial secrets; (c) it has favoured a speculative business policy which again has required expropriation; (d) apart from any considerations of technical rationality, expropriation has been favoured by the bargaining superiority which management, by virtue of its possession of property, has enjoyed, both on the labour market in relation to the worker, and in the commodity market, by virtue of its capital accounting, and its command over capital goods and credit. In these ways it is superior to any type of competitor operating on a lower level of rationality in methods of calculation or less well situated with respect to capital and credit resources. The upshot of all these considerations is that the maximum of formal rationality in capital accounting is possible only where the workers are subjected to the authority of business management. This is a further specific element of substantive irrationality[7] in the modern economic order; (e) finally, free labour and the complete appropriation of the means of production create the most favourable conditions for discipline.

The Expropriation of Workers from the Means of Production—(Continued)

The expropriation of *all* the workers from the means of production may have the following effects in practice: (1) That management is in the hands of the administrative staff of a corporate group. This would be true very particularly of any rationally organized socialistic economy. The expropriation of all the workers would be retained and merely brought to completion by the expropriation of private owners; (2) that the managerial functions are, by virtue of their appropriation of the means of production, exercised by the owners or by persons they appoint. The appropriation of control over the persons exercising managerial authority by the interests of ownership may have the following con-

___

7. Attention should be called again to Weber's peculiar use of the term "irrational." He means that the maximum of formal rationality in his specific sense can be attained only in a structure which is in conflict with certain important values or ideas of welfare.—ED.

sequences: (a) Management by one or more entrepreneurs who are at the same time owners —the immediate appropriation of managerial functions. This situation, however, does not exclude the possibility that a wide degree of control over the policies of management may rest in hands outside the organization, by virtue of their powers over credit or financing; for instance, the bankers who finance the enterprise; (b) the separation of managerial functions from appropriated ownership, especially through limitations of the functions of owners to the appointment of management and to the free appropriation of shares of the profits, these powers exercised by the owners of capital shares. From this situation to the purely personal type of appropriation there are all manner of gradual transitions. The separation of ownership and management is formally rational in the sense that, as contrasted with the case of permanent and hereditary appropriation of managerial functions, it permits the selection for managerial posts of the persons best qualified from the standpoint of profitability. But this can have various different practical consequences. By virtue of their ownership, control over managerial positions may rest in the hands of property interests outside the organization as such. They may be shareholders who are, above all, concerned with maximizing their investment returns. Or control over managerial positions may lie, by virtue of a temporary market situation, in the hands of speculative interests outside the organization, such as shareholders who are interested in profits from the sale of their shares. Or, finally, control over managerial positions may be in the hands of other business interests, such as banks or others, which by virtue of their power over markets or over credit are in a position to exercise control. These may pursue their own interests, which are often foreign to those of the organization as such.

Interests are spoken of as "outside the firm" so far as they are not primarily oriented to the long-run profitability of the enterprise. This may be true of all sorts of property interests. It is particularly true, however, of interests having control of the plant and capital goods of the enterprise or of a share in it, which is not exercised as a permanent investment, but as a means of making a speculative profit. The types of outside interest which are most readily reconciled with those of the enterprise are those of pure investment; they are, that is, interests in long-run profitability.

The ways in which these outside interests play into the modes of control over managerial position constitutes another specific element of substantive irrationality in the modern economic order. This is the more true the higher the degree of rationality exercised in selection. It is possible for entirely private property interests to exercise control, or others which are oriented to ends having no connexion with the organization, or finally, those concerned only with gambling. By gaining control of shares, these can control the appointment of the managing personnel and, more important, the business policies they pursue. The influence exercised on the market situation, especially that for capital goods, and in turn on the orientation of production of goods for profit, by speculative interests outside the producing organizations themselves, is *one* of the sources of the phenomena known as the "crises" of the modern market economy. This cannot, however, be further discussed here.

3. *Budgetary Management and Profit-Making*

BY MAX WEBER

THE RATIONALITY OF MONETARY ACCOUNTING:
MANAGEMENT AND BUDGETING

FROM A PURELY technical point of view, money is the most "efficient" means of eco-

Reprinted from Max Weber, *The Theory of Social and Economic Organization*, trans. A. M. Henderson and Talcott Parsons, ed. Talcott Parsons (Glencoe, Ill.: The Free Press, 1947), pp. 186–203. Copyright 1947 by Oxford University Press.

nomic accounting. That is, it is formally the most rational means of orienting economic activity. Accounting in terms of money, and not its actual use, is thus the specific means of rational, economic provision. So far as it is completely rational, money accounting has the following primary consequences:

(1) The valuation of all the means of achieving a productive purpose in terms of the present or expected market situation. This includes everything

which is needed at present or it is expected may be needed in the future; everything actually in the actor's control, which he may come to control or may acquire by exchange from the control of others; everything lost, or in danger of damage or destruction; all types of utilities of means of production or any other sort of economic advantages.

(2) The numerical statement of (a) the prospects of every projected course of economic action and (b) assessment of the results of every completed action in the form of an account comparing costs and returns in money and comparing the estimated net profit to be gained from alternative lines of action by means of these calculations.

(3) A periodical comparison of all the goods and other assets controlled by an economic unit at a given time with those controlled at the beginning of a period, both in terms of money.

(4) A previous estimate and subsequent verification of receipts and expenditures, either those in money itself, or those which can be valued in money, which the economic unit is likely to have available for its use during a period, if it maintains the money value of the means at its disposal intact.

(5) The orientation of provision for consumption to these data by the use of money available during the accounting period for the acquisition of the requisite utilities in accordance with the principle of marginal utility.

The continual use and provision by an economic unit, whether through production or exchange, of goods either for its own consumption or to procure other goods to be consumed, will be called "budgetary management" (*Haushalt*).[1] Where rationality is maximized, its basis for an individual or for a group economically oriented in this way is the "budget" (*Haushaltsplan*), which states systematically in what way the means which are expected to be used within the unit for an accounting period— needs for utilities or for means of production—can be covered by the anticipated income.

The "income" of a "budgetary unit" is the total of goods valued in money, which, as estimated according to the principle stated above in number 4, has been available during a previous period or, on the availability of which the unit is likely to be able to count by rational calculations for the present or for a future period. The total estimated value of the goods at the disposal of a budgetary unit, which are

normally used immediately or as a source of income, will be called its "resources" (*Vermögen*).[2] The possibility of complete money budgeting for the budgetary unit is dependent on the possibility that its income and resources consist either in money or in goods which are at any time subject to exchange for money; that is, which are in the highest degree marketable.

A rational type of management and budgeting of a budgetary unit is possible where calculation is carried out in kind, as will be further discussed below. It is true that in that case there is no such thing as a single sum of "resources" capable of being estimated in money nor is there a single income. Calculations must be worked out in terms of "possession" of concrete goods and, where acquisition is limited to peaceful means, of concrete "receipts" from the direct outlay of available goods and services. These receipts will then be administered with a view to attaining the optimum provision for the satisfaction of wants. If the wants are strictly given, this involves a comparatively simple problem from the technical point of view so long as the situation does not require a very precise estimate of the comparative utility to be gained from the allocation of the available resources to each of a large number of very heterogeneous modes of use. If the situation is markedly different, even the simple self-sufficient household is faced with problems which are only to a very limited degree subject to a formally exact solution by calculation. The actual solution is usually found partly by the application of purely traditional standards, partly by making very rough estimates, which, however, may be quite adequate where both the wants concerned and the conditions of provision for them are well known and readily comparable. When possessions consist in heterogeneous goods, as must be the case in the absence of exchange, a formally exact calculable comparison of the state of possession at the beginning and the end of a period, or of the comparison of different possible ways of securing receipts, is possible only with categories of goods which are qualitatively similar. The typical result is that all the available goods are treated as forming a totality of possessions in kind and certain goods are treated as available for consumption so long as it appears that this will not in the long run diminish the available re-

1. The concept *Haushalt*, as distinguished from *Erwerb*, is central to Weber's analysis in this context. He means by it essentially what Aristotle meant by the "management of a household" (Jowett's translation). It is a question of rational allocation of resources in providing for a given set of needs. The concept of budget and budgetary management seems to be the closest English equivalent in common use.—Ed.

2. Corresponding to the distinction of *Haushalt* and *Erwerb*, Weber distinguishes *Vermögen* and *Kapital*. They are, of course, classes of property distinguished, however, in terms of their function in the management of an economic unit. There is no English equivalent of *Vermögen* in this sense, and it has seemed necessary to employ the more general term "resources." Where there is danger of confusion, it will be amplified as "budgetary resources." —Ed.

sources. But every change in the conditions of production—as, for instance, through a bad harvest—or any change in wants necessitates a new allocation since it alters the scale of relative marginal utilities. Under conditions which are simple and adequately understood, this adaptation may be carried out without much difficulty. Otherwise, it is technically more difficult than if money terms could be used. For then any change in the price situation in principle influences the satisfaction only of the wants which are marginal on the scale of relative urgency, which are thus met with the final (variable) increments of income.

As far as accounting in kind becomes more and more rational, and is thus emancipated from tradition, the estimation of marginal utilities in terms of the relative urgency of wants encounters grave complications; whereas, if it were carried out in terms of money resources and income, it would be relatively simple. In the latter case the question is merely whether to apply more labour or whether to satisfy or sacrifice, as the case may be, one or more wants, rather than others. For when the problems of budgetary management are expressed in money terms, this is the form that "costs" take. But where calculations are in kind, it is necessary, in addition to having a scale of urgency of wants, to estimate (1) the various possible modes of use of the means of production, including their value in terms of previous labour applied to them; that is, it is necessary to evaluate a variant and changeable relationship between want satisfaction and expenditure of resources. This involves further (2) estimating the amount of labour which it would be necessary to expend in order to secure various forms of new receipts; and (3) the ways in which the various resources could be used in carrying out each of a series of potential productive processes. It is one of the most important tasks of economic theory to analyse the various possible ways in which these evaluations can be rationally carried out. It is, on the other hand, a task for economic history to follow out the ways in which the budgetary management of resources in kind has actually worked out in the course of various historical epochs. In general, the following may be said: (1) that the degree of formal rationality has, generally speaking, fallen short of the level which was even empirically possible, to say nothing of the theoretical maximum. As a matter of necessity, the accounting of nonmonetary budgetary management units has in the great majority of cases remained strongly bound to tradition. (2) In the larger units of this type, precisely because an expansion and refinement of everyday wants has not taken place, there has been

a tendency to employ surpluses for uses outside the everyday standard of living, above all, for artistic purposes. This is an important basis of the tendency of societies with an economy on a low level of the use of money to develop cultures with a strong emphasis on style and an artistic type of orientation.

1. The category of "resources" includes more than physical goods. It also includes all the economic advantages over which the budgetary unit has an assured control, whether that control is due to custom, to the play of interests, to convention, or to law. The clientèle of a profit-making organization, whether it be a medical or legal practice, or a retail shop, belongs to the resources of the owner if it is for whatever reason relatively stable. In case such resources are legally appropriated, they may, according to the definition in Chapter 1, sec. 10, constitute part of its property.

2. Money accounting is found without the actual use of money or with its use limited to the settlement of balances which cannot be paid in kind in the goods being exchanged on both sides. Evidence of this is common in the Egyptian and Babylonian records. The use of money accounting as a measure of payments in kind is found in the code of Hammurabi and in the late Roman and early Medieval law, in the permission for a debtor to pay an amount due in whatever form he is able. The establishment of equivalents may in such cases have been carried out on the basis of traditional prices or of prices laid down by decree.

3. Apart from this, the above discussion contains only commonplaces, which are introduced to facilitate the formulation of a precise concept of the rational budgetary unit as distinguished from that of a rational profit-making enterprise—the latter will be discussed presently. It is important to state explicitly that both can take rational forms. The satisfaction of needs is not something more "primitive" than profit-seeking; "resources" is not necessarily a more primitive category than capital; income, than profit. It is, however, true that historically the budgetary unit has been prior and has been the dominant form in most periods of the past.

4. It is indifferent what unit is the bearer of a budgetary management economy. Both the budget of a state and the family budget of a worker fall under the same category.

5. Empirically the administration of budgetary units and profit-making are not mutually exclusive alternatives. The business of a consumers' cooperative, for instance, is normally oriented to the economical provision for wants; but in the form of its activity, it tends to be a profit-making business without being oriented to profit as a substantive end.

In the action of an individual, the two elements may be so intimately intertwined, and in the past have typically been so, that only the conclusion of the course of action, whether its product was sold or consumed, can serve as a basis for interpreting the meaning of the action. This has been particularly true of small peasants. Exchange may well be a part of the process of budgetary management where it is a matter of acquiring consumption goods by exchange and of disposing of surpluses. On the other hand, the budgetary economy of a prince or a landowner may, at least in part in the sense of the following discussion, be a profit-making enterprise. This has been true on a large scale in earlier times. Whole industries have developed out of the heterocephalous and heteronomous enterprises which landowners, monasteries, princes, etc., have established to exploit the products of their lands. All sorts of profit-making enterprises to-day are part of the economy of such units as local authorities or even states. In these cases it is legitimate to include in the "income" of the units, if they are rationally administered, only the net profits of these enterprises. Conversely, it is possible for profit-making enterprises to establish various types of heteronomous budgetary units under their direction for such purposes as providing subsistence for slaves or wage workers— among them are "welfare" organizations, housing and eating facilities. Net profits are money surpluses after the deduction of all money costs. See above, para. 2 of this section.

6. It has been possible here to give only the most elementary starting points for analysing the significance of economic calculations in kind for general social development.

The Concept and Types of Profit-Making. The Role of Capital

"Profit-making" (*Erwerben*)[3] is activity which is oriented to opportunities for seeking new powers of control over goods on a single occasion, repeatedly, or continuously. "Profit-making activity" is activity which is partly oriented to profit-making. Profit-making is economic if it is oriented to acquisition by peaceful methods. It may be oriented to the exploitation of market situations. "Means of profit" (*Erwerbsmittel*) are those goods and other economic advantages which are used in the interests of economic profit-making. Exchange for profit is that

which is oriented to market situations in order to increase control over goods, rather than to secure means for consumption. Credit may be extended as a means of increasing control over the necessary requisites of profit-making activity.

There is a form of monetary accounting which is peculiar to rational economic profit-making; namely, "capital accounting." Capital accounting is the valuation and verification of opportunities for profit and of the success of profit-making activity. It involves the valuation of the total assets of the enterprise, whether these consist in goods in kind or in money, at the beginning of a period of activity; and the comparison of this with a similar valuation of the assets still present or newly acquired, at the end of the process. In the case of a profit-making organization operating continuously, it is a matter of accounting periods. But in any case, a balance is drawn between the initial and final states of the enterprise. "Capital" is the sum of money in terms of which the means of profit-making which are available to the enterprise are valued. "Profit," and correspondingly "loss," is the difference between the valuations as revealed by the initial balance and that drawn at the conclusion of the period. "Capital risk" is the estimated probability of loss as expressed in terms of a balance. A profit-making "enterprise" (*Unternehmen*) is a system of action capable of autonomous orientation to capital accounting. This orientation takes place by means of calculation. On the one hand, there is a calculation, prior to actual action, of the probable risks and chances of profit; on the other hand, at the conclusion of a measure, verification of the actual profit or loss resulting. "Profitability" (*Rentabilität*) means, in the rational case, one of two things: (1) the amount of profit estimated as possible by previous calculations, the attainment of which is made an objective of the entrepreneur's activity; or (2) that which an audit shows actually to have been earned in a given period and which is available for the consumption uses of the entrepreneur, without prejudice to his future chances of profit making. In both cases it is usually expressed in ratios—to-day, percentages—in relation to the capital of the initial balance.

Enterprises based on capital accounting may be oriented to the exploitation of opportunities of acquisition afforded by the market or they may be oriented toward other channels of acquisition, such as exploitation of the ability to use force, as in the case of tax farming or the sale of offices.

Each individual operation undertaken by a rational profit-making enterprise is oriented to estimated profitability by means of calculation. In the case of profit-making activities on the market, capital accounting requires: (1) that there exist, subject

---

3. In common usage the term *Erwerben* would perhaps best be translated as "acquisition." This has not, however, been used as Weber is here using the term in a technical sense as the antithesis of *Haushalten*. "Profit-Making" brings out this specific meaning much more clearly.—ED.

to estimate beforehand, adequately extensive and assured opportunities for sale of the goods which the enterprise produces; that is, normally a high degree of marketability. (2) That, similarly, the means of carrying on the enterprise such as instruments of production and the services of labour are available in the market at costs which can be estimated with an adequate degree of certainty. Finally, (3) that the technical and legal conditions to which the process is subjected, from the acquisition of the means of production to final sale, including transport, manufacturing operations, storage, etc., can be taken account of as calculable money costs.

The extraordinary importance of the highest possible degree of calculability as the basis for efficient capital accounting will be evidenced again and again throughout the discussion of the sociological conditions of economic activity. It is far from the case that only economic factors are important to it. On the contrary, it will be shown that the most various sorts of external and subjective barriers have existed to account for the fact that capital accounting has arisen as a basic form of economic calculation only in the Western World.

As distinguished from the calculation appropriate to a budgetary unit, the capital accounting and calculation of the market entrepreneur, are oriented not to marginal utility, but to profitability. To be sure, the probabilities of profit are in the last analysis dependent on the income of consumption units and, through this, on the marginal utility of the available income of the final consumers of consumption goods. As it is usually put, it depends on their "purchasing power" for the relevant commodities. But from a technical point of view, the accounting calculations of a profit-making enterprise and of a consumption unit differ as fundamentally as do the ends of want satisfaction and of profit-making which they serve. For purposes of economic theory, it is the marginal consumer who determines the direction of production. In actual fact, given the actual distribution of power this is only true in a limited sense for the modern situation. To a large degree, even if the consumer is in a position to buy, his wants are "awakened" and "directed" by the entrepreneur.

In a market economy every form of rational calculation, hence, especially, of capital accounting, is oriented to expectations of prices and their changes as they are determined by the conflicts of interests in bargaining and competition and the resolution of these conflicts. In the estimation of profitability this is made particularly clear by the form of bookkeeping, the double entry type, which is the most highly developed from a technical point of view. For here,

in the system of accounting, there is introduced the fiction of exchange transactions between the different parts of a single enterprise; or, between different accounts in order to develop a technique of estimating the bearing of each particular measure on the profitability of the enterprise. Thus the highest degree of rational capital accounting presupposes the existence of competition on a large scale. And this in turn involves a further very specific condition. It is not possible in *any* economic system for subjective wants to correspond directly to effective demand; that is, to that which enters into calculations for provision by the acquisition of goods. For whether or not a subjective want can be satisfied depends, on the one hand, on its place in the scale of relative urgency; on the other hand, on the goods which are actually or potentially estimated to be available for its satisfaction. Satisfaction does not take place if the utilities needed for it are applied to other more urgent uses, or if they either cannot be procured at all, or only by such sacrifices of labour and goods that future wants, which are still, from a present point of view, adjudged more urgent, could not be satisfied. This is true of consumption in every kind of economic system including a communistic one.

In an economy which makes use of capital accounting and which is thus characterized by the appropriation of the means of production by individual units, that is by property, profitability depends on the prices which the "consumers," according to the marginal utility of money in relation to their income, can and will pay. It is only possible to produce profitably for those consumers who, in these terms, have sufficient income. A need may fail to be satisfied, not only when an individual's own demand for other goods takes precedence, but also when the greater purchasing power of others, in relation to any kind of demand, withdraws the relevant good from the market. Thus the fact that competition on the market is an essential condition of the existence of rational money accounting further implies that the outcome of the economic process is decisively influenced by the ability of persons who are plentifully supplied with money to outbid the others, and of those more favourably situated for production to underbid their rivals on the selling side. The latter are particularly those well supplied with goods essential to production or with money. In particular, rational money accounting presupposes the existence of effective prices and not merely of fictitious prices conventionally employed for technical accounting purposes. These, in turn, presuppose money which functions as an effective circulating medium of exchange and in demand as such, and not merely as a technical accounting unit.[4] Thus the orientation of action to money prices and to profit has the following consequences: (1) that the distribution of the amount of money or of marketable goods at the disposal of the different parties in the market is decisive in determining the direction taken by the production of goods, so far as it is carried on by profit-making enterprises. For it is only demand which is made effective through purchasing power which is and can be satisfied. Further, (2) the question, what type of demand is to be satisfied by the production of goods, becomes in turn dependent on the profitability of production itself. Production is, to be sure, in formal terms a rational process of want satisfaction. But it does not respond to actual wants unless their possessors are in a position to make them effective by sufficient purchasing power on the market.

"Capital goods," as distinguished from ordinary possessions or the resources of a budgetary unit, are all such goods as are administered and so long as they are administered on the basis of capital accounting. "Interest on capital," as distinct from various other possible kinds of interest on loans, is: (1) what is estimated to be the minimum normal profitability of the use of material means to profit making; (2) the rate of interest at which profit-making enterprises can obtain money or capital goods.

1. The concept of capital has been defined strictly with reference to the individual enterprise and in accordance with accounting practice, which was, indeed, the most convenient method for present purposes. This usage is much less in conflict with everyday speech than with the usual scientific use of the term, which, furthermore, has by no means been consistent. In order to test the usefulness of the present accounting term, which is being increasingly employed in scientific writings again, it is necessary only to ask the following simple questions: (1) What does it mean when we say that a company has an original capital of a million pounds? When (2) that capital is "written down"? When (3) laws dealing with financing make rules which lay down what may and may not be included in original capital? The first question means that when profit is being divided, it is only when the excess of credits over debits as stated in the balance

sheet exceeds a million pounds, that it can be treated as profit and divided among the shareholders to do what they like with. In the case of a one man enterprise, it means that only this surplus may be used for his private expenditures. The second question concerns the situation where there have been heavy losses. It means that the division of profit need not be postponed until a surplus of over a million pounds has been accumulated but that the division of "profits" may begin at a lower figure. In order to do this, it is necessary to "write down" the capital and this is the purpose of the operation. Finally, the purpose of rules as to how capital liability can be "covered" by acquisition of assets and when and how it can be written down or up is to give creditors and shareholders a guarantee that the division of profits will be carried out correctly according to the rules of the enterprise; in such a way, that is, (a) that profitability is maintained, and (b) that the security of the creditors is not impaired. The rules as to what may be entered in the balance sheet are concerned essentially with how objects may be reckoned as capital. (4) What does it mean when we say that as a result of unprofitability "capital turns to other channels of investment"? The statement may refer to the resources of a budgetary unit, for "investment" may be a category of the administration of budgetary resources, as well as of profit-making enterprise. But it may mean that capital goods partly have ceased to be such by being sold, for instance as scrap or junk, partly are transferred to other uses as capital. (5) What is meant when we speak of the "power of capital"? We mean that the possessors of control over the means of production and of economic advantages which can be used as capital goods in a profit-making enterprise enjoy, by virtue of this control and of the orientation of economic action to the principles of capitalistic acquisition, a specific position of power in relation to others.

In the earliest beginnings of rational profit-making activity capital appears, though not under this name, as a sum of money used in accounting. Thus in the "commenda" relationship various types of goods were entrusted to a travelling merchant to sell in a foreign market, and possibly he was also commissioned to purchase other goods wanted for sale at home. The profit or loss was then divided in a particular proportion between the travelling merchant and the entrepreneur who advanced the capital. But for this to take place it was necessary to value the goods in money; that is, to strike balances at the beginning and the conclusion of an enterprise. The "capital" of the commenda relationship or the *societas maris* was simply this

---

4. Since Weber wrote, there has been an extensive discussion of the problem of whether rational allocation of resources was possible in a completely socialistic economy in which there were no independent, competitively determined prices. The principal weight of technical opinion seems at present to take the opposite position from that which Weber defends here. A recent discussion of the problem will be found in the book on the *Economic Theory of Socialism*, edited by B. E. Lippincott. This book includes a bibliography on the subject.—Ed.

money valuation, which served only the purpose of settling accounts between the parties and no other.

What is meant when the term "capital market" is used? It means that goods, especially money, are in demand in order to be used as capital goods. Furthermore, it means that there are profit-making enterprises, especially various kinds of "banks," which make profits by the provision of goods, especially money, for this purpose as a regular business. In the case of so-called "loan capital," which consists in handing over money in lieu of a promise to return the same amount at a later time with or without the addition of "interest," the term capital will only be used if lending is the object of a profit-making enterprise. Otherwise, the term "money loans" will be used. Everyday speech tends to use the term capital in so far as "interest" is paid because the latter is usually reckoned as a proportion of the nominal value of the loan. It is only because of this basis of calculation that we speak of the amount of a loan or a deposit as capital. It is true that this is the origin of the term. *Capitale* was the principal sum of a loan which is said, though it cannot be proved, to derive from the heads counted in a loan of cattle. But this is irrelevant. Even in very early times a loan of goods in kind was reckoned in money terms; and it was on this basis that interest was calculated, so that even in such cases capital goods and capital accounting are typically related, as has been true in later times. In the case of an ordinary loan, which is made simply as a phase in the administration of a budgetary unit and so far as it is employed for the needs of the budgetary unit, the term "loan capital" will not be used. The same, of course, applies to the lender.

The concept of a profit-making enterprise is in accord with ordinary usage, except for the fact that the orientation to capital accounting, which is usually taken for granted, is made explicit. This is done in order to emphasize that not every case of search for profit as such constitutes an "enterprise," but only when it is capable of orientation to capital accounting, regardless of whether it is on a large or a small scale. At the same time it is indifferent whether this capital accounting is in fact rationally carried out according to rational principles. Similarly the terms "profit" and "loss" will be used only as applying to enterprises oriented to capital accounting. The earnings or other modes of acquisition without relation to capital, of such persons as authors, physicians, lawyers, civil servants, professors, clerks, technicians, or workers, is naturally "acquisition" (*Erwerb*), but it is not "profit." Even everyday usage would not call it profit. "Profitability" is a concept which is applicable to

every sort of act which is oriented in terms of business accounting technique to profit and loss, such as the employment of a particular worker, the purchase of a new machine, the determination of rest periods in the working day, etc.

It is not expedient in defining the concept of interest on capital to start with interest on any type of loan. If somebody helps out a peasant by giving him seed and demands an increment on its return, or if the same is done in the case of money loaned to a household to be returned with interest, it is not expedient to call this a "capitalistic" process. It is possible, where action is rational, for the lender to secure an additional amount because his creditor is in a position to expect benefits from the use of the loan greater than the amount of the interest he pays; when, that is, the situation is seen in terms of what it would be if he had had to do without the loan. Similarly, the lender, being aware of the situation, is in a position to exploit it, in that for him the marginal utility of his present control over the goods he lends is exceeded by the marginal utility at the relevant future time of the repayment with the addition of the interest. This is essentially a matter of the administration of budgetary units and their resources, not of capital accounting. Even a person who secures a loan for his urgent personal needs from a "usurer" is not for purposes of the present discussion said to be paying interest on capital, nor does the lender receive such interest. It is rather a case of return for the loan. But the person who makes a business of lending calculates interest, in case he acts rationally, in terms of its relation to his business capital, and must consider that he has suffered a "loss" if the returns from loans do not come up to the requisite rate of profitability. This is a case of interest on capital; the former is simply interest. Thus for the present terminological purposes, interest on capital is always that which is calculated on the basis of capital, not that which is a return for capital. It is always oriented to money valuations, and thus to the sociological fact that disposal over means to making profit, whether through the market or not, is in private hands; that is, appropriated. Without this, capital accounting, and thus calculation of interest, would be unthinkable.

In a rational profit-making enterprise, the interest, which is charged on the books to a capital sum, is the minimum of profitability. It is in terms of whether or not this minimum is reached that a judgment of the advisability of this particular mode of use of capital goods is arrived at. Advisability in this context is naturally conceived from the point of view of maximizing profit. The rate for this minimum profitability is, it is well known, only approximately that at which it is possible to secure credit on the capital market at the time. But nevertheless, the existence of the capital market is the reason why calculations are made on this basis, just as the existence of market exchange is the basis for making entries against the different accounts. It is one of the fundamental phenomena of a capitalistic economy that entrepreneurs are permanently willing to pay interest for loans. This phenomenon can only be explained by understanding how it is that the average entrepreneur may hope in the long run to earn a profit, or that entrepreneurs on the average in fact do earn it, over and above what they have to pay as interest on loans.

Economic theory approaches this problem in terms of the relative marginal utilities of goods under present and under future control. No objection is to be made to this procedure. But the sociologist wishes to know in addition how this supposed relation of marginal utilities affects human action so that actors are in a position and willing to make differences in time preference a basis of the payment of interest. For it is by no means obvious that this would happen at all times and places. In fact, it is a phenomenon specific to profit-making economies. The primary basis of it is the economic market structure which mediates between the profit-making enterprises, on the one hand, and the budgetary units on the other, which not only consume the goods offered on the market but also provide certain essential means of production, notably labour. It is only where there is such a market that profit-making enterprises are founded and administered permanently with a capitalistic orientation. Such enterprises are further dependent on an expectation of earning the minimum rate of interest on capital. In terms of economic theory, which is subject to numerous variations, it might well be said that this type of exploitation of the situation was a consequence of positions of power deriving from private property in the means of production and in the products. It is only this type of economically-acting individuals who are in a position to orient their economic activity to interest payments.

2. The budgetary administration of resources and profit-making enterprises may be outwardly so similar as to appear identical. They are in fact in the analysis only distinguishable in terms of the difference in meaningful orientation of the corresponding economic activities. In the one case, it is oriented to maintaining and improving profitability and the market position of the enterprise; in the other, to the security and increase of resources and income. It is, however, by no means necessary

that this fundamental orientation should always, in a concrete case, be decisively turned in either direction; and sometimes it is impossible to decide it. In cases where the private resources of the entrepreneur are identical with his business control over its business resources and his private income is identical with the profit of the business, the two things seem to go entirely hand in hand. All manner of personal considerations may in such a case cause the entrepreneur to enter upon business policies which, in terms of the rational maximization of profit, are irrational. But very generally, private resources and those of the business are not identical. Furthermore, such factors as personal indebtedness of the proprietor, his personal demand for a higher present income, and the like, often exert what is, in terms of business considerations, a highly irrational influence on the business. Such situations often lead to measures intended to eliminate these influences altogether, as in the incorporation of family businesses.

The tendency to separate the sphere of private affairs from the business is thus not fortuitous. It is a consequence of the fact that, from the point of view of business interest, the interest in maintaining the private resources of the owner is often irrational, as is his interest in income receipts at any given time from the point of view of the profitability of the enterprise. Considerations relevant to the profitability of a business are also not identical with those governing the private interests of persons who are related to it as workers or as consumers. Conversely, the interests growing out of the private fortunes and income of persons or corporate groups having powers of control over an enterprise, do not necessarily lie in the same direction as the long-run considerations of maximizing its profitability and its market position. This is definitely, even especially, true when a profit-making enterprise is controlled by a producers' co-operative association. The objective interests of rational management of a business enterprise and the personal interest of the individuals who control it, are by no means identical and are often opposed. This fact implies the distinction in principle of the budgetary unit and the enterprise, even where both, with respect to powers of control and objects controlled, are identical.

It is essential for purposes of a clear and convenient terminology to maintain a sharp distinction between the budgetary unit and the profit-making enterprise. The purchase of securities on the part of a private investor who wishes to consume the proceeds, is not an investment of capital but of personal resources. A money loan made by a private individual for obtaining the interest is, when regarded from the standpoint of the lender, entirely different from one made by a bank to the same borrower. On the other hand, a loan made to a consumer and one to an entrepreneur for business purposes are quite different from the point of view of the borrower. The bank is investing capital and the entrepreneur is borrowing capital; but in the first case, it may be for the borrower a matter simply of borrowing for purposes of budgetary management; in the second it may be, for the lender, a case of investment of his private resources. This distinction between private resources and capital, between the budgetary unit and the profit-making enterprise, is of far-reaching importance. In particular, without it, it is impossible to understand the economic development of the ancient world and the limitations on the development of capitalism in those times.

3. By no means all profit-making enterprises with capital accounting are doubly oriented to the market in that they both purchase means of production on the market and sell their product there. Tax farming and all sorts of financial operations have been carried on with capital accounting but without selling any products. The very important consequences of this will be discussed later. It is a case of capitalistic profit-making which is not oriented to the market.

4. For reasons of convenience, acquisitive activity and profit-making enterprise have been distinguished. Anyone is engaged in acquisitive activity so far as he seeks, among other things, in given ways to acquire goods—money or others—which he does not yet possess. Thus it includes the official and the worker, no less than the entrepreneur. But the term "profit-making enterprise" will be confined to those types of acquisitive activity which are continually oriented to market advantages by virtue of the fact that goods are used as means to secure profit, either (a) through the production and sale of goods in demand, or (b) through the offer of services in demand in exchange for money, which may occur through free exchange or through the exploitation of appropriated advantages, as has been pointed out above. The person who is a mere investor is, in the present terminology, not engaged in profit-making, no matter how rationally he administers his resources.

5. It goes without saying that in terms of economic theory the direction in which goods can be profitably produced by profit-making enterprises is determined by their marginal utilities for final consumers in conjunction with the latter's incomes. But from a sociological point of view, it should not be forgotten that, to a large extent, in a capitalistic economy (a) new wants are created and others allowed to disappear and (b) capitalistic enterprises, through their aggressive advertising policies, exercise an important influence on the demand functions of consumers. Indeed, these are essential traits of a capitalistic economy. It is true that this does not apply primarily to wants of the highest degree of necessity, but even types of food provision and housing are importantly determined by the producers in a capitalistic economy.

4. Industrial Organization

BY ALFRED MARSHALL

WRITERS on social science from the time of Plato downwards have delighted to dwell on the increased efficiency which labour derives from organization. But in this, as in other cases, Adam Smith gave a new and larger significance to an old doctrine, by the philosophic thoroughness with which he explained it, and the practical knowledge with which he illustrated it. After insisting on the advantages of the division of labour, and pointing out how they render it possible for increased numbers to live in comfort on a limited territory, he argued that the pressure of population on the means of subsistence tends to weed out those races who through want of organization or for any other cause are unable to turn to the best account the advantages of the place in which they live.

Reprinted from Alfred Marshall, *Principles of Economics* (London: Macmillan & Co., 1890), I, 300–1, 310–11, 314–17, 318–19, 322–25, 339–42, 344–46, 353–56, 359–66, 368–73.

Before Adam Smith's book had yet found many readers, biologists were already beginning to make great advances towards understanding the real nature of the differences in organization which separate the higher from the lower animals; and before two more generations had elapsed Malthus' historical account of man's struggle for existence set Darwin thinking as to the effects of the struggle for existence in the animal world. Since that time biology has more than repaid her debt; and economists have in their turn owed much to the many profound analogies which have been discovered between social and especially industrial organization on the one side, and the physical organization of the higher animals on the other. In a few cases indeed the apparent analogies disappeared on closer inquiry: but many of those which seemed at first sight most fanciful, have gradually been supplemented by others, and have at last established their claim to illustrate a fundamental unity of action between the laws of nature in the physical and in the moral world. This central unity is set forth in the general rule, to which there are not very many exceptions, that the development of the organism, whether social or physical, involves a greater subdivision of functions between its separate parts on the one hand, and on the other a more intimate connection between them. Each part gets to be less and less self-sufficient, to depend for its well-being more and more on other parts, so that no change can take place in any part of a highly developed organism without affecting others also.

This increased subdivision of functions, or "differentiation" as it is called, manifests itself with regard to industry in such forms as the division of labour, and the development of specialized skill, knowledge and machinery: while "integration," that is, a growing intimacy and firmness of the connections between the separate parts of the industrial organism, shows itself in such forms as the increase of security of commercial credit, and of the means and habits of communication by sea and road, by railway and telegraph, by post and printing-press.

*   *   *

The Division of Labour and the Influence of Machinery

The first condition of an efficient organization of industry is that it should keep every one employed at such work as his abilities and training fit him to do well, and should equip him with the best machinery and other appliances for his work. We shall leave on one side for the present the distribution of functions between those who carry out the details of production on the one hand, and those who manage its general arrangement and undertake its risks on the other; and confine ourselves to the division of labour between different classes of operations, with special reference to the influence of machinery. In the following chapter we shall consider the reciprocal effects of division of labour and localization of industry; in a third chapter we shall inquire how far the advantages of division of labour depend upon the aggregation of large capitals into the hands of single individuals or firms, or, as is commonly said, on production on a large scale; and lastly we shall examine the growing specialization of the work of business management.

Every one is familiar with the fact that "practice makes perfect," that it enables an operation, which at first seemed difficult, to be done after a time with comparatively little exertion, and yet much better than before; and physiology in some measure explains this fact. For it gives reasons for believing that the change is due to the gradual growth of new habits of more or less "reflex" or automatic action. Perfectly reflex actions, such as that of breathing during sleep, are performed by the responsibility of the local nerve centres without any reference to the supreme central authority of the thinking power, which is supposed to reside in the cerebrum. But all deliberate movements require the attention of the chief central authority: it receives information from the nerve centres or local authorities and perhaps in some cases direct from the sentient nerves, and sends back detailed and complex instructions to the local authorities or in some cases direct to muscular nerves, and so co-ordinates their action as to bring about the required results.

*   *   *

Again, in the wood and the metal industries, a man who has to perform exactly the same operations over and over again on the same piece of material gets into the habit of holding it exactly in the way in which it is wanted, and of arranging the tools and other things which he has to handle in such positions that he is able to bring them to work on one another with the least possible loss of time and of force in the movements of his own body. Accustomed to find them always in the same position and to take them in the same order, his hands work in harmony with one another almost automatically: and as his practice increases, his expenditure of nervous force diminishes even more rapidly than his expenditure of muscular force. But when the action has thus been reduced to routine it has nearly arrived at the stage at which it can be taken over by machinery. The chief difficulty to be overcome is that of getting the machinery to hold the material firmly in exactly the position in which the machine tool can be brought to bear on it in the right way, and without wasting meanwhile too much time in taking grip of it. But this can generally be contrived when it is worth while to spend some labour and expense on it; and then the whole operation can often be controlled by a worker who, sitting before the machine, takes with the left hand a piece of wood or metal from a heap and puts it in a socket, while with the right he draws down a lever, or in some other way sets the machine tool at work, and finally with his left hand throws on to another heap the material which has been cut or punched or drilled or planed exactly after a given pattern. It is in these industries especially that we find the reports of modern trades unions to be full of complaints that unskilled labourers, and even their wives and children, are put to do work which used to require the skill and judgment of a trained mechanic, but which has been reduced to mere routine by the improvement of machinery and the ever-increasing minuteness of the subdivision of labour.

We are thus led to a general rule, the action of which is more prominent in some branches of manufacture than others, but which applies to all. It is, that any manufacturing operation that can be reduced to uniformity, so that exactly the same thing has to be done over and over again in the same way, is sure to be taken over sooner or later by machinery. There may be delays and difficulties; but if the work to be done by it is on a sufficient scale, money and inventive power will be spent without stint on the task till it is achieved.

New machinery, when just invented, generally requires a great deal of care and attention. But the work of its attendant is always being sifted; that which is uniform and monotonous is gradually taken over by the machine, which thus becomes steadily more and more automatic and self-acting; till at last there is nothing for the hand to do, but to supply the material at certain intervals and to take away the work when finished. There still remains the responsibility for seeing that the machinery is in good order and working smoothly; but even this task is often made light by the introduction of an automatic movement, which brings the machine to a stop the instant anything goes wrong.

Nothing could be more narrow or monotonous than the occupation of a weaver of plain stuffs in the old time. But now one woman will manage four or more looms, each of which does many times as much work in the course of the day as the old hand loom did; and her work is much less monotonous and calls for much more judgment than his did. So that for every hundred yards of cloth that are woven, the purely monotonous work done by human beings is probably not a twentieth part of what it was.

Thus the two movements of the improvement of machinery and the growing subdivision of labour have gone together and are in some measure connected. But the connection is not so close as is generally supposed. It is the largeness of markets, the increased demand for great numbers of things of the same kind, and in some cases of things made with great accuracy, that leads to subdivision of labour; the chief effect of the improvement of machinery is to cheapen and make more accurate the work which would anyhow have been subdivided. For instance, "in organizing the works at Soho, Boulton and Watt found it necessary to carry division of labour to the furthest practical point. There were no slide-lathes, planing machines or boring tools, such as now render mechanical accuracy of construction almost a matter of certainty. Everything depended on the individual mechanic's accuracy of hand and eye; yet mechanics generally were much less skilled then than they are now. The way in which Boulton and Watt contrived partially to get over the difficulty was to confine their workmen to special classes of work, and make them as expert in them as possible. By continued practice in handling the same tools and fabricating the same articles, they thus acquired great individual proficiency." Thus machinery constantly supplants and renders unnecessary that purely manual skill, the attainment of which was, even up to Adam Smith's time, the chief advantage of division of labour. But this influence is more than countervailed by its tendency to increase the scale of manufactures and to make them more complex; and therefore to increase the opportunities for division of labour of all kinds, and especially in the matter of business management.

* * *

The influences which machinery exerts over the character of modern industry are well illustrated in the manufacture of watches. A few years ago the chief seat of this business was in French Switzerland; where the subdivision of labour was carried far, though a great part of the work was done by a more or less scattered population. There were about fifty distinct branches of trade each of which did one small part of the work. In almost all of them a highly specialized manual skill was required, but very little judgment; the earnings were generally low, because the trade had been established too long for those in it to have anything like a monopoly, and there was no difficulty in bringing up to it any child with ordinary intelligence. But this industry is now yielding ground to the American system of making watches by machinery, which requires very little specialized manual skill. In fact the machinery is becoming every year more and more automatic, and is getting to require less and less assistance from the human hand. But the more delicate the machine's power, the greater is the judgment and carefulness which is called for from those who see after it. Take for instance a beautiful machine which feeds itself with steelwire at one end, and delivers at the other tiny screws of exquisite form; it displaces a great many operatives who had indeed acquired a very high and specialized manual skill, but who lived sedentary lives, straining their eyesight through microscopes, and finding in their work very little scope for any faculty except a mere command over the use of their fingers. But the machine is intricate and costly, and the person who minds it must have an intelligence, and an energetic sense of responsibility, which go a long way towards making a fine character; and which, though more common than they were, are yet sufficiently rare to be able to earn a very high rate of pay. No doubt this is an extreme case; and the greater part of the work done in a watch factory is much simpler. But a great deal of it requires higher faculties than the old system did, and those engaged in it earn on the average higher wages; at the same time that it has already brought the price of a trustworthy watch within the range of the poorest classes of the community and is showing signs of being able soon to accomplish the very highest class of work.

*   *   *

Now looking at all this we are struck on the one hand by the power of mechanical and scientific appliances to attain results that would be impossible without them: and on the other hand by the persistent way in which they take over work that used to require manual skill and dexterity, but not much judgment; while they leave for man's hand all those parts which do require the use of judgment, and open up all sorts of new occupations in which there is a great demand for it. Every improvement and cheapening of the printer's appliances increases the demand for the judgment and discretion and literary knowledge of the reader, for the skill and taste of those who know how to set up a good title page, or how to make ready a sheet on which an engraving is to be printed, so that light and shade will be distributed properly. It increases the demand for the gifted and highly-trained artists who draw or engrave on wood and stone and metal, and for those who know how to give an accurate report

in ten lines of the substance of a speech that occupied ten minutes—an intellectual feat the difficulty of which we underrate, because it is so frequently performed. And again, it tends to increase the work of photographers and electrotypers, and stereotypers, of the makers of printer's machinery, and many others who get a higher training and a higher income from their work than did those layers on and takers off, and those folders of newspapers who have found their work taken over by iron fingers and iron arms.

We may now pass to consider the effects which machinery has in relieving that excessive muscular strain which a few generations ago was the common lot of more than half the working men even in such a country as England. The most marvellous instances of the power of machinery are seen in large iron works, and especially in those for making armour plates, where the force to be exerted is so great that man's muscles count for nothing, and where every movement, whether horizontal or vertical, has to be effected by hydraulic or steam force, and man stands by governing the machinery and occasionally clearing away ashes or performing some such secondary task. Machinery of this class has increased our command over nature, but it has not directly altered the character of man's work very much; for that which it does he could not have done without it. Let us then look at work such as that of house carpenters who make things of the same kind as those used by our forefathers, but with much less toil for themselves. They now give themselves chiefly to those parts of the task which are most pleasant and most interesting; while in every country town and almost every village there are found steam mills for sawing, planing and moulding, which relieve them of that grievous fatigue which not very long ago used to make them prematurely old.

Facts of this kind are to be found in the recent history of many trades: and they are of great importance when we are considering the way in which the modern organization of industry is tending to narrow the scope of each person's work, and thereby to render it monotonous. For those trades in which the work is most subdivided are those in which the chief muscular strain is most certain to be taken off by machinery; and thus the chief evil of monotonous work is much diminished. As Roscher says, it is monotony of life much more than monotony of work that is to be dreaded: monotony of work is an evil of the first order only when it involves monotony of life. Now when a person's employment requires much physical exertion, he is fit for nothing after his work; and unless his mental faculties are called forth in his work, they have little chance of being developed at all. But the nervous force is not very much exhausted in the ordinary work of a factory, at all events where there is not excessive noise, and where the hours of labour are not too long. The social surroundings in the factory and out of it stimulate mental activity; and even those workers in it whose occupations are seemingly the most monotonous have much more intelligence and mental resource than has been shown by the English agricultural labourer whose employment has more variety. It is true that the American agriculturist is an able man, and that his children rise rapidly in the world. But he has had better social conditions than the English; he has always had to think for himself, and has long had to use and to repair complex machines; and the English agricultural labourer is following in his steps, and is steadily improving his position.

Perhaps the textile industries afford the best instance of work that used to be done by hand and is now done by machinery. They are especially prominent in England, where they give employment to nearly half a million males and more than half a million females, or more than one in ten of those persons who are earning independent incomes. The strain that is taken off human muscles in dealing even with those soft materials is shewn by the fact that for every one of these million operatives there is used about one horse-power of steam, that is, about ten times as much as they would themselves exert if they were all strong men; and the history of these industries will serve to remind us that many of those who perform the more monotonous parts of manufacturing work are as a rule not skilled workers who have come down to it from a higher class of work, but unskilled workers who have risen to it. A great number of those who work in the Lancashire cotton mills have come there from poverty-stricken districts of Ireland, while others are the descendants of paupers and people of weak physique, who were sent there in large numbers early in the century from the most miserable conditions of life in the poorest agricultural districts, where the labourers were fed and housed almost worse than the animals whom they tended. Again, when regret is expressed that the cotton factory hands of New England have not the high standard of culture which prevailed among them a century ago, we must remember that the descendants of those factory workers have moved up to higher and more responsible posts, and include many of the ablest and wealthiest of the citizens of America. Those who have taken their places are in the process of being raised; they are chiefly French Canadians and Irish, who though they may learn in their new homes some of the vices of civilization, are yet much better off and have on the whole better opportunities of developing the higher faculties of themselves and their children than they had in their old homes.

But passing from this inquiry we must proceed to consider what are the conditions under which the economies in production arising from division of labour can best be secured. It is obvious that the efficiency of specialized machinery or specialized skill is but one condition of its economic use; the other is that sufficient work should be found to keep it well employed. As Babbage pointed out, in a large factory "the master manufacturer by dividing the work to be executed into different processes, each requiring different degrees of skill or force, can purchase exactly that precise quantity of both which is necessary for each process; whereas if the whole work were executed by one workman that person must possess sufficient skill to perform the most difficult and sufficient strength to execute the most laborious of the operations into which the work is divided." And it is to be noticed that the economy of production requires not only that each person should be employed constantly in a narrow range of work, but also that, when it is necessary for him to undertake different tasks, each of these tasks should be such as to call forth as much as possible of his skill and ability. Just in the same way the economy of machinery requires that a powerful turning-lathe when specially arranged for one class of work should be kept employed as long as possible on that work; and if after all it is necessary to employ it on other work, that should be such as to be worthy of the lathe, and not such as could have been done equally well by a much smaller machine.

Here then, so far as the economy of production goes, men and machines stand on much the same footing: but while machinery is a mere implement of production, man's welfare is also its ultimate aim. We have already been occupied with the question whether the human race as a whole gains by carrying to an extreme that specialization of function which causes all the most difficult work to be done by a few people: but we have now to consider it more nearly with special reference to the work of business management. The main drift of the next three chapters is to inquire what are the causes which make different forms of business management the fittest to profit by their environment, and the most likely to prevail over others; but it is well that meanwhile we should have in our minds the question, how far they are severally fitted to benefit their environment.

Many of those economies in the use of specialized skill and machinery which are commonly regarded as within the reach of very large establishments, can be secured in a great measure by the concentration of many small businesses of a similar character in particular localities: or, as is commonly said, by the localization of industry. This subject has such important bearings on much of our future work, that it will be worth while to study it with some care.

The Concentration of Specialized Industries in Particular Localities

In an early stage of civilization every place had to depend on its own resources for most of the heavy wares which it consumed; unless indeed it happened to have special facilities for water carriage. But the slowness with which customs changed, made it easy for producers to meet the wants of consumers with whom they had but very little communication; and it enabled comparatively poor people to buy a few expensive goods from a distance, in the security that they would add to the pleasure of festivals and holidays during a life time, or perhaps even during two or three life times. Consequently the lighter and more expensive articles of dress and personal adornment, together with spices and some kinds of metal implements used by all classes, and many other things for the special use of the rich, often came from astonishing distances. Some of these were produced only in a few places, or even only in one place; and they were diffused all over Europe partly by the agency of fairs and professional pedlars, and partly by the producers themselves, who would vary their work by travelling on foot for many thousand miles to sell their goods and see the world. These sturdy travellers took on themselves the risks of their little businesses; they enabled the production of certain classes of goods to be kept on the right track for satisfying the needs of purchasers far away; and they created new wants among consumers, by showing them at fairs or at their own houses new goods from a distant land.

This concentration of special groups of industry in particular localities, or the "localization of industry" as it is commonly called, began at an early stage in the world's history; and gradually prepared the way for many of the modern developments of division of labour in the mechanical arts and in the task of business management. Even now we find industries of a primitive fashion localized in retired villages of central Europe, and sending their simple wares even to the busiest haunts of modern industry. In Russia the expansion of a family group into a village has often been the cause of a localized industry; and there are an immense number of villages each of which carries on only one branch of production, or even only a part of one. There are for instance over 500 villages devoted to various branches of woodwork; one village makes nothing but spokes for the wheels of vehicles, another nothing but the bodies and so on; and indications of a like state of things are found in the histories of oriental civilizations and in the chronicles of mediæval Europe.

The causes by which localized industries have been originated are various. But the chief of them have been physical conditions; such as the character of the climate and the soil, of mines and quarries in the neighbourhood, or within easy access by land or water. Thus metallic industries have generally been either near mines or in places where fuel was cheap. The iron industries in England first sought those districts in which charcoal was plentiful, and afterwards they went to the neighbourhood of collieries. Staffordshire makes many kinds of pottery, all the materials of which are imported from a long distance; but she has cheap coal and excellent clay for making the heavy "seggars" or boxes in which the pottery is placed while being fired. Straw plaiting has its chief home in Bedfordshire, where straw has just the right proportion of silex to give strength without brittleness; and Buckinghamshire beeches have afforded the material for the Wycombe chairmaking. The Sheffield cutlery trade is due chiefly to the excellent grit of which its grindstones are made.

Another chief cause has been the patronage of a court. The rich folk there assembled make a demand for goods of specially high quality, and this attracts skilled workmen from a distance, and educates those on the spot. When an Eastern potentate changed his residence—and, partly for sanitary reasons, this was constantly done—the deserted town was apt to take refuge in the development of a specialized industry, which had owed its origin to the presence of the court. But very often the rulers deliberately invited artisans from a distance and settled them in a group together. Thus the mechanical faculty of Lancashire is said to be due to the influence of Norman smiths who were settled at Warrington by Hugo de Lupus in William the Conqueror's time. While the greater part of England's manufacturing industry before the era of cotton and steam had its course directed by settlements of Flemish and Huguenot artisans; many of which were made under the immediate direction of Plantagenet and Tudor kings. These immigrants taught us how to weave woollen and worsted stuffs, though for a long time we sent our cloths to the Netherlands to be fulled and dyed. They taught us how to cure herrings, how to manufacture silk, how to make lace, glass, and paper, and to provide for many other of our wants.

But how did these immigrants learn their skill? Their ancestors had no doubt profited by the traditional arts of earlier civilizations on the shores of the Mediterranean and in the far East: for nearly all important knowledge has long deep roots stretching downwards to distant times; and so widely spread have been these roots, so ready to send up shoots of vigorous life, that there is perhaps no part of the old world in which there might not long ago have flourished many beautiful and highly skilled industries, if their growth had been favoured by the character of the people, and by their social and political institutions. This accident or that may have determined whether a particular industry flourished in any one town; the industrial character of a whole country even may have been largely influenced by the richness of her soil and her mines, and her facilities for commerce. Such natural advantages may themselves have stimulated free industry and enterprise: but it is the existence of these last, by whatever means they may have been promoted, which has been the supreme condition for the growth of noble forms of the arts of life. In sketching the history of free industry and enterprise we have already incidentally traced the outlines of the causes which have localized the industrial leadership of the world now in this country and now in that. We have seen how physical nature acts on man's energies, how he is stimulated by an invigorating climate, and how he is encouraged to bold ventures by the opening out of rich fields for his work: but we have also seen how the use he makes of these advantages depends on his ideals of life, and how inextricably therefore the religious, political and economic threads of the world's history are interwoven; while together they have been bent this way or that by great political events and the influence of the strong personalities of individuals.

The causes which determine the economic progress of nations will require further study when we come to discuss the problems of international trade. But for the present we must turn aside from these broader movements of the localization of industry; and follow the fortunes of groups of skilled workers who are gathered within the narrow boundaries of a manufacturing town or a thickly peopled industrial district.

When then an industry has once chosen a locality for itself, it is likely to stay there long: so great are the advantages which people following the same skilled trade get from near neighbourhood to one another. The mysteries of the trade become no mysteries; but are as it were in the air, and children learn many of them unconsciously. Good work is rightly appreciated, inventions and improvements in machinery, in processes and the general organization of the business have their merits promptly discussed; if one man starts a new idea it is taken up by others and combined with suggestions of their own; and thus becomes the source of yet more new ideas.

And subsidiary trades grow up in the neighbourhood, supplying it with implements and materials, organizing its traffic, and in many ways conducing to the economy of its material.

Again the economic use of expensive machinery can sometimes be attained in a very high degree in a district in which there is a large aggregate production of the same kind, even though no individual capital employed in the trade be very large. For subsidiary industries devoting themselves each to one small branch of the process of production, and working it for a great many of their neighbours, are able to keep in constant use machinery of the most highly specialized character; and to make it pay its expenses, though its original cost may have been high, and its rate of depreciation very rapid.

Again, in all but the earliest stages of economic development a localized industry gains a great advantage from the fact that it offers a constant market for skill. Employers are apt to resort to any place where they are likely to find a good choice of workers with the special skill which they require; while men seeking employment naturally go to places where they expect to find a good market for their skill, in consequence of the presence of many employers who require its aid. The owner of an isolated factory is often put to great shifts for want of some special skilled labour which has suddenly run short; and a skilled workman, when thrown out of employment in it, has no easy refuge. Social forces here co-operate with economic: there are often strong friendships between employers and employed; but neither side likes to feel that in case of any disagreeable incident happening between them, they must go on rubbing against one another: both sides like to be able easily to break off old associations should they become irksome. These difficulties are still very great, though they are being diminished by the railway, the printing press and the telegraph.

On the other hand a localized industry has some disadvantages as a market for labour if the work done in it is chiefly of one kind, such for instance as can be done only by strong men. In those iron districts in which there are no textile or other factories to give employment to women and children, wages are high and the cost of labour dear to the employer, while the average money earnings of each family are low. But the remedy for this evil is obvious, and is found in the growth in the same neighbourhood of industries of a supplementary character. Thus textile industries are constantly found congregated in the neighbourhood of mining and engineering industries, in some cases having been attracted by almost imperceptible steps; in others, as for instance at Barrow, having been started deliberately on a large scale in order to give variety of employment in a place where previously there had been but little demand for the work of women and children.

The advantages of variety of employment are combined with those of localized industries in some of our manufacturing towns, and this is a chief cause of their continued growth. But on the other hand the value which the central sites of a large town have for trading purposes, enables them to command much higher ground-rents than the situations are worth for factories, even when account is taken of this combination of advantages: and there is a similar competition for dwelling space between the employés of the trading houses, and the factory workers. The result is that factories now congregate in the outskirts of large towns and in manufacturing districts in their neighbourhood rather than in the towns themselves.

A district which is dependent chiefly on one industry is liable to extreme depression, in case of a falling off in the demand for its produce, or of a failure in the supply of the raw material which it uses. This evil again is in a great measure avoided by those large towns, or large industrial districts in which several distinct industries are strongly developed. If one of them fails for a time, the others are likely to support it in many ways, chiefly indirect; one of these being that they keep in heart the local shopkeepers, who are thus enabled to continue their assistance longer than they otherwise could, to the work-people in those trades that happen to be depressed.

Every cheapening of the means of communication, every new facility for the free interchange of ideas between distant places alters the action of the forces which tend to localize industries. Speaking generally we may say that a lowering of tariffs, or of freights for the transport of goods, tends to make each locality buy more largely from a distance what it requires; and thus tends to concentrate particular industries in special localities: but on the other hand every thing that increases people's readiness to migrate from one place to another, tends to bring skilled artisans to ply their crafts

near to the consumers who will purchase their wares. These two opposing tendencies are well illustrated by the recent history of the English people.

On the one hand the steady cheapening of freights, the opening of railways from the agricultural districts of America and India to the seaboard, and the adoption by England of a free-trade policy, have led to a great increase in her importation of raw produce. But on the other hand the growing cheapness, rapidity and comfort of foreign travel, are inducing her trained business men and her skilled artisans to pioneer the way for new industries in other lands, and to help them to manufacture for themselves goods which they have been wont to buy from England. English mechanics have taught people in almost every part of the world how to use English machinery, and even how to make the machinery like it; and English miners have opened out mines of ore which have diminished the foreign demand for many of England's products.

One of the most striking movements towards the specialization of a country's industries, which history records, is the rapid increase of the non-agricultural population of England in recent times.

Production on a Large Scale

The advantages of production on a large scale are best shown in manufacture; under which head we may include all businesses engaged in working up material into forms in which it will be adapted for sale in distant markets: the characteristic of manufacturing industries which makes them offer generally the best illustrations of the advantages of production on a large scale, is their power of choosing freely the locality in which they will do their work. They are thus contrasted on the one hand with agriculture and other extractive industries, (mining, quarrying, fishing etc.), the geographical distribution of which is determined by nature; and on the other hand with industries that make or repair things to suit the special needs of individual consumers, from whom they cannot be far removed, at all events without great loss.

The chief advantages of production on a large scale are economy of skill, economy of machinery and economy of materials: but the last of these is rapidly losing importance relatively to the other two. It is true that an isolated workman often throws away a number of small things which would have been collected and turned to good account in a factory; but waste of this kind can scarcely occur in a localized manufacture even if it is in the hands of small men; and there is not very much of it in any branch of industry in modern England, except perhaps in agriculture and in domestic cooking. No doubt many of the most important advances of recent years have been due to the utilizing of what had been a waste product; but this has been generally due to a distinct invention, either chemical or mechanical, the use of which has been indeed promoted by minute subdivision of labour, but has not been directly dependent on it. Again it is true that when a hundred suits of furniture, or of clothing, have to be cut out on exactly the same pattern, it is worth while to spend great care on so planning the cutting out of the boards or the cloth, that only a few small pieces are wasted. But this is properly an economy of skill; one planning is made to suffice for many tasks, and therefore can be done well and carefully. We may pass then to the economy of machinery.

In spite of the aid which subsidiary industries can give to small manufactures, where many in the same branch of trade are collected in one neighbourhood, they are still placed under a great disadvantage by the growing variety and expensiveness of machinery. For in a large establishment there are often many expensive machines each made specially for one small use. Each of them requires space in a good light, and thus stands for something considerable in the rent and general expenses of the factory; and independently of interest and the expense of keeping it in repair a heavy allowance must be made for depreciation in consequence of its being probably improved upon before long. A small manufacturer must therefore have many things done by hand or by imperfect machinery, though he knows how to have them done better and cheaper by special machinery, if only he could find constant employment for it.

But next, a small manufacturer may not always be acquainted with the best machinery for his purpose. It is true that if the industry in which he is engaged has been long established on a large scale, his machinery will be well up to the mark, provided he can afford to buy the best in the market. In agriculture and the cotton industries for instance, improvements in machinery are devised almost exclusively by machine makers, and are accessible to all, at any rate on paying a royalty for patent right. But this is not the case in industries that are as yet in an early stage of development or are rapidly changing their form; such as the chemical industries, the watchmaking industry and some branches of the jute and silk manufactures; and in a host of trades that are constantly springing up to supply some new want or to work up some new material.

In all such trades new machinery and new processes are for the greater part devised by manufac-turers for their own use. Each new departure is an experiment which may fail; those which succeed must pay for themselves and for the failure of others; and though a small manufacturer may think he sees his way to an improvement, he must reckon on having to work it out tentatively, at considerable risk and expense and with much interruption to his other work; and even if he should be able to perfect it, he is not likely to be able to make the most of it. For instance, he may have devised a new specialty, which would get a large sale if it could be brought under general notice: but to do this would perhaps cost many thousand pounds; and if so he will probably have to turn his back on it. For it is almost impossible for him to discharge, what Roscher calls the characteristic task of the modern manufacturer, that of creating new wants by showing people something which they had never thought of having before; but which they want to have as soon as the notion is suggested to them. In the pottery trade for example the small manufacturer cannot afford even to make experiments with new patterns and designs except in a very tentative way. His chance is better with regard to an improvement in making things for which there is already a good market. But even here he cannot get the full benefit of his invention unless he patents it; and sells the right to use it; or borrows some capital and extends his business; or lastly changes the character of his business and devotes his capital to that particular stage of the manufacture to which his improvement applies. But after all such cases are exceptional: the growth of machinery in variety and expensiveness presses hard on the small manufacturer everywhere. It has already driven him completely out of some trades and is fast driving him out of others.

*   *   *

The large manufacturer has a much better chance than a small one has, of getting hold of men with exceptional natural abilities, to do the most difficult part of his work—that on which the reputation of his establishment chiefly depends. This is occasionally important as regards mere handiwork in trades which require much taste and originality, as for instance that of a house decorator, and in those which require exceptionally fine workmanship, as for instance that of a manufacturer of delicate mechanism. But in most businesses, its chief importance lies in the facilities which it gives to the employer for the selection of able and tried men, men whom he trusts and who trust him, to be his foremen and heads of departments. We are thus brought to the central problem of the modern organization of industry, viz. that which relates to the advantages and disadvantages of the subdivision of the work of business management.

The head of a large business can reserve all his strength for the broadest and most fundamental problems of his trade: he must indeed assure himself that his managers, clerks and foremen are the right men for their work, and are doing their work well; but beyond this he need not trouble himself much about details. He can keep his mind fresh and clear for thinking out the most difficult and vital problems of his business; for studying the broader movements of the markets, the yet undeveloped results of current events at home and abroad; and for contriving how to improve the organization of the internal and external relations of his business.

For much of this work the small employer has not the time if he has the ability; he cannot take so broad a survey of his trade, or look so far ahead; he must often be content to follow the lead of others. And yet he must spend much of his time on work that is below him; for if he is to succeed at all, he must have a good deal of originating and organizing force; his mind must be in some respects of a high quality; and his strength is wasted when he occupies himself, as he must do to a great extent, with easy but tedious routine work.

On the other hand the small employer has great advantages of his own. The master's eye is everywhere; there is no shirking by his foremen or workmen. Again by keeping things himself under lock and key, and in other ways, he can save much of the book-keeping, and nearly all of the cumbrous system of checks that are necessary in the business of a large firm. The gain from this source is of very great importance in trades which use the more valuable metals and other expensive materials.

And though he must always remain at a great disadvantage in getting information and in making experiments; yet in this matter the general course of progress is on his side. For newspapers, and trade and technical publications of all kinds are perpetually scouting for him and bringing him much of the knowledge he wants—knowledge which a little while ago would have been beyond the reach of anyone who could not afford to have well-paid agents in many distant parts. Again it is to his interest also that the secrecy of business is on the whole diminishing, and that the most important improvements in method seldom remain secret for long after they have passed from the experimental stage. It is to his advantage that changes in manufacture depend less on mere rules of thumb and more on broad developments of scientific principle; and that many of these are made by students in the pursuit of knowledge for its own sake, and are promptly published in the general interest. Although therefore the small manufacturer can seldom be in the front of the race of progress, he need not be far from it, if he has the time and the ability for availing himself of the modern facilities for obtaining knowledge. But it is true that he must be exceptionally strong if he can do this without neglecting the minor but necessary details of the business.

*   *   *

Business Management

Business may be taken to include all provision for the wants of others which is made in the expectation of payment direct or indirect from those who are to be benefitted. It is thus contrasted with the provision for our own wants which each of us makes for himself, and with those kindly services which are prompted by family affection and the desire to promote the well-being of others. Business management or undertaking has always had many different forms, and their number and variety was never so great as in England now. Relics remain of almost every form that has ever been in use; while new forms are constantly being developed.

The primitive handicraftsman managed his whole business for himself; but since his customers were with few exceptions his immediate neighbours, since he required very little capital, since the plan of production was arranged for him by custom, and since he had no labour to superintend outside of his own household, these tasks did not involve any very great mental strain. He was far from enjoying unbroken prosperity; war and scarcity were constantly pressing on him and his neighbours, hindering his work and stopping their demand for his wares. But he was inclined to take good and evil fortune, like sunshine and rain, as things beyond his control: his fingers worked on, but his brain was seldom weary.

Even in modern England we find now and then a village artisan who adheres to primitive methods, and makes things on his own account for sale to his neighbours; managing his own business and undertaking all its risks. But such cases are rare: the most striking instances of an adherence to old-fashioned methods of business are supplied by the learned professions; for a physician or a solicitor manages as a rule his own business and does all its work. This plan is not without its disadvantages: much valuable activity is wasted or turned to but slight account by some professional men of first-rate ability, who have not the special aptitude required for obtaining a business connection; they would be better paid, would lead happier lives, and would do more good service for the world if their work could be arranged for them by some sort of a middleman. But yet on the whole things are probably best as they are: there are sound reasons behind the popular instinct which distrusts the intrusion of the middleman in the supply of those services which require the highest and most delicate mental qualities, and which can have their full value only when there is complete personal confidence.

English solicitors however act, if not as employers or undertakers, yet as agents for hiring that branch of the legal profession which ranks highest, and whose work involves the hardest mental strain. Again many of the best instructors of youths sell their services, not directly to the consumer, but to the governing body of a college or school, or to a head master, who arranges for their purchase: the employer supplies to the teacher a market for his labour; and is supposed to give to the purchaser, who may not be a good judge himself, some sort of guarantee as to the quality of the teaching supplied.

Again, artists of every kind, however eminent, often find it to their advantage to employ some one else to arrange for them with customers; while those of less established repute are sometimes dependent for their living on capitalist traders, who are not themselves artists, but who understand how to sell artistic work to the best advantage.

But we have already seen how unsuitable the primitive pattern is for the greater part of the business of the modern world. The task of directing production so that a given effort may be most effective in supplying human wants is so difficult under the complex conditions of modern life, that it has to be broken up and given into the hands of a specialized body of employers, or to use a more general term, of business men; who "adventure" or "undertake" its risks; who bring together the capital and the labour required for the work; who arrange or "engineer" its general plan, and who superintend its minor details. Looking at business men from one point of view we may regard them as a highly skilled industrial grade, from another as middlemen intervening between the manual worker and the consumer.

There are some kinds of business men who undertake great risks, and exercise a large influence over the welfare both of the producers and of the consumers of the wares in which they deal, but who are not to any considerable extent direct employers of labour. The extreme type of these is the dealer on the stock exchange or the produce markets, whose daily purchases and sales are of vast dimensions, and who yet has neither factory nor warehouse, but at most an office with a few clerks in it. The good and the evil effects of the action of speculators such as these are however so complex themselves, and are so intimately interwoven with fluctuations of commercial credit and the changes of the money market that they cannot be conveniently discussed in this place. It is true that there is an element of speculation in almost every kind of business: but in this early stage of our inquiry it is best that we should give our chief attention to those forms of business in which administration counts for most and the subtler forms of speculation for least. Let us then take some illustrations of the more common types of business, and watch the relations in which the undertaking of risks stands to the rest of the work of the business man.

The building trade will serve our purpose well, partly because it adheres in some respects to primitive methods of business. Late in the Middle Ages it was quite common for a private person to build a house for himself without the aid of a master builder; and the habit is not even now altogether extinct. A person who undertakes his own building must hire separately all his workmen, he must watch their work and check their demands for payment; he must buy his materials from many quarters, and he must dispense with the use of expensive machinery unless he happens to be able to hire it. In the result he probably pays more than the current wages; but as others gain what he loses, there is no resultant waste so far. There is however great waste in the time he spends in bargaining with the men and testing and directing their work by his imperfect knowledge; and again in the time that he spends in finding out what kinds and quantities he wants of different materials, and where to get them best, and so on. This waste is avoided by that division of labour which assigns to the professional builder the task of superintending details, and to the professional architect the task of drawing plans.

The division of labour is often carried still further when houses are built not at the expense of those who are to live in them, but as a building speculation. When this is done on a large scale, as for instance in opening out a new suburb, the stakes at issue are so large as to offer an attractive field to powerful capitalists with a very high order of general business ability, but perhaps with not much technical knowledge of the building trade. They rely on their own judgment of the decision as to what are likely to be the coming relations of demand and supply for different kinds of houses; but they intrust to others the management of details. They employ architects and surveyors to make plans in accordance with their general directions; and then enter in to contracts with professional builders for carrying them out. But they themselves undertake the chief risks of the business, and control its general direction.

*   *   *

When the profits of business are under discussion they are generally connected in people's minds with the employer of labour: "the employer" is often taken as a term practically coextensive with the receiver of business profits. But the instances which we have just considered are sufficient to illustrate the truth that the superintendence of labour is but one side, and often not the most important side of business work; and that the employer who undertakes the whole risks of his business really performs two entirely distinct services on behalf of the community, and requires a twofold ability.

The ideal manufacturer for instance, if he makes goods not to meet special orders but for the general market, must, in his first rôle as merchant and organizer of production, have a thorough knowledge of *things* in his own trade. He must have the power of forecasting the broad movements of production and consumption, of seeing where there is an opportunity for supplying a new commodity that will meet a real want or improving the plan of producing an old commodity. He must be able to judge cautiously and undertake risks boldly; and he must of course understand the materials and machinery used in his trade.

But secondary in his rôle of employer he must be a natural leader of *men*. He must have a power of first choosing his assistants rightly and then trusting them fully; of interesting them in the business and of getting them to trust him, so as to bring out whatever enterprise and power of origination there is in them; while he himself exercises a general control over everything, and preserves order and unity in the main plan of the business.

The abilities required to make an ideal employer are so great and so numerous that very few persons can exhibit them all in a very high degree. Their relative importance however varies with the nature of the industry and the size of the business; and while one employer excels in one set of qualities, another excels in another; scarcely any two owe their success to exactly the same combination of advantages. Some men make their way by the use of none but noble qualities, while others owe their prosperity to qualities in which there is very little that is really admirable except sagacity and strength of purpose.

Such then being the general nature of the work of business management, we have next to inquire what opportunities different classes of people have of developing business ability; and, when they have obtained that, what opportunities they have of getting command over the capital required to give it scope. This inquiry may conveniently be combined with some examination of the different "forms of business management." Hitherto we have considered almost exclusively that form in which the whole responsibility and control rests in the hands

of a single individual. But this form is yielding ground to others in which the supreme authority is distributed among several partners or even a great number of shareholders. Private firms and joint stock companies, co-operative societies and public corporations are taking a constantly increasing share in the management of business; and one chief reason of this is that they offer an attractive field to people who have good business abilities, but have not inherited any great business opportunities.

The son of a man already established in business has certainly very great advantages over others. He has from his youth up special facilities for obtaining the knowledge and developing the faculties that are required in the management of his father's business: he learns quietly and almost unconsciously about men and manners in his father's trade and in those from which that trade buys and to which it sells; he gets to know the relative importance and the real significance of the various problems and anxieties which occupy his father's mind: and he acquires a technical knowledge of the processes and the machinery of the trade. Some of what he learns will be applicable only to his father's trade; but the greater part will be serviceable in any trade that is in any way allied with that; while those general faculties of judgment and resource, of enterprise and caution, of firmness and courtesy, which are trained by association with those who control the larger issues of any one trade, will go a long way towards fitting him for managing almost any other trade. Further the sons of successful business men start with more material capital than almost any one else except those who by nurture and education are likely to be disinclined for business and unfitted for it: and if they continue their father's work, they have also the vantage ground of established trade connections. It would therefore at first sight seem likely that business men should constitute a sort of caste; dividing out among their sons the chief posts of command, and founding hereditary dynasties, which should rule certain branches of trade for many generations together. But the actual state of things is very different.

As a matter of fact when a man has got together a great business, his descendants, in spite of all their great advantages, often fail to develop the high abilities and the special turn of mind and temperament required for carrying it on with equal success. He himself was probably brought up by parents of strong earnest character; and was educated by their personal influence and by struggle with difficulties in early life. But his children, at all events if they were born after he became rich, and in any case his grand-children, are perhaps left a good deal to the care of domestic servants who are not of the same strong fibre as the parents by whose influence he was educated. And while his highest ambition was probably success in business, they are likely to be at least equally anxious for social or academic distinction.

For a time indeed all may go well. His sons find a firmly established trade connection and, what is perhaps even more important, a well chosen staff of subordinates with a generous interest in the business. By mere assiduity and caution, availing themselves of the traditions of the firm, they may hold together for a long time. But when a full generation has passed, when the old traditions are no longer a safe guide, and when the bonds that held together the old staff have been dissolved, then the business almost invariably falls to pieces unless it is practically handed over to the management of new men who have meanwhile risen to partnership in the firm.

But in most cases his descendants arrive at this result by a shorter route. They prefer an abundant income coming to them without effort on their part, to one which though twice as large could be earned only by incessant toil and anxiety; and they sell the business to private persons or a joint stock company; or they become sleeping partners in it; that is sharing in its risks and in its profits, but not taking part in its management: in either case the active control over their capital falls chiefly into the hands of new men.

The oldest and simplest plan for renovating the energies of a business is that of taking into partnership some of its ablest employés. The autocratic owner and manager of a large manufacturing or trading concern finds that, as years go on, he has to delegate more and more responsibility to his chief subordinates; partly because the work to be done is growing heavier, and partly because his own strength is becoming less than it was. He still exercises a supreme control, but much must depend on their energy and probity: so, if his sons are not old enough, or for any other reason are not ready to take part of the burden off his shoulders, he decides to stimulate the zeal of one or more of his trusted assistants by taking them into partnership: he thus lightens his own labours, at the same time that he secures that the task of his life will be carried on by those whose habits he has moulded, and for whom he has perhaps acquired something like a fatherly affection. Much of the happiest romance of life, much that is most pleasant to dwell upon in the social history of England from the Middle Ages up to our own day is connected with the story of private partnerships of this class.

But there are now, and there always have been private partnerships on more equal terms, two or more people of about equal wealth and ability combining their resources for a large and difficult undertaking. In such cases there is often a distinct partition of the work of management: in manufactures for instance one partner will sometimes give himself almost exclusively to the work of buying raw material and selling the finished product, while the other is responsible for the management of the factory: and in a trading establishment one partner will control the wholesale and the other the retail department. In these and other ways private partnership is capable of adapting itself to a great variety of problems: it is very strong and very elastic; it has played a great part in the past, and it is full of vitality now.

But the expansion of old trades and the growth of new trades have long tended to outgrow the capitals that can easily be obtained by private companies; and from the end of the Middle Ages to the present time there has been a movement of constantly increasing force towards the substitution of public joint stock companies, the shares of which can be sold to anybody in the open market, for private companies, the shares in which are not transferable without the leave of all concerned; and various plans, with which we need not occupy ourselves just now, have been adopted in different countries for enabling the shareholders to limit their risks to their shares. The effect of this change has been to induce people, many of whom have no special knowledge of trade, to give their capital into the hands of others employed by them: and there has thus arisen a new distribution of the various parts of the work of business management.

The ultimate undertakers of the risks incurred by a joint stock company are the shareholders; but as a rule they do not take much active part in engineering the business and controlling its general policy; and they take no part in superintending its details. After the business has once got out of the hands of its original promoters, the control of it is left chiefly in the hands of Directors; who, if the company is a very large one, probably own but a very small proportion of its shares, while the greater part of them have not much technical knowledge of the work to be done. They are not generally expected to give their whole time to it; but they are supposed to bring wide general knowledge and sound judgment to bear on the broader problems of its policy; and at the same time to make sure that the "Managers" of the company are doing their work thoroughly. To the Managers and their assistants is left a great part of the work of engineering the business, and the whole of the work of superintending it: but they are not required to bring any capital into it; and they are supposed to be promoted from the lower ranks to the higher according to their zeal and ability. Since the joint stock companies in the United Kingdom have an aggregate income of £100,000,000, and do a tenth of the business of all kinds that is done in the country, they offer very large opportunities to men with natural talents for business management, who have not inherited any material capital, or any business connection.

Joint stock companies have great elasticity and can expand themselves without limit when the work to which they have set themselves offers a wide scope; and they are gaining ground in nearly all directions. But they have one great source of weakness in the absence of any adequate knowledge of the business on the part of the shareholders who undertake its chief risks. It is true that the head of a large private firm undertakes the chief risks of the business, while he intrusts many of its details to others; but his position is secured by his power of forming a direct judgment as to whether his subordinates serve his interests faithfully and discreetly. If those to whom he has intrusted the buying or selling of goods for him take commissions from those with whom they deal, he is in a position to discover and punish the fraud. If they show favouritism and promote incompetent relations or friends of their own, or if they themselves become idle and shirk their work, or even if they do not fulfil the promise of exceptional ability which induced him to give them their first lift, he can discover what is going wrong and set it right.

But in all these matters the great body of the shareholders of a joint stock company are, save in a few exceptional instances, almost powerless; though a few of the larger shareholders often exert themselves to find out what is going on; and are thus able to exercise an effective and wise control over the general management of the business. It is a strong proof of the marvellous growth in recent times of a spirit of honesty and uprightness in commercial matters, that the leading officers of great public companies yield as little as they do to the vast temptations to fraud which lie in their way. If they showed an eagerness to avail themselves of opportunities for wrong-doing at all approaching that of which we read in the commercial history of earlier civilization, their wrong uses of the trusts imposed in them would have been on so great a scale as to prevent the development of this democratic form of business. There is every reason to hope that the progress of trade morality will continue, aided in the future as it has been in the past, by a diminution of trade secrecy and by increased publicity in every form; and thus collective and democratic forms of business management may be able to extend themselves safely in many directions in which they have hitherto failed, and may

far exceed the great services they already render in opening a large career to those who have no advantages of birth.

The same may be said of the undertakings of governments imperial and local: they also may have a great future before them, but up to the present time the tax-payer who undertakes the ultimate risks has not generally succeeded in exercising an efficient control over the businesses, and in securing officers who will do their work with as much energy and enterprise as is shown in private establishments. The problem of government undertakings involves however many important side issues, which will require our careful attention later on.

* * *

In speaking of the difficulty that a working man has in rising to a post in which he can turn his business ability to full account, the chief stress is commonly laid upon his want of capital: but this is not always his chief difficulty. For instance the co-operative distributive societies have accumulated a vast capital, on which they find it difficult to get a good rate of interest; and which they would be rejoiced to lend to any set of working men who could show that they had the capacity for dealing with difficult business problems. Co-operators who have firstly a high order of business ability and probity, and secondly the "personal capital" of great reputation among their fellows for these qualities, will have no difficulty in getting command of enough material capital for a considerable undertaking: the real difficulty is to convince a sufficient number of those around them that they have these rare qualities. And the case is not very different when an individual endeavours to obtain from the ordinary sources the loan of the capital required to start him in business.

It is true that in almost every business there is a constant increase in the amount of capital required to make a fair start; but there is a much more rapid increase in the amount of capital which is owned by people who do not want to use it themselves, and are so eager to lend it out that they will accept a constantly lower and lower rate of interest for it. Much of this capital passes into the hands of bankers and others, people of keen intellect and restless energy; people who have no class prejudices and care nothing for social distinctions; and who would promptly lend it to any one of whose business ability and honesty they were convinced. To say nothing of the credit that can be got in many businesses from those who supply the requisite raw material or stock in trade, the opportunities for direct borrowing are now so great that an increase in the amount of capital required for a start in business is no very serious obstacle in the way of a person who has once got over the initial difficulty of earning a reputation for being likely to use it well.

And perhaps a greater though not so conspicuous hindrance to the rise of the working man is the growing complexity of business. The head of a business has now to think of many things about which he never used to trouble himself in earlier days; and these are just the kind of difficulties for which the training of the workshop affords the least preparation. Against this must be set the rapid improvement of the education of the working man not only at school, but what is more important, in after life by newspapers and from the work of co-operative societies and trades unions, and in other ways.

About three-fourths of the whole population of England belong to the wage-earning classes; and at all events when they are well fed, properly housed and educated, they have their fair share of that nervous strength which is the raw material of business ability. Without going out of their way they are all consciously or unconsciously competitors for posts of business command. The ordinary workman if he shows ability generally becomes a foreman, from that he may rise to be a manager, and to be taken into partnership with his employer. Or having saved a little of his own he may start one of those small shops which still can hold their own in a working man's quarter, stock it chiefly on credit, and let his wife attend to it by day, while he gives his evenings to it. In these or in other ways he may increase his capital till he can start a small workshop, or factory. Once having made a good beginning he will find the banks eager to give him generous credit. He must have time; and since he is not likely to start in business till after middle age he must have a long as well as a strong life; but if he has this and has also "patience, genius and good fortune" he is pretty sure to command a large capital before he dies. In a factory those who work with their hands, have better opportunities of rising to posts of command than the book-keepers and many others to whom social tradition has assigned a higher place. But in trading concerns it is otherwise; what manual work is done in them has as a rule no educating character, while the experience of the office is better adapted for preparing a man to manage a commercial than a manufacturing business.

There is then on the whole a broad movement from below upwards. There are perhaps not so many who rise at once from the position of working men to that of employers: but there are more who get on sufficiently far to give their sons a good chance of attaining to the highest posts. The com-

plete rise is not so very often accomplished in one generation; it is more often spread over two; but the total volume of the movement upwards is probably greater than it has ever been. And it may be remarked in passing that it is better for society as a whole that the rise should be distributed over two generations. The workmen who at the beginning of this century rose in such large numbers to become employers were seldom fit for posts of command: they were too often harsh and tyrannical; they lost their self-control, and were neither truly noble nor truly happy; while their children were often haughty, extravagant, and self-indulgent, squandering their wealth on low and vulgar amusements, having the worst faults of the older aristocracy without their virtues. The foreman or superintendent who has still to obey as well as to command, but who is rising and sees his children likely to rise further, is in some ways more to be envied than the small master. His success is less conspicuous, but his work is often higher and more important for the world, while his character is more gentle and refined and not less strong. His children are well-trained; and if they get wealth, they are likely to make a fairly good use of it.

When a man of great ability is once at the head of an independent business, whatever be the route by which he has got there, he will with moderate good fortune, soon be able to show such evidence of his power of turning capital to good account as to enable him to borrow in one way or another almost any amount that he may need. Making good profits he adds to his own capital, and this extra capital of his own is a material security for further borrowings; while the fact that he has made it himself tends to make lenders less careful to insist on a full security for their loans. Of course fortune tells for much in business: a very able man may find things going against him; the fact that he is losing money may diminish his power of borrowing. If he is working partly on borrowed capital, it may even make those who have lent it, refuse to renew their loans, and may thus cause him to succumb to what would have been but a passing misfortune, if he had been using no capital but his own: and in fighting his way upwards he may have a chequered life full of great anxieties, and even misfortunes. But he can show his ability in misfortune as well as in success: human nature is sanguine; and it is notorious that men are abundantly willing to lend to those who have passed through commercial disaster without loss to their business reputation. Thus, in spite of vicissitudes, the able business man generally finds that in the long run the capital at his command grows in proportion to his ability.

Meanwhile he, who with small ability is in command of a large capital, speedily loses it: he may perhaps be one who could and would have managed a small business with credit, and left it stronger than he had found it: but if he has not the genius for dealing with large problems, the larger it is the more speedily will he break it up. For as a rule a large business can be kept going only by transactions which, after allowing for ordinary risks, leave but a very small percentage of gain. A small profit on a large turn-over quickly made, will yield a rich income to able men: and in those businesses which are of such a nature as to give scope to very large capitals, competition generally cuts the rate of profits on the turn-over very fine. A village trader may make five per cent. less profits on his turn-over than his abler rival, and yet be able to hold his head above water. But in those large manufacturing and trading businesses in which there is a quick return and a straightforward routine, the whole profits on the turn-over are often so very small that a person who falls behind his rivals by even a small percentage loses a large sum at every turn-over; while in those large businesses which are difficult and do not rely on routine, and which afford high profits on the turn-over to really able management, there are no profits at all to be got by anyone who attempts the task with only ordinary ability.

These two sets of forces, the one increasing the capital at the command of able men, and the other destroying the capital that is in the hands of weaker men, bring about the result that there is a far more close correspondence between the ability of business men and the size of the businesses which they own than at first sight would appear probable. And when to this fact we add all the many routes, which we have already discussed, by which a man of great natural business ability can work his way up high in some private firm or public company, we may conclude that wherever there is work on a large scale to be done in such a country as England, the ability and the capital required for it are pretty sure to be speedily forthcoming.

Further, just as industrial skill and ability are getting every day to depend more and more on the broad faculties of judgment, promptness, resource, carefulness and steadfastness of purpose—faculties which are not specialized to any one trade, but which are more or less useful in all—so it is with regard to business ability. In fact business ability consists more of these general and non-specialized faculties than do industrial skill and ability in the lower grades: and the higher the grade of business ability the more various are its applications.

Since then business ability in command of capital moves with great ease horizontally from a trade which is overcrowded to one which offers good openings for it: and since it moves with great ease vertically, the abler men rising to the higher posts in their own trade, we may conclude than in modern England the supply of business ability in command of capital accommodates itself, as a general rule, to the demand for it.

V–ECONOMIC DEVELOPMENT

---

1. A Historical Survey of Industrial Systems

BY KARL BÜCHER

IN ECONOMIC and social matters most people have very definite opinions on what *should be,* often much more definite than on what *is.* What in their view should be is by no means an ideal state of affairs, an imaginative creation that has never been realized. Very frequently indeed it is a conception drawn from the conditions that prevailed in times more or less remote, which long custom has led us to consider normal.

Such is the case, if we mistake not, with many of our contemporaries regarding what we call *handicraft* and the so-called handicraft problem. One has become accustomed to look upon handi-

Reprinted from Karl Bücher, *Industrial Evolution,* trans. S. M. Wickett (New York: Henry Holt & Co., 1901), chap. iv, pp. 150–84.

craft as the normal form of industry, after it has dominated five centuries or more of the life of the burgher class of Germany. The proverb says "Handicraft stands on golden ground"; and observation teaches us that this ground is, according to present-day valuation, no longer golden. We ask ourselves how that happy condition can be restored, how handicraft can be "resuscitated."

But what right has one to regard handicraft as the normal form of industry and thus as it were to strive after an ideal whose realization belongs to the past?

The earlier political economists represent handicraft as the original form of industrial production. "In a tribe of hunters or shepherds," says Adam Smith, "a particular person makes bows and arrows with more readiness and dexterity than any other. He frequently exchanges them for cattle or venison with his companions; and he finds at last he can in this manner get more cattle and venison than if he himself went to the field to catch them." Finally, "the making of bows and arrows grows to be his chief business and he becomes a sort of armourer." If we follow this historical progress a couple of stages further, the original handicraftsman will after a time probably take an apprentice, and when the latter has learned his trade, a second, while the first becomes his journeyman.

Seek as we may, we find nothing added by subsequent development. When we speak of a craftsman to-day we have in mind a business undertaker on a small scale, who has passed by regular stages of transition from apprentice to journeyman and from journeyman to master workman, who produces with his own hand and his own capital for a locally limited circle of customers, and into whose hands flows undiminished the whole product of his labour. Everything that one can demand of an industrial system founded on justice seems realized in the life of the typical craftsman—gradual social progress, independence, an income corresponding to services rendered. And those forms of industry that vary from this primal type, namely, house industry and factory production, may readily appear abnormal; and the social stratification of those employed, and the accompanying unequal distribution of income out of harmony with the idea of economic justice.

Even later economists are rarely free from this popular conception. In contrasting the three industrial systems that they recognise, handicraft, house industry, and factory production, they almost unwittingly draw from the fundamental institutions of handicraft the criterion for judging the others. Until quite recently house industry was for many of them merely a degenerate handicraft or a transi-

tional form, and the factory a necessary evil of the age of machinery. This narrowness of view was prejudicial to the scientific understanding of even modern industrial methods, open as these are to direct observation.

An historically constructive view, such as we will here present, must from the start shake off the idea that any particular form in any department of economic activity can be the norm for all times and peoples. Even handicraft is for it only one phenomenon in the great stream of history, with its origin, continuance, and success dependent upon certain given economic conditions. It is neither the original nor even a necessary form in the historical evolution of industrial production. It is, in other words, just as little necessary that the industry of a country shall have passed through the handicraft phase before arriving at house industry or factory manufacture as that every people shall have been hunters or nomads before passing over to settled agriculture. Among us handicraft has been preceded by other industrial systems, which, indeed, even in Europe, still exist in part.

The great historical significance of these primitive industrial forms in the evolution of economic conditions has hitherto been almost wholly ignored, although they shaped for thousands of years the economic life of the nations and left lasting marks upon their social organizations. Only a comparatively small portion of the history of industry, namely, that part which written laws have enabled us to know, has been at all cleared up; and this, too, much more on its formal side than as regards its inner life, its method of operation. Even the guild handicraft of the Middle Ages, to which in recent times so much persevering and penetrating labour has been devoted, has, on the side of its actual operation, enjoyed scarcely more accurate investigation. In this domain arbitrary theoretical constructions based upon the postulates and concepts of modern commercial economy still widely prevail.

Our "historical" political economy, it is true, has a wealth of material for the economic history of the classical and modern peoples. But it has hardly yet been duly noted that the complex nature of all social phenomena renders it just as difficult for the investigator of to-day to reconstruct the economic conditions of the life of the nations of antiquity and of the Middle Ages as to forecast even with the most lively and powerful imagination the ultimate consequences of the "socialist State of the future." We shall not arrive at an understanding of whole epochs of early economic history until we study the economic side of the life of primitive and uncivilized peoples of the present with the care we to-day devote to Englishmen and Americans. Instead of sending our young political economists on journeys of investigation to these latter, we should rather send them to the Russians, the Rumanians, or the South Slavs; we should study the characteristic features of primitive economic life and the legal conceptions of the peoples of our newly acquired colonies before such features and conceptions disappear under the influence of European trade.

It is almost a fortunate circumstance that such external influences rarely affect deeply the real life of the people, but are confined chiefly to the more privileged classes. Hence it is that in extensive regions of eastern and northern Europe, which the unheeding traveller courses through by rail, there may still be observed among the rural population primitive forms of production that modern commerce has caused to vary but slightly.

In the attempt made in the following pages to give a compact presentation of what we know of the industrial methods of such "backward" tribes and the present conclusions of industrial history, our sole aim is to present in clear outline the chief stages of development. In order to have a guiding thread through the perplexing variety and wealth of forms of individual ethnographical observations, it is most necessary to separate typical and casual, to disregard subsidiary and transitional forms, and to consider a new phase of development as beginning only where changes in industrial technique call forth economic phenomena that imply a radical alteration in the organization of society. In this way we arrive at five main systems of industry. In historical succession they are:

1. Housework (Domestic Work).
2. Wage-work.
3. Handicraft.
4. Commission Work (House Industry).
5. Factory Work.

We shall first attempt to give a concise outline of the characteristic economic peculiarities of these industrial systems, merely indicating the socio-historical import of the whole development. The filling out of occasional gaps and the explanation of the transitions from one system to the other may be left to detailed investigation. In our sketch we shall, naturally, devote most time to the two industrial systems precedent to handicraft, while for the later a brief account may suffice. We begin with housework.

Housework is industrial production in and for the house from raw materials furnished by the household itself. In its original and purest form it presupposes the absence of exchange, and the ability of each household to satisfy by its own labour

the wants of its members. Each commodity passes through all the stages of production in the establishment in which it is to be consumed. Production is consequently undertaken only according to the needs of the house itself. There is still neither circulation of goods nor capital. The wealth of the house consists entirely in consumption goods in various stages of completion, such as corn, meal, bread, flax, yarn, cloth, and clothes. It also possesses auxiliary means of production, such as the handmill, the axe, the distaff, and the weaver's loom, but no goods with which it could procure other goods by process of exchange. All it has it owes to its own labour, and it is scarcely possible to separate the operations of the household from those of production.

In the form of housework, industry is older than agriculture. Wherever explorers of new countries have come into contact with primitive peoples, they have found many forms of industrial skill, such as the making of bow and arrow, the weaving of mats and vessels out of reeds, bast, and tough roots, a primitive pottery, tanning skins, crushing farinaceous grains on the grinding-stone, smelting iron ore, the building of houses. To-day the hunting tribes of North America, the fisher tribes of the South Sea, the nomad hordes of Siberia, and the agricultural negro tribes of Africa make similar display of varied technical skill without possessing actual artisans. Even the wretched naked forest tribes of Central Brazil make their clubs and bows and arrows, build houses and bark canoes, make tools of bone and stone, weave baskets for carrying and storing, scoop out gourd dishes, spin, knit, and weave, form artistically ornamented clay vessels without knowledge of the potter's wheel, carve ornamented digging-sticks, stools, flutes, combs, and masks, and prepare many kinds of ornaments out of feathers, skins, etc.

In the temperate and colder countries with the advance to the use of the plough, this activity loses more and more the character of the accidental; the whole husbandry acquires a settled character; the mild period of the year must be devoted to the procuring of raw material and to outdoor work; in winter the working up of this material clusters the members of the household around the hearth. For each kind of work there is developed a definite method which is incorporated into the domestic life according to the natural and imperative demands of economy; about it custom weaves its fine golden ethical thread; it enriches and ennobles the life of men among whom, with its simple technique and archaic forms, it is transmitted from generation to generation. As people labour only for their own requirements, the interest of the producer in the work of his hands long survives the completion of the work. His highest technical skill and his whole artistic sense are embodied in it. It is for this reason that the products of domestic work throughout Germany have become for our age of artistic industry such a rich mine of models of popular style.

The Norwegian peasant is not merely his own smith and joiner, like the Westphalian *Hofschulze* in Immermann's "Münchhausen"; with his own hands he also builds his wooden house, makes his field-implements, wagons and sleighs, tans leather, carves from wood various kinds of house utensils, and even makes metal ones. In Iceland the very peasants are skilful workers in silver. In the Highlands of Scotland, up to the close of last century, every man was his own weaver, fuller, tanner, and shoemaker. In Galicia and Bukowina, in many parts of Hungary and Siebenbürgen, in Rumania, and among the southern Slav peoples there could scarcely be found, down to recent times, any other craftsman than the smith, and he was usually a gypsy. In Greece and other lands of the Balkan peninsula the only additional craftsmen were occasional wandering builders. Numberless examples of a similar kind might be adduced from other peoples. The wonderful adroitness and dexterity of the Russian and Swedish peasants, to cite a striking instance, has its undoubted origin in the varied technical tasks of their own households. The industrial employments of women in ancient and modern times, such as spinning, weaving, baking, etc., are too well known to call for further reference.

In order to obtain an idea of the wealth of domestic industrial skill that characterizes the life of less civilized peoples a detailed description would be necessary. Lack of space unfortunately forbids that here. It will suffice, however, to reproduce the following sentences from an account of household work in Bukowina:

"In the narrow circle of the family, or at least within the limits of his little village, the Bukowina countryman supplies all his own necessaries. In building a house the husband, as a rule, can do the work of carpenter, roofer, etc., while the wife must attend to plastering the woven and slatted walls or stopping the chinks in the log walls with moss, pounding out of the floor, and many other related duties. From the cultivation of the plant from which cloth is spun or the raising of sheep down to the making of bed and other clothes out of linen, wool or furs, leather, felt, or plaited straw, the Bukowina country folk produce everything, including dyes from plants of their own culture, as well as the necessary though, indeed, extremely primitive utensils. The same holds in general of the food-supply. With a rather heavy expenditure of labour

the peasant cultivates his field of maize, and with his handmill grinds the kukuruz meal used by him in baking mamaliga, his chief article of food, which resembles polenta. His simple farming implements, the dishes and utensils for household and kitchen, he, or, if not he, some self-taught villager, is also able to make. The working of iron, alone, a substance that the native population uses in exceedingly small quantities, he generally leaves to the gypsies scattered through the country."

Yet whatever the industrial skill developed by the self-sufficing household, such a method of supply was destined to prove inadequate when the household diminished to the smaller circle of blood-relations, which we call the family. The ancient family group, it is true, was broader than our present family; but just at the time when wants are increasing in extent and variety, the tribal organization of many peoples breaks down and a more minute division of labour among the members of the household is rendered impossible. The transition to specialized production and a system of exchange would at this point have been unavoidable had it not been possible, by adopting slaves or by utilizing serf labour, to enlarge artificially the household circle. The greater the number of these unfree members of the household, the easier it is to introduce a varied division of labour among them and to train each person for a definite industrial employment.

Thus we find among the house-slaves of the wealthy Greeks and Romans industrial workers of various kinds; and in the famous instructions of Charles the Great regarding the management of his country estates we have definite rules prescribing what kinds of unfree workers shall be maintained at each villa. "Each steward," we read, "shall have in his service good workmen, such as smiths, workers in gold and silver, shoemakers, turners, carpenters, shield-makers, fishers, fowlers, soap-boilers, brewers of mead (*siceratores*), bakers, and net-makers." Copious evidence of a similar kind is available for the manors of the nobility and the monasteries. The handicraftsmen maintained by them are at their exclusive service; in some cases they are merely domestic servants receiving their board and lodging in the manor-house, in others they are settled and gain their living on their own holdings, and in return render villein services in that branch of labour in which they have special skill. In token that they are engaged to hold their skill at the service of the manor, they bear the title *officiales, officiati*, i.e., officials.

Housework, we see, has here obtained an extensive organization, which allows the lord of the manor a relatively large and varied consumption of industrial products.

But housework does not remain mere production for direct consumption. At a very early stage inequality of natural endowment causes a varied development of technical skill. One tribe produces pottery, stone implements, or arrows, and a neighbouring tribe does not. Such industrial products are then scattered among other tribes as gifts of hospitality, or as spoils of war, and later as the objects of exchange. Among the ancient Greeks wealthy slave-owners caused a considerable number of their dependent labourers, whom they did not need for their own estates, to be trained for a special industry, and then to produce for the market. In a similar fashion peasant families exchange the surplus products of their household industry more frequently than the surpluses from their agriculture or cattle-raising. As in the Old Testament it is one of the good qualities of the virtuous wife to dispose of the wares that her own hands have produced, so to-day the negro wife in Central Africa carries to the weekly market the pots or basketware she produces in order to exchange them for salt or pearls. In like manner, in many parts of Germany the rural population have from the beginning of the Middle Ages sold their linen cloths at the town markets and fairs; and in the era of mercantilism measures were taken by the government in Silesia and Westphalia to facilitate the export of home-made linen. So also in the Baltic provinces during the Middle Ages the coarse woollen cloth, *Vadhmâl,* which is still woven by the peasant women, was one of the best known articles of trade, and actually served as money. Similarly among many African peoples domestic products made by neighbouring tribes serve as general mediums of exchange. In almost every villager's house in Japan yarn is spun and cloth woven out of cotton grown in his own fields, and of this a portion comes into exchange. In Sweden the West Goths and Smalanders wander through almost the whole country offering for sale home-woven stuffs. In Hungary, Galicia, Rumania, and the southern Slav countries, everywhere one can meet with peasants offering for sale at the weekly town markets their earthen and wooden wares, and peasant women selling, along with vegetables and eggs, aprons, embroidered ribbons, and laces which they themselves have made.

It is especially when the land owned by a family becomes divided up and no longer suffices for its maintenance, that a part of the rural population take up a special branch of housework and produce for the market in exactly the same way as our small

peasants in South Germany produce wine, hops, or tobacco. At first the necessary raw material is gained from their own land or drawn from the communal forests; later on, if need be, it is also purchased. All sorts of allied branches of production are added; and thus there develops out of housework, as in many parts of Russia, an endlessly varied system of peasant industry on a small scale.

But the evolution may take another course, and an independent professional class of industrial labourers arise, and with them our second industrial system—*wage-work.* Whereas all industrial skill has hitherto been exercised in close association with property in land and tillage, the adept house-labourer now frees himself from this association, and upon his technical skill founds for himself an existence that gradually becomes independent of property in land. But he has only his simple tools for work; he has no business capital. He therefore always exercises his skill upon raw material furnished him by the producer of the raw material, who is at the same time the consumer of the finished product.

Here again two distinct forms of this relationship are possible. In one case the wage-worker is taken temporarily into the house, receives his board and, if he does not belong to the place, his lodging as well, together with the daily wage; and leaves when the needs of his customer are satisfied. In South Germany we call this going on one's intinerancy (*auf die Stör gehen*), and may accordingly designate the whole industrial phase as that of *itinerancy* (*Stör*), and the labourer carrying on work in this manner as the *itinerant* (*Störer*). The dressmakers and seamstresses whom our women in many places are accustomed to take into the house may serve as an illustration.

On the other hand, the wage-worker may have his own place of business, and the raw material be given out to him. For working it up he receives piece-work wage. In the country the linen-weaver, the miller, and the baker working for a wage are examples. We will designate this form of work *home work* (*Heimwerk*). It is met with chiefly in industries that demand permanent means of production difficult to transport, such as mills, ovens, weavers' looms, forges, etc.

Both forms of wage-work are still very common in all parts of the world. Examples might be drawn from India and Japan, from Morocco and the Sudan, and from almost all European countries. The system can be traced in Babylonian temple records and in ancient Egypt; it can be followed in literature from Homer down through ancient and mediæval times to the present day. The whole conception of the relation of the customer to the independent (personally free or unfree) artisan in early Greek and Roman law rests upon wage-work; and only by it are numerous ordinances of mediæval guild law to be explained.

In the Alpine lands it is still the predominant industrial method in the country. The Styrian writer P. K. Rosegger has, in an interesting book, given a picture of his experiences as apprentice to a peripatetic tailor carrying on his trade among the peasants. "The peasant craftsmen," he says in the preface, "such as the cobbler, the tailor, the weaver, the cooper (in other places also the saddler, the wheelwright, the carpenter, and, in general, all artisan builders), are in many Alpine districts a sort of nomad folk. Each of them has, indeed, a definite abode somewhere, either in his own little house or in the rented room of a peasant's home, where his family lives, where he has safekeeping for his possessions, and where he spends his Sundays and holidays. On Monday morning, however, he puts his tools upon his back or in his pocket and starts out upon his rounds; that is, he goes out for work and takes up his quarters in the home of the peasant by whom he has been engaged, and there remains until he has satisfied the household needs. Then he wends his way to another farm. The handicraftsman in his temporary abode is looked upon as belonging to the family." Every peasant's house has a special room with a "handicraftsman's bed" for his quarters overnight; wherever he has been working during the week, he is invited to Sunday dinner.

We find described in almost the same words the industrial conditions of rural Sweden and many parts of Norway. In Russia and the southern Slav countries there are hundreds of thousands of wageworkers, belonging especially to the building and clothing trades, who lead a continuous migratory life and who, on account of the great distances travelled, often remain away from home half a year or more.

From the point of view of development these two forms of wage-work have different origins. Itinerant labour is based upon the exclusive possession of aptitude for a special kind of work, homework upon the exclusive possession of fixed means of production. Upon this basis there now arises all sorts of *mixed forms* between housework and wage-work.

The *itinerant* labourer is at first an experienced neighbour whose advice is sought in carrying out an important piece of work, the actual work, however, still being performed by the members of the household. Even later it is long the practice for the members of the customer's family to give the necessary assistance to the craftsman and his journeyman; and this is still met with in the country, for example, in the raising of a frame building.

In the case of *homework* the later tradesman is at first merely the owner of the business plant and technical director of the production, the customer doing the actual work. This frequently remains true in the country to-day with oil-presses, flaxmills, mills for husking barley and oats, and cidermills.

In many North German towns the mediæval maltsters and brewers were merely the owners of malt-kilns and brewing-houses, who for a fee gave the citizens the opportunity of malting their own barley and brewing their own beer. In the flourmills the customer at least supplied the handler who attended to the sifting of the meal. Even to-day it is customary in many localities for the peasant's wife, after kneading the dough, to mould the breadloaves in her own house; the baker simply places his oven at her disposal, heats it and attends to the baking. In French and western Swiss towns the public washing places are managed in much the same fashion, merely providing their customers with washing-apparatus and hot water, and frequently a drying-place in addition, while the work is done by the servants or female members of the customer's household. These afterwards bring the washed and dried linen to the mangle to be smoothed out, in which process the owner assists by working the handle. Payment is made by the hour. In Posen and West Prussia until recently it was the custom for the owner of a smithy merely to supply fire, tools, and iron, leaving the actual work to his customers.

From the economic point of view the essential feature of the wage-work system is that there is no business capital. Neither the raw material nor the finished industrial product is for its producer ever a means of profit. The character and extent of the production are still determined in every case by the owner of the soil, who produces the raw material; he also superintends the whole process of production. The peasant grows, threshes, and cleans the rye and then turns it over to the miller to be ground, paying him in kind; the meal is given to the baker, who delivers, on receipt of a baker's wage and indemnification for the firing, a certain number of loaves made from it. From the sowing of the seed until the moment the bread is consumed the product has never been capital, but always a mere article for use in course of preparation. No earnings of management and interest charges or middleman's profits attach to the finished product, but only wages for work done.

Under certain social conditions, and where needs are very simple, this is a thoroughly economic method of production and, like housework, secures the excellence of the product and the complete adjustment of supply to demand. It avoids exchange, where this would lead only to a round-about method of supplying the producer of the raw material with wares prepared from his own products. But it also forces the consumer to run the risk attaching to industrial production, as only those needs that can be foreseen can find suitable and prompt satisfaction, while a sudden need must often remain unsatisfied because the wage-worker happens at the very time to be elsewhere engaged. In the case of homework there is the additional danger that a portion of the material furnished may be embezzled or changed. The system has also many disadvantages for the wage-worker. Amongst these are the inconveniences and loss of time suffered in his itinerancy from place to place; also the irregularity of employment, which leads now to the overwork, now to the complete idleness, of the workman. Both forms of wage-work thus act satisfactorily only when the unoccupied hours can be turned to account in some allied branch of agriculture.

In the Middle Ages, when this could be done, wage-work greatly facilitated the emancipation of the artisan from serfdom and feudal obligations, as it required practically no capital to start an independent business. It is a great mistake still common to look upon the class of guild handicraftsmen of the Middle Ages as a class of small capitalists. It was in essence rather an industrial labouring class, distinguished from the labourers of to-day by the fact that each worked not for a single employer but for a large number of consumers. The supplying of the material by the customer is common to almost all mediæval handicrafts; in many instances, indeed, it continues for centuries, even after the customer has ceased to produce the raw material himself and must buy it, as, for example, the leather for the shoemaker and the cloth for the tailor. The furnishing of the material by the master workman is a practice that takes slow root; at first it holds only for the poorer customers, but later for the wealthy as well. Thus arises *handicraft* in the sense in which it is generally understood to-day; but alongside it wage-work maintains itself for a long time, even entering, in many cases, into the service of handicraft. Thus the tanner is wage-worker for the shoemaker and saddler, the miller for the baker, the woolbeater, the dyer, and the fuller wage-workers for the cloth-maker.

In the towns itinerancy is the first of two forms of wage-work to decline. This decline is considerably hastened by the interference of the guilds.[1] The itinerancy was too suggestive of early villenage. In it the workman is, so to speak, only a special kind of day-labourer, who must temporarily become a subordinate member of another household. Consequently from the fourteenth century on we find the guild ordinances frequently prohibiting the master from working in private houses. To the same cause is to be ascribed the hatred displayed by the town craftsmen towards those of the country, because the migratory labour of the latter could not well be forbidden. Eventually *itinerant* or *botcher* (*Bönhase*), becomes a general term of contempt for those who work without regular credentials from the guilds. In the North German towns the guild masters claimed the right of entering the houses of their customers to ferret out the itinerant artisans and call them to account,—the so-called "botcher-hunt"; and the public authorities were often weak enough to wink at this breach of the domestic rights of the citizen.

But the guilds did not everywhere have such an easy task in supplanting one industrial system by another. As early as the middle of the fourteenth century the sovereign authority in the Austrian duchy takes vigorous measures against them. In the statutes of the electorate of Saxony for the year 1482 shoemakers, tailors, furriers, joiners, glaziers, and other handicraftsmen who shall refuse without sufficient reason to work in the house of their customer are made liable to a fine of three florins, a high sum for those times. In Basel a definite statute governing house tailors was enacted in 1526 for the maintenance of "ancient and honourable customs." In many German territories definite ordinances were made regulating the charges of the various kinds of wage-workers. Thus in many crafts, especially in the building trade, wage-work has persisted down to the present time.

In the majority, however, its place has been taken by the industrial system that to-day is customarily designated *handicraft*, whose nature we have indicated at the beginning of the present chapter. It might also be called *price-work* (*Preiswerk*), which would mark the contrast with wage-work. For the handicraftsman is distinguished from the wage-worker only by the fact that he possesses all the means of production, and sells for a definite price the finished article which is the product of his own

1. In this connection it may not be out of place to point out that, in the industrial limitation of those entitled to the privileges of the guild, the old housework was at the same time affected. In very many of the guild ordinances we find the regulation that the non-guildsman may do handicraftsman's work, but only in so far as the needs of his household demand, not for purposes of sale. The surplus house production for the market described above was thereby made impossible.

raw material and his own incorporated labour, while the wage-worker merely receives a recompense for his labour.

All the important characteristics of handicraft may be summed up in the single expression *custom production*. It is the method of sale that distinguishes this industrial system from all later ones. The handicraftsman always works for the consumer of his product whether it be that the latter by placing separate orders affords the occasion for the work, or that the two meet at the weekly or yearly market. Ordered work and work for the market must supplement each other if "dull times" are to be avoided. As a rule the region of sale is local, namely, the town and its more immediate neighbourhood. The customer buys at first hand, the handicraftsman sells to the actual consumer. This assures a proper adjustment of supply and demand and introduces an ethical feature into the whole relationship; the producer in the presence of the consumer feels responsibility for his work.

With the rise of handicraft a wide cleft, so to speak, appears in the economic process of production. Hitherto the owner of the land, though perhaps calling in the aid of other wage-workers, had conducted this whole process; now there are two classes of economic activity, each of which embraces only a part of the process of production, one producing the raw material, the other the manufactured article. It is a principle that handicraft endeavoured to carry out wherever possible— an article should pass through all the stages of its preparation in the same workshop. In this way the needed capital is diminished and frequent additions of profit to price avoided. By the acquisition of an independent business capital the artisan class is changed from a mere wage-earning class of labourers into a capitalistic producing class; and the movable property now, dissociated from land-ownership, accumulates in its hands and becomes the basis of an independent social and political reputability which is embodied in the burgher class.

The direct relationship between the handicraftsman and the consumer of his products makes it necessary that the business remain small. Whenever any one line of handicraft threatens to become too large, new handicrafts split off from it and appropriate part of its sphere of production. This is the mediæval division of labour, which continually creates new and independent trades and which led later to that jealous delimitation of the spheres of work that caused a large portion of the energy of the guild system to be consumed in internal bickerings.

Handicraft is a phenomenon peculiar to the town. Peoples which, like the Russians, have developed no real town life, know likewise no national handicraft. And this also explains why, with the formation of large centralized States and unified commercial territories, handicraft was doomed to decline. In the seventeenth and eighteenth centuries there was developed a new industrial system, based no longer on the local but on the national and international market. Our ancestors have denoted this system by the two names *manufactories* and *factories*, without distinguishing between the two terms. When viewed more closely these are seen to indicate two quite distinct industrial systems. The one hitherto characterized by the misleading phrase *house industry* we prefer to call the *commission system* (*Verlag*), the other is our *factory system*. Both systems undertake the work of supplying a wide market with industrial products, and both require for this purpose a large number of labourers; they differ only in the manner in which they accomplish the work and organize the labourers.

In this respect the method of the commission system is the simplest. In the first place, it leaves the existing method of production quite undisturbed and confines itself to organizing the market. The business undertaker is a commercial entrepreneur who regularly employs a large number of labourers in their own homes, away from his place of business. These labourers are either former handicraftsmen who now produce for a single *tradesman* instead of for a number of consumers, or former wage-workers who now receive their raw material, not from the consumer, but from the merchant; or, finally, they are peasant families, the former products of whose domestic work are now produced as market wares and by the entrepreneur introduced into the markets of the world.

In some cases the entrepreneur advances to the small producers, who at first enjoy a fairly independent position, the purchase price of their products; in some cases he furnishes them with the raw material, and then pays piecework wage; while in others he owns even the principal machinery, such as the weaver's loom, the embroidering machine, etc. As the small producers have only the *one* customer they gradually sink into ever-greater dependence. The entrepreneur becomes their employer, and they are employees, even when they supply the raw material themselves.

It is scarcely necessary to describe in detail the commission system and its contingent method of work, house industry. We have plenty of examples in the mountain districts of Germany, for instance, the straw-plaiting and the clock and brush industries in the Black Forest, the wood-carving of Upper Bavaria, the toy manufacture in the Meiningen Oberland, the embroidery of the Voigtland, the lace-making of the Erzgebirge, etc. The history and present condition of these industries have been fairly well investigated in recent times. But we can no more enter into them than into the great variety of phases presented by this form of industry.

The essential feature is ever the transformation of the industrial product, before it reaches the consumer, into capital—that is, into a means of acquisition for one or more intermediary merchants. Whether the entrepreneur place the product on the general market, or keep a town wareroom from which to sell it; whether he receive the wares from the houseworker ready for sale, or himself subject them to a last finishing process; whether the workman call himself master and keep journeymen, or whether he be a tiller of the soil as well—the house workman is always far removed from the real market of his product and from a knowledge of market conditions, and therein lies the chief cause of his hopeless weakness.

If under the commission system capital has merely assumed control of the marketing of the products, under the *factory system* it grasps the whole process of production. The former system, in order to accomplish the productive task falling to it, draws loosely together a large number of homogeneous labourers, imparts to their production a definite direction, approximately the same for each, and causes the product of their labour to flow, as it were, into a great reservoir before distributing it in all directions. The factory system organizes the whole process of production; it unites various kinds of workers, by mutual relations of control and subjection, into a compact and well-disciplined body, brings them together in a special business establishment, provides them with an extensive and complex outfit of the machinery of production, and thereby immensely increases their productive power. The factory system is as distinguishable from the commission system as the well-organized, uniformly equipped regular army from the motley volunteer militia.

Just as in an army corps ready for battle, troops of varied training and accoutrement—infantry, cavalry, and artillery regiments, pioneers, engineers, ammunition columns and commissariat are welded into one, so under the factory system groups of workers of varied skill and equipment are united together and enabled to accomplish the most difficult tasks of production.

The secret of the factory's strength as an institution for production thus lies in the *effective utilization of labour*. In order to accomplish this it takes a peculiar road, which at first sight appears circuitous. It divides as far as possible all the work necessary to a process of production into its simplest elements, separates the difficult from the easy, the mechanical from the intellectual, the skilled from the rude. It thus arrives at a system of successive functions, and is enabled to employ simultaneously and successively human powers of the most varied kind—trained and untrained men, women and children, workers with the hand and head, workers possessing technical, artistic and commercial skill. The restriction of each individual to a small section of the labouring process effects a mighty increase in the volume of work turned out. A hundred workmen in a factory accomplish in a given process of production more than a hundred independent master craftsmen, although each of the latter understands the whole process, while none of the former understands more than a small portion of it. As far as the struggle between handicraft and factory is fought out on the ground of technical skill, it is an evidence how the weak overcome the strong when guided by superior intellectual power.

The machine is not the essential feature of the factory, although the *subdivision of work* just described has, by breaking up the sum of labour into simple movements, endlessly assisted and multiplied the application of machinery. From early times machines for performing tasks and for furnishing power have been employed in industry. In connection with the factory, however, their application attained its present importance only when men succeeded in securing a motive power that would work unintermittently, uniformly and ubiquitously, namely, steam; and even here its full importance is felt only in connection with the peculiar industrial form of factory manufacture.

An example will serve to illustrate what has just been said. In the year 1787 the canton of Zurich had 34,000 male and female hand-spinners producing cotton yarn. After the introduction of the English spinning-machines a few factories produced an equal or greater quantity of thread, and the number of their workers (chiefly women and children) fell to scarcely a third of what it had been before. What is the explanation? The machines? But was not the then-existing spinning-wheel a machine? Certainly it was; and, moreover, a very ingenious one. Machine was thus ousted by machine. Or better, what had hitherto been done by the woman hand-spinner with her wheel was now done by successive collaboration of a whole series of various kinds of workers and machines. The entire spinning process had been decomposed into its simplest elements, and perfectly new operations had arisen for which even immature powers could in part be utilized.

In the subdivision of work originate these further peculiarities of factory production—the necessity of manufacture on a large scale, the requirement of a large capital, and the economic dependence of the workman.

With regard to the two last points we easily perceive an important difference between the factory and the commission system. Its *large fixed capital* assures to factory work greater steadiness in production. Under the commission system the house-workers can at any moment be deprived of employment without the entrepreneur running any risk of losing capital; but the manufacturer must in like case go on producing, because he fears loss of interest and shrinkage in the value of his fixed capital, and because he cannot afford to lose his trained body of workmen. This is the reason why it is probable that the commission system will long maintain itself alongside factory production in those branches of industry in which the demand is liable to sudden change, and in which the articles produced are of great variety.

If, in conclusion, we were briefly to characterize these five industrial systems, we might say that housework is production for one's own needs, wage-work is custom work, handicraft is custom production, commission work is decentralized, and factory labour centralized production of wares. As no economic phenomenon stands isolated, each of these systems of industry is at the same time but a section of a great economic and social order. Housework is the transformation of materials in the autonomous household economy; wage-work belongs to the period of transition from independent household economy to town economy; the heyday of handicraft coincides with the period when town economy reached its full development; the commission system is a connecting link between town economy and national economy (independent State economy), and the factory system is the industrial system of fully developed national economy.

It would lead us too far to explain in this chapter how each industrial system fits organically into the contemporary method of production and how it is mutually determined by a series of allied phenomena in the spheres of agriculture, personal services, trade and transportation. It can scarcely escape the observant eye that all the elements of the evolution here broadly sketched are contained in the primitive cell of society, the family; or, in economic phrase, in the conditions of production in the independent household. From this primitive social

unit, teeming with life and swallowing up all individual existence, parts have continually detached themselves through differentiation and integration, and become more and more independent. Wage-work is only a sprout from the root of the tree of independent household economy; handicraft still needs its protection in order to flourish; commission work makes the marketing of products a special business, while production sinks back almost to the first stages of development. Factory manufacture, on the other hand, permeates with the entrepreneur principle the whole process of production; it is an independent economic system freed from all elements of consumption, and separated as regards commodities and locality from the household life of those engaged in it.

The position of the worker changes in a similar way. With the commencement of wage-work the industrial worker separates himself personally from the independent household economy of the landed proprietor; with the transition to handicraft he also becomes, through the elimination of business capital, materially free and independent. Through the commission system he enters into a fresh personal subjection, he falls into dependence upon the capitalistic entrepreneur; under the factory system he becomes also materially dependent upon him. By four stages of evolution he passes from manorial servitude to factory servitude.

There is a sort of parallelism in this evolution. The relation between the unfree houseworker and the ancient landowner bears a certain resemblance to the relation between the factory hand and the modern manufacturer; and the wage-worker occupies much the same position with regard to the economy of the landed proprietor that the worker engaged in house industry does to the entrepreneur giving out commission work. In the middle of this ascending and descending series stands handicraft as its foundation and corner-stone. From housework to handicraft we see the gradual emancipation of the worker from the soil and the formation of capital; from handicraft to the factory system a gradual separation of capital from work, and the subjection of the worker to capital.

At the stage of housework capital has not yet emerged; there are only consumption goods at various stages of ripeness. Everything belongs to the household—raw material, tools, the manufactured article, often the worker himself. In the case of wage-work the tools are the only capital in the hands of the worker; the raw and auxiliary materials are household stores not yet ready for consumption; the work-place belongs, under the system of migratory labour, to the domestic establishment that is to consume the finished product, or, under the housework system, to the worker who produces the article. In the case of handicraft the tools, work-place, and raw material are capital in the possession of the worker; the latter is master of the product, though he invariably sells it to the immediate consumer. In the commission system the product also becomes capital—not the capital of the worker, however, but of quite a new figure on the scene, the commercial entrepreneur; the worker either retains all his means of production, or he loses possession successively of his goods, capital, and his implements of production. Thus all the elements of capital finally unite in the hand of the manufacturer, and serve him as a foundation for the reorganization of industrial production. In his hands even the worker's share in the product becomes a part of the business capital.

This share of the worker consists, at the stage of housework, in a participation in the consumption of the finished products; in the case of wage-work it consists in board, together with a time- or piece-work wage, which even at this point includes compensation for wear and tear of tools; in handicraft it consists in the full returns from production. Under the commission system the commercial undertaker takes away a portion of the latter as profit on his business capital; under the factory system all the elements of production which can be turned into capital become crystallizing centres for further profits on capital, while for the worker there remains only the stipulated wage.

We must not, however, imagine the historical evolution of the industrial system to have been such that each new industrial method absolutely superseded its predecessor. That would be just as far astray as, for example, to suppose that a new means of communication supplants those already existing. Railways have done away neither with conveyances on the highways, nor with transportation by means of ships, pack-animals or the human back; they have only confined each of these older methods of transportation to the field in which it can best develop its peculiar advantages: it is probable that not only absolutely but relatively more horses and men are employed in the work of transportation in our civilized countries to-day than there were in the year 1830.

The very same causes that have produced such an enormous increase in traffic are also at work in the sphere of industry; and in spite of the continual improvement of the mechanical means of production they demand an ever-increasing number of persons. From two quarters, however, the sphere of productive industry is constantly receiving accessions; first, from the old household economy and agriculture, from which even to-day parts are

always separating themselves and becoming independent branches of industry; secondly, from the continual improvement[2] and increase in range of articles serving for the satisfaction of our wants.

As regards the first point, there have sprung in the industrial world during the last generation dozens of new trades for taking over such kinds of work as used formerly to fall to the women of the household or to the servants, such as vegetable and fruit preserving, fancy baking and preparation of meats, making and mending women's and children's clothes, cleaning windows, feather beds and curtains, chemical cleaning and dyeing, painting and polishing floors, gas and water installation, etc. Under the heading "Art and Market Gardening," the latest statistics of trades in the German Empire give thirty-five, and under the heading "Stock-raising," thirty-one, independent occupations, many of which are of very recent origin.

With regard to the second point, we will mention only the bicycle industry, which within a short time has not only necessitated the erection of a great number of factories, but has already given rise to special repair-shops and separate establishments for the manufacture of rubber tires, cyclometers and bicycle spokes. A still more striking example is afforded by the application of electricity. In the industrial census of 1895 there are enumerated names of twenty-two electrical occupations that did not exist in 1882. The production of electrical machines, apparatus and plant in the German Empire gave employment in 1895 to 14,494 persons, with 18,449 members of their families and servants—thus furnishing a living for nearly 33,000 persons. In metal-work, in the manufacture of machinery, chemicals, paper, in the building industries, the clothing and cleaning industries the number of recorded occupations more than doubled itself between 1882 and 1895. It is, at the same time, to be remembered not only that specialization has made immense strides, but that in many instances subsidiary articles of production and trade which have hitherto been produced by the businesses using them are the objects of separate enterprises. In these fields industry not only meets demand but frequently outruns it, as has at all times been the case. In the patent lists we find significant expression of this effort to improve the world of commodities; and though many of the new inventions prove deficient in vitality, there

---

2. In reply to a criticism of this expression in the Revue d'économie po'itique for November, 1892, (p. 1228, note), we will not omit making it more definite by saying that we do not mean by it the improvement of the quality of already existing species of goods, but the supplanting of existing goods by others which better and more cheaply supply the demand.

always remains a considerable number whereby life is permanently enriched.

If we were able statistically to bring together the whole sum of industrial products produced yearly in Germany in such a way that we could separate the output of factories, of house industry, and of handicraft, wage-work and housework, we should without doubt find that the greater part of the factory wares embraces goods which were never produced under any of the other industrial systems, and that handicraft produces to-day an absolutely greater quantity than ever before. The commission and factory systems, it is true, have completely absorbed some of the lesser handicrafts and robbed many others of portions of their sphere of production. But all the great guild handicrafts that existed at the close of the 18th century with perhaps the single exception of weaving, still exist to-day. Handicraft is constantly being displaced by the more perfect industrial systems, just as in mediæval times housework and wage-work were ousted by handicraft, only now it occurs in a less violent manner, on the field of free competition. This competition of all with all, supported as it is by a perfected system of transportation and communication, often compels the transition from custom to wholesale production, even where from the technical standpoint the former might still have been possible. Many independent master workmen enter the service of the entrepreneur carrying on commission or factory work just as their predecessors a thousand years ago became manorial labourers.

Handicraft has thus been relegated economically and socially to a secondary position. But even if it will no longer flourish in the large towns, it has in compensation spread all the more in the country, and here called forth, in combination with agriculture, numerous industries upon which the eye of the philanthropist can rest with delight. Handicraft, it may be said with certainty, will no more disappear than wage-work and housework have disappeared. What it has won for society in a time of universal feudalization, namely, a robust class of people independent of landed property, whose existence is based upon personal worth and a small amount of movables, and who are a repository of popular morality and uprightness—that will and

must remain a lasting possession, even though the existence of those whom these virtues will in future adorn may rest upon a different basis.

In recent times there has been raised with rare persistence a cry for the uprooting of the older industry. Handicraft, house industry, in general all forms of work on a small scale are, we are told, a drag upon the national productive power; they are "antiquated, superseded, rude, not to say socially impeditive methods of production," which in the best interests of those who follow them must be replaced by a "rational and judicious organization and regulation of human activities on a large scale," if the actual national production is not to lag far behind what is technically possible.

This short-sighted economico-political theorizing is not new. There was once a time when every peasant shoemaker who raised his own potatoes and cabbage was looked upon as a sort of enemy to the highest possible national wealth, and when people would have liked to force him by police regulation to stick to his last, even though at the same time he ran the risk of starving. Truly, it has always been much easier to censure than to understand.

If, instead of such dogmatic pronouncements, a willingness had been shown to make an unbiassed investigation of the conditions governing those older and supposedly antiquated systems of production, the conviction would soon have arisen that in the majority of cases where they still persist they are economically and socially justifiable; and the means for the removal of the existing evils would be sought in the soil in which these industrial forms are rooted instead of such drastic remedies being applied to them. In this way we should undoubtedly preserve the good of each of these individual systems and be striving only to remove their disadvantages.

For, after all, the comforting result of every serious consideration of history is, that no single element of culture which has once entered into the life of men is lost; that even after the hour of its predominance has expired, it continues in some more modest position to coöperate in the realization of the great end in which we all believe, the helping of mankind towards more and more perfect forms of existence.

2. *The Fundamentals of Economic Development*

BY JOSEPH A. SCHUMPETER

WE NOW come to the third of the elements with which our analysis works, namely the "new combination of means of production," and credit. Although all three elements form a whole, the third may be described as the fundamental phenomenon of economic development. The carrying out of new combinations we call "enterprise"; the individuals whose function it is to carry them out we call "entrepreneurs." These concepts are at once broader and narrower than the usual. Broader, because in the first place we call entrepreneurs not only those "independent" businessmen in an exchange economy who are usually so designated, but all who actually fulfil the function by which we define the concept, even if they are, as is becoming the rule, "dependent" employees of a company, like managers, members of boards of directors, and so forth, or even if their actual power to perform the entrepreneurial function has any other foundations, such as the control of a majority of shares. As it is the carrying out of new combinations that constitutes the entrepreneur, it is not necessary that he should be permanently connected with an individual firm; many "financiers," "promotors," and so forth are not, and still they may be entrepreneurs in our sense. On the other hand, our concept is narrower than the traditional one in that it does not include all heads of firms or managers or industrialists who merely may operate an established business, but only those who actually perform that function. Nevertheless I maintain that the above definition does no more than formulate with greater precision what the traditional doctrine really means to convey. In the first place our definition agrees with the usual one on the fundamental point of distinguishing between "entrepreneurs" and "capitalists"—irrespective of whether the latter are regarded as owners of money, claims to money, or material goods. This distinction is common property to-day and has been so for a considerable time. It also settles the question whether the ordinary shareholder as such is an entrepreneur, and disposes of the conception of the entrepreneur as risk bearer.[1] Furthermore, the ordinary characterisation of the entrepreneur type by such expessions as "initiative," "authority," or "foresight" points entirely in our direction. For there is little scope for such qualities within the routine of the circular flow, and if this had been sharply separated from the occurrence of changes in this routine itself, the emphasis in the definition of the function of entrepreneurs would have been shifted automatically to the latter. Finally there are definitions which we could simply accept. There is in particular the well known one that goes back to J. B. Say: the entrepreneur's function is to combine the productive factors, to bring them together. Since this is a performance of a special kind only when the factors are combined for the first time—while it is merely routine work if done in the course of running a business—this definition coincides with ours. When Mataja (in Unternehmergewinn) defines the entrepreneur as one who receives profit, we have only to add the conclusion of the first chapter, that there is no profit in the circular flow, in order to trace this formulation too back to ours.[2]

---

1. Risk obviously always falls on the owner of the means of production or of the money-capital which was paid for them, hence never on the entrepreneur *as such*. A shareholder *may* be an entrepreneur. He may even owe to his holding a controlling interest the power to act as an entrepreneur. Shareholders *per se*, however, are never entrepreneurs, but merely capitalists, who in consideration of their submitting to certain risks participate in profits. That this is no reason to look upon them as anything but capitalists is shown by the facts, first, that the average shareholder has normally no power to influence the management of his company, and secondly, that participation in profits is frequent in cases in which everyone recognises the presence of a loan contract. Compare, for example, the Graeco-Roman *foenus nauticum*. Surely this interpretation is more true to life than the other one, which, following the lead of a faulty legal construction—which can only be explained historically—attributes functions to the average shareholder which he hardly ever thinks of discharging.
2. The definition of the entrepreneur in terms of entrepreneurial profit instead of in terms of the function the performance of which creates the entrepreneurial profit is obviously not brilliant. But we have still another objection to it: we shall see that entrepreneurial profit does not fall to the entrepreneur by "necessity" in the same sense as the marginal product of labor does to the worker.

And this view is not foreign to traditional theory, as is shown by the construction of the *entrepreneur faisant ni bénéfice ni perte,* which has been worked out rigorously by Walras, but is the property of many other authors. The tendency is for the entrepreneur to make neither profit nor loss in the circular flow—that is he has no function of a special kind there, he simply does not exist; but in his stead, there are heads of firms or business managers of a different type which we had better not designate by the same term.

It is a prejudice to believe that the knowledge of the historical origin of an institution or of a type immediately shows us its sociological or economic nature. Such knowledge often leads us to understand it, but it does not directly yield a theory of it. Still more false is the belief that "primitive" forms of a type are also *ipso facto* the "simpler" or the "more original" in the sense that they show their nature more purely and with fewer complications than later ones. Very frequently the opposite is the case, amongst other reasons because increasing specialisation may allow functions and qualities to stand out sharply, which are more difficult to recognise in more primitive conditions when mixed with others. So it is in our case. In the general position of the chief of a primitive horde it is difficult to separate the entrepreneurial element from the others. For the same reason most economists up to the time of the younger Mill failed to keep capitalist and entrepreneur distinct because the manufacturer of a hundred years ago was both; and certainly the course of events since then has facilitated the making of this distinction, as the system of land tenure in England has facilitated the distinction between farmer and landowner, while on the Continent this distinction is still occasionally neglected, especially in the case of the peasant who tills his own soil.[3] But in our case there are still more of such difficulties. The entrepreneur of earlier times was not only as a rule the capitalist too, he was also often—as he still is to-day in the case of small concerns—his own technical expert, in so far as a professional specialist was not called in for special cases. Likewise he was (and is) often his own buying and selling agent, the head of his office, his own personnel manager, and sometimes, even though as a rule he of course employed solicitors, his own legal

adviser in current affairs. And it was performing some or all of these functions that regularly filled his days. The carrying out of new combinations can no more be a *vocation* than the making and execution of strategical decisions, although it is this function and not his routine work that characterises the military leader. Therefore the entrepreneur's essential function must always appear mixed up with other kinds of activity, which as a rule must be much more conspicuous than the essential one. Hence the Marshallian definition of the entrepreneur, which simply treats the entrepreneurial function as "management" in the widest meaning, will naturally appeal to most of us. We do not accept it, simply because it does not bring out what we consider to be the salient point and the only one which specifically distinguishes entrepreneurial from other activities.

Nevertheless there are types—the course of events has evolved them by degrees—which exhibit the entrepreneurial function with particular purity. The "promoter," to be sure, belongs to them only with qualifications. For, neglecting the associations relative to social and moral status which are attached to this type, the promoter is frequently only an agent intervening on commission, who does the work of financial technique in floating the new enterprise. In this case he is not its creator nor the driving power in the process. However, he *may* be the latter also, and then he is something like an "entrepreneur by profession." But the modern type of "captain of industry" corresponds more closely to what is meant here, especially if one recognises his identity on the one hand with, say, the commercial entrepreneur of twelfth-century Venice—or, among later types, with John Law—and on the other hand with the village potentate who combines with his agriculture and his cattle trade, say, a rural brewery, an hotel, and a store. But whatever the type, everyone is an entrepreneur only when he actually "carries out new combinations," and loses that character as soon as he has built up his business, when he settles down to running it as other people run their businesses. This is the rule, of course, and hence it is just as rare for anyone always to remain an entrepreneur throughout the decades of his active life as it is for a businessman never to have a moment in which he is an entrepreneur, to however modest a degree.

Because being an entrepreneur is not a profession and as a rule not a lasting condition, entrepreneurs do not form a social class in the technical sense, as, for example, landowners or capitalists or workmen do. Of course the entrepreneurial function will *lead* to certain class

---

3. Only this neglect explains the attitude of many socialistic theorists towards peasant property. For smallness of the individual possession makes a difference only for the petit-bourgeois, not for the socialist. The criterion of the employment of labor other than that of the owner and his family is economically relevant only from the standpoint of a kind of exploitation theory which is hardly tenable any longer.

positions for the successful entrepreneur and his family. It can also put its stamp on an epoch of social history, can form a style of life, or systems of moral and aesthetic values; but in itself it signifies a class position no more than it presupposes one. And the class position which may be attained is not as such an entrepreneurial position, but is characterised as landowning or capitalist, according to how the proceeds of the enterprise are used. Inheritance of the pecuniary result and of personal qualities may then both keep up this position for more than one generation and make further enterprise easier for descendants, but the function of the entrepreneur itself cannot be inherited, as is shown well enough by the history of manufacturing families.[4]

But now the decisive question arises: why then is the carrying out of new combinations a special process and the object of a special kind of "function"; Every individual carries on his economic affairs as well as he can. To be sure, his own intentions are never realised with ideal perfection, but ultimately his behavior is moulded by the influence on him of the results of his conduct, so as to fit circumstances which do not as a rule change suddenly. If a business can never be absolutely perfect in any sense, yet it in time approaches a relative perfection having regard to the surrounding world, the social conditions, the knowledge of the time, and the horizon of each individual or each group. New possibilities are continuously being offered by the surrounding world, in particular new discoveries are continuously being added to the existing store of knowledge. Why should not the individual make just as much use of the new possibilities as of the old, and, according to the market position as he understands it, keep pigs instead of cows, or even choose a new crop rotation, if this can be seen to be more advantageous? And what kind of special new phenomena or problems, not to be found in the established circular flow, can arise there?

While in the accustomed circular flow every individual can act promptly and rationally because he is sure of his ground and is supported by the conduct, as adjusted to this circular flow, of all other individuals, who in turn expect the accustomed activity from him, he cannot simply do this when he is confronted by a new task. While in the accustomed channels his own ability and experience suffice for the normal individual, when confronted with innovations he needs guidance.

While he swims with the stream in the circular flow which is familiar to him, he swims against the stream if he wishes to change its channel. What was formerly a help becomes a hindrance. What was a familiar datum becomes an unknown. Where the boundaries of routine stop, many people can go no further, and the rest can only do so in a highly variable manner. The assumption that conduct is prompt and rational is in all cases a fiction. But it proves to be sufficiently near to reality, if things have time to hammer logic into men. Where this has happened, and within the limits in which it has happened, one may rest content with this fiction and build theories upon it. It is then not true that habit or custom or non-economic ways of thinking cause a hopeless difference between the individuals of different classes, times, or cultures, and that, for example, the "economics of the stock exchange" would be inapplicable say to the peasants of to-day or to the craftsmen of the Middle Ages. On the contrary the same theoretical picture[5] in its broadest contour lines fits the individuals of quite different cultures, whatever their degree of intelligence and of economic rationality, and we can depend upon it that the peasant sells his calf just as cunningly and egotistically as the stock exchange member his portfolio of shares. But this holds good only where precedents without number have formed conduct through decades and, in fundamentals, through hundreds and thousands of years, and have eliminated unadapted behavior. Outside of these limits our fiction loses its closeness to reality.[6] To cling to it there also, as the traditional theory does, is to hide an essential thing and to ignore a fact which, in contrast with other deviations of our assumptions from reality, is theoretically important and the source of the explanation of phenomena which would not exist without it.

Therefore, in describing the circular flow one must treat combinations of means of production (the production-functions) as data, like natural pos-

4. On the nature of the entrepreneurial function also compare my statement in the article "Unternehmer" in the Handwörterbuch der Staatswissenschaften.

5. The same *theoretical* picture, obviously not the same sociological, cultural, and so forth.

6. How much this is the case is best seen to-day in the economic life of those nations, and within our civilisation in the economics of those individuals, whom the development of the last century has not yet completely drawn into its stream, for example, in the economy of the Central European peasant. This peasant "calculates"; there is no deficiency of the "economic way of thinking" (Wirtschaftsgesinnung) in him. Yet he cannot take a step out of the beaten path; his economy has not changed at all for centuries, except perhaps through the exercise of external force and influence. Why? Because the choice of new methods is not simply an element in the concept of rational economic action, nor a matter of course, but a distinct process which stands in need of special explanation.

sibilities, and admit only small[7] variations at the margins, such as every individual can accomplish by adapting himself to changes in his economic environment, without materially deviating from familiar lines. Therefore, too, the carrying out of new combinations is a special function, and the privilege of a type of people who are much less numerous than all those who have the "objective" possibility of doing it. Therefore, finally, entrepreneurs are a special type,[8] and their behavior

7. Small disturbances which may indeed, as mentioned earlier, in time add up to great amounts. The decisive point is that the businessman, if he makes them, never alters his routine. The usual case is one of small, the exception one of great (*uno actu* great), disturbances. Only in this sense is emphasis put upon "smallness" here. The objection that there can be no difference in principle between small and large disturbances is not effective. For it is false in itself, in so far as it is based upon the disregard of the principle of the infinitesimal method, the essence of which lies in the fact that one can assert of "small quantities" under certain circumstances what one cannot assert of "large quantities." But the reader who takes umbrage at the large-small contrast may, if he wishes, substitute for it the contrast adapting-spontaneous. Personally I am not willing to do this because the latter method of expression is much easier to misunderstand than the former and really would demand still longer explanations.

8. In the first place it is a question of a type of *conduct* and of a type of *person* in so far as this conduct is accessible in very unequal measure and to relatively few people, so that it constitutes their outstanding characteristic. Because the exposition of the first edition was reproached with exaggerating and mistaking the peculiarity of this conduct, and with overlooking the fact that it is more or less open to every businessman, and because the exposition in a later paper ("Wellenbewegung des Wirtschaftslebens," Archiv für Sozialwissenschaft) was charged with introducing an intermediate type ("half-static" businessmen), the following may be submitted. The conduct in question is peculiar in two ways. First, because it is directed towards something different and signifies doing something different from other conduct. One may indeed in this connection include it with the latter in a higher unity, but this does not alter the fact that a theoretically relevant difference exists between the two, and that only one of them is adequately described by traditional theory. Secondly, the type of conduct in question not only differs from the other in its object, "innovation" being peculiar to it, but also in that it presupposes aptitudes differing *in kind* and not only in degree from those of mere rational economic behavior.

Now these aptitudes are presumably distributed in an ethically homogeneous population just like others, that is the curve of their distribution has a maximum ordinate, deviations on either side of which become rarer the greater they are. Similiarly we can assume that every healthy man can sing if he will. Perhaps half the individuals in an ethically homogeneous group have the capacity for it to an average degree, a quarter in progressively diminishing measure, and, let us say, a quarter in a measure above the average; and within this quarter, through a series of continually increasing singing ability and continually diminishing number of people who possess it, we come finally to the Carusos. Only in this quarter are we struck in general by the singing ability, and only in the supreme instances can it become the characterising mark of the person. Although practically all men can sing, singing ability does not cease to be a distinguishable characteristic and attribute of a minority, indeed not exactly of a type, because

a special problem, the motive power of a great number of significant phenomena. Hence, our position may be characterised by three corresponding pairs of opposites. First, by the opposition of two real processes: the circular flow or the tendency towards equilibrium on the one hand, a change in the channels of economic routine or a spontaneous change in the economic data arising from within the system on the other. Secondly, by the opposition of two theoretical *apparatuses:* statics and dynamics.[9] Thirdly, by the opposition

this characteristic—unlike ours—affects the total personality relatively little.

Let us apply this: Again, a quarter of the population may be so poor in those qualities, let us say here provisionally, of economic initiative that the deficiency makes itself felt by poverty of their moral personality, and they play a wretched part in the smallest affairs of private and professional life in which this element is called for. We recognise this type and know that many of the best clerks, distinguished by devotion to duty, expert knowledge, and exactitude, belong to it. Then comes the "half," the "normal." These prove themselves to be better in the things which even within the established channels cannot simply be "dispatched" (erledigen) but must also be "decided" (entscheiden) and "carried out" (durchsetzen). Practically all business people belong here, otherwise they would never have attained their positions; most represent a selection—individually or hereditarily tested. A textile manufacturer travels no "new" road when he goes to a wool auction. But the situations there are never the same, and the success of the business depends so much upon skill and initiative in buying wool that the fact that the textile industry has so far exhibited no trustification comparable with that in heavy manufacturing is undoubtedly partly explicable by the reluctance of the cleverer manufacturers to renounce the advantage of their own skill in buying wool. From there, rising in the scale we come finally into the highest quarter, to people who are a type characterised by super-normal qualities of intellect and will. Within this type there are not only many varieties (merchants, manufacturers, financiers, etc.) but also a continuous variety of degrees of intensity in "initiative." In our argument types of every intensity occur. Many a one can steer a safe course, where no one has yet been; others follow where first another went before; still others only in the crowd, but in this among the first. So also the great political leader of every kind and time is a type, yet not a thing unique, but only the apex of a pyramid from which there is a continuous variation down to the average and from it to the sub-normal values. And yet not only is "leading" a special function, but the leader also something special, distinguishable—wherefore there is no sense in our case in asking: "Where does that type begin then? and then to exclaim: "This is no type at all!"

9. It has been objected against the first edition that it sometimes defines "statics" as a theoretical construction, sometimes as the picture of an actual state of economic life. I believe that the present exposition gives no ground for this opinion. "Static" theory does not assume a stationary economy; it also treats of the effects of changes in data. In itself, therefore, there is no necessary connection between static theory and stationary reality. Only in so far as one can exhibit the fundamental form of the economic course of events with the maximum simplicity in an unchanging economy does this assumption recommend itself to theory. The stationary economy is for uncounted thousands of years, and also in historical times in many places for centuries, an incontrovertible fact, apart from the fact, moreover, which Sombart emphasised, that there

of two types of conduct, which, following reality, we can picture as two types of individuals: mere managers and entrepreneurs. And therefore the "best method" of producing in the theoretical sense is to be conceived as "the most advantageous among the methods which have been empirically tested and become familiar." But it is not the "best" of the methods "possible' at the time. If one does not make this distinction, the concept becomes meaningless and precisely those problems remain unsolved which our interpretation is meant to provide for.

Let us now formulate precisely the characteristic feature of the conduct and type under discussion. The smallest daily action embodies a huge mental effort. Every schoolboy would have to be a mental giant, if he himself had to create all he knows and uses by his own individual activity. And every man would have to be a giant of wisdom and will, if he had in every case to create anew all the rules by which he guides his everyday conduct. This is true not only of those decisions and actions of individual and social life the principles of which are the product of tens of thousands of years, but also of those products of shorter periods and of a more special nature which constitute the particular instrument for performing vocational tasks. But precisely the things the performance of which according to this should involve a supreme effort, in general demand no special individual effort at

---

is a tendency towards a stationary state in every period of depression. Hence it is readily understood how this historical fact and that theoretical construction have allied themselves in a way which led to some confusion. The words "statics" and "dynamics" the author would not now use in the meaning they carry above, where they are simply short expressions for "theory of the circular flow" and "theory of development." One more thing: theory employs two methods of interpretation, which may perhaps make difficulties. If it is to be shown how all the elements of the economic system are determined in equilibrium by one another, this equilibrium system is considered as not yet existing and is built up before our eyes *ab ovo*. This does not mean that its coming into being is genetically explained thereby. Only its existence and functioning are made logically clear by mental dissection. And the experiences and habits of individuals are assumed as existing. How just these productive combinations have come about is not thereby explained. Further, if two contiguous equilibrium positions are to be investigated, then sometimes (not always), as in Pigou's Economics of Welfare, the "best" productive combination in the first is compared with the "best" in the second. And this again need not, but may, mean that the two combinations in the sense meant here differ not only by small variations in quantity but in their whole technical and commercial structure. Here too the coming into being of the second combination and the problems connected with it are not investigated, but only the functioning and the outcome of the already existing combination. Even though justified as far as it goes, this method of treatment passes over our problem. If the assertion were implied that this is also settled by it, it would be false.

all; those which should be especially difficult are in reality especially easy; what should demand superhuman capacity is accessible to the least gifted, given mental health. In particular within the ordinary routine there is no need for leadership. Of course it is still necessary to set people their tasks, to keep up discipline, and so forth; but this is easy and a function any normal person can learn to fulfil. Within the lines familiar to all, even the function of directing other people, though still necessary, is mere "work" like any other, comparable to the service of tending a machine. All people get to know, and are able to do, their daily tasks in the customary way and ordinarily perform them by themselves; the "director" has his routine as they have theirs; and his directive function serves merely to correct individual aberrations.

This is so because all knowledge and habit once acquired becomes as firmly rooted in ourselves as a railway embankment in the earth. It does not require to be continually renewed and consciously reproduced, but sinks into the strata of sub-consciousness. It is normally transmitted almost without friction by inheritance, teaching, upbringing, pressure of environment. Everything we think, feel, or do often enough becomes automatic and our conscious life is unburdened of it. The enormous economy of force, in the race and the individual, here involved is not great enough, however, to make daily life a light burden and to prevent its demands from exhausting the average energy all the same. But it is great enough to make it possible to meet the ordinary claims. This holds good likewise for economic daily life. And from this it follows also for economic life that every step outside the boundary of routine has difficulties and involves a new element. It is this element that constitutes the phenomena of leadership.

The nature of these difficulties may be focussed in the following three points. First, outside these accustomed channels the individual is without those data for his decisions and those rules of conduct which are usually very accurately known to him within them. Of course he must still foresee and estimate on the basis of his experience. But many things must remain uncertain, still others are only ascertainable within wide limits, some can perhaps only be "guessed." In particular this is true of those data which the individual strives to alter and of those which he wants to create. Now he must really to some extent do what tradition does for him in everyday life, viz. consciously plan his conduct in every particular. There will be much more conscious rationality in this than in customary action, which as such does not need to be reflected upon at all; but this plan must necessarily be open not only to errors greater in degree, but also to other kinds of errors than those occurring in customary action. What has been done already has the sharp-edged reality of all the things which we have seen and experienced; the new is only the figment of our imagination. Carrying out a new plan and acting according to a customary one are things as different as making a road and walking along it.

How different a thing this is becomes clearer if one bears in mind the impossibility of surveying exhaustively all the effects and counter-effects of the projected enterprise. Even as many of them as could in theory be ascertained if one had unlimited time and means must practically remain in the dark. As military action must be taken in a given strategic position even if all the data potentially procurable are not available, so also in economic life action must be taken without working out all the details of what is to be done. Here the success of everything depends upon intuition, the capacity of seeing things in a way which afterwards proves to be true, even though it cannot be established at the moment, and of grasping the essential fact, discarding the unessential, even though one can give no account of the principles by which this is done. Thorough preparatory work, and special knowledge, breadth of intellectual understanding, talent for logical analysis, may under certain circumstances be sources of failure. The more accurately, however, we learn to know the natural and social world, the more perfect our control of facts becomes; and the greater the extent, with time and progressive rationalisation, within which things can be simply calculated, and indeed quickly and reliably calculated, the more the significance of this function decreases. Therefore the importance of the entrepreneur type must diminish just as the importance of the military commander has already diminished. Nevertheless a part of the very essence of each type is bound up with this function.

As this first point lies in the task, so the second lies in the psyche of the businessman himself. It is not only objectively more difficult to do something new than what is familiar and tested by experience, but the individual feels reluctance to it and would do so even if the objective difficulties did not exist. This is so in all fields. The history of science is one great confirmation of the fact that we find it exceedingly difficult to adopt a new scientific point of view or method. Thought turns again and again into the accustomed track even if it has become unsuitable and the more suitable innovation in itself presents no particular difficulties. The very nature of fixed habits of thinking, their energy-saving function, is founded upon the fact that they have become subconscious, that they yield their results automatically and are proof against criticism and even against contradiction by individual facts. But precisely because of this they become drag-chains when they have outlived their usefulness. So it is also in the economic world. In the breast of one who wishes to do something new, the forces of habit rise up and bear witness against the embryonic project. A new and another kind of effort of will is therefore necessary in order to wrest, amidst the work and care of the daily round, scope and time for conceiving and working out the new combination and to bring oneself to look upon it as a real possibility and not merely as a day-dream. This mental freedom presupposes a great surplus force over the everyday demand and is something peculiar and by nature rare.

The third point consists in the reaction of the social environment against one who wishes to do something new. This reaction may manifest itself first of all in the existence of legal or political impediments. But neglecting this, any deviating conduct by a member of a social group is condemned, though in greatly varying degrees according as the social group is used to such conduct or not. Even a deviation from social custom in such things as dress or manners arouses opposition, and of course all the more so in the graver cases. This opposition is stronger in primitive stages of culture than in others, but it is never absent. Even mere astonishment at the deviation, even merely noticing it, exercises a pressure on the individual. The manifestation of condemnation may at once bring noticeable consequences in its train. It may even come to social ostracism and finally to physical prevention or to direct attack. Neither the fact that progressive differentiation weakens this opposition —especially as the most important cause of the weakening is the very development which we wish to explain—nor the further fact that the social opposition operates under certain circumstances and upon many individuals as a stimulus, changes anything in principle in the significance of it. Surmounting this opposition is always a special kind of task which does not exist in the customary course of life, a task which also requires a special kind of conduct. In matters economic this resistance manifests itself first of all in the groups threatened by the innovation, then in the difficulty in finding the necessary cooperation, finally in the difficulty in winning over consumers. Even though these elements are still effective to-day, despite the fact that a period of turbulent development has accustomed us to the appearance and the carrying out of innovations, they can be best studied in the beginnings of capitalism. But they are so obvious there that it would be time lost for our purposes to dwell upon them.

There is leadership *only* for these reasons—leadership, that is, as a special kind of function and in contrast to a mere difference in rank, which would exist in every social body, in the smallest as in the largest, and in combination with which it generally appears. The facts alluded to create a boundary beyond which the majority of people do not function promptly by themselves and require help from a minority. If social life had in all respects the relative immutability of, for example, the astronomical world, or if mutable this mutability were yet incapable of being influenced by human action, or finally if capable of being so influenced this type of action were yet equally open to everyone, then there would be no special function of leadership as distinguished from routine work.

The specific problem of leadership arises and the leader type appears only where new possibilities present themselves. That is why it is so strongly marked among the Normans at the time of their conquests and so feebly among the Slavs in the centuries of their unchanging and relatively protected life in the marshes of the Pripet. Our three points characterise the nature of the *function* as well as the *conduct* or behavior which constitutes the leader type. It is no part of his function to "find" or to "create" new possibilities. They are always present, abundantly accumulated by all sorts of people. Often they are also generally known and being discussed by scientific or literary writers. In other cases, there is nothing to discover about them, because they are quite obvious. To take an example from political life, it was not at all difficult to see how the social and political conditions of France at the time of Louis XVI could have been improved so as to avoid a breakdown of the *ancien régime*. Plenty of people as a matter of fact did see it. But nobody was in a position to *do* it. Now, it is this "doing the thing," without which possibilities are dead, of which the leader's function consists. This holds good of all kinds of leadership, ephemeral as well as more enduring ones. The former may serve as an instance. What is to be done in a casual emergency is as a rule quite simple. Most or all people may see it, yet they want someone to speak out, to lead, and to organise. Even leadership which influences merely by example, as artistic or scientific leadership, does not consist simply in finding or creating the new thing but in so impressing the social group with it as to draw it on in its wake. It is, therefore, more by will than by intellect that the leaders fulfil their function, more by "authority," "personal weight," and so forth than by original ideas.

Economic leadership in particular must hence be distinguished from "invention." As long as they are not carried into practice, inventions are economically irrelevant. And to carry any improvement into effect is a task entirely different from the inventing of it, and a task, moreover, requiring entirely different kinds of aptitudes. Although entrepreneurs of course *may* be inventors just as they may be capitalists, they are inventors not by nature of their function but by coincidence and vice versa. Besides, the innovations which it is the function of entrepreneurs to carry out need not necessarily be any inventions at all. It is, therefore, not advisable, and it may be downright misleading, to stress the element of invention as much as many writers do.

The entrepreneurial kind of leadership, as distinguished from other kinds of economic leadership such as we should expect to find in a primitive tribe of a communist society, is of course colored by the conditions peculiar to it. It has none of that glamour which characterises other kinds of leadership. It consists in fulfilling a very special task which only in rare cases appeals to the imagination of the public. For its success, keenness and vigor are not more essential than a certain narrowness which seizes the immediate chance and *nothing else*. "Personal weight" is, to be sure, not without importance. Yet the personality of the capitalistic entrepreneur need not, and generally does not, answer to the idea most of us have of what a "leader" looks like, so much so that there is some difficulty in realizing that he comes within the sociological category of leader at all. He "leads" the means of production into new channels. But this he does, not by convincing people of the desirability of carrying out his plan or by creating confidence in his leading in the manner of a political leader—the only man he has to convince or to impress is the banker who is to finance him—but by buying them or their services, and then using them as he sees fit. He also leads in the sense that he draws other producers in his branch after him. But as they are his competitors, who first reduce and then annihilate his profit, this is, as it were, leadership against one's own will. Finally, he renders a service, the full appreciation of which takes a specialist's knowledge of the case. It is not so easily understood by the public at large as a politician's successful speech or a general's victory in the field, not to insist on the fact that he seems to act—and often harshly—in his individual interest alone. We shall understand, therefore, that we do not observe, in this case, the emergence of all those affective values which are the glory of all other kinds of social leadership. Add to this the precariousness of the economic position both of the individual entrepreneur and of entrepreneurs as a group, and the fact that when his economic success raises him socially he has no cultural tradition or attitude to fall back upon, but moves about in society as an upstart, whose ways are readily laughed at, and we shall understand why this type has never been popular, and why even scientific critique often makes short work of it.[10]

We shall finally try to round off our picture of the entrepreneur in the same manner in which we always, in science as well as in practical life, try to understand human behavior, viz. by analysing the characteristic motives of his conduct. Any attempt to do this must of course meet with all those objections against the economist's intrusion into "psychology" which have been made familiar by a long series of writers. We cannot here enter into the fundamental question of the relation between psychology and economics. It is enough to state that those who on principle object to *any* psychological considerations in an economic argument may leave out what we are about to say without thereby losing contact with the argument of the following chapters. For none of the results to which our analysis is intended to lead stands or falls with our "psychology of the entrepreneur," or could be vitiated by any errors in it. Nowhere is there, as the reader will easily satisfy himself, any necessity for us to overstep the frontiers of observable behavior. Those who do not object to *all* psychology but only to the *kind* of psychology which we know from the traditional textbook, will see that we do not adopt any part of the time-honored picture of the motivation of the "economic man."

In the theory of the circular flow, the importance of examining motives is very much reduced by the fact that the equations of the system of equilibrium may be so interpreted as not to imply any psychic magnitudes at all, as shown by the analysis of Pareto and of Barone. This is the reason why even very defective psychology interferes much less with results than one would expect. There may be rational *conduct* even in the absence of rational *motive*. But as soon as we really wish to penetrate

into motivation, the problem proves by no means simple. Within given social circumstances and habits, most of what people do every day will appear to them primarily from the point of view of duty carrying a social or a superhuman sanction. There is very little of conscious rationality, still less of hedonism and of *individual* egoism about it, and so much of it as may safely be said to exist is of comparatively recent growth. Nevertheless, as long as we confine ourselves to the great outlines of constantly repeated economic action, we may link it up with wants and the desire to satisfy them, on condition that we are careful to recognise that economic motive so defined varies in intensity very much in time; that it is society that shapes the particular desires we observe; that wants must be taken with reference to the group which the individual thinks of when deciding his course of action—the family or any other group, smaller or larger than the family; that action does not promptly follow upon desire but only more or less imperfectly corresponds to it; that the field of individual choice is always, though in very different ways and to very different degrees, fenced in by social habits or conventions and the like: it still remains broadly true that, within the circular flow, everyone adapts himself to his environment so as to satisfy certain *given* wants—of himself or others—as best he can. In *all* cases, the *meaning* of economic action is the satisfaction of wants in the sense that there would be no economic action if there were no wants. In the case of the circular flow, we may also think of satisfaction of wants as the normal *motive*.

The latter is not true for our type. In one sense, he may indeed be called the most rational and the most egotistical of all. For, as we have seen, conscious rationality enters much more into the carrying out of new plans, which themselves have to be worked out before they can be acted upon, than into the mere running of an established business, which is largely a matter of routine. And the typical entrepreneur is more self-centered than other types, because he relies less than they do on tradition and connection and because his characteristic task—theoretically as well as historically—consists precisely in breaking up old, and creating new, tradition. Although this applies primarily to his economic action, it also extends to the moral, cultural, and social consequences of it. It is, of course, no mere coincidence that the period of the rise of the entrepreneur type also gave birth to Utilitarianism.

But his conduct and his motive are "rational" in no other sense. And in *no* sense is his character-

10. It may, therefore, not be superfluous to point out that our analysis of the rôle of the entrepreneur does not involve any "glorification" of the type, as some readers of the first edition of this book seemed to think. We do hold that entrepreneurs *have* an economic function as distinguished from, say, robbers. But we neither style every entrepreneur a genius or a benefactor to humanity, nor do we wish to express any opinion about the comparative merits of the social organisation in which he plays his rôle, or about the question whether what he does could not be effected more cheaply or efficiently in other ways.

istic motivation of the hedonist kind. If we define hedonist motive of action as the wish to satisfy one's wants, we may indeed make "wants" include any impulse whatsoever, just as we may define egoism so as to include all altruistic values too, on the strength of the fact that they also mean something in the way of self-gratification. But this would reduce our definition to tautology. If we wish to give it meaning, we must restrict it to such wants as are capable of being satisfied by the consumption of goods, and to that kind of satisfaction which is expected from it. Then it is no longer true that our type is acting on a wish to satisfy his wants.

For unless we assume that individuals of our type are driven along by an insatiable craving for hedonist satisfaction, the operations of Gossen's law would in the case of business leaders soon put a stop to further effort. Experience teaches, however, that typical entrepreneurs retire from the arena only when and because their strength is spent and they feel no longer equal to their task. This does not seem to verify the picture of the economic man, balancing probable results against disutility of effort and reaching in due course a point of equilibrium beyond which he is not willing to go. Effort, in our case, does not seem to weigh at all in the sense of being felt as a reason to stop. And activity of the entrepreneurial type is obviously an obstacle to hedonist enjoyment of those kinds of commodity which are usually acquired by incomes beyond a certain size, because their "consumption" presupposes leisure. Hedonistically, therefore, the conduct which we usually observe in individuals of our type would be irrational.

This would not, of course, prove the absence of hedonistic motive. Yet it points to another psychology of non-hedonist character, especially if we take into account the indifference to hedonist enjoyment which is often conspicuous in outstanding specimens of the type and which is not difficult to understand.

First of all, there is the dream and the will to found a private kingdom, usually, though not necessarily, also a dynasty. The modern world really does not know any such positions, but what may be attained by industrial or commercial success is still the nearest approach to medieval lordship possible to modern man. Its fascination is specially strong for people who have no other chance of achieving social distinction. The sensation of power and independence loses nothing by the fact that both are largely illusions. Closer analysis would lead to discovering an endless variety within this group of motives, from spiritual ambition down to mere snobbery. But this need

not detain us. Let it suffice to point out that motives of this kind, although they stand nearest to consumers' satisfaction, do not coincide with it.

Then there is the will to conquer: the impulse to fight, to prove oneself superior to others, to succeed for the sake, not of the fruits of success, but of success itself. From this aspect, economic action becomes akin to sport—there are financial races, or rather boxing-matches. The financial result is a secondary consideration, or, at all events, mainly valued as an index of success and as a symptom of victory, the displaying of which very often is more important as a motive of large expenditure than the wish for the consumers' goods themselves. Again we should find countless nuances, some of which, like social ambition, shade into the first group of motives. And again we are faced with a motivation characteristically different from that of "satisfaction of wants" in the sense defined above, or from, to put the same thing into other words, "hedonistic adaptation."

Finally, there is the joy of creating, of getting things done, or simply of exercising one's energy and ingenuity. This is akin to a ubiquitous motive, but nowhere else does it stand out as an independent factor of behavior with anything like the clearness with which it obtrudes itself in our case. Our type seeks out difficulties, changes in order to change, delights in ventures. This group of motives is the most distinctly anti-hedonist of the three.

Only with the first groups of motives is private property as the result of entrepreneurial activity an essential factor in making it operative. With the other two it is not. Pecuniary gain is indeed a very accurate expression of success, especially of *relative* success, and from the standpoint of the man who strives for it, it has the additional advantage of being an objective fact and largely independent of the opinion of others. These and other peculiarities incident to the mechanism of "acquisitive" society make it very difficult to replace it as a motor of industrial development, even if we would discard the importance it has for creating a fund ready for investment. Nevertheless it is true that the second and third groups of entrepreneurial motives may in principle be taken care of by other social arrangements not involving private gain from economic innovation. What other stimuli could be provided, and how they could be made to work as well as the "capitalistic" ones do, are questions which are beyond our theme. They are taken too lightly by social reformers, and are altogether ignored by fiscal radicalism. But they are not insoluble, and may be answered by detailed observation of the psychology of entrepreneurial activity, at least for given times and places.

Section C

Stratification and Mobility

Editorial Foreword, BY TALCOTT PARSONS   *517*

1. *Of Wages and Profit in the Different Employments of Labor and Stock,* BY ADAM SMITH   *518*
2. *The Class Struggle,* BY KARL MARX   *529*
3. *Class and Occupations,* BY EDMOND GOBLOT   *535*
4. *On Superordination and Subordination,* BY GEORG SIMMEL   *540*
5. *The Circulation of Elites,* BY VILFREDO PARETO   *551*
6. *Conspicuous Consumption,* BY THORSTEIN VEBLEN   *558*
7. *Social Stratification,* BY PITIRIM A. SOROKIN   *570*
8. *Social Stratification and Class Structure,* BY MAX WEBER   *573*

Stratification and Mobility

by Talcott Parsons

Though it is prominent in more recent sociology, particularly in the United States, the subject of social stratification did not, in the earlier phases, produce a large volume of notable literature. This section's relative brevity reflects this fact; there are not many writings which were highly influential.

The modern sociological interest in stratification has taken most of its departure from its reference to economic organization as this took shape in Western society during the Industrial Revolution, and the concept has been amplified from there. Hence the initial selection we present is by Adam Smith, though not, this time, with direct reference to the problem of economic organization, except as implicit background. This selection is concerned with the way in which the problem of the distribution of wealth became focused in the classical economics. There are three shares of income that figure in that analysis; and rent became progressively less important as industrial organization began overshadowing agriculture. Hence it is the relation between the businessman's profit (which, in the classical scheme, included interest) and the worker's wages that formed the focus of the important conflict of interest. This was associated with the assumption, discussed in the general Introduction to Part Two, that there was a relatively simple dichotomy between owning-managing family groups and property-less "workers." As noted in the Introduction to Section B, the owner's function was conceived more as "making advances to labor" than as active management.

Into his concept of class struggle, Marx built this broad picture of the structure of industry and its inherent conflict of interest over proceeds. The *Communist Manifesto* itself is the best statement of the Marxist position, and a selection from that presents the position.

Theoretical development occurred essentially through a process of amplification from this economic point of reference. Goblot presents an analysis concentrating on the style-of-life aspect of social class; occupation becomes an essential component, though not the final criterion, of membership. Possibly the style-of-life aspect of occupation may be more important than its effective contribution to society. He is chiefly interested in showing the consequence of the class function—the stabilization of life chances—for the recruitment process (the barrier) and for the inner structure of the class (the level).

The following three selections vary their emphasis somewhat; instead of concentrating on the most general structural picture, they emphasize a more detailed analysis of components in a society's hierarchical structure. Simmel took the general pattern of super- and sub-ordination as a type case of "social form," and attempted to survey the various modes in which this dimension of social relationships could develop. Like Goblot, Simmel reacted strongly against any simple dichotomy concept which could be applied universally to characterize a whole society; but Simmel extended his analysis to include non-occupational bases of hierarchy.

The selections from Pareto and Veblen deal with somewhat more specialized aspects of the problem. Pareto retains the dichotomy between a system's elite and non-elite components, but he broadens the Marxian analysis. He treats elites with different functional positions in the society as, within limits, independently variable—he recognizes the independent significance of the political process, and does not reduce political leadership in a capitalistic age to the status of the "executive committee of the bourgeoisie." Also, Pareto was one of the early authors to emphasize mobility—genetic con-

517

tinuity in kinship terms is not a given; there are complex processes of differentially selective recruitment of elite groups of different sorts. In this respect, Pareto exemplifies an important phase of the revolt against the exclusive economic Marxian emphasis. For Pareto, it was a revolt primarily in favor of the autonomy of political processes.

Veblen was the most important early American theorist in this field. He shared, though with many qualifications, the broad Marxist view of the main conflict of interest in industrial society, and disparaged the pretensions of the upper groups. His treatment of conspicuous consumption, developed in the *Theory of the Leisure Class,* initiated consideration of the interrelations between the analysis of conflicting economic interest in the Marxian tradition, and the symbolic significance of patterns of the style of life that could be applied on a more broadly comparative basis. Perhaps without knowing it, Veblen was subtly challenging the doctrine of the nearly exclusive predominance of economic interest; otherwise, why should the motive of validation of status through the proper style of life be so powerful? Veblen's interests are obviously connected with the "conformity" problem so prominent in current American social science. Veblen, like Pareto, concentrated on a somewhat special case. Pareto dealt with the instability of the late nineteenth-century alliance between a rising business-oriented bourgeoisie and the controllers of political organization. Veblen was concerned with the status-validation of the American business magnates who had risen during the post-Civil War period. Within a generation, however, these problems were to shift so radically that Pareto's and Veblen's empirical interpretations became dated. But in the history of thought, both raised problems which could not be easily solved within the utilitarian-Marxist frame of reference.

The last two selections in this section treat these problems more generally. In his *Social Mobility,* Sorokin considers social stratification as involving a plurality of relatively independent scales of evaluation, of which the economic was only one. Weber's chapter (from *The Theory of Social and Economic Organization*) is only a fragment, the bare beginning of what was obviously intended to be an extended essay, comparable to the essay on types of authority. The most critical point is the distinction between "class" and "status" as foci of social stratification. Here Weber was consciously attempting to make the Marxian emphasis on economic interest relative, and to place the economic factor in a more comprehensive frame of reference. Both selections present phases of the general reaction against economic determinism in favor of a more general analysis of social systems. There is an evident relation between this shift and the evolutionary and comparative interests stressed in Part Two.

1. Of Wages and Profit in the Different Employments of Labor and Stock

BY ADAM SMITH

THE whole of the advantages and disadvantages of the different employments of labour and stock, must, in the same neighbourhood, be either perfectly equal, or continually tending to equality. If in the same neighbourhood, there was any employment evidently either more or less advantageous than the rest, so many people would crowd into it in the one case, and so many would desert it in the other, that its advantages would soon return to the level of other employments. This at least would be the case in a society where things were left to follow their natural course, where there was perfect liberty, and where every man was perfectly free both to chuse what occupation he thought proper, and to change it as often as he thought proper. Every man's interest would prompt him to seek the advantageous, and to shun the disadvantageous employment.

Reprinted from Adam Smith, *An Inquiry into the Nature and Causes of the Wealth of Nations* (7th ed.; London: A. Strahan & T. Cadell, 1793), chap. x, pp. 151–84, 188–89, 200–3, 209.

Pecuniary wages and profit, indeed, are every where in Europe extremely different, according to the different employments of labour and stock. But this difference arises partly from certain circumstances in the employments themselves, which, either really, or at least in the imaginations of men, make up for a small pecuniary gain in some, and counter-balance a great one in others; and partly from the policy of Europe, which no-where leaves things at perfect liberty.

The particular consideration of those circumstances and of that policy will divide this chapter into two parts.

Inequalities Arising from the Nature of the Employments Themselves

The five following are the principal circumstances which, so far as I have been able to observe, make up for a small pecuniary gain in some employments, and counter-balance a great one in others: first, the agreeableness or disagreeableness of the employments themselves; secondly, the easiness and cheapness, or the difficulty and expence of learning them; thirdly, the constancy or inconstancy of employment in them; fourthly, the small or great trust which must be reposed in those who exercise them; and fifthly, the probability or improbability of success in them.

First, the wages of labour vary with the ease or hardship, the cleanliness or dirtiness, the honourableness or dishonourableness of the employment. Thus in most places, take the year round, a journeyman taylor earns less than a journeyman weaver. His work is much easier. A journeyman weaver earns less than a journeyman smith. His work is not always easier, but it is much cleanlier. A journeyman blacksmith, though an artificer, seldom earns so much in twelve hours, as a collier, who is only a labourer, does in eight. His work is not quite so dirty, is less dangerous, and is carried on in daylight, and above ground. Honour makes a great part of the reward of all honourable professions. In point of pecuniary gain, all things considered, they are generally under-recompensed, as I shall endeavour to shew by and by. Disgrace has the contrary effect. The trade of a butcher is a brutal and an odious business; but it is in most places more profitable that the greater part of common trades. The most detestable of all employments, that of public executioner, is, in proportion to the quantity of work done, better paid than any common trade whatever.

Hunting and fishing, the most important employments of mankind in the rude state of society, become in its advanced state their most agreeable amusements, and they pursue for pleasure what they once followed from necessity. In the advanced state of society, therefore, they are all very poor people who follow as a trade, what other people pursue as a pastime. Fishermen have been so since the time of Theocritus. A poacher is every-where a very poor man in Great Britain. In countries where the rigour of the law suffers no poachers, the licensed hunter is not in a much better condition. The natural taste for those employments makes more people follow them than can live comfortably by them, and the produce of their labour, in proportion to its quantity, comes always too cheap to market to afford any thing but the most scanty subsistence to the labourers.

Disagreeableness and disgrace affect the profits of stock in the same manner as the wages of labour. The keeper of an inn or tavern, who is never master of his own house, and who is exposed to the brutality of every drunkard, exercises neither a very agreeable nor a very creditable business. But there is scarce any common trade in which a small stock yields so great a profit.

Secondly, the wages of labour vary with the easiness and cheapness, or the difficulty and expence of learning the business.

When any expensive machine is erected, the extraordinary work to be performed by it before it is worn out, it must be expected, will replace the capital laid out upon it, with at least the ordinary profits. A man educated at the expence of much labour and time to any of those employments, which require extraordinary dexterity and skill, may be compared to one of those expensive machines. The work which he learns to perform, it must be expected, over and above the usual wages of common labour, will replace to him the whole expence of his education, with at least the ordinary profits of an equally valuable capital. It must do this too in a reasonable time, regard being had to the very uncertain duration of human life, in the same manner as to the more certain duration of the machine.

The difference between the wages of skilled labour and those of common labour, is founded upon this principle.

The policy of Europe considers the labour of all mechanics, artificers, and manufacturers, as skilled labour; and that of all country labourers as common labour. It seems to suppose that of the former to be of a more nice and delicate nature than that of the latter. It is so perhaps in some cases; but in the greater part it is quite otherwise, as I shall endeavour to shew by and by. The laws and customs of Europe, therefore, in order to qualify any person for exercising the one species of labour, impose the necessity of an apprenticeship, though with different degrees of rigour in different places. They leave the other free and open to every body. During the continuance of the apprenticeship, the whole labour of the apprentice belongs to his master. In the mean time he must, in many cases, be maintained by his parents or relations, and in almost all cases must be cloathed by them. Some money too is commonly given to the master for teaching him his trade. They who cannot give money, give time, or become bound for more than the usual number of years; a consideration which, though it is not always advantageous to the master, on account of the usual idleness of apprentices, is always disadvantageous to the apprentice. In country labour, on the contrary, the labourer, while he is employed about the easier, learns the more difficult parts of his business, and his own labour maintains him through all the different stages of his employment. It is reasonable, therefore, that in Europe the wages of mechanics, artificers, and manufacturers, should be somewhat higher than those of common labourers. They are so accordingly, and their superior gains make them in most places be considered as a superior rank of people. This superiority, however, is generally very small; the daily or weekly earnings of journeymen in the more common sorts of manufactures, such as those of plain linen and woollen cloth, computed at an average, are, in most places, very little more than the day wages of common labourers. Their employment, indeed, is more steady and uniform, and the superiority of their earnings, taking the whole year together, may be somewhat greater. It seems evidently, however, to be no greater than what is sufficient to compensate the superior expence of their education.

Education in the ingenious arts and in the liberal professions, is still more tedious and expensive. The pecuniary recompence, therefore, of painters and sculptors, of lawyers and physicians, ought to be much more liberal: and it is so accordingly.

The profits of stock seem to be very little affected by the easiness or difficulty of learning the trade in which it is employed. All the different ways in which stock is commonly employed in great towns seem, in reality, to be almost equally easy and and equally difficult to learn. One branch either of foreign or domestic trade, cannot well be a much more intricate business than another.

Thirdly, the wages of labour in different occupations vary with the constancy or inconstancy of employment.

Employment is much more constant in some trades than in others. In the greater part of manufactures, a journeyman may be pretty sure of employment almost every day in the year that he is able to work. A mason or bricklayer, on the contrary, can work neither in hard frost nor in foul weather, and his employment at all other times depends upon the occasional calls of his customers. He is liable, in consequence, to be frequently without any. What he earns, therefore, while he is employed, must not only maintain him while he is idle, but make him some compensation for those anxious and desponding moments which the thought of so precarious a situation must sometimes occasion. Where the computed earnings of the greater part of manufacturers, accordingly, are nearly upon a level with the day wages of common labourers, those of masons and bricklayers are generally from one half more to double those wages. Where common labourers earn four and five shillings a week, masons and bricklayers frequently earn seven and eight; where the former earn six, the latter often earn nine and ten, and where the former earn nine and ten, as in London, the latter commonly earn fifteen and eighteen. No species of skilled labour, however, seems more easy to learn than that of masons and bricklayers. Chairmen in London, during the summer season, are said sometimes to be employed as bricklayers. The high wages of those workmen, therefore, are not so much the recompence of their skill, as the compensation for the inconstancy of their employment.

A house carpenter seems to exercise rather a nicer and more ingenious trade than a mason. In most places, however, for it is not universally so, his day-wages are somewhat lower. His employment, though it depends much, does not depend so entirely upon the occasional calls of his customers; and it is not liable to be interrupted by the weather.

When the trades which generally afford constant employment, happen in a particular place not to do so, the wages of the workmen always rise a good deal above their ordinary proportion to those of common labour. In London almost all journeymen artificers are liable to be called upon and dismissed by their masters from day to day, and from week to week, in the same manner as day-labourers in other places. The lowest order of artificers, journeymen taylors, accordingly, earn there half a crown a day, though eighteen pence may be reckoned the wages of common labour. In small towns and country villages, the wages of journeymen taylors frequently scarce equal those of common labour; but in London they are often many weeks without employment, particulary during the summer.

When the inconstancy of employment is combined with the hardship, disagreeableness, and dirtiness of the work, it sometimes raises the wages of the most common labour above those of the most skilful artificers. A collier working by the piece is supposed at Newcastle to earn commonly about double, and in many parts of Scotland about three times the wages of common labour. His high wages arise altogether from the hardship, disagreeableness, and dirtiness of his work. His employment may, upon most occasions, be as constant as he pleases. The coal-heavers in London exercise a trade which in hardship, dirtiness, and disagreeableness, almost equals that of colliers; and from the unavoidable irregularity in the arrivals of coal ships, the employment of the greater part of them is necessarily very inconstant. If colliers, therefore, commonly earn double and triple the wages of common labour, it ought not to seem unreasonable that coal heavers should sometimes earn four and five times those wages. In the enquiry made into their condition a few years ago, it was found that at the rate at which they were then paid, they could earn from six to ten shillings a day. Six shillings are about four times the wages of common labour in London, and in every particular trade, the lowest common earnings may always be considered as those of the far greater number. How extravagant soever those earnings may appear, if they were more than sufficient to compensate all the disagreeable circumstances of the business, there would soon be so great a number of competitors as, in a trade which has no exclusive privilege, would quickly reduce them to a lower rate.

The constancy or inconstancy of employment cannot affect the ordinary profits of stock in any particular trade. Whether the stock is or is not constantly employed depends, not upon the trade, but the trader.

Fourthly, the wages of labour vary according to the small or great trust which must be reposed in the workmen.

The wages of goldsmiths and jewellers are everywhere superior to those of many other workmen, not only of equal, but of much superior ingenuity; on account of the precious materials with which they are intrusted.

We trust our health to the physician; our fortune, and sometimes our life and reputation, to the lawyer and attorney. Such confidence could not safely be reposed in people of a very mean or low condition. Their reward must be such, therefore, as may give them that rank in the society which so important a trust requires. The long time and the great expence which must be laid out in their education, when combined with this circumstance, necessarily enhance still further the price of their labour.

When a person employs only his own stock in trade, there is no trust; and the credit which he may get from other people depends, not upon the nature of his trade, but upon their opinion of his fortune, probity, and prudence. The different rates of profit, therefore, in the different branches of trade, cannot arise from the different degrees of trust reposed in the traders.

Fifthly, the wages of labour in different employments vary according to the probability or improbability of success in them.

The probability that any particular person shall ever be qualified for the employment to which he is educated, is very different in different occupations. In the greater part of mechanic trades, success is almost certain; but very uncertain in the liberal professions. Put your son apprentice to a shoemaker, there is little doubt of his learning to make a pair of shoes: but send him to study the law, it is at least twenty to one if ever he makes such proficiency as will enable him to live by the business. In a perfectly fair lottery, those who draw the prizes ought to gain all that is lost by those who draw the blanks. In a profession where twenty fail for one that succeeds, that one ought to gain all that should have been gained by the unsuccessful twenty. The counsellor at law who, perhaps, at near forty years of age, begins to make something by his profession, ought to receive the retribution, not only of his own so tedious and expensive education, but of that of more than twenty other who are never likely to make any thing by it. How extravagant soever the fees of counsellors at law may sometimes appear, their real retribution is never equal to this. Compute in any particular place what is likely to be annually gained, and what is likely to be annually spent, by all the different workmen in any common trade, such as that of shoemakers or weavers, and you will find that the former sum will generally exceed the latter. But make the same computation with regard to all the counsellors and students of law, in all the different inns of court, and you will find that their annual gains bear but a very small proportion to their annual expence, even though you rate the former as high, and the latter as low, as can well be done. The lottery of the law, therefore, is very far from being a perfectly fair lottery; and that, as well as many other liberal and honourable professions, is, in point of pecuniary gain, evidently under-recompensed.

Those professions keep their level, however, with other occupations, and, notwithstanding these discouragements, all the most generous and liberal spirits are eager to crowd into them. Two different causes contribute to recommend them. First, the desire of the reputation which attends upon superior excellence in any of them; and, secondly, the natural confidence which every man has more or less, not only in his own abilities, but in his own good fortune.

To excel in any profession, in which but few arrive at mediocrity, is the most decisive mark of what is called genius or superior talents. The public admiration which attends upon such distinguished abilities, makes always a part of their reward; a greater or smaller in proportion as it is higher or lower in degree. It makes a considerable part of that reward in the profession of physic; a still greater, perhaps, in that of law; in poetry and philosophy it makes almost the whole.

There are some very agreeable and beautiful talents, of which the possession commands a certain sort of admiration; but of which the exercise for the sake of gain is considered, whether from reason or prejudice, as a sort of public prostitution. The pecuniary recompence, therefore, of those who exercise them in this manner, must be sufficient, not only to pay for the time, labour, and expence of acquiring the talents, but for the discredit which attends the employment of them as the means of subsistence. The exorbitant rewards of players, opera-singers, opera-dancers, &c. are founded upon those two principles; the rarity and beauty of the talents, and the discredit of employing them in this manner. It seems absurd at first sight that we should despise their persons, and yet reward their talents with the most profuse liberality. While we do the one, however, we must of necessity do the other. Should the public opinion or prejudice ever alter with regard to such occupations, their pecuniary recompence would quickly diminish. More people would apply to them, and the competition would quickly reduce the price of their labour. Such talents, though far from being common, are by no means so rare as is imagined. Many people possess them in great perfection, who disdain to make this use of them; and many more are capable of acquiring them, if any thing could be made honourably by them.

The over-weaning conceit which the greater part of men have of their own abilities, is an ancient evil remarked by the philosophers and moralists of all ages. Their absurd presumption in their own good fortune, has been less taken notice of. It is, however, if possible, still more universal. There is no man living, who, when in tolerable health and spirits, has not some share of it. The chance of gain is by every man more or less over-valued, and the chance of loss is by most men under-valued, and by scarce any man, who is in tolerable health and spirits, valued more than it is worth.

That the chance of gain is naturally overvalued, we may learn from the universal success of lotteries. The world neither ever saw, nor ever will see, a perfectly fair lottery; or one in which the whole gain compensated the whole loss; because the undertaker could make nothing by it. In the state lotteries the tickets are really not worth the price which is paid by the original subscribers, and yet commonly sell in the market for twenty, thirty, and sometimes forty per cent. advance. The vain hope of gaining some of the great prizes is the sole cause of this demand. The soberest people scarce look upon it as a folly to pay a small sum for the chance of gaining ten or twenty thousand pounds; though they know that even that small sum is perhaps twenty or thirty per cent. more than the chance is worth. In a lottery in which no prize exceeded twenty pounds, though in other respects it approached much nearer to a perfectly fair one than the common state lotteries, there would not be the same demand for tickets. In order to have a better chance for some of the great prizes, some people purchase several tickets, and others, small shares in a still greater number. There is not, however, a more certain proposition in mathematics, than that the more tickets you adventure upon, the more likely you are to be a loser. Adventure upon all the tickets in the lottery, and you lose for certain; and the greater the number of your tickets, the nearer you approach to this certainty.

That the chance of loss is frequently undervalued, and scarce ever valued more than it is worth, we may learn from the very moderate profit of insurers. In order to make insurance, either from fire or sea-risk, a trade at all, the common premium must be sufficient to compensate the common losses, to pay the expence of management, and to afford such a profit as might have been drawn from an equal capital employed in any common trade. The person who pays no more than this, evidently pays no more than the real value of the risk, or the lowest price at which he can reasonably expect to insure it. But though many people have made a little money by insurance, very few have made a great fortune; and from this consideration alone, it seems evident enough, that the ordinary balance of profit and loss is not more advantageous in this, than in other common trades by which so many people make fortunes. Moderate, however, as the premium of insurance commonly is, many people despise the risk too much to care to pay it. Taking the whole kingdom at an average, nineteen houses in twenty, or rather, perhaps, ninety-nine in a hundred, are not insured from fire. Sea-risk is more alarming to the greater part of people, and the proportion of ships insured to those not insured is much greater. Many sail, however, at all seasons, and even in time of war, without any insurance. This may sometimes perhaps be done without any imprudence. When a great company, or even a great merchant, has twenty or thirty ships at sea, they may, as it were, insure one another. The premium saved upon them all, may more than compensate such losses as they are likely to meet with in the common course of chances. The neglect of insurance upon shipping, however, in the same manner as upon houses, is in most cases, the effect of no such nice calculation, but of mere thoughtless rashness and presumptuous contempt of the risk.

The contempt of risk and the presumptuous hope of success, are in no period of life more active than at the age at which young people chuse their professions. How little the fear of misfortune is then capable of balancing the hope of good luck, appears still more evidently in the readiness of the common people to enlist as soldiers, or to go to sea, than in the eagerness of those of better fashion to enter into what are called the liberal professions.

What a common soldier may lose is obvious enough. Without regarding the danger, however, young volunteers never enlist so readily as at the beginning of a new war; and though they have scarce any chance of preferment, they figure to themselves, in their youthful fancies, a thousand occasions of acquiring honour and distinction which never occur. These romantic hopes make the whole price of their blood. Their pay is less than that of common labourers, and in actual service their fatigues are much greater.

The lottery of the sea is not altogether so disadvantageous as that of the army. The son of a creditable labourer or artificer may frequently go to sea with his father's consent; but if he enlists as a soldier, it is always without it. Other people see some chance of his making something by the one trade: nobody but himself sees any of his making any thing by the other. The great admiral is less the object of public admiration than the great general; and the highest success in the sea service promises a less brilliant fortune and reputation than equal success in the land. The same difference runs through all the inferior degrees of preferment in both. By the rules of precedency a captain in the navy ranks with a colonel in the army: but he does not rank with him in the common estimation. As the great prizes in the lottery are less, the smaller ones must be more numerous. Common sailors, therefore, more frequently get some fortune and preferment than common soldiers; and the hope of those prizes is what principally recommends the trade. Though their skill and dexterity are much superior to that of almost any artificers, and though their whole life is one continual scene of hardship and danger, yet for all this dexterity and skill, for all those hardships and dangers, while they remain in the condition of common sailors, they receive scarce any other recompence but the pleasure of exercising the one and of surmounting the other. Their wages are not greater than those of common labourers at the port which regulates the rate of seamen's wages. As they are continually going from port to port, the monthly pay of those who fail from all the different ports of Great Britain, is more nearly upon a level than that of any other workmen in those different places; and the rate of the port to and from which the greatest number fail, that is, the port of London, regulates that of all the rest. At London the wages of the greater part of the different classes of workmen are about double those of the same classes at Edinburgh. But the sailors who sail from the port of London seldom earn above three or four shillings a month more than those who sail from the port of Leith, and the difference is frequently not so great. In time of peace, and in the merchant service, the London price is from a guinea to about seven-and-twenty shillings the calendar month. A common labourer in London, at the rate of nine or ten shillings a week, may earn in the calendar month from forty to five-and-forty shillings. The sailor, indeed, over and above his pay, is supplied with provisions. Their value, however, may not perhaps always exceed the difference between his pay and that of the common labourer; and though it sometimes should, the excess will not be clear gain to the sailor, because he cannot share it with his wife and family, whom he must maintain out of his wages at home.

The dangers and hair-breadth escapes of a life of adventures, instead of disheartening young people, seem frequently to recommend a trade to them. A tender mother, among the inferior ranks of people, is often afraid to send her son to school at a sea-port town, lest the sight of the ships and the conversation and adventures of the sailors should entice him to go to sea. The distant prospect of hazards, from which we can hope to extricate ourselves by courage and address, is not disagreeable to us, and does not raise the wages of labour in any employment. It is otherwise with those in which courage and address can be of no avail. In trades which are known to be very unwholesome, the wages of labour are always remarkably high. Unwholesomeness is a species of disagreeableness, and its affects upon the wages of labour are to be ranked under that general head.

In all the different employments of stock, the ordinary rate of profit varies more or less with the certainty or uncertainty of the returns. These are in general less uncertain in the inland than in the foreign trade, and in some branches of foreign trade than in others; in the trade to North America, for example, than in that to Jamaica. The ordinary rate of profit always rises more or less with the risk. It does not, however, seem to rise in proportion to it, or so as to compensate it completely. Bankruptcies are most frequent in the most hazardous trades. The most hazardous of all trades, that of a smuggler. though when the adventure succeeds it is likewise the most profitable, is the infallible road to bankruptcy. The presumptuous hope of success seems to act here as upon all other occasions, and to entice so many adventurers into those hazardous trades, that their competition reduces their profit below what is sufficient to compensate the risk. To compensate it completely, the common returns ought, over and above the ordinary profits of stock, not only to make up for all occasional losses, but to afford a surplus profit to the adventurers of the same nature with the profit of insurers. But if the common returns were sufficient for all this, bankruptcies would not be more frequent in these than in other trades.

Of the five circumstances, therefore, which vary the wages of labour, two only affect the profits of stock; the agreeableness or disagreeableness of the business, and the risk or security with which it is attended. In point of agreeableness or disagreeableness, there is little or no difference in the far greater part of the different employments of stock; but a great deal in those of labour; and the ordinary profit of stock, though it rises with the risk, does not always seem to rise in proportion to it. It should follow from all this, that, in the same society or neighbourhood, the average and ordinary rates of profit in the different employments of stock should be more nearly upon a level than the pecuniary wages of the different sorts of labour. They are so accordingly. The difference between the earnings of a common labourer and those of a well employed lawyer or physician, is evidently much greater than that between the ordinary profits in any two different branches of trade. The apparent difference, besides, in the profits of different trades, is generally a deception arising from our not always distinguishing what ought to be considered as wages, from what ought to be considered as profit.

Apothecaries profit is become a bye-word, denoting something uncommonly extravagant. This great apparent profit, however, is frequently no more than the reasonable wages of labour. The skill of an apothecary is a much nicer and more delicate matter than that of any artificer whatever; and the trust which is reposed in him is of much greater importance. He is the physician of the poor in all cases, and of the rich when the distress or danger is not very great. His reward, therefore, ought to be suitable to his skill and his trust, and it arises generally from the price at which he sells his drugs. But the whole drugs which the best em-

ployed apothecary, in a large market town, will sell in a year, may not perhaps cost him above thirty or forty pounds. Though he should sell them, therefore, for three or four hundred, or at a thousand per cent. profit, this may frequently be no more than the reasonable wages of his labour charged, in the only way in which he can charge them, upon the price of his drugs. The greater part of the apparent profit is real wages disguised in the garb of profit.

In a small sea-port town, a little grocer will make forty or fifty per cent. upon a stock of a single hundred pounds, while a considerable wholesale merchant in the same place will scarce make eight or ten per cent. upon a stock of ten thousand. The trade of the grocer may be necessary for the conveniency of the inhabitants, and the narrowness of the market may not admit the employment of a larger capital in the business. The man, however, must not only live by his trade, but live by it suitably to the qualifications which it requires. Besides possessing a little capital, he must be able to read, write, and account, and must be a tolerable judge too of, perhaps, fifty or sixty different sorts of goods, their prices, qualities, and the markets where they are to be had cheapest. He must have all the knowledge, in short, that is necessary for a great merchant, which nothing hinders him from becoming but the want of a sufficient capital. Thirty or forty pounds a year cannot be considered as too great a recompence for the labour of a person so accomplished. Deduct this from the seemingly great profits of his capital, and little more will remain, perhaps, than the ordinary profits of stock. The greater part of the apparent profit is, in this case too, real wages.

The difference between the apparent profit of the retail and that of the wholesale trade, is much less in the capital than in small towns and country villages. Where ten thousand pounds can be employed in the grocery trade, the wages of the grocer's labour must be a very trifling addition to the real profits of so great a stock. The apparent profits of the wealthy retailer, therefore, are there more nearly upon a level with those of the wholesale merchant. It is upon this account that goods sold by retail are generally as cheap and frequently much cheaper in the capital than in small towns and country villages. Grocery goods, for example, are generally much cheaper; bread and butcher's meat frequently as cheap. It costs no more to bring grocery goods to the great town than to the country village; but it costs a great deal more to bring corn and cattle, as the greater part of them must be brought from a much greater distance. The prime cost of grocery goods, therefore, being the same in both places, they are cheapest where the least profit is charged upon them. The prime cost of bread and butcher's meat is greater in the great town than in the country village; and though the profit is less, therefore they are not always cheaper there, but often equally cheap. In such articles as bread and butcher's meat, the same cause, which diminishes apparent profit, increases prime cost. The extent of the market, by giving employment to greater stocks, diminishes apparent profit; but by requiring supplies from a greater distance, it increases prime cost. This diminution of the one and increase of the other seem, in most cases, nearly to counter-balance one another; which is probably the reason that, though the prices of corn and cattle are commonly very different in different parts of the kingdom, those of bread and butcher's meat are generally very nearly the same through the greater part of it.

Though the profits of stock both in the wholesale and retail trade are generally less in the capital than in small towns and country villages, yet great fortunes are frequently acquired from small beginnings in the former, and scarce ever in the latter. In small towns and country villages, on account of the narrowness of the market, trade cannot always be extended as stock extends. In such places, therefore, though the rate of a particular person's profits may be very high, the sum or amount of them can never be very great, nor consequently that of his annual accumulation. In great towns, on the contrary, trade can be extended as stock increases, and the credit of a frugal and thriving man increases much faster than his stock. His trade is extended in proportion to the amount of both, and the sum or amount of his profits is in proportion to the extent of his trade, and his annual accumulation in proportion to the amount of his profits. It seldom happens, however, that great fortunes are made even in great towns by any one regular, established, and well-known branch of business, but in consequence of a long life of industry, frugality, and attention. Sudden fortunes, indeed, are sometimes made in such places by what is called the trade of speculation. The speculative merchant exercises no one regular, established, or well-known branch of business. He is a corn merchant this year, and a wine merchant the next, and a sugar, tobacco, or tea merchant the year after. He enters into every trade, when he foresees that it is likely to be more than commonly profitable, and he quits it when he foresees that its profits are likely to return to the level of other trades. His profits and losses, therefore, can bear no regular proportion to those of any one established and well-known branch of business. A bold adventurer may sometimes acquire a consider-

able fortune by two or three successful speculations; but is just as likely to lose one by two or three unsuccessful ones. This trade can be carried on no where but in great towns. It is only in places of the most extensive commerce and correspondence that the intelligence requisite for it can be had.

The five circumstances above mentioned, though they occasion considerable inequalities in the wages of labour and profits of stock occasion none in the whole of the advantages and disadvantages, real or imaginary, of the different employments of either. The nature of those circumstances is such, that they make up for a small pecuniary gain in some, and counter-balance a great one in others.

In order, however, that this quality may take place in the whole of their advantages or disadvantages, three things are requisite even where there is the most perfect freedom. First, the employments must be well known and long established in the neighbourhood; secondly, they must be in their ordinary, or what may be called their natural state; and, thirdly, they must be the sole or principal employments of those who occupy them.

First, this quality can take place only in those employments which are well known, and have been long established in the neighbourhood.

Where all other circumstances are equal, wages are generally higher in new than in old trades. When a projector attempts to establish a new manufacture, he must at first entice his workmen from other employments by higher wages than they can either earn in their own trades, or than the nature of his work would otherwise require, and a comfortable time must pass away before he can venture to reduce them to the common level. Manufactures for which the demand arises altogether from fashion and fancy, are continually changing, and seldom last long enough to be considered as old established manufactures. Those, on the contrary, for which the demand arises chiefly from use or necessity, are less liable to change, and the same form or fabric may continue in demand for whole centuries together. The wages of labour, therefore, are likely to be higher in manufactures of the former, than in those of the latter kind. Birmingham deals chiefly in manufactures of the former kind; Sheffield in those of the latter; and the wages of labour in those two different places, are said to be suitable to this difference in the nature of their manufactures.

The establishment of any new manufacture, of any new branch of commerce, or of any new practice in agriculture, is always a speculation, from which the projector promises himself extraordinary profits. These profits sometimes are very great, and sometimes, more frequently, perhaps, they are quite otherwise; but in general they bear no regular proportion to those of other old trades in the neighbourhood. If the project succeeds, they are commonly at first very high. When the trade or practice becomes thoroughly established and well known, the competition reduces them to the level of other trades.

Secondly, this equality in the whole of the advantages and disadvantages of the different employments of labour and stock, can take place only in the ordinary, or what may be called the natural state of those employments.

The demand for almost every different species of labour is sometimes greater and sometimes less than usual. In the one case the advantages of the employment rise above, in the other they fall below the common level. The demand for country labour is greater at hay-time and harvest, than during the greater part of the year; and wages rise with the demand. In time of war, when forty or fifty thousand sailors are forced from the merchant service into that of the king, the demand for sailors to merchant ships necessarily rises with their scarcity, and their wages upon such occasions commonly rise from a guinea and seven-and-twenty shillings, to forty shillings and three pounds a month. In a decaying manufacture, on the contrary, many workmen, rather than quit their old trade, are contented with smaller wages than would otherwise be suitable to the nature of their employment.

The profits of stock vary with the price of the commodities in which it is employed. As the price of any commodity rises above the ordinary or average rate, the profits of at least some part of the stock that is employed in bringing it to market, rise above their proper level, and as it falls they sink below it. All commodities are more or less liable to variations of price, but some are much more so than others. In all commodities which are produced by human industry, the quantity of industry annually employed is necessarily regulated by the annual demand, in such a manner that the average annual produce may, as nearly as possible, be equal to the average annual consumption. In some employments, it has already been observed, the same quantity of industry will always produce the same, or very nearly the same quantity of commodities. In the linen or woollen manufactures, for example, the same number of hands will annually work up very nearly the same quantity of linen and woollen cloth. The variations in the market price of such commodities therefore, can arise only from some accidental variation in the demand. A public mourning raises the price of black cloth. But as the demand for most sorts of plain linen and woollen cloth

is pretty uniform, so is likewise the price. But there are other employments in which the same quantity of industry will not always produce the same quantity of commodities. The same quantity of industry, for example, will, in different years, produce very different quantities of corn, wine, hops, sugar, tobacco, &c. The price of such commodities, therefore, varies not only with the variations of demand, but with the much greater and more frequent variations of quantity, and is consequently extremely fluctuating. But the profit of some of the dealers must necessarily fluctuate with the price of the commodities. The operations of the speculative merchant are principally employed about such commodities. He endeavours to buy them up when he foresees that their price is likely to rise, and to sell them when it is likely to fall.

Thirdly, this equality in the whole of the advantages and disadvantages of the different employments of labour and stock, can take place only in such as are the sole or principal employments of those who occupy them.

When a person derives his subsistence from one employment, which does not occupy the greater part of his time; in the intervals of his leisure he is often willing to work at another for less wages than would otherwise suit the nature of the employment.

There still subsists in many parts of Scotland a set of people called Cotters or Cottagers, though they were more frequent some years ago than they are now. They are a sort of out-servants of the landlords and farmers. The usual reward which they receive from their masters is a house, a small garden for pot-herbs, as much grass as will feed a cow, and, perhaps, an acre or two of bad arable land. When their master has occasion for their labour, he gives them, besides, two pecks of oatmeal a week, worth about sixteen pence sterling. During a great part of the year he has little or no occasion for their labour, and the cultivation of their own little possession is not sufficient to occupy the time which is left at their own disposal. When such occupiers were more numerous than they are at present, they are said to have been willing to give their spare time for a very small recompence to any body, and to have wrought for less wages than other labourers. In ancient times they seem to have been common all over Europe. In countries ill cultivated and worse inhabited, the greater part of landlords and farmers could not otherwise provide themselves with the extraordinary number of hands, which country labour requires at certain seasons. The daily or weekly recompence which such labourers occasionally receive from their masters, was evidently not the whole price of their labour. Their small tenement made a considerable part of it. This daily or weekly recompence, however, seems to have been considered as the whole of it, by many writers who have collected the prices of labour and provisions in ancient times, and who have taken pleasure in representing both as wonderfully low.

The produce of such labour comes frequently cheaper to market than would otherwise be suitable to its nature. Stockings in many parts of Scotland are knit much cheaper than they can any-where be wrought upon the loom. They are the work of servants and labourers, who derive the principal part of their subsistence from some other employment. More than a thousand pair of Shetland stockings are annually imported into Leith, of which the price is from five pence to seven pence a pair. At Learwick, the small capital of the Shetland islands, ten pence a day, I have been assured, is a common price of common labour. In the same islands they knit worsted stockings to the value of a guinea a pair and upwards.

The spinning of linen yarn is carried on in Scotland nearly in the same way as the knitting of stockings, by servants who are chiefly hired for other purposes. They earn but a very scanty subsistence, who endeavour to get their whole livelihood by either of those trades. In most parts of Scotland she is a good spinner who can earn twenty pence a week.

In opulent countries the market is generally so extensive, that any one trade is sufficient to employ the whole labour and stock of those who occupy it. Instances of people's living by one employment, and at the same time deriving some little advantage from another, occur chiefly in poor countries. The following instance, however, of something of the same kind is to be found in the capital of a very rich one. There is no city in Europe, I believe, in which house-rent is dearer than in London, and yet I know no capital in which a furnished apartment can be hired so cheap. Lodging is not only much cheaper in London than in Paris; it is much cheaper than in Edinburgh of the same degree of goodness; and what may seem extraordinary, the dearness of house-rent is the cause of the cheapness of lodging. The dearness of house-rent in London arises, not only from those causes which render it dear in all great capitals, the dearness of labour, the dearness of all the materials of building, which must generally be brought from a great distance, and above all the the dearness of ground-rent, every landlord acting the part of a monopolist, and frequently exacting a higher rent for a single acre of bad land in a town, than can be had for a hundred of the best in the country; but it arises in part from the peculiar manners and customs of the people which oblige every master of a family to hire a whole house from top to bottom. A dwelling-house in England means every thing that is contained under the same roof. In France, Scotland, and many other parts of Europe, it frequently means no more than a single story. A tradesman in London is obliged to hire a whole house in that part of the town where his customers live. His shop is upon the ground-floor, and he and his family sleep in the garret; and he endeavours to pay a part of his house-rent by letting the two middle stories to lodgers. He expects to maintain his family by his trade, and not by his lodgers. Whereas, at Paris and Edinburgh, the people who let lodgings have commonly no other means of subsistence; and the price of the lodging must pay, not only the rent of the house, but the whole expence of the family.

Inequalities Occasioned by the Policy of Europe

Such are the inequalities in the whole of the advantages and disadvantages of the different employments of labour and stock, which the defect of any of the three requisites above-mentioned must occasion, even where there is the most perfect liberty. But the policy of Europe, by not leaving things at perfect liberty, occasions other inequalities of much greater importance.

It does this chiefly in the three following ways. First, by restraining the competition in some employments to a smaller number than would otherwise be disposed to enter into them; secondly, by increasing it in others beyond what it naturally would be; and thirdly, by obstructing the free circulation of labour and stock, both from employment to employment, and from place to place.

First, the policy of Europe occasions a very important inequality in the whole of the advantages and disadvantages of the different employments of labour and stock, by restraining the competition in some employments to a smaller number than might otherwise be disposed to enter into them.

The exclusive privileges of corporations are the principal means it makes use of for this purpose.

The exclusive privilege of an incorporated trade necessarily restrains the competition, in the town where it is established, to those who are free of the trade. To have served an apprenticeship in the town, under a master properly qualified, is commonly the necessary requisite for obtaining this freedom. The bye-laws of the corporation regulate sometimes the number of apprentices which any master is allowed to have, and almost always the number of years which each apprentice is obliged to serve. The intention of both regulations is to restrain the competition to a much smaller number than might otherwise be disposed to enter into the trade. The limitation of the number of apprentices restrains it directly. A long term of apprenticeship restrains it more indirectly, but as effectually, by increasing the expence of education.

*   *   *

The property which every man has in his own labour, as it is the original foundation of all other property, so it is the most sacred and inviolable. The patrimony of a poor man lies in the strength and dexterity of his hands; and to hinder him from employing this strength and dexterity in what manner he thinks proper without injury to his neighbour, is a plain violation of this most sacred property. It is manifest encroachment upon the just liberty both of the workman, and of those who might be disposed to employ him. As it hinders the one from working at what he thinks proper, so it hinders the others from employing whom they think proper. To judge whether he is fit to be employed, may surely be trusted to the discretion of the employers whose interest it so much concerns. The affected anxiety of the law-giver, lest they should employ an improper person, is evidently as impertinent as it is operative.

The institution of long apprenticeships can give no security that insufficient workmanship shall not frequently be exposed to public sale. When this is done it is generally the effect of fraud, and not of inability; and the longest apprenticeship can give no security against fraud. Quite different regulations are necessary to prevent this abuse. The sterling mark upon plate, and the stamps upon linen and woollen cloth, give the purchaser much greater security than any statute of apprenticeship. He generally looks at these, but never thinks it worth while to enquire whether the workmen had served a seven years apprenticeship.

The institution of long apprenticeships has no tendency to form young people to industry. A journeyman who works by the piece is likely to be industrious, because he derives a benefit from every exertion of his industry. An apprentice is likely to be idle, and almost always is so, because he has no immediate interest to be otherwise. In the inferior employments, the sweets of labour consist altogether in the recompence of labour. They who are soonest in a condition to enjoy the sweets of it, are likely soonest to conceive a relish for it, and to acquire the early habit of industry. A young man naturally conceives an aversion to labour, when for a long time he receives no benefit from it. The boys who are put out apprentices from public charities are generally bound for more than the usual

number of years, and they generally turn out very idle and worthless.

*   *   *

People of the same trade seldom meet together, even for merriment and diversion, but the conversation ends in a conspiracy against the public, or in some contrivance to raise prices. It is impossible indeed to prevent such meetings, by any law which either could be executed, or would be consistent with liberty and justice. But though the law cannot hinder people of the same trade from sometimes assembling together, it ought to do nothing to facilitate such assemblies; much less to render them necessary.

A regulation which obliges all those of the same trade in a particular town to enter their names and places of abode in a public register, facilitates such assemblies. It connects individuals who might never otherwise be known to one another, and gives every man of the trade a direction where to find every other man of it.

A regulation which enables those of the same trade to tax themselves in order to provide for their poor, their sick, their widows and orphans, by giving them a common interest to manage, renders such assemblies necessary.

An incorporation not only renders them necessary, but makes the act of the majority binding upon the whole. In a free trade an effectual combination cannot be established but by the unanimous consent of every single trader, and it cannot last longer than every single trader continues of the same mind. The majority of a corporation can enact a bye-law with proper penalties, which will limit the competition more effectually and more durably than any voluntary combination whatever.

The pretence that corporations are necessary for the better government of the trade, is without any foundation. The real and effectual discipline which is exercised over a workman, is not that of his corporation, but that of his customers. It is the fear of losing their employment which restrains his frauds and corrects his negligence. An exclusive corporation necessarily weakens the force of this discipline. A particular set of workmen must then be employed, let them behave well or ill. It is upon this account, that in many large incorporated towns no tolerable workmen are to be found, even in some of the most necessary trades. If you would have your work tolerably executed, it must be done in the suburbs, where the workmen, having no exclusive privilege, have nothing but their character to depend upon, and you must then smuggle it into the town as well as you can.

It is in this manner that the policy of Europe, by restraining the competition in some employments to a smaller number than would otherwise be disposed to enter into them, occasions a very important inequality in the whole of the advantages and disadvantages of the different employments of labour and stock.

Secondly, the policy of Europe, by increasing the competition in some employments beyond what it naturally would be, occasions another inequality of an opposite kind in the whole of the advantages and disadvantages of the different employments of labour and stock.

It has been considered as of so much importance that a proper number of young people should be educated for certain professions, that, sometimes the public, and sometimes the piety of private founders have established many pensions, scholarships, exhibitions, bursaries, &c. for this purpose, which draw many more people into those trades than could otherwise pretend to follow them. In all christian countries, I believe, the education of the greater part of churchmen is paid for in this manner. Very few of them are educated altogether at their own expence. The long, tedious, and expensive education, therefore, of those who are, will not always procure them a suitable reward, the

church being crowded with people who, in order to get employment, are willing to accept of a much smaller recompence than what such an education would otherwise have entitled them to; and in this manner the competition of the poor takes away the reward of the rich. It would be indecent, no doubt, to compare either a curate or a chaplain with a journeyman in any common trade. The pay of a curate or chaplain, however, may very properly be considered as of the same nature with the wages of a journeyman. They are, all three, paid for their work according to the contract which they may happen to make with their respective superiors.

* * *

Thirdly, the policy of Europe, by obstructing the free circulation of labour and stock both from employment to employment, and from place to place, occasions in some cases a very inconvenient inequality in the whole of the advantages and disadvantages of their different employments.

The statute of apprenticeship obstructs the free circulation of labour from one employment to another, even in the same place. The exclusive privileges of corporations obstruct it from one place to another, even in the same employment.

2. *The Class Struggle*

BY KARL MARX

THE HISTORY of all hitherto existing society[1] is the history of class struggles.

Reprinted from Karl Marx, *Manifesto of the Communist Party* (Chicago: Charles H. Kerr, 1888), sec. 1, pp. 12–32.

1. That is, all written history. In 1847, the pre-history of society, the social organization existing previous to recorded history, was all but unknown. Since then Haxthausen discovered common ownership of land in Russia, Maurer proved it to be the social foundation from which all Teutonic races started in history, and by and bye village communities were found to be, or to have been, the primitive form of society everywhere from India to Ireland. The inner organization of this primitive Communistic society was laid bare, in its typical form, by Morgan's crowning discovery of the true nature of the gens and its relation to tribe. With the dissolution of these primaeval communities society begins to be differentiated into separate and finally antagonistic classes. I have attempted to retrace this process of dissolution in: "Der Ursprung der Familie des, Privateigenthums und des Staats," 2nd edit., Stuttgart 1886.

Freemen and slave, patrician and plebeian, lord and serf, guild-master[2] and journeyman, in a word, oppressor and oppressed, stood in constant opposition to one another, carried on an uninterrupted, now hidden, now open fight, a fight that each time ended, either in a revolutionary re-constitution of society at large, or in the common ruin of the contending classes.

In the earlier epochs of history, we find almost everywhere a complicated arrangement of society into various orders, a manifold gradation of social rank. In ancient Rome we have patricians, knights, plebeians, slaves; in the middle ages, feudal lords, vassals, guild-masters, journeymen, apprentices, serfs; in almost all of these classes, again, subordinate gradations.

2. Guild-master, that is a full member of a guild, a master within, not a head of, a guild.

The modern bourgeois[3] society that has sprouted from the ruins of feudal society, has not done away with class antagonisms. It has but established new classes, new conditions of oppression, new forms of struggle in place of the old ones.

Our epoch, the epoch of the bourgeoisie, possesses, however, this distinctive feature; it has simplified the class antagonisms. Society as a whole is more and more splitting up into two great hostile camps, into two great classes directly facing each other: Bourgeoisie and Proletariat.

From the serfs of the middle ages sprang the chartered burghers of the earliest towns. From these burgesses the first elements of the bourgeoisie were developed.

The discovery of America, the rounding of the Cape, opened up fresh ground for the rising bourgeoisie. The East-Indian and Chinese markets, the colonisation of America, trade with the colonies, the increase in the means of exchange and in commodities generally, gave to commerce, to navigation, to industry, an impulse never before known, and thereby, to the revolutionary element in the tottering feudal society, a rapid development.

The feudal system of industry, under which industrial production was monopolised by close guilds, now no longer sufficed for the growing wants of the new markets. The manufacturing system took its place. The guild-masters were pushed on one side by the manufacturing middle-class; division of labour between the different corporate guilds vanished in the face of division of labour in each single workshop.

Meantime the markets kept ever growing, the demand, ever rising. Even manufacture no longer sufficed. Thereupon, steam and machinery revolutionised industrial production. The place of manufacture was taken by the giant, Modern Industry, the place of the industrial middle-class, by industrial millionaires, the leaders of whole industrial armies, the modern bourgeois.

Modern industry has established the world-market, for which the discovery of America paved the way. This market has given an immense development to commerce, to navigation, to communication by land. This development has, in its turn, reacted on the extension of industry; and in proportion as industry, commerce, navigation, railways extended, in the same proportion the bourgeoisie developed, increased its capital, and pushed into the background every class handed down from the Middle Ages.

We see, therefore, how the modern bourgeoisie is itself the product of a long course of development, of a series of revolutions in the modes of production and of exchange.

Each step in the development of the bourgeoisie was accompanied by a corresponding political advance of that class. An oppressed class under the sway of the feudal nobility, an armed and self-governing association in the mediaeval commune,[4] here independent urban republic (as in Italy and Germany), there taxable "third estate" of the monarchy (as in France), afterwards, in the period of manufacture proper, serving either the semi-feudal or the absolute monarchy as a counterpoise against the nobility, and, in fact, corner stone of the great monarchies in general, the bourgeoisie has at last, since the establishment of Modern Industry and of the world-market, conquered for itself, in the modern representative State, exclusive political sway. The executive of the modern State is but a committee for managing the common affairs of the whole bourgeoisie.

The bourgeoisie, historically, has played a most revolutionary part.

The bourgeoisie, wherever it has got the upper hand, has put an end to all feudal patriarchal, idyllic relations. It has pitilessly torn asunder the motley feudal ties that bound man to his "natural superiors," and has left remaining no other nexus between man and man than naked self-interest, than callous "cash payment." It has drowned the most heavenly ecstacies of religious fervour, of chivalrous enthusiasm, of philistine sentimentalism, in the icy water of egotistical calculation. It has resolved personal worth into exchange value, and in place of the numberless indefeasible chartered freedoms, has set up that single, unconscionable freedom—Free Trade. In one word, for political exploitation, veiled by religious and political illusions, it has substituted naked, shameless, direct, brutal exploitation.

The bourgeoisie has stripped of its halo every occupation hitherto honoured and looked up to with reverent awe. It has converted the physician, the lawyer, the priest, the poet, the man of science, into its paid wage-labourers.

The bourgeoisie has torn away from the family

---

3. By bourgeoisie is meant the class of modern Capitalists, owners of the means of social production and employers of wage-labour. By proletariat, the class of modern wage-labourers who, having no means of production of their own, are reduced to selling their labour-power in order to live.

4. "Commune" was the name, taken in France, by the nascent towns even before they had conquered from their feudal lords and masters, local self-government and political rights as "the Third Estate." Generally speaking, for the economical development of the bourgeoisie, England is here taken as the typical country, for its political development, France.

its sentimental veil, and has reduced the family relation to a mere money relation.

The bourgeoisie has disclosed how it came to pass that the brutal display of vigour in the Middle Ages, which Reactionists so much admire, found its fitting complement in the most slothful indolence. It has been the first to shew what man's activity can bring about. It has accomplished wonders far surpassing Egyptian pyramids, Roman aqueducts, and Gothic cathedrals; it has conducted expeditions that put in the shade all former Exoduses of nations and crusades.

The bourgeoisie cannot exist without constantly revolutionising the instruments of production, and thereby the relations of production, and with them the whole relations of society. Conservation of the old modes of production in unaltered form, was, on the contrary, the first condition of existence for all earlier industrial classes. Constant revolutionising of production, uninterrupted disturbance of all social conditions, everlasting uncertainty and agitation distinguish the bourgeois epoch from all earlier ones. All fixed, fast-frozen relations, with their train of ancient and venerable prejudices and opinions, are swept away, all new-formed ones become antiquated before they can ossify. All that is solid melts into air, all that is holy is profaned, and man is at last compelled to face with sober senses, his real conditions of life, and his relations with his kind.

The need of a constantly expanding market for its products chases the bourgeoisie over the whole surface of the globe. It must nestle everywhere, settle everywhere, establish connexions everywhere.

The bourgeoisie has through its exploitation of the world-market given a cosmopolitan character to production and consumption in every country. To the great chagrin of Re-actionists, it has drawn from under the feet of industry the national ground on which it stood. All old-established national industries have been destroyed or are daily being destroyed. They are dislodged by new industries, whose introduction becomes a life and death question for all civilised nations, by industries that no longer work up indigenous raw material, but raw material drawn from the remotest zones; industries whose products are consumed, not only at home, but in every quarter of the globe. In place of the old wants, satisfied by the productions of the country, we find new wants, requiring for their satisfaction the products of distant lands and climes. In place of the old local and national seclusion and self-sufficiency, we have intercourse in every direction, universal inter-dependence of nations. And as in material, so also in intellectual production. The intellectual creations of individual nations become common property. National one-sidedness and narrow-mindedness become more and more impossible, and from the numerous national and local literatures there arises a world-literature.

The bourgeoisie, by the rapid improvement of all instruments of production, by the immensely facilitated means of communication, draws all, even the most barbarian, nations into civilisation. The cheap prices of its commodities are the heavy artillery with which it batters down all Chinese walls, with which it forces the barbarians' intensely obstinate hatred of foreigners to capitulate. It compels all nations, on pain of extinction, to adopt the bourgeois mode of production; it compels them to introduce what it calls civilisation into their midst, i.e., to become bourgeois themselves. In a word, it creates a world after its own image.

The bourgeoisie has subjected the country to the rule of the towns. It has created enormous cities, has greatly increased the urban population as compared with the rural, and has thus rescued a considerable part of the population from the idiocy of rural life. Just as it has made the country dependent on the towns, so it has made barbarian and semi-barbarian countries dependent on the civilised ones, nations of peasants on nations of bourgeois, the East on the West.

The bourgeoisie keeps more and more doing away with the scattered state of the population, of the means of productions, and of property. It has agglomerated population, centralised means of production, and has concentrated property in a few hands. The necessary consequence of this was political centralisation. Independent, or but loosely connected provinces, with separate interests, laws, governments and systems of taxation, became lumped together in one nation, with one government, one code of laws, one national class-interest, one frontier and one customs-tariff.

The bourgeoisie, during its rule of scarce one hundred years, has created more massive and more colossal productive forces than have all preceding generations together. Subjection of Nature's forces to man, machinery, application of chemistry to industry and agriculture, steam-navigation, railways, electric telegraphs, clearing of whole continents for cultivation, canalization of rivers, whole populations conjured out of the ground—what earlier century had even a presentiment that such productive forces slumbered in the lap of social labour?

We see then: the means of production and of exchange on whose foundation the bourgeoisie built itself up, were generated in feudal society.

At a certain stage in the development of these means of production and of exchange, the conditions under which feudal society produced and exchanged, the feudal organisation of agriculture and manufacturing industry, in one word, the feudal relations of property became no longer compatible with the already developed productive forces; they became so many fetters. They had to burst asunder; they were burst asunder.

Into their places stepped free competition, accompanied by a social and political constitution adapted to it, and by the economical and political sway of the bourgeois class.

A similar movement is going on before our own eyes. Modern bourgeois society with its relations of production, of exchange and of property, a society that has conjured up such gigantic means of production and of exchange, is like the sorcerer, who is no longer able to control the powers of the nether world whom he has called up by his spells. For many a decade past the history of industry and commerce is but the history of the revolt of modern productive forces against modern conditions of production, against the property relations that are the conditions for the existence of the bourgeoisie and of its rule. It is enough to mention the commercial crises that by their periodical return put on its trial, each time more threateningly, the existence of the entire bourgeois society. In these crises a great part not only of the existing products, but also of the previously created productive forces, are periodically destroyed. In these crises there breaks out an epidemic that, in all earlier epochs, would have seemed an absurdity—the epidemic of over-production. Society suddenly finds itself put back into a state of momentary barbarism; it appears as if a famine, a universal war of devastation had cut off the supply of every means of subsistence; industry and commerce seem to be destroyed; and why? Because there is too much civilisation, too much means of subsistence, too much industry, too much commerce. The productive forces at the disposal of society no longer tend to further the development of the conditions of bourgeois property; on the contrary, they have become too powerful for these conditions, by which they are fettered, and so soon as they overcome these fetters, they bring disorder into the whole of bourgeois society, endanger the existence of bourgeois property. The conditions of bourgeois society are too narrow to comprise the wealth created by them. And how does the bourgeoisie get over these crises? On the one hand by enforced destruction of a mass of productive forces; on the other, by the conquest of new markets, and by the more thorough exploitation of the old ones. That is to say, by paving the way for more extensive and more destructive crises, and by diminishing the means whereby crises are prevented.

The weapons with which the bourgeoisie felled feudalism to the ground are now turned against the bourgeoisie itself.

But not only has the bourgeoisie forged the weapons that bring death to itself; it has also called into existence the men who are to wield those weapons—the modern working-class—the proletarians.

In proportion as the bourgeoisie, i.e., capital, is developed, in the same proportion is the proletariat, the modern working-class, developed, a class of labourers, who live only so long as they find work, and who find work only so long as their labour increases capital. These labourers, who must sell themselves piecemeal, are a commodity, like every other article of commerce, and are consequently exposed to all the vicissitudes of competition, to all the fluctuations of the market.

Owing to the extensive use of machinery and to division of labour, the work of the proletarians has lost all individual character, and, consequently, all charm for the workman. He becomes an appendage of the machine, and it is only the most simple, most monotonous, and most easily acquired knack that is required of him. Hence, the cost of production of a workman is restricted, almost entirely, to the means of subsistence that he requires for his maintenance, and for the propagation of his race. But the price of a commodity, and also of labour, is equal to its cost of production. In proportion, therefore, as the repulsiveness of the work increases, the wage decreases. Nay more, in proportion as the use of machinery and division of labour increases, in the same proportion the burden of toil also increases, whether by prolongation of the working hours, by increase of the work enacted in a given time, or by increased speed of the machinery, etc.

Modern industry has converted the little workshop of the patriarchal master into the great factory of the industrial capitalist. Masses of labourers, crowded into the factory, are organised like soldiers. As privates of the industrial army they are placed under the command of a perfect hierarchy of officers and sergeants. Not only are they the slaves of the bourgeois class, and of the bourgeois State, they are daily and hourly enslaved by the machine, by the over-looker, and, above all, by the individual bourgeois manufacturer himself. The more openly this despotism proclaims gain to be its end and aim, the more petty, the more hateful and the more embittering it is.

The less the skill and exertion or strength implied in manual labour, in other words, the more modern industry becomes developed, the more is the labour of men superseded by that of women. Differences of age and sex have no longer any distinctive social validity for the working class. All are instruments of labour, more or less expensive to use, according to their age and sex.

No sooner is the exploitation of the labourer by the manufacturer, so far, at an end, that he receives his wages in cash, than he is set upon by the other portions of the bourgeoisie, the landlord, the shopkeeper, the pawnbroker, etc.

The lower strata of the Middle class—the small tradespeople, shopkeepers, and retired tradesmen generally, the handicraftsmen and peasants—all these sink gradually into the proletariat, partly because their diminutive capital does not suffice for the scale on which Modern Industry is carried on, and is swamped in the competition with the large capitalists, partly because their specialised skill is rendered worthless by new methods of production. Thus the proletariat is recruited from all classes of the population.

The proletariat goes through various stages of development. With its birth begins its struggle with the bourgeoisie. At first the contest is carried on by individual labourers, then by the workpeople of a factory, then by the operatives of one trade, in one locality, against the individual bourgeois who directly exploits them. They direct their attacks not against the bourgeois conditions of production, but against the instruments of production themselves; they destroy imported wares that compete with their labour, they smash to pieces machinery, they set factories ablaze, they seek to restore by force the vanished status of the workman of the Middle Ages.

At this stage the labourers still form an incoherent mass scattered over the whole country, and broken up by their mutual competition. If anywhere they unite to form more compact bodies, this is not yet the consequence of their own active union, but of the union of the bourgeoisie, which class, in order to attain its own political ends, is compelled to set the whole proletariat in motion, and is moreover yet, for a time, able to do so. At this stage, therefore, the proletarians do not fight their enemies, but the enemies of their enemies, the remnants of absolute monarchy, the landowners, the non-industrial bourgeois, the petty bourgeoisie. Thus the whole historical movement is concentrated in the hands of the bourgeoisie; every victory so obtained is a victory for the bourgeoisie.

But with the development of industry the proletariat not only increases in number; it becomes concentrated in greater masses, its strength grows, and it feels that strength more. The various interests and conditions of life within the ranks of the proletariat are more and more equalised, in proportion as machinery obliterates all distinctions of labour, and nearly everywhere reduces wages to the same low level. The growing competition among the bourgeois, and the resulting commercial crises, make the wages of the workers ever more fluctuating. The unceasing improvement of machinery, ever more rapidly developing, makes their livelihood more and more precarious; the collisions between individual workmen and individual bourgeois take more and more the character of collisions between two classes. Thereupon the workers begin to form combinations (Trades' Unions) against the bourgeois; they club together in order to keep up the rate of wages; they found permanent associations in order to make provision beforehand for these occasional revolts. Here and there the contest breaks out into riots.

Now and then the workers are victorious, but only for a time. The real fruit of their battles lies, not in the immediate result, but in the ever expanding union of the workers. This union is helped on by the improved means of communication that are created by modern industry, and that place the workers of different localities in contact with one another. It was just this contact that was needed to centralise the numerous local struggles, all of the same character, into one national struggle between classes. But every class struggle is a political struggle. And that union, to attain which the burghers of the Middle Ages, with their miserable highways, required centuries, the modern proletarians, thanks to railways, achieve in a few years.

This organisation of the proletarians into a class, and consequently into a political party, is continually being upset again by the competition between the workers themselves. But it ever rises up again, stronger, firmer, mightier. It compels legislative recognition of particular interests of the workers, by taking advantage of the divisions among the bourgeoisie itself. Thus the ten-hours'-bill in England was carried.

Altogether collisions between the classes of the old society further, in many ways, the course of development of the proletariat. The bourgeoisie finds itself involved in a constant battle. At first with the aristocracy; later on, with those portions of the bourgeoisie itself, whose interests have become antagonistic to the progress of industry; at all times, with the bourgeoisie of foreign countries. In all these battles it sees itself compelled to appeal to the proletariat, to ask for its help, and thus, to drag it into the political arena. The bourgeoisie itself, therefore, supplies the proletariat with its own elements of political and general education, in other words, it furnishes the proletariat with weapons for fighting the bourgeoisie.

Further, as we have already seen, entire sections of the ruling classes are, by the advance of industry, precipitated into the proletariat, or are at least threatened in their conditions of existence. These also supply the proletariat with fresh elements of enlightenment and progress.

Finally, in times when the class-struggle nears the decisive hour, the process of dissolution going on within the ruling class, in fact within the whole range of old society, assumes such a violent, glaring character, that a small section of the ruling class cuts itself adrift, and joins the revolutionary class, the class that holds the future in its hands. Just as, therefore, at an earlier period, a section of the nobility went over to the bourgeoisie, so now a portion of the bourgeoisie goes over to the proletariat, and in particular, a portion of the bourgeois ideologists, who have raised themselves to the level of comprehending theoretically the historical movements as a whole.

Of all the classes that stand face to face with the bourgeoisie to-day, the proletariat alone is a really revolutionary class. The other classes decay and finally disappear in the face of modern industry; the proletariat is its special and essential product.

The lower middle-class, the small manufacturer, the shopkeeper, the artisan, the peasant, all these fight against the bourgeoisie, to save from extinction their existence as fractions of the middle class. They are therefore not revolutionary, but conservative. Nay more, they are reactionary, for they try to roll back the wheel of history. If by chance they are revolutionary, they are so, only in view of their impending transfer into the proletariat, they thus defend not their present, but their future interests, they desert their own standpoint to place themselves at that of the proletariat.

The "dangerous class," the social scum, that passively rotting mass thrown off by the lowest layers of old society, may, here and there, be swept into the movement by a proletarian revolution; its conditions of life, however, prepare it far more for the part of a bribed tool of reactionary intrigue.

In the conditions of the proletariat, those of old society at large are already virtually swamped. The proletarian is without property; his relation to his wife and children has no longer anything in common with the bourgeois family-relations; modern industrial labour, modern subjection to capital, the same in England as in France, in America as in Germany, has stripped him of every trace of national character. Law, morality, religion, are to him so many bourgeois prejudices, behind which lurk in ambush just as many bourgeois interests.

All the preceding classes that got the upper hand, sought to fortify their already acquired status by subjecting society at large to their conditions of appropriation. The proletarians cannot become masters of the productive forces of society, except by abolishing their own previous mode of appropriation, and thereby also every other previous mode of appropriation. They have nothing of their own to secure and to fortify; their mission is to destroy all previous securities for, and insurances of, individual property.

All previous historical movements were movements of minorities, or in the interest of minorities. The proletarian movement is the self-conscious, independent movement of the immense majority, in the interest of the immense majority. The proletariat, the lowest stratum of our present society, cannot stir, cannot raise itself up, without the whole superincumbent strata of official society being sprung into the air.

Though not in substance, yet in form, the struggle of the proletariat with the bourgeoisie is at first a national struggle. The proletariat of each country must, of course, first of all settle matters with its own bourgeoisie.

In depicting the most general phases of the development of the proletariat, we traced the more or less veiled civil war, raging within existing society, up to the point where that war breaks out into open revolution, and where the violent overthrow of the bourgeoisie, lays the foundation for the sway of the proletariat.

Hitherto, every form of society has been based, as we have already seen, on the antagonism of oppressing and oppressed classes. But in order to oppress a class, certain conditions must be assured to it under which it can, at least, continue its slavish existence. The serf, in the period of serfdom, raised himself to membership in the commune, just as the petty bourgeois, under the yoke of feudal absolutism, managed to develop into a bourgeois. The modern labourer, on the contrary, instead of rising with the progress of industry, sinks deeper and deeper below the conditions of existence of his own class. He becomes a pauper, and pauperism develops more rapidly than population and wealth. And here it becomes evident, that the bourgeoisie is unfit any longer to be the ruling class in society, and to impose its conditions of existence upon society as an over-riding law. It is unfit to rule, because it is incompetent to assure an existence to its slave within his slavery, because it cannot help letting him sink into such a state, that it has to feed him, instead of being fed by him. Society can no longer live under this bourgeoisie, in other words, its existence is no longer compatible with society.

The essential condition for the existence, and for the sway of the bourgeois class, is the formation and augmentation of capital; the condition for capital is wage-labour. Wage-labour rests exclusively on competition between the labourers. The advance of industry, whose involuntary promoter is the bourgeoisie, replaces the isolation of the labourers, due to competition, by their involuntary combination, due to association. The development of Modern Industry, therefore, cuts from under its feet the very foundation on which the bourgeoisie produces and appropriates products. What the bourgeoisie therefore produces, above all, are its own gravediggers. Its fall and the victory of the proletariat are equally inevitable.

3. *Class and Occupation*

BY EDMOND GOBLOT

NOTHING STAMPS a man as much as his occupation. Daily work determines the mode of life; even more than the organs of the body, it constrains our ideas, feelings, and tastes. Habits of the body and mind and habits of language combine to give each one of us his occupational type. People of the same occupation know one another, seek each other's company, and frequent one another—by necessity and by choice. Consequently, each imitates the other.

The end result is groups and not classes. Classes, by contrast, influence the choice of occupation. A bourgeois does not become a carpenter, a locksmith, a baker, or a blacksmith. On the other hand, one can very well become a bourgeois by starting from such professions. But if a carpenter's son is to become a lawyer, he must first become a bourgeois in the lycée and in law school.

Men of very different professions are members of the bourgeoisie and treat one another as equals; men of very different trades are all craftsmen. The function of classes is to group occupations and to segregate them. Language reflects this segregation: functions performed by craftsmen are not called professions, but trades. The gradation in meaning subsists even when the terms are inverted. If, instead of saying that a physician or a lawyer is "learned" or "capable," we say that he "knows his job," we are intentionally signifying that he is being judged outside of any class consideration and that we are evaluating in the man only the good workman. If the schools where trades are taught are called "professional schools," rather than trade schools, it is because at their inception it was felt desirable to give them a designation that upgraded them. In these inversions of terms, there is a dash of democratic spirit as well as an implicit recognition of social inequality.

The proverb, "there is no stupid trade, there are only stupid people," is an idea of simple common sense. Why, then, was it necessary to express it, if not to combat a prejudice? Proverbs are often self-evident truths that seem to require restatement, in order to be remembered. Restating them still does not protect them from oblivion. For if this particular proverb were really taken seriously, and applied, it would be the very denial of social classes. In fact, the bourgeois does believe that there are many stupid trades, trades that are low and ridiculous and yet very good and very honorable—but for someone else. Some may even tempt him because they pay well and would fit his tastes and aptitudes, but self-respect must deter him. What are these trades that are taboo for the bourgeois?

First, there are the trades that are repugnant and dirty the hands or the clothing. The hands of the bourgeois are not soiled by the dirt, scratches, and calluses of work. Delicate hands are a sign of class; the bourgeois takes good care of his. He wears gloves.

Then, we have the strenuous trades: carrying loads, manipulating heavy tools, maintaining a tiresome position, or mechanically repeating a monotonous motion are not proper work for

Translated by Jesse Pitts, from Edmond Goblot, *La barrière et le niveau* (Paris: Presses Universitaires de France, 1925), chap. iii, pp. 38–59, with the permission of Presses Universitaires de France.

a bourgeois. His means permit him to escape the slavery of hard labor, where the physical strength of man struggles against the physical strength of things.

Finally, manual trades in general, even if the tool is as light as a pen, or a needle, are below his dignity, as long as they involve docile hands rather than the spirit that conceives or the will that orders.

In these three cases, it seems evident that the exercise of such trades is precluded by class membership. One does not do carpentry in a cutaway or ditchdigging in a top hat. When a man belongs to good society, he does not risk carrying, even after washing, the persistent smell of the substances he has handled all day long. A man may well have dealings with persons of inferior education in order to give them orders, but he cannot live with them in intimacy. It is because he is a bourgeois, because he lives in a bourgeois manner, because he visits in bourgeois society, because he wears in the street and in society the garb of the bourgeois, that he cannot accept work that disfigures or that soils, or that compels mingling with inferiors.

In her house, Madame does not remain inactive; but there are tasks she will not do. She has them done by domestics or mercenaries; for instance, all the cleaning and the heavy work.

The bourgeoisie attaches an extreme importance to keeping one's distance from manual labor. In the country, those employers who have no pretensions to a bourgeois style of life (and who therefore often live all the better) eat at the same table with their servants, wear the same clothes, perhaps of a trifle better quality, speak the same language, and can be distinguished only by the fact that they command. In town, it is the same for the master craftsman in relation to his co-worker and to the apprentices. But in bourgeois life, the distances between master and servants are all the more clearly marked as they live under the same roof. Servants are generally treated with humanity. They are well fed; they are cared for when they are sick. Feelings of personal fondness grow for those who are devoted and faithful. There used to be, in practically every bourgeois household, old retainers attached to their masters, who spent their lives and died in their shadows after having raised several generations of children. They were loved; they truly belonged to the family; but they did not live a bourgeois life. The clothes and the language indicated the inequality between those whose condition it was to serve and those who had the advantage and the right to be served. It is perhaps because the more recent bourgeoisie has too strongly accentuated these distances that these old and faithful servants have practically disappeared.

The bourgeois also separates himself from those who serve him outside the house. A lady speaks of her tradesman with a distinct tone of voice, somewhat in the style of a great lady of the *ancien régime* who used to say "my people." She does not like to meet them or their wives socially; she is not of the same social rank as those to whom she gives orders. These tradesmen may be capitalists, be good businessmen, even be much wealthier than their customers. They are not bourgeois if they themselves wait on their customers. The retailer or the industrialist is bourgeois only if he is a manager, if he has personnel to weigh, wrap, and receive money, and if he shows up in the store only to supervise and give orders. The bourgeois of the *ancient régime* was above all a merchant; the bourgeois of the new regime can still be a merchant, but not a shopkeeper.

Thus, self-respect forbids the bourgeois to attend personally to repugnant or too-strenuous tasks, as well as to serve others for money. For his style of life is to be fashionable and to be waited upon.

But would not the reverse be correct? Can we not say that the bourgeois class is the totality of persons lucky enough to be able to leave the "stupid trades" to others? And is not bourgeois life simply the adoption of the mores, the customs, clothing, language, manners, and even ideas, opinions, and feelings of professional-type occupations?

Besides, the negative prestige attached to manual and subordinate labor is not a trait specific to the modern French bourgeoisie; we meet it everywhere where castes and classes exist. Every superiority of social rank translates itself and expresses itself by the power to be waited on, not so much in order to avoid fatigue as to mark social rank. For it is imperative that rank be recognizable and, if possible, at first glance. In China, the nails of the mandarin, as long as his fingers, wellgroomed, supple, transparent, spiraled, are manifest proof that he does nothing with his hands. Is it not also to signify that he would not demean himself to servile tasks that our bourgeois wears a costume in which these tasks would be impossible? He feels the need to have it known, at a glance, that he is not a common laborer, a hired hand, or a servant. Is it social class that determines the occupation? Is it not rather the occupation that classes?

It is both. Whoever has recognized the falsity, the absurdity, and often the revolting injustice of the principles underlying certain class attitudes and the customs which they support, and who would try to renounce them, meets the nearly invincible resistance of the social milieu to which he belongs. There are cases where it is absolutely necessary "to do like everybody else"; that is, like one's equals, like people of the same occupation. Hence, it is the occupation, once selected, that imposes the style of life. But, on the other hand, class precedes occupation; before choosing a career, a man already belongs to a class by virtue of his family, his connections, his education, and his culture. He has not chosen his social rank any more than he has chosen his family. He was born there; he was raised there; he is owned by his class. He chose his profession, but the choice was limited; a bourgeois can only choose a bourgeois occupation. True, occupation is the most common means for climbing socially. But he will only be a *parvenu* if he does not become a bourgeois at the same time, and even beforehand.

The bourgeois does not fear physical effort any more than the next man if this effort is voluntary and gratuitous, but he would blush to find there his means of existence. Not that he be indifferent to money. The revenues of his trading house, factory, or bank seem to him the just reward of his efforts, energy, foresight, and good behavior. These virtues bringing cash benefits are those which he praises the most. He is not afraid to sell or rent his intelligence, knowledge, advice, supervision, his mere presence, and even, if it has a cash value, his name; but he does not rent his hands, shoulders, or back. He requires payment for his time, work, and responsibility; but he does not earn his bread by "the sweat of his brow." However, he will work with his hands when witnesses, if there are any, will believe or know that he is not compelled to do so and that it brings him no return. He will not hide to dig in his garden, or to split wood, or to do carpentry, as long as it is believed he is doing it for his pleasure or for his health. Certain sports demand more physical efforts and more endurance than many manual trades. The bourgeois would not cross the square with a basket; yet he goes on a hike loaded with an enormous sack, and he does it voluntarily. He does not fear the strain, but the humiliation. He does not want to seem constrained, either by someone's authority or the necessity of earning a living, to endure the fatigues of manual labor.

It is quite honorable for a lady to busy herself in her home with the care of her linen, and to make her own hats and her dresses. But, if ladies grouped in a salon busy their fingers while talking or listening to music, it is not to darn socks; it must be for some "lady-like work,"—some useless embroidery, some superfluous tapestry, or sewing for the poor.

Intellectual work is as tiresome as many manual trades. "Getting used to it" is as necessary for the one as it is for the others. An intellectual would not stand for one hour the task that a laborer bears for eight hours; but then how many laborers would stand one hour's serious reading? Every lecturer knows that one hour is the maximum of intellectual effort that one may request from an adult audience, even an intelligent and learned audience.

However, it seems that the work of the mind elevates one's status as much as the other degrades it. Could the value judgments that make for the distinction between classes be reduced to the superiority of mind over matter, of intellectual and moral life over physical life? There was once a bourgeois philosophy; upper class people had to be spiritualists; for them materialism was always "crude." This superiority of the spiritual over the corporal is at once in the tradition of classical antiquity and in the tradition of Christianity; our civilization is completely permeated by it. Manual work assimilates man to a beast of toil; one uses the handy man as one uses a horse, an ox, or a dog, each according to its natural aptitudes. A man and an ox are two servants, the bones, muscles, organs, and perceptions of which are differently constituted and differently available. With progress, one replaces advantageously the human servant as well as the animal servant by a machine.

According to this logic, the bourgeoisie would monopolize the professions of initiative, command, and intelligence, and would leave to the lower classes the trades of execution, obedience, and physical effort. The former are those which were exercised in antiquity by the freemen, hence, the name of liberal professions. The popular trades would correspond to the servile arts of ancient times. There would be, in our class division, something of a "survival"—very indirect, and very remote, it is true—of antique slavery. Of course, our legal code no longer allows persons without rights or without family to be bought and sold as commodities, but if manual labor and subordinate work are still considered signs of social inferiority, it must mean that, however many revolutions, the division of labor has in its essential features, remained unchanged.

No one will deny that there are in the lower classes persons who are very superior—intellectually and morally—to many bourgeois, and more capable and worthy to exercise the better professions. A social class cannot prevent the birth, in its midst, of weak characters, of mediocre or worse than mediocre minds, of inferior personalities who will never exercise authority because nobody would obey them, and of men of dubious morality, to whom nobody cares to trust his interests. These children are the despair and the shame of their families. It may be possible, eventually, to place them; they are found some subordinate employment that retains the appearance of a bourgeois profession. But it is the threat and even the first step of downward mobility. In the lower classes, there is no shortage of gifted men who, while remaining in their trades, become leaders, run their businesses well, and become financially independent, without, for all that, adopting a bourgeois profession and a bourgeois style of life. But it is the first step of social climbing; their children will be ladies and gentlemen. It is more frequent to become a bourgeois through one's father's merits than through one's own.

The liberal professions could, then, be said to be the touchstone of the bourgeois class, if we agree that it is through those professions that one reaches and maintains bourgeois status and it is through failure to be capable or worthy to exercise them that one begins to fall downward. With equality before the law, the most important and definitive conquest of the Revolution was the abolition of the privileges of birth and the access of all to all occupations.

But if the modern bourgeoisie were of superior intellect and culture, those who have been named, recently, the *intellectuals,* would form a class superior to the bourgeoisie or, at least, a subclass occupying a superior status within the bourgeoisie. It is nothing of the kind. Intellectual professions do not constitute special classes and even less one class. Intellectuals are bourgeois, but of a comparatively low social rank if they are bourgeois only because of their intelligence. The respect one has for them is somewhat equivocal: one does not know very well if these professions are common or superior, coveted or disdained. The way they are judged, if judgment is not corrected by reflection, is often colored by some disfavor and even condescending pity. We admire that such enlightened men assume so much work for so little profit. The first impulse is to think that their choice was a blunder and another blunder to persevere in it. As an afterthought, one bows to their disinterestedness.

Intellectual work is, at least in part, disinterested, because those who give themselves to it, feeling rewarded for their effort by personal satisfaction, are content with comparatively low monetary remunerations. Every university professor feels a certain pride in thinking that his salary does not represent the value of his services. The judge, the soldier, and the priest have the same feeling. The mediocrity of their financial situation is a guarantee that they do not sell science, or justice, or the sacrifices of their lives, or the salvation of souls. Naturally, intellectuals are bourgeois if they were already so by their income, their family, and the

social milieu from which they came. If they are bourgeois only by their professions, they are rather mediocre bourgeois.

Indeed, it is impossible for class distinction to be based upon fundamental characteristics requiring subtle evaluation, such as intelligence, morality, or character. The advantages in being a member of a class are precisely that the outward signs of class membership certify, rightly or wrongly, to merits which, without these signs, would escape detection. The bourgeoisie which believes itself to be and wants to look like an elite, cannot tolerate another elite forming above it and stealing its advantage. It honors talent, knowledge, and virtue; it welcomes intellectuals. It cannot reject them, for its whole *raison d'etre,* its sole appearance of legitimacy is the superiority of its culture. But personal merit, by the very fact that it is personal, is a dissolvent of class, a perpetual danger to its existence. By vital necessity, bourgeois society upholds the talent that emerges from itself and from below itself, and attempts to absorb it, to color itself entirely with its reflection and its diffusion, so as to make it appear an emanation and a natural flowering of its own essence. If the intellectual professions should withdraw from its midst, if the world of science, letters, and arts, on the one hand, and the world of business, on the other, although having received a similar general culture, could not, because of their later specialization, remain on the same level, the bourgeoisie would disappear.

To be exact, the superiority of the bourgeoisie is neither intellectual or moral. Intellectual work is deemed more honorable than the work of the body, but it is even more honorable not to work at all and to live on one's income. And of all the spiritual and moral qualities, the most honored are those rewarded by increase in wealth. Practical and calculating wisdom, prudence, order, economy, regularity in work—those are the bourgeois virtues. The most degrading vices are those that disturb the world of business or the enjoyment of revenues: dishonesty, theft, swindling, deception. Bankruptcy declasses and dishonors, even when it is more a misfortune than a personal failure. We know the severity of juries for crimes against property, their indulgence for crimes against the person. Although debauchery is severely judged when it results in ruin and downward mobility, it is a very minor sin when it is carefully regulated and limited. The bourgeois has no great esteem for pure thought, science, and philosophy; he does not like doctrinaires and ideologues; he is suspicious of engineers who are too learned—pure theoreticians, and bad practitioners. This fear of ideas is a characteristic of the bourgeois mind. He is also afraid of imagination and afraid of sentiment. He prides himself on being practical; he is a utilitarian. Hence, he has only a moderate taste for art, poetry, literature. In this latter respect, he has in due time gone to schools which have partly corrected this attitude. Under Louis Philippe, the bourgeoisie was obstinately against the "addition of the skilled" to the electorate: and this triggered the Revolution of 1848. Later, the bourgeoisie became aware that practically all of the artistic world and a part of the literary world were outside of it, in that it was ignoring them shamefully. Arts and letters then became fashionable; otherwise, another elite would have formed outside of the bourgeoisie and would have constituted, of course, the best elite.

Hence, we shall not find in the superiority of intelligence and culture a sufficient explanation for the division of society in classes; like income, occupations rank but do not classify. They rank on an infinite variety of levels. In a public administration, in a large private enterprise—whether of rural, industrial or commercial character—in an industry such as the building, clothing, or food, industries, work is not only specialized, it is more or less integrated in a hierarchy. Within these various hierarchies, one can, almost without hesitating, trace the demarkation between bourgeois professions and popular trades. In general, the occupation is ranked more highly when it requires more intelligence and more independence, when it has more scope, and when it brings more revenue. There is a line above which the occupation is liberal and bourgeois; below that limit it remains common. The social scale of occupations and the social scale of fortunes do not class because they are both continuous. But this scale is cut in two by the frontier of class. Above this frontier, one admits a sort of equivalence between the most various occupations, or an equality or community of class even where there is inequality of rank. This is the level. One can see without difficulty that the engineer deems himself superior to the road-worker; and the superior court judge, to the process-server. But why is the engineer superior to the process-server, to whom he is not the superior and to whom he does not give any orders, in the same way as the judge is superior to the road worker? And why are the engineer and the superior court judge of the same bourgeois class, the process-server and the road-worker of the same working class? Why, finally, in the public and private occupations, does the inequality of ranks, so clearly indicated by hierarchy, not result in an inequality of classes? Occupationally unequal, why are some people socially equal?

In the continuum of occupations, as in the continuum of incomes, class distinction seems to operate through a single variable upon which all the others depend: liberal professions versus servile trades; intellectual work versus physical work; scientific education versus manual apprenticeship; initiative versus compliance; commandment versus obedience; etc. This variable is the concrete and easily grasped fact that the preparation for liberal professions lasts until about the age of twenty-five. The bourgeois begins to earn his living ten years later than the common man. As a result, his family must be able to advance him funds. At twenty-five years of age, the young bourgeois is a human capital that has not produced yet any interest; it is in this sense that the bourgeois can be called a capitalist. These advances are considerable; they exceed by far specific tuition costs. Scholarships give a very efficacious aid to the poor bourgeois and favor the ascension to the bourgeoisie of some gifted children of the lower classes. The elements thus preserved or acquired by the upper classes are generally the best. But scholarships are never sufficient. As a result, they are very rarely sought by the lower classes, for whom they are nearly useless. For even if prolonged studies are necessary, they are far from sufficient to enable one to break through the barrier of class, be it only for the reason that, except for rare exceptions, one does not break through this barrier alone. Family solidarity is a very crucial factor.

It is not sufficient that the social climber possess intelligence, knowledge, aptitudes, and the virtues necessary to his profession. He—and his family—must be able to live in a social milieu that corresponds to his profession. In the Second Empire, which was, far more than the reign of Louis Philippe, the apex of the bourgeoisie, social factors were greatly emphasized in the promotion of civil servants: the manner in which they entertained, how they behaved in a drawing room, and the behavior of their wives, their kin, and the kin of their wives were taken into account. The ministries were informed of all this by special memorandums. The lieutenant who "cut his bread" at the table would never reach the higher ranks. The republican civil service cares less about these details of private life, but the bourgeois class defends itself against outsiders and opposes to them a subtly complicated fence, constantly kept up and repaired, so as to insure that only those who can be treated as equals will be able to break through it.

In principle, the liberal professions are those supposing qualities of intelligence, knowledge, culture, character, and authority; in a word, qualities of personal worth. Because of this, it is impossible that they should constitute a class. The bourgeoisie appropriates these qualities by associating intellectual and moral qualities with the superficial characteristics that constitute and distinguish it. Its ways of judging, feeling, acting—in a word, its mores—can be understood as efforts to maintain the opinion that personal merit is naturally found among its members and that it is found only rarely outside its boundaries.

4. *On Superordination and Subordination*

BY GEORG SIMMEL

Introduction

1. DOMINATION, A FORM OF INTERACTION

NOBODY, in general, wishes that his influence completely determine the other individual. He rather wants this influence, this determination of the other, to act back upon *him*. Even the abstract will-to-dominate, therefore, is a case of interaction. This will draws its satisfaction from the fact that the acting or suffering of the other, his positive or negative condition, offers itself to the dominator as the product of *his* will. The significance of this solipsistic exercise of domination (so to speak) consists, for the superordinate himself, exclusively in the consciousness of his efficacy. Sociologically speaking, it is only a rudimentary form. By virtue of it alone, sociation occurs as little as it does between a sculptor and his statue, although the statue, too, acts back on the artist through his consciousness of his own creative power. The practical function of this desire for domination, even in this sublimated form, is not so much the exploitation of the other as the mere consciousness of this possibility. For the rest, it does not represent the extreme case of egoistic inconsiderateness. Certainly, the desire for domination is designed to break the *internal* resistance of the subjugated (whereas egoism usually aims only at the victory over his *external* resistance). But still, even the desire for domination has some interest in the other person, who constitutes a value for it. Only when egoism does not even amount to a desire for domination; only when the other is absolutely indifferent and a mere means for purposes which lie beyond him, is the last shadow of any sociating process removed.

The definition of later Roman jurists shows, in a relative way, that the elimination of *all* independent significance of one of the two interacting parties annuls the very notion of society. This definition was to the effect that the *societas leonina* must not be conceived of as a social contract. ["sociation with a lion," that is, a partnership in which all the advantage is on one side—Tr.] A comparable statement has been made regarding the lowest-paid workers in modern giant enterprises which preclude all effective competition among rivaling entrepreneurs for the services of these laborers. It has been said that the difference in the strategic positions of workers and employers is so overwhelming that the work contract ceases to be a "contract" in the ordinary sense of the word, because the former are unconditionally at the mercy of the latter. It thus appears that the moral maxim never to use a man as a mere means is actually the formula of every sociation. Where the significance of the one party sinks so low that its effect no longer enters the relationship with the other, there is as little ground for speaking of sociation as there is in the case of the carpenter and his bench.

Within a relationship of subordination, the exclusion of all spontaneity whatever is actually rarer than is suggested by such widely used popular expressions as "coercion," "having no choice," "absolute necessity," etc. Even in the most oppressive and cruel cases of subordination, there is still a considerable measure of personal freedom. We merely do not become aware of it, because its manifestation would entail sacrifices which we usually never think of taking upon ourselves. Actually, the "absolute" coercion which even the most cruel tyrant imposes upon us is always distinctly relative. Its condition is our desire to escape from the threatened punishment or from other consequences of our disobedience. More precise analysis shows that the super-subordination relationship

Reprinted from *The Sociology of Georg Simmel*, ed. and trans., Kurt H. Wolff. (Glencoe, Ill.: The Free Press, 1950), from Part III, chap. i, pp. 181–89; chap. iv, 250–67; with the permission of The Free Press.

destroys the subordinate's freedom only in the case of direct physical violation. In every other case, this relationship only demands a price for the realization of freedom—a price, to be sure, which we are not willing to pay. It can narrow down more and more the sphere of external conditions under which freedom is clearly realized, but, except for physical force, never to the point of the complete disappearance of freedom. The moral side of this analysis does not concern us here, but only its sociological aspect. This aspect consists in the fact that interaction, that is, action which is mutually determined, action which stems exclusively from personal origins, prevails even where it often is not noted. It exists even in those cases of superordination and subordination—and therefore makes even those cases *societal* forms—where according to popular notions the "coercion" by one party deprives the other of every spontaneity, and thus of every real "effect," or contribution to the process of interaction.

2. AUTHORITY AND PRESTIGE

Relationships of superordination and subordination play an immense role in social life. It is therefore of the utmost importance for its analysis to clarify the spontaneity and co-efficiency of the subordinate subject and thus to correct their widespread minimization by superficial notions about them. For instance, what is called "authority" presupposes, in a much higher degree than is usually recognized, a freedom on the part of the person subjected to authority. Even where authority seems to "crush" him, it is based not *only* on coercion or compulsion to yield to it.

The peculiar structure of "authority" is significant for social life in the most varied ways; it shows itself in beginnings as well as in exaggerations, in acute as well as in lasting forms. It seems to come about in two different ways. A person of superior significance or strength may acquire, in his more immediate or remote milieu, an overwhelming weight of his opinions, a faith, or a confidence which have the character of objectivity. He thus enjoys a prerogative and an axiomatic trustworthiness in his decisions which excel, at least by a fraction, the value of mere subjective personality, which is always variable, relative, and subject to criticism. By acting "authoritatively," the quantity of his significance is transformed into a new quality; it assumes for his environment the physical state—metaphorically speaking—of objectivity.

But the same result, authority, may be attained in the opposite direction. A super-individual power—state, church, school, family or military organizations—clothes a person with a reputation,

a dignity, a power of ultimate decision, which would never flow from his individuality. It is the nature of an authoritative person to make decisions with a certainty and automatic recognition which logically pertain only to impersonal, objective axioms and deductions. In the case under discussion, authority descends upon a person from above, as it were, whereas in the case treated before, it arises from the qualities of the person himself, through a *generatio aequivoca*. ["Equivocal birth" or "spontaneous generation."—Tr.] But evidently, at this point of transition and change-over [from the personal to the authoritative situation], the more or less voluntary faith of the party subjected to authority comes into play. This transformation of the value of personality into a super-personal value gives the personality something which is beyond its demonstrable and rational share, however slight this addition may be. The believer in authority himself achieves the transformation. He (the subordinate element) participates in a sociological event which requires his spontaneous cooperation. As a matter of fact, the very feeling of the "oppressiveness" of authority suggests that the autonomy of the subordinate party is actually presupposed and never wholly eliminated.

Another nuance of superiority, which is designated as "prestige," must be distinguished from "authority." Prestige lacks the element of super-subjective significance; it lacks the identity of the personality with an objective power or norm. Leadership by means of prestige is determined entirely by the strength of the individual. This individual force always remains conscious of itself. Moreover, whereas the average type of leadership always shows a certain mixture of personal and superadded-objective factors, prestige leadership stems from pure personality, even as authority stems from the objectivity of norms and forces. Superiority through prestige consists in the ability to "push" individuals and masses and to make unconditional followers of them. Authority does not have this ability to the same extent. The higher, cooler, and normative character of authority is more apt to leave room for criticism, even on the part of its followers. In spite of this, however, prestige strikes us as the more voluntary homage to the superior person. Actually, perhaps, the recognition of authority implies a more profound freedom of the subject than does the enchantment that emanates from the prestige of a prince, a priest, a military or spiritual leader. But the matter is different in regard to the *feeling* on the part of those led. In the face of authority, we are often defenseless, whereas the *élan* with which we follow a given prestige always contains a consciousness of spontaneity. Here, precisely because devotion is only to the wholly personal, this devotion seems to flow only from the ground of personality with its inalienable freedom. Certainly, man is mistaken innumerable times regarding the measure of freedom which he must invest in a certain action. One reason for this is the vagueness and uncertainty of the explicit conception by means of which we account for this inner process. But in whatever way we interpret freedom, we can say that some measure of it, even though it may not be the measure we suppose, is present wherever there is the feeling and the conviction of freedom.

3. LEADER AND LED

The seemingly wholly passive element is in reality even more active in relationships such as obtain between a speaker and his audience or between a teacher and his class. Speaker and teacher appear to be nothing but leaders; nothing but, momentarily, superordinate. Yet whoever finds himself in such or a similar situation feels the determining and controlling re-action on the part of what seems to be a purely receptive and guided mass. This applies not only to situations where the two parties confront one another physically. All leaders are also led; in innumerable cases, the master is the slave of his slaves. Said one of the greatest German party leaders referring to his followers: "I am their leader, therefore I must follow them."

In the grossest fashion, this is shown by the journalist. The journalist gives content and direction to the opinions of a mute multitude. But he is nevertheless forced to listen, combine, and guess what the tendencies of this multitude are, what it desires to hear and have confirmed, and whither it wants to be led. While apparently it is only the public which is exposed to *his* suggestions, actually he is as much under the sway of the *public's* suggestion. Thus, a highly complex interaction (whose two, mutually spontaneous forces, to be sure, appear under very different forms) is hidden here beneath the semblance of the pure superiority of the one element and a purely passive being-led of the other.

The content and significance of certain personal relations consist in the fact that the exclusive function of one of the two elements is service for the other. But the perfect measure of this devotion of the first element often depends on the condition that the other element surrenders to the first, even though on a different level of the relationship. Thus, Bismarck remarked concerning his relation to William I: "A certain measure of devotion is determined by law; a greater measure, by political

conviction; beyond this, a personal feeling of *reciprocity* is required.—My devotion had its principal ground in my loyalty to royalist convictions. But in the special form in which this royalism existed, it is after all possible only under the impact of a certain reciprocity—the reciprocity between master and servant." The most characteristic case of this type is shown, perhaps, by hypnotic suggestion. An outstanding hypnotist pointed out that in every hypnosis the hypnotized has an effect upon the hypnotist; and that, although this effect cannot be easily determined, the result of the hypnosis could not be reached without it. Thus here, too, appearance showns an absolute influence, on the one side, and an absolute being-influenced, on the other; but it conceals an interaction, an exchange of influences, which transforms the pure one-sidedness of superordination and subordination into a *sociological* form.

4. INTERACTION IN THE IDEA OF "LAW"

I shall cite some cases of superordination and subordination in the field of law. It is easy to reveal the interaction which actually exists in what seems a purely unilateral situation. If the absolute despot accompanies his orders by the threat of punishment or the promise of reward, this implies that he himself wishes to be bound by the decrees he issues. The subordinate is expected to have the right to request something of him; and by establishing the punishment, no matter how horrible, the despot commits himself not to impose a more severe one. Whether or not afterward he actually abides by the punishment established or the reward promised is a different question: the *significance* of the relation is that, although the superordinate wholly determines the subordinate, the subordinate nevertheless is assured of a claim on which he can insist or which he can waive. Thus even this extreme form of the relationship still contains some sort of spontaneity on his part.

The motive of interaction within an apparently one-sided and passive subordination appears in a peculiar modification in a medieval theory of the state. According to this theory, the state came into existence because men mutually obligated one another to submit to a common chief. Thus, the ruler —including, apparently, the unconditional ruler— is appointed on the basis of a mutual contract among his subjects. Whereas contemporaneous theories of domination saw its reciprocal character in the contract between ruler and ruled, the theory under discussion located this mutual nature of domination in its very basis, the people: the obligation to the prince is conceived to be the mere articulation, expression, or technique of a reciprocal relation among the individuals of whom his people is composed. In Hobbes, in fact, the ruler has no means of breaking the contract with his subjects because he has not made one; and the corollary to this is that the subject, even if he rebels against his ruler, does not thereby break a contract concluded with *him,* but only the contract he has entered with all other members of the society, to the effect of letting themselves be governed by this ruler.

It is the *absence* of this reciprocity which accounts for the observation that the tyranny of a group over its own members is worse than that of a prince over his subjects. The group—and by no means the political group alone—conceives of its members, not as confronting it, but as being included by it as its own links. This often results in a peculiar inconsiderateness toward the members, which is very different from a ruler's personal cruelty. Wherever there is, formally, confrontation (even if, contentually, it comes *close* to submission), there is interaction; and, in principle, interaction always contains some limitation of *each* party to the process (although there may be individual exceptions to this rule). Where superordination shows an extreme inconsiderateness, as in the case of the group that simply *disposes* of its members, there no longer is any confrontation with its form of interaction, which involves spontaneity, and hence limitation, of both superordinate and subordinate elements.

This is very clearly expressed in the original conception of Roman law. In its purity, the term "law" implies a submission which does not involve any spontaneity or counter-effect on the part of the person subordinate to the law. And the fact that the subordinate has actually cooperated in making it—and more, that *he* has given himself the law which binds him—is irrelevant. For in doing so, he has merely decomposed himself into the subject and object of lawmaking; and the law which the subject applies to the object does not change its significance only by the fact that both subject and object are accidentally lodged in the same physical person. Nevertheless, in their conception of law, the Romans directly allude to the idea of interaction. For originally, "*lex*" means "contract," even though in the sense that the conditions of the contract are fixed by its proponent, and the other party can merely accept or reject it in its totality. In the beginning, the *lex publica populi romani* implied that the King proposed this legislation, and the people were its acceptors. Hence the very concept which most of all seems to exclude interaction is, nevertheless, designed to refer to it by its linguistic expression. In a certain sense this is revealed in the

prerogative of the Roman king that he alone was allowed to speak to the people. Such a prerogative, to be sure, expressed the jealously guarded exclusiveness of his rulership, even as in ancient Greece the right of everybody to speak to the people indicated complete democracy. Nevertheless, this prerogative implies that the significance of speaking to the people, and, hence, of the people themselves, was recognized. Although the people merely *received* this one-sided action, they were nonetheless a *contractor* (whose party to the contract, of course, was only a single person, the king).

The purpose of these preliminary remarks was to show the properly sociological, social-formative character of superordination and subordination even where it appears as if a social relationship were replaced by a purely mechanical one—where, that is, the position of the subordinate seems to be that of a means or an object for the superordinate, without any spontaneity. It has been possible, at least in many cases, to show the sociologically decisive *reciprocal effectiveness,* which was concealed under the one-sided character of influence and being-influenced.

*   *   *

Subordination under a Principle

1. SUBORDINATION UNDER A PRINCIPLE VS. A PERSON

I now come, finally, to the third typical form of subordination, subordination neither to an individual nor to a plurality, but to an impersonal, objective principle. The fact that here a real interaction, at least an immediate interaction, is precluded, seems to deprive this form of the element of freedom. The individual who is subordinate to an objective law feels himself determined by it; while he, in turn, in no way determines the law, and has no possibility of reacting to it in a manner which could influence it—quite in contrast to even the most miserable slave, who, in some fashion at least, can still in this sense react to his master. For if one simply does not obey the law, one is, to this extent, not *really* subjected to it; and if one changes the law, one is not subordinate to the old law at all, but is again, in the same entirely unfree manner, subject to the new law. In spite of this, however, for modern, objective man, who is aware of the difference between the spheres of spontaneity and of obedience, subordination to a law which functions as the emanation of impersonal, uninfluenceable powers, is the more dignified situation. This was quite different at a time when the personality could preserve its self-esteem only in situations characterized by full spontaneity, which even in case of complete subordination were still associated with inter-personal effect and counter-effect. For this reason, as late as in the sixteenth century, princes in France, Germany, Scotland, and the Netherlands often met with considerable resistance, if they let their countries be ruled by administrative bodies or erudite substitutes—that is, more nearly by laws. The ruler's order was felt to be something personal; the individual wanted to lend him obedience only from personal devotion; and personal devotion, in spite of its unconditional character, is always in the form of free reciprocity.

This passionate personalism of the subordination relationship almost becomes its own caricature in the following circumstance, reported from Spain at the beginning of the modern period. An impoverished nobleman who became a cook or lackey, did not thereby definitely lose his nobility: it only became latent and could be awakened again by a favorable turn of fate. But once he became a craftsman, his nobility was destroyed. This is entirely contrary to the modern conception, which separates the person from his achievement and, therefore, finds personal dignity to be preserved best if the content of subordination is as objective as possible. Thus, an American girl, who would work in a factory without the slightest feeling of humiliation, would feel wholly degraded as a family cook. Already in thirteenth-century Florence, the *lower* guilds comprised occupations in the immediate service of persons, such as cobblers, hosts, and school teachers; whereas the *higher* guilds were composed of occupations which, though still serving the public, were yet more objective and less dependent on particular individuals—for instance, clothiers and grocers. On the other hand, in Spain, where knightly traditions, with their engagement of the whole person in all activity, were still alive, every relationship which (in any sense) took place between person and person, was bound to be considered at least bearable; while every subordination to more objective claims, every integration into a system of impersonal duties (impersonal, because serving many and anonymous persons), was bound to be regarded as wholly disgraceful. An aversion to the objectivity of law can still be felt in the legal theories of Althusius: the *summus magistratus* legislates, but he does so, not because he represents the state, but because he is appointed by the people. The notion that the ruler could be designated as the representative of the state by appointment through law, not by personal appointment (actual or presumed) by the people—is still alien to Althusius.

In antiquity, on the contrary, subordination to law appeared thoroughly adequate, precisely because of the idea that law is free from any personal characteristics. Aristotle praised law as "*tó méson*," that is, as that which is moderate, impartial, free from passions. Plato, in the same sense, had already recognized government by impersonal law as the best means for counteracting selfishness. His, however, was only a psychological motivation. It did not touch the core of the question, namely, the fundamental transition of the relationship of obedience from personalism to objectivism, a transition which cannot be derived from the anticipation of utilitarian consequence. Yet, in Plato, we also find this other theory: that, in the ideal state, the insight of the ruler stands above the law; and as soon as the welfare of the whole seems to require it of the ruler, he must be able to act even against the laws laid down by him. There must be laws which may not be broken under any circumstances, only if there are no true statesmen. The law, therefore, appears here as the lesser evil—but not, as in the Germanic feeling, mentioned before, because subordination under a person has an element of freedom and dignity in comparison with which all obedience to laws has something mechanical and passive. Rather, it is the rigidity of the law which is felt to be its weakness: in its rigidity, it confronts the changing and unforeseeable claims of life in a clumsy and inadequate way; and this is an evil from which only the entirely unprejudiced insight of a personal ruler can escape; and only where there is no such insight, does law become relatively advantageous. Here, therefore, it is always the *content* of the law, its physical state, as it were, which determines its value or disvalue as compared with subordination under persons. The fact that the relationship of obedience is totally different in its inner principle and in terms of the whole feeling of life, on the part of the obeyer, according to whether it originates in a person or in a law—this fact does not enter these considerations. The most general, or formal relation between government by law and government by person can (of course) be expressed in a preliminary, practical manner by saying that where the law is not forceful or broad enough, a person is necessary, and where the person is inadequate, the law is required. But, far beyond this, whether rule by man is considered as something provisional in lieu of rule by perfect law, or, inversely, rule by law is considered a gap-filler or an inferior substitute for government by a personality which is absolutely qualified to rule—this choice depends upon decisions of ultimate, indiscussable feelings concerning sociological values.

2. SUBORDINATION UNDER OBJECTS

There is still another form in which an objective principle may become the turning point in the relationship between superordinates and subordinates, namely, when neither a law nor an ideal norm, but rather a concrete object governs the domination, as, for instance, in the principle of patrimony. Here —most radically under the system of Russian bondage—bonded subjects are only appurtenances of the land—"the air bonds the people." The terrible hardship of bondage at least excluded personal slavery which would have permitted the sale of the slave. Instead, it tied subordination to the land in such a way that the bondsman could be sold only along with the land. In spite of all contentual and quantitative differences, nevertheless, sometimes this same form occurs in the case of the modern factory worker, whose own interest, through certain arrangements, binds him to a given factory. For instance, the acquisition of his house was made possible for him, or he participated out of his own purse in certain welfare expenditures, and all these benefits are lost once he leaves the factory, etc. He is thus bound, merely by objects, in a way which in a very specific manner makes him powerless in respect to the entrepreneur. Finally, it was this same form of domination which, under the most primitive patriarchal conditions, was governed not by a merely spatial, but by a living object: children did not belong to the father because he was their progenitor, but because the mother belonged to him (as the fruits of the tree belong to the tree's owner); therefore, children begotten by other fathers were no less his property.

This type of domination usually involves a humiliatingly harsh and unconditional kind of subordination. For, inasmuch as a man is subordinate by virtue of belonging to a thing, he himself psychologically sinks to the category of mere thing. With the necessary reservations, one could say that where law regulates domination, the superordinate belongs in the sphere of objectivity; while, where a *thing* regulates it, the *subordinate* does. The condition of the subordinate, therefore, is usually more favorable in the first case, and more unfavorable in the second, than in many cases of purely personal subordination.

3. CONSCIENCE

Immediate sociological interest in subordination under an objective principle attaches to two chief cases of it. One case is when this ideal, superordinate principle can be interpreted as a psychological crystallization of an actual social power. The other is when, among those who are commonly subject to it, it produces particular and characteristic relationships. The first case must be taken into consideration, above all, when dealing with moral imperatives. In our moral consciousness, we feel

subordinate to a command which does not seem to derive from any human, personal power. The voice of conscience we hear only in ourselves, although in comparison with all subjective egoism, we hear it with a force and decisiveness which apparently can stem only from a tribunal *outside* the individual. An attempt has been made, as is well-known, to solve this contradiction by deriving the contents of morality from social norms. What is useful to the species and the group, the argument runs, and what the group, therefore, requests of its members for the sake of its own maintenance, is gradually bred into the individual as an instinct. He thus comes to contain it in himself, as his own, autonomous feeling, in addition to his personal feelings properly speaking, and thus often in contrast to them. This, it is alleged, explains the dual character of the moral command: that on the one hand, it confronts us as an impersonal order to which we simply have to submit, but that, on the other, no external power, but only our most private and internal impulses, imposes it upon us. At any rate, here is one of the cases where the individual, within his own consciousness, repeats the relationships which exist between him, as a total personality, and the group. It is an old observation that the conceptions of the single individual, with all their relations of association and dissociation, differentiation, and unification, behave in the same way in which individuals behave in regard to one another. It is merely a peculiar case of this correspondence that those intrapsychological relations are repeated, not only between individuals in general, but also between the individual and his group. All that society asks of its members—adaptation and loyalty, altruism and work, self-discipline and truthfulness—the individual also asks of himself.

In all this, several very important motives cut across one another. Society confronts the individual with precepts. He becomes habituated to their compulsory character until the cruder and subtler means of compulsion are no longer necessary. His nature may thereby be so formed or deformed that he acts by these precepts as if on impulse, with a consistent and direct will which is not conscious of any law. Thus, the pre-Islamic Arabs were without any notion of an objectively legal compulsion; in all instances, purely personal decision was their highest authority, although this decision was thoroughly imbued with tribal consciousness and the requirements of tribal life, which gave it its norms. Or else, the law, in the form of a command which is carried by the authority of the society, does live in the individual consciousness, but irrespective of the question whether society actually backs it with its compulsory power or even itself supports it solely with its explicit will. Here then, the individual represents society to himself. The external confrontation, with its suppressions, liberations, changing accents, has become an interplay between his social impulses and the ego impulses in the stricter sense of the word; and both are included by the ego in the larger sense.

But this is not yet the really objective lawfulness, indicated above, in whose consciousness of which no trace of any historical-social origin is left. At a certain higher stage of morality, the motivation of action lies no longer in a real-human, even though super-individual power; at this stage, the spring of moral necessities flows beyond the contrast between individual and totality. For, as little as these necessities derive from society, as little do they derive from the singular reality of individual life. In the free conscience of the actor, in individual reason, they only have their bearer, the locus of their efficacy. Their power of obligation stems from these necessities themselves, from their inner, super-personal validity, from an objective ideality which we must recognize, whether or not we want to, in a manner similar to that in which the validity of a truth is entirely independent of whether or not the truth becomes real in any consciousness. The *content,* however, which fills these forms is (not necessarily but often) the societal requirement. But this requirement no longer operates by means of its social impetus, as it were, but rather as if it had undergone a metapsychosis into a norm which must be satisfied for its own sake, not for my sake nor for yours.

We are dealing here with differences which not only are psychologically of the greatest delicacy, but whose boundaries are also constantly blurred in practice. Yet this mixture of motivations in which psychic reality moves, makes it all the more urgent that it be isolated analytically. Whether society and individual confront one another like two powers and the individual's subordination is effected by society through energy which seems to flow from an uninterrupted source and constantly seems to renew itself; or whether this energy changes into a psychological impulse in the very individual who considers himself a social being and, therefore, fights and suppresses those of his impulses that lean toward his "egoistic" part; or whether the Ought, which man finds above himself as an actuality as objective as Being, is merely filled with the content of societal life conditions— these are constellations which only begin to exhaust the kinds of individual subordination to the group. In them, the three powers which fill historical life—society, individual, and objectivity—become norm-giving, in this order. But they do so

in such a way that each of them absorbs the social content, the quantity of superordination of society over the individual; in a specific manner, each of them forms and presents the power, the will, and the necessities of society.

4. SOCIETY AND "OBJECTIVITY"

Among these three potencies, objectivity can be defined as the unquestionably valid law which is enthroned in an ideal realm above society and the individual. But it can also be defined in still another dimension, as it were. Society often is the third element, which solves conflicts between the individual and objectivity or builds bridges where they are disconnected. As regards the genesis of cognition, the concept of society has liberated us from an alternative characteristic of earlier times, namely, that a cultural value either must spring from an individual or must be bestowed upon mankind by an objective power. Practically speaking, it is societal labor by means of which the individual can satisfy his claims upon the objective order. The cooperation of the many, the efforts of society as a unit, both simultaneously and successively, wrest from nature not only a greater quantity of need-satisfactions than can be achieved by the individual, but also new qualities and types of need-satisfactions which the labor of the individual alone cannot possibly attain. This fact is merely a symbol of the deeper and fundamental phenomenon of society standing between individual man and the sphere of general natural laws. As something psychologically concrete, society blends with the individual; as something general, it blends with nature. It is the general, but it is not abstract. To be sure, every historical group is an individual, as is every historical human being; but it is this only in relation to other groups; for its members, it is super-individual. But it is super-individual, not as a concept is in regard to its single, concrete realizations, where the concept synthesizes what is common to all of them. The group is super-individual, rather, in a specific manner of generality—similar to the organic body, which is "general" above its organs, or to "room furniture," which is "general" above table, chair, chest, and mirror. And this specific generality coincides with the specific objectivity which society possesses for its members as subjects.

But the individual does not confront society as he confronts nature. The objectivity of nature denotes the irrelevance of the question of whether or not the subject spiritually participates in nature; whether he has a correct, a false, or no conception of it. Its being exists, and its laws are valid, independently of the significance which either of them may have for any subject. Certainly, society, likewise, transcends the individual and lives its own life which follows its own laws; it, too, confronts the individual with a historical, imperative firmness. Yet, society's "in front of" the individual is, at the same time, a "within." The harsh indifference toward the individual also is an interest: social objectivity needs general individual subjectivity, although it does not need any particular individual subjectivity. It is these characteristics which make society a structure intermediate between the subject and an absolutely impersonal generality and objectivity.

The following observation, for instance, points in this direction. As long as the development of an economy does not yet produce objective prices, properly speaking; as long as knowledge and regulation of demand, offer, production costs, amounts at risk, gain, etc., do not yet lead to the idea that a given piece of merchandise is worth so much and must have such and such a fixed price—so long is the immediate interference of society and its organs and laws with the affairs of commerce (particularly in regard to the price and stability of commerce) much more strong and rigorous than under other conditions. Price taxes, the surveillance of quantity and quality of production, and, in a larger sense, even sumptuary laws and consumers' obligations, often emerged at that stage of economic development at which the subjective freedom of commerce strove after stable objectivity, without, however, yet being able to attain any pure, abstract objectivity in determining prices. It is at this stage that the concrete generality, the living objectivity of society enters, often clumsily, obstructively, schematically, but yet always as a super-subjective power which supplies the individual with a norm before he derives this norm directly from the structure of the matter at issue and its understood regularity.

On a much larger scale, this same formal development, from subordination under society to subordination under objectivity, occurs in the intellectual sphere. All of intellectual history shows to what extent the individual intellect fills the content of its truth-concepts only with traditional, authoritative conceptions which are "accepted by all," long before he confronts the object directly and derives the content of the truth-concepts from its objectivity. Initially, the support and the norm of the inquiring mind are not the object, whose immediate observation and interpretation the mind is entirely unable to manipulate, but the general opinion of the object. It is this general opinion which mediates theoretical conceptions, from the silliest superstition to the subtlest prejudices, which almost entirely conceal the lacking independence of their recipient and the un-objective nature of their contents. It seems as if

man could not easily bear looking the object in the eye; as if he were equal neither to the rigidity of its lawfulness nor to the freedom which the object, in contrast to all coercion coming from men, gives him. By comparison, to bow to the authority of the many or their representatives, to traditional opinion, to socially accepted notions, is something intermediate. Traditional opinion, after all, is more modifiable than is the law of the object; in it, man can feel some psychological mediation; it transmits, as it were, something which is already digested psychologically. At the same time, it gives us a hold, a relief from responsibility—the compensation for the lack of that autonomy which we derive from the purely intrinsic relationship between ego and object.

The concept of objective justice, no less than the concept of truth, finds its intermediate stage, which leads toward the objective sense of "justice," in social behavior. In the field of criminal law, as well as in all other regulations of life, the correlation between guilt and expiation, merit and reward, service and counter-service, is first, evidently, a matter of social expediency or of social impulses. Perhaps the equivalence of action and reaction, in which justice consists, is never an analytical equivalence directly resulting from these elements, but always requires a third element, an ideal, a purpose, a norm-setting situation, in which the first two elements create or demonstrate their mutual correspondence synthetically. Originally, this third element consists in the interests and forms of the general life which surrounds the individuals, that is, the subjects of the realization of justice. This general life creates, and acts on, the criteria of justice or injustice in the relation between action and reaction—of justice or injustice which cannot be ascertained in the action-and-reaction in isolation. Above this process, and mediated by it, there rises, at an objectively and historically later stage, the necessity of the "just" correspondence between action and reaction, a correspondence which emerges in the comparison of these two elements themselves. This higher norm, which perhaps even in this later phase continues to determine weight and counter-weight according to its own scale, is completely absorbed by the elements themselves; it has become a value which seems to originate with them and operates out of them. Justice now appears as an objective relationship which follows necessarily from the intrinsic significance of sin and pain, good deed and happiness, offer and response. It must be realized for its own sake: *fiat justitia, pereat mundus*. It was, by contrast, the very preservation of the world which, from the earlier standpoint, constituted the ground of justice. Whatever the ideal sense of justice may be (which is not the topic of discussion here), the *objective* law, in which justice, purely for its own sake, embodies itself, and which claims compliance in its own right, is historically and psychologically a later stage of development. It is preceded, prepared, and mediated by the claim to justice stemming from merely *social* objectivity.

This same development, finally, prevails within the moral sphere, in the stricter sense of this term. The original content of morality is of an altruistic-social nature. The idea is not that morality has its own life independent of this content and merely absorbs it. Rather, the devotion of the "I" to the "thou" (in the singular or plural) is the very idea, the definition, of the moral. Philosophical doctrines of ethics represent, by comparison, a much later phase. In them, an absolutely objective Ought is separated from the question of "I" and "thou." If it is important to Plato that the Idea of the Good be realized; to Kant, that the principle of individual action be suitable as a general law; to Nietzsche, that the human species transcend its momentary stage of development; then, occasionally, these norms may also refer to reciprocal relations among individuals. But, essentially this is no longer important. What is important is the realization of an objective law, which not only leaves behind the subjectivity of the actor but also the subjectivity of the individuals whom the action may concern. For, now, even the reference to the societal complex of the subjects is merely an accidental satisfaction of a much more general norm and obligation, which may legitimate socially and altruistically oriented action, but may also refuse to do so. In the development of the individual as of the species, ethical obedience to the claims of the "thou" and of society characterizes the first emergence from the pre-ethical stage of naïve egoism. Innumerable individuals never go beyond obedience to the "thou." But, in principle, this stage is preparatory and transitory to subordination under an objectively ethical law, which transcends the "I" as much as the "thou," and only on its own initiative admits the interests of the one or the other as ethical contents.

5. THE EFFECT OF SUBORDINATION UNDER A PRINCIPLE UPON THE RELATIONS BETWEEN SUPERORDINATES AND SUBORDINATES

The second sociological question in regard to subordination under an impersonal-ideal principle concerns the effect of this common subordination upon the reciprocal relations among the subordinates. Here, also, it must above all be remembered that ideal subordination is often preceded by real subordination. We frequently find that a person or

class exerts superordination in the name of an ideal principle to which the person or class themselves are allegedly subordinated. This principle, therefore, seems to be logically prior to the social arrangement; the actual organization of domination among people seems to develop in consequence of that ideal dependency. Historically, however, the road has usually run in the opposite direction. Superordinations and subordinations develop out of very real, personal power relations. Through the spiritualization of the superordinate power or through the enlargement and de-personalization of the whole relationship, there gradually grows an ideal, objective power over and above these superordinations and subordinations. The superordinate then exerts his power merely in the capacity of the closest representative of this ideal, objective force.

These successive processes are shown very distinctly in the development of the position of *pater familias* among the Aryans. Originally—this is how the type is presented to us—his power was unlimited and wholly subjective. That is, the *pater familias* decided all arrangements by momentary whim and in terms of personal advantage. Yet this arbitrary power was gradually replaced by a feeling of responsibility. The unity of the family group, embodied (for instance) in the *spiritus familiaris*, became an ideal force, in reference to which even the master of the whole felt himself to be merely an executor and obeyer. It is in this sense that custom and habit, rather than subjective preference, determined his actions, his decisions, and judicial decrees; that he no longer behaved as the unconditional master of the family property, but rather as its administrator in the interest of the whole; that his position had more the character of an office than that of an unlimited right. The relation between superordinates and subordinates was thus placed upon an entirely new basis. Whereas, at the first stage, the subordinates constituted, so to speak, only at a personal appurtenance of the superordinates, later there prevailed the objective idea of the family which stands above all individuals and to which the leading patriarch is as much subordinated as is every other member. The patriarch can give orders to the other members of the family only in the name of that ideal unit.

Here we encounter an extremely important form-type, namely, that the very commander subordinates himself to the law which he has made. The moment his will becomes law, it attains objective character, and thus separates itself from its subjective-personal origin. As soon as the ruler gives the law as law, he documents himself, to this extent, as the organ of an ideal necessity. He merely reveals a norm which is plainly valid on the ground of its inner sense and that of the situation, whether or not the ruler actually enunciates it. What is more, even if instead of this more or less distinctly conceived legitimation, the will of the ruler itself becomes law, even then the ruler cannot avoid transcending the sphere of subjectivity: for in this case, he carries the super-personal legitimation *a priori* in himself, so to speak. In this way, the inner form of law brings it about that the law-giver, in giving the law, subordinates himself to it as a person, in the same way as all others. Thus, the Privileges of the medieval Flemish cities stated expressly that the jurors must give everybody a fair trial, including even the Count who had bestowed this privilege upon the city. And such a sovereign ruler as the Great Elector introduced a head-tax without asking the estates for their consent—but then he not only made his court pay it, but he also paid it himself.

The most recent history gives an example of the growth of an objective power, to which the person, who is originally and subsequently in command, must subordinate himself in common with his subordinates. The example is formally related to the case cited from the history of the family. In modern economic production, objective and technical elements dominate over personal elements. In earlier times, many superordinations and subordinations had a personal character, so that in a given relationship, one person simply was superordinate, and the other subordinate. Many of these super-subordinations have changed in the sense that both superordinates and subordinates alike stand under an objective purpose; and it is only within this common relationship to the higher principle that the subordination of the one to the other continues to exist as a technical necessity. As long as the relationship of wage labor is conceived of as a rental contract (in which the worker is rented), it contains as an essential element the worker's subordination to the entrepreneur. But, once the work contract is considered, not as the renting of a person, but as the purchase of a piece of merchandise, that is, labor, then this element of personal subordination is eliminated. In this case, the subordination which the employer requests of the worker is only—so it has been expressed—subordination "under the cooperative process, a subordination as compulsive for the entrepreneur, once he engages in any activity at all, as for the worker." The worker is no longer subject as a person but only as the servant of an objective, economic procedure. In this process, the element which in the form of entrepreneur or manager is superordinated to the worker, operates no longer as a personal element

but only as one necessitated by objective requirements.

The increased self-feeling of the modern worker must, at least partly, be connected with this process, which shows its purely sociological character also in the circumstance that it often has no influence upon the material welfare of the laborer. He merely sells a quantitatively defined service, which may be smaller or larger than what was required of him under the earlier, personal arrangement. As a man, he thus frees himself from the relationship of subordination, to which he belongs only as an element in the process of production; and to this extent, he is coordinate with those who direct the production. This technical objectivity has its symbol in the legal objectivity of the contract relation: once the contract is concluded, it stands as an objective norm above *both* parties. In the Middle Ages, this phenomenon marked the turning point in the condition of the journeyman, which originally implied full personal subordination under the master: the journeyman was generally called "servant" [*Knecht*]. The gathering of journeymen in their own estate was centered upon the attempt at transforming the personal-service relationship into a contractual relationship: as soon as the organization of the "servants" was achieved, their name, most characteristically, was replaced by that of "journeymen." In general, it is relative coordination, instead of absolute subordination, which is correlated with the contractual form, no matter what the material content of the contract may be.

This form further strengthens its objective character if the contract is not concluded between individuals, but consists in collective regulations between a group of workers on the one side, and a group of employers on the other. It has been developed especially by the English Trade Unions, which in certain, highly advanced industries conclude contracts regarding wage rates, working time, overtime, holidays, etc., with associations of entrepreneurs. These contracts may not be ignored by any sub-contract that might be made between individual members of these larger categories. In this manner, the impersonality of the labor relationship is evidently increased to an extraordinary degree. The objectivity of this relationship finds an appropriate instrument and expression in the super-individual collectivity. This objective character, finally, is assured in an even more specific manner if the contracts are concluded for very brief periods. English Trade Unions have always urged this brevity, in spite of the increased insecurity which results from it. The explanation of the recommendation has been that the worker distinguishes himself from the slave by the right to leave his place of work; but, if he surrenders this right for a long time, he is, for the whole duration of this period, subject to all conditions which the entrepreneur imposes upon him, with the exception of those expressly stipulated; and he has lost the protection offered him by his right to suspend the relationship. Instead of the breadth, or comprehensiveness, of the bond which in earlier times committed the total personality, there emerges, if the contract lasts very long, the length, or duration, of the bond. In the case of short contracts, objectivity is guaranteed, not by something positive, but only by the necessity of preventing the objectively regulated contractual relationship from changing into a relationship determined by subjective arbitrariness—whereas in the case of long contracts there is no corresponding, sufficient protection.

In the condition of domestic servants—at least, on the whole, in contemporary central Europe—it is still the total individual, so to speak, who enters the subordination. Subordination has not yet attained the objectivity of an objectively, clearly circumscribed service. From this circumstance derive the chief inadequacies inherent in the institution of domestic service. This institution does approach that more perfect form when it is replaced by services of persons who perform only certain, objective functions in the house, and who are, to this extent, coordinated with the housewife. The earlier, but still existing, relationship involved them as total personalities and obliged them—as is most strikingly shown by the concept of the "all-around girl" ["*Mädchen für alles*"]—to "unlimited services": they became subordinate to the housewife as a person, precisely because there were no objective delimitations. Under thoroughly patriarchal (as contrasted with contemporary) conditions, the "house" is considered an objective, intrinsic purpose and value, in behalf of which housewife and servants cooperate. This results, even if there is a completely personal subordination, in a certain coordination sustained by the interest which the servant, who is solidly and permanently connected with the house, usually feels for it. The "thou," used in addressing him, on the one hand, gives expression to his personal subordination, but on the other, makes him comparable to the children of the house and thus ties him more closely to its organization. Strangely enough, it thus appears that in some measure, obedience to an objective idea occurs at the extreme stages in the development of obedience: under the condition of full patriarchal subordination, where the house still has, so to speak, an absolute value, which is served by the work of the housewife (though in a higher position) as well as by that of the servant; and then, under the condition of complete differentiation, where service and reward are objectively pre-determined, and the personal attachment, which characterizes the stage of an undefined quantity of subordination, has become extraneous to the relationship. The contemporary position of the servant who shares his master's house, particularly in the large cities, has lost the first of these two kinds of objectivity, without having yet attained the second. The total personality of the servant is no longer claimed by the objective idea of the "house"; and yet, in view of the general way in which his services are requested, it cannot really separate itself from it.

Finally, this form-type may be illustrated by the relationship betwen officers and common soldiers. Here, the cleavage between subordination within the organization of the group, and coordination which results from common service in defense of one's country, is as wide as can be imagined. Understandably enough, the cleavage is most noticeable at the front. On the one hand, discipline is most merciless there, but on the other hand, fellowship between officers and privates is furthered, partly by specific situations, partly by the general mood. During peacetime, the army remains arrested in the position of a means which does not attain its purposes; it is, therefore, inevitable for its technical structure to grow into a psychological ultimate aim, so that super-subordination, on which the technique of the organization is based, stands in the foreground of consciousness. The peculiar sociological mixture with coordination, which results from the common subordination under an objective idea, becomes important only when the changed situation calls attention to this idea, as the real purpose of the army.

Within the group organization of his specific content of life, the individual thus occupies a superordinate or subordinate position. But the group as a whole stands under a dominating idea which gives each of its members an equal, or nearly equal, position in comparison with all outsiders. Hence, the individual has a double role which makes his purely formal, sociological situation the vehicle for peculiarly mixed life-feelings. The employee of a large business may have a leading position in his firm, which he lets his subalterns feel in a superior and imperious way. But, as soon as he confronts the public, and acts under the idea of his business as a whole, he will exhibit serviceable and devout behavior. In the opposite direction, these elements are interwoven in the frequent haughtiness of subalterns, servants in noble houses, members of decimated intellectual or social circles, who actually stand at the periphery of these groups, but to the outsider represent all the more energetically the dignity of the whole circle and of its idea. For, the kind of positive relation to the circle which they have, gives them only a semi-solid position in it, internally and externally; and they seek to improve it in a negative way, by differentiating themselves from others. The richest formal variety of this type is offered, perhaps, by the Catholic hierarchy. Although every member of it is bound by a blind obedience which admits of no contradiction, nevertheless, in comparison with the layman, even the lowest member stands at an absolute elevation, where the idea of the eternal God rises above all temporal matters. At the same time, the highest member of this hierarchy confesses himself to be the "servant of servants." The monk, who within his order may have absolute power, dresses himself in deepest humility and servility in the face of a beggar; but the lowest brother of an order is superior to the secular prince by all the absolute sovereignty of church authority.

5. *The Circulation of Elites*

BY VILFREDO PARETO

2026. *Social* élites *and their circulation.*[1] Suppose we begin by giving a theoretical definition of the thing we are dealing with, making it as exact as possible, and then go on to see what practical considerations we can replace it with to get a first approximation. Let us for the moment completely disregard considerations as to the good or bad, useful or harmful, praiseworthy or reprehensible character of the various traits in individuals, and confine ourselves to degrees—to whether, in other words, the trait in a given case be slight, average, intense, or more exactly, to the index that may be assigned to each individual with reference to the degree, or intensity, in him of the trait in question.

2027. Let us assume that in every branch of human activity each individual is given an index which stands as a sign of his capacity, very much the way grades are given in the various subjects in examinations in school. The highest type of lawyer, for instance, will be given 10. The man who does not get a client will be given 1—reserving zero for the man who is an out-and-out idiot. To the man who has made his millions—honestly or dishonestly as the case may be—we will give 10. To the man who has earned his thousands we will give 6; to such as just manage to keep out of the poor-house, 1, keeping zero for those who get in. To the woman "in politics," such as the Aspasia of Pericles, the Maintenon of Louis XIV, the Pompadour of Louis XV, who has managed to infatuate a man of power and play a part in the man's career, we shall give some higher number, such as 8 or 9; to the strumpet who merely satisfies the senses of such a man and exerts no influence on public affairs, we shall give zero. To a clever rascal who knows how to fool people and still keep clear of the penitentiary, we shall give 8, 9, or 10, according to the number of geese he has plucked and the amount of money he has been able to get out of them. To the sneak-thief who snatches a piece of silver from a restaurant table and runs away into the arms of a policeman, we shall give 1. To a poet like Carducci we shall give 8 or 9 according to our tastes; to a scribbler who puts people to rout with his sonnets we shall give zero. For chess-players we can get very precise indices, noting what matches, and how many, they have won. And so on for all the branches of human activity.

2028. We are speaking, remember, of an actual, not a potential, state. If at an English examination

---

Reprinted from Vilfredo Pareto, *The Mind and Society,* ed. Arthur Livingston, trans. Andrew Bongiorno and Arthur Livingston (New York: Harcourt, Brace & Co., 1935), Vol. III, §§ 2026-59; Vol. IV, §§ 2233-36, with the permission of The Pareto Fund.

1. Kolabinska, *La circulation des élites en France,* p. 5: "The outstanding idea in the term 'élite' is 'superiority.' That is the only one I keep. I disregard secondary connotations of appreciation or as to the utility of such superiority. I am not interested here in what is desirable. I am making a simple study of what is. In a broad sense I mean by the *élite* in a society people who possess in marked degree qualities of intelligence, character, skill, capacity, of whatever kind. . . . On the other hand I entirely avoid any sort of judgment on the merits and utility of such classes." [The phrase "circulation of *élites*" is well established in Continental literature. Pareto himself renders it in Italian as "circulation of the élite (selected, chosen, ruling, "better") classes." It is a cumbersome phrase and not very exact, and I see no reason for preferring it to the more natural and, in most connexions, the more exact, English phrase, class-circulation.—A. L.]

a pupil says: "I could know English very well if I chose to; I do not know any because I have never seen fit to learn," the examiner replies: "I am not interested in your alibi. The grade for what you know is zero." If, similarly, someone says: "So-and-so does not steal, not because he couldn't but because he is a gentleman," we reply: "Very well, we admire him for his self-control, but his grade as a thief is zero."

2029. There are people who worship Napoleon Bonaparte as a god. There are people who hate him as the lowest of criminals. Which are right? We do not choose to solve that question in connexion with a quite different matter. Whether Napoleon was a good man or a bad man, he was certainly not an idiot, nor a man of little account, as millions of others are. He had exceptional qualities, and that is enough for us to give him a high ranking, though without prejudice of any sort to questions that might be raised as to the ethics of his qualities or their social utility.

2030. In short, we are here as usual resorting to scientific analysis, which distinguishes one problem from another and studies each one separately. As usual, again, we are replacing imperceptible variations in absolutely exact numbers with the sharp variations corresponding to groupings by class, just as in examinations those who are passed are sharply and arbitrarily distinguished from those who are "failed," and just as in the matter of physical age we distinguish children from young people, the young from the aged.

2031. So let us make a class of the people who have the highest indices in their branch of activity, and to that class give the name of *élite*.

2032. For the particular investigation with which we are engaged, a study of the social equilibrium, it will help if we further divide that class into two classes: a *governing élite*, comprising individuals who directly or indirectly play some considerable part in government, and a *non-governing élite*, comprising the rest.[2]

2033. A chess champion is certainly a member of the *élite*, but it is no less certain that his merits as a chess-player do not open the doors to political influence for him; and hence unless he has other qualities to win him that distinction, he is not a member of the governing *élite*. Mistresses of

absolute monarchs have oftentimes been members of the *élite*, either because of their beauty or because of their intellectual endowments; but only a few of them, who have had, in addition, the particular talents required by politics, have played any part in government.

2034. So we get two strata in a population: (1) A lower stratum, the *non-élite*, with whose possible influence on government we are not just here concerned; then (2) a higher stratum, *the élite*, which is divided into two: (*a*) a governing *élite*; (*b*) a non-governing *élite*.

2035. In the concrete, there are no examinations whereby each person is assigned to his proper place in these various classes. That deficiency is made up for by other means, by various sorts of labels that serve the purpose after a fashion. Such labels are the rule even where there are examinations. The label "lawyer" is affixed to a man who is supposed to know something about the law and often does, though sometimes again he is an ignoramus. So, the governing *élite* contains individuals who wear labels appropriate to political offices of a certain altitude —ministers, Senators, Deputies, chief justices, generals, colonels, and so on—making the opposite exceptions for those who have found their way into that exalted company without possessing qualities corresponding to the labels they wear.

2036. Such exceptions are much more numerous than the exceptions among lawyers, physicians, engineers, millionaires (who have made their own money), artists of distinction, and so on; for the reason, among others, that in these latter departments of human activity the labels are won directly by each individual, whereas in the *élite* some of the labels—the label of wealth, for instance—are hereditary. In former times there were hereditary labels in the governing *élite* also—in our day hardly more than the label of king remains in that status; but if direct inheritance has disappeared, inheritance is still powerful indirectly; and an individual who has inherited a sizable patrimony can easily be named Senator in certain countries, or can get himself elected to the parliament by buying votes or, on occasion, by wheedling voters with assurances that he is a democrat of democrats, a Socialist, an Anarchist. Wealth, family, or social connexions also help in many other cases to win the label of the *élite* in general, or of the governing *élite* in particular, for persons who otherwise hold no claim upon it.

2037. In societies where the social unit is the family the label worn by the head of the family also benefits all other members. In Rome, the man who became Emperor generally raised his freedom to the higher class, and oftentimes, in fact, to the

---

2. Kolabinska, *Op. cit.*, p. 6: "We have just enumerated different categories of individuals comprising the *élite*. They may also be classified in many other ways. For the purpose I have in view in this study it is better to divide the *élite* into two parts: one, which I will call *M*, will contain those individuals in the *élite* who share in the government of the state, who make up what may be more or less vaguely called 'the governing class.' The other part, *N*, will be made up of the remainder of the *élite* when the part *M* has been set off from it."

governing *élite*. For that matter, now more, now fewer, of the freemen taking part in the Roman government possessed qualities good or bad that justified their wearing the labels which they had won through imperial bounty. In our societies, the social unit is the individual; but the place that the individual occupies in society also benefits his wife, his children, his connexions, his friends.

2038. If all these deviations from type were of little importance, they might be disregarded, as they are virtually disregarded in cases where a diploma is required for the practice of a profession. Everyone knows that there are persons who do not deserve their diplomas, but experience shows that on the whole such exceptions may be overlooked.

2039. One might, further, from certain points of view at least, disregard deviations if they remained more or less constant quantitatively—if there were only a negligible variation in proportions between the total of a class and the people who wear its label without possessing the qualities corresponding.

2040. As a matter of fact, the real cases that we have to consider in our societies differ from those two. The deviations are not so few that they can be disregarded. Then again, their number is variable, and the variations give rise to situations having an important bearing on the social equilibrium. We are therefore required to make a special study of them.

2041. Furthermore, the manner in which the various groups in a population intermix has to be considered. In moving from one group to another an individual generally brings with him certain inclinations, sentiments, attitudes, that he has acquired in the group from which he comes, and that circumstance cannot be ignored.

2042. To this mixing, in the particular case in which only two groups, the *élite* and the non-*élite*, are envisaged, the term "circulation of élites" has been applied[3]—in French, *circulation des élites* [or in more general terms "class-circulation"].

2043. In conclusion we must pay special attention (1), in the case of one single group, to the proportions between the total of the group and the number of individuals who are nominally members of it but do not possess the qualities requisite for effective membership; and then (2), in the case of various groups, to the ways in which transitions from one group to the other occur, and to the in-

tensity of that movement—that is to say, to the velocity of the circulation.

2044. Velocity in circulation has to be considered not only absolutely but also in relation to the supply of and the demand for certain social elements. A country that is always at peace does not require many soldiers in its governing class, and the production of generals may be overexuberant as compared with the demand. But when a country is in a state of continuous warfare many soldiers are necessary, and though production remains at the same level it may not meet the demand. That, we might note in passing, has been one of the causes for the collapse of many aristocracies.[4]

2045. Another example. In a country where there is little industry and little commerce, the supply of individuals possessing in high degree the qualities requisite for those types of activity exceeds the demand. Then industry and commerce develop and the supply, though remaining the same, no longer meets the demand.

2046. We must not confuse the state of law with the state of fact. The latter alone, or almost alone, has a bearing on the social equilibrium. There are many examples of castes that are legally closed, but into which, in point of fact, new-comers make their way, and often in large numbers. On the other hand, what difference does it make if a caste is legally open, but conditions *de facto* prevent new accessions to it? If a person who acquires wealth thereby becomes a member of the governing class, but no one gets rich, it is as if the class were closed; and if only a few get rich, it is as if the law erected serious barriers against access to the caste. Something of that sort was observable towards the end of the Roman Empire. People who acquired wealth entered the order of the curials. But only a few individuals made any money. Theoretically we might examine any number of groups. Practically we have to confine ourselves to the more important. We shall proceed by successive approximations, starting with the simple and going on to the complex.

2047. *Higher class and lower class in general.* The least we can do is divide society into two strata: a higher stratum, which usually contains the rulers, and a lower stratum, which usually controls the ruled. That fact is so obvious that it has always

3. And most inappropriately, for, in this sense, the phrase never meant more than circulation within the *élite*. Furthermore, the *élite* is not the only class to be considered, and the principles that apply to circulation within the *élite* apply to circulation within such lower classes as one may choose for one purpose or another to consider.—A.L.

4. Kolabinska, *Op. cit.,* p. 10: "Inadequate recruiting in the *élite* does not result from a mere numerical proportion between new members and old. Account has to be taken of the number of persons who possess the qualities required for membership in the governing *élite* but are refused admittance; or else, in an opposite direction, the number of new members the *élite* might require but does not get. In the first case, the production of persons possessing unusual qualities as regards education may far surpass the number of such persons that the *élite* can accommodate, and then we get what has been called an 'intellectual proletariat.' "

forced itself even upon the most casual observation, and so for the circulation of individuals between the two strata. Even Plato had an inkling of class-circulation and tried to regulate it artificially. The "new man," the upstart, the *parvenu*, has always been a subject of interest, and literature has analyzed him unendingly. Here, then, we are merely giving a more exact form to things that have long been perceived more or less vaguely. We noted a varying distribution of residues in the various social groupings, and chiefly in the higher and the lower class. Such heterogeneousness is a fact perceived by the most superficial glance.

2048. Changes in Class I and Class II residues occurring within the two social strata have an important influence in determining the social equilibrium. They have been commonly observed by laymen under a special form, as changes in "religious" sentiments, so called, in the higher stratum of society. It has often been noted that there were times when religious sentiments seemed to lose ground, others when they seemed to gain strength, and that such undulations corresponded to social movements of very considerable scope. The uniformity might be more exactly described by saying that in the higher stratum of society Class II residues gradually lose in strength, until now and again they are reinforced by tides updwelling from the lower stratum.[5]

2049. Religious sentiments were very feeble in the higher classes in Rome towards the end of the Republic; but they gained notably in strength thereafter, through the rise to the higher classes of men from the lower, of foreigners that is, freedmen, and others, whom the Roman Empire raised in station. They gained still further in intensity in the days of the decadent Roman Empire, when the government passed into the hands of a military plebs and a bureaucracy originating in the lower classes. That was a time when a predominance of Class II residues made itself manifest in a decadence in literature and in the arts and sciences, and in invasions by Oriental religions and especially Christianity.

2050. The Protestant Reformation in the sixteenth century, the Puritan Revolution in Cromwell's day in England, the French Revolution of 1789, are examples of great religious tides originating in the lower classes and rising to engulf the sceptical higher classes. An instance in our day would be the United States of America, where this

---

5. Many writers who are not equipped with this general conception fall into contradictions. Sometimes the clarity of the facts forces itself upon them; then again preconceptions will blur their view of things. Taine is an example. In the *Ancien régime* he well notes (Chap. III) that the mind of the masses at large is steeped in prejudices (is, in our terms, under the sway of Class II residues). On that basis he should go on and conclude that the French Revolution was a particular case of the religious revolution, where popular faith overwhelms the scepticism of the higher classes. But, consciously or otherwise, he succumbs to the influence of the preconception that the higher classes are educators of the masses, and views unbelief and impiety in the nobility, the Third Estate, and the higher clergy as among the main causes of the Revolution. He notes the difference between France and England in that regard and seems on the verge of ascribing to that circumstance the fact that the revolution which occurred in France did not occur in England. Says he, Bk. IV, Chap. II, sec. I (Vol. II, p. 118): "In England [the higher class] speedily perceived the danger. Philosophy was precocious in England, native to England. That does not matter. It never got acclimated there. Montesquieu wrote in his travel note-book in 1729 (*Notes sur l'Angleterre*, p. 352): 'No religion in England. . . . If anyone brings up the subject of religion, he is laughed at.' Fifty years later the public mind has about-faced: 'all those who have a tight roof over their heads and a good coat on their backs' [The expression is Macaulay's.] have seen what these new doctrines mean. In any event they feel that speculations in the library must not become preachings on the streets. [They and Taine therefore believe in the efficacy of such preachings.] Impiety seems to them bad manners. They regard religion as the cement that holds public order together. That is because they are themselves public men,

interested in doing things, participating in the government and well taught by daily personal experience. . . . [Yet a few lines before that Taine had refuted himself:] When you talk religion or politics with people, you find their minds almost always made up. Their preconceptions, their interests, their situation in life, have convinced them already, and they will listen to you only if you tell them aloud things they have been thinking in silence." If that is so, the "preachings in the street" to which Taine alludes ought not to be very effective, and if they are, it cannot be that people "will listen to you only if you tell them aloud things they have been thinking in silence." As a matter of fact, it is these latter hypotheses that the more closely approximate experience. The mental state of the French people towards the end of the eighteenth century had been but little affected by the impiety of the higher classes, any more than the mental state of the Romans had been affected by the impiety of the contemporaries of Lucretius, Cicero, and Caesar, or the mental state of the European masses by the impiety of the nobility and higher clergy at the time of the Reformation. Belin, *La commerce des livres prohibés à Paris de 1750 à 1789*, pp. 104–05: "One may assert that the works of the philosophers did not directly reach the masses or the lower *bourgeoisie*. The working-men, the tradesmen, did not know Voltaire and Rousseau until the time of the Revolution, when their tribunes began to gloss them in inflammatory harangues or to translate their maxims into legislation. When they stepped into the limelight they had certainly not read the great books of the century, though they could not have missed entirely the more celebrated of the literary quarrels. The true disciples of the *philosophes*, the faithful patrons of the pedlars of forbidden literature, were the nobles, the abbés, the members of the privileged classes, idlers about the parlours of society who were on the look-out for some distraction from their relentless tedium and threw themselves headlong into philosophical discussions and soon let themselves be vanquished by the new spirit [That is all borne out by the experience; the following less so.], without foreseeing the remoter consequences of the premises that they were adopting so gaily. . . . [Belin makes a further point:] The privileged for that matter were the only ones who could afford the exorbitant prices that any lover of forbidden books had to pay."

upward thrust of members of lower classes strong in Class II residues is very intense; and in that country one witnesses the rise of no end of strange and wholly unscientific religions—such as Christian Science—that are utterly at war with any sort of scientific thinking, and a mass of hypocritical laws for the enforcement of morality that are replicas of laws of the European Middle Ages.

2051. The upper stratum of society, the *élite*, nominally contains certain groups of people, not always very sharply defined, that are called aristocracies. There are cases in which the majority of individuals belonging to such aristocracies actually possess the qualities requisite for remaining there; and then again there are cases where considerable numbers of the individuals making up the class do not possess those requisites. Such people may occupy more or less important places in the governing *élite* or they may be barred from it.

2052. In the beginning, military, religious, and commercial aristocracies and plutocracies—with a few exceptions not worth considering—must have constituted parts of the governing *élite* and sometimes have made up the whole of it. The victorious warrior, the prosperous merchant, the opulent plutocrat, were men of such parts, each in his own field, as to be superior to the average individual. Under those circumstances the label corresponded to an actual capacity. But as time goes by, considerable, sometimes very considerable, differences arise between the capacity and the label; while on the other hand, certain aristocracies originally figuring prominently in the rising *élite* end by constituting an insignificant element in it. That has happened especially to military aristocracies.

2053. Aristocracies do not last. Whatever the causes, it is an incontestable fact that after a certain length of time they pass away. History is a graveyard of aristocracies. The Athenian "People" was an aristocracy as compared with the remainder of a population of resident aliens and slaves. It vanished without leaving any descent. The various aristocracies of Rome vanished in their time. So did the aristocracies of the Barbarians. Where, in France, are the descendents of the Frankish conquerors? The genealogies of the English nobility have been very exactly kept; and they show that very few families still remain to claim descent from the comrades of William the Conqueror. The rest have vanished. In Germany the aristocracy of the present day is very largely made up of descendants of vassals of the lords of old. The populations of European countries have increased enormously during the past few centuries. It is as certain as certain can be that the aristocracies have not increased in proportion.

2054. They decay not in numbers only. They decay also in quality, in the sense that they lose their vigour, that there is a decline in the proportions of the residues which enabled them to win their power and hold it. The governing class is restored not only in numbers, but—and that is the more important thing—in quality, by families rising from the lower classes and bringing with them the vigour and the proportions of residues necessary for keeping themselves in power. It is also restored by the loss of its more degenerate members.

2055. If one of those movements comes to an end, or worse still, if they both come to an end, the governing class crashes to ruin and often sweeps the whole of a nation along with it. Potent cause of disturbance in the equilibrium is the accumulation of superior elements in the lower classes and, conversely, of inferior elements in the higher classes. If human aristocracies were like thoroughbreds among animals, which reproduce themselves over long periods of time with approximately the same traits, the history of the human race would be something altogether different from the history we know.

2056. In virtue of class-circulation, the governing *élite* is always in a state of slow and continuous transformation. It flows on like a river, never being today what it was yesterday. From time to time sudden and violent disturbances occur. There is a flood—the river overflows its banks. Afterwards, the new governing *élite* again resumes its slow transformation. The flood has subsided, the river is again flowing normally in its wonted bed.

2057. Revolutions come about through accumulations in the higher strata of society—either because of a slowing-down in class-circulation, or from other causes—of decadent elements no longer possessing the residues suitable for keeping them in power, and shrinking from the use of force; while meantime in the lower strata of society elements of superior quality are coming to the fore, possessing residues suitable for exercising the functions of government and willing enough to use force.

2058. In general, in revolutions the members of the lower strata are captained by leaders from the higher strata, because the latter possess the intellectual qualities required for outlining a tactic, while lacking the combative residues supplied by the individuals from the lower strata.

2059. Violent movements take place by fits and starts, and effects therefore do not follow immediately on their causes. After a governing class, or a nation, has maintained itself for long periods of time on force and acquired great wealth, it may subsist for some time still without using force, buying off its adversaries and paying not only in gold, but also in terms of the dignity and respect that it had formerly enjoyed and which constitute, as it were, a capital. In the first stages of decline, power is maintained by bargainings and concessions, and people are so deceived into thinking that that policy can be carried on indefinitely. So the decadant Roman Empire brought peace of the Barbarians with money and honours. So Louis XVI, in France, squandering in a very short time an ancestral inheritance of love, respect, and almost religious reverence for the monarchy, managed, by making repeated concessions, to be the King of the Revolution. So the English aristocracy managed to prolong its term of power in the second half of the nineteenth century down to the dawn of its decadence, which was heralded by the "Parliament Bill" in the first years of the twentieth.

*   *   *

Suppose we put in one category, which we may call *S*, individuals whose incomes are essentially variable and depend upon the person's wide-awakeness in discovering sources of gain. In that group, generally speaking and disregarding exceptions, will be found those promoters of enterprise—those *entrepreneurs*—whom we were considering some pages back; and with them will be stockholders in industrial and commercial corporations (but not bondholders, who will more fittingly be placed in our group next following). Then will come owners of real estate in cities where building speculation is rife; and also landowners—on a similar condition that there be speculation in the lands about them; and then stock-exchange speculators and bankers who make money on governmental, industrial, and commercial loans. We might further add all persons depending upon such people—lawyers, engineers, politicians, working-people, clerks—and deriving advantage from their operations. In a word, we are putting together all persons who directly or indirectly speculate and in one way or another manage to increase their incomes by ingeniously taking advantage of circumstances.

2234. And let us put into another category, which we may call *R*, persons who have fixed or virtually fixed incomes not depending to any great extent on ingenious combinations that may be conceived by an active mind. In this category, roughly, will be found persons who have savings and have deposited them in savings-banks or invested them in life-annuities; then people living on incomes from government bonds, certificates of the funded debt, corporation bonds, or other securities with fixed interest-rates; then owners of real estate and lands in places where there is no speculation; then farmers, working-people, clerks, depending upon such

persons and in no way depending upon speculators. In a word, we so group together here all persons who neither directly nor indirectly depend on speculation and who have incomes that are fixed, or virtually fixed, or at least are but slightly variable.[6]

2235. Just to be rid of the inconvenience of using mere letters of the alphabet, suppose we use the term "speculators" for members of category *S* and the French term *rentiers* for members of category *R*.[7] Within the two groups of persons we shall find analogous conflicts, economic and social, between them. In the speculator group Class I residues predominate, in the *rentier* group, Class II residues. That that should be the case is readily understandable. A person of pronounced capacity for economic combinations is not satisfied with a fixed income, often a very small one. He wants to earn more, and if he finds a favourable opportunity, he moves into the *S* category. The two groups perform functions of differing utility in society. The *S* group is primarily responsible for change, for eco-

---

6. Monographs along the lines of Le Play's would be of great use in determining the character of the persons belonging in our *S* group, and those belonging to our *R* group. Here is one such, contributed by Prezzolini: *La Francia e i francesi del secolo XX osservati da un italiano.* I know it as quoted by E. Cesari in the *Vita italiana,* Oct. 15, 1917, pp. 367–70. The person in question is a well-known member of the French parliament—we suppress the proper name: for us here, he is not a person, but just a type. The figures given by Prezzolini are those publicly declared by the member himself, Monsieur *X.* *X*'s fixed income yields a total of 17,500 francs, of which 15,000 are salary as a member of the parliament and 2,500 interest on his wife's dowry. Only the latter sum belongs in category *R*—the salary belongs rather in category *S,* because to get such a thing one must have the ability and the good fortune to be elected. *X*'s expense-account shows a total of 64,200 francs, divided as follows: household expenses, 33,800; office expenses, 22,550; expenses for his election district (avowable expenses), 7,850. There ought, therefore, to be a deficit of 45,700 francs; but the deficit is not only covered but changes into a surplus in view of the following revenues: contributions to newspapers and other publications, 12,500 francs; honorarium as general agent of the *A.B.C.* Company, 21,000 francs; commissions on sales, 7,500. In this connexion, Prezzolini notes that *X,* reporting on the war budget, enters 100,000 francs for supplies delivered to himself, as general agent of the *A.B.C.* Company: that gives *X* his "sales commissions." Finally, because of the influence that he enjoys, our member, *X,* receives a stipend of 18,000 francs from a newspaper. In all, these revenues, which clearly belong in the category *S,* yield a total of 50,000 francs. Prezzolini adds that the member in question is not the only one, nor the least, of his species. He is just a better-known and an honester type.

7. It might be well to repeat that our use of such terms is not based on their ordinary senses, nor upon their etymologies. We are to use them strictly in the sense defined in §§ 2233–34, and the reader must refer to those definitions whenever he encounters them in the remainder of this volume. [I keep the term "speculator." English ordinarily analyzes the matter embraced under Pareto's term, especially in slang. Pareto's "speculator" is our "hustler," "man of pep," "wide-awake individual," "live-wire," and so on.—A. L.]

nomic and social progress. The R group, instead, is a powerful element in stability, and in many cases counteracts the dangers attending the adventurous capers of the S's. A society in which R's almost exclusively predominate remains stationary and, as it were, crystallized. A society in which S's predominate lacks stability, lives in a state of shaky equilibrium that may be upset by a slight accident from within or from without.

Members of the R group must not be mistaken for "conservatives," nor members of the S group for "progressives," innovators, revolutionaries. They may have points in common with such, but there is no identity. There are evolutions, revolutions, innovations, that the R's support, especially movements tending to restore to the ruling classes certain residues of group-persistence that had been banished by the S's. A revolution may be made against the S's—a revolution of that type founded the Roman Empire, and such, to some extent, was the revolution known as the Protestant Reformation. Then too, for the very reason that sentiments of group-persistence are dominant in them, the R's may be so blinded by sentiment as to act against their own interests. They readily allow themselves to be duped by anyone who takes them on the side of sentiment, and time and time again they have been the artisans of their own ruin. If the old feudal lords, who were endowed with R traits in a very conspicuous degree, had not allowed themselves to be swept off their feet by a sum of sentiments in which religious enthusiasm was only one element, they would have seen at once that the Crusades were to be their ruin. In the eighteenth century, had the French nobility living on income, and that part of the French *bourgeoisie* which was in the same situation, not succumbed to the lure of humanitarian sentiments, they would not have prepared the ground for the Revolution that was to be their undoing. Not a few among the victims of the guillotine had for long years been continually, patiently, artfully grinding the blade that was to cut off their heads. In our day those among the R's who are known as "intellectuals" are following in the footprints of the French nobles of the eighteenth century and are working with all their might to encompass the ruin of their own class.

Nor are the categories R and S to be confused with groupings that might be made according to economic occupation. There again we find points of contact, but not full coincidence. A retail merchant often belongs to the R group, and a wholesale merchant too, but the wholesaler will more likely belong to the S group. Sometimes one same enterprise may change in character. An individual of the S type founds an industry as a result of for-

tunate speculations. When it yields or seems to be yielding a good return, he changes it into a corporation, retires from business, and passes over into the R group. A large number of stockholders in the new concern are also R's—the ones who bought stock when they thought they were buying a sure thing. If they are not mistaken, the business changes in character, moving over from the S type to the R type. But in many cases the best speculation the founder ever made was in changing his business to a corporation. It is soon in jeopardy, with the R's standing in line to pay for the broken crockery. There is no better business in this world than the business of fleecing the lambs—of exploiting the inexperience, the ingenuousness, the passions, of the R's. In our societies the fortunes of many many wealthy individuals have no other foundations.[8]

2236. The differing relative proportions in which S types and R types are combined in the governing

8. Many people conclude that such facts are enough to condemn our social organization, and hold it responsible for most of the pains from which we suffer. Others think that they can defend our present order only by denying the facts or minimizing their significance. Both are right from the ethical standpoint, wrong from the standpoint of social utility experimentally considered. Obviously, if it be posited as an axiom that men *ought,* whatever happens, to observe certain rules, those who do not observe them necessarily stand condemned. If one goes on to say that the organization so condemned is in the main injurious to society, one must logically fall back on some premise that confuses morality and utility. On the other hand, if premises of those types are granted and one would, notwithstanding, still defend or approve the organization of our societies, there is nothing left but to deny the facts or say they are not significant. The experimental approach is altogether different. Anyone accepting it grants no axioms independent of experience, and therefore finds it necessary to discuss the premises of the reasonings mentioned. On so doing one soon perceives that it is a question of two phenomena that do indeed have points in common but are in no sense identical, and that in every particular case experience has to be called in to decide whether one is dealing with a point of contact or a point of divergence. An instant's reflection is enough to see that if one accepts certain conclusions one adopts by that fact the premises to which they are indissolubly bound. But the power of sentiment and the influence of habitual manners of reasoning are such that people disregard the force of logic entirely and establish conclusions without reference to the premises or, at the very best, accept the premises as axioms not subject to discussion. Another effect of such power and such influence will be that in spite of the warnings we have given and over and over again repeated, there will always be someone to carry the import of the remarks that he is here reading on the R's and S's beyond the limits we have so strictly specified, interpreting all that we have been saying against one of those groups as implying that the influence of the group is, on the whole, harmful to society and the group itself "condemnable"; and all that we have been saying in its favour as a proof that the influence of the group is, in general, beneficial to society and the group itself worthy of praise. We have neither the means nor the least desire to prevent the fabrication of such interpretations. We are satisfied with recognizing them as one variety of our derivations.

class correspond to differing types of civilization; and such proportions are among the principal traits that have to be considered in social heterogeneity. Going back, for instance, to the protectionist cycle, we may say that in modern democratic countries industrial protection increases the proportion of S's in the governing class. That increase in turn serves to intensify protection, and the process would go on indefinitely if counter-forces did not come into play to check it.

6. Conspicuous Consumption

BY THORSTEIN VEBLEN

THE DISTINCTION BETWEEN exploit and drudgery is an invidious distinction between employments. Those employments which are to be classed as exploit are worthy, honourable, noble; other employments, which do not contain this element of exploit, and especially those which imply subservience or submission, are unworthy, debasing, ignoble. The concept of dignity, worth, or honour, as applied either to persons or conduct, is of first-rate consequence in the development of classes and of class distinctions, and it is therefore necessary to say something of its derivation and meaning. Its psychological ground may be indicated in outline as follows.

As a matter of selective necessity, man is an agent. He is, in his own apprehension, a centre of unfolding impulsive activity—"teleological" activity. He is an agent, seeking in every act the accomplishment of some concrete, objective, impersonal end. By force of his being such an agent he is possessed of a taste for effective work, and a distaste for futile effort. He has a sense of the merit of serviceability or efficiency and of the demerit of futility, waste, or incapability. This aptitude or propensity may be called the instinct of workmanship. Wherever the circumstances or traditions of life lead to an habitual comparison of one person with another in point of efficiency, the instinct of workmanship works out in an emulative or invidious comparison of persons. The extent to which this result follows depends in some considerable degree on the temperament of the population. In any community where such an invidious comparison of persons is habitually made, visible success becomes an end sought for its own utility as a basis of esteem. Esteem is gained and dispraise is avoided by putting one's efficiency in evidence. The result is that the instinct of workmanship works out in an emulative demonstration of force.

During that primitive phase of social development, when the community is still habitually peaceable, perhaps sedentary, and without a developed system of individual ownership, the efficiency of the individual can be shown chiefly and most consistently in some employment that goes to further the life of the group. What emulation of an economic kind there is between the members of such a group will be chiefly emulation in industrial serviceability. At the same time the incentive to emulation is not strong, nor is the scope for emulation large.

When the community passes from peaceable savagery to a predatory phase of life, the conditions of emulation change. The opportunity and the incentive to emulation increase greatly in scope and urgency. The activity of the men more and more takes on the character of exploit; and an invidious comparison of one hunter or warrior with another grows continually easier and more habitual. Tangible evidences of prowess—trophies—find a place in men's habits of thought as an essential feature of the paraphernalia of life. Booty, trophies of the chase or of the raid, come to be prized as evidence of preëminent force. Aggression becomes the accredited form of action, and booty serves as *prima facie* evidence of successful aggression. As accepted at this cultural stage, the accredited, worthy form of self-assertion is contest; and useful articles or services obtained by seizure or compulsion, serve as a conventional evidence of successful contest. Therefore, by contrast, the obtaining of goods by other methods than seizure comes to be accounted unworthy of man in his best estate. The performance

Reprinted from Thorstein Veblen, *The Theory of the Leisure Class* (New York: Macmillan Co., 1899), pp. 15–21, 25–34. 68–89. 97–101 of productive work, or employment in personal service, falls under the same odium for the same reason. An invidious distinction in this way arises between exploit and acquisition by seizure on the one hand and industrial employment on the other hand. Labour acquires a character of irksomeness by virtue of the indignity imputed to it.

With the primitive barbarian, before the simple content of the notion has been obscured by its own ramifications and by a secondary growth of cognate ideas, "honourable" seems to connote nothing else than assertion of superior force. "Honourable" is "formidable"; "worthy" is "prepotent." A honorific act is in the last analysis little if anything else than a recognised successful act of aggression; and where aggression means conflict with men and beasts, the activity which comes to be especially and primarily honourable is the assertion of the strong hand. The naïve, archaic habit of construing all manifestations of force in terms of personality or "will power" greatly fortifies this conventional exaltation of the strong hand. Honorific epithets, in vogue among barbarian tribes as well as among peoples of a more advanced culture, commonly bear the stamp of this unsophisticated sense of honour. Epithets and titles used in addressing chieftains, and in the propitiation of kings and gods, very commonly impute a propensity for overbearing violence and an irresistible devastating force to the person who is to be propitiated. This holds true to an extent also in the more civilised communities of the present day. The predilection shown in heraldic devices for the more rapacious beasts and birds of prey goes to enforce the same view.

Under the common-sense barbarian appreciation of worth or honour, the taking of life—the killing of formidable competitors, whether brute or human —is honourable in the highest degree. And this high office of slaughter, as an expression of the slayer's prepotence, casts a glamour of worth over every act of slaughter and over all the tools and accessories of the act. Arms are honourable, and the use of them, even in seeking the life of the meanest creatures of the fields, becomes a honorific employment. At the same time, employment in industry becomes correspondingly odious, and, in the common-sense apprehension, the handling of the tools and implements of industry falls beneath the dignity of ablebodied men. Labour becomes irksome.

It is here assumed that in the sequence of cultural evolution primitive groups of men have passed from an initial peaceable stage to a subsequent stage at which fighting is the avowed and characteristic employment of the group. But it is not implied that there has been an abrupt transition from unbroken peace and good-will to a later or higher phase of life

in which the fact of combat occurs for the first time. Neither is it implied that all peaceful industry disappears on the transition to the predatory phase of culture. Some fighting, it is safe to say, would be met with at any early stage of social development. Fights would occur with more or less frequency through sexual competition. The known habits of primitive groups as well as the habits of the anthropoid apes, argue to that effect and the evidence from the well-known promptings of human nature enforces the same view.

It may therefore be objected that there can have been no such initial stage of peaceable life as is here assumed. There is no point in cultural evolution prior to which fighting does not occur. But the point in question is not as to the occurrence of combat, occasional or sporadic, or even more or less frequent and habitual; it is a question as to the occurrence of an habitual bellicose frame of mind—a prevalent habit of judging facts and events from the point of view of the fight. The predatory phase of culture is attained only when the predatory attitude has become the habitual and accredited spiritual attitude for the members of the group; when the fight has become the dominant note in the current theory of life; when the common-sense appreciation of men and things has come to be an appreciation with a view to combat.

The substantial difference between the peaceable and the predatory phase of culture, therefore, is a spiritual difference, not a mechanical one. The change in spiritual attitude is the outgrowth of a change in the material facts of the life of the group, and it comes on gradually as the material circumstances favourable to a predatory attitude supervene. The inferior limit of the predatory culture is an industrial limit. Predation cannot become the habitual, conventional resource of any group or any class until industrial methods have been developed to such a degree of efficiency as to leave a margin worth fighting for, above the subsistence of those engaged in getting a living. The transition from peace to predation therefore depends on the growth of technical knowledge and the use of tools. A predatory culture is similarly impracticable in early times, until weapons have been developed to such a point as to make man a formidable animal. The early development of tools and of weapons is of course the same fact seen from two different points of view.

The life of a given group would be characterised as peaceable so long as habitual recourse to combat has not brought the fight into the foreground in men's everyday thoughts, as a dominant feature of the life of man. A group may evidently attain such a predatory attitude with a greater or less degree of completeness, so that its scheme of life and canons of conduct may be controlled to a greater or less extent by the predatory animus. The predatory phase of culture is therefore conceived to come on gradually, through a cumulative growth of predatory aptitudes, habits, and traditions; this growth being due to a change in the circumstances of the group's life, of such a kind as to develop and conserve those traits of human nature and those traditions and norms of conduct that make for a predatory rather than a peaceable life.

The evidence for the hypothesis that there has been such a peaceable stage of primitive culture is in great part drawn from psychology rather than from ethnology, and cannot be detailed here. It will be recited in part in a later chapter, in discussing the survival of archaic traits of human nature under the modern culture.

*		*		*

The end of acquisition and accumulation is conventionally held to be the consumption of the goods accumulated—whether it is consumption directly by the owner of the goods or by the household attached to him and for this purpose identified with him in theory. This is at least felt to be the economically legitimate end of acquisition, which alone it is incumbent on the theory to take account of. Such consumption may of course be conceived to serve the consumer's physical wants—his physical comfort—or his so-called higher wants—spiritual, æsthetic, intellectual, or what not; the latter class of wants being served indirectly by an expenditure of goods, after the fashion familiar to all economic readers.

But it is only when taken in a sense far removed from its naïve meaning that consumption of goods can be said to afford the incentive from which accumulation invariably proceeds. The motive that lies at the root of ownership is emulation; and the same motive of emulation continues active in the further development of the institution to which it has given rise and in the development of all those features of the social structure which this institution of ownership touches. The possession of wealth confers honour; it is an invidious distinction. Nothing equally cogent can be said for the consumption of goods, nor for any other conceivable incentive to acquisition, and especially not for any incentive to the accumulation of wealth.

It is of course not to be overlooked that in a community where nearly all goods are private property the necessity of earning a livelihood is a powerful and ever-present incentive for the poorer members of the community. The need of subsistence and of an increase of physical comfort may for a time be the dominant motive of acquisition for those classes who are habitually employed at manual labour, whose subsistence is on a precarious footing, who possess little and ordinarily accumulate little; but it will appear in the course of the discussion that even in the case of these impecunious classes the predominance of the motive of physical want is not so decided as has sometimes been assumed. On the other hand, so far as regards those members and classes of the community who are chiefly concerned in the accumulation of wealth, the incentive of subsistence or of physical comfort never plays a considerable part. Ownership began and grew into a human institution on grounds unrelated to the subsistence minimum. The dominant incentive was from the outset the invidious distinction attaching to wealth, and, save temporarily and by exception, no other motive has usurped the primacy at any later stage of the development.

Property set out with being booty held as trophies of the successful raid. So long as the group had departed but little from the primitive communal organisation, and so long as it still stood in close contact with other hostile groups, the utility of things or persons owned lay chiefly in an invidious comparison between their possessor and the enemy from whom they were taken. The habit of distinguishing between the interests of the individual and those of the group to which he belongs is apparently a later growth. Invidious comparison between the possessor of the honorific booty and his less successful neighbours within the group was no doubt present early as an element of the utility of the things possessed, though this was not at the outset the chief element of their value. The man's prowess was still primarily the group's prowess, and the possessor of the booty felt himself to be primarily the keeper of the honour of his group. This appreciation of exploit from the communal point of view is met with also at later stages of social growth, especially as regards the laurels of war.

But so soon as the custom of individual ownership begins to gain consistency, the point of view taken in making the invidious comparison on which private property rests will begin to change. Indeed, the one change is but the reflex of the other. The initial phase of ownership, the phase of acquisition by naïve seizure and conversion, begins to pass into the subsequent stage of an incipient organisation of industry on the basis of private property (in slaves); the horde develops into a more or less self-sufficing industrial community; possessions then come to be valued not so much as evidence of successful foray, but rather as evidence of the prepotence of the possessor of these goods over other individuals within the community. The invidious comparison now becomes primarily a comparison of the owner with the other members of the group. Property is still of the nature of trophy, but, with the cultural advance, it becomes more and more a trophy of successes scored in the game of ownership carried on between the members of the group under the quasi-peaceable methods of nomadic life.

Gradually, as industrial activity further displaces predatory activity in the community's everyday life and in men's habits of thought, accumulated property more and more replaces trophies of predatory exploit as the conventional exponent of prepotence and success. With the growth of settled industry, therefore, the possession of wealth gains in relative importance and effectiveness as a customary basis of repute and esteem. Not that esteem ceases to be awarded on the basis of other, more direct evidence of prowess; not that successful predatory aggression or warlike exploit ceases to call out the approval and admiration of the crowd, or to stir the envy of the less successful competitors; but the opportunities for gaining distinction by means of this direct manifestation of superior force grow less available both in scope and frequency. At the same time opportunities for industrial aggression, and for the accumulation of property by the quasi-peaceable methods of nomadic industry, increase in scope and availability. And it is even more to the point that property now becomes the most easily recognised evidence of a reputable degree of success as distinguished from heroic or signal achievement. It therefore becomes the conventional basis of esteem. Its possession in some amount becomes necessary in order to any reputable standing in the community. It becomes indispensable to accumulate, to acquire property, in order to retain one's good name. When accumulated goods have in this way once become the accepted badge of efficiency, the possession of wealth presently assumes the character of an independent and definitive basis of esteem. The possession of goods, whether acquired aggressively by one's own exertion or passively by transmission through inheritance from others, becomes a conventional basis of reputability. The possession of wealth, which was at the outset valued simply as an evidence of efficiency, becomes, in popular apprehension, itself a meritorious act. Wealth is now itself intrinsically honourable and confers honour on its possessor. By a further refinement, wealth acquired passively by transmission from ancestors or other antecedents presently becomes even more honorific than wealth acquired by the possessor's own effort; but this distinction belongs at a later stage in the evolution of the pecuniary culture and will be spoken of in its place.

Prowess and exploit may still remain the basis of award of the highest popular esteem, although the possession of wealth has become the basis of commonplace reputability and of a blameless social standing. The predatory instinct and the consequent approbation of predatory efficiency are deeply ingrained in the habits of thought of those peoples who have passed under the discipline of a protracted predatory culture. According to popular award, the highest honours within human reach may, even yet, be those gained by an unfolding of extraordinary predatory efficiency in war, or by a quasi-predatory efficiency in statecraft; but for the purposes of a commonplace decent standing in the community these means of repute have been replaced by the acquisition and accumulation of goods. In order to stand well in the eyes of the community, it is necessary to come up to a certain, somewhat indefinite, conventional standard of wealth; just as in the earlier predatory stage it is necessary for the barbarian man to come up to the tribe's standard of physical endurance, cunning and skill at arms. A certain standard of wealth in the one case, and of prowess in the other, is a necessary condition of reputability, and anything in excess of this normal amount is meritorious.

Those members of the community who fall short of this, somewhat indefinite, normal degree of prowess or of property suffer in the esteem of their fellow-men; and consequently they suffer also in their own esteem, since the usual basis of self-respect is the respect accorded by one's neighbours. Only individuals with an aberrant temperament can in the long run retain their self-esteem in the face of the disesteem of their fellows. Apparent exceptions to the rule are met with especially among people with strong religious convictions. But these apparent exceptions are scarcely real exceptions, since such persons commonly fall back on the putative approbation of some supernatural witness of their deeds.

So soon as the possession of property becomes the basis of popular esteem therefore it becomes also a requisite to that complacency which we call self-respect. In any community where goods are held in severalty it is necessary, in order to his own peace of mind that an individual should possess as large a portion of goods as others with whom he is accustomed to class himself; and it is extremely gratifying to possess something more than others. But as fast as a person makes new acquisitions, and becomes accustomed to the resulting new standard of wealth, the new standard forthwith ceases to afford appreciably greater satisfaction than the earlier standard did. The tendency in any case is constantly to make the present pecuniary standard the point of departure for a fresh increase of wealth; and this in turn gives rise to a new standard of sufficiency and a new pecuniary classification of one's self as compared with one's neighbours. So far as concerns the present question, the end sought by accumulation is to rank high in comparison with the rest of the community in point of pecuniary strength. So long as the comparison is distinctly unfavourable to himself, the normal, average individual will live in chronic dissatisfaction with his present lot; and when he has reached what may be called the normal pecuniary standard of the community, or of his class in the community, this chronic dissatisfaction will give place to a restless straining to place a wider and ever-widening pecuniary interval between himself and this average standard. The invidious comparison can never become so favourable to the individual making it that he would not gladly rate himself still higher relatively to his competitors in the struggle for pecuniary reputability.

In the nature of the case, the desire for wealth can scarcely be satiated in any individual instance, and evidently a satiation of the average or general desire for wealth is out of the question. However widely, or equally, or "fairly," it may be distributed, no general increase of the community's wealth can make any approach to satiating this need, the ground of which is the desire of every one to excel every one else in the accumulation of goods. If, as is sometimes assumed, the incentive to accumulation were the want of subsistence or of physical comfort, then the aggregate economic wants of a community might conceivably be satisfied at some point in the advance of industrial efficiency; but since the struggle is substantially a race for reputability on the basis of an invidious comparison, no approach to a definitive attainment is possible.

What has just been said must not be taken to mean that there are no other incentives to acquisition and accumulation than this desire to excel in pecuniary standing and so gain the esteem and envy of one's fellow-men. The desire for added comfort and security from want is present as a motive at every stage of the process of accumulation in a modern industrial community; although the standard of sufficiency in these respects is in turn greatly affected by the habit of pecuniary emulation. To a great extent this emulation shapes the methods and selects the objects of expenditure for personal comfort and decent livelihood.

Besides this, the power conferred by wealth also affords a motive to accumulation. That propensity for purposeful activity and that repugnance to all futility of effort which belong to man by virtue of his character as an agent do not desert him when he emerges from the naïve communal culture where the dominant note of life is the unanalysed and un-

differentiated solidarity of the individual with the group with which his life is bound up. When he enters upon the predatory stage, where self-seeking in the narrower sense becomes the dominant note, this propensity goes with him still, as the pervasive trait that shapes his scheme of life. The propensity for achievement and the repugnance to futility remain the underlying economic motive. The propensity changes only in the form of its expression and in the proximate objects to which it directs the man's activity. Under the régime of individual ownership the most available means of visibly achieving a purpose is that afforded by the acquisition and accumulation of goods; and as the self-regarding antithesis between man and man reaches fuller consciousness, the propensity for achievement—the instinct of workmanship—tends more and more to shape itself into a straining to excel others in pecuniary achievement. Relative success, tested by an invidious pecuniary comparison with other men, becomes the conventional end of action. The currently accepted legitimate end of effort becomes the achievement of a favourable comparison with other men; and therefore the repugnance to futility to a good extent coalesces with the incentive of emulation. It acts to accentuate the struggle for pecuniary reputability by visiting with a sharper disapproval all shortcoming and all evidence of shortcoming in point of pecuniary success. Purposeful effort comes to mean, primarily, effort directed to or resulting in a more creditable showing of accumulated wealth. Among the motives which lead men to accumulate wealth, the primacy, both in scope and intensity, therefore, continues to belong to this motive of pecuniary emulation.

In making use of the term "invidious," it may perhaps be unnecessary to remark, there is no intention to extol or depreciate, or to commend or deplore any of the phenomena which the word is used to characterise. The term is used in a technical sense as describing a comparison of persons with a view to rating and grading them in respect of relative worth or value—in an æsthetic or moral sense—and so awarding and defining the relative degrees of complacency with which they may legitimately be contemplated by themselves and by others. An invidious comparison is a process of valuation of persons in respect of worth.

*   *   *

Conspicuous Consumption

In what has been said of the evolution of the vicarious leisure class and its differentiation from the general body of the working classes, reference has been made to a further division of labour,— that between different servant classes. One portion of the servant class, chiefly those persons whose occupation is vicarious leisure, come to undertake a new, subsidiary range of duties—the vicarious consumption of goods. The most obvious form in which this consumption occurs is seen in the wearing of liveries and the occupation of spacious servants' quarters. Another, scarcely less obtrusive or less effective form of vicarious consumption, and a much more widely prevalent one, is the consumption of food, clothing, dwelling, and furniture by the lady and the rest of the domestic establishment.

But already at a point in economic evolution far ante-dating the emergence of the lady, specialised consumption of goods as an evidence of pecuniary strength had begun to work out in a more or less elaborate system. The beginning of a differentiation in consumption even antedates the appearance of anything that can fairly be called pecuniary strength. It is traceable back to the initial phase of predatory culture, and there is even a suggestion that an incipient differentiation in this respect lies back of the beginnings of the predatory life. This most primitive differentiation in the consumption of goods is like the later differentiation with which we are all so intimately familiar, in that it is largely of a ceremonial character, but unlike the latter it does not rest on a difference in accumulated wealth. The utility of consumption as an evidence of wealth is to be classed as a derivative growth. It is an adaptation to a new end, by a selective process, of a distinction previously existing and well established in men's habits of thought.

In the earlier phases of the predatory culture the only economic differentiation is a broad distinction between an honourable superior class made up of the able-bodied men on the one side, and a base inferior class of labouring women on the other. According to the ideal scheme of life in force at that time it is the office of the men to consume what the women produce. Such consumption as falls to the women is merely incidental to their work; it is a means to their continued labour, and not a consumption directed to their own comfort and fulness of life. Unproductive consumption of goods is honourable, primarily as a mark of prowess and a perquisite of human dignity; secondarily it becomes substantially honourable in itself, especially the consumption of the more desirable things. The consumption of choice articles of food, and frequently also of rare articles of adornment, becomes tabu to the women and children; and if there is a base (servile) class of men, the tabu holds also for them. With a further advance in culture this tabu may change into simple custom of a more or less rigorous character; but whatever be the theoretical basis of the distinction which is maintained, whether it be a tabu or a larger conventionality, the features of the conventional scheme of consumption do not change easily. When the quasi-peaceable stage of industry is reached, with its fundamental institution of chattel slavery, the general principle, more or less rigorously applied, is that the base, industrious class should consume only what may be necessary to their subsistence. In the nature of things, luxuries and the comforts of life belong to the leisure class. Under the tabu, certain victuals, and more particularly certain beverages, are strictly reserved for the use of the superior class.

The ceremonial differentiation of the dietary is best seen in the use of intoxicating beverages and narcotics. If these articles of consumption are costly, they are felt to be noble and honorific. Therefore the base classes, primarily the women, practise an enforced continence with respect to these stimulants, except in countries where they are obtainable at a very low cost. From archaic times down through all the length of the patriarchal régime it has been the office of the women to prepare and administer these luxuries, and it has been the perquisite of the men of gentle birth and breeding to consume them. Drunkenness and the other pathological consequences of the free use of stimulants therefore tend in their turn to become honorific, as being a mark, at the second remove, of the superior status of those who are able to afford the indulgence. Infirmities induced by over-indulgence are among some peoples freely recognised as manly attributes. It has even happened that the name for certain diseased conditions of the body arising from such an origin has passed into everyday speech as a synonym for "noble" or "gentle." It is only at a relatively early stage of culture that the symptoms of expensive vice are conventionally accepted as marks of a superior status, and so tend to become virtues and command the deference of the community; but the reputability that attaches to certain expensive vices long retains so much of its force as to appreciably lessen the disapprobation visited upon the men of the wealthy or noble class for any excessive indulgence. The same invidious distinction adds force to the current disapproval of any indulgence of this kind on the part of women, minors, and inferiors. This invidious traditional distinction has not lost its force even among the more advanced peoples of to-day. Where the example set by the leisure class retains its imperative force in the regulation of the conventionalities, it is observable that the women still in great measure practise the same traditional continence with regard to stimulants.

This characterisation of the greater continence

in the use of stimulants practised by the women of the reputable classes may seem an excessive refinement of logic at the expense of common sense. But facts within easy reach of any one who cares to know them go to say that the greater abstinence of women is in some part due to an imperative conventionality; and that this conventionality is, in a general way, strongest where the patriarchal tradition—the tradition that the woman is a chattel—has retained its hold in greatest vigour. In a sense which has been greatly qualified in scope and rigour, but which has by no means lost its meaning even yet, this tradition says that the woman, being a chattel, should consume only what is necessary to her sustenance,—except so far as her further consumption contributes to the comfort or the good repute of her master. The consumption of luxuries, in the true sense, is a consumption directed to the comfort of the consumer himself, and is, therefore, a mark of the master. Any such consumption by others can take place only on a basis of sufferance. In communities where the popular habits of thought have been profoundly shaped by the patriarchal tradition we may accordingly look for survivals of the tabu on luxuries at least to the extent of a conventional deprecation of their use by the unfree and dependent class. This is more particularly true as regards certain luxuries, the use of which by the dependent class would detract sensibly from the comfort or pleasure of their masters, or which are held to be of doubtful legitimacy on other grounds. In the apprehension of the great conservative middle class of Western civilisation the use of these stimulants is obnoxious to at least one, if not both, of these objections; and it is a fact too significant to be passed over that it is precisely among these middle classes of the Germanic culture, with their strong surviving sense of the patriarchal proprieties, that the women are to the greatest extent subject to a qualified tabu on narcotics and alcoholic beverages. With many qualifications—with more qualifications as the patriarchal tradition has gradually weakened —the general rule is felt to be right and binding that women should consume only for the benefit of their masters. The objection of course presents itself that expenditure on women's dress and household paraphernalia is an obvious exception to this rule; but it will appear in the sequel that this exception is much more obvious than substantial.

During the earlier stages of economic development, consumption of goods without stint, especially consumption of the better grades of goods,—ideally all consumption in excess of the subsistence minimum,—pertains normally to the leisure class. This restriction tends to disappear, at least formally, after the later peaceable stage has been reached, with private ownership of goods and an industrial system based on wage labour or on the petty household economy. But during the earlier quasi-peaceable stage, when so many of the traditions through which the institution of a leisure class has affected the economic life of later times were taking form and consistency, this principle has had the force of a conventional law. It has served as the norm to which consumption has tended to conform, and any appreciable departure from it is to be regarded as an abberant form, sure to be eliminated sooner or later in the further course of development.

The quasi-peaceable gentleman of leisure, then, not only consumes of the staff of life beyond the minimum required for subsistence and physical efficiency, but his consumption also undergoes a specialisation as regards the quality of the goods consumed. He consumes freely and of the best, in food, drink, narcotics, shelter, services, ornaments, apparel, weapons and accoutrements, amusements, amulets, and idols or divinities. In the process of gradual amelioration which takes place in the articles of his consumption, the motive principle and the proximate aim of innovation is no doubt the higher efficiency of the improved and more elaborate products for personal comfort and well-being. But that does not remain the sole purpose of their consumption. The canon of reputability is at hand and seizes upon such innovations as are, according to its standard, fit to survive. Since the consumption of these more excellent goods is an evidence of wealth, it becomes honorific; and conversely, the failure to consume in due quantity and quality becomes a mark of inferiority and demerit.

This growth of punctilious discrimination as to qualitative excellence in eating drinking, etc., presently affects not only the manner of life, but also the training and intellectual activity of the gentleman of leisure. He is no longer simply the successful, aggressive male,—the man of strength, resource, and intrepidity. In order to avoid stultification he must also cultivate his tastes, for it now becomes incumbent on him to discriminate with some nicety between the noble and the ignoble in consumable goods. He becomes a connoisseur in creditable viands of various degrees of merit, in manly beverages and trinkets, in seemly apparel and architecture, in weapons, games, dances, and the narcotics. This cultivation of the æsthetic faculty requires time and application, and the demands made upon the gentleman in this direction therefore tend to change his life of leisure into a more or less arduous application to the business of learning how to live a life of ostensible leisure in a becoming way. Closely related to the requirement that the gentleman must consume freely and of the right kind of goods, there is the requirement that he must know how to consume them in a seemly manner. His life of leisure must be conducted in due form. Hence arise good manners in the way pointed out in an earlier chapter. High-bred manners and ways of living are items of conformity to the norm of conspicuous leisure and conspicuous consumption.

Conspicuous consumption of valuable goods is a means of reputability to the gentleman of leisure. As wealth accumulates on his hands, his own unaided effort will not avail to sufficiently put his opulence in evidence by this method. The aid of friends and competitors is therefore brought in by resorting to the giving of valuable presents and expensive feasts and entertainments. Presents and feasts had probably another origin than that of naïve ostentation, but they acquired their utility for this purpose very early, and they have retained that character to the present; so that their utility in this respect has now long been the substantial ground on which these usages rest. Costly entertainments, such as the potlatch or the ball, are peculiarly adapted to serve this end. The competitor with whom the entertainer wishes to institute a comparison is, by this method, made to serve as a means to the end. He consumes vicariously for his host at the same time that he is a witness to the consumption of that excess of good things which his host is unable to dispose of single-handed, and he is also made to witness his host's facility in etiquette.

In the giving of costly entertainments other motives, of a more genial kind, are of course also present. The custom of festive gatherings probably originated in motives of conviviality and religion; these motives are also present in the later development, but they do not continue to be the sole motives. The latter-day leisure-class festivities and entertainments may continue in some slight degree to serve the religious need and in a higher degree the needs of recreation and conviviality, but they also serve an invidious purpose; and they serve it none the less effectually for having a colourable non-invidious ground in these more avowable motives. But the economic effect of these social amenities is not therefore lessened, either in the vicarious consumption of goods or in the exhibition of difficult and costly achievements in etiquette.

As wealth accumulates, the leisure class develops further in function and structure and there arises a differentiation within the class. There is a more or less elaborate system of rank and grades. This differentiation is furthered by the inheritance of wealth and the consequent inheritance of gentility. With the inheritance of gentility goes the inheritance of obligatory leisure; and gentility of a sufficient potency to entail a life of leisure may be inherited without the complement of wealth required to maintain a dignified leisure. Gentle blood may be transmitted without goods enough to afford a reputably free consumption at one's ease. Hence results a class of impecunious gentlemen of leisure, incidentally referred to already. These half-caste gentlemen of leisure fall into a system of hierarchical gradations. Those who stand near the higher and the highest grades of the wealthy leisure class, in point of birth, or in point of wealth, or both, outrank the remoter-born and the pecuniarily weaker. These lower grades, especially the impecunious or marginal gentlemen of leisure, affiliate themselves by a system of dependence or fealty to the great ones; by so doing they gain an increment of repute, or of the means with which to lead a life of leisure, from their patron. They become his courtiers or retainers, servants; and being fed and countenanced by their patron they are indices of his rank and vicarious consumers of his superfluous wealth. Many of these affiliated gentlemen of leisure are at the same time lesser men of substance in their own right; so that some of them are scarcely at all, others only partially, to be rated as vicarious consumers. So many of them, however, as make up the retainers and hangers-on of the patron may be classed as vicarious consumers without qualification. Many of these again, and also many of the other aristocracy of less degree, have in turn attracted to their persons a more or less comprehensive group of vicarious consumers in the persons of their wives and children, their servants, retainers, etc.

Throughout this graduated scheme of vicarious leisure and vicarious consumption the rule holds that these offices must be performed in some such manner, or under some such circumstance or insignia, as shall point plainly to the master to whom this leisure or consumption pertains, and to whom therefore the resulting increment of good repute of right inures. The consumption and leisure executed by these persons for their master or patron represents an investment on his part with a view to an increase of good fame. As regards feasts and largesses this is obvious enough, and the imputation of repute to the host or patron here takes place immediately, on the ground of common notoriety. Where leisure and consumption is performed vicariously by henchmen and retainers, imputation of the resulting repute to the patron is effected by their residing near his person so that it may be plain to all men from what source they draw. As the group whose good esteem is to be secured in this way grows larger, more patent means are required to indicate the imputation of credit for the leisure performed, and to this end uniforms, badges, and liveries come into vogue. The wearing of uniforms or liveries implies a considerable degree of dependence, and may even be said to be a mark of servitude, real or ostensible. The wearers of uniforms and liveries may be roughly divided into two classes—the free and the servile, or the noble and the ignoble. The services performed by them are likewise divisible into noble and ignoble. Of course the distinction is not observed with strict consistency in practice; the less debasing of the base services and the less honorific of the noble functions are not infrequently merged in the same person. But the general distinction is not on that account to be overlooked. What may add some perplexity is the fact that this fundamental distinction between noble and ignoble, which rests on the nature of the ostensible service performed, is traversed by a secondary distinction into honorific and humiliating, resting on the rank of the person for whom the service is performed or whose livery is worn. So, those offices which are by right the proper employment of the leisure class are noble; such are government, fighting, hunting, the care of arms and accoutrements, and the like,—in short, those which may be classed as ostensibly predatory employments. On the other hand, those employments which properly fall to the industrious class are ignoble; such as handicraft or other productive labour, menial services, and the like. But a base service performed for a person of very high degree may become a very honorific office; as for instance the office of a Maid of Honour or of a Lady in Waiting to the Queen, or the King's Master of the Horse or his Keeper of the Hounds. The two offices last named suggest a principle of some general bearing. Whenever, as in these cases, the menial service in question has to do directly with the primary leisure employments of fighting and hunting, it easily acquires a reflected honorific character. In this way great honour may come to attach to an employment which in its own nature belongs to the baser sort.

In the later development of peaceable industry, the usage of employing an idle corps of uniformed men-at-arms gradually lapses. Vicarious consumption by dependents bearing the insignia of their patron or master narrows down to a corps of liveried menials. In a heightened degree, therefore, the livery comes to be a badge of servitude, or rather of servility. Something of a honorific character always attached to the livery of the armed

retainer, but this honorific character disappears when the livery becomes the exclusive badge of the menial. The livery becomes obnoxious to nearly all who are required to wear it. We are yet so little removed from a state of effective slavery as still to be fully sensitive to the sting of any imputation of servility. This antipathy asserts itself even in the case of the liveries or uniforms which some corporations prescribe as the distinctive dress of their employees. In this country the aversion even goes the length of discrediting—in a mild and uncertain way—those government employments, military and civil, which require the wearing of a livery or uniform.

With the disappearance of servitude, the number of vicarious consumers attached to any one gentleman tends, on the whole, to decrease. The like is of course true, and perhaps in a still higher degree, of the number of dependents who perform vicarious leisure for him. In a general way, though not wholly nor consistently, these two groups coincide. The dependent who was first delegated for these duties was the wife, or the chief wife; and, as would be expected, in the later development of the institution, when the number of persons by whom these duties are customarily performed gradually narrows, the wife remains the last. In the higher grades of society a large volume of both these kinds of service is required; and here the wife is of course still assisted in the work by a more or less numerous corps of menials. But as we descend the social scale, the point is presently reached where the duties of vicarious leisure and consumption devolve upon the wife alone. In the communities of the Western culture, this point is at present found among the lower middle class.

And here occurs a curious inversion. It is a fact of common observation that in this lower middle class there is no pretence of leisure on the part of the head of the household. Through force of circumstances it has fallen into disuse. But the middle-class wife still carries on the business of vicarious leisure, for the good name of the household and its master. In descending the social scale in any modern industrial community, the primary fact—the conspicuous leisure of the master of the household—disappears at a relatively high point. The head of the middle-class household has been reduced by economic circumstances to turn his hand to gaining a livelihood by occupations which often partake largely of the character of industry, as in the case of the ordinary business man of to-day. But the derivative fact—the vicarious leisure and consumption rendered by the wife, and the auxiliary vicarious performance of leisure by menials—remains in vogue as a conventionality which the demands of reputability will not suffer to be slighted. It is by no means an uncommon spectacle to find a man applying himself to work with the utmost assiduity, in order that his wife may in due form render for him that degree of vicarious leisure which the common sense of the time demands.

The leisure rendered by the wife in such cases is, of course, not a simple manifestation of idleness or indolence. It almost invariably occurs disguised under some form of work or household duties or social amenities, which prove on analysis to serve little or no ulterior end beyond showing that she does not and need not occupy herself with anything that is gainful or that is of substantial use. As has already been noticed under the head of manners, the greater part of the customary round of domestic cares to which the middle-class housewife gives her time and effort is of this character. Not that the results of her attention to household matters, of a decorative and mundificatory character, are not pleasing to the sense of men trained in middle-class proprieties; but the taste to which these effects of household adornment and tidiness appeal is a taste which has been formed under the selective guidance of a canon of propriety that demands just these evidences of wasted effort. The effects are pleasing to us chiefly because we have been taught to find them pleasing. There goes into these domestic duties much solicitude for a proper combination of form and colour, and for other ends that are to be classed as æsthetic in the proper sense of the term; and it is not denied that effects having some substantial æsthetic value are sometimes attained. Pretty much all that is here insisted on is that, as regards these amenities of life, the housewife's efforts are under the guidance of traditions that have been shaped by the law of conspicuously wasteful expenditure of time and substance. If beauty or comfort is achieved,—and it is a more or less fortuitous circumstance if they are,—they must be achieved by means and methods that commend themselves to the great economic law of wasted effort. The more reputable, "presentable" portion of middle-class household paraphernalia are, on the other hand, apparatus for putting in evidence the vicarious leisure rendered by the housewife.

The requirement of vicarious consumption at the hands of the wife continues in force even at a lower point in the pecuniary scale than the requirement of vicarious leisure. At a point below which little if any pretence of wasted effort, in ceremonial cleanness and the like, is observable, and where there is assuredly no conscious attempt at ostensible leisure, decency still requires the wife to consume some goods conspicuously for the reputability of the household and its head. So that, as the latter-day outcome of this evolution of an archaic institution, the wife, who was at the outset the drudge and chattel of the man, both in fact and in theory,—the producer of goods for him to consume,—has become the ceremonial consumer of goods which he produces. But she still quite unmistakably remains his chattel in theory; for the habitual rendering of vicarious leisure and consumption is the abiding mark of the unfree servant.

This vicarious consumption practised by the household of the middle and lower classes can not be counted as a direct expression of the leisure-class scheme of life, since the household of this pecuniary grade does not belong within the leisure class. It is rather that the leisure-class scheme of life here comes to an expression at the second remove. The leisure class stands at the head of the social structure in point of reputability; and its manner of life and its standards of worth therefore afford the norm of reputability for the community. The observance of these standards, in some degree of approximation, becomes incumbent upon all classes lower in the scale. In modern civilized communities the lines of demarcation between social classes have grown vague and transient, and wherever this happens the norm of reputability imposed by the upper class extends its coercive influence with but slight hindrance down through the social structure to the lowest strata. The result is that the members of each stratum accept as their ideal of decency the scheme of life in vogue in the next higher stratum, and bend their energies to live up to that ideal. On pain of forfeiting their good name and their self-respect in case of failure, they must conform to the accepted code, at least in appearance.

The basis on which good repute in any highly organised industrial community ultimately rests is pecuniary strength; and the means of showing pecuniary strength, and so of gaining or retaining a good name, are leisure and a conspicuous consumption of goods. Accordingly, both of these methods are in vogue as far down the scale as it remains possible; and in the lower strata in which the two methods are employed, both offices are in great part delegated to the wife and children of the household. Lower still, where any degree of leisure, even ostensible, has become impracticable for the wife, the conspicuous consumption of goods remains and is carried on by the wife and children. The man of the household also can do something in this direction, and, indeed, he commonly does; but with a still lower descent into the levels of indigence—along the margin of the slums—the man, and presently also the children, virtually cease to consume valuable goods for appearances, and the woman remains virtually the sole exponent of the household's pecuniary decency. No class of society, not even the most abjectly poor, forgoes all customary conspicuous consumption. The last items of this category of consumption are not given up except under stress of the direst necessity. Very much of squalor and discomfort will be endured before the last trinket or the last pretence of pecuniary decency is put away. There is no class and no country that has yielded so abjectly before the pressure of physical want as to deny themselves all gratification of this higher or spiritual need.

From the foregoing survey of the growth of conspicuous leisure and consumption, it appears that the utility of both alike for the purposes of reputability lies in the element of waste that is common to both. In the one case it is a waste of time and effort, in the other it is a waste of goods. Both are methods of demonstrating the possession of wealth, and the two are conventionally accepted as equivalents. The choice between them is a question of advertising expediency simply, except so far as it may be affected by other standards of propriety, springing from a different source. On grounds of expediency the preference may be given to the one or the other at different stages of the economic development. The question is, which of the two methods will most effectively reach the persons whose convictions it is desired to affect. Usage has answered this question in different ways under different circumstances.

So long as the community or social group is small enough and compact enough to be effectually reached by common notoriety alone,—that is to say, so long as the human environment to which the individual is required to adapt himself in respect of reputability is comprised within his sphere of personal acquaintance and neighbourhood gossip,—so long the one method is about as effective as the other. Each will therefore serve about equally well during the earlier stages of social growth. But when the differentiation has gone farther and it becomes necessary to reach a wider human environment, consumption begins to hold over leisure as an ordinary means of decency. This is especially true during the later, peaceable economic stage. The means of communication and the mobility of the population now expose the individual to the observation of many persons who have no other means of judging of his reputability than the display of goods (and perhaps of breeding) which he is able to make while he is under their direct observation.

The modern organisation of industry works in the same direction also by another line. The exigencies of the modern industrial system frequently place individuals and households in juxtaposition between whom there is little contact in any other sense than that of juxtaposition. One's neighbours, mechanically speaking, often are socially not one's neighbours, or even acquaintances; and still their transient good opinion has a high degree of utility. The only practicable means of impressing one's pecuniary ability on these unsympathetic observers of one's everyday life is an unremitting demonstration of ability to pay. In the modern community there is also a more frequent attendance at large gatherings of people to whom one's everyday life is unknown; in such places as churches, theatres, ballrooms, hotels, parks, shops, and the like. In order to impress these transient observers, and to retain one's self-complacency under their observation, the signature of one's pecuniary strength should be written in characters which he who runs may read. It is evident, therefore, that the present trend of the development is in the direction of heightening the utility of conspicuous consumption as compared with leisure.

It is also noticeable that the serviceability of consumption as a means of repute, as well as the insistence on it as an element of decency, is at its best in those portions of the community where the human contact of the individual is widest and the mobility of the population is greatest. Conspicuous consumption claims a relatively larger portion of the income of the urban than of the rural population, and the claim is also more imperative. The result is that, in order to keep up a decent appearance, the former habitually live hand-to-mouth to a greater extent than the latter. So it comes, for instance, the American farmer and his wife and daughters are notoriously less modish in their dress, as well as less urbane in their manners, than the city artisan's family with an equal income. It is not that the city population is by nature much more eager for the peculiar complacency that comes of a conspicuous consumption, nor has the rural population less regard for pecuniary decency. But the provocation to this line of evidence, as well as its transient effectiveness, are more decided in the city. This method is therefore more readily resorted to, and in the struggle to outdo one another the city population push their normal standard of conspicuous consumption to a higher point, with the result that a relatively greater expenditure in this direction is required to indicate a given degree of pecuniary decency in the city. The requirement of conformity to this higher conventional standard becomes mandatory. The standard of decency is higher, class for class, and this requirement of decent appearance must be lived up to on pain of losing caste.

Consumption becomes a larger element in the standard of living in the city than in the country. Among the country population its place is to some extent taken by savings and home comforts known through the medium of neighbourhood gossip sufficiently to serve the like general purpose of pecuniary repute. These home comforts and the leisure indulged in—where the indulgence is found —are of course also in great part to be classed as items of conspicuous consumption; and much the same is to be said of the savings. The smaller amount of the savings laid by by the artisan class is no doubt due, in some measure, to the fact that in the case of the artisan the savings are a less effective means of advertisement, relative to the environment in which he is placed, than are the savings of the people living on farms and in the small villages. Among the latter, everybody's affairs, especially everybody's pecuniary status, are known to everybody else. Considered by itself simply—taken in the first degree—this added provocation to which the artisan and the urban labouring classes are exposed may not very seriously decrease the amount of savings; but in its cumulative action, through raising the standard of decent expenditure, its deterrent effect on the tendency to save cannot but be very great.

*   *   *

The use of the term "waste" is in one respect an unfortunate one. As used in the speech of everyday life the word carries an undertone of deprecation. It is here used for want of a better term that will adequately describe the same range of motives and of phenomena, and it is not to be taken in an odious sense, as implying an illegitimate expenditure of human products or of human life. In the view of economic theory, the expenditure in question is no more and no less legitimate than any other expenditure. It is here called "waste" because this expenditure does not serve human life or human well-being on the whole, not because it is waste or misdirection of effort or expenditure as viewed from the standpoint of the individual consumer who chooses it. If he chooses it, that disposes of the question of its relative utility to him, as compared with other forms of consumption that would not be deprecated on account of their wastefulness. Whatever form of expenditure the consumer chooses, or whatever end he seeks in making his choice, has utility to him by virtue of his preference. As seen from the point of view of the individual consumer, the question of wasteful-

ness does not arise within the scope of economic theory proper. The use of the word "waste" as a technical term, therefore, implies no deprecation of the motives or of the ends sought by the consumer under this canon of conspicuous waste.

But it is, on other grounds, worth noting that the term "waste" in the language of everyday life implies deprecation of what is characterised as wasteful. This common-sense implication is itself an outcropping of the instinct of workmanship. The popular reprobation of waste goes to say that in order to be at peace with himself the common man must be able to see in any and all human effort and human enjoyment an enhancement of life and well-being on the whole. In order to meet with unqualified approval, any economic fact must approve itself under the test of impersonal usefulness—usefulness as seen from the point of view of the generically human. Relative or competitive advantage of one individual in comparison with another does not satisfy the economic conscience, and therefore competitive expenditure has not the approval of this conscience.

In strict accuracy nothing should be included under the head of conspicuous waste but such expenditure as is incurred on the ground of an invidious pecuniary comparison. But in order to bring any given item or element in under this head it is not necessary that it should be recognised as waste in this sense by the person incurring the expenditure. It frequently happens that an element of the standard of living which set out with being primarily wasteful, ends with becoming, in the apprehension of the consumer, a necessary of life; and it may in this way become as indispensable as any other item of the consumer's habitual expenditure. As items which sometimes fall under this head, and are therefore available as illustrations of the manner in which this principle applies, may be cited carpets and tapestries, silver table service, waiter's services, silk hats, starched linen, many articles of jewellery and of dress. The indispensability of these things after the habit and the convention have been formed, however, has little to say in the classification of expenditures as waste or not waste in the technical meaning of the word. The test to which all expenditure must be brought in an attempt to decide that point is the question whether it serves directly to enhance human life on the whole—whether it furthers the life process taken impersonally. For this is the basis of award of the instinct of workmanship, and that instinct is the court of final appeal in any question of economic truth or adequacy. It is a question as to the award rendered by a dispassionate common sense. The question is therefore, not whether, under the existing circumstances of individual habit and social custom, a given expenditure conduces to the particular consumer's gratification or peace of mind; but whether, aside from acquired tastes and from the canons of usage and conventional decency, its result is a net gain in comfort or in the fulness of life. Customary expenditure must be classed under the head of waste in so far as the custom on which it rests is traceable to the habit of making an invidious pecuniary comparison—in so far as it is conceived that it could not have become customary and prescriptive without the backing of this principle of pecuniary reputability or relative economic success.

It is obviously not necessary that a given object of expenditure should be exclusively wasteful in order to come in under the category of conspicuous waste. An article may be useful and wasteful both, and its utility to the consumer may be made up of use and waste in the most varying proportions.

Consumable goods, and even productive goods, generally show the two elements in combination, as constituents of their utility; although, in a general way, the element of waste tends to predominate in articles of consumption, while the contrary is true of articles designed for productive use. Even in articles which appear at first glance to serve for pure ostentation only, it is always possible to detect the presence of some, at least ostensible, useful purpose; and on the other hand, even in special machinery and tools contrived for some particular industrial process, as well as in the rudest appliances of human industry, the traces of conspicuous waste, or at least of the habit of ostentation, usually become evident on a close scrutiny. It would be hazardous to assert that a useful purpose is ever absent from the utility of any article or of any service, however obviously its prime purpose and chief element is conspicuous waste; and it would be only less hazardous to assert of any primarily useful product that the element of waste is in no way concerned in its value, immediately or remotely.

7. *Social Stratification*

BY PITIRIM A. SOROKIN

CONCEPTIONS AND DEFINITIONS

SOCIAL stratification means the differentiation of a given population into hierarchically superposed classes. It is manifested in the existence of upper and lower layers. Its basis and very essence consist in an unequal distribution of rights and privileges, duties and responsibilities, social values and privations, social power and influences among the members of a society. Concrete forms of social stratification are different and numerous. If the economic status of the members of a society is unequal, if among them there are both wealthy and poor, the society is *economically stratified*, regardless of whether its organization is communistic or capitalistic, whether in its constitution it is styled "the society of equal individuals" or not. Labels,

signboards and "speech reactions" cannot change nor obliterate the real fact of the economic inequality manifested in the differences of incomes, economic standards, and in the existence of the rich and the poor strata. If the social ranks within a group are hierarchically superposed with respect to their authority and prestige, their honors and titles; if there are the rulers and the ruled, then whatever are their names (monarchs, executives, masters, bosses), these things mean that the group is *politically stratified*, regardless of what is written in its constitution or proclaimed in its declarations. If the members of a society are differentiated into various occupational groups, and some of the occupations are regarded as more honorable than others, if the members of an occupational group are divided into bosses of different authority and into members who are subordinated to the bosses, the group is *occupationally stratified*, independently of the fact whether the bosses are elected or

Reprinted from Pitirim A. Sorokin, *Social Mobility*, in *Social and Cultural Mobility* (Glencoe, Ill.: The Free Press, 1959), chap. ii, pp. 11–17, with the permission of The Free Press.

appointed, whether their position is acquired by social inheritance or personal achievement.

PRINCIPAL FORMS OF SOCIAL STRATIFICATION AND THEIR INTERRELATIONS

Concrete forms of social stratification are numerous. The majority of them may, however, be reduced to three principal classes: the economic, the political, and the occupational stratification. As a general rule, these forms are closely intercorrelated with each other. Usually, those who occupy the upper strata in one respect happen to be in the upper strata also in other respects, and *vice versa*. The men who dwell in the upper economic layers happen also to be in the upper political and occupational strata. The poor, as a rule, are politically disfranchised and dwell in the lowest strata of the occupational hierarchy. Such is the general rule, though there are, however, many exceptions to it. Not always are the wealthiest men at the apex of the political or occupational pyramid; and not always are the poor men the lowest in the political or the occupational gradations. This means that the intercorrelation among the three forms of stratification is far from being perfect; the strata of each form do not coincide completely with one another. There is always a certain degree of overlapping among them. This fact does not permit us to analyze in a summary way all three fundamental forms of social stratification. For the sake of a greater accuracy each form has to be studied separately. A real picture of social stratification in any society is very complex. In order to make its analysis easier, only the most fundamental traits must be taken. Many details must be omitted, and the situation simplified, without, however, disfiguring it. This is done in any science and has to be done especially here where the problem is so complex and so little studied. In such cases the Roman *minima non curat prætor* is completely justified.

SOCIAL STRATIFICATION IS A PERMANENT CHARACTERISTIC OF ANY ORGANIZED SOCIAL GROUP

Any organized social group is always a stratified social body. There has not been and does not exist any permanent social group which is "flat," and in which all members are equal. Unstratified society, with a real equality of its members, is a myth which has never been realized in the history of mankind. This statement may sound somewhat paradoxical and yet it is accurate. The forms and proportions of stratification vary, but its essence is permanent, as far as any more or less permanent and organized social group is concerned. This is true not only in human society, but even in plant and animal communities. Let us consider the principal corroborations.

Plant and Animal Communities.—As far as it is possible to apply the conceptions of human sociology to plant and animal communities, social stratification may be said to exist here also. In the plant communities there are different "social" classes, the phenomena of parasitism and exploitation, suppression and domination, different "economic" standards of living (the amount of air, sunlight, moisture, and soil ingredients consumed) and so on. Of course, these phenomena are but roughly analogous to those of social stratification in human society; and yet they signify clearly that the plant community is in no way a community of "equal units," whose positions are equal and whose interrelations are identical within the community.

With still greater reason the same may be said of animal societies. Within them social stratification is manifested in: (*a*) the existence of different and sharply divided classes in the communities of bees, ants, and other insects; (*b*) the existence of leaders among gregarious mammals; (*c*) the general facts of parasitism, exploitation, domination, subordination, and so on. In brief, one cannot find here any society which may be styled an unstratified group.

Pre-literate Human Tribes.—Except, perhaps, the few cases where the members of a population are leading an isolated life, where no permanent social life and interaction exist, where, therefore, we do not have a social organization in the proper sense of the word, as soon as organization begins primitive social groups exhibit the trait of stratification. It is manifested in various forms. First, in the existence of the sex and age groups with quite different privileges and duties. Second, in the existence of a privileged and influential group of the tribe's leaders. Third, in the existence of the most influential chieftain or headman. Fourth, in the existence of outcasts and outlawed men. Fifth, in the existence of inter- and intratribal division of labor. Sixth, in the existence of different economic standards, and in that of economic inequality generally. Traditional opinion about primitive groups as communistic societies which do not have any commerce or private property, or economic inequality, or inheritance of fortune, are far from being correct. "The primitive economy (*Urwirtschaft*) is neither an economy of isolated individuals searching for food (as K. Bücher thinks), nor the economy of communism or collective production. What we really have is the economic group composed of mutually dependent and economically active individuals and of the smaller parts of the group which have a system of commerce and barter with each other."[1] If in many tribes economic differentiation is very slight, and customs of mutual aid approach communism, this is due only to the general poverty of the group. These facts support the contention that primitive groups also are stratified bodies.

More Advanced Societies and Groups.—If we cannot find a non-stratified society among the most primitive groups, it is useless to try to find it among more advanced, larger and compound societies. Here, without any single exception the fact of stratification is universal. Its forms and proportions vary; its essence has existed everywhere and at all times. Among all agricultural and, especially, industrial societies social stratification has been conspicuous and clear. The modern democracies also do not present any exception to the rule. Though in their constitutions it is said that "all men are equal," only a quite naïve person may infer from this a non-existence of social stratification within these societies. It is enough to mention the gradations: from Henry Ford to a beggar; from the President of the United States to a policeman; from a foreman to the most subordinate worker; from the president of a university to a janitor; from an "LL.D." or "Ph.D." to a "B.A."; from a "leading authority" to an average man; from a commander-in-chief of an army to a soldier; from a president of a board of directors of a corporation to its common laborer; from an editor-in-chief of a newspaper to a simple reporter; it is enough to mention these various ranks and social gradations to see that the best democracies have social stratification scarcely less than the non-democratic societies.

It is needless to insist on these obvious facts. What should be stressed here is, that not only large social bodies, but any organized social group whatever, once it is organized, is inevitably stratified to some degree.

Gradations, hierarchies, shining leaders, cumulative aspirations—all these appear spontaneously whenever men get together, whether for play, for mutual help, for voluntary association, or for the great compulsory association of the State. Every Englishman is said to love a lord; every American is said to love a title.[2]

Family, church, sect, political party, faction, business organization, gang of brigands, labor union, scientific society—in brief, any organized social group is stratified at the price of its permanency and organization. The organization even of groups of ardent levelers, and the permanent failure of all attempts to build a non-stratified group, testify to the imminency and unavoidability of stratification in an organized social group. This remark may appear somewhat strange to many people who, under the influence of high-sounding phraseology, may believe that, at least, the societies of the levelers themselves are non-stratified. This belief, as many another one, is utterly wrong. Different attempts to exterminate social feudalism have been successful, in the best cases, only in ameliorating some of the inequalities, and in changing the concrete forms of stratification. They have never succeeded in annihilating stratification itself. And the regularity with which all these efforts have failed once more witnesses the "natural" character of stratification. Christianity started its history with an attempt to create an equal society; very soon, especially after 313 A.D., it already had a complicated hierarchy, and soon finished by the creation of a tremendous pyramid, with numerous ranks and titles, beginning with the omnipotent pope and ending with that of a lawless heretic. The institution of Fratres Minorum was organized by St. Francis of Assisi on the principle of perfect equality. Seven years later equality disappeared. Without any exceptions, all attempts of the most ardent levelers in the history of all countries have had the same fate. They could not avoid it even when the faction of the levelers has been victorious. The failure of the Russian Communism is only an additional example in a long series of similar experiments performed on small and large scale, sometimes peacefully, as in many religious sects, sometimes violently, as in social revolutions of the past and present. If many forms of stratification were destroyed for a moment, they regularly reappeared again in the old or in a modified form, often being built by the hands of the levelers themselves.

Present democracies and Socialist, Communist, Syndicalist, and other organizations, with their slogan of "equality" do not present any exception to the rule. In regard to democracies this has been shown above. The inner organization of different socialist and similar groups pleading "equality" shows that perhaps in no other organization does such an enormous hierarchy and "bossism" exist as in these groups of levelers. "The Socialist leaders regard the masses only as the passive tools in their hands, as a series of zeros destined only to increase the significance of the figure on the left" (the

1. Somló, F., *Der Güterverkehr in der Urgesellschaft, Inst. of Solvay,* pp. 65–67, 155, 177 ff., 1909. See also Panskow, H., "Betrachtungen über das Wirtschaftsleben der Natürvölker," *Zeitschrift der Gesellschaft für Erdkunde zu Berlin,* Vol. XXXI, 1896; Maunier, R., "Vie Religieuse et vie économique," *Revue International de Sociologie,* December, 1907, January and February, 1908; Lowie, R. H., *Primitive Society,* Chap. IX, New York, 1920; Thurnwald, R., *Die Gestaltung d. Wirtschaftsentwicklung aus ihren Aufangen heraus,* 1923; Malinowski, B., "The Argonauts in the West Pacific," *Economics Journal,* March, 1921.

2. Taussig, F. W., *Inventors and Money Makers,* p. 126, New York, 1915.

importance of the leaders themselves), says E. Fournière, himself one of these socialists.[3] If in the statement there is an exaggeration, it is hardly considerable. At least, the best and the most competent investigators of the situation are unanimous in their conclusions of an enormous development of oligarchy and stratification within all these groups. The enormous potential taste for inequality of numerous "levelers" becomes at once conspicuous, as soon, indeed, as they happen to be victorious. In such cases they often exhibit a greater cruelty and contempt toward the masses than former kings and rulers. This has been repeated regularly in victorious revolutions where the levelers become dictators. Classical descriptions of the situation given by Plato and Aristotle, on the basis of the ancient Greek social revolutions, may be literally applied to all such cases, including the Bolshevist experiment.

To sum up: social stratification is a permanent characteristic of any organized society. "Varying in form, social stratification has existed in all societies which proclaimed the equality of men."[4]

Feudalism and oligarchy continue to exist in science and arts, in politics and administration, in a gang of bandits, in democracies, among the levelers, everywhere.

This, however, does not mean that the stratification quantitatively or qualitatively is identical in all societies and at all times. In its concrete forms, defects or virtues, it certainly varies. The problem to be discussed now is these quantitative and qualitative variations. Begin with the quantitative aspect of social stratification in its three forms; economic, political and occupational. This is what is meant by the height and the profile of social stratification, and, correspondingly, the height and the profile of a "social building." How high is it? How long is the distance from the bottom to the top of a social cone? Of how many stories is it composed? Is its profile steep, or does it slope gradually? These are the problems of the quantitative analysis of social stratification. It deals, so to speak, exclusively with the exterior architecture of a social building. Its inner structure, in its entirety, is the object of the qualitative analysis. The study should begin with the height and the profile of the social pyramid. After that the pyramid should be entered and an investigation of its inner organization made from the standpoint of stratification.

---

3. Fournière, E., *La Sociocratie*, p. 117, 1910.
4. Pareto, V., *Traité de sociologie générale*, Vol. I, p. 613, Paris, 1917–1919.

8. *Social Stratification and Class Structure*

BY MAX WEBER

The Concepts of Class and Class Status

THE TERM "class status"[1] will be applied to the typical probability that a given state of (a) provision with goods, (b) external conditions of life, and (c) subjective satisfaction or frustration will be possessed by an individual or a group. These probabilities define class status in so far as they are

Reprinted from Max Weber, *The Theory of Social and Economic Organization*, trans. A. M. Henderson and Talcott Parsons, ed. Talcott Parsons (Glencoe, Ill.: The Free Press, 1947), pp. 424–29. Copyright 1947 by Oxford University Press.

1. Weber uses the term "class" (*Klasse*) in a special sense, which is defined in this paragraph and which, in particular, he contrasts with *Stand*. There seems no other alternative translation of *Klasse*, but it should be kept in mind that it is being used in a special sense.—Ed.

dependent on the kind and extent of control or lack of it which the individual has over goods or services and existing possibilities of their exploitation for the attainment of income or receipts within a given economic order.

A "class" is any group of persons occupying the same class status. The following types of classes may be distinguished: (a) A class is a "property class" when class status for its members is primarily determined by the differentiation of property holdings; (b) a class is an "acquisition class" when the class situation of its members is primarily determined by their opportunity for the exploitation of services on the market; (c) the "social class" structure is composed of the plurality of class statuses between which an interchange of individuals on a personal basis or in the course of generations is readily possible and typically observable. On the basis of any of the three types of class status, associative relationships between those sharing the same class interests, namely, corporate class organizations may develop. This need not, however, necessarily happen. The concepts of class and class status as such designate only the fact of identity or similarity in the typical situation in which a given individual and many others find their interests defined. In principle control over different combinations of consumers goods, means of production, investments, capital funds or marketable abilities constitute class statuses which are different with each variation and combination. Only persons who are completely unskilled, without property and dependent on employment without regular occupation, are in a strictly identical class status. Transitions from one class status to another vary greatly in fluidity and in the ease with which an individual can enter the class. Hence the unity of "social" classes is highly relative and variable.

The primary significance of a positively privileged property class lies in the following facts: (i) Its members may be able to monopolize the purchase of high-priced consumers goods. (ii) They may control the opportunities of pursuing a systematic monopoly policy in the sale of economic goods. (iii) They may monopolize opportunities for the accumulation of property through unconsumed surpluses. (iv) They may monopolize opportunities to accumulate capital by saving, hence, the possibility of investing property in loans and the related possibility of control over executive positions in business. (v) They may monopolize the privileges of socially advantageous kinds of education so far as these involve expenditures.

Positively privileged property classes typically live from property income. This may be derived from property rights in human beings, as with slaveowners, in land, in mining property, in fixed equipment such as plant and apparatus, in ships, and as creditors in loan relationships. Loans may consist of domestic animals, grain, or money. Finally they may live on income from securities.

Class interests which are negatively privileged with respect to property belong typically to one of the following types: (a) They are themselves objects of ownership, that is they are unfree. (b) They are "outcasts" that is "proletarians" in the sense meant in Antiquity. (c) They are debtor classes and, (d) the "poor."

In between stand the "middle" classes. This term includes groups who have all sorts of property, or of marketable abilities through training, who are in a position to draw their support from these sources. Some of them may be "acquisition" classes.

Entrepreneurs are in this category by virtue of essentially positive privileges; proletarians, by virtue of negative privileges. But many types such as peasants, craftsmen, and officials do not fall in this category. The differentiation of classes on the basis of property alone is not "dynamic," that is, it does not necessarily result in class struggles or class revolutions. It is not uncommon for very strongly privileged property classes such as slaveowners, to exist side by side with such far less privileged groups as peasants or even outcasts without any class struggle. There may even be ties of solidarity between privileged property classes and unfree elements. However, such conflicts as that between creditors and debtors, the latter often being a question of urban patricians as opposed to either rural peasants or urban craftsmen, may lead to revolutionary conflict. Even this, however, need not necessarily aim at radical changes in economic organization. It may, on the contrary, be concerned in the first instance only with a redistribution of wealth. These may be called "property revolutions."

A classic example of the lack of class antagonism has been the relation of the "poor white trash," originally those not owning slaves, to the planters in the Southern States of the United States. The "poor whites" have often been much more hostile to the Negro than the planters who have frequently had a large element of patriarchal sentiment. The conflict of outcast against the property classes, of creditors and debtors, and of landowners and outcasts are best illustrated in the history of Antiquity.

The Significance of Acquisition Classes

The primary significance of a positively privileged acquisition class is to be found in two directions. On the one hand it is generally possible to go far toward attaining a monopoly of the management of productive enterprises in favour of the members of the class and their business interests. On the other hand, such a class tends to insure the security of its economic position by exercising influence on the economic policy of political bodies and other groups.

The members of positively privileged acquisition classes are typically entrepreneurs. The following are the most important types: merchants, shipowners, industrial and agricultural entrepreneurs, bankers and financiers. Under certain circumstances two other types are also members of such classes, namely, members of the "liberal" professions with a privileged position by virtue of their abilities or training, and workers with special skills commanding a monopolistic position, regardless of how far they are hereditary or the result of training.

Acquisition classes in a negatively privileged situation are workers of the various principal types. They may be roughly classified as skilled, semi-skilled and unskilled.

In this connexion as well as the above, independent peasants and craftsmen are to be treated as belonging to the "middle classes." This category often includes in addition officials, whether they are in public or private employment, the liberal professions, and workers with exceptional monopolistic assets or positions.

Examples of "social classes" are (a) the "working" class as a whole. It approaches this type the more completely mechanized the productive process becomes. (b) The "lower middle" classes.[2] (c) The "intelligentsia" without independent property and the persons whose social position is primarily dependent on technical training such as engineers, commercial and other officials, and civil servants. These groups may differ greatly among themselves, in particular according to costs of training. (d) The classes occupying a privileged position through property and education.

The unfinished concluding section of Karl Marx's *Kapital* was evidently intended to deal with the problem of the class unity of the proletariat, which he held existed in spite of the high degree of qualitative differentiation. A decisive factor is the increase in the importance of semi-skilled workers who have been trained in a relatively short time directly on the machines themselves, at the expense of the older type of "skilled" labour and also of unskilled. However, even this type of skill may often have a monopolistic aspect. Weavers are said to attain the highest level of productivity only after five years' experience.

At an earlier period every worker could be said to have been primarily interested in becoming an independent small bourgeois, but the possibility of realizing this goal is becoming progressively smaller. From one generation to another the most readily available path to advancement both for skilled and semi-skilled workers is into the class of technically trained individuals. In the most highly privileged classes, at least over the period of more than one generation, it is coming more and more to be true that money is overwhelmingly decisive. Through the banks and corporate enterprises members of the lower middle class and the salaried groups have certain opportunities to rise into the privileged class.

Organized activity of class groups is favoured by the following circumstances: (a) the possibility of concentrating on opponents where the immediate conflict of interests is vital. Thus workers organize against management and not against security holders who are the ones who really draw income without working. Similarly peasants are not apt to organize against landlords. (b) The existence of a class status which is typically similar for large masses of people. (c) The technical possibility of being easily brought together. This is particularly true where large numbers work together in a small area, as in the modern factory. (d) Leadership directed to readily understandable goals. Such goals are very generally imposed or at least are interpreted by persons, such as intelligentsia, who do not belong to the class in question.

Social Strata and Their Status

The term of "social status"[3] will be applied to a typically effective claim to positive or negative privilege with respect to social prestige so far as it rests on one or more of the following bases: (a) mode of living, (b) a formal process of education which may consist in empirical or rational training and the acquisition of the corresponding modes of life, or (c) on the prestige of birth, or of an occupation.

The primary practical manifestations of status with respect to social stratification are conubium, commensality, and often monopolistic appropriation of privileged economic opportunities and also prohibition of certain modes of acquisition. Finally, there are conventions or traditions of other types attached to a social status.

Stratificatory status may be based on class status directly or related to it in complex ways. It is not, however, determined by this alone. Property and managerial positions are not as such sufficient to lend their holder a certain social status, though they may well lead to its acquisition. Similarly, poverty is not as such a disqualification for high social status though again it may influence it.

Conversely, social status may partly or even wholly determine class status, without, however, being identical with it. The class status of an officer, a civil servant, and a student as determined by their income may be widely different while their social status remains the same, because they adhere to the same mode of life in all relevant respects as a result of their common education.

A social "*stratum*" *stand* is a plurality of individuals who, within a larger group, enjoy a particular kind and level of prestige by virtue of their position

---

2. Like the French "petite bourgeoisie," the German term *Kleinbürgertum* has a somewhat more specific meaning than the English "lower-middle class." It refers particularly to economically independent elements not employed in large-scale organizations. The typical example are the small shopkeeper and the proprietor of a small handicraft workshop.—ED.

3. *Ständische Lage.*—ED.

and possibly also claim certain special monopolies.

The following are the most important sources of the development of distinct strata: (a) The most important is by the development of a peculiar style of life including, particularly, the type of occupation pursued. (b) The second basis is hereditary charisma arising from the successful claim to a position of prestige by virtue of birth. (c) The third is the appropriation of political or hierocratic authority as a monopoly by socially distinct groups.

The development of hereditary strata is usually a form of the hereditary appropriation of privileges by an organized group or by individual qualified persons. Every well-established case of appropriation of opportunities and abilities, especially of exercising imperative powers, has a tendency to lead to the development of distinct strata. Conversely, the development of strata has a tendency in turn to lead to the monopolistic appropriation of governing powers and of the corresponding economic advantages.

Acquisition classes are favoured by an economic system oriented to market situations, whereas social strata develop and subsist most readily where economic organization is of a monopolistic and liturgical character and where the economic needs of corporate groups are met on a feudal or patrimonial basis. The type of class which is most closely related to a stratum is the "social" class, while the "acquisition" class is the farthest removed. Property classes often constitute the nucleus of a stratum.

Every society where strata play a prominent part is controlled to a large extent by conventional rules of conduct. It thus creates economically irrational conditions of consumption and hinders the development of free markets by monopolistic appropriation and by restricting free disposal of the individual's own economic ability. This will have to be discussed further elsewhere.[4]

---

4. This chapter breaks off at this point but is obviously incomplete. There is, however, no other part of Weber's published work in which the subject is systematically developed, although aspects of it are treated in different connexions at many points.—ED.

Section D

Political Organization and Authority

Editorial Foreword, BY TALCOTT PARSONS   579

I–POWER AND INEQUALITY

1. *The Withering Away of the State,* BY NICOLAI LENIN   580

2. *The Use of Force in Society,* BY VILFREDO PARETO   589

3. *On the Ruling Class,* BY GAETANO MOSCA   598

4. *The Sociological Character of Political Parties,* BY ROBERT MICHELS   603

II–SOME PATTERNS OF POLITICAL ORGANIZATION
AND AUTHORITY

1. *The Idea of Corporation,* BY OTTO VON GIERKE   611

2. *The Types of Authority,* BY MAX WEBER   626

3. *The Theory of Authority,* BY CHESTER I. BARNARD   632

Political Organization and Authority

by Talcott Parsons

IN CONSIDERING THE POLITICAL aspect of social structure, one is faced—as in the economic case, though not in that of stratification—with a plethora of materials from which to choose. In both the political and the economic cases, this situation is a result of the existence of social science disciplines which had become firmly established before sociology emerged, and developed a very important literature independent of sociology. We have touched on this literature at various points; but the present section is, with only two exceptions, confined to selections whose major direct reference is sociological. This decision is justified by our limited available space and by the extent to which political theory figures in our general historical prolegomena, as shown in Part One, Section A.

Orientation to the utilitarian-Marxist point of view is a major axis of organization for this Reader. One aspect of this tradition—that we deliberately use as a counterfoil—has been its allegedly "hard" and "realistic" emphasis on economic interest. The obverse is the tradition's utopian element—Locke's postulation of the "natural identity of interests," as Halevy called it, was an early version of this.[1] In its political context, this utopian element culminates in the Marxist doctrine of the "withering away of the state"—which had precedents in Godwinian "anarchism" and similar pre-Marxian movements. We have begun this section of selections with a violent contrast. First, we present the selection, from Lenin's *State and Revolution*, incorporating the doctrine of "withering away" in the strong form which has become canonical for the Communist movement. This

is followed by a selection from Pareto that—in this area, as distinct from the economic—presents a sharply "realistic" view of the inevitability of the use of force in social affairs. This juxtaposition presents the fundamental problem of the conditions of order. In modern thought, this problem's first classical formulation occurred in the conflict between Hobbes and Locke, as outlined above in the Introduction to Part One, Section A. In its relation to collective goal-attainment this is the fundamental setting of the political problem, viewed from our sociological perspective.

The questions of political equality, and of the senses in which various kinds of inequality are functional necessities, are involved deeply here. The so-called "élitist" theorists of the early twentieth century were especially concerned with the problem. The theme of the integration of the class structure with political authority and leadership was developed in a particularly well-rounded and sophisticated way by Mosca, whose analysis has been very influential in subsequent political thinking. The second selection relevant here is from Michels' book on political parties, stressing the oligarchic element existing in party leadership whatever the party's program. In general, these views were consequences of disillusionment with the more utopian convictions of the democratic liberalism of the intellectual circles of the political left in Europe during the later nineteenth century. They indicated important problems concerning the realistic structure of political systems as these were integrated with other elements of the social structure.

The second subsection is concerned less with the conflict between ideals of equality and the elements of political structure making for inequality; it is

---

1. In the interpretive literature on Marxism, the most insightful discussion of this component known to us is by Ernest Troeltsch, *Der Historismus und Seine Probleme* (Tübingen: J. C. B. Mohr), Chap. III, section 4.

more concerned with positive institutionalization in the area of political function. Much political theory has dealt with problems which, like that of "sovereignty," treat the direct relation of the individual to the state as a whole. However, the great German legal historian, Otto von Gierke, presented the classic analysis of the development of the corporation as a type of collectivity sanctioned in law, standing between the individual and the state, having privileges of acting responsibly in concert, holding property, etc. This indicates especially that many private and semi-public collectivities are not the atomistic associations of discrete individuals that much of utilitarian theory postulated. By the same token, the "state," conceived as the over-all collectivity structure of a society, is not a simple aggregation of individuals; but individuals' relations to the higher authorities are mediated by a complex network of more or less corporate subcollectivities.

Since all sophisticated law in the Western world is based on the Roman model, it is particularly important that Roman Law was, on normative grounds, hostile to corporate collectivities within the state that could possibly serve as a focus of alienation from over-all loyalty to the state—a hostility based on the pattern of the Greek *polis*. Gierke's most important direct contribution was showing how, in Europe, the corporate idea that derived from Germanic and feudal sources gradually attained a permanent place in the normative structure of Western society—a place which fundamentally distinguishes Western society from the society of classical antiquity. This emphasis is significant for the major theme of structural differentiation that has been one of our major guides in treating social morphology.

The last two selections in this section are chosen on the same principle as those dealing with the problem of inequality. The first, from Max Weber, concerns the broadest bases of the society-wide organization of political authority. The second, from Barnard, deals with the problem at the level of a more specific type of collectivity within the society.

Weber's classification of three major types of "authority" (in German, *legitime Herrschaft*) has probably influenced political science more than any other single contribution from sociology. Its primary theme concerns modes of legitimizing the right to make collective decisions which are binding on a societal collectivity as a whole. It fits in a comparative and in an evolutionary perspective. Weber did not himself fully clarify the status of these concepts—the three cases are not on the same level. Working out this problem is, however, the task of a generation of theorists later than Weber's. His classification has proved a focus for much fruitful comparative analysis and for integration with a variety of non-political phenomena.

The last selection is the chapter on authority from Chester I. Barnard's *Functions of the Executive*. Barnard was a business executive when he wrote it, and he refers primarily to business organizations. His analysis is, however, on such a general level that it presents a prototype for analyzing this problem, with special reference to the collectivity which, like those with which Gierke is concerned, stands between the individual and the state.

I–POWER AND INEQUALITY

---

1. *The Withering Away of the State*

BY NICOLAI LENIN

IN THE USUAL debates about the State, it is constantly forgotten that the destruction of the State involves also the destruction of democracy;

Reprinted from Nicolai Lenin, *State and Revolution,* trans. Moissaye J. Olgin (New York: International Publishers, 1932), chap. v, pp. 84–105, with the permission of International Publishers.

that the withering away of the State also means the withering away of Democracy. At first sight such a statement seems exceedingly strange and incomprehensible. Indeed, perhaps some one or other may begin to fear lest we be expecting the advent of such an order of society in which the principle of majority rule will not be respected—for is not a

Democracy just the recognition of this principle?

No, Democracy is not identical with majority rule. No, Democracy is a *State* which recognizes the subjection of the minority to the majority, that is, an organization for the systematic use of *violence* by one class against the other, by one part of the population against another.

We set ourselves, as our final aim, the task of the destruction of the State, that is, of every organized and systematic violence, every form of violence against man in general. We do not expect the advent of an order of society in which the principle of the submission of the minority to the majority will not be observed. But, striving for Socialism, we are convinced that it will develop further into Communism, and, side by side with this, there will vanish all need for force, for the *subjection* of one man to another, of one section of society to another, since people will *grow accustomed* to observing the elementary conditions of social existence *without force and without subjection.*

In order to emphasize this element of habit, Engels speaks of a *new* generation, "brought up under new and free social conditions which will prove capable of throwing on the dustheap all the useless old rubbish of State Organization"—*every* sort of State, including even the democratic republican State.

For the elucidation of this, we must examine the question of the economic foundations of the withering away of the State.

A most detailed elucidation of this question is given by Marx in his *Criticism of the Gotha Programme* (letter to Bracke, May 15th, 1875, printed as late as 1891 in the *Neue Zeit,* ix. 1). The polemical part of this remarkable work consisting of a criticism of Lassalleanism has, so to speak, overshadowed its positive part, namely the analysis of the connection between the development of Communism and the withering away of the State.

The Formulation of the Question by Marx

From a superficial comparison of the letter of Marx to Bracke (May 15th, 1875) with Engels' letter to Bebel (March 28th, 1875), discussed above, it might appear that Marx was much more of an upholder of the State than Engels, and that the difference of opinion between them on the question of the State is very considerable.

Engels suggests to Bebel that all the chatter about the State should be thrown overboard; that the word "State" should be eliminated from the programme and replaced by "Commonwealth"; Engels even declares that the Commune was really no longer a State in the proper sense of the word.

Whereas Marx even speaks of the "future State in Communist society," that is, apparently recognizing the necessity of a State even under Communism.

But such a view would be fundamentally incorrect; and a closer examination shows that Marx's and Engels' views on the State and its decay were completely identical, and that Marx's expression quoted above refers merely to the *decaying* State.

It is clear that there can be no question of defining the exact moment of the *future* "withering away"—the more so as it must obviously be a prolonged process. The apparent difference between Marx and Engels is due to the different subjects they dealt with, the different aims they were pursuing. Engels set forth the problem in a plain, bold, and large outline in order to show Bebel all the absurdity of the current superstitions concerning the State, shared to no small degree by Lassalle himself. Marx only touches upon *this* question in passing, being interested mainly in another subject—the *evolution* of Communist society. The whole theory of Marx is an application of the theory of evolution—in its most consistent, complete, well-thought-out and fruitful form—to modern Capitalism. Naturally, for Marx there arose the question of the application of this theory both to the *coming* crash of Capitalism and to the *future* development of *future* Communism.

On what foundation of facts can the future development of future Communism be based? It can be based on the fact that *it has its origin* in Capitalism, that it develops historically from Capitalism, that it is the result of the action of social forces to which Capitalism *has given birth.* There is no shadow of an attempt on Marx's part to fabricate a Utopia, idly to guess that which cannot be known. Marx treats the question of Communism in the same way as a naturalist would treat the question of the development of, say, a new biological variety, if he knew that such and such was its origin, and such and such is the direction in which it changes its form.

Marx, first of all, brushes aside the confusion which is introduced by the Gotha programme into the question of the mutual relations of State and of Society.

Contemporary society, [he writes] is capitalist society, which exists in all civilized countries, freed, to a greater or lesser extent, from admixture of mediaevalism, more or less varying in type according to the peculiar historical conditions of development of each country, more or less fully developed. The "contemporary State," on the contrary, varies with every State boundary. In the Prusso-German Empire it is quite a different thing from that in Switzerland; in

582 Part Two, Sec. D—Political Organization and Authority

England quite different from that in the United States. The "contemporary State" is, therefore a fiction.

"However, in spite of the motley variety of their forms, the different forms of the State in the different civilized countries have this in common—they are all based on contemporary bourgeois society, more or less capitalistically developed. They have, therefore, certain fundamental traits in common. In this sense one can speak of the "contemporary State" in contradistinction to that future time when its present root, namely, capitalist society, will have perished.

"The question is then put thus: To what transformation will the forms of government be subjected in communist society? In other words, what social functions will there remain, then, analogous to the present functions of the State? This question can only be answered with the help of the scientific method; and however many thousands of times the word "people" is combined with the word "State," this will not bring us one iota nearer its solution. . . .

Having thus ridiculed all the talk of a "People's State," Marx formulates the question and warns us, as it were, that for a scientific answer to it one can only rely on firmly established scientific facts.

The first fact that has been established with complete exactness by the whole theory of evolution, indeed, by the whole of science—a fact which the utopians forgot, however, and which is now forgotten by the present Opportunists, afraid of the Socialist revolution—is that, historically, there must undoubtedly be a special stage or epoch of *transition* from Capitalism to Communism.

The Transition from Capitalism to Communism

Between capitalist and communist society, [Marx continues] there lies a period of revolutionary transformation from the former to the latter. A stage of political transition corresponds to this period, and the State during this period can be no other than the *revolutionary dictatorship of the proletariat.*

This conclusion Marx bases on an analysis of the role played by the proletariat in modern capitalist society, on the facts of the development of this society and on the irreconcilability of the antagonistic interests of the proletariat and the capitalist class.

Earlier the question was put thus: To attain its emancipation the proletariat must overthrow the capitalist class, conquer political power and establish its own revolutionary dictatorship. Now the question is put somewhat differently: The transition from capitalist society developing towards Communism, to a communist Society, is impossible without a period of "political transition," and the State in this period can only be the revolutionary dictatorship of the proletariat.

What, then, is the relation of this dictatorship to democracy?

We saw that the *Communist Manifesto* simply places side by side the two ideas: the "conversion of the proletariat into the ruling class" and the "conquest of Democracy." On the basis of all that has been said above, one can define more exactly how democracy changes in the transition from Capitalism to Communism.

In capitalist society, under the conditions most favorable to its development, we have a more or less complete democracy in the form of a democratic republic. But this democracy is always bound by the narrow framework of capitalist exploitation, and, consequently, always remains, in reality, a democracy only for the minority, only for the possessing classes, only for the rich. Freedom in capitalist society always remains more or less the same as it was in the ancient Greek republics, that is, freedom for the slave owners. The modern wage-slaves, in virtue of the conditions of capitalist exploitation, remain to such an extent crushed by want and poverty that they "cannot be bothered with democracy," have "no time for politics"; that, in the ordinary peaceful course of events, the majority of the population is debarred from participating in public political life.

The accuracy of this statement is perhaps most clearly proved by Germany, just because in this state constitutional legality has lasted and remained stable for a remarkably long time—for nearly half a century (1871–1914); and the Social-Democracy during this time has been able, far better than has been the case in other countries, to make use of "legality" in order to organize into a political party a larger proportion of the working class than has occurred anywhere else in the world.

What, then, is this highest proportion of politically conscious, and active wage-slaves that has so far been observed in capitalist society? One million members of the Social-Democratic Party out of fifteen millions of wage-workers! Three millions industrially organized out of fifteen millions!

Democracy for an insignificant minority, democracy for the rich—that is the democracy of capitalist society. If we look more closely into the mechanism of capitalist democracy, everywhere—in the so-called "petty" details of the suffrage (the residential qualification, the exclusion of women, etc.), in the technique of the representative institutions, in the actual obstacles to the right of meeting (public buildings are not for the "poor"), in the purely capitalist organization of the daily press, etc., etc.—on all sides we shall see restrictions upon restrictions of Democracy. These restrictions, exceptions, exclusions, obstacles for the poor, seem light—especially in the eyes of one who has himself never known want, and has never lived in close contact with the oppressed classes in their herd life, and nine-tenths, if not ninety-nine hundredths, of the bourgeois publicists and politicians are of this class! But in their sum these restrictions exclude and thrust out the poor from politics and from an active share in democracy. Marx splendidly grasped the *essence* of capitalist democracy, when, in his analysis of the experience of the Commune, he said that the oppressed are allowed, once every few years, to decide which particular representatives of the oppressing class are to represent and repress them in Parliament!

But from this capitalist democracy—inevitably narrow, stealthily thrusting aside the poor, and therefore to its core, hypocritical and treacherous—progress does not march along a simple, smooth and direct path to "greater and greater democracy," as the Liberal professors and the lower middle-class Opportunists would have us believe. No, progressive development—that is, towards Communism—marches through the dictatorship of the proletariat; and cannot do otherwise, for there is no one else who can *break the resistance* of the exploiting capitalists, and no other way of doing it.

And the dictatorship of the proletariat—that is, the organization of the advance-guard of the oppressed as the ruling class, for the purpose of crushing the oppressors—cannot produce merely an expansion of democracy. *Together* with an immense expansion of democracy—for the first time becoming democracy for the poor, democracy for the people, and not democracy for the rich folk—the dictatorship of the proletariat will produce a series of restrictions of liberty in the case of the oppressors, exploiters and capitalists. We must crush them in order to free humanity from wage-slavery; their resistance must be broken by force. It is clear that where there is suppression there most also be violence, and there cannot be liberty or democracy.

Engels expressed this splendidly in his letter to Bebel when he said, as the reader will remember, that "the proletariat needs the State, not in the interests of liberty, but for the purpose of crushing its opponents; and, when one will be able to speak of freedom, the State will have ceased to exist."

Democracy for the vast majority of the nation, and the suppression by force—that is, the exclusion from democracy—of the exploiters and oppressors of the nation: this is the modification of democracy which we shall see during the *transition* from Capitalism to Communism.

Only in Communist Society, when the resistance of the capitalists has finally been broken, when the

capitalists have disappeared, when there are no longer any classes (that is, when there is no difference between the members of society in respect of their social means of production), *only then* "does the State disappear *and one can speak of freedom.*" Only then will be possible and will be realized a really full democracy, a democracy without any exceptions. And only then will democracy itself begin to wither away in virtue of the simple fact that, freed from capitalist slavery, from the innumerable horrors, savagery, absurdities and infamies of capitalist exploitation, people will gradually *become accustomed* to the observation of the elementary rules of social life, known for centuries, repeated for thousands of years in all sermons. They will become accustomed to their observance without force, without constraint, without subjection, without the *special apparatus* for compulsion which is called the State.

The expression "the State withers away," is very well chosen, for it indicates the gradual and elemental nature of the process. Only habit can, and undoubtedly will, have such an effect: for we see around us millions of times how readily people get accustomed to observe the necessary rules of life in common, if there is no exploitation, if there is nothing that causes indignation, that calls forth protest and revolt and has to be suppressed.

Thus, in capitalist society, we have a democracy that is curtailed, wretched, false; a democracy only for the rich, for the minority. The dictatorship of the proletariat, the period of transition to Communism, will, for the first time, produce a democracy for the people, for the majority, side by side with the necessary suppression of the minority constituted by the exploiters. Communism alone is capable of giving a really complete democracy, and the fuller it is the more quickly will it become unnecessary and wither away of itself. In other words, under Capitalism we have a State in the proper sense of the word: that is, a special instrument for the suppression of one class by another, and of the majority by the minority at that. Naturally, for the successful discharge of such a task as the systematic suppression by the minority of exploiters of the majority of exploited, the greatest ferocity and savagery of suppression is required, and seas of blood are needed, through which humanity has to direct its path, in a condition of slavery, serfdom and wage labor.

Again, during the *transition* from Capitalism to Communism, suppression is *still* necessary; but in this case it is the suppression of the minority of exploiters by the majority of exploited. A special instrument, a special machine for suppression—that is, the "State"—is necessary, but this is now a transitional State, no longer a State in the ordinary sense of the term. For the suppression of the minority of exploiters by the majority of those who were *but yesterday* wage slaves, is a matter comparatively so easy, simple and natural that it will cost far less bloodshed than the suppression of the risings of the slaves, serfs or wage laborers, and will cost the human race far less. And it is compatible with the diffusion of democracy over such an overwhelming majority of the nation that the need for any *special machinery* for suppression will gradually cease to exist. The exploiters are unable, of course, to suppress the people without a most complex machine for performing this duty; but *the people* can suppress the exploiters even with a very simple "machine"—almost without any "machine" at all, without any special apparatus— by the simple *organization of the armed masses* (such as the Councils of Workers' and Soldiers' Deputies, we may remark, anticipating a little).

Finally, only under Communism will the State become quite unnecessary, for there will be *no one* to suppress—"no one" in the sense of a *class,* in the sense of a systematic struggle with a definite section of the population. We are not utopians, and we do not in the least deny the possibility and inevitability of excesses by *individual persons,* and equally the need to suppress such excesses. But, in the first place, for this no special machine, no special instrument of repression is needed. This will be done by the armed nation itself, as simply and as readily as any crowd of civilized people, even in modern society, parts a pair of combatants or does not allow a woman to be outraged. And, secondly, we know that the fundamental social cause of excesses which violate the rules of social life is the exploitation of the masses, their want and their poverty. With the removal of this chief cause, excesses will inevitably begin to "wither away." We do not know how quickly and in what stages, but we know that they will be withering away. With their withering away, the State will also wither away. Marx, without plunging into Utopia, defined more fully what can *now* be defined regarding this future epoch: namely, the difference between the higher and lower phases (degrees, stages) of Communist society.

The First Phase of Communist Society

In the *Criticism of the Gotha Programme* Marx disproves in detail the Lassallean idea of the receipt by the workers under Socialism of the "undiminished" or "full product of their labor." Marx shows that out of the whole of the social labor of society, it will be necessary to deduct a reserve fund, a fund for the expansion of industry, the replacement of "worn-out" machinery, and so on; then, also, out of the collective product, a fund for the expenses of management, for schools, hospitals, homes for the aged, and so forth.

Instead of the hazy, obscure, general phrase of Lassalle—"the full product of his labor for the worker"—Marx gives a sober estimate as to how exactly a Socialist society will have to manage its affairs. Marx takes up a *concrete* analysis of the conditions of life of a society in which there will be no capitalism, and says: "We have to deal here" (analyzing the programme of the Party), "not with a Communist society which has *developed* on its own foundations, but with one which has just *issued* actually from capitalist society, and which in consequence, in all respects—economic, moral, and intellectual—still bears the stamp of the old society, from the womb of which it came." And it is this Communist society—a society which has just come into the world out of the womb of Capitalism, and which, in all respects, bears the stamp of the old society—that Marx terms the first, or lower, phase of Communist society.

The means of production are now no longer the private property of individuals. The means of production belong to the whole of society. Every member of society, performing a certain part of socially-necessary labor, receives a certificate from society that he has done such and such a quantity of work. According to this certificate, he receives from the public stores of articles of consumption a corresponding quantity of products. After the deduction of that proportion of labor which goes into the public fund, every worker, therefore, receives from society as much as he has given it.

"Equality" seems to reign supreme. But when Lassalle, having in view such a social order (generally called "Socialism," but termed by Marx the first phase of Communism) speaks of this as "just distribution," and says that this is "the equal right of each to an equal share of the products of labor," Lassalle is mistaken, and Marxism explains his error.

Equal right [says Marx], we indeed have here; but it is *still* a "bourgeois right," which, like every right, *presupposes inequality.* Every "right" is an application of the *same* measure to *different* people who, as a matter of fact, are not similar and are not equal one to another; and, therefore, "equal right" is really a violation of equality, and an injustice. In effect, every man having done as much social labor as every other, receives an equal share of the social products (with the above-mentioned deductions). Notwithstanding this, different people are not equal to one another. One is strong, another is weak; one is married, the other is not. One has more children, another has less, and so on.

With equal labor [Marx concludes], and therefore with an equal share in the public stock of articles of consumption, one will, in reality, receive more than another, will find himself richer, and so on. To avoid all this, "rights," instead of being equal, should be unequal.

The first phase of Communism, therefore, still cannot produce justice and equality; differences, and unjust differences, in wealth will still exist, but the *exploitation* of one man by many, will have become impossible, because it will be impossible to seize as private property, the *means of production,* the factories, machines, land, and so on. While tearing to tatters Lassalle's small bourgeois, confused phrase about "equality" and "justice" *in general,* Marx at the same time shows the *line of development* of Communist society, which is forced at first to destroy *only* the "injustice" that the means of production are in the hands of private individuals. *It is not capable* of destroying at once the further injustice which is constituted by the distribution of the articles of consumption according to "work performed" (and not according to need).

The vulgar economists, including the bourgeois professors (such as "our" Tugan-Baranowsky), constantly reproach the Socialists with forgetting the inequality of mankind and with "dreaming" of destroying this inequality. Such a reproach, as we see, only proves the extreme ignorance of the bourgeois ideologists.

Marx not only, with the greatest care, takes into account the inevitable inequalities of men; he also takes cognizance of the fact that the mere conversion of the means of production into the common property of the whole of society—"Socialism" in the generally accepted sense of the word—*does not remove* the shortcomings of distribution and the inequality of "bourgeois justice," which continue to exist as long as the products are divided according to the quantity of "work performed."

But these defects [Marx continues] are unavoidable in the first phase of Communist society, in the form in which it comes forth, after the prolonged travail of birth, from capitalist society. Justice can never be in advance of its stage of economic development, and of the cultural development of society conditioned by the latter.

And so, in the first phase of Communist society (generally called Socialism) "bourgeois justice" is *not* abolished in its entirety, but only in part, only in proportion to the economic transformation so far attained, that is, only in respect of the means of production. "Bourgeois law" recognizes them as the private property of separate individuals. Social-

ism converts them into common property, and to that extent and only to that extent, does "bourgeois law" die out. But it continues to live as far as its other part is concerned, in the capacity of regulator or adjuster dividing labor and allotting the products among the members of society.

"He who does not work neither shall he eat"—this Socialist principle is *already* realized. "For an equal quantity of labor an equal quantity of products"—this Socialist principle is also already realized. Nevertheless, this is not yet Communism, and this does not abolish "bourgeois law," which gives to unequal individuals, in return for an unequal (in reality) amount of work, an equal quantity of products.

This is a "defect," says Marx, but it is unavoidable during the first phase of Communism; for, if we are not to land in Utopia, we cannot imagine that, having overthrown Capitalism, people will at once learn to work for society *without any regulations by law;* indeed, the abolition of Capitalism does not *immediately* lay the economic foundations for such a change.

And there is no other standard yet than that of "bourgeois law." To this extent, therefore, a form of State is still necessary, which, while maintaining the public ownership of the means of production, preserves the equality of labor and equality in the distribution of the products. The State is withering away in so far as there are no longer any capitalists, any classes, and, consequently, any *class* whatever to suppress. But the State is not yet dead altogether, since there still remains the protection of "bourgeois law," which sanctifies actual inequality. For the complete extinction of the State complete Communism is necessary.

The Highest Phase of Communist Society

Marx continues:

In the highest phase of Communist society, after the disappearance of the enslavement of man caused by his subjection to the principle of division of labor; when, together with this, the opposition between brain and manual work will have disappeared; when labor will have ceased to be a mere means of supporting life and will itself have become one of the first necessities of life; when, with the all-round development of the individual, the productive forces, too, will have grown to maturity, and all the forces of social wealth will be pouring an uninterrupted torrent—only then will it be possible wholly to pass beyond the narrow horizon of bourgeois laws, and only then will Society be able to inscribe on its banner: "From each according to his ability; to each according to his needs."

Only now can we appreciate the full justice of Engels' observations when he mercilessly ridiculed all the absurdity of combining the words "freedom" and "State." While the State exists there can be no freedom. When there is freedom there will be no State.

The economic basis for the complete withering away of the State is that high stage of development of Communism when the distinction between brain and manual work disappears; consequently, when one of the principal sources of modern *social* inequalities will have vanished—a source, moreover, which it is impossible to remove immediately by the mere conversion of the means of production into public property, by the mere expropriation of the capitalists.

This expropriation will make it possible gigantically to develop the forces of production. And seeing how incredibly, even now, Capitalism *retards* this development, how much progress could be made even on the basis of modern technique at the level it has reached, we have a right to say, with the fullest confidence, that the expropriation of the capitalists will result inevitably in a gigantic development of the productive forces of human society. But how rapidly this development will go forward, how soon it will reach the point of breaking away from the division of labor, of the destruction of the antagonism between brain and manual work, of the transformation of work into a "first necessity of life"—this we do not and *cannot* know.

Consequently, we are right in speaking solely of the inevitable withering away of the State, emphasizing the protracted nature of this process, and its dependence upon the rapidity of development of the *higher phase* of Communism; leaving quite open the question of lengths of time, or the concrete forms of this withering away, since material for the solution of such questions is not available.

The State will be able to wither away completely when Society has realized the formula: "From each according to his ability; to each according to his needs"; that is, when people have become accustomed to observe the fundamental principles of social life, and their labor is so productive, that they will voluntarily work *according to their abilities*. "The narrow horizon of bourgeois law," which compels one to calculate, with the pitilessness of a Shylock, whether one has not worked half an hour more than another, whether one is not getting less pay than another—this narrow horizon will then be left behind. There will then be no need for any exact calculation by Society of the quantity of products to be distributed to each of its members; each will take freely "according to his needs."

From the capitalist point of view, it is easy to declare such a social order a "pure Utopia," and to sneer at the Socialists for promising each the right to receive from society, without any control of the labor of the individual citizens, any quantity of truffles, motor cars, pianos, and so forth. Even now, most bourgeois "*savants*" deliver themselves of such sneers, but thereby they only display at once their ignorance and their material interest in defending Capitalism. Ignorance—for it has never entered the head of any Socialist "to promise" that the highest phase of Communism will actually arrive, while the *anticipation* of the great Socialists that it *will* arrive, assumes *neither the present* productive powers of labor, *nor the present* unthinking "man in the street" capable of spoiling, without reflection, the stores of social wealth and of demanding the impossible. As long as the "highest" phase of Communism has not arrived, the Socialists demand the *strictest* control, *by Society and by the State,* of the quantity of labor and the quantity of consumption; only this control must *start* with the expropriation of the capitalists, with the control of the workers over the capitalists, and must be carried out, not by a Government of bureaucrats, but by a Government of the *armed workers*.

The interested defence of Capitalism by the capitalist ideologists (and their hangers-on like Tseretelli, Tchernoff and Co.) consists just in that they *substitute* their disputes and discussions about the far future for the essential, imperative questions *of the day*: the expropriation of the capitalists, the conversion of *all* citizens into workers and employees of *one* huge "syndicate"—the whole State —and the complete subordination of the whole of the work of this syndicate to a really democratic State—to the *State consisting of the Councils of Workers' and Soldiers' Deputies.* In reality, when a learned professor, and in his train, some philistine, and in his wake Messrs. Tseretelli and Tchernoff, talk of the unreasonable Utopias, of the demagogic promises of the Bolsheviks, of the impossibility of "bringing in" Socialism, it is the highest stage or phase of Communism which they have in mind, and which no one has not only not promised, but never even thought of trying to "bring in," because, in any case, it is altogether impossible to "bring it in."

And here we come to that question of the scientific difference between Socialism and Communism, upon which Engels touched in his discussion cited above on the incorrectness of the name "Social Democrat." The political difference between the first, or lower, and the higher phase of Communism will in time, no doubt, be tremendous; but it would be ridiculous to emphasize it now, under Capitalism, and only, perhaps, some isolated Anarchist could invest it with primary importance,—that is, if there are still people among the Anarchists who have learned nothing from the Plekhanoff-like conversion of the Kropotkins, the Graves, the Cornelisens, and other "leading lights" of Anarchism to Social-Chauvinism or Anarcho-*Jusquauboutism* as one of the few Anarchists still preserving their honor (Gay) has expressed it.

But the scientific difference between Socialism and Communism is clear. That which is generally called Socialism is termed by Marx the first or lower phase of Communist society. In so far as the means of production become public property, the word Communism is also applicable here, providing that we do not forget that it is not full Communism. The great importance of Marx's explanation is this: that here, too, he consistently applies materialist dialectics, the theory of evolution, looking upon Communism as something which evolves *out* of Capitalism.

Instead of artificially elaborate and scholastic definitions and profitless disquisitions on the meanings of words ("what Socialism is," "what Communism is"), Marx gives us an analysis of what may be called the stages in the economic growth of Communism.

In its first phase or first stage Communism *cannot* as yet be economically mature and quite free of all tradition and of all taint of Capitalism. Hence we see the interesting phenomenon of the first phase of Communism retaining "the narrow horizon of bourgeois law." Bourgeois law, in respect of the distribution of articles of consumption, presupposes inevitably the capitalist State, for law is nothing without the organization for *forcing* people to obey it. Consequently, for a certain time not only bourgeois law, but even the capitalist State may remain under Communism without the capitalist class.

This may appear to some a paradox, a piece of intellectual subtlety, of which Marxism is often accused by people who would not put themselves out to study its extraordinarily profound teachings. But, as a matter of fact, the Old surviving in the New confronts us in life at every step in nature as well as in Society. It is not Marx's own sweet will which smuggled a scrap of bourgeois law into Communism; he simply indicated what is economically and politically inevitable in a society issuing from the *womb of Capitalism*.

Democracy is of great importance in the working-class struggle for freedom against the capitalists. But Democracy is not a limit one may not overstep; it is merely one of the stages in the course of development from Feudalism to Capitalism, and from Capitalism to Communism.

Democracy implies equality. The immense significance of the struggle of the proletariat for equality and the power of attraction of such a battle-cry are obvious, if we but rightly interpret it as meaning the *annihilation of classes*. But the equality of Democracy is *formal* equality—no more; and immediately after the attainment of the equality of all members of society in respect to the ownership of the means of production, that is, of equality of labor and equality of wages, there will inevitably arise before humanity the question of going further from equality which is formal to equality which is real, and of realizing in life the formula "From each according to his ability; to each according to his needs." By what stages, by means of what practical measures humanity will proceed to this higher aim —this we do not and cannot know. But it is important that one should realize how infinitely mendacious is the usual capitalist representation of Socialism as something lifeless, petrified, fixed once for all. In reality, it is *only* with Socialism that there will commence a rapid, genuine, real mass advance, in which first the majority and then the *whole* of the population will take part—an advance in all domains of social and individual life.

Democracy is a form of the State—one of the varieties of the State; and, consequently, like every State, it stands as an organized, systematic application of force against mankind. That is its one aspect. But, on the other hand, it is the formal recognition of the equality of all citizens, the equal right of all to determine the structure and administration of the State. Out of this formal recognition there arises, in its turn, a stage in the development of Democracy, when it first rallies the proletariat as a revolutionary class against Capitalism, and gives it an opportunity to crush, to break to atoms, to wipe off the face of the earth the capitalist government machine—even the republican variety: the standing army, police, and bureaucracy. Second, it enables it to substitute for all this a more democratic, but still a *State* machinery in the shape of armed masses of the working class, which then become transformed into a universal participation of the people in a militia.

Here "quantity passes into quality." Such a degree of Democracy carries with it the abandonment of the framework of capitalist society, and the beginning of its Socialist reconstruction. If *everyone really* takes part in the administration of the State, Capitalism cannot retain its hold. As a matter of fact, Capitalism as it develops, itself prepares the ground for everyone to be able really to take part in the administration of the State.

We may class as part of this preparation of the ground the universal literacy of the population, already realized in most of the more progressive capitalist countries; then the education and discipline inculcated upon millions of workers by the huge, complex, and socialized apparatus of the post, railways, big factories, large-scale commerce, banking, and so on, and so forth.

With such an *economic* groundwork it is quite possible, immediately, within twenty-four hours, to pass to the overthrow of the capitalists and bureaucrats, and to replace them, in the control of production and distribution, in the business of apportioning labor and products, by the armed workers, or the people in arms. The question of control and book-keeping must not be confused with the question of the scientifically educated staff of engineers, agriculturists, and so on. These gentlemen work today owing allegiance to the capitalists: they will work even better tomorrow, owing it to the armed workers. Book-keeping and control—these are the chief things necessary for the smooth and correct functioning of the *first phase* of Communist society. *All* the citizens are here transformed into the hired employees of the State, which then is the armed workers. *All* citizens become the employees and workers of *one* national *State* "syndicate." It simply resolves itself into a question of all working to an equal extent, of all carrying out regularly the measure of work apportioned to them, and of all receiving equal pay.

The book-keeping and control necessary for this have been simplified by capitalism to the utmost, till they have become the extraordinarily simple operations of watching, recording, and issuing receipts, within the reach of anybody who can read and write and knows the first four arithmetical rules. (When most of the functions of the State are reduced to this book-keeping and control by the workers themselves it ceases to be a "political" State. Then "the public functions are converted from political into simple administrative functions.") When the majority of the citizens themselves begin everywhere to keep such accounts and maintain such control over the capitalists, now converted into employees, and over the intellectual gentry, who still retain capitalist habits, this control will, indeed, become universal, pervading, rational: it will be ubiquitous, and there will be no way of escaping it.

The whole of society will have become one office and one factory, with equal work and equal pay. But this "factory" discipline, which the proletariat will extend to the whole of society on the defeat of Capitalism and the overthrow of the exploiters, is by no means our ideal, and is far from our final aim. It is but a foothold as we press on to the radical cleansing of society from all the brutality and foulness of capitalist exploitation: we leave it behind as we move on.

When all, or be it even only the greater part of society, have learnt how to govern the State, have taken this business into their own hands, have established a control over the insignificant minority of capitalists, over the gentry with capitalist leanings, and workers thoroughly demoralized by capitalism —from this moment the need for any government begins to vanish. The more complete the Democracy, the nearer the moment when it ceases to be necessary. The more democratic the "State" consisting of armed workers, which is "no longer really a State in the ordinary sense of the term," the more rapidly does every form of the State begin to decay. For when all have learnt to manage, and really do manage, socialized production, when all really do keep account and control of the idlers, gentlefolk, swindlers, and suchlike "guardians of capitalist traditions," the escape from such general registration and control will inevitably become so increasingly difficult, so much the exception, and will probably be accompanied by such swift and severe punishment (for the armed workers are very practical people, not sentimental intellectuals, and they will scarcely allow anyone to trifle with them), that very soon the *necessity* of observing the simple, fundamental rules of any kind of social life will become a habit. The door will then be wide open for the transition from the first phase of Communist society to its second and higher phase, and along with it to the complete withering away of the State.

2. *The Use of Force in Society*

BY VILFREDO PARETO

2170. Societies in general subsist because alive and vigorous in the majority of their constituent members are sentiments corresponding to residues of sociality. But there are also individuals in human societies in whom some at least of those sentiments are weak or indeed actually missing. That fact has two interesting consequences which stand in apparent contradiction, one of them threatening the dissolution of a society, the other making for its progress in civilization. What at bottom is there is continuous movement, but it is a movement that may progress in almost any direction.

2171. It is evident that if the requirement of uniformity were so strongly active in all individuals in a given society as to prevent even one of them from breaking away in any particular from the uniformities prevalent in it, such a society would have no internal causes for dissolution; but neither would it have any causes for change, whether in the direction of an increase, or of a decrease, in the utility of the individuals or of the society. On the other hand if the requirement of uniformity were to fail, society would not hold together, and each individual would go on his own way, as lions and tigers, birds of prey, and other animals do. Societies that endure and change are therefore situated in some intermediate condition between those two extremes.

2172. A homogeneous society might be imagined in which the requirement of uniformity would be the same in all individuals, and would correspond to the intermediate state just mentioned. But observation shows that that is not the case with human societies. Human societies are essentially heterogeneous, and the intermediate state is attained because the requirement of uniformity is very strong in some individuals, moderately strong in others, very feeble in still others, and almost entirely absent in a few. The average is found not in each individual, but in the group comprising them all. One may add as a datum of fact that the number of individuals in whom the requirement of uniformity is stronger than the average requisite of the intermedi-

ate state in which the society is situated is much greater than the number of individuals in whom the requirement is weaker than that average, and very very much greater than the number in whom it is entirely missing.

2173. For the reader who has followed us thus far it is needless to add that, in view of the effects of this greater or lesser potency of the sentiments of uniformity, one may foresee out of hand that two theologies will put in an appearance, one of which will glorify the immobility of one or another uniformity, real or imaginary, the other of which will glorify movement, progress, in one direction or another. That is what has actually happened in history. There have been popular Olympuses where the gods fixed and determined once and for all how human society was to be; and then, too, Olympuses of utopian reformers, who derived from their exalted minds conceptions of forms from which human society was never more to deviate. On the other hand from the days of ancient Athens down to our own, the lord gods of Movement in a Certain Direction have listened to the prayers of their faithful and now sit triumphant in our latter-day Olympus, where Progress Optimus Maximus reigns in sovereign majesty. So that intermediate situation of society has usually been attained as the resultant of many forces, prominent among them the two categories mentioned, which envisage different imaginary goals and correspond to different classes of residues.

2174. To ask whether or not force ought to be used in a society, whether the use of force is or is not beneficial, is to ask a question that has no meaning; for force is used by those who wish to preserve certain uniformities and by those who wish to overstep them; and the violence of the ones stands in contrast and in conflict with the violence of the others. In truth, if a partisan of a governing class disavows the use of force, he means that he disavows the use of force by insurgents trying to escape from the norms of the given uniformity. On the other hand, if he says he approves of the use of force, what he really means is that he approves of the use of force by the public authority to constrain insurgents to conformity. Conversely, if a partisan of the subject class says he detests the use of force

Reprinted from Vilfredo Pareto, *The Mind and Society*. ed. Arthur Livingston, trans. Andrew Bongiorno and Arthur Livingston (New York: Harcourt, Brace & Co., 1935) Vol. IV, §§ 2170–75, 2179–220, with the permission of The Pareto Fund.

in society, what he really detests is the use of force by constituted authorities in forcing dissidents to conform; and if, instead, he lauds the use of force, he is thinking of the use of force by those who would break away from certain social uniformities.

2175. Nor is there any particular meaning in the question as to whether the use of violence to enforce existing uniformities is beneficial to society, or whether it is beneficial to use force in order to over-step them; for the various uniformities have to be distinguished to see which of them are beneficial and which deleterious to society. Nor, indeed, is that enough; for it is further necessary to determine whether the utility of the uniformity is great enough to offset the harm that will be done by using violence to enforce it, or whether detriment from the uni-formity is great enough to overbalance the damage that will be caused by the use of force in subverting it; in which detriment and damage we must not for-get to reckon the very serious drawback involved in the anarchy that results from any frequent use of violence to abolish existing uniformities, just as among the benefits and utilities of maintaining frankly injurious uniformities must be counted the strength and stability they lend to the social order. So, to solve the problem as to the use of force, it is not enough to solve the other problem as to the utility, in general, of certain types of social organi-zation; it is essential also and chiefly to compute all the advantages and all the drawbacks, direct and in-direct. Such a course leads to the solution of a scien-tific problem; but it may not be and oftentimes is not the course that leads to an increase in social utility. It is better, therefore, if it be followed only by peo-ple who are called upon to solve a scientific problem or, to some limited extent, by certain individuals belonging to the ruling class; whereas social utility is oftentimes best served if the members of the sub-ject class, whose function is not to lead but to act, accept one of the two theologies according to the case—either the theology that enjoins preservation of existing uniformities, or the theology that coun-sels change.

2178. What now are the correlations that subsist between this method of applying force and other social facts? We note, as usual, a sequence of actions and reactions, in which the use of force appears now as cause, now as effect. As regards the governing class, one gets, in the main, five groups of facts to consider: 1. A mere handful of citizens, so long as they are willing to use violence, can force their will upon public officials who are not inclined to meet violence with equal violence. If the reluctance of the officials to resort to force is primarily motivated by humanitarian sentiments, that result ensues very readily; but if they refrain from violence because

they deem it wiser to use some other means, the effect is often the following: 2. To prevent or resist violence, the governing class resorts to "diplomacy," fraud, corruption—governmental authority passes, in a word, from the lions to the foxes. The governing class bows its head under the threat of violence, but it surrenders only in appearances, trying to turn the flank of the obstacle it cannot demolish in frontal attack. In the long run that sort of procedure comes to exercise a far-reaching influence on the selection of the governing class, which is now recruited only from the foxes, while the lions are blackballed. The individual who best knows the arts of sapping the strength of the foes of "graft" and of winning back by fraud and deceit what seemed to have been sur-rendered under pressure of force, is now leader of leaders. The man who has bursts of rebellion, and does not know how to crook his spine at the proper times and places, is the worst of leaders, and his presence is tolerated among them only if other dis-tinguished endowments offset that defect. 3. So it comes about that the residues of the combination-instinct (Class I) are intensified in the governing class, and the residues of group-persistence debili-tated; for the combination-residues supply, pre-cisely, the artistry and resourcefulness required for evolving ingenious expedients as substitutes for open resistance, while the residues of group-persist-ence stimulate open resistance, since a strong senti-ment of group-persistence cures the spine of all tendencies to curvature. 4. Policies of the governing class are not planned too far ahead in time. Predom-inance of the combination instincts and enfeeble-ment of the sentiments of group-persistence result in making the governing class more satisfied with the present and less thoughtful of the future. The individual comes to prevail, and by far, over family, community, nation. Material interests and interests of the present or a near future come to prevail over the ideal interests of community or nation and in-terests of the distant future. The impulse is to enjoy the present without too much thought for the mor-row. 5. Some of these phenomena become observ-able in international relations as well. Wars become essentially economic. Efforts are made to avoid con-flicts with the powerful and the sword is rattled only before the weak. Wars are regarded more than any-thing else as speculations. A country is often un-wittingly edged towards war by nursings of eco-nomic conflicts which, it is expected, will never get out of control and turn into armed conflicts. Not seldom, however, a war will be forced upon a country by peoples who are not so far advanced in the evolution that leads to the predominance of Class I residues.

2179. As regards the subject class, we get the following relations, which correspond in part to the preceding: 1. When the subject class contains a number of individuals disposed to use force and with capable leaders to guide them, the governing class is, in many cases, overthrown and another takes its place. That is easily the case where governing classes are inspired by humanitarian sentiments primarily, and very very easily if they do not find ways to assimilate the exceptional individuals who come to the front in the subject classes. A humanitarian aristocracy that is closed or stiffly exclusive represents the maximum of insecurity. 2. It is far more difficult to overthrow a governing class that is adept in the shrewd use of chicanery, fraud, corruption; and in the highest degree difficult to overthrow such a class when it successfully assimilates most of the individuals in the subject class who show those same talents, are adept in those same arts, and might therefore become the leaders of such plebeians as are disposed to use violence. Thus left without leadership, without talent, disorganized, the subject class is almost always powerless to set up any lasting régime. 3. So the combination-residues (Class I) become to some extent enfeebled in the subject class. But that phenomenon is in no way comparable to the corresponding reinforcement of those same residues in the governing class; for the governing class, being composed, as it is, of a much smaller number of individuals, changes considerably in character from the addition to it or withdrawal from it of relatively small numbers of individuals; whereas shifts of identical numbers produce but slight effects in the enormously greater total of the subject class. For that matter the subject class is still left with many individuals possessed of combination-instincts that are applied not to politics or activities connected with politics but to arts and trades independent of politics. That circumstance lends stability to societies, for the governing class is required to absorb only a small number of new individuals in order to keep the subject class deprived of leadership. However, in the long run the differences in temperament between the governing class and the subject class become gradually accentuated, the combination-instincts tending to predominate in the ruling class, and instincts of group-persistence in the subject class. When that difference becomes sufficiently great, revolution occurs. 4. Revolution often transfers power to a new governing class, which exhibits a reinforcement in its instincts of group-persistence and so adds to its designs of present enjoyment aspirations towards ideal enjoyments presumably attainable at some future time—scepticism in part gives way to faith. 5. These considerations must to some extent be applied to international relations. If the combination-instincts are reinforced in a given country beyond a certain limit, as compared with the instincts of group-persistence, that country may be easily vanquished in war by another country in which that change in relative proportions has not occurred. The potency of an ideal as a pilot to victory is observable in both civil and international strife. People who lose the habit of applying force, who acquire the habit of considering policy from a commercial standpoint and of judging it only in terms of profit and loss, can readily be induced to purchase peace; and it may well be that such a transaction taken by itself is a good one, for war might have cost more money than the price of peace. Yet experience shows that in the long run, and taken in connexion with the things that inevitably go with it, such practice leads a country to ruin. The combination-instincts rarely come to prevail in the whole of a population. More commonly that situation arises in the upper strata of society, there being few if any traces of it in the lower and more populous classes. So when a war breaks out one gazes in amazement on the energies that are suddenly manifested by the masses at large, something that could in no way have been foreseen by studying the upper classes only. Sometimes, as happened in the case of Carthage, the burst of energy may not be sufficient to save a country, because a war may have been inadequately prepared for and be incompetently led by the ruling classes, and soundly prepared for and wisely led by the ruling classes of the enemy country. Then again, as happened in the wars of the French Revolution, the energy in the masses may be great enough to save a country because, though the war may have been badly prepared for by its ruling classes, preparations and leadership have been even worse in the ruling classes of the enemy countries, a circumstance that gives the constituent members of the lower strata of society time to drive their ruling class from power and replace it with another of greater energy and possessing the instincts of group-persistence in greater abundance. Still again, as happened in Germany after the disaster at Jena, the energy of the masses may spread to the higher classes and spur them to an activity that proves most effective as combining able leadership with enthusiastic faith.

2180. These, then, are the main, the outstanding phenomena, but other phenomena of secondary or incidental importance also figure. Notable among such is the fact that if a ruling class is unable or unwilling or incompetent to use force to eradicate violations of uniformities in private life, anarchic action on the part of the subject class tends to make up for the deficiency. It is well known to history that the private vendetta languishes or recurs in proportion as public authority continues or ceases to replace it. It has been seen to recur in the form of lynchings in the United States, and even in Europe. Whenever the influence of public authority declines, little states grow up within the state, little societies within society. So, whenever judicial process fails, private or group justice replaces it, and *vice versa*. In international relations, the tinselling of humanitarian and ethical declamation is just a dressing for an underlying force. The Chinese considered themselves the superiors in civilization of the Japanese, and perhaps they were, but they lacked a military aptitude that the Japanese, in virtue of a surviving remnant of feudal "barbarism," possessed in abundance. So the poor Chinese were attacked by hordes of Europeans—whose exploits in China, as Sorel well says, remind one of the feats of the Spanish *conquistadores* in the Americas. They suffered murder, rapine, and pillage at European hands, and then paid an indemnity into the bargain; whereas the Japanese came off victorious over the Russians and now exact respect from everybody. A few centuries back, the subtle diplomacy of the Christian lords of Constantinople did not save them from ruin under the impact of the fanaticism and might of the Turks; and now, in this year 1913, on the very same spot, the victors show that they have deteriorated in their fanaticism and in their power and, in their turn reposing illusory hopes in the diplomatic arts, are defeated and overthrown by the vigour of their sometime subjects. Grievous the hallucination under which those statesmen labour who imagine that they can replace the use of force with unarmed law. Among the many examples that one might point to are Sulla's constitution in ancient Rome and the conservative constitution of the Third Republic in France. Sulla's constitution fell because the armed force that might have compelled respect for it was not maintained. The constitution of Augustus endured because his successors were in a position to rely on the might of the legions. When the Commune had been defeated and overthrown, Thiers decided that his government ought to find its support rather in the law than in armed force. As a result his laws were scattered like leaves before the hurricane of democratic plutocracy. We need say nothing of Louis XVI of France, who thought he could halt the Revolution with his royal veto, for his was the illusion of a spineless weakling who was soon to lose what little head he had.

2181. All such facts as a rule present themselves in the guise of derivations. In one direction we get theories that condemn the use of violence by the subject class in whatever case, in the other direction theories that censure its use by public authority.

2182. Ruling-class theories, when the requirement of logic is not too keenly felt, appeal simply to sentiments of veneration for holders of power, or for abstractions such as "the state," and to sentiments of disapprobation for individuals who try to disturb or subvert existing orders (§ 2192). Then when it is deemed advisable to satisfy the need of logic, the effort is to create a confusion between the violation of an established uniformity for the individual's exclusive profit and a violation designed to further some collective interest or some new uniformity. The aim in such a derivation is to carry over to the social or political act the reprobation that is generally visited upon common crime. Frequent in our day are reasonings in some way connected with the theology of Progress. Not a few of our modern governments have revolutionary origins. How condemn the revolutions that might be tried against them without repudiating the forefathers? That is attended to by invoking a new divine right: Insurrection was legitimate enough against governments of the past, where authority was based on force; it is not legitimate against modern governments, where the authority is based on "reason." Or else: Insurrection was legitimate against kings and oligarchies; it is never legitimate against "the People." Or again: Rebellion is justifiable where there is no universal suffrage, but not where that panacea is the law of the land. Or again: Revolt is useless and therefore reprehensible in all countries where "the People" are able to express their "will." Then finally—just to give some little satisfaction to their Graces, the Metaphysicists: Insurrection cannot be tolerated where a "state of law" exists. I hope I shall be excused if I do not define that very sweet entity here. For all of most painstaking researches on my part, it remains an entity altogether unknown to me, and I should much rather be asked to give the zoological pedigree of the Chimaera.

2183. Again as usual, no one of these derivations has any exact meaning. All governments use force, and all assert that they are founded on reason. In the fact, whether universal suffrage prevails or not, it is always an oligarchy that governs, finding ways to give to the "will of the people" that expression which the few desire, from the "royal law" that bestowed the *imperium* on the Roman Emperors down to the votes of a legislative majority elected in one way or another, from the plebiscite that gave the empire to Napoleon III down to the universal suffrage that is shrewdly bought, steered, and manipulated by our "speculators." Who is this new god called Universal Suffrage? He is no more exactly definable, no less shrouded in mystery, no less beyond the pale of reality, than the hosts of other divinities; nor are there fewer and less patent contradictions in his theology than in theirs. Worshippers of Universal Suffrage are not led by their god. It is they who lead him—and by the nose, determining the forms in which he must manifest himself. Oftentimes, proclaiming the sanctity of "majority rule," they resist "majority rule" by obstructionist tactics, even though they form but small minorities, and burning incense to the goddess Reason, they in no wise disdain, in certain cases, alliances with Chicanery, Fraud, and Corruption.

2184. Substantially such derivations express the sentiments felt by people who have climbed into the saddle and are willing to stay there—along with the far more general sentiment that social stability is a good thing. If, the moment a group, large or small, ceased to be satisfied with certain norms established in the community of which it is a part, it flew to arms to abolish them, organized society would fall to pieces. Social stability is so beneficial a thing that to maintain it it is well worth while to enlist the aid of fantastic ideals and this or that theology—among the others, the theology of universal suffrage—and be resigned to putting up with certain actual disadvantages. Before it becomes advisable to disturb the public peace, such disadvantages must have grown very very serious; and since human beings are effectively guided not by the sceptical reasonings of science but by "living faiths" expressed in ideals, theories such as the divine right of kings, the legitimacy of oligarchies, of "the people," of "majorities," of legislative assemblies, and other such things, may be useful within certain limits, and have in fact proved to be, however absurd they may be from the scientific standpoint.

2185. Theories designed to justify the use of force by the governed are almost always combined with theories condemning the use of force by the public authority. A few dreamers reject the use of force in general, on whatever side; but their theories either have no influence at all or else serve merely to weaken resistance on the part of people in power, so clearing the field for violence on the part of the governed. In view of that we may confine ourselves to considering such theories, in general, in the combined form.

2186. No great number of theories are required to rouse to resistance and to the use of force people who are, or think they are, oppressed. The derivations therefore are chiefly designed to incline people who would otherwise be neutral in the struggle to condemn resistance on the part of the governing powers, and so to make their resistance less vigorous; or at a venture, to persuade the rulers themselves in that sense, a thing, for that matter, that is not likely to have any great success in our day save with those whose spinal columns have utterly rotted from the bane of humanitarianism. A few centuries

ago some results might have been achieved in our Western countries by working with religious derivations upon sincere Christians; and, in other countries, by working upon firm believers with derivations of the religion prevailing in the given case. Since humanitarianism is a religion, like the Christian, the Moslem, or any other, we may say, in general, that one may sometimes secure the aid of neutrals and weaken resistance on the part of people in power by using derivations of the religion, whatever it may be, in which they sincerely believe. But since derivations readily lend themselves to proving the pro and contra, that device is often of scant effect even when it is not a mere mask for interests.

2187. In our times conflicts are chiefly economic. If a government therefore sets out to protect employers or strike-breakers from violence by strikers, it is accused of "interfering" in an economic matter that does not properly concern it. If the police do not allow their heads to be broken without using their weapons, they are said to have "shown poor judgment," to have acted "impulsively," "nervously." Like strike-breakers, they must be denied the right to use arms whenever they are attacked by strikers, for otherwise some striker might be killed, and the crime of assault, assuming but not conceding that there has been such a crime, does not deserve the penalty of death. Court decisions are impugned as "class decisions"; at any rate, they are always too severe. Amnesties, finally, must wipe out all remembrance of such unpleasantness. One might suppose that since the interests of employers and strike-breakers are directly contrary to the interests of the strikers, they would use the opposite derivations. But that is not the case, or if they do, they do it in a very mild, apologetic way. The reason is, as regards the "strike-breaker," the "scab," that he has, as a class, very little spirit. He is not inspired by any lofty ideal, he is almost ashamed of what he is doing, and does it with as little talk as possible. As regards employers of labour, the reason is that many of them are "speculators" who hope to make up for their losses in a strike through government aid and at the expense of consumer or taxpayer. Their quarrels with strikers are quarrels between accomplices over the division of the loot. The strikers belong to the masses, where there is a wealth of Class II residues. They have not only interests but ideals. Their "speculator" employers belong to a class that has grown rich in its aptitude for combinations. They are well supplied, over-supplied, with residues from Class I and so have interests chiefly, and few or no ideals. They spend their time in activities that are far more lucrative than the manufacture of theories. Among them are not a few plutocratic demagogues who are artists at the trick of turning to their advantage strikes that are in all appearances directed against them. There are general considerations, furthermore, that apply to both domestic and international conflicts. They come down, in brief, to an appeal to sentiments of pity for the sufferings that are caused by the use of force, disregarding entirely the reasons for which the force is used and the utility or the harm that results from using or not using it. They are often filled out with expressions of reverence, or at least of compassion, for the proletariat, which can never do wrong or at the very least is excusable for whatever it does. In a day gone by, similar derivations, corresponding to the very same sentiments, were used in favour now of royal, now of theocratic, now of aristocratic, rule.

2188. It is interesting, as in keeping with the essentially sentimental character of derivations, that theories that would be the soundest from the logico-experimental standpoint are as a rule neglected. In the Middle Ages an excellent argument might have been put forward in favour of the ecclesiastical power at a time when it was at war with imperial, royal, or baronial powers—the fact that it was virtually the only counterbalance to those other powers, and almost the only refuge of intelligence, science, and cultivation against ignorant brutal force. But that argument was seldom, if ever, used. People preferred to rely on derivations based on the doctrine of revelation and quotations from Scripture. Now employers who themselves enjoy economic protection manifest great indignation at strikers for trying to rid themselves of the competition of non-union workers. The rejoinder is never made that they are trying to keep others from doing what they are doing themselves, and that they fail to show how and why free competition is good for the workingman and bad for the employer of labour. An individual tries to slip across the Italian frontier with a few bags of saccharin. Customs officers come running and violently prevent such competition with Italian manufacturers of beet-sugar, going, on occasion, so far as to use their guns and sometimes to kill the smuggler whom nobody mourns. All the same it is owing to just such violence and such murders that now a few Italian "sugar men" have managed to amass considerable fortunes and win public esteem, national honours, and even seats among the law-makers. One still has to be shown why violence cannot be used in the same way to increase wages.

2189. It may be objected that the violence that safe-guards the interests of the employer is legal and the violence used by the strikers on "scabs" illegal. That transfers the question from the utility of the violence to the utility of the manner in which violence is applied—a matter of considerable importance, no one will deny. Legal violence is the consequence of the norms established in a society, and in general resort to it is more beneficial or at least less harmful than resort to private violence, which is designed as a rule to overthrow prevailing norms. The strikers might answer, and in fact sometimes do, that they are using illegal violence because they are cut off from using the legal variety. If the law were to constrain people by use of legal violence to give them what they demand, they would not need to resort to illegal violence. The same argument would serve in many other cases. People who use illegal violence would ask for nothing better than to be able to transmute it into legal violence.

2190. But the matter is not yet exhausted, and we now come to the salient point in question. Let us set the particular case aside and look at the problem in its general form. The dispute is really as to the relative merits of shrewdness and force, and to decide it in the sense that never, not even in the exceptional case, is it useful to meet wits with violence, it would be necessary first to show that the use of cunning is always, without exception, more advisable than the use of force. Suppose a certain country has a governing class, A, that assimilates the best elements, as regards intelligence, in the whole population. In that case the subject class, B, is largely stripped of such elements and can have little or no hope of ever overcoming the class A so long as it is a battle of wits. If intelligence were to combine with force, the dominion of the A's would be perpetual, for as Dante says, *Inferno*, XXXVI, vv. 55–57 (Fletcher translation):

> "For if the machination of the mind
> To evil-will be added and to might,
> Of no defence is competent mankind."

But such a happy combination occurs only for a few individuals. In the majority of cases people who rely on their wits are or become less fitted to use violence, and *vice versa*. So concentration in the class A of the individuals most adept at chicanery leads to a concentration in class B of the individuals most adept at violence; and if that process is long continued, the equilibrium tends to become unstable, because the A's are long in cunning but short in courage to use force and in the force itself; whereas the B's have the force and the courage to use it, but are short in the skill required for exploiting those advantages. But if they chance to find leaders who have the skill—and history shows that such leadership is usually supplied by dissatisfied A's—they have all they need for driving the A's from power. Of just that development history affords countless examples from remotest times all the way down to the present.

2191. In general terms, a revolution of that type is beneficial to a community—more so when a governing class is tending more and more towards humanitarianism, less so when it is made up of individuals who are tending more and more to use combinations instead of force, especially if the combinations result, even indirectly, in the material prosperity of the community.

Let us imagine a country where the governing class, *A*, is inclining more and more in the direction of humanitarianism, is fostering, in other words, only the more harmful group-persistences, rejecting the others as outworn prejudices, and, while awaiting the advent of the "reign of reason," is becoming less and less capable of using force and is so shirking the main duty of a ruling class. Such a country is on its way to utter ruin. But lo, the subject class, *B*, revolts against the class *A*. In fighting *A* it uses the humanitarian derivations so dear to the *A*'s, but underlying them are quite different sentiments, and they soon find expression in deeds. The *B*'s apply force on a far-reaching scale, and not only overthrow the *A*'s but kill large numbers of them— and, in so doing, to tell the truth, they are performing a useful public service something like ridding the country of a baneful animal pest. They bring with them to the seats of power a great abundance of group-persistences; and little it matters, if it matters at all, that these group-persistences be different in outward forms from the old. The important thing is that now they are functioning in the governing class and that owing to them the social fabric is acquiring stability and strength. The country is saved from ruin and is reborn to a new life.

If one judges superficially, one may be tempted to dwell more especially on the slaughter and pillaging that attend a revolution, without thinking to ask whether such things may not be manifestations —as regrettable as one may wish—of sentiments, of social forces, that are very salutary. If one should say that, far from being reprehensible, the slaughter and robbery are signs that those who were called upon to commit them deserved power for the good of society, he would be stating a paradox, for there is no relationship of cause and effect, nor any close and indispensable correlation, between such outrages and social utility; but the paradox would still contain its modicum of truth, in that the slaughter and rapine are external symptoms indicating the advent of strong and courageous people to places formerly held by weaklings and cowards. In all that we have been describing in the abstract many revolutions that have actually occurred in the concrete, from the revolution which gave imperial rule to Augustus down to the French Revolution of '89. If the class governing in France had had the faith that counsels use of force and the will to use force, it would never have been overthrown and, procuring its own advantage, would have procured the advantage of France. Since it failed in that function it was salutary that its rule should give way to rule by others; and since, again, it was the resort to force that was wanting, it was in keeping with very general uniformities that there should be a swing to another extreme where force was used even more than was required. Had Louis XVI not been a man of little sense and less courage, letting himself be floored without fighting, and preferring to lose his head on the guillotine to dying weapon in hand like a man of sinew, he might have been the one to do the destroying. If the victims of the September massacres, their kinsmen and friends, had not for the most part been spineless humanitarians without a particle of courage or energy, they would have annihilated their enemies instead of waiting to be annihilated themselves. It was a good thing that power should pass into the hands of people who showed that they had the faith and the resolve requisite for the use of force.

The advantage of the use of force to a society is less apparent when the governing class is made up of persons in whom the combination instincts are prevalent, and within certain limits there may be no advantage. But when a governing class divests itself too completely of the sentiments of group-persistence, it easily reaches a point where it is unfit to defend, let alone its own power, what is far worse the independence of its country. In such a case, if the independence is to be deemed an advantage, it must also be deemed an advantage to be rid of a class that has become incompetent to perform the functions of defence. As a rule it is from the subject class that individuals come with the faith and the resolve to use force and save a country.

2192. The governing class, *A*, tries to defend its power and avert the danger of an uprising of the *B*'s in various ways. It may try to take advantage of the strength of the *B*'s, and that is the most effective policy. Or it may try to prevent its disaffected members from becoming leaders of the *B*'s, or rather, of that element among the *B*'s which is disposed to use force; but that is a very difficult thing to achieve. And the *A*'s use derivations to keep the *B*'s quiet (§2182), telling them that "all power comes from God," that it is a "crime" to resort to violence, that there is no reason for using force to obtain what, if it is "just," may be obtained by "reason." The main purpose of such derivations is to keep the *B*'s from giving battle on their own terrain, the terrain of force, and to lead them to other ground—the field of cunning—where their defeat is certain, pitted as they will be against the *A*'s, who are immensely their superiors in wits. But as a rule the effectiveness of such derivations depends largely upon the pre-existing sentiments that they express, and only to a slight extent upon sentiments that they create.

2193. Those derivations have to be met with other derivations of equal effectiveness, and it will be better if some of them play upon sentiments that are acceptable to people who imagine that they are neutral, though in reality they may not be, who would prefer not to take sides with either the *A*'s or the *B*'s but to think solely of what is "just" and "honest." Such sentiments are chiefly available in the group manifested by residues of sociality (Class IV) and more especially the sentiments of pity. For that reason, most of the derivations favouring the use of violence by the subject class defend it not so much directly as indirectly—condemning resistance on the part of the governing class in the name of sociality, pity, and repugnance to sufferings in others. These latter sentiments are almost the only ones that are exploited by many pacifists who can think of no other way to defend their thesis than by describing the "horrors of war." Derivations relating to the social struggle often have recourse, further, to sentiments of asceticism, which sometimes influence individuals among the *A*'s and so prove to be of no mean advantage to the *B*'s.

2194. At bottom all such derivations express in chief, the sentiments of individuals who are eager for change in the social order, and they are therefore beneficial or harmful according as the change is beneficial or harmful. If one is going to assert that change is always for the worse, that stability is the supreme good, one ought to be ready to show either that it would have been to the advantage of human societies always to have remained in a state of barbarism, or that the transition from barbarism to civilization has been achieved, or *might have* been achieved, without wars and revolutions. This latter assertion is so grossly at variance with the facts as we learn them from history that it is absurd even to discuss it. So only the first is left, and it might be defended by giving a special meaning to the term, "utility" and adopting the theories that have sung the joys of a "state of nature." If one is unwilling to go as far as that, one cannot hold to the first proposition either; and so one is forced by the facts and by logic to admit that wars and revolutions have sometimes been beneficial (which does not mean that they have always been so). And once that is admitted for the past, no bias whatever remains for showing that things will be otherwise in the future.

2195. So there we are again, and as usual, driven from the qualitative field, where derivations predominate, into the quantitative field of logico-experimental science. One cannot assert in general that stability is always beneficial or that change is always beneficial. Every case has to be examined on its particular merits and the utility and the detriment appraised to see whether the first overbalances the second, or *vice versa*.

2196. We have already found that in many cases stability is beneficial. We should find cases no fewer in number where violations of existing norms have also proved beneficial, provided we consider norms of an intellectual order along with norms of a material order. But keeping them separate, it will be apparent that—especially as regards violations by small numbers of individuals—many are the cases where violations of intellectual norms by individuals or by a few individuals prove advantageous, few the cases where violations of norms of a material order prove beneficial. For that reason, the implications of the formula stated in §2176, whereby violations of norms of a material order should be the more vigorously suppressed, the more exclusively they are the work of individuals, the less so, the more they are the work of groups, do not in many cases take us too far astray from the maximum of social utility, as they would do if the formula were applied to violations of norms of an intellectual order. That, substantially, is the chief argument that can be advanced in favour of what is called "freedom of thought."

2197. Derivations do not run that way. Dissenters defend their opinions because they are "better" than the opinions held by the majority; and it is a good thing that they have that faith, for it alone can supply them with the energy they need to resist the persecutions that they almost always incur. So long as they are few in numbers, they ask just for a little place in the Sun for their sect. In reality they are panting for the moment when they can turn from persecuted to persecutor, a thing that infallibly happens as soon as they have become numerous enough to enforce their will. At that moment the advantage of their past dissent is at an end, and the detriment resulting from their new orthodoxy begins to assert itself.

2198. In considering the use of force there is a stronger temptation than in other social connexions to think only of relationships of cause and effect; nor in many cases do we go very far wide of the mark in that. After all, in the sequence of actions and reactions that confronts one, the action of this or that force as producing this or that effect occupies a very considerable place. However, it is better not to stop at that, but go on to see whether phenomena that are more general should not be taken into account.

2199. We have previously compared the revolution in Rome at the time of Augustus with the revolution in France at the time of Louis XVI; and we saw that to understand those two events we had to look beyond the derivations to the sentiments and interests that the derivations represented. Advancing one step further, one notes that both in the fall of the Roman Republic and in the fall of the French monarchy, the respective governing classes were either unwilling or unable to use force, and were overthrown by other classes that were both willing and able to do that (§2191). Both in ancient Rome and in France the victorious element rose from the people and was made up in Rome of the legions of Sulla, Caesar, and Octavius, in France of the revolutionary mobs that routed a very feeble royal power, and then of an army that vanquished the very inefficient troops of the European potentates. The leaders of the victors spoke Latin, of course, in Rome, and French in France, and no less naturally used derivations that were suitable to the Romans and the French respectively. The Roman people was fed on derivations conforming with a feeling that substance might be changed so long as forms were kept, the French masses, on derivations inspired by the religion of "Progress," a faith surpassing dear to the French of that day. Not otherwise, in the days of the Puritan Revolution, did Cromwell and other foes of the Stuarts use biblical derivations.

2200. The French derivations are more familiar than the Roman not only because more documents have come down to us, but also, as seems very probable, because they were supplied in greater abundance. Had Octavius long continued in his rôle as defender of the Senate, he might have made very lavish use of them; but when, before Bologna, he came to an understanding with Antony and Lepidus, his fortunes came to rest altogether on the might of his legions; so he laid his derivations away in his arsenals as weapons no longer needed, not taking them out again till after his victory, when it was a question of smoothing the fur of old-timers in Rome, which might have been ruffled by the change in régime. Something of the same sort took place in France as regards Napoleon I; but before his time the Jacobins, who opened the road for him, found it impossible to play only the lion and had to resort to the tricks of the fox. With his own prestige as commander, Octavius had made sure of the support of an armed force, and at first with his own money, later on

with the money that he was in a position to extort by force from others. The French revolutionary leaders were unable to do anything like that, in the beginning. They had to recruit their revolutionary army with derivations, which, expressing as they did the sentiments of many of the government's enemies, brought them in a flock to their standards, and, expressing also the sentiments of almost all members of the ruling classes, further served as an opiate to their already listless vigilance, and broke down their already feeble resistance. Later on, as soon as the revolution got possession of power, its leaders imitated the Roman triumvirs and many other masterful men of the same type, distributing among their followers the money and property of their adversaries.

2201. If the effects of derivations are much less considerable than the effects of residues, they are not, as we have many times seen, altogether without influence, serving primarily to give greater strength and effectiveness to the residues that they express. It would not therefore be exact to say that the historians who have made the derivations of the French Revolution their exclusive or at least their main concern have dealt with an entirely irrelevant aspect of that episode. They may be said to have erred in regarding as primary an aspect that was merely secondary. It has been a more serious error on their part not to consider the rôle played by force and the reasons why force was used by some parties, and not by others. The few who have considered the rôle of force at all have gone astray in assuming that this or that man in power refrained from using force in deference to derivations, whereas both derivations and the aversion to use of force had a common origin in the sentiments of those men. And yet—if one examines closely—the whole thing seems clear, with the proof and the counter-proof. Louis XVI fell because he was unwilling, unable, incompetent, to use force; the revolutionists triumphed because they were willing and able and competent. Not by any cogency in their theories but by sheer might of their followings did now this and now that revolutionary faction climb to power. Even the Directory, which had saved itself by resorting to force in conflicts with weaker factions, succumbed to force in its struggle with Bonaparte, made the man of the hour by his victorious troops. And Napoleon lasts until he is worn down under the superior force of the Allies. And then—over again: a succession of régimes in France, each falling because unwilling, unable, incompetent, to use force, and others rising on the use of force. That was observable on the fall of Charles X, on the fall of Louis Philippe, on the advent of Napoleon III; and one may go on and say that if the government of Versailles in 1871 managed to keep its feet in the face of the Commune, it was because it had a strong army at its disposal and knew enough to use it.

3. On the Ruling Class

BY GAETANO MOSCA

IN SOCIETIES in which religious beliefs are strong and ministers of the faith form a special class a priestly aristocracy almost always arises and gains possession of a more or less important share of the wealth and the political power. Conspicuous examples of that situation would be ancient Egypt (during certain periods), Brahman India and medieval Europe. Oftentimes the priests not only perform religious functions. They possess legal and scientific knowledge and constitute the class of highest intellectual culture. Consciously or unconsciously, priestly hierarchies often show a tendency to monopolize learning and hamper the dissemination of the methods and procedures that make the acquisition of knowledge possible and easy. To that tendency may have been due, in part at least, the painfully slow diffusion of the demotic alphabet in ancient Egypt, though that alphabet was infinitely more simple than the hieroglyphic script. The Druids in Gaul were acquainted with the Greek alphabet but would not permit their rich store of sacred literature to be written down, requiring their pupils to commit it to memory at the cost of untold effort. To the same outlook may be attributed the stubborn and frequent use of dead languages that we find in ancient Chaldea, in India, and in medieval Europe. Sometimes, as was the case in India, lower classes have been explicitly forbidden to acquire knowledge of sacred books.

Specialized knowledge and really scientific culture, purged of any sacred or religious aura, become important political forces only in a highly advanced stage of civilization, and only then do they give access to membership in the ruling class to those who possess them. But in this case too, it is not so much learning in itself that has political

Reprinted by permission from Gaetano Mosca, The Ruling Class, trans. Hannah D. Kahn (New York: McGraw-Hill, 1939), chap. ii, secs. 6–8, pp. 59–69. Copyright 1939. McGraw-Hill Book Company, Inc.

value as the practical applications that may be made of learning to the profit of the public or the state. Sometimes all that is required is mere possession of the mechanical processes that are indispensable to the acquisition of a higher culture. This may be due to the fact that on such a basis it is easier to ascertain and measure the skill which a candidate has been able to acquire—it is easier to "mark" or grade him. So in certain periods in ancient Egypt the profession of scribe was a road to public office and power, perhaps because to have learned the hieroglyphic script was proof of long and patient study. In modern China, again, learning the numberless characters in Chinese script has formed the basis of the mandarin's education. In present-day Europe and America the class that applies the findings of modern science to war, public administration, public works and public sanitation holds a fairly important position, both socially and politically, and in our western world, as in ancient Rome, an altogether privileged position is held by lawyers. They know the complicated legislation that arises in all peoples of long-standing civilization, and they become especially powerful if their knowledge of law is coupled with the type of eloquence that chances to have a strong appeal to the taste of their contemporaries.

There are examples in abundance where we see that long-standing practice in directing the military and civil organization of a community creates and develops in the higher reaches of the ruling class a real art of governing which is something better than crude empiricism and better than anything that mere individual experience could suggest. In such circumstances aristocracies of functionaries arise, such as the Roman senate, the Venetian nobility and to a certain extent the English aristocracy. Those bodies all stirred John Stuart Mill to admiration and certainly they all three developed governments that were distinguished for carefully considered policies and for great steadfastness and sagacity in carrying them out. This art of governing is not political science, though it has, at one time or another, anticipated applications of a number of the postulates of political science. However, even if the art of governing has now and again enjoyed prestige with certain classes of persons who have long held possession of political functions, knowledge of it has never served as an ordinary criterion for admitting to public offices persons who were barred from them by social station. The degree of mastery of the art of governing that a person possesses is, moreover, apart from exceptional cases, a very difficult thing to determine if the person has given no practical demonstration that he possesses it.

In some countries we find hereditary castes. In such cases the governing class is explicitly restricted to a given number of families, and birth is the one criterion that determines entry into the class or exclusion from it. Examples are exceedingly common. There is practically no country of long-standing civilization that has not had a hereditary aristocracy at one period or another in its history. We find hereditary nobilities during certain periods in China and ancient Egypt, in India, in Greece before the wars with the Medes, in ancient Rome, among the Slavs, among the Latins and Germans of the Middle Ages, in Mexico at the time of the Discovery and in Japan down to a few years ago. In this connection two preliminary observations are in point. In the first place, all ruling classes tend to become hereditary in fact if not in law. All political forces seem to possess a quality that in physics used to be called the force of inertia. They have a tendency, that is, to remain at the point and in the state in which they find themselves. Wealth and military valor are easily maintained in certain families by moral tradition and by heredity. Qualification for important office—the habit of, and to an extent the capacity for, dealing with affairs of consequence—is much more readily acquired when one has had a certain familiarity with them from childhood. Even when academic degrees, scientific training, special aptitudes as tested by examinations and competitions, open the way to public office, there is no eliminating that special advantage in favor of certain individuals which the French call the advantage of *positions déjà prises*. In actual fact, though examinations and competitions may theoretically be open to all, the majority never have the resources for meeting the expense of long preparation, and many others are without the connections and kinships that set an individual promptly on the right road, enabling him to avoid the gropings and blunders that are inevitable when one enters an unfamiliar environment without any guidance or support.

The democratic principle of election by broad-based suffrage would seem at first glance to be in conflict with the tendency toward stability which, according to our theory, ruling classes show. But it must be noted that candidates who are successful in democratic elections are almost always the ones who possess the political forces above enumerated, which are very often hereditary. In the English, French and Italian parliaments we frequently see the sons, grandsons, brothers, nephews and sons-in-law of members and deputies, ex-members and ex-deputies.

In the second place, when we see a hereditary caste established in a country and monopolizing political power, we may be sure that such a status de jure was preceded by a similar status de facto. Before proclaiming their exclusive and hereditary right to power the families or castes in question must have held the scepter of command in a firm grasp, completely monopolizing all the political forces of that country at that period. Otherwise such a claim on their part would only have aroused the bitterest protests and provoked the bitterest struggles.

Hereditary aristocracies often come to vaunt supernatural origins, or at least origins different from, and superior to, those of the governed classes. Such claims are explained by a highly significant social fact, namely that every governing class tends to justify its actual exercise of power by resting it on some universal moral principle. This same sort of claim has come forward in our time in scientific trappings. A number of writers, developing and amplifying Darwin's theories, contend that upper classes represent a higher level in social evolution and are therefore superior to lower classes by organic structure. Gumplowicz we have already quoted. That writer goes to the point of maintaining that the divisions of populations into trade groups and professional classes in modern civilized countries are based on ethnological heterogeneousness.[1]

Now history very definitely shows the special abilities as well as the special defects—both very marked—which have been displayed by aristocracies that have either remained absolutely closed or have made entry into their circles difficult. The ancient Roman patriciate and the English and German nobilities of modern times give a ready idea of the type we refer to. Yet in dealing with this

---

1. *Der Rassenkampf*. This notion transpires from Gumplowicz's whole volume. It is explicitly formulated in book II, chap. XXXIII.

fact, and with the theories that tend to exaggerate its significance, we can always raise the same objection—that the individuals who belong to the aristocracies in question owe their special qualities not so much to the blood that flows in their veins as to their very particular upbringing, which has brought out certain intellectual and moral tendencies in them in preference to others.

Among all the factors that figure in social superiority, intellectual superiority is the one with which heredity has least to do. The children of men of highest mentality often have very mediocre talents. That is why hereditary aristocracies have never defended their rule on the basis of intellectual superiority alone, but rather on the basis of their superiorities in character and wealth.

It is argued, in rebuttal, that education and environment may serve to explain superiorities in strictly intellectual capacities but not differences of a moral order—will power, courage, pride, energy. The truth is that social position, family tradition, the habits of the class in which we live, contribute more than is commonly supposed to the greater or lesser development of the qualities mentioned. If we carefully observe individuals who have changed their social status, whether for better or for worse, and who consequently find themselves in environments different from the ones they have been accustomed to, it is apparent that their intellectual capacities are much less sensibly affected than their moral ones. Apart from a greater breadth of view that education and experience bring to anyone who is not altogether stupid, every individual, whether he remains a mere clerk or becomes a minister of state, whether he reaches the rank of sergeant or the rank of general, whether he is a millionaire or a beggar, abides inevitably on the intellectual level on which nature has placed him. And yet with changes of social status and wealth the proud man often becomes humble, servility changes to arrogance, an honest nature learns to lie, or at least to dissemble, under pressure of need, while the man who has an ingrained habit of lying and bluffing makes himself over and puts on an outward semblance at least of honesty and firmness of character. It is true, of course, that a man fallen from high estate often acquires powers of resignation, self-denial and resourcefulness, just as one who rises in the world sometimes gains in sentiments of justice and fairness. In short, whether a man change for the better or for the worse, he has to be exceptionally level-headed if he is to change his social status very appreciably and still keep his character unaltered. Mirabeau remarked that, for any man, any great climb on the social ladder produces a crisis that cures the ills he has and creates new ones that he never had before.[2]

Courage in battle, impetuousness in attack, endurance in resistance—such are the qualities that have long and often been vaunted as a monopoly of the higher classes. Certainly there may be vast natural and—if we may say so—innate differences between one individual and another in these respects; but more than anything else traditions and environmental influences are the things that keep them high, low or just average, in any large group of human beings. We generally become indifferent to danger or, perhaps better, to a given type of danger, when the persons with whom we daily live speak of it with indifference and remain cool and imperturbable before it. Many mountaineers or sailors are by nature timid men, yet they face unmoved, the ones the dangers of the precipice, the others the perils of the storm at sea. So peoples and classes that are accustomed to warfare maintain military virtues at the highest pitch.

So true is this that even peoples and social classes which are ordinarily unaccustomed to arms acquire the military virtues rapidly when the individuals who compose them are made members of organizations in which courage and daring are traditional, when—if one may venture the metaphor—they are cast into human crucibles that are heavily charged with the sentiments that are to be infused into their fiber. Mohammed II recruited his terrible Janizaries in the main from boys who had been kidnapped among the degenerate Greeks of Byzantium. The much despised Egyptian fellah, unused for long centuries to war and accustomed to remaining meek and helpless under the lash of the oppressor, became a good soldier when Mehemet Ali placed him in Turkish or Albanian regiments. The French nobility has always enjoyed a reputation for brilliant valor, but down to the end of the eighteenth century that quality was not credited in anything like the same degree to the French bourgeoisie. However, the wars of the Republic and the Empire amply proved that nature had been uniformly lavish in her endowments of courage upon all the inhabitants of France. Proletariat and bourgeoisie both furnished good soldiers and, what is more, excellent officers, though talent for command had been considered an exclusive prerogative of the nobility. Gumplowicz's theory that differentiation in social classes depends very largely on ethnological antecedents requires proof at the very least. Many facts to the contrary readily occur to one—among others the obvious fact that branches of the

---

2. *Correspondance entre le comte de Mirabeau et le comte de La Marck*, vol. II, p. 228.

same family often belong to widely different social classes.

Finally, if we were to keep to the idea of those who maintain the exclusive influence of the hereditary principle in the formation of ruling classes, we should be carried to a conclusion somewhat like the one to which we were carried by the evolutionary principle: The political history of mankind ought to be much simpler than it is. If the ruling class really belonged to a different race, or if the qualities that fit it for dominion were transmitted primarily by organic heredity, it is difficult to see how, once the class was formed, it could decline and lose its power. The peculiar qualities of a race are exceedingly tenacious. Keeping to the evolutionary theory, acquired capacities in the parents are inborn in their children and, as generation succeeds generation, are progressively accentuated. The descendants of rulers, therefore, ought to become better and better fitted to rule, and the other classes ought to see their chances of challenging or supplanting them becomes more and more remote. Now the most commonplace experience suffices to assure one that things do not go in that way at all.

What we see is that as soon as there is a shift in the balance of political forces—when, that is, a need is felt that capacities different from the old should assert themselves in the management of the state, when the old capacities, therefore, lose some of their importance or changes in their distribution occur—then the manner in which the ruling class is constituted changes also. If a new source of wealth develops in a society, if the practical importance of knowledge grows, if an old religion declines or a new one is born, if a new current of ideas spreads, then, simultaneously, far-reaching dislocations occur in the ruling class. One might say, indeed, that the whole history of civilized mankind comes down to a conflict between the tendency of dominant elements to monopolize political power and transmit possession of it by inheritance, and the tendency toward a dislocation of old forces and an insurgence of new forces; and this conflict produces an unending ferment of endosmosis and exosmosis between the upper classes and certain portions of the lower. Ruling classes decline inevitably when they cease to find scope for the capacities through which they rose to power, when they can no longer render the social services which they once rendered, or when their talents and the services they render lose in importance in the social environment in which they live. So the Roman aristocracy declined when it was no longer the exclusive source of higher officers for the army, of

administrators for the commonwealth, of governors for the provinces. So the Venetian aristocracy declined when its nobles ceased to command the galleys and no longer passed the greater part of their lives in sailing the seas and in trading and fighting.

In inorganic nature we have the example of our air, in which a tendency to immobility produced by the force of inertia is continuously in conflict with a tendency to shift about as the result of inequalities in the distribution of heat. The two tendencies, prevailing by turn in various regions on our planet, produce now calm, now wind and storm. In much the same way in human societies there prevails now the tendency that produces closed, stationary, crystallized ruling classes, now the tendency that results in a more or less rapid renovation of ruling classes.

The Oriental societies which we consider stationary have in reality not always been so, for otherwise, as we have already pointed out, they could not have made the advances in civilization of which they have left irrefutable evidence. It is much more accurate to say that we came to know them at a time when their political forces and their political classes were in a period of crystallization. The same thing occurs in what we commonly call "aging" societies, where religious beliefs, scientific knowledge, methods of producing and distributing wealth have for centuries undergone no radical alteration and have not been disturbed in their everyday course by infiltrations of foreign elements, material or intellectual. In such societies political forces are always the same, and the class that holds possession of them holds a power that is undisputed. Power is therefore perpetuated in certain families, and the inclination to immobility becomes general through all the various strata in that society.

So in India we see the caste system become thoroughly entrenched after the suppression of Buddhism. The Greeks found hereditary castes in ancient Egypt, but we know that in the periods of greatness and renaissance in Egyptian civilization political office and social status were not hereditary. We possess an Egyptian document that summarizes the life of a high army officer who lived during the period of the expulsion of the Hyksos. He had begun his career as a simple soldier. Other documents show cases in which the same individual served successively in army, civil administration and priesthood.

The best-known and perhaps the most important example of a society tending toward crystallization is the period in Roman history that used to be called the Low Empire. There, after several centuries of almost complete social immobility, a division between two classes grew sharper and sharper, the one made up of great landowners and high officials, the other made up of slaves, farmers and urban plebeians. What is even more striking, public office and social position became hereditary by custom before they became hereditary by law, and the trend was rapidly generalized during the period mentioned.[3]

On the other hand it may happen in the history of a nation that commerce with foreign peoples, forced emigrations, discoveries, wars, create new poverty and new wealth, disseminate knowledge of things that were previously unknown or cause infiltrations of new moral, intellectual and religious currents. Or again—as a result of such infiltrations or through a slow process of inner growth, or from both causes—it may happen that a new learning arises, or that certain elements of an old, long forgotten learning return to favor so that new ideas and new beliefs come to the fore and upset the intellectual habits on which the obedience of the masses has been founded. The ruling class may also be vanquished and destroyed in whole or in part by foreign invasions, or, when the circumstances just mentioned arise, it may be driven from power by the advent of new social elements who are strong in fresh political forces. Then, naturally, there comes a period of renovation, or, if one prefer, of revolution, during which individual energies have free play and certain individuals, more passionate, more energetic, more intrepid or merely shrewder than others, force their way from the bottom of the social ladder to the topmost rungs.

Once such a movement has set in, it cannot be stopped immediately. The example of individuals who have started from nowhere and reached prominent positions fires new ambitions, new greeds, new energies, and this molecular rejuvenation of the ruling class continues vigorously until a long period of social stability slows it down again. We need hardly mention examples of nations in such periods of renovation. In our age that would be superfluous. Rapid restocking of ruling classes is a frequent and very striking phenomenon in countries that have been recently colonized. When social life begins in such environments, there is no ready-made ruling class, and while such a class is in process of formation, admittance to it is gained very easily.

Monopolization of land and other agencies of production is, if not quite impossible, at any rate more difficult than elsewhere. That is why, at least during a certain period, the Greek colonies offered a wide outlet for all Greek energy and enterprise. That is why, in the United States, where the colonizing of new lands continued through the whole nineteenth century and new industries were continually springing up, examples of men who started with nothing and have attained fame and wealth are still frequent—all of which helps to foster in the people of that country the illusion that democracy is a fact.

Suppose now that a society gradually passes from its feverish state to calm. Since the human being's psychological tendencies are always the same, those who belong to the ruling class will begin to acquire a group spirit. They will become more and more exclusive and learn better and better the art of monopolizing to their advantage the qualities and capacities that are essential to acquiring power and holding it. Then, at last, the force that is essentially conservative appears—the force of habit. Many people become resigned to a lowly station, while the members of certain privileged families or classes grow convinced that they have almost an absolute right to high station and command.

A philanthropist would certainly be tempted to inquire whether mankind is happier—or less unhappy—during periods of social stability and crystallization, when everyone is almost fated to remain in the social station to which he was born, or during the directly opposite periods of renovation and revolution, which permit all to aspire to the most exalted positions and some to attain them. Such an inquiry would be difficult. The answer would have to take account of many qualifications and exceptions, and might perhaps always be influenced by the personal preferences of the observer. We shall therefore be careful not to venture on any answer of our own. Besides, even if we could reach an undebatable conclusion, it would have a very slight practical utility; for the sad fact is that what the philosophers and theologians call free will—in other words, spontaneous choice by individuals—has so far had, and will perhaps always have, little influence, if any at all, in hastening either the ending or the beginning of one of the historical periods mentioned.

3. Marquardt, *Manuel des antiquités romaines;* Fustel de Coulanges, *Nouvelles recherches sur quelques problèmes d'histoire.*

4. The Sociological Character of Political Parties

BY ROBERT MICHELS

THE POLITICAL PARTY, etymologically and logically, can embrace only a part of the citizenry, politically organized. The party is a fraction; it is *pars pro toto*. Let us endeavor briefly to analyze its causal origin and its behavior.

According to Max Weber, the political party has a dual teleology. It is a spontaneous society of propaganda and of agitation seeking to acquire power, in order to procure thereby for its active militant adherents chances, ideal and material, for the realization either of objective aims or of personal advantages, or of both. Consequently, the general orientation of the political party, whether in its personal or impersonal aspect, is that of *Machstreben* (striving to power).

Kinds of Political Parties

In the personal aspect, parties are often based on the protection accorded inferiors by a strong man. In the Prussian diet of 1855, which was composed of a large number of political groups, each was given the name of its leader. There were the groups of Count de Schlieffen, of Count Arnim, of Tietz, of Karl, of von Patow, of von Vincke, of von Bethmann-Hollweg, of Reichensperger and Mallinkrodt (the last being Catholic). The only group which was called by its true name was a national one, the Polish party.

The history of the labor movement shows that the socialists have not abandoned this "bourgeois" tradition. The socialist parties, on the contrary, have often so completely identified themselves with a leader that they have more or less officially assumed his name, as though to proclaim that they were his property. In Germany, between 1863 and 1875, the rival socialist factions, courting the favor of the mass of workingmen, were the Marxists and the Lassallians. In France, more recently, the great current of socialism was divided into the Broussists, the Allemanists, the Blanquists, the Guesdists, and the Jaurèsists. It is true that the men who so gave their names to different separatist movements personified as completely as possible the ideas and the

disposition with which the party was inspired, and which guided them throughout the whole course of their evolution; but it must be admitted, on the other hand, that when the party assumes the name of its leader it is carrying the regard of the herd for its shepherd a bit too far.

Perhaps there is here an analogy between political party and religious sects or monastic orders. Yves-Guyot justly remarked that the individual belonging to a modern party acts after the same fashion as did the mediaeval monks, who, faithful as they were to the precepts of their masters, called themselves after St. Dominicus,, St. Benedictus, St. Augustinius, and St. Franciscus, respectively, the Dominicans, the Benedictines, the Augustines, and the Franciscans. These are the types of party which one may designate as the parties of patronage. If the leader exercises his influence over his followers by qualities so striking that they seem to them supernatural, one can call him a charismatic chief.

This sort of party, the charismatic, takes on varying forms. Ferdinand Lassalle himself, the leader of the Lassallians, was officially merely president of the Allgemeiner Deutscher Arbeiterverein. But he was its president for life. All the main characteristics of leadership were united in him: force of will, wide knowledge, ambition and self-sufficiency, reputation for disinterestedness, celebrity, persuasive oratorship. It pleased him to encourage his followers in idolatry of which he was made the object by the delirious masses and the white-clad virgins who chanted praises to him and offered him bouquets. But not only was, in the case of Lassalle, the charismatic faith the ripe fruit of a psychology which was exuberant and megalomaniacal, but it also was in agreement with the theoretical conception of the hero. We must, he said to the workingmen of the Rhine, in offering them his ideas on the organization of the political party, out of all our scattered desires forge a hammer and place it in the hands of a man whose intelligence, character, and devotion would be to us a guaranty that with the hammer he will strike hard. That is the hammer of the dictator, as he was in fact.

In later periods of history, when the masses demanded at least a simulacrum of democracy and group control in party affairs, and when especially

Reprinted from Robert Michels, *First Lectures in Political Sociology*, trans. Alfred De Grazia (Minneapolis: University of Minnesota Press, 1949), pp. 134–54, with the permission of the University of Minnesota Press.

the burning jealousy among the ever-increasing number of leaders admitted no longer, in the socialist movement, the dictatorship of one man, the striking individualities among the leaders, such as August Bebel and Jean Jaurès, were obliged to restrain, as much as possible, these desires and jealousies. Surely, Bebel and Jaurès, were two quite different types of charismatic leaders. The one was an orphan of a Pomeranian sergeant, the other a university professor of southern France. The former possessed hauteur and was as imperious as his cousin, the Kaiser (whence the nickname "Kaiser Bebel" which Gustave Hervé attempted to fix upon him); the latter was an orator without peer, fiery, romantic as well as realistic, seeking to surmount difficulties by seriating problems and to resolve them as fast as they presented themselves. Yet the two great leaders, at once friends and enemies, had in common an indomitable faith both in the efficacy of their action and in the historical destiny of the cohorts whose standard-bearers they were. So both became deified—the Prussian, still during his lifetime; the Frenchman, only, alas, after his death.

Moreover, the present offers to discreet sociologists another example of a great leader of a party which regards him as apostle and seer. In Italy, Benito Mussolini differs from the other men whom we have just mentioned in this: he is not only the leader of a great party, he has become also the leader of a great state. With him the axiom, "The party, it is I," has assumed, not only with regard to powerfulness and consciousness, but also with regard to responsibility and assiduous labor, its maximum development. It is very interesting to see how far the masses understand and develop Mussolini's ideals even beyond'his own concept. When, after having barely escaped (only some hours before) an attempt on his life, Mussolini, from the balcony of the Palazzo Chigi, harangued an agitated crowd of ten thousand people, explaining to them Italy's situation and the dangers she would have encountered if he had been killed, a voice was raised from the edge of the throng—immediately to be drowned by thunderous applause: "*Tu sei l'Italia*" ("But you are Italy itself"). With these words the interrupter meant to say (and the applauding crowd accentuated the sentiment) that there is really no difference between Mussolini the man and Italy the country, and that the death of the one would undoubtedly be followed by the complete ruin of the other. The leader of the Fascist party himself openly manifested the charismatic quintessence of his character when, after another attempt on his life, he sent a telegram to his Fascist comrades at Bologna urging them to be certain, absolutely certain, that nothing serious could happen to him before he had completed his task.

We do not here have to indicate the dangers such an idea involves in politics. We shall, however, make one strictly sociological observation. It is evident that charismatic leadership like this bears within itself political dynamics of the utmost vigor. The great Saint-Simon on his deathbed told his disciples, it must be remembered, that in order to do great things one must be impassioned. But to be zealous means to have the gift of inciting the zeal of others. It is, in effect, a formidable goad. This is the advantage of charismatic parties over parties with a well-defined program and a class interest. It is true, on the other hand, that the duration of the former is often circumscribed by the duration of their verve and enthusiasm, which sometimes furnish only a very fragile basis. So we see the charismatic parties induced to rest their appeal, in addition to enthusiasm, as much as possible on institutions more durable than human emotions, such, for example, as protective, workers', and professional organizations and interests.

Charism thus lends itself to all political views, no matter of what complexion. All political parties can be provided with charismatic chiefs. Particularly is this true of young, ardent, doctrinaire parties, although, to be sure, charismatic chiefs are sometimes found in parties of more flexible beliefs. In general, charismatic leaders are, as regards political parties, primary phenomena. In other words, they are the founders of them; it is they who engender and start parties. But the history of political parties demonstrates also that there is a certain number of inverse cases. Then it is the party which is the primary phenomenon. From the chronological point of view the leaders are then secondary; that is to say, they appear later, when the party is already active. But that in no way diminishes the intensity of their force, once acknowledged, provided that the pre-existing party is without other leaders of equal value.

In the second place, there are parties which have for their bases, *a priori,* interests of economic and social classes. And these are especially workers' parties or parties of peasants or of the lower middle class—what the French call "les petites gens"—since the bourgeoisie cannot, by itself, form a party. It is necessary to add still a third category composed of political parties which have been inspired by political or moral ideas—general and abstract—of a *Weltanschauung.* When this conception rests on a more developed and minutely elaborated dogma, one can speak of doctrinaire parties whose doctrines are, however, a privilege of leaders. Here we are in the presence of parties of free trade or protection, or of those which speak of the rights of liberty or of justice (To each the fruit of his labor; or, To each according to his abilities; or, To each according to his needs), or, again, of those which speak of authority.

It is, however, evident that this differentiation into parties of patronage, parties of social or economic interest, and parties of doctrinaire consistency is neither sharp nor final. It is not sharp, for the simple reason that past and present parties represent, in large degree, intermediate nuances or combinations, in which the competent observer will not fail immediately to recognize the existence, sometimes in very unequal proportions, of constituent elements of all three categories. At all events, there is no doubt that the program (which is, so to speak, the codification of political beliefs that have given birth to organization) can, in the first category—based as it is entirely on the faith and authority of a single person—be rudimentary; while it is undeniable that the two other categories, and the second, perhaps, still more than the third, require well developed programs. But even for the doctrinaire parties it may be true to say, with P. Orman Ray, that the principles of a party are apt to be most conspicuous in its early or formative period, while in its later history politics are likely to overshadow principles.

It seems to us, however, that there are still two categories of political parties which, while approaching in a certain sense parties based on principles, have nevertheless characteristics belonging to other types of party that distinguish them somewhat from their analogues. These are the confessional parties and the national parties. The former profess to have, not merely a *Weltanschauung* (theory of life) but an *Ueberweltanschauung* (theory of metaphysical life, a belief). They are the parties seeking to adapt the needs of life here below, envisaged as a preparatory phase, to the immortal life of the soul. The latter, the nationalist parties, may assuredly have ideas both general and universal; they may, for example, proclaim, with the Italian Irredentists, with Stanislao Mancini and Terenzio Mamiani, the principle of nationality, understood in its true sense as the right of each people, and of each fraction of a people, to complete, unconditioned sovereignty. However, at least ever since 1870, the national parties practicing this ideal have transformed themselves into nationalistic parties. These are, in a sense, more limited and devoid of general principles, because one cannot conceive of a general principle which stops at the frontier, or, still worse, which crosses it only to refuse to other nationalities the claims to liberty and

freedom which they jealously reserve for themselves.

It is, nevertheless, equally true that many other political principles in the course of time function in a manner exactly opposite to their original and general aims, e.g., the principle of freedom of thought. One can say that optimists are, in general, extremist theoreticians. The consequences of this have been well put by Georges Sorel in writing of the Jacobins: "If, unfortunately, they find themselves armed with great political power allowing them to realize an ideal that they have conceived, optimists may lead their country to worse catastrophes. They are not long in recognizing, indeed, that social transformations are not achieved with the facility they had expected; they attribute their disappointments to their contemporaries, rather than explain the march of events in terms of historic necessity; thus they end by attempting to remove those people whose evil desires seem to them dangerous to the welfare of mankind. During the Terror, the men who spilt most blood were exactly those who had the keenest desire to enable their fellow-creatures to enjoy the golden age of which they had dreamed, and who had the strongest sympathy for human misery. Optimistic, idealistic, and sensitive, as they were, these men showed themselves the more inexorable as they had a greater thirst for universal well-being."

But if the unconscious identification of finalities—material or immaterial, it matters little—with the general good seems to be an absolute law of our spirit; it is none the less true that of all the social groups it is the national political party which uses and abuses this principle the most. For each nation believes that it must accomplish missions, either of liberty (the French in the Revolution), or of order (the Germans under William II), or of civilization (the "white man's burden"), or of discipline, or of morality, or of other ideals. All of these occur in endowing them with presumptive rights over neighboring peoples, who are judged incapable of facing their jobs without being forced to obey orders issued by the missionary people. The good faith, which very often springs from this idea of a mission, communicating itself to national collectivities, gives them the aplomb and energy of which they have need in order to achieve their goals. This is as much as to say that those critics who estimate that in their aggressive actions national groups are fundamentally ferocious and savage are profoundly wrong. At bottom, this ferocity and savagery which cause people to trample under foot and wipe out the interests and aspirations of others are only the forms in which the missionary—and almost always the visionary—

conviction manifests itself. Missionary peoples are ferocious and savage not in their feelings but in their actions.

However, as I have attempted to prove in one of my books, the need for organization (what Americans call machinery) and the ineluctable tendencies of human psychology, individual and group, cause distinctions of origin in the main to disappear. The political party as such has its own peculiar soul, independent of the programs and rules which it possesses and the eternal principles with which it is embued. The psychology of the crowd is fairly the same in the socialists and the nationalists, in the liberals and the conservatives. In group movements, with rare exceptions everything proceeds naturally, and not "artificially." The fact that the people follow their leader is quite a natural phenomenon. "To use the term exactly," Rousseau has said, "there has never existed a true democracy, and none can ever exist. It is against natural order that the great number should govern and that the few should be governed." Our consistent knowledge of the political life of the principal civilized nations of the world authorizes us to assert that the tendency toward oligarchy constitutes one of the historic necessities, one of the iron laws of history, from which the most democratic modern societies and, within those societies, the most advanced parties, have been unable to escape.

By giving themselves leaders, the workers create with their own hands new masters, whose principal means of domination consists in their technical and intellectual superiority and in the inability of the masses to control the execution of their commands to the leaders. In this respect, the intellectual has played a role in party politics which has many times been the subject of profound study. Moreover, the mechanism of the socialist party offers to the workers, thanks to the numerous salaried and honorary positions of which it disposes, a possibility of making a career, which exercises on them a force of considerable attraction. Now, to the degree that the political calling becomes complicated and the rules of social legislation multiplied, there is imposed on the leaders of political parties an existence more and more professionalized, based on a continuously widening knowledge, savoir-faire, routine, and sometimes delicate finesse. This is why the distance between the leaders and the led grows constantly greater. Thus one can place one's finger upon the flagrant contradiction which exists, in mature parties, between democratic declarations and intentions, on the one hand, and the concrete oligarchic reality, on the other. Hence the continuous raising of conflicts, often Shakespearian in character, in which the comic borders upon the

tragic. It may, therefore, be said that the organization constitutes precisely the source whence conservative currents debouch upon the plain of democracy, causing devastating inundations which render that plain unrecognizable.

Such a *Götterdämmerung* can in no way surprise analytic and alert spirits. Long ago Adam Smith's teacher, the Scottish philosopher Hutcheson, remarked that the patience of the people has always been too great and its veneration for its leaders too inept. Furthermore, for Pareto, the contemporary era is in no way characterized by the augmentation of sociality and the diminution of individualism. Fundamentally, it can be only a question of a quadrille chassé-croisé. For example, the sentiment of subordination, whicn was manifested in former days by the subjection, more or less voluntary, of inferior classes to superior classes, has today merely been replaced by the submission of the inferior classes to the leader of their party, the syndicate and the strike, and by the submission, less apparent, of the superior classes to the scum of the people, who have never been the object of so much flattery as in the present. And Gabriel Tarde has referred to two correlative sentiments of modern times, namely, the morbid mistrust of the democratic public for its master, and the fear, the malice, the insipidity of the so-called master who submits to all the orders of his inferiors. Naturally, experience informs us that the sycophant and demagogic chief himself considers flattery merely as a means, his aim being always that of dominating the crowd. The democracy clings to the lofty rungs of the orator's ladder, Charles Maurras has said, just like a woman—for the mob is feminine—whose imagination greets with transport the element which is able to excite her. And Thomas Carlyle well stated before him: "No British man can attain to be a statesman or chief of workers till he has first proved himself a chief of talkers."

The Democratic Appeals

Democracy is of a massive nature. Therefore it cannot function without masses. Parliamentarism presupposes electionism, electionism implies electoral masses. It follows from this that political parties are in vain partly aristocratic in origin and in aim; for it is none the less true that they are forced to make use of the masses. At election time, the *aristoi* candidates deign to descend from their mansions and to bestir themselves among the yokels in order to obtain the majority in their districts. That is not astonishing. They are not indeed ridiculous enough to speak in these solemn and decisive moments for the privilege of minorities, and to restrict themselves to accepting exclusively the votes of that portion of their fellow men who are sole possessors of the governing vocation. Inasmuch as they must rely upon the medium of election, the aristocratic parties make the best of a bad job. After all, the aristocrats cling to the hope of persuading the masses indirectly to renounce their own rights by their own votes. It is, at bottom, the ideal of the Prussian Junkers and the French aristocrats, who, to democratize themselves, discard the cast-off garments of royalty. Moreover, parties of huge economic and social classes or interests also follow this method of camouflage very closely. The majority parties also take care, in political elections, to address themselves not alone to their associates. In democracy every one appeals to the people, to every one of the people, without discrimination. The Socialist party—the most strictly proletarian —does not hesitate to solicit openly, at the proper time, the suffrage of artisans, peasants, and petty bourgeoisie. A Socialist who before the elections, and afterward, has only a very narrow conception of what is meant by the working class, loves, during the campaign, to stretch the theoretical extent of this class to the point of including capitalists, providing, of course, that they are not too refractory to accord to their employees, in such a case, some small wage increment.

This tendency, immanent in contemporary political life, and which a wag would be tempted to denominate a game of hide-and-seek, manifests itself even in the names that political parties are accustomed to give themselves in democratic countries. Indeed, in a democracy, political parties tend to envelop themselves in a very thick terminological fog, and one of nearly even color. Here are a few modern political nomenclatures. In France, the Liberal Action, the Progressive Republicans, the Republican Union, the Democratic Left, the Radical Left, the Radical-Socialist Republicans, the Socialist Republicans. In Germany, the German Popular party, the German People's National party, the German People's party, the Democratic party, the Social Democratic party, and the Christian People's party. In Switzerland the names of political parties differ scarcely at all from those used among their larger neighbors. One would say that no party is distinguishable from the others. All the German and French parties are more or less equally "popular," "democratic," and "national." This tendency is a beautiful example, indeed, of the application of Darwin's law of adaptation to environment carried over into the political field. It is almost cryptic mimicry. In the French elections

of 1848 the candidates of almost all shades of political opinion liked to call themselves workers and socialists, in homage to the first universal suffrage. Nowadays they are all democratic.

The influence which the omnibus tendency exerts on political parties is also very distinctly apparent in the tactics of the confessional parties. Let us remember, for example, that in the most important countries of Europe, where there is a Catholic party it has the habit of carefully concealing its essential character by the designations it uses. None ventures to call itself Catholic. In Italy, the Catholic party calls itself, quite simply, "Popular"; in Germany, it becomes the "Center party." But further: the latter party offers strong inducements to have among its members, even among its official representatives, a certain number of Protestants. In Italy, at the congress held by the Catholic party at Easter, 1923, in Turin, Don Sturzo, under the pretext that a party truly Catholic is a *contradictio in adjecto* (the word Catholic signifying universal, and the word party signifying partial), advanced the thesis that his party should be strongly non-confessional. This omnibus tendency has penetrated even into parliament. If this needs demonstration, it will suffice to cite, in France, the paradoxical existence in the Palais Bourbon, in addition to the politically constituted groups, of a "group of deputies not enrolled in any group," which includes men of every shade of opinion, and which even names a bureau.

There is, of course, among political parties a differentiating tendency, which we shall designate a centrifugal tendency, by which they are induced to distinguish themselves one from another, whether in their program and theoretical basis or in their daily manifestations. Moreover, this tendency seems to be repressed and often diverted by a much stronger tendency inherent in all political parties. This is the integrative tendency of the numerical maximum, mortal enemy to all freedom of program and of thought. It is a centripetal tendency, and, in fact, only the logical consequence of the fundamental tendency that dominates the life of political parties, namely, the tendency toward the conquest of the state. Where there are only two parties, as in America, this system is already the extreme expression of the victory of the centripetal tendency over the centrifugal. This victory seems still more manifest considering the fact that the Democrats and the Republicans are at present almost devoid of theoretical or programmatical differences, so that they can both address themselves to the electorate without any "ballast" of differentiating ideas.

False Party Classifications

In truth, the *raison d'être* of the political party is the push for power. Here the objectives certainly differ, some wishing to reach their goal in a peaceful fashion, without agitation (evolutionary as it were). Others, believing that by evolutionary methods they may never attain their ends, prefer an action or a series of actions more vigorous and rapid, by tactics called revolutionary. And it is likewise obvious that the conceptions of political parties are no more identical in the action to be taken after success—action which will depend, at least in principle, on conceptions which they have formed of the role of the state, and which may, in theory, even contemplate its abolition. For to destroy, it is necessary first to capture. At any rate, the first stage of the political party is determined by its ardent desire to absorb power, to become the state. Also the final goal of the party consists in statization. This is why, while awaiting utopia, the party will try to establish at the outset as much as possible a little state within the state. One may thus sustain the thesis that the most accomplished political party will be that one which will have created in its own ranks all the organizing and intellectual details of a nature to make it capable some day to assume the functions of the state, in complete form, just as Minerva issued fully armed from the brain of Jupiter.

It will be worth while to deal briefly with Vilfredo Pareto's theory of political parties. Like Max Weber, the author of these lines, and others, Pareto begins with the premise that political parties seek power. He then divides parties into two essential groups. First, there are the parties which devote themselves to government. This group embraces alike the party in power and those that do not hold it but aspire to it with good chance, and that meanwhile form the parties of opposition. Second, there are the intransigent parties which would hardly attain power. These last contain a greater number of fanatics, but also of honest men, than the other parties which are less ferocious but likewise more depraved. Let us note in passing that, according to an axiom of Italian juridical sociology, it is not a universal supposition that a government is composed of honest men. An eminent Italian sociologist, Gaetano Mosca, considers it even difficult for an honest man, having achieved the realization of his political ambitions, to resist deterioration of his moral sense, and seems to prefer that the honest man remain and act outside of the government, though capable of influencing public opinion.

We should not dare to say, however, that the differentiation of Pareto is impeccable. In the first

place, his point of view is, in my opinion, erroneous. To divide political parties into those that have "arrived" and those that have not or do not wish to do so, is to set up chance as a criterion, unless one considers that there are political parties which have amused themselves in being intransigent out of pure whimsy, which is inadmissible. For if there are parties that, at a given moment, refuse to take office, even when it is offered to them like a ripe fruit, this refusal does not signify a renunciation forever—a thing which would be for them equivalent to suicide. The refusal, on the contrary, is inspired in these cases by the fear either of not yet being ready to assume with impunity the responsibilities of government, or of being uncertain of the obedience of their adherents, divided by differences of opinion on the tactics to be followed; or, again, because they fear accepting but a Trojan horse and falling into an ambush or a trap which their enemies have laid for them. It is certain that such refusals (recent examples have been furnished by the Italian and French socialist parties) may be judged in a very different manner, as approaching a "policy of missed occasions and of tardy repentance." Whatever it is, these refusals to assume power have, as we have seen, an accidental and casuistical political causation, and always imply the party's hope of being able at an early maturity to redeem the mortgage on government and to conquer the state under political constellations more lucky and more promising.

In the second place, by identifying the party "arrived" and the party transigent, Pareto implies a relation between conquest of power and political compromise which certainly can often be verified, but which, nevertheless, is very far from forming a sovereign law capable of comprehending the extremely varied history of modern political parties.

Here, still another question arises. May one, perhaps, distinguish political parties according to whether their aspirations are fixed in past history or in political progressivism? Are there not, indeed, retrogressive and reactionary parties and progressive parties? There resides in this nomenclature a modicum of truth. One can undoubtedly discern parties tending toward a re-establishment of political and social institutions which have existed and which are judged superior and more suitable than the state of things which has replaced them. Parenthetically, we may add that, pursuant to this uniquely historical criterion of time—which involves neither the idea of liberty, nor that of authority, nor yet that of any other principle of political or philosophic order—one should logically designate as retrogressive, for example, the anti-Bolshevist parties in Russia, as well as the liberal anti-Fascist parties in Italy, the monarchist parties of France and Germany, and the irredentist parties in the countries detached from their fatherlands. Of course, this criterion gives us a most incongruous collection of political organizations in which are found joined together mortal enemies bound to one another by but a single tie: their common aspiration toward a pre-existing state of things, whatever it may have been. On the other hand, there is a group of political parties certainly no less incongruous than the collection we have just examined. These are the progressive parties, envisaging a new state of things which has never existed in history, but which they deem possible, desirable, and practicable. The prototypes of these parties are the socialist parties in central and western Europe.

It would, however, not be exact to classify political parties in two categories, those of the past and those of the future. This is true, in the first place, because whoever dares to range himself along with partisans of Giambattista Vico's philosophy of history—the kernel of which consists in the cyclical theory of *corsi e ricorsi*—would not at all doubt the thesis that the present is merely a contradictory parenthesis between the past and the future, with the result that the future often possesses a greater affinity with the past than it does with the present. In the next place, one lacks the historic sense if one supposes it possible completely to restore the past. Epochs of history do not lend themselves to photographic reproduction. In the process, something has been altered, some one has moved, as regards congruity of situation and agreement of will. This is why parties of the past should not imagine themselves able to re-establish the *tempora acta* as they were. The future must perforce be influenced by the durable changes which have been produced, the "reactionary" party must take account, not only of the real advantages evolved by the disliked present order which it is trying to eliminate, but also of the new fundamental interests which this régime has created. Let us cite two examples. In France, the defeat of the great Revolution and of the fulfillment (though incomplete) which it found in Napoleon I, even while involving the return of the Bourbons and the so-called Restoration, did not—despite the promises of indemnity made to the émigrés—at all restore the old great landed estates. The reaction interfered but slightly with the new peasant class, which, through *fas aut nefas,* had been called into being by means of the redistribution of confiscated property of the aristocrats. Although it is somewhat undesirable, and indeed hazardous, to predict a future enveloped in the mists of the unknown, it

seems clear that the fall of Bolshevism, uncertain though it be, will end in enormous transformations within the legal and economic constitution of Russia, but will leave intact the new forms of small agrarian property which, at the expense of the nobility, have replaced the *latifundia.*

A word more on the question, terminological in the extreme, of parties called revolutionary. Too often is assigned to the term "revolutionary" special historical significance derived from the memory men preserve of the great French Revolution, which is generally considered the prototype of revolutions. It follows that one attaches the word only to the struggles for liberty undertaken by inferior social classes against their superiors. And in addition to this, the popular interpretation of the term involves the existence of violence and bloodletting; whereas, from the purely logical point of view, the word implies only a fundamental change of a legal order, no matter what means are employed to consummate it. Hence one can sustain the thesis that the terms "revolution" and "counter-revolution" are, after all, equivalent. There is only a moral difference between them, and this difference is merely subjective.

In 1831, a Prussian historian, Friedrich von Raumer, wrote from Paris these sensible words: "For liberals, the word 'revolutionary' signifies the suppression of a decrepit and obsolete social order, pernicious and ignominious; while 'counter-revolution' is in their eyes equivalent to a leaning toward injustice and an outworn order. On the contrary, their opponents, the conservatives, understand by the word 'revolution' the aggregate of all follies and delinquencies; while the word 'counter-revolution' is for them a synonym for order, authority, and religion." It is, then, a question of words that express only sentiments and evaluations perhaps quite appreciable but entirely personal and arbitrary. Political science should not countenance such kinds of terminology.

Certainly what may appear to some the debacle of democracy and a sad, nearly irremediable, lesion of its eternal principles can seem to others the confirmation of a salutary law. This law prescribes that men, in every enterprise requiring collective action, must submit their particular movements to the rule of the single will of a leader, and that, of the two possible attitudes, loyalty and mistrust, to be assumed toward that leader—to whom democracies must have recourse—the former is the only one that is constructive and generous.

Since the World War, two new parties, inspired by the ideas of August Blanqui on minorities, and still more by the severe and diversified conceptions of the French syndicalist movement under the spiritual direction of Georges Sorel (Pareto's friend), have arisen. The parties have a new basis, that of the elite. Both consequently find themselves in deep-seated contrast with the current democratic and electionist theories. In Russia, bolshevism, while seizing the central power with an unheard-of violence, has imposed on the majority of the population the domination of a proletarian minority. In Italy, fascism, gifted with the same *élan vital,* snatched the power from weak hands and called to itself, in the name of the country, the minority of active and energetic men who are always to be found.

Moreover, the anti-democratic and theoretically minority elite is rather unable to set completely aside the principle of the masses. For more than a century, liberalism, democracy, and socialism have daily addressed themselves to all classes of the people equally. Let us add to this the method of modern patriotism, which we know to be of a revolutionary nature both by its origin and by its tactics, and which has never ceased to attract to it or to try to fascinate the very last molecule of the national community. Indeed, on the eve of the Revolution, France was (or seemed to the democrats to be) merely an assemblage of people badly united, in part strangers to one another. In spite of a constant tendency toward unity, this France of the *ancien régime* appeared to exhibit only diversity, disorder, heterogeneity; to contemporaries it offered the aspect of chaos. France was united neither in civil legislation (which included more than three hundred local systems of law, often contradictory), nor in administration, nor in judicature, nor in military arrangements, nor in communal life, nor in anything at all. Also, in order to voice in this disunited country the sentiment of *la patrie moderne,* one must give to the whole of France, urban and rural, leave to speak. Heaven knows how much she made use of it in the cahiers of 1789.

Now, with the awakening of the laboring and peasant masses which followed thereupon for nearly a century and a half, the phenomenology of the facts which unroll continually before our eyes demonstrates that today the elite is no longer able to maintain its power without the explicit or tacit consent of the masses upon which it in numerous ways depends. There is, then, between the party, monopolistic and so far master of the state as to be confounded with it, on the one hand, and the masses, deprived of so-called political rights, on the other a social constraint at all points reciprocal. So, at least in Italy, the party of the elite, the Fascists, could but solicit, secure, and conserve the sympathy of the masses. In pursuing this end, the Fascist party was also led by political necessity, i.e, the need of proving to the neighboring states— that, although theoretically a minority, it fully represents the authentic and autochthonous popular will. From this results the adoption of the consensual theory which rests (more than upon the popular vote) upon a public opinion mensurable less by the liberty of the press than by the number of adherents and political and economico-social organizations. It is to some extent popular enthusiasm which serves the parties of the elite as justification of their acquired rights. In relying upon it the party of the elite loses very little of its theoretical purity because an elite, theoretically sure as it is both of its calling and its power, will, by definition, be self-sufficient. There is no need for the elite to have the majority in agreement with it.

And this is truly the antinomy of anti-democracy, an antinomy not necessarily tragic but dangerous, consisting in a dilemma that appears in a form which one might liken to that of an accordion. For the parties of the elite describe, in their applied political life, a perpetual oscillatory movement, stimulated alternately by fortuities, such as the suitability of the situation, and still more by the two inherent tendencies, that is, by their doctrinaire stereotypes and by their political interests. Indeed, the parties of the elite, turn by turn, swell their structures excessively up to the point of embracing nearly the whole nation and boast of their millions of political and syndical assessed members, and then suddenly contract their frames by expelling the excess, attempting to become again minority parties, properly so called, namely, the parties of election and of choice, sometimes even in proportion to a *numerus clausus.* Between these two extreme limits, the one signalized by the indispensability of the authority of numbers, and the other fixed by the principle of homogeneity and of the strength which flows therefrom, the pendulum oscillates unceasingly.

II–SOME PATTERNS OF POLITICAL ORGANIZATION AND AUTHORITY

1. *The Idea of Corporation*

BY OTTO VON GIERKE

I

THE INTERPRETATION of the material set down in the *Corpus juris civilis,* by the flourishing science of law in medieval Italy, called forth theoretical reflections about the legal nature of corporate groups [*Verbaende*]. Thus, a learned theory of corporations came into being.

Its foundations were laid by the glossators of secular law. The extant legal writings of the pre-Bologna period, as well as the writings of the Lombard school of law, fail to show even a faint trace of a theory of corporations. The glossators, however, by their thorough scholarly preoccupation with the sources, were necessarily led to resume the theoretical considerations about the legal nature of corporate groups already made by the Romans. Furthermore, making the rediscovered ideas of a vanished era the objects of their own thinking, they supplied the modern science of law with a speculative element that was alien to Roman jurisprudence. They were the first to raise questions about the "legal nature" and the "essence of the thing." They posed the fundamental question as to whether, and to what extent, the *universitas,* or corporate body, is essentially identical with the sum of its members and the whole with the sum of its parts. The raising of these questions sowed the seed for all future speculation on the nature of the subjectivity of corporate groups. [*Verbandssubjektivitaet*].

Yet the glossators and their immediate successors did not go beyond the beginnings of a theory of corporations. Its dogmatic elaboration and full expression took place only around the middle of the thirteenth century, and—as we shall see—it was largely in the hands of the canonists. In two

respects, however, the foundations laid in this preparatory stage by the civilistic glossators remained crucial for the entire medieval theory of corporations.

First of all, the glossators had a major share in introducing Roman legal views of corporate groups into medieval thinking. They adhered as closely as possible to the text of the sources, much more closely than their successors. They took no account of the specific features of the legal customs of their own time whenever they had, or believed to have, an unequivocal decision of the sources before them. To the extent that they understood the sources correctly, the glossators inevitably revived Roman legal notions, although this revival was at first limited only to the community of scholars.

On the other hand, they themselves had already brought into the theory of corporations an abundance of medieval Germanic elements. Here, more than in any other area, the source material, difficult and incomplete as it was, defied their full comprehension. The principle behind the separate statements of the sources remained hidden to them; the historical context escaped them; the actual bases of the Roman [legal] abstractions remained strange to them. The distinction between legal subjectivity of public law and the personality of private law—so fundamental for Roman legal thought—must especially have been beyond their comprehension. They frequently tended to make obvious reinterpretations and misinterpretations and ingenious emendations. But wherever they acted in such an involuntarily independent way, the glossators read into the sources the point of view of the earlier, still essentially Germanic, Middle Ages, whose children they themselves were.

Through the medium of the Longobard law and particularly the Longobard feudal law, the Italian statutes, and some laws of the German emperors, the glossators acquired a wealth of positive Germanic legal material, which was often incorporated

Translated by Ferdinand Kolegar, from Otto von Gierke, *Das deutsche Genossenschaftsrecht* (Berlin: Weidmannsche Buchlandlung, 1881), Book III, chap. xii, pp. 188–238.

into their system. But the whole intellectual climate of medieval Italy and the realities of the state and legal life surrounding them influenced the intellectual form into which they shaped Roman legal materials. With respect to the gamut of political ideas and styles, inseparable from corporation law, it goes without saying that the law which predominated in Italy in the period of glossators was the Germanic law. It is thus understandable that the ideas of Germanic law infiltrated the glossators' theory of corporations.

But the [legal] elements of ancient Rome and of the Germanic Middle Ages were not amalgamated in the glossators' doctrine. From the onset, an inner cleavage was implanted in corporation theory that has never been entirely healed. The contradiction and conflict of these two conceptions led to many confusions and misunderstandings, but they also gave impetus to a rich theoretical development.

The glossators themselves were not fully aware of the contradiction between the divergent conceptions with which they operated. Nevertheless, they discerned the point which was at the root of the basic predicament of the theory and of the cleavage of the conceptions. They took pains to answer the question they had introduced into jurisprudence, namely, the question of the conceptual relationship between the group as a whole and the sum of its parts. Yet, as we shall demonstrate, they did not succeed in finding a satisfactory answer. We search in vain through their writings for a cogently formulated principle that was consciously applied to all particulars. They covered up resulting contradictions by blunting the unpleasant edge of this or that rule or completely ignoring, as if by a tacit consensus, this or that logical difficulty. Only over relatively unimportant points do the differences crystallize into explicit controversies.

In its foundations, the glossators' theory of corporations is incomplete, inconclusive, and ambiguous. This is true not only of the form in which we encounter this theory in the compilation of *Glossa ordinaria,* but also of its formulation in the extant writings of the mid-thirteenth century.

We shall now attempt to reconstruct this first stage of the medieval theory of corporations. It is apparent that the corporation theory of the glossators and their successors contains the beginnings of a juridical conception of state and ecclesiastic corporate groups. But at the point where, in the glossators' own view, the genuine state sphere begins, the medieval philosophic conception of the universal spiritual-temporal association of mankind rises above the legal conception evolved from the corporation law. This is the meeting ground of the ideas of Romanistic jurisprudence developed on the basis of the revived Roman law, the theorems derived from the doctrine of the church, political ideas formulated in the struggle between the church and the state, and philosophical reflections about state and church stemming from the renascence of ancient philosophy. Therefore, both here and in the subsequent stages of development of the medieval theory of corporations, we shall discuss the relevant aspects of the theoretical system of the jurists only so far as necessary for our understanding and, later on, for a comprehensive presentation of the public-law theories of the Middle Ages.

The glossators' concept of the corporation is extraordinarily broad and vague. It coincided substantially, in their own time and during the whole Middle Ages, with the concept of the corporate group as a legal subject. The glossators did not find in the sources any other generic term to denote a subjective unit that cannot be dissolved into a simple communal or societal relationship among the many [*Gemeinschafts- oder Gesellschaftsverhaeltnis unter Mehreren*], nor did they coin such a concept themselves.

Consequently, the glossators subsume every corporate unit that is a subject of public and private rights—including the church and the state—under the one concept of corporation. The term they prefer most to denote it is *universitas,* but they often use terms like *corpus, collegium,* and even *societas* co-extensively. They nevertheless try to establish a more precise and consistent terminology. Thus, while emphasizing the general meaning of the word *universitas,* they want to regard *collegium* only as an association of *"simul cohabitantes";* *societas* as an association of *"non cohabitantes";* and *corpus* as any one of both instances. But they themselves do not carry out this arbitrary differentiation, whose legal insignificance has been already noted by Baldus.

The definitions of the concept of corporation preserved from this time are so general as to be applicable to any organized human corporate group. The *Glossa ordinaria* does not contain any definition at all. On the other hand, the definitions of Pillius (*Summa* to *Cod.* 11, 17, No. 1) and of Hugolinus (*Summa* to *Dig.* 3, 4 No. 1), later attributed to Azo, were held in great respect. Yet Pillius says: *"Collegium est personarum plurium in corpus unum quasi conjunctio vel collectio: quod generali sermone universitas appellatur, corpus quoque, vulgariter apud nos consortium vel schola."* The definition of Hugolinus is even more general. Lumping together the universalities of persons and of things and quoting a reference from 1. 30 D. 41, 3, he defines: *"universitas est plurium corporum collectio inter se distantium, uno nomine specialiter eis deputato."* The words *"plurium collectio"* are used to indicate the difference from the *individuum* (such as *"bos vel Socrates"*) which consists of parts; the words *"inter se distantium"* are meant to exclude the *totum integrale,* the compound things (such as *armarium vel carruca*); and the words *"specialiter eis deputato,"* to indicate that a generic term (such as *homo*) of itself does not denote a *universitas.* As a subspecies of the *universitas,* Hugolinus regards the *universitas rationabilis,* which alone is meant by the Digest title, despite the rubric word *"cujusque."* A corporation to him, then, is any human corporate group that is outwardly characterized as a separate entity by means of a special corporate name.

Not only were all the then existing communities and associations included under this generic concept. It was also applied to institutions [*Anstalten*] and foundations [*Stiftungen*], which we have come to think of in contrast to the corporation. Herein the glossators followed the example of the sources. But they treated the idea of corporation earnestly, in a way quite different than in late Roman law with the institutionalized corporation concept. All temporal and ecclesiastic groups were not only classified but also treated as *universitates.* This could be done because the corporate element in fact was never quite lacking in the temporal groups of that time, and it was also present, at least as a norm, in the ecclesiastic groups.

The church especially, in so far as it was discussed as a legal subject, was subsumed under the concept of the corporation. The glossators came to realize that the word *ecclesia* has several meanings. In particular, one had to distinguish three meanings of it: the general or universal, the spatial, and the particular church. The *ecclesia universalis* was conceived of as an *universitas* endowed with rights and privileges. There was no need of a more precise specification of the nature of the church, since the ownership of the church property and, thus, the legal subjectivity in accordance with secular law were ascribed to the individual churches. With regard to the individual churches, the linguistic usage that introduced the *"locus pius"* or *"locus religiosus"* as a subject continues. An attempt is even made to construe the legal subjectivity of the church as a personification of a thing [*Sachpersonifikation*]. We read about an *"archiepiscopus Moyses,"* who advanced the view that *ecclesia* is always *"locus consecratus et parietibus circumdatus";* that the church in this spatial sense has property and possessions (*"quod ipse locus possideat"*); and that, therefore, especially after a complete cessation of clerical fellowship, the church property is held together by walls (*quod parietes possessionem retineant"*), since in reality *"etiam durante collegio parietes possideant."* According to the gloss, it might be said in support of Moyses that the sources actually understood the *ecclesia* mostly in terms of the church building. Yet, at the same time, the church was regarded as having the right, having possession, and being the proper plaintiff in an action for recovery. But this conception, which might have led to a genuine concept of institution [*Anstalt*], was not understood, and there were even many who rejected it as absurd.

The prevailing view ascribed rights and privileges to the church in the spatial sense, but these were only special privileges of all consecrated places, such as the right of asylum, etc. The idea of God's ownership of the church property expressed in one gloss and the popular view of ownership by a particular patron saint of the church were insufficient from the legal standpoint, and the glossators had recourse to the third meaning of *ecclesia,* i.e., *ecclesia* as a local corporate group. This must be understood whenever the church is discussed as a legal subject. Considering the conditions of that time, the local corporate group [*lokaler Verband*] was not conceived of as the congregation [*Gemeinde*], but only as the clerical fellowship [*Genossenschaft*]. In this way, the glossators arrived at a definition such as the one formulated by Placentinus: *"ecclesia dicitur collectio vel coadunatio virorum vel mulierum in aliquo sacro loco constitutorum vel constitutarum ad serviendum Deo."* Thus, the church was actually brought into the corporate schema as a legal subject, and thus the *ecclesia* could be counted forthwith among the *universitates* and *collegia* and be subjected to the same rules of law. Moreover, since it was the most privileged of corporations, the church could not be deprived of any right ascribable to a corporation. Consequently, it was put on the same level with the *respublica* and *civitas.*

This corporate concept of the church was completely applicable to the collegiate churches and monasteries. One always thought primarily of such churches, and the legists generally refer to cathedral churches and cloisters for the purpose of exemplification in corporation law. But this concept becomes inadequate once the collegiate arrangement is lacking or is left out of consideration. As soon as one is fully aware that this subsumption is inappropriate, one cannot help but apply the corporation law anyway. Typical in this respect is the glossators' treatment of the controversial question: *"an episcopus, abbas aut similes personae juramentum calumniae ipsi subire debeant."* A legal dispute about the components of church property is obviously assumed. In such a case, the prelate acts alone, not as a head of the collegiate body or with the collegiate body co-acting. There is a dispute over whether, in such an instance, the prelate can be represented in taking the oath. The right to swear through a *syndicus* or *actor* is regarded as a privilege of the *universitas*. Several legists, notably Aldricus, refuse to grant this right to the bishop or abbot, "*quia isti non sunt universi nec universitas,*" (or as a gloss says: "*quia ipse nec univ. nec corpus nec coll. est*"), and because they are represented by a regular *procurator* without the rights of a *syndicus*. In spite of this, the opposite view of Johannes Bassianus, i.e., the application of the corporation law, became prevalent. The reasoning was that the prelate does not litigate on behalf of himself but on behalf of the *ecclesia* and is, thus, on an equal footing with a guardian or a similar "*legitimus administrator.*" But it remained unanswered what the represented *ecclesia* really is.

As a rule, little attention was paid to churches employing only one clergyman. Only Azo, who is generally commendably precise, tried to formulate a church concept comprehensive enough to include such churches. He defines *ecclesia* as "*persona constituta ad serviendum Deo vel collectio personarum plurium ad idem destinata.*" But he obviously designates thereby only the outward form of the ideal legal subject and leaves unsolved the question of the nature of this subject in case of its being represented by *una persona*. In his further discussion, Azo, like other glossators, makes the assumption that the church acts as a *collegium*.

Charitable endowments did not evoke a special concept of institution or foundation as an addition to the concept of corporation. On the one hand, as church institutes, they were classed together with the *ecclesiae;* on the other hand, they were subsumed under the generic concept of *collegia* and *corpora*. This classification is a result of the old conception according to which even the *personae miserabiles* in the hospital or poorhouse constitute a *collegium*.

The fact that the legists subsumed the churches and ecclesiastical institutions under the corporation of Roman law had an important consequence, namely, that the canonists, in their turn, could incorporate the Roman corporation law into the church doctrine of ecclesiastical institutions. In this medley of the elements of fellowship [*Genossenschaftlich*] and of institutions [*anstaltlich*], the legists gave precedence to the idea of fellowship, whereas the canonists embraced the institutional idea.

No less important was the fact that the glossators subsumed the organs of the state of their time under the concept of corporation and consequently under Roman corporation law. In strict adherence to the classical texts, the glossators apply the Roman concept of the state only to the empire (*Reich*) of their time, identifying it with the Roman empire of the Caesarean era. For all other corporate groups, be they kingdoms or independent republics, they retain the concept of *universitas*.

However, the glossators would hardly have reproved the later conception, which saw in the empire (*Reich*) itself only the most supreme and most inclusive *universitas*. But they do not yet make such an explicit subsumption. Rather they uphold in their theory the contrariety between the empire and other corporate groups as they found it in the sources. They put into the Roman concept of corporation a content that makes it possible for it to be used for theoretical construction of entities having all the characteristics of the state, save formal sovereignty.

The glossators insist that the Roman Empire is the only state in the sense of the sources. They claim the plenitude of power of the state only for the Emperor. This plenitude of power follows from his exclusive possession of the *imperium* conferred upon him by the *populus Romanus*. And wherever the senate and the people are mentioned as bearers of state rights, in addition to the Emperor, the glossators apply these passages literally to the Roman senate and Roman people of their own day and treat the urban community of medieval Rome as the privileged *respublica Romana* and as the capital of the empire. In their view, there is no temporal sovereign but the Emperor, no real *respublica* but the *respublica Romana*. They regard all other holders of public authority, including kings and princes, as Roman magistrates with a derivative *imperium;* and their lands, as Roman provinces and city districts. Every self-contained commonalty—vaguely defined as *populus*, as *civitas*, or as *respublica*—fits into the framework of the Roman *universitas*, no matter whether it is compared, as in the monarchical constitution, to the *universitas provinciae* under the *praeses provinciae*, or, as in a republican constitution, to the Roman *municipium*.

Nevertheless, the idea of a true disestablishment of the territorial and municipal corporate groups was not contained in the teachings of the glossators. No matter how much the glossators tried to enhance the imperial power, the medieval empire [*Kaiserreich*] was much too removed from a genuine and exclusive state to make it plausible for them to resuscitate, though only in theory, the Roman conception of public law concentrated in the sphere of one single will. And it was impossible to deny independent publicistic legal subjectivity to the more or less independent territories and municipalities, which contained the beginnings of the state structure to a far greater extent than was the case in the Reich, and especially to the powerful city republics of Italy, in whose midst the glossators themselves lived. If the medieval lands and cities were to be regarded as provinces and municipal towns of the Roman law, the compelling nature of these facts forced an expansion of these concepts that was alien to the sources. This occurred in such a way that all fundamental concepts of the Roman law of state were unconsciously assimilated by the glossators to the medieval point of view. Roman offices came to be regarded as official prerogatives, jurisdictions as privileges, the *imperium merum* and *mixtum* and the *jurisdictio* as patrimonial or feudal property of their owners. The conception according to which public power was an object of acquired rights was thus brought into the sources. The associations [*engere Verbaende*] or their heads obtained many publicistic power rights that could be traced to enfeoffment of superior power, but which were thought of as independently acquired subjective rights even with regard to the grantor of the fief. Indeed, the internal corporate rights were regarded as original attributes of the entity of every corporate group. The *universitas* thus became a self-contained body; its very concept held the quintessence of a public community [*oeffentliches Gemeinwesen*], and it was capable of absorbing all the constituents of the state.

In principle, however, the glossators do not agree to applying the name of the public community to the associations [*engere Verbaende*]. Following the sources, they assert that the terms "*res publica*," "*jus publicum*," "*bona publica*" can be rightly applied only to the empire and the city of Rome, other commonalties being "*loco privatorum*." They also uphold the lasting validity of the internal and external provincial and municipal law of the Justinian era. For this reason, they attribute to the cities only the importance of the Roman *municipia,* and explain the independent status of the Italian cities, which is inconsistent with that notion, mostly as usurpation. In all jurisdictions that, according to Roman administrative organization, are in some way permanently connected with provincial or municipal administration, the glossators see the rights of such corporate groups, loaned one and for all and hence vested rights. For them, these corporate groups [*Verbaende*] are the equivalents of provinces and *municipia*. They concede the possibility of an enlargement of a thus constituted

normal sphere of authority by special privileges of the Emperor or by other legitimate legal titles, from which they naturally let follow other acquired rights. On the basis of misunderstood passages, they finally grant to any recognized *universitas* autonomy, jurisdiction, election of the head, and other rights of self-administration. Actually, they elevate the associations [*engere Verbaende*] of the empire to public communities. The glossators increasingly apply the concept and the right of *res-publica*, of *jus publicum,* and of *bona publica* to the individual *populi* and *civitates*, with the usual provisos. Indeed, the glossators sometimes openly admit that they ascribe to the corporation a public-law sphere of its own.

Yet, having taken from the Romans the terms *publicus* and *privatus*, the glossators do not make the complete separation of public and private rights in fact. Under the influence of medieval views, they constantly apply many public-law principles to situations included under Roman private law. Consider the continual confusion of dominance [*Herrschaft*] and property right [*Vermoegensrecht*] in the concept of *dominium!* Thus, the glossators are in the position to inject public-law content into allegedly private rights of corporations.

In fact, then, the glossators' doctrine of corporations contains a fair amount of theory concerning public or constitutional law.

II

In view of such an expansion of the concept of corporation, the glossators were little prepared to comprehend the nature of the corporation as it was understood in the classical texts, since the sources did not contain an explicit formulation of fundamental Roman ideas. Because the separation of publicistic and property-law aspects of the corporate groups did not occur to them, the glossators lacked the key to a full comprehension of the various definitions contained in the sources. They applied anything stated in the sources about the public functions of a group or its head, uncritically to the sphere of the legal person as assumed in private law, and the other way round. In all their fumbling attempts at a conceptualization of the nature of corporativeness, the glossators take it for granted that the group [*Verbandsganze*] is in precisely the same way a subject as to property and as to power [*Vermoegenssubjekt und Machtsubjekt*].

In this sense, the glossators take from the sources the general idea that the corporate group, as such, is a unitary legal subject [*einheitliches Rechtssubjekt*]. By defining the *universitas* as an association "*in corpus unum*" and comparing its members to the limbs of the human body, they conceive of the corporation as a unified whole made up of many parts. They ascribe to this whole its own legal subjectivity, by maintaining—following the classical texts—that the *universitas* does not change with the exchange of its members, that it can last perpetually, and that it has a right different from that of the *singuli*.

The glossators did not succeed in building a foundation for corporate legal subjectivity, since they failed to make the decisive step, which was the application of the concept of personality to the *universitas*. Not once does one find in the writings of the glossators the word and the concept of "juristic person." The gloss characteristically refrains from any comment on the famous *lex mortuo* and on other passages of the classical texts that later led to the discovery of the personality of the corporate group. This fact makes it unnecessary to speculate about the nature of the corporate-group personality. Similarly, the theory of fictions was then not yet established. The first legist to write about the nature of the corporate legal subjectivity lived in the first half of the thirteenth century and was also a canonist. His name was Roffredus of Benevant. In the qu. 27 of his *Questiones sabbatinae,* Roffredus discusses the question of the right of recovery of a sponsor of a *universitas* against the *singuli* and, with a precision unusual at that time, evolves the distinction between the *universitas* and the *singuli*. In this connection, he raises the question as to whether anybody could represent a *pars universitatis* in a lawsuit. He declares that this is logically impossible because the "*universitas est quoddam individuum, unde partes non habet,*" since—according to Aristotle—the individual is indivisible. The manner in which the idea of an indivisible individuality of the corporation is expressed shows clearly that Roffredus was not yet familiar with the concept of *persona ficta.* This concept was to gain currency soon thereafter.

So the glossators did not go beyond the idea that the corporate legal subject is identical with the totality [of members] [*Gesammtheit*]. And they were then confronted with an even more ponderous question concerning the relationship of the totality as a unity to the totality as a multiplicity.

They did not reach an unequivocal decision on this cardinal question. The text of the sources has drawn them to the Roman conception, which held the *universitas* as a unitary legal subject to be an artificial "individual" quite distinct from the totality of its members. But the glossators were far from expressing and pursuing such a conception. They were much more profoundly influenced by

the Germanic view holding the unity as a group-person, which is immanent to organized commonalty, to be elevated above the individual persons. But they were unable to come out with a legal explication and clarification of this view. They remain prisoners of the then prevalent sensory-concrete way of thinking, which views the totality as a unity with assembled multiplicity as identical with the totality as a multiplicity with a dispersed unity. This accounts for the fact that they put forth many mutually contradictory statements that were to perplex even their successors in a later period. On the one hand, they make varied use of the Roman dictum "*quod universitatis est non est singulorum,*" from which it follows that the *universitas* is not identical with the sum of all its members. But, on the other hand, they steadfastly maintain that the *universitas* is a sum total of the individuals. If necessary, the word "*singulorum*" could be translated as "of individual" rather than "of the individual," so that either "*omnes singuli*" or "*universitas*" could be construed as an antithesis of the "*singuli*." The gloss to 1. 7 par. D. h.t., thus says: "*universitas nihil aliud est, nisi singuli homines qui ibi sunt.*" The gloss to 1. 15 par. 1 D. *de dolo malo* 4, 3, explains "municipes" in terms of "*sc. omnes generaliter.*" The gloss to 1. 1 par. 1 D. h. t., says about the "*syndicus*" that he is a representative of an *universitas* and acts always "*pro pluribus,*" never "*pro uno,*" which is substantiated by a strange etymology: "*nam dicitur syndicus quasi singulorum causam dicens.*"

Similar views emerge in other rulings and interpretations, although they are usually not expressed so bluntly. There is only one passage which suggests a solution for the inevitable contradictions: in the gloss to 1. par. 1 D. de coll. et corp. 47, 22 v., "*competit*" appears to be introducing, in its last sentence, the distinction between the totality in the collective, and the totality in the distributive, sense. The view of the *universitas* as a collective unity elevated to the status of a legal subject represents, in effect, the basic conception of the glossators.

It may be concluded that the glossators were as yet not even aware of the difference between the corporation, on the one hand, and the communal or societal relationships, on the other hand. They protected themselves against outright confusion by closely following the classical texts, which on this very point are unambiguous. The glossators accordingly treat the *universitas* as a legal subject, while at the same time avoiding the assumption of legal subjectivity on the part of a *societas* or *communio.* The nonchalance with which they lump together the corporate and societal elements betrays the fact that the glossators had not yet discovered the criterion for distinguishing between them.

As the glossators' view of the nature of a corporation oscillates between the Roman and the Germanic conceptions, the details of the theory of corporations fluctuate correspondingly in both directions. Depending on which is determining—the clear language of the classical texts or the medieval-Germanic viewpoint of the commentators—the individual decisions and rulings point to opposite basic principles.

III

To establish a corporate group, the glossators posit above all the requirement of recognition by the state. They even venture a supposition that no association is allowed for which there is not a specific proof of approval by the state.

The glossators never expound the distinction between a public-law permission or a permission issued by the police, on the one hand, and the granting of a legal subjectivity, on the other hand. By governmental approval, a society [*Verein*] becomes *collegium licitum* and obtains corporate rights, whereas a society [*Verein*] without an approval, and thus as a *collegium illicitum,* not only is punishable but is devoid of the legal capacity to have rights and duties [*Rechtsfaehigkeit*]. *Collegia licita* without legal subjectivity are as unknown to the glossators as are *collegia illicita* with legal subjectivity.

Although they call this required approval a "special" one, the glossators do not mean by this a special licensing of each individual society [*Verein*], but rather the permission of entire categories of corporations by a general rule of law. Such a rule they find expressed in the common written law favoring all types of corporations mentioned by the *Corpus juris*—either explicitly or in the opinion of its interpreters—as *collegia licita*. Therefore, they ascribe the corporate right to all churches and church institutions; to all local communities, including rural ones (on this only seldom was there a divergent view); to the town councils; to the artisans' guilds explicitly mentioned in the sources; etc. But the glossators do not hesitate to expand these categories whenever they feel a special need for it. Thus, for example, they declare as *collegia* approved by law (on the basis of 1. 7 C. *de jurisd. omn. jud.* 3, 13, which is actually little suited for this purpose) all fellowships [*Genossenschaften*] of business men and artisans. On the same level with these fellowships, they put the collectivity of university teachers. There was a dispute as to whether the *universitas scholarium* was approved by common law. Some denied it and questioned the right of

election of the rector appertaining to the *universitas scholarium* in Bologna, on the ground that the *scholares* themselves do not practice a profession but are comparable to the pupils of the practitioners and, consequently, to the apprentices of a trade. Other glossators again drew an opposite conclusion from the classical texts. And, according to a widespread opinion, every fellowship [*Genossenschaft*] dedicated to protection of common rights was regarded as *universitas approbata*. Thus, Hugolinus concludes his enumeration of *collegia licita* with the words: "*et ut generalius loquar, omnis congregatio potest dici licita, quae fit pro conservanda cuique sua justitia.*" And the gloss to 1. 1 par. 2 D. h. t. v. "*aliorum*" takes up this category of "*quaelibet congregatio pro justitia conservanda,*" cites as an example the "*congregatio scholarium Tuscorum vel universitatis totius,*" and in the end even ascribes to every "*societas quinque vel sex scholarium in uno hospitio*"—the right to appoint a *syndicus* for *causae societatis*.

No matter how broadly or how narrowly the categories of the corporations recognized by common law are conceived, one can still think of situations in which a corporately constituted group could not be subsumed under these categories. In such cases, the necessary approval was found in a special "*privilegium principis*." Herein was the root and beginning of the doctrine of the necessity of a character [*Koncessionslehre*], which became fully developed only later on.

The glossators have little to say about other requirements for the foundation of a corporation. They merely reiterate the rules contained in the sources that demand a union [*Verein*] of at least three persons and tacitly assume the necessity of a constitution and a president.

The glossators do not divide corporations according to whether their coming into existence was indispensable or whether they were voluntarily created, nor do they distinguish conceptually between purely personal corporations and those determined territorially or by material circumstances.

IV

In regard to the legal capacity of the corporation, the glossators borrow from the classical texts the proposition that the corporation is capable of owning property. They equate this with the individual person's capability of owning property and go beyond the Roman law to the extent that they overlook the restrictions on corporate capability of acquiring property on death by bequest and device, restrictions that were upheld even by Justinian. They regard each *collegium licitum* as fully capable of acquiring property from the institution of an heir. They also ascribe to the corporations the capacity for specific medieval rights—particularly public rights—regarding property. At the same time, they claim for the corporations of their time all the private-law privileges entrusted to certain kinds of corporations by the Roman law. They are disposed to transfer the privileges of fiscus, of the churches, and of the cities to all corporations or certain types of them. This gave rise to numerous controversies, such as those concerning the statute of the period of limitations, the *restitutio in integrum,* the taking of possession without "immemorial usage," the debt privileges, and letting out on bail. We shall be concerned with these controversies only in so far as they had a direct bearing on the nature of the corporation.

In accordance with the Roman law, the glossators treat the corporate property as ordinary individual property, the subject of which is the *universitas* as such.

This idea of corporate property had to overweigh the residual influence, noticeable both in the Roman and the German law, of another conception which negates, completely or partially, the idea of ownership as regards public property. The often unclear terminology of the sources with reference to derelict, common, and public things was a cause of many difficulties to the glossators. They extricate themselves from some of these difficulties by labeling the Roman category of *res nullius* as ambiguous and vague. In their view, the category of *res nullius* in the narrower sense comprises only the ownerless things that can be occupied; in the broader sense it negates only the property of individuals, but it comprises also the *res sacrae, religiosae et sanctae,* since their real owner is God ("*sed sunt in bonis Dei, hominum censura sive dispositione*"). Furthermore, it comprises the common, public, and corporate things, since they belong to human groups but to no single individual as such ("*quia esse possunt et sunt hominum, licet non hominis singularis; nullius, i.e., hominis privati, sed communitatis*"). As to the latter, one has to distinguish the *res communae* and the true *res publicae* from the *res universitatis.* Both former categories exclude ownership, not only by individuals, but also by any corporate group. Only the right of "*populus totius mundi*" is applicable to them. The *res communes* are common in terms of usage and ownerless in terms of ownership, whereas the *res publicae* are the property of all mankind. In contrast to these, the *res universitatis* are characterized by the fact that they belong to a distinct corporate group; they are, in the glossators' opinion, "*res unius populi*" and, therefore, they, too, are some-

times called *res publicae,* although not in the strict sense of that word.

Among the *res universitatis,* the gloss distinguishes two kinds of property, depending on whether it is used publicly or not. The latter, the glossators agreed, are just as much "*in patrimonio universitatis*" as similar pieces of property are in the possession of individuals. But the old controversy with regard to the *res universitatis* left to public use persisted. Placentinus maintained that only the right of use [*Gebrauchsrecht*] but not of property [*Eigentum*] itself appertains to an *universitas.* This view was supported by citing particularly the restrictions on sale and the exclusion of adverse possession [*Ausschluss der Ersitzung*]. And it was on this view that Roffredus based his decision in an extremely interesting *quaestio* about the possibility of executive requisition of "*forum, theatrum, viae publicae, fontes et flumina,*" on account of communal debts. But, on the whole, the opposite opinion of Azo prevailed, assuming a *dominium* of the *universitas.* Azo notes that the difference between both types of the *res universitatis* lies in the fact that things destined for public use are both in *dominium* and in *usus,* whereas the other things are in *dominium* and *fructus,* but not in *usus* of the *universitas.* The identification of the *universitas* with the totality [*Gesammtheit*] in this statement is apparent. The latter usage that made the distinction between *res in patrimonio universitatis* and true *res universitatis* and that included under the *res universitatis* those assets that—as "civic property" [*Buergervermoegen*] or "people's property" [*Genossengut*]—we usually place in contraposition to the "true" corporation property [*Korporationsvermoegen*] is thus made understandable. The idea of individual corporate property [*korporatives Individualvermoegen*], which by definition negates the concept of shares in Roman law, had to contend with the then firmly ingrained Germanic idea of the property of the community. The glossators mistakenly read into the sources a contradiction which they sensed in themselves. They maintained that the many variations on the theme "*quod universitatis est non est singulorum,*" in the classical texts, are contradicted by other statements which patently contained the opposite idea: "*quod est collegii est singulorum.*" They particularly pointed out to 1. 1 par. 1 i. f. D. *de coll. et corp.,* according to which the resigning member can claim his share. They also referred to 1.3 *eod.,* according to which the right of the division of property granted to *collegia illicita* in case of their dissolution must be automatically granted also to *collegia licita.* And they referred also to the least relevant Nov. 123 c. 36, which rules that the bishop divides the property whenever monks and nuns are assigned to separate cloisters. In all these instances, the glossators said, the shares of *singuli* are recognized, but they cannot be reconciled, according to other passages (arg. 1. 25 pr. D. *de V.S.* and 1. 5 D. *de leg.* I) with the conception of the property of the *universitas* as distinguished from the right of *singuli:* "*quod ergo erat collegii, erat singulorum*" Whereas some glossators strictly adhered to the Roman conception, in spite of the ostensibly contradictory statements, others among them regarded the applications cited in the *Corpus juris* as mere singularities, and sought to substantiate the assumption of the shares by the individuals with the idea that members who were leaving were by right always replaced by substitutes. Gradually, they reached the very significant opinion that the solution is not to be sought in the rejection of one or the other rule but in the distinction between various types of assets, each of which is subsumable under a different principle or rule. Already in the *Glossa ordinaria* this opinion is considered to be the correct one. But this distinction was then obviously novel and as yet insufficiently formulated. Evidence of this is to be found in the inappropriate examples cited by the gloss for one or the other kind of assets, e.g., recognizing the shares of the *singuli* in property built by contributions, but denying them with regard to assets bequeathed to the corporation. The distinction between the various types of assets was then not yet applied to the actual conditions of joint ownership of commons; and it is not mentioned in the question of an individual's capacity to give legal evidence in matters of the *universitas,* although it plays an important role later on.

In any case, the first foundation was laid for the later [legal] constructions which attempted to incorporate the ideas about the legal relations in commons and similar local communities as found in the German law into the Romanistic doctrine of corporate property.

As to corporate debts, the glossators began with the Roman ruling that *universitas* itself is liable for debts to the exclusion of its single members. But they supplemented it by the general rule according to which a propertyless *universitas* could be compelled to procure the property necessary to meet its obligations by imposing a levy on its members. In the back of this, of course, there was the concept of the susidiary liability of the *singuli.*

V

Moreover, the glossators altered the content of the sources in two ways. First, by postulating a special publicistic legal capacity of corporate groups. Secondly, by identifying the subject of corporate power rights with the subject of corporate property rights.

The glossators constantly assume that a *universitas* can acquire public rights on ground of special claims to the same extent as can an individual. The dispute about the alienability [*Verueusserlichkeit*] and prescriptibility [*Verjaehrbarkeit*] of the rights of the empire [*Reichsrechte*] will be discussed in a later section of this work on publicistic theories.

Of particular interest here is the fact that the glossators derive from the nature of the corporation a number of privileges characterizing the corporation as a social organism with its own special and independent sphere of communal life [*Gemeinleben*]. They also conclude that the corporation is a community [*Gemeinwesen*] endowed with authority over its members. While subscribing to the views of their time, the glossators "rediscovered" their ideas in the *Corpus juris,* to which the idea of specific and aboriginal inner corporate rights was unknown.

Only occasionally do the glossators say that they regard the rights of assemblage, admission of new members, election of the board, and taxation as self-evident attributes of the corporation. By citing misunderstood passages from the classical texts, they substantiate emphatically and thoroughly the rights of corporate autonomy and corporate jurisdiction.

As far as autonomy was concerned, one found an explicit recognition of "*statuta municipalia,*" in those passages that defined the *jus civile* as "*jus quod quisque populus ipse sibi constituit*" or as "*jus proprium civitatis,*" in contradistinction to the *jus gentium.* The controversial right of territorial legislation [*Recht partikulaerer Gesetzgebung*] for various categories of territorial rulers and municipal authorities was derived from the official privileges of Roman magistrates, mixing the concepts of jurisdiction and legislation. And, by assuming or postulating the participation of the people [*Volk*] or its representatives, the territorial corporate group [*territorialer Verband*] as such was regarded as the proper subject of the right of territorial legislation. The maxim which ruled out autonomy: "*soli principi legem facere licet,*" was brushed aside in making the assumption that it refers only to *lex generalis* and leaves local legislation free. In other cases, the glossators made the even bolder interpretation that this rule only means that "*solus Imperator solus legem facere potest,*" so that the participation of others is always necessary.

The right of autonomy was in no way restricted

to territorial communities, but was also conceded to voluntarily created fellowships [*gewillkuerte Genossenschaften*], at least in handling their internal affairs (*inter se*). It was esay to concede the broadest measure of autonomy, in supposed agreement with the classical texts, since autonomy has always been put on par with customary law. It was taught that the distinction between *statutum* and *consuetudo* implies merely the distinction between an explicit and a tacit consensus, so that *consuetudo* is a *statutum tacitum*. Although this theory was subjected to devastating criticism by Johannes Basianus, Azo, and Accursius, both sources of law were subordinated to the communal standpoint of contract. Under such circumstances, the cause of local autonomy benefited from the struggle waged for the derogative power of local *consuetudo* in relation to common written law.

The glossators succeeded in deducing the right of corporate jurisdiction from the *Corpus juris,* although the basis for this was very tenuous. They applied particularly 1. 7 C. *de jurisd. omn. jud.* 3. 13, which deals with the subordination of tradesmen and artisans to certain special laws, in that elected heads of the fellowship [*Genossenschaft*] were simply regarded as judges. Inversely, the glossators deduced from the stipulations (in Nov. 15) regarding the election of the *defensor civitatis* that his office is a judicature of the community, performed in the name and mandate of the citizens. The glossators argued that the confirmation by the *praefectus praetorio,* as decreed by the supplementary law, merely grants permission to the performance of *jurisdictio:* the *jurisdictio* itself is instituted by municipal election. The glossators proceeded to state that, in general, every *universitas* will establish a normal jurisdiction by electing a board, and consequently the Roman rule "*consensus privatorum non facit judicem*" does not imply the "*consensus universitatis.*"

VI

The glossators' understanding of the classical texts, with regard to the story of the corporation's capacity to act and to have will of its own [*Willens- und Handlungsfaehigkeit*], was even more influenced by their Germanic conception and point of view than their understanding of the theory of legal capacity [*Rechtsfaehigkeit*].

Since they undoubtedly thought that the unanimous will of all was the same thing as the corporate will [*Korporationswille*], the glossators regarded the corporation as capable of having a will of its own [*willensfaehig*]. And since every communal action of all, such as occurred during elec-

tions and acts of assemblies, appeared to them as an action of the corporation, the corporation itself had to be regarded as having capacity to act [*handlungsfaehig*].

The glossators could not comprehend the true meaning of the contradictory statements of the classical texts, because they failed to distinguish between the sphere of the public law and that of the private law. They helped themselves out by seeing in these contradictions mere indication of actual difficulties which the plural nature [*Vielkoepfigkeit*] of the *universitas* and the human propensity to differences in opinion pose to the unitary will and action of a totality [*Gesamtheit*]. This occasioned the oft-repeated excuse to the effect that in the Roman rule, "*universi consentire non possunt,*" one has to insert the word "*facile*"; and that, likewise, wherever a "*facere*" of the *universitas* seems to be described as impossible, what is really meant is that it is difficult. The glossators also claim that they can cite in their support other passages from the classical texts in which the capacity of the *universitas* to act and to have a will of its own is expressly recognized. And with characteristic frankness and simplicity, they also include the "*consensus universorum,*" which the emperor [*Kaiser*] promised to consider, in the *lex humana,* before enacting new laws.

Informed by such a conception, the glossators see in those institutions that, in our eyes, constitute the corporate organization only a series of expedients, necessitated by the difficulty of bringing about unanimous co-operation, on the one hand, and by the inability of an assemblage to undertake certain acts, on the other hand. For this reason, they leave the specific legal concepts of the corporate constitution and of corporate organs as undeveloped as the Roman jurists had left them. They do not go beyond the elaboration and exposition of positive rules contained in the classical texts. The unrelated conception which the glossators brought into these texts has a modifying effect. But the actual state of the corporate constitutional law of their time was decisive.

The two elements to which they reduce all these institutions assert themselves also in the glossators' categorization of these institutions according to two distinct criteria. Those institutions owing their existence to the fact that unanimous joint action is difficult are put into one group. They are the institutions where the will of the majority is important and where there is a representation of the totality by an assembly of the representatives [*Repraesentantenversammlung*]. The glossators believed that both of these types of institutions are essentially based on a legal fiction, by virtue of which an action not willed or done by all is regarded *as if* "all" willed or did it. It is in this connection that the word "fiction" appears in the medieval theory of corporations for the first time.

In the other group are those institutions that enable the corporation to undertake such actions as can be, by their nature, undertaken only by individuals and not at all by assemblies. These are the institutions of corporate board, of other corporate officialdom, and of an individual's authority to represent the corporation. Essential to these institutions, according to the glossators, is the principle of agency [*Stellvertretung*]. The idea of fiction, by virtue of which the actions of individuals were regarded as direct joint actions, seems to be inappropriate in this context, because the glossators were mainly concerned with things that the totality cannot do. The principle of agency, on the other hand, could be applied more easily, since the medieval jurists were free from the Roman restrictions on the concept of representation. The glossators thus put forward the rule that the *universitas*, like an individual, can act "*per se*" as well as "*per alium*." And while regarding the action of all, or the action of a majority, or of a committee of representatives [*Repraesentantenkolleg*] as the actual or fictitious action of the *universitas* "per se," the actions of heads, officials, and authorized agents were regarded as actions of the *universitas* "*per alium*."

If we look at the former of the two just-mentioned groups, we see that the glossators borrowed from the Roman sources the principle of majority as a legal rule applicable to all corporations. The views of some glossators about the mode of reckoning a majority already betray the influence of canon law. To substantiate why the minority should be bound by the decision of the majority, the glossators cite explicitly and exclusively a legal fiction and argue as follows: since it is difficult to achieve an agreement of all it should be decreed by law that whatever the majority wills or does is to be regarded as if all willed or did it. The glossators do not yet think of explaining this rule in terms of the nature of the corporation; they are not yet aware of its specifically corporate constitution and cite, in a veritable hodge-podge, instances of unanimity in purely communal conditions as exceptions to the general rule, and instances of majority will outside of the corporations as confirmations of the rule!

Nevertheless, in two respects, the principle of majority became a starting-point for a clearer comprehension of the concept of the corporation.

First of all, the glossators put forth the rule that not any decision of a majority, but only a decision arrived at in a proper manner, is valid as a decision of the *universitas*. By generalizing the Roman rules concerning the decurion assemblies, the glossators required that all members be summoned to meet —be it singly, be it in the usual public form ("*per tubam vel campanam vel voce praeconia*")—and that two-thirds of them actually appear. If this is the case, and rejecting a different interpretation of the sources, the majority of those present was deemed to be sufficient, since the two-thirds present are tantamount to the whole body. But now, if majority resolutions were contingent on an assembly following a determinate set of rules, the question arose as to whether the situation is any different in case of complete unanimity of all. This question, the answer to which is of singular importance for the concept of the corporation, was actually raised by the glossators. But this very occasion demonstrated that they hardly made the conceptual distinction between the unified joint will [*Gesamtwille*] and the sum of individual wills, between the constituted assembly and the sum of its members. In answering the question: "*quid si quilibet de universitate tibi intulit injuriam? Numquid universitas dicetur hoc fecisse et poterit a te conveniri?*" they assert "*videtur quod non, quia non ut universitas, sc. concilio habito et campana sonata vel alias eis convocatis, fecisset, sed quilibet, suo motu.*" But the ruling of the *Glossa ordinaria* is as follows: "*econtra quod sic; quia universitas nihil aliud est nisi singuli homines, qui ibi sunt.*"

Secondly, the glossators state that the majority resolutions [*Mehrheitsbeschluesse*] are valid only within the area of corporate affairs, but they can never take any individual rights away from the members, nor can they impose individual burdens on them. This was the point of departure for the general idea that the entire activity of the corporation is restricted to a sphere defined by the constitution and determined by its purpose, whereas the individual legal spheres of the members of a corporate group are not at all affected.

On an equal footing with the principle of the majority, the glossators put the principle of representation [*Repraesentativprincip*]. In a way alien to the Romans, they developed this principle as a general institution of corporation law from the law of decurions. They formulated the rule that, wherever the assembly of all is difficult or impracticable, a *collegium* of elected representatives of its majority can make and carry out corporate resolutions instead of the majority of all members. But even this rule they based upon a legal fiction, by virtue of which everything that such representatives willed or did was to be regarded as if all members willed or did. This conception, of course, did not prevent them from simultaneous-developing the idea that full powers [*Vollmacht*] of all members were bestowed by the election. Since the glossators had in mind especially the town-councils of their time, in which representative and administrative functions were combined, they generally interpreted that rule in favor of those who "govern," "administer," or "preside over" a corporate group. But whatever the actions of heads or managers [*Vorsteher*] are thus characterized as actions of the "*universitas ipsa*," what is understood are never individual managers but rather council-like *collegia*. No fixed rules were as yet formulated in regard to the extent to which the assemblage of members can be replaced by the assemblage of representatives. Generally, in congruence with the idea of fiction, the glossators were inclined to make a considerable extension of the principle. This meant that wherever the majority resolutions of all would have been sufficient, in case of doubt the acts of the assembly of representatives could be attributed to the totality [*Gesamtheit*].

These institutions oriented to a fictitious construction of an action of the *universitas ipsa* were then contrasted by the glossators with another group of institutions in which an action of the *universitas per alium* was assumed. Here, again, the glossators altered the content of the classical texts in two respects. On the one hand, they uncritically carried out the principle of free agency [*freie Stellvertretung*], based on a contract or the law, with regard to public-law and private-law acts. On the other hand, they conceived of the relationship between the *universitas* and its heads [*Vorsteher*], officials, and representatives—not merely with regard to its possible consequences for the rights of property, but above all with regard to its publicistic content—as a reciprocal legal relationship. Instead of talking about mere distribution of deportments [*Kompetenz*], they made the assignment of their own proper powers [*Befugnissphaeren*], which, even though they were freely founded and bestowed by the *universitas*, constituted the object of vested rights of their carriers.

Above all, the glossators take it for granted that each *universitas* has a head, a "*rector*," or "*praeses*." Using the Germanic constitutional arrangements as a model, the head of secular corporations, in their view, was the judicial-governmental director [*Vorsteher*]; in the ecclesiastic corporations, it was the prelate or rector *ecclesiae*. They considered this head of the corporate group to be the bearer of the powers of public authority [*obrigkeitliche Befugnisse*], related to the group in question, powers to which they ascribe—under the Roman names of *imperium merum* and *mixtum* or

of a mere *jurisdictio*—the content of Germanic public authorities. However, the exercise of these powers generally called for a single individual. The totality, in so far as it was independent, could acquire such powers, but it could not keep and exercise them and was compelled to transfer them to an individual. And, in so far as the authority in question originated not from the group itself but had its origin in the enfeoffment of superior power [*hoehere Verleihung*], it was entrusted at the outset to the head of the totality. Thus, according to medieval jurisprudence, the board [*Vorsteherschaft*] was regarded as a sphere of power [*Befugnissphaere*] separated from the legal sphere of the totality [*Gesamtheit*] and independent on that totality. In every case, the *rector universitatis* was to some extent a monarchical subject with public authority of his own, regardless of the fact that his position and right could be traced back to a choice and a mandate of the totality. Conversely, even the actual monarch was, in medieval jurisprudence, always regarded as a head of a corporation, whose sphere of power in the last analysis was only a separate and independent piece in the sphere of totality, regardless of the fact that enfeoffment of superior and ultimately divine power was thought to be the source of his power. Thus, in diverse groups, the head of the group and the totality of the group [*Verbandsgesamtheit*] confront each other as two distinct legal subjects as far as their special rights and duties are concerned, while being, as it were, the head and the limbs of one body corporate in the affairs of the community.

Hence, an actual split of the corporate personality into an institutional board or directorate and an associational body, as we often encounter in canonic and publicistic doctrine, was made possible. Although the head of the group and the totality of the group appear collectively as one corporate legal subject, one head is at the same time regarded as the carrier of a special legal personality over and above the totality, while the totality in its turn, even without the head, is regarded as a corporation and, consequently, as a separate juristic person.

A similar position, in a less comprehensive sense, was assigned to other officials of the corporation. They, too, had to perform legal acts on behalf of the *universitas*, that is to say, acts which the totality could not perform at all or only with difficulty. This is true especially of the officials responsible for the current management of property matters and for the conduct of legal cases. Hence, they were regarded as representatives who stood beside the *universitas* rather than in it, and who in fact did not have to belong to the *universitas* at all. Their spheres of power also could be seen as more or less independent in relationship to the corporation.

Finally, the *universitas* was in the position to appoint all kinds of representatives [*Bevollmaechtigte*] for both private and public law affairs, which could then represent the *universitas* in actions which the totality could not, or did not want to, attend directly.

The jurisdictional powers of all those persons who act in behalf of the *universitas* were delineated on the basis of general principles regarding representation. They were determined partly by the powers of attorney conferred by the totality, but on the other hand, if necessary, their content was defined by law. In this latter connection, one spoke of a *"legitima administratio"* and meticulous care was exercised in defining its scope.

In elaboration of the idea contained in the classical texts, the *"legitima administratio"* of the directors, syndics, and administrators was thought of as a guardianship [*Vormundschaft*] under which the *universitas* was placed, in analogy to the *tutela, cura,* or paternal supervision. Consequently, the *universitas* itself was thought of as a minor. Hence, it was entitled also to the benefits [*Rechtswohltaten*] accorded to minors. In fact, instances in which the *universitas* was not equated with the *"pupillus"* were regarded as exceptions. In the old controversy about the time limit of the *"restitutio in integrum"* granted the corporations, some teachers of law took the comparison of the *universitas* with the *minor* so literally that they wanted to allow the *universitas* a perpetual delay, since it will remain forever under age. And when the opinion prevailed that restitution is to be made only *"intra quadrennium a die lesionis,"* most of them adduced only reasons of expediency (*"ratione infinitatis vitandae"*). The view of Azo that the *universitas,* though having the rights of minors, is not really *minor et pupilla* was isolated and had no effect.

Yet this conception of the *universitas* as a minor obviously meant a partial limitation of its capacity to act and to have will of its own. The view of the glossators was that the *universitas* is capable to will and to act, but that this capacity extends only so far as the totality can be directly active in corporate affairs, either actually or by virtue of a fiction. On the other hand, in so far as direct action of an assembly is not possible, the *universitas* seemed to them to be incapable to act and in need of being represented by a guardian. Since in every *universitas* there are some legal transactions that can be performed only by representatives, the *universitas* seemed to belong to the class of subjects held in tutelage, subjects who *"de necessitate per alios agunt."*

To this were added further restrictions on corporate capacity to act, which the glossators imposed by accepting the concept of state and/or ecclesiastical general superintendence rights as they found it in the classical texts. Although they came close to public-law viewpoints and to suggesting the idea of paramount guardianship [*Obervormundschaft*], they did not develop any concise principle, nor did they go beyond proclaiming Roman rules as a valid law. They were only slightly concerned with the problem of how all these rules about the duties of decurions, the *decretum judicis,* the required permission of the *praeses provinciae,* of the *praefectus praetorio,* or of the *princeps* himself were to be carried out in the real-life situations of their time.

VII

When we examine the theory of corporate capacity to act as it was applied to various spheres of activity, we find a confirmation of what we said above in regard to the publicistic sphere. In so far as the assembly of members or a representative committee are directly involved, such as in elections, in the admission of new members, statutes, appointments of officials, etc., the action of the *"universitas ipsa"* is assumed. In so far as the director performs functions of public power, or in so far as other officials or agents act within their spheres of competence, then a direct representation on behalf of the *universitas* is given.

In many cases, the participation or permission of a superior power is necessary for such actions to be considered valid.

Similarly, the corporation was thought to be capable of acting in the pecuniary sphere, e.g., of acquiring possession, concluding contracts, coming into a legacy, accomplishing sales, and release on bond. Here, too, it could act both by itself and through a representative, but for the current management of property matters it needed permanent *"administratores,"* to whom a certain jurisdictional sphere belonged by right. In case of a sale, gift, relinquishment, or settlement, special formalities and assistance of public power were necessary. In this respect, the glossators repeated and often generalized the positive rules contained in the classical texts, especially those pertaining to cities and churches, in spite of numerous controversies and uncertainties.

In applying many of these legal rules to corporations, the glossators did not understand the difficulties that the Roman law had to overcome, since they did not have any reservations that would be rooted in the assumption of absolute capacity to act on the part of the *universitas,* on the one hand, and the limited right of representation, on the other. The glossators regarded the theoretical doubts expressed on the question of the acquisition of property as mistakes that were repudiated later on, and they overlooked other pertinent ideas on this problem. They take as valid law only the positive limitation of the capacity to assume obligation by way of loan, as it was ruled for the cities and churches by the *lex civitas* (1. 27 D. *de R. C.*) and its emendations. Yet, although the glossators are disposed to extend this rule to all corporations and to all kinds of obligations incurred by the receipt of money, they do not think of explaining it in terms of the legal person. Nor do they attempt, as later writers did, to explain away all fundamental peculiarities contained in the *lex civitas* by interpreting them and reshaping them in the desired direction. Rather, they view it as a positive ruling of a special type.

The glossators believed that the *universitas* could take an oath, since the *"universitas ipsa"* seemed to be taking an oath whenever all members, or the majority of members or just the majority of representatives took an oath in a unanimous manner. In this connection, the glossator referred to 1. 97 D. *de cond. et dem.* 35, 1, in applying the jurist's doubt about the possibility to fulfill the condition *"si jurassent municipes"* to the material difficulties of such an oath. Thus the famous controversy of the glossators concerning the corporate oath of calumny centered not around the possibility of corporate oath as such, but only around the extent to which the corporation can be represented in taking the oath.

Whereas Martinus, Aldricus, Placentinus, and others required, on the basis of 1. 2, par. 5 C. *de jur.* cal. 2, 59, that this oath be taken by all members or their majority, most of the teachers of law interpreted the passage of the Codex, in accordance with Pillius, Azo, and Hugolinus, so as to mean that in this instance, too, the oath of the representing authority or its majority is sufficient. Beyond that, on the basis of *"legitima administratio"* and by drawing an analogy with the guardians, special representatives of the corporations in a lawsuit were generally admitted to the oath of calumny on behalf of the *universitas.* In this circumstance, one saw clearly one of the main differences between such representatives and the regular *procuratores.* To substantiate this power of representation, the glossators never argued that the *universitas* as such was unable to take an oath but always pointed to the actual, material difficulties of a collective oath.

VIII

The corporation's power to sue and to be sued was never doubted. But it is precisely before a court of justice that the totality itself cannot appear, either directly or through a representative. Hence, in this area, in the opinion of the glossators, the corporation had to be represented: it had to *"agere et excipere per alium."* In the absence of a legitimate representative, the *universitas* was thought to be tantamount to a *"pupillus indefensus."*

The head of a corporation can act as its representative in a lawsuit. But a special corporate representation in a lawsuit can be established permanently or for individual disputes by means of an election by the totality or its representatives, by a mandate of the directors or administrators, by a decree of the statutes, or through custom. But, according to the glossators, neither the *universitas* itself, nor its directors or administrators can appoint a regular *"procurator,"* since that is reserved only to the representation of an individual person litigating his own case. For procedural representation of a corporation, one can engage the offices of a *"syndicus,"* *"actor,"* and *"oeconomus."* These three kinds of representatives are carefully distinguished from each other, in that the *"syndicus"* is only a representative of the *universitas,* the *"actor"* is a representative both of the *universitas* and of individuals, and the *"oeconomus"* can only be a representative of the bishopric. Actual differences in their legal status are hardly noticeable, the *"syndicus"* and the *"actor"* particularly being treated as equals. All three categories represent an antithesis to the *"procurator,"* being distinguished from him by greater scope of power to act in a lawsuit, based on their *"legitima administratio."*

In any case, the difference between the procedural representative of a corporation and attorneys acting for an individual is only of a qualitative, nature. The representatives of a corporation also belong to the *"procuratores"* in the broader sense, and, like regular *procurators,* they are not a party to a lawsuit, but only representatives of the absent party. Therefore, in certain cases, even though the lawsuit may be conducted through a *"syndicus,"* *"actor,"* or *"oeconomus,"* one has to consider the *universitas* as the true party. Consequently, according to the glossators, in order to put the *universitas* as such in contempt of court, the summons must reach the corporation while it is in assembly. This is closely connected with the conception of the criminal consequences of contumacy, a conception that dominated the whole doctrine. Likewise, the confession of a principal or syndic should be binding on the *universitas* only when it is made in the presence or with the approval of the totality.

Finally, the penalty should be imposed not on the sentenced representative but directly on the property of the corporation.

The above conception of procedural representatives of a corporation as mere independent procurators explains, perhaps, the fact that the older writings on lawsuit overlooked completely, or almost completely, the important doctrine about the procedural situation of legal persons. The first writer on trials to put forth a detailed theoretical statement of this doctrine, containing a special discussion *"de syndico et actore,"* is the canonist Tancredus in his *Ordo judiciarius,* written about 1216. Even later, it was chiefly the canonists who elaborated this theory.

IX

No wonder, then, that the glossators regarded the corporation as capable of committing the tort. In fact, they proclaim without any hesitation that every *universitas,* every local community, yes, every *ecclesia* can be judged delinquent, and to this end they exploit every allusion contained in the *Corpus juris,* while eliminating the antithetical 1. 15 par. 1 D. *de dolo,* by inserting the word *"facile,"* as mentioned above.

They assume that a corporation committed a tort as soon as the totality had acted directly. The view obtained that a wrong committed by everybody for himself was committed by all and consequently by the *universitas.* Yet this opinion was countered by the statement, later generally accepted, that the *universitas,* as such, is delinquent only when all act *"ut universitas,"* i.e., in corporate assembly under corporate forms. Furthermore, in case of unlawful actions as well as in legal transactions, one assumed that the totality was represented by the majority and even by a representative committee, such as, for example, a municipal council. Finally, unlawful actions of the directors, administrators, and other representatives were not supposed to be attributed to the *universitas* any more than the delicts of a guardian are ascribed to the pupil. However, the glossators held that in such a case one could not only bring an action for unjust enrichment against the corporation—and here they were in agreement with the classical texts—but they wanted to impute the delict directly to the corporation, at least when the unlawful action was commissioned or sanctioned after the act by the totality.

The same principles were applied to churches in a way characteristic of the then prevailing conception of the church. The glossators reaffirmed the canonical rules: *"delictum personae non nocet ecclesiae,"* and *"ecclesia non patitur damnum propter culpam praelati."* But not only were the exceptions to this rule postulated, particularly in case of a felony by the prelate of an enfeoffed church, but it was generally assumed that this rule applied only to actions of a superior or of an individual clergyman, and that the opposite held true as soon as the totality of clergymen employed by the church in question acted or took part in the action of the prelate. Such a delict then is a delict committed by the *ecclesia* itself and has the usual consequences.

The glossators found support for this conception in a very artificial interpretation of the 1. 10 C. *de ss. ecclesiis* 1, 2 (*lex jubemus*), threatening with the confiscation of a ship which was not given to the disposal of the state, under some pretext, such as the use of the ship for religious purposes. Whereas some maintained that the confiscation with which the church was threatened constituted a breaking of the rule, *"delictum praelati non nocet ecclesiae,"* the opinion of the glossators was that in this passage the participation of the *collegium* of clergymen in the refusal was presupposed, and, hence, the delict of the church as such was assumed and punished.

There is no doubt that the glossators regarded punishment of the corporation as permissible. The Germanic rules about decreeing a ban against communities, then widely used in Italy, were to them quite unobjectionable. It was precisely here that the Germanic concept of fellowship [*Genossenschaft*] with its identification of unity [*Einheit*] and totality [*Gesamtheit*] made its influence felt in a conspicuous way.

X

As far as the termination [*Beeindingung*] of the corporate was concerned, the glossators assume that in itself every *universitas,* as such, can be permanent. In this connection, they bring up the limitation of the duration of its *ususfructus,* although there was an old controversy as to whether this rule was analogously applicable to the bequest of an annual rent or whether the rent was to be paid perpetually. But the glossators also mention that a corporation can cease to exist in a natural way. They cannot dismiss the explicit ruling of the sources that the corporation continues to exist in a single member. They are aware of the contradiction between this ruling and their own basic conception, and they try to resolve it by claiming that in such a case the *universitas* no longer really exists, since one person cannot constitute a totality, but that one person retains the rights of the *uni-*

versitas. They also discuss what the consequences would be should all members cease to exist (*"si nullus omnino remanserit"*). In the church view, the existing legal subject can continue to exist even then, since the possession [*Besitz*] and title [*Eigentum*] remain attached to the building of the institution [*Anstaltsgebäude*], which was the true subject even *"durante collegio."* The glossators resolutely reject this view as entirely irreconcilable with their own conception. They declare emphatically that the corporation is dissolved when its members "fall away" and that its property becomes ownerless and derelict. Yet, in the eventuality of a reconstitution of the corporation by a competent authority, by means of some legal stratagem, they want to use the fiction—by analogy with the universal succession in case of heritage—that in the new corporation the rights of the old one are perpetuated (*"sed tamen si postea auctoritate domini Papae vel ejus, ad quem spectat cura ejusdem collegii, instituatur in eodem collegio, juris artificio fingitur istius fuisse"*).

In discussing the settlement of property of the *universitas,* the glossators assert that, since the classical sources decreed a distribution of a *collegium illicitum,* this ruling must hold with an even greater force for the *collegia licita.* When all members "fall away," however, the glossators assume that the title of the extinct corporation goes as abandoned to the fiscus or to the Pope (*"verumtamen id esse videtur, ut nullo modo dicantur esse ullius, scil. ab eo tempore, quo solutum est collegium: sed ipso jure sint fisco vel Papae quasita"*), while the possessions become extinct (*"et hoc quantum ad dominium, secus quantum ad possessionem"*).

2. *The Types of Authority*

BY MAX WEBER

I. *The Basis of Legitimacy*

THE DEFINITION, CONDITIONS, AND TYPES OF IMPERATIVE CONTROL

"IMPERATIVE CO-ORDINATION" was defined as the probability that certain specific commands (or all commands) from a given source will be obeyed by a given group of persons. It thus does not include every mode of exercising "power" or "influence" over other persons. The motives of obedience to commands in this sense can rest on considerations varying over a wide range from case to case; all the way from simple habituation to the most purely rational calculation of advantage. A criterion of every true relation of imperative control, however, is a certain minimum of voluntary submission; thus an interest (based on ulterior motives or genuine acceptance) in obedience.

Not every case of imperative co-ordination makes use of economic means; *still less* does it always have economic objectives. But normally (not always) the imperative co-ordination of the action of a considerable number of men requires control of a staff of persons. It is necessary, that is, that there should be a relatively high probability that the action of a definite, supposedly reliable group of persons will be primarily oriented to the execution of the supreme authority's general policy and specific commands.

The members of the administrative staff may be bound to obedience to their superior (or superiors) by custom, by affectual ties, by a purely material complex of interests, or by ideal (*wertrational*) motives. *Purely* material interests and calculations of advantage as the basis of solidarity between the chief and his administrative staff result, in this as in other connexions, in a relatively unstable situation. Normally other elements, affectual and ideal, supplement such interests. In certain exceptional, temporary cases the former may be alone decisive. In everyday routine life these relationships, like others, are governed by custom and in addition, material calculation of advantage. But these factors, custom and personal advantage, purely affectual or ideal motives of solidarity, do not, even taken to-

Reprinted from Max Weber, *The Theory of Social and Economic Organization,* trans. A. M. Henderson and Talcott Parsons, ed. Talcott Parsons (Glencoe, Ill.: Free Press, 1947), pp. 324–36. Copyright 1947 by Oxford University Press.

gether, form a sufficiently reliable basis for a system of imperative co-ordination. In addition there is normally a further element, the belief in legitimacy.

It is an induction from experience that no system of authority voluntarily limits itself to the appeal to material or affectual or ideal motives as a basis for guaranteeing its continuance. In addition every such system attempts to establish and to cultivate the belief in its "legitimacy." But according to the kind of legitimacy which is claimed, the type of obedience, the kind of administrative staff developed to guarantee it, and the mode of exercising authority, will all differ fundamentally. Equally fundamental is the variation in effect. Hence, it is useful to classify the types of authority according to the kind of claim to legitimacy typically made by each. In doing this it is best to start from modern and therefore more familiar examples.

1. The choice of this rather than some other basis of classification can only be justified by its results. The fact that certain other typical criteria of variation are thereby neglected for the time being and can only be introduced at a later stage is not a decisive difficulty. The "legitimacy" of a system of authority has far more than a merely "ideal" significance, if only because it has very definite relations to the legitimacy of property.

2. Not every "claim" which is protected by custom or by law should be spoken of as involving a relation of authority. Otherwise the worker, in his claim for fulfilment of the wage contract, would be exercising "authority" over his employer because his claim can, on occasion, be enforced by order of a court. Actually his formal status is that of party to a contractual relationship with his employer, in which he has certain "rights" to receive payments. At the same time, the concept of a relation of authority naturally does not exclude the possibility that it has originated in a formally free contract. This is true of the authority of the employer over the worker as manifested in the former's rules and instructions regarding the work process; and also of the authority of a feudal lord over a vassal who has freely entered into the relation of fealty. That subjection to military discipline is formally "involuntary" while that to the discipline of the factory is voluntary does not alter the fact that the latter is also a case of subjection to authority. The position of a bureaucratic official is also entered into by contract and can be freely resigned, and even the status of "subject" can often be freely entered into and (in certain circumstances) freely repudiated. Only in the limiting case of the slave is formal subjection to authority absolutely involuntary.

Another case, in some respects related, is that of economic "power" based on monopolistic position; that is, in this case, the possibility of "dictating" the terms of exchange to contractual partners. This will not, taken by itself, be considered to constitute "authority" any more than any other kind of "influence" which is derived from some kind of superiority, as by virtue of erotic attractiveness, skill in sport or in discussion. Even if a big bank is in a position to force other banks into a cartel arrangement, this will not alone be sufficient to justify calling it a relation of imperative co-ordination. But if there is an immediate relation of command and obedience such that the management of the first bank can give orders to the others with the claim that they shall, and the probability that they will, be obeyed purely as such regardless of particular content, and if their carrying out is supervised, it is another matter. Naturally, here as everywhere the transitions are gradual; there are all sorts of intermediate steps between mere indebtedness and debt slavery. Even the position of a "salon" can come very close to the borderline of authoritarian domination and yet not necessarily constitute a system of authority. Sharp differentiation in concrete fact is often impossible, but this makes clarity in the analytical distinctions all the more important.

3. Naturally, the legitimacy of a system of authority may be treated sociologically only as the probability that to a relevant degree the appropriate attitudes will exist, and the corresponding practical conduct ensue. It is by no means true that every case of submissiveness to persons in positions of power is primarily (or even at all) oriented to this belief. Loyalty may be hypocritically simulated by individuals or by whole groups on purely opportunistic grounds, or carried out in practice for reasons of material self-interest. Or people may submit from individual weakness and helplessness because there is no acceptable alternative. But these considerations are not decisive for the classification of types of imperative co-ordination. What is important is the fact that in a given case the particular claim to legitimacy is to a significant degree and according to its type treated as "valid"; that this fact confirms the position of the persons claiming authority and that it helps to determine the choice of means of its exercise.

Furthermore a system of imperative co-ordination may—as often occurs in practice—be so completely assured of dominance, on the one hand by the obvious community of interests between the chief and his administrative staff as opposed to the subjects (bodyguards, Pretorians, "red" or "white" guards), on the other hand by the helplessness of the latter, that it can afford to drop even the pretence of a claim to legitimacy. But even then the mode of legitimation of the relation between chief and his staff may vary widely according to the type of basis of the relation of authority between them, and, as will be shown, this variation is highly significant for the structure of imperative co-ordination.

4. "Obedience" will be taken to mean that the action of the person obeying follows in essentials such a course that the content of the command may be taken to have become the basis of action for its own sake. Furthermore, the fact that it is so taken is referable only to the formal obligation, without regard to the actor's own attitude to the value or lack of value of the content of the command as such.

5. Subjectively, the causal sequence may vary, especially as between "submission" and "sympathetic agreement." This distinction is not, however, significant for the present classification of types of authority.

6. The scope of determination of social relationships and cultural phenomena by authority and imperative co-ordination is considerably broader than appears at first sight. For instance, the authority exercised in the school has much to do with the determination of the forms of speech and of written language which are regarded as orthodox. The official languages of autonomous political units, hence of their ruling groups, have often become in this sense orthodox forms of speech and writing and have even led to the formation of separate "nations" (for instance, the separation of Holland from Germany). The authority of parents and of the school, however, extends far beyond the determination of such cultural patterns which are perhaps only apparently formal, to the formation of the character of the young, and hence of human beings generally.

7. The fact that the chief and his administrative staff often appear formally as servants or agents of those they rule, naturally does nothing whatever to disprove the authoritarian character of the relationship. There will be occasion later to speak of the substantive features of so-called "democracy." But a certain minimum of assured power to issue commands, thus of "authority," must be provided for in nearly every conceivable case.

THE THREE PURE TYPES OF LEGITIMATE
AUTHORITY

There are three pure types of legitimate authority. The validity of their claims to legitimacy may be based on:

1. Rational grounds—resting on a belief in the "legality" of patterns of normative rules and the right of those elevated to authority under such rules to issue commands (legal authority).

2. Traditional grounds—resting on an established belief in the sanctity of immemorial traditions and the legitimacy of the status of those exercising authority under them (traditional authority); or finally,

3. Charismatic grounds—resting on devotion to the specific and exceptional sanctity, heroism or exemplary character of an individual person, and of the normative patterns or order revealed or ordained by him (charismatic authority).

In the case of legal authority, obedience is owed to the legally established impersonal order. It extends to the persons exercising the authority of office under it only by virtue of the formal legality of their commands and only within the scope of authority of the office. In the case of traditional authority, obedience is owed to the *person* of the chief who occupies the traditionally sanctioned position of authority and who is (within its sphere) bound by tradition. But here the obligation of obedience is not based on the impersonal order, but is a matter of personal loyalty within the area of accustomed obligations. In the case of charismatic authority, it is the charismatically qualified leader as such who is obeyed by virtue of personal trust in him and his revelation, his heroism or his exemplary qualities so far as they fall within the scope of the individual's belief in his charisma.

1. The usefulness of the above classification can only be judged by its results in promoting systematic analysis. The concept of "charisma" (the gift of grace") is taken from the vocabulary of early Christianity. For the Christian religious organization, Rudolf Sohm, in his *Kirchenrecht,* was the first to clarify the substance of the concept, even though he did not use the same terminology. Others (for instance, Hollin, *Enthusiasmus und Bussgewalt*) have clarified certain important consequences of it. It is thus nothing new.

2. The fact that none of these three ideal types, the elucidation of which will occupy the following pages, is usually to be found in historical cases in "pure" form, is naturally not a valid objection to attempting their conceptual formulation in the sharpest possible form. In this respect the present case is no different from many others. Later on the transformation of pure charisma by the process of routinization will be discussed and thereby the relevance of the concept to the understanding of empirical systems of authority considerably increased. But even so it may be said of every empirically historical phenomenon of authority that it is not likely to be "as an open book." Analysis in terms of sociological types has, after all, as

compared with purely empirical historical investigation, certain advantages which should not be minimized. That is, it can in the particular case of a concrete form of authority determine what conforms to or approximates such types as "charisma," "hereditary charisma," "the charisma of office," "patriarchy," "bureaucracy" the authority of status groups [*Ständische*], and in doing so it can work with relatively unambiguous concepts. But the idea that the whole of concrete historical reality can be exhausted in the conceptual scheme about to be developed is as far from the author's thoughts as anything could be.

II. *Legal Authority with a Bureaucratic Administrative Staff*

LEGAL AUTHORITY: THE PURE TYPE WITH EMPLOYMENT OF A BUREAUCRATIC ADMINISTRATIVE STAFF

The effectiveness of legal authority rests on the acceptance of the validity of the following mutually inter-dependent ideas.

1. That any given legal norm may be established by agreement or by imposition, on grounds of expediency or rational values or both, with a claim to obedience at least on the part of the members of the corporate group. This is, however, usually extended to include all persons within the sphere of authority or of power in question—which in the case of territorial bodies is the territorial area—who stand in certain social relationships or carry out forms of social action which in the order governing the corporate group have been declared to be relevant.

2. That every body of law consists essentially in a consistent system of abstract rules which have normally been intentionally established. Furthermore, administration of law is held to consist in the application of these rules to particular cases; the administrative process in the rational pursuit of the interests which are specified in the order governing the corporate group within the limits laid down by legal precepts and following principles which are capable of generalized formulation and are approved in the order governing the group, or at least not disapproved in it.

3. That thus the typical person in authority occupies an "office." In the action associated with his status, including the commands he issues to others, he is subject to an impersonal order to which his actions are oriented. This is true not only for persons exercising legal authority who are in the usual sense "officials," but, for instance, for the elected president of a state.

4. That the person who obeys authority does so, as it is usually stated, only in his capacity as a "member" of the corporate group and what he obeys is only "the law." He may in this connexion be the member of an association, of a territorial commune, of a church, or a citizen of a state.

5. In conformity with point 3, it is held that the members of the corporate group, in so far as they obey a person in authority, do not owe this obedience to him as an individual, but to the impersonal order. Hence, it follows that there is an obligation to obedience only within the sphere of the rationally delimited authority which, in terms of the order, has been conferred upon him.

The following may thus be said to be the fundamental categories of rational legal authority:—

(1) A continuous organization of official functions bound by rules.

(2) A specified sphere of competence. This involves (a) a sphere of obligations to perform functions which has been marked off as part of a systematic division of labour. (b) The provision of the incumbent with the necessary authority to carry out these functions. (c) That the necessary means of compulsion are clearly defined and their use is subject to definite conditions. A unit exercising authority which is organized in this way will be called an "administrative organ" [*Behörde*].

There are administrative organs in this sense in large-scale private organizations, in parties and armies, as well as in the state and the church. An elected president, a cabinet of ministers, or a body of elected representatives also in this sense constitute administrative organs. This is not, however, the place to discuss these concepts. Not every administrative organ is provided with compulsory powers. But this distinction is not important for present purposes.

(3) The organization of offices follows the principle of hierarchy; that is, each lower office is under the control and supervision of a higher one. There is a right of appeal and of statement of grievances from the lower to the higher. Hierarchies differ in respect to whether and in what case complaints can lead to a ruling from an authority at various points higher in the scale, and as to whether changes are imposed from higher up or the responsibility for such changes is left to the lower office, the conduct of which was the subject of complaint.

(4) The rules which regulate the conduct of an office may be technical rules or norms. In both cases, if their application is to be fully rational, specialized training is necessary. It is thus normally true that only a person who has demonstrated an adequate technical training is qualified to be a member of the administrative staff of such an or-

ganized group, and hence only such persons are eligible for appointment to official positions. The administrative staff of a rational corporate group thus typically consists of "officials," whether the organization be devoted to political, religious, economic—in particular, capitalistic—or other ends.

(5) In the rational type it is a matter of principle that the members of the administrative staff should be completely separated from ownership of the means of production or administration. Officials, employees, and workers attached to the administrative staff do not themselves own the non-human means of production and administration. These are rather provided for their use in kind or in money, and the official is obligated to render an accounting of their use. There exists, furthermore, in principle complete separation of the property belonging to the organization, which is controlled within the sphere of office, and the personal property of the official, which is available for his own private uses. There is a corresponding separation of the place in which official functions are carried out, the "office" in the sense of premises, from living quarters.

(6) In the rational type case, there is also a complete absence of appropriation of his official position by the incumbent. Where "rights" to an office exist, as in the case of judges, and recently of an increasing proportion of officials and even of workers, they do not normally serve the purpose of appropriation by the official, but of securing the purely objective and independent character of the conduct of the office so that it is oriented only to the relevant norms.

(7) Administrative acts, decisions, and rules are formulated and recorded in writing, even in cases where oral discussion is the rule or is even mandatory. This applies at least to preliminary discussions and proposals, to final decisions, and to all sorts of orders and rules. The combination of written documents and a continuous organization of official functions constitutes the "office" which is the central focus of all types of modern corporate action.

(8) Legal authority can be exercised in a wide variety of different forms which will be distinguished and discussed later. The following analysis will be deliberately confined for the most part to the aspect of imperative co-ordination in the structure of the administrative staff. It will consist in an analysis in terms of ideal types of officialdom or "bureaucracy."

In the above outline no mention has been made of the kind of supreme head appropriate to a system of legal authority. This is a consequence of certain considerations which can only be made entirely understandable at a later stage in the analysis. There are very important types of rational

imperative co-ordination which, with respect to the ultimate source of authority, belong to other categories. This is true of the hereditary charismatic type, as illustrated by hereditary monarchy and of the pure charismatic type of a president chosen by plebiscite. Other cases involve rational elements at important points, but are made up of a combination of bureaucratic and charismatic components, as is true of the cabinet form of government. Still others are subject to the authority of the chief of other corporate groups, whether their character be charismatic or bureaucratic; thus the formal head of a government department under a parliamentary regime may be a minister who occupies his position because of his authority in a party. The type of rational, legal administrative staff is capable of application in all kinds of situations and contexts. It is the most important mechanism for the administration of everyday profane affairs. For in that sphere, the exercise of authority and, more broadly, imperative co-ordination, consists precisely in administration.

LEGAL AUTHORITY: THE PURE TYPE WITH EMPLOYMENT OF A BUREAUCRATIC ADMINISTRATIVE STAFF—(*Continued*)

The purest type of exercise of legal authority is that which employs a bureaucratic administrative staff. Only the supreme chief of the organization occupies his position of authority by virtue of appropriation, of election, or of having been designated for the succession. But even *his* authority consists in a sphere of legal "competence." The whole administrative staff under the supreme authority then consists, in the purest type, of individual officials who are appointed and function according to the following criteria:

(1) They are personally free and subject to authority only with respect to their impersonal official obligations.

(2) They are organized in a clearly defined hierarchy of offices.

(3) Each office has a clearly defined sphere of competence in the legal sense.

(4) The office is filled by a free contractual relationship. Thus, in principle, there is free selection.

(5) Candidates are selected on the basis of technical qualifications. In the most rational case, this is tested by examination or guaranteed by diplomas certifying technical training, or both. They are *appointed*, not elected.

(6) They are remunerated by fixed salaries in money, for the most part with a right to pensions. Only under certain circumstances does the employ-

ing authority, especially in private organizations, have a right to terminate the appointment, but the official is always free to resign. The salary scale is primarily graded according to rank in the hierarchy; but in addition to this criterion, the responsibility of the position and the requirements of the incumbent's social status may be taken into account.

(7) The office is treated as the sole, or at least the primary, occupation of the incumbent.

(8) It constitutes a career. There is a system of 'promotion' according to seniority or to achievement, or both. Promotion is dependent on the judgment of superiors.

(9) The official works entirely separated from ownership of the means of administration and without appropriation of his position.

(10) He is subject to strict and systematic discipline and control in the conduct of the office.

This type of organization is in principle applicable with equal facility to a wide variety of different fields. It may be applied in profit-making business or in charitable organizations, or in any number of other types of private enterprises serving ideal or material ends. It is equally applicable to political and to religious organizations. With varying degrees of approximation to a pure type, its historical existence can be demonstrated in all fields.

1. For example, this type of bureaucracy is found in private clinics, as well as in endowed hospitals or the hospitals maintained by religious orders. Bureaucratic organization has played a major role in the Catholic Church. It is well illustrated by the administrative role of the priesthood [*Kaplanokratie*] in the modern church, which has expropriated almost all of the old church benefices, which were in former days to a large extent subject to private appropriation. It is also illustrated by the conception of the universal Episcopate, which is thought of as formally constituting a universal legal competence in religious matters. Similarly, the doctrine of Papal infallibility is thought of as in fact involving a universal competence, but only one which functions "ex cathedra" in the sphere of the office, thus implying the typical distinction between the sphere of office and that of the private affairs of the incumbent. The same phenomena are found in the large-scale capitalistic enterprise; and the larger it is, the greater their role. And this is not less true of political parties, which will be discussed separately. Finally, the modern army is essentially a bureaucratic organization administered by that peculiar type of military functionary, the "officer."

2. Bureaucratic authority is carried out in its purest form where it is most clearly dominated by the principle of appointment. There is no such

thing as a hierarchy of elected officials in the same sense as there is a hierarchical organization of appointed officials. In the first place, election makes it impossible to attain a stringency of discipline even approaching that in the appointed type. For it is open to a subordinate official to compete for elective honours on the same terms as his superiors, and his prospects are not dependent on the superior's judgment.

3. Appointment by free contract, which makes free selection possible, is essential to modern bureaucracy. Where there is a hierarchical organization with impersonal spheres of competence, but occupied by unfree officials—like slaves or dependents, who, however, function in a formally bureaucratic manner—the term "patrimonial bureaucracy" will be used.

4. The role of technical qualifications in bureaucratic organizations is continually increasing. Even an official in a party or a trade-union organization is in need of specialized knowledge, though it is usually of an empirical character, developed by experience, rather than by formal training. In the modern state, the only "offices" for which no technical qualifications are required are those of ministers and presidents. This only goes to prove that they are "officials" only in a formal sense, and not substantively, as is true of the managing director or president of a large business corporation. There is no question but that the "position" of the capitalistic entrepreneur is as definitely appropriated as is that of a monarch. Thus, at the top of a bureaucratic organization, there is necessarily an element which is at least not purely bureaucratic. The category of bureaucracy is one applying only to the exercise of control by means of a particular kind of administrative staff.

5. The bureaucratic official normally receives a fixed salary. By contrast, sources of income which are privately appropriated will be called "benefices" [*Pfründen*]. Bureaucratic salaries are also normally paid in money. Though this is not essential to the concept of bureaucracy, it is the arrangement which best fits the pure type. Payments in kind are apt to have the character of benefices, and the receipt of a benefice normally implies the appropriation of opportunities for earnings and of positions. There are, however, gradual transitions in this field with many intermediate types. Appropriation by virtue of leasing or sale of offices or the pledge of income from office are phenomena foreign to the pure type of bureaucracy.

6. "Offices" which do not constitute the incumbent's principal occupation, in particular "honorary" offices, belong in other categories. The

typical "bureaucratic" official occupies the office as his principal occupation.

7. With respect to the separation of the official from ownership of the means of administration, the situation is essentially the same in the field of public administration and in private bureaucratic organizations, such as the large-scale capitalistic enterprise.

8. Collegial bodies at the present time are rapidly decreasing in importance in favour of types of organization which are in fact, and for the most part formally as well, subject to the authority of a single head. For instance, the collegial "governments" in Prussia have long since given way to the monocratic "district president" [*Regierungs präsident*]. The decisive factor in this development has been the need for rapid, clear decisions, free of the necessity of

compromise between different opinions and also free of shifting majorities.

9. The modern army officer is a type of appointed official who is clearly marked off by certain class distinctions. In this respect such officers differ radically from elected military leaders, from charismatic condottieri, from the type of officers who recruit and lead mercenary armies as a capitalistic enterprise, and, finally, from the incumbents of commissions which have been purchased. There may be gradual transitions between these types. The patrimonial "retainer," who is separated from the means of carrying out his function, and the proprietor of a mercenary army for capitalistic purposes have, along with the private capitalistic entrepreneur, been pioneers in the organization of the modern type of bureaucracy.

3. *The Theory of Authority*

BY CHESTER I. BARNARD

IN THIS CHAPTER we consider a subject which in one aspect relates to the "willingness of individuals to contribute to organizations," the element of organization presented in the preceding chapter; and in a second aspect is the most general phase of the element "communication."

The Source of Authority

If it is true that all complex organizations consist of aggregations of unit organizations and have grown only from unit organizations, we may reasonably postulate that, whatever the nature of authority, it is inherent in the simple organization unit; and that a correct theory of authority must be consistent with what is essentially true of these unit organizations. We shall, therefore, regard the observations which we can make of the actual conditions as at first a source for discovering what is essential in elementary and simple organizations.

I

Now a most significant fact of general observation relative to authority is the extent to which it is ineffective in specific instances. It is so ineffective that the violation of authority is accepted as a matter of course and its implications are not considered. It is true that we are sometimes appalled at the extent of major criminal activities; but we pass over very lightly the universal violations, particularly of sumptuary laws, which are as "valid" as any others. Even clauses of constitutions and statutes carrying them "into effect," such as the Eighteenth Amendment, are violated in wholesale degrees.

Violation of law is not, however, peculiar to our own country. I observed recently in a totalitarian state under a dictator, where personal liberty is supposed to be at a minimum and arbitrary authority at a maximum, many violations of positive law or edict, some of them open and on a wide scale; and I was reliably informed of others.

Nor is this condition peculiar to the authority of the state. It is likewise true of the authority of churches. The Ten Commandments and the prescriptions and prohibitions of religious authority are repeatedly violated by those who profess to acknowledge their formal authority.

These observations do not mean that all citizens are lawless and defy authority; nor that all Christians are godless or their conduct unaffected by the tenets of their faith. It is obvious that to a large extent citizens are governed; and that the conduct of Christians is substantially qualified by the prescriptions of their churches. What is implied is merely that which specific laws will be obeyed or disobeyed by the individual citizen are decided by him under the specific conditions pertinent. This is what we mean when we refer to individual responsibility. It implies that which prescriptions of the church will be disobeyed by the individual are determined by him at a given time and place. This is what we mean by moral responsibility.

It may be thought that ineffectiveness of authority in specific cases is chiefly exemplified in matters of state and church, but not in those of smaller organizations which are more closely knit or more concretely managed. But this is not true. It is surprising how much that in theory is authoritative, in the best of organizations in practice lacks authority—or, in plain language, how generally orders are disobeyed. For many years the writer has been interested to observe this fact, not only in organizations with which he was directly connected, but in many others. In all of them, armies, navies, universities, penal institutions, hospitals, relief organizations, corporations, the same conditions prevail —dead laws, regulations, rules, which no one dares bury but which are not obeyed; obvious disobedience carefully disregarded; vital practices and major institutions for which there is no authority, like the Democratic and Republican parties, not known to the Constitution.

II

We may leave the secondary stages of this analysis for later consideration. What we derive from it is an approximate definition of authority for our purpose: Authority is the character of a communication (order) in formal organization by virtue of which it is accepted by a contributor to or "member" of the organization as governing the action he contributes; that is, as governing or determining what he does or is not to do so far as the organization is concerned. According to this definition, authority involves two aspects: first, the subjective, the personal, the *accepting* of a communication as authoritative, the aspects which I shall present in this section; and, second, the objective aspect—the character in the communication by virtue of which it is accepted—which I present in the second section, "The System of Coördination."

If a directive communication is accepted by one to whom it is addressed, its authority for him is confirmed or established. It is admitted as the basis of action. Disobedience of such a communication is a denial of its authority for him. Therefore, under this definition the decision as to whether an order has authority or not lies with the persons to whom it is addressed, and does not reside in "persons of authority" or those who issue these orders.

This is so contrary to the view widely held by informed persons of many ranks and professions, and so contradictory to legalistic conceptions, and will seem to many so opposed to common experience, that it will be well at the outset to quote two opinions of persons in a position to merit respectful attention. It is not the intention to "argue from authorities"; but before attacking the subject it is desirable at least to recognize that prevalent notions are not universally held. Says Roberto Michels in the monograph "Authority" in the *Encyclopaedia of the Social Sciences*,[1] "Whether authority is of personal or institutional origin it is created and maintained by public opinion, which in its turn is conditioned by sentiment, affection, reverence or fatalism. Even when authority rests on mere physical coercion it is *accepted*[2] by those ruled, although the acceptance may be due to a fear of force."

Again, Major-General James G. Harbord, of long and distinguished military experience, and since his retirement from the Army a notable business executive, says on page 259 of his *The American Army in France:*[3]

A democratic President had forgotten that the greatest of all democracies is an Army. Discipline and morale influence the inarticulate vote that is instantly taken by masses of men when the order comes to move forward—a variant of the crowd psychology that inclines it to follow a leader, but the Army does not move forward until the motion has "carried." "Unanimous consent" only follows cooperation between the *individual* men in the ranks.

These opinions are to the effect that even though physical force is involved, and even under the extreme condition of battle, when the regime is nearly absolute, authority nevertheless rests upon the acceptance of consent of individuals. Evidently such conceptions, if justified, deeply affect an appropriate understanding of organization and especially of the character of the executive functions.

Our definition of authority, like General Harbord's democracy in an army, no doubt will appear

---

1. New York: Macmillan.
2. Italics mine.
3. Boston: Little, Brown and Co., 1936.

to many whose eyes are fixed only on enduring organizations to be a platform of chaos. And so it is —exactly so in the preponderance of attempted organizations. They fail because they can maintain no authority, that is, they cannot secure sufficient contributions of personal efforts to be effective or cannot induce them on terms that are efficient. In the last analysis the authority fails because the individuals in sufficient numbers regard the burden involved in accepting necessary orders as changing the balance of advantage against their interest, and they withdraw or withhold the indispensable contributions.

III

We must not rest our definition, however, on general opinion. The necessity of the assent of the individual to establish authority *for him* is inescapable. A person can and will accept a communication as authoritative only when four conditions simultaneously obtain: (*a*) he can and does understand the communication; (*b*) *at the time of his decision* he believes that it is not inconsistent with the purpose of the organization; (*c*) *at the time of his decision*, he believes it to be compatible with his personal interest as a whole; and (*d*) he is able mentally and physically to comply with it.

(*a*) A communication that cannot be understood *can* have no authority. An order issued, for example, in a language not intelligible to the recipient is no order at all—no one would so regard it. Now, many orders are exceedingly difficult to understand. They are often necessarily stated in general terms, and the persons who issued them could not themselves apply them under many conditions. Until interpreted they have no meaning. The recipient either must disregard them or merely do anything in the hope that that is compliance.

Hence, a considerable part of administrative work consists in the interpretation and reinterpretation of orders in their application to concrete circumstances that were not or could not be taken into account initially.

(*b*) A communication believed by the recipient to be incompatible with the purpose of the organization, as he understands it, could not be accepted. Action would be frustrated by cross purposes. The most common practical example is that involved in conflicts of orders. They are not rare. An intelligent person will deny the authority of that one which contradicts the purpose of the effort as *he* understands it. In extreme cases many individuals would be virtually paralyzed by conflicting orders. They would be literally unable to comply—for example, an employee of a water system ordered to

blow up an essential pump, or soldiers ordered to shoot their own comrades. I suppose all experienced executives know that when it is necessary to issue orders that will appear to the recipients to be contrary to the main purpose, especially as exemplified in prior habitual practice, it is usually necessary and always advisable, if practicable, to explain or demonstrate why the appearance of conflict is an illusion. Otherwise the orders are likely not to be executed, or to be executed inadequately.

(*c*) If a communication is believed to involve a burden that destroys the net advantage of connection with the organization, there no longer would remain a net inducement to the individual to contribute to it. The existence of a net inducement is the only reason for accepting *any* order as having authority. Hence, if such an order is received it must be obeyed (evaded in the more usual cases) as utterly inconsistent with personal motives that are the basis of accepting any orders at all. Cases of voluntary resignation from all sorts of organizations are common for this sole reason. Malingering and intentional lack of dependability are the more usual methods.

(*d*) If a person is unable to comply with an order, obviously it must be disobeyed, or, better, disregarded. To order a man who cannot swim to swim a river is a sufficient case. Such extreme cases are not frequent; but they occur. The more usual case is to order a man to do things only a little beyond his capacity; but a little impossible is still impossible.

IV

Naturally the reader will ask: How is it possible to secure such important and enduring coöperation as we observe if in principle and in fact the determination of authority lies with the subordinate individual? It is possible because the decisions of individuals occur under the following conditions: (*a*) orders that are deliberately issued in enduring organizations usually comply with the four conditions mentioned above; (*b*) there exists a "zone of indifference" in each individual within which orders are acceptable without conscious questioning of their authority; (*c*) the interests of the persons who contribute to an organization as a group result in the exercise of an influence on the subject, or on the attitude of the individual, that maintains a certain stability of this zone of indifference.

(*a*) There is no principle of executive conduct better established in good organizations than that orders will not be issued that cannot or will not be obeyed. Executives and most persons of experience who have thought about it know that to do so destroys authority, discipline, and morale.[4] For reasons to be stated shortly, this principle cannot ordinarily be formally admitted, or at least cannot be professed. When it appears necessary to issue orders which are initially or apparently unacceptable, either careful preliminary education, or persuasive efforts, or the prior offering of effective inducements will be made, so that the issue will not be raised, the denial of authority will not occur, and orders will be obeyed. It is generally recognized that those who least understand this fact—newly appointed minor or "first line" executives—are often guilty of "disorganizing" their groups for this reason, as do experienced executives who lose self-control or become unbalanced by a delusion of power or for some other reason. Inexperienced persons take literally the current notions of authority and are then said "not to know how to use authority" or "to abuse authority." Their superiors often profess the same beliefs about authority in the abstract, but their successful practice is easily observed to be inconsistent with their professions.

(*b*) The phrase "zone of indifference" may be explained as follows: If all the orders for actions reasonably practicable be arranged in the order of

---

4. Barring relatively few individual cases, when the attitude of the individual indicates in advance likelihood of disobedience (either before or after connection with the organization), the connection is terminated or refused before the formal question arises.

It seems advisable to add a caution here against interpreting the exposition in terms of "democracy," whether in governmental, religious, or industrial organizations. The dogmatic assertion that "democracy" or "democratic methods" are (or are not) in accordance with the principles here discussed is not tenable. As will be more evident after the consideration of objective authority, the issues involved are much too complex and subtle to be taken into account in *any* formal scheme. Under many conditions in the political, religious, and industrial fields democratic processes create artificial questions of more or less logical character, in place of the real questions, which are matters of feeling and appropriateness and of informal organization. By oversimplification of issues this may destroy objective authority. No doubt in many situations formal democratic processes may be an important element in the maintenance of authority, i.e., of organization cohesion, but may in other situations be disruptive, and probably never could be, in themselves, sufficient. On the other hand the solidarity of some coöperative systems (General Harbord's army, for example) under many conditions may be unexcelled, though requiring formally autocratic processes.

Moreover, it should never be forgotten that authority in the aggregate arises from *all* the contributors to a coöperative system, and that the weighting to be attributed to the attitude of individuals varies. It is often forgotten that in industrial (or political) organizations measures which are acceptable at the bottom may be quite unacceptable to the substantial proportion of contributors who are executives, and who will no more perform their essential functions than will others, if the conditions are, to them, impossible. The point to be emphasized is that the maintenance of the contributions necessary to the endurance of an organization requires the authority of *all* essential contributors.

their acceptability to the person affected, it may be conceived that there are a number which are clearly unacceptable, that is, which certainly will not be obeyed; there is another group somewhat more or less on the neutral line, that is, either barely acceptable or barely unacceptable; and a third group unquestionably acceptable. This last group lies within the "zone of indifference." The person affected will accept orders lying within this zone and is relatively indifferent as to what the order is so far as the question of authority is concerned. Such an order lies within the range that in a general way was anticipated at time of undertaking the connection with the organization. For example, if a soldier enlists, whether voluntarily or not, in an army in which the men are ordinarily moved about within a certain broad region, it is a matter of indifference whether the order to go to A or B, C or D, and so on; and goings to A, B, C, D, etc., are in the zone of indifference.

The zone of indifference will be wider or narrower depending upon the degree to which the inducements exceed the burdens and sacrifices which determine the individual's adhesion to the organization. It follows that the range of orders that will be accepted will be very limited among those who are barely induced to contribute to the system.

(*c*) Since the efficiency of organization is affected by the degree to which individuals assent to orders, denying the authority of an organization communication is a threat to the interests of all individuals who derive a net advantage from their connection with the organization, unless the orders are unacceptable to them also. Accordingly, at any given time there is among most of the contributors an active personal interest in the maintenance of the authority of all orders which to them are within the zone of indifference. The maintenance of this interest is largely a function of informal organization. Its expression goes under the names of "public opinion," "organization opinion," "feeling in the ranks," "group attitude," etc. Thus the common sense of the community informally arrived at affects the attitude of individuals, and makes them, as individuals, loath to question authority that is within or near the zone of indifference. The formal statement of this common sense is the fiction that authority comes down from above, from the general to the particular. This fiction merely establishes a presumption among individuals in favor of the acceptability of orders from superiors, enabling them to avoid making issues of such orders without incurring a sense of personal subserviency or a loss of personal or individual status with their fellows.

Thus the contributors are willing to maintain

the authority of communications because, where care is taken to see that only acceptable communications in general are issued, most of them fall within the zone of personal indifference; and because communal sense influences the motives of most contributors most of the time. The practical instrument of this sense is the fiction of superior authority, which makes it possible normally to treat a personal question impersonally.

The fiction[5] of superior authority is necessary for two main reasons:

(1) It is the process by which the individual delegates upward, or to the organization, responsibility for what is an organization decision—an action which is depersonalized by the fact of its coördinate character. This means that if an instruction is disregarded, an executive's risk of being wrong must be accepted, a risk that the individual cannot and usually will not take unless in fact his position is at least as good as that of another with respect to correct appraisal of the relevant situation. Most persons are disposed to grant authority because they dislike the personal responsibility which they otherwise accept, especially when they are not in a good position to accept it. The practical difficulties in the operation of organization seldom lie in the excessive desire of individuals to assume responsibility for the organization action of themselves or others, but rather lie in the reluctance to take responsibility for their own actions in organization.

(2) The fiction gives impersonal notice that what is at stake is the good of the organization. If objective authority is flouted for arbitrary or merely temperamental reasons, if, in other words, there is deliberate attempt to twist an organization requirement to personal advantage, rather than properly to safeguard a substantial personal interest, then there is a deliberate attack on the organization itself. To remain outside an organization is not necessarily to be more than not friendly or not interested. To fail in an obligation intentionally is an act of hostility. This no organization can permit; and it must respond with puntive action if it can, even to the point of incarcerating or executing the culprit. This is rather generally the case where a person has agreed in advance in general what he will do. Leaving an organization in the lurch is not often tolerable.

The correctness of what has been said above will perhaps appear most probable from a consideration of the difference between executive ac-

tion in emergency and that under "normal" conditions. In times of war the disciplinary atmosphere of an army is intensified—it is rather obvious to all that its success and the safety of its members are dependent upon it. In other organizations, abruptness of command is not only tolerated in times of emergency, but expected, and the lack of it often would actually be demoralizing. It is the sense of the justification which lies in the obvious situation which regulates the exercise of the veto by the final authority which lies at the bottom. This is a commonplace of executive experience, though it is not a commonplace of conversation about it.

The System of Coördination

Up to this point we have devoted our attention to the subjective aspect of authority. The executive, however, is predominantly occupied not with this subjective aspect, which is fundamental, but with the objective character of a communication which induces acceptance.

I

Authority has been defined in part as a "character of a communication in a formal organization." A "superior" is not in our view an authority nor does he have authority strictly speaking; nor is a communication authoritative except when it is an effort or action of organization. This is what we mean when we say that individuals are able to exercise authority only when they are acting "officially," a principle well established in law, and generally in secular and religious practice. Hence the importance ascribed to time, place, dress, ceremony, and authentication of a communication to establish its official character. These practices confirm the statement that authority relates to a communication "in a formal organization." There often occur occasions of compulsive power of individuals and of hostile groups; but authority is always concerned with something *within* a definitely organized system. Current usage conforms to the definition in this respect. The word "authority" is seldom employed except where formal organization connection is stated or implied (unless, of course, the reference is obviously figurative).

These circumstances arise from the fact that the character of authority in organization communications lies in the *potentiality of assent* of those to whom they are sent. Hence, they are only sent to contributors or "members" of the organization. Since all authoritative communications are official and relate only to organization action, they have no meaning to those whose actions are not included within the coöperative system. This is clearly in ac-

---

5. The word "fiction" is used because from the standpoint of logical construction it merely explains overt acts. Either as a superior officer or as a subordinate, however, I know nothing that I actually regard as more "real" than "authority."

cord with the common understanding. The laws of one country have no authority for citizens of another, except under special circumstances. Employers do not issue directions to employees of other organizations. Officials would appear incompetent who issued orders to those outside their jurisdiction.

A communication has the presumption of authority when it originates at sources of organization information—a communications center—better than individual sources. It loses this presumption, however, if not within the scope or field of this center. The presumption is also lost if the communication shows an absence of adjustment to the actual situation which confronts the recipient of it.

Thus men impute authority to communications from superior positions, provided they are reasonably consistent with advantages of scope and perspective that are credited to those positions. This authority is to a considerable extent independent of the personal ability of the incumbent of the position. It is often recognized that though the incumbent may be of limited personal ability his advice may be superior solely by reason of the advantage of position. This is the *authority of position.*

But it is obvious that some men have superior ability. Their knowledge and understanding regardless of position command respect. Men impute authority to what they say in an organization for this reason only. This is the *authority of leadership.* When the authority of leadership is combined with the authority of position, men who have an established connection with an organization generally will grant authority, accepting orders far outside the zone of indifference. The confidence engendered may even make compliance an inducement in itself.

Nevertheless, the determination of authority remains with the individual. Let these "positions" of authority in fact show ineptness, ignorance of conditions, failure to communicate what ought to be said, or let leadership fail (chiefly by its concrete action) to recognize implicitly its dependence upon the essential character of the relationship of the individual to the organization, and the authority if tested disappears.

This objective authority is only maintained if the positions or leaders continue to be adequately informed. In very rare cases persons possessing great knowledge, insight, or skill have this adequate information without occupying executive position. What they say ought to be done or ought not to be done will be accepted. But this is usually personal advice at the risk of the taker. Such persons have influence rather than authority. In most cases genuine leaders who give advice concerning organized efforts are required to accept positions of responsibility; for knowledge of the applicability of their special knowledge or judgment to concrete *organization* action, not to abstract problems, is essential to the worth of what they say as a basis of organization authority. In other words, they have an organization personality, as distinguished from their individual personality, commensurate with the influence of their leadership. The common way to state this is that there cannot be authority without corresponding responsibility. A more exact expression would be that objective authority cannot be imputed to persons in organization positions unless subjectively they are dominated by the organization as respects their decisions.

It may be said, then, that the maintenance of objective authority adequate to support the fiction of superior authority and able to make the zone of indifference an actuality depends upon the operation of the system of communication in the organization. The function of this system is to supply adequate information to the positions of authority and adequate facilities for the issuance of orders. To do so it requires commensurate capacities in those able to be leaders. High positions that are not so supported have weak authority, as do strong men in minor positions.

Thus authority depends upon a coöperative personal attitude of individuals on the one hand; and the system of communication in the organization on the other. Without the latter, the former cannot be maintained. The most devoted adherents of an organization will quit it, if its system results in inadequate, contradictory, inept orders, so that they cannot know who is who, what is what, or have the sense of effective coördination.

This system of communication, or its maintenance, is a primary or essential continuing problem of a formal organization. Every other practical question of effectiveness or efficiency—that is, of the factors of survival—depends upon it. In technical language the system of communication of which we are now speaking is often known as the "lines of authority."

II

The requirements of communication determine the size of unit organizations, the grouping of units, the grouping of groups of unit organizations. We may now consider the controlling factors in the character of the communication system as a system of objective authority.

(a) The first is that *channels of communication should be definitely known.* The language in which this principle is ordinarily stated is, "The lines of authority must be definitely established." The method of doing so is by assigning each individual to his position; by general announcements; by organization charts; by educational effort, and most of all by habituation, that is, by securing as much permanence of system as is practicable. Emphasis is laid either upon the position, or upon the persons; but usually the fixing of authority is made both to positions and, less emphatically, to persons.

(b) Next, we may say that *objective authority requires a definite formal channel of communication to every member of an organization.* In ordinary language this means "everyone must report to someone" (communication in one direction) and "everyone must be subordinate to someone" (communication in the other direction). In other words, in formal organizations everyone must have definite formal relationship to the organization.

(c) Another factor is that *the line of communication must be as direct or short as possible.* This may be explained as follows: Substantially all formal communication is verbal (written or oral). Language as a vehicle of communication is limited and susceptible of misunderstanding. Much communication is necessarily without preparation. Even communications that are carefully prepared require interpretation. Moreover, communications are likely to be in more general terms the more general —that is, the higher—the position. It follows that something may be lost or added by transmission at each stage of the process, especially when communication is oral, or when at each stage there is combination of several communications. Moreover, when communications go from high positions down they often must be made more specific as they proceed; and when in the reverse direction, usually more general. In addition, the speed of communication, other things equal, will be less the greater the number of centers through which it passes. Accordingly, the shorter the line the greater the speed and the less the error.

How important this factor is may be indicated by the remarkable fact that in great complex organizations the number of levels of communication is not much larger than in smaller organizations. In most organizations consisting of the services of one or two hundred men the levels of communication will be from three to five. In the Army the levels are: President, (Secretary of War), General, Major-General, Brigadier-General, Colonel, Major, Captain, Lieutenant, Sergeant, men—that is, nine or ten. In the Bell Telephone System, with over 300,000 working members, the number is eight to ten.[6] A similar shortness of the line of communication is noteworthy in the Catholic Church viewed from the administrative standpoint.

Many organization practices or inventions are used to accomplish this end, depending upon the purpose and technical conditions. Briefly, these methods are: The use of expanded executive organizations at each stage; the use of the staff department (technical, expert, advisory); the division of executive work into functional bureaus; and processes of delegating responsibility with automatic coördination through regular conference procedures, committees for special temporary functions, etc.

(d) Another factor is that, in principle, *the complete line of communication should usually be used.* By this is meant that a communication from the head of an organization to the bottom should pass through every stage of the line of authority. This is due to the necessity of avoiding conflicting communications (in either direction) which might (and would) occur if there were any "jumping of the line" of organization. It is also necessary because of the need of interpretation, and to maintain responsibility.[7]

(e) Again, the *competence of the persons serving as communication centers, that is, officers, supervisory heads, must be adequate.* The competence required is that of more and more *general* ability with reference to the work of the entire organization the more central the office of communication and the larger the organization. For the function of the center of communication in an organization is to translate incoming communications concerning external conditions, the progress of activity, successes, failures, difficulties, dangers, into outgoing communications in terms of new activities, preparatory steps, etc., all shaped according to the ultimate as well as the immediate purposes to be served. There is accordingly required more or less mastery of the technologies involved, of the capabilities of the personnel, of the informal organization situation, of the character and status of the subsidiary organizations, of the principles of action relative to purpose, of the interpretation of environmental factors, and a power of discrimination between communications that can possess authority because they are recognizably compatible with *all* the pertinent conditions and those which will not possess authority because they will not or cannot be accepted.

It is a fact, I think, that we hardly nowadays expect individual personal ability adequate to posi-

---

6. Disregarding the corporate aspects of the organization, and not including boards of directors.

7. These by no means exhaust the considerations. The necessity of maintaining personal prestige of executives as an *inducement to them* to function is on the whole an important additional reason.

tional requirements of communication in modern large-scale organization. The limitations of individuals as respects time and energy alone preclude such personal ability, and the complexity of the technologies or other special knowledge involved make it impossible. For these reasons each major center of communication is itself organized, sometimes quite elaborately. The immediate staff of the executive (commanding officer), consisting of deputies, or chief clerks, or adjutants, or auxiliaries with their assistants, constitute an executive unit of organization only one member of which is perhaps an "executive," that is, occupies the *position* of authority; and the technical matters are assigned to staff departments or organizations of experts. Such staff departments often are partly "field" departments in the sense that they directly investigate or secure information on facts or conditions external to the organizations; but in major part in most cases they digest and translate information from the field, and prepare the plans, orders, etc., for transmission. In this capacity they are advisory or adjutant to the executives. In practice, however, these assistants have the function of semi-formal advice under regulated conditions to the organizations as a whole. In this way, both the formal channels and the informal organization are supplemented by intermediate processes.

In some cases the executive (either chief or some subordinate executive) may be not a person but a board, a legislature, a committee. I know of no important organizations, except some churches and some absolute governments in which the highest objective authority is not lodged in an *organized* executive group, that is, a "highest" unit of organization.

(*f*) Again, *the line of communication should not be interrupted during the time when the organization is to function.* Many organizations (factories, stores) function intermittently, being closed or substantially so during the night, Sundays, etc. Others, such as army, police, railroad systems, telephone systems, never cease to operate. During the times when organizations are at work, in principle the line of authority must never be broken; and practically this is almost, if not quite, literally true in many cases. This is one of the reasons which may be given for the great importance attached to hereditary succession in states, and for the elaborate provision that is made in most organizations (except possibly small "personal" organizations) for the temporary filling of offices automatically during incapacity or absence of incumbents. These provisions emphasize the non-personal and communication character of organization authority, as does the persistent emphasis upon the *office* rather than

the *man* that is a matter of indoctrination of many organizations, especially those in which "discipline" is an important feature.

The necessity for this is not merely that specific communications cannot otherwise be attended to. It is at least equally that the *informal* organization disintegrates very quickly if the formal "line of authority" is broken. In organization parlance, "politics" runs riot. Thus, if an officer were vacant, but the fact were not known, an organization might function for a considerable time without serious disturbance, except in emergency. But if known, it would quickly become disorganized.

(*g*) The final factor I shall mention is that *every communication should be authenticated.* This means that the person communicating must be known actually to occupy the "position of authority" concerned; that the position includes the type of communication concerned—that is, it is "within its authority"; and that it actually is an authorized communication from this office. The process of authentication in all three respects varies in different organizations under different conditions and for different positions. The practice is undergoing rapid changes in the modern technique, but the principles remain the same. Ceremonials of investiture, inaugurations, swearing-in, general orders of appointment, induction, and introduction, are all essentially appropriate methods of making known who actually fills a position and what the position includes as authority. In order that these *positions* may function it is often necessary that the filling of them should be dramatized, an essential process to the creation of authority *at the bottom*, where only it can be fundamentally—that is, it is essential to inculcate the "sense of organization." This is merely stating that it is essential to "organization loyalty and solidarity" as it may be otherwise expressed. Dignifying the superior position is an important method of dignifying *all* connection with organization, a fact which has been well learned in both religious and political organizations where great attention to the subjective aspects of the "membership" is the rule.

This statement of the principles of communication systems of organizations from the viewpoint of the maintenance of objective authority has necessarily been in terms of complex organizations, since in a simple unit organization the concrete applications of these principles are fused. The principles are with difficulty isolated under simple conditions. Thus, as a matter of course, in unit organizations the channels of communication are known, indeed usually obvious; they are definite; they are the shortest possible; the only lines of authority are complete lines; there is little question of authentication. The doubtful points in unit organization are the competence of the leader, never to be taken for granted even in simple organizations, and whether he is functioning when the organization is in operation. Yet as a whole the adequately balanced maintenance of these aspects of simple leadership is the basis of objective authority in the unit organization, as the maintenance of the more formal and observable manifestations of the same aspects in the basis of authority in the complex organizations.

Reconciliation with Legalistic Conceptions

Legalistic conceptions of authority, at least somewhat different from those we have presented, seem to have support in the relations between superior and subsidiary organizations. A corporate organization, for example, is subject to the law of the state. Is not this a case where authority actually does come down from the top, from the superior organizations? Only in exactly the same sense that individuals accept objective authority, as we have described it. A subsidiary or dependent organization must accept law to give law its authority. Units of organization, integrated complexes of organization, and dependent organizations, make and must make the subjective decision of authority just as individuals do. A corporation may and often does quit if it cannot obey the law and still have a net reason for existence. It is no more able to carry out an unintelligible law than an individual, it can no more do the impossible than an individual, it will show the same inability to conform to conflicting laws as the individual. The only difference between subsidiary, or dependent, unit and group organizations and individuals is that the denial of authority can be made directly by the individual, and either directly or indirectly by the unit, group, or dependent or subsidiary complex. When it is direct, the effect of the law or order upon the organization as a whole is in point; when it is indirect the effect is on the individuals of whose efforts the whole is made up. Thus no complex can carry out a superior order if its members (either unit organizations or individuals) will not enable it to do so. For example, to order by law working conditions which will not be accepted by individual employees, even though the employer is willing, is futile; its authority is in fact denied. The employees quit, then the organization ends.

But in the final analysis the differences are not important, except occasionally in the concrete case. The subsidiary organization in point of fact derives most of its authority for most of its action from its own "members" individually. They may quit

if they do not accept the orders, no matter what the "ultimate" authority; and no absolute or external authority can compel the necessary effort beyond a minimum insufficient to maintain efficient or effective organization performance. An important effect of the ascription of legalistic origin of a part of the formal authority of subsidiary and independent organizations has been its obscuring of the nature of the real authority that governs the greater part of the coöperative effort of such organizations.

There is, however, a considerable quantitative difference in the factor of informal organization, that is, the factor of public opinion, general sentiment. This is not a difference of principle, but merely one of the relationship of the size of the informal organization relative to the individual or formal group. A strong individual can resist the domination of opinion if it is confined to a small number; but rarely if there is in question the opinion of an overwhelming number, actively and hostilely expressed. Now the size of any subsidiary organization is small compared with the informal organization that permeates the State; and this wide informal organization will usually support "law and order" regardless of merits if the question at issue is minor from its point of view. The pressure on the subjective attitude of individuals or on that of subsidiary or dependent organizations is strong ordinarily to induce acceptance of law in an "orderly" society.

But this informal support of objective authority of the State depends upon essentially the same principles as in the case of ordinary organizations. Inappropriateness of law and of government administration, lack of understanding of the ultimate basis of authority, indifference to the motives governing individual support, untimely or impossible legislation, as is well known destroy "respect for law and order," that is, destroy objective political authority. In democracies the normal reaction is to change law and administration through political action. But when majorities are unable to understand that authority rests fundamentally upon the consent of minorities as well as of majorities, or when the system is autocratic or absolute, the liquidation of attempted tyranny is through revolution or civil war. Authority lies always with him to whom it applies. Coercion creates a contrary illusion; but the use of force *ipso facto* destroys the authority postulated. It creates a new authority, a new situation, a new objective, which is granted when the force is accepted. Many men have destroyed all authority as to themselves by dying rather than yield.

At first thought it may seem that the element

of communication in organization is only in part related to authority; but more thorough consideration leads to the understanding that communication, authority, specialization, and purpose are all aspects comprehended in coördination. All communication relates to the formulation of purpose and the transmission of coördinating prescriptions for action and so rests upon the ability to communicate with those willing to coöperate.

Authority is another name for the willingness and capacity of individuals to submit to the necessities of coöperative systems. Authority arises from the technological and social limitations of coöperative systems on the one hand, and of individuals on the other. Hence the status of authority in a society is the measure both of the development of individuals and of the technological and social conditions of the society.

Section E

Religion and Social Structure

Editorial Foreword, BY TALCOTT PARSONS   *645*

1. *The Theological Stage,* BY AUGUSTE COMTE   *646*
2. *Of Superstition and Enthusiasm,* BY DAVID HUME   *656*
3. *The Gods of the City,* BY FUSTEL DE COULANGES   *659*
4. *Jehovah and the Prophets,* BY W. ROBERTSON SMITH   *661*
5. *Church and Sect,* BY ERNST TROELTSCH   *664*
6. *Trends in Western Monasticism,* BY ADOLF VON HARNACK   *670*
7. *Religion and Society,* BY EMILE DURKHEIM   *677*

Religion and Social Structure

by Talcott Parsons

THE PRINCIPAL SOCIAL THINK-ers leading up to the developments of our special interest were largely concerned with the economic and political aspects of social systems. Besides this main trend, however, an important group of "mavericks" wrote with great insight about the religious aspects of social organization.

Prominent among them is the founder of the special concept of sociology, Auguste Comte. Comte was among the rationalists and positivists who believed that religion could not form a stable permanent component in human orientation but would eventually be completely replaced by science. (This general issue will be further discussed in the Introduction to Part Four.) Comte, as noted, was one of the earliest proponents of a theory of social evolution. It is in this connection that he made his most important positive contributions to the understanding of the role of religion. In his famous "law of the three stages," he placed the theological stage first. He thus recognized the fact that the political and the religious components of the leadership elements of early societies have usually not been differentiated from each other in a structural sense, at least involving collectivities. However, Comte extends his theological stage through the earlier history of Western Christianity through the Middle Ages, thus obscuring the fundamentally important event of the differentiation of church and state. Though we cannot agree with him that religion is becoming obsolete as an important focus of social structure, Comte made an important contribution to the statement of the problems of religion's place in social evolution.

The second selection antedates Comte; it follows his selection here because it is more specialized. This is David Hume's essay on "superstition" and "enthusiasm." Hume was one of the great skeptics in history. The title of his essay shows his distance from any personal commitment to the religious positions he was analyzing. Yet this essay, like so much of Hume's work, contains extraordinarily shrewd observations about the characters of the social organization of the Catholic Church and of the Methodist movement. Hume was writing during the second half of the eighteenth century, when the rise of Methodism was the most important religious change occurring in the British Isles since the seventeenth century. In an important sense, it was a kind of counterfoil to the impact of the Enlightenment, in which Hume himself was very much involved. In many respects, Hume's analysis anticipates the Weber-Troeltsch distinction of church and sect that appears in a later selection.

The next two selections are by writers who were important immediate precursors of the crystallization of interest in the sociology of religion that occurred in the generation with which we are concerned. Fustel de Coulanges was one of Durkheim's teachers, and his *Cité Antique* was certainly a major source of the latter's orientation to the sociological problems of religion. Fustel gave the classic account of the fusion of religion and civic commitment in the *polis;* it served as a model for Durkheim's analysis of Australian Totemism. Since Western society has dual religio-cultural roots in Greek and Semitic sources, it seems significant that the second relatively direct precursor of Durkheim's ideas, W. Robertson Smith, was the most eminent scholar in his time of early Semitic religion. A selection from his more famous work, the *Religion of the Semites,* is included in Part Four; this section contains his discussion of the Prophets of Israel.

In a theoretical sense, Robertson Smith probably had a more direct influence on Durkheim than on Weber. Yet Weber's analysis of the relation between Western Christianity and the Oriental religions starts from the significance he attributes to Prophetic Judaism. These two selections thus express a particularly important "crossroads" of intellectual influence that helps very much to explain the common factors underlying the convergence between Durkheim and Weber—a convergence occurring in spite of their mutual unawareness and their disparate national allegiances.

Next, two eminent authors are represented who belong to the relevant generation. Ernst Troeltsch is perhaps the most eminent sociologically oriented historian of Western Christianity, and his *Social Teachings of the Christian Churches* (1913) is a major classic. Our space has allowed inclusion of only one selection from this rich work, that outlines his typological distinction between church and sect. This generalized Hume's theme, and delineated the most important single basis of differentiation of religious types of organization within the Christian tradition. The second selection is from another German historian, Adolf von Harnack. From his extensive researches we have chosen his treatment of the place of monasticism within the Western church, especially of the ways in which the monastic orders prepared and served as "bases of operation" for the exertion of leverage on secular society from the point of view of Christian ethics. They constituted critical mechanisms for the movement in the direction of a Christian society that Troeltsch delineated.

This section ends on a note of general theory with the concluding chapter of Durkheim's *Elementary Forms of the Religious Life* (1912). This book constitutes one primary landmark in the history of analysis of the relation between religion and society. Even this late in his career, Durkheim had not yet fully freed himself from the limitations of his positivistic orientation. He had, however, fully overcome the bias of the positivistic evolutionists that relegated the role of religion exclusively to the early stages of social development. Above all, he clearly stated the essential connection between religion and the paramount values of a society— the *conscience collective*. His statement constitutes a primary point of reference for all subsequent discussion of this range of problems.

We have faced a particularly difficult problem in drawing the line between this last section of Part Two, and the first subsection in Section B of Part Four on the religious and magical aspects of value and belief patterns; and the separation is partially arbitrary. This difficulty is a result of our treatment of religion as the focal point of the articulation and hence interpenetration of social systems and culture. It therefore may be regarded from the point of view either of the morphology of the social system or of the social implications of cultural orientations.

Max Weber's primary interest in the sociology of religion was conceived from the latter point of view; therefore the selections from this part of his work are included in Part Four rather than here. In general, the comparative significance of religious variation emerges particularly clearly in that context. The final selection in the second subsection of Section B in Part Four, from Weber, on religion and social status, brings the analysis full circle, to the religious orientations' roots in the structure of societies. This very important selection might with equal relevance have been included at either point.

1. The Theological Stage

BY AUGUSTE COMTE

THE THEOLOGICAL PERIOD of humanity could begin no otherwise than by a complete and usually very durable state of pure Fetichism, which allowed free exercise to that tendency of

Reprinted from Auguste Comte, *The Positive Philosophy*, trans. and ed. Harriet Martineau (London: George Bell & Sons, 1896), II, 545–61.

our nature by which Man conceives of all external bodies as animated by a life analogous to his own, with differences of mere intensity. This primitive character of human speculation is established by the biological theory of Man in the *à-priori* way; and in the opposite way, by all the precise information that we can obtain of the earliest social period;

and again, the study of individual development confirms the analysis of the collective. Some philosophers set out in the inquiry, as a matter of course, with the supposition that polytheism was the first stage; and some have been so perverse as to place monotheism furthest back, and fetichism as a corruption of polytheism: but such inversions are inconsistent with both the laws and the facts of human history.

The real starting-point is, in fact, much humbler than is commonly supposed, Man having everywhere begun by being a fetich-worshipper and a cannibal. Instead of indulging our horror and disgust of such a state of things by denying it, we should admit a collective pride in that human progressiveness which has brought us into our present state of comparative exaltation, while a being less nobly endowed than Man would have vegetated to this hour in his original wretched condition. Another supposition involves an error less grave, but still requiring notice. Some philosophers suppose a state prior even to fetichism; a state in which the human species was altogether material, and incapable of any speculation whatever;—in that lowest condition in which they now conclude the natives of Tierra del Fuego and some of the Pacific Islanders to be. If this were true, there must have been a time when intellectual wants did not exist in Man: and we must suppose a moment when they began to exist, without any prior manifestation;—a notion which is in direct contradiction to biological principles, which show that the human organism, in all times and places, has manifested the same essential needs, differing only in their degree of development and corresponding mode of satisfaction. This is proof enough of the error of the supposition: and all our observation of the lowest idiocy and madness in which Man appears to be debased below the higher brutes, assures us that a certain degree of speculative activity exists, which obtains satisfaction in a gross fetichism. The error arises from the want of knowing what to look for; and hence, the absence of all theological ideas is hastily concluded wherever there is no organized worship or distinct priesthood. Now, we shall see presently that fetichism may obtain a considerable development, even to the point of star-worship, before it demands a real priesthood; and when arrived at star-worship, it is on the threshold of polytheism. The error is natural enough, and excusable in inquirers who are unfurnished with a positive theory which may obviate or correct any vicious interpretation of facts.

On the ground of this hypothesis, it is said that Man must have begun like the lower animals. The fact is so,—allowing for superiority of organization; but perhaps we may find in the defects of the inference a misapprehension of the mental state of the lower animals themselves. Several species of animals afford clear evidence of speculative activity: and those which are endowed with it certainly attain a kind of gross fetichism, as Man does,—supposing external bodies, even the most inert, to be animated by passion and will, more or less analogous to the personal impressions of the spectator. The difference in the case is that Man has ability to raise himself out of this primitive darkness, and that the brutes have not,—except some few select animals, in which a beginning to polytheism may be observed,—obtained, no doubt, by association with Man. If, for instance, we exhibit a watch to a child or a savage, on the one hand, and a dog or a monkey, on the other, there will be no great difference in their way of regarding the new object, further than their form of expression:—each will suppose it a sort of animal, exercising its own tastes and inclinations: and in this they will hold a common fetichism,—out of which the one may rise, while the other can not. And thus the allegation about the starting-point of the human species turns out to be a confirmation of our proposition, instead of being in any way inconsistent with it.

It is so difficult to us to conceive of any but a metaphysical theology, that we are apt to fall into perpetual mistakes in contemplating this, its gross origin. Fetichism has even been usually confounded with polytheism, when the latter has been called Idolatry,—a term which applies only to the former; and the priests of Jupiter and Minerva would doubtless have repelled the trite reproach of the adoration of images as justly as Catholic priests do now, when subject to the same charge from Protestants. But, though we are too distant from fetichism to form a just conception of it, each one of us may find in his own earliest experience a more or less faithful representation of it. The celebrated phrase of Bosseut, applied to the starting-point of the human mind, describes the elementary simplicity of theology:—*Everything was God, except God himself;* and from that moment forward, the number of gods steadily decreased. We may reorganize some features of that state in our own conditions of mind when we are betrayed into searching after the mode of production of phenomena, of whose natural laws we are ignorant. We then instinctively conceive of the production of unknown effects according to the passions and affections of the corresponding being regarded as alive; and this is the philosophical principle of fetichism. A man who smiles at the folly of the savage in taking the watch for an animal may, if wholly ignorant of watch-making, find himself surprised into a state not so far superior, if any unforeseen and inexplicable effects should arise from some unperceived derangement of the mechanism. But for a widely analogous experience, preparing him for such accidents and their interpretation, he could hardly resist the impression that the changes were tokens of the affections or caprices of an imaginary being.

Thus is Fetichism the basis of the theological philosophy,—deifying every substance or phenomenon which attracts the attention of nascent humanity, and remaining traceable through all its transformations to the very last. The Egyptian theocracy, whence that of the Jews was evidently derived, exhibited, in its best days, the regular and protracted coexistence of the three religious periods in the different castes of its sacerdotal hierarchy—the lowest remaining in mere fetichism, while those above them were in full possession of a marked polytheism, and the highest rank had probably attained an incipient monotheism. Moreover, a direct analysis will disclose to us very marked traces, at all times, of the original fetichism, however it may be involved in metaphysical forms in subtle understandings. The conception among the ancients of the Soul of the universe, the modern notion that the earth is a vast living animal, and, in our own time, the obscure pantheism which is so rife among German metaphysicians, is only fetichism generalized and made systematic, and throwing a cloud of learned words as dust into the eyes of the vulgar. These evidences show that fetichism is no theological aberration, but the source of theology itself,—of that primitive theology which exhibits a complete spontaneousness, and which required from Man in his apathetic state no trouble in creating supernatural agents, but permitted him passively to yield to his propensity to transfer to outward objects the sense of existence which served him for an explanation of his own phenomena, and therefore for an absolute explanation of all out of himself. At first it was only inanimate nature that was the object in its more conspicuous phenomena,—even the negative ones, such as shadows, which no doubt terrified the nascent race as they now alarm individual children and some animals: but the spontaneous theology soon extended to embrace the animal kingdom, producing the express adoration of brutes, when they presented any aspect of mystery: that is, when Man did not find the corresponding equivalent of their qualities in himself,—whether it were the exquisite superiority of the sense of smell, or any other sense in animals, or that their organic sus-

ceptibility made them aware, sooner than himself, of atmospheric changes, etc., etc.

That philosophy was as suitable to the moral as to the intellectual state of the infant human race. The preponderance of the affective over the intellectual life, always conspicuous, was in its full strength in the earliest stages of the human mind. The empire of the passions over the reason, favorable to theology at all times, is yet more favorable to fetich theology than to any other. All substances being immediately personified, and endowed with passions, powerful in proportion to the energy of the phenomena, the external world presented to the observer a spectacle of such perfect harmony as has never been seen since: of a harmony which yielded him a satisfaction to which we can not even give a name, from our inability to feel it, however strenuously we may endeavor to carry our minds back into that cradle of humanity. It is easy to see how this exact correspondence between the universe and Man must attach us to fetichism, which, in return, specially protracts the appropriate moral state. In more advanced periods, evidence of this appears when organizations or situations show us any overwhelming action of the affective part of Man's nature. Men who may be said to think naturally with the hinder part of the head, or who find themselves so disposed for the moment, are not preserved even by high intellectual culture from the danger of being plunged by some passion of hope or fear, into the radical fetichism,—personifying, and then deifying, even the most inert objects that can interest their roused sensibilities. From such tendencies in our own day, we may form some idea of the primitive force of such a moral condition, which, being at once complete and normal, was also permanent and universal.

The metaphorical constitution of human language is, in my eyes, a remarkable and eternal testimony to the primitive condition of Man. There can be no doubt that the main body of human language has descended from that remotest period, which must probably have endured much longer than any other, from the special slowness of such progress as it could admit of. The common opinion which attributes the use of figurative expressions to a dearth of direct signs is too rational to be admissible with regard to any but a very advanced period. Up to that time, and during the ages which must have mainly influenced the formation or rather the development, of language, the excessive abundance of figures belonged naturally to the prevalent philosophy, which, likening all phenomena to human acts, must introduce as faithful description expressions which must seem metaphorical when that state had passed away in which they were literal. It is an old observation that the tendency diminishes as the human mind expands: and we may remark that the nature of metaphors is gradually transformed with the lapse of time:— in the early ages men transferred to the external world the expressions proper to human acts; whereas now we apply to the phenomena of life terms originally appropriated to inert nature, thus showing that the scientific spirit, which looks from without inward, is more and more influencing human language.

Looking now to the influence of the primitive theological philosophy on human progression, we observe that fetichism is the most intense form of theology—at least, as regards the individual; that is, the fetich form of that order of ideas is the one which most powerfully influences the mental system. If we are surprised at the number of pagan gods that we are continually meeting with in ancient books, there is no saying how we might be impressed if we could for a moment see the multitude of deities that the pure fetich-worshipper must live in the midst of. And again, the primitive man could see and know nothing but through his theological conceptions, except some very few practical notions of natural phenomena, furnished by experience, and little superior to the knowledge obtained by the higher animals by the same means. In no other religious period could theological ideas be so completely adherent to the sensations, which were incessantly presenting those ideas; so that it was almost impossible for the reason to abstract them in any degree, or for a single moment. It does not follow that the social influence of this form of theology was at all in proportion to its effect on individuals. On the contrary, the political influence of the theological philosophy will be seen, as we proceed, to strengthen as it becomes more abstract in the human mind.

It is not difficult to perceive why fetichism was a feeble instrument of civilization, notwithstanding its wide intellectual dominion; and this will disclose to us what its social influence really was.

In the first place, sacerdotal authority is indispensable to render available the civilizing quality of theological philosophy. All doctrine must have special organs, to direct its social application; and the necessity is strongest in the case of religious doctrine, on account of its indefinite character, which compels a permanent exercise of active discipline, to keep the vagueness and indefiniteness within bounds. The experience of the last three centuries shows us how, when sacerdotal authority is broken up, religious ideas become a source of discord instead of union: and this may give us some notion of the small social influence of a theology

which anticipated all priesthoods, though it might be the first concern of every member of that infant society. Why fetichism admitted of no priesthood, properly so called, is obvious. Its gods were individual; and each resided fixedly in a particular object; whereas, the gods of polytheism are more general by their nature, and have a more extended dominion and residence. The fetich gods had little power to unite men, or to govern them. Though there were certainly fetiches of the tribe, even of the nation, the greater number were domestic, or even personal; and such deities could afford little assistance to the development of common ideas. And again, the residence of each deity in a material object left nothing for a priesthood to do, and therefore gave no occasion for the rise of a distinct speculative class. The worship, incessant and pervading as it was, when every act of a man's life had its religious aspect, was of a kind that required every man to be his own priest, free from intervention between himself and gods that were constantly accessible. It was the subsequent belief in gods that were invisible, more or less general, and distinct from the substances which they ruled, that originated and developed a real priesthood, enjoying high social influence, in its character of mediator between the worshipper and his deity. In the most triumphant periods of Greek and Roman polytheism, we meet with evidence of the contrasted character of the two theological phases, in the Lares and Penates, the domestic gods which had survived the fetich multitude, and which were served, not by any priest, but by each believer; or, at most, by the head of the family, as their spontaneous priest.

The beginning of a priesthood may, however, be discerned in the professions of soothsayers, conjurers, etc., which exist among the fetich tribes of Africa: but a close inquiry into their state, as into that of the first societies of men, will show that, in such cases, fetichism has reached its highest elevation, and become star-worship. This astrolatry is the introduction to polytheism; and it has qualities which instigate the development of a genuine priesthood. There is a character of generality about the stars which fits them to be common fetiches: and sociological analysis shows us that this was in fact their destination among populations of any extent. And again, when their inaccessible position was understood (which was not so soon as is commonly thought) the need of special intermediaries began to be felt. These two circumstances, the superior generality and the inaccessible position of the stars, are the reasons why the adoration of them, without changing the character of the universal fetichism, determined the formation of an organized worship and a distinct priesthood: and thus the advent of astrolatry was not only a symptom, but a powerful means of social progress in its day, though, from its extreme and mischievous protraction, we are apt to condemn it as universally a principle of human degradation. It must have been long, however, before star-worship obtained a marked ascendency over other branches of fetichism, so as to impart a character of real astrolatry to the whole region. The human mind was long engrossed with what lay nearest; and the stars held no prominent place in comparison with many terrestrial objects, as, for instance, meteorological effects, which indeed furnished the attributes of supernatural power through nearly the whole of the theological period. While magicians could control the moon and stars, no one supposed they could have anything to do with the government of the thunder. A long series of gradual modifications in human conceptions was therefore necessary to invert the primitive order, and place the stars at the head of natural bodies, while still subordinated to the earth and Man, according to the spirit of theological philosophy at its highest perfection. But, it was only when fetichism rose to the elevation of astrolatry that it could exercise any great social influence, for the reasons thus given. And this is the rational explanation of the singular characteristic of the theological spirit— that its greater intellectual extension is coincident with its smaller social influence. Thus, not only does fetichism share the common condition of all philosophies, that of not extending to moral and social considerations till it has embraced all simpler speculations, but there are special reasons for the retardation of the time when it can acquire any political consistency, notwithstanding its vast preparatory intellectual extension. The further we proceed in our review of the social operation of the theological spirit, the more we shall perceive how great is the mistake of supposing that religious belief is the only basis of human association, to the exclusion of all other orders of common conceptions. We have now seen that the political attribute did not disclose itself in the period of the greatest mental prevalence of the religious system: and we shall presently find that polytheism, and yet more monotheism, exhibits the necessary connection between the intellectual decline of the theological spirit and the perfect realization of its civilizing faculty: and this will confirm our conclusion that this social destination could be attributed to it only provisionally, while awaiting the advent of more direct and more permanent principles.—If, however, fetichism is not adapted to the development of the theological polity, its social influence has nevertheless been very extensive, as may be easily shown.

In a purely philosophical view,—that is, in regard to its function of directing human speculation,—this earliest form of religious belief manifests in the smallest possible degree the theological quality of attacking the original torpor of the human faculties, by furnishing some aliment to our conceptions, and some bond between them. Having done this, fetichism obstructs all advance in genuine knowledge. It is in this form, above all others, that the religious spirit is most directly opposed to the scientific, with regard to the simplest phenomena; and all idea of natural laws is out of the question when every object is a divinity with a will of its own. At this period of intellectual infancy, imaginary facts wholly overwhelm real ones; or rather, there is no phenomenon which can be distinctly seen in its genuine aspect. The mind is in a state of vague pre-occupation with regard to the external world, which, universal and natural as it is, is not the less a kind of permanent hallucination, proceeding from such a preponderance of the affective over the intellectual life, that the most absurd beliefs impair all direct observation of natural phenomena. We are too apt to treat as imposture exceptional sensations which we have long ceased to be able to understand, but which have always been well known to magicians and fortunetellers in the stage of fetichism; but, if we try, we may picture to ourselves how it is that, in the absence of all conception of natural laws, nothing can appear monstrous, and Man is pretty sure to see what he is disposed to see, by illusions which appear to me strongly analogous to those which are experienced by brutes, through their gross fetichism. However familiar we may now be with the conception of the regularity of natural events, and however this conception may be now the basis of our whole mental system, it is certainly not an innate idea, as each of us can almost assign the very date of its formation in his own mind. Setting ourselves back to a time before its existence among men, we can not wonder at the hallucinations produced by an intellectual activity so at the mercy of the passions, or of natural stimulants affecting the human frame; and our surprise is rather that the radical integrity of the mind of Man should have restrained as far as it did the tendency to illusion which was encouraged by the only theories then possible.

The influence of fetichism was less oppressive in regard to the fine arts. It is evident that a philosophy which endowed the whole universe with life must favor the expansion of imagination, which was then supreme among the faculties. Thus, it is certain that the origin of all the fine arts, not excepting poetry, is to be referred to the fetich period. When I treat of the relation of polytheism to the fine arts, I shall have occasion to glance at that of fetichism also; and I therefore leave it now; observing only that the fact to be shown is that, in social as in individual life, the rise and expansion of human faculties begins with the faculties of expression, so as gradually to lead on the evolution of the superior and less marked faculties, in accordance with the connection established among them by our organization.

As to the industrial development of the race, it is certain that Man began his conquests over external nature in the fetich period. We do not give their due to those primitive times when we forget that it was then that men learned to associate with tamed animals, and to use fire, and to employ mechanical forces, and even to affect some kind of commerce by the nascent institution of a currency. In short, the germs of almost all the arts of life are found in that period. Moreover, Man's activity prepared the ground for the whole subsequent evolution of the race by the exercise of his destructive propensities, then in their utmost strength. The chase not only brought separate families into association when nothing else could have done it, but it cleared the scene of social operations from the encumbrance of an inconvenient multitude of brutes. So great was the destruction, that it is now believed to have concurred with some geological causes in obliterating certain races of animals, and especially some of the largest: in the same way that the superfluous vegetation is believed to have been got rid of by the devastation attending a pastoral mode of life. It is not easy however to settle how much of the industrial advance of the period is to be attributed to its fetichism. At the first glance, it might seem that the direct consecration of external objects must forbid Man to modify the world around him: and it is certain that too long a protraction of fetichism could not but have that effect, if the human mind were always or ever thoroughly consistent, and if there were no conflict between beliefs and instincts, in which the first must give way. But there is to be considered, besides, the theological quality which is so favorable to the incitement of human activity in the absence of all knowledge of natural laws,— the assurance given to Man that he is supreme in Nature. Though his supremacy is unavailing without the intervention of divine agents, the constant sense of this supreme protection can not but be the best support to human energy at a period when Man is surrounded by immense obstacles, which he would not otherwise venture to attack. Up to a very recent date in human history, when the knowledge of natural laws had become a sufficient groundwork for wise and bold action, the imperfect and precarious theological stimulus continued to act. Its function was all the more appropriate to fetichism, that it offered the hope of almost unlimited empire by an active use of religious resources. The more we contemplate those primitive ages, the more clearly we shall see that the great move was rousing the human mind from animal torpor; and it would have been extremely difficult, physically and morally, if the theological philosophy, in the form of fetichism, had not opened the only possible issue. When we examine, from the right point of view, the characteristic illusions of that age about controlling the courses of the stars, lulling or exciting storms, etc., we are less disposed to an unphilosophical contempt than to mark in these facts the first symptoms of the awakening of human intelligence and activity.

As to its social influence, fetichism effected great things for the race, though less than the subsequent forms of the theological spirit. We are apt to underrate these services, because the most religious persons of our own time are unable to do justice to the effects of a belief which is extinct. It is only the positive philosophy which enables us to estimate the share borne by the religious spirit in the social, as well as the intellectual progression of the human race. Now, it is plain that moral efforts must, from our organizations, be almost always in conflict, more or less, with the strongest impulses of our nature; and what but the theological spirit could afford a ground for social discipline at a time when foresight, collective and individual, was far too restricted to sustain any influence of rationality? Even at more advanced periods, institutions which are justified by reason, remain long under theological tutelage before they can be freely committed to their true sanctions; as, for instance, when sanitary precepts are diffused and established by religious prescription. An irresistible induction shows us the necessity of a similar consecration of social changes in which we are at present least disposed to look for it. We should not, for instance, suspect any religious influence to be concerned in the institution of property; yet there are some aspects of society, in which we find it; as, for instance, in the famous *Taboo* of the Pacific Islands, which I regard as a valuable trace of the participation of theology in that first consolidation of territorial property which takes place when hunting or pastoral tribes pass into the agricultural stage. It seems probable, too, that religious influences contributed to establish, and yet more to regulate, the permanent use of clothing, which is regarded as one of the chief marks of nascent civilization, both because it stimulates industrial aptitudes and because its moral operation is good in encouraging Man to improve his own nature by giving reason control over the propensities.

It is a great and injurious mistake to conceive of this theological influence as an artifice applied by the more enlightened men to the government of the less. We are strangely apt to ascribe eminent political ability to dissimulation and hypocrisy; but it is happily rendered incontestable, by all experience and all study, that no man of superior endowments has ever exercised any great influence over his fellows without being first, for his own part, thoroughly convinced. It is not only that there must be a sufficient harmony of feeling and inclinations between himself and them, but his faculties would be paralyzed by the effort to guide his thoughts in the two opposite ways,—the real and the affected,—either of which would separately be as much as he could manage. If theological theories entered into the simplest speculations of men, in the age of fetichism, they must have governed social and political meditations, the complexity of which rendered religious resources peculiarly necessary. The legislators of that age must have been as sincere in their theological conceptions of society as of everything else; and the dreadful practical extravagances into which they too often fell under that guidance are unquestionable evidence of their general sincerity. We must consider, too, that the earliest theological polity naturally afforded suggestions which were coincident with corresponding social needs. The coincidence arose partly from that general property of all religious phases,—the vagueness of all faiths, which adapts them to be modified by all political exigencies, and thus to appear to sanction a suggestion when they merely respond to a want; and partly from the fact, special in each case, that the beliefs of any society must be mainly determined by the existing modifications of that society; so that opinions must necessarily present certain attributes in special harmony with corresponding social circumstances; and without this they could not retain their influence. By the first property an organization under a priesthood was rendered necessary, to prevent opinions so capable of abuse from being committed to the vulgar; and by the second, theological theories could not only consecrate all valuable suggestions, but could frequently produce some which were suitable to the contemporary social state. The first corresponds to what is vague and uncontrollable in each religious system; and the other to what is definite and susceptible of regulation; and the two supply each other's deficiencies. As belief becomes simpli-

fied and organized, its social influence diminishes under the first aspect, on account of the restriction on speculation; but it is ever increasing under the second aspect, as we shall presently see, permitting superior men to make the utmost use of the civilizing virtue of this primitive philosophy. It is clear that the first of these modes of social action of any theology must prevail eminently in fetichism; and this agrees with our observation of the absence or imperfection of any religious organization; but this fact renders all analysis inextricable, from the difficulty of discerning how much of the religious element was incorporated with the intricate web of a life which our familiar conceptions are so little adapted to unravel. We can only verify by some decisive examples the necessary reality of our theory; a thing which is easily done. As to the second mode, though it operated little during the fetich period, its precise nature enables us to obtain a better hold of it. An example or two will show its effect on the social progress of the race.

All philosophers are agreed about the supreme importance of the institution of agricultural life, without which no further human progress would have been possible; but all do not see how religion was concerned in the transition. War, which is the chief temporal instrument of early civilization, has no important social influence till the nomade condition is left behind. The fierce conflicts of hunting, and even of pastoral tribes, are like those of carnivorous animals, and only exercise activity and prepare for progress without producing immediate political results. The importance of subjecting Man to a fixed residence is thus obvious enough, on the one hand, and, on the other, the difficulty attending a change so little compatible in many ways with the character of infant humanity. There can be no doubt that a wandering life was natural to primitive Man, as we see it to be now to individuals below the reach of culture. This shows us how the intervention of spiritual influences may have been necessary to so great a change. It is usual to suppose that the condensation of numbers, as the race increased, would compel the tillage of the soil, as it had before compelled the keeping of flocks. But the explanation, though true as far as it goes, is insufficient; for, as we have seen before, want does not produce faculty. No social exigency will find its satisfaction if Man is not already disposed to provide it; and all experience shows that men will, in the most urgent cases, rather palliate each suffering as it arises, than resolve on a total change of condition which is repugnant to their nature. We know by observation what dreadful expedients men would adopt to reduce the excess of population, rather than exchange a nomade for an agricultural life, before their intellectual and moral nature was duly prepared for it. The progression of the human being therefore caused the change, though the precise date of its accomplishment must depend on external requirements; and above all, on the numbers needing food. Now, as agricultural life was certainly instituted before fetichism passed away, it is clear that there must be in fetichism something favorable to the change, though we may not know precisely what it was. But I have no doubt about the essential principle. The worship of the external world must be especially directed to the objects which are nearest and commonest; and this must tend to develop the originally feeble affection of men for their native soil. The moving lamentations of vanquished warriors for their tutelary gods were not about Jupiter, Minerva, or other abstract and general deities, whom they could find everywhere, but for their domestic gods; that is, pure fetiches. These were the special divinities whom the captives wept to leave behind, almost as bitterly as the tombs of their fathers, which were also involved in the universal fetichism. Among nations which had reached polytheism before becoming agricultural, the religious influence necessary to the change was chiefly due, no doubt, to the remains of fetichism, which held a conspicuous place in polytheism, up to a very advanced period. Such an influence then is an essential property of the first theological phase; and it would not have been strong enough in the subsequent religions if the great material change had not by that time been so well established on other grounds as to be able to relinquish the original one which was passing away. The reaction of the change upon theology is, at the same time, worthy of notice. It was then that fetichism assumed that highest form,—that of star-worship,—which was the transition stage to polytheism. It is plain that the settled abode of agricultural peoples must fix their speculative attention upon the heavenly bodies, while their labors remarkably disclosed the influences of the sky: whereas, the only astronomical observations to be expected of a wandering tribe are of the polar star which guides their nocturnal course. Thus there is a double relation between the development of fetichism and the final establishment of agricultural life.

Another instance of the influence of fetichism on social progress is its occasioning the systematic preservation of serviceable animals, and also of vegetables. It has been shown that the first action of Man on the external world must be in the form of devastation; and his destructive propensities do their work in clearing the field for future operations. A propensity so marked among men as rude as they were vehement threatened the safety of all races, before the utility of any was known. The most valuable organic species were the most exposed; and they must almost inevitably have perished if the first intellectual and moral advance of the human race had not intervened to restrain the tendency to indiscriminate destruction. Fetichism performed this office, not only by introducing agricultural life, but directly; and if it was done by a method which afterward became excessively debased—the express worship of animals, it may be asked how else the thing could have been done. Whatever evils belonged afterward to fetichism, it should be remembered how admirably it was adapted to preserve the most valuable animals and vegetables, and indeed all material objects requiring special protection. Polytheism rendered the same service, by placing everything under the care of some deity or other; but this was a less direct method than that of fetichism, and would not have sufficed in the first instance. No provision of the kind is to be found in monotheism; but neither is it so necessary in the more advanced stage of human progress to which it is adapted: yet the want of regular discipline in this order of relations is found to be a defect to this day, and one which is only imperfectly repaired by purely temporal measures. There can be no doubt that the moral effect of Man's care of animals contributed largely to humanize him. His carnivorous constitution is one of the chief limitations of his pacific capabilities, favorable as is the growing subdivision of employments to the milder inclinations of the majority of society; and, honorable as is the Utopia of Pythagoras, imagined in an age when the destructive tendency prevailed in the highest portion of society, it is not the less opposed to Man's nature and destiny, which oblige him to increase in all directions his natural ascendency over the whole of the animal kingdom. On this account, and for the regulation of this power, laws are essential, as in every other case of power possessed; and fetichism must be regarded as having first indicated, in the only way then possible, an exalted kind of human institution, for the regulation of the general political relations of all,— those of Man toward the external world, and especially the animal part of it. The selfishness of kind could not prevail among these relations without serious danger; and it must become moderate in proportion as the organisms rise to an increasing resemblance to our own. When the positive philosophy shall regulate these relations, it will be by constituting a special department of external nature, in regard to which a familiar knowledge of our interest in the zoological scale will have trained us in our duty to all living beings.

Such were, as nearly as we can estimate, the

social influences of fetichism. We must now observe how it passed into polytheism.

There can be no doubt of the direct derivation of polytheism from fetichism, at all times and in all places. The analysis of individual development, and the investigation of the corresponding degrees of the social scale, alike disclose this constant succession. The study of the highest antiquity, when illustrated by sound sociological theories, verifies the same fact. In most theogonies the prior existence of fetichism is necessary to the formation of the gods of polytheism. The Greek gods that issued from the Ocean and the Earth, issued from the two principal fetiches; and we have seen how, in its maturity, polytheism incorporates strong remains of fetichism. Speculatively regarded, this transformation of the religious spirit is perhaps the most radical that it has ever undergone, though we are unable, through its remoteness, to appreciate with any steadiness its extent and difficulty. From the comparative nearness and social importance of the transition to monotheism, we naturally exaggerate its relative importance; but, in truth, the interval to be passed was much narrower in the later case than in the earlier. If we reflect that fetichism supposed matter to be, in all forms, actually alive, while polytheism declared it to be nearly inert, and passively subject to the arbitrary will of a divine agent, it seems hardly imaginable how such a transition of views could be gradually made. Both are equally remote from the positive view,—that of the operation of natural laws; but they are no less opposed to each other, except in the one point of some express will being the cause of every incident: and thus it is a matter of the highest philosophical interest to ascertain the spontaneous mode of this memorable transition.

The intervention of the scientific spirit has only recently been direct and explicit; but not the less has it been concerned in all the successive modifications of the religious spirit. If Man had been no more capable than monkeys and carnivorous animals of comparing, abstracting, and generalizing, he would have remained for ever in the rude fetichism which their imperfect organization forbids their surmounting. Man, however, can perceive likeness between phenomena, and observe their succession: and when these characteristic faculties had once found aliment and guidance under the first theological instigation, they gathered strength perpetually, and by their exercise reduced, more and more rapidly, the influence of the religious philosophy by which they had been cherished. The first general result of the rise of this spirit of observation and induction seems to me to have been the passage from fetichism to polytheism, beginning, as all such changes do, with the highest order of minds, and reaching the multitude at last. To understand this, we must bear in mind that, as all fetich faith relates to some single and determinate object, the belief is of an individual and concrete nature. This quality suits well with the particular and unconnected character of the rudely-material observations proper to an infant state of the human mind: so that the exact accordance between the conception and the investigation that is found wherever our understandings are at work, is evident in the present case. The expansion of the spirit of observation caused by the first theory, imperfect as it was, must destroy the balance which, at length, can not be maintained at all but by some modification of the original philosophy. Thus the great revolution which carried men on from fetichism to polytheism is due to the same mental causes, though they may not be so conspicuous, that now produce all scientific revolutions,—which always arise out of a discordance between facts and principles. Thus did the growing generalization of human observations necessitate the same process in regard to the corresponding theological conceptions, and occasion the transformation of fetichism into simple polytheism; for the difference between the divinities of the two systems is the essential one that the gods, properly so called, have, from their indeterminate residence, a more general and abstract character. Each undertakes a special order of phenomena, but in a great number of bodies at the same time; so that each rules a department of some extent; whereas the fetich is inseparable from the one object in which it resides. When certain phenomena appeared alike in various substances, the corresponding fetiches must have formed a group, and at length coalesced into one principal one, which thus became a god; that is, an ideal and usually invisible agent, whose residence is no longer rigorously fixed. Thus, when the oaks of a forest, in their likeness to each other, suggested certain general phenomena, the abstract being in whom so many fetiches coalesced was no fetich, but the god of the forest. Thus, the intellectual transition from fetichism to polytheism is neither more nor less than the ascendency of specific over individual ideas, in the second stage of human childhood, social as well as personal. As every essential disposition is, on our principles, inherent in humanity from the beginning, this process must have already taken place, in certain cases; and the transition was thus, no doubt, much facilitated; as it was only necessary to extend and imitate what had already been done. Polytheism itself may have been primitive in certain cases, where the individual had a strong natural tendency to abstraction, while his contemporaries, being more impressible than reasonable, were more struck by differences than resemblances. As this exceptional condition does not indicate any general superiority, and the cases must have been few and restricted, my theory is not affected by them. They are interesting to us only as showing how the human mind was subjected to its first great philosophical transition, and carried through it. Thus it is that the purely theological nature of the primitive philosophy was preserved, in the conception that phenomena were governed by Will and not by laws; while, again, it was profoundly modified by the view of matter being no longer alive but inert, and obtaining all its activity from an imaginary external being. The intellectual and social consequences of the change will appear hereafter. The remark that occurs in this place is that the decline of the mental influence of the religious spirit, while its political influence is rising, may be distinctly perceived at this stage. When each individual thing lost its character of essential life and divineness, it became accessible to the scientific spirit, which might be humble enough in its operation, but was no longer excluded by theological intervention. The change is evidenced by the corresponding steady diminution of the number of divinities, while their nature was becoming more abstract and their dominion more extended. Each god took the place of a troop of fetiches, which were thenceforth permitted, or reduced, to serve as his escort. We shall hereafter recognise the same process, in the succession of monotheism to polytheism.

The particular issue by which the transition was effected is easily found, when we consider that it must be through the phenomenon which appears the most general and abstract, and the most universal in its influence. The stars answer to this description, when once their isolated and inaccessible position had fixed men's attention, in preference to the nearer objects which had at first engrossed it. The difference in conception between a fetich and a god must be smaller in the case of a star than of any other body; and it was this which made astrolatry, as I observed before, the natural intermediary state between the two first theological phases. Each sidereal fetich, powerful and remote, was scarcely distinguishable from a god; and especially in an age when men did not trouble themselves with nice distinctions. The only thing necessary to get rid of the individual and concrete character altogether, was to liberate the divinity from his imprisonment in one place and function, and to connect him by some real or apparent analogy with more general functions; thus making him a god, with a star for his preferred abode. This last transformation was so little necessary that,

throughout nearly the whole polytheistic period, it was only the planets that, on account of their special variations, were subjected to it. The fixed stars remained true fetiches till they were included with everything in the universal monotheism.

In order to complete our estimate of this part of the human evolution, in which all the principles of subsequent progress must be implicated, I must point out the manifestations of the metaphysical spirit which here present themselves. If the theological philosophy is modified by the scientific spirit, this is done only through the metaphysical spirit, which rises with the decline of the theological, till the positive prevails over them both. The more recent dominion of the metaphysical spirit may be the most engrossing to us; but perhaps its operation when it was a mere gradation of the theological philosophy might appear to be of higher importance, if we could estimate the change wrought by it, and were in possession of any precise evidence. When bodies ceased to be divinely alive by their own nature, they must have some abstract property which rendered them fit to receive the action of the supernatural agent—an action which could not be immediate when the agent had a wider influence and an unfixed abode. Again, when a group of fetiches yield up their common attributes to a single god, and that god is regarded as living, in spite of his abstract origin, the conception is metaphysical in its whole character—recognising, as it does, personified abstractions. For the universal characteristic of the metaphysical state, as a transitional condition of the understanding, is a radical confusion between the abstract and the concrete point of view, alternately assumed to modify theological conceptions; now to render abstract what was before concrete, when each generalization is accomplished, and now to prepare for a new concentration the conception of more general existences, which was hitherto only abstract. Such is the operation of the metaphysical spirit on the theological philosophy, whose fictions had offered the only intelligible ground to human understanding, while all that it could do was to transfer to everything out of itself its own sense of active existence. Distinct from every substance, though inseparable from it, the metaphysical entity is more subtile and less definite than the corresponding supernatural action from which it emanates; and hence its aptitude to effect transitions which are invariably a decline, in an intellectual sense, of the theological philosophy. The action is always critical, as it preserves theology while undermining its intellectual basis; and it can appear organic only when it is not too preponderant, and in as far as it contributes to the gradual modification of the theological philosophy, to which, especially in a social view, must be referred whatever may appear to be organic in the metaphysical philosophy. These explanations must at first appear obscure; but the applications we shall have to make of them will render them unquestionable as we proceed. Meantime, it was impossible to defer them, and to neglect the true origin of the metaphysical influence, concerned as it is in the great transition from fetichism to polytheism.

Besides the immediate scientific necessity, it is certainly desirable to trace from the cradle of humanity upward, that spontaneous and constant rivalry, first intellectual and then political, between the theological and the metaphysical spirit, which, protracted to the present moment, and necessary till the preparatory revolution is accomplished, is the main cause of our disturbed and conflicting condition.

2. *Of Superstition and Enthusiasm*

BY DAVID HUME

THAT[1] *the corruption of the best things produces the worst,* is grown into a maxim, and is commonly proved, among other instances, by the pernicious effects of *superstition* and *enthusiasm,* the corruptions of true religion.

These two species of false religion, though both pernicious, are yet of a very different, and even of a contrary nature. The mind of man is subject to certain unaccountable terrors and apprehensions, proceeding either from the unhappy situation of private or public affairs, from ill health, from a gloomy and melancholy disposition, or from the concurrence of all these circumstances. In such a state of mind, infinite unknown evils are dreaded from unknown agents; and where real objects of terror are wanting, the soul, active to its own prejudice, and fostering its predominant inclination, finds imaginary ones, to whose power and malevolence it sets no limits. As these enemies are entirely invisible and unknown, the methods taken to appease them are equally unaccountable, and consist in ceremonies, observances, mortifications, sacrifices, presents, or in any practice, however absurd or frivolous, which either folly or knavery recommends to a blind and terrified credulity. Weakness, fear, melancholy, together with ignorance, are, therefore, the true sources of Superstition.

But the mind of man is also subject to an unaccountable elevation and presumption, arising from prosperous success, from luxuriant health, from strong spirits, or from a bold and confident disposition. In such a state of mind, the imagination swells with great, but confused conceptions, to which no sublunary beauties or enjoyments can correspond. Every thing mortal and perishable vanishes as unworthy of attention. And a full range is given to the fancy in the invisible regions or world of spirits, where the soul is at liberty to indulge itself in every imagination, which may best suit its present taste and disposition. Hence arise raptures, transports and surprising flights of fancy; and confidence and presumption still increasing, these raptures, being altogether unaccountable, and seeming quite beyond the reach of our ordinary faculties, are attributed to the immediate inspiration of that Divine Being, who is the object of devotion. In a little

Reprinted from David Hume, *Essays: Moral, Political, and Literary* (London: Longmans Green & Co., 1882), Essay X, pp. 144–50.

1. Some of the opinions, delivered in these Essays, with regard to the public transactions in the last century, the Author, on more accurate examination, found reason to retract in his *History of Great Britain.* And as he would not enslave himself to the systems of either party, neither would he fetter his judgment by his own preconceived opinions and principles; nor is he ashamed to acknowledge his mistakes. [This note does not occur in any edition prior to M. A and B add the following paragraph to the text:—As violent Things have not commonly so long a Duration as moderate, we actually find, that the *Jacobite* Party is almost entirely vanish'd from among us, and that the Distinction of *Court* and *Country,* which is but creeping in at London, is the only one that is ever mention'd in this *kingdom.* Beside the Violence and Openness of the Jacobite party, another Reason has, perhaps, contributed to produce so sudden and so visible an Alteration in this part of Britain. There are only two Ranks of Men among us; Gentlemen, who have some Fortune and Education, and the meanest slaving Poor; without any considerable Number of that middling Rank of Men, which abounds more in England, both in Cities and in the Country, than in any other Part of the World. The slaving Poor are incapable of any Principles: Gentlemen may be converted to true Principles, by Time and Experience. The middling Rank of Men have Curiosity and Knowledge enough to form Principles, but not enough to form true ones, or correct any Prejudices that they may have imbib'd: And 'tis among the middling Rank, that Tory Principles do at present prevail most in England.]

time, the inspired person comes to regard himself as a distinguished favourite of the Divinity; and when this frenzy once takes place, which is the summit of enthusiasm, every whimsy is consecrated: Human reason, and even morality are rejected as fallacious guides: And the fanatic madman delivers himself over, blindly, and without reserve, to the supposed illapses of the spirit, and to inspiration from above. Hope, pride, presumption, a warm imagination, together with ignorance, are, therefore, the true sources of Enthusiasm.

These two species of false religion might afford occasion to many speculations; but I shall confine myself, at present, to a few reflections concerning their different influence on government and society.

² My first reflection is, *That superstition is favour-*

---

2. [In Editions A and B, this and the three next paragraphs were written as follows: My first Reflection is, that Religions, which partake of Enthusiasm are, on their first Rise, much more furious and violent than those which partake of Superstition; but in a little Time become much more gentle and moderate. The Violence of this Species of Religion, when excited by Novelty, and animated by Opposition, appears from numberless Instances; of the *Anabaptists* in *Germany*, the *Camisars* in *France*, the *Levellers* and other Fanaticks in *England*, and the *Covenanters* in *Scotland*. As Enthusiasm is founded on strong Spirits and a presumptuous Boldness of Character, it naturally begets the most extreme Resolutions; especially after it rises to that Height as to inspire the deluded Fanaticks with the Opinion of Divine Illuminations, and with a Contempt of the common Rules of Reason, Morality and Prudence.

'Tis thus Enthusiasm produces the most cruel Desolation in human Society: But its Fury is like that of Thunder and Tempest, which exhaust themselves in a little Time, and leave the Air more calm and serene than before. The Reason of this will appear evidently, by comparing Enthusiasm to Superstition, the other Species of false Religion; and tracing the natural Consequences of each. As Superstition is founded on Fear, Sorrow, and a Depression of Spirits, it represents the Person to himself in such despicable Colours, that he appears unworthy, in his own Eyes, of approaching the Divine Presence, and naturally has Recourse to any other Person, whose Sanctity of Life, or, perhaps, Impudence and Cunning, have made him be supposed to be more favoured by the Divinity. To him they entrust their Devotions: To his Care they recommend their Prayers, Petitions, and Sacrifices: And, by his Means, hope to render their Addresses acceptable to their incensed Deity. Hence the Origin of *Priests*, who may justly be regarded as one of the grossest Inventions of a timorous and abject Superstition, which, ever diffident of itself, dares not offer up its own Devotions, but ignorantly thinks to recommend itself to the Divinity, by the Mediation of his supposed Friends and Servants. As Superstition is a considerable Ingredient of almost all Religions, even the most fanatical; there being nothing but Philosophy able to conquer entirely these unaccountable Terrors; hence it proceeds, that in almost every Sect of Religion there are Priests to be found: But the stronger Mixture there is of Superstition, the higher is the Authority of the Priesthood. Modern Judaism and Popery, especially the latter, being the most barbarous and absurd Superstitions that have yet been known in the World, are the most enslav'd by their Priests. As the Church of England may justly be said to retain a strong Mixture of Popish Superstition, it partakes also, in its original Constitution, of a Propensity to Priestly Power and Dominion; particularly in the Respect it exacts

able to priestly power, and enthusiasm not less or rather more contrary to it, than sound reason and philosophy. As superstition is founded on fear, sorrow, and a depression of spirits, it represents the man to himself in such despicable colours, that he appears unworthy, in his own eyes, of approaching the divine presence, and naturally has recourse to any other person, whose sanctity of life, or, perhaps, impudence and cunning, have made him be supposed more favoured by the Divinity. To him the superstitious entrust their devotions: To his care they recommend their prayers, petitions, and sacrifices: And by his means, they hope to render their addresses acceptable to their incensed Deity.

to the Priest. And though, according to the Sentiments of that Church, the Prayers of the Priest must be accompanied with those of the Laity; yet is he the mouth of the Congregation, his Person is sacred, and without his Presence few would think their public Devotions, or the Sacraments, and other Rites, acceptable to the Divinity. On the other Hand, it may be observed, That all Enthusiasts have been free from the Yoke of Ecclesiastics, and have exprest a great Independence in their Devotion; with a contempt of Forms, Tradition and Authorities. The *Quakers* are the most egregious, tho', at the same Time, the most innocent, Enthusiasts that have been yet known; and are, perhaps, the only Sect, that have never admitted Priests among them. The *Independents*, of all the English Sectaries, approach nearest to the Quakers in Fanaticism, and in their Freedom from Priestly Bondage. The *Presbyterians* follow after, at an equal Distance in both these Particulars. In short, this Observation is founded on the most certain Experience; and will also appear to be founded on Reason, if we consider, that as Enthusiasm arises from a presumptuous Pride and Confidence, it thinks itself sufficiently qualified to *approach* the Divinity without any human Mediator. Its rapturous Devotions are so fervent, that it even imagines itself *actually* to *approach* him by the Way of Contemplation and inward Converse; which makes it neglect all those outward Ceremonies and Observances, to which the Assistance of the Priests appears so requisite in the Eyes of their superstitious Votaries. This Fanatick consecrates himself, and bestows on his own Person a sacred Character, much superior to what Forms and ceremonious Institutions can confer on any other.

'Tis therefore an infallible Rule, That Superstition is favourable to Priestly Power, and Enthusiasm as much, or rather more, contrary to it than sound Reason and Philosophy. The Consequences are evident. When the first Fire of Enthusiasm is spent, Men naturally, in such fanatical Sects, sink into the greatest Remissness and Coolness in Sacred Matters; there being no Body of Men amongst them, endow'd with sufficient Authority, whose Interest is concerned, to support the religious Spirit. Superstition, on the contrary, steals in gradually and insensibly; renders Men tame and submissive; is acceptable to the Magistrate, and seems inoffensive to the People: Till at last the Priest, having firmly establish'd his Authority, becomes the Tyrant and Disturber of human Society, by his endless Contentions, Persecutions, and religious Wars. How smoothly did the *Romish* Church advance in their Acquisition of Power? But into what dismal Convulsions did they throw all Europe, in order to maintain it? On the other Hand, our Sectaries, who were formerly such dangerous Bigots, are now become our greatest Freethinkers; and the *Quakers* are, perhaps, the only regular Body of *Deists* in the Universe, except the *Literati* or Disciples of *Confucius* in *China*.]

Hence the origin of Priests,[3] who may justly be regarded as an invention of a timorous and abject superstition, which, ever diffident of itself, dares not offer up its own devotions, but ignorantly thinks to recommend itself to the Divinity, by the mediation of his supposed friends and servants. As superstition is a considerable ingredient in almost all religions, even the most fanatical; there being nothing but philosophy able entirely to conquer these unaccountable terrors; hence it proceeds, that in almost every sect of religion there are priests to be found: But the stronger mixture there is of superstition, the higher is the authority of the priesthood.[4]

On the other hand, it may be observed, that all enthusiasts have been free from the yoke of ecclesiastics, and have expressed great independence in their devotion; with a contempt of forms, ceremonies, and traditions. The *quakers* are the most egregious, though, at the same time, the most innocent enthusiasts that have yet been known; and are, perhaps, the only sect, that have never admitted priests amongst them. The *independents,* of all the English sectaries, approach nearest to the *quakers* in fanaticism, and in their freedom from priestly bondage. The *presbyterians* follow after, at an equal distance in both particulars. In short this observation is founded in experience; and will also appear to be founded in reason, if we consider, that, as enthusiasm arises from a presumptuous pride and confidence, it thinks itself sufficiently qualified to *approach* the Divinity, without any human mediator. Its rapturous devotions are so fervent, that it even imagines itself *actually* to *approach* him by the way of contemplation and inward converse; which makes it neglect all those outward ceremonies and observances, to which the assistance of the priests appears so requisite in the eyes of their superstitious votaries. The fanatic

3. [The following note is appended in Editions D to N: By *Priests,* I here mean only the pretenders to power and dominion, and to a superior sanctity of character, distinct from virtue and good morals. These are very different from *clergymen,* who are set apart *by the laws,* to the care of sacred matters, and to the conducting our public devotions with greater decency and order. There is no rank of men more to be respected than the latter.]

4. [Here D to P add: Modern Judaism and popery, especially the latter) being the most unphilosophical and absurd superstitions which have yet been known in the world, are the most enslaved by their priests. As the church of England may justly be said to retain some mixture of Popish superstition, it partakes also, in its original constitution, of a propensity to priestly power and dominion; particularly in the respect it exacts to the sacerdotal character. And though, according to the sentiments of that Church, the prayers of the priest must be accompanied with those of the laity; yet is he the mouth of the congregation, his person is sacred, and without his presence few would think their public devotions, or the sacraments, and other rites, acceptable to the divinity.]

consecrates himself, and bestows on his own person a sacred character, much superior to what forms and ceremonious institutions can confer on any other.

My *second* reflection with regard to these species of false religion is, *that religions, which partake of enthusiasm are, on their first rise, more furious and violent than those which partake of superstition; but in a little time become more gentle and moderate.* The violence of this species of religion, when excited by novelty, and animated by opposition, appears from numberless instances; of the *anabaptists* in Germany, the *camisars* in France, the *levellers* and other fanatics in England, and the *covenanters* in Scotland. Enthusiasm being founded on strong spirits, and a presumptuous boldness of character, it naturally begets the most extreme resolutions; especially after it rises to that height as to inspire the deluded fanatic with the opinion of divine illuminations, and with a contempt for the common rules of reason, morality, and prudence.

It is thus enthusiasm produces the most cruel disorders in human society; but its fury is like that of thunder and tempest, which exhaust themselves in a little time, and leave the air more calm and pure than before. When the first fire of enthusiasm is spent, men naturally, in all fanatical sects, sink into the greatest remissness and coolness in sacred matters; there being no body of men among them, endowed with sufficient authority, whose interest is concerned to support the religious spirit: No rites, no ceremonies, no holy observances, which may enter into the common train of life, and preserve the sacred principles from oblivion. Superstition, on the contrary, steals in gradually and insensibly; renders men tame and submissive; is acceptable to the magistrate, and seems inoffensive to the people: Till at last the priest, having firmly established his authority, becomes the tyrant and disturber of human society, by his endless contentions, persecutions, and religious wars. How smoothly did the Romish church advance in her acquisition of power? But into what dismal convulsions did she throw all Europe, in order to maintain it? On the other hand, our sectaries, who were formerly such dangerous bigots, are now become very free reasoners; and the *quakers* seem to approach nearly the only regular body of *deists* in the universe, the *literati,* or the disciples of Confucius in China.[5]

My *third* observation on this head is *that superstition is an enemy to civil liberty, and enthusiasm a*

5. The Chinese Literati have no priests or ecclesiastical establishment. [This note is not in D and K, which read in the text: and the quakers seem to approach nearly the only regular body of deists in the universe, the *literati,* or the disciples of *Confucius* in China.]

friend to it. As superstition groans under the dominion of priests, and enthusiasm is destructive of all ecclesiastical power, this sufficiently accounts for the present observation. Not to mention, that enthusiasm, being the infirmity of bold and ambitious tempers, is naturally accompanied with a spirit of liberty; as superstition, on the contrary, renders men tame and abject, and fits them for slavery. We learn from English history, that, during the civil wars, the *independents* and *deists,* though the most opposite in their religious principles; yet were united in their political ones, and were alike passionate for a commonwealth. And since the origin of *whig* and *tory,* the leaders of the *whigs* have either been *deists* or profest *latitudinarians* in their principles; that is, friends to toleration, and indifferent to any particular sect of *christians:* While the sectaries, who have all a strong tincture of enthusiasm, have always, without exception, concurred with that party, in defence of civil liberty. The resemblance in their superstitions long united the highchurch *tories,* and the *Roman*

catholics, in support of prerogative and kingly power; though experience of the tolerating spirit of the *whigs* seems of late to have reconciled the *catholics* to that party.

The *molinists* and *jansenists* in France have a thousand unintelligible disputes, which are not worthy the reflection of a man of sense: But what principally distinguishes these two sects, and alone merits attention, is the different spirit of their religion. The *molinists* conducted by the *jesuits,* are great friends to superstition, rigid observers of external forms and ceremonies, and devoted to the authority of the priests, and to tradition. The *jansenists* are enthusiasts, and zealous promoters of the passionate devotion, and of the inward life; little influenced by authority; and, in a word, but half catholics. The consequences are exactly conformable to the foregoing reasoning. The *jesuits* are the tyrants of the people, and the slaves of the court: And the *jansenists* preserve alive the small sparks of the love of liberty, which are to be found in the French nation.

3. *The Gods of the City*

BY FUSTEL DE COULANGES

TO UNDERSTAND the truth about the Greeks and Romans, it is wise to study them without thinking of ourselves, as if they were entirely foreign to us; with the same disinterestedness, and with the mind as free, as if we were studying ancient India or Arabia.

Thus observed, Greece and Rome appear to us in a character absolutely inimitable; nothing in modern times resembles them; nothing in the future can resemble them. We shall attempt to show by what rules these societies were regulated, and it will be freely admitted that the same rules can never govern humanity again.

Whence comes this? Why are the conditions of human government no longer the same as in earlier times? The great changes which appear from time to time in the constitution of society can be the effect neither of chance nor of force alone.

Reprinted from Fustel de Coulanges, *The Ancient City,* trans. Willard Small (Boston: Lee and Shepard, 1874), pp. 10–13, 164–67.

The cause which produces them must be powerful, and must be found in man himself. If the laws of human association are no longer the same as in antiquity, it is because there has been a change in man. There is, in fact, a part of our being which is modified from age to age; this is our intelligence. It is always in movement; almost always progressing; and on this account, our institutions and our laws are subject to change. Man has not, in our day, the way of thinking that he had twenty-five centuries ago; and this is why he is no longer governed as he was governed then.

The history of Greece and Rome is a witness and an example of the intimate relation which always exists between men's ideas and their social state. Examine the institutions of the ancients without thinking of their religious notions, and you find them obscure, whimsical, and inexplicable. Why were there patricians and plebeians, patrons, and clients, eupatrids and thetes; and whence came the native and ineffaceable differences which we find between these classes? What was the meaning of those Lacedæmonian institutions which appear to us so contrary to nature? How are we to explain those unjust caprices of ancient private law; at Corinth and at Thebes, the sale of land prohibited; at Athens and at Rome, an inequality in the succession between brother and sister? What did the jurists understand by *agnation,* and by *gens?* Why those revolutions in the laws, those political revolutions? What was that singular patriotism which sometimes effaced every natural sentiment? What did they understand by that liberty of which they were always talking? How did it happen that institutions so very different from anything of which we have an idea to-day, could become established and reign for so long a time? What is the superior principle which gave them authority over the minds of men?

But by the side of these institutions and laws place the religious ideas of those times, and the facts at once become clear, and their explanation is no longer doubtful. If, on going back to the first ages of this race,—that is to say, to the time when its institutions were founded,—we observe the idea which it had of human existence, of life, of death, of a second life, of the divine principle, we perceive a close relation between these opinions and the ancient rules of private law; between the rites which spring from these opinions and their political institutions.

A comparison of beliefs and laws shows that a primitive religion constituted the Greek and Roman family, established marriage and paternal authority, fixed the order of relationship, and consecrated the right of property, and the right of inheritance. This same religion, after having enlarged and extended the family, formed a still larger association, the city, and reigned in that as it had reigned in the family. From it came all the institutions, as well as all the private law, of the ancients. It was from this that the city received all its principles, its rules, its usages, and its magistracies. But, in the course of time, this ancient religion became modified or effaced, and private law and political institutions were modified with it. Then came a series of revolutions, and social changes regularly followed the development of knowledge.

It is of the first importance, therefore, to study the religious ideas of these peoples, and the oldest are the most important for us to know. For the institutions and beliefs which we find at the flourishing periods of Greece and Rome are only the development of those of an earlier age; we must seek the roots of them in the very distant past. The Greek and Italian population are many centuries older than Romulus and Homer. It was at an epoch

more ancient, in an antiquity without date, that their beliefs were formed, and that their institutions were either established or prepared.

*   *   *

It happened, in the course of time, the divinity of a family having acquired a great prestige over the imaginations of men, and appearing powerful in proportion to the prosperity of this family, that a whole city wished to adopt him, and offer him public worship, to obtain his favors. This was the case with the Demeter of the Eumolpidæ, the Athene of the Butadæ, and the Hercules of the Potitii. But when a family consented thus to share its god, it retained at least the priesthood. We may remark that the dignity of priest, for each god, was during a long time hereditary, and could not go out of a certain family. This is a vestige of a time when the god himself was the property of this family; when he protected it alone, and would be served only by it.

We are correct, therefore, in saying that this second religion was at first in unison with the social condition of men. It was cradled in each family, and remained long bounded by this narrow horizon. But it lent itself more easily than the worship of the dead to the future progress of human association. Indeed, the ancestors, heroes, and manes were gods, who by their very nature could be adored only by a very small number of men, and who thus established a perpetual and impassable line of demarcation between families. The religion of the gods of nature was more comprehensive. No rigorous laws opposed the propagation of the worship of any of these gods. There was nothing in their nature that required them to be adored by one family only, and to repel the stranger. Finally, men must have come insensibly to perceive that the Jupiter of one family was really the same being or the same conception as the Jupiter of another, which they could never believe of two Lares, two ancestors, or two sacred fires.

Let us add, that the morality of this new religion was different. It was not confined to teaching men family duties. Jupiter was the god of hospitality; in his name came strangers, suppliants, "the venerable poor," those who were to be treated "as brothers." All these gods often assumed the human form, and appeared among mortals; sometimes, indeed, to assist in their struggles and to take part in their combats; often, also, to enjoin concord, and to teach them to help each other.

As this second religion continued to develop, society must have enlarged. Now, it is quite evident that this religion, feeble at first, afterwards assumed large proportions. In the beginning it was, so to speak, sheltered under the protection of its older sister, near the domestic hearth. There the god had obtained a small place, a narrow *cella,* near and opposite to the venerated altar, in order that a little of the respect which men had for the sacred fire might be shared by him. Little by little, the god, gaining more authority over the soul, renounced this sort of guardianship, and left the domestic hearth. He had a dwelling of his own, and his own sacrifices. This dwelling (ναὸς, from ναίω, to inhabit) was, moreover, built after the fashion of the ancient sanctuary; it was, as before, a *cella* opposite a hearth; but the *cella* was enlarged and embellished, and became a temple. The holy

fire remained at the entrance of the god's house, but appeared very small by the side of this house. What had at first been the principal, had now become only an accessory. It ceased to be a god, and descended to the rank of the god's altar, an instrument for the sacrifice. Its office was to burn the flesh of the victim, and to carry the offering with men's prayers to the majestic divinity whose statue resided in the temple.

When we see these temples rise and open their doors to the multitude of worshippers, we may be assured that human associations have become enlarged.

4. Jehovah and the Prophets

BY W. ROBERTSON SMITH

THE PRIMARY difference between the religion of Israel and that of the surrounding nations does not lie in the idea of a theocracy, or in a philosophy of the invisible world, or in the external forms of religious service, but in a personal difference between Jehovah and other gods. That difference, again, is not of a metaphysical but of a directly practical nature; it was not defined once for all in a theological dogma, but made itself felt in the attitude which Jehovah actually took up towards Israel in those historical dealings with His nation to which the word of the prophets supplied a commentary. Everything that befell Israel was interpreted by the prophets as a work of Jehovah's hand, displaying His character and will— not an arbitrary character or a changeable will, but a fixed and consistent holy purpose, which has Israel for its object and seeks the true felicity of the nation, but at the same time is absolutely sovereign over Israel, and will not give way to Israel's desires or adapt itself to Israel's convenience. No other religion can show anything parallel to this. The gods of the nations are always conceived either as arbitrary and changeful, or as themselves subordinate to blind fate, or as essentially capable of being bent into sympathy with whatever is for the time being the chief desire of their worshippers, or, in some

more speculative forms of faith, introduced when these simpler conceptions broke down, as escaping these limitations only by being raised to entire unconcern in the petty affairs of man. In Israel alone does Jehovah appear as a God near to man, and yet maintaining an absolute sovereignty of will, a consistent independence of character. And the advance of the Old Testament religion is essentially identified with an increasing clearness of perception of the things which this character of the Deity involves. The name of Jehovah becomes more and more full of meaning as faith in His sovereignty and self-consistency is put to successive tests in the constantly changing problems presented by the events of history.

Now, when we speak of Jehovah as displaying a consistent character in His sovereignty over Israel, we necessarily imply that Israel's religion is a moral religion, that Jehovah is a God of righteousness, whose dealings with His people follow an ethical standard. The ideas of right and wrong among the Hebrews are forensic ideas; that is, the Hebrew always thinks of the right and the wrong as if they were to be settled before a judge. Righteousness is to the Hebrew not so much a moral quality as a legal status. The word "righteous" (*çaddîk*) means simply "in the right," and the word "wicked" (*râshâ‘*) means "in the wrong." "I have sinned this time," says Pharaoh, "Jehovah is in the right (A.V. righteous), and I and my people are

Reprinted from W. Robertson Smith, *The Prophets of Israel* (New York: D. Appleton Co., 1882), pp. 70–75, 78–83.

in the wrong (A.V. wicked)," Exod. ix. 27. Jehovah is always in the right, for He is not only sovereign but self-consistent. He is the fountain of righteousness, for from the days of Moses He is the judge as well as the captain of His people, giving forth law and sentence from His sanctuary. In primitive society the functions of judge and lawgiver are not separated, and reverence for law has its basis in personal respect for the judge. So the just consistent will of Jehovah is the law of Israel, and it is a law which as King of Israel He Himself is continually administering.

Now, in every ancient nation, morality and law (including in this word traditional binding custom) are identical and in every nation law and custom are a part of religion, and have a sacred authority. But in no other nation does this conception attain the precision and practical force which it has in the Old Testament, because the gods themselves, the guardians of law, do not possess a sharply-defined consistency of character such as Jehovah possesses. The heathen gods are guardians of law, but they are something else at the same time; they are not wholly intent on righteousness, and righteousness is not the only path to their favour, which sometimes depends on accidental partialities, or may be conciliated by acts of worship that have nothing to do with morality. And here be it observed that the fundamental superiority of the Hebrew religion does not lie in the particular system of social morality that it enforces, but in the more absolute and self-consistent righteousness of the Divine Judge. The abstract principles of morality—that is, the acknowledged laws of social order—are pretty much the same in all parts of the world in corresponding stages of social development. Heathen nations at the same general stage of society with the Hebrews will be found to acknowledge all the duties of man to man laid down in the decalogue; and on the other hand there are many things in the social order of the Hebrews, such as polygamy, blood revenge, slavery, the treatment of enemies, which do not correspond with the highest ideal morality, but belong to an imperfect social state, or, as the gospel puts it, were tolerated for the hardness of the people's hearts. But, with all this, the religion of Jehovah put morality on a far sounder basis than any other religion did, because in it the righteousness of Jehovah as a God enforcing the known laws of morality was conceived as absolute, and as showing itself absolute, not in a future state, but upon earth. I do not, of course, mean that this high view of Jehovah's character was practically present to all His worshippers. On the contrary, a chief complaint of the prophets is that it was not so, or,

in other words, that Israel did not know Jehovah. But the higher view is never put forth by the prophets as a novelty; they regard it as the very foundation of the religion of Jehovah from the days of Moses downwards, and the people never venture to deny that they are right. In truth they could not deny it, for the history of the first creation of Israel, which was the fundamental evidence as to the true character of Jehovah's relation to His people, gave no room for such mythological conceptions as operate in the heathen religions to make a just conception of the Godhead impossible. Heathen religions can never conceive of their gods as perfectly righteous, because they have a natural as well as a moral side, a physical connection with their worshippers, physical instincts and passions, and so forth. The Old Testament brings out this point with great force of sarcasm when Elijah taunts the prophets of Baal, and suggests that their god may be asleep, or on a journey, or otherwise busied with some human avocation. In fact, all this was perfectly consistent with the nature of Baal. But the Hebrews knew Jehovah solely as the King and Judge of Israel. He was this, and this alone; and therefore there was no ground to ascribe to Him less than absolute sovereignty and absolute righteousness. If the masses lost sight of those great qualities, and assimilated His nature to that of the Canaanite deities, the prophets were justified in reminding them that Jehovah was Israel's God before they knew the Baalim, and that He had then showed Himself a God far different from these.

But religion cannot live on the mere memory of the past, and the faith of Jehovah had to assert itself as the true faith of Israel by realising a present God who still worked in the midst of the nation as He had worked of old. No nation can long cleave to a God whose presence and power are not actually with them in their daily life. If Jehovah was Israel's God, He must manifest Himself as still the King and the Judge of His people, and these names must acquire more and more full significance through the actual experience of deeds of sovereignty and righteousness. Without such deeds no memory of the days of Moses could long have saved the God of the Hebrews from sinking to the level of the gods of the nations, and we have now to see that such deeds were not wanting, and not without fruit for the progress of the Old Testament faith.

*   *   *

The prophets were never patriots of the common stamp, to whom national interests stand higher than the absolute claims of religion and morality.

Had Elijah been merely a patriot, to whom the state stood above every other consideration, he would have condoned the faults of a king who did so much for the greatness of his nation; but the things for which Elijah contended were of far more worth than the national existence of Israel, and it is a higher wisdom than that of patriotism which insists that divine truth and civil righteousness are more than all the counsels of statecraft. Judged from a mere political point of view Elijah's work had no other result than to open a way for the bloody and unscrupulous ambition of Jehu, and lay bare the frontiers of the land to the ravages of the ferocious Hazael; but with him the religion of Jehovah had already reached a point where it could no longer be judged by a merely national standard, and the truths of which he was the champion were not the less true because the issue made it plain that the cause of Jehovah could not triumph without destroying the old Hebrew state. Nay, without the destruction of the state the religion of Israel could never have given birth to a religion for all mankind, and it was precisely the incapacity of Israel to carry out the higher truths of religion in national forms which brought into clearer and clearer prominence those things in the faith of Jehovah which are independent of every national condition, and make Jehovah the God not of Israel alone but of all the earth. This, however, is to anticipate what will come out more clearly as we proceed. Let us for the present confine our attention to what Elijah himself directly saw and taught.

The ruling principle in Elijah's life was his consuming jealousy for Jehovah the God of hosts (1 Kings xix. 14); or, to put the idea in another and equally Biblical form, Jehovah was to him preeminently a jealous God who could endure no rival in His land or in the affections of His people. There was nothing novel in this idea; the novelty lay in the practical application which gave to the idea a force and depth which it had never shown before. To us it seems obvious that Ahab had broken the first commandment in giving Baal a place in his land, but to Ahab and the mass of his contemporaries the thing could hardly be so clear. There are controversies enough even among modern commentators as to the exact force of the "before me" of the first commandment; and, even if we are to suppose that practical religious questions were expressly referred to the words of this precept, it would not have been difficult to interpret them in a sense that meant only that no other god should have the pre-eminence over Israel's King. But no doubt these things were judged of less by the letter of the decalogue than by habitual feeling and usage. Hitherto all Israel's interest in Jehovah had had practical reference to His contests with the gods of hostile nations, and it was one thing to worship deities who were felt to be Jehovah's rivals and foes, and quite another thing to allow some recognition to the deity of an allied race. But Elijah saw deeper into the true character of the God of Israel. Where He was worshipped no other god could be acknowledged in any sense. This was a proposition of tremendous practical issues. It really involved the political isolation of the nation, for as things then stood it was impossible to have friendship and alliance with other peoples if their gods were proscribed in Israel's land. It is not strange that Ahab as a politician fought with all his might against such a view; for it contained more than the germ of that antagonism between Israel and all the rest of mankind which made the Jews appear to the Roman historian as the enemies of the human race, and brought upon them an unbroken succession of political misfortunes and the ultimate loss of all place among the nations. It is hard to say how far the followers of Elijah or indeed the prophet himself perceived the full consequences of the position which he took up. But the whole history of Elijah testifies to the profound impression which he made. The air of unique grandeur that surrounds the prophet of Gilead proves how high he stood above the common level of his time. It is Jehovah and Elijah not against Ahab alone, but against and above the world.

The work of Elijah, in truth, was not so much that of a great teacher as of a great hero. He did not preach any new doctrine about Jehovah, but at a critical moment he saw what loyalty to the cause of Jehovah demanded, and of that cause he became the champion, not by mere words, but by his life. The recorded words of Elijah are but few, and in many cases have probably been handed down with the freedom that ancient historians habitually use in such matters. His importance lies in his personality. He stands before us as the representative of Jehovah's personal claims on Israel. The word of Jehovah in his mouth is not a word of doctrine, but of kingly authority, and to him pre-eminently applies the saying of Hosea: "I have hewed them by the prophets; I have slain them by the word of My mouth: and My judgments were as the light that goeth forth" (Hosea vi. 5).

This view of the career of Elijah, which is that naturally derived from the Biblical narrative, is pretty much an exact inversion of the common representation of the function of the prophets. The traditional view which we have from the Rabbins makes the prophets mere interpreters of the Law, and places the originality of their work entirely in their predictions. In that case Elijah would be the least original of prophets, for he gave no

Messianic prediction. But in reality Jehovah did not first give a complete theoretical knowledge of Himself and then raise up prophets to enforce the application of the theoretical scheme in particular circumstances. That would not have required a prophet; it would have been no more than is still done by uninspired preachers. The place of the prophet is in a religious crisis where the ordinary interpretation of acknowledged principles breaks down, where it is necessary to go back, not to received doctrine, but to Jehovah Himself. The word of Jehovah through the prophet is properly a declaration of what Jehovah as the personal King of Israel commands in this particular crisis, and it

is spoken with authority, not as an inference from previous revelation, but as the direct expression of the character and will of a personal God, who has made Himself personally audible in the prophet's soul. General propositions about divine things are not the basis but the outcome of such personal knowledge of Jehovah, just as in ordinary human life a general view of a man's character must be formed by observation of his attitude and action in a variety of special circumstances. Elijah's whole career, and not his words merely, contained a revelation of Jehovah to Israel—that is, made them feel that through this man Jehovah asserted Himself as a living God in their midst.

5. *Church and Sect*

BY ERNST TROELTSCH

Sect-Type and Church-Type Contrasted

THE IMPORTANCE of this element is the fact that at this point, alongside of the Church-type produced by Christianity in its sociological process of self-development, there appears the new type of the sect.

At the outset the actual differences are quite clear. The Church is that type of organization which is overwhelmingly conservative, which to a certain extent accepts the secular order, and dominates the masses; in principle, therefore, it is universal, i.e., it desires to cover the whole life of humanity. The sects, on the other hand, are comparatively small groups; they aspire after personal inward perfection, and they aim at a direct personal fellowship between the members of each group. From the very beginning, therefore, they are forced to organize themselves in small groups, and to renounce the idea of dominating the world. Their attitude towards the world, the State, and Society may be indifferent, tolerant, or hostile, since they have no desire to control and incorporate these forms of social life; on the contrary, they tend to avoid them; their aim is usually either to tolerate their presence alongside of their own body, or even

to replace these social institutions by their own society.

Further, both types are in close connection with the actual situation and with the development of Society. The fully developed Church, however, utilizes the State and the ruling classes, and weaves these elements into her own life; she then becomes an integral part of the existing social order; from this standpoint, then, the Church both stabilizes and determines the social order; in so doing, however, she becomes dependent upon the upper classes, and upon their development. The sects, on the other hand, are connected with the lower classes, or at least with those elements in Society which are opposed to the State and to Society; they work upwards from below, and not downwards from above.

Finally, too, both types vary a good deal in their attitude towards the supernatural and transcendent element in Christianity, and also in their view of its system of asceticism. The Church relates the whole of the secular order as a means and a preparation to the supernatural aim of life, and it incorporates genuine asceticism into her structure as one element in this preparation, all under the very definite direction of the Church. The sects refer their members directly to the supernatural aim of life, and in them the individualistic, directly religious character of asceticism, as a means of union

Reprinted from Ernst Troeltsch, *The Social Teaching of the Christian Churches*, trans. Olive Wyon (New York: Macmillan Co., 1931), I, 331–43, with the permission of George Allen & Unwin, London.

with God, is developed more strongly and fully; the attitude of opposition to the world and its powers, to which the secularized Church now also belongs, tends to develop a theoretical and general asceticism. It must, however, be admitted that asceticism in the Church, and in ecclesiastical monasticism, has a different meaning from that of the renunciation of or hostility to the world which characterizes the asceticism of the sects.

The asceticism of the Church is a method of acquiring virtue, and a special high watermark of religious achievement, connected chiefly with the repression of the senses, or expressing itself in special achievements of a peculiar character; otherwise, however, it presupposes the life of the world as the general background, and the contrast of an average morality which is on relatively good terms with the world. Along these lines, therefore, ecclesiastical asceticism is connected with the asceticism of the redemption cults of late antiquity, and with the detachment required for the contemplative life; in any case, it is connected with a moral dualism.

The ascetism of the sects, on the other hand, is merely the simple principle of detachment from the world, and is expressed in the refusal to use the law, to swear in a court of justice, to own property, to exercise dominion over others, or to take part in war. The sects take the Sermon on the Mount as their ideal; they lay stress on the simple but radical opposition of the Kingdom of God to all secular interests and institutions. They practise renunciation only as a means of charity, as the basis of a thorough-going communism of love, and, since their rules are equally binding upon all, they do not encourage extravagant and heroic deeds, nor the vicarious heroism of some to make up for the worldliness and average morality of others. The ascetic ideal of the sects consists simply in opposition to the world and to its social institutions, but it is not opposition to the sense-life nor to the average life of humanity. It is therefore only related with the asceticism of monasticism in so far as the latter also creates special conditions, within which it is possible to lead a life according to the Sermon on the Mount, and in harmony with the ideal of the communism of love. In the main, however, the ascetic ideal of the sects is fundamentally different from that of monasticism, in so far as the latter implies emphasis upon the mortification of the senses, and upon works of supererogation in poverty and obedience for their own sake. In all things the ideal of the sects is essentially not one which aims at the destruction of the sense life and of natural self-feeling, but a union in love which is not affected by the social inequalities and struggles of the world.

All these differences which actually existed between the late Mediaeval Church and the sects, must have had their foundation in some way or another within the interior structure of the twofold sociological edifice. If, then, in reality both types claim, and rightly claim, a relationship with the Primitive Church, it is clear that the final cause for this dualistic development must lie within primitive Christianity itself. Once this point becomes clear, therefore, it will also shed light upon the whole problem of the sociological understanding of Christianity in general. Since it is only at this point that the difference between the two elements emerges very clearly as a permanent difference, only now have we reached the stage at which it can be discussed. It is also very important to understand this question thoroughly at this stage, since it explains the later developments of Church History, in which the sect stands out ever more clearly alongside of the Church. In the whole previous development of the Church this question was less vital, for during the early centuries the Church itself fluctuated a great deal between the sect and the Church-type; indeed, it only achieved the development of the Church-type with the development of sacerdotal and sacramental doctrine; precisely for that reason, in its process of development up to this time, the Church had only witnessed a sect development alongside of itself to a small extent, and the differences between them and the Church were still not clear. The problem first appears clearly in the opposition between the sacramental-hierarchical Church conception of Augustine and the Donatists. But with the disappearance of African Christianity this opposition also disappeared, and it only reappeared in a decisive form after the completion of the idea of the Church in the Gregorian church reform.

The word "sect," however, gives an erroneous impression. Originally the word was used in a polemical and apologetic sense, and it was used to describe groups which separated themselves from the official Church, while they retained certain fundamental elements of Christian thought; by the very fact, however, that they were outside the corporate life of the ecclesiastical tradition—a position, moreover, which was usually forced upon them—they were regarded as inferior side-issues, one-sided phenomena, exaggerations or abbreviations of ecclesiastical Christianity. That is, naturally, solely the viewpoint of the dominant churches, based on the belief that the ecclesiastical type alone has any right to exist. Ecclesiastical law within the modern State definitely denotes as "sects" those religious groups which exist along-side of the official privileged State Churches, by law established, groups which the State either does not recognize at all, or, if it does recognize them, grants them fewer rights and privileges than the official State Churches. Such a conception, how-ever, confuses the actual issue. Very often in the so-called "sects" it is precisely the essential ele-ments of the Gospel which are fully expressed; they themselves always appeal to the Gospel and to Primitive Christianity, and accuse the Church of having fallen away from its ideal; these impulses are always those which have been either suppressed or undeveloped in the official churches, of course for good and characteristic reasons, which again are not taken into account by the passionate party polemics of the sects. There can, however, be no doubt about the actual fact: the sects, with their greater independence of the world, and their con-tinual emphasis upon the original ideals of Chris-tianity, often represent in a very direct and char-acteristic way the essential fundamental ideas of Christianity; to a very great extent they are a most important factor in the study of the development of the sociological consequences of Christian thought. This statement is proved conclusively by all those who make a close study of the sect move-ments, which were especially numerous in the latter mediaeval period—movements which played their part in the general disintegration of the mediaeval social order. This comes out very clearly in the great works of Sebastian Franck, and especially of Gottfried Arnold, which were written later in defence of the sects.

The main stream of Christian development, how-ever, flows along the channel prepared by the Church-type. The reason for this is clear: the Church-type represents the longing for a universal all-embracing ideal, the desire to control great masses of men, and therefore the urge to dominate the world and civilization in general. Paulinism, in spite of its strongly individualistic and "enthusias-tic" features, had already led the way along this line: it desired to conquer the world for Christ; it came to terms with the order of the State by interpreting it as an institution ordained and per-mitted by God; it accepted the existing order with its professions and its habits and customs. The only union it desired was that which arose out of a common share in the energy of grace which the Body of Christ contained; out of this union the new life ought to spring up naturally from within through the power of the Holy Spirit, thus prepar-ing the way for the speedy coming of the Kingdom of God, as the real universal end of all things. The more that Christendom renounced the life of this

supernatural and eschatological fulfilment of its universal ideal, and tried to achieve this end by missionary effort and organization, the more was it forced to make its Divine and Christian character independent of the subjective character and service of believers; henceforth it sought to concentrate all its emphasis upon the objective possession of re-ligious truth and religious power, which were con-tained in the tradition of Christ, and in the Divine guidance of the Church which fills and penetrates the whole Body. From this objective basis subjective energies could ever flow forth afresh, exerting a renewing influence, but the objective basis did not coincide with these results. Only thus was it possible to have a popular Church at all, and it was only thus that the relative acceptance of the world, the State, of Society, and of the existing culture, which this required, did no harm to the objective founda-tion. The Divine nature of the Church was retained in its objective basis, and from this centre there welled up continually fresh streams of vital spiritual force. It was the aim of the leaders of the Church to render this basis as objective as possible, by means of tradition, priesthood, and sacrament; to secure in it, objectively, the sociological point of contact; if that were once firmly established the subjective influence of the Church was considered secure; it was only in detail that it could not be controlled. In this way the fundamental religious sense of possessing something Divinely "given" and "redeeming" was ensured, while the universalizing tendency was also made effective, since it estab-lished the Church, the organ of Divine grace, in the supreme position of power. When to that was added the Sacrament of Penance, the power of spiritual direction, the law against heretics, and the general supervision of the faith, the Church was then able to gain an inward dominion over the hearts of men.

Under these circumstances, however, the Church found it impossible to avoid making a compromise with the State, with the social order, and with econ-omic conditions, and the Thomist doctrine worked this out in a very able, comprehensive theory, which vigorously maintained the ultimate supernatural orientation of life. In all this it is claimed that the whole is derived, quite logically, from the Gospel; it is clear that this point of view became possible as soon as the Gospel was conceived as a universal way of life, offering redemption to all, whose influence radiates from the knowledge given by the Gospel, coupled with the assurance of salvation given by the Church. It was precisely the develop-ment of an objective sociological point of refer-ence, its establishment on a stable basis, and its endeavour to go forward from that point to organize the conquest of the world, which led to this development. It is, however, equally obvious that in so doing the radical individualism of the Gospel, with its urge towards the utmost personal achievement, its radical fellowship of love, uniting all in the most personal centre of life, with its heroic indifference towards the world, the State and civilization, with its mistrust of the spiritual danger of distraction and error inherent in the possession of or the desire for great possessions, has been given a secondary place, or even given up altogether; these features now appear as mere factors within the system; they are no longer ruling principles.

It was precisely this aspect of the Gospel, however, which the sects developed still farther, or, rather, it was this aspect which they were continually re-emphasizing and bringing into fresh prominence. In general, the following are their characteristic features: lay Christianity, personal achievement in ethics and in religion, the radical fellowship of love, religious equality and brotherly love, indifference towards the authority of the State and the ruling classes, dislike of technical law and of the oath, the separation of the religious life from the economic struggle by means of the ideal of poverty and frugality, or occasionally in a charity which becomes communism, the directness of the personal religious relationship, criticism of official spiritual guides and theologians, the appeal to the New Testament and to the Primitive Church. The sociological point of contact, which here forms the starting-point for the growth of the religious community, differs clearly from that upon which the Church has been formed. Whereas the Church assumes the objective concrete holiness of the sacerdotal office, of Apostolic Succession, of the *Depositum fidei* and of the sacraments, and appeals to the extension of the Incarnation which takes place permanently through the priesthood, the sect, on the other hand, appeals to the ever new common performance of the moral demands, which, at bottom, are founded only upon the Law and the Example of Christ. In this, it must be admitted that they are in direct contact with the Teaching of Jesus. Consciously or unconsciously, therefore, this implies a different attitude to the early history of Christianity, and a different conception of Christian doctrine. Scripture history and the history of the Primitive Church are permanent ideals, to be accepted in their literal sense, not the starting-point, historically limited and defined, for the development of the Church. Christ is not the God-Man, eternally at work within the Church, leading it into all Truth, but He is the direct Head of the Church, binding the Church to Himself through His Law in the Scriptures. On the one hand, there is develop-

ment and compromise, on the other literal obedience and radicalism.

It is this point of view, however, which makes the sects incapable of forming large mass organizations, and limits their development to small groups, united on a basis of personal intimacy; it is also responsible for the necessity for a constant renewal of the ideal, their lack of continuity, their pronounced individualism, and their affinity with all the oppressed and idealistic groups within the lower classes. These also are the groups in which an ardent desire for the improvement of their lot goes hand in hand with a complete ignorance of the complicated condition of life, in which therefore an idealistic orthodoxy finds no difficulty in expecting to see the world transformed by the purely moral principles of love. In this way the sects gained on the side of intensity in Christian life, but they lost in the spirit of universalism, since they felt obliged to consider the Church as degenerate, and they did not believe that the world could be conquered by human power and effort; that is why they were always forced to adopt eschatological views. On the side of personal Christian piety they score, and they are in closer touch with the radical individualism of the Gospel, but they lose spontaneity and the spirit of grateful surrender to the Divine revelation of grace; they look upon the New Testament as the Law of God, and, in their active realization of personal fellowship in love, they tend towards legalism and an emphasis upon "good works." They gain in specific Christian piety, but they lose spiritual breadth and the power to be receptive, and they thus revise the whole vast process of assimilation which the Church had completed, and which she was able to complete because she had placed personal Christian piety upon an objective basis. The Church emphasizes the idea of Grace and makes it objective; the sect emphasizes and realizes the idea of subjective holiness. In the Scriptures the Church adheres to the source of redemption, whereas the sect adheres to the Law of God and of Christ.

Although this description of the sect-type represents in the main its prevailing sociological characteristics, the distinctive significance of the sect-type contrasted with the Church-type still has a good concrete basis. (There is no need to consider here the particular groups which were founded purely upon dogma; they were indeed rare, and the pantheistic philosophical sects of the Middle Ages merge almost imperceptibly into sects of the practical religious kind. In reality, the sects are essentially different from the Church and the churches. The word "sect," however, does not mean that these movements are undeveloped expressions of the Church-type; it stands for an independent sociological type of Christian thought.

The essence of the Church is its objective institutional character. The individual is born into it, and through infant baptism he comes under its miraculous influence. The priesthood and the hierarchy, which hold the keys to the tradition of the Church, to sacramental grace and ecclesiastical jurisdiction, represent the objective treasury of grace, even when the individual priest may happen to be unworthy; this Divine treasure only needs to be set always upon the lampstand and made effective through the sacraments, and it will inevitably do its work by virtue of the miraculous power which the Church contains. The Church means the eternal existence of the God-Man; it is the extension of the Incarnation, the objective organization of miraculous power, from which, by means of the Divine Providential government of the world, subjective results will appear quite naturally. From this point of view compromise with the world, and the connection with the preparatory stages and dispositions which it contained, was possible; for in spite of all individual inadequacy the institution remains holy and Divine, and it contains the promise of its capacity to overcome the world by means of the miraculous power which dwells within it. Universalism, however, also only becomes possible on the basis of this compromise; it means an actual domination of the institution as such, and a believing confidence in its invincible power of inward influence. Personal effort and service, however fully they may be emphasized, even when they go to the limits of extreme legalism, are still only secondary; the main thing is the objective possession of grace and its universally recognized dominion; to everything else these words apply: *et cetera adjicientur vobis*. The one vitally important thing is that every individual should come within the range of the influence of these saving energies of grace; hence the Church is forced to dominate Society, compelling all the members of Society to come under its sphere and influence; but, on the other hand, her stability is entirely unaffected by the fact of the extent to which her influence over all individuals is actually attained. The Church is the great educator of the nations, and like all educators she knows how to allow for various degrees of capacity and maturity, and how to attain her end only by a process of adaptation and compromise.

Compared with this institutional principle of an objective organism, however, the sect is a voluntary community whose members join it of their own free will. The very life of the sect, therefore, depends on actual personal service and co-operation; as an independent member each individual has his part within the fellowship; the bond of union has not been indirectly imparted through the common possession of Divine grace, but it is directly realized in the personal relationships of life. An individual is not born into a sect; he enters it on the basis of conscious conversion; infant baptism, which, indeed, was only introduced at a later date, is almost always a stumbling-block. In the sect spiritual progress does not depend upon the objective impartation of Grace through the Sacrament, but upon individual personal effort; sooner or later, therefore, the sect always criticizes the sacramental idea. This does not mean that the spirit of fellowship is weakened by individualism; indeed, it is strengthened, since each individual proves that he is entitled to membership by the very fact of his services to the fellowship. It is, however, naturally a somewhat limited form of fellowship, and the expenditure of so much effort in the maintenance and exercise of this particular kind of fellowship produces a certain indifference towards other forms of fellowship which are based upon secular interests; on the other hand, all secular interests are drawn into the narrow framework of the sect and tested by its standards, in so far as the sect is able to assimilate these interests at all. Whatever cannot be related to the group of interests controlled by the sect, and by the Scriptural ideal, is rejected and avoided. The sect, therefore, does not educate nations in the mass, but it gathers a select group of the elect, and places it in sharp opposition to the world. In so far as the sect-type maintains Christian universalism at all, like the Gospel, the only form it knows is that of eschatology; this is the reason why it always finally revives the eschatology of the Bible. That also naturally explains the greater tendency of the sect towards "ascetic" life and thought, even though the original ideal of the New Testament had not pointed in that direction. The final activity of the group and of the individual consists precisely in the practical austerity of a purely religious attitude towards life which is not affected by cultural influences. That is, however, a different kind of asceticism, and this is the reason for that difference between it and the asceticism of the Church-type which has already been stated. It is not the heroic special achievement of a special class, restricted by its very nature to particular instances, nor the mortification of the senses in order to further the higher religious life; it is simply detachment from the world, the reduction of worldly pleasure to a minimum, and the highest possible development of fellowship in love; all this is interpreted in the old Scriptural sense. Since the sect-type is rooted in the teaching of Jesus, its asceticism also is that of primitive Christianity and of the Sermon on the Mount, not that of the Church and of the contemplative life; it is narrower and more scrupulous than that of Jesus, but, literally understood, it is still the continuation of the attitude of Jesus towards the world. The concentration on personal effort, and the sociological connection with a practical ideal, makes an extremely exacting claim on individual effort, and avoidance of all other forms of human association. The asceticism of the sect is not an attempt to popularize and universalize an ideal which the Church had prescribed only for special classes and in special circumstances. The Church ideal of asceticism can never be conceived as a universal ethic; it is essentially unique and heroic. The ascetic ideal of the sect, on the contrary, is, as a matter of course, an ideal which is possible to all, and appointed for all, which, according to its conception, united the fellowship instead of dividing it, and according to its content is also capable of a general realization in so far as the circle of the elect is concerned.

Thus, in reality we are faced with two different sociological types. This is true in spite of the fact (which is quite immaterial) that incidentally in actual practice they may often impinge upon one another. If objections are raised to the terms "Church" and "Sect," and if all sociological groups which are based on and inspired by monotheistic, universalized, religious motives are described (in a terminology which is in itself quite appropriate) as "Churches," we would then have to make the distinction between institutional churches and voluntary churches. It does not really matter which expression is used. The all-important point is this: that both types are a logical result of the Gospel, and only conjointly do they exhaust the whole range of its sociological influence, and thus also indirectly of its social results, which are always connected with the religious organization.

In reality, the Church does not represent a mere deterioration of the Gospel, however much that may appear to be the case when we contrast its hierarchical organization and its sacramental system with the teaching of Jesus. For wherever the Gospel is conceived as primarily a free gift, as pure grace, and wherever it is offered to us in the picture which faith creates of Christ as a Divine institution, wherever the inner freedom of the Spirit, contrasted with all human effort and organization, is felt to be the spirit of Jesus, and wherever His splendid indifference towards secular matters is felt, in the sense of a spiritual and inner independence, while these secular things are used outwardly, there the institution of the Church may be regarded as a natural continuation and transformation of the

Gospel. At the same time, with its unlimited universalism, it still contains the fundamental impulse of the evangelic message; the only difference is that whereas the Gospel had left all questions of possible realization to the miraculous coming of the Kingdom of God, a Church which had to work in a world which was not going to pass away had to organize and arrange matters for itself, and in so doing it was forced into a position of compromise.

On the other hand, the essence of the sect does not consist merely in a one-sided emphasis upon certain vital elements of the Church-type, but it is itself a direct continuation of the idea of the Gospel. Only within it is there a full recognition of the value of radical individualism and of the idea of love; it is the sect alone which instinctively builds up its ideal of fellowship from this point of view, and this is the very reason why it attains such a strong subjective and inward unity, instead of merely external membership in an institution. For the same reason the sect also maintains the original radicalism of the Christian ideal and its hostility towards the world, and it retains the fundamental demand for personal service, which indeed it is also able to regard as a work of grace: in the idea of grace, however, the sect emphasizes the subjective realization and the effects of grace, and not the objective assurance of its presence. The sect does not live on the miracles of the past, nor on the miraculous nature of the institution, but on the constantly renewed miracle of the Presence of Christ, and on the subjective reality of the individual mastery of life.

The starting-point of the Church is the Apostolic Message of the Exalted Christ, and faith in Christ the Redeemer, into which the Gospel has developed; this constitutes its objective treasure which it makes still more objective in its sacramental-sacerdotal institution. To this extent the Church can trace its descent from Paulinism, which contained the germ of the sacramental idea, which, however, also contained some very unecclesiastical elements in its pneumatic enthusiasm, and in its urgent demand for the personal holiness of the "new creature."

The sect, on the contrary, starts from the teaching and the example of Jesus, from the subjective work of the apostles and the pattern of their life of poverty, and unites the religious individualism preached by the Gospel with the religious fellowship, in which the office of the ministry is not based upon ecclesiastical ordination and tradition, but upon religious service and power, and which therefore can also devolve entirely upon laymen. The Church administers the sacraments without reference to the personal worthiness of the priests; the sect distrusts the ecclesiastical sacraments, and either permits them to be administered by laymen, or makes them dependent upon the personal character of the celebrant, or even discards them altogether. The individualism of the sect urges it towards the direct intercourse of the individual with God; frequently, therefore, it replaces the ecclesiastical doctrine of the sacraments by the Primitive Christian doctrine of the Spirit and by "enthusiasm." The Church has its priests and its sacraments; it dominates the world and is therefore also dominated by the world. The sect is lay Christianity, independent of the world, and is therefore inclined towards asceticism and mysticism. Both these tendencies are based upon fundamental impulses of the Gospel. The Gospel contains the idea of an objective possession of salvation in the knowledge and revelation of God, and in developing this idea it becomes the Church. It contains, however, also the idea of an absolute personal religion and of an absolute personal fellowship, and in following out this idea it becomes a sect. The teaching of Jesus, which cherishes the expectation of the End of the Age and the Coming of the Kingdom of God, which gathers into one body all

who are resolute in their determination to confess Christ before men and to leave the world to its fate, tends to develop the sect-type. The apostolic faith which looks back to a miracle of redemption and to the Person of Jesus, and which lives in the powers of its heavenly Lord: this faith which leans upon something achieved and objective, in which it unites the faithful and allows them to rest, tends to develop the Church-type. Thus the New Testament helps to develop both the Church and the sect; it has done so from the beginning, but the Church had the start, and its great world mission. Only when the objectification of the Church had been developed to is fullest extent did the sectarian tendency assert itself and react against this excessive objectification. Further, just as the objectification of the Church was achieved in connection with the feudal society of the Early Middle Ages, the reappearance of the tendency to form sects was connected with the social transformation, and the new developments of city-civilization in the central period of the Middle Ages and in its period of decline—with the growth of individualism and the gathering of masses of people in the town themselves—and with the reflex effect of this city formation upon the rural population and the aristocracy.

6. *Trends in Western Monasticism*

BY ADOLPH VON HARNACK

IN THE TENTH CENTURY it appeared as if monasticism had well-nigh played its part in the West: it seemed—a few houses, chiefly nunneries, being disregarded—as if Western monasticism had succumbed to the danger which in the East could not possibly in this way arise—it had become worldly, and vulgarly worldly, not by a hair's breadth higher than the world at large. In the tenth century, Pope, Church and monastery alike seemed to have reached the last stage of decrepitude.

Reprinted from Adolph von Harnack, *Monasticism: Its Ideals and History & The Confessions of St. Augustine,* (London: Williams & Norgate, 1901), pp. 81–116.

I

And yet there had already begun a second movement in the Church; a second revival of monasticism. This revival started in France. The monastery of Cluny, founded so early as the tenth century, became the home of that great reform of the Church which the West experienced in the eleventh. Begun by monks, it was at first supported by pious and intelligent princes and bishops as a counterpoise to the secularised Papacy; but later the great Hildebrand took it up, and alike as Cardinal and as Pope opposed it to the princes and the secularised clergy. The West gained by it an effective reformation of the Church; a reformation, however, not of Evangelical but on Catholic lines. The aims of this new movement were in the first instance a restoration of the old discipline, of true renunciation and piety in the monasteries themselves; but later, first, a subjection of the secular clergy to the regulars, and, secondly, the dominion of the whole spirituality, as regulated by the monks, over the laity—princes and nations alike. The great reform of the monks of Cluny and of their mighty Pope presents itself first as the energetic attempt to conform the life of the whole spirituality to monastic ordinances. In this movement Western monasticism for the first time puts forth the decisive claim to pose as the only Christian life for all adult believers, and to ensure the general recognition of this claim. Monasticism in the West must inevitably come again and again into contact with the secular Church, for the reason that it can never cease itself to put forth claims on the whole of Christendom or to serve the Church. The Christian freedom at which it aims is to it, in spite of all vacillation, not only a freedom of the individual *from* the world, but the freedom of Christendom for the service of God *in* the world. We Evangelicals can even today still judge this great movement with sympathy: for in it expression is given to the consciousness that within the Church there can be only one morality and only one ideal of life, and that to this therefore all adult Christians are pledged. If monasticism is really the highest form of Christianity, it comes to this, that all adult confessors should be subjected to the monastic rule, and all Christians in their nonage—*i.e.,* in the mediæval view all the laity—should be urged at least to obedience. Such were the ideas that dominated Cluny and Cluny's great Pope. Hence the stern enforcement of the celibacy of the clergy; hence the struggle against the secularisation of the spirituality, and specially against simony; hence the monastic discipline of the priests. And what about his effort after political supremacy? Though it might from this point of view be looked on as a mere *parergon* which was to last because, and only so long as, the true conversion of the world was incomplete, yet here begin the points of difference between monasticism and the reformed secular Church. It is possible so to represent the ideas of Hildebrand and those of his more earnest friends as to make them appear to differ only by a shade. Yet this shade of difference led to policies totally opposed. From the very first voices were heard, even among the most zealous supporters of the Pope, crying that it was enough to reform manners and to cherish piety: it was not for the Church to rule in the style and with the weapons of the State. These voices

demanded a true return to apostolic life, and a renewal of the Early Church. It is incorrect to describe these efforts of the monks as if they betokened a retrogression to the standard of the Greek Church, and thus fell outside the circle of Western Catholicism. The real truth is, these monks had a positive aim—*Christian life* for the *whole* of Christendom. But since tradition offered to them a conception of a supernaturally renewed Empire, which they did not renounce the hope of realising on earth, they conceived an almost invincible mistrust of the "parergon," which the Roman Bishop held out and for which he strove. In this mistrust was included that shrinking from everything in the Church that recalled political or legal ordinances. Repugnance to public law and to the State is in the Western monasticism as characteristic as in the East the reason is plain why Greek ascetics show no such repugnance. But in the eleventh century devotion to the Church and her ruler was powerful enough to prevent an open conflict between the reformed clergy and the monks. In the Sacrament of Penance the Church possessed the strongest means of binding even the monks to herself. With conscience stained and courage broken, many bowed to the will of the great monastic Pope. And it was precisely those that had most willingly dedicated their whole life to God whom he drew out of the quiet of the monastery. He knew well that only that monk will help to subjugate the world who shuns it and strives to free himself from it. Renunciation of the world in the service of a world-ruling Church—such is the amazing problem that Gregory solved for the next century and a half. But Gregory's aims, and those of the reformed bishops, with all their political character, were spiritual also. Only as spiritual did they transform the masses, and inflame them against the worldly clergy in upper Italy, or against simoniacal princes throughout Europe. A new religious zeal stirred the nations, and specially the Romance nations, of the West. The enthusiasm of the Crusades was the direct fruit of the monastic reform of the eleventh century. That religious revival which Europe experienced is expressed most vividly in them. The dominion of the Church is to be consummated on earth. It was the ideas of the world-ruling monk of Cluny that led the van of the Crusades; and the Crusaders brought back from the Holy Land and the Holy Places a new, or at least till now rare form of Christian piety—that of absorption in the sufferings and in the Via Dolorosa of Christ. Asceticism, once negative, received a positive form and a new positive aim, that of becoming one with the Redeemer by fervent love and perfect imitation. A personal element, working from heart to heart, began to vivify the hitherto unimpassioned and aimless struggle of self-abnegation, and to awaken the sleeping subjectivity. Even to monasticism, though as a rule only in a few isolated cases, it lent an inner impulse. The great number of new Orders that were founded at this time, specially in France, bears witness to the general enthusiasm. It was then that arose the Carthusians, the Cistercians, the Præmonstratensians, the Carmelites, and many other Orders. But the constant appearance of fresh Orders only shows that monasticism, in alliance with the secular Church, was ever losing its special character. Each new Order sought to call back the monks to their old austerity and to drag them away from secularisation; but in the very act of subjecting itself to the secular Church, it was annexed and exploited by the Church. It shows the illusions in which men moved that the Orders which were founded to restore the original monasticism, by the very terms of their foundation expressly announced their subjection to the bishops, and thenceforward renounced not only the care of souls, but all special programmes within the Church and for the Church. In the twelfth century the dependence of Christendom, and thus also of monasticism, on the Church is still a very *naïve* one: the contradiction between the actual form of the world-ruling Church and the Gospel which she preaches is felt indeed but always suppressed, and criticism of the claims and of the constitution of the Church is as yet ineffective. We need only mention the name of a single man, that of Bernard of Clairvaux, in order to see as in a picture alike all the greatness which this second monastic reform of the Church introduced, and its limitations and illusions. The same monk who in the quiet of his cell speaks a new language of devotion, who dedicates his soul entirely to the Bridegroom, who urges Christendom to forsake the world, who tells the Pope that he is called to the chair of Peter not for dominion but for service: this same man was yet imbued with all the hierarchical prejudices of his time, and himself led the politics of the world-ruling Church. But it was precisely because monasticism in that age went with the Church that it was able to do so great a work for her. It roused, it is true, a reform in the Church; but this reform, in the long run, came to strengthen the political power of the Church, and so to increase her secularisation—a strange and yet easily intelligible result. The domain in which Church and cloister found constantly their common ground was the contest with all the claims of the laity, and specially of the princes, on the Church. Western monasticism took this to be a "liberation from the world," and therefore offered its services in the struggle to the Church. Only by

observing this can we understand how one and the same man in that age could be at once an upright monk and a prince of the Church, or how he could deceive himself and others, or even be uncertain, as to the final aims of this opposition to the State.

II

A new age arose, with which the old conceptions did not harmonise. The Church had attained to political world-dominion; she had either actually overcome, or was on the point of overcoming, the Empire and the old State order. The aims and results of the mighty efforts put forth by the Church in the eleventh and twelfth centuries had now been made manifest; but now a movement began among the laity and in the nations to emancipate themselves from the tutelage of the hierarchy. In social movements, in religious sectarianism, in pious unions which failed to find satisfaction in official piety, in the endeavours of nations and princes to order their own concerns independently, was heralded the approach of a new era. For a whole century the secular Church succeeded in holding back the tide; and in doing so she was aided by a fresh phenomenon in monasticism which is marked by the foundation of the mendicant Orders.

The figure of the tenderest and most loveable of all monks, the quaint saint of Assisi, stands out brilliantly in the history of the Middle Ages. Here, however, we are not asking what was his character, but what were his aims in devoting himself to the service of God and of his brethren. In the first place he desired to renew the life of the Apostles by imitating the poverty of their life and their preaching of the Gospel. This preaching was to arouse penitence in Christendom and to make Christendom effectively that which she already was through her possession of the Holy Sacraments. A society of brethren was to be formed which, like the Apostles, should possess nothing but penitence, faith, and love, and which should own no other aim than to serve others and to win souls. St. Francis never clearly defined how far this society was to extend itself. He was no politician, and never intruded on the domain of government. But what could converts, made by the preaching of the poor brethren, have become, but themselves brethren, serving itinerant preachers, in their turn? For them St. Francis himself laid down fixed and settled rules. Neither individuals nor even the society, united as it was for a truly Christ-like life, was to possess property of any kind. "Go sell all that thou hast." Life in God, suffering along with His Son, love for His creatures, human and other, service even to the sacrifice of one's own life, the riches of the soul, which possesses nothing but the Saviour—such was the Gospel of St. Francis. If any man ever realised in his life what he preached, St. Francis was that man. And—what is the characteristic mark of this Western movement—intense as this asceticism was, heartfelt as this religion was, it did not drive its disciples into solitude or the desert, but the reverse. Christendom, nay, the whole world, was to be won for this new and yet old Christianity of repentance, renunciation, and love. A Christian world—this conception, at the beginning of the thirteenth century, had a quite other content than in the sixth and eleventh; not only because the geographical horizon had extended itself for the West, but to a higher degree because the poor and the ordinary man were now to be reckoned as part of that world. Western monasticism, down to the end of the twelfth century, had been essentially an aristocratic institution; the privileges of the monasteries were in most cases conditioned by the descent of their inmates. The monastic schools were as a rule open only to the nobility. To the coarse and common people the monastery remained as inaccessible as the castle. There were no popular Orders and few popular monks. St. Francis did not break down the walls of the noble monasteries but raised alongside them huts for poor and rich. He thus restored the Gospel to the people, who had hitherto possessed only the priest and the Sacrament. But the saint of Assisi was the most submissive son of the Church and of the Pope in history. His labours were devoted to the service of the Church. Thus he was the first to give to monasticism—for a monasticism his brotherhood became, little as he meant it—special tasks for Christianity as a whole, but in the bosom of the Church: for care for the Church is care for salvation. Cluny and its monks had exclusively devoted themselves to the reform of the spiritualty. St. Francis would know no distinctions. We may say without exaggeration that he wished not to found a new order of monks but to revolutionise the world—to make the world a fair garden, colonised by men who follow Christ, who need nothing, in whose hearts is God. It was love that enlarged his horizon: his fancy neither grew rankly luxuriant, nor did it become barren through his stern asceticism: his determination to serve Church and Christianity remained to the end strong and powerful, though he was constrained with pain to see how the Church corrected and narrowed his creation. Hundreds of thousands flocked to him. But what were thousands when it was a question of millions? The emergence of the so-called Tertiary Brethren by the side of the strict monastic order is on one side, of course, an indication that this Gospel does not penetrate into human society without compromise, but on the other a shining example of the far-reaching influence of the Franciscan preaching. The Tertiaries kept up their secular callings, their marriages and their possessions; but they adapted themselves as far as possible to the monastic life, held themselves aloof from public affairs, and devoted themselves, as far as they could, to asceticism and works of piety. This institution, which formed itself without any recognised founder, is a striking proof of the universal character of the Franciscan movement. Sects had led the way; but the brotherhood remained true to the Church. Nay, the interest of the laity in the life and in the sacraments of *the Church* was awakened by them; through them the idea grew slowly effective that a layman, sincerely obedient to the Church and inwardly pious, has a right to share in the highest good which the Church can communicate. The conception of a double morality differing in value, could on this basis be transformed into another more tolerable conception of a morality differing only in kind. An *active* Christian life may be of equal value with the contemplative; the latter is only a more direct path to salvation.

A newly moulded piety, dominated by the surrender of the soul to Christ, spread forth from Assisi and made itself master of the Church. It was religious individuality and freedom that had been awakened; Christianity as the *religion* of poverty and love was to come by its own as opposed to the degeneracy in morality and politics.

The finest of mediæval hymns, the mightiest of mediæval sermons, belong to the Franciscan Order or to the nearly-related Dominicans. But to art and science also these Orders gave a new impulse. All the important schoolmen of the thirteenth century —a Thomas Aquinas, a Bonaventura, an Albertus Magnus—were mendicant monks. The noblest paintings of the old Italian school are inspired by the new spirit, the spirit of absorption in the sufferings of Christ, of a holy sorrow and a transcendental strength. A Dante, a Giotto, and again a Tauler, and a Berthold of Ratisbon—all these, in their feelings, thoughts, and creations, lived in the religious ideas of the mendicant Orders. But—what is more significant—these monks stooped to the populace and to individuals. They had an eye for their sorrows and an ear for their complaints. They lived with the people, they preached to the people in their own language, and they brought them a consolation they could understand. What the sacrament and the services had hitherto failed to give—a certainty of salvation—the mysticism of the Orders aimed at producing: but not outside of the Church means of grace. The eye must learn to see the Saviour; the soul must attain peace by sensuous perception of

His presence. But the 'theology,' which here arose, proclaimed also the religious freedom and blessedness of souls lifted above the world and conscious of their God. If by this idea it did not actually begin the Evangelical Reformation, it made the path straight for it.

By the help of the mendicant Orders, of which she availed herself to the full, the Church was able in the thirteenth century to maintain herself at the height of her dominion. She won back the hearts of the faithful; but at the same time, through the activity of the monks, she ordered and brought to perfection her hold on the goods of the world, science, art, and law. It was then that the body of canon law was completed, which regulates all the relations of life from the standpoint of the Church's world-dominion, and of an asceticism devoted to her service. This canon law is no longer recognized in civilised states, but its ideas still bear fruit. To a much higher degree are philosophy and theology, as well as social politics, still dependent on the mode of thought which in the thirteenth century, in the mendicant Orders, led to the masterly development of great scholastic systems. Through these Orders, again, the Church succeeded in overcoming the sectarian movements that had taken hold of the laity. It was the mendicants who with furious zeal conquered the heretical, but, alas! also free-spirited and evangelical, movements of the thirteenth century. Thus here also they made common cause with the world-ruling Church, the Church of politics and of the sword: nay, they became precisely the most favoured clerical servants of the Popes, who endowed them with the highest privileges, and permitted them everywhere to interfere with the regular administration of the Church and with the cure of souls. In the mendicant Orders, the Roman Pope found a tool wherewith to weld the national churches of the country more closely to his see, and to crush the independence of the Bishops. Thus they had the largest share in the Romanising of the Catholic Church in Europe, and also influenced in many ways the older foundations which sprang out of the Benedictine Rule. But they became secularised as speedily as any other Order before them. The connection with the secular Church proved once again fatal to monasticism. That connection had been from the first extraordinarily close—Francis had been compelled to yield as if to a decree of Fate—and the ruin was all the more rapid. What was meant to raise them above the world—their poverty—proved but an occasion of specific secularisation to those who no longer took poverty seriously. They saw themselves led to speculate on the coarseness, the superstition, and the sluggishness of the masses;

and they became, like the masses, coarse, superstitious, and sluggish.

Yet the high ideal set before Christendom by St. Francis could not disappear without shaking to their foundations the Church and the Order founded by him. When one party in the Order urged a modification of the strictness of the regulations imposing poverty, another, faithful to the Master, arose to defend them. When the Popes took up the cause of the former, the zealous party turned their criticism upon the Papacy and the secular Church. Complaints of the corruption of the Church had long been uttered by individual monks, but they had always died away again. The strife of the Church against the states and their claims had hitherto constantly enticed monasticism to recognise in the programme of the Church the beginning of the realisation of its own. But now arose the idea which had always lain dormant in monasticism and had again and again been suppressed. The tie with Church and papacy was sundered: ancient apocalyptic ideas emerged; the Papal Church appeared as Babylon, as the Kingdom of Antichrist, who has falsified the true Christianity of renunciation and poverty. The whole history of the Church appeared suddenly in the light of a monstrous apostasy; and the Pope no longer as the successor of Peter but as the heir of Constantine. It was hopeless to attempt to move the Church to turn back. Nothing but a new revelation of the Spirit could avail to save her, and men accordingly looked for a future final Gospel of Christian perfection. With all the means in her power the Church suppressed this dangerous uprising. She pronounced the teachings of the Franciscans on the poverty of Christ and the Apostles to be heresy, and she demanded submission. A bitter struggle was the result. Christendom witnessed the new spectacle of the secular Church in arms against a doctrine of renunciation that had become aggressive. With the courage of men who had sacrificed all, the Spirituals preached to Pope and Bishop their doctrine of poverty, and sealed their testimony at the stake. At the end of the fourteenth century the secular Church came forth, victorious and unchanged, from her strife with poverty. Thus once again, at the end of the Middle Ages, the sleeping but ever reviving antagonism between the aims of the Church and the aims of monasticism had come to light in a terrible crisis. But monasticism was vanquished. The foundation of the mendicant Orders was its last great attempt in the Middle Ages to assert itself and its ideal in the Church as a whole while maintaining its connection with the history and constitution of that Church. But the development of the Franciscan Order was twofold. The one party, from the very first, resigned its original ideal, subjected itself completely to the Church, and became speedily secularised; the other sought to maintain its ideal, made that ideal stricter, set it up even against the Church, and exhausted itself, until it succumbed, in fantastic pursuits. This development will to some appear an unredeemed tragedy; but it will perhaps not seem an unmixed evil to those who recognise that individuals of the Order which strove to emancipate itself from the Church, sought deliverance at the hands of the State, and, in opposition to the claims of the Church, which they no longer or only partially admitted, began to defend the independence and ordinances of the State. It was the Franciscans who, in the fourteenth century, discovered a scientific foundation for the Hohenstaufen theory of politics. Western monasticism, as we learn from this astonishing volte-face, is unable to exist for any length of time without a close alliance with the forces of society. When the Church is not available it seeks even the State. Yet this movement was but transitory. In the fifteenth century a deathly stillness reigns in the Order, which is now in entire subjection to the Church; attempts at reform were feeble, and resulted in no fresh life. In the age of the Renascence monasticism—with a few honourable exceptions—seemed to have condemned itself to inaction and uselessness. Yet the new culture, whose supporters, it is true, frequently spent their shafts of ridicule on the ignorant, slavish, and hypocritical monks, was not utterly hostile to ascetic ideals. Rather did the vision reappear of a wise and pious man, absorbed in the enjoyment of a quiet contemplation of heaven, without neglecting the world, in peaceful detachment from the noises of the day; who needs nothing because in spirit he possesses all. The attempt was even made to revive this ideal in the traditional forms of cloister-life; nor did it everywhere fail. But it was only given to isolated individuals to unite the rule of the convent with the study of Cicero or Plato, and to be sufficient for both. The scholar who was at the same time a man of the world, and who at his desk became enthusiastic for Stoical indifference or for Franciscan independence of externals, was anything but a monk; and the Church, in spite of all classical and edifying dissertations, remained as she was. The poor, as in the days before St. Francis had shown them the way, sought to secure their salvation in pious and enthusiastic unions of every kind, which were, it is true, of occasional service to the Church, but nevertheless were to her a constant danger.

III

What was left? What new form of monasticism remained possible after all these attempts? None—

or rather, perhaps, one, which in truth is no longer one, and yet became the last and in a true sense the authentic word of Western monasticism. It remained possible to begin with reversing the relations between asceticism and ecclesiastical service; to keep at once in the eye, as the purposed and highest aim, the ideal which had always floated before the gaze of Western monasticism, but had never been taken up save with hesitation. It remained possible to find, instead of an ascetic union with ecclesiastical tendencies, a society that should pursue no other aim than to strengthen and extend the dominion of the Church. The glory of recognising this possibility, and of understanding the lessons of history, belongs to the Spaniard, Ignatius Loyola. His creation, the Society of Jesus, which he set up against the Reformation, is no monasticism in the oldest sense of the word, nay, it appears as a downright protest against the monasticism of a St. Anthony or a St. Francis. True, the Society is equipped with all the rules of the older Orders; but its first principle is that which they had uncertainly viewed as a side-purpose, or which they had unwillingly allowed to be imposed upon them by circumstances. To the Jesuits all asceticism, all renunciation, is but a means to an end. Emancipation from the world extends only so far as such emancipation helps towards domination over the world—a domination exercised *politically* by means of the Church. The professed aim of the Order is the dominion of the Church over the world. Religious enthusiasm, culture and barbarism, splendour and squalor, diplomacy and simplicity, all alike are employed by this Order to attain the one purpose to which it has dedicated itself. In it, Western Catholicism, so to speak, neutralised monasticism, and gave it a turn by which it made the aims of monasticism its own. And yet the Society was not the work of a cunning, calculating intelligence merely. As it arose, it was the product of a high enthusiasm, but of an enthusiasm from within that Church which had already rejected any sort of evangelical reform, and which had resolved to maintain itself for ever in the form given to it, in the course of a long history, by worldly wisdom and policy.

On the other side, the Jesuit Order is the last and authentic word of Western monasticism. Its rise, no less than its nature, lies entirely on the lines which we have traced from Benedict to Bernard, and from Bernard to the mendicants. The Society of Jesus has solved the problems to which they were unequal, and has attained the objects for which they strove. It produced a new form of piety, and gave to that piety a special expression and a methodical form, and in this respect it made a successful appeal to the whole of Catholic Christianity. It has known how to interest the laity in the Church, and has opened to them in its mysticism that which hitherto had been denied to them. It has penetrated the life of the Church in all its domains, and brought the faithful to the feet of the Pope. But not only has the Order constantly pursued objects of its own in the service of the Church; it has also known how to maintain itself at all times in a certain independence of her. While it has not seldom corrected the policy of the Popes in accordance with the programme of the Papacy, it to-day rules the Church by its peculiar Christianity, its fantastic and sensuous mode of worship, and its political morality. It never became a mere tool in the hand of the Church, and it never, like the earlier Orders, sank into mere insignificance. It never transformed itself into a department of the Church; rather did the Church fall under the domination of the Jesuits. In the Society of Jesus, in fact, monasticism has actually won the victory over the secular Church of the West.

Monasticism, then, prevailed; but what form of monasticism? Not that of St. Francis; but one which had previously made the programme of the Church its own, and thus emptied and renounced its own essence. In it asceticism and renunciation have become mere political forms and instruments; diplomacy and a sensuous mysticism have taken the place of a simple piety and moral discipline. This monasticism can no longer materially maintain its genuineness except by its opposition to states and their culture, and by making small account of the individual. Under the supremacy of the Jesuits the Church has become specifically and definitively secularized; she opposes to the world, to history, and to civilisation, *her own* worldly possessions, which are the legacy of the Middle Ages. Her consciousness of "other-worldliness" she strengthens to-day mainly by her opposition to the culture of the Renascence and of the Reformation; but she draws her strength from the failings and defects of that culture and from the mistakes of its protectors. If we regard the negative attitude of the Church to the modern State as the expression of her "other-worldly" sentiment, then monasticism has indeed conquered in her; but if we see, in the manner in which she to-day maintains this attitude, an essential secularisation, then it is precisely the Jesuitic monasticism which is to be made answerable therefor. As historical factors, the other Orders are to-day nearly without importance. The Society of Jesus influenced the older and the younger almost without exception. Whether they returned, like the Trappists, to an Oriental silence, or whether some of them, in the style of the old Egyptian monks, have

come to view even ecclesiastical learning with mistrust, and to declaim against it; whether they continue their existence divided between the world and asceticism, though it be to the attainment of something notable in social usefulness or in the salvation of individuals—in any case they have ceased to be an historical factor. Their place has been taken by the Jesuits, and by the "Congregations," those elastic and pliant creations in which the spirit of the Jesuitic Order has found a point of contact with the needs and institutions of modern society. The Congregations, directed in the spirit of the Society of Jesus, and the innumerable "free" Catholic associations which work in the same spirit, and which are at need secular or spiritual, free or "tied"; these are the real Catholic monasticism of modern times.

In the Church of the West, which set before herself moral and political aims, monasticism in its original form, and the ideals of that monasticism, have had in the long run but sporadic effects. So far as it decided to bear its part in the secular mission of the Church, it had to transform itself into that society which betokens its freedom from the world by a worldly and political reaction against culture and history, and which thus brought to completion the secularisation of the Church. Monasticism in the East maintained its independence at the cost of stagnation; monasticism in the West remained effectual at the cost of losing its essential principle. In the East it was shattered, because it thought it could despise moral effort for the benefit of the world; and in the West it succumbed, because it subjected itself to a Church that devoted religion and morality to the service of politics. But there, as here, it was the Church herself that engendered monasticism and appointed its ideals; and thus in East and West alike, though after long vacillation and severe struggles, monasticism came finally to be the protector of ecclesiastical tradition and the guardian of ecclesiastical empiricism; and so its original aims were transformed into their opposites.

Even to-day, to certain hearts weary of the world, monasticism may indeed bring peace; but the view of history passes beyond monasticism to the message of Luther, that man begins the imitation of Christ when, in his calling and in his sphere of life, he aids in the work of God's kingdom by faith and ministering love. Even this ideal is not simply identical with the content of the Gospel message; but it points out the lines along which the Christian must move, and secures him against insincerity and self-deception. Like all ideals, it was set up when men were striving to escape from an intolerable position; and, like them, it was soon falsified and tainted by the world. But if it aims to be no more than the confession that no man attains to the perfection of life which is set before us in the Gospel; and if it expresses the fact that in any condition the Christian may rely on the divine help and grace; then it will be the strength of the weak, and in the strife of creeds it may yet be a signal of peace.

7. *Religion and Society*

BY EMILE DURKHEIM

THE THEORISTS who have undertaken to explain religion in rational terms have generally seen in it before all else a system of ideas, corresponding to some determined object. This object has been conceived in a multitude of ways: nature, the infinite, the unknowable, the ideal, etc.; but these differences matter but little. In any case, it was the conceptions and beliefs which were considered as the essential elements of religion. As for the rites, from this point of view they appear to be only an external translation, contingent and material, of these internal states which alone pass as having any intrinsic value. This conception is so commonly held that generally the disputes of which religion is the theme turn about the question whether it can conciliate itself with science or not, that is to say, whether or not there is a place beside our scientific knowledge for another form of thought which would be specifically religious.

But the believers, the men who lead the religious life and have a direct sensation of what it really is, object to this way of regarding it, saying that it does not correspond to their daily experience. In fact, they feel that the real function of religion is not to make us think, to enrich our knowledge, nor to add to the conceptions which we owe to science others of another origin and another character, but rather, it is to make us act, to aid us to live. The believer who has communicated with his god is not merely a man who sees new truths of which the unbeliever is ignorant; he is a man who is *stronger*. He feels within him more force, either to endure the trials of existence, or to conquer them. It is as though he were raised above the miseries of the world, because he is raised above his condition as a mere man; he believes that he is saved from evil, under whatever form he may conceive this evil. The first article in every creed is the belief in salvation by faith. But it is hard to see how a mere idea could have this efficacy. An idea is in reality only a part of ourselves; then how could it confer upon us powers superior to those which we have of our own nature? Howsoever rich it might be in affective virtues, it could add nothing to our natural vitality; for it could only release the motive powers which are within us, neither creating them nor increasing them. From the mere fact that we consider an object worthy of being loved and sought after, it does not follow that we feel ourselves stronger afterwards; it is also necessary that this object set free energies superior to these which we ordinarily have at our command and also that we have some means of making these enter into us and unite themselves to our interior lives. Now for that, it is not enough that we think of them; it is also indispensable that we place ourselves within their sphere of action, and that we set ourselves where we may best feel their influence; in a word, it is necessary that we act, and that we repeat the acts thus necessary every time we feel the need of renewing their effects. From this point of view, it is readily seen how that group of regularly repeated acts which form the cult get their importance. In fact, whoever has really practised a religion knows very well that it is the cult which gives rise to these impressions of joy, of interior peace, of serenity, of enthusiasm which are, for the believer, an experimental proof of his beliefs. The cult is not simply a system of signs by which the faith is outwardly translated; it is a collection of the means by which this is created and recreated periodically. Whether it consists in material acts or mental operations, it is always this which is efficacious.

Our entire study rests upon this postulate that the unanimous sentiment of the believers of all times cannot be purely illusory. Together with a recent

Reprinted from Emile Durkheim, *Elementary Forms of the Religious Life,* trans. Joseph W. Swain (Glencoe, Ill.: The Free Press, 1954), from "Conclusion," sec. 1, pp. 416–27, with the permission of The Free Press.

apologist of the faith[1] we admit that these religious beliefs rest upon a specific experience whose demonstrative value is, in one sense, not one bit inferior to that of scientific experiments, though different from them. We, too, think that "a tree is known by its fruits,"[2] and that fertility is the best proof of what the roots are worth. But from the fact that a "religious experience," if we choose to call it this, does exist and that it has a certain foundation— and, by the way, is there any experience which has none?—it does not follow that the reality which is its foundation conforms objectively to the idea which believers have of it. The very fact that the fashion in which it has been conceived has varied infinitely in different times is enough to prove that none of these conceptions express it adequately. If a scientist states it as an axiom that the sensations of heat and light which we feel correspond to some objective cause, he does not conclude that this is what it appears to the senses to be. Likewise, even if the impressions which the faithful feel are not imaginary, still they are in no way privileged intuitions; there is no reason for believing that they inform us better upon the nature of their object than do ordinary sensations upon the nature of bodies and their properties. In order to discover what this object consists of, we must submit them to an examination and elaboration analogous to that which has substituted for the sensuous idea of the world another which is scientific and conceptual.

This is precisely what we have tried to do, and we have seen that this reality, which mythologies have represented under so many different forms, but which is the universal and eternal objective cause of these sensations *sui generis* out of which religious experience is made, is society. We have shown what moral forces it develops and how it awakens this sentiment of a refuge, of a shield and of a guardian support which attaches the believer to his cult. It is that which raises him outside himself; it is even that which made him. For that which makes a man is the totality of the intellectual property which constitutes civilization, and civilization is the work of society. Thus is explained the preponderating rôle of the cult in all religions, whichever they may be. This is because society cannot make its influence felt unless it is in action, and it is not in action unless the individuals who compose it are assembled together and act in common. It is by common action that it takes consciousness of itself and realizes its position; it is before all else an active co-operation. The collective ideas and sentiments are even possible only owing to these exterior movements which symbolize them, as we have established. Then it is action which dominates the religious life, because of the mere fact that it is society which is its source.

In addition to all the reasons which have been given to justify this conception, a final one may be added here, which is the result of our whole work. As we have progressed, we have established the fact that the fundamental categories of thought, and consequently of science, are of religious origin. We have seen that the same is true for magic and consequently for the different processes which have issued from it. On the other hand, it has long been known that up until a relatively advanced moment of evolution, moral and legal rules have been indistinguishable from ritual prescriptions. In summing up, then, it may be said that nearly all the great social institutions have been born in religion.[3] Now in order that these principal aspects of the collective life may have commenced by being only varied aspects of the religious life, it is obviously necessary that the religious life be the eminent form and, as it were, the concentrated expression of the whole collective life. If religion has given birth to all that is essential in society, it is because the idea of society is the soul of religion.

Religious forces are therefore human forces, moral forces. It is true that since collective sentiments can become conscious of themselves only by fixing themselves upon external objects, they have not been able to take form without adopting some of their characteristics from other things: they have thus acquired a sort of physical nature; in this way they have come to mix themselves with the life of the material world, and then have considered themselves capable of explaining what passes there. But when they are considered only from this point of view and in this rôle, only their most superficial aspect is seen. In reality, the essential elements of which these collective sentiments are made have been borrowed by the understanding. It ordinarily seems that they should have a human character only when they are conceived under human forms;[4] but even the most impersonal and the most anonymous are nothing else than objectified sentiments.

---

1. William James, *The Varieties of Religious Experience.*
2. Quoted by James, *op. cit.,* p. 20.

3. Only one form of social activity has not yet been expressly attached to religion: that is economic activity. Sometimes processes that are derived from magic have, by that fact alone, an origin that is indirectly religious. Also, economic value is a sort of power or efficacy, and we know the religious origins of the idea of power. Also richness can confer *mana;* therefore it has it. Hence it is seen that the ideas of economic value and of religious value are not without connection. But the question of the nature of these connections has not yet been studied.
4. It is for this reason that Frazer and even Preuss set impersonal religious forces outside of, or at least on the threshold of religion, to attach them to magic.

It is only by regarding religion from this angle that it is possible to see its real significance. If we stick closely to appearances, rites often give the effect of purely manual operations: they are anointings, washings, meals. To consecrate something, it is put in contact with a source of religious energy, just as to-day a body is put in contact with a source of heat or electricity to warm or electrize it; the two processes employed are not essentially different. Thus understood, religious technique seems to be a sort of mystic mechanics. But these material manœuvres are only the external envelope under which the mental operations are hidden. Finally, there is no question of exercising a physical constraint upon blind and, incidentally, imaginary forces, but rather of reaching individual consciousnesses, of giving them a direction and of disciplining them. It is sometimes said that inferior religions are materialistic. Such an expression is inexact. All religions, even the crudest, are in a sense spiritualistic: for the powers they put in play are before all spiritual, and also their principal object is to act upon the moral life. Thus it is seen that whatever has been done in the name of religion cannot have been done in vain: for it is necessarily the society that did it, and it is humanity that has reaped the fruits.

But, it is said, what society is it that has thus made the basis of religion? Is it the real society, such as it is and acts before our very eyes, with the legal and moral organization which it has laboriously fashioned during the course of history? This is full of defects and imperfections. In it, evil goes beside the good, injustice often reigns supreme, and the truth is often obscured by error. How could anything so crudely organized inspire the sentiments of love, the ardent enthusiasm and the spirit of abnegation which all religions claim of their followers? These perfect beings which are gods could not have taken their traits from so mediocre, and sometimes even so base a reality.

But, on the other hand, does someone think of a perfect society, where justice and truth would be sovereign, and from which evil in all its forms would be banished for ever? No one would deny that this is in close relations with the religious sentiment; for, they would say, it is towards the realization of this that all religions strive. But that society is not an empirical fact, definite and observable; it is a fancy, a dream with which men have lightened their sufferings, but in which they have never really lived. It is merely an idea which comes to express our more or less obscure aspirations towards the good, the beautiful and the ideal. Now these aspirations have their roots in us; they come from the very depths of our being; then there is nothing outside of us which can account for them. Moreover, they are already religious in themselves; thus it would seem that the ideal society presupposes religion, far from being able to explain it.[5]

But, in the first place, things are arbitrarily simplified when religion is seen only on its idealistic side: in its way, it is realistic. There is no physical or moral ugliness, there are no vices or evils which do not have a special divinity. There are gods of theft and trickery, of lust and war, or sickness and of death. Christianity itself, howsoever high the idea which it has made of the divinity may be, has been obliged to give the spirit of evil a place in its mythology. Satan is an essential piece of the Christian system; even if he is an impure being, he is not a profane one. The anti-god is a god, inferior and subordinated, it is true, but nevertheless endowed with extended powers; he is even the object of rites, at least of negative ones. Thus religion, far from ignoring the real society and making abstraction of it; is in its image; it reflects all its aspects, even the most vulgar and the most repulsive. All is to be found there, and if in the majority of cases we see the good victorious over evil, life over death, the powers of light over the powers of darkness, it is because reality is not otherwise. If the relation between these two contrary forces were reversed, life would be impossible; but, as a matter of fact, it maintains itself and even tends to develop.

But if, in the midst of these mythologies and theologies we see reality clearly appearing, it is none the less true that it is found there only in an enlarged, transformed and idealized form. In this respect, the most primitive religions do not differ from the most recent and the most refined. For example, we have seen how the Arunta place at the beginning of time a mythical society whose organization exactly reproduces that which still exists to-day; it includes the same clans and phratries, it is under the same matrimonial rules and it practices the same rites. But the personages who compose it are ideal beings, gifted with powers and virtues to which common mortals cannot pretend. Their nature is not only higher, but it is different, since it is at once animal and human. The evil powers there undergo a similar metamorphosis: evil itself is, as it were, made sublime and idealized. The question now raises itself of whence this idealization comes.

Some reply that men have a natural faculty for idealizing, that is to say, of substituting for the real world another different one, to which they transport themselves by thought. But that is merely changing the terms of the problem; it is not resolving it or even advancing it. This systematic idealization is an essential characteristic of religions. Explaining them

---

5. Boutroux, *Science et Religion*, pp. 206–207.

by an innate power of idealization is simply replacing one word by another which is the equivalent of the first; it is as if they said that men have made religions because they have a religious nature. Animals know only one world, the one which they perceive by experience, internal as well as external. Men alone have the faculty of conceiving the ideal, of adding something to the real. Now where does this singular privilege come from? Before making it an initial fact or a mysterious virtue which escapes science, we must be sure that it does not depend upon empirically determinable conditions.

The explanation of religion which we have proposed has precisely this advantage, that it gives an answer to this question. For our definition of the sacred is that it is something added to and above the real: now the ideal answers to this same definition; we cannot explain one without explaining the other. In fact, we have seen that if collective life awakens religious thought on reaching a certain degree of intensity, it is because it brings about a state of effervescence which changes the conditions of psychic activity. Vital energies are over-excited, passions more active, sensations stronger; there are even some which are produced only at this moment. A man does not recognize himself; he feels himself transformed and consequently he transforms the environment which surrounds him. In order to account for the very particular impressions which he receives, he attributes to the things with which he is in most direct contact properties which they have not, exceptional powers and virtues which the objects of every-day experience do not possess. In a word, above the real world where his profane life passes he has placed another which, in one sense, does not exist except in thought, but to which he attributes a higher sort of dignity than to the first. Thus, from a double point of view it is an ideal world.

The formation of the ideal world is therefore not an irreducible fact which escapes science; it depends upon conditions which observation can touch; it is a natural product of social life. For a society to become conscious of itself and maintain at the necessary degree of intensity the sentiments which it thus attains, it must assemble and concentrate itself. Now this concentration brings about an exaltation of the mental life which takes form in a group of ideal conceptions where is portrayed the new life thus awakened; they correspond to this new set of physical forces which is added to those which we have at our disposition for the daily tasks of existence. A society can neither create itself nor recreate itself without at the same time creating an ideal. This creation is not a sort of work of supererogation for it, by which it would complete itself, being already

formed; it is the act by which it is periodically made and remade. Therefore when some oppose the ideal society to the real society, like two antagonists which would lead us in opposite directions, they materialize and oppose abstractions. The ideal society is not outside of the real society; it is a part of it. Far from being divided between them as between two poles which mutually repel each other, we cannot hold to one without holding to the other. For a society is not made up merely of the mass of individuals who compose it, the ground which they occupy, the things which they use and the movements which they perform, but above all is the idea which it forms of itself. It is undoubtedly true that it hesitates over the manner in which it ought to conceive itself; it feels itself drawn in divergent directions. But these conflicts which break forth are not between the ideal and reality, but between two different ideals, that of yesterday and that of to-day, that which has the authority of tradition and that which has the hope of the future. There is surely a place for investigating whence these ideals evolve; but whatever solution may be given to this problem, it still remains that all passes in the world of the ideal.

Thus the collective ideal which religion expresses is far from being due to a vague innate power of the individual, but it is rather at the school of collective life that the individual has learned to idealize. It is in assimilating the ideals elaborated by society that he has become capable of conceiving the ideal. It is society which, by leading him within its sphere of action, has made him acquire the need of raising himself above the world of experience and has at the same time furnished him with the means of conceiving another. For society has constructed this new world in constructing itself, since it is society which this expresses. Thus both with the individual and in the group, the faculty of idealizing has nothing mysterious about it. It is not a sort of luxury which a man could get along without, but a condition of his very existence. He could not be a social being, that is to say, he could not be a man, if he had not acquired it. It is true that incarnating themselves in individuals, collective ideals tend to individualize themselves. Each understands them after his own fashion and marks them with his own stamp; he suppresses certain elements and adds others. Thus the personal ideal disengages itself from the social ideal in proportion as the individual personality develops itself and becomes an autonomous source of action. But if we wish to understand this aptitude, so singular in appearance, of living outside of reality, it is enough to connect it with the social conditions upon which it depends.

Therefore it is necessary to avoid seeing in this theory of religion a simple restatement of historical materialism: that would be misunderstanding our thought to an extreme degree. In showing that religion is something essentially social, we do not mean to say that it confines itself to translating into another language the material forms of society and its immediate vital necessities. It is true that we take it as evident that social life depends upon its material foundation and bears its mark, just as the mental life of an individual depends upon his nervous system and in fact his whole organism. But collective consciousness is something more than a mere epiphenomenon of its morphological basis, just as individual consciousness is something more than a simple efflorescence of the nervous system. In order that the former may appear, a synthesis *sui generis* of particular consciousnesses is required. Now this synthesis has the effect of disengaging a whole world of sentiments, ideas and images which, once born, obey laws all their own. They attract each other, repel each other, unite, divide themselves, and multiply, though these combinations are not commanded and necessitated by the condition of the underlying reality. The life thus brought into being even enjoys so great an independence that it sometimes indulges in manifestations with no purpose or utility of any sort, for the mere pleasure of affirming itself. We have shown that this is often precisely the case with ritual activity and mythological thought.

But if religion is the product of social causes, how can we explain the individual cult and the universalistic character of certain religions? If it is born *in foro externo*, how has it been able to pass into the inner conscience of the individual and penetrate there ever more and more profoundly? If it is the work of definite and individualized societies, how has it been able to detach itself from them, even to the point of being conceived as something common to all humanity?

In the course of our studies, we have met with the germs of individual religion and of religious cosmopolitanism, and we have seen how they were formed; thus we possess the more general elements of the reply which is to be given to this double question.

We have shown how the religious force which animates the clan particularizes itself, by incarnating itself in particular consciousnesses. Thus secondary sacred beings are formed; each individual has his own, made in his own image, associated to his own intimate life, bound up with his own destiny; it is the soul, the individual totem, the protecting ancestor, etc. These beings are the object of rites which the individual can celebrate by himself, outside of any group; this is the first form of the individual cult. To be sure, it is only a very rudimentary cult; but since the personality of the individual is still only slightly marked, and but

little value is attributed to it, the cult which expresses it could hardly be expected to be very highly developed as yet. But as individuals have differentiated themselves more and more and the value of an individual has increased, the corresponding cult has taken a relatively greater place in the totality of the religious life and at the same time it is more fully closed to outside influences.

Thus the existence of individual cults implies nothing which contradicts or embarrasses the sociological interpretation of religion; for the religious forces to which it addresses itself are only the individualized forms of collective forces. Therefore, even when religion seems to be entirely within the individual conscience, it is still in society that it finds the living source from which it is nourished. We are now able to appreciate the value of the radical individualism which would make religion something purely individual: it misunderstands the fundamental conditions of the religious life. If up to the present it has remained in the stage of theoretical aspirations which have never been realized, it is because it is unrealizable. A philosophy may well be elaborated in the silence of the interior imagination, but not so a faith. For before all else, a faith is warmth, life, enthusiasm, the exaltation of the whole mental life, the raising of the individual above himself. Now how could he add to the energies which he possesses without going outside himself? How could *he surpass himself merely by his own forces?* The only source of life at which we can morally reanimate ourselves is that formed by the society of our fellow beings; the only moral forces with which we can sustain and increase our own are those which we get from others. Let us even admit that there really are beings more or less analogous to those which the mythologies represent. In order that they may exercise over souls the useful direction which is their reason for existence, it is necessary that men believe in them. Now these beliefs are active only when they are partaken by many. A man cannot retain them any length of time by a purely personal effort; it is not thus that they are born or that they are acquired; it is even doubtful if they can be kept under these conditions. In fact, a man who has a veritable faith feels an invincible need of spreading it: therefore he leaves his isolation, approaches others and seeks to convince them, and it is the ardour of the convictions which he arouses that strengthens his own. It would quickly weaken if it remained alone.

It is the same with religious universalism as with this individualism. Far from being an exclusive attribute of certain very great religions, we have found it, not at the base, it is true, but at the summit of the Australian system. Bunjil, Daramulun or

Baiame are not simple tribal gods; each of them is recognized by a number of different tribes. In a sense, their cult is international. This conception is therefore very near to that found in the most recent theologies. So certain writers have felt it their duty to deny its authenticity, howsoever incontestable this may be.

And we have been able to show how this has been formed.

Neighbouring tribes of a similar civilization cannot fail to be in constant relations with each other. All sorts of circumstances give an occasion for it; besides commerce, which is still rudimentary, there are marriages; these international marriages are very common in Australia. In the course of these meetings, men naturally become conscious of the moral relationship which united them. They have the same social organization, the same division into phratries, clans and matrimonial classes; they practise the same rites of initiation, or wholly similar ones. Mutual loans and treaties result in reinforcing these spontaneous resemblances. The gods to which these manifestly identical institutions were attached could hardly have remained distinct in their minds. Everything tended to bring them together and consequently, even supposing that each tribe elaborated the notion independently, they must necessarily have tended to confound themselves with each other. Also, it is probable that it was in inter-tribal assemblies that they were first conceived. For they are

chiefly the gods of initiation, and in the initiation ceremonies, the different tribes are usually represented. So if sacred beings are formed which are connected with no geographically determined society, that is not because they have an extra-social origin. It is because there are other groups above these geographically determined ones, whose contours are less clearly marked: they have no fixed frontiers, but include all sorts of more or less neighbouring and related tribes. The particular social life thus created tends to spread itself over an area with no definite limits. Naturally the mythological personages who correspond to it have the same character; their sphere of influence is not limited; they go beyond the particular tribes and their territory. They are the great international gods.

Now there is nothing in this situation which is peculiar to Australian societies. There is no people and no state which is not a part of another society, more or less unlimited, which embraces all the people and all the States with which the first comes in contact, either directly or indirectly; there is no national life which is not dominated by a collective life of an international nature. In proportion as we advance in history, these international groups acquire a greater importance and extent. Thus we see how, in certain cases, this universalistic tendency has been able to develop itself to the point of affecting not only the higher ideas of the religious system, but even the principles upon which it rests.

PART THREE

Personality and the Social System

Introduction

BY JESSE R. PITTS

THE PRECEDING PARTS OF THIS Reader have been concerned with the internal structure of social systems. The remaining parts will concentrate upon the relationship of the social system to the other analytical systems of behavioral science: in Part Three the personality system and the organic system; in Part Four the cultural system. Finally, Part Five deals with the study of social change, which is essentially the study of the process in which the equilibrium of social systems is broken and new equilibrium regained.

In Part Three, we will consider primarily the relations between the personality and the social system, touching only secondarily on the relations between the organism and the social system. This is more the result of our comparative ignorance of the latter relations than of any theoretical position regarding their importance. The relations between organism and social structure have led to few investigations, largely because we take the organism, like the one-to-one sex ratio, to be a constant. Such matters as the effect of the lengthened life span on social structure still await systematic investigation.

We shall begin in Section A by analyzing the notion of society and the relation of individuals to social order: how is it that individuals, each unique, can harmonize their actions, often effortlessly, so as to reach their goals without disconcerting, surprising, and destroying one another? A major aspect of this problem is the existence of consensus. From the broader theoretical standpoint, consensus implies the existence of structures common to both personality and social systems: each, while distinct from the other, enters into the constitution of the other.

Section B examines the general conditions under which these common structures can be created. This involves the problem of learning. From the

sociologist's viewpoint, the discussion here indicates the manner in which the general properties of the personality system limit the kinds of consensus that are possible. The second subsection of Section B goes on to attempt a more specific description of those units of the personality that are the "motivational fuel" of social roles.

Section C, which deals with socialization, will present some analyses of the process whereby these personality units are differentiated through interaction with authoritative figures and groups. Section D will proceed to show how, on the basis of socialized motivation, tendencies for deviance originate, how these tendencies are checked, how their consequences are minimized, how finally the consensus, which is the basis of the personality-society relationship, is maintained and reinforced.

"SOCIETY IS IN THE MIND OF INDIVIDUALS"

The concept of society has a long history, in the common language, as a convenient term used in describing historical events, or in describing the pressures for conformity an individual encounters in his daily life. As a scientific concept "society" has a comparatively short existence. In the period between approximately 1890 and 1930, students of human affairs often tried to reduce society to the elements that had a longer academic tradition. Those who, like the French sociologist Worms, adopted the biologically oriented view of society generally treated values or norms as dependent variables. Those who took a philosophical approach and adopted the emanationist view tended to ignore

685

interaction in favor of the inner logic of ideological or ultimate value systems.

The authors excerpted here owe some of their greatness to their ability to break through the limits of the intellectual traditions from which they stemmed. The major intellectual problems that preoccupied them, in relating the individual to society, were the nature and origin of society's constraining power; the limits and possibilities of individual freedom in a progressively more liberal society; and the source of the individual's commitment, not only to the total society, but also to the many smaller communities within it.

Prior to 1890 those, like Karl Marx and Spencer, who had come closest to a distinct and not immediately reducible conception of society, had done so in the context of a belief that society limited the free realization of rational man. The utopian hope, for Spencer, was that society as a constraining force would wither away, leaving gentlemen of the English type free to enter into utilitarian contract; for Marx, it was a garden of plenty, in which a communist man could fulfill himself without the restrictions imposed by the division of labor. The history of societies, marked by inevitable oppression and injustice, would be replaced eventually by the history of individuals. The sociology of Auguste Comte is certainly not free of this Messianism.

A common characteristic of Durkheim, Weber, Freud, G. H. Mead, W. I. Thomas is that they have abandoned the utopian wish.[1] They see society irrevocably as both limiting and enriching for the individual personality. In fact, Durkheim sees society as indispensable for restraining the desires of man, which otherwise would expand limitlessly, condemning him to limitless frustration. Reason is a characteristic not of individuals but of social order; it balances obligations and gratifications and keeps them within possible bounds, thus permitting a harmonious development of the individual. The individual is essentially a physical organism, whose "spirituality" and rationality derive from his participation in the social system. Durkheim retains Spencer's concept of society as an organic whole that differentiates through the division of labor, but does not agree that this organic whole depends for its continued existence upon certain transient fears or scarcities.[2] Society is a reality *sui generis,* independent of the members that constitute it. If society has insufficient control over the individual, the result is *anomie,* which is felt as psychic pain.

What is the source of society's constraining force? Durkheim answers: the sharing by individuals of a common set of representations, which prescribe and proscribe certain types of behavior, and which, because they are shared, create solidarity among those who share them—create, that is, a desire to be mutually helpful and to avoid conflict.[3] The sharing of these ideas is not explicable in terms of their utility to the individual organism; nor can it be explained as being the result of a social contract *à la* Rousseau. The individual is not free to refuse the constraint of these representations, because they arouse in him the nonrational feeling of "moral respect."

What, then, is the source of moral respect? Durkheim's explanation seems somehow to involve a concept of mass: (a) the constraining power of a representation seems directly proportional to the number of people who share it—a positivistic explanation that still does not explain how or why the sharing began; and (b) what involves two or more individuals has greater survival value than what involves only one. Social utilitarianism has replaced individual utilitarianism.

With all its insufficiencies, Durkheim's approach to the relations between the individual and society remains very rich in theoretical potential. Society is essentially a set of ideas shared by individuals. Social facts are *things,* but things that exist only in the minds of individuals. Society, like religion, is abstract, normative, and emotional. As an object of investigation it is influenced by physical facts, size of collectivity, existential values, complexity of the division of labor, and the characteristics of individual psychology, but it is not reducible to any one of these factors. The maintenance of consensus and the maintenance of order are the organizing principles of Durkheim's society. He saw the development of new representations, of new social forms, as the result of a unilinear evolutionary force, with the maximum welfare of the society playing the role that adaptation had played in Darwinian evolution. Hence the specific value content of the collective representations is, for Durkheim, somewhat secondary. Each society will have the collective representations and the values that it needs in order to operate in its milieu. Society has an inherent authority.

For Max Weber, on the other hand, it is the reverse: society exists where there is an authority

1. Vilfredo Pareto should certainly be added to this list, although we have not had the space to reprint an excerpt of his work in this first section of Part Three.
2. Cf. Durkheim, *Division of Labor,* Chapter VII.

3. See "Organic Solidarity and Contract," Part Two, Section B, II, Selection 6, in this Reader. Durkheim also calls our attention to a fact that is often overlooked in the evaluation of the functions of an institution: the institution serves as a symbol of consensus. Technical improvements may impair this function if they change the *emblème* valence.

that, in a sense, precedes it. And this authority is attached to ideas that fulfill the individual's needs for ultimate meaning.[4] In return for this fulfillment the individual grants legitimate authority to a leader or to a ruling apparatus. What forms a corporate group or a society? Weber answers: the presence of individuals around a leader. Durkheim avoids the problem of political authority; for Weber it is crucial. According to Weber, a society is an organization of men who *share* a similar granting of legitimate authority to a leader. "Leader" and "organization" are terms used in referring to the fact that a society is a means for implementing the values that determine its pattern of legitimacy. This implementation is determined both by the content of the values, the kind of answers they provide to the problems of ultimate meaning—the existence of evil, the meaning of life and death—and the conditions of action given by the material and non-material environments. The most important aspect of the nonmaterial environment is the psychology of individuals. Weber does not describe this psychology directly: only very rarely is he concerned with total systems, either social or psychological. Rather he describes four types of action of which individuals are capable. (1) "Substantive rationality" refers to the inner logic of value commitments that ignore questions of comparative costs. This contrasts with (2) "formal rationality," in which the choice of values is determined by their comparative costs. Two somewhat residual categories of action are: (3) "affectual action," which is the capacity for random emotional reaction; and (4) "traditional action," which is an equivalent of the inertia principle or of habit.

These explain the different types of legitimate authority and social organization. Substantive rationality and perhaps affectual action are behind the gift of the individual to the charismatic leader. The interplay between substantive rationality and formal rationality largely dictates the forms under which charisma will be routinized.[5] Because of substantive rationality the commitment of the individual to certain religious values blocks other value commitments that are meaningfully incompatible with them. On the other hand, the individual's experience in certain economic and political roles influences the terms in which he poses to himself the questions of ultimate meaning: hence the differ-

ential "vulnerability" of various individuals to religious systems. Formal rationality feeds back upon substantive rationality: it implements, it countors, it influences, the choice of its initial direction.[6]

According to Durkheim, the great contribution of society to the individual is order and control—a sort of French reasonableness that guarantees the individual his only chance of *bonheur;* society, according to Weber, offers the individual the "enchantment" of final answers to the insoluble problems of his life, and the occasions to implement, in cooperation with others, the values implied in these final answers.

For Weber, then, the source of social order is in the individual's need to give himself to something beyond himself. Durkheim agrees and attempts to give a mechanistic explanation for this need, which he describes as the attitude of moral respect: the exalting nature of ideas shared by all the members of a group. This is not very satisfactory. Weber takes this need as a datum and gives it what many will feel is an unduly romantic formulation. It remained for Freud to make here a decisive contribution to social science.

For Freud, the attitude of moral respect is the result of the differentiation of the *superego* in the personality of the child, in response to the exigencies of the group in which he finds himself, that is, the family. He points to the long dependency of the child upon his parents; to his competition with the father for possession of the mother; and to his resolution of the conflict by internalizing the father figure, thus forming the superego. The characteristics of this superego are essentially the denial of pleasure (utility) and unquestioning obedience to the commands of the *internalized* figure, which is omnipotent and omniscient. Thus is explained the nonrational aspects of the attitude of moral respect. The superego, once established, can vary only in content, not in structure—it is immune to dilution by the temptations of expediency. Major collectivities, like Church, State, or Army, can replace the parental figures that the growing adolescent finds wanting in omnipotence and omniscience. Hence the origin of the Weberian pattern of legitimacy is the father image. In relating the personality to the outside world two principles are operative: one is the pleasure principle embodied in the id; the other is the superego's prohibition on certain behavior. Between the id and the superego, the ego follows the reality principle, which Weber would call formal rationality, consisting primarily of adaptation to *social* situations.

---

4. This is the trend of thought in Weber's *Religionssozi-ologie*. This summary of Weber's thought without doubt does some injustice to its nuances and complexities, well illustrated in the excerpts reprinted in Parts One and Two.

5. Cf. Part One, Section C, Selection 6; Part Two, Section D, II, Selection 2: and Part Five, Section B, Selection

6. This shows that Weber did not, as is often thought, propound the sole causality of religious values. Cf. Part Four, Section B, II, Selection 9.

Freud's second contribution to the problem of social order was his interpretation of the force that permits individuals to form solidary collectivities [7] capable of resiliency. The internalization of the same object—Durkheim would say, the sharing of an identical representation—by group members leads to their identification with one another, with consequent positive feelings and cooperation. The "object" in most cases is, of course, the leader, whom Durkheim would see as the symbol of the collectivity. This problem—of how order is achieved without immediate reference to consensus on the sacred—is one that Durkheim had approached at one time through the concept of "organic solidarity." In the *Division of Labor,* Durkheim had fallen back for explanation upon mutual dependency, expediency, and habit. Freud gives a nonrational explanation: the love that group members have for one another.

Another aspect of Freud's analysis locates a source of social order in the theory of *lost objects.* The ego, according to Freud, is a precipitate of objects to which an immediate gratifying relationship—an object cathexis—has been lost.[8] Through an effort to maintain the old relationship in fantasy, Alter's role becomes a part of Ego's personality. Thus the lost object is reinstated within the ego, which becomes *like* the object. The relationship can then be continued on a narcissistic level, and the internalized object becomes the guide to new cathexes. However, incompatible internalizations will result in conflict within the personality system; social disorder leads to personality disorder. The theory of lost objects shows how the individual comes to want what the society needs, not only in terms of ultimate values, but in terms of operating procedures, that is, in terms of doing what the loved one is doing. This becomes much clearer if we follow the lead of G. H. Mead in stressing the fact that the object internalized is not a concrete person, but a *role relationship* between the ego and the person (alter). The process of generalization is Mead's equivalent of Freud's process of internalization through object loss. It transforms the specific relationship with Alter into a capacity for relating in a patterned way with others. Thus, the unconditional and limitless character of the gratifications secured by the child from his first cathexis are soon transformed, through a process in which language plays a vital part, into an internalized set of rules. Hence what the personality internalizes is an object system, a *role-expectation for the self*

and for Alter. This role-expectation is the basic unit of the social system. Two or more complementary role-expectations make up a *role-system,* the smallest type of social system studied by sociology.

We now have a more developed version of the relation between individual and society. The facet of the personality that deals with the outside world is derived from the role structure of society: wanting something, or, in Freudian terms, cathecting an object, is above all wanting to play a role. But each internalized role-expectation includes an idiosyncratic personality component, involving the sediment of past internalizations and an output from the organism, that provides the energy for social action. In this way, personality in its biographical sense enters, through the self component of the role-expectation, into the constitution of the social system. The social system constantly responds to the needs of the individual, even as it molds those needs to insure some reliability and order. The *definition of the situation,* a concept offered by W. I. Thomas, was most convenient for handling this flexibility and ambiguity in the relation of man to society.

Since then, the relevant action systems have been more strictly defined. The concept of the individual has been differentiated into the concepts of organism and personality, while society has been differentiated into the cultural and social systems. Instead of the biological model of subject (man) adjusting to an object (nature), sociological theorists today accept, at least implicitly, the concept of *interpenetration.* By interpenetration we mean that two or more different systems of analysis —each with its own principle of organization— are all part of the same concrete data at the same time. This interaction involves both personality and social systems; not only must each be analyzed separately but the relationship between them must be sorted out in order to explain any concrete event. Another aspect of interpenetration is the fact that a unit of the social system—the role-expectation— is a component of the personality system. What are some of the implications of the concept?

First, the concept of interpenetration casts a new light on the problem or order. In one sense, the forces making for integrated action on the part of "individuals" who are members of the same society are stronger than the nineteenth-century thinkers had believed possible, in view of the spread of industrialization. For the goals of the personality are, above all, to act out valued roles within collectivities. Hence, the major problem of order is not the degree to which operating motivational components independently conform to society's

7. *Group Psychology and the Analysis of the Ego* (New York: Liveright, 1922).
8. Cf. the excerpt from *The Ego and the Id,* Part Three, Section A, Selection 4.

rules, but the ways in which role systems within society intermesh; the problem is one of structural analysis. This does not exhaust the problem, since the concept of interpenetration also underlines the subjective component in the internalized role-expectation. Thus, no two role-expectations can ever be quite the same. The solidarity of the corporate group (in Freud's terms, the love that members have for one another) is the force that makes for the mutual adjustment of discrepant role-expectations. This could be called "the libidinal component of order."

This force is all the more necessary if, following Freud, we consider cathexes to be functions of internalized role-expectations: these internalizations are necessarily made in terms of the past. According to the theory of "lost objects," the relationships that are internalized are those that have been interrupted; and these interrupted relationships become the source of future cathexes and role behavior. In one sense, then, internalized role-systems are always oriented to a world that is no longer there. In terms of the demands of the present, they are "regressive." They can account for the continuity of social structure—the tendency to preserve the past and re-create it in the present (Weber's traditional action)—but they cannot account for change toward higher levels of value implementation, nor even for adjustive change.[9] The latter can be explained in terms of the libidinal component of order described above. The Freudian superego, on the other hand, seemed largely confined to a negative, censorship, function.

A force for change that is not "structurally frozen" is *culture,* which has its own set of relationships with the personality. Even though Freud provides the best explanations of how the attitude of moral respect arises, he does not explain how the objects that replace the parental figures in the superego are chosen. Culture must provide the Weberian pattern of legitimacy, and we still lack a theory explaining the way the child develops, through social participation, the capacity for cultural participation.

On the other hand, the theory of the internalization of lost objects does explain the fact that personalities cannot internalize any and every role-system. The choice of object for cathexis, necessary for an eventual internalization, is limited by past internalizations, which themselves are part of the individual biography. Furthermore, the organic system intervenes by affording differential capacities to different personalities within a given collectivity.

To understand social order, we must conclude that personalities will share the internalizations both of the broad collectivities like sex ("we men") or nation ("we Americans") mediated by the parents, and of a culture that has its own value emphasis and strain toward self-consistency (substantive rationality). Different roles will link personalities of varying capacity to the same lost objects, in the process of institutionalization. Internalization, however, is an aspect of the broader concept of learning, which we shall examine in the next section.

An important consequence of the concept of interpenetration is that it defines at once the possibilities and the limits of an analysis of the relationship between personality and social system. Since society is *in the minds of individuals,* it is *meaning* that acts upon personality rather than an objectively defined set of social conditions. One can presume the likelihood of a certain event having a certain meaning; one cannot guarantee it. Constantly we are tempted to ascribe middle-class meanings to events occurring in a lower-class or upper-class context, not forgetting, of course, the differences in meaning created by the existence of different national references for the observer and the observed; these are inherent risks of social science research.

Some of the challenging problems in relation to social order and consensus are those created by panic and mob actions. In certain forms of panic the individual is temporarily "desocialized": the stimulus is suddenly threatening, and there is no social reference for coping with it. It is as if society had deserted the individual in his hour of greatest need. Hence he deserts society: the regression of the personality system is so deep that meaningful social interaction becomes impossible. The individual either goes into a state of passive shock or escapes into headlong flight. Combat has given many such examples, where the soldier will flee on half-torn limbs, to be stopped only by death or exhaustion, unaware of the damage that this heedless flight was doing to his own organism, if not to his platoon. On the other hand, most cases of so-called panic are only the development of a withdrawal consensus in a situation that has become ambiguous. Flight has become an act of conformity to the peer group rather than the convergent actions of frightened men. The same consensus, reversing direction, can lead the same men to extraordinary feats of heroism, for men are usually more afraid to live alone than to die together.

---

9. Freud has mentioned several times the concept of the ego-ideal, a sort of structure halfway between the ego and the superego that would have a positive, change-oriented force. Nevertheless, the concept is not extensively developed in his writings.

THE ELEMENTS OF LEARNED
MOTIVATION

This section will consider how the structural aspects of the personality have consequences for the structure of the social system. The first part will attempt to outline some of the motivational units that must somehow be integrated into role behavior.

The Nature of Learning

One might question the rationale behind the order of this presentation—should not learning follow an outline of the basic properties of the personality system rather than vice versa? As a matter of fact, the scientific study of the personality seems to have received a decisive impetus from learning studies, which provided the first effective models for "before and after" observations of an objective nature.

In the period covered by this Reader, social science was struggling to differentiate itself from ideology. Those who regarded divine intervention in man's affairs as an overriding explanatory factor tended to emphasize the importance of human consciousness as a "free" agent irreducible to physico-chemical causality. Final causes found a new support in the study of instincts as perfectly adapted behavior, requiring no experience. From the atheistic side came the radical positivists, such as LeDantec,[10] who saw in consciousness an epiphenomenon, having no relevance to the effective causality of behavior. Superposed on this quarrel was the heredity-environment controversy, the conservatives holding for the importance of heredity—a new source of legitimacy for the bourgeois dynasties that aspire to replace the "degenerate" aristocracies—and the liberals claiming that environment is the crucial factor in determining behavior.

Psychologists who wanted their discipline to become a cumulative science believed they had to do the following: isolate themselves from the metaphysical problems of consciousness; give up introspective data, which were hopelessly heterogeneous and as such unfit for quantitative treatment; and reduce the scope of their concern to problems easily set in operational terms. Animal learning seemed to provide this opportunity. It stressed plasticity and determinism, where instinctual theories had stressed miraculous perfection and immutability. In the best Darwinian tradition it pointed to the animal nature of man and to the existence of laws governing not only the anatomy and physiology

but also the behavior of all animal species. It avoided the problem of subjective meaning, since there was no language with which the animal could convey the existence of thought in his brain. Experiments on animals did not raise serious ethical problems that would interfere with the application of measuring devices to the operation, and to the control of the pre- and postexperimental life of the subject.

Within this narrowed frame of reference we find two main schools of learning theory, the school of Pavlov and the American school, which derives its experimental orientation from Thorndike and its philosophy from Watson. The Pavlovian school solves the problem of subjectivism by calling its members physiologists rather than psychologists. They are interested in the activity of the brain as a source of conditioned reflexes, whereby the organism furthers its adaptation by responding to *signals* rather than by responding only to unconditioned stimuli, such as food in the mouth or a shock to the paw. In the heredity-environment controversy, the Pavlovian school tends to support the environmentalist position: the associations that originate conditioned reflexes are given either by nature or by the experimenter. The organism, including its unconditioned reflexes, is essentially passive.

Americans, however, could not bring themselves to conceive of the human organism as lacking any autonomy. Thorndike introduced the concept of satisfaction which is an up-to-date version of utilitarianism: random responses to the environment (stimulus) become selected by the organism on the basis of the fact that some responses will result in satisfaction for the organism, while other responses result in dissatisfaction.

In the learning theory of Hull the concept of satisfaction became that of *drive reduction*. The needs of the organism determined "primary drives," which were at the origin of reward. "Secondary drives," less directly related to metabolic needs, were grafted upon primary drives through a process of association. The subjectivity of satisfaction has been replaced by the objectivity of drive reduction. On the other hand the concept of *cue* (Pavlov's signal) becomes a means for reintroducing into the model those influencers of action that are not immediately explainable in terms of metabolic needs.

The Hullian approach has been very popular in American psychology, partly because it did represent a higher level of conceptual differentiation, and also because it has permitted many experiments susceptible of mathematical analysis, with small animals as subjects. Although dogs, pigeons, cats, or mice are very frequently the subjects, man is the real focus of these animal experiments, under

10. French biologist and philosopher (1869–1917).

the assumption that the result can be directly extrapolated to him. This extrapolation, in turn, implied two major theoretical positions. The structure of the experimental situation raises no problems; the definition of the learning problem set for the rat, and the interpretation of his responses, are projections of meaning by the experimenter, as if he were in the rat's position. Thrown out the front door, meaning and purpose tend to come back through the window. The other theoretical position is that the object of these experiments is essentially the *physiology* of learning. The proponents of this position have been moving in the direction of psychophysiology.

Certain social scientists (for example, John Dollard, Neal E. Miller, Leonard W. Doob, George Murdock, John Whiting, Robert Sears) have used modified Hullian models in analyzing the processes of socialization, imitation, kinship terminology, and the diffusion of incest taboos, as well as various phenomena of deviance. Using Hull's differentiation of the behaving individual into *drive* and *response,* and of the environment into *cue* and *reward,* they were able to "relativize" the response of the personality in terms of the environmental cues and rewards present at the time of observation. Under different settings the same drive could be satisfied by a different set of responses. Thus they promoted more understanding of the *interactional* aspect of human behavior, even if this interaction was sometimes considered in the framework of a semi-Darwinian model of individual *versus* nature-society. Hullian learning theory was an important force in getting the behavioral sciences out of the heredity-environment controversy.

The counterpart of this relativism is the assumption that the personality—which is not clearly differentiated from the organism—has great plasticity: all that is needed in order to stamp habits into or out of the organism is either regularity of, or lack of, reward, respectively. These writers who did recognize the regularities of reward as a property of the social system sometimes forgot that the personality also has structural requirements as a system. Their analysis was often equivalent to saying that a society that gives great rewards to the winners of foot races will have good runners. As the notion of personality system became clearer, often under the impact of Freudian psychoanalysis, the application of learning theory models became less tautological: certain patterns, once learned, could favor or hinder the learning of other patterns. From more or less systematic descriptions we move closer to testable theoretical propositions.

A difficulty, however, was encountered by the users of Hullian learning theory: as they came to give structure to the personality and to identify certain mechanisms, such as frustration-aggression, they tended to ignore or to abandon their earlier perceptions of the environment as structured. Again, they saw little problem as to what should be defined as frustration or aggression. The result has been a search for behavioral universals unaffected by differences created by the integration of these traits into different social systems and subsequent changes in their meaning for the personality.[11] The associationist tradition of classical learning theory, when transposed to the level of culture, results in trait atomism. It is here that the Gestalt theories of learning bring their contribution.

The *Gestalt* school, represented in our selections by Köhler, has stressed what the behaviorists tried to abandon: the autonomous activity of the mind, whether in animals or in men. The behaviorists have thought in terms of relatively discrete stimulus-response connections; the Gestaltists have thought in terms of perceptual systems, in which the meaning of any given stimulus depends upon the field in which it is perceived. *Insight* was a reorganization of the perceptual field that would give meaning to objects, leading to the most direct solution to a problem. Insight can be regarded as a transposition of the "principle of least effort"[12] to problem solving. The field is reorganized so as to permit goal attainment with the minimum of motion.

Some Gestaltists thought insight resulted from the inner harmony of the environment, which forces itself upon the mind. This explained the confluence of individual insights to one model. Again, there was no concept of interpenetration.

Others saw in insight an independent creation of the mind in terms of its idiosyncratic needs: the perceiver gives structure to the environment. It is one of the rationales behind the development of the projective tests, which have turned out to be a major tool in determining the need structure of the individual personality.

The Gestalt approach, tending to a nominalism of meaningful situations, has produced some arresting descriptions of creative thinking, but few theorems that have broad applicability.[13] It is in the tradition of German intuitionism and emanationism.

---

11. Durkheim had already warned about this pitfall in his *Elementary Forms,* pp. 94–95.

12. The same idea appears in Weber, who described it as "formal rationality," and in Freud, who mentions it as the "economic" principle of the ego.

13. With the exception of Kurt Lewin's Field Theory, which stems from the Gestalt theory and has been a seminal contribution to social science, especially in the study of small groups.

Various Syntheses and Additional Developments

Several psychologists have tried to combine the cognitive approach of the Gestalt school with the objectivity and measurements of the behaviorists. Tolman used the concept of the "cognitive map" as an intervening variable between drives, cues, and the final overt behavior. The cognitive map is not directly connected with a specific goal object, but is a general adaptive facility, susceptible of modification for future performance.

Progress in learning theory seemed to have been promoted by a clearer definition of system reference and an abandonment of reductionism. Tolman, for instance, was not prevented by his concept of the cognitive map from stressing the importance of purely organic factors in learning. Others tried to combine Hullian learning theory and Freudian psychoanalysis—which can be considered one variant of the Gestalt approach—in order to show the facilities and hindrances to adult learning that are created by child learning. Psychoanalytical theory forced the notion of personality structure upon an approach that had taken for granted the infinite plasticity of a relatively undifferentiated personality-organism entity.

Adorno and others [14] have given an elaborate version of the cognitive map in the concept of the "authoritarian personality," which has special capacities for the learning of antidemocratic ideology. Regardless of the eventual worth of the concept, it was one of the major efforts to relate systematically the personality system to the cultural system without reductionism. Furthermore, the efforts of Tolman, of the neo-Hullians, and of the "authoritarian personality" group did help to bring back to the study of human learning a psychology surer of its scientific standing.

Indeed, until recently learning theory was able to give the social scientist little help—in analyzing the interchanges between the personality or the organism and the social system—beyond the concepts of reward, repetition (Thorndike's law of use), insight, and cognitive map. Reward and repetition were most useful in explaining the acquisition of instrumental skills, while insight and the cognitive map helped to explain the learning of general meanings.[15]

The sociologist would like to know how to determine when deprivation increases the drive power of a learned response and when, on the contrary, it tends to extinguish it. Here we have the contradictory findings of D. M. Levy, who shows pups, deprived of sucking, fixating a strong sucking need, and the experiments of R. R. Sears and G. M. Wise on small children, which supports the more classic reinforcement theory: children weaned early do not suck their fingers.[16]

Recent research on the problem of the strengthening or weakening of drives under deprivation has been done under the leadership of Hebb.[17] Here, some of the Pavlovian learning experiments, with their attempt to control the dog so that he would be sure to react to the laboratory stimulus only, have been extended to the attempt to deprive a human subject of all stimulus. The apparent success of Soviet "brain washing" techniques may have led to the conception of these experiments. The results of experiments in sensory deprivation seem to imply the need for a certain rate of sensory stimulation in order to maintain adequate reality testing. Below this rate the boundaries of the ego may weaken with the consequent development of hallucination. The narrowing of the perceptual field created by deprivation may result in regression; in this case the one stimulus made active assumes enormous reward power, and, in the hands of a skillful manipulator, this stimulus can lead to extensive learning. Whether this learning is sign-learning or essentially instrumental (expedient) is another question.[18] Sleep deprivation experiments tend to suggest that rather than the dream defending sleep—as Freud has said—it may be sleep that defends the dream. The latter may have more importance to the equilibrium of the personality than sleep may have for the equilibrium of the organism. Both sensory and sleep deprivation experiments may lead to a better understanding of the

14. T. W. Adorno, Else Frenkel-Brunswick, D. J. Levinson, and R. N. Sanford, *The Authoritarian Personality* (New York: Harper, 1950).

15. O. H. Mower, "A Disorder of Conditioning or Problem Solving," *Annals of The New York Academy of Sciences,* LVI (1953), 273–288.

16. D. M. Levy, "Experiments on the Sucking Reflex and Social Behavior of Dogs," *American Journal of Orthopsychiatry,* IV (1934), 203–224; R. R. Sears and G. M. Wise, "Relations of Cup Feeding in Infancy to Thumb Sucking and Oral Drive," *American Journal of Orthopsychiatry,* XX (1950), 123–128. See James Olds, *The Growth and Structure of Motives* (Glencoe: The Free Press, 1956), pp. 70–71, for an interesting attempt to synthesize these contradictory results.

17. D. O. Hebb, "Drives and the CNS," *Psychological Review,* LXII (1955), 243–254; W. H. Bexton, W. Heron, and T. H. Scott, "Effects of Decreased Variation in the Sensory Environment," *Canadian Journal of Psychology,* VIII (1954), 70–76; W. Heron, B. K. Dohne, and T. H. Scott, "Visual Disturbances after Prolonged Perceptual Isolation," *Canadian Journal of Psychology,* X (1956), 13–18.

18. Cf. E. H. Shein, "The Chinese Indoctrination Program for Prisoners of War: a Study of Attempted Brainwashing," *Psychiatry,* XIX (1956), 149–172.

impact upon the personality of such social situations as isolation, whether geographical or induced by guilt or rejection; isolation promoted by social planning (in a doctor's waiting room for instance), by the foreigner role, by long periods of passive but attentive waiting in some industrial or military situations. And thus learning theory leads to the objective analysis of general personality-dynamics.

Another discovery in learning theory that has important implications to the social scientist is James Olds' discovery of the pleasure center.[19] The existence of a pleasure center in the brain challenges the Hullian concept that learning reinforcement is a direct function of drive reduction. Pleasure, instead of being merely a signal or epiphenomenon, becomes a structural mechanism of the personality, perhaps its first organizing principle. It is probably the presence and easy stimulation of this non-metabolic erotic factor in the human personality that makes man capable of such a wide range of symbolic learning: pleasure is probably the major factor behind stimulus generalization.

This hypothesis could have some bearing on early socialization theory. One of the aspects of early socialization is that the baby's metabolic needs are rarely allowed to develop very strong drive force. The more diffuse sensory-motor needs, not having the competition of the metabolic needs, may on the contrary develop a reward primacy that promotes the initial mother-child role system: the baby learns to do the things that insure the greatest sensory-motor stimulation. It is also possible that sensory-motor stimulation allows for greater differentiation: there are more shades of plus and minus, while metabolic needs are more an all or none affair.[20] Thus *pattern* transcends stimulus.

The pleasure center probably also plays a crucial role in establishing internalized object-systems as sources of narcissistic rewards and tension management. Thus, the discovery of the pleasure center supports Freud's theory that the id follows the pleasure principle quite independently of the organism's requirements for survival.[21] Only the pleasure investment in the mother-child pattern can override the homeostatic pressures of *early* motiva-

tional systems. Freud emphasizes the attachment of libido (cathexes) to social objects, the transformation of the cathexes into personality structure, and the capacity of libido to detach itself from objects that are no longer consistent with the structure. In this way, he accounts, much better than "secondary conditioning" can, for the progressive differentiation and greater complexity of motivational structure within the personality. Only by neglecting structure and its resistance to change could learning theory have been led to use mere contiguity and amount of reinforcement as the primary mechanisms of personality development.

The Freudian Approach

Psychoanalysis is perhaps the most comprehensive theory of *human* learning that we now possess. Early psychoanalysis stressed the reorganization of the cognitive map through the development of insight, and also showed how past learning could preclude the formation of insight. In its later developments, the theory stressed the necessity, for the development of insight in problem-solving, of abreacting motivational energy that had been fixated upon imperfectly internalized and badly integrated objects—for example, parents toward whom there was much aggression or unrequited love. Freud's learning theory is most relevant when we analyze the problems of socialization. But even for adult learning, Freudian theory offers important guide lines, especially when this learning involves a reorganization of the personality structure—such as occurs in psychotherapy, in assuming an occupation, in coming to terms with old age. In these learning situations certain identifications[22] (role systems), in which participation had heretofore been legitimate, must be given up and transformed into internalizations, so as to free libido for a new cathexis. This requires a shift of libido from the obsolete role systems to an *intermediary and superior figure* who stands for the broader social values. This is possible because, besides making greater superego demands, the new identification (transference) offers much unconditional support. It is tolerant of one's failures, yet denies reciprocity for attempts to re-create the obsolete relationship; it gives differential rewards for adequate performance, and esteem for one's commitment to a higher plateau of value

19. Cf. James Olds, "Self Stimulation of the Brain," *Science* (1958) 1–27:315. Technically speaking, there are apparently several pleasure centers. For our purposes, however, the distinction is not necessary.

20. This hypothesis might also be used to explain some of the findings of marasmus in institutionalized babies. Cf. Rene Spitz, "Hospitalism," in *The Psychoanalytical Study of the Child* (New York: International Universities Press, 1945–46), Vols. I and II.

21. The latter are mediated to the personality by the ego and its "reality principle."

22. Cf. the discussion in Section A, Selection 4. It seems preferable, in order to avoid confusion, to reserve the word "cathexis" for "wanting to have," "identification" for "wanting to be with," and "internalization" for "wanting to be like." The common usage tends to give to "identification" the meaning of "wanting to be like."

achievement.[23] The superior figure involved in the relationship may be a person, a group, and may rarely intervene directly in the learning process.

Freud has also brought out that among the reactions to a learning situation, even strongly cathected, will be found regression, attempts to leave the field, and aggression against the "teacher." The sociologist will find in this model many cues for analyzing the impact upon the personality of various memberships that put high learning pressures on their members, at certain phases of membership or as a continuing stress.

We have briefly reviewed four major approaches to the problem of learning: the stimulus-response approach, which strove for objectivity while treating the problem of social and personality structure as residual; the Gestalt approach, which stressed structure but confused system references and had no place for interpenetration; the Tolman approach, which combined the stimulus-response attempts at objectivity with the Gestalt stress upon meaning and purpose; and the Parsonian review of some implications of Freudian psychoanalysis.

It is a common feature of these four major approaches that the content of the personality does not enter into the description of learning problems. Though theories attempting to describe mechanisms of the personality might seem entitled to ignore content, the very concept of interpenetration implies that role-content becomes an intrinsic part of structure. Freud discusses the content of early role-participation, especially as affecting the preoedipal child; but in classical Freudian analysis, several factors militated against a more extensive use of content. One was the residual use of "racial memory traces," which obviated the need for a more refined structural analysis of the learning situation. Another was the primarily punitive concept of the superego, making any superordinate figure in the superego remain relatively external to the personality's center of action. Finally, Freud remained somewhat committed to the older concept of motivation, the instinct concept. No effective theory of the superego was possible without both a concept of role-playing and a better understanding of the social system than was available to Freud.

The introduction of role-content in the analysis of personality structure would focus upon the logico-meaningful integration of the role commitments of the personality. The problem would be to delineate the congruence of early son or daughter roles with school, peer group, and status roles on the one hand, with their future specifications and unfolding into marital, parental, occupational, community, and recreational roles on the other hand. Since we are dealing with the interpenetrations of two action systems, there can be no direct equivalence between the logic of the social system (role integration) and the logic of the personality system (role-orientation and role-expectation integration). Finding discrepancies would, however, aid in the determination of the specificities of the personality; thus we are led to the conclusion that development of personality science depends upon parallel development of social system science. Without parallel development, role requirements will continue to be described as preferences of personality types.

The nature of the learning process draws the sociologist's attention to the time dimension in social change. Social change means learning for the members of the community, and these members have differential capacity for learning. A barely explored categorization[24] of this learning differential is the concept of generation. In relation to certain social experiences, generations are not a continuum but rather a discontinuity: war, depression, defeat, are not equally shared within the same population.

We cannot leave learning theory without mentioning the relationship between organism and social structure. The logic of treating social action as the interaction among four major analytical systems—organism, personality, social structure, and culture—requires a direct interchange between organism and social structure. So far, it has been easier to regard organic "needs" as mediated to the social structure through the personality; but in certain cases, the direct relationships deserve attention. The treatment of illness provides one example of such a direct relationship. It is also very likely that the nuclear family could not have developed as a tension-management center without a general increase in people's life expectancy. Because of this increase, the nuclear family in the Western world has attained much greater reliability as a protective and nurturant center for the personalities of its members. Children are more likely to have both parents in their formative years. The social scientist who wishes to take into account the needs of the personality system for tension management, or the metabolic needs of the organism, may settle for making the nuclear family the unit

23. For a more detailed analysis of the synthesis of learning theory and of the psychoanalytical therapeutic model, see Talcott Parsons and Robert Bales, *Family, Socialization and Interaction Process* (Glencoe: The Free Press, 1955), Chap. 2.

24. Cf., however, S. N. Eisenstadt, *From Generation to Generation* (Glencoe: The Free Press, 1956).

of action, rather than using the classical "individual." Since the nuclear family is, in many civilizations, the main provider of the metabolic needs and of the needs for tension reduction, it will mediate, through its own role exigencies, the organic and personality needs that we cannot as yet evaluate meaningfully.[25]

THE ORGANIZATION OF MOTIVATION

The determination of the motivational units of the personality has been one of the most frustrating tasks encountered by social science. This is where, of course, the confusion between what belongs to the social system and what belongs to the personality system is greatest. On the basis of observable behavior it is easier to infer complementary role-expectations than to infer the needs of the personality. There can be many "reasons" for performing a role; the role may remain the same and yet the motivational forces that activate it may change. What began as a crusade ends by being a job. On the surface, at least, the same motions are performed, the same problems are solved; their meaning to the individual personality is no longer the same. The sociologist cannot ignore this fact because it bears upon the problems of deviance and social change. If, for some reason, the role requirements become ambiguous, they start to serve as a sort of projective test, and the definition of the situation by the actor becomes a measure of his personality needs. These needs may be regressive—that is, oriented to immediate gratification regardless of the general value standards; they may be, on the contrary, highly value-oriented and result in behavior that sets role expectations higher than they had been heretofore. The sociological problem becomes: when and how do roles become ambiguous, or rather, more ambiguous than usual? On the basis of past recruitment patterns, is it possible to predict the reinterpretations that will take place in the personalities of the individuals, resulting in an attempt to institutionalize new role expectations?

Another problem is the evaluation of the "demands" that a role makes on the personality and the question of whether all personalities called on to fulfill this role will have the motivational resources—the needs—that dovetail into these demands, and whether these motivational resources are likely to be available over a long period of time. Student nurses, for instance, bring to the job a level of commitment that they are unlikely to maintain once they have become married. When student nurses become registered nurses employed in an organization, they join a professional peer group where established procedures become symbols of membership and consensus as well as techniques susceptible of improvement. Their critical spirit, their eagerness for the better technique tends to decline.[26]

The above reasoning is based on the assumption of a sort of hydraulic model of the personality: a personality is capable of just so much cathexis. If peer-group roles increase their claims—through clique warfare for instance—there is less energy available for client-oriented problem solving. We follow Freud in believing that personalities that share a common cathexis—the nursing role and the general nursing values—will identify with one another, this identification being the basis for the development of peer groups and peer-group roles.

Robert Park, in fact, takes for granted this tendency of the personality even when there is a great difference in the level of problem solving, as in the master and slave relationship. Thus, "the intimate association of master and slave may be said steadily to have corrupted the institution of slavery and in so doing hastened it on its course to its predestined extinction."[27] Caste etiquette, by creating distance, prevented this intimacy from developing to the point where control of the slave for economic purposes would have escaped the master completely.

It is interesting to note that the descriptions of "human nature" that the sociologist has been able to use most fruitfully are often those that are the most literary. Literary descriptions have the advantages of being shrewd, imprecise, and global. Scientific descriptions are narrow, precise, and often irrelevant to the problems of the sociologist. Psychoanalytic descriptions combine the best and the worst of these characteristics. The social scientist can usually find a table of needs that will fit the needs of his model. It is precisely this lack of resistance of the personality material that preoccupies the reader. The American behaviorist used questionnaires and tests to locate specific personality attributes. The more sophisticated

25. Cf. Talcott Parsons, "Social Structure and the Development of Personality," *Psychiatry*, XXI (1958), 321–40.

26. At least it has to be divided between multiple role contexts. The opportunity of the student nurse is that the sacred rituals and myths of the peer group are still largely distinct from specific nursing procedures. Some of the eagerness for change was in fact more a channel for the discharge of aggression generated by the learning pressures —"our floor supervisors are not really competent"—than an effective concern with progress.

27. R. E. Park, "The Etiquette of Race Relations in the South," in *Race and Culture* (Glencoe: The Free Press, 1950), p. 179.

studies tried to relate attitudes to one another, approaching the issue of personality structure through the study of attitude compatibilities. However, they often overlooked the fact that any behavioral sequence involves several "instincts," "sentiments," "needs," or "attributes," and in this they were often less sophisticated than McDougall and the classic introspectionists.[28] Social behavior as observed, and test behavior as measured,[29] are both forms of role behavior. And role behavior—in Tolman's term, molar behavior—goes through several phases of problem solving, spread over time.[30] Using its system-properties model, action theory describes these four role phases as follows: *adaptive, goal-consummatory, integrative, pattern maintenance.*

The *adaptive* phase is characterized by the attempt to secure facilities through cognition and manipulation. The "attitudes" required in this phase are affective neutrality and specificity—that is, orientation to an object is made dispassionately and exclusively on the basis of its immediate suitability or unsuitability as a facility.

In the second phase, *goal-consummation,* there is a single-minded concentration on effective securing of the goal; the functional "attitude" complex combines specificity and affectivity.

There are two other phases, usually overlooked in attitude studies: the *integrative* phase, in which commitment is made to the particular relationship in which a gratification occurred; and the *pattern-maintenance* phase, in which the enacted role is made congruent with the internalized role as object system. In the integrative phase, the most functional "attitude" complex is one of diffused affectivity, in contrast with the specific affectivity of the goal-consummation phase. Ego ascribes, to a significant Alter or Alters, those qualities which imply a role *complementarity* for the future. The relationship with Alter becomes the promise of goal gratification. This is the process of identification ("wanting to be with," as distinguished from "wanting to be like") discussed briefly in the preceding section.[31]

Finally, in the pattern-maintenance phase, the congruence of the acted-out role-system with the internalized object system[32] requires an attitude complex that combines an affective neutrality with the type of generalization found in diffuseness—since here we are dealing with an evaluative judgment about whether the cathected role-system fits with one's internalized values.

Any *enacted* role can be seen as a series of behavioral systems, each triggering off the other until the goal of the role has been secured. Each of these behavioral systems will go through the four phases, and each of these phases will call for its successful accomplishment mainly (though not solely) on *one* of the attitude complexes described above. Each behavioral system will vary as to the type of system problem—adaptive, goal consummatory, integrative, pattern maintenance—that is central to it. By adding up the behavioral systems that compose a role one could draw both a problem-primacy profile and a motivational-primacy profile in terms of the differential primacy of each of the four attitude complexes.

To return to these attitude complexes: what are they, and why are there four of them? First, there are four of them because the personality is also a system and must therefore meet the four system problems. So far this is only the tautology of action theory. Two sets of pattern variables—affective neutrality-affectivity, specificity-diffuseness—give four possible combinations. A more striking statement, by Talcott Parsons,[33] is that these attitude complexes each define one of four basic need-dispositions,[34] which themselves result from the *internalization of the nuclear family.* This is a good example of the theory of interpenetration.[35]

From the *conformity* need-disposition stems the combination of affective neutrality and diffuseness needed for pattern-maintenance in role-systems. This necessary combination results from the internalization of the father-self role, where Ego acts out the father's role-expectation toward the self (Ego takes the role of the father vis à vis itself).[36]

The *nurturance* need-disposition results in the combination of affectivity and specificity most functional for goal consummation. This combination derives from the internalization of the mother-self role, where Ego acts out the mother's role-

28. T. Ribot, *Physiologie des Sentiments* (Paris: Felix Alcan, 1907).

29. This would include the projective test, which supposedly offers no interactive stimulus from the experimentor to the subject.

30. Cf. Talcott Parsons and Robert F. Bales, "The Dimensions of Action Space," in *Working Papers in the Theory of Action* (Glencoe: The Free Press, 1953), Chap. 3.

31. Cf. footnote 22, above.

32. We use this term as synonymous with "internalized role-system," for, in this context, it permits us to follow the parallelism with Freud's thought a little bit more closely.

33. Parsons and Bales, *op. cit.,* Chap. 3.

34. "Need" refers to the narcissistic aspect of this psychological "unit"; "disposition" refers to the performance component—it is the disposition to act.

35. Cf. p. 688.

36. In classical psychoanalysis this personality component would be called the superego.

expectation toward the self (Ego takes the role of the mother vis à vis itself).

The *adequacy* need-disposition results in the combination of affective neutrality and specificity necessary for solving the adaptive problems of role-systems. Here the necessary complex results from the internalization of the father-self role, where Ego acts out the role-expectation *complementary* to father's demand for specific performance. Here, Father is the cathected object of a son role orientation.[37]

The *security* need-disposition produces the combination of affectivity and diffuseness that is most functional for solving integrative problems. This combination results from the internalization of the mother-self role, where Ego acts out the role-expectation *complementary* to the mother's nurturance. This is a daughter role orientation. Its external manifestation is the giving of love.

These four basic need-dispositions thus correspond to the structure of the nuclear family comprising father, mother, son, daughter. The personality of any one member of the family will have all four need-dispositions: hence we have a new basis for bisexuality of the personality. Girls will have adequacy and conformity needs, just as boys will have nurturance and security needs. Of course, the organism intervenes, facilitating the development of those need-dispositions that are better supported by one's physical type; but in this schema, femininity or masculinity depends on role-experience as much as upon physical sexual characteristics.

The four basic need-dispositions, under the impact of pressures for participation in complex roles, are each going to differentiate into an attitude complex formed of various units, just as the various embryonic tissues differentiate in phase but independently of one another. Child, adolescent, and adult roles will utilize "units" in each of the attitude complexes, in varying combinations, and perhaps even units not belonging to the same complexity of differentiation.[38] Role participation will lead to the internalization of role systems that contain a rhythm of tension and satisfaction for the attitude complexes and their units. These role systems will appear in the personality as relatively stable role-orientations and role-expectations. In turn, each of these role orientations guides and

limits the role participation that is possible for a given individual.

Action theory attempts to use role analysis in the determination of personality units without falling into reductionism. It has offered a theory of differentiation. So far, however, the sixteen categories that result from the differentiation of the four initial need-dispositions are too many and too broad to permit easy handling by the researcher. Further, to this writer's knowledge, there have not been many attempts to spell out in role terms the differentiation of any one of the four need-dispositions beyond the oedipal state, where Parsons left them.

Before this attempt by action theory to delineate personality units, there were various approaches to personality structure that have had their moments of popularity and have left a sediment of knowledge. Somewhat parallel to the four needs of action theory are the four wishes of W. I. Thomas;[39] the instinct theory of McDougall; the frustration-aggression theory of Miller and Dollard; the libido and death wish theory of classical psychoanalysis; the oral, anal, and urethral characters described by Abraham, Jones, Fenichel; the need-press theory of H. A. Murray, which rivals action theory in complexity but has the advantage of having developed some operational criteria; and more recently the authoritarian personality (Adorno et al.), which tried to isolate a general disposition of the personality toward prejudice, rigid thought patterns, and antidemocratic ideology.

One treatment of the personality that has had great success with social scientists has been Freud's description of the qualities of cathexis known as ambivalence and fixation. Ambivalence refers to the fact that any object relationship will contain a certain component of negative affect. Parsons has made of this structural aspect of the personality a crucial element of his theory of deviance. In the phenomenon of fixation, large amounts of libido are blocked on primitive role systems, leaving insufficient motivation for higher level roles. Since high frustration or, on the contrary, excessive gratification lead to fixation signalled by anxiety reactions, there have been attempts to recognize the socialization practices that would tend to produce such fixations.[40]

Even more popular, and in fact nearly universally accepted today, are Freud's descriptions of the homeostatic mechanisms of the personality systems known as "the mechanisms of ego-

37. The "achievement motive" studied by McClelland seems a close relative of the adequacy need-disposition. Cf. David C. McClelland, John W. Atkinson, Russel A. Clark, and Edgar L. Lowell, *The Achievement Motive* (New York: Appleton-Century-Crofts, 1953).

38. The father role, for instance, will involve some units that are relatively undifferentiated, that is, the old internalized child roles.

39. Cf. Part Three, Section A, Selection 6.

40. Cf. John W. R. Whiting, and Irvin L. Child, *Child Training and Personality: A Cross-Cultural Study* (New Haven: Yale University Press, 1953), Chaps. 7–10.

defense." This popularity has not been without its pitfalls as when social scientists speak of a *group displacing* aggression, or a *group projecting* hostility upon an out-group. Unless this is a shorthand expression, there is a danger of confusing system references. Nevertheless it would be hard to understand the development of ideology in situations of role conflict if the personality of group members did not find *"rationalization"* a useful means of coping with their individual experience of stress.[41]

Classical psychoanalysis has also attributed to all the mechanisms of defense, except sublimation, a pathogenic quality. Ego-psychology rejects this view as too narrow and, with action theory, has stressed the fact that *regression* can actually serve the ego.[42] Better understanding of the personality meaning of certain role participations, as in entertainment, religious ritual, sports, has been opened up by this approach.

THE PROCESSES OF SOCIALIZATION

It is with the study of socialization that the social scientist finds his first major opportunity to relate systematically the personality system and the social system. During the period covered by this book, the major contributions were made by two students of the personality as a process of growth: Freud and Piaget. Piaget's genetic theory has concentrated on problems of cognition, while psychoanalysis has focused on problems of emotion and conation. Psychoanalysis has been more popular than genetic psychology because of its success in providing explanatory schemes for the behavior of the pre-school child, including, in fact, a richer account of childhood phantasy than was provided by the more formal genetic approach. Both theories have a concept of personality development by stages. Both bring into their model the action of social factors: Piaget, the peer group, and Freud, the nuclear family.

A popular use of Freudian socialization theory has been to show social integration through personality integration: adult society was explainable by childhood experiences—the boys were fathers to the men. Some have reinterpreted psychoanalytical concepts along the lines of classical learning theory, retaining only the mechanisms and ascribing little importance to the structure of the situation—i.e., society. For instance, attempts have been made to explain national character as a consequence of early socialization practices resulting in oral or anal fixations. This approach is based on two misconceptions: (1) that the understanding of social action could be reached by merely adding up individual reactions; and (2) that the adult's complex role-behavior could be adequately explained by pre-oedipal psychological structures. The "real" experiences of the infant—"permissive" or "harsh" weaning[43] or toilet-training, or experiences of swaddling—were considered to determine a society's political, religious or economic system, or the "paranoid" quality of a given culture.

These explanations of adult behavior by means of the pre-oedipal experiences of the child were first derived from the study of non-literate societies, whose social structure does not appear, at first glance, to be extremely complex. The temptation was very strong to find, in very early family experience, the origins of religious beliefs or of hierarchical structure; for, in such simple societies, socialization appears to be ended at puberty, and socialization in the latency period is apparently aimed at only the acquisition of technological concepts or folklore—which could be explained on a straight learning theory basis.

But, applied to the study of complex societies, the "basic personality" approach has often produced results that belong more properly to the realms of literature or of wartime propaganda than to the realm of social science.[44] This approach has led to neglecting organizational considerations in favor of a dynamic of "basic attitudes." For instance, studies of national character have obscured the fact of social class differences in implementing the common societal value system.

The concept of "national character" correctly points to the fact that differences between societal structures are likely to be reflected in differences

---

41. Nor should we forget that ideology may be an *embleme* of group membership rather than an effective commitment to implementation on the part of the members acting singly or collectively.

42. The names to be mentioned here are those of Anna Freud, *The Ego and the Mechanism of Defence* (London: Hogarth Press, 1937); H. Hartmann, "Ego Psychology and the Problem of Adaptation," in D. Rapaport, *Organization and Pathology of Thought* (New York: Columbia University Press, 1951); H. Hartmann, E. Kris, and R. Lowenstein, "Comments on the Formation of Psychic Structure," in *The Psychoanalytic Study of the Child* (New York: International Universities Press, 1946), Vol. II.

43. For some good examples of this approach, see A. Kardiner, *Psychological Frontiers of Society* (New York: Columbia University Press, 1945), and G. Gorer and John Rickman, *The People of Great Russia* (New York: Chanticleer Press, 1950).

44. For a good review of national character studies, see A. Inkeles and D. J. Levinson, "National Character: The Study of Modal Personality and Sociocultural Systems," in G. Lindzey, ed., *Handbook of Social Psychology* (Cambridge: Addison-Wesley, 1954), Vol. II.

between the distributions of personality types that "act out" each national society. "National character" implies that individuals in a given nation reach adulthood with certain capacities and incapacities for organizational behavior, and with certain general ways of defining unstructured situations where communication and order must somehow be maintained. However, it seems very unlikely that these capacities and incapacities are formed in the first six years of the individual's life, for the environment of the child during that period is everywhere the nuclear family; and if we accept psychoanalytical theory's description of early socialization, we must conclude that the structures differentiated in the pre-oedipal child's personality are universal. They involve the incest taboo, met in every society; and the basic differentiation of sex-roles into instrumental or expressive primacies, which also appear to be universal.[45] In short, the child of six is probably available for socialization in *any* culture and society. What establishes the national character is not early socialization; it is experiences in latency, puberty, and adolescence. However, psychoanalytical theory has least to say precisely when dealing with these ages. Too many national-character studies have made this gap a matter of principle, instead of recognizing it as a deficiency.

Erikson[46] is, with Harry S. Sullivan, one of the few psychoanalysts who have paid attention to the phased development of the personality beyond puberty. If we are to understand latency and post-latency socialization, we must study the structure of the institutions in which the child participates— e.g., the nuclear family, the extended family, the school, the church, peer groups, dyadic friendships, cross-sex relationships, and the broad community relationships available for participation by the future citizen.

We have stated that each of the four need disposition systems—conformity, adequacy, security, and nurturance—existed at the oedipal stage, within the child's personality. In fact, the existence of all four was essential to the child's capacity to enter into new familial and extra-familial roles.[47] Role-participation results in interaction among these four need systems, and in two additional differentiations within each of them. These two differentiations arise from the necessity to internalize two bases of object categorization—the universalism-particularism category, and the performance-quality category.

The universalism-particularism category seems to be internalized mainly in the latency stage. Piaget has described this process, particularly in connection with what action theory would describe as the conformity and adequacy need systems. Broadly, it refers to the transformation of "experience" into role-facilities with increasing self-control on the part of the individual, because he learns the classification of objects. *Time* is one concept that becomes crucial in the universalism-particularism categorization, as does the distinction between those role-systems in which Ego participates, and those which are outside his referability. Furthermore, the child is taught the hierarchy of role-participation with a strong valuation on membership in his nation and his peer group. Durkheim[48] had great insight when he perceived that the concepts "inclusion," "unit," and "interchangeable unit" related directly to the organization of roles within a given society. Time enters in in so far as universalistic categories are connected with the most future-oriented perceptions, requiring strengthening of the notion of the relevant community and moral rule.

The second major object categorization is that of quality versus performance, corresponding to the ascription-achievement polarity in social structure terms. This object categorization apparently occurs between puberty and the end of adolescence. as the individual comes to understand the legitimate limits to reciprocity. When is Ego entitled to hold Alter strictly to his end of the bargain? When may the latter's past performance be transformed into an ascription of quality to Alter?

Another dimension of this categorization is the margin of autonomy that is available to the individual in implementing values. Indeed, this categorization contains many of the elements we associate in current language with *maturity*.

Though these modes of object categorization affect all four families of need disposition, we may say that the particularism-universalism polarity more particularly affects the security and adequacy need dispositions, while the quality-performance categorization more particularly affects the conformity and nurturance need dispositions. In the first case, school, peer groups, and extended family provide the basic pressures leading to differentiation. In the second case, the differentiation is supported by cross-sex relationships, intimate friend-

---

45. See Zeldich, in Parsons and Bales, *op. cit.*
46. Eric H. Erikson, *Childhood and Society* (NewYork: W. W. Norton, 1950) Chap. 7.
47. The schools have become increasingly aware of the "emotional" balance that is necessary for the acquisition of reading skills and number manipulation.

---

48. Cf. Durkheim, "Quelques formes de classification primitive," translated and reprinted in Part Four, Section B, I, Selection 4, "Social Structure and the Structure of Thought."

ships, and the relationship to the community in occupational and proto-occupational roles.

We come now to the question that must have occurred to our readers: What about primitive societies or comparatively undifferentiated societies—do they result in undifferentiated personalities?

Most of the primitive societies that have been described in sufficient detail have a functional equivalent of our school system. When he is about six, the child is separated from his family and enters an intensive period of being trained in tribal lore and skills, paralleled by the development of strong peer groups. Often paternal or maternal uncles become the child's task-masters, leaving to the parents the roles of support and of expressive rewarding.[49]

However, in primitive societies the period of adolescence is more likely to be cut short; it frequently ends within two or three years after puberty. This raises the question of whether the quality-performance differentiation is made as completely in primitive as in literate societies. Primitive societies certainly provide opportunities for individual achievement in securing desirable brides, or in gaining prestige for skilful hunting, farming, or fighting; nevertheless, the margin is much narrower than in literate societies. Primitive societies recognize fewer performances which can be evaluated and rewarded on their merits without committing the actor to a whole nexus of relationships. This is one reason that market relationships partake more of gift exchange than of true exchange.

In literate societies, this situation may be approximated in the lower class, where schooling is frequently ended shortly after puberty [50] and the margin for personal achievement is comparatively small. The effective social system for the lower class is relatively undifferentiated. We may suggest that the failure to differentiate the performance-quality object categories is responsible for the rigidities in the thinking process described under the syndrome of the *authoritarian personality*. Hence, although under certain conditions these thought patterns will be met at any social level, they are more endemic to the lower class.[51]

The complexity of a social system, as an index of the range of roles available to the personality, cannot be analytically determined by the apparent number and complexity of visible organizations. A single organization, like the extended family, may provide several different types of role-participation for the personality. In fact, an undifferentiated social system may require more varied role-participation by the same individual than would a differentiated social system, which might keep all but a few specialists from participating actively in certain roles, because these roles, to be compatible with order, need be performed at a relatively high level of skill.

Each society is probably characterized by the centrality of different role-systems in its total institutional picture: occupational and family roles in the United States; political and occupational roles in the Soviet Union; family and peer-group roles in France. Hence, in each society, there is a special motivational complex which functions best—i.e., which is able to secure maximum satisfaction for the individual while contributing the maximum utility to the society. The post-oedipal socialization process is intended to produce the optimum motivational complex in as many citizens as possible. This is the logic behind the concept of national character.

Then do we assume that a society with political primacy will tend to create personalities with goal-consummation primacy? Only within certain limits. The motivational complexes of those men who are essentially used as facilities need not be the same as the motivational complexes of those who make the decisions about how these facilities are to be used. Thus, we again meet the problem of structural differentiation—the different national characters existing in the same society depend, in part, upon the different class memberships of individuals.

In analyzing national character, we may use several ways of breaking down the concept into variables that can be systematically manipulated. We can analyze the ways the *solidarity norms* of a given society are transmitted. Solidarity norms are those which are fundamental to the functioning of any kind of social organization—e.g., honesty, loyalty, or reliability. National-character analysis will not find that people in a given society are *more* honest, reliable, or loyal than those in another; but it will find that the situations in which one is expected to be honest, loyal, or reliable in one nation are different from the situations in which, in another country, the same performance is expected. This is because of differences in the categorization of objects, especially the universalism-particularism categorization, as well as the differential ranking of roles, by the value systems in different societies.

The second variable may be described as the *system values* of the society. These values refer more directly to those over-all goals of the society

49. Such seems to have been the case in the Trobriand Islands. See Malinowski, *The Sexual Life of Savages* (London: George Routledge and Sons, 1932), pp. 2–7.

50. In Western society, this was, until recently, the norm rather than the exception.

51. Cf. S. Stouffer, *Communism, Conformity and Civil Liberties* (New York: Doubleday, 1955).

that distinguish it from other societies—e.g., the gentleman's way of life, concern with a particular type of religious salvation—in short, the answers to the Weberian problem of ultimate meaning. The commitment to these system values is established with increasing irrevocability in latency and adolescence, though rarely perceived by nationals except through the opposition (and superiority) of their style of living to that of other nationals. System values may be a divinity known only to social scientists: they are abstractions from the pervasive patterning of culture. In fact, the very language transmits system values simply through its structure and its way of conceptualizing the world. As Whorf has shown,[52] a language has areas of conceptual richness and areas of conceptual poverty. It has a real, though unclear, influence upon the cognitive facilities available to the personality. Sentence structure influences the rhythm, the mode of thought, and the interaction between individuals. It fosters or hinders certain differentiations.

Another major way that the personality internalizes the society's system values is through the series of memberships the child assumes during his latency period. School membership, for instance, implies the acceptance of an explicit value system, even though solidarity norms may be emphasized more than system values. The child's peer group is another crucial socialization agency—the American peer group is much more open than the French, but in America one's membership is conditional on one's contribution to a group purpose that is legitimate according to adult values. French peer groups are much more oriented to the tension reduction of their members than to implementing social values. They have little or no opportunity for autonomous achievement along lines approved by adults, since the French child is emphatically taught that legitimate goals of action are pursued only by established collectivities like family, state, and school. The implicit lesson of the American peer group is the reverse: a legitimate purpose may be served by any organization; the established collectivities have no monopoly on positive achievement.

The teachings of the peer group have a great influence on the child's definition of situations along the universalistic-particularistic variable. He learns under what circumstances he should behave only to increase the group's solidarity; and when, on the contrary, his behavior should be guided by general

values, and membership considerations should be relatively secondary. Social science has barely begun to investigate these less obvious but pervasive patterns of socialization.

DEVIANCE AND THE MAINTENANCE
OF CONFORMITY

Illness, Error, Crime, and Sin

We have analyzed the process of socialization that creates, in the human personality, the motivational structure necessary for the assumption of adult roles. We shall now examine the process whereby these psychological structures are maintained and developed to increase conformity with the role-systems constituting social structure. This process is commonly known as "social control," and is often regarded as only a function of specialized agencies, like the police or the courts; but in fact, *every* role-reciprocity involves an element of social control, by acting as a sanction, negative or positive, for behavior in conformity with role-expectations. The specialized agencies do not relieve the individual of all responsibility for enforcing social sanctions.

As was mentioned previously, any role can be viewed as an example of a social system, with four major subsystems specialized in solving problems of (1) adaptation; (2) goal-attainment; (3) integration; and (4) pattern maintenance. We may assume that each subsystem will have its particular focus of failure. Solution of the adaptive problem means the transformation of the environment into the maximum amounts of generalized facilities at the cost of the least expenditure of system resources, i.e., efficiency; deviance from this norm is waste. Goal-attainment requires conformity to the norm of effectiveness, i.e., mobilizing and using the facilities in order to attain system goals; deviance means failure to achieve the goal. Solution of the integrative problem requires solidarity and harmony; deviance is nonreciprocity and disorder. Pattern maintenance requires the commitment to system values; failure is lack of motivational commitment to these values.

If we now look at the failures of the personality system that parallel those on the social system level, we shall find that an adaptive failure would be the failure to transform the organism and the personality into role facilities, motivational and nonmotivational: this would be *illness*, either physical or mental. The failure to reach desired

52. Benjamin Lee Whorf, "Science and Linguistics," *Technology Review*, XLIV (1940), pp. 229–48. See also D. D. Lee, "A Primitive System of Values," *Philosophy of Science*, VII (1940), pp. 355–65. Both articles are reprinted in T. M. Newcomb and E. L. Hartley (eds.), *Readings in Social Psychology*, New York: Henry Holt, 1947.

goals is ascribed to *error*. Nonreciprocity is defined as *crime* of varying seriousness. Lack of commitment to system values could be called *sin*. Sin differs from crime in that it may be potential rather than virtual: reciprocity can be maintained by an individual for the wrong reasons. Treason is a form of sin.

Error and illness are two forms of deviance that apparently derive exclusively from failures to reach efficiency and/or effectiveness. In error, failure is due to ignorance or to lack of control over the elements of action. Illness is also a lack of control—a lack of control over the body and the mind that renders the individual incapable of realizing his value commitments and of fulfilling his share of solidarity obligations. Even though error and illness appear "unmotivated," they will nevertheless be sanctioned negatively, especially in role-systems that have adaptive or goal-consummatory primacy. For example, the frequently sick individual is not hired for positions that demand stamina and for which replacements are difficult to secure. Nor is error tolerated when it dissipates the resources of the community.

Yet a distinction must somehow be made between the error resulting from failure to control situational factors that no one could have controlled, and the error resulting from failure to assimilate available knowledge. The first we shall call "normal error"; the second, "presumption." Normal error may be forgiven as long as it is clearly perceived as such by all; but presumption cannot be forgiven. The sanctions brought to bear against the author of the presumption include an imputation of negative personalities—"stupid," "rash," and "incompetent" are among the commonly applied epithets; they will also usually entail, through market or political mechanisms, a reduction in his status. He will be shifted, at least until he demonstrates an improved capacity to fulfill his former role, to roles that have fewer responsibilities and opportunities for personal choice, and where any future errors he makes will not have so disruptive an impact on the social order. Unsuccessful entrepreneurs become employees; defeated generals are shifted to training centers or service commands.

Like error, illness is regarded as an "undesired" failure to control the organism, or, in the case of mental illness, to control the personality. Whenever an individual seems to violate the norm of least effort by systematically acting so as to increase his pain and decrease his pleasure, we ascribe his behavior to mental illness. This ascription is based on a rationalistic concept of man. Freud, however, has shown that the economics of the personality

are more complex than had been realized, and that neurosis and even psychosis can have important "secondary gains." Even "completely physical" illness can be an escape from onerous duty; error, too, can be the expression of a motivational system that is consciously inhibited but can find ways of securing its goals under the camouflage of "unmotivated" error.

If error and illness are defined as undesired failures to achieve efficiency and effectiveness, "crime" and "sin" refer to failures to cooperate within the valued collectivities of the community or to demonstrate commitment to societal values. They are more severely punished than error or illness because the likelihood of their harming society is usually greater. There is a gradient of deviance in which the sinner occupies the top echelon. The sinner is bound eventually to show nonreciprocity; in fact he is likely to do so when the consequences of this nonreciprocity are most destructive of wealth and social order. The habitual criminal falls into the category of the sinner. The nonhabitual criminal, on the other hand, remains committed to social values. Sooner or later he will return to loyal membership in the community. The person in error destroys facilities and fails expectations while not threatening the basic framework of order. The sick person harms mainly himself, rather than the society.

How a role failure will be interpreted in terms of the responsibility of the individual will depend less on the objective intent of the individual than on the society's level of role-differentiation and on the over-all threat to the community that the deviance represents. An examination of error in economic and political action will clarify this statement.

"Error" in Economic and Political Action

Among economic acts, bankruptcy provides a good example of a type of deviance whose definition has changed so that the relative immunity of "error" is more likely to be granted to the deviant than formerly. In nineteenth-century America, and in the first half of the twentieth century in Europe, bankruptcy was still considered a source of dishonor—it was akin to stealing, since it dissipated the property of creditors. Since capital was scarcer, its loss was much more serious both to society and to the status of the owner's family.

In addition, economic efficacy was considered as a mysterious quality of the entrepreneur's personality, one that he could transmit to his descendants through special family training and trade secrets.

This notion is typical of an economy where production roles, embedded in the family firm, are not yet segregated from pattern-maintenance and integrative structures. The growth and differentiation of economic structures result in a more rational depiction of the economic situation. Economic problems are no longer considered soluble by special magical powers (the secret of the firm); rather, they may be resolved by knowledge acquired through universalistic procedures (business science, economics). Increased understanding of the economic situation reveals the many factors of uncertainty that do exist, and the fact that not all these factors can be controlled with the techniques available at the time. Thus the chance for normal error in all economic decisions is discovered to be large. Even though nonreciprocity may follow an economic action (e.g., customers fail to buy the goods offered at a certain price), the sanction valence of this nonreciprocity no longer extends to an indication of the individual's dishonesty or over-all incompetence. It has become restricted to indicating erroneous judgment—which may well have been due to normal error—or, at worst, to presumption. Although it may impair confidence in the entrepreneur's business acumen, bankruptcy is no longer a black mark upon his whole character, and certainly not a stigma upon the character of his relatives.

Another reason for the redefinition of bankruptcy is the wider collectivity's acceptance of a share in the responsibility for bankruptcy. Once economic action has become differentiated from the kinship unit and the narrow territorial community, it ceases to be dominated by tradition. In undifferentiated economies, the entrepreneur is a deviant who must prove the legitimacy of his deviancy by being successful; but in a differentiated economy ruled by economic rationality there is an imperative for change—the present state of affairs is, by definition, unsatisfactory in relation to the economic ideal. The entrepreneur is no longer the deviant; on the contrary, he is the leader in the search for greater efficiency. As leader, he is entitled to co-operation—from the investors, in the form of their trusting him with their money; from the suppliers, who provide him with the raw materials; and from the workers and executives, in the form of their labor. All realize that any "gain" can only follow a "venture," and that risk-taking is part of the dignity of economic action, just as facing danger is part of the dignity of soldiering. The bankrupt entrepreneur *may be* one who merely took more risks than other members of the community—then his failure, paradoxically, testifies to his entrepreneurial virtues, even though the immediate outcome was unfortunate.

Finally, capital becomes less scarce, so that the consequences of failure are not so drastic for the collectivity. In sum, there are four basic factors in the acceptance of normal error in the economy: (1) the differentiation of economic roles from other role-contexts; (2) the rationalization of economic roles; (3) the imperative of entrepreneurship that exposes one to risk; and (4) limitations on the consequences of error for the welfare of the collectivity.

Unlike economic enterprise, political enterprise as yet does not provide so much immunity. A political leader's failure to solve the group problem may initially raise the question: was the technique of leadership he used an efficacious one? Such a question bears only upon the "technological" capacity of the leader; it permits him to retire with some honor from the field.

If other leaders fail at the same task, thus demonstrating that the explanation by error (presumption) is unsatisfactory, different questions may be raised. These might include the following: Did the collectivity provide the leader with sufficient facilities? Was the goal of the collectivity at all attainable in the present external circumstances? Was the pursuit of this goal compatible with the pursuit of other goals dear to the collectivity? Was the goal legitimate in terms of the collectivity's basic value commitments?

These questions pose a much more direct threat to the equilibrium of collectivity members' personalities. If the collectivity proves incapable of achieving a goal desirable and legitimate in terms of its value commitments, a reorganization of the various roles may be necessary; thus, role-expectations which were in harmony with the need dispositions of the individual will have to be abandoned. This threat to the homeostatic integration of the personality (the hierarchy of role-commitments) and to its identity (the level of value commitment) causes a "neurotic" anxiety, as distinct from the "true" anxiety caused by technological failure.[53]

This threat itself will cause neurotic anxiety in the collectivity members most directly affected by the failure to achieve the goal; in addition, some of the solutions that present themselves may prove as traumatic as the failure. For example, people may feel tempted to shift membership, i.e., to desert the collectivity. Another way of neutralizing or coping with their neurotic anxiety is to project blame only on the unsuccessful leader, holding that he deceived his constituents by pretending a competence which he did not possess. More serious is the imputation of insincerity in his devotion to the commonweal: he

---

53. See below, selection from Freud's *Problem of Anxiety*, Part Three, Section B, II, Selection 4.

should have demanded more facilities, even if it meant some unpopularity.

To a certain extent, insincerity may be considered an aspect of presumption: to boast of one's capacities, to be so sensitive to the rewards of political power that one cannot bear to risk losing office through unpopular but necessary policies, is "human." Boasting and opportunism are the occupational hazards of the politician. When the citizen acknowledges this, he is close to acknowledging his own boasting and his own opportunism; he has relinquished the image of an omnipotent and pure leader and made a more realistic appraisal of the political situation.

An effort to retain this image results in more projection of neurotic anxiety, and the reactions toward the unsuccessful leader are likely to be even more severe. The collectivity's failure will be explained as resulting from the fact that the leader did not want the group to succeed in the first place, i.e., that he was disloyal. Similarly, when a particular goal's compatibility with other collectivity goals is questioned, as well as the over-all efficacy of a cultural tradition (a pattern-maintenance problem), the leader may be accused not of mere insincerity, but of treason. It is hoped that the expulsion and/or destruction of the leader-traitor will permit the problem to be solved easily with the facilities at hand, and without undue disturbance to the present equilibrium in role-commitment: the sin of the leader restores the innocence of the members of the collectivity.

Often, after having eliminated the leader "guilty" of disloyalty, the collectivity may be more willing to face the more or less drastic reorganization of roles that the achievement of collectivity goals seems to require. The aggression toward the leader —in its milder forms, it is expressed as common grumbling—has abreacted the regressive reactions characteristic of any learning situation.

The collectivity's participation in the entrepreneur's economic risk-taking makes the collectivity more willing to grant him, in case of bankruptcy, the immunities of "normal error" or the limited reprisals attached to presumption. In the same way, it is possible that participation by the citizens in making collective political decisions results in an increased capacity to allow political leaders a comparable tolerance. On the other hand, this trend has been hampered by the lagging of political science behind economic science, and by the fact that there has been no increase in political security comparable to the growth of capital resources that has helped to "desensitize" economic action.

"Illness" in French and American Society

As in the case of "error," a society's definition of a deviance as "illness" implies the granting of immunity from the more severe sanctions enforced against "crime." It is interesting to compare the French and the American societies in their respective willingness to grant the immunities of the definition of various patterns of deviance as "illness."

In France, with the greater political and economic importance of family lineage and the hedonistic bias of French values, "legitimate" illness and "legitimate" crime both have wider ranges than in the United States. "Legitimate," applied to illness, indicates that there is much less tendency to question the motivation behind it, and to regard it as accidental. And criminal behavior which brings a palpable advantage to the perpetrator and to his family will be accepted as comprehensible, even though it is illegal. Adultery or stable pre- or protomarital relations which act as safeguards for the extended family will be conceded a measure of "legitimacy"; so will crimes which discharge feelings of anger and jealousy or eliminate rivals for inheritance or for trade. The criminal has simply gone too far in asserting his self-interest or in securing his pleasure; he has lacked *mesure* (restraint) and consequently must be restrained by others and punished. The rationale for punishment is the violation of public order more than the motivational state of the actor. Consequently, the prosecution of crime is subordinate to the requirement of public order, which at times may justify impunity for the delinquent. But once his breach of public order has become an objective fact, there is little inquiry into the criminal's motivation or concern about reforming him. His rights of *habeas corpus* are minimal, for the criminal is an enemy of the broader society and must be rendered innocuous.

Illness, on the other hand, is not lack of *mesure;* it is the essence of powerlessness. In a civilization which does not stress the conquest of nature, illness is perceived as an expression of nature's power over man. Illness also seems too obviously an intrinsic deprivation to be open to the suspicion of secondary gain. Besides being physically painful, it deprives one of pleasures like good food and sociable conversation in a society which considers such civilized pleasure as one of the major goals of the socialized individual.

In American society, however, the impact of illness on the organization of the group is more readily perceived—the person who falls ill "lets the other members down." Furthermore, in a society stressing the spirit's mastery over matter, illness is considered, not as inevitable, but as a failure of the will.

Americans see, in illness, not so much the onset of pain and the lack of pleasure, but the lack of activity. Illness is enforced passivity, but passivity nevertheless. Thus, illness strikes much more deeply at the values of American society. The ill person is more alienated from his society than he would be in France, where the will's failure in the face of nature is expected as part of the order of things. In American society, the patient must *earn* his immunity from the suspicion of alienation by taking vigorous steps to get well. Otherwise he will be suspected of malingering (secondary gain). In this context, popular acceptance of the Freudian theory of illness has increased the pressure on the individual.

Such a conception of illness is apt to embrace the whole field of deviance. Rather than granting the criminal the "legitimacy" of a rational interest contradictory to the requirements of morality and of social order, American society tends to undercut any such claim by granting his deviance the legitimacy of mental illness. By declaring the criminal mentally ill, the society declares it unthinkable for any sane individual to be alienated from the wider community of Americans and uncommitted to its Puritan values. Far from representing a dissolution of the value base from which deviancy is assessed, the American conception of deviance as illness becomes a way to reassert the Puritan tradition that there can be no human behavior that is not an active search for secularized salvation and in the service of the commonwealth of true believers.

This society asks, about someone who is physically or mentally ill and/or has committed "irrational" crimes, "Is he motivated to get well?" If the answer is positive and the deviant "confesses" to his illness, much energy will be expended to permit him to recover control over his physical and mental capacities. If the answer is negative, he will be isolated from the community of the loyal and well-meaning, under a "sentence" that will probably be much longer and more immune to "fixing" than a prison sentence.

As a society differentiates and gains greater margins of security in the economic and political spheres, the error and illness concepts of deviance become progressively more prevalent. They provide the incumbent of a specialized role with the immunities necessary for risking the independent judgments that his tasks may require. They also may make more imperative his conformity to basic value commitments. Extending higher education to larger proportions of each new generation results in a higher level of participation in the dominant culture and a broader commitment to societal values. On the other hand, among the lower social classes, which do not benefit as much as the upper classes either in the level of education or in the level of general security, a definition of deviance as illness will often meet with skepticism, if not actual indignation: a case of deviance is more likely to appear as a political challenge, to be controlled by force and by physically eradicating the deviant.

Finally, the illness concept of deviance helps cope with the fact that, in a differentiated society, successful performance is less defined in advance—even if unsuccessful performance is more visible, because of the growing "rationality of the market." (In Weber's terms, "rationality of the market" expresses both the market's effectiveness as an indication of societal utility, and the greater reliability and pervasiveness of the price system. Cost accounting is a by-product of this growing rationality.) Both the immunity accorded to normal error and the immunity granted to illness mitigate the membership consequences of failure, while avoiding pressures upon the norms of judgment.

White-Collar Crime

The phenomenon of white-collar crime provides another illustration of the way social structure shapes definitions of deviance. Sutherland[54] defines "white-collar crime" as crime "committed by a person of respectability and high social status in the course of his occupation." One may also stress the fact that the latter has many opportunities for utilizing the situations of power given by the ignorance of the customer and the lack of alternative sources of supply. White-collar crime is less likely to meet retribution than is lower-class crime, largely because the former does not arouse the same level of indignation as the more obvious forms of robbery, and because the offender's class status protects him to a large degree.

The concept of white-collar crime involves a major ambiguity: it includes crimes, like abortion, that escape detection because of the structure of an occupation but are considered crimes by everyone within the occupation; and it includes alleged crimes that persons of good faith within the occupation seriously question defining *as* crimes. This is the case in "fee splitting" in medical practice, or in the misrepresentation of interest rates by bankers. In such situations, the attitude of the white-collar criminal is as follows: even if his action violates the letter of some law, he is justified in redefining the situation in terms that maximize his power, for his professional position makes him responsible for implementing the more general rules in situations where

54. Edwin H. Sutherland, *White Collar Crime* (New York: Dryden Press, 1949), p. 9.

the letter of the law cannot apply. Within the medical profession, fee splitting becomes a secret device for re-allocating income more "justly," and preventing the surgeon from being the sole beneficiary of a bargaining advantage usually denied the general practitioner. The banker may believe he does a better job of utilizing his customers' money for the benefit of society than the customers are likely to do, so that ambiguous or deceptive advertising that maximizes the bank's profit is morally justifiable.

White-collar crime is, thus, one of the more common forms of the "class struggle," centering in the maximization through power of profit-making opportunities, the proceeds of which may, in some cases, be used for the implementation of societal goals. As the concept of class interest becomes less particularistic—whether through a growing dedication to societal membership rather than to the narrower class membership, or through a concept of *noblesse oblige*—the incidence of the second type of white-collar crime should decline. In a United States where Cornelius Vanderbilt had said "The public be damned," the relative decline of the great bourgeois dynasties by the early twentieth century allowed the development, among employers, of a broader concept of the relevant community; and the professionalization of management has replaced the paternalistic *noblesse oblige* attitude. The desensitization of social hierarchies, the greater tolerance for error, and the broadening of illness categories of deviance have compensated upper-status groups for the breakdown of class barriers and for the less relentless waging of the "class struggle."

This discussion has indicated that the categorization of deviance as error, illness, crime, white-collar crime or sin depends more on social aspects of the deviance situation than on the deviant's personal motivation. This is the *major* source of the patterning of deviance: society recognizes and classifies deviance in the categories with which it can cope.

The Structure of Deviant Behavior

The regularities of motivational content provide another source for the analysis of deviance. Both Robert K. Merton and Talcott Parsons have made classifications of deviance based on certain broad characteristics of the personality.[55] Merton analyzes deviance as an individual's response to structural conflict between emphasized and general cultural goals ("success") and the scarcity of institutional-

ized means for achieving those goals (capital, profit-making opportunities). It may be useful to reprint this table, reminding the reader that the plus signs imply conformity and the minus signs imply rejection.

A TYPOLOGY OF MODES OF INDIVIDUAL ADAPTATION[56]

Modes of Adaptation	Culture Goals	Institutional Means
I. Conformity	+	+
II. Innovation	+	—
III. Ritualism	—	+
IV. Retreatism	—	—
V. Rebellion	±	±

This has been a seminal contribution, dominating work in the field for more than twenty years. Not only did it attempt to specify the types of deviance to which different social classes are prone, but it also pointed out that ritualism could be considered a form of deviance, while to most observers it seems, in fact, to be the acme of conformity. Ritualism is defined as the renunciation of the higher levels of achievement promoted by the culture, and a concentration of energy upon the faultless conformity with institutionalized means at the level where the individual finds himself.

It is true that all cultures, and not merely American culture, foster an imperative of maximizing one's level of achievement in relation to the system of values of the society. These values may be religious salvation and involve little or no social mobility, as in classical India, or, on the contrary, may refer to increasing levels of contribution to the society's wealth and power. In the latter case, the increasing levels of contribution are manifested by an increase in the achiever's control over wealth and power. Even though American values put greater stresses than most on the obligation to "make something of yourself"— i.e., in the old Puritanical statement, "to render the best possible account of the gifts God has entrusted to you"—the specific goals of this striving are usually kept at a realistic level. The norms for achievement are derived from one's own "reference group," not from the contemplation of upper-class standards or the emulation of exceptional success; the norm for a skilled worker is certainly not becoming head of a large corporation. Keeping one's level of aspiration within the scope of one's achievement would not be adequately described as "ritualism." Nor should we neglect the real achievement involved in *maintaining* one's level of achievement in the face of the normal frustrations and fatigues of everyday life. The lower-middle-class person, whom Merton considers "ritualism-

---

55. Merton calls his categories types of more or less enduring response, not types of personality organization. See Robert K. Merton, *Social Theory and Social Structure* (rev. ed.), (Glencoe: The Free Press, 1952), Chap. 4.

56. Merton, *op. cit.*, p. 140.

prone," has to maintain middle-class standards with comparatively low financial means, and often from a lower-class starting point. His most difficult achievement is the complete break from lower-class attitudes toward immediate gratification, apathy toward community affairs, education, sexuality, aggression and work. Many of his commitments to middle-class values will have the characteristics of reaction formation. Their rigidity may not permit, in fact, the type of productive innovation that secures rewards at the upper-middle-class levels. It may, in fact, take a whole generation to consolidate a commitment to middle-class values and pay off the mortgage on the split-level home.

The point at issue here is that the conformity with institutionalized means is unlikely to be in conflict with the commitment to culture goals, since the former are *by and large* the institutionalization of the latter.[57] There is, after all, great achievement in remaining an honest bank clerk. Where there is conflict we are more likely to be in the presence of *sin,* rather than ritualism. Alienation hides itself under surface conformity often in order to hide a total lack of commitment—itself a violation of the spirit of the employment contract—or to strike all the more efficaciously at the organization through sabotage. The point will be explored further in the discussion of Parsons' classification.

There is a scarcity of time, talent, and space in relation to the achievement of cultural goals—this is an ineluctable characteristic of social structure. Normally, status groups mitigate the tensions created by the general desirability of cultural goals and the differential availability of the means for reaching them. They do this by increasing the flow of facilities to their members, crippling outsiders, and by acting as reference groups that translate the cultural goals into more specific norms that are relatively accessible to their members, given the supply of facilities.

There may be, in fact, an interesting situation in American society due to the relative weakness of the extended family, and to the permeability of neighborhood and status groups. It is possible that these two factors have lowered the capacity of these groups to place limits on their members' ambition and to punish the use of illegal means by candidates for admission. In one sense, easy entry into a higher status group destroys the lower echelon reference points for evaluating one's success. "The local boy who made good" finds that he is not a local boy anymore; he "can't go home again." Thus it is more difficult, in such a society, to know whether one is really a success or merely an escapee from failure. The old Calvinist anxiety about one's state of eternal grace has been secularized. This is Durkheim's meaning of *anomie* from a psychological standpoint: the lack of limitation of one's desires that leads one to an equally immoderate frustration.

We may then approach the problem of deviance from the standpoint of determining either what will diminish the capacity of the status groups to stabilize the motivation of their members, or what past role-participations make it more likely that the members will not accept adequate group controls. Talcott Parsons' approach deals more with the second problem.

A Typology of Deviant Behavior

Holding role-expectation as a constant, Parsons has described the relationship (see the accompanying table[58]) between general need-dispositions of the personality and categories of deviant behavior as seen from the social system standpoint.

In later writings[59] Parsons has attempted to link the three dimensions of the deviance paradigm—conformity-alienation, activity-passivity, focus on norms *versus* focus on social objects—to his analysis of the differentiation of the personality system. Conformity-alienation would be rooted in the constitution of the primary mother-child identity with its attendant subordination of organic needs to the rules of the mother-child role system. A failure to develop a strong mother-child identity would result in a general psychopathic propensity, pervasive of the whole personality, with little capacity for foregoing immediate satisfaction in favor of long-range system goals. Activity-passivity would refer to the differentiation of the primary mother-child identity into an autonomy need-disposition and a dependency need-disposition. Passivity would imply a strong dependency dominance. Activity would imply a strong autonomy dominance.[60] Finally the focus of deviant motivation upon pattern or social objects would depend upon the third level of personality differentiation, which gave rise to the four

---

57. In formal organization it is possible to have conflict between the imperatives to get along with others and to please the boss—all part of the culture—and the "ideals" of the organization. The Mertonian paradigm finds a narrower, and perhaps richer, application to the theory of formal organization.

58. T. Parsons, *The Social System* (Glencoe: The Free Press, 1952), Chap. 7.

59. T. Parsons and R. Bales, *op. cit.* pp. 145–146.

60. Alienation and inappropriate passivity or activity need not result in deviant behavior if they are hidden by strong reaction-formations. The latter, however, tend to "spill over" into compulsive excesses.

	ACTIVITY		PASSIVITY	
	Compulsive Performance Orientation		Compulsive Acquiescence	
Conformative Dominance	Focus on Social Objects	Focus on Norms	Focus on Social Objects	Focus on Norms
	Dominance	Compulsive Enforcement	Submission	Perfectionistic Observance (Merton's ritualism)
Alienative Dominance	Rebelliousness		Withdrawal	
	Aggressiveness toward Social Objects	Incorrigibility	Compulsive Independence	Evasion

basic need-dispositions: conformity, nurturance, adequacy, security. The focus on norms would imply a dominance in the motivational system of the adequacy need,[61] the focus on objects a dominance of the security need.

The value of any classification must be measured by the clarification it brings to the problem and to the insights it promotes. The motivation behind deviant behavior is as complex as that behind conforming behavior, and the difficulty of inferring personality meaning from observed role events is ever present.

Parsons' classification is suggestive in several directions. First, it gives a genetic theory of deviant motivation. If the sociologist could isolate groups in which the child is likely to encounter defective infant ties to the mother, excessive reinforcement of dependency or autonomy needs, he could conceivably predict a propensity to deviance among the juveniles and the adults issued from this group. Lower-class groups show a higher percentage of broken homes,[62] and the earlier the home is broken the more *difficult* it is for the child to internalize the nuclear family and differentiate, in proper pro-

portions, the basic four need-dispositions mentioned earlier. Difficult does not mean impossible. The meaning of a home broken by death is different from that of a home broken by divorce or desertion. An uncle, an elder brother, a cousin, a neighbor, a friendly policeman or grocer, can often make up for the lack of a biological father. Sometimes even the peer group can take the meaning of the father image for a child. The presence of the father figure need not be continuous in order to be an effective force for personality differentiation.

True enough, the lower-class family often lives in relative social isolation. When low achievement leads to self-doubt, the presence of one's kind is a reminder of one's own degradation. The lower-class family is apt to experience that meaning of *anomie* which American sociology has extended to the phenomenon Durkheim had described as leading to *suicide egoiste:* the isolation of the individual from significant memberships, which could compensate for the deficiencies of the nuclear family.[63]

The Parsonian typology also accounts for the way in which each sex tends to deviate from institutionalized norms: men tend more to acts of violence and sabotage (incorrigibility); women tend more to sexual offenses (if we wish to say that promiscuity has a high component of *compulsive independence*) and to illness, which Parsons has described as a form of deviance having a high component of *evasion.*[64]

61. Parsons, *The Social System*, p. 261. In *Family, Socialization . . .* , pp. 145–146, Parsons focuses more on the dominance, in the case of deviance toward a pattern, of *affectively neutral* need-dispositions that are predominant in both the adequacy and conformity need-dispositions. In the case of deviance toward social objects, there is "over-emphasis on the affective ones," which dominate in nurturance and security.

62. A. B. Hollingshead and F. C. Redlich, in their book, *Social Class and Mental Illness* (New York: John Wiley and Sons, 1958), p. 124, state that forty per cent of the children under seventeen years of age, in class V (the lowest class), "live in homes that have been disrupted by death, desertion, separation, or divorce."

63. Cf. Part One, Section C, Selection 4. It is interesting to note that Durkheim had seen social isolation as more of a problem for the upper classes and intellectuals than for the lower classes.

64. Granted that many of the deviancies of women escape public notice because they take place within the confines of the nuclear family.

Parsons' use of the concept of ambivalence has also led him to approach the problem of deviance from the point of view of the "too much" as well as that of the "not enough." When ambivalence exceeds a certain intensity, behavior will follow a compulsively conforming direction, characterized frequently by excessive zeal. Here the "perfectionistic observance" of the passively inclined compulsive conformer takes its full meaning. It often will result in error and dysfunctional rigidities of behavior. For the compulsive conformer, the normal innovations of role performance resemble too much the temptations of alienation. This motivational set is, of course, dominated by the mechanism of reaction formation.[65]

One of the most fruitful consequences of Parsons' classification has been the insight as to the inevitable ambivalence of all alienation, which after all can exist only if there has been an initial commitment to the valued role-expectation. Starting from the inevitable ambivalence of the "criminal" or of the "sinful," it has added to our understanding of the tendency of the deviant to try to gratify both aspects of his motivation: by joining a deviant group he can act out the alienative disposition toward society and yet display great conformity to his group, which, in fact, often claims value superiority in relation to the general society.[66]

For instance the primary-school child must commit himself to roles that imply acceptance of the societal values as best exemplified by teachers, principals, traffic policemen, George Washington and Abraham Lincoln. His failure to implement this initial commitment creates the problems from which alienation may spring—whether the failure be in deportment, in language, or in developing such basic "tool skills" as reading and writing. If the personality cannot find a "low achiever" role congruent with its still earlier masculine role-commitments, deviance will probably occur. If alienation combines with passivity, withdrawal will result. If alienation combines with activity, the result will be rebelliousness, as in the delinquent subculture described by A. K. Cohen.[67] This delinquent subculture presents a relatively clear case of ambivalent alienation that has taken refuge in a cult of primitive masculinity, defined as the capacity for aggression and sex. Other themes for the delinquent subculture are the "reverse English" of vandalism as a reply to the values of production, and of systematic idleness and hedonism as a

counterpart to the values of work.[68] The problem of who is likely to join a gang as an active member is, of course, a problem of individual psychology, although it is related to family role participation.[69]

From the analysis of ambivalent alienation leading to membership in the delinquent group, with its two apparently contradictory contributions to the personality, it is interesting to consider the reverse process: how membership in noncompatible groups leads the member to a deviance-prone condition known as *marginality*. Here the concepts of ambivalence, compulsive conformity, and compulsive alienation will be particularly useful.

The Case of Marginality

The concept of marginality is a contribution made by Robert Park and his pupil Stonequist to the understanding of deviance.[70] Its original meaning describes an enduring conflict between broad role-commitments associated with incompatible collectivity memberships. Our description of cathexes as deriving from past internalizations might lead us to think that there should be an automatic integration between new role cathexes and past internalization. This is largely so. But the initial cathexis is rarely to a role that is clearly spelled out; it is more to a collectivity whose purposes seem, at first glance, to be one's own. Once inside the collectivity, the member may discover, too late, that roles are assigned to him that contradict his past commitments. How well these contradictions are resolved determines whether the new member "belongs" or remains "marginal."

SOURCES OF MARGINALITY

In a way, some marginality is inherent in the very structure of all role-behavior, and especially in roles

---

65. Part Three, Section B, II, Selection 5.
66. Cf. Parsons, *The Social System*, pp. 284–297.
67. A. K. Cohen, *Delinquent Boys* (Glencoe: The Free Press, 1955).

68. Cf. Walter B. Miller's vivid description of "Lower-Class Culture as a Generating Milieu of Gang Delinquency," *Journal of Social Issues*, XIV (1958), 3–19. However, there is too much evidence of ambivalence among delinquents to believe that the lower class is so autonomous and ignorant of the middle-class values as Miller makes it out to be. While A. K. Cohen stresses the frequent non-utilitarian aspect of the gang's activities, Herbert Bloch and Arthur Niederhoffer, *The Gang: a Study in Adolescent Behavior* (New York: Philosophical Library, 1958) stress the Mertonian, "innovation" oriented ways of the gang to secure money. For a description of gang types and a general discussion of the field see R. A. Cloward and L. E. Ohlin, *Delinquency and Opportunity* (Glencoe: The Free Press, 1960).
69. Cf. J. McCord and W. McCord, "The Effort of Parental Role Model on Criminality," in *The Journal of Social Issues*, XIV (1958), 66–75. The whole issue of this journal deserves careful reading.
70. [Robert E. Park and] Everett V. Stonequist, *The Marginal Man* (New York: Charles Scribner's Sons, 1937).

where Ego must control Alter—Alter, even an "evil" Alter, must somehow be internalized. In this sense, a soldier is always fighting "the enemy within." Colonial administrators, policemen, jailers, and ambassadors are also subject to this kind of marginality.

Among the more transient sources of marginality is subordination to dual authorities differing in their definitions of the situation or in their policies. In a mental hospital, for instance, a conflict between the policies of the treating psychiatrist and of the psychiatrist administering the ward frequently results in exciting the patient, who does not know to which role-system he belongs and should give reciprocity.[71] This situation increases the secondary gains of illness as compared with the torments of therapeutic commitments; and the patient is likely to get worse. A less dramatic example is the employee who is exposed to two sources of conflicting orders. Committed to the values of the organization, he ought to resolve the conflict by obeying the source which is more strategic for the smooth functioning of the organization; but conflict of authority does not promote conditions for making such constructive decisions. The conflict is likely to generate, in the worker, a certain amount of antagonism toward the organization, which does not know what it wants; second, the employee is not always able to determine what the best interests of the organization are. As a result, his personality tends to reassert its regressive needs; and he will support whichever source of orders is more compatible with them. In organizational terms, this support will be translated into the worker's support of routine and his sabotage of measures that aim to increase economic and political rationality.

On the more general structural level, some occupational roles—such as chiropractor, optometrist, or veterinarian—create marginality in their incumbents by being on the fringes of professional status, yet unable to claim commensality with the traditional professions of medicine, ministry, law, and university teaching.

Still another level of marginality is exemplified by the adult immigrant. This marginality is often mitigated by the immigrant's being able to limit his participation in his adopted country to a few relatively clear roles—e.g., worker, taxpayer, consumer—whose contents are determined universalistically by measurable performance rather than by membership in status groups or by the knowledge of complex symbol systems. These roles involve adjustive techniques which do not imply an alteration in the basic age, sex, and status roles internal-

71. Alfred H. Stanton and Morris S. Schwartz, *The Mental Hospital* (New York: Basic Books, 1954).

ized by the personality. For emotional support and tension reduction, the immigrant can usually turn to his family and to peer groups of the same nationality.

For the second-generation family, however, the problem is more complex. As the school and peer groups are socializing the second-generation child in the age, sex, and status roles functional to participation in the larger community, his parents and their friends are trying to socialize him in the age, sex, and status roles functional to participation in the immigrant community which was so helpful in their adjustment to the new country. The language, the gestures, the valued symbols, the conceptions of authority, the limits of solidarity, the relations between boys and girls, the conception of property—all these are different in the immigrant community. And the child cannot help internalizing some of the roles functional to immigrant societies, if only because his parents represent his basic concept of masculinity and femininity and remain two powerful sources of sanctions.

Another source of marginality is intermarriage between different nationality or ethnic groups and/or social classes. The very fact of such a marriage reflects a certain alienation, on the part of each spouse, from his or her original milieu; without such alienation, each could have found a counterpart to his internalized female role, and to her internalized male role, in the local youth. Intermarriage may permit one to stabilize commitment to a milieu that is defined as "higher" in some scale of values. On the other hand, the motivation of one of the spouses may change after the marriage: the aggression against the milieu of origin may disappear, abreacted by the "acting out" implied by the intermarriage. Then one's differences from one's spouse are reinterpreted negatively and the child of such a marriage may have difficulty learning what memberships he must assume in order to realize his sex and status role-commitments. The mother tries to re-create, in her son, a masculine role which is at variance with what his father appears to be. Even when this occurs with the father's approval, it creates fundamental ambiguity. In one way, the son is "superior" to his father, and this superiority may weaken the father prematurely in the son's eyes; or, in order to resolve this conflict, he may over-identify with his father, and be strongly aggressive against what his mother represents.

ANTICIPATORY SOCIALIZATION

The motivational forces making for marginality may be reinforced by the group's attitude toward the individual in whom signs of incompatible membership have been recognized. The group in which he claims membership may not accept him—or it may accept him partially, allowing him only a small range of error, compared to the range of error allowed in a "regular" member. Since there is always a second frame of reference available for interpreting the marginal man's action (not only by the other group members, but, more important, by the actor himself), his error can always be explained coherently as the expression of an alien allegiance prescribing hostile acts against the group. This interpretation is particularly likely to be made when the marginal man's past and present membership groups are currently antagonistic to each other. Since the marginal person implies, by his very existence, the possibility of deviance from the norms of the group, he can never be so fully a member as the others. A status group, for example, can never accept a social climber as a full member, because his motivation has not been completely tested by his mere financial success. Only after the financially successful family has demonstrated, through the raising of their children, that their hierarchy of values has changed to full conformity with the upper-class emphasis on civic duty and "cultural" interests—only then will the children, or even the grandchildren, be accepted as full-fledged members. Until then, the marginal family is expected to demonstrate conspicuously its allegiance to the upper-status group by a somewhat fundamentalist attachment to its causes and to its style of life.

RESOLUTIONS OF MARGINALITY

In coping with marginality—which, in its wider sense, has been described as conflicts between role-orientations—the personality appears to have several patterns of role-participation available. The first is aggressive projection: the role-orientations incompatible with the personality's dominant commitments are projected outward onto the group whence they originated, and the personality is systematically aggressive against this group. The marginal individual becomes an unusually active "defender of the faith." This is the attitude of some of the "100 per cent Americans" descended from various immigrant groups.

Fighting against a part of himself, the marginal man will often evince a keen sensitivity to the threats presented by the out-group. For him, the danger is always real; for the in-group, the danger may be objectively rather slight. But in situations where peril is generally recognized, the marginal man may even become a leader of the in-group. Aggressive projection could be described as the "political" solution to the problem of marginality.

Another solution for the marginal man is to proselytize the out-group instead of being aggressively against it: he will show the out-group that its members should abandon it and join the ranks of the faithful. Thus, instead of fighting his deviant role-orientation through projection and aggression, the marginal man will reinforce, in himself, the dominant commitments, through teaching and therapy. Some projection probably is still involved in this complex mechanism, but the approach to reality is likely to be more flexible, since the fostering of change is desired and expected. Furthermore, the role-orientations to be dissolved do not appear so threatening as they do in the case of aggressive projection—teaching and therapy imply an optimistic bias. This could be described as the "pattern-maintenance" solution of marginality.

A third solution is to compromise between incompatible role-orientations by finding a structural position where one can successively enact both role-orientations. This is the role of the diplomat: he represents his country to a certain foreign country, and represents the foreign country to his own. Another example is the foreman, who participates in the working-class peer group *and* in the managerial organization. One might anticipate that the marginal personality would shy away from marginal situations in order not to activate his conflict; but, on the contrary, he tends to choose occupational roles which can utilize his marginality. Situations like this activate the conflicting role-orientations, but resolve their incompatibility by enclosing them in a single role-expectation made legitimate by society. The role of patient is an example of such a single role-expectation, combining both excessive dependency and the commitment to health and activity. This is the "integrative" solution of marginality.

The political, pattern-maintenance, and integrative solutions to marginality provide motivational resources for the functioning of agencies of social control. For example, roles of political control seem to utilize best the type of motivation characterized by aggressive projection. Police work, custodial roles in penitentiaries, and the control of the mentally ill in old-style hospitals provide outlets for such marginal personality types. This does not mean that such personality types are the only ones to assume police or custodial roles; it means only that, in these roles, aggressive projection can be an asset, as long as the aggression does not become excessive.

Modern psychiatric hospitals attempt to develop staff roles that are integrative and oriented to pattern-maintenance rather than politically oriented. The integrative approach utilizes the patient's role to the maximum, developing those aspects most similar to the "normal" citizen and peer-group roles through patient self-government and "group activities." This requires the staff members to have the capacity to "identify," without panic, with the patients, and to center the hospital organization around the new patient role. Friendships with patients are recommended; and the physical dangerousness of the aggressive patient is minimized. The staff become the leaders of the patient community, mediating the needs of the patients to the surrounding local community and vice versa.

Many penitentiaries have a similar regime, in which the staff work out a *modus vivendi* with the convicts' peer group.[72] Some policemen, too, interpret their roles as integrative, developing friendships with criminals, exchanging small favors, avoiding trouble and crusading zeal, with the desired result that the underworld may keep its activities below the level which would trigger reform movements.[73] The legal profession also sees itself as mainly devoted to reconciling the client's interests with the requirements of order.[74] In addition to exegesis and interpretation, this involves some socialization of the client into behavior which may be less "profitable" than his first impulse. Indeed, this is an example of role-behavior utilizing both the pattern-maintenance and the integrative solutions of marginality.

Therapy and teaching roles are other examples. They require intimate participation in the delinquent or immature role-orientations, in order to promote in Alter the learning necessary to change the content and structure of his motivation. Consequently, they also require a stronger hold upon reality and morality, in order not to be seduced by the delinquent or immature Alter: seduction is the semi-Newtonian reaction to socialization action. Very powerful professional peer groups are necessary, to support this hold on reality and morality while permitting the expeditions into Hades that psychotherapy, for instance, may require.

Thus we come to a somewhat paradoxical conclusion. The organizations of social control aim to limit the activities of overt deviants and to recuperate them for adult social roles; and they also are means for controlling the activities of their staffs—thus, police work keeps certain policemen honest; psychotherapy keeps some psychiatrists sane. Similarly, even parents need children in order

to remain adult. To attain an effective understanding of the organizations of social control, we must remember that one of their major functions is to maintain conformity in their own staffs. Changing the staff's role-orientations, from a political to an integrative or a pattern-maintenance primacy, requires that the personalities of the staff members abandon aggressive projection as a means of resolving their own problems of marginality. Because they forgot this aspect of the socio-psychology of "normals," many efforts at reform, whether in mental hospitals, in penitentiaries, or in personnel management, have come to naught.

THE MODES OF SOCIAL CONTROL

Discussing the ways by which personalities and collectivities mitigate the strains of marginality raises the more general issue of social control. "Social control" applies to the structural devices whose objects are to prevent the onset of deviance, and to limit its scope and effects when it does occur. The main procedures are those of (1) tension management, (2) reinforcing socialization pressure, and (3) labelling and isolating deviants.

Tension management. The failure of role-behavior to satisfy the needs of the personality results in tensions which change the economy of purposive behavior and make the individual more likely to attempt to gain need satisfaction in socially unacceptable ways. Reduction of these tensions for all its members is one of the basic functions of the modern conjugal family. This function is accomplished through great permissiveness for regressive behavior which, being isolated by the family from the wider social system, does not lead to social sanctions. The married couple find their level of mutual permissiveness, within which each is free of guilt and secure in the other's understanding. Modern marriage, more oriented to reducing tension than past marriages, requires the matching of personalities by mutual choice. In turn, this presupposes greater freedom and equality in the socialization experience of the teen-age girl, and greater opportunity for the wife who assumes superordinate roles within the family system. Vis-à-vis their children, parents find opportunities for tension reduction in acting out fantasies of omnipotence or in gratifying the dependent needs of the internalized child while gratifying the flesh-and-blood child. Parenthood also permits the parents to realize their frustrated ambitions through the careers of their children. The presence of children lengthens the time span during which parents reap the rewards of conformity, and diminishes the gains secured from deviance—for parents who want their children to

72. Cf. Sykes, G. M., *The Society of Captives* (Princeton: Princeton University Press, 1959).
73. The process is very well described in William Foote Whyte, *Street Corner Society* (Chicago: University of Chicago Press, 1945), pp. 123–146.
74. See Talcott Parsons, *Essays in Sociological Theory* (rev. ed.; Glencoe: The Free Press, 1954), Chap. 18.

succeed will think twice before engaging in deviant behavior that might handicap their children.[75]

Organized religion works to reduce tensions on somewhat the same principle, by providing a wider time span for the realization of value.[76] In organized religion, salvation in the after-life is secured through the basic dedication of the soul to social values, regardless of the worldly success one has in implementing these values. As long as the sinner sincerely confesses to Jesus Christ and attempts to improve his performance, all sins are reduced to error and need not alienate him from the broadest community of man, nor prevent him from attempting to implement the common values through a performance for which he has so far received little or no reward.

Another major source of tension reduction is entertainment. Basically, entertainment reduces tensions by acting as a reward, symbolizing publicly one's accomplishment of valued performances and one's concomitant accumulation of rights to gratification. Entertainment's cathartic effect has been described by Aristotle. Identification with fictional characters permits the abreaction of aggressive, sexual, or dependent tendencies that are not functional to legitimate role-expectation; or the tribulations of fictional characters can make one's own frustrations appear minimal by comparison. Soap opera, for example, enhances this feeling of "relative gratification" in its listeners.

Entertainment can also reduce tensions by providing—e.g., in sports, hobbies, or amateur theatricals—opportunities for capacities not ordinarily employable in economic and political structures. Such entertainment roles are insulated simultaneously from the economic and political structures, for they are not "taken seriously." Similarly, participation in certain other forms of entertainment allows one to behave irresponsibly without concomitant repercussions for one's regular roles: thus, the citizen may safely abreact his aggression against the government—in a letter to a newspaper; the office worker may safely insult his boss—at an office party. And the drunk is allowed his expressions of aggression, sexuality, and dependency only because he is implicitly committed when sober, not to make these demands.

Reinforcement of socialization pressure. After tension management, society's second mode of social control is the reinforcement of socialization pressure. Little need be added to the description given by Durkheim and G. H. Mead of the socializing functions of ritual and of punitive justice. Besides providing tension reduction, rituals act as powerful reinforcers of the more general beliefs necessary to social order.

It is commonly considered that, outside of churches, ritual rarely occurs in modern society because of the increasing rationalization of life. But if we define ritual as a pattern of *behavior which is invariant and immune to criticism based on the criteria of efficiency and effectiveness, and which has the purpose of expressing motivational conformity and solidarity,* we find many rituals that disguise themselves as staff conferences, pep talks, seminars, political conventions, televised fireside chats, P.T.A. meetings, etc. These rituals are as real as those of Memorial Day or Independence Day. Each occupation has its own rituals; it is part of the skill that a new member must acquire to distinguish between situations when communication based on criteria of efficiency and effectiveness is in order, and situations when the group happens to be in a sort of a collective trance during which creative comment would be strongly resented by all.

Of all the means for reinforcing socialization pressures, punitive justice—the capture, trial, and condemnation of the criminal—is still among the most dramatic and efficacious. Its main impact is not on the criminal but on the rest of the public, for whom it creates a learning situation. First, the state's action against the violator of the norm proves that the norm violated is an important one. For all those who are tempted toward rationalizing that this crime is not so serious any more, the prosecution and condemnation of the culprit guilty of the specific crime make the situation unambiguous. Furthermore, the punishment of the guilty acts as a relative reward for those who have managed to remain innocent. Relative reward is important for those who are most exposed to the temptation of delinquency. Thus, some of the lower-status groups of the community, in particular "the poor but honest," are most eager to see the criminal punished severely. This harsh punishment implies high rank for the values that "the poor but honest" are managing to implement. A great deal of criminality tends to prey on the lower classes, who have less police protection and are closer in social space to the criminal. Some sections of the upper classes, for which this type of criminality is no temptation, are likely to be more lenient toward the criminal, especially since they are rarely his victims.

A third means of reinforcing socialization is commercial entertainment, especially in that it also acts as a means of tension reduction. Some believe

75. This mechanism of social control depends on the "injustices" inherent in family identification, where both the good qualities and the defects of parents are ascribed to their children.

76. We do not mean to imply that tension management exhausts the functions or meaning of religion.

that the public, and especially children, are being socialized into criminal behavior by comic books and movies featuring violence.[77] They ignore the tension-reducing effect of catharsis and dismiss the moral message as ineffectual. On the second score, the pessimist may be right. The message of many movies and TV shows is: do not take direct action when confronted by exploitation; trust to the law to set matters right. As in much advertising, this moral propaganda touches only those who already were convinced. It gives them a greater feeling of legitimacy, by glorifying the product they have already bought. On the other hand, the movies have undoubtedly had a great influence in socializing the lower-class to middle-class standards of manners and consumption.

Integration through labelling and isolation. The unknown is often more threatening than the dangerous.[78] Consequently, one of the best means of insuring conformity and limiting deviance is to give each individual a label, a stereotype that indicates what roles he is likely to perform at what level of competence and with what motivational style. This label is provided by the symbols of social class and, within this social class, by the status group to which the individual belongs. Order is also maintained by the fact that the status group is a peer group whose members aid and protect each other in order to maintain a certain level of value achievement. For example, in factory peer groups like those described by Roethlisberger and Dickson,[79] the output of the worker actually becomes a group affair; the faster workers help the slower ones to maintain the level of production defined as a "fair day's work." In return for the protection of the status group, the individual commits himself to a certain level of performance, to shared values, and to automatic reciprocity to legitimate action by another group member. As a result, the status group becomes, both for its members and for the rest of society, a center of order and reliable performance. Members who either surpass this level of performance or consistently fail to achieve it must leave this status group for others more appropriate to them. Class membership sanctions conformity.

Thus social class isolates from one another individuals committed to different levels of performance in relation to societal values, and it reduces the traumas of uncertainty and the conflicts of incompatible role-expectation between Ego and Alter. Isolation, labelling, and reliability are the reasons that it is much less dangerous for society to have its deviants grouped in organizations of their own. To be sure, these organizations are committed to the promotion of deviance, and their unity may make them seem more noxious; but, on the other hand, their action is more predictable, and can be counteracted more reliably than can the independent actions of individual deviants.

The paradox is that society has more to fear from the anarchic deviant than it has to fear from groups promoting deviant subcultures. A good example is provided by the inexperienced criminal who takes unnecessary risks (and who is thus unpredictable from a rational standpoint) for petty gain (again, unpredictable from a rational standpoint). Once in prison, he will have a chance to learn his trade and become a fully socialized member of the underworld. Not all criminals, however, are integrated to what might be called the "industrial underworld." Some criminals are deterred by their jail experience from persevering in a life of crime, either because they perceive that society "means it," or because they see the gain from deviance as not being worth the risks. The data are rather scanty; nevertheless, it appears that perhaps one-quarter of all first-timers manage to stay out of jails for the rest of their lives.[80] The murderer of a "loved one" is a particularly good risk. Of the remainder, some join small criminal enterprises specializing in swindling, stealing furs and jewelry, etc.; and some join "syndicates" specializing in larger-scale crimes. Whether he has joined a syndicate or a "small operation," if the "unreformed" criminal did not belong to the underworld before his jail experience, he will very likely belong to it afterwards; he will then learn its scale of prestige, its mores, and its definitions of "outlaws" e.g., the

77. See Frederick Wertham, *Seduction of the Innocent* (New York: Rinehart & Co., 1954). See also Wertham's *The Circle of Guilt* (New York: Rinehart & Co., 1956), chaps. iii, iv.

78. Professor Garfinkel, at the University of California in Los Angeles, has constructed some experiments concerning personal reactions to incongruous situations: his students may suddenly thrust their faces within six inches of a person with whom they are holding a routine conversation, or insist on treating a fellow customer in a store as if he were a clerk without listening to his disclaimer. The emotion aroused in the victims of these experiments is often disproportionately intense—which leads to the conclusion that neurotic anxiety is triggered by the student's unexpected behavior. When the victim cannot immediately classify this behavior and respond accordingly to it, he is left defenseless against regressive temptations.

79. Roethlisberger and Dickson, *Management and the Worker* (Cambridge: Harvard University Press, 1941). Cf. the selection reprinted in Part Two, Section Ic.

80. Cf. Sheldon and Eleanor Glueck, *After-conduct of Discharged Offenders* (London: Macmillan and Co., 1945). The Gluecks state that about 80% or 422 of the 500 young adult offenders, about whom much information could be obtained, continued to commit crimes. In *Juvenile Delinquents Grown Up* (New York: The Commonwealth Fund, 1940) the Gluecks state "By the end of the third follow-up period (15 years), when they had reached an average age of twenty-nine years, more than a third (of 1000 juvenile delinquents) had reformed" (p. 74).

"stool-pigeon," the sex criminal, the kidnapper, and the cop-killer. And some criminals remain unsocialized, their criminal actions appearing as occasional explosions in otherwise law-abiding lives.

Righteous citizens will avoid normal contact with those individuals who have been labelled "convicts"; reciprocally, the ex-convict will restrict his interaction to other criminals. His contact with "honest people" will be limited to legitimate buyer-seller relations or to exploitative behavior in circumstances exciting a minimum of anguish and anxiety within the general public. As a matter of fact, many underworld organizations specialize in furnishing services which are illegitimate in terms of the society's values, but highly valuable in terms of tension reduction—such as prostitution, drugs, and gambling. The exploitation of the public is made through an "overcharge," which in turn acts as a penalty for use. The identifiably criminal source of the service makes clear the moral dubiousness of the gratification—which may not deter the "regular customers," but affects the potential customer on the margin of temptation.

Thus the prison often *isolates* the criminal—not only in the immediate sense of locking him up for the term of his sentence, but also in the long-range sense of making him a member of the criminal subsociety. This subsociety has regularized modes of interaction with the broader society; and, by enforcing its own norms of behavior on its members, it makes their behavior more predictable and thus controllable.

Similarly, isolation and stereotyping are still the major means of coping with the lower-class psychotic. His first admission to a mental hospital or to a prison is a rite of passage, in that it separates, forever, the patient or the prisoner from the rest of the community. He who wants to "pass" must afterward demonstrate unswerving conformity. The mental hospital defines a deviancy as "mental illness" to the patient himself, to his family, to his work companions, and to the local community Upon his discharge from the hospital, the patient has two choices: he may leave the protection of the patient role and try to "pass," which is not difficult in a large city; or he may retain the protection of the role, which permits the ex-patient to be treated as a fragile object by the community and by the patient himself. Even the "passer" will preserve the benefit of careful handling by his intimates. The result is that about 50 per cent[81] of adult psychotics who are first admissions to hospitals leave and never "need" to return there. Whether he has recommitted himself to breadwinning and family

roles, or whether his home has been transformed into a hospital away from the hospital, the psychotic has been reintegrated into society.

Besides the prison and the hospital, which both operate to label and isolate the deviant, there is also the less obvious (but not less efficacious) means provided by the fringe organization. Fringe organizations are usually involved in promoting policies that are sharply at variance with the political principles of the society or imply at least a drastic change in the hierarchy of social values. Examples of such fringe organizations are Communist and Trotskyite groups, on the Left; Silver Shirts and anti-Semitic groups, on the Right. Other fringe groups, like those particularly numerous in Southern California, profess various exotic religious revelations or more specific causes, like anti-vivisection.

These organizations attract people who feel a sense of alienation from their major role-participation—who feel that they are not receiving, from the community, the type of reciprocity to which they are entitled. Adolescents and young adults with strong value commitments but few organizational participations, technicians barred by lack of diplomas from better prestige and earning opportunities, writers without audiences, middle-aged women with weak family ties—in general, all kinds of people lacking in peer group skills and meaningful membership will feel drawn toward fringe organizations. A general characteristic of fringe organizations is the members' conviction that their group alone promotes the true values of the society; in the group, its members find a new reason for self-respect. The group turns their personal experiences of alienation into certificates of "special" value conformity. Relations with the outside world—the world of the squares, of the greedy capitalists, of the heartless persecutors of animals, of the blind sinners against the true God—must be limited to proselytizing, martyrdom, and/or direct aggression. The delinquent gang is a variation of the fringe organization.

Once they have recognized themselves and one another as members of the true faith, the members make a contract of reciprocity toward one another, either a new or long-forgotten event in their lives. Solidarity is strong, because the group must defend itself against the rest of society. Members learn reciprocity, forbearance, compliance with leadership, and frustration of immediate needs in order to serve the interest of the organization. In struggling with the wider society, the organization's leadership is compelled to be realistic when assessing possibilities for implementing the organization's

81. This is an "educated guess" derived from the Warren State figures and the author's own research.

purpose and when enforcing their decisions on the membership. They are helped in maintaining discipline by defining the situation in terms of peril or high urgency for achieving the maximum objectives. Thus the organization compels alienated personalities to experience a high intensity of interaction that will undo the motivational basis of alienation for many of the members.

The fringe organization tends to be what Goffman[82] has called a "total institution," i.e., one which includes as many of the member's roles as is possible. It often organizes recreational activities; it may even attempt to provide food, clothing, and shelter. Participation in such an organization resembles the roles the member played in the pre-oedipal nuclear family. Participation permits the member to regress to a state of great dependency and trust in a powerful "parental" figure, the organization. The initial phase is one of enthusiastic—compulsive—conformity: for the member the organization is the value incarnate, and membership gives the personality a consecration which it previously lacked. Precisely because of this consecration, the needs of the individual gain in legitimacy, and the member learns dissent—or, at least, the fact that his continued membership necessitates compromising between organizational needs and his personality needs. Like the child who discovers that his parents are not perfect, the member discovers the discrepancy between the Utopian values of the group and the limits of its organization. He realizes that the in-groupers are

neither worse nor better than the out-groupers, and any participation in out-group activities increases his resistance to the organization's tendency to monopolize his existence. Soon the member is ready to leave the organization and rejoin the ranks of the wider community. Participation in the group has served as a therapeutic experience, permitting the member to work out some oedipal and post-oedipal problems which had made it very difficult for him to assume adult status and sex roles.

Hence the high turnover in the membership of these fringe organizations: members leave either because they are cured, or because they shift to another organization in the hopeless search for a perfect group. For others, however, membership in the organization becomes a crutch indispensable for participation in breadwinning and/or homemaking roles.

Meanwhile, the fringe organization has served society in another way: it has channelled many diverse deviant motivations into a predictable pattern of deviant behavior which can be controlled by standard countermeasures. The fact that the deviance is shared by a collectivity which accepts the rules of political struggle implies that, in the last analysis, this collectivity is committed to the basic welfare of the society. In Durkheim's terms,[83] the deviant collectivity becomes an alternative pattern available if conditions should change and require a new response. For the capacity to tolerate deviance is also a measure of a society's capacity to progress.

82. Erving Goffman, "The Characteristics of Total Institutions" in *Symposium on Preventive and Social Psychiatry* (Walter Reed Army Institute of Research; Washington, D.C.: U.S. Government Printing Office, 1958). See pp. 43–84.

83. See *Rules of the Sociological Method* (Glencoe: The Free Press, 1950), reprinted in Part Three, Section D, I.

Section A

The Definition of the Situation
and the Internalization of Objects

Editorial Foreword, BY JESSE R. PITTS   *719*

1. *Society and Individual Consciousness,* BY EMILE DURKHEIM   *720*
2. *Ideas and Religious Interests,* BY MAX WEBER   *724*
3. *The Libido's Attachment to Objects,* BY SIGMUND FREUD   *729*
4. *The Ego and the Superego,* BY SIGMUND FREUD   *733*
5. *Taking the Role of the Other,* BY GEORGE H. MEAD   *739*
6. *The Four Wishes and the Definition of the Situation,* BY WILLIAM
    I. THOMAS   *741*

The Definition of the Situation and the Internalization of Objects

by Jesse R. Pitts

I<small>T SEEMED FITTING TO BEGIN</small> Part Three with a selection from the *Elementary Forms of the Religious Life* where *Durkheim* expressed his most mature view of the relation between individual and society. Society constrains the individual through the attitude of moral respect. This moral respect is not derived from intrinsic properties of the ideas that are shared, but from the fact that they are shared. Durkheim adheres to a positivistic though anti-utilitarian explanation for the attitude of moral respect. In this view, the power of the idea is derived from the reverberation of ideas within the minds of individuals assembled in large and compact groups. This sharing is often objectified through the orator who is inspired by his audience and who, in turn, becomes a symbol of group consensus. The crucial importance of this excerpt resides in the paradox of a society as a phenomenon *sui generis,* with a specific type of causality, which is nevertheless present in the minds of individuals and only there.

For *Weber,* it is not the group that determines the sacred and its particular characteristics, it is the sacred that determines the nature of the group. The answers to the problems of ultimate meaning that are given by the world religions have pervasive consequences for the forms of social organization and even for activities which seem to be remote from religious preoccupations—such as economic action. In this selection, Weber analyzes the consequences of religious interests shaped by Puritan ideas for the development of modern capitalism. This is not simple emanationism, for such ideas as Calvinistic predestination suffer many alterations in the process of becoming satisfactorily meaningful for the mass of faithful: a good example of the relationship between culture, personality, and social structure.

Freud, on the other hand, introduces the organism as a crucial component in relating the individual to his society. The organism is the source of the libido, the pleasure oriented force which drives the individual toward other individuals. This force is essentially non-rational since, of itself, it is incapable of recognizing, in the cathexes of objects, those situations which will result in the destruction of the organism or in the disease of the personality. It does not have even the wisdom of the body since libido is largely independent of metabolic needs. When this libido becomes structured into the superego, it retains essentially the non-rational characteristic; this explains the rigid and uncompromising demands of conscience. Freud has never been very clear as to how superego differentiation occurred. One theme is that the wish for the mother has to be repressed under threat of castration, and that the child transforms his hostility toward the father-interloper into wanting to be like him through reaction-formation. The hostility felt toward the father is turned against the ego when it violates the wishes of the father. A straight "lost object" explanation would have to explain why the dual parental image has to be given up before it can be internalized and how the mother's love disappears as an attribute of the superego.[1]

As distinguished from structure, the content of the superego is given by the father image, and "the masters which follow after him." On the other hand,

---

1. For the "lost object" approach, see: S. Freud, *New Introductory Lecture on Psycho-analysis* (New York: Norton, 1933), pp. 88–96, and 150.

men are bound to one another, i.e., achieve solidarity through the fact that they share the same superego identification. Here Freud and Durkheim agree: solidarity results from the sharing of certain ideas. Freud, however, has moved from a theory of constraint to a theory of internalization.

For *G. H. Mead,* the internalization of social control takes place without Freudian drama. The essence of all human experience is social; hence perception and communication are social. The internalization of the other, or as Mead puts it, the "taking the role of the other," is an intrinsic aspect of human thinking. Leadership becomes the prerogative of the multiple participator and communications facilitator. Implicit in G. H. Mead's thinking is the idea that the unit of the social system is not the "individual" but the dyadic role expectation which involves expectations from self and alter: this is the social "me."

It remained for *W. I. Thomas* to give the growing understanding of the relationship between personality and social structure one of its more workable analytical tools: the concept of *the definition of the situation.* W. I. Thomas makes more clearly than most the distinction between personality, culture, and social structure as independent but interpenetrating variables. Personality provides the wishes to be satisfied. Culture gives external objects their value. The *social definition of the situation* copes with the Darwinian competition of individuals and the needs of the community for order. It determines the terms under which values can be secured. It is the procedure for attaining simultaneously maximum order and maximum individual satisfaction, and is the backbone of social structure. In the same time, the inexorably subjective aspect of any definition of the situation opens up an avenue for the analysis of individual variations and deviance.

1. *Society and Individual Consciousness*

BY EMILE DURKHEIM

IN A GENERAL WAY, it is unquestionable that a society has all that is necessary to arouse the sensation of the divine in minds, merely by the power that it has over them; for to its members it is what a god is to his worshippers. In fact, a god is, first of all, a being whom men think of as superior to themselves, and upon whom they feel that they depend. Whether it be a conscious personality, such as Zeus or Jahveh, or merely abstract forces such as those in play in totemism, the worshipper, in the one case as in the other, believes himself held to certain manners of acting which are imposed upon him by the nature of the sacred principle with which he feels that he is in communion. Now society also gives us the sensation of a perpetual dependence. Since it has a nature which is peculiar to itself and different from our individual nature, it pursues ends which are likewise special to it; but, as it cannot attain them except through our intermediacy, it imperiously demands our aid. It re-

Reprinted from Emile Durkheim, *The Elementary Forms of Religions Life,* trans. Joseph Swan (Glencoe, Ill.: The Free Press, 1954), pp. 206–14, with the permission of The Free Press.

quires that, forgetful of our own interests, we make ourselves its servitors, and it submits us to every sort of inconvenience, privation and sacrifice, without which social life would be impossible. It is because of this that at every instant we are obliged to submit ourselves to rules of conduct and of thought which we have neither made nor desired, and which are sometimes even contrary to our most fundamental inclinations and instincts.

Even if society were unable to obtain these concessions and sacrifices from us except by a material constraint, it might awaken in us only the idea of a physical force to which we must give way of necessity, instead of that of a moral power such as religions adore. But as a matter of fact, the empire which it holds over consciences is due much less to the physical supremacy of which it has the privilege than to the moral authority with which it is invested. If we yield to its orders, it is not merely because it is strong enough to triumph over our resistance; it is primarily because it is the object of a venerable respect.

We say that an object, whether individual or collective, inspires respect when the representation expressing it in the mind is gifted with such a force that it automatically causes or inhibits actions, *without regard for any consideration relative to their useful or injurious effects.* When we obey somebody because of the moral authority which we recognize in him, we follow out his opinions, not because they seem wise, but because a certain sort of physical energy is imminent in the idea that we form of this person, which conquers our will and inclines it in the indicated direction. Respect is the emotion which we experience when we feel this interior and wholly spiritual pressure operating upon us. Then we are not determined by the advantages or inconveniences of the attitude which is prescribed or recommended to us; it is by the way in which we represent to ourselves the person recommending or prescribing it. This is why commands generally take a short, peremptory form leaving no place for hesitation; it is because, in so far as it is a command and goes by its own force, it excludes all idea of deliberation or calculation; it gets its efficacy from the intensity of the mental state in which it is placed. It is this intensity which creates what is called a moral ascendancy.

Now the ways of action to which society is strongly enough attached to impose them upon its members, are, by that very fact, marked with a distinctive sign provocative of respect. Since they are elaborated in common, the vigour with which they have been thought of by each particular mind is retained in all the other minds, and reciprocally. The representations which express them within each of us have an intensity which no purely private states of consciousness could ever attain; for they have the strength of the innumerable individual representations which have served to form each of them. It is society who speaks through the mouths of those who affirm them in our presence; it is society whom we hear in hearing them; and the voice of all has an accent which that of one alone could never have. The very violence with which society reacts, by way of blame or material suppression, against every attempted dissidence, contributes to strengthening its empire by manifesting the common conviction through this burst of ardour. In a word, when something is the object of such a state of opinion, the representation which each individual has of it gains a power of action from its origins and the conditions in which it was born, which even those feel who do not submit themselves to it. It tends to repel the representations which contradict it, and it keeps them at a distance; on the other hand, it commands those acts which will realize it, and it does so, not by a material coercion or by the perspective of something of this sort, but by the simple radiation of the mental energy which it con-

tains. It has an efficacy coming solely from its psychical properties, and it is by just this sign that moral authority is recognized. So opinion, primarily a social thing, is a source of authority, and it might even be asked whether all authority is not the daughter of opinion.[1] It may be objected that science is often the antagonist of opinion, whose errors it combats and rectifies. But it cannot succeed in this task if it does not have sufficient authority, and it can obtain this authority only from opinion itself. If a people did not have faith in science, all the scientific demonstrations in the world would be without any influence whatsoever over their minds. Even to-day, if science happened to resist a very strong current of public opinion, it would risk losing its credit there.[2]

Since it is in spiritual ways that social pressure exercises itself, it could not fail to give men the idea that outside themselves there exist one or several powers, both moral and, at the same time, efficacious, upon which they depend. They must think of these powers, at least in part, as outside themselves, for these address them in a tone of command and sometimes even order them to do violence to their most natural inclinations. It is undoubtedly true that if they were able to see that these influences which they feel emanate from society, then the mythological system of interpretations would never be born. But social action follows ways that are too circuitous and obscure, and employs psychical mechanisms that are too complex to allow the ordinary observer to see whence it comes. As long as scientific analysis does not come to teach it to them, men know well that they are acted upon, but they do not know by whom. So they must invent by

---

1. This is the case at least with all moral authority recognized as such by the group as a whole.
2. We hope that this analysis and those which follow will put an end to an inexact interpretation of our thought, from which more than one misunderstanding has resulted. Since we have made constraint the *outward sign* by which social facts can be the most easily recognized and distinguished from the facts of individual psychology, it has been assumed that according to our opinion, physical constraint is the essential thing for social life. As a matter of fact, we have never considered it more than the material and apparent expression of an interior and profound fact which is wholly ideal: this is *moral authority.* The problem of sociology— if we can speak of *a* sociological problem—consists in seeking, among the different forms of external constraint, the different sorts of moral authority corresponding to them and in discovering the causes which have determined these latter. The particular question which we are treating in this present work has as its principal object, the discovery of the form under which that particular variety of moral authority which is inherent in all that is religious has been born, and out of what elements it is made. It will be seen presently that even if we do make social pressure one of the distinctive characteristics of sociological phenomena, we do not mean to say that it is the only one. We shall show another aspect of the collective life, nearly opposite to the preceding one, but none the less real.

themselves the idea of these powers with which they feel themselves in connection, and from that, we are able to catch a glimpse of the way by which they were led to represent them under forms that are really foreign to their nature and to transfigure them by thought.

But a god is not merely an authority upon whom we depend; it is a force upon which our strength relies. The man who has obeyed his god and who, for this reason, believes the god is with him, approaches the world with confidence and with the feeling of an increased energy. Likewise, social action does not confine itself to demanding sacrifices, privations and efforts from us. For the collective force is not entirely outside of us; it does not act upon us wholly from without; but rather, since society cannot exist except in and through individual consciousness,[3] this force must also penetrate us and organize itself within us; it thus becomes an integral part of our being and by that very fact this is elevated and magnified.

There are occasions when this strengthening and vivifying action of society is especially apparent. In the midst of an assembly animated by a common passion, we become susceptible of acts and sentiments of which we are incapable when reduced to our own forces; and when the assembly is dissolved and when, finding ourselves alone again, we fall back to our ordinary level, we are then able to measure the height to which we have been raised above ourselves. History abounds in examples of this sort. It is enough to think of the night of the Fourth of August, 1789, when an assembly was suddenly led to an act of sacrifice and abnegation which each of its members had refused the day before, and at which they were all surprised the day after. This is why all parties, political, economic or confessional, are careful to have periodical reunions where their members may revivify their common faith by manifesting it in common. To strengthen those sentiments which, if left to themselves, would soon weaken, it is sufficient to bring those who hold them together and to put them into closer and more active relations with one another. This is the explanation of the particular attitude of a man speaking to a crowd, at least if he has succeeded in entering into communion with it. His language has a grandiloquence that would be ridiculous in ordinary circumstances; his gestures show a certain domination; his very thought is impatient of all rules, and easily falls into all sorts of excesses. It is because he feels within him an abnormal oversupply of force which overflows and tries to burst

out from him; sometimes he even has the feeling that he is dominated by a moral force which is greater than he and of which he is only the interpreter. It is by this trait that we are able to recognize what has often been called the demon of oratorical inspiration. Now this exceptional increase of force is something very real; it comes to him from the very group which he addresses. The sentiments provoked by his words come back to him, but enlarged and amplified, and to this degree they strengthen his own sentiment. The passionate energies he arouses re-echo within him and quicken his vital tone. It is no longer a simple individual who speaks; it is a group incarnate and personified.

Beside these passing and intermittent states, there are other more durable ones, where this strengthening influence of society makes itself felt with greater consequences and frequently even with greater brilliancy. There are periods in history when, under the influence of some great collective shock, social interactions have become much more frequent and active. Men look for each other and assemble together more than ever. That general effervescence results which is characteristic of revolutionary or creative epochs. Now this greater activity results in a general stimulation of individual forces. Men see more and differently now than in normal times. Changes are not merely of shades and degrees; men become different. The passions moving them are of such an intensity that they cannot be satisfied except by violent and unrestrained actions, actions of superhuman heroism or of bloody barbarism. This is what explains the Crusades, for example, or many of the scenes, either sublime or savage, of the French Revolution. Under the influence of the general exaltation, we see the most mediocre and inoffensive bourgeois become either a hero or a butcher. And so clearly are all these mental processes the ones that are also at the root of religion that the individuals themselves have often pictured the pressure before which they thus gave way in a distinctly religious form. The Crusaders believed that they felt God present in the midst of them, enjoining them to go to the conquest of the Holy Land; Joan of Arc believed that she obeyed celestial voices.

But it is not only in exceptional circumstances that this stimulating action of society makes itself felt; there is not, so to speak, a moment in our lives when some current of energy does not come to us from without. The man who has done his duty finds, in the manifestations of every sort expressing the sympathy, esteem or affection which his fellows have for him, a feeling of comfort, of which he does not ordinarily take account, but which sustains him, none the less. The sentiments which so-

---

3. Of course this does not mean to say that the collective consciousness does not have distinctive characteristics of its own.

ciety has for him raise the sentiments which he has for himself. Because he is in moral harmony with his comrades, he has more confidence, courage and boldness in action, just like the believer who thinks that he feels the regard of his god turned graciously towards him. It thus produces, as it were, a perpetual sustenance for our moral nature. Since this varies with a multitude of external circumstances, as our relations with the groups about us are more or less active and as these groups themselves vary, we cannot fail to feel that this moral support depends upon an external cause; but we do not perceive where this cause is nor what it is. So we ordinarily think of it under the form of a moral power which, though immanent in us, represents within us something not ourselves: this is the moral conscience, of which, by the way, men have never made even a slightly distinct representation except by the aid of religious symbols.

In addition to these free forces which are constantly coming to renew our own, there are others which are fixed in the methods and traditions which we employ. We speak a language that we did not make; we use instruments that we did not invent; we invoke rights that we did not found; a treasury of knowledge is transmitted to each generation that it did not gather itself, etc. It is to society that we owe these varied benefits of civilization, and if we do not ordinarily see the source from which we get them, we at least know that they are not our own work. Now it is these things that give man his own place among things; a man is a man only because he is civilized. So he could not escape the feeling that outside of him there are active causes from which he gets the characteristic attributes of his nature and which, as benevolent powers, assist him, protect him and assure him of a privileged fate. And of course he must attribute to these powers a dignity corresponding to the great value of the good things he attributes to them.

Thus the environment in which we live seems to us to be peopled with forces that are at once imperious and helpful, august and gracious, and with which we have relations. Since they exercise over us a pressure of which we are conscious, we are forced to localize them outside ourselves, just as we do for the objective causes of our sensations. But the sentiments which they inspire in us differ in nature from those which we have for simple visible objects. As long as these latter are reduced to their empirical characteristics as shown in ordinary experience, and as long as the religious imagination has not metamorphosed them, we entertain for them no feeling which resembles respect, and they contain within them nothing that is able to raise us outside ourselves. Therefore, the repre-

sentations which express them appear to us to be very different from those aroused in us by collective influences. The two form two distinct and separate mental states in our consciousness, just as do the two forms of life to which they correspond. Consequently, we get the impression that we are in relations with two distinct sorts of reality and that a sharply drawn line of demarcation separates them from each other: on the one hand is the world of profane things, on the other, that of sacred things.

Also, in the present day just as much as in the past, we see society constantly creating sacred things out of ordinary ones. If it happens to fall in love with a man and if it thinks it has found in him the principal aspirations that move it, as well as the means of satisfying them, this man will be raised above the others and, as it were, deified. Opinion will invest him with a majesty exactly analogous to that protecting the gods. This is what has happened to so many sovereigns in whom their age had faith: if they were not made gods, they were at least regarded as direct representatives of the deity. And the fact that it is society alone which is the author of these varieties of apotheosis, is evident since it frequently chances to consecrate men thus who have no right to it from their own merit. The simple deference inspired by men invested with high social functions is not different in nature from religious respect. It is expressed by the same movements: a man keeps at a distance from a high personage; he approaches him only with precautions; in conversing with him, he uses other gestures and language than those used with ordinary mortals. The sentiment felt on these occasions is so closely related to the religious sentiment that many peoples have confounded the two. In order to explain the consideration accorded to princes, nobles and political chiefs, a sacred character has been attributed to them. In Melanesia and Polynesia, for example, it is said that an influential man has *mana,* and that his influence is due to this *mana.* However, it is evident that his situation is due solely to the importance attributed to him by public opinion. Thus the moral power conferred by opinion and that with which sacred beings are invested are at bottom of a single origin and made up of the same elements. That is why a single word is able to designate the two.

In addition to men, society also consecrates things, especially ideas. If a belief is unanimously shared by a people, then, for the reason which we pointed out above, it is forbidden to touch it, that is to say, to deny it or to contest it. Now the prohibition of criticism is an interdiction like the others and proves the presence of something sacred. Even to-day, howsoever great may be the liberty which we accord to others, a man who should totally deny progress or ridicule the human ideal to which modern societies are attached, would produce the effect of a sacrilege. There is at least one principle which those the most devoted to the free examination of everything tend to place above discussion and to regard as untouchable, that is to say, as sacred: this is the very principle of free examination.

This aptitude of society for setting itself up as a god or for creating gods was never more apparent than during the first years of the French Revolution. At this time, in fact, under the influence of the general enthusiasm, things purely laïcal by nature were transformed by public opinion into sacred things: these were the Fatherland, Liberty, Reason. A religion tended to become established which had its dogmas, symbols, altars and feasts. It was to these spontaneous aspirations that the cult of Reason and the Supreme Being attempted to give a sort of official satisfaction. It is true that this religious renovation had only an ephemeral duration. But that was because the patriotic enthusiasm which at first transported the masses soon relaxed. The cause being gone, the effect could not remain. But this experiment, though short-lived, keeps all its sociological interest. It remains true that in one determined case we have seen society and its essential ideas become, directly and with no transfiguration of any sort, the object of a veritable cult.

All these facts allow us to catch glimpses of how the clan was able to awaken within its members the idea that outside of them there exist forces which dominate them and at the same time sustain them, that is to say in fine, religious forces: it is because there is no society with which the primitive is more directly and closely connected. The bonds uniting him to the tribe are much more lax and more feebly felt. Although this is not at all strange or foreign to him, it is with the people of his own clan that he has the greatest number of things in common; it is the action of this group that he feels the most directly; so it is this also which, in preference to all others, should express itself in religious symbols.

But this first explanation has been too general, for it is applicable to every sort of society indifferently, and consequently to every sort of religion. Let us attempt to determine exactly what form this collective action takes in the clan and how it arouses the sensation of sacredness there. For there is no place where it is more easily observable or more apparent in its results.

2. *Ideas and Religious Interests*

BY MAX WEBER

The Religious Foundations of Worldly Asceticism

IT WOULD ALMOST SEEM as though we had best completely ignore both the dogmatic foundations and the ethical theory and confine our attention to the moral practice so far as it can be determined. That, however, is not true. The various different dogmatic roots of ascetic morality did no doubt die out after terrible struggles. But the original connection with those dogmas has left behind

Reprinted from Max Weber, *The Protestant Ethic and the Spirit of Capitalism*, trans. Talcott Parsons (New York: Charles Scribner's Sons, 1930), pp. 97, 105–7, 108–10, 111–12, 115, 117, 121–22, 124–25, 156–59, 163–64, 170–72, with the permission of Charles Scribner's Sons and George Allen and Unwin, Ltd.

important traces in the later undogmatic ethics; moreover, only the knowledge of the original body of ideas can help us to understand the connection of that morality with the idea of the after-life which absolutely dominated the most spiritual men of that time. Without its power, overshadowing everything else, no moral awakening which seriously influenced practical life came into being in that period.

We are naturally not concerned with the question of what was theoretically and officially taught in the ethical compendia of the time, however much practical significance this may have had through the influence of Church discipline, pastoral work, and preaching. We are interested rather in something entirely different: the influence of those psychological sanctions which, originating in religious belief and the practice of religion, gave a direction to practical conduct and held the individual to it.

* * *

That great historic process in the development of religions, the elimination of magic from the world which had begun with the old Hebrew prophets and, in conjunction with Hellenistic scientific thought, had repudiated all magical means to salvation as superstition and sin, came here to its logical conclusion. The genuine Puritan even rejected all signs of religious ceremony at the grave and buried his nearest and dearest without song or ritual in order that no superstition, no trust in the effects of magical and sacramental forces on salvation, should creep in.

There was not only no magical means of attaining the grace of God for those to whom God had decided to deny it, but no means whatever. Combined with the harsh doctrines of the absolute transcendentality of God and the corruption of everything pertaining to the flesh, this inner isolation of the individual contains, on the one hand, the reason for the entirely negative attitude of Puritanism to all the sensuous and emotional elements in culture and in religion, because they are of no use toward salvation and promote sentimental illusions and idolatrous superstitions. Thus it provides a basis for a fundamental antagonism to sensuous culture of all kinds. On the other hand, it forms one of the roots of that disillusioned and pessimistically inclined individualism which can even to-day be identified in the national characters and the institutions of the peoples with a Puritan past, in such a striking contrast to the quite different spectacles through which the Enlightenment later looked upon men. We can clearly identify the traces of the influence of the doctrine of predestination in the elementary forms of conduct and attitude toward life in the era with which we are concerned, even where its authority as a dogma was on the decline. It was in fact only the most extreme form of that exclusive trust in God in which we are here interested. It comes out for instance in the strikingly frequent repetition, especially in the English Puritan literature, of warnings against any trust in the aid of friendship of men. Even the amiable Baxter counsels deep distrust of even one's closest friend, and Bailey directly exhorts to trust no one and to say nothing compromising to anyone. Only God should be your confidant. In striking contrast to Lutheranism, this attitude toward life was also connected with the quiet disappearance of the private confession, of which Calvin was suspicious only on account of its possible sacramental misinterpretation, from all the regions of fully developed Calvinism. That was an occurrence of the greatest importance. In the first place it is a symptom of the type of influence this religion

exercised. Further, however, it was a psychological stimulus to the development of their ethical attitude. The means to a periodical discharge of the emotional sense of sin was done away with.

Of the consequences for the ethical conduct of everyday life we speak later. But for the general religious situation of a man the consequences are evident. In spite of the necessity of membership in the true Church for salvation, the Calvinist's intercourse with his God was carried on in deep spiritual isolation. To see the specific results of this peculiar atmosphere, it is only necessary to read Bunyan's *Pilgrim's Progress,* by far the most widely read book of the whole Puritan literature. In the description of Christian's attitude after he had realized that he was living in the City of Destruction and he had received the call to take up his pilgrimage to the celestial city, wife and children cling to him, but stopping his ears with his fingers and crying, "life, eternal life," he staggers forth across the fields. No refinement could surpass the naïve feeling of the tinker who, writing in his prison cell, earned the applause of a believing world, in expressing the emotions of the faithful Puritan, thinking only of his own salvation.

* * *

It seems at first a mystery how the undoubted superiority of Calvinism in social organization can be connected with this tendency to tear the individual away from the closed ties with which he is bound to this world. But, however strange it may seem, it follows from the peculiar form which the Christian brotherly love was forced to take under the pressure of the inner isolation of the individual through the Calvinistic faith. In the first place it follows dogmatically. The world exists to serve the glorification of God and for that purpose alone. The elected Christian is in the world only to increase this glory of God by fulfilling His commandments to the best of his ability. But God requires social achievement of the Christian because He wills that social life shall be organized according to His commandments, in accordance with that purpose. The social activity of the Christian in the world is solely activity *in majorem gloriam Dei*. This character is hence shared by labour in a calling which serves the mundane life of the community. Even in Luther we found specialized labour in callings justified in terms of brotherly love. But what for him remained an uncertain, purely intellectual suggestion became for the Calvinists a characteristic element in their ethical system. Brotherly love, since it may only be practised for the glory of God and not in the service of the flesh, is expressed in the first place in the fulfilment of the daily tasks given by the *lex naturae;* and in the process this fulfilment assumes a peculiarly objective and impersonal character, that of service in the interest of the rational organization of our social environment. For the wonderfully purposeful organization and arrangement of this cosmos is, according both to the revelation of the Bible and to natural intuition, evidently designed by God to serve the utility of the human race. This makes labour in the service of impersonal social usefulness appear to promote the glory of God and hence to be willed by Him. The complete elimination of the theodicy problem and of all those questions about the meaning of the world and of life, which have tortured others, was as self-evident to the Puritan as, for quite different reasons, to the Jew, and even in a certain sense to all the non-mystical types of Christian religion.

To this economy of forces Calvinism added another tendency which worked in the same direction. The conflict between the individual and the ethic (in Sören Kierkegaard's sense) did not exist for Calvinism, although it placed the individual entirely on his own responsibility in religious matters. This is not the place to analyse the reasons for this fact, or its significance for the political and economic rationalism of Calvinism. The source of the utilitarian character of Calvinistic ethics lies here, and important peculiarities of the Calvinistic idea of the calling were derived from the same source as well. But for the moment we must return to the special consideration of the doctrine of predestination.

For us the decisive problem is: How was this doctrine borne in an age to which the after-life was not only more important, but in many ways also more certain, than all the interests of life in this world? The question, Am I one of the elect? must sooner or later have arisen for every believer and have forced all other interests into the background. And how can I be sure of this state of grace?

*   *   *

It was impossible, at least so far as the question of a man's own state of grace arose, to be satisfied with Calvin's trust in the testimony of the expectant faith resulting from grace, even though the orthodox doctrine had never formally abandoned that criterion. Above all, practical pastoral work, which had immediately to deal with all the suffering caused by the doctrine, could not be satisfied. It met these difficulties in various ways. So far as predestination was not reinterpreted, toned down, or fundamentally abandoned, two principal, mutually connected, types of pastoral advice appear. On the one hand it is held to be an absolute duty to consider oneself chosen, and to combat all doubts as temptation of the devil, since lack of self-confidence is the result of insufficient faith, hence of imperfect grace. The exhortation of the apostle to make fast one's own call is here interpreted as a duty to attain certainty of one's own election and justification in the daily struggle of life. In the place of the humble sinners to whom Luther promises grace if they trust themselves to God in penitent faith are bred those self-confident saints whom we can rediscover in the hard Puritan merchants of the heroic age of capitalism and in isolated instances down to the present. On the other hand, in order to attain that self-confidence intense worldly activity is recommended as the most suitable means. It and it alone disperses religious doubts and gives the certainty of grace.

*   *   *

In practice this means that God helps those who help themselves. Thus the Calvinist, as it is sometimes put, himself creates his own salvation, or, as would be more correct, the conviction of it. But this creation cannot, as in Catholicism, consist in a gradual accumulation of individual good works to one's credit, but rather in a systematic self-control which at every moment stands before the inexorable alternative, chosen or damned. This brings us to a very important point in our investigation.

*   *   *

The rationalization of the world, the elimination of magic as a means to salvation, the Catholics had not carried nearly so far as the Puritans (and before them the Jews) had done. To the Catholic the absolution of his Church was a compensation for his own imperfection. The priest was a magician who performed the miracle of transubstantiation, and who held the key to eternal life in his hand. One could turn to him in grief and penitence. He dispensed atonement, hope of grace, certainty of forgiveness, and thereby granted release from that tremendous tension to which the Calvinist was doomed by an inexorable fate, admitting of no mitigation. For him such friendly and human comforts did not exist. He could not hope to atone for hours of weakness or of thoughtlessness by increased good will at other times, as the Catholic or even the Lutheran could. The God of Calvinism demanded of his believers not single good works, but a life of good works combined into a unified system. There was no place for the very human Catholic cycle of sin, repentance, atonement, release, followed by renewed sin. Nor was there any balance of merit for a life as a whole which could be adjusted by temporal punishments or the Churches' means of grace.

The moral conduct of the average man was thus deprived of its planless and unsystematic character and subjected to a consistent method for conduct as a whole.

*   *   *

Sebastian Franck struck the central characteristic of this type of religion when he saw the significance of the Reformation in the fact that now every Christian had to be a monk all his life. The drain of asceticism from everyday worldly life had been stopped by a dam, and those passionately spiritual natures which had formerly supplied the highest type of monk were now forced to pursue their ascetic ideals within mundane occupations.

But in the course of its development Calvinism added something positive to this, the idea of the necessity of proving one's faith in worldly activity. Therein it gave the broader groups of religiously inclined people a positive incentive to asceticism. By founding its ethic in the doctrine of predestination, it substituted for the spiritual aristocracy of monks outside of and above the world the spiritual aristocracy of the predestined saints of God within the world. It was an aristocracy which, with its *character indelebilis,* was divided from the eternally damned remainder of humanity by a more impassable and in its invisibility more terrifying gulf, than separated the monk of the Middle Ages from the rest of the world about him, a gulf which penetrated all social relations with its sharp brutality. This consciousness of divine grace of the elect and holy was accompanied by an attitude toward the sin of one's neighbour, not of sympathetic understanding based on consciousness of one's own weakness, but of hatred and contempt for him as an enemy of God bearing the signs of eternal damnation.

* * *

As he observed his own conduct, the later Puritan also observed that of God and saw His finger in all the details of life. And, contrary to the strict doctrine of Calvin, he always knew why God took this or that measure. The process of sanctifying life could thus almost take on the character of a business enterprise. A thoroughgoing Christianization of the whole of life was the consequence of this methodical quality of ethical conduct into which Calvinism as distinct from Lutheranism forced men. That this rationality was decisive in its influence on practical life must always be borne in mind in order rightly to understand the influence of Calvinism.

Asceticism and the Spirit of Capitalism

Baxter was a Presbyterian and an apologist of the Westminster Synod, but at the same time, like so many of the best spirits of his time, gradually grew away from the dogmas of pure Calvinism. At heart he opposed Cromwell's usurpation as he would any revolution. He was unfavourable to the sects and the fanatical enthusiasm of the saints, but was very broad-minded about external peculiarities and objective towards his opponents. He sought his field of labour most especially in the practical promotion of the moral life through the Church. In the pursuit of this end, as one of the most successful ministers known to history, he placed his services at the disposal of the Parliamentary Government, of Cromwell, and of the Restoration, until he retired from office under the last, before St. Bartholomew's day. His *Christian Directory* is the most complete compendium of Puritan ethics, and is continually adjusted to the practical experiences of his own ministerial activity. In comparison we shall make use of Spener's *Theologische Bedenken,* as representative of German Pietism, Barclay's *Apology* for the Quakers, and some other representatives of ascetic ethics, which, however, in the interest of space, will be limited as far as possible.

* * *

Examples of the condemnation of the pursuit of money and goods may be gathered without end from Puritan writings, and may be contrasted with the late mediæval ethical literature, which was much more open-minded on this point.

Moreover, these doubts were meant with perfect seriousness; only it is necessary to examine them somewhat more closely in order to understand their true ethical significance and implications. The real moral objection is to relaxation in the security of possession, the enjoyment of wealth with the consequence of idleness and the temptations of the flesh, above all of distraction from the pursuit of a righteous life. In fact, it is only because possession involves this danger of relaxation that it is objectionable at all. For the saints' everlasting rest is in the next world; on earth man must, to be certain of his state of grace, "do the works of him who sent him, as long as it is yet day." Not leisure and enjoyment, but only activity serves to increase the glory of God, according to the definite manifestations of His will.

Waste of time is thus the first and in principle the deadliest of sins. The span of human life is infinitely short and precious to make sure of one's own election. Loss of time through sociability, idle talk, luxury, even more sleep than is necessary for health, six to at most eight hours, is worthy of absolute moral condemnation. It does not yet hold, with Franklin, that time is money, but the proposition is true in a certain spiritual sense. It is infinitely valuable because every hour lost is lost to labour for the glory of God. Thus inactive contemplation is also valueless, or even directly reprehensible if it is at the expense of one's daily work. For it is less pleasing to God than the active performance of His will in a calling. Besides, Sunday is provided for that, and, according to Baxter, it is always those who are not diligent in their callings who have no time for God when the occasion demands it.

Accordingly, Baxter's principal work is dominated by the continually repeated, often almost passionate preaching of hard, continuous bodily or mental labour. It is due to a combination of two different motives. Labour is, on the one hand, an approved ascetic technique, as it always has been in the Western Church, in sharp contrast not only to the Orient but to almost all monastic rules the world over. It is in particular the specific defence against all those temptations which Puritanism united under the name of the unclean life, whose rôle for it was by no means small. The sexual asceticism of Puritanism differs only in degree, not in fundamental principle, from that of monasticism; and on account of the Puritan conception of marriage, its practical influence is more far-reaching than that of the latter. For sexual intercourse is permitted, even within marriage, only as the means willed by God for the increase of His glory according to the commandment, "Be fruitful and multiply." Along with a moderate vegetable diet and cold baths, the same prescription is given for all sexual temptations as is used against religious doubts and a sense of moral unworthiness: "Work hard in your calling." But the most important thing was that even beyond that labour came to be considered in itself the end of life, ordained as such by God. St. Paul's "He who will not work shall not eat" holds unconditionally for everyone. Unwillingness to work is symptomatic of the lack of grace.

*   *   *

Wealth is thus bad ethically only in so far as it is a temptation to idleness and sinful enjoyment of life, and its acquisition is bad only when it is with the purpose of later living merrily and without care. But as a performance of duty in a calling it is not only morally permissible, but actually enjoined. The parable of the servant who was rejected because he did not increase the talent which was entrusted to him seemed to say so directly. To wish to be poor was, it was often argued, the same as wishing to be unhealthy; it is objectionable as a glorification of works and derogatory to the glory of God. Especially begging, on the part of one able to work, is not only the sin of slothfulness, but a violation of the duty of brotherly love according to the Apostle's own word.

The emphasis on the ascetic importance of a fixed calling provided an ethical justification of the modern specialized division of labour. In a similar way the providential interpretation of profit-making justified the activities of the business man. The superior indulgence of the *seigneur* and the parvenu ostenta-

tion of the *nouveau riche* are equally detestable to asceticism. But, on the other hand, it has the highest ethical appreciation of the sober, middle-class, self-made man. "God blesseth His trade" is a stock remark about those good men who had successfully followed the divine hints. The whole power of the God of the Old Testament, who rewards His people for their obedience in this life, necessarily exercised a similar influence on the Puritan who, following Baxter's advice, compared his own state of grace with that of the heroes of the Bible, and in the process interpreted the statements of the Scriptures as the articles of a book of statutes.

*   *   *

Man is only a trustee of the goods which have come to him through God's grace. He must, like the servant in the parable, give an account of every penny entrusted to him, and it is at least hazardous to spend any of it for a purpose which does not serve the glory of God but only one's own enjoyment. What person, who keeps his eyes open, has not met representatives of this view-point even in the present? The idea of a man's duty to his possessions, to which he subordinates himself as an obedient steward, or even as an acquisitive machine, bears with chilling weight on his life. The greater the possessions the heavier, if the ascetic attitude toward life stands the test, the feeling of responsibility for them, for holding them undiminished for the glory of God and increasing them by restless effort. The origin of this type of life also extends in certain roots, like so many aspects of the spirit of capitalism, back into the Middle Ages. But it was in the ethic of ascetic Protestantism that it first found a consistent ethical foundation. Its significance for the development of capitalism is obvious.

This worldly Protestant asceticism, as we may recapitulate up to this point, acted powerfully against the spontaneous enjoyment of possessions; it restricted consumption, especially of luxuries. On the other hand, it had the psychological effect of freeing the acquisition of goods from the inhibitions of traditionalistic ethics. It broke the bonds of the impulse of acquisition in that it not only legalized it, but (in the sense discussed) looked upon it as directly willed by God. The campaign against the temptations of the flesh, and the dependence on external things, was, as besides the Puritans the great Quaker apologist Barclay expressly says, not a struggle against the rational acquisition, but against the irrational use of wealth.

But this irrational use was exemplified in the outward forms of luxury which their code condemned as idolatry of the flesh, however natural they had appeared to the feudal mind. On the other hand, they approved the rational and utilitarian uses of wealth which were willed by God for the needs of the individual and the community. They did not wish to impose mortification on the man of wealth, but the use of his means for necessary and practical things. The idea of comfort characteristically limits the extent of ethically permissible expenditures. It is naturally no accident that the development of a manner of living consistent with that idea may be observed earliest and most clearly among the most consistent representatives of this whole attitude toward life. Over against the glitter and ostentation of feudal magnificence which, resting on an unsound economic basis, prefers a sordid elegance to a sober simplicity, they set the clean and solid comfort of the middle-class home as an ideal.

On the side of the production of private wealth, asceticism condemned both dishonesty and impulsive avarice. What was condemned as covetousness, Mammonism, etc., was the pursuit of riches for their own sake. For wealth in itself was a temptation. But here asceticism was the power "which ever seeks the good but ever creates evil"; what was evil in its sense was possession and its temptations. For, in conformity with the Old Testament and in analogy to the ethical valuation of good works, asceticism looked upon the pursuit of wealth as an end in itself as highly reprehensible; but the attainment of it as a fruit of labour in a calling was a sign of God's blessing. And even more important: the religious valuation of restless, continuous, systematic work in a worldly calling, as the highest means to asceticism, and at the same time the surest and most evident proof of rebirth and genuine faith, must have been the most powerful conceivable lever for the expansion of that attitude toward life which we have here called the spirit of capitalism.

3. *The Libido's Attachment to Objects*

BY SIGMUND FREUD

IN EVERY WAY analogous to *hunger,* libido is the force by means of which the instinct, in this case the sexual instinct, as, with hunger, the nutritional instinct, achieves expression.

Keep in view at the moment the idea that the sexual life—the *libido-function,* as we call it—does not first spring up in its final form, does not even expand along the lines of its earliest forms, but goes through a series of successive phases unlike one another; in short, that many changes occur in it, like those in the development of the caterpillar into the butterfly. The turning-point of this development is the *subordination of all the sexual component-instincts under the primacy of the genital zone* and, together with this, the enrolment of sexuality in the service of the reproductive function. Before this happens the sexual life is, so to say, disparate—independent activities of single component-impulses each seeking *organ-pleasure* (pleasure in a bodily organ). This anarchy is modified by attempts at

Reprinted from Sigmund Freud, *Introductory Lectures on Psychoanalysis,* trans. Joan Riviere (London: George Allen & Unwin, 1922), pp. 263, 276, 344–52, with the permission of George Allen & Unwin and W. W. Norton & Company, Inc.

pre-genital "organizations," of which the chief is the sadistic-anal phase, behind which is the oral, perhaps the most primitive. In addition there are the various processes, about which little is known as yet, which effect the transition from one stage of organization to the next above it. Of what significance this long journey over so many stages in the development of the libido is for comprehension of the neuroses we shall learn later on.

The Theory of the Libido: Narcissism

We have repeatedly, and again quite recently, referred to the distinction between the sexual and the ego-instincts. First of all, repression showed how they can oppose each other, how the sexual instincts are then apparently brought to submission, and required to procure their satisfaction by circuitous regressive paths, where in their impregnability they obtain compensation for their defeat. Then it appeared that from the outset they each have a different relation to the task-mistress, Necessity, so that their developments are different and they acquire different attitudes to the reality-principle. Finally we believe we can observe that the sexual instincts are connected by much closer ties with the affective state of anxiety than are the ego-instincts—a conclusion which in one important point only still seems incomplete. In support of it we may bring forward the further remarkable fact that want of satisfaction of hunger or thirst, the two most elemental of the self-preservative instincts, never results in conversion of them into anxiety, whereas the conversion of unsatisfied libido into anxiety is, as we have heard, a very well-known and frequently observed phenomenon.

Our justification for distinguishing between sexual and ego-instincts can surely not be contested; it is indeed assumed by the existence of the sexual instinct as a special activity in the individual. The only question is what significance is to be attached to this distinction, how radical and decisive we intend to consider it. The answer to this depends upon what we can ascertain about the extent to which the sexual instincts, both in their bodily and their mental manifestations, conduct themselves differently from the other instincts which we set against them; and how important the results arising from these differences are found to be. We have of course no motive for maintaining any difference in the fundamental nature of the two groups of instincts, and, by the way, it would be difficult to apprehend any. They both present themselves to us merely as descriptions of the sources of energy in the individual, and the discussion whether fundamentally they are one, or essentially different, and if one, when they became separated from each other, cannot be carried through on the basis of these concepts alone, but must be grounded on the biological facts underlying them. At present we know too little about this, and even if we knew more it would not be relevant to the task of psycho-analysis.

We should clearly also profit very little by emphasizing the primordial unity of all the instincts, as Jung has done, and describing all the energies which flow from them as "libido." We should then be compelled to speak of sexual and asexual libido, since the sexual function is not to be eliminated from the field of mental life by any such device. The name libido, however, remains properly reserved for the instinctual forces of the sexual life, as we have hitherto employed it.

In my opinion, therefore, the question how far the quite justifiable distinction between sexual and self-preservative instincts is to be carried has not much importance for psycho-analysis, nor is psycho-analysis competent to deal with it. From the biological point of view there are certainly various indications that the distinction is important. For the sexual function is the only function of a living organism which extends beyond the individual and secures its connection with its species. It is undeniable that the exercise of this function does not always bring advantage to the individual, as do his other activities, but that for the sake of an exceptionally high degree of pleasure he is involved by this function in dangers which jeopardize his life and often enough exact it. Quite peculiar metabolic processes, different from all others, are probably required in order to preserve a portion of the individual's life as a disposition for posterity. And finally, the individual organism that regards itself as first in importance and its sexuality as a means like any other to its own satisfaction is from a biological point of view only an episode in a series of generations, a short-lived appendage to a germ-plasm which is endowed with virtual immortality, comparable to the temporary holder of an entail that will survive his death.

We are not concerned with such far-reaching considerations, however, in the psycho-analytic elucidation of the neuroses. By means of following up the distinction between the sexual and the ego-instincts we have gained the key to comprehension of the group of transference neuroses. We were able to trace back their origin to a fundamental situation in which the sexual instincts had come into conflict with the self-preservative instincts, or—to express it biologically, though at the same time less exactly—in which the ego in its capacity of independent individual organism had entered into opposition with itself in its other capacity as a member of a series of generations. Such a dissociation perhaps only exists in man, so that, taken all in all, his superiority over the other animals may come down to his capacity for neurosis. The excessive development of his libido and the rich elaboration of his mental life (perhaps directly made possible by it) seem to constitute the conditions which give rise to a conflict of this kind. It is at any rate clear that these are the conditions under which man has progressed so greatly beyond what he has in common with the animals, so that his capacity for neurosis would merely be the obverse of his capacity for cultural development. However, these again are but speculations which distract us from the task in hand.

Our work so far has been conducted on the assumption that the manifestations of the sexual and the ego-instincts can be distinguished from one another. In the transference neuroses this is possible without any difficulty. We called the investments of energy directed by the ego towards the object of its sexual desires "libido," and all the other investments proceeding from the self-preservative instincts its "interest"; and by following up the investments with libido, their transformations, and their final fates, we were able to acquire our first insight into the workings of the forces in mental life. The transference neuroses offered the best material for this exploration. The ego, however,—its composition out of various organizations with their structure and mode of functioning—remained undiscovered; we were led to believe that analysis of other neurotic disturbances would be required before light could be gained on these matters.

The extension of psycho-analytic conceptions on to these other affections was begun in early days. Already in 1908 K. Abraham expressed the view after a discussion with me that the main characteristic of dementia præcox (reckoned as one of the psychoses) is that in this disease *the investments of objects with libido is lacking.* (*The Psycho-Sexual Differences between Hysteria and Dementia Præcox.*) But then the question arose: what happens to the libido of dementia patients when it is diverted from its objects? Abraham did not hesitate to answer that it is turned back upon the ego, and that *this reflex reversion of it is the source of the delusions of grandeur in dementia præcox.* The delusion of grandeur is in every way comparable to the well-known overestimation of the object in a love-relationship. Thus we came for the first time to understand a feature of a psychotic affection by bringing it into relation to the normal mode of loving in life.

I will tell you at once that these early views of Abraham's have been retained in psycho-analysis and have become the basis of our position regarding the psychoses. We became slowly accustomed to the conception that the libido, which we find attached to certain objects and which is the expression of a desire to gain some satisfaction in these objects, can also abandon these objects and set the ego itself in their place; and gradually this view developed itself more and more consistently. The name for this utilization of the libido—NARCISSISM—we borrowed from a perversion described by P. Näcke, in which an adult individual lavishes upon his own body all the caresses usually expended only upon a sexual object other than himself.

Reflection then at once disclosed that if a fixation of this kind to the subject's own body and his own person can occur it cannot be an entirely exceptional or meaningless phenomenon. On the contrary, it is probable that this *narcissism* is the universal original condition, out of which *object-love* develops later without thereby necessarily effecting a disappearance of the narcissism. One also had to remember the evolution of object-libido, in which to begin with many of the sexual impulses are gratified on the child's own body—as we say, auto-erotically—and that this capacity for auto-eroticism

accounts for the backwardness of sexuality in learning to conform to the reality-principle. Thus it appeared that auto-eroticism was the sexual activity of the narcissistic phase of direction of the libido.

To put it briefly, we formed an idea of the relation between the ego-libido and the object-libido which I can illustrate to you by a comparison taken from zoology. Think of the simplest forms of life consisting of a little mass of only slightly differentiated protoplasmic substances. They extend protrusions which are called pseudopodia into which the protoplasm overflows. They can, however, again withdraw these extensions of themselves and re-form themselves into a mass. We compare this extending of protrusions to the radiation of libido on to the objects, while the greatest volume of libido may yet remain within the ego; we infer that under normal conditions ego-libido can transform itself into object-libido without difficulty and that this can again subsequently be absorbed into the ego.

*   *   *

Two observations are in place here. First, how is the concept "narcissism" distinguished from "egoism"? In my opinion, narcissism is the libidinal complement of egoism. When one speaks of egoism one is thinking only of the *interests* of the person concerned, narcissism relates also to the satisfaction of his libidinal needs. It is possible to follow up the two separately for a considerable distance as practical motives in life. A man may be absolutely egoistic and yet have strong libidinal attachments to objects, in so far as libidinal satisfaction in an object is a need of his ego: his egoism will then see to it that his desires towards the object involve no injury to his ego. A man may be egoistic and at the same time strongly narcissistic (i.e., feel very little need for objects), and this again either in the form taken by the need for direct sexual satisfaction, or in those higher forms of feeling derived from the sexual needs which are commonly called "love," and as such are contrasted with "sensuality." In all these situations egoism is the self-evident, the constant element, and narcissism the variable one. The antithesis of egoism, "altruism," is not an alternative term for the investment of an object with libido; it is distinct from the latter in its lack of the desire for sexual satisfaction in the object. But when the condition of love is developed to its fullest intensity altruism coincides with the investment of an object with libido. As a rule the sexual object draws to itself a portion of the ego's narcissism, which becomes apparent in what is called the "sexual overestimation" of the object. If to this is added an altruism directed towards the object and derived from the egoism of the lover, the sexual object becomes supreme; it has entirely swallowed up the ego.

* * *

Certain conditions—organic illness, painful accesses of stimulation, an inflammatory condition of an organ—have clearly the effect of loosening the libido from its attachment to its objects. The libido which has thus been withdrawn attaches itself again to the ego in the form of a stronger investment of the diseased region of the body. Indeed, one may venture the assertion that in such conditions the withdrawal of the libido from its objects is more striking than the withdrawal of the egoistic interests from their concerns in the outer world. This seems to lead to a possibility of understanding hypochondria, in which some organ, without being perceptibly diseased, becomes in a very similar way the subject of a solicitude on the part of the ego. I shall, however, resist the temptation to follow this up, or to discuss other situations which become explicable or capable of exposition on this assumption of a return of the object-libido into the ego; for I feel bound to meet two objections which I know have all your attention at the moment. First of all, you want to know why when I discuss sleep, illness, and similar conditions, I insist upon distinguishing between libido and "interests," sexual instincts and ego-instincts, while the observations are satisfactorily explained by assuming a single uniform energy which is freely mobile, can invest either object or ego, and can serve the purposes of the one as well as of the other. Secondly, you will want to know how I can be so bold as to treat the detachment of the libido from its objects as the origin of a pathological condition, if such a transformation of object-libido into ego-libido—or into ego-energy in general—is a normal mental process repeated every day and every night.

The answer is: Your first objection sounds a good one. Examination of the conditions of sleep, illness, and falling in love would probably never have led to a distinction between ego-libido and object-libido, or between libido and "interests." But in this you omit to take into account the investigations with which we started, in the light of which we now regard the mental situations under discussion. The necessity of distinguishing between libido and "interests," between sexual and self-preservative instincts, has been forced upon us by our insight into the conflict from which the transference neuroses arise. We have to reckon with this distinction henceforth. The assumption that object-libido can transform itself into ego-libido, in other words, that we shall also have to reckon with an ego-libido, appears to be the only one capable of solving the riddle

of what are called the narcissistic neuroses, e.g., dementia præcox, or of giving any satisfactory explanation of their likeness to hysteria and obsessions and differences from them. We then apply what we have found undeniably proved in these cases to illness, sleep, and the condition of intense love. We are at liberty to apply them in any direction and see where they will take us. The single conclusion which is not directly based on analytical experience is that libido is libido and remains so, whether it is attached to objects or to the ego itself, and is never transformed into egoistic "interests," and vice versa. This statement, however, is another way of expressing the distinction between sexual instincts and ego-instincts which we have already critically examined and which we shall hold to from heuristic motives until such time as it may prove valueless.

Your second objection too raises a justifiable question, but it is directed to a false issue. The withdrawal of object-libido into the ego is certainly not pathogenic; it is true that it occurs every night before sleep can ensue, and that the process is reversed upon awakening. The protoplasmic animalcule draws in its protrusions and sends them out again at the next opportunity. But it is quite a different matter when a definite, very forcible process compels the withdrawal of the libido from its objects. The libido that has then become narcissistic can no longer find its way back to its objects, and this obstruction in the way of the free movement of the libido certainly does prove pathogenic. It seems that an accumulation of narcissistic libido over and above a certain level becomes intolerable. We might well imagine that it was this that first led to the investment of objects, that the ego was obliged to send forth its libido in order not to fall ill of an excessive accumulation of it. If it were part of our scheme to go more particularly into the disorder of dementia præcox I would show you that the process which detaches the libido from its objects and blocks the way back to them again is closely allied to the process of repression, and is to be regarded as a counterpart of it. In any case you would recognize familiar ground under your feet when you found that the preliminary conditions giving rise to these processes are almost identical, so far as we know at present, with those of repression. The conflict seems to be the same and to be conducted between the same forces. Since the outcome is so different from that of hysteria, for instance, the reason can only lie in some difference in the disposition. The weak point in the libido-development in these patients is found at a different phase of the development; the decisive fixation which, as you will remember, enables the process of symptom-formation to break out is at another point, probably at the stage of primary narcissism, to which dementia præcox finally returns. It is most remarkable that for all the narcissistic neuroses we have to assume fixation-points of the libido at very much earlier phases of development than those found in hysteria or the obsessional neurosis. You have heard, however, that the concepts we have elicited from the study of the transference neuroses also suffice to show us our bearings in the narcissistic neuroses, which are in practice so much more severe. There is a very wide community between them; fundamentally they are phenomena of a single class. You may imagine how hopeless a task it is for anyone to attempt to explain these disorders (which properly belong to psychiatry) without being first equipped with the analytical knowledge of the transference neuroses.

The picture formed by the symptoms of dementia præcox, incidentally a very variable one, is not determined exclusively by the symptoms arising from

the forcing of the libido back from the objects and the accumulation of it as narcissism in the ego. Other phenomena occupy a large part of the field, and may be traced to the efforts made by the libido to reach its objects again, which correspond therefore to attempts at restitution and recovery. These are in fact the conspicuous, clamorous symptoms; they exhibit a marked similarity to those of hysteria, or more rarely of the obsessional neurosis; they are nevertheless different in every respect. It seems that in dementia præcox the efforts of the libido to get back to its objects, that is, to the mental idea of its objects, do really succeed in conjuring up something of them, something that at the same time is only the shadow of them—namely, the verbal images, the words, attached to them. This is not the place to discuss this matter further but in my opinion this reversed procedure on the part of the libido gives us an insight into what constitutes the real difference between a conscious and an unconscious idea.

4. *The Ego and the Superego*

BY SIGMUND FREUD

THE FUNCTIONAL IMPORTANCE of the ego is manifested in the fact that normally control over the approaches to motility devolves upon it. Thus in its relation to the id it is like a man on horseback, who has to hold in check the superior strength of the horse; with this difference, that the rider seeks to do so with his own strength while the ego uses borrowed forces. The illustration may be carried further. Often a rider, if he is not to be parted from his horse, is obliged to guide it where it wants to go; so in the same way the ego constantly carries into action the wishes of the id as if they were its own.

It seems that another factor, besides the influence of the system Pcpt, has been at work in bringing about the formation of the ego and its differentiation from the id. The body itself, and above all its surface, is a place from which both external and internal perceptions may spring. It is seen in the same way as any other object, but to the touch it

yields two kinds of sensations, one of which is equivalent to an internal perception. Psychophysiology has fully discussed the manner in which the body attains its special position among other objects in the world of perception. Pain seems also to play a part in the process, and the way in which we gain new knowledge of our organs during painful illnesses is perhaps a prototype of the way by which in general we arrive at the idea of our own body.

The ego is first and foremost a body-ego; it is not merely a surface entity, but it is itself the projection of a surface.[1] If we wish to find an anatomical analogy for it we can easily identify it with the "cortical homunculus" of the anatomists, which stands on its head in the cortex, sticks its heels into the air, faces backwards and, as we know has its speech-area on the left-hand side.

The relation of the ego to consciousness has been

1. *I.e.*, the ego is ultimately derived from bodily sensations, chiefly from those springing from the surface of the body. It may thus be regarded as a mental projection of the surface of the body, besides, as we have seen above, representing the superficies of the mental apparatus. —Authorized note by the Translator.

Reprinted from Sigmund Freud, *The Ego and the Id*, trans. Joan Riviere (London: Hogarth Press, 1950), pp. 30–53, with the permission of the publisher.

gone into repeatedly; yet there are still some important facts in this connection which remain to be described. Accustomed as we are to taking our social or ethical standard of values along with us wherever we go, we feel no surprise at hearing that the scene of the activities of the lower passions is in the unconscious; we expect, moreover, that the higher any mental function ranks in our scale of values the more easily it will find access to consciousness assured to it. Here, however, psychoanalytic experience disappoints us. On the one hand, we have evidence that even subtle and intricate intellectual operations which ordinarily require strenuous concentration can equally be carried out preconsciously and without coming into consciousness. Instances of this are quite incontestable; they may occur, for instance, during sleep, as is shown when some one finds immediately after waking that he knows the solution of a difficult mathematical or other problem with which he had been wrestling in vain the day before.[2]

There is another phenomenon, however, which is far stranger. In our analyses we discover that there are people in whom the faculties of self-criticism and conscience—mental activities, that is, that rank as exceptionally high ones—are unconscious and unconsciously produce effects of the greatest importance; the example of resistances remaining unconscious during analysis is therefore by no means unique. But this new discovery, which compels us, in spite of our critical faculties, to speak of an "unconscious sense of guilt," bewilders us far more than the other and sets us fresh problems, especially when we gradually come to see that in a great number of neuroses this unconscious sense of guilt plays a decisive economic part and puts the most powerful obstacles in the way of recovery. If we come back once more to our scale of values, we shall have to say that not only what is lowest but also what is highest in the ego can be unconscious. It is as if we were thus supplied with a proof of what we have just asserted of the conscious ego: that it is first and foremost a body-ego.

If the ego were merely the part of the id that is modified by the influence of the perceptual system, the representative in the mind of the real external world, we should have a simple state of things to deal with. But there is a further complication.

The considerations that led us to assume the existence of a differentiating grade within the ego, which may be called the ego-ideal or super-ego.

have been set forth elsewhere. They still hold good.[3] The new proposition which must now be gone into is that this part of the ego is less closely connected with consciousness than the rest.

At this point we must widen our range a little. We succeeded in explaining the painful disorder of melancholia by supposing that, in those suffering from it, an object which was lost has been reinstated within the ego; that is, that an object-cathexis has been replaced by an identification. When this explanation was first proposed, however, we did not appreciate the full significance of the process and did not know how common and how typical it is. Since then we have come to understand that this kind of substitution has a great share in determining the form taken on by the ego and that it contributes materially towards building up what is called its "character."

At the very beginning, in the primitive oral phase of the individual's existence, object-cathexis and identification are hardly to be distinguished from each other. We can only suppose that later on object-cathexes proceed from the id, in which erotic trends are felt as needs. The ego, which at its inception is still far from robust, becomes aware of the object-cathexes, and either acquiesces in them or tries to defend itself against them by the process of repression.[4]

When it happens that a person has to give up a sexual object, there quite often ensues a modification in his ego which can only be described as a reinstatement of the object within the ego, as it occurs in melancholia; the exact nature of this substitution is as yet unknown to us. It may be that, by undertaking this introjection, which is a kind of regression to the mechanism of the oral phase, the ego makes it easier for an object to be given up or renders that process possible. It may even be that this identification is the sole condition under which the id can give up its objects. At any rate the process, especially in the early phases

2. I was quite recently told an instance of this which was, in fact, brought up as an objection against my description of the "dream-work."

3. Except that I seem to have been mistaken in ascribing the function of testing the reality of things to this super-ego—a point which needs correction. The view that the testing of reality is rather one of the functions of the ego itself would fit in perfectly with what we know of the relations of the ego to the world of perception. Some earlier suggestions about a "nucleus of the ego," never very definitely formulated, also require to be put right, since the system Pcpt-Cs alone can be regarded as the nucleus of the ego.

4. An interesting parallel to the replacement of object-choice by identification is to be found in the belief of primitive peoples, and in the taboos based upon it, that the attributes of animals which are assimilated as nourishment survive as part of the character of the persons who eat them. As is well known, this belief is one of the roots of cannibalism and its effects can be traced down to the Holy Communion. The consequences ascribed by this belief to oral mastery of the object do in fact follow in the case of the later sexual object-choice.

of development, is a very frequent one, and it points to the conclusion that the character of the ego is a precipitate of abandoned object-cathexes and that it contains a record of past object-choices. It must, of course, be admitted from the outset that there are varying degrees of capacity for resistance, as shown by the extent to which the character of any particular person accepts or resists the influences of the erotic object-choices through which he has lived. In women who have had many love affairs there seems to be no difficulty in finding vestiges of their object-cathexes in the traits of their character. We must also take into consideration the case of simultaneous object-cathexis and identification, *i.e.,* in which the alteration in character occurs before the object has been given up. In such a case the alteration in character would be able to survive the object-relation and in certain sense to conserve it.

From another point of view it may be said that this transformation of an erotic object-choice into a modification of the ego is also a method by which the ego can obtain control over the id and deepen its relations with it—at the cost, it is true, of acquiescing to a large extent in the id's experiences. When the ego assumes the features of the object, it forces itself, so to speak, upon the id as a love-object and tries to make good the loss of that object by saying, "Look, I am so like the object, you can as well love me."

The transformation of object-libido into narcissistic libido which thus takes place obviously implies an abandonment of sexual aims, a process of desexualization; it is consequently a kind of sublimation. Indeed, the question arises, and deserves careful consideration, whether this is not always the path taken in sublimation, whether all sublimation does not take place through the agency of the ego, which begins by changing sexual object-libido into narcissistic libido and then, perhaps, goes on to give it another aim.[5] We shall later on have to consider whether other instinctual vicissitudes may not also result from this transformation, whether, for instance, it may not bring about a defusion of the instincts that are fused together.

Although it is a digression from our theme, we cannot avoid giving our attention for a moment longer to the ego's object-identifications. If they obtain the upper hand and become too numerous, unduly intense and incompatible with one another, a pathological outcome will not be far off. It may

come to a disruption of the ego in consequence of the individual identifications becoming cut off from one another by resistances; perhaps the secret of the cases of so-called multiple personality is that the various identifications seize possession of consciousness in turn. Even when things do not go so far as this, there remains the question of conflicts between the different identifications into which the ego is split up, conflicts which cannot after all be described as purely pathological.

But, whatever the character's capacity for resisting the influences of abandoned object-cathexes may turn out to be in after years, the effects of the first identifications in earliest childhood will be profound and lasting. This leads us back to the origin of the ego-ideal; for behind the latter there lies hidden the first and most important identification of all, the identification with the father,[6] which takes place in the prehistory of every person. This is apparently not in the first instance the consequence or outcome of an object-cathexis; it is a direct and immediate identification and takes place earlier than any object-cathexis. But the object-choices belonging to the earliest sexual period and relating to the father and mother seem normally to find their outcome in an identification of the kind discussed, which would thus reinforce the primary one.

The whole subject, however, is so complicated that it will be necessary to go into it more minutely. The intricacy of the problem is due to two factors: the triangular character of the Oedipus situation and the constitutional bisexuality of each individual.

In its simplified form the case of the male child may be described as follows. At a very early age the little boy develops an object-cathexis of his *mother,* which originally related to the mother's breast and is the earliest instance of an object-choice on the anaclitic model; his *father* the boy deals with by identifying himself with him. For a time these two relationships exist side by side, until the sexual wishes in regard to the mother becomes more intense and the father is perceived as an obstacle to them; this gives rise to the Oedipus complex. The identification with the father then takes on a hostile colouring and changes into

---

5. Now that we have distinguished between the ego and the id, we must recognize the id as the great reservoir of libido mentioned in my introductory paper on narcissism (*Collected Papers,* Vol. IV.). The libido which flows into the ego owing to the identifications described above brings about its "secondary narcissism."

6. Perhaps it would be safer to say "with the parents"; for before a child has arrived at definite knowledge of the difference between the sexes, the missing penis, it does not distinguish in value between its father and its mother. I recently came across the instance of a young married woman whose story showed that, after noticing the lack of a penis in herself, she had supposed it to be absent not in all women, but only in those whom she regarded as inferior, and had still supposed that her mother possessed one.

In order to simplify my presentment I shall discuss only identification with the father.

a wish to get rid of the father in order to take his place with the mother. Henceforward the relation to the father is ambivalent; it seems as if the ambivalence inherent in the identification from the beginning had become manifest. An ambivalent attitude to the father and an object-relation of a purely affectionate kind to the mother makes up the content of the simple positive Oedipus complex in the boy.

Along with the dissolution of the Oedipus complex the object-cathexis of the mother must be given up. Its place may be filled by one of two things: either an identification with the mother or an intensified identification with the father. We are accustomed to regard the latter outcome as the more normal; it permits the affectionate relation to the mother to be in a measure retained. In this way the passing of the Oedipus complex would consolidate the masculinity in the boy's character. In a precisely analogous way, the outcome of the Oedipus attitude in the little girl may be an intensification of the identification with her mother (or such an identification may thus be set up for the first time)—a result which will stamp the child's character in the feminine mould.

These identifications are not what our previous statements would have led us to expect, since they do not involve the absorption of the abandoned object into the ego: but this alternative outcome may also occur; it is more readily observed in girls than in boys. Analysis very often shows that a little girl, after she has had to relinquish her father as a love-object, will bring her masculinity into prominence and identify herself wtih her father, that is, with the object which has been lost, instead of with her mother. This will clearly depend on whether the masculinity in her disposition—whatever that may consist of—is strong enough.

It would appear, therefore, that in both sexes the relative strength of the masculine and feminine sexual dispositions is what determines whether the outcome of the Oedipus situation shall be an identification with the father or with the mother. This is one of the ways in which bisexuality takes a hand in the subsequent vicissitudes of the Oedipus complex. The other way is even more important. For one gets the impression that the simple Oedipus complex is by no means its commonest form, but rather represents a simplification or schematization which, to be sure, is often enough adequate for practical purposes. Closer study usually discloses the more complete Oedipus complex, which is twofold, positive and negative, and is due to the bisexuality originally present in children: that is to say, a boy has not merely an ambivalent attitude towards his father and an affectionate

object-relation towards his mother, but at the same time he also behaves like a girl and displays an affectionate feminine attitude to his father and a corresponding hostility and jealousy towards his mother. It is this complicating element introduced by bisexuality that makes it so difficult to obtain a clear view of the facts in connection with the earliest object-choices and identifications, and still more difficult to describe them intelligibly. It may even be that the ambivalence displayed in the relations to the parents should be attributed entirely to bisexuality and that it is not, as I stated just now, developed out of an identification in consequence of rivalry.

In my opinion it is advisable in general, and quite especially where neurotics are concerned, to assume the existence of the complete Oedipus complex. Analytic experience then shows that in a number of cases one or the other of its constituents disappears, except for barely distinguishable traces, so that a series can be formed with the normal positive Oedipus complex at one end and the inverted negative one at the other, while its intermediate members will exhibit the complete type with one or other of its two constituents preponderating. As the Oedipus complex dissolves, the four trends of which it consists will group themselves in such a way as to produce a father-identification and a mother-identification. The father-identification will preserve the object-relation to the mother which belonged to the positive complex and will at the same time take the place of the object-relation to the father which belonged to the inverted complex: and the same will be true, *mutatis mutandis,* of the mother-identification. The relative intensity of the two identifications in any individual will reflect the preponderance in him of one or other of the two sexual dispositions.

The broad general outcome of the sexual phase governed by the Oedipus complex may, therefore, be taken to be the forming of a precipitate in the ego, consisting of these two identifications in some way combined together. This modification of the ego retains its special position; it stands in contrast to the other constituents of the ego in the form of an ego-ideal or super-ego.

The super-ego is, however, not merely a deposit left by the earliest object-choices of the id; it also represents an energetic reaction-formation against those choices. Its relation to the ego is not exhausted by the precept: "You *ought to be* such and such (like your father)"; it also comprises the prohibition: "You *must not be* such and such (like your father); that is, you may not do all that he does; many things are his prerogative." This double aspect of the ego-ideal derives from the fact that the ego-ideal had the task of effecting the repression of the Oedipus complex, indeed, it is to that revolutionary event that it owes its existence. Clearly the repression of the Oedipus complex was no easy task. The parents, and especially the father, were perceived as the obstacle to realization of the Oedipus wishes; so the child's ego brought in a reinforcement to help in carrying out the repression by erecting this same obstacle within itself. The strength to do this was, so to speak, borrowed from the father, and this loan was an extraordinarily momentous act. The super-ego retains the character of the father, while the more intense the Oedipus complex was and the more rapidly it succumbed to repression (under the influence of discipline, religious teaching, schooling and reading) the more exacting later on is the domination of the super-ego over the ego—in the form of conscience or perhaps of an unconscious sense of guilt. I shall later on bring forward a suggestion about the source of the power it employs to dominate in this way, the source, that is, of its compulsive character which manifests itself in the form of a categorical imperative.

If we consider once more the origin of the super-ego as we have described it, we shall perceive it to be the outcome of two highly important factors, one of them biological and the other historical: namely, the lengthy duration in man of the helplessness and dependence belonging to childhood, and the fact of his Oedipus complex, the repression of which we have shown to be connected with the interruption of libidinal development by the latency period and so with the twofold onset of activity characteristic of man's sexual life.[7] According to the view of one psychoanalyst, the last-mentioned phenomenon, which seems peculiar to man, is a heritage of the cultural development necessitated by the glacial epoch. We see, then, that the differentiation of the super-ego from the ego is no matter of chance; it stands as the representative of the most important events in the development both of the individual and of the race; indeed, by giving permanent expression to the influence of the parents it perpetuates the existence of the factors to which it owes its origin.

Psycho-analysis has been reproached time after time with ignoring the higher, moral, spiritual side of human nature. The reproach is doubly unjust, both historically and methodologically. For, in the first place, we have from the very beginning attributed the function of instigating repression to the moral and aesthetic tendencies in the ego, and

secondly, there has been a general refusal to recognize that psycho-analytic research could not produce a complete and finished body of doctrine, like a philosophical system, ready-made, but had to find its way step by step along the path towards understanding the intricacies of the mind by making an analytic dissection of both normal and abnormal phenomena. So long as the study of the repressed part of the mind was our task, there was no need for us to feel any agitated apprehensions about the existence of the higher side of mental life. But now that we have embarked upon the analysis of the ego we can give an answer to all those whose moral sense has been shocked and who have complained that there must surely be a higher nature in man: "Very true," we can say, "and here we have that higher nature, in this ego-ideal or super-ego, the representative of our relation to our parents. When we were little children we knew these higher natures, we admired them and feared them; and later we took them into ourselves."

The ego-ideal, therefore, is the heir of the Oedipus complex and thus it is also the expression of the most powerful impulses and most important vicissitudes experienced by the libido in the id. By setting up this ego-ideal the ego masters its Oedipus complex and at the same time places itself in subjection to the id. Whereas the ego is essentially the representative of the external world, of reality, the super-ego stands in contrast to it as the representative of the internal world, of the id. Conflicts between the ego and the ideal will, as we are now prepared to find, ultimately reflect the contrast between what is real and what is mental, between the external world and the internal world.

Through the forming of the ideal, all the traces left behind in the id by biological developments and by the vicissitudes gone through by the human race are taken over by the ego and lived through again by it in each individual. Owing to the way in which it is formed, the ego-ideal has a great many points of contact with the phylogenetic endowment of each individual—his archaic heritage. And thus it is that what belongs to the lowest depths in the minds of each one of us is changed, through this formation of the ideal, into what we value as the highest in the human soul. It would be vain, however, to attempt to localize the ego-ideal, even in the sense in which we have localized the ego, or to work it into any of those analogies with the help of which we have tried to picture the relation between the ego and the id.

It is easy to show that the ego-ideal answers in every way to what is expected of the higher

---

7. This sentence represents a slight modification of the original text in accordance with direct instructions from the author.—Trans.

nature of man. In so far as it is a substitute for the longing for a father, it contains the germ from which all religions have evolved. The self-judgement which declares that the ego falls short of its ideal produces the sense of worthlessness with which the religious believer attests his longing. As a child grows up, the office of father is carried on by masters and by others in authority; the power of their injunctions and prohibitions remains vested in the ego-ideal and continues, in the form of conscience, to exercise the censorship of morals. The tension between the demands of conscience and the actual attainments of the ego is experienced as a sense of guilt. Social feelings rest on the foundation of identifications with others, on the basis of an ego-ideal in common with them.

Religion, morality, and a social sense—the chief elements of what is highest in man—were originally one and the same thing. According to the hypothesis which I have put forward in *Totem und Tabu* they were acquired phylogenetically out of the father-complex: religion and moral restraint by the actual process of mastering the Oedipus complex itself, and social feeling from the necessity for overcoming the rivalry that then remained between the members of the younger generation. It seems that the male sex has taken the lead in developing all of these moral acquisitions; and that they have then been transmitted to women by cross-inheritance. Even to-day the social feelings arise in the individual as a superstructure founded upon impulses of jealousy and rivalry against his brothers and sisters. Since the enmity cannot be gratified there develops an identification with the former rival. The study of mild cases of homosexuality confirms the suspicion that in this instance, too, the identification is a substitute for an affectionate object-choice which has succeeded the hostile, aggressive attitude.

With the mention of phylogenesis, however, fresh problems arise, from which one is tempted to shrink back dismayed. But there is no help for it, the attempt must be made; in spite of a fear that it will lay bare the inadequacy of the whole structure that we have so arduously built up. The question is: which was it, the ego of primitive man or his id, that acquired religion and morality in those early days out of the father complex? If it was his ego, why do we not speak simply of these things being inherited by the ego? If it was the id, how does that agree with the character of the id? Or are we wrong in carrying the differentiation between ego, super-ego, and id back into such early times? Or should we not honestly confess that our

whole conception of the processes within the ego is of no help in understanding phylogenesis and cannot be applied to it?

Let us answer first what is easiest to answer. The differentiation betwen ego and id must be attributed not only to primitive man but even to much simpler forms of life, for it is the inevitable expression of the influence of the external world. The super-ego, according to our hypothesis, actually originated from the experiences that led to totemism. The question whether it was the ego or the id that experienced and acquired these things soon ceases to have any meaning. Reflection at once shows us that no external vicissitudes can be experienced or undergone by the id, except by way of the ego, which is the representative of the outer world to the id. Nevertheless it is not possible to speak of direct inheritance by the ego. It is here that the gulf between the actual individual and the conception of the species becomes evident. Moreover, one must not take the difference between ego and id in too hard-and-fast a sense, nor forget that the ego is a part of the id which has been specially modified. The experiences undergone by the ego seem at first to be lost to posterity; but, when they have been repeated often enough and with sufficient intensity in the successive individuals of many generations, they transform themselves, so to say, into experiences of the id, the impress of which is preserved by inheritance. Thus in the id, which is capable of being inherited, are stored up vestiges of the existences led by countless former egos; and, when the ego forms its super-ego out of the id, it may perhaps only be reviving images of egos that have passed away and be securing them a resurrection.

The way in which the super-ego came into being explains how it is that the earlier conflicts of the ego with the object-cathexes of the id can be carried on and continued in conflicts with their successor, the super-ego. If the ego has not succeeded in mastering the Oedipus complex satisfactorily, the energic cathexis of the latter, springing from the id, will find an outlet in the reaction-formations of the ego-ideal. The very free communication possible between the ideal and these Ucs instinctual trends explains how it is that the ideal itself can be to a great extent unconscious and inaccessible to the ego. The struggle which once raged in the deepest strata of the mind, and was not brought to an end by rapid sublimation and identification, is now carred on in a higher region like the Battle of the Huns which in Kaulbach's painting is being fought out in the sky.

5. Taking the Role of the Other

BY GEORGE H. MEAD

The Social Foundations and Functions of Thought and Communication

IN THE SAME socio-physiological way that the human individual becomes conscious of himself he also becomes conscious of other individuals; and his consciousness both of himself and of other individuals is equally important for his own self-development and for the development of the organized society or social group to which he belongs.

The principle which I have suggested as basic to human social organization is that of communication involving participation in the other. This requires the appearance of the other in the self, the identification of the other with the self, the reaching of self-consciousness through the other. This participation is made possible through the type of communication which the human animal is able to carry out—a type of communication distinguished from that which takes place among other forms which have not this principle in their societies. I discussed the sentinel, so-called, that may be said to communicate his discovery of the danger to the other members, as the clucking of the hen may be said to communicate to the chick. There are conditions under which the gesture of one form serves to place the other forms in the proper attitude toward external conditions. In one sense we may say the one form communicates with the other, but the difference between that and self-conscious communication is evident. One form does not know that communication is taking place with the other. We get illustrations of that in what we term mob-consciousness, the attitude which an audience will take when under the influence of a great speaker. One is influenced by the attitudes of those about him, which are reflected back into the different members of the audience so that they come to respond as a whole. One feels the general attitude of the whole audience. There is then communication in a real sense, that is, one form communicates to the other an attitude which the other assumes toward a certain part of the environment that is of importance to them both. That level of communication is found in forms of society which are of lower type than the social organization of the human group.

In the human group, on the other hand, there is not only this kind of communication but also that in which the person who uses this gesture and so communicates assumes the attitude of the other individual as well as calling it out in the other. He himself is in the rôle of the other person whom he is so exciting and influencing. It is through taking this rôle of the other that he is able to come back on himself and so direct his own process of communication. This taking the rôle of the other, an expression I have so often used, is not simply of passing importance. It is not something that just happens as an incidental result of the gesture, but it is of importance in the development of cooperative activity. The immediate effect of such rôle-taking lies in the control which the individual is able to exercise over his own response. The control of the action of the individual in a co-operative process can take place in the conduct of the individual himself if he can take the rôle of the other. It is this control of the response of the individual himself through taking the rôle of the other that leads to the value of this type of communication from the point of view of the organization of the conduct in the group. It carries the process of co-operative activity farther than it can be carried in the herd as such, or in the insect society.

And thus it is that social control, as operating in terms of self-criticism, exerts itself so intimately and extensively over individual behavior or conduct, serving to integrate the individual and his actions with reference to the organized social process of experience and behavior in which he is implicated. The physiological mechanism of the human individual's central nervous system makes it possible for him to take the attitudes of other individuals, and the attitudes of the organized social group of which he and they are members, toward himself, in terms of his integrated social relations to them and to the group as a whole; so that the general social process of experience and behavior which the group is carrying on is directly presented to him

Reprinted from George H. Mead, *Mind, Self and Society* (Chicago: University of Chicago Press, 1934), pp. 253–57, with the permission of the University of Chicago Press.

in his own exprience, and so that he is thereby able to govern and direct his conduct consciously and critically, with reference to his relations both to the social group as a whole and to its other individual members, in terms of this social process. Thus he becomes not only self-conscious but also self-critical; and thus, through self-criticism, social control over individual behavior or conduct operates by virtue of the social origin and basis of such criticism. That is to say, self-criticism is essentially social criticism, and behavior controlled by self-criticism is essentially behavior controlled socially. Freud's conception of the psychological "censor" represents a partial recognition of this operation of social control in terms of self-criticism, a recognition, namely, of its operation with reference to sexual experience and conduct. But this same sort of censorship or criticism of himself by the individual is reflected also in all other aspects of his social experience, behavior, and relations—a fact which follows naturally and inevitably from our social theory of the self. Hence social control, so far from tending to crush out the human individual or to obliterate his self-conscious individuality, is, on the contrary, actually constitutive of and inextricably associated with that individuality; for the individual is what he is, as a conscious and individual personality, just in as far as he is a member of society, involved in the social process of experience and activity, and thereby socially controlled in his conduct.

The very organization of the self-conscious community is dependent upon individuals taking the attitude of the other individuals. The development of this process, as I have indicated, is dependent upon getting the attitude of the group as distinct from that of a separate individual—getting what I have termed a "generalized other." I have illustrated this by the ball game, in which the attitudes of a set of individuals are involved in a co-operative response in which the different rôles involve each other. In so far as a man takes the attitude of one individual in the group, he must take it in its relationship to the action of the other members of the group; and if he is fully to adjust himself, he would have to take the attitudes of all involved in the process. The degree, of course, to which he can do that is restrained by his capacity, but still in all intelligent processes we are able sufficiently to take the rôles of those involved in the activity to make our own action intelligent. The degree to which the life of the whole community can get into the self-conscious life of the separate individuals varies enormously. History is largely occupied in tracing out the development which could not have been present in the actual experience of the members of the community at the time the historian is writing about. Such an account explains the importance of history. One can look back over that which took place, and bring out changes, forces, and interests which nobody at the time was conscious of. We have to wait for the historian to give the picture because the actual process was one which transcended the experience of the separate individuals.

Occasionally a person arises who is able to take in more than others of an act in process, who can put himself into relation with whole groups in the community whose attitudes have not entered into the lives of the others in the community. He becomes a leader. Classes under a feudal order may be so separate from each other that, while they can act in certain traditional circumstances, they cannot understand each other; and then there may arise an individual who is capable of entering into the attitudes of the other members of the group. Figures of that sort become of enormous importance because they make possible communication between groups otherwise completely separated from each other. The sort of capacity we speak of is in politics the attitude of the statesman who is able to enter into the attitudes of the group and to mediate between them by making his own experience universal, so that others can enter into this form of communication through him.

6. *The Four Wishes and the Definition of the Situation*

BY WILLIAM I. THOMAS

THE VARIETY OF EXPRESSIONS of behavior is as great as the variety of situations arising in the external world, while the nervous system represents only a general mechanism for action. We can however approach the problem of behavior through the study of the forces which impel to action, namely, the wishes, and we shall see that these correspond in general with the nervous mechanism.

The human wishes have a great variety of concrete forms but are capable of the following general classification:

1. The desire for new experience.
2. The desire for security.
3. The desire for response.
4. The desire for recognition.

THE DESIRE FOR NEW EXPERIENCE

Men crave excitement, and all experiences are exciting which have in them some resemblance to the pursuit, flight, capture, escape, death which characterized the earlier life of mankind. Behavior is an adaptation to environment, and the nervous system itself is a developmental adaptation. It represents, among other things, a hunting pattern of interest. "Adventure" is what the young boy wants, and stories of adventure. Hunting trips are enticing; they are the survival of natural life. All sports are of the hunting pattern; there is a contest of skill, daring, and cunning. It is impossible not to admire the nerve of a daring burglar or highwayman. A fight, even a dog fight, will draw a crowd. In gambling or dice throwing you have the thrill of success or the chagrin of defeat. The organism craves stimulation and seeks expansion and shock even through alcohol and drugs. "Sensations" occupy a large part of the space in newspapers. Courtship has in it an element of "pursuit." Novels, theaters, motion pictures, etc., are partly an adaptation to this desire, and their popularity is a sign of its elemental force.

*   *   *

There is also in the hunting pattern of interest an intellectual element. Watson does not note curiosity

Reprinted from *The Unadjusted Girl* in *Social Behavior and Personality: Contributions of W. I. Thomas to Theory and Social Research,* ed. E. H. Volkart (Social Science Research Council, 1951), pp. 121–44, with deletions, with permission of the Social Science Research Council.

among the instincts because it does not manifest itself at birth, but it appears later as the watchful and exploratory attitude which determines the character of action,—whether, for example, it shall be attack or flight. The invention of the bow and arrow, the construction of a trap, the preparation of poison, indicated a scientific curiosity in early man. Activities of this kind were interesting because they implied life or death. The man who constructed the poisoned arrow visualized the scene in which it was to be used, saw the hunt in anticipation. The preparation for the chase was psychologically part of the chase. The modern scientific man uses the same mental mechanism but with a different application. He spends long months in his laboratory on an invention in anticipation of his final "achievement." The so-called "instinct for workmanship" and the "creative impulse" are "sublimations" of the hunting psychosis. The making of a trap was a "problem," and any problem is interesting, whether the construction of a wireless or the solving of a puzzle. Modern occupations or "pursuits" are interesting or irksome to the degree that they have or have not a problematical element.

*   *   *

THE DESIRE FOR SECURITY

The desire for security is opposed to the desire for new experience. The desire for new experience is, as we have seen, emotionally related to anger, which tends to invite death, and expresses itself in courage, advance, attack, pursuit. The desire for new experience implies, therefore, motion, change, danger, instability, social irresponsibility. The individual dominated by it shows a tendency to disregard prevailing standards and group interests. He may be a social failure on account of his instability, or a social success if he converts his experiences into social values,—puts them into the form of a poem, makes them a contribution to science. The desire for security, on the other hand, is based on fear, which tends to avoid death and expresses itself in timidity, avoidance, and flight. The individual dominated by it is cautious, conservative, and apprehensive, tending also to regular habits, systematic work, and the accumulation of property.

The social types known as "bohemian" and "philistine" are determined respectively by the domination of the desire for new experience and the desire for security. The miser represents a case where the means of security has become an end in itself.

* * *

THE DESIRE FOR RESPONSE

Up to this point I have described the types of mental impressionability connected with the pursuit of food and the avoidance of death, which are closely connected with the emotions of anger and fear. The desire for response, on the other hand, is primarily related to the instinct of love, and shows itself in the tendency to seek and to give signs of appreciation in connection with other individuals.

There is first of all the devotion of the mother to the child and the response of the child, indicated in the passage from Watson above, and in the following passage from Thorndike.

All women possess originally, from early childhood to death, some interest in human babies, and a responsiveness to the instinctive looks, calls, gestures and cries of infancy and childhood, being satisfied by childish gurglings, smiles and affectionate gestures, and moved to instinctive comforting acts by childish signs of pain, grief and misery. Brutal habits may destroy, or competing habits overgrow, or the lack of exercise weaken, these tendencies, but they are none the less as original as any fact in human nature.

This relation is of course useful and necessary since the child is helpless throughout a period of years and would not live unless the mother were impelled to give it her devotion. This attitude is present in the father of the child also but is weaker, less demonstrative, and called out more gradually.

In addition, the desire for response between the two sexes in connection with mating is very powerful. An ardent courtship is full of assurances and appeals for reassurance. Marriage and a home involve response but with more settled habits, more routine work, less of new experience. Jealousy is an expression of fear that the response is directed elsewhere. The flirt is one who seeks new experience through the provocation of response from many quarters.

In some natures this wish, both to receive and to give response, is out of proportion to the other wishes, "over-determined," so to speak, and interferes with a normal organization of life. And the fixation may be either on a child or a member of either sex.

* * *

In general the desire for response is the most social of the wishes. It contains both a sexual and a gregarious element. It makes selfish claims, but on the other hand it is the main source of altruism. The

devotion to child and family and devotion to causes, principles, and ideals may be the same attitude in different fields of application. It is true that devotion and self-sacrifice may originate from any of the other wishes also—desire for new experience, recognition, or security—or may be connected with all of them at once. Pasteur's devotion to science seems to be mainly the desire for new experience,—scientific curiosity; the campaigns of a Napoleon represent recognition (ambition) and the self sacrifice of such characters as Maria Spiridonova, Florence Nightingale, Jane Addams is a sublimation of response. The women who demanded Juvenile Courts were stirred by the same feeling as the mother in document No. 11, whereas the usual legal procedure is based on the wish to have security for life and property.

THE DESIRE FOR RECOGNITION

This wish is expressed in the general struggle of men for position in their social group, in devices for securing a recognized, enviable, and advantageous social status. Among girls dress is now perhaps the favorite means of securing distinction and showing class. A Bohemian immigrant girl expressed her philosophy in a word: "After all, life is mostly what you wear." Veblen's volume, "Theory of the Leisure Class," points out that the status of men is established partly through the show of wealth made by their wives. Distinction is sought also in connection with skillful and hazardous activities, as in sports, war, and exploration. Playwriters and sculptors strive for public favor and "fame." In the "achievement" of Pasteur (case 6) and of similar scientific work there is not only the pleasure of the "pursuit" itself, but the pleasure of public recognition. Boasting, bullying, cruelty, tyranny, "the will to power" have in them a sadistic element allied to the emotion of anger and are efforts to compel a recognition of the personality. The frailty of women, their illness, and even feigned illness, is often used as a power-device, as well as a device to provoke response. On the other hand, humility, self-sacrifice, saintliness, and martyrdom may lead to distinction. The showy motives connected with the appeal for recognition we define as "vanity"; the creative activities we call "ambition."

The importance of recognition and status for the individual and for society is very great. The individual not only wants them but he needs them for the development of his personality. The lack of them and the fear of never obtaining them are probably the main source of those psychopathic disturbances which the Freudians treat as sexual in origin.

On the other hand society alone is able to confer

status on the individual and in seeking to obtain it he makes himself responsible to society and is forced to regulate the expression of his wishes. His dependence on public opinion is perhaps the strongest factor impelling him to conform to the highest demands which society makes upon him.

* * *

The general pattern of behavior which a given individual tends to follow is the basis of our judgment of his character. Our appreciation (positive or negative) of the character of the individual is based on his display of certain wishes as against others and on his modes of seeking their realization. Whether given wishes tend to predominate in this or that person is dependent primarily on what is called temperament, and apparently this is a chemical matter, dependent on the secretions of the glandular systems. Individuals are certainly temperamentally predisposed toward certain classes of the wishes. But we know also, and I shall illustrate presently, that the expression of the wishes is profoundly influenced by the approval of the man's immediate circle and of the general public. The conversions of wild young men to stable ways, from new experience to security, through marriage, religion, and business responsibility, are examples of this. We may therefore define character as an expression of the organization of the wishes resulting from temperament and experience, understanding by "organization" the general pattern which the wishes as a whole tend to assume among themselves.

The significant point about the wishes as related to the study of behavior is that they are the motor element, the starting point of activity. Any influences which may be brought to bear must be exercised on the wishes.

We may assume also that an individual life cannot be called normal in which all the four types of wishes are not satisfied in some measure and in some form.

* * *

The Regulation of the Wishes

One of the most important powers gained during the evolution of animal life is the ability to make decisions from within instead of having them imposed from without. Very low forms of life do not make decisions, as we understand this term, but are pushed and pulled by chemical substances, heat, light, etc., much as iron filings are attracted or repelled by a magnet. They do tend to behave properly in given conditions—a group of small crustaceans will flee as in a panic if a bit of strychnia is placed in the basin containing them and will rush toward a drop of beef juice like hogs crowding around swill—but they do this as an expression of organic affinity for the one substance and repugnance for the other, and not as an expression of choice or "free will." There are, so to speak, rules of behavior but these represent a sort of fortunate mechanistic adjustment of the organism to typically recurring situations, and the organism cannot change the rule.

On the other hand, the higher animals, and above all man, have the power of refusing to obey a stimulation which they followed at an earlier time. Response to the earlier stimulation may have had painful consequences and so the rule or habit in this situation is changed. We call this ability the power of inhibition, and it is dependent on the fact that the nervous system carries memories or records of past experiences. At this point the determination of action no longer comes exclusively from outside sources but is located within the organism itself.

Preliminary to any self-determined act of behavior there is always a stage of examination and deliberation which we may call *the definition of the situation*. And actually not only concrete acts are dependent on the definition of the situation, but gradually a whole life-policy and the personality of the individual himself follow from a series of such definitions.

But the child is always born into a group of people among whom all the general types of situation which may arise have already been defined and corresponding rules of conduct developed, and where he has not the slightest chance of making his definitions and following his wishes without interference. Men have always lived together in groups. Whether mankind has a true herd instinct or whether groups are held together because this has worked out to advantage is of no importance. Certainly the wishes in general are such that they can be satisfied only in a society. But we have only to refer to the criminal code to appreciate the variety of ways in which the wishes of the individual may conflict with the wishes of society. And the criminal code takes no account of the many unsanctioned expressions of the wishes which society attempts to regulate by persuasion and gossip.

There is therefore always a rivalry between the spontaneous definitions of the situation made by the member of an organized society and the definitions which his society has provided for him. The individual tends to a hedonistic selection of activity, pleasure first; and society to a utilitarian selection, safety first. Society wishes its member to be laborious, dependable, regular, sober, orderly, self-sacrificing; while the individual wishes less of this and more of new experience. And organized society seeks also to regulate the conflict and competition inevitable between its members in the pursuit of of their wishes. The desire to have wealth for example, or any other socially sanctioned wish, may not be accomplished at the expense of another member of the society,—by murder, theft, lying, swindling, blackmail, etc.

It is in this connection that a moral code arises, which is a set of rules or behavior norms, regulating the expression of the wishes, and which is built up by successive definitions of the situation. In practice the abuse arises first and the rule is made to prevent its recurrence. Morality is thus the generally accepted definition of the situation, whether expressed in public opinion and the unwritten law, in a formal legal code, or in religious commandments and prohibitions.

Section B

The Elements of Learned Motivation

Editorial Foreword, BY JESSE R. PITTS   *747*

I–THE NATURE OF LEARNING

1. *The Principal Instincts of Man,* BY WILLIAM MC DOUGALL   *751*
2. *On Behaviorism,* BY JOHN B. WATSON   *758*
3. *The Law of Effect,* BY EDWARD L. THORNDIKE   *762*
4. *On Conditioned Reflexes,* BY IVAN P. PAVLOV   *764*
5. *On Drive,* BY CLARK L. HULL   *770*
6. *On Insight,* BY WOLFGANG KÖHLER   *772*
7. *A Summary Discussion of Purposive Behavior,* BY EDWARD C. TOLMAN   *777*

II–THE ORGANIZATION OF MOTIVATIONAL SYSTEMS

1. *Combinations and Group Persistence,* BY VILFREDO PARETO   *780*
2. *Faithfulness and Gratitude,* BY GEORG SIMMEL   *787*
3. *On Valence,* BY KURT LEWIN   *794*
4. *Anxiety as Motivation,* BY SIGMUND FREUD   *799*
5. *Mechanisms of Defense,* BY SIGMUND FREUD   *808*

The Elements of Learned Motivation

by Jesse R. Pitts

I. THE NATURE OF LEARNING

Much of the early think-ing on the problem of learning took place within the framework of the heredity-environment con-troversy, itself an offshoot of Darwinian and Lamarkian concepts of evolution. *McDougall's* instinct theory is one of the extreme expressions of the heredity side of the controversy, just as Pavlov's theory is one of the extreme expressions of the environment viewpoint. McDougall found in instincts, and in the combination of instincts, a sort of molecular theory of behavior which by-passed the problem of social structure.

The concept of instinct is rather discredited to-day, even though Freud and many others have taken the concept very seriously. From the point of view of theory development, it provided an easy way to handle glaring gaps in knowledge and to achieve a certain degree of system closure. Instincts were ul-timately replaced by more complex structures in psychology, sociology, or economic theory, where the acquisitive instinct had led a long and useful life. The ultimate molecules, the units of theoretical systems were thereby pushed farther and farther from common-sense experience. And from *instinct*, there developed the concepts of *tropism, drive, need, national character, authoritarian* or *humani-tarian personality*, or the *need-dispositions* of action theory. Sometimes a change of label does not announce a new wine.

McDougall was probably the last representative of that interesting mixture of introspectionism and positivism we find in Shand, Hobhouse, Ribot, and Wundt. After the behaviorist manifestos of *Watson*, this psychology found fewer and fewer supporters.

Watson's behaviorism is a militant attempt to make psychology into a science on the model of biology, chemistry, or physics. The selection by Watson pre-sents not only the basic aspects of the doctrine, but also the interesting concept of inner thought proc-esses as a covert language response. This is as far as behaviorism was willing to go in taking "ideas" into its schema. As a consequence of this movement, American psychology concentrated heavily on the problems of learning. Since behaviorists did not treat ideation as a useful datum, it was difficult to impute invisible purpose to action. The social en-vironment, made essentially of meanings, was by-passed in favor of the physical environment.

Although marginal to behaviorism, *Thorndike* believed, for instance, that the organism discharges energy (responses) at random. The responses which are reinforced are selected through the *law of effect:* the response which has resulted in satisfaction will, "other things being equal, be more firmly connected with the situation . . ." This proc-ess has become known as *trial and error learning.* For Thorndike, the adjustment of the organism is not conditional on its possession of the right in-stincts, but on its capacity to retain the procedures which secure its satisfaction. Since the behavior of the organism is initially random, the implicit con-clusion is that, for all practical purposes, the organ-ism has an infinite plasticity.

In the heredity *vs.* environment controversy, Thorndike tended to regard the environment as the independent variable. However, the recognition of directionality on the part of the organism was started by Thorndike's finding that the organism learned faster under the stimulus of satisfaction than under the stimulus of dissatisfaction induced through punishment. Teachers' colleges took note.

Indeed, *Pavlov's* learning theory is more radically environment-oriented than is Thorndike's. It limits the assumption of infinite plasticity through the determination of certain organic givens: the *unconditioned reflexes,* which are triggered by *unconditioned stimuli.* Food triggers salivation; electric shock triggers the lifting of the paw. Behavior develops by attaching, through simple contiguity, a conditioned stimulus to the unconditioned reflex, in order to obtain the same reflex—to make it a conditioned reflex: the dog begins to salivate at the sound of the metronome. If a black square is presented to the dog at the same time as the metronome ticks away, it can, of itself, become a signal for salivation. Thus we have a process of second-order conditioning which, in human beings, particularly through language, can be extended to fifth or sixth order conditioning. As opposed to the trial and error learning of Thorndike, the conditioned learning of Pavlov is a progress because it takes into account the structure of the organism. It gives an external description of the process of symbolization and generalization which takes place in the brain. However, it assumes too easily the equivalence of the conditioned reflex and the unconditioned reflex on the basis of external similarities—an assumption into which it is forced by Pavlov's refusal to deal with the problem of purpose.

Hull has made an effort to synthesize Thorndike and Pavlov through his theory of *drive.* From Thorndike he takes the concept of satisfaction and defines it in terms of an organic *need* manifested by a theoretical construct called *drive.* Drive is not as complex as instinct nor as specific as unconditioned reflex or even need. Nor does it pattern behavior directly. It is more an intensity than a steering device. The organism responds to a stimulus, and the response has no preordained efficiency, as instinct would have. This is still trial and error. If a particular response reduces a drive, i.e., if it secures a suitable object for the organism, the association between the stimulus and the response is "reinforced." The relatively vague and rather subjective notion of "satisfaction" no longer explains the retaining of a response; rather, it is retained because it reduces a drive with a direct organic referent.

Thus Hull sees trial and error learning (also known as instrumental learning) and conditioned learning as aspects of the same fundamental process which is described by *drive, cue, response,* and *reward.* The concept of stimulus has been differentiated into an inner component, drive, and an environmental component, the cue. A stimulus may have both a drive function which relates to its intensity and a cue function which relates to its distinctiveness. Hullian theory has been used in such

a way, however, that the drive component of the learning paradigm tends to be secondary to the cue component. What replaces the unconditioned reflexes of Pavlov are the *primary drives*—hunger, thirst, pain, sex, upon which *secondary drives,* which include fear, can be grafted like so many conditioned reflexes.

The selection by *Köhler* deals with *insight* and is in sharp contrast to trial and error learning and to conditioned learning. The argument that the suddenness of insight is proof that it is not connected with trial and error would not be accepted today. In fact, the "S" curve of learning described by Culler (1928) accepts rather well the application of the concept of insight; one could say that failures bombard the gestalt of the monkey as so many frustrations and subsequently decrease his commitment to this gestalt; eventually its components are reorganized into a new gestalt which becomes fixated by the successes which follow its synthesis in the mind of the subject. Learning would thus appear as a series of discontinuities, with insights marking the sharp improvements of performance.

This synthesis between trial and error learning and Gestalt theory was in fact made by *Tolman* and is summarized in his "Summary for Psychologists and Philosophers." One of the forces which led Tolman to this synthesis was a series of experiments on "latent learning," where animals seemed to become familiar with a maze even though there was no reward for its exploration. This familiarity resulted in much faster learning when specific rewards were offered. The hypothesis of a sign-gestalt—what W. I. Thomas would call a "definition of the situation" —explains *latent learning* in a way that Thorndike with his law of effect and his law of use (practice makes perfect and longer lasting) could not match. Latent learning "reinforced" Tolman's belief in the necessity of an intermediary between stimulus and response: Köhler's insight became Tolman's sign gestalt.

Tolman postulated three sets of behavior determinants: capacities, which include past training; immanent determinants; and behavior adjustments.

Immanent determinants are inferred from docile variations (behavior is docile when it responds to successful or unsuccessful consequences) resulting from experimentally controlled conditions. The cognitions include *means-end-readinesses,* also known as *sign-gestalt-readinesses,* and a specific *expectation* aroused by the actually presented stimuli.

Behavior adjustments are the non-observable equivalents for "an actual running-back-and-forth." Tolman, in the tradition of Watson, cites sub-vocal speech as an example of behavior adjustments. As to what the *purposes* of behavior are, Tolman is not as specific as Hull and his theory of drives. Tolman finds it sufficient to reject the built-in purposes of McDougall and the randomness of Thorndike. He refers to his *molar behaviorism,* with its relatively complex sequences of action—such as a psychologist's reciting nonsense syllables in the laboratory in order to get an offer from another university. This is contrasted with Watson's molecular behaviorism. For Tolman, goals are an essential part of the behavioral systems he wishes to study. Others are free to study something else, and that is that. Sometimes science-making demands such arbitrariness. For Tolman, subjective purpose has returned into learning theory. Behaviorism has come of age.

II. THE ORGANIZATION OF MOTIVATIONAL STATES

In the preceding section, the selections dealt with the basic elements of learned motivation. The present section contains selections describing motivational systems closer to the requirements of social system analysts. In fact, they are often constructed ad hoc to justify or to complement a social structural analysis.

Pareto first constructs a typology of psychological forces and analyzes various states of *social equilibrium* as the results of the various combinations into which these forces can enter. Residues and derivations do not in fact pretend to describe the essence of these psychological forces. Rather, they are indices, manifestations, of these forces, the residues being the more stable indicators, the derivations being the more variable.

Of the six residues distinguished by Pareto, the first two, *the instinct of combinations and the persistence of aggregates,* have been most crucial to his sociological theories. For Pareto, the residues remain invariant once established in the personality. Ideally an understanding of a given state of social equilibrium would be the knowledge of the quantitative composition of the residues brought to the society by its individual members. Hence, the major importance of those movements whereby the percentage of residues, especially of Class I and Class II, is made to vary, either in the total society through invasions, or in the governing elite through *circulation of elites* or revolution.

Simmel is also concerned with the motivational background of social equilibrium. He is concerned with why the personality should commit itself to relationships which outlive their initial usefulness. Simmel argues in terms of *inertia.* There is an inertia of the personality system which corresponds to the inertia of the social system. A relationship once undertaken will maintain itself unless some negative force is made to bear upon it. This, to a large extent, is the counterpart of Pareto's residue of the persistence of aggregates. Another strand in Simmel's discussion describes faithfulness as a principle of generalization, a diffuse feeling projecting the experience of the past upon the future. Faithfulness maintains a relationship undisturbed by fluctuations on the outside and in the personalities of the participants.

It is in the discussion of gratitude that Simmel makes the most of this diffuse quality of feeling which exceeds the limits of the immediate situation. While faithfulness exists regardless of need satisfaction, gratitude exists because of need satisfaction but transcends immediate gratification. It is the emotional background of reciprocity. Gratitude is an open commitment for the future, a promise of co-operation. It is more "practical" than faithfulness, "it may yet engender new actions."

Simmel is probably the sociologist who went furthest in analyzing social forces as combinations of sentiments and of "presentations of self." Whatever the arbitrariness of his initial concepts, there is here a hard residue of knowledge that more systematic theories of behavior must integrate.

While Simmel describes the organizations of motivation that contribute to the inertia or integration of social relationships, *Lewin's* selection is concerned with the problem of goal attainment. Lewin was certainly one of the great psychologists of our times, and only categorical restraints from our publisher have prevented us from presenting more extensive selections from his work. "Life space," "valence," "barrier," "levels of aspiration," are concepts which have brought a new richness to our understanding of personality and social structure in microcosmic situations. *Valence* is different from *value* in that valence is a force in a given life space (subject plus human and non-human environment) which represents an active commitment of the personality to the outside world—whether in attraction or repulsion. Leaving aside the problem of why a particular valence should exist, Lewin is concerned with the behavior that results from the complex economy of valences, barriers, and the change in the field of forces which the movement of the individual will create. The principle of least motion for maximum gain, which was utilized by Köhler for the description of insight, is implicitly utilized for the analysis of the individual's performance in situations of decision. These situations always involve, *from the standpoint of the observer,* an algebraic summation of valences and barriers.

While Simmel's gratitude generalizes in the direction of inclusion, *Freud's anxiety* generalizes in the direction of exclusion. Anxiety serves three specific functions: it serves as a signal that a threat to the personality's equilibrium is present; it orients the reaction of the personality to the threat by reinforcing the pleasure principle; libido which is not discharged because of the threat that its cathexis represents for the personality as an integrated system, is transformed into anxiety.

In later developments of his thinking, Freud tended to abandon the idea that blocked libido could be transformed into anxiety. Anxiety is seen more specifically as a homeostatic reaction, and certainly not as an instinctual reaction to specific stimuli. Anxiety is an alarm reaction of personality organization. On the other hand, the painful character of anxiety helps to explain how symptom formation can still satisfy the pleasure principle. The patient flies into neurosis to avoid overwhelming anxiety. Only if we take into account the pain of anxiety that he is trying to avoid, will the "economy"—in a sense the lack of economy—of his symptoms make sense.

The classical *Freudian mechanisms of defense* are part of the structure of the ego. They are means whereby the ego avoids anxiety and assimilates stimuli. Their existence depends upon the property of libido described as *displacement*. When displacement results in the channeling of an impulse into an adequate discharge congruent with social values, then we have the process of *sublimation* which Freud considers as the prototype of healthy mental activity. If the impulse is channeled otherwise, we have the mechanisms of defense which classical psychoanalysis saw as likely to be pathogenic.

Today we tend to see the mechanisms of defense not only as means to ward off threats to the ego, but more generally as the means whereby the ego relates to all the stimuli. The classical list of defense mechanisms includes repression, regression, reaction-formation, isolation, projection, introjection. *Introjection* is the most archaic form of internalization of the object through swallowing it. In *regression*, mastery of reality is replaced by behavior oriented to obsolete role participation. Its role is important in the so-called identification with the hero in fiction. Other mechanisms of defense less often cited are: *denial* where the ego, through a semi-hallucinatory process, refuses to integrate the stimulus; *intellectualization*, whereby the cathectic weaving of a stimulus is blunted; *rationalization*, an effort at the reintegration of behavior by syllogistic chains.[1]

Reaction-formation is one of the most important mechanisms of defense; yet it is one which Freud explains very little. Reaction-formation is a mechanism whereby the ego follows a behavior pattern opposite to its cathectic impulse. Usually reaction-formation results in the transformation of aggressive impulses into patience, forbearance, or even nurturance. Yet there may be the transformation of nurturant impulses into an aggressive approach to the desired object: the gruff person "with a heart of gold" is an example of reaction-formation in the aggressive direction. The bigot obsessed with the dangers created by obscene literaure is another example of reaction-formation. In the face of the normal ambivalence toward stimulus, systematization of behavior will require some reaction-formation. It will be the "compulsive" resolution of ambivalence.

Another aspect of reaction-formation fits well with the Mead-Parsons conception of the internalization of role. In passive reaction-formations, the ego acts out the part of the victim. But the reciprocity of aggression exists within the actor. Hence, the reaction-formation is successful at the cost of reinforcing within the self the disposition which is consciously distasteful to the actor. Eventually the disposition will reveal itself through organic *conversions* or destructive errors.

---

1. For further discussion, cf. Otto Fenichel, *The Psychoanalytic Theory of Neuroses*, New York: W. W. Norton, 1945.

1–THE NATURE OF LEARNING

1. *The Principal Instincts of Man*

BY WILLIAM MCDOUGALL

WE MAY, then, define an instinct as an inherited or innate psycho-physical disposition which determines its possessor to perceive, and to pay attention to, objects of a certain class, to experience an emotional excitement of a particular quality upon perceiving such an object, and to act in regard to it in a particular manner, or, at least, to experience an impulse to such action.

*   *   *

Before we can make any solid progress in the understanding of the complex emotions and impulses that are the forces underlying the thoughts and actions of men and of societies, we must be able to distinguish and describe each of the principal human instincts and the emotional and conative tendencies characteristic of each one of them. This task will be attempted in the present chapter.

*   *   *

In considering the claim of any human emotion or impulse to rank as a primary emotion or simple instinctive impulse, we shall find two principles of great assistance. First, if a similar emotion and impulse are clearly displayed in the instinctive activities of the higher animals, that fact will afford a strong presumption that the emotion and impulse in question are primary and simple; on the other hand, if no such instinctive activity occurs among the higher animals, we must suspect the affective state in question of being either a complex composite emotion or no true emotion. Secondly, we must inquire in each case whether the emotion and impulse in question occasionally appear in human beings with morbidly exaggerated intensity, apart from such general hyper-excitability as is displayed in mania. For it would seem that each instinctive disposition, being a relatively independent functional unit in the constitution of the mind, is capable of morbid hypertrophy or of becoming ab-

normally excitable, independently of the rest of the mental dispositions and functions. That is to say, we must look to comparative psychology and to mental pathology for confirmation of the primary character of those of our emotions that appear to be simple and unanalysable.[1]

The Instinct of Flight and the Emotion of Fear

The instinct to flee from danger is necessary for the survival of almost all species of animals, and in most of the higher animals the instinct is one of the most powerful. Upon its excitement the locomotory apparatus is impelled to its utmost exertions, and sometimes the intensity and long duration of these exertions is more than the visceral organs can support, so that they are terminated by utter exhaustion or death. Men also have been known to achieve extraordinary feats of running and leaping under this impulse; there is a well-known story of a great athlete who, when pursued as a boy by a savage animal, leaped over a wall which he could not again "clear" until he attained his full stature and strength. These locomotory activities are accompanied by a characteristic complex of symptoms, which in its main features is common to man and to many of the higher animals, and which, in conjunction with the violent efforts to escape, constitutes so unmistakable an expression of the emotion of fear that no one hesitates to in-

Reprinted from William McDougall, *An Introduction to Social Psychology* (Boston: John W. Luce & Co., 1950), pp. 29, 45, 48–50, 57–70, 72–73, 81–84, 85–86, 87–89, with the permission of John W. Luce & Co.

1. That the emotion as a fact of consciousness may properly be distinguished from the cognitive process which it accompanies and qualifies is, I think, obvious and indisputable. The propriety of distinguishing between the conative element in consciousness, the impulse, appetite, desire, or aversion, and the accompanying emotion is not so obvious. For these features are most intimately and constantly associated, and introspective discrimination of them is usually difficult. Nevertheless they show a certain degree of independence of one another; e.g., with frequent repetition of a particular emotional situation and reaction, the affective aspect of the process tends to become less prominent, while the impulse grows stronger.

terpret it as such; hence popular speech recognizes the connection of the emotion with the instinct that determines the movements of flight in giving them the one name *fear*. Terror, the most intense degree of this emotion, may involve so great a nervous disturbance, both in men and animals, as to defeat the ends of the instinct by inducing general convulsions or even death. In certain cases of mental disease the patient's disorder seems to consist essentially in an abnormal excitability of this instinct and a consequent undue frequency and intensity of its operation; the patient lives perpetually in fear, shrinking in terror from the most harmless animal or at the least unusual sound, and surrounds himself with safeguards against impossible dangers.

*   *   *

The Instinct of Curiosity and the Emotion of Wonder

The instinct of curiosity is displayed by many of the higher animals, although its impulse remains relatively feeble in most of them. And, in fact, it is obvious that it could not easily attain any considerable strength in any animal species, because the individuals that displayed a too strong curiosity would be peculiarly liable to meet an untimely end. For its impulse is to approach and to examine more closely the object that excites it—a fact well known to hunters in the wilds, who sometimes by exciting this instinct bring the curious animal within the reach of their weapons. The native excitant of the instinct would seem to be any object similar to, yet perceptibly different from, familiar objects habitually noticed. It is therefore not easy to distinguish in general terms between the excitants of curiosity and those of fear; for we have seen that one of the most general excitants of fear is whatever is strange or unfamiliar. The difference seems to be mainly one of degree, a smaller element of the strange or unusual exciting curiosity, while a larger and more pronounced degree of it excites fear. Hence the two instincts, with their opposed impulses of approach and retreat, are apt to be excited in animals and very young children in rapid alternation, and simultaneously in ourselves. Who has not seen a horse, or other animal, alternately approach in curiosity, and flee in fear from, some such object as an old coat upon the ground? And who has not experienced a fearful curiosity in penetrating some dark cave or some secret chamber of an ancient castle? The behaviour of animals under the impulse of curiosity may be well observed by any one who will lie down in a field where sheep or cattle are grazing and repeat at short intervals some pe-

culiar cry. In this way one may draw every member of a large flock nearer and nearer until one finds oneself the centre of a circle of them, drawn up at a respectful distance, of which every pair of eyes and ears is intently fixed upon the strange object of their curiosity.

In the animals nearest to ourselves, namely, the monkeys, curiosity is notoriously strong, and them it impels not merely to approach its object and to direct the senses attentively upon it, but also to active manipulation of it. That a similar impulse is strong in children, no one will deny. Exception may perhaps be taken to the use of wonder as the name for the primary emotion that accompanies this impulse; for this word is commonly applied to a complex emotion of which this primary emotion is the chief but not the sole constituent.[2] But, as was said above, some specialisation for technical purposes of words in common use is inevitable in psychology and in this instance it is, I think, desirable and justifiable owing to the lack of any more appropriate word.

This instinct being one whose exercise is not of prime importance to the individual, exhibits great individual differences as regards its innate strength; and these differences are apt to be increased during the course of life, the impulse growing weaker for lack of use in those in whom it is innately weak, stronger through exercise in those in whom it is innately strong. In men of the latter type it may become the main source of intellectual energy and effort; to its impulse we certainly owe most of the purely disinterested labours of the highest types of intellect. It must be regarded as one of the principal roots of both science and religion.

The Instinct of Pugnacity and the Emotion of Anger

This instinct though not so nearly universal as fear, being apparently lacking in the constitution of the females of some species, ranks with fear as regards the great strength of its impulse and the high intensity of the emotion it generates. It occupies a peculiar position in relation to the other instincts and cannot strictly be brought under the definition of instinct proposed in the first chapter. For it has no specific object or objects the perception of which constitutes the initial stage of the instinctive process. The condition of its excitement is rather any opposition to the free exercise of any impulse, any obstruction to the activity to which the creature is impelled by any one of the other instincts. And its impulse is to break down any such

---

2. A form of admiration in which curiosity (or wonder in the sense in which the word is here used) predominates.

obstruction and to destroy whatever offers this opposition. This instinct thus presupposes the others; its excitement is dependent upon, or secondary to, the excitement of the others and is apt to be intense in proportion to the strength of the obstructed impulse. The most mean-spirited cur will angrily resent any attempt to take away its bone if it is hungry; a healthy infant very early displays anger, if his meal is interrupted; and all through life most men find it difficult to suppress irritation on similar occasions. In the animal world the most furious excitement of this instinct is provoked in the male of many species by any interference with the satisfaction of the sexual impulse; since such interference is the most frequent occasion of its excitement, and since it commonly comes from other male members of his own species, the actions innately organised for securing the ends of this instinct are such actions as are most effective in combat with his fellows. Hence, also, the defensive apparatus of the male is usually like the lion's or the stallion's mane, especially adapted for defence against attacks of his fellows. But the obstruction of every other instinctive impulse may in its turn become the occasion of anger. We see how among the animals even the fear-impulse, the most opposed in tendency to the pugnacious, may on obstruction give place to it; for the hunted creature when brought to bay—*i.e.,* when its impulse to flight is obstructed—is apt to turn upon its pursuers and to fight furiously, until an opportunity for escape presents itself.

Darwin has shown the significance of the facial expression of anger, of the contracted brow and raised upper lip; and man shares with many of the animals the tendency to frighten his opponent by loud roars or bellowings. As with most of the other human instincts, the excitement of this one is expressed in its purest form by children. Many a little boy has, without any example or suggestion, suddenly taken to running with open mouth to bite the person who has angered him, much to the distress of his parents. As the child grows up, as self-control becomes stronger, the life of ideas richer, and the means we take to overcome obstructions to our efforts more refined and complex, this instinct ceases to express itself in its crude natural manner, save when most intensely excited, and becomes rather a source of increased energy of action towards the end set by any other instinct; the energy of its impulse adds itself to and reinforces that of other impulses and so helps us to overcome our difficulties. In this lies its great value for civilised man. A man devoid of the pugnacious instinct would not only be incapable of anger, but would lack this great source of reserve energy which is called into play in most of us by any difficulty in our path. In this respect also it is the opposite of fear, which tends to inhibit all other impulses than its own.

THE INSTINCTS OF SELF-ABASEMENT (OR SUBJECTION) AND OF SELF-ASSERTION (OR SELF-DISPLAY), AND THE EMOTIONS OF SUBJECTION AND ELATION (OR NEGATIVE AND POSITIVE SELF-FEELING)

These two instincts have attracted little attention, and the two corresponding emotions have, so far as I know, been adequately recognised by M. Ribot alone, whom I follow in placing them among the primary emotions. Ribot names the two emotions negative and positive self-feeling respectively, but since these names are awkward in English, I propose, in the interests of a consistent terminology, to call them the emotions of subjection and elation. The clear recognition and understanding of these instincts, more especially of the instinct of self-display, is of the first importance for the psychology of character and volition, as I hope to show in a later chapter. At present I am only concerned to prove that they have a place in the native constitution of the human mind.

The instinct of self-display is manifested by many of the higher social or gregarious animals, especially, perhaps, though not only, at the time of mating. Perhaps among mammals the horse displays it most clearly. The muscles of all parts are strongly innervated the creature holds himself erect, his neck is arched, his tail lifted, his motions become superfluously vigorous and extensive, he lifts his hoofs high in the air, as he parades before the eyes of his fellows. Many animals, especially the birds, but also some of the monkeys are provided with organs of display that are specially disposed on these occasions. Such are the tail of the peacock and the beautiful breast of the pigeon. The instinct is essentially a social one, and is only brought into play by the presence of spectators. Such self-display is popularly recognised as implying pride; we say "How proud he looks!" and the peacock has become the symbol of pride. By psychologists pride is usually denied the animals, because it is held to imply self-consciousness, and that, save of the most rudimentary kind, they probably have not. But this denial arises from the current confusion of the emotions and the sentiments. The word "pride" is no doubt most properly to be used as the name of one form of the self-regarding sentiment, and such sentiment does imply a developed self-consciousness such as no animal can be credited with. Nevertheless, popular opinion is, I think, in the right in attributing to the animals in their moments of self-display the germ of the emotion that is the most essential constituent of pride. It is this primary emotion which may be called positive self-feeling or elation, and which might well be called pride, if that word were not required to denote the sentiment of pride. In the simple form, in which it is expressed by the self-display of animals, it does not necessarily imply self-consciousness.

Many children clearly exhibit this instinct of self-display; before they can walk or talk the impulse finds its satisfaction in the admiring gaze and plaudits of the family circle as each new acquirement is practised; a little later it is still more clearly expressed by the frequently repeated command, "See me do this," or "See how well I can do so-and-so;" and for many a child more than half the delight of riding on a pony, or of wearing a new coat, consists in the satisfaction of this instinct, and vanishes if there be no spectators. A little later, with the growth of self-consciousness the instinct may find expression in the boasting and swaggering of boys, the vanity of girls; while, with almost all of us, it becomes the most important constituent of the self-regarding sentiment and plays an all-important part in the volitional control of conduct, in the way to be discussed in a later chapter.

The situation that more particularly excites this instinct is the presence of spectators to whom one feels oneself for any reason, or in any way, superior, and this is perhaps true in a modified sense of the animals; the "dignified" behaviour of a big dog in the presence of small ones, the stately strutting of a hen among her chicks, seem to be instances in point. We have, then, good reason to believe that the germ of this emotion is present in the animal world, and, if we make use of our second criterion of the primary character of an emotion, it answers well to the test. For in certain mental diseases, especially in the early stages of that most terrible disorder, general paralysis of the insane, exaggeration of this emotion and of its impulse of display is the leading symptom. The unfortunate patient is perpetually in a state of elated self-feeling, and his behaviour corresponds to his emotional state; he struts before the world, boasts of his strength, his immense wealth, his good looks, his luck, his family, when, perhaps, there is not the least foundation for his boastings.

As regards the emotion of subjection or negative self-feeling, we have the same grounds for regarding it as a primary emotion that accompanies the excitement of an instinctive disposition. The impulse of this instinct expresses itself in a slinking, crestfallen behaviour, a general diminution of muscular tone, slow restricted movements, a hanging down of the head, and sidelong glances. In the dog the picture is completed by the sinking of the tail between the legs. All these features express submissiveness, and are calculated to avoid attracting attention or to mollify the spectator. The nature of the instinct is sometimes very completely expressed in the behaviour of a young dog on the approach of a larger, older dog; he crouches or crawls with legs so bent that his belly scrapes the ground, his back hollowed, his tail tucked away, his head sunk and turned a little on one side, and so approaches the imposing stranger with every mark of submission.

The recognition of this behaviour as the expression of a special instinct of self-abasement and of a corresponding primary emotion enables us to escape from a much-discussed difficulty. It has been asked, "Can animals and young children that have not attained to self-consciousness feel shame?" And the answer usually given is, "No; shame implies self-consciousness." Yet some animals, notably the dog, sometimes behave in a way which the popular mind interprets as expressing shame. The truth seems to be that, while fully-developed shame, shame in the full sense of the word, does imply self-consciousness and a self-regarding sentiment, yet in the emotion that accompanies this impulse to slink submissively we may see the rudiment of shame; and, if we do not recognise this instinct, it is impossible to account for the genesis of shame or of bashfulness.

In children the expression of this emotion is often mistaken for that of fear; but the young child sitting on his mother's lap in perfect silence and with face averted, casting sidelong glances at a stranger, presents a picture very different from that of fear.

Applying, again, our pathological test, we find that it is satisfied by this instinct of self-abasement. In many cases of mental disorder the exaggerated influence of this instinct seems to determine the leading symptoms. The patient shrinks from the observation of his fellows, thinks himself a most wretched, useless, sinful creature, and, in many cases he develops delusions of having performed various unworthy or even criminal actions; many such patients declare they are guilty of the unpardonable sin, although they attach no definite meaning to the phrase—that is to say, the patient's intellect endeavours to justify the persistent emotional state, which has no adequate cause in his relations to his fellow-men.

THE PARENTAL INSTINCT AND THE
TENDER EMOTION

As regards the parental instinct and tender emotion, there are wide differences of opinion. Some of the authors who have paid most attention to the psychology of the emotions, notably Mr. A. F. Shand, do not recognize tender emotion as a primary; others, especially Mr. Alex Sutherland and M. Ribot recognize it as a true primary and see in its impulse the root of all altruism; Mr. Sutherland, however, like Adam Smith and many other writers, has confused tender emotion with sympathy, a serious error of incomplete analysis, which Ribot has avoided.

The maternal instinct, which impels the mother to protect and cherish her young, is common to almost all the higher species of animals. Among the lower animals the perpetuation of the species is generally provided for by the production of an immense number of eggs or young (in some species of fish a single adult produces more than a million eggs), which are left entirely unprotected, and are so preyed upon by other creatures that on the average but one or two attain maturity. As we pass higher up the animal scale, we find the number of eggs or young more and more reduced, and the diminution of their number compensated for by parental protection. At the lowest stage this protection may consist in the provision of some merely physical shelter, as in the case of those animals that carry their eggs attached in some way to their bodies. But, except at this lowest stage, the protection afforded to the young always involves some instinctive adaptation of the parent's behaviour. We may see this even among the fishes, some of which deposit their eggs in rude nests and watch over them, driving away creatures that might prey upon them. From this stage onwards protection of offspring becomes increasingly psychical in character, involves more profound modification of the parent's behaviour and a more prolonged period of more effective guardianship. The highest stage is reached by those species in which each female produces at a birth but one or two young and protects them so efficiently that most of the young born reach maturity; the maintenance of the species thus becomes in the main the work of the parental instinct. In such species the protection and cherishing of the young is the constant and all-absorbing occupation of the mother, to which she devotes all her energies, and in the course of which she will at any time undergo privation, pain, and death. The instinct becomes more powerful than any other, and can override any other, even fear itself; for it works directly in the service of the species, while the other instincts work primarily in the service of the individual life, for which Nature cares little. All this has been well set out by Sutherland, with a wealth of illustrative detail, in his work on "The Origin and Growth of the Moral Instinct."

When we follow up the evolution of this instinct to the highest animal level, we find among the apes the most remarkable examples of its operation. Thus in one species the mother is said to carry her young one clasped in one arm uninterruptedly for several months, never letting go of it in all her wanderings. This instinct is no less strong in many human mothers, in whom, of course, it becomes more or less intellectualised and organised as the most essential constituent of the sentiment of parental love. Like other species, the human species is dependent upon this instinct for its continued existence and welfare. It is true that reason, working in the service of the egoistic impulses and sentiments, often circumvents the ends of this instinct and sets up habits which are incompatible with it. When that occurs on a large scale in any society, that society is doomed to rapid decay. But the instinct itself can never die out, save with the disappearance of the human species itself; it is kept strong and effective just because those families and races and nations in which it weakens become rapidly supplanted by those in which it is strong.

It is impossible to believe that the operation of this, the most powerful of the instincts, is not accompanied by a strong and definite emotion; one may see the emotion expressed unmistakably by almost any mother among the higher animals, especially the birds and the mammals—by the cat, for example, and by most of the domestic animals; and it is impossible to doubt that this emotion has in all cases the peculiar quality of the tender emotion provoked in the human parent by the spectacle of her helpless offspring. This primary emotion has been very generally ignored by the philosophers and psychologists; that is, perhaps, to be explained by the fact that this instinct and its emotion are in the main decidedly weaker in men than in women, and in some men, perhaps, altogether lacking. We may even surmise that the philosophers as a class are men among whom this defect of native endowment is relatively common.

It may be asked, How can we account for the fact that men are at all capable of this emotion and of this disinterested protective impulse? For in its racial origin the instinct was undoubtedly primarily maternal. The answer is that it is very common to see a character, acquired by one sex to meet its special needs, transmitted, generally imperfectly and with large individual variations, to the members of the other sex. Familiar examples of such transmission of sexual characters are afforded by the horns and antlers of some species of sheep and deer. That the parental instinct is by no means altogether lacking in men is probably due in the main to such transference of a primarily maternal instinct, though it is probable that in the human species natural selection has confirmed and increased its inheritance by the male sex.

To this view, that the parental tenderness of human beings depends upon an instinct phylogenetically continuous with the parental instinct of the higher animals, it might be objected that the very widespread prevalence of infanticide among existing savages implies that primitive man lacked this instinct and its tender emotion. But that would be a most mistaken objection. There is no feature of savage life more nearly universal than the kindness and tenderness of savages, even of savage fathers, for their little children. All observers are agreed upon this point. I have many a time watched with interest a bloodthirsty head-hunter of Borneo spending a day at home tenderly nursing his infant in his arms. And it is a rule, to which there are few exceptions among savage people, that an infant is only killed during the first hours of its life. If the child is allowed to survive but a few days, then its life is safe; the tender emotion has been called out in fuller strength and has begun to be organised into a sentiment of parental love that is too strong to be overcome by prudential or purely selfish considerations.

*   *   *

Like the other primary emotions, the tender emotion cannot be described; a person who had not experienced it could no more be made to understand its quality than a totally colour-blind person can be made to understand the experience of colour-sensation. Its impulse is primarily to afford physical protection to the child, especially by throwing the arms about it; and that fundamental impulse persists in spite of the immense extension of the range of application of the impulse and its incorporation in many ideal sentiments.[3]

Like all other instinctive impulses, this one, when its operation meets with obstruction or opposition, gives place to, or is complicated by, the pugnacious or combative impulse directed against the source of the obstruction; and, the impulse being essentially protective, its obstruction provokes anger perhaps more readily than the obstruction of any other. In almost all animals that display it, even in those which in all other situations are very timid, any attempt to remove the young from the protecting parent, or in any way to hurt them, provokes a fierce and desperate display of all their combative resources. By the human mother the same prompt yielding of the one impulse to the other is displayed on the same plane of physical protection, but also

on the higher plane of ideal protection; the least threat, the smallest slight or aspersion (*e.g.,* the mere speaking of the baby as "it," instead of as "he" or "she"), the mere suggestion that it is not the most beautiful object in the world, will suffice to provoke a quick resentment.

This intimate alliance between tender emotion and anger is of great importance for the social life of man, and the right understanding of it is fundamental for a true theory of the moral sentiments; for the anger evoked in this way is the germ of all moral indignation, and on moral indignation justice and the greater part of public law are in the main founded. Thus, paradoxical as it may seem, beneficence and punishment alike have their firmest and most essential root in the parental instinct. For the understanding of the relation of this instinct to moral indignation, it is important to note that the object which is the primary provocative of tender emotion is, not the child itself, but the child's expression of pain, fear, or distress of any kind, especially the child's cry of distress; further, that this instinctive response is provoked by the cry, not only of one's own offspring, but of any child. Tender emotion and the protective impulse are, no doubt, evoked more readily and intensely by one's own offspring, because about them a strongly organised and complex sentiment grows up. But the distress of any child will evoke this response in a very intense degree in those in whom the instinct is strong. These are women—and men also, though fewer—who cannot sit still, or pursue any occupation, within sound of the distressed cry of a child; if circumstances compel them to restrain their impulse to run to its relief, they yet cannot withdraw their attention from the sound, but continue to listen in painful agitation.

*   *   *

SOME OTHER INSTINCTS OF LESS WELL-DEFINED EMOTIONAL TENDENCY

The seven instincts we have now reviewed are those whose excitement yields the most definite of the primary emotions; from these seven primary emotions together with feelings of pleasure and pain (and perhaps also feelings of excitement and of depression) are compounded all, or almost all, the affective states that are popularly recognised as emotions, and for which common speech has definite names. But there are other human instincts which, though some of them play but a minor part in the genesis of the emotions, have impulses that are of great importance for social life; they must therefore be mentioned.

Of these by far the most important is the sexual instinct or *instinct of reproduction.* It is un-

---

3. It is, I think, not improbable that the impulse to kiss the child, which is certainly strong and seems to be innate, is a modification of the maternal impulse to lick the young which is a feature of the maternal instinct of so many animal species.

necessary to say anything of the great strength of its impulse or of the violence of the emotional excitement that accompanies its exercise. One point of interest is its intimate connection with the parental instinct. There can, I think, be little doubt that this connection is an innate one, and that in all (save debased) natures it secures that the object of the sexual impulse shall become also the object in some degree of tender emotion.[4] The biological utility of an innate connection of this kind is obvious. It would prepare the way for that co-operation between the male and female in which, even among the animals, a lifelong fidelity and mutual tenderness is often touchingly displayed.

This instinct, more than any other, is apt in mankind to lend the immense energy of its impulse to the sentiments and complex impulses into which it enters, while its specific character remains submerged and unconscious. It is unnecessary to dwell on this feature, since it has been dealt with exhaustively in many thousands of novels. From the point of view of this section the chief importance of this instinct is that it illustrates, in a manner that must convince the most obtuse, the continuity and the essential similarity of nature and function between the human and the animal instincts.

In connection with the instinct of reproduction a few words must be said about *sexual jealousy* and *female coyness*. These are regarded by some authors as special instincts, but perhaps without sufficiently good grounds. Jealousy in the full sense of the word is a complex emotion that presupposes an organised sentiment, and there is no reason to regard the hostile behavior of the male animal in the presence of rivals as necessarily implying any such complex emotion or sentiment. The assumption of a specially intimate innate connection between the instincts of reproduction and of pugnacity will account for the fact that the anger of the male, both in the human and in most animal species, is so readily aroused in an intense degree by any threat of opposition to the operation of the sexual impulse; and perhaps the great strength of the sexual impulse sufficiently accounts for it.

The coyness of the female in the presence of the male may be accounted for in similar fashion by the assumption that in the female the instinct of reproduction has specially intimate innate relations to the instincts of self-display and self-abasement, so that the presence of the male excites these as well as the former instinct.

The desire for food that we experience when hungry, with the impulse to seize it, to carry it to the mouth, to chew it and swallow it, must, I think, be regarded as rooted in a true instinct. In many of the animals the movements of feeding exhibit all the marks of truly instinctive behaviour. But in ourselves the instinct becomes at an early age so greatly modified through experience, on both its receptive and its executive sides, that little, save the strong impulse, remains to mark the instinctive nature of the process of feeding.

The *gregarious* instinct is one of the human instincts of greatest social importance, for it has played a great part in moulding societary forms. The affective aspect of the operation of this instinct is not sufficiently intense or specific to have been given a name. The instinct is displayed by many species of animals, even by some very low in the scale of mental capacity. Its operation in its simplest form implies none of the higher qualities of mind, neither sympathy nor capacity for mutual aid. Mr. Francis Galton has given the classical description of the operation of the crude instinct. Describing the South African ox in Damaraland, he says he displays no affection for his fellows, and hardly seems to notice their existence, so long as he is among them; but, if he becomes separated from the herd, he displays an extreme distress that will not let him rest until he succeeds in rejoining it, when he hastens to bury himself in the midst of it, seeking the closest possible contact with the bodies of his fellows. There we see the working of the gregarious instinct in all its simplicity, a mere uneasiness in isolation and satisfaction in being one of a herd. Its utility to animals liable to the attacks of beasts of prey is obvious.

* * *

The gregarious instinct is no exception to the rule that the human instincts are liable to a morbid hypertrophy under which their emotions and impulses are revealed with exaggerated intensity. The condition known to alienists as agoraphobia seems to result from the morbidly intense working of this instinct—the patient will not remain alone, will not cross a wide empty space, and seeks always to be surrounded by other human beings. But of the normal man also it is true that, as Professor James says: "To be alone is one of the greatest of evils for him. Solitary confinement is by many regarded as a mode of torture too cruel and unnatural for civilised countries to adopt. To one long pent up on a desert island the sight of a human footprint or a human form in the distance would be the most tumultuously exciting of experiences."

* * *

Two other instincts of considerable social importance demand a brief mention. The impulse to

---

4. In so far, of course, as the impulse is not completely thwarted.

collect and hoard various objects is displayed in one way or another by almost all human beings, and seems to be due to a true instinct; it is manifested by many animals in the blind, unintelligent manner that is characteristic of crude instinct. And, like other instinctive impulses of man, it is liable to become morbidly exaggerated, when it appears, in a mild form, as the collecting mania and, in greater excess, as miserliness and kleptomania. Like other instincts, it ripens naturally and comes into play independently of all training. Statistical inquiry among large numbers of children has shown that very few attain adult life without having made a collection of objects of one kind or another, usually without any definite purpose; such collecting is no doubt primarily due to the ripening of an *instinct of acquisition.*

We seem to be justified in assuming in man an *instinct of construction.* The playful activities of children seem to be in part determined by its impulse; and in most civilised adults it still survives, though but little scope is allowed it by the circumstances of the majority. For most of us the satisfaction of having actually made something is very real, quite apart from the value or usefulness of the thing made. And the simple desire to make something, rooted in this instinct, is probably a contributing motive to all human constructions from a mud-pie to a metaphysical system or a code of laws.

The instincts enumerated above, together with a number of minor instincts, such as those that prompt to crawling and walking, are, I think, all that we can recognise with certainty in the constitution of the human mind. Lightly to postulate an indefinite number and variety of human instincts is a cheap and easy way to solve psychological problems, and is an error hardly less serious and less common than the opposite error of ignoring all the instincts. How often do we not hear of the religious instinct! Renan asserted that the religious instinct is as natural to man as the nest-building instinct is to birds, and many authors have written of it as one of the fundamental attributes of the human mind. But, if we accept the doctrine of the evolution of man from animal forms, we are compelled to seek the origin of religious emotions and impulses in instincts that are not specifically religious. And consideration of the conditions, manifestations, and tendencies of religious emotions must lead to the same search. For it is clear that religious emotion is not a simple and specific variety, such as could be conditioned by any one instinct; it is rather a very complex and diversified product of the co-operation of several instincts, which bring forth very heterogeneous manifestations, differing from one another as widely as light from darkness, according to the degree and kind of guidance afforded by imagination and reason.

2. *On Behaviorism*

BY JOHN B. WATSON

Scientific Procedure

THE DETAILED SUBJECT MATTER OF SCIENTIFIC PSYCHOLOGY

AS A SCIENCE psychology puts before herself the task of unraveling the complex factors involved in the development of human behavior from infancy to old age, and of finding the laws for the regulation of behavior. At first sight it may

seem that this program leaves out many of the factors with which psychology ought to be concerned. Historically considered, this is true, but when we are confronted both with the practical and scientific needs of life we are ready to admit that, after all, what we seek to have psychology busy herself with is just this matter of *environmental adjustment;* what man can do apart from his training; what he can be trained to do, and what the best methods for training are; and finally, how, when the varied systems of instincts and habits have sufficiently developed, we can arrange the conditions for calling out appropriate action upon de-

Reprinted from John B. Watson, *Psychology from the Point of View of the Behaviorist* (Philadelphia: J. B. Lippincott Co., 1919), pp. 8–15, 38–41.

mand. To solve such problems we must necessarily study the simple and complex things which call out action in man; how early in life he can react to the various simple and complex sense stimuli; at what age he usually puts on the various instincts, and what the situations are which call them out. Just what is the pattern of his instinctive acts—that is, does the human being, apart from training, do any complex acts instinctively as do the lower animals? If so, what is man's full equipment of instincts? When does emotional activity manifest itself? and what are the situations which call it out? and what special acts can be observed in emotional behavior? How soon can we observe the beginnings of habit in infants? What special methods can we develop for rapidly and securely implanting and retaining the body and speech habits which society demands? Do we find special and individual equipments in infants, and do these develop, and, later, form the basis for their entering one kind of vocation or another, or developing into one or another type of personality? Are there such factors as habit and instinct conflicts, distortion of habits and emotions? How do they manifest themselves? and is it possible to develop methods for shaping the environment of the individual so that such conflicts will not arise? What in general are the factors which affect the functioning of habits once they are acquired?

STIMULUS AND RESPONSE

This general description of the subject matter of psychology helps us very little as regards the analysis of particular problems in conduct and behavior. In order to plan an experimental attack upon any problem in psychology we must first reduce it to its simplest terms. If we look over the list of problems in human behavior given in the preceding paragraph, and at our practical examples, we shall see that there are common factors running through all forms of human acts. In each adjustment there is always both a *response or act* and a *stimulus or situation* which call out that response. Without going too far beyond our facts, it seems possible to say that the stimulus is always provided by the environment, external to the body, or by the movements of man's own muscles and the secretions of his glands; finally, that the responses always follow relatively immediately upon the presentation or incidence of the stimulus. These are really assumptions, but they seem to be basal ones for psychology. Before we finally accept or reject them we shall have to examine into both the nature of the stimulus or situation, and of the response. If we provisionally accept them we may say that the goal of psychological study is the *ascertaining of such data and laws that, given the stimulus, psychology can predict what the response will be; or, on the other hand, given the response, it can specify the nature of the effective stimulus.*

USE OF THE TERM "STIMULUS"

We use the term *stimulus* in psychology as it is used in physiology. Only in psychology we have to extend somewhat the usage of the term. In the psychological laboratory, when we are dealing with relatively simple factors, such as the effect of ether waves of different lengths, the effect of sound waves, etc., and are attempting to isolate their effects upon the adjustments of men, we speak of stimuli. On the other hand, when the factors leading to reactions are more complex, as, for example, in the social world, we speak of *situations*. A situation is, of course, upon final analysis, resolvable into a complex group of stimuli. As examples of stimuli we may name such things as rays of light of different wave lengths, sound waves differing in amplitude, length, phase, and combination; gaseous particles given off in such small diameters that they affect the membrane of the nose; solutions which contain particles of matter of such size that the taste buds are thrown into action; solid objects which affect the skin and mucous membrane; radiant stimuli which call out temperature response; noxious stimuli, such as cutting, pricking, and those injuring tissue generally. Finally, movements of the muscles and activity in the glands themselves serve as stimuli by acting upon the afferent nerve endings in the moving muscles.

It must be emphasized here that only under the rarest experimental conditions can we stimulate the organism with a single stimulus. Life presents stimuli in confusing combinations. As you write you are stimulated by a complex system—perspiration pours from your brow, the pen has a tendency to slip from your grasp; the words you write are focussed upon your retinæ; the chair offers stimulation, and finally the noises from the street constantly impinge upon your ear-drum. But far more important, delicate instruments would show that, though you are not speaking aloud, your vocal mechanisms—tongue, throat and laryngeal muscles—are in constant motion, moving in habitual trains: these laryngeal and throat movements serve largely as the stimuli for releasing the writing movements of the hands. The fact that you are here in the lecture room, facing your instructor and surrounded by your classmates, is another very important element. The world of stimulation is thus seen to be exceedingly complex. It is convenient to speak of a total mass of stimulating factors, which lead man to react as a whole, as a situation. Situations can be of the simplest kind or of the greatest complexity. It should be noted here, finally, that there are many forms of physical energy which do not directly affect our sense organs. As examples we may cite the facts that ether waves longer than $760\mu\mu$ or shorter than $397\mu\mu$ do not lead to visual reactions, and that many of the wave motions in the air are of such length or amplitude that they do not produce auditory stimulation. The inability of the human organism to respond to many possible forms of stimulation will be discussed later.

THE GENERAL NATURE OF RESPONSE

In a similar way we employ in psychology the physiological term "response," but again we must slightly extend its use. The movements which result from a tap on the patellar tendon, or from stroking the soles of the feet are "simple" responses which are studied both in physiology and in medicine. In psychology our study, too, is sometimes concerned with simple responses of these types, but more often with several complex responses taking place simultaneously. In the latter case we sometimes use the popular term "act" or adjustment, meaning by that that the whole group of responses is integrated in such a way (instinct or habit) that the individual does something which we have a name for, that is, "takes food," "builds a house," "swims," "writes a letter," "talks."[1] Psychology is not concerned with the goodness or badness of acts, or with their successfulness, as judged by occupational or moral standards. Because a man fails by his separate acts to get his food, to build his house, to work out his mathematical problem, or to live in harmony with his wife, is no reason for rejecting him as a psychological subject. We study him for his *reaction possibilities and without prejudice;* the discovery of the fact that he will make only abortive attempts to meet and control certain aspects of his environment is an important part of our task; just as important as being able to state that he can make certain other types of adjustment. "Successful" adjustments, "good" acts, "bad" acts, are terms really which society uses. Every social age sets up certain standards of action, but these standards change from cultural epoch to cultural epoch. Hence they are not psychological standards. Reaction possibilities, however, on the average probably remain about the same from eon to eon. It lies well within the bounds of probability that if we were able to obtain a new-born baby belonging to the dynasty of the Pharaohs, and were to bring him up along with other lads in Boston, he would develop into the same kind of college youth that we find among the other Harvard students. His chances for success in life would probably not be at all different from those of his classmates. The results obtained from the scientific analysis of reaction in the human being should fit any cultural age. It is part of the function of the psychologist to tell whether a given individual has the reaction possibilities within him to meet the standards of that cultural age, and the most rapid way of bringing him to act in accordance with them. The fact that social values (group *mores*) change puts ever new burdens upon the psychologist, because every change in the *mores* means a different situation, to which man has to respond by a different combination of acts, and any new set of acts must be incorporated into and integrated with the rest of the action systems of the individual. The problems put up to psychology are those of deciding whether the individual can meet the new standards, and for determining and developing methods of instructing him.

Motor and Glandular Indicators of Response.— What is it that the psychologist can observe? *Behavior,* of course. But behavior on analysis is the separate systems of reactions that the individual makes to his environment. When we come to study the mechanics of such adjustments we find that they depend upon the integration of reflexes connecting the receptors with the muscles and glands. It should be emphasized here that objective psychology does not analyze such integrations to the bitter end except where the problem demands it. Concrete, whole activities are as important to the behaviorist as to other psychologists. . . .

* * *

THE GENERAL CLASSIFICATION OF RESPONSES

The various possibilities of reaction are thus seen to be vast; so vast, indeed, that it would seem at first sight as though any classification would be impossible. We can at least find a convenient grouping which will serve both for discussion and for setting experimental problems. Most reactions may be looked upon as falling into one of four main classes:

1. Explicit habit responses: as examples we cite unlocking a door, tennis playing, violin playing, building houses, talking easily to people, staying on good terms with the members of your own and the opposite sex.

2. Implicit habit responses: *"thinking,"* by *which we mean subvocal talking,* general body

---

1. But it should be well understood that whatever the man does under stimulation is a response or adjustment— blushing, increased heart-beat, change in respiration, etc., are definite part adjustments. We have names for only a few thousand of the total possible number of such adjustments. The term adjustment is used by most writers to refer to the doing of one of these *named acts.* In this volume the terms adjustment, response, and reaction are used almost interchangeably.

language habits, bodily sets or attitudes which are not easily observable without instrumentation or experimental aid; the system of conditioned reflexes in the various glands and unstriped muscular mechanisms—for example, conditioned salivary reflexes.

3. Explicit hereditary responses: including man's observable instinctive and emotional reactions as seen, for example, in grasping, sneezing, blinking and dodging, and in fear, rage, love.

4. Implicit hereditary responses: this includes, of course, the whole system of endocrine or ductless gland secretions, changes in circulation, etc., so largely studied by physiology. Here again instrumentation or experimental aid is necessary before observation can be made.

These various types of response will be studied in detail in later chapters. The classification as a whole should be clear, with the possible exception of 2 (implicit habit responses). This group is so important and so generally neglected in discussion that we shall single it out here for brief mention in advance of the chapter in which it is entered into with some care.

WHAT MAN IS DOING WHEN NOT OVERTLY ACTING

With a highly specialized organism like man, even careful observation often fails to show any overt response. A man may sit motionless at his desk with pen in hand and paper before him. In popular parlance we may say he is idle or "thinking," but our *assumption* is that his muscles are really as active and possibly more active than if he were playing tennis. But what muscles? Those muscles which have been trained to act when he is in such a situation, his laryngeal, tongue, and speech muscles generally.[2] Those muscles are as active and are carrying out as orderly a system of movements as if he were executing a sonata on the piano; they are doing it well or ill, depending upon the training he has had along the particular lines which engage him. While we cannot at present watch the play of this implicit stream of words, there is no reason for hypothecating a mystery about it. Could we bring "thinking" out for observation as readily as we can tennis playing or rowing, the need of "explaining" it would disappear. We shall see later that efforts have been made to bring such responses under experimental control. But entirely apart from our present unreadiness to make observation on implicit habits, we find a certain way of arriving indirectly at the same end: *implicit language habits,* by methods which we shall study, come to issue finally in overt action.

---

2. Indeed, the whole glandular and muscular systems are contributory.

By watching the easily observable explicit habits and instincts of an individual keenly enough, and for a sufficient stretch of time, and under varying enough conditions, we can obtain the necessary data for most psychological requirements.

* * *

Verbal Report Methods

INTRODUCTION

The methods so far discussed have dealt with the integrated motor and glandular behavior of individuals other than ourselves. The methods have been largely developed by and have come into prominence through the study of animal behavior and infant human subjects. Indeed, in these fields we must depend largely upon such methods, since the observation of the happenings in their own bodies and the verbal reports of the same are impossible in the case of animals, or very imperfect in the case of abnormal individuals. Man is above all an animal which reacts most often and most complexly with speech reactions. The notion has somehow gained ground that objective psychology does not deal with speech reactions. This, of course, is a mistake. It would be foolish and one-sided to an absurd degree to neglect man's vocal behavior. Often the sole observable reaction in man is speech. In other words, his adjustments to situations are made more frequently by speech than through action of the remaining motor mechanisms. We shall in a later chapter develop our notion of the implicit and explicit language adjustments. We wish here mainly to show the use of speech reactions as a part of general psychological methods. As an illustration of the use of the verbal report method in an actual experiment we may glance for a moment at the tests on sensitivity to warmth and cold on a given area of the skin. We first mark off a small area and go over it with a warm and a cold cylinder: we say to the subject, "Tell us each time the cold cylinder is applied and each time the warm cylinder is applied." If the area touched is sensitive to cold he *responds with the word "cold,"* and similarly when the warm cylinder is applied with the word *"warm."* The verbal report or response is put down in our records of the results of the experiment and is used exactly as the conditioned reflex responses would be used had we adopted that form of experimentation in our test.

IS THERE A VERBAL REPORT METHOD DISTINCT FROM OTHER OBSERVABLE METHODS?

Up to the present time psychologists have employed the verbal report method in a somewhat different sense from that used here. Without entering into this bitterly contested and controversial field, we can briefly outline the position of this text in regard to it. The question: Can I make the same observations upon myself that I make on other individuals? brings home the difficulties. The answer is, of course, "yes," but it will be remembered that . . . we stated that all we can observe in another individual is his behavior, and we defined behavior as the integrated responses of muscles and glands. The question now becomes simpler: Can I observe the movements of my own muscles and glands and their integration? For example, that I am writing, that my face is flushed, etc.? Who would deny it?

At this point we diverge for a moment to correct a misconception which has arisen with reference to objective psychology. The misconception lies in the fact that a good many psychologists have misunderstood the behaviorist's position. They insist that he is only observing the individual movements of the muscles and glands; that he is interested in the muscles and glands in exactly the same way the physiologist is interested in them. This is not the whole statement. *The behaviorist is interested in integrations and total activities of the individual.* At one moment we ask the question: What is the individual doing? We observe that he is typewriting, searching for a lost pocket-book or "reacting" to an emotional stimulus. If the latter happens to be true and we are interested in the way his emotional life as a whole hangs together, we may go on to show why the individual reacts in an emotional way to this particular stimulus. We may show how his fear reactions to certain situations arose in his infancy and how they have affected his whole personality and more highly organized habit activities.

To illustrate this we may give a hypothetical example: Through some injury (or other emotional happening) in youth, occasioned by a rapidly moving mechanical toy, the individual cannot be induced to enter an automobile or motor boat or to ride in a train if it can possibly be avoided. In the occupations and activities of individuals we do not stop as a rule to reduce the total activity to muscle twitches. We can do it if necessary and we do it at times when it becomes necessary to study the various part reactions. Surely objective psychology can study brick-laying, house building, playing games, marriage or emotional activity without being accused of reducing everything to muscle twitch or the secretion of a gland. It is just as fair to accuse the behaviorist, or indeed the conventional psychologist as far as that goes, of reducing everything to the ionic constitution of matter. All of us believe that matter is constituted as the physicists would have us believe, but his formulation does not help us very much in specific psychological problems. On the psychological side, we can describe a man's behavior in selecting and marrying a wife. We can show how that event has influenced his whole life after marriage. In detail, how the increased responsibility stabilized certain emotional mal-adjustments, how the added financial burden led him to work longer hours and to study the details of his profession so that his salary would be increased and his number of business connections enlarged. It would not help us very much in the present state of science to be able to trace the molecular changes in cell constitution— they certainly exist, but are aside from our problem. Our problem is the effect of marriage upon the general behavior of this one individual.

3. *The Law of Effect*

BY EDWARD L. THORNDIKE

THE INTELLECT, character and skill possessed by any man is the product of certain original tendencies and the training which they have received. His eventual nature is the development of his original nature in the environment which it has had. Human nature in general is the result of the original nature of man, the laws of learning, and the forces of nature amongst which man lives and learns.

In a previous volume[1] the original tendencies of

Reprinted from Edward L. Thorndike, *The Psychology of Learning* (New York: Teachers College, Columbia University, 1913), II, pp. 1–5.

1. *Educational Psychology, Vol. I, The Original Nature of Man.*

man as a species were listed and described. It was shown that these constitute an enormous fund of *connections* or *bonds* of varying degrees of directness and strength between the *situations* furnished by physical forces, plants, animals and the behavior of other men and the *responses* of which the human creature is capable. Many of these tendencies are notably modifiable; and some of them—such as vocalization, manipulation, curiosity, "doing something to have something happen," and "making a variety of responses to an annoying state of affairs which continues in spite of this, that and the other responses"—are veritable hot-beds for the growth of learned habits.

These original human tendencies include also certain ones whereby modifiability or learning itself is possible. These are best thought of in the form of the three laws of Readiness, Exercise and Effect. The Law of Readiness is: When any conduction unit is in readiness to conduct, for it to do so is satisfying. When any conduction unit is not in readiness to conduct, for it to conduct is annoying. When any conduction unit is in readiness to conduct, for it *not* to do so is annoying. By a satisfying state of affairs is meant one which the animal does nothing to avoid, often doing things which maintain or renew it. By an annoying state of affairs is meant one which the animal does nothing to preserve, often doing things which put an end to it.

The Law of Exercise comprises the laws of *Use* and *Disuse*.

The Law of Use is: When a modifiable connection is made[2] between a situation and a response, that connection's strength is, other things being equal, increased. By the strength of a connection is meant roughly the probability that the connection will be made when the situation recurs. Greater probability that a connection will be made means a greater probability for the same time, or an equal probability, but for a longer time.[3] This probability in any case would be for the recurrence of the connection, supposing all other conditions—of general health, general or special fatigue, interest, time of day, distraction by competing tendencies, and the like—to be equal. Furthermore, in certain cases, where the probability that the connection will be made as the result of the mere presence

of the situation is zero, the connection still may exist with a measurable degree of strength, shown by the fact that it can be re-made more readily.[4] Also, in certain cases in each of which the probability that the connection will be made is 100 per cent, the connections still may exist with different degrees of strength, shown by the fact that the probability of 100 per cent will hold for a week only or for a year; will succumb to a slight, or prevail over a great, distraction; or will otherwise show little or much strength. Thus, if the reader will read and repeat *miscob raltof* once or twice he may be apparently as able to supply the *raltof* when *miscob* is presented as if he had read and repeated these words a thousand times: but the future history of the two connections would reveal their differences in strength.

Ultimately degrees of strength of a connection in behavior will be defined as degrees of some anatomical or physiological fact whereby synapses between neurones differ in intimacy.

Varying symptoms that we now refer to the "strength" of a connection will then each appear as a consequence of this difference in the neurones concerned. For the present, greater strength has to mean either a greater percentage of occurrence under equal conditions outside of itself; or an equal percentage of occurrence for a longer time, or against greater competition; or a readier reëstablishment to equal strength (tested in any of the above ways); or some even more subtle and indirect effects on behavior.

It should be borne in mind also that the connection is often a compound of several connections each having possibly a different degree of strength. Thus, the connection between the situation, *Understanding of and desire to fulfill the command, "Write that man's full name,"* and the response of writing *Jonathan Edwards Leighton* is multiple. One of the names may be remembered and the other not; the bond productive of the general structure of the name may be strong, but all the others very weak, with the result that *Timothy Williams Damon* is the best that can be done; similarly for many variations in completeness, spelling, and so on. The actual physiological bond in even the apparently most single connections is doubtless a compound, and subject to variation by varying unevenly in its different parts as well as by an equal strengthening or weakening of them all.

The Law of Disuse is: When a modifiable connection is *not* made between a situation and a re-

---

2. The vigor and duration of each "making" of the connection count, as well as the number of times that it is made.

3. Thus, a certain greater strength of the connection between the situation. *"What is the square of 16?"* and the response, *"256,"* may mean that the probability of that response to that situation is now ninety out of a hundred instead of sixty out of a hundred; or that it is ninety-nine out of a hundred for fifty days hence instead of for twenty days hence.

4. Thus, though a man was utterly unable to give the English equivalents of a hundred Greek words, both on January 1, 1905, and on Jan. 1, 1910, he might have been able to relearn them in thirty minutes in 1905, but only in sixty minutes in 1910.

sponse during a length of time, that connection's strength is decreased. The explanations and qualifications stated in connection with the Law of Use apply here also.

The Law of Effect is: When a modifiable connection between a situation and a response is made and is accompanied or followed by a satisfying state of affairs, that connection's strength is increased: When made and accompanied or followed by an annoying state of affairs, its strength is decreased. The strengthening effect of satisfyingness (or the weakening effect of annoyingness) upon a bond varies with the closeness of the connection between it and the bond. This closeness or intimacy of association of the satisfying (or annoying) state of affairs with the bond in question may be the result of nearness in time or of attentiveness to the situation, response and satisfying event in question. "Strength" means the same here as in the case of the Law of Use.

These laws were briefly explained and illustrated in the previous volume. By their action original tendencies are strengthened, preserved, weakened, or altogether abolished; old situations have new responses bound to them and old responses are bound to new situations; and the inherited fund of instincts and capacities grows into a multitude of habits, interests and powers. They are the agents by which man acquires connections productive of behavior suitable to the environment in which he lives. *Adaptation, adjustment, regulative change,* and all other similar terms descriptive of successful learning, refer to their effects. The consideration of their action in detail and of the results to which it leads is one task of this volume.

A man's intellect, character and skill is the sum of his tendencies to respond to situations and elements of situations. The number of different situation-response connections that make up this sum would, in an educated adult, run well up into the millions. Consequently, in place of any list of these detailed tendencies to make responses r_1, r_2, r_3, etc. to each particular situation, we may summarize the man in terms of broader traits or functions, such as "knowledge of German," "honesty," "speed in writing," "love of music," "memory for figures," "fidelity of visual images of faces," and the like.

In educational theories of human learning, and still more in the actual control of it by school practice, these larger traits or functions—these knowledges, powers, conducts, interests and skills—rather than the elementary connections and readinesses of which they are composed, are commonly the subjects of discussion and experiment. Psychological theory and experimentation have also been engaged with traits or functions each of which denotes a group of elementary tendencies, though the traits or functions or abilities which have been investigated by psychologists are usually narrower than those just listed. For example, amongst the functions which have been somewhat elaborately studied are "rapidity in tapping as with a telegraph key," "the delicacy of discrimination of pitch," "ability to grasp and retain a series of nonsense syllables," "skill in tossing balls," and "interest in puzzles."

Facts concerning the nature of such "traits" or "functions" or "abilities" and their improvement by practice have been accumulating very rapidly in the course of the last fifteen years. To present and interpret these facts is the second task of this volume, and the one to which the majority of its pages will be assigned.

4. On Conditioned Reflexes

BY IVAN P. PAVLOV

THE AGGREGATE of reflexes constitutes the foundation of the nervous activities both of men and of animals. It is therefore of great im-

Reprinted from Ivan P. Pavlov, *Conditioned Reflexes,* trans. G. V. Anrep (London: Oxford University Press, 1927), pp. 11–15, 23–26, 27, 28–29, 30–32, 395, with the permission of Oxford University Press.

portance to study in detail all the fundamental reflexes of the organism. Up to the present, unfortunately, this is far from being accomplished, especially, as I have mentioned before, in the case of those reflexes which have been known vaguely as "instincts." Our knowledge of these latter is very limited and fragmentary. Their classification under such headings as "alimentary," "defensive," "sexual," "parental" and "social" instincts, is thoroughly inadequate. Under each of these heads is assembled often a large number of individual reflexes. Some of these are quite unidentified; some are confused with others; and many are still only partially appreciated. I can demonstrate from my own experience to what extent the subject remains inchoate and full of gaps. In the course of the researches which I shall presently explain, we were completely at a loss on one occasion to find any cause for the peculiar behaviour of an animal. It was evidently a very tractable dog, which soon became very friendly with us. We started off with a very simple experiment. The dog was placed in a stand with loose loops round its legs, but so as to be quite comfortable and free to move a pace or two. Nothing more was done except to present the animal repeatedly with food at intervals of some minutes. It stood quietly enough at first, and ate quite readily, but as time went on it became excited and struggled to get out of the stand, scratching at the floor, gnawing the supports, and so on. This ceaseless muscular exertion was accompanied by breathlessness and continuous salivation, which persisted at every experiment during several weeks, the animal getting worse and worse until it was no longer fitted for our researches. For a long time we remained puzzled over the unusual behaviour of this animal. We tried out experimentally numerous possible interpretations, but though we had had long experience with a great number of dogs in our laboratories we could not work out a satisfactory solution of this strange behaviour, until it occurred to us at last that it might be the expression of a special *freedom reflex,* and that the dog simply could not remain quiet when it was constrained in the stand. This reflex was overcome by setting off another against it—the reflex for food. We began to give the dog the whole of its food in the stand. At first the animal ate but little, and lost considerably in weight, but gradually it got to eat more, until at last the whole ration was consumed. At the same time the animal grew quieter during the course of the experiments: the freedom reflex was being inhibited. It is clear that the freedom reflex is one of the most important reflexes, or, if we use a more general term, reactions, of living beings. This reflex has even yet to find its final recognition. In James's writings it is not even enumerated among the special human "instincts." But it is clear that if the animal were not provided with a reflex of protest against boundaries set to its freedom, the smallest obstacle in its path would interfere with the proper fulfilment of its natural functions. Some animals as we all know have this freedom reflex

to such a degree that when placed in captivity they refuse all food, sicken and die.

As another example of a reflex which is very much neglected we may refer to what may be called the *investigatory reflex.* I call it the "What-is-it?" reflex. It is this reflex which brings about the immediate response in man and animals to the slightest changes in the world around them, so that they immediately orientate their appropriate receptor organ in accordance with the perceptible quality in the agent bringing about the change, making full investigation of it. The biological significance of this reflex is obvious. If the animal were not provided with such a reflex its life would hang at every moment by a thread. In man this reflex has been greatly developed with far-reaching results, being represented in its highest form by inquisitiveness—the parent of that scientific method through which we may hope one day to come to a true orientation in knowledge of the world around us.

Still less has been done towards the elucidation of the class of negative or inhibitory reflexes (instincts) which are often evoked by any strong stimulus or even by weak stimuli, if unusual. Animal hypnotism, so-called, belongs to this category.

As the fundamental nervous reactions both of men and of animals are inborn in the form of definite reflexes, I must again emphasize how important it is to compile a complete list comprising all these reflexes with their adequate classification. For, as will be shown later on, all the remaining nervous functions of the animal organism are based upon these reflexes. Now, although the possession of such reflexes as those just described constitutes the fundamental condition for the natural survival of the animal, they are not in themselves sufficient to ensure a prolonged, stable and normal existence. This can be shown in dogs in which the cerebral hemispheres have been removed. Leaving out of account the internal reflexes, such a dog still retains the fundamental external reflexes. It is attracted by food; it is repelled by nocuous stimuli; it exhibits the investigatory reflex, raising its head and pricking up its ears to sound. In addition it exhibits the freedom reflex, offering a powerful resistance to any restraint. Nevertheless it is wholly incapable of looking after itself, and if left to itself will very soon die. Evidently something important is missing in its present nervous make-up. What nervous activities can it have lost? It is easily seen that, in this dog, the number of stimuli evoking reflex reaction is considerably diminished; those remaining are of an elemental, generalized nature, and act at a very short range. Consequently the dynamic equilibrium between the inner forces of the animal system and the external forces in its environment has become elemental as compared with the exquisite adaptability of the normal animal, and the simpler balance is obviously inadequate to life.

Let us return now to the simplest reflex from which our investigations started. If food or some rejectable substance finds its way into the mouth, a secretion of saliva is produced. The purpose of this secretion is in the case of food to alter it chemically, in the case of a rejectable substance to dilute and wash it out of the mouth. This is an example of a reflex due to the physical and chemical properties of a substance when it comes into contact with the mucous membrane of the mouth and tongue. But, in addition to this, a similar reflex secretion is evoked when these substances are placed at a distance from the dog and the receptor organs affected are only those of smell and sight. Even the vessel from which the food has been given is sufficient to evoke an alimentary reflex complete in all its details; and, further, the secretion may be provoked even by the sight of the person who brought the vessel, or by the sound of his footsteps. All these innumerable stimuli falling upon the several finely discriminating distance receptors lose their power for ever as soon as the hemispheres are taken from the animal, and those only which have a direct effect on mouth and tongue still retain their power. The great advantage to the organism of a capacity to react to the former stimuli is evident, for it is in virtue of their action that food finding its way into the mouth immediately encounters plenty of moistening saliva, and rejectable substances, often nocuous to the mucous membrane, find a layer of protective saliva already in the mouth which rapidly dilutes and washes them out. Even greater is their importance when they evoke the motor component of the complex reflex of nutrition, *i.e.,* when they act as stimuli to the reflex of seeking food.

Here is another example—the reflex of self-defence. The strong carnivorous animal preys on weaker animals, and these if they waited to defend themselves until the teeth of the foe were in their flesh would speedily be exterminated. The case takes on a different aspect when the defence reflex is called into play by the sights and sounds of the enemy's approach. Then the prey has a chance to save itself by hiding or by flight.

How can we describe, in general, this difference in the dynamic balance of life between the normal and the decorticated animal? What is the general mechanism and law of this distinction? It is pretty evident that under natural conditions the normal animal must respond not only to stimuli which themselves bring immediate benefit or harm, but also to other physical or chemical agencies—waves of sound, light, and the like—which in themselves only *signal* the approach of these stimuli; though it is not the sight and sound of the beast of prey which is in itself harmful to the smaller animal, but its teeth and claws.

Now although the *signalling stimuli* do play a part in those comparatively simple reflexes we have given as examples, yet this is not the most important point. The essential feature of the highest activity of the central nervous system, with which we are concerned and which in the higher animals most probably belongs entirely to the hemispheres, consists not in the fact that innumerable signalling stimuli do initiate reflex reactions in the animal, but in the fact that under different conditions these same stimuli may initiate quite different reflex reactions; and conversely the same reaction may be initiated by different stimuli.

In the above-mentioned example of the salivary reflex, the signal at one time is one particular vessel, at another time another; under certain conditions one man, under different conditions another—strictly depending upon which vessel had been used in feeding and which man had brought the vessel and given food to the dog. This evidently makes the machine-like responsive activities of the organism still more precise, and adds to it qualities of yet higher perfection. So infinitely complex, so continuously in flux, are the conditions in the world around, that that complex animal system which is itself in living flux, and that system only, has a chance to establish dynamic equilibrium with the environment. Thus we see that the fundamental and the most general function of the hemispheres is that of reacting to signals presented by innumerable stimuli of interchangeable signification.

*   *   *

Our next step will be to consider the question of the nature of signalization and of its mechanism from a purely physiological point of view. It has been mentioned already that a reflex is an inevitable reaction of the organism to an external stimulus, brought about along a definite path in the nervous system. Now it is quite evident that in signalization all the properties of a reflex are present. In the first place an external stimulus is required. This was given in our first experiment by the sounds of a metronome. These sounds falling on the auditory receptor of the dog caused the propagation of an impulse along the auditory nerve. In the brain the impulse was transmitted to the secretory nerves of the salivary glands, and passed thence to the glands, exciting them to active secretion. It is true that in the experiment with the metronome an interval of several seconds elapsed between the beginning of the stimulus and the beginning of the salivary secretion, whereas the time interval for the inborn reflex secretion was only 1 to 2 seconds. The longer latent period was, however, due to some special conditions of the experiment, as will come out more clearly as we proceed. But generally speaking the reaction to signals under natural conditions is as speedy as are the inborn reflexes. We shall be considering the latent period of signalization in fuller detail in a further lecture.

In our general survey we characterized a reflex as a necessary reaction following upon a strictly definite stimulus under strictly defined conditions. Such a definition holds perfectly true also for signalization; the only difference is that the type of the effective reaction to signals depends upon a greater number of conditions. But this does not make signalization differ fundamentally from the better known reflexes in any respect, since in the latter, variations in character or force, inhibition and absence of reflexes, can also be traced to some definite change in the conditions of the experiment.

Thorough investigation of the subject shows that accident plays no part whatever in the signalizing activity of the hemispheres, and all experiments proceed strictly according to plan. In the special laboratory I have described, the animal can frequently be kept under rigid experimental observation for 1 to 2 hours without a single drop of saliva being secreted independently of stimuli applied by the observer, although in the ordinary type of physiological laboratory experiments are very often distorted by the interference of extraneous and uncontrolled stimuli.

All these conditions leave no grounds for regarding the phenomena which we have termed "signalization" as being anything else than reflex. There is, however, another aspect of the question which at a first glance seems to point to an essential difference between the better known reflexes and signalization. Food, through its chemical and physical properties, evokes the salivary reflex in every dog right from birth, whereas this new type claimed as reflex—"the signal reflex"—is built up gradually in the course of the animal's own individual existence. But can this be considered as a fundamental point of difference, and can it hold as a valid argument against employing the term "reflex" for this new group of phenomena? It is certainly a sufficient argument for making a definite distinction between the two types of reflex and for considering the signal reflex in a group distinct from the inborn reflex. But this does not invalidate in any way our right logically to term both "reflex," since the point of distinction does not concern the character of the response on the part of the organism, but only the mode of formation of the reflex mechanism. We may take the telephonic installation as an

illustration. Communication can be effected in two ways. My residence may be connected directly with the laboratory by a private line, and I may call up the laboratory whenever it pleases me to do so; or on the other hand, a connection may have to be made through the central exchange. But the result in both cases is the same. The only point of distinction between the methods is that the private line provides a permanent and readily available cable, while the other line necessitates a preliminary central connection being established. In the one case the communicating wire is always complete, in the other case a small addition must be made to the wire at the central exchange. We have a similar state of affairs in reflex action. The path of the inborn reflex is already completed at birth; but the path of the signalizing reflex has still to be completed in the higher nervous centres. We are thus brought to consider the mode of formation of new reflex mechanisms. A new reflex is formed inevitably under a given set of physiological conditions, and with the greatest ease, so that there is no need to take the subjective state of the dog into consideration. With a complete understanding of all the factors involved, the new signalizing reflexes are under the absolute control of the experimenter; they proceed according to as rigid laws as do any other physiological processes, and must be regarded as being in every sense a part of the physiological activity of living beings. I have termed this new group of reflexes conditioned reflexes to distinguish them from the inborn or unconditioned reflexes. The term "conditioned" is becoming more and more generally employed, and I think its use is fully justified in that, compared with the inborn reflexes, these new reflexes actually do depend on very many conditions, both in their formation and in the maintenance of their physiological activity. Of course the terms "conditioned" and "unconditioned" could be replaced by others of arguably equal merit. Thus, for example, we might retain the term "inborn reflexes," and call the new type "acquired reflexes"; or call the former "species reflexes" since they are characteristic of the species, and the latter "individual reflexes" since they vary from animal to animal in a species, and even in the same animal at different times and under different conditions. Or again we might call the former "conduction reflexes" and the latter "connection reflexes."

There should be no theoretical objection to the hypothesis of the formation of new physiological paths and new connections within the cerebral hemispheres. Since the especial function of the central nervous system is to establish most complicated and delicate correspondences between the organism and its environment we may not un-naturally expect to find there, on the analogy of the methods used by the technician in everyday experience, a highly developed connector system superimposed on a conductor system. The physiologist certainly should not object to this conception seeing that he has been used to employing the German conception of "Bahnung," which means a laying down of fresh physiological paths in the centres. Conditioned reflexes are phenomena of common and widespread occurrence: their establishment is an integral function in everyday life. We recognize them in ourselves and in other people or animals under such names as "education," "habits," and "training;" and all of these are really nothing more than the results of an establishment of new nervous connections during the post-natal existence of the organism. They are, in actual fact, links connecting definite extraneous stimuli with their definite responsive reactions. I believe that the recognition and the study of the conditioned reflex will throw open the door to a true physiological investigation probably of all the highest nervous activities of the cerebral hemispheres, and the purpose of the present lectures is to give some account of what we have already accomplished in this direction.

We come now to consider the precise conditions under which new conditioned reflexes or new connections of nervous paths are established. The fundamental requisite is that any external stimulus which is to become the signal in a conditioned reflex must overlap in point of time with the action of an unconditioned stimulus.

*   *   *

Further, it is not enough that there should be overlapping between the two stimuli; it is also and equally necessary that the conditioned stimulus should begin to operate before the unconditioned stimulus comes into action.

If this order is reversed, the unconditioned stimulus being applied first and the neutral stimulus second, the conditioned reflex cannot be established at all. Dr. Krestovnikov performed these experiments with many different modifications and controls, but the effect was always the same.

*   *   *

As regards the condition of the hemispheres themselves, an alert state of the nervous system is absolutely essential for the formation of a new conditioned reflex. If the dog is mostly drowsy during the experiments, the establishment of a conditioned reflex becomes a long and tedious process, and in extreme cases is impossible to accomplish. The hemispheres must, however, be free from any other nervous activity, and therefore in building up a new conditioned reflex it is important to avoid foreign stimuli which, falling upon the animal, would cause other reactions of their own. If this is not attended to, the establishment of a conditioned reflex is very difficult, if not impossible. Thus, for example, if the dog has been so fastened up that anything causes severe irritation, it does not matter how many times the combination of stimuli is repeated, we shall not be able to obtain a conditioned reflex. A somewhat similar case was described in the first lecture—that of the dog which exhibited the *freedom reflex* in an exaggerated degree. It can also be stated as a rule that the establishment of the first conditional reflex in an animal is usually more difficult than the establishment of succeeding ones. It is obvious that this must be so, when we consider that even in the most favourable circumstances the experimental conditions themselves will be sure to provoke numerous different reflexes—*i.e.*, will give rise to one or other disturbing activity of the hemispheres. But this statement must be qualified by remarking that in cases where the cause of these uncontrolled reflexes is not found out, so that we are not able to get rid of them, the hemispheres themselves will help us. For if the environment of the animal during the experiment does not contain any powerful disturbing elements, then practically always the extraneous reflexes will with time gradually and spontaneously weaken in strength.

The third factor determining the facility with which new conditioned reflexes can be established is the health of the animal. A good state of health will ensure the normal functioning of the cerebral hemispheres, and we shall not have to bother with the effects of any internal pathological stimuli.

The fourth, and last, group of conditions has to do with the properties of the stimulus which is to become conditioned, and also with the properties of the unconditioned stimulus which is selected. Conditioned reflexes are quite readily formed to stimuli to which the animal is more less indifferent at the outset, though strictly speaking no stimulus within the animal's range of perception exists to which it would be absolutely indifferent. In a normal animal the slightest alteration in the environment—even the very slightest sound or faintest odour, or the smallest change in intensity of illumination—immediately evokes the reflex which I referred to in the first lecture as the investigatory reflex—"What is it?"—manifested by a very definite motor reaction. However, if these neutral stimuli keep recurring, they spontaneously and rapidly weaken in their effect upon the hemispheres, thus bringing about bit by bit the removal of this obstacle to the establishment of a conditional reflex. But if the extraneous stimuli are strong or unusual, the formation of a conditioned reflex will be difficult, and in extreme cases impossible.

* * *

Successful transformation of the unconditioned stimulus for one reflex into the conditioned stimulus for another reflex can be brought about only when the former reflex is physiologically weaker and biologically of less importance than the latter. We are led to this conclusion from a consideration of Dr. Eroféeva's experiments. A nocuous stimulus applied to the dog's skin was transformed into a conditioned stimulus for the alimentary reflex. This, we consider, was due to the fact that the alimentary reflex is in such cases stronger than the defence reflex. In the same way we all know that when dogs join in a scuffle for food they frequently sustain skin wounds, which however play no dominant part as stimuli to any defence reflex, being entirely subordinated to the reflex for food. Nevertheless there is a certain limit—there are stronger reflexes than the alimentary reflex. One is the reflex of self-preservation, of existence or non-existence, life or death. To give only one example, it was found impossible to transform a defence reaction into an alimentary conditioned reflex when the stimulus to the unconditioned defence reaction was a strong electric current applied to skin overlying bone with no muscular layer intervening. This signifies that the afferent nervous impulses set up by injury to the skin, cannot acquire even a temporary connection with the part of the brain from which the alimentary reflex is controlled. Nevertheless, on the whole, the foregoing considerations emphasize the advantage of using the alimentary reflex for most of our experiments, since in the hierarchy of reflexes this holds a very high place.

While, as we have seen, very strong and even specialized stimuli can under certain conditions acquire the properties of conditioned stimuli, there is, on the other hand, a minimum strength below which stimuli cannot be given conditioned properties. Thus a thermal stimulus of 45° C. applied to the skin can be made into an alimentary conditioned reflex, whereas at 38° to 39° C. (approximately 2° C. above the skin temperature in the dog) a thermal stimulus is ineffective [experiments of Dr. Solomonov]. Similarly, while with the help of a very strong unconditioned stimulus it is possible to convert a very unsuitable stimulus—for example, one which naturally evokes a different unconditioned reflex—into a conditioned stimulus, it is exceedingly difficult or even impossible with the help of only a weak unconditioned stimulus to transform even a very favourable neutral stimulus

into a conditioned stimulus. Even where such a conditioned reflex is successfully established, its occurrence results only in a very small reflex response. Some unconditioned stimuli may be permanently weak, others may display a weakness which is only temporary—varying with the condition of the animal. As an example of the last we may take food. In the hungry animal food naturally brings about a powerful unconditioned reflex, and the conditioned reflex develops quickly. But in a dog which has not long been fed the unconditioned stimulus has only a small effect, and alimentary conditioned reflexes either are not formed at all or are established very slowly.

By complying with all the conditions which I have enumerated—which is not a very difficult task—a new conditioned reflex is infallibly obtained. We apply to the receptors of the animal rigidly defined stimuli; these stimuli necessarily result in the formation of a new connection in the hemispheres with a consequent development of a typical reflex reaction.

To sum up, we may legitimately claim the study of the formation and properties of conditioned reflexes as a special department of physiology. There is no reason for thinking about all these events in any other way, and it is my belief that in these questions prejudices blunt the intellect and that generally speaking the preconceptions of the human mind stand in the way of any admission that the highest physiological activity of the hemispheres is rigidly determined. The difficulty is mainly due to the tremendous complexity of our subjective states; and, of course, these cannot yet be traced to their primary causations.

* * *

THE EXPERIMENTAL RESULTS OBTAINED WITH ANIMALS IN THEIR APPLICATION TO MAN

In applying to man the results of investigation of the functions of the heart, digestive tract and other organs in the higher animals, allied as these organs are to the human in structure, great reserve must be exercised and the validity of comparisons must be verified at every step. Obviously even greater caution must be used in attempting similarly to apply our recently acquired knowledge concerning the higher nervous activity in the dog—the more so, since the incomparably greater development of the cerebral cortex in man is pre-eminently that factor which has raised man to his dominant position in the animal world. It would be the height of presumption to regard these first steps in elucidating the physiology of the cortex as solving the intricate problems of the higher psychic activities in man, when in fact at the present stage of our work no detailed application of its results to man is yet permissible.

Nevertheless, inasmuch as the higher nervous activity exhibited by the cortex rests, undoubtedly, on the same foundation in man as in the higher animals, some very general and tentative inferences can even now be drawn from the latter to the former. In the future it may confidently be expected that a full and detailed knowledge of at least the elementary facts of this activity will be obtained as regards both normal and pathological states.

5. On Drive

BY CLARK L. HULL

WE SAW in an earlier chapter that when a condition arises for which action on the part of the organism is a prerequisite to optimum probability of survival of either the individual or the species, a state of need is said to exist. Since a need, either actual or potential, usually precedes and accompanies the action of an organism, the need is often said to motivate or drive the associated activity. Because of this motivational characteristic of needs they are regarded as producing primary animal *drives*.

DRIVES ARE TYPICAL INTERVENING VARIABLES

It is important to note in this connection that the general concept of drive (D) tends strongly to have the systematic status of an intervening variable or X, never directly observable. The need of food, ordinarily called hunger, produces a typical primary drive. Like all satisfactory intervening variables, the presence and the amount of the hunger drive are susceptible of a double determination on the basis of correlated events which are themselves directly observable. Specifically, the amount of the food need clearly increases with the number of hours elapsed since the last intake of food; here the amount of hunger drive (D) is a function of observable *antecedent* conditions, i.e., of the need which is measured by the number of hours of food privation. On the other hand, the amount of energy which will be expended by the organism in the securing of food varies largely with the intensity of the hunger drive existent at the time; here the amount of "hunger" is a function of observable events which are its *consequence*. As usual with

observables, the determination of the exact quantitative functional relationship of the intervening variable to both the antecedent and the consequent conditions presents serious practical difficulties. This probably explains the paradox that despite the almost universal use of the concepts of need and drive, this characteristic functional relationship is not yet determined for any need, though some preliminary work has been done in an attempt to determine it for hunger.

INNATE BEHAVIOR TENDENCIES VARY ABOUT A CENTRAL RANGE

With our background of organic evolution we must believe that the behavior of newborn organisms is the result of unlearned, i.e., inherited, neural connections between receptors and effectors ($_sU_R$) which have been selected from fortuitous variations or mutations throughout the long history of the species. Since selection in this process has been on the intensely pragmatic basis of survival in a life-and-death struggle with multitudes of factors in a considerable variety of environments, it is to be expected that the innate or reflex behavior of young organisms will, upon the whole, be reasonably well adapted to the modal stimulating situations in which it occurs.

It may once have been supposed by some students of animal behavior, e.g., by Pavlov and other Russian reflexologists, that innate or reflex behavior is a rigid and unvarying neural connection between a single receptor discharge and the contraction of a particular muscle or muscle group. Whatever may have been the views held in the past, the facts of molar behavior, as well as the general dynamics of behavioral adaptation, now make it very clear not only that inherited behavior tendencies ($_sU_R$)

Reprinted from *Principles of Behavior* by Clark L. Hull, pp. 57–61. Copyright 1943, D. Appleton-Century Co., Inc. By permission of Appleton-Century-Crofts, Inc.

are not strictly uniform and invariable, but that rigidly uniform reflex behavior would not be nearly so effective in terms of survival in a highly variable and unpredictable environment as would a *behavior tendency*. By this expression is meant behavior which will vary over a certain range, the frequency of occurrence at that segment of the range most likely to be adaptive being greatest, and the frequency at those segments of the range least likely to be adaptive being, upon the whole, correspondingly rare. Thus in the expression $_sU_R$, R represents not a single act but a considerable range of more or less alternative reaction potentialities.

The neurophysiological mechanism whereby the type of flexible receptor-effector dynamic relationship could operate is by no means wholly clear, but a number of factors predisposing to variability of reaction are evident. First must be mentioned the spontaneous impulse discharge of individual nerve cells, discussed above. This, in conjunction with the principle of neural interaction operating on efferent neural impulses (*efferent neural interaction*), would produce a certain amount of variability in any reaction. Secondly, the variable proprioceptive stimulation arising from the already varying reaction would, by afferent neural interaction, clearly increase the range of variability in the reaction. Finally, as the primary exciting (drive) stimulus increases in intensity, it is to be expected that the effector impulses will rise above the thresholds of wider and wider ranges of effectors until practically the entire effector system may be activated.

Consider the situation resulting from a foreign object entering the eye. If the object is *very* small the stimulation of its presence may result in little more than a slightly increased frequency of lid closure and a small increase in lachrymal secretion, two effector processes presenting no very conspicuous range of variability except quantitatively. But if the object be relatively large and rough, and if the stimulation continues after the first vigorous blinks and tear secretions have occurred, the muscles of the arm will move the hand to the point of stimulation and a considerable variety of manipulative movements will follow, all more or less likely to contribute to the removal of the acutely stimulating object but none of them *precisely* adapted to that end.

In the case of a healthy human infant, which is hungry or is being pricked by a pin, we have the same general picture, though the details naturally will differ to a certain extent. If the need be acute, the child will scream loudly, opening its mouth very wide and closing its eyes; both legs will kick vigor-

ously in rhythmic alternation, and the arms will flail about in a variety of motions which have, however, a general focus at the mouth and eyes. In cases of severe and somewhat protracted injurious stimulation the back may be arched and practically the entire musculature of the organism may be thrown into more or less violent activity.

SOME PRIMARY NEEDS AND THE MODAL REACTIONS TO THEM

The major primary needs or drives are so ubiquitous that they require little more than to be mentioned. They include the need for foods of various sorts (hunger), the need for water (thirst), the need for air, the need to avoid tissue injury (pain), the need to maintain an optimal temperature, the need to defecate, the need to micturate, the need for rest (after protracted exertion), the need for sleep (after protracted wakefulness), and the need for activity (after protracted inaction). The drives concerned with the maintenance of the species are those which lead to sexual intercourse and the need represented by nest building and care of the young.

The primary core or mode of the range of innate or reflex tendencies to action must naturally vary from one need to another if the behavior is to be adaptive. In cases where the rôle of chance as to what movements will be adaptive is relatively small, the behavior tendency may be relatively simple and constant. For example, the acute need for oxygen may normally be satisfied (terminated) by inspiration; the need represented by pressure in the urinary bladder is normally terminated by micturition. It is not accidental that these relatively stereotyped and invariable reactions are apt to concern mainly those portions of the external environment which are highly constant and, especially, the internal environment which is characteristically constant and predictable.

In the case of mechanical tissue injury, withdrawal of the injured part from the point where the injury began is the characteristic reflex form of behavior, and the probability of the effectiveness of such action is obvious. Environmental temperatures considerably below the optimum for the organism tend to evoke shivering and a posture presenting a minimum of surface exposed to heat loss. Temperatures above the optimum tend to produce a general inactivity, a postulate yielding a maximum surface for heat radiation, and rapid panting. In certain relatively complex situations such as those associated with the need for food, water, or reproduction, the factor of search is apt to be included as a preliminary. Since extensive search involves locomotion, the preliminary activities arising from these three needs will naturally be much alike.

ORGANIC CONDITIONS WHICH INITIATE THREE TYPICAL PRIMARY DRIVE BEHAVIORS

During recent years physiologists and students of behavior have made important advances in unraveling the more immediate conditions which are associated with the onset of the activities characteristic of the three most complex primary drives —thirst, hunger, and sex. Thirst activities appear from these studies to be initiated by a dryness in the mouth and throat caused by the lack of saliva, which in its turn is caused by the lack of available

water in the blood. The hunger drive seems to be precipitated, at least in part, by a rhythmic and, in extreme cases, more or less protracted contraction of the stomach and adjacent portions of the digestive tract presumably caused by the lack of certain nutritional elements in the blood. Copulatory and maternal drives appear to be most complex of all and are not too well understood as yet. It is known that female copulatory receptivity (oestrum) is precipitated by the presence in the blood of a specific hormone secreted periodically, and that male copulatory activity is dependent upon the presence in the blood of a male hormone. Just how these hormones bring about the actual motivation is not yet entirely clear.

6. On Insight

BY WOLFGANG KÖHLER

IN THIS BOOK, no theory of intelligent behaviour is to be developed. Since, however, we have to decide whether chimpanzees ever behave with insight, we must at least discuss certain interpretations which cannot be accepted without the observations at the same time losing all their value in regard to this question. This will at least prevent any quite arbitrary treatment of the facts, and the direct meaning of the experiments will appear with more force and certainty. Perhaps finally it will be possible to make this meaning rest on its own merits, instead of allowing it to disappear in the solvent of general and indefinite principles.

*   *   *

How one is to explain that the field as a whole, the relations of the parts of the situation to one another, etc., determine the solution, belong to the theory. Here we have only to exclude the idea that the behaviour of the animals is to be explained by the assumption according to which the solution will be accomplished without regard to the structure of the situation, as a sequence of chance parts, that is to say, without intelligence.

In the description of these experiments it should have been apparent enough that what is lacking for this explanation is that most necessary thing, a composition of the solutions out of chance parts. It is certainly not a characteristic of the chimpanzee, when he is brought into an experimental situation, to make any chance movements, out of which, among other things, a non-genuine solution could arise. He is very seldom seen to attempt anything which would have to be considered accidental in relation to the situation (excepting, of course, if his interest is turned away from the objective to other things). As long as his efforts are directed to the objective, all distinguishable stages of his behaviour (as with human beings in similar situations), tend to appear as complete attempts at solutions, *none* of which appears as the product of accidentally arrayed parts. This is true, most of all, of the solution which is finally successful. Certainly, it often follows upon a period of perplexity or quiet (often a period of survey), but in real and convincing cases, the solution never appears in a disorder of blind impulses. It is one continuous smooth action, which can be resolved into parts *only by abstract thinking* by the onlooker; in *reality* they do *not* appear independently. But that in so many "genuine" cases as have been described, these solutions *as wholes* should have arisen from mere chance, is an entirely inadmissible supposition, which the theory cannot

Reprinted from Wolfgang Köhler, *The Mentality of Apes*, trans. from the 2d rev. ed. by Ella Winter (New York: Harcourt, Brace & Co., London: Kegan Paul, Trench, Trubner and Co., 1926), pp. 186, 191–92, 194–96, 198–99, 202–8, with the permission of Humanities Press and Routledge & Kegan Paul.

allow without renouncing what is considered its chief merit.

*   *   *

If one does not watch attentively, the crude stupidities of the animals, already referred to several times, might be taken as proofs that the chimpanzee does, after all, perform senseless actions, a sequence of which may, by chance, give rise to apparent solutions.

The chimpanzee commits three kinds of errors:—

1. *"Good errors,"* of which more will be said later. In these, the animal does not make a stupid, but rather an almost favourable impression, if only the observer can get right away from preoccupation with human achievements, and concentrate only on the nature of the behaviour observed.

2. *Errors caused by complete lack of comprehension of the conditions of the task.* This can be seen when the animals, in putting a box higher up, will take it from a statically good position and put it into a bad one. The impression one gets in such cases is that of a certain innocent limitation.

3. *Crude stupidities arising from habit* in situations which the animal ought to be able to survey (e.g. dragging the box to the railings—Sultan). Such behaviour is extremely annoying—it almost makes one angry.

Here we are dealing with the third class, and it is easily seen that these mistakes are not at all liable to confirm the chance theory. This kind of behaviour never arises unless a similar procedure often took place beforehand as a real and genuine solution. The stupidities are not accidental "natural" fractions, from which *primarily* apparent solutions can arise—I know of no case in which such an interpretation is even possible—they are the *after-effects* of former genuine solutions, which were often repeated, and so developed a tendency to appear *secondarily* in later experiments, without much consideration for the special situation. The preceding conditions for such mistakes seem to be drowsiness, exhaustion, colds, or even excitement. For instance, a chimpanzee, when he performs an experiment for the first time and cannot reach the objective lying outside the bars without an implement, will never have the "accidental impulse" to drag a box to the bars, and even get up on it. On the other hand, one may see that actually, after frequent repetition of a solution originally arrived at genuinely, and in the consequent mechanization of the proceeding, such stupidities are easily committed. Not infrequently have I demonstrated an experiment to interested observers, and, for the sake of simplicity, usually chose the opening of a door, in front of the hinge side of which the objective was hanging. After the

animal had done this about twenty times since the first solution, and always at the same place, there began to appear a tendency to fetch down objectives hung high up with the help of a door, even when other methods were more obvious, and the use of a door had been made very difficult, in fact, almost impossible. And if attempts at other solutions developed, they were more or less under the influence, or magnetic power, of the door. Chica, for instance, made out of the jumping-stick method, which she had in its simple form completely mastered, a combination of this and the door-method; and quite unnecessarily, because it was by no means an improvement. Before the door had come into intelligent use for the first time, the chimpanzees had paid no attention to it in any experiment, not even when the experiment took place opposite to it.

According to this, processes, originally very valuable, have a disagreeable tendency to sink to a lower rank with constant repetition. This *secondary self-training* is usually supposed to bring about a great saving, and it may be so, both in man and in anthropoid apes. But one must never forget what a startling resemblance there is between these crude stupidities of the chimpanzees arising from habit, and certain empty and meaningless repetitions of moral, political, and other principles in men. Once all these meant more, one cared about the "solution" in a predicament deeply felt or much thought about; but later the situation does not matter so much, and the statement of the principle becomes a cliché.

It should now be clear enough that these meaningless reproductions of originally genuine and correct solutions have absolutely nothing to do with the accidental and confused production of "natural" impulses of theory discussed above.

*   *   *

For one who has actually watched the experiments, discussions like the above have something comic about them. For instance, when one has seen for oneself, how in the first experiment of her life it did not dawn on Tschego for hours to push the obstructing box out of the way, how she merely stretched out her arm uselessly, or else sat down quietly, but then, fearing the loss of her food, suddenly seized the obstacle, and pushed it to one side, thus solving the task in a second—when one has watched that, then to "secure these facts against misinterpretation" seems almost pedantic. But the living impression will not be reproduced, and many a question can be raised on the words of a report, which would not even occur to anyone after some observation. Nevertheless, it may be that after these discussions, the description of a further experiment carried out as a model will be

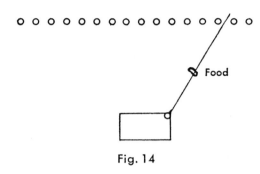

Fig. 14

particularly instructive; an experiment which is characterized both by its simplicity and its unequivocal relation to several theories.

A heavy box is standing upright at some distance on the other side of the oft-mentioned bars; one end of a stout string is affixed to it, and the string itself is laid down obliquely so that its free end lies between the vertical bars of the railings. Half-way between the box and the bars fruit is tied to the string (cf. Fig. 14); it cannot be reached from the bars as it is, but only if the string is laid straight. (19.6.1914) First of all, Chica pulls in the direction in which the string is lying, and so hard that the board of the box breaks, the string is freed, and the objective can be pulled to her. The box is then replaced by a heavy stone and the string tied round it. As the simple solution by pulling is no longer possible, Chica takes the string in one hand, passes it round the bar to her other, which she puts through the next space, and so on, passing it thus until the string is at right angles to the bars, and the objective can be seized.

Grande seems at first not to see the string, which is grey and lying on a grey ground. She drags stones about senselessly—an after-effect of earlier experiments—tries to detach an iron rod from the wall, which she presumably wants to use as a stick, and at last sees the string. After this the experiment runs as with Chica, a solution without any hesitations.

*   *   *

Do the animals arrive at the solution in accordance with the theory we have discussed? If so, we should expect to find in all cases the appearance of a large number of impulses which might, in some of the chimpanzees, perhaps, accidentally contain the right "fragments" in the right succession. In reality Grande is the only animal that does anything senseless, and that in the form of a habit stupidity, when she had not yet thoroughly surveyed the possibilities of the problem; when she sees the string, a new stage of behaviour sets in, and immediately after-

wards a perfectly clear solution is achieved. Altogether only two movements ("impulses" may occur in lizards, but rarely in chimpanzees) really take place with regard to the objective. These two movements are:—

1. *Pulling in the direction of the string,* i.e. a sensible proceeding, the practicability of which Chica once proves. No man, still less a chimpanzee, can otherwise find out if the string will not really come loose from box or stone.

2. Pulling at the string, or continuous passing of the rope hand-over-hand—in both cases in the *right direction for a solution.*

Not in a single animal was anything approaching a direction midway between these two observed, much less a third quite new one, etc. Where the more primitive tendency appeared first (in the direction of the string), the jump to the other one was yet made quite abruptly.

I should imagine that everybody must feel that we have here a very clear, though peculiar occurrence, and one which has nothing at all to do with the postulates of that theory. Are we to squeeze and force the facts to make them fit in with that theory, just to suit the so-called principle of scientific economy? In this case the observer is forced to the conclusion that attempts 1 and 2, appearing as wholes, yet each on its own, are a direct result of a visual survey of the situation. A certain scientific attitude, which one might also formulate as a principle, the "principle of maximum scientific fertility," would lead one to begin the theoretical considerations with this character of the observations, and not to eliminate it at whatever cost as the theory of chance does.

There would be no need to discuss this theory further if the previous life of the chimpanzees we have tested were known to us in all details, from birth to the moment of testing. But unfortunately this is not the case; and even if the possibility that in the *experiment* the solutions arise by chance be excluded, yet the possibility remains that they were developed *before,* within the scope of the theory, by accident, that they were repeated and improved, and now seem to appear as genuine solutions.

It is always difficult to contend against arguments which are outside the domain of possible proof. In this case, however, not even the overstepping of the bounds of experience will be a weakness in the argument, for naturally the chimpanzees we tested had passed several years as lively animals, uncontrolled, in the jungle of the West Coast, and, while there, came into contact with several objects similar to those employed in some of our experiments. Thus it becomes necessary to consider whether this circumstance does not influence the significance and the factual value of the experiments.

But two points must be kept rigidly in mind, if the object of the discussion is not to be lost:—

1. The fact that the animals have had to deal with single objects or situations prior to the experiments, has not necessarily any direct connexion with our problem. It is only when, exactly according to the theory, during this previous period, meaningless but successful chains of actions, externally like the behaviour observed here, have been formed—accidentally, and selected by success—that "previous experience" speaks against the value of these experiments. I am far from asserting that the animals tested in the second chapter have never had a stick, or anything like that, in their hands before the experiment. On the contrary, I take it for granted that every chimpanzee above a certain very low age has had some such experience; he will have seized a branch in play, scratched on the ground with it, and so on. Exactly the same thing is very frequently observed in small children of less than a year, so that these, too, had their "experience" with sticks, before they used them as implements to pull things towards them that they could not otherwise reach. But just as this does not at all prove that they get accustomed to the use of implements in the mere play of chance and quite without insight, reproducing it again without insight at two, four, or twenty years of age, so also it does not follow for the chimpanzee, whose test-stick is not the first he has ever had in his hand.

2. I am by no means trying in this work to prove that the chimpanzee is a marvel of intelligence: on the contrary, the narrow limit of his powers (as compared to man's) has often been demonstrated. All that has to be decided is whether *any* of his actions have ever the characteristics of insight, and the answer to this question of principle is at present far more important than an exact determination of *degrees* of intelligence. On the other hand, the theory of chance, discussed here as a general principle of interpretation has no interest in the mere *diminution* of the *number* of intelligent acts in experiment, but, in order to be convincing, the theory must explain *all* tests, without exception, consistently with itself. And it fails when, even though some results observed are explained by it, others are not. In the latter case, when the general application collapses, there will be less temptation to explain certain kinds of behaviour as products of accident, which, by their nature, do not invite such an interpretation, though they may be forced under this theory.

The past history of these animals, before the tests, is not altogether unknown. Since at least the beginning of the year 1913, they have been carefully watched, and for a further six months before that date, we can rest assured that any practice in a number of test-situations was impossible, because the animals were confined in the narrowest cages, with no "objects" in them (in Cameroon, on the voyage, in Tenerife). According to the information of my predecessor, E. Teuber, during the year of observation *before* these tests, Sultan and Rana did not get beyond using ordinary sticks (without any complications) for lengthening of the arm, and jumping—the others did not even achieve this much; occasional throwing of stones was observed, and in one case the fabrication of an implement as described above when Sultan takes the shoe-cleaner to pieces.

In any case, the following circumstance is important: when it is a question of the principal decision, whether insight occurs or not, then for any explanation to be in accordance with the chance theory, *not the slightest trace of insight* must occur, not in the most hidden, or in the most innocent, disguise. Therefore since everything, to the smallest details, was to be put together out of chance combinations of elements, and rehearsed, until it could *seem* to appear as a single and intelligent action in the experiments, so we shall, in general, have to assume, not *one sole* former occasion in a similar situation, but a *series of repetitions* of such occasions. Only then somebody might say with conviction that this procedure or that, or rather *all* the lines of action here observed have had their origin and development, in accordance with the principles of the theory.

I remarked above that the general principles of higher psychology often had a tendency to hide rather than to clarify the things to be explained. For instance, when we say that the objectively-useful employment of a stick, as a means of reaching otherwise inaccessible objects, developed by accident and the selective working of success, it will sound very precise and satisfactory. When we look closer, however, our satisfaction with the general principle is soon diminished, if we are really serious in making the condition "without a trace of insight." Let us assume, for instance, that the animal seized a little stick *by accident* at a time when some food, otherwise unattainable, lay at some distance. As, for the ape, the stick and the objective have nothing to do with each other, we have to ascribe it to chance also, if, among a large number of other possibilities, the animal brings the stick into the vicinity of the object desired. For, of course, we must not assume that this action occurs all at once, as one. With one of its ends in the neighbourhood of the objective, the stick has still nothing at all to do with the objective, as far as the animal is concerned, he "does not know" that he has arrived objectively a little nearer to the attainment of the goal. The stick may be dropped, or pulled back, or pointed in all the directions of a sphere with the animal as centre; and chance will now have to work hard until from all the possibilities *one* emerges, namely that the end of the stick is put down behind the objective. But again, this position of the stick tells the unintelligent animal nothing; as before, the most various "impulses" may appear and chance might well have reached the limit of its capacity, if the animal now makes an accidental movement which brings the goal a little nearer to it. But this again the animal does not understand as an improvement of the situation; for it understands nothing at all, and poor, exhausted chance, which has to do all the work that the animal itself is unable to do directly, must now prevent the stick from being dropped, drawn back, and so forth, and must bring it about that the animal keeps the right direction in further chance impulses. It may be said that there are very various sequences or combinations of impulses containing, for instance, as their last constituents "stick behind objective," and after that "the objectively fitting impulse." That is correct, and the possibilities open to chance, if it is to do this great work, become thereupon more numerous. And yet even now nothing is spared to it; for the majority of these combinations contain, of course, factors objectively quite meaningless, which only follow upon each other in such a way that the whole series *finally leads to the two elements mentioned above.* Therefore, if the first favourable combinations, of which these elements form the end, contain such objectively-meaningless components, chance must later complete the work by means of a large number of other favourable cases, until a perfectly smooth, and *seemingly intelligent,* procedure matures with the help of the (at first, probably extremely rare) successes; for as the use of the stick is observed here for the first time, it contains in no case a thoroughly false component, even if (as with Koko) weakness of the arm and clumsiness act as somewhat of a hindrance.

At this juncture it will probably be objected that the desire for the objective, the general *urge of the instinct* in its direction, is being left out of consideration. To this we reply: in the first place, to conform to the theory, we assume that this "instinct" is perfectly blind, that *the animal is not in any way aware that he is nearing its goal* by taking this direction—for otherwise the theory would be untrue to itself; secondly, according to the theory, this instinct exists *for the body of the animal,* and for the innervations of his limbs, *not for the stick* he happens to hold in his hand. I want to know therefore: if the animal, following that impulse, moves his arm in the direction of the objective in order to catch hold of it, why should he keep the stick, of which his instinct knows nothing, in his hand, rather than open his hand to seize the objective, as at other times, and thus let go of the stick? For, all this time, the stick has, in the animal's eyes, *nothing to do with the objective.* Should he, however, contrary to this demand of the chance theory, continue holding the stick in his hand, that would, with his lack of any trace of insight, be possible in a variety of very different ways. It may be held right in the centre, so that the stick is parallel to his front and sideways, or it may be grasped at the extreme end, the other end pointing back towards the animal, upwards to the sky, or down to the ground, etc. For if nothing is assumed but the impulse of instinct in the direction of the objective, and accidental movements—*intelligence,* to the contrary, remaining wholly *excluded,* one way of holding the stick is as good as another and the different possibilities are limited only by the animal's muscular power; because success will have its selecting effect at the earliest after *one* favourable combination only. And so chance which has already, in opposition to the theory, left the stick in the animal's hand, has still plenty to do before it succeeds in obtaining the right manner of holding the stick, in eliminating the false elements by the help of chance *successes,* and obtaining a mode of procedure, superficially similar to intelligent behavior.

7. *A Summary Discussion of Purposive Behavior*

BY EDWARD C. TOLMAN

THE VARIABLES

OUR SYSTEM has been presented. It conceives mental processes as functional variables intervening between stimuli, initiating physiological states, and the general heredity and past training of the organism, on the one hand, and final resulting responses, on the other. These intervening variables it defines as behavior-determinants. And these behavior-determinants it subdivides further into (1) immanent purposive and cognitive determinants, (2) capacities and (3) behavior-adjustments. All three of these types of determinant are to be discovered, in the last analysis, by behavior experiments. They have to be inferred "back" from behavior. They are precipitated out from the empirical correlations which can be observed between specific stimuli and initiating physiological states, on the one hand, and specific resultant acts, on the other. They are to behavior as electrons, waves, or whatever it may be, are to the happenings in inorganic matter. There is nothing private or "mentalistic" about them. They are pragmatically conceived, objective variables the concepts of which can be altered and changed as proves most useful. They are not the dictates of any incontrovertible moments of immediacy.

We must finally bring out, however, certain general characteristics of the system which, though implied in all the foregoing, have not, perhaps, been sufficiently stressed.

PURPOSIVE BEHAVIORISM CONCERNS ITSELF WITH DOCILE BEHAVIOR ONLY

The first of these general characteristics to be emphasized is the fact that this system concerns itself with, and is valid for, docile behavior only. This point is implicit in all the preceding, and needs only a little reiteration. It has been implied throughout that, only in so far as behavior is docile, can it be said to be purposive and cognitive. It is only docile behavior which can be examined for immanent sign-gestalts and hierarchies of demands. In so far as behavior is not docile, but goes off willy nilly by virtue of invariable reflex stimulus-response con-

nections, a description of it in terms of immanent sign-gestalt-readinesses and -expectations and hierarchies of demands, and the like, would be both silly and meaningless.

The empirical question, therefore, arises with regard to each species as to in what degree its acts are docile or in what degree they are reflex. And the answer to this empirical question is, of course, as yet far from completely known. The lower the organism, or the more internal and physiological the response, the more likely, it would seem, that a given act is non-docile, i.e., of a purely reflex or tropistic variety. But many more observations need to be made. There is some evidence of learning, or at any rate of modifiability, the exact nature of which needs further analysis, even in protozoa, not to mention earthworms and the lower insects.

THE ROLES OF PHYSIOLOGY AND NEUROLOGY

The other general characteristic of the present system which needs perhaps to be further emphasized concerns the relation of purposive behaviorism to physiology and neurology. In how far are we, as mere psychologists—i.e., mere purposive behaviorists—interested in, and dependent upon a knowledge of the underlying neurology and physiology of behavior? Inasmuch as the ultimate ends of all behavior are, we assume, the physiological states of disturbance and quiescence, we are necessarily interested in discovering and listing, if we can, these ultimate types of physiological disturbance and quiescence. And in so far as the immanent determinants, the capacities and the behavior-adjustments, are ultimately dependent upon matters of neurology, we are likewise interested in all that the most advanced work can tell us about such neurology.

But, first and foremost, and this is a point which it is important to stress, our task, *as psychologists*, is the collecting and ordering of the *molar behavior* facts per se. And this task can, in large part, be performed in relative ignorance of both physiology and neurology. Our task is to find out the behavior facts and the appetite and the aversion facts which are to be explained, before attempting too much explanation. Let us not, in short, be misled, as we believe many of the simple stimulus-response psychologists of the immediate past have been, into substituting inadequate and, if Lashley and Franz and Coghill be correct, arrantly erroneous, neurological explanations in place of a direct and adequate account and systematization of the immediate behavior data themselves. Behavior is a stimulus response affair. But it is not for that reason a simple aggregation of mere reflexes as a premature neurologizing misled the early behaviorists into supposing. Furthermore, these early behaviorists were distracted from honestly and open-mindedly continuing to observe the behavior facts at their own truly behavioristic (i.e., molar) level. They were misled when, for example, they were observing the behavior of a rat in a maze, into seeing it as simply, and as possessing as few hesitations and hitches, as though it were the action of a simple billiard ball caroming on a pool table.

RELATION TO OTHER SYSTEMS

As our next question, let us consider the affinities of the present system to other psychological systems. Ours we have called a Purposive Behaviorism. And this name summarizes at once two of its affinities; viz., that with purposivism and that with behaviorism. But it has, of course, a third affinity which we were unable to include in the title; viz., that with Gestalt Psychology. Let us briefly summarize each of these three relationships. We begin with the relation to behaviorism.

WHEREIN THE PRESENT SYSTEM IS A BEHAVIORISM

By way of introduction to the question of the relations of the present system to behaviorism, we may recall McDougall's entertaining division of all behaviorists into *Strict Behaviorists, Near Behaviorists,* and *Purposive Behaviorists.* As has been remarked the present system owes its title to McDougall and falls into the last category; and our question becomes: Wherein does a purposive behaviorism differ from a strict behaviorism? A Purposive Behaviorism agrees with a strict behaviorism in asserting that organisms, their behavior and the environmental and organic conditions which induce the latter, are all that there is to be studied. It differs from a strict behaviorism such as that of Watson, Weiss, or of Meyer—in that for a purposive behaviorism behavior *qua* molar has characteristic descriptive properties all its own. For us, behavior has emergent patterns and meanings which are other than the patterns and meanings of the gland secretions and muscle contractions which underlie it, though no doubt they are completely dependent upon the latter. For a Purposive Behaviorism, behavior, as we have seen, is purposive, cognitive, and molar, i.e., "gestalted." Purposive Behaviorism is a molar, not a molecular, behaviorism, but it is none the less a behaviorism. Stimuli and responses and the behavior-determinants of responses are all that it finds to study.

WHEREIN THE PRESENT SYSTEM IS A GESTALT-ISM

Next, it may be asked in how far the present system, asserting as it does that behavior has meaning, is molar, and does not break up into atomistically defined reflex units, is a Gestalt Psychology. Undoubtedly, the final answer to this second question must be stated by the Gestalt Psychologists themselves. What is to be admitted as a brand of Gestalt Psychology, the Gestaltists themselves, in the last analysis, alone can say. We, however, it should be noted, would be proud to be admitted to their fold. There are certain features of our system, however, which in all honesty and fairness should be brought to the Gestalt-ists' attention as possible blemishes, which may unfit us, in their eyes, for being enclosed in their exclusive corral.

A first blemish will consist, perhaps, in our emphasis upon inference back from behavior and stimuli as the way to get at mind, rather than by introspection. But this difference from what would seem their point of view may well be more a matter of terminology and historical accident than anything fundamental and logical. The Gestalt Psychologists began life as orthodox mentalists and introspectionists. They started, that is, with the notion of mental phenomena as immediate introspective givens (Köhler's "direct experience"[1]). And, although they have thrown an atomistic description of this immediately mental overboard, they often seem to have retained mentalistically conceived gestalts, and along with the latter a psychophysical parallelism between these introspectively given "mental" gestalts, on the one hand, and physical, neurological gestalts, on the other. It is possible, however, that such an inference accords more with their words than their sense. We, on the other hand, starting life as crass stimulus-response behaviorists, who saw, to begin with, nothing between stimulus and response but neurology, have come only gradually, and perforce by much travail, to the concept of objectively defined capacities, immanent determinants and behavior-adjustments. But it may well be that our emphasis on all these determinants rather than upon "direct experiences" is but a hangover from our initial crassness. It may be that our capacities, immanent determinants and behavior-adjustments and their directly experienced gestalts will, in the end, turn out to have one and the same final, methodological and metaphysical status.

The second feature of our system which may, perhaps, be abhorrent to true Gestalt-ists is that we

1. Cf. W. Köhler, *Gestalt Psychology* (New York, Horace Liveright, 1929). Esp. Chapter 1.

have included among these determining variables not only the immanent sign-gestalts and the behavior-adjustments but also: (a) a variety of preceding determinants; viz., capacities and (b) a series of *analyzed* variables within the sign-gestalts; viz., means-end-readinesses and means-end-expectations, and discriminanda- and manipulanda-readinesses and -expectations.

That is, we have found it necessary, for purposes of discourse and prediction, to look *behind* and *within* the gestalts to independently distinguishable variables to be treated as the determiners and components of such gestalts. These "behind-variables" and "within-variables" do not, of course, ever occur and operate in insulation one from another, i.e., outside of the sign-gestalt wholes. But they can and must, none the less, be torn and analyzed out for the purposes of discourse and of predictive science. Now, such tearing apart and out often appears abhorrent to the Gestalt Psychologists. However, here again, the difference is probably one more of words than of meaning. The Gestalt-ists themselves really have their own part-variables—their figures vs. grounds, their contours, their accents, etc., etc. What the Gestalt Psychologists have, in fact, really been contending against seems not so much analysis per se, but what they conceive to have been the incorrect and erroneous analyses of their predecessors. So that the final question becomes rather in how far the "behind-variables" and the "within-variables," which we find, are or are not translatable into the contours, accents, groupings, etc., of Gestalt Psychology. Here again we must leave the issue for the future to decide.

Finally, the third possible blemish, from the Gestalt point of view, which may leave us as mere maverick outsiders, is our emphasis on the purposive structure of all gestalts—though in the light of Lewin's construance of purposive concepts to gestalt ends, this should hardly prove a final difficulty. For it is again to be emphasized that all *gestalts* are for us sign-gestalts—and all relations, in the last analysis, means-end-relations. Types of organization of the environmental field are for us always held together by, threaded upon, means-end-strands. Up and down, right and left, good and bad, near and far, figure and ground, are for us ultimately but *means-end* affairs.

WHEREIN THE PRESENT SYSTEM IS A PURPOSIVISM

We turn now to a consideration of the third affinity of the present system; viz., its relationship to a thorough-going purposivism, such, for example, as

McDougall's. McDougall's psychology, called by him a "hormic" psychology, bases all behavior and all mental activity of whatever sort upon the functioning of certain fundamental "instincts." Now it is obvious that McDougall's "instincts" are in many ways similar to what we have called the appetites and aversions. It must be emphasized, however, that whereas, for McDougall, the hormic drives, and their dependent purposes and cognitions, which are resident in the instincts, seem to be in the last analysis, mentalistic, introspectively defined affairs for us, they are, as has been emphasized perhaps *ad nauseam*, but functionally defined entities—quite objective variables invented to be inserted into the objectively definable equations which exist between stimuli on the one side and responses on the other. Thus, whereas for McDougall the objective behavior facts of purpose and cognition are a mere external testimony—a testimony to a probably ultimate dualism in nature—a testimony to the fact that mind is somehow, in some degree, metaphysically other than body—for us, these same facts of purpose and cognition are but an expression of certain very complex activities in organic bodies.

Our purposivism is, in short, not a fundamental or metaphysical purposivism. The purposes we have been talking about were purely objectively determined entities. In discovering purposes (and cognitions) in organisms, we have been asserting nothing about the ultimate texture of the universe. We have been neither asserting nor denying that there is some fundamental purpose (or mind) running through all nature.

And, even should it finally turn out, on a basis of further experiments, that there is for the behavior of organisms, just as for the behavior of electrons, some principle of ultimate indeterminateness (i.e., a kind of Heisenberg's uncertainty principle), this need not lead us to assume or suppose any metaphysically "other" as "butting in" to the course of organic nature. The finding of such an uncertainty principle would, to be sure, mean important and exciting things. It would mean that we must talk in terms of probabilities, of statistical averages, rather than in terms of unique individual cases. It would not mean, or at any rate would not need to mean, however, any metaphysical bifurcation or dualism—any breakdown in the possibility of final deterministic, descriptions per se.

In a word, the fact of purpose, as we conceive it, is an objective fact. It is the fact that behavior is docile relative to objectively determinable ends. Our psychology is a purposivism; but it is an objective, behavioristic purposivism, not a mentalistic one.

II–THE ORGANIZATION OF MOTIVATIONAL SYSTEMS

1. Combinations and Group Persistence

BY VILFREDO PARETO

842. SINCE SOCIAL PHENOMENA appear in complex form in the concrete, we saw at once that it would be helpful to divide them into at least two elements, distinguishing logical from non-logical conduct; and that gave us a first conception of the nature of non-logical conduct and of its importance in human society. But at that point a question arose: If non-logical conduct plays such an important role in human life, why has it been so generally neglected? We found in reply that almost all writers on social or political subjects have indeed observed such conduct, or at least caught glimpses of it. Many elements, therefore, of the theory we are framing in these volumes are to be found scattered about here and there in the works of various writers, though often under hardly recognizable forms.

843. But we saw that all such writers had ideas of their own to which they very expressly attached capital importance—ideas on religion, morality, law, and the like, which have been battle-grounds for centuries. So, if they did recognize non-logical conduct implicitly, explicitly they glorified logical conduct, and most of them regarded it as the only conduct worth considering in social phenomena. We were therefore called upon to see what truth there was in theories of that type, and to decide whether we were to abandon the course on which we had set out or take heart and push on.

We then proceeded to examine those various manners of considering social phenomena, and we saw that from the logico-experimental standpoint they were devoid of all exactness and of any strict accord with the facts; though from another standpoint, we could not deny the great importance that

they had had in history and in determining the social equilibrium. That discovery lent force to a suspicion which had already occurred to us, and which will acquire greater and greater prominence in the course of these volumes: that the experimental "truth" of certain theories is one thing and their social "utility" quite another, and that the two things are not only not one and the same but may, and often do, stand in flat contradiction.

844. We found that it was as important to separate those two things as it had been to distinguish logical from non-logical conduct, and our inductive survey showed that the failure to make such a distinction had been the main cause of error, from the scientific standpoint, in most social theories.

845. So we looked at them a little more closely and saw how and why they went astray, and how and why, though fallacious, they enjoyed and still enjoy such great prestige. In the course of that investigation we came upon things which we had not thought of at the outset. But we went on analyzing, distinguishing, and soon we observed another distinction that struck us as being quite as important as the others we had made—on the one hand an instinctive, non-logical element that was constant, on the other, a deductive element that was designed to explain, justify, demonstrate, the constant element. Arriving at that point, we found that induction had given us the elements of a theory.

846. Here, now, we are called upon to frame it, that is to say, we must now drop the inductive for the deductive method, and see what consequences result from the principles that we have found, or think we have found. After that we shall have to compare our inferences with the facts. If they fit, we shall keep our theory. If they fail to fit, we shall discard it.

847. In this chapter (and since the subject is a vast one, in the next two) we are to study the constant element *a*, going on, after that, to the deduc-

Reprinted from Vilfredo Pareto, *The Mind and Society,* ed. Arthur Livingston, trans. Andrew Bongiorno and Arthur Livingston (New York: Harcourt, Brace & Co., 1935), Vol. II, §§ 842–87, with the permission of The Pareto Fund.

tive element *b*. But we are dealing with a very difficult matter, and a few more remarks in general on the elements *a* and *b*, and their resultant *c*, will not come amiss.

848. We saw in [an earlier section] that in the theories of the logico-experimental sciences one may discern a basic element *A*, and a deductive element *B*, which in some respects are analogous to, in some respects different from, the elements *a* and *b* in theories that are not strictly logico-experimental.

The social sciences as hitherto cultivated show elements that bear a closer resemblance to *a* than to *A*, through their failure to avoid intrusions of sentiments, prejudices, creeds, or other predilections, tendencies, postulates, principles, that carry the thinker outside the logico-experimental domain.

849. The deductive element in the social sciences as hitherto cultivated sometimes comes very close to *B*, and there are cases where the logic is so adequate that coincidence with *B* would be exact were it not for a lack of definiteness in the premises *a*, which deprives the reasoning of strict validity. But oftentimes in the social sciences the deductive element stands very close to *b*, as containing many non-logical and non-experimental principles and showing great susceptibility to inclinations, bias, and the like.

850. So let us make the elements *a* and *b* our main concern. The element *a* corresponds, we may guess, to certain instincts of man, or more exactly, men, because *a* has no objective existence and differs in different individuals; and it is probably because of its correspondence to instincts that it is virtually constant in social phenomena. The element *b* represents the work of the mind in accounting for *a*. That is why *b* is much more variable, as reflecting the play of the imagination.[1]

851. But if the element *a* corresponds to certain instincts, it is far from reflecting them all; and that is evident from the very manner in which we found it. We analyzed specimens of thinking on the look-out for a constant element. We may therefore have found only the instincts that underlay those reasonings. There was no chance of our meeting along that road instincts which were not so logicalized. Unaccounted for still would be simple appetites, tastes, inclinations, and in social relationships the very important class called "interests."

852. We may also have found only a part of one of the things *a*, the other part being a mere appetite. If the sex instinct tended only to unite the sexes it

would not figure in our investigations. But that instinct is often enough logicalized and dissembled under guise of asceticism; there are people who preach virtue as a way of lingering, in their thoughts, on sex matters. Examining their thinking, we accordingly find an element *a* corresponding to the sex instinct, and an element *b* that is the reasoning under which it hides. Diligent search might reveal similar elements corresponding to the appetites for food and drink. But in those cases the role played by simple instinct is far more considerable, at any rate, than in the case of sex.

853. The fact of being provident or improvident depends upon certain instincts, certain tastes, and from that point of view it would not figure in *a*. But in the United States the improvident instinct has fathered a theory that people ought to spend all they can earn; and so analysis of that theory yields a quantum *a*, which will be improvidence.

854. A politician is inspired to champion the theory of "solidarity" by an ambition to obtain money, power, distinctions. Analysis of that theory would reveal but scant trace of his motives, which are, after all, the motives of virtually all politicians, whether they preach white or black. First prominence would be held by principles *a* that are effective in influencing others. If the politician were to say, "Believe in 'solidarity' because if you do it means money for me," he would get many laughs and few votes. He therefore has to take his stand on principles that are acceptable to his prospective constituents.

If we stopped at that, it might seem that in the case before us the *a*'s were located not in the principles that suggested championing the theory to the politician, but in the principles that inspired acceptance of it by his hearers. But going a little deeper, such a distinction is seen not to hold. Oftentimes the person who would persuade others begins by persuading himself; and even if he is moved in the beginning by thoughts of personal advantage, he comes eventually to believe that his real interest is the welfare of others. Unbelieving apostles are rare and ineffective, but ubiquitous and ubiquitously effective is the apostle who believes, and he is the more effective, the more sincere his belief. The element *a* in a theory *c* is present both in the persons who accept and in the persons who propound it, but not to be overlooked in either case are the advantages accruing from the theory *c*, to the ones and the others.

855. In analyzing a theory *c*, we must keep the objective standpoint sharply distinguished from the subjective. The two researches are very often confused, and so two errors, in chief, arise. In the first place, as we have so often cautioned, the logico-

---

1. As we have already seen, the part *b* has in its turn to be subdivided, since it varies all the way from one extreme, where it is pure logic, to another extreme where it is pure instinct and fancy.

experimental value of a theory is not kept distinct from its persuasive force or its social utility. Then again—and this is a peculiarly modern error—the objective study of a theory is replaced by a subjective research as to how and why it was evolved or adopted by its author. This second research certainly has its importance, but it ought to supplement the other, not replace it. Whether a theorem of Euclid is true or false, and how and why he came to discover it, are two separate questions, and the one does not preclude the other. If the *Principia* of Newton had been written by an unknown writer, would that in any way affect the value of the book? So two of the aspects under which a writer's theory may be considered become confused: (1) his manner of thinking, his psychic state, and how he came by it; (2) what he meant in a given passage. The first aspect, which is personal, subjective to him, is mixed in with the second, which is impersonal, objective. A factor in the confusion oftentimes is regard for the writer's authority. In deference to that sentiment it is assumed *a priori* that everything he thinks and believes must necessarily be "true," and that to determine his thought is tantamount to testing the "truth" (or when the logico-experimental sciences are concerned, the accord with experience) of what he thought.

856. Long prevalent was an inclination to consider theories exclusively from the standpoint of their intrinsic merit (sometimes their logico-experimental soundness), which, much more often, was determined with reference to the sentiments of the critic or to certain metaphysical or theological principles. Nowadays the tendency is to consider them exclusively from the extrinsic standpoint, as to the manner of their genesis, that is, and the reasons for their acceptance. Both methods, if used exclusively, are equally incomplete and to that extent erroneous.

857. The second error (§ 855) is the opposite of the first. The first considered only the intrinsic merit of the theory; the second only its extrinsic merit. It appears in the abuse of the historical method, which is frequent enough nowadays, especially in the social and economic sciences. In the beginning, in their eagerness to free their science of contingencies of time and place, the fathers of political economy made the mistake of viewing their findings as absolutes. It was a salutary reaction, therefore, when just such contingencies came to be taken into account, and from that point of view the historical method was a notable contribution to the progress of science. And a forward step no less important was taken when the effort to derive the forms of social institutions from dogmatic absolutes was abandoned in favour of historical studies that made it

possible to learn how institutions had developed, and their bearing on other social phenomena. We are altogether within the domain of logico-experimental science when we ask not what the family ought to be, but what it has actually been. But the historical study is to be thought of as supplementing, not as replacing, our inquiry into the relations between the constitution of the family and other social phenomena. It is useful to know how, historically, theories of income have been evolved; but it is also useful to know the relations of such theories to the facts—their logico-experimental value.

858. However, this latter type of research is much more difficult than the mere writing of history; and there are plenty of people who are utterly incapable of understanding, let alone of creating, a logico-experimental theory in political economy, yet who blithely presume to write histories of that science.

859. In the literary field historical studies often degenerate into mere collections of anecdotes that are easy to write and agreeable to read. To find out what a writer ate and drank, how he slept, the clothes he wore, is intellectually and scientifically easier than to deal with the relations between his theories and experimental realities. And if a critic can find something to say about a writer's love affairs, he is certain to make a very entertaining book indeed.

860. To study the element b is to study the subjective element in a theory. But the subjective element may be further subdivided into two: the general causes and the special causes that account for the genesis and success of a theory. General causes would be causes operative over fairly extensive periods of time and affecting considerable numbers of individuals. Special causes operate in an essentially contingent manner. If a theory comes into vogue because it serves the interests of a social class it has, in that fact, a general cause. If a writer invents a theory because he is paid to do so or because he wants to spite a rival, the cause is special.

861. Things that exert powerful effects upon the social order give rise to theories, and we shall find them, therefore, in the course of our quest for a's. In addition to such a's there are, as we have just seen, appetites and interests. Taking them all together we have the sum of the things that operate to any appreciable extent towards determining the social order (§ 851), bearing in mind of course that the social order reacts upon them, so that we are all along dealing not with a relationship of cause and effect, but with an interrelation or a relationship of interdependence. If we assume, as in fact seems probable, that animals have no theories, they cannot have an element *a* of any kind and perhaps not even interests—all that is left in their case is instincts. Uncivilized peoples, however close to animals they may seem to stand, do have theories of one sort or another, and an element *a* has to be considered in dealing with them. And beyond a doubt they have instincts and interests. Civilized peoples have theories for very very many of their instincts and interests. An element *a* figures through virtually the whole range of their social life.

862. In this volume we are to go looking for the element *a*. In many cases already we have distinguished *a* elements and *b* elements that we found combined and confused in some single phenomenon, *c*. That was in itself a start towards finding a norm for making such analyses. Suppose we get a still clearer view of the method from an example or two and then proceed with our systematic study.

863. *Example I.* Christians have the custom of baptism. If one knew the Christian procedure only one would not know whether and how it could be analyzed. Moreover, we have an explanation of it: We are told that the rite of baptism is celebrated in order to remove original sin. That still is not enough. If we had no other facts of the same class to go by, we should find it difficult to isolate the elements in the complex phenomenon of baptism. But we do have other facts of that type. The pagans too had lustral water, and they used it for purposes of purification. If we stopped at that, we might associate the use of water with the fact of purification. But other cases of baptism show that the use of water is not a constant element. Blood may be used for purification, and other substances as well. Nor is that all; there are numbers of rites that effect the same result. In cases where taboos have been violated, certain rites remove the pollution that a person has incurred in one set of circumstances or another. So the circle of similar facts widens, and in the great variety of devices and in the many explanations that are given for their use the thing which remains constant is the feeling, the sentiment, that the integrity of an individual which has been altered by certain causes, real or imaginary, can be restored by certain rites. The given case, therefore, is made up of that constant element, *a*, and a variable element, *b*, the latter comprising the means that are used for restoring the individual's integrity and the reasonings by which the efficacy of the means is presumably explained. The human being has a vague feeling that water somehow cleanses moral as well as material pollutions. However, he does not, as a rule, justify his conduct in that manner. The explanation would be far too simple. So he goes looking for something more

complicated, more pretentious, and readily finds what he is looking for.

864. The nucleus *a*, now that we have found it, is seen to be made up of a number of elements: first of all an instinct for combinations; people want "to do something about it"—they want to combine certain things with certain acts. It is a curious fact, also, that the ties so imagined persist in time. It would be easy enough to try some new combination every day. Instead there is one combination, fantastic though it be, that tends to prevail and sometimes does prevail over all competitors. Discernible, finally, is an instinct which inclines people to believe that certain combinations are suited to attaining certain objectives.[2]

865. *Example II.* We have seen many cases where people believed that they could raise or avert tempests. If we knew only one such case, we could make little or nothing of it. However, we know many cases and can identify a constant nucleus in them. Ignoring, for the moment, the element in the nucleus that relates, as in the case of baptism, to the persistence of certain combinations and the faith in their efficacy, we find a constant element, *a*, corresponding to the feeling, the sentiment, that a divinity exists and that, by a variable means, *b*, he (or "it") may be made to interfere and influence the weather. And then, right away, there is another sort of belief, the belief that it is possible to produce the desired effect by certain rites or practices, which mean nothing in themselves—the practice, for instance, of tearing a white cock asunder and carrying the two halves around a field to protect it from drought. So the circle widens, and another constant *a* appears: an instinct for combinations, whereby things and acts designed for producing given effects are brought together haphazard.

866. *Example III.* Catholics believe that Friday is a day of evil omen as—so it is averred—the day of the Passion. If we knew just that, and nothing else of the kind, it would be difficult to determine which of the two facts, the evil omen or the Passion, was the main, and which the secondary, fact. But we do have other facts of the kind, many of them. The Romans had their "black" or "vicious" days (*dies atri* or *vitiosi*), which were days of evil omen—for instance, the eighteenth of July, the anniversary of their defeat by the Gauls at Allia,

2. As for "causes" or "origins," we might guess that actually effective combinations, such as striking a flint to get a fire, may have led people to believe in the efficiency of imaginary combinations. But we need not, for the present, concern ourselves with that explanation or any other. We can rest content with establishing the fact, and stop at that. In some other connexion we might try to go further and explain the fact by other facts, then the latter by others still, and so on.

A.U.C. 365. That is one kind of *a*—the feeling that the day which is associated with some catastrophe is a day of evil omen. But there are other facts. Both the Romans and the Greeks had days of evil omen and days of good omen without there being any special causes in the nature of public successes or disasters. Hence there has to be a more comprehensive class of *a*'s, which includes the *a* just mentioned and expresses an impulse to combine days (and other things too) with good or evil omens.

867. These examples give us an inkling as to how a composite situation, *c,* may be broken up into *a* elements and *b* elements.[3]

868. Before going any farther it might perhaps be advisable to give word-names to the things we have been calling *a, b,* and *c.* To designate them by mere letters of the alphabet in a measure embarrasses our discussion and makes it harder to follow. For that reason, and for no other, suppose we call the things *a, residues,* the things *b, derivations,* and the things *c, derivatives.* But we must always and at all times remember that nothing, absolutely nothing, is to be inferred from the proper meanings of those words or their etymologies, that they mean respectively the things *a, b,* and *c* and nothing else.

869. As we have already seen, the residues *a* constitute a multifarious mass of facts, which have to be classified according to the mutual analogies they present. In that way we get "classes," "genera," and "species." And so for the derivations *B.*

870. Residues correspond to certain instincts in human beings, and for that reason they are usually wanting in definiteness, in exact delimitation. That trait, indeed, nearly always serves to distinguish them from scientific facts or principles *A,* which otherwise bear some resemblance to them. Many times *A*'s have come out of *a*'s as a result of making the *a*'s more exact. The term "warm" is indefinite. Using it, it has been possible to say that well-water is "warm" in winter and "cold" in summer. But as used by physicists the term "warm" corresponds to certain degrees of heat as registered by a thermometer; it is definite. That made it evident that the water in wells is not in that sense warmer in winter than in summer, for a thermometer lowered into a well registers about the same temperature in winter as in summer, or if anything a lower one.

871. Curious the number of different meanings the term "warm" has in Macrobius, *Saturnalia,* VII, 6–8, all of them showing as their residue the sentiments that the term "warm" awakens in the minds now of this, now of that, individual. The doctors say that wine is warm; but a character in the *Saturnalia* disagrees, finding wine by nature cold. A woman's body, says another, contains a large amount of cold. No, answers a companion, the female body is naturally warmer than the male—it is so warm, in fact, that when is was the custom to dispose of dead bodies by cremation, a female corpse was commonly burned with each ten males so that the latter might more quickly be consumed. Women have so much heat in their bodies that they are able to wear light clothing in winter. Heat, moreover, is the principle of conception. All that is disputed by another, except as regards conception, the cause of which seems really to be heat. Why is it that in a very hot country wine has the property of cold instead of heat? The reson is that when the air is hot it drives the cold into the ground. The air is always hot in Egypt, so the cold permeates the soil and reaches the vine-roots, imparting its own properties to the wine. And we are told why a fan cools.

872. That is the type of the metaphysical reasoning, whether ancient or modern. The premises contain terms altogether devoid of exactness, and from the premises, as from mathematical axioms presumably trustworthy, conclusions are drawn by strict logic. They serve, after all, to probe not things but the notions that given individuals have of things.[4]

873. The Macrobius example again shows how inexact terms may readily be used to prove both the pro and the contra. Women can wear lighter clothing than men because of the heat in their bodies. No, someone objects, it is because of the cold in their bodies.

874. In general terms, it is the indefiniteness of the residues *a,* chiefly, that unsuits them to serve as premises in strict reasonings, whereas *A* propositions can be and are constantly being so used in the sciences.

875. The residues *a* must not be confused with the sentiments or instincts to which they correspond. The residues are the manifestations of sentiments and instincts just as the rising of the mercury in a thermometer is a manifestation of the

3. [Pareto makes no very extensive use of the term "derivative," probably because its functions are filled just as well by the term "theory," or better, "non-logico-experimental theory." Etymologically, a "residue" would be "what is left" (the constant element) when the variable elements have been eliminated from an action or a reasoning by a comparative analysis. It is always reducible to the synonymous phrase: "principle underlying a non-logical action or reasoning."—A. L.]

4. Some people are willing as an extreme concession to bar that type of reasoning from the physical sciences, but insist on retaining it for the social sciences. If we keep within experimental limits, however, there is nothing to justify any such distinction.

rise in temperature. Only elliptically and for the sake of brevity do we say that residues, along with appetites, interests, etc. are the main factors in determining the social equilibrium, just as we say that water boils at 100° Centigrade. The completed statements would be: "The sentiments or instincts that correspond to residues, along with those corresponding to appetites, interests, etc., are the main factors in determining the social equilibrium." "Water boils when its calorific state attains the temperature of 100° as registered by a Centigrade thermometer."

876. It is only by way of analysis and for the sole purposes of study that we distinguish various residues $a1$, $a2$, $a3$. . . . What is at work in the individual is sentiments corresponding to the groups (a_1, a_2, a_3); (a_1, a_3, a_4); (a_3, a_5); and so on. These are composites as compared with the residues $a1$, $a2$ . . . which are simpler. We might go on and break up $a1$, $a2$ . . . as well into simpler elements; but we must know how to stop in time, because if made too general propositions end by meaning nothing. So the multifarious circumstances conditioning life on our globe may, in general, be reduced to solar light, the presence of an atmosphere, and so on; but the biologist needs conditions that are much less general than that as a basis for a greater number of biological laws.

877. It sometimes happens that a derivative, c, reached from a residue, a, by way of derivation, b, becomes in its turn the residue of other phenomena and itself subject to deviations. The bad omen, for instance, that is associated with the presence of thirteen persons at a table may be a derivative from a sentiment of horror at Judas's betrayal followed by his suicide; but that derivative has become a residue by this time, and people feel ill at ease at a table of thirteen without the least thought of Judas.

878. All the pointers just given must be kept in mind at all times in the investigations following. Anyone forgetting them will get everything askew.

879. This research as so far outlined has certain points of analogy with the ordinary researches of philology that deal with the roots and derivatives in which the words of a language originate. The analogy is not altogether artificial. It arises in the fact that products of the mental activity of the human being are involved in both cases, that their processes are the same. Take, for instance, Greek. The words in that language may be grouped in families, each family having its own root. There are the nouns meaning "anchor" (ἄγχυρα), "fish-hook" (ἄγκιστρον), "curved object" (ἀγκαλη), "bent arm" (ἀγκαλίς), "bend of the arm" (ἀγκύλη), "elbow" (ἀγκών); the adjectives "curved" (ἀγκυλος)

and "hook-shaped" (ἀγκιστρωτός,-ή-όν); the verbs "to fish with a hook" (ἀγκιστρεύω) and "to bend" (ἀγκυλῶ). They all have the same root (residue) ἀγκ, which originates in, and expresses, the rather vague notion of something curved, hooked, crooked. By processes of derivation, which have their rules, words are derived from these roots, just as the derivatives, c, are derived from the residues, a. We find combinations of roots just as we find combinations of residues. The adjective "biting a hook" (ἀγκιστροφάγος has ἀγκ and φαγ for its roots, the first referring to something vaguely hook-shaped, the second to eating. There are some very common derivations in Greek. The suffix μᾱτ, for instance, combining with various roots, gives large numbers of words designating the effects of the actions indicated by the roots. So in social phenomena, certain derivations are very common. The Will of the Divinity, for instance, serves to justify no end of prescriptions. Combined with the residue of filial love, it yields the precept: "Honour thy father and thy mother, for God so ordains."

880. Actually observable in society are certain derivatives, c, that derive from residues, a, by way of derivations, b. Other derivatives (γ) may be as regularly deducible from the residues as the c's but are not observable in the concrete.

881. That situation has its philological counterpart in regular and irregular verbs. In point of fact such terms must not be taken literally. A so-called irregular verb is as regular as any other. The difference lies in the differing methods of derivation. A process of derivation used for certain roots gives a class of verbs that actually occur in the language. Used for other roots, it gives verbs that do not occur in the language. Conversely, the process of derivation used for these second roots yields verbs that occur in the language, but non-existent verbs when used for the other roots.

882. Derivatives treated as residues have their counterparts in language. The word αγκιστροφάγος ("biting a hook") was not derived directly from the roots ἀγκ and φαγ, but from ἀγκιστρον and φαγετν. Inflections, conjugations, comparatives, superlatives, locatives, to mention only a few, are examples of derivations based on other derivations.

883. That is not all. The philologists of our time know that the language is an organism which has developed according to its own laws and is not an artificial invention. Only a relatively few technical terms, such as "oxygen," "meter," "thermometer," and the like, are products of logical activity on the part of scholars. Such terms would correspond to "logical actions" in society. The majority of the words in ordinary usage correspond in their formation to "non-logical" actions.[5]

884. We have noted these analogies merely to facilitate a clear comprehension of the theories that we are expounding. They of course are not and could not be offered as proofs. Proof must come from direct examination of the facts and in no other way. The method that relies on analogies is a very bad method.

885. Investigations into the "origins" of social phenomena, which have so far concerned sociology in the main, have oftentimes been, though their authors were not aware of the fact, searches for residues. It was taken for granted, more or less vaguely, that the simple must have preceded the complex—that the residue must have been anterior to the derivative. When Herbert Spencer locates the chronological origin of religion in the deification of human beings, he thinks he has found the residue of all religious phenomena, the simple phenomenon from which the complex religious observable in our day derive.

886. Two criticisms are to be made of that view. 1. No proof is offered of the hypothesis that knowledge of the residue is chronologically anterior to knowledge of the derivative. That has been the case in some instances, but certainly not in others. So

in chemistry certain chemical compounds have been discovered later in time than the elements of which they are compounded, but many other compounds have been known earlier in time. In sociology the "latent" principles of law are an excellent example of derivatives that were known before their residues. An illiterate peasant woman in the mountains around Pistoia knows the conjugations of many Italian verbs by practice perfectly well and much better than any number of educated people; but she has not the remotest idea of the rules that govern the derivation of those conjugations from their roots. 2. Even if knowledge of the residue is anterior in time to knowledge of the derivative, it is better to follow a course directly opposite to the one that has so far been followed. A chronological quest for the residue *a* is difficult, often impossible, because there are no documents for times so remote from ours; and it is illegitimate to take the imagination and the "common sense" of the modern man as substitutes for them. Imagination and common sense may, to be sure, yield fascinating theories, but they have little or nothing to do with the facts. To try to discover in primitive periods the residue, *a,* from which the phenomena, *c,* observable today, are derived is to try to explain the known by the unknown. To the precise contrary, the less well known must be inferred from the better known; one must try to discover the residues, *a,* in the phenomena, *c,* that are observable today and then see whether there are traces of *a* in documents of the past. If in so doing we find that *a* existed before *c* was known we might conclude that *a* is anterior in time to *c,* and that, in the particular case, the *origin* is one and the same with the *residue.* Where such proof is lacking no such identity can legitimately be assumed.

887. So far in these volumes we have tried, and we shall continue at all times trying, to explain facts of the past by other facts that we are able to observe in the present; and in any event, we shall always be at the greatest pains to work from the better known to the less known. We are not dealing with "origins" here, not because origins are not important historically, but because the question of origins has little or no bearing on the inquiry into the conditions determining the social equilibrium with which we are at present engaged. Of great moment, instead, are the instincts and sentiments that correspond to residues.

---

5. It is high time that sociology were making some progress and trying to get to the level that philology has already reached. Many other analogies between the two sciences might be noted—to mention just one, the analogy between the abuse of the historical method in sociology and of hypercriticism of texts in philology. Reinach, *Manuel de philologie,* Vol. I, § 3, p. 48: "Boeckh has very properly called attention to a vicious circle to which philological criticism is not immune. In order to explain a text it has to be read under a certain form, and to read it under that form *without change* one has to be able to understand it and explain it. Hence a tendency in many scholars to correct or suppress all passages they do not understand. [That is a way also with writers interested in the 'origins' of (social or historical) phenomena.] Says Nauck, in Schneidewin's edition of Sophocles: 'The conjecture that can claim plausibility is the conjecture that best realizes from every point of view what the most exacting mind would like to find in a Greek tragic author.' Boeckh seems almost to have been writing for Nauck's benefit when he said: 'The Athenians, at the suggestion of Lycurgus, had forbidden any alteration in the texts of the tragic authors. One could almost wish the ancient classics were protected by a similar law today.'" Nowadays, in the quest for "origins" everybody takes account of the facts that agree with his notions, and nothing else. Show me if you can the humanitarian who will accept an account of facts that runs counter to his beliefs, or the Marxian who does not test all facts by his doctrine of capitalism!

2. *Faithfulness and Gratitude*

BY GEORG SIMMEL

FAITHFULNESS is one of those very general modes of conduct that may become important in all interactions among men, no matter how different they may be materially or sociologically. In superordinations, subordinations, coordinations; in collective hostilities toward third parties as in collective friendships; in families and in regard to the state; in love as well as in one's relation to one's occupational group—in all these structures, examined purely in their sociological constellations, faithfulness and its opposite become important. But faithfulness is significant as a sociological form of the second order, as it were, as the instrument of relations which already exist and endure. In its general form, the connection between faithfulness and the sociological forms it supports is, in a certain sense, like the connection between these forms and the material contents and motives of social life.

Without the phenomenon we call faithfulness, society could simply not exist, as it does, for any length of time. The elements which keep it alive —the self-interest of its members, suggestion, coercion, idealism, mechanical habit, sense of duty, love, inertia—could not save it from breaking apart if they were not supplemented by this factor. Its measure and significance, however, cannot be determined in the given case, because its practical effect always consists in replacing some other feeling, which hardly ever disappears completely. The contribution of this feeling is inextricably interwoven with that of faithfulness itself, in a composite result that resists quantitative analysis.

Because of the supplementary character of faithfulness, such a term as "faithful love," for instance, is somewhat misleading. If love continues to exist in a relationship between persons, why does it need faithfulness? If the partners are not, from the beginning, connected by it but, rather, by the primary and genuine psychological disposition of love, why must faithfulness, as the guardian of the relationship, be added after ten years if, by definition, love remains identical even then, and still on its own strength has its initial binding power? If linguistic usage understands by *faithful* love what

is simply *enduring* love, there is no objection, of course. Words do not concern us here; what is important is the existence of a specific psychic and sociological state, which insures the continuance of a relationship beyond the forces that first brought it about; which survives these forces with the same synthesizing effect they themselves had originally; and which we cannot help but designate as faithfulness, although this term also has a very different meaning, namely, the perseverance of these forces themselves. Faithfulness might be called the inertia of the soul. It keeps the soul on the path on which it started, even after the original occasion that led it onto it no longer exists.[1]

It is a fact of the greatest sociological importance that innumerable relationships preserve their sociological structure unchanged, even after the feeling or practical occasion, which originally gave rise to them, has ended. That destruction is easier than construction, is not unqualifiedly true of certain human relations, however indubitable it is otherwise. The rise of a relationship, to be sure, requires certain positive and negative conditions, and the absence of even one of them may, at once, preclude its development. Yet once started, it is by no means always destroyed by the subsequent disappearance of that condition which, earlier, it could not have overcome. An erotic relation, for instance, begun on the basis of physical beauty, may well survive the decline of this beauty and its change into ugliness. What has been said of states—that they are maintained only by the means by which they were founded—is only a very incomplete truth, and anything but an all-pervasive principle of sociation generally. Sociological connectedness, no matter what its origin, develops a self-preservation and autonomous existence of its form that are independent of its initially connecting motives. Without this inertia of existing sociations, society as a whole would constantly collapse, or change in an unimaginable fashion.

The preservation of social units is psychologically

Reprinted from *The Sociology of Georg Simmel*, trans. and ed. Kurt Wolff (Glencoe, Ill.: The Free Press, 1950), pp. 379–95, with the permission of The Free Press.

1. It goes without saying that I always speak here of faithfulness only as a purely psychic disposition operating from "inside out," not as behavior such as marital faithfulness in the legal sense, for instance, which refers to nothing positive at all, but only to the non-occurrence of unfaithfulness.

sustained by many factors, intellectual and practical, positive and negative. Faithfulness is the *affective* factor among them; or better, faithfulness in the form of feeling, in its projection upon the plane of feeling, is this affective factor. The quality of this feeling will be ascertained here only in its psychic reality, whether or not one accepts it as an adequate definition of the idea of faithfulness. Every beginning relationship is accompanied by a specific feeling, interest, impulse, directed toward it by its participants. If the relation continues, there develops a particular feeling in interaction with this continuance—or, better, often, though not always, the original psychic states change into a particular form which we call faithfulness. It is a psychological reservoir, as it were, an over-all or unitary mold for the most varied interests, affects, and motives of reciprocal bonds. In spite of all variety of origin, the original psychic states attain, in the form of faithfulness, a certain similarity, which understandably promotes the permanence of faithfulness itself. In other words, the discussion here does not concern so-called "faithful love," "faithful attachment," etc., which refer to certain modes or temporal quantities of feelings already defined: what I mean is that faithfulness itself is a specific psychic state, which is directed toward the continuance of the relation as such, independently of any particular affective or volitional elements that sustain the content of this relation. This psychic state of the individual is one of the *a priori* conditions of society which alone make society possible (at least as we know it), in spite of the extraordinary differences of degree in which this psychic state exists. It can probably never reach zero: the absolutely unfaithful person—the person for whom it is impossible to transform feelings that engender relationships into the feeling designed to preserve the relationship—is not a thinkable phenomenon.

Faithfulness, thus, might be called "induction by feeling." At such and such a moment a relation existed. In formal analogy to theoretical induction, feeling concludes that, therefore, the relation also exists at a later moment. And, just as in intellectual induction, the later instance need no longer be ascertained as fact, so to speak (because induction precisely means that we may do without this ascertainment), so here, very often, the later moment no longer shows a real feeling or interest, but only the inductively developed state called faithfulness. In the consideration of a great many relations and connections among men, one must count with the fact (a fundamental sociological fact) that mere habitual togetherness, the mere existence of a relation over a period of time, produces this induction by feeling.

This broadens the concept of faithfulness by adding a very important element. The external sociological situation of togetherness appropriates the particular feelings that properly correspond to it, as it were, even though they did not justify the beginnings of the relationship. In a certain sense, the process of faithfulness here runs backward. The psychical motives which produced the relation allow the specific feeling of faithfulness toward this relation to develop, or they transform themselves into this feeling. Although the relationship may have been brought about for external reasons (or at best, for intimate ones that are extrinsic to its meaning), it nevertheless develops its own faithfulness which, in turn, gives rise to deeper and more adequate feeling states: the relation is legitimated, so to speak, *per subsequens matrimonium animarum* [through the subsequent marriage of the souls].

The banal wisdom one often hears in reference to marriages that were concluded on conventional or other external grounds—that love will come later, during the marriage—is sometimes actually quite apt. For once the existence of the relationship has found its psychological correlate, faithfulness, then faithfulness is followed, eventually, also by the feelings, affective interests, and inner bonds that properly belong to the relationship. Only, instead of appearing at the beginning, as we should "logically" expect, they reveal themselves as its end product. But this development cannot come to pass without the mediation of faithfulness, of the affect which is directed toward the preservation of the relationship as such. In psychological association in general, once imagination B is tied to imagination A, there also develops the opposite effect: A is called into consciousness wherever B is. Analogously, the sociological form of a given relationship produces, in the manner indicated, the inner state of feeling that corresponds to it, although ordinarily the process runs in the opposite direction.

An example will illustrate this. In order to restrict, as much as possible, the exposing of children and their being given over to foundlings' homes, France introduced, in the middle of the nineteenth century, the *"secours temporaires,"* that is, fairly adequate subsidies for unmarried mothers who kept their children under their own care. On the basis of abundant observational material, the originators of this measure pointed out in favor of it that, in the overwhelming majority of cases, once the mother could be persuaded to keep the child for any length of time, there was no danger any longer of her giving it up. The natural emotional tie between mother and child should make her wish to keep it, but obviously does not always. Yet, if she can be swayed to do so even for a while, if only for external reasons, to secure the advantage of that temporary subsidy, this external relationship creates its own emotional underpinning.

These psychological constellations appear especially intensified in the phenomenon of the *renegade*. He exhibits a characteristic loyalty to his new political, religious, or other party. The awareness and firmness of this loyalty (other things being equal) surpass those of persons who have belonged to the party all along. In sixteenth- and seventeenth-century Turkey, this went so far that very often born Turks were not allowed to occupy high government positions, which were filled only by Janizaries, that is, born Christians, either voluntarily converted to Islam or stolen from their parents as children and brought up as Turks. They were the most loyal an energetic subjects. The special loyalty of the renegade seems to me to rest on the fact that the circumstances under which he enters the new relationship, have a longer and more enduring effect than if he had naïvely grown into it, so to speak, without breaking with a previous one.

As far as it concerns us here, faithfulness or loyalty is the emotional reflection of the autonomous life of the relation, unperturbed by the possible disappearance of the motives which originally engendered the relation. But the longer these motives survive, and the less seriously the power of pure form alone (of the relationship itself) is put to test, the more energetic and certain is the effect of faithfulness. This is particularly true of the renegade because of his sharp awareness that he cannot go back: the old relationship, with which he has irrevocably broken, remains for him, who has a sort of heightened discriminatory sensitivity, the background of the relation now existing. It is as if he were repelled by the old relationship and pushed into the new one, over and over again. Renegade loyalty is so strong because it includes what loyalty in general can dispense with, namely, the conscious continuance of the motives of the relationship. This continuance here fuses more permanently with the formal power of the relationship itself than in cases without contrasting past and without absence of alternative paths, of return, or in other directions.

The very conceptual structure of faithfulness shows that it is a sociological, or (if one will) a sociologically oriented, feeling. Other feelings, no matter how much they may tie person to person, have yet something more solipsistic. After all, even love, friendship, patriotism, or the sense of social duty, essentially occur and endure in the individual himself, immanently—as is perhaps revealed most strikingly in Philine's question: "In what way does it concern *you* that I love you?" In spite of their

extraordinary sociological significance, these feelings remain, above all, subjective states. To be sure, they are engendered only by the intervention of other individuals or groups, but they do so even before the intervention has changed into interaction. Even where they are directed toward other *individuals* the *relation* to these individuals is, at least not *necessarily*, their true presupposition or content.

But precisely this is the meaning of faithfulness —at least as here discussed, although linguistic usage also gives it other meanings. Faithfulness refers to the peculiar feeling which is not directed toward the possession of the other as the possessor's eudaemonistic good, nor toward the other's welfare as an extrinsic, objective value, but toward the preservation of the *relationship* to the other. It does not engender this relationship; therefore, unlike these other affects, it cannot be pre-sociological: it pervades the relation once it exists and, as its inner self-preservation, makes the individuals-in-relation hold fast to one another. This specific sociological character is connected with the fact that faithfulness, more than other feelings, is accessible to our moral intentions. Other feelings overcome us like sunshine or rain, and their coming and going cannot be controlled by our will. But *un*faithfulness entails a more severe reproach than does absence of love or social responsibility, beyond their merely obligatory manifestations.

Moreover, its particular sociological significance makes faithfulness play a unifying role in connection with a basic dualism that pervades the fundamental form of all sociation. The dualism consists in the fact that a relation, which is a fluctuating, constantly developing life-process, nevertheless receives a relatively stable external form. The sociological forms of reciprocal behavior, of unification, of presentation toward the outside, cannot follow, with any precise adaptation, the changes of their inside, that is, of the processes that occur in the individual in regard to the other. These two layers, relation and form, have different tempi of development; or it often is the nature of the external form not to develop properly at all.

Evidently, the strongest external measure for fixing internally variable relations is law. Examples are the marital form, which unyieldingly confronts changes in personal relationship; the contract between two associates, which continues to divide business profit evenly between them, although one of them does all the work, and the other none; membership in an urban or religious community that has become completely alien or anti-pathetic to the member. But even beyond these obvious cases, inter-individual as well as inter-group relations, which have hardly begun, can constantly be observed to have an immediate tendency toward solidifying their form. The form thus comes to constitute a more or less rigid handicap for the relation in its further course, while the form itself is incapable of adapting to the vibrating life and the more or less profound changes of this concrete, reciprocal relation.

But this is only the repetition of a discrepancy within the individual himself. Our inner life, which we perceive as a stream, as an incessant process, as an up and down of thoughts and moods, becomes crystallized, even for ourselves, in formulas and fixed directions often merely by the fact that we verbalize this life. Even if this leads only rarely to specific inadequacies; even if, in fortunate cases, the fixed external form constitutes the center of gravity or indifference above and below which our life evenly oscillates; there still remains the fundamental, formal contrast between the essential flux and movement of the subjective psychic life and the limitations of its forms. These forms, after all, do not express or shape an ideal, a contrast with life's reality, but this life itself.

Whether they are the forms of individual or social life, they do not flow like our inner development does, but always remain fixed over a certain period of time. For this reason, it is their nature sometimes to be ahead of the inner reality and sometimes to lag behind it. More specifically, when the life, which pulsates beneath outlived forms, breaks these forms, it swings into the opposite extreme, so to speak, and creates forms ahead of itself, forms which are not yet completely filled out by it. To take an instance from the field of personal relations: among friends the *Sie* [polite form of address] is often felt to be a stiffness that is incommensurate with the warmth of the relation; but when it finally comes to the *Du* [intimate form of address], this too, at least in the beginning, strikes them just as often as something slightly "too much," as the anticipation of full intimacy which has yet to be achieved. Another example is the change of a political constitution, by which obsolete forms that have become unbearably oppressive are replaced by freer and larger ones, while the reality of the political and economic forces is not always ripe for them: an overly narrow frame is replaced by one which, for the time being, is still too wide.

In regard to these conditions of social life, faithfulness (in the sense discussed) has the significance that, by virtue of it, for once the personal, fluctuating inner life actually adopts the character of the fixed, stable form of a relation. Or vice versa: this sociological fixity, which remains outside life's immediacy and subjective rhythm, here actually becomes the content of subjective, emotionally

determined life. Irrespective of the innumerable modifications, deflections, intermixtures of concrete destinies, faithfulness bridges and reconciles that deep and essential dualism which splits off the life-form of individual internality [*Innerlichkeit*] from the life-form of sociation that is nevertheless borne by it. Faithfulness is that constitution of the soul (which is constantly moved and lives in a continuous flux), by means of which it fully incorporates into itself the stability of the super-individual form of relation and by means of which it admits to life, as the meaning and value of life, a content which, though created by the soul itself, is in its form, nevertheless bound to contradict the rhythm or un-rhythm of life as actually lived.

Although in the feeling called *gratitude* the sociological character emerges much less directly, its sociological importance can hardly be overestimated. Only the external insignificance of its concrete acts—which contrasts, however, with the immense sphere of its application—has thus far apparently concealed the circumstance that the life and the cohesion of society would be unforeseeably changed without this phenomenon.

Gratitude, in the first place, supplements the legal order. All contacts among men rest on the schema of giving and returning the equivalence. The equivalence of innumerable gifts and performances can be enforced. In all economic exchanges in legal form, in all fixed agreements concerning a given service, in all obligations of legalized relations, the legal constitution enforces and guarantees the reciprocity of service and return service—social equilibrium and cohesion do not exist without it. But there also are innumerable other relations, to which the legal form does not apply, and in which the enforcement of the equivalence is out of the question. Here gratitude appears as a supplement. It establishes the bond of interaction, of the reciprocity of service and return service, even where they are not guaranteed by external coercion. Gratitude is, thus, a supplementation of the legal form in the same sense that I showed *honor* to be.[2]

In order to appraise the specific nature of this connection correctly, it is necessary (above all) to realize that personal action among men by means of things—as, for instance, in robbery and gift, the primitive forms of property exchange—becomes objectified in *exchange*. Exchange is the objectification of human interaction. If an individual gives a thing, and another returns one of the same value, the purely spontaneous character [*Seelenhaftigkeit*] of their relation has become projected into objects.

---

2. On pp. 403–6 of the same chapter of *Soziologie* from which the present *"Exkurs"* is taken (VIII, *"Die Selbsterhaltung der sozialen Gruppe,"* The Self-Preservation of the Social Group).

This objectification, this growth of the relationship into self-contained, movable things, becomes so complete that, in the fully developed economy, personal interaction recedes altogether into the background, while goods gain a life of their own. Relations and value balances between them occur automatically, by mere computation: men act only as the executors of the tendencies toward shifts and equilibriums that are inherent in the goods themselves. The objectively equal is given for the objectively equal, and man himself is really irrelevant, although it goes without saying that he engages in the process for his own interest. The relation among men has become a relation among objects.

Gratitude likewise originates from interaction, and in interaction, between men. But it does so in the same manner, toward the inside, as the relation of things originates from it, toward the outside. While interaction is lifted out of the spontaneous act of correlation through the exchange of things, this act in its consequences, subjective meanings, and psychic echoes, sinks into the soul through gratitude. Gratitude, as it were, is the moral memory of mankind. In this respect, it differs from faithfulness by being more practical and impulsive: although it may remain, of course, something purely internal, it may yet engender new actions. It is an ideal bridge which the soul comes across again and again, so to speak, and which, upon provocations too slight to throw a *new* bridge to the other person, it uses to come closer to him.

Beyond its first origin, all sociation rests on a relationship's effect which survives the emergence of the relationship. An action between men may be engendered by love or greed of gain, obedience or hatred, sociability or lust for domination alone, but this action usually does not exhaust the creative mood which, on the contrary, somehow lives on in the sociological situation it has produced. Gratitude is definitely such a continuance. It is an ideal living-on of a relation which may have ended long ago, and with it, the act of giving and receiving. Although it is a purely personal affect, or (if one will) a lyrical affect, its thousandfold ramifications throughout society make it one of the most powerful means of social cohesion. It is a fertile emotional soil which grows concrete actions among particular individuals. But much more: although we are often unaware of its fundamentally important existence, and although it is interwoven with innumerable other motivations, nevertheless, it gives human actions a unique modification or intensity: it connects them with what has gone before, it enriches them with the element of personality, it gives them the continuity of interactional life. If every grateful action, which lingers on from good turns received in the past, were suddenly eliminated, society (at least as we know it) would break apart.[3]

All external and internal motives that bind individuals together may be examined with respect to their implementation of the exchange which not only holds society together once it is formed but, in large measure, forms it. From such an examination, gratitude emerges as the motive which, for inner reasons, effects the return of a benefit where there is no external necessity for it. But "benefit" is not limited to a person's giving things to another: we also thank the artist or poet who does not even know us. This fact creates innumerable connections, ideal and concrete, loose and firm, among those who are filled with gratitude toward the same giver. In fact, we do not thank somebody only for what he *does:* the feeling with which we often react to the mere existence of a person, must itself be designated as gratitude. We are grateful to him only because he exists, because we experience him. Often the subtlest as well as firmest bonds among men develop from this feeling. It is independent of any particular act of receiving; it offers our whole personality to the other, as if from a duty of gratitude to *his* total personality.

The concrete content of gratitude, that is, of the responses it induces, calls forth modifications of interaction whose delicacy does not lessen their significance for the structure of our relationships. The intimate character of these relations receives an extraordinary wealth of nuances when the psychological situation makes it necessary for a gift received to be returned with a gift of an essentially different kind. Thus an individual, perhaps, gives "spirit," that is, intellectual values, while the other shows his gratitude by returning affective values. Another offers the aesthetic charms of his personality, for instance, and the receiver, who happens to be the stronger nature, compensates him for it by injecting will power into him, as it were, or firmness and resoluteness. There is, probably, not a single interaction in which the things that go back and forth, in the reciprocity of giving and taking, are exactly equal, although the examples given are

3. Giving, itself, is one of the strongest sociological functions. Without constant giving and taking within society—outside of exchange, too—society would not come about. For, giving is by no means only a simple effect that one individual has upon another: it is precisely what is required of all sociological functions, namely, interaction. By either accepting or rejecting the gift, the receiver has a highly specific effect upon the giver. The manner of his acceptance, gratefully or ungratefully, having expected the gift or being surprised by it, being satisfied or dissatisfied, elevated or humiliated—all this keenly acts back upon the giver, although it can, of course, not be expressed in definite concepts and measures. Every act of giving is, thus, an interaction between giver and receiver.

extreme intensifications of this inevitable difference between gifts and return gifts among men.

If this difference is striking and is accompanied by its own awareness, it constitutes a problem for what might be called "inner sociology," a problem which is equally difficult ethically and theoretically. For, when an individual offers his intellectual possessions, but is not very emotionally involved in the relation, while the other can return nothing but his love, there often is a slight note of inner incommensurateness; in fact, for our feelings, all cases of this sort have something fatal: they somehow resemble a purchase. Purchase—and this distinguishes it from exchange in general—implies that the exchange, which actually takes place under its name, concerns two entirely heterogeneous things that can be juxtaposed and compared only by means of a common monetary value. Thus, if earlier, prior to the use of metal money, some handiwork was purchased with a cow or goat, these wholly heterogeneous things were juxtaposed and became exchangeable by virtue of the economic, abstract-general value contained in each of them.

This heterogeneity reaches its peak in modern money economy. Because money expresses the general element contained in all exchangeable objects, that is, their exchange value, it is incapable of expressing the individual element in them. Therefore, objects insofar as they figure as salable things, become degraded: the individual in them is leveled down to the general which is shared by everything salable, particularly by money itself. Something of this basic heterogeneity occurs in the cases I mentioned. Two individuals offer one another different parts of their inner lives. Gratitude for the gift is realized in a different coin, as it were, and thus injects something of the character of purchase into the exchange, which is inappropriate in principle. One buys love with what one gives of spirit. One buys the charm of a person one wants to enjoy, and pays for it with one's superior power of suggestion or will, which the other either wishes to feel over himself or by which he allows himself to be inspired.

This feeling of a certain inadequacy or indignity, however, arises only if the reciprocal offerings appear as isolated objects of exchange, if the mutual gratitude concerns only the benefits, the exchanged contents themselves, so to speak. But man is not the merchant of himself; and particularly not in the relationships discussed here. His qualities, the powers and functions which emanate from him, do not simply lie before him like merchandise on a counter. It is most important to realize that, even if an individual gives only a particular item, offers only one side of his personal-

ity, he may yet wholly *be* in this side, may yet give his personality completely in the form of this single energy, or attribute, as Spinoza would say. This disproportion appears only if the relation has become differentiated to a point where the gift is severed from the giver's total personality. If this is *not* so, however, it is precisely in these cases that a wonderfully pure instance of a phenomenon emerges which is, otherwise, not very frequent: of gratitude as the reaction equally to the benefit and to the benefactor. Man's plasticity allows him both to offer and to accept, by means of the apparently objective response to the gift which consists in another gift, all of the subjectivity of gift and giver.

The most profound instance of this kind occurs when the whole inner mood, which is oriented toward the other person in the particular manner called gratitude, is *more* than an enlarged projection (as it were) of the actually well-defined reaction of thankfulness upon our total psychic disposition: but when, instead, the goods and other obligations we receive from the other, merely strike us as an occasion upon which our relation to him, predetermined as it is in our inner nature, is realized. What we usually call gratitude and what has given this feeling its name in terms of single benefits, here goes much below the ordinary form of thanks for gifts. One might say that here gratitude actually consists, not in the return of a gift, but in the consciousness that it cannot be returned, that there is something which places the receiver into a certain permanent position with respect to the giver, and makes him dimly envisage the inner infinity of a relation that can neither be exhausted nor realized by any finite return gift or other activity.

This touches upon a further deep-lying incommensurability, which is an essential characteristic of the relationships subsumed under the category of gratitude. Once we have received something good from another person, once he has preceded us with his action ["*vorgeleistet*"], we no longer can make up for it completely, no matter how much our own return gift or service may objectively or legally surpass his own. The reason is that his gift, because it was first, has a voluntary character which no return gift can have. For, to return the benefit we are obliged ethically; we operate under a coercion which, though neither social nor legal but moral, is still a coercion. The first gift is given in full spontaneity; it has a freedom without any duty, even without the duty of gratitude. By his bold identification of doing one's duty with freedom, Kant ruled this character of duty out of court, but thereby confused the negative side of freedom with its positive side. We are apparently free to do or not to do the duty we feel above us as an ideal; but, actually, complete freedom exists only in regard to *not* doing it, since to do it follows from a psychic imperative, from a coercion which is the inner equivalent of the legal coercion of society. Complete freedom does not lie on the side of doing, but only on that of not-doing, for, to *do* I am obligated because it is a duty—I am caused to return a gift, for instance, by the mere fact that I received it. Only when we give first are we free, and this is the reason why, in the first gift, which is not occasioned by any gratitude, there lies a beauty, a spontaneous devotion to the other, an opening up and flowering from the "virgin soil" of the soul, as it were, which cannot be matched by any subsequent gift, no matter how superior its content. The difference involved here finds expression in the feeling (apparently often unjustified in regard to the concrete *content* of the gift) that we *cannot* return a gift; for it has a freedom which the return gift, because it is *that,* cannot possibly possess.

This, perhaps, is the reason why some people do not like to accept, and try to avoid as much as possible being given gifts. Their attitude would be ununderstandable if gift and gratitude concerned objects only: for, merely by returning the gift, everything could be balanced and the inner obligation redeemed. Actually, however, these people act on the instinct, perhaps, that the return gift cannot possibly contain the decisive element of the original, namely, freedom; and that, in accepting it, therefore, they would contract an irredeemable obligation.[4] As a rule such people have a strong impulse to independence and individuality; and this suggests that the condition of gratitude easily has a taste of bondage, that it is a moral *character indelebilis* [inextinguishable element]. A service, a sacrifice, a benefit, once accepted, may engender an inner relation which can never be eliminated completely, because gratitude is perhaps the only feeling which, under all circumstances, can be morally demanded and rendered. If by itself or in response to some external reality, our inner life has made it impossible for us to continue loving, revering, esteeming a person (aesthetically or ethically or intellectually), we can still be grateful to him, since he once gained our gratitude. To *this* demand we are (or could be) unconditionally subject: in regard to no fault of feeling is an un-

mitigated sentence as appropriate as in regard to ingratitude.

Even intimate faithfulness is more remissible. There are relationships which, from their very beginning, operate only with a limited capital of feeling (so to speak) and, after a time, inevitably use it up. Thus their termination does not involve any unfaithfulness, properly speaking. In their initial stages, however, it is difficult to distinguish these from other relations, which (continuing the metaphor) live off interest only and in which no passionate and unreserved giving makes inroads into the capital. It is certainly one of the most common errors of man to think that something which actually is capital is only interest, and, for this reason, so to construct a relationship that its breach does become an act of unfaithfulness. But this act is not then a delinquency committed in full freedom, but only the logical outcome of a development based all along on erroneous factors. Nor does unfaithfulness appear any more avoidable where not the discovery of a mistake, but an actual change in the individuals, alters the presuppositions of their relationship. Perhaps the greatest tragedy of human conditions springs from (among other things) the utterly unrationalizable and constantly shifting mixture of the stable and variable elements of our nature. Even when we have entered a binding relationship with our whole being, we may yet remain in the same mood and inclination as before with some of our aspects—perhaps with those that are turned outward, but possibly even with some internal ones. But other aspects develop into entirely new interests, aims, capacities, and thus come to throw our total existence into new directions. In doing so, they turn us away from earlier conditions[5] with a sort of unfaithfulness, which is neither quite innocent, since there still exist some bonds which must now be broken, nor quite guilty, since we are no longer the persons we were when we entered the relationship; the subject to whom the unfaithfulness could be imputed has disappeared.

When our feeling of gratitude gives out, our sentiments admit of no such exoneration on inner grounds. For, gratitude seems to reside in a point in us which we do not allow to change; of which we demand constancy with more right, than we do of more passionate, even of deeper, feelings. Gratitude is peculiarly irredeemable. It maintains its claim even after an equal or greater return gift has been made, and it may, in fact, claim both parties to the relation, the first and the second giver (a possibility which is indirectly due perhaps, to that freedom of the initial gift which is missing in

---

4. This, of course, is an extreme statement, but its remoteness from reality is inevitable in analyses which try to isolate, and thus make visible, elements of phychic reality that actually are mixed in a thousand ways, are constantly deflected, and exist almost exclusively in embryonic forms.

5. By conditions, of course, only purely internal ones are understood here, not those of external duty.

the return gift with only its moral necessity). This irredeemable nature of gratitude shows it as a bond between men which is as subtle as it is firm. Every human relationship of any duration produces a thousand occasions for it, and even the most ephemeral ones do not allow their increment to the reciprocal obligation to be lost. In fortunate cases, but sometimes even in cases abundantly provided with counter-instances, the sum of these incre-ments produces an atmosphere of generalized obligation (the saying that one is "obliged" ["*verbunden*"] to somebody who has earned our thanks is quite apt), which can be redeemed by no accomplishments whatever. This atmosphere of obligation belongs among those "microscopic," but infinitely tough, threads which tie one element of society to another, and thus eventually all of them together in a stable collective life.

3. On Valence

BY KURT LEWIN

Environmental Structure and Needs

AN ANALYSIS of environmental factors must start from a consideration of the total situation. Such an analysis hence presupposes an adequate comprehension and presentation in dynamic terms of the total psychological situation as its most important task.

Loeb's theory, by and large, identifies the biological environment with the physical environment: the dynamic factors of the environment consist of light of specific wave length and intensity, gravity, and others of similar nature. Others, notably von Uexküll, have shown, on the contrary, that the biological environment is to be characterized quite differently, namely, as a complex of foods, enemies, means of protection, etc. The same physical situation must thus be described for different species of animals as a specifically different phenomenal and functional world ["*Merk- und Wirkwelt*"].

In child psychology, also, the same physical environment must be quite differently characterized according to the age, the individual character, and the momentary condition of the child. The life-space of the infant is extremely small and undifferentiated. This is just as true of its perceptual as of its effective space. With the gradual extension and differentiation of the child's life-space, a larger environment and essentially different facts acquire psychological existence, and this is true also with respect to dynamic factors. The child learns in increasing degree to control the environment. At the same time—and no less important—it becomes psychologically dependent upon a growing circle of environmental events.

When, for example, one breaks a doll a few feet away from a baby, the latter is unaffected, while the same procedure with a three-year-old usually calls forth energetic intervention.

The later extension of the child's space-time beyond the room and the family also means not only an intellectual survey of wider relations but, above all, an extension of the environmental objects and events upon which the child is psychologically immediately dependent.

The mere *knowledge* of something (*e.g.*, of the geography of a foreign country, of the economic and political situation, or even of immediate family affairs) does not necessarily change the child's life-space more than superficially. On the other hand, psychologically critical facts of the environment, such as the friendliness or unfriendliness of a certain adult, may have fundamental significance for the child's life-space without the child's having a clear intellectual appreciation of the fact.

For the investigation of dynamic problems we are forced to start from the psychologically real environment of the child.

In the "objective" sense, the existence of a social bond is a necessary condition of the viability of an infant not yet able itself to satisfy its biologically important needs. This is usually a social bond with the mother in which, functionally, the needs of the baby have primacy.

But social facts, as essential constituents of the *psycho-biological* environment, very early acquire

Reprinted by permission from Kurt Lewin, *A Dynamic Theory of Personality*, trans. D. K. Adams and K. E. Zener (New York: McGraw-Hill Book Co., 1935), pp. 73–85. Copyright 1935. McGraw-Hill Book Company, Inc.

dominant significance. This does not mean, of course, that when the child of three months reacts specifically to the human voice and to a friendly smile the relation to certain individuals has already become a stable constituent of the child's psychological environment. The age at which this will occur depends essentially upon the individual endowment and the experiences of the child.

The fact that certain activities (e.g., playing with certain toys) are allowed and others forbidden (*e.g.,* throwing things or touching certain objects belonging to grown-ups) begins very early—certainly before the age of two—to play an important dynamic part in the structure of the child's environment. With the growth of the child social facts usually acquire more and more significance for the structure of the psychological environment.

Social facts such as friendship with another child, dependence upon an adult, etc., must also be regarded, from the dynamic point of view, as no less real than physical facts. Of course, in the description of the child's psychological environment one may not take as a basis the immediately objective social forces and relations as the sociologist or jurist, for example, would list them. One must, rather, describe the social facts as they affect the particular individual concerned. For the objective social factors have no more an unambiguous relation to the psychological individual than objective physical factors have. Exactly the same physical object may have quite different sorts of psychological existence for different children and for the same child in different situations. A wooden cube may be one time a missile, again a building block, and a third time a locomotive. What a thing is at any time depends upon the total situation and the momentary condition of the child involved. Similar considerations hold also for the social factors.

In this dependence there becomes clear a matter of fundamental psychological importance, namely, *the direct relationship between the momentary state of the individual and the structure of his psychological environment.* That the psychological environment, even when objectively the same, depends not only upon the individual character and developmental stage of the child concerned but also upon its momentary condition becomes clear when we consider the relation between environment and needs.

Beside the quasi-physical and quasi-social environment, a mental task or a phantasy must sometimes be characterized from the dynamic point of view as environment. Activities (*e.g.,* a game) may have the character of a region into or out of which the child may go. In the same sense a mathematical problem may have this character. The description of the child's environment would be incomplete without including the whole world of phantasy which is so important for the child's behavior and so closely connected with its ideals and with its ideal goals.

In the environment there are, as we have seen, many objects and events of quasi-physical and quasi-social nature, such as rooms, halls, tables, chairs, a bed, a cap, knife and fork, things that fall down, turn over, can start and go of themselves; there are dogs, friends, grown-ups, neighbors, someone who rarely gets cross, and someone who is always strict and disagreeable. There are places where one is safe from rain, others where one is safe from adults, and still others where one may not go under any circumstances. All these things and events are defined for the child partly by their appearance but above all by their *functional possibilities* (the *Wirkwelt* in von Uexküll's sense). The stairs are something that one can (or cannot yet) go up and down, or something that one climbed yesterday for the first time. Thus history, as the child has experienced it, is also a psychologically essential constituent of the things of the environment.

With all these, however, there remain certain critical properties of the psychological environment still undescribed. Objects are not neutral to the child, but have an immediate psychological effect on its behavior. Many things attract the child to eating, others to climbing, to grasping, to manipulation, to sucking, to raging at them, etc. These imperative environmental facts—we shall call them valences[1] [*Aufforderungscharaktere*]—determine the direction of the behavior. Particularly from the standpoint of dynamics, the valences, their kind (sign), strength, and distribution, must be regarded as among the most important properties of the environment.

The valence of an object usually derives from the fact that the object is a means to the satisfaction of a need, or has indirectly something to do with the satisfaction of a need. The kind (sign) and strength of the valence of an object or event thus depends directly upon the momentary condition of the needs of the individual concerned; the valence

1. These valences are not to be confused with what is generally understood by "stimulus," as the term is used in speaking of a stimulus-reaction process. The effect of the valence corresponds dynamically much more nearly to a command, a summons, or a request.

A fairly precise translation of *Aufforderungscharakter* is the term "demand value," which Tolman [E. C. TOLMAN, *Purposive Behavior*, Appleton-Century, New York, 1932] uses for the same concept. In order to avoid unnecessary misunderstandings, Professor Tolman and Lewin have agreed to use the same term and at Tolman's suggestion have chosen "valence."

of environmental objects and the needs of the individual are correlative. Even with objective identity of environment, the strength and the appearance of the valences are quite other for a hungry child than for a satisfied one, for a healthy child than for a sickly one.

The correlation between valence and environment leads to a fundamental change in the latter with the changing needs of increasing age. The objects bearing valences are different for the baby, the toddler, the kindergartener, and the pubescent.

The valences change also with the *momentary state* of the needs. When the need for nourishment, for playing with a doll, or for reading history is in a hungry or unsatisfied condition, a bit of food, a doll, or the history book attracts the child, that is, has a positive valence; whereas, when this need is in a stage or state of satisfaction, the object is indifferent to the child; and, in the stage of over-satiation of the need, it becomes disagreeable to the child, that is, it acquires a negative valence.

Since the psychological environment, especially for the child, is not identical with the physical or social environment, one cannot, in investigating environmental forces, proceed from the physical forces as Loeb, for example, does in biology. If we start primarily from the psychobiological environment and pay due attention to its dependence upon the actual momentary condition of the individual involved, it is quite possible to discover universally valid principles of the dynamic effects of the environment. To be sure, it will always be necessary to keep in mind the total structure of the existing situation.[2]

Psychological environmental forces [*Umweltkräfte*] may be defined empirically and functionally, excluding all metaphysical problems, by their effect upon the behavior of the child.[3] They are equally applicable to the momentary situation and to the permanent environment of the child.

In summary: to understand or predict the psychological behavior (*B*) one has to determine for every kind of psychological event (actions, emotions, expressions, etc.) the momentary whole situation, that is, the momentary structure and the state of the person (*P*) and of the psychological environment (*E*). $B = f(PE)$. Every fact that exists psychobiologically must have a position in this field and only facts that have such position have dynamic effects (are causes of events). The environment is for all of its properties (directions,

distances, etc.) to be defined not physically but *psychobiologically,* that is, according to its quasi-physical, quasi-social, and quasi-mental structure.

It is possible to represent the dynamic structure of the person and of the environment by means of mathematical concepts. The coordination between the mathematical representation and its psychodynamic meaning has to be strict and without exception.

We shall first describe the psychological field forces and their mode of operation, without consideration of the question whether the object in any particular case has acquired its valence through some previous experience or in some other way.

The Region of Freedom of Movement. Forces and Fields of Force

The first presupposition for the understanding of the child is the determination of the psychological place at which the child concerned is and of his region of freedom of movement, that is, of the regions that are accessible to him and of those regions that psychologically exist for the child but are inaccessible to him by reason of the social situation (prohibition by the adult, limitation by other children, etc.) or because of the limitations of his own social, physical, and intellectual abilities. Whether his region of freedom of movement is large or small is of decisive significance for the whole behavior of the child.

One can characterize these possible and not possible psycho-dynamic locomotions (quasi-bodily, quasi-social, and quasi-mental locomotions) at every point of the environment with the help of the concept of topology, which is a nonquantitative discipline about the possible kinds of connections between "spaces" and their parts.

The basis for the coordination between mathematical and psychodynamic concepts so far as environmental questions are concerned is the coordination of topological path and psychodynamic locomotion. The topological description determines which points the different paths lead to and which regions these paths cross. The region which a child cannot reach one can characterize by means of barriers between these regions and their neighboring regions. The barrier corresponds as a dynamic concept to the mathematical concept of boundary. One must distinguish between different strengths of barriers.

FUNDAMENTAL PROPERTIES OF FIELD FORCES

To determine not only which locomotions (paths) are possible but which of the possible locomotions will occur at a given moment one has to use the concept of *force.*

---

2. By situation is meant the psychological situation, with particular reference to its dynamic properties.

3. The fundamental concepts of psychological dynamics are thus for the present to be defined purely from the point of view of psychology and biology. Whether they agree in their formal logical structure with the fundamental dynamic concepts of physics need not here be discussed.

A force is defined through three properties: (1) direction, (2) strength, and (3) point of application. The first and second properties are to be represented through the mathematical concept *vector*. The point of application is indicated in the figures (as is the custom in physics) by the point of the arrow.

Dynamically the force is correlated with psychobiological locomotions in a one-to-one correspondence. "The real locomotion must occur in every case according to the direction and the strength of the resultant of the momentary forces" and "In any case of locomotion there exists a resultant of forces in its direction."

The direction which the valence imparts to the child's behavior varies extremely, according to the content of the wants and needs. Nevertheless, one may distinguish two large groups of valences according to the sort of initial behavior they elicit: the positive valences $(+)$, those effecting approach; and the negative $(-)$, or those producing withdrawal or retreat.

The *actions* in the direction of the valence may have the form of uncontrolled impulsive behavior or of directed voluntary activity; they may be "appropriate" or "inappropriate."

Those processes which make an especially goal-striving impression are usually characterized dynamically by a reference to a positive valence.

One has to distinguish between *driving* forces, which correspond to positive or negative valences, and *restraining* forces, which correspond to barriers.

Direction of the Field Force. That the valence is not associated merely with a subjective experience of direction, but that a directed force, determinative of the behavior, must be ascribed to it, may be seen in the fact that a change in the position of the attractive object brings about (other things being equal) a change in the direction of the child's movements.

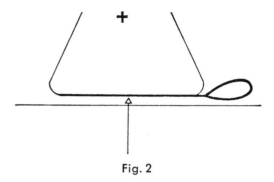

Fig. 2

An especially simple example of an action in the direction of a positive valence is illustrated in Figs. 1 and 2. A six-months-old infant stretches arms, legs, and head toward a rattle or a spoonful of porridge in accordance with the direction of the vector (V).

The direction of the field forces plays an important part in such intelligent behavior as has to do with detour [*Umweg*] problems. The child perhaps wants to get a piece of chocolate on the other side of a bench (see Fig. 3). The difficulty of such a

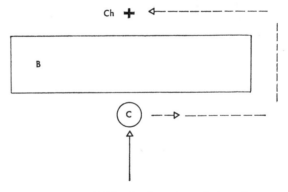

Fig. 3—C, child; Ch, chocolate; B, bench.

problem consists primarily not in the length of the detour (D) but in the fact that the initial direction of the appropriate route does not agree with that of the vector from the valence. The detour is the more difficult, other things being equal, the more the barrier makes it necessary for the child in making the detour to start off in a direction opposed to the direction of the valence (Fig. 4).

The situation is similar when the child wants to take a ring off a stick, while the stick stands so that the ring cannot be pulled directly toward the child, but must first be moved upward or away from himself. Similar factors are operative when a child at a certain age may have difficulties in sitting

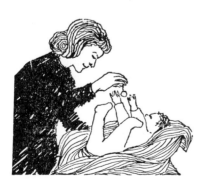

Fig. 1

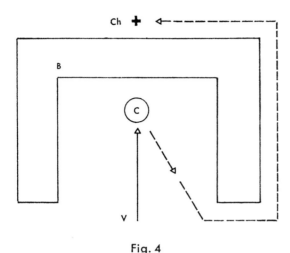

Fig. 4

down on a chair or a stone. The child approaches with his face toward the stone (*S*). In order to sit down he must turn around, that is, execute a movement opposed to the direction of the field force (Fig. 5).

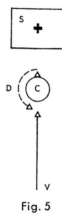

Fig. 5

When the child finds the solution of such a detour problem, it happens by reason of a restructuring of the field. There occurs a perception of the total situation of such a kind that the path to the goal becomes a unitary whole. The initial part of the route, which objectively is still a moment away from the goal (see Fig. 4), thereby loses psychologically that character and becomes the first phase of a general movement toward the goal.[4]

How critically important the question of *direction* is in this case is indicated by the fact that one

cannot force a solution of the detour by increasing the *strength* of the valence. If the attraction is much too weak, it is, to be sure, unfavorable, because the child does not concern himself sufficiently with the affair.[5] But if we continue to strengthen the valence, the solution of the task ceases to be facilitated and instead becomes more difficult. The strength of the attraction then makes it doubly difficult for the child to start in a direction opposed to the field force. Instead, the child will execute, with all its energy, affective meaningless actions in the direction of the valence.[6] Above all, that relative detachment and inward retirement from the valence which are so favorable to perception of the whole situation and hence to the transformation [*Umstrukturierung*] of the total field, which occurs in the act of insight, are made much more difficult. For the same reason, the prospect of an especially intense reward or punishment may impede the solution of intellectual tasks.

To older children of normal intelligence the preceding examples of detour problems offer no difficulty, because they already have a sufficient survey of such situations or corresponding experiences. For them it no longer requires a special act of intelligence in order that, instead of the spatial directions, the *functional* directions become decisive for the movement.

We may at this point remark a circumstance of general importance: direction in the psychobiological field is not necessarily to be identified with physical direction, but must be defined primarily in psychological terms. The difference between psychological and physical direction appears more prominently in older children. When the child fetches a tool or applies to the experimenter for help, the action does not mean, even when it involves a physical movement in a direction opposite to the goal, a turning away from the goal but an approach to it. Such indirect approaches are more rare among babies. This is due to the slighter functional differentiation of their environment and to the fact that *social* structure has not yet the overwhelming significance for them that it has for older children.

Fajans found, for example, that in a certain situation in which three- and four-year-old children usually applied to the experimenter for help (indirect approach), the corresponding turning of the

---

4. Frequently this transformation is not immediately complete, and the first part of the route retains a sort of double character.

5. Bogen found, even among school children who were working on such tasks voluntarily, that solutions were found more frequently if the valence of the goal was strengthened by the addition of a piece of chocolate (see H. BOGEN and O. LIPMANN, *Naïve Physik. Handeln*, Barth, Leipzig, 1923).

6. The impulsive struggles of Thorndike's cats may have been due in part to such a situation (see E. L. THORNDIKE, *Animal Intelligence*, Macmillan, New York, 1911).

baby to its mother was more a withdrawal from failure than a seeking for help.

In the cases mentioned, the direction of the field forces is determined by objects which, by reason of visual or auditory distance perceptions, have a definite place in the environment. In the case of newborn children, it is possible to speak of such precisely directed field forces only in so far as the psychological environment has sufficient structure and solidity.

Directed action in response to certain forms of tactile stimulation may be observed very early. Touching the child's cheek with the nipple may elicit a turning of the head in the corresponding direction.

Also among older children the (psychological) *separation of the self from the valence* remains in many respects a necessary condition for the directedness of the action upon the valence. Fairly often

the action does not proceed immediately to the use of the object, but the field force disappears (or is at least very much weakened) as soon as the object comes into the "possession" of the individual involved. An example from our films: a nine-month-old child before which two rattles are laid does not begin to play after getting one of them, but is interested only in the rattle that he does not have. The close relation between directed field forces and the separation of the self from the goal object can also be demonstrated in various ways with older children.

Strength of the Field Forces. For the strength of the valences, internal factors, especially the actual momentary state of the child's needs, are of crucial significance. In addition, the strength of the field force going out from a valence depends also upon the position of the valence relative to the individual and upon the presence or absence of other valences.

4. *Anxiety as Motivation*

BY SIGMUND FREUD

WHAT WE HAVE LEARNED about anxiety in the phobias is applicable also to compulsion neurosis. It is not difficult to reduce the situation of the compulsion neurosis to that of the phobia. The motive force behind all later symptom formation is here clearly the ego's fear of its superego. The hostility of the superego is the danger situation which the ego must avoid. Here any semblance of projection is lacking; the danger is wholly internalized. But when we ask what it is that the ego fears at the hands of the superego, the conclusion is forced upon us that the punishment meted out by the superego is an extension of the punishment of castration. Just as the superego is the father become impersonalized, so the dread of the castration which he threatened has become converted into indefinite social anxiety or dread of conscience. But this anxiety is insured against; the ego escapes it by carrying out obediently the commands, the preventive measures and the penances imposed upon it. If it is impeded in doing this, there im-

mediately ensues an extremely distressing sense of discomfort in which we may perceive the equivalent of anxiety and which the patient himself equates with anxiety. What we have arrived at is therefore the following: Anxiety is the reaction to a situation of danger; and it is circumvented by the ego's doing something to avoid the situation or retreat from it. One might say, then, that symptoms are created in order to avoid the development of anxiety, but such a formulation does not go below the surface. It is more accurate to say that symptoms are created in order to avoid the *danger situation* of which anxiety sounds the alarm. In the cases so far considered this danger was castration or a derivative of it.

* * *

According to all that we know of the structure of the simpler neuroses of everyday life, it is very reasonable that a neurosis should come about only by reason of the objective fact of exposure to danger without the participation of the deeper unconscious strata of the mental apparatus. In the unconscious, however, there is nothing to give content to our conception of the destruction of life. Castration becomes, as it were, imaginable through

Reprinted from Sigmund Freud, *The Problem of Anxiety*, trans. Henry A. Bunker (New York: W. W. Norton & Co., 1936), pp. 85–110, 146–59, with the permission of *The Psychoanalytic Quarterly*.

the daily experience of parting with the contents of the bowel and through the loss of the mother's breast which is experienced in weaning; but nothing similar to death has ever been experienced, or if it has been, it has left, like fainting, no demonstrable trace. I therefore maintain that the fear of death is to be regarded as an analogue of the fear of castration, and that the situation to which the ego reacts is the state of being forsaken or deserted by the protecting superego—by the powers of destiny—which puts an end to security against every danger. It is also to be taken into account that in the experiences which result in traumatic neurosis the external protective mechanism against stimuli of excessive strength is broken down and excessive quanta of excitation gain access to the mental apparatus, so that here the second possibility exists that anxiety is not only employed as an affective signal but is also newly created in response to the economic demands of the situation.

With the above formulation—namely, that through regularly repeated losses of objects the ego has been prepared for castration—we have arrived at a new conception of anxiety. If we have thus far considered it as an affective signal of danger, it now appears to us, since it is so frequently a matter of the danger of castration, as the reaction to a loss, to a separation. Though various considerations which immediately occur to one seem also to tell against this conclusion, we must nevertheless be struck by a phenomenon which is in very remarkable agreement with it. The first anxiety experience, of the human being at least, is birth; and this means, objectively, separation from the mother, and could be likened to a castration of the mother (in accordance with the equation: child = penis). Now it would be very satisfactory if anxiety as the symbol of a separation were to be repeated on the occasion of every subsequent separation, but unfortunately the applicability of the agreement I have just spoken of is discounted by the fact that, subjectively, birth is not at all experienced as a separation from the mother, since the mother, in the role of object, is entirely unknown to the completely narcissistic fœtus. Another consideration that would apply is that affective reactions to a separation are known to us, and that we experience them as grief and mourning, not as anxiety. We recall, to be sure, that in our discussion of mourning we were also unable to understand why mourning is so painful.

An Analysis of Anxiety

It is time to take stock. What we are seeking, it is apparent, is an insight which shall reveal the nature of anxiety, an "either-or" which shall distinguish truth from error in regard to it. But this is difficult of attainment; anxiety is not a simple thing to grasp. Thus far we have arrived at nothing but contradictions, from among which no unbiased choice was possible. I now propose to order it otherwise; we will bring together in unprejudiced manner everything that can be said about anxiety, while renouncing at the same time the expectation of achieving an immediate synthesis of the problem.

Anxiety, then, is in the first place something felt. We call it an affective state, although we are equally ignorant of what an affect is. As a feeling it is of most obviously unpleasurable character, but this is not by any means a complete description of its quality; not every state of unpleasure (*Unlust*) may we call anxiety. There are other feelings of unpleasurable character (mental tension, sorrow, grief), and anxiety must have other characteristics besides this quality of unpleasure. Shall we ever succeed, one cannot help asking, in understanding the differences between these various affects of unpleasure?

Of the feeling of anxiety we can after all learn something. Its character of unpleasure seems to possess a particular note of its own—a thing difficult to demonstrate but none the less probable, nor would it be at all surprising if it were so. But in addition to this special characteristic so difficult to define, we perceive more definite physical sensations, which we refer to specific organs, as accompanying anxiety. Since the physiology of anxiety does not interest us here, it will suffice to draw attention to specific examples of these sensations, such as those referable to the respiratory organs and the heart, which are the most common and the most definite of them. They are evidence that motor innervations, efferent processes, take part in the total phenomenon of anxiety. The analysis of the anxiety state gives us, then, as its attributes: (1) a specific unpleasurable quality, (2) efferent or discharge phenomena, and (3) the perception of these.

The second and third of the foregoing supply in themselves a distinction from similar affective states, such as for example grief and sorrow, for of these latter, motor manifestations do not form an integral part; when such are present, they are definitely distinguishable as not constituting essential constituents of the total phenomenon but consequences of or reactions to the emotional state in question. Anxiety, therefore, is a specific state of unpleasure accompanied by motor discharge along definite pathways. In accordance with our general outlook, we shall believe that an increase of excitation underlies anxiety, an increase which on the one hand is responsible for its unpleasurable character and on the other is relieved through the discharge referred to. This purely physiological summary will scarcely satisfy us, however; we are tempted to presume that there is an historical element present which binds the afferent and the efferent components of anxiety firmly together; in other words, that the anxiety state is the reproduction of an experience which contains within itself the requisite conditions for the increase in stimulation just mentioned, and for its discharge via given pathways; and it is in virtue of this, therefore, that the unpleasure element in anxiety acquires its specific character. As the prototypic experience of such a sort, we think in the case of the human being of birth, and on this account we are inclined to see in the anxiety state a reproduction of the trauma of birth.

In doing so we have claimed nothing which would assign to anxiety an exceptional position among affective states. For we hold that other affects as well are reproductions of past experiences of a character vital to the organism, experiences possibly even antedating the individual; and we draw a comparison between these, as universal, specific, congenital hysterical attacks, and the seizures of the hysterical neurosis, later and individually acquired, the genesis and significance of which as memory symbols have been made clearly manifest by analysis. It would of course be most desirable to be able to demonstrate the validity of this conception for a number of other affects, but at the present time we are far from being in a position to do this.

The tracing back of anxiety to the birth experience needs justification in the face of certain obvious objections. Anxiety is a reaction characteristic of probably all organisms, certainly of all the higher ones, but birth is experienced only by mammals, and it is open to question whether for all of these birth has a traumatic significance. There is, therefore, such a thing as anxiety without a prototype in birth. But this objection takes us from psychology into biology. Precisely because anxiety, as a reaction to situations of danger, has a biologically indispensable function to fulfill it may have been contrived in different organisms in different ways. We do not know, moreover, whether in creatures at a further remove from man anxiety has the same content, afferently and efferently, as in the human being. All this does not prevent it from being the case, therefore, that anxiety, in the human being, takes the birth process as its prototype.

If this is the structure and origin of anxiety, the question arises: What is its function? On what occasions is it reproduced? The answer seems obvious and inescapable. Anxiety arose as a response to a situation of *danger;* it will be regularly reproduced thenceforward whenever such a situation recurs.

But there is more than this to be said. The motor impulses accompanying the original anxiety state had probably as much meaning and utility as the muscular movements of the initial hysterical attack. If one would explain the hysterical seizure, one needs only, indeed, to look for the situation in which the movements in question were part of the behavior appropriate to that situation. Thus, during birth, it is probable that the directing of nerve impulses to the organs of respiration has made preparation in advance for the functioning of the lungs, the acceleration of the heart beat tended to counteract the accumulation of toxic substances in the blood. This teleology of function is of course absent from the subsequent reproduction of the anxiety state as affect, just as it is also lacking in the recurrent hysterical seizure. If therefore the individual encounters a danger situation new to him, his responding with the anxiety that constitutes the reaction to an earlier danger, instead of with the reaction appropriate to the present one, may easily become inexpedient. The suitability of the reaction reappears, however, if the danger is perceived as imminent and forewarning of it given through the outbreak of anxiety. The anxiety can then be immediately replaced by more appropriate measures for dealing with the danger. Two possibilities with regard to the appearance of anxiety, therefore, may at once be distinguished: the one, inappropriate and inexpedient, in response to a new situation of danger; the other, a useful one, as a means of giving warning of and averting such a situation.

But what is a "danger"? In the act of birth there is an objective danger to the preservation of life; we know what that means in the reality sense. But psychologically it has no meaning at all. The danger attending birth has still no psychic content. For certainly we cannot imagine as existing in the fœtus anything which in the least approaches any sort of knowledge of the possibility of death as an outcome. The fœtus can be aware of nothing beyond a gross disturbance in the economy of its narcissistic libido. Large amounts of excitation press upon it, giving rise to novel sensations of unpleasure; numerous organs enforce increased cathexes in their behalf, as it were a prelude to the object-cathexis soon to be initiated; what is there in all this that can be regarded as bearing the stamp of a "danger situation?"

Unfortunately, we know far too little of the mental make-up of the newborn to be able to answer such a question directly. I cannot even vouch for the usefulness of the description I have just given. It is easy to say that the newborn infant will repeat the affect of anxiety in every situation which reminds it of the birth situation. The real question, however, is by what and of what it is reminded.

There is left us hardly any other course to pursue than to study the occasions on which the infant or the slightly older child gives evidence of a readiness to develop anxiety. In his book, *The Trauma of Birth,* Rank has made a very vigorous attempt to demonstrate a relationship between the earliest phobias of the child and the impression which the birth experience has made upon it, but I cannot consider the attempt a very happy one. Two criticisms can be brought against it, of which the first is that it makes the assumption that in the process of birth the child has been the recipient of sense impressions, particularly visual ones, the renewal of which may evoke the memory of the birth trauma and therewith a reaction of anxiety. This assumption is entirely unproved and very improbable; it is not credible that the child has preserved any other than tactile and general sensations from the act of birth. If, then, the child later shows a fear of small animals which disappear into holes or come out of them, Rank explains this reaction as its perception of an analogy which, however, would not strike the child. Secondly, in appraising these later anxiety situations Rank holds responsible the memory either of the happy existence within the uterus or of its traumatic disturbance, entirely according to the necessities of the case, thus throwing the door wide open to arbitrariness of interpretation. Individual instances of this childhood anxiety flatly contradict the Rankian principle. If the child is brought into darkness and solitude, we should expect that it would welcome this restoration of the intrauterine situation; and if the fact that in precisely these circumstances the child reacts with anxiety is ascribed to the memory of the interruption of the happy state through birth, one may be pardoned for failing to appreciate the appositeness of such reasoning.

I am forced to the conclusion that the earliest phobias of childhood do not permit of being directly traced to the impression made upon the child by the act of birth, and that they have thus far, in fact, defied all explanation. A certain predisposition to anxiety on the part of the infant is indubitable. It is not at its maximum immediately after birth, to diminish gradually thereafter, but first makes its appearance later on with the progress of psychic development, and persists over a certain period of childhood. When early phobias of this sort continue beyond such a period, they give rise to the suspicion of a neurotic disturbance, although their relationship to the definite neuroses of later childhood is in no wise clear.

Only a few instances of the expression of anxiety in infancy are intelligible to us; we shall have to keep to these. Thus, the three situations of being left alone, being in the dark, and finding a strange person in place of the one in whom the child has confidence (the mother), are all reducible to a single situation, that of feeling the loss of the loved (longed for) person. From this point forwards the way is clear to an understanding of anxiety and to the reconciling of the contradictions which seem to be connected with it.

The memory picture of the person longed for is certainly cathected in very intense degree, probably at first in hallucinatory fashion. But this is without result, and now it appears as if this longing were transformed into anxiety. It decidedly seems as if this anxiety were an expression of helplessness, as if the still very undeveloped creature did not know what else to do with his longing. Anxiety thus seems to be a reaction to the perception of the absence of the object, and there at once spring to mind the analogies that castration anxiety has also separation from a highly valued object as its content and that the most basic anxiety of all, the "primal anxiety" of birth, arises in connection with separation from the mother.

The next consideration takes us beyond this emphasis upon loss of the object. If the infant longs for the sight of the mother, it does so, surely, only because it already knows from experience that she gratifies all its needs without delay. The situation which the infant appraises as "danger," and against which it desires reassurance, is therefore one of not being gratified, of an *increase of tension arising from non-gratification of its needs*—a situation against which it is powerless. I believe that from this standpoint everything falls into place, the situation of privation, in which stimuli reach an unpleasurable magnitude and intensity without an ability to cope with them psychically and thus provide for their discharge, must represent to the infant a situation analogous to the birth experience, a repetition of the danger situation; what the two situations have in common is the economic disturbance brought about by an increase in stimuli demanding some disposition made of them, this common factor hence being the very essence of the "danger." In both cases the reaction of anxiety appears, a reaction which still in the infant proves to the purpose since the discharge of the anxiety via the respiratory and vocal musculature now calls the mother to the infant's side, just as earlier it aroused respiratory activity to get rid of internal stimuli. More than this sign of danger the child does not need to have preserved from birth.

Along with the experiencing of the fact that an external and perceptible object may put an end to the danger situation reminiscent of birth, there takes place a displacement of the content of the danger from the economic situation to that which occasions it, namely, object loss. The perception of the absence of the mother now becomes the danger at the appearance of which the infant gives the signal of anxiety, even before the economic situation which is feared has arisen. This change represents a first great step in advance in the economy of self-preservation, and includes at the same time the transition from the automatically unpurposed creation *de novo* of anxiety to its purposeful reproduction as a signal of danger.

In both respects, alike as an automatic phenomenon and as a safety signal, anxiety proves to be a product of the psychic helplessness of the infant which is the obvious counterpart of its biological helplessness. The striking coincidence that both birth anxiety and the anxiety of the infant alike claim separation from the mother as their prerequisite needs no psychological interpretation; it is simply enough explicable biologically by the fact that the mother, who in the beginning had satisfied all the needs of the fœtus through her body mechanisms, continues after birth as well to exercise in some measure this same function, although by other means. Intrauterine life and early infancy form a continuum to a far greater extent than the striking cæsura of the act of birth would lead us to believe. The psychic mother object replaces for the child the biological fœtal situation. Hence we should not forget that during intrauterine life the mother was not an object, and that there were no objects at all at that period.

It is easy to see that in this continuum there is no room for an abreacting of the birth trauma, and that any other function of anxiety than that of a signal for avoiding a situation of danger is not discoverable. Object loss as the precondition of anxiety now has some further implications. For the next transformation of anxiety, the castration anxiety which makes its appearance in the phallic phase, is a separation anxiety also, and is similarly conditioned. The danger here is separation from the genital. A seemingly entirely legitimate line of thought of Ferenczi's enables us to recognize clearly here the point of connection with the earlier content of the danger situation. The high narcissistic value attaching to the penis may be referable to the fact that the possession of this organ contains a guaranty of reunion with the mother (or mother

substitute) in the act of coitus. Deprivation of this member is tantamount to a second separation from the mother, and thus has again the significance (as in the case of birth) of being delivered over helpless to the unpleasurable tension arising from the non-gratification of a need. This need, of which the increase is feared, is now, however, a specialized one, a need of the genital libido, and no longer an undifferentiated one, as in infancy. I would add here that the fantasy of returning to the uterus is the substitute for coitus which we find in impotent men (those inhibited by the threat of castration). In the spirit of Ferenczi's formulation one may say that the individual who wished to have his genital organ act as a proxy in his return to the uterus in fact regressively substitutes for this organ his whole body.

The various steps in the development of the child, its increased independence, the sharper differentiation of its mental apparatus into various agencies, the appearance of its new needs—all these cannot remain without their effect upon the content of the danger situation. We have followed the change in the content of the latter from loss of the maternal object to castration, and we now see the next step therein as caused by the power of the superego. With the impersonalization of the parental authority at whose hands castration was feared, the danger becomes more indefinite. Fear of castration develops into dread of conscience, into social anxiety. It is now no longer easy to state what it is that there is fear of. The formula, "separation, exclusion from the horde," applies only to that more lately developed portion of the superego which was patterned after social models, not to the nucleus thereof which corresponds to the introjected parental authority. Expressed in more general terms, it is the anger, the punishment, of the superego, the loss of its love, which the ego apprehends as a danger and to which it responds with the signal of anxiety. The final transformation undergone by this fear of the superego has appeared to me to consist of death- (life-) anxiety, fear felt for the projection of the superego upon the powers of destiny.

Formerly I attached a certain value to the proposition that the cathexis withdrawn in repression finds employment as a discharge in the form of anxiety. This seems to me today of very little interest. The difference consists in the fact that formerly I believed anxiety to orginate in every instance automatically through an economic process, whereas the present conception of anxiety as a signal intended by the ego for the purpose of influencing the pleasure-pain mechanism renders us independent of this economic restriction. It does not contradict this supposition, of course, that for the arousing of affect the ego employs precisely the energy set free by the withdrawal of cathexis in repression, but it has become unimportant to distinguish with which moiety of energy this is accomplished.

Another assertion I once made now demands re-examination in the light of our new conception. I refer to the statement that the ego is the real seat of anxiety; I think that this statement will prove to be correct. That is to say, we have no reason to ascribe any expression of anxiety to the superego. But when it is a matter of an "anxiety of the id," one does not have so much to contradict this as to emend an infelicitous expression. Anxiety is an affective state which can of course be experienced only by the ego. The id cannot be afraid, as the ego can; it is not an organization, and cannot estimate situations of danger. On the contrary, it is of extremely frequent occurrence that processes are initiated or executed in the id which give the ego occasion to develop anxiety; as a matter of fact, the repressions which are probably the earliest are motivated, like the majority of all later ones, by such fear on the part of the ego of this or that process in the id. We have good grounds here for once again distinguishing the two cases: that in which something happens in the id which activates one of the danger situations to which the ego is sensitive, causing the latter to give the anxiety signal for inhibition; and that in which there develops in the id a situation analogous to the birth trauma, which automatically brings about a reaction of anxiety. The two cases are brought into closer approximation to each other if it is emphasized that the second corresponds to the initial and original situation of danger, whereas the first corresponds to one of the anxiety-occasioning situations subsequently derived from it. Or, to relate the matter to actually existing disorders: the second case is that which is operative in the ætiology of the "actual" neuroses, the first is characteristic of the psychoneuroses.

We now see that we need not dismiss earlier formulations as without value but have merely to bring them into line with our newer understanding. It is undeniable that in abstinence, in perverted interference with the normal discharge of sexual excitation, or in the diverting of the latter from its psychic elaboration, anxiety arises directly out of libido; that is to say, there is brought about that state of helplessness of the ego in the face of excessive tension arising from ungratified need which results, as in birth, in the development of anxiety, so that there is again a possibility, which although obvious is of no great consequence, that it is precisely the excess of unutilized libido that finds its discharge in the form of anxiety. We know that

psychoneuroses develop with particular readiness on the basis of these "actual" neuroses; and this may mean that the ego makes attempts to minimize and to fix by means of symptoms the anxiety which it has learned to hold temporarily in suspension. Probably analysis of the traumatic war neuroses (although this term includes a wide variety of disorders, certainly) would have shown that a certain proportion of them share the characteristics of "actual" neuroses.

When we represented the various danger situations as developing out of the original prototype of birth, we were far from maintaining that every later anxiety-occasioning situation simply renders inoperative those which were earlier effective in giving rise to anxiety. The progressive development of the ego contributes, it is true, to depriving of value and relegating to unimportance the earlier danger situation, so that it may be said that to a given period of development is assigned the anxiety-occasioning situation which is, so to speak, appropriate to it. Psychic helplessness is the danger which is consonant with the period of immaturity of the ego, as object loss is the danger appertaining to the state of dependence of early childhood, the danger of castration to the phallic phase, and dread of the superego to the latency period. And yet all these danger situations and anxiety determinants may persist alongside one another and cause the ego to react with anxiety at a later period also than the appropriate one; or several of them may become operative simultaneously. Possibly there also exists a close relationship between the danger situation which is effective in the given case and the form of the neurosis which develops in consequence.[1]

---

1. Since the differentiation between the ego and the id was made, our interest in the problems of repression has necessarily undergone a revival. Until then we were satisfied to dwell upon those of its elements which are referable to the ego—namely, the keeping of the repressed material out of consciousness and its withholding from motor discharge, and the creating of substitute (symptom) formations; of the repressed instinctual impulse itself we assumed that it persisted unchanged for an indefinite period in the unconscious. Now our interest shifts to the fate of the repressed, and we begin to feel that this persistence, unchanged and unchanging, is not a matter of course, is perhaps not even the rule. The original impulse has in any case been inhibited and deflected from its aim. But has its root persisted in the unconscious, having proved resistant to the modifying and depreciatory influence of life? Do there therefore still exist the old desires, of the earlier existence of which analysis informs us? The answer appears obvious and certain: The old repressed desires must still persist in the unconscious, since we find their lineal descendants, the symptoms, still active. But this answer is inadequate; it does not make it possible to distinguish between the two possibilities that, on the one hand, the old desire now operates only through its descendants, to which it has transferred all its cathectic energy, or, on the other hand, that the desire itself persists in addition. If it was its destiny to be expended in the cathexis of its descendants, there remains the third pos-

When in an earlier chapter of this inquiry we encountered the significance of the danger of castration in more than one neurotic disorder, we warned ourselves against overestimating this factor, since it assuredly could not be the crucial one in the female sex, the sex certainly more predisposed to neurosis. We see now that we are in no danger of taking castration anxiety to be the sole motive force behind the defense processes resulting in neurosis. I have explained elsewhere how the development of the little girl is guided to tender object-cathexis through the castration complex. It is precisely in the female that object loss seems to remain the most effective situation of danger. As to that which gives rise to her anxiety, we may introduce the slight modification that it is no longer a matter of feeling the absence, or of the loss in reality, of the object, but rather of the loss of the object's love. Since it is certainly true that hysteria has a greater affinity with femininity, just as compulsion neurosis has with masculinity, the idea suggests itself that, as a determinant of anxiety, loss of love plays a role in hysteria similar to that of the threat of castration in the phobias and of dread of the superego in compulsion neurosis.

* * *

SUPPLEMENTARY REMARKS ON ANXIETY

There are certain characteristics possessed by the affect of anxiety, the investigation of which gives promise of further enlightenment. Anxiety is undeniably related to expectation; one feels anxiety *lest* something occur.[2] It is endowed with a certain character of indefiniteness and objectlessness; correct usage even changes its name when it has found an object, and in that case speaks instead of *dread*. Anxiety has, moreover, in addition to its relation to danger, a relation to neurosis, over the clarification of which we have expended much labor. For there arises the question why it is that not all anxiety reactions are neurotic, why we recognize so many of them as normal; and, finally, the distinction between true anxiety (*Realangst*) and neurotic anxiety needs to be properly evaluated.

Let us start with the latter task. The progress we

have made has consisted in tracing a backward path from the reaction of anxiety to the situation of danger. If we apply the same process to the problem of true anxiety, its solution becomes simple. A *real* danger is a danger which we know, a true anxiety the anxiety in regard to such a known danger. Neurotic anxiety is anxiety in regard to a danger which we do not know. The neurotic danger must first be sought, therefore: analysis has taught us that it is an instinctual danger. By bringing into consciousness this danger of which the ego is unaware, we obliterate the distinction between true and neurotic anxiety and are able to treat the latter as we would the former.

In the case of a true danger we develop two reactions: an affective one, the outbreak of anxiety, and action looking to protection from the danger. Presumably the same thing happens in the case of instinctual danger. We are acquainted with the instance of the purposeful coöperation of the two reactions, wherein one of them gives the signal for the initiation of the other, but we know also of a useless and inexpedient form, namely, paralysis through fear, in which the one is promulgated at the expense of the other.

There are cases in which the attributes of true and of neurotic anxiety are intermingled. The danger is known and of the real type, but the anxiety in regard to it is disproportionately great, greater than in our judgment it ought to be. It is by this excess that the neurotic element stands revealed. But these cases contribute nothing which is new in principle. Analysis shows that involved with the known reality danger is an unrecognized instinctual danger.

It would be better not to be satisfied even with reducing anxiety to danger. What is the kernel, what is the true significance, of the danger situation? Evidently it is the estimation of our strength in comparison with its magnitude, the admission of our helplessness in the face of it—of material helplessness in the case of a true danger, of psychic helplessness in that of instinctual danger. Our judgment in this regard will be guided by actual experience; whether one is mistaken in one's evaluation makes no difference to the result. Let us call our experience in a situation of helplessness of this kind a *traumatic* situation; we then have a sufficient basis for distinguishing the *traumatic* from the *danger* situation.

Now it is an important advance in self-protection when this traumatic situation of helplessness is not merely awaited but is foreseen, anticipated. Let us call the situation in which resides the cause of this anticipation the danger situation; it is in this latter that the signal of anxiety is given. What this means is: I anticipate that a situation of helplessness will

sibility that in the course of the neurosis the wish was reactivated through regression, so out of accord with the present may it be. One need not regard these considerations as otiose; there is much in the phenomena of both the morbid and the normal life of the psyche which seems to demand the raising of such questions. In my study of the breakdown of the œdipus complex I became mindful of the distinction between the mere repression and the true disappearance of an old desire or impulse.

2. That is, the German usage is: *Angst* vor *etwas*—literally, anxiety *before* something, instead of *of* something. TRANSLATOR'S NOTE.

come about, or the present situation reminds me of one of the traumatic experiences which I have previously undergone. Hence I will anticipate this trauma; I will act as if it were already present as long as there is still time to avert it. Anxiety, therefore, is the expectation of the trauma on the one hand, and on the other, an attenuated repetition of it. The two characteristics which have struck us with regard to anxiety have therefore a different origin: its relation to expectation pertains to the danger situation, its indefiniteness and objectlessness to the traumatic situation of helplessness which is anticipated in the danger situation.

Having developed this series: anxiety—danger—helplessness (trauma), we may summarize the matter as follows: The danger situation is the recognized, remembered and anticipated situation of helplessness. Anxiety is the original reaction to helplessness in the traumatic situation, which is later reproduced as a call for help in the danger situation. The ego, which has experienced the trauma passively, now actively repeats an attenuated reproduction of it with the idea of taking into its own hands the directing of its course. We know that the child behaves in such a manner towards all impressions which he finds painful, by reproducing them in play; through this method of transition from passivity to activity the child attempts to cope psychically with its impressions and experiences. If this is what is meant by "abreacting a trauma," no objection can be made to it. But the crux of the matter is the initial displacement of the anxiety reaction from its origin in the situation of helplessness to the anticipation of the latter, the danger situation. There then ensue the further displacements from the danger itself to that which occasions the danger, namely, object loss and the modifications thereof already mentioned.

"Spoiling" young children has the undesirable result that the danger of object loss—the object being the protection against all situations of helplessness—is overemphasized in comparison with all other dangers. It therefore encourages persistence in that childhood state of which both motor and psychic helplessness is characteristic.

We have so far had no occasion to regard true anxiety differently from neurotic anxiety. We know the difference between them; a real danger is one which threatens from some external object, neurotic danger from an instinctual demand. In so far as this instinctual demand is a piece of reality, neurotic anxiety as well may be considered as founded on reality. We have understood that the seemingly extremely intimate relation between anxiety and neurosis derives from the fact that the ego protects itself against an instinctual danger in the same manner as against an external reality danger, but that in con-

sequence of an imperfection of the psychic apparatus this defensive activity eventuates in neurosis. We have become convinced also that instinctual demands often become an (internal) danger only because of the fact that their gratification would bring about an external danger—because, therefore, this internal danger represents an external one.

On the other hand, the external (reality) danger must have undergone internalization if it is to become significant for the ego; its relation to a situation of helplessness which has been lived through must be recognized.[3] An instinctive recognition of dangers threatening from without does not seem to have been among Nature's gifts to man, save to a very moderate degree. Small children are always doing things which endanger their lives, and for that reason alone cannot do without the protecting object. In relation to the traumatic situation, against which one is helpless, external and internal danger, reality danger and instinctual demand, coincide. Whether in the one case the ego experience a grief which will not be assuaged, or in the other a pent-up need incapable of gratification, the economic situation is in both cases the same and motor helplessness finds expression in psychic helplessness.

The enigmatic phobias of early childhood deserve mention once again at this point. Certain of them—the fear of being alone, of the dark, of strangers—we can understand as reactions to the danger of object loss; with regard to others—fear of small animals, thunderstorms, etc.—there is the possibility that they represent the atrophied remnants of an innate preparedness against reality dangers such as is so well developed in other animals. It is the part of this archaic heritage having to do with object loss which alone has utility for man. If such childhood phobias become fixed, grow more intense, and persist into a later period of life, analysis demonstrates that their content has become connected with instinctual demands, has become the representative of internal dangers also.

ANXIETY, GRIEF AND MOURNING

So little is known of the psychology of the emotions that the diffident remarks which follow may bespeak critical indulgence. It is at the point immediately to be referred to that the problem confronts us. We were forced to the conclusion that

---

3. It may also be quite often the case that in a danger situation which is correctly assessed as such a modicum of instinctual anxiety is superadded to the reality anxiety. The instinctual demand from the gratification of which the ego shrinks back would then be the masochistic one, the destructive impulse turned against the subject's own person. Perhaps this superadded element explains the case of the anxiety reaction becoming excessive and inexpedient, paralyzing. The fear of high places might have this origin; its hidden feminine significance is suggestive of masochism.

anxiety is the reaction to the danger of object loss. Now we already know of a reaction to object loss —namely, mourning. Therefore the question is, when do we have the one, when the other? With regard to mourning, with which we have dealt on a previous occasion, one of its characteristics remained completely obscure—its especial painfulness. That separation from the object is painful seems sufficiently self-evident. But the problem is more complicated; thus: When does separation from the object give rise to anxiety, when to mourning, and when merely perhaps to grief?

Let us say at once that there is no prospect of supplying an answer to these questions. We shall resign ourselves to marking out certain boundary lines and discovering a few suggestions.

Our point of departure shall once again be the one situation which we believe we understand, that of the infant who sees a strange person in place of his mother. He then manifests the anxiety which we have interpreted as due to the danger of object loss. But the situation is more complicated than this and merits a more detailed discussion. As to the infant's anxiety there is, to be sure, no doubt, but his facial expression and the fact of his crying lead one to suppose that in addition he feels pain. It seems as though in him something were fused together which later will be separated. He is not yet able to distinguish temporary absence from permanent loss; when he fails to see his mother on a given occasion, he behaves as though he would never see her again, and it requires repeated consoling experiences before he learns that such a disappearance on his mother's part is usually followed by her reappearance. The mother promotes this knowledge, so important to him, by playing with him the familiar game of covering her face and then to his joy revealing it again. Thus he is enabled, as it were, to experience longing without an accompaniment of despair.

The situation in which he misses his mother is not, owing to his miscomprehension, a danger situation for him but a traumatic one, or, more correctly, it is a traumatic one if he experiences at that juncture a need which his mother ought to gratify; it changes into a danger situation when this need is not immediate. The initial cause of anxiety, which the ego itself introduces, is therefore loss of perception of the object, which becomes equated with loss of the object. Loss of love does not yet enter into the situation. Later on, experience teaches that the object may continue to be present but may have become angry with the child, and now loss of love on the part of the object becomes a new and far more enduring danger and occasion for anxiety.

The traumatic situation of missing the mother differs in one crucial respect from the traumatic situation of birth. On that occasion there was no object present who could be missed. Anxiety was still the only reaction which took place. Subsequent thereto, repeated situations in which gratification was experienced have created out of the mother the object who is the recipient, when a need arises, of an intense cathexis which we may call "longingful." It is to this innovation that the reaction of grief is referable. Grief is therefore the reaction specific to object loss, anxiety to the danger which this object loss entails, or, by a further displacement, to the danger of object loss itself.

Of pain, likewise, we know very little. Its only certain meaning derives from the fact that pain—primarily and as a rule—occurs if a stimulus impinging on the periphery breaks through the defenses that oppose stimuli of excessive strength and hence acts like a continuous instinctual stimulus against which otherwise efficacious muscular activity such as serves to remove the stimulated region from the stimulus remains powerless. If the pain does not originate from a point on the skin but from an internal organ, this does not alter the situation in any way; it is only that a bit of the internal periphery has replaced the external. The child has obviously occasion to experience pain of this kind which is independent of his experiencing of needs. This mode of origin of pain seems to have very little in common with the loss of an object, however, and further, the factor of peripheral stimulation, essential in the case of pain, is entirely lacking in the child's situation of longing. And it certainly cannot be without significance that language has created the concept of inward, of psychic, pain, and has equated the sensations attendant upon object loss with physical pain.[4]

In the case of physical pain there arises an intense cathexis, which may be termed narcissistic, of the painful region of the body—a cathexis which increases progressively and which acts upon the ego in a so to speak evacuative manner. It is a familiar fact that when we feel pain in the internal organs we experience spatial and other impressions of these organs which otherwise would not be registered in consciousness at all. Furthermore, the remarkable fact that the most intense physical pain fails of its full effect (here one may not say, "remains unconscious") when we are distracted by some different interest is to be explained on the ground of the concentration of the cathexis upon the psychic representative of the painful body area. Now it is in this point that the analogy seems to consist which has allowed the transference of the sensation of pain to the mental sphere. The intense and, owing to its un-

---

4. That is, by using the same word (*Schmerz*) for both. —TRANSLATOR'S NOTE,

appeasability, ever-increasing longingful cathexis of the missed (lost) object creates the same economic conditions as the painful cathexis of the injured body area, and makes it possible to disregard the peripheral determination of the physical pain. The transition from physical pain to psychic corresponds to the change from narcissistic to object-cathexis. The idea of the object, highly cathected out of need, plays the role of the body area cathected by increased stimulation. The continuous and uninhibitable character of the cathectic process brings about the same state of psychic helplessness. If the unpleasurable sensation which then arises bears the specific stamp, not necessitating more exact description, of pain, instead of being expressed in the form of anxiety, the obvious thing is to hold responsible for this a factor which has heretofore been made far too little use of in our efforts at explanation—namely, the high level of cathexis and libido-binding at which these processes resulting in sensations of unpleasure take place.

We know of still another emotional reaction to object loss—namely, mourning. Its elucidation, however, does not involve any additional difficulties. Mourning originates under the influence of reality testing, which demands categorically that one must part from the object because the object no longer exists. Now it is the task of mourning to carry out this retreat from the object in all the situations in which the object was the recipient of an intense cathexis. The painful character of this separation accords with the explanation just given—that is, it is explained by the intense and unrealizable longingful cathexis of the object during the reproduction of the situations in which the tie to the object has to be dissolved.

5. Mechanisms of Defense

BY SIGMUND FREUD

A. On Repression*

ONE of the vicissitudes an instinctual impulse may undergo is to meet with resistances which seek to make it inoperative. Under certain conditions, which we shall presently investigate more closely, the impulse then passes into the state of "repression" [*Verdrängung*]. If what was in question was the operation of an external stimulus, the appropriate method to adopt would obviously be flight; with an instinct, flight is of no avail, for the ego cannot escape from itself. At some later period, rejection based on judgement (*condemnation*) will be found to be a good method to adopt against an instinctual impulse. Repression is a preliminary stage of condemnation, something between flight and condemnation; it is a concept which could not have been formulated before the time of psycho-analytic studies.

It is not easy in theory to deduce the possibility of such a thing as repression. Why should an instinctual impulse undergo a vicissitude like this? A necessary condition of its happening must clearly be that the instinct's attainment of its aim should produce unpleasure instead of pleasure. But we cannot well imagine such a contingency. There are no such instincts: satisfaction of an instinct is always pleasurable. We should have to assume certain peculiar circumstances, some sort of process by which the pleasure of satisfaction is changed into unpleasure.

In order the better to delimit repression, let us discuss some other instinctual situations. It may happen that an external stimulus becomes internalized—for example, by eating into and destroying some bodily organ—so that a new source of constant excitation and increase of tension arises. The stimulus thereby acquires a far-reaching similarity to an instinct. We know that a case of this sort is experienced by us as *pain*. The aim of this pseudo-instinct, however, is simply the cessation of the change in the organ and of the unpleasure accompanying it. There is no other direct pleasure to be attained by cessation of pain. Further, pain is imperative; the only things to which it can yield are removal by some toxic agent or the influence of mental distraction.

The case of pain is too obscure to give us any help in our purpose. Let us take the case in which an instinctual stimulus such as hunger remains unsatisfied. It then becomes imperative and can be allayed by nothing but the action that satisfies it; it keeps up a constant tension of need. Nothing in

* Reprinted from *The Standard Edition of the Complete Psychological Works of Sigmund Freud* (London: Hogarth Press, 1958), XIV, 146–56; XX, 91–95, with the permission of the Hogarth Press and The Macmillan Co.

the nature of a repression seems in this case to come remotely into question.

Thus repression certainly does not arise in cases where the tension produced by lack of satisfaction of an instinctual impulse is raised to an unbearable degree. The methods of defence which are open to the organism against that situation must be discussed in another connection.

Let us rather confine ourselves to clinical experience, as we meet with it in psycho-analytic practice. We then learn that the satisfaction of an instinct which is under repression would be quite possible, and further, that in every instance such a satisfaction would be pleasurable in itself; but it would be irreconcilable with other claims and intentions. It would, therefore, cause pleasure in one place and unpleasure in another. It has consequently become a condition for repression that the motive force of unpleasure shall have acquired more strength than the pleasure obtained from satisfaction. Psycho-analytic observation of the transference neuroses, moreover, leads us to conclude that repression is not a defensive mechanism which is present from the very beginning, and that it cannot arise until a sharp cleavage has occurred between conscious and unconscious mental activity—that *the essence of repression lies simply in turning something away and keeping it at a distance, from the conscious*. This view of repression would be made more complete by assuming that, before the mental organization reaches this stage, the task of fending off instinctual impulses is dealt with by the other vicissitudes which instincts may undergo— e.g. reversal into the opposite or turning round upon the subject's own self.

It seems to us now that, in view of the very great extent to which repression and what is unconscious are correlated, we must defer probing more deeply into the nature of repression until we have learnt more about the structure of the succession of psychical agencies and about the differentiation between what is unconscious and conscious. Till then, all we can do is to put together in a purely descriptive fashion a few characteristics of repression that have been observed clinically, even though we run the risk of having to repeat unchanged much that has been said elsewhere.

We have reason to assume that there is a *primal repression,* a first phase of repression, which consists in the psychical (ideational) representative of the instinct being denied entrance into the conscious. With this a *fixation* is established; the representative in question persists unaltered from then onwards and the instinct remains attached to it. This is due to the properties of unconscious processes of which we shall speak later.

The second stage of repression, *repression proper,* affects mental derivatives of the repressed representative, or such trains of thought as, originating elsewhere, have come into associative connection with it. On account of this association, these ideas experience the same fate as what was primarily repressed. Repression proper, therefore, is actually an after-pressure. Moreover, it is a mistake to emphasize only the repulsion which operates from the direction of the conscious upon what is to be repressed; quite as important is the attraction exercised by what was primally repressed upon everything with which it can establish a connection. Probably the trend towards repression would fail in its purpose if these two forces did not cooperate, if there were not something previously repressed ready to receive what is repelled by the conscious.

Under the influence of the study of the psychoneuroses, which brings before us the important effects of repression, we are inclined to overvalue their psychological bearing and to forget too readily that repression does not hinder the instinctual representative from continuing to exist in the unconscious, from organizing itself further, putting out derivatives and establishing connections. Repression in fact interfers only with the relation of the instinctual representative to *one* psychical system, namely, to that of the conscious.

Psycho-analysis is able to show us other things as well which are important for understanding the effects of repression in the psychoneuroses. It shows us, for instance, that the instinctual representative develops with less interference and more profusely if it is withdrawn by repression from conscious influence. It proliferates in the dark, as it were, and takes on extreme forms of expression, which when they are translated and presented to the neurotic are not only bound to seem alien to him, but frighten him by giving him the picture of an extraordinary and dangerous strength of instinct. This deceptive strength of instinct is the result of an uninhibited development in phantasy and of the damming-up consequent on frustrated satisfaction. The fact that this last result is bound up with repression points the direction in which the true significance of repression has to be looked for.

Reverting once more, however, to the opposite aspect of repression, let us make it clear that it is not even correct to suppose that repression withholds from the conscious *all* the derivatives of what was primally repressed. If these derivatives have become sufficiently far removed from the repressed representative, whether owing to the adoption of distortions or by reason of the number of intermediate links inserted, they have free access to the conscious. It is as though the resistance of the conscious against them was a function of their distance from what was originally repressed. In carrying out the technique of psycho-analysis, we continually require the patient to produce such derivatives of the repressed as, in consequence either of their remoteness or of their distortion, can pass the censorship of the conscious. Indeed, the associations which we require him to give without being influenced by any conscious purposive idea and without any criticism, and from which we reconstitute a conscious translation of the repressed representative—these associations are nothing else than remote and distorted derivatives of this kind. During this process we observe that the patient can go on spinning a thread of such associations, till he is brought up against some thought, the relation of which to what is repressed becomes so obvious that he is compelled to repeat his attempt at repression. Neurotic symptoms, too, must have fulfilled this same condition, for they are derivatives of the repressed, which has, by their means, finally won the access to consciousness which was previously denied to it.

We can lay down no general rule as to what degree of distortion and remoteness is necessary before the resistance on the part of the conscious is removed. A delicate balancing is here taking place, the play of which is hidden from us; its mode of operation, however, enables us to infer that it is a question of calling a halt when the cathexis of the unconscious reaches a certain intensity—an intensity beyond which the unconscious would break through to satisfaction. Repression acts, therefore, in a *highly individual* manner. Each single derivative of the repressed may have its own special vicissitude; a little more or a little less distortion alters the whole outcome. In this connection we can understand how it is that the objects to which men give most preference, their ideals, proceed from the same perceptions and experiences as the objects which they most abhor, and that they were originally only distinguished from one another through slight modifications. Indeed, as we found in tracing the origin of the fetish, it is possible for the original instinctual representative to be split in two, one part undergoing repression, while the remainder, precisely on account of this intimate connection, undergoes idealization.

The same result as follows from an increase or a decrease in the degree of distortion may also be achieved at the other end of the apparatus, so to speak, by a modification in the condition for the production of pleasure and unpleasure. Special techniques have been evolved, with the purpose of bringing about such changes in the play of mental forces that what would otherwise give rise to un-

pleasure may on this occasion result in pleasure; and, whenever a technical device of this sort comes into operation, the repression of an instinctual representative which would otherwise be repudiated is removed. These techniques have till now only been studied in any detail in jokes. As a rule the repression is only temporarily removed and is promptly reinstated.

Observations like this, however, enable us to note some further characteristics of repression. Not only is it, as we have just shown, *individual* in its operation, but it is also exceedingly *mobile*. The process of repression is not to be regarded as an event which takes place *once,* the results of which are permanent, as when some living thing has been killed and from that time onward is dead; repression demands a persistent expenditure of force, and if this were to cease the success of the repression would be jeopardized, so that a fresh act of repression would be necessary. We may suppose that the repressed exercises a continuous pressure in the direction of the conscious, so that this pressure must be balanced by an unceasing counter-pressure. Thus the maintenance of a repression involves an uninterrupted expenditure of force, while its removal results in a saving from an economic point of view. The mobility of repression, incidentally, also finds expression in the psychical characteristics of the state of sleep, which alone renders possible the formation of dreams. With a return to waking life the repressive cathexes which have been drawn in are once more sent out.

Finally, we must not forget that after all we have said very little about an instinctual impulse when we have established that it is repressed. Without prejudice to its repression, such an impulse may be in widely different states. It may be inactive, i.e. only very slightly cathected with mental energy; or it may be cathected in varying degrees, and so enabled to be active. True, its activation will not result in a direct removal of the repression, but it will set in motion all the processes which end in a penetration by the impulse into consciousness along circuitous paths. With unrepressed derivatives of the unconscious the fate of a particular idea is often decided by the degree of its activity or cathexis. It is an everyday occurrence that such a derivative remains unrepressed so long as it represents only a small amount of energy, although its content would be calculated to give rise to a conflict with what is dominant in consciousness. The quantitative factor proves decisive for this conflict: as soon as the basically obnoxious idea exceeds a certain degree of strength, the conflict becomes a real one, and it is precisely this activation that leads to repression. So that, where repression is concerned, an increase of energic cathexis operates in the same sense as an approach to the unconscious, while a decrease of that cathexis operates in the same sense as remoteness from the unconscious or distortion. We see that the repressive trends may find a substitute for repression in a weakening of what is distasteful.

In our discussion so far we have dealt with the repression of an instinctual representative, and by the latter we have understood an idea or group of ideas which is cathected with a definite quota of psychical energy (libido or interest) coming from an instinct. Clinical observation now obliges us to divide up what we have hitherto regarded as a single entity; for it shows us that besides the idea, some other element representing the instinct has to be taken into account, and that this other element undergoes vicissitudes of repression which may be quite different from those undergone by the idea. For this other element of the psychical representative the term *quota of affect* has been generally adopted. It corresponds to the instinct in so far as the latter has become detached from the idea and finds expression, proportionate to its quantity, in processes which are sensed as affects. From this point on, in describing a case of repression, we shall have to follow up separately what, as the result of repression, becomes of the *idea,* and what becomes of the instinctual energy linked to it.

We should be glad to be able to say something general about the vicissitudes of both; and having taken our bearings a little we shall in fact be able to do so. The general vicissitude which overtakes the *idea* that represents the instinct can hardly be anything else than that it should vanish from the conscious if it was previously conscious, or that it should be held back from consciousness if it was about to become conscious. The difference is not important; it amounts to much the same thing as the difference between my ordering an undesirable guest out of my drawing-room (or out of my front hall), and my refusing, after recognizing him, to let him cross my threshold at all.[1] The *quantitative* factor of the instinctual representative has three possible vicissitudes, as we can see from a cursory survey of the observations made by psycho-analysis: either the instinct is altogether suppressed, so that no trace of it is found, or it appears as an affect which is in some way or other qualitatively coloured, or it is changed into anxiety. The two latter possibilities set us the task of taking into ac-

count, as a further instinctual vicissitude, the *transformation* into *affects,* and especially into *anxiety,* of the psychical energies of *instincts.*

We recall the fact that the motive and purpose of repression was nothing else than the avoidance of unpleasure. It follows that the vicissitude of the quota of affect belonging to the representative is far more important than the vicissitude of the idea, and this fact is decisive for our assessment of the process of repression. If a repression does not succeed in preventing feelings of unpleasure or anxiety from arising, we may say that it has failed, even though it may have achieved its purpose as far as the ideational portion is concerned. Repressions that have failed will of course have more claim on our interest than any that may have been successful; for the latter will for the most part escape our examination.

We must now try to obtain some insight into the *mechanism* of the process of repression. In particular we want to know whether there is a single mechanism only, or more than one, and whether perhaps each of the psychoneuroses is distinguished by a mechanism of repression peculiar to it. At the outset of this enquiry, however, we are met by complications. The mechanism of a repression becomes accessible to us only by our deducing that mechanism from the *outcome* of the repression. Confining our observations to the effect of repression on the ideational portion of the representative, we discover that as a rule it creates a *substitutive formation.* What is the mechanism by which such a substitute is formed? Or should we distinguish several mechanisms here as well? Further, we know that repression leaves *symptoms* behind it. May we then suppose that the forming of substitutes and the forming of symptoms coincide, and, if this is so on the whole, is the mechanism of forming symptoms the same as that of repression? The general probability would seem to be that the two are widely different, and that it is not the repression itself which produces substitutive formations and symptoms, but that these latter are indications of a *return of the repressed* and owe their existence to quite other processes. It would also seem advisable to examine the mechanisms by which substitutes and symptoms are formed before considering the mechanisms of repression.

Obviously this is no subject for further speculation. The place of speculation must be taken by a careful analysis of the results of repression observable in the different neuroses. I must, however, suggest that we should postpone this task, too, until we have formed reliable conceptions of the relation of the conscious to the unconscious. But, in order that the present discussion may not be entirely

1. This simile, which is thus applicable to the process of repression, may also be extended to a characteristic of it which has been mentioned earlier: I have merely to add that I must set a permanent guard over the door which I have forbidden this guest to enter, since he would otherwise burst it open.

unfruitful, I will say in advance that (1) the mechanism of repression does not in fact coincide with the mechanism or mechanisms of forming substitutes, (2) there are a great many different mechanisms of forming substitutes and (3) the mechanisms of repression have at least this one thing in common: *a withdrawal of the cathexis of energy* (or of *libido,* where we are dealing with sexual instincts).

Further, restricting myself to the three best-known forms of psychoneurosis, I will show by means of some examples how the concepts here introduced find application to the study of repression.*

From the field of *anxiety hysteria* I will choose a well-analysed example of an animal phobia. The instinctual impulse subjected to repression here is a libidinal attitude towards the father, coupled with fear of him. After repression, this impulse vanishes out of consciousness: the father does not appear in it as an object of libido. As a substitute for him we find in a corresponding place some animal which is more or less fitted to be an object of anxiety. The formation of the substitute for the ideational portion [of the instinctual representative] has come about by *displacement* along a chain of connections which is determined in a particular way. The quantitative portion has not vanished, but has been transformed into anxiety. The result is fear of a wolf, instead of a demand for love from the father. The categories here employed are of course not enough to supply an adequate explanation of even the simplest case of psychoneurosis: there are always other considerations to be taken into account. A repression such as occurs in an animal phobia must be described as radically unsuccessful. All that it has done is to remove and replace the idea; it has failed altogether in sparing unpleasure. And for this reason, too, the work of the neurosis does not cease. It proceeds to a second phase, in order to attain its immediate and more important purpose. What follows is an attempt at flight—the formation of the *phobia proper,* of a number of avoidances which are intended to prevent a release of the anxiety. More specialized investigation enables us to understand the mechanism by which the phobia achieves its aim.

We are obliged to take quite another view of the process of repression when we consider the picture of a true *conversion hysteria.* Here the salient point is that it is possible to bring about a total disappearance of the quota of affect. When this is so, the patient displays towards his symptoms what Charcot called "*la belle indifférence des hystériques.*" In other cases this suppression is not so completely successful: some distressing sensations may attach to the symptoms themselves, or it may prove impossible to prevent some release of anxiety, which in turn sets to work the mechanism of forming a phobia. The ideational content of the instinctual representative is completely withdrawn from consciousness; as a substitute—and at the same time as a symptom—we have an over-strong innervation (in typical cases, a somatic one), sometimes of a sensory, sometimes of a motor character, either as an excitation or an inhibition. The over-innervated area proves on a closer view to be a part of the repressed instinctual representative itself—a part which, as though by a process of *condensation,* has drawn the whole cathexis on to itself. These remarks do not of course bring to light the whole mechanism of a conversion hysteria; in especial the factor of *regression,* which will be considered in another connection, has also to be taken into account. In so far as repression in [conversion] hysteria is made possible only by the extensive formation of substitutes, it may be judged to be entirely unsuccessful; as regards dealing with the quota of affect, however, which is the true task of repression, it generally signifies a total success. In conversion hysteria the process of repression is completed with the formation of the symptom and does not, as in anxiety hysteria, need to continue to a second phase—or rather, strictly speaking, to continue endlessly.

The main characteristics of the formation of symptoms have long since been studied and, I hope, established beyond dispute. A symptom is a sign of, and a substitute for, an instinctual satisfaction which has remained in abeyance; it is a consequence of the process of repression. Repression proceeds from the ego when the latter—it may be at the behest of the super-ego—refuses to associate itself with an instinctual cathexis which has been aroused in the id. The ego is able by means of repression to keep the idea which is the vehicle of the reprehensible impulse from becoming conscious. Analysis shows that the idea often persists as an unconscious formation.

So far everything seems clear; but we soon come upon difficulties which have not as yet been solved. Up till now our account of what occurs in repression has laid great stress on this point of exclusion from consciousness. But it has left other points open to uncertainty. One question that arose was, what happened to the instinctual impulse which had been activated in the id and which sought satisfaction? The answer was an indirect one. It was that owing

---

* Freud's third example—obsessional neurosis—has been omitted from this selection.

to the process of repression the pleasure that would have been expected from satisfaction had been transformed into unpleasure. But we were then faced with the problem of how the satisfaction of an instinct could produce unpleasure. The whole matter can be clarified, I think, if we commit ourselves to the definite statement that as a result of repression the intended course of the excitatory process in the id does not occur at all; the ego succeeds in inhibiting or deflecting it. If this is so the problem of "transformation of affect" under repression disappears. At the same time this view implies a concession to the ego that it can exert a very extensive influence over processes in the id, and we shall have to find out in what way it is able to develop such surprising powers.

It seems to me that the ego obtains this influence in virtue of its intimate connections with the perceptual system—connections which, as we know, constitute its essence and provide the basis of its differentiation from the id. The function of this system, which we have called *Pcpt.-Cs.*, is bound up with the phenomenon of consciousness. It receives excitations not only from outside but from within, and endeavours, by means of the sensations of pleasure and unpleasure which reach it from these quarters, to direct the course of mental events in accordance with the pleasure principle. We are very apt to think of the ego as powerless against the id; but when it is opposed to an instinctual process in the id it has only to give a "*signal of unpleasure*" in order to attain its object with the aid of that almost omnipotent institution, the pleasure principle. To take this situation by itself for a moment, we can illustrate it by an example from another field. Let us imagine a country in which a certain small faction objects to a proposed measure the passage of which would have the support of the masses. This minority obtains command of the press and by its help manipulates the supreme arbiter, "public opinion," and so succeeds in preventing the measure from being passed.

But this explanation opens up fresh problems. Where does the energy come from which is employed for giving the signal of unpleasure? Here we may be assisted by the idea that a defence against an unwelcome *internal* process will be modelled upon the defence adopted against an *external* stimulus, that the ego wards off internal and external dangers alike along identical lines. In the case of external danger the organism has recourse to attempts at flight. The first thing it does is to withdraw cathexis from the perception of the dangerous object; later on it discovers that it is a better plan to perform muscular movements of such a sort as will render perception of the dangerous object impossible even in the absence of any refusal to perceive it—that it is a better plan, that is, to remove itself from the sphere of danger. Repression is an equivalent of this attempt at flight. The ego withdraws its (preconscious) cathexis from the instinctual representative that is to be repressed and uses that cathexis for the purpose of releasing unpleasure (anxiety). The problem of how anxiety arises in connection with repression may be no simple one; but we may legitimately hold firmly to the idea that the ego is the actual seat of anxiety and give up our earlier view that the cathectic energy of the repressed impulse is automatically turned into anxiety. If I expressed myself earlier in the latter sense, I was giving a phenomenological description and not a metapsychological account of what was occurring.

This brings us to a further question: how is it possible, from an economic point of view, for a mere process of withdrawal and discharge, like the withdrawing of a preconscious ego-cathexis, to produce unpleasure or anxiety, seeing that, according to our assumptions, unpleasure and anxiety can only arise as a result of an *increase* in cathexis? The reply is that this causal sequence should not be explained from an economic point of view. Anxiety is not newly created in repression; it is reproduced as an affective state in accordance with an already existing mnemic image. If we go further and enquire into the origin of that anxiety—and of affects in general—we shall be leaving the realm of pure psychology and entering the borderland of physiology. Affective states have become incorporated in the mind as precipitates of primaeval traumatic experiences, and when a similar situation occurs they are revived like mnemic symbols. I do not think I have been wrong in likening them to the more recent and individually acquired hysterical attack and in regarding them as its normal prototypes. In man and the higher animals it would seem that the act of birth, as the individual's first experience of anxiety, has given the affect of anxiety certain characteristic forms of expression. But, while acknowledging this connection, we must not lay undue stress on it nor overlook the fact that biological necessity demands that a situation of danger should have an affective symbol, so that a symbol of this kind would have to be created in any case. Moreover, I do not think that we are justified in assuming that whenever there is an outbreak of anxiety something like a reproduction of the situation of birth goes on in the mind. It is not even certain whether hysterical attacks, though they were originally traumatic reproductions of this sort, retain that character permanently.

As I have shown elsewhere, most of the repressions with which we have to deal in our therapeutic work are cases of *after*-pressure. They presuppose the operation of earlier, *primal repressions* which exert an attraction on the more recent situation. Far too little is known as yet about the background and preliminary stages of repression. There is a danger of overestimating the part played in repression by the super-ego. We cannot at present say whether it is perhaps the emergence of the super-ego which provides the line of demarcation between primal repression and after-pressure. At any rate, the earliest outbreaks of anxiety, which are of a very intense kind, occur before the super-ego has become differentiated. It is highly probable that the immediate precipitating causes of primal repressions are quantitative factors such as an excessive degree of excitation and the breaking through of the protective shield against stimuli.

This mention of the protective shield sounds a note which recalls to us the fact that repression occurs in two different situations—namely, when an undesirable instinctual impulse is aroused by some external perception, and when it arises internally without any such provocation. We shall return to this difference later. But the protective shield exists only in regard to external stimuli, not in regard to internal instinctual demands.

So long as we direct our attention to the ego's attempt at flight we shall get no nearer to the subject of symptom-formation. A symptom arises from an instinctual impulse which has been detrimentally affected by repression. If the ego, by making use of the signal of unpleasure, attains its object of completely suppressing the instinctual impulse, we learn nothing of how this has happened. We can only find out about it from those cases in which repression must be described as having to a greater or less extent failed. In this event the position, generally speaking, is that the instinctual impulse has found a substitute in spite of repression, but a substitute which is very much reduced, displaced and inhibited and which is no longer recognizable as a satisfaction. And when the substitutive impulse is carried out there is no sensation of pleasure; its carrying out has, instead, the quality of a compulsion.

In thus degrading a process of satisfaction to a symptom, repression displays its power in a further respect. The substitutive process is prevented, if possible, from finding discharge through motility; and even if this cannot be done, the process is forced to expend itself in making alterations in the subject's own body and is not permitted to impinge upon the external world. It must not be transformed into action. For, as we know, in repression the ego is operating under the influence of external reality and therefore it debars the substitutive process from having any effect upon that reality.

Just as the ego controls the path to action in regard to the external world, so it controls access to consciousness. In repression it exercises its power in both directions, acting in the one manner upon the instinctual impulse itself and in the other upon the [psychical] representative of that impulse. At this point it is relevant to ask how I can reconcile this acknowledgement of the might of the ego with the description of its position which I gave in *The Ego and the Id.* In that book I drew a picture of its dependent relationship to the id and to the super-ego and revealed how powerless and apprehensive it was in regard to both and with what an effort it maintained its show of superiority over them. This view has been widely echoed in psycho-analytic literature. Many writers have laid much stress on the weakness of the ego in relation to the id and of our rational elements in the face of the daemonic forces within us; and they display a strong tendency to make what I have said into a corner-stone of a psycho-analytic *Weltanschauung.* Yet surely the psycho-analyst, with his knowledge of the way in which repression works, should, of all people, be restrained from adopting such an extreme and one-sided view.

B. On Displacement*

In the case of the complicated and confused dreams with which we are now concerned, condensation and dramatization alone are not enough to account for the whole of the impression that we gain of the dissimilarity between the content of the dream and the dream-thoughts. We have evidence of the operation of a third factor, and this evidence deserves careful sifting.

First and foremost, when by means of analysis we have arrived at a knowledge of the dream-thoughts, we observe that the manifest dream-content deals with quite different material from the latent thoughts. This, to be sure, is no more than an appearance, which evaporates under closer examination, for we find ultimately that the whole of the dream-content is derived from the dream-thoughts, and that almost all the dream-thoughts are represented in the dream-content. Nevertheless, something of the distinction still remains. What stands out boldly and clearly in the dream as its essential content must, after analysis, be satisfied with playing an extremely subordinate role among the dream-

* Reprinted from *The Standard Edition of the Complete Psychological Works of Sigmund Freud* (London: Hogarth Press, 1958), V. 654–657 with the permission of The Hogarth Press and W. W. Norton & Co., Inc.

thoughts; and what, on the evidence of our feelings, can claim to be the most prominent among the dream-thoughts is either not present at all as ideational material in the content of the dream or is only remotely alluded to in some obscure region of it. We may put it in this way: *in the course of the dream-work the psychical intensity passes over from the thoughts and ideas to which it properly belongs on to others which in our judgement have no claim to any such emphasis.* No other process contributes so much to concealing the meaning of a dream and to making the connection between the dream-content and the dream-thoughts unrecognizable. In the course of this process, which I shall describe as "dream-displacement," the psychical intensity, significance or affective potentiality of the thoughts is, as we further find, transformed into sensory vividness. We assume as a matter of course that the most distinct element in the manifest content of a dream is the most important one; but in fact [owing to the displacement that has occurred] it is often an *indistinct* element which turns out to be the most direct derivative of the essential dream-thought.

What I have called dream-displacement might equally be described [in Nietzsche's phrase] as "a transvaluation of psychical values." I shall not have given an exhaustive estimate of this phenomenon, however, unless I add that this work of displacement or transvaluation is performed to a very varying degree in different dreams. There are dreams which come about almost without any displacement. These are the ones which make sense and are intelligible, such, for instance, as those which we have recognized as undisguised wishful dreams. On the other hand, there are dreams in which not a single piece of the dream-thoughts has retained its own psychical value, or in which everything that is essential in the dream-thoughts has been replaced by something trivial. And we can find a complete series of transitional cases between these two extremes. The more obscure and confused a dream appears to be, the greater the share in its construction which may be attributed to the factor of displacement.

Our specimen dream exhibits displacement to this extent at least, that its content seems to have a different *centre* from its dream-thoughts. In the foreground of the dream-content a prominent place is taken by a situation in which a woman seems to be making advances to me; while in the dream-thoughts the chief emphasis is laid on a wish for once to enjoy unselfish love, love which "costs nothing"—an idea concealed behind the phrase about "beautiful eyes" and the far-fetched allusion to "spinach."

If we undo dream-displacement by means of analysis, we obtain what seems to be completely trustworthy information on two much-disputed problems concerning dreams: as to their instigators and as to their connection with waking life. There are dreams which immediately reveal their derivation from events of the day; there are others in which no trace of any such derivation is to be discovered. If we seek the help of analysis, we find that every dream without any possible exception goes back to an impression of the past few days, or, it is probably more correct to say, of the day immediately preceding the dream, of the "dream-day." The impression which plays the part of dream-instigator may be such an important one that we feel no surprise at being concerned with it in the daytime, and in that case we rightly speak of the dream as carrying on with the significant interests of our waking life. As a rule, however, if a connection is to be found in the content of the dream with any impression of the previous day, that impression is so trivial, insignificant and unmemorable, that it is only with difficulty that we ourselves can recall it. And in such cases the content of the dream itself, even if it is connected and intelligible, seems to be concerned with the most indifferent trivialities, which would be unworthy of our interest if we were awake. A good deal of the contempt in which dreams are held is due to the preference thus shown in their content for what is indifferent and trivial.

Analysis does away with the misleading appearance upon which this derogatory judgement is founded. If the content of a dream puts forward some indifferent impression as being its instigator, analysis invariably brings to light a significant experience, and one by which the dreamer has good reason to be stirred. This experience has been replaced by the indifferent one, with which it is connected by copious associative links. Where the content of the dream treats of insignificant and uninteresting ideational material, analysis uncovers the numerous associative paths connecting these trivialities with things that are of the highest psychical importance in the dreamer's estimation. *If what make their way into the content of dreams are impressions and material which are indifferent and trivial rather than justifiably stirring and interesting, that is only the effect of the process of displacement.* If we answer our questions about dream-instigators and the connection between dreaming and daily affairs on the basis of the new insight we have gained from replacing the manifest by the latent content of dreams, we arrive at these conclusions: *dreams are never concerned with things which we should not think it worth while to be concerned with during the day, and trivialities which do not affect us during the day are unable to pursue us in our sleep.*

What was the dream-instigator in the specimen that we have chosen for analysis? It was the definitely insignificant event of my friend giving me *a drive in a cab free of cost*. The situation in the dream at the table d'hôte contained an allusion to this insignificant precipitating cause, for in my conversation I had compared the taximeter cab with a table d'hôte. But I can also point to the important experience which was represented by this trivial one. A few days earlier I had paid out a considerable sum of money on behalf of a member of my family of whom I am fond. No wonder, said the dream-thoughts, if this person were to feel grateful to me: love of that sort would not be "free of cost." Love that is free of cost, however, stood in the forefront of the dream-thoughts. The fact that not long before I had had several *cab-drives* with the relative in question, made it possible for the cab-drive with my friend to remind me of my connections with this other person.

The indifferent impression which becomes a dream-instigator owing to associations of this kind is subject to a further condition which does not apply to the true source of the dream: it must always be a *recent* impression, derived from the dream-day.

I cannot leave the subject of dream-displacement without drawing attention to a remarkable process which occurs in the formation of dreams and in which condensation and displacement *combine* to produce the result. In considering condensation we have already seen the way in which two ideas in the dream-thoughts which have something in common, some point of contact, are replaced in the dream-content by a composite idea, in which a relatively distinct nucleus represents what they have in common, while indistinct subordinate details correspond to the respects in which they differ from each other. If displacement takes place in addition to condensation, what is constructed is not a composite idea but an "intermediate common entity," which stands in a relation to the two different elements similar to that in which the resultant in a parallelogram of forces stands to its components. For instance, in the content of one of my dreams there was a question of an injection with *propyl*. To begin with, the analysis only led me to an indifferent experience which had acted as dream-instigator, and in which a part was played by *amyl*. I was not yet able to justify the confusion between amyl and propyl. In the group of ideas behind this same dream, however, there was also a recollection of my first visit to Munich, where I had been struck by the *Propylaea*.[1] The details of the analysis made it plausible to sup-

pose that it was the influence of this second group of ideas upon the first one that was responsible for the displacement from amyl to propyl. *Propyl* is as it were an intermediate idea between *amyl* and *Propylaea*, and found its way into the content of the dream as a kind of *compromise*, by means of simultaneous condensation and displacement.[2]

C. On Projection* . . . .

In my *Three Essays on the Theory of Sexuality*, I have expressed the opinion that each stage in the development of psychosexuality affords a possibility of "fixation" and thus of a dispositional point. People who have not freed themselves completely from the stage of narcissism—who, that is to say, have at that point a fixation which may operate as a disposition to a later illness—are exposed to the danger that some unusually intense wave of libido, finding no other outlet, may lead to a sexualization of their social instincts and so undo the sublimations which they had achieved in the course of their development. This result may be produced by anything that causes the libido to flow backwards (i.e. that causes a "regression"): whether, on the one hand, the libido becomes collaterally reinforced owing to some disappointment over a woman, or is directly dammed up owing to a mishap in social relations with other men—both of these being instances of "frustration;" or whether, on the other hand, there is a general intensification of the libido, so that it becomes too powerful to find an outlet along the channels which are already open to it, and consequently bursts through its banks at the weakest spot. Since our analyses show that paranoics endeavour to protect themselves against any such *sexualization of their social instinctual cathexes*, we are driven to suppose that the weak spot in their development is to be looked for somewhere between the stages of auto-erotism, narcissism and homosexuality, and that their disposition to illness (which may perhaps be susceptible of more precise definition) must be located in that region. A similar disposition would have to be assigned to patients suffering from Kraepelin's dementia praecox or (as Bleuler has named it) *schizophrenia;* and we shall hope later on to find clues which will enable

---

1. A ceremonial portico on the Athenian model.

2. The dream from which this detail is taken was the first one to be exhaustively analyzed by Freud. It is reported at length in *The Interpretation of Dreams*.

* Reprinted from *The Standard Edition of the Complete Psychological Works of Sigmund Freud* (London: Hogarth Press, 1958) XII, 61–66, with the permission of The Hogarth Press.

us to trace back the differences between the two disorders (as regards both the form they take and the course they run) to corresponding differences in the patients' dispositional fixations.

In taking the view, then, that what lies at the core of the conflict in cases of paranoia among males is a homosexual wishful phantasy of *loving a man,* we shall certainly not forget that the confirmation of such an important hypothesis can only follow upon the investigation of a large number of instances of every variety of paranoic disorder. We must therefore be prepared, if need be, to limit our assertion to a single type of paranoia. Nevertheless, it is a remarkable fact that the familiar principal forms of paranoia can all be represented as contradictions of the single proposition: "*I* (a man) *love him* (a man)," and indeed that they exhaust all the possible ways in which such contradictions could be formulated.

The proposition "I (a man) love him" is contradicted by:

(*a*) Delusions of *persecution;* for they loudly assert:

"I do not *love* him—I *hate* him."

This contradiction, which must have run thus in the unconscious, cannot, however, become conscious to a paranoic in this form. The mechanism of symptom-formation in paranoia requires that internal perceptions—feelings—shall be replaced by external perceptions. Consequently the proposition "I hate him" becomes transformed by *projection* into another one: "He *hates* (persecutes) *me,* which will justify me in hating him." And thus the impelling unconscious feeling makes its appearance as though it were the consequence of an external perception:

"I do not *love* him—I *hate* him, because HE PERSECUTES ME."

Observation leaves room for no doubt that the persecutor is some one who was once loved.

(*b*) Another element is chosen for contradiction in *erotomania,* which remains totally unintelligible on any other view:

"I do not love *him*—I love *her.*"

And in obedience to the same need for projection, the proposition is transformed into: "I observe that *she* loves me."

"I do not love *him*—I love *her,* because SHE LOVES ME."

Many cases of erotomania might give an impression that they could be satisfactorily explained as being exaggerated or distorted heterosexual fixations, if our attention were not attracted by the circumstance that these infatuations invariably be-

gin, not with any internal perception of loving, but with an external perception of being loved. But in this form of paranoia the intermediate proposition "I love *her*" can also become conscious, because the contradiction between it and the original proposition is not a diametrical one, not so irreconcilable as that between love and hate: it is, after all, possible to love *her* as well as *him.* It can thus come about that the proposition which has been substituted by projection ("*she loves me*") may make way again for the "basic language" proposition "I love *her.*"

(*c*) The third way in which the original proposition can be contradicted would be by delusions of *jealousy* which we can study in the characteristic forms in which they appear in each sex.

(1) Alcoholic delusions of jealousy. The part played by alcohol in this disorder is intelligible in every way. We know that that source of pleasure removes inhibitions and undoes sublimations. It is not infrequently disappointment over a woman that drives a man to drink—but this means, as a rule, that he resorts to the public-house and to the company of men, who afford him the emotional satisfaction which he has failed to get from his wife at home. If now these men become the objects of a strong libidinal cathexis in his unconscious, he will ward it off with the third kind of contradiction:

"It is not *I* who love the man—*she* loves him," and he suspects the woman in relation to all the men whom he himself is tempted to love.

Distortion by means of projection is necessarily absent in this instance, since, with the change of the subject who loves, the whole process is in any case thrown outside the self. The fact that the woman loves the men is a matter of external perception to him; whereas the facts that he himself does not love but hates, or that he himself loves not this but that person, are matters of internal perception.

(2) Delusions of jealousy in women are exactly analogous.

"It is not *I* who love the women—*he* loves them." The jealous woman suspects her husband in relation to all the women by whom she is herself attracted owing to her homosexuality and the dispositional effect of her excessive narcissism. The influence of the time of life at which her fixation occurred is clearly shown by the selection of the love-objects which she imputes to her husband; they are often old and quite inappropriate for a real love relation —revivals of the nurses and servants and girls who were her friends in childhood, or sisters who were her actual rivals.

Now it might be supposed that a proposition consisting of three terms, such as "*I love him,*" could only be contradicted in three different ways. Delusions of jealousy contradict the subject, delusions of persecution contradict the verb, and erotomania contradicts the object. But in fact a fourth kind of contradiction is possible—namely, one which rejects the proposition as a whole:

"*I do not love at all—I do not love any one.*" And since, after all, one's libido must go somewhere, this proposition seems to be the psychological equivalent of the proposition: "I love only myself." So that this kind of contradiction would give us megalomania, which we may regard as a *sexual overvaluation of the ego* and may thus set beside the overvaluation of the love-object with which we are already familiar.

It is of some importance in connection with other parts of the theory of paranoia to notice that we can detect an element of megalomania in most other forms of paranoic disorder. We are justified in assuming that megalomania is essentially of an infantile nature and that, as development proceeds, it is sacrificed to social considerations. Similarly, an individual's megalomania is never so vehemently suppressed as when he is in the grip of an overpowering love:

Denn wo die Lieb' erwachet, stirbt
   das Ich, der finstere Despot.[1]

After this discussion of the unexpectedly important part played by homosexual wishful phantasies in paranoia, let us return to the two factors in which we expected from the first to find the distinguishing marks of paranoia, namely, the mechanisms *by which the symptoms are formed* and the mechanism *by which repression is brought about.*

We certainly have no right to begin by assuming that these two mechanisms are identical, and that symptom-formation follows the same path as repression each proceeding along it, perhaps, in an opposite direction. Nor does there seem to be any great probability that such an identity exists. Nevertheless, we shall refrain from expressing any opinion on the subject until we have completed our investigation.

The most striking characteristics of symptom-formation in paranoia is the process which deserves the name of *projection.*

---

1. From the *Ghazals* of Muhammad ibn Muhammad (Jalāl al-Dīn) *Rūmī,* translated by Rückert.
   [For when the flames of love arise,
      Then Self, the Gloomy tyrant, dies.
   In Rückert's version the word '*dunkele*' ('dark') appears in place of '*finstere*'.]

Section C

Processes of Socialization

Editorial Foreword, BY JESSE R. PITTS   *821*

1. *The Social Self,* BY CHARLES H. COOLEY   *822*
2. *Internalized Others and the Self,* BY GEORGE H. MEAD   *829*
3. *On Intellectual Growth,* BY JEAN PIAGET   *830*
4. *Moral Realism,* BY JEAN PIAGET   *835*
5. *On Object-Relations and Psycho-Sexual Stages,* BY SIGMUND FREUD   *838*
6. *On the Internalization of the Sex Role: The Feminine Case,*
   BY SIGMUND FREUD   *852*
7. *On the Learning of Discipline,* BY EMILE DURKHEIM   *860*

Processes of Socialization

by Jesse R. Pitts

AMERICAN WRITERS, TO A greater extent than most, have perceived the subtle by-play between society and the individual, how the individual develops a sense of self through participation in social interaction, and yet how this sense of self requires a feeling of separation from others. J. M. Baldwin[1] gave an early expression of the idea that "the real self is the bipolar self, the social self, the socius." With *Cooley,* we have the idea that the self is a mirror of others, that it is through the perception of others and the control of others that the child develops a self capable of autonomous action. Cooley had a clear idea of the specificity of the social fact and of its ideal nature. In fact, he could have paraphrased Durkheim by stating that society is in the minds of individuals through the ideas they have of one another.

G. H. Mead's emphasis is more behavioristic but develops essentially the same views. The excerpt in this section should be read in conjunction with the excerpt from the same author in Section B of Part One. Mead offers a more developed theory of the growth of the self through the use of language and gestures to participation in the play and the game. The interactional process gives rise to the symbolic process. The more complex the society in which the self participates, the more differentiated the symbolic process.

With *Piaget,* some of the principles of the relationship between social participation and the cognitive structure of the personality begin to be spelled out. Egocentrism leads to defects in logic and to moral realism. Increasing co-operation with peers permits the development of rationalized conformity, which Durkheim would have described as *organic*

solidarity. Piaget thus brings out the educative importance of the peer group, a factor which is often overlooked in the stress on parental authority and school curriculum. What we miss in Piaget is a motivational force behind co-operation and the surrender of egocentrism. How does the child come to differentiate between the cognitive valence and the cathectic valence of an object? Does not moral realism remain an intrinsic feature of the adult personality both as a regressive potential, and as the non-rational element of value commitment?

Freudian psychology, for all its focus on motivation, does not contradict Piaget's description of child thought. Autism, of course, is a concept created by Bleuler, the author of the great classic text in schizophrenia. Primary process and oral omnipotence are concepts that are somewhat equivalent to autism and egocentrism. Freud, however, attaches himself to the cathectic meaning of children's behavior and verbalizations, rather than to logical cohesion. While Piaget's stages of the child's growth are given in terms of thought processes, Freud describes these stages in terms of the primacy of certain erogenous zones—oral, anal, and phallic. Freud sees the transition from one stage to the other as a self-contained development, like embryological growth. Somehow the libido contained in love makes the object choice which integrates with the tensions of the dominant erogenous zone. Otherwise we have neurosis. Even though Freud was highly aware of the social factors which made essential the frustration of sexual libido and the necessity of the incest taboo, in 1904 he still held to an organic theory of stages.

The excerpt on the psychology of women was published nearly thirty years later and gives a much larger part to the social factor, especially to the family relationship. We may not accept *penis envy*

---

1. J. M. Baldwin: *Social and Ethical Interpretations,* New York: Macmillan Co., 1897, chap. i.

as a special cause of the strong ambivalence of the girl toward her mother who is seen, supposedly, as responsible for the daughter's being born without a penis. On the other hand, the special relation of the girl to the oedipus conflict seems a most valuable insight. The girl is helped in giving up her ambivalent attachment to the mother by the sensualization of her relationship to the father. Because of the libidinal nature of this second tie, she can never reach the boy's level in the repression of dependent cathexes. Nor is her superego as fully formed, since the processes of reaction-formation are relatively little involved in her relation to the father, who intruded upon her possession of the mother. The reader may note that in describing how the girl takes the role of the mother "whom she has set aside," Freud comes very close to the role concept of the internalized object.

The section on socialization would not be complete without *Durkheim's discussion of discipline*. It undoubtedly suffers from certain obsolete psychological premises. Nevertheless, it brings out a crucial point often overlooked by pseudo-Freudian educational theories: discipline is indispensable to the equilibrium of the child. What the child loses in random frustrations he gains in the stabilization of the outside environment and of his own motivational system. As Freud might have put it: discipline is an aspect of the pleasure principle. In fact, it removes much of the sting of the immediate frustration by making the latter a preparation for and a guarantee of a future satisfaction. Discipline organizes internalized objects into a meaningful whole. Without discipline, unlimited desires interfere with one another and condemn the personality to the boundless frustration of *anomie*.

1. *The Social Self*

BY CHARLES H. COOLEY

IT IS WELL to say at the outset that by the word "self" in this discussion is meant simply that which is designated in common speech by the pronouns of the first person singular, "I," "me," "my," "mine," and "myself." "Self" and "ego" are used by metaphysicians and moralists in many other senses, more or less remote from the "I" of daily speech and thought, and with these I wish to have as little to do as possible. What is here discussed is what psychologists call the empirical self, the self that can be apprehended or verified by ordinary observation. I qualify it by the word social not as implying the existence of a self that is not social—for I think that the "I" of common language always has more or less distinct reference to other people as well as the speaker—but because I wish to emphasize and dwell upon the social aspect of it.

*   *   *

The distinctive thing in the idea for which the pronouns of the first person are names is apparently

a characteristic kind of feeling which may be called the my-feeling or sense of appropriation. Almost any sort of ideas may be associated with this feeling, and so come to be named "I" or "mine," but the feeling, and that alone it would seem, is the determining factor in the matter. As Professor James says in his admirable discussion of the self, the words "me" and "self" designate "all the things which have the power to produce in a stream of consciousness excitement of a certain peculiar sort." This view is very fully set forth by Professor Hiram M. Stanley, whose work, "The Evolutionary Psychology of Feeling," has an extremely suggestive chapter on self-feeling.

I do not mean that the feeling aspect of the self is necessarily more important than any other, but that it is the immediate and decisive sign and proof of what "I" is; there is no appeal from it; if we go behind it it must be to study its history and conditions, not to question its authority. But, of course, his study of history and conditions may be quite as profitable as the direct contemplation of self-feeling. What I would wish to do is to present each aspect in its proper light.

The emotion or feeling of self may be regarded as instinctive, and was doubtless evolved in con-

Reprinted from *The Two Major Works of Charles H. Cooley: Human Nature and the Social Order & Social Organization* (Glencoe, Ill.: The Free Press, 1956), Part II, pp. 168–70, 171, 179–85, 187–88, 189–92, 193–94, 196–200, 202–7, with the permission of The Free Press.

nection with its important function in stimulating and unifying the special activities of individuals.[1] It is thus very profoundly rooted in the history of the human race and apparently indispensable to any plan of life at all similar to ours. It seems to exist in a vague though vigorous form at the birth of each individual, and, like other instinctive ideas or germs of ideas, to be defined and developed by experience, becoming associated, or rather incorporated, with muscular, visual, and other sensations; with perceptions, apperceptions, and conceptions of every degree of complexity and of infinite variety of content; and, especially, with personal ideas. Meantime the feeling itself does not remain unaltered, but undergoes differentiation and refinement just as does any other sort of crude innate feeling. Thus, while retaining under every phase its characteristic tone or flavor, it breaks up into innumerable self-sentiments. And concrete self-feeling, as it exists in mature persons, is a whole made up of these various sentiments, along with a good deal of primitive emotion not thus broken up. It partakes fully of the general development of the mind, but never loses that peculiar gusto of appropriation that causes us to name a thought with a first-personal pronoun.

* * *

The social self is simply any idea, or system of ideas, drawn from the communicative life, that the mind cherishes as its own. Self-feeling has its chief scope *within* the general life, not outside of it; the special endeavor or tendency of which it is the emotional aspect finds its principal field of exercise in a world of personal forces, reflected in the mind by a world of personal impressions.

As connected with the thought of other persons the self idea is always a consciousness of the peculiar or differentiated aspect of one's life, because that is the aspect that has to be sustained by purpose and endeavor, and its more aggressive forms tend to attach themselves to whatever one finds to be at once congenial to one's own tendencies and at variance with those of others with whom one is in mental contact. It is here that they are most needed to serve their function of stimulating characteristic activity, of fostering those personal variations which the general plan of life seems to require. Heaven, says Shakespeare, doth divide

"The state of man in divers functions, Setting endeavor in continual motion,"

and self-feeling is one of the means by which this diversity is achieved.

Agreeably to this view we find that the aggressive self manifests itself most conspicuously in an appropriativeness of objects of common desire, corresponding to the individual's need of power over such objects to secure his own peculiar development, and to the danger of opposition from others who also need them. And this extends from material objects to lay hold, in the same spirit, of the attentions and affections of other people, of all sorts of plans and ambitions, including the noblest special purposes the mind can entertain, and indeed of any conceivable idea which may come to seem a part of one's life and in need of assertion against some one else. The attempt to limit the word self and its derivatives to the lower aims of personality is quite arbitrary; at variance with common sense as expressed by the emphatic use of "I" in connection with the sense of duty and other high motives, and unphilosophical as ignoring the function of the self as the organ of specialized endeavor of higher as well as lower kinds.

That the "I" of common speech has a meaning which includes some sort of reference to other persons is involved in the very fact that the word and the ideas it stands for are phenomena of language and the communicative life. It is doubtful whether it is possible to use language at all without thinking more or less distinctly of some one else, and certainly the things to which we give names and which have a large place in reflective thought are almost always those which are impressed upon us by our contact with other people. Where there is no communication there can be no nomenclature and no developed thought. What we call "me," "mine," or "myself" is, then, not something separate from the general life, but the most interesting part of it, a part whose interest arises from the very fact that it is both general and individual. That is, we care for it just because it is that phase of the mind that is living and striving in the common life, trying to impress itself upon the minds of others. "I" is a militant social tendency, working to hold and enlarge its place in the general current of tendencies. So far as it can it waxes, as all life does. To think of it as apart from society is a palpable absurdity of which no one could be guilty who really *saw* it as a fact of life.

"Der Mensch erkennt sich nur im Menschen, nur Das Leben lehret jedem was er sei."[2]

If a thing has no relation to others of which one is conscious he is unlikely to think of it at all, and if he does think of it he cannot, it seems to me, re-

---

1. It is, perhaps, to be thought of as a more general instinct, of which anger, etc., are differentiated forms, rather than as standing by itself.

2. "Only in man does man know himself; life alone teaches each one what he is."—Goethe, *Tasso*, act 2, sc. 3.

gard it as emphatically *his*. The appropriative sense is always the shadow, as it were, of the common life, and when we have it we have a sense of the latter in connection with it. Thus, if we think of a secluded part of the woods as "ours," it is because we think, also, that others do not go there. As regards the body I doubt if we have a vivid my-feeling about any part of it which is not thought of, however vaguely, as having some actual or possible reference to some one else. Intense self-consciousness regarding it arises along with instincts or experiences which connect it with the thought of others. Internal organs, like the liver, are not thought of as peculiarly ours unless we are trying to communicate something regarding them, as, for instance, when they are giving us trouble and we are trying to get sympathy.

"I," then, is not all of the mind, but a peculiarly central, vigorous, and well-knit portion of it, not separate from the rest but gradually merging into it, and yet having a certain practical distinctness, so that a man generally shows clearly enough by his language and behavior what his "I" is as distinguished from thoughts he does not appropriate. It may be thought of, as already suggested, under the analogy of a central colored area on a lighted wall. It might also, and perhaps more justly, be compared to the nucleus of a living cell, not altogether separate from the surrounding matter, out of which indeed it is formed, but more active and definitely organized.

The reference to other persons involved in the sense of self may be distinct and particular, as when a boy is ashamed to have his mother catch him at something she has forbidden, or it may be vague and general, as when one is ashamed to do something which only his conscience, expressing his sense of social responsibility, detects and disapproves; but it is always there. There is no sense of "I," as in pride or shame, without its correlative sense of you, or he, or they. Even the miser gloating over his hidden gold can feel the "mine" only as he is aware of the world of men over whom he has secret power; and the case is very similar with all kinds of hid treasure. Many painters, sculptors, and writers have loved to withhold their work from the world, fondling it in seclusion until they were quite done with it; but the delight in this, as in all secrets, depends upon a sense of the value of what is concealed.

*   *   *

In a very large and interesting class of cases the social reference takes the form of a somewhat definite imagination of how one's self—that is any idea he appropriates—appears in a particular mind, and the kind of self-feeling one has is determined by the attitude toward this attributed to that other mind. A social self of this sort might be called the reflected or looking-glass self:

> "Each to each a looking-glass
> Reflects the other that doth pass."

As we see our face, figure, and dress in the glass, and are interested in them because they are ours, and pleased or otherwise with them according as they do or do not answer to what we should like them to be; so in imagination we perceive in another's mind some thought of our appearance, manners, aims, deeds, character, friends, and so on, and are variously affected by it.

A self-idea of this sort seems to have three principal elements: the imagination of our appearance to the other person; the imagination of his judgment of that appearance and some sort of self-feeling, such as pride or mortification. The comparison with a looking-glass hardly suggests the second element, the imagined judgment, which is quite essential. The thing that moves us to pride or shame is not the mere mechanical reflection of ourselves, but an imputed sentiment, the imagined effect of this reflection upon another's mind. This is evident from the fact that the character and weight of that other, in whose mind we see ourselves, makes all the difference with our feeling. We are ashamed to seem evasive in the presence of a straightforward man, cowardly in the presence of a brave one, gross in the eyes of a refined one, and so on. We always imagine, and in imagining share, the judgments of the other mind. A man will boast to one person of an action—say some sharp transaction in trade—which he would be ashamed to own to another.

*   *   *

As suggested in the previous chapter, self-feeling may be regarded as in a sense the antithesis, or better perhaps, the complement, of that disinterested and contemplative love that tends to obliterate the sense of a divergent individuality. Love of this sort has no sense of bounds, but is what we feel when we are expanding and assimilating new and indeterminate experience, while self-feeling accompanies the appropriating, delimiting, and defending of a certain part of experience; the one impels us to receive life, the other to individuate it. The self, from this point of view, might be regarded as a sort of citadel of the mind, fortified without and containing selected treasures within, while love is an undivided share in the rest of the universe. In a healthy mind each contributes to the growth of the other: what we love intensely or for a long time we are likely to bring within the citadel, and to assert as part of ourself. On the other hand, it is only on the basis of a substantial self that a person is capable of progressive sympathy or love.

*   *   *

The view that "self" and the pronouns of the first person are names which the race has learned to apply to an instinctive attitude of mind, and which each child in turn learns to apply in a similar way, was impressed upon me by observing my child M. at the time when she was learning to use these pronouns. When she was two years and two weeks old I was surprised to discover that she had a clear notion of the first and second persons when used possessively. When asked, "Where is your nose?" she would put her hand upon it and say "my." She also understood that when some one else said "my" and touched an object, it meant something opposite to what was meant when she touched the same object and used the same word. Now, any one who will exercise his imagination upon the question how this matter must appear to a mind having no means of knowing anything about "I" and "my" except what it learns by hearing them used, will see that it should be very puzzling. Unlike other words, the personal pronouns have, apparently, no uniform meaning, but convey different and even opposite ideas when employed by different persons. It seems remarkable that children should master the problem before they arrive at considerable power of abstract reasoning. How should a little girl of two, not particularly reflective, have discovered that "my" was not the sign of a definite object like other words, but meant something different with each person who used it? And, still more surprising, how should she have achieved the correct use of it with reference to herself which, it would seem, *could not be copied from any one else,* simply because no one else used it to describe what belonged to her? The meaning of words is learned by associating them with other phenomena. But how is it possible to learn the meaning of one which, as used by others, is never associated with the same phenomenon as when properly used by one's self? Watching her use of the first person, I was at once struck with the fact that she employed it almost wholly in a possessive sense, and that, too, when in an aggressive, self-assertive mood. It was extremely common to see R. tugging at one end of a plaything and M. at the other, screaming, "My, my." "Me" was sometimes nearly equivalent to "my," and was also employed to call attention to herself when she wanted something done for her. Another common use of "my" was to demand something she did not have at all. Thus if R. had something the like of which she wanted, say a cart, she would exclaim, "Where's *my* cart?"

It seemed to me that she might have learned the use of these pronouns about as follows. The self-feeling had always been there. From the first week she had wanted things and cried and fought for them. She had also become familiar by observation and opposition with similar appropriative activities on the part of R. Thus she not only had the feeling herself, but by associating it with its visible expression had probably divined it, sympathized with it, resented it, in others. Grasping, tugging, and screaming would be associated with the feeling in her own case and would recall the feeling when observed in others. They would constitute a language, precedent to the use of first-personal pronouns, to express the self-idea. All was ready, then, for the word to name this experience. She now observed that R., when contentiously appropriating something, frequently exclaimed, "*my*," "*mine*," "give it to *me*," "*I* want it," and the like. Nothing more natural, then, than that she should adopt these words as names for a frequent and vivid experience with which she was already familiar in her own case and had learned to attribute to others. Accordingly it appeared to me, as I recorded in my notes at the time, that " 'my' and 'mine' are simply names for concrete images of appropriativeness," embracing both the appropriative feeling and its manifestation. If this is true the child does not at first work out the I-and-you idea in an abstract form. The first-personal pronoun is a sign of a concrete thing after all, but that thing is not primarily the child's body, or his muscular sensations as such, but the phenomenon of aggressive appropriation, practised by himself, witnessed in others, and incited and interpreted by a hereditary instinct. This seems to get over the difficulty above mentioned, namely, the seeming lack of a common content between the meaning of "my" when used by another and when used by one's self. This common content is found in the appropriative feeling and the visible and audible signs of that feeling. An element of difference and strife comes in, of course, in the opposite actions or purposes which the "my" of another and one's own "my" are likely to stand for. When another person says "mine" regarding something which I claim, I sympathize with him enough to understand what he means, but it is a hostile sympathy, overpowered by another and more vivid "mine" connected with the idea of drawing the object my way.

In other words, the meaning of "I" and "mine" is learned in the same way that the meanings of hope, regret, chagrin, disgust, and thousands of other words of emotion and sentiment are learned: that is, by having the feeling, imputing it to others in connection with some kind of expression, and hearing the word along with it. As to its communication and growth the self-idea is in no way peculiar that I see, but essentially like other ideas. In its more complex forms, such as are expressed by "I" in conversation and literature, it is a social sentiment, or type of sentiments, defined and developed by intercourse, in the manner suggested in a previous chapter.

* * *

I imagine, then, that as a rule the child associates "I" and "me" at first only with those ideas regarding which his appropriative feeling is aroused and defined by opposition. He appropriates his nose, eye, or foot in very much the same way as a plaything—by antithesis to other noses, eyes, and feet, which he cannot control. It is not uncommon to tease little children by proposing to take away one of these organs, and they behave precisely as if the "mine" threatened were a separable object—which it might be for all they know. And, as I have suggested, even in adult life, "I," "me," and "mine" are applied with a strong sense of their meaning only to things distinguished as peculiar to us by some sort of opposition or contrast. They always imply social life and relation to other persons. That which is most distinctively mine is very private, it is true, but it is that part of the private which I am cherishing in antithesis to the rest of the world, not the separate but the special. The aggressive self is essentially a militant phase of the mind, having for its apparent function the energizing of peculiar activities, and, although the militancy may not go on in an obvious, external manner, it always exists as a mental attitude.

* * *

The process by which self-feeling of the looking-glass sort develops in children may be followed without much difficulty. Studying the movements of others as closely as they do they soon see a connection between their own acts and changes in those movements, that is, they perceive their own influence or power over persons. The child appropriates the visible actions of his parent or nurse, over which he finds he has some control, in quite the same way as he appropriates one of his own members or a plaything, and he will try to do things with this new possession, just as he will with his hand or his rattle. A girl six months old will attempt in the most evident and deliberate manner to attract attention to herself, to set going by her actions some of those movements of other persons that she has appropriated. She has tasted the joy of being a cause, of exerting social power, and wishes more of it. She will tug at her mother's skirts, wriggle, gurgle, stretch out her arms, etc., all the time watching for the hoped-for effect. These performances often give the child, even at this age,

an appearance of what is called affectation, that is, she seems to be unduly preoccupied with what other people think of her. Affectation, at any age, exists when the passion to influence others seems to overbalance the established character and give it an obvious twist or pose. It is instructive to find that even Darwin was, in his childhood, capable of departing from truth for the sake of making an impression. "For instance," he says in his autobiography, "I once gathered much valuable fruit from my father's trees and hid it in the shrubbery, and then ran in breathless haste to spread the news that I had discovered a hoard of stolen fruit."[3]

The young performer soon learns to be different things to different people, showing that he begins to apprehend personality and to foresee its operation. If the mother or nurse is more tender than just she will almost certainly be "worked" by systematic weeping. It is a matter of common observation that children often behave worse with their mother than with other and less sympathetic people. Of the new persons that a child sees it is evident that some make a strong impression and awaken a desire to interest and please them, while others are indifferent or repugnant. Sometimes the reason can be perceived or guessed, sometimes not; but the fact of selective interest, admiration, prestige, is obvious before the end of the second year. By that time a child already cares much for the reflection of himself upon one personality and little for that upon another. Moreover, he soon claims intimate and tractable persons as *mine*, classes them among his other possessions, and maintains his ownership against all comers. M., at three years of age, vigorously resented R.'s claim upon their mother. The latter was "*my* mamma," whenever the point was raised.

Strong joy and grief depend upon the treatment this rudimentary social self receives. In the case of M. I noticed as early as the fourth month a "hurt" way of crying which seemed to indicate a sense of personal slight. It was quite different from the cry of pain or that of anger, but seemed about the same as the cry of fright. The slightest tone of reproof would produce it. On the other hand, if people took notice and laughed and encouraged, she was hilarious. At about fifteen months old she had become "a perfect little actress," seeming to live largely in imaginations of her effect upon other people. She constantly and obviously laid traps for attention, and looked abashed or wept at any signs of disapproval or indifference. At times it would seem as if she could not get over these repulses, but would cry long in a grieved way, refusing to

3. Life and Letters of Charles Darwin, by F. Darwin, p. 27.

be comforted. If she hit upon any little trick that made people laugh she would be sure to repeat it, laughing loudly and affectedly in imitation. She had quite a repertory of these small performances, which she would display to a sympathetic audience, or even try upon strangers. I have seen her at sixteen months, when R. refused to give her the scissors, sit down and make-believe cry, putting up her under lip and snuffling, meanwhile looking up now and then to see what effect she was producing.

In such phenomena we have plainly enough, it seems to me, the germ of personal ambition of every sort. Imagination co-operating with instinctive self-feeling has already created a social "I," and this has become a principal object of interest and endeavor.

Progress from this point is chiefly in the way of a greater definiteness, fulness, and inwardness in the imagination of the other's state of mind. A little child thinks of and tries to elicit certain visible or audible phenomena, and does not go back of them; but what a grown-up person desires to produce in others is an internal, invisible condition which his own richer experience enables him to imagine, and of which expression is only the sign. Even adults, however, make no separation between what other people think and the visible expression of that thought. They imagine the whole thing at once, and their idea differs from that of a child chiefly in the comparative richness and complexity of the elements that accompany and interpret the visible or audible sign. There is also a progress from the naïve to the subtle in socially self-assertive action. A child obviously and simply, at first, does things for effect. Later there is an endeavor to suppress the appearance of doing so; affection, indifference, contempt, etc., are simulated to hide the real wish to affect the self-image. It is perceived that an obvious seeking after good opinion is weak and disagreeable.

I doubt whether there are any regular stages in the development of social self-feeling and expression common to the majority of children. The sentiments of self develop by imperceptible gradations out of the crude appropriative instinct of new-born babes, and their manifestations vary indefinitely in different cases. Many children show "self-consciousness" conspicuously from the first half-year; others have little appearance of it at any age. Still others pass through periods of affectation whose length and time of occurrence would probably be found to be exceedingly various. In childhood, as at all times of life, absorption in some idea other than that of the social self tends to drive "self-consciousness" out.

*   *   *

Sex-difference in the development of the social self is apparent from the first. Girls have, as a rule, a more impressible social sensibility; they care more obviously for the social image, study it, reflect upon it more, and so have even during the first year an appearance of subtlety, *finesse,* often of affectation, in which boys are comparatively lacking. Boys are more taken up with muscular activity for its own sake and with construction, their imaginations are occupied somewhat less with persons and more with things. In a girl *das ewig Weibliche,* not easy to describe but quite unmistakable, appears as soon as she begins to take notice of people, and one phase of it is certainly an ego less simple and stable, a stronger impulse to go over to the other person's point of view and to stake joy and grief on the image in his mind. There can be no doubt that women are as a rule more dependent upon immediate personal support and corroboration than are men. The thought of the woman needs to fix itself upon some person in whose mind she can find a stable and compelling image of herself by which to live. If such an image is found, either in a visible or an ideal person, the power of devotion to it becomes a source of strength. But it is a sort of strength dependent upon this personal complement, without which the womanly character is somewhat apt to become a derelict and drifting vessel. Men, being built more for aggression, have, relatively, a greater power of standing alone. But no one can really stand alone, and the appearance of it is due simply to a greater momentum and continuity of character which stores up the past and resists immediate influences. Directly or indirectly the imagination of how we appear to others is a controlling force in all normal minds.

The vague but potent phases of the self associated with the instinct of sex may be regarded, like other phases, as expressive of a need to exert power and as having reference to personal function. The youth, I take it, is bashful precisely because he is conscious of the vague stirring of an aggressive instinct which he does not know how either to effectuate or to ignore. And it is perhaps much the same with the other sex: the bashful are always aggressive at heart; they are conscious of an interest in the other person, of a need to be something to him. And the more developed sexual passion, in both sexes, is very largely an emotion of power, domination, or appropriation. There is no state of feeling that says "mine, mine," more fiercely. The need to be appropriated or dominated which, in women at least, is equally powerful, is of the same nature at bottom, having for its object the attracting to itself of a masterful passion. "The desire of the man is for the woman, but the desire of the woman is for the desire of the man."[4]

Although boys have generally a less impressionable social self than girls, there is great difference among them in this regard. Some of them have a marked tendency to *finesse* and posing, while others have almost none. The latter have a less vivid personal imagination; they are unaffected chiefly, perhaps, because they have no vivid idea of how they seem to others, and so are not moved to seem rather than to be; they are unresentful of slights because they do not feel them, not ashamed or jealous or vain or proud or remorseful, because all these imply imagination of another's mind. I have known children who showed no tendency whatever to lie; in fact, could not understand the nature or object of lying or of any sort of concealment, as in such games as hide-and-coop. This excessively simple way of looking at things may come from unusual absorption in the observation and analysis of the impersonal, as appeared to be the case with R., whose interest in other facts and their relations so much preponderated over his interest in personal attitudes that there was no temptation to sacrifice the former to the latter. A child of this sort gives the impression of being non-moral; he neither sins nor repents, and has not the knowledge of good and evil. We eat of the tree of this knowledge when we begin to imagine the minds of others, and so become aware of that conflict of personal impulses which conscience aims to allay.

Simplicity is a pleasant thing in children, or at any age, but it is not necessarily admirable, nor is affectation altogether a thing of evil. To be normal, to be at home in the world, with a prospect of power, usefulness, or success, the person must have that imaginative insight into other minds that underlies tact and *savoir-faire,* morality and beneficence. This insight involves sophistication, some understanding and sharing of the clandestine impulses of human nature. A simplicity that is merely the lack of this insight indicates a sort of defeat. There is, however, another kind of simplicity, belonging to a character that is subtle and sensitive, but has sufficient force and mental clearness to keep in strict order the many impulses to which it is open, and so preserve its directness and unity. One may be simple like Simple Simon, or in the sense that Emerson meant when he said, "To be simple is to be great." Affectation, vanity, and the like, indicate the lack of proper assimilation of the influences arising from our sense of what others think of us. Instead of these influences working

4. Attributed to Mme. de Staël.

upon the individual gradually and without disturbing his equilibrium, they overbear him so that he appears to be not himself, posing, out of function, and hence silly, weak, contemptible. The affected smile, the "foolish face of praise" is a type of all affectation, an external, put-on thing, a weak and fatuous petition for approval. Whenever one is growing rapidly, learning eagerly, preoccupied with strange ideals, he is in danger of this loss of equilibrium; and so we notice it in sensitive children, especially girls, in young people between fourteen and twenty, and at all ages in persons of unstable individuality.

This disturbance of our equilibrium by the outgoing of the imagination toward another person's point of view means that we are undergoing his influence. In the presence of one whom we feel to be of importance there is a tendency to enter into and adopt, by sympathy, his judgment of ourself, to put a new value on ideas and purposes, to recast life in his image. With a very sensitive person this tendency is often evident to others in ordinary conversation and in trivial matters. By force of an impulse springing directly from the delicacy of his perceptions he is continually imagining how he appears to his interlocutor, and accepting the image, for the moment, as himself. If the other appears to think him well-informed on some recondite matter, he is likely to assume a learned expression; if thought judicious he looks as if he were, if accused of dishonesty he appears guilty, and so on. In short, a sensitive man, in the presence of an impressive personality, tends to become, for the time, his interpretation of what the other thinks he is. It is only the heavy-minded who will not feel this to be true, in some degree, of themselves. Of course it is usually a temporary and somewhat superficial phenomenon; but it is typical of all ascendancy, and helps us to understand how persons have power over us through some hold upon our imaginations, and how our personality grows and takes form by divining the appearance of our present self to other minds.

So long as a character is open and capable of growth it retains a corresponding impressibility, which is not weakness unless it swamps the assimilating and organizing faculty. I know men whose careers are a proof of stable and aggressive character who have an almost feminine sensitiveness regarding their seeming to others. Indeed, if one sees a man whose attitude toward others is always assertive, never receptive, he may be confident that man will never go far, because he will never learn much. In character, as in every phase of life, health requires a just union of stability with plasticity.

2. *Internalized Others and the Self*

BY GEORGE H. MEAD

The Background of the Genesis of the Self

THE PROBLEM now presents itself as to how, in detail, a self arises. We have to note something of the background of its genesis. First of all there is the conversation of gestures between animals involving some sort of co-operative activity. There the beginning of the act of one is a stimulus to the other to respond in a certain way, while the beginning of this response becomes again a stimulus to the first to adjust his action to the oncoming response. Such is the preparation for the completed act, and ultimately it leads up to the conduct which is the outcome of this preparation. The conversation of gestures, however, does not carry with it the reference of the individual, the animal, the organism, to itself. It is not acting in a fashion which calls for a response from the form itself, although it is conduct with reference to the conduct of others. We have seen, however, that there are certain gestures that do affect the organism as they affect other organisms and may, therefore, arouse in the organism responses of the same character as aroused in the other. Here, then, we have a situation in which the individual may at least arouse responses in himself and reply to these responses, the condition being that the social stimuli have an effect on the individual which is like that which they have on the other. That, for example, is what is implied in language; otherwise language as significant symbol would disappear, since the individual would not get the meaning of that which he says.

*   *   *

Another set of background factors in the genesis of the self is represented in the activities of play and the game.

Among primitive people, as I have said, the necessity of distinguishing the self and the organism was recognized in what we term the "double": the individual has a thing-like self that is affected by the individual as it affects other people and which is distinguished from the immediate organism in that it can leave the body and come back to it. This is the basis for the concept of the soul as a separate entity.

We find in children something that answers to this double, namely, the invisible, imaginary companions which a good many children produce in their own experience. They organize in this way the responses which they call out in other persons and call out also in themselves. Of course, this playing with an imaginary companion is only a peculiarly interesting phase of ordinary play. Play in this sense, especially the stage which precedes the organized games, is a play at something. A child plays at being a mother, at being a teacher, at being a policeman; that is, it is taking different rôles, as we say. We have something that suggests this in what we call the play of animals: a cat will play with her kittens, and dogs play with each other. Two dogs playing with each other will attack and defend, in a process which if carried through would amount to an actual fight. There is a combination of responses which checks the depth of the bite. But we do not have in such a situation the dogs taking a definite rôle in the sense that a child deliberately takes the rôle of another. This tendency on the part of the children is what we are working with in the kindergarten where the rôles which the children assume are made the basis for training. When a child does assume a rôle he has in himself the stimuli which call out that particular response or group of responses. He may, of course, run away when he is chased, as the dog does, or he may turn around and strike back just as the dog does in his play. But that is not the same as playing at something. Children get together to "play Indian." This means that the child has a certain set of stimuli which call out in itself the responses that they would call out in others, and which answer to an Indian. In the play period the child utilizes his own responses to these stimuli which he makes use of in building a self. The response which he has a tendency to make to these stimuli organizes them. He plays that he is, for instance, offering himself something, and he buys it; he gives a letter to himself and takes it away; he addresses himself as a parent, as a teacher; he arrests himself as a policeman. He has a set of stimuli which call out in himself the sort of responses they call out in others. He takes this group of responses and organizes them into a certain whole. Such is the simplest form of

Reprinted from George H. Mead, *Mind, Self and Society,* ed. Charles Morris (Chicago: University of Chicago Press, 1934), pp. 144–45, 149–52, with the permission of the University of Chicago Press. Copyright 1934 by the University of Chicago.

being another to one's self. It involves a temporal situation. The child says something in one character and responds in another character, and then his responding in another character is a stimulus to himself in the first character, and so the conversation goes on. A certain organized structure arises in him and in his other which replies to it, and these carry on the conversation of gestures between themselves.

If we contrast play with the situation in an organized game, we note the essential difference that the child who plays in a game must be ready to take the attitude of everyone else involved in that game, and that these different rôles must have a definite relationship to each other. Taking a very simple game such as hide-and-seek, everyone with the exception of the one who is hiding is a person who is hunting. A child does not require more than the person who is hunted and the one who is hunting. If a child is playing in the first sense he just goes on playing, but there is no basic organization gained. In that early stage he passes from one rôle to another just as a whim takes him. But in a game where a number of individuals are involved, then the child taking one rôle must be ready to take the rôle of everyone else. If he gets in a ball nine he must have the responses of each position involved in his own position. He must know what everyone else is going to do in order to carry out his own play. He has to take all of these rôles. They do not all have to be present in consciousness at the same time, but at some moments he has to have three or four individuals present in his own attitude, such as the one who is going to throw the ball,

the one who is going to catch it, and so on. These responses must be, in some degree, present in his own make-up. In the game, then, there is a set of responses of such others so organized that the attitude of one calls out the appropriate attitudes of the other.

This organization is put in the form of the rules of the game. Children take a great interest in rules. They make rules on the spot in order to help themselves out of difficulties. Part of the enjoyment of the game is to get these rules. Now, the rules are the set of responses which a particular attitude calls out. You can demand a certain response in others if you take a certain attitude. These responses are all in yourself as well. There you get an organized set of such responses as that to which I have referred, which is something more elaborate than the rôles found in play. Here there is just a set of responses that follow on each other indefinitely. At such a stage we speak of a child as not yet having a fully developed self. The child responds in a fairly intelligent fashion to the immediate stimuli that come to him, but they are not organized. He does not organize his life as we would like to have him do, namely, as a whole. There is just a set of responses of the type of play. The child reacts to a certain stimulus, and the reaction is in himself that is called out in others, but he is not a whole self. In his game he has to have an organization of these rôles; otherwise he cannot play the game. The game represents the passage in the life of the child from taking the rôle of others in play to the organized part that is essential to self-consciousness in the full sense of the term.

3. *On Intellectual Growth*

BY JEAN PIAGET

EGO-CENTRISM must not be confused with secrecy. Reflexion in the child does not admit of privacy. Apart from thinking by images or autistic symbols which cannot be directly communicated, the child up to an age, as yet undetermined

Reprinted from Jean Piaget, *The Language and Thought of the Child* (New York: Harcourt, Brace & Co., 1926), pp. 38–42, 231–38, with permission of Harcourt, Brace & Co.

but probably somewhere about seven, is incapable of keeping to himself the thoughts which enter his mind. He says everything. He has no verbal continence. Does this mean that he socializes his thought more than we do? That is the whole question, and it is for us to see to whom the child really speaks. It may be to others. We think on the contrary that, as the preceding study shows, it is first and foremost to himself, and that speech, before it can be used to socialize thought, serves to accompany and reinforce individual activity. Let us try to examine more closely the difference between thought which is socialized but capable of secrecy, and infantile thought which is ego-centric but incapable of secrecy.

The adult, even in his most personal and private occupation, even when he is engaged on an enquiry which is incomprehensible to his fellow-beings, thinks socially, has continually in his mind's eye his collaborators or opponents, actual or eventual, at any rate members of his own profession to whom sooner or later he will announce the result of his labours. This mental picture pursues him throughout his task. The task itself is henceforth socialized at almost every stage of its development. Invention eludes this process, but the need for checking and demonstrating calls into being an inner speech addressed throughout to a hypothetical opponent, whom the imagination often pictures as one of flesh and blood. When, therefore, the adult is brought face to face with his fellow-beings, what he announces to them is something already socially elaborated and therefore roughly adapted to his audience, i.e., it is comprehensible. Indeed, the further a man has advanced in his own line of thought, the better able is he to see things from the point of view of others and to make himself understood by them.

The child, on the other hand, placed in the conditions which we have described, seems to talk far more than the adult. Almost everything he does is to the tune of remarks such as "I'm drawing a hat," "I'm doing it better than you," etc. Child thought, therefore, seems more social, less capable of sustained and solitary research. This is so only in appearance. The child has less verbal continence simply because he does not know what it is to keep a thing to himself. Although he talks almost incessantly to his neighbours, he rarely places himself at their point of view. He speaks to them for the most part as if he were alone, and as if he were thinking aloud. He speaks, therefore, in a language which disregards the precise shade of meaning in things and ignores the particular angle from which they are viewed, and which above all is always making assertions, even in argument, instead of justifying them. Nothing could be harder to understand than the note-books which we have filled with the conversation of Pie and Lev. Without full commentaries, taken down at the same time as the children's remarks, they would be incomprehensible. Everything is indicated by allusion, by pronouns and demonstrative articles—"he, she, the, mine, him, etc."—which can mean anything in turn, regardless of the demands of clarity or even of intel-

ligibility. . . . In a word, the child hardly ever even asks himself whether he has been understood. For him, that goes without saying, for he does not think about others when he talks. He utters a "collective monologue." His language only begins to resemble that of adults when he is directly interested in making himself understood; when he gives orders or asks questions. To put it quite simply, we may say that the adult thinks socially, even when he is alone, and that the child under 7 thinks ego-centrically, even in the society of others.

What is the reason for this? It is, in our opinion, twofold. It is due, in the first place, to the absence of any sustained social intercourse between the children of less than 7 or 8, and in the second place to the fact that the laguage used in the fundamental activity of the child—play—is one of gestures, movement and mimicry as much as of words. There is, as we have said, no real social life between children of less than 7 or 8 years. The type of children's society represented in a class-room of the *Maison des Petits* is obviously of a fragmentary character, in which consequently there is neither division of work, centralization of effort, nor unity of conversation. We may go further, and say that it is a society in which, strictly speaking, individual and social life are not differentiated. An adult is at once far more highly individualized and far more highly socialized than a child forming part of such a society. He is more individualized, since he can work in private without perpetually announcing what he is doing, and without imitating his neighbours. He is more socialized for the reasons which have just given. The child is neither individualized, since he cannot keep a single thought secret, and since everything done by one member of the group is repeated through a sort of imitative repercussion by almost every other member, nor is he socialized, since this imitation is not accompanied by what may properly be called an interchange of thought, about half the remarks made by children being ego-centric in character. If, as Baldwin and Janet maintain, imitation is accompanied by a sort of confusion between one's own action and that of others, then we may find in this fragmentary type of society based on imitation some sort of explanation of the paradoxical character of the conversation of children who, while they are continually announcing their doings, yet talk only for themselves, without listening to anyone else.

Social life at the *Maison des Petits* passes, according to the observations of Mlles Audemars and Lafendel, through three stages. Up till the age of about 5, the child almost always works alone. From 5 to about 7½, little groups of two are formed, like that of Pie and Ez (cf. the remarks taken down under the heading "adapted information.") These groups are transitory and irregular. Finally, between 7 and 8 the desire manifests itself to work with others. Now it is in our opinion just at this age that ego-centric talk loses some of its importance, and it is at this age, as we shall see in the next chapter, that we shall place the higher stages of conversation properly so-called as it takes place between children. It is also at this age, (cf. Chapter III) that children begin to understand each other in spoken explanations, as opposed to explanations in which gestures play as important a part as words.

*   *   *

In what circumstances do the first "whys" appear? Approximately at the same age as the three following fundamental phenomena: 1° The formation of two distinct planes of reality. Up till the age of 3, the real may be said to be simply what is desired. There is, indeed, after 1;9 or 2 a yes and a no, a real and an unreal, but without any further shade of difference. At about 3, on the other hand, the imagined is something distinct from the real. According to Stern, this is the age when we first meet with such words as "perhaps," etc., which are precisely those which mark a divergence between the imagined and the real. Again, to quote Stern, there appear at the same date such verbs as "to think," "to believe," etc. As we take it, the advent of these words, whatever may be said to the contrary, in no way indicates a distinction between the psychical and the physical, or between thought and thing, but a distinction between what is imagined and what is perceived. 2° It is at about the same period (2;9 and 3;10) that Scupin detected the earliest lies, or, as P. Janet has so excellently described them, "beliefs about the future" as opposed to beliefs about the present. 3° Finally, it is also at about the age of three that grammatical accident makes its first appearance. Cases and tenses of a certain complexity, the simpler forms of subordinate prepositions—in a word, the whole necessary apparatus for the beginnings of formulated reasoning begins to be incorporated into the language of the subject. Now the function of this reasoning is to construct, over and above the immediate world of sensation, a reality supposedly deeper than the merely given world. And all these transformations have this fundamental trait in common, that they indicate an act of conscious realization. From now onwards the child distinguishes between the real as it appears immediately to his senses, and something which precedes events and underlies all phenomena. Let us describe this something by the very comprehensive term—intention. The intentions of

people and of things sometimes conform to the wishes of the child, sometimes they do not; hence the distinction between the imagined or desired and the real. Hence, also, the resistance put up by reality which necessitates lying. Intentions can sometimes be detected at once, and fit in spontaneously with the events; at other times they cannot, whence the necessity of reconstructing them, of supposing their presence behind things, in a word, or reasoning instead of simply looking on.

These changes, contemporaneous with the earliest "whys," are not altogether unrelated to this type of question. Up till this age, reality coincided almost entirely with desire, and existed on a single plane, so to speak, without the child having ever become clearly conscious of intentions contrary to its own, or definitely independent of them. The questions asked relate simply to the names of objects and to the place which they occupied after they have disappeared. Roughly speaking, the child takes cognizance at about three years old of the resistance set up by things and people; discord arises between desire and its realization. For a mentality that has not yet learnt to distinguish between thought and things, between animate and inanimate, between ego and non-ego, this discord can only be conceived as an intentional resistance on the part of the people and things. The real, henceforth, becomes crowded with intentions ascribed first to other people, then to things, whether these things are thought of as autonomous or dependent upon persons. Thus the whole world becomes peopled in various degrees—not, it is true, with personified spirits, because at this age the child is still unconscious of its own personal unity, and does not think of ascribing intentions to definite 'I's'—but with intentions that are impersonal, so to speak, or at any rate improperly localized and multiform. Hence the earliest "whys," "why" being the specific question for seeking the intention hidden behind an action or an event.

The earliest "whys" are generally asked in connexion with human actions. The first "why" noted by Scupin in the case of "Bubi" is of this order. The child's mother was lying on the ground. The boy wants to get her up: "Du bis ya nicht tot warum stehste nicht immersu auf?" The second one appears when the child is forbidden to pull the petals off flowers. "Warum denn?" But even where children begin with a "why of explanation," it is difficult not to see in the expected explanation not only a precausal explanation, but one in which precausality is almost entirely confused with psychological or intentional causality. "Why do trees have leaves?"

It is these intentions ascribed to people and to things which will give rise to the types of question corresponding to the principal categories of child thought. These categories will therefore have an intentionalistic origin, *i.e.*, they will arise from the conscious realization of psychological operations relative to intentions, and not from a mere observation of the world given in perception. Moreover, the earlier categories of name and place, etc., will join themselves to these categories of intention, and together with them will form a single whole.

This intentionalism gives rise to two fundamental categories or primitive functions of thought: the *explicatory function* and the *implicatory function*. These do not represent two separate departments of the mind, but describe two moments which are present in all mental activity. The explicatory function is the centrifugal moment, in which the mind turns to the external world; the implicatory function is the centripetal, in which the mind turns inwards to the analysis of intentions and of their relations.

The explicatory functions arise out of the need felt by the child, as soon as he becomes conscious of intentions, to project these into the world around him. On the one hand, he finds himself surrounded by people whose actions can be foreseen and whose motives can be detected; on the other hand, he is faced by a world of phenomena and events which up till now have never resisted his thought and therefore required no explanation, but which have now become as great obstacles to his fantasy as are people themselves. This duality has to be abolished; since there is a "why" to human actions, the same treatment must be applied to everything which presents itself. Hence this universal desire for precausal explanation which comes from confusing psychological intentionalism with physical causality. Thus the explicatory function has two poles—psychological explanation and material explanation. These two poles are close together at first and not easily distinguishable, but as time goes on they grow more and more distinct, though always held together by the fact that both are rooted in one and the same desire for explanation.

Owing to the fact, moreover, that the idea of intention first appears through the resistance of reality, and in particular through the resistance of persons, everything seems to the child to obey some sort of necessity which is both moral and physical. Everything seems to him to be as it should be. So that the child's tendency will be, not only to project intentions into every object so as to explain events, but also to seek to account for everything, to justify every event, and to look for the connexions existing between intentions. Hence

the implicatory function. The explicatory function was centrifugal in this sense, that from the intention it sought to draw out the material consequence, the resultant act or event. The direction of the implicatory function is, on the contrary, centripetal, in the sense that from the intention, the mind seeks to trace its way back to the directing motive or idea. The explicatory function tends towards things, the implicatory function tends towards ideas or judgments. And the child mind, being at its origin equally removed from things and from thought, occupies an intermediate position between the two.

Thus the implicatory function also has two poles. First a psychological pole which it shares with the explicatory function and which causes the child to ask: "Why do people do so? etc." The "whys of justification" which we collected from Del are naturally of a much later date than these primitive questions, although they constitute a special case of the "whys" concerning what ought to be. The other pole is made up of questions about names, definitions, the reason for judgments, in a word, about everything concerning logical justification. Just as between psychological and physical explanation there are innumerable transitional cases, so also between the implication of psychological actions (justification) and the implication of names, classes and later on of numbers, there is every type of intermediate example. Thus the pole which is common to both functions, *i.e.*, the psychological pole (psychological justification and explanation) serves both as a starting point and as a point of divergence for the two functions, explicatory and implicatory, which are at first confused and then grow more and more distinct. We shall call mixed, that function of psychological justification and explanation which partakes of the nature of explication and implication.

This schema may be thought to apply only to "whys," but it is obvious that other types of question, even of earlier date, such as those of place ("where is . . . ?" etc.) and of name ("who is . . . ?") are more or less incorporated in it. As the explicatory function develops, questions of place come more and more to resemble the great group of questions of reality and history, to which the desire for explanation gives its chief impetus. Questions about names are originally independent, and belong as such neither to the desire for explanation nor to that for justification or implication; but their function is modified concomitantly with the development of the implicatory function. The child finds that names which originally were bound up in his mind with the object can be subjected to an increasingly logical justification (childish etymologies). This in itself tightens the bond between questions of names and the implicatory function. The same thing happens to questions of classification and definition, definitions being at first, as is well known, purely utilitarian, and then becoming increasingly logical.

The main categories of child thought between the years of 3 and 7–8 are therefore represented by the following table:

Explicatory function $\begin{cases} \text{Causality.} \\ \text{Reality, time and place.} \end{cases}$

Mixed function . . . $\begin{cases} \text{Motivation of actions.} \\ \text{Justification of rules.} \end{cases}$

Implicatory function $\begin{cases} \text{Classification. Names.} \\ \text{Number. Logical relations.} \end{cases}$

To bring this chapter to an end, we must now try very briefly to connect the results we have obtained with the factors established in the earlier chapters, and particularly with the ego-centrism of child thought.

In this chapter special stress has been laid on the importance of precausality and consequently of intellectual realism; in other words, we have emphasized the paradoxical fact that child thought is equally removed from dealing with strictly causal explanation as it is from dealing with logical justification properly so called. The whole mechanism of children's questions, as we have studied it, can be accounted for by this fundamental fact.

What relation could there be between this fact and the ego-centrism of child thought? A fairly close one of mutual dependence, since precausality tends to disappear at the same age as ego-centrism, viz., between 7 and 8. For in every strictly causal explanation there is an effort to adapt oneself to the external world, an effort to objectify, and, one might almost say, to depersonalize one's thought. Without this effort, the mind tends to project intentions into everything, or connect everything together by means of relations not based on observations, as is apparent from the childish habit of justifying everything and of conceiving nothing as fortuitous. Now ego-centrism certainly hinders this effort towards the adaptation and depersonalization

of thought. It interferes with it directly, in the first place, because the more the ego is made the centre of interests, the less will the mind be able to depersonalize its thought, and to get rid of the idea that in all things are intentions either favourable or hostile (animism, artificialism, etc.). But ego-centrism is also an indirect hindrance, for in so far as he is ego-centric, the child will not trouble to pit his own ideas against those of others, and thus prove what he has come to believe. He will therefore give way to the primitive impulse of all thought, *i.e.*, he will substitute for things as they are, a fragmentary world of his own making in which everything has an aim, and in which everything can be justified. But there is also in the logical habit an effort towards internal coherence and direction of thought, which is not spontaneously given to the primitive mind, but is a gradual conquest of reason. Here again, ego-centrism is a real obstacle to the acquisition of this desire for implication or logical systematization. It is a direct obstacle, because all ego-centrism is designed by its structure to stand half-way between autistic thought which is "undirected," *i.e.*, which as in day-dreaming hovers about at the mercy of every whim, and "directed" intelligence. Ego-centrism is therefore obedient to the self's good pleasure and not to the dictates of impersonal logic. It is also an indirect obstacle, because only the habits of discussion and social life will lead to the logical point of view, and ego-centrism is precisely what renders these habits impossible.

We can now see that ego-centrism, while it does not exactly explain the child's incapacity for true causal explanation and logical justification, is nevertheless closely connected with it. And we can understand how, as a result of this, the child mind is always hovering between these convergent paths, and is also equally removed from both. This it is that gives rise to the phenomena of precausality and intellectual position. And this it is also that gives rise to that tendency in children to justify things at any price, or to connect everything with everything else, which we have dealt with at length in the course of this last chapter.

4. *Moral Realism*

BY JEAN PIAGET

THIS CONCORDANCE of our results with those of historico-critical or logico-sociological analysis brings us to a second point: the parallelism existing between moral and intellectual development. Everyone is aware of the kinship between logical and ethical norms. Logic is the morality of thought just as morality is the logic of action. Nearly all contemporary theories agree in recognizing the existence of this parallelism—from the *a priori* view which regards pure reason as the arbiter both of theoretical reflection and daily practice, to the sociological theories of knowledge and of ethical values. It is therefore in no way surprising that the analysis of child thought should bring to the fore certain particular aspects of this general phenomenon.

One may say, to begin with, that in a certain sense neither logical nor moral norms are innate in the individual mind. We can find, no doubt, even before language, all the elements of rationality and morality. Thus sensori-motor intelligence gives rise to operations of assimilation and construction, in which it is not hard to see the functional equivalent of the logic of classes and of relations. Similarly the child's behaviour towards persons shows signs from the first of those sympathetic tendencies and affective reactions in which one can easily see the raw material of all subsequent moral behaviour. But an intelligent act can only be called logical and a good-hearted impulse moral from the moment that certain norms impress a given structure and rules of equilibrium upon this material. Logic is not co-extensive with intelligence, but consists of the sum-total of rules of control which intelligence makes use of for its own direction. Morality plays a similar part with regard to the affective life. Now there is nothing that allows us to affirm the existence of such norms in the pre-social behaviour occurring before the appearance of language. The control characteristic of sensori-motor intelligence is of external origin: it is things themselves that constrain the organism to select which steps it will take; the initial intellectual activity does actively seek for truth. Similarly, it is persons external to him who canalize the child's

elementary feelings, those feelings do not tend to regulate themselves from within.

This does not mean that everything in the *a priori* view is to be rejected. Of course the *a priori* never manifests itself in the form of a ready-made innate mechanisms. The *a priori* is the obligatory element, and the necessary connections only impose themselves little by little, as evolution proceeds. It is at the end of knowledge and not in its beginnings that the mind becomes conscious of the laws immanent to it. Yet to speak of directed evolution and asymptotic advance towards a necessary ideal is to recognize the existence of a something which acts from the first in the direction of this evolution. But under what form does this "something" present itself? Under the form of a structure that straightway organizes the contents of consciousness, or under the form of a functional law of equilibrium, unconscious as yet because the mind has not yet achieved this equilibrium, and to be manifested only in and through the multitudinous structures that are to appear later? There seems to us to be no doubt about the answer. There is in the very functioning of sensori-motor operations a search for coherence and organization. Alongside, therefore, of the incoherence that characterizes the successive steps taken by elementary intelligence we must admit the existence of an ideal equilibrium, indefinable as structure but implied in the functioning that is at work. Such is the *a priori*: it is neither a principle from which concrete actions can be deduced nor a structure of which the mind can become conscious as such, but it is a sum-total of functional relations implying the distinction between the existing states of disequilibrium and an ideal equilibrium yet to be realized.

How then will the mind extract norms in the true sense from this functional equilibrium? It will form structures by means of an adequate conscious realization (*prise de conscience*). To ensure that the functional search for organization exhibited by the initial sensori-motor and affective activity give rise to rules of organization properly so called, it is sufficient that the mind should become conscious of this search and of the laws governing it, thus translating into structure what till then had been function and nothing more.

Reprinted from Jean Piaget, *The Moral Judgment of the Child* (Glencoe, Ill.: The Free Press, 1948), pp. 404–11, with the permission of The Free Press.

But this coming into consciousness or conscious realization is not a simple operation and is bound up with a whole set of psychological conditions. It is here that psycho-sociological research becomes indispensable to the theory of norms and that the genetic parallelism existing between the formation of the logical and of the moral consciousness can be observed.

In the first place it should be noticed that the individual is not capable of achieving this conscious realization by himself, and consequently does not straight away succeed in establishing norms properly so-called. It is in this sense that reason in its double aspect, both logical and moral, is a collective product. This does not mean that society has conjured up rationality out of the void, nor that there does not exist a spirit of humanity that is superior to society because dwelling both within the individual and the social group. It means that social life is necessary if the individual is to become conscious of the functioning of his own mind and thus to transform into norms properly so called the simple functional equilibria immanent to all mental and even all vital activity.

For the individual, left to himself, remains egocentric. By which we mean simply this—Just as at first the mind, before it can dissociate what belongs to objective laws from what is bound up with the sum of subjective conditions, confuses itself with the universe, so does the individual begin by understanding and feeling everything through the medium of himself before distinguishing what belongs to things and other people from what is the result of his own particular intellectual and affective perspective. At this stage, therefore, the individual cannot be conscious of his own thought, since consciousness of self implies a perpetual comparison of the self with other people. Thus from the logical point of view egocentrism would seem to involve a sort of alogicality, such that sometimes affectivity gains the ascendant over objectivity, and sometimes the relations arising from personal activity prove stronger than the relations that are independent of the self. And from the moral point of view, egocentrism involves a sort of anomy such that tenderness and disinterestedness can go hand in hand with a naïve selfishness, and yet the child not feel spontaneously himself to be better in one case than the other. Just as the ideas which enter his mind appear from the first in the form of beliefs and not of hypotheses requiring verification, so do the feelings that arise in the child's consciousness appear to him from the first as having value and not as having to be submitted to some ulterior evaluation. It is only through contact with the judgments and evaluations of others that this in-

tellectual and affective anomy will gradually yield to the pressure of collective logical and moral laws.

In the second place, the relations of constraint and unilateral respect which are spontaneously established between child and adult contribute to the formation of a first type of logical and moral control. But this control is insufficient of itself to eliminate childish egocentrism. From the intellectual point of view this respect of the child for the adult gives rise to an "annunciatory" conception of truth: the mind stops affirming what it likes to affirm and falls in with the opinion of those around it. This gives birth to a distinction which is equivalent to that of truth and falsehood: some affirmations are recognized as valid while others are not. But it goes without saying that although this distinction marks an important advance as compared to the anomy of egocentric thought, it is none the less irrational in principle. For if we are to speak of truth as rational, it is not sufficient that the contents of one's statements should conform with reality: reason must have taken active steps to obtain these contents and reason must be in a position to control the agreement or disagreement of these statements with reality. Now, in the case under discussion, reason is still very far removed from this autonomy: truth means whatever conforms with the spoken word of the adult. Whether the child has himself discovered the propositions which he asks the adult to sanction with his authority, or whether he merely repeats what the adult has said, in both cases there is intellectual constraint put upon an inferior by a superior, and therefore heteronomy. Thus, far from checking childish egocentrism at its source, such a submission tends on the contrary partly to consolidate the mental habits characteristic of egocentrism. Just as, if left to himself, the child believes every idea that enters his head instead of regarding it as a hypothesis to be verified, so the child who is submissive to the word of his parents believes without question everything he is told, instead of perceiving the element of uncertainty and search in adult thought. The self's good pleasure is simply replaced by the good pleasure of a supreme authority. There is progress here, no doubt, since such a transference accustoms the mind to look for a common truth, but this progress is big with danger if the supreme authority be not in its turn criticized in the name of reason. Now, criticism is born of discussion, and discussion is only possible among equals: cooperation alone will therefore accomplish what intellectual constraint failed to bring about. And indeed we constantly have occasion throughout our schools to notice the combined effects of this constraint and of intellectual egocentrism. What is "verbalism," for example, if not the joint result of oral authority and the syncretism peculiar to the egocentric language of the child? In short, in order to really socialize the child, cooperation is necessary, for it alone will succeed in delivering him from the mystical power of the word of the adult.

An exact counterpart of these findings about intellectual constraint is supplied by the observations on the effect of moral constraint contained in the present book. Just as the child believes in the adult's omniscience so also does he unquestioningly believe in the absolute value of the imperatives he receives. This result of unilateral respect is of great practical value, for it is in this way that there is formed an elementary sense of duty and the first normative control of which the child is capable. But it seemed to us clear that this acquisition was not sufficient to form true morality. For conduct to be characterized as moral there must be something more than an outward agreement between its content and that of the commonly accepted rules: it is also requisite that the mind should tend towards morality as to an autonomous good and should itself be capable of appreciating the value of the rules that are proposed to it. Now in the case under discussion, the good is simply what is in conformity with heteronomous commands. And as in the case of intellectual development, moral constraint has the effect of partly consolidating the habits characteristic of egocentrism. Even when the child's behaviour is not just a calculated attempt to reconcile his individual interest with the letter of the law, one can observe (as we had occasion to do in the game of marbles) a curious mixture of respect for the law and of caprice in its application. The law is still external to the mind, which cannot therefore be transformed by it. Besides, since he regards the adult as the source of the law, the child is only raising up the will of the adult to the rank of the supreme good after having previously accorded this rank to the various dictates of his own desires. An advance, no doubt, but again an advance charged with doubtful consequences if cooperation does not come and establish norms sufficiently independent to subject even the respect due to the adult to this inner ideal. And indeed so long as unilateral respect is alone at work, we see a "moral realism" developing which is the equivalent of "verbal realism." Resting in part on the externality of rules, such a realism is also kept going by all the other forms of realism peculiar to the egocentric mentality of the child. Only cooperation will correct this attitude, thus showing that in the moral sphere, as in matters of intelligence, it plays a liberating and a constructive role.

Hence a third analogy between moral and intellectual evolution: cooperation alone leads to autonomy. With regard to logic, cooperation is at first a source of criticism; thanks to the mutual control which it introduces, it suppresses both the spontaneous conviction that characterizes egocentrism and the blind faith in adult authority. Thus, discussion gives rise to reflection and objective verification. But through this very fact cooperation becomes the source of constructive values. It leads to the recognition of the principles of formal logic in so far as these normative laws are necessary to common search for truth. It leads, above all, to a conscious realization of the logic of relations, since reciprocity on the intellectual plane necessarily involves the elaboration of those laws of perspective which we find in the operations distinctive of systems of relations.

In the same way, with regard to moral realities, cooperation is at first the source of criticism and individualism. For by comparing his own private motives with the rules adopted by each and sundry, the individual is led to judge objectively the acts and commands of other people, including adults. Whence the decline of unilateral respect and the primacy of personal judgment. But in consequence of this, cooperation suppresses both egocentrism and moral realism, and thus achieves an interiorization of rules. A new morality follows upon that of pure duty. Heteronomy steps aside to make way for a consciousness of good, of which the autonomy results from the acceptance of the norms of reciprocity. Obedience withdraws in favour of the idea of justice and of mutual service, now the source of all the obligations which till then had been imposed as incomprehensible commands. In a word, cooperation on the moral plane brings about transformations exactly parallel to those of which we have just been recalling the existence in the intellectual domain.

5. On Object-Relations and Psycho-Sexual Stages

BY SIGMUND FREUD

THE PERIOD OF SEXUAL LATENCY IN CHILDHOOD AND ITS INTERRUPTIONS

THE remarkably frequent reports of what are described as irregular and exceptional sexual impulses in childhood, as well as the uncovering in neurotics of what have hitherto been unconscious memories of childhood, allow us to sketch out the sexual occurrences of that period in some such way as this.[1]

There seems no doubt that germs of sexual impulses are already present in the new-born child and that these continue to develop for a time, but are then overtaken by a progressive process of suppression; this in turn is itself interrupted by periodical advances in sexual development or may be held up by individual peculiarities. Nothing is known for certain concerning the regularity and periodicity of this oscillating course of development. It seems, however, that the sexual life of children usually emerges in a form accessible to observation round about the third or fourth year of life.

Sexual Inhibitions.—It is during this period of total or only partial latency that are built up the mental forces which are later to impede the course of the sexual instinct and, like dams, restrict its flow—disgust, feelings of shame and the claims of aesthetic and moral ideals. One gets an impression from civilized children that the construction of these dams is a product of education, and no doubt education has much to do with it. But in reality this development is organically determined and fixed by heredity, and it can occasionally occur without any help at all from education. Education will not be trespassing beyond its appropriate domain if it limits itself to following the lines which have already been laid down organically and to impressing them somewhat more clearly and deeply.

Reaction-Formation and Sublimation.—What is it that goes to the making of these constructions which are so important for the growth of a civilized and normal individual? They probably emerge at the cost of the infantile sexual impulses themselves. Thus the activity of those impulses does not cease even during this period of latency, though their energy is diverted, wholly or in great part, from their sexual use and directed to other ends. Historians of civilization appear to be at one in assuming that powerful components are acquired for every kind of cultural achievement by this diversion of sexual instinctual forces from sexual aims and their direction to new ones—a process which deserves the name of "sublimation." To this we would add, accordingly, that the same process plays a part in the development of the individual and we would place its beginning in the period of sexual latency of childhood.[2]

It is possible further to form some idea of the mechanism of this process of sublimation. On the one hand, it would seem, the sexual impulses cannot be utilized during these years of childhood, since the reproductive functions have been deferred—a fact which constitutes the main feature of the period of latency. On the other hand, these impulses would seem in themselves to be perverse—that is, to arise from erotogenic zones and to derive their activity from instincts which, in view of the direction of the subject's development, can only arouse unpleasurable feelings. They consequently evoke opposing mental forces (reacting impulses) which, in order to suppress this unpleasure effectively, build up the mental dams that I have already mentioned—disgust, shame and morality.[3]

Reprinted from Sigmund Freud, *Three Essays on the Theory of Sexuality* in *The Standard Edition of the Complete Psychological Works of Sigmund Freud,* trans. James Strachey (London: Hogarth Press and the Institute for Psychoanalysis, 1956), VII, 176–93, 196–200, 207–12, 219–30, with the permission of The Hogarth Press and The Macmillan Co.

1. We are able to make use of the second of these two sources of material since we are justified in expecting that the early years of children who are later to become neurotic are not likely in this respect to differ *essentially* from those of children who are to grow up into normal adults, [added 1915:] but only in the intensity and clarity of the phenomena involved.

2. Once again, it is from Fliess that I have borrowed the term "period of sexual latency."

3. [*Footnote added* 1915:] In the case which I am here discussing, the sublimation of sexual instinctual forces takes place along the path of reaction-formation. But in general it is possible to distinguish the concepts of sublimation and reaction-formation from each other as two different processes. Sublimation can also take place by other and simpler mechanisms. [Further theoretical discussions of sublimation will be found in Section III of Freud's paper on narcissism (1914c) and at several points in *The Ego and the Id* (1932b, Chapters III, IV and V).]

Interruptions of the Latency Period.—We must not deceive ourselves as to the hypothetical nature and insufficient clarity of our knowledge concerning the processes of the infantile period of latency or deferment; but we shall be on firmer ground in pointing out that such an application of infantile sexuality represents an educational ideal from which individual development usually diverges at some point and often to a considerable degree. From time to time a fragmentary manifestation of sexuality which has evaded sublimation may break through; or some sexual activity may persist through the whole duration of the latency period until the sexual instinct emerges with greater intensity at puberty. In so far as educators pay any attention at all to infantile sexuality, they behave exactly as though they shared our views as to the construction of the moral defensive forces at the cost of sexuality, and as though they knew that sexual activity makes a child ineducable: for they stigmatize every sexual manifestation by children as a "vice," without being able to do much against it. We, on the other hand, have every reason for turning our attention to these phenomena which are so much dreaded by education, for we may expect them to help us to discover the original configuration of the sexual instincts.

THE MANIFESTATIONS OF INFANTILE SEXUALITY

Thumb-Sucking.—For reasons which will appear later, I shall take thumb-sucking (or sensual sucking) as a sample of the sexual manifestations of childhood. (An excellent study of this subject has been made by the Hungarian paediatrician, Lindner, 1879.[4]

Thumb-sucking appears already in early infancy and may continue into maturity, or even persist all through life. It consists in the rhythmic repetition of a sucking contact by the mouth (or lips). There is no question of the purpose of this procedure being the taking of nourishment. A portion of the lip itself, the tongue, or any other part of the skin within reach—even the big toe—may be taken as the object upon which this sucking is carried out. In this connection a grasping-instinct may appear and may manifest itself as a simultaneous rhythmic tugging at the lobes of the ears or a catching hold of some part of another person (as a rule the ear) for the same purpose. Sensual sucking involves a complete absorption of the attention and leads either to sleep or even to a motor reaction in the nature of an orgasm.[5] It is not infrequently combined with rubbing some sensitive part of the body such as the breast or the external genitalia. Many children proceed by this path from sucking to masturbation.

Lindner himself clearly recognized the sexual nature of this activity and emphasized it without qualification. In the nursery, sucking is often classed along with the other kinds of sexual "naughtiness" of children. This view has been most energetically repudiated by numbers of paediatricians and nerve-specialists, though this is no doubt partly due to a confusion between "sexual" and "genital." Their objection raises a difficult question and one which cannot be evaded: what is the general characteristic which enables us to recognize the sexual manifestations of children? The concatenation of phenomena into which we have been given an insight by psycho-analytic investigation justifies us, in my opinion, in regarding thumb-sucking as a sexual manifestation and in choosing it for our study of the essential features of infantile sexual activity.

Auto-Erotism.—We are in duty bound to make a thorough examination of this example. It must be insisted that the most striking feature of this sexual activity is that the instinct is not directed towards other people, but obtains satisfaction from the subject's own body. It is "auto-erotic," to call it by a happily chosen term introduced by Havelock Ellis (1910).

Furthermore, it is clear that the behaviour of a child who indulges in thumb-sucking is determined by a search for some pleasure which has already been experienced and is now remembered. In the simplest case he proceeds to find this satisfaction by sucking rhythmically at some part of the skin or mucous membrane. It is also easy to guess the occasions on which the child had his first experiences of the pleasure which he is now striving to renew. It was the child's first and most vital activity, his sucking at his mother's breast, or at substitutes for it, that must have familiarized him with this pleasure. The child's lips, in our view, behave like an erotogenic zone, and no doubt stimulation by the warm flow of milk is the cause of the pleasurable sensation. The satisfaction of the erotogenic zone is associated, in the first instance, with the satisfaction of the need for nourishment. To begin with, sexual activity attaches itself to functions serving the purpose of self-

---

4. [There seems to be no nursery word in English equivalent to the German "*lutschen*" and "*ludeln*," used by Freud alongside "*wonnesaugen*" ("*sensual sucking*"). Conrad in *Struwwelpeter* was a "*Lutscher*"; but, as will be seen from the context, "suck-a-thumbs" and "thumb-sucking" have in fact too narrow a connotation for the present purpose.]

5. Thus we find at this early stage, what holds good all through life, that sexual satisfaction is the best soporific. Most cases of nervous insomnia can be traced back to lack of sexual satisfaction. It is well known that unscrupulous nurses put crying children to sleep by stroking their genitals.

preservation and does not become independent of them until later. No one who has seen a baby sinking back satiated from the breast and falling asleep with flushed cheeks and a blissful smile can escape the reflection that this picture persists as a prototype of the expression of sexual satisfaction in later life. The need for repeating the sexual satisfaction now becomes detached from the need for taking nourishment—a separation which becomes inevitable when the teeth appear and food is no longer taken in only by sucking, but is also chewed up. The child does not make use of an extraneous body for his sucking, but prefers a part of his own skin because it is more convenient, because it makes him independent of the external world, which he is not yet able to control, and because in that way he provides himself, as it were, with a second erotogenic zone, though one of an inferior kind. The inferiority of this second region is among the reasons why at a later date he seeks the corresponding part—the lips—of another person. ("It's a pity I can't kiss myself," he seems to be saying.)

It is not every child who sucks in this way. It may be assumed that those children do so in whom there is a constitutional intensification of the erotogenic significance of the labial region. If that significance persists, these same children when they are grown up will become epicures in kissing, will be inclined to perverse kissing, or, if males, will have a powerful motive for drinking and smoking. If, however, repression ensues, they will feel disgust at food and will produce hysterical vomiting. The repression extends to the nutritional instinct owing to the dual purpose served by the labial zone. Many of my women patients who suffer from disturbances of eating, *globus hystericus,* constriction of the throat and vomiting, have indulged energetically in sucking during their childhood.

Our study of thumb-sucking or sensual sucking has already given us the three essential characteristics of an infantile sexual manifestation. At its origin it attaches itself to one of the vital somatic functions; it has as yet no sexual object, and is thus auto-erotic; and its sexual aim is dominated by an erotogenic zone. It is to be anticipated that these characteristics will be found to apply equally to most of the other activities of the infantile sexual instincts.

THE SEXUAL AIM OF INFANTILE SEXUALITY

Characteristics of Erotogenic Zones.—The example of thumb-sucking shows us still more about what constitutes an erotogenic zone. It is a part of the skin or mucous membrane in which stimuli of a certain sort evoke a feeling of pleasure possessing a particular quality. There can be no doubt that the stimuli which produce the pleasure are governed by special conditions, though we do not know what those are. A rhythmic character must play a part among them and the analogy of tickling is forced upon our notice. It seems less certain whether the character of the pleasurable feeling evoked by the stimulus should be described as a "specific" one—a "specific" quality in which the sexual factor would precisely lie. Psychology is still so much in the dark in questions of pleasure and unpleasure that the most cautious assumption is the one most to be recommended. We may later come upon reasons which seem to support the idea that the pleasurable feeling does in fact possess a specific quality.

The character of erotogenicity can be attached to some parts of the body in a particularly marked way. There are predestined erotogenic zones, as is shown by the example of sucking. The same example, however, also shows us that any other part of the skin or mucous membrane can take over the functions of an erotogenic zone, and must therefore have some aptitude in that direction. Thus the quality of the stimulus has more to do with producing the pleasurable feeling than has the nature of the part of the body concerned. A child who is indulging in sensual sucking searches about his body and chooses some part of it to suck—a part which is afterwards preferred by him from force of habit; if he happens to hit upon one of the predestined regions (such as the nipples or genitals) no doubt it retains the preference. A precisely analogous tendency to displacement is also found in the symptomatology of hysteria. In that neurosis repression affects most of all the actual genital zones and these transmit their susceptibility to stimulation to other erotogenic zones (normally neglected in adult life), which then behave exactly like genitals. But besides this, precisely as in the case of sucking, any other part of the body can acquire the same susceptibility to stimulation as is possessed by the genitals and can become an erotogenic zone. Erotogenic and hysterogenic zones show the same characteristics.

The Infantile Sexual Aim.—The sexual aim of the infantile instinct consists in obtaining satisfaction by means of an appropriate stimulation of the erotogenic zone which has been selected in one way or another. This satisfaction must have been previously experienced in order to have left behind a need for its repetition; and we may expect that Nature will have made safe provisions so that this experience of satisfaction shall not be left to chance. We have already learnt what the contrivance is that fulfils this purpose in the case of the labial zone: it is the simultaneous connection which links this part of the body with the taking in of food. We shall come across other, similar contrivances as sources of sexuality. The state of being in need of a repetition of the satisfaction reveals itself in two ways: by a peculiar feeling of tension, possessing, rather, the character of unpleasure, and by a sensation of itching or stimulation which is centrally conditioned and projected on to the peripheral erotogenic zone. We can therefore formulate a sexual aim in another way: it consists in replacing the projected sensation of stimulation in the erotogenic zone by an external stimulus which removes that sensation by producing a feeling of satisfaction. This external stimulus will usually consist in some kind of manipulation that is analogous to the sucking.

The fact that the need can also be evoked peripherally, by a real modification of the erotogenic zone, is in complete harmony with our physiological knowledge. This strikes us as somewhat strange only because, in order to remove one stimulus, it seems necessary to adduce a second one at the same spot.

MASTURBATORY SEXUAL MANIFESTATIONS

It must come as a great relief to find that, when once we have understood the nature of the instinct arising from a single one of the erotogenic zones, we shall have very little more to learn of the sexual activity of children. The clearest distinctions as between one zone and another concern the nature of the contrivance necessary for satisfying the instinct; in the case of the labial zone it consisted of sucking, and this has to be replaced by other muscular actions according to the position and nature of the other zones.

Activity of the Anal Zone.—Like the labial zone, the anal zone is well suited by its position to act as a medium through which sexuality may attach itself to other somatic functions. It is to be presumed that the erotogenic significance of this part of the body is very great from the first. We learn with some astonishment from psycho-analysis of the transmutations normally undergone by the sexual excitations arising from this zone and of the frequency with which it retains a considerable amount of susceptibility to genital stimulation throughout life. The intestinal disturbances which are so common in childhood see to it that the zone shall not lack intense excitations. Intestinal catarrhs at the tenderest age make children "nervy," as people say, and in cases of later neurotic illness they have a determining influence on the symptoms in which the neurosis is expressed, and they put at its disposal the whole range of intestinal disturbances. If we bear in mind the erotogenic

significance of the outlet of the intestinal canal, which persists, at all events in a modified form, we shall not be inclined to scoff at the influence of haemorrhoids, to which old-fashioned medicine used to attach so much importance in explaining neurotic conditions.

Children who are making use of the susceptibility to erotogenic stimulation of the anal zone betray themselves by holding back their stool till its accumulation brings about violent muscular contractions and, as it passes through the anus, is able to produce powerful stimulation of the mucous membrane. In so doing it must no doubt cause not only painful but also highly pleasurable sensations. One of the clearest signs of subsequent eccentricity or nervousness is to be seen when a baby obstinately refuses to empty his bowels when he is put on the pot—that is, when his nurse wants him to—and holds back that function till he himself chooses to exercise it. He is naturally not concerned with dirtying the bed, he is only anxious not to miss the subsidiary pleasure attached to defaecating. Educators are once more right when they describe children who keep the process back as "naughty."

The contents of the bowels, which act as a stimulating mass upon a sexually sensitive portion of mucous membrane, behave like forerunners of another organ, which is destined to come into action after the phase of childhood. But they have other important meanings for the infant. They are clearly treated as a part of the infant's own body and represent his first "gift": by producing them he can express his active compliance with his environment and, by withholding them, his disobedience. From being a "gift" they later come to acquire the meanings of "baby"—for babies, according to one of the sexual theories of children, are acquired by eating and are born through the bowels.

The retention of the faecal mass, which is thus carried out intentionally by the child to begin with, in order to serve, as it were, as a masturbatory stimulus upon the anal zone or to be employed in his relation to the people looking after him, is also one of the roots of the constipation which is so common among neuropaths. Further, the whole significance of the anal zone is reflected in the fact that few neurotics are to be found without their special scatological practices, ceremonies, and so on, which they carefully keep secret.[6]

6. [*Footnote added* 1920:] Lou Andreas-Salomé (1916), in a paper which has given us a very much deeper understanding of the significance of anal erotism, has shown how the history of the first prohibition which a child comes across—the prohibition against getting pleasure from anal activity and its products—has a decisive effect on his whole development. This must be the first occasion on which the infant has a glimpse of an environment hostile to his instinctual impulses, on which he learns to separate

Activity of the Genital Zones.—Among the erotogenic zones that form part of the child's body there is one which certainly does not play the opening part, and which cannot be the vehicle of the oldest sexual impulses, but which is destined to great things in the future. In both male and female children it is brought into connection with micturition (in the glans and clitoris) and in the former is enclosed in a pouch of mucous membrane, so that there can be no lack of stimulation of it by secretions which may give an early start to sexual excitation. The sexual activities of this erotogenic zone, which forms part of the sexual organs proper, are the beginning of what is later to become "normal" sexual life. The anatomical situation of this region, the secretions in which it is bathed, the washing and rubbing to which it is subjected in the course of a child's toilet, as well as accidental stimulation (such as the movement of intestinal worms in the case of girls), make it inevitable that the pleasurable feeling which this part of the body is capable of producing should be noticed by children even during their earliest infancy, and should give rise to a need for its repetition. If we consider this whole range of contrivances and bear in mind that both making a mess and measures for keeping clean are bound to operate in much the same way, it is scarcely possible to avoid the conclusion that the foundations for the future primacy over sexual activity exercised by this erotogenic zone are established by early infantile masturbation, which scarcely a single individual escapes. The action which disposes of the stimulus and brings about satisfaction consists in a rubbing movement with the hand or in the application of pressure (no doubt on the lines of a pre-existing reflex) either from the hand or by bringing the thighs together. This last method is by far the more common in the case of girls. The preference for the hand which is shown by boys is already evidence of the important contribution which the instinct for mastery is destined to make to masculine sexual activity.[7]

It will be in the interests of clarity if I say at

once that three phases of infantile masturbation are to be distinguished. The first of these belongs to early infancy, and the second to the brief efflorescence of sexual activity about the fourth year of life; only the third phase corresponds to pubertal masturbation, which is often the only kind taken into account.

Second Phase of Infantile Masturbation.—The masturbation of early infancy seems to disappear after a short time; but it may persist uninterruptedly until puberty, and this would constitute the first great deviation from the course of development laid down for civilized men. At some point of childhood after early infancy, as a rule before the fourth year, the sexual instinct belonging to the genital zone usually revives and persists again for a time until it is once more suppressed, or it may continue without interruption. This second phase of infantile sexual activity may assume a variety of different forms which can only be determined by a precise analysis of individual cases. But all its details leave behind the deepest (unconscious) impressions in the subject's memory, determine the development of his character, if he is to remain healthy, and the symptomatology of his neurosis, if he is to fall ill after puberty. In the latter case we find that this sexual period has been forgotten and that the conscious memories that bear witness to it have been displaced. (I have already mentioned that I am inclined to relate normal infantile amnesia to this infantile sexual activity.) Psycho-analytic investigation enables us to make what has been forgotten conscious and thus do away with a compulsion that arises from the unconscious psychical material.

Return of Early Infantile Masturbation.—During the years of childhood with which I am now dealing, the sexual excitation of early infancy returns, either as a centrally determined tickling stimulus which seeks satisfaction in masturbation, or as a process in the nature of a nocturnal emission which, like the nocturnal emissions of adult years, achieves satisfaction without the help of any action by the subject. The latter case is the more frequent with girls and in the second half of childhood; its determinants are not entirely intelligible and often, though not invariably, it seems to be conditioned by a period of earlier *active* masturbation. The symptoms of these sexual manifestations are scanty; they are mostly displayed on behalf of the still undeveloped sexual apparatus by the *urinary* apparatus, which thus acts, as it were, as the former's trustee. Most of the so-called bladder disorders of this period are sexual disturbances: nocturnal enuresis, unless it represents an epileptic fit, corresponds to a nocturnal emission.

The reappearance of sexual activity is determined

---

his own entity from this alien one and on which he carries out the first "repression" of his possibilities for pleasure. From that time on, what is "anal" remains the symbol of everything that is to be repudiated and excluded from life. The clear-cut distinction between anal and genital processes which is later insisted upon is contradicted by the close anatomical and functional analogies and relations which hold between them. The genital apparatus remains the neighbour of the cloaca, and actually [to quote Lou Andreas-Salomé] "in the case of women is only taken from it on lease."

7. [*Footnote added* 1915:] Unusual techniques in carrying out masturbation in later years seem to point to the influence of a prohibition against masturbation which has been overcome.

by internal causes and external contingencies, both of which can be guessed in cases of neurotic illness from the form taken by their symptoms and can be discovered with certainty by psycho-analytic investigation. I shall have to speak presently of the internal causes; great and lasting importance attaches at this period to the accidental *external* contingencies. In the foreground we find the effects of seduction, which treats a child as a sexual object prematurely and teaches him, in highly emotional circumstances, how to obtain satisfaction from his genital zones, a satisfaction which he is then usually obliged to repeat again and again by masturbation. An influence of this kind may originate either from adults or from other children. I cannot admit that in my paper on "The Aetiology of Hysteria" (1896c) I exaggerated the frequency or importance of that influence, though I did not then know that persons who remain normal may have had the same experiences in their childhood, and though I consequently overrated the importance of seduction in comparison with the factors of sexual constitution and development. Obviously seduction is not required in order to arouse a child's sexual life; that can also come about spontaneously from internal causes.

Polymorphously Perverse Disposition.—It is an instructive fact that under the influence of seduction children can become polymorphously perverse, and can be led into all possible kinds of sexual irregularities. This shows that an aptitude for them is innately present in their disposition. There is consequently little resistance towards carrying them out, since the mental dams against sexual excesses —shame, disgust, and morality—have either not yet been constructed at all or are only in course of construction, according to the age of the child. In this respect children behave in the same kind of way as an average uncultivated woman in whom the same polymorphously perverse disposition persists. Under ordinary conditions she may remain normal sexually, but if she is led on by a clever seducer she will find every sort of perversion to her taste, and will retain them as part of her own sexual activities. Prostitutes exploit the same polymorphous, that is, infantile, disposition for the purposes of their profession; and, considering the immense number of women who are prostitutes or who must be supposed to have an aptitude for prostitution without becoming engaged in it, it becomes impossible not to recognize that this same disposition to perversions of every kind is a general and fundamental human characteristic.

Component Instincts.—Moreover, the effects of seduction do not help to reveal the early history of the sexual instinct; they rather confuse our view

of it by presenting children prematurely with a sexual object for which the infantile sexual instinct at first shows no need. It must, however, be admitted that infantile sexual life, in spite of the preponderating dominance of erotogenic zones, exhibits components which from the very first involve other people as sexual objects. Such are the instincts of scopophilia, exhibitionism and cruelty, which appear in a sense independently of erotogenic zones; these instincts do not enter into intimate relations with genital life until later, but are already to be observed in childhood as independent impulses, distinct in the first instance from erotogenic sexual activity. Small children are essentially without shame, and at some periods of their earliest years show an unmistakable satisfaction in exposing their bodies, with especial emphasis on the sexual parts. The counterpart of this supposedly perverse inclination, curiosity to see other people's genitals, probably does not become manifest until somewhat later in childhood, when the obstacle set up by a sense of shame has already reached a certain degree of development. Under the influence of seduction the scopophilic perversion can attain great importance in the sexual life of a child. But my researches into the early years of normal people, as well as of neurotic patients, force me to the conclusion that scopophilia can also appear in children as a spontaneous manifestation. Small children whose attention has once been drawn—as a rule by masturbation—to their own genitals usually take the further step without help from outside and develop a lively interest in the genitals of their playmates. Since opportunities for satisfying curiosity of this kind usually occur only in the course of satisfying the two kinds of need for excretion, children of this kind turn into *voyeurs,* eager spectators of the processes of micturition and defaecation. When repression of these inclinations sets in, the desire to see other people's genitals (whether of their own or the opposite sex) persists as a tormenting compulsion, which in some cases of neurosis later affords the strongest motive force for the formation of symptoms.

The cruel component of the sexual instinct develops in childhood even more independently of the sexual activities that are attached to erotogenic zones. Cruelty in general comes easily to the childish nature, since the obstacle that brings the instinct for mastery to a halt at another person's pain— namely a capacity for pity—is developed relatively late. The fundamental psychological analysis of this instinct has, as we know, not yet been satisfactorily achieved. It may be assumed that the impulse of cruelty arises from the instinct for mastery and appears at a period of sexual life at which the genitals have not yet taken over their later role. It then dominates a phase of sexual life which we shall later describe as a pregenital organization. Children who distinguish themselves by special cruelty towards animals and playmates usually give rise to a just suspicion of an intense and precocious sexual activity arising from erotogenic zones; and, though all the sexual instincts may display simultaneous precocity, *erotogenic* sexual activity seems, nevertheless, to be the primary one. The absence of the barrier of pity brings with it a danger that the connection between the cruel and the erotogenic instincts, thus established in childhood, may prove unbreakable in later life. Ever since Jean Jacques Rousseau's *Confessions,* it has been well known to all educationalists that the painful stimulation of the skin of the buttocks is one of the erotogenic roots of the *passive* instinct of cruelty (masochism). The conclusion has been rightly drawn by them that corporal punishment, which is usually applied to this part of the body, should not be inflicted upon any children whose libido is liable to be forced into collateral channels by the later demands of cultural education.

*   *   *

Theories of Birth.—Many people can remember clearly what an intense interest they took during the prepubertal period in the question of where babies come from. The anatomical answers to the question were at the time very various: babies come out of the breast, or are cut out of the body, or the navel opens to let them through. Outside analysis, there are very seldom memories of any similar researches having been carried out in the *early* years of childhood. These earlier researches fell a victim to repression long since, but all their findings were of a uniform nature: people get babies by eating some particular thing (as they do in fairy tales) and babies are born through the bowel like a discharge of faeces. These infantile theories remind us of conditions that exist in the animal kingdom—and especially of the cloaca in types of animals lower than mammals.

Sadistic View of Sexual Intercourse.—If children at this early age witness sexual intercourse between adults—for which an opportunity is provided by the conviction of grown-up people that small children cannot understand anything sexual—they inevitably regard the sexual act as a sort of ill-treatment or act of subjugation: they view it, that is, in a sadistic sense. Psycho-analysis also shows us that an impression of this kind in early childhood contributes a great deal towards a predisposition to a subsequent sadistic displacement of the sexual aim. Furthermore, children are much concerned with the problem of what sexual intercourse—or,

as they put it, being married—consists in: and they usually seek a solution of the mystery in some common activity concerned with the function of micturition or defaecation.

Typical Failure of Infantile Sexual Research.—We can say in general of the sexual theories of children that they are reflections of their own sexual constitution, and that in spite of their grotesque errors the theories show more understanding of sexual processes than one would have given their creators credit for. Children also perceive the alterations that take place in their mother owing to pregnancy and are able to interpret them correctly. The fable of the stork is often told to an audience that receives it with deep, though mostly silent, mistrust. There are, however, two elements that remain undiscovered by the sexual researches of children: the fertilizing role of semen and the existence of the female sexual orifice—the same elements, incidentally, in which the infantile organization is itself undeveloped. It therefore follows that the efforts of the childish investigator are habitually fruitless, and end in a renunciation which not infrequently leaves behind it a permanent injury to the instinct for knowledge. The sexual researches of these early years of childhood are always carried out in solitude. They constitute a first step towards taking an independent attitude in the world, and imply a high degree of alienation of the child from the people in his environment who formerly enjoyed his complete confidence.

THE PHASES OF DEVELOPMENT OF THE
SEXUAL ORGANIZATION

The characteristics of infantile sexual life which we have hitherto emphasized are the facts that it is essentially auto-erotic (i.e. that it finds its object in the infant's own body) and that its individual component instincts are upon the whole disconnected and independent of one another in their search for pleasure. The final outcome of sexual development lies in what is known as the normal sexual life of the adult, in which the pursuit of pleasure comes under the sway of the reproductive function and in which the component instincts, under the primacy of a single erotogenic zone, form a firm organization directed towards a sexual aim attached to some extraneous sexual object.

Pregenital Organizations.—The study, with the help of psycho-analysis, of the inhibitions and disturbances of this process of development enables us to recognize abortive beginnings and preliminary stages of a firm organization of the component instincts such as this—preliminary stages which themselves constitute a sexual régime of a sort. These phases of sexual organization are normally passed through smoothly, without giving more than a hint of their existence. It is only in pathological cases that they become active and recognizable to superficial observation.

We shall give the name of "pregenital" to organizations of sexual life in which the genital zones have not yet taken over their predominant part. We have hitherto identified two such organizations, which almost seem as though they were harking back to early animal forms of life.

The first of these is the oral or, as it might be called, cannibalistic pregenital sexual organization. Here sexual activity has not yet been separated from the ingestion of food; nor are opposite currents within the activity differentiated. The *object* of both activities is the same; the sexual *aim* consists in the incorporation of the object—the prototype of a process which, in the form of identification, is later to play such an important psychological part. A relic of this constructed phase of organization, which is forced upon our notice by pathology, may be seen in thumb-sucking, in which the sexual activity, detached from the nurtritive activity, has substituted for the extraneous object one situated in the subject's own body.[8]

A second pregenital phase is that of the sadistic-anal organization. Here the opposition between two currents, which runs through all sexual life, is already developed: they cannot yet, however, be described as "masculine" and "feminine," but only as "active" and "passive." The *activity* is put into operation by the instinct for mastery through the agency of the somatic musculature; the organ which, more than any other, represents the *passive* sexual aim is the erotogenic mucous membrane of the anus. Both of these currents have objects, which, however, are not identical. Alongside these, other component instincts operate in an auto-erotic manner. In this phase, therefore, sexual polarity and an extraneous object are already observable. But organization and subordination to the reproductive function are still absent.

Ambivalence.—This form of sexual organization can persist throughout life and can permanently attract a large portion of sexual activity to itself. The predominance in it of sadism and the cloacal part played by the anal zone give it a quite peculiarly archaic colouring. It is further characterized by the fact that in it the opposing pairs of instincts are developed to an approximately equal extent, a state

of affairs described by Bleuler's happily chosen term "ambivalence."

The assumption of the existence of pregenital organizations of sexual life is based on the analysis of the neuroses, and without a knowledge of them can scarcely be appreciated. Further analytic investigation may be expected to provide us with far more information on the structure and development of the normal sexual function.

In order to complete our picture of infantile sexual life, we must also suppose that the choice of an object, such as we have shown to be characteristic of the pubertal phase of development, has already frequently or habitually been effected during the years of childhood: that is to say, the whole of the sexual currents have become directed towards a single person in relation to whom they seek to achieve their aims. This then is the closest approximation possible in childhood to the final form taken by sexual life after puberty. The only difference lies in the fact that in childhood the combination of the component instincts and their subordination under the primacy of the genitals have been effected only very incompletely or not at all. Thus the establishment of that primacy in the service of reproduction is the last phase through which the organization of sexuality passes.

Diphasic Choice of Object.—It may be regarded as typical of the choice of an object that the process is diphasic, that is, that it occurs in two waves. The first of these begins between the ages of two and five, and is brought to a halt or to a retreat by the latency period; it is characterized by the infantile nature of the sexual aims. The second wave sets in with puberty and determines the final outcome of sexual life.

Although the diphasic nature of object-choice comes down in essentials to no more than the operation of the latency period, it is of the highest importance in regard to disturbances of that final outcome. The resultants of infantile object-choice are carried over into the later period. They either persist as such or are revived at the actual time of puberty. But as a consequence of the repression which has developed between the two phases they prove unutilizable. Their sexual aims have become mitigated and they now represent what may be described as the "affectionate current" of sexual life. Only psycho-analytic investigation can show that behind this affection, admiration and respect there lie concealed the old sexual longings of the infantile component instincts which have now become unserviceable. The object-choice of the pubertal period is obliged to dispense with the objects of childhood and to start afresh as a "sensual current." Should these two currents fail to converge, the

---

8. [*Footnote added* 1920:] For remnants of this phase in adult neurotics, cf. Abraham (1916). [*Added* 1924:] In another, later work (1924) the same writer has divided both this oral phase, and also the later sadistic-anal one, into two sub-divisions, which are characterized by differing attitudes towards the object.

result is often that one of the ideals of sexual life, the focusing of all desires upon a single object, will be unattainable.

*   *   *

The Transformations of Puberty

With the arrival of puberty, changes set in which are destined to give infantile sexual life its final, normal shape. The sexual instinct has hitherto been predominantly auto-erotic; it now finds a sexual object. Its activity has hitherto been derived from a number of separate instincts and erotogenic zones, which, independently of one another, have pursued a certain sort of pleasure as their sole sexual aim. Now, however, a new sexual aim appears, and all the component instincts combine to attain it, while the erotogenic zones become subordinated to the primacy of the genital zone.[9] Since the new sexual aim assigns very different functions to the two sexes, their sexual development now diverges greatly. That of males is the more straightforward and the more understandable, while that of females actually enters upon a kind of involution. A normal sexual life is only assured by an exact convergence of the affectionate current and the sensual current, both being directed towards the sexual object and sexual aim. (The former, the affectionate current, comprises what remains over of the infantile efflorescence of sexuality.) It is like the completion of a tunnel which has been driven through a hill from both directions.

The new sexual aim in men consists in the discharge of the sexual products. The earlier one, the attainment of pleasure, is by no means alien to it; on the contrary, the highest degree of pleasure is attached to this final act of the sexual process. The sexual instinct is now subordinated to the reproductive function; it becomes, so to say, altruistic. If this transformation is to succeed, the original dispositions and all the other characteristics of the instincts must be taken into account in the process. Just as on any other occasion on which the organism should by rights make new combinations and adjustments leading to complicated mechanisms, here too there are possibilities of pathological disorders if these new arrangements are not carried out. Every pathological disorder of sexual life is rightly to be regarded as an inhibition in development.

---

9. [*Footnote added* 1915:] The schematic picture I have given in the text aims at emphasizing differences. I have already shown on [p. 845] the extent to which infantile sexuality, owing to its choice of object and to the development of the phallic phase, approximates to the final sexual organization.

THE PRIMACY OF THE GENITAL ZONES AND FORE-PLEASURE

The starting-point and the final aim of the process which I have described are clearly visible. The intermediate steps are still in many ways obscure to us. We shall have to leave more than one of them as an unsolved riddle.

The most striking of the processes at puberty has been picked upon as constituting its essence: the manifest growth of the external genitalia. (The latency period of childhood is, on the other hand, characterized by a relative cessation of their growth.) In the meantime the development of the internal genitalia has advanced far enough for them to be able to discharge the sexual products or, as the case may be, to bring about the formation of a new living organism. Thus a highly complicated apparatus has been made ready and awaits the moment of being put into operation.

This apparatus is to be set in motion by stimuli, and observation shows us that stimuli can impinge on it from three directions: from the external world by means of the excitation of the erotogenic zones with which we are already familiar, from the organic interior by ways which we have still to explore, and from mental life, which is itself a storehouse for external impressions and a receiving-post for internal excitations. All three kinds of stimuli produce the same effect, namely a condition described as "sexual excitement," which shows itself by two sorts of indication, mental and somatic. The mental indications consist in a peculiar feeling of tension of an extremely compelling character; and among the numerous somatic ones are first and foremost a number of changes in the genitals, which have the obvious sense of being preparations for the sexual act—the erection of the male organ and the lubrication of the vagina.

Sexual Tension.—The fact that sexual excitement possesses the character of tension raises a problem the solution of which is no less difficult than it would be important in helping us to understand the sexual processes. In spite of all the differences of opinion that reign on the subject among psychologists, I must insist that a feeling of tension necessarily involves unpleasure. What seems to me decisive is the fact that a feeling of this kind is accompanied by an impulsion to make a change in the psychological situation, that it operates in an urgent way which is wholly alien to the nature of the feeling of pleasure. If, however, the tension of sexual excitement is counted as an unpleasurable feeling, we are at once brought up against the fact that it is also undoubtedly felt as pleasurable. In every case in which tension is produced by sexual processes it is accompanied by pleasure; even in the preparatory changes in the genitals a feeling of satisfaction of some kind is plainly to be observed. How, then, are this unpleasurable tension and this feeling of pleasure to be reconciled?

Everything relating to the problem of pleasure and unpleasure touches upon one of the sorest spots of present-day psychology. It will be my aim to learn as much as possible from the circumstances of the instance with which we are at present dealing, but I shall avoid any approach to the problem as a whole.

Let us begin by casting a glance at the way in which the erotogenic zones fit themselves into the new arrangement. They have to play an important part in introducing sexual excitation. The eye is perhaps the zone most remote from the sexual object, but it is the one which, in the situation of wooing an object, is liable to be the most frequently stimulated by the particular quality of excitation whose cause, when it occurs in a sexual object, we describe as beauty. (For the same reason the merits of a sexual object are described as "attractions.") The stimulation is on the one hand already accompanied by pleasure, while on the other hand it leads to an increase of sexual excitement or produces it if it is not yet present. If the excitation now spreads to another erotogenic zone—to the hand, for instance, through tactile sensations—the effect is the same: a feeling of pleasure on the one side, which is quickly intensified by pleasure arising from the preparatory changes [in the genitals], and on the other side an increase of sexual tension, which soon passes over into the most obvious unpleasure if it cannot be met by a further accession of pleasure. Another instance will perhaps make this even clearer. If an erotogenic zone in a person who is not sexually excited (e.g. the skin of a woman's breast) is stimulated by touch, the contact produces a pleasurable feeling; but it is at the same time better calculated than anything to arouse a sexual excitation that demands an increase of pleasure. The problem is how it can come about that an experience of pleasure can give rise to a need for greater pleasure.

The Mechanism of Fore-Pleasure.—The part played in this by the erotogenic zones, however, is clear. What is true of one of them is true of all. They are all used to provide a certain amount of pleasure by being stimulated in the way appropriate to them. This pleasure then leads to an increase in tension which in its turn is responsible for producing the necessary motor energy for the conclusion of the sexual act. The penultimate stage of that act is once again the appropriate stimulation of an erotogenic zone (the genital zone itself, in the glans penis) by the appropriate object (the mucous

membrane of the vagina); and from the pleasure yielded by this excitation the motor energy is obtained, this time by a reflex path, which brings about the discharge of the sexual substances. This last pleasure is the highest in intensity, and its mechanism differs from that of the earlier pleasure. It is brought about entirely by discharge: it is wholly a pleasure of satisfaction and with it the tension of the libido is for the time being extinguished.

This distinction between the one kind of pleasure due to the excitation of erotogenic zones and the other kind due to the discharge of the sexual substances deserves, I think, to be made more concrete by a difference in nomenclature. The former may be suitably described as "fore-pleasure" in contrast to the "end-pleasure" or pleasure of satisfaction derived from the sexual act. Fore-pleasure is thus the same pleasure that has already been produced, although on a smaller scale, by the infantile sexual instinct; end-pleasure is something new and is thus probably conditioned by circumstances that do not arise till puberty. The formula for the new function of the erotogenic zones runs therefore: they are used to make possible, through the medium of the fore-pleasure which can be derived from them (as it was during infantile life), the production of the greater pleasure of satisfaction.

I was able recently to throw light upon another instance, in a quite different department of mental life, of a slight feeling of pleasure similarly making possible the attainment of a greater resultant pleasure, and thus operating as an "incentive bonus." In the same connection I was also able to go more deeply into the nature of pleasure.[10]

Dangers of Fore-Pleasure.—The connection between fore-pleasure and infantile sexual life is, however, made clearer by the pathogenic part which it can come to play. The attainment of the normal sexual aim can clearly be endangered by the mechanism in which fore-pleasure is involved. This danger arises if at any point in the preparatory sexual processes the fore-pleasure turns out to be too great and the element of tension too small. The motive for proceeding further with the sexual process then disappears, the whole path is cut short, and the preparatory act in question takes the place of the normal sexual aim. Experience has shown that the precondition for this damaging event is that the erotogenic zone concerned or the corresponding

10. See my volume on *Jokes and their Relation to the Unconscious* which appeared in 1905 [near the end of Chapter IV]. The "fore-pleasure" attained by the technique of joking is used in order to liberate a greater pleasure derived from the removal of internal inhibitions. [In a later paper, on creative writing (1908e), Freud attributed a similar mechanism to aesthetic pleasure.]

component instinct shall already during childhood have contributed an unusual amount of pleasure. If further factors then come into play, tending to bring about a fixation, a compulsion may easily arise in later life which resists the incorporation of this particular fore-pleasure into a new context. Such is in fact the mechanism of many perversions, which consist in a lingering over the preparatory acts of the sexual process.

This failure of the function of the sexual mechanism owing to fore-pleasure is best avoided if the primacy of the genitals too is adumbrated in childhood; and indeed things seem actually arranged to bring this about in the second half of childhood (from the age of eight to puberty). During these years the genital zones already behave in much the same way as in maturity; they become the seat of sensations of excitation and of preparatory changes whenever any pleasure is felt from the satisfaction of other erotogenic zones, though this result is still without a purpose—that is to say, contributes nothing to a continuation of the sexual process. Already in childhood, therefore, alongside of the pleasure of satisfaction there is a certain amount of sexual tension, although it is less constant and less in quantity. We can now understand why, in discussing the sources of sexuality, we were equally justified in saying of a given process that it was sexually satisfying or sexually exciting. It will be noticed that in the course of our enquiry we began by exaggerating the distinction between infantile and mature sexual life, and that we are now setting this right. Not only the deviations from normal sexual life but its normal form as well are determined by the infantile manifestations of sexuality.

*　　*　　*

THE DIFFERENTIATION BETWEEN
MEN AND WOMEN

As we all know, it is not until puberty that the sharp distinction is established between the masculine and feminine characters. From that time on, this contrast has a more decisive influence than any other upon the shaping of human life. It is true that the masculine and feminine dispositions are already easily recognizable in childhood. The development of the inhibitions of sexuality (shame, disgust, pity, etc.) takes place in little girls earlier and in the face of less resistance than in boys; the tendency to sexual repression seems in general to be greater; and, where the component instincts of sexuality appear, they prefer the passive form. The auto-erotic activity of the erotogenic zones is, however, the same in both sexes, and owing to this uniformity there is no possibility of a distinction between the two sexes such as arises after puberty. So far as the auto-erotic

and masturbatory manifestations of sexuality are concerned, we might lay it down that the sexuality of little girls is of a wholly masculine character. Indeed, if we were able to give a more definite connotation to the concepts of "masculine" and "feminine," it would even be possible to maintain that libido is invariably and necessarily of a masculine nature, whether it occurs in men or in women and irrespectively of whether its object is a man or a woman.[11]

Since I have become acquainted with the notion of bisexuality I have regarded it as the decisive factor, and without taking bisexuality into account I think it would scarcely be possible to arrive at an understanding of the sexual manifestations that are actually to be observed in men and women.

Leading Zones in Men and Women.—Apart from this I have only the following to add. The leading erotogenic zone in female children is located at the clitoris, and is thus homologous to the masculine genital zone of the glans penis. All my experience concerning masturbation in little girls has related to the clitoris and not to the regions of the external genitalia that are important in later sexual functioning. I am even doubtful whether a female child can be led by the influence of seduction to anything other than clitoridal masturbation. If such a thing occurs, it is quite exceptional. The spontaneous discharges of sexual excitement which oc-

---

11. [Before 1924 the words from "libido" to the end of the sentence were printed in spaced type.—*Footnote added* 1915:] It is essential to understand clearly that the concepts of "masculine" and "feminine," whose meaning seems so unambiguous to ordinary people, are among the most confused that occur in science. It is possible to distinguish at least three uses. "Masculine" and "feminine" are used sometimes in the sense of activity and passivity, sometimes in a biological, and sometimes, again, in a sociological sense. The first of these three meanings is the essential one and the most serviceable in psycho-analysis. When, for instance, libido was described in the text above as being "masculine," the word was being used in this sense, for an instinct is always active even when it has a passive aim in view. The second, or biological, meaning of "masculine" and "feminine" is one whose applicability can be determined most easily. Here "masculine" and "feminine" are characterized by the presence of spermatozoa or ova respectively and by the functions proceeding from them. Activity and its concomitant phenomena (more powerful muscular development, aggressiveness, greater intensity of libido) are as a rule linked with biological masculinity; but they are not necessarily so, for there are animal species in which these qualities are on the contrary assigned to the female. The third, or sociological, meaning receives its connotation from the observation of actually existing masculine and feminine individuals. Such observation shows that in human beings pure masculinity or femininity is not to be found either in a psychological or a biological sense. Every individual on the contrary displays a mixture of the character-traits belonging to his own and to the opposite sex; and he shows a combination of activity and passivity whether or not these last character-traits tally with his biological ones. [A later discussion of this point will be found in a footnote at the end of Chapter IV of *Civilization and Its Discontents* (1930a).]

cur so often precisely in little girls are expressed in spasms of the clitoris. Frequent erections of that organ make it possible for girls to form a correct judgment, even without any instruction, of the sexual manifestations of the other sex: they merely transfer on to boys the sensations derived from their own sexual processes.

If we are to understand how a little girl turns into a woman, we must follow the further vicissitudes of this excitability of the clitoris. Puberty, which brings about so great an accession of libido in boys, is marked in girls by a fresh wave of *repression,* in which it is precisely clitoridal sexuality that is affected. What is thus overtaken by repression is a piece of masculine sexuality. The intensification of the brake upon sexuality brought about by pubertal repression in women serves as a stimulus to the libido in men and causes an increase of its activity. Along with this heightening of libido there is also an increase of sexual overvaluation which only emerges in full force in relation to a woman who holds herself back and who denies her sexuality. When at last the sexual act is permitted and the clitoris itself becomes excited, it still retains a function: the task, namely, of transmitting the excitation to the adjacent female sexual parts, just as—to use a simile—pine shavings can be kindled in order to set a log of harder wood on fire. Before this transference can be effected, a certain interval of time must often elapse, during which the young woman is anaesthetic. This anaesthesia may become permanent if the clitoridal zone refuses to abandon its excitability, an event for which the way is prepared precisely by an extensive activity of that zone in childhood. Anaesthesia in women, as is well known, it often only apparent and local. They are anaesthetic at the vaginal orifice but are by no means incapable of excitement originating in the clitoris or even in other zones. Alongside these erotogenic determinants of anaesthesia must also be set the psychical determinants, which equally arise from repression.

When erotogenic susceptibility to stimulation has been successfully transferred by a woman from the clitoris to the vaginal orifice, it implies that she has adopted a new leading zone for the purposes of her later sexual activity. A man, on the other hand, retains his leading zone unchanged from childhood. The fact that women change their leading zone in this way, together with the wave of repression at puberty, which, as it were, puts aside their childish masculinity, are the chief determinants of the greater proneness of women to neurosis and especially to hysteria. These determinants, therefore, are intimately related to the essence of femininity.

THE FINDING OF AN OBJECT

The processes at puberty thus establish the primacy of the genital zones; and, in a man, the penis, which has now become capable of erection, presses forward insistently towards the new sexual aim—penetration into a cavity in the body which excites his genital zone. Simultaneously on the psychical side the process of finding an object, for which preparations have been made from earliest childhood, is completed. At a time at which the first beginnings of sexual satisfaction are still linked with the taking of nourishment, the sexual instinct has a sexual object outside the infant's own body in the shape of his mother's breast. It is only later that the instinct loses that object, just at the time, perhaps, when the child is able to form a total idea of the person to whom the organ that is giving him satisfaction belongs. As a rule the sexual instinct then becomes auto-erotic, and not until the period of latency has been passed through is the original relation restored. There are thus good reasons why a child sucking at his mother's breast has become the protype of every relation of love. The finding of an object is in fact a refinding of it.[12]

The Sexual Object during Early Infancy.—But even after sexual activity has become detached from the taking of nourishment, an important part of this first and most significant of all sexual relations is left over, which helps to prepare for the choice of an object and thus to restore the happiness that has been lost. All through the period of latency children learn to feel for other people who help them in their helplessness and satisfy their needs a love which is on the model of, and a continuation of, their relation as sucklings to their nursing mother. There may perhaps be an inclination to dispute the possibility of identifying a child's affection and esteem for those who look after him with sexual love. I think, however, that a closer psychological examination may make it possible to establish this identity beyond any doubt. A child's intercourse with anyone responsible for his care affords him an unending source of sexual excitation and satisfaction from his erotogenic zones. This is especially so since the person in charge of him, who, after all, is as a rule his mother, herself regards him with feelings that are derived from her own sexual life: she strokes him, kisses him, rocks him and quite clearly treats him as a sub-

---

12. [*Footnote added* 1915:] Psycho-analysis informs us that there are two methods of finding an object. The first, described in the text, is the "anaclitic" or "attachment" one, based on attachment to early infantile prototypes. The second is the narcissistic one, which seeks for the subject's own ego and finds it again in other people. This latter method is of particularly great importance in cases where the outcome is a pathological one, but it is not relevant to the present context.

stitute for a complete sexual object.[13] A mother would probably be horrified if she were made aware that all her marks of affection were rousing her child's sexual instinct and preparing for its later intensity. She regards what she does as asexual, "pure" love, since, after all, she carefully avoids applying more excitations to the child's genitals than are unavoidable in nursery care. As we know, however, the sexual instinct is not aroused only by direct excitation of the genital zone. What we call affection will unfailingly show its effects one day on the genital zones as well. Moreover, if the mother understood more of the high importance of the part played by instincts in mental life as a whole—in all its ethical and psychical achievements—she would spare herself any self-reproaches even after her enlightenment. She is only fulfilling her task in teaching the child to love. After all, he is meant to grow up into a strong and capable person with vigorous sexual needs and to accomplish during his life all the things that human beings are urged to do by their instincts. It is true that an excess of parental affection does harm by causing precocious sexual maturity and also because, by spoiling the child, it makes him incapable in later life of temporarily doing without love or of being content with a smaller amount of it. One of the clearest indications that a child will later become neurotic is to be seen in an insatiable demand for his parents' affection. And on the other hand neuropathic parents, who are inclined as a rule to display excessive affection, are precisely those who are most likely by their caresses to arouse the child's disposition to neurotic illness. Incidentally, this example shows that there are ways more direct than inheritance by which neurotic parents can hand their disorder on to their children.

Infantile Anxiety.—Children themselves behave from an early age as though their dependence on the people looking after them were in the nature of sexual love. Anxiety in children is originally nothing other than an expression of the fact that they are feeling the loss of the person they love. It is for this reason that they are frightened of every stranger. They are afraid in the dark because in the dark they cannot see the person they love; and their fear is soothed if they can take hold of that person's hand in the dark. To attribute to bogeys and blood-curdling stories told by nurses the responsibility for making children timid is to over-estimate their efficacy. The truth is merely that children who are inclined to be timid are affected by stories which

would make no impression whatever upon others, and it is only children with a sexual instinct that is excessive or has developed prematurely or has become vociferous owing to too much petting who are inclined to be timid. In this respect a child, by turning his libido into anxiety when he cannot satisfy it, behaves like an adult. On the other hand an adult who has become neurotic owing to his libido being unsatisfied behaves in his anxiety like a child: he begins to be frightened when he is alone, that is to say when he is away from someone of whose love he had felt secure, and he seeks to assuage this fear by the most childish measures.[14]

The Barrier Against Incest.—We see, therefore, that the parents' affection for their child may awaken his sexual instinct prematurely (i.e. before the somatic conditions of puberty are present) to such a degree that the mental excitation breaks through in an unmistakable fashion to the genital system. If, on the other hand, they are fortunate enough to avoid this, then their affection can perform its task of directing the child in his choice of a sexual object when he reaches maturity. No doubt the simplest course for the child would be to choose as his sexual objects the same persons whom, since his childhood, he has loved with what may be described as damped-down libido.[15] But, by the postponing of sexual maturation, time has been gained in which the child can erect, among other restraints on sexuality, the barrier against incest, and can thus take up into himself the moral precepts which expressly exclude from his object-choice, as being blood-relations, the persons whom he has loved in his childhood. Respect for this barrier is essentially a cultural demand made by society. Society must defend itself against the danger that the interests which it needs for the establishment of higher social

---

13. Anyone who considers this "sacrilegious" may be recommended to read Havelock Ellis's views [1913, 18] on the relation between mother and child, which agree almost completely with mine.

14. For this explanation of the origin of infantile anxiety I have to thank a three-year-old boy whom I once heard calling out of dark room: "Auntie, speak to me! I'm frightened because it's so dark." His aunt answered him: "What good would that do? You can't see me." "That doesn't matter," replied the child, "if anyone speaks, it gets light." Thus what he was afraid of was not the dark, but the absence of someone he loved; and he could feel sure of being soothed as soon as he had evidence of that person's presence. [*Added* 1920:] One of the most important results of psycho-analytic research is this discovery that neurotic anxiety arises out of libido, that it is the product of a transformation of it, and that it is thus related to it in the same kind of way as vinegar is to wine. A further discussion of this problem will be found in my *Introductory Lectures on Psycho-Analysis* (1916–17), Lecture XXV, though even there, it must be confessed, the question is not finally cleared up. [For Freud's latest views on the subject of anxiety see his *Inhibitions, Symptoms and Anxiety* (1926*d*) and his *New Introductory Lectures* (1933*a*), Chapter XXXII.]

15. [*Footnote added* 1915:] Cf. what has been said [earlier] about children's object-choice and the "affectionate current."

units may be swallowed up by the family; and for this reason, in the case of every individual, but in particular of adolescent boys, it seeks by all possible means to loosen their connection with their family —a connection which, in their childhood, is the only important one.[16]

It is in the world of ideas, however, that the choice of an object is accomplished at first; and the sexual life of maturing youth is almost entirely restricted to indulging in phantasies, that is, in ideas that are not destined to be carried into effect. In these phantasies the infantile tendencies invariably emerge once more, but this time with intensified pressure from somatic sources. Among these tendencies the first place is taken with uniform frequency by the child's sexual impulses towards his parents, which are as a rule already differentiated owing to the attraction of the opposite sex—the son being drawn towards his mother and the daughter towards her father. At the same time as these plainly incestuous phantasies are overcome and repudiated, one of the most significant, but also one of the most painful, psychical achievements of the pubertal period is completed: detachment from parental authority, a process that alone makes possible the opposition, which is so important for the progress of civilization, between the new generation and the old. At every stage in the course of development through which all human beings ought by rights to pass, a certain number are held back; so there are some who have never got over their parents' authority and have withdrawn their affection from them either very incompletely or not at all. They are mostly girls, who, to the delight of their parents, have persisted in all their childish love far beyond puberty. It is most instructive to find that it is precisely these girls who in their later marriage lack the capacity to give their husbands what is due to them; they make cold wives and remain sexually anaesthetic. We learn from this that sexual love and what appears to be non-sexual love for parents are fed from the same sources; the latter, that is to say, merely corresponds to an infantile fixation of the libido.

The closer one comes to the deeper disturbances of psycho-sexual development, the more unmistak-

ably the importance of incestuous object-choice emerges. In psychoneurotics a large portion or the whole of their psychosexual activity in finding an object remains in the unconscious as a result of their repudiation of sexuality. Girls with an exaggerated need for affection and an equally exaggerated horror of the real demands made by sexual life have an irresistible temptation on the one hand to realize the ideal of asexual love in their lives and on the other hand to conceal their libido behind an affection which they can express without self-reproaches, by holding fast throughout their lives to their infantile fondness, revived at puberty, for their parents or brothers and sisters. Psychoanalysis has no difficulty in showing persons of this kind that they are *in love,* in the everyday sense of the word, with these blood-relations of theirs; for, with the help of their symptoms and other manifestations of their illness, it traces their unconscious thoughts and translates them into conscious ones. In cases in which someone who has previously been healthy falls ill after an unhappy experience in love it is also possible to show with certainty that the mechanism of his illness consists in a turning-back of his libido on to those whom he preferred in his infancy.

After-Effects of Infantile Object-Choice. Even a person who has been fortunate enough to avoid an incestuous fixation of his libido does not entirely escape its influence. It often happens that a young man falls in love seriously for the first time with a mature woman, or a girl with an elderly man in a position of authority; this is clearly an echo of the phase of development that we have been discussing, since these figures are able to re-animate pictures of their mother or father. There can be no doubt that every object-choice whatever is based, though less closely, on these prototypes. A man, especially, looks for someone who can represent his picture of his mother, as it has dominated his mind from his earliest childhood; and accordingly, if his mother is still alive, she may well resent this new version of herself and meet her with hostility. In view of the importance of a child's relations to his parents in determining his later choice of a sexual object, it can easily be understood that any disturbance of those relations will produce the gravest effects upon his adult sexual life. Jealousy in a lover is never without an infantile root or at least an infantile reinforcement. If there are quarrels between the parents or if their marriage is unhappy, the ground will be prepared in their children for the severest predisposition to a disturbance of sexual development or to a neurotic illness.

A child's affection of his parents is no doubt the most important infantile trace which, after being revived at puberty, points the way to his choice of

---

16. [*Footnote added* 1915:] The barrier against incest is probably among the historical acquisitions of mankind, and, like other moral taboos, has no doubt already become established in many persons by organic inheritance. (Cf. my *Totem and Taboo,* 1912–13.) Psycho-analytic investigation shows, however, how intensely the individual struggles with the temptation to incest during his period of growth and how frequently the barrier is transgressed in phantasies and even in reality.—[Though this is its first published appearance, the "horror of incest" had been discussed by Freud on May 31, 1897 (Draft N in Freud, 1950*a*)—some months, that is, before his first revelation of the Oedipus complex. In that draft too he accounts for it on the ground that incest is "antisocial."]

an object; but it is not the only one. Other starting-points with the same early origin enable a man to develop more than one sexual line, based no less upon his childhood, and to lay down very various conditions for his object-choice.[17]

Prevention of Inversion.—One of the tasks implicit in object-choice is that it should find its way to the opposite sex. This, as we know, is not accomplished without a certain amount of fumbling. Often enough the first impulses after puberty go astray, though without any permanent harm resulting. Dessoir [1894] has justly remarked upon the regularity with which adolescent boys and girls form sentimental friendships with others of their own sex. No doubt the strongest force working against a permanent inversion of the sexual object is the attraction which the opposing sexual characters exercise upon one another. Nothing can be said within the framework of the present discussion to throw light upon it. This factor is not in itself, however, sufficient to exclude inversion; there are no doubt a variety of other contributory factors. Chief among these is its authoritative prohibition by society. Where inversion is not regarded as a crime it will be found that it answers fully to the sexual

inclinations of no small number of people. It may be presumed, in the next place, that in the case of men a childhood recollection of the affection shown them by their mother and others of the female sex who looked after them when they were children contributes powerfully to directing their choice towards women, on the other hand their early experience of being deterred by their father from sexual activity and their competitive relation with him deflect them from their own sex. Both of these two factors apply equally to girls whose sexual activity is particularly subject to the watchful guardianship of their mother. They thus acquire a hostile relation to their own sex which influences their object-choice decisively in what is regarded as the normal direction. The education of boys by male persons (by slaves, in antiquity) seems to encourage homosexuality. The frequency of inversion among the present-day aristocracy is made somewhat more intelligible by their employment of menservants, as well as by the fact that their mothers give less personal care to their children. In the case of some hysterics it is found that the early loss of one of their parents, whether by death, divorce or separation, with the result that the remaining parent absorbs the whole of the child's love, determines the sex of the person who is later to be chosen as a sexual object, and may thus open the way to permanent inversion.

17. [*Footnote added* 1915:] The innumerable peculiarities of the erotic life of human beings as well as the compulsive character of the process of falling in love itself are quite unintelligible except by reference back to childhood and as being residual effects of childhood.

6. On the Internalization of the Sex Role: the Feminine Case

BY SIGMUND FREUD

IN APPROACHING the study of the sexual development of women we start with two preconceptions: firstly, that, as is the case of men, the constitution will not adapt itself to its function without a struggle; and secondly, that the decisive changes will have been set in motion or completed before puberty. Both of these preconceptions turn out to be justified. Further, a comparison with what happens in the case of the boy shows us that the development of the little girl into a normal woman is

more difficult and more complicated; for she has two additional tasks to perform, to which there is nothing corresponding in the development of the man. Let us follow the parallel from the very beginning. Certainly the original material is different in the boy and the girl; it does not require psychoanalysis to find that out. The difference in the formation of their genital organs is accompanied by other bodily differences, which are too familiar for me to need to mention them. In their instinctual disposition, as well, there are differences which foreshadow the later nature of the woman. The little girl is as a rule less aggressive, less defiant, and less self-sufficient; she seems to have a greater need for

Reprinted from Sigmund Freud, *New Introductory Lectures*, trans. W. J. H. Sprott (New York: W. W. Norton & Co., 1933), pp. 159–85, with the permission of W. W. Norton & Co., Inc., and Hogarth Press, Ltd.

affection to be shown her, and therefore to be more dependent and docile. The fact that she is more easily and more quickly taught to control her excretions is very probably only the result of this docility; urine and stool are, as we know, the first gifts that the child can offer to those who look after it, and control over them is the first concession which can be wrung from the instinctual life of the child. One gets the impression, too, that the little girl is more intelligent and more lively than the boy of the same age; she is more inclined to meet the external world half way, and, at the same time, she makes stronger object-cathexes. I do not know whether the view that she gets a start in development has been confirmed by more exact observations, but in any case it is quite clear that the little girl cannot be called intellectually backward. But these sexual differences are of no great importance; they can be out-balanced by individual variations. For the purposes which we have immediately in view they may be left on one side.

Both sexes seem to pass through the early phases of libidinal development in the same way. One might have expected that already in the sadistic-anal phase we should find that the girl showed less aggressiveness; but this is not the case. Women analysts have found from the analysis of children's play that the aggressive impulses of little girls leave nothing to be desired as regards copiousness and violence. With the onset of the phallic phase the difference between the sexes becomes much less important than their similarities. We are now obliged to recognise that the little girl is a little man. As we know, in the boy this phase is characterised by the fact that he has discovered how to obtain pleasurable sensations from his little penis, and associates its state of excitation with his ideas about sexual intercourse. The little girl does the same with her even smaller clitoris. It seems as though with her, all her masturbatory actions center round this penis-equivalent, and that the actual female vagina is still undiscovered by both sexes. It is true that, here and there, reports have been made that tell us of early vaginal sensations as well; but it cannot be easy to discriminate between these and anal sensations or from sensations of the vaginal vestibule; in any case they·cannot play a very important rôle. We may assume that, in the phallic phase of the girl, the clitoris is the dominant erotogenic zone. But it is not destined to remain so; with the change to femininity, the clitoris must give up to the vagina its sensitivity, and, with it, its importance, either wholly or in part. This is one of the two tasks which have to be performed in the course of the woman's development; the more fortunate man has only to continue at the time of his sexual maturity what he has already practised during the period of early sexual expansion.

We shall return to the part played by the clitoris, but shall now pass on to the second task with which the girl's development is burdened. The first love-object of the boy is his mother, and she remains as such in the formation of his Oedipus-complex, and, ultimately, throughout his whole life. For the little girl, too, her mother must be her first object (together with figures of nurses and other attendants that merge into hers); the first object-cathexes, indeed, follow the lines of the satisfaction of the great and simple needs of life, and the circumstances in which the child is nursed are the same for both sexes. In the Oedipus situation, however, the father has become the little girl's love-object, and it is from him that, in the normal course of development, she should find her way to her ultimate object-choice. The girl has, then, in the course of time to change both her erotogenic zone and her object, while the boy keeps both of them unchanged. The question then arises of how this comes about. In particular, how does the little girl pass from an attachment to her mother to an attachment to her father? or, in other words, how does she pass from her masculine phase into the feminine phase which has been biologically marked out for her?

Now it would provide us with an ideally simple solution of the problem if we could assume that, from a certain age onwards, the elementary influence of hetero-sexual attraction makes itself felt, and draws the little girl towards men, while the same principle allows the boy to keep to his mother. One could even assume further, that, in doing this, children are following a hint given them by the sexual preferences of their parents. But things are not so convenient as this. We hardly know whether we can seriously believe in the mysterious and unanalysable force, of which the poets sing so enthusiastically. Painstaking investigations have resulted in findings of quite a different kind, the material for which, at all events, was easily obtainable. You must know that the number of women who until late in life remain tenderly attached to father-objects, or indeed to their real fathers, is very large. We have made the most surprising discoveries about these women who display intense and prolonged father-fixations. We knew, of course, that there had been an earlier stage in which they were attached to their mother; but we did not know that it was so rich in content, that it persisted so long, and that it could leave behind it so many occasions for fixations and predispositions. During this time, their father is no more than an irksome rival. In many cases the attachment to the mother lasts beyond the fourth year; almost everything that we find later in the father-relation was already present in that attachment, and has been subsequently transferred on to the father. In short, we gain the conviction that one cannot understand women, unless one estimates this *pre-oedipal attachment to the mother* at its proper value.

Now we should very much like to know what the libidinal relations of the little girl to her mother are. The answer is that they are manifold. Since they pass through all the three phases of infantile sexuality, they take on the characteristics of each separate phase, and express themselves by means of oral, sadistic-anal, and phallic wishes. These wishes represent active as well as passive impulses; if one relates them to the differentiation of the sexes which comes about later (which one should avoid doing as far as possible), one can speak of them as masculine and feminine. They are, in addition, completely ambivalent—both of a tender and of a hostile-aggressive nature. It often happens that the hostile wishes only become apparent after they have been turned into anxiety-ideas. It is not always easy to point out the way in which these early sexual wishes are formulated. What is most clearly expressed is the desire to get the mother with child as well as the corresponding one, to have a child by the mother; both belong to the phallic phase, and seem sufficiently strange, though their existence is established beyond all doubt by analytic observation. The attraction of these investigations lies in the extraordinary facts which they bring to light. Thus, for instance, one discovers the fear of being murdered or poisoned, which may later on form the nucleus of a paranoic disorder, already present in this pre-oedipal stage and directed against the mother. Or, to take another case. You will remember that interesting episode in the history of analytical research which caused me so many painful hours? At the time when my main interest was directed on to the discovery of infantile sexual traumas, almost all my female patients told me that they had been seduced by their fathers. Eventually I was forced to the conclusion that these stories were false, and thus I came to understand that hysterical symptoms spring from phantasies and not from real events. Only later was I able to recognise in this phantasy of seduction by the father the expression of the typical Oedipus-complex in woman. And now we find, in the early pre-oedipal history of girls, the seduction-phantasy again; but the seducer is invariably the mother. Here, however, the phantasy has a footing in reality; for it must in fact have been the mother who aroused (perhaps for the first time) pleasurable sensations in the child's genitals in the ordinary course of attending to its bodily needs.

I dare say that you are prepared to suspect that this description of the richness and strength of the sexual relations of the little girl to her mother is very much exaggerated. One has, after all, plenty of opportunity of watching little girls, and one notices nothing of the sort. But the objection cannot be sustained. One can see enough of such things in children, if one understands how to observe them, and, besides this, you must consider how little the child is able to give preconscious expression to its sexual wishes, and how little it can communicate them. We are therefore acting entirely within our rights in studying the subsequent traces and consequences of this emotional field in persons in whom these developmental processes show a particularly clear, or even exaggerated, growth. Pathology, as you know, has always assisted us, by isolation and exaggeration, in making recognisable things which would normally remain hidden. And since our researches have been carried out on people who are by no means grossly abnormal, we may, I think, consider the results of them worthy of belief.

We will now turn our attention to the question of why this strong attachment of the girl to her mother comes to grief. We are aware that that is what usually happens to it; it is fated to give way to an attachment to her father. And here we stumble on a fact which points in the right direction. This step in development is not merely a question of a change of object. The turning away from the mother occurs in an atmosphere of antagonism; the attachment to the mother ends in hate. Such a hatred may be very marked and may persist throughout an entire lifetime; it may later on be carefully overcompensated; as a rule, one part of it is overcome, while another part persists. The outcome is naturally very strongly influenced by the actual events of later years. We will confine ourselves to studying this hatred at the actual time at which the turn towards the father takes place, and to inquiring into its motives. We are then met by a long list of complaints and grievances, levelled at the mother, which are intended to justify the antagonistic feelings of the child; they vary much in value, and we shall examine them further. Many are obvious rationalisations, and we have yet to find the true source of the antagonism. I hope you will bear with me, if on this occasion I conduct you through all the details of a psychoanalytical investigation.

The complaint against the mother that harks back furthest, is that she has given the child too little milk, which is taken as indicating a lack of love. Now this complaint has a certain justification in the civilised human family. The mothers often have not enough nourishment for their children, and content themselves with nursing them for nine months or six or even less. Among primitive peoples children remain at the breast for as long as two or three years. The figure of the wet-nurse is as a rule merged in that of the mother; where this does not take place, the complaint against the mother takes another form, namely, that she sent the nurse, who was so ready to feed the child, away too soon. But whatever may have been the true state of affairs, it is impossible that the child's complaint can be as often justified as it is met with. It looks far more as if the desire of the child for its first form of nourishment is altogether insatiable, and as if it never got over the pain of losing the mother's breast. I should not be at all surprised if an analysis of a member of a primitive race, who must have sucked the mother's breast when he could already run and talk, brought the same complaint to light. It is probable, too, that the fear of poisoning is connected with weaning. Poison is the nourishment that makes one ill. Perhaps, moreover, the child traces his early illnesses back to this frustration. It requires a good deal of intellectual training before we can believe in chance; primitive and uneducated people, and certainly children, can give a reason for everything that happens. Perhaps this reason was originally a motive (in the animistic sense). In many social strata, even to this day, no one can die, without having been done to death by some one else, preferably by the doctor. And the regular reaction of a neurotic to the death of some one intimately connected with him is to accuse himself of being the cause of the death.

The next accusation against the mother flares up when the next child makes its appearance in the nursery. If possible this complaint retains the connection with oral frustration: the mother could not or would not give the child any more milk, because she needed the nourishment for the new arrival. In cases where the two children were born so close together that lactation was interfered with by the second pregnancy, this complaint has a real foundation. It is a remarkable fact that even when the difference between the children's ages is only eleven months, the older one is nevertheless able to take in the state of affairs. But it is not only the milk that the child grudges the undesired interloper and rival, but all the other evidences of motherly care. It feels that it has been dethroned, robbed and had its rights invaded, and so it directs a feeling of jealous hatred against its little brother or sister, and develops resentment against its faithless mother, which often finds expression in a change for the worse in its behaviour. It begins to be "naughty," irritable, intractable, and unlearns the control which it has acquired over its excretions. All this has been known for a long time, and is accepted as self-evident, but we seldom form a right idea of the strength of these jealous impulses, of the tenacious hold they have on the child, and the amount of influence they exert on

its later development. These jealous feelings are particularly important because they are always being fed anew during the later years of childhood, and the whole shattering experience is repeated with the arrival of every new brother or sister. Even if the child remains its mother's favourite, things are not very different; its demands for affection are boundless; it requires exclusive attention and will allow no sharing whatever.

A potent source of the child's antagonism against its mother is found in its many sexual wishes, which change with its libidinal phases. These cannot, for the most part, be satisfied. The strongest of these frustrations occurs in the phallic stage, when the mother forbids pleasurable activities centering round the genital organs—often with an accompaniment of harsh threats and every indication of disapproval—activities to which, after all, she herself stimulated the child. It might be thought that we had here motives enough for the little girl's alienation from her mother. In that case it might be our view that estrangement follows inevitably from the nature of infantile sexuality, from the child's unlimited demands for love and the unfulfillable nature of its sexual wishes. One might even believe that this first love relation of the child is doomed to extinction for the very reason that it is the first, for these early object-cathexes are always ambivalent to a very high degree; alongside the child's intense love there is always a strong aggressive tendency present, and the more passionately the child loves an object, the more sensitive it will be to disappointments and frustrations coming from it. In the end, the love is bound to capitulate to the accumulated hostility. Or, on the other hand, one might reject the idea of a fundamental ambivalence of this kind in the libidinal cathexes, and point to the fact that it is the peculiar nature of the mother-child relationship which leads, equally inevitably, to the disturbance of the child's love, since even the mildest form of education cannot avoid using compulsion and introducing restrictions, and every such encroachment on its freedom must call forth as a reaction in the child a tendency to rebellion and aggressiveness. A discussion of these possibilities might, I think, be very interesting, but at this point an objection suddenly arises, which forces our attention in another direction. All of these factors—slights, disappointments in love, jealousy and seduction followed by prohibition—operate as well in the relationship between the boy and his mother, and yet are not sufficient to alienate him from the mother-object. If we do not find something which is specific for the girl, and which is not present at all, or not present in the same way in the case of the boy, we shall not have explained the ending of the girl attachment to her mother.

I think that we have discovered this specific factor, in a place where we might indeed have expected it, but in a surprising form. In a place where we might have expected it, I say, for it lies in the castration complex. The anatomical distinction between the sexes must, after all, leave its mark in mental life. It was a surprise, however, to discover from analyses that the girl holds her mother responsible for her lack of a penis, and never forgives her for that deficiency.

You will note that we ascribe a castration-complex to the female sex as well as to the male. We have good grounds for doing so, but that complex has not the same content in girls as in boys. In the boy the castration-complex is formed after he has learnt from the sight of the female genitals that the sexual organ which he prizes so highly is not a necessary part of every human body. He remembers then the threats which he has brought on himself by his playing with his penis, he begins to believe in them, and thence forward he comes under the influence of *castration-anxiety,* which supplies the strongest motive force for his further development. The castration-complex in the girl, as well, is started by the sight of the genital organs of the other sex. She immediately notices the difference, and—it must be admitted—its significance. She feels herself at a great disadvantage, and often declares that she would "like to have something like that too," and falls a victim to *penis-envy,* which leaves ineradicable traces on her development and character-formation, and, even in the most favourable instances, is not overcome without a great expenditure of mental energy. That the girl recognises the fact that she lacks a penis, does not mean that she accepts its absence lightly. On the contrary, she clings for a long time to the desire to get something like it, and believes in that possibility for an extraordinary number of years; and even at a time when her knowledge of reality has long since led her to abandon the fulfilment of this desire as being quite unattainable, analysis proves that it still persists in the unconscious, and retains a considerable charge of energy. The desire after all to obtain the penis for which she so much longs may even contribute to the motives that impel a grown-up woman to come to analysis; and what she quite reasonably expects to get from analysis, such as the capacity to pursue an intellectual career, can often be recognised as a sublimated modification of this repressed wish.

One cannot very well doubt the importance of penis-envy. Perhaps you will regard the hypothesis that envy and jealousy play a greater part in the mental life of women than they do in that of men as an example of male unfairness. Not that I think that these characteristics are absent in men, or that they have no other origin in women except envy of the penis, but I am inclined to ascribe the greater amount of them to be found in women to this latter influence. Many analysts, however, tend to minimize the importance of this first wave of penis-envy in the phallic phase. They think that the signs one comes across of this attitude in women are in the main a secondary formation, which has come about through regression to the early infantile impulse in question on the occasion of some subsequent conflict. Now this is one of the general problems of depth psychology. In the case of many pathological —or merely unusual—instinctual attitudes, for example with all sexual perversions, the question arises how much of their force is to be attributed to early infantile fixations and how much to the influence of later experiences and developments. It is almost always a question of complemental series, such as we have postulated when dealing with the aetiology of the neuroses. Both sets of factors share in the causation in a varying proportion; a less in the one set will be balanced by a more in the other. The infantile factor in every case paves the way; it is not always the decisive force, though it often is. But with regard to the particular case of penis-envy, I should like to come down decidedly in favour of the preponderance of the infantile factor.

The discovery of her castration is a turning-point in the life of the girl. Three lines of development diverge from it; one leads to sexual inhibition or to neurosis, the second to a modification of character in the sense of masculinity complex, and the third to normal femininity. We have learnt a good deal, though not everything, about all three. The fundamental content of the first is that the little girl, who has hitherto lived a masculine life, and has been able to obtain pleasure through the excitation of her clitoris, and has connected this behaviour with the sexual wishes (often of an active character) which she has directed towards her mother, finds her enjoyment of phallic sexuality spoilt by the influence of penis-envy. She is wounded in her self-love by the unfavourable comparison with the boy who is so much better equipped, and therefore gives up the masturbatory satisfaction which she obtained from her clitoris, repudiates her love towards her mother, and at the same time often represses a good deal of her sexual impulses in general. No doubt this turning away from her mother does not come to pass at one blow, for at first the girl looks on her castration as a personal misfortune, and only gradually extends it to other females, and eventually to her mother. Her love had as its object the phallic mother; with the discovery that the mother is castrated it becomes possible to drop her as a love-object, so that the incentives to hostility which have been so long accumulating, get the upper hand. This means, therefore, that as a result of the discovery of the absence of a penis, women are as much depreciated in the eyes of the girl as in the eyes of the boy, and later, perhaps, of the man.

You all know what an overwhelming aetiological importance is attributed by neurotics to their masturbatory practices. They make them responsible for all their troubles, and we have the greatest difficulty in getting them to believe that they are wrong. But as a matter of fact we ought to admit that they are in the right, for masturbation is the executive agent of infantile sexuality, from the faulty development of which they are suffering. The difference is that what the neurotics are blaming is the masturbation of the pubertal stage; the infantile masturbation, which is the one that really matters, has for the most part been forgotten by them. I wish I could find an opportunity for giving you a circumstantial account of how important all the factual details of early masturbation are in determining the subsequent neurosis or character of the individual concerned—such details as whether it was discovered or not, how the parents combated it or whether they permitted it, and whether the subject succeeded in suppressing it himself. All these details will have left indelible traces upon his development. But in fact I am relieved that it is not necessary for me to do this; it would be a difficult and weary task, and at the end you would embarrass me because you would quite certainly ask for some practical advice as to how one should behave towards the masturbation of small children as a parent or educator. The history of the development of girls, which is the subject I am telling you about, offers an instance of the child itself striving to free itself from masturbation. But it does not always succeed. Where penis-envy has aroused a strong impulse against clitoritic masturbation, but where the latter will not give way, there follows a fierce battle for freedom, in which the girl herself takes over, as it were, the rôle of the mother whom she has set aside, and expresses her whole dissatisfaction with the inferior clitoris, by striving against the gratification derived from it. Many years later, when her masturbatory activity has long ago been suppressed, we may find an interest persisting which we must interpret as a defence against the temptation, which she still fears. It finds expression in feelings of sympathy for persons to whom she ascribes similar difficulties; it may enter into her motives for marriage, and may indeed determine her choice of a husband or lover. The settling of the problem of infantile masturbation is truly no easy or unimportant task.

When the little girl gives up clitoritic masturbation, she surrenders a certain amount of activity. Her passive side has now the upper hand, and in turning to her father she is assisted in the main by passive instinctual impulses. You will see that a step in development, such as this one, which gets rid of phallic activity, must smooth the path for femininity. If in the process not too much is lost through repression, this femininity may prove normal. The wish with which the girl turns to her father, is, no doubt, ultimately the wish for the penis, which her mother has refused her and which she now expects from her father. The feminine situation is, however, only established when the wish for the penis is replaced by the wish for a child—the child taking the place of the penis, in accordance with the old symbolic equation. It does not escape us that at an earlier stage the girl has already desired a child, before the phallic phase was interfered with; that was the meaning of her playing with dolls. But this play was not really an expression of her femininity, it served, in identifying her with her mother, the purpose of substituting activity for passivity. She was the mother, and the doll was herself; now she could do everything to the doll that her mother used to do with her. Only with the onset of the desire for a penis does the doll-child become a child by the father, and, thenceforward, the strongest feminine wish. Her happiness is great indeed when this desire for a child one day finds a real fulfilment; but especially is this so if the child is a little boy, who brings the longed-for penis with him. In the idea of having a child by the father, the accent is often enough placed on the child, and not on the father. Thus the old masculine wish for the possession of a penis still shows under the completely developed femininity. But perhaps we should rather think of this desire for a penis as something essentially feminine in itself.

With the transference of the child-penis wish on to her father, the girl enters into the situation of the Oedipus-complex. The hostility against her mother, which did not require to be newly created, now receives a great reinforcement, for her mother becomes a rival, who gets everything from her father that she herself wants. The girl's Oedipus-complex has long concealed from us the pre-oedipal attachment to her mother which is so important and which leaves behind it such lasting fixations. For the girl, the Oedipus situation is the conclusion of a long and difficult period of development, it is a kind of temporary solution of her problem, a state of equilibrium which is not lightly to be given up, especially as the onset of the latency period is not far off. And here we notice a difference between the two sexes in the relation between the Oedipus-complex and the castration-complex, a difference which is probably a momentous one. The boy's Oedipus-complex, in which he desires his mother, and wants to get rid of his father as a rival, develops naturally out of the phase of phallic sexuality. The threat of castration, however, forces him to give up this attitude. Under the influence of the danger of losing his penis, he abandons his Oedipus-complex; it is repressed and in the most normal cases entirely destroyed, while a severe super-ego is set up as its heir. What happens in the case of the girl is almost the opposite. The castration-complex prepares the way for the Oedipus-complex instead of destroying it; under the influence of her penis-envy the girl is driven from her attachment to her mother, and enters the Oedipus situation, as though it were a haven of refuge. When the fear of castration disappears, the primary motive is removed, which has forced the boy to overcome his Oedipus-complex. The girl remains in the Oedipus situation for an indefinite period, she only abandons it late in life, and then incompletely. The formation of the super-ego must suffer in these circumstances; it cannot attain the strength and independence which give it its cultural importance and feminists are not pleased if one points to the way in which this factor affects the development of the average feminine character.

Let us now go back a little. We have mentioned, as the second possible reaction after the discovery of female castration, the development of a strong masculinity complex. What is meant by this is that the girl refuses, as it were, to accept the unpalatable fact, and, in an outburst of defiance, exaggerates still further the masculinity which she has displayed hitherto. She clings to her clitoritic activities, and takes refuge in an identification either with the phallic mother, or with the father. What is the determinant which leads to this state of affairs? We can picture it as nothing other than a constitutional factor: the possession of a greater degree of activity, such as is usually characteristic of the male. The essential thing about the process is, after all, that at this point of development the onset of passivity, which makes possible the change over to femininity, is avoided. The most extreme achievement of this masculinity complex seems to occur when it influences the girl's object-choice in the direction of manifest homosexuality. Analytic experience teaches us, it is true, that female homosexuality is seldom or never a direct continuation of infantile masculinity. It seems to be characteristic of female homosexuals that they too take the father as love-object for a while, and thus become implicated in the Oedipus situation. Then, however, they are driven by the inevitable disappointments

which they experience from the father into a regression to their early masculinity complex. One must not overestimate the importance of these disappointments; girls who eventually achieve femininity also experience them without the same results. The preponderance of the constitutional factor seems undeniable, but the two phases in the development of female homosexuality are admirably reflected in the behaviour of homosexuals, who just as often and just as obviously play the parts of mother and child towards each other as those of man and wife.

What I have been telling you is what one might call the pre-history of women. It is an achievement of the last few years, and you may have been interested in it as an example of detailed work in analysis. Since women are our theme, I am going to permit myself to mention by name a few women to whom this investigation owes important contributions. Dr. Ruth Mack Brunswick was the first to describe a case of neurosis which went back to a fixation on the pre-oedipal state, and in which the Oedipus situation was not reached at all. It took the form of paranoia with delusions of jealousy, and proved accessible to treatment. Dr. Jeanne Lamplde Groot has from her own unequivocal observations established the fact of the girl's phallic activities towards her mother which seem so hard to believe. Dr. Helene Deutsch has shown that the erotic behaviour of homosexual woman reproduces the mother-child relationship.

It is not my intention to trace the further course of femininity through puberty up to the time of maturity. Our views on the subject are indeed not complete enough for me to do so. In what follows, I will merely mention a few separate points. Bearing in mind the early history of femininity, I will emphasise the fact that its development remains open to disturbance from the traces left behind by the previous masculine period. Regressions to fixations at these pre-oedipal phases occur very often; in many women we actually find a repeated alternation of periods in which either masculinity or femininity has obtained the upper hand. What we men call "the enigma of woman" is probably based in part upon these signs of bi-sexuality in female life. But another question seems to have become ripe for discussion in the course of these investigations. We have called the motor force of sexual life "libido." This sexual life is dominated by the polarity, masculine-feminine; one is therefore tempted to consider the relation of the libido to this polarity. It would not be surprising if it turned out that each form of sexuality had its own special form of libido, so that one kind of libido pursued the aims of the masculine sexual life, and the other those of the feminine. Nothing of the sort, however, is the case. There is only one libido which is as much in the service of the male as of the female sexual function. To it itself we can assign no sex; if, in accordance with the conventional analogy between activity and masculinity, we choose to call it masculine, we must not forget that it also includes impulses with passive aims. Nevertheless the phrase "feminine libido" cannot possibly be justified. It is our impression that more violence is done to the libido when it is forced into the service of the female function; and that—to speak teleologically—Nature has paid less careful attention to the demands of the female function than to those of masculinity. And—again speaking teleologically—this may be based on the fact that the achievement of the biological aim is entrusted to the aggressiveness of the male, and is to some extent independent of the co-operation of the female.

The sexual frigidity of women, the frequency of which seems to confirm this last point, is still a phenomenon which is insufficiently understood. Sometimes it is psychogenic, and, if so, it is accessible to influence; but in other cases one is led to assume that it is constitutionally conditioned or even partly caused by an anatomical factor.

I have promised to put before you a few more of the mental characteristics of mature femininity, as we find them in our analytical observation. We do not claim for these assertions more than that they are true on the whole; and it is not always easy to distinguish between what is due to influence of the sexual function and what to social training. We attribute to women a greater amount of narcissism (and this influences their object-choice) so that for them to be loved is a stronger need than to love. Their vanity is partly a further effect of penis-envy, for they are driven to rate their physical charms more highly as a belated compensation for their original sexual inferiority. Modesty, which is regarded as a feminine characteristic *par excellence,* but is far more a matter of convention than one would think, was, in our opinion, originally designed to hide the deficiency in her genitals. We do not forget that, later on, it takes over other functions. People say that women contributed but little to the discoveries and inventions of civilisation, but perhaps after all they did discover one technical process, that of plaiting and weaving. If this is so, one is tempted to guess at the unconscious motive at the back of this achievement. Nature herself might be regarded as having provided a model for imitation, by causing pubic hair to grow at the period of sexual maturity so as to veil the genitals.

The step that remained to be taken was to attach the hairs permanently together, whereas in the body they are fixed in the skin and only tangled with one another. If you repudiate this idea as being fantastic, and accuse me of having an *idée fixe* on the subject of the influence exercised by the lack of a penis upon the development of femininity, I cannot of course defend myself.

The conditions of object-choice in women are often enough made unrecognisable by social considerations. Where that choice is allowed to manifest itself freely, it often occurs according to the narcissistic ideal of the man whom the girl would have liked to be. If the girl has remained attached to her father, if that is to say she has remained in the Oedipus-complex, then she chooses according to a father-type. Since, when she turned from her mother to her father, the antagonistic part of her ambivalent feelings remained directed on to her mother, such a choice should ensure a happy marriage. But very often a factor emerges which in general imperils such solutions of the ambivalence-conflict. The antagonism which has been left behind may follow in the wake of the positive attachment, and extend to the new object. The husband, who had in the first instance inherited his position from the father, comes in the course of time to inherit the position of the mother as well. In this way it may easily occur that the second part of a woman's life is taken up with a struggle against her husband, just as the shorter earlier part was occupied with rebellion against her mother. After this reaction has been lived out, a second marriage may easily turn out far more satisfactorily. Another change in a woman's nature, for which neither husband nor wife are prepared, may come about after the first child has been born. Under the influence of her own motherhood, her identification with her mother may be revived (an identification against which she has struggled up to the time of her marriage) and may attract to itself all the libido that she has at her disposal, so that the repetition-compulsion may reproduce an unhappy marriage of the parents. That the old factor of lack of penis has not even yet forfeited its power is seen in the different reactions of the mother according to whether the child born is a son or a daughter. The only thing that brings a mother undiluted satisfaction is her relation to a son; it is quite the most complete relationship between human beings, and the one that is the most free from ambivalence. The mother can transfer to her son all the ambition which she has had to suppress in herself, and she can hope to get from him the satisfaction of all that has remained to her of her masculinity complex. Even a marriage is not firmly assured until the woman has succeeded in making her husband into her child and in acting the part of a mother towards him.

The mother-identification of the woman can be seen to have two levels, the pre-oedipal, which is based on the tender attachment to the mother and which takes her as a model, and the later one, derived from the Oedipus-complex, which tries to get rid of the mother and replace her in her relationship with the father. Much of both remains over for the future. One is really justified in saying that neither is overcome to any adequate extent during the process of development. But the phase of tender pre-oedipal attachment is the decisive one; it paves the way for her acquisition of those characteristics which will later enable her to play her part in the sexual function adequately, and carry out her inestimable social activities. In this identification, too, she acquires that attractiveness for the man which kindles his oedipal attachment to his mother into love. Only what happens so often is, that it is not he himself who gets what he wanted, but his son. One forms the impression that the love of man and the love of woman are separated by a psychological phase-difference.

It must be admitted that women have but little sense of justice, and this is no doubt connected with the preponderance of envy in their mental life; for the demands of justice are a modification of envy; they lay down the conditions under which one is willing to part with it. We say also of women that their social interests are weaker than those of men, and that their capacity for the sublimation of their instincts is less. The former is no doubt derived from the unsocial character which undoubtedly attaches to all sexual relationships. Lovers find complete satisfaction in each other, and even the family resists absorption into wider organisations. The capacity for sublimation is subject to the greatest individual variations. In spite of this I cannot refrain from mentioning an impression which one receives over and over again in analytic work. A man of about thirty seems a youthful, and, in a sense, an incompletely developed individual, of whom we expect that he will be able to make good use of the possibilities of development, which analysis lays open to him. But a woman of about the same age frequently staggers us by her psychological rigidity and unchangeability. Her libido has taken up its final positions, and seems powerless to leave them for others. There are no paths open to her for further development; it is as though the whole process had been gone through, and remained inaccessible to influence for the future; as though, in fact, the difficult development which leads to femininity had exhausted all the possibilities of the individual. As therapeutists we deplore this state of affairs, even when we are successful in removing her sufferings by solving her neurotic conflict.

That is all I had to say to you about the psychology of women. It is admittedly incomplete and fragmentary, and sometimes it does not sound altogether flattering. You must not forget, however, that we have only described women in so far as their natures are determined by their sexual function. The influence of this factor is, of course, very far-reaching, but we must remember that an individual woman may be a human being apart from this. If you want to know more about femininity, you must interrogate your own experience, or turn to the poets, or else wait until Science can give you more profound and more coherent information.

7. On the Learning of Discipline

BY EMILE DURKHEIM

AFTER HAVING ISOLATED the different components of morality, we shall try to find out how they can be implanted or developed in the child. We shall begin with the first component we have isolated, which is the spirit of discipline.

The very nature of the problem determines the method that we shall follow. We know the goal to be reached, that is, the goal to which the child must be led, but the manner in which he must be led and the road through which he must travel, depend neces-

Translated by Jesse Pitts, from Emile Durkheim, l'Education Morale (Paris: Felix Alcan, 1925), pp. 147, 148, 149, 151–64. This section is from the ninth in a series of lectures given by Durkheim in 1902–3.

sarily upon what type of person he is at the beginning. Actually, educative action never starts with a clean slate. The child has his own personality, and since it is this personality which must be taught, we should first try to understand it if we wish our action to be effective. We first have to ask ourselves to what extent and in what ways the child is ready for the state of mind we wish to develop in him; among his native abilities, what are those upon which we can draw in order to obtain the desired result. The moment has come to inquire into the psychology of the particular child, which is, at this point, the only source of the necessary information.

We said, in our first lesson, that the mental states which education must develop in the child exist in him only as very general potentialities, very different from the fully developed forms they will eventually assume. It is easy to verify this proposition in the case of the child's capacity for disciplined action. Indeed, one could say that none of its components are present in a final form in the child's mind.

These components are two in number:

First is the desire for a regular existence. Because one's duty is always the same under the same conditions, and because the main conditions of one's life are determined once and for all by his sex, age, profession, and social class, it is impossible to enjoy doing one's duty if one is impatient of all that is regular habit. All moral order is based upon this regularity. For collective living could not function harmoniously if each of those who have a social function of any sort, domestic, political, or professional, did not behave in the right manner at the right time. On the other hand, what characterizes the child's activity is the complete irregularity of its expression. The child passes from one mood to another with extraordinary speed. His disposition is not durable; anger is aroused and appeased with the same suddenness; tears follow laughter; friendliness follows hatred, or inversely, without any objective reason, or at best, in response to the smallest stimulus. The game which occupies him at one moment will not retain him long; he tires quickly and passes to another. We find the same motility in the tireless curiosity with which the child harasses his parents and teachers. Some have seen there a primitive form of the scientific instinct. The comparison cannot be accepted without some reservations. Doubtlessly, when the child asks questions, it is because he feels the need to classify the things he sees, the sensations he feels, in this little system of ideas in the process of formation which constitutes his mind; and this need to relate is indeed the basis of scientific knowledge. But, in the child, how frivolous and unstable is this need! Whatever was

the object which drew our little observer's attention, it held it for only a few moments. He does not persist until he has reached or until he has been given a concept which satisfies him. The answer has hardly had the time to be uttered that already his mind is on something else. . . . Indeed, what predominates in the child's curiosity is instability and lability.

From a second point of view, the attitude of discipline is, we have said, moderation of one's desires and self-control. Common experience is sufficient to prove that this is completely lacking until rather late in the growth process. The child has nowhere the feeling that there are normal bounds to his needs; when he likes something, he wants it to the point of satiation. He will not stop by himself, nor will he easily accept being stopped. He is not even checked by the notion, shared by adults, that one cannot escape the consequences of the laws of nature. He cannot distinguish the possible from the impossible, and, consequently, he does not realize that reality offers insuperable barriers to his desires. He believes that everything should give in to him and becomes impatient with the resistance offered by things, as well as with the resistance offered by humans. There is one emotion in particular which points up this aspect of the child's personality in the most striking way; it is anger.

As we know, anger is very frequent in the child, and often takes on the most extreme forms. "When young children are angry," says Darwin, "they roll on the ground, on their back, on their stomach, screaming, kicking, scratching, hitting anything within reach." One might think that they cannot produce enough activity to relieve themselves. Indeed, there is no mental state which is more sharply opposed to the self-control implied by discipline than anger, for it consists precisely in a temporary disintegration of the personality. We say of someone in anger that he does not know himself. For there are few passions more exclusive; when anger bursts, especially if it is intense, it expels all other passions; it expels all the various perceptions which might restrain it; it occupies all of consciousness. Hence, there is nothing to neutralize it; this fact explains its tendency to grow beyond all limits. It keeps going forward until it burns itself out. The frequency and violence of anger in the child proves his innate lack of moderation better than any other observation. In fact, here again, the child does but reproduce a very well known trait of the primitive mind. We know indeed the untamed quality of passions among primitives, their incapacity to control themselves, their natural tendency to all sorts of excesses.

The distance between the point from which the child starts and the point to which we must bring him is great indeed; on the one hand, a mind perpetually in motion, a true kaleidoscope which does not remain the same from one moment to the next, and passionate impulses which charge forward until they are exhausted; on the other hand, the wish for a regular and organized activity. Education must make the child cover in a few years the enormous distance traveled by mankind in many centuries. Thus, it is not a mere question of developing the capacity for action and of stimulating latent trends just waiting for the chance to express themselves and grow. Rather, we must organize from nothing new psychic structures[1] which are not latent in the original constitution of the child. However, even if nature does not orient him in advance in a way which would leave us only to watch and supervise a normal process of growth; if nature has left us with practically everything to do, it is also evident that we could not succeed in our task if we had everything in the child against us, and if he was absolutely rebellious to the bent which we must impress upon him. Nature is not such a malleable thing that we can impose shapes upon it which it is in no way ready to assume. Even if the structures we aim to build are not present, there must be in the child at least general predispositions which we can use to reach our goal and which act as the levers through which educative action is carried to the depths of the child's mind. Without them, his mind would be closed to us. We might force the child from outside to perform given acts; but the springs of his inner life would escape us. We might tame the child; we would not educate him.

There are, indeed, at least two fundamental predispositions, two constitutional characteristics of the child's nature, which open it to our influence; there are: (1) the child's traditionalism and (2) his receptiveness to suggestion, especially imperative suggestion.

By a contradiction which may seem odd, but which is nonetheless certain, and which we shall explain in a few moments, the child which we have just seen as the incarnation of mobility, is in the same time a real formalist. Once he has adopted habits, they have over him a greater hold than they might have upon an adult. When he has repeated the same act several times, he feels the need to reproduce it in exactly the same way as before; the slightest variation exasperates him. We know, for instance, how the organization of his meals becomes sacred to him once established. He pushes the respect of custom to the heights of mania. He wants his cup or his plate always at the same place;

he wants to be served by the same person. The smallest change disturbs him.

A while ago, we noticed with what ease the child passes from one game to another. But, on the other hand, once he has become used to a particular game, he will repeat it endlessly. He will read over the same book or will stare at the same picture without fatigue or boredom. How many times have we told our children the same traditional stories! One might think they were always new to them. Anything new, if it implies some change in their daily habits, makes them withdraw. . . . "One of the things which disconcerts the child most," says Sully, "is a sudden change of locale." At a very early age, the child shows no fear when he is taken to a new room; but later on, after he has become accustomed to a certain room, he will have a feeling of strangeness if carried somewhere else." A change in the circle of people who ordinarily surround him will have the same effect. . . . Thus the child in the same time is both unstable and a real conservative.[2]

It is not only of his own habits that the child is so respectful, but also of those which he observes in the people who surround him. When he notices that everyone about him always behaves in the same way in the same circumstances, he believes that it is impossible to behave otherwise. Any transgression of custom is to him a scandal, which arouses a surprise into which feelings of revolt and indignation enter easily. True, the adult is also prone to these fetishisms; but the child is even more so. Gestures, even the most insignificant ones, if they are always repeated in front of him in the same fashion, will become, in his eyes, basic elements of an immutable order which must not be disturbed.

This is the origin of the child's appreciation of ceremonial formalism. His parents embrace him in a certain way; he will embrace the dolls that are his children in the same fashion. This traditionalism has a higher meaning than the first form, because it is more general. The child applies it not only to himself but to all the aspects of his little world. He practically comes to see in it a sort of general rule applicable to all humanity.

However surprising this co-existence of conservatism and instability may seem, it is not particular to the child. We also find it among primitives. This is because extreme mobility and extreme routine only appear to be mutually exclusive. Indeed, transitory ideas or feelings, precisely because they do not last, and because they are immediately replaced by other ideas and feelings, are unable to

---

1. [Durkheim says "*des états*,"—literally "states of mind." The word "structure" translates the meaning but gives it a contemporary flavor not found in the original.]

2. [We translate thus the word *misonéiste*, which means "hater of innovation."]

resist habit formation. For there is in a habit a strength accumulated by repetition, which cannot be overcome by states-of-mind so evanescent and fickle that they disappear as soon as they are born, shoving each other out of the focus of consciousness, and contradicting and neutralizing each other. If we compare these feeble strands composed of fluid and ephemeral states-of-mind with the density of a well established habit, we can easily understand why the subject must go in the direction which habit gives him. Habit rules because it is the only constituted power.

It is, in a way, a mechanical necessity that the center of gravity of behavior should be located in the region of habits. If the adult, and particularly the cultured adult, is not to some extent under the domination of his habits, it is because the ideas and sentiments which pass through his mind have more coherence and persistence, and are not mere flickers which disappear as soon as they are born. They stay in consciousness over an appreciable period; they are real forces which can oppose and contain habits. Because the activity of the mind has more consistency and is not continually disrupted, habit is no longer the sole master. Consequently, excessive mobility, far from being incompatible with routine, gives it its chance and reinforces its domination.

Although this tendency toward traditionalism is not in itself a moral structure, it does serve as a leverage point for the action which we must exercise upon the child. The power which habit holds over him through the instability of his psychic life can be used to correct and limit this instability itself. It suffices to make him assume regular habits for all that concerns the principle circumstances of his waking day. When this has happened, his life no longer offers the paradoxical spectacle of extreme mobility alternating with a nearly compulsive routine; the evanescent and changing becomes fixed; his life becomes a regular and organized entity, which is already a sort of first initiation to morality. In this attachment of the child to his habitual ways of doing things, in the malaise he feels when he does not find familiar objects and persons in their accustomed places, there is already an obscure feeling that there is but a single order of things which is normal and rooted in nature. Consequently, this order is opposed to accidental sequences and must be preferred to them. It is precisely a distinction of this type which is at the basis of the moral order. Of course, a notion so confused and so unconscious of its own existence, must be made precise, elaborated, and consolidated. Nevertheless, we have here an opening through which specifically moral action will be initiated in

the mind of the child, and we have detected one of the springs of his inner life which can be used to orient him in the desired direction.

But the taste for regular living is not, as we know, exactly the same as the spirit of discipline. The latter includes also the taste for harmony, the habit of restraining one's impulses, and the realization of one's normal limits. It is not enough that the child be accustomed to repeat the same actions in the same circumstances; he must also have the feeling that there are moral forces outside of him which set limits to his own forces, with which he has to deal and before which his will must bend. The child, however, cannot see these forces with the eyes of the body, since they are moral forces. There are no senses which make it possible for him to apprehend the distinctive features of a moral authority. Here is a world which surrounds him completely and which is still, in a way, invisible to him. No doubt he sees clearly the material bodies of the people and things which fill his immediate surroundings, i.e., his family; he knows that its adults, i.e., his parents, can force their will upon him. But this physical constraint could not, in any way, give him the sensation of that attraction *sui generis* which flows from moral forces, and which makes our will defer to them by a movement of respectful and spontaneous acquiescence, rather than by surrender to material coercion. How can we arouse in him this crucial sensation? By utilizing his great receptivity to all sorts of suggestions.

Guyau was the first to point out that the child finds himself placed by nature in a mental situation very analogous to that of hypnosis. What are, indeed, the conditions of hypnotic suggestion? There are two main ones: (1) The hypnotized subject is in a state of passivity as complete as possible. His will is paralyzed; his mind is like a flat surface; he sees and listens only through his hypnotist. Everything that happens around him leaves him indifferent. The idea which is suggested in these circumstances settles in his conscience with all the more weight because it meets no resistance. It is not counterbalanced by any other idea since a perfect psychic vacuum has been created. Hence, it tends to act itself out spontaneously. For an idea is not a pure intellectual and speculative state; it always contains the beginning of the action sequence essential to its realization, and the action thus begun continues if no contrary state come to inhibit it. (2) However, if the suggested act is to be put into effect with precision, this first condition is not ordinarily sufficient. The hypnotist must say: "I want you to do such and such." He must convey the fact that a refusal is out of question and that the subject must obey. If he weakens, if he starts to argue, his power disappears.

Both of these conditions are fulfilled in the child's relationships with parents and teachers. (1) He finds himself placed by nature in the same condition of passivity which hypnosis induces artificially. Although his mind is not a clean slate, it lacks specific representations and motivations. Hence, any new idea introduced into this psychic milieu of low density meets little resistance and consequently tends to work itself out in action. This is why the child is so easily accessible to the contagion of example, and is so prone to imitate others. When he witnesses an act, the representation perceived by his mind tends spontaneously to put itself into effect in a similar action.

(2) The second condition is fulfilled simply through the commanding tone with which the educator gives his orders. If his will is to dominate, it must be relentless and affirmed relentlessly. True enough, it is only in the early stages that educative suggestion draws all its action potential, all its power, from these external manifestations. When the child has succeeded in understanding more clearly the state of moral dependence in which he finds himself in relation to his parents and teachers, then their intellectual superiority and the worth of that superiority, the ascendency with which they now become permanently invested, diffuses to all their prescriptions and reinforces them. It is nevertheless true that the imperative character of suggestion is the original source of its efficacy and that it will retain a very important function for a long time to come.

Messrs. Binet and Henry have demonstrated this natural suggestibility of the child in an interesting experiment. Their procedure was as follows: Lines of different length were drawn on a blackboard and shown to school children who looked at them carefully. Once they had become fully familiar with them, they were asked to find their equivalent on another blackboard on which were drawn lines of the same length mixed with lines of a greater or shorter length. When the child believed he had found and designated the line which corresponded to the one shown on the first blackboard, the observer asked without any emphasis, this simple question: "Are you sure this is the only right one?"

This question alone was sufficient to determine 89 per cent of these grammar school children to change their first answer. In the middle grades and in the superior grades, the proportions were respectively 80 per cent and 54 per cent. Even a considerable percentage—56 per cent—of these who had given the right answer abandoned their first opinion.

In this last case, the reversal is completely due to suggestion. We notice, furthermore, the unequal suggestibility of the child according to his age. As his mind becomes more learned, it also acquires greater resistance.

This fact is now established, and it is no longer contested by educators. The suprising credulity, the docility, the willingness to please, the obedience, and the low will-consistency which the child demonstrates through a multitude of little incidents, recall the phenomena observed in the hypnotized adult. If, for instance, to a two-and-a-half year old child who has just taken the first bite from his cookie and is on the verge of taking another, I say categorically without any explanation and with a self-assurance that allows no contradiction, in a loud voice but without frightening the child: "The child has now eaten sufficiently, he does not want any more," the child is likely to stop biting his cookie, take it away from his mouth, put it on the table, and end his meal right there. It is easy to convince children, even those of three or four years, that the pain suffered from a blow has gone away, that they are no more thirsty, or no more tired, if . . . the assertion opposed to their complaints be absolutely final.

Here is, then, an external brake which can be opposed to the desires and passions of the child; and through this brake, we can train him to contain and moderate himself; we can make him feel that he must not surrender to his impulses altogether, but that there is always a limit beyond which he must not go. And the child feels distinctly, in this case, that he is under the influence of a force which does not act like a physical force, but which has very specific characters. He must have a clear realization that this force is, in a way, external to him, that he would not have acted in the same way had he complete control over his action since he has complied with the command; but, on the other hand, he knows he did not suffer any material constraint. The determinant of his act was not physical pressure, as when such and such a gesture is forced upon him, but a state of mind, i.e., a suggested idea; and the power of this idea was determined by intrinsic characteristics. It is with these elements that mankind in the past built up, and children today build up, their first conception of what we call a moral force or moral authority. Moral authority has precisely the characteristic feature that it acts upon us from outside, without any material coercion, either actual or virtual, and through the intermediary of a state-of-mind. Of course, around this primal nucleus, many other elements immediately start to cluster. Already, by the sole effect of having obeyed the commands of the same person several times, the child is naturally led to give to this person attributes commensurate to the action exercised upon him; he sees him as having a power *sui generis* which gives him a special place in his imagination. But we do not have to follow the evolution of the idea at the moment; it is enough to show what its anchoring point is in the child's constitution.

Consequently, we are far from being defenseless. Thanks to the hold that habit acquires so easily upon the mind of the child, we can accustom him to regularity, and make him like it; thanks to his suggestibility, we can, at the same time, give him a sort of first impression of the moral forces which surround him and upon which he depends. Thus, we have in our hands two powerful levers, so powerful that they must be handled with the greatest of care. When we think of the child's mind, how vulnerable it is, of the ease with which it keeps the imprint of any pressure, ever so slight and unsustained, one comes to fear possible abuses of power rather than the weakness of the educator.

All sorts of precautions must be taken in order to protect the freedom of the child against the omnipotence of education. How can we think, as some did recently, of letting the child spend his entire formative years in the hands of a single teacher? Such an education is bound to become soul-crushing. The child could not fail to reproduce passively the only model under his eyes. The only way to prevent this enslavement and to prevent the child from becoming a copy of the teacher's defects is to multiply the teachers, so that they may complement one another, and thus insure that the diversity of influences will preclude any one from becoming too exclusively dominant.

However powerful our means of action may be, we are still far from our goal. Between this very general receptivity of the child to habit and suggestion on the one hand, and his attaining a clear representation of the moral rule on the other, there is a wide margin. If these vague predispositions, these formless tendencies, are to become the well-defined and complex sentiments that the child needs, education has to fecundate and transform them.

Section D

Social Structure and the Motivation of Deviant and Conforming Behavior

Editorial Foreword, BY JESSE R. PITTS   *869*

I–THE ELEMENTS OF DEVIANCE AND SOCIAL CONTROL

1. *On the Normality of Crime*, BY EMILE DURKHEIM   *872*
2. *The Psychology of Punitive Justice*, BY GEORGE H. MEAD   *876*
3. *The Psychopathology of Everyday Life*, BY SIGMUND FREUD   *887*
4. *Analytic Therapy and Transference*, BY SIGMUND FREUD   *896*
5. *Analysis Terminable and Interminable*, BY SIGMUND FREUD   *903*

II–THE STRUCTURE OF DEVIANT BEHAVIOR

1. *Anomic Suicide*, BY EMILE DURKHEIM   *916*
2. *Social Patterns and the Gang*, BY FREDERIC M. THRASHER   *929*

III–THE MOTIVATION OF DEVIANCE

1. *Three Types of Personality*, BY WILLIAM I. THOMAS AND FLORIAN
   ZNANIECKI   *934*
2. *Internal Sources of Behavioral Instability and Their Control*, BY
   SIGMUND FREUD   *940*
3. *Cultural Conflict and the Marginal Man*, BY ROBERT E. PARK   *944*

IV–THE MAINTENANCE OF CONFORMITY

1. *Death and the Reintegration of the Group*, BY BRONISLAW MALINOWSKI   *947*
2. *On the Rites of Passage*, BY ARNOLD VAN GENNEP   *950*
3. *On Taboo*, BY A. R. RADCLIFFE-BROWN   *951*
4. *On Communal Ritual*, BY EMILE DURKHEIM   *959*

Social Structure and the Motivation
of Deviant and Conforming Behavior

by Jesse R. Pitts

I. THE ELEMENTS OF DEVIANCE
AND SOCIAL CONTROL

MAN HAS OFTEN DREAMED OF a society in which there would be no more crime and order would be perfect without being stultifying. *Durkheim,* in the selection from the *Rules of Sociological Method,* shows how utopian this wish must remain. Modern readers may feel that the part of the argument which is based on formal logic is belabored. On the other hand, he will be impressed with the demonstration that the existence of crime is essential to the adaptive capacity of the society, and that we could not have the deviancy of innovation if we did not have the deviancy of crime.

"The Psychology of Punitive Justice" by *G. H. Mead* has kept, after more than forty years, a freshness that is a sad commentary on the lack of progress of our ideas on social control. There are several strands of thought in this article. On the one hand, Mead concurs with Durkheim's statement that punitive justice reinforces the solidarity of the group and the commitment of the innocent to legality. On the other hand, he asserts that the aggressive stance of punitive justice promotes rigidity in the institutional patterns, the defects of which may be partly responsible for the deviance of the criminal.

By stressing the fact that successful individuals are less aggressive toward deviants, Mead opens the way for a further elaboration of his argument: what strata of society feel the need for punitive justice and toward what crimes—a problem already evoked

in the Introduction to Part Three. It is intimately related to another problem raised by Mead, which has plagued organizations of social control that seek to rehabilitate the offender: the tension between the custodial functions and the therapeutic procedures. Here the differences in culture and class status between the custodial personnel and the therapeutic staff becomes highly relevant.

Furthermore, there is an aspect of therapy that is always a threat to the maintenance of order: if we are to secure the commitment of the deviant to the therapeutic relationship, it is necessary to prove to him that the therapist is on his side. A "gratuitous" reward, a favor, granted at the beginning of the relationship can help secure the trust of the subject, but at the cost of threatening the normal conditionality of rewards prevailing in the institution as well as in normal society. Here it is the deviant who, *because of his deviance,* does get the attention, the support, the protection of professional people. Prison psychologists and sociologists often show more friendliness to the convicts than they do to their guards. Eager psychiatric residents sometimes reserve their hostility for the nurses and attendants, who "compete" with them for the possession of the patients. Some professional sympathy for the deviant may be a cover for a regressive identification with one who has challenged middle-class morality and the limits set by social order.

As to the constitutive elements of deviance, it is *Freud* who gives us the most insightful remarks. The *Psychopathology of Everyday Life* points to the fact that the unavoidable ambivalence of human relations must result in deviances, the aggressive intent of which will often remain unconscious for the

869

perpetrator. Hence, behind error and illness there may be other factors than a mere "technical" failure of control.

In the discussion of "Analytic Therapy and Transference" which follows, Freud gives us elements of deviance which go beyond the unsublimated aspects of the sexual and aggressive "instincts." In the discussion of the transference neuroses, we have a problem not so much of instinct as of structure: the individual regresses to a level of organization that is not in harmony with his normal age, sex, and status roles. Thus we have the projection upon alter—the therapist in the least disruptive case—of infantile wishes which can result in deviant behavior either through the seeking for illegitimate reciprocity (seduction), or through the "misperceiving" of alter and subsequent failure in communication.

Freud has given us, in his analysis of transference, the key to social control through therapeutic re-education. In this and in the following excerpt the reader will find some of the main elements of the psychoanalytical theory of learning, implicit in the description of the therapeutic process. One may reject the Freudian instinct or developmental theories, but still follow an analytical model in the treatment of patients. In the case of impaired adult personalities it is always a lengthy process, demanding great skill and self-control on the part of the therapist. The use of psychotherapy in the treatment of lower-class deviants, so far minimal, is increasing.

In "Analysis Terminable and Interminable" Freud alludes to the problem of secondary gain, of growing concern to all psychotherapy. It is not possible to take for granted the desire of the deviant to become normal and/or to conform. For some the sick role is a refuge from social obligations. Others, such as many homosexuals, alcoholics, and drug addicts, cannot bear the anxieties of psychotherapy. Some cannot "give up" the support of the transference. Freud also mentions the importance of passive trends in men and of "masculine protest" in women as a crucial element in the constitution of some neuroses and character disorders. This parallels Parsons' use of the dimensions of passivity-activity in the paradigm of deviance. It also raises some interesting questions as to the meaning of homosexuality in prisons.

II. THE STRUCTURE OF DEVIANT BEHAVIOR

By the *structure* of deviant behavior we are referring to the fact that deviant behavior can manifest itself as the addition of "individual responses" to strain, or as the organized patterns of the delinquent subcultures. *Durkheim*'s excerpt from *Suicide* is a model for the analysis of deviance that may occur when institutional patterns fail to provide meaningful guides to the personality. When *anomie* prevails, social action loses its value as a cue and a reward for the personality. Durkheim went beyond the analysis of anomic situations to an implicit prediction of how individuals would react under high intensities of such a stress. His theory of personality made suicide the obvious way out of unendurable pain created by the frustration of boundless desires. Today, the pattern of deviant response is not regarded as so clear-cut. The personality intervenes as a more complex independent variable: suicide is only one possible reaction; others are mental illness, physical illness, accidents, and, on the organization level, intensified clique ethnocentrism.

Excerpts from *W. I. Thomas and F. Znaniecki*, in Part Five, deal with the concept of "social disorganization," a close relative of Durkheim's "anomie," which influenced the ecological school of Chicago and, in particular, Clifford Shaw. *Thrasher*, in analyzing the delinquent gang, tries to reconcile this conception with the realities of gang organization.

III. THE MOTIVATION OF DEVIANCE

One approach to the motivation of deviance has been to describe it as the action of character types —and this, in fact, is the approach of common sense. *W. I. Thomas and Florian Znaniecki* offer two fundamental patterns of deviance from the ideal of the "creative type," the *Philistine* and the *Bohemian*. In the Philistine, there is an excess of rigidity and a refusal to develop new attitudes and definitions of the situation. In the Bohemian, there is an unwillingness to organize existence so as to provide reliable behavior toward others. One may add that in strange ways, Philistines and Bohemians tend to complement each other: Philistines show extreme rigidity because of the weaknesses in their personality organization which make them near relatives to the Bohemians they abhor; Bohemians are often no less "compulsive" in their cult of spontaneity. An imbalance in the distribution of the personality between the four needs outlined in Section A results in a propensity to deviance.

Freud provides us with an analysis of deviance in terms of personality dynamics which stresses the pressures of both the id and the superego upon the ego. To use W. I. Thomas' characterology, super-ego-dominated personalities produce Philistine types; id dominated personalities became Bohemian types. The personalities having a strong ego would be called "creative." For the greater bulk of mankind, which avoids either extreme without reaching great heights in creativity, the maintenance of ego mastery over both the impulses of the id and the harsh demands of the superego, is a constant problem. In fact, Freud marvelled that man could succeed as well as he did, given the power of the forces arraigned against the ego. This is because Freud still thinks of the personality as deriving its energy and most of its goals from instincts competing first for dominance with the personality, and second for object cathexis in a competitive world. Not all of the instinctual libido can be sublimated into socially useful purposes.

Against an instinctual theory of deviance, *Robert Park* provides us with a socio-cultural analysis of the sources of deviance. The *Marginal Man*, as described in reference to George Santayana, comes out more as an intellectual innovator and creator than as a negative deviant. The marginal man, however, is also a potential traitor, an embezzler. The alienation which assists in the achievement of independence from stereotypes can be a source of sin or crime. As Robert Park reminds us, the sources of marginality are many; and we could add that few individuals are not marginal in relation to at least one social system, and hence deviance-prone in relation to it.

IV. THE MAINTENANCE OF CONFORMITY

To a certain extent, all institutions have a social control dimension which is exercised through the spelling out of the specifications of conforming behavior and the reinforcement of the wish to conform through the rewarding of conformity and the punishment of deviance. Another way to control deviance is to drain residual impulses before they can result in the disruption of regular role patterns. Thus the nuclear family as well as certain professional situations—doctor-patient and lawyer-client relationships, or the church revival—operate as privileged sanctuaries for tension management.

Bronislaw Malinowski's discussion of the *funeral ritual* provides an example of the special sanctuary for the expression of grief, and shows how the fu-neral increases social pressure and reasserts group membership at a time of role disruption.

Arnold Van Gennep's rites of passage are other forms of ritual which separate the individual from roles that have become unsuitable for his age, sex, or status. The rites of passage make it very clear to the individual that he cannot regress to the roles he assumed before the puberty ceremonies or the ceremony of marriage. The whole community is witness to the individual's new role commitments. Often the prohibition of regression is made all-powerful by the statement in the ritual that the ante-initiation individual has died and that he is reborn to a new status. Another aspect of the *rite-de-passage* not covered by Van Gennep is the *humiliation of the impetrant,* which makes clear the differences in prestige of the ante-initiation role as compared to the post-initiation role.

For *Radcliffe-Brown,* the maintenance of conformity is achieved through the transformation of important articulating events or things into sacred occasions marked by taboo. Radcliffe-Brown's analysis may seem narrowly functional to some. Taboos seem to arise in situations that are relatively indifferent as well as in crucial ones. What seems determinant is the need of the society to create a consensus and to insure the awareness of that consensus on the part of the individual. Taboos, in fact, are often private rituals: by following the interdict, the individual secures the satisfaction of being a member of society in good standing. Taboo forces the abandonment by the individual of a utilitarian approach to the object in favor of a social one marked by a component of sacrifice on his part. The sacrifice may be comparatively slight and may focus merely on the abandonment of spontaneity in favor of the restraints of ceremony.

Durkheim insists to a greater extent on the collective aspect of ritual, which unites the group in a single locale and thus reinforces the constraining power of the collective representation upon the individual. We do not need Durkheim's contagion psychology in order to accept the soundness of his insight. Collective ritual makes clearer the terms of consensus. It makes also very clear the power of the group as against the weakness of the individual, and it imparts this power to the symbols and values of the ceremony. Thus the individual shares in the power of the group in direct proportion to his conformity to the group's beliefs. The group protects him at the condition of his compliance. To use Freudian terms. ritual is a moment of controlled regression to early parent-child role expectations, whereby the superego derives from primary id structures a new strength for the days to come.

I–THE ELEMENTS OF DEVIANCE AND SOCIAL CONTROL

1. On the Normality of Crime

BY EMILE DURKHEIM

IF THERE is any fact whose pathological character appears incontestable, that fact is crime. All criminologists are agreed on this point. Although they explain this pathology differently, they are unanimous in recognizing it. But let us see if this problem does not demand a more extended consideration.

We shall apply the foregoing rules. Crime is present not only in the majority of societies of one particular species but in all societies of all types. There is no society that is not confronted with the problem of criminality. Its form changes; the acts thus characterized are not the same everywhere; but, everywhere and always, there have been men who have behaved in such a way as to draw upon themselves penal repression. If, in proportion as societies pass from the lower to the higher types, the rate of criminality, i.e., the relation between the yearly number of crimes and the population, tended to decline, it might be believed that crime, while still normal, is tending to lose this character of normality. But we have no reason to believe that such a regression is substantiated. Many facts would seem rather to indicate a movement in the opposite direction. From the beginning of the [nineteenth] century, statistics enable us to follow the course of criminality. It has everywhere increased. In France the increase is nearly 300 per cent. There is, then, no phenomenon that presents more indisputably all the symptoms of normality, since it appears closely connected with the conditions of all collective life. To make of crime a form of social morbidity would be to admit that morbidity is not something accidental, but, on the contrary, that in certain cases it grows out of the fundamental constitution of the living organism; it would result in wiping out all distinction between the physiological and the pathological. No doubt it is possible that

crime itself will have abnormal forms as, for example, when its rate is unusually high. This excess is, indeed, undoubtedly morbid in nature. What is normal, simply, is the existence of criminality, provided that it attains and does not exceed, for each social type, a certain level, which it is perhaps not impossible to fix in conformity with the preceding rules.[1]

Here we are, then, in the presence of a conclusion in appearance quite paradoxical. Let us make no mistake. To classify crime among the phenomena of normal sociology is not to say merely that it is an inevitable, although regrettable phenomenon, due to the incorrigible wickedness of men; it is to affirm that it is a factor in public health, an integral part of all healthy societies. This result is, at first glance, surprising enough to have puzzled even ourselves for a long time. Once this first surprise has been overcome, however, it is not difficult to find reasons explaining this normality and at the same time confirming it.

In the first place crime is normal because a society exempt from it is utterly impossible. Crime, we have shown elsewhere, consists of an act that offends certain very strong collective sentiments. In a society in which criminal acts are no longer committed, the sentiments they offend would have to be found without exception in all individual consciousnesses, and they must be found to exist with the same degree as sentiments contrary to them. Assuming that this condition could actually be realized, crime would not thereby disappear; it would only change its form, for the very cause which would thus dry up the sources of criminality would immediately open up new ones.

Reprinted from Emile Durkheim, *The Rules of Sociological Method*, trans. Sarah Solovay and John Mueller, ed. George E. G. Catlin (Glencoe, Ill.: The Free Press, 1950), pp. 65–75, with the ⸱⸱⸱ᵣᵐission of The Free Press.

1. From the fact that crime is a phenomenon of normal sociology, it does not follow that the criminal is an individual normally constituted from the biological and psychological points of view. The two questions are independent of each other. This independence will be better understood when we have shown, later on, the difference between psychological and sociological facts.

Indeed, for the collective sentiments which are protected by the penal law of a people at a specified moment of its history to take possession of the public conscience or for them to acquire a stronger hold where they have an insufficient grip, they must acquire an intensity greater than that which they had hitherto had. The community as a whole must experience them more vividly, for it can acquire from no other source the greater force necessary to control these individuals who formerly were the most refractory. For murderers to disappear, the horror of bloodshed must become greater in those social strata from which murderers are recruited; but, first it must become greater throughout the entire society. Moreover, the very absence of crime would directly contribute to produce this horror; because any sentiment seems much more respectable when it is always and uniformly respected.

One easily overlooks the consideration that these strong states of the common consciousness cannot be thus reinforced without reinforcing at the same time the more feeble states, whose violation previously gave birth to mere infraction of convention —since the weaker ones are only the prolongation, the attenuated form of the stronger. Thus robbery and simple bad taste injure the same single altruistic sentiment, the respect for that which is another's. However, this same sentiment is less grievously offended by bad taste than by robbery; and since, in addition, the average consciousness has not sufficient intensity to react keenly to the bad taste, it is treated with greater tolerance. That is why the person guilty of bad taste is merely blamed, whereas the thief is punished. But, if this sentiment grows stronger, to the point of silencing in all consciousnesses the inclination which disposes man to steal, he will become more sensitive to the offenses which, until then, touched him but lightly. He will react against them, then, with more energy; they will be the object of greater opprobrium, which will transform certain of them from the simple moral faults that they were and give them the quality of crimes. For example, improper contracts, or contracts improperly executed, which only incur public blame or civil damages, will become offenses in law.

Imagine a society of saints, a perfect cloister of exemplary individuals. Crimes, properly so called, will there be unknown; but faults which appear venial to the layman will create there the same scandal that the ordinary offense does in ordinary consciousnesses. If, then, this society has the power to judge and punish, it will define these acts as criminal and will treat them as such. For the same reason, the perfect and upright man judges his smallest failings with a severity that the majority reserve for acts more truly in the nature of an offense. Formerly, acts of violence against persons were more frequent than they are today, because respect for individual dignity was less strong. As this has increased, these crimes have become more rare; and also, many acts violating this sentiment have been introduced into the penal law which were not included there in primitive times.[2]

In order to exhaust all the hypotheses logically possible, it will perhaps be asked why this unanimity does not extend to all collective sentiments without exception. Why should not even the most feeble sentiment gather enough energy to prevent all dissent? The moral consciousness of the society would be present in its entirety in all the individuals, with a vitality sufficient to prevent all acts offending it—the purely conventional faults as well as the crimes. But a uniformity so universal and absolute is utterly impossible; for the immediate physical milieu in which each one of us is placed, the hereditary antecedents, and the social influences vary from one individual to the next, and consequently diversify consciousnesses. It is impossible for all to be alike, if only because each one has his own organism and that these organisms occupy different areas in space. This is why, even among the lower peoples, where individual originality is very little developed, it nevertheless does exist.

Thus, since there cannot be a society in which the individuals do not differ more or less from the collective type, it is also inevitable that, among these divergences, there are some with a criminal character. What confers this character upon them is not the intrinsic quality of a given act but that definition which the collective conscience lends them. If the collective conscience is stronger, if it has enough authority practically to suppress these divergences, it will also be more sensitive, more exacting; and, reacting against the slightest deviations with the energy it otherwise displays only against more considerable infractions, it will attribute to them the same gravity as formerly to crimes. In other words, it will designate them as criminal.

Crime is, then, necessary; it is bound up with the fundamental conditions of all social life and by that very fact it is useful, because these conditions of which it is a part are themselves indispensable to the normal evolution of morality and law.

Indeed, it is no longer possible today to dispute the fact that law and morality vary from one social type to the next, nor that they change within the same type if the conditions of life are modified. But, in order that these transformations may be possible, the collective sentiments at the basis of

---

2. Calumny, insults, slander, fraud, etc.

morality must not be hostile to change, and consequently must have but moderate energy. If they were too strong, they would no longer be plastic. Every pattern is an obstacle to new patterns, to the extent that the first pattern is inflexible. The better a structure is articulated, the more it offers a healthy resistance to all modification; and this is equally true of functional, as of anatomical, organization. If there were no crimes this condition could not have been fulfilled; for such a hypothesis presupposes that collective sentiments have arrived at a degree of intensity unexampled in history. Nothing is good indefinitely and to an unlimited extent. The authority which the moral conscience enjoys must not be excessive; otherwise no one would dare criticize it, and it would too easily congeal into an immutable form. To make progress, individual originality must be able to express itself. In order that the originality of the idealist whose dreams transcend his century may find expression, it is necessary that the originality of the criminal, who is below the level of his time, shall also be possible. One does not occur without the other.

Nor is this all. Aside from this indirect utility, it happens that crime itself plays a useful role in this evolution. Crime implies not only that the way remains open to necessary changes but that in certain cases it directly prepares these changes. Where crime exists, collective sentiments are sufficiently flexible to take on a new form, and crime sometimes helps to determine the form they will take. How many times, indeed, it is only an anticipation of future morality—a step toward what will be! According to Athenian law, Socrates was a criminal, and his condemnation was no more than just. However, his crime, namely the independence of his thought, rendered a service not only to humanity but to his country. It served to prepare a new morality and faith which the Athenians needed, since the traditions by which they had lived until then were no longer in harmony with the current conditions of life. Nor is the case of Socrates unique; it is reproduced periodically in history. It would never have been possible to establish the freedom of thought we now enjoy if the regulations prohibiting it had not been violated before being solemnly abrogated. At that time, however, the violation was a crime, since it was an offense against sentiments still very keen in the average conscience. And yet this crime was useful as a prelude to reforms which daily became more necessary. Liberal philosophy had as its precursors the heretics of all kinds who were justly punished by secular authorities during the entire course of the Middle Ages and until the eve of modern times.

From this point of view the fundamental facts of criminality present themselves to us in an entirely new light. Contrary to current ideas, the criminal no longer seems a totally unsociable being, a sort of parasitic element, a strange and unassimilable body, introduced into the midst of society.[3] On the contrary, he plays a definite role in social life. Crime, for its part, must no longer be conceived as an evil that cannot be too much suppressed. There is no occasion for self-congratulation when the crime rate drops noticeably below the average level, for we may be certain that this apparent progress is associated with some social disorder. Thus, the number of assault cases never falls so low as in times of want.[4] With the drop in the crime rate, and as a reaction to it, comes a revision, or the need of a revision in the theory of punishment. If, indeed, crime is a disease, its punishment is its remedy and cannot be otherwise conceived; thus, all the discussions it arouses bear on the point of determining what the punishment must be in order to fulfil this role of remedy. If crime is not pathological at all, the object of punishment cannot be to cure it, and its true function must be sought elsewhere.

It is far from the truth, then, that the rules previously stated have no other justification than to satisfy an urge for logical formalism of little practical value, since, on the contrary, according as they are or are not applied, the most essential social facts are entirely changed in character. If the foregoing example is particularly convincing—and this was our hope in dwelling upon it—there are likewise many others which might have been cited with equal profit. There is no society where the rule does not exist that the punishment must be proportional to the offense; yet, for the Italian school, this principle is but an invention of jurists, without adequate basis.

For these criminologists the entire penal system, as it has functioned until the present day among all known peoples, is a phenomenon contrary to nature. We have already seen that, for M. Garofalo, the criminality peculiar to lower societies is not at

---

3. We have ourselves committed the error of speaking thus of the criminal, because of a failure to apply our rule (*Division du travail social,* pp. 395–96).

4. Although crime is a fact cf normal sociology, it does not follow that we must not abhor it. Pain itself has nothing desirable about it; the individual dislikes it as society does crime, and yet it is a function of normal physiology. Not only is it necessarily derived from the very constitution of every living organism, but it plays a useful role in life, for which reason it cannot be replaced. It would, then, be a singular distortion of our thought to present it as an apology for crime. We would not even think of protesting against such an interpretation, did we not know to what accusations and misunderstandings one exposes oneself when one undertakes to study moral facts objectively and to speak of them in a different language from that of the layman.

all natural. For socialists it is the capitalist system, in spite of its wide diffusion, which constitutes a deviation from the normal state, produced, as it was, by violence and fraud. Spencer, on the contrary, maintains that our administrative centralization and the extension of governmental powers are the radical vices of our societies, although both proceed most regularly and generally as we advance in history. We do not believe that scholars have ever systematically endeavored to distinguish the normal or abnormal character of social phenomena from their degree of generality. It is always with a great array of dialectics that these questions are partly resolved.

Once we have eliminated this criterion, however, we are not only exposed to confusions and partial errors, such as those just pointed out, but science is rendered all but impossible. Its immediate object is the study of the normal type. If, however, the most widely diffused facts can be pathological, it is possible that the normal types never existed in actuality; and if that is the case, why study the facts? Such study can only confirm our prejudices and fix us in our errors. If punishment and the responsibility for crime are only the products of ignorance and barbarism why strive to know them in order to derive the normal forms from them? By such arguments the mind is diverted from a reality in which we have lost interest, and falls back on itself in order to seek within itself the materials necessary to reconstruct its world. In order that sociology may treat facts as things, the sociologist must feel the necessity of studying them exclusively.

The principle object of all sciences of life, whether individual or social, is to define and explain the normal state and to distinguish it from its opposite. If, however, normality is not given in the things themselves—if it is, on the contrary, a character we may or may not impute to them—this solid footing is lost. The mind is then complacent in the face of a reality which has little to teach it; it is no longer restrained by the matter which it is analyzing, since it is the mind, in some manner or other, that determines the matter.

The various principles we have established up to the present are, then, closely interconnected. In order that sociology may be a true science of things, the generality of phenomena must be taken as the criterion of their normality.

Our method has, moreover, the advantage of regulating action at the same time as thought. If the social values are not subjects of observation but can and must be determined by a sort of mental calculus, no limit, so to speak, can be set for the free inventions of the imagination in search of the best. For how may we assign to perfection a limit? It escapes all limitation, by definition. The goal of humanity recedes into infinity, discouraging some by its very remoteness and arousing others who, in order to draw a little nearer to it, quicken the pace and plunge into revolutions. This practical dilemma may be escaped if the desirable is defined in the same way as in health and normality and if health is something that is defined as inherent in things. For then the object of our efforts is both given and defined at the same time. It is no longer a matter of pursuing desperately an objective that retreats as one advances, but of working with steady perseverance to maintain the normal state, of re-establishing it if it is threatened, and of rediscovering its conditions if they have changed. The duty of the statesman is no longer to push society toward an ideal that seems attractive to him, but his role is that of the physician: he prevents the outbreak of illnesses by good hygiene, and he seeks to cure them when they have appeared.[5]

5. From the theory developed in this chapter, the conclusion has at times been reached that, according to us, the increase of criminality in the course of the nineteenth century was a normal phenomenon. Nothing is farther from our thought. Several facts indicated by us apropos of suicide (see *Suicide*, pp. 420 ff.) tend, on the contrary, to make us believe that this development is in general morbid. Nevertheless, it might happen that a certain increase of certain forms of criminality would be normal, for each state of civilization has its own criminality. But on this, one can only formulate hypotheses.

2. The Psychology of Punitive Justice

BY GEORGE H. MEAD

THE STUDY of instincts on the one side and of the motor character of human conduct upon the other has given us a different picture of human nature from that which a dogmatic doctrine of the soul and an intellectualistic psychology presented to an earlier generation.

The instincts even in the lower animal forms have lost their rigidity. They are found to be subject to modification by experience, and the nature of the animal is found to be not a bundle of instincts but an organization within which these congenital habits function to bring about complex acts—acts which are in many cases the result of instincts which have modified each other. Thus new activities arise which are not the simple expression of bare instincts. A striking illustration of this is found in play, especially among young animal forms, in which the hostile instinct is modified and held in check by the others that dominate the social life of the animals. Again the care which the parent form gives to the infant animal admits of hostile features which, however, do not attain the full expression of attack and destruction usually involved in the instinct from which they arise. Nor is this merging and interaction of such divergent instinctive acts a process of alternate dominance of now one and now another instinct. Play and parental care may be and generally are of a piece, in which the inhibition of one tendency by the others has entered into the structure of the animal's nature and seemingly even of its congenital nervous organization. Another illustration of such a merging of divergent instincts is found in the elaborate wooing of the female among the birds.

Back of all this type of organization of instinctive conduct lies the social life within which there must be co-operation of the different individuals, and therefore a continual adjustment of the responses to the changing attitudes of the animals that participate in the corporate acts. It is this body of organized instinctive reactions to one another which makes up the social nature of these forms, and it is from a social nature of this kind exhibited in the conduct of lower forms that our human nature is evolved. An elaborate analysis of this is still in the making, but certain great features in it stand out with sufficient clearness to warrant comment. We find two opposing groups of instincts, those which we have named hostile and those which may be termed friendly, the latter being largely combinations of the parental and sexual instincts. The import of a herding instinct lying back of them all is still very uncertain if not dubious. What we do find is that individuals adjust themselves to each other in common social processes, but come into conflict with each other frequently in the process, that the expression of this individual hostility within the whole social act is primarily that of the destructive hostile type, modified and molded by the organized social reaction, that where this modification and control breaks down, as, e.g., in the rivalry of males in the herd or pack, the hostile instinct may assert itself in its native ruthlessness.

If we turn to the human nature that has developed out of the social nature of lower animals, we find in addition to the organization of social conduct that I have indicated a vast elaboration of the process of adjustment of individuals to each other. This elaboration of gesture, to use Wundt's generalized term, reaches its most developed expression in language. Now language was first the attitude, glance of the eye, movement of the body and its parts indicating the oncoming social act to which the other individuals must adjust their conduct. It becomes language in the narrower sense when it is a common speech of whatever form; that is when through his gesture the individual addresses *himself* as well as the others who are involved in the act. His speech is their speech. He can address himself in their gestures and thus present to himself the whole social situation within which he is involved, so that not only is conduct social but consciousness becomes social as well.

It is out of this conduct and this consciousness that human society grows. What gives it its human character is that the individual through language addresses himself in the rôle of the others in the group and thus becomes aware of them in his own conduct. But while this phase of evolution is perhaps the most critical in the development of man, it

Reprinted from George H. Mead, "The Psychology of Punitive Justice," *The American Journal of Sociology,* XXIII (1918), 577–602, by permission of The University of Chicago Press. Copyright 1918 by The University of Chicago Press.

is after all only an elaboration of the social conduct of lower forms. Self-conscious conduct is only an exponent which raises the possible complications of group activity to a higher degree. It does not change the character of the social nature that is elaborated and complicated, nor does it change the principles of its organization. Human nature still remains an organization of instincts which have mutually affected each other. Out of such fundamental instincts as those of sex, parenthood, and hostility has arisen an organized type of social conduct, the conduct of the individual within the group. The attack upon the other individuals of the group has been modified and softened so that the individual asserts himself as over against the others in play, in courting, in care of the young, in certain common attitudes of attack and defense, without the attempted destruction of the individuals attacked. If we use the common terminology we shall account for these modifications by the process of trial and error within the evolution out of which has arisen the social form. Out of the hostile instinct has arisen conduct modified by the social instincts that has served to delimit the conduct springing from sex, parenthood, and mutual defense and attack. It has been the function of the hostile instinct to provide the reaction by which the individual asserts himself within a social process, thus modifying that process while the hostile conduct is itself modified *pro tanto*. The result is the appearance of new individuals, certain types of sex mates, playmates, parent and child forms, mates in fight and mates in defense. While this assertion of the individual within the social process delimits and checks the social act at various points, it leads to a modified social response with a new field of operation which did not exist for the unmodified instincts. The source of these higher complexes of social conduct appears suddenly when through a breakdown of the organization of the social act there is enacted a crime of passion, the direct outcome of self-assertion within sex, family, or other group responses. Unmodified self-assertion under these conditions means the destruction of the individual attacked.

When now, through the exponent of self-consciousness, the complexities of social conduct are raised to the *n*th power, when the individual addresses himself as well as the others, by his gestures, when in the rôle of another he can respond to his own stimulus, all the range of possible activities is brought within the field of social conduct. He finds himself within groups of varied sorts. The size of the group to which he can belong is limited only by his ability to co-operate with its members. Now the common control over the food process lifts these

instincts out of the level of the mechanical response to biologically determined stimuli and brings them within the sweep of self-conscious direction inside of the larger group activity. And these varied groupings multiply the occasions of individual oppositions. Here again the instinct of hostility becomes the method of self-assertion, but while the oppositions are self-conscious the process of readjustment and the molding of the hostile attitudes by the larger social process remains in principle the same, though the long road of trial and error may be at times abandoned for the short cuts which the symbolism of language provides.

On the other hand the consciousness of self through consciousness of others is responsible for a more profound sense of hostility—that of the members of the groups to those opposed to it, or even to those merely outside it. And this hostility has the backing of the whole inner organization of the group. It provides the most favorable condition for the sense of group solidarity because in the common attack upon the common enemy the individual differences are obliterated. But in the development of these group hostilities we find the same self-assertion with the attempted elimination of the enemy giving way before the larger social whole within which the conflicting groups find themselves. The hostile self-assertion passes over into functional activities in the new type of conduct as it has taken place in play even among lower animal forms. The individual becomes aware of himself, not through the conquest of the other, but through the distinction of function. It is not so much that the actual hostile reactions are themselves transformed as that the individual who is conscious of himself as over against the enemy finds other opportunities for conduct which remove the immediate stimuli for destroying the enemy. Thus the conqueror who realized himself in his power of life or death over the captive found in the industrial value of the slave a new attitude which removed the sense of hostility and opened the door to that economic development which finally placed the two upon the same ground of common citizenship.

It is in so far as the opposition reveals a larger underlying relationship within which the hostile individuals arouse non-hostile reactions that the hostile reactions themselves become modified into a type of self-assertion which is balanced against the self-assertion of those who had been enemies, until finally these oppositions become the compensating activities of different individuals in a new social conduct. In other words the hostile instinct has the function of the *assertion* of the social self when this self comes into existence in the evolution of human behavior. The man who has achieved an economic, a legal, or any type of social triumph does not feel the impulse to physically annihilate his opponent, and ultimately the mere sense of the security of his social position may rob the stimulus to attack of all of its power.

The moral of this is, and one is certainly justified in emphasizing it at this time of a profound democratic movement in the midst of a world-war, that advance takes place in bringing to consciousness the larger social whole within which hostile attitudes pass over into self-assertions that are functional instead of destructive.

The following pages discuss the hostile attitude as it appears especially in punitive justice.

In the criminal court it is the purpose of the proceeding to prove that the defendant did or did not commit a certain act, that in case the defendant did commit the act this act falls under such and such a category of crime or misdemeanor as defined by the statute, and that, as a consequence, he is subject to such and such punishment. It is the assumption of this procedure that conviction and punishment are the accomplishment of justice and also that it is for the good of society, that is, that it is both just and expedient, though it is not assumed that in any particular case the meting out to a criminal of the legal recompense of his crime will accomplish an immediate social good which will outweigh the immediate social evil that may result to him, his family, and society itself from his conviction and imprisonment. Galsworthy's play *Justice* turns upon the wide discrepancy between legal justice and social good in a particular case. On the other side lies the belief that without this legal justice with all its miscarriages and disintegrating results society itself would be impossible. In the back of the public mind lie both these standards of criminal justice, that of retribution and that of prevention. It is just that a criminal should suffer in proportion to the evil that he has done. On the other hand it is just that the criminal should suffer so much and in such a manner that his penalty will serve to deter him and others from committing the like offense in the future. There has been a manifest shift in the emphasis upon these two standards. During the Middle Ages, when courts of justice were the antechambers to chambers of torture, the emphasis lay upon the nice proportioning of the suffering to the offense. In the grand epic manner Dante projected this torture chamber, as the accomplishment of justice, against the sphere of the heavens, and produced those magnificent distortions and magnifications of human primitive vengeance that the mediaeval heart and imagination accepted as divine.

There existed, however, even then no commensurability between retributory sufferings and the evil for which the criminal was held responsible. In the last analysis he suffered until satisfaction had been given to the outraged sentiments of the injured person, or of his kith and kin, or of the community, or of an angry God. To satisfy the latter an eternity might be too short, while a merciful death ultimately carried away from the most exacting community the victim who was paying for his sin in the coin of his own agony. Commensurability does not exist between sin and suffering but does exist roughly between the sin and the amount and kind of suffering that will satisfy those who feel themselves aggrieved and yet it has become the judgment of our common moral consciousness that satisfaction in the suffering of the criminal has no legitimate place in assessing his punishment. Even in its sublimated form, as a part of righteous indignation, we recognize its legitimacy only in resenting and condemning injury, not in rendering justice for the evil done. It was therefore natural that in measuring the punishment the emphasis should shift from retribution to prevention, for there is a rough quantitative relation between the severity of the penalty and the fear which it inspires. This shift to the standard of expediency in determining the severity of the penalty does not mean that retribution is no longer the justification for punishment either in the popular mind or in legal theory, for however expedient it may be to visit crimes with condign punishments in the interest of the welfare of society, the justification for inflicting the suffering at all is found in the assumption that the criminal owes retributive suffering to the community; a debt which the community may collect in the form and amount which is most expedient to itself.

This curious combination of the concepts of retributive suffering which is the justification for punishment but may not be the standard for the amount and degree of the punishment, and of a social expediency which may not be the justification for the punishment itself but is the standard of the amount and kind of punishment inflicted, is evidently not the whole story. If retribution were the only justification for punishment it is hard to believe that punishment would not itself have disappeared when society came to recognize that a possible theory of punishment could not be worked out or maintained on the basis of retribution; especially when we recognize that a system of punishments assessed with reference to their deterrent powers not only works very inadequately in repressing crime but also preserves a criminal class. This other part of the story, which neither retribution nor social expediency tells, reveals itself in the assumed solemnity of criminal court procedure, in the majesty of the law, in the supposedly impartial and impersonal character of justice. These characters are not involved in the concept of retribution nor in that of deterrence. Lynch law is the very essence of retribution and is inspired with the grim assurance that such summary justice must strike terror into the heart of the prospective criminal, and lynch law lacks solemnity, and majesty, and is anything but impersonal or impartial. These characters inhere, not in the primitive impulses out of which punitive justice has arisen nor in the cautious prudence with which society devises protection for its goods, but in the judicial institution which theoretically acts on rule and not upon impulse and whose justice is to be done though the heavens fall. What, then, are these values evidenced in and maintained by the laws of punitive justice? The most patent value is the theoretically impartial enforcement of the common will. It is a procedure which undertakes to recognize and protect the individual in the interest of the common good and by the common will. In his acceptance of the law and dependence upon it the individual is at one with the community, while this very attitude carries with it the recognition of his responsibility to obey and support the law in its enforcement. So conceived the common law is an affirmation of citizenship. It is, however, a grave mistake to assume that the law itself and men's attitudes toward it can exist *in abstracto*. It is a grave mistake, for too often the respect for law as law is what we demand of members of the community, while we are able to regard with comparative indifference defects both in the concrete laws and in their administration. It is not only a mistake, it is also a fundamental error, for all emotional attitudes—and even respect for law and a sense of responsibility are emotional attitudes—arise in response to concrete impulses. We do not respect law in the abstract but the values which the laws of the community conserve. We have no sense of responsibility as such but an emotional recognition of duties which our position in the community entails. Nor are these impulses and emotional reactions less concrete because they are so organized into complex habits that some slight but appropriate stimulus sets a whole complex of impulses into operation. A man who defends an apparently unimportant right on principle is defending the whole body of analogous rights which a vast complex of social habits tends to preserve. His emotional attitude, which is seemingly out of proportion to the immediate issue, answers to all of those social goods toward which the different impulses in the organized body of habits are directed. Nor may we assume that because our emotions answer to concrete impulses they are therefore necessarily egoistic or self-regarding. No small portion of the impulses which make up the human

individual are immediately concerned with the good of others. The escape from selfishness is not by the Kantian road of an emotional response to the abstract universal, but by the recognition of the genuinely social character of human nature. An important instance of this illusory respect for abstract law appears in our attitude of dependence upon the law and its enforcement for the defense of our goods and those of others with whom we identify our interests.

A threatened attack upon these values places us in an attitude of defense, and as this defense is largely intrusted to the operation of the laws of the land we gain a respect for the laws which is in proportion to the goods which they defend. There is, however, another attitude more easily aroused under these conditions which is, I think, largely responsible for our respect for law as law. I refer to the attitude of hostility to the lawbreaker as an enemy to the society to which we belong. In this attitude we are defending the social structure against an enemy with all the animus which the threat to our own interests calls out. It is not the detailed operation of the law in defining the invasion of rights and their proper preservation that is the center of our interest but the capture and punishment of the personal enemy, who is also the public enemy. The law is the bulwark of our interests, and the hostile procedure against the enemy arouses a feeling of attachment due to the means put at our disposal for satisfying the hostile impulse. The law has become the weapon for overwhelming the thief of our purses, our good names, or even of our lives. We feel toward it as we feel toward the police officer who rescues us from a murderous assault. The respect for the law is the obverse side of our hatred for the criminal aggressor. Furthermore the court procedure, after the man accused of the crime is put under arrest and has been brought to trial, emphasizes this emotional attitude. The state's attorney seeks a conviction. The accused must defend himself against this attack. The aggrieved person and the community find in this officer of the government their champion. A legal battle takes the place of the former physical struggle which led up to the arrest. The emotions called out are the emotions of battle. The impartiality of the court who sits as the adjudicator is the impartiality of the umpire between the contending parties. The assumption that contending parties will each do his utmost to win, places upon each, even upon the state's attorney, the obligation to get a verdict for his own side rather than to bring about a result which will be for the best interests of all concerned. The doctrine that the strict enforcement of the law in this fashion is for the best interest of all concerned has no bearing upon the point which I am trying to emphasize. This point is that the emotional attitude of the injured individual and of the other party to the proceedings—the community—toward the law is that engendered by a hostile enterprise in which the law has become the ponderous weapon of defense and attack.[1]

There is another emotional content involved in this attitude of respect for law as law, which is perhaps of like importance with the other. I refer to that accompanying stigma placed upon the criminal. The revulsions against criminality reveal themselves in a sense of solidarity with the group, a sense of being a citizen which on the one hand excludes those who have transgressed the laws of the group and on the other inhibits tendencies to criminal acts in the citizen himself. It is this emotional reaction against conduct which excludes from society that gives to the moral taboos of the group such impressiveness. The majesty of the law is that of the angel with the fiery sword at the gate who can cut one off from the world to which he belongs. The majesty of the law is the dominance of the group over the individual, and the paraphernalia of criminal law serves not only to exile the rebellious individual from the group, but also to awaken in law-abiding members of society the inhibitions which make rebellion impossible to them. The formulation of these inhibitions is the basis of criminal law. The emotional content that accompanies them is a large part of the respect for law as law. In both these elements of our respect for law as law, in the respect for the common instrument of defense from and attack upon the enemy of ourselves and of society, and in the respect for that body of formulated custom which at once identifies us with the whole community and excludes those who break its commandments, we recognize concrete impulses—those of attack upon the enemy of ourselves and at the same time of the community,

and those of inhibition and restraint through which we feel the common will, in the identity of prohibition and of exclusion. They are concrete impulses which at once identify us with the predominant whole and at the same time place us on the level of every other member of the group, and thus set up that theoretical impartiality and evenhandedness of punitive justice which calls out in no small degree our sense of loyalty and respect. And it is out of the universality that belongs to the sense of common action springing out of these impulses that the institutions of law and of regulative and repressive justice arise. While these impulses are concrete in respect of their immediate object, i.e., the criminal, the values which this hostile attitude toward the criminal protects either in society or in ourselves are negatively and abstractly conceived. Instinctively we estimate the worth of the goods protected by the procedure against the criminal and in terms of this hostile procedure. These goods are not simply the physical articles but include the more precious values of self-respect, in not allowing one's self to be overridden, in downing the enemy of the group, in affirming the maxims of the group and its institutions against invasions. Now in all of this we have our backs toward that which we protect and our faces toward the actual or potential enemy. These goods are regarded as valuable because we are willing to fight and even die for them in certain exigencies, but their intrinsic value is neither affirmed nor considered in the legal proceeding. The values thus obtained are not their values in use but sacrifice values. To many a man his country has become infinitely valuable because he finds himself willing to fight and die for it when the common impulse of attack upon the common enemy has been aroused, and yet he may have been, in his daily life, a traitor to the social values he is dying to protect because there was no emotional situation within which these values appeared in his consciousness. It is difficult to bring into commensurable relationship to each other a man's willingness to cheat his country out of its legitimate taxes and his willingness to fight and die for the same country. The reactions spring from different sets of impulses and lead to evaluations which seem to have nothing in common with each other. The type of valuation of social goods that arises out of the hostile attitude toward the criminal is negative, because it does not present the positive social function of the goods that the hostile procedure protects. From the standpoint of protection one thing behind the wall has the same import as anything else that lies behind the same defense. The respect for law as law thus is found to be a respect for a social organization of defense against the enemy of the group and a legal

---

1. I am referring here to criminal law and its enforcement, not only because respect for the law and the majesty of the law have reference almost entirely to criminal justice, but also because a very large part, perhaps the largest part, of civil law proceedings are undertaken and carried out with the intent of defining and readjusting social situations without the hostile attitudes which characterize the criminal procedure. The parties to the civil proceedings belong to the same group and continue to belong to this group, whatever decision is rendered. No stigma attaches to the one who loses. Our emotional attitude toward this body of law is that of interest, of condemnation and approval as it fails or succeeds in its social function. It is not an institution that must be respected even in its disastrous failures. On the contrary it must be changed. It is hedged about in our feelings by no majesty. It is efficient or inefficient and as such awakens satisfaction or dissatisfaction and an interest in its reform which is in proportion to the social values concerned.

and judicial procedure that are oriented with reference to the criminal. The attempt to utilize these social attitudes and procedures to remove the causes of crime, to assess the kind and amount of punishment which the criminal should suffer in the interest of society, or to reinstate the criminal as a law-abiding citizen has failed utterly. For while the institutions which inspire our respect are concrete institutions with a definite function, they are responsible for a quite abstract and inadequate evaluation of society and its goods. These legal and political institutions organized with reference to the enemy or at least the outsider give a statement of social goods which is based upon defense and not upon function. The aim of the criminal proceeding is to determine whether the accused is innocent, i.e., still belongs to the group or whether he is guilty, i.e., is put under the ban which criminal punishment carries with it. The technical statement of this is found in the loss of the privileges of a citizen, in sentences of any severity, but the more serious ban is found in the fixed attitude of hostility on the part of the community toward a jailbird. One effect of this is to define the goods and privileges of the members of the community as theirs in virtue of their being law-abiding, and their responsibilities as exhausted by the statutes which determine the nature of criminal conduct. This effect is not due alone to the logical tendency to maintain the same definition of the institution of property over against the conduct of the thief and that of the law-abiding citizen. It is due in far greater degree to the feeling that we all stand together in the protection of property. In the positive definition of property, that is in terms of its social uses and functions, we are met by wide diversity of opinion, especially where the theoretically wide freedom of control over private property, asserted over against the thief, is restrained in the interest of problematic public goods. Out of this attitude toward the goods which the criminal law protects arises that fundamental difficulty in social reform which is due, not to mere difference in opinion nor to conscious selfishness, but to the fact that what we term opinions are profound social attitudes which, once assumed, fuse all conflicting tendencies over against the enemy of the people. The respect for law as law in its positive use in defense of social goods becomes unwittingly a respect for the conceptions of these goods which the attitude of defense has fashioned. Property becomes sacred not because of its social uses but because all the community is as one in its defense, and this conception of property, taken over into the social struggle to make property serve its functions in the community, becomes the bulwark of these in possession, *beati possidentes.*

Beside property other institutions have arisen, that of the person with its rights, that of the family with its rights, and that of the government with its rights. Wherever rights exist, invasion of those rights may be punished, and a definition of these institutions is formulated in protecting the right against trespass. The definition is again the voice of the community as a whole proclaiming and penalizing the one whose conduct has placed him under the ban. There is the same unfortunate circumstance that the law speaking against the criminal gives the sanction of the sovereign authority of the community to the negative definition of the right. It is defined in terms of its contemplated invasion. The individual who is defending his own rights against the trespasser is led to state even his family and more general social interests in abstract individualistic terms. Abstract individualism and a negative conception of liberty in terms of the freedom from restraints become the working ideas in the community. They have the prestige of battle cries in the fight for freedom against privilege. They are still the countersigns of the descendants of those who cast off the bonds of political and social restraint in their defense and assertion of the rights their forefathers won. Wherever criminal justice, the modern elaborate development of the taboo, the ban, and their consequences in a primitive society, organizes and formulates public sentiment in defense of social goods and institutions against actual or prospective enemies, there we find that the definition of the enemies, in other words the criminals, carries with it the definition of the goods and institutions. It is the revenge of the criminal upon the society which crushes him. The concentration of public sentiment upon the criminal which mobilizes the institution of justice, paralyzes the undertaking to conceive our common goods in terms of their uses. The majesty of the law is that of the sword drawn against a common enemy. The even-handedness of justice is that of universal conscription against a common enemy, and that of the abstract definition of rights which places the ban upon anyone who falls outside of its rigid terms.

Thus we see society almost helpless in the grip of the hostile attitude it has taken toward those who break its laws and contravene its institutions. Hostility toward the lawbreaker inevitably brings with it the attitudes of retribution, repression, and exclusion. These provide no principles for the eradication of crime, for returning the delinquent to normal social relations, nor for stating the transgressed rights and institutions in terms of their positive social functions.

On the other side of the ledger stands the fact that the attitude of hostility toward the lawbreaker has the unique advantage of uniting all members of the community in the emotional solidarity of aggression. While the most admirable of humanitarian efforts are sure to run counter to the individual interests of very many in the community, or fail to touch the interest and imagination of the multitude and to leave the community divided or indifferent, the cry of thief or murder is attuned to profound complexes, lying below the surface of competing individual effort, and citizens who have separated by divergent interests stand together against the common enemy. Furthermore, the attitude reveals common, universal values which underlie like a bedrock the divergent structures of individual ends that are mutually closed and hostile to each other. Seemingly without the criminal the cohesiveness of society would disappear and the universal goods of the community would crumble into mutually repellent individual particles. The criminal does not seriously endanger the structure of society by his destructive activities, and on the other hand he is responsible for a sense of solidarity, aroused among those whose attention would be otherwise centered upon interests quite divergent from those of each other. Thus courts of criminal justice may be essential to the preservation of society even when we take account of the impotence of the criminal over against society, and the clumsy failure of criminal law in the repression and suppression of crime. I am willing to admit that this statement is distorted, not however in its analysis of the efficacy of the procedure against the criminal, but in its failure to recognize the growing consciousness of the many common interests which is slowly changing our institutional conception of society, and its consequent exaggerated estimate upon the import of the criminal. But it is important that we should realize what the implications of this attitude of hostility are within our society. We should especially recognize the inevitable limitations which the attitude carries with it. Social organization which arises out of hostility at once emphasizes the character which is the basis of the opposition and tends to suppress all other characters in the members of the group. The cry of "stop thief" unites us all as property owners against the robber. We all stand shoulder to shoulder as Americans against a possible invader. Just in proportion as we organize by hostility do we suppress individuality. In a political campaign that is fought on party lines the members of the party surrender themselves to the party. They become simply members of the party whose conscious aim is to defeat the rival organization. For this purpose the party member becomes merely a republican or a democrat. The party symbol expresses everything. Where simple

social aggression or defense with the purpose of eliminating or encysting an enemy is the purpose of the community, organization through the common attitude of hostility is normal and effective. But as long as the social organization is dominated by the attitude of hostility the individuals or groups who are the objectives of this organization will remain enemies. It is quite impossible psychologically to hate the sin and love the sinner. We are very much given to cheating ourselves in this regard. We assume that we can detect, pursue, indict, prosecute, and punish the criminal and still retain toward him the attitude of reinstating him in the community as soon as he indicates a change in social attitude himself, that we can at the same time watch for the definite transgression of the statute to catch and overwhelm the offender, and comprehend the situation out of which the offense grows. But the two attitudes, that of control of crime by the hostile procedure of the law and that of control through comprehension of social and psychological conditions, cannot be combined. To understand is to forgive and the social procedure seems to deny the very responsibility which the law affirms, and on the other hand the pursuit by criminal justice inevitably awakens the hostile attitude in the offender and renders the attitude of mutual comprehension practically impossible. The social worker in the court is the sentimentalist, and the legalist in the social settlement in spite of his learned doctrine is the ignoramus.

While then the attitude of hostility, either against the transgressor of the laws or against the external enemy, gives to the group a sense of solidarity which most readily arouses like a burning flame and which consumes the differences of individual interests, the price paid for this solidarity of feeling is great and at times disastrous. Though human attitudes are far older than any human institutions and seem to retain identities of structure that make us at home in the heart of every man whose story has come down to us from the written and unwritten past, yet these attitudes take on new forms as they gather new social contents. The hostilities which flamed up between man and man, between family and family, and fixed the forms of old societies have changed as men came to realize the common whole within which these deadly struggles were fought out. Through rivalries, competitions, and co-operations men achieved the conception of a social state in which they asserted themselves while they at the same time affirmed the status of the others, on the basis not only of common rights and privileges but also on the basis of differences of interest and function, in an organization of more varied individuals. In the modern economic world a man is able to assert himself much more effectively against others through his acknowledgment of common property rights underlying their whole economic activity; while he demands acknowledgment for his individual competitive effort by recognizing and utilizing the varied activities and economic functions of others in the whole business complex.

This evolution reaches a still richer content when the self-assertion appears in the consciousness of social contribution that obtains the esteem of the others whose activities it complements and renders possible. In the world of scientific research rivalries do not preclude the warm recognition of the service which the work of one scientist renders to the whole co-operative undertaking of the *monde savant*. It is evident that such a social organization is not obtainable at will, but is dependent upon the slow growth of very varied and intricate social mechanisms. While no clearly definable set of conditions can be presented as responsible for this growth, it will I think be admitted that a very necessary condition, perhaps the most important one, is that of overcoming the temporal and spatial separations of men so that they are brought into closer interrelation with each other. Means of intercommunications have been the great civilizing agents. The multiple social stimulation of an indefinite number of varied contacts of a vast number of individuals with each other is the fertile field out of which spring social organizations, for these make possible the larger social life that can absorb the hostilities of different groups. When this condition has been supplied there seems to be an inherent tendency in social groups to advance from the hostile attitudes of individuals and groups toward each other through rivalries, competitions, and co-operations toward a functional self-assertion which recognizes and utilizes other selves and groups of selves in the activities in which social human nature expresses itself. And yet the attitude of hostility of a community toward those who have transgressed its laws or customs, i.e., its criminals, and toward the outer enemies has remained as a great solidifying power. The passionate appreciation of our religious, political, property, and family institutions has arisen in the attack upon those who individually or collectively have assailed or violated them, and hostility toward the actual or prospective enemies of our country has been the never-failing source of patriotism.

If then we undertake to deal with the causes of crime in a fundamental way, and as dispassionately as we are dealing with the causes of disease, and if we wish to substitute negotiation and international adjudication for war in settling disputes between nations, it is of some importance to consider what

sort of emotional solidarity we can secure to replace that which the traditional procedures have supplied. It is in the juvenile court that we meet the undertaking to reach and understand the causes of social and individual breakdown, to mend if possible the defective situation and reinstate the individual at fault. This is not attended with any weakening of the sense of the values that are at stake, but a great part of the paraphernalia of hostile procedure is absent. The judge sits down with the child who has been committed to the court, with members of the family, parole officers, and others who may help to make the situation comprehensible and indicates what steps can be taken to bring matters to a normal condition. We find the beginnings of scientific technique in this study in the presence of the psychologist and medical officer who can report upon the mental and physical condition of the child, of the social workers who can report upon the situation of the families and neighborhood involved. Then there are other institutions beside the jails to which the children can be sent for prolonged observation and change of immediate environment. In centering interest upon reinstatement the sense of forward-looking moral responsibility is not only not weakened but is strengthened, for the court undertakes to determine what the child must do and be to take up normal social relations again. Where the responsibility rests upon others this can be brought out in much greater detail and with greater effect since it is not defined under abstract legal categories and the aim in determining responsibility is not to place punishment but to obtain future results. Out of this arises a much fuller presentation of the facts that are essential for dealing with the problem than can possibly appear in a criminal court procedure that aims to establish simply responsibility for a legally defined offense with the purpose of inflicting punishment. Of far greater importance is the appearance of the values of family relations, of schools, of training of all sorts, of opportunities to work, and of all the other factors that go to make up that which is worth while in the life of a child or an adult. Before the juvenile court it is possible to present all of these and all of them can enter the consideration of what action is to be taken. These are the things that are worth while. They are the ends that should determine conduct. It is impossible to discover their real import unless they can all be brought into relationship with each other.

It is impossible to deal with the problem of what the attitude and conduct of the community should be toward the individual who has broken its laws, or what his responsibility is in terms of future action, unless all the facts and all the values with reference to which the facts must be interpreted are there and can be impartially considered, just as it is impossible to deal scientifically with any problem without recognizing all the facts and all the values involved. The attitude of hostility which places the criminal under the ban, and thus takes him out of society, and prescribes a hostile procedure by which he is secured, tried, and punished can take into account only those features of his conduct which constitute infraction of the law, and can state the relation of the criminal and society only in the terms of trial for fixing guilt and of punishment. All else is irrelevant. The adult criminal court is not undertaking to readjust a broken-down social situation, but to determine by the application of fixed rules whether the man is a member of society in good and regular standing or is an outcast. In accordance with these fixed rules what does not come under the legal definition not only does not naturally appear but it is actually excluded. Thus there exists a field of facts bearing upon the social problems that come into our courts and governmental administrative bureaus, facts which cannot be brought into direct use in solving these problems. It is with this material that the social scientist and the voluntary social worker and his organizations are occupied. In the juvenile court we have a striking instance of this material forcing its way into the institution of the court itself and compelling such a change in method that the material can be actually used. Recent changes of attitude toward the family permit facts bearing upon the care of children which earlier lay outside the purview of the court to enter into its consideration.

Other illustrations could be cited of this change in the structure and function of institutions by the pressure of data which the earlier form of the institution had excluded. One may cite the earlier theory of charity that it was a virtue of those in fortunate circumstances which is exercised toward the poor whom we have always with us, in its contrast with the conception of organized charity whose aim is not the exercise of an individual virtue but such a change in the condition of the individual case and of the community within which the cases arise that a poverty which requires charity may disappear. The author of a mediaeval treatise on charity considering the lepers as a field for good works contemplated the possibility of their disappearance with the ejaculation "which may God forbid!" The juvenile court is but one instance of an institution in which the consideration of facts which had been regarded as irrelevant or exceptional has carried with it a radical change in the institution. But it is of particular interest because the court is the objective form of the attitude of hostility on the part of the community toward the one who transgresses its laws and customs, and it is of further interest because it throws into relief the two types of emotional attitudes which answer to two types of social organization. Over against the emotional solidarity of the group opposing the enemy we find the interests which spring up around the effort to meet and solve a social problem. These interests are at first in opposition to each other. The interest in the individual delinquent opposes the interest in property and the social order dependent upon it. The interest in the change of the conditions which foster the delinquent is opposed to that identified with our positions in society as now ordered, and the resentment at added responsibilities which had not been formerly recognized or accepted.

But the genuine effort to deal with the actual problem brings with it tentative reconstructions which awaken new interests and emotional values. Such are the interests in better housing conditions, in different and more adequate schooling, in playgrounds and small parks, in controlling child labor and in vocational guidance, in improved sanitation and hygiene, and in community and social centers. In the place of the emotional solidarity which makes us all one against the criminal there appears the cumulation of varied interests unconnected in the past which not only bring new meaning to the delinquent but which also bring the sense of growth, development, and achievement. This reconstructive attitude offers the cumulative interest which comes with interlocking diversified values. The discovery that tuberculosis, alcoholism, unemployment, school retardation, adolescent delinquency, among other social evils, reach their highest percentages in the same areas not only awakens the interest we have in combatting each of these evils, but creates a definite object, that of human misery, which focuses endeavor and builds up a concrete object of human welfare which is a complex of values. Such an organization of effort gives rise to an individual or self with a new content of character, a self that is effective since the impulses which lead to conduct are organized with reference to a clearly defined object.

It is of interest to compare this self with that which responds to the community call for defense of itself or its institutions. The dominant emotional coloring of the latter is found in the standing together of all the group against the common enemy. The consciousness which one has of others is stripped of the instinctive oppositions which in varying forms are aroused in us by the mere presence of others. These may be merely the slight rivalries and differences of opinion and of social attitude and position, or just the reserves which we all preserve over against those about us. In the common cause these can disappear. Their disappearance means a removal of resistance and friction and adds exhilaration and enthusiasm to the expression of one of the most powerful of human impulses. The result is a certain enlargement of the self in which one seems to be at one with everyone else in the group. It is not a self-consciousness in the way of contrasting one's self with others. One loses himself in the whole group in some sense, and may attain the attitude in which he undergoes suffering and death for the common cause. In fact just as war removes the inhibitions from the attitude of hostility so it quickens and commends the attitude of self-assertion of a self which is fused with all the others in the community. The ban upon self-assertion which the consciousness of others in the group to which one belongs carries with it disappears when the assertion is directed against an object of common hostility or dislike. Even in times of peace we feel as a rule little if any disapproval of arrogance toward those of another nationality, and national self-conceit and the denigration of the achievements of other peoples may become virtues. The same tendency exists in varying degree among those who unite against the criminal or against the party foe. Attitudes of difference and opposition between members of the community or group are in abeyance and there is given the greater freedom for self-assertion against the enemy. Through these experiences come the powerful emotions which serve to evaluate for the time being what the whole community stands for in comparison with the interests of the individual who is opposed to the group. These experiences, however, serve only to set off against each other what the group stands for and the meager birthright of the individual who cuts himself off from the group.

What we all fight for, what we all protect, what we all affirm against the detractor, confers upon each in some measure the heritage of all, while to be outside the community is to be an Esau without heritage and with every man's hand against him. Self-assertion against the common enemy, suppressing as it does the oppositions of individuals within the group and thus identifying them all in a common effort, is after all the self-assertion of the fight in which the opposing selves strive each to eliminate the other, and in so doing are setting up their own survival and the destruction of the others as the end. I know that many ideals have been the ends of war, at least in the minds of many of the fighters; that in so far the fighting was not to destroy the fighters but some pernicious institution, such as slavery, that many have fought bloody wars for liberty and freedom. No champions however, of

such causes have ever failed to identify the causes in the struggle with themselves. The battle is for the survival of the right party and the death of the wrong. Over against the enemy we reach the ultimate form of self-assertion, whether it is the patriotic national self, or the party, or the schismatic self, or the institutional self, or simply the self of the hand to hand mêlée. It is the self whose existence calls for the destruction, or defeat, or subjection, or reduction of the enemy. It is a self that finds expression in vivid, concentrated activity and under appropriate conditions of the most violent type. The instinct of hostility which provides the structure for this self when fully aroused and put in competition with the other powerful human complexes of conduct, those of sex, of hunger, and of parenthood and of possession has proved itself as more dominant than they. It also carries with it the stimulus for readier and, for the time being, more complete socialization than any other instinctive organization. There is no ground upon which men get together so readily as that of a common enemy, while a common object of the instinct of sex, of possession, or of hunger leads to instant opposition, and even the common object of the parental instinct may be the spring of jealousy. The socializing agency of common hostility is marked, as I have above indicated, by its own defects. In so far as it is the dominant instinct it does not organize the other instincts for its object. It suppresses or holds the others in abeyance. While hostility itself may be a constituent part of the execution of any instinct, for they all involve oppositions, there is no other instinctive act of the human self which is a constituent part of the immediate instinctive process of fighting, while struggle with a possible opponent plays its part in the carrying out of every other instinctive activity. As a result those who fight together against common enemies instinctively tend to ignore the other social activities within which oppositions between the individuals engage normally arise.

It is this temporary relief from the social frictions which attend upon all other co-operative activities which is largely responsible for the emotional upheavals of patriotism, of mob consciousness, and the extremes of party warfare, as well as for the gusto of malicious gossiping and scandalmongering. Furthermore, in the exercise of this instinct success implies the triumph of the self over the enemy. The achievement of the process is the defeat of certain persons and the victory of others. The end takes the form of that sense of self-enlargement and assurance which comes with superiority of the self over others. The attention is directed toward the relative position of the self toward others. The values involved are those that only can be expressed in terms of interests and relations of the self in its differences from others. From the standpoint of one set of antagonists their victory is that of efficient civilization while the other regards their victory as that of liberal ideas. All the way from the Tamerlanes who create a desert and call it peace to the idealistic warriors who fight and die for ideas, victory means the survival of one set of personalities and the elimination of others, and the ideas and ideals that become issues in the contest must perforce be personified if they are to appear in the struggles that arise out of the hostile instinct. War, whether it is physical, economic, or political, contemplates the elimination of the physical, economic, or political opponent. It is possible to confine the operation of this instinct within certain specific limitations and fields. In the prize fights as in the olden tourneys the annihilation of the enemy is ceremonially halted at a fixed stage in the struggle. In a football game the defeated team leaves the field to the champion. Successful competition in its sharpest form eliminates its competitor. The victor at the polls drives the opponent from the field of political administration. If the struggle can be *à outrance* within any field and contemplates the removal of the enemy from that field, the instinct of hostility has this power of uniting and fusing the contesting groups, but since victory is the aim of the fight and it is the victory of one party over the other, the issues of battle must be conceived in terms of the victor and the vanquished.

Other types of social organization growing out of the other instincts, such as possession, hunger, or parenthood, imply ends which are not as such identified with selves in their oppositions to other selves, though the objects toward which these instinctive activities are directed may be occasion for the exercise of the hostile instinct. The social organizations which arise about these objects are in good part due to the inhibitions placed upon the hostile impulse, inhibitions which are exercised by the other groups of impulses which the same situations call out. The possession by one individual in a family or clan group of a desirable object is an occasion for an attack on the part of other members of the group, but his characters as a member of the group are stimuli to family and clan responses which check the attack. It may be mere repression with smoldering antagonisms, or there may be such a social reorganization that the hostility can be given a function under social control, as in the

party, political, and economic contests, in which certain party, political, and economic selves are driven from the field leaving others that carry out the social activity. Here the contest being restricted the most serious evils of the warfare are removed, while the contest has at least the value of the rough selection. The contest is regarded in some degree from the standpoint of the social function, not simply from that of the elimination of an enemy. As the field of constructive social activity widens the operation of the hostile impulse in its instinctive form decreases. This does not, however, mean that the reactions that go to make up the impulse or instinct have ceased to function. It does mean that the impulse ceases to be an undertaking to get rid of the offending object by injury and destruction, that is, an undertaking directed against another social being with capacities for suffering and death —physical, economical or political—like his own. It becomes in its organization with other impulses an undertaking to deal with a situation by removing obstacles. We will speak of him as fighting against his difficulties. The force of the original impulse is not lost but its objective is no longer the elimination of a person, but such a reconstruction that the profounder social activities may find their continued and fuller expression. The energy that expressed itself in burning witches as the causes of plagues expends itself at present in medical research and sanitary regulations and may still be called a fight with disease.

In all these changes the interest shifts from the enemy to the reconstruction of social conditions. The self-assertion of the soldier and conqueror becomes that of the competitor in industry or business or politics, of the reformer, the administrator, of the physician or other social functionary. The test of success of this self lies in the change and construction of the social conditions which make the self possible, not in the conquest and elimination of other selves. His emotions are not those of mass consciousness dependent upon suppressed individualities, but arise out of the cumulative interest of varied undertakings converging upon a common problem of social reconstruction. This individual and his social organization are more difficult of accomplishment and subject to vastly greater friction than those which spring out of war. Their emotional content may not be so vivid, but they are the only remedy for war, and they meet the challenge which the continued existence of war in human society has thrown down to human intelligence.

3. The Psychopathology of Everyday Life

BY SIGMUND FREUD

Erroneously Carried-out Actions

I SHALL GIVE another passage from Meringer and Mayer (p. 98):

"Lapses in speech do not stand entirely alone. They resemble the errors which often occur in our other activities and are quite foolishly termed 'forgetfulness.'"

I am therefore in no way the first to presume that there is a sense and purpose behind the slight functional disturbances of the daily life of healthy people.

If the lapse in speech, which is without doubt a motor function, admits of such a conception, it is quite natural to transfer to the lapses of our other motor functions the same expectation. I have here formed two groups of cases; all these cases in which the faulty effect seems to be the essential element—that is, the deviation from the intention—I denote as erroneously carried-out actions (*Vergreifen*); the others, in which the entire action appears rather inexpedient, I call "symptomatic and chance actions." But no distinct line of demarcation can be formed; indeed, we are forced to conclude that all divisions used in this treatise are of only descriptive significance and contradict the inner unity of the sphere of manifestation.

The psychologic understanding of erroneous actions apparently gains little in clearness when we place it under the head of "ataxia," and especially under "cortical ataxia." Let us rather try to trace the individual examples to their proper determinants. To do this I shall again resort to personal observations, the opportunities for which I could not very frequently find in myself.

(*a*) In former years, when I made more calls at the homes of patients than I do at present, it often happened, when I stood before a door where I should have knocked or rung the bell, that I would pull the key of my own house from my pocket, only to replace it, quite abashed. When I investigated in what patients' homes this occured, I had to admit that the faulty action—taking out my key instead of ringing the bell—signified paying a certain tribute to the house where the error occurred. It was equivalent to the thought "Here I feel at home," as it happened only where I possessed the patient's regard. (Naturally, I never rang my own doorbell.)

The faulty action was therefore a symbolic representation of a definite thought which was not accepted consciously as serious; for in reality the neurologist is well aware that the patient seeks him only so long as he expects to be benefited by him, and that his own excessively warm interest for his patient is evinced only as a means of psychic treatment.

An almost identical repetition of my experience is described by A. Maeder ("Contrib. à la psychopathologie de la vie quotidienne," *Arch. de Psychol.*, vi., 1906): "*Il est arrivé a chacun de sortir son trousseau, en arrivant à la porte d'un ami particulièrement cher, de se surprendre pour ainsi dire, en train d'ouvrir avec sa clé comme chez soi. C'est un retard, puisqu'il faut sonner malgré tout, mais c'est une preuve qu'on se sent—ou qu'on voudrait se sentir—comme chez soi, auprès de cet ami.*"

Jones speaks as follows about the use of keys.[1] "The use of keys is a fertile source of occurrences of this kind, of which two examples may be given. If I am disturbed in the midst of some engrossing work at home by having to go to the hospital to carry out some routine work, I am very apt to find myself trying to open the door of my laboratory there with the key of my desk at home, although the two keys are quite unlike each other. The mistake unconsciously demonstrates where I would rather be at the moment.

"Some years ago I was acting in a subordinate position at a certain institution, the front door of which was kept locked, so that it was necessary to ring for admission. On several occasions I found myself making serious attempts to open the door with my house key. Each one of the permanent visiting staff, of which I aspired to be a member, was provided with a key to avoid the trouble of having to wait at the door. My mistake thus expressed the desire to be on a similar footing and to be quite 'at home' there."

Reprinted from Sigmund Freud, *Psychopathology of Everyday Life*, trans. A. A. Brill (New York: The Macmillan Co., 1935), pp. 90–108, by permission of the publisher.

1. Ernest Jones, *Papers on Psychoanalysis*, p. 79.

A similar experience is reported by Dr. Hans Sachs of Vienna: "I always carry two keys with me, one for the door of my office and one for my residence. They are not by any means easily interchanged, as the office key is at lease three times as big as my house key. Besides, I carry the first key in my trouser pocket and the other in my vest pocket. Yet it often happened that I noticed on reaching the door that while ascending the stairs I had taken out the wrong key. I decided to undertake a statistical examination; as I was daily in about the same emotional state when I stood before both doors, I thought that the interchanging of the two keys must show a regular tendency, if they were differently determined psychically. Observation of later occurrences showed that I regularly took out my house key before the office door. Only on one occasion was this reversed: I came home tired, knowing that I would find there a guest. I made an attempt to unlock the door with the, naturally too big, office key."

(*b*) At a certain time twice a day for six years I was accustomed to wait for admission before a door in the second story of the same house, and during this long period of time it happened twice (within a short interval) that I climbed a story higher. On the first of these occasions I was in an ambitious daydream, which allowed me to "mount always higher and higher." In fact, at that time I heard the door in question open as I put my foot on the first step of the third flight. On the other occasion I again went too far "engrossed in thought." As soon as I became aware of it, I turned back and sought to snatch the dominating fantasy; I found that I was irritated over a criticism of my works, in which the reproach was made that I "always went too far," which I replaced by the less respectful expression "climbed too high."

(*c*) For many years a reflex hammer and a tuning-fork lay side by side on my desk. One day I hurried off at the close of my office hours, as I wished to catch a certain train, and despite broad daylight, put the tuning-fork in my coat pocket in place of the reflex hammer. My attention was called to the mistake through the weight of the object drawing down my pocket. Any one unaccustomed to reflect on such slight occurrences would without hesitation explain the faulty action by the hurry of the moment, and excuse it. In spite of that, I preferred to ask myself why I took the tuning-fork instead of the hammer. The haste could just as well have been a motive for carrying out the action properly in order not to waste time over the correction.

"Who last grasped the tuning-fork?" was the question which immediately flashed through my mind. It happened that only a few days ago an idiotic child, whose attention to sensory impressions I was testing, had been so fascinated by the tuning-fork that I found it difficult to tear it away from him. Could it mean, therefore, that I was an idiot? To be sure, so it would seem, as the next thought which associated itself with the hammer was *chamer* (Hebrew for "ass").

But what was the meaning of this abusive language? We must here inquire into the situation. I hurried to a consultation at a place on the Western railroad to see a patient who, according to the anamnesis which I received by letter, had fallen from a balcony some months before, and since then had been unable to walk. The physician who invited me wrote that he was still unable to say whether he was dealing with a spinal injury or traumatic neurosis—hysteria. That was what I was to decide. This could therefore be a reminder to be particularly careful in this delicate differential diagnosis. As it is, my colleagues think that hysteria is diagnosed far too carelessly where more serious matters are concerned. But the abuse is not yet justified. Yes, the next association was that the small railroad station is the same place in which, some years previous, I saw a young man who, after a certain emotional experience, could not walk properly. At that time I diagnosed his malady as hysteria, and later put him under psychic treatment; but it afterward turned out that my diagnosis was neither incorrect nor correct. A large number of the patient's symptoms were hysterical, and they promptly disappeared in the course of treatment. But back of these was a visible remnant that could not be reached by therapy, and could be referred only to a multiple sclerosis. Those who saw the patient after me had no difficulty in recognizing the organic affection. I could scarcely have acted or judged differently, still the impression was that of a serious mistake; the promise of a cure which I had given him could naturally not be kept.

The mistake in grasping the tuning-fork instead of the hammer could therefore be translated into the following words: "You fool, you ass, get yourself together this time, and be careful not to diagnose again a case of hysteria where there is an incurable disease, as you did in this place years ago in the case of the poor man!" And fortunately for this little analysis, even if unfortunately for my mood, this same man, now having a very spastic gate, had been to my office a few days before, one day after the examination of the idiotic child.

We observe that this time it is the voice of self-criticism which makes itself perceptible through the mistake in grasping. The erroneously carried-out action is specially suited to express self-reproach. The present mistake attempts to represent the mistake which was committed elsewhere.

(*d*) It is quite obvious that grasping the wrong thing may also serve a whole series of other obscure purposes. Here is a first example: It is very seldom that I break anything. I am not particularly dexterous, but by virtue of the anatomic integrity of my nervous and muscular apparatus there are apparently no grounds in me for such awkward movements with undesirable results. I can recall no object in my home the counterpart of which I have ever broken. Owing to the narrowness of my study it has often been necessary of me to work in the most uncomfortable position among my numerous antique clay and stone objects, of which I have a small collection. So much is this true that onlookers have expressed fear lest I topple down something and shatter it. But it never happened. Then why did I brush to the floor the cover of my simple inkwell so that it broke into pieces?

My inkstand is made of a flat piece of marble which is hollowed out for the reception of the glass inkwell; the inkwell has a marble cover with a knob of the same stone. A circle of bronze statuettes with terra-cotta figures is set behind this inkstand. I seated myself at the desk to write, I made a remarkably awkward outward movement with the hand holding the pen-holder, and so swept the cover of the inkstand, which already lay on the desk, to the floor.

It is not difficult to find the explanation. Some hours before my sister had been in the room to look at some of my new acquisitions. She found them very pretty, and then remarked: "Now the desk really looks very well, only the inkstand does not match. You must get a prettier one." I accompanied my sister out and did not return for several hours. But then, as it seems, I performed the execution of the condemned inkstand.

Did I perhaps conclude from my sister's words that she intended to present me with a prettier inkstand on the next festive occasion, and did I shatter the unsightly old one in order to force her to carry out her signified intention? If that be so, then my swinging motion was only apparently awkward; in reality it was most skillful and designed, as it understood how to avoid all the valuable objects located near it.

I actually believe that we must accept this explanation for a whole series of seemingly accidental awkward movements. It is true that on the surface these seem to show something violent and irregular, similar to spastic-ataxic movements, but on examination they seem to be dominated by some intention, and they accomplish their aim with a certainty that cannot be generally credited to conscious arbitrary motions. In both characteristics, the force as well as the sure aim, they show besides a resemblance to the motor manifestations of the hysterical neurosis, and in part also to the motor accomplishments of somnambulism, which here as well as there point to the same unfamiliar modification of the functions of innervation.

In latter years, since I have been collecting such observations, it has happened several times that I have shattered and broken objects of some value, but the examination of these cases convinced me that it was never the result of accident or of my unintentional awkwardness. Thus, one morning while in my bathrobe and straw slippers I followed a sudden impulse as I passed a room, and hurled a slipper from my foot against the wall so that it brought down a beautiful little marble Venus from its bracket. As it fell to pieces I recited quite unmoved the following verse from Busch:

> "Ach! Die Venus ist perdü—[2]
> Klickeradoms—von Medici!"

This crazy action and my calmness at the sight of the damage is explained in the then existing situation. We had a very sick person in the family, of whose recovery I had personally despaired. That morning I had been informed that there was a great improvement; I know that I had said to myself, "After all she will live." My attack of destructive madness served therefore as the expression of a grateful feeling toward fate, and afforded me the opportunity of performing an "act of sacrifice," just as if I had vowed, "If she gets well I will give this or that as a sacrifice." That I chose the Venus of Medici as this sacrifice was only gallant homage to the convalescent. But even today it is still incomprehensible to me that I decided so quickly, aimed so accurately, and struck no other object in close proximity.

Another breaking, in which I utilized a penholder falling from my hand, also signified a sacrifice, but this time it was a pious offering to avert some evil. I had once allowed myself to reproach a true and worthy friend for no other reason than certain manifestations which I interpreted from his unconscious activity. He took it amiss and wrote me a letter in which he bade me not to treat my friends by psychoanalysis. I had to admit that he was right and appeased him with my answer. While writing this letter I had before me my latest acquisition—a small, handsome, glazed Egyptian figure. I broke it in the manner mentioned, and then immediately knew that I had caused this mischief to avert a greater one. Luckily, both the friendship

---

2. Alas! the Venus of Medici is lost!

and the figure could be so cemented that the break would not be noticed.

A third case of breaking had a less serious connection; it was only a disguised "execution," to use an expression from Th. Vischer's *Auch Einer*, of an object that no longer suited my taste. For quite a while I had carried a cane with a silver handle; through no fault of mine the thin silver plate was once damaged and poorly repaired. Soon after the cane was returned I mirthfully used the handle to angle for the leg of one of my children. In that way it naturally broke, and I got rid of it.

The difference with which we accept the resulting damage in all these cases may certainly be taken as evidence for the existence of an unconscious purpose in their execution.

(*e*) As can sometimes be demonstrated by analysis, the dropping of objects or the overturning and breaking of the same are very frequently utilized as the expression of unconscious streams of thought, but more often they serve to represent the superstitious or odd significances connected therewith in popular sayings. The meanings attached to the spilling of salt, the overturning of a wine glass, the sticking of a knife dropped to the floor, and so on, are well known. I shall discuss later the right to investigate such superstitious interpretations; here I shall simply observe that the individual awkward acts do not by any means always have the same meaning, but, depending on the circumstances, they serve to represent now this or that purpose.

Recently we passed through a period in my house during which an unusual number of glass and china dishes were broken. I myself largely contributed to this damage. This little endemic was readily explained by the fact that it preceded the public betrothal of my eldest daughter. On such festivities it is customary to break some dishes and utter at the same time some felicitating expression. This custom may signify a sacrifice or express any other symbolic sense.

When servants destroy fragile objects through dropping them, we certainly do not think in the first place of a psychologic motive for it; still, some obscure motives are not improbable even here. Nothing lies farther from the uneducated than the appreciation of art and works of art. Our servants are dominated by a foolish hostility against these productions, especially when the objects, whose worth they do not realize, become a source of a great deal of work for them. On the other hand, persons of the same education and origin employed in scientific institutions often distinguish themselves by great dexterity and reliability in the handling of delicate objects, as soon as they begin to identify

themselves with their masters and consider themselves an essential part of the staff.

I shall here add the report of a young mechanical engineer, which gives some insight into the mechanism of damaging things.

"Some time ago I worked with many others in the laboratory of the High School on a series of complicated experiments on the subject of elasticity. It was a work that we undertook of our own volition, but it turned out that it took up more of our time than we expected. One day, while going to the laboratory with F., he complained of losing so much time, especially on this day, when he had so many other things to do at home. I could only agree with him, and he added half jokingly, alluding to an incident of the previous week: 'Let us hope that the machine will refuse to work, so that we can interrupt the experiment and go home earlier.'

"In arranging the work, it happened that F. was assigned to the regulation of the pressure valve, that is, it was his duty to carefully open the valve and let the fluid under pressure flow from the accumulator into the cylinder of the hydraulic press. The leader of the experiment stood at the manometer and called a loud 'Stop!' when the maximum pressure was reached. At this command F. grasped the valve and turned it with all his force—to the left (all valves, without any exception, are closed to the right). This caused a sudden full pressure in the accumulator of the press, and as there was no outlet, the connecting pipe burst. This was quite a trifling accident to the machine, but enough to force us to stop our work for the day and go home.

"It is characteristic, moreover, that some time later, on discussing this occurrence, my friend F. could not recall the remark that I positively remember his having made."

Similarly, to fall, to make a misstep, or to slip need not always be interpreted as an entirely accidental miscarriage of a motor action. The linguistic double meaning of these expressions points to diverse hidden fantasies, which may present themselves through the giving up of bodily equilibrium. I recall a number of lighter nervous ailments in women and girls which made their appearance after falling without injury, and which were conceived as traumatic hysteria as a result of the shock of the fall. At that time I already entertained the impression that these conditions had a different connection, that the fall was already a preparation of the neurosis, and an expression of the same unconscious fantasies of sexual content which may be taken as the moving forces behind the symptoms. Was not this very thing meant in the proverb which says, "When a maiden falls, she falls on her back?"

We can also add to these mistakes the case of one who gives a beggar a gold piece in place of a copper or a silver coin. The solution of such mishandling is simple: it is an act of sacrifice designed to mollify fate, to avert evil, and so on. If we hear a tender mother or aunt express concern regarding the health of a child, directly before taking a walk during which she displays her charity, contrary to her usual habit, we can no longer doubt the sense of this apparently undesirable accident. In this manner our faulty acts make possible the practice of all those pious and superstitious customs which must shun the light of consciousness, because of the strivings against them of our unbelieving reason.

(*f*) That accidental actions are really intentional will find no greater credence in any other sphere than in sexual activity, where the border between the intention and accident hardly seems discernible. That an apparently clumsy movement may be utilized in a most refined way for sexual purposes I can verify by a nice example from my own experience. In a friend's house I met a young girl visitor who excited in me a feeling of fondness which I had long believed extinct, this putting me in a jovial, loquacious, and complaisant mood. At that time I endeavored to find out how this came about, as a year before this same girl made no impression on me.

As the girl's uncle, a very old man, entered the room, we both jumped to our feet to bring him a chair which stood in the corner. She was more agile than I and also nearer the object, so that she was the first to take possession of the chair. She carried it with its back to her, holding both hands on the edge of the seat. As I got there later and did not give up the claim to carrying the chair, I suddenly stood directly back of her, and with both my arms was embracing her from behind, and for a moment my hands touched her lap. I naturally solved the situation as quickly as it came about. Nor did it occur to anybody how dexterously I had taken advantage of this awkward movement.

Occasionally I have had to admit to myself that the annoying, awkward stepping aside on the street, whereby for some seconds one steps here and there, yet always in the same direction as the other person, until finally both stop facing each other, that this "barring one's way" repeats an ill-mannered, provoking conduct of earlier times and conceals erotic purposes under the mask of awkwardness. From my psychoanalysis of neurotics I know that the so-called naïveté of young people and children is

frequently only such a mask, employed in order that the subject may say or do the indecent without restraint.

W. Stekel has reported similar observations in regard to himself: "I entered a house and offered my right hand to the hostess. In a most remarkable way I thereby loosened the bow which held together her loose morning-gown. I was conscious of no dishonorable intent, still I executed this awkward movement with the agility of a juggler."

(*g*) The effects which result from mistakes of normal persons are, as a rule, of a most harmless nature. Just for this reason it would be particularly interesting to find out whether mistakes of considerable importance, which could be followed by serious results, as, for example, those of physicians or druggists, fall within the range of our point of view.

As I am seldom in a position to deal with active medical matters, I can only report one mistake from my own experience. I treated a very old woman, whom I visited twice daily for several years. My medical activities were limited to two acts which I performed during my morning visits: I dropped a few drops of an eye lotion into her eyes and gave her a hypodermic injection of morphine. I prepared regularly two bottles—a blue one, containing the eye lotion, and a white one, containing the morphine solution. While performing these duties my thoughts were mostly occupied with something else, for they had been repeated so often that the attention acted as if free. One morning I noticed that the automaton worked wrong; I had put the dropper into the white instead of into the blue bottle, and had dropped into the eyes the morphine instead of the lotion. I was greatly frightened, but then calmed myself through the reflection that a few drops of a *two per cent* solution of morphine would not likely do any harm even if left in the conjunctival sac. The cause of the fright manifestly belonged elsewhere.

In attempting to analyze the slight mistake I first thought of the phrase, "to seize the old woman by mistake," which pointed out the short way to the solution. I had been impressed by a dream which a young man had told me the previous evening, the contents of which could be explained only on the basis of sexual intercourse with his own mother.[3] The strangeness of the fact that the Oedipus legend takes no offense at the age of Queen Jocasta seemed to me to agree with the assumption

---

3. The Oedipus dream, as I was wont to call it, because it contains the key to the understanding of the legend of King Oedipus. In the text of Sophocles the relation of such a dream is put in the mouth of Jocasta (cf. *The Interpretation of Dreams*, pp. 222–4, etc.).

that in being in love with one's mother we never deal with the present personality, but with her youthful memory picture carried over from our childhood. Such incongruities always show themselves where one fantasy fluctuating between two periods is made conscious, and is then bound to one definite period.

Deep in thoughts of this kind, I came to my patient of over ninety; I must have been well on the way to grasp the universal character of the Oedipus fable as the correlation of the fate which the oracle pronounces, for I made a blunder in reference to or on the old woman. Here, again, the mistake was harmless; of the two possible errors, taking the morphine solution for the eye, or the eye lotion for the injection, I chose the one by far the least harmful. The question still remains open whether in mistakes in handling things which may cause serious harm we can assume an unconscious intention as in the cases here discussed.

The following case from Brill's experience corroborates the assumption that even serious mistakes are determined by unconscious intentions: "A physician received a telegram informing him that his aged uncle was very sick. In spite of important family affairs at home he at once repaired to that distant town because his uncle was really his father, who had cared for him since he was one and a half years old, when his own father had died. On reaching there he found his uncle suffering from pneumonia, and, as the old man was an octogenarian, the doctors held out no hope for his recovery. 'It was simply a question of a day or two,' was the local doctor's verdict. Although a prominent physician in a big city, he refused to co-operate in the treatment, as he found that the case was properly managed by the local doctor, and he could not suggest anything to improve matters.

"Since death was daily expected, he decided to remain to the end. He visited a few days, but the sick man struggled hard, and although there was no question of any recovery, because of the many new complications which had arisen, death seemed to be deferred for a while. One night before retiring he went into the sickroom and took his uncle's pulse. As it was quite weak, he decided not to wait for the doctor, and administered a hypodermic injection. The patient grew rapidly worse and died within a few hours. There was something strange in the last symptoms, and on later attempting to replace the tube of hypodermic tablets into the case, he found to his consternation that he had taken out the wrong tube, and instead of a small dose of digitalis he had given a large dose of hyoscine.

"This case was related to me by the doctor after he read my paper on the Oedipus Complex.[4] We agreed that this mistake was determined not only by his impatience to get home to his sick child, but also by an old resentment and unconscious hostility toward his uncle (father)."

It is known that in the more serious cases of psychoneuroses one sometimes finds self-mutilations as symptoms of the disease. That the psychic conflict may end in suicide can never be excluded in these cases. Thus I know from experience, which some day I shall support with convincing examples, that many apparently accidental injuries happening to such patients are really self-inflicted. This is brought about by the fact that there is a constantly lurking tendency to self-punishment, usually expressing itself in self-reproach, or contributing to the formation of a symptom, which skillfully makes use of an external situation. The required external situation may accidently present itself or the punishment tendency may assist it until the way is open for the desired injurious effect.

Such occurrences are by no means rare even in cases of moderate severity, and they betray the portion of unconscious intention through a series of special features—for example, through the striking presence of mind which the patients show in the pretended accidents.[5]

I will report exhaustively one in place of many such examples from my professional experience. A young woman broke her leg below the knee in a carriage accident so that she was bedridden for weeks. The striking part of it was the lack of any manifestation of pain and the calmness with which she bore her misfortune. This calamity ushered in a long and serious neurotic illness, from which she was finally cured by psychotherapy. During the treatment I discovered the circumstances surrounding the accident, as well as certain impressions which preceded it. The young woman with her jealous husband spent some time on the farm of her married sister, in company with her numerous other brothers and sisters with their wives and husbands. One evening she gave an exhibition of one of her talents before this intimate circle: she danced artistically the "cancan," to the great delight of her relatives, but to the great annoyance of her husband, who afterward whispered to her, "Again you have behaved like a prostitute." The words

4. *New York Medical Journal,* September, 1912. Reprinted in large form as Chapter X of *Psychoanalysis,* etc. Saunders, Philadelphia.

5. The self-inflicted injury which does not entirely tend toward self-annihilation has, moreover, no other choice in our present state of civilization than to hide itself behind the accidental, or to break through in a simulation of spontaneous illness. Formerly, it was a customary sign of mourning; at other times it expressed itself in ideas of piety and renunciation of the world.

took effect; we will leave it undecided whether it was just on account of the dance. That night she was restless in her sleep, and the next forenoon she decided to go out driving. She chose the horses herself, refusing one team and demanding another. Her youngest sister wished to have her baby with its nurse accompany her, but she opposed this vehemently. During the drive she was nervous; she reminded the coachman that the horses were getting skittish, and as the fidgety animals really produced a momentary difficulty she jumped from the carriage in fright and broke her leg, while those remaining in the carriage were uninjured. Although after the disclosure of these details we can hardly doubt that this accident was really contrived, we cannot fail to admire the skill which forced the accident to mete out a punishment so suitable to the crime. For as it happened "cancan" dancing with her became impossible for a long time.

Concerning self-inflicted injuries of my own experience, I cannot report anything in calm times, but under extraordinary conditions I do not believe myself incapable of such acts. When a member of my family complains that he or she has bitten his tongue, bruised her finger, and so on, instead of the expected sympathy I put the question, "Why did you do that?" But I have most painfully squeezed my thumb, after a youthful patient acquainted me during the treatment with his intention (naturally not to be taken seriously) of marrying my eldest daughter, while I knew that she was then in a private hospital in extreme danger of losing her life.

One of my boys, whose vivacious temperament was wont to put difficulties in the management of nursing him in his illness, had a fit of anger one morning because he was ordered to remain in bed during the forenoon, and threatened to kill himself: a way out suggested to him by the newspapers. In the evening he showed me a swelling on the side of his chest which was the result of bumping against the door knob. To my ironical question why he did it, and what he meant by it, the eleven-year-old child explained, "That was my attempt at suicide which I threatened this morning." However, I do not believe that my views on self-inflicted wounds were accessible to my children at that time.

Whoever believes in the occurrence of semi-intentional self-inflicted injury—if this awkward expression be permitted—will become prepared to accept through it the fact that aside from conscious intentional suicide there also exists semi-intentional annihilation—with unconscious intention—which is capable of aptly utilizing a threat against life and masking it as a casual mishap. Such mechanism is by no means rare. For the tendency to self-destruction exists to a certain degree in many more persons than in those who bring it to completion. Self-inflicted injuries are, as a rule, a compromise between this impulse and the forces working against it, and even where it really comes to suicide the inclination has existed for a long time with less strength or as an unconscious and repressed tendency.

Even suicide consciously committed chooses its time, means, and opportunity; it is quite natural that unconscious suicide should wait for a motive to take upon itself one part of the causation and thus free it from its oppression by taking up the defensive forces of the person.[6] These are in no way idle discussions which I here bring up; more than one case of apparently accidental misfortune (on a horse or out of a carriage) has become known to me whose surrounding circumstances justified the suspicion of suicide.

For example, during an officers' horse race one of the riders fell from his horse and was so seriously injured that a few days later he succumbed to his injuries. His behavior after regaining consciousness was remarkable in more than one way, and his conduct previous to the accident was still more remarkable. He had been greatly depressed by the death of his beloved mother, had crying spells in the society of his comrades, and to his trusted friend had spoken of the *taedium vitae*. He had wished to quit the service in order to take part in a war in Africa which had no interest for him.[7] Formerly a keen rider, he had later evaded riding whenever possible. Finally, before the horse race, from which he could not withdraw, he expressed a sad foreboding, which most expectedly in the light of our conception came true. It may be contended that it

---

6. The case is then identical with a sexual attack on a woman, in whom the attack of the man cannot be warded off through the full muscular strength of the woman because a portion of the unconscious feelings of the one attacked meets it with ready acceptance. To be sure, it is said that such a situation paralyzes the strength of a woman; we need only add the reasons for this paralysis. Insofar the clever sentence of Sancho Panza, which he pronounced as governor of his island, is psychologically unjust (*Don Quixote*, vol. ii. chap. xlv). A woman hauled before the judge a man who was supposed to have robbed her of her honor by force of violence. Sancho indemnified her with a full purse which he took from the accused, but after the departure of the woman he gave the accused permission to follow her and snatch the purse from her. Both returned wrestling, the woman priding herself that the villain was unable to possess himself of the purse. Thereupon Sancho spoke: "Had you shown yourself so stout and valiant to defend your body (nay, but half so much) as you have done to defend your purse, the strength of Hercules could not have forced you."

7. It is evident that the situation of a battlefield is such as to meet the requirement of conscious suicidal intent which, nevertheless, shuns the direct way. Cf. in *Wallenstein* the words of the Swedish captain concerning the death of Max Piccolomini: "They say he wished to die."

is quite comprehensible without any further cause that a person in such a state of nervous depression cannot manage a horse as well as on normal days. I quite agree with that, only I should like to look for the mechanism of this motor inhibition through "nervousness" in the intention of self-destruction here emphasized.

Dr. Ferenczi has left to me for publication the analysis of an apparently accidental injury by shooting which he explained as an unconscious attempt at suicide. I can only agree with his deduction:

"J. Ad., 22 years old, carpenter, visited me on the 18th of January, 1908. He wished to know whether the bullet which had pierced his left temple March 20, 1907, could or should be removed by operation. Aside from occasional, not very severe, headaches, he felt quite well, also the objective examination showed nothing besides the characteristic powder wound on the left temple, so that I advised against an operation. When questioned concerning the circumstances of the case he asserted that he injured himself accidentally. He was playing with his brother's revolver, and *believing that it was not loaded* he pressed it with his left hand against the left temple (he is not left-handed), put his finger on the trigger, and the shot went off. *There were three bullets in the six-shooter.*

"I asked him how he came to carry the revolver, and he answered that it was at the time of his army conscription, that he took it to the inn the evening before because he feared fights. At the army examination he was considered unfit for service on account of varicose veins, which caused him much mortification. He went home and played with the revolver. He had no intention of hurting himself, but the accident occurred. On further questioning whether he was otherwise satisfied with his fortune, he answered with a sigh, and related a love affair with a girl who loved him in return, but nevertheless left him. She emigrated to America out of sheer avariciousness. He wanted to follow her, but his parents prevented him. His lady-love left on the 20th of January, 1907, just two months before the accident.

"Despite all these suspicious elements the patient insisted that the shot was an 'accident.' I was firmly convinced, however, that the neglect to find out whether the revolver was loaded before he began to play with it, as well as the self-inflicted injury, were psychically determined. He was still under the depressing effects of the unhappy love affair, and apparently wanted 'to forget everything' in the army. When this hope, too, was taken away from him he resorted to playing with the weapon—that is, to an unconscious attempt at suicide. The fact

that he did not hold the revolver in the right but in the left hand speaks conclusively in favor of the fact that he was really only 'playing'—that is, he did not wish consciously to commit suicide."

Another analysis of an apparently accidental self-inflicted wound, detailed to me by an observer, recalls the saying, "He who digs a pit for others falls in himself."[8]

"Mrs. X., belonging to a good middle-class family, is married and has three children. She is somewhat nervous but never needed any strenuous treatment, as she could sufficiently adapt herself to life. One day she sustained a rather striking though transitory disfigurement of her face in the following manner: She stumbled in a street that was in process of repair and struck her face against the house wall. The whole face was bruised, the eyelids blue and edematous, and as she feared that something might happen to her eyes she sent for the doctor. After she was calmed I asked her, 'But why did you fall in such a manner?' She answered that just before this accident she warned her husband, who had been suffering for some months from a joint affection, to be very careful in the street, and she often had the experience that in some remarkable way those things occurred to her against which she warned others.

"I was not satisfied with this as the determination of her accident, and asked her whether she had not something else to tell me. Yes, just before the accident she noticed a nice picture in a shop on the other side of the street, which she suddenly desired as an ornament for her nursery, and wished to buy it at once. She thereupon walked across to the shop without looking at the street, stumbled over a heap of stones, and fell with her face against the wall without making the slightest effort to shield herself with her hands. The intention to buy the picture was immediately forgotten, and she walked home in haste.

" 'But why were you not more careful?' I asked.

" 'Oh!' she answered, 'perhaps it was only a punishment for that episode which I confided to you!'

" 'Has this episode still bothered you?'

" 'Yes, later I regretted it very much; I considered myself wicked, criminal, and immoral, but at the time I was almost crazy with nervousness.'

"She referred to an abortion which was started by a quack and had to be brought to completion by a gynecologist. This abortion was initiated with the consent of her husband, as both wished, on ac-

8. "Selbstbestrafung wegen Abortus" by Dr. J. E. G. van Emden, Haag (Holland), *Zentralb. f. Psychoanalyse,* ii. 12.

count of their pecuniary circumstances, to be spared from being additionally blessed with children.

"She said: 'I had often reproached myself with the words, "You really had your child killed," and I feared that such a crime could not remain unpunished. Now that you have assured me that there is nothing seriously wrong with my eyes I am quite assured I have already been sufficiently punished.'

"This accident, therefore, was, on the one hand, a retribution for her sin, but, on the other hand, it may have served as an escape from a more dire punishment which she had feared for many months. In the moment that she ran to the shop to buy the picture the memory of this whole history, with its fears (already quite active in her unconscious at the time she warned her husband), became overwhelming and could perhaps find expression in words like these: 'But why do you want an ornament for the nursery?—you who had your child killed! You are a murderer! The great punishment is surely approaching!'

"This thought did not become conscious, but instead of it she made use of the situation—I might say of the psychologic moment—to utilize in a commonplace manner the heap of stones to inflict upon herself this punishment. It was for this reason that she did not even attempt to put out her arms while falling and was not much frightened. The second, and probably lesser, determinant of her accident was obviously the self-punishment for her unconscious wish to be rid of her husband, who was an accessory to the crime in this affair. This was betrayed by her absolutely superfluous warning to be very careful in the street on account of the stones. For, just because her husband had a weak leg, he was very careful in walking."

If such a rage against one's integrity and one's own life can be hidden behind apparently accidental awkwardness and motor insufficiency, then it is not a big step forward to grasp the possibility of transferring the same conception to mistakes which seriously endanger the life and health of others. What I can put forward as evidence for the validity of this conception was taken from my experience with neurotics, and hence does not fully meet the demands of this situation. I will report a case in which it was not an erroneously carried-out action, but what may be more aptly termed a symbolic or chance action that gave me the clue which later made possible the solution of the patient's conflict.

I once undertook to improve the marriage relations of a very intelligent man, whose differences with his tenderly attached young wife could surely be traced to real causes, but as he himself admitted could not be altogether explained through them. He continually occupied himself with the thought of a separation, which he repeatedly rejected because he dearly loved his two small children. In spite of this he always returned to that resolution and sought no means to make the situation bearable to himself. Such an unsettlement of a conflict served to prove to me that there were unconscious and repressed motives which enforced the conflicting conscious thoughts, and in such cases I always undertake to end the conflict by psychic analysis. One day the man related to me a slight occurrence which had extremely frightened him. He was sporting with the older child, by far his favorite. He tossed it high in the air and repeated his tossing till finally he thrust it so high that its head almost struck the massive gas chandelier. Almost, but not quite, or say "just about!" Nothing happened to the child except that it became dizzy from fright. The father stood transfixed with the child in his arms, while the mother merged into an hysterical attack. The particular facility of this careless movement, with the violent reaction in the parents, suggested to me to look upon this accident as a symbolic action which gave expression to an evil intention toward the beloved child.

I could remove the contradiction of the actual tenderness of his father for his child by referring the impulse to injure it to the time when it was the only one, and so small that as yet the father had no occasion for tender interest in it. Then it was easy to assume that this man, so little pleased with his wife at that time, might have thought: "If this small being for whom I have no regard whatever should die, I would be free and could separate from my wife." The wish for the death of this much loved being must therefore have continued unconsciously. From here it was easy to find the way to the unconscious fixation of this wish.

There was indeed a powerful determinant in a memory from the patient's childhood: it referred to the death of a little brother, which the mother laid to his father's negligence, and which led to serious quarrels with threats of separation between the parents. The continued course of my patient's life, as well as the therapeutic success, confirmed my analysis.

4. Analytic Therapy and Transference

BY SIGMUND FREUD

THE AIM of our efforts may be expressed in various formulas—making conscious the unconscious, removing the repressions, filling in the gaps in memory; they all amount to the same thing. But perhaps you are dissatisfied with this declaration; you imagined the recovery of a nervous person rather differently, that after he had been subjected to the laborious process of psychoanalysis he would emerge a different person altogether, and then you hear that the whole thing only amounts to his having a little less that is unconscious and a little more that is conscious in him than before. Well, you probably do not appreciate the importance of an inner change of this kind. A neurotic who has been cured has really become a different person, although at bottom of course he remains the same—that is, he has become his best self, what he would have been under the most favourable conditions. That, however, is a great deal. Then when you hear of all that has to be done, of the tremendous exertion required to carry out this apparently trifling change in his mental life, the significance attached to these differences between the various mental levels will appear more comprehensible to you.

I will digress a moment to enquire whether you know what "a causal therapy" means? This name is given to a procedure which puts aside the manifestations of a disease and looks for a point of attack in order to eradicate the cause of the illness. Now is psycho-analysis a causal therapy or not? The answer is not a simple one, but it may give us an opportunity to convince ourselves of the futility of such questions. In so far as psycho-analytic therapy does not aim immediately at removing the symptoms it is conducted like a causal therapy. In other respects you may say it is not, for we have followed the causal chain back far beyond the repressions to the instinctive predispositions, their relative intensity in the constitution, and the aberrations in the course of their development. Now suppose that it were possible by some chemical means to affect this mental machinery, to increase or decrease the amount of Libido available at any

given moment, or to reinforce the strength of one impulse at the expense of another—that would be a causal therapy in the literal sense, and our analysis would be the indispensable preliminary work of reconnoitring the ground. As you know, there is at present no question of any such influence upon the processes of the Libido; our mental therapy makes its attack at another point in the concatenation, not quite at the place where we perceive the manifestations to be rooted, but yet comparatively far behind the symptoms themselves, at a place which becomes accessible to us in very remarkable circumstances.

What then have we to do in order to bring what is unconscious in the patient into consciousness? At one time we thought that would be very simple; all we need do would be to identify this unconscious matter and then tell the patient what it was. However, we know already that that was a short-sighted mistake. Our knowledge of what is unconscious in him is not equivalent to his knowledge of it; when we tell him what we know, he does not assimilate it *in place of* his own unconscious thoughts, but *alongside* of them, and very little has been changed. We have rather to regard this unconscious material topographically; we have to look for it in his memory at the actual spot where the repression of it originally ensued. This repression must be removed, and then the substitution of conscious thought for unconscious thought can be effected straightaway. How is a repression such as this to be removed? Our work enters upon a second phase here; first, the discovery of the repression, and then the removal of the resistance which maintains this repression.

How can this resistance be got rid of? In the same way: by finding it out and telling the patient about it. The resistance too arises in a repression, either from the very one which we are endeavouring to dispel, or in one that occurred earlier. It is set up by the counter-charge which rose up to repress the repellent impulse. So that we now do just the same as we were trying to do before; we interpret, identify, and inform the patient; but this time we are doing it at the right spot. The counter-charge or the resistance is not part of the Unconscious, but of the Ego which co-operates with us, and this is so, even if it is not actually conscious. We know that a difficulty arises here in the ambiguity of the word "unconscious," on the one hand, as a phenomenon, on the other hand, as a system. That sounds very obscure and difficult; but after all it is only a repetition of what we have said before, is it not? We have come to this point already long ago.—Well then, we expect that this resistance will be abandoned, and the counter-charge withdrawn, when we have made the recognition of them possible by our work of interpretation. What are the instinctive propelling forces at our disposal to make this possible? First, the patient's desire for recovery, which impelled him to submit himself to the work in co-operation with us, and secondly, the aid of his intelligence which we reinforce by our interpretation. There is no doubt that it is easier for the patient to recognize the resistance with his intelligence, and to identify the idea in his Unconscious which corresponds to it, if we have first given him an idea which rouses his expectations in regard to it. If I say to you: "Look up at the sky and you will see a balloon," you will find it much more quickly than if I merely tell you to look up and see whether you can see anything; a student who looks through a microscope for the first time is told by the instructor what he is to see; otherwise he sees nothing, although it is there and quite visible.

And now for the fact! In quite a number of the various forms of nervous illness, in the hysterias, anxiety-conditions, obsessional neuroses, our hypothesis proves sound. By seeking out the repression in this way, discovering the resistances, indicating the repressed, it is actually possible to accomplish the task, to overcome the resistances, to break down the repression, and to change something unconscious into something conscious. As we do this we get a vivid impression of how, as each individual resistance is being mastered, a violent battle goes on in the soul of the patient—a normal mental struggle between two tendencies on the same ground, between the motives striving to maintain the counter-charge and those which are ready to abolish it. The first of these are the old motives which originally erected the repression; among the second are found new ones more recently acquired, which it is hoped will decide the conflict in our favour. We have succeeded in revivifying the old battle of the repression again, in bringing the issue, so long ago decided, up for revision again. The new contribution we make to it lies, first of all, in demonstrating that the original solution led to illness and in promising that a different one would pave the way to health, and secondly, in pointing out that the circumstances have all changed immensely since the time of that original repudiation of these impulses. Then, the

Ego was weak, infantile, and perhaps had reason to shrink with horror from the claims of the Libido as being dangerous to it. To-day it is strong and experienced and moreover has a helper at hand in the physician. So we may expect to lead the revived conflict through to a better outcome than repression; and, as has been said, in hysteria, anxiety-neurosis, and the obsessional neurosis success in the main justifies our claims.

There are other forms of illness, however, with which our therapeutic treatment never is successful, in spite of the similarity of the conditions. In them also there was originally a conflict between Ego and Libido, leading to repression—although this conflict may be characterized by topographical differences from the conflict of the transference neuroses; in them too it is possible to trace out the point in the patient's life at which the repressions occurred; we apply the same method, are ready to make the same assurances, offer the same assistance by telling the patient what to look out for; and here also the interval in time between the present and the point at which the repressions were established is all in favour of a better outcome of the conflict. And yet we cannot succeed in overcoming one resistance or in removing one of the repressions. These patients, paranoiacs, melancholics, and those suffering from dementia præcox, remain on the whole unaffected, proof against psycho-analytic treatment. What can be the cause of this? It is not due to lack of intelligence; a certain degree of intellectual capacity must naturally be stipulated for analysis, but there is no deficiency in this respect in, for instance, the very quick-witted deductive paranoiac. Nor are any of the other propelling forces regularly absent: melancholics, for instance, in contrast to paranoiacs, experience a very high degree of realization that they are ill and that their sufferings are due to this; but they are not on that account any more accessible to influence. In this we are confronted with a fact that we do not understand, and are therefore called upon to doubt whether we have really understood all the conditions of the success possible with the other neuroses.

When we keep to consideration of hysterical and obsessional neurotics we are very soon confronted with a second fact, for which we were quite unprepared. After the treatment has proceeded for a while we notice that these patients behave in a quite peculiar manner towards ourselves. We thought indeed that we had taken into account all the motive forces affecting the treatment and had reasoned out the situation between ourselves and the patient fully, so that it balanced like a sum in arithmetic; and then after all something seems to slip in which was quite left out of our calculation. This new and unexpected feature is in itself many-sided and complex; I will first of all describe some of its more frequent and simpler forms to you.

We observe then that the patient, who ought to be thinking of nothing but the solution of his own distressing conflicts, begins to develop a particular interest in the person of the physician. Everything connected with this person seems to him more important than his own affairs and to distract him from his illness. Relations with the patient then become for a time very agreeable; he is particularly docile, endeavours to show his gratitude wherever he can, exhibits a fineness of character and other good qualities which we had perhaps not anticipated in him. The analyst thus forms a very good opinion of the patient and values his luck in being able to render assistance to such an admirable personality. If the physician has occasion to see the patient's relatives he hears with satisfaction that this esteem is mutual. The patient at home is never tired of praising the analyst and attributing new virtues to him. "He has quite lost his head over you; he puts implicit trust in you; everything you say is like a revelation to him," say the relatives. Here and there one among this chorus having sharper eyes will say: "It is positively boring the way he never speaks of anything but you: he quotes you all the time."

We will hope that the physician is modest enough to ascribe the patient's estimate of his value to the hopes of recovery which he has been able to offer him, and to the widening in the patient's intellectual horizon consequent upon the surprising revelations entailed by the treatment and their liberating influence. The analysis too makes splendid progress under these conditions, the patient understands the suggestions offered to him, concentrates upon the tasks appointed by the treatment, the material needed—his recollections and associations—is abundantly available; he astonishes the analyst by the sureness and accuracy of his interpretations, and the latter has only to observe with satisfaction how readily and willingly a sick man will accept all the new psychological ideas that are so hotly contested by the healthy in the world outside. A general improvement in the patient's condition, objectively confirmed on all sides, also accompanies this harmonious relationship in the analysis.

But such fair weather cannot last for ever. There comes a day when it clouds over. There begin to be difficulties in the analysis; the patient says he cannot think of anything more to say. One has an unmistakable impression that he is no longer interested in the work, and that he is casually ignoring the injunction given him to say everything that comes into his mind and to yield to none of the critical objections that occur to him. His behaviour is not dictated by the situation of the treatment; it is as if he had not made an agreement to that effect with the physician; he is obviously preoccupied with something which at the same time he wishes to reserve to himself. This is a situation in which the treatment is in danger. Plainly a very powerful resistance has risen up. What can have happened?

If it is possible to clear up this state of things, the cause of the disturbance is found to consist in certain intense feelings of affection which the patient has transferred on to the physician, not accounted for by the latter's behaviour nor by the relationship involved by the treatment. The form in which this affectionate feeling is expressed and the goal it seeks naturally depend upon the circumstances of the situation between the two persons. If one of them is a young girl and the other still a fairly young man, the impression received is that of normal love; it seems natural that a girl should fall in love with a man with whom she is much alone and can speak of very intimate things, and who is in the position of an adviser with authority—we shall probably overlook the fact that in a neurotic girl some disturbance of the capacity for love is rather to be expected. The farther removed the situation between the two persons is from this supposed example, the more unaccountable it is to find that nevertheless the same kind of feeling comes to light in other cases. It may be still comprehensible when a young woman who is unhappily married seems to be overwhelmed by a serious passion for her physician, if he is still unattached, and that she should be ready to seek a divorce and give herself to him, or, where circumstances would prevent this, to enter into a secret love-affair with him. That sort of thing, indeed, is known to occur outside psychoanalysis. But in this situation girls and women make the most astonishing confessions which reveal a quite peculiar attitude on their part to the therapeutic problem: they had always known that nothing but love would cure them, and from the beginning of the treatment they had expected that this relationship would at last yield them what life had so far denied them. It was only with this hope that they had taken such pains over the analysis and had conquered all their difficulties in disclosing their thoughts. We ourselves can add: "and had understood so easily all that is usually so hard to accept." But a confession of this kind astounds us; all our calculations are blown to the winds. Could it be that we have omitted the most important element in the whole problem?

And actually it is so; the more experience we gain the less possible does it become for us to contest this new factor, which alters the whole problem and puts our scientific calculations to shame. The first few times one might perhaps think that the analytic treatment had stumbled upon an obstruction in the shape of an accidental occurrence, extraneous to its purpose and unconnected with it in origin. But when it happens that this kind of attachment to the physician regularly evinces itself in every fresh case, under the most unfavourable conditions, and always appears in circumstances of a positively grotesque incongruity—in elderly women, in relation to grey-bearded men, even on occasions when our judgment assures us that no temptations exist —then we are compelled to give up the idea of a disturbing accident and to admit that we have to deal with a phenomenon in itself essentially bound up with the nature of the disease.

The new fact which we are thus unwillingly compelled to recognize we call TRANSFERENCE. By this we mean a transference of feelings on to the person of the physician, because we do not believe that the situation in the treatment can account for the origin of such feelings. We are much more disposed to suspect that the whole of this readiness to develop feeling originates in another source; that it was previously formed in the patient, and has seized the opportunity provided by the treatment to transfer itself on to the person of the physician. The transference can express itself as a passionate petitioning for love, or it can take less extreme forms; where a young girl and an elderly man are concerned, instead of the wish to be wife or mistress, a wish to be adopted as a favourite daughter may come to light, the libidinous desire can modify itself and propose itself as a wish for an everlasting, but ideally platonic friendship. Many women understand how to sublimate the transference and to mould it until it acquires a sort of justification for its existence; others have to express it in its crude, original, almost impossible form. But at bottom it is always the same, and its origin in the same source can never be mistaken.

Before we enquire where we are to range this new fact, we will amplify the description of it a little. How is it with our male patients? There at least we might hope to be spared the troublesome element of sex difference and sex attraction. Well, the answer is very much the same as with women. The same attachment to the physician, the same overestimation of his qualities, the same adoption of his interests, the same jealousy against all those connected with him. The sublimated kinds of transference are the forms more frequently met with between man and man, and the directly sexual declaration more rarely, in the same degree to which the manifest homosexuality of the patient is subordinated to the other ways by which this component-instinct can express itself. Also, it is in

male patients that the analyst more frequently observes a manifestation of the transference which at the first glance seems to controvert the description of it just given—that is, the hostile or *negative* transference.

First of all, let us realize at once that the transference exists in the patient from the beginning of the treatment, and is for a time the strongest impetus in the work. Nothing is seen of it and one does not need to trouble about it as long as its effect is favourable to the work in which the two persons are co-operating. When it becomes transformed into a resistance, attention must be paid to it; and then it appears that two different and contrasting states of mind have supervened in it and have altered its attitude to the treatment: first, when the affectionate attraction has become so strong and betrays signs of its origin in sexual desire so clearly that it was bound to arouse an inner opposition against itself; and secondly, when it consists in antagonistic instead of affectionate feeling. The hostile feelings as a rule appear later than the affectionate and under cover of them; when both occur simultaneously they provide a very good exemplification of that ambivalence in feeling which governs most of our intimate relationships with other human beings. The hostile feelings therefore indicate an attachment of feeling quite similar to the affectionate, just as defiance indicates a similar dependence upon the other person to that belonging to obedience, though with a reversed prefix. There can be no doubt that the hostile feelings against the analyst deserve the name of "transference," for the situation in the treatment certainly gives no adequate occasion for them; the necessity for regarding the negative transference in this light is a confirmation of our previous similar view of the positive or affectionate variety.

Where the transference springs from, what difficulties it provides for us, how we can overcome them, and what advantage we can finally derive from it, are questions which can only be adequately dealt with in a technical exposition of the analytic method; I can merely touch upon them here. It is out of the question that we should yield to the demands made by the patient under the influence of his transference; it would be nonsensical to reject them unkindly, and still more so, indignantly. The transference is overcome by showing the patient that his feelings do not originate in the current situation, and do not really concern the person of the physician, but that he is reproducing something that had happened to him long ago. In this way we require him to transform his *repetition* into *recollection*. Then the transference which, whether affectionate or hostile, every time seemed the greatest menace to the cure becomes its best instrument, so that with its help we can unlock the closed doors in the soul. I should like, however, to say a few words to dispel the unpleasant effects of the shock that this unexpected phenomenon must have been to you. After all, we must not forget that this illness of the patient's which we undertake to analyse is not a finally accomplished, and as it were consolidated thing; but that it is growing and continuing its development all the time like a living thing. The beginning of the treatment puts no stop to this development; but, as soon as the treatment has taken a hold upon the patient, it appears that the entire productivity of the illness henceforward becomes concentrated in one direction—namely, upon the relationship to the physician. The transference then becomes comparable to the cambium layer between the wood and the bark of a tree, from which proceeds the formation of new tissue and the growth of the trunk in diameter. As soon as the transference has taken on this significance the work upon the patient's recollection recedes far into the background. It is then not incorrect to say that we no longer have to do with the previous illness, but with a newly-created and transformed neurosis which has replaced the earlier one. This new edition of the old disease has been followed from its inception, one sees it come to light and grow, and is particularly familiar with it since one is oneself its central object. All the patient's symptoms have abandoned their original significance and have adapted themselves to a new meaning, which is contained in their relationship to the transference; or else only those symptoms remain which were capable of being adapted in this way. The conquest of this new artificially-acquired neurosis coincides with the removal of the illness which existed prior to the treatment, that is, with accomplishing the therapeutic task. The person who has become normal and free from the influence of repressed instinctive tendencies in his relationship to the physician remains so in his own life when the physician has again been removed from it.

The transference has this all-important, absolutely central significance for the cure in hysteria, anxiety-hysteria, and the obsessional neurosis, which are in consequence rightly grouped together as the "transference neuroses." Anyone who has grasped from analytic experience a true impression of the fact of transference can never again doubt the nature of the suppressed impulses which have manufactured an outlet for themselves in the symptoms; and he will require no stronger proof of their libidinal character. We may say that our conviction of the significance of the symptoms as a substitutive gratification of the Libido was only finally and definitely established by evaluating the phenomenon of transference.

Now, however, we are called upon to correct our former dynamic conception of the process of cure and to bring it into agreement with the new discovery. When the patient has to fight out the normal conflict with the resistances which we have discovered in him by analysis, he requires a powerful propelling force to influence him towards the decision we aim at, leading to recovery. Otherwise it might happen that he would decide for a repetition of the previous outcome, and allow that which had been raised into consciousness to slip back again under repression. The outcome in this struggle is not decided by his intellectual insight—it is neither strong enough nor free enough to accomplish such a thing—but solely by his relationship to the physician. In so far as his transference bears the positive sign, it clothes the physician with authority, transforms itself into faith in his findings and in his views. Without this kind of transference or with a negative one, the physician and his arguments would never even be listened to. Faith repeats the history of its own origin; it is a derivative of love and at first it needed no arguments. Not until later does it admit them so far as to take them into critical consideration if they have been offered by someone who is loved. Without this support arguments have no weight with the patient, never do have any with most people in life. A human being is therefore on the whole only accessible to influence, even on the intellectual side, in so far as he is capable of investing objects with Libido; and we have good cause to recognize, and to fear, in the measure of his narcissism a barrier to his susceptibility to influence, even by the best analytic technique.

The capacity for the radiation of Libido towards other persons in object-investment must, of course, be ascribed to all normal people; the tendency to transference in neurotics, so-called, is only an exceptional intensification of a universal characteristic. Now it would be very remarkable if a human character-trait of this importance and universality had never been observed and made use of. And this has really been done. Bernheim, with unerring perspicacity, based the theory of hypnotic manifestations upon the proposition that all human beings are more or less open to suggestion, are "suggestible." What he called suggestibility is nothing else but the tendency to transference, rather too narrowly circumscribed so that the negative transference did not come within its scope. But Bernheim could never say what suggestion actually was nor how it arises; it was an axiomatic fact to him and he could give no explanation of its origin. He did not recognize the dependence of "suggestibility" on sexuality, on the functioning of the Libido. And we have to admit that we have only abandoned hypnosis in our methods in order to discover suggestion again in the shape of transference.

* * *

In the light of the knowledge we have obtained through psycho-analysis, the difference between hypnotic and psycho-analytic suggestion may be described as follows: The hypnotic therapy endeavours to cover up and as it were to whitewash something going on in the mind, the analytic to lay bare and to remove something. The first works cosmetically, the second surgically. The first employs suggestion to interdict the symptoms; it reinforces the repressions, but otherwise it leaves unchanged all the processes that have led to symptom-formation. Analytic therapy takes hold deeper down nearer the roots of the disease, among the conflicts from which the symptoms proceed; it employs suggestion to change the outcome of these conflicts. Hypnotic therapy allows the patient to remain inactive and unchanged, consequently also helpless in the face of every new incitement to illness. Analytic treatment makes as great demands for efforts on the part of the patient as on the physician, efforts to abolish the inner resistances. The patient's mental life is permanently changed by overcoming these resistances, is lifted to a higher level of development, and remains proof against fresh possibilities of illness. The labour of overcoming the resistances is the essential achievement of the analytic treatment; the patient has to accomplish it and the physician makes it possible for him to do this by suggestions which are in the nature of an *education*. It has been truly said therefore, that psycho-analytic treatment is a kind of *re-education*.

I hope I have now made clear to you the difference between our method of employing suggestion therapeutically and the method which is the only possible one in hypnotic therapy. Since we have traced the influence of suggestion back to the transference, you also understand the striking capriciousness of the effect in hypnotic therapy, and why analytic therapy is within its limits dependable. In employing hypnosis we are entirely dependent upon the condition of the patient's transference and yet we are unable to exercise any influence upon this condition itself. The transference of a patient being hypnotized may be negative, or, as most commonly, ambivalent, or he may have guarded himself against his transference by adopting special attitudes; we gather nothing about all this. In psycho-analysis we work upon the transference itself, dissipate whatever stands in the

way of it, and manipulate the instrument which is to do the work. Thus it becomes possible for us to derive entirely new benefits from the power of suggestion; we are able to control it; the patient alone no longer manages his suggestibility according to his own liking, but in so far as he is amenable to its influence at all, we guide his suggestibility.

Now you will say that, regardless of whether the driving force behind the analysis is called transference or suggestion, the danger still remains that our influence upon the patient may bring the objective certainty of our discoveries into doubt; and that what is an advantage in therapy is harmful in research. This is the objection that has most frequently been raised against psycho-analysis; and it must be admitted that, even though it is unjustified, it cannot be ignored as unreasonable. If it were justified, psycho-analysis after all would be nothing else but a specially well-disguised and particularly effective kind of suggestive treatment; and all its conclusions about the experiences of the patient's past life, mental dynamics, the Unconscious, and so on, could be taken very lightly. So our opponents think; the significance of sexual experiences in particular, if not the experiences themselves, we are supposed to have "put into the patient's mind," after having first concocted these conglomerations in our own corrupt minds. These accusations are more satisfactorily refuted by the evidence of experience than by the aid of theory. Anyone who has himself conducted psycho-analyses has been able to convince himself numberless times that it is impossible to suggest things to a patient in this way. There is no difficulty, of course, in making him a disciple of a particular theory, and thus making it possible for him to share some mistaken belief possibly harboured by the physician. He behaves like anyone else in this, like a pupil; but by this one has only influenced his intellect, not his illness. The solving of his conflicts and the overcoming of his resistances succeeds only when what he is told to look for in himself corresponds with what actually does exist in him. Anything that has been inferred wrongly by the physician will disappear in the course of the analysis; it must be withdrawn and replaced by something more correct. One's aim is, by a very careful technique, to prevent temporary successes arising through suggestion; but if they do arise no great harm is done, for we are not content with the first result. We do not consider the analysis completed unless all obscurities in the case are explained, the gaps in memory filled out, and the original occasions of the repressions discovered. When results appear prematurely, one regards them as obstacles rather than as furtherances of the analytic work, and one destroys them again by continually exposing the transference on which they are founded. Fundamentally it is this last feature which distinguishes analytic treatment from that of pure suggestion, and which clears the results of analysis from the suspicion of being the results of suggestion. In every other suggestive treatment the transference is carefully preserved and left intact; in analysis it is itself the object of the treatment and is continually being dissected in all its various forms. At the conclusion of the analysis the transference itself must be dissolved; if success then supervenes and is maintained it is not founded on suggestion, but on the overcoming of the inner resistances effected by the help of suggestion, on the inner change achieved within the patient.

That which probably prevents single effects of suggestion from arising during the treatment is the struggle which is incessantly being waged against the resistances, which know how to transform themselves into a negative (hostile) transference. Nor will we neglect to point to the evidence that a great many of the detailed findings of analysis, which would otherwise be suspected of being produced by suggestion, are confirmed from other, irreproachable sources. We have unimpeachable witnesses on these points, namely, dements and paranoiacs, who are of course quite above any suspicion of being influenced by suggestion. All that these patients relate in the way of phantasies and translations of symbols, which have penetrated through into their consciousness, corresponds faithfully with the results of our investigations into the Unconscious of transference neurotics, thus confirming the objective truth of the interpretations made by us which are so often doubted. I do not think you will find yourselves mistaken if you choose to trust analysis in these respects.

We now need to complete our description of the process of recovery by expresing it in terms of the Libido theory. (The neurotic is incapable of enjoyment or of achievement—the first because his Libido is attached to no real object, the last because so much of the energy which would otherwise be at his disposal is expended in maintaining the Libido under repression, and in warding off its attempts to assert itself.) He would be well if the conflict between his Ego and his Libido came to an end, and if his Ego again had the Libido at its disposal. The task of the treatment, therefore, consists in the task of loosening the Libido from its previous attachments, which are beyond the reach of the Ego, and in making it again seviceable to the Ego. Now where is the Libido of a neurotic? Easily found: it is attached to the symptoms, which offer it the substitutive satisfaction that is all it can obtain as things are. We must master the symptoms then, dissolve them—just

what the patient asks of us. In order to dissolve the symptom it is necessary to go back to the point at which they originated, to review the conflict from which they proceeded, and with the help of propelling forces which at that time were not available to guide it towards a new solution. This revision of the process of repression can only partially be effected by means of the memory-traces of the processes which led up to repression. The decisive part of the work is carried through by creating—in the relationship to the physician, in "the transference"—new editions of those early conflicts, in which the patient strives to behave as he originally behaved, while one calls upon all the available forces in his soul to bring him to another decision. The transference is thus the battlefield where all the contending forces must meet.

All the Libido and the full strength of the opposition against it are concentrated upon the one thing, upon the relationship to the physician; thus it becomes inevitable that the symptoms should be deprived of their Libido; in place of the patient's original illness appears the artificially-acquired transference, the transference-disorder; in place of a variety of unreal objects of his Libido appears the one object, also "phantastic," of the person of the physician. This new struggle which arises concerning this object is by means of the analyst's suggestions lifted to the surface, to the higher mental levels, and is there worked out as a normal mental conflict. Since a new repression is thus avoided, the opposition between the Ego and the Libido comes to an end; unity is restored within the patient's mind. When the Libido has been detached from its temporary object in the person of the physician it cannot return to its earlier objects, but is now at the disposal of the Ego. The forces opposing us in this struggle during the therapeutic treatment are on the one hand the Ego's aversion against certain tendencies on the part of the Libido, which had expressed itself in repressing tendencies; and on the other hand the tenacity or "adhesiveness" of the Libido, which does not readily detach itself from objects it has once invested.

The therapeutic work thus falls into two phases; in the first all the Libido is forced away from the symptoms into the transference and there concentrated, in the second the battle rages round this new object and the Libido is made free from it. The change that is decisive for a successful outcome of this renewed conflict lies in the preclusion of repression, so that the Libido cannot again withdraw itself from the Ego by a flight into the Unconscious. It is made possible by changes in the Ego ensuing as a consequence of the analyst's suggestions. At the expense of the Unconscious the Ego becomes wider by the work of interpretation which brings the unconscious material into consciousness; through education it becomes reconciled to the Libido and is made willing to grant it a certain degree of satisfaction; and its horror of the claims of its Libido is lessened by the new capacity it acquires to expend a certain amount of the Libido in sublimation. The more nearly the course of the treatment corresponds with this ideal description the greater will be the success of the psycho-analytic therapy. Its barriers are found in the lack of mobility in the Libido, which resists being released from its objects, and in the rigidity of the patient's narcissism, which will not allow more than a certain degree of object-transference to develop. Perhaps the dynamics of the process of recovery will become still clearer if we describe it by saying that, in attracting a part of it to ourselves through transference, we gather in the whole amount of the Libido which has been withdrawn from the Ego's control.

It is as well here to make clear that the distributions of the Libido which ensue during and by means of the analysis afford no direct inference of the nature of its disposition during the previous illness. Given that a case can be successfully cured by establishing and then resolving a powerful father-transference to the person of the physician, it would not follow that the patient had previously suffered in this way from an unconscious attachment of the Libido to his father. The father-transference is only the battlefield on which we conquer and take the Libido prisoner; the patient's Libido has been drawn hither away from other "positions." The battlefield does not necessarily constitute one of the enemy's most important strongholds; the defence of the enemy's capital city need not be conducted immediately before its gates. Not until after the transference has been again resolved can one begin to reconstruct in imagination the dispositions of the Libido that were represented by the illness.

5. *Analysis Terminable and Interminable*

BY SIGMUND FREUD

BEFORE THE WAR, I myself had already tried another way of speeding up analysis. I had undertaken to treat a young Russian, a rich man spoilt by riches, who had come to Vienna in a state of complete helplessness, accompanied by physician and attendant. It was possible in the course of several years to restore to him a considerable measure of independence, and to awaken his interest in life, while his relations to the principal people in his life were adjusted. But then we came to a full stop. We made no progress in clearing up his childhood's neurosis, which was the basis of his later illness, and it was obvious that the patient found his present situation quite comfortable and did not intend to take any step which would bring him nearer to the end of his treatment. It was a case of the treatment obstructing itself: the analysis was in danger of failing as a result of its —partial—success. In this predicament I resorted

to the heroic remedy of fixing a date for the conclusion of the analysis. At the beginning of a period of treatment I told the patient that the coming year was to be the last of his analysis, no matter what progress he made or failed to make in the time still left to him. At first he did not believe me, but, once he was convinced that I was in dead earnest, the change which I had hoped for began to take place. His resistances crumbled away, and in the last months of treatment he was able to produce all the memories and to discover the connecting links which were necessary for the understanding of his early neurosis and his recovery from the illness from which he was then suffering. When he took leave of me at mid-summer, 1914, unsuspecting as we all were, of what was so shortly to happen, I believed that his cure was complete and permanent.

In a postscript to this patient's case history (1923*d*) I have already reported that I was mistaken. When, towards the end of the war, he returned to Vienna, a refugee and destitute, I had to help him master a part of the transference which

Reprinted from Sigmund Freud, *Collected Papers*, trans. Joan Riviere (London: Hogarth Press, 1950), V, 317–48, 354–57, with the permission of Hogarth Press & Basic Books.

had remained unresolved. Within a few months this was successfully accomplished and I was able to conclude my postscript with the statement that "since then the patient has felt normal and has behaved unexceptionably, in spite of the war having robbed him of his home, his possessions, and all his family relationships." Fifteen years have passed since then, but this verdict has not proved erroneous, though certain reservations have had to be made. The patient has remained in Vienna and has made good, although in a humble social position. Several times, however, during this period, his satisfactory state of health has broken down, and the attacks of neurotic illness from which he has suffered could be construed only as offshoots of his original neurosis. Thanks to the skill of one of my pupils, Dr. Ruth Mack Brunswick, a short course of treatment has sufficed on each occasion to clear up these attacks. I hope Dr. Mack Brunswick herself will report on this case before long. Some of these relapses were caused by still unresolved residues of the transference; short-lived though the attacks were, they were distinctly paranoic in character. In other instances, however, the pathogenic material consisted of fragments from the history of the patient's childhood, which had not come to light while I was analysing him and which now came away (the comparison is obvious) like sutures after an operation or small pieces of necrotic bone. I have found the history of this man's recovery almost as interesting as that of his illness.

Since then I have employed the method of fixing a date for the termination of analysis in other cases and I have also inquired about the experience of other analysts in this respect. There can be only one verdict about the value of this blackmailing device. The measure is effective, provided that one hits the right time at which to employ it. But it cannot be held to guarantee perfect accomplishment of the task of psychoanalysis. On the contrary, we may be quite sure that, while the force of the threat will have the effect of bringing part of the material to light, another part will be held back and become buried, as it were, and will be lost to our therapeutic efforts. Once the date for discontinuing the treatment has been fixed we must not extend the time; otherwise the patient will lose all his faith in the analyst. The most obvious way out would be to let him continue his treatment with another analyst, although we know that a change of this sort involves a fresh loss of time and the sacrifice of some of the results of the work already done. Nor can any general rule be laid down as to the right time for resorting to this forcible technical method: the analyst must use his own

tact in the matter. A mistake, once made, cannot be rectified. The saying that the lion springs once and once only must hold good here.

The discussion of the technical problem of how to accelerate the slow progress of an analysis suggests another, more deeply interesting question: is there such a thing as a natural end to an analysis or is it really possible to conduct it to such an end? To judge by the ordinary talk of analysts we should presume that it is, for we often hear them say, when deploring or excusing the admitted imperfection of some fellow-mortal: "His analysis was not finished" or "He was not completely analysed."

Now we must first decide what is meant by the ambiguous term, "the end of an analysis." From the practical standpoint it is easily defined. An analysis is ended when analyst and patient cease to meet for the analytic session. This happens when two conditions have been approximately fulfilled. First, the patient must no longer be suffering from his former symptoms and must have overcome his various anxieties and inhibitions and, secondly, the analyst must have formed the opinion that so much repressed material has been brought into consciousness, so much that was inexplicable elucidated, and so much inner resistance overcome that no repetition of the patient's specific pathological processes is to be feared. If for external reasons one is prevented from reaching this goal, it is more correct to say that an analysis is imperfect than to say that it has not been completed.

The second definition of the "end" of an analysis is much more ambitious. According to it we have to answer the question whether the effect upon the patient has been so profound that no further change would take place in him if this analysis were continued. The implication is that by means of analysis it is possible to attain to absolute psychical normality and to be sure that it will be maintained, the supposition that all the patient's repressions have been lifted and every gap in his memory filled. Let us first consult our experience and see whether such things do in fact happen, and then examine our theory and learn whether there is any *possibility* of their happening.

Every analyst will have treated some cases with this gratifying outcome. He has succeeded in clearing up the patient's neurosis, there has been no relapse and no other nervous disturbance has succeeded it. We know something of what determines these results. No noticeable modification had taken place in the patient's ego and the causation of his illness was pre-eminently traumatic. The aetiology of all neuroses is indeed a mixed one; either the patient's instincts are excessively strong and refuse to submit to the taming influence of his ego or else he is suffering from the effects of premature traumas, by which I mean traumas which his immature ego was unable to surmount. Generally there is a combination of the two factors: the constitutional and the accidental. The stronger the constitution factor the more readily will a trauma lead to fixation, with its sequel in a disturbance of development; the stronger the trauma the more certain is it that it will have injurious effects even when the patient's instinctual life is normal. There can be no doubt that, when the aetiology of the neurosis is traumatic, analysis has a far better chance. Only when the traumatic factor predominates can we look for what psycho-analysis can achieve in such a masterly fashion, namely, the replacement (owing to the strengthening of the ego) of the inadequate decision made in infancy by a correct solution. Only in such a case can one speak of a definitive end to an analysis. When such a result has been attained analysis has done all that can be required of it and need not be continued. If the patient who has made such a good recovery never produces any more symptoms calling for analysis, it still, of course, remains an open question how much of this immunity is due to a benevolent fate which spares him too searching a test.

The factors which are prejudicial to analysis and may cause it to be so long-drawn-out as to be really interminable are a constitutional strength of instinct and an unfavourable modification of the ego in the defensive conflict, a modification comparable to a dislocation or crippling. One is tempted to make the first factor—the strength of the instincts—responsible for the second—the modification of the ego—but it seems that the latter has its own aetiology and indeed it must be admitted that our knowledge of these relations is as yet imperfect. They are only just becoming the object of analytic investigation. I think that here the interest of analysts is quite wrongly orientated. Instead of inquiring *how* analysis effects a cure (a point which in my opinion has been sufficiently elucidated) we should ask what are the obstacles which this cure encounters.

This brings me to two problems which arise directly out of psycho-analytic practice, as I hope to show by the following examples. A certain man, who had himself been a most successful practitioner of analysis, came to the conclusion that his relations with men as well as with women—the men who were his rivals and the woman whom he loved—were not free from neurotic inhibitions, and he therefore had himself analysed by an analyst whom he regarded as his superior. This critical exploration of his own personality was entirely success-ful. He married the woman whom he loved and became the friend and teacher of the men whom he had regarded as rivals. Many years passed, during which his relation to his former analyst remained unclouded. But then, for no demonstrable external reason, trouble arose. The man who had been analysed adopted an antagonistic attitude to his analyst and reproached him for having neglected to complete the analysis. The analyst, he said, ought to have known and to have taken account of the fact that a transference-relation could never be merely positive; he ought to have considered the possibilities of a negative transference. The analyst justified himself by saying that, at the time of the analysis, there was no sign of a negative transference. But, even supposing that he had failed to observe some slight indication of it, which was quite possible considering the limitations of analysis in those early days, it was still doubtful, he thought, whether he would have been able to activate a psychical theme or, as we say, a "complex," by merely indicating it to the patient, so long as it was not at that moment an actuality to him. Such activation would certainly have necessitated real unfriendly behaviour on the analyst's part. And, he added, every happy relation between an analyst and the subject of his analysis, during and after analysis, was not to be regarded as transference; there were friendly relations with a real basis, which were capable of persisting.

I now pass on to my second example, which raises the same problem. A girl who had left her childhood behind her had, since puberty, been cut off from life by an inability to walk, owing to acute pain in her legs. Her condition was obviously hysterical in character and it had resisted various kinds of treatment. After an analysis lasting nine months the trouble disappeared and the patient, whose character was truly sound and estimable, was able once more to take her place in life. In the years following her recovery she was consistently unfortunate: there were disasters in her family, they lost their money and, as she grew older, she saw every hope of happiness in love and marriage vanish. But this woman, who had formerly been an invalid, stood her ground valiantly and in difficult times was a support to her people. I cannot remember whether it was twelve or fourteen years after the end of her analysis that she had to undergo a gynaecological examination on account of profuse haemorrhages. A myoma was discovered which made a complete hysterectomy advisable. From the time that this operation took place she relapsed into neurosis. She fell in love with the surgeon and was overwhelmed by masochistic phantasies of the dreadful internal changes which had taken place in her—phantasies in which she disguised her romance. She proved inaccessible to a further attempt at analysis, and to the end of her life she remained abnormal. The successful analytic treatment took place so long ago that we could not expect too much from it; it was in the first years of my work as an analyst. It is no doubt possible that the patient's second neurosis sprang from the same root as the first, which had been successfully overcome, and that it was a different manifestation of repressed tendencies which the analysis had only partially resolved. But I am inclined to think that, but for the fresh trauma, there would have been no second outbreak of neurosis.

These two cases, purposely selected from a large number of similar ones, will suffice to set going a discussion of the problems we are considering. The sceptical, the optimistic and the ambitious will draw very different conclusions from them. Sceptics will say that they prove that even a successful analysis does not prevent the patient who is cured for the time being from subsequently developing another neurosis, or even a neurosis springing from the same instinctual root, that is to say, from a recurrence of his former trouble. The others will maintain that this is not proved. They will object that both the cases I have cited date from the early days of analysis, twenty and thirty years ago, respectively, and that since then we have acquired deeper insight and wider knowledge and, in adapting our technique to our new discoveries, we have modified it in many respects. To-day, they will argue, we may demand and expect that an analytic cure shall be permanent, or at least, that if a patient falls ill again, his fresh neurosis shall not turn out to be a revival of his earlier instinctual disturbance, manifesting itself in a new guise. Our experience, they will say, is not such that we must limit so severely the demands which we may legitimately make upon psychoanalytic therapy.

Now, of course, my reason for selecting these particular cases as illustrations was precisely that they date so far back. It is obvious that the more recent the result of an analysis the less valuable is it for our theoretical discussion since we have no means of predicting what will happen later to a patient who has been cured. Clearly the expectations of the optimist presuppose a number of things which are not exactly a matter of course. In the first place he assumes that it is really possible to resolve an instinctual conflict (or, more accurately, a conflict between the ego and an instinct) finally and for all time. Secondly, that when we are dealing with one such conflict in a patient, we can, as it were, inoculate him against the possibility of any other instinctual conflicts in the future. And thirdly, that we

have the power, for purposes of prophylaxis, to stir up a pathogenic conflict of this sort, when at the moment there is no indication of it, and that it is wise to do so. I merely suggest these questions: I do not propose to answer them now. In any case a definite answer is perhaps not possible at the present time.

Probably some light may be thrown on the subject from the theoretical standpoint. But already another point has become clear: if we wish to fulfill the more exacting demands which are now made upon therapeutic analysis, we shall not shorten its duration whether as a means or an end.

My analytic experience, extending now over several decades, and the change which has taken place in the nature and mode of my work encourage me to attempt an answer to the questions before us. In earlier days I dealt with a comparatively large number of patients, who, as was natural, wanted to be cured as quickly as possible. Of late years I have been mainly engaged in training-analyses and I have also had a relatively small number of patients suffering from severe neuroses, whose treatment has been carried on continuously, though with longer or shorter intermissions. In these cases the therapeutic aim is no longer the same as before. There is no question of shortening the treatment: the object has been completely to exhaust the possibilities of illness and to bring about a radical change in the personality.

Of the three factors which, as we have seen, determine the result of analysis—the effect of traumas, the constitutional strength of the instincts and the modification of the ego—we are at this point concerned with the second only: the strength of the instincts. Reflection immediately suggests a doubt as to whether it is necessary to use the qualifying adjective "constitutional" (or "congenital"). It is true that from the very beginning the constitutional factor is of crucial importance, but it is yet conceivable that the same effects might ensue from a reinforcement of instinctual energy at some later period in life. If this were so, we should have to modify our formula and say "the strength of the instincts at a given moment" rather than "the constitutional strength of the instincts." Now the first of our questions was this: is it possible for analysis permanently and definitively to resolve a conflict between instinct and ego or to settle a pathogenic instinctual demand upon the ego? To avoid misunderstanding we must perhaps define more exactly what we mean by the phrase: "a permanent settlement of an instinctual demand." We certainly do not mean that we cause the demand to disappear, so that it never makes itself felt again. As a rule this is impossible and not even desirable. No, we mean something else, something which may be roughly described as the "taming" of the instinct. That is to say, it is brought into harmony with the ego and becomes accessible to the influence of the other trends in the ego, no longer seeking for independent satisfaction. If we are asked how and by what means this result is achieved, we do not find it easy to answer. There is nothing for it but to "summon help from the Witch"[1]—the Witch Metapsychology. Without metapsychology speculation and theorizing—I had almost said "phantasy"—we shall not get a step further. Unfortunately, here as elsewhere, what our Witch reveals is neither very clear nor very exact. We have only a single clue to follow—but a clue the value of which cannot be exaggerated—namely, the antithesis between the primary and the secondary processes, and to this I must refer here.

Reverting to our first question, we find that our new approach to the problem makes a particular conclusion inevitable. The question was as follows: is it possible permanently and definitively to resolve an instinctual conflict—that is to say, to "tame" the instinctual demand? Formulated thus, the question contains no mention whatever of the strength of the instinct, but it is precisely this which determines the issue. Let us assume that what analysis achieves for neurotics is only what normal people accomplish for themselves without its help. But everyday experience teaches us that in a normal person any solution of an instinctual conflict holds good only for a particular strength of instinct, or rather, only where there is a particular relation between the strength of the instinct and the strength of the ego.[2] If the latter becomes enfeebled, whether through illness, exhaustion or for some similar cause, all the instincts which have so far been successfully tamed may renew their demands and strive in abnormal ways after substitutive satisfactions.[3] We have irrefutable proof of this statement in what takes place in dreams, when the reaction to the ego's condition in sleep is the awakening of instinctual demands.

The material relating to the strength of the instincts is equally unambiguous. Twice in the course

of the development of the individual certain instincts are powerfully reinforced: at puberty and at the menopause in women. We are not in least surprised if people who were normal before become neurotic at these times. When the instincts were not so strong these individuals succeeded in taming them, but they can no longer do so when the instincts acquire this new strength. The repressions behave like dams in time of flood. What occurs regularly at these two periods, when for physiological reasons the instincts become stronger, may occur sporadically as the result of accidental influences at any other period in life. Factors contributing to the reinforcement of instinct are: fresh traumas, the infliction of frustration and collateral interaction between the various instincts. The result is always the same and it confirms the irresistible importance of the quantitative factor in the causation of illness.

I feel as if I ought to be ashamed of so much ponderous exposition, seeing that all I have said has long been familiar and self-evident. It is a fact that we have always behaved as if we knew these things, yet for the most part our theoretical concepts have failed to give the same importance to the economic as to the dynamic and topographical aspects of the case. So my excuse must be that I am drawing attention to this omission.

Before we decide on an answer to our question, however, we must listen to an objection the force of which lies in the fact that we are very likely predisposed in its favour. It will be contended that our arguments are all deduced from the spontaneous processes that take place between ego and instinct and that we are assuming that analytic therapy can accomplish nothing which does not occur spontaneously under favourable normal conditions. But is this really so? Is not the claim of our theory precisely that analysis produces a state which never does occur spontaneously within the ego and the creation of which constitutes the main difference between a person who has been analysed and a person who has not? Let us consider on what this claim is based. All repressions take place in early childhood; they are primitive defensive measures adopted by the immature, feeble ego. In later years there are no fresh repressions, but the old ones persist and are used by the ego for the purpose of further mastering instinct. New conflicts are resolved by what we call "after-repression." To these infantile repressions our general statement applies that they depend entirely on the relative strength of the various psychical forces and cannot withstand an increase in the strength of the instincts. But analysis enables the mature ego, which by this time has attained a greater strength, to review these old repressions, with the result that some are lifted, while others are accepted

---

1. "*So muss denn doch die Hexe dran.*" [Goethe, *Faust*, Part I.]

2. Or, to be perfectly accurate, where that relation falls within particular limits.

3. Here we have a justification of the claim to aetiological importance of such unspecific factors as overwork, shock, etc. These have always been certain of general recognition and psycho-analysis has had to force them into the background. It is impossible to define health except in terms of metapsychology, *i.e.*, of the dynamic relations between those agencies of the psychical apparatus, the existence of which psychoanalysis has discovered, or, if it is preferred, has deduced or conjectured.

but reconstructed from more solid material. These new dams have a greater tenacity than the earlier ones; we may be confident that they will not so easily give way before the floodtide of instinct. Thus the real achievement of analytic therapy would be the subsequent correction of the original process of repression, with the result that the supremacy of the quantitative factor is brought to an end.

So far our theory, to which we must adhere unless we are irresistibly compelled to abandon it. And what is the testimony of our *experience?* Perhaps it is not yet wide enough to enable us to come to a definite decision. Quite often it justifies our expectations, but not always. Our impression is that we must not be surprised if the difference between a person who has not and a person who has been analysed is, after all, not so radical as we endeavour to make it and expect and assert that it will be. Thus analysis does indeed sometimes succeed in counteracting the effect of increases in the strength of instinct, but it does not invariably do so. Sometimes its effect is simply to raise the power of the resistance put up by inhibitions, so that after analysis they are equal to a much heavier strain than before the analysis took place or if it had never taken place at all. I really cannot commit myself to a decision on this point nor do I know whether at the present time a decision is possible.

There is another angle from which we may approach this problem of the variability of the effect of analysis. We know that the first step towards the intellectual mastery of the world in which we live is the discovery of general principles, rules and laws which bring order into chaos. By such mental operations we simplify the world of phenomena, but we cannot avoid falsifying it in so doing, especially when we are dealing with processes of development and change. We are trying to discern a qualitative alteration and as a rule we neglect, at any rate at first, the quantitative factor. In reality transitional and intermediate stages are far more common than sharply differentiated opposite states. In studying various developments and changes we focus our attention entirely on the result and we readily overlook the fact that such processes are usually more or less incomplete, that is to say, the changes that take place are really only partial. A shrewd satirist of the old Austria, Johann Nestroy, once said: "Every advance is only half as great as it looks at first." One is tempted to think that this malicious dictum is universally valid. There are almost always vestiges of what has been and a partial arrest at a former stage. When an open-handed Maecenas surprises us by some isolated trait of miserliness or a person whose kind-heartedness has been excessive suddenly indulges in some unfriendly act, these are "vestiges"

and are of priceless value for genetic research. They show that these praiseworthy and valuable qualities are based on compensation and overcompensation which, as was only to be expected, have not been absolutely and completely successful. Our first account of libidinal development was that an original oral phase was succeeded by a sadistic-anal, and this in its turn by a phallic-genital phase. Later investigation has not contradicted this view, but we must now qualify our statement by saying that the one phase does not succeed the other suddenly but gradually, so that part of the earlier organization always persists side by side with the later, and that even in normal development the transformation is never complete, the final structure often containing vestiges of earlier libidinal fixations. We see the same thing in quite different connections. There is not one of the erroneous and superstitious beliefs of mankind that are supposed to have been superseded but has left vestiges at the present day in the lower strata of civilised peoples or even in the highest strata of cultivated society. All that has once lived clings tenaciously to life. Sometimes one feels inclined to doubt whether the dragons of primaeval ages are really extinct.

Applying these remarks to our particular problem, I would say that the answer to the question how we explain the variable results of our analytic therapy might well be that our success in replacing insecure repressions by reliable and ego-syntonic controls is not always complete, *i.e.* is not radical enough. A change does occur but it is often only partial: parts of the old mechanisms remain untouched by analysis. It is difficult to prove that this is really so. We can only judge it by the result which it is supposed to explain. But the impressions we receive during our analytic work do not contradict this hypothesis—rather, they confirm it. We have to be careful not to imagine that the clarity of our own insight is a measure of the conviction we produce in the mind of the patient. This conviction may lack "depth," so to speak; the point in question is always that quantitative factor which is so easily overlooked. If we now have the correct answer to our question, we may say that analysis is always right in theory in its claim to cure neurosis by ensuring control over instinct but that in practice its claim is not always justified. This is because it does not always succeed in laying sufficiently firm foundations for that control. The reason for this partial failure is easy to discover. The quantitative factor of instinctual strength in the past opposed the efforts of the patient's ego to defend itself, and now that analysis has been called in to help, that same factor sets a limit to the efficacy of this new attempt. If the instincts are excessively strong the ego fails in its task, although it is now mature and has the support of analysis, just as it failed in earlier days in its helpless state; its control over instinct is greater but not complete, because the change in the defensive mechanism is only partial. This is not surprising, for the power of analysis is not infinite; it is limited, and the final result always depends on the relative strength of the conflicting psychical agencies.

No doubt it is desirable to shorten analytic treatment, but we shall achieve our therapeutic purpose only when we can give a greater measure of analytic help to the patient's ego. At one time it seemed that hypnotic influence was a splendid way of achieving our end; the reasons why we had to abandon that method are well known. Hitherto no substitute for hypnosis has been discovered, but we can understand from this how such a master of analysis as Ferenczi came to devote his last years to therapeutic experiments which were, alas! in vain.

The two further questions—whether, when dealing with one instinctual conflict, we can guard a patient against future conflicts and whether it is practicable and advisable to stir up for purposes of prophylaxis a conflict which is not at the moment manifest—must be treated together; for obviously the first task can be accomplished only if one performs the second, *i.e.* if one turns a possible future conflict into an actual one and then brings analytic influence to bear upon it. This new problem is really only an extension of the earlier one. In the first instance we were considering how to guard against the return of the *same* conflict: now we are considering the possible substitution of a second conflict for the first. This sounds a very ambitious proposal, but we are in fact only trying to make clear what limits are set to the efficacy of analytic therapy.

Tempting as it may be to our therapeutic ambition to propose such tasks for itself, experience bids us reject them out of hand. If an instinctual conflict is not an actual one and does not manifest itself in any way, it cannot be influenced by analysis. The warning that we should "let sleeping dogs lie"—which we have so often heard in connection with our investigation of the psychical underworld—is peculiarly inapposite when applied to the conditions existing in mental life. For if the instincts are causing disturbances it is a proof that the dogs are not sleeping and if they seem really to be sleeping, we have not the power to wake them. This last statement, however, does not seem entirely accurate and we must consider it in greater detail. Let us consider the means we have at our disposal for transforming a latent into an actual instinctual conflict. Clearly there are only two things we can do: either we can

bring about situations in which the conflict becomes actual or we can content ourselves with discussing it in analysis and pointing out that it may possibly arise. The first of these two alternatives can be accomplished in two different ways, either in reality, or in the transference. In either case we expose the patient to a measure of real suffering through frustration and the damming-up of libido. Now it is true that in ordinary analytic practice we do make use of this technique. Otherwise, what would be the meaning of the rule that analysis must be carried through "in a state of abstinence"? But we use it when we are dealing with a conflict which is already present. We try to bring this conflict to a head and to develop it in its most acute form in order to increase the instinctual energy available for its solution. Analytic experience has taught us that the better is always the enemy of the good and that in every phase of the patient's restoration we have to combat his intertia, which disposes him to be content with a partial solution of his conflicts.

If, however, our aim is the prophylactic treatment of instinctual conflicts which are not actual but merely possible, it is not enough to deal with the suffering which the patient is inevitably undergoing. We must make up our minds to conjure up fresh suffering—a thing which we have so far quite rightly left to fate. We should receive protests from all sides against the presumption of vying with fate in putting wretched human beings to such cruel experiments. And what sort of experiments would they be? Could we, for purposes of prophylaxis, take the responsibility of destroying a happy marriage or causing a patient to give up work upon which his livelihood depended? Fortunately there is no question of having to justfy such interference with real life. We have not the plenary powers which such intervention would demand and most certainly the object of this therapeutic experiment would refuse to co-operate in it. In practice then, this method may be said to be excluded and there are, besides, theoretical objections to it, for the work of analysis progresses best when the patient's pathogenic experiences belong to the past so that the ego can stand at a distance from them. In conditions of acute crisis it is, to all intents and purposes, impossible to use analysis. In such states the whole interest of the ego is concentrated on the painful reality, and resists analysis, which seeks to penetrate below the surface and to discover the influences to which the patient has been exposed in the past. Thus to create a fresh conflict will only make the analysis longer and more difficult.

It may be objected that all this discussion is quite superfluous. Nobody imagines that a latent instinctual conflict can be treated by purposely conjuring up a fresh painful situation. As a prophylactic achievement this would not be much to boast of. Let us take an example: we know that when a patient recovers from scarlet fever he has become immune to a recurrence of that illness. But it never occurs to a physician on that account to infect a patient with scarlet fever in order to make him immune. It is not the business of prophylactic treatment to produce the same dangerous situation as that of the illness itself but only something much more mild, as in the case of vaccination and many similar procedures. Similarly, in the analytic prophylaxis of instinctual conflicts the only methods which we need really consider are the other two: the artificial production of new conflicts in the transference (conflicts which lack the character of reality) and the rousing of such conflicts in the imagination of the patient by talking to him about them and telling him that they may possibly arise.

I do not know if we can assert that the first of these two less drastic procedures is out of the question in analysis. No experiments have been made in this particular direction. But some difficulties at once suggest themselves which make the success of such an undertaking very problematic. In the first place the choice of such situations for the transference is very limited. The patient himself cannot embody all his conflicts in the transference, nor can the transference-situation be so employed by the analyst as to rouse all the instinctual conflicts in which the patient may possibly become engaged. We may incite him to jealousy or inflict upon him the pain of disappointed love, but no special technical design is necessary for that purpose. These things happen spontaneously in most analyses. But in the second place we must not overlook the fact that any such deliberate procedure would necessitate unkind behaviour on the part of the analyst towards the patient and this would have an injurious effect upon his affectionate attitude towards the analyst, *i.e.* upon the positive transference, which is the patient's strongest motive for co-operating in the work of analysis. So we shall not form any high expectation of the results of such a technique.

This leaves only the other method, which is probably the only one originally contemplated. The analyst will tell the patient about possible instinctual conflicts which may occur and will lead him to expect that they may occur in himself. This is done in the hope that the information and warning will have the effect of activating in the patient one of these conflicts in a moderate degree and yet sufficiently for it to be dealt with. But here experience speaks with no uncertain voice. The result hoped for is not achieved. The patient hears what we say

but it rouses no response in his mind. He probably thinks to himself: "That is very interesting, but I see no sign of it in myself." We have increased his knowledge but effected no other change in his mind. We have much the same situation when people read psycho-analytical writings. The reader is "stimulated" only by those passages which he feels apply to himself, *i.e.* which refer to conflicts that are active in him. Everything else leaves him cold. I think we have a similar experience when we enlighten children on matters of sex. I am far from maintaining that this is a harmful or unnecessary thing to do, but it is clear that the prophylactic effect of this liberal measure has been vastly overestimated. After such enlightenment the children know something that they did not know before but they make no use of the new knowledge imparted to them. We come to the conclusion that they are by no means ready to sacrifice those sexual theories which may be said to be a natural growth and which they have constructed in harmony with and in dependence on their undeveloped libidinal organization—theories about the part played by the stork, about the nature of sexual intercourse and about the way in which children are born. For a long time after they have been enlightened on these subjects they behave like primitive races who have had Christianity thrust upon them and continue in secret to worship their old idols.

Our starting-point was the question of how to shorten the tediously long duration of an analysis and, still pursuing the question of time, we went on to consider whether we can achieve permanent cure or prevent illness in the future by prophylactic treatment. We saw that the success of our therapeutic work depended on the influence of traumatic factors in the aetiology of the neurosis, on the relative strength of the instincts which have to be controlled and on something which we called modification of the ego. Only the second of these factors has been discussed in any detail and we have had occasion in so doing to recognize the paramount importance of the quantitative factor and to stress the claim of the metapsychological standpoint to be taken into account in any attempt at explanation.

Of the third factor, the modification of the ego, we have as yet said nothing. The first impression received when we turn our attention to it is that there is much to ask and to answer, and that what we can say on the subject will prove very inadequate. This impression is confirmed when we go into the problem further. We know that the essence of the analytic situation is that the analyst enters into an alliance with the ego of the patient to subdue certain uncontrolled parts of his id, *i.e.* to include them in the synthesis of the ego. The fact that in the case of psychotics this co-operation is never successful brings us to our first definite conclusion. If we want to make a compact with the patient's ego, that ego must be normal. But such a normal ego is, like normality in general, an ideal fiction. The abnormal ego, which is of no use for our purpose, is unfortunately no fiction. Now every normal person is only approximately normal: his ego resembles that of the psychotic in one point or another, in a greater or lesser degree, and its distance from one end of the scale and proximity to the other may provisionally serve as a measure of what we have indefinitely spoken of as "modification of the ego."

If we ask what is the source of the great variety of kinds and degrees of ego-modification we cannot escape the first obvious alternative that such modifications are either congenital or acquired. The second case will be the easier to treat. If they are acquired it must certainly have been during the individual's development from the very beginning of his life. From the very outset the ego has to try to fulfil its task of acting as an intermediary between the id and the external world in the service of the pleasure principle, to protect the id from the dangers of the external world. If, while thus endeavouring, the ego learns to adopt a defensive attitude towards its own id and to treat the instinctual demands of the latter like external dangers, this is at any rate partly because it understands that satisfaction of instinct would lead to conflicts with the external world. Under the influence of its upbringing, the child's ego accustoms itself to shift the scene of the battle from outside to inside and to master the *inner* danger before it becomes *external*. Probably it is generally right in so doing. In this battle on two fronts—later there is a third front as well—the ego makes use of various methods of fulfilling its task, *i.e.*, to put it in general terms, of avoiding danger, anxiety and unpleasure. We call these devices *defensive* mechanisms. Our knowledge of them is as yet incomplete. Anna Freud's book (1936) has given us our first insight into their multiplicity and their manifold significance.

One of these mechanisms, that of repression, provided the starting-point for the study of neurotic processes in general. There was never any doubt that repression was not the only method which the ego could employ for its purposes. Nevertheless, repression is something quite peculiar, more sharply differentiated from the other mechanisms than these are from one another. I should like to make its relation to these other mechanisms clear

by an analogy, but I know that analogies never carry us very far in such matters.

Let us imagine what might have happened to a book at the time when books were not printed in editions but written out separately by hand. We will imagine that such a book contained statements which at a later time were regarded as undesirable—as, for instance, according to Robert Eisler (1929), the writings of Flavius Josephus must have contained passages about Jesus Christ which were offensive to later Christendom. At the present day the only defensive mechanism to which the official censorship would resort would be the confiscation and destruction of every copy of the whole edition. At that time other methods were employed to render the book innocuous. Either the offensive passages were heavily scored through, so that they were illegible, in which case they could not be transcribed and the next copyist of the book produced a text to which no exception could be taken but which had gaps in certain places, probably making the passages in question unintelligible. Or, not satisfied with this, the authorities tried to conceal any indication that the text had been mutilated. They therefore proceeded to tamper with the text. Single words here and there were left out or replaced by others and whole new sentences were interpolated; at best, the passage was completely erased and replaced by another in exactly the opposite sense. When the book was next transcribed the text aroused no suspicion, but had, in fact, been falsified. It no longer contained the author's statement and very probably the correction was not in the interests of truth.

Without pressing the analogy too closely we may say that repression is to the other methods of defence what the omission of words or passages is to the corruption of a text, and in the various forms of this falsification we can discover parallels to the manifold ways in which the ego may be modified. It may be objected that this analogy breaks down in an essential particular, for the corruption of a text is the work of a purposeful censorship to which we have no counterpart in the development of the ego. But this is not so, for this purpose is amply represented by the compelling force of the pleasure principle. The psychical apparatus is intolerant of unpleasure and strives to ward it off at all costs and, if the perception of reality involves unpleasure, that perception—*i.e.* the truth—must be sacrificed. For quite a long time flight and an avoidance of a dangerous situation serve as expedients in the face of external danger, until the individual is finally strong enough to remove the menace by actively modifying reality. But one cannot flee from oneself and no flight avails against danger from within; hence the ego's defensive mechanisms are condemned to falsify the inner perception, so that it transmits to us only an imperfect and travestied picture of our id. In its relations with the id the ego is paralysed by its restrictions or blinded by its errors, and the result in the sphere of psychical events may be compared to the progress of a poor walker in a country which he does not know.

The purpose of the defensive mechanisms is to avert dangers. It cannot be disputed that they are successful; it is doubtful whether the ego can altogether do without them during its development, but it is also certain that they themselves may become dangerous. Not infrequently it turns out that the ego has paid too high a price for the services which these mechanisms render. The expenditure of energy necessary to maintain them and the ego-restrictions which they almost invariably entail prove a heavy burden on the psychical economy. Moreover these mechanisms are not relinquished after they have helped the ego through the difficult years of its development. Of course, no individual makes use of all the possible mechanisms of defence: each person merely selects certain of them, but these become fixated in his ego, establishing themselves as regular modes of reaction for that particular character, which are repeated throughout life whenever a situation occurs similar to that which originally evoked them. They are, in fact, infantilisms and share the fate of so many institutions which struggle to maintain themselves when they have outlived their usefulness. *"Verunuft wird Unsinn, Wohltat Plage,"*[4] as the poet laments. The adult ego with its greater strength continues to defend itself against dangers which no longer exist in reality and even finds itself impelled to seek out real situations which may serve as a substitute for the original danger, so as to be able to justify its clinging to its habitual modes of reaction. Thus the defensive mechanisms produce an ever-growing alienation from the external world and a permanent enfeeblement of the ego and we can easily understand how they pave the way for and precipitate the outbreak of neurosis.

For the moment, however, we are not concerned with the pathogenic role of the defensive mechanisms. Our purpose is to discover how our therapeutic work is affected by the ego-modification they produce. The material for the answer to this question is contained in Anna Freud's work, to which I have already referred. The main point is that the patient repeats these modes of reaction during analysis itself, exhibiting them, as it were, before our eyes; in fact, that is the only means we

---

4. ["Reason becomes unreason, kindness torment." Goethe, *Faust*, Part I.]

have of learning about them. This must not be taken to imply that they make analysis impossible. On the contrary, they constitute half of our analytic task. The other half, the first to be tackled by analysis in its early days, is the revelation of that which is hidden in the id. Our therapeutic work swings to and fro during the treatment like a pendulum, analysing now a fragment of the id and now a fragment of the ego. In the one case our aim is to bring a part of the id into consciousness and in the other to correct something in the ego. The crux of the matter is that the mechanisms of defence against former dangers recur in analysis in the shape of *resistances* to cure. It follows that the ego treats recovery itself as a new danger.

The therapeutic effect of analysis depends on the making conscious what is, in the widest sense, repressed within the id. We prepare the way for this operation by our interpretations and constructions, but so long as the ego clings to its former defences and refuses to abandon its resistances we have interpreted merely for ourselves and not for the patient. Now these resistances, although they belong to the ego, are nevertheless unconscious and, in a certain sense, they are segregated within the ego. The analyst recognizes them more easily than the hidden material in the id; one would suppose it would be enough to treat them as parts of the id and to bring them into relation with the rest of the ego by making them conscious. This would mean that half of our analytic task had been accomplished: we are hardly prepared for a resistance to the discovery of resistances. But what takes place is as follows. While we are analysing the resistances, the ego—more or less of set purpose—breaks the compact upon which the analytic situation is based. It ceases to support us in our efforts to reveal the id, it opposes those efforts, disobeys the fundamental rule of analysis and suffers no further derivatives of repressed material to emerge into consciousness. It is too much to expect that the patient should have a firm conviction of the curative power of analysis, but he may have come to the analyst with a certain amount of confidence and this, reinforced by the various factors in the positive transference which it is our business to evoke, makes him capable of doing his share. The effect of the unpleasurable impulses which he feels stirring in him when his defensive conflicts are once more roused may be that negative transferences gain the upper hand and break up the whole analytic situation. The patient now regards the analyst simply as an alien personality who makes disagreeable demands upon him and he behaves towards him exactly like a child who does not like a stranger and has no confidence in him. If the analyst tries to explain to the patient one of the distortions which his defence has produced and to correct it, he meets with a complete lack of comprehension and an imperviousness to valid arguments. We see then that there really *is* a resistance to the discovery of resistances and that the defensive mechanisms do deserve the name which we originally gave them before they had been more closely examined: they are resistances not only to the bringing of id-contents into consciousness but also to the whole process of analysis and so to cure.

The effect which the defensive activities produce within the ego is rightly described as "modification of the ego," if by that we understand the deviation of the ego from an imaginary normal ego which would guarantee unswerving loyalty to the analytic compact. We can well believe what our daily experience suggests, that the outcome of an analysis depends principally upon the strength and depth of the roots of the resistances constituting the ego-modification. Once more we realize the importance of the quantitative factor and once more we are reminded that analysis has only certain limited quantities of energy which it can employ to match against the hostile forces. And it does seem as if victory were really for the most part with the big battalions.

Our next question will be whether all modification of the ego (in the sense in which we are using the term) is acquired during the defensive conflicts of early childhood. There can be no doubt about the answer. We have no reason to dispute the existence and importance of primary congenital variations in the ego. A single fact is decisive, namely, that every individual selects only *certain* of the possible defensive mechanisms and invariably employs those which he has selected. This suggests that each individual ego is endowed from the beginning with its own peculiar dispositions and tendencies, though it is true that we cannot predicate their nature and conditioning factors. Moreover, we know that we must not exaggerate the difference between inherited and acquired characteristics into an antithesis; what was acquired by our ancestors is certainly an important part of what we inherit. When we speak of our "archaic heritage" we are generally thinking only of the id and we apparently assume that no ego is yet in existence at the beginning of the individual's life. But we must not overlook the fact that id and ego are originally one, and it does not imply a mystical over-valuation of heredity if we think it credible that, even before the ego exists, its subsequent lines of development, tendencies and reactions are already determined. The psychological peculiarities of families, races and nations, even in

their attitude towards analysis, admit of no other explanation. Indeed, analytic experience convinces us that particular psychical contents, such as symbolism, have no other source than hereditary transmission, and research in various fields of social psychology seems to justify the assumption that there are other, no less specialized, deposits from primitive human development present in our archaic heritage.

When we recognize that the peculiarities of the ego which we detect in the form of resistances may be not only acquired in defensive conflicts but determined by heredity, the topographical differentiation between ego and id loses much of its value for our investigations. When we advance a step further in analytic experience we come upon resistances of another type, which we can no longer localize and which seem to be conditioned by certain fundamental characteristics of the mental apparatus. I can give only a few examples of the type of resistance to which I refer: this whole field of inquiry is still bewilderingly strange and has not been sufficiently explored. We come across people, for instance, of whom we could say that they display a peculiar "adhesiveness of libido." The processes which their analysis sets in motion are so much slower than in other people because they apparently cannot make up their minds to detach libidinal cathexes from one object and displace them to another, although we can find no particular reasons for this cathectic fidelity. Then we meet the opposite type, in which libido seems specially mobile: it readily enters upon the new cathexes suggested by the analysis, abandoning its former ones for these. The difference between the two types is comparable to that experienced by a sculptor according as he works in hard stone or soft clay. Unfortunately in the latter type the results of analysis often prove very evanescent; the new cathexes are soon abandoned and one feels not as if one had been working in clay but as if one had been writing on water. "*Wie gewonnen, so zerronnen,*" ("Light come, light go.") as the proverb says.

In another group of patients we are surprised by an attitude which we can only put down to a loss of the plasticity we should expect, an exhaustion of the capacity for change and development. We are indeed prepared for a certain degree of psychical inertia in analysis; when new paths are pointed out for the instinctual impulses, we almost invariably see an obvious hesitation in entering upon them. We have described this attitude, though perhaps not quite rightly, as "resistance from the id." But in the cases which I have in mind all the mental processes, relations and distributions of energy are immutable, fixed and rigid. One finds the same state of affairs in very old people, when it is explained by what is described as force of habit, the exhaustion of receptivity through a kind of psychical entropy; but I am thinking of people who are still young. Our theoretical knowledge does not seem adequate to explain these types. Probably some element of a temporal nature is at work here, changes in some rhythm in the development of psychical life which we have not yet apprehended.

In yet another group of cases the patients' resistance to analysis and the obstacles in the way of therapeutic success are probably due to variations in the ego which spring from another and even deeper root. Here we come to the ultimate phenomena to which psychological research has penetrated —the behaviour of the two primal instincts, their distribution, fusion and defusion, things which we cannot imagine to be confined to a single province of the mental apparatus, whether it be id, ego or super-ego. Nothing impresses us more strongly in connection with the resistances encountered in analysis than the feeling that there is a force at work which is defending itself by all possible means against recovery and is clinging tenaciously to illness and suffering. We have recognized that part of this force is the sense of guilt and the need for punishment, and that is undoubtedly correct; we have localized it in the ego's relation to the super-ego. But this is only one element in it, which may be described as psychically bound by the super-ego and which we thus perceive. We may suppose that other portions of the same force are at work, either bound or free, in some unspecified region of the mind. If we consider the whole picture made up of the phenomena of the masochism inherent in so many people, of the negative therapeutic reaction and of the neurotic's sense of guilt, we shall have to abandon the belief that mental processes are governed exclusively by a striving after pleasure. These phenomena are unmistakable indications of the existence of a power in mental life which, according to its aim, we call the aggressive or destructive instinct and which we derive from the primal death-instinct of animate matter. It is not a question of an optimistic as opposed to a pessimistic theory of life. Only by the concurrent or opposing action of the two primal instincts—Eros and the death-instinct— never by one or the other alone, can the motley variety of vital phenomena be explained.

How the elements of these two species of instinct combine to fulfil the various vital functions, under what conditions such combinations grow looser and break up, what disturbances correspond to these changes and what feelings they evoke in the perceptual scale of the pleasure principle—these are problems whose elucidation would be the most valuable achievement of psychological research. For the moment we must bow to those superior forces which foil our efforts. Even to exert a psychical influence upon a simple case of masochism is a severe tax on our powers.

In studying the phenomena which testify to the activity of the instinct of destruction we are not confined to the observation of pathological material. There are countless facts in normal mental life which require this explanation, and the keener the power of our discernment the greater the abundance in which they present themselves to our notice. The subject is too novel and too important to be treated as a side-issue in this discussion; I will content myself with selecting a few specimens of these phenomena.

Here is an example: It is well known that at all times there have been, as there still are, human beings who can take as their sexual objects persons of either sex without the one trend interfering with the other. We call these people bisexual and accept the fact of their existence without wondering much at it. But we have come to know that all human beings are bisexual in this sense and that their libido is distributed between objects of both sexes, either in a manifest or a latent form. But the following point strikes us. While in the individuals I first mentioned the libidinal impulses can take both directions without producing a clash, in the other and more frequent cases the result is an irreconcilable conflict. A man's heterosexuality will not tolerate homosexuality, and vice versa. If the former tendency is the stronger, it succeeds in keeping the latter in a state of latency and preventing its attaining satisfaction in actuality. On the other hand there is no greater danger for a man's heterosexual function than disturbance by latent homosexuality. We might explain these facts by saying that each individual has only a given quantity of libido at his disposal and that the two rival trends have to contend for it. But it is not clear why these rivals should not regularly divide between them the available quantity of libido, according to their relative strength, since that is what does in fact happen in some cases. We are forced to conclude that there is something peculiar in the tendency to conflict, something which introduces a new element into the situation, independently of the quantity of libido. It is difficult to account for this spontaneous tendency to conflict except as the intervention of an element of free aggressiveness.

If we recognize that the case which I have just described is a manifestation of the destructive or aggressive instinct we are at once confronted with the question whether this notion should not be extended to apply to other instances of conflict, or, indeed, whether we ought not to review all our knowledge or psychical conflict from this new angle. After all, we assume that, in the course of the development of human beings from their primitive state to civilization a considerable part of their aggressiveness is internalized or turned inwards; and, if this is so, internal conflicts would certainly be the correct equivalent of the external conflicts which have now ceased. I am well aware that the dualistic theory, according to which an instinct of death, destruction or aggression claims equal partnership with Eros as manifested in libido, has met with little general acceptance and has not really established itself even among psycho-analysts.

*   *   *

Both in the therapeutic and character-analyses we are struck by the prominence of two themes which give the analyst an extraordinary amount of trouble. It soon becomes clear that some general principle is at work here. These two themes are connected with the difference between the sexes: one is characteristic of men and the other equally characteristic of women. In spite of the difference in their content there is an obvious correspondence between the two. Some factor common to both sexes is forced, by the difference between them, to express itself differently in the one and in the other.

The two corresponding themes are, in women, envy for the penis—the striving after the possession of a male genital—and, in men, the struggle against their passive or feminine attitude towards other men. What is common to these two themes was singled out by early psycho-analytic nomenclature as an attitude to the castration complex. Subsequently Alfred Adler brought the term "masculine protest" into current use. It fits the case of men perfectly; but I think that, from the first, "repudiation of femininity" would have been the correct description of this remarkable feature in the psychical life of mankind.

Supposing that we now try to introduce this notion into the structure of psycho-analytical theory we shall find that, by its very nature, this factor cannot occupy the same place in the case of both sexes. In males the masculine striving is from the beginning and throughout entirely ego-syntonic; the passive attitude, since it implies an acceptance of castration, is energetically repressed, and often the only indications of its existence are exaggerated over-compensations. In females also the striving after masculinity is ego-syntonic at a certain period, namely, in the phallic phase, before development in the direction of femininty has set in. But later it succumbs to that momentous process of repression, the outcome of which (as has often been pointed out) determines the fortunes of the woman's femininity. A great deal depends upon

whether a sufficient amount of her masculinity-complex escapes repression and exercises a lasting influence on her character. Normally, large portions of that complex undergo transformation and contribute to the development of femininity: the unsatisfied wish for a penis should be converted into a wish for a child and for a man, who possesses a penis. Very often indeed, however, we find that the wish for masculinity persists in the unconscious and, in its repressed state, exercises a disturbing influence.

As is plain from what has just been said, in both cases it is the attitude belonging to the sex opposite to the subject's own which succumbs to repression. I have stated elsewhere[5] that it was Wilhelm Fliess who called my attention to this point. Fliess was inclined to regard the difference between the sexes as the true cause and original motive of repression. I can only repeat that I do not accept this view: I do not think we are justified in sexualizing repression in this way—that is to say, in explaining it on a biological instead of a purely psychological basis.

The paramount importance of these two themes —the wish for a penis in women and, in men, the struggle against passivity—did not escape the notice of Ferenczi. In the paper that he read in 1927 he laid it down as a principle that in every successful analysis these two complexes must have been resolved.[6] From my own experience I would observe that in this I think Ferenczi was asking a very great deal. At no point in one's analytic work does one suffer more from the oppressive feeling that all one's efforts have been in vain and from the suspicion that one is "talking to the winds" than when one is trying to persuade a female patient to abandon her wish for a penis on the ground of its being unrealizable, or to convince a male patient that a passive attitude towards another man does not always signify castration and that in many relations in life it is indispensable. The rebellious over-compensation of the male produces one of the strongest transference-resistances. A man will not be subject to a father-substitute or owe him anything and he therefore refuses to accept his cure from the physician. There is no analogous form of transference which can arise from the feminine wish for a penis, but it is the source of attacks of acute depression, because women patients feel an inner conviction

<hr>

5. ' "A Child is being Beaten" ' (1919), *Collected Papers,* 2, 172.

6. ". . . in every male patient the sign that his castration-anxiety has been mastered must be forthcoming, and this sign is a sense of equality of rights with the analyst; and every female patient, if her cure is to rank as complete and permanent, must have finally conquered her masculinity-complex and become able to submit without bitterness to thinking in terms of her feminine role." (Ferenczi, 1928, 8.)

that the analysis will avail them nothing and that they will be none the better for it. We can only agree with them when we discover that their strongest motive in coming for treatment was the hope that they might somehow still obtain a male organ, the lack of which is so painful to them.

All this shows that the form of the resistance is immaterial: it does not matter whether it appears as a transference or not. The vital point is that it prevents any change from taking place—everything remains as it was. We often feel that, when we have reached the wish for a penis and the masculine protest, we have penetrated all the psychological strata and reached "bedrock" and that our task is accomplished. And this is probably correct, for in the psychical field the biological factor is really the rock-bottom. The repudiation of femininity must surely be a biological fact, part of the great riddle of sex.[7] Whether and when we have succeeded in mastering this factor in an analysis is hard to determine. We must console ourselves with the certainty that everything possible has been done to encourage the patient to examine and to change his attitude to the question.

---

7. We must not be misled by the term "masculine protest" into supposing that what the man repudiates is the *attitude* of passivity, or, as we may say, the social aspect of femininity. Such a notion is speedily contradicted by the observation that the attitude such men display towards women is often masochistic or actually slavish. What they reject is not passivity in general but passivity in relation to *men*. That is to say, the "masculine protest" is in fact nothing other than fear of castration.

II—THE STRUCTURE OF DEVIANT BEHAVIOR

1. *Anomic Suicide*

BY EMILE DURKHEIM

BUT SOCIETY is not only something attracting the sentiments and activities of individuals with unequal force. It is also a power controlling them. There is a relation between the way this regulative action is performed and the social suicide-rate.

I

It is a well-known fact that economic crises have an aggravating effect on the suicidal tendency.

In Vienna, in 1873 a financial crisis occurred which reached its height in 1874; the number of suicides immediately rose. From 141 in 1872, they rose to 153 in 1873 and 216 in 1874. The increase in 1874 is 53 per cent above 1872 and 41 per cent above 1873. What proves this catastrophe to have been the sole cause of the increase is the special prominence of the increase when the crisis was

Reprinted from Emile Durkheim, *Suicide*, trans. John A. Spaulding and George Simpson (Glencoe, Ill.: The Free Press, 1951), pp. 241–42, 243–44, 245, 246–51, 252–54, 257, 258–61, 262–64, 265–66, 267–68, 269–72, with the permission of The Free Press.

acute, or during the first four months of 1874. From January 1 to April 30 there had been 48 suicides in 1871, 44 in 1872, 43 in 1873; there were 73 in 1874. The increase is 70 per cent (In 1874 over 1873.) The same crisis occurring at the same time in Frankfurt-on-Main produced the same effects there. In the years before 1874, 22 suicides were committed annually on the average; in 1874 there were 32, or 45 per cent more.

The famous crash is unforgotten which took place on the Paris Bourse during the winter of 1882. Its consequences were felt not only in Paris but throughout France. From 1874 to 1886 the average annual increase was only 2 per cent; in 1882 it was 7 per cent. Moreover, it was unequally distributed among the different times of year, occurring principally during the first three months or at the very time of the crash. Within these three months alone 59 per cent of the total rise occurred. So distinctly is the rise the result of unusual circumstances that it not only is not encountered in 1881 but has disappeared in 1883, although on the whole the latter year had a few more suicides than the preceding one:

	1881	1882	1883
Annual total	6,741	7,213 (plus 7%)	7,267
First three months	1,589	1,770 (plus 11%)	1,604

This relation is found not only in some exceptional cases, but is the rule. The number of bankruptcies is a barometer of adequate sensitivity, reflecting the variations of economic life. When they increase abruptly from year to year, some serious disturbance has certainly occurred. From 1845 to 1869 there were sudden rises, symptomatic of crises, on three occasions. While the annual increase in the number of bankruptcies during this period is 3.2 per cent, it is 26 per cent in 1847, 37 per cent in 1854 and 20 per cent in 1861. At these three moments, there is also to be observed an unusually rapid rise in the number of suicides. While the average annual increase during these 24 years was only 2 per cent, it was 17 per cent in 1847, 8 per cent in 1854 and 9 per cent in 1861.

But to what do these crises owe their influence? Is it because they increase poverty by causing public wealth to fluctuate? Is life more readily renounced as it becomes more difficult? The explanation is seductively simple; and it agrees with the popular idea of suicide. But it is contradicted by facts.

*   *   *

So far is the increase in poverty from causing the increase in suicide that even fortunate crises, the effect of which is abruptly to enhance a country's prosperity, affect suicide like economic disasters.

The conquest of Rome by Victor-Emmanuel in 1870, by definitely forming the basis of Italian unity, was the starting point for the country of a process of growth which is making it one of the great powers of Europe. Trade and industry received a sharp stimulus from it and surprisingly rapid changes took place. Whereas in 1876, 4,459 steam boilers with a total of 54,000 horse-power were enough for industrial needs, the number of machines in 1887 was 9,983 and their horse-power of 167,000 was threefold more. Of course the amount of production rose proportionately during the same time. Trade followed the same rising course; not only did the merchant marine, communications and transportation develop, but the number of persons and things transported doubled. As this generally heightened activity caused an increase in salaries (an increase of 35 per cent is estimated to have taken place from 1873 to 1889), the material comfort of workers rose, especially since the price of bread was falling at the same time. Finally, according to calculations by Bodio, private wealth rose from 45 and a half billions on the average during the period 1875–80 to 51 billions during the years 1880–85 and 54 billions and a half in 1885–90.

Now, an unusual increase in the number of suicides is observed parallel with this collective renaissance. From 1866 to 1870 they were roughly stable; from 1871 to 1877 they increased 36 per cent. There were in

1864–70	29	suicides per million
1871	31	suicides per million
1872	33	suicides per million
1873	36	suicides per million
1874	37	suicides per million
1875	34	suicides per million
1876	36.5	suicides per million
1877	40.6	suicides per million

And since then the movement has continued. The total figure, 1,139 in 1877, was 1,463 in 1889, a new increase of 28 per cent. . . .

On the morrow of the war of 1870 a new accession of good fortune took place. Germany was unified and placed entirely under Prussian hegemony. An enormous war indemnity added to the public wealth; commerce and industry made great strides. The development of suicide was never so rapid. From 1875 to 1886 it increased 90 per cent, from 3,278 cases to 6,212.

*   *   *

What proves still more conclusively that economic distress does not have the aggravating influence often attributed to it, is that it tends rather to produce the opposite effect. There is very little suicide in Ireland, where the peasantry leads so wretched a life. Poverty-stricken Calabria has almost no suicides; Spain has a tenth as many as France. Poverty may even be considered a protection. In the various French departments the more people there are who have independent means, the more numerous are suicides.

Departments Where, per 100,000 Inhabitants, Suicides Were Committed (1878–1887)		Average Number of Persons of Independent Means per 1,000 Inhabitants in Each Group of Departments (1886)
Suicides	Number of Departments	
From 48 to 43	5	127
From 38 to 31	6	73
From 30 to 24	6	69
From 23 to 18	15	59
From 17 to 13	18	49
From 12 to 8	26	49
From 7 to 3	10	42

*   *   *

If therefore industrial or financial crises increase suicides, this is not because they cause poverty, since crises of prosperity have the same result; it is because they are crises, that is, disturbances of the collective order.[1] Every disturbance of equilibrium, even though it achieves greater comfort and a heightening of general vitality, is an impulse to voluntary death. Whenever serious readjustments take place in the social order, whether or not due to a sudden growth or to an unexpected catastrophe, men are more inclined to self-destruction. How is this possible? How can something considered generally to improve existence serve to detach men from it?

For the answer, some preliminary considerations are required.

II

No living being can be happy or even exist unless his needs are sufficiently proportioned to his means. In other words, if his needs require more than can be granted, or even merely something of a different sort, they will be under continual friction and can only function painfully. Movements incapable of production without pain tend not to be reproduced. Unsatisfied tendencies atrophy, and as the impulse to live is merely the result of all the rest, it is bound to weaken as the others relax.

In the animal, at least in a normal condition, this equilibrium is established with automatic spontaneity because the animal depends on purely material conditions. All the organism needs is that the supplies of substance and energy constantly employed in the vital process should be periodically renewed by equivalent quantities; that replacement be equivalent to use. When the void created by existence in its own resources is filled, the animal, satisfied, asks nothing further. Its power of reflection is not sufficiently developed to imagine other ends than those implicit in its physical nature. On the other hand, as the work demanded of each organ itself depends on the general state of vital energy and the needs of organic equilibrium, use is regulated in turn by replacement and the balance is automatic. The limits of one are those of the other; both are fundamental to the constitution of the existence in question, which cannot exceed them.

This is not the case with man, because most of his needs are not dependent on his body or not to the same degree. Strictly speaking, we may consider that the quantity of material supplies necessary to the physical maintenance of a human life is subject to computation, though this be less exact than in the preceding case and a wider margin left for the free combinations of the will; for beyond the indispensable minimum which satisfies nature when instinctive, a more awakened reflection suggests better conditions, seemingly desirable ends craving fulfillment. Such appetites, however, admittedly sooner or later reach a limit which they cannot pass. But how determine the quantity of well-being, comfort or luxury legitimately to be craved by a human being? Nothing appears in man's organic nor in his psychological constitution which sets a limit to such tendencies. The functioning of individual life does not require them to cease at one point rather than at another; the proof being that they have constantly increased since the beginnings of history, receiving more and more complete satisfaction, yet with no weakening of average health. Above all, how establish their proper variation with different conditions of life, occupations, relative importance of services, etc.? In no society are they equally satisfied in the different stages of the social hierarchy. Yet human nature is substantially the same among all men, in its essential qualities. It is not human nature which can assign the variable limits necessary to our needs. They are thus unlimited so far as they depend on the individual alone. Irrespective of any external regulatory force, our capacity for feeling is in itself an insatiable and bottomless abyss.

But if nothing external can restrain this capacity, it can only be a source of torment to itself. Unlimited desires are insatiable by definition and insatiability is rightly considered a sign of morbidity. Being unlimited, they constantly and infinitely surpass the means at their command; they cannot be quenched. Inextinguishable thirst is constantly renewed torture. It has been claimed, indeed, that human activity naturally aspires beyond assignable limits and sets itself unattainable goals. But how can such an undetermined state be any more reconciled with the conditions of mental life than with the demands of physical life? All man's pleasure in acting, moving and exerting himself implies the sense that his efforts are not in vain and that by walking he has advanced. However, one does not advance when one walks toward no goal, or—which is the same thing—when his goal is infinity. Since the distance between us and it is always the same, whatever road we take, we might as well have made the motions without progress from the spot. Even our glances behind and our feeling of pride at the distance covered can cause only deceptive satisfaction, since the

---

1. To prove that an increase in prosperity diminishes suicides, the attempt has been made to show that they become less when emigration, the escape-valve of poverty, is widely practiced (See Legoyt, pp. 257–259). But cases are numerous where parallelism instead of inverse proportions exist between the two. In Italy from 1876 to 1890 the number of emigrants rose from 76 per 100,000 inhabitants to 335, a figure itself exceeded between 1887 and 1889. At the same time suicides did not cease to grow in numbers.

remaining distance is not proportionately reduced. To pursue a goal which is by definition unattainable is to condemn oneself to a state of perpetual unhappiness. Of course, man may hope contrary to all reason, and hope has its pleasures even when unreasonable. It may sustain him for a time; but it cannot survive the repeated disappointments of experience indefinitely. What more can the future offer him than the past, since he can never reach a tenable condition nor even approach the glimpsed ideal? Thus, the more one has, the more one wants, since satisfactions received only stimulate instead of filling needs. Shall action as such be considered agreeable? First, only on condition of blindness to its uselesness. Secondly, for this pleasure to be felt and to temper and half veil the accompanying painful unrest, such unending motion must at least always be easy and unhampered. If it is interfered with only restlessness is left, with the lack of ease which it, itself, entails. But it would be a miracle if no insurmountable obstacle were never encountered. Our thread of life on these conditions is pretty thin, breakable at any instant.

To achieve any other result, the passions first must be limited. Only then can they be harmonized with the faculties and satisfied. But since the individual has no way of limiting them, this must be done by some force exterior to him. A regulative force must play the same role for moral needs which the organism plays for physical needs. This means that the force can only be moral. The awakening of conscience interrupted the state of equilibrium of the animal's dormant existence; only conscience, therefore, can furnish the means to re-establish it. Physical restraint would be ineffective; hearts cannot be touched by physio-chemical forces. So far as the appetites are not automatically restrained by physiological mechanisms, they can be halted only by a limit that they recognize as just. Men would never consent to restrict their desires if they felt justified in passing the assigned limit. But, for reasons given above, they cannot assign themselves this law of justice. So they must receive it from an authority which they respect, to which they yield spontaneously. Either directly and as a whole, or through the agency of one of its organs, society alone can play this moderating role; for it is the only moral power superior to the individual, the authority of which he accepts. It alone has the power necessary to stipulate law and to set the point beyond which the passions must not go. Finally, it alone can estimate the reward to be prospectively offered to every class of human functionary, in the name of the common interest.

As a matter of fact, at every moment of history there is a dim perception, in the moral consciousness of societies, of the respective value of different social services, the relative reward due to each, and the consequent degree of comfort appropriate on the average to workers in each occupation. The different functions are graded in public opinion and a certain coefficient of well-being assigned to each, according to its place in the hierarchy. According to accepted ideas, for example, a certain way of living is considered the upper limit to which a workman may aspire in his efforts to improve his existence, and there is another limit below which he is not willingly permitted to fall unless he has seriously bemeaned himself. Both differ for city and country workers, for the domestic servant and the day-laborer, for the business clerk and the official, etc. Likewise the man of wealth is reproved if he lives the life of a poor man, but also if he seeks the refinements of luxury overmuch. Economists may protest in vain; public feeling will always be scandalized if an individual spends too much wealth for wholly superfluous use, and it even seems that this severity relaxes only in times of moral disturbance.[2] A genuine regimen exists, therefore, although not always legally formulated, which fixes with relative precision the maximum degree of ease of living to which each social class may legitimately aspire. However, there is nothing immutable about such a scale. It changes with the increase or decrease of collective revenue and the changes occurring in the moral ideas of society. Thus what appears luxury to one period no longer does so to another; and the well-being which for long periods was granted to a class only by exception and supererogation, finally appears strictly necessary and equitable.

Under this pressure, each in his sphere vaguely realizes the extreme limit set to his ambitions and aspires to nothing beyond. At least if he respects regulations and is docile to collective authority, that is, has a wholesome moral constitution, he feels that it is not well to ask more. Thus, an end and goal are set to the passions. Truly, there is nothing rigid nor absolute about such determination. The economic ideal assigned each class of citizens is itself confined to certain limits, within which the desires have free range. But it is not infinite. This relative limitation and the moderation it involves, make men contented with their lot while stimulating them moderately to improve it; and this average contentment causes the feeling of calm, active happiness, the pleasure in existing and living which characterizes health for societies as well as for individuals. Each person is then at least, generally speaking, in harmony with

2. Actually, this is a purely moral reprobation and can hardly be judicially implemented. We do not consider any reestablishment of sumptuary laws desirable or even possible.

his condition, and desires only what he may legitimately hope for as the normal reward of his activity. Besides, this does not condemn man to a sort of immobility. He may seek to give beauty to his life; but his attempts in this direction may fail without causing him to despair. For, loving what he has and not fixing his desire solely on what he lacks, his wishes and hopes may fail of what he has happened to aspire to, without his being wholly destitute. He has the essentials. The equilibrium of his happiness is secure because it is defined, and a few mishaps cannot disconcert him.

But it would be of little use for everyone to recognize the justice of the hierarchy of functions established by public opinion, if he did not also consider the distribution of these functions just. The workman is not in harmony with his social position if he is not convinced that he has his deserts. If he feels justified in occupying another, what he has would not satisfy him. So it is not enough for the average level of needs for each social condition to be regulated by public opinion, but another, more precise rule, must fix the way in which these conditions are open to individuals. There is no society in which such regulation does not exist. It varies with times and places. Once it regarded birth as the almost exclusive principle of social classification; today it recognizes no other inherent inequality than hereditary fortune and merit. But in all these various forms its object is unchanged. It is also only possible, everywhere, as a restriction upon individuals imposed by superior authority, that is, by collective authority. For it can be established only by requiring of one or another group of men, usually of all, sacrifices and concessions in the name of the public interest.

*   *   *

It is not true, then, that human activity can be released from all restraint. Nothing in the world can enjoy such a privilege. All existence being a part of the universe is relative to the remainder; its nature and method of manifestation accordingly depend not only on itself but on other beings, who consequently restrain and regulate it. Here there are only differences of degree and form between the mineral realm and the thinking person. Man's characteristic privilege is that the bond he accepts is not physical but moral; that is, social. He is governed not by a material environment brutally imposed on him, but by a conscience superior to his own, the superiority of which he feels. Because the greater, better part of his existence transcends the body, he escapes the body's yoke, but is subject to that of society.

But when society is disturbed by some painful crisis or by beneficent but abrupt transitions, it is momentarily incapable of exercising this influence; thence come the sudden rises in the curve of suicides which we have pointed out above.

In the case of economic disasters, indeed, something like a declassification occurs which suddenly casts certain individuals into a lower state than their previous one. Then they must reduce their requirements, restrain their needs, learn greater self-control. All the advantages of social influence are lost so far as they are concerned; their moral education has to be recommenced. But society cannot adjust them instantaneously to this new life and teach them to practice the increased self-repression to which they are unaccustomed. So they are not adjusted to the condition forced on them, and its very prospect is intolerable; hence the suffering which detaches them from a reduced existence even before they have made trial of it.

It is the same if the source of the crisis is an abrupt growth of power and wealth. Then, truly, as the conditions of life are changed, the standard according to which needs were regulated can no longer remain the same; for it varies with social resources, since it largely determines the share of each class of producers. The scale is upset; but a new scale cannot be immediately improvised. Time is required for the public conscience to reclassify men and things. So long as the social forces thus freed have not regained equilibrium, their respective values are unknown and so all regulation is lacking for a time. The limits are unknown between the possible and the impossible, what is just and what is unjust, legitimate claims and hopes and those which are immoderate. Consequently, there is no restraint upon aspirations. If the disturbance is profound, it affects even the principles controlling the distribution of men among various occupations. Since the relations between various parts of society are necessarily modified, the ideas expressing these relations must change. Some particular class especially favored by the crisis is no longer resigned to its former lot, and, on the other hand, the example of its greater good fortune arouses all sorts of jealousy below and about it. Appetites, not being controlled by a public opinion become disoriented, no longer recognize the limits proper to them. Besides, they are at the same time seized by a sort of natural erethism simply by the greater intensity of public life. With increased prosperity desires increase. At the very moment when traditional rules have lost their authority, the richer prize offered these appetites stimulates them and makes them more exigent and impatient of control. The state of de-regulation or anomy is thus further heightened by passions being less disciplined, precisely when they need more disciplining.

But then their very demands make fulfillment impossible. Overweening ambition always exceeds the results obtained, great as they may be, since there is no warning to pause here. Nothing gives satisfaction and all this agitation is uninterruptedly maintained without appeasement. Above all, since this race for an unattainable goal can give no other pleasure but that of the race itself, if it is one, once it is interrupted the participants are left empty-handed. At the same time the struggle grows more violent and painful, both from being less controlled and because competition is greater. All classes contend among themselves because no established classification any longer exists. Effort grows, just when it becomes less productive. How could the desire to live not be weakened under such conditions?

This explanation is confirmed by the remarkable immunity of poor countries. Poverty protects against suicide because it is a restraint in itself. No matter how one acts, desires have to depend upon resources to some extent; actual possessions are partly the criterion of those aspired to. So the less one has the less he is tempted to extend the range of his needs indefinitely. Lack of power, compelling moderation, accustoms men to it, while nothing excites envy if no one has superfluity. Wealth, on the other hand, by the power it bestows, deceives us into believing that we depend on ourselves only. Reducing the resistance we encounter from objects, it suggests the possibility of unlimited success against them. The less limited one feels, the more intolerable all limitation appears. Not without reason, therefore, have so many religions dwelt on the advantages and moral value of poverty. It is actually the best school for teaching self-restraint. Forcing us to constant self-discipline, it prepares us to accept collective discipline with equanimity, while wealth, exalting the individual, may always arouse the spirit of rebellion which is the very source of immorality. This, of course, is no reason why humanity should not improve its material condition. But though the moral danger involved in every growth of prosperity is not irremediable, it should not be forgotten.

III

If anomy never appeared except, as in the above instances, in intermittent spurts and acute crisis, it might cause the social suicide-rate to vary from time to time, but it would not be a regular, constant factor. In one sphere of social life, however—the sphere of trade and industry—it is actually in a chronic state.

* * *

Industrial and commercial functions are really among the occupations which furnish the greatest number of suicides. Almost on a level with the liberal professions, they sometimes surpass them; they are especially more afflicted than agriculture, where the old regulative forces still make their appearance felt most and where the fever of business has least penetrated. Here is best recalled what was once the general constitution of the economic order. And the divergence would be yet greater if, among the suicides of industry, employers were distinguished from workmen, for the former are probably most stricken by the state of anomy. The enormous rate of those with independent means (720 per million) sufficiently shows that the possessors of most comfort suffer most. Everything that enforces subordination attenuates the effects of this state. At least the horizon of the lower classes is limited by those above them, and for this same reason their desires are more modest. Those who have only empty space above them are almost inevitably lost in it, if no force restrains them.

* * *

Anomy, therefore, is a regular and specific factor in suicide in our modern societies; one of the springs from which the annual contingent feeds. So we have here a new type to distinguish from the others. It differs from them in its dependence, not on the way in which individuals are attached to society, but on how it regulates them. Egoistic suicide results from man's no longer finding a basis for existence in life; altruistic suicide, because this basis for existence appears to man situated beyond life itself. The third sort of suicide, the existence of which has just been shown, results from man's activity's lacking regulation and his consequent sufferings. By virtue of its origin we shall assign this last variety the name of *anomic suicide*.

Certainly, this and egoistic suicide have kindred ties. Both spring from society's insufficient presence in individuals. But the sphere of its absence is not the same in both cases. In egoistic suicide it is deficient in truly collective activity, thus depriving the latter of object and meaning. In anomic suicide, society's influence is lacking in the basically individual passions, thus leaving them without a check-rein. In spite of their relationship, therefore, the two types are independent of each other. We may offer society everything social in us, and still be unable to control our desires; one may live in an anomic state without being egoistic, and vice versa. These two sorts of suicide therefore do not draw their chief recruits from the same social environments; one has its principal field among intellectual careers, the world of thought—the other, the industrial or commercial world.

Table I—Comparison of European States from the Point of View of
Both Divorce and Suicide

	Annual Divorces per 1,000 Marriages	Suicides per Million Inhabitants
I. COUNTRIES WHERE DIVORCE AND SEPARATION ARE RARE		
Norway	0.54 (1875–80)	73
Russia	1.6 (1871–77)	30
England and Wales	1.3 (1871–79)	68
Scotland	2.1 (1871–81)	....
Italy	3.05 (1871–73)	31
Finland	3.9 (1875–79)	30.8
Averages	2.07	46.5
II. COUNTRIES WHERE DIVORCE AND SEPARATION ARE OF AVERAGE FREQUENCY		
Bavaria	5.0 (1881)	90.5
Belgium	5.1 (1871–80)	68.5
Holland	6.0 (1871–80)	35.5
Sweden	6.4 (1871–80)	81
Baden	6.5 (1874–79)	156.6
France	7.5 (1871–79)	150
Wurttemberg	8.4 (1876–78)	162.4
Prussia	...	133
Averages	6.4	109.6
III. COUNTRIES WHERE DIVORCE AND SEPARATION ARE FREQUENT		
Kingdom of Saxony	26.9 (1876–80)	299
Denmark	38 (1871–80)	258
Switzerland	47 (1876–80)	216
Averages	37.3	257

IV

But economic anomy is not the only anomy which may give rise to suicide.

The suicides occurring at the crisis of widowhood, of which we have already spoken are really due to domestic anomy resulting from the death of husband or wife. A family catastrophe occurs which affects the survivor. He is not adapted to the new situation in which he finds himself and accordingly offers less resistance to suicide.

But another variety of anomic suicide should draw greater attention, both because it is more chronic and because it will serve to illustrate the nature and functions of marriage.

In the *Annales de demographie internationale* (September 1882), Bertillon published a remarkable study of divorce, in which he proved the following proposition: throughout Europe the number of suicides varies with that of divorces and separations.

If the different countries are compared from this twofold point of view, this parallelism is apparent (see Table I). Not only is the relation between the averages evident, but the single irregular detail of any importance is that of Holland, where suicides are not as frequent as divorces.

The law may be yet more vigorously verified if we compare not different countries but different provinces of a single country. Notably, in Switzerland the agreement between the two series of phenomena is striking (see Table II). The Protestant cantons have the most divorces and also the most suicides. The mixed cantons follow, from both points of view, and only then come the Catholic cantons. Within each group the same agreements appear.

*   *   *

One must seek the cause of this remarkable relation, not in the organic predispositions of people but in the intrinsic nature of divorce. As our first proposition here we may assert: in all countries for which we have the necessary data, suicides of divorced people are immensely more numerous than those of other portions of the population.

Table II—Comparison of Swiss Cantons from the Point of View of Divorce and Suicide

	Divorces and Separations per 1,000 Marriages	Suicides per Million		Divorces and Separations per 1,000 Marriages	Suicides per Million
I. CATHOLIC CANTONS					
French and Italian					
Tessino	7.6	57	Freiburg	15.9	119
Valais	4.0	47			
Averages	5.8	50	Averages	15.9	119
German					
Uri	...	60	Solothurn	37.7	205
Upper Unterwalden	4.9	20	Inner Appenzell	18.9	158
Lower Unterwalden	5.2	1	Zug	14.8	87
Schwyz	5.6	70	Luzern	13.0	100
Averages	3.9	37.7	Averages	21.1	137.5
II. PROTESTANT CANTONS					
French					
Neufchâtel	42.4	560	Vaud	43.5	352
German					
Bern	47.2	229	Schaffhausen	106.0	602
Basel (city)	34.5	323	Outer Appenzell	100.7	213
Basel (country)	33.0	288	Glaris	83.1	127
			Zurich	80.0	288
Averages	38.2	280	Averages	92.4	307
III. CANTONS MIXED AS TO RELIGION					
Argau	40.0	195	Geneva	70.5	360
Grisons	30.9	116	Saint Gall	57.6	179
Averages	36.9	155	Averages	64.0	269

Thus, divorced persons of both sexes kill themselves between three and four times as often as married persons, although younger (40 years in France as against 46 years), and considerably more often than widowed persons in spite of the aggravation resulting for the latter from their advanced age. What is the explanation?

There is no doubt that the change of moral and material regimen which is a consequence of divorce is of some account in this result. But it does not suffi-

Suicides in a Million

	Unmarried Above 15 Years		Married		Widowed		Divorced	
	Men	Women	Men	Women	Men	Women	Men	Women
Prussia (1887–1889) *	360	120	430	90	1,471	215	1,875	290
Prussia (1883–1890) *	388	129	498	100	1,552	194	1,952	328
Baden (1885–1893)	458	93	460	85	1,172	171	1,328	...
Saxony (1847–1858)	...	...	481	120	1,242	240	3,102	312
Saxony (1876)		555.18†	821	146	.....	...	3,252	389
Wurttemberg (1846–1860)	...	...	226	52	530	97	1,298	281
Wurttemberg (1873–1892)	251	...	218†		405†		796†	

* There appears to be some error in the figures for Prussia here.—Ed

† Men and women combined.—Ed.

ciently explain the matter. Widowhood is indeed as complete a disturbance of existence as divorce; it usually even has much more unhappy results, since it was not desired by husband and wife, while divorce is usually a deliverance for both. Yet divorced persons who, considering their age, should commit suicide only one half as often as widowed persons, do so more often everywhere, even twice as often in certain countries. This aggravation, to be represented by a coefficient between 2.5 and 4, does not depend on their changed condition in any way.

Let us refer to one of the propositions established above to discover the causes of this fact. In the third chapter of Book II, we saw that in a given society the tendency of widowed persons to suicide was a function of the corresponding tendency of married persons. While the latter are highly protected, the former enjoy an immunity less, to be sure, but still considerable, and the sex best protected by marriage is also that best protected in the state of widowhood. Briefly, when conjugal society is dissolved by the death of one of the couple, the effects which it had with reference to suicide continue to be felt in part by the survivor. Then, however, is it not to be supposed that the same thing takes place when the marriage is interrupted, not by death, but by a judicial act, and that the aggravation which afflicts divorced persons is a result not of the divorce but

of the marriage ended by divorce? It must be connected with some quality of the matrimonial society, the influence of which the couple continue to experience even when separated. If they have so strong an inclination to suicide, it is because they were already strongly inclined to it while living together and by the very effect of their common life.

Admitting so much, the correspondence between divorces and suicides becomes explicable. Actually, among the people where divorce is common, this peculiar effect of marriage in which divorce shares must necessarily be very wide-spread; for it is not confined to households predestined to legal separation. If it reaches its maximum intensity among them, it must also be found among the others, or the majority of the others, though to a lesser degree. For just as where there are many suicides, there are many attempted suicides, and just as mortality cannot grow without morbidity increasing simultaneously, so wherever there are many actual divorces there must be many households more or less close to divorce. The number of actual divorces cannot rise, accordingly, without the family condition predisposing to suicide also developing and becoming general in the same degree, and thus the two phenomena naturally vary in the same general direction.

Not only does this hypothesis agree with every-

Table III—Influence of Divorce on the Immunity of Married Persons

| Country | Suicides per Million Persons | | Coefficient of Preservation of Married with Reference to Unmarried Men |
	Unmarried Men Above 15 Years	Married Men	
Where divorce does not exist			
Italy (1884–88)	145	88	1.64
France (1863–68) *	273	245.7	1.11
Where divorce is common			
Baden (1885–93)	458	460	0.99
Prussia (1883–90)	388	498	0.77
Prussia (1887–89)	364	431	0.83

	Per one hundred suicides of every marital status.		
	Unmarried men	Married men	
Where divorce is very	27.5	52.5	0.63
frequent †	Per one hundred male inhabitants of every marital status.		
Saxony (1879–80)	Unmarried men	Married men	
	42.10	52.47	

* We take this distant period because divorce did not exist at all at the time. The law of 1884 re-establishing it seems, however, up to the present, to have had no perceptible effects on the suicides of married men; their coefficient of preservation had not appreciably changed in 1888–92; an institution does not produce its effects in so short a time.

† For Saxony we have only the relative numbers given above and taken from Oettingen; they are enough for the purpose. In Legoyt (p. 171) other data will be found likewise proving that in Saxony married persons have a higher rate than unmarried. Legoyt himself notes this with surprise.

thing demonstrated above but it is susceptible of direct proof. Indeed, if it is well-founded, married persons in countries where divorces are numerous must have less immunity against suicide than where marriage is indissoluble. This is the net result of the facts, at least *so far as husbands are concerned* as appears from Table III. Italy, a Catholic country in which divorce is unknown, is also the country with the highest coefficient of preservation for husbands; it is less in France, where separations have always been more frequent, and can be seen to diminish as we pass to countries where divorce is more widely practiced.

* * *

This is one more proof that the large number of suicides in countries where divorce is widespread has no reference to any organic predisposition, especially to the number of unstable people. For if such were the real cause, it would affect unmarried as well as married men. Now the latter are actually those most affected. The origin of the evil is therefore undoubtedly to be sought, as we have supposed, in some peculiarity either of marriage or of family life. It remains for us to choose between the last two hypotheses. Is the lesser immunity of husbands due to the condition of domestic society, or to that of matrimonial society? Is the family morale inferior or the conjugal bond not all that it should be?

A first fact which makes the former explanation improbable is that among peoples where divorce is most frequent the birth-rate is very high and, consequently, the density of the domestic group is also very high. Now we know that where the family is dense, family spirit is usually strong. There is reason to believe, then, that the cause of the phenomenon is to be sought in the nature of marriage.

Actually, if it were imputable to the constitution of the family, wives should also be less protected from suicide in countries where divorce is current than in those where it is rare; for they are as much affected by the poor state of domestic relations as husbands. Exactly the reverse is the truth. The coefficient of preservation of married women rises proportionately to the fall of that of husbands, or in proportion as divorces are more frequent and vice versa. The more often and easily the conjugal bond is broken, the more the wife is favored in comparison with the husband (see Table IV).

The inversion between the two series of coefficients is remarkable. In countries where there is no divorce, the wife is less protected than the husband; but her inferiority is greater in Italy than in France, where the matrimonial tie has always been more easily broken. On the contrary, wherever divorce is practiced (Baden), the husband is less protected than the wife, and the latter's advantage increases regularly with the increase in the frequency of divorce.

* * *

Comparison of the Seine with other French departments confirms this law in a striking manner. In the provinces, where there is less divorce, the average coefficient of married women is only 1.49; it is therefore only half the average coefficient of husbands, which is 2.88. In the Seine the relation is reversed. The immunity of men is only 1.56 and

Table IV—Influence of Divorce on the Immunity of Married Women*

	Suicides per Million		Coefficient of Preservation		How Many Times Husbands' Coefficient Above Wives'	How Many Times Wives' Coefficient Above Husbands'
	Unmarried Women Over 16 Years	Wives	Wives	Husbands		
Italy	21	22	0.95	1.64	1.72	....
France	59	62.5	0.96	1.11	1.15	....
Baden	93	85	1.09	0.99	....	1.10
Prussia	129	100	1.29	0.77	....	1.67
Prussia (1887–89)	120	90	1.33	0.83	....	1.60

	Per 100 suicides of every marital status.					
	Unmarried Women	Wives				
Saxony	35.3	42.6				
	Per 100 inhabitants of every marital status.					
	Unmarried Women	Wives				
	37.97	49.74	1.19	0.63	....	1.73

* The periods are the same as in Table III.

Provinces Containing, per 100,000 Married Persons

From 810 to 405 Divorced	Coefficient of Preservation of Wives	From 371 to 324 Divorced	Coefficient of Preservation of Wives	From 229 to 116 Divorced	Coefficient of Preservation of Wives
Berlin	1.72	Pomerania	1	Posen	1
Brandenburg	1.75	Silesia	1.18	Hesse	1.44
East Prussia	1.50	West Prussia	1	Hanover	0.90
Saxony	2.08	Schleswig	1.20	Rhineland	1.25
				Westphalia	0.80

even 1.44 if we omit the uncertain figures referring to the period of from 20 to 25 years; the immunity of women is 1.79. The woman's situation in relation to the husband's there is thus more than twice as good as in the departments.

The same result is obtained by comparing the various provinces of Prussia:

All the coefficients of the first group are distinctly above those of the second, and the lowest are found in the third. The only anomaly is Hesse, where, for unknown reasons, married women have a considerable immunity although divorced persons are few in number. (It has been necessary to classify these provinces by the number of divorced persons recorded, the number of annual divorces not having been available.)

*   *   *

Accordingly, the following law may be regarded as beyond dispute: *From the standpoint of suicide, marriage is more favorable to the wife the more widely practiced divorce is; and vice versa.*

From this proposition, two consequences flow.

First, only husbands contribute to the rise in the suicide rate observable in societies where divorces are frequent, wives on the contrary committing suicide more rarely than elsewhere. If, then, divorce can only develop with the improvement of woman's moral situation, it cannot be connected with an unfavorable state of domestic society calculated to aggravate the tendency to suicide; for such an aggravation should occur in the case of the wife, as well as of the husband. A lowering of family morale cannot have such opposite effects on the two sexes: it cannot both favor the mother and seriously afflict the father. Consequently, the cause of the phenomenon which we are studying is found in the state of marriage and not in the constitution of the family. And indeed, marriage may very possibly act in an opposite way on husband and wife. For though they have the same object as parents, as partners their interests are different and often hos-

tile. In certain societies therefore, some peculiarity of the matrimonial institution may very well benefit one and harm the other. All of the above tends to show that this is precisely the case with divorce.

Secondly, for the same reason we have to reject the hypothesis that this unfortunate state of marriage, with which divorces and suicides are closely connected, is simply caused by more frequent domestic disputes; for no such cause could increase the woman's immunity, any more than could the loosening of the family tie. If, where divorce is common, the number of suicides really depends on the number of conjugal disputes, the wife should suffer from them as much as the husband. There is nothing in this situation to afford her exceptional immunity. The hypothesis is the less tenable since divorce is usually asked for by the wife from the husband (in France, 60 per cent of divorces and 83 per cent of separations). Accordingly, domestic troubles are most often attributable to the man. Then, however, it would not be clear why, in countries of frequent divorce, the husband kills himself with greater frequency because he causes his wife more suffering, and the wife kills herself less often because her husband makes her suffer more. Nor is it proven that the number of conjugal dissensions increases in the same measure with divorce.

If we discard this hypothesis, only one other remains possible. The institution of divorce must itself cause suicide through its effect on marriage.

After all, what is marriage? A regulation of sexual relations, including not merely the physical instincts which this intercourse involves but the feelings of every sort gradually engrafted by civilization on the foundation of physical desire. For among us love is a far more mental than organic fact. A man looks to a woman, not merely to the satisfaction of the sexual impulse. Though this natural proclivity has been the germ of all sexual evolution, it has become increasingly complicated with aesthetic and moral feelings, numerous and varied, and today it is only the smallest element of the total complex process to which it has given birth. Under the influence of these intellectual elements it has itself been partially freed from its physical nature and assumed something like an intellectual one. Moral reasons as well as physical needs impel love. Hence, it no longer has the regular, automatic periodicity which it displays in animals. A psychological impulse may awaken it at any time: it is not seasonal. But just because these various inclinations, thus changed, do not directly depend upon organic necessities, social regulation becomes necessary. They must be restrained by society since the organism has no means of restraining them. This is the function of marriage. It completely regulates the life of passion, and monogamic marriage more strictly than any other. For by forcing a man to attach himself forever to the same woman it assigns a strictly definite object to the need for love, and closes the horizon.

This determination is what forms the state of moral equilibrium from which the husband benefits. Being unable to seek other satisfactions than those permitted, without transgressing his duty, he restricts his desires to them. The salutary discipline to which he is subjected makes it his duty to find his happiness in his lot, and by doing so supplies him with the means. Besides, if his passion is forbidden to stray, its fixed object is forbidden to fail him; the obligation is reciprocal. Though his enjoyment is restricted, it is assured and this certainty forms his mental foundation. The lot of the unmarried man is different. As he has the right to form attachment wherever inclination leads him, he aspires to everything and is satisfied with nothing. This morbid desire for the infinite which everywhere accompanies anomy may as readily assail this as any other part of our consciousness; it very often assumes a sexual form which was described by Musset. (See *Rolla* and in *Namouna* the portrait of Don Juan.) When one is no longer checked, one becomes unable to check one's self. Beyond experienced pleasures one senses and desires others; if one happens almost to have exhausted the range of what is possible, one dreams of the impossible; one thirsts for the non-existent. How can the feelings not be exacerbated by such unending pursuit? For them to reach that state, one need not even have infinitely multiplied the experiences of love and lived the life of a Don Juan. The humdrum existence of the ordinary bachelor suffices. New hopes constantly awake, only to be deceived, leaving a trail of weariness and disillusionment behind them. How can desire, then, become fixed, being uncertain that it can retain what it attracts; for the anomy is twofold. Just as the person makes no definitive gift of himself, he has defini-

tive title to nothing. The uncertainty of the future plus his own indeterminateness therefore condemns him to constant change. The result of it all is a state of disturbance, agitation and discontent which inevitably increases the possibilities of suicide.

Now divorce implies a weakening of matrimonial regulation. Where it exists, and especially where law and custom permit its excessive practice, marriage is nothing but a weakened simulacrum of itself; it is an inferior form of marriage. It cannot produce its useful effects to the same degree. Its restraint upon desire is weakened; since it is more easily disturbed and superceded, it controls passion less and passion tends to rebel. It consents less readily to its assigned limit. The moral calmness and tranquility which were the husband's strength are less; they are replaced to some extent by an uneasiness which keeps a man from being satisfied with what he has. Besides, he is the less inclined to become attached to his present state as his enjoyment of it is not completely sure: the future is less certain. One cannot be strongly restrained by a chain which may be broken on one side or the other at any moment. One cannot help looking beyond one's own position when the ground underfoot does not feel secure. Hence, in the countries where marriage is strongly tempered by divorce, the immunity of the married man is inevitably less. As he resembles the unmarried under this regime, he inevitably loses some of his own advantages. Consequently, the total number of suicides rises.

But this consequence of divorce is peculiar to the man and does not affect the wife. Woman's sexual needs have less of a mental character because, generally speaking, her mental life is less developed. These needs are more closely related to the needs of the organism, following rather than leading them, and consequently find in them an efficient restraint. Being a more instinctive creature than man, woman has only to follow her instincts to find calmness and peace. She thus does not require so strict a social regulation as marriage, and particularly as monogamic marriage. Even when useful, such a discipline has its inconveniences. By fixing the conjugal state permanently, it prevents all retreat, regardless of consequences. By limiting the horizon, it closes all egress and forbids even legitimate hope. Man himself doubtless suffers from this immutability; but for him the evil is largely compensated by the advantages he gains in other respects. Custom, moreover, grants him certain privileges which allow him in some measure to lessen the strictness of the regime. There is no compensation or relief for the woman. Monogamy is strictly obligatory for her, with no qualification of any sort, and, on the other hand, marriage is not in the same degree useful to her for limiting her desires, which are naturally limited, and for teaching her to be contented with her lot; but it prevents her from changing it if it becomes intolerable. The regulation therefore is a restraint to her without any great advantages. Consequently, everything that makes it more flexible and lighter can only better the wife's situation. So divorce protects her and she has frequent recourse to it.

*   *   *

The state of conjugal anomy, produced by the institution of divorce, thus explains the parallel development of divorces and suicides. Accordingly, the suicides of husbands which increase the number of voluntary deaths in countries where there are many divorces, form a division of anomic suicide. They are not the result of the existence of more bad husbands or bad wives in these societies, that is, of more unhappy households. They result from a moral structure *sui generis,* itself caused by a weakening of matrimonial regulation. This structure, established by marriage, by surviving it produces the exceptional tendency to suicide shown by divorced men. But we do not mean that this enervation of the regulation is created out of whole cloth by the legal establishment of divorce. Divorce is never granted except out of respect for a pre-existing state of customs. If the public conscience had not gradually decided that the indissolubility of the conjugal bond is unreasonable, no legislator would ever have thought of making it easier to break up. Matrimonial anomy may therefore exist in public opinion even without being inscribed in law. On the other hand, only when it has assumed a legal form, can it produce all its consequences. So long as the marriage law is unmodified, it at least serves considerably to restrict the passions; above all, it opposes the increase of the taste for anomy merely by reproof. That is why anomy has pronounced and readily recognizable effects only where it has become a legal institution.

*   *   *

Finally, several facts established in Chapter III[3] of this very book are explained by the theory just set forth and consequently help to verify it.

We saw in that chapter that marriage in France, by itself and irrespective of family, gives man a coefficient of preservation of 1.5. We know now to what this coefficient corresponds. It represents the advantages obtained by a man from the regulative influence exerted upon him by marriage, from the moderation it imposes on his inclinations and from his consequent moral well-being. But at the same time we noted that in the same country the condition of a married woman was, on the contrary, made worse with respect to suicide unless the advent of children corrects the ill effects of marriage for her. We have just stated the reason. Not that man is naturally a wicked and egoistic being whose role in a household is to make his companion suffer. But in France where, until recently, marriage was not weakened by divorce, the inflexible rule it imposed on women was a very heavy, profitless yoke for them. Speaking generally, we now have the cause of that antagonism of the sexes which prevents marriage favoring them equally: their interests are contrary; one needs restraint and the other liberty.

Furthermore, it does seem that at a certain time of life man is affected by marriage in the same way as woman, though for different reasons. If, as we have shown, very young husbands kill themselves much more often than unmarried men of the same age, it is doubtless because their passions are too vehement at that period and too self-confident to be subjected to so severe a rule. Accordingly, this rule seems to them an unendurable obstacle against which their desire dashes and is broken. This is probably why marriage produces all its beneficent effects only when age, supervening, tempers man somewhat and makes him feel the need of discipline.[4]

Finally, in this same Chapter III we saw that where marriage favors the wife rather than the husband, the difference between the sexes is always less than when the reverse is true. This proves that, even in those societies where the status of matrimony is wholly in the woman's favor, it does her less service than it does man where it is he that profits more by it. Woman can suffer more from marriage if it is unfavorable to her than she can benefit by it if it conforms to her interest. This is be-

---

3. Chapter III dealt with Egoistic Suicide [N.D.E.]

4. It is even probable that marriage in itself produces a prophylactic effect only later, after the age of thirty. Actually, until that age, childless married men commit as many suicides in absolute numbers as married men with children, 6.6 from 20 to 25 years, for both, and from 25 to 30 years, 33 for the former and 34 for the latter. Of course, however, marriages with children are much more common than infertile marriages at this period. The tendency of the husbands of the latter marriages to suicide must therefore be several times as strong as that of husbands with children; or very close in intensity to that of unmarried men. Unfortunately we can only form hypotheses on the subject; for, as the census does not give the population of husbands without children for each age, as distinct from husbands with children, we cannot calculate separately the rate of each for each period of life. We can give only the absolute numbers, as we have them from the Ministry of Justice for 1889–91. We have reproduced them in a special table to be found at the close of this work. This gap in census-taking is most regrettable.

cause she has less need of it. This is the assumption of the theory just set forth. The results obtained previously and those arising from the present chapter therefore combine and check each other mutually.

Thus we reach a conclusion quite different from the current idea of marriage and its role. It is supposed to have been originated for the wife, to protect her weakness against masculine caprice. Monogamy, especially, is often represented as a sacrifice made by man of his polygamous instincts, to raise and improve woman's condition in marriage. Actually, whatever historical causes may have made him accept this restriction, he benefits more by it. The liberty he thus renounces could only be a source of torment to him. Woman did not have the same reasons to abandon it and, in this sense, we may say

that by submitting to the same rule, it was she who made a sacrifice.[5]

> 5. The above considerations show that there is a type of suicide the opposite of anomic suicide, just as egoistic and altruistic suicides are opposites. It is the suicide deriving from excessive regulation, that of persons with futures pitilessly blocked and passions violently choked by oppressive discipline. It is the suicide of very young husbands, of the married woman who is childless. So, for completeness' sake, we should set up a fourth suicidal type. But it has so little contemporary importance and examples are so hard to find aside from the cases just mentioned that it seems useless to dwell upon it. However it might be said to have historical interest. Do not the suicides of slaves, said to be frequent under certain conditions (See Corre, *Le crime en pays creoles*, p. 48), belong to this type, or all suicides attributable to excessive physical or moral despotism? To bring out the ineluctible and inflexible nature of a rule against which there is no appeal, and in contrast with the expression "anomy" which has just been used, we might call it *fatalistic suicide*.

2. *Social Patterns and the Gang*

BY FREDERIC M. THRASHER

IN THOSE INTERSTITIAL sections of Chicago where neglect and suppression of boyhood combine to produce gangs, there abound adult social patterns of crime and vice which are naturally reflected in the activities of the unsupervised gang or gang club. In the poverty belt, the deteriorating neighborhood, and the slum there is little understanding of the interests of boys or the situations they meet in everyday life. So far as immigrant communities are concerned the parents were reared for the most part in rural or semirural Old World communities controlled by tradition and with few new and disturbing situations to be met. Their children on the streets of Chicago come into contact with a motley collection of diverse customs on the one hand and new situations on the other. Hence, they have needs of which their parents never heard.

The larger community of gangland is no better able to provide for the boy than is the immigrant family. While the mobility of these areas affords him a considerable range of contacts, these are in the main demoralizing. Attempts of the American

community to deal with the situation have taken the form of settlements and various boys' clubs, but while the work of such agencies has been constructive, they are far too few in number to meet the needs of such a vast territory.

Hence, without wholesome direction for the most part from the home or the larger community, the gang adopts the patterns which have prestige in its own social environment, selecting those which appeal to it and setting them up to be followed by its own members in so far as the group controls them.

THE ISOLATION OF GANGLAND

Some degree of isolation is common to almost every vocational, religious, or cultural group of a large city. Each develops its own sentiments, attitudes, codes, even its own words, which are at best only partially intelligible to others. Between gangland and the conventionalized American community exists this barrier of unsympathetic social blindness, this inability of either to enter understandingly into the life of the other. The social world of the gang boy suffers from this isolation and the boy himself lacks contacts which would help prepare him for participation in the activities of a conventional social order.

Reprinted from Frederic M. Thrasher, *The Gang* (2d rev. ed.; Chicago: University of Chicago Press, 1927), pp. 252–56, 265, 277–79, 280, 281, 284, 286, 291–92, 293–95, 297–98, 304–6, with the permission of the author.

A large part of this isolation is due to the fact that in Chicago he usually lives in an immigrant colony, which is itself an isolated social world. Immigrant participation in American life is not encouraged by the American community. Contacts with Americans are usually superficial and disheartening and for the child are limited to certain official contact with school teachers, employers, or police. It often happens also that the immigrant community resists Americanization in order to exalt the values of a nationality that has been oppressed abroad. Hence, the children of the foreign born do not come into contact with the best in American life, but, when they escape parental control and follow their own impulses, become Americanized only with reference to our vices.

The significance of this lack of cultural communion with the world at large can hardly be overemphasized in explaining the life and organization of the gang. Almost everything—history, geography, art, music, and government—that is the common knowledge of the schoolboy of the middle classes, is entirely beyond the ken and experience of the gang boy. He moves only in his own universe and other regions are clothed in nebulous mystery. He is only vaguely aware of them, for they rarely cut his plane. There are exceptions, of course, for some gangs are less isolated than others, but this description is characteristic of the great majority.

As a result, the gang boy does not participate in civic affairs, nor does he have much part in the life of his own isolated community. He knows little of the outside world except its exteriors. He views it usually as a collection of influences that would suppress him and curtail his activities with laws and police, cells and bars. In one way or another he is denied effective access to the larger cultural heritages of the dominant social order.

SOCIAL PATTERNS AND THE MORALITY OF THE GANG

In developing their own organization, gang boys cannot go beyond their experiences, and hence their codes and chosen activities must be studied with reference to the moral codes and activities they meet in the communities where they live. Gang morality develops from the interpretation or definition which the gang, in the light of its previous experience, puts upon events.

The definition of the situation, which in its social aspects represents morality, has been stated by William I. Thomas. Every self-determined act is performed in the light of the individual's examination and deliberation; this results in the individual definition of the situation. Definitions of the situation have already been established, however, by the groups into which the child is born and there is little chance to change these to meet individual whims. There is always, therefore, a conflict between individual wishes and the definitions, which have been worked out as the result of social experience for the safety of the group. Thus moral codes arise to curb the individual pursuit of pleasure. "Morality is thus the generally accepted definition of the situation, whether expressed in public opinion and unwritten law, in a formal legal code, or in religious commandments and prohibitions."[1]

The definition of the situation for the gang boy must emanate largely from the disorderly life of the economic, moral, and cultural frontiers of which gangland is a manifestation. The problem of gang morality, therefore, may be stated largely in terms of the patterns which prevail in the immediate social environment.

The mechanism by which the gang boy molds his life according to the patterns he knows by experience is not wholly one of rational choice. The process is common to all social life and is found in the adoption by children of the ways of their parents. It is the same unreflective process by which the child builds up the verbal habit organization represented in language.

Likewise, the play of children generally tends to follow the adult patterns. In Spain, for example, the boys play at bullfighting rather than at baseball, while the Ku Klux Klan has had its infantile counterpart in the play of American children.[2]

So, also, the exploits of the gang tend to follow patterns in its own social world. The underlying principles and mechanisms of gang behavior are the same for all groups of this type, but there are sharp contrasts in the nature of gang activities in different environments. This is strikingly brought out in comparing the gangs of a lumbering community with those of Chicago.

*   *   *

INFORMAL EDUCATION

Many writers have conceived of education in too narrow a sense. The effective education of the boy, so far as the development of character and personality are concerned, takes place far more vitally outside the schoolroom in those informal contacts which escape conventional supervision. These are periods of freedom, and it is probably this very fact of spontaneous and self-directed activity that makes

1. William I. Thomas, *The Unadjusted Girl*, pp. 42–43.
2. "Cyril Stoddart, ten years old, is under physician's care, suffering from shock and minor injuries, and police are hunting for a gang of small boys who, wearing masks and said to be playing Ku Klux Klan Monday night, attacked the boy, tied him to a telephone pole, and gagged him. He was rescued after being tied up for three hours."— *Chicago Tribune*, September 27, 1925.

them so much more effective than the formal contacts that are presumed to be the truly educative ones. The education of the street, to which practically every boy in gangland is subject, is basic in the development of tastes and habits, ambitions and ideals.

Group Control in the Gang

Although gang activities and gang morality are, in part at least, a reflection of the gang's disorganized social world, they find a supplementary explanation in the conception of the gang as an elementary society, which, unhampered by conventional controls, tends to develop its own organization and codes in an independent or spontaneous fashion. The codes of the gang are enforced upon its members in a variety of ways—some definitely directed, others almost entirely unreflective. Thus, the gang defines the situation for its members (illustrated in the initiation of newcomers and "pledges" or probationers) and secures more or less harmonious group action.

THE UNITY OF THE GANG

The execution of collective enterprises and activities necessitates harmony and mutual aid within the gang. The following are types of corporate behavior which require unity and co-operation.

Gang fighting	Games
Outwitting enemies	Predatory activities
Raiding	Playing pranks
Robbing	Maintaining club-
Defending hang-out	rooms
Pursuing	Planning
Getting shagged	Discussing
Attacking	Junking
Athletic contests	Building something
Dances	Vandalism
Picnics	Criminal Projects
Camping	Charitable enterprises
Hiking and ranging	

Effective collective action and continued corporate existence require that the gang control its members. Hence, the group, both through planned and unreflective methods, attempts to incorporate them, to subordinate each to the demands of the whole, and to discipline the unruly. Although the gang is not always unified and harmonious within,[3] discord is usually eliminated by the conditions which collective action imposes.

This unity of the gang rests upon a certain consensus or community of habits, sentiments, and attitudes, which enable the gang members to feel as one, to subordinate themselves and their personal wishes to the gang purposes, and to accept the common objectives, beliefs, and symbols of the gang as their own. The *esprit de corps* of the gang, which is characteristic even of the diffuse type, is evident in many of its collective enterprises—in the enthusiasm of talk-fests, in its play together, its dances, its drinking bouts.

MORALE AND SOLIDARITY

A stable unity does not develop in the diffuse type of gang, however, until it becomes solidified through conflict. It learns eventually to formulate a policy and pursue a more or less consistent course of action despite deterring circumstances. Then it may be said to have acquired morale, which reinforces fellowship and enthusiasm in time of crisis.

* * *

The Flannigan Gang

The Flannigan gang, composed of boys between fourteen and sixteen, has as its natural leader, Edward Flannigan, the best athlete and fighter in the gang. When the neighborhood recreational center advertised for boys to play on its baseball team, the whole gang reported along with other boys. It was decided to elect a captain and let him choose his team. Flannigan was elected and proceeded to choose his players all from his own gang. When remonstrated with he said that these other boys were members of other gangs, and if the social center was not satisfied with his players, the whole gang would quit....

During the winter the Railroad gang tried to use their rendezvous located in an old house near the tracks. This provoked a fight with brickbats, stones, etc., which resulted in a victory for the Flannigans. The boys were intensely loyal, standing by each other in a fight or backing those of their fellows who got into trouble. At their meetings at the center, none of the gang would express an opinion until the leader had had an opportunity to speak; then the gang accepted his opinion and voted accordingly.[4]

This superior solidarity creates a serious problem for the church, settlement, playground, or similar agency which attempts to use, to incorporate, or to supervise the gang. It is sometimes so well developed as to wreck a larger conventionalized organization in which it becomes a unit.

* * *

PLANNING AND CO-OPERATION

The unity of the group is further aided by the individual slogans, words, traditions, and so on, which

---

3. Compare Charles H. Cooley, *Social Organization*, pp. 24–25. Cooley presents in his statement an entirely too idealistic view with reference to the behavior of the average gang.

4. From a manuscript by a former member of the group.

are developed by the gang and which symbolize in common terms its objectives. The gang's planning must be carried on in terms of the common meanings which these symbols make possible. The name of the gang is of particular significance as a means of social control. It affords a common stimulus or value to which all members of the gang may respond with common sentiments. It is the rallying and unifying stimulus in a conflict situation. Since each member of the group is more or less identified with the group name, it becomes a matter of common pride to defend and exalt it.

*   *   *

THE CODE OF THE GANG

Every gang tends to develop its own code of conduct, of which its members are more or less aware and which may be more or less rigidly enforced upon them. The code of the gang is in part reflected from the patterns of behavior in its own social world, in part the result of the development of primary group sentiments, and in part the product of the individual group in its own special environment. The following cases illustrate these three factors, as well as other points with reference to group control.

*   *   *

A Gang Code

My gang, which had about ten members, had as its main object the stealing of ice-cream from the parties attended by the girls of our acquaintance. The leader was a hard rock.

The first principle and most important rule of the group was not to squeal on another member.

The gang swiped ice-cream, not because its members could not afford to buy this luxury, but because we enjoyed the excitement. One evening we managed to get away with a gallon can. Not having anything to eat it with, we used silver dollars and the crystals of our watches. For this escapade a fine of $25 was assessed against the member of our party who was caught and dragged into police court. He did not give our names, but we came to his rescue and paid the fine.

Another rule of the gang was that each member was to carry a package of Duke's Mixture tobacco in his shirt pocket with the tag always hanging out. That I did not smoke made no difference; I had to have the "makins" if some other member of the gang happened to want them.

We had a strict rule against any associations with girls.

Another rule was to protect the property of a widow and a blind couple on Hallowe'en. We not only observed this ourselves but we kept other gangs in line also.

The gang was completely broken up by being expelled bodily from school. One of the boys had put glue on the chair of the manual training teacher. He was punished. In retaliation the gang "stacked" the high school; that is, put all movable objects together into one huge pile.

*   *   *

MECHANISMS OF CONTROL IN THE GANG

The individual member of a gang is almost wholly controlled by the force of group opinion. The way everybody in the gang does or thinks is usually sufficient justification or dissuasion for the gang boy. In such cases he is really feeling the pressure of public opinion in that part of his own social world which is most vital to him and in which he wishes to maintain status.[5] This sort of sanction will make almost any kind of conduct right or wrong within the group. It will also make a boy one person when under group influence and quite another when apart from it.

Opinion in the gang manifests its pressure in the variety of mechanisms through which group control is exerted such as applause, preferment, and hero-worshiping as well as ridicule, scorn, and ostracism. Physical punishment is not uncommon. The leader has considerable power over his subordinates so long as he does not abuse it. Many of the influences that determine the behavior of the gang and its members, however, are unplanned and unreflective, and, as in the crowd, arise out of the very nature of collective action.

PUNISHMENT

One of the chief mechanisms of control in the gang is the fear of violence or physical punishment. In the fraternity this takes the form of "hazing," ducking in cold water, and paddling, especially for probationers. In the gang the member who has broken the code may be subjected to a beating or in extreme cases may be marked for death.

*   *   *

RIDICULE AND APPLAUSE

Another important mechanism of social control within the gang is ridicule, commonly known to the boys as "razzing." It includes "making fun" of the nonconformer, "riding" him, teasing him, mocking him, laughing at him, and calling him by opprobrious epithets. It varies all the way from the subtlest allusions in conversation, the sliest winks and titters, to the coarsest pantomime, the crudest horse laugh, and the most stinging sarcasm. Only one who has been made the target for it by some

5. See W. I. Thomas, *The Unadjusted Girl*, p. 32. One reason the individual responds to social control is that he has a fundamental wish for status, which society alone is in a position to confer.

intimate group in which he has had to live can understand its constant and merciless pressure in the direction of enforcing conformity. This is one of the chief weapons in the hands of the American fraternity, the German "corporation," and the gang of every nationality in assimilating new members.

The use of epithets of derision constitutes one compelling element in razzing. The sort that are most effective for control are the so-called "humilific." The gang boy has his own epithets for those who fail to measure up to his standards. The coward receives the hated appellation of "yellow" or "yellow belly." The traitor is a "snitcher," or "stooler." The boy who hangs back or is not game is a "baby." The boy who plays with girls or assumes any niceties of dress or behavior is a "sissie." A real gang boy would prefer to take almost any punishment rather than to be called by one of these names; for to be so called is an indication that he has lost caste in the group which is most vital to his happiness. These collective representations of the gang get their meaning from actual life situations; like the social virtues in the gang, they are defined in interaction.

Ridicule defines what the boy must not do if he wishes to maintain his status. There is, however, a positive method of control which contributes to his desire for recognition; this is applause and hero worshiping. To gain the praise and flattery of his pals and such rewards as prizes, preferment, honors, and leadership, the gang boy conforms to types of behavior which are consonant with the ideals and policies of the group.

*   *   *

THE SUBTLER FORMS OF CONTROL

Interpretations by members of a gang of the more delicate and subtle changes in the behavior of other members may be regarded as important for crowd control. It is by the reading of these less perceptible signs that one person is able to respond to the sentiment and attitude of another. In a face-to-face group changes in facial expression, slight gestures, and the like, although largely in the field of unverbalized reactions, enable an individual to sense a situation instantly. Thus, they define the situation and promote rapport.

The gang, as an intimate primary group, develops an excellent basis for control through rapport. Life together over a more or less extended period results in a common social heritage shared by every member of the group. Common experience of an intimate and often an intense nature prepares the way for close sympathy—for mutual interpretation of subtle signs indicating changes in sentiment or atti-

tude. Collective representations embodied in signs, symbols (such as the badge in a fraternity), secret grips and words, and the argot of the group, all promote mutual responsiveness in the more subtle forms of communication. Peculiarities of dress or physique serve the same purpose; for example, a peculiar sort of hair cut as identifying members of a certain gang or the wearing of certain types of blouses or ties.

This rapport is sometimes so complete in a gang (and in a college fraternity also) that one receives the impression of interpenetration of personalities, if such a mystical conception is permissible. The consensus of habits, sentiments, and attitudes becomes so thoroughly unified in some of these cases that individual differences seem swallowed up.

*   *   *

THE LIMITATIONS OF GANG MORALITY

Certain writers have been somewhat too idealistic with regard to the educational value of the gang for the boy. They have emphasized the fact that the gang teaches its members the great human virtues. Some have even suggested that the gang is a desirable institution for the boy apart from all supervision.

VALUES IN LACK OF SUPERVISION

I have the theory that the gang develops the boy in many important ways. This sort of spontaneous growth is so valuable to his personality, that I am not sure that there should ever be any supervision. The boys learn to settle their differences in an equitable way. In this way the group develops the boy into a real person. I think every boy should have his gang.[6]

Other workers with boys have concluded that these so-called "guerrilla virtues" are a great asset to any social agency that would turn the energies of the gang into wholesome channels.

As preparation for life in a larger world, however, it is doubtful if the gang as such does enough. The gang virtues which have been so exalted as ideal patterns for humanity at large hold only for members of the in-group and the rest of the world may quite normally be looked upon as lawful prey. The sense of fair play which tends to govern relationships of the boys to each other does not extend to outsiders.

The ethnocentrism which marked the small groups of primitive life and tribal society, is also characteristic of the gang. The Greek-letter fraternity, which is akin to the gang in many respects, presents a good example of the same thing. A current attitude among members of such societies is

---

6. Interview with a leading Chicago boys' worker.

expressed in such words as "We belong; we are the Greeks; we are the cultured. You do not belong; you are the barbarians; you are rude and untutored."

In another sense, moreover, the gang does too much; for along with the virtues, it inculcates in its members the primary-group vices. Revenge, which is characteristic of many detached primary groups,

is the law of the gang. The amity which prevails among members of the same group is often accompanied by this antithetical sentiment of hatred toward outsiders. In extreme cases this manifests itself in the most abandoned types of retaliation and often does not stop short of murder. In the more vicious gangs there develops a lust for blood revenge.

III–THE MOTIVATION OF DEVIANCE

---

1. *Three Types of Personality*

BY WILLIAM I. THOMAS AND FLORIAN ZNANIECKI

THE INDIVIDUAL does not find passively ready situations exactly similar to past situations; he must consciously define every situation as similar to certain past situations, if he wants to apply to it the same solution applied to those situations. And this is what society expects him to do when it requires of him a stable life-organization; it does not want him to react instinctively in the same way to the same material conditions, but to construct reflectively similar social situations even if material conditions vary. The uniformity of behavior it tends to impose upon the individual is not a uniformity of organic habits but of consciously followed *rules*. The individual, in order to control social reality for his needs, must develop not series of uniform reactions, but general *schemes* of situations; his life-organization is a set of rules for definite situations, which may be even expressed in abstract formulas. Moral principles, legal prescription, economic forms, religious rites, social customs, etc., are examples of schemes.

The definiteness of attitudes attained in character and the corresponding schematization of social data in life-organization admit, however, a wide scale of gradation with regard to one point of fundamental importance,—the range of possibilities of

Reprinted from William I. Thomas and Florian Znaniecki, *The Polish Peasant in Europe and America* in *Social Behavior and Personality: Contributions of W. I. Thomas to Theory and Social Research*, ed. Edmund H. Volkart (Social Science Research Council, 1951), pp. 158–70, with the permission of the Social Science Research Council.

further development remaining open to the individual after the stabilization. This depends on the nature of the attitudes involved in the character and of the schemes of life-organization, and also on the way in which both are unified and systematized. And here three typical cases can be distinguished.

The set of attitudes constituting the character may be such as practically to exclude the development of any new attitude in the given conditions of life, because the reflective attitudes of an individual have attained so great a fixity that he is accessible to only a certain class of influences—those constituting the most permanent part of his social milieu. The only possibilities of evolution then remaining open to the individual are the slow changes brought by age in himself and by time in his social milieu, or a change of conditions so radical as to destroy at once the values to whose influence he was adapted and presumably his own character. This is the type which has found its expression in literature as the "Philistine." It is opposed to the "Bohemian," whose possibilities of evolution are not closed, simply because his character remains unformed. Some of his temperamental attitudes are in their primary form, others may have become intellectualized but remain unrelated to each other, do not constitute a stable and systematized set, and do not exclude any new attitude, so that the individual remains open to any and all influences. As opposed to both these types we find the third type of the individual whose character is settled and organized but involves the possibility and even the necessity of evolution, because the reflective attitudes constituting it include a tendency to change, regulated by plans of productive activity, and the individual remains open to such influences as will be in line of his preconceived development. This is the type of the creative individual.

A parallel distinction must be made with regard to the schemes of social situations constituting the life-organization. The ability to define every situation which the individual meets in his experience is not necessarily a proof of intellectual superiority; it may mean simply a limitation of claims and interests and a stability of external conditions which do not allow any radically new situations to be noticed, so that a few narrow schemes are sufficient to lead the individual through life, simply because he does not see problems on his way which demand new schemes. This type of schemes constitutes the common stock of social traditions in which every class of situation is defined in the same way once and forever. These schemes harmonize perfectly with the Philistine's character and therefore the Philistine is always a conformist, usually accepting social tradition in its most stable elements. Of course every important and unexpected change in the conditions of life results for such an individual in a disorganization of activity. As long as he can he still applies the old schemes, and up to a certain point his old definition of new situations may be sufficient to allow him to satisfy his claims if the latter are low, although he cannot compete with those who have higher claims and more efficient schemes. But as soon as the results of his activity become unsuccessful even in his own eyes, he is entirely lost; the situation becomes for him completely vague and undetermined, he is ready to accept any definition that may be suggested to him and is unable to keep any permanent line of activity. This is the case with any conservative and intellectually limited member of a stable community, whatever may be his social class, when he finds himself transferred into another community or when his own group undergoes some rapid and sudden change.

Opposed to this type we find an undetermined variation of schemes in the life of all the numerous species of the Bohemian. The choice of the scheme by a Bohemian depends on his momentary standpoint, and this may be determined either by some outburst of a primary temperamental attitude or by some isolated character-attitude which makes him subject to some indiscriminately accepted influence. In either case inconsistency is the essential feature of his activity. But on the other hand he shows a degree of adaptability to new conditions

quite in contrast with the Philistine, though his adaptability is only provisional and does not lead to a new systematic life-organization.

But adaptability to new situations and diversity of interest are even compatible with a consistency of activity superior to that which tradition can give if the individual builds his life-organization not upon the presumption of the immutability of his sphere of social values, but upon the tendency to modify and to enlarge it according to some definite aims. These may be purely intellectual or aesthetic, and in this case the individual searches for new situations to be defined simply in order to widen and to perfect his knowledge or his aesthetic interpretation and appreciation; or his aims may be "practical," in any sense of the term—hedonistic, economical, political, moral, religious—and then the individual searches for new situations in order to widen the control of his environment, to adapt to his purposes a continually increasing sphere of social reality. This is the creative man.

The Philistine, the Bohemian and the creative man are the three fundamental forms of personal determination toward which social personalities tend in their evolution. None of these forms is ever completely and absolutely realized by a human individual in all lines of activity; there is no Philistine who lacks completely Bohemian tendencies, no Bohemian who is not a Philistine in certain respects, no creative man who is fully and exclusively creative and does not need some Philistine routine in certain lines to make creation in other lines practically possible, and some Bohemianism in order to be able to reject occasionally such fixed attitudes and social regulations as hinder his progress, even if he should be unable at the time to substitute for them any positive organization in the given line. But while pure Philistinism, pure Bohemianism and pure creativeness represent only ideal limits of personal evolution, the process of personal evolution grows to be more and more definite as it progresses, so that, while the form which a human personality will assume is not determined in advance, either by the individual's temperament or by his social milieu, his future becomes more and more determined by the very course of his development; he approaches more and more to Philistinism, Bohemianism or creativeness and thereby his possibilities of becoming something else continually diminish.

These three general types—limits of personal evolution—include, of course, an indefinite number of variations, depending on the nature of the attitudes by which characters are constituted and on the schemes composing the life-organization of social individuals. If we wished therefore to classify human personalities on the ground of the limits of development to which they tend, our task would be very difficult, if not impossible, for we should have to take characters and life-organizations separately in all their varieties into account. In each of these three fundamental types similar characters may correspond to indefinitely varying life-organizations and similar life-organizations to indefinitely varying characters. But, as we have seen, the problem is to study characters and life-organizations not in their static abstract form, but in their dynamic concrete development. And both character and life-organization—the subjective and the objective side of the personality—develop together. For an attitude can become stabilized as a part of the reflective character only under the influence of a scheme of behavior, and *vice versa,* the construction or acceptance of a scheme demands that an attitude be stabilized as a part of character. Every process of personal evolution consists, therefore, in a complex evolutionary series in which social schemes, acting upon pre-existing attitudes, produce new attitudes in such a way that the latter represent a determination of the temperamental tendencies with regard to the social world, a realization in a conscious form of the character-possibilities which the individual brings with him; and these new attitudes, with their intellectual continuity, acting upon pre-existing sets of social values in the sphere of individual experiences produce new values in such a way that every production of a value represents at the same time a definition of some vague situation, and this is a step toward the constitution of some consistent scheme of behavior. In the continual interaction between the individual and his environment we can say neither that the individual is the product of his milieu nor that he produces his milieu; or rather, we can say both. For the individual can indeed develop only under the influence of his environment, but on the other hand during his development he modifies this environment by defining situations and solving them according to his wishes and tendencies. His influence upon the environment may be scarcely noticeable socially, may have little importance for others, but it is important for himself, since, as we have said, the world in which he lives is not the world as society or the scientific observer sees it but as he sees it himself. In various cases we may find various degrees of dependence upon the environment, conditioned by the primary qualities of the individual, and the type of social organization. The individual is relatively dependent upon society in his evolution if he develops mainly such attitudes as lead to dependence, which is then due both to his temperamental dispositions and to the fact that the organization of society is such as to enforce by various

means individual subjection; he is relatively independent if in his evolution he develops attitudes producing independence, which again results from certain primary tendencies determined by a social organization which favors individual spontaneity. And thus both dependence and independence are gradual products of an evolution which is due originally to reciprocal interaction; the individual cannot become exclusively dependent upon society without the help of his own disposition, nor become independent of society without the help of social influences. The fundamental principles of personal evolution must be sought therefore both in the individual's own nature and in his social milieu.

We find, indeed, two universal traits manifested in all individual attitudes, instinctive or intellectual, which form the condition of both development and conservatism. In the reflex system of all the higher organisms are two powerful tendencies which in their most distinct and explicit form manifest themselves as curiosity and fear. Without curiosity, that is, and interest in new situations in general, the animal would not live; to neglect the new situation might mean either that he was about to be eaten or that he was missing his chance for food. And fear with its contrary tendency to avoid certain experiences for the sake of security is equally essential to life. To represent these two permanent tendencies as they become parts of character in the course of the social development of a personality we shall use the terms ("*desire for new experience*" and "*desire for stability.*") These two tendencies in every permanent attitude manifest themselves in the rhythmical form which conscious life assumes in every line. When consciousness embraces only a short span of activities, the rhythm expresses itself in the alternation of single wishes or appetites with repose. The satisfaction of hunger or of sexual desire and the subsequent wish for uninterrupted calm are the most general examples. On a higher level these tendencies manifest themselves with regard to much more complex and longer series of facts. The desire for stability extends to a whole period of regular alternations of activity and rest from which new experiences are relatively excluded; the desire for new experience finds its expression in the break of such a whole line of regulated activities. And the range and complexity of both stability and change may have many degrees. Thus, for example, stability may mean the possibility of a single series of satisfactions of hunger in a certain restaurant, of a week's relation with an individual of the other sex, of a few days' stay in one place during travel, of a certain kind of work in an office; or it may lie in the possibility of such an organization of money-affairs as gives the certainty of always getting food, of a permanent marriage-relation, settling permanently in one place, a life career, etc. And new experience may mean change of restaurant, change of the temporary sexual relation, change of the kind of work within the same office, the resuming of travel, the acquiring of wealth, getting a divorce, developing a Don Juan attitude toward women, change of career or speciality, development of amateur or sporting interests, etc.

On the individual side, then, alternation of the desire for new experience and of the desire for security is the fundamental principle of personal evolution, as including both the development of a character and of a life-organization. On the social side the essential point of this evolution lies in the fact that the individual living in society has to fit into a pre-existing social world, to take part in the hedonistic, economic, political, religious, moral, aesthetic, intellectual activities of the group. For these activities the group has objective *systems,* more or less complex sets of schemes, organized either by traditional association or with a conscious regard to the greatest possible efficiency of the result, but with only a secondary, or even with no interest in the particular desires, abilities and experiences of the individuals who have to perform these activities. The latter feature of the social systems results, of course, from the fact that the systems have to regulate identically the activities of many individuals at once, and that they usually last longer than the period of activity of an individual, passing from generation to generation. The gradual establishment of a determined relation between these systems which constitute together the social organization of the civilized life of a group, and individual character and life-organization in the course of their progressive formation, is the central problem of the social control of personal evolution. And social control—which, when applied to personal evolution, may be called "social education"—manifests itself also in the duality of two opposite tendencies: the tendency to suppress in the course of personal evolution, any attitudes or values which are either directly in disharmony with the existing social organization or seem to be the starting-points of lines of genesis which are expected to lead to socially disharmonious consequences; and the tendency to develop by adequately influencing personal evolution features of character and schemes of situations required by the existing social systems.

There is, of course, no pre-existing harmony whatever between the individual and the social factors of personal evolution, and the fundamental tendencies of the individual are always in some disaccordance with the fundamental tendencies of social control. Personal evolution is always a struggle between the individual and society—a struggle for self-expression on the part of the individual, for his subjection on the part of society—and it is in the total course of this struggle that the personality—not as a static "essence" but as a dynamic, continually evolving set of activities—manifests and constructs itself. The relative degree of the desire for new experience and the desire for stability necessary for and compatible with the progressive incorporation of a personality into a social organization is dependent on the nature of individual interests and of the social systems. Thus, different occupations allow for more or less change, as in the cases of the artist and the factory workman; and a many-sided dilettante needs and can obtain more new experiences than a specialist; single life usually makes more new experiences along certain lines possible and demands less stabilization than married life; political co-operation with the conservative part of a group brings less change than taking part in a revolutionary movement. And in modern society in general there is an increasing tendency to appreciate change, as compared with the appreciation of stability in the ancient and mediaeval worlds. For every system within a given group and at a certain time there is a maximum and a minimum of change and of stability permissible and required. The widening of this range and the increase of the variety of systems are, of course, favorable to individual self-expression within the socially permitted limits. Thus, the whole process of development of the personality as ruled in various proportions by the desire for new experience and the desire for stability on the individual side, by the tendency to suppress and the tendency to develop personal possibilities on the social side, includes the following parallel and interdependent processes:

(1) Determination of the character on the ground of the temperament;

(2) Constitution of a life-organization which permits a more or less complete objective expression of the various attitudes included in the character;

(3) Adaptation of the character to social demands put upon the personality;

(4) Adaptation of individual life-organization to social organization.

1. We know already that the development of temperamental attitudes into character-attitudes can assume many different directions, so that, if the proper influences were exercised from the beginning, a wide range of characters, theoretically any possible character, might be evolved out of any temperament. But the directions which evolution must take in order to produce a determined atti-

tude out of a pre-existing one become more and more limited with the fixation of character; in a systematically unified "consistent" character every fixed attitude would exclude the contrary one, and some degree of consistency appears as soon as the character begins to be formed. With the progressive evolution of the personality the means of developing a given character become therefore less and less numerous and it may be finally practically impossible to carry the development of certain attitudes to their end, for the process necessary to develop them might be so long and complicated as to be impracticable. Thus, it might be possible to produce a sweet and even a meek character out of an irascible temperament by developing first, for example, a strong altruistic disposition, to which in turn the way might lead through the desire for social response. But if in the development of the personality other attitudes were gradually formed contrary to the desire for response or to altruism, such as desire for solitude, pride, etc., the original irascibility might be still subdued by other influences, but certainly it would be impossible to produce sweetness. Assuming now that we are determined to produce the latter, then we must be careful not to allow any temperamental possibilities to realize themselves which may be contrary either to this attitude itself or to any of the attitudes which the individual must evolve in order to attain this stage. The more opposition there is between the original temperamental attitude and the one that we want to develop, the longer the process, the more the intermediary stages to be passed, and the greater the number of necessary suppressions.

But in actual social life the mechanism of suppression is not used in this detailed way and the motives of suppression are not in the main those which we have outlined. The possible attitudes which the members of the group wish to suppress are usually those whose direct expression in action would, in the social opinion, be harmful, rather than those which are contrary to the development of other useful ones. The control exercised by the group is negative much more than positive, tends to destroy much more than to construct, for reasons which we shall investigate presently. And even when it wishes to construct, it often assumes, implicitly or explicitly, that when an undesirable attitude is suppressed, the contrary desirable one will develop. And, of course, if there is in individual temperament a possiblity of the desirable attitude, this supposition may be true. But the point is that by suppressing an attitude, whether for the sake of some other more desirable one or through fear of its undesirable manifestations, we suppress at the same time all the possible lines of a further evolu-

tion that may have started from the suppressed attitude and resulted in something very desirable. The earlier the suppression, the greater the number of possibilities destroyed and the greater the resulting limitation of the personality. Well-known examples are the suppression of the adventurous spirit and of the critical tendency in children.

The mechanism of suppression is double. A temperamental possibility not yet conscious is suppressed if given no opportunity to manifest itself in any situation, for only through such manifestations can it become explicit and be evolved into a character-attitude. This form of suppression is attained by an isolation of the individual from all experiences that may give stimulation to endeavors to define situations by the undesirable tendency. The suppression of sexual attitudes and of free thought in religious matters are good examples of this mechanism. The second course, used when an attitude is already manifested, in order to prevent its further development and stabilization, is suppression by negative sanction; a negative value—punishment or blame—is attached to the manifestation of the attitude, and by lack of manifestation the attitude cannot evolve. But both mechanisms are in fact only devices for postponing the development of the undesirable attitude until a character is fixed including the contrary attitudes, and it is only this fixation which does suppress the undesirable attitude definitively.

But suppression is not always a necessary consequence of the evolution of character from temperament. Attitudes need to be suppressed only when they are inadequately qualified and thus interfere with more desirable ones when meeting in the same field of social experience. For example, unqualified spirit of adventure and a tendency to regulated life, unqualified sexual desire and claims of social respectability, unqualified wish for pleasures and recognition of familial obligations are, indeed, more or less irreconcilable with each other. But one of the fundamental points of the development of character from temperament is precisely the qualification of attitudes with respect to definite social contents, and if this qualification begins in time and the attitudes are determined with sufficient precision, there may be no opposition between them at all and none of them needs to be socially harmful.

The principle that permits the harmonizing of opposite attitudes without impairing the consistency of character is, in general, distinction of applicability of attitudes. The situations involved must, of course, be classed in advance so that certain features of a given complex of values may be a sufficient criterion for the application of one attitude or another. Many criteria are given by social tradition; the conventionalization of certain attitudes in certain circumstances permits of their preservation together with others to which they are opposed. The criteria are of various kinds. They may consist, for example, in a time-limitation. Vacation is considered a time when some of the spirit of adventure suppresssed during the year may be expressed. Or it may be a limitation in space, as when certain behavior is permitted at a certain place, like the dropping of social forms and the relative freedom of relations between the sexes at bathing resorts. Sometimes the occasion is ceremonial, as in the hilarity of evening parties and the drinking at social meetings. On other occasions a certain attitude is assumed to be excluded from situations to which without the conventionalization it would apply. Thus, the sexual attitude is theoretically not applied to passages in the Bible bearing on sexual questions, or to an artist's model, or in medical studies and investigations and in legal works. More important cases of conventionalization are found when a whole line of organized activities, with the corresponding attitudes, is permitted under circumstances carefully circumscribed and usually designated by some social symbol. Thus, marriage is a conventionalization of the woman's—to some extent also the man's—system of sexual attitudes, besides being a familial organization. War is the conventionalization of murder, plundering and arson, diplomacy a conventionalization of cheating and treachery. Freedom of theoretic investigation has attained a social conventionalization in the physical sciences but not yet in human sciences—philosophy, sociology, history, history of literature, economics.

In every case the dividing line between the fields of applicability of two contrary attitudes can be drawn by or for the individual even if no general rules of division are laid down by society. The only difficulty is that every attitude if allowed to develop freely tends to an exclusive domination of the whole field of experience to which it can be applied. Of course this is not true of every attitude of every individual, but there is probably not a single attitude which does not in somebody tend to assume such an importance as to conflict with others. The principle of right measure and harmony of virtues, developed by Greek ethics, expressed precisely the need of such a limitation of attitudes. But it is evident that with a proper limitation no attitude needs to be suppressed and all the temperamental possibilities can be allowed to develop without leading to internal contradictions and impairing the consistency of character. The principle through which any attitude can be made not only socially harm-

less but even useful, is *sublimation*. It consists in turning the attitude exclusively toward situations that have in them an element endowed with social sacredness. We cannot analyze the latter concept now; we shall do it another time. At present it is enough to point out that an object is socially sacred when it provokes in members of the group an attitude of reverence and when it can be profaned in the eyes of social opinion, by being connected with some other object. There are many degrees of social sacredness; an object that may appear as sacred in comparison with another may be itself a source of profanation of a third. Thus, business has a feature of sacredness which becomes manifest when it is interfered with by frivolous things like drinking or the company of women of the demi-monde; but its sacredness is not very high since it can easily appear as profane when it interferes with scientific or religious interests. And even so highly sacred an object as a scientific congress or a formal religious meeting may seem profane as compared with a particularly eager and difficult pursuit by the individual of the solution of a great theoretic problem, the ecstasy of a mystic, or the preservation of the society itself from destruction or devastation by an alien enemy. And of course the degree of sacredness attached to different objects varies from group to group and from time to time, and some still current contrarieties, such as the fight for superiority of sacredness between art and morality, religion and science, patriotism and internationalism, show that in certain lines a general understanding even within a single group may be hardly possible at a given moment. But in spite of all these variations of sacredness there are, from this point of view, higher and lower forms possible for every attitude, dependent on the relative degree of sacredness of the situations which it defines. Thus, the spirit of adventure may manifest itself in a criminal's career, in a cow-boy's or trapper's life, in the activity of a detective, in geographical or ethnographical exploration; the desire for money, in stealing, gambling, "living by one's wits," commercial activity, great industrial organization; the sexual attitude may manifest itself in association with prostitutes, in relations, short but not devoid of individualization, with many girls and married women, in an ordinary marriage for the sake of the regulation of sexual life; in romantic love, in artistic creation, in religious mysticism. Even such attitudes as seem essentially harmful, as the desire of shedding blood, may become sublimated; the butcher's activity represents a lower degree of sublimation, surgery the highest.

To sublimate an attitude we must develop an appreciation of its higher forms, which then becomes a factor of evolution and eventually results in a depreciation of its lower manifestations. The feeling of social sacredness can arise in the individual only in close contact with a group which has definite standards of sacredness; more than any other feeling it needs a continual and permeating influence of social opinion and is likely to be lost without the support of the environment. But the social group does not always provide ready methods for the sublimation of all the attitudes which need this stimulation; its standards of sacredness are incomplete, often contradictory, and not extended to *all* the values to which they ought to be applied. The individual's own initiative must therefore supplement the social influences. When the feeling of social sacredness is once strongly developed with regard to a larger number of values the individual will be able to sublimate spontaneously social attitudes whose sublimation is not provided for by social tradition, by extending old standards of social sacredness to new values or by creating new standards. And as he needs social support to maintain his new valuations, he will try to convert his environment, to impart to others his reverence for things whose sacredness they have failed to recognize.

The principles of discrimination of situations to which contrary attitudes should be applied and of sublimation of socially forbidden attitudes allow a rich and consistent character to develop without suppressions from any source, temperamental or social. The individual spontaneously tries to preserve his temperamental attitudes, and as he can do this only by removing contradictions between attitudes contending for supremacy and by sublimating attitudes that can find no expression in his milieu, and since society never gives him all the ready conventions and the whole hierarchy of sacredness that he needs, he is naturally led to create new discriminations and new valuations, and becomes a creative type simply by fully developing all of his possibilities. The only task of social culture is to prepare him for this creation by teaching him the mechanism of discrimination and sublimation in general, and not interfering with his efforts to preserve all that he is able to preserve of his individuality. (It is the suppression that produces the two other fundamental characters, the Philistine and the Bohemian.) If society is successful in repressing all the possibilities that seem directly or indirectly dangerous until a character is formed which excludes them once and forever, then the product tends to be an individual for whom there are no problems of self-development left, no internal contradictions to solve, no external oppositions to overcome—a limited, stable, self-satisfied Philistine. If, on the contrary, the suppression is unsuccessful and the rebellious attitudes break out before a sufficiently stable set of contrary attitudes is formed, the individual is unprepared to meet the problems that arise, unable to discriminate or to sublimate, and an inconsistent, non-conformist, Bohemian type develops, which in its highest form, as artist, thinker, religious reformer, social revolutionist, may even succeed in producing, but whose products will always lack the internal harmony and social importance of the true creative type.

2. *Internal Sources of Behavioral Instability and Their Control*

BY SIGMUND FREUD

AS HAS BEEN SAID repeatedly, the ego is formed to a great extent out of identification taking the place of cathexes on the part of the id which have been abandoned; the earliest of these identifications always fulfil a special office in the ego and stand apart from the rest of the ego in the

Reprinted from Sigmund Freud, *The Ego and the Id,* trans. Joan Riviere (London: Hogarth Press, 1950), pp. 68–83, with the permission of Hogarth Press.

form of a super-ego, while later on, as it grows stronger, the ego may become more able to withstand the effects of identifications. The super-ego owes its special position in the ego, or in regard to the ego, to a factor which must be considered from two sides: to the fact that on the one hand it was the first identification and one which took place while the ego was still feeble, and that on the other hand it was the heir to the Oedipus complex and thus incorporated into the ego objects of far greater significance than any others. The super-ego's relation to the subsequent modifications effected in the ego is roughly that of the primary sexual period in childhood to full-grown sexual activity after puberty. Although it is amenable to every later influence, it preserves throughout life the character given to it by its derivation from the father-complex, namely, the capacity to stand apart from the ego and to rule it. It is a memorial of the former weakness and dependence of the ego and the mature ego remains subject to its domination. As the child was once compelled to obey its parents, so the ego submits to the categorical imperative pronounced by its super-ego.

The descent of the super-ego from the first object-cathexes of the id, from the Oedipus complex, however, signifies even more for it. This descent, as we have already described, connects it with the phylogenetic acquisitions of the id and makes it a reincarnation of former ego-structures which have left their precipitates behind in the id. Thus the super-ego is always in close touch with the id and can act as its representative in relation to the ego. It reaches deep down into the id and is for that reason farther from consciousness than the ego.[1]

We can best appreciate these relations by turning our attention to certain clinical facts, which have long since lost their novelty but which still await theoretical discussion.

There are certain people who behave in a quite peculiar fashion during the work of analysis. When one speaks hopefully to them or expresses satisfaction with the progress of the treatment, they show signs of discontent and their condition invariably becomes worse. One begins by regarding this as defiance and as an attempt to prove their superiority to the physician, but later one comes to take a deeper and truer view. One becomes convinced, not only that such people cannot endure any praise or appreciation, but that they react inversely to the progress of the treatment. Every partial solution that ought to result, and in other people does result, in an improvement or a temporary suspension of symptoms produces in them for the time being an exacerbation of their illness; they get worse during the treatment instead of getting better. They exhibit the so-called negative therapeutic reaction.

There is no doubt that there is something in these people that sets itself against their recovery and dreads its approach as though it were a danger. We are accustomed to say that the need for illness has got the upper hand in them over the desire for health. If we analyse this resistance in the usual way—then, even after we have subtracted from it the defiant attitude towards the physician and the fixation on the various kinds of advantage which the patient derives from the illness, the greater part of it is still left over; and this reveals itself as the most powerful of all obstacles to recovery, more powerful even than such familiar ones as narcissistic inaccessibility, the assumption of a negative attitude towards the physician or a clinging to the advantages of the illness.

In the end we come to see that we are dealing with what may be called a "moral" factor, a sense of guilt, which is finding atonement in the illness and is refusing to give up the penalty of suffering. We are justified in regarding this rather disheartening explanation as conclusive. But as far as the patient is concerned this sense of guilt is dumb; it does not tell him he is guilty; he does not feel guilty, he simply feels ill. This sense of guilt expresses itself only as a resistance to recovery which it is extremely difficult to overcome. It is also particularly difficult to convince the patient that this motive lies behind his continuing to be ill; he holds fast to the more obvious explanation that treatment by analysis is not the right remedy for his case.[2]

The description we have given applies to the most extreme instances of this state of affairs, but in a lesser measure this factor has to be reckoned with in very many cases, perhaps in all severe cases of neurosis. In fact it may be precisely this

---

1. It may be said that the psycho-analytical or metapsychological ego stands on its head no less than the anatomical ego—the "cortical homunculus."

2. The battle with the obstacle of an unconscious sense of guilt is not made easy for the analyst. Nothing can be done against it directly, and nothing indirectly but the slow procedure of unmasking its unconscious repressed roots, and of thus gradually changing it into a conscious sense of guilt. One has a special opportunity for influencing it when this Ucs sense of guilt is a "borrowed" one, *i.e.*, when it is the product of an identification with some other person who was once the object of an erotic cathexis. When the sense of guilt has been adopted in this way it is often the sole remaining trace of the abandoned love-relation and not at all easy to recognize as such. (The likeness between this process and what happens in melancholia is unmistakable.) If one can unmask this former object-cathexis behind the Ucs sense of guilt, the therapeutic success is often brilliant, but otherwise the outcome of one's efforts is by no means certain. It depends principally on the intensity of the sense of guilt; there is often no counteracting force of similar strength which the treatment can put in motion against it. Perhaps it may depend, too, on whether the personality of the analyst allows of the patient's putting him in the place of his ego-ideal, and this involves a temptation for the analyst to play the part of prophet, saviour, and redeemer to the patient. Since the rules of analysis are diametrically opposed to the physician's making use of his personality in any such manner, it must be honestly confessed that here we have another limitation to the effectiveness of analysis; after all, analysis does not set out to abolish the possibility of morbid reactions, but to give the patient's ego *freedom* to choose one way or the other.

element in the situation, the attitude of the ego-ideal, that determines the severity of a neurotic illness. We shall not hesitate, therefore, to discuss rather more fully the way in which the sense of guilt expresses itself under different conditions.

An explanation of the normal conscious sense of guilt (conscience) presents no difficulties; it is due to tension between the ego and the ego-ideal and is the expression of a condemnation of the ego pronounced by its criticizing function. The feelings of inferiority so well known in neurotics are presumably closely related to it. In two very familiar maladies the sense of guilt is over-strongly conscious; in them the ego-ideal displays particular severity and often rages against the ego with the utmost cruelty. The attitude of the ego-ideal in these two diseases, the obsessional neurosis and melancholia, presents, alongside of this similarity, differences that are no less significant.

In certain forms of the obsessional neurosis the sense of guilt expresses itself loudly but cannot justify itself to the ego. Consequently the patient's ego rebels against this imputation of guilt and seeks the physician's support in repudiating it. It would be folly to acquiesce in this, for to do so would have no effect. Analysis shows that the super-ego is being influenced by processes that have remained hidden from the ego. It is possible to discover the repressed impulses which really occasion the sense of guilt. The super-ego is thus proved to have known more than the ego about the unconscious id.

In melancholia the impression that the super-ego has obtained a hold upon consciousness is even stronger. But in this case the ego ventures no objection; it admits the guilt and submits to the punishment. The explanation of this difference is plain. In the obsessional neurosis the reprehensible impulses which are being criticized by the super-ego have never formed part of the ego, while in melancholia the object of the super-ego's wrath has become part of the ego through identification.

It is certainly not clear why the sense of guilt reaches such an extraordinary intensity in these two neurotic disorders; and indeed, the main problem presented in this state of affairs lies in another direction. We shall postpone discussion of it until we have dealt with the other cases—in which the sense of guilt remain unconscious.

It is essentially in hysteria and in states of a hysterical type that this condition is found. The mechanism by which the sense of guilt is kept unconscious is easy to discover. The hysterical type of ego defends itself from the painful perception which the criticisms of its super-ego threaten to produce in it by the same means that it uses to defend itself from an unendurable object-cathexis—

by an act of repression. It is the ego, therefore, that is responsible for the sense of guilt remaining unconscious. We know that as a rule the ego carries out repressions in the service and at the behest of its super-ego; but this is a case in which it has turned the same weapon against its harsh taskmaster. In the obsessional neurosis, as we know, the phenomena of reaction-formation predominate; but here the ego contents itself with keeping at a distance the material to which the sense of guilt refers.

One may go further and venture the hypothesis that a great part of the sense of guilt must normally remain unconscious, because the origin of conscience is closely connected with the Oedipus complex which belongs to the unconscious. If any one were inclined to put forward the paradoxical proposition that the normal man is not only far more immoral than he believes but also far more moral than he has any idea of, psycho-analysis, which is responsible for the first half of the assertion, would have no objection to raise against the second half.[3]

It was a surprise to find that exacerbation of this Ucs sense of guilt could turn people into criminals. But it is undoubtedly a fact. In many criminals, especially youthful ones, it is possible to detect a very powerful sense of guilt which existed before the crime, and is not therefore the result of it but its motive. It is as if it had been a relief to be able to fasten this unconscious sense of guilt on to something real and immediate.

In all these situations the super-ego displays its independence of the conscious ego and the closeness of its relations with the unconscious id. And now, having regard to the importance we ascribed to preconscious verbal residues in the ego, the question arises whether the super-ego, if it is in part unconscious, can consist in such verbal images, or, if not, in what it does consist. Our answer, though it does not carry us very far, will be that it cannot possibly be disputed that the super-ego, no less than the ego, is derived from auditory impressions; it is part of the ego and remains to a great extent accessible to consciousness by way of these verbal images (concepts, abstractions), but the cathectic energy of these elements of the super-ego does not originate from the auditory perceptions, instruction, reading, etc., but from sources in the id.

The question which we postponed answering runs thus: How is it that the super-ego manifests itself essentially as a sense of guilt (or rather, as criticism —for the sense of guilt is the perception in the ego which corresponds to the criticism) and at the same

---

3. This proposition is only apparently a paradox; it simply states that human nature has a far greater capacity, both for good and for evil, than it thinks it has, *i.e.*, than it is aware of through the conscious perceptions of the ego.

time develops such extraordinary harshness and severity towards the ego? If we turn to melancholia first, we find that the excessively strong super-ego which has obtained a hold upon consciousness rages against the ego with merciless fury, as if it had taken possession of the whole of the sadism available in the person concerned. Following our view of sadism, we should say that the destructive component had entrenched itself in the super-ego and turned against the ego. What is now holding sway in the super-ego is, as it were, a pure culture of the death-instinct, and in fact it often enough succeeds in driving the ego into death, if the latter does not protect itself from the tyrant in time by a revulsion into mania.

The reproaches of conscience in certain forms of obsessional neurosis are just as painful and tormenting, but here the situation is less perspicuous. It is remarkable that the obsessional neurotic, in contrast to the melancholiac, never takes the step of self-destruction; he is as if immune against the danger of suicide, and is far better protected from it than the hysteric. We can see that what guarantees the safety of the ego is the fact that the object has been retained. In the obsessional neurosis it has become possible, through a regression to the pregenital organization, for the love-impulses to transform themselves into impulses of aggression against the object. Here again the instinct of destruction has been set free and it aims at destroying the object, or at least it appears to have this aim. These tendencies have not been adopted by the ego; it struggles against them with reaction-formations and precautionary measures, and they remain in the id. The super-ego, however, behaves as if the ego were responsible for them and shows by its zeal in chastising these destructive intentions that they are no mere semblance evoked by regression but an actual substitution of hate for love. Helpless in either direction, the ego defends itself vainly, alike against the instigations of the murderous id and against the reproaches of the punishing conscience. It succeeds in holding in check at least the most brutal actions of both sides; the first outcome is interminable self-torment, and eventually there follows a systematic torturing of the object, in so far as it is within reach.

The activity of the dangerous death-instincts within the individual organism is dealt with in various ways; in part they are rendered harmless by being fused with erotic components, in part they are diverted towards the external world in the form of aggression, while for the most part they undoubtedly continue their inner work unhindered. How is it then that in melancholia the super-ego can become a kind of gathering-place for the death-instincts?

From the point of view of morality, the control and restriction of instinct, it may be said of the id that it is totally non-moral, of the ego that it strives to be moral, and of the super-ego that it can be hyper-moral and then becomes as ruthless as only the id can be. It is remarkable that the more a man checks his aggressive tendencies towards others the more tyrannical, that is aggressive, he becomes in his ego-ideal. The ordinary view sees the situation the other way round: the standard set up by the ego-ideal seems to be the motive for the suppression of aggressiveness. The fact remains, however, as we have stated it: the more a man controls his aggressiveness, the more intense become the aggressive tendencies of his ego-ideal against his ego. It is like a displacement, a turning round upon the self. But even ordinary normal morality has a harshly restraining, cruelly prohibiting quality. It is from this, indeed, that the conception arises of an inexorable higher being who metes out punishment.

I cannot go further in my consideration of these questions without introducing a fresh assumption. The super-ego arises, as we know, from an identification with the father regarded as a model. Every such identification is in the nature of a desexualization or even of a sublimation. It now seems as though when a transformation of this kind takes place there occurs at the same time an instinctual defusion. After sublimation the erotic component no longer has the power to bind the whole of the destructive elements that were previously combined with it, and these are released in the form of inclinations to aggression and destruction. This defusion would be the source of the general character of harshness and cruelty exhibited by the ideal—its dictatorial "Thou shalt."

Let us again consider the obsessional neurosis for a moment. The state of affairs is different here. The defusion of love into aggressiveness has not been effected by the agency of the ego, but is the result of a regression which has come about in the id. But this process has extended beyond the id to the super-ego, which now increases its tyranny over the innocent ego. It would seem, however, that in this case no less than in that of melancholia, the ego, having gained possession of the libido by means of identification, is punished for doing so by the super-ego through the instrumentality of the aggressiveness which had before been mixed with the libido.

Our ideas about the ego are beginning to clear, and its various relationships are gaining distinctness. We now see the ego in its strength and in its weaknesses. It is entrusted with important functions. By virtue of its relation to the perceptual system it arranges the processes of the mind in a temporal order and tests their correspondence with reality. By interposing the process of thinking it secures a postponement of motor discharges and controls the avenues to motility. This last office is, to be sure, a question more of form than of fact; in the matter of action the ego's position is like that of a constitutional monarch, without whose sanction no law can be passed but who hesitates long before imposing a veto on any measure put forward by Parliament. All the experiences of life that originate from without enrich the ego; the id, however, is another outer world to it, which it strives to bring into subjection to itself. It withdraws libido from the id and transforms the object-cathexes of the id into ego-constructions. With the aid of the super-ego, though in a manner that is still obscure to us, it draws upon the experiences of past ages stored in the id.

There are two paths by which the contents of the id can penetrate into the ego. The one is direct, the other leads by way of the ego-ideal; which of these two paths they take may, for many mental activities, be of decisive importance. The ego develops from perceiving instincts to controlling them, from obeying instincts to curbing them. In this achievement a large share is taken by the ego-ideal, which indeed is partly a reaction-formation against the instinctual processes in the id. Psycho-analysis is an instrument to enable the ego to push its conquest of the id further still.

From the other point of view, however, we see this same ego as a poor creature owing service to three masters and consequently menaced by three several dangers: from the external world, from the libido of the id, and from the severity of the super-ego. Three kinds of anxiety correspond to these three dangers, since anxiety is the expression of a recoil from danger. Like the dweller in a borderland that it is, the ego tries to mediate between the world and the id, to make the id comply with the world's demands and, by means of muscular activity, to accommodate the world to the id's desires. In point of fact it behaves like the physician during treatment by analysis; it offers itself to the id as a libidinal object in view of its power of adaptation to the real world, and aims at attaching the id's libido to itself. It is not only the ally of the id; it is also a submissive slave who courts the love of his master. Whenever possible, it tries to remain on good terms with the id; it draws the veil of its Pcs rationalizations over the id's Ucs demands; it pretends that the id is showing obedience to the mandates of reality, even when in fact it is remaining obdurate and immovable; it throws a disguise over the id's conflicts with reality and, if possible, over its conflicts with the super-ego too. Its position midway between the id and reality tempts it only too often to become sycophantic, opportunist and false, like a politician who sees the truth but wants to keep his place in popular favour.

3. Cultural Conflict and the Marginal Man

BY ROBERT E. PARK

WILLIAM GRAHAM SUMNER, in what is probably the most frequently quoted passage in the *Folkways*, tells us that we should conceive primitive society as a congeries of small ethnocentric groups scattered over a territory. In such a society each group thinks of itself in the first person and regards itself as "the center of everything." It is a "we-group." Others are outsiders. They are part of the landscape.

The size of such a group is determined "by the conditions of the struggle for existence, and its in-

ternal organization corresponds to its size but is further conditioned by its relations with all the others. This is because order and discipline in each 'we-group' or 'in-group' depends upon the exigencies of war and peace with the 'other-groups' or 'out-groups.' " Thus society, primitive society at least, turns out to be "a group of groups," in which the normal relation of each to every other is "one of war and plunder, except so far as agreements have modified it." Under these circumstances "the relation of comradeship and peace in the we-group and that of hostility and war towards others-groups are correlative to each other." The loyalties that bind together the members of the little world—the world of the family, the clan and the tribe—are in direct

Reprinted with the permission of Charles Scribner's Sons from *The Marginal Man* by E. V. Stonequist, copyright 1937 Charles Scribner's Sons, pp. xiii–xviii [from Robert E. Park's "Introduction"].

proportion to the intensity of the fears and hatreds with which they view their enemies and rivals in the larger intertribal and international world outside.

In the course of the long historical process from which the modern world has emerged this picture of primitive society has been progressively altered. Now that the aeroplane has wellnigh abolished the distances that once separated the nations and peoples and the radio has converted the world into one vast whispering gallery, the great world—intertribal, interracial, and international—the world of business and politics—has grown at the expense of the little world, the world of intimate, personal loyalties in which men were bound together by tradition, custom, and natural piety.

Nevertheless the general patterns of primitive society still persist and human nature is, on the whole, what it has been. It is still in the family and under the influence of the tribe, the sect or the local community, as Cooley insisted, that the individual acquires those habits, sentiments, attitudes and other personality traits that characterize him as human.

On the other hand, it was and is in the market place where men from distant places come together to chaffer and bargain, that men first learn the subtleties of commerce and exchange; the necessity for cool calculation, even in human affairs, and the freedom to act, as individuals, in accordance with interests, rather than sentiments. It is with the expansion of the market, as a matter of fact, that intellectual life has prospered and local tribal cultures have been progressively integrated into that wider and more rational social order we call civilization.

Thus the vast expansion of Europe during the last four hundred years has brought about changes more devastating than in any earlier period in the world's history. Europeans have invaded every part of the world, and no part of the earth has escaped the disturbing, even if vivifying, contacts of European commerce and culture. The movements and migrations incident to this expansion have brought about everywhere an interpenetration of peoples and a fusion of cultures. Incidentally it has produced, at certain times and under certain conditions, a personality type, a type which if not wholly new is at any rate peculiarly characteristic of the modern world. It is a type to which some of us, including the author of this volume [Stonequist], have given the title "The Marginal Man."

The marginal man, as here conceived, is one whom fate has condemned to live in two societies and in two, not merely different but antagonistic, cultures. Thus, the individual whose mother is a Jew and whose father is a Gentile is fatally condemned to grow up under the influence of two tra-

ditions. In that case, his mind is the crucible in which two different and refractory cultures may be said to melt and, either wholly or in part, fuse. One runs across individuals who are caught in this conflict of cultures in the most unlikely places.

Readers of George Santayana's *The Last Puritan* will hardly fail to discover—even if the subtitle, "A Memoir in the Form of a Novel," did not advertise the fact—that the story it tells, if not an autobiography, is nevertheless, in some subtle and symbolic way, autobiographical. Obviously the two leading characters, Oliver and Mario, are the symbols of the two cultures, which the author united in his own person, and the almost mystical friendship which, in spite of differences of temperament and tradition, unites them indicates how intimately the traditions they represent were related in the mind of the author.

In the epilogue the author refers to this novel as a "fable," and Mario, with whom he represents himself as discussing the import of the fable, adds, that "perhaps there is a better philosophy in it than in your other books."

Perhaps the best philosophy is one that achieves, as in the case of Plato, its fullest and happiest expression in fables. In any case a man's philosophy is always an aspect, if not an integral part, of his personality, and Santayana's philosophy reflects the effect, upon a mind conscious of a conflict in its natural loyalties, of an effort to achieve an inner harmony and consistency; such a harmony and consistency as is essential to that "life of reason" which he has so persuasively set forth in the volumes he has written under that title.

Santayana was born in Spain of Spanish parents, but fate ordained that he should get his education and live most of his life in America and England. It is evident from his account of life in Boston, that he lived there with his mother, as he did in fact in Spain with his father, more or less as an alien, always conscious of a different tradition and of intimate and indissoluble connections with another and a different world. In fact his life in both Spain and America seems to have been that of the typical "stranger," as described by Simmel in his *Sociology;* that is, one who lives in intimate association with the world about him but never so completely identified with it that he is unable to look at it with a certain critical detachment. In Santayana's case this detachment has become, as Edman expresses it, an intimate but "compassionate understanding" of his world.

In an article, contributed to a symposium on the subject of contemporary American philosophy, Santayana[1] has described "the mixed associations"

---

1. Irwin Edman, *The Philosophy of Santayana*, pp. 1–20.

under which his "opinions" came into existence, subjected as they were to the strain of his "complex allegiances." He says: "My philosophy may be regarded as a synthesis of these various traditions, or an attempt to view them from a level from which their several deliverances may be justly understood."

Of himself a little later, he adds: "I felt like a foreigner in Spain, more acutely so than in America, although for more trivial reason. . . . English had become my only possible instrument, and I deliberately put away everything that might confuse me in that medium. English, and the whole Anglo-Saxon tradition in literature and philosophy, have always been a medium to me rather than a scholarship, and learning of any sort seemed to me a means, not an end. . . . Thus in renouncing everything else for the sake of English letters I might be said to have been guilty, quite unintentionally, of a little stratagem, as if I had set out to say plausibly in English as many un-English things as possible."[2]

The Last Puritan, whether is be an "indirect memoir" of the author, as Edman assumes, or a philosophy in the form of a fable, as Santayana himself suggests, is in any case for the student of human nature a human document in which the conflict and fusion of cultures, as it actually takes place under certain circumstances and in certain minds, is clearly reflected.

The fundamental notion upon which this present study of the so-called marginal man is based is, I should say, the conviction that the individual's personality, while based on instincts, temperament and the endocrine balance, achieves its final form under the influence of the individual's conception of himself. The conception which each individual inevitably forms of himself is determined by the rôle which fate assigns to him in some society, and upon

the opinion and attitude which persons in that society form of him—depends, in short, upon his social status. The individual's conception of himself is, in this sense, not an individual but a social product.

The marginal man is a personality type that arises at a time and a place where, out of the conflict of races and cultures, new societies, new peoples and cultures are coming into existence. The fate which condemns him to live, at the same time, in two worlds is the same which compels him to assume, in relation to the worlds in which he lives, the rôle of a cosmopolitan and a stranger. Inevitably he becomes, relatively to his cultural milieu, the individual with the wider horizon, the keener intelligence, the more detached and rational viewpoint. The marginal man is always relatively the more civilized human being. He occupies the position which has been, historically, that of the Jew in the Diaspora. The Jew, particularly the Jew who has emerged from the provincialism of the ghetto, has everywhere and always been the most civilized of human creatures.

From what has been said one may infer that the marginal man is an incidental product of a process of acculturation, such as inevitably ensues when peoples of different cultures and different races come together to carry on a common life. He is, as I have suggested, an effect of imperialism, economic, political and cultural; an incident of the process by which civilization, as Spengler has said, grows up at the expense of earlier and simpler cultures.

The Marginal Man is concerned finally and fundamentally less, as the title might suggest, with a personality type, than with a social process, the process of acculturation. The distinction is that, in the latter case, the author has chosen to investigate the process less from the point of view of the person than of the society of which he is a part; less from the point of view of custom and culture than from habit and personality.

---

2. *Philosophy of Santayana,* pp. 4–5.

IV–THE MAINTENANCE OF CONFORMITY

1. Death and the Reintegration of the Group

BY BRONISLAW MALINOWSKI

OF ALL SOURCES of religion, the supreme and final crisis of life—death—is of the greatest importance. Death is the gateway to the other world in more than the literal sense. According to most theories of early religion, a great deal, if not all, of religious inspiration has been derived from it—and in this orthodox views are on the whole correct. Man has to live his life in the shadow of death, and he who clings to life and enjoys its fullness must dread the menace of its end. And he who is faced by death turns to the promise of life. Death and its denial—Immortality—have always formed, as they form today, the most poignant theme of man's forebodings. The extreme complexity of man's emotional reactions to life finds necessarily its counterpart in his attitude to death. Only what in life has been spread over a long space and manifested in a succession of experiences and events is here at its end condensed into one crisis which provokes a violent and complex outburst of religious manifestations.

Even among the most primitive peoples, the attitude at death is infinitely more complex and, I may add, more akin to our own, than is usually assumed. It is often stated by anthropologists that the dominant feeling of the survivors is that of horror at the corpse and of fear of the ghost. This twin attitude is even made by no less an authority than Wilhelm Wundt the very nucleus of all religious belief and practice. Yet this assertion is only a half-truth, which means no truth at all. The emotions are extremely complex and even contradictory; the dominant elements, love of the dead and loathing of the corpse, passionate attachment to the personality still lingering about the body and a shattering fear of the gruesome thing that has been left over, these two elements seem to mingle and play into each other. This is reflected in the spontaneous behavior and in the ritual proceedings at death. In the tending of the corpse, in the modes of its disposal, in the post-funerary and commemorative ceremonies, the nearest relatives, the mother mourning for her son, the widow for her husband, the child for the parent, always show some horror and fear mingled with pious love, but never do the negative elements appear alone or even dominant.

The mortuary proceedings show a striking similarity throughout the world. As death approaches, the nearest relatives in any case, sometimes the whole community, forgather by the dying man, and dying, the most private act which a man can perform, is transformed into a public, tribal event. As a rule, a certain differentiation takes place at once, some of the relatives watching near the corpse, others making preparations for the pending end and its consequences, others again performing perhaps some religious acts at a sacred spot. Thus in certain parts of Melanesia the real kinsmen must keep at a distance and only relatives by marriage perform the mortuary services, while in some tribes of Australia the reverse order is observed.

As soon as death has occurred, the body is washed, anointed and adorned, sometimes the bodily apertures are filled, the arms and legs tied together. Then it is exposed to the view of all, and the most important phase, the immediate mourning begins. Those who have witnessed death and its sequel among savages and who can compare these events with their counterpart among other uncivilized peoples must be struck by the fundamental similarity of the proceedings. There is always a more or less conventionalized and dramatized outburst of grief and wailing in sorrow, which often passes among savages into bodily lacerations and the tearing of hair. This is always done in a public display and is associated with visible signs of mourning, such as black or white daubs on the body, shaven or dishevelled hair, strange or torn garments.

The immediate mourning goes on round the corpse. This, far from being shunned or dreaded, is usually the center of pious attention. Often there are

Reprinted from Bronislaw Malinowski, *Magic, Science, and Religion* (Glencoe, Ill.: The Free Press, 1948), pp. 29–35, with the permission of the Free Press.

ritual forms of fondling or attestations of reverence. The body is sometimes kept on the knees of seated persons, stroked and embraced. At the same time these acts are usually considered both dangerous and repugnant, duties to be fulfilled at some cost to the performer. After a time the corpse has to be disposed of. Inhumation with an open or closed grave; exposure in caves or on platforms, in hollow trees or on the ground in some wild desert place; burning or setting adrift in canoes—these are the usual forms of disposal.

This brings us to perhaps the most important point, the two-fold contradictory tendency, on the one hand to preserve the body, to keep its form intact, or to retain parts of it; on the other hand the desire to be done with it, to put it out of the way, to annihilate it completely. Mummification and burning are the two extreme expressions of this two-fold tendency. It is impossible to regard mummification or burning or any intermediate form as determined by mere accident of belief, as a historical feature of some culture or other which has gained its universality by the mechanism of spread and contact only. For in these customs is clearly expressed the fundamental attitude of mind of the surviving relative, friend or lover, the longing for all that remains of the dead person and the disgust and fear of the dreadful transformation wrought by death.

One extreme and interesting variety in which this double-edged attitude is expressed in a gruesome manner is sarco-cannibalism, a custom of partaking in piety of the flesh of the dead person. It is done with extreme repugnance and dread and usually followed by a violent vomiting fit. At the same time it is felt to be a supreme act of reverence, love, and devotion. In fact it is considered such a sacred duty that among the Melanesians of New Guinea, where I have studied and witnessed it, it is still performed in secret, although severely penalized by the white Government. The smearing of the body with the fat of the dead, prevalent in Australia and Papuasia is, perhaps, but a variety of this custom.

In all such rites, there is a desire to maintain the tie and the parallel tendency to break the bond. Thus the funerary rites are considered as unclean and soiling, the contact with the corpse as defiling and dangerous, and the performers have to wash, cleanse their body, remove all traces of contact, and perform ritual lustrations. Yet the mortuary ritual compels man to overcome the repugnance, to conquer his fears, to make piety and attachment triumphant, and with it the belief in a future life, in the survival of the spirit.

And here we touch on one of the most important functions of religious cult. In the foregoing analysis I have laid stress on the direct emotional forces created by contact with death and with the corpse, for they primarily and most powerfully determine the behavior of the survivors. But connected with these emotions and born out of them, there is the idea of the spirit, the belief in the new life into which the departed has entered. And here we return to the problem of animism with which we began our survey of primitive religious facts. What is the substance of a spirit, and what is the psychological origin of this belief?

The savage is intensely afraid of death, probably as the result of some deep-seated instincts common to man and animals. He does not want to realize it as an end, he cannot face the idea of complete cessation, of annihilation. The idea of spirit and of spiritual existence is near at hand, furnished by such experiences as are discovered and described by Tylor. Grasping at it, man reaches the comforting belief in spiritual continuity and in the life after death. Yet this belief does not remain unchallenged in the complex, double-edged play of hope and fear which sets in always in the face of death. To the comforting voice of hope, to the intense desire of immortality, to the difficulty, in one's own case, almost the impossibility, of facing annihilation there are opposed powerful and terrible forebodings. The testimony of the senses, the gruesome decomposition of the corpse, the visible disappearance of the personality—certain apparently instinctive suggestions of fear and horror seem to threaten man at all stages of culture with some idea of annihilation, with some hidden fears and forebodings. And here into this play of emotional forces, into this supreme dilemma of life and final death, religion steps in, selecting the positive creed, the comforting view, the culturally valuable belief in immortality, in the spirit independent of the body, and in the continuance of life after death. In the various ceremonies at death, in commemoration and communion with the departed, and worship of ancestral ghosts, religion gives body and form to the saving beliefs.

Thus the belief in immortality is the result of a deep emotional revelation, standardized by religion, rather than a primitive philosophic doctrine. Man's conviction of continued life is one of the supreme gifts of religion, which judges and selects the better of the two alternatives suggested by self-preservation—the hope of continued life and the fear of annihilation. The belief in spirits is the result of the belief in immortality. The substance of which the spirits are made is the full-blooded passion and desire for life, rather than the shadowy stuff which haunts his dreams and illusions. Religion saves man from a surrender to death and destruction, and in doing this it merely makes use of the observations of dreams, shadows, and visions. The real nucleus of animism lies in the deepest emotional fact of human nature, the desire for life.

Thus the rites of mourning, the ritual behavior immediately after death, can be taken as pattern of the religious act, while the belief in immortality, in the continuity of life and in the nether world, can be taken as the prototype of an act of faith. Here, as in the religious ceremonies previously described, we find self-contained acts, the aim of which is achieved in their very performance. The ritual despair, the obsequies, the acts of mourning, express the emotion of the bereaved and the loss of the whole group. They endorse and they duplicate the natural feelings of the survivors; they create a social event out of a natural fact. Yet, though in the acts of mourning, in the mimic despair of wailing, in the treatment of the corpse and in its disposal, nothing ulterior is achieved, these acts fulfil an important function and possess a considerable value for primitive culture.

What is this function? The initiation ceremonies we have found fulfil theirs in sacralizing tradition; the food cults, sacrament and sacrifice bring man into communion with providence, with the beneficent forces of plenty; totemism standardizes man's practical, useful attitude of selective interest towards his surroundings. If the view here taken of the biological function of religion is true, some such similar role must also be played by the whole mortuary ritual.

The death of a man or woman in a primitive group, consisting of a limited number of individuals, is an event of no mean importance. The nearest relatives and friends are disturbed to the depth of their emotional life. A small community bereft of a member, especially if he be important, is severely mutilated. The whole event breaks the normal course of life and shakes the moral foundations of society. The strong tendency on which we have insisted in the above description: to give way to fear and horror, to abandon the corpse, to run away from the village, to destroy all the belongings

of the dead one—all these impulses exist, and if given way to would be extremely dangerous, disintegrating the group, destroying the material foundations of primitive culture. Death in a primitive society is, therefore, much more than the removal of a member. By setting in motion one part of the deep forces of the instinct of self-preservation, it threatens the very cohesion and solidarity of the group, and upon this depends the organization of that society, its tradition, and finally the whole culture. For if primitive man yielded always to the disintegrating impulses of his reaction to death, the continuity of tradition and the existence of material civilization would be impossible.

We have seen already how religion, by sacralizing and thus standardizing the other set of impulses, bestows on man the gift of mental integrity. Exactly the same function it fulfils also with regard to the whole group. The ceremonial of death which ties the survivors to the body and rivets them to the place of death, the beliefs in the existence of the spirit, in its beneficent influences or malevolent intentions, in the duties of a series of commemorative or sacrificial ceremonies—in all this religion counteracts the centrifugal forces of fear, dismay, demoralization, and provides the most powerful means of reintegration of the group's shaken solidarity and of the re-establishment of its morale.

In short, religion here assures the victory of tradition and culture over the mere negative response of thwarted instinct.

With the rites of death we have finished the survey of the main types of religious acts. We have followed the crises of life as the main guiding thread of our account, but as they presented themselves we also treated the side issues, such as totemism, the cults of food and of propagation, sacrifice and sacrament, the commemorative cults of ancestors and the cults of the spirits. To one type already mentioned we still have to return—I mean, the seasonal feasts and ceremonies of communal or tribal character—and to the discussion of this subject we proceed now.

2. *On the Rites of Passage*

BY ARNOLD VAN GENNEP

ONCE THE CLASSIFICATION of ritual mechanism has been established, it becomes relatively easy to understand the *raisons d'etre* of ceremonial sequences. Here again, let us note that the theorists have shown little interest in classifying these sequences. We have some excellent works on a particular element of a sequence, but very few which follow a whole sequence from beginning to end, and even fewer where the sequences are studied in their relations to one another. It is to an attempt of this sort that the present volume is dedicated, and I have tried to group all the ceremonial sequences which accompany the passage from one situation into another, and from one cosmic or social world to another.

Given the importance of these passages, I believe it is legitimate to distinguish a special category of *Rites of Passage,* which can be broken down into *Rites of Separation, Rites of Marginality,* and *Rites of Aggregation.* These three sub-categories are not developed equally within a given society nor even within a given ceremonial. The rites of separation are more important in the funeral ceremonies; the rites of aggregation are more important in the marriage ceremonies; as far as the rites of marginality are concerned, they may be important, for example in pregnancy and engagement or be reduced to a minimum in adoption, the second parturition, remarriage, the passage from the second to the third age-group, etc. . . . Hence, even if the concept of rites of passage theoretically includes *preliminary* rites (separation), *liminary* rites (margin), and *postliminary* rites (aggregation), in practice they are far from being equivalent, whether in their respective importance, or for their level of elaboration.

Furthermore, when the marginality is sufficiently developed to constitute an autonomous stage, the concept can be subdivided once more. Thus, engagement is certainly a marginal period between adolescence and marriage; but the passage from adolescence to engagement includes a special series of rites of separation, marginality, and aggregation

to the marginal state; and from engagement to marriage, there is a series of rites of separation from the marginal state—of marginality and aggregation—to marriage. This interlocking can be also noted in the complex constituted by the rites of pregnancy, parturition, and birth. While trying to group all these rites with the utmost precision, one should not deny that, since we are dealing with human action, it is impossible to obtain in these matters as rigorous a classification as can be obtained in botany, for example.

I am also far from pretending that all the rites of birth, initiation, marriage, etc. . . . are but rites of passage. For, outside their general purpose, which is to secure a change of estate or the passage from one magico-religious or lay society to another one, each of the ceremonies has a concern of its own. Thus, the marriage ceremonies include fecundity rites—rites of birth, protection, and divining rites; funerals include rites of defence; initiation ceremonies include propitiation rites; and those of ordination, rites of appropriation by the divinity. All these rites, which have specific and present purpose, are co-existent to or combine with the rites of passage, sometimes in such an intimate way that it is hard to know whether a given element is, for example, a rite of protection or a rite of separation. . . .

This leads me to speak rapidly of what could be called the mythical sweep of the notion of sacred. The sacred, and the rites which correspond to it, has the characteristic of being an alternance. Indeed, it is not an absolute value, but a value which is attached to specific situations. A man who lives at home, in his clan, lives with the profane; he lives in the sacred as soon as he goes traveling and finds himself, as a stranger, close to an unknown camp. Every woman, being congenitally impure, is sacred in relation to all the adult men; if she is pregnant, she becomes, in addition, sacred for all the other women of the clan, with the exception of her close kin; in relation to herself, these women, plus the young and adult men, will constitute a profane world. Every Brahman lives, by the fact of his birth, in a sacred world, but there is a hierarchy of Brahman families which are sacred one to another. Finally, by accomplishing rites of purifica-

Translated, with deletions, by Jesse Pitts, from Arnold Van Gennep, *Les rites de passage* (Paris: E. Nourry, 1909), pp. 13–17.

tion, the woman who has given birth does re-enter society through specific sections of it, her sex group, her family, etc. . . . and she remains sacred in relation to the initiated men and the magico-religious ceremonies. Hence, alternatively, according to the situation one assumes among the various sections of the society, there is a displacement of magic circles. He who passes through these alternatives during his life-span finds himself at a given moment, by the very change of concepts and classifications, turning around and staring at the sacred instead of at the profane and vice versa. Such changes of state are not accomplished without troubling social and individual life, and it is the purpose of a certain number of rites of passage to check their noxious effects. That these changes should be considered as real and awesome is demonstrated by the recurrence, in great ceremonies and among the most different societies, of the rites of death to the antecedent world, and resurrection to the new world . . . , rites which constitute the most dramatic form of the rites of passage.

3. On Taboo

BY A. R. RADCLIFFE-BROWN

I HAVE PURPOSELY CHOSEN from our society two examples of ritual avoidances which are of very different kinds. The rule against eating meat on Friday or in Lent is a rule of religion, as is the rule, where it is recognised, against playing golf or tennis on Sunday. The rule against spilling salt, I suppose it will be agreed, is non-religious. Our language permits us to make this distinction very clearly, for infractions of the rules of religion are sins, while the non-religious avoidances are concerned with good and bad luck. Since this distinction is so obvious to us it might be thought that we should find it in other societies. My own experience is that in some of the societies with which I am acquainted this distinction between sinful acts and acts that bring bad luck cannot be made. Several anthropologists, however, have attempted to classify rites into two classes, religious rites and magical rites.

For Emile Durkheim the essential distinction is that religious rites are obligatory within a religious society or church, while magical rites are optional. A person who fails in religious observances is guilty of wrong-doing, whereas one who does not observe the precautions of magic or those relating to luck is simply acting foolishly. This distinction is of considerable theoretical importance. It is difficult to apply in the study of the rites of simple societies.

Sir James Frazer defines religion as "a propitiation or conciliation of superhuman powers which are believed to control nature and man," and regards magic as the erroneous application of the notion of causality. If we apply this to ritual prohibitions, we may regard as belonging to religion those rules the infraction of which produces a change of ritual status in the individual by offending the superhuman powers, whereas the infraction of a rule of magic would be regarded as resulting immediately in a change of ritual status, or in the misfortune that follows, by a process of hidden causation. Spilling salt, by Sir James Frazer's definition, is a question of magic, while eating meat on Friday is a question of religion.

An attempt to apply this distinction systematically meets with certain difficulties. Thus with regard to the Maori Sir James Frazer states that "the ultimate sanction of the taboo, in other words, that which engaged the people to observe its commandments, was a firm persuasion that any breach of those commandments would surely and speedily be punished by an *atua* or ghost, who would afflict the sinner with a painful malady till he died." This would seem to make the Polynesian taboo a matter of religion, not of magic. But my own observation of the Polynesians suggests to me that in general the native conceives of the change in his ritual status as taking place as the immediate result of such an act as touching a corpse, and that it is only when he proceeds to rationalise the whole system of taboos that he thinks of the gods and spirits—

Reprinted from A. R. Radcliffe-Brown, *Structure and Function in Primitive Society* (Glencoe, Ill.: The Free Press, 1952), pp. 136–52, with the permission of The Free Press.

the *atua*—as being concerned. Incidentally it should not be assumed that the Polynesian word *atua* or *otua* always refers to a personal spiritual being.

Of the various ways of distinguishing magic and religion I will mention only one more. For Professor Malinowski a rite is magical when "it has a definite practical purpose which is known to all who practise it and can be easily elicited from any native informant," while a rite is religious if it is simply expressive and has no purpose, being not a means to an end but an end in itself. A difficulty in applying this criterion is due to uncertainty as to what is meant by "definite practical purpose." To avoid the bad luck which results from spilling salt is, I suppose, a practical purpose though not very definite. The desire to please God in all our actions and thus escape some period of Purgatory is perhaps definite enough, but Professor Malinowski may regard it as not practical. What shall we say of the desire of the Polynesian to avoid sickness and possible death which he gives as his reason for not touching chiefs, corpses and newly-born babies?

Seeing that there is this absence of agreement as to the definitions of magic and religion and the nature of the distinction between them, and seeing that in many instances whether we call a particular rite magical or religious depends on which of the various proposed definitions we accept, the only sound procedure, at any rate in the present state of anthropological knowledge, is to avoid as far as possible the use of the terms in question until there is some general agreement about them. Certainly the distinctions made by Durkheim and Frazer and Malinowski may be theoretically significant, even though they are difficult to apply universally. Certainly, also, there is need for a systematic classification of rites, but a satisfactory classification will be fairly complex and a simple dichotomy between magic and religion does not carry us very far towards it.

Another distinction which we make in our own society within the field of ritual avoidances is between the holy and the unclean. Certain things must be treated with respect because they are holy, others because they are unclean. But, as Robertson Smith and Sir James Frazer have shown, there are many societies in which this distinction is entirely unrecognised. The Polynesian, for example, does not think of a chief or a temple as holy and a corpse as unclean. He thinks of them all as things dangerous. An example from Hawaii will illustrate this fundamental identity of holiness and uncleanness. There, in former times, if a commoner committed incest with his sister he became *kapu* (the Hawaiian form of tabu). His presence was dangerous in the extreme for the whole community, and since he

could not be purified he was put to death. But if a chief of high rank, who, by reason of his rank was, of course, sacred (*kapu*), married his sister he became still more so. An extreme sanctity or untouchability attached to a chief born of a brother and sister who were themselves the children of a brother and sister. The sanctity of such a chief and the uncleanness of the person put to death for incest have the same source and are the same thing. They are both denoted by saying that the person is *kapu*. In studying the simpler societies it is essential that we should carefully avoid thinking of their behaviour and ideas in terms of our own ideas of holiness and uncleanness. Since most people find this difficult it is desirable to have terms which we can use that do not convey this connotation. Durkheim and others have used the word "sacred" as an inclusive term for the holy and the unclean together. This is easier to do in French than in English, and has some justification in the fact that the Latin *sacer* did apply to holy things such as the gods and also to accursed things such as persons guilty of certain crimes. But there is certainly a tendency in English to identify sacred with holy. I think that it will greatly aid clear thinking if we adopt some wide inclusive term which does not have any undesirable connotation. I venture to propose the term "ritual value."

Anything—a person, a material thing, a place, a word or name, an occasion or event, a day of the week or a period of the year—which is the object of a ritual avoidance or taboo can be said to have ritual value. Thus in Polynesia chiefs, corpses and newly-born babies have ritual value. For some people in England salt has ritual value. For Christians all Sundays and Good Friday have ritual value, and for Jews all Saturdays and the Day of Atonement. The ritual value is exhibited in the behaviour adopted towards the object or occasion in question. Ritual values are exhibited not only in negative ritual but also in positive ritual, being possessed by the objects towards which positive rites are directed and also by objects, words or places used in the rites. A large class of positive rites, those of consecration or sacralisation, have for their purpose to endow objects with ritual value. It may be noted that in general anything that has value in positive ritual is also the object of some sort of ritual avoidance or at the very least of ritual respect.

The word "value," as I am using it, always refers to a relation between a subject and an object. The relation can be stated in two ways by saying either that the object has a value for the subject, or that the subject has an interest in the object. We can use the terms in this way to refer to any act of behaviour towards an object. The relation is exhibited in and defined by the behaviour. The words "interest" and "value" provide a convenient shorthand by which we can describe the reality, which consists of acts of behaviour and the actual relations between subjects and objects which those acts of behaviour reveal. If Jack loves Jill, then Jill has the value of a loved object for Jack, and Jack has a recognisable interest in Jill. When I am hungry I have an interest in food, and a good meal has an immediate value for me that it does not have at other times. My toothache has a value to me that it does not have at other times. My toothache has a value for me as something that I am interested in getting rid of as quickly as possible.

A social system can be conceived and studied as a system of values. A society consists of a number of individuals bound together in a network of social relations. A social relation exists between two or more persons when there is some harmonisation of their individual interests, by some convergence of interest and by limitation or adjustment of divergent interests. An interest is always the interest of an individual. Two individuals may have similar interests. Similar interests do not in themselves constitute a social relation; two dogs may have a similar interest in the same bone and the result may be a dog-fight. But a society cannot exist except on the basis of a certain measure of similarity in the interests of its members. Putting this in terms of value, the first necessary condition of the existence of a society is that the individual members shall agree in some measure in the values that they recognise.

Any particular society is characterised by a certain set of values—moral, aesthetic, economic, etc. In a simple society there is a fair amount of agreement amongst the members in their evaluations, though of course the agreement is never absolute. In a complex modern society we find much more disagreement if we consider the society as a whole, but we may find a closer measure of agreement amongst the members of a group or class within the society.

While some measure of agreement about values, some similarity of interests, is a prerequisite of a social system, social relations involve more than this. They require the existence of common interests and of social values. When two or more persons have a common interest in the same object and are aware of their community of interest a social relation is established. They form, whether for a moment or for a long period, an association, and the object may be said to have a social value. For a man and his wife the birth of a child, the child itself and its well-being and happiness or its death, are objects of a common interest which binds them

together and they thus have, for the association formed by the two persons, social value. By this definition an object can only have a social value for an association of persons. In the simplest possible instance we have a triadic relation; Subject 1 and Subject 2 are both interested in the same way in the Object and each of the Subjects has an interest in the other, or at any rate in certain items of the behaviour of the other, namely those directed towards the object. To avoid cumbersome circumlocutions it is convenient to speak of the object as having a social value for any one subject involved in such a relation, but it must be remembered that this is a loose way of speaking.

It is perhaps necessary for the avoidance of misunderstanding to add that a social system also requires that persons should be objects of interest to other persons. In relations of friendship or love each of two persons has a value for the other. In certain kinds of groups each member is an object of interest for all the others, and each member therefore has a social value for the group as a whole. Further, since there are negative values as well as positive, persons may be united or associated by their antagonism to other persons. For the members of an anti-Comintern pact the Comintern has a specific social value.

Amongst the members of a society we find a certain measure of agreement as to the ritual value they attribute to objects of different kinds. We also find that most of these ritual values are social values as defined above. Thus for a local totemic clan in Australia the totem-centres, the natural species associated with them, i.e. the totems, and the myths and rites that relate thereto, have a specific social value for the clan; the common interest in them binds the individuals together into a firm and lasting association.

Ritual values exist in every known society, and show an immense diversity as we pass from one society to another. The problem of a natural science of society (and it is as such that I regard social anthropology) is to discover the deeper, not immediately perceptible, uniformities beneath the superficial differences. This is, of course, a highly complex problem which will require the studies begun by Sir James Frazer and others to be continued by many investigators over many years. The ultimate aim should be, I think, to find some relatively adequate answer to the question—*What is the relation of ritual and ritual values to the essential constitution of human society?* I have chosen a particular approach to this study which I believe to be promising—to investigate in a few societies studied as thoroughly as possible the relations of ritual values to other values including moral and aesthetic values. In the present lecture, however, it is only one small part of this study in which I seek to interest you—the question of a relation between ritual values and social values.

One way of approaching the study of ritual is by the consideration of the purposes or reasons for the rites. If one examines the literature of anthropology one finds this approach very frequently adopted. It is by far the least profitable, though the one that appeals most to common sense. Sometimes the purpose of a rite is obvious, or a reason may be volunteered by those who practise it. Sometimes the anthropologist has to ask the reason, and in such circumstances it may happen that different reasons are given by different informants. What is fundamentally the same rite in two different societies may have different purposes or reasons in the one and in the other. The reasons given by the members of a community for any custom they observe are important data for the anthropologist. But it is to fall into grievous error to suppose that they give a valid explanation of the custom. What is entirely inexcusable is for the anthropologist, when he cannot get from the people themselves a reason for their behaviour which seems to him satisfactory, to attribute to them some purpose or reason on the basis of his own preconceptions about human motives. I could adduce many instances of this from the literature of ethnography, but I prefer to illustrate what I mean by an anecdote.

A Queenslander met a Chinese who was taking a bowl of cooked rice to place on his brother's grave. The Australian in jocular tones asked if he supposed that his brother would come and eat the rice. The reply was "No! We offer rice to people as an expression of friendship and affection. But since you speak as you do I suppose that you in this country place flowers on the graves of your dead in the belief that they will enjoy looking at them and smelling their sweet perfume."

So far as ritual avoidances are concerned the reasons for them may vary from a very vague idea that some sort of misfortune or ill-luck, not defined as to its kind, is likely to befall anyone who fails to observe the taboo, to a belief that non-observance will produce some quite specific and undesirable result. Thus an Australian aborigine told me that if he spoke to any woman who stood in the relation of mother-in-law to him his hair would turn grey.[1]

The very common tendency to look for the explanation of ritual actions in their purpose is the result of a false assimilation of them to what may be called technical acts. In any technical activity an adequate statement of the purpose of any particular act or series of acts constitutes by itself a sufficient explanation. But ritual acts differ from technical acts in having in all instances some expressive or symbolic element in them.

A second approach to the study of ritual is therefore by a consideration not of their purpose or reason but of their meaning. I am here using the words symbol and meaning as coincident. Whatever has a meaning is a symbol and the meaning is whatever is expressed by the symbol.

But how are we to discover meanings? They do not lie on the surface. There is a sense in which people always know the meaning of their own symbols, but they do so intuitively and can rarely express their understanding in words. Shall we therefore be reduced to guessing at meanings as some anthropologists have guessed at reasons and purposes? I think not. For as long as we admit guess-work of any kind social anthropology cannot be a science. There are, I believe, methods of determining, with some fair degree of probability, the meanings of rites and other symbols.

There is still a third approach to the study of rites. We can consider the effects of the rite—not the effects that it is supposed to produce by the people who practise it but the effects that it does actually produce. A rite has immediate or direct effects on the persons who are in any way directly concerned in it, which we may call, for lack of a better term, the psychological effects. But there are also secondary effects upon the social structure, i.e. the network of social relations binding individuals together in an ordered life. These we may call the social effects. By considering the psychological effects of a rite we may succeed in defining its psychological function; by considering the social effects we may discover its social function. Clearly it is impossible to discover the social function of a rite without taking into account its usual or average psychological effects. But it is possible to discuss the psychological effects while more or less completely ignoring the more remote sociological effects, and this is often done in what is called "functional anthropology."

Let us suppose that we wish to investigate in Australian tribes the totemic rites of a kind widely distributed over a large part of the continent. The ostensible purpose of these rites, as stated by the

---

1. In case it may be thought that this is an inadequate supernatural punishment for a serious breach of rules of proper behaviour a few words of explanation are necessary. Grey hair comes with old age and is thought to be usually associated with loss of sexual potency. It is thus premature old age with its disadvantages but without the advantages that usually accompany seniority that threatens

the man who fails to observe the rules of avoidance. On the other hand when a man's hair is grey and his wife's mother has passed the age of child-bearing the taboo is relaxed so that the relatives may talk together if they wish.

natives themselves, is to renew or maintain some part of nature, such as a species of animal or plant, or rain, or hot or cold weather. With reference to this purpose we have to say that from our point of view the natives are mistaken, that the rites do not actually do what they are believed to do. The rain-making ceremony does not, we think, actually bring rain. In so far as the rites are performed for a purpose they are futile, based on erroneous belief. I do not believe that there is any scientific value in attempts to conjecture processes of reasoning which might be supposed to have led to these errors.

The rites are easily perceived to be symbolic, and we may therefore investigate their meaning. To do this we have to examine a considerable number of them and we then discover that there is a certain body of ritual idiom extending from the west coast of the continent to the east coast with some local variations. Since each rite has a myth associated with it we have similarly to investigate the meanings of the myths. As a result we find that the meaning of any single rite becomes clear in the light of a cosmology, a body of ideas and beliefs about nature and human society, which, so far as its most general features are concerned, is current in all Australian tribes.

The immediate psychological effects of the rites can be to some extent observed by watching and talking to the performers. The ostensible purpose of the rite is certainly present in their minds, but so also is that complex set of cosmological beliefs by reference to which the rite has a meaning. Certainly a person performing the rite, even if, as sometimes happens, he performs it alone, derives therefrom a definite feeling of satisfaction, but it would be entirely false to imagine that this is simply because he believes that he has helped to provide a more abundant supply of food for himself and his fellow-tribesmen. His satisfaction is in having performed a ritual duty, we might say a religious duty. Putting in my own words what I judge, from my own observations, to express what the native feels, I would say that in the performance of the rite he has made that small contribution, which it is both his privilege and his duty to do, to the maintenance of that order of the universe of which man and nature are interdependent parts. The satisfaction which he thus receives gives the rite a special value for him. In some instances with which I am acquainted of the last survivor of a totemic group who still continues to perform the totemic rites by himself, it is this satisfaction that constitutes apparently the sole motive for his action.

To discover the social function of the totemic rites we have to consider the whole body of cosmological ideas of which each rite is a partial expression. I believe that it is possible to show that the social structure of an Australian tribe is connected in a very special way with these cosmological ideas and that the maintenance of its continuity depends on keeping them alive, by their regular expression in myth and rite.

Thus any satisfactory study of the totemic rites of Australia must be based not simply on the consideration of their ostensible purpose and their psychological function, or on an analysis of the motives of the individuals who perform the rites, but on the discovery of their meaning and of their social function.

It may be that some rites have no social function. This may be the case with such taboos as that against spilling salt in our own society. Nevertheless, the method of investigating rites and ritual values that I have found most profitable during work extending over more than thirty years is to study rites as symbolic expressions and to seek to discover their social functions. This method is not new except in so far as it is applied to the comparative study of many societies of diverse types. It was applied by Chinese thinkers to their own ritual more than twenty centuries ago.

In China, in the fifth and sixth centuries B.C., Confucius and his followers insisted on the great importance of the proper performance of ritual, such as funeral and mourning rites and sacrifices. After Confucius there came the reformer Mo Ti who taught a combination of altruism—love for all men—and utilitarianism. He held that funeral and mourning rites were useless and interfered with useful activities and should therefore be abolished or reduced to a minimum. In the third and second centuries B.C., the Confucians, Hsün Tze and the compilers of the *Li Chi* (Book of Rites), replied to Mo Ti to the effect that though these rites might have no utilitarian purpose they none the less had a very important social function. Briefly the theory is that the rites are the orderly (the *Li Chi* says the beautified) expression of feelings appropriate to a social situation. They thus serve to regulate and refine human emotions. We may say that partaking in the performance of rites serves to cultivate in the individual sentiments on whose existence the social order itself depends.

Let us consider the meaning and social function of an extremely simple example of ritual. In the Andaman Islands when a woman is expecting a baby a name is given to it while it is still in the womb. From that time until some weeks after the baby is born nobody is allowed to use the personal name of either the father or the mother; they can be referred to by teknonymy, i.e. in terms of their relation to the child. During this period both the parents are required to abstain from eating certain foods which they may freely eat at other times.

I did not obtain from the Andamanese any statement of the purpose or reason for this avoidance of names. Assuming that the act is symbolic, what method, other than that of guessing, is there of arriving at the meaning? I suggest that we may start with a general working hypothesis that when, in a single society, the same symbol is used in different contexts or on different kinds of occasions there is some common element of meaning, and that by comparing together the various uses of the symbol we may be able to discover what the common element is. This is precisely the method that we adopt in studying an unrecorded spoken language in order to discover the meanings of words and morphemes.

In the Andamans the name of a dead person is avoided from the occurrence of the death to the conclusion of mourning; the name of a person mourning for a dead relative is not used; there is avoidance of the name of a youth or girl who is passing through the ceremonies that take place at adolescence; a bride or bridegroom is not spoken of or to by his or her own name for a short time after the marriage. For the Andamanese the personal name is a symbol of the social personality, i.e. of the position that an individual occupies in the social structure and the social life. The avoidance of a personal name is a symbolic recognition of the fact that at the time the person is not occupying a normal position in the social life. It may be added that a person whose name is thus temporarily out of use is regarded as having for the time an abnormal ritual status.

Turning now to the rule as to avoiding certain foods, if the Andaman Islanders are asked what would happen if the father or mother broke his taboo the usual answer is that he or she would be ill, though one or two of my informants thought it might perhaps also affect the child. This is simply one instance of a standard formula which applies to a number of ritual prohibitions. Thus persons in mourning for a relative may not eat pork and turtle, the most important flesh foods, and the reason given is that if they did they would be ill.

To discover the meaning of this avoidance of foods by the parents we can apply the same method as in reference to the avoidance of their names. There are similar rules for mourners, for women during menstruation, and for youths and girls during the period of adolescence. But for a full demonstration we have to consider the place of foods in Andamanese ritual as a whole, and for an examination of this I must refer to what I have already written on the subject.

I should like to draw your attention to another point in the method by which it is possible to test our hypotheses as to the meanings of rites. We take the different occasions on which two rites are associated together, for example the association of the avoidance of a person's name with the avoidance by that person of certain foods, which we find in the instance of mourners on the one hand and the expectant mother and father on the other. We must assume that for the Andamanese there is some important similarity between these two kinds of occasions—birth and death—by virtue of which they have similar ritual values. We cannot rest content with any interpretation of the taboos at childbirth unless there is a parallel interpretation of those relating to mourners. In the terms I am using here we can say that in the Andamans the relatives of a recently dead person, and the father and mother of a child that is about to be, or has recently been, born, are in an abnormal ritual status. This is recognised or indicated by the avoidance of their names. They are regarded as likely to suffer some misfortune, some bad luck, if you will, unless they observe certain prescribed ritual precautions of which the avoidance of certain foods is one. In the Andaman Islands the danger in such instances is thought of as the danger of illness. This is the case also with the Polynesian belief about the ritual status of anyone who has touched a corpse or a newly-born baby. It is to be noted that for the Polynesians as well as for the Andamanese the occasion of a birth has a similar ritual value to that of a death.

The interpretation of the taboos at childbirth at which we arrive by studying it in relation to the whole system of ritual values of the Andamanese is too complex to be stated here in full. Clearly, however, they express, in accordance with Andamanese ritual idiom, a common concern in the event. The parents show their concern by avoiding certain foods; their friends show theirs by avoiding the parents' personal names. By virtue of these taboos the occasion acquires a certain social value, as that term has been defined above.

There is one theory that might seem to be applicable to our example. It is based on a hypothesis as to the psychological function of a class of rites. The theory is that in certain circumstances the individual human being is anxious about the outcome of some event or activity because it depends to some extent on conditions that he cannot control by any technical means. He therefore observes some rite which, since he believes it will ensure good luck, serves to reassure him. Thus an aeronaut takes with him in a plane a mascot which he believes will protect him from accident and thus carries out his flight with confidence.

The theory has a respectable antiquity. It was perhaps implied in the *Primus in orbe deos fecit timor* of Petronius and Statius. It has taken various forms from Hume's explanation of religion to Malinowski's explanation of Trobriand magic. It can be made so plausible by a suitable selection of illustrations that it is necessary to examine it with particular care and treat it with reasonable scepticism. For there is always the danger that we may be taken in by the plausibility of a theory that ultimately proves to be unsound.

I think that for certain rites it would be easy to maintain with equal plausibility an exactly contrary theory, namely, that if it were not for the existence of the rite and the beliefs associated with it the individual would feel no anxiety, and that the psychological effect of the rite is to create in him a sense of insecurity or danger. It seems very unlikely that an Andaman Islander would think that it is dangerous to eat dugong or pork or turtle meat if it were not for the existence of a specific body of ritual the ostensible purpose of which is to protect him from those dangers. Many hundreds of similar instances could be mentioned from all over the world.

Thus, while one anthropological theory is that magic and religion give men confidence, comfort and a sense of security, it could equally well be argued that they give men fears and anxieties from which they would otherwise be free—the fear of black magic or of spirits, fear of God, of the Devil, of Hell.

Actually in our fears or anxieties as well as in our hopes we are conditioned (as the phrase goes) by the community in which we live. And it is largely by the sharing of hopes and fears, by what I have called common concern in events or eventualities, that human beings are linked together in temporary or permanent associations.

To return to the Andamanese taboos at childbirth, there are difficulties in supposing that they are means by which parents reassure themselves against the accidents that may interfere with a successful delivery. If the prospective father fails to observe the food taboo it is he who will be sick, according to the general Andamanese opinion. Moreover, he must continue to observe the taboos after the child is safely delivered. Further, how are we to provide a parallel explanation of the similar taboos observed by a person mourning for a dead relative?

The taboos associated with pregnancy and parturition are often explained in terms of the hypothesis I have mentioned. A father, naturally anxious at the outcome of an event over which he does not have a technical control and which is subject to

hazard, reassures himself by observing some taboo or carrying out some magical action. He may avoid certain foods. He may avoid making nets or tying knots, or he may go round the house untying all knots and opening any locked or closed boxes or containers.

I wish to arouse in your minds, if it is not already there, a suspicion that both the general theory and this special application of it do not give the whole truth and indeed may not be true at all. Scepticism of plausible but unproved hypotheses is essential in every science. There is at least good ground for suspicion in the fact that the theory has so far been considered in reference to facts that seem to fit it, and no systematic attempt has been made, so far as I am aware, to look for facts that do not fit. That there are many such I am satisfied from my own studies.

The alternative hypothesis which I am presenting for consideration is as follows. In a given community it is appropriate that an expectant father should feel concern or at least should make an appearance of doing so. Some suitable symbolic expression of his concern is found in terms of the general ritual or symbolic idiom of the society, and it is felt generally that a man in that situation ought to carry out the symbolic or ritual actions or abstentions. For every rule that *ought* to be observed there must be some sort of sanction or reason. For acts that patently affect other persons the moral and legal sanctions provide a generally sufficient controlling force upon the individual. For ritual obligations conformity and rationalisation are provided by the ritual sanctions. The simplest form of ritual sanction is an accepted belief that if rules of ritual are not observed some undefined misfortune is likely to occur. In many societies the expected danger is somewhat more definitely conceived as a danger of sickness or, in extreme cases, death. In the more specialised forms of ritual sanction the good results to be hoped for or the bad results to be feared are more specifically defined in reference to the occasion or meaning of the ritual.

The theory is not concerned with the historical origin of ritual, nor is it another attempt to explain ritual in terms of human psychology; it is a hypothesis as to the relation of ritual and ritual values to the essential constitution of human society, i.e. to those invariant general characters which belong to all human societies, past, present and future. It rests on the recognition of the fact that while in animal societies social coaptation depends on instinct, in human societies it depends upon the efficacy of symbols of many different kinds. The theory I am advancing must therefore, for a just estimation of its value, be considered in its place in a general theory of symbols and their social efficacy.

By this theory the Andamanese taboos relating to childbirth are the obligatory recognition in a standardised symbolic form of the significance and importance of the event to the parents and to the community at large. They thus serve to fix the social value of occasions of this kind. Similarly I have argued in another place that the Andamanese taboos relating to the animals and plants used for food are means of affixing a definite social value to food, based on its social importance. The *social* importance of food is not that it satisfies hunger, but that in such a community as an Andamanese camp or village an enormously large proportion of the activities are concerned with the getting and consuming of food, and that in these activities, with their daily instances of collaboration and mutual aid, there continuously occur those inter-relations of interests which bind the individual men, women and children into a society.

I believe that this theory can be generalised and with suitable modifications will be found to apply to a vast number of the taboos of different societies. My theory would go further for I would hold, as a reasonable working hypothesis, that we have here the primary basis of all ritual and therefore of religion and magic, however those may be distinguished. The primary basis of ritual, so the formulation would run, is the attribution of ritual value to objects and occasions which are either themselves objects of important common interests linking together the persons of a community or are symbolically representative of such objects. To illustrate what is meant by the last part of this statement two illustrations may be offered. In the Andamans ritual value is attributed to the cicada, not because it has any social importance itself but because it symbolically represents the seasons of the year which do have importance. In some tribes of Eastern Australia the god Baiame is the personification, i.e. the symbolical representative, of the moral law of the tribe, and the rainbow-serpent (the Australian equivalent of the Chinese dragon) is a symbol representing growth and fertility in nature. Baiame and the rainbow-serpent in their turn are represented by the figures of earth which are made on the sacred ceremonial ground of the initiation ceremonies and at which rites are performed. The reverence that the Australian shows to the image of Baiame or towards his name is the symbolic method of fixing the social value of the moral law, particularly the laws relating to marriage.

In conclusion let me return once more to the work of the anthropologist whom we are here to honour. Sir James Frazer, in his *Psyche's Task* and in his other works, set himself to show how, in his own words, taboos have contributed to build up the complex fabric of society. He thus initiated that functional study of ritual to which I have in this lecture and elsewhere attempted to make some contribution. But there has been a shift of emphasis. Sir James accounted for the taboos of savage tribes as the application in practice of beliefs arrived at by erroneous processes of reasoning, and he seems to have thought of the effects of these beliefs in creating or maintaining a stable orderly society as being accidental. My own view is that the negative and positive rites of savages exist and persist because they are part of the mechanism by which an orderly society maintains itself in existence, serving as they do to establish certain fundamental social values. The beliefs by which the rites themselves are justified and given some sort of consistency are the rationalisations of symbolic actions and of the sentiments associated with them. I would suggest that what Sir James Frazer seems to regard as the accidental results of magical and religious beliefs really constitute their essential function and the ultimate reason for their existence.

4. On Communal Ritual

BY EMILE DURKHEIM

BUT IF THIS THEORY of totemism has enabled us to explain the most characteristic beliefs of this religion, it rests upon a fact not yet explained. When the idea of the totem, the emblem of the clan, is given, all the rest follows; but we must still investigate how this idea has been formed. This is a double question and may be subdivided as follows: What has led the clan to choose an emblem? and why have these emblems been borrowed from the animal and vegetable worlds, and particularly from the former?

That an emblem is useful as a rallying-centre for any sort of a group it is superfluous to point out. By expressing the social unity in a material form, it makes this more obvious to all, and for that very reason the use of emblematic symbols must have spread quickly when once thought of. But more than that, this idea should spontaneously arise out of the conditions of common life; for the emblem is not merely a convenient process for clarifying the sentiment society has of itself: it also serves to create this sentiment; it is one of its constituent elements.

In fact, if left to themselves, individual consciousnesses are closed to each other; they can communicate only by means of signs which express their internal states. If the communication established between them is to become a real communion, that is to say, a fusion of all particular sentiments into one common sentiment, the signs expressing them must themselves be fused into one single and unique resultant. It is the appearance of this that informs individuals that they are in harmony and makes them conscious of their moral unity. It is by uttering the same cry, pronouncing the same word, or performing the same gesture in regard to some object that they become and feel themselves to be in unison. It is true that individual representations also cause reactions in the organism that are not without importance; however, they can be thought of apart from these physical reactions which accompany them or follow them, but which do not constitute them. But it is quite another matter with

collective representations. They presuppose that minds act and react upon one another; they are the product of these actions and reactions which are themselves possible only through material intermediaries. These latter do not confine themselves to revealing the mental state with which they are associated; they aid in creating it. Individual minds cannot come in contact and communicate with each other except by coming out of themselves; but they cannot do this except by movements. So it is the homogeneity of these movements that gives the group consciousness of itself and consequently makes it exist. When this homogeneity is once established and these movements have once taken a stereotyped form, they serve to symbolize the corresponding representations. But they symbolize them only because they have aided in forming them.

Moreover, without symbols, social sentiments could have only a precarious existence. Though very strong as long as men are together and influence each other reciprocally, they exist only in the form of recollections after the assembly has ended, and when left to themselves, these become feebler and feebler; for since the group is now no longer present and active, individual temperaments easily regain the upper hand. The violent passions which may have been released in the heart of a crowd fall away and are extinguished when this is dissolved, and men ask themselves with astonishment how they could ever have been so carried away from their normal character. But if the movements by which these sentiments are expressed are connected with something that endures, the sentiments themselves become more durable. These other things are constantly bringing them to mind and arousing them; it is as though the cause which excited them in the first place continued to act. Thus these systems of emblems, which are necessary if society is to become conscious of itself, are no less indispensable for assuring the continuation of this consciousness.

So we must refrain from regarding these symbols as simple artifices, as sorts of labels attached to representations already made, in order to make them more manageable: they are an integral part of them. Even the fact that collective sentiments

Reprinted from Emile Durkheim, *The Elementary Forms of the Religious Life,* trans. Joseph W. Swain (Glencoe, Ill.: The Free Press, 1954), pp. 230–31, with the permission of The Free Press.

are thus attached to things completely foreign to them is not purely conventional: it illustrates under a conventional form a real characteristic of social facts, that is, their transcendence over individual minds. In fact, it is known that social phenomena are born, not in individuals, but in the group. Whatever part we may take in their origin, each of us receives them from without. So when we represent them to ourselves as emanating from a material object, we do not completely misunderstand their nature. Of course they do not come from the specific thing to which we connect them, but nevertheless, it is true that their origin is outside of us. If the moral force sustaining the believer does not come from the idol he adores or the emblem he venerates, still it is from outside of him, as he is well aware. The objectivity of its symbol only translates its externalness.

PART FOUR

Culture and the Social System

Introduction

BY TALCOTT PARSONS

Part four concerns the second of the most salient "boundary-zones" of social systems—that in which the patterning of social interaction articulates with the cultural system, which is itself one of the primary subsystems of the general system of action. The main frame of reference in which we conceive their relations was presented in the second essay of the General Introduction to the Reader; we will take this concept as our point of departure here.[1]

According to that concept, human action is organized through and in terms of the patterning of the "meanings" of objects and of orientations to objects in the world of human experience.[2]

"Meaning," in the present technical usage, should be understood as a *relational* category. In philosophical terms, it implies both a "knowing" (or, to avoid a cognitive bias, an "orienting") subject or actor, and an object—or, more generally, a *system* comprising a plurality both of actors and of objects. Orientations to objects are conceived as structured or, in the term commonly used in the cultural context, as "patterned." In other words, there are elements of "consistency," "order," or "coherence"—between orientations *to* different discrete objects and classes of objects; and between the orientations *of* different actors and classes of actors. In this sense, the structure of cultural meanings constitutes the "ground" of any system of action, as distinguished from the set of situational conditions to which its functioning is subject.

In the second essay of the General Introduction, the distinction between external and internal references for the analysis of any system of action was presented as one of the two main axes of the analysis of systems of action in general. The importance of this axis is a consequence of the general concept that a system of action, like all living systems, is an "open" system continually interacting with an external situation or environment through interchanging outputs and inputs. One example of such interaction is the body's nutritional and respiratory inputs, and its output of physical energy in the skeletal-muscular manipulation of environmental objects.

Any such system, considered both as a whole and in different ways through its structurally differentiated units, becomes involved in these processes of interchange. Some of its structures and functions become specialized in relation to interchanges with the situation; these are the externally oriented structures and functions that we have located on the contexts of goal-attainment and adaptation. Other structures and functions become specialized with reference to the internal states of the system, in ways that are relatively insulated from the more immediate impact of the situation. These structures and functions are concerned, first, with maintaining the *states* of the units serving as conditions of their effective interaction with other units and with the external situation; and second, with the interaction of units in relation to each other, in terms of their mutual compatibility and reinforcement—i.e., with what we have called pattern-maintenance and integration. The two sets of structures and functions are interdependent; but each set is discrete.

Using "meaning," as above defined, as the master category of the cultural reference, we can, in one sense, treat the familiar and fundamental distinction between the knowing subject and the object known as a special case of the internal-external distinction. However, the subject-object distinction has been used most extensively in analyzing cognitive structures, i.e., in the analysis of "knowledge." In order to avoid any appearance of a cognitive

---

1. In connection with this Introduction, I am particularly indebted to Dr. Robert N. Bellah. Many of the ideas presented here developed from discussions with him, and his stimulating criticism of the first draft of the manuscript led to major revisions.

2. The German term *Sinnzusammenhänge*, though difficult to translate, is particularly expressive in this connection.

bias, we shall speak of *orientation* in terms of meaning; and shall use the distinction between the meanings of *objects* oriented *to* (the external aspect of a cultural system), and the meanings of *orientations by* actors (the internal aspect) as our major frame of reference.

Two of our four dimensions of the variation of cultural systems may thus be formulated as dimensions of the meaning of objects to orienting actors. The other two are dimensions of the meaning of orientations as such—of strucured states of orienting "subjects," abstracted from the particularities of objects and specific classes of them to which they orient.

An additional point is a preliminary to the discussion of cultural systems. A great deal of the treatment of culture has emphasized the element of *pattern* as such, considering culture as a system of "eternal objects."[3] Culture conceived exclusively in these terms, however important its part in the determination of action might be, would be deprived of the status of being a *system* of action in the same sense that behavioral organisms, personalities, and social systems are action systems. This pattern element is an authentically central aspect of culture, but is not exhaustive. Broadly, it comprises the *structural* component of cultural systems; the "content" of their pattern-maintenance subsystems and subsystems. The analysis of this cultural structure as such is, in our opinion, the task area of formal disciplines such as logic, mathematics, structural linguistics, the systematics of stylistic form, the purely logical structure of a theological system, and the formal analysis of legal norms.

How a cultural system is also a system of action in the direct sense is best shown through a comparison with the social system. Like all other action systems, a social system involves the organization of *all* the components which in any sense enter into action. A social system is distinctive, not in its ultimate components, but in focusing the organization of these ultimate components around the exigencies of the functioning of systems of social interaction as such—analytically, independently of the exigencies of personality functioning or of cultural integrity as such, though interdependent with them. From the general premises of action theory it follows that, if the functions of culture are as essential as they seem to be, the important patterns of culture, i.e., complexes of meaning, could not be created and/or maintained as available resources

for action in the other systems of action unless there were processes of action primarily oriented to their creation and/or maintenance. These processes may be part of a "society," just as the life of an individual as personality may be; but analytically, the subsystem of action focused in this way should be distinguished from the social system as focused on interaction relationships. The maintenance of a religious orientation through the functioning of a church would be considered as a case of interpenetration of cultural and social system; but a church as such would be regarded as a collectivity with cultural primacy, i.e., as first, a cultural "system of action," and second, a social system. Similarly, the organization of scientific research is, in the first instance, cultural in focus, and secondarily social, because it must meet exigencies of interaction.

Cultural patterns as such will be considered as forming the focus of organization for a set of subsystems in the action system. The primacy of this focus distinguishes a cultural system from a social system, a personality system, or a behavioral organism.

THE DIMENSIONS OF CULTURAL
VARIATION

First, we shall discuss the two externally oriented dimensions of the cultural system—i.e., those concerned with categories of the meanings of objects, as distinguished from the patterns of orientation *to* objects. These externally oriented dimensions correspond to, or are special cases of, the dimensions of adaptation and goal-attainment, as these concepts are often used in the general theory of action. In dealing with the meanings of objects, however, one must remember that these aspects or subsystems of cultural systems are parts of a larger whole. The meanings in question are not simply intrinsic; like all categories of human culture, they are inherently "relational." That is, they concern categories of the meaning of objects for human "interests," as "perceived" by these interests.

The first of the externally oriented dimensions concerns orientation to objects as objects of cognition in the empirical sense—i.e., as objects of scientific knowledge, or of the kinds of common sense preceding and underlying the scientific level of sophisticated knowledge.

Points or zones in this dimension can be defined and distinguished on the basis of levels of cultural generality of the components of a body of scientific

---

3. The phrase is Whitehead's. This was the view taken by the author, both in *The Structure of Social Action* and, in collaboration with Shils, in *Toward a General Theory of Action*. It no longer seems adequate in the light of further theoretical developments, and has been modified along the lines sketched in the following paragraphs.

knowledge; i.e., the structural component of empirically cognitive systems. This scale of levels is a special case of the hierarchy of control, in the cybernetic sense prominently used in the second essay of the General Introduction. In this case, the distinctions are based in well-established concepts in the field of the methodology of science.

The lowest-order culturally structured component of a body of empirical knowledge is the body of ordered, or in some sense codified (i.e., classified) knowledge of facts (i.e., data which are somehow empirically validated). In these terms, facts are *statements* about empirical phenomena, not the phenomena themselves—the phenomena belong to the external situation of the cultural system; they are parts of the objects to which the knower is oriented, and not the *meanings* of the objects.

The second-order component consists in the solutions of empirical problems. Data, or statements of fact, can be organized to refer beyond the phenomena and to the validity of the facts themselves. This involves reference to a particular basis of interest in external phenomena or object-systems; and, also, reference to the meaning of the problems in terms of the scientifically relevant basic system of cultural order, i.e., the order involved in systems of theory. The available data form the raw material through which problem solutions can be achieved; but the facts do not speak for themselves—they must be organized, processed, and related to theory.

The third-order component is the structure of theory itself. This, as noted, is the system of cultural order relevant to this dimension of the organization of cultural systems. Its primary function with respect to empirical knowledge is integration. It is the primary basis on which different facts, referring to different objects and their aspects, can be related to one another in an ordered system, and thereby form a *corpus* of knowledge, as distinct from a catalogue of discrete items of factual information.

An additional distinction must be made, between theory itself and the higher-order premises on which a system of theory rests. The higher-order premises are the "primitive" concepts which are not subject to empirical validation, but are assumed to underlie the meaning of the problems which are posed for investigation. These premises lead into the logical and epistemological problem areas where science has its major direct connections with philosophy. In one set of terms, this level constitutes the frame of reference within which a theoretical scheme "makes sense." Theory is a body of interrelated generalized propositions about empirical phenomena within a frame of reference. The frame of reference of classical mechanics, involving such concepts as particle, mass, motion, velocity within space and time, is one example. Another example is the "action" frame of reference, with such concepts as actor, situation, goals, values, etc.

These four components of the methodology of science constitute more than a list or catalogue. They may be organized in at least three different ways. The most important to us is the hierarchy which has been used as the basis of the above exposition. Data concerning them constitute the lowest-order level of meaning of external objects in this cognitive reference. Problems, then, constitute the next level of meaning; the data's significance for problems forms the basis for organizing a plurality of statements of fact into a higher-order complex. For investigation as a process, the problem-statement is the immediate basis for marshalling known factual information, and then for undertaking to determine new facts at the points where gaps in knowledge exist. However, problems may have various meanings in a larger cultural system, and different orders of relation to each other. In so far as the meaning has scientific primacy, however, the significance of the problem's solution for a system of theory is the primary basis of the meaning of the problems, and especially of different problems in relation to each other. Finally, theory itself is relative to the level of the frame of reference that is not empirically provable, but is necessary in order to give meaning to problems and to theory itself. This hierarchical order is one of *levels of generality of conceptual components*. It is also a hierarchy of control, in that the meaning of problems controls interest in the meaning of facts; the place in theory controls the meaning or significance of particular problems; and the frame of reference controls the significance of the system of theory. But the obverse conditional relation also holds. So far as it is scientifically significant, a problem not solved on the basis of validated data is not scientifically solved; a theory not validated by solutions of the principal empirical problems deriving from it has no scientific status; and a frame of reference which cannot serve as a framework for empirically scientific theory and its related problems has no place in science.

The second basis of organizing the components concerns the external-internal distinction as applied to this subsystem of culture, rather than to culture as a whole. The first two components in the order presented constitute the *empirical* components of a scientific system of knowledge; these are consistently emphasized by "empiricists." They are the "power" or "high-energy" subsystems of the empirical cognitive aspect of culture, the conditions without which higher-order development is impossible. Theories and frames of reference, however, constitute the theoretical⁴ components. They are "low-energy" components: alone, they do not solve any empirical scientific problems nor yield any data; but they control and organize these essential processes. From the cultural point of view, theory and frames of reference are the internal components of the cultural subsystem of empirical cognition.

The third mode of organization is a special case of the distinction between the instrumental and the consummatory aspects of action systems. In empirical cognition, it may be described as the distinction between "methodological" elements and "results." In the investigative process, there are two levels of "methodology." One constitutes the standards and procedures for gathering data and validation; the other, the "logic of science," concerns the criteria for the formulation of frames of reference and their use, in particular relation to theory but also to the other components. Methods, however, are of no great significance taken by themselves; their meaning is instrumental to the results to which they contribute. There are two major classes of scientifically important results—the solution of particular empirical problems, and the construction of theory. The success of investigative endeavors must be evaluated by these outcomes.

The above analysis is based on a classification of the components of systems of empirical cognition. As such it cuts across another important classification in this area, the classification of *objects* of empirical cognition. From the perspective of the theory of action, these objects may be classified, in ascending hierarchical order, as physical, biological, psychological, social, and cultural. This also is a cybernetic hierarchy. It is remarkable how closely the categories which seem appropriate now correspond to those proposed by Comte in his classification of the sciences more than a century ago.

In the later nineteenth century, Western science underwent a phase in which "reductionism" was popular, leading to the contention that all empirical phenomena could be "ultimately" explained in terms of the theory and frame of reference of physics. A variety of changes have made this seem progressively less likely. Among them are the newer developments of evolutionary thinking in biology; the development of information theory and cybernetics, with their utilization of the concepts of function and goal or purpose; and the more independent development of theory in psychology and the social and cultural sciences.

In accord with the general relational character of all cultural systems and subsystems, the distinctions among these categories must be regarded in two ways. One aspect concerns the "intrinsic" basis of the distinctions; here, that basis is *levels of organization* of systems. In other words, organisms are organizations of physico-chemical components. Personalities are organizations of the components of the behavior of organisms; societies, of the interaction of personalities; etc. Physical phenomena are not per se components of action systems, but constitute their conditional substratum. Organisms, in relation to the physical environment, constitute the adaptive subsystem of action; personalities, its goal-attaining subsystem; societies, its integrative subsystem; and cultural systems, its pattern-maintenance subsystem.

The other aspect of the relational character of this object classification concerns the basis of *interest* in these different categories of objects. As subsequent discussion will indicate, this has both cathectic and evaluative aspects, which will be amplified upon in connection with these dimensions of the organization of culture.

Seen in these terms, cultural objects stand at the top of the hierarchy. Their structure consists in the *pattern* element of the relevant cultural action system. In the case of empirical object systems, this cultural pattern element is the theory of the relevant sciences, or the protoscientific patterns of generalized conceptualization defining orientations toward empirical objects as objects of cognition rather than of cathexis. This cultural object component falls into two important subclasses: the "formal" theoretical content of the conceptual schemes of the empirical sciences as such; and the content of the formal disciplines as outlined above.

Considered in terms of its place in the more general system of culture, theory becomes acceptable on the basis of its grounding in the orientations of meaning in the system. It is here that it must find its philosophical grounding in logic and epistemology. At this point, science inherently depends on nonscientific considerations for defining its meanings in human action. There are also the ultimate realities of the empirical world. For present purposes, this is interpreted as the definition of the boundary-relation of this subsystem of the cultural system vis-à-vis the other subsystems of action and, through them, the physical world.

The other dimension defining relations of cultural systems to external objects also involves the relative

---

4. There is an ambiguity in the common use of "theory"—the term is often used to designate what I have above called the solution of a problem, e.g. a "theory of juvenile delinquency." By "theory" in the present context I mean a logical system of abstract propositions which as such have no direct empirical content at all. A prototype is the system of differential equations constituting the theory of classical mechanics.

primacy of different components in the meaning of objects. In this case, however, it involves their meaning as objects of *goal*-orientation of action systems. In other words, objects are regarded in terms of their significance for the immediate stabilization of a condition of disturbance or tension in the relation between a system of action and relevant parts of its situation or environment. In psychology this is often described as the "cathexis" of objects. We shall use this term more generally, to refer to any category of the meaning of an object with respect to which its significance in terms of goal-attainment or of blocking such attainment is paramount.

An attempt at the present order of theoretical systematization in this field is somewhat unfamiliar. For this reason we will first propose a set of categories which formulate the relation between basic orientations and the modalities of the relevant objects at the *general* action system level. This formulation will use terminology related to the psychological, using in particular *cathexis* as a key term. We will then attempt to translate the results into terms appropriate to the level of the cultural system where the appropriate objects are *expressive symbols*.

At the level of the general action system, then, the lowest level of the "cathectic meaning" of an object is its treatment as a "means-object" or, in economic terminology, as an object of utility. The next level is its treatment as "goal-object" for the personality—the acting system's attainment and/or maintenance of a specific *relation* to this object has "consummatory" significance for the system. The actor may become "attached" to such an object. These two categories of cathectic meaning are important at the most elementary level of unit relations or interaction.

As the first essay of the General Introduction indicated, however, cathectic system relations are not limited to these two levels—the more extensive and time-extended the system, the less its cathectic relations are so limited. The level above the "consummatory" is the level of "inclusion" or "adherence." This is best illustrated by the interaction of individual persons. Though Alter (as person in role) may be "cathected" by Ego, as an object with minimal involvement of higher-level cultural components, if a "serious," long-term, and stable relationship is established, it will necessarily generate a normative structure of *shared* meanings. One aspect of this is that Ego and Alter combine to constitute a *collectivity,* in the sociological sense. Then, in addition to Alter's meaning as a discrete person, there is, for Ego, the meaning of their common membership in or adherence to the collectivity comprised by Ego and Alter together.[5] The principle involved in this interaction between people may be generalized to apply to any case of a system of action related to an object in its environment. We must consider both the meaning of the complementary object standing on the same level of cathectic meaning as the actor of reference; and the meaning of the object constituted by both of them, and possibly others, through their interaction. This latter is the meaning of inclusion, adherence, or membership, as distinguished from the meaning of attachment or consummation.

The order comprised by any given interaction process—whether of organisms, persons, or collectivities—is always part of a larger system in which it is treated as, or has the "meaning of being," a subsystem. Therefore, cathexis has one higher level—of the object constituted by the interaction process, and also of some conception of an object (or set of objects) conceived as standing "above" this interaction and, in some normative sense, controlling it. For the society as system, this concerns the source of the legitimation of its values and norms. Cognitively, it is usually conceived as non-empirical; and, cathectically, as an object of generalized respect perhaps even of worship. For social systems of a lower order than the society, it is essentially the paramount object of motivational commitment, which takes precedence over and regulates lower-order commitments. Relations to the prescription of obligations may vary enormously, from minute details to the most general orientations. However, for the existence of detailed norms, analytically some special mechanism must be postulated, e.g., "revelation." Always, the object as conceived has a generalized aspect that is analytically separable from these. Hence, this highest level may be described as the cathexis of the object of *generalized respect,* at a level above the level of legitimation of the detailed system of obligations governing the actions of the units under consideration.

A general principle is involved in the "highest" level of each scale of generality outlined for each cultural dimension. In the case of empirical cognitive patterns, there must be some kind of non-empirical basis for empirical knowledge. For cathectic meaning, cathexis of an order or of a source of legitimation is no longer "purely" cathectic. A parallel interpretation may be made in the two cases. The ultimate basis of empirical cognitive meaning cannot itself be empirical; it merges into the orientational foundation of meaning. Similarly, the ultimate basis of cathectic meaning is inseparable from

5. The importance of this distinction of more than one level of "identification" for the process of socialization of the individual has been discussed in Parsons, "Social Structure and the Development of Personality," *Psychiatry,* November, 1958.

a basis in evaluative orientation, which will be discussed presently.

There is, therefore, a dimension of cultural systems constituted by the order of precedence or importance of the meanings of objects of cathexis. Objects which are to be "used" as means to unit goals beyond themselves are lowest in this order. Just above these are objects on the same level as the acting system, "attachment" to which is a goal—a relation implying *reciprocity* of cathectic meaning, as exemplified by a love relationship between people. Next higher is the more "inclusive" object of adherence, comprised by two or more interacting subsystems; the social collectivity is the prototype of this. Highest is the superordinate object, transcending the interactive system, that is the source of the legitimation of norms and the object of generalized respect. This is the dimension of *level of generality of cathectic attachment*.

The cross-cutting between the components of empirical cognition and the classification of objects, discussed above, bears an important relation to the hierarchy of cathectic or expressive pattern-components. This relation derives from goal-attainment's special significance for people. It may be inferred from this that the prototypal object of attachment is another person; therefore the attachment level of cathexis or motivational commitment particularly concerns personalities as objects. This suggests that objects of utility are typically biological and physical objects; the individual's own body, considered as a set of facilities for attaining the personality's goals, is the prototypal case. This distinction seems to underlie the very general sentiment against treating people primarily as means to an end instead of as ends in themselves; whereas treating physical objects as means is usually considered legitimate.

Objects of inclusion are prototypally social objects, e.g., collectivities. Objects of generalized respect are cultural objects that often may be connected with a non-empirical status in the cognitive mode.

The problem of the status of these categories of objects becomes closely connected with the subject of symbolism. Symbolism will be discussed later; our concern now is with the major categories of meaning of objects in the mode of cathexis or goal-attainment for action. In this area, the prototypal relation to the general classification of objects obtains. As will be discussed later, other categories of objects also can serve as symbols in any and all of these meaning modes.

Like the components of empirical cognition, the categories of cathectic meaning of objects can be ranked on bases other than levels of generality. Two

other bases are significant. The first is a special case of the external-internal line of differentiation. The lower-order components, the treatment of objects as utilities and as objects of attachment, are categorically external. Freud's concept of cathexis is directly applicable here, first to the category of attachment. However, it has been shown, particularly by Olds, that the motive force deriving from a goal-cathexis is generalized to the cathexis of means-objects instrumental to attaining the goal.[6]

In the relevant respects, the other two categories stand on a different level, which can be regarded as a case of the internal reference. They are not categories of the direct meaning of objects as sources of gratification or of utility; they are categories of the cultural framework within which particular gratifications acquire meaning. Particular attachments to persons must, to be consistently meaningful, occur in the framework of socially organized collectivities; and these collectivities must be "legitimized" in terms of objects of generalized respect. Freud's term, "identification," as distinct from cathexis or object-attachment, may be appropriated for this category of meanings.[7]

The second basis of organization uses the instrumental-consummatory distinction. For the two external categories, it is the prototypal example of that distinction, since this is precisely the motivational or cathectic meaning of objects of goal-attainment and of utility. It might also be described in terms of the distinction between rewards and facilities. However, in one sense inclusion is also a category of reward, the reward of "acceptance," whereas relations to objects of generalized respect cannot in the same sense have consummatory meaning, which is, rather, a basis of energizing action. In the religious context, it is often described as a source of "strength."

The above categories have been formulated at the level of the general structure of action, without taking into account the special features which develop when the concern is at the cultural level as such. In the cultural case the focus is on *meaning* as such rather than on the empirical features of the concrete object-relation; it concerns *symbols* rather than actual objects of cathexis, utility etc. A symbol must, as we shall see later, be meaningfully related to its "real" referent, but if the relation of the orienting actor to both were identical the distinction between

---

6. See James Olds, *The Growth and Structure of Motives,* Free Press, 1957, Chap. III. Also Parsons, "The Theory of Symbolism in Relation to Action," *Working Papers in the Theory of Action,* Free Press, 1953, Chap. II.

7. The argument for choosing this term has been developed in Parsons, "Social Structure and the Development of Personality," *loc. cit.*

symbol and referent would become redundant. Thus if the conception of the "fatherhood" of God is symbolic, there must of course be a sense in which the relation of a believer to his God is *analogous* to that of a child to his father, but it can be a true symbol *only* if it is *not* in fact a father-child relationship in the empirical sense.

The cultural categories which belong here, therefore, are categories of expressive *symbolism*, as distinguished from the intrinsic cathectic interest in "real" objects. If we take expressive symbolization as in some sense parallel to empirical knowledge, then we can suggest a classification of components of systems of such symbolization. The focal category will be that of symbolic *content*, as such, the symbols which are expected to be the objects of cathexis in place of "real" objects; an example would be the Madonna and Child of Renaissance painting as the portrayal of a realistic social relationship type of great importance in the society of the time, but as "meaning" more than a pictorial representation of an actual mother and child. The facilities which are necessary to build up such a symbolic representation are the technical devices and procedures utilized by the artist which, like the facts of the scientist, are organized and codified, not merely ad hoc "play" with canvas, pigments and brushes. But this technically produced symbol acquires its artistic meaning by virtue of its incorporation in still higher-order meaning or pattern systems. This seems to be the kind of thing that art historians and critics speak of when they refer to questions of "form" and "style." In a sense not directly reducible to the levels of content and technique, these are the specifically "aesthetic" components of the symbolization, by virtue of which it acquires expressive significance beyond the particular case or its realistic references.

The external-internal axis of differentiation is essentially that between concrete symbolizations on the one hand and the codes in which their meaning must be interpreted on the other. This is a distinction which will be seen presently to be of very general importance in connection with the problems of language. The instrumental-consummatory line of differentiation on the other hand is parallel to that between methods and results in the case of science. Here it may be spoken of as the distinction between the primary resources at the disposal of the artist, namely techniques and normative patterns of style, and the results at which he aims which are respectively effective concrete symbol-formations and form-patterns which generalize the relations between whole complexes of more specific symbols.

In the two dimensions just outlined, components of meaning as object, intrinsic or symbolic, take precedence over meaning in the mode of orientation, i.e., the "disposition" of the acting system. In considering this latter aspect of the cultural "picture," we will discriminate between two dimensions which constitute the application of the more general concepts of integration and of pattern-maintenance, respectively, to the cultural field.

In its reference to culture, integration is essentially the orientation-mode we call "evaluation." In regarding the object-world, integration comprises (1) the evaluation of costs, i.e., of the utilities of means-objects, *in relation* to their empirical properties, i.e., their conditions of production and utilization; and (2) evaluation of action-goals, i.e., the relative importance of different goal-objects as intrinsically desirable or undesirable. On the cultural level the crucial categories are the *standards* applied to such judgments of evaluation.

These two contexts of evaluation, however, are subordinate to higher-order contexts, concerned primarily with the rank-ordering of the moral principles or standards according to which the evaluation of particularized goals and facilities become meaningful.

These moral principles are essentially those appropriate, respectively, to the "interests" of each in turn of the four major components or dimensions of cultural orientation. Thus where empirical cognition has primacy it is a matter of standards of empirical validity; in the context of expressive symbolization it is those of expressive adequacy; in that of evaluation as such, of moral integrity and in that of the grounding of ultimate meanings, of what may be called philosophical adequacy and depth. It should be noted that, from the point of view of the cultural system more generally, these are all of *moral* significance, since they concern the priority system of the commitments assumed by culturally oriented actors.

In addition, the highest level of evaluation involves reference to the possibilities of interpreting the meanings of experience or reality, in a way transcending each of these different levels of evaluative standard. In the evaluative context, this last category leads to the core problems of meaning on which Weber based his analysis of the sociology of religion. Like other zenithal levels, the highest level of evaluative orientation necessarily involves references which transcend evaluation as such.

The third dimension of cultural variation thus comprises a hierarchy of patterns of evaluation, i.e., of *levels of evaluative priority*. Evaluations of cost *within* a given operative subsystem of action are at the base of this hierarchy; next come evaluations of goals within the given system. Evaluations of the standards governing the pursuit of these goals in terms of relative priority are above these. At the peak of the hierarchy is the evaluation of the different possible modes of meaning of reality— e.g., as a field of opportunity for "worldly" achievement, as a system of order into which human action should be fitted, etc.

The evaluative subsystem is peculiarly related to the classification of objects, through the subcategory of the evaluation of the spheres of life. These spheres are defined, within the field of action itself, as the subsystems of the more general system of action. Primacy can then be given to "interests" centering in the organism, the personality, the society, or the culture. Various complexities of interrelation occur, but the minimum pattern or organization involves some scale of priorities whose bearing on the evaluation of action-goals and of costs must be defined. This delineation will provide the framework for the evaluative sanctioning of motivational commitments through cathexes and identifications.

This aspect of cultural systems is particularly important to sociology. It is at this point that the cultural facet of value systems must be analyzed in order to provide a groundwork for the concept of a social value system that, as discussed in the General Introduction, is the highest-level category of the structure of social systems.

Besides the hierarchy of levels of generality, there are two other bases of organizing evaluative patterns, corresponding to those discussed for the other two cases. The external-internal distinction, in the present case, is a distinction between imperatives of action, and patterns of choice or selection. The former categories concern the consequences of the higher-order choices made in the latter. These consequences must be affected by the particularities of actual situations of choice, whereas the evaluative components of choices may abstract from these particularities. Commitment to particular goals, then, implies the necessity to incur the costs, especially in the form of sacrificing other goals which might have been attainable had the commitment not been made.

The instrumental-consummatory distinction applicable here is that between patterns of evaluative rationality and patterns of purpose. One type or level of rationality concerns maximizing results at minimum cost—this is what Weber meant by *Zweckrationalität*. It includes economic rationality and rationality in the pursuit and use of political power. The other type of rationality, concerning the expression in action of types of ultimate meaning, is what Weber meant by *Wertrationalität;* it is literal ac-

ceptance of the implications of an ultimate value-commitment.

Action-goals are valued purposes. However, commitments to alternative moral principles become comparable at a normatively higher level— namely, they are commitments to give priority to the interests of one or another basic type of cultural pattern or interest.

The fourth dimension of cultural variation essentially concerns the *grounds* of the orientations of meaning themselves. It concerns the most general world-views or definitions of the human condition that underlie orientations to more particular problems. These orientations may also be arranged in a hierarchy, according to the bases of meaning. The lowest category concerns orientation defining the meaning of performance or achievement, individual or collective. Weber's analysis of the concept of work in a "calling" as fulfilling the injunction to glorify God through contributing to the building of His kingdom on earth is a classical example in this field. In other religious traditions, devotional or ascetic practice has taken primacy among meaningful types of performance.

The second level in the hierarchy concerns the meaning of the different spheres in which the performances or achievements just mentioned may be implemented or acted out. Thus the injunction to implement the Divine Will by action may be interpreted as action in devotional exercises or in attempts to restructure the organization of "this world" by contributing to the building of the Kingdom of God on Earth. Another alternative is to work on the "perfection" of the individual personality, without special reference to the social context of his life. Conceptions of meaning at this level are necessarily rooted in a third and still higher level, namely, a concept of the nature of *order,* in the humanly normative sense, in the universe. That is, there must be an ultimately meaningful concept of what constitutes conforming with the nature of things and of what constitutes disorder.[8]

The highest level of the problems of meaning, is that of the conceptions of ultimate reality, in the religio-philosophical sense. This concerns the major premises in which the non-empirical components of a culture's total belief system are rooted.

This level must be characterized as a limit of the intelligible. Logically, it involves the premises on which lower-order commitments of meaning must rest; but the relevance of any such ultimate ground-

---

8. A classic analysis of the structure and implications of the conception of meaningful order in the present sense is given by Kenneth Burke, "On the First Three Chapters of Genesis," *Daedalus,* Summer, 1958.

ing of meaning need not be confined to a cognitive context. The highest level signifies the limiting point at which cognition, cathexis, and evaluation merge, because they are all somehow modes of *differentiation* from a common matrix.

In this case, as in the other three, there is a four-stage hierarchy of ultimate grounds of meaning. These four levels are: the meaning of performance; of performance in the different spheres of life; of the order sanctioning such selection of spheres; and of the basic foundation which supersedes and underlies all others, including the legitimizing order.

In this case, the external-internal distinction is between patterns defining the meanings of different types of empirical (or, in a religious sense, worldly) performance, and patterns defining the transcendental bases of the meaning of such performances. There are widely varied kinds of achievements; but each is a meaningful action of existing empirical actors, whether it be highly utilitarian or ascetic or devotional—an achievement is something people do. On the other hand, concepts of order and of being are not things people can do; they are concepts of the grounds on which people's actions and the concrete situations in which they occur can ultimately be made meaningful and justifiable.

The instrumental-consummatory distinction in this case is between grounds of commitment and grounds of legitimacy. Legitimation occurs at two levels. The higher level is that of the most general concept of order, as analyzed by Kenneth Burke in his discussion of the Book of Genesis. For effectiveness in concrete action, however, this must be amplified by specifying classes of object carrying legitimate authority, which at the highest level of meaning may be the will of a divinity, or a "dialectic of history." Commitments, similarly, are at the level of the concept of being. that may be something like religious faith; and at the level of courses of action, of what one is expected to do.

Any given pattern of cultural orientation is characterized by "positions" on all four of these ranges of variation and, implicitly or explicitly, by components at all the hierarchical levels distinguished above. It is, however, possible to derive a variety of typologies from such a classification. For example, where the cognitive meanings of objects as such have primacy over the other components, it is an *empirical belief* system. Where the cathectic meanings of objects have primacy, it is an *expressive* symbol system; and where the evaluative aspects of orientation have primacy, *value-patterns* are involved. In systems of *existential belief,* the grounds of meaning-orientation have primacy over the other components of cultural orientation in general.

LANGUAGE AS A GROUNDWORK OF CULTURE

Before entering into a more general analysis of the interpenetration and interdependence of the social and cultural components of action systems, we shall attempt to apply the above outline of the dimensions of cultural systems to the fundamental cultural phenomenon of language, and to lead from that into a few essential ideas about symbolism. The intimacy of the relations between language and human society is demonstrated by the completely social character of language—no isolated individual can develop a language—and by the fact that human social systems are universally dependent on linguistic symbolization and communication.

Language is the most general and elementary mechanism of communication, and so of social integration, at the cultural level of the organization of action. Language constitutes the most important single matrix from which other generalized mechanisms have been differentiated, though not necessarily the only such matrix; visual art and music seem relatively independent of language. Language should, therefore, have a structure directly comparable to the structure of other such mechanisms which, in this connection, are better known to sociologists—e.g., money.

Commonly, language is considered to have two primary functions, expression and communication. In the present context, communication clearly has priority over expression. Because language is the primary medium of cultural-level communication, it can also serve as a medium of expression. Communication is primarily a function in social systems; expression, a function of the personality as a system.

The comparison of language with money suggests another first-order distinction applicable to language. Since the classical economists, it has been customary to distinguish between money as a medium of exchange and money as a measure of value. As a medium of exchange, money circulates—it is spent by one social unit and acquired by another. Through this process of circulation, the allocation of resources, so far as it is a function of the market, is carried out but the medium itself is not consumed. By spending, one unit in the society makes commitments which influence the actions of other units. Similarly, through language, utterances are made, messages are transmitted from one unit of the social system to others. An utterance, made in circumstances where others can understand it, has consequences which are irrevocable. An actor inevitably spends his store of things utterable—that is, once having said certain things, he finds that his freedom to say anything further he pleases is automatically constrained; he will to some degree be held responsible for the content and implications of his previous utterances. Messages, therefore, constitute a kind of "circulating medium." But "the language" is not "consumed" by its use. In this sense it is not a resource.

Money, however, is not only a circulating medium; it is also a measure of value. It is an institutionalized set of forms and rules by which intentions are expressed and commitments made and accepted. It has integrative functions in the social system: it is through monetary standards, i.e., the meanings of the monetary unit, that the values of physically and otherwise diverse goods and services are rendered comparable, thus making possible their more or less rational allocation between different claimants.

At an even more generalized—in that it is diffuse and undifferentiated—level, language also contains a set of rules and forms by which intentions are expressed and commitments made and accepted or rejected in social intercourse. A monetary offer, to be valid, must be in the institutionalized medium, in coin of the realm or its equivalent. Similarly, a linguistic utterance, to be relevant, must be expressed in the language of the culture; otherwise it will not be understood. This necessitates conforming to the normative patterns of the language—i.e., not uttering combinations and sequences of sounds that are not appropriately organized.

Thus the distinction between money's functions as medium of exchange and as measure of value corresponds to the distinction linguists usually make between language's functions as message and as code.

There is another important parallel. As a social phenomenon, money is essentially a mechanism of communication; like other forms of communication, it must operate through physical media. The classical physical medium is one or more precious metals. However, trade in precious metals is not per se monetary exchange. The units traded must be standardized and categorized as "coins" belonging to a system of denominations. In other words, the standardized unit of metal must function in terms of its monetary meaning, rather than only because of its physical properties and commodity value—to use Durkheim's term, monetary value is a kind of "superadded element" relative to the commodity value of the metal. When the abstraction goes far enough, the coin becomes a symbol.

The monetary unit is a highly generalized category of meaning, e.g., *the* dollar or *the* pound sterling. The dissociation of meaning from the physical base is important; in modern monetary systems, only a small fraction of actual exchange transactions are negotiated with coins, or even "cash." The principal component of cash, the note, is a letter addressed "to whom it may concern." But the process of circulation of bank deposits and other credit instruments, where the physical media are purely linguistic (if accounting be included in language, as it must be), is more important. The parallel with language is patent. All language initially employs the processes of producing and organizing sound as its medium. With the development of writing, there is transfer to a wholly different physical medium. Yet no linguist would say that spoken and written English are two different languages.

In mechanisms of communication—both money and language—there is a physical medium. For language, this is initially the phonetic system, where patterns of *organization* occur that go beyond simply utilizing given physical possibilities on to a highly controlled system of their organized use. This organization of the physical processes is then systematically articulated with an organization at the level of *meaning*. Only because the physical acts —i.e., producing organized patterns of sound, and transferring possession of specially standardized pieces of metal or other media—have patterned meanings can they be utterances which transmit messages, or monetary transactions which create or absolve obligations. If these acts of utterance or transfer are to have meaning, they must fit into a systematically organized normative system which may be abstracted from the particular acts of sound production or of metal transfer.

The processes by which messages are conveyed through physical media are, for language, phonetic media—the area of *interpenetration* between the phonetic system and the semantic system. Correspondingly, for money the processes of concrete transaction—whether the medium be metal, cash notes, or manipulation of entries on accounts—are the area of interpenetration between the physical medium of exchange and the meaning-content of the monetary institution. When linguists discuss speech, they include both interpenetrating aspects; similarly, when economists speak of money as a medium of exchange, they refer to phenomena which include both the physical media and the meaning of the facets of process using these media.

The phenomenon, however, is not confined to this area of interpenetration for either money or language. For money, there is the measure of value aspect. An elaborate statistical estimate of gross national product is stated in monetary terms—production at the rate of X billion dollars annually. But in this use of money, no transactions occur, no dollars change hands. Similarly a linguist can analyze what is implied in patterns of utterance, without actually communicating anything. In linguistics, the distinction is between the use of a language and the level of "metalanguage,"[9] where the language is used to *talk about*, rather than to *say things in*, the language. Money "says things" in the ordinary processes of the economy, but economists also talk about the economy in monetary terms.

There is another parallel between money and language. Within each of the two levels which have been distinguished, a further distinction can be made. For money, there are two main aspects at the medium level. One is the availability of money as a generalized medium, and hence as a facility which can be utilized for an indefinite variety of purposes. This involves the standardization of the monetary unit and the interchangeability of concrete units, so that their minor variations in detail are ignored; e.g., a dollar is a dollar, whether the bill be old or new, wrinkled or smooth. Similarly the utterance of a word is the same word, e.g., "cat," within a considerable range of variations of the actual phonetic processes. In other words, a medium functioning in communication in a generalized system must be sufficiently standardized so that both parties using it communicatively know with what they are dealing without having to make an elaborate preliminary investigation of the particularities. This is illustrated by the "displacement upward" of the problem of meaning. In diplomatic communication, the words and sentences uttered are on the record—reference to the record can usually settle a dispute about what they are. The issue then is what they mean, what the speaker intended. Similarly, in modern monetary systems there are, for the most part, no disputes about how many dollars were really offered or received; but problems remain about what certain credit forms, securities, etc., are worth.

One major facet of this level is the medium's generalized standardization as a physical-semantic integrate. Another is the medium's flexible capacity to meet the particularized needs of varying occasions and situations. The fact that there is a standardized phonetic-semantic system in a language is not important to a speaker unless it enables him to say what he wants to say to particular interlocutors in particular situations, and thereby to elicit responses meaningful to him. In other words, the system must have combinatorial flexibility, so that particular goals can be achieved by utilizing facilities available in specific combinations in the specific situation. Stated in the terms of our foregoing discussion, there must be both an adaptive aspect and a goal-attainment aspect of such a medium.

The power of such a medium in facilitating communication depends on the *combination* of these two aspects. In the case of money, this power can most directly be demonstrated by contrasting monetary exchange with barter. In barter, the holder of a commodity valued by others may secure something he values through exchange. To do so, he must, in a specific situation and time range, find someone who both has what he wants and wants what he has, who wants to make the exchange at the particular time, and who will agree to the particular terms. The effect of money in creating a market system is the introduction of an entirely new set of degrees of freedom into the situation of exchange partners.

When money is used, there are four such degrees of freedom. The acceptor of money is not committed to spend it for any particular commodity or service at the time. Second, he is not committed to procure the commodity or service from any particular source of supply; he is free to shop around. Third, he is not committed to spend the money at any particular time or within a specified period; he is free to wait. Finally, he is not committed in advance to accept any particular terms; he can settle the terms according to the particular situation and the relevant circumstances.

The appropriate comparison for language is between linguistic and prelinguistic sign communication. Genuine and important communication can occur without the use of linguistic symbols. But if the acts conveying meaning are not part of a standardized code, but must be interpreted ad hoc according to their specific behavioral and physical properties in the particular context, the degrees of freedom that language makes possible will not be present. Let us consider the problem at what some linguists call the "lexical" level—morphemically significant and organized components of utterances that, taken by themselves, have intelligible meaning and can be defined. Possessing (i.e., knowing) such lexical symbols as part of his linguistic repertoire does not commit the speaker of a language to use the word or phrase in only one particular way, i.e., to convey a specific meaning to a specific interlocutor. The word or phrase is an interchangeable part; it can be fitted into many different messages, in different ways, and addressed to different people. Second, the elements of a lexical repertoire can be used to elicit responses from an indefinite range of interlocutors, i.e., potentially all the other speakers of the language. Third, the repertoire's use is not specifically temporally limited; the speaker is free to choose his time of speaking. Fourth, conversation is a process of mutual adjustment, where a standard-

---

9. Roman Jakobson and Morris Halle, *Fundamentals of Language* (The Hague: Mouton & Co., 1956).

ized set of linguistic tools, common to both partners, can be adapted to highly particularized goals of communicating specific messages and reaching particularized understandings. The *combination* of the standardized repertoire and its flexible adaptability to particularized uses underlies gaining the essential degrees of freedom through which the limitations of prelinguistic sign communication are transcended.

There are problems about the exactness of correspondence. Speaking on the semantic level, Jakobson and Halle[10] discuss a phonemic level and a lexical level of the organization of language. This corresponds roughly to the sense in which money funds constitute a highly generalized resource or facility largely independent of any particular use, and to the sense in which more particularized combinations bringing in the relevance of more specific terms can be assembled. The difference between money and language here is that, while language is the most general cultural-level mechanism of communication, money is a highly specialized one; so that many distinctions necessary in the analysis of language are not important in the analysis of money, which, being so specialized, is relatively simple in its structure.

The above discussion has concerned the components of messages, the sense in which components of language and of money respectively are parts of messages. For the general analysis of culture, this is the sense in which they constitute *objects* to which actors are oriented. But considered as a system, such components can be fully cultural only when organized as a set of pattern components which are components of orientation and not, as such, objects. In the case of money, this involves the measure of value aspect, which can be divided again into (1) measure of value as such, and (2) measure of cost. The statement of a calculation of gross national product is an example of the use of money as a measure of value. It uses the monetary concept as the logical frame for stating a quantitative fact about the economy. Dollars as objects are not involved. However, in a monetary economy there must be a way of mediating between this level and the processes of actual expenditure and dollar acquisition by units in the course of the economic process. The functional context is the one, familiar in economic theory, of allocation of resources, in which money functions as a *standard of allocation* e.g. in the case of an expectation of solvency. Real monetary units, as objects, control the allocation of resources in the economist's sense; but these monetary units themselves must be allocated. Goods and factors of production are scarce—and so, nec-

essarily, is money as an object. Monetary cost thus provides the primary criteria for allocating certain fundamental categories of fluid resources in the social process. This allocation may be influenced by many non-economic factors, but it is a channel through which these influences must operate. This facet of money is fundamentally associated with the institutional complexes of contract, employment, and property.

The aspects of linguistic structure parallel to these two aspects of money are the "style" or primary "form-pattern" of a language as Whorf and his followers deal with it, or the "phraseological" pattern, as Jakobson and Halle describe it; and what Jakobson and Halle call the "syntactical" level, which includes grammar. With respect to the first, the primary form-pattern, since Whorf a language has generally been considered to categorize its users' world of experience distinctively, but on a level independent of the particularities of the language's morphemes, lexicon, and phonology. For the structure of language, this level is probably comparable to the level of paramount values for a social system. Since it is not specific either to function within the system or to particular uses and situations, the fact that it is an essential aspect of structure is often overlooked. Whorf's analysis of the contrast between Hopi and the European languages at this level is classic.

However, this kind of spirit, or most general orientation, of a language does not immediately determine the processes of speech. There must be an intermediate level of the rules for the uses and combinations of lexical elements. These rules constitute a normative structure which is the basis for organizing these components—including processes of modifying their own forms, as in the grammatical categories of gender and case. As phraseology, in language, is analogous to values, in the social system, the syntactical level in language seems analogous to institutionalized norms in the social system —most formally developed and codified in the content of the legal system—and to money as standard of allocation.

In addition to the specific categories which have been formulated about the dimensions of cultural systems and points along them, there are three primary ways in which these components may be organized: the hierarchy of control, the external-internal axis, and the instrumental-consummatory axis. We shall now try to apply this more general analysis of cultural systems to language.

If language is considered first as a semantic system in terms of categories of meaning, there is a general correspondence with our way of analyzing culture. Linguists have not reached consensus on

10. *Ibid.*, p. 77.

many of the important points, but the existence of a hierarchy of control in our sense is beyond doubt. The formulation closest to our scheme is that of Jakobson and Halle, who refer to a hierarchy, running from lower to higher levels, that comprises morphemic, lexical, syntactic, and phraseological elements of language. This corresponds almost exactly with the four functional categories already described.

A corresponding hierarchy operates in the field of phonology. Dr. Dell W. Hymes, in formulating this, distinguishes the categories of sounds, phonemes, (phonemic) syllables, and intonation patterns, in an ascending order. The morpheme constitutes the main point of articulation between phonetic and semantic systems, in that it is a *sound* pattern which carries a component of a message. (Technically, this would concern morphophonemics, the study of the phonemic shapes of morphemes.) Therefore it may be said to belong in both classifications.

Beyond this, however, Jakobson and Halle, and Hymes, in slightly different ways, stress the distinction between two different aspects of the organization of linguistic systems. In slightly different contexts, Jakobson and Halle use three different pairs of terms to designate this distinction: contiguity-similarity; combination-selection; and metonymy-metaphor. We suggest that the axis of organization they designate as contiguity, combination, or metonymy corresponds very closely to the external-internal axis as that has been employed in the above discussion, whereas the axis of similarity, selection, or metaphor corresponds to the instrumental-consummatory axis.

As a first indication, Jakobson and Halle speak of words (or other lexical, and presumably also morphemic, units) as deriving their more precise meaning from the "context" in which they are used—i.e., the ways in which they are built into higher-order linguistic organizations through the normative order of the language. This relation to context is the focus of one of the two types of aphasia which they discuss (contiguity disturbances). However, on both higher and lower contiguity or contextual levels, those components which per se are not organized for any particular uses but are "resources" of the language must be organized, through selective processes, to form coherent messages. The other type of aphasic disturbance, similarity disorder, focuses in this axis of organization.

Hymes (personal communication) emphasizes the distinction between the mode of organization by which components co-occur in a higher-order unit *simultaneously*, e.g., distinctive features in phonemes, morphemes in words, which we assume to be equivalent to the relations of contiguity; and where they occur *hierarchically*, e.g., phonemes in syllables, or syntactical constructions within an utterance. Furthermore, there is at least the suggestion that these two modes of organization are salient at alternative steps in the more general hierarchy of control. If closer analysis bears out these suggestions, the general analysis of the components of cultural systems set forth above seems fully applicable to language.

The framework within which we have been considering language as a prototypal cultural system can clarify the question of the concept symbol. First, the term symbol has been used ambiguously, treated as an object, and as a category of "meaning." The distinction between the object aspect and the orientational aspect of the cultural frame of reference, as of action generally, is one of the major axes of the analysis presented here. Within this framework, strong reasons are presented for restricting the technical use of the concept symbol to categories of objects, and not using it to designate categories of orientation pattern.

But not all objects are symbols. Symbols should be treated as a very special category of objects that are precisely distinguished by their place in *cultural* systems. They are objects *with meaning on a particular minimum level of generality* in the requisite meaning system. This generalization of meaning emancipates a symbol from being bound to the particularities of context, in the same sense as discussed in connection with the degrees of freedom involved in monetary exchange and in speech. A symbol must be an object with sufficiently generalized meaning so that its production and its observation, can fit into combinational patterns of great diversity, and do so in such a way that the specific symbols are not dependent for their meaning on the particularities of the context of use, but must be interpreted according to their place in a culturally generalized code.

From this point of view, the morphemic and the lexical elements of language constitute systems of symbols; the syntactic and the phraseological elements do not. The linguistic symbol is the prototypal object of generalized meaning, since the sound combination (or visual object, in written language) is nearly meaningless apart from the conventions of the language. Because of this, they cannot function as symbols—express and convey meaning—without reference to the non-symbolic orientational component of the language.

In one sense, therefore, an object's status as symbol is dependent on its meaning's dissociation from the intrinsic significance of the properties of the object itself. As Durkheim expresses it, its meaning must be superadded to this intrinsic significance. For example, the "father" as symbol is a symbol precisely in that it is *not* simply functionally equivalent to the actual father, but, relative to the father-child relationship as an empirical social category, represents things which are *not* characteristic of that relation. The difference is one of level of generality. In action theory terms, relative to the particularism of the actual father-child relationship, the *meaning* of a "father-figure" is universalistic; the father-figure does not, in the same sense, need to stand in a particularistic relation to the subject. The symbol of "God, the Father" is the prototypal example of the use of the word "father" as a symbol. *Because* a realistic kinship relation with the deity is impossible, a *symbolization* of the relationship becomes necessary and is meaningful.

In one sense, it is legitimate to follow general usage and consider a symbol as a special class of sign—treating, however, a sign as also an object with meaning. But signs as such need not have the level of generality of meaning central to the concept of symbols. Most signs are involved in communicative "barter"; they are peculiar to the relatively immediate context of the relationship among those communicating.

The place of language in systems of action, lies especially in the relation between culture and the social system. The focal consideration is that language is the most generalized mechanism mediating human communication. In the general system of action, its primary function is social, since communication and social interaction are inseparable. Language thus underlies the range of the interpenetration of social and cultural systems.

The cultural system's primary input to the social system is of the cultural patterns or schemata on which the organization of empirical knowledge depends. The social system's primary reciprocal output is the institutionalization of these patterns, i.e., their automatic acceptance as the way of thinking and communicating of members of the society. Language is the principal mechanism for mediating this interchange. The pattern structure of the language, i.e., its orientational components, is the primary cultural contribution; the meanings of linguistic symbols, i.e., the lexical and phonemic components, are primarily a societal contribution.

In the course of societal evolution, other more specialized mechanisms for mediating interaction have differentiated from language. One basis of the difference is that mechanisms like money and political power are both more specialized, and are primarily intrasocietal rather than cultural in character and function. But these mechanisms depend on the attainment of "symbolic" levels of cultural generalization, which in turn depends on the emancipation of the resources they control from ascriptive fixation. The general nature of this process for money is well known. Historically, there have been two major steps—the development of markets for exhanging consumers' goods through money, and the development of markets for the factors of production. In the case of political power, the equivalent of consumers' goods are specific decisions made by collective leadership. Power can emerge as a generalized medium only when there is institutionalized generalization of support for such leadership, and the supporting elements can choose between genuine alternatives of policy and leadership.

Language's role as a matrix from which more specialized mechanisms have developed in sociocultural history is paralleled in the life history of the individual. Here, the relation between language learning and the other aspects of the child's socialization is striking. The nature and importance of the process of early identification with the mother—the matrix from which a more differentiated motivational system develops—has become relatively well established. Since this process normally culminates toward the end of the first year of life, it is interesting that it tends to be followed almost immediately by the learning of language. Successful identification seems to be the primary condition of capacity to learn language. Spoken language becomes the foundation of cognitive learning and the behavioral skills most directly associated with it. This type of sequence is then repeated, in literate societies; the next major motivational reorganization of the personality system, the Oedipal transition, is followed by the acquisition of *written* language as the cultural foundation of the higher-order cognitive learning and skills. This, even though many qualifications must be made in detail, is an authentic case of the "ontogeny recapitulates phylogeny" relation which is firmly established in biological theory.

SOME RELATIONS OF CULTURAL TO SOCIAL SYSTEMS

The complexity of both social and cultural systems necessitates the foregoing discussion of problems about the latter before considering the systems' interdependence and interpenetration. These relations are inevitably complex also. It will be possible here to discuss only a few major ones.

Two propositions are most fundamental as points of departure for analyzing these interrelations. The first is that, of the major components of the cultural system, the evaluative component is strategically most crucial to the society. Cultural values form the major cultural component of the structure of social systems. The second proposition is that a value-pattern, to become a structural part of a social system—i.e., for its relation to the control of inter-action to be stabilized—it must become *institutionalized*.

The place of language as a matrix of cultural systems provides a sufficient basis for insisting on the social character of all higher-order culture. *Communication* is the action process which is the source and the bearer of cultural creation and maintenance. Without plurality of units and complex organization, complex communication systems and, hence, cultural patterning of the media and content, are not possible. In the cultural system, the evaluative components are those parts shaped by their relation to the function of integrating the eternal object, the pattern aspect of cultural systems, with the exigencies of actual communication. In the general system of action, social systems have the parallel position, especially as the mediating, inte-grating structure and processes of action standing between cultural systems and the personalities of individuals. Evaluative patterns are critical for insti-tutionalization in social systems, while cathectic patterns and expressive symbolization have a par-allel significance as the primary cultural compo-nents internalized in personalities. This theme is too complex to pursue farther here.

In the nature of our concept of the structure of cultural systems, evaluative patterns in this sense cannot stand alone; though regulating integration, they must themselves also be integrated, first, at the cultural content level, with other components of the same cultural system, and second, with the exigen-cies of operative effectiveness in action systems other than the cultural. "Institutionalization" is the fulfilment of these conditions of integration as an effectively operative part of an empirical system of action.

The most significant relation for the pattern con-tent of the cultural system itself is the relation to the underlying orientations of meaning, since, in hierarchical terms, these are on a higher level than values. These are the cultural premises of social system values, the concepts at the level of orienta-tional meaning in whose terms the evaluative com-mitments formulated in the value system itself are intelligible. There are, however, three other crucial conditions which must be fulfilled if a value-pattern is to be both fully meaningful and an operative basis of the control of action. First, the nature of the objects evaluated and their empirical relations to

each other must be clarified. The General Introduc-tion emphasized that societal values are distin-guished from other values by the concept of the society as the *object* of evaluation. In order to evalu-ate determinately, it is necessary to have criteria or standards, and also to have an adequately clear con-ception of the objects concerned—i.e., of *what* is being evaluated. Then, for an evaluation to be more than a conception of the desirable, people must be motivationally *committed* to implementing the pat-tern of value in concrete action. This problem con-cerns the internalization of values in personalities. Finally, for implementing the value-pattern, *be-havioral* resources must be mobilizable—especially the resources of the organism in relation to its physical environment.

The relations to the cultural premises operate through specification of the *implications* of the higher-order meaning premises for situations—i.e., object-complexes—which *sui generis* limit the rele-vance of levels of higher generalization. Thus a human society is inevitably composed of mortal human beings, who are born as infants who must be cared for and socialized, and who must be interde-pendent with others throughout their strictly limited life spans. There may be aspects of the orientation of meaning for which these exigencies are irrelevant; but if these premises are to be the bases of values that are intelligible to real human beings, they must somehow "solve" the problems raised by these exigencies. Thus the problem of death is an ineluc-table one for *all* religious systems. If there were no biological mortality and if death were not empiri-cally inevitable, a new range of possible values would be opened. But just as no really institutional-ized religion has pretended to conquer death—as distinguished from "transcending" it—so no science has yet pretended to have the capacity to eliminate death and make real living human beings literally immortal.

Specification consists in the *orderly* introduction of considerations of the relevance of the funda-mental exigencies to which the implementation of an orientation of meaning is subject. Evaluation is critical in this series of specifications, because it is the point at which the balancing of the importance of the inevitable variety of more specific exigencies must be done. Thus the human individual's life is in-evitably limited to "three-score years and ten," more or less; while a society has a possible span of indenti-fiable continuity far beyond this. When sacrificing the individual life might contribute to the society's continuity, under what circumstances would this sacrifice be justified on value grounds?

This order of questions must link cultural premises and institutionalized patterns of value.

When the culture is institutionalized in social systems, these problems have a very important double reference. Fairly definite evaluations must be justified or legitimized by reference to the culture's higher-order meaning-orientations, however these may be articulated. However, a social system, like any other action system, is a "going concern"—a system continuing through time, always seeing interests, from a long-run perspective, that transcend the shorter-range interests of various units and subsystems. There is hence a central interest in the *continuity* of the major cultural components of the system. For a society, a basic change in values is a major crisis, because it implies restructuring everywhere. A social system therefore looks upward to the sources of its values' legitimation in terms of meaning, and backward (and forward) in terms of the problem of temporal continuity—and, hence, the sense in which the traditions of the past may still be adequate guides for meeting the complex problems in which any society is involved in the present and prospective future.

The first major reference of a value system is its intelligibility in terms of higher-order meaning orientations and of continuity with the society's traditions. Second, however, is the fact that, as noted, a determinate evaluative orientation cannot exist unless the definition of *what* is being evaluated is clear. This definition includes the cognitively formulated properties and qualities of the specific object of evaluation, and the rest of the empirical manifold in which this object fits. As noted above, for social values the social system as object (in our primary case, the society of reference) is the center of this "definition of the situation" problem. But first the society must be regarded in determinate (i.e., ordered) relations to the other categories of objects in the empirical world—for social systems, personalities, organisms, and the physical world—and to any non-empirical limiting matrix which may be conceived in such ways as to be cognitively significant. These considerations imply that something of the order of a "social theory," in an empirical sense, must be part of the larger system of cultural orientations of which a societal value-system is also a part. Such a theory, so far as it is directly linked to values as a set of presumptively valid prescriptions for the implementation of the values, together with the "rationalization" of these prescriptions, may be described as a science-value integrate.[11] The set of beliefs linking the value system with its bases in the higher-order orientations of meaning—in their cultural premises—can be described as the underlying *philosophy* of the cultural system.

The third centrally significant component of the institutionalization of a social value-system is the cultural element in the motivational commitment of individual persons to the implementation of the values. The central mechanisms for securing this commitment is the *internalization,* during the process of socialization of the individual, of the social object-systems of the society—as this was analyzed in the Introduction to Part Three. These social object-systems, constituting the social environment of the socialization process, are conceived as structured; and the patterning of this structure comprises the institutionalized values of the society.

From the above, it follows that the process of cathexis of successively more complex (and hence higher-order) systems of social objects is, so far as the object systems do in fact become internalized, *ipso facto* the process of building the normative culture involved in these object-systems into the structure of the constituent personalities.

"Ideological distortions" can easily develop in the field of the cognitive definitions of valued objects. In the internalization of normative culture, there is opportunity for the development of much alienation and consequent motivation to deviant or variant behavior—whether this be regressive, or toward creative innovations.

The final field of institutionalization concerns the values of utility and the facilities available to the social system for implementing its values. We suggest that this concerns structuring the organisms's plasticity in the direction of maximum scope for socially useful skills. Since this component is lowest in the hierarchy of control, these skills have less direct relevance to value-implementation than any other components of institutionalization so far reviewed. Nevertheless, a personality committed to implementing certain values cannot do so effectively unless, confronting actual situations, he has the skills necessary for translating his motivational commitments into decisions and real behavior. One very important skill is the skill of communication.

The institutionalization of cultural systems is not a one-way process. Social systems are dependent on the cultural systems which in part are institutionalized in them; but influence in the reverse direction is also crucially important. Under the pressure of strains in the structure of personalities and of the society, alienation frequently occurs from commitments to implement institutionalized values; this leads to various types of deviance in the society. In a growing society—even if the higher-order value-system is undisturbed—structures at lower levels

---

11. Where this culturally grounded integrate is characterized by further selection and distortion attributable to structured strains in the society I would speak of an "ideology." See Parsons, "An Approach to the Sociology of Knowledge," *Proceedings of the Fourth World Congress of Sociology,* Vol. IV, 1961.

may become unable to meet the exigencies of the situation, necessitating a process of structural differentiation. This implies value-change at the lower levels of specification, and consequent strain, alienation, and shifting of commitments. At all levels, and most conspicuously at the higher ones, the tensions involved in commitments and structural strains may make it difficult to maintain an ordered cognitive picture of the system. Ideological *distortion* presumably reflects some imbalance between the cognitive standards of the culture, and the motivational imperatives of balancing commitments with other components of personality and with each other. Similar influences from society must be analyzed in relation to the rationalization of the patterns of meaning of institutionalized values.

In a sense, a social system can be considered as suspended in a web of cultural definitions, whose pressures are by no means uniform or mutually coordinated in different directions. There may be an inherent direction of change in the meaning-premises of the central value-system. The cognitive definitions of the system as object may be subject to many types of change or distortion. Commitments in different classes of personalities are not static. The relations of the society to the skills of the organism and the understanding of the environment are culturally patterned. In each of these contexts there is interaction and not merely a one-way process; and all the relevant factors have complex feedback effects on each other.

Later in this Introduction we shall discuss the possibility of making any general statements about the problem of direction of change in the cultural and social systems taken together. We shall also discuss, later, the bearing that our type of analysis of the interdependence of the two types of system has on the problems of the sociology of knowledge.

THE CLASSIFICATION OF
CULTURAL MATERIALS

It is difficult to classify the components of a cultural system on a basis which can serve as a rationale for the classification of the selections presented in this Part of the Reader. The difficulty is the same type that has arisen in connection with the other parts of the Reader—a classification developed according to a currently acceptable conceptual scheme may not be appropriate for a selection, because the author had another conceptual scheme according to which one must order and interpret his treatment of the relevant topics. Nevertheless, it is possible to develop a scheme which seems to fit fairly well.

Our main classification includes two major divisions, the subject matters of Sections A and B. These deal respectively with the foundations of culture as a component of human action systems, and with functionally differentiated parts of the cultural system that impinge differently on societies.

Section A has two parts. The first is composed of selections dealing with general problems of the nature of symbolism and of the process of communication. The second deals with the general concept of patterns of culture, which has become a major constitutive reference point for virtually all theoretical consideration of human action.

As suggested in the Introduction to Part Two, the theoretical treatment of these subjects and of the functionally differentiated parts of the cultural system had not proceeded so far as it had in the analysis of social structure. This is still true now. Hence it will be impossible to present an outline of the problem area going as far beyond the basic orienting considerations as did the outline of social structure.

The Cultural Groundwork of Interaction

The most important starting point in this area is the one associated especially with G. H. Mead—the involvement of the problem of meanings, and hence of the functions of signs and symbols, in the elementary processes of social interaction. This is the focal point of departure for considering the cultural level of meanings. In order to function as a stabilizing mechanism in the processes of interaction, the cultural system must be capable of sufficient particularization of designation and prescription to fit the particular demands of the situations and tasks in which an individual actor is placed and is expected to perform. In the same interaction process, it must be possible to adapt to the all-important differentiation in the roles and tasks performed by the interacting participants. These particularized meanings of signs and symbols must, however, also be mutually comprehensible to the performer of a differentiated role and to his role-partners. Only on this assumption is it possible to match sanction to performance and vice versa, which is the very essence of the integration of an interaction system.

Mutual comprehensibility and the matching of sanction and performance (the punishment fitting the crime, to paraphrase Gilbert) imply a common component of cultural meaning shared by the particularities in question. This component consists in common categories, class concepts, etc.; and above those, the grammatical, syntactical and phraseological components constituting the structure of the languages through which interaction is mediated. In the empirical cultural reference, this is precisely the theoretical component of the cultural structures involved. There must be comparable elements of "generalized pattern" in the other, functionally more differentiated, components.

An important general perspective emerges from these considerations. All cultural systems must structure a *range* of relations of particularity and generality of meaning; and there must be a point on this range at which the relevant break between subject-orientation and object-modality occurs. This break is typically found at the transition point between the symbolic reference to particularities (i.e., objects and classes of objects) and the "meaning" reference to orientational patterns and grounds. For the structure of the social system, this is the critical distinction between the role and collectivity levels of its organization involving regulation of the behavior of actual specifiable persons, and the level of institutionalized patterns (e.g., the normative content of legal systems) and institutionalized values, which tend to favor *types* of behavior without specific reference to particular groups, persons or acts.

In this context, the essential thesis (which was stated in the General Introduction) is that the higher-order components in the structure of the social system *consist* in institutionalized culture, specifically in the evaluative "mode." Hence this same basic line of division can be expected to run through all the other aspects and components of cultural systems, since social structure is, culturally, a special case. The dividing line does run through language. It is relevant to the methodology of science. The ancient controversy about the importance of theory involves this general frame of reference. The empirical element of science, itself complex in levels as well as in designative reference, consists in the detailed facts about the properties of objects and about the discriminations between objects and classes of objects. This detailed knowledge can be ordered only in terms of a level of theory transcending this more particularized level of reference by introducing a level of conceptualization concerned with relational patterns and the underlying assumptions on which they rest. This might almost be considered the mathematical aspect of the structure of a system of theory.[12]

Mathematics is a particularly significant prototypal case. It is a kind of metalanguage; it contains no designative nouns, but only abstract symbols which can refer to any arbitrarily selected categories of data concerning objects fulfilling the formal definitional requirements. A mathematical

system is thus one in which the orientational component of cultural content is maximized toward some limit. It must have its x's and y's, but these are at the highest possible level of contentless abstraction. Mathematics merges into any systematization of the formal content of conceptual schemes.

There seem to be certain uniform characteristics in cultural systems that must be taken into account as an explicit frame of reference for the analysis of any action system, notably any other than the cultural. This is especially true of the ones rooted in the basic distinction between object-reference and orientational-reference, as outlined above, with the implication that the orientational components are always higher in the scale of generality than the object-references, in the sense in which "higher" has been used here. As indicated, the problem of the nature of symbolism is involved in this question.

Patterns of Culture

The second part of Section A is concerned with the central features of "patterns of culture." In this aspect, it is essential that a cultural system be a mode of *organizing* the components of a system of action with reference to the axis of the higher-order *meanings* of the lower-order components. If this criterion is applied to any cultural element of the social system, it indicates that the first essential property of a cultural subsystem is the *sharedness* of the relevant meanings among operative units of the social system. Impairment of this sharedness is ipso facto an element of malintegration of the social system. This sharedness cannot be taken for granted, as evidenced by the common phenomenon of people's "talking past each other" instead of genuinely communicating.

Meanings, however, are not only, at any given moment, more or less fully shared. They may be communicated from one unit of a system to another, and from system to system. Communication of meaning has a special property not shared by other processes of transfer or interchange that occur in the course of social interaction. This property is that the acquisition of meaning, e.g., understanding, occurs without loss to the transferring agent. What the General Introduction called "real commitments" do not have this quality. Thus property rights cannot be simultaneously transferred to others and retained; nor can various mechanisms which mediate transactions, like money. But in imparting information to another, one does not cease to know it; and the same seems to hold for all processes of the learning—correlatively, teaching—of meanings. This implies that a communication of meaning, if directed at a unit not previously "knowing" its content, ipso facto extends the range of the sharedness just mentioned. In so far as the "possession" of a pattern of meaning is a mode of organizing a system of action, diffusion of meaning implies an extension of the pattern of organization. It must be remembered that diffusion, in this sense, must be interpreted, and that it is dependent on specifiable conditions.[13]

As a criterion of cultural patterns, "sharability" implies components containing an element of generality or uniformity. As a mechanism of organizing orientations to situations, i.e., to systems of objects, it must also have elements of differentiation. Even though meanings be shared, in the sense that signs and symbols are understandable, the utilization of these signs and symbols in the processes of action and interaction implies discrimination of their appropriateness to particular objects and occasions. Hence the importance of the component of particularity as well as that of generality. Furthermore, a cultural system must have some capacity for increasing differentiation. Otherwise it will not be adequate for performing the function of control in a progressively differentiating system of action—a system undergoing change that is not merely random, but directional, in bringing within the same pattern of organization a progressively more extensive and more complex set of object-components in the situation of action. The further implication of such a process of differentiation is that the orientational components of the system, as well as the object-focused ones, must become differentiated at a given time and be capable of further differentiation. The simple addition of new words to designate new classes of objects is not sufficient, if the development of a language is to be adequate to an increasingly complex society and culture. Involving syntactical and phraseological levels, there must be new *ways* of saying things if sufficiently complicated *new things* are to be said. Correspondingly, in the development of science it is not enough to accumulate increasingly large aggregates of particularized facts; the body of knowledge reaching

into its higher-order theoretical structure must be *reorganized*. Thus, though crucial stages in the development of a science are often marked by new "discoveries" of fact, in the relatively particularized sense, if they are really critical they lead to major reorganizations on the higher theoretical levels.

These considerations lead to the last general property of cultural systems, a property which has played a central part in the thinking about the subject that is represented in our selections. This is the capacity of cultural systems for *cumulative* development.

Here it is important that the modern social sciences' concern with the problems of culture is rooted, at least in Western Europe, largely in the biological theory of evolution, and gave rise to a series of evolutionary interpretations of the processes of social change. The first major theoretical task was to dissentangle the cultural factors in human evolution from the biological. In this, a development of biological theory itself proved vitally important —the concept that acquired characteristics could not be inherited. It became much more feasible to introduce a clear distinction between genetic inheritance and what was then sometimes called "social heredity," however difficult it may have been to continue the discrimination in many detailed empirical fields.

The transmission of culture without loss at the generalized pattern level, and at the more particularized levels through learning, is one of the fundamental conditions of its cumulative possibilities. Through the socialization of the oncoming generations in the culture, the innovations of previous generations can be preserved to provide the foundations for further innovations.

The above analysis suggests that the most critical basis of the cumulative development of culture is its capacity to reach to progressively higher levels of generality in precisely the *orientational* pattern components of any given cultural system or subsystem. That is, a higher-level cultural system, in this sense, would have developed a pattern system capable of comprising a more *extensive* range of particularized meanings than a lower-order one, and a more *differentiated* system of meanings—i.e., a range both "wider" and involving what, qualitatively speaking, are more different *kinds* of particularized meanings.

The best analyzed and understood example of this process available is the development of scientific knowledge in relation to the structure of theory. Science is par excellence the cumulative component of higher-order sophisticated cultural systems. In speaking of the generality problem in scientific

---

13. A centrally important point of the above discussion of language in relation to money is the distinction between the cultural structure aspect of mechanisms of communication, and certain conditions and consequences of their operative use. Cultural structure and meanings can certainly be transmitted without loss; for langauge, this clearly includes particularized messages, not merely knowledge of the language itself. But in the context of concrete social interaction, saying things, orally or in writing, has consequences. Hence a speaker's freedom to say what he likes is not without most important constraints. In other words, speech as realistic process involves *costs;* something in the way of open alternatives is sacrificed when commitment to particular statements has been made. Thus breach of contract or breach of promise may be actionable offences, as is libel. These are analogous to the sense in which money spent is no longer possessed.

theory, we wish particularly to stress the element of relative discontinuity in levels of generality—the component of a body of scientific knowledge that does not accord with the conception, prevalent until quite recently, of scientific advance as a process of purely additive accumulation of more and more discrete items of factual knowledge. Though this additive component is important, it is only one aspect—the one to which we have referred as the extensive aspect—of a larger and more complex cultural system. We are now focusing attention on the aspect of a level of generality of theoretical orientation, one discontinuous with lower and higher levels, in that going from a lower to a higher level implies the *reorganization* of the body of knowledge. This kind of discontinuity is implied in the succession of *systems* of theory in the history of science—e.g., the transition from the Ptolemaic astronomy to the Copernican-Newtonian, and from that to the Einsteinian. Thus the famous Michelson-Morley experiment was crucial not because it produced one more previously unknown item of factual knowledge, but because it showed the imperativeness of a major theoretical reorganization, by providing a factual item which could not be made to fit the previously ascendant theoretical pattern.

There has been a strong tendency to contend, often more implicitly than explicitly, that cumulation is a property only possessed by science, and by the protoscientific empirical components of knowledge. This prevalent view has been conditioned partially by the kind of empiricist methodology mentioned, that has treated cumulation as the kind of quantitatively additive or linear process outlined. The recognition of the importance of the distinction of levels of organization in scientific knowledge itself should cast some doubt on this point.

If this discussion is to go farther, however, the problem of the internal differentiation of systems of culture must be reviewed. This brings us to the organization of the selections included in Section B of Part Four. After discussing that, we will return to the more general question of cumulativeness.

THE FUNCTIONAL DIFFERENTIATION
OF CULTURAL SYSTEMS

Our functional classification here is based on the scheme of dimensions of the variation of cultural systems outlined earlier in this Introduction. Each major type of cultural subsystem is character-

ized by its primacy of attention to the problems focusing on the relevant dimension. These dimensions are cognitive generality, level of generality of cathectic meaning, evaluative level, and level of ultimacy of the grounding of meanings.

Prototypal cultural subsystems giving primacy to the dimension of cognitive generality are bodies of scientific knowledge, with special reference to their theoretical components. The same principles used in the General Introduction and the Introduction to Part Two apply to the differentiation of scientific systems from the other cultural subsystems. In the process of the development of societies and cultures, a progressively higher level of this differentiation is usually reached. The more epistemological themes Durkheim dealt with in the *Elementary Forms* suggest that both scientific knowledge and philosophical thought have developed from a matrix of religious orientations; we agree, subject to making the qualifications proper for the many detailed problems involved in tracing any such evolution. Another example is provided by the set of controversies which have raged in the Western world during the past fifty years, in the social science field, about the place of values in social science, notably about the discrimination between the value-position held by the investigator and the canons of objectivity of his judgments. Earlier, the problem of discriminating evaluative culture from that which is empirically cognitive did not clearly arise for the field of human behavior. During the past fifty years, however, the requisite empirical disciplines have reached a stage of development at which the differentiation becomes of paramount importance. Like many other processes of differentiation of institutionalized structures, however, this one has not been painless. On this basis, more than any other, as will be noted in the last section of this Introduction, the sociology of knowledge has become a centrally important problem area.

For present purposes, the order of treatment will be different from the one used in the early section. Instead of a consideration of the common factor of external orientation to the object world, scientific systems will be compared to the orientations in the grounds of meaning, which share, with empirical cognition, the "instrumental" relation to action. Empirical cognitive systems and meaning-orientation systems share what may be called an "existential" reference—though for the meaning systems, the reference is non-empirical or philosophical. They are thus instrumental, in that they do not per se gratify the interests of action-system units, as both expressive symbols and integrations do gratify them.

These subsystems of culture formulate, in Weber's sense, answers to the "problems of meaning" underlying the major religious and philosophical systems. Existential patterns of orientation to problems of meaning are, then, a second major type of subsystem of a culture. These patterns constitute the major premises of whatever the configurational structure of the culture may be. Only on the highest levels of cultural differentiation in the relevant directions are they clearly and explicitly differentiated from other components—particularly values and various elements of expressive symbolism. In general, they are, in Kluckhohn's terms, part of implicit culture, though in major philosophical and theological movements they have sometimes been made explicit.

The aspect of culture of primarily motivational or consummatory significance is the type of subsystem that is most a facet of orientation (as distinguished from relation to objects)—called, above, patterns of evaluation. This component of cultural systems has been particularly prominent throughout our discussions, because of its special and critical relation to the structure of social systems. Clarification of that relation is dependent on the clear analytical discrimination between cultural and social systems in general, and between the different subsystems of culture. It is particularly important because of, rather than in spite of, the interpenetration of cultural and social systems. But it is imperative to maintain a clear distinction between value-patterns and other subsystems of the same cultural system—even though, as is often true in particular social systems, these may not in many empirical cases be clearly differentiated from the other types.

In summary, our previous discussion has shown value patterns as patterns embodying evaluations of problems of cost, of the action goals of operative units of action systems, of the more generalized moral principles by which action is guided and, at the highest level of generality, of the different components of the "reality" in which meaning itself is rooted. Evaluative patterns involve orientation toward objects; and these evaluations of action systems as objects, especially of the society itself, constitute the systems of societal values that form such a crucial reference point for our theoretical analysis.

The final major class of cultural subsystem is concerned with the primacy of expressions of cathectic attachment to objects and classes of objects. The general considerations regarding the importance and functions of signs and symbols, and their relations to generalized orientational components, apply to this class also. On the grounds discussed above we think of this category of subsystem of culture as that of *expressive symbolization*. In differentiated cases, the prototypal examples are the arts. They may be located in this way through elimination of the other three categories. In sophisticated cultures, works of art are clearly differentiated from scientific knowledge. They purport to reflect or "describe" empirical reality only on certain limiting fringes; and even there, not in patterns organized through the analytical generalization of scientific theory. Second, in relation to patterns of value, art does not primarily carry evaluative judgements or commitments; it may be appreciated or enjoyed for its own sake. Finally, though like all patterns of orientation, art is in some sense ultimately rooted in orientations of meaning; works of art per se are not attempts to articulate these grounds—this belongs to philosophy and theology as *cognitive* disciplines—but rather to create forms of expression which are adequate, and to manipulate objects in creating these forms of expression.

Art, like all other components of cultural systems, involves particularized signs and symbols, and generalized patterns that somehow organize and govern their use. The most common words for these generalized patterns are "form" and "style," which are, as we have suggested, analogous to the grammar, syntax, and phraseology of language.

The general place of religion in the field of action has special importance in our area of concern. We do not consider religion to "belong" in any one of the primary subsystems of action, but to be a phenomenon relating, and thus in a sense integrating, three of these subsystems—cultural systems, personality systems, and social systems. The organism and the physical environment are not directly involved in religion, but are factors conditioning it and potentially facilitating and/or interfering with it. Also, in less differentiated socio-cultural systems what is usually called "religion" occupies, actually, a very different place from what is usually described as "religion" in more highly differentiated systems.

Religion, as organizing the highest levels of the orientation of action more generally, is rooted in the most generalized orientations of meaning. In so far as action is specifically concerned with the articulation of these orientations "for their own sake," however, it is philosophical rather than religious. Religious orientation transcends this, in that it involves "commitment" in real action contexts; it is not just "theorizing" or "speculation." This seems to be what Durkheim meant in his famous dictum about religion, "*c'est de la vie sérieuse.*"

These commitments occur in two directions. One

is commitment of the personality, which, ipso facto, must have cathectic primacy. The religiously relevant is the highest of the levels of personal commitment in this sense—the level involving the attitude of "generalized respect" or, in religious terminology, of "worship." From the point of view of the personality, then, religious orientation involves an attitude of personal commitment to a highest "object" of respect, an object or system of them which, relative to empirical objects, must be an entity which can only be *symbolized,* not "described," by empirical objects. The focal attitude which is considered appropriate is generally called "faith"; the reciprocal input to the personality, "justification."

The second direction of commitment is the moral or evaluative. Since the primary focus of evaluative culture is always the values institutionalized in the society, the problem of the moral legitimacy of societal values is always critical for systems of religious orientation. However, though the religious orientation may be accepting or rejecting of these values, their basis is never wholly internal to the social system; it always involves a generality of reference in which personal, organic, and cultural, and in some sense non-empirical, considerations are involved. The concept "eternity" seems to be the expression of the highest level of relativity of all things "temporal" that can be articulated. Spinoza's famous formula of seeing things *sub specie aeternitatis* is, therefore, a formulation of the religious attitude toward moral problems.

Perhaps we are saying that religion is a phenomenon of the *general* system of action, one which cannot be broken down as particularly cultural, personal, or social. Its primary focus, however, in the present frame of reference is cultural.

According to the above outline, Section B of Part Four is truncated. It deals with only three of the four major categories distinguished, empirical existential patterns, patterns of value, and "religious beliefs." Even this last category is not—as the considerations reviewed above demonstrate—a "pure" category; it deviates from pure patterns of meaning-orientation in the religious direction, and is partially combined with patterns of value. This emphasis is justified by the fact that anything approaching the pure case is rare in the available materials, and has not been treated in terms easily connected with sociological problems. The problems of meaning and orientations to meanings have impinged massively on societies and their value systems, and thus conceivably constituted an important influence on their development, primarily through religious beliefs.

The analytical category of patterns of value is partly included here. It has in part already been adequately treated, notably in Section E of Part Two, dealing with the integration of religion in social structure, and also as a major theme running through Part Two, as well as in the discussion of socialization and of deviance and social control in Part Three. For logical symmetry, it would have been desirable to include selections dealing with this area apart from religious or philosophical beliefs. There is, however, another important difficulty. Only very recently, after the generation of writers from whose works we have drawn most of our selections, can we speak of the emergence of clear distinctions between cultural values themselves, and their involvements in social structures through institutionalization and in personalities through internalization.[14] For reasons of this sort, a number of the selections in Section A of Part Four contain discussions relevant to the problems of values, as do selections in the first subsection of Section B. Also, understandably, relevant materials are contained in Part Five—especially those dealing with Weber's concept of *Charisma* and its routinization.

Section C is relatively brief and deals with expressive symbolism.[15] As theory directly relevant to the purposes of this Reader, expressive symbolism is, for the period we cover, the least developed of the branches of cultural systems; indeed, it remains the least developed today. However, we consider it to be a field of very great importance, and have thus tried to include the most important points of reference for the incipient development of theory in it. We have included a small number of selections representative of the most important currents of thought that may be expected to provide fruitful starting points.

THE PROBLEM OF CULTURAL
ACCUMULATION

There was reference earlier to the problem of the senses in which culture does and does not contain the potentialities of cumulative development. Then

---

14. See the brief memorandum on the genesis and importance of this distinction between cultural and social systems, by Kroeber and Parsons, *American Sociological Review,* October, 1958.

15. Here, the editors are indebted to Dr. Clifford Geertz of the University of California, at Berkeley, who strongly urged the importance of including materials on expressive symbolism and helped us in the choice of selections.

discussion was concerned with scientific knowledge as the fully differentiated form of cognitive empirical culture. Traditionally, this has been the prototypal example of accumulation. However, part of this case has rested upon the untenable view that the process of accumulation in this field is exclusively, or even primarily, the additive accumulation of discrete items of factual knowledge. We argued that the problem presented by the need for successive reorganizations of the corpus of knowledge on the level of generalized theory substantially complicated this picture, and that it introduced a pattern characterized by qualitatively discrete levels of generalization in place of the purely linear concept of continuous accumulation. However, this complication does not impair the general conviction of the reality and importance of scientific advance. On the contrary, we feel that the concept is thereby given a far more solid grounding than the additive concept could give it. Obviously, the Newtonian cosmology was an advance beyond the Ptolemaic; but their respective conceptual schemes were differently *structured*.

The tendency has been to regard the three realms of culture other than scientific knowledge as noncumulative. None of them, in its course of development, is additive in the linear sense. There is a bewildering succession of art forms, of value systems, and of non-empirical belief systems.

Max Weber provides the most important exception to the tendency to accept either linear cumulation or complete discontinuity. He has often been interpreted as a radical relativist, particularly with reference to values and orientations of the grounding of meaning. But he postulated a single fundamental type of "primitive" religion, which may here be interpreted as that preceding any philosophic breakthrough. Further, he thought in terms of a definite process of rationalization which permeated, in different ways, all branches of culture. He definitely did not postulate a single linear process of cultural development, but had a "branching tree" concept. When considering the most fundamental religious orientations, however, he did not conceive of this branching as eventuating in a random collection of unrelated types. He rather formulated at least the outline of a systematic typology. The primary axes of this typology were otherworldly and innerworldly orientation in his specific senses, and asceticism and mysticism. He thus treated Calvinism as the polar possibility of innerworldly asceticism, and Buddhism as its polar opposite, otherworldly mysticism. Weber's extension of the concept of rationalization, even to the arts, is exemplified by his essay on the development of

Western music, placing a special emphasis on rationalization.[16]

Thus Weber's work has definite reference points for a concept of cumulation in cultural development —a decidedly complex, not simple, concept. Durkheim also had definite ideas in this area, though they were neither so fully articulated nor comprehensive over such a broad comparative scope as Weber's.[17]

Kroeber presents another important line of thought when, in his *Configurations of Culture Growth,* he demonstrates the importance in the history of science of relatively discontinuous phases of development, suggesting the importance of the qualitative elements which have been discussed here, and suggesting closer comparability with the arts than has usually been envisaged. Thus, for example, the late sixteenth through the seventeenth centuries saw, in the Kepler–Copernicus–Galileo–Newton sequence, the completion of a phase of theoretical reorganization of physical science that established a pattern. This pattern was not substantially modified until Clerk Maxwell's work, in the nineteenth century, started a new phase, which in turn did not reach culmination until the advent of Einstein's theory of relativity and the quantum theory. These may be regarded as convergent indications that there is a deeper similarity of pattern between these different realms of culture than is initially apparent.

The Introduction to Part Two presented an explicitly evolutionary point of view in treating the problems of ordering the materials available for the analysis of social structures. In this treatment, there are two crucial propositions, partly explicit, partly implicit. First, the structure of social systems consists in institutionalized patterns of culture. Second, the focus of this culture lies in systems of value. Early social evolutionists, like Condorcet, Comte, and Spencer, tended to take science as the prototype of culture, especially from the developmental point of view, and did not clearly discriminate the empirically cognitive, evaluative, etc., components of cultural systems.

If the institutionalized values of the society do form the primary focus of the articulation of cultural and social systems, then a concept of social *evolution*—which inherently implies a cumulative directionality—is unrealistic unless value-systems, in their cultural capacity, can demonstrably evolve. The denial of this possibility in the name of "cultural relativity" is the basic fallacy of the recent

---

16. Max Weber, *Wirtschaft und Gesellschaft,* 2d ed.; Tübingen: J. C. B. Mohr, 1956.
17. On this phase of Durkheim's work, see Robert N. Bellah, "Durkheim and History," *American Sociological Review,* 1959.

school of anthropological theory that has taken this name—combining the culturalism of the Benedictine persuasion and the functionalism associated especially (though with dubious validity) with Radcliffe-Brown. This type of emphasis has been justified in the interest of studying the particularities of different value systems on different levels and in different concrete social settings. This is analogous to the historian of science giving careful attention to the particularities of different theoretical systems. It does not, however, justify the view that there is no relation of developmental progression between systems of cultural values, any more than the elements of discontinuity in the relation of theoretical systems in science would justify the inference that there is no such thing as scientific "advancement."

The frame of reference for the analysis of an evolutionary sequence of value systems is presented in the concept—proposed in the early part of this Introduction—of a scale of levels of generality of evaluative priorities. Essentially, the progression may be formulated in terms of the emergence and handling of evaluative problems, including the problem of extent of concern with the spread of evaluative scope. For example: are many phenomena of physical nature to be assumed as simply "given," as part of "man's fate"; or are they to be evaluated in the context of the possibility of control? Then, do other societies simply "happen" as part of the environment in which the society of reference lives; or are the ways in which their way of life can be *meaningfully* related to ours a salient problem of evaluation?[18]

Beyond certain points, this kind of extension ceases to be meaningful unless it is accompanied and guided by a process of differentiation—of discrimination in the categorizing of different parts of the object world, like the discrimination between physical and social objects; and, within the latter category, between "motivated" personalities and social systems which do not, in the same sense, "act" on their own. Finally, any such process of differentiation leads to problems of integration. In cultural terms, integration of newly differentiated components implies rising to a higher *level* in the generalized organization of the cultural components concerned. It is a process of "upgrading" through the series of "levels of generality" emphasized throughout this discussion. Our argument

is that this general paradigm applies to systems of evaluation as much as it does to systems of empirical cognition. But this upgrading is directly constitutive of the structure of the society.

The two are interdependent, in two senses. Empirically considered, they are parts of the same cultural system; and they are integrated, through institutionalization and internalization, in the same non-cultural systems of action of societies and personalities. It would be strange if the empirically cognitive subsystem of the cultural system were highly differentiated in terms of levels of generality, while the value-system were a totally flat structure with no such differentiation of levels. Hence there must have been, in the course of social evolution, a process of upgrading value systems that is parallel with the upgrading of systems of empirical knowledge.

This, however, must not be understood to repeat the "positivistic" error—the suppression of any analytical distinction between scientific knowledge and value systems.[19] The latter are integrated with the non-cultural components of social systems in ways that scientific systems are not—especially with the exigencies of the behavior of organisms and with the motivational exigencies of personalities. There is also a secondary relation: on certain levels of socio-cultural development, social systems themselves can become objects of systematically codified empirical knowledge, as already indicated.

If this critical extension of the general principle of accumulation from systems of empirical knowledge to institutionalized value systems is accepted, then it is logical to extend it still farther, to the other two principal aspects of cultural systems. Weber pioneered in bringing out the intimate connections between value-systems—particularly in relation to economic functions within societies—and their roots in orientations in terms of the problems of meaning; this was the major theme of Weber's grand design for the comparative study of religion and society.

There are not only qualitative differences in these basic orientations; they must also, for satisfying cultural analysis, be ordered on a scale of levels of generality along the kind of lines suggested by our

---

18. Thus ethnocentrism may be described as a characteristic feature of "primitive" societies, linked with non-literacy, dominance of kinship in the social structure, etc. By "ethnocentrism," we mean taking for granted that "our way of life" is the naturally right and proper one in general.

19. The common "positivistic" idea of the feasibility of "scientific ethics" is not implied in the position we have taken. To say that the pattern of cumulation through the reaching of higher levels of generality is shared by science and evaluative concepts is not to say that the latter can be adequately *based* on the former, in the sense of being logically derivable from scientific generalizations as postulates. "Ethics," we conceive, on the cultural level as such, to be part of a much more ramified system of cultural content which is partly independent of, but also interdependent with, not only science, but also cathectic patternings and commitments and orientations of meaning.

above formulation of the dimension of the grounding of meanings. Thus there must be meanings of means-objects, of goals, of systems of order, and of the ultimate roots of the latter. Moreover, the range of considerations must be upgraded more in an advanced system than in more primitive systems. Dr. Robert Bellah has referred to the process of "philosophic breakthrough"[20] underlying the development of the major "world religions"; this seems precisely such a process of the *reorganization* of the orientations of meaning at the highest level of cultural generality. The existential *malaise* of our time may well be related to the occurrence of a comparable process, whose structural outlines are at present only dimly comprehensible, if at all.[21]

The question of cumulation in the field of expressive symbolization, i.e., of the arts, has been deliberately left until now because it has so generally been cited as the prototypal case of complete irrelevance of the idea of cumulative development. It is the most difficult to analyze in this way, because, in all systems of action, the cathectic relation to situational objects is the most highly particularized of all essential relations. In contrast, the instrumental relation to means, e.g., to objects of utility, has more generalized meaning—as does, in a quite different direction, the justification of cathexes in relation to the integrative problems of the system to which they relate, i.e., in the case of the social system to its institutionalized norms.

Cathectic-artistic generalization can therefore be expected to assume special forms clearly differentiated from those of empirical cognition, meaning-orientation, and even evaluation. A special mode of "condensation" of meaning seems to be a keynote of aesthetic or appreciative patterns, in this sense. Since the reference is object-oriented, it may reasonably be assumed that this has tended particularly to emphasize symbols, and hence generalization through the patterning of symbols rather than the symbolization of patterns. For one particular case of special relevance to the personality system, the symbolism of dreams as treated by Freud is probably a prototype of artistic symbolism—it is the highly condensed expression of a profusely rich set of associations of the content of experience and of expectations.[21a]

One difficulty in seeing the element of generalization in the arts may derive from the common tendency to emphasize the importance of artistic symbolism as such. If, beyond the general particularity of reference of the cathectic field of meaning, one of the lower levels of generality of any cultural subsystem is stressed, then it is easy to overlook the elements corresponding to the syntactical and phraseological levels in the case of language, or to general theory in the case of science.

For the arts, these are form and style. It is fairly commonplace in this area for even works that are called "realistic" to be far from direct representations of their subject-matter. Through selection, condensation, symbolization, and patterned arrangement of components, much more meaning can be condensed in a small compass than could be in real life—except in the most crucial experiences and events.

The development of art forms cannot be understood as an additive process of inventing new symbols one at a time. Symbols are critically important to the arts; and one major task of their analysis is the clarification of the characteristics of artistic symbols as distinguished from the characteristics which figure most prominently in science and philosophy.

One most important point about artistic symbolism is vividly indicated by Burke.[22] This is the multiplicity of references involved in the same symbol and symbolic complex. Burke emphasizes the simultaneous involvement of the civic level in Greek tragedy, and the religious level which in some sense is, relative to the former, an "archaic" substratum of meaning. This order of multiple reference of symbols seems to maintain for cathectic symbolization in the personality field, as found in the Freudian type of interpretation of dreams and used generally to interpret material produced during psychoanalysis. It is essentially to the patterns of order involved in the *organization* of these multiple symbolic references that one must look for the elements of generalized patterning involved in systems of expressive symbolism.

The central problems concern the senses in which such pattern systems can be arranged in

---

20. In an unpublished paper, "Religion and Politics in Modern Asia." This term has been used by cultural historians and historians of philosophy, like Henri Frankfort and Georg Misch.

21. Essentially, the above argument introduces a concept of the "relativity of relativity" for all three of the cultural subsystems discussed. This means that they must be conceived to be integrated with each other at broadly comparable levels of generality. Thus modern science cannot be conceived as part of the same cultural system as a primitive religion, but is definitely linked with Western Christianity, especially ascetic Protestantism, and its later cultural derivatives.

21a. An as yet unpublished manuscript of Kenneth Burke, *Poetics,* in which he uses the tragedies of Sophocles as his point of departure, seems one of the most highly sophisticated analyses both of the elaborate ramifications of the association of meanings on several different levels, and of the importance of the factor of generalization. A comparably rich analysis of such ramifications, strongly oriented from an aesthetic point of view, is presented in Erik H. Erikson, *Young Man Luther.*

22. *Ibid.*

series of levels of generality, and how they are linked with the other components of the cultural system as a whole. For the latter problem, the most immediately significant and tangible set of links are those to the religious belief and symbol system. The case analyzed by Burke may be considered prototypal; in artistic systems, there is always a more manifest level of the centrality of symbolization, and a substratum which, in terms of the development of the culture, is historically earlier—on the scale of "sophistication," less general, and closer to religious traditions than the higher levels.

The ways in which art differentiates from a religious matrix are closely related to this. The patterns of form which were differentiated from a religious matrix are, in the present sense, more general than those embedded in religion. These considerations are advanced to help to place the arts more completely in the general process of structural differentiation of systems of action, since this underlies the higher-level patterns of integration associated with the concept of upgrading. Essentially, the phenomenon of the "relativizing of relativity" (noted with reference to the other three subsystems of culture) is the key to the problem of cumulation in the field of expressive symbolization. The impression of planless pluralism derives largely from the treatment of style patterns in isolation both from the cultural system of which they are a part and from the society. When both contexts are carefully considered and theoretically analyzed, comparatively and in developmental perspective, the inevitable conclusion is that expressive symbolism is an integral part of the total socio-cultural complex.

Perhaps one example is in order.[23] European music underwent a major transformation in the transition from Handel and Mozart, through Beethoven, to the patterns of the nineteenth century. Beethoven did much more than invent a few new musical tricks or gadgets unknown to his predecessors. He introduced a major reorganization of musical form, most conspicuous in the symphonic form and illustrated by the contrast of the *Eroica* with his first two, much more Mozartian, symphonies. This produced a range and power for expression, especially of intense emotion and conflict, that had been absent from the highly integrated but more restricted style of eighteenth-century music. As often remarked, this cultural change was connected with the French Revolution and the Napoleonic era—i.e., with the dissolution of the aristocratic society of the Old Regime in Europe. Beethoven, in one of the major arts, revealed possibilities of expressing emotion that were in certain respects com-

parable with those Freud, nearly a century later, opened on the level of science.

The general analysis of cultural systems provides foundation for the view that a principle of cumulative development is inherent in the nature of cultural systems as a whole, and not only of their empirically cognitive components and subsystems. However, this development is not a simple additive or linear process; seen in relation to levels of generality, it is, in one set of respects, a "stepwise" process—and probably, seen in terms of the inevitably complex relations between the different subsystems of a larger cultural system, it is in some sense a "spiral" process. Some such complication would follow from the dependence of these subsystems on their complex relations of interdependence with the other, non-cultural subsystems of action. This is not the place to attempt to analyze these many complications of interrelationship. Neglecting them was the major sin of omission committed by the early theorists of evolution in the cultural and in the social fields. The fact that they are inevitably complicated is, however, no basis for asserting categorically that their analysis has no proper place in social science. On the contrary, taking them properly into account will prove to be one of the main bases on which social science can advance beyond its present state—which, in certain theoretical respects, seems to be stuck on a dead level.

The relevance of these considerations transcends the concerns of sociology. The crucial significance of a proper understanding of the main outlines of the nature, structure, and functioning of cultural systems for the theory of social systems should, however, be clear. In closing this Introduction, we shall attempt to combine a few of these implications for the analysis of social in relation to cultural systems, by a brief discussion of a field of study which has attracted a good deal of attention from sociologists—the "sociology of knowledge."

THE "SOCIOLOGY OF KNOWLEDGE"
AND THE SOCIOLOGY OF CULTURE

The sociology of knowledge has, since the latter part of the main period on which our attention in these volumes has been concentrated, been the most important single focus of the discussion of problems of the interrelations of culture and social systems in sociology. This field, originating in Germany and called the "sociology of knowledge" (*Wissenssoziologie*), has been associated especially

---

23. This example was suggested by Dr. Clifford Geertz in a personal communication.

with Karl Mannheim. Some of the considerations discussed in the Introduction to Section A of Part One indicate why this should have been a particularly salient problem area in Germany; its salience grows directly from the background of the version predominant there of the collectivistic tradition in sociology on the background of idealistic philosophy.

In idealistic historicism, the more extreme positions tended to identify cultural and social systems completely, resulting, as in the cases of Dilthey and Sombart, in a kind of cultural emanationism treating a *Geist* as "actualizing itself" through the "historical process." The first major challenge to this tendency came with the Marxian conception of historical materialism, which postulated both the independence and the predominance of the complex of factors that Marx summed up in the formula of the relations of production (*Produktionsverhältnisse*) and that were rather vaguely and indeterminately related to a "superstructure" of beliefs, values, ideologies, etc. The problem of the relations between *Idealfaktoren* and *Realfaktoren* in this sense came to dominate sociological discussion in Germany, in the work, for example, of Max Weber, Max Scheler, and Alfred Weber.

The various introductory materials presented in these volumes indicate our opinion that Max Weber made by far the most significant contribution to this problem. This is especially so in that he attempted to support his version of an analytical distinction between these factors by a set of comparative studies guided by the concept of the logic of experimental method—i.e., the attempt at empirical demonstration of independent variation. He thereby broke through the prevailing German tendency to insist that tracing historical sequences, and the related tendency to insist on the inherent "individuality" of the phenomena in a sense precluding the relevance of comparative method, were the only requirements necessary or even possible for "understanding." Even though Weber's conceptual refinements have been enormously elaborated in many ways, however, the heritage of his work still leaves many more fundamental theoretical problems unsolved. These issues' relevance to the problem of cultural cumulativeness as discussed in the last section of the present Introduction is clear. Weber himself vacillated on some of these points.

It was almost in the nature of the "definition of the intellectual situation" that consideration of the problem should be carried back to its philosophical foundations. Here Mannheim's epistemological relativism struck at a very sensitive point in the conceptual structure. One might almost say that this was a last-ditch defense of the basic historical rel-

ativism which increasingly emerged from the general idealistic tradition, at the same time becoming involved in mounting difficulties. Mannheim's relativism—however justified with respect to particular conceptual patterns, especially in the realms of ideology and of religious beliefs—if taken in a radical epistemological sense, leads to an untenable position completely incompatible with the foundations of science in the fields of human action. Mannheim vacillated on this basic point, but Max Weber was entirely clear and was fundamentally right, even though he did not develop his position to its ultimate conclusion.[24]

Seen in the perspective of the whole development of social thought over the past 150 years, the similarity between the logical structure of this dilemma and that of the famous problem of heredity and environment is striking. There has been the same logic of dichotomy, the same tendency to pose the problem in terms of *versus*—to attempt to prove that *either* one *or* the other is "really" important. In general, two major types of development indicate the way out of this kind of impasse—developments already illustrated, e.g., in connection with the problem of the independence of patterns of culture from biological heredity itself. The first essential development is recognition of the *analytical* character of the categories at issue and the concomitant untenability of reifying them as concrete entities excluding the involvement, in the same concrete empirical systems, of other factors. Thus the fact that the planet Earth is a particle, in the sense of analytical mechanics, does not preclude its surface from being at the same time a physical environment for living species. It is futile to argue whether one or the other conceptualization describes earth's "true character." The second essential is that further progress requires differentiation in the conceptual schemes employed in the area concerned, and on *both* sides of the initial dichotomy.

These two points will be the keynote of our approach to the problem of the sociology of knowledge. The primary starting point is the existence of a valid distinction between cultural and social systems. In the traditional German treatment of *Realfaktoren*, however, the social system aspect has often been confused with physical, biological, and psychological components.[25] This is evidenced by

24. A classic discussion of these issues, which unfortunately has never been translated into English, is Alexander von Schelting, *Max Webers Wissenschaftslehre*, which devotes an extensive discussion to the problem of "sociological relativity" in the work of Mannheim.

25. Thus, for understandable reasons, historically the problems of personality were not salient in this German historical tradition. It was *Kultur* or *Geist* vis-à-vis *Gesellschaft*.

the many ambiguities of the terms "material" and "materialistic." The point therefore is that it is important to distinguish between cultural systems and social systems, and also between these and the other systems of action, namely, personalities and behavioral organisms, and, beyond these, the "physical" world.

Second, treating the distinction as analytical makes it possible to develop a conception which considers cultural and social systems, not as completely "concrete" systems, nor merely as "interdependent," but as *interpenetrating*. The failure to clarify the problem of interpenetration is one of the major sources of the difficulties in which discussions about the sociology of knowledge have become enmeshed. The key to the relation is the proposition already reiterated—the patterning of the structure of social systems *consists* in institutionalized culture. If this be granted, the question of "which is more important" becomes nonsensical on a certain level.

The obverse relation also exists. It may be formulated as follows: the cultural *problems* posed by the fact that human beings are organized in social systems cannot be formulated from a "purely" cultural point of view; they involve the detailed exigencies of the operation of social systems as such— just as much a category of reality as is anything one might say about "hard, tough physical matter." The essential point is that certain aspects of cultural systems cannot be understood without reference to the facts about social systems; and, vice versa, social systems cannot be analyzed without reference to the cultural focus. In this sense, cultural and social systems cannot be "separated," but they *can be distinguished* and treated as analytically independent. The endless ambiguities which have arisen about the Marxist formula of the "relations of production" constitute a classic example of the problem. It culminates in the undoubted fact that, by Marx's own account, the normative structure of the legal system must be included in the relations of production. But is this a "material factor?" In our opinion, the dichotomy of material and ideal simply does not apply concretely at this level. Legal norms form a component of *institutionalized culture*. As institutionalized legal norms, they are part of the social system; as culture, they are "ideal"—in this case, in the normative sense. The tendency of the real-ideal dichotomy has been to obscure what is, in many respects, the central feature of the social system, its being a set of mechanisms by which cultural factors are in fact involved in empirical, and hence in some sense "material," systems of reality—it is the interpenetration and the relations of control and of "conditioning" between the two that are in one aspect the *central* feature of systems of action.[26]

The problem of conceptual differentiation is third. The discussion of the sociology of knowledge has tended to treat culture, as a whole, as an undifferentiated category. At least at times, the tendency has been to consider expressive symbolization— with its accentuation, relative to other components, of individuality and of cathectic attachment as distinguished from more instrumental orientations— as the prototype of culture. If any selectivity is to occur within the general structure of cultural systems, as we have outlined it, this emphasis would maximize the element of relativism.

The element of cultural systems that has the most direct structural or constitutive significance for social systems is the evaluative element, with particular reference to social system values. This component is somewhat less relativistic than is expressive symbolization, but it is more closely assimilated to the latter in some value systems than in others. While assessing the importance of such variability, however, we shall continue to emphasize the strategic significance of the evaluative aspect of culture for the social system, and also the importance of the distinction between the evaluative and the expressive components of cultural systems.

For our analysis, however, a further distinction is crucially needed. The very terminology of the discussion directs attention to it, namely, the term "sociology of *knowledge*." The word "knowledge" is one of many commonly used in this field that are very ambiguous. Sometimes it connotes all culture, but most usages exclude artistic expression and its appreciation from the category, and the importance of the suggestion that evaluating and "knowing" should be distinguished is there. In English, "knowledge" is strongly associated with science, with *empirical* knowledge. In German, however, the word *Wissen* has broader meaning, and is almost equivalent, in its modified form of *Wissenschaft*, to "discipline." *Wissenschaft* might thus almost be equated with sophisticated analysis of, or in terms of, *any* subsystem of culture. But in terms of our above scheme, two vital distinctions must still be made. The first is between the primarily (but not exclusively) non-cognitive (expressive and evaluative) branches of culture; the second, between the empirically cognitive and those formulating orientations in terms of the grounds of meaning. It is especially confusing to identify cultural orientations to empirical objects, in the sciences of action, with the structures of the orientation of meaning, in Weber's sense.

---

26. The central contribution of Durkheim was probably that he fully understood and clarified this relation.

These distinctions constitute only the first stage of a process of conceptual differentiation of culture that is essential for any clear-cut and important analysis of the sociology of culture, here interpreted as the analysis of the interdependence and interpenetration of social and cultural systems or their subsystems, is to develop. But if conceptual differentiation on the cultural system is essential, it is equally so for the social system.

Mannheim was so preoccupied with what he regarded as his great discovery of certain patterns of interdependence, that he tended to adopt and work with the Marxian level of analysis of the structure and functioning of social systems (the *Realfaktoren*). He did not even seriously utilize the much higher level of theoretical differentiation in this field that Max Weber's work made available. Above all, Mannheim tended to regard social class as too exclusively central a concept. In one particular theme, however, Mannheim built on Weber—his ideas about the special features of the "intellectuals" in modern society. Though he did not fully analyze this, Mannheim did make an important and interesting contribution.

We have presented a considerable range, of different types of conceptual refinement in the social system field that we think are essential for further progress, in the General Introduction and in the introductory materials for Parts One, Two, and Three. In this Introduction, we have presented, in outline, the main lines of differentiation of cultural systems internally, in relation to the social system, and in relation to the other subsystems of action.

In our view, any adequate treatment of the "sociology of culture" must take explicit cognizance of these differentiations on both sides of the relation, as well as of the inevitably complex interrelations involved in the interdependence and interpenetration of the two systems. In conclusion, we can suggest only a few lines of analysis that have already been partly developed and seem promising for the future.

Particularly in the English-speaking world, the least confusion understandably reigns where empirical knowledge is the aspect of culture on which attention is concentrated. As will be demonstrated, Malinowski's clear differentiation between magical and religious orientations, and between the primitive prototypes of science and rational technology, provided a major orientation here. Important beginnings in this field in Weber's work have been developed by Merton, Barber, and others.[27]

It is important here to note that three different aspects of the sociology of scientific knowledge must be distinguished in general, apart from particular content. One aspect concerns the conditions involved in maintaining a given level of scientific knowledge, in the purely cultural tradition, and at the command of sufficiently large and strategically placed elements of the population. This is most directly involved with the pattern-maintenance complex of the society, the culture, and—in relation to particular population elements—the socialization process in its educational aspect. A second complex is the technological, concerning the sociological conditions of the implementation of empirical knowledge in areas of the social structure that are not, as such, primarily concerned with its creation or with its preservation. E.g., the field of health provides abundant evidence of how common are the conditions which block the use of knowledge that is "readily" available.[28] Above all, it is essential to know and remember that, in the last century or so, the development of technology—with its enormous impact on the routine lives of millions of people—is not a simple result of the availability of the basic knowledge; it is a function of complex sets of conditions in the social system, conditions associated with the structural characteristics of "industrial societies."[29]

The third aspect of the sociology of science concerns the conditions of scientific creativity. This involves subtle relations to the level of personality; but the importance of "genius" must not obscure the co-existent importance of the social setting of research. This setting is intimately interdependent with cultural factors outside science itself, probably especially with the definitions of the situation in terms of meaning. The connections between Puritanism and physical science, suggested by Weber and developed by Merton, provide a striking example.

A special development and complication in this field becomes involved when the objects of scientific observation and analysis are the behavior of human beings—particularly their personality, social, and cultural systems. Naegele's analysis of the conditions prerequisite to the emergence of sociology, as presented in the first essay of the General Introduction, constitutes an excellent example of work in the field of the sociology of knowledge in this area. Another classic example is the self-observation of the individual person, or "introspection." The radical behaviorists of a generation ago

27. Robert K. Merton, *Science, Technology and Society in Seventeenth-Century England*, Bruges: Osiris History of Science Monographs, 1938; Bernard Barber, *Science and the Social Order*, Glencoe: The Free Press, 1952.

28. An impressive compendium of such evidence is found in B. D. Paul (ed.), *Health, Culture and Community*, New York: Russell Sage Foundation, 1955.

29. See Parsons, *Structure and Process in Modern Societies*, Free Press, 1959, Chap. IV.

denied it any scientific status; but this denial no longer provides any grounds for rejecting its status. Successful introspection, however, is just as dependent on definable conditions as the pursuit of any other type of objective empirical knowledge. More generally, as we have emphasized, the development of scientific knowledge of the field of human action is necessarily a late and especially difficult part of the evolution of empirical scientific culture.

One major source of difficulty of behavioral science—and also one of its main foci of problems and of opportunity—lies in its relations to ideology. Ideology as indicated above, should be regarded as a mode of the patterning of orientation that links empirical cognition in the action field with evaluative components. This is validly the historical center of the problems of the sociology of knowledge. The difficulty of reconciling the "intrusion" of the evaluative component into the field of objective science was one vital impetus to Mannheim's relativism.

Values occupy a very central place in the area of interpenetration of social and cultural systems. This component of culture is truly most directly constitutive of the social system itself. If sociology is to be a science, there must be a thorough development of thinking about the basic relations between the treatment of social systems as objects of scientific observation and analysis, and about the consideration of the values of social scientists as members of societies who *orient* their own behavior in terms of the values institutionalized in their societies—especially when they feel in opposition to the currently dominant values. Mannheim therefore indicated the truly crucial center of the problem of the interrelations between social science as itself a social phenomenon, and simultaneously, in its cultural references, as a subsystem of the culture, independent of the society in which it can occur. The problem of ideology is, at the level of the institutionalization of culture, the functional problem of social systems—directly analogous to Durkheim's problem of organic solidarity treated at the level of the internal organization of the social system itself. However, a much more differentiated scheme of analysis than Mannheim or his more immediate followers commanded is necessary to carry through the task presented to sociology by this central problem of ideology.

In this connection, it is particularly important to distinguish two levels of considering the problem. The first level concerns the relation between values and the scientific analysis of the society in which those values are institutionalized *at the level of the integration of the cultural system itself*. This prob-

lem area corresponds closely to what Mannheim called the "general problem of ideology." However, using terms derived from Max Weber and von Schelting, we may state that, if it is to be integrated with the institutionalized value-system of a society, there must be selectivity in the structure of the relevant body of social science according to criteria of the significance the problems have for those values; this is what Weber called the principle of *Wertbeziehung,* which may be translated as "value-relevance." Second, this element of relativity to values does not imply that the scientific canons of objectivity are inapplicable. The element of relativity concerns selectivity in terms of the significance of *problems,* and not distortion in the standards for evaluating the *solution* of those problems. The process of validation is subject to what Weber called the "logical schema of proof," which is not culturally relative in the same sense. To avoid confusion with the second area of problems to be discussed we suggest that the word "ideology" should not be used in this connection, but that a term like the "value-science integrate" of the culture be employed instead.

The second set of problems concerns the interaction between cultural and social systems, and not the structure of the cultural system as such. Because of structured strains in the social system, it is possible to demonstrate and explicate the elements of selection in the structure of the concept of the social system, and, beyond this, the elements of distortion. The criteria for asserting the existence of this "secondary" selection and of distortion must be the standards of the social disciplines as formulated in terms of the value-science integrate. The word "ideology," corresponding to Mannheim's "particular ideology," will be reserved for an evaluative concept of the social system, or its aspects or subsystems that, according to these standards, *deviate* from the "ideal type" of the value-science integrate in the particular culture. Explanation of ideological selection and distortion then must be found in selective and partial institutionalization of values within the social system, and in interrelations between these values and other components of the social system, e.g., motivational "interests," integrative communication and its exigencies, etc.[30]

The type of problem of higher-level cultural

---

30. This concept of ideology is employed, e.g., by Sutton, Harris, Kaysen, and Tobin in their important book, *The American Business Creed* (Cambridge: Harvard University Press, 1957). I have attempted to work out, in more detail than the limitations of space of the present Introduction permit, the basis of the above discrimination of problem areas and certain main lines of analysis both within each and with respect to their interdependence, in 'An Approach to the Sociology of Knowledge," *loc. cit.*

references involved in physical science, exemplified in the relation of Puritanism to science in seventeenth-century England, is parallel to the relation of values to the religious foundations on which, in the orientational sense, they rest. Weber, in his analysis of the relations of the ethic of ascetic Protestantism, to "capitalism," and to the whole value-complex underlying and institutionalized in modern industrial societies, has most fruitfully posed the problem. Sufficient comparative study has now been done to show that the relation between ascetic Protestantism and social organization is not a simple or exclusive one.[31] This, however, is not a valid reason for denying that there is any significant relationship.

Weber comprehensively documented his own acute awareness of the obverse relationship in his long discussion of the relations between religion and social status (Section B below). Different types of social groups are differentially sensitive to the appeals of different types of religious orientations, and especially to their being rooted in different concepts of the grounds of meaning. But this is one of many cases in which showing that one set of factors is dependent on another in no way provides a source of objection to emphasizing the importance of *inter*dependence—in Weber's words, of analyzing "the other side of the causal chain."

In discussing the general place of religion in the complex of the relations of cultural and social systems, we suggested that there is a particularly important triangular relation among the aspects of culture in which orientations of meaning are based, the place of these orientations in the legitimation of individuals' moral commitments, and the society's institutionalized values. At the high cultural level, this presents a complex of relations analogous to Durkheim's problem of mechanical solidarity, at the level of the society's internal structure and mechanisms of social control. Here, as much as in any other field, the sociology of culture must take account of the complex interrelations between society and culture, through the bases of societal values, and also of the ways in which this grounding depends on the commitments of individuals. In this connection, the major position of the sociology of religion as a branch of the sociology of culture can best be understood.

The sociology of religion (and much of philosophy) concerns the problem of "knowledge" (*Wissen*) in one of its German meanings, i.e., orientation in the context of "problems of meaning." It also simultaneously involves the problems of the fourth of our major subsystems of culture, expressive symbolization. We have argued that the peak of the heirarchy of objects of cathexis is the concept of objects of "generalized respect" or of "worship." The implications of this placing would probably lead into the problems of the sociology of the arts—but also of more general demands toward experience.

We hope that this discussion, which takes its departure from the problems of the sociology of knowledge, has served to indicate the relevance of some of the analytical considerations, proposed in earlier parts of this Introduction, to the more contemporary problems involved in the sociology of culture—i.e., the interdependence and interpenetration of social and cultural systems. Mannheim's contribution made salient a very critical problem area in this field—the problem of ideology as the most important field of the relations between social science and the value-systems of societies, and the importance of the concomitant problems of methodology. This was a continuation of the discussion in which Weber's essay on the objectivity of knowledge in the social sciences[32] was such an important landmark. It also focused attention on an axis of the whole complex of problems different from the axis in Weber's discussion of the religious problems of meaning as foundations of value-systems and of the personal commitments ("religious interests") of individuals. In our view, neither the sociology of knowledge nor Weber's type of sociology of religion constitute, taken alone, adequate foundations for a more general analytical scheme. Both need to be fitted into a more general sociology of culture, in which all the components of both systems reviewed here are treated as systematically interdependent with each other.

31. See especially Bellah, *Tokugawa Religion,* Free Press; Clifford Geertz, *Religion in Java,* Free Press, 1960; and David S. Landes, *Religion and Enterprise: The Case of the French Textile Industry,* unpublished manuscript.

32. Max Weber, "The Meaning of 'Ethical Neutrality' in Sociology and Economics," *Max Weber on the Methodology of the Social Sciences* (trans. and ed. by E. A. Shils and H. A. Finch, Glencoe, Ill.: Free Press, 1949).

Section A

Symbolic Processes and the Cultural Heritage

Editorial Foreword, BY TALCOTT PARSONS   *997*

I—SYMBOLISM AND COMMUNICATION

1. *From Gesture to Symbol,* BY GEORGE H. MEAD   *999*
2. *Ideational Content of the Sign,* BY ERNST CASSIRER   *1004*
3. *On Sacred Objects as Symbols,* BY EMILE DURKHEIM   *1008*
4. *Dream-Work,* BY SIGMUND FREUD   *1010*
5. *How Words Change Their Meanings,* BY ANTOINE MEILLET   *1013*
6. *Symbolism,* BY EDWARD SAPIR   *1018*

II—PATTERNS OF CULTURE

1. *The Factors of Social Phenomena,* BY HERBERT SPENCER   *1021*
2. *On Biological and Cultural Factors,* BY FRANZ BOAS   *1024*
3. *On Culture,* BY ALFRED L. KROEBER   *1032*
4. *On the Mores,* BY WILLIAM GRAHAM SUMNER   *1037*
5. *On the Patterns of Culture,* BY RUTH BENEDICT   *1047*

Symbolic Processes and the Cultural Heritage

by Talcott Parsons

As indicated in its general Introduction, Part Four has been divided into three main sections. The first deals with certain fundamentals of cultural systems essential for understanding their involvement in social systems; the second deals with two categories of cultural subsystems and their specific relevance to societies. Section A is subdivided into a first subsection, containing selections from writings introducing the modern discussion of the nature of communication, signs and symbols, language, etc.; the second subsection concerns the more general character of cultural patterns.

Because of its relevance to sociological theory, it seemed appropriate to begin with a selection, from the work of G. H. Mead, analyzing the conditions of the genesis of symbolization and the capacity for higher-order communication in the process of social interaction. In Mead's discussion, the concept "gesture" is a special case of the use of signs to guide action and interaction—a use which can lead to symbolic levels of meaning-orientation and be incorporated in symbolic systems. Though many other authors have discussed these problems, Mead probably placed them most squarely in the context of their relation to the process of social interaction. His work makes the main point of the inherent interpenetration of the symbolic level of cultural organization and the social process of interaction through communication. Symbolization provides the indispensable medium of higher-level communication; however, extension, differentiation, and upgrading of symbolic systems cannot occur without social interaction. Symbolic systems are not "inventions" of individuals that are put at the disposal of social groups. Whatever the critical role of individuals in initiating innovations, a cultural level of symbol-meaning has been established

only if it has become shared as part of the communicative resources of an interaction system. Purely autistic sign-formation is not culture. In Mead's work and elsewhere, the importance of these considerations in establishing the concept of role is patent.

The excerpt from Cassirer's work deals with the more philosophical task of establishing the basis of symbolic structures. More than any other philosopher of the period, Cassirer paid extensive and systematic attention to this problem; and his work has provided an indispensable foundation for later discussion.

The next two selections deal with the role of symbolization in two critically important contexts, specifically, the contexts of religion and of the unconscious layers of the personality's structure. Durkheim's clear insight into the importance of symbolization in religion is one of the features of his *Elementary Forms* which establish the high importance of the work. As noted above, both the animism of Tylor and the "naturism" of Max Müller had attempted to "explain" the currency of ideas such as the "soul" and the deification of the forces of nature by the "intrinsic reasonableness" of the associations. From this point of view, the "primitive man" occupying so much of the thought of the second half of the nineteenth century was an early scientist, diagnosing, as best he could, what might account for mysterious aspects of his experience. The effect was the complete assimilation of religious symbolization to that of empirical science, blocking the development of the type of differentiation within the system of culture emphasized in the general Introduction to Part Four.

Durkheim started with the concept that the enormous variety of objects treated as sacred precluded any explanation in terms of a common factor of "intrinsic" correctness, e.g., that the fearsome impressiveness of the storm made storm gods prevalent in some societies. Durkheim started at the other end, using the "arbitrary" connection between symbol and meaning so characteristic of language. Instead of asking what the intrinsic properties of the sacred object suggest as the most important context of meaning, the question became, What, in the total context of the society and culture, can be isolated as the functional *problems* likely to produce a religious response, and, hence, how are the objects actually treated as sacred related to these problems? Though there is no intrinsic resemblance between a species of animal or bird and a clan, a symbolic relationship between a totem species and the clan can certainly occur. This does not preclude other associations in the total symbolic complex; in particular, it frees one from adhering to Durkheim's view that *the* important meaning-reference of the totem symbol is to a social group as such. Nevertheless, Durkheim's analysis of the symbolic character of sacred objects opened a new range of possible relationships.

Similar things can be said about Freud's concept of the symbolic content of dreams in his *The Interpretation of Dreams*. This book was the first in which Freud presented the major outlines of his concept of personality. It is not fortuitous that symbolism, here assumed to be fundamentally a category of culture, played such a prominent part in this concept.

Many interpreters of Freud have treated this symbolism, particularly the part dealing with erotic content and the body references involved, as simply a manifestation of "sexual instincts." However, we do not believe that authentic symbolization exists on non-cultural levels of the organization of action. There may be hereditary components of "predisposition" to select certain object-references as symbols in this connection, but in our view, the predominant content is, psychologically speaking, learned; and the symbolism even of the id, to use Freud's later concept, is authentically cultural. Thus, in one sense, Durkheim and Freud introduced the idea of symbolic process at the two poles of the structure of action systems: at the pole closest to the ultimate orientations of meaning; and at the pole closest to the most "primitive" (in the Freudian sense, "deepest") level of the motivational organization of the individual personality.

Freud's work also serves as an important illustration of the dangers of a rigid either/or attitude toward analytical problems in this field. Certainly, in contrast to the notion of intrinsic understandability of the symbol, i.e., object, as the "cause" of meaning—the common assumption of animism and naturism—Durkheim was completely right in emphasizing the arbitrariness of the association. But Freud reminds us that, despite crucial differences, various elements of physical and other resemblance do enter into the structure of symbolic systems, especially those with expressive primacy. Thus, the famous proposition that elongated objects generally serve as penis-symbols must not be cavalierly dismissed on the grounds that the combination of sounds represented by the symbol "book" in no discernable way resembles the class of physical objects (which are, of course, not only physical) which it signifies. On such grounds, it is not legitimate to reject the interpretation that snakes, including the serpent of the Book of Genesis, are frequently penis-symbols.

This type of consideration is applicable to language itself, as is vividly indicated by the selection from Meillet. In his exploration of the relations between the symbolic content of words and the detailed structure of social systems, Meillet was, in our opinion, far in advance of his time in the science of linguistics. Clearly, the language of a society does not remain totally unchanged when the structure of the society changes. That the two poles of emphasis in the theory of symbolism, illustrated by Durkheim and Freud, are not inherently incompatible is brought out by the fact that Meillet was a student of Durkheim.

The first subsection closes with the article which Edward Sapir wrote on Symbolism for the *Encyclopedia of the Social Sciences*. Sapir was an unusual figure, a pioneer both in technical linguistics and in cultural anthropology. He certainly raised the level of thinking on this range of problems to a height which, at the time, few had attained.

The second subsection of Section A deals with patterns of culture as discussed in our more general Introduction to this Part. The initial theme is the possibility of distinguishing a distinctively "cultural" or, as we would now be more inclined to say, "socio-cultural," component within the more general framework of the theory of evolution. Here a particularly appropriate point of departure for the sociologist is Herbert Spencer's concept of the "superorganic," which came to be considered as analogous to the genetic constitution of the organism, as an element often described as "social heredity." The problem of cumulativeness, accorded much prominence in the Introduction to Part Four, is a central problem for Spencer. It merits a genuine revival of attention, but on a more theoretically sophisticated basis.

A selection from Franz Boas follows the opening selection from Spencer. Boas was especially important as the builder of bridges between the biological and the social sciences, and between German and American thinking in this area. He began his professional career as a biologist and entered anthropology rather late. This transition coincided with the transition from the German phase of his career to the American. From the point of view of the present orientation, it may be said that Boas strongly reinforced the importance of the distinction between biological and socio-cultural components in behavior; he also served as the most important single channel through which German historicist-idealistic concepts influenced American social science, particularly anthropology.

Here Spencer's tradition of evolutionary tendency collided with the inherently anti-evolutionary influence of the German tradition. Boas' influence was clearly anti-evolutionary, even "atomistic." In American anthropology, he is the father of the "trait" theory, or of what is sometimes called the "historical school."

In the tradition emphasizing patterns of culture, Kroeber is perhaps the most important mediator between the two viewpoints. In his early and justly famous essay on the "Superorganic," he built directly on Spencer; we have here reproduced his more recent views on the subject. We have already noted the important contribution he made to the problem of cumulation by his analysis of common components in the configurations of cultural growth.

William Graham Sumner is another influential figure who bridged the notions of evolution and cultural relativity; though a sociologist, he emphasized culture, in our meaning of the term, more than social systems. In his more general framework, Sumner might be regarded as almost a pure Spencerian, going even farther than his master in emphasizing the ineluctible determinism of natural selection. However, he considered mores to be highly relativistic; indeed, he is credited with the dictum that the mores can "make anything right." It is the latter side of Sumner that is represented in the selection on the concept of the mores. In spite of his relativism, however, Sumner was well aware of the importance of the normative component in the culture institutionalized in a society. The mores were specifically given moral sanction, and hence were embodiments of institutionalized patterns of evaluation.

The final selection in this subsection, from Ruth Benedict's *Patterns of Culture,* represents the extreme point which cultural relativism reached in American anthropology. Though possibly not so analytically sophisticated as some of its German counterparts (particularly, Dilthey's work), it has been an important landmark in the social sciences. The positive contribution of such work must not be underestimated; though the relativistic position implied cannot be accepted here, it deserves representation in this collection.

I–SYMBOLISM AND COMMUNICATION

1. *From Gesture to Symbol*

BY GEORGE H. MEAD

IN THE CASE of the vocal gesture the form hears its own stimulus just as when this is used by other forms, so it tends to respond also to its own stimulus as it responds to the stimulus of other forms. That is, birds tend to sing to themselves, ba-

Reprinted from George H. Mead, *Mind, Self and Society,* ed. Charles W. Morris (Chicago: University of Chicago Press, 1934), pp. 65, 66, 67–68, 68–70, 70–76, 78, with the permission of the University of Chicago Press. Copyright 1934 by the University of Chicago.

bies to talk to themselves. The sounds they make are stimuli to make other sounds. Where there is a specific sound that calls out a specific response, then if this sound is made by other forms it calls out this response in the form in question. If the sparrow makes use of this particular sound then the response to that sound will be one which will be heard more frequently than another response. In that way there will be selected out of the sparrow's repertoire those elements which are found in the song of the canary, and gradually such selection would build up in the song of the sparrow those elements which are common to both, without assuming a particular tendency of imitation. There is here a selective process by which is picked out what is common. "Imitation" depends upon the individual influencing himself as others influence him, so that he is under the influence not only of the other but also of himself in so far as he uses the same vocal gesture.

The vocal gesture, then, has an importance which no other gesture has. We cannot see ourselves when our face assumes a certain expression. If we hear ourselves speak we are more apt to pay attention. One hears himself when he is irritated using a tone that is of an irritable quality, and so catches himself. But in the facial expression of irritation the stimulus is not one that calls out an expression in the individual which it calls out in the other. One is more apt to catch himself up and control himself in the vocal gesture than in the expression of the countenance.

*   *   *

If there is any truth in the old axiom that the bully is always the coward, it will be found to rest on the fact that one arouses in himself that attitude of fear which his bullying attitude arouses in another, so that when put into a particular situation which calls his bluff, his own attitude is found to be that of the others. If one's own attitude of giving way to the bullying attitude of others is one that arouses the bullying attitude, he has in that degree aroused the attitude of bullying in himself. There is a certain amount of truth in this when we come back to the effect upon one's self of the gesture of which he makes use. In so far as one calls out the attitude in himself that one calls out in others, the response is picked out and strengthened. That is the only basis for what we call imitation. It is not imitation in the sense of simply doing what one sees another person doing. The mechanism is that of an individual calling out in himself the response which he calls out in another, consequently giving greater weight to those responses than to the other responses, and gradually building up those sets of responses into a dominant whole. That may be done, as we say, unconsciously. The sparrow does not know it is imitating the canary. It is just a gradual picking up of the notes which are common to both of them. And that is true wherever there is imitation.

*   *   *

I have contrasted two situations to show what a long road[1] speech or communication has to travel

from the situation where there is nothing but vocal cries over to the situation in which significant symbols are utilized. What is peculiar to the latter is that the individual responds to his own stimulus in the same way as other people respond. Then the stimulus becomes significant; then one is saying something. As far as a parrot is concerned, its "speech" means nothing, but where one significantly says something with his own vocal process he is saying it to himself as well as to everybody else within reach of his voice. It is only the vocal gesture that is fitted for this sort of communication, because it is only the vocal gesture to which one responds or tends to respond as another person tends to respond to it. It is true that the language of the hands is of the same character. One sees one's self using the gestures which those who are deaf make use of. They influence one the same way as they influence others. Of course, the same is true of any form of script. But such symbols have all been developed out of the specific vocal gesture, for that is the basic gesture which does influence the individual as it influences others. Where it does not become significant is in the vocalization of the two birds. Nevertheless, the same type of process is present, the stimulus of the one bird tending to call out the response in another bird which it tends to call out, however slightly, in the bird itself.

*   *   *

Thought

We are more or less unconsciously seeing ourselves as others see us. We are unconsciously addressing ourselves as others address us; in the same way as the sparrow takes up the note of the canary we pick up the dialects about us. Of course, there must be these particular responses in our own mechanism. We are calling out in the other person something we are calling out in ourselves, so that unconsciously we take over these attitudes. We are unconsciously putting ourselves in the place of others and acting as others act. I want simply to isolate the general mechanism here, because it is of very fundamental importance in the development of what we call self-consciousness and the appearance of the self. We are, especially through the use of the vocal gestures, continually arousing in ourselves those responses which we call out in other persons, so that we are taking the attitudes of the other persons into our own conduct. The critical importance of language in the development of human experience lies in this fact that the stimulus is one that can react upon the speaking individual as it reacts upon the other.

---

1. In the preceding pages Mead has been discussing what happens when a sparrow is put in a cage with a canary [eds. of this volume].

A behaviorist, such as Watson, holds that all of our thinking is vocalization. In thinking we are simply starting to use certain words. That is in a sense true. However, Watson does not take into account all that is involved here, namely, that these stimuli are the essential elements in elaborate social processes and carry with them the value of those social processes. The vocal process as such has this great importance, and it is fair to assume that the vocal process, together with the intelligence and thought that go with it, is not simply a playing of particular vocal elements against each other. Such a view neglects the social context of language.[2]

The importance, then, of the vocal stimulus lies in this fact that the individual can hear what he says and in hearing what he says is tending to respond as the other person responds.

* * *

In seeking for an explanation of this, we ordinarily assume a certain group of centers in the nervous system which are connected with each other, and which express themselves in the action. If we try to find in a central nervous system something that answers to our word "chair," what we should find would be presumably simply an organization of a whole group of possible reactions so connected that if one starts in one direction one will carry out one process, if in another direction one will carry out another process. The chair is primarily what one sits down in. It is a physical object at a distance. One may move toward an object at a distance and then enter upon the process of sitting down when one reaches it. There is a stimulus which excites certain paths which cause the individual to go toward that object and to sit down. Those centers are in some degree physical. There is, it is to be noted, an influence of the later act on the earlier act. The later process which is to go on has already been initiated and that later process has its influence on the earlier process (the one that takes place before this process, already

initiated, can be completed). Now, such an organization of a great group of nervous elements as will lead to conduct with reference to the objects about us is what one would find in the central nervous system answering to what we call an object. The complications are very great, but the central nervous system has an almost infinite number of elements in it, and they can be organized not only in spatial connection with each other, but also from a temporal standpoint. In virtue of this last fact, our conduct is made up of a series of steps which follow each other, and the later steps may be already started and influence the earlier ones. The thing we are going to do is playing back on what we are doing now. That organization in the neural elements in reference to what we call a physical object would be what we call a conceptual object stated in terms of the central nervous system.

In rough fashion it is the initiation of such a set of organized sets of responses that answers to what we call the idea or concept of a thing. If one asked what the idea of a dog is, and tried to find that idea in the central nervous system, one would find a whole group of responses which are more or less connected together by definite paths so that when one uses the term "dog" he does tend to call out this group of responses. A dog is a possible playmate, a possible enemy, one's own property or somebody else's. There is a whole series of possible responses. There are certain types of these responses which are in all of us, and there are others which vary with the individuals, but there is always an organization of the responses which can be called out by the term "dog." So if one is speaking of a dog to another person he is arousing in himself this set of responses which he is arousing in the other individual.

It is, of course, the relationship of this symbol, this vocal gesture, to such a set of responses in the individual himself as well as in the other that makes of that vocal gesture what I call a significant symbol. A symbol does tend to call out in the individual a group of reactions such as it calls out in the other, but there is something further that is involved in its being a significant symbol: this response within one's self to such a word as "chair," or "dog" is one which is a stimulus to the individual as well as a response. This is what, of course, is involved in what we term the meaning of a thing, or its significance.[3] We often act with reference to objects in

2. Gestures, if carried back to the matrix from which they spring, are always found to inhere in or involve a larger social act of which they are phases. In dealing with communication we have first to recognize its earliest origins in the unconscious conversation of gestures. Conscious communication—conscious conversation of gestures—arises when gestures become signs, that is, when they come to carry for the individuals making them and the individuals responding to them, definite meanings or significations in terms of the subsequent behavior of the individuals making them; so that, by serving as prior indications, to the individuals responding to them, of the subsequent behavior of the individuals making them, they make possible the mutual adjustment of the various individual components of the social act to one another, and also, by calling forth in the individuals making them the same responses implicitly that they call forth explicitly in the individuals to whom they are made, they render possible the rise of self-consciousness in connection with this mutual adjustment.

3. The inclusion of the matrix or complex of attitudes and responses constituting any given social situation or act, within the experience of any one of the individuals implicated in that situation or act (the inclusion within his experience of his attitudes toward other individuals, of their responses to his attitudes toward them, of their attitudes toward him, and of his responses to these attitudes) is all that an *idea* amounts to; or at any rate is the only basis

what we call an intelligent fashion, although we can act without the meaning of the object being present in our experience. One can start to dress for dinner, as they tell of the absent-minded college professor, and find himself in his pajamas in bed. A certain process of undressing was started and carried out mechanically; he did not recognize the meaning of what he was doing. He intended to go to dinner and found he had gone to bed. The meaning involved in his action was not present. The steps in this case were all intelligent steps which controlled his conduct with reference to later action, but he did not think about what he was doing. The later action was not a stimulus to his response, but just carried itself out when it was once started.

When we speak of the meaning of what we are doing we are making the response itself that we are on the point of carrying out a stimulus to our action. It becomes a stimulus to a later stage of action which is to take place from the point of view of this particular response. In the case of the boxer the blow that he is starting to direct toward his opponent is to call out a certain response which will open up the guard of his opponent so that he can strike. The meaning is a stimulus for the preparation of the real blow he expects to deliver. The response which he calls out in himself (the guarding reaction) is the stimulus to him to strike where an opening is given. This action which he has initiated already in himself thus becomes a stimulus for his later response. He knows what his opponent is going to do, since the guarding movement is one which is already aroused, and becomes a stimulus to strike where the opening is given. The meaning would not have been present in his conduct unless it became a stimulus to strike where the favorable opening appears.

Such is the difference between intelligent conduct on the part of animals and what we call a reflective individual. We say the animal does not think. He does not put himself in a position for which he is responsible; he does not put himself in the place of the other person and say, in effect, "He will act in such a way and I will act in this way." If the individual can act in this way, and the attitude which

he calls out in himself can become a stimulus to him for another act, we have meaningful conduct. Where the response of the other person is called out and becomes a stimulus to control his action, then he has the meaning of the other person's act in his own experience. That is the general mechanism of what we term "thought," for in order that thought may exist there must be symbols, vocal gestures generally, which arouse in the individual himself the response which he is calling out in the other, and such that from the point of view of that response he is able to direct his later conduct. It involves not only communication in the sense in which birds and animals communicate with each other, but also an arousal in the individual himself of the response which he is calling out in the other individual, a taking of the rôle of the other, a tendency to act as the other person acts. One participates in the same process the other person is carrying out and controls his action with reference to that participation. It is that which constitutes the meaning of an object, namely, the common response in one's self as well as in the other person, which becomes, in turn, a stimulus to one's self.

If you conceive of the mind as just a sort of conscious substance in which there are certain impressions and states, and hold that one of those states is a universal, then a word becomes purely arbitrary —it is just a symbol.[4] You can then take words and pronounce them backwards, as children do; there seems to be absolute freedom of arrangement and language seems to be an entirely mechanical thing that lies outside of the process of intelligence. If you recognize that language is, however, just a part of a co-operative process, that part which does lead to an adjustment to the response of the other so that the whole activity can go on, then language has only a limited range of arbitrariness. If you are

for its occurrence or existence "in the mind" of the given individual.

In the case of the unconscious conversation of gestures, or in the case of the process of communication carried on by means of it, none of the individuals participating in it is conscious of the meaning of the conversation—that meaning does not appear in the experience of any one of the separate individuals involved in the conversation or carrying it on; whereas, in the case of the conscious conversation of gestures, or in the case of the process of communication carried on by means of it, each of the individuals participating in it is conscious of the meaning of the conversation, precisely because that meaning does appear in his experience, and because such appearance is what consciousness of that meaning implies.

4. Müller attempts to put the values of thought into language; but this attempt is fallacious, because language has those values only as the most effective mechanism of thought merely because it carries the conscious or significant conversation of gestures to its highest and most perfect development. There must be some sort of an implicit attitude (that is, a response which is initiated without being fully carried out) in the organism making the gesture—an attitude which answers to the overt response to the gesture on the part of another individual, and which corresponds to the attitude called forth or aroused in this other organism by the gesture—if thought is to develop in the organism making the gesture. And it is the central nervous system which provides the mechanism for such implicit attitudes or responses.

The identification of language with reason is in one sense an absurdity, but in another sense it is valid. It is valid, namely, in the sense that the process of language brings the total social act into the experience of the given individual as himself involved in the act, and thus makes the process of reason possible. But though the process of reason is and must be carried on in terms of the process of language—in terms, that is, of words—it is not simply constituted by the latter.

talking to another person you are, perhaps, able to scent the change in his attitude by something that would not strike a third person at all. You may know his mannerism, and that becomes a gesture to you, a part of the response of the individual. There is a certain range possible within the gesture as to what is to serve as the symbol. We may say that a whole set of separate symbols with one meaning are acceptable; but they always are gestures, that is, they are always parts of the act of the individual which reveal what he is going to do to the other person so that when the person utilizes the clue he calls out in himself the attitude of the other. Language is not ever arbitrary in the sense of simply denoting a bare state of consciousness by a word. What particular part of one's act will serve to direct co-operative activity is more or less arbitrary. Different phases of the act may do it. What seems unimportant in itself may be highly important in revealing what the attitude is. In that sense one can speak of the gesture itself as unimportant, but it is of great importance as to what the gesture is going to reveal. This is seen in the difference between the purely intellectual character of the symbol and its emotional character. A poet depends upon the latter; for him language is rich and full of values which we, perhaps, utterly ignore. In trying to express a message in something less than ten words, we merely want to convey a certain meaning, while the poet is dealing with what is really living tissue, the emotional throb in the expression itself. There is, then, a great range in our use of language; but whatever phase of this range is used is a part of a social process, and it is always that part by means of which we affect ourselves as we affect others and mediate the social situation through this understanding of what we are saying. That is fundamental for any language; if it is going to be language one has to understand what he is saying, has to affect himself as he affects others.

Meaning

We are particularly concerned with intelligence on the human level, that is, with the adjustment to one another of the acts of different human individuals within the human social process; an adjustment which takes place through communication: by gestures on the lower planes of human evolution, and by significant symbols (gestures which posess meanings and are hence more than mere substitute stimuli) on the higher planes of human evolution.

The central factor in such adjustment is "meaning." Meaning arises and lies within the field of the relation between the gesture of a given human organism and the subsequent behavior of this organism as indicated to another human organism by that gesture. If that gesture does so indicate to another organism the subsequent (or resultant) behavior of the given organism, then it has meaning. In other words, the relationship between a given stimulus—as a gesture—and the later phases of the social act of which it is an early (if not the initial) phase constitutes the field within which meaning originates and exists. Meaning is thus a development of something objectively there as a relation between certain phases of the social act; it is not a psychical addition to that act and it is not an "idea" as traditionally conceived. A gesture by one organism, the resultant of the social act in which the gesture is an early phase, and the response of another organism to the gesture, are the relata in a triple or threefold relationship of gesture to first organism, of gesture to second organism, and of gesture to subsequent phases of the given social act; and this threefold relationship constitutes the matrix within which meaning arises, or which develops into the field of meaning. The gesture stands for a certain resultant of the social act, a resultant to which there is a definite response on the part of the individuals involved therein; so that meaning is given or stated in terms of response. Meaning is implicit—if not always explicit—in the relationship among the various phases of the social act to which it refers, and out of which it develops. And its development takes place in terms of symbolization at the human evolutionary level.

*   *   *

Symbolization constitutes objects not constituted before, objects which would not exist except for the context of social relationships wherein symbolization occurs. Language does not simply symbolize a situation or object which is already there in advance; it makes possible the existence or the appearance of that situation or object, for it is a part of the mechanism whereby that situation or object is created. The social process relates the responses of one individual to the gestures of another, as the meanings of the latter, and is thus responsible for the rise and existence of new objects in the social situation, objects dependent upon or constituted by these meanings. Meaning is thus not to be conceived, fundamentally, as a state of consciousness, or as a set of organized relations existing or subsisting mentally outside the field of experience into which they enter; on the contrary, it should be conceived objectively, as having its existence entirely within this field itself. The response of one organism to the gesture of another in any given social act is the meaning of that gesture, and also is in a sense responsible for the appearance or coming into being of the new object—or new content of an old object

—to which that gesture refers through the outcome of the given social act in which it is an early phase. For, to repeat, objects are in a genuine sense constituted within the social process of experience, by the communication and mutual adjustment of behavior among the individual organisms which are involved in that process and which carry it on. Just as in fencing the parry is an interpretation of the thrust, so, in the social act, the adjustive response of one organism to the gesture of another is the interpretation of that gesture by that organism—it is the meaning of that gesture.

2. *Ideational Content of the Sign*

BY ERNST CASSIRER

SO FAR we have aimed at a kind of critical "deduction," an explanation and justification of the concept of representation, in the belief that the representation of one content in and through another is an essential premise for the structure and formal unity of consciousness. The following study, however, will not deal with this general logical significance of the representative function. We shall seek to pursue the problem of signs, not backward to its ultimate "foundations," but forward to its concrete unfolding and configuration in the diverse cultural spheres.

We have acquired a new foundation for such an investigation. We must go back to "natural" symbolism, to that representation of consciousness as a whole which is necessarily contained or at least projected in every single moment and fragment of consciousness, if we wish to understand the artificial symbols, the "arbitrary" signs which consciousness creates in language, art, and myth. The force and effect of these mediating signs would remain a mystery if they were not ultimately rooted in an original spiritual process which belongs to the very essence of consciousness. We can understand how a sensuous particular, such as the spoken sound, can become the vehicle of a purely intellectual meaning, only if we assume that the basic function of signification is present and active before the individual sign is produced, so that this producing does not create signification, but merely stabilizes it, applies it to the particular case. Since every particular content of consciousness is situated in a network of diverse relations, by virtue of which its simple

existence and self-representation contain *reference* to other and still other contents, there can and must be certain formations of consciousness in which the pure form of reference is, as it were, sensuously embodied. From this follows the characteristic twofold nature of these formations: their bond with sensibility, which however contains within it a freedom from sensibility. In every linguistic "sign," in every mythical or artistic "image," a spiritual content, which intrinsically points beyond the whole sensory sphere, is translated into the form of the sensuous, into something visible, audible or tangible. An independent mode of configuration appears, a specific activity of consciousness, which is differentiated from any datum of immediate sensation or perception, but makes use of these data as vehicles, as means of expression. Thus the "natural" symbolism which we have found embedded as a fundamental characteristic of consciousness is on the one hand utilized and retained, while on the other hand it is surpassed and refined. For in this "natural" symbolism, a certain partial content of consciousness, though distinct from the whole, retained the power to represent this whole and in so doing to reconstitute it in a sense. A present content possessed the power of evoking another content, which was not immediately given but merely conveyed by it. It is not the case, however, that the symbolic signs which we encounter in language, myth, and art first "are" and then, beyond this "being," achieve a certain meaning; their being arises from their signification. Their content subsists purely and wholly in the function of signification. Here consciousness, in order to apprehend the whole in the particular, no longer requires the stimulus of the particular itself, which must be given as such; here consciousness *creates* definite concrete

Reprinted from Ernst Cassirer, *The Philosophy of Symbolic Forms*, trans. Ralph Mannheim (New Haven: Yale University Press; and London: Geoffrey Camberlege, Oxford University Press, 1953), I, 105–14, with the permission of Yale University Press.

sensory contents as an expression for definite complexes of meaning. And because these contents which consciousness creates are entirely in its power, it can, through them, freely "evoke" all those meanings at any time. When, for example, we link a given intuition or idea with an arbitrary linguistic sound, we seem, at first sight, to have added nothing whatever to its content. And yet, on closer scrutiny, the content itself takes on a different "character" for consciousness through the creation of the linguistic sign: it becomes more definite. Its sharp and clear intellectual "reproduction" proves to be inseparable from the act of linguistic "production." For the function of language is not merely to *repeat* definitions and distinctions which are already present in the mind, but to formulate them and make them intelligible as such. Thus in every sphere, it is through the freedom of spiritual action that the chaos of sensory impressions begins to clear and take on fixed form for us. The fluid impression assumes form and duration for us only when we *mould* it by symbolic action in one direction or another. In science and language, in art and myth, this formative process proceeds in different ways and according to different principles, but all these spheres have this in common: that the product of their activity in no way resembles the mere *material* with which they began. It is in the basic symbolic function and its various directions that the spiritual consciousness and the sensory consciousness are first truly differentiated. It is here that we pass beyond passive receptivity to an indeterminate outward material, and begin to place upon it our independent imprint which articulates it for us into diverse spheres and forms of reality. Myth and art, language and science, are in this sense configurations *towards* being: they are not simple copies of an existing reality but represent the main directions of the spiritual movement, of the ideal process by which reality is constituted for us as one and many —as a diversity of forms which are ultimately held together by a unity of meaning.

Only when we are oriented towards this goal do the specifications of the various systems of signs, and the use which the intelligence makes of them, become intelligible. If the sign were nothing but a repetition of a determinate and finished, particular intuitive or ideational content, we should be faced with two questions. What would be accomplished by a mere copy of something already present? And how could such an exact copy be accomplished? For it is obvious that a copy can never approach the original and can never replace it for the eye of the spirit. If we took an exact reproduction as our norm, we should be driven to an attitude of fundamental skepticism toward the value of the sign as such. If,

for example, we regarded it as the true and essential function of language to express once again, but merely in a different medium, the very same reality that lies ready-made before us in particular sensations and intuitions—we should be struck at once by the vast inadequacy of all languages. Measured by the limitless richness and diversity of intuitive reality, all linguistic symbols would inevitably seem empty; measured by its individual concretion, they would inevitably seem abstract and vague. If language attempts to compete with sensation or intuition in *this* respect, it cannot but fall far behind. The $\pi\rho\hat{\omega}\tau o\nu$ $\psi\epsilon\nu\delta\acute{o}s$ of the skeptical critique of language is precisely that it takes this standard as the only valid and possible one. In reality the analysis of language—particularly if it starts not from the mere particular of the word, but from the unity of the *sentence*—shows that all linguistic expression, far from being a mere copy of the given world of sensation or intuition, possesses a definite independent character of "signification."

And the same relation applies to signs of the most diverse type and origin. In a sense it can be said of them all that their value consists not so much in what they stabilize of the concrete, sensuous content and its immediate factuality, as in the part of this immediate factuality which they suppress and pass over. Similarly, artistic delineation becomes what it is and is distinguished from a mere mechanistic reproduction, only through what it omits from the "given" impression. It does not reflect this impression in its sensuous totality, but rather selects certain "pregnant" factors, i.e., factors through which the given impression is amplified beyond itself and through which the artistic-constructive fantasy, the synthetic spatial imagination, is guided in a certain direction. What constitutes the true force of the sign, here as in other fields, is precisely this: that as the immediate, determinate contents recede, the general factors of form and relation become all the sharper and clearer. The particular as such is seemingly limited; but precisely thereby that operation which we have called "integration" is effected the more clearly and forcefully. We have seen that the particular of consciousness "exists" only in so far as it potentially contains the whole and is, as it were, in constant transition towards the whole. But the use of the sign liberates this potentiality and enables it to become true actuality. Now, *one* blow strikes a thousand connected chords which all vibrate more or less forcefully and clearly in the sign. In positing the sign, consciousness detaches itself more and more from the direct *substratum* of sensation and sensory intuition: but precisely therein it reveals its inherent, original power of synthesis and unification.

Perhaps this tendency is most clearly manifested in the functioning of the *scientific* systems of signs. The abstract chemical "formula," for example, which is used to designate a certain substance, contains nothing of what direct observation and sensory perception teach us about this substance; but, instead, it places the particular body in an extraordinarily rich and finely articulated complex of relations, of which perception as such knows nothing. It no longer designates the body according to its sensuous content, according to its immediate sensory data, but represents it as a sum of potential "reactions," of possible chains of causality which are defined by general rules. In the chemical formula the totality of these necessary relations fuses with the expression of the particular, and gives this expression of the particular an entirely new and characteristic imprint. Here as elsewhere, the sign serves as an intermediary between the mere "substance" of consciousness and its spiritual "form." Precisely because it is without any sensuous mass of its own, because, in a manner of speaking, it hovers in the pure ether of meaning, it has the power to represent not the mere particulars of consciousness but its complex general movements. It does not reflect a fixed content of consciousness but defines the direction of such a general movement. Similarly, the spoken word, considered from the standpoint of physical substance, is a mere breath of wind; but in this breath there lies an extraordinary force for the dynamic of ideas and thought. This dynamic is both intensified and regulated by the sign. It is one of the essential advantages of the sign—as Leibniz pointed out in his *Characteristica generalis,* that it serves not only to represent, but above all to *discover* certain logical relations—that it not only offers a symbolic abbreviation for what is already known, but opens up new roads into the unknown. Herein we see confirmed from a new angle the synthetic power of consciousness as such, by virtue of which every concentration of its contents impels it to extend its limits. The concentration provided by the sign not only permits us to look backward, but at the same time opens up new perspectives. It sets a relative limit, but this limit itself embodies a challenge to advance and opens up the road to this advance by disclosing its general rule. This is eminently borne out by the history of science, which shows how far we have progressed toward solving a given problem or complex of problems, once we have found a fixed and clear "formula" for it. For example: Most of the questions solved in Newton's concept of fluxion and in the algorism of Leibniz' differential calculus were known before Leibniz and Newton and approached from the most diverse directions—from

the angles of algebraic analysis, geometry, and mechanics. But all these problems were truly mastered only when a unified and comprehensive symbolic *expression* was found for them: for now they no longer formed a loose and fortuitous sequence of separate questions; the common principle of their origin was designated in a definite, universally applicable *method,* a basic operation whose rules were established.

In the symbolic function of consciousness, an antithesis which is given and grounded in the simple concept of consciousness is represented and mediated. All consciousness appears to us in the form of a temporal process—but in the course of this process certain types of "form" tend to detach themselves. The factor of constant change and the factor of duration tend to merge. This universal tendency is realized in different ways in the products of language, myth and art, and in the intellectual symbols of science. All these forms seem to be an immediate part of the living, constantly renewed process of consciousness; yet, at the same time, they reveal a spiritual striving for certain fixed points or resting places in this process. In them consciousness retains a character of constant flux; yet it does not flow indeterminately, but articulates itself around fixed centers of form and meaning. In its pure specificity, each such form is an αὐτὸ καθ᾽ αὑτό in the Platonic sense, detached from the mere stream of ideas—but at the same time in order to be manifested, to exist "for us," it must in some way be represented in this stream. In the creation and application of the various groups and systems of symbolic signs, both conditions are fulfilled, since here indeed a particular sensory content, without ceasing to be such, acquires the power to represent a universal for consciousness. Here neither the sensationalist axiom, "Nihil est in intellectu, quod non ante fuerit in sensu," nor its intellectualistic reversal applies. We no longer ask whether the "sensory" precedes or follows the "spiritual," for we are dealing with the revelation and manifestation of basic spiritual functions in the sensory material itself.

What would seem to constitute the bias of "empiricism" as well as abstract "idealism" is precisely that neither of them fully and clearly develops this fundamental relation. One posits a concept of the given particular but fails to recognize that any such concept must always, explicitly or implicitly, encompass the *defining* attributes of some universal; the other asserts the necessity and validity of these attributes but fails to designate the medium through which they can be represented in the given psychological world of consciousness. If, however, we start not with abstract postulates but from the concrete basic form of spiritual life, this dualistic antithesis is resolved. The illusion of an original division between the intelligible and the sensuous, between "idea" and "phenomenon," vanishes. True, we still remain in a world of "images"—but these are not images which reproduce a self-subsistent world of "things"; they are image-worlds whose principle and origin are to be sought in an autonomous creation of the spirit. Through them alone we see what we call "reality," and in them alone we possess it: for the highest objective truth that is accesible to the spirit is ultimately the form of its own activity. In the totality of its own achievements, in the knowledge of the specific rule by which each of them is determined and in the consciousness of the context which reunites all these special rules into *one* problem and one solution: in all this, the human spirit now perceives itself and reality. True, the question of what, apart from these spiritual functions, constitutes absolute reality, the question of what the "thing in itself" may be in *this* sense, remains unanswered, except that more and more we learn to recognize it as a fallacy in formulation, an intellectual phantasm. The true concept of reality cannot be squeezed into the form of mere abstract being; it opens out into the diversity and richness of the forms of spiritual *life*—but of a spiritual life which bears the stamp of inner necessity and hence of objectivity. In this sense each new "symbolic form"—not only the conceptual world of scientific cognition but also the intuitive world of art, myth, and language—constitutes, as Goethe said, a revelation sent outward from within, a "synthesis of world and spirit," which truly assures us that the two are originally one.

And here new light is cast upon a last fundamental antithesis, with which modern philosophy has struggled since its beginnings and which it has formulated with increasing sharpness. Its "subjective" trend has led philosophy more and more to focus the totality of its problems in the concept of *life* rather than the concept of being. But though this seemed to appease the antithesis of subjectivity and objectivity in the form manifested by dogmatic ontology, and to prepare the way for its ultimate reconciliation—now, in the sphere of life itself, a still more radical antithesis appeared. The truth of life seems to be given only in its pure *immediacy,* to be enclosed in it—but any attempt to understand and apprehend life seems to endanger, if not to negate, this immediacy. True, if we start from the dogmatic concept of being, the dualism of being and thought becomes more and more pronounced as we advance in our investigations—but here there remains some hope that the picture of being developed by cognition will retain at least a remnant of the truth of being. Not all being, to be sure, but

at least a *part* of it would seem to enter into this picture—the substance of being would seem to penetrate the substance of cognition and in it create a more or less faithful reflection of itself. But the pure immediacy of life admits of no such partition. It, apparently, must be seen wholly or not at all; it does not enter into our mediate representations of it, but remains outside them, fundamentally different from them and opposed to them. The original content of life cannot be apprehended in any form of *representation,* but only in pure *intuition.* It would seem, therefore, that any understanding of spiritual life must choose between the two extremes. We are called upon to decide whether to seek the substance of the human spirit in its pure originality, which *precedes* all mediate configurations—or whether to surrender ourselves to the richness and diversity of these mediate forms. Only in the first approach do we seem to touch upon the true and authentic center of life, which however appears as a simple, self-enclosed center; in the second, we survey the entire drama of spiritual developments, but as we immerse ourselves in it, it dissolves more and more manifestly into a mere drama, a reflected image, without independent truth and essence. The cleavage between these two antitheses—it would seem—cannot be bridged by any effort of mediating thought which itself remains entirely on one side of the antithesis: the farther we advance in the direction of the symbolic, the merely figurative, the farther we go from the primal source of pure intuition.

Philosophical mysticism has not been alone in its constant confrontation of this problem and this dilemma; the pure logic of idealism has repeatedly seen it and formulated it. Plato's remarks in his *Seventh Epistle* on the relation of the "idea" to the "sign" and on the necessary inadequacy of this relation, strike a motif which has recurred in all manner of variations. In Leibniz' methodology of knowledge, "intuitive knowledge" is sharply distinguished from mere "symbolic" knowledge. Even for the author of the *characteristica universalis,* all knowledge through mere symbols becomes "blind knowledge" (*cogitatio caeca*) when measured by intuition, as the pure vision, the true "sight" of the idea. True, *human* knowledge can nowhere dispense with symbols and signs; but it is precisely this that characterizes it as human, i.e., limited and finite in contradistinction to the ideal of the perfect, archetypal and divine intellect. Even Kant, who assigned its exact logical position to this idea by defining it as a mere borderline concept of cognition, and who believed that in so doing he had critically mastered it—even Kant, in a passage which constitutes the purely methodical climax of the *Critique of Judgment,* once again sharply develops the antithesis between the *intellectus archetypus* and the *intellectus ectypus,* between the intuitive, archetypal intellect and the discursive intellect "which is dependent on images." From the standpoint of this antithesis it would seem to follow that the richer the *symbolic content* of cognition or of any other cultural form becomes, the more its *essential content* must diminish. All the many images do not designate, but cloak and conceal the imageless One, which stands behind them and towards which they strive in vain. Only the negation of all finite figuration, only a return to the "pure nothingness" of the mystics can lead us back to the true primal source of being. Seen in a different light, this antithesis takes the form of a constant tension between "culture" and "life." For it is the necessary destiny of culture that everything which it creates in its constant process of configuration and education* removes us more and more from the originality of life. The more richly and energetically the human spirit engages in its formative activity, the farther this very activity seems to remove it from the primal source of its own being. More and more, it appears to be imprisoned in its own creations—in the words of language, in the images of myth or art, in the intellectual symbols of cognition, which cover it like a delicate and transparent, but unbreachable veil. But the true, the profoundest task of a *philosophy* of culture, a philosophy of language, cognition, myth, etc., seems precisely to consist in raising this veil—in penetrating from the mediate sphere of mere meaning and characterization to the original sphere of intuitive vision. But on the other hand the specific *organ* of philosophy—and it has no other at

* The German *Bildung* means both formation and education. *Trans.*

its disposal—rebels against this task. To philosophy, which finds its fulfillment only in the sharpness of the concept and in the clarity of "discursive" thought, the paradise of mysticism, the paradise of pure immediacy, is closed. Hence it has no other solution than to reverse the *direction* of inquiry. Instead of taking the road back, it must attempt to continue forward. If all culture is manifested in the creation of specific image-worlds, of specific symbolic forms, the aim of philosophy is not to go behind all these creations, but rather to understand and elucidate their basic formative principle. It is solely through awareness of this principle that the content of life acquires its true form. Then life is removed from the sphere of mere given natural existence: it ceases to be a part of this natural existence or a mere biological process, but is transformed and fulfilled as a form of the "spirit." In truth, the negation of the symbolic forms would not help us to apprehend the essence of life; it would rather destroy the spiritual form with which for us this essence proves to be bound up. If we take the opposite direction, we do not pursue the idea of a passive intuition of spiritual reality, but situate ourselves in the midst of its activity. If we approach spiritual life, not as the static contemplation of being, but as functions and energies of formation, we shall find certain common and typical principles of formation, diverse and dissimilar as the forms may be. If the philosophy of culture succeeds in apprehending and elucidating such basic principles, it will have fulfilled, in a new sense, its task of demonstrating the unity of the spirit as opposed to the multiplicity of its manifestations—for the clearest evidence of this unity is precisely that the diversity of the *products* of the human spirit does not impair the unity of its *productive process,* but rather sustains and confirms it.

3. On Sacred Objects as Symbols

BY EMILE DURKHEIM

BUT COLLECTIVE REPRESENTA-tions very frequently attribute to the things to which they are attached qualities which do not

Reprinted from Emile Durkheim, *Elementary Forms of the Religious Life,* trans. Joseph Ward Swain (Glencoe, Ill.: The Free Press, 1954), pp. 228–29, with the permission of The Free Press.

exist under any form or to any degree. Out of the commonest object, they can make a most powerful sacred being.

Yet the powers which are thus conferred, though purely ideal, act as though they were real; they determine the conduct of men with the same degree of necessity as physical forces. The Arunta who has been rubbed with his churinga feels himself stronger; he is stronger. If he has eaten the flesh of an animal which, though perfectly healthy, is forbidden to him, he will feel himself sick, and may die of it. Surely the soldier who falls while defending his flag does not believe that he sacrifices himself for a bit of cloth. This is all because social thought, owing to the imperative authority that is in it, has an efficacy that individual thought could never have; by the power which it has over our minds, it can make us see things in whatever light it pleases; it adds to reality or deducts from it according to the circumstances. Thus there is one division of nature where the formula of idealism is applicable almost to the letter: this is the social kingdom. Here more than anywhere else, the idea is the reality. Even in this case, of course, idealism is not true without modification. We can never escape the duality of our nature and free ourselves completely from physical necessities: in order to express our own ideas to ourselves, it is necessary, as has been shown above, that we fix them upon material things which symbolize them. But here the part of matter is reduced to a minimum. The object serving as support for the idea is not much in comparison with the ideal superstructure, beneath which it disappears, and also, it counts for nothing in the superstructure. This is what that pseudo-delirium consists in, which we find at the bottom of so many collective representations: it is only a form of this essential idealism.[1] So it is not properly called a delirium, for the ideas thus objectified are well founded, not in the nature of the material things upon which they settle themselves, but in the nature of society.

We are now able to understand how the totemic principle, and in general, every religious force, comes to be outside of the object in which it resides. It is because the idea of it is in no way made up of the impressions directly produced by this thing

upon our senses or minds. Religious force is only the sentiment inspired by the group in its members, but projected outside of the consciousnesses that experience them, and objectified. To be objectified, they are fixed upon some object which thus becomes sacred; but any object might fulfil this function. In principle, there are none whose nature predestines them to it to the exclusion of all others; but also there are none that are necessarily impossible.[2] Everything depends upon the circumstances which lead the sentiment creating religious ideas to establish itself here or there, upon this point or upon that one. Therefore, the sacred character assumed by an object is not implied in the intrinsic properties of this latter: *it is added to them.* The world of religious things is not one particular aspect of empirical nature; *it is superimposed upon it.*

This conception of the religious, finally, allows us to explain an important principle found at the bottom of a multitude of myths and rites, and which may be stated thus: when a sacred thing is subdivided, each of its parts remains equal to the thing itself. In other words, as far as religious thought is concerned, the part is equal to the whole; it has the same powers, the same efficacy. The debris of a relic has the same virtue as a relic in good condition. The smallest drop of blood contains the same active principle as the whole thing. The soul, as we shall see, may be broken up into nearly as many pieces as there are organs or tissues in the organism; each of these partial souls is worth a whole soul. This conception would be inexplicable if the sacredness of something were due to the constituent properties of the thing itself; for in that case, it should vary with this thing, increasing and decreasing with it. But if the virtues it is believed to possess are not intrinsic in it, and if they come from certain sentiments which it brings to mind and symbolizes, though these originate outside of it, then, since it has no need of determined dimensions to play this rôle of reminder, it will have the same value whether it is entire or not. Since the part makes us think of the whole, it evokes the same sentiments as the whole. A mere fragment of the flag represents the fatherland just as well as the flag itself: so it is sacred in the same way and to the same degree.[3]

---

1. Thus we see how erroneous those theories are which, like the geographical materialism of Ratzel (see especially his *Politische Geographie*), seek to derive all social life from its material foundation (either economic or territorial). They commit an error precisely similar to the one committed by Maudsley in individual psychology. Just as this latter reduced all the psychical life of the individual to a mere epiphenomenon of his physiological basis, they seek to reduce the whole psychical life of the group to its physical basis. But they forget that ideas are realities and forces, and that collective representations are forces even more powerful and active than individual reprensentations. On this point, see our *Représentations individuelles et représentations collectives,* in the *Revue de Métaphysique et de Morale,* May, 1898.

2. Even the *excreta* have a religious character. See Preuss, *Der Ursprung der Religion und Kunst,* especially ch. ii, entitled *Der Zauber der Defäkation* (*Globus,* LXXXVI, pp. 325 ff.).

3. This principle has passed from religion into magic: it is the *totem ex parte* of the alchemists.

4. Dream-Work

BY SIGMUND FREUD

EVERY ATTEMPT that has hitherto been made to solve the problem of dreams has dealt directly with their *manifest* content as it is presented in our memory. All such attempts have endeavoured to arrive at an interpretation of dreams from their manifest content or (if no interpretation was attempted) to form a judgement as to their nature on the basis of that same manifest content. We are alone in taking something else into account. We have introduced a new class of psychical material between the manifest content of dreams and the conclusions of our enquiry: namely, their *latent* content, or (as we say) the "dream-thoughts," arrived at by means of our procedure. It is from these dream-thoughts and not from a dream's manifest content that we disentangle its meaning. We are thus presented with a new task which had no previous existence: the task, that is, of investigating the relations between the manifest content of dreams and the latent dream-thoughts, and of tracing out the processes by which the latter have been changed into the former.

The dream-thoughts and the dream-content are presented to us like two versions of the same subject-matter in two different languages. Or, more properly, the dream-content seems like a transcript of the dream-thoughts into another mode of expression, whose characters and syntactic laws it is our business to discover by comparing the original and the translation. The dream-thoughts are immediately comprehensible, as soon as we have learnt them. The dream-content, on the other hand, is expressed as it were in a pictographic script, the characters of which have to be transposed individually into the language of the dream-thoughts. If we attempted to read these characters according to their pictorial value instead of according to their symbolic relation, we should clearly be led into error. Suppose I have a picture-puzzle, a rebus, in front of me. It depicts a house with a boat on its roof, a single letter of the alphabet, the figure of a running

man whose head has been conjured away, and so on. Now I might be misled into raising objections and declaring that the picture as a whole and its component parts are nonsensical. A boat has no business to be on the roof of a house, and a headless man cannot run. Moreover, the man is bigger than the house; and if the whole picture is intended to represent a landscape, letters of the alphabet are out of place in it since such objects do not occur in nature. But obviously we can only form a proper judgement of the rebus if we put aside criticisms such as these of the whole composition and its parts and if, instead, we try to replace each separate element by a syllable or word that can be represented by that element in some way or other. The words which are put together in this way are no longer nonsensical but may form a poetical phrase of the greatest beauty and significance. A dream is a picture-puzzle of this sort and our predecessors in the field of dream-interpretation have made the mistake of treating the rebus as a pictorial composition: and as such it has seemed to them nonsensical and worthless.

The Work of Condensation

The first thing that becomes clear to anyone who compares the dream-content with the dream-thoughts is that a work of *condensation* on a large scale has been carried out. Dreams are brief, meagre and laconic in comparison with the range and wealth of the dream-thoughts. If a dream is written out it may perhaps fill half a page. The analysis setting out the dream-thoughts underlying it may occupy six, eight or a dozen times as much space. This relation varies with different dreams; but so far as my experience goes its direction never varies. As a rule one underestimates the amount of compression that has taken place, since one is inclined to regard the dream-thoughts that have been brought to light as the complete material, whereas if the work of interpretation is carried further it may reveal still more thoughts concealed behind the dream. It is in fact never possible to be sure that a dream has been completely interpreted. Even if the solution seems satisfactory and without gaps,

Reprinted from Sigmund Freud, *The Interpretation of Dreams* ("The Complete Psychological Works of Sigmund Freud," Vol. IV [London: Hogarth Press, 1953]), chap. vi, pp. 277–78, 279–80, 295–96, 305–8, 218–26, and from *The Interpretation of Dreams*, translated by James Strachey (Basic Books, 1955), with the permission of the Hogarth Press and Basic Books, Inc.

the possibility always remains that the dream may have yet another meaning. Strictly speaking, then, it is impossible to determine the amount of condensation.

There is an answer, which at first sight seems most plausible, to the argument that the great lack of proportion between the dream-content and the dream-thoughts implies that the psychical material has undergone an extensive process of condensation in the course of the formation of the dream. We very often have an impression that we have dreamt a great deal all through the night and have since forgotten most of what we dreamt. On this view, the dream which we remember when we wake up would only be a fragmentary remnant of the total dream-work; and this, if we could recollect it in its entirety, might well be as extensive as the dream-thoughts. There is undoubtedly some truth in this: there can be no question that dreams can be reproduced most accurately if we try to recall them as soon as we wake up and that our memory of them becomes more and more incomplete towards evening. But on the other hand it can be shown that the impression that we have dreamt a great deal more than we can reproduce is very often based on an illusion, the origin of which I shall discuss later. Moreover the hypothesis that condensation occurs during the dream-work is not affected by the possibility of dreams being forgotten, since this hypothesis is proved to be correct by the quantities of ideas which are related to each individual piece of the dream which has been retained. Even supposing that a large piece of the dream has escaped recollection, this may merely have prevented our having access to another group of dream-thoughts. There is no justification for supposing that the lost pieces of the dream would have related to the same thoughts which we have already reached from the pieces of the dream that have survived.[1]

In view of the very great number of associations produced in analysis to each individual element of the content of a dream, some readers may be led to doubt whether, as a matter of principle, we are justified in regarding as part of the dream-thoughts all the associations that occur to us during the subsequent analysis—whether we are justified, that is, in supposing that all these thoughts were already active during the state of sleep and played a part in the formation of the dream. Is it not more probable that new trains of thought have arisen in the course of the analysis which had no share in forming the dream? I can only give limited assent to this argu-

ment. It is no doubt true that some trains of thought arise for the first time during the analysis. But one can convince oneself in all such cases that these new connections are only set up between thoughts which were already linked in some other way in the dream-thoughts. The new connections are, as it were, loop-lines or short-circuits, made possible by the existence of other and deeper-lying connecting paths.

* * *

The work of condensation in dreams is seen at its clearest when it handles words and names. It is true in general that words are treated in dreams as though they were concrete things, and for that reason they are apt to be combined in just the same way as presentations of concrete things.[2] Dreams of this sort offer the most amusing and curious neologisms.[3]

On one occasion a medical colleague had sent me a paper he had written, in which the importance of a recent physiological discovery was, in my opinion, overestimated, and in which, above all, the subject was treated in too emotional a manner. The next night I dreamt a sentence which clearly referred to this paper: "*It's written in a positively norekdal style.*" The analysis of the word caused me some difficulty at first. There could be no doubt that it was a parody of the [German] superlatives "*kolossal*" and "*pyramidal*"; but its origin was not so easy to guess. At last I saw that the monstrosity was composed of the two names "Nora" and "Ekdal"—characters in two well-known plays of Ibsen's. [*A Doll's House* and *The Wild Duck.*] Some time before, I had read a newspaper article on Ibsen by the same author whose latest work I was criticizing in the dream.

* * *

The Work of Displacement

In making our collection of instances of condensation in dreams, the existence of another relation, probably of no less importance, had already become evident. It could be seen that the elements which stand out as the principal components of the manifest content of the dream are far from playing the same part in the dream-thoughts. And, as a corollary, the converse of this assertion can be af-

---

1. [*Footnote added* 1914:] The occurrence of condensation in dreams has been hinted at by many writers. Du Prel (1885, 85) has a passage in which he says it is absolutely certain that there has been a process of condensation of the groups of ideas in dreams.

2. [The relation between presentations of words and of things was discussed by Freud very much later, in the last pages of his paper on the Unconscious.]

3. [A dream involving a number of verbal conceits is reported by Freud in Chapter V (10) of his *Psychopathology of Everyday Life.*]

firmed: what is clearly the essence of the dream-thoughts, need not be represented in the dream at all. The dream is, as it were, differently centered from the dream-thoughts—its content has different elements as its central point. Thus in the dream of the botanical monograph, for instance, the central point of the dream-content was obviously the element "botanical"; whereas the dream-thoughts were concerned with the complications and conflicts arising between colleagues from their professional obligations, and further with the charge that I was in the habit of sacrificing too much for the sake of my hobbies. The element "botanical" had no place whatever in this core of the dream-thoughts, unless it was loosely connected with it by an antithesis—the fact that botany never had a place among my favourite studies. In my patient's *Sappho* dream the central position was occupied by climbing up and down and being up above and down below; the dream-thoughts, however, dealt with the dangers of sexual relations with people of an inferior social class. So that only a single element of the dream-thoughts seems to have found its way into the dream-content, though that element was expanded to a disproportionate extent. Similarly, in the dream of the may-beetles, the topic of which was the relations of sexuality to cruelty, it is true that the factor of cruelty emerged in the dream-content; but it did so in another connection and without any mention of sexuality, that is to say, divorced from its context and consequently transformed into something extraneous. Once again, in my dream about my uncle, the fair beard which formed its centre-point seems to have had no connection in its meaning with my ambitious wishes which, as we saw, were the core of the dream-thoughts. Dreams such as these give a justifiable impression of "displacement." In complete contrast to these examples, we can see that in the dream of Irma's injection the different elements were able to retain, during the process of constructing the dream, the approximate place which they occupied in the dream-thoughts. This further relation between the dream-thoughts and the dream-content, wholly variable as it is in its sense or direction, is calculated at first to create astonishment. If we are considering a psychical process in normal life and find that one out of its several component ideas has been picked out and has acquired a special degree of vividness in consciousness, we usually regard this effect as evidence that a specially high amount of psychical value—some particular degree of interest —attaches to this predominant idea. But we now discover that, in the case of the different elements of the dream-thoughts, a value of this kind does not persist or is disregarded in the process of dream-formation. There is never any doubt as to which of the elements of the dream-thoughts have the highest psychical value; we learn that by direct judgement. In the course of the formation of a dream these essential elements, charged, as they are with intense interest, may be treated as though they were of small value, and their place may be taken in the dream by other elements, of whose small value in the dream-thoughts there can be no question. At first sight it looks as though no attention whatever is paid to the psychical intensity[4] of the various ideas in making the choice among them for the dream, and as though the only thing considered is the greater or less degree of multiplicity of their determination. What appears in dreams, we might suppose, is not what is *important* in the dream-thoughts but what occurs in them several times over. But this hypothesis does not greatly assist our understanding of dream-formation, since from the nature of things it seems clear that the two factors of multiple determination and inherent physical value must necessarily operate in the same sense. The ideas which are most important among the dream-thoughts will almost certainly be those which occur most often in them, since the different dream-thoughts will, as it were, radiate out from them. Nevertheless a dream can reject elements which are thus both highly stressed in themselves and reinforced from many directions, and can select for its content other elements which possess only the second of these attributes.

In order to solve this difficulty we shall make use of another impression derived from our enquiry into the overdetermination of the dream-content. Perhaps some of those who have read that enquiry may already have formed an independent conclusion that the overdetermination of the elements of dreams is no very important discovery, since it is a self-evident one. For in analysis we start out from the dream-elements and note down all the associations which lead off from them; so that there is nothing surprising in the fact that in the thought-material arrived at in this way we come across these same elements with peculiar frequency. I cannot accept this objection; but I will myself put into words something that sounds not unlike it. Among the thoughts that analysis brings to light are many which are relatively remote from the kernel of the dream and which look like artificial interpolations made for some particular purpose. That purpose is easy to divine. It is precisely *they* that constitute a connection, often a forced and far-fetched one, be-

---

4. *Psychical* intensity or value or the degree of interest of an idea is of course to be distinguished from *sensory* intensity or the intensity of the image presented.

tween the dream-content and the dream-thoughts; and if these elements were weeded out of the analysis the result would often be that the component parts of the dream-content would be left not only without overdetermination but without any satisfactory determination at all. We shall be led to conclude that the multiple determination which decides what shall be included in a dream is not always a primary factor in dream-construction but is often the secondary product of a psychical force which is still unknown to us. Nevertheless multiple determination must be of importance in choosing what particular elements shall enter a dream, since we can see that a considerable expenditure of effort is used to bring it about in cases where it does not arise from the dream-material unassisted.

It thus seems plausible to suppose that in the dream-work a psychical force is operating which on the one hand strips the elements which have a high psychical value of their intensity, and on the other hand, *by means of overdetermination,* creates from elements of low psychical value new values, which afterwards find their way into the dream-content. If that is so, *a transference and displacement of psychical intensities* occurs in the process of dream-formation, and it is as a result of these that the difference between the text of the dream-content and that of the dream-thoughts comes about. The process which we are here presuming is nothing less than the essential portion of the dream-work; and it deserves to be described as "dream-displacement." Dream-displacement and dream-condensation are

the two governing factors to whose activity we may in essence ascribe the form assumed by dreams.

Nor do I think we shall have any difficulty in recognizing the psychical force which manifests itself in the facts of dream-displacement. The consequence of the displacement is that the dream-content no longer resembles the core of the dream-thoughts and that the dream gives no more than a distortion of the dream-wish which exists in the unconscious. But we are already familiar with dream-distortion. We traced it back to the censorship which is exercised by one psychical agency in the mind over another. Dream-displacement is one of the chief methods by which that distortion is achieved. *Is fecit cui profuit.*[5] We may assume, then, that dream-displacement comes about through the influence of the same censorship—that is, the censorship of endopsychic defence.

The question of the interplay of these factors—of displacement, condensation and overdetermination—in the construction of dreams, and the question which is a dominant factor and which a subordinate one—all of this we shall leave aside for later investigation. But we can state provisionally a second condition which must be satisfied by those elements of the dream-thoughts which make their way into the dream: *they must escape the censorship imposed by resistance.* And henceforward in interpreting dreams we shall take dream-displacement into account as an undeniable fact.

5. [The old legal tag: "He did the deed who gained by it."]

5. *How Words Change Their Meanings*

BY ANTOINE MEILLET

THE GROUP of linguistic facts where the action of social causes has been definitely established is that of changes in the meanings given to the same words . . . though it is often impossible to determine, through lack of data, the causes of a specific change in meaning, the general characteristics of the phenomenon are now fairly well under-

Translated by Jesse Pitts from Antoine Meillet, "How Words Change Their Meaning," *Année Sociologique,* 1905–6, pp. 6–7, 8, 9, 11, 13, 14, 15, 16, 17, 18, 19, 20, 23, 24, 25, 33.

stood. A systematic classification of the cases observed so far, and of their scientific explanations, is enough to suggest that, under the label of "change in meaning," we are dealing with facts that are fundamentally heterogeneous, derived from different processes, the study of which could not be covered by one single chapter of linguistics.

Before listing the processes that lead to changes in meaning, we must remember that linguistic phenomena are specific and that the efficient causes, which we shall analyze, do not act alone, but rather through their impact upon a definite type of facts—the linguistic facts.

First, the essential discontinuity of language transmission must be taken into account. The child who learns to speak does not receive his language ready-made as it were; he must recreate it entirely anew for his personal use from what he hears about him, and it is a fact of common experience that little children begin by giving to words a very different meaning from that which they have for the adults who taught them. Hence, if one of the causes that we are going to analyze is brought to bear, and if, as a consequence, a word becomes frequently used in a new way in the adult language, it is this common usage that comes to the child's attention, and the old meaning of the word, which still prevails for the adult mind, disappears in the new generation. Let us take, for instance, the word *saoul* (drunk), the old meaning of which is "satiated." The word came to be applied to inebriated people, who are "satiated of drink"; the first people who used the word *saoul* in this manner were expressing themselves with a sort of ironical forbearance and were avoiding the bluntness of the epithet *ivre* (inebriated), but the child who heard them simply associated the idea of an inebriated man to that of the word *saoul*, and that is how *saoul* became the synonym of the word for inebriated, and even replaced it in the familiar vernacular. Thus, the word *saoul* is the word that today expresses the condition with the greatest crudity. This discontinuous character of language transmission could not, by itself, explain anything, but, without it, all the causes of change would probably have been powerless to transform the meaning of words as radically as often as has been the case. In a general way, the discontinuity in transmission is the precondition of the possibility and of the modalities of all linguistic changes; one theoretician even went so far as to try to explain by discontinuity all the linguistic changes. (See E. Herzog, *Streitfragen der romanischen Philologie,* Vol. I.)

With regard to changes in meaning, another important fact is that the word, whether spoken or heard, almost never evokes the image of the object or act of which it is a sign; as Mr. Paulhan, quoted by Mr. Leroy (*Le langage,* p. 97) rightly said: "to understand a word or a sentence is not to have in mind the image of the real objects represented by this word or sentence, but rather to feel in oneself a vague stirring of all the tendencies which would be aroused by the actual seeing of the objects represented by the word." An image, evoked so feebly and with so little precision, is thus apt to be modified without much resistance.

All the changes in form or usage undergone by

words contribute indirectly to changes in meaning. As long as a word remained associated to a definite group of linguistic forms, it was held by the general value of the group, and hence its meaning maintains a certain stability; but, if for some reason the group breaks up, its various constituent elements, no more supporting one another, become exposed to the impact of the various influences that make for change in meaning. For instance, the Latin word *vivus* is, in Latin, inseparable from the verb *vivere,* from the substantive *vita* etc., and thus, could never lose the meaning of "alive." But from the day when pronunciation, as in French, separated the adjective *vif* from the verb *vivere* and made unnoticeable the community of linguistic forms whose radical was the word *vie,* a nuance of meaning, which had already existed in Latin and which referred to "mobile," "animated," was able to become predominant. . . . But whether we are dealing with discontinuity of language transmission or with the segregation of certain words, the linguistic conditions are never simply negative conditions, as it were: they create the linguistic possibilities of a change in meaning, though they are insufficient to determine it; they are the necessary conditions, but not the sufficient ones, and it remains to analyze the efficient causes of changes in meaning.

These causes can be reduced to three major types, which constitute three different kinds of action. In each of the three cases, the result is a change in meaning, and, for this reason, the linguist is apt to confuse them. However, they are definitely distinct and have in common only their end result; thus, in a really scientific study, they must be analyzed separately.

* * *

A certain type of change, of rather rare occurrence, proceeds from purely linguistic causes: such changes derive from the structure of certain sentences, where a given word seems to play a special role. . . .

A second type of change in meaning is one where the things represented by words undergo inner transformation—the French words *père* and *mère* are the exact continuation of the Indo-European words that indicated the father and the mother. Yet the French words are not associated to the same representation: these Indo-European words used to designate well-defined social relationships rather than the physiological aspects of fatherhood and motherhood, the latter being expressed by words that in Latin are *genitor and genitrix;* but social structure having changed and the Indo-European patriarchal family having disappeared, the words *père* and *mère* express above all physiological fatherhood and motherhood; and henceforth one is led to apply the words of *père* and *mère* to animals. In popular French, a *père* is a "male" and a *mère*, a "female," and this meaning is so well developed that there are French idioms where the local forms for *père* and *mère* mean merely the "male" or "female" in animals and where one resorts to the official French forms to refer correctly to "mother" and "father"; in the ancient Indo-European languages, the words corresponding to the Latin *pater* and *mater* do not permit this usage. . . .

* * *

The effect upon the meaning of words of the division of society into distinct classes has been frequently noted by the authors who have dealt with semantics, and Mr. Bréal, in particular, has analyzed it with great precision:

Insofar as a civilization gains in variety and wealth, the occupations, the actions, the interests that confine social life are allocated among different groups of men: neither the state of mind, nor the direction of activity are the same for the priest, the soldier, the politician, the farmer. Though they have inherited the same language, words are, for each of these men, colored with a specific shade of meaning, which sticks and finally becomes fixed to them. . . . When the word *operation* is uttered by a surgeon, we see a patient, a wound, instruments for cutting and slicing; if it is spoken by a military man, we think of armies in the field; if it is a businessman speaking, we understand that we are dealing with capital transfers; . . . Each science, each art, each trade, in elaborating its terminology, marks its imprint upon the words of everyday language. (*See Essai de sémantique*, 3d ed., p. 285 f.)

Hence, the crucial fact is that words that have a wide application in the general language, when used within the smaller groups that compose the society, tend to become restricted to a smaller range of objects. Mr. Meninger says very aptly (*Indogermanische Forschungen*, XVIII, 232): "A word extends its meaning when it passes from a narrow circle to a wider one; it restricts it when it passes from a wide circle to a narrower one." The example of the word "operation" illustrates this principle well enough to make elaboration unnecessary; at any rate, the fact is of common observation. Each group of men utilizes the general resources of the language in a particular manner.

It is not only among professional groups that the meaning of words becomes more precise. Any agglomeration of individuals that has, from any standpoint, a particular situation within a given society comes to share special knowledge and follow conventions specific to the small group that it temporarily or permanently constitutes; moreover, the meaning of a word is defined by the totality of the concepts with which the word is associated, and the associations vary, of course, according to the group where the word is used. The vocabulary of women is not identical to that of men: the word *habiller* (to dress) has, in French, a different feeling tone among women and among men, because it applies to an act having vastly different character and importance for each sex. In other cases, it is because of etiquette that women use words different from those used by men. One may cite, for instance, a Servian dialect where women avoid the correct word for oxen, *Kurjak*, used by men, because the word has also the meaning of penis and hence they use other words. We use, in fact, a special terminology at the army camp, in a student group, in a sports group, and, it is important to note, the same individuals belong simultaneously or successively to several of these groups, so that they fall under various influences either all at once or at different periods of their lives.

Men who exercise the same profession have to name a great number of objects and concepts for which the common language has no nouns because they do not enter the sphere of the common man's interests. Many of these word-signs are obtained by attributing to certain objects the name of other objects with which they have a more or less remote resemblance; thus a machine for carrying goes under the name of *chèvre* (goat); the English *cat* refers also to a hook for holding the anchor (from the claws of the cat, etc.); the intent is merely to note vague analogies, and very often instead of keeping the word itself, they use a derivative: the *manette* (handle) is different from the *main* (hand) —this process of derivation is the rule in Russian where the "beak" of a coffee pot is a *nosik* and not a *nos* (nose). (See Boyer and Spéranski, *Manuel de russe*, p. 113, n. 4.)

Whatever the kind of group considered, the meaning of words is apt to vary, not only because of the particular circumstances in which it is used, as happens, for instance, in the case of the word "operation," but also because the group may be more or less isolated, more or less closed, more or less antonomous from the rest of society. For the alteration in the vocabulary is not limited to what is required by the very nature of the group: it is intentionally accentuated by the tendency, shown by each group, to signal its independence and its unique character. While the influence of the total society tends to standardize a language, the influence of the particular groups tends to differentiate, if not the pronunciation and grammar, which remain basically the same, at least the vocabulary of its individual members. We have here two contradictory trends, which express, on the one hand, characteristics of the general language and, on the other, the special role played by particular sublanguages.

The language of particular groups thus became jargons, and these jargons may grow into artificial languages, through systematic alteration, as, in France, the jargon of the butchers, the *loucherbème.* The fact that this process is found in completely different languages shows this to be a very general phenomenon. Mr. Chéon describes the jargon of the pig-dealers, cereal merchants, sailors, singers, etc. . . . of the Tonking, each of which is a deformation of the Annamite language. (See *Bulletin de l'École Française d'Extrème-Orient,* Vol. XLVII f.)

The action of the trend toward changed meanings in these particular languages is further facilitated by several circumstances. In a group of limited membership, the same issues are raised again and again; the association of ideas are the same among the various members; and they understand one another without needing many details. What, to an outsider, would be obscure, is clear to the group members as soon as certain modes of speech and a certain style have become current.

Thus can be explained the characteristic feature of change of meaning in slang, which is derivation by synonyms. (See Schwab and Guieysse, *Mémoires de la Société de Linguistique,* VII, 33 f.) If a word *A* has simultaneously two meanings, one, *x*, in the current language, the other, *y*, in slang, all the approximate synonyms of the word *A* to the meaning of *x* in the current language will be accepted in slang as having the meaning, *y*, of slang. For instance, if *polir* (to polish) is used in slang with the meaning of *to steal*—as we already find in Villon—one may use in the same way *fourbir* (to furbish), *brunir* (to darken), *nettoyer* (to clean); if *battre* (to beat) ever comes in slang to mean *to mislead,* the same meaning will be given to *taper* (to hit), *estamper* (to stamp in) etc. The necessity that words remain unintelligible to the common man explains much of the considerable development this process has experienced in slang; but the principle itself is not peculiar to slang in the narrow sense of the word, and the process is found, more or less prevalent, in all the languages of particular subgroups. For instance, in a group where adverbs such as *terribly* are used to express what the common language means by *very,* one is led eventually to use all the approximate synonyms such as *frightfully, horribly,* or adverbs of the same ilk in the same way. . . . Such modification in the meaning of words through synonymous derivations can be found only in closed groups: the resistance to linguistic innovations, normal for the society as a whole, can be broken on a particular point, within the small group, by the individual member who can thus affirm all the better his solidarity with his group by differentiating himself linguistically from the total society.

One of the reasons why particular subgroups are highly inclined to modify their vocabulary is that their constitutive elements frequently are not homogeneous from the language standpoint, and that, furthermore, they come under outside influences. Indeed, the groups which form within a society, and notably the professional groups, are composed of people who do not come necessarily from the same locality, nor from the same region, and hence their languages are not quite identical. Leaving aside the action of any of these local dialects, this lack of homogeneity is, by itself, a cause of instability and uncertainty, and it is one of the main causes—the main one perhaps—of all linguistic changes, those affecting pronunciation and grammar as well as those affecting the vocabulary, those coming under the heading of spontaneous change as well as the instances of borrowing.

Foreign members tend to introduce to us the group language forms from their native tongue: thus, the language of German students contains words from many different dialects; in his *Studentensprache* (p. 65), Mr. Kluge gives some examples, notably the substitution of the Low German *Gnote* for the High German *Genosse* (companion). Mr. Horn makes the same remark with regard to the language of the German soldiers in his *Soldatensprache* (p. 9f.). In the special tongue of the first Christians, the "elder" who was the "priest" was called by the word πρεσβυτερος in Greek; in the group of Latin-speaking Christians, which had many Hellenic or Hellenized members, the word was kept as it was; one says *presbiter,* which survived in French under the form *prêtre,* as well as *prouvoire* in early French.

The influence of foreign elements is often evidenced by translators. In Armenia the word *erêc* (elder) has thus received the meaning of "priest." Or one may give a foreign meaning to a native word: at the time of Knut, the Anglo-Saxon *eorl* (free man who goes to war, noble) was given the meaning of the Scandinavian *jarl* (viceroy, governor of province), the latter word being recognised by the speaker as similar to the English word; under the Norman rule, the same *eorl* was used as equivalent to the French *comte* (count), and it is the meaning which earl has kept in modern English.

As a result of this double process of borrowing

and translation of foreign terms, the vocabularies of particular groups, which are in contact with similar groups in other countries, will normally present many similitudes—the military vocabulary, for instance, is approximately the same across the width of Europe.

This uniformity is particularly marked in groups made up of scientists, or where science as such plays an important role. Scientists who deal with ideas that must be given concrete expression are very prone to create special vocabularies, which spread quickly in their respective countries. And, since science is eminently international, the particular terms invented by scientists are either reproduced or translated in groups sharing the most varied mother tongues. A very good example of this process can be seen in the language of the Scholastics, which had an eminently European character, and to which Europe owes the greatest part of whatever unity of vocabulary and meaning has emerged from a variety of native tongues. . . .

When, as happened relatively frequently throughout history, the dominant elements of a nation have spoken a language different from that of the other groups, the people who approach the ruling caste and who, of necessity, learn some of its language, will constitute for themselves a vocabulary containing a good number of foreign terms, especially those covering concepts important to the caste—the old English word *here* (army) was eliminated in the language of the people who worked with the Norman aristocracy, in favor of the words of French origin, *army* and *host*.

Within a given language, defined by a given pronunciation and foremostly by certain grammatical forms, there are in reality as many particular vocabularies as there exist social groups having an autonomous existence within the society that speaks this language. Each constituted group of men has special terms to describe not only what is particular to it, but also the numerous things that it shares with the members of wider groups in which these men also play certain roles.

*   *   *

The changes in meaning that we have discussed summarily do not remain confined to their circles of origin. Once beyond the boundaries of their particular groups, individuals do not escape from the habits contracted there, and even when dealing with outsiders, they are apt to use words with their private group meaning. If these groups have prestige, such as aristocratic or scientific groups, outsiders will enjoy reproducing their customs and especially their vocabulary. . . .

The particular meanings that were born in small enclosed groups hence have many occasions to be passed on to the common language, through the pressure of either fashion or necessity; we have here examples of real borrowing that can take place *inside* a given language.

If words are borrowed by the common language only to express the concepts for which they were created, there is nothing more to say: they will remain as more or less foreign bodies, as technical terms, and act only as accessory elements; this is the situation that first drew the attention of linguists, but its importance is relatively secondary.

Borrowed words can penetrate the common language and gain current usage only if they undergo a change of meaning; precise and rigorous word meanings depend upon the small size of a milieu where there is community of interests and where one does not need to spell out everything in order to be understood. Outside of this small milieu that gave it its special meaning, the word immediately loses precision and tends to become more and more vague. Let us take, for instance, the Latin word *caussa* (*causa*): in the language of the Roman courts it meant "a judicial case, a law suit"; passing into the common language, it came merely to mean an *affaire* (a matter of business) and finally a *chose* (thing), so that it could be applied not only to business but to any object and *chose* has become one of the vaguest terms of the French language. The same word borrowed, in a learned context, from the particular language of scholars with the meaning of "cause," which was the general meaning of the word in Latin, has also passed into the common language, but with a more and more indefinite meaning, and it is no longer used to designate the efficient cause or the final cause, but now signifies any motive of action—"because?" is equal to "why?" in the popular language. . . .

Just as use in a particular language determines a change in meaning, loans made by the general languages to a particular one lead to another change, although in a totally different direction. And this is but a consequence of the way in which the meaning of words is established; Mr. Wundt (*Sprache*, 2d ed., II, 484 ff.) shows that a word does not necessarily refer to a general idea: for each individual the word refers most often simply to certain given objects that are part of his private experience. Yet the word is used by other members of the community, for whom it refers to other but more or less similar objects. Through this process it sheds all of its narrowly particular quality and keeps only the role of sign for the characteristics common to all the objects referred to by this word as used in a given social group: the child who learns the word *dog* is naturally prone to apply it exclusively to the dog of the household; it is only as he hears the same word applied to other animals that he strips it of its concrete character and gives it a general value. One sees, from this example, that the general value of words is, in large measure, a social fact, and that the generality of the meaning of a word will often be proportional to the size of the group: in the dialect of a village of shepherds, the *dog* is truly the shepherd's dog; but in a language such as French, the word *dog* excludes any special connection to a given breed and refers in an abstract way to an animal species.

It seems, then, that the essential principle of change in meaning is to be found in the existence of social groupings within the milieu where a language is spoken—in short, in a fact of social structure. It would be excessive to pretend that it is possible, at the present time, to explain all the transformations of meaning by this principle; a great number of facts would resist this explanation, and their interpretation would require arbitrary and often farfetched assumptions. The history of words is not sufficiently elaborated, in any given language, to permit the analysis of all possible cases, showing that they can be explained without exception by the principle evoked here. Usually it is only by extrapolation that it is possible to trace the curve followed by the meaning of a word as it continues to change. But if it is true that a change in meaning can only take place if provoked by a specific action, and this is the postulate necessary to any sound theory of semantics, then the principle outlined here is the only principle known and conceivable which acts powerfully enough to proceed explanations for most of the observed instances of change; and, furthermore, the hypothesis is always verified when conditions permit following the phenomenon step by step. . . .

6. Symbolism

BY EDWARD SAPIR

THE TERM SYMBOLISM covers a great variety of apparently dissimilar modes of behavior. In its original sense it was restricted to objects or marks intended to recall or to direct special attention to some person, object, idea, event or projected activity associated only vaguely or not at all with the symbol in any natural sense. By gradual extensions of meaning the terms symbol and symbolism have come to include not merely such trivial objects and marks as black balls, to indicate a negative attitude in voting, and stars and daggers, to remind the reader that supplementary information is to be found at the bottom of the page, but also more elaborate objects and devices, such as flags and signal lights, which are not ordinarily regarded as important in themselves but which point to ideas and actions of great consequence to society. Such complex systems of reference as speech, writing and mathematical notation should also be included under the term symbolism, for the sounds and marks used therein obviously have no meaning in themselves and can have significance only for those who know how to interpret them in terms of that to which they refer. A certain kind of poetry is called symbolic or symbolistic because its apparent content is only a suggestion for wider meanings. In personal relations too there is much behavior that may be called symbolic, as when a ceremonious bow is directed not so much to an actual person as to a status which that person happens to fill. The psychoanalysts have come to apply the term symbolic to almost any emotionally charged pattern of behavior which has the function of unconscious fulfilment of a repressed tendency, as when a person assumes a raised voice of protest to a perfectly indifferent stranger who unconsciously recalls his father and awakens the repressed attitude of hostility toward the father.

Amid the wide variety of senses in which the word is used there seem to emerge two constant characteristics. One of these is that the symbol is always a substitute for some more closely intermediating type of behavior, whence it follows that all symbolism implies meanings which cannot be derived directly from the contexts of experience. The second characteristic of the symbol is that it expresses a condensation of energy, its actual significance being out of all proportion to the appar-

Reprinted from Edward Sapir, "Symbolism," in *Encyclopaedia of the Social Sciences* (New York: Macmillan Co., 1930), pp. 492–95, with the permission of The Macmillan Co.

ent triviality of meaning suggested by its mere form. This can be seen at once when the mildly decorative function of a few scratches on paper is compared with the alarming significance of apparently equally random scratches which are interpreted by a particular society as meaning "murder" or "God." This disconcerting transcendence of form comes out equally well in the contrast between the involuntary blink of the eye and the crudely similar wink which means "He does not know what an ass he is, but you and I do."

It seems useful to distinguish two main types of symbolism. The first of these, which may be called referential symbolism, embraces such forms as oral speech, writing, the telegraph code, national flags, flag signaling and other organizations of symbols which are agreed upon as economical devices for purposes of reference. The second type of symbolism is equally economical and may be termed condensation symbolism, for it is a highly condensed form of substitutive behavior for direct expression, allowing for the ready release of emotional tension in conscious or unconscious form. Telegraphic ticking is virtually a pure example of referential symbolism; the apparently meaningless washing ritual of an obsessive neurotic, as interpreted by the psychoanalysts, would be a pure example of condensation symbolism. In actual behavior both types are generally blended. Thus specific forms of writing, conventionalized spelling, peculiar pronunciations and verbal slogans, while ostensibly referential, easily take on the character of emotionalized rituals and become highly important to both individual and society as substitutive forms of emotional expression. Were writing merely referential symbolism, spelling reforms would not be so difficult to bring about.

Symbols of the referential type undoubtedly developed later as a class than condensation symbols. It is likely that most referential symbolisms go back to unconsciously evolved symbolisms saturated with emotional quality, which gradually took on a purely referential character as the linked emotion dropped out of the behavior in question. Thus shaking the fist at an imaginary enemy becomes a dissociated and finally a referential symbol for anger when no enemy, real or imaginary, is actually intended. When this emotional denudation takes place, the symbol becomes a comment, as it were, on anger itself and a preparation for something like language. What is ordinarily called language may have had its ultimate root in just such dissociated and emotionally denuded cries, which originally released emotional tension. Once referential symbolism had been established as a by-product of behavior, more conscious symbols of reference could

be evolved by the copying in abbreviated or simplified form of the thing referred to, as in the case of pictographic writing. On still more sophisticated levels referential symbolism may be attained by mere social agreement, as when a numbered check is arbitrarily assigned to a man's hat. The less primary and associational the symbolism, the more dissociated from its original context, and the less emotionalized it becomes, the more it takes on the character of true reference. A further condition for the rich development of referential symbolism must not be overlooked—the increased complexity and homogeneity of the symbolic material. This is strikingly the case in language, in which all meanings are consistently expressed by formal patterns arising out of the apparently arbitrary sequences of unitary sounds. When the material of a symbolic system becomes sufficiently varied and yet homogeneous in kind, the symbolism becomes more and more richly patterned, creative and meaningful in its own terms, and referents tend to be supplied by a retrospective act of rationalization. Hence it results that such complex systems of meaning as a sentence form or a musical form mean so much more than they can ever be said to refer to. In highly evolved systems of reference the relation between symbol and referent becomes increasingly variable or inclusive.

In condensation symbolism also richness of meaning grows with increased dissociation. The chief developmental difference, however, between this type of symbolism and referential symbolism is that while the latter grows with formal elaboration in the conscious, the former strikes deeper and deeper roots in the unconscious and diffuses its emotional quality to types of behavior or situations apparently far removed from the original meaning of the symbol. Both types of symbols therefore begin with situations in which a sign is dissociated from its context. The conscious elaboration of form makes of such dissociation a system of reference, while the unconscious spread of emotional quality makes of it a condensation symbol. Where, as in the case of a national flag or a beautiful poem, a symbolic expression which is apparently one of mere reference is associated with repressed emotional material of great importance to the ego, the two theoretically distinct types of symbolic behavior merge into one. One then deals with symbols of peculiar potency and even danger, for unconscious meanings, full of emotional power, become rationalized as mere references.

It is customary to say that society is peculiarly subject to the influence of symbols in such emotionally charged fields as religion and politics. Flags and slogans are the type examples in the field of politics, crosses and ceremonial regalia in the field of religion. But all culture is in fact heavily charged with symbolism, as is all personal behavior. Even comparatively simple forms of behavior are far less directly functional than they seem to be, but include in their motivation unconscious and even unacknowledged impulses, for which the behavior must be looked upon as a symbol. Many, perhaps most reasons are little more than ex post facto rationalizations of behavior controlled by unconscious necessity. Even an elaborate, well documented scientific theory may from this standpoint be little more than a symbol of the unknown necessities of the ego. Scientists fight for their theories not because they believe them to be true but because they wish them to be so.

It will be useful to give examples of some of the less obvious symbolisms in socialized behavior. Etiquette has at least two layers of symbolism. On a relatively obvious plane of symbolism etiquette provides the members of society with a set of rules which, in condensed and thoroughly conventionalized form, express society's concern for its members and their relation to one another. There is another level of etiquette symbolism, however, which takes little or no account of such specific meanings but interprets etiquette as a whole as a powerful symbolism of status. From this standpoint to know the rules of etiquette is important, not because the feelings of friends and strangers are becomingly observed but because the manipulator of the rule proves that he is a member of an exclusive group. By reason of the richly developed meanings which inhere in etiquette, both positive and negative, a sensitive person can actually express a more bitter hostility through the frigid observance of etiquette than by flouting it on an obvious wave of hostility. Etiquette, then, is an unusually elaborate symbolic play in which individuals in their actual relationships are the players and society is the bogus referee.

Education is also a thoroughly symbolic field of behavior. Much of its rationale cannot be tested as to direction or value. No one knows or can discover just how much Latin, French, mathematics or history is good for any particular person to acquire. The tests of the attainment of such knowledge are themselves little more than symbolic gestures. For the social psychologist education, whatever else it may be or do, stands out as a peculiarly massive and well articulated set of symbols which express the needs of the individual in society and which help him to orient himself in his relations to his fellow men. That an individual possesses the bachelor's degree may or may not prove that he knows, or once knew, something about Roman

history and trigonometry. The important thing about his degree is that it helps him to secure a position which is socially or economically more desirable than some other position which can be obtained without the aid of this degree. Society has misgivings about the function of specific items in the educational process and has to make symbolic atonement by inventing such notions as the cultivation of the mind.

It is important to observe that symbolic meanings can often be recognized clearly for the first time when the symbolic value, generally unconscious or conscious only in a marginal sense, drops out of a socialized pattern of behavior and the supposed function, which up to that time had been believed to be more than enough to explain it and keep it going, loses its significance and is seen to be little more than a paltry rationalization. Chairmanship of a committee, for instance, has symbolic value only in a society in which two things are believed: that administrative functions somehow stamp a person as superior to those who are being directed; and that the ideal society is a democratic one and that those who are naturally more able than others somehow automatically get into positions of administrative advantage. Should people come to feel that administrative functions are little more than symbolic automatisms, the chairmanship of a committee would be recognized as little more than a petrified symbol and the particular value that is now felt to inhere in it would tend to disappear.

An important field for investigation is that of personal symbolisms in the use of cultural patterns. Personal symbolisms are often the more valuable as they are hidden from consciousness and serve as the springs of effective behavior. Interest in a particular science may be an elaborately sublimated symbol of an unconscious emotional attachment to what a man who is significant in one's personal development is believed to be linked up with, such as the destruction of religion or the discovery of God, these grandiose preferences in turn serving as symbols of repressed hate or love. Much charitable endeavor is animated by an unconscious desire to peer into lives that one is glad to be unable to share. Society itself, perfecting its rigid mechanisms of charitable activity, cannot in every case or even in the vast majority of cases subject the charitable act to a pragmatic critique but must rest content for the most part with charity organization as its symbolic gesture toward alleviating suffering. Thus individual and society, in a never ending interplay of symbolic gestures, build up the pyramided structure called civilization. In this structure very few bricks touch the ground.

II–PATTERNS OF CULTURE

1. The Factors of Social Phenomena

BY HERBERT SPENCER

1. THE BEHAVIOR of a single inanimate object depends on the co-operation between its own forces and the forces to which it is exposed: instance a piece of metal, the molecules of which keep the solid state or assume the liquid state, according partly to their natures and partly to the heat-waves falling on them. Similarly with any groups of inanimate objects. Be it a cart-load of bricks shot down, a barrowful of gravel turned over, or a boy's bag of marbles emptied, the behaviour of the assembled masses—here standing in a heap with steep sides, here forming one with sides much less inclined, and here spreading out and rolling in all directions—is in each case determined partly by the properties of the individual members of the group, and partly by the forces of gravitation, impact, and friction, they are subjected to.

It is equally so when the discrete aggregate consists of organic bodies, such as the members of a species. For a species increases or decreases in numbers, widens or contracts its habitat, migrates or remains stationary, continues an old mode of life or falls into a new one, under the combined influences of its intrinsic nature and the environing actions, inorganic and organic.

It is thus, too, with aggregates of men. Be it rudimentary or be it advanced, every society displays phenomena that are ascribable to the characters of its units and to the conditions under which they exist. Here, then, are the factors as primarily divided.

2. These factors are re-divisible. Within each there are groups of factors that stand in marked contrasts.

Beginning with the extrinsic factors, we see that from the outset several kinds of them are variously operative. We have climate; hot, cold, or temperate, moist or dry, constant or variable. We have surface; much or little of which is available, and the avail-

able part of which is fertile in greater or less degree; and we have configuration of surface, as uniform or multiform. Next we have the vegetal productions; here abundant in quantities and kinds, and there deficient in one or both. And besides the Flora of the region we have its Fauna, which is influential in many ways; not only by the numbers of its species and individuals, but by the proportion between those that are useful and those that are injurious. On these sets of conditions, inorganic and organic, characterizing the environment, primarily depends the possibility of social evolution.

When we turn to the intrinsic factors we have to note first, that, considered as a social unit, the individual man has physical traits, such as degrees of strength, activity, endurance, which affect the growth and structure of the society. He is in every case distinguished by emotional traits which aid, or hinder, or modify, the activities of the society, and its developments. Always, too, his degree of intelligence and the tendencies of thought peculiar to him, become co-operating causes of social quiescence or social change.

Such being the original sets of factors, we have now to note the secondary or derived sets of factors, which social evolution itself brings into play.

3. First may be set down the progressive modifications of the environment, inorganic and organic, which societies effect.

Among these are the alterations of climate caused by clearing and by drainage. Such alterations may be favourable to social growth, as where a rainy region is made less rainy by cutting down forests, or a swampy surface rendered more salubrious and fertile by carrying off water;* or they may be un-

* It is worth noting that drainage increases what we may figuratively call terrestrial respiration; and that on terrestrial respiration the lives of land-plants, and therefore of land-animals, and therefore of men, depend. Every change of atmospheric pressure produces exits or entrances of the air into all the interstices of the soil. The depth to which these irregular inspirations and expirations reach, is increased by freedom from water; since interstices occupied by water cannot be filled by air. Thus those chemical de-

Reprinted from Herbert Spencer, *The Priciples of Sociology* (New York: D. Appleton & Co., 1897), I, 8–15.

favourable, as where, by destroying the forests, a region already dry is made arid: witness the seat of the old Semitic civilizations, and, in a less degree, Spain.

Next come the changes wrought in the kinds and quantities of plant-life over the surface occupied. These changes are three-fold. There is the increasing culture of plants conducive to social growth, replacing plants not conducive to it; there is the gradual production of better varieties of these useful plants, causing, in time, great divergences from their originals; and there is, eventually, the introduction of new useful plants.

Simultaneously go on the kindred changes which social progress works in the Fauna of the region. We have the diminution or destruction of some or many injurious species. We have the fostering of useful species, which has the double effect of increasing their numbers and making their qualities more advantageous to society. Further, we have the naturalization of desirable species brought from abroad.

It needs but to think of the immense contrast between a wolf-haunted forest or a boggy moor peopled with wild birds, and the fields covered with crops and flocks which eventually occupy the same area, to be reminded that the environment, inorganic and organic, of a society, undergoes a continuous transformation during the progress of the society; and that this transformation becomes an all-important secondary factor in social evolution.

4. Another secondary factor is the increasing size of the social aggregate, accompanied, generally, by increasing density.

Apart from social changes otherwise produced, there are social changes produced by simple growth. Mass is both a condition to, and a result of, organization. It is clear that heterogeneity of structure is made possible only by multiplicity of units. Division of labour cannot be carried far where there are but few to divide the labour among them. Complex co-operations, governmental and industrial, are impossible without a population large enough to supply many kinds and gradations of agents. And sundry developed forms of activity, both predatory and peaceful, are made practicable only by the power which large masses of men furnish.

Hence, then, a derivative factor which, like the rest, is at once a consequence and a cause of social progress, is social growth. Other factors co-operate to produce this; and this joins other factors in working further changes.

5. Among derived factors we may next note the

compositions effected by the air that is renewed with every fall and rise of the barometer, are extended to a greater depth by drainage; and the plant-life depending on such decompositions is facilitated.

reciprocal influence of the society and its units— the influence of the whole on the parts, and of the parts on the whole.

As soon as a combination of men acquires permanence, there begin actions and reactions between the community and each member of it, such that either affects the other in nature. The control exercised by the aggregate over its units, tends ever to mould their activities and sentiments and ideas into congruity with social requirements; and these activities, sentiments, and ideas, in so far as they are changed by changing circumstances, tend to remould the society into congruity with themselves.

In addition, therefore, to the original nature of the individuals and the original nature of the society they form, we have to take into account the induced natures of the two. Eventually, mutual modification becomes a potent cause of transformation in both.

6. Yet a further derivative factor of extreme importance remains. I mean the influence of the super-organic environment—the action and reaction between a society and neighbouring societies.

While there exist only small, wandering, unorganized hordes, the conflicts of these with one another work no permanent changes of arrangement in them. But when there have arisen the definite chieftainships which frequent conflicts tend to initiate, and especially when the conflicts have ended in subjugations, there arise the rudiments of political organization; and, as at first, so afterwards, the wars of societies with one another have all-important effects in developing social structures, or rather, certain of them. For I may here, in passing, indicate the truth to be hereafter exhibited in full, that while the industrial organization of a society is mainly determined by its inorganic and organic environments, its governmental organization is mainly determined by its super-organic environment—by the actions of those adjacent societies with which it carries on the struggle for existence.

7. There remains in the group of derived factors one more, the potency of which can scarcely be over-estimated. I mean that accumulation of super-organic products which we commonly distinguish as artificial, but which, philosophically considered, are no less natural than all other products of evolution. There are several orders of these.

First come the material appliances, which, beginning with roughly-chipped flints, end in the complex automatic tools of an engine-factory driven by steam; which from boomerangs rise to eighty-ton guns; which from huts of branches and grass grow to cities with their palaces and cathedrals. Then we have language, able at first only to eke out gestures in communicating simple ideas, but eventually becoming capable of expressing involved conceptions with precision. While from that stage in which it conveys thoughts only by sounds to one or a few persons, we pass through picture-writing up to steam-printing: multiplying indefinitely the numbers communicated with, and making accessible in voluminous literatures the ideas and feelings of countless men in various places and times. Concomitantly there goes on the development of knowledge, ending in science. Numeration on the fingers grows into far-reaching mathematics; observation of the moon's changes leads in time to a theory of the solar system; and there successively arise sciences of which not even the germs could at first be detected. Meanwhile the once few and simple customs, becoming more numerous, definite, and fixed, end in systems of laws. Rude superstitions initiate elaborate mythologies, theologies, cosmogonies. Opinion getting embodied in creeds, gets embodied, too, in accepted codes of ceremony and conduct, and in established social sentiments. And then there slowly evolve also the products we call æsthetic; which of themselves form a highly-complex group. From necklaces of fishbones we advance to dresses elaborate, gorgeous, and infinitely varied; out of discordant war-chants come symphonies and operas; cairns develop into magnificent temples; in place of caves with rude markings there arise at length galleries of paintings; and the recital of a chief's deeds with mimetic accompaniment gives origin to epics, dramas, lyrics, and the vast mass of poetry, fiction, biography, and history.

These various orders of super-organic products, each developing within itself new genera and species while growing into a larger whole, and each acting on the other orders while reacted on by them, constitute an immensely-voluminous, immensely-complicated, and immensely-powerful set of influences. During social evolution they are ever modifying individuals and modifying society, while being modified by both. They gradually form what we may consider either as a non-vital part of the society itself, or else as a secondary environment, which eventually becomes more important than the primary environments—so much more important that there arises the possibility of carrying on a high kind of social life under inorganic and organic conditions which originally would have prevented it.

8. Such are the factors in outline. Even when presented under this most general form, the combination of them is seen to be of an involved kind.

Recognizing the primary truth that social phenomena depend in part on the natures of the individuals and in part on the forces the individuals are subject to, we see that these two fundamentally-distinct sets of factors, with which social changes commence, give origin to other sets as social changes advance. The pre-established environing influences, inorganic and organic, which are at first almost unalterable, become more and more altered by the actions of the evolving society. Simple growth of population brings into play fresh causes of transformation that are increasingly important. The influences which the society exerts on the natures of its units, and those which the units exert on the nature of the society, incessantly co-operate in creating new elements. As societies progress in size and structure, they work on one another, now by their war-struggles and now by their industrial intercourse, profound metamorphoses. And the ever-accumulating, ever-complicating super-organic products, material and mental, constitute a further set of factors which become more and more influential causes of change. So that, involved as the factors are at the beginning, each step in advance increases the involution, by adding factors which themselves grow more complex while they grow more powerful.

2. On Biological and Cultural Factors

BY FRANZ BOAS

THE SCIENCE of anthropology has grown up from many distinct beginnings. At an early time men were interested in foreign countries and in the lives of their inhabitants. Herodotus reported to the Greeks what he had seen in many lands. Caesar and Tacitus wrote on the customs of the Gauls and Germans. In the middle ages Marco Polo, the Venetian, and Ibn Batuta, the Arab, told of the strange peoples of the Far East and of Africa. Later on, Cook's journeys excited the interest of the world. From these reports arose gradually a desire to find a general significance in the multifarious ways of living of strange peoples. In the eighteenth century Rousseau, Schiller and Herder tried to form, out of the reports of travelers, a picture of the history of mankind. More solid attempts were made about the middle of the nineteenth century, when the comprehensive works of Klemm and Waitz were written.

Biologists directed their studies towards an understanding of the varieties of human forms. Linnaeus, Blumenbach, Camper are a few of the names that stand out as early investigators of these problems, which received an entirely new stimulus when Darwin's views of the instability of species were accepted by the scientific world. The problem of man's origin and his place in the animal kingdom became the prime subject of interest. Darwin, Huxley and Haeckel are outstanding names representing this period. Still more recently the intensive study of heredity and mutation has given a new aspect to inquiries into the origin and meaning of race.

The development of psychology led to new problems presented by the diversity of the racial and social groups of mankind. The question of mental characteristics of races, which at an earlier period had become a subject of discussion with entirely inadequate methods—largely stimulated by the desire to justify slavery—was taken up again with the more refined technique of experimental psychology, and particular attention is now being paid to the mental status of primitive man and of mental

Reprinted from Franz Boas, *Race, Language and Culture* (New York: Macmillan Co., 1940), pp. 243–59. Address of the president of the American Association for the Advancement of Science, Atlantic City, December, 1932, with the permission of The Macmillan Co.

life under pathological conditions. The methods of comparative psychology are not confined to man alone, and much light may be thrown on human behavior by the study of animals. The attempt is being made to develop a genetic psychology.

Finally sociology, economics, political science, history and philosophy have found it worth while to study conditions found among alien peoples in order to throw light upon our modern social processes.

With this bewildering variety of approaches, all dealing with racial and cultural forms, it seems necessary to formulate clearly what the objects are that we try to attain by the study of mankind.

We may perhaps best define our objective as the attempt to understand the steps by which man has come to be what he is, biologically, psychologically and culturally. Thus it appears at once that our material must necessarily be historical material, historical in the widest sense of the term. It must include the history of the development of the bodily form of man, his physiological functions, mind and culture. We need a knowledge of the chronological succession of forms and an insight into the conditions under which changes occur. Without such data progress seems impossible and the fundamental question arises as to how such data can be obtained.

Ever since Lamarck's and Darwin's time the biologist has been struggling with this problem. The complete paleontological record of the development of plant and animal forms is not available. Even in favorable cases gaps remain that cannot be filled on account of the lack of intermediate forms. For this reason indirect proofs must be resorted to. These are based partly on similarities revealed by morphology and interpreted as proof of genetic relationship, partly on morphological traits observed in prenatal life, which suggest relationship between forms that as adults appear quite distinct.

Caution in the use of morphological similarities is required, because there are cases in which similar forms develop in genetically unrelated groups, as in the marsupials of Australia, which show remarkable parallelism with higher mammal forms, or in the white-haired forms of the Arctic and of high altitudes, which occur independently in many genera and species, or in the blondness and other abnormal hair forms of domesticated mammals which develop regardless of their genetic relations.

As long as the paleontological record is incomplete we have no way of reconstructing the history of animals and plants except through morphology and embryology.

This is equally true of man, and for this reason the eager search for early human and prehuman forms is justified. The finds of the remains of the Pithecanthropus in Java, the Sinanthropus in China, of the Heidelberg jaw and of the later types of the glacial period are so many steps advancing our knowledge. It requires the labors of the enthusiastic explorer to furnish us with the material that must be interpreted by careful morphological study. The material available at the present time is sadly fragmentary. It is encouraging to see that it is richest in all those countries in which the interest in the paleontology of man has been keenest, so that we may hope that with the increase of interest in new fields the material on which to build the evolutionary history of man will be considerably increased.

It is natural that with our more extended knowledge of the evolutionary history of the higher mammals certain points stand out that will direct the labors of the explorer. Thus on the basis of our knowledge of the distribution of ape forms, nobody would search for the ancestors of humanity in the New World, although the question when the earliest migration of man into America took place is still one of the problems that is prominent in researches on the paleontology of the glacial period of America.

The skeletal material of later periods is more abundant. Still it is difficult to establish definitely the relation of early skeletal remains and of modern races, because many of their most characteristic traits are found in the soft parts of the body that have not been preserved. Furthermore, the transitions from one race to another are so gradual that only extreme forms can be determined with any degree of definiteness.

On account of the absence of material elucidating the history of modern races, it is not surprising that for many years anthropologists have endeavored to classify races, basing their attempts on a variety of traits, and that only too often the results of these classifications have been assumed as expressions of genetic relationship, while actually they have no more than a descriptive value, unless their genetic significance can be established. If the same metric proportions of the head recur in all races they cannot be a significant criterion of fundamental racial types, although they may be valuable

indications of the development of local strains within a racial group. If, on the other hand, a particular hair form is a trait well-nigh universal in extensive groups of mankind, and one that does not recur in other groups, it will in all probability represent an ancient hereditary racial trait, the more so, if it occurs in a geographically continuous area. It is the task of the anthropologist to search out these outstanding traits and to remember that the exact measurement of features which are not exclusive racial characteristics will not answer the problems of the evolution of fundamental types, but can be taken only as an indication of independent, special modifications of late origin within the large racial groups.

From this point of view the general question of the occurrence of parallel development in genetically unrelated lines assumes particular importance. We have sufficient evidence to show that morphological form is subject to environmental influences that in some cases will have similar effects upon unrelated forms. Even the most skeptical would admit this for size of the body.

Changes due to environment that occur under our eyes, such as minute changes in size and proportion of the body, are probably not hereditary, but merely expressions of the reaction of the body to external conditions and subject to new adjustments under new conditions.

However, one series of changes, brought about by external conditions are undoubtedly hereditary. I mean those developing in domestication. No matter whether they are due to survival of aberrant forms or directly conditioned by domestication, they are found in similar ways in all domesticated animals, and because man possesses all these characteristics he proves to be a domesticated form. Eduard Hahn was probably the first to point out that man lives like a domesticated animal; the morphological points were emphasized by Eugen Fischer, B. Klatt and myself.

The solution of the problem of the origin of races must rest not only on classificatory studies and on those of the development of parallel forms, but also on the consideration of the distribution of races, of early migrations and consequent intermingling or isolation.

On account of the occurrence of independent development of parallel forms it seems important to know the range of variant local forms that originate in each race, and it might seem plausible that races producing local variants of similar types are closely related. Thus Mongoloids and Europeans occasionally produce similar forms in regions so wide apart that it would be difficult to interpret them as effects of intermingling.

The biological foundations of conclusions based on this type of evidence are, to a great extent, necessarily speculative. Scientific proof would require a knowledge of the earliest movements of mankind, an intimate acquaintance with the conditions under which racial types may throw off variants and the character and extent of variations that may develop as mutants.

The solution of these problems must extend beyond morphological description of the race as a whole. Since we are dealing to a great extent with forms determined by heredity, it seems indispensable to found the study of the race as a whole on that of the component genetic lines and of their variants, and on inquiries into the influence of environment and selection upon bodily form and function. The race must be studied not as a whole but in its genotypical lines as developing under varying conditions.

In the study of racial forms we are too much inclined to consider the importance of races according to the number of their representatives. This is obviously an error, for the important phenomenon is the occurrence of stable morphological types, not the number of individuals representing each. The numerical strength of races has changed enormously in historic times, and it would be quite erroneous to attribute an undue importance to the White race or to the East Asiatics, merely because they have outgrown in numbers all other racial types. Still, in descriptive classifications the local types of a large race are given undue prominence over the less striking subdivisions of lesser groups. As an example, I might mention Huxley's divisions of the White race as against his divisions of other races.

We are interested not only in the bodily form of races but equally in the functioning of the body, physiologically as well as mentally. The problems presented by this class of phenomena present particular difficulties on account of the adjustability of function to external demands, so that it is an exceedingly precarious task to distinguish between what is determined by the biological make-up of the body and what depends upon external conditions. Observations made on masses of individuals in different localities may be explained equally well by the assumption of hereditary racial characteristics and by that of changes due to environmental influences. A mere description of these phenomena will never lead to a result. Different types, areas, social strata and cultures exhibit marked differences in physiological and mental function. A dogmatic assertion that racial type alone is responsible for these differences is a pseudo-science. An adequate treatment requires a weighing of the diverse factors.

Investigators are easily misled by the fact that the hereditary, biologically determined endowment of an individual is intimately associated with the functioning of his body. This appears most clearly in cases of bodily deficiency or of unusually favorable bodily development. It is quite a different matter to extend this observation over whole populations or racial groups in which are represented a great variety of hereditary lines and individuals, for the many forms of bodily make-up found in each group allow a great variety of functioning. Hereditary characteristics are pronounced in genetic lines, but a population—or to use the technical term, a phenotype—is not a genetic line and the great variety of genotypes within a race forbids the application of results obtained from a single hereditary line to a whole population in which the diversity of the constituent lines is bound to equalize the distribution of diverse genetic types in the populations considered. I have spoken so often on this subject that you will permit me to pass on to other questions.

While paleontological evidence may give us a clue to the evolution of human forms, only the most superficial evidence can be obtained for the development of function. A little may be inferred from size and form of the brain cavity and that of the jaw, in so far as it indicates the possibility of articulate speech. We may obtain some information on the development of erect posture, but the physiological processes that occurred in past generations are not accessible to observation. All the conclusions that we may arrive at are based on very indirect evidence.

The mental life of man also can be studied experimentally only among living races. It is, however, possible to infer some of its aspects by what past generations have done. Historical data permit us to study the culture of past times, in a few localities, as in the eastern Mediterranean area, India, China as far back as a few thousand years—and a limited amount of information on the mental life of man may be obtained from these data. We may even go farther back and extend our studies over the early remains of human activities. Objects of varied character, made by man and belonging to periods as early as the Quaternary, have been found in great quantities, and their study reveals at least certain aspects of what man has been able to do during these times.

The data of prehistoric archeology reveal with progress of time a decided branching out of human activities. While from earliest periods nothing remains but a few simple stone implements, we see an increasing differentiation of form of implements used by man. During the Quaternary the use of fire had been discovered, artistic work of high esthetic value had been achieved, and painted records of human activities had been made. Soon after the beginning of the recent geological period the beginnings of agriculture appear and the products of human labor take on new forms at a rapidly accelerating rate. While in early Quaternary times we do not observe any change for thousands of years, so that the observer might imagine that the products of human hands were made according to an innate instinct, like the cells of a beehive, the rapidity of change becomes the greater the nearer we approach our time, and at an early period we recognize that the arts of man cannot be instinctively determined, but are the cumulative result of experience.

It has often been claimed that the very primitiveness of human handiwork of early times proves organic mental inferiority. This argument is certainly not tenable, for we find in modern times isolated tribes living in a way that may well be paralleled with early conditions. A comparison of the psychic life of these groups does not justify the belief that their industrial backwardness is due to a difference in the types of organism, for we find numbers of closely related races on the most diverse levels of cultural status. This is perhaps clearest in the Mongoloid race, where by the side of the civilized Chinese are found the most primitive Siberian tribes, or in the American group, where the highly developed Maya of Yucatan and the Aztecs of Mexico may be compared with the primitive tribes of our western plateaus. Evidently historic and prehistoric data give us little or no information on the biological development of the human mind.

How little the biological, organic determinants of culture can be inferred from the state of culture appears clearly if we try to realize how different the judgment of racial ability would have been at various periods of history. When Egypt flourished, northern Europe was in primitive conditions, comparable to those of American Indians or African Negroes, and yet northern Europe of our day has far outdistanced those people, who at an earlier time were the leaders of mankind. An attempt to find biological reasons for these changes would necessitate innumerable unprovable hypotheses regarding changes of the biological make-up of these peoples, hypotheses that could be invented only for the purpose of sustaining an unproved assumption.

A safer mode of approaching the problems at issue would seem to lie in the application of experimental psychology which might enable us to determine the psychophysical and also some of the mental characteristics of various races. As in the case of biological inquiry it would be equally necessary in this study to examine genotypical lines rather than populations, because so many different lines are contained in the mass.

A serious difficulty is presented by the dependence of the results of all psychophysical or mental tests upon the experiences of the individual who is the subject of the tests. His experiences are largely determined by the culture in which he lives. I am of the opinion that no method can be devised by which this all-important element is eliminated, but that we always obtain a result which is a mixed impression of culturally determined influences and of bodily build. For this reason I quite agree with those critical psychologists who acknowledge that for most mental phenomena we know only European psychology and no other.

In the few cases in which the influence of culture upon mental reaction of populations has been investigated it can be shown that culture is a much more important determinant than bodily build. I repeat that in individuals a somewhat close relation between mental reaction and bodily build may be found, which is all but absent in populations. Under these circumstances it is necessary to base the investigation of the mental life of man upon a study of the history of cultural forms and of the interrelations between individual mental life and culture.

This is the subject-matter of cultural anthropology. It is safe to say that the results of the extensive materials amassed during the last fifty years do not justify the assumption of any close relation between biological types and form of culture.

As in the realm of biology our inferences must be based on historical data, so it is in the investigation of cultures. Unless we know how the culture of each group of man came to be what it is, we cannot expect to reach any conclusions in regard to the conditions controlling the general history of culture.

The material needed for the reconstruction of the biological history of mankind is insufficient on account of the paucity of remains and the disappearance of all soft, perishable parts. The material for the reconstruction of culture is ever so much more fragmentary because the largest and most important aspects of culture leave no trace in the soil; language, social organization, religion—in short, everything that is not material—vanishes with the life of each generation. Historical information is available only for the most recent phases of cultural life and is confined to those peoples who had the art of writing and whose records we can read. Even this information is insufficient because many aspects of culture find no expression in literature. Is it then necessary to resign ourselves and to consider the problem as insoluble?

In biology we supplement the fragmentary paleontological record with data obtained from comparative anatomy and embryology. Perhaps an analogous procedure may enable us to unravel some of the threads of cultural history.

There is one fundamental difference between biological and cultural data which makes it impossible to transfer the methods of the one science to the other. Animal forms develop in divergent directions, and an intermingling of species that have once become distinct is negligible in the whole developmental history. It is otherwise in the domain of culture. Human thoughts, institutions, activities may spread from one social unit to another. As soon as two groups come into close contact their cultural traits will be disseminated from the one to the other.

Undoubtedly there are dynamic conditions that mould in similar forms certain aspects of the morphology of social units. Still we may expect that these will be overlaid by extraneous elements that have no organic relation to the dynamics of inner change.

This makes the reconstruction of cultural history easier than that of biological history, but it puts the most serious obstacles in the way of discovering the inner dynamic conditions of change. Before morphological comparison can be attempted the extraneous elements due to cultural diffusion must be eliminated.

When certain traits are diffused over a limited area and absent outside of it, it seems safe to assume that their distribution is due to diffusion. In some rare cases even the direction of diffusion may be determined. If Indian corn is derived from a Mexican wild form and is cultivated over the larger part of the two Americas we must conclude that its cultivation spread from Mexico north and south; if the ancestors of African cattle are not found in Africa, they must have been introduced into that continent. In the majority of cases it is impossible to determine with certainty the direction of diffusion. It would be an error to assume that a cultural trait had its original home in the area in which it is now most strongly developed. Christianity did not originate in Europe or America. The manufacture of iron did not originate in America or northern Europe. It was the same in early times. We may be certain that the use of milk did not originate in Africa, nor the cultivation of wheat in Europe.

For these reasons it is well-nigh impossible to base a chronology of the development of specific cultures on the observed phenomena of diffusion. In a few cases it seems justifiable to infer from

the worldwide diffusion of a particular cultural achievement its great antiquity. This is true when we can prove by archeological evidence its early occurrence. Thus, fire was used by man in early Quaternary times. At that period man was already widely scattered over the world and we may infer that either the use of fire was carried along by him when he migrated to new regions or that it spread rapidly from tribe to tribe and soon became the property of mankind. This method cannot be generalized, for we know of other inventions of ideas that spread with incredible rapidity over vast areas. An example is the spread of tobacco over Africa, as soon as it was introduced on the coast.

In smaller areas attempts at chronological reconstruction are much more uncertain. From a cultural center in which complex forms have developed, elements may radiate and impress themselves upon neighboring tribes, or the more complex forms may develop on an old, less differentiated basis. It is seldom possible to decide which one of these alternatives offers the correct interpretation.

Notwithstanding all these difficulties, the study of geographical distribution of cultural phenomena offers a means of determining their diffusion. The outstanding result of these studies has been the proof of the intricate interrelation of people of all parts of the world. Africa, Europe and the greater part of Asia appear to us as a cultural unit in which one area cannot be entirely separated from the rest. America appears as another unit, but even the New World and the Old are not entirely independent of each other, for lines of contact have been discovered that connect northeastern Asia and America.

As in biological investigations the problem of parallel independent development of homologous forms obscures that of genetic relationship, so it is in cultural inquiry. If it is possible that analogous anatomical forms develop independently in genetically distinct lines, it is ever so much more probable that analogous cultural forms develop independently. It may be admitted that it is exceedingly difficult to give absolutely indisputable proof of the independent origin of analogous cultural data. Nevertheless, the distribution of isolated customs in regions far apart hardly admits of the argument that they were transmitted from tribe to tribe and lost in intervening territory. It is well known that in our civilization current scientific ideas give rise to independent and synchronous inventions. In an analogous way primitive social life contains elements that lead to somewhat similar forms in many parts of the world. Thus the dependence of the infant upon the mother necessitates at least a temporary difference in the mode of life of the sexes and makes woman less movable than man. The long dependence of children on their elders leaves also an inevitable impress upon social form. Just what these effects will be depends upon circumstances. Their fundamental cause will be the same in every case.

The number of individuals in a social unit, the necessity or undesirability of communal action for obtaining the necessary food supply constitute dynamic conditions that are active everywhere and that are germs from which analogous cultural behavior may spring.

Besides these, there are individual cases of inventions or ideas in lands far apart that cannot be proved to be historically connected. The fork was used in Fiji and invented comparatively recently in Europe; the spear, projected by a thong wound spirally about the shaft, was used on the Admiralty Islands and in ancient Rome. In some cases the difference in time makes the theory of a transfer all but unthinkable. This is the case, for instance, with the domestication of mammals in Peru, the invention of bronze in Peru and Yucatan and that of the zero in Yucatan.

Some anthropologists assume that, if a number of cultural phenomena agree in regions far apart, these must be due to the presence of an exceedingly ancient substratum that has been preserved notwithstanding all the cultural changes that have occurred. This view is not admissible without proof that the phenomena in question remain stable not only for thousands of years, but even so far back that they have been carried by wandering hordes from Asia to the extreme southern end of South America. Notwithstanding the great tenacity of cultural traits, there is no proof that such extreme conservatism ever existed. The apparent stability of primitive types of culture is due to our lack of historical perspective. They change much more slowly than our modern civilization, but wherever archeological evidence is available we do find changes in time and space. A careful investigation shows that those features that are assumed as almost absolutely stable are constantly undergoing changes. Some details may remain for a long time, but the general complex of culture cannot be assumed to retain its character for a very long span of time. We see people who were agricultural become hunters, others change their mode of life in the opposite direction. People who had totemic organization give it up, while others take it over from their neighbors.

It is not a safe method to assume that all analogous cultural phenomena must be historically related. It is necessary to demand in every case proof of historical relation, which should be the more rigid the less evidence there is of actual recent or early contact.

In the attempt to reconstruct the history of modern races we are trying to discover the earlier forms preceding modern forms. An analogous attempt has been demanded of cultural history. To a limited extent it has succeeded. The history of inventions and the history of science show to us in course of time constant additions to the range of inventions, and a gradual increase of empirical knowledge. On this basis we might be inclined to look for a single line of development of culture, a thought that was pre-eminent in anthropological work of the end of the past century.

The fuller knowledge of to-day makes such a view untenable. Cultures differ like so many species, perhaps genera, of animals, and their common basis is lost forever. It seems impossible, if we disregard invention and knowledge, the two elements just referred to, to bring cultures into any kind of continuous series. Sometimes we find simple, sometimes complex, social organizations associated with crude inventions and knowledge. Moral behavior, except in so far as it is checked by increased understanding of social needs, does not seem to fall into any order.

It is evident that certain social conditions are incompatible. A hunting people, in which every family requires an extended territory to insure the needed food supply, cannot form large communities, although it may have intricate rules governing marriage. Life that requires constant moving about on foot is incompatible with the development of a large amount of personal property. Seasonal food supply requires a mode of life different from a regular, uninterrupted food supply.

The interdependence of cultural phenomena must be one of the objects of anthropological inquiry, for which material may be obtained through the study of existing societies.

Here we are compelled to consider culture as a whole, in all its manifestations, while in the study of diffusion and of parallel development the character and distribution of single traits are more commonly the objects of inquiry. Inventions, economic life, social structure, art, religion, morals are all interrelated. We ask in how far are they determined by environment, by the biological character of the people, by psychological conditions, by historical events or by general laws of interrelation.

It is obvious that we are dealing here with a different problem. This is most clearly seen in our use of language. Even the fullest knowledge of the history of language does not help us to understand how we use language and what influence language has upon our thought. It is the same in other phases of life. The dynamic reactions to cultural environment are not determined by its history, although they are a result of historical development. Historical data do give us certain clues that may not be found in the experience of a single generation. Still, the psychological problem must be studied in living societies.

It would be an error to claim, as some anthropologists do, that for this reason historical study is irrelevant. The two sides of our problem require equal attention, for we desire to know not only the dynamics of existing societies, but also how they came to be what they are. For an intelligent understanding of historical processes a knowledge of living processes is as necessary as the knowledge of life processes for the understanding of the evolution of life forms.

The dynamics of existing societies are one of the most hotly contested fields of anthropological theory. They may be looked at from two points of view, the one, the interrelations between various aspects of cultural form and between culture and natural environment; the other the interrelation between individual and society.

Biologists are liable to insist on a relation between bodily build and culture. We have seen that evidence for such an interrelation has never been established by proofs that will stand serious criticism. It may not be amiss to dwell here again on the difference between races and individuals. The hereditary make-up of an individual has a certain influence upon his mental behavior. Pathological cases are the clearest proof of this. On the other hand, every race contains so many individuals of different hereditary make-up that the average differences between races freed of elements determined by history cannot readily be ascertained, but appear as insignificant. It is more than doubtful whether differences free of these historic elements can ever be established.

Geographers try to derive all forms of human culture from the geographical environment in which man lives. Important though this may be, we have no evidence of a creative force of environment. All we know is that every culture is strongly influenced by its environment, that some elements of culture cannot develop in an unfavorable geographical setting, while others may be advanced. It is sufficient to see the fundamental differences of culture that thrive one after another in the same environment, to make us understand the limitations of environmental influences. The aborigines of Australia live in the same environment in which the White invaders live. The nature and location of Australia have remained the same during human history, but they have influenced different cultures. Environment can affect only an existing culture, and it is worth while to study its influence in detail. This has been clearly recognized by critical geographers, such as Hettner.

Economists believe that economic conditions control cultural forms. Economic determinism is proposed as against geographic determinism. Undoubtedly the interrelation between economics and other aspects of culture is much more immediate than that between geographical environment and culture. Still it is not possible to explain every feature of cultural life as determined by economic status. We do not see how art styles, the form of ritual or the special form of religious belief could possibly be derived from economic forces. On the contrary, we see that economics and the rest of culture interact as cause and effect, as effect and cause.

Every attempt to deduce cultural forms from a single cause is doomed to failure, for the various expressions of culture are closely interrelated and one cannot be altered without having an effect upon all the others. Culture is integrated. It is true that the degree of integration is not always the same. There are cultures which we might describe by a single term, that of modern democracies as individualistic-mechanical; or that of a Melanesian island as individualization by mutual distrust; or that of our Plains Indians as overvaluation of intertribal warfare. Such terms may be misleading, because they overemphasize certain features, still they indicate certain dominating attitudes.

Integration is not often so complete that all contradictory elements are eliminated. We rather find in the same culture curious breaks in the attitudes of different individuals, and, in the case of varying situations, even in the behavior of the same individual.

The lack of necessary correlations between various aspects of culture may be illustrated by the cultural significance of a truly scientific study of the heavenly bodies by the Babylonians, Maya and by Europeans during the Middle Ages. For us the necessary correlation of astronomical observations is with physical and chemical phenomena; for them the essential point was their astrological significance, i.e., their relation to the fate of man, an attitude based on the general historically conditioned culture of their times.

These brief remarks may be sufficient to indicate the complexity of the phenomena we are studying, and it seems justifiable to question whether any generalized conclusions may be expected that will be applicable everywhere and that will reduce the data of anthropology to a formula which may be applied to every case, explaining its past and predicting its future.

I believe that it would be idle to entertain such hopes. The phenomena of our science are so individualized, so exposed to outer accident that no set of laws could explain them. It is as in any other science dealing with the actual world surrounding us. For each individual case we can arrive at an understanding of its determination by inner and outer forces, but we cannot explain its individuality in the form of laws. The astronomer reduces the movement of stars to laws, but unless given an unexplainable original arrangement in space, he cannot account for their present location. The biologist may know all the laws of ontogenesis, but he cannot explain by their means the accidental forms they have taken in an individual species, much less those found in an individual.

Physical and biological laws differ in character on account of the complexity of the objects of their study. Biological laws can refer only to biological forms, as geological laws can refer only to the forms of geological formations. The more complex the phenomena, the more special will be the laws expressed by them.

Cultural phenomena are of such complexity that it seems to me doubtful whether valid cultural laws can be found. The causal conditions of cultural happenings lie always in the interaction between individual and society, and no classificatory study of societies will solve this problem. The morphological classification of societies may call to our attention many problems. It will not solve them. In every case it is reducible to the same source, namely, the interaction between individual and society.

It is true that some valid interrelations between general aspects of cultural life may be found, such as between density and size of the population constituting a community and industrial occupations; or solidarity and isolation of a small population and their conservatism. These are interesting as static descriptions of cultural facts. Dynamic processes also may be recognized, such as the tendency of customs to change their significance according to changes in culture. Their meaning can be understood only by a penetrating analysis of the human elements that enter into each case.

In short, the material of anthropology is such that it needs must be a historical science, one of the sciences the interest of which centers in the attempt to understand the individual phenomena rather than in the establishment of general laws which, on account of the complexity of the material, will be necessarily vague and, we might almost

say, so self-evident that they are of little help to a real understanding.

The attempt has been made too often to formulate a genetic problem as defined by a term taken from our own civilization, either based on analogy with forms known to us or contrasted to those with which we are familiar. Thus concepts, like war, the idea of immortality, marriage regulations, have been considered as units and general conclusions have been derived from their forms and distributions. It should be recognized that the subordination of all such forms, under a category with which we are familiar on account of our own cultural experience, does not prove the historical or sociological unity of the phenomenon. The ideas of immortality differ so fundamentally in content and significance that they can hardly be treated as a unit and valid conclusions based on their occurrence cannot be drawn without detailed analysis.

A critical investigation rather shows that forms of thought and action which we are inclined to consider as based on human nature are not generally valid, but characteristic of our specific culture. If this were not so, we could not understand why certain aspects of mental life that are characteristic of the Old World should be entirely or almost entirely absent in aboriginal America. An example is the contrast between the fundamental idea of judicial procedure in Africa and America; the emphasis on oath and ordeal as parts of judicial procedure in the Old World, their absence in the New World.

The problems of the relation of the individual to his culture, to the society in which he lives have received too little attention. The standardized anthropological data that inform us of customary behavior, give no clue to the reaction of the individual to his culture, not to an understanding of his influence upon it. Still, here lie the sources of a true interpretation of human behavior. It seems a vain effort to search for sociological laws disregarding what should be called social psychology, namely, the reaction of the individual to culture. They can be no more than empty formulas that can be imbued with life only by taking account of individual behavior in cultural settings.

Society embraces many individuals varying in mental character, partly on account of their biological make-up, partly due to the special social conditions under which they have grown up. Nevertheless, many of them react in similar ways, and there are numerous cases in which we can find a definite impress of culture upon the behavior of the great mass of individuals, expressed by the same mentality. Deviations from such a type result in abnormal social behavior and, although throwing light upon the iron hold of culture upon the average individual, are rather subject-matter for the study of individual psychology than of social psychology.

If we once grasp the meaning of foreign cultures in this manner, we shall also be able to see how many of our lines of behavior that we believe to be founded deep in human nature are actually expressions of our culture and subject to modification with changing culture. Not all our standards are categorically determined by our quality as human beings, but may change with changing circumstances. It is our task to discover among all the varieties of human behavior those that are common to all humanity. By a study of the universality and variety of cultures anthropology may help us to shape the future course of mankind.

3. On Culture

BY ALFRED L. KROEBER

PRIMARY, it seems to me, is the recognition of culture as a "level" or "order" or "emergent" of natural phenomena, a level marked by a certain distinctive organization of its characteristic phenomena. The emergence of phenomena of life from previous inorganic existence is the presumably earliest and most basic segregation of an order or level. Such emergence does not mean that physical and chemical processes are abrogated but that new organizations occur on the new level: organic manifestations, which need study in their own right or biologically, as well as physicochemically, because they possess a certain, though not an absolute, autonomy. For instance, phenomena of reproduction are intelligible, only on the organic level, in organic terms. Since Lloyd Morgan, many biologists have argued for this partial autonomy of the organic. A superorganic or superindividual social level was asserted, adumbrated, or implied by Spencer, Tarde, and Durkheim. Recognition of a supra-societal level of culture goes back to Spencer, who spoke of the immensely powerful accumulation of superorganic products commonly called "artificial" which constitute a secondary environment more important than the primary one; though in practice Spencer operated rather scantily on this level. Anthropologists have, on the whole, dealt more outrightly with cultural phenomena than any other group of scientists or scholars but have tended to concern themselves with its manifestations while taking it for granted. Tylor defined culture, Boas estimated very justly many of its properties and influences, but the thesis of a distinctive cultural level interested neither of them. Indeed, it has largely been left to myself and then to Leslie White to propound it explicitly.

The risk in a high degree of consciousness of a separate order is that of going on to reify its organization and phenomena into an autonomous sort of substance with its own inner forces—life, mind, society, or culture. I have probably at times in the past skirted such lapsing and have at any rate been charged with mysticism. However, mysticism is by no means a necessary ingredient of level recognition. The value of the recognition is largely methodological. It is only by a *de facto* cultural approach to cultural phenomena that some of their most fundamental properties can be ascertained. How far such a "pure" approach can be pursued without explicit consciousness of it probably varies according to personal factors. However, if one is going to be broadly theoretical or philosophic about culture, it seems to me that its acceptance as a distinctive order of phenomena in nature cannot be evaded.

In second place I would put the related principle that it is of the nature of culture to be heavily conditioned by its own cumulative past, so that the most fruitful approach to its understanding is a historical one. I recognize the distinction of nomothetic and idiographic method, but not as an absolute dichotomy between science as investigation of nature and history as the study of man or spirit or culture. Both approaches, I hold, contrariwise, can be applied to any level of phenomena—as the simple example of historical sciences like astronomy and geology shows—and should ultimately be applied. But on the basic inorganic level it is the mathematically formulable, experimentally verifiable, analytic approach that is most immediately rewarding. On the upper levels, especially on the uppermost one of culture, it is the qualitative and the contextual associations of phenomena that are important, and isolation of specific causal factors tends to be both difficult and, so far as we can see, of less significance. After all, the history of a particular civilization has obvious meaning; the history of a particular stone on the beach, or even of a particular volcano as such, has very little meaning as history. The significance of pebbles or volcanoes is as examples of processes that form or produce them. A "physics" or "physiology" of culture would be desirable enough and may ultimately and gradually be attainable. But to transfer the method of the physicochemical sciences of the inorganic to culture would be a fallacy. By eliminating the history of a cultural situation, we cut off its largest component or dimension.

The essential quality of the historical approach as a method of science I see as its integration of phenomena into an ever widening phenomenal context, with as much preservation as possible—instead of analytic resolution—of the qualitative organization of the phenomena dealt with. The context includes the placing in space and time and therefore, when knowledge allows, in sequence. But I see narrative as incidental rather than as essential to the method of history in the wider sense. Recognition of quality and of organizing pattern seems much more important. This is unorthodox but appears to me to be cardinal.

All history, whether political or stellar, reconstructs. The reconstruction is part of the characteristic process of integration into context. Linguists, who operate with sharper intellectual tools than most of us, have always felt free to reconstruct. Organic evolutionists reconstruct and interpolate; their findings would otherwise be but sorry tatters. Similarly, the history of human culture is being reconstructed—in part by archaeological exploration, in part by recognition of cultural forms and patterns, in part by growing understanding of cultural process. Developed further, this last can grow into a nomothetic or processual analytic "science" of culture complementary to its "history" as just defined.

Patterns or configurations or Gestalts are what it seems most profitable and productive to distinguish and formulate in culture. On this point I stand with Ruth Benedict, although I differ from her in practice at several points. I agree with her that the formulation of whole-culture patterns of quality is desirable and worth while. I agree also that one kind of whole-culture characterization is in psychological terms of temperament or ethos; but this should not abrogate or displace formulations in cultural terms.

I also hold that her proceeding from whole-cultural characterizations to consideration of the effects of cultures on their members as regards conformity and deviancy passes on to a separate set of problems which have returned largely to a subcultural level. Finally, I advocate going on from Benedict's essentially static and nonhistorical conception of cultures to considerations of both stylistic and whole-culture flow, as in the historic "configurations" or profiles of movement which I have tried to define for certain cultural activities. These remarks are made less in stricture of Benedict than by way of ready definition. I recognize my affinity to her.

That values constitute an essential ingredient of culture is coming to be increasingly accepted. That they are subjectively held is nothing to prevent their being objectively described, examined for their interassociations, and compared. After all, ideologies and religious beliefs are subjective too. What probably brought it about that values were shied off from so long in culture studies is their affective side. A myth or a dogma can be stated in coherent form, where a value is often a quality of suffusion of something else. Nevertheless, values are too integral in culture to be left out of consideration.

The principle of cultural relativism has long been standard anthropological doctrine. It holds that any cultural phenomenon must be understood and evaluated in terms of the culture of which it forms part. The corresponding assumption in the organic field is so obvious that biologists have scarcely troubled to formulate it. The difference is that we, the students of culture, live in our culture, are attached to its values, and have a natural human inclination to become ethnocentric over it, with the result that, if unchecked, we would perceive, describe, and evaluate other cultures by the forms, standards, and values of our own, thus preventing fruitful comparison and classification. Realization of relativism can be shocking to the tender-minded, through taking away the affective security which seeming absolutes render. Basically, of course, relativism is no more than desire for inquiry coupled with readiness to undergo unrestricted comparison.

Beyond this, there is a real and profounder problem: that of fixed, pan-human, if not absolute, values. This problem is only beginning to come to the consciousness of anthropologists, who have perhaps done most to stress the relativistic principle. It is touched only by implication in the present book. My conviction is that value-judgments as between the values of different cultures are possible, though not by any majority poll or with absolute finality, and probably with a pluralistic outcome. It is not to be expected that any one culture will differ from all other imperfect ones in having developed perfect values. The important requisite in this problem of transcending values would seem, paradoxically, to be prolonged and increasingly deep comparison of value-systems—in other words, of cultures. The more prematurely this balancing comparison is abandoned in favor of a choice between value-systems, the shallower will such choice be, the greater the risk of a naïve return to ethnocentrism in the guise of a determination of more-than-relative values.

The recurrent insistence on comparison in the foregoing paragraphs may have been noted and may recall "the comparative method" of nineteenth-century anthropologists. The difference is that these earlier students too often disregarded and violated the natural, actual context of the phenomena they compared, in their ardor of developing logical but speculative constructs which they considered evolutionary. The comparison here advocated respects both the structural and the historical context of the cultural phenomena dealt with, in much the way that truly evolutionary biologists respect context structurally and historically in their organic phenomena.

Culture-wholes present a series of problems: as to their distinctness or continuity, for instance; as to their degree of internal consistency or integration and its nature; and as to what makes for such discontinuities and integrations as they possess. Anthropologists have acquired considerable skill in presenting culture-wholes of tribal size as discrete units—also in tracing the passage of material and forms between cultures; but they have concerned themselves little with the problems of outward segregation and inner consistency, especially of large civilizations. Interest among other students, while occasionally vivid, has been spottily rare and diverse. I am convinced that this somewhat special set of problems forms part of those on the general nature of culture.

Any theory that specializes on culture must of course recognize that, in the case of man, society and culture always co-occur, so that the phenomena available necessarily have both a social and a cultural aspect. Since societies comprise individuals and especially since individuals are heavily shaped by their culture, there is also a third aspect or factor immediately involved in the phenomena, that of psychology or personality—apart from more remote considerations, such as the biological nature of people and the subhuman environment in which they operate. It is of course possible to try to study the cultural, social, and psychological aspects simultaneously and interwoven, as they occur. Such a meshed understanding is obviously the broadest and is therefore desirable in principle. However, it is

also much the most difficult to attain, because more variable factors are involved. Also it is plain that the most valid and fruitful synthesis, other things being equal, must be the one which is based on the most acute preceding analysis. Such analysis is going to be more effective if directed at an isolable set of factors than at several interacting ones. Premature and short-circuiting synthesizing is thus avoided by discrimination between the aspects or levels that come associated in phenomena, and by unraveling, out of the snarl with which actuality presents us, the factors of one level at a time and seeing how far they can be traced as such, before retying them into a web of larger understanding with the other strands.

The level which I have personally chosen or become addicted to is the cultural one. This is not the only way of proceeding, but it is my way, and it seems the most consistent with an integrative-contextual or "historical" approach. It is hard to judge one's self, but I do seem more consciously and single-heartedly to separate out the purely cultural aspects and individual factors, than, for instance, my American colleagues Boas, Lowie, Radin, Linton, Spier, Redfield, or Murdock, and certainly more than Hallowell or Kluckhohn or Mead, or than British anthropologists such as Evans-Pritchard, Firth, Forde, or Nadel. This is a limitation, but it also results in certain gains. Thus the kind of general problems I treated in *Configurations of Cultural Growth* could hardly have been even defined except in terms of assuming races and individuals to be uniform in mass effect. Thereafter, it was possible to explore more clearly the "movements" and "behavior" of the civilizational phenomena treated. The questions of how the civilizations of Asia and Europe have been interdependent in their development and to what degree the cultures of native America are derivative from those of Eurasia are particular problems of historical fact and are not in themselves general or theoretical. But they are certainly broad problems which may have import on theory. And it is plain that they can be settled only on cultural and environmental evidence, since individual psychological considerations are evidently so remote as to be practically irrelevant, and so are "social" phenomena except for their cultural facies.

It is because of this bent or warp that I came to realize the significance of the simultaneity of many inventions and discoveries. In the historical process of cultural development, an invention is a single act or event and, within a given situation, likely to be more or less inevitable. It is only from the point of view of the several individuals involved that simultaneity and co-occurrence exist. The distinction is simple enough, once the concept of culture has been grasped. It was long in being made because of the conventional historical habit of treating general sociocultural factors and individual personal factors on the single amalgamated or undifferentiated level on which the phenomena of history are ordinarily received, perceived, and dealt with.

Similarly, the clustering of great minds, which has been recognized as a fact for two thousand years, though as a wanton one, takes on a meaning in terms of culture. Genius is seen as a product which is a function of cultural growth. This growth, in developing a style-like pattern, evokes or releases the required innate individual talents or creative abilities which presumably are always potentially present in larger quantity than utilized. As the pattern is realized, a culmination is attained; with its exhaustion, decline sets in, until a new pattern is evolved. With this culture-level approach, we have at least made a beginning of understanding how civilizations come to be and develop, instead of merely taking them for granted as miracles or accidents or deriving them from impossibly remote causes like physical environment.

The phenomena of fashion, again, seem wholly random until approached from the angle of superpersonal—impersonal, one might almost say—style patterns of culture. Stimulus diffusion is a concept for probing certain intercultural similarities whose historic connection is tenuous or lost. One or more individuals necessarily enter each situation, but only as a cog in the mechanism of intercultural transfer, stimulus, and creativity.

It is true that, in the study of culture by deliberate suppression of individuals as individuals, the element of human behavior is also eliminated. One investigates, provisionally, the interrelation of collective and patterned products of the behavior of personalities, with these personalities and their behavior no longer taken into account. For myself, I have carried out this methodological suppression without qualms. Having begun with an interest in the forms of culture, I remained interested in the continued development of ways of analyzing the relations of these forms. The injection into anthropology of the concept of behavior, first developed as a corrective in the internal emancipation or purification of psychology, sprang from quite different motives and touched me little or belatedly. Writers of history, it is true, have always dealt with behavior in treating of individuals and events, just as they have implicitly dealt with culture in recognizing institutions. But, as has already been said, historians thrive on eating and digesting their phenomena raw. Those who want culture as such have to smelt it out of an ore.

The cultural view is not only collective, it is also almost inevitably long-range, because the dimension of time adds so much, imparting to the phenomena the quality of dynamism or flow or growth. This is why archaeology has so wide and persistent an appeal. The element of antiquity in its discoveries directly stimulates the imagination with overtones of elapsement and change; and, before long, historic problems formulate themselves. As these are prosecuted, individuals necessarily recede from sight, and even their collective behavior, no longer observable, becomes only remotely inferable. Time and decay have strained out, from what was once lived by human beings, almost everything but the cultural forms that archaeology restores. From the angle of culture, archaeological data come ready to hand as the purest there are, with language probably second. In archaeology facts are certainly less mixed, not only than in history, but than in ethnography.

With long range, the individual, even the outstanding one, necessarily fades from view, just as, even in synchronous collocation of nations, he begins to shrink. It is only now and then that an Alexander, Jenghiz Khan, Napoleon, or Hitler stands out as a landmark in the collective submergence. With this recognition, a deterministic view tends to creep in. Before long, one finds himself a determinist, like Tolstoy. I was consciously so, for decades. I am less sure now. When one has acquired the habit of viewing the millennial sweeps and grand contours, and individuals have shrunk to insignificance, it is very easy to deny them consequential influence, even any influence—and therewith one stands in the gateway of belief in undefined immanent forces; a step more, and the forces have become mysterious. But from close by, at the moment, it is the individuals that loom as active; and no viewing them as blind controlled pawns, still less as wound-up clockworks, really helps to understand their activities. Actually, of course, the question of free or determined will is a metaphysical, theological, ethical, or practical one. It has apparently no scientific answer and is therefore not a scientific question. After all, I might have realized this long ago instead of in 1948. My own theory of "deterministic" pattern realization and exhaustion contains a concealed factor of striving and will, in the individuals through whom the realization is achieved. A creative urge and spark must be accorded them, and potentialities of the same to all men, no matter how much the concept of creativity has in the past been abused and vulgarized, and may at the outset set on edge the teeth of scholar and scientist. A good modern definition of "creativity," probably in terms of cultural values relativistically and precisely conceived, and at any rate with all "spirituality" wholly excluded, is a genuine desideratum.

For that matter, my old comparison of culture to a coral reef should have warned me against too facile a determinism. To the geologist, as to the mariner, the reef is a massive, ancient accumulation of secretions, a great product and influence in its own right. But it concerns the zoölogist as a collection of living polyps, resting on reef but making more reef through their physiologies. The free will of a polyp may be minute and his individuation somewhat limited, but his activity is definite.

This brings us to the troublesome question of causes in culture. My opinions have varied on this matter; and I am still not too sure precisely where I stand. About 1917, I thought I stood at the threshold of glimpsing vague, grand forces of pre-destination, not so different perhaps from the "fate" that Spengler was soon to proclaim. Thirty years later, I was not so sure that cause could be found, or was worth looking for, in cultural situations. On some points I seem to have had strong intuitions early, almost as a boy; such as that all search for "origins" is vain, and that alleged simple, specific causes for cultural and historical phenomena, whether particular or general, were almost certain to be false. I am still sure of these two things. Also I am convinced that, on the cultural level and in any "historic" approach as defined above, recognition of pattern is the suitable and fruitful aim of nearer understanding. Causation should not be denied because it is hard to determine; but to put its isolation into the forefront of endeavor, as if we were operating in old-fashioned mechanics, is naïve. Spengler, with all his dogmatism and maniac exaggeration, was not wholly wide of the mark when he rejected nineteenth-century causality for culture and its history. And his "destiny," if deflated of its absolutism and quality of tragic doom —it is already externally nonteleological—shrivels to something not too different from the larger patterning of culture-wholes.

One other thing is clear. Much more of the culture native to any given group is the product not of that living population but of its preceding generations. Likewise, the majority of the content of any culture has normally been developed by other groups and introduced and accepted. These facts do not seriously matter when attention is focused on momentary or short-term changes, on social interrelations within the group, or on personality developments, because in such considerations old and recent components of the culture tend to function and to be reacted to alike. In any diachronic approach, however, or in any broadly comparative or contextual one, age does enter into consideration, and the majority of the impinging causality is therefore somewhat like an iceberg—below the surface of the present. With ancient and recent, outside and internal, factors all at work and of an indefinitely great variety of ages and proveniences, it is easy to see why the causality of cultures, viewed historically, should be both intricate and diffuse.

Finally, while culture is essentially limited to man and is the only order of phenomena so limited, it is as much a part of nature as any other phenomenal order or level, and, in spite of its highly special properties, it must always be construed as within nature. Moreover, being distinctive of man to a greater degree than the society and mind which man shares with other animals, culture is that aspect of him which almost surely will be most significant of the determination and understanding of man's place in nature as that place and relation gradually become worked out more clearly. Anthropology is recognized and admitted as a natural science not so much because it includes that human branch of biology called "physical" or "racial anthropology" but really rather because of its very nonbiological, extra-somatic portion concerned with culture. This cultural segment of the science of man is the larger, is much the more distinctive, and is dominant, and therefore calls urgently for more avowed treatment as part of nature. As a mere animal, cultureless man was one of many, and not of the strongest; with culture, he began, and has continued increasingly, to dominate life on the planet and to control its future. Therewith the evolutionary lead has clearly passed from the organic order to the cultural order. It seems more than questionable whether any wholly genetically based new forms of life can ever overcome the competitive head-start already conferred on us by our culture. All this is part of a natural process and must increasingly be seen in the context of nature.

On the other side, much of culture, especially its history, its values, and its indispensable symbolic mechanism of speech, have long been studied, even though often anthropocentrically, by the scholars in the humanities. This body of intensive, organized knowledge is not only lying available; it is waiting to be absorbed into the naturocentric context of natural science. The obvious bridge to that absorption is acceptance of the concept of culture.

4. On the Mores

BY WILLIAM GRAHAM SUMNER

Difference between Mores and Some Cognate Things.—Products of intentional investigation or of rational and conscious reflection, projects formally adopted by voluntary associations, rational methods consciously selected, injunctions and prohibitions by authority, and all specific conventional arrangements are not in the mores. They are differentiated by the rational and conscious element in them. We may also make a distinction between usages and mores. Usages are folkways which contain no principle of welfare, but serve convenience so long as all know what they are expected to do. For instance, Orientals, to show respect, cover the head and uncover the feet; Occidentals do the opposite. There is no inherent and necessary connection between respect and either usage, but it is an advantage that there should be a usage and that all should know and observe it. One way is as good as another, if it is understood and established. The folkways as to public decency belong to the mores, because they have real connection with welfare which determines the only tenor which they can have. The folkways about propriety and modesty are sometimes purely conventional and sometimes inherently real. Fashions, fads, affectations, poses, ideals, manias, popular delusions, follies, and vices must be included in the mores. They have characteral qualities and characteral effect. However frivolous or foolish they may appear to people of another age, they have the form of attempts to live well, to satisfy some interest, or to win some good. The ways of advertisers who exaggerate, use tricks to win attention, and appeal to popular weakness and folly; the ways of journalism; electioneering devices; oratorical and dithyrambic extravagances in politics; current methods of humbug and sensationalism—are not properly part of the mores but symptoms of them. They are not products of the concurrent and coöperative effort of all members of the society to live well. They are devices made with conscious ingenuity to exert suggestion on the minds of others. The mores are rather the underlying facts in regard to the faiths, notions, tastes, desires, etc., of that society at that time, to which

Reprinted from William Graham Sumner, *Folkways* (Boston: Ginn & Co., 1906), §§ 64, 67, 68, 80, 82–84, 88, 91–93, 97–100, 102–3, 105, 112, 114, 117–21, with the permission of Ginn & Co.

all these modes of action appeal and of whose existence they are evidence.

*   *   *

Ritual.—The process by which mores are developed and established is ritual. Ritual is so foreign to our mores that we do not recognize its power. In primitive society it is the prevailing method of activity, and primitive religion is entirely a matter of ritual. Ritual is the perfect form of drill and of the regulated habit which comes from drill. Acts which are ordained by authority and are repeated mechanically without intelligence run into ritual. If infants and children are subjected to ritual they never escape from its effects through life. Galton says that he was, in early youth, in contact with the Mohammedan ritual idea that the left hand is less worthy than the right, and that he never overcame it.

*   *   *

The Ritual of the Mores.—The mores are social ritual in which we all participate unconsciously. The current habits as to hours of labor, meal hours, family life, the social intercourse of the sexes, propriety, amusements, travel, holidays, education, the use of periodicals and libraries, and innumerable other details of life fall under this ritual. Each does as everybody does. For the great mass of mankind as to all things, and for all of us for a great many things, the rule to do as all do suffices. We are led by suggestion and association to believe that there must be wisdom and utility in what all do. The great mass of the folkways give us discipline and the support of routine and habit. If we had to form judgments as to all these cases before we could act in them, and were forced always to act rationally, the burden would be unendurable. Beneficent use and wont save us this trouble.

*   *   *

The Mores Have the Authority of Facts.—The mores come down to us from the past. Each individual is born into them as he is born into the atmosphere, and he does not reflect on them, or criticise them any more than a baby analyzes the atmosphere before he begins to breathe it. Each one is subjected to the influence of the mores, and formed by them, before he is capable of reasoning about them. It may be objected that nowadays, at least, we criticise all traditions, and accept none just because they are handed down to us. If we take up cases of things which are still entirely or almost entirely in the mores. we shall see that this is not so. There are sects of free-lovers amongst us who want to discuss pair marriage. They are not simply people of evil life. They invite us to discuss rationally our inherited customs and ideas as to marriage, which, they say, are by no means so excellent and elevated as we believe. They have never won any serious attention. Some others want to argue in favor of polygamy on grounds of expediency. They fail to obtain a hearing. Others want to discuss property. In spite of some literary activity on their part, no discussion of property, bequest, and inheritance has ever been opened. Property and marriage are in the mores. Nothing can ever change them but the unconscious and imperceptible movement of the mores. Religion was originally a matter of the mores. It became a societal institution and a function of the state. It has now to a great extent been put back into the mores. Since laws with penalties to enforce religious creeds or practices have gone out of use any one may think and act as he pleases about religion. Therefore it is not now "good form" to attack religion. Infidel publications are now tabooed by the mores, and are more effectually repressed than ever before. They produce no controversy. Democracy is in our American mores. It is a product of our physical and economic conditions. It is impossible to discuss or criticise it. It is glorified for popularity, and is a subject of dithyrambic rhetoric. No one treats it with complete candor and sincerity. No one dares to analyze it as he would aristocracy or autocracy. He would get no hearing and would only incur abuse. The thing to be noticed in all these cases is that the masses oppose a deaf ear to every argument against the mores. It is only in so far as things have been transferred from the mores into laws and positive institutions that there is discussion about them or rationalizing upon them. The mores contain the norm by which, if we should discuss the mores, we should have to judge the mores. We learn the mores as unconsciously as we learn to walk and eat and breathe. The masses never learn how we walk, and eat, and breathe, and they never know any reason why the mores are what they are. The justification of them is that when we wake to consciousness of life we find them facts which already hold us in the bonds of tradition, custom, and habit. The mores contain embodied in them notions, doctrines, and maxims, but they are facts. They are in the present tense.

They have nothing to do with what ought to be, will be, may be, or once was, if it is not now.

* * *

The Mores Are Unrecorded.—A society is never conscious of its mores until it comes in contact with some other society which has different mores, or until, in higher civilization, it gets information by literature. The latter operation, however, affects only the literary classes, not the masses, and society never consciously sets about the task of making mores. In the early stages mores are elastic and plastic; later they become rigid and fixed. They seem to grow up, gain strength, become corrupt, decline, and die, as if they were organisms. The phases seem to follow each other by an inherent necessity, and as if independent of the reason and will of the men affected, but the changes are always produced by a strain towards better adjustment of the mores to conditions and interests of the society, or of the controlling elements in it. A society does not record its mores in its annals, because they are to it unnoticed and unconscious. When we try to learn the mores of any age or people we have to seek our information in incidental references, allusions, observations of travelers, etc. Generally works of fiction, drama, etc., give us more information about the mores than historical records. It is very difficult to construct from the Old Testament a description of the mores of the Jews before the captivity. It is also very difficult to make a complete and accurate picture of the mores of the English colonies in North America in the seventeenth century. The mores are not recorded for the same reason that meals, going to bed, sunrise, etc., are not recorded, unless the regular course of things is broken.

Inertia and Rigidity of the Mores.—We see that we must conceive of the mores as a vast system of usages, covering the whole of life, and serving all its interests; also containing in themselves their own justification by tradition and use and wont, and approved by mystic sanctions until, by rational reflection, they develop their own philosophical and ethical generalizations, which are elevated into "principles" of truth and right. They coerce and restrict the newborn generation. They do not stimulate to thought, but the contrary. The thinking is already done and is embodied in the mores. They never contain any provision for their own amendment. They are not questions, but answers, to the problem of life. They present themselves as final and unchangeable, because they present answers which are offered as "the truth." No world philosophy, until the modern scientific world philosophy, and that only within a generation or two, has ever presented itself as perhaps transitory, certainly incomplete, and liable to be set aside to-morrow by more knowledge. No popular world philsophy or life policy ever can present itself in that light. It would cost too great a mental strain. All the groups whose mores we consider far inferior to our own are quite as well satisfied with theirs as we are with ours. The goodness or badness of mores consists entirely in their adjustment to the life conditions and the interests of the time and place. Therefore it is a sign of ease and welfare when no thought is given to the mores, but all coöperate in them instinctively. The nations of southeastern Asia show us the persistency of the mores, when the element of stability and rigidity in them becomes predominant. Ghost fear and ancestor worship tend to establish the persistency of the mores by dogmatic authority, strict taboo, and weighty sanctions. The mores then lose their naturalness and vitality. They are stereotyped. They lose all relation to expediency. They become an end in themselves. They are imposed by imperative authority without regard to interests or conditions (caste, child marriage, widows). When any society falls under the dominion of this disease in the mores it must disintegrate before it can live again. In that diseased state of the mores all learning consists in committing to memory the words of the sages of the past who established the formulæ of the mores. Such words are "sacred writings," a sentence of which is a rule of conduct to be obeyed quite independently of present interests, or of any rational considerations.

Persistency.—Asiatic fixity of the mores is extreme, but the element of persistency in the mores is always characteristic of them. They are elastic and tough, but when once established in familiar and continued use they resist change. They give stability to the social order when they are well understood, regular, and undisputed. In a new colony, with a sparse population, the mores are never fixed and stringent. There is great "liberty." As the colony always has traditions of the mores of the mother country, which are cherished with respect but are never applicable to the conditions of a colony, the mores of a colony are heterogeneous and are always in flux. That is because the colonists are all the time learning to live in a new country and have no traditions to guide them, the traditions of the old country being a hindrance. Any one bred in a new country, if he goes to an old country, feels the "conservatism" in its mores. He thinks the people stiff, set in their ways, stupid, and unwilling to learn. They think him raw, brusque, and uncultivated. He does not know the ritual, which can be written in no books, but knowl-edge of which, acquired by long experience, is the mark of fit membership in the society.

* * *

Variability.—No less remarkable than the persistency of the mores is their changeableness and variation. There is here an interesting parallel to heredity and variation in the organic world, even though the parallel has no significance. Variation in the mores is due to the fact that children do not perpetuate the mores just as they received them. The father dies, and the son whom he has educated, even if he continues the ritual and repeats the formulæ, does not think and feel the same ideas and sentiments as his father. The observance of Sunday; the mode of treating parents, children, servants, and wives or husbands; holidays; amusements; arts of luxury; marriage and divorce; wine drinking,—are matters in regard to which it is easy to note changes in the mores from generation to generation, in our own times. Even in Asia, when a long period of time is taken into account, changes in the mores are perceptible. The mores change because conditions and interests change. It is found that dogmas and maxims which have been current do not verify; that established taboos are useless or mischievous restraints; that usages which are suitable for a village or a colony are not suitable for a great city or state; that many things are fitting when the community is rich which were not so when it was poor; that new inventions have made new ways of living more economical and healthful. It is necessary to prosperity that the mores should have a due degree of firmness, but also that they should be sufficiently elastic and flexible to conform to changes in interests and life conditions. A herding or an agricultural people, if it moves into a new country, rich in game, may revert to a hunting life. The Tunguses and Yakuts did so as they moved northwards. In the early days of the settlement of North America many whites "Indianized"; they took to the mode of life of Indians. The Iranians separated from the Indians of Hindostan and became agriculturists. They adopted a new religion and new mores. Men who were afraid of powerful enemies have taken to living in trees, lake dwellings, caves, and joint houses. Mediæval serfdom was due to the need of force to keep the peasant on his holding, when the holding was really a burden to him in view of the dues which he must pay. He would have run away if he had not been kept by force. In the later Middle Ages the villain had a valuable right and property in his holding. Then he wanted security of tenure so that he could not be driven away from it. In the early period it was the duty of the lord to kill the game and protect the peasant's crops. In the later period it became the monopoly right of the lord to kill game. Thus the life conditions vary. The economic conjuncture varies. The conpetition of life varies. The interests vary with them. The mores all conform, unless they have been fixed by dogma with mystic sanctions so that they are ritual obligations, as is, in general, the case now in southeastern Asia. The rights of the parties, and the right and wrong of conduct, after the mores have conformed to new life conditions, are new deductions. The philosophers follow with their systems by which they try to construe the whole new order of acts and thoughts with reference to some thought fabric which they put before the mores, although it was found out after the mores had established the relations. In the case in which the fixed mores do not conform to new interests and needs crises arise. Moses, Zoroaster, Manu, Solon, Lycurgus, and Numa are either mythical or historical culture heroes, who are said to have solved such crises by new "laws," and set the society in motion again. The fiction of the intervention of a god or a hero is necessary to account for a reconstruction of the mores of the ancestors without crime.

*   *   *

Possibility of Modifying Mores.—The combination in the mores of persistency and variability determines the extent to which it is possible to modify them by arbitrary action. It is not possible to change them, by any artifice or device, to a great extent, or suddenly, or in any essential element; it is possible to modify them by slow and long-continued effort if the ritual is changed by minute variations. The German emperor Frederick II was the most enlightened ruler of the Middle Ages. He was a modern man in temper and ideas. He was a statesman and he wanted to make the empire into a real state of the absolutist type. All the mores of his time were ecclesiastical and hierocratic. He dashed himself to pieces against them. Those whom he wanted to serve took the side of the papacy against him. He became the author of the laws by which the civil institutions of the time were made to serve ecclesiastical domination. He carried the purpose of the crusades to a higher degree of fulfillment than they ever reached otherwise, but this brought him no credit or peace. The same drift in the mores of the time bore down the Albigenses when they denounced the church corporation, the hierarchy, and the papacy. The pope easily stirred up all Europe against them. The current opinion was that every state must be a Christian state according to the mores of the time. The people could not conceive of a state which could answer its purpose if it was not such. But a "Christian state" meant

one which was in harmony with the pope and the ecclesiastical organization. This demand was not affected by the faults of the organization, or the corruption and venality of the hierarchy. The popes of the thirteenth century rode upon this tide, overwhelming opposition and consolidating their power. In our time the state is charged with the service of a great number of interests which were then intrusted to the church. It is against our mores that ecclesiastics should interfere with those interests. There is no war on religion. Religion is recognized as an interest by itself, and is treated with more universal respect than ever before, but it is regarded as occupying a field of its own, and if there should be an attempt in its name to encroach on any other domain, it would fail, because it would be against the mores of our time.

Russia.—When Napoleon said: "If you scratch a Russian you find a Tartar," what he had perceived was that, although the Russian court and the capital city have been westernized by the will of the tsars, nevertheless the people still cling to the strongly marked national mores of their ancestors. The tsars, since Peter the Great, have, by their policing and dragooning, spoilt one thing without making another, and socially Russia is in the agonies of the resulting confusion. Russia ought to be a democracy by virtue of its sparse population and wide area of unoccupied land in Siberia. In fact all the indigenous and most ancient usages of the villages are democratic. The autocracy is exotic and military. It is, however, the only institution which holds Russia together as a unit. On account of this political interest the small intelligent class acquiesce in the autocracy. The autocracy imposes force on the people to crush out their inherited mores, and to force on them western institutions. The policy is, moreover, vacillating. At one time the party which favored westernizing has prevailed at court; at another time the old Russian or pan-Slavic party. There is internal discord and repression. The ultimate result of such an attempt to control mores by force is an interesting question of the future. It also is a question which affects most seriously the interests of western civilization. The motive for the westernizing policy is to get influence in European politics. All the interference of Russia in European politics is harmful, menacing, and unjustifiable. She is not, in character, a European power, and she brings no contribution to European civilization, but the contrary. She has neither the capital nor the character to enable her to execute the share in the world's affairs which she is assuming. Her territorial extensions for two hundred years have been made at the cost of her internal strength. The latter has never been at all proportioned to the former. Consequently the debt and taxes due to her policy of expansion and territorial greatness have crushed her peasant class, and by their effect on agriculture have choked the sources of national strength. The people are peaceful and industrious, and their traditional mores are such that they would develop great productive power and in time rise to a strong civilization of a truly indigenous type, if they were free to use their powers in their own way to satisfy their interests as they experience them from the life conditions which they have to meet.

Emancipation in Russia and the United States.— In the time of Peter the Great the ancient national mores of Russia were very strong and firmly established. They remain to this day, in the mass of the population, unchanged in their essential integrity. There is, amongst the upper classes, an imitation of French ways, but it is unimportant for the nation. The autocracy is what makes "Russia," as a political unit. The autocracy is the apex of a military system, by which a great territory has been gathered under one control. That operation has not affected the old mores of the people. The tsar Alexander II was convinced by reading the writings of the great literary coterie of the middle of the nineteenth century that serfdom ought to be abolished, and he determined that it should be done. It is not in the system of autocracy that the autocrat shall have original opinions and adopt an independent initiative. The men whom he ordered to abolish serfdom had to devise a method, and they devised one which was to appear satisfactory to the tsar, but was to protect the interests which they cared for. One is reminded of the devices of American politicians to satisfy the clamor of the moment, but to change nothing. The reform had but slight root in public opinion, and no sanction in the interests of the influential classes; quite the contrary. The consequence is that the abolition of serfdom has thrown Russian society into chaos, and as yet reconstruction upon the new system has made little growth. In the United States the abolition of slavery was accomplished by the North, which had no slaves and enforced emancipation by war on the South, which had them. The mores of the South were those of slavery in full and satisfactory operation, including social, religious, and philosophical notions adapted to slavery. The abolition of slavery in the northern states had been brought about by changes in conditions and interests. Emancipation in the South was produced by outside force against the mores of the whites there. The consequence has been forty years of economic, social, and political discord. In this case free institutions and mores in which free individual initiative is a leading element

allow efforts towards social readjustment out of which a solution of the difficulties will come. New mores will be developed which will cover the situation with customs, habits, mutual concessions, and coöperation of interests, and these will produce a social philosophy consistent with the facts. The process is long, painful, and discouraging, but it contains its own guarantees.

* * *

Reforms of Joseph II.—The most remarkable case of a reform attempted by authority, and arbitrary in its method, is that of the reforms attempted by Joseph II, emperor of Germany. His kingdoms were suffering from the persistence of old institutions and mores. They needed modernizing. This he knew and, as an absolute monarch, he ordained changes, nearly all of which were either the abolition of abuses or the introduction of real improvements. He put an end to survivals of mediæval clericalism, established freedom of worship, made marriage a civil contract, abolished class privilege, made taxation uniform, and replaced serfdom in Bohemia by the form of villanage which existed in Austria. In Hungary he ordered the use of the German language instead of Latin, as the civil language. Interferences with language act as counter suggestion. Common sense and expediency were in favor of the use of the German language, but the order to use it provoked a great outburst of national enthusiasm which sought demonstration in dress, ceremonies, and old usages. Many of the other changes made by the emperor antagonized vested interests of nobles and ecclesiastics, and he was forced to revoke them. He promulgated orders which affected the mores, and the mental or moral discipline of his subjects. If a man came to enroll himself as a deist a second time, he was to receive twenty-four blows with the rod, not because he was a deist, but because he called himself something about which he could not know what it is. No coffins were to be used, corpses were to be put in sacks and buried in quicklime. Probably this law was wise from a purely rational point of view, but it touched upon a matter in regard to which popular sentiment is very tender even when the usage is most irrational. "Many a usage and superstition was so closely interwoven with the life of the people that it could not be torn away by regulation, but only by education." Non-Catholics were given full civil rights. None were to be excluded from the cemeteries. The unilluminated Jews would have preferred that there should be no change in the laws. Frederick of Prussia said that Joseph always took the second step without having taken the first. In the end the emperor revoked all his changes and innovations except the abolition of serfdom and religious toleration. Some of his measures were gradually realized through the nineteenth century. Others are now an object of political effort.

Adoption of Mores of Another Age.—The Renaissance was a period in which an attempt was made by one age to adopt the mores of another, as the latter were known through literature and art. The knowledge was very imperfect and mistaken, as indeed it necessarily must be, and the conceptions which were formed of the model were almost as fantastic as if they had been pure creations of the imagination. . . .

. . . The New England Puritans, in the seventeenth century, tried to build a society on the Bible, especially the books of Moses. The attempt was in every way a failure. It may well be doubted if any society ever existed of which the books referred to were a description, and the prescriptions were found ill adapted to seventeenth-century facts. The mores made by any age for itself are good and right for that age, but it follows that they can suit another age only to a very limited extent.

What Changes are Possible.—All these cases go to show that changes which run with the mores are easily brought about, but that changes which are opposed to the mores require long and patient effort, if they are possible at all. The ruling clique can use force to warp the mores towards some result which they have selected, especially if they bring their effort to bear on the ritual, not on the dogmas, and if they are contented to go slowly. The church has won great results in this way, and by so doing has created a belief that religion, or ideas, or institutions, make mores. The leading classes, no matter by what standard they are selected, can lead by example, which always affects ritual. An aristocracy acts in this way. It suggests standards of elegance, refinement, and nobility, and the usages of good manners, from generation to generation, are such as have spread from the aristocracy to other classes. Such influences are unspoken, unconscious, unintentional. If we admit that it is possible and right for some to undertake to mold the mores of others, of set purpose, we see that the limits within which any such effort can succeed are very narrow, and the methods by which it can operate are strictly defined. The favorite methods fail because they do not affect ritual, and because they always aim at great results in a short time. Above all, we can judge of the amount of serious attention which is due to plans for "reorganizing society," to get rid of alleged errors and inconveniences in it. We might as well plan to reorganize our globe by redistributing the elements in it.

Dissent from the Mores; Group Orthodoxy.—

Since it appears that the old mores are mischievous if they last beyond the duration of the conditions and needs to which they were adapted, and that constant, gradual, smooth, and easy readjustment is the course of things which is conducive to healthful life, it follows that free and rational criticism of traditional mores is essential to societal welfare. We have seen that the inherited mores exert a coercion on every one born in the group. It follows that only the greatest and best can react against the mores so as to modify them. It is by no means to be inferred that every one who sets himself at war with the traditional mores is a hero of social correction and amelioration. The trained reason and conscience never have heavier tasks laid upon them than where questions of conformity to, or dissent from, the mores are raised. It is by the dissent and free judgment of the best reason and conscience that the mores win flexibility and automatic readjustment. Dissent is always unpopular in the group. Groups form standards of orthodoxy as to the "principles" which each member must profess and the ritual which each must practice. Dissent seems to imply a claim of superiority. It evokes hatred and persecution. Dissenters are rebels, traitors, and heretics. We see this in all kinds of subgroups. Noble and patrician classes, merchants, artisans, religious and philosophical sects, political parties, academies and learned societies, punish by social penalties dissent from, or disobedience to, their code of group conduct. The modern trades union, in its treatment of a "scab," only presents another example. The group also, by a majority, adopts a programme of policy and then demands of each member that he shall work and make sacrifices for what has been resolved upon for the group interest. He who refuses is a renegade or apostate with respect to the group doctrines and interests. He who adopts the mores of another group is a still more heinous criminal. The mediæval definition of a heretic was one who varied in life and conversation, dress, speech, or manner (that is, the social ritual) from the ordinary members of the Christian community. The first meaning of "Catholic" in the fourth century was a summary of the features which were common to all Christians in social and ecclesiastical behavior; those were Catholic who conformed to the mores and were characteristic of Christians. If a heretic was better than the Catholics, they hated him more. That never excused him before the church authorities. They wanted loyalty to the ecclesiastical corporation. Persecution of a dissenter is always popular in the group which he has abandoned. Toleration of dissent is no sentiment of the masses.

*   *   *

Social Policy.—In Germany an attempt has been made to develop social policy into an art (*Socialpolitik*). Systematic attempts are made to study demographical facts in order to deduce from them conclusions as to the things which need to be done to make society better. The scheme is captivating. It is one of the greatest needs of modern states, which have gone so far in the way of experimental devices for social amelioration and rectification, at the expense of tax payers, that those devices should be tested and that the notions on which they are based should be verified. So far as demographical information furnishes these tests it is of the highest value. When, however, the statesmen and social philosophers stand ready to undertake any manipulation of institutions and mores, and proceed on the assumption that they can obtain data upon which to proceed with confidence in that undertaking, as an architect or engineer would obtain data and apply his devices to a task in his art, a fallacy is included which is radical and mischievous beyond measure. We have, as yet, no calculus for the variable elements which enter into social problems and no analysis which can unravel their complications. The discussions always reveal the dominion of the prepossessions in the minds of the disputants which are in the mores. We know that an observer of nature always has to know his own personal equation. The mores are a societal equation. When the mores are the thing studied in one's own society, there is an operation like begging the question. Moreover, the convictions which are in the mores are "faiths." They are not affected by scientific facts or demonstration. We "believe in" democracy, as we have been brought up in it, or we do not. If we do, we accept its mythology. The reason is because we have grown up in it, are familiar with it, and like it. Argument would not touch this faith. In like manner the people of one state believe in "the state," or in militarism, or in commercialism, or in individualism. Those of another state are sentimental, nervous, fond of rhetorical phrases, full of group vanity. It is vain to imagine that any man can lift himself out of these characteristic features in the mores of the group to which he belongs, especially when he is dealing with the nearest and most familiar phenomena of everyday life. It is vain to imagine that a "scientific man" can divest himself of prejudice or previous opinion, and put himself in an attitude of neutral independence towards the mores. He might as well try to get out of gravity or the pressure of the atmosphere. The most learned scholar reveals all the philistinism and prejudice of the man-on-the-curbstone when mores are in discussion. The most elaborate discussion only consists in resolving on

one's own axis. One only finds again the prepossessions which he brought to the consideration of the subject, returned to him with a little more intense faith. The philosophical drift in the mores of our time is towards state regulation, militarism, imperialism, towards petting and flattering the poor and laboring classes, and in favor of whatever is altruistic and humanitarian. What man of us ever gets out of his adopted attitude, for or against these now ruling tendencies, so that he forms judgments, not by his ruling interest or conviction, but by the supposed impact of demographic data on an empty brain. We have no grounds for confidence in these ruling tendencies of our time. They are only the present phases in the endless shifting of our philosophical generalizations, and it is only proposed, by the application of social policy, to subject society to another set of arbitrary interferences, dictated by a new set of dogmatic prepossessions that would only be a continuation of old methods and errors.

Degenerate and Evil Mores. Mores of Advance and Decline.—The case is somewhat different when attempts are made by positive efforts to prevent the operation of bad mores, or to abolish them. The historians have familiarized us with the notion of corrupt or degenerate mores. Such periods as the later Roman empire, the Byzantine empire, the Merovingian kingdom, and the Renaissance offer us examples of evil mores. We need to give more exactitude to this idea. Bad mores are those which are not well fitted to the conditions and needs of the society at the time. But, as we have seen, the mores produce a philosophy of welfare, more or less complete, and they produce taboos which are concentrated inhibitions directed against conduct which the philosophy regards as harmful, or positive injunctions to do what is judged expedient and beneficial. The taboos constitute morality or a moral system which, in higher civilization, restrains passion and appetite, and curbs the will. Various conjunctures arise in which the taboos are weakened or the sanctions on them are withdrawn. Faith in the current religion may be lost. Then its mystic sanctions cease to operate. The political institutions may be weak or unfit, and the civil sanctions may fail. There may not be the necessary harmony between economic conditions and political institutions, or the classes which hold the social forces in their hands may misuse them for their selfish interest at the expense of others. The philosophical and ethical generalizations which are produced by the mores rise into a realm of intellect and reason which is proud, noble, and grand. The power of the intelligence is a human prerogative. If the power is correctly used the scope of achievement in the satisfaction of needs is enormously extended. The penalty of error in that domain is correspondingly great. When the mores go wrong it is, above all, on account of error in the attempt to employ the philosophical and ethical generalizations in order to impose upon mores and institutions a movement towards selected and "ideal" results which the ruling powers of the society have determined to aim at. Then the energy of the society may be diverted from its interests. Such a drift of the mores is exactly analogous to a vice of an individual, i.e. energy is expended on acts which are contrary to welfare. The result is a confusion of all the functions of the society, and a falseness in all its mores. Any of the aberrations which have been mentioned will produce evil mores, that is, mores which are not adapted to welfare, so that a group may fall into vicious mores just as an individual falls into vicious habits.

*   *   *

The Correction of Aberrations.—It is impossible to arrest or avert such an aberration in the mores at its beginning or in its early stages. It is, however, very difficult to do so, and it would be very difficult to find a case in which it has been done. Necessarily the effort to do it consists in a prophecy of consequences. Such prophecy does not appeal to any one who does not himself foresee error and harm. Prophets have always fared ill, because their predictions were unwelcome and they were unpopular. The pension system which has grown up in the United States since the civil war has often been criticised. It is an abuse of extreme peril in a democracy. Demagogues easily use it to corrupt voters with their own money. It is believed that it will soon die out by its own limitations. There is, however, great doubt of this. It is more likely to cause other evil measures, in order that it may not die out. If we notice the way in which, in this case, people let a thing go in order to avoid trouble, we may see how aberrant mores come in and grow strong.

*   *   *

Antagonism between an Individual and the Mores.—The case of dissent from the mores, which was considered above (§100), is the case in which the individual voluntarily sets himself in antagonism to the mores of the society. There are cases in which the individual finds himself in involuntary antagonism to the mores of the society, or of some subgroup to which he belongs. If a man passes from one class to another, his acts show the contrast between the mores in which he was bred and those in which he finds himself. The satirists have made fun of the *parvenu* for centuries. His mistakes and misfortunes reveal the nature of the mores, their power over the individual, their pertinacity against

later influences, the confusion in character produced by changing them, and the grip of habit which appears both in the persistence of old mores and the weakness of new ones. Every emigrant is forced to change his mores. He loses the sustaining help of use and wont. He has to acquire a new outfit of it. The traveler also experiences the change from life in one set of mores to life in another. The experience gives him the best power to criticize his native mores from a standpoint outside of them. In the north American colonies white children were often stolen by Indians and brought up by them in their ways. Whether they would later, if opportunity offered, return to white society and white mores, or would prefer to remain with the Indians, seems to have depended on the age at which they were captured. Missionaries have often taken men of low civilization out of the society in which they were born, have educated them, and taught them white men's mores. If a single clear and indisputable case could be adduced in which such a person was restored to his own people and did not revert to their mode of life, it would be a very important contribution to ethnology. We are forced to believe that, if a baby born in New England was taken to China and given to a Chinese family to rear and educate, he would become a Chinaman in all which belongs to the mores, that is to say, in his character, conduct and code of life.

*   *   *

Antagonism between Groups in Respect to Mores.—When different groups come in contact with each other their mores are brought into contrast and antagonism. Some Australian girls consider that their honor requires that they shall be knocked senseless and carried off by the men who thereby become their husbands. If they are the victims of violence, they need not be ashamed. Eskimo girls would be ashamed to go away with husbands without crying and lamenting, glad as they are to go. They are shocked to hear that European women publicly consent in church to be wives, and then go with their husbands without pretending to regret it. In Homer girls are proud to be bought and to bring to their fathers a bride price of many cows. In India *gandharva* marriage is one of the not-honorable forms. It is love marriage. It rests on passion and is considered sensual; moreover, it is due to a transitory emotion. If property is involved in marriage the institution rests on a permanent interest and is guaranteed. Kaffirs also ridicule Christian love marriage. They say that it puts a woman on a level with a cat, the only animal which, amongst them, has no value. Where polygamy prevails women are ashamed to be wives of men who can afford only one each; under monogamy they think it a disgrace to be wives of men who have other wives. The Japanese think the tie to one's father the most sacred. A man who should leave father and mother and cleave to his wife would become an outcast. Therefore the Japanese think the Bible immoral and irreligious. Such a view in the mores of the masses will long outlast the "adoption of western civilization." The Egyptians thought the Greeks unclean. Herodotus says that the reason was because they ate cow's flesh. The Greeks, as wine drinkers, thought themselves superior to the Egyptians, who drank beer. A Greek people was considered inferior if it had no city life, no agora, no athletics, no share in the games, no group character, and if it kept on a robber life. The real reason for the hatred of Jews by Christians has always been the strange and foreign mores of the former. When Jews conform to the mores of the people amongst whom they live prejudice and hatred are greatly diminished, and in time will probably disappear. The dislike of the colored people in the old slave states of the United States and the hostility to whites who "associate with negroes" is to be attributed to the difference in the mores of whites and blacks. Under slavery the blacks were forced to conform to white ways, as indeed they are now if they are servants. In the North, also, where they are in a small minority, they conform to white ways. It is when they are free and form a large community that they live by their own mores. The civil war in the United States was due to a great divergence in the mores of the North and the South, produced by the presence or absence of slavery. The passionate dislike and contempt of the people of one section for those of the other was due to the conception each had formed of the other's character and ways. Since the abolition of slavery the mores of the two sections have become similar and the sectional dislike has disappeared. The contrast between the mores of English America and Spanish America is very great. It would long outlast any political combination of parts of the two, if such should be brought about.

*   *   *

Modification of the Mores by Agitation.—To this point all projects of missions and reform must come. It must be recognized that what is proposed is an arbitrary action on the mores. Therefore nothing sudden or big is possible. The enterprise is possible only if the mores are ready for it. The conditions of success lie in the mores. The methods must conform to the mores. That is why the agitator, reformer, prophet, reorganizer of society, who has found out "the truth" and wants to "get a law passed" to realize it right away, is only a mischief-maker. He has won considerable prestige

in the last hundred years, but if the cases are examined it will be found that when he had success it was because he took up something for which the mores were ready. Wilberforce did not overthrow slavery. Natural forces reduced to the service of man and the discovery of new land set men "free" from great labor, and new ways suggested new sentiments of humanity and ethics. The mores changed and all the wider deductions in them were repugnant to slavery. The free-trade agitators did not abolish the corn laws. The interests of the English population had undergone a new distribution. It was the redistribution of population and political power in the United States which made the civil war. Witchcraft and trial by torture were not abolished by argument. Critical knowledge and thirst for reality made them absurd. In Queen Anne's reign prisons in England were frightful sinks of vice, misery, disease, and cruel extortion. "So the prisons continued until the time of Howard," seventy-five years later. The mores had then become humanitarian. Howard was able to get a response.

Capricious Interest of the Masses.—Whether the masses will think certain things wrong, cruel, base, unjust, and disgusting; whether they will think certain pleas and demands reasonable; whether they will regard certain projects as sensible, ridiculous, or fantastic, and will give attention to certain topics, depends on the convictions and feelings which at the time are dominant in the mores. No one can predict with confidence what the response will be to any stimulus which may be applied. . . .

How the Group becomes Homogeneous.—The only way in which, in the course of time, remnants of foreign groups are apparently absorbed and the group becomes homogeneous, is that the foreign element dies out. In like manner people who live by aberrant mores die. The aberrant forms then cease to be, and the mores become uniform. In the meantime, there is a selection which determines which mores shall survive and which perish. This is accomplished by syncretism.

Syncretism.—Although folkways for the same purpose have a great similarity in all groups, yet they present variations and characteristic differences from group to group. These variations are sometimes due to differences in the life conditions, but generally causes for them are unascertainable, or the variations appear capricious. Therefore each in-group forms its own ways, and looks with contempt and abhorrence upon the ways of any outgroup. Dialectical differences in language or pronunciation are a sufficient instance. They cannot be accounted for, but they call out contempt and ridicule, and are taken to be signs of barbarism and inferiority. When groups are compounded by inter-marriage, intercourse, conquest, immigration, or slavery, syncretism of the folkways takes place. One of the component groups takes precedence and sets the standards. The inferior groups or classes imitate the ways of the dominant group, and eradicate from their children the traditions of their own ancestors. . . .

The Art of Societal Administration.—It is not to be inferred that reform and correction are hopeless. Inasmuch as the mores are a phenomenon of the society and not of the state, and inasmuch as the machinery of administration belongs to the state and not to the society, the administration of the mores presents peculiar difficulties. Strictly speaking, there is no administration of the mores, or it is left to voluntary organs acting by moral suasion. The state administration fails if it tries to deal with the mores, because it goes out of its province. The voluntary organs which try to administer the mores (literature, moral teachers, schools, churches, etc.) have no set method and no persistent effort. They very often make great errors in their methods. In regard to divorce, for instance, it is idle to set up stringent rules in an ecclesiastical body, and to try to establish them by extravagant and false interpretation of the Bible, hoping in that way to lead opinion; but the observation and consideration of cases which occur affect opinion and form convictions. The statesman and social philosopher can act with such influences, sum up the forces which make them, and greatly help the result. The inference is that intelligent art can be introduced here as elsewhere, but that it is necessary to understand the mores and to be able to discern the elements in them, just as it is always necessary for good art to understand the facts of nature with which it will have to deal. It belongs to the work of publicists and statesmen to gauge the forces in the mores and to perceive their tendencies. The great men of a great epoch are those who have understood new currents in the mores. The great reformers of the sixteenth century, the great leaders

of modern revolutions, were, as we can easily see, produced out of a protest or revulsion which had long been forming under and within the existing system. The leaders are such because they voice the convictions which have become established and because they propose measures which will realize interests of which the society has become conscious. A hero is not needed. Often a mediocre, commonplace man suffices to give the critical turn to thought or interest. "A Gian Angelo Medici, agreeable, diplomatic, benevolent, and pleasure-loving, sufficed to initiate a series of events which kept the occidental races in perturbation through two centuries." (Symonds, *Catholic Reaction*, I, 144.) Great crises come when great new forces are at work changing fundamental conditions, while powerful institutions and traditions still hold old systems intact. The fifteenth century was such a period. It is in such crises that great men find their opportunity. The man and the age react on each other. The measures of policy which are adopted and upon which energy is expended become components in the evolution. The evolution, although it has the character of a nature process, always must issue by and through men whose passions, follies, and wills are a part of it but are also always dominated by it. The interaction defies our analysis, but it does not discourage our reason and conscience from their play on the situation, if we are content to know that their function must be humble. Stoll boldly declares that if one of us had been a judge in the times of the witch trials he would have reasoned as the witch judges did, and would have tortured like them. (Stoll, *Suggestion und Hypnotismus*, 248.) If that is so, then it behooves us by education and will, with intelligent purpose, to criticise and judge even the most established ways of our time, and to put courage and labor into resistance to the current mores where we judge them wrong. It would be a mighty achievement of the science of society if it could lead up to an art of societal administration which should be intelligent, effective, and scientific.

5. On the Patterns of Culture

BY RUTH BENEDICT

A CHIEF of the Digger Indians, as the Californians call them, talked to me a great deal about the ways of his people in the old days. He was a Christian and a leader among his people in the planting of peaches and apricots on irrigated land, but when he talked of the shamans who had transformed themselves into bears before his eyes in the bear dance, his hands trembled and his voice broke with excitement. It was an incomparable thing, the power his people had had in the old days. He liked best to talk of the desert foods they had eaten. He brought each uprooted plant lovingly and with an unfailing sense of its importance. In those days his people had eaten "the health of the desert," he said, and knew nothing of the insides of tin cans and the things for sale at butcher shops. It was such innovations that had degraded them in these latter days.

One day, without transition, Ramon broke in upon his descriptions of grinding mesquite and preparing acorn soup. "In the beginning," he said, "God gave to every people a cup, a cup of clay, and from this cup they drank their life." I do not know whether the figure occurred in some traditional ritual of his people that I never found, or whether it was his own imagery. It is hard to imagine that he had heard it from the whites he had known at Banning; they were not given to discussing the ethos of different peoples. At any rate, in the mind of this humble Indian the figure of speech was clear and full of meaning. "They all dipped in the water," he continued, "but their cups were different. Our cup is broken now. It has passed away."

Our cup is broken. These things that had given significance to the life of his people, the domestic rituals of eating, the obligations of the economic system, the succession of ceremonials in the villages, possession in the bear dance, their standards of right and wrong—these were gone, and with them the shape and meaning of their life. The old man was still vigorous and a leader in relationships with the whites. He did not mean that there was any question of the extinction of his people. But

he had in mind the loss of something that had value equal to that of life itself, the whole fabric of his people's standards and beliefs. There were other cups of living left, and they held perhaps the same water, but the loss was irreparable. It was no matter of tinkering with an addition here, lopping off something there. The modelling had been fundamental, it was somehow all of a piece. It had been their own.

Ramon had had personal experience of the matter of which he spoke. He straddled two cultures whose values and ways of thought were incommensurable. It is a hard fate. In Western civilization our experiences have been different. We are bred to one cosmopolitan culture, and our social sciences, our psychology, and our theology persistently ignore the truth expressed in Ramon's figure.

The course of life and the pressure of environment, not to speak of the fertility of human imagination, provide an incredible number of possible leads, all of which, it appears, may serve a society to live by. There are the schemes of ownership, with the social hierarchy that may be associated with possessions; there are material things and their elaborate technology; there are all the facets of sex life, parenthood and post-parenthood; there are the guilds or cults which may give structure to the society; there is economic exchange; there are the gods and super-natural sanctions. Each one of these and many more may be followed out with a cultural and ceremonial elaboration which monopolizes the cultural energy and leaves small surplus for the building of other traits. Aspects of life that seem to us most important have been passed over with small regard by peoples whose culture, oriented in another direction, has been far from poor. Or the same trait may be so greatly elaborated that we reckon it as fantastic.

It is in cultural life as it is in speech; selection is the prime necessity. The numbers of sounds that can be produced by our vocal cords and our oral and nasal cavities are practically unlimited. The three or four dozen of the English language are a selection which coincides not even with those of such closely related dialects as German and French. The total that are used in different languages of the world no one has ever dared to estimate. But each language must make its selection and abide by it

Reprinted from Ruth Benedict, *Patterns of Culture* (Boston: Houghton Mifflin Co., 1935), chap. ii, pp. 33–40, with the permission of Houghton Mifflin Co. and Routledge & Kegan Paul, Ltd.

on pain of not being intelligible at all. A language that used even a few hundreds of the possible—and actually recorded—phonetic elements could not be used for communication. On the other hand a great deal of our misunderstanding of languages unrelated to our own has arisen from our attempts to refer alien phonetic systems back to ours as a point of reference. We recognize only one *k*. If other people have five *k* sounds placed in different positions in the throat and mouth, distinctions of vocabulary and of syntax that depend on these differences are impossible to us until we master them. We have a *d* and an *n*. They may have an intermediate sound which, if we fail to identify it, we write now *d* and now *n*, introducing distinctions which do not exist. The elementary prerequisite of linguistic analysis is a consciousness of these incredibly numerous available sounds from which each language makes its own selections.

In culture too we must imagine a great arc on which are ranged the possible interests provided either by the human age-cycle or by the environment or by man's various activities. A culture that capitalized even a considerable proportion of these would be as unintelligible as a language that used all the clicks, all the glottal stops, all the labials, dentals, sibilants, and gutturals from voiceless to voiced and from oral to nasal. Its identity as a culture depends upon the selection of some segments of this arc. Every human society everywhere has made such selection in its cultural institutions. Each from the point of view of another ignores fundamentals and exploits irrelevancies. One culture hardly recognizes monetary values; another has made them fundamental in every field of behaviour. In one society technology is unbelievably slighted even in those aspects of life which seem necessary to ensure survival; in another, equally simple, technological achievements are complex and fitted with admirable nicety to the situation. One builds an enormous cultural superstructure upon adolescence, one upon death, one upon after-life.

The case of adolescence is particularly interesting, because it is in the limelight in our own civilization and because we have plentiful information from other cultures. In our own civilization a whole library of psychological studies has emphasized the inevitable unrest of the period of puberty. It is in our tradition a physiological state as definitely characterized by domestic explosions and rebellion as typhoid is marked by fever. There is no question of the facts. They are common in America. The question is rather of their inevitability.

The most casual survey of the ways in which different societies have handled adolescence makes one fact inescapable: even in those cultures which have made most of the trait, the age upon which they focus their attention varies over a great range of years. At the outset, therefore, it is clear that the so-called puberty institutions are a misnomer if we continue to think of biological puberty. The puberty they recognize is social, and the ceremonies are a recognition in some fashion or other of the child's new status of adulthood. This investiture with new occupations and obligations is in consequence as various and as culturally conditioned as the occupations and obligations themselves. If the sole honourable duty of manhood is conceived to be deeds of war, the investiture of the warrior is later and of a different sort from that in a society where adulthood gives chiefly the privilege of dancing in a representation of masked gods. In order to understand puberty institutions, we do not most need analyses of the necessary nature of *rites de passage;* we need rather to know what is identified in different cultures with the beginning of adulthood and their methods of admitting to the new status. Not biological puberty, but what adulthood means in that culture conditions the puberty ceremony.

Adulthood in central North America means warfare. Honour in it is the great goal of all men. The constantly recurring theme of the youth's coming-of-age, as also of preparation for the warpath at any age, is a magic ritual for success in war. They torture not one another, but themselves: they cut strips of skin from their arms and legs, they strike off their fingers, they drag heavy weights pinned to their chest or leg muscles. Their reward is enhanced prowess in deeds of warfare.

In Australia, on the other hand, adulthood means participation in an exclusively male cult whose fundamental trait is the exclusion of women. Any woman is put to death if she so much as hears the sound of the bull-roarer at the ceremonies, and she must never know of the rites. Puberty ceremonies are elaborate and symbolic repudiations of the bonds with the female sex; the men are symbolically made self-sufficient and the wholly responsible element of the community. To attain this end they use drastic sexual rites and bestow supernatural guaranties.

The clear physiological facts of adolescence, therefore, are first socially interpreted even where they are stressed. But a survey of puberty institutions makes clear a further fact: puberty is physiologically a different matter in the life-cycle of the male and the female. If cultural emphasis followed the physiological emphasis, girls' ceremonies would be more marked than boys'; but it is not so. The ceremonies emphasize a social fact: the adult prerogatives of men are more far-reaching in every culture than women's, and consequently, as in the above instances, it is more common for societies to take note of this period in boys than in girls.

Girls' and boys' puberty, however, may be socially celebrated in the same tribe in identical ways. Where, as in the interior of British Columbia, adolescent rites are a magical training for all occupations, girls are included on the same terms as boys. Boys roll stones down mountains and beat them to the bottom to be swift of foot, or throw gambling-sticks to be lucky in gambling; girls carry water from distant springs, or drop stones down inside their dresses that their children may be born as easily as the pebble drops to the ground.

In such a tribe as the Nandi of the lake region of East Africa, also, girls and boys share an even-handed puberty rite, though, because of the man's dominant rôle in the culture, his boyhood training period is more stressed than the woman's. Here adolescent rites are an ordeal inflicted by those already admitted to adult status upon those they are now forced to admit. They require of them the most complete stoicism in the face of ingenious tortures associated with circumcision. The rites for the two sexes are separate, but they follow the same pattern. In both the novices wear for the ceremony the clothing of their sweethearts. During the operation their faces are watched for any twinge of pain, and the reward of bravery is given with great rejoicing by the lover, who runs forward to receive back some of his adornments. For both the girl and the boy the rites mark their *entrée* into a new sex status: the boy is now a warrior and may take a sweetheart, the girl is marriageable. The adolescent tests are for both a premarital ordeal in which the palm is awarded by their lovers.

Puberty rites may also be built upon the facts of girls' puberty and admit of no extension to boys. One of the most naïve of these is the institution of the fatting-house for girls in Central Africa. In the region where feminine beauty is all but identified with obesity, the girl at puberty is segregated, sometimes for years, fed with sweet and fatty foods, allowed no activity, and her body rubbed assiduously with oils. She is taught during this time her future duties, and her seclusion ends with a parade of her corpulence that is followed by her marriage to her proud bridegroom. It is not regarded as necessary for the man to achieve pulchritude before marriage in a similar fashion.

The usual ideas around which girls' puberty institutions are centred, and which are not readily extended to boys', are those concerned with menstruation. The uncleanness of the menstruating woman is a very widespread idea, and in a few regions first menstruation has been made the focus of all the associated attitudes. Puberty rites in these cases are of a thoroughly different character from any of which we have spoken. Among the Carrier Indians of British Columbia, the fear and horror of a girl's puberty was at its height. Her three or four years of seclusion was called "the burying alive," and she lived for all that time alone in the wilderness, in a hut of branches far from all beaten trails. She was a threat to any person who might so much as catch a glimpse of her, and her mere footstep defiled a path or a river. She was covered with a great headdress of tanned skin that shrouded her face and breasts and fell to the ground behind. Her arms and legs were loaded with sinew bands to protect her from the evil spirit with which she was filled. She was herself in danger and she was a source of danger to everybody else.

Girls' puberty ceremonies built upon ideas associated with the menses are readily convertible into what is, from the point of view of the individual concerned, exactly opposite behaviour. There are always two possible aspects to the sacred: it may be a source of peril or it may be a source of blessing. In some tribes the first menses of girls are a potent supernatural blessing. Among the Apaches I have seen the priests themselves pass on their knees before the row of solemn little girls to receive from them the blessing of their touch. All the babies and the old people come also of necessity to have illness removed from them. The adolescent girls are not segregated as sources of danger, but court is paid to them as to direct sources of supernatural blessing. Since the ideas that underlie puberty rites for girls, both among the Carrier and among the Apache, are founded on beliefs concerning menstruation, they are not extended to boys, and boys' puberty is marked instead, and lightly, with simple tests and proofs of manhood.

The adolescent behaviour, therefore, even of girls was not dictated by some physiological characteristic of the period itself, but rather by marital or magic requirements socially connected with it. These beliefs made adolescence in one tribe serenely religious and beneficent, and in another so dangerously unclean that the child had to cry out in warning that others might avoid her in the woods. The adolescence of girls may equally, as we have seen, be a theme which a culture does not institutionalize. Even where, as in most of Australia, boys' adolescence is given elaborate treatment, it may be that the rites are an induction into the status of manhood and male participation in tribal matters, and female adolescence passes without any kind of formal recognition.

These facts, however, still leave the fundamental question unanswered. Do not all cultures have to cope with the natural turbulence of this period, even though it may not be given institutional expression? Dr. Mead has studied this question in Samoa. There the girl's life passes through well-marked periods. Her first years out of babyhood are passed in small neighbourhood gangs of age mates from which the little boys are strictly excluded. The corner of the village to which she belongs is all-important, and the little boys are traditional enemies. She has one duty, that of baby-tending, but she takes the baby with her rather than stays home to mind it, and her play is not seriously hampered. A couple of years before puberty, when she grows strong enough to have more difficult tasks required of her and old enough to learn more skilled techniques, the little girls' play group in which she grew up ceases to exist. She assumes woman's dress and must contribute to the work of the household. It is an uninteresting period of life

to her and quite without turmoil. Puberty brings no change at all.

A few years after she has come of age, she will begin the pleasant years of casual and irresponsible love affairs that she will prolong as far as possible into the period when marriage is already considered fitting. Puberty itself is marked by no social recognition, no change of attitude or of expectancy. Her pre-adolescent shyness is supposed to remain unchanged for a couple of years. The girl's life in Samoa is blocked out by other considerations than those of physiological sex maturity, and puberty falls in a particularly unstressed and peaceful period during which no adolescent conflicts manifest themselves. Adolescence, therefore, may not only be culturally passed over without ceremonial; it may also be without importance in the emotional life of the child and in the attitude of the village toward her.

Section B

Value and Belief Patterns

Editorial Foreword, BY TALCOTT PARSONS   *1053*

I–KNOWLEDGE AND RATIONALITY

1. *Rational Mastery of the Environment,* BY BRONISLAW MALINOWSKI   *1056*
2. *On Logical and Non-Logical Action,* BY VILFREDO PARETO   *1061*
3. *Types of Rationality,* BY MAX WEBER   *1063*
4. *Social Structure and the Structure of Thought,* BY EMILE DURKHEIM
   AND MARCEL MAUSS   *i065*
5. *On the Origins of the Idea of Force,* BY EMILE DURKHEIM   *1068*
6. *The Positive Role of the Sociology of Knowledge,* BY KARL MANNHEIM *1070*

II–RELIGION AND MAGIC

1. *Types of Magic,* BY SIR JAMES G. FRAZER   *1077*
2. *On Magic and the Unknown,* BY MARCEL MAUSS AND H. HUBERT   *1088*
3. *On the Social Functions of Religion,* BY BRONISLAW MALINOWSKI   *1091*
4. *On Sacrifice,* BY W. ROBERTSON SMITH   *1096*
5. *The Tao,* BY MARCEL GRANET   *1098*
6. *Confucianism and Puritanism,* BY MAX WEBER   *1101*
7. *On Eastern and Western Christianity,* BY ADOLF HARNACK   *1111*
8. *On Religious Rejection of the World,* BY MAX WEBER   *1120*
9. *Religion and Social Status,* BY MAX WEBER   *1138*

Value and Belief Patterns

by Talcott Parsons

THE PRIMARY CONSIDERATION here is delineating and discriminating the components into which cultural systems may differentiate. As observed in the general Introduction to Part Four, because of the literature available in our main period of emphasis, it has not been possible to present a set of selections displaying the whole range of differentiated types. We have therefore limited ourselves to a truncated classification consolidating our four major analytically distinguished types into two, which are not even completely distinguished from each other. We consider the two most clearly differentiated points of reference to be empirical rationality in its relation to science, and religious belief in its relation to patterns of evaluation; the two subsections below are organized around these types. Each case, however, ranges from the primary point of reference into closely related areas of cultural concern.

Because of the special relation of empirical knowledge to the history of theory in this field, selections dealing with the problem of empirical knowledge have been placed first. In view of the ways that this problem has been interwoven with that of the role of culture in social evolution, it seems appropriate to begin subsection I with the selection from Malinowski's work. As noted, there was an early tendency to try to assimilate all of early cultural orientation to the model of science, to treat magical and animistic conceptions as a kind of primitive science in that the differences in the cultural patterns from science patterns were attributed exclusively to the relative "ignorance" of the primitive peoples accepting them.

The "holistic" view that developed, especially in France, opposed this interpretation. The holistic concept was that primitive man had a totally "prelogical" mentality, and consequently, nothing in "primitive psychology" could be regarded as a gen-uine precursor of modern empirical orientations. The best-known proponent of this view was Lévy-Bruhl (*La mentalité primitive*).

Malinowski, especially within the anthropological tradition, was the one who, emphasizing the situation among non-literate peoples, first insisted on the *differentiation* of the orientation of "primitive man" between different aspects of his experience. In his famous book, *Magic, Science and Religion*, Malinowski used a double distinction of great significance here. He insisted that, though his Trobrianders were prolific users of magical procedures and firm believers in their efficacy and indispensability, they were also, in slightly different connections, entirely "empirically rational" and in this capacity, so far as the problems were cognitive, "protoscientists." The line of distinction he drew is a double one. When the situation is one that makes the emotional problem mainly a "matter of fact"—i.e., one where the practical interest in effectiveness coincides with sufficient certainty to make the relations between effort, skill, and outcome reasonably stable—the native tends to act in terms of technical rationality. On the other hand, when he has strong emotional interest in the outcome but the outcome is, for reasons beyond his control, highly uncertain, he tends to resort to magic. Even here, however, though inherently competing with each other, rational techniques and magic are not confused. Rather, magic is believed to be a necessary *addition* to doing one's rational best. The second line of distinction is that, in the rational technique, consequences are believed to follow their antecedents by "natural" processes; in magic, the tendency is to invoke some kind of "supernatural" agencies.

However, Malinowski carefully distinguished the religious from magical processes in this sense. He felt the religious was involved when *no* empirical goal for the individual could be subserved by the action. For example, the dead could not be brought back to life by funeral ritual. But what we would now call latent functions, for both the individual and the social system, could be subserved by this ritual action. For the individual, ritual action was, above all, resolving the ambivalent conflicts aroused by the death of a close associate in the direction of reinforcing role obligations; for the social system, it reinforced the institutionalized patterns of its organization in the face of the disturbance occasioned by the loss of a member.

Pareto was concerned with the importance of empirically rational or logical orientations of behavior—not as a question of *the* important mode, but as one within a differentiated manifold. He, at nearly the same time as Malinowski, but in a different context, raised the point in his distinction between the logical and non-logical components of action. Pareto's major interest was developing a scheme for the analysis of action in social systems. His primary model was the use of the concept of rationality in the formulations of economic theory. He clarified this model's implications by using the methodological standards of empirical science as the source of his main criteria of the "logical" component in action. An action was logical in so far as the end would be effected by the means, as predicted by the criteria of empirical knowledge. Pareto in this produced a category broader than that of economic rationality; however, he did not clearly define this category beyond these two major reference points.

To Pareto, non-logical action was a residual category. But the very fact that he proceeded as he did advanced beyond the attempt to constrict all cultural orientation into the single category of empirical knowledge; it thus matched Malinowski's version, on its different level. At the same time, Pareto's non-logical category did not remain simply residual; he himself distinguished between the elements involved in "pseudoscientific" theories and the "theories which transcend experience." The latter concept was a first positivistic approach to a concept of orientations of the bases of meaning in their relations to values. Many insights in the field of expressive symbolization, overlapping with Malinowski's treatment of magic, were contained, though not analytically separated, in the latter.

The selection from Max Weber on the types of rationality represents a farther step toward differentiating conceptualization of the relation of social action to cultural patterns. In Weber's concept of *Zweckrationalität* economic rationality is used as a point of reference in the same way Pareto used it, and Weber makes the same kind of attempt to broaden the concept beyond this to include certain types of technical and political rationality. Similarly, the concept of *Wertrationalität* involves the orientations to problems of meaning, but does not clearly discriminate between the evaluative and the grounding aspects. However, Weber's two types of rationality were incorporated into a wider classification of types of social action, including the "traditional" and "affective" types. As a whole, the classification did not clearly distinguish between the cultural and the social systems, nor did it clarify the extent to which cultural patterns, e.g., expressive symbolization, were involved in affective orientations, and to what order of "rationalization" these might or might not be subject. However, the classification was an immense advance beyond earlier treatment of these problems. Above all, it transcended the tendency to reduce problems to the "logic of dichotomies," a tendency discussed a number of times in our introductory materials.

The next selection, the essay of Durkheim and Mauss on forms of primitive classification, introduces the evolutionary problem again. This essay was the most important precursor of Durkheim's fuller development of these themes in the *Elementary Forms*. In it, Durkheim and Mauss consider the problem of a diffuse matrix of cultural orientation within which the more specialized cultural components are fused in primitive cultures (and, in certain ways, in special types of sophisticated cultures, e.g., the Chinese), and from which they differentiate during cultural evolution. One of the most famous lines of development suggested (developed later by Durkheim), is the emergence, from this religious matrix, of the categories of understanding, including such concepts as force, as they later became constitutive of empirical knowledge. Therefore, a selection is included, from the *Elementary Forms*, in which Durkheim develops this concept.

The last of the selections in the first subsection is from Karl Mannheim, on the sociology of knowledge. In the general Introduction to Part Four, the place of this theme in the development of the sociology of culture, and the concomitant importance of the problem of ideology, have been discussed. Mannheim raised this problem to prominence in the post-Marxian period; any treatment of the problems of empirical rationality and its limitations in a sociological context would be incomplete without Mannheim's statement of position.

The second subsection of Section B contains selections emphasizing the orientational and value aspects, more than the object-oriented aspect, of cultural systems. However, these are so closely intermingled that it is often difficult to make the distinction. Thus the two selections which begin the subsection deal with magic, though they represent two different traditions of thought. Sir James G. Frazer's selection is in the English tradition, dominated by utilitarian patterns of thought; it is true to form in treating primitive man as a protoscientist—a tradition from which Malinowski, partly in reaction against Frazer, broke sharply. In this selection from Frazer, however, the emphasis is not on this aspect of his views; he emphasizes the factors of the differentiation of different types of magic—sympathetic, homeopathic, etc. He reveals the involvement of components other than the purely cognitive in the magical patterns. This aspect of magic raises questions about magic's relation to expressive symbolization generally, and links it, at least implicitly, to Freud's concept. Mauss and Hubert stress similar components in magic in the background of the Durkheimian tradition in France.

The theme of expressive symbolization in ritual is, however, even more striking in one of the early classics of the sociology of religion, *The Religion of the Semites* by W. Robertson Smith. This is the source of the section on the sacrifice. Smith, who was one of Durkheim's most important predecessors, discusses an almost universal symbolic theme in the expressive field, one that Durkheim considered in his own analyses of the totemic sacrifice in relation to the Australian material. It is of particular sociological significance, in that it is a focal center in the relation of the individual to any collectivity or higher-order focus of authority—the surrender of centrifugal, lower-order interests in favor of a normative order. So far as religion is socially institutionalized, this is a perennial problem; it seems in general to be involved in the ritual system, in terms of some form of sacrifice.

Malinowski was particularly concerned with the balance between the functional requirements of a society and the psychological needs of individuals. Whatever objections be raised to his particular way of theoretically handling this problem,[1] Malinowski's interest was of the first importance. It culminates in Malinowski's own treatment of religion, because here the social group's interest in the stability of the emotional balance held by its members is so obvious. In spite of their many differences, Malinowski and Durkheim converge here.

The emphasis of the next set of selections shifts from the object aspect of religio-magical subsystems of culture, and their relations to the individuals' motivational problems, to the orientational

aspect and its relation to the evolutionary position and modes of differentiating the larger cultural systems. From the many writings in this field, we have chosen four selections that are clearly stated contributions to the problem.

The first is from Marcel Granet's notable book, *La pensée chinoise.* Granet was one of Durkheim's students; he became a leading Sinologist of his time. Following some of the leads provided by Durkheim and Mauss, he developed one of the most sophisticated analyses of a system of cultural orientation in sharp contrast with the Western that can be found in the literature. Granet denied that the master "conceptions" of the historic Chinese tradition could legitimately be called "concepts" in the Graeco-Western philosophical sense, and he introduced the use of the term *emblème* to designate these highest-order orientational patterns. Our selection considers the *emblème* at the highest level of all—usually transliterated as *Tao,* which, very roughly translated, means "the Way"—which summarizes the Chinese orientation of Being in the modern philosophical sense of that term.

One of the classic comparative analyses is next: Weber's contrast between Confucianism and Puritanism, with which he closes his analysis of the *Religion of China.* Here Weber is concerned with the background of the ostensible paradox that, though it is exceedingly "worldly" from many points of view, the Chinese orientation provided no basis for the thoroughgoing utilitarian "rationalization" of everyday conduct; whereas Puritanism, with its transcendental orientation, did provide one. Weber's succinct formula, "Confucianism was a doctrine of rational adaptation *to* the world; Puritanism was a doctrine of rational mastery *over* the world," will remain a classic statement of differentiation between major cultural orientations.

The selection from Harnack deals with a more narrow reference of cultural variation, the one between Eastern and Western Christianity. It provides, however, the same order of clear formulation of an essential contrast that may be presumed to have been of historic significance. In his era, Harnack was one of the German students of religion who, with Troeltsch and Weber, had a most sensitive appreciation of the significance of basic differences in orientations of meaning—however little these differences interest the "man in the street" on a routine basis of social organization.

The eighth selection is Weber's essay on religious rejections of the world, written as the Introduction to his study of the *Religion of India.* It was designed to help the Westerner understand the radical difference in the assumptions about the meaning of life underlying the great religious movements of

1. Parsons, "Malinowski and the Theory of Social Systems," in Raymond Firth (ed.), *Man and Culture* (London: Routledge & Kegan Paul, 1957).

India, especially Brahmanic Hinduism and Buddhism, from anything known in the West. It is dominated by the question of how an "irrational"—from the Western viewpoint—orientation to life can nevertheless serve as the basis of a far-reaching process of rationalization, in working through the philosophical problems, systematizing their answers, and drawing conclusions for the conduct of life. These four selections represent, in overlapping ways, analyses of a considerable proportion of the main orientations in terms of meaning that have underlain the differentiation of the great historic civilizations from each other.

The last selection in Part Four is the long section on Religion and Social Status in Weber's general survey of the problems of the sociology of religion in *Wirtschaft und Gesellschaft*.[2] The preceding four selections have all dealt with the cultural side of the relation between orientations of meaning and social action; here, Weber turns to the other side.

His general theme is the analysis of the ways in which different kinds of social groups—e.g., aristocracies, military groups, peasants, urban craftsmen, merchants, etc.—are selectively predisposed to be accessible to the appeal of different types of religious orientation. It is one of the extraordinary comparative surveys that Weber carried out in so many different fields. It seems appropriate to end this section on this note, while reminding our readers that we are dealing with a relation of interdependence and interpenetration and not with one-way causation. Weber himself, most frequently in connection with the *Protestant Ethic,* has often been charged with believing that religion somehow single-handedly "created" types of social system. That this interpretation of Weber is incorrect and that such a view is untenable should be clear from the Introductions to Section A of Part One and to Part Four. This selection should effectively end the misinterpretation of Weber himself, and should give the reader of the whole second subsection of Section B a strong impression of the complex interrelations between the cultural and the social factors involved in these problems.

---

2. It is the final section of that very long essay and is entitled, in German, *Stände, Klassen und Religion*. The entire essay is unfortunately not available in English, though we understand that a translation is to be published by the Beacon Press.

I—KNOWLEDGE AND RATIONALITY

---

1. *Rational Mastery of the Environment*

BY BRONISLAW MALINOWSKI

THE PROBLEM of primitive knowledge has been singularly neglected by anthropology. Studies on savage psychology were exclusively confined to early religion, magic and mythology. Only recently the work of several English, German, and French writers, notably the daring and brilliant speculations of Professor Lévy-Bruhl, gave an impetus to the student's interest in what the savage does in his more sober moods. The results were startling indeed: Professor Lévy-Bruhl tells us, to put it in a nutshell, that primitive man has no sober moods at all, that he is hopelessly and completely immersed in a mystical frame of mind. Incapable

of dispassionate and consistent observation, devoid of the power of abstraction, hampered by "a decided aversion towards reasoning," he is unable to draw any benefit from experience, to construct or comprehend even the most elementary laws of nature. "For minds thus orientated there is no fact purely physical." Nor can there exist for them any clear idea of substance and attribute, cause and effect, identity and contradiction. Their outlook is that of confused superstition, "pre-logical," made of mystic "participations" and "exclusions." I have here summarized a body of opinion, of which the brilliant French sociologist is the most decided and competent spokesman, but which numbers besides, many anthropologists and philosophers of renown.

But there are also dissenting voices. When a

Reprinted from Bronislaw Malinowski, *Magic, Science and Religion* (Glencoe, Ill.: The Free Press, 1948), pp. 8–18, with the permission of The Free Press.

scholar and anthropologist of the measure of Professor J. L. Myres entitles an article in *Notes and Queries* "Natural Science," and when we read there that the savage's "knowledge based on observation is distinct and accurate," we must surely pause before accepting primitive man's irrationality as a dogma. Another highly competent writer, Dr. A. A. Goldenweiser, speaking about primitive "discoveries, inventions and improvements"—which could hardly be attributed to any pre-empirical or pre-logical mind—affirms that "it would be unwise to ascribe to the primitive mechanic merely a passive part in the origination of inventions. Many a happy thought must have crossed his mind, nor was he wholly unfamiliar with the thrill that comes from an idea effective in action." Here we see the savage endowed with an attitude of mind wholly akin to that of a modern man of science!

To bridge over the wide gap between the two extreme opinions current on the subject of primitive man's reason, it will be best to resolve the problem into two questions.

First, has the savage any rational outlook, any rational mastery of his surroundings, or is he, as M. Lévy-Bruhl and his school maintain, entirely "mystical"? The answer will be that every primitive community is in possession of a considerable store of knowledge, based on experience and fashioned by reason.

The second question then opens: Can this primitive knowledge be regarded as a rudimentary form of science or is it, on the contrary, radically different, a crude empiry, a body of practical and technical abilities, rules of thumb and rules of art having no theoretical value? This second question, epistemological rather than belonging to the study of man, will be barely touched upon at the end of this section and a tentative answer only will be given.

In dealing with the first question, we shall have to examine the "profane" side of life, the arts, crafts and economic pursuits, and we shall attempt to disentangle in it a type of behavior, clearly marked off from magic and religion, based on empirical knowledge and on the confidence in logic. We shall try to find whether the lines of such behavior are defined by traditional rules, known, perhaps even discussed sometimes, and tested. We shall have to inquire whether the sociological setting of the rational and empirical behavior differs from that of ritual and cult. Above all we shall ask, do the natives distinguish the two domains and keep them apart, or is the field of knowledge constantly swamped by superstition, ritualism, magic or religion?

Since in the matter under discussion there is an appalling lack of relevant and reliable observations, I shall have largely to draw upon my own material, mostly unpublished, collected during a few years' field-work among the Melanesian and Papuo-Melanesian tribes of Eastern New Guinea and the surrounding archipelagoes. As the Melanesians are reputed, however, to be specially magic-ridden, they will furnish an acid test of the existence of empirical and rational knowledge among savages living in the age of polished stone.

These natives, and I am speaking mainly of the Melanesians who inhabit the coral atolls to the N.E. of the main island, the Trobriand Archipelago and the adjoining groups, are expert fishermen, industrious manufacturers and traders, but they rely mainly on gardening for their subsistence. With the most rudimentary implements, a pointed digging-stick and a small axe, they are able to raise crops sufficient to maintain a dense population and even yielding a surplus, which in olden days was allowed to rot unconsumed, and which at present is exported to feed plantation hands. The success in their agriculture depends—besides the excellent natural conditions with which they are favored—upon their extensive knowledge of the classes of the soil, of the various cultivated plants, of the mutual adaptation of these two factors, and, last not least, upon their knowledge of the importance of accurate and hard work. They have to select the soil and the seedlings, they have appropriately to fix the times for clearing and burning the scrub, for planting and weeding, for training the vines of the yam-plants. In all this they are guided by a clear knowledge of weather and seasons, plants and pests, soil and tubers, and by a conviction that this knowledge is true and reliable, that it can be counted upon and must be scrupulously obeyed.

Yet mixed with all their activities there is to be found magic, a series of rites performed every year over the gardens in rigorous sequence and order. Since the leadership in garden work is in the hands of the magician, and since ritual and practical work are intimately associated, a superficial observer might be led to assume that the mystic and the rational behavior are mixed up, that their effects are not distinguished by the natives and not distinguishable in scientific analysis. Is this so really?

Magic is undoubtedly regarded by the natives as absolutely indispensable to the welfare of the gardens. What would happen without it no one can exactly tell, for no native garden has ever been made without its ritual, in spite of some thirty years of European rule and missionary influence and well over a century's contact with white traders. But certainly various kinds of disaster, blight, unseasonable droughts and rains, bush-pigs and locusts, would destroy the unhallowed garden made without magic.

Does this mean, however, that the natives attribute all the good results to magic? Certainly not. If you were to suggest to a native that he should make his garden mainly by magic and scamp his work, he would simply smile on your simplicity. He knows as well as you do that there are natural conditions and causes, and by his observations he knows also that he is able to control these natural forces by mental and physical effort. His knowledge is limited, no doubt, but as far as it goes it is sound and proof against mysticism. If the fences are broken down, if the seed is destroyed or has been dried or washed away, he will have recourse not to magic, but to work, guided by knowledge and reason. His experience has taught him also, on the other hand, that in spite of all his forethought and beyond all his efforts there are agencies and forces which one year bestow unwonted and unearned benefits of fertility, making everything run smooth and well, rain and sun appear at the right moment, noxious insects remain in abeyance, the harvest yield a super-abundant crop; and another year again the same agencies bring ill-luck and bad chance, pursue him from beginning till end and thwart all his most strenuous efforts and his best-founded knowledge. To control these influences and these only he employs magic.

Thus there is a clear-cut division: there is first the well-known set of conditions, the natural course of growth, as well as the ordinary pests and dangers to be warded off by fencing and weeding. On the other hand there is the domain of the unaccountable and adverse influences, as well as the great unearned increment of fortunate coincidence. The first conditions are coped with by knowledge and work, the second by magic.

This line of division can also be traced in the social setting of work and ritual respectively. Though the garden magician is, as a rule, also the leader in practical activities, these two functions are kept strictly apart. Every magical ceremony has its distinctive name, its appropriate time and its place in the scheme of work, and it stands out of the ordinary course of activities completely. Some of them are ceremonial and have to be attended by the whole community, all are public in that it is known when they are going to happen and anyone can attend them. They are performed on selected plots within the gardens and on a special corner of this plot. Work is always tabooed on such occasions, sometimes only while the ceremony lasts, sometimes for a day or two. In his lay character the leader and magician directs the work, fixes the dates for starting, harangues and exhorts slack or careless gardeners. But the two roles never overlap or interfere: they are always clear, and any native will inform you without hesitation whether the man acts as magician or as leader in garden work.

What has been said about gardens can be paralleled from any one of the many other activities in which work and magic run side by side without ever mixing. Thus in canoe-building empirical knowledge of material, of technology, and of certain principles of stability and hydrodynamics, function in company and close association with magic, each yet uncontaminated by the other.

For example, they understand perfectly well that the wider the span of the outrigger the greater the stability yet the smaller the resistance against strain. They can clearly explain why they have to give this span a certain traditional width, measured in fractions of the length of the dug-out. They can also explain, in rudimentary but clearly mechanical terms, how they have to behave in a sudden gale, why the outrigger must be always on the weather side, why the one type of canoe can and the other cannot beat. They have, in fact, a whole system of principles of sailing, embodied in a complex and rich terminology, traditionally handed on and obeyed as rationally and consistently as is modern science by modern sailors. How could they sail otherwise under eminently dangerous conditions in their frail primitive craft?

But even with all their systematic knowledge, methodically applied, they are still at the mercy of powerful and incalculable tides, sudden gales during the monsoon season and unknown reefs. And here comes in their magic, performed over the canoe during its construction, carried out at the beginning and in the course of expeditions and resorted to in moments of real danger. If the modern seaman, entrenched in science and reason, provided with all sorts of safety appliances, sailing on steel-built steamers, if even he has a singular tendency to superstition—which does not rob him of his knowledge or reason, nor make him altogether pre-logical—can we wonder that his savage colleague, under much more precarious conditions, holds fast to the safety and comfort of magic?

An interesting and crucial test is provided by fishing in the Trobriand Islands and its magic. While in the villages on the inner lagoon fishing is done in an easy and absolutely reliable manner by the method of poisoning, yielding abundant results without danger and uncertainty, there are on the shores of the open sea dangerous modes of fishing and also certain types in which the yield varies according to whether shoals of fish appear beforehand or not. It is most significant that in the Lagoon fishing, where man can rely completely upon his knowledge and skill, magic does not exist, while in the open-sea fishing, full of danger and uncertainty, there is extensive magical ritual to secure safety and good results.

Again, in warfare the natives know that strength, courage, and agility play a decisive part. Yet here also they practice magic to master the elements of chance and luck.

Nowhere is the duality of natural and supernatural causes divided by a line so thin and intricate, yet, if carefully followed up, so well marked, decisive, and instructive, as in the two most fateful forces of human destiny: health and death. Health to the Melanesians is a natural state of affairs and, unless tampered with, the human body will remain in perfect order. But the natives know perfectly well that there are natural means which can affect health and even destroy the body. Poisons, wounds, burns, falls, are known to cause disablement or death in a natural way. And this is not a matter of private opinion of this or that individual, but it is laid down in traditional lore and even in belief, for there are considered to be different ways to the nether world for those who died by sorcery and those who met "natural" death. Again, it is recognized that cold, heat, overstrain, too much sun, over-eating, can all cause minor ailments, which are treated by natural remedies such as massage, steaming, warming at a fire and certain potions. Old age is known to lead to bodily decay and the explanation is given by the natives that very old people grow weak, their oesophagus closes up, and therefore they must die.

But besides these natural causes there is the enormous domain of sorcery and by far the most cases of illness and death are ascribed to this. The line of distinction between sorcery and the other causes is clear in theory and in most cases of practice, but it must be realized that it is subject to what could be called the personal perspective. That is, the more closely a case has to do with the person who considers it, the less will it be "natural," the more "magical." Thus a very old man, whose pending death will be considered natural by the other members of the community, will be afraid only of sorcery and never think of his natural fate. A fairly sick person will diagnose sorcery in his own case, while all the others might speak of too much betel nut or over-eating or some other indulgence.

But who of us really believes that his own bodily infirmities and the approaching death is a purely natural occurrence, just an insignificant event in the infinite chain of causes? To the most rational of civilized men health, disease, the threat of death, float in a hazy emotional mist, which seems to become denser and more impenetrable as the fateful forms approach. It is indeed astonishing that "savages" can achieve such a sober, dispassionate outlook in these matters as they actually do.

Thus in his relation to nature and destiny, whether he tries to exploit the first or to dodge the second, primitive man recognizes both the natural and the supernatural forces and agencies, and he tries to use them both for his benefit. Whenever he has been taught by experience that effort guided by knowledge is of some avail, he never spares the one or ignores the other. He knows that a plant cannot grow by magic alone, or a canoe sail or float without being properly constructed and managed, or a fight be won without skill and daring. He never relies on magic alone, while, on the contrary, he sometimes dispenses with it completely, as in fire-making and in a number of crafts and pursuits. But he clings to it, whenever he has to recognize the impotence of his knowledge and of his rational technique.

I have given my reasons why in this argument I had to rely principally on the material collected in the classical land of magic, Melanesia. But the facts discussed are so fundamental, the conclusions drawn of such a general nature, that it will be easy to check them on any modern detailed ethnographic record. Comparing agricultural work and magic, the building of canoes, the art of healing by magic and by natural remedies, the ideas about the causes of death in other regions, the universal validity of what has been established here could easily be proved. Only, since no observations have methodically been made with reference to the problem of primitive knowledge, the data from other writers could be gleaned only piecemeal and their testimony though clear would be indirect.

I have chosen to face the question of primitive man's rational knowledge directly: watching him at his principal occupations, seeing him pass from work to magic and back again, entering into his mind, listening to his opinions. The whole problem might have been approached through the avenue of language, but this would have led us too far into questions of logic, semasiology, and theory of primitive languages. Words which serve to express general ideas such as *existence, substance,* and *attribute, cause* and *effect,* the *fundamental* and the *secondary;* words and expressions used in complicated pursuits like sailing, construction, measuring and checking; numerals and quantitative descriptions, correct and detailed classifications of natural phenomena, plants and animals—all this would lead us exactly to the same conclusion: that primitive man can observe and think, and that he possesses, embodied in his language, systems of methical though rudimentary knowledge.

Similar conclusions could be drawn from an examination of those mental schemes and physical contrivances which could be described as diagrams or formulas. Methods of indicating the main points of the compass, arrangements of stars into constellations, co-ordination of these with the seasons, naming of moons in the year, of quarters in the moon—all these accomplishments are known to the simplest savages. Also they are all able to draw diagrammatic maps in the sand or dust, indicate arrangements by placing small stones, shells, or sticks on the ground, plan expeditions or raids on such rudimentary charts. By co-ordinating space and time they are able to arrange big tribal gatherings and to combine vast tribal movements over extensive areas. The use of leaves, notched sticks, and similar aids to memory is well known and seems to be almost universal. All such "diagrams" are means of reducing a complex and unwieldy bit of reality to a simple and handy form. They give man a relatively easy mental control over it. As such are they not—in a very rudimentary form no doubt—fundamentally akin to developed scientific formulas and "models," which are also simple and handy paraphrases of a complex or abstract reality, giving the civilized physicist mental control over it?

This brings us to the second question: Can we regard primitive knowledge, which, as we found, is both empirical and rational, as a rudimentary stage of science, or is it not at all related to it? If by science be understood a body of rules and conceptions, based on experience and derived from it by logical inference, embodied in material achievements and in a fixed form of tradition and carried on by some sort of social organization—then there is no doubt that even the lowest savage communities have the beginnings of science, however rudimentary.

Most epistemologists would not, however, be satisfied with such a "minimum definition" of science, for it might apply to the rules of an art or craft as well. They would maintain that the rules of science must be laid down explicitly, open to control by experiment and critique by reason. They must not only be rules of practical behavior, but theoretical laws of knowledge. Even accepting this stricture, however, there is hardly any doubt that many of the principles of savage knowledge are scientific in this sense. The native shipwright knows

not only practically of buoyancy, leverage, equilibrium, he has to obey these laws not only on water, but while making the canoe he must have the principles in his mind. He instructs his helpers in them. He gives them the traditional rules, and in a crude and simple manner, using his hands, pieces of wood, and a limited technical vocabulary, he explains some general laws of hydrodynamics and equilibrium. Science is not detached from the craft, that is certainly true, it is only a means to an end, it is crude, rudimentary, and inchoate, but with all that it is the matrix from which the higher developments must have sprung.

If we applied another criterion yet, that of the really scientific attitude, the disinterested search for knowledge and for the understanding of causes and reasons, the answer would certainly not be in a direct negative. There is, of course, no widespread thirst for knowledge in a savage community, new things such as European topics bore them frankly and their whole interest is largely encompassed by the traditional world of their culture. But within this there is both the antiquarian mind passionately interested in myths, stories, details of customs, pedigrees, and ancient happenings, and there is also to be found the naturalist, patient and painstaking in his observations, capable of generalization and of connecting long chains of events in the life of animals, and in the marine world or in the jungle. It is enough to realize how much European naturalists have often learned from their savage colleagues to appreciate this interest found in the native for nature. There is finally among the primitives, as every field-worker well knows, the sociologist, the ideal informant, capable with marvelous accuracy and insight to give the *raison d'être,* the function, and the organization of many a simpler institution in his tribe.

Science, of course, does not exist in any uncivilized community as a driving power, criticizing, renewing, constructing. Science is never consciously made. But on this criterion, neither is there law, nor religion, nor government among savages.

The question, however, whether we should call it *science* or only *empirical and rational knowledge* is not of primary importance in this context. We have tried to gain a clear idea as to whether the savage has only one domain of reality or two, and we found that he has his profane world of practical activities and rational outlook besides the sacred region of cult and belief.

2. On Logical and Non-Logical Action

BY VILFREDO PARETO

146. THIS is the first step we take along the path of induction. If we were to find, for instance, that all human actions[1] corresponded to logico-experimental theories, or that such actions were the most important, others having to be regarded as phenomena of social pathology deviating from a normal type, our course evidently would be entirely different from what it would be if many of the more important human actions proved to correspond to theories that are not logico-experimental.

147. Let us accordingly examine actions from the standpoint of their logico-experimental character. But in order to do that we must first try to classify them, and in that effort we propose to follow the principles of the classification called natural in botany and zoology, whereby objects on the whole presenting similar characteristics are grouped together. In the case of botany Tournefort's classification was wisely abandoned. It divided plants into "herbs" and "trees," and so came to separate entities that as a matter of fact present close resemblances. The so-called natural method nowadays preferred does away with all divisions of that kind and takes as its norm the characteristics of plants in the mass, putting like with like and keeping the unlike distinct. Can we find similar groupings to classify the actions of human beings?

148. It is not actions as we find them in the concrete that we are called upon to classify, but the elements constituting them. So the chemist classifies elements and compounds of elements, whereas in nature what he finds is mixtures of compounds. Concrete actions are synthetic—they originate in mixtures, in varying degrees, of the elements we are to classify.

149. Every social phenomenon may be considered under two aspects: as it is in reality, and as it presents itself to the mind of this or that human being. The first aspect we shall call *objective,* the second *subjective.* Such a division is necessary, for we cannot put in one same class the operations performed by a chemist in his laboratory and the operations performed by a person practising magic; the conduct of Greek sailors in plying their oars to drive their ship over the water and the sacrifices they offered to Poseidon to make sure of a safe and rapid voyage. In Rome the Laws of the XII Tables punished anyone casting a spell on a harvest. We choose to distinguish such an act from the act of burning a field of grain.

We must not be misled by the names we give to the two classes. In reality both are subjective, for all human knowledge is subjective. They are to be distinguished not so much by any difference in nature as in view of the greater or lesser fund of factual knowledge that we ourselves have. We know, or think we know, that sacrifices to Poseidon have no effect whatsoever upon a voyage. We therefore distinguish them from other acts which (to our best knowledge, at least) are capable of having such effect. If at some future time we were to discover that we have been mistaken, that sacrifices to Poseidon are very influential in securing a favourable voyage, we should have to reclassify them with actions capable of such influence. All that of course is pleonastic. It amounts to saying that when a person makes a classification, he does so according to the knowledge he has. One cannot imagine how things could be otherwise.

150. There are actions that use means appropriate to ends and which logically link means with ends. There are other actions in which those traits are missing. The two sorts of conduct are very different according as they are considered under their objective or their subjective aspect. From the subjective point of view nearly all human actions

---

Reprinted from Vilfredo Pareto, *The Mind and Society,* ed. Arthur Livingston, trans. Andrew Bongiorno and Arthur Livingston (New York: Harcourt, Brace & Co., 1935), Vol. I, §§ 146–54, 160–61, with the permission of The Pareto Fund.

1. Pareto, following Bentham, invariably uses the word "actions" (*azioni*) where ordinary English parlance uses "conduct" or "behaviour." Such phrases as "logical actions" and "non-logical actions" often lead to syntactical and other paradoxes in Pareto's text that have contributed not a little to his occasional obscurity. For mere convenience *azioni* is rendered here by "conduct," "behaviour," "acts," "actions," more or less interchangeably. The literally-minded reader can always recover the feel of the original Italian by understanding those words as "actions" with constructions in the plural. More troublesome still to the translator is Pareto's use of the phrase "non-logical actions" for "the sentiments (or "impulses" or "residues") underlying non-logical actions," or for "the principles of non-logical actions." There is no extricating him from that situation, and in it as a rule I leave him.—A. L.

belong to the logical class. In the eyes of the Greek mariners sacrifices to Poseidon and rowing with oars were equally logical means of navigation. To avoid verbosities which could only prove annoying, we had better give names to these types of conduct.[2] Suppose we apply the term *logical actions* to actions that logically conjoin means to ends not only from the standpoint of the subject performing them, but from the standpoint of other persons who have a more extensive knowledge—in other words, to actions that are logical both subjectively and objectively in the sense just explained. Other actions we shall call *non-logical* (by no means the same as "illogical"). This latter class we shall subdivide into a number of varieties.

151. A synoptic picture of the classification will prove useful:

GENERA AND SPECIES	HAVE THE ACTIONS LOGICAL ENDS AND PURPOSES:	
	Objectively?	Subjectively?

CLASS I. LOGICAL ACTIONS
(The objective end and the subjective purpose are identical.)

	Yes	Yes

CLASS II. NON-LOGICAL ACTIONS
(The objective end differs from the subjective purpose.)

Genus 1	No	No
Genus 2	No	Yes
Genus 3	Yes	No
Genus 4	Yes	Yes

SPECIES OF THE GENERA 3 AND 4

3α, 4α	The objective end would be accepted by the subject if he knew it.
3β, 4β	The objective end would be rejected by the subject if he knew it.

The ends and purposes here in question are immediate ends and purposes. We choose to disregard the indirect. The objective end is a real one, located within the field of observation and experience, and not an imaginary end, located outside that field. An imaginary end may, on the other hand, constitute a subjective purpose.

152. Logical actions are very numerous among civilized peoples. Actions connected with the arts and sciences belong to that class, at least for artists and scientists. For those who physically perform

them in mere execution of orders from superiors, there may be among them non-logical actions of our II-4 type. The actions dealt with in political economy also belong in very great part in the class of logical actions. In the same class must be located, further, a certain number of actions connected with military, political, legal, and similar activities.

153. So at the very first glance induction leads to the discovery that non-logical actions play an important part in society. Let us therefore proceed with our examination of them.

154. First of all, in order to get better acquainted with these non-logical actions, suppose we look at a few examples. Many others will find their proper places in chapters to follow. Here are some illustrations of actions of Class II:

Genera 1 and 3, which have no subjective purpose, are of scant importance to the human race. Human beings have a very conspicuous tendency to paint a varnish of logic over their conduct. Nearly all human actions therefore work their way into genera 2 and 4. Many actions performed in deference to courtesy and custom might be put in genus 1. But very very often people give some reason or other to justify such conduct, and that transfers it to genus 2. Ignoring the indirect motive involved in the fact that a person violating common usages incurs criticism and dislike, we might find a certain number of actions to place in genera 1 and 3.

Says Hesiod: "Do not make water at the mouth of a river emptying into the sea, nor into a spring. You must avoid that. Do not lighten your bowels there, for it is not good to do so." The precept not to befoul rivers at their mouths belongs to genus 1. No objective or subjective end or purpose is apparent in the avoidance of such pollution. The precept not to befoul drinking-water belongs to genus 3. It has an objective purpose that Hesiod may not have known, but which is familiar to moderns: to prevent contagion from certain diseases.

It is probable that not a few actions of genera 1 and 3 are common among savages and primitive peoples. But travellers are bent on learning at all costs the reasons for the conduct they observe. So in one way or another they finally obtain answers that transfer the conduct to genera 2 and 4.

*   *   *

160. Another very important difference between human conduct and the conduct of animals lies in the fact that we do not observe human conduct wholly from the outside as we do in the case of animals. Frequently we know the actions of human beings through the judgments that people pass upon them, through the impressions they make, and in

---

2. It would perhaps be better to use designations that have no meanings in themselves, such as letters of the alphabet. On the other hand, such a system would impair the clarity of our argument. We must therefore resign ourselves to using terms of ordinary speech; but the reader must bear in mind that such words, or their etymologies, in no way serve to describe the things they stand for. Things have to be examined directly. Names are just labels to help us keep track of them.

the light of the motives that people are pleased to imagine for them and assign as their causes. For that reason, actions that would otherwise belong to genera 1 and 3 make their way into 2 and 4.

Operations in magic when unattended by other actions belong to genus 2. The sacrifices of the Greeks and Romans have to be classed in the same genus—at least after those peoples lost faith in the reality of their gods. Hesiod, *Opera et dies*, vv. 735–39, warns against crossing a river without first washing one's hands in it and uttering a prayer. That would be an action of genus 1. But he adds that the gods punish anyone who crosses a river without so washing his hands. That makes it an action of genus 2.

This rationalizing procedure is habitual and very wide-spread. Hesiod says also, vv. 780–82, that grain should not be sown on the thirteenth of a month, but that that day is otherwise very auspicious for planting, and he gives many other precepts of the kind. They all belong to genus 2. In Rome a soothsayer who had observed signs in the heavens was authorized to adjourn the *comitia* to some other day.[3] Towards the end of the Republic, when all faith in augural science had been lost, that was a logical action, a means of attaining a desired end.

3. Cicero, *De legibus,* II, 12, 31: "If we are thinking of prerogative, what prerogative more extreme than to be able to adjourn assemblies and councils called by the supreme authorities, the highest magistrates, or to annul their enactments if they have already been held? And what more important than that business in course should be postponed if a single augur cries, *Alio die!?*"

But when people still believed in augury, it was an action of genus 4. For the soothsayers who, with the help of the gods, were so enabled to forestall some decision that they considered harmful to the Roman People, it belonged to our species 4a, as is apparent if one consider that in general such actions correspond, very roughly to be sure, to the provisions used in our time for avoiding ill-considered decisions by legislative bodies: requirements of two or three consecutive readings, of approvals by two houses, and so on.

Most acts of public policy based on tradition or on presumed missions of peoples or individuals belong to genus 4. William I, King of Prussia, and Napoleon III, Emperor of the French, both considered themselves "men of destiny." But William I thought his mission lay in promoting the welfare and greatness of his country, Louis Napoleon believed himself destined to achieve the happiness of mankind. William's policies were of the 4a type; Napoleon's, of the 4B.

Human beings as a rule determine their conduct with reference to certain general rules (morality, custom, law), which give rise in greater or lesser numbers to actions of our 4a and even 4B varieties.

161. Logical actions are at least in large part results of processes of reasoning. Non-logical actions originate chiefly in definite psychic states, sentiments, subconscious feelings, and the like. It is the province of psychology to investigate such psychic states. Here we start with them as data of fact, without going beyond that.

3. *Types of Rationality*

BY MAX WEBER

SOCIAL ACTION, like other forms of action, may be classified in the following four types according to its mode of orientation (1) in terms of rational orientation to a system of discrete individual ends (*zweckrational*), that is, through expectations as to the behaviour of objects in the external situation and of other human individuals,

Reprinted from Max Weber, *The Theory of Social and Economic Organization,* trans. A. M. Henderson and Talcott Parsons, ed. Talcott Parsons (Glencoe, Ill.: The Free Press, 1947), 115–17. Copyright 1947 by Oxford University Press.

making use of these expectations as "conditions" or "means" for the successful attainment of the actor's own rationally chosen ends; (2) in terms of rational orientation to an absolute value (*wertrational*); involving a conscious belief in the absolute value of some ethical, aesthetic, religious, or other form of behaviour, entirely for its own sake and independently of any prospects of external success; (3) in terms of affectual orientation, especially emotional, determined by the specific affects and states of feeling of the actor; (4) traditionally oriented, through the habituation of long practice.[1]

1. Strictly traditional behaviour, like the reactive type of imitation discussed above, lies very close to the borderline of what can justifiably be called meaningfully oriented action, and indeed often on the other side. For it is very often a matter of almost automatic reaction to habitual stimuli which guide behaviour in a course which has been repeatedly followed. The great bulk of all everyday action to which people have become habitually accustomed approaches this type. Hence, its place in a systematic classification is not merely that of a limiting case because, as will be shown later, attachment to habitual forms can be upheld with varying degrees of self-consciousness and in a variety of senses. In this case the type may shade over into number two (*Wertrationalität*).

2. Purely affectual behaviour also stands on the borderline of what can be considered "meaningfully" oriented, and often it, too, goes over the line. It may, for instance, consist in an uncontrolled reaction to some exceptional stimulus. It is a case of sublimation when affectually determined action

occurs in the form of conscious release of emotional tension. When this happens it is usually, though not always, well on the road to rationalization in one or the other or both of the above senses.

3. The orientation of action in terms of absolute value is distinguished from the affectual type by its clearly self-conscious formulation of the ultimate values governing the action and the consistently planned orientation of its detailed course to these values. At the same time the two types have a common element, namely that the meaning of the action does not lie in the achievement of a result ulterior to it, but in carrying out the specific type of action for its own sake. Examples of affectual action are the satisfaction of a direct impulse to revenge, to sensual gratification, to devote oneself to a person or ideal, to contemplative bliss, or, finally, toward the working off of emotional tensions. Such impulses belong in this category regardless of how sordid or sublime they may be.

Examples of pure rational orientation to absolute values would be the action of persons who, regardless of possible cost to themselves, act to put into practice their convictions of what seems to them to be required by duty, honour, the pursuit of beauty, a religious call, personal loyalty, or the importance of some "cause" no matter in what it consists. For the purposes of this discussion, when action is oriented to absolute values, it always involves "commands" or "demands" to the fulfilment of which the actor feels obligated. It is only in cases where human action is motivated by the fulfilment of such unconditional demands that it will be described as oriented to absolute values. This is empirically the case in widely varying degrees, but for the most part only to a relatively slight extent. Nevertheless, it will be shown that the occurrence of this mode of action is important enough to justify its formulation as a distinct type; though it may be remarked that there is no intention here of attempting to formulate in any sense an exhaustive classification of types of action.

4. Action is rationally oriented to a system of discrete individual ends (*zweckrational*) when the end, the means, and the secondary results are all rationally taken into account and weighed. This involves rational consideration of alternative means to the end, of the relations of the end to other prospective results of employment of any given means, and finally of the relative importance of different possible ends. Determination of action, either in affectual or in traditional terms, is thus incompatible with this type. Choice between alternative and conflicting ends and results may well be determined by considerations of absolute value. In that case, action is rationally oriented to a system of

---

1. The two terms *zweckrational* and *wertrational* are of central significance to Weber's theory, but at the same time present one of the most difficult problems to the translator. Perhaps the keynote of the distinction lies in the absoluteness with which the values involved in *Wertrationalität* are held. The sole important consideration to the actor becomes the realization of the value. In so far as it involves ends, rational considerations, such as those of efficiency, are involved in the choice of means. But there is no question either of rational weighing of this end against others, nor is there a question of "counting the cost" in the sense of taking account of possible results other than the attainment of the absolute end. In the case of *Zweckrationalität*, on the other hand, Weber conceives action as motivated by a plurality of relatively independent ends, none of which is absolute. Hence, rationality involves on the one hand the weighing of the relative importance of their realization, on the other hand, consideration of whether undesirable consequences would outweigh the benefits to be derived from the projected course of action. It has not seemed possible to find English terms which would express this distinction succinctly. Hence the attempt has been made to express the ideas as clearly as possible without specific terms.

It should also be pointed out that, as Weber's analysis proceeds, there is a tendency of the meaning of these terms to shift, so that *Wertrationalität* comes to refer to a system of ultimate ends, regardless of the degree of their absoluteness, while *Zweckrationalität* refers primarily to considerations respecting the choice of means and ends which are in turn means to further ends, such as money. What seems to have happened is that Weber shifted from a classification of ideal types of action to one of elements in the structure of action. In the latter context "expediency" is often an adequate rendering of *Zweckrationalität*. This process has been analysed in the editor's *Structure of Social Action*, chap. xvi.

The other two terms *affektuell* and *traditional* do not present any difficulty of translation. The term affectual has come into English psychological usage from the German largely through the influence of psychoanalysis.

discrete individual ends only in respect to the choice of means. On the other hand, the actor may, instead of deciding between alternative and conflicting ends in terms of a rational orientation to a system of values, simply take them as given subjective wants and arrange them in a scale of consciously assessed relative urgency. He may then orient his action to this scale in such a way that they are satisfied as far as possible in order of urgency, as formulated in the principle of "marginal utility." The orientation of action to absolute values may thus have various different modes of relation to the other type of rational action, in terms of a system of discrete individual ends. From the latter point of view, however, absolute values are always irrational. Indeed, the more the value to which action is oriented is elevated to the status of an absolute value, the more "irrational" in this sense the corresponding action is. For, the more unconditionally the actor devotes himself to this value

for its own sake, to pure sentiment or beauty, to absolute goodness or devotion to duty, the less is he influenced by considerations of the consequences of his action. The orientation of action wholly to the rational achievement of ends without relation to fundamental values is, to be sure, essentially only a limiting case.

5. It would be very unusual to find concrete cases of action, especially of social action, which were oriented *only* in one or another of these ways. Furthermore, this classification of the modes of orientation of action is in no sense meant to exhaust the possibilities of the field, but only to formulate in conceptually pure form certain sociologically important types, to which actual action is more or less closely approximated or, in much the more common case, which constitute the elements combining to make it up. The usefulness of the classification for the purposes of this investigation can only be judged in terms of its results.

4. *Social Structure and the Structure of Thought*

BY EMILE DURKHEIM AND MARCEL MAUSS

PRIMITIVE CLASSIFICATIONS are not exceptional phenomena bearing no resemblance to those commonly found among the more civilized populations; on the contrary, they appear as direct ancestors of the first scientific systems of classification. Although they differ profoundly from the latter in certain respects, they share all of their most essential features. First, like all scientific classifications, they are systems of concepts arranged in hierarchical order. Things are not simply placed in groups isolated from one another; rather, these groups have specific relationships with one another, and all of them combine into a single entity. Furthermore, these primitive systems, just as the scientific ones, have an exclusively speculative function. Their purpose is not to facilitate action, but to further understanding, to render intelligible the relationships that exist between beings. Once certain fundamental concepts are given, the human mind feels the need to integrate with them

the ideas it has about the rest of things. Such classifications are then, above all, destined to link ideas together and to unify knowledge. In this context, it is permissible to say that they are works of science and constitute the beginnings of a cosmology. The Australian divides the world between the totems of his tribe not in order to pattern his behavior or even to justify his ritual; because the idea of totem is fundamental for him, it is essential that he situate all the rest of his knowledge in relation to it. It is likely, then, that the conditions under which these very ancient classifications were elaborated have played an important role in the birth of the classifying function in general.

Furthermore, it appears from this study that these conditions are social. Far from it being the logical relationships between things that give the basis for the social relationships between men—as Mr. Frazer seems to assume—in reality, the reverse is true. According to Frazer, men divided themselves in clans following a prior classification of things. In reality, they have classified things because they were divided into clans.

Translated by Jesse Pitts, from Emile Durkheim and Marcel Mauss, "Quelques formes de classification primitives," *Année Sociologique*, VI (1901–2), pp. 66–72.

We have seen how these classifications were modeled after the earliest and most fundamental social organization. To state the point more emphatically: society was not merely a model from which classificatory thought took its departure; its very framework was used as the framework of the system. The first logical categories were social categories; the first classes of things were classes of men, into which these things were integrated. It is because men lived in groups and thought of themselves as groups that they have abstractly grouped everything else, and the two types of groups began by being so fused as to be inseparable. Phratries were the first genera; the clans, the first species. Things were supposed to be integral parts of the society, and it was their place in society that determined their place in nature. We may even wonder if the schematic way in which the genera are ordinarily conceived does not result in part from the same influences. It is a fact of common observation that the things included in genera are generally imagined as located in a sort of ideal milieu, the space dimensions of which are more or less clearly defined. It is certainly not without reason that concepts and their relationships have so often been represented by circles—concentric or excentric, inside or outside one another, etc. Could not this tendency of ours to represent purely logical groups under a form that so contrasts their true nature come from the fact that they were first conceived under the form of social groups, which occupy a definite area in space? And have we not observed this spacial localization of genera and species in a relatively large number of widely different societies?

Not only the external definition of these categories but also their interrelationships with one another are of social origin. It is because human groups contain one another—the clan contains the subclan; the phratry, the clan; and the tribe, the phratry—that groups of things are disposed in the same order. Their extension, regularly decreasing as we pass from genus to species, from the species to the variety, etc., comes from the similarly decreasing extension that we find in social groupings as we leave the largest and most ancient to approach the most recent and differentiated. If the totality of things is conceived as one unique system, it is because society itself is conceived in the same way. It is an entity, or, rather, it is the unique entity to which everything else is referred. Thus, the logical hierarchy is but another aspect of social hierarchy, and the unity of knowledge is but the very unity of the community, extrapolated to the universe.

The ties that bind the beings of the same group, or the different groups to one another, are conceived of as social ties. Earlier, we recalled that the expressions by which we still name these relationships have a moral meaning; although for us they are merely metaphors, at the beginning, these expressions retained all their meaning. The things of the same class were really considered as kin to the individuals of the same social groups, and hence as kin to one another. They are "of the same flesh" —of the same family. Hence, logical relationships are, in a way, domestic relationships. Sometimes, as we have seen, they are even on all points comparable to those existing between the master and the thing he possesses, between the chief and his subordinates. We might even wonder whether the notion—so distasteful from a positivistic standpoint— of the superiority of the genus to the species did not find here its first rudimentary form. As, for the realist, the general concept is stronger than the individual, so the clan totem dominates that of the subclans and, even more, the personal totem of each individual. In the societies where the phratry has kept its primitive cohesion, it has a sort of primacy over its subdivisions and the individuals comprising the latter. Among the Zuni, the animals that symbolize the six fundamental clans have sovereignty over their respective subclans and the beings of all sorts that they include.

We may have explained how the notion of classes integrated within one and the same system was born, but we still do not know what forces drove men to distribute things between these classes in the way they did. Even if the external framework of classification was given by society, it does not necessarily follow that the way in which this framework was used can be explained by social factors. A priori, it is very possible that altogether different forces have determined the way in which beings were assembled and assimilated to one another, or, on the other hand, were differentiated and came to oppose each other.

However, the striking conception of logical relationships that prevails in these early stages permits us to set aside this hypothesis. We have seen that logical relationships are represented in the form of family ties, or as relations of economic or political subordination: the same feelings, then, which are at the basis of social and domestic organization, also presided at this logical sorting of things. The latter relations attract or oppose one another in the same way as men are linked by kinship or opposed in vendetta. They unite as the members of a family unite in common thinking. That which makes certain things subordinate to others is somewhat analogous to that which makes the subject inferior to his master. Consequently, it is the states of the collective mind that have given birth to these groupings; furthermore, these states are obviously of an affective nature. There are sentimental affinities between things as between individuals, and it is after these affinities that they are classified.

We thus arrive at this conclusion: it is possible to classify other things than concepts, and otherwise than through the laws of pure reason. For if concepts can be ordered systematically for reasons of sentiment, they cannot be pure ideas, but must be themselves works of sentiment. Indeed, for those we call primitives, a species of things is not a mere object of knowledge but above all is related to certain emotional attitudes. All sorts of affective elements participate in the representation that is made of it. Religious emotions, notably, not only give it a special feeling tone but are also responsible for its most essential attributes. Things are above all sacred or profane, pure or impure, friendly or hostile, favorable or unfavorable; that is to say, their most fundamental characteristics do but evidence the manner in which they affect the social senses. The differences and resemblances determining the manner in which they are grouped are more affective than intellectual. This is why the nature of things changes, in a way, from one society to the other; they affect the feelings of different groups differently. What is here conceived as perfectly homogeneous is represented elsewhere as essentially heterogeneous. For us, space is formed of identical parts, interchangeable one with the other. We have seen, however, that for many peoples space is profoundly differentiated, depending on the region considered. This is because each region has its own affective value. Under the influence of various sentiments, a particular region of space is referred back to a specific religious principle; in consequence, it is endowed with virtues *sui generis,* which distinguish it from any other region. It is this emotional value of concepts that plays a primordial role in the manner with which ideas approach one another or diverge. It is the dominant guide to the classification.

It has often been said that man began to represent things by referring them back to himself. The preceding developments permit analysis of the components of this anthropocentrism, which could be better called *sociocentrism.* The center of the first cosmogony is not the individual, but society. It is society that realizes itself. Nothing is clearer in this context than the way in which the Sioux Indians make the tribal space contain the whole world, and we have seen how universal space itself is nothing else than the tribe's own location, but infinitely extended beyond its effective limits. It is this same

mental attitude which has led so many peoples to place the center of the world, "the navel of the world," in their political or religious capital; that is, where the center of their spiritual life is to be found. Similarly, although on another plane, the creative force of the universe and of all that it includes was primitively conceived as the mythical ancestor, fathering the whole society.

This is why the conception of logical classification has had so much difficulty in getting started. A logical classification is a classification of concepts; the concept is the notion of a group of beings that is sharply defined, and its limits can be traced with precision. Emotion, on the other hand, is essentially vaporous and boundless. Its contagious influence diffuses well beyond its point of origin to all that surrounds it, with no definite barrier to its powers of ramification. All states of emotional nature necessarily share these characteristics. No precise beginning nor ending can be ascribed to them: they join together, mixing their properties so that they cannot be categorized with any rigor. Furthermore, in order to mark the boundaries of a class, it is necessary to have analyzed the characteristics by which the beings assembled in this class are identified and segregated. Emotion is naturally resistant to analysis, or, at least, because of its complexity, very hard to cope with. It defies critical and reasoned analysis, particularly when it has a collective origin. The pressure exercised by the social group upon each of its members does not permit individuals to judge freely the concepts that the society itself has elaborated and where it has put something of its character. Such constructions are sacred to the citizen. Furthermore, the history of scientific classification is, in the last analysis, the very history of the steps through which this element of social affect has progressively weakened, leaving more and more room for the reflective thinking of individuals. However, these ancient influences have certainly not ceased to make themselves felt. They have left behind them a pervasive effect: it is the basic framework of all classification, it is the whole set of mental habits that makes us represent beings and facts under the form of groups that are coordinated and subordinated one to the other.

It is possible to see in this example what light sociology can shed upon the genesis, and hence the functioning, of logical operations. What we have tried to do for classification could also be tried for the other functions or the basic categories of human reason. We have already had occasion to indicate how ideas—even as abstract as those of Time and Space—are, at each moment of their history, in close relationship with their corresponding social organizations. The same method could help us to understand the way in which the ideas of cause, substance, the different forms of reasoning, etc., have been formed. All these questions, so long debated by metaphysicians and psychologists, will at last be freed from tedious cliches when they are posed in sociological terms. This, at least, is a new approach which deserves to be tried.

5. *On the Origins of the Idea of Force*

BY EMILE DURKHEIM

THE FIRST THING which is implied in the notion of the causal relation is the idea of efficacy, of productive power, of active force. By cause we ordinarily mean something capable of producing a certain change. The cause is the force before it has shown the power which is in it; the effect is this same power, only actualized. Men have always thought of causality in dynamic terms. Of course certain philosophers had refused all objective value to this conception; they see in it only an arbitrary construction of the imagination, which corresponds to nothing in the things themselves. But, at present, we have no need of asking whether it is founded in reality or not; it is enough for us to state that it exists and that it constitutes and always has constituted an element of ordinary mentality; and this is recognized even by those who criticize it. Our immediate purpose is to seek, not what it may be worth logically, but how it is to be explained.

Now it depends upon social causes. Our analysis of facts has already enabled us to see that the prototype of the idea of force was the mana, wakan, orenda, the totemic principle or any of the various names given to collective force objectified and projected into things. The first power which men have thought of as such seems to have been that exercised by humanity over its members. Thus reason confirms the results of observation; in fact, it is even possible to show why this notion of power, efficacy or active force could not have come from any other source.

In the first place, it is evident and recognized by all that it could not be furnished to us by external experience. Our senses only enable us to perceive phenomena which coexist or which follow one another, but nothing perceived by them could give us

the idea of this determining and compelling action which is characteristic of what we call a power or force. They can touch only realized and known conditions, each separate from the others; the internal process uniting these conditions escapes them. Nothing that we learn could possibly suggest to us the idea of what an influence or efficaciousness is. It is for this very reason that the philosophers of empiricism have regarded these different conceptions as so many mythological aberrations. But even supposing that they all are hallucinations, it is still necessary to show how they originated.

If external experience counts for nothing in the origin of these ideas, and it is equally inadmissible that they were given us ready-made, one might suppose that they come from internal experience. In fact, the notion of force obviously includes many spiritual elements which could only have been taken from our psychic life.

Some have believed that the act by which our will brings a deliberation to a close, restrains our impulses and commands our organism, might have served as the model of this construction. In willing, it is said, we perceive ourselves directly as a power in action. So when this idea had once occurred to men, it seems that they only had to extend it to things to establish the conception of force.

As long as the animist theory passed as a demonstrated truth, this explanation was able to appear to be confirmed by history. If the forces with which human thought primitively populated the world really had been spirits, that is to say, personal and conscious beings more or less similar to men, it was actually possible to believe that our individual experience was enough to furnish us with the constituent elements of the notion of force. But we know that the first forces which men imagined were, on the contrary, anonymous, vague and diffused powers which resemble cosmic forces in their impersonality, and which are therefore most sharply con-

Reprinted from Emile Durkheim, *Elementary Forms of the Religious Life,* trans. Joseph Ward Swain (Glencoe, Ill.: The Free Press, 1954), pp. 363–67, with the permission of The Free Press.

trasted with the eminently personal power, the human will. So it is impossible that they should have been conceived in its image.

Moreover, there is one essential characteristic of the impersonal forces which would be inexplicable under this hypothesis: this is their communicability. The forces of nature have always been thought of as capable of passing from one object to another, of mixing, combining and transforming themselves into one another. It is even this property which gives them their value as an explanation, for it is through this that effects can be connected with their causes without a break of continuity. Now the self has just the opposite characteristic: it is incommunicable. It cannot change its material substratum or spread from one to another; it spreads out in metaphor only. So the way in which it decides and executes its decisions could never have suggested the idea of an energy which communicates itself and which can even confound itself with others and, through these combinations and mixings, give rise to new effects.

Therefore, the idea of force, as implied in the conception of the causal relation, must present a double character. In the first place, it can come only from our internal experience; the only forces which we can directly learn about are necessarily moral forces. But, at the same time, they must be impersonal, for the notion of an impersonal power was the first to be constituted. Now the only ones which satisfy these two conditions are those coming from life together: they are collective forces. In fact, these are, on the one hand, entirely psychical; they are made up exclusively of objectified ideas and sentiments. But, on the other hand, they are impersonal by definition, for they are the product of a co-operation. Being the work of all, they are not the possession of anybody in particular. They are so slightly attached to the personalities of the subjects in whom they reside that they are never fixed there. Just as they enter them from without, they are also always ready to leave them. Of themselves, they tend to spread further and further and to invade ever new domains: we know that there are none more contagious, and consequently more communicable. Of course physical forces have the same property, but we cannot know this directly; we cannot even become acquainted with them as such, for they are outside us. When I throw myself against an obstacle, I have a sensation of hindrance and trouble; but the force causing this sensation is not in me, but in the obstacle, and is consequently outside the circle of my perception. We perceive its effects, but we cannot reach the cause itself. It is otherwise with social forces: they are a part of our internal life, as we know, more than the products of their action; we see them acting. The force isolating the

sacred being and holding profane beings at a distance is not really in this being; it lives in the minds of the believers. So they perceive it at the very moment when it is acting upon their wills, to inhibit certain movements or command others. In a word, this constraining and necessitating action, which escapes us when coming from an external object, is readily perceptible here because everything is inside us. Of course we do not always interpret it in an adequate manner, but at least we cannot fail to be conscious of it.

Moreover, the idea of force bears the mark of its origin in an apparent way. In fact, it implies the idea of power which, in its turn, does not come without those of ascendancy, mastership and domination, and their corollaries, dependence and subordination; now the relations expressed by all these ideas are eminently social. It is society which classifies beings into superiors and inferiors, into commanding masters and obeying servants; it is society which confers upon the former the singular property which makes the command efficacious and which makes *power*. So everything tends to prove that the first powers of which the human mind had any idea were those which societies have established in organizing themselves: it is in their image that the powers of the physical world have been conceived. Also, men have never succeeded in imagining themselves as forces mistress over the bodies in which they reside, except by introducing concepts taken from social life. In fact, these must be distinguished from their physical doubles and must be attributed a dignity superior to that of these latter; in a word, they must think of themselves as souls. As a matter of fact, men have always given the form of souls to the forces which they believe that they are. But we know that the soul is quite another thing from a name given to the abstract faculty of moving, thinking and feeling; before all, it is a religious principle, a particular aspect of the collective force. In fine, a man feels that he has a soul, and consequently a force, because he is a social being. Though an animal moves its members just as we do, and though it has the same power as we over its muscles, nothing authorizes us to suppose that it is conscious of itself as an active and efficacious cause. This is because it does not have, or, to speak more exactly, does not attribute to itself a soul. But if it does not attribute a soul to itself, it is because it does not participate in a social life comparable to that of men. Among animals, there is nothing resembling a civilization.*

But the notion of force is not all of the principle

---

* Of course animal societies do exist. However, the word does not have exactly the same sense when applied to men and to animals. The institution is a characteristic fact of human societies; but animals have no institutions of causality. This consists in a judgment stating that every force develops in a definite manner, and that the state in which it is at each particular moment of its existence predetermines the next state. The former is called cause, the latter, effect, and the causal judgment affirms the existence of a necessary connection between these two moments for every force. The mind posits this connection before having any proofs of it, under the empire of a sort of constraint from which it cannot free itself; it postulates it, as they say, *a priori*.

Empiricism has never succeeded in accounting for this apriorism and necessity. Philosophers of this school have never been able to explain how an association of ideas, reinforced by habit, could produce more than an expectation or a stronger or weaker predisposition on the part of ideas to appear in a determined order. But the principle of causality has quite another character. It is not merely an imminent tendency of our thought to take certain forms; it is an external norm, superior to the flow of our representations, which it dominates and rules imperatively. It is invested with an authority which binds the mind and surpasses it, which is as much as to say that the mind is not its artisan. In this connection, it is useless to substitute hereditary habit for individual habit, for habit does not change its nature by lasting longer than one man's life; it is merely stronger. An instinct is not a rule.

The rites which we have been studying allow us to catch a glimpse of another source of this authority, which, up to the present, has scarcely been sus-pected. Let us bear in mind how the law of causality, which the imitative rites put into practice, was born. Being filled with one single preoccupation, the group assembles: if the species whose name it bears does not reproduce, it is a matter of concern to the whole clan. The common sentiment thus animating all the members is outwardly expressed by certain gestures, which are always the same in the same circumstances, and after the ceremony has been performed, it happens, for the reason set forth, that the desired result seems obtained. So an association arises between the idea of this result and that of the gestures preceding it; and this association does not vary from one subject to another; it is the same for all the participators in the rite, since it is the product of a collective experience. However, if no other factor intervened, it would produce only a collective expectation; after the imitative gestures had been accomplished, everybody would await the subsequent appearance of the desired event, with more or less confidence; an imperative rule of thought could never be established by this. But since a social interest of the greatest importance is at stake, society cannot allow things to follow their own course at the whim of circumstances; it intervenes actively in such a way as to regulate their march in conformity with its needs. So it demands that this ceremony, which it cannot do without, be repeated every time that it is necessary, and consequently, that the movements, a condition of its success, be executed regularly: it imposes them as an obligation.

6. *The Positive Role of the Sociology of Knowledge*

BY KARL MANNHEIM

ONCE we realize that although epistemology is the basis of all the empirical sciences, it can only derive its principles from the data supplied by them and once we realize, further, the extent to which epistemology has hitherto been profoundly influenced by the ideal of the exact sciences, then it is clearly our duty to inquire how the problem will be affected when other sciences are taken into consideration. This suggests the following arguments:

Reprinted from Karl Mannheim, *Ideology and Utopia* (New York: Harcourt, Brace & Co.; and London: Kegan Paul, Trench, Trubner & Co., 1936), pp. 262–75, with the permission of Harcourt, Brace & Co., Inc. and Routledge & Kegan Paul, Ltd.

REVISION OF THE THESIS THAT THE GENESIS OF A PROPOSITION IS UNDER ALL CIRCUMSTANCES IRRELEVANT TO ITS TRUTH

The abrupt and absolute dualism between "validity" and "existence"—between "meaning" and "existence"—between "essence" and "fact" is, as has often been pointed out, one of the axioms of the "idealistic" epistemology and noology prevailing to-day. It is regarded as impregnable and is the most immediate obstacle to the unbiased utilization of the findings of the sociology of knowledge.

Indeed, if the type of knowledge represented by

the example $2 \times 2 = 4$ is subjected to examination, then the correctness of this thesis is fairly well demonstrated. It is true of this type of knowledge that its genesis does not enter into the results of thought. From this it is only a short step to construct a sphere of truth in itself in such a manner that it becomes completely independent of the knowing subject. Moreover, this theory of the separability of the truth-content of a statement from the conditions of its origin had great value in the struggle against psychologism, for only with the aid of this theory was it possible to separate the known from the act of knowing. The observation that the genesis of an idea must be kept separate from its meaning applies also in the domain of explanatory psychology. It is only because in this realm it could be demonstrated in certain cases that the psychological processes which produce meanings are irrelevant to their validity, that this statement was legitimately incorporated into the truths of noology and epistemology. Between, for instance, the laws of the mechanism of association and the judgment arrived at by this associative mechanism, there exists a gap, which makes it plausible that a genesis of that kind does not contribute anything to the evaluation of meaning. There are, however, types of genesis which are not void of meaning, the peculiarities of which have until now never been analysed. Thus, for example, the relationship between existential position and the corresponding point of view may be considered as a genetic one, but in a sense different from that used previously. In this case, too, the question of genesis is involved, since there can be no doubt that we are here dealing with the conditions of emergence and existence of an assertion. If we speak of the "position behind a point of view" we have in mind a complex of conditions of emergence and existence which determine the nature and development of an assertion. But we would be falsely characterizing the existential situation of the assertor if we failed to take into account its meaning for the validity of the assertion. A position in the social structure carries with it, as we have seen, the probability that he who occupies it will think in a certain way. It signifies existence oriented with reference to certain meanings (*Sinnausgerichtetes Sein*). Social position cannot be described in terms which are devoid of social meanings as, for example, by mere chronological designation. As a chronological date, 1789 is wholly meaningless. As historical designation, however, this date refers to a set of meaningful social events which in themselves demarcate the range of a certain type of experiences, conflicts, attitudes, and thoughts. Historical-social position can only be adequately characterized by meaningful designations (as, for in-

stance, by such designations as "liberal position," "proletarian conditions of existence," etc.). "Social existence" is thus an area of being, or a sphere of existence, of which orthodox ontology which recognizes only the absolute dualism between being devoid of meaning on the one hand and meaning on the other hand takes no account. A genesis of this sort could be characterized by calling it a "meaningful genesis" (*Sinngenesis*) as contrasted with a "factual-genesis" (*Faktizitätsgenesis*). If a model of this sort had been kept in mind in stating the relationship between being and meaning, the duality of being and validity would not have been assumed as absolute in epistemology and noology. Instead, there would have been a series of gradations between these two poles, in which such intermediate cases as "being invested with meaning" and "being oriented to meaning" would have found a place and been incorporated into the fundamental conception.

The next task of epistemology, in our opinion, is to overcome its partial nature by incorporating into itself the multiplicity of relationships between existence and validity (*Sein und Geltung*) as discovered by the sociology of knowledge, and to give attention to the types of knowledge operating in a region of being which is full of meaning and which affects the truth-value of the assertions. Thereby epistemology is not supplanted by the sociology of knowledge but a new kind of epistemology is called for which will reckon with the facts brought to light by the sociology of knowledge.

FURTHER CONSEQUENCES OF THE SOCIOLOGY OF KNOWLEDGE FOR EPISTEMOLOGY

Having seen that most of the axioms of the prevailing noology and epistemology have been taken over from the quantifiable natural sciences and are, so to speak, mere extensions of the tendencies singularly characteristic of this form of knowledge, it becomes clear that the noological problem must be reformulated with reference to the counter model of more or less existentially determined varieties of knowledge. We intend now in a few words to state the new formulation of the problem which is deemed necessary once we have recognized the partial character of the older noology.

The Discovery of the Activistic Element in Knowledge

That in the "idealistic" conception of knowledge knowing is regarded mostly as a purely "theoretical" act in the sense of pure perception, has its origins, in addition to the above-mentioned orientation toward mathematical models, in the fact that in the background of this epistemology there lies the philosophical ideal of the "contemplative life." We cannot concern ourselves here with the history of this ideal or the manner in which purely contemplative conception of knowledge first penetrated into epistemology. (This would require examination of the pre-history of scientific logic and of the development of the philosopher from the seer, from whom the former took over the ideal of the "mystic vision.") It suffices for us to point out that this great esteem for the contemplatively perceived is not the outcome of the "pure" observation of the act of thinking and knowing, but springs from a hierarchy of values based on a certain philosophy of life. The idealistic philosophy, which represents this tradition, insisted that knowledge was pure only when it was purely theoretical. Idealistic philosophy was not upset by the discovery that the type of knowledge represented by pure theory was only a small segment of human knowledge, that in addition there can be knowledge where men, while thinking, are also acting, and finally, that in certain fields knowledge arises only when and in so far as it itself is action, i.e. when action is permeated by the intention of the mind, in the sense that the concepts and the total apparatus of thought are dominated by and reflect this activist orientation. Not purpose *in addition* to perception but purpose *in* perception itself reveals the qualitative richness of the world in certain fields. Also the phenomenologically demonstrable fact that in these fields the activist genesis penetrates into the structure of the perspective and is not separable from it could not deter the older noology and epistemology either from overlooking this type of knowledge, which is integrated with action, or from seeing in it only an "impure" form of knowledge. (It is interesting to note that the connotations of the designation "impure knowledge" seems to point to a magical origin of the term.) The problem henceforth consists not in rejecting this type of knowledge from the very beginning, but in considering the manner in which the concept of knowing must be reformulated so that knowledge can be had even where purposeful action is involved. This reformulation of the noological problem is not intended to open the gates to propaganda and value-judgments in the sciences. On the contrary, when we speak of the fundamental intent of the mind (*intentio animi*) which is inherent in every form of knowledge and which affects the perspective, we refer to the irreducible residue of the purposeful element in knowledge which remains even when all conscious and explicit evaluations and biases have been eliminated. It is self-evident that science (in so far as it is free from

evaluation) is not a propagandistic device and does not exist for the purpose of communicating evaluations, but rather for the determination of facts. What the sociology of knowledge seeks to reveal is merely that, after knowledge has been freed from the elements of propaganda and evaluation, it still contains an activist element which, for the most part, has not become explicit, and which cannot be eliminated, but which, at best, can and should be raised into the sphere of the controllable.

THE ESSENTIALLY PERSPECTIVISTIC ELEMENT IN CERTAIN TYPES OF KNOWLEDGE

The second point of which we must take cognizance is that in certain areas of historical-social knowledge it should be regarded as right and inevitable that a given finding should contain the traces of the position of the knower. The problem lies not in trying to hide these perspectives or in apologizing for them, but in inquiring into the question of how, granted these perspectives, knowledge and objectivity are still possible. It is not a source of error that in the visual picture of an object in space we can, in the nature of the case, get only a perspectivistic view. The problem is not how we might arrive at a nonperspectivistic picture but how, by juxtaposing the various points of view, each perspective may be recognized as such and thereby a new level of objectivity attained. Thus we come to the point where the false ideal of a detached, impersonal point of view must be replaced by the ideal of an essentially human point of view which is within the limits of a human perspective, constantly striving to enlarge itself.

THE PROBLEM OF THE SPHERE OF TRUTH AS SUCH

In examining the philosophy of life, which furnishes the background for the idealistic epistemology and noology, it became clear that the ideal of a realm of truth as such (which, so to speak, pre-exists independently of the historical-psychological act of thought, and in which every concrete act of knowing merely participates) is the last offshoot of the dualistic world-view which, alongside of our world of concrete immediate events, created a second world by adding another dimension of being.

The positing of a sphere of truth which is valid in itself (an offshoot of the doctrine of ideas) is intended to do the same for the act of knowing as the notion of the beyond or the transcendental did for dualistic metaphysics in the realm of ontology, namely to postulate a sphere of perfection which does not bear the scars of its origins and, measured by which, all events and processes are shown to be finite and incomplete. Furthermore, just as in this extreme spiritualistic metaphysics the quality of "being human" was conceived as "merely being human"—which had been stripped of everything vital, corporeal, historical, or social—so an attempt was made to set forth a conception of knowledge in which these human elements would be submerged. It is necessary to raise the question time and again whether we can imagine the concept of knowing without taking account of the whole complex of traits by which man is characterized, and how, without these presuppositions we can even think of the concept of knowing, to say nothing of actually engaging in the act of knowing.

In the realm of ontology, in modern times, this dualistic view (which originated for the purpose of proving the inadequacy of "this" world) was, furthermore, gradually broken down in the course of empirical research. In noology and epistemology, however, it is still a force. But since here the basic presuppositions in the field of the theory of science are not quite so transparent, it was believed that this ideal of a superhuman, supertemporal sphere of validity was not a possible construction arising out of one's world-view, but an essential datum and prerequisite for the interpretation of the phenomenon of "thinking." Our discussion here is intended to show that from the point of view of the phenomenology of thought, there is no necessity to regard knowledge as though it were an intrusion from the sphere of actual happenings into a sphere of "truth in itself." Such a construction at best is of a heuristic value for such modes of thought as are represented by the example $2 \times 2 = 4$. Our reflections aim, on the contrary, to show that the problem of knowing becomes more intelligible if we hold strictly to the data presented by the real factual thinking that we carry on in this world (which is the only kind of thinking known to us, and which is independent of this ideal sphere) and if we accept the phenomenon of knowing as the act of a living being. In other words, the sociology of knowledge regards the cognitive act in connection with the models to which it aspires in its existential as well as its meaningful quality, not as insight into "eternal" truths, arising from a purely theoretical, contemplative urge, or as some sort of participation in these truths (as Scheler still thought), but as an instrument for dealing with life-situations at the disposal of a certain kind of vital being under certain conditions of life. All these three factors, the nature and structure of the process of dealing with life-situations, the subjects' own make-up (in his biological as well as historical-social aspects), and the peculiarity of the conditions of life, especially the place and position of the thinker—all these influence the results of thought. But they also condition the ideal of truth

which this living being is able to construct from the products of thought.

The conception of knowledge as an intellectual act, which is only then complete when it no longer bears the traces of its human derivation, has, as we have already indicated, its greatest heuristic value in those realms where, as in the example $2 \times 2 = 4$, the above-mentioned characteristics can phenomenologically, with greater or less justification, be shown actually to exist. It is misleading, however, and tends to obscure fundamental phenomena in those broader realms of the knowable where, if the human historical element is overlooked, the results of thought are completely denatured.

Only the phenomenological evidence derived from the existing models of thought may be used as an argument for or against certain concepts involved in knowledge. Disguised motives, arising out of a certain outlook on the world, have no bearing on the matter. There is no reason for retaining in our noology the disdain for corporeal, sensual, temporal, dynamic, and social things characteristic of the type of human being presupposed in the "idealistic" philosophy. At the present moment there are confronting each other two types of knowledge which are of representative significance, and correspondingly there are two possibilities of noological and epistemological explanations of knowledge. For the moment it would be well to keep these two approaches separate and to make the differences between them stand out rather than to minimize them. Only in the process of trial and error will it become clear which of these bases of interpretation is the more sound and whether we get farther if, as has been done hitherto, we take the situationally detached type of knowledge as our point of departure and treat the situationally conditioned as secondary and unimportant or contrariwise, whether we regard the situationally detached type of knowledge as a marginal and special case of the situationally conditioned.

If we were to inquire into the possible directions of epistemology if it followed the last-mentioned model of thought and recognized the inherent "situational determination" of certain types of knowledge and made it the basis for its further reflections, we should be confronted with two possible alternatives. The scientist, in this case has the task, first of all, of making explicit the possibilities of the further implications of his problem and to point out all the eventualities that are likely to come into his range of vision. He should content himself with asserting only what, in his present stage of penetration into the problem, he can honestly determine. The function of the thinker is not to pronounce judgment at any cost when a new problem first arises, but rather, in full awareness of the fact that research is still under way, to state only that which has become definitely perceivable. There are two alternatives that he may follow once he has arrived at this stage.

THE TWO DIRECTIONS IN EPISTEMOLOGY

One of the two directions taken by epistemology emphasizes the prevalence of situational determination, maintaining that in the course of the progress of social knowledge this element is ineradicable, and that, therefore, even one's point of view may always be expected to be peculiar to one's position. This would require revision of the theoretical basis of knowledge by setting up the thesis of the inherently relational structure of human knowledge (just as the essentially perspectivistic nature of visually perceived objects is admitted without question).

This solution does not imply renunciation of the postulate of objectivity and the possibility of arriving at decisions in factual disputes; nor does it involve an acceptance of illusionism according to which everything is an appearance and nothing can be decided. It does imply rather that this objectivity and this competence to arrive at decisions can be attained only through indirect means. It is not intended to assert that objects do not exist or that reliance upon observation is useless and futile but rather that the answers we get to the questions we put to the subject-matter are, in certain cases, in the nature of things, possible only within the limits of the observer's perspective. The result even here is not relativism in the sense of one assertion being as good as another. Relationism, as we use it, states that every assertion can only be relationally formulated. It becomes relativism only when it is linked with the older static ideal of eternal, unperspectivistic truths independent of the subjective experience of the observer, and when it is judged by this alien ideal of absolute truth.

In the case of situationally conditioned thought, objectivity comes to mean something quite new and different: (*a*) there is first of all the fact that in so far as different observers are immersed in the same system, they will, on the basis of the identity of their conceptual and categorical apparatus and through the common universe of discourse thereby created, arrive at similar results, and be in a position to eradicate as an error everything that deviates from this unanimity; (*b*) and recently there is a recognition of the fact that when observers have different perspectives, "objectivity" is attainable only in a more roundabout fashion. In such a case, what has been correctly but differently perceived by

the two perspectives must be understood in the light of the differences in structure of these varied modes of perception. An effort must be made to find a formula for translating the results of one into those of the other and to discover a common denominator for these varying perspectivistic insights. Once such a common denominator has been found, it is possible to separate the necessary differences of the two views from the arbitrarily conceived and mistaken elements, which here too should be considered as errors.

The controversy concerning visually perceived objects (which, in the nature of the case, can be viewed only in perspective) is not settled by setting up a non-perspectivist view (which is impossible). It is settled rather by understanding, in the light of one's own positionally determined vision, why the object appeared differently to one in a different position. Likewise, in our field also, objectivity is brought about by the translation of one perspective into the terms of another. It is natural that here we must ask which of the various points of view is the best. And for this too there is a criterion. As in the case of visual perspective, where certain positions have the advantage of revealing the decisive features of the object, so here pre-eminence is given to that perspective which gives evidence of the greatest comprehensiveness and the greatest fruitfulness in dealing with empirical materials.

The theory of knowledge can also pursue a second course by emphasizing the following facts: The impetus to research in the sociology of knowledge may be so guided that it will not absolutize the concept of "situational determination"; rather, it may be directed in such a fashion that precisely by discovering the element of situational determination in the views at hand, a first step will be taken towards the solution of the problem of situational determination itself. As soon as I identify a view which sets itself up as absolute, as representing merely a given angle of vision, I neutralize its partial nature in a certain sense. Most of our earlier discussion of this problem moved quite spontaneously in the direction of the neutralization of situational determination by attempting to rise above it. The idea of the continuously broadening basis of knowledge, the idea of the continuous extension of the self and of the integration of various social vantage points into the process of knowledge—observations which are all based on empirical facts—and the idea of an all-embracing ontology which is to be sought for—all move in this direction. This tendency in intellectual and social history is closely connected with the processes of group contact and interpenetration. In its first stage, this tendency neutralizes the various conflicting points of view (i.e. deprives them of their absolute character); in its second stage, it creates out of this neutralization a more comprehensive and servicable basis of vision. It is interesting to note that the construction of a broader base is bound up with a higher degree of abstractness and tends in an increasing degree to formalize the phenomena with which we are concerned. This formalizing tendency consists in relegating to a subordinate position the analysis of the concrete qualitative assertions which lead in a given direction, and substituting in place of the qualitative and configurative description of phenomena a purely functional view modelled after a purely mechanical pattern. This theory of increasing abstractness will be designated as the theory of the social genesis of abstraction. According to this sociological derivation of abstraction (which is clearly observable in the emergence of the sociological point of view itself), the trend towards a higher stage of abstraction is a correlate of the amalgamation of social groups. The corroboration of this contention is found in the fact that the capacity for abstraction among individuals and groups grows in the measure that they are parts of heterogeneous groups and organizations in more inclusive collective units, capable of absorbing local or otherwise particular groups. But this tendency towards abstraction on a higher level is still in accord with the theory of the situational determination of thought, for the reason that the subject that engages in this thinking is by no means an absolutely autonomous "mind in itself," but is rather a subject which is ever more inclusive and which neutralizes the earlier particular and concrete points of view.

All the categories justifiably formulated by formal sociology are products of this neutralizing and formalizing operation. The logical conclusion of this approach is that, in the end, it sees only a formal mechanism in operation. Thus, to cite an illustration from formal sociology, domination is a category which can only be abstracted from the concrete positions of the persons involved (i.e. the dominator and the dominated), because it contents itself with emphasizing the structural inter-relationship (the mechanism, so to speak) of the behaviour involved in the process of interaction. This it does by operating with concepts like sub- and super-ordination, force, obedience, subjectibility, etc. The qualitative content of domination in the concrete (which would immediately present "domination" in an historical setting) is not accessible through this formula, and could be adequately portrayed only if the dominated as well as the dominator were to tell what their experiences actually were in the situations in which they live. For not even the

formal definitions that we discover float in thin air; they arise rather out of the concrete problems of a situation. At this point the notion arises, which of course needs detailed verification, that the problem of perspectivism concerns primarily the qualitative aspect of a phenomenon. Because, however, the content of social-intellectual phenomena is primarily meaningful and because meaning is perceived in acts of understanding and interpretation, we may say that the problem of perspectivism in the sociology of knowledge refers, first of all, to what is understandable in social phenomena. But in this we are by no means denoting a narrowly circumscribed realm. The most elementary facts in the social sphere surpass in complexity the purely formal relations, and they can only be understood in referring to qualitative contents and meanings. In short, the problem of interpretation is a fundamental one.

Even where formalization has gone farthest and where we are concerned with mere relations, so to speak, there is still a minimum of evidence of the investigator's general direction of interest which could not be entirely eliminated. For example, when Max Weber, in classifying types of conduct, distinguished between "purposeful-rational" and "traditional" conduct, he was still expressing the situation of a generation in which one group had discovered and given evaluative emphasis to the rationalistic tendencies in capitalism, while another, demonstrably impelled by political motives, discovered the significance of tradition and emphasized it as over against the former. The interest in the problem of a typology of conduct itself arises out of this particular social situation. And when we find that precisely these types of conduct were singled out and formalized in precisely this direction, we must seek the source of this tendency towards abstraction in the concrete social situation of the epoch which was preoccupied with the phenomenon of conduct as seen from this angle. If another age had attempted a formal systematization of the types of conduct, it would no doubt have arrived at quite another typology. In another historical situation, different abstractions would have been found and singled out from the total complex of events. In our judgment the sociology of knowledge, by virtue of its premises, does not need to deny the existence or possibility of formalized and abstract thought. It need show only that, in this respect, too, thought is not independent of "existence," for it is not a super-social, super-human subject which is expressing itself in "as such" categories in this typology. Rather the neutralizations of the qualitative differences in the varying points of view, arising in certain definite situations, result in a scheme of orientation which allows only certain formal and structural components of the phenomena to emerge into the foreground of experience and thought. In a rudimentary form this process is already observable in the rules of etiquette and social intercourse which arise spontaneously in the contact between different groups. There, too, the more fleeting the contacts the less concern there is with the qualitative understanding of the mutual relationship, which is formalized to such an extent that it becomes a "formal sociological category" indicating, so to speak, only the specific role of the relationship. The other party is regarded merely as an "ambassador," "stranger," or "train conductor." In social intercourse we react to the other only with reference to these characteristics. In other words, the formalization in such cases is itself an expression of certain social situations, and the direction which formalization takes (whether we pick out, as we do in the case of the "ambassador," his function as a political representative or whether, as we do in the case of the "stranger," single out his ethnic traits) is dependent on the social situation, which enters, even though in a diluted form, into the categories that we use. In a similar vein, the observation may be made that in jurisprudence formalized law takes the place of informal justice, which arises out of concrete issues and represents a qualitative judgment derived from the situation and expressing the sense of right of a community, whenever an exchange economy reaches the point where its very existence depends on knowing in advance what the law will be. Henceforth, it is less important to do full justice to each case in its absolute uniqueness than to be able more and more correctly to classify and subsume each case under pre-established formalized categories.

As already indicated, we are not yet in a position to-day to decide the question as to which of the two above-mentioned alternatives the nature of the empirical data will force a scientific theory of knowledge to follow. In either case, however, we will have to reckon with situational determination as an inherent factor in knowledge, as well as with the theory of relationism and the theory of the changing basis of thought. In either case we must reject the notion that there is a "sphere of truth in itself" as a disruptive and unjustifiable hypothesis. It is instructive to note that the natural

sciences seem to be, in many respects, in a closely analogous situation, especially if we use as our basis for comparison the interpretation of their present plight that has been so skilfully presented by W. Westphal. According to this view, once it was discovered that our conventional standards for measurement, such as clocks, etc., and the everyday language associated with them are possible and usable only for this everyday, common sense scheme of orientation, it began to be understood that in the quantum theory, for instance, where we are dealing with the measurement of electrons, it is impossible to speak of a result of measurement which can be formulated independently of the measuring instrument used. For in the latter case the measuring instrument is interpreted as an object which itself relevantly influences the position and velocity of the electrons to be measured. Thus the thesis arose that position and velocity measurements are expressible only in "indeterminate relations" (Heisenberg) which specify the degree of indeterminacy. Furthermore, the next step from this idea was the denial of the assertion, which was closely allied to the older method of thinking, that the electrons *in themselves* must in reality have well-defined paths, on the ground that such "as such" assertions belong to that type of completely contentless assertion which, to be sure, do communicate a sort of intuitively derived image, but which are completely devoid of content, since no consequences can be drawn from them. The same was held to apply to the assumption that bodies in motion must have an absolute velocity. But since, according to Einstein's relativity this is, in principle, not determinable, this assumption in the light of modern theory belongs quite as much with these empty assertions as the thesis that in addition to our world there exists another world which is, in the nature of the case, inaccessible to our experience.

If we followed this trend of thought, which in its unformulated relationism is surprisingly similar to our own, then the setting-up of the logical postulate that a sphere of "truth in itself" exists and has validity seems as difficult to justify as all of the other empty existential dualisms just mentioned. Because, as long as we see only relational determinabilities in the whole realm of empirical knowledge, the formulation of an "as such" sphere has no consequences whatsoever for the process of knowing.

II–RELIGION AND MAGIC

1. *Types of Magic*

BY SIR JAMES G. FRAZER

WHEN WE HAVE SAID that the ancient kings were commonly priests also, we are far from having exhausted the religious aspect of their office. In those days the divinity that hedges a king was no empty form of speech, but the expression of a sober belief. Kings were revered, in many cases not merely as priests, that is, as intercessors between man and god, but as themselves gods, able to bestow upon their subjects and worshippers those blessings which are commonly supposed to be beyond the reach of man, and are sought, if at all, only by prayer and sacrifice offered to superhuman and invisible beings. Thus kings are often expected to give rain and sunshine in due season, to make the crops grow, and so on. Strange as this expectation appears to us, it is quite of a piece with early modes of thought. A savage hardly conceives the distinction commonly drawn by more advanced peoples between the natural and the supernatural. To him the world is to a great extent worked by supernatural agents, that is, by personal beings acting on impulses and motives like his own, liable like him to be moved by appeals to their pity, their hopes, and their fears. In a world so conceived he sees no limit to his power of influencing the course of nature to his own advantage. Prayers, promises, or threats may secure him fine weather and an abundant crop from the gods; and if a god should happen, as he sometimes believes, to become incarnate in his own person, then he need appeal to no higher being; he, the savage, possesses in himself all the powers necessary to further his own well-being and that of his fellow-men.

This is one way in which the idea of a man-god is reached. But there is another. Side by side with the view of the world as pervaded by spiritual forces, primitive man has another conception in which we may detect a germ of the modern notion of natural law or the view of nature as a series of events occurring in an invariable order without the intervention of personal agency. The germ of which I speak is involved in that sympathetic magic, as it may be called, which plays a large part in most systems of superstition.

Manifold as are the applications of this crude philosophy—for a philosophy it is as well as an art—the fundamental principles on which it is based would seem to be reducible to two; first, that like produces like, or that an effect resembles its cause; and second, that things which have once been in contact, but have ceased to be so, continue to act on each other as if the contact still persisted. From the first of these principles the savage infers that he can produce any desired effect merely by imitating it; from the second he concludes that he can influence at pleasure and at any distance any person of whom, or any thing of which, he possesses a particle. Magic of the latter sort, resting as it does on the belief in a certain secret sympathy which unites indissolubly things that have once been connected with each other, may appropriately be termed sympathetic in the strict sense of the term. Magic of the former kind, in which the supposed cause resembles or simulates the supposed effect, may conveniently be described as imitative or mimetic.[1] But inasmuch as the efficacy even of imitative magic must be supposed to depend on a certain physical influence or sympathy linking the imaginary cause or subject to the imaginary effect or object, it seems desirable to retain the name sympathetic magic as a general designation to include both branches of the art. In practice the two are often conjoined; or, to speak more exactly, while imitative magic may be practised by itself, sympathetic magic in the strict sense will generally be found to involve an application of the mimetic principle. This will be more readily understood from the examples with which I will now illustrate

---

Reprinted from Sir James G. Frazer, *The Golden Bough* (London: Macmillan Co., 1900), I, 8–11, 49–51, 60–81.

1. I have adopted the suggestion of a writer (Mr. E. S. Hartland?) in *Folklore*, viii. (1897), p. 65. The expression "imitative magic" was used incidentally in the first edition of this work (vol. ii. p. 268).

both branches of the subject, beginning with the imitative.

Perhaps the most familiar application of the principle that like produces like is the attempt which has been made by many peoples in many ages to injure or destroy an enemy by injuring or destroying an image of him, in the belief that, just as the image suffers, so does the man, and that when it perishes he must die. A few instances out of many may be given to prove at once the wide diffusion of the practice over the world and its remarkable persistence through the ages. For thousands of years ago it was known to the sorcerers of ancient India, Babylon, and Egypt as well as of Greece and Rome,[2] and at this day it is still resorted to by cunning and malignant savages in Australia, Africa, and Scotland. Thus, for example, when an Ojebway Indian desires to work evil on any one, he makes a little wooden image of his enemy and runs a needle into its head or heart, or he shoots an arrow into it, believing that wherever the needle pierces or the arrow strikes the image, his foe will the same instant be seized with a sharp pain in the corresponding part of his body; but if he intends to kill the person outright, he burns or buries the puppet, uttering certain magic words as he does so.[3]

A Malay charm of the same sort is as follows. Take parings of nails, hair, eyebrows, spittle, and so forth of your intended victim, enough to represent every part of his person, and then make them up into his likeness with wax from a deserted bees' comb. Scorch the figure slowly by holding it over a lamp every night for seven nights, and say:

"It is not wax that I am scorching,
   It is the liver, heart, and spleen of So-and-so
      that I scorch."

After the seventh time burn the figure, and your victim will die. Another form of the Malay charm, which resembles the Ojebway practice still more closely, is to make a corpse of wax from an empty bees' comb and of the length of a footstep: then pierce the eye of the image, and your enemy is blind; pierce the stomach, and he is sick; pierce

the head, and his head aches; pierce the breast, and his breast will suffer. If you would kill him outright, transfix the image from the head downwards; enshroud it as you would a corpse; pray over it as if you were praying over the dead; then bury it in the middle of a path where your victim will be sure to step over it. In order that his blood may not be on your head, you should say:

"It is not I who am burying him,
   It is Gabriel who is burying him."

Thus the guilt of the murder will be laid on the shoulders of the archangel Gabriel, who is a great deal better able to bear it than you are.[4] In eastern Java an enemy may be killed by means of a likeness of him drawn on a piece of paper, which is then incensed or buried in the ground.[5]

Thus far we have been considering that branch of sympathetic magic which may be called mimetic or imitative. Its leading principle, as we have seen, is that like produces like, or, in other words, that an effect resembles its cause. On the other hand, sympathetic magic in the strict sense of the word proceeds upon the assumption that things which have once been conjoined must remain ever afterwards, even when quite dissevered from each other, in such a sympathetic relation that whatever is done to the one must similarly affect the other. The most familiar example is the magic sympathy which is supposed to exist between a man and any severed portion of his person, as his hair or nails; so that whoever gets possession of human hair or nails may work his will, at any distance, upon the person from whom they were cut. This superstition is world-wide; instances of it in regard to hair and nails will be noticed later on. Here it may suffice to illustrate the general principle by a few beliefs and customs concerned with other parts of the body.

Among the Australian tribes it was a common practice to knock out one or more of a boy's front teeth at those ceremonies of initiation to which every male member had to submit before he could enjoy the rights and privileges of a full-grown man. The reason of the practice is obscure; all that concerns us here is the evidence of a belief that a sympathetic relation continued to exist between the lad and his teeth after the latter had been extracted from his gums. Thus among some of the tribes about the river Darling, in New South Wales, the extracted tooth was placed under the bark of a tree near a river or water-hole; if the

2. For the Greek and Roman practice, see Theocritus, *Id.* ii.; Virgil, *Ecl.* viii. 75–82; Ovid, *Heroides*, vi. 91 *sq.; id., Amores*, iii. 7. 29 *sq.*

3. Peter Jones, *History of the Ojebway Indians*, p. 146; J. G. Kohl, *Kitschi-Gami*, ii. 80. Similar practices are reported among the Illinois, the Mandans, and the Hidatsas of North America (Charlevoix, *Histoire de la Nouvelle France, vi.* 88; Maximilian, Prinz zu Wied, *Reise in das Innere Nord-America*, ii. 188; Washington Matthews, *Ethnography and Philology of the Hidatsa Indians*, p. 50), and the Aymaras of Bolivia and Peru (D. Forbes, "On the Aymara Indians of Bolivia and Peru," *Journal of the Ethnological Society of London*, ii. (1870), p. 236).

4. W. W. Skeat, *Malay Magic* (London, 1900), pp. 570–72.

5. J. Kreemer, "Regenmaken, Oedjoeng, Tooverij onder de Javanen," *Mededeelingen van wege het Nederlandsche Zendinggenootschap*, xxx. (1886), p. 117 *sq.*

bark grew over the tooth or if the tooth fell into the water, all was well; but if it were exposed and the ants ran over it, the natives believed that the boy would suffer from a disease of the mouth. Among certain Victorian tribes the tree in which the teeth had thus been concealed was ever afterwards in some sense held sacred. It was made known only to certain persons of the tribe, and the youth himself was never allowed to learn where his teeth had been deposited. If he died, the foot of the tree was stripped of its bark, and the tree itself was killed by kindling a fire about it, "so that it might remain stricken and sere, as a monument of the deceased." This latter custom points to a belief that even after being severed from the body the teeth remained so intimately united with it by a secret sympathy, that when it perished they too must be destroyed. Among the Murring and other tribes of New South Wales the extracted tooth was at first taken care of by an old man, and then passed from one headman to another, until it had gone all round the community, when it came back to the lad's father, and finally to the lad himself. But however it was thus conveyed from hand to hand, it might on no account be placed in a bag containing magical substances, for to do so would, they believed, put the owner of the tooth in great danger.[6] Mr. A. W. Howitt once acted as custodian of the teeth which had been extracted from some novices at a ceremony of initiation, and the old men earnestly besought him not to carry them in a bag in which they knew that he had some quartz crystals. They declared that if he did so the magic of the crystals would pass into the teeth, and so injure the boys. Nearly a year after Mr. Howitt's return from the ceremony he was visited by one of the principal men of the Murring tribe, who had travelled about three hundred miles from his home to fetch back the teeth. This man explained that he had been sent for them because one of the boys had fallen into ill health, and it was believed that the teeth had received some injury which had affected him. He was assured that the teeth had been kept in a box apart from any substances, like quartz crystals, which could influence them; and he returned home bearing the teeth with him carefully wrapt up and concealed. Among the Dieri tribe of South Australia the teeth knocked out at initiation were bound up in emu feathers, and kept by the boy's father or his next of kin until the mouth had healed, and even for long afterwards. Then the father, accompanied by a few old men, performed a ceremony for the purpose of taking all the supposed life out of the

teeth. He made a low rumbling noise without uttering any words, blew two or three times with his mouth, and jerked the teeth through his hand to some little distance. After that he buried them about eighteen inches under ground. The jerking movement was meant to show that he thereby took all the life out of the teeth. Had he failed to do so, the boy would, in the opinion of the natives, have been liable to an ulcerated and wry mouth, impediment in speech, and ultimately a distorted face. This ceremony is interesting as a rare instance of an attempt to break the sympathetic link between a man and a severed part of himself by rendering the part insensitive.

*　　*　　*

These examples may suffice to illustrate the general principles of sympathetic magic both in the wider and the narrower sense of the term. In a few of the cases cited we have seen that the operation of spirits is assumed, and that an attempt is made to win their favour by prayer and sacrifice. But these cases are exceptional; they exhibit magic tinged and alloyed with religion. Wherever sympathetic magic occurs in its pure unadulterated form, it assumes that in nature one event follows another necessarily and invariably without the intervention of any spiritual or personal agency. Thus its fundamental conception is identical with that of modern science; underlying the whole system is a faith, implicit but real and firm, in the order and uniformity of nature. The magician does not doubt that the same causes will always produce the same effects, that the performance of the proper ceremony, accompanied by the appropriate spell, will inevitably be attended by the desired results, unless, indeed, his incantations should chance to be thwarted and foiled by the more potent charms of another sorcerer. He supplicates no higher power; he sues the favour of no fickle and wayward being; he abases himself before no awful deity. Yet his power, great as he believes it to be, is by no means arbitrary and unlimited. He can weild it only so long as he strictly conforms to the rules of his art, or to what may be called the laws of nature as conceived by him. To neglect these rules, to break these laws in the smallest particular is to incur failure, and may even expose the unskilful practitioner himself to the utmost pearl. If he claims a sovereignty over nature, it is a constitutional sovereignty rigorously limited in its scope and exercised in exact conformity with ancient usage. Thus the analogy between the magical and the scientific conceptions of the world is close. In both of them the succession of events is perfectly regular and certain, being determined by immutable laws, the operation of which can be foreseen and calculated

6. A. W. Howitt, in *Journal of the Anthropological Institute*, xiii. (1884), p. 456 *sq.*

precisely; the elements of caprice, of chance, and of accident are banished from the course of nature. Both of them open up a seemingly boundless vista of possibilities to him who knows the causes of things and can touch the secret springs that set in motion the vast and intricate mechanism of the world. Hence the strong attraction which magic and science alike have exercised on the human mind; hence the powerful stimulus that both have given to the pursuit of knowledge. They lure the weary inquirer, the footsore seeker, on through the wilderness of disappointment in the present by their endless promises of the future; they take him up to the top of an exceeding high mountain and show him, beyond the dark clouds and rolling mists at his feet, a vision of the celestial city, far off, it may be, but radiant with unearthly splendour, bathed in the light of dreams.

The fatal flaw of magic lies not in its general assumption of a succession of events determined by law, but in its total misconception of the nature of the particular laws which govern that succession. If we analyse the various cases of sympathetic magic which have been passed in review in the preceding pages, and which may be taken as fair samples of the bulk, we shall find them to be all mistaken applications of one or other of two great fundamental laws of thought, namely, the association of ideas by similarity and the association of ideas by contiguity in space or time. A mistaken association of similar ideas produces imitative or mimetic magic; a mistaken association of contiguous ideas produces sympathetic magic in the narrower sense of the word. The principles of association are excellent in themselves, and indeed absolutely essential to the working of the human mind. Legitimately applied they yield science; illegitimately applied they yield magic, the bastard sister of science. It is therefore a truism, almost a tautology, to say that all magic is necessarily false and barren; for were it ever to become true and fruitful, it would no longer be magic but science. From the earliest times man has been engaged in a search for general rules whereby to turn the order of natural phenomena to his own advantage, and in the long search he has scraped together a great hoard of such maxims, some of them golden and some of them mere dross. The true or golden rules constitute the body of applied science which we call the arts; the false are magic.

If magic is thus next of kin to science, we have still to inquire how it stands related to religion. But the view we take of that relation will necessarily be coloured by the idea which we have formed of the nature of religion itself; hence a writer may reasonably be expected to define his conception of religion before he proceeds to investigate its relation to magic. There is probably no subject in the world about which opinions differ so much as the nature of religion, and to frame a definition of it which would satisfy every one must obviously be impossible. All that a writer can do is, first, to say clearly what he means by religion, and afterwards to employ the word consistently in that sense throughout his work. By religion, then, I understand a propitiation or conciliation of powers superior to man which are believed to direct and control the course of nature and of human life. In this sense it will readily be perceived that religion is opposed in principle both to magic and to science. For all conciliation implies that the being conciliated is a conscious or personal agent, that his conduct is in some measure uncertain, and that he can be prevailed upon to vary it in the desired direction by a judicious appeal to his interests, his appetites, or his emotions. Conciliation is never employed towards things which are regarded as inanimate, nor towards persons whose behaviour in the particular circumstances is known to be determined with absolute certainty. Thus in so far as religion assumes the world to be directed by conscious agents who may be turned from their purpose by persuasion, it stands in fundamental antagonism to magic as well as to science, both of which take for granted that the course of nature is determined, not by the passions or caprice of personal beings, but by the operation of immutable laws acting mechanically.[7] In magic, indeed, the assumption is only implicit, but in science it is explicit. It is true that magic often deals with spirits, which are personal agents of the kind assumed by religion; but whenever it does so in its proper form, it treats them exactly in the same fashion as it treats inanimate agents—that is, it constrains or coerces instead of conciliating or propitiating them as religion would do. In ancient Egypt, for example, the magicians claimed the power of compelling even the highest gods to do their bidding, and actually threatened them with destruction in case of disobedience. Similarly in India at the present day the great Hindoo trinity itself of Brahma, Vishnu, and Siva is subject to the sorcerers, who, by means of their spells,

7. The opposition of principle between magic and religion is well brought out by Sir A. C. Lyall in his *Asiatic Studies*, First Series (London, 1899), i. 99 *sqq.* It is also insisted on by Mr. F. B. Jevons in his *Introduction to the History of Religion* (London, 1896). The distinction is clearly apprehended and sharply maintained by Professor H. Oldenberg in his notable book *Die Religion des Veda* (Berlin, 1894); see especially pp. 58 *sq.*, 311 *sqq.*, 476 *sqq.* When I wrote this book originally I failed to realise the extent of the opposition, because I had not formed a clear general conception of the nature of religion, and was disposed to class magic loosely under it.

exercise such an ascendency over the mightiest deities, that these are bound submissively to execute on earth below, or in heaven above, whatever commands their masters the magicians may please to issue. This radical conflict of principle between magic and religion sufficiently explains the relentless hostility with which in history the priest has often pursued the magician. The haughty self-sufficiency of the magician, his arrogant demeanour towards the higher powers, and his unabashed claim to exercise a sway like theirs could not but revolt the priest, to whom, with his awful sense of the divine majesty, and his humble prostration in presence of it, such claims and such a demeanour must have appeared an impious and blasphemous usurpation of prerogatives that belong to God alone. And sometimes, we may suspect, lower motives concurred to whet the edge of the priest's hostility. He professed to be the proper medium, the true intercessor between God and man, and no doubt his interests as well as his feelings were often injured by a rival practitioner, who preached a surer and smoother road to fortune than the rugged and slippery path of divine favour.

Yet this antagonism, familiar as it is to us, seems to have made its appearance comparatively late in the history of religion. At an earlier stage the functions of priest and sorcerer were often combined or, to speak perhaps more correctly, were not yet differentiated from each other. To serve his purpose man wooed the good-will of gods or spirits by prayer and sacrifice, while at the same time he had recourse to ceremonies and forms of words which he hoped would of themselves bring about the desired result without the help of god or devil. In short, he performed religious and magical rites simultaneously; he uttered prayers and incantations almost in the same breath, knowing or recking little of the theoretical inconsistency of his behaviour, so long as by hook or crook he contrived to get what he wanted. Instances of this fusion or confusion of magic with religion have already met us in the practices of Melanesians and of some East Indian islanders. So far as the Melanesians are concerned, the general confusion cannot be better described than in the words of Dr. R. H. Codrington:—"That invisible power which is believed by the natives to cause all such effects as transcend their conception of the regular course of nature, and to reside in spiritual beings, whether in the spiritual part of living men or in the ghosts of the dead, being imparted by them to their names and to various things that belong to them, such as stones, snakes, and indeed objects of all sorts, is that generally known as *mana*. Without some understanding of this it is impossible to understand the religious beliefs and practices of the Melanesians; and this again is the active force in all they do and believe to be done in magic, white or black. By means of this men are able to control or direct the forces of nature, to make rain or sunshine, wind or calm, to cause sickness or remove it, to know what is far off in time and space, to bring good luck and prosperity, or to blast and curse." "By whatever name it is called, it is the belief in this supernatural power, and in the efficacy of the various means by which spirits and ghosts can be induced to exercise it for the benefit of men, that is the foundation of the rites and practices which can be called religious; and it is from the same belief that everything which may be called Magic and Witchcraft draws its origin. Wizards, doctors, weather-mongers, prophets, diviners, dreamers, all alike, everywhere in the islands, work by this power. There are many of these who may be said to exercise their art as a profession; they get their property and influence in this way. Every considerable village or settlement is sure to have some one who can control the weather and the waves, some one who knows how to treat sickness, some one who can work mischief with various charms. There may be one whose skill extends to do all these branches, but generally one man knows how to do one thing, and one another. This various knowledge is handed down from father to son, from uncle to sister's son, in the same way as is the knowledge of the rites and methods of sacrifice and prayer; and very often the same man who knows the sacrifice knows also the making of the weather, and of charms for many purposes besides. But as there is no order of priests, there is also no order of magicians or medicine-men. Almost every man of consideration knows how to approach some ghost or spirit, and has some secret of occult practices."[8]

The same confusion of magic and religion has survived among peoples that have risen to higher levels of culture. It was rife in ancient India and ancient Egypt; it is by no means extinct among European peasantry at the present day. With regard to ancient India we are told by an eminent Sanscrit scholar that "the sacrificial ritual at the earliest period of which we have detailed information is pervaded with practices that breathe the spirit of the most primitive magic."[9] Again, the same writer observes that "the ritual of the very sacrifices for which the metrical prayers were composed is described in the other Vedic texts as saturated from beginning to end with magical practices which were to be carried out by the sacrificial priests." In particular he tells us that

8. R. H. Codrington, *The Melanesians*, p. 191 *sq.*
9. H. Oldenberg, *Die Religion des Veda.* p. 59.

the rites celebrated on special occasions, such as marriage, initiation, and the anointment of a king, "are complete models of magic of every kind, and in every case the forms of magic employed bear the stamp of the highest antiquity."[10] Speaking of the importance of magic in the East, and especially in Egypt, Professor Maspero remarks that "we ought not to attach to the word magic the degrading idea which it almost inevitably calls up in the mind of a modern. Ancient magic was the very foundation of religion. The faithful who desired to obtain some favour from a god had no chance of succeeding except by laying hands on the deity, and this arrest could only be effected by means of a certain number of rites, sacrifices, prayers, and chants, which the god himself had revealed, and which obliged him to do what was demanded of him."[11] According to another distinguished Egyptologist "the belief that there are words and actions by which man can influence all the powers of nature and all living things, from animals up to gods, was inextricably interwoven with everything the Egyptians did and everything they left undone. Above all, the whole system of burial and of the worship of the dead is completely dominated by it. The wooden puppets which relieved the dead man from toil, the figures of the maid-servants who baked bread for him, the sacrificial formulas by the recitation of which food was procured for him, what are these and all the similar practices but magic? And as men cannot help themselves without magic, so neither can the gods; the gods also wear amulets to protect themselves, and use magic spells to constrain each other."[12] But though we can perceive the union of discrepant elements in the faith and practice of the ancient Egyptians, it would be rash to assume that the people themselves did so. "Egyptian religion," says Professor Wiedemann, "was not one and homogeneous; it was compounded of the most heterogeneous elements, which seemed to the Egyptian to be all equally justified. He did not care whether a doctrine or a myth belonged to what, in modern scholastic phraseology, we should call faith or superstition; it was indifferent to him whether we should rank it as religion or magic, as worship or sorcery. All such classifications were foreign to the Egyptian. To him no one doctrine seemed more or less justified than another. Nay, he went so far as

to allow the most flagrant contradictions to stand peaceably side by side."[13]

Among the ignorant classes of modern Europe the same confusion of ideas, the same mixture of religion and magic, crops up in various forms. Thus we are told that in France "the majority of the peasants still believe that the priest possesses a secret and irresistible power over the elements. By reciting certain prayers which he alone knows and has the right to utter, yet for the utterance of which he must afterwards demand absolution, he can, on an occasion of pressing danger, arrest or reverse for a moment the action of the eternal laws of the physical world. The winds, the storms, the hail, and the rain are at his command and obey his will. The fire also is subject to him, and the flames of a conflagration are extinguished at his word."[14] For example, French peasants used to be, perhaps are still, persuaded that the priests could celebrate, with certain special rites, a "Mass of the Holy Spirit," of which the efficacy was so miraculous that it never met with any opposition from the divine will; God was forced to grant whatever was asked of Him in this form, however rash and importunate might be the petition. No idea of impiety or irreverence attached to the rite in the minds of those who, in some of the great extremities of life, sought by this singular means to take the kingdom of heaven by storm. The secular priests generally refused to say the "Mass of the Holy Spirit"; but the monks, especially the Capuchin friars, had the reputation of yielding with less scruple to the entreaties of the anxious and distressed.[15] In the constraint thus supposed by Catholic peasantry to be laid by the priest upon the deity we seem to have an exact counterpart of the power which, as we saw, the ancient Egyptians ascribed to their magicians. Again, to take another example, in many villages of Provence the priest is still reputed to possess the faculty of averting storms. It is not every priest who enjoys this reputation; and in some villages when a change of pastors takes place, the parishioners are eager to learn whether the new incumbent has the power (pouder), as they call it. At the first sign of a heavy storm they put him to the proof by inviting him to exorcise the threatening clouds; and if the result answers to their hopes, the new shepherd is assured of the sympathy and respect of his flock. In some parishes, where the reputation of the curate in this respect stood higher than that of his rector, the relations between the two have been so strained

10. *Ibid.* p. 477. For particular examples of the blending of magical with religious ritual in ancient India see pp. 311 *sqq.*, 369 *sq.*, 476 *sqq.*, 522 *sq.* of the same work.

11. G. Maspero, *Etudes de mythologie et d'archéologie égyptienne* (Paris, 1893), i. 106.

12. A. Erman, *Aegypten und aegyptisches Leben im Altertum*, p. 471.

13. A. Wiedemann, "Ein altägyptischer Weltschöpfungsmythus," *Am Urquell*, N. F., ii. (1898), p. 95 *sq.*

14. J. Lecœur, *Esquisses du Bocage Normand*, ii. 78.

15. Amélie Bosquet, *La Normandie romanesque et merveilleuse* (Paris and Rouen, 1845), p. 308.

in consequence, that the bishop has had to translate the rector to another benefice. Again, Gascon peasants believe that to revenge themselves on their enemies bad men will sometimes induce a priest to say a mass called the Mass of Saint Sécaire. Very few priests know this mass, and three-fourths of those who do know it would not say it for love or money. None but wicked priests dare to perform the gruesome ceremony, and you may be quite sure that they will have a very heavy account to render for it at the last day. No curate or bishop, not even the archbishop of Auch, can pardon them; that right belongs to the pope of Rome alone. The Mass of Saint Sécaire may be said only in a ruined or deserted church, where owls mope and hoot, where bats flit in the gloaming, where gypsies lodge of nights, and where toads squat under the desecrated altar. Thither the bad priest comes by night with his light o'love, and at the first stroke of eleven he begins to mumble the mass backwards, and ends just as the clocks are knelling the midnight hour. His leman acts as clerk. The host he blesses is black and has three points; he consecrates no wine, but instead he drinks the water of a well into which the body of an unbaptized infant has been flung. He makes the sign of the cross, but it is on the ground and with his left foot. And many other things he does which no good Christian could look upon without being struck blind and deaf and dumb for the rest of his life. But the man for whom the mass is said withers away little by little, and nobody can say what is the matter with him; even the doctors can make nothing of it. They do not know that he is slowly dying of the Mass of Saint Sécaire.

Yet though magic is thus found to fuse and amalgamate with religion in many ages and in many lands, there are some grounds for thinking that this fusion is not primitive, and that there was a time when man trusted to magic alone for the satisfaction of such wants as transcended his immediate animal cravings. In the first place a consideration of the fundamental notions of magic and religion may incline us to surmise that magic is older than religion in the history of humanity. We have seen that on the one hand magic is nothing but a mistaken application of the very simplest and most elementary processes of the mind, namely the association of ideas by virtue of resemblance or contiguity; and on the other hand that religion assumes the operation of conscious or personal agents, superior to man, behind the visible screen of nature. Obviously the conception of personal agents is more complex than a simple recognition of the similarity or contiguity of ideas; and a theory which assumes that the course of nature is determined by conscious agents is more abstruse and

recondite, and requires for its apprehension a far higher degree of intelligence and reflection than the view that things succeed each other simply by reason of their contiguity or resemblance. The very beasts associate the ideas of things that are like each other or that have been found together in their experience; and they could hardly survive for a day if they ceased to do so. But who attributes to the animals a belief that the phenomena of nature are worked by a multitude of invisible animals or by one enormous and prodigiously strong animal behind the scenes? It is probably no injustice to the brutes to assume that the honour of devising a theory of this latter sort must be reserved for human reason. Thus, if magic be deduced immediately from elementary processes of reasoning, and be, in fact, an error into which the mind falls almost spontaneously, while religion rests on conceptions which the merely animal intelligence can hardly be supposed to have yet attained to, it becomes probable that magic arose before religion in the evolution of our race, and that man essayed to bend nature to his wishes by the sheer force of spells and enchantments before he strove to coax and mollify a coy, capricious, or irascible deity by the soft insinuation of prayer and sacrifice.

The conclusion which we have thus reached deductively from a consideration of the fundamental ideas of religion and magic is confirmed inductively by what we know of the lowest existing race of mankind. To the student who investigates the development of vegetable and animal life on our globe, Australia serves as a sort of museum of the past, a region in which strange species of plants and animals, representing types that have long been extinct elsewhere, may still be seen living and thriving, as if on purpose to satisfy the curiosity of these later ages as to the fauna and flora of the antique world. This singularity Australia owes to the comparative smallness of its area, the waterless and desert character of a large part of its surface, and its remote situation, severed by wide oceans from the other and greater continents. For these causes, by concurring to restrict the number of competitors in the struggle for existence, have mitigated the fierceness of the struggle itself; and thus many a quaint old-fashioned creature, many an antediluvian oddity, which would long ago have been rudely elbowed and hustled out of existence in more progressive countries, has been suffered to jog quietly along in this preserve of Nature's own, this peaceful garden, where the hand on the dial of time seems to move more slowly than in the noisy bustling world outside. And the same causes which have favoured the survival of antiquated types of plants and animals in Australia, have conserved the aboriginal race at a lower level of mental and social development than is now occupied by any other set of human beings spread over an equal area elsewhere. Without metals, without houses, without agriculture, the Australian savages represent the stage of material culture which was reached by our remote ancestors in the Stone Age; and the rudimentary state of the arts of life among them reflects faithfully the stunted condition of their minds. Now in regard to the question of the respective priority of magic or religion in the evolution of thought, it is very important to observe that among these rude savages, while magic is universally practised, religion in the sense of a propitiation or conciliation of the higher powers seems to be nearly unknown. Roughly speaking, all men in Australia are magicians, but not one is a priest; everybody fancies he can influence his fellows or the course of nature by sympathetic magic, but nobody dreams of propitiating gods or spirts by prayer and sacrifice.[16] "It may be truly affirmed," says a recent

writer on the Australians, "that there was not a solitary native who did not believe as firmly in the power of sorcery as in his own existence; and while anybody could practise it to a limited extent, there were in every community a few men who excelled in pretension to skill in the art. The titles of these magicians varied with the community, but by unanimous consent the whites have called them 'doctors,' and they correspond to the medicine-men and rain-makers of other barbarous nations. The power of the doctor is only circumscribed by the range of his fancy. He communes with spirits, takes aerial flights at pleasure, kills or cures, is invulnerable and invisible at will, and controls the elements."[17]

But if in the most primitive state of human society now open to observation on the globe we find magic thus conspicuously present and religion conspicuously absent, may we not reasonably conjecture that the civilised races of the world have also at some period of their history passed through a similar intellectual phase, that they attempted to force the great powers of nature to do their pleasure before they thought of courting their favour by offerings and prayer—in short that, just as on the material side of human culture there has everywhere been an Age of Stone, so on the intellectual side there has everywhere been an Age of Magic?[18] There are reasons for answering this question in the affirmative. When we survey the existing races of mankind from Greenland to Tierra del Fuego, or from Scotland to Singapore, we observe that they are distinguished one from the other by a great variety of religions, and that these distinctions are not, so to speak, merely coterminous with the broad distinctions of race, but descend into the minuter subdivisions of states and commonwealths, nay, that

16. In the south-eastern parts of Australia, where the conditions of life in respect of climate, water, and vegetation are more favourable than elsewhere, some faint beginnings of religion appear in the shape of a slight regard for the comfort of departed friends. Thus some Victorian tribes are said to have kindled fires near the bodies of their dead in order to warm the ghost, but "the recent custom of providing food for it is derided by the intelligent old aborigines as 'white fellow's gammon' " (J. Dawson, *Australian Aborigines,* p. 50 sq.). Some tribes in this south-eastern region are further reported to believe in a supreme spirit, who is regarded sometimes as a benevolent, but more frequently as a malevolent being (A. W. Howitt in *Journal of the Anthropological Institute,* xiii. (1884), p. 191). Brewin, the supreme being of the Kurnai, was at first identified by two intelligent members of the tribe with Jesus Christ, but on further reflection they thought he must be the devil (L. Fison and A. W. Howitt, *Kamilaroi and Kurnai,* p. 255). But whether viewed as gods or devils, it does not seem that these spirits were ever worshipped. See A. W. Howitt in *Journal of the Anthropological Institute,* xiii. (1884), p. 459. It is worth observing that in the same districts which thus exhibit the germs of religion, the organisation of society and the family has also made the greatest advance. The cause is probably the same in both cases, namely a more plentiful supply of food, due to the greater fertility of the soil. See A. W. Howitt in *Journal of the Anthropological Institute,* xviii. (1889), p. 32 *sq.* On the other hand, in the parched and barren regions of Central Australia, where magic attains its highest importance, religion seems to be entirely wanting. See Spencer and Gillen, *Native Tribes of Central Australia.* The traces of a higher faith in Australia, where they occur, are probably sometimes due to European influence. "I am strongly of opinion," says one who knew the aborigines well, "that those who have written to show that the Blacks had some knowledge of God, practised prayer, and believed in places of reward and punishment beyond the grave, have been imposed upon, and that until they had learnt something of Christianity from missionaries and others, the Blacks had no beliefs or practices of the sort. Having heard the missionaries, however, they were not slow to invent what I may call kindred statements with aboriginal accessories, with a view to please and surprise the whites" (E. M. Curr, *The Australian Race,* i. 45). Sometimes too the reported belief of the natives in a Great or Good Spirit may rest merely on a misunderstanding. Mr. Lorimer Fison

informs me (in a letter dated 3rd June 1899) that a German missionary, Mr. Siebert, resident in the Dieri tribe of Central Australia, has ascertained that their Mura Mura, which Mr. Gason explained to be the Good Spirit (*Native Tribes of South Australia,* p. 260), is nothing more or less than the ancestors in the "dream times." There are male and female Mura Mura—husbands, wives, and children—just as among the Dieri at the present day. Mr. Fison adds: "The more I learn about savage tribes the more I am convinced that among them the ancestors grow into gods."

17. J. Mathew, *Eaglehawk and Crow,* p. 142. Similarly among the Fuegians, another of the lowest races of mankind, almost every old man is a magician, who is supposed to have the power of life and death, and to be able to control the weather. But the members of the French scientific expedition to Cape Horn could detect nothing worthy the name of religion among these savages. See *Mission Scientifique du Cap Horn,* vii. "Anthropologie, Ethnographie," par P. Hyades et J. Deniker (Paris, 1891), pp. 253–257.

18. The suggestion has been made by Prof. H. Oldenberg (*Die Religion des Veda,* p. 59), who seems, however, to regard a belief in spirits as part of the raw material of magic. If the view which I have put forward tentatively is correct, faith in magic is probably older than a belief in spirits.

they honeycomb the town, the village, and even the family, so that the surface of society all over the world is cracked and seamed, wormed and sapped with rents and fissures and yawning crevasses opened up by the disintegrating influence of religious dissension. Yet when we have penetrated through these differences, which affect mainly the intelligent and thoughtful part of the community, we shall find underlying them all a solid stratum of intellectual agreement among the dull, the weak, the ignorant, and the superstitious, who constitute, unfortunately, the vast majority of mankind. One of the great achievements of the century which is now nearing its end is to have run shafts down into this low mental stratum in many parts of the world, and thus to have discovered its substantial identity everywhere. It is beneath our feet—and not very far beneath them—here in Europe at the present day, and it crops up on the surface in the heart of the Australian wilderness and wherever the advent of a higher civilisation has not crushed it under ground. This universal faith, this truly Catholic creed, is a belief in the efficacy of magic. While religious systems differ not only in different countries, but in the same country in different ages, the system of sympathetic magic remains everywhere and at all times substantially alike in its principles and practice. Among the ignorant and superstitious classes of modern Europe it is very much what it was thousands of years ago in Egypt and India, and what it now is among the lowest savages surviving in the remotest corners of the world. If the test of truth lay in a show of hands or a counting of heads, the system of magic might appeal, with far more reason than the Catholic Church, to the proud motto, "Quod semper, quod ubique, quod ab omnibus," as the sure and certain credential of its own infallibility.

It is not our business here to consider what bearing the permanent existence of such a solid layer of savagery beneath the surface of society, and unaffected by the superficial changes of religion and culture, has upon the future of humanity. The dispassionate observer, whose studies have led him to plumb its depths, can hardly regard it otherwise than as a standing menace to civilisation. We seem to move on a thin crust which may at any moment be rent by the subterranean forces slumbering below. From time to time a hollow murmur underground or a sudden spirt of flame into the air tells of what is going on beneath our feet. Now and then the polite world is startled by a paragraph in a newspaper which tells how in Scotland an image has been found stuck full of pins for the purpose of killing an obnoxious laird or minister, how a woman has been slowly roasted to death as a witch in Ireland, or how a girl has been murdered and chopped up in Russia to make those candles of human tallow by whose light thieves hope to pursue their midnight trade unseen. But whether the influences that make for further progress, or those that threaten to undo what has already been accomplished, will ultimately prevail; whether the kinetic energy of the minority or the dead weight of the majority of mankind will prove the stronger force to carry us up to higher heights or to sink us into lower depths, are questions rather for the sage, the moralist, and the statesman, whose eagle vision scans the future, than for the humble student of the present and the past. Here we are only concerned to ask how far the uniformity, the universality, and the permanence of a belief in magic, compared with the endless variety and the shifting character of religious creeds, raises a presumption that the former represents a ruder and earlier phase of the human mind, through which all the races of mankind have passed or are passing on their way to religion and science.

If an Age of Religion has thus everywhere, as I venture to surmise, been preceded by an Age of Magic, it is natural that we should inquire what causes have led mankind, or rather a portion of them, to abandon magic as a principle of faith and practice and to betake themselves to religion instead. When we reflect upon the multitude, the variety, and the complexity of the facts to be explained, and the scantiness of our information regarding them, we shall be ready to acknowledge that a full and satisfactory solution of so profound a problem is hardly to be hoped for, and that the most we can do in the present state of our knowledge is to hazard a more or less plausible conjecture. With all due diffidence, then, I would suggest that a tardy recognition of the inherent falsehood and barrenness of magic set the more thoughtful part of mankind to cast about for a truer theory of nature and a more fruitful method of turning her resources to account. The shrewder intelligences must in time have come to perceive that magical ceremonies and incantations did not really effect the results which they were designed to produce, and which the majority of their simpler fellows still believed that they did actually produce. This great discovery of the inefficacy of magic must have wrought a radical though probably slow revolution in the minds of those who had the sagacity to make it. The discovery amounted to this, that men for the first time recognised their inability to manipulate at pleasure certain natural forces which hitherto they had believed to be completely within their control. It was a confession of human ignorance and weakness. Man saw that he had taken for causes what were no causes, and that all his efforts to work by means of these imaginary causes had been vain. His painful toil had been wasted, his curious ingenuity had been squandered to no purpose. He had been pulling at strings to which nothing was attached; he had been marching, as he thought, straight to his goal, while in reality he had only been treading in a narrow circle. Not that the effects which he had striven so hard to produce did not continue to manifest themselves. They were still produced, but not by him. The rain still fell on the thirsty ground; the sun still pursued his daily, and the moon her nightly journey across the sky; the silent procession of the seasons still moved in light and shadow, in cloud and sunshine across the earth; men were still born to labour and sorrow, and still, after a brief sojourn here, were gathered to their fathers in the long home hereafter. All things indeed went on as before, yet all seemed different to him from whose eyes the old scales had fallen. For he could no longer cherish the pleasing illusion that it was he who guided the earth and the heaven in their courses, and that they would cease to perform their great revolutions were he to take his feeble hand from the wheel. In the death of his enemies and his friends he no longer saw a proof of the resistless potency of his own or of hostile enchantments; he now knew that friends and foes alike had succumbed to a force stronger than any that he could wield, and in obedience to a destiny which he was powerless to control.

Thus cut adrift from his ancient moorings and left to toss on a troubled sea of doubt and uncertainty, his old happy confidence in himself and his powers rudely shaken, our primitive philosopher must have been sadly perplexed and agitated till he came to rest, as in a quiet haven after a tempestuous voyage, in a new system of faith and practice, which seemed to offer a solution of his harassing doubts and a substitute, however precarious, for that sovereignty over nature which he had reluctantly abdicated. If the great world went on its way without the help of him or his fellows, it must surely be because there were other beings, like himself, but far stronger, who, unseen themselves, directed its course and brought about all the varied series of events which he had hitherto believed to be dependent on his own magic. It was they, as he now believed, and not he himself, who made the stormy wind to blow, the lightning to flash, and the thunder to roll; who had laid the foundations of the solid earth and set bounds to the restless sea that it might not pass; who caused all the glorious lights of heaven to shine; who gave the fowls of the air their meat and the wild beasts of the desert their prey; who bade the fruitful land to bring forth in abundance, the high hills to be clothed with forests, the

bubbling springs to rise under the rocks in the valleys, and green pastures to grow by still waters; who breathed into man's nostrils and made him live, or turned him to destruction by famine and pestilence and war. To these mighty beings, whose handiwork he traced in all the gorgeous and varied pageantry of nature, man now addressed himself, humbly confessing his dependence on their invisible power, and beseeching them of their mercy to furnish him with all good things, to defend him from the perils and dangers by which our mortal life is compassed about on every hand, and finally to bring his immortal spirit, freed from the burden of the body, to some happier world beyond the reach of pain and sorrow, where he might rest with them and with the spirits of good men in joy and felicity for ever.

In this, or some such way as this, the deeper minds may be conceived to have made the great transition from magic to religion. But even in them the change can hardly ever have been sudden; probably it proceeded very slowly, and required long ages for its more or less perfect accomplishment. For the recognition of man's powerlessness to influence the course of nature on a grand scale must have been gradual; he cannot have been shorn of the whole of his fancied dominion at a blow. Step by step he must have been driven back from his proud position; foot by foot he must have yielded, with a sigh, the ground which he had once viewed as his own. Now it would be the wind, now the rain, now the sunshine, now the thunder, that he confessed himself unable to wield at will; and as province after province of nature thus fell from his grasp, till what had once seemed a kingdom threatened to shrink into a prison, man must have been more and more profoundly impressed with a sense of his own helplessness and the might of the invisible beings by whom he believed himself to be surrounded. Thus religion, beginning as a slight and partial acknowledgement of powers superior to man, tends with the growth of knowledge to deepen into a confession of man's entire and absolute dependence on the divine; his old free bearing is exchanged for an attitude of lowliest prostration before the mysterious powers of the unseen. But this deepening sense of religion, this more perfect submission to the divine will in all things, affect only those higher intelligences who have breadth of view enough to comprehend the vastness of the universe and the littleness of man. Small minds cannot grasp great ideas; to their narrow comprehension, their purblind vision, nothing seems really great and important but themselves. Such minds hardly rise into religion at all. They are, indeed, drilled by their betters into an outward conformity with its precepts and a verbal profession of its tenets; but at heart they cling to their old magical superstitions, which may be discountenanced and forbidden, but cannot be eradicated by religion, so long as they have their roots deep down in the mental framework and constitution of the great majority of mankind.

The reader may well be tempted to ask, How was it that intelligent men did not sooner detect the fallacy of magic? How could they continue to cherish expectations that were invariably doomed to disappointment? With what heart persist in playing venerable antics that led to nothing, and mumbling solemn balderdash that remained without effect? Why cling to beliefs which were so flatly contradicted by experience? How dare to repeat experiments that had failed so often? The answer seems to be that the fallacy was far from easy to detect, the failure by no means obvious, since in many, perhaps in most cases, the desired event did actually follow, at a longer or shorter interval, the performance of the rite which was designed to bring it about; and a mind of more than common acuteness was needed to perceive that, even in these cases, the rite was not necessarily the cause of the event. A ceremony intended to make the wind blow or the rain fall, or to work the death of an enemy, will always be followed, sooner or later, by the occurrence it is meant to bring to pass; and primitive man may be excused for regarding the occurrence as a direct result of the ceremony, and the best possible proof of its efficacy. Similarly, rites observed in the morning to help the sun to rise, and in spring to wake the dreaming earth from her winter sleep, will invariably appear to be crowned with success, at least within the temperate zones; for in these regions the sun lights his golden fire in the east every morning, and year by year the vernal earth decks herself afresh with a rich mantle of green. Hence the practical savage, with his conservative instincts, might well turn a deaf ear to the subtleties of the theoretical doubter, the philosophic radical, who presumed to hint that sunrise and spring might not, after all, be direct consequences of the punctual performance of certain daily or yearly devotions, and that the sun might perhaps continue to rise and trees to blossom though the devotions were occasionally intermitted, or even discontinued altogether These sceptical doubts would naturally be repelled by the other with scorn and indignation as airy reveries subversive of the faith, and manifestly contradicted by experience. "Can anything be plainer," he might say, "than that I light my twopenny candle on earth and that the sun then kindles his great fire in heaven? I should be glad to know whether, when I have put on my green robe in spring, the trees do not afterwards do the same? These are facts patent to everybody, and on them I take my stand. I am a

plain practical man, not one of your theorists and splitters of hairs and choppers of logic. Theories and speculation and all that may be very well in their way, and I have not the least objection to your indulging in them, provided, of course, you do not put them in practice. But give me leave to stick to facts; then I know where I am." The fallacy of this reasoning is obvious to us, because it happens to deal with facts about which we have long made up our minds. But let an argument of precisely the same calibre be applied to matters which are still under debate, and it may be questioned whether a British audience would not applaud it as sound and esteem the speaker who used it a safe man— not brilliant or showy, perhaps, but thoroughly sensible and hard-headed. If such reasonings could pass muster among ourselves, need we wonder that they long escaped detection by the savage?

The patient reader may remember—and the impatient reader who has quite forgotten is respectfully reminded—that we were led to plunge into the labyrinth of magic, in which we have wandered for so many pages, by a consideration of two different types of man-god. This is the clue which has guided our devious steps through the maze, and brought us out at last on higher ground, whence, resting a little by the way, we can look back over the path we have already traversed and forward to the longer and steeper road we have still to climb.

As a result of the foregoing discussion, the two types of human gods may conveniently be distinguished as the religious and the magical man-god respectively. In the former, a being of an order different from and superior to man is supposed to become incarnate, for a longer or a shorter time, in a human body, manifesting his superhuman power and knowledge by miracles wrought and prophecies uttered through the medium of the fleshly tabernacle in which he has deigned to take up his abode. This may also appropriately be called the inspired or incarnate type of man-god. In it the human body is merely a frail earthly vessel filled with a divine and immortal spirit. On the other hand, a man-god of the magical sort is nothing but a man who possesses in an unusually high degree powers which most of his fellows arrogate to themselves on a smaller scale; for in rude society there is hardly a person who does not dabble in magic. Thus, whereas a man-god of the former or inspired type derives his divinity from a deity who has stopped to hide his heavenly radiance behind a dull mask of earthly mould, a man-god of the latter type draws his extraordinary power from a certain physical sympathy with nature. He is not merely the receptacle of a divine spirit. His whole being, body and soul, is so delicately attuned to the harmony of the world that a touch of his hand or a turn of his head may send a thrill vibrating through the universal framework of things; and conversely his divine organism is acutely sensitive to such slight changes of environment as would leave ordinary mortals wholly unaffected. But the line between these two types of man-god, however sharply we may draw it in theory, is seldom to be traced with precision in practice, and in what follows I shall not insist on it.

To readers long familiarised with the conception of natural law, the belief of primitive man that he can rule the elements must be so foreign that it may be well to illustrate it by examples. When we have seen that in early society men who make no pretence at all of being gods, do nevertheless commonly believe themselves to be invested with powers which to us would seem supernatural, we shall have the less difficulty in comprehending the extraordinary range of powers ascribed to persons who are actually regarded as divine.

2. *On Magic and the Unknown*

BY MARCEL MAUSS AND H. HUBERT

WE CALL "MAGIC" any ritual that is not part of an organized cult, such as the private ritual, which is secret, mysterious, and tending at one extreme toward the prohibited. From the definition is derived a first approximation of the concept. We are not defining magic by the content of its rituals, but by the conditions under which they take place and which determine their function within the complex of social habits.

We have succeeded step by step in circumscribing this new element that magic superposes over these impersonal concepts—sympathetic and intrinsic properties—and the concepts of spirit. We now conceive of it as superior to these two orders of concepts and of such a character that, if given, the two others are but derivatives of it.

This complex concept includes first the idea of power, or still better of "magical potential," as it has been called. It is the idea of a force, of which the force of the magician, the force of the ritual, the force of the spirit are but different expressions, according to the actual components of any given magic. For each of these components does not act of itself, but only in so far as it is endowed, by invention or by special rites, with this very character of being a force that is not mechanical but magical. Furthermore, the concept of magic force is, from this standpoint, very comparable to our concept of mechanical force. As we name "force" the cause of observable motions, so magic force is specifically the cause of magical efforts—sickness and death, happiness and health, etc.

This concept includes also the idea of a milieu where such powers are exercised. In this mysterious milieu, events do not take place as in the tangible world of our senses. Distance does not preclude contact. Forms and wishes are immediately concretized. It is the world of the spiritual and also the world of the spirits: everything being spiritual, everything may also become spirit. However boundless the power may be, and however elevated the milieu, events nevertheless follow laws that are the relations necessary to the interaction of things—the relations of words and signs to the objects signified, laws of sympathetic resonance, and laws of properties susceptible of being codified through classifications (similar to these which have been studied in the *Année Sociologique*). This concept of force and the concept of milieu are inseparable; they coincide entirely and express themselves simultaneously, through the same means. Indeed, the ritual forms, i.e., the dispositions that aim to create magical force, are also those that create and separate the milieu before, during, and after the ceremony. Hence, if our analysis is correct, we shall find at the basis of magic a particularly confused idea, altogether foreign to the minds of European adults. . . .

This composite idea of force and milieu is beyond the rigid and abstract categories of our reason and language. From the viewpoint of an intellectualistic psychology of the individual, it is an absurdity. Let us see whether a non-intellectualistic psychology of

Translated by Jesse Pitts, from Marcel Mauss and H. Hubert, "Esquisse d'une théorie générale de la magie," *Année Sociologique*, VI (1902–3), 16, 99–101, 101–3, 105, 111–12, 113–15, 118–20.

man in society will not be able to accept and explain the existence of such a concept.

The Mana

Such a concept indeed exists in a certain number of societies, and, from the standpoint of mere logic, the fact that it operates under its own name in the relatively differentiated magics of two of the ethnic groups that we are studying tends to support our analysis.

This concept is that which in Melanisia goes under the name of "mana." Nowhere can it be observed more easily, and, luckily enough, it has been admirably observed and described by Mr. Codrington (*The Melanisians*, p. 119ff., p. 191ff., etc.). The word "mana" is common to all specifically Melanisian languages and even to most of the Polynesian languages. Mana is not merely a force, a being; it is also an action, a quality, and a state of affairs. The idea of mana is one of these confused ideas that we believe we have gotten rid of, and, consequently, find hard to imagine. It is a notion obscure and vague and yet surprisingly specific as to the proper conditions of its use. It is abstract and general and yet full of concrete elements. Its primitive nature, i.e., complex and indeterminate, precludes any logical analysis; hence, we must be content to describe it. For Mr. Codrington, it covers the whole of magical and religious ritual, the whole of the magical and religious spirits and all the persons and things that intervene in each and every ritual. Mana is exactly what gives value to things and people—magical value, religious and even social value. The social rating of an individual is in direct relation to the importance of his mana—very specifically, his position in the secret society. The importance and severity of the property taboos depend upon the mana of the individual who imposes them. Wealth is supposed to be an effect of mana; in certain islands the word "mana" may even designate money.

The idea of mana is composed of a series of unstable ideas that merge into one another. It is successively and simultaneously quality, substance, and activity. In the first place, it is a quality. It is something possessed by the thing mana; it is not the thing itself. It can be described by saying that it is power and heaviness: at Saa, it is the warm; at Tanna, it is the strange, the indelible, the resistant, the extraordinary. In the second instance, mana is a thing, a substance, an essence that can be controlled but has also a life of its own, which is why it can be handled only by mana individuals in mana actions, that is to say, by qualified individuals and in the framework of a ritual. It is by nature transmissible and contagious; one may communi-cate the mana contained in a harvest stone to other stones, by putting them into contact. It is represented as material: it can be heard; it can be seen issuing from the things where it resides; mana rustles in the leaves; it escapes under the form of clouds or flames. It may specialize: there is mana which renders one rich and mana for killing. . . . In the third place, mana is a force, specifically, of a spiritual nature, that is to say, the force of the ancestral souls and of the spirits of nature. It is this force which makes magical beings of them. Indeed, it does not belong to all spirits indiscriminately. The natural spirits are intrinsically possessed of mana, but this is not the case for all souls of the dead. Mana is possessed by *tindalos*, i.e., efficacious spirits, the souls of the chiefs, at best the souls of the family heads, and even more specifically the souls of those who manifested mana during their lifetime or through miracles after their death. Those alone deserve the name of potent spirit, the others being lost in the multitude of empty shadows. . . .

Mana is thus given as something not only mysterious but also separate. In short, mana is first a certain type of action, that is, the long distance spiritual action that takes place between beings in resonance with one another. It is also a sort of ether, imponderable, communicable, which spreads of itself. . . .

This concept accounts well for what takes place in magic. It is the source of the useful idea of a world above reality, where ritual takes place, where the magician penetrates, populated by spirits and saturated by magical fluids. Furthermore, it legitimizes the power of the magician, it justifies the need for formal acts, the creative power of words, sympathetic connections, the transfers of qualities and influences. It explains the presence of spirits and their intervention, since it conceives of all magical force as being spiritual. Finally, it motivates the general belief in magic, since magic, when shorn of its outside appearances, is essentially mana; and it feeds this same belief, since it is mana that animates all the forms that magic may take.

Through mana, the efficacy of magic is established beyond discussion, and doubt itself intervenes in its favor. This concept is indeed the very condition of magical experimentation, and permits interpretation of the most negative events as supporting the belief. In fact, the belief is beyond any critical examination. It is given *a priori,* prior to any experiencing of life. Properly speaking, mana is not an aspect of magic, as are sympathetic resonance, demons, and magical properties. Rather, it rules all magical aspects; it is their condition, their necessary form. It functions as a category does; it renders possible magical ideas, as logical categories render possible human ideas. This role of unconscious category of man's understanding, which we are positing here, is well demonstrated by the facts. We have seen how rarely it reaches the threshold of consciousness, and rarer still that it should find there a clear expression. This is because mana is as inherent to magic as the Euclidian postulate is inherent to our conception of space.

However, it should be understood that this category is not inherent in the individual's mind, as are the categories of time and space. The proof of this resides in the fact that it could have been seriously weakened by the progress of civilization and that it varies in content from one society to the other, as well as with the various phases through which these same societies go. If it exists in the minds of individuals, it is only because of the existence of society, which is also true for the ideas of justice or value; we might well say that mana is a category of collective thought.

It appears from our analysis that the notion of mana is of the same order as the notion of the sacred. First, in a certain number of cases the two notions are combined: for instance, the idea of manito among the Algonquins, the idea of Orenda among the Iroquois, and the idea of mana in Melanisia, belong as much to religion as they do to magic. Furthermore, we have seen that, in Melanisia, there are connections between the idea of mana and the idea of taboo; we have seen that a certain number of things having mana were taboo, but that taboo could only apply to mana things. Similarly among the Algonquins, if all gods are manitos, all manitos are not gods. Consequently, not only is the notion of mana more general than that of the sacred, but the latter is comprised in the former and is derived from it. It is probably correct to say that the sacred is a specie of the genus mana. Thus, beneath the magical rituals, we shall have found not only the notion of sacred but also its origin.

Either magic is a social phenomenon and the notion of sacred is a social phenomenon, or magic is not a social phenomenon and neither is the notion of sacred. Without wishing to go into considerations on the intrinsic nature of the sacred, we nevertheless can make a few remarks that will point to the social character of both the notions of magic and mana. The qualities of mana and of sacred attach to objects sharing a very special place in society, to the extent that they are very often considered as outside the common domain and usage. These objects play a considerable part in magic; they are its very core.

The souls of the dead and all that touches death are beings and objects that are eminently magic: witness the highly magical character of the universal practice of evoking the dead, witness the capacity everywhere attributed to the contact with the hand of the dead to render one as invisible as the dead, and a thousand other instances. These same dead are equally the object of funeral rites—sometimes of ancestor cults—which make very clear how their condition is different from that of the living. It may be objected that in certain societies magic does not deal with all of the dead, but foremostly with those that have suffered a violent death and, particularly, criminals. It is an additional proof for the argument; for the latter are the objects of beliefs and rituals that make of them beings highly differentiated, not only from the living, but also from the rest of the dead. However, in general, all dead—corpses and spirits—form a special world, from which the magician derives his deadly powers and evil spells.

Furthermore, if women, whose role in magic is supposedly so important, are believed to be magicians and to hold special powers, it is because of the peculiarity of their social position. They are reputed qualitatively different from men and endowed with certain powers: menstruations, the mysterious processes of sex and gestation, are but the signs of these qualities. Society, as far as men are concerned, shares toward women intense convictions, which the latter respect and share as well. Hence, the differentiation or inferiority of their legal and especially of their religious status. On the other hand, this is precisely the reason why they are given to magic and why magic gives them a status inverse to that which they occupy in religion. Women exhude constantly morbid fluids. *Nirrtir hi stri,* "woman is death" the old Brahmanic texts say (*Maitrayani samhita,* 1, 10, 11). They bring misery and witchcraft. They have the evil eye. This is why, even though the activity of women in magic is less than what the men have made of it, it is greater than their activity in religion.

As these two examples show, the magical value of things results from their relative position within the society or in relation to it. The two concepts of magical power and social position coincide, in so far as it is the one that creates the other. In the last analysis, we are still dealing in magic with the values recognized by society. These values are not derived from the intrinsic qualities of objects and persons, but from the place and the rank attributed to them by the convictions of sovereign public opinion. Values are social and not inherent to experience. This is very well shown by the magical power of words and the fact that often the magical power of things is due to their name; whence it results that, being in strict dependance of dialects and languages, the said values are tribal and national. Therefore, objects, beings, and actions are ordered hierarchically, some commanding the others. It is according to this order that magical actions occur, as they go from magician to a certain class of spirits, from the latter to another class, and so on until the final effect. What we did like in the expression "magical potentiality," which Mr. Hewitt applies to the notions of mana and *orenda,* is that it does precisely imply the existence of a sort of magical potential, and indeed this is what we have just described. What we have called "relative position" or "specific value of things," we might call as well "differential potential." For it is in virtue of these differentials that they act upon one another. Hence, it is not enough to say that the quality of mana attaches itself to certain objects by virtue of their relative positions in society. We must add that the idea of mana is nothing but the idea of these magnitudes, and differences in the magnitude of this potential. That is the crucial aspect of the notion on which magic is based, and hence, of magic itself. It goes without saying that such a notion has no purpose outside of society, that it is absurd from the standpoint of pure reason, and that it has for sole origin the functioning of collective life.

We do not see, in this hierarchy of notions dominated by the idea of mana, the product of many artificial conventions arrived at between individuals —laymen and magicians—which would then become part of the traditional heritage in view of their efficacy, although they were originally marred by various errors. Quite the contrary. We believe that magic, like religion, is a matter of sentiment. We shall say, more exactly, and to employ the abstruse language of modern theology, that magic, like religion, is a set of "value judgments," i.e., of effective aphorisms attributing various qualities to the various objects entering its system. But these value judgments are not the work of individual minds; they are the expression of social sentiments that have developed—sometimes of necessity and universally, sometimes fortuitously—toward certain things arbitrarily chosen, for the most part, among plants and animals, occupations and sexes, planets, meteors, elements, physical phenomena, irregularities of terrain, substances, etc. The notion of mana, like the notion of the sacred, is finally that category of collective thought which is at the basis of these judgments, which imposes a classification of things, separates some, unites others, and establishes lines of influences or boundaries for segregation.

3. *On the Social Functions of Religion*

BY BRONISLAW MALINOWSKI

The Three Aspects of Religion

RELIGION IS a difficult and refractory subject of study. It seems futile to question that which contains the answers to all problems. It is not easy to dissect with the cold knife of logic what can only be accepted with a complete surrender of heart. It seems impossible to comprehend with reason that which encompasses mankind with love and supreme wisdom.

Nor is it easier for an atheist to study religion than for a deeply convinced believer. The rationalist denies the reality of religious experience. To

Reprinted from Bronislaw Malinowski, *Foundations of Faith and Morals,* Riddell Lectures (London: Humphrey Milford, 1936), chap. i, pp. 1–8, and chap. vii, pp. 58–62, and used with the permission of Humphrey Milford.

him, the very fact of religion is a mystery over which he may smile, or by which he may be puzzled, but which, by his very admission, he is not qualified to fathom; it is difficult to study seriously facts which appear merely a snare, a delusion, or a trickery. Yet how can even a rationalist lightly dismiss those realities which have formed the very essence of truth and happiness to millions and hundreds of millions over thousands of years?

In another away the believer, too, is debarred from impartial study. For him one religion, his own, presents no problems. It is the Truth, the whole Truth, and nothing but the Truth. Especially if he be a fundamentalist, that is, unable to understand the foundations of human faith, he will simply disregard most religious phenomena as "superstitions" and will uphold his own views as Absolute Truth. And yet every one, the bigoted fundamentalist always excepted, might well pause and reflect on the way of his Providence which has vouchsafed the Truth to a small part of humanity, and has kept the rest of mankind in a state of perpetual darkness and error and thus condemned them to eternal perdition. Yet there may perhaps be room for a humble approach to all facts of human belief, in which the student investigates them with a sympathy which makes him almost a believer, but with an impartiality which does not allow him to dismiss all religions as erroneous whilst one remains true.

It is in this spirit that the Anthropologist must approach the problems of primitive religion if they are to be of use in the understanding of the religious crises of our modern world. We must always keep in sight the relation of faith to human life, to the desires, difficulties, and hopes of human beings. Beliefs, which we so often dismiss as "superstition," as a symptom of savage crudeness or "prelogical mentality," must be understood; that is, their culturally valuable core must be brought to light. But belief is not the alpha and omega of religion: it is important to realize that man translates his confidence in spiritual powers into action; that in prayer and ceremonial, in rite and secrament, he always attempts to keep in touch with that supernatural reality, the existence of which he affirms in his dogma. Again, we shall see that every religion, however humble, carries also instructions for a good life; it invariably provides its followers with an ethical system.

Every religion, primitive or developed, presents then three main aspects, dogmatic, ritual, and ethical. But the mere division or differentiation into three aspects is not sufficient. It is equally important to grasp the essential interrelation of these three aspects, to recognize that they are really only three facets of the same essential fact. In his dogmatic system, man affirms that Providence or Spirits or Supernatural Powers exist. In his religious ritual he worships those entities and enters into relation with them, for revelation implies that such a relation is possible and necessary. Spirits, ancestral ghosts, or gods refuse to be ignored by man, and he in turn is in need of their assistance. The dependence on higher powers implies further the mutual dependence of man on his neighbour. You cannot worship in common without a common bond of mutual trust and assistance, that is, of charity and love. If God has created man in His own image, one image of God may not debase, defile, or destroy the other.

In discussing dogmatics, especially in primitive relations, we shall be met by what might be described as the mystery of myth. In all religions, Christianity and Judaism not excepted, we find that every tenet of belief, every dogmatic affirmation, has a tendency to be spun out into a long narrative.

In other words, the abstract system of dogmatic principles is invariably bound up with a sacred history.

Minor characteristics, extravagances, and peculiarities of mythology have mostly attracted the interest of the student in the past and aroused his passion to explain them. The stories are at times crude, in some cases even obscene. This, within the general scope of our analysis, we shall not find difficult to understand: religious beliefs enter deeply into the essential facts of life, of which fertility and procreation are an essential part. Another peculiarity of myth is the frequent reference to natural phenomena, to features of the landscape, to quaint habits of animals and plants. This has often been accounted for in learned theories by the assumption that mythology is primitive science, and that its main function is to explain natural phenomena and the mysteries of the Universe. Such theories we shall to a large extent have to dismiss or at least to correct. Primitive man has his science as well as his religion; a myth does not serve to explain phenomena but rather to regulate human actions.

The main problem of myth is, in my opinion, its relation to dogma; the fact that myth is an elaboration of an act of faith into an account of a definite concrete miracle. Why is this necessary? In the course of our analysis I hope to show that this is due to the very nature of life and faith. Faith is always based on primeval revelation, and revelation is a concrete event. In revelation, God, or ancestral spirits, or culture heroes create and mould the Universe, manifest their will and power to man. All this is a temporal process, a concrete sequence of activities, a set of dramatic performances. Man in turn reacts to this manifestation of supernatural power, he rebels and sins, gains knowledge, loses grace and regains it once more. Small wonder, then, that most of the dogmatic systems of mankind occur as a body of sacred tradition, as a set of stories stating the beginning of things and thus vouching for their reality. Again, since in myth we have an account of how Providence created man and revealed its reality to him, we usually find that myth contains also the prescription of how man has to worship Providence in order to remain in contact with it.

Thus the discussion of myth leads us directly to the riddle of ritual. Here, again, we shall not tarry over the sensational peculiarities of detail. We shall proceed at once to the central and fundamental problem: "Why ritual?" We may start here with the extreme Puritan's scorn and rejection of all ritualism, for this represents the voice of reason against the sensuous, almost physiological attitude of naïve faith. Incense, pictures, processions, fireworks are as incomprehensible, hence repugnant, to the highly refined and relective type of religious consciousness as they are to the anti-religious rationalist. Ritualism is to reason, pure, or sublimated in religious feeling, always a form of idolatry, a return to magic. To the dispassionate student of all religions, who is not prepared to discount Roman Catholicism because he feels a deep admiration for the religion of Friends, nor to dismiss Totemism because he appreciates its distance from the religion of Israel, ritual still remains a problem. Why has man to express such simple affirmations as the belief in the immortality of the soul, in the reality of a spiritual world, by antics, dramatized performances, by dancing, music, incense, by an elaboration, richness, and an extensiveness of collective action which often consumes an enormous amount of tribal or national energy and substance?

Here, again, our argument will not be a mere tilting at windmills. The usual scientific treatment of ritual, primitive and civilized, does not seem to me to be quite satisfactory. The conception, for instance, of primitive magic as "a false scientific technique" does not do justice to its cultural value. Yet one of the greatest contemporary anthropologists, Sir James Frazer, has to a certain extent given countenance to this conception. Freud's theory that magic is man's primitive belief in the "omnipotence of thought" would also dismiss primitive ritual as a colossal piece of pragmatic self-deception. The views here advanced will be that every ritual performance, from a piece of primitive Australian magic to a Corpus Christi procession, from an initiation ceremony to the Holy Mass, is a traditionally enacted miracle. In such a miracle the course of human life or of natural events is re-modelled by the action of supernatural forces, which are released in a sacred, traditionally standardized act of the congregation or of the religious leader. The fact that every religious rite must contain an element of the miraculous will not appear to us an outgrowth of human childishness, of primeval stupidity (*Urdummheit*), nor yet a blind alley of primitive pseudo-science. To us it represents the very essence of religious faith. Man needs miracles not because he is benighted through primitive stupidity, through the trickery of a priesthood, or through being drugged with "the opiate for the masses," but because he realizes at every stage of his development that the powers of his body and of his mind are limited. It is rather the recognition of his practical and intellectual limitations, and not the illusion of the "omnipotence of thought," which leads man into ritualism; which makes him re-enact miracles, the feasibility of which he has accepted from his mythology.

The enigma of ethics, the question why every

religion carries its own morals, is simpler. Why, in order to be decent and righteous, must man believe in the Devil as well as in God, in demons as well as in spirits, in the malice of his ancestral ghosts as well as in their benevolence? Here, once more, we have a host of theoretical conceptions, or misconceptions, dictated by hostility to religion or by the partisanship of sectarians. In order to safeguard ourselves against invented hell-fire so as to cow believers into doing what it wishes, we shall have to make an attempt at a real understanding of the phenomena. For, with all our sympathy for the religious attitude, we shall also have to reject the theological view that morality must be associated with dogma, because both have been vouchsafed to mankind by the One True Revelation. The correct answer to our problem lies in the social character of religion. That every organized belief implies a congregation, must have been felt by many thinkers instructed by scholarship and common sense. Yet, here again, science was slow to incorporate the dictates of simple and sound reason. Tylor and Bastian, Max Müller and Mannhardt treat religious systems as if initiative in putting the sociological aspect of religion on the scientific map came from the Scottish divine and scholar, Robertson Smith. It was elaborated with precision, but also with exaggeration, by the French philosopher and sociologist, Durkheim.

The essentially sound methodological principle is that worship always happens in common because it touches common concerns of the community. And here, as our analysis will show, enters the ethical element intrinsically inherent in all religious activities. They always require efforts, discipline, and submission on the part of the individual for the good of the community. Taboos, vigils, religious exercises are essentially moral, not merely because they express submission of man to spiritual powers, but also because they are a sacrifice of man's personal comfort for the common weal. But there is another ethical aspect which, as we shall see, makes all religions moral in their very essence. Every cult is associated with a definite congregation: ancestor-worship is primarily based on the family; at times even on a wider group, the clan; at times it becomes tribal, when the ancestor spirit is that of a chief. The members of such a group of worshippers have natural duties towards each other. The sense of common responsibility, of reciprocal charity and goodwill, flows from the same fundamental idea and sentiment which moves clansmen, brothers, or tribesmen to common worship. I am my tribesman's brother, or my clansman's totemic kinsman, because we are all descended from the same being whom we worship in our ceremonies, to whom we sacrifice, and to whom we pray. We have only to change the word *descended* into *created* in order to pass to those religions which maintain as a fundamental principle the brotherhood of man, because he owes his existence to a Creator whom he addresses as "Our Father which art in Heaven." The conception of the Church as a big family is rooted in the very nature of religion.

These conclusions may seem simple, once they are stated directly. Fundamental scientific truths in physics and biology, as in the science of man, are never sophisticated. Yet, even now anthropologist and missionary alike deny ethics to the heathen.

Conclusions on the Anatomy and Pathology of Religion

The scientific analysis of religion is systems as regards substance, form, and function. Every organized faith must carry its specific apparatus, by which it expresses its substance. There must be a dogmatic system backed by mythology or sacred tradition; a developed ritual in which man acts on his belief and communes with the powers of the unseen world; there must also be an ethical code of rules which binds the faithful and determines their behaviour towards each other and towards the things they worship. This structure or form of religion can be traced in Totemism and Animism, in ancestor-worship as well as in the most developed monotheistic systems.

We find, moreover, that there exists an intrinsically appropriate subject-matter in every religious system, a subject-matter which finds its natural expression in the religious technique of ritual and ethnics, and its validation in sacred history. This subject-matter can be summed up as the twin beliefs in Providence and in Immortality. By belief in Providence we understand the mystical conviction that there exist in the universe forces or persons who guide man, who are in sympathy with man's destinies, and who can be propitiated by man. This concept completely covers the Christian's faith in God, One and Indivisible though present in Three Persons, who has created the world and guides it to-day. It embraces also the many forms of polytheistic paganism: the belief in ancestor ghosts and guardian spirits. Even the so-called totemic religions, based on the conviction that man's social and cultural order is duplicated in a spiritual dimension, through which he can control the natural forces of fertility and of the environment, are but a rude version of the belief in Providence. For they allow man to get in touch with the spiritual essence of animal or plant species, to honour them and

fulfil duties towards them, in return for their yielding to his needs. The belief in Immortality in our higher religions is akin to that of private creeds, some of which only affirm a limited continuance after death, while others assume an immortality consisting in repeated acts of reincarnation.

The substance of all religion is thus deeply rooted in human life; it grows out of the necessities of life. In other words, religion fulfils a definite cultural function in every human society. This is not a platitude. It contains a scientific refutation of the repeated attacks on religion by the less enlightened rationalists. If religion is indispensable to the integration of the community, just because it satisfies spiritual needs by giving man certain truths and teaching him how to use these truths, then it is impossible to regard religion as a trickery, as an "opiate for the masses," as an invention of priests, capitalists, or any other servants of vested interests.

The scientific treatment of religion implies above all a clear analysis of how it grows out of the necessities of human life. One line of approach consists in the study of sacraments, that is, those religious acts which consecrate the crises of human life, at birth, at puberty, at marriage, and above all at death. In these religion gives a sense and a direction to the course of life and to the value of personality. It binds the individual to the other members of his family, his clan or tribe, and it keeps him in constant relation with the spiritual world.

Another empirical approach shows how magical and religious phenomena are directly dictated to man by the stresses and strains of life, and the necessity of facing heavy odds; how faith and ritual must follow the darker, more dangerous, and more tragic aspects of man's practical labours. Here the material foundations of man's life ought to be scrutinized. Agriculture, with its principal condition of rainfall and sunshine, leads to the magic of fertility, to an elaborate ritual of sowing, flowering, harvest, and first-fruits, and to the institution of divine kings and chiefs. Primitive food-gathering produces ceremonies of the Intichiuma type. Hazardous pursuits, such as hunting and fishing, sailing and distant trading, yield their own type of ritual, belief, and ethical rules. The vicissitudes of war and love are also rich in magical concomitants. Religion, no doubt, combines all these elements in a great variety of designs or mosaics. It is the object of science to discover the common elements in them, though it may be the task of the artist or of the mystic to depict or to cherish the individual phenomenon. But I venture to affirm that in not a single one of its manifestations can religion be found without its firm roots in human emotion, which again always grows out of desires and vicissitudes connected with life.

Two affirmations, therefore, preside over every ritual act, every rule of conduct, and every belief. There is the affirmation of the existence of powers sympathetic to man, ready to help him on condition that he conforms to the traditional lore which teaches how to serve them, conjure them, and propitiate them. This is the belief in Providence, and this belief assists man in so far as it enhances his capacity to act and his readiness to organize for action, under conditions where he must face and fight not only the ordinary forces of nature, but also chance, ill luck, and the mysterious, ever incalculable designs of destiny.

The second belief is that beyond the brief span of natural life there is compensation in another existence. Through this belief man can act and calculate far beyond his own forces and limitations, looking forward to his work being continued by his successors in the conviction that, from the next world, he will still be able to watch and assist them. The sufferings and efforts, the injustices and inequalities, of this life are thus made up for. Here again we find that the spiritual force of this belief not only integrates man's own personality, but is indispensable for the cohesion of the social fabric. Especially in the form which this belief assumes in ancestor-worship and the communion with the dead do we perceive its moral and social influence.

In their deepest foundations, as well as in their final consequences, the two beliefs in Providence and Immortality are not independent of one another. In the higher religions man lives in order to be united to God. In the simpler forms, the ancestors worshipped are often mystically identified with environmental forces, as in Totemism. At times they are both ancestors and carriers of fertility, as the Kachina of the Pueblos. Or again the ancestor is worshipped as the divinity, or at least as a culture hero.

The unity of religion in substance, form, and function is to be found everywhere. Religious development consists probably in the growing predominance of the ethical principle and in the increasing fusion of the two main factors of all belief, the sense of Providence and the faith in Immortality.

The conclusions to be drawn with regard to con-temporary events I shall leave to the reader's own reflection. Is religion, in the sense in which we have just defined it—the affirmation of an ethical Providence, of Immortality, of the transcendental value and sense of human life—is such religion dead? Is it going to make way for other creeds, perhaps less exacting, perhaps more immediately repaying and grossly satisfactory, but creeds which, nevertheless, fail to satisfy man's craving for the Absolute; fail to answer the riddle of human existence, and to convey the ethical message which can only be received from a Being or Beings regarded as beyond human passions, strife, and frailties? Is religion going to surrender its own equipment of faith, ritual, and ethics to cross-breeds between superstition and science, between economics and credulity, between politics and national megalomania? The dogmatic affirmations of these new mysticisms are banal, shallow, and they pander directly to the lowest instincts of the multitude. This is true of the belief in the absolute supremacy of one race and its right to bully all others; the belief in the sanctity of egoism in one's own nationality; the conviction of the value of war and collective brutality; the belief that only manual labour gives the full right to live and that the whole culture and public life of a community must be warped in the interests of the industrial workers.

Those of us who believe in culture and believe in the value of religion, though perhaps not in its specific tenets, must hope that the present-day misuse of the religious apparatus for partisan and doctrinaire purposes is not a healthy development of religion, but one of the many phenomena in the pathology of culture which seem to threaten the immediate development of our post-war western society. If this be so, these new pseudo-religions are doomed to die. Let us hope that our whole society will not be dragged with them to destruction. Let us work for the maintenance of the eternal truths which have guided mankind out of barbarism to culture, and the loss of which seems to threaten us with barbarism again. The rationalist and agnostic must admit that even if he himself cannot accept these truths, he must at least recognize them as indispensable pragmatic figments without which civilization cannot exist.

4. On Sacrifice

BY W. ROBERTSON SMITH

IN ACTS OF WORSHIP we expect to find the religious ideal expressed in its purest form and we cannot easily think well of a type of religion whose ritual culminates in a jovial feast. It seems that such a faith sought nothing higher than a condition of physical *bien être,* and in one sense this judgment is just. The good things desired of the gods were the blessings of earthly life, not spiritual but carnal things. But Semitic heathenism was redeemed from mere materialism by the fact that religion was not the affair of the individual but of the community. The ideal was earthly, but it was not selfish. In rejoicing before his god a man rejoiced with and for the welfare of his kindred, his neighbours and his country, and, in renewing by a solemn act of worship the bond that united him to his god, he also renewed the bonds of family, social and national obligation. We have seen that the compact between the god and the community of his worshippers was not held to pledge the deity to make the private cares of each member of the community his own. The gods had their favourites no doubt, for whom they were prepared to do many things that they were not bound to do; but no man could approach his god in a purely personal matter with that spirit of absolute confidence which I have described as characteristic of antique religions; it was the community, and not the individual, that was sure of the permanent and unfailing help of its deity. It was a national not a personal providence that was taught by ancient religion. So much was this the case that in purely personal concerns the ancients were very apt to turn, not to the recognised religion of the family or of the state, but to magical superstitions. The gods watched over a man's civic life, they gave him his share in public benefits, the annual largess of the harvest and the vintage, national peace or victory over enemies, and so forth, but they were not sure helpers in every private need, and above all they would not help him in matters that were against the interests of the community as a whole. There was therefore a whole region of possible needs and desires for which religion could and would do nothing; and if supernatural help was sought in such things it had to be sought through magical ceremonies,

designed to purchase or constrain the favour of demoniac powers with which the public religion had nothing to do. Not only did these magical superstitions lie outside religion, but in all well-ordered states they were regarded as illicit. A man had no right to enter into private relations with supernatural powers that might help him at the expense of the community to which he belonged. In his relations to the unseen he was bound always to think and act with and for the community, and not for himself alone.

With this it accords that every complete act of worship—for a mere vow was not a complete act till it was fulfilled by presenting a sacrifice—had a public or quasi-public character. Most sacrifices were offered on fixed occasions, at the great communal or national feasts, but even a private offering was not complete without guests, and the surplus of sacrificial flesh was not sold but distributed with an open hand. Thus every act of worship expressed the idea that man does not live for himself only but for his fellows, and that this partnership of social interests is the sphere over which the gods preside and on which they bestow their assured blessing.

The ethical significance which thus appertains to the sacrificial meal, viewed as a social act, received particular emphasis from certain ancient customs and ideas connected with eating and drinking. According to antique ideas, those who eat and drink together are by this very act tied to one another by a bond of friendship and mutual obligation. Hence when we find that in ancient religions all the ordinary functions of worship are summed up in the sacrificial meal, and that the ordinary intercourse between gods and men has no other form, we are to remember that the act of eating and drinking together is the solemn and stated expression of the fact that all who share the meal are brethren, and that the duties of friendship and brotherhood are implicitly acknowledged in their common act. By admitting man to his table the god admits him to his friendship; but this favour is extended to no man in his mere private capacity; he is received as one of a community, to eat and drink along with his fellows, and in the same measure as the act of worship cements the bond between him and his god, it cements also the bond between him and his brethren in the common faith.

Reprinted from W. Robertson Smith, *Lectures on the Religion of the Semites* (new ed.; London: Adam & Charles Black, 1907), pp. 263–68.

We have now reached a point in our discussion at which it is possible to form some general estimate of the ethical value of the type of religion which has been described. The power of religion over life is twofold, lying partly in its association with particular precepts of conduct, to which it supplies a supernatural sanction, but mainly in its influence on the general tone and temper of men's minds, which it elevates to higher courage and purpose, and raises above a brutal servitude to the physical wants of the moment, by teaching men that their lives and happiness are not the mere sport of the blind forces of nature, but are watched over and cared for by a higher power. As a spring of action this influence is more potent than the fear of supernatural sanctions, for it is stimulative, while the other is only regulative. But to produce a moral effect on life the two must go together; a man's actions must be not only supported by the feeling that the divine help is with him, but regulated by the conviction that that help will not accompany him except on the right path. In ancient religion, as it appears among the Semites, the confident assurance of divine help belongs, not to each man in his private concerns, but to the community in its public functions and public aims; and it is this assurance that is expressed in public acts of worship, where all the members of the community meet together to eat and drink at the table of their god, and so renew the sense that he and they are altoegther at one. Now, if we look at the whole community of worshippers as absolutely one, personify them and think of them as a single individual, it is plain that the effect of this type of religion must be regarded as merely stimulative and not regulative. When the community is at one with itself and at one with its god, it may, for anything that religion has to say, do exactly what it pleases towards all who are outside it. Its friends are the god's friends, its enemies the god's enemies; it takes its god with it in whatever it chooses to do. As the ancient communities of religion are tribes or nations, this is as much as to say that, properly speaking, ancient religion has no influence on intertribal or international morality—in such matters the god simply goes with his own nation or his own tribe. So long as we consider the tribe or nation of common religion as a single subject, the influence of religion is limited to an increase of the national self-confidence—a quality very useful in the continual struggle for life that was waged between ancient communities, but which beyond this has no moral value.

But the case is very different when we look at the religious community as made up of a multitude of individuals, each of whom has private as well as public purposes and desires. In this aspect it is the regulative influence of ancient religion that is predominant, for the good things which religion holds forth are promised to the individual only in so far as he lives in and for the community. The conception of man's chief good set forth in the social act of sacrificial worship is the happiness of the individual in the happiness of the community, and thus the whole force of ancient religion is directed, so far as the individual is concerned, to maintain the civil virtues of loyalty and devotion to a man's fellows at a pitch of confident enthusiasm, to teach him to set his highest good in the prosperity of the society of which he is a member, not doubting that in so doing he has the divine power on his side and has given his life to a cause that cannot fail. This devotion to the common weal was, as every one knows, the mainspring of ancient morality and the source of all the heroic virtues of which ancient history presents so many illustrious examples. In ancient society, therefore, the religious ideal expressed in the act of social worship and the ethical ideal which governed the conduct of daily life were wholly at one, and all morality—as morality was then understood—was consecrated and enforced by religious motives and sanctions.

These observations are fully applicable only to the typical form of ancient religion, when it was still strictly tribal or national. When nationality and religion began to fall apart, certain worships assumed a character more or less cosmopolitan. Even in heathenism, therefore, in its more advanced forms, the gods, or at least certain gods, are in some measure the guardians of universal morality, and not merely of communal loyalty. But what was thus gained in comprehensiveness was lost in intensity and strength of religious feeling, and the advance towards ethical universalism, which was made with feeble and uncertain steps, was never sufficient to make up for the decline of the old heroic virtues that were fostered by the narrower type of national faith.

5. *The Tao*

BY MARCEL GRANET

THE MYTHICAL MODE of thought—and with it the various techniques that aim to order the world—is steeped in the belief that physical things can be controlled by their images. The theoreticians of the divining arts, by giving to the mythical mode of thought a systematic formulation, succeeded in reinforcing this disposition of the Chinese mind. By conceiving of the Tao as a principle of Order that rules both mental activity and the life of the universe, one is led to admit that the changes that can be noted in things are identical to the substitution of symbols that take place in the process of thought.

Once this axiom is accepted, neither causality nor contradiction can be used as guiding principles—not because Chinese thought runs to confusion, but, on the contrary, because the idea of an efficient and pervasive Order dominates it completely, embracing both the concept of causality and the concept of gender. If one starts from the ideas of mutation and efficacious Virtue, there is no need for a formal logic of extension or for experimental physics; and one gains, through the refusal to invent parameters, the advantage of not removing from time and space their concrete characteristics.

The idea of mutation removes all philosophical interest from an inventory of nature, where an attempt would be made to order facts through a distinction between antecedents and consequences.

Instead of registering sequences of phenomena, the Chinese register cyclical changes in their aspect. If two aspects seem tied together, it is not by way of cause and effect; rather, they seem to be *paired* as are inside and outside, or—to use a metaphor current as early as the period of Hi Ts'eu—as are paired echo and sound, or shadow and light.

The conviction that the Whole and each of the self-enclosed units composing it have a cyclical nature and can be explained as alternations dominates thinking so thoroughly that the idea of *sequence* is always overshadowed by that of *interdependence*. Hence, there will be no objection to *ex post facto* explanation. Such-and-such a lord could not, *while alive,* obtain supremacy, for, it is said, *after his death,* human sacrifices were

made in his honor. Political failure and nefarious funeral rites are solidary aspects of one and the same reality, which is the prince's lack of Virtue, or, better, they are equivalent signs of this lack.

What Chinese thought likes to record are not causes and effects but, the order of appearance being of little importance, phenomena conceived of as peculiar, although issuing from the same root: *equally demonstrative, they seem substitutable one for the other.* A river that runs dry, a landslide, a man who changes into a woman—all may announce the approaching end of a dynasty. These are four aspects of the same event: an obsolete order disappears to make room for a new order. Everything deserves to be noted down, as a precursive sign or as confirmation of a sign—or of a series of signs—but nothing encourages the search of an efficacious cause.

When one writes a report, one never thinks of *measuring* the elements brought together. It is not natural phenomena that are being observed, and there is no need to consider their relative magnitude. We are dealing here only with signals, for which the quantitative estimates of size and frequency are irrelevant. The most useful of precursive signs are, in fact, the most peculiar, the most minute, the rarest, the least obvious ones. A bird that destroys its nest indicates a breakdown—both physical and moral—in the Empire that is most alarming, since the sentiment of domestic piety is lacking even among the smallest of animals. The purpose of the catalogue is not to discover *sequences; its* aim is rather to reveal *solidarities.* Instead of considering the stream of events as a series of phenomena that may be measured and then related, the Chinese see in perceptible facts a mass of concrete signals. The duty to list them falls not upon physicists but upon chroniclers.

Far from trying to isolate facts from their time and place references, the Chinese see them only as signs revealing the qualities specific to a given Time and to a given Space. They do not try to register them by reference to a standard and stable set of variables. They try to omit nothing of what may reveal their *local meaning.* In describing them, they use indications of time, space, and size that are suitable to a definite period, to a definite area, or to a given nomenclature. They multiply the

---

Translated by Jesse Pitts, from Marcel Granet, *La pensée chinoise* (Paris: Albin Michel, 1934), pp. 329–39 with few deletions, with the permission of Albin Michel.

systems of classification, and they multiply the cross references between these systems. They avoid all that could permit comparisons and emphasize only what seems substitutable on a symbolic level. In indicating measurements, they avoid what might lead to measurement by abstract units. Numbers are used less as means of adding together equal units, than as concrete representations, to describe and situate so as to suggest the possibility of mutations justified by the identity or equivalence of the numerical symbols. The principle is to identify by referring to nomenclatures, without abstracting or generalizing and, if anything, by singularizing; while reserving, through the polyvalence of symbolism, wide possibilities of substitution. The concrete solidarities are infinitely more important than the abstract cause-effect relationship.

Knowledge means the constitution of collections of evocative singularities. The king's garden or his hunting park must contain all the animal and vegetal curiosities of the universe. Animals no hunter was able to capture must nevertheless be concretely present, i.e., as drawings or sculptures. Collections aim to be complete; the monstrosities, especially, must be present because they are assembled less for the sake of knowledge, than for the sake of control, and the most efficacious collections comprise not actual beasts but symbols. He who possesses the symbol can act upon the real. The symbol replaces the real. . . .

When a concrete form seems to call forth another form, the Chinese believe themselves to be in the presence of two congruent signs, which evoke one another by a simple effect of resonance: they both testify to the same condition or, rather, to the same aspect of the Universe. When a form changes into another form, the mutation acts like a signal, to which other signals must respond in unison. It indicates the advent of another *concrete situation,* which comprises an indefinite number of congruent manifestations. The manner in which this substitution, which is not a change in our sense, comes about is explained by the belief that any mutation bears upon the Whole and thus partakes of all of its features. There is no common measure to be found between two symbols that testify to the existence of two concrete aspects of the whole world. The consideration of second causes presents no interest for it has no applications. What accounts for all the details of a form is not a detail of causes, but the sole Tao.

The Tao is not in itself a first cause. It is but an efficacious Whole, a center of responsibility, or, better still, an accountable milieu. It is not creative. Nothing is created in the World, and the World was not created. The heroes who most resemble gods are content to put some order into the Universe. The sovereigns are *responsible* for the Order of the World, but they are not its creators. When they have Efficacy, they succeed within specified areas and a specified era—specified in function of their Authority—in maintaining an Order of civilization with which the Order of nature is solidary. Tao is but the exalted state of this Efficacy and of this Order. To give a ruling principle for action and to render the world intelligible, it is not necessary to distinguish between forces, substances, and causes and to burden oneself with problems imminent to the ideas of matter, motion, and work. Being conscious of the interdependence between symbolic realities and their concrete expressions is of itself sufficient. It promotes the recognition of solidarities and responsibilities. It dispenses not only with conceiving of a Cause, but also with looking for causes.

These ways of thinking did not prevent the ancient Chinese from showing great mechanical abilities: the perfection of their archery and of their carriages proves it. But this is how they conceived of the growth of an invention: when one of their philosophers wants to explain the invention of the wheel, he states that the idea was given by the flying seeds whirling in the air. Adverse to mechanical explanations, Chinese thought does not attempt to apply itself to the domain of motion and quantity. It remains resolutely shut within a world of symbols, which it does not wish to separate from the actual universe. To become informed about the universe it is enough to list symbols. If, on the one hand, it is true that one single reality corresponds to each symbol, on the other hand, each symbol possesses an indefinite power of evocation. It arouses, by a sort of direct effect, many realities and symbols that can be substituted for one another. This contagious quality of symbols differs radically from the articulations that may exist between ideas. There are no limits to the potentialities of various symbols. Hence, there is no advantage to classifying ideas on things by gender and species. Since it has no reference points, the principle of contradiction becomes useless. Instead of classifying concepts, one tries to order things, or, rather, their symbols, which appear more real since they are more powerful; and one tries to order them in a hierarchical order by taking into account their differential power.

The distinction between Same and Different is superseded by the antithesis Equivalent versus Opposite. Things and symbols evoke one another by plain resonance when they are equivalent, by rhythm when they are opposite. The world and the spirit both obey the same rule, which seems to resolve in two formulas: not that the similar produces the similar, and that the contrary springs from the contrary, but that equivalence goes with equivalence, and the opposite with opposite. These two formulas, which imply neither the idea of gender nor the idea of species, both express the same conviction: each appearance of the Universe or of the process of thought results, like the Universe itself, from the interdependence of two complementary aspects.

The Yin and the Yang are not opposed in the way of Being and Non-Being, or even as two genders would be. Far from conceiving a contradiction between two aspects, Yin and Yang, it is believed that they complete and perfect (*tch'eng*) one another, in reality as well as in thought. In the multiplicity of appearances, these aspects that can manifest themselves simultaneously and are linked by a simple and far reaching solidarity are equivalent (*t'ong*) and attract one another without losing their identity; the others—which contrast—oppose one another, but are united by an intimate interdependence evidenced by their cyclical sequence (*cheng-cheng*). The Chinese can avoid delegating to the principle of contradiction the task of ordering thought. They attribute this function to the principle of harmony (*ho:* harmonious union) of the contrasts. The efficacious order that rules thought and action is made of contrasts, but excludes the possibility of contradictions in a relative as well as in an absolute sense. There is no need for making up genders and species. Order is realized by constituting groups of symbols having the value of an active nomenclature. All these nomenclatures relay one another in the task, the different Elements alternating their reign, as well as the Yin and the Yang. The most detailed classifications serve only to give a more complex sentiment of Order, and an analysis—more thorough but without ever becoming abstract—of the rhythmical realizations of this Order in a Space and Time made of concrete elements.

The Chinese concept of the Universe is neither monistic nor dualistic nor even pluralistic. It is derived from the idea that the Whole distributes itself into hierarchical groups, where it is contained entirely. These groupings are differentiated only by the power of the Efficacious that is specific to each one. Tied to *Space-Time* units that are hierarchically ranked as well as incommensurable, they differ by their content, and even more by their tension: they are seen as realizations, more or less complex, more or less diluted, more or less concentrated, of the Efficacious. Knowledge has for first and last object a plan of organization of the Universe, which seems to be realized, thanks to a hierarchical arrangement of concrete nomenclatures. In the same way that they abstain from thinking conceptually by gender and species, the Chinese have no taste for syllogisms—of what use anyway would syllogistic deduction be for a thought that refuses to deprive Space and Time from their concrete character?

How can one state that Socrates, being a man, is mortal? In the coming times and in other spaces, is it sure that men die? On the other hand, one may say: Confucius is dead, hence I shall die; there is little hope that anyone deserves a span of life greater than was allotted to the greatest among wise men. Chinese logic is a logic of Order, or, if you wish, a logic of Efficacy, a logic of Hierarchy. The type of reasoning preferred by the Chinese has been compared to the Sorites.* However, except among a few dialecticians, and among the first Taoists who were trying to draw from the ancient ideal of Totality the notion of the Infinite, or at least of the Indefinite, this reasoning does not end in a series of conditions; it tends to render manifest the circulation of a principle of order among different realizations, more or less perfect and hence susceptible of being counted hierarchically, of this Totality that must be found in each of its manifestations. (Doing without inductive or deductive reasoning the Chinese try to put order in their thought in the same way that they introduce it in the world, that is, in Society. They give to their symbols and to their nomenclature a hierarchical arrangement, through which is expressed the Authority specific to each one.)

Neither the principle of contradiction nor the principle of causality possess the power given to imperative rules. Chinese thought does not break these rules systematically, nor does it feel the need to give them a special philosophical dignity. The Chinese strive to distinguish as they strive to coordinate. But, rather than isolate by abstraction genders and species, they try to establish a hierarchy of Efficacities or of Responsibilities. The techniques of reasoning or experimentation do not seem to deserve as much credit as the art of noting signs concretely and listing their resonances. They do not try to represent reality by conceiving of relationships and analyzing mechanics. They start from concrete representation and keep a concrete value for all their symbols, even for numerical nomenclatures.

---

* An abridged series of syllogisms in a series of propositions so arranged that the predicate of the first is the subject of the second, and so on, the conclusion uniting the subject of the first proposition with the predicate of the last. (*Webster's New Collegiate Dictionary*, 2d ed.; Springfield, Mass.: G. & C. Merriam Co., 1950.)

These symbols and these nomenclatures are used to stimulate meditation and to arouse a sense for responsibilities and solidarities. In the last analysis, they conceive of the world as if it were ruled by a protocol and they presume to arrange it like a ceremonial. Their morality, their physics, their logic are but aspects of a knowledge in action which is Etiquette.

When they mediate on events, they do not try to determine the general, nor to calculate the probable: they concentrate on spotting the transient and the peculiar. But, by so doing, they strive to perceive the indexes of metamorphoses that affect the whole of appearances, for they concentrate on detail only so as to bask in the feeling of Order. Because it moves in a world of symbols and gives full concreteness to symbols and to hierarchies of symbols, Chinese thought is oriented toward a sort of conventional or scholastic rationalism. But, on the other hand, it is fired with a passion for empiricism, which has stimulated it to an exhaustive observation of the concrete, which in turn has doubtless led to fruitful remarks. (If we were better informed on the pharmacy and the chemistry of the Chinese, and especially on their invention in agriculture and stock-breeding, it might then appear that Chinese empiricism and the pedagogical value of the idea of mutation is not devoid of value. We have been certainly too sarcastic toward the Chinese intellectual, who, in the nineteenth century and of course through nationalistic fervor, insisted that discoveries comparable to those of Western science were implicit on the Yi King.)

The greatest merit of Chinese thought is that it never separated the human from the natural and always conceptualized the human in a social context. If the idea of law did not develop, and if, consequently, the observation of nature was left to empiricism while the organization of society was left to a regime of compromise; the idea of Rule, or, better still, the concept of Models, by allowing the Chinese to keep a flexible conception of Order, prevented them from imagining a world of transcendental realities above the human kind. Deeply infused with a concrete approach to nature, their wisdom is definitely humanistic.

6. *Confucianism and Puritanism*

BY MAX WEBER

IN THIS CONTEXT we may best gain perspective on the foregoing by clarifying the relationship between Confucian rationalism—for the name is appropriate—and what is geographically and historically closest to us, namely, Protestant rationalism.

To judge the level of rationalization a religion represents we may use two primary yardsticks which are in many ways interrelated. One is the degree to which the religion has divested itself of magic; the other is the degree to which it has systematically unified the relation between God and the world and therewith its own ethical relationship to the world. In the former respect the varying expressions of ascetic Protestantism represent a last phase. The most characteristic forms of Protestantism have liquidated magic most completely. In principle, magic was eradicated even in the sublimated form of sacraments and symbols, so much so that the strict Puritan had the corpses of his loved ones dug under without any formality in order to assure the complete elimination of superstition. That meant, in this context, cutting off all trust in magical manipulations. Nowhere has the complete disenchantment of the world been carried through with greater consistency, but that did not mean freedom from what we nowadays customarily regard as "superstition." Witch trials also flourished in New England. Still while Confucianism left untouched the significance of magic for redemption, Puritanism came to consider all magic as devilish. Only ethical rationalism was defined as religiously valuable, i.e., conduct according to God's commandment and at that, proceeding from a God-fearing attitude. Finally, from our presentation it should be perfectly clear that in the magic garden

Reprinted from Max Weber, *The Religion of China*, trans. and ed. Hans H. Gerth (Glencoe, Ill.: The Free Press, 1951), chap. viii, pp. 226–49, with the permission of The Free Press.

of heterodox doctrine (Taoism) a rational economy and technology of modern occidental character was simply out of the question. For all natural scientific knowledge was lacking, partly as a cause and partly as an effect of these elemental forces: the power of chronomancers, geomancers, hydromancers, meteoromancers; and a crude, abstruse, universist conception of the unity of the world. Furthermore, Taoism was interested in the income opportunities of prebendal office, the bulwark of magical tradition.

The preservation of this magic garden, however, was one of the tendencies intimate to Confucian ethics. To this, internal reasons were added which prevented any shattering of Confucian power.

In strong contrast to the naïve stand of Confucianism toward things of this world, Puritan ethics construed them as a tremendous and grandiose tension toward the "world." As we shall see further in detail, every religion finds itself at some point in a state of tension with the irrationalities of the world. These tensions with individual religions set in at very different points, and the nature and intensity of the tension varies accordingly. With the individual religions this depends largely on the path of salvation as defined by metaphysical promises. We must note that the degree of religious devaluation of the world is not identical with the degree of its rejection in actual practice.

Confucianism, we have seen as (in intent) a rational ethic which reduced tension with the world to an absolute minimum. This was true of its religious depreciation as well as its practical rejection. The world was the best of all possible worlds; human nature was disposed to the ethically good. Men, in this as in all things, differed in degree but being of the same nature and capable of unlimited perfection, they were in principle adequate for fulfilling the moral law. Philosophical-literary education based upon the old classics was the universal means of self-perfection, and insufficient education along with its main cause, insufficient economic provision, were the only sources of shortcoming. Such faults, however, and especially the faults of government, were the essential reason for all misfortunes since they caused the unrest of the purely magically-conceived spirits. The right path to salvation consisted in adjustment to the eternal and supra-divine orders of the world, Tao, and hence to the requirements of social life, which followed from cosmic harmony. Pious conformism with the fixed order of secular powers reigned supreme. The corresponding individual ideal was the elaboration of the self as a universal and harmoniously balanced personality, in this sense a microcosm. For the Confucian ideal man, the gentleman, "grace and dignity" were expressed in fulfilling traditional obligations. Hence, the cardinal virtue and goal in selfperfection meant ceremonial and ritualist propriety in all circumstances of life. The appropriate means to this goal were watchful and rational self-control and the repression of whatever irrational passions might cause poise to be shaken.

The Confucian desired "salvation" only from the barbaric lack of education. As the reward for virtue he expected only long life, health, and wealth in this world and beyond death the retention of his good name. Like for truly Hellenic man all transcendental anchorage of ethics, all tensions between the imperatives of a supra-mundane God and a creatural world, all orientation toward a goal in the beyond, and all conception of radical evil were absent. He who complied with the commandments, fashioned for the man of average ability, was free of sin. In vain Christian missionaries tried to awaken a feeling of sin where such presuppositions were taken for granted. Then, too, an educated Chinese would simply refuse to be continually burdened with "sin." Incidentally, the concept of "sin" is usually felt as rather shocking and lacking in dignity by genteel intellectuals everywhere. Usually it is replaced by conventional, or feudal, or aesthetically formulated variants such as "indecent" or "not in good taste." There were sins, certainly, but in the field of ethics, these consisted of offenses against traditional authorities, parents, ancestors, and superiors in the hierarchy of office. For the rest they were magically precarious infringements of inherited customs, of the traditional ceremonial, and, finally, of the stable social conventions. All these were of equal standing. "I have sinned" corresponded to our "I beg your pardon" in violating a convention. Asceticism and contemplation, mortification and escape from the world were not only unknown in Confucianism but were despised as parasitism. All forms of congregational and redemptory religiosity were either directly persecuted and eradicated, or were considered a private affair and little esteemed, as were the orphic priests by the noble Hellenic men of classic time. This ethic of unconditional affirmation of and adjustment to the world presupposed the unbroken and continued existence of purely magical religion. It applied to the position of the emperor who, by personal qualification, was responsible for the good conduct of the spirits and the occurrence of rain and good harvest weather; it applied to ancestor worship which was equally fundamental for official and popular religiosity; and it applied to unofficial (Taoist) magical therapy and the other survival forms of animist compulsion of spirits (i.e., anthropo- and herolatric belief in functional deities).

Like the educated Hellene, the educated Confucian adhered to magical conceptions with a mixture of skepticism while occasionally submitting to demonology. But the mass of the Chinese, whose way of life was influenced by Confucianism, lived in these conceptions with unbroken faith. With regard to the beyond the Confucian might say with old Faust, "Fool who turns his eyes blinking in that direction"; but like Faust he would have to make the reservation, "If only I could remove magic from my path . . ." Also the high Chinese officials, educated in the old Chinese way, did not hesitate to be edified by the stupidest miracle. Tension toward the "world" had never arisen because, as far as known, there had never been an ethical prophecy of a supramundane God who raised ethical demands. Nor was there a substitute for this in the "spirits" who raised demands and insisted upon faithful fulfillment of contract. For it was always a matter of specific duty placed under the spirits' guardianship, oath, or whatever it happened to be; never did it involve inner formation of the personality per se nor the person's conduct of life. The leading intellectual stratum, officials and candidates for office, had consistently supported the retention of ancestor worship as absolutely necessary for the undisturbed preservation of bureaucratic authority. They suppressed all upheavals arising from religions of redemption. Besides Taoist divination and sacramental grace, the only religion of salvation permitted was that of the Buddhist monks for, being pacifist, it was not dangerous. In China, its practical effect was to enrich the scope of psychic experience by certain nuances of moody inwardness, as we shall see. For the rest, it was a further source of magical-sacramental grace and tradition-strengthening ceremony.

This means that such an ethic of intellectuals was necessarily limited in its significance for the broad masses. First, local and, above all, social differences in education were enormous. The traditionalist and, until modern times, strongly subsistence-oriented pattern of consumption among the poorer strata of the people was maintained by an almost incredible virtuosity in thrift (in consumption matters), which has nowhere been surpassed and which precluded any intimate relation to the gentleman ideals of Confucianism.

As usual, only the gestures and forms of external conduct among the master stratum became the object of general diffusion. In all probability, the educated stratum has decisively influenced the way of life of the masses. This influence seems to have been consummated especially through negative effects: on the one hand, completely blocking the emergence of any prophetic religiosity, and on the other hand, eradicating almost all orgiastic elements in the animist religion. It is possible that at least part of the traits which some authors are occasionally wont to refer to as the racial qualities of the Chinese are co-determined by these factors. Nowadays, here as elsewhere, even experienced and knowing men can say nothing definite about the extent to which biological heredity is influential. For us, however, there is an important observation which can easily be made and is confirmed by eminent sinologists. In the traits relevant for us, the further back one goes in history the more similar the Chinese and Chinese culture appear to what is found in the Occident. The old popular beliefs, the old anchorets, the oldest songs of the *Shi Ching,* the old warrior kings, the antagonisms of the philosophical schools, feudalism, the beginnings of capitalist developments in the Period of the Warring States—all of which are considered characteristic—are more closely related to occidental phenomena than are the traits of Confucian China. Hence, one has to reckon with the possibility that many of the Chinese traits which are considered innate may be the products of purely historical and cultural influences.

Regarding such traits, the sociologist essentially depends upon the literature of missionaries. This certainly varies in value but in the last analysis remains relatively the most authentic. Always emphasized are such observations as these: the striking lack of "nerves" in the specifically modern European meaning of the word; the unlimited patience and controlled politeness; the strong attachment to the habitual; the absolute insensitivity to monotony; the capacity for uninterrupted work and the slowness in reacting to unusual stimuli, especially in the intellectual sphere. All this seems to constitute a coherent and plausible unit but other seemingly sharp contrasts appear. There is an extraordinary and unusual horror of all unknown and not immediately apparent things which finds expression in ineradicable distrust. There is the rejection or lack of intellectual curiosity about things not close at hand and immediately useful. These traits stand in contrast to an unlimited and good-natured credulity in any magical swindle, no matter how fantastic it may be. In the same way, the strong lack of genuine sympathy and warmth, often even among people who are personally close, stands in apparent contrast to the great and close-knit cohesion of social organizations. The absolute docility and ceremonial piety of the adult toward his parents hardly seems compatible with the alleged lack of love and respect for authority in small children. Likewise what is repeatedly maintained as the incomparable dishonesty of the Chinese, even toward their own defense attorneys, could scarcely be reconciled with the obviously remarkable reliability of merchants in big business—compared to countries with a feudal past such as Japan, for example. Retail trade, to be sure, seems to know little of such honesty; the "fixed" prices appear to be fictitious even among native Chinese. The typical distrust of the Chinese for one another is confirmed by all observers. It stands in sharp contrast to the trust and honesty of the faithful brethren in the Puritan sects, a trust shared by outsiders as well. Finally, the unity and unshakability of the general psycho-physical bearing contrasts sharply with the often reported instability of all those features of the Chinese way of life which are not regulated from without by fixed norms. Most traits, however, are so fixed. More sharply formulated, the bondage of the Chinese, which is produced by their innumerable conventions, contrasts basically with the absence of an inward core, of a unified way of life flowing from some central and autonomous value position. How can all this be explained?

The absence of hysteria-producing, asceticist religious practices and the rather thorough elimination of toxic cults could not fail to influence the nervous and psychic constitution of a human group. As regards the use of toxics the Chinese belong to the relatively "sober" peoples. This has been since the pacification as compared to the former carousing in the old long house and at princely courts. Frenzy and orgiastic "obsession" were divested of the charismatic value attaching to sacredness and were only considered symptomatic of demonic rule. Confucianism rejected the use of alcohol except for rudimentary use at sacrifices. That the alcoholic orgy was not rare among the lower strata of the people in China, as elsewhere, does not change the *relative* significance of the difference. Opium, the toxic considered specifically Chinese, has been imported only in modern times. As is well known, it was imposed by war from without, despite the sharpest resistance of the ruling strata. Its effects, moreover, lie in the direction of apathetic ecstasy, a straight continuation of the line of "*wu wei*," and not in the direction of heroic frenzy or the unchaining of active passions. The Hellenic *sophrosyne* did not prevent Plato in "*Phaidros*" from considering beautiful ecstasy as the source of everything great. In this the rationalist Roman nobility of office—who translated "*ekstasis*" as "*superstitio*"—and the educated stratum of China were of different mind. The "naïveté," as well as what is felt to

be indolence, is perhaps partly connected with this complete lack of Dionysion element in Chinese religion, a lack which resulted from the deliberate sobering of the cult by the bureaucracy. In the bureaucracy nothing existed and nothing was allowed that might bring the psyche out of its equilibrium. Every inordinate passion, especially wrath, *ch'i,* produced evil charms; thus, on feeling any pain, the first question to ask was to what *ch'i* it might be ascribed. Animistic magic, as the only remaining form of popular religion, determined the traditionalist fear of any innovation which might bring evil charms or stir up the spirits. To be sure, this magic was despised by the educated Chinese; but it was the form of religion supported because of the character of the official cults. The preservation of this animistic magic explains the great credulity of the Chinese. Thus, magical also is the belief that disease and misfortune are symptoms of divine wrath which the individual has brought upon himself. In turn this belief facilitated a certain inhibition of those sympathetic emotions which, in the face of suffering, usually originate from the we-feeling of salvation religions. These emotions have always strongly governed popular ethics in India.

From the retention of magic in China there also resulted the specifically cool temper of Chinese humanity and formal kindliness toward one's fellow man. Even in intra-familial relationships there was a ceremonious punctilio and a selfish fear of the spirits.

Immeasurable ceremonial fetters surround the life of the Chinese, from the stage of the embryo to the cult of the dead. In their unexampled elaborateness and inviolability of detail they constitute a treasure house for folklorist research. W. Grube's works have especially exploited this material. Part of this ceremonial is evidently magical, especially apotropaic in origin. Part is to be attributed to Taoism and popular Buddhism, to be discussed elsewhere. Both Taoism and popular Buddhism have left profound traces in the workaday life of the masses. But there remains a very considerable residue of the purely conventional and ceremonial. Ceremonial prescription regulated questions and answers, indispensable offers as well as the exact manner of grateful decline, also visits, presents, expressions of respect, condolence and joyful sympathy. This surpassed anything preserved from ancient peasant tradition, such as is found in Spain where that tradition was influenced by feudalism and probably also by Islamism. In the field of gesture and of "face" one may assume Confucian origins to be predominant even where the origin cannot be traced.

While the Confucian ideal of propriety did not always exert its influence in the form of prevailing customs it revealed itself in the "spirit" in which they were practiced. The aesthetically cool temper caused all duties bequeathed from feudal times, especially duties of charity, to be frozen into a symbolic ceremonial. On the other hand, the belief in spirits bound the sib members more closely together. Undoubtedly, as in Egypt, the much bewailed dishonesty was partly a direct product of that patrimonial fiscalism which everywhere proved a training ground for dishonesty. For both in Egypt and China the process of tax collection involved raids, flogging, assistance of sib members, howlings of the oppressed, fear of the oppressors, and compromise. To this must certainly be added the exclusive cult of ceremonial and conventional propriety in Confucianism. Still there were lacking the feudal instincts which branded all trade with the adage *"Qui trompe t'on?"* Among the monopolistically secure and cultured status group of wealthy oversea traders of the *Ko Hang* guild, a much vaunted business integrity could develop out of the exigencies of their interest-situation. This honesty, if it existed, seems to have been a factor of acculturation rather than an internal development like the Puritan ethic. This, however, applies to all ethical traits of the Chinese.

A true prophecy creates and systematically orients conduct toward one internal measure of value. In the face of this the "world" is viewed as material to be fashioned ethically according to the norm. Confucianism in contrast meant adjustment to the outside, to the conditions of the "world." A well-adjusted man, rationalizing his conduct only to the degree requisite for adjustment, does not constitute a systematic unity but rather a complex of useful and particular traits. In Chinese popular religion the animistic ideas which perpetuate the belief in plural souls of the individual could almost stand as a symbol of this fact. Not reaching beyond this world, the individual necessarily lacked an autonomous counterweight in confronting this world. Confucianism facilitated the taming of the masses as well as the dignified bearing of the gentleman, but the style of life thus achieved must necessarily be characterized by essentially negative traits. Such a way of life could not allow man an inward aspiration toward a "unified personality," a striving which we associate with the idea of personality. Life remained a series of occurrences. It did not become a whole placed methodically under a transcendental goal.

The contrast between this socio-ethical position and the whole religious ethic of the Occident was unbridgeable. Outwardly some patriarchical aspects of the Thomist and the Lutheran ethic might appear to resemble Confucianism, but this is merely an external impression. The Confucian system of radical world-optimism succeeded in removing the basic pessimistic tension between the world and the supra-mundane destination of the individual. But no Christian ethic, however entangled in mundane compromises, could attain this.

Completely absent in Confucian ethic was any tension between nature and deity, between ethical demand and human shortcoming, consciousness of sin and need for salvation, conduct on earth and compensation in the beyond, religious duty and socio-political reality. Hence, there was no leverage for influencing conduct through inner forces freed of tradition and convention. Family piety, resting on the belief in spirits, was by far the strongest influence on man's conduct. Ultimately family piety facilitated and controlled, as we have seen, the strong cohesion of the sib associations. This was likewise true of the above-mentioned cooperative associations which may be considered as enlarged family enterprises with specialization of labor. This firm cohesion was in its way religiously motivated and the strength of the truly Chinese economic organization was roughly co-extensive with these personal associations controlled by piety. Chinese ethic developed its strongest motives in the circle of naturally grown, personalist associations or associations affiliated with or modeled after them. This contrasts sharply with the Puritan ethic which amounts to an objectification of man's duties as a creature of God. The religious duty toward the hidden and supra-mundane God caused the Puritan to appraise all human relations—including those naturally nearest in life—as mere means and expression of a mentality reaching beyond the organic relations of life. The religious duty of the pious Chinese, in contrast, enjoined him to develop himself within the organically given, personal relations. Mencius rejected the universal "love of man" with the comment that it would extinguish piety and justice and that it is the way of animals to have neither father nor brother. In substance, the duties of a Chinese Confucian always consisted of piety toward concrete people whether living or dead, and toward those who were close to him through their position in life. The Confucian owed nothing to a supra-mundane God; therefore, he was never bound to a sacred "cause" or an "idea." For Tao was neither; it was simply the embodiment of the binding, traditional ritual, and its command was not "action" but "emptiness." For the economic mentality, the personalist principle was undoubtedly as great a barrier to impersonal rationalization as it was generally to impersonal matter of factness. It tended to tie the individual ever anew to his sib members and to bind him to the manner of the sib, in any case to "persons" instead of functional tasks ("enterprises"). This barrier was intimately connected with the nature of Chinese religion, as our whole presentation has shown. For it was an obstacle to rationalizing the religious ethic, an obstacle which the ruling and educated stratum maintained in the interest of their position. It is of considerable economic consequence whether or not confidence, which is basic to business, rests upon purely personal, familial, or semi-familial relationships as was largely the case in China.

The great achievement of ethical religions, above all of the ethical and asceticist sects of Protestantism, was to shatter the fetters of the sib. These religions established the superior community of faith and a common ethical way of life in opposition to the community of blood, even to a large extent in opposition to the family. From the economic viewpoint it meant basing business confidence upon the ethical qualities of the individual proven in his impersonal, vocational work. The economic ramifications of universal and mutual distrust must probably be rated high, though we have no yardstick for this. Thus, universal distrust resulted from the official and exclusive sway of conventional dishonesty and from the Confucian emphasis on keeping face.

Confucianism and Confucian mentality, deifying "wealth," could facilitate political-economic measures of a sort comparable to the worldliness of the Renaissance in the Occident. At this point, however, one can observe the limited significance of economic policy as compared to economic mentality. In no other civilized country has material welfare ever been so exalted as the supreme good. The politico-economic views of Confucianism were comparable to those of our Cameralists. The oldest document of Chinese political economy is a tract by the Confucian Ssu-ma Ch'ien on the "balance of trade" in which the usefulness of wealth, including commercial profit, is emphasized. Economic policy alternated between fiscal and *laissez-faire* measures; in any case it was not deliberately anti-chrematistic. The merchants of the occidental Middle Ages were and are "despised" by German literati just as in China. Still economic policy did not create the economic mentality of capitalism. The money profits of the traders in the Period of the Warring States were political profits of commissioners to the state. The great mining *corvées* were used to search gold. Still no intermediate link led from Confucianism and its ethic—as firmly rooted as Christianity—to a civic and methodical way of life. This was all-important. Puritanism did

create it, and unintentionally at that. This strange reversion of the "natural," which is strange only on first, superficial glance, instructs us in the paradox of unintended consequences: i.e., the relation of man and fate, of what he intended by his acts and what actually came of them.

Puritanism represents the polar opposite type of rational dealing with the world, a somewhat ambiguous concept as we have shown elsewhere. The *"ecclesia pura,"* in practice and in true meaning, represented the Christian communion at the Lord's Supper in honor of God and purged of all morally rejected participants. This honor might have a Calvinist or Baptist foundation, its church constitution might be more synodical or more congregationalist. Broadly understood, Puritanism may refer to the morally rigoristic and Christian asceticist lay communities in general. This includes the Baptist, Mennonite, Quaker, ascetic Pietist, and Methodist communities which had spiritual mystical beginnings.

As against the Confucian type, it was peculiar to these types that they should oppose the flight from the world in order to rationalize it, despite or indeed because of their asceticist rejection of the world. Men are equally wicked and fail ethically; the world is a vessel of sin; and there can be no differences in creatural wickedness in the face of the Lord. Adjustment to vanity fair would be a sign of rejection; self-perfection in the sense of Confucianism would be idolatrous blasphemy. Wealth and surrender to its enjoyment would be the specific temptation, reliance on philosophy and literary education would be sinful and creatural pride; all trust in magical coercion of spirits and deities would be not only despicable superstition but impudent blasphemy. All things reminiscent of magic, all vestigial ritualism and priestly powers were eradicated. The Quakers, in theory, did not even have an appointed preacher; the majority of the Protestant sects had no paid professional preacher. In the small and light meeting halls of the Quakers the last traces of religious emblems are gone. Men were held to be equally sinful by nature even though their religious opportunities were not equal but highly unequal, temporarily and for all time. Either this was the result of arbitrary predestination as with the Calvinists, the particularist Baptists, the Whitefield Methodists, and the reformed Pietists; or it was the result of differing disposition for spiritual endowment. Finally, inequality of religious opportunity was due to the varying intensity and success of the endeavor to attain "conversion" (decisive with the old Pietists), "penitance," "winning through," or whatever the nature of rebirth might be. However, besides the unreasoning, unmerited, "free" grace of a supra-mundane God, Providence was always instrumental in these differences. Thus the belief in predestination was but one, though by far the most consistent, dogmatic form of this religion of virtuosi.

Only a few of the *massa perditionis* were called to attain the holy whether they alone were destined for it by virtue of a predestination of yore, or whether all—according to the Quakers this included non-Christians—had received the offer but only a small company, capable of seizing it, could reach the goal. According to some Pietist doctrines, salvation was offered only once in a lifetime; according to others, the so-called Terminists, it was offered once and for all. Man always had to prove himself capable of grasping the holy. Hence, everything was directed toward God's free grace and the destiny in the beyond; life in the here and now was either a vale of tears or a mere transition. Therefore, a tremendous emphasis was placed upon this tiny span of time and upon what happened during it. This was perhaps encompassed by Carlyle's words: "Millennia had to pass ere thou camest to life and millennia wait in silence for what thou shalt do with this thy life." It was not that it was possible to attain eternal grace by one's own achievement. The latter was impossible. The individual could receive and above all recognize his call to salvation only through consciousness of a central and unitary relation of this short life toward the supra-mundane God and His will in "sanctification." Sanctification in turn could prove itself only through God-ordained activities, and as in all active asceticism, through an ethical conduct blessed by God. Thus, the individual could gain certainty of salvation only in being God's tool. The strongest premium imaginable was thereby placed upon a rational and moral way of life. Only life conduct abided by firm principles and controlled at a unitary center could be considered a God-pleasing way of life. Though naïve surrender to the world unconditionally led away from salvation, nevertheless the creatural world and creatural man were God's creation and to them He addressed certain demands. According to Calvinist conception God had created the world "in His honor." Therefore, however creaturally wicked men might be, He wished to see His honor realized by subduing sin, possibly also sufferance and wished to subject them to ethical discipline through rational order. To "work the works of him that sent me, while it is day" here became a duty and the works posited were not ritual but rational-ethical in nature.

The contrast to Confucianism is clear: both ethics had their irrational anchorages, the one in magic, the other in the ultimately inscrutable resolves of a supra-mundane God. But from magic there followed the inviolability of tradition as the proven magical means and ultimately all bequeathed forms of life-conduct were unchangeable if the wrath of the spirits were to be avoided. From the relation between the supra-mundane God and the creaturally wicked, ethically irrational world there resulted, however, the absolute unholiness of tradition and the truly endless task of ethically and rationally subduing and mastering the given world, i.e., rational, objective "progress." Here, the task of the rational transformation of the world stood opposed to the Confucian adjustment to the world. Confucianism demanded constant and vigilant self-control in order to maintain the dignity of the universally accomplished man of the world; Puritan ethics demanded this self-control in order methodically to concentrate man's attitudes on God's will. The Confucian ethic intentionally left people in their personal relations as naturally grown or given by relations of social super- and subordination. Confucianism hallowed alone those human obligations of piety created by inter-human relations, such as prince and servant, higher and lower official, father and son, brother and brother, teacher and pupil, friend and friend. Puritan ethic, however, rather suspected these purely personal relationships as pertaining to the creatural; but Puritanism, of course, did allow for their existence and ethically controlled them so far as they were not against God. The relation to God had precedence in all circumstances. Overly intensive idolatrous relations of men *per se* were by all means to be avoided. Trust in men, and precisely in those closest to one by nature, would endanger the soul. Thus, the Calvinist Duchess Renate d'Este might curse her next of kin if she knew them rejected by God through arbitrary predestination. From this, very important practical differences of the two ethical conceptions resulted even though we shall designate both of them as rationalist in their practical turn of mind and although both of them reached "utilitarian" conclusions. These differences did not alone result from the autonomy of the laws of political structures. In part the cohesion of the sibs was an essential result of forms of political and economic organization which were themselves tied to personal relations. To a striking degree they lacked rational matter-of-factness, impersonal rationalization, and the nature of an abstract, impersonal, purposive association. True "communities" were absent, especially in the cities, because there were no economic and managerial forms of association or enterprise which were purely purposive. Almost none of these originated from purely Chinese roots. All communal action remained engulfed and conditioned by purely personal, above all, by kinship relations. This applied also to occupational associations. Whereas Puritanism objectified everything and transformed it into rational enterprise, dissolved everything into the pure business relation, and substituted rational law and agreement for tradition, in China, the pervasive factors were tradition, local custom, and the concrete personal favor of the official. Another factor seems still more important. In conjunction with the tremendous density of population in China, a calculating mentality and self-sufficient frugality of unexampled intensity developed under the influence of worldly-minded utilitarianism and belief in the value of wealth as a universal means of moral perfection. The Chinese shopkeeper haggled for and reckoned with every penny, and he daily counted over his cash receipts. Reliable travelers reported that the conversation of the native Chinese was about money and money affairs, apparently to an extent seldom found elsewhere. But it is very striking that out of this unceasing and intensive economic ado and the much bewailed crass "materialism" of the Chinese, there failed to originate on the economic plane those great and methodical business conceptions which are rational in nature and are presupposed by modern capitalism. Such conceptions have remained alien to China, except, for instance, in Canton where past or present foreign influence and the incessant advance of occidental capitalism have taught them to the Chinese.

In the past, especially in times of political division, political capitalism arose independently in the form of usury connected with office, emergency loans, wholesale trade and industrial *ergasteria.* This Chinese political capitalism was comparable to the capitalism of late Antiquity, Egypt, and Islam. Recently there has also been the usual dependency upon the merchant and buyer. In general, however, the Chinese lacked the strict organization of the *sistema domestico,* such as existed even during the late Middle Ages in the Occident. But in spite of the rather intensive internal and, for a time at least, considerable foreign trade, there existed no bourgeois capitalism of the modern or even late Medieval type. There were no rational forms of late Medieval and scientific European capitalist enterprise in industry, and no formation of capital in the European manner. Chinese capital, which took part in exploiting modern opportunities, was predominantly the capital of mandarins; hence, it was capital accumulated through extortionist practices in office. There was no rational method of organized enterprise in the European fashion, no truly rational organization of commercial news services, no rational money system—the development of the

money economy did not even equal that of Ptolemean Egypt. There were only beginnings of legal institutions and these compare with our law of firms, of commercial companies, of checks, bonds, shares. (These beginnings were characterized essentially by their technical imperfection.) The numerous technical inventions were little used for economic purposes. Finally, there was no genuine, technically valuable system of commercial correspondence, accounting, or bookkeeping.

Thus, we meet with conditions very similar to those of Mediterranean Antiquity, though in consequence of the pacification of the empire slavery was insignificant. In some respects, however, these conditions were even more remote from the "spirit" of modern capitalism and its institutions than those of Antiquity. In spite of all the heresy trials, there was extensive religious tolerance, at least compared to the intolerance of Calvinist Puritanism. Peace existed and there was a far reaching freedom of commodity trade, freedom of mobility, freedom of occupational choice and methods of production. There was no tabooing whatsoever of the shopkeeper spirit. All of this has not favored the rise of modern capitalism in China. In this typical land of profiteering, one may well see that by themselves neither "acquisitiveness," nor high and even exclusive esteem for wealth, nor utilitarian "rationalism" have any connection as yet with modern capitalism. The Chinese petty and middle class business man, as well as the big business man who adhered to the old tradition, ascribed success and failure, like the Puritan, to divine powers. The Chinese, however, ascribed them to the Taoistic god of wealth. For him success and failure in business were not symptomatic of a state of grace but of magically and ceremonially significant merit or offense, and compensation was sought in terms of ritually "good" works. The Chinese lacked the central, religiously determined, and rational method of life which came from within and which was characteristic of the classical Puritan. For the latter, economic success was not an ultimate goal or end in itself but a means of proving one's self. The Chinese did not deliberately cut himself off from the impressions and influences of the "world"—a world which the Puritan sought to control, just as he did himself, by means of a definite and one-sided rational effort of will. The Puritan was taught to suppress the petty acquisitiveness which destroys all rational, methodical enterprise—an acquisitiveness which distinguishes the conduct of the Chinese shopkeeper. Alien to the Confucian was the peculiar confinement and repression of natural impulse which was brought about by strictly volitional and ethical rationalization and ingrained in the Puritan.

For the Confucian the pruning of freely expressed and original impulse was of a different nature. The watchful self-control of the Confucian was to maintain the dignity of external gesture and manner, to keep "face." This self-control was of an aesthetic and essentially negative nature. Dignified deportment, in itself devoid of definite content, was esteemed and desired. The equally vigilant self-control of the Puritan had as its positive aim a definitely qualified conduct and, beyond this, it had as an inward aim the systematic control of one's own nature which was regarded as wicked and sinful. The consistent Pietist would take inventory, a sort of bookkeeping practiced daily even by such an *Epigonus* as Benjamin Franklin, for the supra-mundane, omniscient God saw the central internal attitude. However, the world to which the Confucian adjusted merely observed the graceful gesture. The Confucian gentleman, striving simply for dignified bearing, distrusted others as generally as he believed others distrusted him. This distrust handicapped all credit and business operations and contrasted with the Puritan's trust, especially his economic trust in the absolutely unshakable and religiously determined righteousness of his brother in faith. Faced with the creatural wickedness of the world and of man, especially of those in high places, this confidence just sufficed to prevent his profoundly realistic and thoroughly unrespecting pessimism from becoming a blockage to the credit indispensable for capitalist commerce. It merely caused him to assess soberly the objective external and internal ability of the partner, to take stock of the constancy of motives indispensable for business according to the adage "honesty is the best policy."

The Confucian's word was a beautiful and polite gesture as an end in itself; the Puritan's word was an impersonal and businesslike communication, short and absolutely reliable: "Yea, yea; Nay, nay: for whatsoever is more than these cometh of evil."

The thriftiness of the Confucian was narrowly circumscribed by the status proprieties of the gentleman. The excessive thrift found in the mystically determined humility of Lao-tzu and some other Taoists was fought by the Confucian school. Thrift, for the Chinese petty bourgeois classes, meant hoarding. This was fundamentally comparable to the peasant's way of hoarding wealth in his stocking. It served to safeguard burial rites and good name, honor and enjoyment of possession *per se,* as is usual where asceticism has not yet broken the enjoyment of wealth.

For the Puritan, however, possessions were as great a temptation as they were for the monk. Like the income of monasteries, his income was a secondary result and symptom of successful asceticism.

John Wesley said: "We have no choice but to recommend that men be pious, and that means," as an unavoidable effect, "getting rich." But obviously the dangerous nature of riches for the pious individual was the same as it had been for the monasteries. Wesley expressly focused upon the observed and apparent paradox between the rejection of the world and acquisitive virtuosity.

For the Confucian, as a statement handed down by the Master expressly teaches, wealth was the most important means for a virtuous, i.e., dignified life and for the ability to dedicate oneself to self-perfection. Hence inquiry as to means of improving men was answered by, "enrich them," for only a rich man could live according to rank and station. However, for the Puritan, income was an unintended result, an important symptom of virtue. The expenditure of wealth for purposes of personal consumption easily constituted idolatrous surrender to the world. Confucius might not disdain the acquisition of riches but wealth seemed insecure and could upset the equilibrium of the genteel soul. Thus, all truly economic and vocational work was the Philistine activity of expert professionals. For the Confucian, the specialistic expert could not be raised to truly positive dignity, no matter what his social usefulness. The decisive factor was that the "cultured man" (gentleman) was "not a tool"; that is, in his adjustment to the world and in his self-perfection he was an end unto himself, not a means for any functional end. This core of Confucian ethics rejected professional specialization, modern expert bureaucracy, and special training; above all, it rejected training in economics for the pursuit of profit.

To this "idolatrous" maxim Puritanism contrasts the task of proving oneself in vocational life and in the special functions of the world. The Confucian was the man of literary education, more precisely the man of bookish education, a man of scripture in the highest form. Confucianism was as foreign to the Hellenic valuation and development of speech and conversation as it was to the energy of rational action in military or economic affairs. Though they did so with differential intensity most Puritan denominations opposed philosophic literary education since it conflicted with an indispensable grounding in the Bible. The Bible was cherished as a sort of book of statutes and a managerial doctrine. Thus, philosophical literary education, the highest ornament of the Confucian, was, for the Puritan, an idle waste of time and a danger to religion. Scholasticism and dialectics, Aristotle and his derivatives, were a horror and a menace to the Puritan; thus Spener, for instance, preferred mathematically-founded Cartesian rational philosophy.

Useful and naturalist knowledge, especially empirical knowledge of natural sciences, geographical orientation as well as the sober clarity of a realist mind and specialized expert knowledge were first cultivated as planned educational ends by Puritans —in Germany particularly by Pietist circles.

Such knowledge was the only avenue to knowledge of God's glory and the providence embodied in His creation. On the other hand, such knowledge served as a means of rationally mastering the world in one's vocation and it enabled one to do one's duty in honor of God. Hellenism and, essentially also, the Renaissance at its height were equally distant from both Confucianism and Puritanism. The indispensable ethical qualities of the modern capitalist entrepreneur were: radical concentration on God-ordained purposes; the relentless and practical rationalism of the asceticist ethic; a methodical conception of matter-of-factness in business management; a horror of illegal, political, colonial, booty, and monopoly types of capitalism which depended on the favor of princes and men as against the sober, strict legality and the harnessed rational energy of routine enterprise; the rational calculation of the technically best way, of practical solidity and expediency instead of the traditionalist enjoyment of transmitted skill or the beauty of product characteristic of the old artisan craftsman. This must be added to the pious worker's special will for work. The relentlessly and religiously systematized utilitarianism peculiar to rational asceticism, to live "in" the world and yet not be "of" it, has helped to produce superior rational aptitudes and therewith the spirit of the vocational man which, in the last analysis, was denied to Confucianism. That is to say, the Confucian way of life was rational but was determined, unlike Puritanism, from without rather than from within. The contrast can teach us that mere sobriety and thriftiness combined with acquisitiveness and regard for wealth were far from representing and far from releasing the "capitalist spirit," in the sense that this is found in the vocational man of the modern economy.

The typical Confucian used his own and his family's savings in order to acquire a literary education and to have himself trained for the examinations. Thus he gained the basis for a cultured status position. The typical Puritan earned plenty, spent little, and reinvested his income as capital in rational capitalist enterprise out of an asceticist compulsion to save. "Rationalism"—and this is our second lesson—was embodied in the spirit of both ethics. But only the Puritan rational ethic with its supra-mundane orientation brought economic rationalism to its consistent conclusion. This happened merely because nothing was further from the conscious Puritan intention. It happened because inner-worldly work was simply expressive of the striving for a transcendental goal. The world, as promised, fell to Puritanism because the Puritans alone "had striven for God and his justice." In this is vested the basic difference between the two kinds of rationalism. Confucian rationalism meant rational adjustment to the world; Puritan rationalism meant rational mastery of the world. Both the Puritan and the Confucian were "sober men." But the rational sobriety of the Puritan was founded in a mighty enthusiasm which the Confucian lacked completely; it was the same enthusiasm which inspired the monk of the Occident. The rejection of the world by occidental asceticism was insolubly linked to its opposite, namely, its eagerness to dominate the world. In the name of a supra-mundane God the imperatives of asceticism were issued to the monk and, in variant and softened form, to the world. Nothing conflicted more with the Confucian ideal of gentility than the idea of a "vocation." The "princely" man was an aesthetic value; he was not a tool of a god. But the true Christian, the other-worldly and inner-worldly asceticist, wished to be nothing more than a tool of his God; in this he sought his dignity. Since this is what he wished to be he was a useful instrument for rationally transforming and mastering the world.

The Chinese in all probability would be quite capable, probably more capable than the Japanese, of assimilating capitalism which has technically and economically been fully developed in the modern culture area. It is obviously not a question of deeming the Chinese "naturally ungifted" for the demands of capitalism. But compared to the Occident, the varied conditions which externally favored the origin of capitalism in China did not suffice to create it. Likewise capitalism did not originate in occidental or oriental Antiquity, or in India, or where Islamism held sway. Yet in each of these areas different and favorable circumstances seemed to facilitate its rise. Many of the circumstances which could or had to hinder capitalism in China similarly existed in the Occident and assumed definite shape in the period of modern capitalism. Thus, there were the patrimonial traits of occidental rulers, their bureaucracy, and the fact that the money economy was unsettled and undeveloped. The money economy of Ptolemaic Egypt was carried through much more thoroughly than it was in fifteenth or sixteenth century Europe. Circumstances which are usually considered to have been obstacles to capitalist development in the Occident had not existed for thousands of years in China. Such circumstances as the fetters of feudalism, landlordism and, in part also, the guild system were lacking there. Besides, a considerable part of the various trade-restricting monopolies which were characteristic of the Occident did not apparently exist in China. Also, in the past, China knew time and again the political conditions arising out of preparation for war and warfare between competing states. In ancient Babylon and in Antiquity, there were conditions conducive to the rise of political capitalism which the modern period also shares with the past. It might be thought that modern capitalism, interested in free trading opportunity, could have gained ground once the accumulation of wealth and profit from political sources became impossible. This is perhaps comparable to the way in which, in recent times, North America has offered the freest space for the development of high capitalism in the almost complete absence of organization for war.

Political capitalism was common to occidental Antiquity until the time of the Roman emperors, to the Middle Ages, and to the Orient. The pacification of the Empire explains, at least indirectly, the non-existence of political capitalism but it does not explain the non-existence of modern capitalism in China. To be sure the basic characteristics of the "mentality," in this case the practical attitudes toward the world, were deeply co-determined by political and economic destinies. Yet, in view of their autonomous laws, one can hardly fail to ascribe to these attitudes effects strongly counteractive to capitalist development.

7. On Eastern and Western Christianity

BY ADOLF HARNACK

The Christian Religion in Greek Catholicism

I MUST INVITE you to descend several centuries with me and to look at the Greek Church as it is to-day, and as it has been preserved, essentially unaltered, for more than a thousand years. Between the third and the nineteenth century the history of the Church of the East nowhere presents any deep gulf. Hence we may take up our position in the present. Here, in turn, we ask the three following questions:—

What did this Greek Catholicism achieve?
What are its characteristics?
What modifications did the Gospel here undergo and how did it hold its own?

What did this Greek Catholicism achieve? Two facts may be cited on this point: firstly, in the great domain which it embraces, the countries of the eastern part of the Mediterranean and northwards to the Arctic Ocean, it made an end of heathenism and polytheism. The decisive victory was accomplished from the third to the sixth century, and so effectually accomplished that the gods of Greece really perished—perished unwept and unmourned. Not in any great battle did they die, but from sheer exhaustion, and without offering any resistance worth mention. I may just point out that before dying they transferred a considerable portion of their power to the Church's saints. But what is more important, with the death of the gods, Neoplatonism, the last great product of Greek philosophy, was also vanquished. The religious philosophy of the Church proved the stronger. The victory over Hellenism is an achievement of the Eastern Church on which it still subsists. Secondly, this Church managed to effect such a fusion with the individual nations which it drew into its bosom that religion and church became to them national palladia, nay, palladia pure and simple. Go amongst Greeks, Russians, Armenians, etc., and you will everywhere find that religion and nationality are inseparable, and the one element exists only in and alongside of the other. Men of these nationalities will, if need be, suffer themselves be cut in pieces for their religion. This is no mere consequence of the pressure exercised by the hostile power of Mohammedanism; the Russians are not subject to this pressure. Nor is it only—shall I say?—in the Moscow press that we can see what a firm and intimate connexion exists between Church and nation in these peoples, in spite of "sects" which are not wanting here either; to

Reprinted from Adolf Harnack, *What Is Christianity?* trans. Thomas Bailey Saunders (New York: G. P. Putnam's Sons, 1901) pp. 217–30 237–38, 239–41, 244–53, 254–62.

convince ourselves of it we must read—to take an instance at random—Tolstoi's *Village Tales*. They bring before the reader a really touching picture of the deep influence of the Church, with its message of the Eternal, of self-sacrifice, of sympathy and fraternity, on the national mind. That the clergy stand low in the social scale, and frequently encounter contempt, must not delude us into supposing that as the representatives of the Church they do not occupy an incomparably high station. In Eastern Europe the monastic ideal is deeply rooted in the national soul.

But the mention of these two points includes everything that can be said about the achievements of this Church. To add that it has disseminated a certain amount of culture would involve pitching our standard of culture very low. In comparison with Islam, too, it is no longer so successful in doing what it has done in the past and still does in regard to polytheism. The missions of the Russian Church are still overthrowing polytheism even to-day; but large territories have been lost to Islam, and the Church has not recovered them. Islam has extended its victories as far as the Adriatic and in the direction of Bosnia. It has won over numerous Albanian and Slav tribes which were once Christian. It shows itself to be at least a match for the Church, although we must not forget that in the heart of its dominions there are Christian nations who have maintained their creed.

Our second question was, What are the characteristics of this Church? The answer is not easy; for as it presents itself to the spectator this Church is a highly complex structure. The feelings, the superstitions, the learning, and the devotional philosophy of hundreds, nay, of thousands of years, are built into it. But, further; no one can look at this Church from outside, with its forms of worship, its solemn ritual, the number of its ceremonies, its relics, pictures, priests, monks and the philosophy of its mysteries, and then compare it on the one hand with the Church of the first century, and on the other with the Hellenic cults in the age of Neoplatonism, without arriving at the conclusion that it belongs not to the former but to the latter. *It takes the form, not of a Christian product in Greek dress, but of a Greek product in Christian dress.* It would have done battle with the Christians of the first century just as it did battle with the worship of Magna Mater and Zeus Soter. There are innumerable features of this Church which are counted as sacred as the Gospel, and towards which not even a tendency existed in primitive Christianity. Of the whole performance of the chief religious service, nay, even of many of the dogmas, the same thing may, in the last resort, be said: if certain words, like Christ, etc.,

are omitted, there is nothing left to recall the original element. In its external form as a whole this Church is nothing more than a continuation of the history of Greek religion under the alien influence of Christianity, parallel to the many other alien influences which have affected it. We might also describe it as the natural product of the union between Hellenism, itself already in a state of oriental decay, and Christian teaching; it is the transformation which history effects in a religion by "natural" means, and, as was here the case, was bound to effect between the third and the sixth century. In this sense it is *a natural religion*. The conception admits of a double meaning. It is generally understood as an abstract term covering all the elementary feelings and processes traceable in every religion. Whether there are any such elements, or, on the other hand, whether they are sufficiently stable and articulate to be followed as a whole, admits, however, of a doubt. The conception "natural religion" may be better applied to the growth which a religion produces when the "natural" forces of history have ceased playing on it. At bottom these forces are everywhere the same, although differing in the way in which they are mounted. They mould religion until it answers their purpose; not by expelling what is sacred, venerable, and so on, but by assigning it the place and allowing it the scope which they consider right. They immerse everything in a uniform medium,—that medium which, like the air, is the first condition of their "natural" existence. In this sense, then, the Greek Church is a *natural* religion; no prophet, no reformer, no genius, has arisen in its history since the third century to disturb the ordinary process by which a religion becomes naturalised into common history. The process attained its completion in the sixth century and asserted itself victoriously against severe assaults in the eighth and ninth. The Church has since been at rest, and no further essential, nay, not even any unessential, change has taken place in the condition which it then reached. Since then, apparently, the nations belonging to this Church have undergone nothing to make it seem intolerable to them and to call for any reform in it. They still continue, then, in this "natural" religion of the sixth century.

I have, however, advisedly spoken of the Church in its external form. Its complex character is partly due to the fact that we cannot arrive at its inner condition by simple deduction from its outer. It is not sufficient to observe, although the observation is correct, that this Church is part of the history of Greek religion. It exercises influences which from this point of view are not easily intelligible. We cannot form a correct estimate of it unless we dwell more closely on the factors which lend it its character.

The first factor which we encounter is *tradition,* and the observance of it. The sacred and the divine do not exist in free action—we shall see later to what reservations this statement is subject—but are put, as it were, into a storehouse, in the form of an immense capital. The capital is to provide for all demands, and to be coined in the precise way in which the Fathers coined it. Here, it is true, we have an idea which can be traced to something already existing in the primitive age. We read in the Acts of the Apostles that "They continued steadfastly in the apostles' doctrine." But what became of this practice and this obligation? Firstly, everything was designated "apostolic" which was deposited in this Church in the course of the succeeding centuries; or, rather, what the Church considered necessary to possess in order to suit the historical position in which it was placed, it called apostolic, because it fancied that otherwise it could not exist, and what is necessary for the Church's existence *must* be simply apostolic. Secondly, it has been established as an irrefragable fact that the "continuing steadfastly in the apostles' doctrine" applies, first and foremost, to the punctilious observance of every direction as to ritual: the sacred element is bound up with *text* and *form.* Both are conceived in a thoroughly antique way. That the divine is, so to speak, stored up as though it were an actual commodity, and that the supreme demand which the Deity makes is the punctilious observance of a ritual, were ideas that in antiquity were perfectly familiar and admitted of no doubt. Tradition and ceremony are the conditions under which the Holy alone existed and was accessible. Obedience, respect, reverence, were the most important religious feelings. Whilst they are doubtless inalienable features of religion, it is only as accompaniments of an active feeling quite different in its character that they possess any value, and that further presumes that the object to which they are directed is a worthy one. Traditionalism and the ritualism so closely connected with it are prominent characteristics of the Greek Church, but this is just what shows how far it has departed from the Gospel.

The second point that fixes the character of this Church is the value which it attaches to *orthodoxy,* to sound doctrine. It has stated and re-stated its doctrines with the greatest precision and often enough made them a terror to men of different creed. No one, it claims, can be saved who does not possess the correct doctrine; the man who does not possess it is to be expelled and must forfeit all his rights; if he be a fellow-countryman, he must be treated as a leper and lose all connexion with his nation. This fanaticism, which still flares up here and there in the Greek Church even to-day and in principle has not been abandoned, is not Greek, although a certain inclination towards it was not lacking in the ancient Greeks; still less did it originate in Roman law; it is the result, rather, of an unfortunate combination of several factors. When the Roman empire became Christian, the hard fight for existence which the Church had waged with the Gnostics was not yet forgotten; still less had the Church forgotten the last bloody persecutions which the State had inflicted upon it in a kind of despair. These two circumstances would in themselves be sufficient to explain how the Church came to feel that it had a right of reprisal, and was at the same time bound to suppress heretics. But, in addition, there had now appeared in the highest place, since the days of Diocletian and Constantine, the absolutist conception, derived from the East, of the unlimited right and the unlimited duty of the ruler in regard to his "subjects." The unfortunate factor in the great change was that the Roman Emperor was at once, and almost in the same moment, a Christian Emperor and an oriental despot. The more conscientious he was, the more intolerant he was bound to be; for the deity had committed to his care not only men's bodies but their souls as well. Thus arose the aggressive and all-devouring orthodoxy of State and Church, or, rather, of the State-Church. Examples which were to hand from the Old Testament completed and sanctified the process.

Intolerance is a new growth in the land of the Greeks and cannot be roundly laid to their charge; but the way in which doctrine developed, namely, as a philosophy of God and the world, was due to their influence; and the fact that religion and doctrine were directly identified is also a product of the Greek spirit. No mere reference to the significance which doctrine already possessed in the apostolic age, and to the tendencies operating in the direction of bringing it into a speculative form, is sufficient to explain the change. These are matters, as I hope that I have shown in the previous lectures, which are rather to be understood in a different sense. It is in the second century, and with the apologists, that Intellectualism commences; and, supported by the struggle with the Gnostics and by the Alexandrian school of religious philosophers in the Church, it manages to prevail.

But it is not enough to assess the teachings of the Greek Church by its formal side alone, and ascertain in what way and to what extent it is exhibited, and what is the value to be placed upon it. We must also examine its substance; for it possesses two elements which are quite peculiar to it and separate it from the Greek philosophy of religion—*the idea of the creation*, and the doctrine of the *God-Man nature of the Saviour*. We shall treat of these two elements in our next lecture, and, further, of the two other elements which, side by side with tradition and doctrine, characterise the Greek Church; namely, the form of worship and the order of monkhood.

So far we have established the fact that Greek Catholicism is characterised as a religion by two elements: by *traditionalism* and by *intellectualism*. According to traditionalism, the reverent preservation of the received inheritance, and the defence of it against all innovation, is not only an important duty, but is itself the practical proof of religion. That is an idea quite in harmony with antiquity and foreign to the Gospel; for the Gospel knows absolutely nothing of intercourse with God being bound up with reverence for tradition itself. But the second element, intellectualism, is also of Greek origin. The elaboration of the Gospel into a vast philosophy of God and the world, in which every conceivable kind of material is handled; the conviction that because Christianity is the absolute religion it must give information on all questions of metaphysics, cosmology, and history; the view of revelation as a countless multitude of doctrines and explanations, all equally holy and important—this is Greek intellectualism. According to it, *Knowledge* is the highest good, and spirit is spirit only in so far as it knows; everything that is of an æsthetical, ethical and religious character must be converted into some form of knowledge, which human will and life will then with certainty obey. The development of the Christian faith into an all-embracing theosophy, and the identification of faith with theological knowledge, are proofs that the Christian religion on Greek soil entered the proscribed circle of the native religious philosophy and has remained there.

But in this vast philosophy of God and the world, which possesses an absolute value as the "substance of what has been revealed" and as "orthodox doctrine," there are two elements which radically distinguish it from Greek religious philosophy and invest it with an entirely original character. I do not mean the appeal which it makes to revelation —for to that the Neoplatonists also appealed—but the *idea of creation* and the doctrine of *the God-Man nature of the Saviour*. They traverse the scheme of Greek religious philosophy at two critical points, and have therefore always been felt to be alien and intolerable by its genuine representatives.

The idea of creation we can deal with in a few words. It is undoubtedly an element which is as important as it is in thorough keeping with the Gospel. It abolishes all intertwining of God and world, and gives expression to the power and actuality of the living God. Attempts were not wanting, it is true, among Christian thinkers on Greek soil— just because they were Greeks—to conceive the Deity only as the uniform power operating in the fabric of the world, as the unity in diversity, and as its goal. Traces of this speculative idea are even still to be found in the Church doctrine; the idea of creation, however, triumphed, and therewith Christianity won a real victory.

The subject of the God-Man nature of the Saviour is one on which it is much more difficult to arrive at a correct opinion. It is indubitably the central point in the whole dogmatic system of the Greek Church. It supplied the doctrine of the Trinity. In the Greek view these two doctrines together make up Christian teaching *in nuce*. When a Father of the Greek Church once said, as he did say: "The idea of the God-Man nature, the idea of God becoming a man, is what is new in the new, nay, is the only new thing under the sun," not only did he correctly represent the opinion of all his fellow-believers, but he also at the same time strikingly expressed their view that, while sound intelligence and earnest reflection yield all the other points of doctrine of themselves, this one lies beyond them. The theologians of the Greek Church are convinced that the only real distinction between the Christian creed and natural philosophy is that the former embraces the doctrine of the God-Man nature, including the Trinity. Side by side with this, the only other doctrine that can at most come in question is that of the idea of creation.

*   *   *

But with traditionalism and intellectualism a further element is associated, namely, ritualism. If religion is presented as a complex system of traditional doctrine, to which the few alone have any real access, the majority of believers cannot practise it at all except as ritual. Doctrine comes to be administered in stereotyped formulas accompanied by symbolic acts. Although no inner understanding of it is thus possible, it produces the feeling of something mysterious. The very deification which the future is expected to bring, and which in itself is something that can neither be described nor conceived, is now administered as though it were an earnest of what is to come, by means of ritual acts. An imaginative mood is excited, and disposes to its reception; and this excitement, when enhanced, is its seal.

Such are the feelings which move the members

of the Greek Catholic Church. Intercourse with God is achieved through the cult of a mystery, and by means of hundreds of efficacious formulas small and great, signs, pictures, and consecrated acts, which, if punctiliously and submissively observed, communicate divine grace and prepare the Christian for eternal life. Doctrine as such is for the most part something unknown; if it appears at all, it is only in the form of liturgical aphorisms. For ninety-nine per cent of these Christians, religion exists only as a ceremonious ritual, in which it is externalised. But even for Christians of advanced intelligence all these ritual acts are absolutely necessary, for it is only in them that doctrine receives its correct application and obtains its due result.

*   *   *

Over the vast area of Greek and Oriental Christendom religion has been almost stifled by ritualism. It is not that religion has sacrificed one of its essential elements. No! it has entered an entirely different plane; it has descended to the level where religion may be described as a cult and nothing but a cult.

Nevertheless, Greek and Oriental Christianity contains within itself an element which for centuries has been capable of offering, and still offers here and there to-day, a certain resistance to the combined forces of traditionalism, intellectualism, and ritualism—I mean monasticism. To the question, Who is in the highest sense of the word a Christian? the Greek Christian replies: the monk. The man who practises silence and purity, who shuns not only the world but also the Church of the world, who avoids not only false doctrine but any statement about the true, who fasts, gives himself up to contemplation, and steadily waits for God's glorious light to dawn upon his gaze, who attaches no value to anything but tranquillity and meditation on the Eternal, who asks nothing of life but death, and who from such utter unselfishness and purity makes mercy arise—this is the Christian. To him not even the Church and the consecration which it bestows is an absolute necessity. For such a man the whole system of sanctified secularity has vanished. Over and over again in ascetics of this kind the Church has seen in its ranks figures of such strength and delicacy of religious feeling, so filled with the divine, so inwardly active in forming themselves after certain features of Christ's image, that we may, indeed, say: here there is a living religion, not unworthy of Christ's name. We Protestants must not take direct offence at the form of monasticism. The conditions under which our Churches arose have made a harsh and one-sided opinion of it a kind of duty. And although for the present, and in view

of the problems which press on us, we may be justified in retaining this opinion, we must not summarily apply it to other circumstances. Nothing but monasticism could provide a leaven and a counterpoise in that traditionalistic and ritualistic secular Church, such as the Greek Church was and still is. Here there was freedom, independence, and vivid experience; here the truth that it is only what is experienced and comes from within that has any value in religion carried the day.

And yet, the invaluable tension which in this part of Christendom existed between the secular Church and monasticism has unhappily almost disappeared, and of the blessing which it established there is scarcely a trace left. Not only has monasticism become subject to the Church and is everywhere bent under its yoke, but the secular spirit has in a special degree invaded the monastries. Greek and oriental monks are now, as a rule, the instruments of the lowest and worst functions of the Church, of the worship of pictures and relics, of the crassest superstition and the most imbecile sorcery. Exceptions are not wanting, and it is still to the monks that we must pin our hopes of a better future; but it is not easy to see how a Church is to be reformed which, teach what it will, is content with its adherents finding the Christian *faith* in the observance of certain ceremonies, and Christian *morality* in keeping fast-days correctly.

*   *   *

Side by side with the Church the Gospel exercises its own influence on individuals. This influence, however, takes shape in a type of religion exhibiting the very characteristics which we have shown to be most distinctive of Jesus' message. Thus on the ground occupied by this Church the Gospel has not completely perished. Here, too, human souls find a dependence on God and a freedom in Him, and when they have found these, they speak the language which every Christian understands, and which goes to every Christian's heart.

The Christian Religion in Roman Catholicism

The Roman Church is the most comprehensive and the vastest, the most complicated and yet at the same time the most uniform structure which, as far as we know, history has produced. All the powers of the human mind and soul, and all the elemental forces at mankind's disposal, have had a hand in creating it. In its many-sided character and severe cohesion Roman Catholicism is far in advance of Greek. We ask, in turn:—

What did the Roman Catholic Church achieve?
What are its characteristics?
What modifications has the Gospel suffered in this Church, and how much of it has remained?
What did the Roman Catholic Church achieve?

Well, in the first place, it educated the Romano-Germanic nations, and educated them in a sense other than that in which the Eastern Church educated the Greeks, Slavs, and Orientals. However much their original nature, or primitive and historical circumstances, may have favoured those nations and helped to promote their rise, the value of the services which the Church rendered is not thereby diminished. It brought Christian civilisation to young nations, and brought it, not once only, so as to keep them at its first stage—no! it gave them something which was capable of exercising a progressive educational influence, and for a period of almost a thousand years it itself led the advance. Up to the fourteenth century it was a leader and a mother; it supplied the ideas, set the aims, and disengaged the forces. Up to the fourteenth century—thenceforward, as we may see, those whom it educated became independent, and struck out paths which it did not indicate, and on which it is neither willing nor able to follow them. But even so, however, during the period covered by the last six hundred years, it has not fallen so far behind as the Greek Church. With comparatively brief interruptions it has proved itself fully a match for the whole movement of politics—we in Germany know that well enough!—and even in the movement of thought it still has an important share. The time, of course, is long past since it was a leader; on the contrary, it is now a drag; but, in view of the mistaken and precipitate elements in modern progress, the drag which it supplies is not always the reverse of a blessing.

In the second place, however, this Church upheld the idea of religious and ecclesiastical independence in Western Europe in the face of the tendencies, not lacking here either, towards State-omnipotence in the spiritual domain. In the Greek Church, as we saw, religion has become so intimately allied with nationality and the State that, public worship and monasticism apart, it has no room left for independent action. On Western ground it is otherwise; the religious element and the moral element bound up with it occupy an independent sphere and jealously guard it. This we owe in the main to the Roman Church.

These two facts embrace the most important piece of work this Church achieved and in part still achieves. We have already indicated the bounds which must be set to the first. To the second also

a sensible limitation attaches, and we shall see what it is as we proceed.

What are the characteristics of the Roman Church? This was our second question. Unless I am mistaken, the Church, complicated as it is, may be resolved into three chief elements. The first, *Catholicism,* it shares with the Greek Church. The second is the *Latin spirit* and the *Roman World-Empire* continuing in the Roman Church. The third is the spirit and religious fervour of *St. Augustine.* So far as the inner life of this Church is religious life and religious thought, it follows the standard which St. Augustine authoritatively fixed. Not only has he arisen again and again in his many successors, but he has awakened and kindled numbers of men who, coming forward with independent religious and theological fervour, are nevertheless spirit of his spirit.

These three elements, the Catholic, the Latin in the sense of the Roman World-Empire, and the Augustinian, constitute the peculiar character of the Roman Church.

So far as the first is concerned, you may recognise its importance by the fact that the Roman Church to-day receives every Greek Christian, nay, at once effects a "union" with every Greek ecclesiastical community, without more ado, as soon as the Pope is acknowledged and submission is made to his apostolic supremacy. Any other condition that may be exacted from the Greek Christians is of absolutely no moment; they are even allowed to retain divine worship in their mother tongue, and married priests. If we consider what a "purification" Protestants have to undergo before they can be received into the bosom of the Roman Church, the difference is obvious. Now a Church cannot make so great a mistake about itself as to omit any essential condition in taking up new members, especially if they come from another confession. The element which the Roman Church shares with the Greek must, then, be of significant and critical importance, when it is sufficient to make union possible on the condition that the papal supremacy is recognized. As a matter of fact, the main points characteristic of Greek Catholicism are all to be found in Roman as well, and are, on occasion, just as energetically maintained here as they are there. Traditionalism, orthodoxy, and ritualism play just the same part here as they do there, so far as "higher considerations" do not step in; and the same is true of monasticism also.

So far as "higher considerations" do not step in—here we have already passed to the examination of the second element, namely, the Latin Spirit in the sense of the Roman World-dominion. In the Western half of Christendom the Latin spirit, the spirit of Rome, very soon effected certain distinct modifications in the general Catholic idea. As early as the beginning of the third century we see the thought emerging in the Latin Fathers that salvation, however effected and whatever its nature, is bestowed in the form of a contract under definite conditions, and only to the extent to which they are observed; it is *salus legitima;* in fixing these conditions the Deity manifested its mercy and indulgence, but it guards their observance all the more jealously. Further, the whole contents of revelation are *lex,* the Bible as well as tradition. Again, this tradition is attached to a class of officials and to their correct succession. The "mysteries," however, are "sacraments"; that is to say, on the one hand, they are binding acts; on the other, they contain definite gifts of grace in a carefully limited form and with a specific application. Again, the discipline of penance is a procedure laid down by law and akin to the process adopted in a civil action or a suit in defense of honour. Lastly, the Church is a *legal institution;* and it is so, not side by side with its function of preserving and distributing salvation, but it is a legal institution for the sake of this very function.

But it is in its constitution as a Church that it is a legal establishment. We must briefly see how things stand in regard to this constitution, as its foundations are common to the Eastern and the Western Church. When the monarchical episcopate had developed, the Church began to approximate its constitution to State government. The system of uniting sees under a metropolitan who was, as a rule, the bishop of the provincial capital, corresponded with the distribution of the Empire into provinces. Above and beyond this, the ecclesiastical constitution in the East was developed a step further when it adapted itself to the division of the Empire introduced by Diocletian, by which large groups of provinces were united. Thus arose the constitution of the patriarchate, which was not, however, strictly enforced, and was in part counteracted by other considerations.

In the West no division into patriarchates came about; but on the other hand something else happened: in the fifth century the Western Roman Empire perished of internal weakness and through the inroads of the barbarians. What was left of what was Roman took refuge in the Roman Church —civilisation, law, and orthodox faith as opposed to the Arian. The barbarian chiefs, however, did not venture to set themselves up as Roman Emperors, and enter the vacant shrine of the *imperium;* they founded empires of their own in the provinces. In these circumstances the Bishop of Rome appeared as the guardian of the past and the shield of the future. All over the provinces occupied by the barbarians, even in those which had previously maintained a defiant independence in the face of Rome, bishops and laity looked to him.

Whatever Roman elements the barbarians and Arians left standing in the provinces—and they were not few—were ecclesiasticised and at the same time put under the protection of the Bishop of Rome, who was the chief person there after the Emperor's disappearance.

But in Rome the episcopal throne was occupied in the fifth century by men who understood the signs of the times and utilised them to the full *The Roman Church in this way privily pushed itself into the place of the Roman World-Empire, of which it is the actual continuation;* the empire has not perished, but has only undergone a transformation. If we assert, and mean the assertion to hold good even of the present time, that the Roman Church is the old Roman Empire consecrated by the Gospel, that is no mere "clever remark," but the recognition of the true state of the matter historically, and the most appropriate and fruitful way of describing the character of this Church. It still governs the nations; its Popes rule like Trajan and Marcus Aurelius; Peter and Paul have taken the place of Romulus and Remus; the bishops and archbishops, of the proconsuls; the troop of priests and monks correspond to the legions; the Jesuits, to the imperial body-guard. The continued influence of the old Empire and its institutions may be traced in detail, down to individual legal ordinances, nay, even in the very clothes. That is no Church like the evangelical communities, or the national Churches of the East; it is a political creation, and as imposing as a World-Empire, because the continuation of the Roman Empire. The Pope, who calls himself "King" and "Pontifex Maximus," is Cæsar's successor. The Church, which as early as the third and fourth century was filled with the Roman spirit, has re-established in itself the Roman Empire.

* * *

I cannot here show what immense results follow from the fact that the Catholic Church is the Roman Empire. Let me mention only a few conclusions which the Church itself draws. It is just as essential to this Church to exercise governmental power as to proclaim the Gospel. The phase "Christus vincit, Christus regnat, Christus triumphat," must be understood in a political sense. He rules on earth by the fact that his Roman-directed Church rules, and rules, too, by law and by force; that is to say, it employs all the means of which States avail themselves. Accordingly it recognises no form of religious fervour which does not first of all submit to this papal Church, is approved by it, and remains in constant dependence upon it. This Church, then, teaches its "subjects" to say: "Though I understand all mysteries, and though I have all faith, and though I bestow all my goods to feed the poor, and though I give my body to be burned, and have not unity in love which alone floweth from unconditional obedience to the Church, it profiteth me nothing." Outside the pale of the Church, all faith, all love, all the virtues, even martyrdoms, are of no value whatever. Naturally; for even an earthly State appreciates only those services which a man has rendered for its sake. But here the State identifies itself with the kingdom of Heaven, in other respects proceeding just like other States. From this fact you can yourselves deduce all the Church's claims; they follow without difficulty. Even the most exorbitant demand appears quite natural as soon as you only admit the truth of the two leading propositions: "The Roman Church is the kingdom of God," and "The Church must govern like an earthly State." It is not to be denied that Christian motives have also had a hand in this development—the desire to bring the Christian religion into a real connexion with life, and to make its influence felt in every situation that may arise, as well as anxiety for the salvation of individuals and of nations. How many earnest Catholic Christians there have been who had no other real desire than to establish Christ's rule on earth and build up his kingdom! But while there can be no doubt that their intention, and the energy with which they put their hands to the work, made them superior to the Greeks, there can be as little that it is a serious misunderstanding of Christ's and the apostles' injunctions to aim at establishing and building up the kingdom of God by political means. The only forces which this kingdom knows are religious and moral forces, and it rests on a basis of freedom. But when a Church comes forward with the claims of an earthly State, it is bound to make use of all the means at the disposal of that State, including, therefore, crafty diplomacy and force; for the earthly State, even a State governed by law, must on occasion become a State that acts contrary to law. The course of development which this Church has followed as an earthly State was, then, bound to lead logically to the absolute monarchy of the Pope and his infallibility; for in an earthly theocracy infallibility means, at bottom, nothing more than full sovereignty means in a secular State. That the Church has not shrunk from drawing this last conclusion is a proof of the extent to which the sacred element in it has become secularized.

That this second element was bound to produce a radical change in the characteristic features of Catholicism in Western Europe, in its traditionalism, its orthodoxy, its ritualism, and its monasticism, is obvious. Traditionalism holds the same position after the change as it did before; but when any element in it has become inconvenient, it is dropped and its place taken by the papal will. "La tradition, c'est moi," as Pius IX. is reported to have said. Further, "sound doctrine" is still a leading principle, but, as a matter of fact, it can be altered by the ecclesiastical policy of the Pope; subtle distinctions have given many a dogma a new meaning. New dogmas, too, are promulgated. In many respects doctrine has become more arbitrary, and a rigid formula in a matter of dogma may be set aside by a contrary injunction in a matter of ethics and in the confessional. The hard and fast lines of the past can be everywhere relaxed in favour of the needs of the present. The same holds good of ritualism, as also of monasticism. The extent to which the old monasticism has been altered, by no means always to its disadvantage alone, and has even in some important aspects been transformed into its flat opposite, I cannot here show. In its organisation this Church possesses a faculty of adapting itself to the course of history such as no other Church possesses; it always remains the same old Church, or seems to do so, and is always becoming a new one.

The third element determining the character of the spirit prevalent in the Church is opposed to that which we have just discussed, and yet has held its own side by side with the second; it goes by the names of Augustine and Augustinianism. In the fifth century, as the very time when the Church was setting itself to acquire the inheritance of the Roman Empire, it came into possession of a religious genius of extraordinary depth and power, accepted his ideas and feelings, and up to the present day has been unable to get rid of them. That the Church became at one and the same time Cæsarian and Augustinian is the most important and marvellous act in its history. What kind of a spirit, however, and what kind of a tendency, did it receive from Augustine?

Well, in the first place, Augustine's theology and his religious fervour denote a special resuscitation of the Pauline experience and doctrine of sin and grace, of guilt and justification, of divine predestination and human servitude. In the centuries that had elapsed since the apostle's day this experience and the doctrine embodying it had been lost, but Augustine went through the same inner experiences as Paul, gave them the same sort of expression, and clothed them in definite conceptions. There was no question here of mere imitation; the individual differences between the two cases are of the utmost importance, especially in the way in which the doctrine of justification is conceived. With Augustine, it was represented as a constant process, continuing until love and all the virtues completely filled the heart; but, as with Paul, it is all a matter of individual experience and inner life. If you read Augustine's *Confessions* you will acknowledge that in spite of all the rhetoric—and rhetoric there is—it is the work of a genius who has felt God, the God of the Spirit, to be the be-all and the end-all of his life; who thirsts after Him and desires nothing beside Him. Further, all the sad and terrible experiences which he had had in his own person, all the rupture with himself, all the service of transient things, the "crumbling away into the world bit by bit," and the egoism for which he had to pay in loss of strength and freedom, he reduces to the one root, *sin;* that is to say, lack of communion with God, godlessness. Again, what released him from the entanglements of the world, from selfishness and inner decay, and gave him strength, freedom, and a consciousness of the Eternal, he calls, with Paul, *grace*. With him he feels too, that grace is wholly the work of God, but that it is obtained through and by Christ, and possessed as forgiveness of sins and as the spirit of love. He is much less free and more beset with scruples in his view of sin than the great apostle; and it is this which gives his religious language and everything that proceeded from him quite a peculiar colour. "Forgetting those things which are behind, and reaching forth unto those things which are before"—the apostolic maxim is not Augustine's. *Consolation for the misery of sin* —this is the complexion of his entire Christianity. Only rarely was he capable of soaring to the sense of the glorious liberty of the children of God; and, where he was so capable, he could not testify to it in the same way as Paul. But he could express the sense of consolation for the misery of sin with a strength of feeling and in words of an overwhelming force such as no one before him ever displayed; nay, more: he has managed by what he has written to go so straight to the souls of millions, to describe so precisely their inner condition, and so impressively and overpoweringly to put the consolation before them, that what he felt has been felt again and again for fifteen hundred years. Up to the day in which we live, so far as Catholic Christians are concerned, inward and vivid religious fervour, and the expression which it takes, are in their whole character Augustinian. It is by what he felt that they are kindled, and it is his thoughts that they think. Nor is it otherwise with many Protestants, and those not of the worst kind. This juxtaposition of sin and grace, this interconnexion

of feeling and doctrine, seems to possess an indestructible power which no lapse of time is able to touch; this feeling of mixed pain and bliss is an unforgettable possession with those who have once experienced it; and even though they may have subsequently emancipated themselves from religion it remains for them a sacred memory.

The Western Church opened, and was compelled to open, its doors to this Augustine at the very moment when it was preparing to enter upon its dominion. It was defenceless in face of him; it had so little of any real value to offer from its immediate past that it weakly capitulated. Thus arose the astonishing "complexio oppositorum" which we see in Western Catholicism: the Church of rites, of law, of politics, of world-dominion, and the Church in which a highly individual, delicate, sublimated sense and doctrine of sin and grace is brought into play. The external and the internal elements are supposed to unite! To speak frankly, this has been impossible from the beginning; internal tension and conflict were bound to arise at once; the history of Western Catholicism is full of it. Up to a certain point, however, these antitheses admit of being reconciled; they admit of it at least so far as the same men are concerned. That is proved by no less a person than Augustine himself, who, in addition to his other characteristics, was also a staunch Churchman; nay, who in such matters as power and prestige promoted external interests of the Church, and its equipment as a whole, with the greatest energy. I cannot here explain how he managed to accomplish this work, but that there could be no lack of internal contradictions in it is obvious. Only let us be clear about two facts: firstly, that the outward Church is more and more forcing the inward Augustinianism into the background, and transforming and modifying it, without, however, being able wholly to destroy it; secondly, that all the great personalities who have continued to kindle religious fervour afresh in the Western Church, and to purify and deepen it, have directly or indirectly proceeded from Augustine and formed themselves on him. The long chain of Catholic reformers, from Agobard and Claudius of Turin in the ninth century down to the Jansenists in the seventeenth and eighteenth, and beyond them, is Augustinian. And if the Council of Trent may be in many respects rightly called a Council of Reform; if the doctrine of penance and grace was formulated then with much more depth and inwardness than could be expected from the state of Catholic theology in the fourteenth and fifteenth centuries, that is only owing to the continued influence of Augustine. With the doctrine of grace taken from Augustine, the Church has, indeed, associated a practice of the confessional which threatens to make that doctrine absolutely ineffective. But, however far it may stretch its bounds so as to keep all those within its pale who do not revolt against its authority, it after all not only tolerates such as take the same view of sin and grace as Augustine, but it also desires that, wherever possible, everyone may feel as strongly as he the gravity of sin and the blessedness of belonging to God.

Such are the essential elements of Roman Catholicism. There is much else that might be mentioned, but what has been said denotes the leading points.

8. On Religious Rejection of the World

BY MAX WEBER

IN STRONGEST CONTRAST to the case of China, Indian religiosity, which we are about to consider, is the cradle of those religious ethics which have abnegated the world, theoretically, practically, and to the greatest extent. It is also in India that the "technique" which corresponds to such abnegation has been most highly developed. Monkhood, as well as the typical ascetic and contemplative manipulations, were not only first but also most consistently developed in India. And it was perhaps from India that this rationalization set out on its historical way throughout the world at large.

Motives for the Rejection of the World: The Meaning of Their Rational Construction

Before turning to this religiosity it may be expedient to clarify briefly, in a schematic and theoretical way, the motives from which religious ethics of world abnegation have originated, and the directions they have taken. In this way we may clarify their possible "meaning."

The constructed scheme, of course, only serves the purpose of offering an ideal typical means of orientation. It does not teach a philosophy of its own. The theoretically constructed types of conflicting "life orders" are merely intended to show that at certain points such and such internal conflicts are possible and "adequate." They are not intended to show that there is no standpoint from which the conflicts could not be held to be resolved in a higher synthesis. As will readily be seen, the individual

Reprinted from *From Max Weber: Essays in Sociology,* trans. and ed. H. H. Gerth and C. Wright Mills (New York: Oxford University Press, 1958), chap. xiii, pp. 323–59, with the permission of Oxford University Press.

spheres of value are prepared with a rational consistency which is rarely found in reality. But they *can* appear thus in reality and in historically important ways, and they have. Such constructions make it possible to determine the typological locus of a historical phenomenon. They enable us to see if, in particular traits or in their total character, the phenomena approximate one of our constructions: to determine the degree of approximation of the historical phenomenon to the theoretically constructed type. To this extent, the construction is merely a technical aid which facilitates a more lucid arrangement and terminology. Yet, under certain conditions, a construction might mean more. For the rationality, in the sense of logical or teleological "consistency," of an intellectual-theoretical or practical-ethical attitude has and always has had power over man, however limited and unstable this power is and always has been in the face of other forces of historical life.

Religious interpretations of the world and ethics of religions created by intellectuals and meant to be rational have been strongly exposed to the imperative of consistency. The effect of the *ratio,* especially of a teleological deduction of practical postulates, is in some way, and often very strongly, noticeable among all religious ethics. This holds however little the religious interpretations of the world in the individual case have complied with the demand for consistency, and however much they might integrate points of view into their ethical postulates which could *not* be rationally deduced. Thus, for substantive reasons, we may hope to facilitate the presentation of an otherwise immensely multifarious subject matter by expediently constructed rational types. To do this we must prepare and emphasize the internally most "consistent" forms of practical conduct that can be deduced from fixed and given presuppositions.

Above all, such an essay in the sociology of religion necessarily aims at contributing to the typology and sociology of rationalism. This essay therefore proceeds from the most rational forms reality *can* assume; it attempts to find out how far certain rational conclusions, which can be established theoretically, have been drawn in reality. And perhaps we will find out why not.

Typology of Asceticism and of Mysticism

The great importance of the conception of the supra-mundane God and Creator for religious ethics has been touched upon. This conception has been especially important for the active and asceticist direction of the quest for salvation. It has not been so important for the contemplative and mystical quest, which has an internal affinity with the depersonalization and immanence of the divine power. However, this intimate connection, which E. Troeltsch has repeatedly and rightly stressed, between the conception of a supra-mundane God and active asceticism is not absolute; the supra-mundane God has not, as such, determined the direction of Occidental asceticism, as will be seen from the following reflections. The Christian Trinity, with its incarnate Savior and the saints, represented a conception of God which fundamentally was rather less supra-mundane than was the God of Jewry, especially of later Jewry, or the Allah of Islamism.

Jewry developed mysticism, but it developed hardly any asceticism of the Occidental type. And early Islamism directly repudiated asceticism. The peculiarity of Dervish religiosity stemmed from quite different sources than from the relation to a supra-mundane God and Creator. It stemmed from mystic, ecstatic sources and in its inner essence it was remote from Occidental asceticism. Important though it was, the conception of a supra-mundane God, in spite of its affinity to emissary prophecy and active asceticism, obviously did not operate alone but always in conjunction with other circumstances. The nature of religious promises and the paths of salvation which they determined were paramount among these circumstances. This matter has to be discussed in connection with particular cases.

We have had repeatedly to use the terms "asceticism" and "mysticism" as polar concepts. In order to elucidate this terminology we shall here further differentiate these terms.

In our introductory comments we contrasted, as abnegations of the world, the active asceticism that is a God-willed *action* of the devout who are God's

tools, and, on the other hand, the contemplative *possession* of the holy, as found in mysticism. Mysticism intends a state of "possession," not action, and the individual is not a tool but a "vessel" of the divine. Action in the world must thus appear as endangering the absolutely irrational and otherworldly religious state. Active asceticism operates within the world; rationally active asceticism, in mastering the world, seeks to tame what is creatural and wicked through work in a worldly "vocation" (inner-worldly asceticism). Such asceticism contrasts radically with mysticism, if the latter draws the full conclusion of fleeing from the world (contemplative flight from the world).

The contrast is tempered, however, if active asceticism confines itself to keeping down and to overcoming creatural wickedness in the actor's own nature. For then it enhances the concentration on the firmly established God-willed and active redemptory accomplishments to the point of avoiding any action in the orders of the world (asceticist flight from the world). Thereby active asceticism in external bearing comes close to contemplative flight from the world.

The contrast between asceticism and mysticism is also tempered if the contemplative mystic does not draw the conclusion that he should flee from the world, but, like the inner-worldly asceticist, remain in the orders of the world (inner-worldly mysticism).

In both cases the contrast can actually disappear in practice and some combination of both forms of the quest for salvation may occur. But the contrast may continue to exist even under the veil of external similarity. For the true mystic the principle continues to hold: the creature must be silent so that God may speak. He "is" in the world and externally "accommodates" to its orders, but only in order to gain a certainty of his state of grace in opposition to the world by resisting the temptation to take the ways of the world seriously. As we can see with Lao-tse, the typical attitude of the mystic is one of a specifically broken humility, a minimization of action, a sort of religious incognito existence in the world. He proves himself *against* the world, against his action in the world. Inner-worldly asceticism, on the contrary, proves itself *through* action. To the inner-worldly asceticist the conduct of the mystic is an indolent enjoyment of self; to the mystic the conduct of the (inner-worldly active) asceticist is an entanglement in the godless ways of the world combined with complacent self-righteousness. With that "blissful bigotry," usually ascribed to the typical Puritan, inner-worldly asceticism executes the positive and divine resolutions whose ultimate meaning remains concealed. Asceticism executes these resolutions as given in the God-ordained rational orders of the creatural. To the mystic, on the contrary, what matters for his salvation is only the grasping of the ultimate and completely irrational meaning through mystic experience. The forms in which both ways of conduct flee from the world can be distinguished by similar confrontations. But we reserve the discussion of these for monographic presentation.

Directions of the Abnegation of the World

We shall now consider in detail the tensions existing between religion and the world. We shall proceed from the reflections of the introduction, but we shall now give them a somewhat different turn.

We have said that these modes of behavior, once developed into a methodical way of life, formed the nucleus of asceticism as well as of mysticism, and that they originally grew out of magical presuppositions. Magical practices were engaged in, either for the sake of awakening charismatic qualities or for the sake of preventing evil charms. The first case has, of course, been more important for historical developments. For even at the threshold of its appearance, asceticism showed its Janus-face: on the one hand, abnegation of the world, and on the other, mastery of the world by virtue of the magical powers obtained by abnegation.

The magician has been the historical precursor of the prohpet, of the exemplary as well as of the emissary prophet and savior. As a rule the prophet and the savior have legitimized themselves through the possession of a magical charisma. With them, however, this has been merely a means of securing recognition and followers for the exemplary significance, the mission, or the savior quality of their personalities. For the substance of the prophecy or of the savior's commandment is to direct a way of life to the pursuit of a sacred value. Thus understood, the prophecy or commandment means, at least relatively, to systematize and rationalize the way of life, either in particular points or totally. The latter has been the rule with all true "religions of salvation," that is, with all religions that hold out deliverance from suffering to their adherents. This is more likely to be the case the more sublimated, the more inward, and the more principled the essence of suffering is conceived. For then it is important to put the follower into a *permanent* state which makes him inwardly safe against suffering. Formulated abstractly, the rational aim of redemption religion has been to secure for the saved a holy state, and thereby a habitude that assures salvation. This takes the place of an acute and extraordinary, and thus a holy, state which is transitorily attained by means of orgies asceticism, or contemplation.

Now if a religious community emerges in the wake of a prophecy or of the propaganda of a savior, the control of regular conduct first falls into the hands of the charismatically qualified successors, pupils, disciples of the prophet or of the savior. Later, under certain very regularly recurrent conditions, which we shall not deal with here, this task falls into the hands of a priestly, hereditary, or official hierocracy. Yet, as a rule, the prophet or the savior personally has stood in opposition to the traditional hierocratic powers of magicians or of priests. He has set his personal charisma against their dignity consecrated by tradition in order to break their power or force them to his service.

In the aforementioned discussion, we have taken for granted and presupposed that a large and, for the historical development, an especially important fraction of all cases of prophetic and redemptory religions have lived not only in an acute but in a permanent state of tension in relation to the world and its orders. This goes without saying, according to the terminology used here. The more the religions have been true religions of salvation, the greater has this tension been. This follows from the meaning of salvation and from the substance of the prophetic teachings as soon as these develop into an ethic. The tension has also been the greater, the more rational in principle the ethic has been, and the more it has been oriented to *inward* sacred values as means of salvation. In common language, this means that the tension has been the greater the more religion has been sublimated from ritualism and towards "religious absolutism." Indeed, the further the rationalization and sublimation of the external and internal possession of—in the widest sense—"things worldly" has progressed, the stronger has the tension on the part of religion become. For the rationalization and the conscious sublimation of man's relations to the various spheres of values, external and internal, as well as religious and secular, have then pressed towards making conscious the *internal and lawful autonomy* of the individual spheres; thereby letting them drift into those tensions which remain hidden to the originally naive relation with the external world. This results quite generally from the development of inner- and other-worldly values towards rationality, towards conscious endeavor, and towards sublimation by *knowledge.* This consequence is very important for the history of religion. In order to elucidate the typical phenomena which recur in connection with greatly varying religious ethics, we shall consider a series of these values.

Wherever prophecies of salvation have created religious communities, the first power with which they have come into conflict has been the natural sib. The sib has had to fear devaluation by the prophecy. Those who cannot be hostile to members of the household, to father and to mother, cannot be disciples of Jesus. "I came not to send peace, but a sword" (Matthew x, 34) was said in this connection, and, it should be noted, solely in this connection. The preponderant majority of all religions have, of course, regulated the inner-worldly bonds of piety. Yet the more comprehensive and the more inward the aim of salvation has been, the more it has been taken for granted that the faithful should ultimately stand closer to the savior, the prophet, the priest, the father confessor, the brother in the faith than to natural relations and to the matrimonial community.

Prophecy has created a new social community, particularly where it became a soteriological religion of congregations. Thereby the relationships of the sib and of matrimony have been, at least relatively, devalued. The magical ties and exclusiveness of the sibs have been shattered, and within the new community the prophetic religion has developed a religious ethic of brotherliness. The ethic has simply taken over the original principles of social and ethical conduct which the "association of neighbors" had offered, whether it was the community of villagers, members of the sib, the guild, or of partners in seafaring, hunting, and warring expeditions. These communities have known two elemental principles: first, the dualism of in-group and out-group morality; second, for in-group morality, simple reciprocity: "As you do unto me I shall do unto you." From these principles the following have resulted for economic life: For in-group morality the principled obligation to give brotherly support in distress has existed. The wealthy and the noble were obliged to loan, free of charge, goods for the use of the propertyless, to give credit free of interest, and to extend liberal hospitality and support. Men were obliged to render services upon the request of their neighbors, and likewise, on the lord's estate, without compensation other than mere sustenance. All this followed the principle: your want of today may be mine of tomorrow. This principle was not, of course, rationally weighed, but it played its part in sentiment. Accordingly, higgling in exchange and loan situations, as well as permanent enslavement resulting, for instance, from debts, were confined to out-group morality and applied only to outsiders.

The religiosity of the congregation transferred this ancient economic ethic of neighborliness to the relations among brethren of the faith. What had previously been the obligations of the noble and the wealthy became the fundamental imperatives of all ethically rationalized religions of the world: to aid widows and orphans in distress, to care for the sick and impoverished brother of the faith, and to give alms. The giving of alms was especially required of the rich, for the holy minstrels and magicians as well as the ascetics were economically dependent upon the rich.

The principle that constituted the communal relations among the salvation prophecies was the suffering common to all believers. And this was the case whether the suffering actually existed or was a constant threat, whether it was external or internal. The more imperatives that issued from the ethic of reciprocity among neighbors were raised, the more rational the conception of salvation became, and the more it was sublimated into an ethic of absolute ends. Externally, such commands rose to a communism of loving brethren; internally they rose to the attitude of *caritas,* love for the sufferer *per se,* for one's neighbor, for man, and finally for the enemy. The barrier to the bond of faith and the existence of hatred in the face of a world conceived to be the locus of undeserved suffering seem to have resulted from the same imperfections and depravities of empirical reality that originally caused the suffering. Above all, the peculiar euphoria of all types of sublimated religious ecstasy operated psychologically in the same general direction. From being "moved" and edified to feeling direct communion with God, ecstasies have always inclined men towards the flowing out into an objectless acosmism of love. In religions of salvation, the profound and quiet bliss of all heroes of acosmic benevolence has always been fused with a charitable realization of the natural imperfections of all human doings, including one's own. The psychological tone as well as the rational, ethical interpretation of this inner attitude can vary widely. But its ethical demand has always lain in the direction of a universalist brotherhood, which goes beyond all barriers of social associations, often including that of one's own faith.

The religion of brotherliness has always clashed with the orders and values of this world, and the more consistently its demands have been carried through, the sharper the clash has been. The split has usually become wider the more the values of the world have been rationalized and sublimated in terms of their own laws. And that is what matters here.

The Economic Sphere

The tension between brotherly religion and the world has been most obvious in the economic sphere.

All the primeval magical or mystagogic ways of influencing spirits and deities have pursued special interests. They have striven for wealth, as well as long life, health, honor, progeny and, possibly, the improvement of one's fate in the hereafter. The Eleusian mysteries promised all this, just as did the Phoenician and Vedic religions, the Chinese folk-religion, ancient Judaism, and ancient Islam; and it was the promise held out to the pious Hindu and Buddhist laymen. The sublimated religions of salvation, however, have been increasingly tense in their relationships with rationalized economies.

A rational economy is a functional oragnization oriented to money-prices which originate in the interest-struggles of men in the *market*. Calculation is not possible without estimation in money prices and hence without market struggles. Money is the most abstract and "impersonal" element that exists in human life. The more the world of the modern capitalist economy follows its own immanent laws, the less accessible it is to any imaginable relationship with a religious ethic of brotherliness. The more rational, and thus impersonal, capitalism becomes, the more is this the case. In the past it was possible to regulate ethically the personal relations between master and slave precisely because they were personal relations. But it is not possible to regulate—at least not in the same sense or with the same success—the relations between the shifting holders of mortgages and the shifting debtors of the banks that issue these mortgages: for in this case, no personal bonds of any sort exist. If one nevertheless tried to do so, the results would be the same as those we have come to know from China, namely, stifling formal rationality. For in China, formal rationality and substantive rationality were in conflict.

As we have seen, the religions of salvation have had a tendency to depersonalize and objectify love in the unique sense of acosmism. Yet these same religions have watched with profound suspicion the deployment of economic forces which, in a different sense, have likewise been impersonal, and because of this they have been specifically opposed to brotherliness.

The Catholic *Deo placere non potest* has always been the characteristic attitude of salvation religions towards the profit economy; with all rational methods of salvation the warnings against attachment to money and goods have pushed to the height of tabooing goods and money. The dependence of religious communities themselves, and of their propaganda and maintenance, upon economic means, and their accommodation to cultural needs and the everyday interests of the masses, have compelled them to enter compromises of which the history of the interdiction of interests is but one example. Yet,

ultimately no genuine religion of salvation has overcome the tension between their religiosity and a rational economy.

Externally, the ethic of religious virtuosos has touched this tense relation in the most radical fashion: by rejecting the possession of economic goods. The ascetic monk has fled from the world by denying himself individual property; his existence has rested entirely upon his own work; and, above all, his needs have been correspondingly restricted to what was absolutely indispensable. The paradox of all rational asceticism, which in an identical manner has made monks of all ages stumble, is that rational asceticism itself has created the very wealth it rejected. Temples and monasteries have everywhere become the very *loci* of rational economies.

Contemplative seclusion as a principle has only been able to establish the rule that the propertyless monk must enjoy only what nature and men voluntarily offer: berries, roots, and free alms. Labor was something which distracted the monk from concentration upon the contemplated value of salvation. Yet even contemplative seclusion has made its compromises by establishing districts for begging, as in India.

There have been only two consistent avenues for escaping the tension between religion and the economic world in a principled and *inward* manner: First, the paradox of the Puritan ethic of "vocation." As a religion of virtuosos, Puritanism renounced the universalism of love, and testing one's state of grace. God's will in its ultimate meaning was quite incomprehensible, yet it was the only positive will that could be known. In this respect, Puritanism accepted the routinization of the economic cosmos, which, with the whole world, it devalued as creatural and depraved. This state of affairs appeared as God-willed, and as material and given for fulfilling one's duty. In the last resort, this meant in principle to renounce salvation as a goal attainable by man, that is, by everybody. It meant to renounce salvation in favor of the groundless and always only particularized grace. In truth, this standpoint of unbrotherliness was no longer a genuine "religion of salvation." A genuine religion of salvation can exaggerate brotherliness to the height of the mystic's acosmism of love.

Mysticism is the other consistent avenue by which the tension between economics and religion has been escaped. This way is represented quite purely in the mystic's "benevolence," which does not at all enquire into the man to whom and for whom it sacrifices. Ultimately, mysticism is not interested in his person. Once and for all, the benevolent mystic gives his shirt when he is asked for his coat, by anybody who accidentally happens to come his way—

and merely because he happens to come his way. Mysticism is a unique escape from this world in the form of an objectless devotion to anybody, not for man's sake but purely for devotion's sake, or, in Baudelaire's words, for the sake of "the soul's sacred prostitution."

The Political Sphere

The consistent brotherly ethic of salvation religions has come into an equally sharp tension with the *political* orders of the world. This problem did not exist for magic religiosity or for the religion of functional deities. The ancient god of war as well as the god who guaranteed the legal order were functional deities who protected the undoubted values of everyday routine. The gods of locality, tribe, and polity were only concerned with the interests of their respective associations. They had to fight other gods like themselves, just as their communities fought, and they had to prove their divine powers in this very struggle.

The problem only arose when these barriers of locality, tribe, and polity were shattered by universalist religions, by a religion with a unified God of the entire world. And the problem arose in full strength only when this God was a God of "love." The problem of tensions with the political order emerged for redemption religion out of the basic demand for brotherliness. And in politics, as in economics, the more rational the political order became the sharper the problems of these tensions became.

The bureaucratic state apparatus, and the rational *homo politicus* integrated into the state, manage affairs, including the punishment of evil, when they discharge business in the most ideal sense, according to the rational rules of the state order. In this, the political man acts just like the economic man, in a matter-of-fact manner "without regard to the person," *sine ira et studio,* without hate and therefore without love. By virtue of its depersonalization, the bureaucratic state, in important points, is less accessible to substantive moralization than were the patriarchal orders of the past, however many appearances may point to the contrary. The patriarchal orders of the past were based upon personal obligations of piety, and the patriarchal rulers considered the merit of the concrete, single case precisely with "regard to the person." In the final analysis, in spite of all "social welfare policies," the whole course of the state's inner political functions, of justice and administration, is repeatedly and unavoidably regulated by the objective pragmatism of "reasons of state." The state's absolute end is to safeguard (or to change) the external and internal distribution of power; ultimately, this end must seem meaningless

to any universalist religion of salvation. This fact has held and still holds, even more so, for foreign policy. It is absolutely essential for every political association to appeal to the naked violence of coercive means in the face of outsiders as well as in the face of internal enemies. It is only this very appeal to violence that constitutes a political association in our terminology. The state is an association that claims the monopoly of the *legitimate use of violence,* and cannot be defined in any other manner.

The Sermon on the Mount says "resist no evil." In opposition, the state asserts: "You *shall* help right to triumph by the use of *force,* otherwise you too may be responsible for injustice." Where this factor is absent, the "state" is also absent; the "anarchism" of the pacifist will have then come to life. According to the inescapable pragmatism of all action, however, force and the threat of force unavoidably breed more force. "Reasons of state" thus follow their own external and internal laws. The very success of force, or of the threat of force, depends ultimately upon power relations and not on ethical "right," even were one to believe it possible to discover objective criteria for such "right."

In contrast to naive, primitive heroism, it is typical of the rational state systems for groups or rulers to line up for violent conflict, all quite sincerely believing themselves to be "in the right." To any consistent religious rationalization, this must seem only an aping of ethics. Moreover, to draw the Lord's name into such violent political conflict must be viewed as a taking of His name in vain. In the face of this, the cleaner and only honest way may appear to be the complete elimination of ethics from political reasoning. The more matter-of-fact and calculating politics is, and the freer of passionate feelings, of wrath, and of love it becomes, the more it must appear to an ethic of brotherliness to be estranged from brotherliness.

The mutual strangeness of religion and politics, when they are both completely rationalized, is all the more the case because, in contrast to economics, politics may come into direct competition with religious ethics at decisive points. As the consummated threat of violence among modern polities, war creates a pathos and a sentiment of community. War thereby makes for an unconditionally devoted and sacrificial community among the combatants and releases an active mass compassion and love for those who are in need. And, as a mass phenomenon, these feelings break down all the naturally given barriers of association. In general, religions can show comparable achievements only in heroic communities professing an ethic of brotherliness.

Moreover, war does something to the warrior which, in its concrete meaning, is unique: it makes him experience a consecrated meaning of death which is characteristic only of death in war. The community of the army standing in the field today feels itself—as in the times of the war lords "following"—to be a community unto death, and the greatest of its kind. Death on the field of battle differs from death that is only man's common lot. Since death is a fate that comes to everyone, nobody can ever say why it comes precisely to him and why it comes just when it does. As the values of culture increasingly unfold and are sublimated to immeasurable heights, such ordinary death marks an end where only a beginning seems to make sense. Death on the field of battle differs from this merely unavoidable dying in that in war, and in this massiveness *only* in war, the individual can *believe* that he knows he is dying "for" something. The why and the wherefore of his facing death can, as a rule, be so indubitable to him that the problem of the "meaning" of death does not even occur to him. At least there may be no presuppositions for the emergence of the problem in its universal significance, which is the form in which religions of salvation are impelled to be concerned with the meaning of death. Only those who perish "in their callings" are in the same situation as the soldier who faces death on the battlefield.

This location of death within a series of meaningful and consecrated events ultimately lies at the base of all endeavors to support the autonomous dignity of the polity resting on force. Yet the way in which death can be conceived as meaningful in such endeavors points in directions that differ radically from the direction in which the theodicy of death in a religion of brotherliness may point. The brotherliness of a group of men bound together in war must appear devalued in such brotherly religions. It must be seen as a mere reflection of the technically sophisticated brutality of the struggle. And the inner-worldly consecration of death in war must appear as a glorification of fratricide. The very extraordinary quality of brotherliness of war, and of death in war, is shared with sacred charisma and the experience of the communion with God, and this fact raises the competition between the brotherliness of religion and of the warrior community to its extreme height. As in economics, the only two consistent solutions of this tension are those of puritanism and of mysticism.

Puritanism, with its particularism of grace and vocational asceticism, believes in the fixed and revealed commandments of a God who is otherwise quite incomprehensible. It interprets God's will to mean that these commandments should be imposed upon the creatural world by the means of this world, namely, violence—for the world is subject to violence and ethical barbarism. And this means at least barriers which resist the obligation of brotherliness in the interest of God's "cause."

On the other hand, there is the solution of the mystic's radical antipolitical attitude, his quest for redemption with its acosmic benevolence and brotherliness. With its "resist no evil" and with its maxim "then turn the other cheek," mysticism is necessarily vulgar and lacking in dignity in the eyes of every self-assured worldly ethic of heroism. It withdraws from the pragma of violence which no political action can escape.

All other solutions to the tensions of politics and religion are full of compromises or of presuppositions which must necessarily appear dishonest or inacceptable to the genuine ethic of brotherliness. Some of these solutions are nevertheless interesting in principle and as types.

Every organization of salvation by a compulsory and universalist *institution* of grace feels responsible before God for the souls of everyone, or at least of all the men entrusted to it. Such an institution will therefore feel entitled, and in duty bound, to oppose with ruthless force any danger through misguidance in faith. It feels bound to promote the diffusion of its saving means of grace.

When salvation aristocracies are charged by the command of their God to tame the world of sin, for His glory, they give birth to the 'crusader.' Such was the case in Calvinism and, in a different form, in Islamism. At the same time, however, salvation aristocracies separate "holy" or "just" wars from other, purely secular, and therefore profoundly devalued, wars. The just war is engaged in for the sake of executing God's commandment, or for the sake of faith, which in some sense always means a war of religion. Therefore, salvation aristocracies reject the compulsion to participate in those wars of the political authorities which are not clearly established as holy wars corresponding to God's will, that is, wars not affirmed by one's own conscience. The victorious army of Cromwell's Saints acted in this way when it took a stand against compulsory military service. Salvation aristocracies prefer mercenary armies to compulsory service. In case men violate God's will, especially on behalf of the faith, the faithful draw conclusions in favor of an active religious revolution, by virtue of the sentence that one should obey God rather than man.

Churchly Lutheranism, for instance, has taken the very opposite stand. It has rejected the crusade and the right to active resistance against any secular coercion in matters of faith; it has considered such coercion an arbitrary wilfulness, which entangles salvation in the pragmatism of violence. In this field Lutheranism has known only passive resistance. It has, however, accepted obedience to secular authority as unobjectionable, even when this authority has given the order for war, because the responsibility for war is on the secular authority and not on the individual and because the ethical autonomy of the secular authority, in contrast to the inwardly universalist (Catholic) institution of grace, was recognized. The insertion of mystic religiosity peculiar to Luther's personal Christianity stopped short of drawing the full conclusions in this matter.

The religious virtuosos' genuinely mystic and charismatic search for salvation has naturally and everywhere been apolitical or anti-political in nature. Such quests for salvation have readily recognized the autonomy of the temporal order, but they have done so only in order to infer consistently its radically diabolical character, or at least to take that standpoint of absolute indifference in the face of the world which has been expressed in the sentence: "Render unto Caesar the things which are Caesar's" (for what is the relevance of these things for salvation?).

The widely varying empirical stands which historical religions have taken in the face of political action have been determined by the entanglement of religious organizations in power interests and in struggles for power, by the always unavoidable collapse of even the highest states of tension with the world in favor of compromises and relativities, by the usefulness and the use of religious organizations for the political taming of the masses and, especially, by the need of the powers-that-be for the religious consecration of their legitimacy. As we may see from history, almost all the platforms of religious organizations have been religiously relative so far as sacred values, ethical rationality, and lawful autonomy are concerned. In practice, the most important type of these relative forms has been the "organic" social ethics. This type has been diffused in many forms and its conception of vocational work has been, in principle, the most important contrast to the idea of "calling," as found in inner-worldly asceticism.

Organic social ethics, where religiously substructured, stands on the soil of "brotherliness," but, in contrast to mystic and acosmic love, is dominated by a cosmic, rational demand for brotherliness. Its point of departure is the experience of the inequality of religious charisma. The very fact that the holy should be accessible only to some and not to all is unbearable to organic social ethics. It therefore attempts to synthesize this inequality of charismatic qualifications with secular stratification by status, into a cosmos of God-ordained services which are specialized in function. Certain tasks are given to every individual and every group according to their personal charisma and their social and economic position as determined by fate. As a rule, these tasks stand in the service of the realization of a condition which in spite of its compromise nature, is pleasing to God. This condition is interpreted as being at the same time utilitarian, social, and providential. In the face of the wickedness of the world, such a condition facilitates at least a relative taming of sin and of suffering; the preservation and salvation of as many souls as possible for the kingdom of God is thereby facilitated. We shall soon learn of a theodicy of far greater pathos, which the Indian doctrine of Kharma has imparted to the organic doctrine of society from the standpoint of redemptory pragmatism oriented solely to the interests of the individual. Without this very special linkage, every organic social ethic unavoidably represents an accommodation to the interests of the privileged strata of this world. At least that is the view of the radical, mystical ethic of religious brotherliness. From the standpoint of inner-wordly asceticism, the organic ethic lacks the inward drive for an ethical and thorough rationalization of individual life. In such matters, it has no premium for the rational and methodological patterning of personal life in the interest of the individual's own salvation.

The organic pragmatism of salvation must consider the redemptory aristocracy of inner-worldly asceticism, with its rational depersonalization of life orders, as the hardest form of lovelessness and lack of brotherliness. It must consider the redemptory pragmatism of mysticism as a sublimated and, in truth, unbrotherly indulgence of the mystic's own charisma. The mystic's unmethodical and planless acosmism of love is viewed as a mere selfish means in the search for the mystic's own salvation. Both inner-worldly asceticism and mysticism ultimately condemn the social world to absolute meaninglessness, or at least they hold that God's aims concerning the social world are utterly incomprehensible. The rationalism of religious and organic doctrines of society cannot stand up under this idea; for it seeks to comprehend the world as an at least relatively rational cosmos in spite of all its wickedness; the world is held to bear at least traces of the divine plan of salvation. For the absolute charisma of virtuoso religiosity, this relativization is indeed objectionable and estranged from the holy.

As economic and rational political actions follow laws of their own, so every other rational action within the world remains inescapably bound to worldly conditions. These conditions are remote from brotherliness and must serve as means or as ends of rational action. Hence all rational action somehow comes to stand in tension with the ethic of brotherliness, and carries within itself a profound tension. For there seems to exist no means of deciding even the very first question: Where, in the individual case, can the ethical value of an act be determined In terms of success, or in terms of some intrinsic value of the act *per se?* The question is whether and to what extent the responsibility of the actor for the results sanctifies the means, or whether the value of the actor's intention justifies him in rejecting the responsibility for the outcome, whether to pass on the results of the act to God or to the wickedness and foolishness of the world which are permitted by God. The absolutist sublimation of religious ethic will incline men towards the latter alternative: "The Christian does right and leaves success to God." In this, however, the actor's own conduct when it is really consistent, and not the lawful autonomy of the world, is condemned as irrational in its effects. Theoretically this is most consistently carried through in the *Bhagavad-Gita,* as we shall see. In the face of this, a sublimated and thoroughgoing search for salvation may lead to an acosmism increasing to the point where it rejects purposive-rational action *per se,* and hence, all action in terms of means-ends relations, for it considers them tied to worldly things and thus estranged from God. We shall see how this has occurred with varying consistency, from the Biblical parable of the lilies in the field to the more principled formulations, for instance, of Buddhism.

The organic ethic of society is everywhere an eminently conservative power and hostile to revolution. Under certain conditions, however, revolutionary consequences may follow from a genuine virtuoso religiosity. Naturally, this occurs only when the pragmatism of force, calling forth more force and leading merely to changes in personnel, or at best to changes in methods of ruling by force, is not recognized as a permanent quality of the creaturely. According to the coloration of the virtuoso religion, its revolutionary turn may in principle assume two forms. One form springs from inner-worldly asceticism, wherever this asceticism is capable of opposing an absolute and divine "natural law" to the creaturely, wicked, and empirical orders of the world. It then becomes a religious duty to realize this divine natural law, according to the sentence that one must obey God rather than men, which in some sense holds for all rational religions. The genuine Puritan revolutions, whose counterparts can be found elsewhere, are typical. This attitude absolutely corresponds to the obligation to crusade.

It is a different matter with the mystic. The psychological turn from possession of God to possession by God is always possible and with the mystic it is consummated. This is meaningful and possible when eschatological expectations of an immediate beginning and of the millennium of acosmic brotherliness are flaming up, hence, when the belief is dropped that an everlasting tension exists between the world and the irrational metaphysical realm of salvation. The mystic then turns into a savior and prophet. The commands, however, which he enunciates have no rational character. As products of his charisma, they are revelations of a concrete sort and the radical rejection of the world easily turns into radical *anomism.* The commands of the world do not hold for the man who is assured in his obsession with God: 'πάντα μοι εξεστιν.' All chiliasm, up to the revolution of the Anabaptists, rested somehow upon this substructure. For him who "possesses God" and is thereby saved, the manner of action is without significance for salvation. We shall find that similar states hold in the case of the Indian djivanmukhti.

The Esthetic Sphere

The religious ethic of brotherliness stands in dynamic tension with any purposive-rational conduct that follows its own laws. In no less degree, this tension occurs between the religious ethic and "this-worldly" life-forces, whose character is essentially non-rational or basically anti-rational. Above all, there is tension between the ethic of religious brotherliness and the spheres of esthetic and erotic life.

Magical religiosity stands in a most intimate relation to the esthetic sphere. Since its beginnings, religion has been an inexhaustible fountain of opportunities for artistic creation, on the one hand, and of stylizing through traditionalization, on the other. This is shown in a variety of objects and processes: in idols, icons, and other religious artifacts; in the stereotyping of magically proved forms, which is a first step in the overcoming of naturalism by a fixation of "style"; in music as a means of ecstasy, exorcism, or apotropaic magic; in sorcerers as holy singers and dancers; in magically proved and therefore magically stereotyped tone relations —the earliest preparatory stages in the development of tonal systems; in the magically proved dance-step as one of the sources of rhythm and as an ecstasy technique; in temples and churches as the largest of all buildings, with the architectural task becoming stereotyped (and thus style-forming) as a consequence of purposes which are established once for all, and with the structural forms becoming stereotyped through magical efficacy; in paraments and church implements of all kinds which have served as objects of applied art. All these processes and objects have been displayed in connection with the churches' and temples' wealth flowing from religious zeal.

For the religious ethic of brotherliness, just as for *a priori* ethical rigorism, art as a carrier of magical effects is not only devalued but even suspect. The sublimation of the religious ethic and the quest for salvation, on the one hand, and the evolution of the inherent logic of art, on the other, have tended to form an increasingly tense relation. All sublimated religions of salvation have focused upon the meaning alone, not upon the form, of the things and actions relevant for salvation. Salvation religions have devalued form as contingent, as something creaturely and distracting from meaning. On the part of art, however, the naive relation to the religious ethic of brotherliness can remain unbroken or can be repeatedly restored as long and as often as the conscious interest of the recipient of art is naively attached to the content and not to the form as such. The relationship between a religious ethic and art will remain harmonious as far as resulting either from a charisma of "ability" (originally magic) or from spontaneous play.

The development of intellectualism and the rationalization of life change this situation. For under these conditions, art becomes a cosmos of more and more consciously grasped independent values which exist in their own right. Art takes over the function of a this-worldly salvation, no matter how this may be interpreted. It provides a *salvation* from the routines of everyday life, and especially from the increasing pressures of theoretical and practical rationalism.

With this claim to a redemptory function, art begins to compete directly with salvation religion. Every rational religious ethic must turn against this inner-worldly, irrational salvation. For in religion's eyes, such salvation is a realm of irresponsible indulgence and secret lovelessness. As a matter of fact, the refusal of modern men to assume responsibility for moral judgments tends to transform judgments of moral intent into judgments of taste ("in poor taste" instead of "reprehensible"). The inaccessibility of appeal from esthetic judgments excludes discussion. This shift from the moral to the esthetic evaluation of conduct is a common characteristic of intellectualist epochs; it results partly from subjectivist needs and partly from the fear of appearing narrow-minded in a traditionalist and Philistine way.

The ethical norm and its "universal validity" create a community, at least in so far as an individual might reject the act of another on moral grounds and yet still face it and participate in the common life. Knowing his own creaturely weakness, the individual places himself under the common norm. In contrast with this ethical attitude, the escape from the necessity of taking a stand on rational, ethical grounds by resorting to esthetic evaluations *may* very well be regarded by salvation religion as a very base form of unbrotherliness. To the creative artist, however, as well as to the esthetically excited and receptive mind, the ethical norm as such may easily appear as a coercion of their genuine creativeness and innermost selves.

The most irrational form of religious behavior, the mystic experience, is in its innermost being not only alien but hostile to all form. Form is unfortunate and inexpressible to the mystic because he believes precisely in the experience of exploding all forms, and hopes by this to be absorbed into the "All-oneness" which lies beyond any kind of determination and form. For him the indubitable psychological affinity of profoundly shaking experiences in art and religion can only be a symptom of the diabolical nature of art. Especially music, the most "inward" of all the arts, can appear in its purest form of instrumental music as an irresponsible *Ersatz* for primary religious experience. The internal logic of instrumental music as a realm not living "within" appears as a deceptive pretension to religious experience. The well-known stand of the Council of Trent may in part have stemmed from this sentiment. Art becomes an "idolatry," a competing power, and a deceptive bedazzlement; and the images and the allegory of religious subjects appear as blasphemy.

In empirical, historical reality, this psychological affinity between art and religion has led to ever-renewed alliances, which have been quite significant for the evolution of art. The great majority of religions have in some manner entered such alliances. The more they wished to be universalist mass religions and were thus directed to emotional propaganda and mass appeals, the more systematic were their alliances with art. But all genuine virtuoso religions have remained very coy when confronting art, as a consequence of the inner structure of the contradiction between religion and art. This holds true for virtuoso religiosity in its active asceticist bent as well as in its mystical turn. The more religion has emphasized either the supra-worldliness of its God or the other-worldliness of salvation, the more harshly has art been refuted.

The Erotic Sphere

The brotherly ethic of salvation religion is in profound tension with the greatest irrational force of life: sexual love. The more sublimated sexuality is, and the more principled and relentlessly consistent the salvation ethic of brotherhood is, the sharper is the tension between sex and religion.

Originally the relation of sex and religion was very intimate. Sexual intercourse was very frequently part of magic orgiasticism or was an unintended result of orgiastic excitement. The foundation of the Skoptsy (Castrators) sect in Russia evolved from an attempt to do away with the sexual result of the orgiastic dance (radjeny) of the *Chlyst,* which was evaluated as sinful. Sacred harlotry has had nothing whatsoever to do with an alleged "primitive promiscuity," it has usually been a survival of magical orgiasticism in which every ecstasy was considered "holy." And profane heterosexual, as well as homosexual, prostitution is very ancient and often rather sophisticated. (The training of tribades occurs among so-called *aborigines.*)

The transition from such prostitution to legally constituted marriage is full of all sorts of intermediary forms. Conceptions of marriage as an economic arrangement for providing security for the wife and legal inheritance for the child; as an institution which is important (because of the death sacrifices of the descendants) for destiny in the beyond; and as important for the begetting of children—these conceptions of marriage are pre-prophetic and universal. They therefore have had nothing to do with asceticism as such. And sexual life, *per se,* has had its ghosts and gods as has every other function.

A certain tension between religion and sex came to the fore only with the temporary cultic chastity of priests. This rather ancient chastity may well have been determined by the fact that from the point of view of the strictly stereotyped ritual of the regulated community cult, sexuality was readily considered to be specifically dominated by demons. Furthermore, it was no accident that subsequently the prophetic religions, as well as the priest-controlled life orders, have, almost without significant exception, regulated sexual intercourse in favor of *marriage.* The contrast of all rational regulation of life with magical orgiasticism and all sorts of irrational frenzies is expressed in this fact.

The tension of religion and sex has been augmented by evolutionary factors on both sides. On the side of sexuality the tension has led through sublimation into "eroticism," and therewith into a consciously cultivated, and hence, a non-routinized sphere. Sex has been non-routinized not solely or necessarily in the sense of being estranged from conventions, for eroticism is a contrast to the sober naturalism of the peasant. And it was precisely eroticism which the conventions of knighthood usually made the object of regulation. These conventions, however, charcteristically regulated eroticism by veiling the natural and organic basis of sexuality.

The extraordinary quality of eroticism has consisted precisely in a gradual turning away from the naive naturalism of sex. The reason and significance of this evolution, however, involve the universal rationalization and intellectualization of culture. We wish to present, in a few sketches, the phases of this development. We shall proceed with examples from the Occident.

The total being of man has now been alienated from the organic cycle of peasant life; life has been increasingly enriched in cultural content, whether this content is evaluated as intellectually or otherwise supra-individual. All this has worked, through the estrangement of life-value from that which is merely naturally given, toward a further enhancement of the special position of eroticism. Eroticism was raised into the sphere of conscious enjoyment (in the most sublime sense of the term). Nevertheless, indeed because of this elevation, eroticism appeared to be like a gate into the most irrational and thereby real kernel of life, as compared with the mechanisms of rationalization. The degree and the manner in which a value-emphasis was thus placed upon eroticism as such has varied enormously throughout history.

To the unrestrained feelings of a warriordom, the possession of and the fight for women has ranked about equally with the fight for treasure and the conquest of power. At the time of pre-classic Hellenism, in the period of knighthood romance, an erotic disappointment could be considered by Archilochos as a significant experience of lasting relevance, and the capture of a woman could be considered the incomparable incident of a heroic war.

The tragedians knew sexual love as a genuine power of destiny, and their lore incorporated lingering echoes of the myths. On the whole, however, a woman, Sappho, remained unequalled by man in the capacity for erotic feeling. The classic Hellenic period of the Hoplite army, conceived of erotic matters in a relatively and unusually sober manner. As all their self-revelations prove, these men were even more sober than the educated stratum of the Chinese. Yet it is not true that this period did not know the deadly earnestness of sexual love. Rather, the contrary was characteristic of Hellenic love. We should remind ourselves—despite Aspasia— of Pericles' speech and finally of the well-known statement of Demosthenes.

To the exclusively masculine character of this epoch of "democracy," the treatment of erotic experience with women as "life-fate"—to speak in our vocabulary—would have appeared as almost sophomoric and sentimental. The "comrade," the boy, was the object demanded with all the ceremony of love, and this fact stood precisely in the center of Hellenic culture. Thus, with all its magnificence, Plato's eros is nevertheless a strongly tempered feeling. The beauty of Bacchian passion as such was not an official component of this relation.

The possibility of problems and of tragedy of a principled character came about in the erotical sphere, at first, through certain demands for responsibility, which, in the Occident, stem from Christianity. However, the value-accentuation of the erotic sensation as such evolved primarily and before all else under the cultural conditioning of feudal notions of honor. This happened by a carrying over of the symbols of knightly vassalship into the erotically sublimated sexual relation. Eroticism was given a value-accent most frequently when, during the fusion of vassalship and erotic relations, there occurred a combination with crypto-erotic religiosity, or directly with asceticism as during the Middle Ages. The troubadour love of the Christian Middle Ages is known to have been an erotic service of vassals. It was not oriented towards girls, but exclusively towards the wives of other men; it involved (in theory!) abstentious love nights and a casuistic code of duties. Therewith began the "probation" of the man, not before his equals but in the face of the erotic interest of the "lady."

The conception of the "lady" was constituted solely and precisely by virtue of her judging function. The masculinity of Hellenism is in strict contrast to this relation of the vassal to the "lady."

A further enhancement of the specifically sensational character of eroticism developed with the transition from the conventions of the Renaissance to the increasingly non-military intellectualism of salon culture. Despite the great differences between the conventions of Antiquity and the Renaissance, the latter were essentially masculine and agonistic; in this respect, they were closely related to antiquity. This was due to the fact that by the time of the Cortegiano and of Shakespeare, the Renaissance conventions had cast off the asceticism of Christian knighthood.

Salon culture rested upon the conviction that inter-sexual conversation is valuable as a creative power. The overt or latent erotic sensation and the agonistic probation of the cavalier before the lady became an indispensable means of stimulating this conversation. Since the *Lettres Portugaises*, the actual love problems of women became a specific intellectual market value, and feminine love correspondence became "literature."

The last accentuation of the erotical sphere oc-

curred in terms of intellectualist cultures. It occurred where this sphere collided with the unavoidably ascetic trait of the vocational specialist type of man. Under this tension between the erotic sphere and rational everyday life, specifically extramarital sexual life, which had been removed from everyday affairs, could appear as the only tie which still linked man with the natural fountain of all life. For man had now been completely emancipated from the cycle of the old, simple, and organic existence of the peasant.

A tremendous value emphasis on the specific sensation of an inner-worldly salvation from rationalization thus resulted. A joyous triumph over rationality corresponded in its radicalism with the unavoidable and equally radical rejection by an ethics of any kind of other- or supra-worldly salvation. For such ethics, the triumph of the spirit over the body should find its climax precisely here, and sexual life could even gain the character of the only and the ineradicable connection with animality. But this tension between an inner-worldly and an other-worldly salvation from rationality must be sharpest and most unavoidable precisely where the sexual sphere is systematically prepared for a highly valued erotic sensation. This sensation reinterprets and glorifies all the pure animality of the relation, whereas the religion of salvation assumes the character of a religion of love, brotherhood, and neighborly love.

Under these conditions, the erotic relation seems to offer the unsurpassable peak of the fulfilment of the request for love in the direct fusion of the souls of one to the other. This boundless giving of oneself is as radical as possible in its opposition to all functionality, rationality, and generality. It is displayed here as the unique meaning which one creature in his irrationality has for another, and only for this specific other. However, from the point of view of eroticism, this meaning, and with it the value-content of the relation itself, rests upon the possibility of a communion which is felt as a complete unification, as a fading of the "thou." It is so overpowering that it is interpreted "symbolically": as a sacrament. The lover realizes himself to be rooted in the kernel of the truly living, which is eternally inaccessible to any rational endeavor. He knows himself to be freed from the cold skeleton hands of rational orders, just as completely as from the banality of everyday routine. This consciousness of the lover rests upon the ineffaceability and inexhaustibleness of his own experience. The experience is by no means communicable and in this respect it is equivalent to the "having" of the mystic. This is not only due to the intensity of the lover's experience, but to the immediacy of the possessed reality. Knowing "life itself" joined to him, the lover stands opposite what is for him the objectless experiences of the mystic, as if he were facing the fading light of an unreal sphere.

As the knowing love of the mature man stands to the passionate enthusiasm of the youth, so stands the deadly earnestness of this eroticism of intellectualism to chivalrous love. In contrast to chivalrous love, this mature love of intellectualism reaffirms the natural quality of the sexual sphere, but it does so consciously, as an embodied creative power.

A principled ethic of religious brotherhood is radically and antagonistically opposed to all this. From the point of view of such an ethic, this inner, earthly sensation of salvation by mature love competes in the sharpest possible way with the de-devotion of a mystical bursting of individuation, of an ethically rational order of God, or with the devotion of a mystical bursting of individuation, which alone appear "genuine" to the ethic of brotherhood.

Certain psychological interrelations of both spheres sharpen the tension between religion and sex. The highest eroticism stands psychologically and physiologically in a mutually substitutive relation with certain sublimated forms of heroic piety. In opposition to the rational, active asceticism which rejects the sexual as irrational, and which is felt by eroticism to be a powerful and deadly enemy, this substitutive relationship is oriented especially to the mystic's union with God. From this relation there follows the constant threat of a deadly sophisticated revenge of animality, or of an unmediated slipping from the mystic realm of God into the realm of the All-Too-Human. This psychological affinity naturally increases the antagonism of inner meanings between eroticism and religion.

From the point of view of any religious ethic of brotherhood, the erotic relation must remain attached, in a certain sophisticated measure, to brutality. The more sublimated it is, the more brutal. Unavoidably, it is considered to be a relation of conflict. This conflict is not only, or even predominantly, jealousy and the will to possession, excluding third ones. It is far more the most intimate coercion of the soul of the less brutal partner. This coercion exists because it is never noticed by the partners themselves. Pretending to be the most humane devotion, it is a sophisticated enjoyment of oneself in the other. No consummated erotic communion will know itself to be founded in any way other than through a mysterious *destination* for one another: *fate,* in this highest sense of the

word. Thereby, it will know itself to be "legitimized" (in an entirely amoral sense).

But, for salvation religion, this "fate" is nothing but the purely fortuitous flaming up of passion. The thus established pathological obsession, idiosyncrasy, and shifting of perspectives and of every objective justice must appear to salvation religion as the most complete denial of all brotherly love and of bondage to God. The euphoria of the happy lover is felt to be "goodness"; it has a friendly urge to poeticize all the world with happy features or to bewitch all the world in a naive enthusiasm for the diffusion of happiness. And always it meets with the cool mockery of the genuinely religiously founded and radical ethic of brotherhood. The psychologically most thorough portions of Tolstoi's early work may be cited in this connection. In the eyes of this ethic, the most sublimated eroticism is the counter-pole of all religiously oriented brotherliness, in these aspects: it must necessarily be exclusive in its inner core; it must be subjective in the highest imaginable sense; and it must be absolutely incommunicable.

All this, of course, is quite apart from the fact that the passionate character of eroticism as such appears to the religion of brotherhood as an undignified loss of self-control and as the loss of orientation towards either the rationality and wisdom of norms willed by God or the mystic "having" of godliness. However, for eroticism, genuine "passion" *per se* constitutes the type of *beauty,* and its rejection is blasphemy.

For psychological reasons and in accordance with its meaning, the erotic frenzy stands in unison only with the orgiastic and charismatic form of religiosity. This form is, however, in a special sense, inner-worldly. The acknowledgment of the *act* of marriage, of the *copula carnalis,* as a "sacrament" of the Catholic Church is a concession to this sentiment. Eroticism enters easily into an unconscious and unstable relation of surrogateship or fusion with other-worldly and extraordinary mysticism. This occurs with very sharp inner tension between eroticism and mysticism. It occurs because they are psychologically substitutive. Out of this fusion the collapse into orgiasticism follows very readily.

Inner-worldly and rational asceticism (vocational asceticism) can accept only the rationally regulated marriage. This type of marriage is accepted as one of the divine ordinations given to man as a creature who is hopelessly wretched by virtue of his "concupiscence." Within this divine order it is given to man to live according to the rational purposes laid down by it and only according to them: to procreate and to rear children, and mutually to further one another in the state of grace. This inner-worldly rational asceticism must reject every sophistication of the sexual into eroticism as idolatry of the worst kind. In its turn, this asceticism gathers the primal, naturalist, and *un*sublimated sexuality of the peasant into a rational order of man as creature. All elements of "passion," however, are then considered as residues of the Fall. According to Luther, God, in order to prevent worse, peeks at and is lenient with these elements of passion. The otherworldly rational asceticism (active asceticism of the monk) also rejects these passionate elements, and with them all sexuality, as a diabolic power endangering salvation. The ethic of the Quakers (as it is displayed in William Penn's letters to his wife) may well have achieved a genuinely humane interpretation of the inner and religious values of marriage. In this respect the Quaker ethic went beyond the rather gross Lutheran interpretation of the meaning of marriage.

From a purely inner-worldly point of view, only the linkage of marriage with the thought of ethical responsibility for one another—hence a category heterogeneous to the purely erotic sphere—can carry the sentiment that something unique and supreme might be embodied in marriage; that it might be the transformation of the feeling of a love which is conscious of responsibility throughout all the nuances of the organic life process, "up to the pianissimo of old age," and a mutual granting of oneself to another and the becoming indebted to each other (in Goethe's sense). Rarely does life grant such value in pure form. He to whom it is given may speak of fate's fortune and grace—not of his own "merit."

The Intellectual Sphere

The rejection of all naive surrender to the most intensive ways of experiencing existence, artistic and erotical, is as such only a negative attitude. But it is obvious that such rejection could increase the force with which energies flow into rational achievement, both the ethical as well as the purely intellectual. It must be noted, however, that the self-conscious tension of religion is greatest and most principled where religion faces the sphere of intellectual knowledge.

There is a unity in the realm of magic and in the purely magical image of the world, as we have noted in the case of Chinese thought. A far-going and mutual recognition is also possible between religion and purely metaphysical speculation, although as a rule this speculation easily leads to skepticism. Religion, therefore, frequently considers purely empirical research, including that of natural science, as more reconcilable to religious interests

than it does philosophy. This is the case above all in ascetic Protestantism.

The tension between religion and intellectual knowledge definitely comes to the fore wherever rational, empirical knowledge has consistently worked through to the disenchantment of the world and its transformation into a causal mechanism. For then science encounters the claims of the ethical postulate that the world is a God-ordained, and hence somehow *meaningfully* and ethically oriented, cosmos. In principle, the empirical as well as the mathematically oriented view of the world develops refutations of every intellectual approach which in any way asks for a "meaning" of inner-worldly occurrences. Every increase of rationalism in empirical science increasingly pushes religion from the rational into the irrational realm; but only today does religion become *the* irrational or anti-rational supra-human power. The extent of consciousness or of consistency in the experience of this contrast, however, varies widely. Athanasius won out with his formula—completely absurd when viewed rationally—in his struggle against the majority of the Hellenic philosophers of the time; it does not seem inconceivable, as has been said, that among other reasons he really wanted to compel them expressly to make the intellectual sacrifice and to fix a limit to rational discussion. Soon afterwards, however, the Trinity itself was rationally argued and discussed.

Because of this apparently irreconcilable tension, prophetic as well as priestly religions have repeatedly stood in intimate relation with rational intellectualism. The less magic or merely contemplative mysticism and the more "doctrine" a religion contains, the greater is its need of rational apologetics. The sorcerers everywhere have been the typical keepers of myths and heroic sagas, because they have participated in educating and training young warriors in order to awaken them for heroic ecstasy and heroic regeneration. From them the priesthood, as the only agents capable of conserving tradition, took over the training of youth in the law and often also in purely administrative technologies, and, above all, in writing and in calculus. The more religion became book-religion and doctrine, the more literary it became and the more efficacious it was in provoking rational lay-thinking, freed of priestly control. From the thinking laymen, however, emerged the prophets, who were hostile to priests; as well as the mystics, who searched salvation independently of priests and sectarians; and finally the skeptics and philosophers, who were hostile to faith.

A rationalization of priestly apologetics reacted against all of these developments. Anti-religious skepticism, *per se*, was represented in China, in Egypt, in the Vedas, in post-exilic Jewish literature. In principle, it was just as it is today; almost no new arguments have been added. Therefore, the central question of power for the priesthood became the monopolization of the education of youth.

With the increasing rationalization of political administration, the power of the priesthood could increase. In the early times of Egypt and Babylon, the priesthood alone procured the scribes for the state. It was the same for the medieval prince when administration based on documents began. Of the great systems of pedagogy, only Confucianism and that of Mediterranean Antiquity have known how to escape the power of priesthood. The former succeeded by virtue of its powerful state bureaucracy the latter through the absolute lack of bureaucratic administration. With the elimination of priests from education, priestly religion itself was eliminated in these cases. With these exceptions, however, the priesthoods have regularly furnished and controlled the personnel of schools.

It has not only been these genuinely priestly interests that have made for ever-renewed connections between religion and intellectualism. It has also been the inward compulsion of the rational character of religious ethics and the specifically intellectualist quest for salvation. In effect, every religion in its psychological and intellectual substructure and in its practical conclusions has taken a different stand towards intellectualism, without however allowing the ultimate inward tension to disappear. For the tension rests on the unavoidable disparity among ultimate forms of images of the world.

There is absolutely no "unbroken" religion working as a vital force which is not compelled at *some* point to demand the *credo non quod, sed quia absurdum*—the "sacrifice of the intellect."

It is hardly necessary and it would be impossible to treat in detail the stages of the tension between religion and intellectual knowledge. Redemptory religion defends itself against the attack of the self-sufficient intellect. It does so, of course, in the most principled fashion, by raising the claim that religious knowledge moves in a different sphere and that the nature and meaning of religious knowledge is entirely different from the accomplishments of the intellect. Religion claims to offer an ultimate stand toward the world by virtue of a direct grasp of the world's "meaning." It does not claim to offer intellectual knowledge concerning what is or what should be. It claims to unlock the meaning of the world not by means of the intellect but by virtue of a charisma of illumination. This charisma is said to be imparted only to those who make use of the

respective technique and free themselves from the misleading and deceptive surrogates which are given out as knowledge by the confused impressions of the senses and the empty abstractions of the intellect. Religion believes that these are in truth irrelevant for salvation. By freeing himself from them, a religious man is said to make himself ready for the reception of the all-important grasp of the meaning of the world and of his own existence. In all the endeavors of philosophy to make this ultimate meaning, and the (practical) stand which follows from grasping, demonstrable redemptory religion will see nothing but the intellect's desire to escape its own lawful autonomy. The same view is held of philosophical attempts to gain any intuitive knowledge, which, although concerned with the "being" of things, has a dignity which principally differs from that of religious knowledge. Above all, religion sees all this as a specific product of the very rationalism that intellectualism, by these endeavors, would very much like to escape.

Salvation religion, however, viewed from its own position, is to be blamed for equally inconsistent trespasses as soon as it surrenders the unassailable incommunicability of mystic experiences. If it is consistent, such religion can only have the means of bringing mystic experiences about as *events;* it has no means of adequately communicating and demonstrating them. Every attempt to influence the world must entice mystical religion to run this danger, as soon as the attempt assumes the character of propaganda. The same holds for every attempt to interpret the meaning of the universe rationally, but nevertheless the attempt has been made again and again.

Religious postulates can come into conflict with the "world" from differing points of view, and the point of view involved is always of the greatest importance for the direction and for the way in which *salvation* will be striven for. At all times and in all places, the need for salvation—consciously cultivated as the substance of religiosity—has resulted from the endeavor of a systematic and practical rationalization of life's realities. To be sure, this connection has been maintained with varying degrees of transparency: on this level, all religions have demanded as a specific presupposition that the course of the world be somehow *meaningful,* at least in so far as it touches upon the interests of men. As we have seen, this claim naturally emerged first as the customary problem of unjust suffering, and hence as the postulate of a just compensation for the unequal distribution of individual happiness in the world. From here, the claim has tended to progress step by step towards an ever-increasing devaluation of the world. For the more intensely rational thought has seized upon the problem of a just and retributive compensation, the less an entirely inner-worldly solution could seem possible, and the less an other-worldly solution could appear probable or even meaningful.

In so far as appearances show, the actual course of the world has been little concerned with this postulate of compensation. The ethically unmotivated inequality in the distribution of happiness and misery, for which a compensation has seemed conceivable, has remained irrational; and so has the brute fact that suffering exists. For the universal diffusion of suffering could only be replaced by another and still more irrational problem, the question of the origin of sin, which, according to the teaching of prophets and priests, is to explain suffering as a punishment or as a means of discipline. A world created for the committing of sin must appear still less ethically perfect than a world condemned to suffering. In any case, the absolute imperfection of this world has been firmly established as an ethical postulate. And the futility of worldly things has seemed to be meaningful and justified only in terms of this imperfection. Such justification, however, could appear suitable for devaluating the world even further. For it was not only, or even primarily, the worthless which proved to be transitory. The fact that death and ruin, with their leveling effects, overtake good men and good works, as well as evil ones, could appear to be a depreciation of precisely the supreme values of this world—once the idea of a perpetual duration of time, of an eternal God, and an eternal order had been conceived. In the face of this, values—and precisely the most highly cherished values—have been hallowed as being "timelessly" valid. Hence, the significance of their realization in "culture" has been stated to be independent of the temporal duration of their concretion. Thereupon the ethical rejection of the empirical world could be further intensified. For at this point onto the religious horizon could enter a train of thoughts of far greater significance than were the imperfection and futility of worldly things, because these ideas were fit to indict precisely the "cultural values" which usually rank highest.

These values have borne the stigma of a deadly sin, of an unavoidable and specific burden of guilt. They have proved to be bound to the charisma of the mind or of taste. Their cultivation has seemed inevitably to presuppose modes of existence which run counter to the demand for brotherliness and which could only be adapted to this demand by self-deception. The barriers of education and of esthetic cultivation are the most intimate and the most insuperable of all status differences. Religious guilt

could now appear not only as an occasional concomitant, but as an integral part of all culture, of all conduct in a civilized world, and finally, of all structured life in general. And thereby the ultimate values which this world offered have seemed burdened with the greatest guilt.

Wherever the external order of the social community has turned into the culture community of the state it obviously could be maintained only by brutal force, which was concerned with justice only nominally and occasionally and in any case only so far as reasons of state have permitted. This force has inevitably bred new deeds of violence against external and internal enemies; in addition, it has bred dishonest pretexts for such deeds. Hence it has signified an overt, or what must appear worse, a pharisaically veiled, absence of love. The routinized economic cosmos, and thus the rationally highest form of the provision of material goods which is indispensable for all worldly culture, has been a structure to which the absence of love is attached from the very root. All forms of activity in the structured world have appeared to be entangled in the same guilt.

Veiled and sublimated brutality, idiosyncrasy hostile to brotherliness, as well as illusionist shifts of a just sense of proportion have inevitably accompanied sexual love. The more powerfully the forces of sexual love are deployed the less they are noticed by the participants, and the more veiled they are in a Pharisaic way. Ethical religiosity has appealed to rational knowledge, which has followed its own autonomous and innerworldly norms. It has fashioned a cosmos of truths which no longer had anything to do with the systematic postulates of a rational religious ethic; with the result that the world as a cosmos must satisfy the demands of a religious ethic or evince some "meaning." On the contrary, rational knowledge has had to reject this claim in principle. The cosmos of natural causality and the postulated cosmos of ethical, compensatory causality have stood in irreconcilable opposition.

Science has created this cosmos of natural causality and has seemed unable to answer with certainty the question of its own ultimate presuppositions. Nevertheless science, in the name of "intellectual integrity," has come forward with the claim of representing the only possible form of a reasoned view of the world. The intellect, like all culture values, has created an aristocracy based on the possession of rational culture and independent of all personal ethical qualities of man. The aristocracy of intellect is hence an unbrotherly aristocracy. Worldly man has regarded this possession of culture as the highest good. In addition to the burden of ethical guilt, however, something has adhered to this cultural value which was bound to depreciate it with still greater finality, namely, senselessness—if this cultural value is to be judged in terms of its own standards.

The purely inner-worldly perfection of self of a man of culture, hence the ultimate value to which "culture" has seemed to be reducible, is meaningless for religious thought. This follows for religious thought from the obvious meaninglessness of death, meaningless precisely when viewed from the inner-worldly standpoint. And under the very conditions of "culture," senseless death has seemed only to put the decisive stamp upon the senselessness of life itself.

The peasant, like Abraham, could die "satiated with life." The feudal landlord and the warrior hero could do likewise. For both fulfilled a cycle of their existence beyond which they did not reach. Each in his way could attain an inner-worldly perfection as a result of the naive unambiguity of the substance of his life. But the "cultivated" man who strives for self-perfection, in the sense of acquiring or creating "cultural values," cannot do this. He can become "weary of life" but he cannot become "satiated with life" in the sense of completing a cycle. For the perfectibility of the man of culture in principle progresses indefinitely, as do the cultural values. And the segment which the individual and passive recipient or the active co-builder can comprise in the course of a finite life becomes the more trifling the more differentiated and multiplied the cultural values and the goals for self-perfection become. Hence the harnessing of man into this external and internal cosmos of culture can offer the less likelihood that an individual would absorb either culture as a whole or what in any sense is "essential" in culture. Moreover there exists no definitive criterion for judging the latter. It thus becomes less and less likely that "culture" and the striving for culture can have any inner-worldly meaning for the individual.

The "culture" of the individual certainly does not consist of the quantity of "cultural values" which he amasses; it consists of an articulated *selection* of culture values. But there is no guarantee that this selection has reached an end that would be meaningful to him at the "accidental" time of his death. He might even turn his back to life with an air of distinction: "I have enough—life has offered (or denied) all that made living worthwhile for *me*." This proud attitude to the religion of salvation must appear as a disdainful blasphemy of the God-ordained ways of life and destinies. No redemption religion positively *approves* of "death by one's own hand," that is, a death which has been hallowed only by philosophies.

Viewed in this way, all "culture" appears as man's emancipation from the organically prescribed cycle of natural life. For this very reason culture's every step forward seems condemned to lead to an ever more devastating senselessness. The advancement of cultural values, however, seems to become a senseless hustle in the service of worthless, moreover self-contradictory, and mutually antagonistic ends. The advancement of cultural values appears the more meaningless the more it is made a holy task, a "calling."

Culture becomes ever more senseless as a locus of imperfection, of injustice, of suffering, of sin, of futility. For it is necessarily burdened with guilt, and its deployment and differentiation thus necessarily become ever more meaningless. Viewed from a purely ethical point of view, the world has to appear fragmentary and devalued in all those instances when judged in the light of the religious postulate of a divine "meaning" of existence. This devaluation results from the conflict between the rational claim and reality, between the rational ethic and the partly rational, and partly irrational values. With every construction of the specific nature of each special sphere existing in the world, this conflict has seemed to come to the fore ever more sharply and more insolubly. The need for "salvation" responds to this devaluation by becoming more other-worldly, more alienated from all structured forms of life, and, in exact parallel, by confining itself to the specific religious essence. This reaction is the stronger the more systematic the thinking about the "meaning" of the universe becomes, the more the external organization of the world is rationalized, and the more the conscious experience of the world's irrational content is sublimated. And not only theoretical thought, disenchanting the world, led to this course, but also the very attempt of religious ethics practically and ethically to rationalize the world.

The specific intellectual and mystical attempts at salvation in the face of these tensions succumb in the end to the world dominion of unbrotherliness. On the one hand, their charisma is *not* accessible to everybody. Hence, in intent, mystical salvation definitely means aristocracy; it is an aristocratic religiosity of redemption. And, in the midst of a culture that is rationally organized for a vocational workaday life, there is hardly any room for the cultivation of acosmic brotherliness, unless it is among strata who are economically carefree. Under the technical and social conditions of rational culture, an imitation of the life of Buddha, Jesus, or Francis seems condemned to failure for purely external reasons.

The Three Forms of Theodicy

The individual redemption ethics of the past which have rejected the world have applied their rejection of the world at very different points of this purely rationally constructed scale. This has depended upon numerous concrete circumstances which cannot be ascertained by a theoretical typology. Besides these circumstances, a rational element has played its part, namely, the structure of a special *theodicy*. The metaphysical need responded to the awareness of existing and unbridgeable tensions, and through theodicy it tried to find a common meaning in spite of all.

Among the three types of theodicy we have already designated as alone consistent, *dualism* could well serve this need. Dualism maintains that always the powers of light and truth, purity and goodness coexist and conflict with the powers of darkness and falsehood, impurity and evil. In the last analysis this dualism is only a direct systematization of the magical pluralism of the spirits with their division of good (useful) and evil (harmful) spirits which represent the preliminary stages of the antagonism between deities and demons.

Zoroastrism was the prophetic religiousness which realized this conception most consistently. Here dualism set out with the magical contrast between "clean" and "unclean." All virtues and vices were integrated into this contrast. It involved renouncing the omnipotence of a god whose power was indeed limited by the existence of a great antagonist. The contemporary followers (the Parsees) have actually given up this belief because they could not endure this limitation of divine power. In the most consistent eschatology, the world of purity and the world of impurity, from the mixture of which the fragmentary empirical world emanated, separated again and again into two unrelated realms. The more modern eschatological hope, however, makes the god of purity and benevolence triumph, just as Christianity makes the Savior triumph over the devil. This less consistent form of dualism is the popular, world-wide conception of heaven and hell, which restores God's sovereignty over the evil spirit who is His creature, and thereby believes that divine omnipotence is saved. But, willy-nilly, it must then, overtly or covertly, sacrifice some of the divine love. For if omniscience is maintained, the creation of a power of radical evil and the admission of sin, especially in communication with the eternity of hell's punishments for one of God's own and finite creatures and for finite sins, simply does not correspond to divine love. In that case, only a renunciation of benevolence is consistent.

The belief in *predestination* realizes this renunciation, in fact and with full consistency. Man's acknowledged incapacity to scrutinize the ways of God means that he renounces in a loveless clarity man's accessibility to any meaning of the world. This renunciation brought all problems of this sort to an end. Outside of the circle of eminent virtuosos the belief in this consistency has not been permanently endured. This was the case because the belief in predestination—in contrast to the belief in the irrational power of "fate"—demands the assumption of a providential, and hence a somehow rational, destination of the condemned, not only to doom but to evil, while demanding the "punishment" of the condemned and therewith the application of an ethical category.

We have dealt with the significance of the belief in predestination [elsewhere]. We shall deal with Zoroastrian dualism later, and only briefly—because the number of the believers is small. It might be omitted entirely were it not for the influence of the Persian ideas of final judgment, as well as of the doctrine of demons and angels, upon late Judaism. Because of such influences, Zoroastrism is of considerable historical significance.

The third form of theodicy which we are going to discuss was peculiar to the religiosity of Indian intellectuals. It stands out by virtue of its consistency as well as by its extraordinary metaphysical achievement: It unites virtuoso-like self-redemption by man's own effort with universal accessibility of salvation, the strictest rejection of the world with organic social ethics, and contemplation as the paramount path to salvation with an inner-worldly vocational ethic.

9. *Religion and Social Status*

BY MAX WEBER

The Religion of the Peasantry

THE FATE of the peasant is so intimately bound to nature, so deeply dependent upon organic processes and natural events, and economically so little adapted to rational systematization that, in general, he turns to religion only when he is threatened with enslavement or proletarianization through internal—fiscal or manorial—or external—political—powers. Both instances—first external threat, then opposition to manorial and simultaneously urban powers, as was always the case in antiquity—pertained, for example, to the religion of the ancient Israelites. The oldest documents, especially the Song of Deborah, show that the struggle that had its center of gravity in the peasant confederations was directed against the town-dwelling Philistine and Canaanite land lords—knights fighting from iron chariots who were (as it was said of Goliath) "trained warriors from youth," and who sought to render tribute from the peasants of the mountain slopes down which "milk and honey flow." The confederations of the peasants are somewhat similar to those of the Aetolians, the Samnites, and the Swiss. They are also comparable to the Swiss to the degree that the great trade route from Egypt to the Euphrates created a situation having characteristics resembling those of Switzerland as a "thoroughfare state" (early money economy and cultural contact). That this struggle, just as the consolidation of the status groups and the expansion of the Mosaic Period, again and again took place under religious leaders in the name of Yahweh (Moschuach, Messiahs as the "judges," such as Gideon and others like him, were called) was a combination of factors of great importance. By means of this relationship, a religious pragmatism was introduced into the old peasant piety, which went beyond the level of the ordinary peasant cults. The cult of Yahweh, coupled with the Mosaic social laws, first became an intrinsically ethical religion in the polis of Jerusalem. As is shown by the social impact of the prophets, to be sure, this occurred under the in-fluence of the social moralism of farming townsmen pitted against the urban landlords and moneyholders and in the name of the Mosaic decrees for the reconciliation of status groups. Prophetic religions, however, are not specifically influenced by the peasantry. A typically plebian fate was co-responsible for the moralism of Hesiod, the first and only theologian of official Hellenic literature. But Hesiod certainly was not a typical "peasant." The more deeply a cultural development is peasant-oriented—be it in the Occident in Rome, the Far East in India, or in the Near East in Egypt—the more profoundly traditional is the population in its orientation and the more the religion of the common people lacks ethical rationalization. In the later Jewish and Christian religious developments, the peasant is either unconcerned with, or directly opposed to, rational ethical currents; in Judaism and in Christianity, such currents appear only in exceptional cases and then in communistic-revolutionary form. The puritanical Donatist sect in Romanized Africa—a province of the heaviest concentration of land ownership, to be sure—seems to have been very widespread in peasant circles, but this is the only such example in antiquity. The Taborites, in as much as they came from peasant circles, as well as the proponents of the doctrine of "divine right" in the German peasant wars, the English radical petty peasant communists, and, above all, the Russian peasant sectarians regularly have agrarian communist starting points in more or less pronounced communal institutions. They are threatened with proletarianization and turn against the official church, at first in its capacities as collector of tithes and pillar of fiscal and manorial powers. Such an involvement with religious demands is possible only on the basis of a pre-existing ethical religion containing specific expectations that can serve as connecting links to revolutionary doctrines of natural rights—the origin of which we shall treat subsequently. Such movements, however, did not originate in Asia, where a combination of religious expectations and revolutionary currents (in China) appears in a very different way and not essentially as a peasant movement. The peasants are very rarely the stratum that initially has had any kind of non-magical religion.

Translated by Christine Kayser, from Max Weber, "Stände, Klassen und Religion," in *Wirtschaft und Gesellschaft* (Tübingen: J. G. B. Mohr (Paul Siebeck), 1956), I, 285–314, with the permission of J. G. B. Mohr.

To be sure, to all appearances, the prophecy of Zoroaster appeals to (relative) rationalism in respect to ordered agricultural work and stock-breeding. It does this in opposition to the animal-torturing, orgiastic cults of false prophets—presumably like the intoxication cults with the bacchanalian mutilation of cattle, which Moses combatted. Since Parsiism considered only cultivated land as magically "pure," considered only agriculture, that is, as absolutely pleasing to God, it retained a pronouncedly agrarian and, in consequence, antiurban bent in its social ethics, even after profoundly transforming adaptations to the mundane world—which was contrasted to the original prophecy. In as much as Zoroastrianism activated economic interests for itself, these were initially more the interests of the princes and the landlords in their peasants' ability to pay rents and perform services, than they were the interests of the peasants themselves. In general, the peasantry remains oriented to weather incantations and animistic magic or ritualism, but when its orientation is based on an ethical religion it is a severely formalistic ethic of *quid pro quo* with God and priest.

The Urban Location of Early Christian Religion

The evaluation of the peasant as an individual who is particularly pious and pleasing to God is a thoroughly modern phenomenon. The very few exceptions to this include Zoroastrianism and isolated cases of opposition to city culture and its consequences, which are found among feudal-patriarchical groups and, conversely, intellectual, world-weary literati. None of the more significant religions of salvation in East Asia know anything of this. In Indian salvation religions, most completely in Buddhism, the peasant is religiously suspicious or directly tabooed (because of *ahimsa,* the prohibition on killing any living thing. Preprophetic Judaism is a religion that is still strong in peasant orientation. On the other hand, the post-exilic glorification of agriculture as the pleasure of God represents a literary and patriarchical opposition to urban developments. At that time, true religion already had a different appearance and later on, during the time of the Pharisees, it was completely changed. Within the late Jewish communal piety of the Cherubim, "countryman" was identical with "godless." The non-city dweller was religiously, as well as politically, a second-class Jew. For according to Jewish ritual law—as well as Buddhist and Hindu—it was practically impossible to live a really

correct life as a peasant. The post-exilic theology, particularly that of the Talmud, has practical consequences that are directly in conflict with the needs of peasant life. The Zionist settlement of Palestine still, for example, confronts an absolute barrier in the late Jewish theology of the Sabbatical Year.[1] For this, the east-European rabbis—in an attitude which contrasts with the doctrinaire one of German orthodoxy—first had to construe a dispensation based on the assumption of a specific divine sanction for this settlement.

In early Christianity, the heathen was designated simply as "countryman" (paganus). Moreover, the churches of the Middle Ages, in their official doctrine (Thomas Aquinas) treated the peasant basically as a Christian of inferior grade; in any case, their attitude toward him was extremely derogatory. The religious idealization of the peasant and the belief in the unique value of his piety are products of a very modern development. They appear first in Lutheranism, in very marked opposition to Calvinism and most of the Protestant sects, and then in the modern Russian religion that bears Slavophilic influences. They are connected, therefore, with church communities which, in their organizational form, to a very great degree are tied to, and dependant on, authoritarian interests of princes and nobles. The predominant interest of modernized Lutheranism (for this was not the position of Luther himself) was the battle against intellectual rationalism and political liberalism. In the case of Slavophilic religion idealizing the peasantry, the predominant interest was the fight against capitalism and modern socialism; whereas the "Narodniki," through the transformation of Russian sectarianism, hoped to connect the antirationalistic protest of intellectuals with the revolt of the proletarianized peasantry, against the bureaucratic church serving the ruling powers. They hoped, thereby, to religiously transform both. In any event, reactions against the development of modern rationalism, which was deemed to be the product of the cities, were involved to a large extent. In the past, in complete contrast to this, the city was considered to be the seat of piety. Even in the seventeenth century, Baxter perceived a marked furtherance of the development of piety among the weavers of Kidderminster in their relations to the metropolis of London—which were brought about by the development of putting-out industry. Early Christian religion is, indeed, an urban religion. As Harnack convincingly shows, the significance of Christianity increases, all other things equal, with increase in the size of the city. Loyalty to the Church in the

---

1. This text was written *circa* 1910, that is when the Zionist settlement of Palestine was just beginning. Trans.

Middle Ages developed most strongly in the cities, as did sectarian religion. It is highly improbable that an organized communal religion, such as early Christianity became, could have developed as it did outside of an urban—and that means, in the occidental sense, an "urbane"—communal life. Such a development presupposes the dissolution of barriers between tribes set by taboos, as well as the presence of the concept of "office" and the interpretation of the community as an "association" of corporate structure serving objective purposes. Early Christianity, for its part, very sharply facilitated the resumption of the already given conceptions and strengthened them during the incipient urban developments of the Middle Ages. These conceptions, however, were really fully developed exclusively in the area of Mediterranean culture. Their locus was particularly the Hellenistic world, but their culmination was found in Roman municipal law. Also, the qualities specific to Christianity, as an ethical religion of salvation and as an attitude of personal piety, found their genuine sustenance in the city; and again and again from there have generated new impulses against the ritualistic, magical, or formalistic reinterpretations encouraged by the preponderance of feudal influences.

The Knight of the Faith

The military nobility and all feudal powers are unlikely to be the bearers of a system of rational religious ethics. Neither the thought of a merciful Providence nor that of the systematic ethical demands of a transcendental God is congenial to the military way of life. Concepts such as "sin," "salvation," and religious "humility" are not only far removed from, but also deleterious to, the feelings of dignity of all politically dominant strata and above all to those of the military nobility. To accept a religion with such conceptions and to genuflect before the prophet or the priest would necessarily have seemed base and undignified to the military hero or to the aristocratic man—to the Roman noble, as late as the time of Tacitus, or to the Confucian mandarin. For the warrior, it was a commonplace to stand innerly steadfast before death and the irrationalities of human fate. His life is filled by the risks and adventures of temporal existence in such a way that he does not demand from religion and accepts from it only unwillingly anything more than protection against bad magic and ritual, ceremonially adequate to his sense of dignity and to the ethos of his social status. At most, he demands priestly prayers for victory or for an auspicious death leading to the heroes' paradise. The cultivated Greek also, at least in spirit, always

remained a warrior. The simple animistic belief in souls—which leaves the nature of the other world and even of this one completely undecided, but which, at any rate, is quite certain that even the most meager worldly existence is preferable to any existence in the realm of Hades—remained the normal belief of the Greeks until the time of complete depolitization. A way out was offered, relative to this belief, only by the mysteries, with their tender of means to the ritualistic improvement—to a certain degree—of the lots in this and the next world; a radical solution was present only in the Orphic communities with their doctrine of the transmigration of souls. To be sure, strong prophetic or reformatory religious fervor attracts also, and particularly, the nobility to the support of prophetic ethical religion, because it breaks through all status and class strata and because the nobility is usually first to adopt secular education. When the stage of the secularization of prophetic religion is reached, however, the nobility usually quickly drops out of the group which maintains religious fervor. The time of the religious wars in France already shows the conflict over ethical questions between the Huguenot synods and a leader like Condé. The Scottish nobility—like the French and English—finally almost completely abandoned Calvinism, within which it, or at least some of its strata, had initially played an important role.

Where religious benefits are specifically contingent on defending the faith, the dignity of feudal strata may indeed be compatible with prophetic religion. This conception presupposes an exclusive relationship to a universal God, together with the moral depravity of the infidels as His enemies, whose unregenerate existence excites His justified wrath. This conception is therefore absent in ancient occidental, as in all Asiatic, religion until the time of Zoroaster. Even in Zoroastrianism, however, there is no direct connection between the fight against the infidels and religious rewards. This connection was first established in Islam. The rudiments, indeed the pattern, for this were the promises of the Jewish God to His people—as they were understood and reinterpreted by Mohammad at a time after he, from a conventicle leader in Mecca, had become the podestá of Jathrib-Medina and, as a prophet, had been conclusively rejected by the Jews. The old wars of the Israelite confederations, led in the name of Yahweh, were transmitted to posterity as "holy wars." Holy war, that is, war in the name of a god, for the specific atonement of a sacrilege with its consequences of expulsion and complete destruction of the enemies and all of their possessions, was also not unknown in antiquity, especially to the Greeks. In contrast to antiquity, the specific phenomenon here, however, is that Yahweh commissioned His chosen people to enhance His own prestige by vanquishing His enemies. Because Yahweh became the universal God, the prophecy and the religion of the Psalms created, instead of the expectation of possession of the Promised Land, the more far-reaching expectation of the elevation of Israel, as the Chosen people, over all other people, who were, at some future time, to be compelled to serve Yahweh and to lie at the feet of Israel. From this, Mohammad created the injunction to holy war, which would terminate only in the subjugation of the infidels to the political power and tributory dominion of the faithful. Their extermination, in as much as they belonged to "religions of the Book" was not demanded; on the contrary, their preservation was enjoined—from financial interests, to be sure. The Christian holy war was the first to adduce the Augustinian formula, *coge intrare:* the infidels or heretics were permitted only the choice between conversion and extermination. The Islamic holy war, to a greater extent than that of the crusaders, was an undertaking oriented essentially to the feudal interests in rents from territorial acquisition, because it was more explicit about this. Pope Urban, nevertheless, very pointedly brought home to the crusaders the need of expansion for the sake of acquisition of feudal fiefs for their progeny. Under Turkish law, participation in holy war is still, in the rules for the distribution of Spahi benefices, an important qualification for preferential claims. Apart from the position of dominance, even in Islam, the expectations linked to war propaganda, especially that of Islamic paradise as a reward for death in a holy war, are, in the intrinsic sense of the word, as little expectations of salvation as are the expectations of Valhalla and of the heroes' paradise on the part of the Indian Kshatriya who falls in battle, or that of the war hero who becomes satiated with life as soon as he sees the son of his son, or the expectations of any other warriors' paradise. The elements of old Islam that represent the character of an ethical religion of salvation recede sharply abreast of the others as long as Islam remains essentially a warriors' religion. The religion of the celibate feudal orders, however, which was first created in the crusades against Islam and which corresponded to that of the Islamlic military orders has, at any rate, in general only formally something to do with salvation religion. This is especially the case of the Templars, just as it is with that of the Indian Sikhs who were driven to the idea of ruthless holy war as a consequence of the combination of Islamic ideas with an initially deeply pacifistic Hinduism. Finally, it is also the case with the warlike orders of Buddhist monks who were at one time

politically important. Here, even formal orthodoxy was often dubious.

Bureaucracy and Religion

Thus, the military strata—such as the feudal knights—stand almost uniformly in conflict with any religion of salvation or any community with a specifically religious organization. On the other hand, there is a different situation in military organizations employing career "officers" in a bureaucratic organization. The Chinese army has—just as every other professional group—its special god, a demigod canonized by the state. And the passionate partisanship of the Byzantine army for the iconoclasts did not stem from puritanical principles, but from the attitudes inculcated in its provinces of recruitment, which were influenced by Islam. Mithraism, however, as the basis of the religious organization of the community—which with its other-worldly expectations, was the rival of Christianity—played a very important role in the Roman army of the Principate, along with certain other favored cults not of interest here. Its role was played predominantly (but not exclusively) among the centurions—thus, essentially among the junior officers with their interests in the financial solvency of the state. In the Mithraic mysteries, the truly ethical pretensions alone are modest and couched in very general terms. Mithraism is essentially a ritualistic purity religion and is exclusively masculine; women, in sharp contrast to Christianity, are excluded. It is, in fact, one of the most masculine doctrines of salvation. At the same time, it is ranked into a hierarchy of initiations and levels of religious attainment and, in contrast to Christianity, is not opposed to participation in other cults and mysteries, which is not, in fact, a rare phenomenon. The cult of Mithras was, therefore, under the protection of the emperors from the time of Commodus, who first took the consecration—similar to the participation of the Prussian kings in Masonic Lodges—to the time of Julian, its last enthusiastic representative. Besides the this-worldly expectations, which were here, as always, connected to other-worldly ones, there were other factors that made this cult attractive to officers. The essentially magical-sacramental character of the dispensation of grace and the hierarchical advancement in the consecrations certainly played a role.

The same considerations made the cult attractive to non-military functionaries, in whose circles it was equally favored. To be sure, dispositions to salvation religion are also to be found elsewhere among civil servants. There are examples of this among the pietistic German civil servants and among the deeply pious generals of the eighteenth and nineteenth centuries, who appear with less frequency. This corresponds to the fact that bourgeois ascetic piety in Germany, as an expression of a specific "bourgeois" style of life, was congenial only to the civil servants and not to the business classes. However, as a rule, this is not the attitude of the ruling bureaucracy to religion. The absolute value standards of such a bureaucracy are always extensive dispassionate rationalism, on the one hand, and ideals of disciplined "order" and calm, on the other. A deep contempt for all irrational religion, combined with an insight into its utility as a means of control, usually characterizes the bureaucracy. This was true of the Roman functionaries in antiquity. It is true today of the bourgeois as well as the military bureaucracy.[2] The specific position of a bureaucracy toward religious things is given in classic form in Confucianism—total lack of any "need for redemption" and, in fact, for anchorage of ethics in anything reaching beyond this world. These are replaced with the conventionalism of a bureaucratic status group, which is purely opportunistic and utilitarian in content but which values aesthetic distinction. All emotional and irrational individual religion that extends beyond traditional animistic beliefs is eradicated. The ancestral cult and filial piety are maintained as the universal basis of subordination. The enlightened functionary "keeps his distance from spirits" and would be contemptuous of magical influence of them, whereas the superstitious functionary participates, the way some people in our culture do in spiritualism. Both are content to let magic thrive as popular (folk) religion, with contemptuous indifference, but both treat it with respect in so far as it enters into the recognized political rituals of their position. The unbroken maintenance of magic as a guarantee of submission, especially in the ancestral cult, made it possible for the bureaucracy to completely inhibit the development of an independent church and of all types of religion that organize the laity. In the interests of control of the masses, the European bureaucracy finds itself forced into official deference to the religion of the established church, although to some extent it usually innerly despises all religion that is taken seriously.

---

2. For example, during my own military service, there was a definite expectation in the officers' club, with the first appearance of Mr. Von Egidy (lieutenant-colonel of the reserves), that His Majesty would take the initiative to reform the military religious services: henceforth we would no longer be regaled with the old fairy tales—which no honest fellow could claim to believe—because the right of the comrades to criticize the orthodox doctrines was taken completely for granted. Because, naturally, nothing of the sort happened, it was not a big step to the suggestion that the church doctrines, just as they were, were the best fare for the recruits.

The Manifold Nature of "Bourgeois" Religion

In the religious position of the strata that are normally most highly privileged—the aristocracy and the bureaucracy—although there are considerable variations, certain tendencies to similarity can be discerned. The truly bourgeois strata show greater contrasts. These contrasts exist irrespective of the extremely sharp social conflicts that these strata develop within themselves. The "merchants," such as the ancient urban patriciate, are sometimes members of the most highly privileged stratum. However, they are sometimes pariahs, such as the propertyless itinerant peddlers. Or they may be a group that is factually powerful, and either privileged—although not in comparison with the aristocracy and the bureaucracy—or unprivileged, or even discriminated against, such as the Roman *equites,* the Greek *metics,* the mediaeval tailors and related traders, the bankers and substantial merchants of Babylon, the Chinese and Indian traders, and finally the "bourgeoisie" of the early modern period.

The attitude of the mercantile patriciate toward religion, independent of such differences of status, shows marked contrasts in all periods. The intense worldliness of their life is incompatible with prophetic or ethical religion. The great merchants of antiquity and the Middle Ages operated a specifically unstable, unsystematic, occasional "trade in money," financing the traveling traders who lacked capital. Historically, they were partly a city-dwelling nobility, which became wealthy through these occasional transactions but whose initial foundation was in real estate and, conversely, partly a merchant class, which acquired real estate with the intention of rising into the nobility. In supplying political demands for money, these great merchants are joined by representatives of capitalism, which is politically oriented to state contracts and credit and by representatives of colonial capitalism. Such capitalism is found in all historical periods. None of these strata has ever been the primary bearer of a religion of salvation or of ethical idealism. The more privileged the position of the merchants, the less they seem to be inclined toward the development of an other-worldly religion. The religion of the noble, plutocratic merchant cities of the Phoenicians was oriented entirely to this world and, as far as we know, was totally unprophetic. On the other hand, the intensity of religion and the anxiety before gods, characterized by somber traits, are very great. In contrast to this, as we see in the *Odyssey,* the ancient Hellenic seafaring and warrior nobility—which was a half-pirate and half-merchant-nobility—shows strong disrespect for the gods. The Chinese Taoist god of riches, which was almost universally revered by merchants, exhibits no ethical traits but has a purely magical character. Even the cult of the Hellenic god of wealth, Pluto, who, to be sure, is a god of agricultural wealth, forms a part of the Eleusinian mysteries, which, apart from purity and freedom from blood guilt, impose no ethical demands. Augustus, by a characteristic policy, tried to make the freedmen, with their very considerable financial resources, the bearers of the imperial cult by creating the ranks of Augustales; this stratum does not intrinsically manifest other directions of religious interest. That part of the Indian merchant class having Hindu religious interests, specifically the bankers who come from the class of large merchants or political money-lenders, are mostly Vallabhacharyas. They are, that is, followers of the Vishnuite priesthood of Goku-lastha Gosains, which was reformed by the swami, Vallabha. They practice a form of erotic devotion to Krishna and Radha, and their ritual meals in honor of the savior have been refined to the form of a sophisticated dinner. The great merchant organizations of the Guelf cities in the Middle Ages, such as Arte de Calimala, were politically good papists, but they often dealt with the problems raised by the church's interdictions against usury by highly formalistic casuistry and sometimes by direct evasion. The great and noble merchants of protestant Holland were, as Arminians, religiously political realists and the principal adversaries of Calvinistic ethical rigorism. Scepticism or equanimity toward religion were and are everywhere widespread attitudes among great merchants and financiers.

In contrast to these easily understandable manifestations, however, the formation of capital, or, to be more precise, the utilization of money possession for the production of capital, especially industrial capital, in a continuous, business-like, rational manner—utilization, therefore, in a specifically modern form—was in the past frequently and strikingly associated with ethically rational religious communities. In India's trade, there is a geographical division between the followers of Zoroaster (the Parsis) and the Jains. The Parsi religion is ethically rigoristic, especially in its unconditional commandment of truthfulness and even in its modernizing tendencies that interpret purity prescriptions as hygienic precepts. Its economic ethic initially recognized only agriculture as pleasing to God and abhorred bourgeois forms of business activity. The Jains, together with the aforementioned Vallabha-charyas, had the most specifically ascetic religion of all cults existing in India. (The Vallabhacharyas,

despite the antirational character of the cult, possess a doctrine of salvation that is the basis of an organized religious community.) Although the evidence is not adequate there seems very frequently to be a close association between the religion of Islamic merchants and that of the dervishes. Even in antiquity, the ethically rational religion of the Jewish communities was one of merchants and money-lenders. To a lesser, although still perceptible, degree in the Christian Middle Ages, the religion of heretical sects or groups bordering on sectarianism, although not necessarily associated with merchant communities, was still a type of bourgeois religion—the more so, the more ethically rational it was. Particularly, all types of eastern and western European Protestantism and sectarian movements, in very different ways of course, have combined most closely with economically rational and, where possible, with capitalistic developments. This includes the Zwinglites, Calvinists, the Reformed, the Baptists, the Mennonites, the Quakers, and also, but to a lesser degree, the reformed Lutheran Pietists and the Methodists, as well as Russian schismatic and heretical sects, especially the Stundists and the Skoptzi. The inclination to adhere to an ethically rational religion, which forms the basis for the organization of communities, becomes, in general, stronger the more one is removed from those strata representing a form of capitalism dependent upon political influence. Such strata have existed ever since the time of Hammurabi, wherever there were tax-farming, profits made from the state, war, sea-piracy, large-scale usury, and colonization. The inclination becomes stronger, the closer one is to those strata that represent modern industrial economy—the strata typical of the business class (in a sense which will be discussed later). The mere existence of "capitalism" of any sort clearly does not suffice to produce in itself a unified ethic, to say nothing of a religion of ethically organized communities.

Let us, for the time being, not raise the question of the type of causal relationship that exists between religiously rational ethics and a particular type of commercial rationalism. Let us only establish the fact that there is an association between economic rationalism, on the one side, and certain forms of ethically rigorous religion, on the other. Only occasionally is this found outside of the Occident, the abode of economic rationalism, but it is very clearly found within the Occident. And, to be sure, the more closely we approach the classical representatives of economic rationalism, the more clearly we observe this association between economic rationalism and certain forms of ethically rigorous religion, which will be more clearly characterized later.

The Atypical Religious Position of the Petty Bourgeoisie

If we now leave the socially and economically privileged strata, there seems to be an increase in the atypical elements of the religious position. Within the petty bourgeois class, especially among artisans, we find a great number of the most contrasting types. Caste taboos and sacramental or orgiastic religion of a magical or mystagogic nature in India; animism in China; dervish religion in Islam; the spiritual-enthusiastic religion of early Christianity, especially in the eastern part of the Roman Empire; deistical demonism together with Dionysian orgies among the ancient Greeks; pharisaical loyalty to the laws in the large cities of ancient Jewry; an essentially idolotrous Christianity, as well as all sorts of sectarian religion, in the Middle Ages; and all kinds of Protestantism at the beginning of modern times—these seem to be the widest conceivable variety of religious types. Early Christianity, to be sure, was from the beginning specifically an artisan religion. Its savior was an artisan from a country town. Its missionaries were itinerant artisans; the greatest of whom was an itinerant tent-maker's apprentice already so alienated from the country that in one of his epistles he uses an obviously false simile from plant-grafting. Finally, as we have previously seen, the Christian community was recruited primarily from the cities, especially from the free and unfree artisans. In the Middle Ages, the petty bourgeoisie was the most pious, if not always the most orthodox, stratum. However, within Christianity, an immense variety of religious types has apparently uniformly found an extraordinarily strong foothold within the petty bourgeois stratum. These types range from unconditional loyalty to the established medieval church, through the mendicant orders and the ancient spirituals who exorcised demons, to certain forms of medieval sectarian religion—such as that of the Orders of Humiliati, long suspected of dubious orthodoxy—and baptist movements of all shades, as well as to the piety of the various churches of the Reformation, including Lutheranism. There was, therefore, a most extensive variety, which at least proves that there never is an unambiguous dependence of artisan religion on economic factors. Nevertheless, the petty bourgeois stratum, compared with that of the peasant, exhibits a pronounced inclination to types of religion emphasizing congregational solidarity and an ethi-

cally rational orientation and also incorporating the idea of salvation. This contrast, it should be remembered, is far from being unambiguous. For example, the baptist movement first expanded into the territory of the open countryside (Friesland) and then, in its socially revolutionary form, found an abode in the city of Münster.

The natural basis of the fact that congregational forms of religion in the Occident are usually closely connected with the petty and middle bourgeoisie lies in the relative recession of blood ties, that is of the ties of the kinship group, within the occidental city. The individual finds substitutes for these ties in voluntary religious and occupational associations, which, in the Occident as everywhere else, are characterized by cults but no longer by elaborate taboos. The economic peculiarities of mere urban living as such, however, do not in and of themselves determine these relationships. The converse, rather, as is easy to see, is often the case. In China, the exceptional significance of the ancestral cult and of clan exogamy holds the individual town-dweller in a permanently fixed relation to his kinship group and his home village. In India, the religious caste taboos make the development of savior-oriented, congregational religions difficult or set limits to their importance in town settlements as well as in the country. In both cases, these phenomena restrict the development of the town into a "community" much more sharply than they restrict the development of the village. But, understandably enough, the petty bourgeois class, on the basis of its economic position, is inclined to an ethically rational religion when the conditions for its formation are given.

The Religion of Artisans

It is clear that the life of a member of the petty bourgeoisie, especially that of the artisan and small merchant, is much less dependent upon nature than that of the peasant. Dependence upon magical influence over the spirits of nature, therefore, cannot play the same role for him as it does for the peasant. On the contrary, his life conditions are essentially more rational, which means that they are more open to calculability and purposive rational influence. Furthermore, the economic position of the artisan and also, under certain conditions, of the merchant suggests to them the idea that honesty is in one's own interest, that loyal work and fulfillment of one's duty bring their own reward, and that honesty, moreover, is "deserving" of its righteous reward. They have, therefore, an ethically rational way of looking at the world, in the sense of keeping a moral ledger, which is attractive to all underprivileged strata. In comparison, the peasant turns to this type of moral calculation only after the destruction of magic through outside forces; whereas the artisan often actively abets this destruction. Above all, it is more congenial to the petty bourgeois when compared with the warrior or the very great money magnate, who is economically interested in wars and political power, both of whom are the least open to the ethically rational elements of religion. The artisan is, to be sure, at the beginning of the differentiation of occupations, very deeply entangled in a web of magical belief. For all sophisticated skills restricted to a few specialized trades tend to be believed to rest on magical powers of a personal or, more generally, of an hereditary character, the acquisition and maintenance of which are guaranteed through magical procedures. The possessor is separated from the community of ordinary people (peasants) by means of totems and taboos, and he is often excluded from the possession of land. The skills left in the hands of the old primary producing peoples, who offer their crafts first as "outsiders" and then as simple resident aliens therefore are condemned to the status of the pariah castes. Moreover, even the technical procedures of the artisans become stereotyped through attributing to them magical significance. Once this situation is broken down, the artisan thinks considerably more rationally about his work, and the small merchant about his business, than does any peasant. This happens most readily in the area of new urban settlements. Moreover, the artisan especially has the time and opportunity to brood during his work, at least during certain kinds of very sedentary work, especially in our climate. This is exemplified by the textile industry, which is everywhere permeated very deeply with sectarian religion. This applies with full force to the textile industry of the past; with limitation it still applies, under certain circumstances, to industry in which the modern mechanical loom is used. Wherever prophets or reformers break down the dependence upon purely magical or ritualistic ideas, the artisans and petty bourgeoisie consequently incline to an ethically and religiously rational view of life, which, to be sure, is often very primitive in nature. They have, moreover, because of their occupational specialization, a specific, markedly uniform "style of life." However, the determination of religion by these general conditions of artisan and petty-bourgeois life is by no means complete. The Chinese small merchants, who are exceedingly "calculating," do not have a rational religion. Neither does the Chinese artisan, as far as we know. In any event, they stick to Buddhist doctrines of Karma along with magic.

This absence of an ethically rational religion is here of primary importance and often seems to have restricted the rationality of their technology in a striking way. The mere existence of artisans and the petty bourgeoisie, in and of itself, never sufficed to bring about the formation of an ethical religion, even if we define the type in most general terms. On the contrary, we saw how caste taboos, together with the belief in the transmigration of souls, influenced and stereotyped the ethics of Indian artisans. Where once a congregational form of religion develops, especially an ethically rational, congregational religion, it can understandably easily gain members from urban, petty-bourgeois circles and then, under certain circumstances, effectively influence their way of life, as has actually happened.

Finally, the strata lowest on the scale of economic privilege—slaves and casual laborers—have never been the originators of a specific religion. The slaves in the old Christian communities were constituent parts of the urban petty bourgeoisie. The Greek slaves and the people of Narcissus, for example, belonged to one of the following groups: the relatively well-situated and independent household retainers or servants of very wealthy men; or, as was the usual case, the independent artisans who paid tribute to their masters and who hoped to save enough to buy their freedom—which was customary in all antiquity and in Russia as late as the nineteenth century; or, finally, the well-situated slaves of the state. It may be conjectured that the people of Narcissus (probably the famous imperial freedmen), who are mentioned in the Epistle to the Romans, belonged to the first-mentioned group. The adherents of Mithraism, as is shown by inscriptions, were also numerous within this stratum.

Ethical Religions of Salvation among the Underprivileged Classes

According to Diesmann's plausible hypothesis, the image of the ransom of the Christians with the blood of the Savior, into freedom from slavery to the Jewish Law and to sin was the product of Paul's reinterpretation of another relationship. This relationship is involved in the fact that the Delphic Apollo (just as surely other gods) indeed functioned as a bank for the deposit of savings, from which the slaves could purchase freedom from their masters. If this is correct—one must also take into consideration the transformation of the Old Testament *gàal* or *padá* as a possible source—then it is understandable how powerfully Christian proselytism appealed to this unfree, yet upwardly mobile, petty bourgeoisie with its economically rational way of life. The "livestock with speech" of the ancient plantations—the lowest slave stratum—on the contrary, was never a fruitful field for a congregational religion or for any kind of religious proselytism. The artisan apprentices of all times, moreover, who are normally separated from the independent petty bourgeoisie only by a lapse of time, have usually participated in religion that was specifically bourgeois. They have done so while often retaining, to be sure, a pronounced inclination to sectarianism. A most fertile field for all forms of sectarian religion was offered by the urban strata of the lower occupational groups—strata which struggled with the needs of the day, the fluctuations in the price of bread and opportunities to earn, and which relied on "fraternal help." The numerous secret or half-tolerated communities of "the poor," with their congregational religion that was sometimes revolutionary, sometimes pacifistic and communistic, and sometimes ethically rational, also regularly include the petty artisan stratum and the apprentices in their membership. This has an important technical basis in the fact that wandering artisan apprentices are the natural missionaries of every congregational faith of the masses. The momentously rapid expansion of Christianity over the formidable distance from the Orient to Rome within a few decades adequately illustrates this.

The modern proletariat, however, in as much as it occupies a special religious position, is distinguished by indifference to, or repudiation of, religion, as are broad strata of the truly modern bourgeoisie. Here, the actual need for reliance on personal achievement is crosscut—and thereby either cancelled out or overshadowed—by consciousness of dependence upon purely social, economic, and political circumstances. With respect to this, as has already been eloquently elucidated by Sombart, every thought of dependence on the course of natural cosmological and meteorological events or those events that can be designated as magical or providential is excluded. Therefore, the rationalism of the proletariat and that of a high capitalistic bourgeoisie cannot easily have a religious character. The rationalism of an high capitalistic bourgeoisie, which is in full possession of economic power, is the counterpart of that of the proletariat. They cannot, easily at least, create a religion. Religion here is normally replaced by other ideal surrogates. It is true that the lowest, and most insecure stratum of the proletariat, which is the least open to rational conceptions, can easily be attracted by emotionally toned evangelism. Sinking petty-bourgeois strata, which are semiproletarian in character or in permanent suffering, can also be attracted by such evangelism. The type of evangelism, however, is always one of a very special

magical character, or, if the true magic has been uprooted, one the character of which offers surrogates for magical orgiastic grace. Such grace is offered in the staging of methodically induced emotional orgies of the sort typical of the Salvation Army. Undoubtedly, emotional elements can far more easily flourish within such strata than can the rational elements of a religious ethic; at any rate, ethical religion is hardly ever the primary attraction.

A specific "class" religion of the underprivileged groups can only exist in a very limited sense. On the other hand, in some religions there are substantive implications for social policy, for example, specific measures that may be divinely ordained. In this connection, we must discuss briefly ethics and the conception of "natural rights." If the character of a religion, as such, comes into consideration, it should be understood that the need for salvation, in the broadest sense of the word, has a place among underprivileged classes. As we shall see later, however, this need does not have an exclusive place nor even the most essential one in the relevant religions. But this need is also far removed from the satiated and privileged classes, at least from the upper military, bureaucratic, and plutocratic groups.

A religion of salvation can, indeed, begin in a socially privileged class. The charisma of the prophet is not linked to status membership; it is normally linked to a certain minimum of intellectual culture. The existence of specifically intellectual prophets adequately proves both of the foregoing statements. But religion regularly changes its character as soon as it shifts to lay circles that do not specifically, according to their professions, concern themselves with intellectualism as such. It changes all the more when it shifts to those underprivileged strata that, for social and economic reasons, are indifferent to intellectual considerations. Indeed, on a general level at least, we can point out a normal characteristic of this transformation that is a product of unavoidable adaptation to the needs of the masses: the coming forth of a personal savior, partly human and partly divine, with whom religious connections are the condition of salvation. We have already recognized the transformation of cultic religion into pure magic as one form of religion adapting to the needs of the masses. Religion centering on a savior is a second typical form of such adaptation and is naturally connected with purely magical transformations in the most diverse ways. The further one descends the social-status ladder, the more radical usually are the forms taken by the need for salvation, once it appears. The Indian Kharba Bajahs, a Vishnuite sect, took the breaking up of the caste taboos with the utmost seriousness. This was theoretically common to many salvation doctrines. This sect established private—not purely cultic—commensality, but, consequently, it is essentially a sect of little people. At the same time, it carries the anthropolotrous reverence for its *guru* to the greatest extreme and thereby to the point of its own exclusiveness. Something similar occurs in other religions, particularly in those that recruit their members from low social-status strata or those that are influenced by these strata. The transmission of salvation doctrines to the masses almost always either provokes the development of a personal savior or increases the emphasis already placed on him. Other phenomena can be mentioned, which are related but which are found only in diverse and atypical forms. Such a phenomenon is the replacement of Buddha, which is an ideal type of intellectual salvation in Nirvana, with Bodisattva. A savior is substituted who descended to earth and who relinquished his own entrance into Nirvana for the sake of the salvation of his fellow men. Other such phenomena are the appearance in the Hindu folk religions, particularly in the Vishnuite religion, of the mediation of saving grace, through the incarnation of God in man, together with the victory of this type of salvation and its magical dispensation of grace over the eminently atheistic salvation of Buddhism and over the old ritualism connected with Vedic learning.

The religious needs of the petty and middle bourgeoisie show themselves everywhere in emotional legends that tend to be intimate and edifying, rather than in forms of expression productive of heroic myths. The appearance of these legends corresponds to the greater importance of household and family life and the gratification involved in it for these classes, in contrast to the dominant classes. This bourgeois transformation of religion into a genre is shown in the appearance of the divine immanence of Bhakti piety in all Indian cults, in the creation of the Bodhisattva figure, as well as in the Krishna cults. It is manifest also in the popularity of the edifying myths, such as those of Dionysius, Osiris, the Christ child, and several similar examples. The appearance of the bourgeoisie as a power which, under the influence of the mendicant monks, codetermined the style of piety meant, at the same time, the supersession of the aristocratic Theotokos—of the imperialistic art of Nicholas Pisano, by the genre pictures of the Holy Family as created by his son, just as the Krishna child is the favorite of the folk cult in India. The myth of salvation through a savior with its God who became human or its savior who became divine is a specifically popular religious conception, as is magic. It is, therefore, a concep-

tion that has been spontaneously developed in the most diverse places. On the other hand, the idea of an impersonal and transcendental ethical order of the cosmos, to which even the gods are subordinated, and the notion of salvation through integration with this order are intellectual conceptions appropriate only for specifically limited groups—groups that have had an ethically rational secular education. But this is also true of the conception of an absolutely transcendental God. All religions and systems of religious ethics, with only the exceptions of Judaism and Protestantism, in the course of their adaptation to the needs of the masses have had to rehabilitate the cults of saints, heroes, or functional gods. Confucianism does this in permitting the coexistence of the Taoist pantheon. Popularized Buddhism tolerates the divinities in the countries into which it expanded as recipients of the cult subordinated to Buddha. Islam and Catholicism have had to admit local, functional, and professional gods as saints who, in the eyes of the people, are the central objects of daily devotion.

Furthermore, the equal acceptance of women is a practice characteristic of the religions of underprivileged classes, which contrasts with the practices of the cults of the military aristocracy. The degree of acceptance of women and of their passive or active participation in religious cults or, conversely, the degree of their exclusion is everywhere a function of the degree of militarization—contemporary or past. The degree is extremely variable. In this connection, the existence of priestesses, the reverence for female soothsayers and magicians, in short, the highest devotion paid to individual women, to whom supernatural powers and charisma are attributed, tells us nothing in the least about the equality of women as such in the cult. Vice versa, in principle, equality in relation to what is considered divine, such as exists in Christianity and Judaism and to a lesser degree in Islam and official Buddhism, can coexist with monopolization by men alone of both priestly functions and the right to active determination of policy in the affairs of the congregation. These men are those who have been admitted to preparatory professional training or who are deemed qualified on other bases. This actually is the case in the aforementioned religions.

The great susceptibility of women to the appeal of all types of religious prophecy that are not exclusively military or political in their orientation is strikingly indicated by the uninhibited freedom in the relation of almost all prophets—of Buddha as well as Christ and perhaps also Pythagoras—to their feminine followers. This susceptibility, however, very rarely maintains itself after the first stages in the development of the community, during which spiritual charisma is evaluated as a sign of specific religious exaltation. A reaction to the spiritual experiences always sets in with the routinization and regulation of relationships within the community. This form of feminine behavior is considered disorderly and even pathological. This was already the case in the time of Paul. Finally, every prophecy, which has a political and military orientation, such as that of Islam, directs itself to men alone. Very often the cult of the military spirit directly serves the task of controlling and plundering the women's households. This is carried out by the inmates of the warriors' quarters organized as a casino or club. This can be seen in the Indian archipelago in the case of the Duk-Duk and in places wherein there have been similar manifestations of heroes' spirits. Wherever ascetic training of the warrior, with "rebirth" of the hero, prevails or has prevailed, women are considered to lack elevated, heroic souls and thus to be religiously inferior. This applies to most aristocratic or specifically militaristic communities organized as cults. Women are completely excluded from the official Chinese cult as well as from the Roman and Brahman cults. Buddhist religion, which is an intellectual one, is also not feminist. Even in the Merovingian period, the Christian synods could doubt the equality of value of the woman's soul. In contrast to this, certain Hindu cults as well as some of the Chinese sects of the Buddhist-Taoist variety have uniformly drawn their missionary strength from interest in, and equality for, women. This was also very true of early Christianity in the Occident and, later on, of the spiritualist and pacifist cults in East and West Europe. When it initially appeared, the Dionysian cult in Greece brought to women who participated in the orgies a completely unprecedented emancipation from all convention. As time went on, to be sure, the freedom became more and more stylized and regulated and thus restricted; it became limited to the processions and other isolated ceremonial acts in the different cults and thus, in its practical significance, completely vanished. The powerful advantage that Christian proselytizing had within the petty bourgeois strata against its most important competitor, Mithraism, was that Mithraism, an extremely masculine cult, excluded women. In a time of universal pacification, the adherents of this cult, in contrast to the adherents of Christianity, were forced to provide religious substitutes in other mysteries for their women, for example in the mysteries of Cybele. The unity and universality of the religious community, even within the family, was disrupted from the beginning. The effect was often similar in the

Gnostic and Manichaean intellectual cults and all other related varieties, even if the principles were not exactly similar. By no means all religions of brotherly love or love of the enemy have arrived at their conceptions through the influence of women nor are they all feministic in character. This was not at all the case in the Indian doctrine of *ahimsa*. The influence of women usually only accentuated the aspects of religion conditioned by emotion and hysteria. This was the case in India. It is certainly not important, however, that salvation religion usually glorifies the non- and antimilitaristic virtues, as this must be congenial to the underprivileged strata and to women.

The Relation of Salvation Religion to Class and Status Groups

The more special significance of salvation religion to the classes that are politically and economically disadvantaged, in contrast to its significance for the privileged classes, can be considered from an even broader point of view. In a discussion of "status groups" and "classes," we have to mention that the feelings of dignity of the most privileged (but not priestly) strata, particularly the aristocracy, that is the "distinguished people," rest on the consciousness of the "perfection" of their way of life as an expression of their qualitative "being." Their "being" is contained in itself, and in the nature of things is capable of being contained in itself and not extending beyond itself. The feelings of dignity of the underprivileged strata, however, rest on a guaranteed religious promise linked to an ascribed "function," "mission," or "vocation." For what they can not pretend "to be," they substitute either the dignity of what they will sometime become or the dignity of what they are fated to be in a future worldly or other-worldly life or (and usually at the same time) of the dignity of that which, providentially considered, they "symbolize" and "achieve." The hunger for a dignity that has not been granted them, according to the way they are and to the way the world is, creates this conception. Out of this conception arises the rationalistic idea of a "Providence," of a significance before a divine court with a different rank ordering of dignity.

These inner attitudes, turned outward toward the other strata, yield some characteristic contrasts concerning what the religions had to "perform" for the different strata. Every requirement for salvation is the expression of a "need." Being subject to social and economic pressure, therefore, although it is by no means the only wellspring of the development of doctrines of salvation, is naturally a very potent one. The socially and economically privileged strata, other things being equal, on their own initiative hardly ever experience the need for salvation. Rather, they ascribe to religion primarily the role of "legitimizing" their way of life and their position in life. This most universal phenomenon is rooted in completely general systems of factors. A person who, relative to the less fortunate, enjoys good fortune is not satisfied with the mere fact of his fortune. He also wishes to have the "right" to his good fortune over the others; he wishes to have the consciousness of having "earned" it, in contrast to the less fortunate who must have somehow "earned" their misfortune.

This spiritual need for the legitimation of fortune is discernible in every commonplace experience, whether it concern political destiny, differences of economic position, physical health, success in erotic competition, or whatever else. "Legitimation," in this inner sense, is what the privileged strata subjectively demand from religion if they demand anything at all. Every privileged strata does not have this need to the same degree. The gods are beings to whom envy is not foreign, especially in warrior heroism. Solon, as well as the ancient Jewish sages, agrees about the danger of high position. The hero claims a position above the workaday world in spite of the gods, not through the gods and often against them. The Homeric epic and part of the ancient Indian epics contain some characteristic contrasts to the chronicles of the Chinese bureaucracy and the Jewish priesthood. In the chronicles, "legitimacy" of fortune is given a much greater emphasis as the reward for virtues that are pleasing to God than it is in the epics. On the other hand, the connection of misfortune with the anger and envy of demons or gods is very widespread. Almost every popular (folk) religion regards physical infirmity as a sign of the magical or moral sinfulness of its victim or (in Judaism) of his ancestors. This is exemplified by the popular religion of the ancient Jews and, to a marked extent, by that of the modern Chinese. In like manner, the person afflicted with physical infirmity or other strokes of misfortune may not appear in the circles of the fortunate—those who enjoy God's favor—during the collective sacrifices of political groups. He may not appear because he is burdened with the wrath of God. Accordingly, in almost every ethical religion of the privileged strata, the individual's social privilege or lack of it is considered as religiously somehow deserved. Only the forms of legitimation of fortune vary.

The attitudes of the underprivileged strata manifest corresponding contrasts. Their specific need is the need for salvation from suffering. They do not always experience the need for salvation in religious form, as is shown, for example, by the modern proletariat. Their religious needs for salvation, where once they exist, can take different forms. The need can unite, especially in a very differently articulated way, with the need for just "compensation"—compensation for one's own good works and retribution for injustice perpetrated by others. Along with, and linked to, magic, an expectation and hope of compensation that are usually rather "calculating" are the most widespread form of belief in the whole world among the masses. Prophecies, which for their own part repudiate at least the mechanical forms of this belief, are again and again reinterpreted when they are popularized and made commonplace. The type and degree of hope for compensation and salvation bring about very different effects, according to the type of expectations awakened by religious promises and, of course, especially different effects when these expectations are projected from the worldly existence of the individual into a future that lies on the other side of his present existence. A particularly important example of the significance of the contents of religious promises is given in the exilic and postexilic religion of the Jews.

Factually since the time of the exile, and formally since the time of the destruction of the Temple, the Jews were a "pariah people." In the sense intended here, this means that they were a special community, which was closed on a hereditary basis and which lacked autonomous political organization. This came about by restrictions toward the outside, based initially on magic, taboo, and ritual in commensal and connubial relationships, on the one hand, and on restrictions on the political and social privileges of the community as well as a far reaching uniqueness of its economic position, on the other.

"Pariah people" is as little identical with the special position of the Indian "pariah caste," as is, for example, the concept of "Kadi justice" identical with the actual principles of justice practiced by the Islamic judge, the Kadi. The underprivileged, occupationally specialized Indian castes, with their closure to the outside guaranteed by taboos and their hereditary obligations to a way of life, are, relatively speaking, most like the Jewish groups, because, in their case also, hopes for salvation are tied to the pariah position as such.

The Indian castes show the same specific effects of a pariah religion as do the Jewish groups. The more the position of the pariah people becomes oppressive, and the more powerful, therefore, become their hopes for salvation—which they link to the divinely ordained fulfillment of religious duty—the more they chain their members to the group and pariah position. Precisely do the lower castes, as has already been mentioned, cling with special fortitude to their caste duties, as the condition for their rebirth in a better position. The more murderous the contempt and persecution heaped on the Jews, the more indissoluble became the tie between Yahweh and His people. For this reason, all of the repeated forced mass conversions of the Jews, which created the privileges of the ruling stratum for them, were in vain. This was a manifest contrast to the case of the oriental Christians, who under the Ommiads flocked in such masses to the privileged religion of Islam that the political powers increased the difficulty of conversion in the interests of the privileged stratum. The fulfillment of the special religious commandments to the pariah people was the only way to salvation for the Indian castes as well as for the Jews. No one could withdraw from these obligations without having to fear bad magic and without endangering his chances in the future and those of his descendants.

The difference between Jewish religion and that of the Hindu castes lies in differences in their hopes for salvation. The Hindu expects an improvement in his personal chances for rebirth from the fulfillment of his religious duties—that is, a reincarnation of his soul in a higher caste. The Jew, on the contrary, expects that his descendants will take part in a messianic kingdom, which will ransom his entire pariah community from its pariah position into one of dominance in the world. For when Yahweh promised that all of the peoples of the world would borrow from the Jews and that the Jews would borrow from no one, He did not mean that this promise would be fulfilled in the figures of small pawn usurers from the ghetto but in the position of a typically powerful ancient urban citizenry—a citizenry whose debtors and debt servants would be the inhabitants of subjugated villages and small cities. Both the Hindu and the Jew work for a future human condition. For the Hindu, this condition has something to do with himself only in terms of the doctrine of the animistic transmigration of souls: he works for the future incarnation of his soul. The Jew works for his corporeal descendants in a relationship to whom his own "worldly immortality" exists—a relationship that is also comprehended animistically. The Hindu does not in any way contest the social-caste structure of the world and the position of his caste in it. He wishes to improve the future lot of his individual soul directly within this same caste order. In contrast to this, the Jew expects his personal salvation in the form of a breakdown of the existing system of social ranks to the benefit of his pariah people. For God has not called and

elected His people to a pariah position but to a position of prestige.

Jewish Religion of Retaliation— Resentment

An element that Nietzsche first observed and that is fully absent in the magical and animistic religions of all caste systems gains great importance in Jewish ethical religion: resentment. Resentment, in Nietzsche's sense, accompanies the religious ethics of underprivileged people. The old beliefs bringing consolation through the assertion that the unequal distribution of worldly fortune is based on the sins and injustices of the privileged groups are directly inverted. The inversion postulates that sooner or later God must take his vengeance on the privileged people. In the form of this theodicy of underprivileged people, moralism serves to legitimize the conscious and unconscious thirst for revenge. Moralism then combines with the "religion of retaliation." If once the religious idea of retaliation exists, then "suffering" as such, can take on the color of something valuable in a purely religious sense, because suffering then conveys powerful hopes for retaliation. Certain ascetic techniques and certain neurotic predispositions can feed into this conception. Religions of suffering take on characteristcs of resentment only under very specific conditions. Hindu and Buddhist religions, for example, are not colored by resentment, because in these religions the individual has brought his suffering on himself. In Judaism, it is different. The religion of the Psalms is replete with the need for vengeance. One finds the same strain in the priestly elaborations of the early Jewish heritage: the majority of the Psalms very tangibly contain moralistic satisfaction in, as well as the legitimation of, the overt or painstakingly repressed needs of a pariah people for revenge. It is unimportant whether or not the relevant passages are perhaps subsequent interpolations into an earlier version that did not contain them.

This resentment occurs in the form of holding God responsible for one's own observances of His commands and for one's own misfortunes, as well as making Him responsible for the godless behavior of the proud and happy heathens who scorn His promises and mock His power. Or it occurs in the form of humbly acknowledging one's own sins, while asking God ultimately to overcome His wrath and again to bestow His grace upon the people that, after all, is His chosen people. Both of these forms contain the hope that God, finally placated, will turn his vengeance compoundedly against the godless enemies, converting them into Israel's footrest. This hope is offered in the priestly accounts of the Canaanite enemies of the people as long as Israel does not arouse God's wrath through disobedience, thus meriting its own abasement beneath the heathen. Some of these Psalms, as modern commentators suggest, may emanate from the wrath of the Pharisaic believers, caused by the persecutions under Alexander Jannaeus. Nevertheless, their selection and preservation is characteristic. Others are quite obviously a reaction to the pariah position as such of the Jews. There is no other universal God in any religion with Yahweh's thirst for vengeance. One can quite precisely spot the historical value of the factual statements in the priestly reworking of history: that the relevant events (such as the battle of Meggido) do not fit into the theodicy of retaliation and vengeance.

Jewish religion became one of retaliation *par excellence*. Divinely prescribed virtue is pursued in the hope of retaliation and, in the first instance, this is collective retaliation. The people as a whole are destined for pre-eminence over their persecutors. Only thereby can the individual regain his honor. Parallel to, and intertwined with, this is the individual theodicy of one's personal destiny, which was always taken for granted. The formulation of the problem of individual theodicy culminates in the Book of Job, which developed out of the elite strata. In renouncing a solution to the problem and in subordination to the absolute sovereignty of God over His creatures, Job anticipates the Puritan idea of predestination. The idea of predestination was bound to emerge as soon as the tension inherent in the idea of eternal damnation was added to the theodicy. But the idea did not develop in Judaism, as is well known, and the meaning intended by the author of Job remained almost fully uncomprehended, because in Judaism the idea of collective retaliation was so solidly established. For the pious Jews, the hope of revenge was unavoidably linked with the moralism of the law, because this hope permeates almost all the Holy Scriptures of the exilic and postexilic periods. For two and a half millennia, it received conscious or unconscious reinforcement in almost every religious ceremony of the people, who were bound in the two unbreakable chains—their religiously sanctioned segregation from the rest of the world and the this-worldly promises of their God. However, this hope of revenge naturally receded again and again in the religious consciousness of the intellectual stratum. Because the Messiah kept them waiting, it receded in favor of mystical communion as such, or in favor of a serene emotional trust in the benevolence of God and readiness for peace with the whole world. This happened especially when the social

position of the community, which was condemned to total political impotence, became somewhat bearable. In periods of persecution, such as during the Crusades, however, the hope of revenge was either again fanned into a piercing, although fruitless, appeal to God for revenge; or it was expressed in the prayer that their souls would "turn to dust" in the presence of the enemies who cursed them, and that their souls would be preserved from evil words and deeds and restricted to the silent fulfillment of God's commandments, and that their hearts would be kept open to Him.

In view of the broad historical changes within Judaism, it would be an unprecedented distortion to single out resentment as the one peculiarly decisive element within it, but one should not, of course, underestimate its influence on the basic characteristics of this religion. Relative to other salvation religions having characteristics in common with Judaism, this is one of Judaism's unique characteristics; resentment does not play such a conspicuous role in any other religion of the underprivileged strata. Of course, the theodicy of the underprivileged, in some form or other, is a part of every salvation religion having its membership in the lower strata. The development of priestly ethics, therefore, confronts this theodicy wherever it becomes a part of the communal religion indigenous to such strata. The almost complete absence of both resentment and socially revolutionary ethics in the religions of the pious Hindus and the Buddhist Asiatics is explained by the nature of the theodicy of rebirth: the caste system as such is eternal and absolutely just. The virtues or sins of a previous life are the reason for birth into a caste, and one's behavior in this life determines the chances for improvement. Therefore, there is no trace of that conspicuous conflict between social pretensions created by the promises of God and a despicable position in reality—the conflict that destroys a carefree life for those who live in constant expectation and fruitless hope.

The religious criticism of the godless heathens, which was returned with pitiless derision, was transformed into attentiveness to their own ritual virtue. This attentiveness was always vigilant and often bitter, because it was continuously threatened with secret self-criticism. To this was added casuistic brooding, which was inculcated over a lifetime, about the religious duties of the fellow believers. The grace of Yahweh ultimately was dependent upon the correct fulfillment of these duties. There was also added a mixture of despair about every meaning of this vain world, genuflections before the chastisements of God, concern about insulting Him through pride, and anxious ritual ethical correctness—a mixture that was characteristically salient in some of the products of the postexilic time. This was forced upon the Jews by the desperate struggle that was no longer for the sake of gaining the respect of others, but for the sake of gaining self-respect and a feeling of dignity. This feeling of dignity—even if the fulfillment of the commandments of Yahweh remained the final measure of one's immediate value in the eyes of God—always became itself precarious and could witness, therefore, the shipwreck of the total meaning of one's entire way of life.

For the ghetto Jews, a more tangible proof of the personal grace of God remained, in fact and to an increasing degree, success in business. However, for the Jews, this alone did not fit into the idea of a "validation" of a "calling" willed by God in the sense in which this idea is acknowledged in this-worldly asceticism. For, in comparison with the Puritans, the benediction of God is to a much lesser degree anchored in systematic, ascetic, rational prescriptions for living as the sole possible source of the certainty of salvation. Not only did sexual ethics remain anti-ascetic and naturalistic; not only was the ancient Jewish economic ethics very traditionalistic in its postulates and filled with an unrestrained and completely non-ascetic respect for wealth; but also the whole sanctification of work was supported by ritual. This sanctification, moreover, was often combined with the emotional overtones characteristic of religions emphasizing faith. As is self-evident, the traditional stipulations of Jewish economic ethics are fully valid only for the fellow believers, not for outsiders. This was the case in all ancient ethics. All in all, however, Yahweh's promises to Judaism, themselves have brought to fruition a strong current of moralism laden with resentment.

It would be very false, however, to represent the need for salvation, as well as either the theodicy or congregational religion, as the outgrowth of resentment alone—as, therefore, simply the result of a "morally expressed revolt of the slaves." This does not apply at all to early Christianity, even though Christianity extended its promises with the greatest vigor directly to the spiritually and materially "poor." In the contrast between the prophecy of Jesus and its immediate effects, one can detect the sort of consequences that had to follow from the devaluation and destruction of the ritual laws, the purpose of which was closure to the outside; one can also detect the consequences of the sequel to this—the dissolution of the yoke between the religion and the believers' position as a pariah people, closed as a caste to the outside. Certainly, the original Christian prophecy contained very specific aspects of "retaliation," in the sense of a future equal-

ization of fortunes and in the sense of the wrath belonging to God alone. This is seen most clearly in the legend of Lazarus. The Kingdom of God, even in this instance is a terrestrial kingdom—a kingdom obviously destined especially or primarily for the Jews who had long believed in the true God. But what is eliminated by the consequences of the new religious promises is precisely the piercing resentment of the pariah people. The danger that wealth presents to the chances for salvation—in those parts of the Bible handed down as Jesus' own gospel, at least—is not caused by asceticism. And that the danger cannot be caused at all by resentment is proved by the traditions pertaining to his transactions, not only with tax collectors (who were usually petty usurers in Palestine), but also with the wealthy people of high social standing. The indifference to worldly interests that is motivated by eschatological expectations is much too great for resentment. To be sure, if the rich youth wants to become "perfect" —that is, to become a disciple—he must unconditionally renounce the "world." But it is expressly said that everything—even the salvation of the rich who cannot decide to relinquish their possessions— although difficult, is nevertheless possible. "Proletarian instincts" are as alien to the prophet of an acosmic love, who brings the joyous message of Heaven's immediate nearness and of freedom from the power of demons to the materially and spiritually poor, as they are to Buddha for whom absolute separation from the world is a condition of salvation.

The limitations of the meaning of "resentment" and the doubtfulness of the all too facile application of the concept of "repression" are nowhere shown as clearly as in the error of Nietzsche who applies the concept to the entirely inappropriate example of Buddhism. Buddhism is the most radical antithesis of moralism of resentment; it is, rather, the salvation doctrine of a proud and aristocratic intellectual stratum that was as contemptuous of the illusions of this-worldly life as of the other-worldly life —a stratum that was recruited in the beginning almost exclusively from the privileged castes, especially from the warrior caste. Buddhism can be compared in social respects with Hellenistic, above all Neoplatonic, Manichaean, or Gnostic doctrines of salvation, as basically different as these are from it. He who does not wish salvation in Nirvana is not begrudged the whole world, including rebirth in paradise, by the Buddhist *bikkshu*. This shows that the needs for salvation and ethical religion have a source other than those of the social position of the underprivileged groups and the rationalism of the bourgeoisie, which is conditioned by the practical exigencies of its life. It has a source in pure intellectualism as such, especially in the metaphysical needs of the spirit that is compelled to brood about ethical and religious questions, not by material need but by its own inner necessity to comprehend the world as a meaningful cosmos and to be able to take a position toward it.

The Impact of the Intellectual Strata on Religion

To an extraordinary degree, the fates of religions have been determined by the different ways in which intellectualism has had an impact on them and by the various ways in which intellectualism has been related to the priesthoods and political powers. These relations, in turn, have been determined by the social extraction of the intellectual stratum. This stratum was, in the first instance, the priesthood itself, especially where the priesthood became a literary guild because the character of the holy scriptures necessitated interpretation and the teaching of the meaning and correct usage of their contents. This never happened in the religions of the ancient city peoples, particularly the Phoenicians, the Greeks, and Romans, on the one hand, or in the ethics of the Chinese, on the other. Consequently the modestly developed thought that was intrinsically theological (Hesiod) and all metaphysical and ethical thought fell into other than priestly hands. To the greatest extent, the contrary was the case in India, Egypt, and Babylonia, in Zoroastrianism and Islam, in ancient and medieval Christianity, and also in the theology of modern Christianity.

Certain priesthoods, to a large extent, have known how to monopolize the development of religious ethics and metaphysics. This was true of the priesthoods of the Egyptians and Zoroastrians, of the early Christians for a time, and of the Brahmans during the Vedic period, that is, prior to the development of lay ascetic philosophy and the philosophy of the Upanishads. It was also true of the Jewish priesthood, but to a lesser degree as there was a strong intrusion of lay prophecy; and also true of the Islamic priesthood, but likewise to a lesser degree as there was a partial intrusion of Sufi speculations. In all branches of Buddhism, Islam, and early and medieval Christianity, along with or in place of the priests, it was the monks or monk-like groups who were really concerned about, and who conserved, not only the theological and ethical thought but also all metaphysical and considerable parts of scientific thought as well as literary works of art.

Because the bards belonged to the people who were important in the cults, the epic, lyric, and satiric poetry of India was incorporated into the

Vedas; and the erotic poetry of Israel, into the holy Scriptures. This brought about the psychological affinity of mystic and spiritual emotions with poetic ones and the role of the mystics in the lyrics of both Orient and Occident. However, we are not concerned here with the literary works and their character, but with the imprint of the influential intellectual strata on religion itself. The influence of the priesthood as such, even where the priesthood was the main custodian of literature, varied greatly relative to the type of non-priestly strata opposing it as well as its own power position. The later developments of Zoroastrian, Egyptian, and Babylonian religions were indeed most strongly influenced by the priests. Judaism of the Deuteronomic and exilic periods was strongly influenced by the prophets and also by the priests. In late Judaism, the rabbi, rather than the priest, was the decisive figure. During antiquity, the high Middle Ages, and again during the Counter Reformation, Christianity was strongly influenced by priests and by monks. Lutheran and early Calvinist religions were greatly influenced by the pastors. To an extraordinary degree, Hinduism was formed and influenced by the Brahmans, at least in the center of its social and institutional aspects, especially in the caste system which developed wherever the Brahmans migrated. The social hierarchy of the caste system is ultimately determined by the positions given by the Brahmans to the various castes. Buddhism in all of its varieties, including especially Lamaism, was influenced throughout by the monks, and, to a lesser degree, so are broad strata within oriental Christianity. But here we are mainly interested in the relationship of the non-priestly groups—the monastic and lay intelligentsia —to the priestly groups, and the relationship of the intellectual strata to religion and their position within the religious community. One must establish the important, basic fact that all of the great Asiatic religious doctrines are creations of intellectuals.

The salvation doctrines of Buddhism and Jainism and all the doctrines related to them were upheld by aristocratic intellectuals with Vedic education (even if not always highly professional), which was the customary aristocratic Indian education. These doctrines were upheld above all by members of the Kshatrya aristocracy, who felt themselves in opposition to the Brahmans. The bearers of Confucian tradition in China, beginning with the founder himself, as well as Lao-Tse who is officially considered the founder of Taoism, were either civil servants with a classical literary education or philosophers with a corresponding education.

Almost all of the principal tendencies of Hellenic philosophy have their counterparts in China as well as in India—although often, to a sure, in a strongly modified form. Confucianism, as a valid set of ethics, had its adherents in the stratum of candidates for the civil service who had a classical literary education, whereas Taoism, of course, became a popular magical exercise. The great reforms of Hinduism were effected by aristocratic intellectuals with Brahmanic education, although to be sure the subsequent formation of the congregation fell partly into the hands of members of the lower castes. This formation of the congregation, therefore, took a different course than did the Catholic Counter Reformation in northern Europe, which was similarly the work of expert, clerically educated men, and the Catholic Counter Reformation, which first found its support in dialectically schooled Jesuits such as Salmeron and Lainez. The formation process of the Hindu congregation also differed from that involved in the transformation of Islamic doctrine (Al Ghazali), which was a process of fusing mysticism and orthodoxy. The leadership of this transformation remained partly in the hands of the official hierarchy and was partly the work of a new, self-made aristocracy of officials who were theologically trained. The Near Eastern salvation doctrines of Manichaeism and Gnosticism, however, are both, in the same manner, very specifically religions of intellectuals, with respect to their founders, their adherents, and the character of their doctrines of salvation.

Despite all the differences between these examples, the upholders of the relevant ethics or doctrines of salvation are the aristocratic intellectual strata with philosophical education—education corresponding to the type offered in the Hellenic schools of philosophy or the most refined sort of monastic or secular-humanistic, university education of the later Middle Ages. Within a given religious situation, the intellectual strata either establish educational organizations somewhat similar to the Platonic Academy and the related Hellenic schools of philosophy—and, as did these schools, take no official position toward the existing religious practices, which outwardly they do not shun but which they adapt to their own philosophical uses—or they simply ignore the religious practices. In turn, the official representatives of the cult—in China, the civil servants bearing the cult obligations and, in India, the Brahmans—evaluate the doctrines of the intellectual strata according to their own criteria of orthodoxy. For example, in China the civil servants considered the materialistic doctrines to be heterodox, just as they did the dualistic Samkhya philosophy in India. These movements, mainly formulated in intellectual terms and only indirectly connected with practical religion, do not concern us more closely in this context. We are concerned, rather, with the other movements that we mentioned above—movements specifically directed to the creation of religious ethics. In occidental antiquity, the closest parallels to these movements are suggested by the Pythagorian and neo-Platonic movements. These are intellectual movements that either develop exclusively within socially privileged strata or that are conducted or primarily influenced by groups derived from such strata.

The socially privileged strata normally are deeply committed to salvation religions when they have been both demilitarized and excluded from the possibility of, or interest in, political activity. Whether they be the aristocratic or the leading bourgeois strata, they turn to salvation religion either when they have been depoliticized by the power of a monolithic state with a bureaucratic and military character or when they themselves, for whatever reason, have withdrawn from politics—when, that is, the development of their intellectual culture to its ultimate cognitive and psychological consequences has primacy over their practical activity in the outer terrestrial world. This is not to say that these conceptions would arise only under such circumstances. On the contrary, under certain conditions, the relevant intellectual conceptions arise exactly during times of political and social disturbance, as a consequence of deliberation that has cut itself loose from conventional premises. But these states of mind are at first submerged. They regularly dominate only when the intellectual groups have been depoliticized.

Confucianism, the ethics of a powerful civil service, rejects doctrines of salvation in any form. Jainism and Buddhism, the radical antitheses to the Confucian adaptation to the world, were tangible expressions of an intellectual attitude that rejected the world and that was radically anti-political and pacifistic. However, we do not know if the once formidable membership of Buddhism and Jainism in India resulted from contemporaneous events that had depoliticizing effects. The small states that existed among the Indian petty princes at the time before Alexander, which were in contrast to the imposing unity of the Brahmans who were then everywhere gradually gaining ground, could not be the objects of an all-absorbing loyalty. These states were inclined to let the intellectually trained nobility seek their interests outside of politics. The Brahman's proscriptive abdication of the world in his old age as a Vanaprastha and the people's holding of his withdrawal as sacred were superseded by the development of the non-Brahman ascetics (Sramanas)—unless the reverse is the case, that is, it is possible that the recommendation to the Brahman who sees the son of his son that he should renounce the world is the more recent of the two phenomena and transmitted from the other. In any case, the Sramanas soon surpassed the official priests as the possessors of ascetic charisma in the popular estimates. A monk-like indifference to political affairs on the part of the aristocratic people in India was endemic in this form since very early times, long before the development of the apolitical doctrines of salvation.

The Near Eastern salvation religions—whether of a mystagogic or prophetic character, whether professed by the oriental and Hellenistic lay intelligentsia, and whether salvation doctrines of a more religious or more philosophical character (in as much as they reach into the socially privileged strata)—almost without exception resulted from the withdrawal of the educated strata from political influence and activity. This withdrawal was either forced upon them or freely accepted. Babylonian religion, which was interspersed with elements of non-Babylonian extraction, first made the switch to salvation religion in Mandaeism. The Near Eastern religions of the intellectuals made the switch first through participation in Mithraic and other savior-oriented cults and then in Gnosticism and Manichaeism. This also occurred after every political interest of the educated stratum had died out. Probably the educated Hellenic stratum always had doctrines of salvation, even before the time of the Pythagorean sects, but these doctrines did not dominate the leading political strata. The success in proselytizing that the salvation cults and the teachers of philosophical salvation had within the distinguished lay circles of late Greece and Rome parallels the final withdrawal of these strata from political activity. That somewhat garrulous, so-called "religious" interest of our German intellectual stratum at the present time is intimately connected with the political disenchantment and concommitant political disinterest of this stratum.

Generally, a disposition to the mysticism of "illumination," coupled with certain intellectual qualifications for grace, which we shall analyze later, is characteristic of the refined yearning for salvation that emerges in the privileged classes. This mysticism severely devaluates whatever is natural, bodily, or sensuous, because these—according to psychological experience—are considered to be temptations to divergence from this particular path to salvation. The heightening, the demanding refinement, and simultaneous repression of normal sexuality in favor of an ersatz abreaction, as conditioned by the way of life of the person who is nothing but an intellectual, may play a role in this context. This seems to be concretely suggested by certain appearances, namely those of the Gnostic mysteries—a subli-

mated auto-erotic substitute for the peasant orgies. This role even today cannot yet be subsumed by psychopathology under unambiguous generalizations. The natural rationalistic need of the intellect to grasp the world as a meaningful cosmos intersects with these purely psychological determinants of the irrationalism of religion. Products of this rationalistic need—which we shall soon discuss—are the Indian doctrine of Karma and its Buddhist variant, as well as the Book of Job in Israel, which presumably derived from aristocratic intellectual circles, and related problems in Egyptian literature, Gnostic speculation, and Manichean dualism.

A regular consequence of the intellectualistic origin of a doctrine of salvation, as well as that of an ethical system, is that when the relevant religion becomes a mass religion, either an esoteric doctrine or a dignified system of status ethics is developed. These are developed to accommodate the needs of the people with an intellectual education within the official religion—which has been popularized and transformed, by magic and the doctrine of salvation through a savior, to accommodate the needs of the non-intellectuals. Thus, the Confucian status ethics of the bureaucracy, which were entirely foreign to salvation, continue to exist together with Taoist magic as well as the Buddhist sacraments and ritual grace, which became petrified as the religion of the people and which were despised by the classically educated people. The salvation ethics of the monks within Buddhism likewise continue to exist along side of the magic and idolatry of the laity, and, similarly, magical taboos accompany new developments of Hindu salvation religion. Religions of intellectuals, however, can also take the form of a mystagogy with a hierarchy of consecrations—such as those of the Gnostics and related cults—from the attainment of which the unenlightened "Pistiker" is excluded.

The salvation for which the intellectual searches is always a salvation from "inner need." It is a salvation that is alien to life, on the one hand, and that, on the other, has a more doctrinaire and systematic character than the salvation from outer need to which the underprivileged strata are inclined. The intellectual searches upon paths, the casuistics of which lead into infinity. He does this in order to bestow upon his way of life a solidly based "meaning,"—a unity with himself, with humanity, and with the cosmos. It is the intellectual who effects the conception of the "world" as a problem of "meaning." The more intellectualism represses belief in magic, and thereby the more the events of the world become disenchanted and devoid of their magical meaning—leaving only "are" and "occur" but no longer " signify"—the more imperative becomes the demand that the world and the "way of life," each as a whole, be significant and "meaningfully" ordered.

The conflicts of this demand with the realities of the world, and its regulations as well as the potentialities for life in it, determine the specifically intellectual flight from the world, which can be either contemplative or actively ascetic and which can reach either for individual salvation or for collective ethical, revolutionary world transformations. This flight can be one into absolute solitude, or—more modernly—into "nature" (witness Rousseau) undisturbed by human arrangement. It can be a flight into a world-abdicating romanticism as well as a flight to be with the "people" (the Russian *umodnichestvo*) undisturbed by human convention. All of these tendencies, to which the apolitical intellect is equally accessible, can appear as religious salvation doctrines, as they have occasionally done. Thus, the particularly other-worldly character of the religions of intellectuals has here one of its sources. This philosophical intellectualism, which has been congenial to classes that on the whole have been socially and economically well off—primarily apolitical aristocrats and rentiers, as well as civil servants and incumbents of church, monastic, and university offices and offices of any other sort—is not the only one of religious relevance and often not the one of the greatest relevance.

Along with upper-class intellectualism, there is semiproletarian intellectualism, which is ubiquitously connected with upper-class intellectualism through gradual transitions and which differs from it only in its frame of mind. Petty civil servants and small benefice-holders of all times, who exist on the border line of subsistence and who have an education of a low level of importance, belong to the semi-proletarian intellectual type. Scribes, who in a time when writing was a special profession did not belong to the privileged strata, also belong to this type, as do primary-school teachers of all varieties, itinerant bards, readers, story-tellers and reciters, as well as people from similar free, semiproletarian occupations. The autodidactic intelligentsia of the underprivileged strata conspicuously belongs here —strata such as are most classically represented in contemporary eastern Europe by the Russian semiproletarian peasant intelligentsia and in the West by the socialist and anarchist proletarian-intelligentsia. The following groups, although with entirely different contents, also belong to this type: the Dutch peasants who retained their famous biblical traditionalism into the first half of the nineteenth century, the English petty-bourgeois Puritans of the seventeenth century, the religiously interested artisan-apprentices of all times and peoples, and, above

all, again in classical form, the pious Jews (Pharisees, Chassidic Jews and, on the whole, the mass of pious Jews who daily read the Law).

In considering "pariah intellectualism," the intensity of this intellectualism—such as that of all semi-proletarian holders of small benefices, the Russian peasants, and the more or less "vagrant" people—rests on the fact that strata that are outside of the social hierarchy or at the bottom end of it stand, to a certain degree, upon the Archimedian point in relation to social conventions and everything concerning the external order as well as customary opinions. People of this type of intellectualism for this reason are capable of taking an original position toward the "meaning" of the cosmos—a meaning unrestrained by convention—and of developing an intense ethical and religious attitude uninhibited by material considerations. In as much as groups belong to the middle classes, as does the religiously autodidactic petty-bourgeois stratum, their religious needs usually take either an ethically rigorous or an occult turn. The intellectualism of the artisan youth stands in the middle of both of these types and has its significance in the qualification of the artisan to go on a journey.

In East Asia and India, a far as is known, there is an almost complete absence of pariah or pettybourgeois intellectualism, because the communal feeling, which is a precondition of petty-bourgeois intellectualism, is missing among the urban citizens; and because the emancipation from magic, which is a precondition of either type of intellectualism, is also missing. Even their Ghatas, who operate among the lower classes, take the forms of religion predominantly from the Brahmans. In China, there is no independent, unofficial intellectualism over against the Confucian culture. Confucianism is the ethics of the "superior person," or the "gentleman" (as Dvŏrak so correctly translated). It is very decidedly a system of status ethics or, to be more precise, a system of etiquette of a superior stratum with a literary education. So far as we know, it was similar in the Orient during antiquity and in Egypt: the intellectualism of the scribes, in as much as it led to ethical religious contemplation, belongs to a type of intellectualism that, under certain conditions, is apolitical but that is always dignified and antibanausic.

In Israel, it is different. The author of the Book of Job presupposed that the aristocratic families were the upholders of religious intellectualism. The wisdom of the Proverbs and all that is related to it show, even in their form, that their character was influenced by a cosmopolitan culture and by a reciprocal influence between the higher apolitical and cultured strata, such as were common in the Orient after Alexander. The Proverbs show themselves to be partially the direct works of a non-Jewish king and all of the literature stamped with "Solomon" has something of the character of cosmopolitan culture. Even when the son of Sirach wishes to emphasize the wisdom of the fathers as against the Hellenization, there is proof of this tendency. As Bousset rightly stresses, according to the Book of Sirach, the "scriptural scholar" of every age is a world-travelled gentleman and a man of culture. Throughout the book, there is—as Meinhold also emphasizes—a markedly antibanausic note, exactly like that of the Greeks: how can the peasant, the smith, and the potter have "wisdom," which can only be unlocked by the leisure to deliberate and to devote oneself to studies?

If Ezra is designated as the "first scriptural scholar," still there are other positions both earlier and more recent. On the one side, the influential position of the monks who were interested only in religion and who congregated around the prophets, the ideologists without whom the codification of Deuteronomy would not have succeeded, is much earlier. On the other side, the towering position of the scriptural scholars—the position of the Hebrew-speaking commentators on the divine commandments, which is practically equivalent to that of the Islamic mufti—is a position considerably more recent than that of this official creator of the theocracy who was commissioned by the Persian king. The social position of the scriptural scholars underwent changes. In the time of the Maccabean kingdom, piety—basically a very sober practical wisdom somewhat like hospitality—and "culture" are identical; this (*musar, paideia*) is the path to virtue and is considered capable of being taught in the same sense as it is by the Greeks. To be sure, the pious intellectual at that time already feels himself sharply opposed to the wealthy and conceited people among whom loyalty to the Law is rare, just as do most of the Psalmists. They belong, however, to a social class of the same rank.

On the other hand, the schools of scriptural scholars of the Herodian times produced a semiproletarian stratum of interpreters of the Law. These interpreters, as spiritual advisors, preachers, and teachers in the synagogues—they also had their representative in the Sanhedrin—had an impact on the popular piety of the community of Jews who were rigorously observant of the Law (*Chaberim*) in the sense of the Peruschim (*Pharisaioi*). They did this with a mounting inner distress and tension resulting from the obvious inevitability of foreign domination. This type of activity was then carried over into the communal civil service of the Rabbinate of the Talmudic Period. As a result of op-

position to them, there ensued an enormous expansion of petty-bourgeois and pariah intellectualism, the like of which cannot be found among any other people: Philo already considered the spread of the art of writing as well as the spread of systematic education in casuistic thinking by a kind of "universal primary school" to be a specific feature of the Jews. It was foremost the influence of the stratum of interpreters of the Law that replaced the activity of the prophets among the Jewish urban citizens with the cult of loyalty to the Law and of religious study of the Law by the Book.

Petty-Bourgeois Intellectualism in Judaism and Early Christianity

This popular Jewish intellectual stratum, to which all mysteries were completely foreign, was decidedly socially inferior to the strata of philosophers and mystagogues of Near Eastern Hellenistic society. No doubt, however, an intellectualism that ramified throughout the different social strata already existed during the pre-Christian era in the Hellenistic Orient. This intellectualism, by means of allegory and speculation, produced similar dogmas concerning a savior in the various sacramental cults of salvation and in the consecrations, as had been done by the Orphics who, indeed, mostly belonged to the middle strata. These mysteries and speculations about salvation through a savior were well known and hated by at least one scriptural scholar of the Diaspora—Paul. The cult of Mithras was spread in Cilicia as the faith of the pirates at the time of Pompey, even if explicit written evidence is given for its existence specifically in Tarsus only after the time of Christ. It is probable, however, that hopes of salvation through a savior of the most diverse forms and origins existed also within Judaism for a long time, especially within provincial Judaism; otherwise the king of the poor people coming upon the beast of burden, along with the future monarch of the dominant Jewish people, would not have already existed in the prophetic time, and the idea of the "Son of Man" (perceptibly a Semitic grammatical construction) would not have been conceived. Lay intellectualism, however, be it either noble or pariah intellectualism, in some way always participates in every complicated doctrine of salvation through a savior—every doctrine that transcends the myths oriented to purely natural events and that transcends the straightforward prophecy of a good king of the future, who already exists somewhere in obscurity; it participates in every such doctrine that unfolds abstractions and opens cosmic perspectives.

.e influence of the scriptural scholars and the .llectualism of the petty bourgeoisie, which it stered, penetrated from Judaism into early Christianity. Paul, an artisan, was a very prominent representative of the type that strongly opposed the antibanausic philosophy of the Sirach Era, as were also apparently many of the later Jewish scholars. Of course, there is something more specific about Paul than just this characteristic: his "spirit," although far removed from what the speculative, Hellenistic-oriental intelligentsia understood by "spirit," nevertheless later on could give a foothold to Marcionism. An element of intellectualism is hidden in the pride that only those who are called by God understand the meaning of the Master's parables. In the case of Paul, this intellectualism is very explicit in the pride that the true recognition is a "vexation to the Jews and a folly to the Greeks." His dualism of "flesh" and "spirit," although imbedded in another conception, has an affinity with the position of typical intellectual doctrines of salvation on sensuality; there seems to exist a presumably somewhat superficial connection to Hellenic philosophy.

Paul's conversion is not only a vision in the sense of an hallucinatory vision; it is simultaneously an inner pragmatic synthesis of the personal destiny of the Resurrected One with the general conceptions of the oriental doctrines concerning a savior and the practices of the cults that were well known to him. Within this synthesis, Paul integrated the promises of the Jewish prophecy. His epistles are extremely typical, in their argumentation, of the dialectics of petty-bourgeois intellectualism; one is astonished at the degree of "logical phantasy" that, in a writing such as the Epistle to the Romans, he presupposes within the strata to which he directs himself. To be sure, nothing is more certain than that it was not really his doctrine of justification that was received at that time, but, rather, his conception of the relation between spirit and the congregation and the manner of relative adaptation to the everyday states of affairs in the surroundings. But the furious wrath, directed against him, by the Jews of the Diaspora—to whom his dialectical method must have appeared as an insolent misuse of scriptural education—only shows how precisely that method corresponded to this type of petty-bourgeois intellectualism. Paul still carried on then in the charismatic position of the teacher (*didaskaloi*) within the old Christian communities (still in the *didache*), and Harnack finds in the Epistle to the Hebrews an example of his method of exposition.

With the gradual appearance of a greater and greater monopolization of the spiritual leadership of the congregation by the bishops and presbyters,

Paul then disappeared. The apologetic intellectuals appeared on the scene. Thereafter, the church fathers and theologians who had received an Hellenistic education and who were almost all members of the clergy, and the theologically dilettante Emperor appeared. Finally, after the iconoclastic struggle, the upper hand was won in the East by the monks who were recruited from the lowest non-Hellenic social strata. The type of formalistic dialectics that was common to all of these circles and that was connected with the half-intellectualistic and half-primitively magical ideal of self-deification was never again competely uprooted in the Eastern church.

The critically important factor for the destiny of early Christianity was that it was a salvation doctrine that, from the beginning, with the greatest awareness and thoroughness opposed intellectualism. Christianity was such a doctrine of salvation in its genesis; it was such a doctrine for its typical adherent. For the adherent, what was decisive was that it was a salvation doctrine in the content of its religious way of life. Christianity was such a doctrine even though it may have borrowed some of the parts of its myth of salvation—which it had in common with the general oriental outlook—and may have directly transformed other parts of its myth, and even though Paul may have taken over the methods of the scriptural scholars. This doctrine opposed the Jewish ritual-legal learnedness as well as the doctrines of salvation of the Gnostic, intellectual aristocracy and finally it completely opposed the ancient philosophy. Christianity is unique in that the Gnostic degradation of the "Pistiker" is rejected, in that the "poor in spirit" are the spiritually blessed and that "learned ones" are not the exemplary Christians. It is unique in its way to salvation. Trained knowledge is not the way—whether this knowledge consist of knowing the Law, knowing the cosmic or psychological foundations of life and suffering, knowing the conditions of life in this world, knowing the secret meanings of the rites, or understanding the future destiny of the soul in the other world. Christianity is also unique by virtue of the fact that quite an essential part of its early church history, including the creation of dogmas, represents self-assertion against intellectualism in all of its forms.

If one wishes to characterize briefly the different strata that were the recipients and propagators of the so-called world religions, then these would be: the bureaucrat who regulates the world for Confucianism; the magician who regulates the world for Hinduism; the mendicant monk who wanders through the world for Buddhism; the warrior who subjugates the world for Islam; the itinerant merchant for Judaism; and the itinerant craftsman for Christianity. These phrases characterize strata, not as exponents of their occupations or of material "class interests," but as ideologists of such ethical systems or doctrines of salvation as could be especially easily espoused within their social positions.

Apart from the official legal and theological schools and the temporary florescence of scientific interests, Islam, within the character of its own specific religion, could have experienced intellectualistic inroads only with a simultaneous penetration of Sufism. But its orientation was not in this direction; precisely the rational element is missing in the popular dervish piety. Only a few isolated, heterodox sects in Islam—although occasionally very influential—have a specifically intellectualistic character. In other respects, Islam developed the beginnings of scholasticism within its universities just as did medieval Christianity.

We cannot dwell here upon the relationship of intellectualism to religion in medieval Christianity. In any case, the religion, in its sociologically relevant effects, was not mainly influenced by intellectualistic elements. The important influence of monastic rationalism lies in the area of its cultural content. This could be clearly elucidated only by a comparison of Western with oriental and Asiatic monasticism, as will be briefly sketched later. This is the case because the peculiarities of the cultural influence of the occidental church are based on the peculiarities of occidental monasticism. During the Middle Ages in the Occident, there was neither lay intellectualism of a petty-bourgeoisie character nor pariah intellectualism, to any important extent. Occasionally, these are found within the sects.

The role of the aristocratic, educated strata was far from negligible within the church development. The educated strata of the Empire during the Carolingian, Ottonian, and Salian-Hohenstaufen periods tended to favor a theocratic type of organization of culture under the emperor, as did the Ossipian monks in Russia during the sixteenth century. The Gregorian Reform Movement and the power struggle of the papacy, however, were highly dependent upon the ideology of an aristocratic, intellectual stratum, which established a common front with the developing bourgeoisie against the feudal powers. The papacy strove to monopolize the distribution of the vast supply of benefices for fiscal reasons and matters of patronage. With this striving of the papacy to monopolize the benefices, which economically sustained the educated stratum, and with the accelerated expansion of university education, this increasingly expanded stratum of beneficiaries turned from the papal power. At first, they turned essentially towards economic-nationalist interests in monopoly. Later, after the schism, this stratum also

turned ideologically against the papal powers and thus belonged to the "bearers" of the Conciliar Reform Movement and later on of humanism. The sociology of the humanists—although interesting, especially the change from a feudal and clerical type of education to education centering in the court and its patronage of learning, and the consequences of this change—cannot be treated here. Predominantly ideological motives determined the ambivalent behavior of this group in the religious schism. Insofar as this group placed itself in the service of education for the Reformation or Counter Reformation Church, it played an important organizing and systematizing role—a role, however, that was never of decisive importance. But insofar as this group was the representative of a specific religion—in fact there was a whole series of religiously separate types —it was without permanent effect.

These classically educated, humanistic strata, corresponding to their standard of living, were generally antibanausic and antisectarian in their attitudes. They were unfriendly to the strife, and, above all, to the demogogy of the priests and preachers. Thus, they were generally Erastian or irenic in their attitudes and, for this reason, condemned to an increasing loss of influence.

Along with their witty skepticism and their rationalistic enlightenment, one finds a religion emphasizing gentle moods among them, especially in the Church of England; or a serious, often ascetic moralism, as in the circles of Port Royal; or an individualistic mysticism, as during the early stages of the movement in Germany and also Italy. But the kind of struggles waged by those groups whose economic and political interests were involved, where not carried on by direct force, were carried on naturally by demogogy. These were struggles the demands of which were beyond the capacities of these circles.

Plebeian Intellectualism and Sectarian Religion

Certainly, at least those churches wishing to have the dominant strata and above all the universities in their service needed the classically educated people —theological apologists and similarly educated preachers. In Lutheranism, corresponding to its alliance with the power of the princes, the combination of education and religious activity quickly retreated in essentials to professional theology. Furthermore, *Hudibras* mocked the Puritan circles because of their philosophical learnedness. But among the Puritans and especially among the Baptist sects, it was not upper-class intellectualism that gave them their unbreakable power of resistance, but rather plebeian and occasionally pariah intellectualism— as with the Baptists in the beginning of their movement, which was spread by itinerant craftsmen and apostles. There was no specific stratum of intellectuals with special living conditions, which was connected with these movements. After the brief period of the itinerant, missionizing preachers, the middle class became permeated with the ideas of these movements. The unprecedented expansion of knowledge of the Bible and interest in the most abstruse and subtle dogmatical controversies, as was found in seventeenth century Puritan circles, extended deeply even into the peasantry. A religious mass intellectualism was created, such as is not found again and which can be compared, in the past, only with late Jewish mass intellectualism and that of the Pauline missionary congregations.

The Communities of the Religiously "Enlightened"

When, in the religious struggle, it appeared that the spheres of power had been tested and fixed, this mass intellectualism rapidly collapsed—at least in England, in contrast to Holland, parts of Scotland, and the American colonies. But the intellectualism of the Anglo-Saxon aristocracy perpetuated from that time on its unique characteristics—namely its traditional deference to a deistic religion of enlightenment, which is conceived of as vaguely liberal but never antagonistic to the Church. We cannot explore this more fully here. These characteristics, however, which have been conditioned both by the traditional position of the politically powerful bourgeoisie and by moralistic interests—by, that is, plebian intellectualism—contrast most sharply with characteristics of the essentially courtly, aristocratic culture of the Romance countries, as this culture developed radical animosity or complete indifference to the Church. Both of these developments, which are equally antimetaphysical in their end results, contrast with the development of German aristocratic culture.

The German culture was determined by very concrete circumstances and only negligibly (mainly negatively) by such sociological ones. This culture was neither oriented toward, nor hostile to, politics, but not without political implications, and metaphysically it was very little oriented to specific religious needs, least of all to needs for "salvation." German plebeian and pariah intellectualism, on the contrary, took an increasingly radical antireligious turn—a tendency that became concrete at the beginning of socialist, economically eschatological belief.

This antireligious tendency was also characteristic of the same types of intellectualism in the Romance countries, but it contrasts with tendencies of those in Anglo-Saxon countries, wherein the most serious religion (since the Puritan Era) did not have an institutional-authoritarian but rather a sectarian character. Only these antireligious sects control a declassed intellectual stratum, which, at least for a time, has the capacity to sustain a semireligious faith in the socialist eschatology. The more the economically interested groups take the representation of their interests into their own hands, the more this "academic" element recedes. The inescapable disenchantment with the almost superstitious glorification of "science" as the possible producer or even prophet of the violent or peaceful social revolution, in the sense of salvation from class domination, does the rest. Consequently, syndicalism—the only variety of socialism in western Europe that can really be viewed as something equivalent to a religious belief—easily falls into the position of becoming a romantic sport of blasé people.

The last great semireligious intellectual movement was that of the Russian revolutionary intelligentsia. This movement has a semireligious character inasmuch as it contained a belief that was shared in its important points even though this belief was not homogeneous. Upper-class academic and noble intellectuals kept company with plebeian intellectuals. The plebeian intellectuals were semiproletarian civil servants, especially those in the autonomous administrative organizations (the so-called "third element"), who were highly trained in their sociological thinking and in their universal cultural interests. They were also journalists, elementary-school teachers, apostles of the revolution, and a peasant intelligentsia that grew out of social conditions peculiar to Russia. This entailed a movement which began in the seventies of the last century with the development of the so-called *Narodnichestvo* (a movement with a romantic conception of the "people"). This movement was oriented by conceptions of natural rights that tended toward agrarian communism. In part, this movement came into marked conflict with Marxian dogmas in the nineties; and in part it merged with them in various ways. Several times attempts were made to bring this philosophy into some kind of vague connection with, first, the religion of the Slavophilic romantics and, then, with mystical religion or religious enthusiasm. Among some intellectual strata—and, to be sure, relatively broad strata—however, this movement, under the influence of Dostoevsky and Tolstoy brought about an ascetic or an acosmic personal way of life. After the catastrophe of the Russian Revolution (of 1906), the manner in which this movement, which is very sharply permeated with the Jewish semiproletarian intelligentsia who are ready to make every sacrifice, will manifest its vitality is indeterminant.

In western Europe, ever since the seventeenth century, the rationalistic religious strata in Anglo-Saxon and, more recently, French cultural areas have created unitarian, deistic or syncretic, aetheistic or religiously independent congregations, within which now and then Buddhist conceptions—or ones that pass for Buddhist—have played a part. Such conceptions have found a permanent foothold in Germany in almost the same circles as did Free Masonry, that is, among the economically disinterested people, and especially among the communal one-vote men as well as the declassed ideologists and separate semi- or totally proletarian educated strata. On the other hand, the Hindu (Brahma-Samaj) and the Persian enlightenment in India is a product of contact with European culture. The practical cultural significance was greater in the past than it is at the present time, at least.

The chances for the development of a religion that could be the basis for a genuine congregation and that would be supported by the intellectuals appear very unfavorable. They are made unfavorable by the interest of the privileged strata in the retention of the existent religion as a means of control and by their need for social distance as well as their aversion to the work of mass enlightenment, which is destructive to their prestige. They are also made unfavorable by the reasoned belief of the privileged strata that a new confession, which would be really literally acceptable to the broad strata, could not be substituted for the traditional creeds. (In any case, everyone always discounts something from the traditional texts—the orthodox, 10 per cent; and the liberals, 90 per cent). Above all, the chances of such a development are made unfavorable by the contemptuous indifference to religious problems and the church on the part of the privileged strata. For them, fulfilling the very few burdensome formalities of the church, in the end, is no heavy sacrifice, since everyone knows that they are mere formalities, best fulfilled by the protectors of orthodoxy and the protectors of status conventions and are fulfilled because the state demands them for one's career. The need, however, of literary, academically respectable intellectuals and of coffeehouse intellectuals not to bypass "religious" feelings in the inventories of their sources of sensation and objects of discussion, the needs of writers to write books about these interesting problems, and the still more effective needs of resourceful publishers to sell such books can counterfeit, to be sure, the appearance of very extensive "religious interests." However, they can do nothing to change the fact that out of such needs of intellectuals and their chattering, a new religion has never yet developed and that the fashion that brought up this subject of conversation and publication will again set it aside.

Section C

Expressive Symbolism

Editorial Foreword, BY TALCOTT PARSONS   *1165*

1. *Expression in Reference to the Body,* BY SIR CHARLES BELL   *1167*
2. *The Expression of the Emotions,* BY CHARLES DARWIN   *1168*
3. *Language in the Phase of Sensuous Expression,* BY ERNST CASSIRER   *1170*
4. *Life-Symbols: The Roots of Sacrament,* BY SUZANNE LANGER   *1179*
5. *The Art of Magic and the Power of Faith,* BY BRONISLAW MALINOWSKI   *1189*
6. *The Nature and Functions of Ceremonials,* BY A. R. RADCLIFFE-BROWN   *1191*
7. *An Incongruous Assortment of Incongruities,* BY KENNETH BURKE   *1200*

Expressive Symbolism

by Talcott Parsons

T HE LAST SECTION OF PART Four is devoted to the difficult subject of expressive symbolism as a component of culture. As noted in the general Introduction to Part Four, this is, theoretically, the least developed field of cultural analysis, in the period from which our selections are drawn and probably at the present time. It is most important to see it in the context of its relations both to the other components of the same cultural systems and to the social system.

We have defined a symbol as an object having meaning at a relatively high level of generality. Objects of experience as such are not symbols unless this element of generalization in their meaning is present. For the instrumental components of cultural systems, this is relatively unproblematical, since it can be formulated in terms of the "conceptual" aspect of meaning—e.g., the abstractly defined properties of objects as these enter into scientific theory. For the evaluative component, the problem is posed in terms of the cultural relativity of values and its involvement in the problem of the sociology of knowledge. Two qualifications are especially relevant here. First, our position in respect to the sociology of knowledge implies that the relativity of values between cultures cannot be absolute; otherwise no theory of societal evolution would be possible. Second, within any given culture there exists a hierarchy of levels of generality of its values; the societal level of the analysis of values is more general than that relevant to the analysis of any given subsystem of the society: Similar considerations apply when we discuss cultural, as distinguished from societal, values.

The relation of expressive symbolism to personalities is parallel to the relation of evaluative patterns to societies. Granted this, then the *meanings* of cathected objects to the same personality system ipso facto cannot be randomly assorted, but must constitute a system. In the hierarchical aspect of the organization of such a system of "personal" symbolism, the lowest order, which is in one sense the "foundation," would be occupied by body symbols. Two sets of these symbols are particularly important—the body symbols of "prowess," which symbolize capacities, e.g., qualities like strength, performance skill, aesthetic qualities of the body, etc.; and the familiar Freudian sexual symbols, which seem to fit in this context, since they utilize the bodily features of the greatest importance in forming certain types of socially significant attachments as the object-categories given generalized meaning.

The next level in the personal system concerns qualities of personality analytically independent of the organism, e.g., "warmth" or affection, aggressiveness, independence-dependence, etc. In the cathexis of persons as objects, these are the typical features that are salient in that they categorize the *kind* of person under consideration as an object of attraction or aversion.

The third level comprises the symbolization of "who" the individual is, in a social sense of inclusion, and the categories of status and membership applying to him. His involvement in the higher-order culture in relation to the problem of generalized respect is also relevant. Such categorizations as "child of God," or even member of a definitely sacralized social community, like Christian or Jew, belongs here. Physical objects obviously enter in, but primarily and initially by virtue of their association with one or more of the above culturally primary categories.

Besides the categorizing of significant types of object of expressive meaning, the second vital aspect of such systems of symbolism is the *cultural* generality of these meanings. In other words, they should be "coded" in a sufficiently generalized set of patternings, and the "understanding" of this coding should be shared by units in a social community. In our sense, expressive symbolism cannot be part of culture, nor constitute symbolism at all, without being shared through communication—unless those using it for expression also have, actually or potentially, an audience of others sensitized to the intended meanings. Expressive symbolism consists of culturally codified generalizations about emotional experience, where the symbolism employed has an order of generality or universality transcending the experience of a particular individual with a particular object. Objects with such meanings in particular contexts are elevated into symbols by precisely such a process of generalization.

In one sense, the range from which selections might have been drawn for this purpose is almost indefinite, particularly if our interest were primarily in illustrating, rather than attempting theoretical generalization. The decision to emphasize the latter limits our choice considerably. In addition, particular attention has been given to views which might be closely connected with the theory of action in its social aspects.

The first two brief selections are from authors in the period preceding that of our principal emphasis. One is from the arts, in 1865, by Sir Charles Bell; the other is from biology in 1872, by Charles Darwin. Both emphasize the use of bodily movements and processes to convey meaning in interaction. Most of these phenomena would be classified as signs rather than as full symbols; but they are deeply involved in human interaction as well as that of animals. They underlie language and the development from gesture to symbol that has already been illustrated in selections from G. H. Mead. (Another author whose writing is relevant to this theme, though space did not allow its inclusion, is W. B. Cannon, particularly in some of the classic studies published in the volume *Bodily Changes in Fear, Hunger, and Rage*.)

The next two selections come from philosophical authors who have made important contributions to clarifying the modes and types of symbolization involved in human communication. The first is a selection from Ernst Cassirer's *Philosophy of Symbolic Forms*. While the earlier Cassirer selection, presented in Section A above, dealt with his more general concept of symbolization, the theme in this selection is the expressive aspect, and the stages of transition from expressive movements and sign language to true symbolization. It is interesting that Cassirer pays such close attention to the structure

of language and incorporates into language the primary criterion of superseding the levels of mimicry, imitation, and analogy in favor of symbolization. To paraphrase, expressions become symbolic only in so far as they are incorporated into a generalized code.

The second of these selections is from Suzanne Langer's *Philosophy in a New Key*. At least in American philosophy, this book marked an important transition from the nearly exclusive preoccupation with the symbolism of science to concern with the arts, with magical and religious ritual, and with various other more expressive fields. After a brief discussion of metaphor as a component of imaginative symbolization, this selection turns to the content of dreams (thus connecting with the selection from Freud's treatment of that subject presented in Section A), and then to the symbolization involved in magical and religious ritual. In this connection, it extends farther some of the themes already introduced in the selections from Robertson Smith and Durkheim in Section B above.

The next pair of selections are from anthropological field studies of ritual. The first, from Malinowski's *Magic, Science and Religion*, analyzes the components involved in a magical rite, with special reference to the importance of the spell as its most efficacious component. The second is from Radcliffe-Brown's *Andaman Islanders*. Beginning with Durkheim's view of ritual, it analyzes especially clearly the combination, in ceremonials, of the sharing of affective states, the psychological supports and conditions involved, and the social obligatory quality of the ritual pattern that differentiates it from spontaneously personalized expression of emotion.

The final selection here is from the sphere of the arts, in this instance literature. Among literary critics, Kenneth Burke has been especially sensitive to the complexity of symbolic systems, and to their intimate relations to general philosophical ideas and to interests in *action*. Few, if any, other writers in this field have been so close, in their theoretical formulations, to the frame of reference of action as we conceive it, while, at the same time, being so keenly aware of the complex ramifications of systems of expressive symbolism on a variety of interconnected levels of generality, particularly in relation to both the personality and the society.

In accord with our policy of trying to limit our selections to writings produced within the period, we have included a selection from Burke's early work, *Permanence and Change*, dealing especially with the problem of incongruity as a means of approaching the analysis of the structure of these complexes. Like Cassirer, Burke is particularly concerned with his themes' relation to the nature and functioning of language.

Under the heading of expressive symbolism, it would have been possible to include selections from the works of many other writers whose names appear in the table of contents of this Reader. Some of the relevant works, like Freud on dream symbolism and Durkheim on religious ritual, have already appeared in earlier sections. In certain cases, e.g., G. H. Mead, the concepts of gesture and symbol are directly involved in the most elementary analysis of interaction, in ways which

are at least partly "expressive" in our sense. Important selections might also have been drawn from Simmel or Scheler; and Max Weber's monograph on the development of music should be mentioned.

However, as noted, the theory of neither the time with which we are dealing nor of our own would provide the basis for a truly systematic selection or arrangement. We have tried to emphasize the importance of this subject by presenting at least a few important selections in a separate section specifically devoted to the theme, without too involved intermingling with others.

1. Expression in Reference to the Body

BY SIR CHARLES BELL

ARE WE NOT NOW authorised to say, that expression is to passion what language is to thought: that as without words to represent ideas, the reasoning faculties of man could not be fully exercised, so there could be no violence or excess of passion merely in the mind, and independent of the action of the body? As our thoughts are embodied and the reasoning powers developed by the instrument of speech, the passions or emotions have also a corresponding organ to give them a determined character and force. The bodily frame, though secondary and inferior, comes in aid of the mind; and the faculties owe their development as much to the operation of the instruments of expression as to the impressions of the outward senses.

It is also curious that expression appears to precede the intellectual operations. The smile that dimples an infant's cheek, which in after-years corresponds with pleasurable and complex emotions, cannot have its origin from such ideas. This expression is not first seen when the infant is awake, but oftener while asleep; and this first beam of pleasure to a mother's eye is met with the cold observation of the wise old women, that it is caused by some internal convulsion. They conclude that the child's intellects are not yet matured to correspond with the expression, and attribute the effect

to some internal irritation. The expression is in fact the spontaneous operation and classification of the muscles, which await the development of the faculties to accompany them closely when they do arise, and in some measure to control them during life. It may be too much to affirm, that without the co-operation of these organs of the frame the mind would remain a blank; but surely the mind must owe something to its connexion with an operation of the features which precedes its own conscious activity, and which is unerring in its exercise from the very commencement.

The expression of pain in an infant is extraordinary in force and caricature; the expression of laughter is pure in the highest possible degree, as indicating unalloyed pleasure, and it will relax by sympathy even the stubborn features of a stranger. Here the rudiments of expression ought to be studied, for in after-life they cease to have the pure and simple source from which they spring in infancy; the feelings are composed and restrained, the mind is in a state of more compound feeling, and the genuine characteristics of passion are to be seen only in unpremeditated bursts of great vehemence.

How much influence the instrument of expression has in first rousing the mind into that state of activity which we call passion or emotion, we may learn from the power of the body to control these affections. "I have often observed," says Burke,

Reprinted from Sir Charles Bell, *The Anatomy and Philosophy of Expression* (London: Henry G. Bohn, 1865), pp. 198–201.

"that on mimicking the looks and gestures of angry, or placid, or frightened, or daring men, I have involuntarily found my mind turned to that passion."

Whether it be possible to mould the body, and thus to steal into another's thoughts, I know not; but it is of more consequence to recollect that we may in this way ascertain our own. As the actions and expressions of the body betray the emotions of the heart, we may be startled and forewarned, as it were, by the reflection of ourselves, and at the same time learn to control our passions by restraining their expression.

As we hold our breath and throw ourselves into an opposite action to restrain the ludicrous idea which would cause us to break out in rude laughter, so may we moderate other rising impulses, by checking the expression of them; and by composing the body, we put a rein upon our very thoughts. The powers of language are so great, and minister in so superior a manner to reason and the higher faculties of the mind, that the language of expression, which attends the development of these powers, is in a manner superseded; good taste and good manners retain it in habitual subordination.

We esteem and honour that man most who subdues the passions which directly refer to himself, and cultivates those which have their source in benevolence—who resists his own gratification, and enters warmly by sympathy into what others feel—who despises direct pleasures, and cultivates those enjoyments in which he participates with others. "Whatever is morally just is beautiful in art": the expression of pain, proceeding from the mere suffering of the body, is repulsive in representation, while the heroic pangs which the artist may raise to the highest degree of expression, in compassion or sympathy with another's sufferings, cannot be too powerfully portrayed, if they be consistent with nature and truth.

In studying expression the artist should attempt all, even that which is disagreeable so that in higher composition he may avoid deformity and every debasing expression, and this not by chance, but by knowing them and avoiding them; by this means—and it was followed by the ancients—his power of representation will be improved, and what is dignified and beautiful in form and expression more certainly attained.

2. *The Expression of the Emotions*

by CHARLES DARWIN

OF ALL EXPRESSIONS, blushing seems to be the most strictly human; yet it is common to all or nearly all the races of man, whether or not any change of colour is visible in their skin. The relaxation of the small arteries of the surface, on which blushing depends, seems to have primarily resulted from earnest attention directed to the appearance of our own persons, especially of our faces, aided by habit, inheritance, and the ready flow of nerve-force along accustomed channels; and afterwards to have been extended by the power of association to a self-attention directed to moral conduct. It can hardly be doubted that many animals are capable of appreciating beautiful colours and even forms, as is shown by the pains which the individuals of one sex take in displaying their

Reprinted from Charles Darwin, *The Expression of the Emotions in Man and Animals* (London: John Murray, 1872), pp. 364–67.

beauty before those of the opposite sex. But it does not seem possible that any animal, until its mental powers had been developed to an equal or nearly equal degree with those of man, would have closely considered and been sensitive about its own personal appearance. Therefore we may conclude that blushing originated at a very late period in the long line of our descent.

From the various facts just alluded to, and given in the course of this volume, it follows that, if the structure of our organs of respiration and circulation had differed in only a slight degree from the state in which they now exist, most of our expressions would have been wonderfully different. A very slight change in the course of the arteries and veins which run to the head, would probably have prevented the blood from accumulating in our eyeballs during violent expiration; for this occurs in extremely few quadrupeds. In this case we should not have displayed some of our most characteristic expressions. If man had breathed water by the aid of external branchiæ (though the idea is hardly conceivable), instead of air through his mouth and nostrils, his features would not have expressed his feelings much more efficiently than now do his hands or limbs. Rage and disgust, however, would still have been shown by movements about the lips and mouth, and the eyes would have become brighter or duller according to the state of the circulation. If our ears had remained movable, their movements would have been highly expressive, as is the case with all the animals which fight with their teeth; and we may infer that our early progenitors thus fought, as we still uncover the canine tooth on one side when we sneer at or defy anyone, and we uncover all our teeth when furiously enraged.

The movements of expression in the face and body, whatever their origin may have been, are in themselves of much importance for our welfare. They serve as the first means of communication between the mother and her infant; she smiles approval, and thus encourages her child on the right path, or frowns disapproval. We readily perceive sympathy in others by their expression; our sufferings are thus mitigated and our pleasures increased; and mutual good feeling is thus strengthened. The movements of expression give vividness and energy to our spoken words. They reveal the thoughts and intentions of others more truly than do words, which may be falsified. Whatever amount of truth the so-called science of physiognomy may contain, appears to depend, as Haller long ago remarked, on different persons bringing into frequent use different facial muscles, according to their dispositions; the development of these muscles being perhaps thus increased, and the lines or furrows on the face, due to their habitual contraction, being thus rendered deeper and more conspicous. The free expression by outward signs of an emotion intensifies it. On the other hand, the repression, as far as this is possible, of all outward signs softens our emotions. He who gives way to violent gestures will increase his rage; he who does not control the signs of fear will experience fear in a greater degree; and he who remains passive when overwhelmed with grief loses his best chance of recovering elasticity of mind. These results follow partly from the intimate relation which exists between almost all the emotions and their outward manifestations; and partly from the direct influence of exertion on the heart, and consequently on the brain. Even the simulation of an emotion tends to arouse it in our minds. Shakespeare, who from his wonderful knowledge of the human mind ought to be an excellent judge, says:—

"Is it not monstrous that this player here,
But in a fiction, in a dream of passion,
Could force his soul so to his own conceit,
That, from her working, all his visage wann'd;
Tears in his eyes, distraction in 's aspect,
A broken voice, and his whole function suiting
With forms to his conceit? And all for nothing!"
                                   Hamlet, act ii. sc. 2.

We have seen that the study of the theory of expression confirms to a certain limited extent the conclusion that man is derived from some lower animal form, and supports the belief of the specific or subspecific unity of the several races; but as far as my judgment serves, such confirmation was hardly needed. We have also seen that expression in itself, or the language of the emotions, as it has sometimes been called, is certainly of importance for the welfare of mankind. To understand, as far as is possible, the source or origin of the various expressions which may be hourly seen on the faces of the men around us, not to mention our domesticated animals, ought to possess much interest for us. From these several causes, we may conclude that the philosophy of our subject has well deserved the attention which it has already received from several excellent observers, and that it deserves still further attention, especially from any able physiologist.

3. *Language in the Phase of Sensuous Expression*

BY ERNST CASSIRER

Language as Expressive Movement: Sign Language and Sound Language

IN DEFINING the distinctive character of any spiritual form, it is essential to measure it by its own standards. The criteria by which we judge it and appraise its achievement, must not be drawn from outside, but must be taken from its own fundamental law of formation. No rigid "metaphysical" category, no definition and classification of being derived elsewhere, however certain and firmly grounded these may seem, can relieve us of the need for a purely immanent beginning. We are justified in invoking a metaphysical category only if, instead of accepting it as a fixed datum to which we accord priority over the characteristic principle of form, we can *derive* it from this principle and understand it in this light. In this sense every new form represents a new "building" of the world, in accordance with specific criteria, valid for it alone. The dogmatic approach, which starts from the being of the world as from a fixed point of unity, is of course disposed to subsume all these inner diversities of the spirit's *spontaneity* under some universal concept of the world's "essence" and so to lose them. It creates rigid segments of being, distinguishing, for example, between an "inward" and "outward," a "psychic" and a "physical" reality, between a world of "things" and a world of "representation"—and within these spheres further divisions of the same sort are made. Consciousness, the reality of the "soul," is also dissected into a number of separate and independent "faculties." It is only through the advancing critique of knowledge that we learn not to take these divisions and distinctions as absolute distinctions, inherent once and for all in things themselves, but to understand them as *mediated* by knowledge itself. Such a critique shows particularly that the opposition of "subject" and "object," of "I" and "world," is not simply to be accepted but must be grounded in the presuppositions of knowledge, by which its meaning is first determined. And this is true not only in the world of cognition; in some sense it holds good for all the truly independent basic functions of spiritual life. Philosophical inquiry into artistic as well as mythical and linguistic expression is in danger of missing its mark if, instead of immersing itself freely in the particular forms and laws of expression, it starts from dogmatic assumptions regarding the relation between "archetype" and "reproduction," "reality" and "appearance," "inner" and "outer" world. The question must rather be whether these distinctions are not determined *through* art, *through* language and *through* myth, and whether each of these forms must not draw its distinctions according to different perspectives, and consequently set up different dividing lines. The idea of a rigid substantial differentiation, of a sharp dualism between "inner" and "outer" world, is in this way thrust more and more into the background. The spirit apprehends itself and its antithesis to the "objective" world only by bringing certain distinctions inherent in itself into its view of the phenomena and, as it were, injecting them into the phenomena.

Language also reveals a noteworthy indifference toward the division of the world into two distinct spheres, into an "outward" and an "inward" reality; so much so, indeed, that this indifference seems inherent in its nature. Spiritual *content* and its sensuous expression are united: the former is not an independent, self-contained entity preceding the latter, but is rather completed in it and with it. The two, content and expression, become what they are only in their interpenetration: the signification they acquire through their relation to one another is not outwardly added to their being; it is this signification which constitutes their being. Here we have to do not with a mediated product but with that fundamental synthesis from which language as a whole arises and by which all its parts, from the most elementary sensuous expression to the supreme spiritual expression, are held together. And not only the formed and articulated language of words, but even the simplest *mimetic* expression of an inner process shows this indissoluble involvement, shows that the process does not in itself form a finished, closed-off sphere, out of which consciousness emerges only accidentally, as it were, for the purpose of conventional communication to others, but that this seeming externalization is an essential fac-

Reprinted from Ernst Cassirer, *The Philosophy of Symbolic Forms*, trans. Ralph Mannheim (New Haven: Yale University Press; and London: Geoffrey Camberlege, Oxford University Press, 1953), pp. 177–97, with the permission of Yale University Press.

tor in its own formation. In this sense the modern psychology of language was right in assigning the problem of language to the general *psychology of expressive movements*. From the purely methodological standpoint this presents an important step forward, since this emphasis on the act of movement and the feeling of movement meant that fundamentally the concepts of the traditional *sensationalist* psychology had already been surpassed. From the sensationalist standpoint, the rigid "state" of consciousness is the first given, indeed in a sense, it is all that is given: the *processes* of consciousness, in so far as they are acknowledged at all in their own character, are reduced to a mere sum, a "combination" of states. However, to regard movement and feeling of movement as an element and a fundamental factor in the structure of consciousness itself, is to acknowledge that here again the dynamic is not based on the static but the static on the dynamic—that all psychological "reality" consists in processes and changes, while the fixation of states is merely a subsequent work of abstraction and analysis. Thus mimetic movement is also an immediate unity of the "inward" and "outward," the "spiritual" and the "physical," for by what it directly and sensuously is, it signifies and "says" something else, which is nonetheless present in it. Here there is no mere "transition," no arbitrary addition of the mimetic sign to the emotion it designates; on the contrary, both emotion and its expression, inner tension and its discharge are given in one and the same act, undivided in time. By a process that can be described and interpreted in purely physiological terms, every inner stimulation expresses itself originally in a bodily movement— and the progressive development consists only in a sharper differentiation of this relation: *specific* movements come to be linked more and more precisely with *specific* stimulations. It is true that at first this form of expression does not seem to be anything more than a "reproduction" of the inward in the outward. An outward stimulus passes from the sensory to the motor function, which however seems to remain within the sphere of mere mechanical reflexes, giving no indication of a higher spiritual "spontaneity." And yet this reflex is itself the first indication of an activity in which a new form of concrete consciousness of the I and of the object begins to develop. In his work on *The Expression of the Emotions in Man and Animals* Darwin attempted to create a biological theory of expressive movements by interpreting them as a vestige of actions which originally served a practical purpose. According to this theory, the expression of a specific emotion would be merely an attenuated form of a previous purposive action; the expression of

anger, for example, would be merely a pale, attenuated image of a former movement of aggression, the expression of fear would be the image of a movement of defense, etc. This view is susceptible of an interpretation which leads beyond the restricted sphere of Darwin's biological formulations and places the question in a more general context. Every elementary expressive movement does actually form a first step in spiritual development, in so far as it is still entirely situated in the immediacy of sensuous life and yet at the same time goes beyond it. It implies that the sensory drive, instead of proceeding directly towards its object, instead of satisfying itself and losing itself in the object, encounters a kind of inhibition and reversal, in which a new *consciousness* of this same drive is born. In this sense the reaction contained in the expressive movement prepares the way for a higher stage of action. In withdrawing, as it were, from the immediate form of activity, action gains a new scope and a new freedom; it is already in transition from the merely "pragmatic" to the "theoretical," from physical to ideal activity.

In the psychological theory of *sign language*, two forms of gesture are usually distinguished, the *indicative* and the *imitative;* these classes can be clearly delimited both as to content and psychological genesis. This indicative gesture is derived biologically and genetically from the movement of grasping. "The arms and hands," Wundt writes,

have from the earliest development of man been active as the organs with which he grasps and masters objects. From this evidently original use of the grasping organs, in which man is superior only in degree but not in kind to the higher animals with analogous activities, there follows one of those gradual transformations, which are at first regressive, but in their consequences provide important components of a progressive development, leading to the first primitive form of pantomimic movement. Genetically considered, this is nothing other than the grasping movement attenuated to an indicative gesture. We still find it among children in every possible intermediary phase from the original to the later form. The child still clutches for objects that he cannot reach because they are too far away. In such cases, the clutching movement changes to a pointing movement. Only after repeated efforts to grasp the objects, does the pointing movement as such establish itself.[1]

And this seemingly so simple step toward the independence of gesture, constitutes one of the most important stages in the development from the animal to the specifically human. For no animal progresses to the characteristic transformation of the grasping movement into the indicative gesture. Even among the most highly developed animals,

1. Wundt, *Die Sprache, Völkerpsychologie*, 2d ed., *I*, 129 ff.

"clutching at the distance," as pointing with the hand has been called, has never gone beyond the first, incomplete beginnings. This simple gentic fact suggests that "clutching at the distance" involves a factor of general spiritual significance. It is one of the first steps by which the perceiving and desiring I removes a perceived and desired content from himself and so forms it into an "object," and "objective" content. In the primitive instinctual stage, to "apprehend" an object is to grasp it immediately with the senses, to take possession of it. The foreign reality is brought into the power of the I—in a purely material sense it is drawn into the sphere of the I. Even the first beginnings of sensory *knowledge* are still entirely within this stage of "pointing there": at this stage man believes, in Plato's characteristic and pregnant term, that he can clutch the object with his hands ($\dot{\alpha}\pi\rho\dot{\iota}\xi$ $\tau\alpha\hat{\iota}\nu$ $\chi\epsilon\rho\sigma\hat{\iota}\nu$).[2] All progress in conceptual knowledge and pure "theory" consists precisely in surpassing this first sensory immediacy. The object of knowledge recedes more and more into the distance, so that for knowledge critically reflecting upon itself, it comes ultimately to appear as an "infinitely remote point," an endless task; and yet, in this apparent distance, it achieves its ideal specification. In the logical concept, in judgment and inference develops that mediate grasp which characterizes "reason." Thus both genetically and actually, there seems to be a continuous transition from physical to conceptual "grasping." Sensory-physical grasping becomes sensory interpretation, which in turn conceals within it the first impulse toward the higher functions of signification manifested in language and thought. We might suggest the scope of this development by saying that it leads from the sensory extreme of mere "indication" (*Weisen*) to the logical extreme of "demonstration" (*Beweisen*). From the mere indication by which an absolutely single thing (a $\tau\acute{o}\delta\epsilon\tau\iota$ in the Aristotelian sense) is designated, the road leads to a progressively general specification: what in the beginning was a mere deictic function becomes the function of "apodeixis." Language itself seems to preserve this connection in the relation between the terms for speaking and saying and those for showing and indicating. In the Indo-Germanic languages, most verbs of "saying" are derived from verbs of "showing": *dicere* stems from the root contained in the Greek $\delta\epsilon\acute{\iota}\kappa\nu\upsilon\mu\iota$ (Gothic * *teihan, ga-teihan,* Old High German *zeigôn*), while the Greek $\phi\eta\mu\acute{\iota}$ $\phi\acute{\iota}\sigma\kappa\omega$ goes back to the root $\phi\alpha$ (Sanskrit *bhâ*), which originally designated glitter, appear, and "make to appear." (Cf. $\phi\alpha\acute{\epsilon}\theta\omega$, $\phi\hat{\omega}\varsigma$, $\phi\alpha\acute{\iota}\nu\omega$ Lat. *fari, fateri,* etc.)

It would seem, however, that we shall have to take a different view of the language of gestures if we start, not with the gestures of indication but with the second fundamental class, those of *imitation*. For imitation as such forms a counterpart to any free form of spiritual activity. In imitation the I remains a prisoner of outward impression and its properties; the more accurately it repeats this impression, excluding all spontaneity of its own, the more fully the aim of imitation has been realized. The richest and most highly differentiated sign languages, those of the primitive peoples, show the strongest bond with outward impression. Along with the immediately sensuous, imitative signs, the sign languages of civilized peoples tend to include an abundance of so-called "symbolic gestures," which do not directly mimic the object or activity to be expressed, but designate it only indirectly. However, such languages—for example that of the Cistercian monks or the Neopolitan sign language described in detail by Jorio[3]—are obviously not primitive forms but highly complex constructions strongly influenced by the spoken language. But as we go back to the true and independent content of the sign languages, mere "concept signs" seem to give way to "thing signs." The ideal of a purely "natural" language in which all arbitrary convention is excluded seems thus to be realized. It is reported that in the sign language of the North American Indians, few gestures are "conventional" in origin, while by far the greater number consist in a simple reproduction of natural phenomena.[4] If we consider only this factor of pantomimic imitation of given objects of sense perception, we do not seem to be on the road to *language* as a free and original activity of the human spirit. However, it must be borne in mind that neither "imitation"—nor "indication"—neither the "mimetic" nor the "deictic" function represents a simple, uniform operation of consciousness, but that elements of diverse origin and significance are intermingled in both of them. Even Aristotle calls the sounds of language "imitations," and says that the human voice is of all organs the best suited to imitation.[5] But for him this mimetic character of the word is not opposed to its purely symbolic character; on the contrary, Aristotle stresses the symbolic character of the word by pointing out that the inarticulate sound expressing

---

2. Cf. Plato, *Theaetetus* 155E.

3. Andrea de Jorio, *La Mimica degli antichi nel Gestire Napolitano* (Napoli, 1832); on the language of the Cistercian monks, see Wundt, *Die Sprache, Völkerpsychologie,* 2d ed., I, 151 ff.
4. Cf. G. Mallery, *Sign Language among North American Indians* (Smithsonian Institution, Bureau of American Ethnology, Washington, Govt. Print. Off., 1881), Annual Report, No. 1, p. 334.
5. Cf. Aristotle, *Rhetoric* iii. 1. 1404a 20: $\tau\grave{\alpha}$ $\gamma\grave{\alpha}\rho$ $\acute{o}\nu\acute{o}\mu\alpha\tau\alpha$ $\mu\iota\mu\acute{\eta}\mu\alpha\tau\acute{\alpha}$ $\acute{\epsilon}\sigma\tau\iota\nu$, $\acute{\upsilon}\pi\hat{\eta}\rho\xi\epsilon$ $\delta\grave{\epsilon}$ $\kappa\alpha\grave{\iota}$ $\acute{\eta}$ $\phi\omega\nu\grave{\eta}$ $\pi\acute{\alpha}\nu\tau\omega\nu$ $\mu\iota\mu\eta\tau\iota\kappa\omega\tau\acute{\alpha}\tau\omega\nu\tau\hat{\omega}\nu$ $\mu\rho\acute{\iota}\omega\nu$ $\acute{\eta}\mu\hat{\iota}\nu$.

sensation, such as we find in the animal world, becomes *linguistic sound* only through its use as a symbol.[6] The two terms merge, for Aristotle here uses "imitation" in a broader, deeper sense: for him it is not only the origin of language, but also of artistic activity. Thus understood μίμησις itself belongs to the sphere of ποίησις, of creative and formative activity. It no longer implies the mere repetition of something outwardly given, but a free project of the spirit: the apparent "reproduction" (*Nachbilden*) actually presupposes an inner "production" (*Vorbilden*). And indeed, it becomes evident on closer scrutiny that this factor which is pure and independent in the form of artistic creation, extends down to the elementary beginnings of all apparently passive reproduction. For this reproduction never consists in retracing, line for line, a specific content of reality; but in selecting a pregnant motif in that content and so producing a characteristic "outline" of its form. But with this, imitation itself is on its way to becoming *representation,* in which objects are no longer simply received in their finished structure, but built up by the consciousness according to their constitutive traits. To reproduce an object in this sense means not merely to compose it from its particular sensuous characteristics, but to apprehend it in its structural relations which can only be truly understood if the consciousness constructively produces them. Sign language represents the germ of this higher form of reproduction; the more highly developed sign languages disclose a transition from the merely imitative to the *representative* gesture, in which, according to Wundt, "the image of an object is more freely formed, in the same sense as creative art is freer than mere mechanical imitation."[7]

But this function of representation emerges in an entirely new freedom and depth, in a new spiritual actuality when for the gesture it substitutes the *word* as its instrument and sensuous basis. In the historical development of language this process of substitution does not take place all at once. Even today, among primitive peoples, the language of gestures not only continues to exist side by side with the language of words, but still decisively affects its formation. Everywhere we find this characteristic permeation, in consequence of which the "verbal concepts" of these languages cannot be fully understood unless they are considered at the same time as mimetic and "manual concepts." The hands are so closely bound up with the intellect that they seem to

form a part of it. Likewise in the development of children's speech, the articulated sound breaks away only very gradually from the totality of mimetic movements; even at relatively advanced stages, it remains embedded in this totality. But once the separation is accomplished, language has acquired a new fundamental principle in the new element in which it now moves. Its truly spiritual spontaneity develops only in the physical medium of articulated sound. The articulation of sounds now becomes an instrument for the articulation of thoughts, while the latter creates for itself a more and more differentiated and sensitive organ in the elaboration and formation of these sounds. Compared to all other means of mimetic expression, the spoken sound has the advantage that it is far more capable of "articulation." Its very fluidity, which differs from the sensuous concreteness of the gesture, gives it an entirely new capacity for configuration, making it capable of expressing not only rigid representative contents, but the most subtle vibrations and nuances of the representative *process.* If with its plastic imitation the gesture seems better adapted to the character of "things" than the disembodied element of the spoken sound, the word gains its inner freedom by the very fact that in it this connection is broken off, that it is a mere becoming, which can no longer immediately reproduce the being of objects. On the objective side, it now becomes capable of serving, not only as an expression of formal relations; on the subjective side, the dynamic of feeling and the dynamic of thought are imprinted upon it. For this dynamic the language of gestures, which is restricted to the medium of space and thus can designate motion only by dividing it into particular and discrete spatial forms, has no adequate organ. In the language of words, however, the particular, discrete element enters into a new relation with speech as a whole. Here the element exists only in so far as it is constantly regenerated: its content is gathered up into the act of its production. But now this act of sound production itself becomes more and more sharply differentiated. To the qualitative differentiation and gradation of sounds is added a dynamic gradation by stress and rhythm. Attempts have been made to prove that this rhythmic articulation, as particularly manifested in primitive work songs, represents an essential factor both of artistic and linguistic development. Here the spoken sound is still immediately rooted in the purely sensuous sphere; yet since what it springs from and serves to express is not merely passive feeling, but a simple sensory activity, it is already on its way to surpassing this sphere. The mere interjection, the expression of emotion produced by an overwhelming momentary impression, now passes into a coherently

---

6. Cf. περὶ ἑρμηνείας (2. 16a 27). A definite distinction between "imitation" and "symbol" (ὁμοίωμα and σύμβολον) is also found for example in Ammonius' *Commentary on Aristotle's* "De interpretatione," ed. A. Busse (Berlin, 1897), p. 100, 15b.

7. Wundt, *Die Sprache, Völkerpsychologie,* 2d ed., *I,* 156.

ordered phonetic sequence, in which the context and order of the activity are reflected. "The ordered unfolding of spoken sounds," writes Jacob Grimm in his essay "On the Origin of Language," "requires us to articulate, and the human language appears as an articulated language; this is borne out by the Homeric epithet for men: οἱ μέροπες, μέροπες ἄνθρωποι or βροτοὶ—from μείρομαι or μερίζω, those who divide, articulate their voice."[8]

Only now is the material of language so constituted that a new form can become imprinted upon it. The sensory-affective state transposes and dissolves itself into mimetic expression; it discharges itself in mimetic expression and therein finds its end. It is only when this immediacy is superseded in the course of further development that the content comes to be stabilized and formed in itself. A higher stage of awareness, a sharper grasp of its inner differentiations is now needed before it can be manifested clearly and concretely in the medium of articulated sounds. Inhibition of the direct outbreak into gestures and inarticulate cries gives rise to an inner measure, a movement within the sphere of sensory appetition and representation. The road leads upwards, more and more clearly, from the mere reflex to the various stages of "reflection." The genesis of the articulated sound, "the noise rounding itself into a tone"—as Goethe put it—presents us with a universal phenomenon which we encounter in different forms in the most divergent fields of function, as it unfolds in accordance with immanent laws, in art, in the mythical-religious consciousness, in language and in cognition.

Mimetic, Analogical, and Symbolic Expression

It is true that, like the theory of art and the theory of knowledge, linguistic theory freed itself only gradually from the constraint of the concept of imitation and the copy theory. The problem of the κυριότης τῶν ὀνομάτων stands at the center of the ancient philosophy of language. And the question of whether language should be regarded as a φύσει or a νόμῳ ὂν was primarily concerned not with the genesis of language but with its truth and reality content.[9] Do language and the word belong exclu-

sively to the sphere of subjective representation and judgment, or is there a profounder bond between the world of names and the world of true being; is there an inner "objective" truth and rightness in names themselves? The Sophists denied and the Stoics affirmed such an objective validity of the word; but whether the answer was positive or negative, the form of the *question* itself remained the same. The basic assumption underlying both answers is that the aim of cognition is to reflect and reproduce the essence of things, while the aim of language is to reflect and reproduce the essence of cognition. The Sophists strive to show that both aims are unattainable: if there is being, says Gorgias, it is inaccessible and unknowable; if it is knowable, it is inexpressible and incommunicable. Just as by their nature, the senses of sight and hearing are restricted to their specific sphere of qualities; just as the one can perceive only brightness and colors and the other can perceive only tones—similarly speech can never transcend itself to apprehend something "other," standing over against it, that is to apprehend "being" and truth.[10] The Stoics sought vainly to avoid this consequence by asserting a natural kinship between being and cognition and a natural accord κατά μίμησιν between word and meaning. The view that the word partly or wholly reflected reality, forming its true ἔτυμον, reduced itself to the absurd by shifting into its opposite in its subsequent development. Not only the relationship of "similarity," but also its converse was now admitted as a basis for etymological explanation: not only ἀναλογία and ὁμοιότης, but also ἐναντίωσις and ἀντίφρασις passed as formative principles of language. *Similitudo* became *contrarium;* "analogy" became "anomaly." The devastating effects of this "explanation by opposites" on the subsequent development of etymology are well known:[11] on the whole, they make it very plain that any explanation of language built on the postulate of similarity must necessarily end in its antithesis and so negate itself.

Even where words are interpreted as imitations not of things but of subjective states of feeling, where, as in Epicurus, they are said to reflect not so much the nature of objects as the ἴδια πάξη of the speaker,[12] the philosophy of language, though it has changed its norm, is still essentially subordinated to the same principle. If the postulate of reproduction as such is sustained, it becomes ultimately indifferent whether what is reproduced is "inward" or "out-

---

8. "Über den Ursprung der Sprache" (1851), in *Kleinere Schriften*, Berlin, 1864, *1*, 266. The etymological connection set forth by Grimm is, to be sure, contested: for details see Curtius, *Grundzüge der griechischen Etymologie*, 5th ed., pp. 110 and 330.

9. For further material concerning this original meaning of the opposition φύσει and νόμῳ, for which φύσει and θέσει were substituted in the Alexandria period, see Steinthal, *Geschichte der Sprachwissenschaft*, 2d ed., *1*, 76 ff., 114 ff., 319 ff.

10. Cf. "Sextus adv. mathematicos," VII, 83 ff. (Diels, *Die Fragmente der Vorsokratiker*, 76B, 554–555).

11. For characteristic examples see Curtius, *Grundzüge der griechischen Etymologie*, 5th ed., pp. 5 ff; Steinthal, *op. cit.*, 1, 353 ff.; L. Lersch, *Sprachphilosophie der Alten* (Bonn, 1838–41), *3*, 47 ff.

12. Cf. above, pp. 148 ff.

ward" whether it is a complex of things or of feelings and representations. Indeed, under the latter assumption a recurrence of skepticism toward language is inevitable, and in its sharpest form. For language can claim to apprehend the immediacy of *life* far less than the immediacy of things. The slightest attempt to express this immediacy merely negates it. "Once the soul speaks, alas, the soul speaks no more." Thus language, by its pure *form* alone is the counterpart of the abundance and concretion of the world of sensation and emotion. Gorgias' contention that "it is the speaker who speaks, not the color or the thing,"[13] applies to a heightened degree if we replace "objective" by "subjective" reality. Subjective reality is characterized by extreme individuality and concretion; while the world of words is characterized by the universality, and that is to say, the indeterminacy and ambiguity, of merely schematic signs. Since the "universal" signification of the word effaces all the differences which characterize real psychological processes, the road of language seems to lead us, not upward into spiritual universality, but downward to the commonplace: for only this, only what is not peculiar to an individual intuition or sensation, but is common to it and others, is accessible to language. Thus language remains a pseudo-value, the mere rule of a game, which becomes more compelling as more players subject themselves to it, but which, as soon as it is critically understood, must renounce all claim to represent, let alone know and understand, any reality, whether of the "inner" or "outer" world.

Fundamentally, however, in the critique of knowledge as of language, this radical skepticism contains within it the transcending of skepticism. Skepticism seeks to expose the nullity of knowledge and language—but what it ultimately demonstrates is rather the nullity of the *standard* by which it measures them. In skepticism the "copy theory" is methodically and consistently demolished by the self-destruction of its basic premises. The farther negation is carried in this point, the more clearly a new positive insight follows from it. The last semblance of any mediate or immediate *identity* between reality and symbol must be effaced, the *tension* between the two must be enhanced to the extreme, for it is precisely in this tension that the specific achievement of symbolic expression and the content of the particular symbolic forms is made evident. For this content cannot be revealed as long as we hold fast to the belief that we possess "reality" as a given, self-sufficient being, as a totality whether of things or of simple sensations, prior to all spiritual formation. If this were true, the forms would indeed have no other purpose than mere reproduction, and such

reproduction would inevitably be inferior to the original. In truth, however, the meaning of each form cannot be sought in what it expresses, but only in the manner and modality, the inner law of the expression itself. In this law of formation, and consequently not in proximity to the immediately given but in progressive *removal* from it, lie the value and the specific character of linguistic as of artistic formation. This *distance* from immediate reality and immediate experience is the condition of their being perceived, of our spiritual awareness of them. Language, too, *begins* only where our immediate relation to sensory impression and sensory affectivity *ceases*. The uttered sound is not yet speech as long as it purports to be mere repetition; as long as the specific factor of signification and the will to "signification" are lacking. The aim of repetition lies in identity—the aim of linguistic designation lies in difference. The synthesis effected can only be a synthesis of different elements, not of elements that are alike or similar in any respect. The more the sound resembles what it expresses; the more it continues to "be" the other, the less it can "signify" that other. The boundary is sharply drawn not only from the standpoint of spiritual content, but biologically and genetically as well. Even among the lower animals we encounter a great number of original sounds expressing feeling and sensation, which in the development to the higher types become more and more differentiated, developing into definitely articulated and distinct "linguistic utterances," cries of fear or warning, lures or mating calls. But between these cries and the sounds of designation and signification characteristic of human speech there remains a gap, a "hiatus" which has been newly confirmed by the sharper methods of observation of modern animal psychology.[14] The step to human speech, as Aristotle stressed, has been taken only when the pure significatory sound has gained primacy over the sounds of affectivity and stimulation: a primacy which in the history of language is expressed by the circumstance that many words of the highly developed languages, which at first sight seem to be mere interjections,

---

13. De Melisso, *Xenophane et Gorgia*, ch. 6, 980 a 20.

14. For the "language" of the highest apes cf., e.g., B. W. Köhler, "Zur Psychologie des Schimpansen," *Psychologische Forschung*, 1 (1921), 27: "It is not easy to describe in detail how animals make themselves understood. It is absolutely certain that their *phonetic* utterances without any exception express 'subjective' states and desires, that they are so-called affective sounds and never aim to delineate or designate the objective. However, so many 'phonetic elements' of human speech occur in the chimpanzee phonetics that it is assuredly not for peripheral reasons that they have remained without language in our sense. The same is true of the facial expressions and gestures of animals: nothing about them designates anything objective or fulfills any 'representative function.'" Cf. Eng. ed., *The Mentality of Apes* (New York: Harcourt, Brace, 1925), App., p. 317.

prove, on close analysis, to be regressions from more complex linguistic structures, from words or sentences with a definite conceptual signification.

In general, language can be shown to have passed through three stages in maturing to its specific form, in achieving its inner freedom. In calling these the mimetic, the analogical, and the truly symbolical stage, we are for the present merely setting up an abstract schema—but this schema will take on concrete content when we see that it represents a functional law of linguistic growth, which has its specific and characteristic counterpart in other fields such as art and cognition. The beginnings of phonetic language seem to be embedded in that sphere of mimetic representation and designation which lies at the base of sign language. Here the sound seeks to approach the sensory impression and reproduce its diversity as faithfully as possible. This striving plays an important part in the speech both of children and "primitive" peoples. Here language clings to the concrete phenomenon and its sensory image, attempting as it were to exhaust it in sound; it does not content itself with general designations but accompanies every particular nuance of the phenomenon with a particular phonetic nuance, devised especially for this case. In Ewe and certain related languages, for example, there are adverbs which describe only *one* activity, *one* state or *one* attribute, and which consequently can be combined only with *one* verb. Many verbs possess a number of qualifying adverbs pertaining to them alone, and most of them are phonetic reproductions of sensory impressions. In his *Grammar of the Ewe Language* Westermann counts no less than thirty-three such phonetic images for the single verb "to walk," each designating a particular manner of walking: slouching or sauntering, limping or dragging the feet, shambling or waddling, energetic or weary. But this, as he adds, does not exhaust the number of adverbs that qualify walking; for most of these can occur in a doubled, usual, or diminutive form, depending on whether the subject is big or little.[15] Although this type of sound painting recedes as language develops, there is no language, however advanced, that has not preserved numerous examples of it. Certain onomatopoeic expressions occur with striking uniformity in all the languages of the globe. They demonstrate extraordinary vitality, resisting phonetic changes which are otherwise almost universal; and moreover, new forms have appeared even in modern times, in the bright light of linguistic history. In view of all this, it is understandable that particularly the empirical linguists have often been inclined to champion the principle of onomatopoeia, so severely chastised by philosophers of language, and to attempt at least a limited rehabilitation of that principle. The sixteenth- and seventeenth-century philosophers of language still supposed that phenomena of onomatopoeia offered the key to the basic and original language of mankind, the lingua adamica. Today, to be sure, the critical progress of linguistics has more and more dispelled this dream; but we still occasionally encounter attempts to prove that in the earliest period of language formation the significatory classes and the phonetic classes corresponded to one another—that the original words were divided into distinct groups, each of which was linked to certain phonetic materials and built up out of them. And even where the hope of arriving in this way at a true reconstruction of the original language has been abandoned, the principle of onomatopoeia is recognized as a means of arriving indirectly at an idea of the relatively oldest strata of language formation. "Despite all change," remarks G. Curtius with regard to the Indo-Germanic languages,

a conservative instinct is also discernible in language. All the peoples of our family from the Ganges to the Atlantic designate the notion of standing by the phonetic group *sta*; in all of them the notion of flowing is linked with the group *plu*, with only slight modifications. This cannot be an accident. Assuredly the same notion has remained associated with the same sounds through all the millennia, because the peoples felt a certain inner connection between the two, i.e., because of an instinct to express this notion by these particular sounds. The assertion that the oldest words presuppose some relation between sounds and the representations they designate has often been ridiculed. It is difficult, however, to explain the origin of language without such assumptions. In any case, the representation lives like a soul even in the words of far more advanced periods.[16]

Since the Stoics, the search for this soul of the individual sounds and sound classes has tempted innumerable linguists and philosophers of language. As late a thinker as Leibniz attempted to investigate the original meanings of particular sounds and sound groups.[17] And after him the subtlest and profoundest students of language attempted to demon-

---

15. D. Westermann, *Grammatik der Ewe-Sprache* (Berlin, D. Reimer, 1907), pp. 83 ff., 129 ff.; Eng. trans. by A. L. Bickford-Smith, *A Study of the Ewe Language* (London, Oxford Univ. Press, 1930), pp. 107 ff., 187 ff. Very similar phenomena are found in the languages of the American natives; cf., e.g., the transition from purely onomatopoeic sounds to universal verbial ar adverbial terms, described by Franz Boas in the Chinook language, in *Handbook of American Indian Languages,* (Smithsonian Institution, Washington, Govt. Print. Off., 1911), Bulletin No. 40, Pt. 1, pp. 575, 655 ff.

16. G. Curtius, *Grundzüge der griechischen Etymologie,* 5th ed. p. 96.

17. See Leibniz, *Nouveaux essais,* Bk. 3, ch. 3.

strate the symbolic value of certain sounds, not only in the material expression of certain isolated concepts, but even in the formal representation of certain grammatical *relations*. Humboldt found this relationship confirmed in the choice of certain sounds for the expression of certain feeling values —he held, for example, that the phonetic group *st* regularly designates the impression of the enduring and stable, the sound *l* that of the melting and fluid, the sound *v* the impression of uneven, vacillating motion. He also saw it in the elements of inflection and gave special attention to this "symbolic character in grammatical sounds."[18] Jacob Grimm also attempted to show that the sounds used in the Indo-Germanic languages for forming words of question and answer were closely related to the spiritual significations of question and answer.[19] The use of certain differences and gradations of vowels to express specific objective gradations, particularly to designate the greater or lesser distance of an object from the speaker, is a phenomenon occurring in the most diverse languages and linguistic groups. Almost always *a, o, u* designate the greater distance, *e* and *i* the lesser. Differences in time interval are also indicated by difference in vowels or by the pitch of vowels. In the same way certain consonants and consonantal groups are used as "natural phonetic metaphors" to which a similar or identical significatory function attaches in nearly all language groups—e.g., with striking regularity the resonant labials indicate direction toward the speaker and the explosive direction away from the speaker, so that the former appear as a "natural" expression of the "I," the latter of the "Thou."

But although these last phenomena seem to retain the color of immediate sensory expression, they nevertheless burst the limits of mere mimicry and imitation. No longer is a single sensuous object or sense impression reproduced by an imitative sound; instead, a qualitatively graduated phonetic sequence serves to express a pure relation. There is no direct material similarity between the form and specificity of this relation and the sounds with which it is rep-

resented, since the mere material of sound as such is in general incapable of reflecting pure relational determinations. The context is rather communicated by a *formal* analogy between the phonetic sequence and the sequence of contents designated; this analogy makes possible a *coordination* of series entirely different in content. This brings us to the second stage which we call the stage of *analogical* as opposed to mere mimetic *expression*. The transition from one to the other is perhaps most clearly revealed in those languages which employ musical tones to differentiate word meanings or express grammatical relations. We still seem close to the mimetic sphere in so far as the pure function of signification remains inextricably bound up with the sensuous sound. Humboldt tells us that in the Indo-Chinese languages the differentiations of pitch and accent between syllables makes speech a kind of song or recitative, and that the tonal gradations in the Siamese, for example are quite comparable to a musical scale.[20] And particularly in the Sudanese languages, the most diverse shades of meaning are expressed by tonal variations, by a high, middle, or low tone, or by composite shadings, such as the low-high rising tone, or high-low falling tone. These variations serve as a basis both for etymological distinctions—i.e., the same syllable serves, according to its tone, to designate entirely different things or actions—and for spatial and quantitative distinctions, i.e., high-pitched words, for example, express long distances and rapidity while low-pitched words, express proximity and slowness, etc. . . . And purely formal relations and oppositions can be expressed in this same way. A mere change in tone can transform the affirmative into the negative form of a verb. Or it may determine the grammatical category of a word; for example, otherwise identical syllables may be identified as nouns or verbs by the manner in which they are pronounced. We are carried one step further by the phenomenon of *vowel harmony* which dominates the whole structure of certain languages and linguistic groups, particularly those of the Ural-Altaic family. Here vowels fall into two sharply separate classes, hard and soft. When a root is augmented by suffixes, the suffix must belong to the same class as that of the root syllable. Here the phonetic assimilation of the components of a word, hence a purely sensuous means, creates a formal link between these components by which they are enabled to progress from relatively loose "agglutination" to a linguistic whole, to a self-contained word or sentence formation. In becoming a phonetic unit through the principle of vowel harmony, the

---

18. Cf. Humboldt, "Einleitung zum Kawi-Werk," *Werke*, 7, No. 1, 76 ff., and the work itself: *Uber die Kawi-Sprache auf der Insel Java* (hereafter cited as *Kawi-Werk*), 2, 111, 153, and elsewhere.

19. See Jacob Grimm, *Deutsche Grammatik*, Bk. 3, ch. 1: "Among all the sounds of the human voice, none is so capable of expressing the essence of the question, which is perceived at the very beginning of the word, as k, the fullest consonant of which the throat is capable. A mere vowel would sound too indefinite, and the labial organ is not as strong as the guttural. T can be produced with the same force, but it is not so much expelled as pronounced and has something more solid about it; it is therefore suited to the expression of the calm, even an indicative *answer*. K questions, inquires, calls; T shows, explains, answers."

20. Humboldt, "Enleitung zum Kawi-Werk," *Werke*, 7, No. 1, 300.

word or word-sentence gains its true significative unity: a relationship which at first applies solely to the quality and physiological production of the particular sounds, becomes a means of combining them into a spiritual whole, a unit of "signification."

This "analogical" correspondence between sound and signification is shown even more distinctly in the function of certain widespread and typical means of language formation, as for example, in the part played by *reduplication* both in morphology and syntax. Reduplication seems at first sight to be governed entirely by the principle of imitation: the doubling of the sound or syllable seems to serve the sole purpose of reflecting as faithfully as possible certain objective characteristics of the thing or event designated. The phonetic repetition conforms closely to a repetition given in the sensuous reality or impression. Reduplication is most at home where a thing presents itself repeatedly to the senses with the same characteristics, or where an event presents a sequence of identical or similar phases. But on this elementary foundation a system of astonishing diversity and subtlety arises. The sensory impression of "plurality" first breaks down into an expression of "collective" and "distributive" plurality. Certain languages which have no designation for the plural in our sense, have instead developed the idea of distributive plurality to the utmost sharpness and concreteness by meticulously distinguishing whether a specific act presents itself as an indivisible whole or falls into several separate acts. If the latter is true, and the act is either performed by several subjects or effected by the same subject in different segments of time, in separate stages, this distributive division is expressed by reduplication. In this exposition of the Klamath language Gatschet has shown how this distinction has actually become the basic category of the language, permeating all its parts and determining its whole "form."[21] In other language groups we can also see how the duplication of a word, which in the beginnings of linguistic history was a simple means of designating quantity, gradually became an intuitive expression for quantities that do not exist as a cohesive whole but are divided into separate groups or individuals. But this is far from exhausting the uses of reduplication. In addition to expressing plurality and repetition, it can serve to represent many other relations, particularly relations of space and size. Scherer calls it an original grammatical form serving essentially to express three basic intuitions: those of force, space

and time.[22] By a ready transition the iterative signification develops into a purely intensive signification, as in the comparative and superlative of adjectives, and in the case of verbs the intensive forms which often subsequently change to causatives. Extremely subtle *modal* differences in an action or event can also be suggested by the very simple means of reduplication: in certain American Indian languages, for example, the reduplicated form of the verb is used to designate a kind of "unreality" in action, to indicate that it exists only in purpose or "idea" and is not practically realized. In all these cases reduplication has clearly passed far beyond the phase of mere sensory description or of a pointing to objective reality. One factor that makes this evident is a peculiar *polarity* in its use: it can be the expression and vehicle not only of different but of directly opposed modalities of signification. Side by side with the intensive signification we often find the exact opposite, an attenuative signification, so that it is used in constituting diminutive forms of adjectives and limitative forms of verbs. In designating temporal stages of an action, it can serve equally well to designate present, past or future. This is the clearest indication that it is not so much a reproduction of a fixed and limited perceptual content as the expression of a specific *approach,* one might say a certain perceptual movement. The purely formal accomplishment of reduplication becomes even more evident where it passes from the sphere of quantitative expression to that of pure relation. It then determines not so much the signification of the word as its general grammatical category. In languages which do not make this category recognizable in the mere word form, a word is often transferred from one category to another, a noun changed to a verb, for example, by the mere reduplication of a sound or syllable. All these phenomena, to which we might easily add others of like nature, make it evident that even where language starts as purely imitative or "analogical" expression, it constantly strives to extend and finally to surpass its limits. It makes a virtue of necessity, that is, of the ambiguity inevitable in the linguistic sign. For this very ambiguity will not permit the sign to remain a mere individual sign; it compels the spirit to take the decisive step from the concrete function of "designation" to the universal and universally valid function of "signification." In this function language casts off, as it were, the sensuous covering in which it has hitherto appeared: mimetic or analogical expression gives way to purely symbolic expression which, precisely in and by virtue of its otherness, becomes the vehicle of a new and deeper spiritual content.

21. A. S. Gatschet, *Grammar of the Klamath Language, Contributions to North American Ethnology, 2* (Washington, Govt. Print. Off., 1890), Pt. 1, pp. 259 ff. On the significance of the "ideal of severalty or distribution," as Gatschet calls it, see below, Chapter 3.

22. Scherer, *Zur Geschichte der deutschen Sprache.*

4. Life-Symbols: The Roots of Sacrament

BY SUZANNE LANGER

IF LANGUAGE is born, indeed, from the profoundly symbolific character of the human mind, we may not be surprised to find that this mind tends to operate with symbols far below the level of speech. Previous studies have shown that even the subjective record of sense experience, the "sense-image," is not a direct copy of actual experience, but has been "projected," in the process of copying, into a new dimension, the more or less stabile form we call a *picture*. It has not the protean, mercurial elusiveness of real visual experience, but a unity and lasting identity that makes it an object of the mind's possession rather than a sensation. Furthermore it is not firmly and fixedly determined by the pattern of natural phenomena, as real sensations are, but is "free," in the same manner as the little noises which a baby produces by impulse and at will. We can call up images and let them fill the virtual space of vision between us and real objects, or on the screen of the dark, and dismiss them again, without altering the course of practical events. They are our own product, yet not part of ourselves as our physical actions are; rather might we compare them with our uttered words (save that they remain entirely private), in that they are objects to us, things that may surprise, even frighten us, experiences that can be contemplated, not merely lived.

In short, images have all the characteristics of symbols. If they were weak sense-experiences, they would confuse the order of nature for us. Our salvation lies in that we do not normally take them for bona fide sensations, but attend to them only in their capacity of *meaning* things, being *images* of things—symbols whereby those things are conceived, remembered, considered, but not encountered.

The best guarantee of their essentially symbolic function is their tendency to become metaphorical. They are not only capable of connoting the things from which our sense-experience originally derived them, and perhaps, by the law of association, the context in which they were derived (as the sight of a bell may cause one to think of "ding-dong"

and also of dinner), but they also have an inalienable tendency to "mean" things that have only a logical analogy to their primary meanings. The image of a rose symbolizes feminine beauty so readily that it is actually harder to associate roses with vegetables than with girls. Fire is a natural symbol of life and passion, though it is one element in which nothing can actually live. Its mobility and flare, its heat and color, make it an irresistible symbol of all that is living, feeling, and active. Images are, therefore, our readiest instruments for abstracting concepts from the tumbling stream of actual impressions. They make our primitive abstractions for us, they are our spontaneous embodiments of general ideas.

Just as verbal symbolism has a natural evolution from the mere suggestive word or "word-sentence" of babyhood to the grammatical edifice we call a language, so presentational symbolism has its own characteristic development. It grows from the momentary, single, static image presenting a simple concept, to greater and greater units of successive images having reference to each other; changing scenes, even visions of things in motion, by which we conceive the passage of events. That is to say, the first thing we *do* with images is to envisage a story; just as the first thing we do with words is to tell something, to make a statement.

Image-making is, then, the mode of our untutored thinking, and stories are its earliest product. We think of things happening, remembered or imaginary or prospective; we see with the mind's eye the shoes we should like to buy, and the transaction of buying them; we visualize the drowning that almost happened by the riverbank. Pictures and stories are the mind's stock-in-trade. Those larger, more complex elements that symbolize events may contain more than merely visual ingredients, kinesthetic and aural and perhaps yet other factors, wherefore it is misleading to call them "story-images"; I will refer to them as "fantasies."

Like all symbols, fantasies are derived from specific experience; even the most elaborately monstrous ones go back to witnessed events. But the original perception—like any item that sticks in the mind—is promptly and spontaneously abstracted, and used symbolically to represent a whole *kind* of actual happening. Every process we perceive, if it is to be retained in memory, must record itself as a fantasy, an envisagement, by virtue of which it can be called up in imagination or recognized when it occurs again. For no actual process happens twice; only we may meet the same *sort* of occasion again. The second time we "know" already what the event is, because we assimilate it to the fantasy abstracted from the previous instance. It will not fit exactly and it need not; the fantasy need only convey certain *general features,* the new case only exemplify these generalities in its own way, to make us apprehend a recurrence of a familiar event.

Suppose a person sees, for the first time in his life, a train arriving at a station. He probably carries away what we should call a "general impression" of noise and mass, steam, human confusion, mighty motion coming to heated, panting rest. Very possibly he has not noticed the wheels going round, but only the rods moving like a runner's knees. He does not instantly distinguish smoke from steam, nor hissing from squeaking, nor freight cars from windowed coaches, nor even boiler, cab, and coal car from each other. Yet the next time he watches a train pull in the process is familiar. His mind retains a fantasy which "means" the general concept, "*a* train arriving at *a* station." Everything that happens the second time is, to him, *like* or *unlike* the first time. The fantasy which we call his conception of a halting train gradually builds itself out of many impressions; but its framework was abstracted from the very first instance, and made the later ones "familiar."

The symbolic status of fantasies (in this technical sense of action-envisagements) is further attested by the regularity with which they follow certain basic laws of symbols. Like words and like images, they have not only literal reference to concepts, but tend to convey metaphorical meanings. Events and actions, motions and emotions, are inexhaustible in our short lives; new experience overwhelms us continually; no mind can conceive in neat literal terms all the challenges and responses, the facts and acts, that crowd in upon it. Yet conception is its essential technique, and conception requires a language of some sort. Among our fantasies there is usually something, at least, that will do as a metaphor, and this something has to serve, just as the nearest word has to serve in a new verbal expression. An arriving train may have to embody nameless dangers coming with a rush to unload their problems before me. Under the pressure of fear and confusion and shrinking, I envisage the engine, and the pursuant cars of unknown content, as a first symbol to shape my unknown concepts. What the arriving train represents is the first aspect of those

dangers that I can grasp. The fantasy that literally means a railroad incident functions here in a new capacity, where its literal generality, its applicability to trains, becomes irrelevant, and only those features that can symbolize the approaching future— power, speed, inevitable direction (symbolized by the track), and so forth— remain significant. The fantasy here is a figure; a metaphor of wordless cognition.

Metaphor is the law of growth of every semantic. It is not a development, but a principle. This is strikingly attested by the fact that the lowest, completely unintentional products of the human brain are madly metaphorical fantasies, that often make no literal sense whatever; I mean the riotous symbolism of dreams.

The first thing we instinctively strive to conceive is simply the experience of being alive. Life is a network of needs and fulfilments and further needs, with temporary frustrations here and there. If its basic needs are long unsatisfied, it ends. Our first consciousness is the sense of need, i.e. desire. Therefore our most elementary conceptions are of objects for desire.

The shapes and relations and names of such objects are unknown to the infant's mind. Food it knows, but not the source of food, beyond the mere touch and vague form of the mother's breast. Comfort and security, human nearness, light and motion —all these objects have neither substance nor fixed identity. The first images that sense impression begets in his mind have to serve for the whole gamut of his desires, for all things absent. Everything soft is a mother; everything that meets his reach is food. Being dropped, even into bed, is terror itself—the first definite form of insecurity, even of death (all our lives we speak of misfortune as a "fall"; we fall into the enemy's hands, fall from grace, fall upon hard times).

In the brief waking spells when his sense organs are learning to make report, when noises overcome his initial deafness and colors or light-spaces arrest his wandering focus, his infantile symbols multiply. Wish and fantasy grow up together. Since the proper function of his mind is conception, he produces ideas without number. He does not necessarily feel desire for everything he can think and dream; desire is only the power behind the mind, which goads it into action, and makes it productive. An overactive mind is uncritical, as a voracious appetite is unfastidious. Children mix dream and reality, fact and fiction, and make impossible combinations of ideas in their haste to capture *everything,* to conceive an overwhelming flood of experiences. Of course the stock of their imagery is always too small for its purpose, so every symbol is a dreamlike, shifting picture, a faery "world."

Something like this may be seen not only in our children, whose free fancy is somewhat hemmed by the literal logic of adults around them, but in primitive societies, where the best thought still bears a childlike stamp. Among certain peoples whom we call "savage," the very use of language exhibits a rampant confusion of metaphorical meanings clinging to every symbol, sometimes to the complete obscurance of any reasonable literal meaning. Cailliet,[1] who made a study of this phenomenon, calls this the "vegetative" stage of thought, likening the tremendous tangle of non-literal symbolism to a jungle where things choke each other in their overgrowth. The cause for this sumptuous prodigality of symbols lies in the intellectual needs of an adolescent race. When new, unexploited possibilities of thought crowd in upon the human mind, the poverty of everyday language becomes acute. Apprehension outruns comprehension so far that every phrase, however homely and literal it may be in its traditional meaning, has a vague aura of further significance. Such a state of mind is peculiarly favorable to the development of metaphorical speech.

It is characteristic of figurative images that their allegorical status is not recognized. Only a mind which can apprehend *both* a literal and a "poetic" formulation of an idea is in a position to distinguish the figure from its meaning. In spontaneous envisagement there is no such duality of form and content. In our most primitive presentations—the metaphorical imagery of dreams—it is the symbol, not its meaning, that seems to command our emotions. We do not know it as a symbol. In dream-experience we very often find some fairly commonplace object—a tree, a fish, a pointed hat, a staircase—fraught with intense value or inspiring the greatest terror. We cannot tell what makes the thing so important. It simply seems to be so in the dream. The emotional reaction is, of course, evoked by the idea embodied in that object, but so long as the idea lives only in this body we cannot distinguish it from its symbolic incarnation which, to literal-minded common sense, seems trivial.

Primitive thought is not far removed from the dream level. It operates with very similar forms. Objects that could function as dream-symbols have a mysterious significance for the waking mind, too, and are viewed with emotion, even though they have never served a practical purpose for good or for evil. The Australian's *churinga,* the Egyptian's scarab, the charms which Greek women carried to the altar, are such objects of indescribable value,

dream-symbols found and treasured in waking life. With their realistic presence, the imaginative process is carried over from dream to reality; fantasy is externalized in the veneration of "sacra."

The study of dreams gives us a clue to the deeper meaning of these bizarre holy articles: they are phallic symbols and death-symbols. We need not consult the psychoanalysts to learn this truth; any student of anthropology or archeology can assure us of it. Life and life-giving, death and the dead, are the great themes of primitive religion. Gods are at first merely emblems of the creative power; fetishes, trees, menhirs. Certain animals are natural symbols to mankind: the snake hidden in earth, the bull strong in his passion, the mysterious long-lived crocodile who metes out unexpected death. When, with the advance of civilization, their images are set up in temples or borne in processions, such images are designed to emphasize their symbolic force rather than their natural shapes. The snake may be horned or crowned or bearded, the bull may have wings or a human head.

Such sacra command a peculiar emotion, which is not the simple joy of possessing something advantageous, e.g. a strong weapon or a new slave; the "rejoicing" of a religious ceremonial is not a spontaneous delight which causes people to raise the cry of triumph, as we shout when we catch a big fish or win a game. The supposed power of the god to protect his worshipers would be no more apt to evoke cries of "hallelujah" than the tacitly accepted power of a father to protect his children. Our children live under the guarantee of our superior strength and have a sense of security in it, but they do not periodically burst into praises of it. Religious rejoicing is bound entirely to set occasions, when the god-symbol—which probably is always there, tucked away in its shrine—is brought forth and officially contemplated. Even this is not enough; someone leads the shouting and makes a demonstration of joy; gradually the feeling develops, and delight seizes the congregation. Their joy is not in an event, but in a presented idea. It centers round objects that are themselves quite passive, and useless for any other purpose than conveying the idea.

The power of conception—of "having ideas"— is man's peculiar asset, and awareness of this power is an exciting sense of human strength. Nothing is more thrilling than the dawn of a new conception. The symbols that embody basic ideas of life and death, of man and the world, are naturally sacred. But naive thinking does not distinguish between symbol and import; it sees only the physical *churinga* or the clay *thesmos,* or, where the symbol is not made by human art, but chosen among natural objects, it sees the actual snake or ibis, oak tree or

---

1. Emile Cailliet, *Symbolisme et âmes primitives* (1936), chap. iv.

arbor vitae. There is no explicit reason why sacredness belongs to such an object, only a strong feeling that in it the luck and hope and power of man is vested. The practical efficacy attributed to sacra is a dream-metaphor for the might of human ideation. Their "mightiness" is thought of as specific efficacy; whatever expresses Life is regarded as a source of life, whatever expresses Death as an agent of death. The savage's alleged stupidity about causal relations rests on this very profound law of mind, which is exemplified not only in primitive religions, but in our own pious beliefs, e.g. that the devil can be averted by holding up a little cross against him, or that a picture of the Virgin Mother protects a house against evil. Such notions rest on a natural identification of symbolic values with practical values, of the expressive with the physical functions of a thing. But this identification is too deeply grounded to be put aside as a "silly" mistake. It is symptomatic of our supreme and constant preoccupation with *ideas,* our spontaneous attention to expressive forms, that causes us to mix their importance with the importance of other activities by which life is carried on.

The contemplation of sacra invites a certain intellectual excitement—intellectual because it centers in a mental activity—the excitement of *realizing* life and strength, manhood, contest, and death. The whole cycle of human emotions is touched by such a contemplation. Undoubtedly the first outward show of sacred emotions is purely self-expressive, an unconscious issue of feelings into shouting and prancing or rolling on the earth, like a baby's tantrum; but soon the outburst becomes a habitual reaction and is used to *demonstrate,* rather than to relieve, the feelings of individuals. Lively demonstration makes an emotion contagious. Shout answers shout, the collective prancing becomes dancing. Even those who are not compelled by inner tension to let off steam just at this moment, fall into step and join the common cry.

But as soon as an expressive act is performed without inner momentary compulsion it is no longer *self-expressive;* it is expressive in the logical sense. It is not a sign of the emotion it conveys, but a symbol of it; instead of completing the natural history of a feeling, it denotes the feeling, and may merely bring it to mind, even for the actor. When an action acquires such a meaning it becomes a *gesture.*[2]

Genuine acts are completed in every detail unless they are forcibly interrupted, but gestures may be quite abortive imitations of acts, showing only their significant features. They are expressive forms, true symbols. Their aspect becomes fixed, they can be deliberately used to communicate an *idea* of the feelings that begot their prototypes. Because they are deliberate gestures, not emotional *acts,* they are no longer subject to spontaneous variation, but bound to an often meticulously exact repetition, which gradually makes their forms as familiar as words or tunes.

With the formalization of overt behavior in the presence of the sacred objects, we come into the field of *ritual.* This is, so to speak, a complement to the life-symbols; for as the latter present the basic facts of human existence, the forces of generation and achievement and death, so the rites enacted at their contemplation formulate and record man's response to those supreme realities. Ritual "expresses feelings" in the logical rather than the physiological sense. It may have what Aristotle called "cathartic" value, but that is not its characteristic; it is primarily an *articulation* of feelings. The ultimate product of such articulation is not a simple emotion, but a complex, permanent *attitude.* This attitude, which is the worshipers' response to the insight given by the sacred symbols, is an emotional pattern, which governs all individual lives. It cannot be recognized through any clearer medium than that of formalized gesture; yet in this cryptic form it *is* recognized, and yields a strong sense of tribal or congregational unity, of rightness and security. A rite regularly performed is the constant reiteration of sentiments toward "first and last things"; it is not a free expression of emotions, but a disciplined rehearsal of "right attitudes."

But emotional attitudes are always closely linked with the exigencies of current life, colored by immediate cares and desires, by specific memories and hopes. Since the sacra are consciously regarded not as symbols of Life and Death, but as life-givers and death-dealers, they are not only revered, but also besought, trusted, feared, placated with service and sacrifice. Their power is invoked for the salvation of worshipers in times of danger. They can break the drought, end famine, stay a pestilence, or turn the tide of battle. The sacred ark going up before the Children of Israel gives them their victory. Held by the Philistines, it visits disease on its captors. Its efficacy is seen in every triumph of the community, every attainment and conquest. Specific events as well as definite feelings become associated with a Holy of Holies, and seek expression round the altar.

This is the source of *mimetic* ritual. The memory of celebrated events is strong in the celebration that

---

2. Cf. L. A. Reid, "Beauty and Significance," *Proceedings of the Aristotelian Society,* N.S. XXIX (1929), 123–154, esp. p. 114: "If an expression, which at first was automatic, is repeated for the sheer joy of expression, at that point it becomes æsthetic. . . . Anger enjoyed in being acted consciously is not mere instinctive anger, but dramatic (sometimes melodramatic) anger, a very different thing."

renders thanks to the saving Power; it enters, perhaps quite unconsciously at first, into the gestures and shouts traditionally conveying such thanks. The story is retold, because it reveals the character of the Holy One, and as the telling soon becomes a formula, the gesticulations that accompany it become traditional gestures, new bodily expressions that can be woven into ritual patterns. The flourish of swords that accompanies the recall of a great exploit is presently carried out at definite points in the narrative, so that the congregation may join in it, as it joins in shouts like "Hallelujah," "Iacchos," or "Amen" at recognized periods. The gesture acquires a swing and rhythm of its own so it can be performed in genuine unison. At the end of the story it may be elaborated into a long demonstration, a "sword-dance."

Another and even more obvious origin of mimetic rites lies not in sacred story, but in supplication. Here conception is even more vivid, more urgent than in memory; an act is to be suggested and recommended to the only Being that can perform it, the Holy One; the suppliants, in their eagerness to express their desire, naturally break into pantomime. Representations of the act mingle with gestures of entreaty. And just as the expressive virtue of sacra is conceived as physical virtue, so the symbolic power of mimetic rites is presently regarded as causal efficacy; hence the world-wide and world-old belief in sympathetic magic. It really sinks to the inane conception of "magic" only when one assumes a *direct* relation between the mimicked event and the expected real one; in so far as the pantomime is enacted before a fetish, a spirit, or God, it is intended to move this divine power to act, and is simply a primitive prayer. We are often told that savage religion begins in magic; but the chances are, I think, that magic begins in religion. Its typical form—the confident, practical *use* of a formula, a brew, and a rite to achieve a physical effect—is the empty shell of a religious act. Confused, inferior minds may retain it, even in a society that no longer thinks in terms of hidden agency, but sees causally connected phenomena; and so we come to the absurd practice of a "magic" that is supposed to *defy* natural law.

Religion is a gradual envisagement of the essential pattern of human life, and to this insight almost any object, act, or event may contribute. There is no ingredient in ritual that may not also be found outside it. Sacred objects are not intrinsically precious, but derive their value from their religious use. Formalized expressive gesture occurs in the most casual social intercourse, in greetings, marks of deference, or mock defiance (like the grimaces school-children make behind the back of an un-

popular teacher, mainly for each other's benefit). As for mimetic gestures, they are the current and often unconscious accompaniment of all dramatic imagination. It need not be of serious or important acts. Mimicry is the natural symbolism by which we represent activities to our minds. It is so obvious a semantic that even where no act is carried out, but every idea merely suggested, pantomime is universally understood. Victor the Wild Boy of Aveyron, and even Wild Peter who was less intelligent, could understand mimetic expression at once, without any training, though neither ever learned language.

Before a symbolic form is put to public religious use—before it serves the difficult art of presenting really profound ideas—it has probably had a long career in a much homelier capacity. Long before men perform *rites* which enact the phases of life, they have learned such acting in *play*. And the play of children is very instructive if we would observe the peculiarly intellectual (non-practical) nature of gesture. If its purpose were, as is commonly supposed, to *learn by imitation,* an oft-repeated enactment should come closer and closer to reality, and a familiar act be represented better than a novel one; instead of that we are apt to find no attempt at *carrying out* the suggested actions of the shared day-dreams that constitute young children's play.

"Now I go away"—three steps away from the center of the game constitute this process. "And you must be crying"—the deserted one puts her hands before her face and makes a little pathetic sound. "Now I sew your fairy dress"—a hand with all five fingertips pressed together describes little circles. But the most convincingly symbolic gesture is that of eating. Children are interested in eating, and this much-desired occasion arises often in their games. Yet their imitation of that process is perhaps their least realistic act. There is no attempt to simulate the use of a spoon or other implement; the hand that carries the imaginary food to the mouth moves with the speed of a short clock-pendulum, the lips whisper "B-b-b-b-b." This sort of imitation would never serve the purpose of learning an activity. It is an abbreviated, schematized form of an action. Whether or no the child could perform the act is irrelevant; eating is an act learned long ago, sewing is probably a total mystery. Yet the imitation of sewing, though clumsy, is not as poor as that of the banquet.

The better an act is understood and the more habitually it is associated with a symbolic gesture, the more formal and cursory may be the movement that represents it. Just as the white settlers of this country first called an Indian feast a "Pow! Wow! Wow!" and later referred to it quite off-handedly as "a pow-wow," so a child's representation of sewing, fighting, or other process will be really imitative at first, but dwindle to almost nothing if the game is played often. It becomes an act of *reference* rather than of representation.

The fact that so much of primitive religious ritual is mimetic, and that mimicry is the typical form of children's play, has misled some excellent philosophers, notably John Dewey, to believe that rites are simply a repetition of practical behavior for the fun of the action itself—a repetition which presently becomes habitual, and has to be dignified by the imputation of magical usefulness. "Men make a game of their fishing and hunting, and turn to the periodic and disciplinary labor of agriculture only when inferiors, women or slaves, cannot be had to do the work. Useful labor is, whenever possible, transformed by ceremonial and ritual accompaniments, subordinated to art that yields immediate enjoyment; otherwise it is attended to under compulsion of circumstance during abbreviated surrenders of leisure. For leisure permits of festivity, in revery, ceremonies and conversation. The pressure of necessity is, however, never wholly lost, and the sense of it led men, as if with uneasy conscience at their respite from work, to impute practical efficacy to play and rites, endowing them with power to coerce events and to purchase the favor of the rulers of events. . . . It was not conscience that kept men loyal to cults and rites, and faithful to tribal myths. So far as it was not routine, it was enjoyment of the drama of life without the latter's liabilities that kept piety from decay. Interest in rites as means of influencing the course of things, and the cognitive or explanation office of myths were hardly more than an embroidery, repeating in pleasant form the pattern which inexpugnable necessities imposed upon practice. When rite and myth are spontaneous rehearsal of the impact and career of practical needs and doings, they must also seem to have practical force."[3]

From this standpoint it is hard to understand why savage rites so often involve terrible tortures—branding, flaying, knocking out teeth, cutting off finger-joints, etc. Puberty-rites, for instance, in which boys sometimes die under the knife or the whip, can hardly be described as "enjoyment of the drama of life without the latter's liabilities." Such actions are far removed from play. Their instrumental value for bringing about victories, fertility, or general good luck is undoubtedly secondary, as Professor Dewey says; but their primary achievement is not entertainment, but *morale*. They are part of man's ceaseless quest for conception and orientation. They embody his dawning notions of power and will, of death and victory, they give ac-

tive and impressive form to his demoniac fears and ideals. Ritual is the most primitive reflection of serious thought, a slow deposit, as it were, of people's imaginative insight into life. That is why it is intrinsically solemn, even though some rites of rejoicing or triumph may degenerate into mere excitement, debauchery, and license.

If men's minds were essentially playful, they could have no "uneasy conscience at their respite from work." Young dogs and young children, to whom play is a necessity, have no such conscience. Only people who feel that play displaces something more vital can disapprove of it; otherwise, if the bare necessities were taken care of, work in itself could command no respect, and we would play with all the freedom in the world, if practical work and sheer enjoyment were our only alternatives.

But the driving force in human minds is fear, which begets an imperious demand for security in the world's confusion: a demand for a world-picture that fills all experience and gives each individual a definite *orientation* amid the terrifying forces of nature and society. Objects that embody such insights, and acts which express, preserve, and reiterate them, are indeed more spontaneously interesting, more serious than work.

The universality of the concepts which religion tries to formulate draws all nature into the domain of ritual. The apparently misguided efforts of savages to induce rain by dancing and drumming are not practical mistakes at all; they are rites in which the rain has a part. White observers of Indian rain-dances have often commented on the fact that in an extraordinary number of instances the downpour really "results." Others, of a more cynical turn, remark that the leaders of the dance know the weather so well that they time their dance to meet its approaching changes and simulate "rain-making." This may well be the case; yet it is not a pure imposture. A "magic" effect is one which *completes a rite.* No savage tries to induce a snowstorm in midsummer, nor prays for the ripening of fruits entirely out of season, as he certainly would if he considered his dance and prayer the physical causes of such events. He dances *with* the rain, he invites the elements to do their part, as they are thought to be somewhere about and merely irresponsive. This accounts for the fact that no evidence of past failures discourages his practices; for if heaven and earth do not answer him, the rite is simply *unconsummated;* it was not therefore a "mistake." Its failure can be redeemed by finding some extenuating circumstance, some "counter-charm" that explains the miscarriage of the usual climax. There is no evil intent in the devices of medicine men to insure, or even to simulate, answers to magi-

---

3. *Experience and Nature* (1925), pp. 78–79.

cal invocations; for the most important virtue of the rite is not so much its practical as its religious success. Rain-making may well have begun in the celebration of an imminent shower after long drought; that the first harbinger clouds would be greeted with entreaty, excitement, and mimetic suggestion is obvious. The ritual evolves while a capricious heaven is making up its mind. Its successive acts mark the stages that bring the storm nearer. Its real import—its power to articulate a relation between man and nature, vivid at the moment—can be recognized only in the metaphorical guise of a physical power to induce the rain.[4]

Sympathetic magic, springing from mimetic ritual, belongs mainly to tribal, primitive religion. There is, however, a type of ceremonial that runs the whole gamut from the most savage to the most civilized piety from blind compulsive behavior, through magical conjuring, to the heights of conscious expression: that is the Sacrament.

The overt form of a sacrament is usually a homely, familiar action, such as washing, eating, drinking; sometimes a more special performance—slaughter, or sexual union—but still an act that is essentially realistic and vital. At first sight it seems strange that the highest symbolic import should attach to the lowliest activities, especially as the more commonplace and frequent of these are the most universal sacraments. But if we consider the genesis of such profound and ancient symbols we can understand their origin in commonplace events.

Before a behavior-pattern can become imbued with secondary meanings, it must be definite, and to the smallest detail familiar. Such forms are naturally evolved only in activities that are *often repeated*. An act that is habitually performed acquires an almost mechanical form, a sequence of motions that practice makes quite invariable. Besides the general repetition of *what* is done there is a repetition of the *way* it is done by a certain person. For instance, two people putting bread into their mouths are *doing* the same thing, but they may do it in widely different manner, according to their

respective temperaments and traditions; their behavior, though purposive and real, contains unconsciously an element of gesture.

This formal element offers high possibilities to the symbol-seeking mind. Just as one person develops personal "ways," so a tribe develops tribal "ways," which are handed down as unconscious mannerisms, until some breach in the usual pattern makes people aware of them, and they are deliberately practiced as "correct forms." As soon as they are thus abstracted, these proper gestures acquire tribal importance; someone sees a secondary meaning in an act which has attained such a formal unity and style. It seems to have a symbolic as well as a practical function; a new, emotional importance attaches to it. In a society whose symbolific impulse is in the riotous "vegetative" stage, a practical act like dividing food, or eating the first new corn of the season, may be so exciting as an *idea* that it actually loses its old material interest in the new, mystical one. Many savages have foods that may be eaten *only* ritually, and there have been Christians who frowned on all washing and bathing that was not incidental to a rite.

These last-named acts of cleansing and purification furnish a good case in point. Washing away dirt is a simple, practical act; but its symbolic value is so striking that one might say the act has a "natural meaning." Eating, likewise, is a daily practice, but is so easily significant of the kinship among those who eat together, and the even closer connection—identification—of the eaters with the eaten, that it has a certain sacramental character for any mind that is capable of general concepts at all. As soon as the symbolical import of (say) eating an animal dawns, the feast is conducted in a new spirit; not food, but *animal characteristics*, constitute its fare. The meat becomes a host; though the indwelling virtue may have no name of its own, and therefore may be thinkable only in terms of this eating, this gathering, this taste and smell and place. Because an *occasion* is the only symbol by which the new virtue is known, that occasion must have permanent form, that it may be repeated, the virtue recalled, reinvoked; and so the abstractable features of the occasion—the manners and mannerisms that were simply learned folk-ways, habitual patterns—are exalted into sacred procedure. The meat must be served in the same order, cut in the same shape and from the same part, every time it is to be eaten ritually. Gradually every detail becomes charged with meaning. Every gesture signifies some step in the acquisition of animal virtue. According to the law of all primitive symbolization, this significance is felt not as such, but as genuine efficacy; the feast not only dramatizes, but actually negotiates the de-

4. The expressive function of ritual is properly distinguished from the practical in an article by Alfred Vierkandt, "Die entwicklungspsychologische Theorie der Zauberei," *Archiv für gesammte Psychologie*, XCVIII (1937), 420–489. Vierkandt treats the causal conception as a superimposed one. "The [mimetic] activity," he says, "appears as a means to the desired end. If this end is all that motivates the rite, then the latter has changed from a purely expressive act to a purposive act. . . . In the course of this change there may be all possible gradations of the relationship between these two structures, from the merest superimposition of a purposive activity to the complete extinction of the expressive need. At the one extreme, the practical end is a mere superstructure, an ideology, while the driving force is the desire for expression. . . . The other extreme is the genuine purposive act, in which the whole is organized according to the categories of means and ends."

sired acquisition. Its performance is magical as well as expressive. And so we have the characteristic blend of power and meaning, mediation and presentation, that belongs to sacraments.[5]

Whether a dim perception of sacramental forces and dangers in the routine actions of life underlies the rigid religious control that almost all primitive societies hold over daily food and drink and housekeeping, we cannot stop to investigate here. What matters in the present context is merely that meaning and magic pervade savage life to such an extent that any behavior-pattern, any striking visual form or musical rhythm, any question or announcement made often enough to become a formula, acquires some symbolic or mystical function; this stage of thinking is the creative period for religion. In it the great life-symbols are established and developed. Concepts which are far beyond the actual grasp of savage or semi-savage minds are apprehended, though not comprehended, in physical embodiments, sacred fetishes, idols, animals; human attitudes, vaguely recognized as reasonable and right, are expressed by actions which are not spontaneous emotional outlets but prescribed modes of participation and assent.

Rites of supplication and offering cannot forever be addressed to a nameless symbol, a mere bundle of sticks, jawbone, grave-mound, or monolith. The Holy One has a part, howbeit a silent part, to play in the ceremony; as the cult develops, the presiding power acquires an epithet expressing this function: "She who Harkens," "He of Appeasement," "He of Sword-play, He of the Sword." The epithet serves as a name, and soon becomes a name; the name fixes a character which gradually finds expression in new physical representations. So the pillar that was once a phallic symbol becomes a "Herm," and the rock that was itself taboo shelters a sacred snake to account for its holiness. The snake can see and hear, respond or retire, strike or spare. The snake can be a forgiver, the Herm can be a watcher.

Of course this is a step from sheer superstition toward theology, toward conceiving gods instead of mere magical cult-objects. But the envisagement of such "gods" is as yet entirely naive; "He of the Sword" may be represented as a sword, and "She who Harkens" may not only have, but be, an ear.[6]

The first idea of a god is not that of an anthropomorphic being that dwells in an object, e.g. in a certain tree; it is simply a notion of the object itself *as a personality,* as an agent participating in the ritual. This participation is what lifts it above mere magical potency to something like a personal will. The might of the cult-objects, charms or sacred arks or holy wells, is simply *efficacy;* that of gods, whether they be trees, animals, statues, or dead men, is *ability.* A charm is made to operate by a correct ritual; a deity is invoked by being pleased, either by service or flattery. The rite may persist for ages, but when the Holy One becomes a god, the keynote of ritual becomes prayer. One cannot simply draw "mana" from him as from the presence of holy things; one has to ask him to exert his talents. Therefore his worshipers recite the catalogue of his virtues—his valor, wisdom, goodness, the wonders of his favor, the terrors of his displeasure. In this way his traits become very definitely and publicly accepted. Every asset his worshipers seek is his, and in his gift. His image tends more and more to express this enhanced character; he is the summary of a human ideal, the ideal of his tribe.

Herein lies the rationale of animal worship, which seems to have preceded, almost universally, the evolution of higher religions. A god who symbolizes moral qualities does well to appear in animal form; for a human incarnation would be confusing. Human personalities are complex, extremely varied, hard to define, hard to generalize; but animals run very true to type. The strength of the bull, the shiftiness of the rabbit, the sinuous mobility of the snake, the solemnity of the owl, are exemplified with perfect definiteness and simplicity by every member of their respective species. Before men can find these traits clearly in themselves they can see them typified in animals. The beast that symbolizes a virtue, physical or moral, is divine to men who see and envy that virtue in it. It is the possessor, hence the possible dispenser, of its peculiar quality. Therefore it is honored, wooed, placated, and sometimes sacramentally eaten by its worshipers.

The man who sees his ideal in an animal calls himself by its name, because, exemplifying his highest aspirations as it does, it is his "true self." We who have higher gods still describe our enemies as the beasts we despise—they are "perfect asses," "just pigs," or on extreme provocation "skunks." Men who still look up to animals bestow analogous titles on human beings in a reverent spirit. Those to whom the swift, intensely vital and prolific hare is a symbol of life and fertility, think of themselves as hares, and attribute even more harishness to their venerated, beatified ancestors. They were the "Great

---

5. For a modern example, consider the following statement by W. H. Frere: "The Eucharist is one homogeneous and continuous action and goes forward, if one may say so, like a drama; it has its prelude, its working up, its climax, its epilogue. . . . The Eucharist was to sum up and supersede all older rites and sacrifices; and it has been from the first the central Christian sacrament, *not significant only, but efficacious." The Principles of Religious Ceremonial* (1928), pp. 37–39 (italics mine).

6. See Jane Harrison, *Prolegomena to the Study of Greek Religion* (1908), p. 187.

Hares." A civilized man would mean this epithet metaphorically, but the primitive mind is always losing its way between symbol and meaning, and freely changes "My earliest ancestor was a 'Hare,' " into "A hare was my first ancestor."

Here is probably the genesis of totemism. The fact that totems feature all kinds of animals and even plants does not preclude such an origin; for once a tribe has adopted an animal form to express its essence, other tribes will follow suit by sheer imitation, without the same motive, choosing different animals to distinguish them from their neighbors. They may have no original notion of any ideal. A tribal ideal is then formed in keeping with the symbol, if at all. But the primary conception of a totem must have sprung from some insight into the human significance of an animal form; perhaps a purely sexual significance, perhaps a sublimer notion of savage virtue.

Such speculation is borne out by the fact that it is the animal *form* rather than any living representative of the species that is preëminently holy. Emile Durkheim, who has made a close study of totemism in *Les formes élémentaires de la vie religieuse,* warns against the fallacy of seeing a simple animal worship in its practices; for in the course of such study, he says, "One comes to the remarkable conclusion that *images of the totem-creature are more sacred than the totem-creature itself.*"[7]

"Here is the real nature of the totem: it is nothing but the material form by which human minds can picture that immaterial substance, that energy diffused throughout all sorts of heterogeneous things, that power which alone is the true object of the cult."[8] Moreover, it is this Power concentrated in the character of the clan—the social influence and authority—which, in M. Durkheim's opinion, is the real divinity.

"The totem is the banner of the clan," he says; and further, "Since the religious Power is nothing else than the collective and nameless Power of the clan, and since this is not capable of representation except through the totem, the totemic emblem is like the visible body of the god. . . . This explains why, in the hierarchy of things sacred, it holds the highest place. . . .

"Why is it forbidden to kill and eat the totem-animal, and why has its flesh these positive virtues which give it its part in ritual? Because this animal resembles the tribal emblem, namely its own image. And as of course it resembles it more closely than man, it has a higher rank than he in the hierarchy of holies."[9]

Durkheim's whole analysis of totemism bears out the contention that it is, like all sacraments, a form of *ideation,* an expression of concepts in purely presentational metaphor.

"Religion is, first and foremost, a system of ideas by means of which individuals can envisage the society of which they are members, and the relations, obscure yet intimate, which they bear to it. That is the primordial task of a faith. And though it be metaphorical and symbolical, it is not therefore untrue. On the contrary, it conveys all that is essential in the relations it claims to portray. . . ."[10]

"The believer is not deceiving himself when he puts his faith in the existence of a moral potency, on which he is dependent, and to which he owes his better part; this Power exists, it is Society. . . . Doubtless, he is mistaken when he believes that the enhancement of his vital strength is the work of a Being that looks like an animal or a plant. But his error lies only in the literal reading of the symbol by which this Being is presented to his mind, the external aspect under which his imagination conveys it, and does not touch the fact of its existence. Behind these figures and metaphors, however gross or refined they may be, there lies a concrete and living reality."[11]

From such primitive sacramentalism to a real theology, a belief in Olympians who lie on beds of asphodel, or in a heavenly Jerusalem where a triune God sits enthroned, may seem so far a call that one may incline to doubt whether human imagination could have passed continuously from one to the other. The mentalities of Australian aborigines and of European worshipers, ancient and modern, appear to be just worlds apart; the Sacred Emu does not give any promise of a future Zeus, nor does a lizard in a cave appear to foreshadow the Christian God of Love. Yet when we trace the histories of such high divinities back to their antecedents in earlier ages, there is an astonishing kinship between those antecedents and the local deities of Australian, African, or American savages. We have no evidence that genuine totemism ever existed in Europe; but of animal cults we have convincing proof. Luck has it that one of the most civilized religions of all time, namely the Greek, has inscribed the whole course of its evolution for us on the places where it flourished—on the temples and households, cemeteries and libraries that tell the story of Hellas from its dawn to its slow destruction; and that a classical scholar with patience and insight has traced that evolution from its earliest recoverable phases to its last decadent forms. For, as Professor Gilbert Murray has said, "In this department as in others, an-

7. *Op. cit.,* p. 189.
8. *Ibid.,* p. 270.
9. *Ibid.,* pp. 315–318.

10. *Ibid.,* p. 323.
11. *Ibid.,* p. 322.

cient Greece has the triumphant if tragic distinction of beginning at the very bottom and struggling, however precariously, to the very summits. There is hardly any horror of primitive superstition of which we cannot find some distant traces in our Greek record. There is hardly any height of spiritual thought attained in the world that has not its archetype or its echo in the stretch of Greek literature that lies between Thales and Plotinus. . . ."[12]

The scholar to whom we are most indebted for a truly coherent picture of religious origins is Jane Harrison, whose *Prolegomena to the Study of Greek Religion* sets forth with all detail the evolution of Olympian and Christian divinities from their humble, zoölatrous beginnings in tombs and snake-holes and chimney-corners. This evolution is a long story. It has been briefly retold by Professor Murray in the book from which the above quotation is taken, and here I can do no more than indicate its beginning, direction, and moral.

Its beginning—contrary to our traditional ideas of the Greek mind—is not at all in bright fancies, lovely anthropomorphic conceptions of the sun, the moon, and the rainbow. Professor Murray remarks this at the outset.

"The things that have misled us moderns in our efforts towards understanding the primitive stage in Greek religion," he says, "have been first the widespread and almost ineradicable error of treating Homer as primitive, and more generally our unconscious insistence on starting with the notion of 'Gods.' . . . The truth is that this notion of a god far away in the sky—I do not say merely a First Cause who is 'without body parts or passions,' but almost any being that we should naturally call a 'god'—is an idea not easy for primitive man to grasp. It is a subtle and rarefied idea, saturated with ages of philosophy and speculation."[13]

The Olympian gods, who seem like free inventions of an innocent, delighted imagination, "are imposed upon a background strangely unlike themselves. For a long time their luminous figures dazzled our eyes; we were not able to see the half-lit regions behind them, the dark primaeval tangle of desires and fears and dreams from which they drew their vitality. The surest test to apply in this question is the evidence of actual cult. Miss Harrison has here shown us the right method. . . ."[14]

Her findings by this method were, in brief, that in the great Greek festivals the Olympian gods played no role at all; their names were quite externally associated with these occasions, and were usually modified by an epithet, to make the connection at least reasonable. Thus the Athenian Diasia is held in honor of "Zeus Meilichios," or "Zeus of Placation."

"A god with an epithet," says Murray, "is always suspicious, like a human being with an 'alias.' Miss Harrison's examination shows that in the rites Zeus has no place at all. Meilichios from the beginning has a fairly secure one. On some of the reliefs Meilichios appears not as a god, but as an enormous, bearded snake, a well-known representation of underworld powers or dead ancestors. . . .

"The Diasia was a ritual of placation, that is, of casting away various elements of pollution or danger and appeasing the unknown wraths of the surrounding darkness. The nearest approach to a god contained in this festival is Meilichios. . . . His name means 'He of appeasement,' and he is nothing else."

"The Thesmophoria formed the great festival of Demeter and her daughter Korê, though here again Demeter appears with a clinging epithet, Thesmophoros. We know pretty clearly the whole course of the ritual. . . . The Olympian Demeter and Persephone dwindle away as we look closer, and we are left with the shadow Thesmophoros, 'She who carries Thesmoi,' not a substantive personal goddess, but merely a personification of the ritual itself; an imaginary charm-bearer generated by so much charm-bearing, just as Meilichios in the Diasia was generated from the ritual of appeasement."[15]

The first entirely anthropomorphic conception seems to have come into Greece with the conquering Achaeans, whose Olympian Zeus, a mountain god, had attained human form, at a time when the native Pelasgian gods still retained their animal shapes or were at best monstrous hybrids; Athena still identified with an owl, or figured as the Diver-Bird or bird-headed "Diver-Maid" of Megara. The effect of this personified Achaean god on the barbarian worship then current in Aegean lands was probably spectacular; for a single higher conception can be a marvellous leaven in the heavy, amorphous mass of human thought. The local gods took shape in the new human pattern, so obvious once it had been conceived; and it is not surprising that this Achaean mountain-god, or rather mountain-dwelling sky-god, became either father or conqueror of those divinities who grew up in his image.

"He had an extraordinary power of ousting or absorbing the various objects of aboriginal worship which he found in his path," says Professor Murray. "The story of Meilichios [whose cult he usurped] is a common one."[16]

But even this great Olympian could not attain his

---

12. *Five Stages of Greek Religion* (1925), pp. 15–16.
13. *Ibid.*, p. 24.
14. *Ibid.*, p. 28.

15. *Ibid.*, pp. 28–31.
16. Murray, *op. cit.*, p. 70.

perfect form, his definite relations to the heavens, the gods, and the human world, until he became a figure in something more than ritual; it is in the great realm of *myth* that human conceptions of divinity really become articulated. A symbol may give identity to a god, a mimetic dance may express his favors, but what really fixes his character is the tradition of his origin, actions, and past adventures. Like the hero of a novel or a drama, he becomes a personality, not by his sheer appearance, but by his story. Moloch, however widely worshiped, has never become an independent being apart from his rites, because if he had any myth, it never became coherent in any systematic account. But Zeus and all his family had their genealogist in Homer, to mention only the greatest myth-maker we know. Herodotus was probably not far from the truth when he said that Homer gave the Greek gods their names and stations and even their shapes.[17] Divinities are

born of ritual, but theologies spring from myth. Miss Harrison, in describing the origin of a *Korê* or primitive earth-goddess, says: "The May-pole or harvest-sheaf is half-way to a harvest Maiden; it is thus . . . that a goddess is made. A song is sung, a story told, and the very telling fixes the outline of the personality. It is possible to worship long in the spirit, but as soon as the story-telling and myth-making instinct awakes you have anthropomorphism and theology.[18]

The "myth-making instinct," however, has a history of its own, and its own life-symbols; though it is the counterpart of sacrament in the making of higher religion, it does not belong to the lower phases; or at least, it has little importance below the level of dawning philosophic thought, which is the last reach of genuine religion, its consummation and also its dissolution.

17. Harrison, *Prolegomena*, p. 64.

18. Harrison, *op. cit.*, p. 80.

5. *The Art of Magic and the Power of Faith*

BY BRONISLAW MALINOWSKI

MAGIC—the very word seems to reveal a world of mysterious and unexpected possibilities! Even for those who do not share in that hankering after the occult, after the short-cuts into "esoteric truth," this morbid interest, nowadays so freely ministered to by stale revivals of half-understood ancient creeds and cults, dished up under the names of "theosophy," "spiritism" or "spiritualism," and various pseudo-"sciences," -ologies and -isms—even for the clear scientific mind the subject of magic has a special attraction. Partly perhaps because we hope to find in it the quintessence of primitive man's longings and of his wisdom—and that, whatever it might be, is worth knowing. Partly because "magic" seems to stir up in everyone some hidden mental forces, some lingering hopes in the miraculous, some dormant beliefs in man's mysterious possibilities. Witness to this is the power which the words *magic, spell, charm, to bewitch,* and *to enchant,* possess in poetry, where the inner

value of words, the emotional forces which they still release, survive longest and are revealed most clearly.

Yet when the sociologist approaches the study of magic, there where it still reigns supreme, where even now it can be found fully developed—that is, among the stone-age savages of to-day—he finds to his disappointment an entirely sober, prosaic, even clumsy art, enacted for purely practical reasons, governed by crude and shallow beliefs, carried out in a simple and monotonous technique. This was already indicated in the definition of magic given above when in order to distinguish it from religion we described it as a body of purely practical acts, performed as a means to an end. Such also we have found it when we tried to disentangle it from knowledge and from practical arts, in which it is so strongly enmeshed, superficially so alike that it requires some effort to distinguish the essentially different mental attitude and the specifically ritual nature of its acts. Primitive magic—every field anthropologist knows it to his cost—is extremely monotonous and unexciting, strictly limited in its

Reprinted from Bronislaw Malinowski, *Magic, Science and Religion* (Glencoe, Ill.: The Free Press, 1948), pp. 50–55, with the permission of The Free Press.

means of action, circumscribed in its beliefs, stunted in its fundamental assumptions. Follow one rite, study one spell, grasp the principles of magical belief, art and sociology in one case, and you will know not only all the acts of the tribe, but, adding a variant here and there, you will be able to settle as a magical practitioner in any part of the world yet fortunate enough to have faith in that desirable art.

The Rite and the Spell

Let us have a look at a typical act of magic, and choose one which is well known and generally regarded as a standard performance—an act of black magic. Among the several types which we meet in savagery, witchcraft by the act of pointing the magical dart is, perhaps, the most widespread of all. A pointed bone or a stick, an arrow or the spine of some animal, is ritually, in a mimic fashion, thrust, thrown, or pointed in the direction of the man to be killed by sorcery. We have innumerable recipes in the oriental and ancient books of magic, in ethnographic descriptions and tales of travellers, of how such a rite is performed. But the emotional setting, the gestures and expressions of the sorcerer during the performance, have been but seldom described. Yet these are of the greatest importance. If a spectator were suddenly transported to some part of Melanesia and could observe the sorcerer at work, not perhaps knowing exactly what he was looking at, he might think that he had either to do with a lunatic or else he would guess that here was a man acting under the sway of uncontrolled anger. For the sorcerer has, as an essential part of the ritual performance, not merely to point the bone dart at his victim, but with an intense expression of fury and hatred he has to thrust it in the air, turn and twist it as if to bore it in the wound, then pull it back with a sudden jerk. Thus not only is the act of violence, or stabbing, reproduced, but the passion of violence has to be enacted.

We see thus that the dramatic expression of emotion is the essence of this act, for what is it that is reproduced in it? Not its end, for the magician would in that case have to imitate the death of the victim, but the emotional state of the performer, a state which closely corresponds to the situation in which we find it and which has to be gone through mimetically.

I could adduce a number of similar rites from my own experience, and many more, of course, from other records. Thus, when in other types of black magic the sorcerer ritually injures or mutilates or destroys a figure or object symbolizing the victim, this rite is, above all, a clear expression of hatred and anger. Or when in love magic the performer has really or symbolically to grasp, stroke, fondle the beloved person or some object representing her, he reproduces the behavior of a heart-sick lover who has lost his common sense and is overwhelmed by passion. In war magic, anger, the fury of attack, the emotions of combative passion, are frequently expressed in a more or less direct manner. In the magic of terror, in the exorcism directed against powers of darkness and evil, the magician behaves as if himself overcome by the emotion of fear, or at least violently struggling against it. Shouts, brandishing of weapons, the use of lighted torches, form often the substance of this rite. Or else in an act, recorded by myself, to ward off the evil powers of darkness, a man has ritually to tremble, to utter a spell slowly as if paralyzed by fear. And this fear gets hold also of the approaching sorcerer and wards him off.

All such acts, usually rationalized and explained by some principle of magic, are *prima facie* expressions of emotion. The substances and paraphernalia used in them have often the same significance. Daggers, sharp-pointed lacerating objects, evil-smelling or poisonous substances, used in black magic; scents, flowers, inebriating stimulants, in love magic; valuables, in economic magic—all these are associated primarily through emotions and not through ideas with the end of the respective magic.

Besides such rites, however, in which a dominant element serves to express an emotion, there are others in which the act does forecast its result, or, to use Sir James Frazer's expression, the rite imitates its end. Thus, in the black magic of the Melanesians recorded by myself, a characteristic ritual way of winding-up the spell is for the sorcerer to weaken the voice, utter a death-rattle, and fall down in imitation of the rigor of death. It is, however, not necessary to adduce any other examples, for this aspect of magic and the allied one of contagious magic has been brilliantly described and exhaustively documented by Frazer. Sir James has also shown that there exists a special lore of magical substances based on affinities, relations, on ideas of similarity and contagion, developed with a magical pseudo-science.

But there are also ritual proceedings in which there is neither imitation nor forecasting nor the expression of any special idea or emotion. There are rites so simple that they can be described only as an immediate application of magical virtue, as when the performer stands up and, directly invoking the wind, causes it to rise. Or again, as when a man conveys the spell to some material substance which afterwards will be applied to the thing or person to be charmed. The material objects used in such ritual are also of a strictly appropriate character—substances best fitted to receive, retain, and transmit magical virtue, coverings designed to imprison and preserve it until it is applied to its object.

But what is the magical virtue which figures not only in the last-mentioned type of act but in every magical rite? For whether it be an act expressing certain emotions or a rite of imitation and foreshadowing or an act of simple casting, one feature they have always in common: the force of magic, its virtue, must always be conveyed to the charmed object. What is it? Briefly, it is always the power contained in the spell, for, and this is never sufficiently emphasized, the most important element in magic is the spell. The spell is that part of magic which is occult, handed over in magical filiation, known only to the practitioner. To the natives knowledge of magic means knowledge of spell, and in an analysis of any act of witchcraft it will always be found that the ritual centers round the utterance of the spell. The formula is always the core of the magical performance.

The study of the texts and formulas of primitive magic reveals that there are three typical elements associated with the belief in magical efficiency. There are, first, the phonetic effects, imitations of natural sounds, such as the whistling of the wind, the growling of thunder, the roar of the sea, the voices of various animals. These sounds symbolize certain phenomena and thus are believed to produce them magically. Or else they express certain emotional states associated with the desire which is to be realized by means of the magic.

The second element, very conspicuous in primitive spells, is the use of words which invoke, state, or command the desired aim. Thus the sorcerer will mention all the symptoms of the disease which he is inflicting, or in the lethal formula he will describe the end of his victim. In healing magic the wizard will give word-pictures of perfect health and bodily strength. In economic magic the growing of plants, the approach of animals, the arrival of fish in shoals are depicted. Or again the magician uses words and sentences which express the emotion under the stress of which he works his magic, and the action which gives expression to this emotion. The sorcerer in tones of fury will have to repeat such verbs as "I break—I twist—I burn—I destroy," enumerating with each of them the various parts of the body and internal organs of his victim. In all this we see that the spells are built very much on the same pattern as the rites and the words selected for the same reasons as the substances of magic.

Thirdly there is an element in almost every spell to which there is no counterpart in ritual. I mean the mythological allusions, the references to ancestors and culture heroes from whom this magic has been received. . . . Tradition . . . gathers in great abundance round magical ritual and cult.

6. *The Nature and Functions of Ceremonials*

BY A. R. RADCLIFFE-BROWN

IN THE PEACE-MAKING CEREMONY of the North Andaman, the meaning is easily discovered; the symbolism of the dance being indeed at once obvious to a witness, though perhaps not quite so obvious from the description given. The dancers are divided into two parties. The actions of the one party throughout are expressions of their aggressive feelings towards the other. This is clear enough in the shouting, the threatening gestures,

Reprinted from A. R. Radcliffe-Brown, *The Andaman Islanders* (Glencoe, Ill.: The Free Press, 1948), pp. 238–57, with the permission of The Free Press.

and the way in which each member of the "attacking" party gives a good shaking to each member of the other party. On the other side what is expressed may be described as complete passivity; the performers stand quite still throughout the whole dance, taking care to show neither fear nor resentment at the treatment to which they have to submit. Thus those of the one side give collective expression to their collective anger, which is thereby appeased. The others, by passively submitting to this, humbling themselves before the just wrath of their enemies, expiate their wrongs. Anger appeased dies down; wrongs expiated are forgiven and forgotten; the enmity is at an end.

The screen of fibre against which the passive participants in the ceremony stand has a peculiar symbolic meaning that will be explained later in the chapter. The only other elements of the ceremony are the weeping together, which will be dealt with very soon, and the exchange of weapons, which is simply a special form of the rite of exchanging presents as an expression of good-will. The special form is particularly appropriate as it would seem to ensure at least some months of friendship, for you cannot go out to fight a man with his weapons while he has yours.

The purpose of the ceremony is clearly to produce a change in the feelings of the two parties towards one another, feelings of enmity being replaced through it by feelings of friendship and solidarity. It depends for its effect on the fact that anger and similar aggressive feelings may be appeased by being freely expressed. Its social function is to restore the condition of solidarity between two local groups that has been destroyed by some act of offence.

The marriage ceremony and the peace-making dance both afford examples of the custom which the Andamanese have of weeping together under certain circumstances. The principal occasions of this ceremonial weeping are as follows: (1) when two friends or relatives meet after having been for some time parted, they embrace each other and weep together; (2) at the peace-making ceremony the two parties of former enemies weep together, embracing each other; (3) at the end of the period of mourning the friends of the mourners (who have not themselves been mourning) weep with the latter; (4) after a death the relatives and friends embrace the corpse and weep over it; (5) when the bones of a dead man or woman are recovered from the grave they are wept over; (6) on the occasion of a marriage the relatives of each weep over the bride and bridegroom; (7) at various stages of the initiation ceremonies the female relatives of a youth or girl weep over him or her.

First of all it is necessary to note that not in any of the above-mentioned instances is the weeping simply a spontaneous expression of feeling. It is always a rite the proper performance of which is demanded by custom. (As mentioned in an earlier chapter, the Andamanese are able to sit down and shed tears at will.) Nor can we explain the weeping as being an expression of sorrow. It is true that some of the occasions are such as to produce sorrowful feelings (4 and 5, for example), but there are others on which there would seem to be no reason for sorrow but rather for joy. The Andamanese do weep from sorrow and spontaneously. A child cries when he is scolded or hurt; a widow weeps thinking of her recently dead husband. Men rarely weep spontaneously for any reason, though they shed tears abundantly when taking part in the rite. The weeping on the occasions enumerated is therefore not a spontaneous expression of individual emotion but is an example of what I have called ceremonial customs. In certain circumstances men and women are required by custom to embrace one another and weep, and if they neglected to do so it would be an offence condemned by all right-thinking persons.

According to the postulate of method laid down at the beginning of the chapter we have to seek such an explanation of this custom as will account for all the different occasions on which the rite is performed, since we must assume that one and the same rite has the same meaning in whatever circumstances it may take place. It must be noted, however, that there are two varieties of the rite. In the first three instances enumerated above the rite is reciprocal, i.e. two persons or two distinct groups of persons weep together and embrace each other, both parties to the rite being active. In the other four instances it is one-sided; a person or group of persons weeps over another person (or the relics of a person) who has only a passive part in the ceremony. Any explanation, to be satisfactory, must take account of the difference between these two varieties.

I would explain the rite as being an expression of that feeling of attachment between persons which is of such importance in the almost domestic life of the Andaman society. In other words the purpose of the rite is to affirm the existence of a social bond between two or more persons.

There are two elements in the ceremony, the embrace and the weeping. We have already seen that the embrace is an expression, in the Andamans as elsewhere, of the feeling of attachment, i.e. the feeling of which love, friendship, affection are varieties. Turning to the second element of the ceremony, we are accustomed to think of weeping as more particularly an expression of sorrow. We are familiar, however, with tears of joy, and I have myself observed tears that were the result neither of joy nor of sorrow but of a sudden overwhelming feeling of affection. I believe that we may describe weeping as being a means by which the mind obtains relief from a condition of emotional tension, and that it is because such conditions of tension are most common in feelings of grief and pain that weeping comes to be associated with painful feelings. It is impossible here to discuss this subject, and I am therefore compelled to assume without proof this proposition on which my explanation of the rite is based. My own conclusion, based on careful observation, is that in this rite the weeping is an expression of what has been called the tender emotion. Without doubt, on some of the occasions of the rite, as when weeping over a dead friend, the participants are suffering a painful emotion, but this is evidently not so on all occasions. It is true, however, as I shall show, that on every occasion of the rite there is a condition of emotional tension due to the sudden calling into activity of the sentiment of personal attachment.

When two friends or relatives meet after having been separated, the social relation between them that has been interrupted is about to be renewed. This social relation implies or depends upon the existence of a specific bond of solidarity between them. The weeping rite (together with the subsequent exchange of presents) is the affirmation of this bond. The rite, which, it must be remembered, is obligatory, compels the two participants to act as though they felt certain emotions, and thereby does, to some extent, produce those emotions in them. When the two friends meet their first feeling seems to be one of shyness mingled with pleasure at seeing each other again. This is according to the statements of the natives as well as my own observation. Now this shyness (the Andamanese use the same word as they do for "shame") is itself a condition of emotional tension, which has to be relieved in some way. The embrace awakens to full activity that feeling of affection or friendship that has been dormant and which it is the business of the rite to renew. The weeping gives relief to the emotional tension just noted, and also reinforces the effect of the embrace. This it does owing to the fact that a strong feeling of personal attachment is always produced when two persons join together in sharing and simultaneously expressing one and the same emotion. The little ceremony thus serves to dispel the initial feeling of shyness and to reinstate the condition of intimacy and affection that existed before the separation.

In the peace-making ceremony the purpose of the whole rite is to abolish a condition of enmity and replace it by one of friendship. The once friendly relations between the two groups have been interrupted by a longer or shorter period of antagonism. We have seen that the effect of the dance is to dispel the wrath of the one group by giving it free expression. The weeping that follows is the renewal of the friendship. The rite is here exactly parallel to that on the meeting of two friends, except that not two individuals but two groups are concerned, and that owing to the number of persons involved the emotional condition is one of much greater intensity. Here therefore also we see that the rite is an affirmation of solidarity or social union, in this instance between the groups, and that the rule is in its nature such as to make the participants feel that they are bound to each other by ties of friendship.

We now come to a more difficult example of the rite, that at the end of mourning. It will be shown later in the chapter that during the period of mourning the mourners are cut off from the ordinary life of the community. By reason of the ties that still bind them to the dead person they are placed, as it were, outside the society and the bonds that unite them to their group are temporarily loosened. At the end of the mourning period they re-enter the society and take up once more their place in the social life. Their return to the community is the occasion on which they and their friends weep together. In this instance also, therefore, the rite may be explained as having for its purpose the renewal of the social relations that have been interrupted. This explanation will seem more convincing when we have considered in detail the customs of mourning. If it be accepted, then it may be seen that in the first three instances of the rite of weeping (those in which the action is reciprocal) we have conditions in which social relations that have been interrupted are about to be renewed, and the rite serves as a ceremony of aggregation.

Let us now consider the second variety of the rite, and first of all its meaning as part of the ceremony of marriage. By marriage the social bonds that have to that time united the bride and bridegroom to their respective relatives, particularly their female relatives such as mother, mother's sister, father's sister and adopted mother, are modified. The unmarried youth or girl is in a position of dependence upon his or her older relatives, and by the marriage this dependence is partly abolished. Whereas the principal duties of the bride were formerly those towards her mother and older female relatives, henceforth her chief duties in life will be towards her husband. The position of the bridegroom is similar, and it must be noted that his social relations with his male relatives are less affected by his marriage than those with his female relatives. Yet, though the ties that have bound the bride and bridegroom to their relatives are about to be modified or partially destroyed by the new ties of marriage with its new duties and rights they will still continue to exist in a weakened and changed condition. The rite of weeping is the expression of this. It serves to make real (by feeling), in those taking part in it, the presence of the social ties that are being modified.

When the mother of the bride or bridegroom

weeps at a marriage she feels that her son or daughter is being taken from her care. She has the sorrow of a partial separation and she consoles herself by expressing in the rite her continued feeling of tenderness and affection towards him in the new condition that he is entering upon. For her the chief result of the rite is to make her feel that her child is still an object of her affection, still bound to her by close ties, in spite of the fact that he or she is being taken from her care.

Exactly the same explanation holds with regard to the weeping at the initiation ceremonies. By these ceremonies the youth (or girl) is gradually withdrawn from a condition of dependence on his mother and older female relatives and is made an independent member of the community. The initiation is a long process that is only completed by marriage. At every stage of the lengthy ceremonies therefore, the social ties that unite the initiate to these relatives are modified or weakened, and the rite of weeping is the means by which the significance of the change is impressed upon those taking part in it. For the mother the weeping expresses her resignation at her necessary loss, and acts as a consolation by making her feel that her son is still hers, though now being withdrawn from her care. For the boy the rite has a different meaning. He realises that he is no longer merely a child, dependent upon his mother, but is now entering upon manhood. His former feelings towards his mother must be modified. That he is being separated from her is, for him, the most important aspect of the matter, and therefore while she weeps he must give no sign of tenderness in return but must sit passive and silent. So also in the marriage ceremony, the rite serves to impress upon the young man and woman that they are, by reason of the new ties that they are forming with one another, severing their ties with their families.

When a person dies the social bonds that unite him to the survivors are profoundly modified. They are not in an instant utterly destroyed, as we shall see better when we deal with the funeral and mourning customs, for the friends and relatives still feel towards the dead person that affection in which they held him when alive, and this has now become a source of deep grief. It is this affection still binding them to him that they express in the rite of weeping over the corpse. Here rite and natural expression of emotion coincide, but it must be noted that the weeping is obligatory, a matter of duty. In this instance, then, the rite is similar to that at marriage and initiation. The man is by death cut off from the society to which he belonged, and association with his friends, but the latter still feel towards him that attachment that bound them to-

gether while he lived, and it is this attachment that they express when they embrace the lifeless corpse and weep over it.

There remains only one more instance of the rite to be considered. When the period of mourning for a dead person is over and the bones are recovered the modification in the relations between the dead and the living, which begins at death, and is, as we shall see, carried out by the mourning customs and ceremonies, is finally accomplished. The dead person is now entirely cut off from the world of the living, save that his bones are to be treasured as relics and amulets. The weeping over the bones must be taken, I think, as a rite of aggregation whereby the bones as representative of the dead person (all that is left of him) are received back into the society henceforth to fill a special place in the social life. It really constitutes a renewal of social relations with the dead person, after a period during which all active social relations have been interrupted owing to the danger in all contact between the living and the dead. By the rite the affection that was once felt towards the dead person is revived and is now directed to the skeletal relics of the man or woman that once was their object. If this explanation seem unsatisfactory, I would ask the reader to suspend his judgment until the funeral customs of the Andamans have been discussed, and then to return to this point.

The proffered explanation of the rite of weeping should now be plain. I regard it as being the affirmation of a bond of social solidarity between those taking part in it, and as producing in them a realisation of that bond by arousing the sentiment of attachment. In some instances the rite therefore serves to renew social relations when they have been interrupted, and in such instances the rite is reciprocal. In others it serves to show the continued existence of the social bond when it is being weakened or modified, as by marriage, initiation or death. In all instances we may say that the purpose of the rite is to bring about a new state of the affective dispositions that regulate the conduct of persons to one another, either by reviving sentiments that have lain dormant, or producing a recognition of a change in the condition of personal relations.

The study of these simple ceremonies has shown us several things of importance. (1) In every instance the ceremony is the expression of an affective state of mind shared by two or more persons. Thus the weeping rite expresses feelings of solidarity, the exchange of presents expresses goodwill. (2) But the ceremonies are not spontaneous expressions of feeling; they are all customary actions to which the sentiment of obligation attaches, which it is the duty of persons to perform on certain definite occasions. It is the duty of everyone in a community to give presents at a wedding; it is the duty of relatives to weep together when they meet. (3) In every instance the ceremony is to be explained by reference to fundamental laws regulating the affective life of human beings. It is not our business here to analyse these phenomena but only to satisfy ourselves that they are real. That weeping is an outlet for emotional excitement, that the free expression of aggressive feelings causes them to die out instead of smouldering on, that an embrace is an expression of feelings of attachment between persons: these are the psychological generalisations upon which are based the explanations given above of various ceremonies of the Andamanese. (4) Finally, we have seen that each of the ceremonies serves to renew or to modify in the minds of those taking part in it some one or more of the social sentiments. The peace-making ceremony is a method by which feelings of enmity are exchanged for feelings of friendship. The marriage rite serves to arouse in the minds of the marrying pair a sense of their obligations as married folk, and to bring about in the minds of the witnesses a change of feeling towards the young people such as should properly accompany their change of social status. The weeping and exchange of presents when friends come together is a means of renewing their feelings of attachment to one another. The weeping at marriage, at initiation, and on the occasion of a death is a reaction of defence or compensation when feelings of solidarity are attacked by a partial breaking of the social ties that bind persons to one another.

In the ceremonial life of the Andamans some part is played by dancing, and it will be convenient to consider next the meaning and function of the dance. It is necessary, however, to deal very briefly with this subject and omit much that would have to be included in an exhaustive study. Thus the ordinary Andaman dance may be looked upon as a form of play; it also shows us the beginnings of the arts of dancing, music and poetry; and therefore in any study pretending to completeness it would be necessary to discuss the difficult problem of the relation between art, play and ceremonial in social life, a subject of too wide a scope to be handled in such an essay as this. For our present purpose we are concerned with the dance only as a form of social ceremonial.

If an Andaman Islander is asked why he dances he gives an answer that amounts to saying that he does so because he enjoys it. Dancing is therefore in general a means of enjoyment. It is frequently a rejoicing. The Andaman Islanders dance after a successful day of hunting; they do not dance if their day has been one of disappointment.

Pleasurable mental excitement finds its natural expression in bodily activity, as we see most plainly in young children and in some animals. And in its turn mere muscular activity is itself a source of pleasure. The individual shouts and jumps for joy; the society turns the jump into a dance, the shout into a song.

The essential character of all dancing is that it is rhythmical, and it is fairly evident that the primary function of this rhythmical nature of the dance is to enable a number of persons to join in the same actions and perform them as one body. In the Andamans at any rate it is clear that the spectacular dance is a late development out of the common dance. And it is probable that the history of the dance is everywhere the same, that it began as a common dance in which all present take some active part, and from this first form (still surviving in our ball-room dances) arose the spectacular dance in which one or more dancers perform before spectators who take no part themselves.

In the Andamans the song is an accompaniment of the dance. The dancing and singing and the marking of the rhythm by clapping and by stamping on the sounding-board are all parts of the one common action in which all join and which for convenience is here spoken of as the dance. It is probable that here again the Andamanese practice shows us the earliest stage in the development of the song, that song and music at first had no independent existence but together with dancing formed one activity. It is reasonable to suppose that the song first came into general use in human society because it provides a means by which a number of persons can utter the same series of sounds together and as with one voice, this being made possible by the fixed rhythm and the fixed pitch of the whole song and of each part of it (i.e. by melody). Once the art of song was in existence its further development was doubtless largely dependent upon the esthetic pleasure that it is able to give. But in the Andamans the esthetic pleasure that the natives get from their simple and monotonous songs seems to me of quite secondary importance as compared with the value of the song as a joint social activity.

The movements of the ordinary Great Andaman dance do not seem to me to be in themselves expressive, or at any rate they are not obviously mimetic like the movements of the dances of many primitive folk. Their function seems to be to bring into activity as many of the muscles of the body as possible. The bending of the body at the hips and of the legs at the knees, with the slightly backward poise of the head and the common position of the arms held in line with the shoulders with the elbows crooked and the thumb and first finger of each hand clasping those of the other, produce a condition of tension of a great number of the muscles of the trunk and limbs. The attitude is one in which all the main joints of the body are between complete flexion and complete extension so that there is approximately an equal tension in the opposing groups of flexor and extensor muscles. Thus the whole body of the dancer is full of active forces balanced one against another, resulting in a condition of flexibility and alertness without strain.

While the dance thus brings into play the whole muscular system of the dancer it also requires the activity of the two chief senses, that of sight to guide the dancer in his movements amongst the others and that of hearing to enable him to keep time with the music. Thus the dancer is in a condition in which all the bodily and mental activities are harmoniously directed to one end.

Finally, in order to understand the function of the Andamanese dance it must be noted that every adult member of the community takes some part in it. All the able-bodied men join in the dance itself; all the women join in the chorus. If anyone through ill-health or old age is unable to take any active part, he or she is at least necessarily a spectator, for the dance takes place in the centre of the village in the open space towards which the huts usually face.

The Andamanese dance (with its accompanying song) may therefore be described as an activity in which, by virtue of the effects of rhythm and melody, all the members of a community are able harmoniously to cooperate and act in unity; which requires on the part of the dancer a continual condition of tension free from strain; and which produces in those taking part in it a high degree of pleasure. We must now proceed to examine very briefly the chief effects on the mental condition of those taking part.

First let us consider some of the effects of rhythm. Any marked rhythm exercises over those submitted to its influence a constraint, impelling them to yield to it and to permit it to direct and regulate the movements of the body and even those of the mind. If one does not yield to this constraining influence it produces a state of restlessness that may become markedly unpleasant. One who yields himself utterly to it, as does the dancer when he joins in the dance, still continues to feel the constraint, but so far from being unpleasant it now produces a pleasure of a quite distinct quality. The first point for us to note therefore is that through

the effect of rhythm the dance affords an experience of a constraint or force of a peculiar kind acting upon the individual and inducing in him when he yields himself to it a pleasure of self-surrender. The peculiarity of the force in question is that it seems to act upon the individual both from without (since it is the sight of his friends dancing and the sound of the singing and marking time that occasions it), and also from within (since the impulse to yield himself to the constraining rhythm comes from his own organism).

A second effect of the rhythm of the dance is due to the well-known fact that a series of actions performed rhythmically produces very much less fatigue than actions not rhythmical requiring the same expenditure of muscular energy. So the dancer feels that in and through the dance he obtains such an increase of his personal energy that he is able to accomplish strenuous exertions with a minimum of fatigue. This effect of rhythm is reinforced by the excitement produced by the rapid movements of the dancers, the loud sounds of the song and clapping and sounding-board, and intensified, as all collective states of emotion are intensified, by reason of being collective; with the result that the Andaman Islanders are able to continue their strenuous dancing through many hours of the night.

There is yet a third most important effect of rhythm. Recent psychology shows that what are called the esthetic emotions are largely dependent upon motor images. We call a form beautiful when, through the movements of the eye in following it, we feel it as movement, and as movement of a particular kind which we can only describe at present by using such a word as "harmonious." Similarly our esthetic appreciation of music seems to be largely dependent on our feeling the music as movement, the sounds appealing not to the ear only but to stored-up unconscious motor memories. With regard to dancing, our pleasure in watching the graceful, rhythmical and harmonious movements of the dancer is an esthetic pleasure of similar nature to that obtained from the contemplation of beautiful shapes or listening to music. But when the individual is himself dancing it does not seem quite fitting to call his pleasure esthetic. Yet the dance, even the simple dance of the Andamans, does make, in the dancer himself, partly by the effect of rhythm, partly by the effect of the harmonious and balanced tension of the muscles, a direct appeal to that motor sense to which the contemplation of beautiful forms and movements makes only an indirect appeal. In other words the dancer actually feels within himself that harmonious action of balanced and directed forces which, in the contemplation of a beautiful form we feel as though it were in the object at which we look. Hence such dancing as that of the Andaman Islanders may be looked upon as an early step in the training of the esthetic sense, and to recognize all that the dance means we must make allowance for this fact that the mental state of the dancer is closely related to the mental state that we call esthetic enjoyment.

Let us now consider the effects of the dance as a social or collective activity. First, the dance affords an opportunity for the individual to exhibit before others his skill and agility and so to gratify his personal vanity. It is very easy to observe the action of this harmless vanity in the dancers, and particularly in the man who takes the place at the sounding-board and acts as soloist or leader of the chorus. The dancer seeks to feel, and does feel, that he is the object of the approbation and admiration of his friends. His self-regarding sentiments are pleasantly stimulated, so that he becomes conscious, in a state of self-satisfaction and elation, of his own personal value. This stimulation of the self-regarding sentiment is an important factor in the total effect produced by the dance.

Secondly, the dance, at the same time that it stimulates pleasantly the self-regarding sentiment, also affects the sentiments of the dancer towards his fellows. The pleasure that the dancer feels irradiates itself over everything around him and he is filled with geniality and good-will towards his companions. The sharing with others of an intense pleasure, or rather the sharing in a collective expression of pleasure, must ever incline us to such expansive feelings. It is certainly a readily observable fact that in the Andamans the dance does produce a condition of warm good-fellowship in those taking part in it. There is no need to enquire more closely into the mental mechanisms by which this is brought about.

The Andaman dance, then, is a complete activity of the whole community, in which every able-bodied adult takes some part, and is also an activity in which, so far as the dancer himself is concerned, the whole personality is involved, by the innervation of all the muscles of the body, by the concentration of attention required, and by its action on the personal sentiments. In the dance the individual submits to the action upon him of the community; he is constrained, by the immediate effect of rhythm as well as by custom, to join in, and he is required to conform in his own actions and movements to the needs of the common activity. The surrender of the individual to this constraint or obligation is not felt as painful, but on the contrary as highly pleasurable. As the dancer loses himself in the dance, as he becomes absorbed in the unified

community, he reaches a state of elation in which he feels himself filled with energy or force immensely beyond his ordinary state, and so finds himself able to perform prodigies of exertion. This state of intoxication, as it might almost be called, is accompanied by a pleasant stimulation of the self-regarding sentiment, so that the dancer comes to feel a great increase in his personal force and value. And at the same time, finding himself in complete and ecstatic harmony with all the fellow-members of his community, experiences a great increase in his feelings of amity and attachment towards them.

In this way the dance produces a condition in which the unity, harmony and concord of the community are at a maximum, and in which they are intensely felt by every member. It is to produce this condition, I would maintain, that is the primary social function of the dance. The well-being, or indeed the existence, of the society depends on the unity and harmony that obtain in it, and the dance, by making that unity intensely felt, is a means of maintaining it. For the dance affords an opportunity for the direct action of the community upon the individual, and we have seen that it exercises in the individual those sentiments by which the social harmony is maintained.

It was formerly the custom, I was told, always to have a dance before setting out to a fight. The reason for this should now be clear. When a group engages in a fight with another it is to revenge some injury that has been done to the whole group. The group is to act as a group and not merely as a collection of individuals, and it is therefore necessary that the group should be conscious of its unity and solidarity. Now we have seen that the chief function of the dance is to arouse in the mind of every individual a sense of the unity of the social group of which he is a member, and its function before setting out to a fight is therefore apparent. A secondary effect of the dance before a fight is to intensify the collective anger against the hostile group, and thereby and in other ways to produce a state of excitement and elation which has an important influence on the fighting quality of the Andaman warrior.

An important feature of the social life of the Andamans in former times was the dance-meetings that were regularly held and at which two or more local groups met together for a few days. Each local group lived for the greater part of the year comparatively isolated from others. What little solidarity there was between neighbouring groups therefore tended to become weakened. Social relations between two groups were for the most part only kept up by visits of individuals from one group to another, but such visits did not constitute a relation between group and group. The function of the dance-meetings was therefore to bring the two groups into contact and renew the social relations between them and in that way to maintain the solidarity between them. Those meetings, apart from the provision of the necessary food, were entirely devoted to the exchange of presents and to dancing, the two or more parties of men and women joining together every night in a dance. We have already seen that the exchange of presents is a means of expressing solidarity of mutual good-will. It is now clear that the dance serves to unite the two or more groups into one body, and to make that unity felt by every individual, so creating for a few days a condition of close solidarity. The effects of the meeting would gradually wear out as months went by, and therefore it was necessary to repeat the meeting at suitable intervals.

Thus it appears that not only the ordinary dance, but also the war-dance, and the dance-meetings owe their place in the life of the Andaman Islanders to the fact that dancing is a means of uniting individuals into a harmonious whole and at the same time making them actually and intensely experience their relation to that unity of which they are the members. The special dances at initiation ceremonies and on other occasions will be dealt with later in the chapter, on the basis of the general explanation given above.

On the occasion of a dance, particularly if it be a dance of some importance, such as a war-dance, or a dance of two groups together, the dancers decorate themselves by putting on various ornaments and by painting their bodies with red paint and white clay. The explanation of the dance cannot therefore be regarded as complete till we have considered the meaning of this personal adornment connected with it.

If the Andaman Islander be asked why he adorns himself for the dance, his reply is invariably that he wishes to look well, to improve his personal appearance. In other words his conscious motive is personal vanity.

One of the features of the dance, and a not unimportant one, is that it offers an opportunity for the gratification of personal vanity. The dancer, painted, and hung over with ornaments, becomes pleasantly conscious of himself, of his own skill and agility, and of his striking or at least satisfactory appearance, and so he becomes also conscious of his relation to others, of their admiration, actual or possible, and of the approval and good-will that go with admiration. In brief, the ornamented dancer is pleasantly conscious of his own personal value. We may therefore say that the most important function of any such adorning of the body is to express or mark the personal value of the decorated individual.

This explanation only applies to certain bodily ornaments and to certain ways of painting the body. It applies to the painting of white clay, with or without red paint, that is adopted at dances and on other ceremonial occasions. It applies to such personal ornaments as those made of netting and *Dentalium* shell which constitute what may be called the ceremonial costume of the Andamanese. It is of these that the natives say that they use them in order to look well.

The occasions on which such personal decoration is used are strictly defined by custom. In other words the society dictates to the individual when and how he shall be permitted to express his own personal value. It is obvious that personal vanity is of great importance in directing the conduct of the individual in his dealings with his fellows, and much more amongst a primitive people such as the Andamanese than amongst ourselves, and it is therefore necessary that the society should have some means of controlling the sentiment and directing it towards social ends. We have seen that the dance is the expression of the unity and harmony of the society, and by permitting at the dance the free expression of personal vanity the society ensures that the individual shall learn to feel, even if only subconsciously, that his personal value depends upon the harmony between himself and his fellows.

The bride and bridegroom are painted with white clay, and wear ornaments of *Dentalium* shell on the day following their marriage. We have seen that marriage involves a change of social status, and we may say that it gives an increased social value to the married pair, the social position of a married man or woman being of greater importance and dignity than that of a bachelor or spinster. They are, after marriage, the objects of higher regard on the part of their fellows than they were before. It is therefore appropriate that the personal value of the bride and bridegroom should be expressed so that both they themselves and their fellows should have their attention drawn to it, and this is clearly the function of the painting and ornaments.

After the completion of any of the more important of the initiation ceremonies, such as the eating of turtle, the initiate is painted with white clay and red paint and wears ornaments of *Dentalium* shell. This is exactly parallel to the painting of the bride and bridegroom. The initiate, by reason of the ceremony he has been through, has acquired

new dignity and importance, and by having fulfilled the requirements of custom has deserved
the approval of his fellows. The decoration of his
body after the ceremony is thus the expression of
his increased social value.

A corpse, before burial, is decorated in the same
manner as the body of a dancer. This, we may
take it, is the means by which the surviving relatives and friends express their regard for the dead,
i.e. their sense of his value. We need not suppose
that they believe the dead man to be conscious of
what they are doing. It is to satisfy themselves that
they decorate the corpse, not to satisfy the spirit.
When a man is painted he feels that he has the
regard and good-will of his fellows, and those who
see him, at any rate in the instance of a bridegroom
or initiate, realise that he has deserved their regard.
So, to express their regard for the dead man they
paint the inanimate body. Hence it is that the
greater the esteem in which the dead man or woman
is held, the greater is the care bestowed on the last
painting.

We may conclude therefore that the painting of
the body with white clay and the wearing of ornaments of *Dentalium* shell is a rite or ceremony by
which the value of the individual to the society is
expressed on appropriate occasions. We shall find
confirmation of this later in the chapter.

Before passing on to consider the meaning of
other methods of decorating the body there is one
matter that is worthy of mention. It is often assumed or stated that both personal ornament and
dancing, amongst uncivilised peoples, are connected with sexual emotion. It is, of course, extremely difficult to disprove a statement of this
sort. So far as the Andamanese are concerned I
was unable to find any trace whatever of a definitely sexual element in either their dances or
their personal adornment. It may be recalled that
both men and women wear exactly the same ornaments on ceremonial occasions, and this is to some
extent evidence that such have no sexual value. It
is possible that some observers might see in the
dance of the women (which is only performed on
rare occasions) a suggestion of something of a
sexual nature. I was unable to find that the natives
themselves consider that there is anything suggestive of sex in either the dance of the men or that
of the women. If it were true that the most important feature of the dance was that it appealed in
some way to sexual feelings it is difficult to see
how we are to explain the different occasions on
which dancing takes place, as before a fight, at the
end of mourning, etc., whereas these are adequately accounted for by the hypothesis that the

dance is a method of expressing the unity and harmony of the society. Similarly the explanation of
personal ornament as being connected with sexual
feeling would fail to account for the occasions on
which it is regarded as obligatory. There is therefore, I believe, no special connection between the
dancing and personal ornament of the Andamanese
and sexual feeling. It would still be possible to hold
that there is a general connection of great importance between the affective dispositions underlying
these and other customs and the complex affective
disposition that we call the sex instinct. The nature
of that connection, important as it is, lies outside
the scope of this work.

I remarked above that the explanation which I
have given of the meaning of personal ornament
does not apply to all the objects that the Andaman
Islanders wear on their body, but only to certain
of them. If an Andaman Islander be asked why
he paints himself with white clay, or why he wears
a belt or necklace of *Dentalium* shell he replies
that he does so in order to look well; but if he be
asked why he wears a string of human bones round
his head or neck or waist, he gives quite a different
answer, to the effect that he does so in order to
protect himself from dangers of a special kind.
According to circumstances he will say either that
he is wearing the bones to cure himself of illness,
or else that he wears them as a protection against
spirits. Thus while some things are worn on the
body in order to improve the personal appearance,
and consequently, as explained above, to give the
individual a sense of his own value, others are
worn because they are believed to have a protective power, and thereby arouse in the person a sense
of security. Exactly the same sort of protective
power is attributed to things that cannot be worn
on the body, such as fire, and it will therefore be
convenient to consider together all the things that
afford this kind of protection, whether they can
be worn on the body or not.

The interpretation here offered is that the customs connected with this belief in the protective
power of objects of various kinds are means by
which is expressed and thereby maintained at the
necessary degree of energy a very important social
sentiment, which, for lack of a better term, I shall
call the sentiment of dependence. In such a primitive society as that of the Andamans one of the
most powerful means of maintaining the cohesion
of the society and of enforcing that conformity to
custom and tradition without which social life is
impossible, is the recognition by the individual
that for his security and well-being he depends entirely upon the society.

7. *An Incongruous Assortment of Incongruities*

BY KENNETH BURKE

THE QUESTION of new meanings or heuristic is confused in its individual trends; and though many men would seem to have merely been breaking down old schemes of orientation, it is probable that with greater or lesser clarity they were doing so in accordance with a new schematization of their own which they were offering as replacement. In some brands of nonsense humor current today, it is hard to distinguish an informing principle other than a general dislike of our great complexity and confusion and indirectness of values, a dislike which the humorists convey by introducing a kind of artificial blindness, a complete vacuity as their new point of view—and the results are often as rich in perspective as are incongruities attained by more systematic methods. Indeed, the nearest approach to a modern art which can appeal to the naïve and the sophisticated alike is perhaps this ambitious and creative nonsense. The explanation may be that the adepts of this organized stumbling are responding to a psychosis common to all. We are all necessarily involved in the momentous discrepancies of our present "order," generated perhaps from that basic economic freak whereby a surplus of products and commodities becomes a national and an international menace—and though we may disagree as to the ways *out of* such an irregular existence, even a paragon of orthodoxy must respond to these disorders as they manifest themselves in the remoter, but highly barometric region of our judgments, tastes, values, and expectancies.

There is, however, even a stage of planned incongruity that goes beyond humor: the grotesque, wherein the perception of discordancies is cultivated without smile or laughter. As compared with the mechanisms underlying the appeal of the grotesque, even the most destructive nonsense is disclosed as an upholder of things as they were. Humor still manifests its respect for our earlier categories of judgment, even while outraging them. Like blasphemy in the sphere of dogmatic religion, it reaffirms the existence of the old gods once more in the very act of denying them. And humor is most

explosive when, besides throwing a shoe among the wheels of our machinery of judgment, it not only leaves one favored judgment completely intact, but deliberately strengthens it. It pits value against value, disposition against disposition, psychotic weighting against psychotic weighting—but it flatters us by confirming as well as destroying. The grotesque is a much more complex matter, and gradually merges into something very much like mysticism. Humor tends to be conservative, the grotesque tends to be revolutionary. Aristophanes was a humorist, excoriating new ways with reference to traditional tests of propriety. Aristophanes was pious, but Socrates had leanings towards the grotesque and impious. The gargoyles of the Middle Ages were typical instances of planned incongruity. The maker of gargoyles who put man's-head on bird-body was offering combinations which were completely rational as judged by his logic of essences. In violating one order of classification, he was stressing another. Considered in this light, Spengler's morphology of history becomes simply a modern gargoyle, a Super-Realist mural, a vast grotesque wherein the writer can soberly picture Kant walking the streets of ancient Athens or bring Petronius to a New York nightclub.

Such considerations also reveal a gargoyle element in Marx's formula of class-consciousness. Class-consciousness is a social therapeutic because it is *reclassification-consciousness*. It is a new perspective that realigns something so profoundly ethical as our categories of allegiance. By this reinterpretative schema, members of the same race or nation who had formerly thought of themselves as *allies* become *enemies,* and members of different races or nations who had formerly thought of themselves as *enemies* become *allies.* The new classification thus has implicit in it a new set of ideas as to what *action* is, and in these ideas are implicit new criteria for deciding what means-selection would be adequate.

A kind of secular mysticism having a distinctly gargoyle quality is to be seen today in the paintings of the Super-Realists, who may show us a watch, dripping over the table like spilled molasses, not merely as an affront to our everyday experience with watches as rigid, but because a *dripping* watch gives us glimpses into a *different symbolism of time.* The outrageous watch is not *funny* at all—nor are

Reprinted from Kenneth Burke, *Permanence and Change* (2d rev. ed.; Los Altos, Cal.: Hermes Publications, 1954), pp. 146–64, with the permission of the author and Hermes Publications.

those "humorous" death-bed scenes in "The Magic Mountain" funny. In their incongruity, they are even terrible.

The notion of perspective by incongruity has obvious bearing upon the grotesques of our dreams. Dreams (and dream-art) seek to connect events by a "deeper" scheme of logic than prevails in our everyday rationale of utility. The symbolism of both dreams and dream-art makes gargoyles of our waking experiences, merging things which common sense had divided and dividing things which common sense had merged. Joyce, blasting apart the verbal atoms of meaning, and out of the ruins making new elements synthetically, has produced our most striking instances of modern linguistic gargoyles. He has accomplished the dangerous feat of dreaming most laxly while most awake. In the portmanteau words of his latest manner, he seems to be attempting to include within the span of one man's work an etymological destiny which may generally take place in the course of many centuries, as the rigidities of education gradually yield to the natural demand that the language of practical utility and the language of "unconscious" utility be brought closer together and their present intense duality be mitigated. The concept of trained incapacity leads me to suspect that his disorders of sight are the reverse aspect of his accomplishments. The self-imposed blindness of Oedipus, who had outraged the most awesome pieties of his tribe, suggests a notable parallel here, since Joyce was profoundly Catholic in his youth, and his adult work, as judged by this Catholic framework, is one mighty monument of heresy. Modern medicine sufficiently recognizes a correspondence between our attitudes and our physical disabilities for one to feel justified in relating Joyce's misfortunes, as well as his attainments, to his intense skill at heretically disintegrating his childhood meanings, to which his exceptional personal sensitiveness (as attested in his "Portrait of the Artist as a Young Man") had fully exposed him. This conflict between his earliest pieties and the reclassifications that went with his later perspective could, in a man whose responses are so thorough, result in a mental concern with disintegration which would have physical counterparts.[1]

We may also consider that semi-art, semi-science, *caricature,* which pursues the course of planned incongruity by a technique of abstraction. In caricature, certain aspects of the object are deliberately omitted, while certain other aspects are overstressed (*caricare*: to overload). Caricatures can almost talk in concepts. Many of Georg Grosz's earlier nudes were a simple choice of vocabulary: mug for mouth, bean for head, lunch-hooks for hands, can for buttocks. Caricature usually reclassifies in accordance with clearly indicated interests.

Dadaism, in many ways the local government out of which Super-Realism grew, revealed an organized hatred of good taste, courted a deliberate flouting of the appropriate, which places it squarely in the movement toward planned incongruity. But dadaism suffered from poor rationalization. Whereas it was pursued by a group of very ambitious and serious-minded writers, many of them extremely well equipped in the traditional lore and especially interested in criticism, they allowed their movement to remain on the basis of mere waywardness, irresponsibility, refusal, which left it with too unpretentious a critical backing. This weakness was inevitable, since their attacks upon the old scheme of the pretentious would naturally apply to their own theorizing as well. But a movement so wicked was forever exposed to a sudden determination to reform. It would make inevitably for the resolve to put away childish things, to take up more serious matters—whereat it seems to have served as a mere opening wedge, a first draft, which some of its adherents later revised as Communism,

---

1. Such a line of thought suggests that, in some cases at least, a cult of perspective carried to extremes which far outstrip the possibilities of communication, or socialization, can have its roots in irrational emotional conflicts. For instance, we know that if a man undergoes an intensely unpleasant experience, neutral environmental facts which happen to be associated with this experience tend to take on the same unpleasant quality. Someone who as a child was badly treated by a man with a wart may subsequently feel ill at ease with anyone who has a wart—or the mere sight of a town in which we were once very unhappy may restore the feeling of unhappiness. Now, if one happens to have been thorough enough for *an entire orientation* to become associated in his mind with a painful experience, in attempting to obliterate the experience he may tend to wipe out the orientation associated with it. It is thus possible that even a wholly rational orientation, which is adequately serving its social purposes, may become discredited in one man's mind, since there are always the possibilities of individual unhappiness—and if the unhappy individual happens to have been so thorough as to associate his whole orientation with his unhappiness, the orientation will take on the unpleasant quality of the unpleasant experience itself. Pain is a great incentive to eloquence, since it provides one with an altar of preoccupation to which he must bring appropriate offerings—and eloquence is a strategy of appeal, a social implement for inducing others to agree with us. In this way individual pain may lead to radical evangelism, as the sufferer attempts to socialize his position by inducing others to repudiate the orientation painful to himself. In classical eras, eras of pronounced social conformity, such anarchistic tendencies of the individual artist or thinker are corrected by the recalcitrance of the social body. In the very act of attempting to socialize his position, the artist is forced to revise his statements to such an extent that he himself is reclaimed in the process. But at times when an orientation is greatly weakened (and particularly under decaying capitalism, when competitive demands place a premium upon the most notable or salient kinds of expression) such normative influences are lacking.

and some as Super-Realism. Since both branches are concerned with new meanings, we can easily appreciate how the earlier systematized incongruities of dadaism proper (with its cry of "*Rien! Rien!*") were an integral step in either of these directions.

Incidentally, since the Dadaists traced their cultural descent from Baudelaire, we might recall an article "L'Erotologie de Baudelaire," by M. Jean Royère, who has noted the great prevalence of metonymy, and "systematic catachreses" in the poems of Baudelaire. He discusses Baudelaire's "systematic use of the most illogical figure of speech, the catachresis (or mixed metaphor), which might be called the metaphor and hyperbole in one." Royère notes the effectiveness of the device particularly in the poem *Beau Navire,* where Baudelaire likens a woman to a boat moving out to sea. The critic selects the word perspective to characterize the result.

In considering the profusion of perspectives, of course, we treat need and opportunity as interchangeable. The crumbling and conflict of values certainly puts new burdens upon the artist—but on the other hand, it facilitates certain kinds of artistic endeavor which, in a stabilized structure, might be possible to the wayward individual but would not be very highly rated by his group. In the confusion of a vocabulary (and of the social texture behind it) writers not only lose old effects but gain new ones. The grotesque flourishes *when it is easiest to imagine the grotesque, or when it is hardest to imagine the classical* (one may take either phrasing, as he prefers). One sees perspectives beyond the structure of a given vocabulary when the structure is no longer firm. Historical conditions cannot wholly account for such a situation. Upon an individual, at any time in history, there may converge a set of factors which strongly differentiate his situation from that of his group. Great liquidity in one's personal life may lead one to see "unclassically" even in an era generally classical. And similarly today, some men have enjoyed cloistered conditions which enable them to retain fixities not there for most of us. The metaphor of the historic stream cannot be taken too literally, unless one is willing to judge a course by its direction through whole millennia, not decades. Furthermore, there is always some quasi-mystical attempt being made to see around the edges of the orientation in which a poet or thinker lives. It is precisely in eras of classical drama, for instance, that the devices of dramatic irony flourish at their best. In cases of dramatic irony we see two conflicting sets of meanings acting simultaneously, as the *dramatis personae* interpret their situation one way and the audience interprets

it another. But in this device of classical drama (it flourishes best when a scheme of orientation is comparatively firm) there is nothing problematical about the audience's knowledge in the matter. The characters are *wrong* and the audience is *right*. The characters think they know, but the audience knows it knows. The characters may be bewildered as to motivation, but the audience is clear.

A Babel of new orientations has arisen in increasing profusion during the last century, until now hardly a year goes by without some brand new model of the universe being offered us. Such interpretative schemes varying in their scope and thoroughness, seem limited only by the time and industry of the heuristically-minded—and our examples have been chosen at random. Out of all this overlapping, conflicting, and supplementing of interpretative frames, what arises as a *totality?* The only thing that all this seems to make for is a reënforcement of the *interpretative attitude* itself. The vast documentation concerning new classifications and characterizations of the events about us may best serve as new case histories, material to be used for the closer study of classification and characterization in general. The myriad orientations will be tragically wasted, the genius of one of the world's most vigorous centuries will be allowed to go unused, unless we can adapt its very welter of interpretations as skeptical grounding for our own certainties. Such an attempt to utilize all past frames of thought, regardless of their apparent divergencies from us, is arising in the science of symbolism, as it extends all the way from new and sharper rigors of lexicography, through the various schemes of individual and group psychoanalysis (as writers like Bentham, Marx, Freud, Jung, and Burrow sought various devices for disclosing the factor of interest as it bears upon our orientation) through the many attempts to found a language divorced from common sense (as with the adherents of symbolic logic, or Bergson's planned incongruity) to methodological speculations (mainly in physics and semeiotic) which lead one close to the edges of a mysticism as arrant as that of any "disorganized" medieval seer. For after all, the language of common sense was not invented for the extremes of heuristic forcing to which our contemporary eschatologists would apply it—hence, any deliberate attempt at analogical extension can be accomplished only by going beyond the conventional categories of speech. The great emphasis upon the test of success is not so despicable as it might seem —for here we have at least a rough and ready corrective to the inventions of new classificatory alignments. The only trouble is, as we have said before, that success itself is a variable—and the tests by which the success of our process-thinking is proved may be as implicated in our ways of process-thinking as the tests of medieval essence-thinking were implicit in their ways of linking events by essence.

In any event, the confluence of scientific revelations, of minute and comprehensive schemes whereby we find new readings for the character of events, is in itself the evidence that Perspective by Incongruity is both needed and extensively practised. Were we to summarize the totality of its effects, advocating as an *exhortation* what has already spontaneously occurred, we might say that planned incongruity should be deliberately cultivated for the purpose of experimentally wrenching apart all those molecular combinations of adjective and noun, substantive and verb, which still remain with us. It should subject language to the same "cracking" process that chemists now use in their refining of oil. If science would be truly atheistic or impious to the last degree, it should try systematically to eradicate every last linkage that remains with us merely as the result of piety or innate propriety, and not because of its rationally established justification. An idea which commonly carries with it diminutive modifiers, for instance, should be treated by magnification, as were one to discuss the heinousness of an extra slice of beef, or the brain storm that rules when one has stumped one's toe. One should be prepared to chart the genesis, flourishing, and decay of a family witticism, precisely as though he were concerned with the broadest processes of cultural change, basic patterns of psychology and history thus being conveniently brought within the scope of the laboratory. One should study one's dog for his *Napoleonic* qualities, or observe mosquitoes for signs of wisdom to which we are forever closed. One should discuss sneezing in the terms heretofore reserved for the analysis of a brilliant invention, as if it were a creative act, a vast synthesis uniting in its simple self a multitude of prior factors. Conversely, where the accepted linkages have been of an imposing sort, one should establish perspective by looking through the reverse end of his glass, converting mastodons into microbes, or human beings into vermin upon the face of the earth. Or perhaps writing a history of medicine by a careful study of the quacks, one should, by the principle of the *lex continui,* extend his observations until they threw light upon the processes of a Pasteur. Or do a history of poetry by going among the odds and ends of Bohemia, asking oneself why some monkey-jumper wore a flowing tie, and letting the answer serve as an explanation of Yeats or Valéry. Or allow the words of children, carefully charted, to humble us by their way of neglecting our profoundest sense of right,—quite as though we had two social words for chair, an *A-chair* designating a chair sat in by negligible people, servants, children, and poor relatives, and a *B-chair* reserved for persons of distinction, such as the father and the mother—and as though a little child, with his "innate iconoclasm," had literally convulsed us by politely saying to the Bishop, "May I offer you this A-chair?"

Or by a schematic shift in the locus of judgment, supply eulogistic words to characterize events usually characterized dyslogistically, or vice versa, or supplement both eulogistic and dyslogistic by words that will be neutral, having no censorious quality whatsoever, but purely indicative of a process. For the friends of a man may discuss his devotion to his business, whereas his enemies may have the same activity in mind when they dicuss his greed, whereby in talking to both we might discuss him somewhat as a stone rolling down a hill, or as illustrating the diversion of man's generic militant, competitive equipment into the specific channels of effort that happen to be singled out by a particular orientation based upon commercial enterprise. Or, just as in the term xy, we may discuss x as a function of y or y as a function of x, let us move about incongruously among various *points de départ* for the discovery of causal connectives, whereby we learn either that free markets were a function of the movement towards emancipation or that the entire cry for emancipation was a mere function of the demand for free markets.

Or let us even deliberately deprive ourselves of available knowledge in the search for new knowledge—as for instance: Imagine that you had long studied some busy and ingenious race of organisms, in the attempt to decide for yourself, from the observing of their ways, what inducements led them to act as they did; imagine next that, after long research with this race which you had thought speechless, you suddenly discovered that they had a vast communicative network, a remarkably complex arrangement of signs; imagine next that you finally succeeded in deciphering these signs, thereby learning of all this race's motives and purposes as they designated them to one another. Would you not be exultant? Would you not feel that your efforts had been rewarded to their fullest? Imagine, then, setting out to study mankind, with whose system of speech you are largely familiar. Imagine beginning your course of study *precisely by depriving yourself of this familiarity,* attempting to understand motives and purposes by avoiding as much as possible the clues handed you ready-made in the texture of the language itself. In this you will have deliberately discarded available data in the interests of a fresh point of view, the heuristic or perspective value of a planned incongruity.

Which suggests that one may even programmatically adopt a postulate known to be false—for the "heuristic value of error" has already been established, as in the fertility of the phlogiston theory, a belief in "fire-particles" which led to the discovery of atomic combinations. So let us, perhaps, discover what is implicit in the proposition that "the presence of heat makes water dislike flowing downhill—and in order to avoid having to 'seek its level' it turns into steam." Let us found a mathematics—or an ethic!—by outraging the law of the excluded middle whereby, instead of saying "A is A; A is not non-A," we may say, "A is either A or non-A." Let us say with Lawrence that the earth's crops make the sun shine, or with James and Lange that we're sad because we cry.

Let us contrive not merely the flat merger of contradictions recommended by Bergson, but also the multitude of imperfect matchings, giving scientific terms for words usually treated sentimentally, or poetic terms for the concepts of science, or discussing disease as an accomplishment, or great structures of thought as an oversight, or considering intense ambition or mighty planetary movements as a mere following of the line of least resistance, a kind of glorified laziness; or using noble epithets for ignoble categories, and borrowing terms for the ephemeral to describe events for which we habitually reserve terms for the enduring. Let us not only discuss a nation as though it were an individual, but also an individual as though he were a nation, depicting massive events trivially, and altering the scale of weeds in a photograph until they become a sublime and towering forest—shifting from the animal, the vegetable, the physical, the mental, "irresponsibly" applying to one category the terms habitual to another, as when Whitehead discerns mere habit in the laws of atomic behavior—or like a kind of Professorial E. E. Cummings who, had he called man an ape, would then study apes to understand Aristotle. "Let us do this?" Everywhere, in our systems for forcing inferences, it is being done.

(The vocabulary of economists, with its abstract and statistical formulations for the description of human conduct, is perhaps the most outstanding instance of incongruity. A man may think of himself as "saving money," but in the economist's categories of description this man may be performing a mere act of "postponed consumption." The economist here says in effect that the savings bank carries in its window a sign reading: "Postpone your consumption, at 3 per cent per annum." Similarly with an "insurance risk." Any particular man who takes out insurance is going to die at a certain date. This is simply a yes-or-no proposition. On such-and-such a date, he will or will not be dead. Yet as member of an insured group he takes on a wholly new attribute: the attribute of *probability*. The *probabilities* are three to one or four to one that on such-and-such a date he will be living or dead. He thus tends to think of himself as possessing this probability, which is solely a character possessed by him as a member of a certain abstract grouping, and does not at all apply to him individually. As an individual (the consideration that really concerns him) his case possesses no probabilities at all: he either will, or will not, be dead. . . . This deceptive attitude towards the whole subject of classification is at present observable in the intense critical battles over proletarian literature. A proletarian is defined, by abstraction, as a worker of a certain sort. But he is obviously many other things as well: a particular endocrine combination, for instance, an "introvert" or "extravert," a man who did or did not have a bad attack of measles in his childhood, etc. All such non-proletarian factors are involved in his make-up —yet critics attempt to find some rigid distinction between proletarian and non-proletarian thinking that will serve as a schema for classifying *all* his expressions. No wonder they are forever detecting in him "bourgeois" or "feudalistic" vestiges.)

La Rochefoucauld says that some things should be seen close at hand and others from a distance. The doctrine of perspective would suggest that perspective is heuristic insofar as we see close at hand the things we had formerly seen from afar, and vice versa. Or Spinoza recommended that we see things *sub specie aeternitatis*—but seeing by the ways of planned incongruity is a deliberate and systematic seeing of things *sub specie temporis,* though undertaken precisely for the ends which Spinoza had in view when speaking of eternity. And Leibniz, who is in many ways our father, has written: "The result of each view of the universe as seen from a different position is a substance which expresses the universe conformably to this view, provided God sees fit to render his thought effective and to produce the substance." God often does see fit—as witness the endless "substances" of the great century of New Meanings.

No wonder so many nineteenth-century writers were prodigious in output. A shift in the angle of approach must disclose an infinity of ways in which our former classifications can be reclassified. After a lifetime of productivity we find Bentham wishing that he could become a dozen selves, since his perspective showed him that he had work for all. Indeed, he has in time become thousands of selves, as Darwin also has.

PART FIVE

Social Change

Introduction

BY KASPAR D. NAEGELE

AT THE GATE OF THE STUDY OF social change stand a host of half-truths. In the middle of the twentieth century, we experience change all about us. We know about population increases; about vast, quiet, or dramatic technological innovations; about migrations between cities and suburbs, between lower and higher social classes, between political systems. Since 1914, we have seen a variety of political shifts and conflicts that, in turn, have in a complicated way been associated with economic, social, and cultural repercussions. They have also involved shifts in inner meanings and psychological dispositions. There have been several wars and some revolutions; dictators and republics have risen and fallen. Older forms of domination, once called imperialism or colonialism, have become elaborated into newer forms, leading to the creation of satellite countries. More recently, the word "satellite" has come to stand for an accomplishment that has considerably increased the spatial dimensions of social arrangements.

In North America during these years, the standard of living has risen steadily. People's participation in the institutions of formal education has increased the world over. Some countries are presently seeking independence from administrative and economic ties to cultures different from theirs. They are, ambiguously, called "underdeveloped." Notions of the welfare state, of individual security, and of the representation of interests, have become subjects of controversy as well as of far-flung institutional arrangements. There have been dramatic shifts, especially in North America, in the proportion of the population living in the country. Suburbs and shopping centers, freeways and motels, are obvious and outward symbols of a style of life nonexistent in 1860. In many places, previous contrasts of status, learning, opportunity, or enjoyment have become reduced or redefined.

For all this, a variety of easy labels have been readily found and easily distributed. Today we can hear about the mass society and the lonely crowd, about modernization and industrialization, about shifts from production to consumption. We can also hear reminders of continuity. We learned from Parmenides and the Greeks that one cannot step in the same river twice, as much because the self changes as because the river changes. We learn from the French that the more things change, the more they stay the same. This is not the place to explore the ironic fact that this paradox was formulated in a culture that, at least in recent years, has experienced a rapid succession of governments.

For every speechmaker who would selectively remind us about change, displaced populations, inner and outer migrations, shifts in the style of life, and requirements to keep up to date, there is another who tells us that fundamental human nature never changes. In fact, the German poet Schiller suggested that hunger and love perennially drive us along.

Such equivocation is surely significant. Change and revolution, evolution and progress, differentiation and continuity, tradition and discontinuity—these are all terms that seem to have a legitimate claim to be included within the analysis of social arrangements. It is precisely the coincidence of stability and flux that clearly characterizes any social arrangements. These terms, as opposites, may well be quite misleading.

Once again, we must return to the distinction between concrete and analytic ideas. Social arrangements, after all, are alive. By definition, being alive, at least in the human domain, involves time, birth, transformation, and death. As an expression, then, social change quickly allows a whole flux of distinctions to crowd in on one. Apart from the *planes* of personal, organizational, or political change, there are its *forms*. Fads and fashions, revolutions and deliberate reorganizations, would be examples. Furthermore, planes and forms of change help distinguish social phenomena *so that* the cause and consequence of that movement or this shift, this unwitting growth or that enacted re-arrangement, can be properly seen and reasonably explained. Ultimately we want to know why there is a shift in some designated pattern, be it a person's political commitment, an organization's size, a country's government in power, or a nation's military technology. In the immediate present, persistence and change per se need no explanation: so, in a manner, Newton would teach us. But their alternations—the demands by some for a different direction, and by others that this direction *not* be taken—these *are* the phenomena demanding explanations.

If this essay remains uncommitted, possibly even remote, within the market-place of counterarguments about the "forces of history," the relative significance of "great men," the specific forms of interdependence between the logically different planes of culture, society, personality, and nature, or even between such orders as those of technical accomplishment and moral assessment, it is because this anthology should contribute to intellectual growth and not to ideological battles. Eclecticism is no solution—at best, it is a lame begging of the questions. Posing the questions, with the benefit of the general pattern of ideas and distinctions constituting the consensus of the editors, may, however, be a step forward. There is, after all, no simple solution.

Yet analysis—be it of meaning, of social relations, or of individual choice—can proceed only on the presumption of some intelligible nexus. If we have put materials on social change at the end of this Reader, we have done so partially because the end of social analysis is an account, in disprovable terms, of the aliveness of social arrangements. Yet, for the time being, this end requires a different beginning. We want to understand why none of those active in 1860 is alive today, while many of the arrangements by which we live today are similar to those inherited a century ago by our predecessors—who, in turn, stand in some line of continuity to their own predecessors.

In introducing the selections of this part of the Reader, I want merely to propose some suggestions for making the requisite minimal distinctions through which the analysis and investigation of social change can become manageable.

SOME QUESTIONS IN THE STUDY
OF SOCIAL CHANGE

In the brief Forewords to each of the three constituent sections into which selections in this part

have been organized, further details concerning the mode and directions of change will be elaborated. In this part of the Reader, the following questions arise:

1) What are the intelligible units of study—within the social and cultural nexus—when one wishes to remain aware of the *historic* character of this nexus? What domains (e.g., economic, political, religious, technological, and other spheres of distinct activity or mutual relations) must one distinguish, to account for change within a given society, a given social organization, or a particular web of social relations?

2) What forms of social change is it necessary or useful to distinguish?

3) What is meant by "social causation"? In what way do the notions of cause, structure, and function mutually imply one another?

4) How does an interest in the variety of forms and causation of social change help distinguish among the different constituent domains of a given society?

5) How must the exploration of personalities and their motives be part of the study of social change? How do the several concerns with the forms, causes, and consequences of social change necessarily involve psychological research and the definition of new questions for such research?

NINETEENTH-CENTURY ROOTS OF
THE STUDY OF CHANGE

Before considering some of these issues and outlining their possible solution, we must place the following selections into a historic context. Today this is more necessary than ever, because now social change is a vivid fact. Yet its vividness is peculiar; it has the characteristics of a crisis. This is not new. Fearful joy, and/or a sense of doom, at the prospect of the end of the world, have long been sources of prophecy in Western civilization—which is only one among several civilizations. In fact, most civilizations have disappeared. Moreover, the image of a good society—or, less collectively, of individual happiness or salvation—directly involves the facts of permanence and change. These facts are, in turn, part of our sense of past and future.

Societies, and circles within them, differ in the manner in which they think the future and the past are connected. We tend, moreover, to distinguish between "conservatives" and others according to the basis on which they put their hopes. For some, heaven or Utopia lies in the future; for others, only the old days were genuinely good. All the writers represented in this anthology confront the discrepancy *arising* from the difference between ideals and accomplishments, hope and possibilities.

All practices embody ideals. The divergence between action and norm occurs because all acts are subject to more than one set of norms, and all norms derive their very potency from their partial vagueness. In any case, the moral consensus of nineteenth-century France, Germany, or England inherited the persistent themes of a Judaeo-Christian ethic, with both its Catholic and Protestant variations, and its degrees of orthodoxy. The consensus was also heir to the succession of humanistic, skeptical, rational, and romantic dispositions linking the nineteenth century to the waning of the Middle Ages. In addition, the nineteenth century included a sequence of revolutions—especially in France, Belgium, and Germany—and drastic reforms, like those in England in the 1830's. Through the writings of Malthus, Wallace, Darwin, Marx, and Engels, it also provided two potent ideas: evolution and dialectic materialism. These ideas have inspired a huge literature—of approval, protest, and/or reformulation. As ideas, they cannot be restricted to the intellectual domain alone.

Evolution

It is essential to distinguish among Darwin's formulated theory of organic evolution, its acceptance or rejection by different intellectual circles, and, finally, its use for the justification of or opposition to a particular direction of political change. As an idea, Darwin's theory can easily be used for justifying rugged individualism and for seeing the market place as the arena for the survival of the shrewdest. However, in the present context, evolution has a different import. We need not decide whether to think of one or of several trees of culture and society. In any case, the notion of evolution suggests a relatively long time perspective; and it contains a variety of modes of social organization that can come to stand in relation to one another, with the help of a process of differentiation —the introductory essay to Part Two of this Reader elaborates this point of view. At best, Darwinian theory is a frame of perception and analysis. It poses questions. As a framework, however, it can help to allow one to maintain a sense of history without becoming limited to a historicist procedure.

In a curious way, the nineteenth-century notion of evolution became associated with the sense of struggle and of nature's virtual ruthlessness, as well as with the sense of hope. It became a symbol for

the ongoing, for the sense of a permanent emergence and hence creativity within the scheme of human arrangements. It stood for open directionality. Weber, as we shall see in the Foreword to the last section of this part of our Reader, developed, among others, the notion of directionality, but in part, at least, he apprehended it pessimistically.

The moral and intellectual import of "social Darwinism" cannot be properly discussed within the confines of this essay. Spencer's work represents one of its forms. He united progress and evolution in his analysis of the stages by which industrial society arrived on the scenes of nature. Perhaps, in retrospect, one can speak of a school of social evolutionists. Today, conditions seem to favor a return to their concerns, for we now have a more firm way to keep separate the notions of evolution, stage, differentiation, progress, natural order, and social order.

Yet the concern with evolution, like the concern with revolution, is easily incorporated into a political philosophy, in the widest sense of that term. These concerns become part of the debate over the proper role of government, the necessary scope of regulation and planning, the character of the processes by which men's capacities and freedoms can and cannot be maintained or enhanced. Today, when the sharp edge of ideological differences has been dulled in the West, these terms' "neutral" values can be differently appreciated.

The selection from Kroeber's work contains, to a degree, a happy combination of older evolutionary concerns with a discriminating sense of the complexities and particularities of history. Its interest in the "super-organic" patterns, considered in abstraction from human individualities, uses an evolutionist interest in species; while its sensibility to works of art and other forms of human accomplishment transcends any simplistic concept of nature. In leaving room for several orders, whatever their ultimate mutual interdependence (as distinct from their intellectual or emotional reducibility), Kroeber also frees us from being constrained to label nature (or society or government) as inherently benevolent or malevolent, as requiring much or almost no interference. A later generation, preparing an anthology like this, will probably be rich in material on evolution and revolution. Our times and our self-imposed time limitations make this less true in our case.

Positivism

Positivism is the second major theme of the aspect of nineteenth-century intellectual consensus directly affecting the analysis and comprehension of social change. As indicated in the General Introduction, positivism as a faith is the belief in science's ultimate adequacy as a mode of knowing and as a guide for action. As a faith, positivism interprets history as successively vindicating the use of human reason over the use of magic, superstition, and theology. It de-emphasizes the differences between social and natural sciences, and perceives the natural and human worlds, including the latter's products, as fully amenable to systematic and, eventually, quantitative exploration and explanation. Combined with notions of evolution, positivism can help sharpen a conflict between religion and science. This conflict is no less sharp for being, in fact, a conflict between two rival faiths. Positivism had limitations, which were discussed above and which Durkheim's later writing at least partially overcame. This overcoming of positivism as an insufficient mode of analysis substantially helped generate the convergence of ideas that we believe connected—without their ever having intended such connection—the work of Durkheim, Weber, Freud, Pareto, and others.

The theory of evolution and the attitude of positivism, like any other potent intellectual accomplishment, became both guide and obstacle. This was the more true because, in the 1890's, these themes were developed concomitantly with a third accomplishment: the theory of historical materialism.

Historical Materialism

Historical materialism united the wish for action with the wish for explanation. It was devoted, especially in its polemic writing, to the causal supremacy of the economic sphere. In retrospect, this single-minded devotion appears as a critique of German Idealism and as the intellectual response to those requirements of "economicalness" that any pattern of human action always poses. It is also much more than that; it is a theory of social stratification, of ideology, of the character of human labor, and of the directionality of human history.

More has been written about Karl Marx than about almost any other social theorist. Rightly or wrongly, his name has become associated with conflicts, political revolution, and regimes that in turn form an inevitable context for contemporary social analysis. An adequate discussion of the antecedents, consequences, contributions, and, from our point of view, limitations of Marx's theories about the structure of society and the history of its transformation would require a separate volume. As a social theory, Marxism responds directly to the combination of economic, technological, political,

and social developments which growing capitalism helped to generate throughout the nineteenth century, especially in England, Germany, and, to a lesser extent, France.

Without these developments, as we have argued in the General Introduction to this Reader, the peculiar distinctions between the human and the non-human realms, and between the impersonal and the personal within the human realm, would not have been made. These distinctions are a strategically necessary, if not sufficient, condition for the development of a systematic study of social institutions.

Whatever his motives and intellectual stimulants, Marx contributed to this analysis with a view of the severalness of spheres within the structure of society. His polemical, more concretely historical, and more generally analytic, writings are not equally guided by a similarly weighted pattern of distinctions. When Marx analyzes the Eighteenth Brumaire, or nineteenth-century revolutionary developments in France, he is more sensitive to what appear to be the impersonal forces, economic or otherwise, than when he writes a more general work on German Idealism. He utilizes the work on Idealism as an opportunity for chastising hypocritical intellectuals or self-interested exploiters whose view of the "truth" is fashioned according to their particular recognition of what is good for them. In any case, Marx contributed several major ideas to the study of social change (as distinct from the pursuit of the philosophy of history, or more conventional and implicit historical analysis).

For the time being, it is irrelevant that each of these major ideas has antecedents in earlier centuries than the nineteenth. Indeed, the study of social change—especially that part dealing with the history of ideas and their bearing on human institutions—frequently inspires the cliché that there is nothing new under the sun. Many people today greet claims of innovation or advance with a wise and superior reminder that Freud or Keynes, Pareto or Sorel, Marx or Weber, Durkheim or Simmel, were all foreshadowed—or even anticipated—by Plato, Aristotle, the Church fathers, Ibn Khaldun, or other thinkers born long before the Renaissance. Frequently, this is partially true; it is also often irrelevant; it is usually rather ambiguous. As Whitehead eloquently reminds us, "Everything of importance has been said before by somebody who did not discover it." Besides, even though sociology as a discipline is more cumulative than history, it is, like the latter, part of a process of revising and rewriting techniques for studying, more productively, the same past events.

Marx regarded society as a historic product,

deeply involved in conflicts among categories of people pursuing different interests. As part of his famous *Communist Manifesto,* he suggested that the history of all hitherto known societies has involved class conflict. By this suggestion, Marx bequeathed a controversial concept and helped make the study of stratification a central, if elusive, concern to which the theory of society is still, and will for a long time remain, bound. The theory of society will be freed from this concern only on the discovery of more probing and clarifying proposals about the alternative modes of distributing wealth, power, privilege, honor, or prestige that different social systems can make possible or find necessary.

Concern with class was part and parcel of the concern with economic forces in society, which Marx saw as the real engines of change. From economic forces he distinguished formulations by which the benefactors of non-socialist economies confirm their positions and obscure the truth.

This separation between the economic sphere and the domain of ideas is as famous as it is tenuous. Surely, economic arrangements involve ideas, be they existential or moral. Indeed, Durkheim and Weber were especially interested in dissecting the mutual contingency between economic and non-economic arrangements within society. Through this, they helped create sociology.

They especially contributed to the analysis of the legal and motivational requisites of economic activity, if the latter term includes a concern with the ends (and means) that people seek. Such seeking implies standards and justifications for choosing ends and means; for decisions made and selections confirmed or defended in the presence, imagined or real, of others. An economic order tends to involve legal arrangements, including contractual ones. These arrangements provide for the possibilities of, and also rationalize, economic patterns. Yet these patterns are always greater than they. Similarly, legal arrangements, including laws, require a consensus and a tradition having an extra-legal root and superstructure. Consequently, in this interdependence of the spheres of society, social change becomes, more than other fields of study, an opportunity (and a necessity) to understand the relations between the domains of society. It is often very difficult to acquire the competence to do so. Besides, social change bears a complex relation to the purposes of men. Among others, Sumner[1] has reminded us of the difference between crescive and enacted change. In truth, the changes characterizing

the institutional arrangements by which we live result—and often ironically, if not pathetically or tragically—both from intention, and from the convergence of unintended consequences of the daily or extraordinary acts or dispositions of specific individuals, acting on their own or as members (or representatives) of corporate structures. No one "intends" the birthrate; but, as a quantitative fact, it obviously bears a relation to men's and women's intentions. No painting can ever be painted without individual intention.

The distinction between enacted and crescive change cuts across the separations that Marx demanded. He saw crescive change in dialectic terms, and hoped for radical resolutions within the sphere of enacted change. Thus he helped force attention toward the conditions under which people seek change (and their methods of attempting to achieve their ends), and the conditions accompanying the resistance to change. The study of social change must at some point involve dissecting vested interests, and separating the demand for change (in the name of an alternative order) from the dislike of the status quo (in the service of a permanent desire to oppose any order). Rebel, revolutionary, apostate, negativist, innovator, entrepreneur, discoverer, creative artist—all represent modes of social action and of social relation whose motives and contributions a theory of society can neither ignore nor leave unassessed.

In Marx, the distinction between the domain of ideas and the domain of economic arrangements is important, especially when it is regarded as one among several necessary distinctions that combine to reveal the domains of society.

The study of change involves a view of the several domains so distinguished. Marx's formulation of the genesis and consequences of ideology provides additional resources for observing change. The somewhat embarrassing issue of the extent to which Marx's theory itself is an example of one of its distinctions is not relevant here. Still, many questions arise from the assumption that people can view the surrounding social world in a manner significantly different, both from the views of others occupying different positions, and also from the point of view of an observer whose perspective of time and place transcends both.

On the plane of social life, this assumption demonstrates what, later, Freud documented within the life of the individual patient. There are differences between Marx's notion of false consciousness and Freud's description of evasions and rationalizations. There are also similarities. Whatever one's ultimate view of the matter, a provisional distinction between more and less adequate concepts of the character

---

1. I am indebted to Daniel Bell, of Columbia University, for reminding me of this and indicating many other omissions in the first draft of this essay, and for challenging, aptly and ably, the noncommital and impersonal character of the present analysis.

of the social world is essential. The distinction itself produces some of the issues of social change.

The correction of incorrect views takes time. The process of correction helps make social affairs into temporal ones. Distinctions between correct and false consciousness have further implications. Today, educated by Durkheim, Weber, and others, we would be forced to make several distinctions within the domain of ideas itself. We would be inclined to distinguish existential from normative ideas; and ideas about empirical matters, susceptible to correction by science, from ideas about non-empirical matters, primarily accessible to the debates of philosophy, theology, and the arts. Besides, we would not regard these distinctions as invidious, but as distinctions among domains within which change is expected to proceed in characteristically different forms. The full exploration of Marx's theory of ideology, therefore, confronts one with many of the chronic issues of sociological analysis.

The concept of ideology also raises the question of the causal status of ideas. Similarly, it points toward a classification of ideas relative to the transformation of social arrangements. Marx regarded the first issue in the light of his historical materialism. He considered the second—helped by a version of positivism which regarded religion as an opiate—to be substantively incorrect in its claims. This is not the place to assert the importance of the difference between cause, assertion, and consequence within the domain of ideas. Theoretically it is now known that differences exist between the motives leading people to assert some propositions, the actual assertions they make, and the possible consequences of the assertions' acceptance or rejection for a variety of persons, institutions, or other phenomena. We know that social reality is malleable enough to enable some prophecies made about it to fulfil themselves through the very act of assertion. We do not yet know how to differentiate between the areas in which prophecies do fulfil themselves, and the areas in which the social nexus is more dense—more self-determined, as it were.

Implicitly or explicitly, Marx raised all these issues. He suggested too that the perception, and also the exploration, of social institutions must be disassociated from certain positions within a given society. With others, he pointed at the more specific process of the worker's alienation from work and the means of production; and also indicated its more general and subtle manifestation within the intellectual community where a certain detachment from reigning interests and conventions has become the precondition for their proper understanding. In formulating historic materialism, Marx also focused on the notion of intent as insufficient for under-

standing the course of history. He thus pointed to the study of the "unintended consequences of purposive social action." Others represented in this Reader, especially Max Weber, have made the same phenomenon the subject of their concern or their observation. In Marx's writings, however, the conception of historical materialism—with its continuous succession of antithetical and conflicting arrangements, heading inevitably toward the establishment of a socialist, stateless, and free society—became also a political cry and program.

THE STUDY OF PERSONALITY

During the turn of the century, the systematic study of personality reached a scope and depth that, at least, in the West, had never been attained before. A succession of great thinkers—e.g., Nietzsche, William James, Marx, Freud, Bergson, Durkheim—deposited a framework of conceptions which yielded a historic attitude toward personality; personality came to be conceived as a historic phenomenon. Many aspects of this development have been discussed or demonstrated in Part Three.

The present has benefited from a general view of personality which would conceive individuality and social embeddedness as complementary, rather than antithetical, dimensions. No account of collective enterprises or more impersonal shifts within human history can proceed now without a relatively detailed sense of human motives.

The historic view of personality emphasizes its capacity for transformation. It poses questions about stages of development, and suggests a process of differentiation occurring within the domain of personal experience. In this perspective, personality becomes itself the causal nexus in which past experiences or intentions have consequences for subsequent intentions and experiences. Personality thus becomes the context for slow and sudden change, shifts in value, allegiance, or taste. But the study and discovery of these changes is not sufficient for the comparable study and discovery of patterns and processes of change on the other planes of social relations, social organization, wider collectivities, or general values—planes that are the more immediate subject matter of this Reader.

Nevertheless, a study of social change emphasizing causation, shift, repetition, novelty, continuity, and discontinuity probably draws directly from the realm of the experience of a personal world more than the complementary study of the steadier features of social systems does. The understanding of personality was enhanced precisely through the study of the succession of thoughts, the association of words, the unlikely combination of ideas. The consideration of the apparent inner flux of the personality makes prominent the inherent combination of permanence and change which, so far as is now known, characterizes all living arrangements. The characteristic of aliveness—and its distinction from the non-alive elements and patterns in the world—lies precisely in the recognition that repetition and constancy are applicable but radically inadequate notions.

Novelty is a fact. However, it is frequently used antithetically with the notion of repetition. This is one thing that has blighted much discussion of social structure and social change. It has drawn these two concepts into the unsatisfactory dichotomy implied by the terms "static" and "dynamic," a dichotomy further compounded by the differences between history and social science.

In any event, a view developed at the end of the last century that considered a personality as a potent mixture of self-known and unconscious strivings, themselves often divided and at war with each other, capable of education, development, and treatment. This view imbued the most immediate plane of society (its constituent individuals) with a dynamic character affecting the perception of the other planes. Similarly, as the distinctions for describing modes of transformation on the planes of social relations, collectivities, and values grow more clear and become better documented, gains made in the study of personality are enhanced and revised.

SOME GENERAL THEMES IN THE ANALYSIS OF SOCIAL CHANGE

As we have presented the analysis of society in these volumes, it has had various relations to history. Its contributors have included both fanatic disciples of relatively deterministic and monocausal views of the character of social transformation, and more cautious and disengaged observers who have either withdrawn from a contemplation of the larger issues and concentrated on the solution of particular questions of historic shifts or liberally proposed an open-minded perspective that, in the extreme, makes a virtue of inconclusiveness.

The beginnings of sociological analysis involved, in a measure, a slow turning from history in favor of focusing on the repetitive and ordered aspects of social phenomena; as sociology has continued to grow it has faced up to history again. The interval represented here—ending in the 1930's—has helped

establish a provisional distinction between static and dynamic concerns—foreshadowed by Spencer, among others, in his terminology and work. The future will probably prove this distinction quite misleading.

On the plane underlying more inclusive historic shifts, the concept "dynamic" has become applied to those special phenomena of more visible or more abrupt change lying in the two realms of collective behavior and long-range, especially quantitative, shifts. The latter became manifest in such areas as rates of birth, death, migration, technological innovation.

The combination of an interest in the conditions of stability with an interest in the direction of transformation of social arrangements is made possible by the distinctions, implicit or explicit, made by the thinkers represented in this Reader. The several planes of personal, social, and cultural coherence then exhibit both independence and continuity. The familiar themes make their appearance once again.

The severalness and coherence of social arrangements. In looking for the common themes running through the writers of the works from which we have made selections, one finds the idea of an institutional order. This order involves a variety of spheres (legal, economic, political, etc.), and implies the several planes of culture, social relations, and individual personality. The institutional order confronts an environment. This environment includes the hereditary constitutions of the constituent members of societies; the constitutions are also subject to change.

Like the concern with order, the concern with change must, then, allow for what are conveniently called creative personalities. Yet the process and products of creation—whether scientific discoveries, poems, pictures, musical compositions, or new architectural styles—involve more than their creators. Moreover, even creative people are, like everyone else, constituted in their humanness within the structure of society. That structure therefore persists by virtue of the changing proportions of traditional, calculating, and charismatic dispositions.

In one sense, all societies, like all languages, contain similar possibilities. They differ, however, in the compromises they make between the characteristic opposing proclivities that govern within the domains of public and private life and the possible relation between them. Social change occurs on two levels: it involves inner shifts *within* any one domain that, combined with the others, constitutes a given society; and it involves shifts *among* the domains, with particular regard to their relative dominance.

Transformation in and transformation of society.
Social arrangements differ in their duration and
durability. Some arrangements, notably those called
societies in this Reader, transcend the life-span
of individuals; this is not automatic. It is made
possible by a multiplicity of arrangements dealing
with the succession and circulation of persons
through a smaller or larger number of the various
structures that, by virtue of tradition and other
requirements, a society at any given time retains
as necessary or given.

As one moves away from a purely personal
perspective, one can perceive a given institutional
complex—e.g., a school—as little changed over a
considerable period—even if it has witnessed the
entrance and graduation of several classes of
students. Change and stability are matters of the
plane of perspective on which they are regarded.
As a corporate structure, a social system can contain a variety of people passing through it who are
not themselves undergoing important transformations (though they may be undergoing them, as
well). A social structure can also encompass
typical repetitive shifts, usually circular, along
dimensions like morale, the relative importance of
internal or external issues, attention to instrumental
or expressive matters, etc.

However, one must also seek for the beginnings
and ends of corporate enterprises. Though corporate enterprises may coincide with some collective withdrawal, withdrawal and engagement on the
part of individuals complexly intersect the temporal extent of social arrangements. Only recent
theoretical developments have systematically begun
distinguishing kinds of nonconformity, rebellion,
deviance, and opposition. These distinctions cut
across the gross distinction between participation
and withdrawal. They also have clearly indicated
that the variousness of opposition to the traditions
of society is both a cost and a gain.

There is a direct continuity between this perspective and Durkheim's famous proposition that
crime is a normal social fact. Full elaboration of
the implications of this proposition for a theoretical
apprehension of the directions and kinds of social
change has now begun.

The distribution of honor and power. Shifts in
the determination of society, the complication of
society through numbers, changes in the division of
labor, multiplication of competing corporate groupings, industrialization, or other forms of cumulative
developments, all involve transformations in creating and ordering categories of individuals. These
categories then become recognized as estates or
castes or classes. Their mutual relations imply a
system of ranking which, itself subject to trans-

formation, in turn becomes a pattern of unequal
participation within the affairs giving shape to
society.

In general, social theory was born and nurtured
during the era that kinship-based ascriptive barriers
were being replaced in favor of a system of recognition of achievement linked mostly to the world of
occupations, and while an ongoing process of professionalization was occurring in the context of a
multiplication of large corporate enterprises. Issues
frequently summed up in slogans—e.g., "the rights
of the common man," "the inalienable birthrights
of equality," "the rule of the people"—thus became vitally important questions for the formula-
tors of a sociological tradition.

Durkheim, Marx, Weber, Simmel, and Pareto
were all, in one way or another, pursued by the
issues implied by "socialism." The reciprocal rights
or powers of individuals or categories of individuals
are, in fact, both natural subjects for moral debate
and appropriate indices for distinguishing among
forms of society. The legitimate and usurpable
resources of power of different individuals or
categories of them—or such corporate enterprises
as the state, trade unions, professional associations,
or legislative assemblies—are the very *objects and
conditions* of social stability and transformation. In
studying them, the founders of sociology made the
analysis of social change a central occupation.

Similarly, by concerns with shifts in the relative
positions of categories of people (e.g., men, women,
or children) or ethnically differentiated groupings,
the continual necessity for distinguishing between
generally acknowledged and unacknowledged patterns of power and influence was introduced into the
consideration of social change. The discrepancy
between these is one source of the difference between appearance and reality that any society
necessarily exhibits. This discrepancy is further
complicated by the differences between communicated and private, displayed and hidden, personal dispositions as these become transformed into
the reciprocities of social relations.

In that sense, societies engender a number of
dimensions. They embody secretiveness as well as
widely understood meanings. The latter are embodied only fragmentarily in the symbols by which
life is carried on.

Directionality of change. Weber and Durkheim
clearly propose a directionality toward increased
complications, increased rational-legal patterns and
standards. To speak of the complication of society,
as a direction of its transformation, as here represented, is one part of a more widespread and collective effort to transcend tradition through rational
and legal plans, formulated by this or that instituted

or self-appointed group, for the sake of understanding and determining an increasingly wider range of affairs. Sociological analysis itself is one aspect of the growth of systematic self-consciousness. Growth is linked to the cumulative growth of science, as well as to the configurations of a wider culture, as one of the selections discusses at length. Parallel directionalities have been proposed in connection with such terms as "secularization."

Very little has been explicitly said, by the central figures in the development of sociological analysis, about the shifts and conflicts in the mutual relationships of growing national and industrialized societies. However, the theme of irreversible social change has been introduced. This theme suggests that the domains of society, whatever their important distinctions, constitute mutual relations which limit lack of change in any one of them. In this regard, social theory becomes a corrective for both conservative and revolutionary idealism. It helps reveal the power of a variety of vested interests, and the balance of forces that both maintain and continually undermine the so-called status quo. On the other hand, Pareto and others have complemented the concept of irreversibility with the concepts of equilibrium and social circulation. Such notions, if taken alone, would constitute a cyclical view of history.

Ideas of the directionality of social change, as already shown, overlap with conceptions of social evolution and of social progress. Even though the notion of progress has the ostensibly narrow moral bias to judge social change in accordance with a standard beyond that change, as a conception it is obviously in itself an important social fact. It is one acknowledgment of the ineradicable purposiveness of human activity.

It has become the office of social theory to show the limits of such purposiveness and the distinction between intended and unintended consequences. The denial of purposiveness, or of a wider meaningfulness of individual or collective events, has become another important social fact. Indeed we may refer to the attempt by Max Weber, included in Part Four above, to order the modes of rejection of the world; in themselves, these are solutions to the question of meaning.

During the nineteenth century, there was a great deal of argument concerning progress. Much of this argument derived from the difficulty of combining a sense of the relativity and variety of moral positions that have informed the efforts of men, with a sense of the generic and chronic issues to which the former can be considered solutions—while the latter, at least partially, arise because of them. Moreover, transformations in domains like

technology, to which one can unequivocally apply criteria of efficiency or destructiveness, were demonstrably marked by an enhancement of such standards over time. Other domains clearly require other models of change; there is no consensus on the details of an over-all model. Yet there seems to be consensus on social systems as subject to increased complication on the plane of societies. A cumulative indirect connection among growing patterns of differentiated domains or social positions seems characteristic of the history of persisting societies. In a manner, this is an evolutionary perspective. Social theory has, however, demanded radical modifications in the assumptions and ideas of a theory of evolution when it is applied to social, rather than biological, phenomena.

There is an apparent but far from ultimate antithesis between a commitment to a view of society as an evolutionary phenomenon and a view of society as a variety of equilibria, each subject to its own mode of circulation of personnel elites. This indicates again the necessity to distinguish between both long-range and short-range changes, as well as between changes in and of society.

The Planes and Confines of Change

The perception of social change is surrounded by the discrepancies between appearance and reality and between permanence and transformation. We see the earth as flat; we know it is round. We experience the world as stationary; we know it is in continuous motion. We see ourselves continuous with our self in the past, and expect to recognize ourselves in the future. Yet we also recognize or claim shifts in our values, in our knowledge and occasionally in our spontaneity. The models for motion easily crowd in on us; they are not neatly distributed among the spheres of change that we recognize. Indeed, the authors represented in this Reader acknowledge a variety of causal nexus, precisely because each admits of a different model of change as most appropriate for its explanation or discovery.

We know that the aging of motors and the aging of organisms, though similar in some important ways, are not the same. Men and metals are both subject to fatigue; yet we assume that, in the realm of conscious being, processes inherited from other realms are associated with matters peculiar to the realms of intention, apprehension, and expectation. Though their boundaries are vague, and their precise determinations are difficult, the transformations associated with social systems are the subject of this Reader.

Despite the rich vocabulary of change—e.g., "growth," "progress," "development," "decay," "accumulation," or "attrition"—immediate experience furnishes only a credible, but not a sufficient, key to understanding social change. Therefore, the exploration of changes in personality has not been extensively represented here. We do not deny that psychological facts are relevant for any attempt to account for changes within social organizations or wider corporate patterns. On the contrary, this Reader is fair proof that changes in and of any society involve changes in the configuration of motives and dispositions characterizing the members of that society. Wide shifts in an economy— e.g., from agricultural to industrial patterns—cannot proceed without changes in people's organization of emotions. This is not the place to discuss the vexing questions of the relative causal status of personality dispositions in such shifts, or to be definitive about the boundaries between psychological cause and effect.

The view of personality that developed in the nineteenth century provided, as noted in Part Three, resources for the explanation of social changes. Also, it was itself a claim that personality, especially as represented by the psychoanalytic tradition, may in part be regarded as a counterweight to the developments of rational and secular thought that form, as this Reader claims, the background of contemporary sociological theory.

The complementarity—as distinct from their mutual reducibility or radical independence—of sociological and psychological modes of analysis has been argued in the introductory essays to Parts One and Three. It is important that charting of the unconscious wellsprings of human conduct necessitated a pattern of systematic clinical observation within the specialized encounter of therapeutic intimacy. Also, the charting required a rationality and literateness capable of clearly formulating the patterns marking the histories of human dispositions. Thus the analysis of the emotions—with their labyrinthine logic—engages capacities that may still be called those of reason. The twin effort has provided a potentially inclusive and penetrating view of human personality. This view demands that all members of societies be regarded as involved in a continuous process of at least potential transformation. Illness, especially emotional disturbance, thus disrupts the continuity of this transformation. Though this plane of transformation has important interrelations with the other planes of social change, it is not directly discussed in the selections following this Introduction. Instead, changes on the planes of social relations, of organizations, and of culture provide the major subject matter.

CHANGE ON THE PLANE OF SOCIAL RELATIONS

The Introduction to Part One discussed lengthily the stubborn distinction, formulated by Toennies and subsequently elaborated by Durkheim, Linton, Redfield, and others, concerning the classification of social relations. Often the classification stands for a view of historic succession. Mechanical and organic solidarity, *Gemeinschaft* and *Gesellschaft*, sacred and secular society, ascribed and achieved social positions—though not identical, these are similar bipolar distinctions making the personal and impersonal components in social life a dichotomy of social reciprocity.

In some hands, this view also became a political program, thriving on the invidious distinction, kept dialectic, between the exploiter and the exploited, and the variety of circles associated with these two categories of persons within capitalistic society. A contrasting view considers society composed of webs of partly overlapping circles which generate conflicts within their members, who thus become more or less precariously balanced representatives of various combinations of attachment and alienation.

Marxian analysis combined a passionate wish to distinguish between reality and illusion, with an equally driving attachment to notions of justice tending to equate all injustice with inequality. In Marxist terms, society was always explored with reference to an image of a good society yet to be established. By the processes of history, the establishment of this society would constitute the end of history. Combined, the notions of evolution, of a positive exploration of human institutions, and of Marx's scheme of analysis provided most of the outstanding features of the intellectual situation from which the founders of the theory of society— notably Durkheim, Weber, Pareto, and Freud— drew their support or their challenge. Yet at the turn of the century, a series of other eminent and important figures made the contemplation of the transformations of history part of the very focus of their thought.

The nineteenth century included Bentham and Nietzsche, Carlyle and Emerson, Thoreau and Sorel, Hegel and John Stuart Mill. They bequeathed us a large view, as did novelists—like Tolstoy, who had the serenity and courage to write about war and peace. The large view has become problematic, if not suspect. Yet we cannot escape being heirs of the nineteenth century. Not many may wish to pursue the past as did a Sorokin or a Toynbee, together with their more immediate or distant predecessors, be they Spengler or Spencer,

Hegel or Kant. Still, they have given us a sense of the range of planes of social change, one that the contemporary concern with limited, more immediate subject matter can now no longer ignore.

The distinction between *Gemeinschaft* and *Gesellschaft* has been stubborn. It suggests that, in the context of a rising capitalism and the proliferation of private enterprises oriented toward the patterns of the market, the growth of the impersonal elements within social arrangements became a noted phenomenon. Subsequent theories, as will be pointed out in the Epilogue, have transcended this dichotomy, but have never quite left it behind. In this Reader, we have filled the wide spaces that it includes with proposals about social differentiation. This concept has been discussed in detail in the Introduction to Part Two above. Similarly, the second essay of the General Introduction to the Reader presented many of the theoretical issues involved in the study of social change.

The paradoxes of the shifts from a presumably more personal nexus of previous societies to a more large-scale and impersonal nexus, and of the development of several kinds of national structures—especially during the nineteenth and twentieth centuries—have not yet been theoretically ordered. All these developments have been involved in an ongoing controversy—the controversy concerning the contrasts between socialist and laissez-faire ideologies, between democratic and totalitarian regimes, between egalitarian sentiments and aristocratic requirements. It concerns itself with the deliberate cultivation of roots and attachments, as well as with the genesis of a wish for individual mobility.

The theories of Marx, Durkheim, Weber, Rousseau, Pareto, and Spengler about the nature of social change are very much part and parcel of that controversy. The terms "left" and "right," arguments between science and religion, between governmental control and individual scope, are additional elements of the same struggle. Hence, especially in recent years, simple proposals about social change are inappropriate.

In the last seventy-five years, the chances of a fair hearing in court, of better medical treatment, of educational and occupational opportunities, or of larger experimentation in the realms of self-knowledge and child raising, have been enhanced—at least in Western society. (This is, of course, not equally true throughout or among any given societies.) At the same time, various forms of social control, of public investigation of private matters, of large-scale cruelties, and of continuous anonymous persuasion, have also increased. These contrasts are embedded in dramatic events—a revolu-

tion in Russia, two world wars, and the rapid advance in military and industrial technology with its far-reaching consequences. Such a foreground obscures the more persistent and generic issues underlying the selections in this last part of the Reader.

As we have seen, the nineteenth century was both optimistic about the growth of society, as consistent with its evolutionary discovery, and concerned about the possibilities of decline. Still, it remains true that most societies outlive by far the life cycle of their constituent members. None of those active in the United States during the 1950's was alive in the 1850's. The distinction between changes *in* a society and changes *of* it remains strategic.

Concern with continuity on this wider scale can lead easily to logical errors. Indeed, the theory of society has only slowly extricated itself from various kinds of extremes, vacillating between theories of the importance of great men and theories of the utter dispensability of individuals. Slowly, a more orderly concern with modes of individual attachment, evasion, rebellion, opposition, retreat, and alienation concerning the traditions of social arrangements, has developed. The substance of tradition has yet to be systematically analyzed.

Social relations always have a past and a future reference. They involve the notion of obligation, though in varying ways. Indeed, the emergence of so-called secondary (as distinct from primary) groupings essentially entails reducing obligations toward the other as a person. But the move from status to contract, as Maine described it in a selection in Part One above, in fact involves replacing the kinds of obligations entailed in a feudal or closed class system by modes of mutual concern mediated through arrangements within and among large groupings and often protected by legal arrangements. It is precisely the permanent juxtaposition—in changing proportion—of the ostensibly opposed notions of ascriptive coherence and individual autonomy, communal bonds and urban anonymity within the *same* social relations, that constitutes the point of departure and guidance for developing the theory of society. In that respect, it is not merely fortuitous that the phenomena of gratitude and sympathy, personal and impersonal mutual obligation, and justification of rules by precedent should be among the recurrent objects of interest within the study of social institutions.

These matters constitute both a calculation of consequence sustained by persons in their capacity as members of various social arrangements, and a body of practices linking present decisions with past events. Similarly, social relations involve expectations. They link the present to the future, especially if continuity is valued.

The writers represented here, however, obviously transcend concern with a web of social relations. They also outline the mutual regard among aggregates of people differing one from another in their economic and other interests. In this connection, social stratification and mobility have become two of the most prominent foci for considering social change. Social mobility between positions implies shifts, by individuals, categories of individuals, or corporate bodies, with regard to other representatives of their kind. Social mobility constitutes a form of change within society. In addition, it can become associated with a change in the very form of society.

This Reader contains analysis both of a growing antagonism between differently placed economic and social groupings, and of the development of new social cleavages within industrialized societies. It also provides the bases for expecting a similarity, in rank order, of occupations (despite sharp ideological differences among nations), the decline of aristocratic settings, and the homogenization of social life, in the twentieth century. This is, of course, oversimplified. Weber's work suggests that, under conditions of social change, the more impersonal bases of social positions, particularly economic ones, are likely to become prominent; while, under conditions of apparent stability and reliability, considerations of honor rather than of economic power, and of style of life rather than of competence, take precedence.

In the past, the proclivity to regard social arrangements under the aspect of dichotomous distinctions helped give impetus to the development of cyclical theories of change. Personal experience is relevant in this regard—old age has similarities to childhood. Cyclical theories, moreover, avoid the "unscientific" notion of progress and the oversimplified implications of a unilinear model of history.

On the other hand, the nineteenth and the early twentieth centuries also saw the development of Michels' famous iron law of oligarchy. This formulation is part of a wider concern with the growth of corporate organizations, which are regarded as imminently involved in the cumulative growth of bureaucratic patterns. Size, co-ordination, and concentration of power, in turn, are perceived as mutually implied developments. Such developments quickly raise ideological issues. So the study of social change becomes, in fact, very closely connected with ideological commitments. By extension, systematic attention to the processes of stability and order can be interpreted as expressing a conserva-

tive commitment. Such linkages tend to confuse factual, logical, and psychological considerations.

For the most part, this Reader presents the theory of society that conceives of social change in relation to the forms of society. It is concerned with the rise of capitalism, the forms of class conflicts, situations in cultural productivity, the general cumulative and rapid growth of technology, and shifts in the opportunities of intimacy, given the facts of the rationalization of life.

Today, we read these selections against a background of more recent concern with the rise of new types of personality, different kinds of social role, new forms of leisure and ecological arrangements, new patterns of entrepreneurship and management, and self-conscious developments of nationalistic autonomy, or large-scale planning for huge populations. Besides, one aspect of social change is precisely the differentiation of societies, under the impact of industrialization, into an increasing number of spheres, circles, and groupings demanding *separate* consideration. The question of rates of change within different domains of a given society always arises here. This concern with rates is one route to distinguishing between personal and social systems, and the realm of values.

The Plane of Culture

According to one view, "culture" is a collective term for patterns of existential and normative assertions. These assertions, in both their form and their content, need not be stated in words. They may take the form of music, art, sculpture, dance, or clothes—to mention only a few classes of human assertions other than literature, language, science, or technology.

It is indisputable that cultures change. Why, how, and in what—if any—orderly fashion they change, is problematic. The culture of ancient Egypt is no more. The pattern of values by which we recognize something as medieval has been displaced. The theory of society represented in this Reader had, as observed above, to extricate itself both from a positivistic impatience, especially with the religious components of cultural configurations; and from a historicist commitment to see the configurations of different periods as a unique succession of transformations, whose every stage could be understood only from within, ultimately through intuition.

The following excerpts are contained within these extremes and progressively transcend them. Two are selected from Spengler and from Kroeber. Each addresses the matter of cultural growth, though Spengler is much more certain and much more analogical. Kroeber is sensitive to birth and decay in the various domains of culture. He considers sculpture as well as national self-consciousness. He is aware of "isolated" geniuses, like the fifteenth-century French poet Villon, or the eighteenth- and early nineteenth-century painter Goya.

Several problems arise on this plane of change. At the beginning, the question of classifying the domains of culture frequently arises. Common sense seems to find little difficulty in seeing differences between philosophy, science, philology, sculpture, painting, drama, literature, and music. These are the domains which Kroeber has made the subject of his lucid exploration of the configurations of culture growth. Men discontented with common sense can then perceive the interrelations among these domains. Yet what is literature? How is one to establish its boundaries?

There are, of course, further planes and further forms of cultural growth—especially obvious when one thinks about fashions and fads. Several more analytic distinctions have been part of intellectual history. In the following selections, MacIver and Alfred Weber in particular are committed—as Ogburn is, in a different form—to the distinction between culture and civilization. This distinction depends upon the difference between cumulative and non-cumulative transformations within the wider history of social arrangements. Civilization is the cumulative component of history. "Accumulation" stands for an image of direct continuity. It considers that present accomplishments proceed from previous accomplishments, while also making them, in a measure, obsolete. Scientific discovery, and particularly technological advance, are presumably classical instances of accumulation.[2]

It would not be difficult to be skeptical of such a formulation. The continuity of products so conceived must be distinguished from a continuity of processes. Still, it seems plausible that Einstein renders Newton obsolete—in a manner in which Kant, though perhaps answering Hume, does not replace Hume. The difference between accumulation and non-cumulative transformations, then, is allied to the differences between cognitive, moral, and aesthetic assertions. It also relates to the distinction between instrumental and expressive modes of engagement in the world.

However, these are all analytic distinctions. Any concrete phenomenon to which they apply is composed of more than one of the terms of the distinctions used. Clothes are both instrumental and expressive: they keep us warm and show our self-conceptions; they express our wish to be part of one circle rather than another, and our willingness to be part of the times. Cultural change is described better as a spiral of oscillating transformations between the poles of simplicity and complexity, than as a straight line. However, the straight-line image does apply better to such accomplishments as the conquest of space and time. But in an area like medicine, where science and art meet, contemporary notions of illness are in some respects more like non-literate conceptions than they are like the nineteenth-century naturalistic notions which they are displacing.

The search for appropriate models of change within the domains of culture continues. Similarly, the search for adequate formulations about the relations among the domains of culture continues—though this section provides evidence of some stimulating landmarks. Kroeber, Spengler, Sorokin, and Toynbee (the list is alphabetical and neutral) all sought to reveal the possible order underlying the succession of cultural accomplishments that has marked civilizations and cultures as alive and dead.

The search for the proper images—dialectic, linear, spiral—to represent transformations in the several domains of culture is one thing. The quest for the conditions and consequences for the forms then described is another. One major theme of Max Weber's work concerns the reasons for the relative absence of the development of science in classical China, compared to the West. He is concerned with the consequences that scientific development, once begun, has for the whole structure of society. The importance of technological change as one form of applying science need no longer be documented. Yet the conditions for maintaining such change, and for change in the wake of technological growth itself, are still understood only partly.

Within the domain of moral commitments and religious attachments, the theory of society has been nourished on a general dissociation between religious and other institutional spheres, and also on the wish to understand precisely the role of religious motivation and religious organization within the process of transformation, particularly of Western society. Similarly, in the question of how a given society (e.g., the American one) can and cannot be described as "the same" over a period of one hundred or one hundred and fifty years, many issues pertaining to the distinction between shifts *of,* and differentiation *in,* systems of value have appropriately arisen.

Forms of Change

The recognition of planes of social change confirms a recognition of the variety of its forms. The

---

2. Some of the more common versions of this distinction have been questioned in the Introduction to Part Four above.

theory of society has, in one way or another, recognized such phenomena as the following: the emergence of new kinds of social positions; the extension of principles of organization (like those of the professions) to more lines of work; shifts in the relative ordering of the public and private spheres of social action, including corporate groupings' extension of control over work and leisure; and shifts among guiding principles (e.g., the emergence of notions of social security—which, as a wit once observed, the nineteenth century might well have adopted if it had thought of them.)

Additional distinctions have slowly emerged. Weber, for instance, in the second part of his observations on society and economy, distinguishes between *Vergemeinschaftung* and *Vergesellschaftung*. He suggests that the internal and external conditions facilitating the relative power of families as units of economic and political force disappear in the course of "cultural development." In that sense, society is regarded as involved in an ongoing process of differentiation, in which the several domains of state and society, community and economy, religious organizations and educational institutions, all become relatively autonomous, while they increasingly sustain between themselves a complicated and indirect division of labor. Such a perspective oscillates between two normative poles. It is sustained by a positive acceptance of the measure of individual freedom and social variety that the process of differentiation demonstrably entails. On the other hand, it approaches contemporary complexity under the aspect of a romantic image of a previous and increasingly lost unity, coherence, and attachment.

Disengaging a view of the differentiation generally entailed in social transformations from these two moral positions is both logically necessary and psychologically difficult. Thus Weber, in discussing rationalization, willingly associated with this process the poet Schiller's expression, "disenchantment of the world." Even if this perspective is balanced with searches for the dialectic of antithetical developments (the emergence of primary groups), the theory of society will probably bypass a vivid sense of the permanent, if unequal, presence of impersonal elements and centrifugal tendencies within *any* and *all* social arrangements.

Forms of change can also be formulated on the basis of their being inherent in social arrangements, as distinct from their being imposed on them; and on the basis of their enhancing or opposing consequences relative to some given tradition. Adaptations (sudden or slow) to changes (abrupt or drawn out) in the external invironment of social systems (e.g., earthquakes, shifts in available resources) are

themselves social facts; but they are not directly engendered by the constitution of social relations. The constitution of social relations, however, as Durkheim has shown, involves both a variety of moral agreements, and intelligible forms of nonconformity with these agreements. Durkheim, as demonstrated in previous selections in this Reader, incorporated into his theory of society the strategic beginnings for an account of individual forms of nonconformity, seen in terms of their social genesis. In studying rates of suicide and in accounting for their unequal distribution among socially meaningful categories of people, he also suggested that the continuity of at least certain social arrangements involves variously placed individuals' withdrawal from life.

On the other hand, Troeltsch and Max Weber, among others, provided the beginnings of an understanding of sects. As a type of social phenomenon, sects involve the formation of new corporate groupings whose corporateness, at least initially, consists in dissatisfaction with other groupings' combination of avowed and enacted beliefs, from which, henceforth, they seek to differ.

In Section D of Part Two, Mosca and Michels discuss political movements, while Pareto and Lenin analyze the questions of force in society and of the possibilities of the disappearance of organized political agencies as they have been known so far. One can equally point to cognate phenomena of individual creativity and the founding of styles and groups of expressions on the planes of cultural accomplishment in music, art, architecture, sculpture, or literature.

The writers represented in this Reader, however, paid less attention to the more "interstitial" or temporary phenomena of apparently sudden enactments—usually in crowds—of distinct, if emotional, patterns (e.g., lynching, demonstrations, riots). These phenomena constitute either a kind of moral holiday, or attempts to take over the law and supersede a more impersonal, anonymous, and slow-working institutional order by rapid, though often well organized, displays.

The realm of ideas provides yet other forms of change. The circumstances surrounding the development of theoretical accomplishments—partially represented by this Reader, for instance—actually included, in refractory but vivid fashion, the growth of rationality, as exhibited by a continuously expanding technology and capitalism, the discovery of unconscious dispositions accompanying any human action, and the founding of political movements devoted to revolutionary qualities and areligiosity. The coincidence of these developments and their consequences have forced themselves upon societies ever since 1914; their "digestion" will continue to be difficult.

Forms of social change are further multiplied by those orders of phenomena which, like the birthrate or any other rate, are the convergent result—in itself not intended—of many intended events. Rates themselves are variable over time, while remaining part of the changing conditions which constitute social arrangements.

Processes and Agencies of Social Change

This whole Reader has been about the processes of *repetition* and *transformation* that mark social arrangements, considered singly or in their mutual relations. It also contains *explanations* of the transformation of social systems. Repeatedly we have noted the themes of the *complication* of society and of the inadequacy of any one model for its representation. Cycles, spirals, straight lines, discontinuous alternation, dialectic zigzags—all have found their places, their critics, and their proper limitations within the several different domains that combine to sustain life in society.

There is no simple consensus concerning the explanation of such phenomena as the French Revolution, the decline of the Roman Empire, the development of the Roman Catholic Church as a social organization, the growth of law governing theft in the eighteenth century, or the rise of the Nazis in the twentieth. But if one temporarily suspends any radical doubts about the genuineness of temporal experience, one perceives that the aliveness of social arrangements lies precisely in their transformation. So far, most of the writers represented here have analyzed them with the help of various contrary ideas. If inconclusive eclecticism be excluded, social theory, as exhibited in this Reader, is observed as always confronted with the problem of being just to impersonal transformations not attributable to any specific individual—presented, e.g., by phenomena like the emergence of occupations and the separation of kinship from corporate economic enterprises—and also to the roles of specific individual intentions and of individualities (in the form of "great persons"). Almost inevitably, the man most concerned with the rise of large-scale transformations (as represented by the rise of capitalism, or the Reformation) was also the man who made so much of the notion of charisma, with its implication of creativity beyond the spheres of established institutional arrangements.

Max Weber has, perhaps irrevocably, stamped upon social theory the notion of the permanent conflict between charisma and institutions. The fact or the possibility of this conflict characterizes societies; it may also destroy them. A theory of change must be able to account for the genesis, the transformation, and the death of social arrangements.

On the plane of personal creativity, the theory of personality—developed by Freud and elaborated into the psychoanalytic tradition—has equally constituted an irrevocable resource for explaining change. It takes seriously—though not at face value —the experiences of inner flux, of association, and of conflict constituting the organism's aliveness as person. This aliveness alternates between various states and degrees of being awake and being asleep. It is constituted in the company of others and in the context of a meaningful universe.

The processes of stability and change in the immediate vicinity and context of personality are palpable enough. They concern the creation of an individuality. Individuality is always involved in "intake" and "output," and in the continuous creation and management of conflicts, whether mild or severe. Concerning the investments of its resources on the plane of social arrangements, stability involves the processes of maintaining the requisite motivational balances. As Durkheim has shown, through his emphasis on ritual, the stability of social arrangements involves periodic representations and reconfirmations of the required moral commitments. For their persistence, societies develop distinct opportunities for withdrawal from one domain of activity into another. Part of the resumability of social activities also involves a variety of ways of replacing individual actors. Societies, then, are —as Durkheim and Weber in particular have shown —structures sustained by persons, but not necessarily continuously by the same persons. They are capable of a continuous transfer of power. Their viability depends on their acceptance of the death, often unpredictable, of individuals.

These two sides are given unequal emphasis by the several authors of the following selections. It is all too easy to omit one, to the other's disavantage. Moreover, social arrangements demand motivated commitments, and they involve the domain of symbols and ideas.

From some points of view, the history of symbols and ideas appears autonomous, especially in the realm of language and the planes of sound or grammar. Yet ideas need men. The inherent divisibility of thought, furthered by this or that wider social context, is likely to create various illusions in this respect. Various imaginary realms can be constituted and given "a misplaced concreteness" belying their abstracted quality. In any case, ideas can grow stale; symbols can suffer attrition. Institutional arrangements help to generate counter-enthusiasms, which sometimes seek their destruction or displacement. Such developments are likely to be mediated both by experiences of deprivation and dissatisfaction, and by that process of alienation inherent in all social arrangements, for they are all compounds of personal and impersonal developments.

Finally, because sources of change have been institutionalized in social transformation's own structure (e.g., science, technology, freedom of enterprise, tolerance for various kinds of individual variation and expression), the continuity, if not the direction, of social transformation is insured. Its rate remains variable.

Continuity and transformation are continually balanced, even in the most rapidly changing circumstances, by the development of personal rigidities, socially embedded vested interests, and the inevitable framework of tradition. Ultimately, the theory of change is confronted by a limiting paradox which arises as part of the ongoing enterprise of self-knowledge and self-determination entailed in the differentiation of society as such. The theory of society represented here developed largely in opposition to explanations by fate, Hegelian dialectic, or divine purposes. In a measure, it is part of that process of rationalization that it helped to discover. That process, however, has led to forms of large-scale planning and control. It has enhanced personal freedom by extending the sphere of considerations of achievement while limiting the sphere of ascriptive calculation. But it also attached conditions of livelihood, for a majority now free to vote, to membership in wide spheres of corporate organization. These conditions are marked by various concentrations of power and authority.

Conditions which enhance self-determination (and knowledge) within social arrangements also present possibilities of control. Similarly, the wish for knowledge, and hence for foreknowledge, eventually proceeds on the assumption that social arrangements are humanly created. Yet sociological knowledge must allow for the realities of choice and of the traditional given attributes of institutions and corporate groups. Moreover, the theory of society has increasingly shown that social reality is, at least in some measure, malleable enough to accommodate the fruits of prophecy—and, in fact, to be partly shaped thereby.

This Reader contains many suggestions about the agencies and processes of social change. These could not be confined to one section. Rather, each part of the Reader is a necessary resource for formulations accounting for the variety of transformations that, among them, the builders of a theory of society have considered—or have to consider.

CONCLUSION

Perhaps more than the other parts of this Reader, this concluding part represents an opening of issues rather than the reporting of confirmed agreements. It is appropriate that we end openly. The heart of the study of society is in understanding its transformations. Such an understanding yields a concept of society's consistent (structural) patterns, whose dissection was exemplified in the first four parts of this Anthology. It also yields a sense of the coincidence of intelligibility and creativity that marks societies in different proportions. This coincidence probably haunts the work of all the thinkers represented here; it is explicitly recognized by most of them.

The analysis of society is free neither from a sense of the irrevocability of the past, nor from a sense of the alternatives open to the future. Yet, though we may continue arrangements for reasons other than those with which we instituted them, we take ourselves along as we leave the past behind. The theory of society will continue to be nourished by the facts that society relies on dependability and helps generate the unexpected.

Section A

Factors of Change

Editorial Foreword, BY KASPAR D. NAEGELE   *1225*

1. *On the Accumulation of Capital,* BY KARL MARX   *1226*
2. *On Protestantism and Capitalism,* BY MAX WEBER   *1253*
3. *On Psychology and History,* BY SIGMUND FREUD   *1265*
4. *The Hypothesis of Cultural Lag,* BY WILLIAM F. OGBURN   *1270*
5. *Fundamentals of Culture-Sociology,* BY ALFRED WEBER   *1274*

Factors of Change

by Kaspar D. Naegele

THE TITLE OF THIS SECTION is eloquent but, without some explanation, misleading. Any theory of society increasingly combines recognition of the distinct character of social arrangements with a recognition of their dependence on cultural and psychological orders, and on non-human orders, including heredity and the physical environment. Other anthologies have collected the writings of those seeking the factors of change along the whole range of domains which somehow impinge on the events comprising history. For instance, one can explain revolutions—even after making a proper distinction between necessary and sufficient, or immediate and approximate, causes—with reference to such diverse considerations as intellectual development, economic conditions, social patterns, political arrangements, constellations of personalities, and fortuitous circumstances.[1]

Like the Reader as a whole, this Section is confined primarily to discussion of matters endemic to social systems and their constituent domains. The selections, taken together, propose distinctions among several domains and characterize these domains according to their relations to change itself. Sporadically, the selections suggest some connections among them. They show alternative ways of allocating priorities to features of human arrangements which are likely to be responsible for far-reaching transformations. To an extent, the selections could also be ordered as voices in an ongoing debate.

The opening selection, from Marx, can be read as an attempt to give pre-eminence to the realm of material conditions that, in dialectic interrelation with the realms of ideas and social relations, provides limits and directions of change.

The second selection, from Max Weber, does not, as is sometimes erroneously believed, suggest the reverse of this position. Weber wishes rather to give religious commitments and changes in religious attitudes a more than derivative status, within the process of historic change. He seeks to demonstrate the association, in the West, between Protestant Christianity and a broad and cumulative process of rationalization. Marx's ambivalence between an assertion of historic determinism issuing from the realm of the means of production and a call for individual self-clarification and revolutionary action is complemented, in Weber's case, by the demand for distinguishing between the moral requirements and psychological prerequisites of specific economic arrangements.

Freud, in the next selection, introduces another theme. He reminds us of the consequences of specific experiences and actions for subsequent choice. Marx, Weber, and Freud would agree that, in attaining or striving for specific ends, we create experiences and conditions exceeding our previous anticipations and yielding consequences that, in turn, become the conditions for subsequent developments. In this way, a theory of society recognizes the impossibility of leaving the past behind. No one ever "starts from scratch." Still, some of our motives do become autonomous. Discontinuity does mark social change.

Ogburn distinguishes (as would Marx and Veblen) between material and non-material culture. Since each is a form of culture, a description of their differences invites a consideration of their similarities. In any event, Ogburn sees, among the phenomena of technology, rates and modes of

---

1. I am indebted for this particular listing to an unpublished memorandum by Harry Eckstein of Princeton University.

change lacking in the realms of law, morality, or social custom. It would be too strong to describe this difference as lag, which would imply that social change in the realm of custom and moral standard is not rapid enough. Ogburn certainly raises the question of the mutual relation between the successive accomplishments in such different realms as art and technology, science and literature. In this connection, much importance has been attributed to the concept of cumulativeness or of displacement of the past by present accomplishment. In the case of technology, such displacement would enhance the scope and intensity of our mastery over nature. No such simple statement is possible in the realms of philosophy or art. Instead, displacement assumes the form of alternative styles that do not stand in unilinear relation to one another.

In Alfred Weber's selection, he makes a proposal for distinguishing between civilization and cultural movement as these occur within society. Civilization, in this view, tends toward impersonal assertions and accomplishments, which are subject to the standards and considerations of logic, rationality, and universality. They presuppose an "external" world that can be discovered or mastered. Civilization leads to inventions—but inventions in the form of machines. As a pattern of products, it is cumulative. Culture is "the opposite." It produces a sequence of "incomparable" configurations of moral commitment or aesthetic accomplishment. Though civilization does not go in a simple, straight, and continuous line, it does have a direction of development, leading to increased mastery. Movements of culture leave no such simple increase in their wake.

1. On the Accumulation of Capital

BY KARL MARX

The Secret of Primitive Accumulation

WE HAVE SEEN how money is changed into capital; how through capital surplus-value is made, and from surplus-value more capital. But the accumulation of capital presupposes surplus-value; surplus-value presupposes capitalistic production; capitalistic production presupposes the pre-existence of considerable masses of capital and of labor-power in the hands of producers of commodities. The whole movement, therefore, seems to turn in a vicious circle, out of which we can only get by supposing a primitive accumulation (previous accumulation of Adam Smith) preceding capitalistic accumulation; an accumulation not the result of the capitalist mode of production, but its starting point.

This primitive accumulation plays in political economy about the same part as original sin in theology. Adam bit the apple, and thereupon sin fell on the human race. Its origin is supposed to be explained when it is told as an anecdote of the past.

Reprinted from Karl Marx, *Capital,* trans. Samuel Moore and Edward Aveling, ed., Frederick Engels (New York: Humboldt Publishing Co., 1886), Part VIII, chaps. xxvi-xxxiii.

In times long gone by there were two sorts of people; one, the diligent, intelligent, and, above all, frugal élite; the other, lazy rascals, spending their substance, and more, in riotous living. The legend of theological original sin tells us certainly how man came to be condemned to eat his bread in the sweat of his brow; but the history of economic original sin reveals to us that there are people to whom this is by no means essential. Never mind! Thus it came to pass that the former sort accumulated wealth, and the latter sort had at last nothing to sell except their own skins. And from this original sin dates the poverty of the great majority that, despite all its labor, has up to now nothing to sell but itself, and the wealth of the few that increases constantly, although they have long ceased to work. Such insipid childishness is every day preached to us in the defence of property. M. Thiers, *e.g.,* had the assurance to repeat it with all the solemnity of a statesman, to the French people, once so *spirituel.* But as soon as the question of property crops up, it becomes a sacred duty to proclaim the intellectual food of the infant as the one thing fit for all ages and for all stages of development. In actual history it is notorious that conquest, enslavement, robbery, murder, briefly force, play the great part. In the tender annals of political economy the idyllic reigns from time immemorial. Right and "labor" were from all time the sole means of enrichment, the present year of course always excepted. As a matter of fact, the methods of primitive accumulation are anything but idyllic.

In themselves, money and commodities are no more capital than are the means of production and of subsistence. They want transforming into capital. But this transformation itself can only take place under certain circumstances, that centre in this, viz., that two very different kinds of commodity-possessors must come face to face and into contact; on the one hand, the owners of money, means of production, means of subsistence, who are eager to increase the sum of values they possess, by buying other people's labor-power; on the other hand, free laborers, the sellers of their own labor-power, and therefore the sellers of labor. Free laborers, in the double sense that neither they themselves form part and parcel of the means of production, as in the case of slaves, bondsmen, etc., nor do the means of production belong to them, as in the case of peasant-proprietors; they are, therefore, free from, unencumbered by, any means of production of their own. With this polarisation of the market for commodities, the fundamental conditions of capitalist production are given. The capitalist system presupposes the complete separation of the laborers from all property in the means by which they can realize their labor. As soon as capitalist production is once on its own legs, it not only maintains this separation, but reproduces it on a continually-extending scale. The process, therefore, that clears the way for the capitalist system can be none other than the process which takes away from the laborer the possession of his means of production; a process that transforms, on the one hand, the social means of subsistence and of production into capital; on the other, the immediate producers into wage-laborers. The so-called primitive accumulation, therefore, is nothing else than the historical process of divorcing the producer from the means of production. It appears as primitive, because it forms the prehistoric stage of capital and of the mode of production corresponding with it.

The economic structure of capitalistic society has grown out of the economic structure of feudal society. The dissolution of the latter set free the elements of the former.

The immediate producer, the laborer, could only dispose of his own person after he had ceased to be attached to the soil and ceased to be the slave, serf, or bondman of another. To become a free seller of labor-power, who carries his commodity wherever he finds a market, he must further have escaped from the regime of the guilds, their rules for apprentices and journeymen, and the impediments of their labor regulations. Hence, the historical movement which changes the producers into wage-workers appears, on the one hand, as their emancipation from serfdom and from the fetters of the guilds, and this side alone exists for our bourgeois historians. But, on the other hand, these new freedmen became sellers of themselves only after they had been robbed of all their own means of production, and of all the guarantees of existence afforded by the old feudal arrangements. And the history of this, their expropriation, is written in the annals of mankind in letters of blood and fire.

The industrial capitalists, these new potentates, had on their part not only to displace the guild masters of handicrafts, but also the feudal lords, the possessors of the sources of wealth. In this respect their conquest of social power appears as the fruit of a victorious struggle both against feudal lordship and its revolting prerogatives, and against the guilds and the fetters they laid on the free development of production and the free exploitation of man by man. The chevaliers d'industrie, however, only succeeded in supplanting the chevaliers of the sword by making use of events of which they themselves were wholly innocent. They have risen by means as vile as those by which the Roman freedman once on a time made himself the master of his *patronus*.

The starting-point of the development that gave rise to the wage-laborer as well as to the capitalist was the servitude of the laborer. The advance consisted in a change of form of this servitude, in the transformation of feudal exploitation into capitalist exploitation. To understand its march, we need not go back very far. Although we come across the first beginnings of capitalist production as early as the fourteenth or fifteenth century, sporadically, in certain towns of the Mediterranean, the capitalistic era dates from the sixteenth century. Wherever it appears, the abolition of serfdom has been long effected, and the highest development of the middle ages, the existence of sovereign towns, has been long on the wane.

In the history of primitive accumulation, all revolutions are epoch-making that act as levers for the capitalist class in course of formation; but, above all, those moments when great masses of men are suddenly and forcibly torn from their means of subsistence, and hurled as free and "unattached" proletarians on the labor market. The expropriation of the agricultural producer, of the peasant, from the soil, is the basis of the whole process. The history of this expropriation, in different countries, assumes different aspects, and runs through its various phases in different orders of succession, and at different periods. In England alone, which we take as our example, has it the classic form.[1]

Expropriation of the Agricultural Population from the Land

In England, serfdom had practically disappeared in the last part of the fourteenth century. The immense majority of the population[2] consisted then, and to a still larger extent in the fifteenth century, of free peasant proprietors, whatever was the feudal title under which their right of property was hidden. In the larger seignorial domains, the old bailiff, himself a serf, was displaced by the free farmer. The wage-laborers of agriculture consisted partly of peasants, who utilized their leisure time by working on the large estates, partly of an independent special class of wage-laborers, relatively and absolutely few in numbers. The latter also were practically at the same time peasant farmers, since, besides their wages, they had allotted to them arable land to the extent of four or more acres, together with their cottages. Besides, they, with the rest of the peasants, enjoyed the usufruct of the common land, which gave pasture to their cattle, furnished them with timber, fire-wood, turf, etc.[3] In all countries

of Europe, feudal production is characterized by division of the soil among the greatest possible number of sub-feudatories. The might of the lord, like that of the sovereign, depended not on the length of his rent-roll, but on the number of his subjects, and the latter depended on the number of peasant proprietors.[4] Although, therefore, the English land, after the Norman conquest, was distributed in gigantic baronies, one of which often included some 900 of the old Anglo-Saxon lordships, it was bestrewn with small peasant properties, only here and there interspersed with great seignorial domains. Such conditions, together with the prosperity of the towns so characteristic of the fifteenth century, allowed of that wealth of the people which Chancellor Fortescue so eloquently paints in his "Laudes legum Angliæ"; but it excluded the possibility of capitalistic wealth.

The prelude of the revolution that laid the foundation of the capitalist mode of production, was played in the last third of the 15th, and the first decade of the 16th, century. A mass of free proletarians was hurled on the labor-market by the breaking up of the bands of feudal retainers, who, as Sir James Steuart well says, "everywhere a product of bourgeois development, in its strife after absolute sovereignty, forcibly hastened on the dissolution of these bands of retainers, it was by no means the sole cause of it. In insolent conflict with king and parliament, the great feudal lords created an incomparably larger proletariat by the forcible driving of the peasantry from the land, to which the latter had the same feudal right as the lord himself, and by the usurpation of the common lands. The rapid rise of the Flemish wool manufactures, and the corresponding rise in the price of wool in England, gave the direct impulse to these evictions. The old nobility had been devoured by the great feudal wars. The new nobility was the child of its time, for which money was the power of all powers. Transformation of arable land into sheep-walks was, therefore, its cry. Harrison, in his "Description of England, prefixed to Holinshed's Chronicle," describes how the expropriation of small peasants is ruining the country. "What care our great encroachers?" The dwellings of the peasants and the cottages of the laborers were razed to the ground or doomed to decay. "If," says Harrison, "the old records of euerie manour be sought . . . it will soon appear that in some manour seventeene, eighteene, or twentie houses are shrunk . . . that England was neuer less furnished with people than at the present.

1. In Italy, where capitalistic production developed earliest, the dissolution of serfdom also took place earlier than elsewhere. The serf was emancipated in that country before he had acquired any prescriptive right to the soil. His emancipation at once transformed him into a free proletarian, who, moreover, found his master ready, waiting for him in the towns, for the most part handed down as legacies from the Roman time. When the revolution of the world-market, about the end of the fifteenth century, annihilated Northern Italy's commercial supremacy, a movement in the reverse direction set in. The laborers of the towns were driven *en masse* into the country, and gave an impulse, never before seen, to the *petite culture*, carried on in the form of gardening.

2. "The petty proprietors, who cultivated their own fields with their own hands, and enjoyed a modest competence, . . . then formed a much more important part of the nation than at present. If we may trust the best statistical writers of that age, not less than 160,000 proprietors who, with their families, must have made up more than a seventh of the whole population, derived their subsistence from little freehold estates. The average income of these small landlords . . was estimated at between £60 and £70 a year. It was computed that the number of persons who tilled their own land was greater than the number of those who farmed the land of others." Macaulay: "History of England," tenth ed., I., pp. 333, 334. Even in the last third of the 17th century, four-fifths of the English people were agricultural. (l. c., p. 413.) I quote Macaulay because, as systematic falsifier of history, he minimises as much as possible facts of this kind.

3. We must never forget that even the serf was not only the owner, if but a tribute-paying owner, of the piece of land attached to his house, but also a co-possessor of the common land. "Le paysan y (in Silesia, under Frederick II.), est serf." Nevertheless, these serfs possess common lands. "On n'a pas pu encore engager les Silésiens au partage des communes, tandis que dans la Nouvelle Marche, il n'y a guère de village où ce partage ne soit exécuté avec le plus grand succès." (Mirabeau: De la Monarchie Prussienne, t. ii. pp. 125, 126. Londres, 1788.)

4. Japan, with its purely feudal organization of landed property and its developed *petite culture*, gives a much truer picture of the European middle ages than all our history books, dictated, as these are, for the most part, by bourgeois prejudices. It is very convenient to be "liberal" at the expense of the middle ages.

. . . Of cities and townes either utterly decaied or more than a quarter or half diminished, though some one be a little increased here or there; of townes pulled downe for sheepe-walks, and no more but the lordships now standing in them . . . I could saie somewhat." The complaints of these old chroniclers are always exaggerated, but they reflect faithfully the impression made on contemporaries by the revolution in the conditions of production. A comparison of the writings of Chancellor Fortescue and Thomas More reveals the gulf between the 15th and 16th century. As Thornton rightly has it, the English working-class was precipitated without any transition from its golden into its iron age.

Legislation was terrified at this revolution. It did not yet stand on that height of civilization where the "wealth of the nation" (*i.e.*—the formation of capital, and the reckless exploitation and impoverishing of the mass of the people) figure as the *ultima Thule* of all state-craft. In his history of Henry VII, Bacon says: "Inclosures at that time (1489) began to be more frequent, whereby arable land (which could not be manured without people and families) was turned into pasture, which was easily rid by a few herdsmen; and tenancies for years, lives, and at will (whereupon much of the yeomanry lived), were turned into demesnes. This bred a decay of people, and (by consequence) a decay of towns, churches, tithes and the like. . . . In remedying of this inconvenience the king's wisdom was admirable, and the parliament's at that time . . . they took a course to take away depopulating inclosures and depopulating pasturage." An Act of Henry VII, 1489, cap. 19, forbad the destruction of all "houses of husbandry" to which at least 20 acres of land belonged. By an Act, 25 Henry VIII, the same law was renewed. It recites, among other things, that many farms and large flocks of cattle, especially of sheep, are concentrated in the hands of a few men, whereby the rent of the land has much risen and tillage has fallen off, churches and houses have been pulled down, and marvellous numbers of people have been deprived of the means wherewith to maintain themselves and their families. The Act, therefore, ordains the rebuilding of the decayed farmsteads, and fixes a proportion between corn land and pasture land, etc. An Act of 1533 recites that some owners possess 24,000 sheep, and limits the number to be owned to 2,000.[5] The cry of the people, and the legislation directed for 150 years after Henry VII

against the expropriation of the small farmers and peasants, were alike fruitless. The secret of their inefficiency Bacon, without knowing it, reveals to us: "The device of King Henry VII," says Bacon in his "Essays, Civil and Moral," Essay 29, "was profound and admirable in making farms and houses of husbandry of a standard—that is, maintained with such a proportion of land unto them as may breed a subject to live in convenient plenty and no servile condition, and to keep the plow in the hands of the owners and not mere hirelings."[6] What the capitalist system demanded was, on the other hand, a degraded and almost servile condition of the mass of the people, the transformation of them into mercenaries, and of their means of labor into capital. During this transformation period, legislation also strove to retain the four acres of land by the cottage of the agricultural wage-laborer, and forbad him to take lodgers into his cottage. In the reign of James I, 1627, Roger Crocker of Front Mill, was condemned for having built a cottage on the manor of Front Mill without four acres of land attached to the same in perpetuity. As late as Charles the First's reign, 1638, a Royal Commission was appointed to enforce the carrying out of the old laws, especially that referring to the four acres of land. Even in Cromwell's time, the building of a house within four miles of London was forbidden unless it was endowed with four acres of land. As late as the first half of the 18th century, complaint is made if the cottage of the agricultural laborer has not an adjunct of one or two acres of land. Nowadays he is lucky if it is furnished with a little garden, or if he may rent, far away from his cottage, a few roods. "Landlords and farmers," says Dr. Hunter, "work here hand in hand. A few

---

5. In his "Utopia" Thomas More says that, in England, "your shepe that were wont to be so meke and tame, and so small eaters, now, as I heare saye, be become so great devourers and so wylde that they eate up and swallow downe the very men themselfes." ("Utopia," transl. by Robinson, ed. Arber, p. 41. London, 1869.)

6. Bacon shows the connection between a free, well-to-do peasantry and good infantry: "This did wonderfully concern the might and mannerhood of the kingdom to have farms as it were of a standard sufficient to maintain an able body out of penury; and did, in effect, amortize a great part of the lands of the kingdom unto the hold and occupation of the yeomanry or middle people of a condition between gentlemen and cottagers and peasants. . . . For it hath been held by the general opinion of men of best judgment in the wars . . . that the principal strength of an army consisteth in the infantry or foot; and, to make good infantry, it requireth men bred, not in a servile or indigent fashion, but in some free and plentiful manner. Therefore, if a State run most to noblemen and gentlemen, and that the husbandmen and ploughmen be but as their workfolk and labourers, or else mere cottagers, which are but hous'd beggars, you may have a good cavalry, but never good, stable bands of foot. . . . And this is to be seen in France and Italy and some other parts abroad where, in effect, all is noblesse or peasantry, . . . insomuch that they are inforced to employ mercenary bands of Switzers and the like for theit battalions of foot; whereby also it comes to pass that those nations have much people and few soldiers." ("The Reign of Henry VII." Verbatim reprint from Kennet's "England," ed. 1719, p. 308. London, 1870.)

acres to the cottage would make the laborers too independent."[7]

The process of forcible expropriation of the people received in the 16th century a new and frightful impulse from the Reformation, and from the consequent colossal spoliation of the church property. The Catholic church was, at the time of the Reformation, feudal proprietor of a great part of the English land. The suppression of the monasteries, etc., hurled their inmates into the proletariat. The estates of the church were to a large extent given away to rapacious royal favorites, or sold at a nominal price to speculating farmers and citizens, who drove out, *en masse,* the hereditary sub-tenants and threw their holdings into one. The legally-guaranteed property of the poorer folk in a part of the church's tithes was tacitly confiscated.[8] "*Pauper ubique jacet,*" cried Queen Elizabeth, after a journey through England. In the forty-third year of her reign, the nation was obliged to recognize pauperism officially by the introduction of a poor-rate. "The authors of this law seem to have been ashamed to state the grounds of it, for [contrary to traditional usage] it has no preamble whatever."[9] By the 16th of Charles I., ch. 4, it was declared perpetual, and, in fact, only in 1834 did it take a new and harsher form.[10] These immediate results

of the Reformation were not its most lasting ones. The property of the church formed the religious bulwark of the traditional conditions of landed property. With its fall these were no longer tenable.[11]

Even in the last decade of the seventeenth century, the yeomanry—the class of independent peasants—were more numerous than the class of farmers. They had formed the backbone of Cromwell's strength, and—even according to the confession of Macaulay—stood in favorable contrast to the drunken squires and to their servants, the country clergy, who had to marry their masters' cast-off mistresses. About 1750, the yeomanry had disappeared,[12] and so had, in the last decade of the eighteenth century, the last trace of the common land of the agricultural laborer. We leave on one side here the purely economic causes of the agricultural revolution. We deal only with the forcible means employed.

After the restoration of the Stuarts, the landed proprietors carried, by legal means, an act of

---

7. "The quantity of land assigned [in the old laws] would now be judged too great for laborers, and rather as likely to convert them into small farmers." (George Roberts: "The Social History of the People of the Southern Counties of England in Past Centuries," pp. 184–185. London, 1856.)

8. "The right of the poor to share in the tithe, is established by the tenor of ancient statutes." [J. D. Tuckett: "A History of the Past and Present State of the Labouring Population," vol. II, pp. 804–805. London, 1846.]

9. William Cobbett: "A History of the Protestant Reformation," § 471.

10. The "spirit" of Protestantism may be seen from the following, among other things: In the south of England certain landed proprietors and well-to-do farmers put their heads together and propounded ten questions as to the right interpretation of the poor-law of Elizabeth. These they laid before a celebrated jurist of that time, Sergeant Snigge (later a judge under James I.), for his opinion. "Question 9 —Some of the more wealthy farmers in the parish have devised a skillful mode by which all the trouble of executing this act (the forty-third of Elizabeth) might be avoided. They have proposed that we shall erect a prison in the parish, and then give notice to the neighborhood that if any persons are disposed to farm the poor of this parish, they do give in sealed proposals, on a certain day, of the lowest price at which they will take them off our hands; and that they will be authorized to refuse to any one unless he be shut up in the aforesaid prison. The proposers of this plan conceive that there will be found in the adjoining counties persons who, being unwilling to labor, and not possessing substance or credit to take a farm or ship, so as to live without labor, may be induced to make a very advantageous offer to the parish. If any of the poor perish under the contractor's care, the sin will lie at his door, as the parish will have done its duty by them. We are, however, apprehensive that the present act (forty-third of Elizabeth) will not warrant a prudential measure of this

kind; but you are to learn that the rest of the freeholders of the county. and the adjoining county of B, will very readily join in instructing their members to propose an Act to enable the parish to contract with a person to lock up and work the poor; and to declare that if any person shall refuse to be so locked up and worked, he shall be entitled to no relief. This, it is hoped will prevent persons in distress from wanting relief, and be the means of keeping down parishes." (R. Blakey: "The History of Political Literature from the Earliest Times," vol. II., pp. 84, 85. London, 1855.) In Scotland, the abolition of serfdom took place some centuries later than in England. Even in 1698, Fletcher of Saltoun declared, in the Scotch Parliament: "The number of beggars in Scotland is reckoned at not less than 200,000. The only remedy that I, a Republican on principle. can suggest, is to restore the old state of serfdom, to make slaves of all those who are unable to provide for their own subsistence." Eden says: "The decrease of villenage seems necessarily to have been the era of the origin of the poor. Manufactures and commerce are the two parents of our national poor." [F. M. Eden: "The State of the Poor," Book I, ch. i, pp. 60–61. London, 1797.] Eden, like our Scotch republican on principle, errs only in this: not the abolition of villenage, but the abolition of the property of the agricultural laborer in the soil made him a proletarian, and eventually a pauper. In France, where the expropriation was effected in another way, the ordonnance of Moulins, 1571, and the Edict of 1656, correspond to the English poor-laws.

11. Professor Rogers, although formerly Professor of Political Economy in the University of Oxford, the hotbed of Protestant orthodoxy, in his preface to the "History of Agriculture" lays stress on the fact of the pauperization of the mass of the people by the Reformation.

12. A letter to Sir T. C. Banbury, Bart., on the "High Price of Provisions." By a Suffolk Gentleman. P. 4. Ipswich, 1795. Even the fanatical advocate of the system of large farms, the author of the "Inquiry into the Connection of Large Farms, etc., London, 1773," p. 133, says: "I most lament the loss of our yeomanry, that set of men who really kept up the independence of this nation; and sorry I am to see their lands now in the hands of monopolizing lords, tenanted out to small farmers, who hold their leases on such conditions as to be little better than vassals, ready to attend a summons on every mischievous occasion."

usurpation effected everywhere on the Continent without any legal formality. They abolished the feudal tenure of land—*i.e.*, they got rid of all its obligations to the State, "indemnified" the State by taxes on the peasantry and the rest of the mass of the people, vindicated for themselves the rights of modern private property in estates to which they had only a feudal title, and finally passed those laws of settlement which, *mutatis mutandis,* had the same effect on the English agricultural laborer as the edict of the Tartar, Boris Godunof, on the Russian peasantry.

The "glorious Revolution" brought into power, along with William of Orange, the landlord and capitalist appropriators of surplus-value.[13] They inaugurated the new era by practising on a colossal scale thefts of State lands—thefts that had been hitherto managed more modestly. These estates were given away, sold at a ridiculous figure, or even annexed to private estates by direct seizure.[14] All this happened without the slightest observation of legal etiquette. The crown lands thus fraudulently appropriated, together with the robbery of the church estates, as far as these had not been lost again during the republican revolution, form the basis of the to-day princely domains of the English oligarchy.[15] The bourgeois capitalists favored the operation, with the view, among others, to promoting free trade in land, to extending the domain of modern agriculture on the large-farm system, and to increasing their supply of the free agricultural proletarians ready to hand. Besides, the new landed aristocracy was the natural ally of the new bankocracy, of the newly-hatched *haute finance,* and of the large manufacturers, then depending on protective duties. The English bourgeoisie acted for its own interest quite as wisely as did the Swedish bourgeoisie who, reversing the process, hand in hand

with their economic allies, the peasantry, helped the kings in the forcible resumption of the crown lands from the oligarchy. This happened since 1604, under Charles X. and Charles XI.

Communal property—always distinct from the State property just dealt with—was an old Teutonic institution which lived on under cover of feudalism. We have seen how the forcible usurpation of this, generally accompanied by the turning of arable into pasture land, begins at the end of the fifteenth and extends into the sixteenth century. But at that time the process was carried on by means of individual acts of violence, against which legislation, for a hundred and fifty years, fought in vain. The advance made by the eighteenth century shows itself in this, that the law itself becomes now the instrument of the theft of the people's land, although the large farmers make use of their little independent methods as well.[16] The parliamentary form of the robbery is that of Acts for enclosures of commons —in other words, decrees by which the landlords grant themselves the people's land as private property, decrees of expropriation of the people. Sir F. M. Eden refutes his own crafty special pleading, in which he tries to represent communal property as the private property of the great landlords who have taken the place of the feudal lords, when he, himself, demands a "general Act of Parliament for the enclosure of commons" (admitting thereby that a Parliamentary *coup d'état* is necessary for its transformation into private property), and moreover calls on the legislature for the indemnification for the expropriated poor.[17]

While the place of the independent yeoman was taken by tenants at will, small farmers on yearly leases, a servile rabble dependent on the pleasure of the landlords, the systematic robbery of the communal lands helped especially, next to the theft of the State domains, to swell those large farms, that were called in the eighteenth century capital farms or merchant farms, and to "set free" the agricultural population as proletarians for manufacturing industry.

The 18th century, however, did not yet recognize as fully as the 19th the identity between national wealth and the poverty of the people. Hence the most vigorous polemic, in the economic literature of that time, on the "inclosure of commons." From

---

13. On the private moral character of this bourgeois hero, among other things: "The large grant of lands in Ireland to Lady Orkney, in 1695, is a public instance of the king's affection and the lady's influence. . . . Lady Orkney's endearing offices are supposed to have been—*fœda labiorum ministeria.*" (In the Sloane Manuscript Collection, at the British Museum. No. 4224. The manuscript is entitled: "The Charakter and Behaviour of King William, Sunderland, etc., as Represented in Original Letters to the Duke of Shrewsbury, from Somers Halifax, Oxford, Secretary Vernon, etc." It is full of curiosa.)

14. "The illegal alienation of the Crown Estates, partly by sale and partly by gift, is a scandalous chapter in English history, . . . a gigantic fraud on the nation." (F. W. Newman: "Lectures on Political Economy," pp. 129, 130. London, 1851.) [For details as to how the present large landed proprietors of England came into their possessions, see "Our Old Nobility. By Noblesse Oblige." London, 1879.—Ed.]

15. Read, *e.g.*, E. Burke's Pamphlet on the Ducal House of Bedford, whose offshoot was Lord John Russell, the "tomtit of Liberalism."

16. "The farmers forbid cottagers to keep any living creatures besides themselves and children, under the pretence that if they keep any beasts or poultry they will steal from the farmers' barns for their support; they also say, keep the cottagers poor and you will keep them industrious, etc.; but the real fact, I believe, is that the farmers may have the whole right of common to themselves." ("A Political Inquiry into the Consequences of Enclosing Waste Lands," p. 75. London, 1785.)

17. Eden, l. c., preface.

the mass of materials that lie before me I give a few extracts that will throw a strong light on the circumstances of the time. "In several parishes of Hertfordshire," writes one indignant person, "24 farms, numbering on the average 50–150 acres, have been melted up into three farms."[18] "In Northamptonshire and Leicestershire the inclosure of common lands has taken place on a very large scale; and most of the new lordships resulting from the inclosure have been turned into pasturage, in consequence of which many lordships have not now 50 acres plowed yearly in which 1,500 were plowed formerly. The ruins of former dwelling-houses, barns, stables," etc., are the sole traces of the former inhabitants. "An hundred houses and families have in some open field villages . . . dwindled to eight or ten. . . . The landholders in most parishes that have been inclosed only fifteen or twenty years are very few in comparison of the numbers who occupied them in their open field state. It is no uncommon thing for four or five wealthy graziers to engross a large inclosed lordship which was before in the hands of twenty or thirty farmers and as many smaller tenants and proprietors. All these are hereby thrown out of their livings, with their families and many other families who were chiefly employed and supported by them."[19] It was not only the land that lay waste, but often land cultivated either in common or held under a definite rent paid to the community, that was annexed by the neighboring landlords under pretext of inclosure. "I have here in view inclosures of open fields and lands already improved. It is acknowledged by even the writers in defense of inclosures that these diminished villages increase the monopolies of farms, raise the prices of provisions, and produce depopulation; . . . and even the inclosure of waste lands, as now carried on, bears hard on the poor by depriving them of a part of their subsistence, and only goes toward increasing farms already too large."[20] "When," says Dr. Price, "this land gets into the hands of a few great farmers, the consequence must be that the little farmers [earlier designated by him "a multitude of little proprietors and tenants who maintain themselves and families by the produce of the ground they occupy, by sheep

kept on a common—by poultry, hogs, etc.—and who, therefore, have little occasion to purchase any of the means of subsistence"] will be converted into a body of men who earn their subsistence by working for others, and who will be under a necessity of going to market for all they want. . . . There will, perhaps, be more labor because there will be more compulsion to it. . . . Towns and manufacturers will increase because more will be driven to them in quest of places and employment. This is the way in which the engrossing of farms naturally operates. And this is the way in which, for many years, it has been actually operating in this kingdom."[21] He sums up the effect of the inclosures thus: "Upon the whole, the circumstances of the lower ranks of men are altered in almost every respect for the worse. From little occupiers of land they are reduced to the state of day laborers and hirelings; and, at the same time, their subsistence in that state has become more difficult."[22] In fact, usurpation of the common lands, and the revolution in agriculture accompanying this, told so acutely on the agricultural laborers that, even according to Eden, between 1765 and 1780, their wages began to fall below the minimum, and to be supplemented by official poor-law relief. Their wages, he says, "were not more than enough for the absolute necessaries of life."

Let us hear for a moment a defender of inclosures and an opponent of Dr. Price: "Nor is it a consequence that there must be depopulation because men are not seen wasting their labor in the open field. . . . If, by converting the little farmers into a body of men who must work for others, more

18. Thomas Wright: "A Short Address to the Public on the Monopoly of Large Farms," pp. 2, 3. 1779.

19. Rev. Addington: "Inquiry Into the Reasons For or Against Enclosing Open Fields," pp. 37, 43, *passim*. London, 1772.

20. Dr. R. Price [: "Observations on Reversionary Payments," 6th Ed. by W. Morgan, Lond., 1803, v. II., p. 155]. Forster, Addington, Kent, Price, and James Anderson should be read and compared with the miserable prattle of Sycophant MacCulloch in his catalogue, "The Literature of Political Economy," London, 1845.

21. Price, l. c., p. 147.

22. Price, l. c., 159. We are reminded of ancient Rome. "The rich had got possession of the greater part of the undivided land. They trusted in the conditions of the time that these possessions would not be again taken from them, and bought, therefore, some of the pieces of land lying near theirs, and belonging to the poor, with the acquiescence of their owners, and took some by force, so that they now were cultivating widely extended domains instead of isolated fields. Then they employed slaves in agriculture and cattle-breeding because freemen would have been taken from labor for military service. The possession of slaves brought them great gain, inasmuch as these, on account of their immunity from military service, could freely multiply and have a multitude of children. Thus, the powerful men drew all wealth to themselves, and all the land swarmed with slaves. The Italians, on the other hand, were always decreasing in number, destroyed as they were by poverty, taxes, and military service. Even when times of peace came, they were doomed to complete inactivity because the rich were in possession of the soil, and used slaves instead of free men in the tilling of it." (Appian, "Civil Wars," I., 7.) This passage refers to the time before the Licinian rogations. Military service, which hastened to so great an extent the ruin of the Roman plebeians, was also the chief means by which, as in a forcing house, Charlemagne brought about the transformation of free German peasants into serfs and bondsmen.

labor is produced, it is an advantage which the nation [to which, of course, the "converted" ones do not belong] should wish for. . . . The produce being greater when their joint labors are employed on one farm, there will be a surplus for manufactures; and, by this means, manufactures, one of the mines of the nation, will increase in proportion to the quantity of corn produced."[23]

The stoical peace of mind with which the political economist regards the most shameless violation of the "sacred rights of property" and the grossest acts of violence to persons, as soon as they are necessary to lay the foundations of the capitalistic mode of production, is shown by Sir F. M. Eden, philanthropist and Tory to boot. The whole series of thefts, outrages, and popular misery that accompanied the forcible expropriation of the people from the last third of the 15th to the end of the 18th century lead him merely to the comfortable conclusion: "The due proportion between arable land and pasture had to be established. During the whole of the 14th and the greater part of the 15th century there was one acre of pasture to two, three, and four of arable land. About the middle of the 16th century the proportion was changed to two acres of pasture to two; later on, of two acres of pasture to one of arable—until at last the just proportion of three acres of pasture to one of arable land was attained."

In the 19th century the very memory of the connection between the agricultural laborer and the communal property had, of course, vanished. To say nothing of more recent times, have the agricultural population received a farthing of compensation for the 3,511,770 acres of common land which, between 1801 and 1831, were stolen from them, and by parliamentary devices presented to the landlords by the landlords?

The last process of wholesale expropriation of the agricultural population from the soil is, finally, the so-called clearing of estates—*i.e.*, the sweeping men off them. All the English methods hitherto considered culminated in "clearing." As we saw in the picture of modern conditions given in a former chapter, where there are no more independent peasants to get rid of, the "clearing" of cottages begins; so that the agricultural laborers do not find on the soil cultivated by them even the spot necessary for their own housing. But what "clearing of estates" really and properly signifies, we learn only in the

Promised Land of modern romance, the Highlands of Scotland. There the process is distinguished by its systematic character, by the magnitude of the scale on which it is carried out at one blow (in Ireland, landlords have gone to the length of sweeping away several villages at once; in Scotland, areas as large as German principalities are dealt with), finally, by the peculiar form of property under which the embezzled lands were held.

The Highland Celts were organized in clans, each of which was the owner of the land on which it was settled. The representative of the clan—its chief or "great man"—was only the titular owner of this property, just as the Queen of England is the titular owner of all the national soil. When the English Government suceeded in suppressing the intestine wars of these "great men" and their constant incursions into the Lowland plains, the chiefs of the clans by no means gave up their time-honored trade as robbers; they only changed its form. On their own authority they transformed their nominal right into a right of private property, and as this brought them into collision with their clansmen, resolved to drive them out by open force. "A king of England might as well claim to drive his subjects into the sea,"[24] says Professor Newman. This revolution, which began in Scotland after the last rising of the followers of the Pretender, can be followed through its first phases in the writings of Sir James Steuart[25] and James Anderson.[26] In the 18th century the hunted-out Gaels were forbidden to emigrate from the country, with a view to driving them by force to Glasgow and other manufacturing towns.[27] As an example of the method[28] obtaining in the 19th cen-

23. "An Inquiry into the Connection between the Present Prices of Provisions," etc., pp. 124, 129. To the like effect, but with an opposite tendency: "Workingmen are driven from their cottages and forced into the towns to seek for employment; but then a larger surplus is maintained, and thus capital is augmented." ("The Perils of the Nation," 2d ed., p. 14. London, 1843.)

24. L. c., p. 132.
25. Steuart says: "If you compare the rent of these lands [he erroneously includes in this economic category the tribute of the taskmen to the clan-chief] with the extent, it appears very small. If you compare it with the numbers fed upon the farm, you will find that an estate in the Highlands maintains, perhaps, ten times as many people as another of the same value in a good and fertile province." (["Principles of Political Economy," Dublin, 1770] vol. I, ch. xvi, p. 104.)
26. James Anderson: "Observations on the Means of Exciting a Spirit of National Industry," etc. Edinburgh, 1777.
27. In 1860 the people expropriated by force were exported to Canada under false pretences. Some fled to the mountains and neighboring islands. They were followed by the police, came to blows with them and escaped.
28. "In the Highlands of Scotland," says Buchanan, the commentator on Adam Smith, 1814, "the ancient state of property is daily subverted. . . . The landlord, without regard to the hereditary tenant [a category used in error here], now offers his land to the highest bidder, who, if he is an improver, instantly adopts a new system of cultivation. The land, formerly overspread with small tenants or laborers, was peopled in proportion to its produce, but under the new system of improved cultivation and increased rents, the largest possible produce is obtained at the least possible expense; and the useless hands being, with this view, re-

tury, the "clearing" made by the Duchess of Sutherland will suffice here. This person, well instructed in
economy, resolved, on entering upon her government, to effect a radical cure, and to turn the
whole country, whose population had already
been, by earlier processes of the like kind, reduced to 15,000, into a sheep-walk. From 1814
to 1820 these 15,000 inhabitants, about 3,000
families, were systematically hunted and rooted
out. All their villages were destroyed and burnt,
all their fields turned into pasturage. British soldiers enforced this eviction, and came to blows
with the inhabitants. One old woman was burnt to
death in the flames of the hut, which she refused
to leave. Thus this fine lady appropriated 794,000
acres of land that had from time immemorial
belonged to the clan. She assigned to the expelled inhabitants about 6,000 acres on the sea-
shore—two acres per family. The 6,000 acres had
until this time lain waste, and brought in no income
to their owners. The Duchess, in the nobility of her
heart, actually went so far as to let these at an
average rent of 2s. 6d. per acre to the clansmen,
who for centuries had shed their blood for her
family. The whole of the stolen clan-land she divided into 29 great sheep farms, each inhabited by
a single family, for the most part imported English
farm-servants. In the year 1835 the 15,000 Gaels
were already replaced by 131,000 sheep. The remnant of the aborigines flung on the seashore, tried
to live by catching fish. They became amphibious
and lived, as an English author says, half on land
and half on water, and withal only half on both.[29]

But the brave Gaels must expiate yet more bitterly their idolatry, romantic and of the mountains,
for the "great men" of the clan. The smell of their
fish rose to the noses of the great men. They scented
some profit in it, and let the seashore to the great
fishmongers of London. For the second time the
Gaels were hunted out.

But, finally, part of the sheep-walks are turned
into deer preserves. Every one knows that there are
no real forests in England. The deer in the parks
of the great are demurely domestic cattle, fat as
London aldermen. Scotland is therefore the last
refuge of the "noble passion." "In the Highlands,"
says Somers in 1848, "new forests are springing up
like mushrooms. Here, on one side of Gaick, you
have the new forest of Glenfeshie; and there on the
other you have the new forest of Ardverikie. In the
same line you have the Black Mount, an immense
waste also recently erected. From east to west—
from the neighborhood of Aberdeen to the crags of
Oban—you have now a continuous line of forests;
while in other parts of the Highlands there are the
new forests of Loch Archaig, Glengarry, Glen-
moriston, etc. Sheep were introduced into glens
which had been the seats of communities of small
farmers; and the latter were driven to seek subsistence on coarser and more sterile tracks of soil.
Now deer are supplanting sheep; and these are once
more dispossessing the small tenants, who will
necessarily be driven down upon still coarser land
and to more grinding penury. Deer forests[30] and the
people cannot co-exist. One or other of the two
must yield. Let the forests be increased in number
and extent during the next quarter of a century,
as they have been in the last, and the Gaels will
perish from their native soil. . . . This movement
among the Highland proprietors is with some a
matter of ambition . . . with some love of sport . . .
while others, of a more practical cast, follow the
trade in deer with an eye to profit. For it is a fact,
that a mountain range laid out in forest is, in many
cases, more profitable to the proprietor than when
let as a sheep-walk. . . . The huntsman who wants
a deer-forest limits his offers by no other calculation than the extent of his purse. . . . Sufferings have
been inflicted in the Highlands scarcely less severe
than those occasioned by the policy of the Norman
kings. Deer have received extended ranges, while
men have been hunted within a narrower and still
narrower circle. . . . One after one the liberties of
the people have been cloven down. . . . And the
oppressions are daily on the increase. . . . The clear-
ance and dispersion of the people is pursued by

moved, the population is reduced, not to what the land will
maintain, but to what it will employ. The dispossessed tenants either seek a subsistence in the neighboring towns,"
etc. (David Buchanan: Observations on, etc., A. Smith's
"Wealth of Nations," vol. IV, p. 144. Edinburgh, 1814.)
"The Scotch grandees dispossess families as they would
grab up coppice-wood, and they treated villages and their
people as Indians harassed with wild beasts do, in their
vengeance, a jungle with tigers. . . . Man is bartered for a
fleece or a carcass of mutton, nay, held cheaper. . . . Why,
how much worse is it than the intention of the Moguls,
who, when they had broken into the northern provinces of
China, proposed in council to exterminate the inhabitants,
and convert the land into pasture. This proposal many
Highland proprietors have effected in their own country
against their own countrymen." (George Ensor: "An Inquiry Concerning the Population of Nations," pp. 215, 216.
London, 1818.)
29. When the present Duchess of Sutherland entertained
Mrs. Beecher-Stowe, authoress of "Uncle Tom's Cabin,"
with great magnificence in London, to show her sympathy
for the negro slaves of the American republic—a sympathy
that she prudently forgot, with her fellow-aristocrats, during the civil war, in which every "noble" English heart beat
for the slave-owner—I gave in the New York Tribune the
facts about the Sutherland slaves. (Epitomized in part by
Cary in "The Slave Trade," pp. 202, 203. London, 1853.)
My article was reprinted in a Scotch newspaper, and led to
a pretty polemic between the latter and the sycophants of
the Sutherlands.

30. The deer-forests of Scotland contain not a single
tree. The sheep are driven from, and then the deer driven
to, the naked hills, and then it is called a deer-forest. Not
even timber-planting and real forest culture.

the proprietors as a settled principle, as an agricultural necessity, just as trees and brushwood are cleared from the wastes of America or Australia; and the operation goes on in a quiet, business-like way, etc."[31]

---

31. Robert Somers: "Letters from the Highlands, or, the Famine of 1847," pp. 12–28 *passim*. London, 1848. These letters originally appeared in the *Times*. The English economists, of course, explained the famine of the Gaels in 1847, by their over-population. At all events, they "were pressing on their food-supply." The "clearing of estates," or as it is called in Germany "Bauernlegen," occurred in Germany especially after the 30 years' war, and led to peasant revolts as late as 1790 in Kursachsen. It obtained especially in East Germany. In most of the Prussian provinces, Frederick II. for the first time secured right of property for the peasants. After the conquest of Silesia he forced the landlords to rebuild the huts, barns, etc., and to provide the peasants with cattle and implements. He wanted soldiers for his army and tax-payers for his treasury. For the rest, the pleasant life that the peasant led under Frederick's system of finance and hodge-podge rule of despotism, bureaucracy, and feudalism, may be seen from the following quotation from his admirer, Mirabeau: "Le lin fait donc une des grandes richesses du cultivateur dans le Nord de l'Allemagne. Malheureusement pour l'espèce humaine, ce n'est qu'une ressource contre la misère et non un moyen de bien-être. Les impôts directs, les corvées, les servitudes de tout genre, écrasent le cultivateur allemand, qui paie encore des impôts indirects dans tout ce qu'il achète . . . et pour comble de ruine, il n'ose pas vendre ses productions où et comme il le veut; il n'ose pas àcheter ce dont il a besoin aux marchands qui pourraient le lui livrer au meilleur prix. Toutes ces causes le ruinent insensiblement, et il se trouverait hors d'état de payer les impôts directs à l'échéance sans la filerie; elle lui offre une ressource, en occupant utilement sa femme, ses enfants, ses servants, ses valets, et lui-même; mais quelle pénible vie, même aidée de ce secours. En été, il travaille comme un forçat au laborage et à la recolte; il se couche à 9 heures et se lève à deux, pous suffire aux travaux; en hiver il devrait réparer ses forces par un plus grand repos; mais il manquera de grains pour le pain et les semailles, s'il se défait des denrées qu'il faudrait vendre pour payer les impôts. Il faut donc filer pour suppléer à ce vide . . . il faut y apporter la plus grande assiduité. Aussi le paysan se couche-t-il en hiver à minuit, une heure, et se lève à cinq ou six; ou bien il se couche à neuf, et se lève à deux, et cela tous les jours de la vie si ce n'est le dimanche, Ces excès de veille et de travail usent la nature humaine, et de là vient qu' hommes et femmes vieillissent beaucoup plûtôt dans les çampagnes que dans les villes." (Mirabeau, l. c., t. III., pp. 212 *sqq*.)

Note to the second edition. In April, 1866, 18 years after the publication of the work of Robert Somers, quoted above, Professor Leone Levi gave a lecture before the Society of Arts on the transformation of sheep-walks into deer-forests, in which he depicts the advance in the devastation of the Scottish Highlands. He says, with other things: "Depopulation and transformation into sheep-walks were the most convenient means for getting an income without expenditure. . . . A deer-forest in place of a sheep-walk was a common change in the Highlands. The land-owners turned out the sheep as they once turned out the men from their estates, and welcomed the new tenants—the wild beasts and the feathered birds. . . . One can walk from the Earl of Dalhousie's estates in Forfarshire to John o' Groats, without ever leaving forest land. . . . In many of these woods the fox, the wild cat, the marten, the polecat, the weasel, and the Alpine hare are common; while the rabbit, the squirrel, and the rat have lately made their way into the country. Immense tracts of land, much of which is de-

---

The spoliation of the church's property, the fraudulent alienation of the State domains, the robbery of the common lands, the usurpation of feudal and clan property, and its transformation into modern private property under circumstances of reckless terrorism, were just so many idyllic methods of primitive accumulation. They conquered the field for capitalistic agriculture, made the soil part and parcel of capital, and created for the town industries the necessary supply of a "free" and outlawed proletariat.

Bloody Legislation Against the Expropriated, from the End of the 15th Century— Forcing Down of Wages by Acts of Parliament

The proletariat created by the breaking up of the bands of feudal retainers and by the forcible expropriation of the people from the soil, this "free" proletariat could not possibly be absorbed by the nascent manufactures as fast as it was thrown upon the world. On the other hand, these men, suddenly dragged from their wonted mode of life, could not as suddenly adapt themselves to the discipline of their new condition. They were turned *en masse* into beggars, robbers, vagabonds, partly from inclination, in most cases from stress of circumstances. Hence, at the end of the 15th and during

---

scribed in the statistical account of Scotland as having a pasturage in richness and extent of very superior description, are thus shut out from all cultivation and improvement, and are solely devoted to the sport of a few persons for a very brief period of the year." *The London Economist* of June 2, 1866, says: "Among the items of news in a Scotch paper of last week, we read. . . . 'One of the finest sheep farms in Sutherlandshire, for which a rent of £1,200 a year was recently offered, on the expiry of the existing lease this year, is to be converted into a deer-forest.' Here we see the modern instincts of feudalism . . . operating pretty much as they did when the Norman Conqueror . . . destroyed 36 villags to create the New Forest. . . . Two millions of acres . . . totally laid waste, embracing within their area some of the most fertile lands of Scotland. The natural grass of Glen Tilt was among the most nutritive in the county of Perth. The deer-forest of Ben Aulder was by far the best grazing ground in the wide district of Badenoch; a part of the Black Mount forest was the best pasture for black-faced sheep in Scotland. Some idea of the ground laid waste for purely sporting purposes in Scotland may be formed from the fact that it embraced an area larger than the whole county of Perth. The resources of the forest of Ben Aulder might give some idea of the loss sustained from the forced desolations. The ground would pasture 15,000 shep, and as it was not more than one-thirtieth part of the old forest ground in Scotland . . . it might etc. . . . All that forest land is as totally unproductive. . . . It might thus as well have been submerged under the waters of the German Ocean. . . . Such extemporized wildernesses or deserts ought to be put down by the decided interference of the Legislature."

the whole of the 16th century, throughout Western Europe a bloody legislation against vagabondage. The fathers of the present working-class were chastised for their enforced transformation into vagabonds and paupers. Legislation treated them as "voluntary" criminals, and assumed that it depended on their own goodwill to go on working under the old conditions that no longer existed.

In England this legislation began under Henry VII.

Henry VII., 1530. Beggars old and unable to work received a beggar's license. On the other hand, whipping and imprisonment for sturdy vagabonds. They are to be tied to the cart-tail and whipped until the blood streams from their bodies, then to swear an oath to go back to their birthplace or to where they have lived the last three years and to "put themselves to labor." What grim irony! In 27 Henry VIII, the former statute is repeated, but strengthened with new clauses. For the second arrest for vagabondage the whipping is to be repeated and half the ear sliced off; but for the third relapse the offender is to be executed as a hardened criminal and enemy of the common weal.

Edward VI.: A statute of the first year of his reign, 1547, ordains that, if any one refuses to work, he shall be condemned as a slave to the person who has denounced him as an idler. The master shall feed his slave on bread and water, weak broth, and such refuse meat as he thinks fit. He has the right to force him to do any work, no matter how disgusting, with whip and chains. If the slave is absent a fortnight, he is condemned to slavery for life, and is to be branded on forehead or back with the letter S; if he runs away thrice, he is to be executed as a felon. The master can sell him, bequeath him, let him out on hire as a slave, just as any other personal chattel or cattle. If the slaves attempt anything against the masters, they are also to be executed. Justices of the peace, on information, are to hunt the rascals down. If it happens that a vagabond has been idling about for three days, he is to be taken to his birth-place, branded with a red-hot iron with the letter V on the breast, and be set to work, in chains, in the streets or at some other labor. If the vagabond gives a false birth-place, he is then to become the slave for life of this place—of its inhabitants or its corporation—and to be branded with an S. All persons have the right to take away the children of the vagabonds and to keep them as apprentices, the young men until the twenty-fourth year, the girls until the twentieth. If they run away, they are to become up to this age the slaves of their masters, who can put them in irons, whip them, etc., if they like. Every master may put an iron ring round the neck, arms, or legs of his slave, by which to know him

more easily and to be more certain of him. The last part of this statute provides that certain poor people may be employed by a place or by persons who are willing to give them food and drink and to find them work. This kind of parish slaves was kept up in England until far into the 19th century under the name of "roundsmen."

Elizabeth, 1572: Unlicensed beggars above 14 years of age are to be severely flogged and branded on the left ear unless some one will take them into service for two years. In case of a repetition of the offense, if they are over 18, they are to be executed, unless some one will take them into service for two years; but, for the third offense, they are to be executed without mercy as felons. Similar statutes: 18 Elizabeth, c. 13, and another of 1597.[32]

James I: Any one wandering about and begging is declared a rogue and a vagabond. Justices of the peace in petty sessions are authorized to have them publicly whipped; and, for the first offense, to imprison them for six months; for the second, for two years. While in prison they are to be whipped as much and as often as the justices of the peace think

---

32. Thomas More says in his "Utopia:" "Therefore that on covetous and unsatiable cormaraunte and very plage of his native countrey maye compasse about and inclose many thousand akers of grounde together within one pale or hedge, the husbandmen be thrust owte of their owne, or els either by coneyne and fraude, or by violent oppression they be put besydes it, or by wrongs and injuries thei be so weried that they be compelled to sell all: by one meanes, therefore, or by other, either by hooke or crooke, they muste needs departe awaye, poore, selye, wretched soules, men, women, husbands, wiues, fatherlesse children, widowes, wofull mothers with their younge babes, and their whole household smal in substance and much in numbre, as husbandrye requireth many hands. Awaye thei trudge, I say, owte of their knowen accustomed houses, fyndynge no place to rest in. All their household stuffe, which is very little woorthe, thoughe it might well abide the sale; yet, beeynge sodainely thruste owte, they be constrayned to sell it for a thing of nought. And, when they haue wandered abrode tyll that be spent, what can they then els doe but steale, and then iustly pardy be hanged, or els go aboute beggyng. And yet then also they be caste in prison as vagabondes because they go aboute and worke not: whom no man wyl set a worke though thei neuer so willyngly profre themselues therto." Of these poor fugitives, of whom Sir Thomas More says that they were forced to thieve, "7,200 great and petty thieves were put to death" in the reign of Henry VIII. (Hollinshed, "Description of England," vol. I., p. 186.) In Elizabeth's time, "rogues were trussed up apace; and that there was not one year commonly wherein three or four hundred were not devoured and eaten up by the gallowes." (Strype's "Annals of the Reformation and Establishment of Religion, and Other Various Occurrences in the Church of England during Queen Elizabeth's Happy Reign," second ed., vol. II. 1725. According to this same Strype, in Somersetshire, in one year, 40 persons were executed, 35 robbers burned in the hand, 37 whipped, and 183 discharged as "incorrigible vagabonds." Nevertheless, he is of opinion that this large number of prisoners does not comprise even a fifth of the actual criminals, thanks to the negligence of the justices and the foolish compassion of the people: and the other counties of England were not better off in this respect than Somersetshire, while some were even worse.

fit. . . . Incorrigible and dangerous rogues are to be branded with an R on the left shoulder and set to hard labor; and, if they are caught begging again, to be executed without mercy. These statutes, legally binding until the beginning of the 18th century, were only repealed by 12 Ann, c. 23.

Similar laws in France where, by the middle of the 17th century, a kingdom of vagabonds (*truands*) was established in Paris. Even at the beginning of Louis VI.'s reign (Ordinance of July 13, 1777) every man in good health from 16 to 60 years of age, if without means of subsistence and not practicing a trade, is to be sent to the galleys. Of the same nature are the statute of Charles V. for the Netherlands (October, 1537), the first edict of the States and towns of Holland (March 10, 1614), the "Plakaat" of the United Provinces (June 26, 1649), etc.

Thus were the agricultural people first forcibly expropriated from the soil, driven from their homes, turned into vagabonds, and then whipped, branded, tortured by laws grotesquely terrible, into the discipline necessary for the wage system.

It is not enough that the conditions of labor are concentrated in a mass, in the shape of capital, at the one pole of society, while at the other are grouped masses of men who have nothing to sell but their labor-power. Neither is it enough that they are compelled to sell it voluntarily. The advance of capitalist production develops a working-class which, by education, tradition, habit, looks upon the conditions of that mode of production as self-evident laws of nature. The organization of the capitalist process of production, once fully developed, breaks down all resistance. The constant generation of a relative surplus-population keeps the law of supply and demand of labor, and therefore keeps wages, in a rut that corresponds with the wants of capital. The dull compulsion of economic relations completes the subjection of the laborer to the capitalist. Direct force, outside economic conditions, is of course still used, but only exceptionally. In the ordinary run of things the laborer can be left to the "natural laws of production"—*i. e.*, to his dependence on capital, a dependence springing from, and guarantied in perpetuity by, the conditions of production themselves. It is otherwise during the historic genesis of capitalist production. The bourgeoisie, at its rise, wants and uses the power of the State to "regulate" wages—*i. e.*, to force them within the limits suitable for surplus-value making —to lengthen the working-day, and to keep the laborer himself in the normal degree of dependence. This is an essential element of the so-called primitive accumulation.

The class of wage-laborers which arose in the latter-half of the 14th century formed then and in the following century only a very small part of the population, well protected in its position by the independent peasant proprietary in the country and the guild organization in the town. In country and town master and workmen stood close together socially. The subordination of labor to capital was only formal—*i. e.*, the mode of production itself had as yet no specific capitalistic character. Variable capital preponderated greatly over constant. The demand for wage-labor grew, therefore, rapidly with every accumulation of capital, while the supply of wage-labor followed but slowly. A large part of the national product, changed later into a fund of capitalist accumulation, then still entered into the consumption fund of the laborer.

Legislation on wage-labor (from the first aimed at the exploitation of the laborer, and, as it advanced, always equally hostile to him)[33] is started in England by the Statute of Laborers of Edward III., 1349. The ordinance of 1350 in France, issued in the name of King John, corresponds with it. English and French legislation run parallel, and are identical in purport. So far as the labor status aim at compulsory extension of the working-day I do not return to them, as this point was treated earlier.

The Statute of Laborers was passed at the urgent instance of the House of Commons. A Tory says naïvely: "Formerly the poor demanded such *high* wages as to threaten industry and wealth. Next their wages are so *low* as to threaten industry and wealth equally and perhaps more, but in another way."[34] A tariff of wages was fixed by law for town and country, for piece-work and day-work. The agricultural laborers were to hire themselves out by the year, the town ones "in open market." It was forbidden, under pain of imprisonment, to pay higher wages than those fixed by the statute; but the taking of higher wages was more severely punished than the giving of them. (So also, in Sections 18 and 19 of the Statute of Apprentices of Elizabeth, ten days' imprisonment is decreed for him that pays the higher wages, but twenty-one days for him that receives them.) A statute of 1360 increased the penalties, and authorized the masters to extort labor at the legal rate of wages by corporal punishment. All combinations, contracts, oaths, etc., by which masons and carpenters reciprocally bound themselves, were declared null and void. Coalition of the laborers is

33. "Whenever the Legislature attempts to regulate the the differences between masters and their workmen, its counsellors are always the masters," says A. Smith. "*L'esprit des lois, c'est la propriété,*" says Linguet.

34. "Sophisms of Free Trade." By a Barrister. P. 53. London, 1850. He adds maliciously,: "We were ready enough to interfere for the employer; can nothing now be done for the employed?"

treated as a heinous crime from the 14th century to 1825, the year of the repeal of the laws against trades' unions. The spirit of the Statute of Laborers of 1349, and of its offshoots, comes out clearly in the fact that, indeed, a maximum of wages is dictated by the State, but on no account a minimum.

In the 16th century, the condition of the laborers had, as we know, become much worse. The money wage rose, but not in proportion to the depreciation of money and the corresponding rise in the prices of commodities. Wages, therefore, in reality fell. Nevertheless, the laws for keeping them down remained in force, together with the ear-clipping and branding of those "whom no one was willing to take into service." By the Statute of Apprentices 5 Elizabeth, c. 3, the justices of the peace were empowered to fix certain wages and to modify them according to the time of the year and the price of commodities. James I. extended these regulations of labor also to weavers, spinners, and all possible categories of workers.[35] George II. extended the laws against coalitions of laborers to manufacturers. In the manufacturing period *par excellence,* the capitalist mode of production had become sufficiently strong to render legal regulation of wages as impracticable as it was unnecessary; but the ruling classes were unwilling in case of necessity to be without the weapons of the old arsenal. Still, 8 George II. forbad a higher day's wage than 2*s.* 7½ *d.* for journeymen tailors in and around London, except in cases of general mourning; still, 13 George III., c. 68, gave the regulation of the wages of silk-weavers to the justices of the peace, still, in 1706, it required two judgments of the higher courts to decide, whether the mandates of justices of the peace as to wages held good also for non-agricul-

tural laborers; still, in 1799, an Act of Parliament ordered that the wages of the Scotch miners should continue to be regulated by a statute of Elizabeth and two Scotch Acts of 1661 and 1671. How completely in the meantime circumstances had changed, is proved by an occurrence unheard of before in the English Lower House. In that place, where for more than 400 years laws had been made for the maximum, beyond which wages absolutely must not rise, Whitbread in 1796 proposed a legal minimum wage for agricultural laborers. Pitt opposed this, but confessed that the "condition of the poor was cruel." Finally, in 1813, the laws for the regulation of wages were repealed. They were an absurd anomaly, since the capitalist regulated his factory by his private legislation, and could by the poor-rates make up the wage of the agricultural laborer to the indispensable minimum. The provisions of the labor statutes as to contracts between master and workman, as to giving notice and the like, which only allow of a civil action against the contract-breaking master, but on the contrary permit a criminal action against the contract-breaking workman, are to this hour (1873) in full force. The barbarous laws against trades' unions fell, in 1825, before the threatening bearing of the proletariat. Despite this, they fell only in part. Certain beautiful fragments of the old statute vanished only in 1859. Finally, the Act of Parliament of June 29, 1871, made a pretence of removing the last traces of this class of legislation by legal recognition of trades' unions. But an Act of Parliament of the same date (an act to amend the criminal law relating to violence, threats, and molestation), re-established, in point of fact, the former state of things in a new shape. By this Parliamentary *escamotage* the means which the laborers could use in a strike or lock-out were withdrawn from the laws common to all citizens, and placed under exceptional penal legislation, the interpretation of which fell to the masters themselves in their capacity as justices of the peace. Two years earlier, the same House of Commons and the same Mr. Gladstone, in the well-known straight-forward fashion, brought in a bill for the abolition of all exceptional penal legislation against the working-class. But this was never allowed to go beyond the second reading, and the matter was thus protracted until at last the "great Liberal party," by an allegiance with the Tories, found courage to turn against the very proletariat that had carried it into power. Not content with this treachery, the "great Liberal party" allowed the English judges, ever complaisant in the service of the ruling classes, to dig up again the earlier laws against "conspiracy," and apply them to coalitions of laborers. We see that only against its will and under the pressure of

---

35. From a clause of Statute 2 James I., c. 6, we can see that certain cloth-makers took upon themselves to dictate, in their capacity of justices of the peace, the official tariff of wages in their own shops. In Germany, especially after the Thirty Years' War, statutes for keeping down wages were general. "The want of servants and laborers was very troublesome to the landed proprietors in the depopulated districts. All villagers were forbidden to let rooms to single men and women; all the latter were to be reported to the authorities and cast into prison if they were unwilling to become servants, even if they were employed at any other work, such as sowing seeds for the peasants at a daily wage, or even buying and selling corn. (Imperial privileges and sanctions for Silesia, I., 25.) For a whole century in the decrees of the small German potentates a bitter cry goes up again and again about the wicked and impertinent rabble that will not reconcile itself to its hard lot, will not be content with the legal wage; the individual landed proprietors are forbidden to pay more than the State had fixed by a tariff. And yet the conditions of service were at times better after the war than 100 years later; the farm servants of Silesia had, in 1652, meat twice a week, while even in our century, districts are known where they have it only three times a year. Further, wages after the war were higher than in the following century." (G. Freitag.)

the masses did the English Parliament give up the laws against strikes and trades' unions, after it had itself, for 500 years, held, with shameless egoism, the position of a permanent trades' union of the capitalists against the laborers.

During the very first storms of the revolution, the French bourgeoisie dared to take away from the workers the right of association but just acquired. By a decree of June 14, 1791, they declared all coalition of the workers as "an attempt against liberty and the declaration of the rights of man," punishable by a fine of 500 livres, together with deprivation of the rights of an active citizen for one year.[36] This law which, by means of State compulsion, confined the struggle between capital and labor within limits comfortable for capital, has outlived revolutions and changes of dynasties. Even the Reign of Terror left it untouched. It was but quite recently struck out of the Penal Code. Nothing is more characteristic than the pretext for this bourgeois *coup d' état*. "Granting," says Chapelier, the reporter of the Select Committee on this law, "that wages ought to be a little higher than they are . . . that they ought to be high enough for him that receives them, to be free from that state of absolute dependence due to the want of the necessaries of life, and which is almost that of slavery," yet the workers must not be allowed to come to any understanding about their own interests, nor to act in common and thereby lessen their "absolute dependence, which is almost that of slavery;" because, forsooth, in doing this they injure "the freedom of their *cidevant* masters, the present *entrepreneurs*," and because a coalition against the despotism of the quondam masters of the corporations is—guess what!—is a restoration of the corporations abolished by the French constitution.[37]

Genesis of the Capitalist Farmer

Now that we have considered the forcible creation of a class of outlawed proletarians, the bloody discipline that turned them into wage-laborers, the disgraceful action of the State which employed the police to accelerate the accumulation of capital by increasing the degree of exploitation of labor, the question remains: Whence came the capitalists originally? For the expropriation of the agricultural population creates, directly, none but great landed proprietors. As far, however, as concerns the genesis of the farmer, we can, so to say, put our hand on it, because it is a slow process evolving through many centuries. The serfs, as well as the free small proprietors, held land under very different tenures, and were therefore emancipated under very different economic conditions. In England the first form of the farmer is the bailiff, himself a serf. His position is similar to that of the old Roman *villicus*, only in a more limited sphere of action. During the second half of the 14th century he is replaced by a farmer, whom the landlord provides with seed, cattle, and implements. His condition is not very different from that of the peasant. Only he exploits more wage-labor. Soon he becomes a métayer, a half-farmer. He advances one part of the agricultural stock, the landlord the other. The two divide the total product in proportions determined by contract. This form quickly disappears in England, to give place to the farmer proper, who makes his own capital breed by employing wage-laborers, and pays a part of the surplus-product, in money or in kind, to the landlord as rent. So long, during the 15th century, as the independent peasant and the farm-laborer working for himself as well as for wages, enriched themselves by their own labor, the circumstances of the farmer, and his field of production, were equally mediocre. The agricultural revolution which commenced in the last third of the 15th century, and continued during almost the whole of the 16th (excepting, however, its last decade), enriched him just as speedily as it impoverished the mass of the agricultural people.[38]

The usurpation of the common lands allowed him to augment greatly his stock of cattle, almost without cost, while they yielded him a richer supply of manure for the tillage of the soil. To this was added, in the sixteenth century, a very important element. At that time the contracts for farms ran for a long time, often for ninety-nine years. The progressive fall in the value of the precious metals, and therefore of money, brought the farmers golden fruit. Apart from all the other circumstances discussed above, it lowered wages. A portion of the latter was now added to the profits of the farm. The continuous rise in the price of corn, wool, meat—in a

36. Article I. of this law runs: "L'anéantissement de toute espèce de corporations du même état et profession étant l'une des bases fondamentales de la constitution Française, il est défendu de les rétablir de fait sous quelque prétexte et sous quelque forme que ce soit." Article IV. declares that of "des citoyens attachés aux mêmes professions, arts et métiers prenaient des délibérations, fasaient entre eux des conventions tendantes à refuser de concert ou à n'accorder qu'à un prix déterminé le secours de leur industrie ou de leurs travaux, les dites délibérations et conventions . . . seront déclarées inconstitutionelles, attentatoires à la liberté et à la declaration des droits de l'homme, etc.;" felony, therefore, as in the old labor-statutes. ("Revolutions de Paris," t. III., p. 523. Paris, 1791.)

37. Buchez et Roux; "Histoire Parliamentaire," t. x., p. 195.

38. Harrison, in his "Description of England," says, "although peradventure foure pounds of old rent be improved to fortie toward the end of his term, if he have not six or seven yeares rent lieng by him, fiftie or a hundred pounds, yet will the farmer thinke his gaines verie small."

word, of all agricultural produce—swelled the money capital of the farmer without any action on his part, while the rent he paid (being calculated on the old value of money) diminished in reality.[39] Thus they grew rich at the expense both of their laborers and their landlords. No wonder, therefore, that England, at the end of the sixteenth century, had a class of capitalist farmers, rich, considering the circumstances of the time.[40]

---

39. On the influence of the depreciation of money in the sixteenth century, on the different classes of society, see "A Compendious or Briefe Examination of Certayne Ordinary Complaints of Diverse of our Countrymen in these our Days." By W. S., Gentlemen. London, 1581. The dialogue form of this work led people for a long time to ascribe it to Shakespeare, and even in 1751 it was published under his name. Its author is William Stafford. In one place the knight reasons as follows:
Knight: "You, my neighbor, the husbandman, you Maister Mercer, and you Goodman Cooper, with other artificers, may save yourselves metely well. For as much as all things are dearer than they were, so much do you arise in the pryce of your wares and occupations that ye sell agayne. But we have nothing to sell whereby we might advance ye price thereof, to countervaile those things that we must buy agayne." In another place the knight asks the doctor: "I pray you, what be those sorts that ye meane? And first, of those that ye thinke should have no losse therebye? Doctor: I mean all those that live by buying and selling, for as they buye deare, they sell thereafter. Knight: What is the next sort that ye say would win by it? Doctor: Marry, all such as have takings of fearmes in their owne manurance [cultivation] at the old rent, where they pay after the olde rate they sell after the newe—that is, they pay for theire lande goode cheape, and sell all things growing thereof deare. What sorte is that which ye sayde should have greater losse hereby than these men had profit? Doctor: It is all noblemen, gentlemen, and all other that live either by a stinted rent or stypend, or do not manure [cultivation] the ground, or doe occupy no buying and selling."
40. In France, the régisseur, steward, collector of dues for feudal lords during the earlier part of the middle ages, soon became an *homme d'affaires*, who, by extortion, cheating, etc., swindled himself into a capitalist. These régisseurs themselves were sometimes noblemen. *E.g.*, "C'est li compte que messire Jacques de Thoraine, chevalier chastelaine sor Besançon tenant les comptes à Dijon pour monseigneur le duc et comte de Bourgoigne, des rentes appartenant à la dite chastellenie, depuis xxve jour de Décembre MCCCLIX jusqu' au xxviiie jour de Décembre MCCCLX. (Alexis Monteil: Histoire des Materiaux Manuscrits, etc, p. 244.) Already it is evident here how in all spheres of social life the lion's share falls to the middleman. In the economic domain, *e.g.*, financiers, stock-exchange speculators, merchants, shopkeepers skim the cream; in civil matters, the lawyer fleeces his clients; in politics the representative is of more importance than the voters, the minister than the sovereign; in religion, God is pushed into the background by the "Mediator," and the latter again is shoved back by the priests, the inevitable middlemen between the good shepherd and his sheep. In France, as in England, the great feudal territories were divided into innumerable small homesteads, but under conditions incomparably more unfavorable for the people. During the fourteenth century arose the farms or *terriers*. Their numbers grew constantly, far beyond 100,000. They paid rents varying from 1/12 to 1/8 of the product, in money or in kind. These farm were fiefs, sub-fiefs, etc., according

---

Reaction of the Agricultural Revolution on Industry—Creation of the Home Market for Industrial Capital

The expropriation and expulsion of the agricultural population, intermittent but renewed again and again, supplied, as we saw, the town industries with a mass of proletarians entirely unconnected with the corporate guilds and unfettered by them; a fortunate circumstance that makes old A. Anderson (not to be confounded with James Anderson), in his "History of Commerce," believe in the direct intervention of Providence. We must still pause a moment on this element of primitive accumulation. The thinning-out of the independent, self-supporting peasants not only brought about the crowding together of the industrial proletariat, in the way that Geoffroy Saint Hilaire explained the condensation of cosmical matter at one place, by its rarefaction at another.[41] In spite of the smaller number of its cultivators, the soil brought forth as much or more produce after as before, because the revolution in the conditions of landed property was accompanied by improved methods of culture, greater co-operation, concentration of the means of production, etc., and because not only were the agricultural wage-laborers put on the strain more intensely,[42] but the field of production on which they worked for themselves became more and more contracted. With the setting free of a part of the agricultural population, therefore, their former means of nourishment were also set free. They were now transformed into material elements of variable capital. The peasant, expropriated and cast adrift, must buy their value in the form of wages, from his new master, the industrial capitalist. That which holds goods of the means of subsistence holds with the raw materials of industry dependent upon home agriculture. They were transformed into an element of constant capital. Suppose, *e.g.*, a part of the Westphalian peasants, who, at the time of Frederic II., all span flax, forcibly expropriated and hunted from the soil; and the other part, that remained, turned into day-laborers of large farmers. At the same time arise large establishments for flax-

---

to the value and extent of the domains, many of them only containing a few acres. But these farmers had rights of jurisdiction in some degree over the dwellers on the soil; there were four grades. The oppression of the agricultural population under all these petty tyrants will be understood. Monteil says that there were once in France 160,000 judges, where to-day 4,000 tribunals, including justices of the peace, suffice.
41. In his "Notions de Philosophie Naturelle." Paris, 1838.
42. A point that Sir James Steuart emphasizes.

spinning and weaving, in which the men "set free" now work for wages. The flax looks exactly as before. Not a fibre of it is changed, but a new social soul has popped into its body. It forms now a part of the constant capital of the master manufacturer. Formerly divided among a number of small producers, who cultivated it themselves, and with their families spun it in retail fashion, it is now concentrated in the hand of one capitalist, who sets others to spin and weave it for him. The extra labor expended in flax-spinning realized itself formerly in extra income to numerous peasant families, or maybe, in Frederic II.'s time, in taxes *pour le roi de Prusse.* It realizes itself now in profit for a few capitalists. The spindles and looms, formerly scattered over the face of the country, are now crowded together in a few great labor-barracks, together with the laborers and the raw material. And spindles, looms, raw material are now transformed, from means of independent existence for the spinners and weavers, into means for commanding them and sucking out of them unpaid labor.[43] One does not perceive, when looking at the large manufactories and the large farms, that they have originated from the throwing into one of many small centres of production, and have been built up by the expropriation of many small independent producers. Nevertheless, the popular intuition was not at fault. In the time of Mirabeau, the lion of the Revolution, the great manufactories were still called *manufactures réunies,* workshops thrown into one, as we speak of fields thrown into one. Says Mirabeau: "We are only paying attention to the grand manufactories, in which hundreds of men work under a director, and which are commonly called *manufactures réunies.* Those where a very large number of laborers work, each separately and on his own account, are hardly considered; they are placed at an infinite distance from the others. This is a great error, as the latter alone make a really important object of national prosperity. . . . The large workshop (*manufacture réunie*) will enrich prodigiously one or two *entrepreneurs* but the laborers will only be journeymen, paid more or less, and will not have any share in the success of the undertaking. In the *discrete* workshop (*manufacture séparée*), on the contrary, no one will become rich, but many laborers will be comfortable; the saving and the industrious will be able to amass a little capital, to put by a little for a birth of a child, for an illness, for themselves or their belongings. The number of saving and industrious laborers will

increase, because they will see in good conduct, in activity, a means of essentially bettering their condition, and not of obtaining a small rise of wages that can never be of any importance for the future, and whose sole result is to place men in the position to live a little better, but only from day to day. . . . The large workshops, undertakings of certain private persons who pay laborers from day to day to work for their gain, may be able to put these private individuals at their ease, but they will never be an object worth the attention of governments. *Discrete* workshops, for the most part combined with cultivation of small holdings, are the only free ones."[44] The expropriation and eviction of a part of the agricultural population not only set free for industrial capital, the laborers, their means of subsistence, and material for labor; it also created the home market.

In fact, the events that transformed the small peasants into wage-laborers, and their means of subsistence and of labor into material elements of capital, created, at the same time, a home-market for the latter. Formerly, the peasant family produced the means of subsistence and the raw materials, which they themselves, for the most part, consumed. These raw materials and means of subsistence have now become commodities; the large farmer sells them, he finds his market in manufactures. Yarn, linen, coarse woolen stuffs—things whose raw materials had been within the reach of every peasant family, had been spun and woven by it for its own use—were now transformed into articles of manufacture, to which the country districts at once served for markets. The many scattered customers, whom stray artisans until now had found in the numerous small producers working on their own account, concentrate themselves now into one great market provided for by industrial capital.[45] Thus, hand in hand with the expropriation of the self-supporting peasants, with their separation from their means of production, goes the destruction of rural domestic industry, the process of separation

43. "Je permettrai," says the capitalist, "que vous avez l'honneur de me servir, à condition que vous me donnez le peu qui vous reste pour la peine que je prends de vous commander. (J. J. Rousseau: "Discours sur l'Economie Politique.")

44. Mirabeau, ll. c., t. III., pp. 20–109 *passim.* That Mirabeau considers the separate workshops more economic and productive than the "combined," and sees in the latter merely artificial exotics under government cultivation, is explained by the position at that time of a great part of the continental manufactures.

45. Twenty pounds of wool converted unobtrusively into the yearly clothing of a laborer's family by its own industry in the intervals of other work, this makes no show; but bring it to market, send it to the factory, thence to the broker, thence to the dealer and you will have great commercial operations, and nominal capital engaged to the amount of twenty times its value. . . . The working-class is thus emerced to support a wretched factory population, a parasitical shop-keeping class, and a fictitious commercial, monetary, and financial system. (David Urquhart [: "Familiar Words," p. 120. London, 1858.])

between manufacture and agriculture. And only the destruction of rural domestic industry can give the internal market of a country that extension and consistence which the capitalist mode of production requires. Still, the manufacturing period, properly so-called, does not succeed in carrying out this transformation radically and completely. It will be remembered that manufacture, properly so-called, conquers but partially the domain of national production, and always rests on the handicrafts of the town and the domestic industry of the rural districts as its ultimate basis. If it destroys these in one form, in particular branches, at certain points, it calls them up again elsewhere, because it needs them for the preparation of raw material up to a certain point. It produces, therefore, a new class of small villagers, who, while following the cultivation of the soil as an accessory calling, find their chief occupation in industrial labor, the products of which they sell to the manufacturers directly, or through the medium of merchants. This is one, though not the chief, cause of a phenomenon which, at first, puzzles the student of English history. From the last third of the fifteenth century he finds continually complaints, only interrupted at certain intervals, about the encroachment of capitalist farming in the country districts, and the progressive destruction of the peasantry. On the other hand, he always finds this peasantry turning up again, although in diminished number, and always under worse conditions.[46] The chief reason is: England is at one time chiefly a cultivator of corn; at another, chiefly a breeder of cattle, in alternate periods, and with these the extent of peasant cultivation fluctuates. Modern industry alone, and finally, supplies, in machinery, the lasting basis of capitalistic agriculture, expropriates radically the enormous majority of the agricultural population, and completes the separation between agriculture and rural domestic industry, whose roots—spinning and weaving—it tears up.[47] It there-

fore, also, for the first time, conquers for industrial capital the entire home market.[48]

Genesis of the Industrial Capitalist

The genesis of the industrial[49] capitalist did not proceed in such a gradual way as that of the farmer. Doubtless many small guild-masters, and yet more independent small artisans, or even wage-laborers, transformed themselves into small capitalists, and (by gradually extending exploitation of wage-labor and corresponding accumulation) into full-blown capitalists. In the infancy of capitalist production, things often happened as in the infancy of mediæval towns, where the question, which of the escaped serfs should be master and which servant, was in great part decided by the earlier or later date of their flight. The snail's-pace of this method corresponded in no wise with the commercial requirements of the new world-market that the great discoveries of the end of the fifteenth century created. But the middle ages had handed down two distinct forms of capital, which mature in the most different economic social formations, and which, before the era of the capitalist mode of production, are considered as capital *grand même*—usurer's capital and merchant's capital.

"At present, all the wealth of society goes first into the possession of the capitalist, . . . he pays the landowner his rent, the laborer his wages, the tax and tithe gatherers their claims, and keeps a large, indeed the largest, and a continually augmenting, share of the annual produce of labor for himself. The capitalist may now be said to be the first owner of all the wealth of the community, though no law has conferred on him the right to this property, . . . this change has been effected by the taking of interest on capital, . . . and it is not a little curious that all the law-givers of Europe endeavored to prevent this by statutes—viz., statutes against usury. . . . The power of the capitalist over all the wealth of the country is a complete change in the right of

---

46. Cromwell's time forms an exception. So long as the Republic lasted, the mass of the English people of all grades rose from the degradation into which they had sunk under the Tudors.

47. Tuckett is aware that the modern woolen industry has sprung, with the introduction of machinery, from manufacture proper and from the destruction of rural and domestic industries. "The plow, the yoke, were 'the invention of the gods, and the occupation of heroes;' are the loom, the spindle, the distaff of less noble parentage? You sever the distaff and the plow, the spindle and the yoke, and you get factories and poorhouses, credit and panics, two hostile nations, agricultural and commercial." (David Urquhart, l. c., p. 122.) But now comes Carey, and cries out upon England, surely not with unreason, that it is trying to turn every other country into a mere agricultural nation, whose manufacturer is to be England. He pretends that in this way Turkey has been ruined, because "the owners and occupants of land have never been permitted by England to strengthen themselves by the formation of that natural

alliance between the plow and the loom, the hammer and the harrow." ("The Slave Trade," p. 125.) According to him, Urquhart himself is one of the chief agents in the ruin of Turkey, where he had made free trade propaganda in the English interest. The best of it is that Carey, a great Russophile, by the way, wants to prevent the process of separation by that very system of protection which accelerates it.

48. Philanthropic English economists, like Mill, Rogers, Goldwin, Smith, Fawcett, etc., and liberal manufacturers like John Bright & Co., ask the English landed proprietors, as God asked Cain after Abel, Where are our thousands of Freeholders gone? But where do *you* come from, then? From the destruction of those Freeholders. Why don't you ask, further, where are the independent weavers, spinners, and artisans gone?

49. Industrial here in contradistinction to agricultural. In the "categoric" sense the farmer is an industrial capitalist as much as the manufacturer.

property; and by what law, or series of laws, was it affected?"[50] The author should have remembered that revolutions are not made by laws.

The money capital formed by means of usury and commerce was prevented from turning into industrial capital in the country by the feudal constitution, in the towns by the guild organization.[51] These fetters vanished with the dissolution of feudal society, with the expropriation and partial eviction of the country population. The new manufactures were established at seaports or at inland points beyond the control of the old municipalities and their guilds. Hence, in England, an embittered struggle of the corporate towns against these new industrial nurseries.

The discovery of gold and silver in America, the extirpation, enslavement, and entombment in mines of the aboriginal population, the beginning of the conquest and looting of the East Indies, the turning of Africa into a warren for the commercial hunting of black-skins, signalized the rosy dawn of the era of capitalist production. These idyllic proceedings are the chief momenta of primitive accumulation. On their heels treads the commercial war of the European nations, with the globe for a theatre. It begins with the revolt of the Netherlands from Spain, assumes giant dimensions in England's anti-Jacobin war, and is still going on in the opium wars against China, etc.

The different momenta of primitive accumulation distribute themselves now more or less in chronological order, particularly over Spain, Portugal, Holland, France, and England. In England, at the end of the 17th century, they arrive at a systematical combination, embracing the colonies, the national debt, the modern mode of taxation, and the protectionist system. These methods depend in part on brute force—*e.g.*, the colonial system. But they all employ the power of the State—the concentrated and organized force of society—to hasten, hot-house fashion, the process of transformation of the feudal mode of production into the capitalist mode, and to shorten the transition. Force is the midwife of every old society pregnant with a new one. It is itself an economic power.

Of the Christian colonial system, W. Howitt, a man who makes a specialty of Christianity, says: "The barbarities and desperate outrages of the so-called Christian race, thoroughout every region of the world, and upon every people they have been able to subdue, are not to be paralleled by those of any other race, however fierce, however untaught, and however reckless of mercy and of shame, in any age of the earth."[52] The history of the colonial administration of Holland—and Holland was the head capitalistic nation of the 17th century—"is one of the most extraordinary relations of treachery, bribery, massacre, and meanness."[53] Nothing is more characteristic than their system of stealing men to get slaves for Java. The men stealers were trained for this purpose. The thief, the interpreter, and the seller were the chief agents in this trade, native princes the chief sellers. The young people stolen were thrown into the secret dungeons of Celebes until they were ready for sending to the slave-ships. An official report says: "This one town of Macassar, *e.g.*, is full of secret prisons, one more horrible than the other, crammed with unfortunates, victims of greed and tyranny, fettered in chains, forcibly torn from their families." To secure Malacca, the Dutch corrupted the Portuguese governor. He let them into the town in 1641. They hurried at once to his house and assassinated him to "abstain" from the payment of £21,875, the price of his treason. Wherever they set foot, devastation and depopulation followed. Banjuwangi, a province of Java, in 1750 numbered over 80,000 inhabitants; in 1811, only 18,000. Sweet commerce!

The English East India Company, as is well known, obtained, besides the political rule in India, the exclusive monopoly of the tea trade as well as of the Chinese trade in general, and of the transport of goods to and from Europe. But the coasting trade of India and between the islands, as well as the internal trade of India, were the monopoly of the higher employés of the company. The monopolies of salt, opium, betel, and other commodities were inexhaustible mines of wealth. The employés themselves fixed the price, and plundered at will the unhappy Hindus. The Governor-General took part in this private traffic. His favorites received contracts under conditions whereby they, cleverer than the alchemists, made gold out of nothing. Great fortunes sprang up like mushrooms in a day; primitive accumulation went on without the advance of a shilling. The trial of Warren Hastings swarms with such cases. Here is an instance: A contract for

50. "The Natural and Artificial Rights of Property Contrasted," pp. 98, 99. London, 1832. Author of the anonymous work: "Th. Hodgskin."

51. Even as late as 1794 the small cloth-makers of Leeds sent a deputation to Parliament with a petition for a law to forbid any merchant from becoming a manufacturer. (Dr. Aikin [: "Description of the country from thirty to forty miles round Manchester." London, 1795.])

52. William Howitt, "Colonization and Christianity, A Popular History of the Treatment of the Natives by the Europeans in All Their Colonies," p. 9. London, 1883. On the treatment of the slaves there is a good compilation in Charles Comte, "Traité de la Législation," 3me éd., Bruxelles, 1837. This subject one must study in detail to see what the bourgeoisie makes of itself and of the laborer wherever it can, without restraint, model the world after its own image.

53. Thomas Stamford Raffles, late Lieut.-Gov. of that island, "History of Java and Its Dependencies." London, 1817.

opium was given to a certain Sullivan at the moment of his departure on an official mission to a part of India far removed from the opium district. Sullivan sold his contract to one Binn for £40,000. Binn sold it the same day for £60,000; and the ultimate purchaser who carried out the contract declared that, after all, he realized an enormous gain. According to one of the lists laid before Parliament, the company and its employés, from 1757–1766, got £6,000,000 from the Indians as gifts. Between 1769 and 1770 the English manufactured a famine by buying up all the rice and refusing to sell it again except at fabulous prices.[54]

The treatment of the aborigines was, naturally, most frightful in plantation colonies destined for export trade only, such as the West Indies, and in rich and well-populated countries, such as Mexico and India, that were given over to plunder. But, even in the colonies properly so-called, the Christian character of primitive accumulation did not belie itself. Those sober *virtuosi* of Protestantism, the Puritans of New England, in 1703, by decrees of their Assembly, set a premium of £40 on every Indian scalp and every captured redskin; in 1720, a premium of £100 on every scalp; in 1744, after Massachusetts Bay had proclaimed a certain tribe as rebels, the following prices—for a male scalp of 12 years and upward, £100 (new currency), for a male prisoner £105, for women and children prisoners £50, for scalps of women and children £50. Some decades later, the colonial system took its revenge on the descendants of the pious pilgrim fathers, who had grown seditious in the meantime. At English instigation, and for English pay, they were tomahawked by redskins. The British Parliament proclaimed bloodhounds and scalping as "means that God and Nature had given into its hand."

The colonial system ripened, like a hot-house, trade and navigation. The "societies Monopolia" of Luther were powerful levers for concentration of capital. The colonies secured a market for the budding manufactures, and, through the monopoly of the market, an increased accumulation. The treasures captured outside Europe by undisguised looting, enslavement, and murder, floated back to the mother country, and were there turned into capital. Holland, which first fully developed the colonial system, in 1648 stood already in the acme of its commercial greatness. It was "in almost exclusive possession of the East Indian trade and the commerce between the south-east and north-west of Europe. Its fisheries, marine, manufactures, surpassed those of any other country. The total capital of the republic was probably more important than that of all the rest of Europe put together." Gülich forgets to add that, by 1648, the people of Holland were more overworked, poorer, and more brutally oppressed than those of all the rest of Europe put together.

To-day, industrial supremacy implies commercial supremacy. In the period of manufacture, properly so-called, it is, on the other hand, the commercial supremacy that gives industrial predominance. Hence the preponderant rôle that the colonial system plays at that time. It was "the strange god" who perched himself on the altar, cheek by jowl with the old gods of Europe, and one fine day, with a shove and kick, chucked them all of a heap. It proclaimed surplus-value making as the sole end and aim of humanity.

The system of public credit, *i.e.*, of national debts, whose origin we discover in Genoa and Venice as early as the middle ages, took possession of Europe generally during the manufacturing period. The colonial system with its maritime trade and commercial wars served as a forcing-house for it. Thus it first took root in Holland. National debts, *i.e.*, the alienation of the state—whether despotic, constitutional, or republican—marked with its stamp the capitalistic era. The only part of the so-called national wealth that actually enters into the collective possessions of modern peoples is—their national debt.[55] Hence, as a necessary consequence, the modern doctrine that a nation becomes the richer the more deeply it is in debt. Public credit becomes the *credo* of capital. And with the rise of national debt-making, want of faith in the national debt takes the place of the blasphemy against the Holy Ghost, which may not be forgiven.

The public debt becomes one of the most powerful levers of primitive accumulation. As with the stroke of an enchanter's wand, it endows barren money with the power of breeding and thus turns it into capital, without the necessity of its exposing itself to the troubles and risks inseparable from its employment in industry or even in usury. The State-creditors actually give nothing away, for the sum lent is transformed into public bonds, easily negotiable, which go on functioning in their hands just as so much hard cash would. But further, apart from the class of lazy annuitants thus created, and from the improvised wealth of the financiers—middlemen between the government and the nation—as also apart from the tax-farmers, merchants, private manufacturers, to whom a good part of every na-

54. In the year 1866 more than a million Hindus died of hunger in the province of Orissa alone. Nevertheless, the attempt was made to enrich the Indian treasury by the prices at which the necessaries of life were sold to the starving people.

55. William Cobbett remarks that in England all public institutions are designated "royal;" as compensation for this, however, there is the "national" debt.

tional loan renders the service of a capital fallen from heaven—the national debt has given rise to joint-stock companies, to dealings in negotiable effects of all kinds, and to agiotage, in a word, to stock-exchange gambling and the modern bankocracy.

At their birth the great banks, decorated with national titles, were only associations of private speculators, who placed themselves by the side of governments, and, thanks to the privileges they received, were in a position to advance money to the State. Hence the accumulation of the national debt has no more infallible measure than the successive rise in the stock of these banks, whose full development dates from the founding of the Bank of England in 1694. The Bank of England began with lending its money to the Government at 8 per cent.; at the same time it was empowered by Parliament to coin money out of the same capital, by lending it again to the public in the form of bank-notes. It was allowed to use these notes for discounting bills, making advances on commodities, and for buying the precious metals. It was not long ere this credit-money, made by the bank itself, became the coin in which the Bank of England made its loans to the State, and paid, on account of the State, the interest on the public debt. It was not enough that the bank gave with one hand and took back more with the other; it remained, even while receiving, the eternal creditor of the nation down to the last shilling advanced. Gradually it became inevitably the receptacle of the metallic hoard of the country, and the centre of gravity of all commercial credit. What effect was produced on their contemporaries by the sudden uprising of this brood of bankocrats, financiers, rentiers, brokers, stock-jobbers, etc., is proved by the writings of that time, e.g., by Bolingbroke's.[56]

With the national debt arose an international credit system, which often conceals one of the sources of primitive accumulation in this or that people. Thus the villainies of the Venetian thieving system formed one of the secret bases of the capital-wealth of Holland, to whom Venice in her decadence lent large sums of money. So also was it with Holland and England. By the beginning of the 18th century the Dutch manufactures were far outstripped. Holland had ceased to be the nation preponderant in commerce and industry. One of its main lines of business, therefore, from 1701–1776, is the lending out of enormous amounts of capital, especially to its great rival England. The same thing is going on to-day between England and the United States. A great deal of capital, which appears to-day in the United States without any certificate of birth, was yesterday, in England, the capitalized blood of children.

As the national debt finds its support in the public revenue, which must cover the yearly payments for interest, etc., the modern system of taxation was the necessary complement of the system of national loans. The loans enable the government to meet extraordinary expenses, without the tax-payers feeling it immediately, but they necessitate, as a consequence, increased taxes. On the other hand, the raising of taxation caused by the accumulation of debts contracted one after another, compels the government always to have recourse to new loans for new extraordinary expenses. Modern fiscality, whose pivot is formed by taxes on the most necessary means of subsistence (thereby increasing their price), thus contains within itself the germ of automatic progression. Over-taxation is not an incident, but rather a principle. In Holland, therefore, where this system was first inaugurated, the great patriot, De Witt, has in his "Maxims" extolled it as the best system for making the wage-laborer submissive, frugal, industrious, and overburdened with labor. The destructive influence that it exercises on the condition of the wage-laborer concerns us less however, here, than the forcible expropriation resulting from it, of peasants, artisans, and in a word, all elements of the lower middle-class. On this there are not two opinions, even among the bourgeois economists. Its expropriating efficacy is still further heightened by the system of protection, which forms one of its integral parts.

The great part that the public debt, and the fiscal system corresponding with it, has played in the capitalization of wealth and the expropriation of the masses, has led many writers, like Cobbett, Doubleday, and others, to seek in this, incorrectly, the fundamental cause of the misery of the modern peoples.

The system of protection was an artificial means of manufacturing manufacturers, of expropriating independent laborers, of capitalizing the national means of production and subsistence, of forcibly abbreviating the transition from the mediæval to the modern mode of production. The European States tore one another to pieces about the patent of this invention, and, once entered into the service of the surplus-value makers, did not merely lay under contribution in the pursuit of this purpose their own people, indirectly through protective duties, directly through export premiums. They also forcibly rooted out, in their dependent countries, all industry, as, e.g., England did with the Irish woolen manufacture. On the continent of Europe, after Colbert's example, the process was much simplified. The primitive industrial capital, here, came in part

56. "Si les Tartares inondaient l'Europe aujourd'hui, il faudrait bein des affaires pour leur faire entendre ce que c'est qu'un financier parmi nous." Montesquieu: Esprit des lois, t. iv., p. 33, ed. Londres, 1769.

directly out of the State treasury. "Why," cries Mirabeau, "why go so far to seek the cause of the manufacturing glory of Saxony before the war? 180,000,000 of debts contracted by the sovereigns!"[57]

Colonial system, public debts, heavy taxes, protection, commercial wars, etc., these children of the true manufacturing period, increase gigantically during the infancy of modern industry. The birth of the latter is heralded by a great slaughter of the innocents. Like the royal navy, the factories were recruited by means of the press-gang. *Blasé* as Sir F. M. Eden is as to the horrors of the expropriation of the agricultural population from the soil, from the last third of the 15th century to his own time; with all the self-satisfaction with which he rejoices in this process, "essential" for establishing capitalistic agriculture and "the due proportion between arable and pasture land"—he does not show, however, the same economic insight in respect to the necessity of child-stealing and child-slavery for the transformation of manufacturing exploitation into factory exploitation, and the establishment of the "true relation" between capital and labor-power. He says: "It may, perhaps, be worthy the attention of the public to consider whether any manufacture which, in order to be carried on successfully, requires that cottages and workhouses should be ransacked for poor children; that they should be employed by turns during the greater part of the night, and robbed of that rest which, though indispensable to all, is most required by the young; and that numbers of both sexes, of different ages and dispositions, should be collected together in such a manner that the contagion of example cannot but lead to profligacy and debauchery—will add to the sum of individual or national felicity."[58]

"In the counties of Derbyshire, Nottinghamshire, and more particularly in Lancashire," says Fielden, "the newly-invented machinery was used in large factories built on the sides of streams capable of turning the water-wheel. Thousands of hands were suddenly required in these places, remote from towns; and Lancashire, in particular, being, till then, comparatively thinly populated and barren, a population was all that she now wanted. The small and nimble fingers of little children being, by very far, the most in request, the custom instantly sprang up of procuring *apprentices* from the different parish workhouses of London, Birmingham, and elsewhere. Many, many thousands of these little hapless creatures were sent down into the north, being from the age of 7 to the age of 13 or 14 years old. The custom was for the master to clothe his apprentices and to feed and lodge them in an "apprentice house" near the factory. Overseers were appointed to see to the works, whose interest it was to work the children to the utmost because their pay was in proportion to the quantity of work that they could exact. Cruelty was, of course, the consequence. . . . In many of the manufacturing districts, but particularly, I am afraid, in the guilty county to which I belong [Lancashire], cruelties the most heartrending were practiced upon the unoffending and friendless creatures who were thus consigned to the charge of master manufacturers. They were harassed to the brink of death by excess of labor; . . . were flogged, fettered, and tortured in the most exquisite refinement of cruelty; . . . they were in many cases starved to the bone while flogged to their work; and . . . even, in some instances, . . . were driven to commit suicide. . . . The beautiful and romantic valleys of Derbyshire, Nottinghamshire, and Lancashire, secluded from the public eye, became the dismal solitudes of torture and of many a murder. The profits of manufactures were enormous; but this only whetted the appetite that it should have satisfied, and, therefore, the manufacturers had recourse to an expedient that seemed to secure to them those profits without any possibility of limit: they began the practice of what is termed "night-working"—that is, having tired one set of hands by working them throughout the day, they had another set ready to go on working throughout the night, the day-set getting into the beds that the night-set had just quitted, and, in their turn again, the night-set getting into the beds that the day-set quitted in the morning. It is common tradition in Lancashire that the beds *never get cold*."[59]

---

57. Mirabeau, l. c., t. VI., p. 101.
58. Eden, l. c., Vol. I., Book II., Ch. I., p 421.

---

59. John Fielden [: "The Curse of the Factory System," pp. 5, 6. London, 1836.] On the Earlier Infamies of the Factory System, cf. Dr. Aikin (1795), l. c., p. 219, and Gisborne, "Enquiry into the Duties of Men," Vol. II., 1795.

When the steam-engine transplanted the factories from the country waterfalls to the middle of towns, the "abstemious" surplus-value maker found the child material ready to his hand without being forced to seek slaves from the workhouses. When Sir R. Peel, father of the "minister of plausibility," brought in his bill for the protection of children, in 1815, Francis Horner, lumen of the Bullion Committee and intimate friend of Ricardo, said in the House of Commons: "It is notorious that, with a bankrupt's effects, a gang, if he might use the word, of these children had been put up to sale, and were advertised publicly as part of the property. A most atrocious instance had been brought before the Court of King's Bench two years before, in which a number of these boys, apprenticed by a parish in London to one manufacturer, had been transferred to another, and had been found by some benevolent persons in a state of absolute famine. Another case more horrible had come to his knowledge while on a [Parliamentary] Committee: . . . that, not many years ago, an agreement had been made between a London parish and a Lancashire manufacturer, by which it was stipulated that, with every twenty sound children, one idiot should be taken."

With the development of capitalist production during the manufacturing period, the public opinion of Europe had lost the last remnant of shame and conscience. The nations bragged cynically of every infamy that served them as a means to capitalistic accumulation. Read, *e.g.*, the *naïve* "Annals of Commerce" of the worthy A. Anderson. Here it is trumpeted forth as a triumph of English statecraft that, at the Peace of Utrecht, England extorted from the Spaniards by the Asiento Treaty the privilege of being allowed to ply the negro trade, until then only carried on between Africa and the English West Indies, between Africa and Spanish America as well. England thereby acquired the right of supplying Spanish America, until 1743, with 4,800 negroes yearly. This threw, at the same time, an official cloak over British smuggling. Liverpool waxed fat on the slave-trade. This was its method of primitive accumulation. And, even to the present day, Liverpool "respectability" is the Pindar of the slave-trade which—compare the work of Aikin (1795) already quoted—"has coincided with that spirit of bold adventure which has characterized the trade of Liverpool, and rapidly carried it to its present state of prosperity; has occasioned vast employment for shipping and sailors, and greatly augmented the demand for the manufactures of the country" (p. 339). Liverpool employed in the slave-trade, in 1730, 15 ships; in 1751, 53; in 1760, 74; in 1770, 96; and, in 1792, 132.

While the cotton industry introduced child slavery in England, it gave in the United States a stimulus to the transformation of the earlier, more or less patriarchal, slavery into a system of commercial exploitation. In fact, the veiled slavery of the wage-workers in Europe needed, for its pedestal, slavery pure and simple in the new world.[60]

Tantae molis erat, to establish the "eternal laws of Nature" of the capitalist mode of production; to complete the process of separation between laborers and conditions of labor; to transform, at one pole, the social means of production and subsistence into capital, at the opposite pole, the mass of the population into wage-laborers—into "free laboring poor"—that artificial product of modern society.[61]

If money, according to Augier,[62] "comes into the world with a congenital blood-stain on one cheek," capital comes dripping from head to foot, from every pore, with blood and dirt.[63]

Historical Tendency of Capitalist Accumulation

What does the primitive accumulation of capital —*i. e.,* its historical genesis—resolve itself into? In so far as it is not immediate transformation of slaves and serfs into wage-laborers, and therefore a mere change of form, it only means the expropriation of the immediate producers—*i. e.,* the dissolution of private property based on the labor of its owner. Private property, as the antithesis to social, collective property, exists only where the means of labor and the external conditions of labor belong to private individuals. But according as these private individuals are laborers or not laborers, private property has a different character. The numberless shades that it at first sight presents correspond to the intermediate stages lying between these two extremes. The private property of the laborer in his means of production is the foundation of petty industry, whether agricultural, manu-

political cant-monger," Edmund Burke, when he called the expression "laboring poor" "execrable political cant." This sycophant, who, in the pay of the English oligarchy, played the romantic *laudator temporis acti* against the French Revolution, just as, in the pay of the North American colonies at the beginning of the American troubles, he had played the Liberal against the English oligarchy, was an out and out vulgar bourgeois. "The laws of commerce are the laws of Nature, and therefore the laws of God." (E. Burke [: "Thoughts and Details on Scarcity," pp. 31, 32. London, 1800.]) No wonder that, true to the laws of God and of Nature, he always sold himself in the best market.

A very good portrait of this Edmund Burke, during his Liberal time, is to be found in the writings of the Rev. Mr. Tucker. Tucker was a parson and a Tory, but, for the rest, an honorable man and a competent political economist. In face of the infamous cowardice of character that reigns to-day, and believes most devoutly in "the laws of commerce," it is our bounden duty again and again to brand the Burkes, who only differ from their successors in one thing, talent.

62. Marie Augier, "Du Crédit Public." Paris, 1842.

63. "Capital is said by a Quarterly Reviewer to fly turbulence and strife and to be timid, which is very true; but this is very incompletely stating the question. Capital eschews no profit, or very small profit, just as Nature was formerly said to abhor a vacuum. With adequate profit, capital is very bold. A certain 10 per cent. will insure its employment anywhere. 20 per cent. certain, will produce eagerness; 50 per cent., positive audacity; 100 per cent. will make it ready to trample on all human laws; 300 per cent., and there is not a crime at which it will scruple, nor a risk it will not run, even to the chance of its owner being hanged. If turbulence and strife will bring a profit, it will freely encourage both. Smuggling and the slave-trade have amply proved all that is here stated." (P. J. Dunning [: "Trades' Unions and Strikes," p. 35. London, 1860.])

60. In 1790, there were in the English West Indies ten slaves for one free man; in the French, fourteen for one; in the Dutch, twenty-three for one. (Henry Brougham, "An Inquiry into the Colonial Policy of the European Powers, Vol. II., p. 74. Edin., 1803.)

61. The phrase "laboring poor" is found in English legislation from the moment when the class of wage-laborers becomes noticeable. This term is used in opposition, on the one hand, to the "idle poor," beggars, etc.; on the other, to those laborers who, pigeons not yet plucked, are still possessors of their own means of labor. From the Statute Book it passed into political economy, and was handed down by Culpeper, J. Child, etc., to Adam Smith and Eden. After this, one can judge of the good faith of the "execrable

facturing, or both. Petty industry again, is an essential condition for the development of social production and of the free individuality of the laborer himself. Of course, this petty mode of production exists also under slavery, serfdom, and other states of dependence. But it flourishes, it lets loose its whole energy, it attains its adequate classical form, only where the laborer is the private owner of his own means of labor set in action by himself—the peasant of the land which he cultivates, the artisan of the tool which he handles as a virtuoso. This mode of production pre-supposes parceling of the soil, and scattering of the other means of production. As it excludes the concentration of these means of production, so also it excludes co-operation, division of labor within each separate process of production, the control over, and the productive application of the forces of nature by society, and the free development of the social productive powers. It is compatible only with a system of production, and a society, moving within narrow and more or less primitive bounds. To perpetuate it would be, as Pecqueur rightly says, "to decree universal mediocrity." At a certain stage of development it brings forth the material agencies for its own dissolution. From that moment new forces and new passions spring up in the bosom of society; but the old social organization fetters them and keeps them down. It must be annihilated; it is annihilated. Its annihilation, the transformation of the individualized and scattered means of production into socially concentrated ones, of the pigmy property of the many into the huge property of the few; the expropriation of the great mass of the people from the soil, from the means of subsistence, and from the means of labor; this fearful and painful expropriation of the mass of the people forms the prelude to the history of capital. It comprises a series of forcible methods, of which we have passed in review only those that have been epoch-making as methods of the primitive accumulation of capital. The expropriation of the immediate producers was accomplished with merciless Vandalism, and under the stimulus of passions the most infamous, the most sordid, the pettiest, the most meanly odious. Self-earned private property, that is based, so to say, on the fusing together of the isolated, independent laboring individual with the conditions of his labor, is supplanted by capitalistic private property, which rests on exploitation of the nominally free labor of others i. e.—on wage-labor.[64]

As soon as this process of transformation has sufficiently decomposed the old society from top to bottom; as soon as the laborers are turned into proletarians, their means of labor into capital; as soon as the capitalist mode of production stands on its own feet; then the further socialization of labor and further transformation of the land and other means of production into socially exploited and, therefore, common means of production, as well as the further expropriation of private proprietors, take a new form. That which is now to be expropriated is no longer the laborer working for himself, but the capitalist exploiting many laborers. This expropriation is accomplished by the action of the immanent laws of capitalistic production itself, by the centralization of capital. One capitalist always kills many. Hand in hand with this centralization, or this expropriation of many capitalists by few, develop, on an ever extending scale, the co-operative form of the labor process, the conscious technical application of science, the methodical cultivation of the soil, the transformation of the instruments of labor into instruments of labor only usable in common, the economizing of all means of production by their use as the means of production of combined, socialized labor, the entanglement of all peoples in the net of the world-market, and with this, the international character of the capitalistic regime. Along with the constantly diminishing number of the magnates of capital, who usurp and monopolize all advantages of this process of transformation, grows the mass of misery, oppression, slavery, degradation, exploitation; but with this too grows the revolt of the working-class, a class always increasing in numbers, and disciplined, united, organized by the very mechanism of the process of capitalist production itself. The monopoly of capital becomes a fetter upon the mode of production, which has sprung up and flourished along with, and under it. Centralization of the means of production and socialization of labor at last reach a point where they become incompatible with their capitalist integument. This integument is burst asunder. The knell of capitalist private property sounds. The expropriators are expropriated.

The capitalist mode of appropriation, the result of the capitalist mode of production, produces capitalist private property. This is the first negation of individual private property, as founded on the labor of the proprietor. But capitalist production begets, with the inexorability of a law of Nature, its own negation. It is the negation of negation. This does not re-establish private property for the producer, but gives him individual property based on the acquisitions of the capitalist era; i. e.—on co-operation and the possession in common of the land and of the means of production.

The transformation of scattered private property,

64. "Nous sommes dans une condition tout-à-fait nouvelle de la société . . . nous tendons à séparer toute espèce de propriété d'avec toute espèce de travail." (Sismondi: Nouveaux Principes de l'Econ. Polit., t. II., p. 434.)

arising from individual labor, into capitalist private
property is, naturally, a process, incomparably more
protracted, violent and difficult than the transformation of capitalistic private property, already
practically resting on socialized production, into
socialized property. In the former case we had the
expropriation of the mass of the people by a few
usurpers; in the latter we have the expropriation of
a few usurpers by the mass of the people.[65]

The Modern Theory of Colonization

Political economy confuses on principle two very
different kinds of private property, of which one
rests on the producers' own labor, the other on the
employment of the labor of others. It forgets that
the latter not only is the direct antithesis of the
former, but absolutely grows on its tomb only. In
Western Europe, the home of political economy,
the process of primitive accumulation is more or
less accomplished. Here the capitalist régime has
either directly conquered the whole domain of national production, or, where economic conditions
are less developed, it, at least, indirectly controls
those strata of society which, though belonging to
the antiquated mode of production, continue to exist side by side with it in gradual decay. To this
ready-made world of capital, the political economist applies the notions of law and of property inherited from a pre-capitalistic world with all the
more anxious zeal and all the greater unction, the
more loudly the facts cry out in the face of his
ideology. It is otherwise in the colonies.[66] There the
capitalist régime everywhere comes into collision
with the resistance of the producer, who, as owner

of his own conditions of labor, employs that labor
to enrich himself, instead of the capitalist. The contradiction of these two diametrically opposed economic systems manifests itself here practically in a
struggle between them. Where the capitalist has at
his back the power of the mother-country, he tries
to clear out of his way by force, the modes of production and appropriation, based on his independent labor of the producer. The same interest, which
compels the sycophant of capital, the political economist, in the mother-country, to proclaim the theoretical identity of the capitalist mode of production
with its contrary, that same interest compels him in
the colonies to make a clean breast of it, and to proclaim aloud the antagonism of the two modes of
production. To this end he proves how the development of the social productive power of labor, co-
operation, division of labor, use of machinery on a
large scale, etc., are impossible without the expropriation of the laborers, and the corresponding
transformation of their means of production into
capital. In the interest of the so-called national
wealth, he seeks for artificial means to insure the
poverty of the people. Here his apologetic armor
crumbles off, bit by bit, like rotten touchwood. It
is the great merit of E. G. Wakefield to have discovered, not anything new about the colonies, but
to have discovered in the colonies the truth as to the
conditions of capitalist production in the mother-
country. As the system of protection at its origin[67]
attempted to manufacture capitalists artificially in
the mother-country, so Wakefield's colonization
theory, which England tried for a time to enforce
by Acts of Parliament, attempted to effect the manufacture of wage-workers in the colonies. This he
calls "systematic colonization."

First of all, Wakefield discovered that in the colonies, property in money, means of subsistence, machines, and other means of production, do not as yet
stamp a man as a capitalist if there be wanting the
correlative—the wage-worker, the other man who
is compelled to sell himself of his own free-will. He
discovered that capital is not a thing, but a social relation between persons established by the instrumentality of things.[68] Mr. Peel, he moans, took with
him from England to Swan River, West Australia,
means of subsistence and of production to the

65. The advance of industry, whose involuntary promoter
is the bourgeoisie, replaces the isolation of the laborers, due
to competition, by their revolutionary combination, due
to association. The development of modern industry, therefore, cuts from under its feet the very foundation on which
the bourgeoisie produces and appropriates products. What
the bourgeoisie therefore produces, above all, are its own
grave-diggers. Its fall and the victory of the proletariat are
equally inevitable. . . . Of all the classes that stand face to
face with the bourgeoisie to-day, the proletariat alone is
a really revolutionary class. The other classes perish and
disappear in the face of modern industry, the proletariat is
its special and essential product. . . . The lower middle
classes, the small manufacturers, the shopkeepers, the artisan, the peasant, all these fight against the bourgeoisie, to
save from extinction their existence as fractions of the
middle class . . . they are reactionary, for they try to roll
back the wheel of history. Karl Marx and Frederick Engels:
"Manifest der Kommunistischen Partei," pp. 9, 11. London.
1847.
66. We treat here of real colonies, virgin soils, colonized
by free immigrants. The United States are, speaking economically, still only a colony of Europe. Besides, to this
category belong also such old plantations as those in which
the abolition of slavery has completely altered the earlier
conditions.

67. Later, it became a temporary necessity in the international competitive struggle. But, whatever its motive, the
consequences remain the same.
68. A negro is a negro. In certain circumstances he becomes a slave. A mule is a machine for spinning cotton.
Only under certain circumstances does it become capital.
Outside these circumstances, it is no more capital than gold
is intrinsically money, or sugar is the price of sugar. . . .
Capital is a social relation of production. It is a historical
relation of production. (Karl Marx, "Lohnarbeit und
Kapital." N. Rh. Z. No. 266, April 7, 1849.)

amount of £50,000. Mr. Peel had the foresight to bring with him, besides, 3,000 persons of the working-class, men, women, and children. Once arrived at his destination, "Mr. Peel was left without a servant to make his bed or fetch him water from the river."[69] Unhappy Mr. Peel who provided for everything except the export of English modes of production to Swan River!

For the understanding of the following discoveries of Wakefield, two preliminary remarks: We know that the means of production and subsistence, while they remain the property of the immediate producer, are not capital. They become capital, only under circumstances in which they serve at the same time as means of exploitation and subjection of the laborer. But this capitalist soul of theirs is so intimately wedded, in the head of the political economist, to their material substance, that he christens them capital under all circumstances, even when they are its exact opposite. Thus it is with Wakefield. Further: the splitting up of the means of production into the individual property of many independent laborers, working on their own account, he calls equal division of capital. It is with the political economist as with the feudal jurist. The latter stuck on to pure monetary relations the labels supplied by feudal law.

"If," says Wakefield, "all the members of the society are supposed to possess equal portions of capital . . . no man would have a motive for accumulating more capital than he could use with his own hands. This is to some extent the case in new American settlements, where a passion for owning land prevents the existence of a class of laborers for hire."[70] So long, therefore, as the laborer can accumulate for himself—and this he can do so long as he remains possessor of his means of production—capitalist accumulation and the capitalistic mode of production are impossible. The class of wage-laborers, essential to these, is wanting. How, then, in old Europe, was the expropriation of the laborer from his conditions of labor, *i. e.,* the co-existence of capital and wage-labor, brought about? By a social contract of a quite original kind. "Mankind have adopted a . . . simple contrivance for promoting the accumulation of capital," which, of course, since the time of Adam, floated in their imagination as the sole and final end of their existence: "they have divided themselves into owners of capital and owners of labor. . . . This division was the result of concert and combination."[71] In one word: the mass of mankind expropriated itself in honor of the "accumula-

tion of capital." Now, one would think, that this instinct of self-denying fanaticism would give itself full fling especially in the colonies, where alone exist the men and conditions that could turn a social contract from a dream to a reality. But why, then, should "systematic colonization" be called in to replace its opposite, spontaneous, unregulated colonization? But—but—"In the Northern States of the American Union, it may be doubted whether so many as a tenth of the people would fall under the description of hired laborers. . . . In England . . . the laboring class compose the bulk of the people."[72] Nay, the impulse to self-expropriation, on the part of laboring humanity, for the glory of capital, exists so little, that slavery, according to Wakefield himself, is the sole natural basis of colonial wealth. His systematic colonization is a mere *pis aller,* since he unfortunately has to do with free men, not with slaves. "The first Spanish settlers in Saint Domingo did not obtain laborers from Spain. But, without laborers, their capital must, have perished, or, at least, must soon have been diminished to that small amount which each individual could employ with his own hands. This has actually occurred in the last Colony founded by Englishmen—the Swan River Settlement—where a great mass of capital, of seeds, implements, and cattle, has perished for want of laborers to use it, and where no settler has preserved much more capital than he can employ with his own hands."[73]

We have seen that the expropriation of the mass of the people from the soil forms the basis of the capitalist mode of production. The essence of a free colony, on the contrary, consists in this—that the bulk of the soil is still public property, and every settler on it therefore can turn part of it into his private property and individual means of production, without hindering the later settlers in the same operation.[74] This is the secret both of the prosperity of the colonies and of their inveterate vice—opposition to the establishment of capital. "Where land is very cheap and all men are free, where every one who so pleases can easily obtain a piece of land for himself, not only is labor very dear, as respects the laborer's share of the produce, but the difficulty is to obtain combined labor at any price."[75]

As in the colonies the separation of the labor from the conditions of labor and their root, the soil, does not yet exist, or only sporadically, or on too limited a scale, so neither does the separation of ag-

69. E. G. Wakefield. "England and America," vol. II., p. 33.
70. L. c., p. 17.
71. L. c., vol. I., p. 18.

72. L. c., pp. 42, 43, 44.
73. L. c., vol. II., p. 5.
74. "Land, to be an element of colonization, must not only be waste, but it must be public property, liable to be converted into private property." (L. c., vol. II., p. 125.)
75. L. c., vol. I., p. 247.

riculture from industry exist, nor the destruction of the household industry of the peasantry. Whence, then, is to come the internal market for capital? "No part of the population of America is exclusively agricultural, excepting slaves and their employers who combine capital and labor in particular works. Free Americans, who cultivate the soil, follow many other occupations. Some portion of the furniture and tools which they use is commonly made by themselves. They frequently built their own houses, and carry to market, at whatever distance, the produce of their own industry. They are spinners and weavers; they make soap and candles, as well as, in many cases, shoes and clothes for their own use. In America the cultivation of land is often the secondary pursuit of a blacksmith, a miller, or a shopkeeper."[76] With such queer people as these, where is the "field of abstinence" for the capitalists?

The great beauty of capitalist production consists in this—that it not only constantly reproduces the wage-worker as wage-worker, but produces always, in proportion to the accumulation of capital, a relative surplus-population of wage-workers. Thus the law of supply and demand of labor is kept in the right rut, the oscillation of wages is penned within limits satisfactory to capitalist exploitation, and lastly, the social dependence of the laborer on the capitalist, that indispensable requisite, is secured; an unmistakeable relation of dependence, which the smug political economist, at home, in the mother country, can transmogrify into one of free contract between buyer and seller, between equally independent owners of commodities, the owner of the commodity capital and the owner of the commodity labor. But in the colonies this pretty fancy is torn asunder. The absolute population here increases much more quickly than in the mother-country, because many laborers enter this world as readymade adults, and yet the labor market is always understocked. The law of the supply and demand of labor falls to pieces. On the one hand, the old world constantly throws in capital, thirsting after exploitation and "abstinence"; on the other, the regular reproduction of the wage-laborer as wage-laborer comes into collision with impediments the most impertinent and in part invincible. What becomes of the production of wage-laborers, supernumerary in proportion to the accumulation of capital? The wage-worker of to-day is to-morrow an independent peasant, or artisan, working for himself. He vanishes from the labor-market, but not into the workhouse. This constant transformation of the wage-laborers into independent producers, who work for themselves instead of for capital, and enrich themselves instead of the capitalist gentry,

re-acts in its turn very perversely on the conditions of the labor-market. Not only does the degree of exploitation of the wage-laborer remain indecently low. The wage-laborer loses into the bargain, along with the relation of dependence, also the sentiment of dependence on the abstemious capitalist. Hence all the inconveniences that our E. G. Wakefield pictures so doughtily, so eloquently, so pathetically.

The supply of wage-labor, he complains, is neither constant, nor regular, nor sufficient. "The supply of labor is always not only small but uncertain."[77] "Though the produce divided between the capitalist and the laborer be large, the laborer takes so great a share that he soon becomes a capitalist. . . . Few, even of those whose lives are unusually long, can accumulate great masses of wealth."[78] The laborers most distinctly decline to allow the capitalist to abstain from the payment of the greater part of their labor. It avails him nothing if he is so cunning as to import from Europe, with his own capital, his own wage-workers. They soon "cease . . . to be laborers for hire; they . . . become independent land owners, if not competitors with their former masters in the labor market."[79] Think of the horror! The excellent capitalist has imported bodily from Europe, with his own good money, his own competitors! The end of the world has come! No wonder Wakefield laments the absence of all dependence and of all sentiment of dependence on the part of the wage-workers in the colonies. On account of the high wages, says his disciple, Merivale, there is in the colonies "the urgent desire for cheaper and more subservient laborers—for a class to whom the capitalist might dictate terms, instead of being dictated to by them. . . . In ancient civilized countries the laborer, though free, is by a law of Nature dependent on capitalists; in colonies this dependence must be created by artificial means."[80]

---

76. L. c., pp. 21, 22.

77. L. c., vol. II., p. 116.
78. L. c., vol. I., p. 131.
79. L. c., vol. II., p. 5.
80. Merivale [: "Lectures on Colonization and Colonies," vol. II, pp. 235, 314, passim. London, 1841.] Even the mild, free-trade, vulgar economist, Molinari, says: "Dans les colonies où l'esclavage a été aboli sans que le travail forcé se trouvait remplacé par une quantité équivalente de travail libre, on a vu s'opérer la contre-partie du fait que se réalise tous les jours sous nos yeux. On a vu les simples travailleurs exploiter à leur tour les entrepreneurs d'industrie, exiger d'eux des salaires hors de toute proportion avec la part légitime que leur revenait dans le produit. Les planteurs, ne pouvant obtenir de leurs sucres un prix suffisant pour couvrir la hausse de salaire, ont été obligés de fournir l'excédant, d'abord sur leurs profits, ensuite sur leurs capitaux mêmes. Une foule de planteurs ont été ruinés de la sorte d'autres ont fermé leurs ateliers pour échapper à une ruine imminente. . . . Sans doute, il vaut mieux voir périr des accumulations de capitaux que des générations d'hommes [how generous of Mr. Molinari!] mais ne vaudrait-il pas mieux que ni les uns ni les autres périssent?" (Molin-

What is now, according to Wakefield, the consequence of this unfortunate state of things in the colonies? A "barbarizing tendency of dispersion" of producers and national wealth.[81] The parceling-out of the means of production among innumerable owners, working on their own account, annihilates, along with the centralization of capital, all the foundations of combined labor. Every long-winded undertaking, extending over several years and demanding outlay of fixed capital, is prevented from being carried out. In Europe, capital invests without hesitating a moment, for the working-class constitutes its living appurtenance, always in excess, always at disposal. But in the colonies! Wakefield tells an extremely doleful anecdote. He was talking with some capitalists of Canada and the State of New York, where the immigrant wave often becomes stagnant and deposits a sediment of "supernumerary" laborers. "Our capital," says one of the characters in the melodrama, "was ready for many operations which require a considerable period of time for their completion; but we could not begin such operations with labor which we knew would soon leave us. If we had been sure of retaining the labor of such emigrants, we should have been glad to have engaged it at once, and for a high price: and we should have engaged it, even though we had been sure it would leave us, provided we had been sure of a fresh supply whenever we might need it."[82]

After Wakefield has contrasted the English capitalist agriculture and its "combined" labor with the scattered cultivation of American peasants, he unwittingly gives us a glimpse at the reverse of the medal. He depicts the mass of the American people as well-to-do, independent, enterprising and comparatively cultured, whilst "the English agricultural laborer is a miserable wretch, a pauper. . . . In what country, except North America and some new colonies, do the wages of free labor employed in agriculture much exceed a bare subsistence for the laborer? . . . Undoubtedly, farm-horses in England being a valuable property, are better fed than English peasants."[83] But, never mind, national wealth is,

once again, by its very nature, identical with misery of the people.

How, then, to heal the anti-capitalistic cancer of the colonies? If men were willing, at a blow, to turn all the soil from public into private property, they would destroy certainly the root of the evil, but also —the colonies. The trick is how to kill two birds with one stone. Let the Government put upon the virgin soil an artificial price, independent of the law of supply and demand, a price that compels the immigrant to work a long time for wages before he can earn enough money to buy land, and turn himself into an independent peasant.[84] The funds resulting from the sale of land at a price relatively prohibitory to the wage-workers—this fund of money extorted from the wages of labor by violation of the sacred law of supply and demand—the Government is to employ, on the other hand, in proportion as it grows, to import have-nothings from Europe into the colonies, and thus keep the wage-labor market full for the capitalists. Under these circumstances, *tout sera pour le mieux dans le meilleur des mondes possibles.* This is the great secret of "systematic colonization." By this plan, Wakefield cries in triumph, "the supply of labor *must* be constant and regular; because, first, as no laborer would be able to procure land until he had worked for money, all immigrant laborers, working for a time for wages and in combination, would produce capital for the employment of more laborers; secondly, because every laborer who left off working for wages and became a land owner, would, by purchasing land, provide a fund for bringing fresh labor to the colony."[85] The price of the soil imposed by the State must, of course, be a "sufficient price," *i.e.*—so high "as to prevent the laborers from becoming independent land owners, until others had followed to take their place."[86] This "sufficient price for the land" is nothing but a euphemistic circumlocution for the ransom which the laborer pays to the capitalist for leave to retire from the wage-labor market to the land. First, he must create for the capitalist "capital," with which the latter may be able to exploit more laborers; then he must place, at his own expense a *locum tenens* on the labor market, whom the Government forwards across the sea for the benefit of his old master, the capitalist.

ari [: Etudes Economiques, pp. 51, 52. Paris, 1846.]) Mr. Molinari, Mr. Molinari! What, then, becomes of the ten commandments, of Moses and the prophets, of the law of supply and demand, if, in Europe, the "*entrepreneur*" can cut down the laborer's legitimate part, and in the West Indies the laborer can cut down the *entrepreneur's?* And what, if you please, is this "legitimate part," which, on your own showing, the capitalist in Europe daily neglects to pay? Over yonder, in the colonies, where the laborers are so "simple" as to "exploit" the capitalist, Mr. Molinari feels a strong itching to set the law of supply and demand, that works elsewhere automatically, on the right road by means of the police.

81. Wakefield, l. c., vol II., p. 52.
82. L. c., pp. 191, 192.
83. L. c., vol. I., pp. 47, 246.

84. "C'est, ajoutez-vous, grâce à l'appropriation du sol et des capitaux que l'homme, qui n' a que ses bras, trouve de l'occupation, et se fait un revenu . . . c'est au contraire, grâce à l'appropriation indivíduelle du sol qu'il se trouve des hommes n'ayant que leurs bras. . . . Quand vous mettez un homme dans le vide, vous vous emparez de l'atmosphère. Ainsi faites-vous, quand vous vous emparez du sol. . . . C'est le mettre dans le vide de richesses, pour ne le laisser vivre qu'à votre volonté." (Colins [: L'Economie Politique, t. III., pp. 268, 271, *passim*.])
85. Wakefield, l. c., vol. II., p. 192.
86. L. c., p. 45.

It is very characteristic that the English Government for years practiced this method of "primitive accumulation," prescribed by Mr. Wakefield expressly for the use of the colonies. The fiasco was, of course, as complete as that of Sir Robert Peel's Bank Act. The stream of emigration was only diverted from the English colonies to the United States. Meanwhile, the advance of capitalistic production in Europe, accompanied by increasing Government pressure, has rendered Wakefield's recipe superfluous. One the one hand, the enormous and ceaseless stream of men, year after year driven upon America, leaves behind a stationary sediment in the east of the United States, the wave of immigration from Europe throwing men on the labor market there more rapidly than the wave of emigration westwards can wash them away. On the other hand, the American Civil War brought in its train a colossal national debt, and, with it, pressure of taxes, the rise of the vilest financial aristocracy, the squandering of a huge part of the public land on speculative companies for the exploitation of railways, mines, etc., in brief, the most rapid centralization of capital. The great republic has, therefore, ceased to be the promised land for emigrant laborers. Capitalistic production advances there with giant strides, even though the lowering of wages and the dependence of the wage-worker are yet far from being brought down to the normal European level. The shameless lavishing of uncultivated colonial land on aristocrats and capitalists by the Government, so loudly denounced even by Wakefield, has produced, especially in Australia,[87] in conjunction with the stream of men that the gold-diggings attract, and with the competition that the importation of English commodities causes even to the smallest artisan, an ample "relative surplus laboring population," so that almost every mail brings the Job's news of a "glut of the Australian labor-market," and prostitution in some places there flourishes as wantonly as in the London Haymarket.

However, we are not concerned here with the condition of the colonies. The only thing that interests us is the secret discovered in the new world by the political economy of the old world, and proclaimed on the house-tops: That the capitalist mode of production and accumulation, and therefore capitalist private property, have for their fundamental condition the annihilation of self-earned private property; in other words, the expropriation of the laborer.

87. As soon as Australia became her own law-giver, she passed, of course, laws favourable to the settlers, but the squandering of the land, already accomplished by the English Government, stands in the way. "The first and main object at which the new Land Act of 1862 aims is to give increased facilities for the settlement of the people." (The Land Law of Victoria, by the Hon. C. G. Duffy, Minister of Public Lands. Lond., 1862.)

2. On Protestantism and Capitalism

BY MAX WEBER

Reprinted from Max Weber, *The Protestant Ethic and the Spirit of Capitalism,* trans. Talcott Parsons (New York: Charles Scribner's Sons, 1930), pp. 13–31, 89–92, 166–83, with the permission of Charles Scribner's Sons and George Allen & Unwin Ltd.

A PRODUCT of modern European civilization, studying any problem of universal history, is bound to ask himself to what combination of circumstances the fact should be attributed that in Western civilization, and in Western civilization only, cultural phenomena have appeared which (as we like to think) lie in a line of development having *universal* significance and value.

Only in the West does science exist at a stage of development which we recognize to-day as valid. Empirical knowledge, reflection on problems of the cosmos and of life, philosophical and theological wisdom of the most profound sort, are not confined to it, though in the case of the last the full development of a systematic theology must be credited to Christianity under the influence of Hellenism, since there were only fragments in Islam and in a few Indian sects. In short, knowledge and observation of great refinement have existed elsewhere, above all in India, China, Babylonia, Egypt. But in Babylonia and elsewhere astronomy lacked—which makes its development all the more astounding—the mathematical foundation which it first received from the Greeks. The Indian geometry had no rational proof; that was another product of the

Greek intellect, also the creator of mechanics and physics. The Indian natural sciences, though well developed in observation, lacked the method of experiment, which was, apart from beginnings in antiquity, essentially a product of the Renaissance, as was the modern laboratory. Hence medicine, especially in India, though highly developed in empirical technique, lacked a biological and particularly a biochemical foundation. A rational chemistry has been absent from all areas of culture except the West.

The highly developed historical scholarship of China did not have the method of Thucydides. Machiavelli, it is true, had predecessors in India; but all Indian political thought was lacking in a systematic method comparable to that of Aristotle, and, indeed, in the possession of rational concepts. Not all the anticipations in India (School of Mimamsa), nor the extensive codification especially in the Near East, nor all the Indian and other books of law, had the strictly systematic forms of thought, so essential to a rational jurisprudence, of the Roman law and of the Western law under its influence. A structure like the canon law is known only to the West.

A similar statement is true of art. The musical ear of other peoples has probably been even more sensitively developed than our own, certainly not less so. Polyphonic music of various kinds has been widely distributed over the earth. The co-operation of a number of instruments and also the singing of parts have existed elsewhere. All our rational tone intervals have been known and calculated. But rational harmonious music, both counterpoint and harmony, formation of the tone material on the basis of three triads with the harmonic third; our chromatics and enharmonics, not interpreted in terms of space, but, since the Renaissance, of harmony; our orchestra, with its string quartet as a nucleus, and the organization of ensembles of wind instruments; our bass accompaniment; our system of notation, which has made possible the composition and production of modern musical works, and thus their very survival; our sonatas, symphonies, operas; and finally, as means to all these, our fundamental instruments, the organ, piano, violin, etc.; all these things are known only in the Occident, although programme music, tone poetry, alternation of tones and chromatics, have existed in various musical traditions as means of expression.

In architecture, pointed arches have been used elsewhere as a means of decoration, in antiquity and in Asia; presumably the combination of pointed arch and cross-arched vault was not unknown in the Orient. But the rational use of the Gothic vault means of distributing pressure and of roofing spaces

of all forms, and above all as the constructive principle of great monumental buildings and the foundation of a *style* extending to sculpture and painting, such as that created by our Middle Ages, does not occur elsewhere. The technical basis of our architecture came from the Orient. But the Orient lacked that solution of the problem of the dome and that type of classic rationalization of all art—in painting by the rational utilization of lines and spatial perspective—which the Renaissance created for us. There was printing in China. But a printed literature, designed *only* for print and only possible through it, and, above all, the press and periodicals, have appeared only in the Occident. Institutions of higher education of all possible types, even some superficially similar to our universities, or at least academies, have existed (China, Islam). But a rational, systematic, and specialized pursuit of science, with trained and specialized personnel, has only existed in the West in a sense at all approaching its present dominant place in our culture. Above all is this true of the trained official, the pillar of both the modern State and of the economic life of the West. He forms a type of which there have heretofore only been suggestions, which have never remotely approached its present importance for the social order. Of course the official, even the specialized official, is a very old constituent of the most various societies. But no country and no age has ever experienced, in the same sense as the modern Occident, the absolute and complete dependence of its whole existence, of the political, technical, and economic conditions of its life, on a specially trained *organization* of officials. The most important functions of the everyday life of society have come to be in the hands of technically, commercially, and above all legally trained government officials.

Organization of political and social groups in feudal classes has been common. But even the feudal state of *rex et regnum* in the Western sense has only been known to our culture. Even more are parliaments of periodically elected representatives, with government by demagogues and party leaders as ministers responsible to the parliaments, peculiar to us, although there have, of course, been parties, in the sense of organizations for exerting influence and gaining control of political power, all over the world. In fact, the State itself, in the sense of a political association with a rational, written constitution, rationally ordained law, and an administration bound to rational rules or laws, administered by trained officials, is known, in this combination of characteristics, only in the Occident, despite all other approaches to it.

And the same is true of the most fateful force in our modern life, capitalism. The impulse to acquisition, pursuit of gain, of money, of the greatest possible amount of money, has in itself nothing to do with capitalism. This impulse exists and has existed among waiters, physicians, coachmen, artists, prostitutes, dishonest officials, soldiers, nobles, crusaders, gamblers, and beggars. One may say that it has been common to all sorts and conditions of men at all times and in all countries of the earth, wherever the objective possibility of it is or has been given. It should be taught in the kindergarten of cultural history that this naïve idea of capitalism must be given up once and for all. Unlimited greed for gain is not in the least identical with capitalism, and is still less its spirit. Capitalism *may* even be identical with the restraint, or at least a rational tempering, of this irrational impulse. But capitalism is identical with the pursuit of profit, and forever *renewed* profit, by means of continuous, rational, capitalistic enterprise. For it must be so: in a wholly capitalistic order of society, an individual capitalistic enterprise which did not take advantage of its opportunities for profit-making would be doomed to extinction.

Let us now define our terms somewhat more carefully than is generally done. We will define a capitalistic economic action as one which rests on the expectation of profit by the utilization of opportunities for exchange, that is on (formally) peaceful chances of profit. Acquisition by force (formally and actually) follows its own particular laws, and it is not expedient, however little one can forbid this, to place it in the same category with action which is, in the last analysis, oriented to profits from exchange. Where capitalistic acquisition is rationally pursued, the corresponding action is adjusted to calculations in terms of capital. This means that the action is adapted to a systematic utilization of goods or personal services as means of acquisition in such a way that, at the close of a business period, the balance of the enterprise in money assets (or, in the case of a continuous enterprise, the periodically estimated money value of assets) exceeds the capital, i.e. the estimated value of the material means of production used for acquisition in exchange. It makes no difference whether it involves a quantity of goods entrusted *in natura* to a travelling merchant, the proceeds of which may consist in other goods *in natura* acquired by trade, or whether it involves a manufacturing enterprise, the assets of which consist of buildings, machinery, cash, raw materials, partly and wholly manufactured goods, which are balanced against liabilities. The important fact is always that a calculation of capital in terms of money is made, whether by modern bookkeeping methods or in any other way, however primitive and crude. Everything is done in terms

of balances: at the beginning of the enterprise an initial balance, before every individual decision a calculation to ascertain its probable profitableness, and at the end a final balance to ascertain how much profit has been made. For instance, the initial balance of a *commenda* transaction would determine an agreed money value of the assets put into it (so far as they were not in money form already), and a final balance would form the estimate on which to base the distribution of profit and loss at the end. So far as the transactions are rational, calculation underlies every single action of the partners. That a really accurate calculation or estimate may not exist, that the procedure is pure guesswork, or simply traditional and conventional, happens even to-day in every form of capitalistic enterprise where the circumstances do not demand strict accuracy. But these are points affecting only the *degree* of rationality of capitalistic acquisition.

For the purpose of this conception all that matters is that an actual adaptation of economic action to a comparison of money income with money expenses takes place, no matter how primitive the form. Now in this sense capitalism and capitalistic enterprises, even with a considerable rationalization of capitalistic calculation, have existed in all civilized countries of the earth, so far as economic documents permit us to judge. In China, India, Babylon, Egypt, Mediterranean antiquity, and the Middle Ages, as well as in modern times. These were not merely isolated ventures, but economic enterprises which were entirely dependent on the continual renewal of capitalistic undertakings, and even continuous operations. However, trade especially was for a long time not continuous like our own, but consisted essentially in a series of individual undertakings. Only gradually did the activities of even the large merchants acquire an inner cohesion (with branch organizations, etc.). In any case, the capitalistic enterprise and the capitalistic entrepreneur, not only as occasional but as regular entrepreneurs, are very old and were very widespread.

Now, however, the Occident has developed capitalism both to a quantitative extent, and (carrying this quantitative development) in types, forms, and directions which have never existed elsewhere. All over the world there have been merchants, wholesale and retail, local and engaged in foreign trade. Loans of all kinds have been made, and there have been banks with the most various functions, at least comparable to ours of, say, the sixteenth century. Sea loans, *commenda,* and transactions and associations similar to the *Kommanditgesellschaft,* have all been widespread, even as continuous businesses. Whenever money finances of public bodies have existed, money-lenders have appeared, as in Babylon, Hellas, India, China, Rome. They have financed wars and piracy, contracts and building operations of all sorts. In overseas policy they have functioned as colonial entrepreneurs, as planters with slaves, or directly or indirectly forced labour, and have farmed domains, offices, and, above all, taxes. They have financed party leaders in elections and *condottieri* in civil wars. And, finally, they have been speculators in chances for pecuniary gain of all kinds. This kind of entrepreneur, the capitalistic adventurer, has existed everywhere. With the exception of trade and credit and banking transactions, their activities were predominantly of an irrational and speculative character, or directed to acquisition by force, above all the acquisition of booty, whether directly in war or in the form of continuous fiscal booty by exploitation of subjects.

The capitalism of promoters, large-scale speculators, concession hunters, and much modern financial capitalism even in peace time, but, above all, the capitalism especially concerned with exploiting wars, bears this stamp even in modern Western countries, and some, but only some, parts of large-scale international trade are closely related to it, to-day as always.

But in modern times the Occident has developed, in addition to this, a very different form of capitalism which has appeared nowhere else: the rational capitalistic organization of (formally) free labour. Only suggestions of it are found elsewhere. Even the organization of unfree labour reached a considerable degree of rationality only on plantations and to a very limited extent in the *Ergasteria* of antiquity. In the manors, manorial workshops, and domestic industries on estates with serf labour it was probably somewhat less developed. Even real domestic industries with free labour have definitely been proved to have existed in only a few isolated cases outside the Occident. The frequent use of day labourers led in a very few cases—especially State monopolies, which are, however, very different from modern industrial organization—to manufacturing organizations, but never to a rational organization of apprenticeship in the handicrafts like that of our Middle Ages.

Rational industrial organization, attuned to a regular market, and neither to political nor irrationally speculative opportunities for profit, is not, however, the only peculiarity of Western capitalism. The modern rational organization of the capitalistic enterprise would not have been possible without two other important factors in its development: the separation of business from the household, which completely dominates modern economic life, and closely connected with it, rational book-keeping. A spatial separation of places of work from those

of residence exists elsewhere, as in the Oriental bazaar and in the *ergasteria* of other cultures. The development of capitalistic associations with their own accounts is also found in the Far East, the Near East, and in antiquity. But compared to the modern independence of business enterprises, those are only small beginnings. The reason for this was particularly that the indispensable requisites for this independence, our rational business book-keeping and our legal separation of corporate from personal property, were entirely lacking, or had only begun to develop. The tendency everywhere else was for acquisitive enterprises to arise as parts of a royal or manorial *household* (of the *oikos*), which is, as Rodbertus has perceived, with all its superficial similarity, a fundamentally different, even opposite, development.

However, all these peculiarities of Western capitalism have derived their significance in the last analysis only from their association with the capitalistic organization of labour. Even what is generally called commercialization, the development of negotiable securities and the rationalization of speculation, the exchanges, etc., is connected with it. For without the rational capitalistic organization of labour, all this, so far as it was possible at all, would have nothing like the same significance, above all for the social structure and all the specific problems of the modern Occident connected with it. Exact calculation—the basis of everything else—is only possible on a basis of free labour.

And just as, or rather because, the world has known no rational organization of labour outside the modern Occident, it has known no rational socialism. Of course, there has been civic economy, a civic food-supply policy, mercantilism and welfare policies of princes, rationing, regulation of economic life, protectionism, and *laissez-faire* theories (as in China). The world has also known socialistic and communistic experiments of various sorts: family, religious, or military communism, State socialism (in Egypt), monopolistic cartels, and consumers' organizations. But although there have everywhere been civic market privileges, companies, guilds, and all sorts of legal differences between town and country, the concept of the citizen has not existed outside the Occident, and that of the bourgeoisie outside the modern Occident. Similarly, the proletariat as a class could not exist, because there was no rational organization of free labour under regular discipline. Class struggles between creditor and debtor classes; landowners and the landless, serfs, or tenants; trading interests and consumers or landlords, have existed everywhere in various combinations. But even the Western mediæval struggles between putters-out and their workers exist elsewhere only in beginnings. The modern conflict of the large-scale industrial entrepreneur and free-wage labourers was entirely lacking. And thus there could be no such problems as those of socialism.

Hence in a universal history of culture the central problem for us is not, in the last analysis, even from a purely economic view-point, the development of capitalistic activity as such, differing in different cultures only in form: the adventurer type, or capitalism in trade, war, politics, or administration as sources of gain. It is rather the origin of this sober bourgeois capitalism with its rational organization of free labour. Or in terms of cultural history, the problem is that of the origin of the Western bourgeois class and of its peculiarities, a problem which is certainly closely connected with that of the origin of the capitalistic organization of labour, but is not quite the same thing. For the bourgeois as a class existed prior to the development of the peculiar modern form of capitalism, though, it is true, only in the Western hemisphere.

Now the peculiar modern Western form of capitalism has been, at first sight, strongly influenced by the development of technical possibilities. Its rationality is to-day essentially dependent on the calculability of the most important technical factors. But this means fundamentally that it is dependent on the peculiarities of modern science, especially the natural sciences based on mathematics and exact and rational experiment. On the other hand, the development of these sciences and of the technique resting upon them now receives important stimulation from these capitalistic interests in its practical economic application. It is true that the origin of Western science cannot be attributed to such interests. Calculation, even with decimals, and algebra have been carried on in India, where the decimal system was invented. But it was only made use of by developing capitalism in the West, while in India it led to no modern arithmetic or book-keeping. Neither was the origin of mathematics and mechanics determined by capitalistic interests. But the *technical* utilization of scientific knowledge, so important for the living conditions of the mass of people, was certainly encouraged by economic considerations, which were extremely favourable to it in the Occident. But this encouragement was derived from the peculiarities of the social structure of the Occident. We must hence ask, from *what* parts of that structure was it derived, since not all of them have been of equal importance?

Among those of undoubted importance are the rational structures of law and of administration. For modern rational capitalism has need, not only of the technical means of production, but of a calculable legal system and of administration in terms of formal rules. Without it adventurous and speculative trading capitalism and all sorts of politically determined capitalisms are possible, but no rational enterprise under individual initiative, with fixed capital and certainty of calculations. Such a legal system and such administration have been available for economic activity in a comparative state of legal and formalistic perfection only in the Occident. We must hence inquire where that law came from. Among other circumstances, capitalistic interests have in turn undoubtedly also helped, but by no means alone nor even principally, to prepare the way for the pre-dominance in law and administration of a class of jurists specially trained in rational law. But these interests did not themselves create that law. Quite different forces were at work in this development. And why did not the capitalistic interests do the same in China or India? Why did not the scientific, the artistic, the political, or the economic development there enter upon that path of rationalization which is peculiar to the Occident?

For in all the above cases it is a question of the specific and peculiar rationalism of Western culture. Now by this term very different things may be understood, as the following discussion will repeatedly show. There is, for example, rationalization of mystical contemplation, that is of an attitude which, viewed from other departments of life, is specifically irrational, just as much as there are rationalizations of economic life, of technique, of scientific research, of military training, of law and administration. Furthermore, each one of these fields may be rationalized in terms of very different ultimate values and ends, and what is rational from one point of view may well be irrational from another. Hence rationalizations of the most varied character have existed in various departments of life and in all areas of culture. To characterize their differences from the view-point of cultural history it is necessary to know what departments are rationalized, and in what direction. It is hence our first concern to work out and to explain genetically the special peculiarity of Occidental rationalism, and within this field that of the modern Occidental form. Every such attempt at explanation must, recognizing the fundamental importance of the economic factor, above all take account of the economic conditions. But at the same time the opposite correlation must not be left out of consideration. For though the development of economic rationalism is partly dependent on rational technique and law, it is at the same time determined by the ability and disposition of men to adopt certain types of practical rational conduct. When these types have been obstructed by spiritual obstacles, the development of rational economic conduct has also met serious inner resistance. The magical and religious forces, and the ethical ideas of duty based upon them, have in the past always been among the most important formative influences on conduct. In the studies collected here we shall be concerned with these forces.

Two older essays have been placed at the beginning which attempt, at one important point, to approach the side of the problem which is generally most difficult to grasp: the influence of certain religious ideas on the development of an economic spirit, or the *ethos* of an economic system. In this case we are dealing with the connection of the spirit of modern economic life with the rational ethics of ascetic Protestantism. Thus we treat here only one side of the causal chain. The later studies on the Economic Ethics of the World Religions attempt, in the form of a survey of the relations of the most important religions to economic life and to the social stratification of their environment, to follow out both causal relationships, so far as it is necessary in order to find points of comparison with the Occidental development. For only in this way is it possible to attempt a causal evaluation of those elements of the economic ethics of the Western religions which differentiate them from others, with a hope of attaining even a tolerable degree of approximation. Hence these studies do not claim to be complete analyses of cultures, however brief. On the contrary, in every culture they quite deliberately emphasize the elements in which it differs from Western civilization. They are, hence, definitely oriented to the problems which seem important for the understanding of Western culture from *this* view-point. With our object in view, any other procedure did not seem possible. But to avoid misunderstanding we must here lay special emphasis on the limitation of our purpose.

In another respect the uninitiated at least must be warned against exaggerating the importance of these investigations. The Sinologist, the Indologist, the Semitist, or the Egyptologist, will of course find no facts unknown to him. We only hope that he will find nothing definitely wrong in points that are essential. How far it has been possible to come as near this ideal as a non-specialist is able to do, the author cannot know. It is quite evident that anyone who is forced to rely on translations, and furthermore on the use and evaluation of monumental, documentary, or literary sources, has to rely himself on a specialist literature which is often highly controversial, and the merits of which he is unable to judge accurately. Such a writer must make modest claims for the value of his work. All the more

so since the number of available translations of real sources (that is, inscriptions and documents) is especially for China, still very small in comparison with what exists and is important. From all this follows the definitely provisional character of these studies, and especially of the parts dealing with Asia. Only the specialist is entitled to a final judgment. And, naturally, it is only because expert studies with this special purpose and from this particular view-point have not hitherto been made, that the present ones have been written at all. They are destined to be superseded in a much more important sense than this can be said, as it can be, of all scientific work. But however objectionable it may be, such trespassing on other special fields cannot be avoided in comparative work. But one must take the consequences by resigning oneself to considerable doubts regarding the degree of one's success.

Fashion and the zeal of the *literati* would have us think that the specialist can to-day be spared, or degraded to a position subordinate to that of the seer. Almost all sciences owe something to dilettantes, often very valuable view-points But dilettantism as a leading principle would be the end of science. He who yearns for seeing should go to the cinema, though it will be offered to him copiously to-day in literary form in the present field of investigation also. Nothing is farther from the intent of these thoroughly serious studies than such an attitude. And, I might add, whoever wants a sermon should go to a conventicle. The question of the relative value of the cultures which are compared here will not receive a single word. It is true that the path of human destiny cannot but appall him who surveys a section of it. But he will do well to keep his small personal commentaries to himself, as one does at the sight of the sea or of majestic mountains, unless he knows himself to be called and gifted to give them expression in artistic or prophetic form. In most other cases the voluminous talk about intuition does nothing but conceal a lack of perspective toward the object, which merits the same judgment as a similar lack of perspective toward men.

Some justification is needed for the fact that ethnographical material has not been utilized to anything like the extent which the value of its contributions naturally demands in any really thorough investigation, especially of Asiatic religions. This limitation has not only been imposed because human powers of work are restricted. This omission has also seemed to be permissible because we are here necessarily dealing with the religious ethics of the classes which were the culture-bearers of their respective countries. We are concerned with the influence which *their* conduct has had. Now it is quite true that this can only be completely known in all its details when the facts from ethnography and folk-lore have been compared with it. Hence we must expressly admit and emphasize that this is a gap to which the ethnographer will legitimately object. I hope to contribute something to the closing of this gap in a systematic study of the Sociology of Religion. But such an undertaking would have transcended the limits of this investigation with its closely circumscribed purpose. It has been necessary to be content with bringing out the points of comparison with our Occidental religions as well as possible.

Finally, we may make a reference to the *anthropological* side of the problem. When we find again and again that, even in departments of life apparently mutually independent, certain types of rationalization have developed in the Occident, and only there, it would be natural to suspect that the most important reason lay in difference of heredity. The author admits that he is inclined to think the importance of biological heredity very great. But in spite of the notable achievements of anthropological research, I see up to the present no way of exactly or even approximately measuring either the extent or, above all, the form of its influence on the development investigated here. It must be one of the tasks of sociological and historical investigation first to analyse all the influences and causal relationships which can satisfactorily be explained in terms of reactions to environmental conditions. Only then, and when comparative racial neurology and psychology shall have progressed beyond their present and in many ways very promising beginnings, can we hope for even the probability of a satisfactory answer to that problem. In the meantime that condition seems to me not to exist, and an appeal to heredity would therefore involve a premature renunciation of the possibility of knowledge attainable now, and would shift the problem to factors (at present) still unknown.

*   *   *

We thus take as our starting-point in the investigation of the relationship between the old Protestant ethic and the spirit of capitalism the works of Calvin, of Calvinism, and the other Puritan sects. But it is not to be understood that we expect to find any of the founders or representatives of these religious movements considering the promotion of what we have called the spirit of capitalism as in any sense the end of his lifework. We cannot well maintain that the pursuit of worldly goods, conceived as an end in itself, was to any of them of positive ethical value. Once and for all it must be remembered that programmes

of ethical reform never were at the centre of interest for any of the religious reformers (among whom, for our purposes, we must include men like Menno, George Fox, and Wesley). They were not the founders of societies for ethical culture nor the proponents of humanitarian projects for social reform or cultural ideals. The salvation of the soul and that alone was the centre of their life and work. Their ethical ideals and the practical results of their doctrines were all based on that alone, and were the consequences of purely religious motives. We shall thus have to admit that the cultural consequences of the Reformation were to a great extent, perhaps in the particular aspects with which we are dealing predominantly, unforeseen and even unwished for results of the labours of the reformers. They were often far removed from or even in contradiction to all that they themselves thought to attain.

The following study may thus perhaps in a modest way form a contribution to the understanding of the manner in which ideas become effective forces in history. In order, however, to avoid any misunderstanding of the sense in which any such effectiveness of purely ideal motives is claimed at all, I may perhaps be permitted a few remarks in conclusion to this introductory discussion.

In such a study, it may at once be definitely stated, no attempt is made to evaluate the ideas of the Reformation in any sense, whether it concern their social or their religious worth. We have continually to deal with aspects of the Reformation which must appear to the truly religious consciousness as incidental and even superficial. For we are merely attempting to clarify the part which religious forces have played in forming the developing web of our specifically worldly modern culture, in the complex interaction of innumerable different historical factors. We are thus inquiring only to what extent certain characteristic features of this culture can be imputed to the influence of the Reformation. At the same time we must free ourselves from the idea that it is possible to deduce the Reformation, as a historically necessary result, from certain economic changes. Countless historical circumstances, which cannot be reduced to any economic law, and are not susceptible of economic explanation of any sort, especially purely political processes, had to concur in order that the newly created Churches should survive at all.

On the other hand, however, we have no intention whatever of maintaining such a foolish and doctrinaire thesis as that the spirit of capitalism (in the provisional sense of the term explained above) could only have arisen as the result of certain effects of the Reformation, or even that capitalism as an economic system is a creation of the Reformation. In itself, the fact that certain important forms of capitalistic business organization are known to be considerably older than the Reformation is a sufficient refutation of such a claim. On the contrary, we only wish to ascertain whether and to what extent religious forces have taken part in the qualitative formation and the quantitative expansion of that spirit over the world. Furthermore, what concrete aspects of our capitalistic culture can be traced to them. In view of the tremendous confusion of interdependent influences between the material basis, the forms of social and political organization, and the ideas current in the time of the Reformation, we can only proceed by investigating whether and at what points certain correlations between forms of religious belief and practical ethics can be worked out. At the same time we shall as far as possible clarify the manner and the general *direction* in which, by virtue of those relationships, the religious movements have influenced the development of material culture. Only when this has been determined with reasonable accuracy can the attempt be made to estimate to what extent the historical development of modern culture can be attributed to those religious forces and to what extent to others.

*   *   *

Let us now try to clarify the points in which the Puritan idea of the calling and the premium it placed upon ascetic conduct was bound directly to influence the development of a capitalistic way of life. As we have seen, this asceticism turned with all its force against one thing: the spontaneous enjoyment of life and all it had to offer. This is perhaps most characteristically brought out in the struggle over the *Book of Sports* which James I and Charles I made into law expressly as a means of counteracting Puritanism, and which the latter ordered to be read from all the pulpits. The fanatical opposition of the Puritans to the ordinances of the King, permitting certain popular amusements on Sunday outside of Church hours by law, was not only explained by the disturbance of the Sabbath rest, but also by resentment against the intentional diversion from the ordered life of the saint, which it caused. And, on his side, the King's threats of severe punishment for every attack on the legality of those sports were motivated by his purpose of breaking the anti-authoritarian ascetic tendency of Puritanism, which was so dangerous to the State. The feudal and monarchical forces protected the pleasure seekers against the rising middle-class morality and the anti-authoritarian ascetic conventicles, just as to-day capitalistic society tends to protect those willing to work

against the class morality of the proletariat and the anti-authoritarian trade union.

As against this the Puritans upheld their decisive characteristic, the principle of ascetic conduct. For otherwise the Puritan aversion to sport, even for the Quakers, was by no means simply one of principle. Sport was accepted if it served a rational purpose, that of recreation necessary for physical efficiency. But as a means for the spontaneous expression of undisciplined impulses, it was under suspicion; and in so far as it became purely a means of enjoyment, or awakened pride, raw instincts or the irrational gambling instinct, it was of course strictly condemned. Impulsive enjoyment of life, which leads away from work in a calling and from religion, was as such the enemy of rational asceticism, whether in the form of seigneurial sports, or the enjoyment of the dance-hall or the public-house of the common man.

Its attitude was thus suspicious and often hostile to the aspects of culture without any immediate religious value. It is not, however, true that the ideals of Puritanism implied a solemn, narrow-minded contempt of culture. Quite the contrary is the case at least for science, with the exception of the hatred of Scholasticism. Moreover, the great men of the Puritan movement were thoroughly steeped in the culture of the Renaissance. The sermons of the Presbyterian divines abound with classical allusions, and even the Radicals, although they objected to it, were not ashamed to display that kind of learning in theological polemics. Perhaps no country was ever so full of graduates as New England in the first generation of its existence. The satire of their opponents, such as, for instance, Butler's *Hudibras,* also attacks primarily the pedantry and highly trained dialectics of the Puritans. This is partially due to the religious valuation of knowledge which followed from their attitude to the Catholic *fides implicita.*

But the situation is quite different when one looks at non-scientific literature, and especially the fine arts. Here asceticism descended like a frost on the life of "Merrie old England." And not only worldly merriment felt its effect. The Puritan's ferocious hatred of everything which smacked of superstition, of all survivals of magical or sacramental salvation, applied to the Christmas festivities and the May Pole and all spontaneous religious art. That there was room in Holland for a great, often uncouthly realistic art proves only how far from completely the authoritarian moral discipline of that country was able to counteract the influence of the court and the regents (a class of *rentiers*), and also the joy in life of the parvenu bourgeoisie, after the short supremacy of the Calvinistic theocracy had been transformed into a moderate national Church, and with it Calvinism had perceptibly lost in its power of ascetic influence.

The theatre was obnoxious to the Puritans, and with the strict exclusion of the erotic and of nudity from the realm of toleration, a radical view of either literature or art could not exist. The conceptions of idle talk, of superfluities, and of vain ostentation, all designations of an irrational attitude without objective purpose, thus not ascetic, and especially not serving the glory of God, but of man, were always at hand to serve in deciding in favour of sober utility as against any artistic tendencies. This was especially true in the case of decoration of the person, for instance clothing. That powerful tendency toward uniformity of life, which to-day so immensely aids the capitalistic interest in the standardization of production had its ideal foundations in the repudiation of all idolatry of the flesh.

Of course we must not forget that Puritanism included a world of contradictions, and that the instinctive sense of eternal greatness in art was certainly stronger among its leaders than in the atmosphere of the Cavaliers. Moreover, a unique genius like Rembrandt, however little his conduct may have been acceptable to God in the eyes of the Puritans, was very strongly influenced in the character of his work by his religious environment. But that does not alter the picture as a whole. In so far as the development of the Puritan tradition could, and in part did, lead to a powerful spiritualization of personality, it was a decided benefit to literature. But for the most part that benefit only accrued to later generations.

Although we cannot here enter upon a discussion of the influence of Puritanism in all these directions, we should call attention to the fact that the toleration of pleasure in cultural goods, which contributed to purely æsthetic or athletic enjoyment, certainly always ran up against one characteristic limitation: they must not cost anything. Man is only a trustee of the goods which have come to him through God's grace. He must, like the servant in the parable, give an account of every penny entrusted to him, and it is at least hazardous to spend any of it for a purpose which does not serve the glory of God but only one's own enjoyment. What person, who keeps his eyes open, has not met representatives of this view-point even in the present? The idea of a man's duty to his possessions, to which he subordinates himself as an obedient steward, or even as an acquisitive machine, bears with chilling weight on his life. The greater the possessions the heavier, if the ascetic attitude toward life stands the test, the feeling of responsibility for them, for holding them undiminished for the glory of God and in-

creasing them by restless effort. The origin of this type of life also extends in certain roots, like so many aspects of the spirit of capitalism, back into the Middle Ages. But it was in the ethic of ascetic Protestantism that it first found a consistent ethical foundation. Its significance for the development of capitalism is obvious.

This worldly Protestant asceticism, as we may recapitulate up to this point, acted powerfully against the spontaneous enjoyment of possessions; it restricted consumption, especially of luxuries. On the other hand, it has the psychological effect of freeing the acquisition of goods from the inhibitions of traditionalistic ethics. It broke the bonds of the impulse of acquisition in that it not only legalized it, but (in the sense discussed) looked upon it as directly willed by God. The campaign against the temptations of the flesh, and the dependence on external things, was, as besides the Puritans the great Quaker apologist Barclay expressly says, not a struggle against the rational acquisition, but against the irrational use of wealth.

But this irrational use was exemplified in the outward forms of luxury which their code condemned as idolatry of the flesh, however natural they had appeared to the feudal mind. On the other hand, they approved the rational and utilitarian uses of wealth which were willed by God for the needs of the individual and the community. They did not wish to impose mortification on the man of wealth, but the use of his means for necessary and practical things. The idea of comfort characteristically limits the extent of ethically permissible expenditures. It is naturally no accident that the development of a manner of living consistent with that idea may be observed earliest and most clearly among the most consistent representatives of this whole attitude toward life. Over against the glitter and ostentation of feudal magnificence which, resting on an unsound economic basis, prefers a sordid elegance to a sober simplicity, they set the clean and solid comfort of the middle-class home as an ideal.

On the side of the production of private wealth, asceticism condemned both dishonesty and impulsive avarice. What was condemned as covetousness, Mammonism, etc., was the pursuit of riches for their own sake. For wealth in itself was a temptation. But here asceticism was the power "which ever seeks the good but ever creates evil"; what was evil in its sense was possession and its temptations. For, in conformity with the Old Testament and in analogy to the ethical valuation of good works, asceticism looked upon the pursuit of wealth as an end in itself as highly reprehensible; but the attainment of it as a fruit of labour in a calling was a sign of God's blessing. And even more important:

the religious valuation of restless, continuous, systematic work in a worldly calling, as the highest means to asceticism, and at the same time the surest and most evident proof of rebirth and genuine faith, must have been the most powerful conceivable lever for the expansion of that attitude toward life which we have here called the spirit of capitalism.

When the limitation of consumption is combined with this release of acquisitive activity, the inevitable practical result is obvious: accumulation of capital through ascetic compulsion to save. The restraints which were imposed upon the consumption of wealth naturally served to increase it by making possible the productive investment of capital. How strong this influence was is not, unfortunately, susceptible of exact statistical demonstration. In New England the connection is so evident that it did not escape the eye of so discerning a historian as Doyle. But also in Holland, which was really only dominated by strict Calvinism for seven years, the greater simplicity of life in the more seriously religious circles, in combination with great wealth, led to an excessive propensity to accumulation.

That, furthermore, the tendency which has existed everywhere and at all times, being quite strong in Germany to-day, for middle-class fortunes to be absorbed into the nobility, was necessarily checked by the Puritan antipathy to the feudal way of life, is evident. English Mercantilist writers of the seventeenth century attributed the superiority of Dutch capital to English to the circumstance that newly acquired wealth there did not regularly seek investment in land. Also, since it is not simply a question of the purchase of land, it did not there seek to transfer itself to feudal habits of life, and thereby to remove itself from the possibility of capitalistic investment. The high esteem for agriculture as a peculiarly important branch of activity, also especially consistent with piety, which the Puritans shared, applied (for instance in Baxter) not to the landlord, but to the yeoman and farmer, in the eighteenth century not to the squire, but the rational cultivator. Through the whole of English society in the time since the seventeenth century goes the conflict between the squirearchy, the representatives of "merrie old England", and the Puritan circles of widely varying social influence. Both elements, that of an unspoiled naïve joy of life, and of a strictly regulated, reserved self-control, and conventional ethical conduct are even to-day combined to form the English national character. Similarly, the early history of the North American colonies is dominated by the sharp contrast of the adventurers, who wanted to set up

plantations with the labour of indentured servants, and live as feudal lords, and the specifically middle-class outlook of the Puritans.

As far as the influence of the Puritan outlook extended, under all circumstances—and this is, of course, much more important than the mere encouragement of capital accumulation—it favoured the development of a rational bourgeois economic life; it was the most important, and above all the only consistent influence in the development of that life. It stood at the cradle of the modern economic man.

To be sure, these Puritanical ideals tended to give way under excessive pressure from the temptations of wealth, as the Puritans themselves knew very well. With great regularity we find the most genuine adherents of Puritanism among the classes which were rising from a lowly status, the small bourgeois and farmers, while the *beati possidentes*, even among Quakers, are often found tending to repudiate the old ideals. It was the same fate which again and again befell the predecessor of this worldly asceticism, the monastic asceticism of the Middle Ages. In the latter case, when rational economic activity had worked out its full effects by strict regulation of conduct and limitation of consumption, the wealth accumulated either succumbed directly to the nobility, as in the time before the Reformation, or monastic discipline threatened to break down, and one of the numerous reformations became necessary.

In fact the whole history of monasticism is in a certain sense the history of a continual struggle with the problem of the secularizing influence of wealth. The same is true on a grand scale of the worldly asceticism of Puritanism. The great revival of Methodism, which preceded the expansion of English industry toward the end of the eighteenth century, may well be compared with such a monastic reform. We may hence quote here a passage from John Wesley himself which might well serve as a motto for everything which has been said above. For it shows that the leaders of these ascetic movements understood the seemingly paradoxical relationships which we have here analysed perfectly well, and in the same sense that we have given them. He wrote:

I fear, wherever riches have increased, the essence of religion has decreased in the same proportion. Therefore I do not see how it is possible, in the nature of things, for any revival of true religion to continue long. For religion must necessarily produce both industry and frugality, and these cannot but produce riches. But as riches increase, so will pride, anger, and love of the world in all its branches. How then is it possible that Methodism, that is, a religion of the heart, though it flourishes now as a green bay tree, should continue in this state? For the Methodists in every place grow diligent and frugal; consequently they increase in goods. Hence they proportionately increase in pride, in anger, in the desire of the flesh, the desire of the eyes, and the pride of life. So, although the form of religion remains, the spirit is swiftly vanishing away. Is there no way to prevent this—this continual decay of pure religion? We ought not to prevent people from being diligent and frugal; *we must exhort all Christians to gain all they can, and to save all they can; that is, in effect, to grow rich.*

There follows the advice that those who gain all they can and save all they can should also give all they can, so that they will grow in grace and lay up a treasure in heaven. It is clear that Wesley here expresses, even in detail, just what we have been trying to point out.

As Wesley here says, the full economic effect of those great religious movements, whose significance for economic development lay above all in their ascetic educative influence, generally came only after the peak of the purely religious enthusiasm was past. Then the intensity of the search for the Kingdom of God commenced gradually to pass over into sober economic virtue; the religious roots died out slowly, giving way to utilitarian worldliness. Then, as Dowden puts it, as in *Robinson Crusoe*, the isolated economic man who carries on missionary activities on the side takes the place of the lonely spiritual search for the Kingdom of Heaven of Bunyan's pilgrim, hurrying through the marketplace of Vanity.

When later the principle "to make the most of both worlds" became dominant in the end, as Dowden has remarked, a good conscience simply became one of the means of enjoying a comfortable bourgeois life, as is well expressed in the German proverb about the soft pillow. What the great religious epoch of the seventeenth century bequeathed to its utilitarian successor was, however, above all an amazingly good, we may even say a pharisaically good, conscience in the acquisition of money, so long as it took place legally. Every trace of the *deplacere vix potest* has disappeared.

A specifically bourgeois economic ethic had grown up. With the consciousness of standing in the fullness of God's grace and being visibly blessed by Him, the bourgeois business man, as long as he remained within the bounds of formal correctness, as long as his moral conduct was spotless and the use to which he put his wealth was not objectionable, could follow his pecuniary interests as he would and feel that he was fulfilling a duty in doing so. The power of religious asceticism provided him in addition with sober, conscientious, and unusually industrious workmen, who clung to their work as to a life purpose willed by God.

Finally, it gave him the comforting assurance that the unequal distribution of the goods of this world was a special dispensation of Divine Providence, which in these differences, as in particular grace, pursued secret ends unknown to men. Calvin himself had made the much-quoted statement that only when the people, i.e., the mass of labourers and craftsmen, were poor did they remain obedient to God. In the Netherlands (Pieter de la Court and others), that had been secularized to the effect that the mass of men only labour when necessity forces them to do so. This formulation of a leading idea of capitalistic economy later emerged into the current theories of the productivity of low wages. Here also, with the dying out of the religious root, the utilitarian interpretation crept in unnoticed, in the line of development which we have again and again observed.

Mediæval ethics not only tolerated begging but actually glorified it in the mendicant orders. Even secular beggars, since they gave the person of means opportunity for good works through giving alms, were sometimes considered an estate and treated as such. Even the Anglican social ethic of the Stuarts was very close to this attitude. It remained for Puritan Asceticism to take part in the severe English Poor Relief Legislation which fundamentally changed the situation. And it could do that, because the Protestant sects and the strict Puritan communities actually did not know any begging in their own midst.

On the other hand, seen from the side of the workers, the Zinzendorf branch of Pietism, for instance, glorified the loyal worker who did not seek acquisition, but lived according to the apostolic model, and was thus endowed with the *charisma* of the disciples. Similar ideas had originally been prevalent among the Baptists in an even more radical form.

Now naturally the whole ascetic literature of almost all denominations is saturated with the idea that faithful labour, even at low wages, on the part of those whom life offers no other opportunities, is highly pleasing to God. In this respect, Protestant Asceticism added in itself nothing new. But it not only deepened this idea most powerfully, it also created the force which was alone decisive for its effectiveness: the psychological sanction of it through the conception of this labour as a calling, as the best, often in the last analysis the only means of attaining certainty of grace. And on the other hand it legalized the exploitation of this specific willingness to work, in that it also interpreted the employer's business activity as a calling. It is obvious how powerfully the exclusive search for the Kingdom of God only through the fulfilment of duty in the calling, and the strict asceticism which Church discipline naturally imposed, especially on the propertyless classes, was bound to affect the productivity of labour in the capitalistic sense of the word. The treatment of labour as a calling became as characteristic of the modern worker as the corresponding attitude toward acquisition of the business man. It was a perception of this situation, new at his time, which caused so able an observer as Sir William Petty to attribute the economic power of Holland in the seventeenth century to the fact that the very numerous dissenters in that country (Calvinists and Baptists) "are for the most part thinking, sober men, and such as believe that Labour and Industry is their duty towards God."

Calvinism opposed organic social organization in the fiscal-monopolistic form which it assumed in Anglicanism under the Stuarts, especially in the conceptions of Laud, this alliance of Church and State with the monopolists on the basis of a Christian-social ethical foundation. Its leaders were universally among the most passionate opponents of this type of politically privileged commercial, putting-out, and colonial capitalism. Over against it they placed the individualistic motives of rational legal acquisition by virtue of one's own ability and initiative. And, while the politically privileged monopoly industries in England all disappeared in short order, this attitude played a large and decisive part in the development of the industries which grew up in spite of and against the authority of the State. The Puritans (Prynne, Parker) repudiated all connection with the large-scale capitalistic courtiers and projectors as an ethically suspicious class. On the other hand, they took pride in their own superior middle-class business morality, which formed the true reason for the persecutions to which they were subjected on the part of those circles. Defoe proposed to win the battle against dissent by boycotting bank credit and withdrawing deposits. The difference of the two types of capitalistic attitude went to a very large extent hand in hand with religious differences. The opponents of the Nonconformists, even in the eighteenth century, again and again ridiculed them for personifying the spirit of shopkeepers, and for having ruined the ideals of old England. Here also lay the difference of the Puritan economic ethic from the Jewish; and contemporaries (Prynne) knew well that the former and not the latter was the bourgeois capitalistic ethic.

One of the fundamental elements of the spirit of modern capitalism, and not only of that but of all modern culture: rational conduct on the basis of the idea of the calling, was born—that is what

this discussion has sought to demonstrate—from the spirit of Christian asceticism. One has only to re-read the passage from Franklin, quoted at the beginning of this essay, in order to see that the essential elements of the attitude which was there called the spirit of capitalism are the same as what we have just shown to be the content of the Puritan worldly asceticism, only without the religious basis, which by Franklin's time had died away. The idea that modern labour has an ascetic character is of course not new. Limitation to specialized work, with a renunciation of the Faustian universality of man which it involves, is a condition of any valuable work in the modern world; hence deeds and renunciation inevitably condition each other to-day. This fundamentally ascetic trait of middle-class life, if it attempts to be a way of life at all, and not simply the absence of any, was what Goethe wanted to teach, at the height of his wisdom, in the *Wanderjahren,* and in the end which he gave to the life of his *Faust.* For him the realization meant a renunciation, a departure from an age of full and beautiful humanity, which can no more be repeated in the course of our cultural development than can the flower of the Athenian culture of antiquity.

The Puritan wanted to work in a calling; we are forced to do so. For when asceticism was carried out of monastic cells into everyday life, and began to dominate worldly morality, it did its part in building the tremendous cosmos of the modern economic order. This order is now bound to the technical and economic conditions of machine production which to-day determine the lives of all the individuals who are born into this mechanism, not only those directly concerned with economic acquisition, with irresistible force. Perhaps it will so determine them until the last ton of fossilized coal is burnt. In Baxter's view the care for external goods should only lie on the shoulders of the "saint like a light cloak, which can be thrown aside at any moment." But fate decreed that the cloak should become an iron cage.

Since asceticism undertook to remodel the world and to work out its ideals in the world, material goods have gained an increasing and finally an inexorable power over the lives of men as at no previous period in history. To-day the spirit of religious asceticism—whether finally, who knows?—has escaped from the cage. But victorious capitalism, since it rests on mechanical foundations, needs its support no longer. The rosy blush of its laughing heir, the Enlightenment, seems also to be irretrievably fading, and the idea of duty in one's calling prowls about in our lives like the ghost of dead religious beliefs. Where the fulfilment of the calling cannot directly be related to the highest spiritual and cultural values, or when, on the other hand, it need not be felt simply as economic compulsion, the individual generally abandons the attempt to justify it at all. In the field of its highest development, in the United States, the pursuit of wealth, stripped of its religious and ethical meaning, tends to become associated with purely mundane passions, which often actually give it the character of sport.

No one knows who will live in this cage in the future, or whether at the end of this tremendous development entirely new prophets will arise, or there will be a great rebirth of old ideas and ideals, or, if neither, mechanized petrification, embellished with a sort of convulsive self-importance. For of the last stage of this cultural development, it might well be truly said: "Specialists without spirit, sensualists without heart; this nullity imagines that it has attained a level of civilization never before achieved."

But this brings us to the world of judgments of value and of faith, with which this purely historical discussion need not be burdened. The next task would be rather to show the significance of ascetic rationalism, which has only been touched in the foregoing sketch, for the content of practical social ethics, thus for the types of organization and the functions of social groups from the conventicle to the State. Then its relations to humanistic rationalism, its ideals of life and cultural influence; further to the development of philosophical and scientific empiricism, to technical development and to spiritual ideas would have to be analysed. Then its historical development from the mediæval beginnings of worldly asceticism to its dissolution into pure utilitarianism would have to be traced out through all the areas of ascetic religion. Only then could the quantitative cultural significance of ascetic Protestantism in its relation to the other plastic elements of modern culture be estimated.

Here we have only attempted to trace the fact and the direction of its influence to their motives in one, though a very important point. But it would also further be necessary to investigate how Protestant Asceticism was in turn influenced in its development and its character by the totality of social conditions, especially economic. The modern man is in general, even with the best will, unable to give religious ideas a significance for culture and national character which they deserve. But it is, of course, not my aim to substitute for a one-sided materialistic an equally one-sided spiritualistic causal interpretation of culture and of history. Each is equally possible, but each, if it does not serve as the preparation, but as the conclusion of an investigation, accomplishes equally little in the interest of historical truth.

3. *On Psychology and History*

BY SIGMUND FREUD

Application

EARLY TRAUMA—Defence—Latency—Outbreak of the Neurosis—Partial return of the repressed material: this was the formula we drew up for the development of a neurosis. Now I will invite the reader to take a step forward and assume that in the history of the human species something happened similar to the events in the life of the individual. That is to say, mankind as a whole also passed through conflicts of a sexual-aggressive nature, which left permanent traces but which were for the most part warded off and forgotten; later, after a long period of latency, they came to life again and created phenomena similar in structure and tendency to neurotic symptoms.

I have, I believe, divined these processes and wish to show that their consequences, which bear a strong resemblance to neurotic symptoms, are the phenomena of religion. Since it can no longer be doubted after the discovery of evolution that mankind had a pre-history, and since this history is unknown (that is to say, forgotten), such a conclusion has almost the significance of an axiom. If

Reprinted from Sigmund Freud, *Moses and Monotheism*, trans. Katherine Jones (New York: Alfred A. Knopf, 1939), pp. 129–48, with the permission of Alfred A. Knopf and The Hogarth Press Ltd.

we should learn that the effective and forgotten traumata relate, here as well as there, to life in the human family, we should greet this information as a highly welcome and unforseen gift which could not have been anticipated from the foregoing discussion.

I have already upheld this thesis a quarter of a century ago, in my book *Totem and Taboo* (1912), and need only repeat what I said there. The argument started from some remarks by Charles Darwin and embraced a suggestion of Atkinson's. It says that in primæval times men lived in small hordes, each under the domination of a strong male. When this was is not known; no point of contact with geological data has been established. It is likely that mankind was not very far advanced in the art of speech. An essential part of the argument is that all primæval men, including, therefore, all our ancestors, underwent the fate I shall now describe.

The story is told in a very condensed way, as if what in reality took centuries to achieve, and during that long time was repeated innumerably, had only happened once. The strong male was the master and father of the whole horde: unlimited in his power, which he used brutally. All females were his property, the wives and daughters in his own horde as well as perhaps also those robbed from other hordes. The fate of the sons was a hard one; if they excited the father's jealousy they were killed or castrated or driven out. They were forced to live in small communities and to provide themselves with wives by robbing them from others. Then one or the other son might succeed in attaining a situation similar to that of the father in the original horde. One favoured position came about in a natural way: it was that of the youngest son who, protected by his mother's love, could profit by his father's advancing years and replace him after his death. An echo of the expulsion of the eldest son, as well as of the favoured position of the youngest, seems to linger in many myths and fairy tales.

The next decisive step towards changing this first kind of "social" organization lies in the following suggestion. The brothers who had been driven out and lived together in a community clubbed together, overcame the father and—according to the custom of those times—all partook of his body. This cannibalism need not shock us; it survived into far later times. The essential point is, however, that we attribute to those primæval people the same feelings and emotions that we have elucidated in the primitives of our own times, our children, by psychoanalytic research. That is to say: they not merely hated and feared their father, but also honoured him as an example to follow; in fact each son wanted to place himself in his father's position. The cannibalistic act thus becomes comprehensible as an attempt to assure one's identification with the father by incorporating a part of him.

It is a reasonable surmise that after the killing of the father a time followed when the brothers quarrelled among themselves for the succession, which each of them wanted to obtain for himself alone. They came to see that these fights were as dangerous as they were futile. This hard-won understanding—as well as the memory of the deed of liberation they had achieved together and the attachment that had grown up among them during the time of their exile—led at last to a union among them, a sort of social contract. Thus there came into being the first form of a social organization accompanied by a renunciation of instinctual gratification; recognition of mutual obligations; institutions declared sacred, which could not be broken—in short the beginnings of morality and law. Each renounced the ideal of gaining for himself the position of father, of possessing his mother or sister. With this the taboo of incest and the law of exogamy came into being. A good part of the power which had become vacant through the father's death passed to the women; the time of the matriarchate followed. The memory of the father lived on during this time of the "brother horde." A strong animal, which perhaps at first was also dreaded, was found as a substitute. Such a choice may seem strange to us, but the gulf which man created later between himself and the animals did not exist for primitive man. Nor does it with our children, whose animal phobias we have been able to explain as dread of the father. The relationship to the totem animal retained the original ambivalency of feeling towards the father. The totem was, on the one hand, the corporeal ancestor and protecting spirit of the clan; he was to be revered and protected. On the other hand, a festival was instituted on which day the same fate was meted out to him as the primæval father had encountered. He was killed and eaten by all the brothers together. (The Totem feast, according to Robertson Smith.) This great day was in reality a feast of triumph to celebrate the victory of the united sons over the father.

Where, in this connection, does religion come in? Totemism, with its worship of a father substitute, the ambivalency towards the father which is evidenced by the totem feast, the institution of remembrance festivals and of laws the breaking of which is punished by death—this totemism, I conclude, may be regarded as the earliest appearance of religion in the history of mankind, and it illustrates the close connection existing from the very beginning of time between social institutions and moral obligations. The further development of religion can be treated here only in a very summary fashion. Without a doubt it proceeded parallel to the cultural development of mankind and the changes in the structure of human social institutions.

The next step forward from totemism is the humanizing of the worshipped being. Human gods, whose origin from the totem is not veiled, take the place previously filled by animals. Either the god is still represented as an animal or at least he bears the countenance of an animal; the totem may become the inseparable companion of the god, or, again, the myth makes the god vanquish just that animal which was nothing but his predecessor. At one period—it is hard to say when—great mother-deities appeared, probably before the male gods, and they were worshipped beside the latter for a long time to come. During that time a great social revolution had taken place. Matriarchy was followed by a restitution of the patriarchal order. The new fathers, it is true, never succeeded to the omnipotence of the primæval father. There were too many of them and they lived in larger communities than the original horde had been; they had to get on with one another and were restricted by social institutions. Probably the mother deities were developed when the matriarchy was being limited, in order to compensate the dethroned mothers. The male gods appear at first as sons by the side of the great mothers; only later do they clearly assume the features of the father. These male gods of polytheism mirror the conditions of patriarchal times. They are numerous, they have to share their authority, and occasionally they obey a higher god. The next step, however, leads us to the topic that interests us here: the return of the one and only father deity whose power is unlimited.

I must admit that this historical survey leaves many a gap and in many points needs further confirmation. Yet whoever declares our reconstruction of primæval history to be fantastic greatly underestimates the richness and the force of the evidence that has gone to make up this reconstruction. Large portions of the past, which are here woven into a whole, are historically proven or even show their traces to this day, such as matriarchal right, totemism and male communities. Others have survived in remarkable replicas. Thus more than one author has been struck by the close resemblance between the rite of Christian Communion—where the believer symbolically incorporates the blood and flesh of his God—and the Totem feast, whose inner meaning it reproduces. Numerous survivals of our forgotten early history are preserved in the legends

and fairy tales of the peoples, and analytic study of the mental life of the child has yielded an unexpectedly rich return by filling up gaps in our knowledge of primæval times. As a contribution towards an understanding of the highly important relation between father and son I need only quote the animal phobias, the fear of being eaten by the father (which seems so strange to the grown mind), and the enormous intensity of the castration complex. There is nothing in our reconstruction that is invented, nothing that is not based on good grounds.

Let us suppose that the presentation here given of primæval history is on the whole credible. Then two elements can be recognized in religious rites and doctrines: on the one hand, fixations on the old family history and survivals of this; on the other hand, reproductions of the past and a return long after of what had been forgotten. It is the latter element that has until now been overlooked and therefore not understood. It will therefore be illustrated here by at least one impressive example.

It is specially worthy of note that every memory returning from the forgotten past does so with great force, produces an incomparably strong influence on the mass of mankind and puts forward an irresistible claim to be believed, against which all logical objections remain powerless—very much like the *credo quia absurdum*. This strange characteristic can only be understood by comparison with the delusions in a psychotic case. It has long been recognized that delusions contain a piece of forgotten truth, which had at its return to put up with being distorted and misunderstood, and that the compulsive conviction appertaining to the delusion emanates from this core of truth and spreads to the errors that enshroud it. Such a kernel of truth—which we might call *historical* truth—must also be conceded to the doctrines of the various religions. They are, it is true, imbued with the character of psychotic symptoms, but as mass phenomena they have escaped the curse of isolation.

No other part of religious history has become so abundantly clear as the establishment of monotheism among the Jewish people and its continuation into Christianity—if we omit the development from the animal totem to the human god with his regular (animal) companion, a development which can be traced without a gap and readily understood. (Each of the four Christian evangelists, by the way, still has his favourite animal.) If we admit for the moment that the rule of Pharaoh's empire was the external reason for the appearance of the monotheistic idea, we see that this idea—uprooted from its soil and transplanted to another people—after a long latency period takes hold of this people, is treasured by them as their most precious possession and for its part keeps this people alive by bestowing on them the pride of being the chosen people. It is the religion of the primæval father and the hope of reward, distinction and finally world sovereignty, is bound up with it. The last-named wish-phantasy —relinquished long ago by the Jewish people— still survives among their enemies in their belief is the conspiracy of the "Elders of Zion." We shall consider in a later chapter how the special peculiarities of a monotheistic religion borrowed from Egypt must have worked on the Jewish people, how it formed their character for good through the disdaining of magic and mysticism and encouraging them to progress in spirituality and sublimations. The people, happy in their conviction of possessing truth, overcome by the consciousness of being the chosen, came to value highly all intellectual and ethical achievements. I shall also show how their sad fate, and the disappointments reality had in store for them, was able to strengthen all these tendencies. At present, however, we shall follow their historical development in another direction.

The restoration to the primæval father of his historical rights marked a great progress, but this could not be the end. The other parts of the prehistoric tragedy also clamoured for recognition. How this process was set into motion it is not easy to say. It seems that a growing feeling of guiltiness had seized the Jewish people—and perhaps the whole of civilization of that time—as a precursor of the return of the repressed material. This went on until a member of the Jewish people, in the guise of a political-religious agitator, founded a doctrine which—together with another one, the Christian religion—separated from the Jewish one. Paul, a Roman Jew from Tarsus, seized upon this feeling of guilt and correctly traced it back to its primæval source. This he called original sin; it was a crime against God that could be expiated only through death. Death had come into the world through original sin. In reality this crime, deserving of death, had been the murder of the Father who later was deified. The murderous deed itself, however, was not remembered; in its place stood the phantasy of expiation and that is why this phantasy could be welcomed in the form of a gospel of salvation (Evangel). A Son of God, innocent himself, had sacrificed himself—and thereby taken over the guilt of the world. It had to be a Son, for the sin had been murder of the Father. Probably traditions from Oriental and Greek mysteries had exerted their influence on the shaping of this phantasy of salvation. The essence of it seems to be Paul's own contribution. He was a man with a gift for religion, in the truest sense of the phrase. Dark

traces of the past lay in his soul, ready to break through into the regions of consciousness.

That the Redeemer sacrificed himself as an innocent man was an obviously tendentious distortion, difficult to reconcile with logical thinking. How could a man who was innocent assume the guilt of the murderer by allowing himself to be killed? In historical reality there was no such contradiction. The "redeemer" could be no one else but he who was most guilty, the leader of the brother horde who had overpowered the Father. Whether there had been such a chief rebel and leader must—in my opinion—remain uncertain. It is quite possible but we must also consider that each member of the brother horde certainly had the wish to do the deed by himself and thus to create for himself a unique position as a substitute for the identification with the father which he had to give up when he was submerged in the community. If there was no such leader, then Christ was the heir of an unfulfilled wish-phantasy; if there was such a leader, then Christ was his successor and his reincarnation. It is unimportant, however, whether we have here a phantasy or the return of a forgotten reality; in any case, here lies the origin of the conception of the hero—he who rebels against the father and kills him in some guise or other. Here we also find the real source of the "tragic guilt" of the hero in drama—a guilt hard to demonstrate otherwise. We can scarcely doubt that in Greek tragedy the hero and the chorus represent this same rebel hero and the brother horde, and it cannot be without significance that in the Middle Ages the theatre began afresh with the story of the Passion.

I have already mentioned that the Christian ceremony of Holy Communion, in which the believer incorporates the flesh and blood of the Redeemer, repeats the content of the old Totem feast; it does so, it is true, only in its tender and adoring sense, not in its aggressive sense. The ambivalency dominating the father-son relationship, however, shows clearly in the final result of the religious innovation. Meant to propitiate the father deity, it ends by his being dethroned and set aside. The Mosaic religion had been a Father religion; Christianity became a Son religion. The old God, the Father, took second place; Christ, the Son, stood in His stead, just as in those dark times every son had longed to do. Paul, by developing the Jewish religion further, became its destroyer. His success was certainly mainly due to the fact that through the idea of salvation he laid the ghost of the feeling of guilt. It was also due to his giving up the idea of the chosen people and its visible sign—circumcision. That is how the new religion could become all-embracing, universal. Although this step might have been determined by

Paul's revengefulness on account of the opposition which his innovation found among the Jews, nevertheless one characteristic of the old Aton religion (universality) was reinstated; a restriction had been abolished which it had acquired while passing on to a new carrier, the Jewish people.

In certain respects the new religion was a cultural regression as compared with the older Jewish religion; this happens regularly when a new mass of people of a lower cultural level effects an invasion or is admitted into an older culture. Christian religion did not keep to the lofty heights of spirituality to which the Jewish religion had soared. The former was no longer strictly monotheistic, took over from the surrounding peoples numerous symbolical rites, re-established the great Mother Goddess and found room for many deities of polytheism in an easily recognizable disguise—though in subordinate positions. Above all it was not inaccessible—as the Aton religion and the subsequent Mosaic religion had been—to the penetration of superstitions, magical and mystical elements which proved a great hindrance to the spiritual development of two following millenia.

The triumph of Christianity was a renewed victory of the Amon priests over the God of Ikhnaton after an interval of a millennium and a half and over a larger region. And yet Christianity marked a progress in the history of religion: that is to say, in regard to the return of the repressed. From now on Jewish religion was, so to speak, a fossil.

It would be worth while to understand why the monotheistic idea should make such a deep impression on just the Jewish people, and why they adhered to it so tenaciously. I believe this question can be answered. The great deed and misdeed of primæval times, the murder of the Father, was brought home to the Jews, for fate decreed that they should repeat it on the person of Moses, an eminent father substitute. It was a case of acting instead of remembering, something which often happens during analytic work with neurotics. They responded to the doctrine of Moses—which should have been a stimulus to their memory—by denying their act, did not progress beyond the recognition of the great Father and barred the passage to the point where later on Paul started his continuation of primæval history. It can scarcely be chance that the violent death of another great man should become the starting point for the creation of a new religion by Paul. This was a man whom a small number of adherents in Judea believed to be the Son of God and the promised Messiah, and who later on took over some of the childhood history that had been attached to Moses. In reality, however, we have hardly more definite knowledge of

him than we have of Moses. We do not know if he was really the great man whom the Gospels depict or whether it was not rather the fact and the circumstances of his death that were the decisive factor in his achieving importance. Paul, who became his apostle, did not himself know him.

The murder of Moses by his people—which Sellin recognized in the traces of tradition and which, strangely enough, the young Goethe had assumed without any evidence—has thus become an indispensable part of our reasoning, an important link between the forgotten deed of primæval times and its subsequent reappearance in the from of Monotheistic religions. It is an attractive suggestion that the guilt attached to the murder of Moses may have been the stimulus for the wish-phantasy of the Messiah, who was to return and give to his people salvation and the promised sovereignty over the world. If Moses was this first Messiah, Christ became his substitute and successor. Then Paul could with a certain right say to the peoples: "See, the Messiah has truly come. He was indeed murdered before your eyes." Then also there is some historical truth in the rebirth of Christ, for he was the resurrected Moses and the returned primæval Father of the primitive horde as well—only transfigured and as a Son in the place of his Father.

The poor Jewish people, who with its usual stiff-necked obduracy continued to deny the murder of their "father," has dearly expiated this in the course of centuries. Over and over again they heard the reproach: you killed our God. And this reproach is true, if rightly interpreted. It says, in reference to the history of religion: you won't *admit* that you murdered God (the archetype of God, the primæval Father and his reincarnations). Something should be added, namely: "It is true, we did the same thing, but we *admitted* it, and since then we have been purified."

Not all accusations with which antisemitism pursues the descendants of the Jewish people are based on such good foundations. There must, of course, be more than one reason for a phenomenon of such intensity and lasting strength as the popular hatred of Jews. A whole series of reasons can be divined: some of them, which need no interpretation, arise from obvious considerations; others lie deeper and spring from secret sources, which one would regard as the specific motives. In the first group the most fallacious is the reproach of their being foreigners, since in many places nowadays under the sway of antisemitism the Jews were the oldest constituents of the population or arrived even before the present inhabitants. This is so, for example, in the town of Cologne, where Jews came with the Romans, before it was colonized by Germanic tribes. Other grounds for antisemitism are stronger, as for example, the circumstance that Jews mostly live as a minority among other peoples, since the feeling of solidarity of the masses—in order to be complete—has need of an animosity against an outside minority and the numerical weakness of the minority invites suppression. Two other peculiarities that the Jews possess, however, are quite unpardonable. The first is that in many respects they are different from their "hosts." Not fundamentally so, since they are not a foreign Asiatic race—as their enemies maintain—but mostly consist of the remnants of Mediterranean peoples and inherit their culture. Yet they are different—although sometimes it is hard to define in what respects—especially from the Nordic peoples, and racial intolerance finds stronger expression—strange to say—in regard to small differences than to fundamental ones. The second peculiarity has an even more pronounced effect. It is that they defy oppression, that even the most cruel persecutions have not succeeded in exterminating them. On the contrary, they show a capacity for holding their own in practical life and, where they are admitted, they make valuable contributions to the surrounding civilization.

The deeper motives of antisemitism have their roots in times long past; they come from the unconscious and I am quite prepared to hear that what I am going to say will at first appear incredible. I venture to assert that the jealousy which the Jews evoked in the other peoples by maintaining that they were the first-born, favourite child of God the Father has not yet been overcome by those others, just as if the latter had given credence to the assumption. Furthermore, among the customs through which the Jews marked off their aloof position, that of circumcision made a disagreeable, uncanny impression on others. The explanation probably is that it reminds them of the dreaded castration idea and of things in their primæval past which they would fain forget. Then there is lastly the most recent motive of the series. We must not forget that all the peoples who now excel in the practice of antisemitism became Christians only in relatively recent times, sometimes forced to it by bloody compulsion. One might say, they all are "badly christened"; under the thin veneer of Christianity they have remained what their ancestors were, barbarically polytheistic. They have not yet overcome their grudge against the new religion which was forced on them, and they have projected it on to the source from which Christianity came to them. The facts that the Gospels tell a story which is enacted among Jews, and in truth treats only of Jews, has facilitated such a projection. The hatred for Judaism is at bottom hatred for Christianity, and it is not surprising that in the German National-Socialist revolution this close connection of the two monotheistic religions finds such clear expression in the hostile treatment of both.

4. The Hypothesis of Cultural Lag

BY WILLIAM F. OGBURN

THIS RAPIDITY OF CHANGE in modern times raises the very important question of social adjustment. Problems of social adjustment are of two sorts. One concerns the adaptation of man to culture or perhaps preferably the adapting of culture to man. This subject is considered in Part V. The other problem is the question of adjustments, occasioned as a result of these rapid social changes, between the different parts of culture, which no doubt means ultimately the adaptation of culture to man. This second problem of adjustment between

Reprinted from William F. Ogburn, *Social Change* (New York: Viking Press, 1932), pp. 200–13, with the permission of Viking Press.

the different parts of culture is the immediate subject of our inquiry.

The thesis is that the various parts of modern culture are not changing at the same rate, some parts are changing much more rapidly than others; and that since there is a correlation and interdependence of parts, a rapid change in one part of our culture requires readjustments through other changes in the various correlated parts of culture. For instance, industry and education are correlated, hence a change in industry makes adjustments necessary through changes in the educational system. Industry and education are two variables, and if the change in industry occurs first and the adjustment through education follows, industry may be referred to as the independent variable and education as the dependent variable. Where one part of culture changes first, through some discovery or invention, and occasions changes in some part of culture dependent upon it, there frequently is a delay in the changes occasioned in the dependent part of culture. The extent of this lag will vary according to the nature of the cultural material, but may exist for a considerable number of years, during which time there may be said to be a maladjustment. It is desirable to reduce the period of maladjustment, to make the cultural adjustments as quickly as possible.

The foregoing account sets forth a problem that occurs when there is a rapid change in a culture of interdependent parts and when the rates of change in the parts are unequal. The discussion will be presented according to the following outlines. First the hypothesis will be presented, then examined and tested by a rather full consideration of the facts of a single instance, to be followed by several illustrations. Next the nature and cause of the phenomenon of cultural maladjustment in general will be analyzed. The extent of such cultural lags will be estimated, and finally the significance for society will be set forth.

A first simple statement of the hypothesis we wish to investigate now follows. A large part of our environment consists of the material conditions of life and a large part of our social heritage is our material culture. These material things consist of houses, factories, machines, raw materials, manufactured products, foodstuffs and other material objects. In using these material things we employ certain methods. Some of these methods are as simple as the technique of handling a tool. But a good many of the ways of using the material objects of culture involve rather larger usages and adjustments, such as customs, beliefs, philosophies, laws, governments. One important function of government, for instance, is the adjustment of the population to the material conditions of life, although there are other governmental functions. Sumner has called many of these processes of adjustments, mores. The cultural adjustments to material conditions, however, include a larger body of processes than the mores; certainly they include the folk ways and social institutions. These ways of adjustment may be called, for purposes of this particular analysis, the *adaptive* culture. The adaptive culture is therefore that portion of the non-material culture which is adjusted or adapted to the material conditions. Some parts of the non-material culture are thoroughly adaptive culture such as certain rules involved in handling technical appliances, and some parts are only indirectly or partially so, as for instance, religion.

The family makes some adjustments to fit changed material conditions, while some of its functions remain constant. The family, therefore, under the terminology used here is a part of the non-material culture that is only partly adaptive. When the material conditions change, changes are occasioned in the adaptive culture. But these changes in the adaptive culture do not synchronize exactly with the change in the material culture. There is a lag which may last for varying lengths of time, sometimes indeed, for many years.

An illustration will serve to make the hypothesis more clearly understood. One class of material objects to which we adjust ourselves is the forests. The material conditions of forestry have changed a good deal in the United States during the past century. At one time the forests were quite plentiful for the needs of the small population. There was plenty of wood easily accessible for fuel, building and manufacture. The forests were sufficiently extensive to prevent in many large areas the washing of the soil, and the streams were clear. In fact, at one time the forests seemed to be too plentiful, from the point of view of the needs of the people. Food and agricultural products were at one time the first need of the people and the clearing of land of trees and stumps was a common undertaking of the community in the days of the early settlers. In some places, the quickest procedure was to kill and burn the trees and plant between the stumps. When the material conditions were like these, the method of adjustment to the forests was characterized by a policy which has been called exploitation. Exploitation in regard to the forests was indeed a part of the mores of the time, and describes a part of the adaptive culture in relation to forests.

As time went on, however, the population grew, manufacturing became highly developed, and the need for forests increased. But the forests were being destroyed. This was particularly true in the Appalachian, Great Lakes and Gulf regions. The policy of exploitation continued. Then rather suddenly it began to be realized in certain centres of thought that if the policy of cutting timber continued at the same rate and in the same manner the forests would in a short time be gone and very soon indeed they would be inadequate to supply the needs of the population. It was realized that the custom in regard to using the forests must be changed and a policy of conservation was advocated. The new policy of conservation means not only a restriction in the amount of cutting down of trees, but it means a more scientific method of cutting, and also reforestation. Forests may be cut in such a way, by selecting trees according to their size, age and location, as to yield a large quantity of timber and yet not diminish the forest area. Also by the proper distribution of cutting plots in a particular area, the cutting can be so timed that by the time the last plot is cut the young trees on the plot first cut will be grown. Some areas when cut leave a land which is well adapted to farming, whereas such sections as mountainous regions when denuded of forests are poorly suited to agriculture. There of course are many other methods of conservation of forests. The science of forestry is, indeed, fairly highly developed in principle, though not in practice in the United States. A new adaptive culture, one of conservation, is therefore suited to the changed material conditions.

That the conservation of forests in the United States should have been begun earlier is quite generally admitted. We may say, therefore, that the old policy of exploitation has hung over longer than it should before the institution of the new policy. In other words, the material conditions in regard to our forests have changed but the old customs of the use of forests which once fitted the material conditions very well have hung over into a period of changed conditions. These old customs are not only not satisfactorily adapted, but are really socially harmful. These customs of course have a utility, since they meet certain human needs; but methods of greater utility are needed. There seems to be a lag in the mores in regard to forestry after the material conditions have changed. Or translated into the general terms of the previous analysis, the material conditions have changed first; and there has been a lag in the adaptive culture, that is, that culture which is adapted to forests. The material conditions changed before the adaptive culture was changed to fit the new material conditions. This

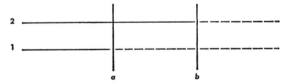

situation may be illustrated by the figure. Line 1 represents the material conditions, in regard to forests in the United States. Line 2 represents the adaptive culture, the policy of using the forests. The continuous lines represent the plentiful forests, with the sparse population and the mores of exploitation, the dotted lines, the new conditions of forests which are small in relation to the population and the new policy of conservation. The space between a and b represents the period when the old adaptive culture or mores exists with the changed material conditions, and is a period of maladjustment.

It is difficult to locate exactly the points a and b. Consider first the location of point b, or the time of

the change from the policy of exploitation to the policy of conservation. The policy of conservation of forests certainly did not begin prior to 1904, when the first National Conservation Congress met. It was during Roosevelt's administration that many active steps in the direction of conservation were taken. Large areas of national forest lands were withdrawn from public entry. Gifford Pinchot was very active in spreading the gospel of conservation, and the House of Governors called by President Roosevelt was in large measure concerned with programmes of conservation. About this time many books and articles in magazines and periodicals were written on the subject. The conservation movement can hardly be said to have started in any extensive manner before this time. It is true that, earlier, papers had been read on the subject before scientific societies and there had been some teaching of scientific forestry, but prior to this time the idea of forest conservation was little known and the movement was certainly not extensive. Nor had the government taken any significant steps in a genuine policy of conservation. Indeed it might be argued with some success that we have not yet adopted fully a policy of conservation. For a great many of the private holdings are still exploited in very much the same old way. Reforestation is still largely a matter of theory in the United States. It is true that the government has taken a number of steps to preserve the forests but the conservationists are far from being satisfied with the progress of the movement to date. Certainly we have not attained the high mark maintained in western Europe.

It is also difficult to locate point a, that is, to determine when we should have started the conservation movement. Some features of conservation probably should have been instituted perhaps early in the last century. Thus the allotment of permanent forest areas might very well have been done coincidently with the extension of our domain; and the destruction of forests on land little suited to agriculture might have been prevented as the population spread to these new regions. At the time of the Civil War the population had become quite large, and shortly afterward the era of railroad-building set in followed by a great development of industry, insuring large population and concentration. It was at this time that the wonderful forests of the Great Lakes region were cut down, and the cuttings in the Appalachian regions increased greatly. Some close observers saw at that time what development of population and industry would take place, but the relation of the forests to such a condition was not appreciated. If scientific forestry had been applied then, many of the unnecessarily wasted forests would still exist and now be furnishing lumber. There would not have been such a washing of soil and the danger of floods would have been less. While some methods of forest conservation might have been applied to advantage shortly after colonial days, the proper time for more extensive developments of conservation was probably in the era following the Civil War. The population was becoming large; the west was being settled; the Pacific coast had been reached; the territorial boundaries had been fixed; industries, railroads, factories, corporations, trusts were all growing with rapidity. The east was in greater need of conservation of forests than the Pacific Northwest or Alaska; nevertheless very probably for the whole country, though its stages of development were unequal, an extensive conservation movement should have been instituted about the middle of the last half of the nineteenth century. It would seem, therefore, that there has been a lag of at least a quarter of a century in changing our forestry policy.

The foregoing discussion of forestry illustrates the hypothesis which it is proposed to discuss. It is desirable to state more clearly and fully the points involved in the analysis. The first point concerns the degree of adjustment or correlation between the material conditions and the adaptive non-material culture. The degree of this adjustment may be only more or less perfect or satisfactory; but we do adjust ourselves to the material conditions through some form of culture; that is, we live, we get along, through this adjustment. The particular culture which is adjusted to the material conditions may be very complex, and, indeed, quite a number of widely different parts of culture may be adjusted to a fairly homogeneous material condition. Of a particular cultural form, such as the family or government, relationship to a particular material culture is only one of its purposes or functions. Not all functions of family organization, as, for instance, the affectional function, are primarily adaptive to material conditions.

Another point to observe is that the changes in the material culture precede changes in the adaptive culture. This statement is not in the form of a universal dictum. Conceivably, forms of adaptation might be worked out prior to a change in the material situation and the adaptation might be applied practically at the same time as the change in the material conditions. But such a situation presumes a very high degree of planning, prediction and control. The collection of data, it is thought, will show that at the present time there are a very large number of cases where the material conditions change and the changes in the adaptive culture follow later. There are certain general theoretical reasons why this is so; but it is not desirable to discuss these until later. For the present, the analysis will only concern those cases where changes in the adaptive culture do not precede changes in the material culture. Furthermore, it is not implied that changes may not occur in non-material culture while the material culture remains the same. Art or education, for instance, may undergo many changes with a constant material culture.

Still another point in the analysis is that the old, unchanged, adaptive culture is not adjusted to the new, changed, material conditions. It may be true that the old adaptive culture is never wholly unadjusted to the new conditions. There may be some degree of adjustment. But the thesis is that the unchanged adaptive culture was more harmoniously related to the old than to the new material conditions and that a new adaptive culture will be better suited to the new material conditions than was the old adaptive culture. Adjustment is therefore a relative term, and perhaps only in a few cases would there be a situation which might be called perfect adjustment or perfect lack of adjustment.

It is desirable, however, not to make the analysis too general until there has been a more careful consideration of particular instances. We now propose, therefore, to test the hypothesis by the facts in a definite case of social change. In attempting to verify the hypothesis in a particular case by measurement, the following series of steps will be followed. The old material conditions will be described, that part of the adaptive culture under consideration will be described, and the degree of adjustment between these two parts of culture shown. Then the changed material conditions and the changed adaptive culture will be defined and the degree of adaptation shown. It is necessary also to show that the unchanged adaptive culture is not as harmoniously adjusted to the new conditions as to the old and not as harmoniously adjusted to the new conditions as is a changed adaptive culture. Having made such a series of descriptions, the next step will be to measure the lag, which should be done by locating the point of change in the material culture and the point of change in the particular adaptive culture.

5. *Fundamentals of Culture-Sociology*

BY ALFRED WEBER

1

IT SEEMS EXPEDIENT for all culture-sociology to distinguish between three different spheres of historical events, namely: social process, civilizational process, and culture-movement.

It is the nature of political as well as economic and social history to examine the destiny of great historical organisms, those great geographic, cultural, and dramatic units of mankind, to examine them with the purpose of clarifying their peculiar destinies by establishing the concrete facts essential to the total process. These disciplines regard the Chinese, Hindu, West-Asiatic-Egyptian, Classical, Arabian, Germano-Roman, and other historical spheres each as a partly "corporeal unit" containing a course of events that gives it temporal and spatial identity; and for the collective destiny of each they assume the task of collecting the principal data. Accordingly they seek to base their version and, in part, their explanation of the major historical events, the portraits of great men and the fate of the masses, upon the body economic, the structural development of political patterns, the social metamorphoses, and upon other corporeal formations and transformations. Their task is concrete historical morphology.[1] The introduction of so-called mental factors and currents does not disturb their essential preoccupation with corporeal destiny. At the same time the histories of art, literature, music, religion, philosophy, and science, in a word, all the parts of culture history which are today separate disciplines (cultural history does not exist as a unified discipline)[2] operate in a profoundly different manner and fairly independently of one another.

For them, corporeal formations of history do not exist as essential objects of examination or data of development. The interpretation of the great cultural emanations and movements with which they are concerned, the mental currents and systems of thought which they seek to expound in principle and bring home to us, proceeds (insofar as they consider it incorrect to restrict themselves to the mere portrayal of form and content) from the disclosure of coherence—coherences, generally speaking, between "problems" to be solved in the cultural field on the one hand (problems in history of philosophy, etc.) and, on the other hand, chiefly the working methods of the various fields, their development and expressive value (development of painting and plastic technique, laws of harmony in music, laws of language development, of literary styles and forms of expression, etc.). The result is a substantiation of a sequence and rhythm of events usually left open for more methodical investigation, substantiation of a conflict of "mental currents," styles, forms, and sundry—always a substantiation of an even progression which, according to its nature, seems to lie either technically or intrinsically within the principles of the cultural field proper. These disciplines, according to the principles of their operation, view cultural history largely as an autonomous historic sphere whose movement and development they seek to explain from within.[3] The political historian thereupon assumes the right to weave somehow the products of all these cultural-historical disciplines into his view of historical events; to place the "mental currents and facts" illuminated by the other disciplines into the setting of "corporeal" events which he in his turn illuminates; to assemble his versions of the destiny of the great historical organisms (*Geschichtskörper*) into a general view, and when he has combined all these general views, to write universal history.

For reasons pertaining not only to the history of science but also necessarily to working technique and methods, it is really a fairly motley, incoherent, at best, a loosely and superficially matched collection of building stones that confronts the sociolo-

---

Reprinted from Alfred Weber, *Fundamentals of Culture-Sociology*, trans. G. H. Weltner and C. F. Hirshman (New York: Columbia University, Department of Social Science and the W.P.A., 1939) pp. 1–33, 42–44, 47.

1. It should be noted that this concept did not originate with Spengler but that it lies implictly at the bottom of all the more recent historiography. Likewise, the "adolescence" and "maturity" of historical organisms have long been ingredients in this point of view.

2. Despite the brilliant personal contribution of Jacob Burckhardt and others.

---

3. We are not overlooking such comprehensive treatments as those of Max Weber and Troeltsch in the history of religion, nor the partly "impromptu" attempts to be found in the numerous recent treatises on the different cultural fields.

gist when, in his turn, he finally undertakes to view things uniformly. For example, let him but try to comprehend as a whole any part of historical fact, like cultural process; let him try to comprehend the necessity by which it grows out of the general movement of history and undertake to establish its typical and lawful connection with this general movement. The same is true if, as sociologist, he tries logically to bind the cultural emanations of the Occident— their essential import—the recurrence or non-recurrence of their typical forms and aspects to the larger collective destiny of the Occident. If he tries to place these emanations in distinct and intelligible relationship with the factual sequences (corporeal sequences) which the various historical disciplines unearth and which mark history's general course, he is confronted at the outset, as we have said, by event-series, factually discrete and, in the general version of history, only superficially connected. Should he wish to connect these series, the difference in objective between himself and the various special disciplines will force him to organize his material accordingly. For his purpose he must attempt a conceptual regrouping of the synthesis. Thus, whatever facts the political, economic and social historians have established concerning the external form of history will necessarily fall into a new perspective. And there will be disclosed to him a great unified social process which, despite the widest variations in the different collective destinies, will reveal typical forms and stages of development. The major events (wars, revolutions, reformations, and the like) will in some typical fashion become incorporated in these forms and stages, and great men will arise not accidentally but necessarily in certain places. Furthermore, he will find that this social process is influenced by the mental sphere, that is, by those facts and processes presented by the cultural disciplines. When he now examines its kernel, he will see it as the form which gives some necessary pattern to the totality of natural human forces of impulse and will (operating as "population" in the various communal destinies), a pattern limited, of course, by certain natural (geographic, climatic, and other) conditions. The impressed pattern, or patterns, will undergo developmental alteration, will oppose and replace one another and in their struggle produce the great *peripeteiai*, the secular historic events. At the same time he will notice how this process in the larger collective destinies, which he likewise views as corporeally closed systems, arises from primitive relationships, residues of gentilic forms, in which they first appear on the historical stage, and passes through similar forms everywhere though, to be sure, in totally different groupings. He will observe

how it seems to lead over spaces of social movement to different final outlets, to a lasting paralysis of form, to senile decay, or to a world expansion of forces, passing through like phases to various outlets which empty into the universal stream of human history. He will see the Chinese and Hindu historical cycles—once their natural conditions and direction of development are given—pursue a necessary social course through the millennia and finally yield to that senile torpor in which they remained through the centuries, and in which they remain today, washed by the tide of Occidental world-expansion. Likewise, by considering the natural conditions of existence (chiefly the systems of canals and irrigation), he will distinctly recognize the type and direction of social development in the West-Asiatic and Egyptian culture-cycle, whose early millennia B.C. he can today reinvestigate by means of unearthed documents. And in terms of these natural conditions of development will he understand the senile torpor in which both were caught during the last millennium B.C. by that new wave of development, the Classical-Mediterranean cycle. He will observe how the conditions of existence, notably the sea, its commerce and "freedom" similarly propel the latter through a given social development—social development in the widest sense, comprising, as suggested, the total corporeal event of the historic cycle—and he will follow its lead to a type of world-expansion wherein must ensue the senile decay of the forms and corporeal identity of the cycle. The historic lapse of the late Classical period in the time of the Caesars is exactly this kind of senile decay. And likewise with reference to the conditions which ushered it in, he will observe the Occidental cycle which followed the Classical and, after the migration of races, carried the scene of history northward; he will observe how it passes through an entirely different yet equally necessary development, one that retains its corporeal identity through many revolutionary stages and convulsions to reach the greatest world-expansion known, embracing the entire globe. And now its inherent forms seem to be dissolving, and the cycle itself is probably passing over into something new: utter decline or the emergence of another historical organism.

In brief, the concrete event-process of the various great historical organisms, their more or less corporeal destiny which the political, economic, and social historians present, will always be viewed by the sociologist as a social evolution, specific but nevertheless fundamentally determined by natural necessity, which undergoes regroupings and realignments of general forms, runs through a predetermined number of stages and reaches a pre-

determined result. In this evolution the universally
given social forces always assume specificity, universally given social forms present a definite and
specific character and urgency, universally given
processes occur in different groupings and with
different results—all of which means that a general
social principle of development functions in different guise. The major events and upheavals substantiated by the historian thus become landmarks
indicating stages of development, or the expression
of the vicissitudes bound up with evolutions, and
the great men seem to rise as shield-bearers and
exponents of new periods.

This is the way the sociologist transforms the
concretely individuated material supplied by the
historian, the "corporeal" development of the different historic cycles, into a new conceptual form
adequate for his mode of thinking—the way he
transforms the mass of historic events pertaining
to these cycles into his view of that sphere, which
I intend to call the "social process."

II

In this process, primarily moved, in his view, by
the natural impulse and will of mankind and primarily determined in form and direction by the
natural conditions peculiar to each historical organism, he will recognize secondary factors which
the other group of historians substantiate: ideas,
"mental currents," artistic views, religious convictions, etc. He must at first be indifferent to their
closer dynamic relation to the stages, vicissitudes,
social formation, and all else pertaining to "corporeal" development, their causal influence on this
development, or the *prius* and *post* of the form and
content of the "mental" and "corporeal" spheres.[4]
What he does see is a mental-cultural sphere existing as a totality in each historical organism along
with the "corporeal." And no matter what he may
think of their mutual interaction, he notes in this
mental-cultural entity, just as in the social process,
certain regularities whose connection with the
corporeal social process is still obscure. He discerns
in it a surge and a decline; he sees parallels between
the destinies of the "cultures" of the various historical organisms, a somehow predetermined appearance of successive developmental stages, a
characteristically recurring rhythm of productivity,
an emergence, variegated yet exhibiting certain
regularities, of the different cultural expressions
(religion, philosophy, art, and within art: music,

epic, lyric, drama, painting, etc.) and modes (classic, romantic, etc.), a characteristic recurrence of
great religious movements and related currents of
ideas under similar conditions, in the social process
of the various "organisms." In short, he notes a
mental-cultural development in the various historical organisms that is related in some fashion, or at
least is somehow parallel to their social process.
He is compelled as a sociologist to view this mental-
cultural development also as a unit, a second sphere
of historic events. For this purpose he has to order
the disconnected facts presented to him by the
different branches of knowledge into a whole historical movement which he sets as a total process
occurring in the various historical organisms side by
side with their social process. He is thereby tempted
—in fact, he now feels it his duty—to clarify the
actual dynamic relationships between these spheres
in the various historical organisms.

But the attempt to fulfill this duty, to scrutinize
the mental-cultural sphere, has a peculiar consequence. He notes that between the social process
and the truly cultural parts of this mental-cultural
sphere with its various aspects and expressions in
religion, art, etc., a third element is interposed, a
mental intermediary realm that is related far more
vitally and distinctly to the shape and course of
the social process than the truly *a postiori* cultural
phenomena (the emergence of religions, systems
of thought, art-periods, etc.)—an intellectual cosmos, in fact, which supplies the social process with
the technical means for its forms and structures
and likewise appears to be one of the grounds
of culture-phenomenology. More accurately expressed: he discovers that the mental-cultural
process of the various historical organisms, viewed
tentatively by him as a unity, is really in its essence,
in its developmental phenomena, and in its relations
to the social process no unity at all, but a duality,
and that it carries within itself two entirely different
spheres of human historical development.

What is revealed upon closer scrutiny is that in
every great historical organism this "mental-cultural" process contains a threefold entity: first,
purely mental and innermost, the development of
a popular consciousness which proves to be the
kernel of the purely mental process of growth and
decline in the historical and cultural organisms
once these are viewed from the mental-cultural
angle. In all the great historic cycles within the
range of his observation, including the Chinese,
Hindu, Classical, and Occidental, the sociologist
can observe that the development of consciousness
proceeds typically toward the clarification of existence. Beginning with primitive stages when the
forms, in which the world and one's own ego are

---

4. Clearly, we are now dealing with marginal questions
of the materialistic interpretation of history. This school's
inquiry into "interest" does not lead to the clarification of
the final categories of cognition.

seen, resemble those of the modern primitive and half-civilized peoples, he will watch consciousness in its development advance to deeper and deeper reflection about existence and discard the totemistic and then the mythical notions, or at any rate, give them a reflectively determined, less naïve place in existence; he will watch it advance from a purely empirical attitude toward world and ego to a more or less scientific or, at least, an intellectual attitude —i.e., determined in some way by intellectual abstractions. He will see how these abstractions are further developed, how at a certain stage every historical organism harbors some rationalized world-view that can be still further elaborated and changed, a world-view into which not only external experience, "the world," but also the personal ego, its emotions, its drives, and its immediate perceptions are woven by a process of systematized, intellectual reflection and given definite though varied forms.

The sociologist discovers that this process, occurring in all the historical organisms under his observations, is intimately bound up with a second and third process within the same unity. The second is an increasing mental domination over nature that presents, parallel to the intellectualization of world and ego, an intellectual structure of utilitarian science, experience, and wisdom, a process which, like the first, tends towards intellectual systematization. Moreover, it remains a self-contained process, retaining its identity through any number of changes in the various historical organisms.

Finally, the third mental process is none other than the actualization and concretion of this second intellectual cosmos; the objectification of this system of practical knowledge through the cultivation of an apparatus of tools and methods, principles of organization, etc., which give concrete structure to existence.

At this point the whole mental sphere, projected in both the above named senses and propelled from within by the development of rational consciousness, impinges upon the social process, influencing it through this technical apparatus. He now sees one distinct and self-contained rationalization-process with only different aspects of expression pervading all the great historical organisms, codetermining their forms and its emanations affecting the inner existence as well as the observational and practical technique of the outer. This rationalization-process has its own laws of development, necessities of growth and conditions of stagnation. Manifestly, it is an essentially different entity from the emergence of religions, systems of thought, works of art, and cultures. It is a unique and vast sphere of development related to the social process quite differently

from these. Once seen as a unity, it breaks up the previously assumed unity of the mental-cultural sphere into a "duality." This process of intellectualization and rationalization which pervades the historical organisms, the intellectual cosmos everywhere set up by this process, its unity which is reflected in its three expressions (inner intellectual enlightenment, bodies of intellectual knowledge, and intellectualized external apparatus), its operations, forms and structures—all these were on the whole not marked by previous historical and sociological thought as a vast and distinct sphere of historical events which should be separated conceptually both from the sphere of social process and from culture-movement proper and investigated as a unity of functions and specific sequences.[5] I propose to call it the civilizational process and to demarcate sharply and fundamentally both the process and its sphere from social process and culture-movement. The latter is also grounded in the social process of the great historical organisms but is related to it quite differently from the civilizational process. As we shall see, it is governed by entirely different laws of development, is of an entirely different nature and has an entirely different place in the course of history. I propose, for the purposes of the culture-sociological approach—perhaps for the sociological approach in general—to resolve the process of history so that the "corporeal" element in its development (that which we have named social process, the realm of originally natural impulse and will and their patterns) can be posited separately and considered, first, as being influenced by the civilizational process, man's sphere of rationalization. Then one can ask how the culture movement proper is related to both and to their interaction, whether it grows in some recognizable fashion out of the interplay of their forms and structures, whether and to what extent it proceeds independently of them, and how much it reacts upon both. I am proposing this kind of trichotomy because this is the way to attain a unified sociological view of the course of history and, especially, (as I believe and intend to prove) a sociological analysis of its culture phenomenology.

III

The civilizational process and culture-movement are, as we have said, intrinsically different; they have divergent forms and laws of development and appear before us in the general course of history as

5. Despite the many points in common between the above and the deductions of Max Weber in his essays on the sociology of religion, the latter derive from a somewhat different point of view which unfortunately does not permit of analysis here.

mutually exclusive phenomenologies. The civilizational process with its various composite parts: its picture of world and ego, formed by the intellect (macrocosmos and microcosmos); its world of pragmatic knowledge; and its intellectually formed equipment for mastering existence may reach entirely different levels in the different historical organisms. It may variously express its world-view, but in every historical organism it always builds, little by little, a cosmos of knowledge whose three indicated parts are merely aspects of the same thing and which, once launched in a certain direction, proceeds by a logic as strict as that of the inherent causal laws underlying the construction of a building. Whatever emerges is a whole and its parts are not "created" but "discovered"; (given the direction of the intellectual movement) they are already there before they are found, that is to say—from the point of view of development—pre-existent. It is as if these parts were merely drawn into the realm of human consciousness, into the illumined sphere of being with which man surrounds himself. This applies to the entire world of practical knowledge in the natural sciences, to every separate "discovery" of natural science, to every theory of knowledge and epistemological insight. But it also applies to the entire technical apparatus: tools, machines, and methodical principles of work and organization. The propositions of Euclidean geometry are "present" prior to "discovery," else they would be undiscoverable; and the same is true of the Copernican formulas for planetary motion and Kant's aprioris to the extent that all these are "correctly" discovered and formulated—and likewise the steam engine, telephone, telegraph, axe, shovel, paper money, division of labor and the whole body of technical means, methods, and principles concerned with the mastery of life and nature. Such are the "objects" of our pragmatic cosmos, those we already possess or shall acquire in the future; all of them are in essence there, i.e., they are "pre-existent" before we have had the chance to attract them into the conscious sphere and put them to use. The total civilizational process that actualizes this whole cosmos and supplies us with all its "objects," including the discoveries of a purely mental nature, merely discloses a world universally "prior" for all mankind and renders it progressively accessible. In this world every part is valid for all mankind. This is proved—I shall soon touch upon apparent deviations—by the fact that the mental and physical concretions of this realm, whenever they are discovered in some historical organism, no matter where, and become a part of conscious life, spread as a matter of course throughout the world as if by natural movement. And they penetrate other historical organisms, to the extent that their social processes are sufficiently developed to receive them and their mental development high enough to "see" them—provided, of course, that intercommunication makes this penetration at all possible. The universality of technical discoveries is well known. But this universality is not restricted to the "technical" cosmos of civilization whose material and mental objects, whose methods and means, from the knowledge of working metals and the use of fire to modern ways of communication and production, have always spread with something akin to the speed of lightning, both in periods of universal communication or isolation. It holds good as well for the realm of intellect, although here the insights in mathematics, astronomy, the natural sciences, etc., may spread at times more slowly, since their reception depends on the level of consciousness attained in the different historical organisms and since many of their practical products, as for instance chronology or accounting, may find no place in the social organization. But this does not prevent them from finally penetrating everywhere in the same measure. And the same universality, with certain modifications in the form and manner of expansion, soon to be discussed in further detail, holds good for the disclosure of new parts of the intellectually shaped view of world and ego, the intellectual results of enlightenment, the clarification of the partly inner aspect of the pre-existent civilization cosmos. The phenomenology of actualization and development of the civilizational cosmos, both in its practical and theoretical aspect, implies, when viewed as a unified historic picture, that the great historical organisms build entirely upon one another in the development of their civilizations and operate as if by agreement in the direction of ultimate unity —this despite wide divergence in their social and cultural development. Indeed, so viewed, the general course of history is really the process of elaborating the unified and universal civilizational cosmos, and mankind, as such, takes control in the halts, gaps, and breaks inherent in the destiny of the different historical organisms. The old West-Asiatic-Egyptian, Classical, Arabian, the modern Occidental, and (less strictly) the Chinese and Hindu cycles, no matter how acutely they deviate in their historic course, social development and culture-movement, all are in this view only links, auxiliary factors in the continuous, logical elaboration of the civilizational cosmos which today is common to all mankind.

The technical parts of this civilizational cosmos first appear in their rational form in the organization of instruments and labor by the Egyptians and Babylonians as far back as 3,000–4,000 B.C. Having evolved in correlation with the historical cycles of India and China (the details of which are not known), this technique became not only the foundation of the whole civilized technical apparatus of the Classical and Arabian historical organisms, but through those of the Occident as well. The latter, taking the lead in technical invention since the 14th century, produced from the 18th century onward the modern apparatus of world-civilization on the world-wide basis previously established.

In like fashion, the mental parts of this worldwide civilizational cosmos, mathematics, astronomy and natural science, apparently had their intellectual inception in the enormous depths of the first and second historical organisms on the Euphrates and the Nile. They are then brought into sharper relief by the Classical, the Arabian and the Chinese organisms, are taken over by the Occident during the period of expansion after the 16th century and carried through the famous "Era of Discovery" to the present universally prevalent conception of the world based on mathematics and the natural sciences, a conception which is valid for all mankind and universally accepted.

The "realm of intellect" which, despite its present diverse forms, by its content is common civilizational possession of mankind, the intellectual notion of world and ego belonging to a single sphere, first seems to have received conscious impulse in the Brahmanic wisdom of the Hindu cycle. It then becomes a subject in the Classical and Arabic as well as the Chinese historical spheres, and, finally, in the Occidental philosophy of the 18th century (Kant), it receives formal principles which seem to show the limitations of knowledge and at the same time bring together the different forms of enlightenment of the various historical spheres, and, insofar as they possess intellectual content, generalize them.

In this gradual emergence of the pre-existent mental and material civilizational cosmos from the darkness into the light of man's collective consciousness, sketched here only in an amateurish and inadequate manner, it is of small moment—nay, it is no more than a "misfortune of a day"—if certain gained knowledge or insights get temporarily lost through historic contingencies, chiefly through the way history has of telescoping the series of historical organisms that become the carriers of enlightenment. Take, for example, the knowledge of the Copernican world-view which, after its discovery during Graeco-Roman antiquity, slumbered in the lap of history until its independent rediscovery by the Occident after the 16th century. It is likewise irrelevant to the nature of the whole process that in the projection of the "technical cosmos" certain technical means of civilization, "accidentally" dis-

covered somewhere, perhaps remain at first unused until their rediscovery somewhere else, when they suddenly receive enormous significance and a universal, practical application. Thus, although the early Chinese discovery of the mechanical clock or the engine was not followed by a social application, their rediscovery in the Occident ushered in the great technical revolution of modern times. These are not changes in the nature of development but the "jests" and curling arabesques that result from the lodgment of the process in the social and cultural movements.

And lastly, it is irrelevant to the essence of the civilizational process as a gradual emergence of a mental type of unity if the development of consciousness underlying it receives a severe set-back in the early "history" of the various historical organisms and if somewhere it has to begin anew from a relatively primitive state. Note the development of the Classical consciousness, succeeding the West-Asiatic-Egyptian. (The migrating and invading Greeks were obviously barbaric compared to the Creto-Mycenaean offshoot of the West-Asiatic-Egyptian cycle which they met.) Note the development of the Arabian consciousness succeeding the Classical and that of the Occidental cycle succeeding both. This merely implies that where there is an influx of new peoples into the general civilizational cosmos of mankind, the "subjective" civilization or "civilized quality" of the new populations must always re-ascend the stages that have already been disclosed and traversed by others within the general objective and subjective civilization cosmos. Here, by the way, the climbing and reaching for old subjective heights of civilization is always considerably facilitated by the fact that the most essential objective elements of civilization are taken over by each new historical organism and also those which are of supreme importance for the association of the subjective process of civilization, the subjective intellectual enlightenment, and the conscious mastery of existence. When, for example, the Classical historical organism took over from the West-Asiatic and Egyptian not only the technical apparatus and the principles and forms of division of labor but also coined money, mathematics, and astronomy, it thereby took over the crucial elements of "objective" civilization which made possible directly a measurable intellectual mastery of existence and enormously facilitated the rationalistic domination of "inner" and "outer" things. They were certainly definite contributory factors in the rapid enlightenment and civilizational development of the "Greek barbarians" that lasted a few centuries after their incursion through the Doric migrations. These civilizational elements also influenced, in the matter of content, the remarkable early rational formulation of their view of world and ego. But this is only in passing. The same thing can be said, for example, of the transmission of the Classical money-accounting to the Occidental cycle after the migrations of the peoples, its effect in terms of development of consciousness and civilization upon this historical organism which had sunk into a vast ignorance and expressed itself only in primitive social forms. We find a general money-accounting and, at the same time, the beginning of "a calculating spirit" in the Graeco-Roman historical organism—as is evident from the *leges barbarorum*—long before the essential importance of a constructed money-exchange economy came to light.

There is no doubt that "subjective civilization" is set back for centuries whenever there emerges a new historical organism, and whenever the new historical process shifts its center of gravity into a new geographical setting in which the historical organism must then grow and go through its social and cultural development. Subjectively, a type of antiquity must always recur, then a middle age, and a modern time. Consequently, the subjective civilizational process of all mankind presents a picture of constantly recurring darkness in certain of the "areas" where man is historically rooted, until gradually the earlier enlightenment reappears and is then surpassed. Unquestionably, however, the preservation of objective civilizational elements and subjective enlightenment in the other undisturbed historical "areas" creates the means whereby the losses of single parts can be speedily recovered and the general enlightenment reintroduced. This general enlightenment is the logically causal, though unevenly graded, disclosure of a new unity valid for all mankind, mankind's universal civilizational cosmos, objectively and subjectively pre-existent.

Which aspect of the enlightenment-process will predominate depends on the specific internal arrangement (I shall not as yet use a more specific or fundamental term) of the various great historical organisms, and (as is recently contended) perhaps also on the spiritual equipment of their populations, shortly to be discussed. The old West-Asiatic-Egyptian organism was led by its arrangement toward practice and technique. On the "theoretical" side it cultivated only the purely quantitative parts that were indispensable for the immediate mastery of existence (astronomy, time-reckoning, accounting, etc.). On the other hand, the Classical organism, prevented, as it were, by its specific arrangement from "seeing" the technical parts of the civilizational cosmos, simply passed them by without special interest. (Except for the arch, no technical invention of Antiquity is worthy of mention.) Its field of attention was restricted to the intellectual and theoretical front, and hence it laid the foundations for mathematics, the natural sciences, philosophy, and all the other disciplines which we now call "sciences." At the same time, the Hindu historical organism with its remarkably appropriate arrangement, wrapped as it was in religious contemplation, chose for its single, and indeed, highly successful objective the philosophical illumination and penetration of the inmost cognition-fields of world and ego, virtually ignoring everything else. Because of specific arrangement and specific means of expression, it is quite reasonable that every historical organism should clothe its insights, especially the most philosophical ones, in forms that do not always immediately reveal their universality and impede their general expansion and application. This is particularly true when the insights, mixed with extra-civilizational elements, appear in religious and metaphysical systems of thoughts, as illustrated by the "epistemological" inferences of the Brahmans. Further, it should be stressed that every historical organism has a repertory of ideas and concepts, consciously or unconsciously operative (which always contains a definite system of mathematics, i.e., a definite structure of temporal and spatial ideas), and that the quality of these ideas and concepts can set quite various limits to enlightenment: without the idea of "function," which appeared first in the Occidental cycle, not only all higher mathematics, but the whole of modern Occidental knowledge could not have been built up. The same relation exists between the Euclidean idea of three-dimensional space and the whole knowledge of Antiquity, and between the Hindu idea that material being is mere "appearance," and all Hindu philosophy. But it was a distinct misapprehension to claim or, at least, to suggest the deduction that the "insights" (in our terminology, the disclosed parts of the intellectual civilizational cosmos) are therefore mere "symbols of the soul" of the various historical organisms, valid only for them, and that there existed, for example, an Occidental-Faustian, Arabian-Magian, or Classical-Appollonian mathematics whose truth and application were correspondingly limited to those organisms. The development of Euclidean geometry may have been a result of the "Apollonian soul" of Hellenism—we shall not dispute the fact here—and, at first, may have been expressed in purely Hellenic form. But its content of truth and knowledge is, in the human sense, eternal, i.e., universally valid and necessary for all mankind. The same is true of the cognitive content of the Faustian infinitesimal calculus and all its consequences, or of the Kantian aprioris or of the Hindu opposition of "Appearance and Reality." It follows that whatever Kant in his test of the formal premises of knowledge excluded from the sphere of pure empirical knowledge and labelled metaphysics must once and for all be excluded from the temples of universal "knowledge," from the temple of civilizational knowledge and therewith from the enlightenment of the universal pre-existent civilizational cosmos, its theory and its practice—not, however, from the temple of "truth" in general. For these metaphysically or religiously conditioned parts of the "mental realm of knowledge" we shall meet again in the realm of culture and culture-movement. As will appear, they possess in this realm—no matter how slight their civilizational (universally valid and necessary) content—a wealth of cultural and, yes, spiritual truth which determines the content and essence of the cultural emanations. But of this later.

Let us now summarize: The phenomenology and apparent form of the civilizational process consist in the logically causal mode of development, the unevenly graded, accummulative clarification of something pre-existent and latent in all mankind, and in the disclosure of this as universally valid and necessary. And the civilizational cosmos is an intellectually formed cosmos of universally valid and necessary things which cohere internally and, considered in their practical aspect, are equally and universally useful (i.e., empirically true) for human ends, and considered in their theoretic aspects, are equally inevitable (i.e., theoretically true) and in the illumination of world and ego, intuitively evident (i.e., true a priori.) This cosmos is the epitome of mankind's increasing enlightenment. Its disclosure proceeds by the laws of logical causality. At every step in the disclosure the concepts, true or untrue, are applicable. And its disclosed and illumined objects bear the stamp of universal validity and necessity, and spread throughout the trafficked world for the very reason that they are pre-existent for all mankind.

IV

Exactly the opposite applies to the culture movement and everything that originates or moves within its sphere. This sphere produces no cosmos of universally valid and necessary things. Rather, everything that is born here remains by its very nature confined and internally bound to its own historical organism. There is produced not an objective cosmos, but a spiritually tempered aggregation of symbols. The following are types of independent symbolic worlds, with runic characters of their own and an ultimately untransferable content. The

Chinese, the Hindu, the Egyptian, the Babylonian, the Classical, the Arabian, and the Occidental. They are all different cultural worlds with differences in all that is truly cultural in them. It is impossible to separate Greek culture from its historical organism, to approximate, transplant, or duplicate its content—despite the often repeated attempts to do so with its plastic arts, its drama, and its sytsems of philosophy. Every renaissance—and there have been many attempted renaissances of Greek culture, from the Augustan in Rome and the Graeco-Buddhistic in the Gandhara region to the Italian, the Empire renaissance and others—every renaissance leads to something radically different from a revival of cultural Hellenism even though certain external forms are always taken over, and content for a similar spiritual redemption is often sought. The content of spiritual redemption as well as the forms of redemption crystallized in works of art and ideas, in other words, the whole new culture is always quite different from the Hellenic; and the alleged renaissance is really a new and distinct creation. The same holds true for the appropriation and dissemination of the purely religious redemption. In the spread of "world-religions" one apparently meets—but only apparently—something similar to the spread of the content of civilizational knowledge, namely, their release from confinement within their native historical organisms and universalization of at least their most important parts for all of mankind. The mental and spiritual universalization of the world-religions, Christianity, Mohammedanism, Buddhism, is an illusion, even granting the limits within which it occured. Viewed more clearly, it may be nothing more than the result of the military expansion of their native historical organisms. For example, the spread of Mohammedanism is almost concomitant with the final expansion of the "Mongoloidized" Arabian historical organism. Or this universalization can be illustrated by the spread of Buddhism to eastern Asia, resulting in a "transvaluational" renaissance of Buddhism in a different historical organism, i.e., essentially one of those "new creations" we have already seen in art. In the case of the "renaissance" of Buddhism there is not even retained a similarly directed spiritual yearning for redemption. For the "Mahayana" that supplied the raw material for Last Asian Buddhism and in this Buddhism received its further development is really an entirely different religion of subjectively beatific instead of cosmologic content, something essentially alien to the true Hindu Buddhism still extant in Ceylon. It applies the intuitive forms of true Buddhism but manifests in all its various guises a different spiritual content.

Or finally, in this apparent universalization, the

powerful expansion of the historical organism and the newly creative transfer of values may combine, as in the case of Christianity and its universal expansion. Born as a spiritual old-age phenomenon of Classical antiquity, Christianity was reborn into something completely different in the Germano-Roman historical cycle at the time of its inner acceptance by the modern world, which did not begin until the year 1000. Since then it has changed not only in its dogma but in its very nature from Oriental Christianity. The latter's spread into Russia also led to a whole series of new creations. And here as in Russia renaissances (called "reformations") have occurred which in the different historical organisms always led to new creeds (Troeltsch quite correctly expresses the opinion that we should call them new religions), to the formation of new sects of quite varied content and apparently quite varied forms of expression. Christianity spread its various forms over the earth at first within the limits of the expanding Occidental organism, and then, since the 18th century, beyond these limits. But even this alleged "universal religion," and notably this, is today a conglomeration of many different religions which co-exist with, and succeed, one another. Each is of equal spiritual truth for its native historical organism; each may express equally well the spiritual situation current in its proper organism. But each in its essence, content, and mode of expansion is actually confined to its own organism.

Moreover, the religious and spiritual expression of culture usually arrays itself in "categories of intuition." It presents itself as "revelation," as "insight," as "certain (immediately intuited) conviction of something unseen" and "knowledge of the invisible" to usurp universal validity and necessity, to evangelize, to convert, and especially, in the case of Christianity, to persecute and burn all those of different faith. But all this merely points to the underlying fact that essentially different expressions of spirit will conflict, bound as they are to spiritual adjustments in the different historical organisms.

What is true of religion is ultimately true of the metaphysical ideas of all philosophical systems, ideas which are always purely and simply a cultural expression of a particular historical organism. It is utterly impossible to convey to the Occidental or any other organism the intrinsic content of Hindu metaphysics, its belief in metempsychosis and its longing for release from individual existence. If we attempt this, we arrive at Schopenhauerianism or theosophy which, although they may externally apply the same or similar forms of concepts or ideas, completely alter their original content. Likewise, it will never be possible to universalize Greek Platonism. It has undergone numerous renaissance in the form of Neo-Platonism, Renaissance Platonism, German Idealism, etc., each of which represents a completely new creation in essence and content.

All cultural emanations in religions, systems of thought and art creations are in complete antithesis to all civilizational expressions; they are confined, so far as their truth-content is concerned, to the time and locality of their native historical organism. Their transfer to other times and other historical organisms is always a mere transfer of their expression and spiritual redemption-values, a transfer of value leading to the so-called "expansion." This has no connection, however, with the logically causal expansion of the illumined parts of the universal civilizational cosmos.

Thus, all cultural emanations are always "creations." They bear the salient traits of all creations, the characteristics of "exclusiveness" and "uniqueness" as opposed to the things disclosed by the civilizational process which always have the characteristic of "discovery" and thereby of universal validity and necessity, the characteristic of having been implicit before disclosure.

Correspondingly, the phenomenology of culture-movement, the type of development in the sphere of culture, differs radically from that of civilization. In the latter, as we have seen, there is a development, broken, of course, and subject to historical contingency but nevertheless occurring by gradations, a unified process of enlightenment covering the whole history of humanity and leading to a definite goal: the total illumination of the pre-existent. In the sphere of culture, on the other hand, we have a bud of productivity cropping out here and there in an apparently inexplicable manner, something suddenly great and unique—an incomparable creation related by no underlying necessity to other things. And if we attempt to observe and establish certain regularities and relations, we arrive not at "gradations of development" but disconnected periods of productivity and unproductivity, periods of decay and stagnation, sudden reversals, conflicting currents—not stages, but expressions of new spiritual situations, an uneasy sea, by turns tempestuous and placid, stirred by this or that "spiritual" wind but having no "constant flow," no destination. So far as we can tell, the term "development" can only apply to the technical means for the expression and elaboration of culture, to the somehow coherent sequence of naturalistic, classical, romantic, and baroque types of expression in the various disparate periods of productivity, to the alternation, somehow conditioned, by more emotional and more rationalized cultural expressions (religions, works of art, etc.), and to the superseding of mythically veiled expressions by unmythical ones at the ageing of the various historical organisms. In short, the term "development" can apply not to the content but to the surface movements which, we must remember, operate independently within each historical organism as if in a separate world.

In the culture-movement of the various historical organisms we are confronted with totally different "worlds" in the making, worlds which come and go along with their respective historical organisms, which are unique and exclusive throughout, and hence are fundamentally different from the uniform cosmos produced by the civilizational process.

Whereas we can apply "intellectual" concepts, modern scientific concepts, to the objects of the universally valid and necessary civilizational process and thereby construct a conscious picture of this process and its consequences, the objects of culture-movement and the various exclusive and unique cultural worlds can only be approached by means of "historical concepts," concepts and ideas dealing in "unique essences." And for the sociological examination of the worlds and movements of culture, it can, therefore, only be a matter of elaborating types, i.e., the comparative presentation of a recurring phenomenology of the surface appearance and an attempt to discover some intelligible connection between this phenomenology, with its unique content, and the general processes of civilization and society in the various historical organisms. Roughly, this is the task of culture-sociology.

*   *   *

Each period of culture that follows from some new life-feeling, since it seeks to shape the stuff of existence and its social and civilizational aggregate and to lend it its own spiritual aspect, naturally reacts upon the corporeal and civilizational aggregate. It creates principles of structure which are conserved and propagated in religions by the Church, and in systems of ideas by mind and the idea. It creates in works of art objective images of eternity, and in great men personified "prototypes" of the life-patterns. Through social and mental channels it impels all these into all the pores of the social and individual structure and over the whole corporeal and mental habitus of the historical sphere in which it arose. In this way it permeates down with its principles of structure into the social and civilizational substratum of historical development and there saturates it. This is exactly its task and purpose as the spiritual mode of expression of the new life-aggregate. It thus influences in most thorough fashion the course of social development and the civilizational process in every historical organ-

ism. Its final development from the natural forces of impulse, will, and intellect is therefore complex —indeed, it is almost always in conflict with cultural formations of the previous aggregate, formations resulting from the very saturation mentioned. (We can recall as historical instance the self-assertion of the early capitalistic aggregate, which was a gigantic naturalism of will in conflict with the psycho-culturally determined medieval life.) At a definite stage culturally acquired structure and rigidity can, in fact, bring the process of re-aggregation to a standstill by the founding of rituals and the chaining of all natural forces (India's religiously fixed caste-system). By means of such ideas bound together by ritual it can congeal the civilizational process. Thus cultural formation becomes relatively an essential element in the concrete structure of society and civilization. But this does not alter the fact that these processes are original and self-moved. They are self-moved in the degree that one (social process) is propelled, within the limits of natural conditions, by natural forces of impulse and will, and in the degree that the other (civilizational process) is propelled by intellectual forces directed toward the mastery of existence. Nor does it alter the fact that each new aggregate thus formed is the source of new tasks and problems for the culture-movement and its inmost centre, the soul. Only then does the concrete solution of these problems create the forms and rigidities in which the historical organisms are from time to time arrested and from which their natural and intellectual forces continually try to liberate them. The result is the creation of ever new spiritual situations, a new soil for cultural productivity. Social process, civilizational process and culture-movement hang together in this correlative, reciprocal, dynamic fashion. But the concrete character of this interrelationship must be elucidated for each historical organism and for each historical instant by further monographic study, though in principle it must always follow the schema development here.

Culture-movement has widely varying degrees of success in drawing the social and civilizational products into its path, depending on the time and the historical organism. Moreover, its desires to do so varies just as widely in different times and periods; for the life-feeling of the soul, which is confronted by a definite life-aggregate and grows out of it, is only capable of this effect within the limits of its own strength. It sees varying degrees of possibility, and in "happier times" necessity, of a complete organization of the stuff of experience.

Section B

Processes of Stabilization and Change

Editorial Foreword, BY KASPAR D. NAEGELE   *1287*

1. *On the Equilibrium of the Social System,* BY VILFREDO PARETO   *1288*
2. *On Disorganization and Reorganization,* BY W. I. THOMAS AND FLORIAN
   ZNANIECKI   *1292*
3. *The Routinization of Charisma,* BY MAX WEBER   *1297*
4. *On the Process of Change in Social Values,* BY EMILE DURKHEIM   *1305*
5. *The Principle of Immanent Change,* BY PITIRIM SOROKIN   *1311*
6. *On Configurations of Culture Growth,* BY ALFRED L. KROEBER   *1321*
7. *On Conflict,* BY GEORG SIMMEL   *1324*

Processes of Stabilization and Change

by Kaspar D. Naegele

THIS SECTION ILLUSTRATES the cardinal importance of distinguishing between change *in* and change *of* society. In the main, it is concerned with analyzing the apprehensible persistence of many institutional arrangements in the light of an equally perceptible continuity of change. The selections suggest a variety of processes whereby, as members of society, we compromise between our wishes—as W. I. Thomas recognized them—for novelty and order. In the intellectual history of the West, the concept of equilibrium, whatever its shortcomings, has combined recognition of the contrary tendencies in individuals and in their collective arrangements. In response, we seek for balance.

The section opens with Pareto, who made the notion of equilibrium centrally important in his dissection of the order by which we carry on.

The selection from W. I. Thomas is taken from the part of his work dealing with migration from one culture to another. Like many others before him, he suggested that any social arrangement imposes strains and costs on its participants in the very act of rewarding them. The strains may be mild or acute, distributed or concentrated. Being alive involves a continuous transcendence of strain (not necessarily its reduction). The reordering of attitudes in the face of shifted contexts of value provides Thomas with an opportunity to understand change within a society—especially one that has made the absorption of immigrants a condition of its own development.

Max Weber indicates the necessity and conflict represented by charismatic claims. Without them, moral and intellectual traditions would die. Yet charismatic leaders wish both to be heard and also to be followed; they seek influence and continuity. The dissociation of charisma from personality and its association with offices that can be filled by a succession of personalities to whom charisma can then become attributed constitutes one important mode of social transformation. As a mode, it also

suggests that demands for stability (subjectively experienced as the reliability of the world) are among the strong and emergent consequences of a dependence on others made possible by the human freedom from relatively specific instincts.

Durkheim's lecture, presented to a gathering of philosophers in Bologna in 1911, restates the central role of value-judgments in the constitution of society. It seeks to demonstrate important similarities between judgments of fact and judgments of value. Both kinds of judgments involve assertions which can be confronted with standards (ideals). If Durkheim had confined himself to that aspect of the matter, the selection would be misplaced in the present context. However, the lecture is relevant to a consideration of social change, because it suggests the existence of "different species of ideals." Our cognitive and moral judgments may simply be different instances of *one* faculty of judgment, the faculty involving a relation both to facts and to ideals. Some judgments, however, are confined to the expression of reality, while others concern the assertion of value. Moral ideals, as a species, are "simply the ideas in terms of which society sees itself." As ideals, however, they imply the facts and processes of commitment and attachment. Moral judgments, therefore, help "*transfigure* the realities to which they relate" (italics mine).

The moral constitution of society ipso facto introduces a pattern of change. Moreover, ideals are not just the private property of insulated individuals— they are part of the relations among individuals. They are also mutually related in constituting a *shared* consensus, which is an object of belief and attachment. Yet for many reasons this consensus cannot coincide fully with the pattern of enacted events that could not have occurred without it. Consensus, furthermore, is subject to renewal and creative revision. It introduces successions, or perhaps cycles, of fervor and indifference, exaltation and exhaustion, routine and special occasion, into the continuities of social life. Finally, the moral constitution of society, with its definition of the desirable (and the possible—in partial contrast to the actual and the past), introduces a permanent disposition of transcendence. With its implication of sacredness, society abets the individual's inclination and ability to surpass himself. This, in turn, contributes to the permanence of change within social arrangements. With the deceptive simplicity characteristic of him, Durkheim thus states a position and many questions essential to the study of social change.

Sorokin and Kroeber are concerned with the dynamics of human creativity in the realms of conscious being. Both perceive a pattern in the cognitive, normative, and aesthetic assertion and accomplishment by which, as members of societies and cultures, we elaborate the conditions of life beyond the point of necessity. We thus bequeath, to successive generations, styles of thought, work, or play. These are composed of contrary tendencies, and so invite change.

In the two brief pages from Simmel, we can contemplate once again the way in which our own inevitable purposiveness becomes both a source of enlightenment about the wider world and a source of error.

1. On the Equilibrium of the Social System

BY VILFREDO PARETO

2063. AN EXHAUSTIVE STUDY of social forms would have to consider at least the chief elements that determine them, disregarding those elements only which seem to be of secondary or incidental influence. But such a study is not at present possible, any more than an exhaustive study of plant or animal forms is possible, and we are therefore obliged to confine ourselves to a study covering a part only of the subject. Fortunately for our project, not a few of the elements have an influence upon human proclivities and sentiments, so that by taking account of residues we indirectly take account of them as well.

2064. The influence of the first group of elements (soil, climate, and so on) is undoubtedly very important. A comparison of the civilizations of peoples of the tropics and peoples of temperate zones would be enough to show that; and many books have been written on the subject, but so far with no great results. We shall make no direct examination of such influences here, but account for them indirectly by taking as data of fact the residues, proclivities, and interests of human beings who are subject to them.

2065. To go farther still in our avoidance of difficulties, we shall confine our investigations to the peoples of Europe and of the Asian and African sections of the Mediterranean basin. That will free us of the many serious—and unsolved—questions that are connected with race. We must necessarily take account of the influences upon a given people of other peoples, for the various peoples of the regions indicated have at no time in history been entirely isolated. But military, political, intellectual, economic, and other kinds of power through which those influences have been exerted depend upon elements such as sentiments, state of knowledge, and interests; and the influences, therefore, may be inferred, in part at least, from those elements.

2066. But however many, however few, the elements that we choose to consider, we assume at any rate that they constitute a system, which we may call the "social system"; and the nature and properties of that system we propose to investigate. The system changes both in form and in character in course of time. When, therefore, we speak of "the social system" we mean that system taken both at a specified moment and in the successive transformations which it undergoes within a specified period of time. So when one speaks of the solar system, one means that system taken both at a specified moment and in the successive moments which go to make up a greater or lesser period of time.

2067. *The state of equilibrium.* If we intend to reason at all strictly, our first obligation is to fix upon the state in which we are choosing to consider the social system, which is constantly changing in form. The real state, be it static or dynamic, of the

Reprinted from Vilfredo Pareto, *The Mind and Society,* ed. Arthur Livingston, trans. Andrew Bongiorno and Arthur Livingston (New York: Harcourt, Brace & Co., 1935) Vol. IV, §§ 2063–79, with the permission of The Pareto Fund.

system is determined by its conditions. Let us imagine that some modification in its form is induced artificially (virtual movements). At once a reaction will take place, tending to restore the changing form to its original state as modified by normal change. If that were not the case, the form, with its normal changes, would not be determined but would be a mere matter of chance.

2068. We can take advantage of that peculiarity in the social system to define the state that we choose to consider and which for the moment we will indicate by the letter X. We can then say that the state X is such a state that if it is artificially subjected to some modification different from the modification it undergoes normally, a reaction at once takes place tending to restore it to its real, its normal, state. That gives us an exact definition of the state X.

2069. The state X is ever in process of change, and we are not able, nor do we care, to consider it that way in all its minute detail. If we desire to figure on the fertility of a piece of land, we do not set out to watch how the grain grows in the sown field every minute, every hour, every day, or even every month. We take the annual crop and let it go at that. If we want to figure on the element of patriotism, we cannot follow each soldier in every move he makes from the day when he is called to arms to the day when he falls on a battle-field. For our purposes it is enough to note the gross fact that so many men have died for their country. Or again, the hand of a watch moves and stops, stops and moves, yet in measuring time we disregard that circumstance and figure as though the movement of the hand were continuous. Let us therefore consider successive states X_1, X_2, X_3 . . . reached at certain intervals of time that we fix on for the purpose of getting at the states which we choose to consider and which are such that each one of the elements that we elect to consider has completed its action. To see the situation more clearly, we might look at a few examples. Pure economics affords a very simple one. Let us take a person who in a given unit of time—every day, we will say—barters bread for wine. He begins with no wine, and stops bartering when he has a certain quantity of wine. In Figure 1, the axis of time is Ot, and ab, bc, cd, de . . . are spaces representing equal units of time. The axis of the quantities of wine is Oq. At the beginning of the first unit of time, the individual has no wine—his position is at a; at the end he has the quantity bX_1 of wine—his position is at X_1. Exactly the same transaction is repeated every day, and at the end of every day, or of every unit of time, the individual's position is at X_1, X_2, X_3. . . . All those points fall within a

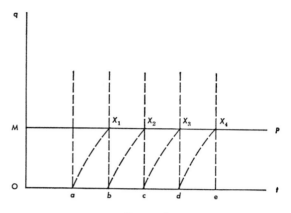

Figure 1

line, MP, parallel to Ot, and the distance between the two lines is equal to the quantity of wine that the individual acquires through exchange each day. The line MP is called the line of equilibrium and, in general, is the line determined by the equations of pure economics. It does not have to be a line parallel to the axis Ot, for there is no reason why exactly the same transaction should be repeated every day. It may, for example, be the line MP in Figure 2: ab, bc, cd . . . are still equal units of time, but at the beginnings of the various periods the individual's position is at a, s, r, d, u . . . and at the ends at X_1, X_2, X_3, X_4, X_5. . . . The line M X_1, X_2, X_3, X_4, X_5 . . . is still called the line of equilibrium. When it is said that pure economics gives the theory of the economic equilibrium, it means that pure economics shows how the final positions, X_1, X_2, X_3 . . . are reached from the points a, s, r, d, u . . . and nothing more. Now let us consider the more general case. In Figure 2, ab, bc, cd . . . are no longer equal to one another, but represent differ-

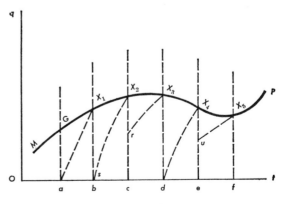

Figure 2

ent periods of time, which we choose in order to examine a phenomenon at the end of each of them, the length of the period being determined by the time required for an element to complete the particular action that we have chosen to consider. The points a, s, r, d, u . . . represent the state of the individual at the beginning of the action; X_1, X_2, X_3 . . . the state of the individual when it is completed. The line $M X_1, X_2$ . . . P is the line of the state X (§2076).

2070. That definition is identical, barring the mere difference in form, with the one given in § 2068. In fact, if we start in the first place with the definition just given of the state X_1, we see that the action of each element having been completed, society cannot of itself assume any form other than the form X_1, and that if it were made artificially to vary from that form, it should tend to resume it; for otherwise, its form would not be entirely determined, as was assumed, by the elements considered. In other words, if society has reached a point, X_1 (Figure 3), following such a path aX_1, that at X_1 the action of the elements which we choose to consider is complete; and if society is artificially made to vary from X_1, the variation can be brought about only: (1) by forcing society to points such as l, n . . . which are located outside the line aX_1; or (2), by forcing it to a point m on the line aX_1. In the first case, society should tend to return to X_1; otherwise its state would not be completely determined, as was assumed, by the elements considered. In the second case, the hypothesis would be in contradiction with our assumption that the action of the elements is complete; for it is complete only at X_1, and is incomplete at m; at the latter point the elements considered are still in action and they carry society from m to X_1.

Using the definition we gave in §2068 as the point of departure, we see, conversely, that if after society has been artificially made to vary from the point X_1, it tends to return to X_1, the phenomenon indicates one of two things: either, as in the first case above, that society has been brought to the points l, n . . . which are different from the points determined by the elements considered, or that society has been brought to a point m, at which the action of the elements considered is incomplete. If instead of reaching the points X_1, X_2, X_3 . . . successively the system were to traverse the line X_1, X_2, X_3 in a continuous movement, there would be nothing to change in the definitions just given. One would need merely to say that if the system were made artificially to deviate from the line X_1, X_2 . . . it would tend at once to return to it; and that if the effect of the elements is to impel the system along that line, their action would not be complete unless the

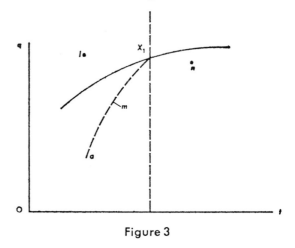

Figure 3

system were located on that line, and on no other.

2071. So we get the precise and rigorous definition that we said . . . we were intending to give of the state we are about to consider. To become more familiar with it let us now look at some analogies, much as one looks at a sphere to get some conception of the shape of the Earth.

For a concrete example, the state X is analogous to the state of a river, and the states X_1, and X_2 . . . to the states of the same river taken day by day. The river is not motionless; it is flowing, and the slightest modification we try to effect in its form and in the manner of its flow is the cause of a reaction that tends to reproduce the original state.

2072. For an abstract case, the state X that we are considering is analogous to the state of dynamic equilibrium in a physical system, the states X_1, X_2 . . . to successive positions of equilibrium in that system. The state X, one might also add, is analogous to the state of equilibrium in a living organism.

2073. We might look for analogies in a field closer to our own. The states X_1, X_2, X_3 . . . are like the states that pure economics considers in an economic system; and the analogy is so close that the states of the economic system may be regarded as particular cases of the general states of the sociological system.

2074. There is another analogy that we cannot disregard if we would go somewhat deeply into this matter. The state X is analogous to the state called a *statistic* equilibrium in the kinetic theory of gases. To make that clearer, suppose we consider a particular case, the consumption, for instance, of cigars of a given quality within a given territory. The states X_1, X_2, X_3 . . . represent hypothetically, the annual consumptions of such cigars. Let us begin by assuming that they are all more or less equal. Then we would say that the consumption of cigars is constant. By that we do not mean that every individual smokes the same number of cigars each year. We know very well that such numbers vary widely. But the variations more or less offset one another, so that the resultant is zero or, to be more exact, approximately zero. To be sure, it may happen that so many of these variations will be in the same direction that the resultant will no longer be approximately zero, but such a probability is so slight that we need not consider it; and that is what we mean when we say that the consumption is constant. If, instead, the probability is not so slight, fluctuations around the constant total of consumption will be observable, such fluctuations following the law of probabilities. But suppose $X_1, X_2, X_3 \ldots$ represent increasing consumptions. We can then repeat, with the proper modifications, everything we have just said. We are in no sense assuming that the individual consumptions are on the increase. We know they are extremely variable. We are speaking of a *statistic* equilibrium, where variations offset one another in such a way that the resultant is an increasing total consumption. And such increasing total consumption may have a probability so great as to eliminate fluctuations depending on probabilities; or a probability not so great, and then fluctuations will occur. So, in preparing ourselves by studying particlular cases of that sort we find it easy to grasp the general significance of $X_1, X_2, X_3 \ldots$ for consumptions varying in any manner whatsoever.

2075. Extend to an entire social system what we have seen to hold for a system of consumers of one brand of cigars, and the result will be a clear conception of the analogy we have in view for the states $X_1, X_2, X_3. \ldots$

2076. We could continue to designate the social states that we elect to consider . . . with the letters X, and $X_1, X_2 \ldots$, but that manner of designating things soon begins to weary and one would prefer to have them given names. We could choose a name at random, but it is perhaps better to borrow it from something more or less like the thing we intend to designate by it. So, stopping at the mechanical analogy, we will call the states X and $X_1, X_2 \ldots$ *states of equilibrium*. But the meaning of the term as we use it has to be sought strictly within the definitions that we gave in §§2068–69, due attention being paid to the argument in §2074.

2077. We have now simplified our problem by deciding to consider certain successive states instead of the numberless imperceptible mutations that lead up to them. We now have to go on along that path and try to reduce the problem of mutual correlations and the number of elements that we are to consider to greater simplicity.

2078. In our study we stop at certain elements, just as the chemist stops at chemical elements; but that in no sense means that the elements at which we stop are not reducible to a smaller number, or even, at a hazard, to one; just as the chemist does not claim that the number of chemical elements is not still further reducible or indeed that some day they may not be recognized as different manifestations of one single element.

2079. *Organization of the social system.* The economic system is made up of certain molecules set in motion by tastes and subject to ties (checks) in the form of obstacles to the acquisition of economic values. The social system is much more complicated, and even if we try to simplify it as far as we possibly can without falling into serious errors, we at least have to think of it as made up of certain molecules harbouring residues, deviations, interests, and proclivities, and which perform, subject to numerous ties, logical and non-logical actions. In the economic system the non-logical element is relegated entirely to tastes and disregarded, since tastes are taken as data of fact. One might wonder whether the same thing might not be done for the social system, whether we might not relegate the non-logical element to the residues, then take the residues as data of fact and proceed to examine the logical conduct that originates in the residues. That, indeed, would yield a science similar to pure, or even to applied, economics. But unfortunately the similarity ceases when we come to the question of correspondences with reality. The hypothesis that in satisfying their tastes human beings perform economic actions which may on the whole be considered logical is not too far removed from realities, and the inferences from those hypotheses yield a general form of the economic phenomenon in which divergences from reality are few and not very great, save in certain cases (most important among them the matter of savings). Far removed from realities, instead, is the hypothesis that human beings draw logical inferences from residues and then proceed to act accordingly. In activity based on residues human beings use derivations more frequently than strictly logical reasonings, and therefore to try to predict their conduct by considering their manners of reasoning would be to lose all contacts with the real. Residues are not, like tastes, merely sources of conduct; they function throughout the whole course of the conduct developing from the source, a fact that becomes apparent in the substitution of derivations for logical reasonings. A science, therefore, based on the hypothesis that logical inferences are drawn from certain given residues would yield a general form of the social phenomenon having little or no contact with reality —it would be a sociology more or less like a non-Euclidean geometry or the geometry of a four-dimensional space. If we would keep within reali-ties, we have to ask experience to acquaint us not only with certain fundamental residues, but with the various ways in which they function in determining the conduct of human beings.

2. On Disorganization and Reorganization

BY WILLIAM I. THOMAS AND FLORIAN ZNANIECKI

THE CHIEF SOCIAL PROBLEM arising with reference to the relation between individual life-organization and social organization is the reconciliation of the stability of social systems with the efficiency of individual activities, and the most significant feature of social evolution in this line is the growing difficulty of maintaining a stable social organization in the face of the increasing importance which individual efficiency assumes in all domains of cultural life.

In early societies we find individual efficiency entirely subordinated to the demand for social stability. All the social schemes of the group are connected, are parts of one whole, one large complex of social tradition, and any innovation is considered a break not only of the one particular scheme which it modifies, but of this entire complex. There is, of course, no objective rational ground whatever for taking the traditional schemes *en bloc,* no finalistic connection between the corresponding activities; the real results of a change of practical methods in a certain line may have little or no bearing on the results of other traditional forms of behavior. Thus, a modification introduced into some social ceremony has nothing to do objectively with the technique of hunting or warfare, a new technical device in constructing houses has no direct effect upon the political organization of the group, etc. But the common bond between all these schemes lies in the character of sacredness which all of them possess in the eyes of the group as parts of the same traditional stock whose unity is ultimately founded on the unity and continuity of the group itself. The individual must make each and all of these schemes his own in order to be a full member of the group. If for the formation of his character the important point is that all his interests are satisfied within the group and therefore are supposed to be founded on his social interest, the essential thing about his life-organization is that he is supposed to share in all the interests of his group and to adopt all social schemes as schemes of his personal behavior. There may be some differentiation between individuals as to the relative importance which certain particular interests assume in their lives, but no specialization in the sense of an absorption by some particular interests to the exclusion of others. Each member of a primary group is by a gradual initiation introduced into all the domains which compose the civilization of the group and is as all-sided in his activities as the stage of civilization which his group has reached permits him to be.

But this all-sidedness is attained at the cost of efficiency. There is a maximum of efficiency in each line which no member of the group can transgress, not because—as is the case on a higher level of culture—a higher efficiency in one particular line would impair his activities in other lines in which he is also expected to be active, but because in each particular line the domination of traditional schemes excludes not only the creation of new and better working schemes, but limits even the possibility of extending old methods to new classes of problems. The only increase of efficiency which is allowed and encouraged is the more and more perfect solution of traditional problems—an increase whose results are well exemplified in the perfection of primitive art and technique, in elaborate religious rituals, in the reliability of information which much of primitive knowledge shows, in the perfect rational order presented by many complex early systems of social and political organization, etc. Under these conditions, spon-

Reprinted from William I. Thomas and Florian Znaniecki, *The Polish Peasant in Europe and America* in *Social Behavior and Personality: Contributions of W. I. Thomas to Theory and Social Research,* ed. Edmund H. Volkart (Social Science Research Council, 1951), with the permission of the Social Science Research Council.

taneous social evolution is possible only by an agglomeration of small changes which are not noticed at once but modify from generation to generation the stock of traditions while leaving the illusion of its identity. When, on the contrary, the primary group is brought rapidly into contact with the outside world with its new and rival schemes, the entire old organization is apt to break down at once, precisely because all the old schemes were interconnected in social consciousness; and the individual whose life-organization was based on the organization of his primary group is apt to become completely disorganized in the new conditions, for the rejection of a few traditional schemes brings with it a general negative attitude toward the entire stock of traditions which he has been used to revere, whereas he is not prepared for the task of reorganizing his life on a new basis. This occurs very frequently with the European peasant who emigrates and we have given in our first two volumes examples showing that the peasants themselves realize the effect which the rejection of certain elements of this stock has on the total personal complex of schemes.

But with the growing social differentiation and the increasing wealth and rationality of social values, the complex of traditional schemes constituting the civilization of a group becomes subdivided into several more or less independent complexes. The individual can no longer be expected to make all these complexes his own; he must specialize. There arises also between the more or less specialized groups representing different more or less systematic complexes of schemes a conscious or half-conscious struggle for the supremacy of the respective complexes or systems in social life, and it happens that a certain system succeeds in gaining a limited and temporary supremacy. Thus, among the ancient Hebrews, in some European countries during and after the Reformation, and in the early American colonies, certain religious systems predominated over all other cultural complexes; in Russia and Prussia, up to the present war, a similarly dominant role was assumed by the state; in Poland and Bohemia during the nineteenth century the concept of nationality, determined mainly by language, historical tradition and the feeling of solidarity, constituted the chief ground of social organization and was supposed to dominate individual life-organization; in societies with a powerful economic development like modern England and America the leading part is played by industrial and commercial schemes. The family system was until lately supposed to be the exclusive foundation of individual life-organization for women. During the present war, military interests have almost everywhere taken the center of attention and imposed far-reaching modifications of the life-organization on all the members of western societies.

But it is clear from the above examples that no special social complex, however wide, rich and consistent, can regulate all the activities which are going on in the group; the predominance of a complex is not only limited in time and space, but always incomplete and relative. Moreover each of the broad complexes which we designate by the terms "religion," "state," "nationality," "industry," "science," "art," etc., splits into many smaller ones and specialization and struggle continue between these. The prevalent condition of our civilization in the past and perhaps in the present can thus be characterized as that of a plurality of rival complexes of schemes each regulating in a definite traditional way certain activities and each contending with others for supremacy within a given group. The antagonism between social stability and individual efficiency is under these circumstances further complicated by the conflicting demands put upon the individual by these different complexes, each of which tends to organize personal life exclusively in view of its own purposes.

Whenever there are many rival complexes claiming individual attention the group representing each complex not only allows for but even encourages a certain amount of creation, of new developments, within the limits of the traditional schemes, for a complex of schemes which excluded new experiences as it does in the primary group would be unable to maintain itself in its implicit or explicit contest with other complexes. Therefore the conservative groups which support any existing schematism want it to be alive, to be as adaptable to the changing conditions of life as is compatible with the existence of the traditional schemes. The amount of efficiency which a scheme makes possible varies, of course, with the nature of the scheme itself, with the rigidity with which the group keeps the mere form, with the rapidity of the social process. And thus society demands from the individual productivity in the line of his career; in morality it is seldom satisfied with passive acceptance of the norms, with their limitation to old and known actions, but usually wants their application to new facts coming under their definition; in custom it is glad to see every extension of tradition; in science or art it greets with satisfaction every new work done in accordance with the traditional system; in religion it meets with joy every revival which proves that the old emotions can stir some modern souls, every theoretic application of dogma which proves that the old conceptions can satisfy some modern intellects; in family life everything is welcome that can enliven the content without changing the form of relation between husband and wife, parents and children; in politics, in law, in economic organization, every reform increasing the efficiency of the existing system without modifying it in the slightest is highly appreciated.

The fact that most if not all social schemes are incorporated in more or less comprehensive and systematic complexes helps to maintain the feeling of their immutability. The unity of many special traditional complexes is still almost as firmly established in modern civilized society as in the unity of its total stock of traditions in a savage primary group. The breakdown of any scheme belonging to a traditional complex seems to imperil the complex itself. And the individual who might easily reject a single scheme will hesitate before rejecting the whole complex. How consciously and masterfully incorporation of the most insignificant schemes into a great system is often made is manifested by such examples as religion and legal state-control. In the Roman Catholic Church disaccordance with the apparently most insignificant detail of the system of beliefs or an infraction of any rule of behavior is supposed to produce estrangement from the congregation, because it involves in social consciousness a break with the whole system; the individual must either admit that he is in error, recant and recognize the scheme—at least in the form of a confession and penance—or consider himself outside the church. In the same way, by breaking any law or ordinance of the state the individual is considered a rebel against the whole system of legal state-control and loses in fact his rights as member of the group, since he may become the object of any violence decreed as punishment for this break; the punishment becomes thus a forcible recognition of the broken scheme. The same method, with only less consistency and less power to enforce obedience, is followed in morality, in class-organization, even in customs, as when one break of social etiquette is sufficient to disqualify a person as member of polite society, or one act opposed to traditional morals sufficient to make all "well-behaved" members of a group disclaim every connection with the offending member.

But such a traditional fixation of special complexes of schemes within which efficiency is required with the condition that all schemes remain recognized does not correspond at all with the spontaneous tendencies of individuals. First of all, the scheme represents for the evolving individual either the minimum of stability which he reaches after a period of changing active experiences, or the minimum of new active experiences which he

reaches after a period of passive security. In other words, as long as the individual evolves, an activity regulated by the scheme and efficient within the limits of this regulation does not represent a definite level; it corresponds always only to an intermediary stage, either of progression from the passive acceptance of socially imposed situations toward a creative activity free from all subordination to schemes, or of regression in the opposition direction. The individual may indeed oscillate, so to speak, from relative passivity to relative creativeness without going far enough in the first direction to become entirely inefficient, and without becoming so efficient as to have to reject the scheme; the less radical these oscillations, the more the individual's conduct approaches the average prescribed by the scheme. Such an individual represents then a social model of behavior in the given sphere; he is the moderately productive conservative, the famous *juste milieu* type. Frequently, however, the individual goes on with a progressively intense and efficient activity, tries continually to find and to define new situations; his efficiency becomes then increasingly dangerous to the scheme, because even if activity begins in perfect conformity with the scheme, the accumulating novelty of experience sooner or later makes the scheme appear insufficient. There are innumerable examples of individuals who began creative activity with the firm intention of keeping within the limits of the traditional schematism and ended by rejecting it altogether. The history of morality, of science, of political and social reform, and particularly of religious heresies is full of such biographies. And therefore the social group which is the bearer of a traditional complex is mistrustful of the individual who is too creative, particularly as the majority is usually composed of personalities whose evolution tends to the opposite limit—to the purely passive acceptance of the formal elements of tradition and the repetition of old activities bordering on habit. In normal times this passivity may be scorned by the active part of the group, but at moments of crisis we find the group condemning all "imprudent" innovations and falling back upon the most abject Philistinism as upon the only absolutely unshakable basis of security.

The second difficulty concerning the adaptation of individual life-organization to the social complexes is the fact that while a complex has to be accepted or rejected in its entirety, since the group does not permit the individual to accept some schemes and to reject others, the individual in his spontaneous development tends to make a selection of schemes from various complexes, thus cutting across social classifications of schemes, and often including in his dynamic life-organization successively, or even simultaneously, elements which from the traditional standpoint may seem contradictory. This difficulty is increased by the fact that many—perhaps most—social complexes are not freely chosen by the individual, but their acceptance is either expected to follow from a position that the individual occupies in the group from birth—as member of a certain class, a certain race, as male or female, handsome or homely, etc.—or from a position which is imposed on him in his early youth through a certain moral code, religion or form of education, or, finally, from a position which he is forced to take in order to satisfy his elementary needs—for example, marriage or choice of a profession. There are complexes prescribed for the son and the daughter, for the bachelor and the married man, for the girl, the wife and the mother, for the society person and the member of a lower class, for the adherent of a religious creed and the atheist, for the professional in any line, for the city and the country inhabitant, for the householder, the tenant of an apartment and the roomer, for the person who eats at home, in a boarding house or in a restaurant, for the pedestrian, the car-passenger and the owner of an automobile, etc. The individual who has a complex imposed upon him or accepts it voluntarily is expected to show the prescribed amount of efficiency—neither more nor less—in all the activities regulated by the schemes belonging to the complex, and is not expected to perform any activities demanded by a rival complex, or to invent any new schemes which may seem to disagree with the accepted ones. More than this, he is often required to abstain from activities which, even if they do not contradict directly the existing schematism, may take his time and energy from the performance of the prescribed activities.

It is obvious that this type of social organization disregards entirely the personal conditions of efficiency. The organization of schemes in a traditionally fixed complex represents usually a degree of methodical perfection sufficient to obtain from individuals an average amount of efficiency, making each individual contribute in some measure to the maintenance of the existing social status, so that an activity organized in accordance with the complex is indubitably more productive socially than an unorganized one. But no socially fixed complex of schemes in whatever line—economic, political, moral, scientific, æsthetic, religious—can obtain from any individual the highest amount of efficiency of which he is capable, not only because it prohibits creation beyond the limits traced by the schemes, but also because it ignores both the differences of personal endowment which make one individual more capable of performing certain activities

than others and the variations of personal evolution which make the individual more efficient in a certain line at one period of his life than at another. The organization of activities demanded by a social complex is both impersonal and changeless, whereas an organization which would fulfil the conditions of the highest individual efficiency would have to be personal and changing.

An unavoidable consequence of the now prevalent social organization is that the immense majority of individuals is forced either into Philistinism or Bohemianism. An individual who accepts any social system in its completeness, with all the schemes involved, is necessarily drifting toward routine and hypocrisy. A part of the system may satisfy his personal needs for a time, particularly as long as he is gradually assimilating and applying certain of its schemes, but the rest of the system will not correspond to his predominant aspirations and may be even opposed to them. If the development of life-organization goes on spontaneously, the individual is gradually led to realize the importance for his chief aims of even activities which originally did not appeal to him—his efficiency in the line of his main interest gradually spreads to many side lines—whereas if a life-organization is socially imposed, the personally uninteresting elements of the social complex cannot become personally attractive by being gradually connected with the interesting ones in the course of a personal evolution, since this evolution is limited. As a consequence, we find the original inefficiency along uninteresting side lines influencing even those activities in which the individual was actually interested at some period of his life, and the whole productivity in the given field drops below the minimum required by the group. In order to remain socially adapted, to avoid active criticism of the group, the individual has then to display in words interests which he does not possess and to invent all kinds of devices in order to conceal his lack of efficiency. This tendency to hypocrisy and pretense is greatly facilitated in such cases by the fact that the majority of the group is in a similar situation and is not only willing to accept any plausible pretension designed to cover individual inefficiency but even often develops a standardized set of "conventional lies" to be used for this purpose, which every one knows to be lies but tacitly agrees to treat as true.

If, on the contrary, the individual either refuses to accept certain of the schemes included in a social complex or develops some positive form of behavior contradicting in the eyes of society some of the schemes of the complex, he is forced to reject the complex in its entirety, and becomes thus, voluntarily or not, a rebel. His situation is then rather difficult, for society has not trained him to develop a life-organization spontaneously and the social organization of the type outlined above opposes innumerable obstacles to such a development. With rare exceptions, he can do nothing but adopt some other ready system instead of the rejected one. But then the same problem repeats itself, and every successive attempt at complete adaptation to a new system after rebellion is usually more difficult than the preceding ones, both because the personal demands of the individual become better defined in opposition to social regulation and because each particular rebellion undermines the prestige of social systems in general. The usual consequence of rebellion is thus Bohemianism, a permanent tendency to pass from one system to another, attracted at first by the personally interesting sides of a system and soon repelled by the personally uninteresting ones. The result is again unproductivity.

Under such conditions the appearance of a really efficient, creative personality is actually a very exceptional social happening, for it needs a very high personal ability and persistence to develop a dynamic individual organization for efficiency instead of adopting a static social organization for stability when social education has exclusively the second purpose in view, and only by a rare concurrence of circumstances individuals who have this high ability of developing without proper educational help happen to be left in peace to pursue their own self-made lines. And it is no wonder that the scarcity of creative individuals has led to the concept of genius, and high efficiency is still treated as a prodigy.

But the direction which social evolution has been gradually assuming in modern times seems to show that though the conditions outlined above are still predominant in civilized society they cannot last long; a different type of social organization is developing which begins to put higher demands on individual efficiency than on individual conformism. First of all, progressing specialization is continually subdividing the old social complexes into more and more narrow systems which can no longer constitute a sufficient basis for individual life-organization in any field. Thus, a modern scientist, business-man, technician, when forced by social division of labor to work in a limited and special line, does not find in this line an organization of even all the intellectual, economic and technical activities which he can and wishes to perform. And on the other hand, there is a continually growing field of common values and common activities over and above the special systems, a political, economic,

intellectual, æsthetic "universe of discourse," in which all the members of a modern society more or less participate; this field is incomparably smaller, in proportion to the totality of the civilization of the group, than it was in an early primary group or in the upper class of an ancient city-state, but it is much wider than it was, for instance, during the middle ages, and it is certainly wide enough to make every specialized individual realize the narrowness of his specialty and to open before him wide horizons of possible new experiences. Thence the increasing tendency of modern society to "vagabondage" in all forms—changes of residence, of profession, of political views, of religion, the decay of the family system as economic, hedonistic and educational institution, Bolshevism in politics and economics. And when vagabondage is in fact impossible, substitutes are sought which satisfy this tendency at least in imagination. This is the chief rôle of the popular literature of adventure, of moving pictures, of daydreams, even, in a large measure, of alcoholism. The task of imposing any particular social systems as definitive frames of individual life-organization is rapidly becoming too difficult for modern society.

And further, the demand for efficiency in every particular line is rapidly growing; efficiency begins to be appreciated even at the cost of conformity. This most important evolution seems to be brought by a radical change of relations between different social complexes, different lines of social activity. Mere specialization of social activity begins to be consciously supplemented by a growing organization of specialized lines. Struggle between social complexes is gradually supplanted by co-operation; the field of application of each complex is more and more frequently defined by distinction from rather than by opposition to other complexes. This evolution is almost completed in the economic field, is rapidly progressing in the fields of science, and is beginning to penetrate everywhere. Thus, the modern state is a highly developed system of the old style, claiming supremacy over other systems, but even there the idea that the state is only an instrument of the national life is being recognized and proclaimed. And when internal struggles lose their traditional form of physical conflict the chief reason for the internal supremacy of the state over other domains of the cultural life of a nation will be gone. Now, wherever co-operation between systems takes the place of struggle, the demand for conformity loses its power in the very measure in which each group engaged in special activities accepts as ultimate aim of these activities not the preservation of a traditional complex against all external influences, but a contribution to the general development of civilization. At the same time co-operation requires that certain results be reached independently of the question whether they are reached by traditional methods or by new ones; calls for efficiency come to every line of social activity from other lines, and the more frequent and insistent they become the more necessary it is to leave to every individual as much freedom as is compatible with efficient co-operation. In certain lines we find, indeed, the division of labor resulting in a separation between inventive and organizing activities on the one hand and mechanical activities on the other hand, but the best sign of the changed social attitudes is that this separation is not accepted calmly by social consciousness but has become one of the great social problems to be solved by conscious efforts.

It is clear that these new characters of modern social evolution require an entirely new standpoint with reference to individual life-organization. The individual must be trained not for conformity, but for efficiency, not for stability, but for creative evolution. And we cannot wait until new educational methods are developed by the slow and groping way of unorganized and unreflective empirical trials. We must realize that social education in the past, viewed from the standpoint of the human personality, has always been a failure and that whatever social progress and whatever personal development has even been achieved was due to the spontaneous constructive power of individuals who succeeded, not thanks to social help but in spite of social hindrances. The best that society has ever done for its members was to put at their disposal materials for creative development by preserving values produced by the past. The task of future society will be not only to remove obstacles preventing spontaneous personal development but to give positive help, to furnish every individual with proper methods for spontaneous personal development, to teach him how to become not a static character and a conformist, but a dynamic, continually growing and continually creative personality. And such methods can be found only by sociopsychological studies of human individuals.

3. The Routinization of Charisma

BY MAX WEBER

IN ITS PURE FORM charismatic authority has a character specifically foreign to everyday routine structures. The social relationships directly involved are strictly personal, based on the validity and practice of charismatic personal qualities. If this is not to remain a purely transitory phenomenon, but to take on the character of a permanent relationship forming a stable community of disciples or a band of followers or a party organization or any sort of political or hierocratic organization, it is necessary for the character of charismatic authority to become radically changed. Indeed, in its pure form charismatic authority may be said to exist only in the process of originating. It

cannot remain stable, but becomes either traditionalized or rationalized, or a combination of both.

The following are the principal motives underlying this transformation: (a) The ideal and also the material interests of the followers in the continuation and the continual reactivation of the community, (b) the still stronger ideal and also stronger material interests of the members of the administrative staff, the disciples or other followers of the charismatic leader in continuing their relationship. Not only this, but they have an interest in continuing it in such a way that both from an ideal and a material point of view, their own status is put on a stable everyday basis. This means, above all, making it possible to participate in normal family relationships or at least to enjoy a secure social position in place of the kind of discipleship which is cut off from ordinary worldly connexions, notably in the family and in economic relationships.

These interests generally become conspicuously

evident with the disappearance of the personal charismatic leader and with the problem of succession, which inevitably arises. The way in which this problem is met—if it is met at all and the charismatic group continues to exist—is of crucial importance for the character of the subsequent social relationships. The following are the principal possible types of solution:—

(a) The search for a new charismatic leader on the basis of criteria of the qualities which will fit him for the position of authority. This is to be found in a relatively pure type in the process of choice of a new Dalai Lama. It consists in the search for a child with characteristics which are interpreted to mean that he is a reincarnation of the Buddha. This is very similar to the choice of the new Bull of Apis.

In this case the legitimacy of the new charismatic leader is bound to certain distinguishing characteristics; thus, to rules with respect to which a tradition arises. The result is a process of traditionalization in favour of which the purely personal character of leadership is eliminated.

(b) By revelation manifested in oracles, lots, divine judgments, or other techniques of selection. In this case the legitimacy of the new leader is dependent on the legitimacy of the technique of his selection. This involves a form of legalization. It is said that at times the *Schofetim* of Israel had this character. Saul is said to have been chosen by the old war oracle.

(c) By the designation on the part of the original charismatic leader of his own successor and his recognition on the part of the followers. This is a very common form. Originally, the Roman magistracies were filled entirely in this way. The system survived most clearly into later times in the appointment of "dictators" and in the institution of the "interrex." In this case legitimacy is acquired through the act of designation.

(d) Designation of a successor by the charismatically qualified administrative staff and his recognition by the community. In its typical form this process should quite definitely not be interpreted as "election" or "nomination" or anything of the sort. It is not a matter of free selection, but of one which is strictly bound to objective duty. It is not to be determined merely by majority vote, but is a question of arriving at the correct designation, the designation of the right person who is truly endowed with charisma. It is quite possible that the minority and not the majority should be right in such a case. Unanimity is often required. It is obligatory to acknowledge a mistake and persistence in error is a serious offence. Making a wrong choice is a genuine wrong requiring expiation. Originally it was a magical offence.

Neverthless, in such a case it is easy for legitimacy to take on the character of an acquired right which is justified by standards of the correctness of the process by which the position was acquired, for the most part, by its having been acquired in accordance with certain formalities, such as coronation. This was the original meaning of the coronation of bishops and kings in the Western World by the clergy or the nobility with the "consent" of the community. There are numerous analogous phenomena all over the world. The fact that this is the origin of the modern conception of "election" raises problems which will have to be gone into later.

(e) By the conception that charisma is a quality transmitted by heredity; thus that it is participated in by the kinsmen of its bearer, particularly by his closest relatives. This is the case of hereditary charisma. The order of hereditary succession in such a case need not be the same as that which is in force for appropriated rights, but may differ from it. It is also sometimes necessary to select the proper heir within the kinship group by some of the methods just spoken of; thus in certain Negro states brothers have had to fight for the succession. In China, succession had to take place in such a way that the relation of the living group to the ancestral spirits was not disturbed. The rule either of seniority or of designation by the followers has been very common in the Orient. Hence, in the house of Osman, it has been obligatory to eliminate all other possible candidates.

Only in Medieval Europe and in Japan universally, elsewhere only sporadically, has the principle of primogeniture, as governing the inheritance of authority, become clearly established. This has greatly facilitated the consolidation of political groups in that it has eliminated struggle between a plurality of candidates from the same charismatic family.

In the case of hereditary charisma, recognition is no longer paid to the charismatic qualities of the individual, but to the legitimacy of the position he has acquired by hereditary succession. This may lead in the direction either of traditionalization or of legalization. The concept of "divine right" is fundamentally altered and now comes to mean authority by virtue of a personal right which is not dependent on the recognition of those subject to authority. Personal charisma may be totally absent. Hereditary monarchy is a conspicuous illustration. In Asia there have been very numerous hereditary priesthoods; also, frequently, the hereditary charisma of kinship groups has been treated as a criterion of social rank and of eligibility for fiefs and benefices.

(f) The concept that charisma may be transmitted by ritual means from one bearer to another or may be created in a new person. The concept was originally magical. It involves a dissociation of charisma from a particular individual, making it an objective, transferrable entity. In particular, it may become the charisma of office. In this case the belief in legitimacy is no longer directed to the individual, but to the acquired qualities and to the effectiveness of the ritual acts. The most important example is the transmission of priestly charisma by anointing, consecration, or the laying on of hands; and of royal authority, by anointing and by coronation. The *caracter indelibilis* thus acquired means that the charismatic qualities and powers of the office are emancipated from the personal qualities of the priest. For precisely this reason, this has, from the Donatist and the Montanist heresies down to the Puritan revolution, been the subject of continual conflicts. The "hireling" of the Quakers is the preacher endowed with the charisma of office.

Concomitant with the routinization of charisma with a view to insuring adequate succession, go the interests in its routinization on the part of the administrative staff. It is only in the initial stages and so long as the charismatic leader acts in a way which is completely outside everyday social organization, that it is possible for his followers to live communistically in a community of faith and enthusiasm, on gifts, "booty," or sporadic acquisition. Only the members of the small group of enthusiastic disciples and followers are prepared to devote their lives purely idealistically to their call. The great majority of disciples and followers will in the long run "make their living" out of their "calling" in a material sense as well. Indeed, this must be the case if the movement is not to disintegrate.

Hence, the routinization of charisma also takes the form of the appropriation of powers of control and of economic advantages by the followers or disciples, and of regulation of the recruitment of these groups. This process of traditionalization or of legalization, according to whether rational legislation is involved or not, may take any one of a number of typical forms.

1. The original basis of recruitment is personal charisma. With routinization, the followers or disciples may set up norms for recruitment, in particular involving training or tests of eligibility. Charisma can only be "awakened" and "tested"; it cannot be "learned" or "taught." All types of magical asceticism, as practiced by magicians and heroes, and all novitiates, belong in this category. These are means of closing the group which constitutes the administrative staff.

Only the proved novice is allowed to exercise authority. A genuine charismatic leader is in a position to oppose this type of prerequisite for membership. His successor is not, at least if he is chosen by the administrative staff. This type is illustrated by the magical and warrior asceticism of the "men's house" with initiation ceremonies and age groups. An individual who has not successfully gone through the initiation, remains a "woman"; that is, is excluded from the charismatic group.

2. It is easy for charismatic norms to be transformed into those defining a traditional social status on a hereditary charismatic basis. If the leader is chosen on a hereditary basis, it is very easy for hereditary charisma to govern the selection of the administrative staff and even, perhaps, those followers without any position of authority. The term "familistic state" (*Geschlechterstaat*) will be applied when a political body is organized strictly and completely in terms of this principle of hereditary charisma. In such a case, all appropriation of governing powers, of fiefs, benefices, and all sorts of economic advantages follow the same pattern. The result is that all powers and advantages of all sorts become traditionalized. The heads of families, who are traditional gerontocrats or patriarchs without personal charismatic legitimacy, regulate the exercise of these powers which cannot be taken away from their family. It is not the type of position he occupies which determines the rank of a man or of his family, but rather the hereditary charismatic rank of his family determines the position he will occupy. Japan, before the development of bureaucracy, was organized in this way. The same was undoubtedly true of China as well where, before the rationalization which took place in the territorial states, authority was in the hands of the "old families." Other types of examples are furnished by the caste system in India, and by Russia before the *Mjestnitschestvo* was introduced. Indeed, all hereditary social classes with established privileges belong in the same category.

3. The administrative staff may seek and achieve the creation and appropriation of individual positions and the corresponding economic advantages for its members. In that case, according to whether the tendency is to traditionalization or legalization, there will develop (a) benefices, (b) offices, or (c) fiefs. In the first case a praebendal organization will result; in the second, patrimonialism or bureaucracy; in the third, feudalism. These become appropriated in the place of the type of provision from gifts or booty without settled relation to the everyday economic structure.

Case (a), benefices, may consist in rights to the proceeds of begging, to payments in kind, or to the proceeds of money taxes, or finally, to the proceeds of fees. Any one of these may result from the regulation of provision by free gifts or by "booty" in terms of rational organization of finance. Regularized begging is found in Buddhism; benefices in kind, in the Chinese and Japanese "rice rents"; support by money taxation has been the rule in all the rationalized conquering states. The last case is common everywhere, especially on the part of priests and judges and, in India, even the military authorities.

Case (b), the transformation of the charismatic mission into an office, may have more of a patrimonial or more of a bureaucratic character. The former is much the more common; the latter is found principally in Mediterranean Antiquity and in the modern Western World. Elsewhere it is exceptional.

In case (c), only land may be appropriated as a fief, whereas the position as such retains its originally charismatic character. On the other hand, powers and authority may be fully appropriated as fiefs. It is difficult to distinguish the two cases. It is, however, rare that orientation to the charismatic character of the position disappears entirely; it did not do so in the Middle Ages.

For charisma to be transformed into a permanent routine structure, it is necessary that its anti-economic character should be altered. It must be adapted to some form of fiscal organization to provide for the needs of the group and hence to the economic conditions necessary for raising taxes and contributions. When a charismatic movement develops in the direction of praebendal provision, the "laity" become differentiated from the "clergy" (Derived from κλῆρος, meaning a "share."); that is, the participating members of the charismatic administrative staff which has now become routinized. These are the priests of the developing "church." Correspondingly, in a developing political body the vassals, the holders of benefices, or officials are differentiated from the "tax payers." The former, instead of being the "followers" of the leader, become state officials, or appointed party officials. This process is very conspicuous in Buddhism and in the Hindu sects. The same is true in all the states resulting from conquest which have become rationalized to form permanent structures; also of parties and other movements which have originally had a purely charismatic character. With the process of routinization the charismatic group tends to develop into one of the forms of everyday authority, particularly the patrimonial form in its decentralized variant or the bureaucratic. Its original peculiarities are apt to be retained in the charismatic standards of honour attendant on the social status acquired by heredity or the holding of office. This applies to all who participate in the process of appropriation, the chief himself and the members of his staff. It is thus a matter of the type of prestige enjoyed by ruling groups. A hereditary monarch by "divine right" is not a simple patrimonial chief, patriarch, or sheik; a vassal is not a mere household retainer or official. Further details must be deferred to the analysis of social stratification.

As a rule the process of routinization is not free of conflict. In the early stages personal claims on the charisma of the chief are not easily forgotten and the conflict between the charisma of office or of hereditary status with personal charisma is a typical process in many historical situations.

1. The power of absolution—that is, the power to absolve from mortal sins—was held originally only by personal charismatic martyrs or ascetics, but became transformed into a power of the office of bishop or priest. This process was much slower in the Orient than in the Occident because in the latter case it was influenced by the Roman conception of office. Revolutions under a charismatic leader, directed against hereditary charismatic powers or the powers of office, are to be found in all types of corporate groups, from states to trade unions. The more highly developed the interdependence of different economic units in a monetary economy, the greater the pressure of the everyday needs of the followers of the charismatic movement becomes. The effect of this is to strengthen the tendency to routinization, which is everywhere operative, and as a rule has rapidly won out. Charisma is a phenomenon typical of prophetic religious movements or of expansive political movements in their early stages. But as soon as the position of authority is well established, and above all as soon as control over large masses of people exists, it gives way to the forces of everyday routine.

2. One of the decisive motives underlying all cases of the routinization of charisma is naturally the striving for security. This means legitimization, on the one hand, of positions of authority and social prestige, on the other hand, of the economic advantages enjoyed by the followers and sympathizers of the leader. Another important motive, however, lies in the objective necessity of adaptation of the patterns of order and of the organization of the administrative staff to the normal, everyday needs and conditions of carrying on administration. In this connexion, in particular, there are always points at which traditions of administrative practice and of judicial decision can take hold; since these are needed both by the normal administrative staff and by those subject to its authority. It is further necessary that there should be some definite order introduced into the organization of the administrative

staff itself. Finally, as will be discussed in detail below, it is necessary for the administrative staff and all its administrative practices to be adapted to everyday economic conditions. It is not possible for the costs of permanent, routine administration to be met by "booty," contributions, gifts, and hospitality, as is typical of the pure type of military and prophetic charisma.

3. The process of routinization is thus not by any means confined to the problem of succession and does not stop when this has been solved. On the contrary, the most fundamental problem is that of making a transition from a charismatic administrative staff, and the corresponding principles of administration, to one which is adapted to everyday conditions. The problem of succession, however, is crucial because through it occurs the routinization of the charismatic focus of the structure. In it, the character of the leader himself and of his claim to legitimacy is altered. This process involves peculiar and characteristic conceptions which are understandable only in this context and do not apply to the problem of transition to traditional or legal patterns of order and types of administrative organization. The most important of the modes of meeting the problem of succession are the charismatic designation of a successor and hereditary charisma.

4. As has already been noted, the most important historical example of designation by the charismatic leader of his own successor is Rome. For the *rex,* this arrangement is attested by tradition; while for the appointment of the "dictator" and of the co-emperor and successor in the principate, it has existed in historical times. The way in which all the higher magistrates were invested with the *imperium* shows clearly that they also were designated as successors by the military commander, subject to recognition by the citizen army. The fact that candidates were examined by the magistrate in office and that originally they could be excluded on what were obviously arbitrary grounds shows clearly what was the nature of the development.

5. The most important examples of designation of a successor by the charismatic followers of the leader are to be found in the election of bishops, and particularly of the Pope, by the original system of designation by the clergy and recognition by the lay community. The investigations of U. Stutz have made it probable that, though it was later altered, the election of the German emperor was modelled on that of the bishops. He was designated by a group of qualified princes and recognized by the "people," that is, those bearing arms. Similar arrangements are very common.

6. The classical case of the development of hereditary charisma is that of caste in India. All occupa-

tional qualifications, and in particular all the qualifications for positions of authority and power, have there come to be regarded as strictly bound to the inheritance of charisma. Eligibility for fiefs, involving governing powers, was limited to members of the royal kinship group, the fiefs being granted by the eldest of the group. All types of religious office, including the extraordinarily important and influential position of *guru,* the *directeur de l'âme,* were treated as bound to hereditary charismatic qualities. The same is true of all sorts of relations to traditional customers and of all positions in the village organization, such as priest, barber, laundryman, watchman, etc. The foundation of a sect always meant the development of a hereditary hierarchy, as was true also of Taoism in China. Also in the Japanese "feudal" state, before the introduction of a patrimonial officialdom on the Chinese model, which then led to praebends and a new feudalization, social organization was based purely on hereditary charisma.

This kind of hereditary charismatic right to positions of authority has been developed in similar ways all over the world. Qualification by virtue of individual achievement has been replaced by qualification by birth. This is everywhere the basis of the development of hereditary aristocracies, in the Roman nobility, in the concept of the *stirps regia,* which Tacitus describes among the Germans, in the rules of eligibility to tournaments and monasteries in the late Middle Ages, and even in the genealogical research carried on on behalf of the parvenu aristocracy of the United States. Indeed, this is to be found everywhere where a differentiation of hereditary social classes has become established.

The following is the principal relation to economic conditions: The process of routinization of charisma is in very important respects identical with adaptation to the conditions of economic life, since this is one of the principal continually-operating forces in everyday life. Economic conditions in this connexion play a leading role and do not constitute merely a dependent variable. To a very large extent the transition to hereditary charisma or the charisma of office serves in this connexion as a means of legitimizing existing or recently acquired powers of control over economic goods. Along with the ideology of loyalty, which is certainly by no means unimportant, allegiance to hereditary monarchy in particular is very strongly influenced by the consideration that all inherited property and all that which is legitimately acquired would be endangered if subjective recognition of the sanctity of succession to the throne were eliminated. It is hence by no means fortuitous that hereditary monarchy is more acceptable to the propertied classes than, for instance, to the proletariat.

Beyond this, it is not possible to say anything in general terms, which would at the same time be substantial and valuable on the relations of the various possible modes of adaptation to the economic order. This must be reserved to a special investigation. The development of a praebendal structure, of feudalism and the appropriation of all sorts of advantages on a hereditary charismatic basis, may in all cases have the same stereotyping effect on the economic order if they develop from charismatic starting points as if they developed from patrimonial or bureaucratic origins. The immediate effect of charisma in economic as in other connexions is usually strongly revolutionary; indeed, often destructive, because it means new modes of orientation. But in case the process of routinization leads in the direction of traditionalism, its ultimate effect may be exactly the reverse.

*   *   *

The Transformation of Charisma in an Anti-Authoritarian Direction

A charismatic principle which originally was primarily directed to the legitimization of authority may be subject to interpretation or development in an anti-authoritarian direction. This is true because the validity of charismatic authority rests entirely on recognition by those subject to it, conditioned as this is by "proof" of its genuineness. This is true in spite of the fact that this recognition of a charismatically qualified, and hence legitimate, person is treated as a duty. When the organization of the corporate group undergoes a process of progressive rationalization, it is readily possible that, instead of recognition being treated as a consequence of legitimacy, it is treated as the basis of legitimacy. Legitimacy, that is, becomes "democratic." Thus, for instance, designation of a successor by an administrative staff may be treated as "election" in advance; while designation by the predecessor is "nomination"; whereas the recognition by the group becomes the true "election." The leader whose legitimacy rested on his personal charisma then becomes leader by the grace of those who follow him since the latter are formally free to elect and elevate to power as they please and even to depose. For the loss of charisma and its proof involves the loss of genuine legitimacy. The chief now becomes the freely elected leader.

Correspondingly, the recognition of charismatic decrees and judicial decisions on the part of the community shifts to the doctrine that the group has

a right to enact, recognize, or repeal laws, according to their own free will, both in general and for an individual case. Under genuinely charismatic authority, on the other hand, it is, to be sure, true that conflicts over the correct law may actually be decided by a vote of the group. But this takes place under the pressure of the feeling that there can be only *one* correct decision and it is a matter of duty to arrive at this. The most important transitional type is the legitimization of authority by plebiscite. The commonest examples are to be found in the party leaders of the modern state. But it is always present in cases where the chief feels himself to be acting on behalf of the masses and where his recognition is based on this. Both the Napoleons are classical examples, in spite of the fact that legitimization by plebiscite took place only after the seizure of power by force. In the case of the second Napoleon, it was confirmed on this basis after a severe loss of prestige. Regardless of how its real value as an expression of the popular will may be regarded, the plebiscite has been formally the specific means of establishing the legitimacy of authority on the basis of the free confidence of those subject to authority, even though it be only formal or possibly a fiction.

Once the elective principle has been applied to the chief by a process of reinterpretation of charisma, it may be extended to the administrative staff. Elective officials whose legitimacy is derived from the confidence of those subject to their authority and to recall if confidence ceases to exist, are typical of certain types of democracies, for instance, the United States. They are not "bureaucratic" types. Because they have an independent source of legitimacy, they are not strongly integrated in a hierarchical order. To a large extent their "promotion" is not influenced by their superiors and, correspondingly, their functions are not controlled. There are analogies in other cases where several charismatic structures, which are qualitatively heterogeneous, exist side by side, as in the relation of the Dalai Lama and the Taschi Lama. An administrative structure organized in this way is, from a technical point of view, a greatly inferior "instrument of precision" as compared with the bureaucratic type consisting of appointed officials.

1. The use of the plebiscite as a means of legitimizing leadership on a democratic basis is the most conspicuous type in which democracy is combined with an important role of leadership. In its fundamental significance it is a type of charismatic authority in which the authoritarian element is concealed, because the traditional position of the leader is held to be dependent on the will of those over whom he exercises authority and to be legitimized only by this will. In actual fact the leader, in this

case the demagogue, is able to influence action by virtue of the devotion and trust his political followers have in him personally. In the first instance his power is only a power over those recruited to his following, but in case, with their aid, he is able to attain positions of wider authority it may extend to the political group as a whole. The type is best illustrated by the "dictators" who have emerged in the revolutions of the ancient world and of modern times. Examples are: the Greek Aisymnetes and the tyrants and demagogues; in Rome the Gracchi and their successors; in the Italian city states the *Capitani del popolo;* and certain types of political leaders in the German cities such as emerged in the democratic dictatorship of Zürich. In modern states the best examples are the dictatorship of Cromwell, and the leaders of the French Revolution and of the First and Second Empire. Wherever attempts have been made to legitimize this kind of power legitimacy has been sought in recognition by the sovereign people through a plebiscite. The leader's personal administrative staff is recruited in a charismatic form usually from able people of humble origin. In Cromwell's case, religious qualifications were taken into account. In that of Robespierre along with personal dependability also certain "ethical" qualities. Napoleon was concerned only with personal ability and adaptibility to the needs of his imperial "rule of genius."

At the height of revolutionary dictatorship the position of a member of the administrative staff tends to be that of a person entrusted with a specific *ad hoc* task subject to recall. This was true of the role of the agents of the "Committee of Public Safety." When a certain kind of communal "dictators" have been swept into power by the reform movements in American cities the tendency has been to grant them freedom to appoint their own staff. Thus both traditional legitimacy and formal legality tend to be equally ignored by the revolutionary dictator. The tendency of patriarchal authorities, in the administration of justice and in their other functions, has been to act in accordance with substantive ideas of justice, with utilitarian considerations and in terms of reasons of state. These tendencies are paralleled by the revolutionary tribunals and by the substantive postulates of justice of the radical democracy of Antiquity and of modern socialism. The process of routinization of revolutionary charisma then brings with it changes similar to those brought about by the corresponding process in other respects. Thus the development of a professional army in England is derived from the principle of free choice in the participation in religious struggles in the days of Cromwell. Similarly, the French system of administration by prefects is derived from

the charismatic administration of the revolutionary democratic dictatorship.

2. The introduction of elected officials always involves a radical alteration in the position of the charismatic leader. He becomes the "servant" of those under his authority. There is no place for such a type in a technically rational bureaucratic organization. He is not appointed by his superiors and the possibility of promotion is not dependent on their judgment. On the contrary, his position is derived from the favour of the persons whose action he controls. Hence he is likely to be little interested in the prompt and strict observance of discipline which would be likely to win the favour of superiors. The tendency is rather for electoral positions to become autocephalous spheres of authority. It is in general not possible to attain a high level of technical administrative efficiency with an elected staff of officials. This is illustrated by a comparison of the elected officials in the individual states in the United States with the appointed officials of the Federal Government. It is similarly shown by comparing the elected communal officials with the administration of the reform mayors with their own appointed staffs. It is necessary to distinguish the type of democracy where positions of authority are legitimized by plebiscite from that which attempts to dispense with leadership altogether. The latter type is characterized by the attempt to reduce to a minimum the control of some men over others.

It is characteristic of the democracy which makes room for leadership (*Führerdemokratie*) that there should in general be a highly emotional type of devotion to and trust in the leader. This accounts for a tendency to favour the type of individual who is most spectacular, who promises the most, or who employs the most effective propaganda measures in the competition for leadership. This is a natural basis for the utopian component which is found in all revolutions. It also indicates the limitations on the level of rationality which, in the modern world, this type of administration can attain. Even in America it has not *always* come up to expectations.

The following are the principal relations to the economic order:

1. The anti-authoritarian direction of the transformation of charisma normally leads into the path of rationality. If a ruler is dependent on recognition by plebiscite he will usually attempt to support his regime by an organization of officials which functions promptly and efficiently. He will attempt to consolidate the loyalty of those he governs either by winning glory and honour in war or by promoting their material welfare, or under certain circumstances, by attempting to combine both. Success in

these will be regarded as proof of the charisma. His first aim will be the destruction of traditional, feudal patrimonial, and other types of authoritarian powers and privileges. His second main aim will have to be to create economic interests which are bound up with his regime as the source of their legitimacy. So far as, in pursuing these policies, he makes use of the formalization and legalization of law he may contribute greatly to the formal rationalization of economic activity.

2. On the other hand, plebiscitary regimes can easily act so as to weaken the formal rationality of economic activity so far as their interests in legitimacy, being dependent on the faith and devotion of the masses, forces them to impose substantive ideas of justice in the economic sphere. This will result in an administration of justice emancipated from formal procedures, and in all sorts of rationing and control of both production and consumption which breaks down the formal character of the judicial process and of administration. This tendency will be dominant so far as the leader is a "social dictator." It is a tendency which is by no means confined to the modern socialist type. When it is and when it is not "socialist" in the modern sense and what are the consequences cannot yet be discussed.

3. The presence of elective officials is a source of disturbance to formally rational economic life. This is true in the first place because such officials are primarily elected according to party affiliations and not technical competence. Secondly, the risks of recall or of failure of re-election make it impossible to pursue a strictly objective course of decision and administration, without regard to such consequences. There is, however, one type of case where the unfavourable effects for the rationality of economic activity are not evident. This is true where there is a possibility of applying the economic and technical achievements of an old culture to new areas. In this case, the means of production are not yet appropriated and there is a sufficiently wide margin so that the almost inevitable corruption of elected officials can be taken account of as one of the cost factors, and large-scale profits still be attained.

The classical example of a favourable effect on economic rationality is to be found in the two Napoleonic regimes. Under Napoleon I the *Code Napoléon* introduced compulsory division of estates by inheritance and destroyed all the traditional authorities in French society. It is true that his regime created what almost amounted to fiefs for his de-

serving followers, and that the soldiers got almost everything, the citizen nothing. But this was compensated for by national glory and on the whole the small bourgeois were relatively well off. Under Napoleon III there was a conscious adoption of the motto of Louis Philippe "enrichissez-vous." Grand scale building was carried out but there was also the *Crédit Mobilier* affair with its well-known scandal.

The tendencies of "social dictatorship" are classically illustrated by the Greek democracy of the Periclean age and of subsequent times. In Rome the jurors who tried a case were bound by the instructions of the Praetor, and decisions followed the formal law. But in the Greek Courts decisions were made in terms of substantive justice. In effect, this meant they were decided by sentimentality, flattery, demagogic invective, and humour. This can be clearly seen in the orations written by the Athenian rhetors. Analogous phenomena are found in Rome only in the case of such political trials as Cicero participated in.

The consequence was that the development of formal law and formal jurisprudence in the Roman sense became impossible. For the Heliaia was a "people's court" directly comparable to the revolutionary tribunals of the French Revolution and of the Soviet phase of the post-war revolution in Germany. The jurisdiction of these lay tribunals was by no means confined to politically relevant cases. On the other hand, no revolutionary movement in England has ever interfered with the administration of justice except in cases of major political significance. It is true that there was a considerable arbitrary element in the decisions of the justices of the peace, but this applied only within a sphere which did not involve the interests of property. It was confined to police cases.

The United States of America is the classical example of the third type of influence. As late as the early 1900's the author inquired of American workers of English origin why they allowed themselves to be governed by party henchmen who were so often open to corruption. The answer was, in the first place, that in such a big country even though millions of dollars were stolen or embezzled there was still plenty left for everybody, and secondly, that these professional politicians were a group which even workers could treat with contempt whereas technical officials of the German type would as a group "lord it over" the workers.

A more detailed discussion of relations to economic activity will have to be left for special treatment.

4. On the Process of Change in Social Values

BY EMILE DURKHEIM

Value Judgments and Judgments of Reality

IN SUBMITTING to the Congress this subject for discussion I am setting myself a double goal: first, to show by specific example how sociology can help to resolve a problem of philosophy, and, secondly, to remove certain prejudices under which so-called positive sociology too often suffers.

When we say that bodies are heavy, that the volume of gas varies in inverse proportion to the pressure applied to it, we make judgments which are limited to the expression of facts. They are judgments which define what is, and for this reason they are called judgments of existence or of reality.

Other judgments do not have for object the nature of things, but rather their worth in relation to persons—i.e. the value which the latter attach—and these are called value judgments. This name is often extended to any judgment which reports an estimation, whatever it may be. This extension of the term makes for confusions against which we must be on our guard.

When I say, "I like hunting," "I prefer beer to wine," "an active life to one of respose" etc., I express judgments which might appear to be based upon estimations but which are, in fact, simple judgments of reality. They merely report my relations with certain objects: that I like this or prefer that. These preferences are facts as much as the heaviness of bodies or the elasticity of gas. Such judgments do not attach value to objects but merely affirm the state of the subject. Also the predilections which are expressed are not communicable. Those who experience them can say that they experience them or, at least, that they think they do; but they cannot communicate their experience to others. It is part of their personality and cannot be divorced from it.

It is quite a different matter when I say: "This man *has* a high moral value, this picture *has* great aesthetic value, this jewel is *worth* so much." In all

these instances I attribute to the people or things in question an objective character quite independent of my own individual feelings at the time of making the judgment. I personally may not attach any value to a jewel; but its value is not the less for that. I as an individual may not be highly moral in my behaviour, but that does not prevent me from recognizing moral value when I see it. By temperament I may not be very sensitive to art, but that is no reason why I should deny that there can be aesthetic value. All these values exist then, in a sense, outside me. Thus when we are in disagreement with others over judgments in such matters we try to communicate our convictions. We are not satisfied with merely affirming their existence; we try to demonstrate their validity by supporting them with impersonal arguments. Implicitly we recognize that these judgments correspond to some objective reality upon which agreement can and should be reached. These *sui generis* realities constitute values, and it is to these realities that value judgments refer.

We must see how it is that such judgments are possible, and the terms of the problem are implicit in what has gone before. On the one hand, all value presupposes appreciation by an individual in relation with a particular sensibility. What has value is in some way good; what is good is desired, and all desire is a psychological state. Nevertheless the values under discussion have the objectivity of things. How can these two characteristics, which at first blush appear contradictory, be reconciled? How, in fact, can a state of feeling be independent of the subject that feels it?

To this problem two contradictory solutions have been given.

I

For many thinkers of heterogeneous schools of thought the difference between these two types of judgment is only apparent. Value, it is said, is inherent in some constituent characteristic of the object to which value is attributed, and a value judgment expresses no more than the effect of this characteristic upon the subject that judges. If this effect is favourable a positive value is ascribed, if unfavourable, a negative value. If life has value

Reprinted from Emile Durkheim, *Sociology and Philosophy*, trans. D. F. Pocock and J. G. Peristiany (Glencoe, Ill.: The Free Press, 1953), pp. 80–97, with the permission of The Free Press.

for a man, it is because man is a living creature and it is in the nature of the living to live. If corn has value it is because it is food and maintains life. If justice is a virtue, it is because justice respects the vital interests; for the opposite reason homicide is a crime. The value of a thing would, in fact, appear to be simply the realization of the effects that it produces as a result of its intrinsic properties.

But what is the *subject* in relation to which the value of these things is, and should be, estimated?

If it is to be the individual, how can we explain the existence of a system of objective values, recognized by all men, or at least by all the men of the same civilization? For, from this point of view, value consists in the effect of the thing upon the sensibility, but the great diversity of individual sensibilities is well known. What pleases some revolts others. Life itself is not desired by all, for there are those who, either out of disgust or duty, throw it away. Above all, there is great variety in the manner of its appreciation. One may like it intense and complex, another's pleasure lies in simplicity. This objection to the utilitarian ethic has been made too often for us to be occupied with it here. We will point out only that it is an objection that applies with equal force to any theory that claims to explain, by purely psychological causes, economic, aesthetic or philosophical values. It might be argued that there is a *mean type* found in the majority of individuals, and that the objective evaluation of things expresses the effect that they have upon the average individual. There is, however, an enormous gap between the way in which values are, in fact, estimated by the ordinary individual and the objective scale of human values which should in principle govern our judgments. The average moral conscience is mediocre; it feels only slightly the commonest duties and hence the corresponding moral values; it is as though it were blind to some of them. We cannot therefore look to the average for a standard of morality. This applies with greater conviction to the aesthetic values that are, for the majority, a dead letter. For economic values the distance, in certain cases, is perhaps less considerable. However, it is obvious that it is not the physical properties of the diamond or the pearl, acting upon the majority of our contemporaries, that explains the present value of these things.

There is, however, another reason why objective evaluation and average evaluation should not be confused: it is that the reactions of the average individual continue to be individual reactions. Because a certain condition is found in a large number of people, it is not for that reason objective. Simply because there are many people who like something in a certain way, it does not follow that

that appreciation has been imposed upon them by some external reality. This phenomenon of unanimity may be entirely due to subjective causes, notably a sufficient homogeneity of individual temperaments. Between "I like this" and "a certain number of us like this" there is no essential difference.

It has been believed possible to escape these difficulties by substituting the society for the individual. As in the preceding theory, it is maintained that value is intrinsic in some element of the thing judged. In this case it is from the way in which the thing affects the collective subject, and no longer the individual, that the value is derived. The estimate becomes objective by being a collective one.

This theory has certain incontestable advantages over the preceding one. Social judgment is objective as compared with individual judgment. The scale of values is thus released from the variable and subjective evaluations of individuals. The latter find outside themselves an established classification which is not their own work, which expresses other than their own personal sentiments, and to which they are bound to conform. The opinion of society derives from its origins a moral authority by virtue of which it imposes itself upon the individual. It resists attempts to disturb it, and reacts against dissentients just as all the world resents the nonconformer. It blames those whose evaluation of moral facts is based on principles other than those it prescribes, and ridicules those whose aesthetic inspiration is different. Whoever tries to obtain something at less than its worth runs up against a resistance similar to that of a material object. Thus may be explained that awareness of external constraint operating when we make a value judgment. We know very well that we are not the masters of our evaluations, that we are bound and constrained. It is the social conscience that binds us.

This aspect of the value judgment is not the only one, for there is another almost opposed to the first. These same values which, on the one hand, have the effect of realities imposed upon us, on the other hand appear to us as things which we like and naturally desire. The fact is that society is at the same time a legislator to whom we owe respect and also the creator and guardian of all those goods of civilization to which we are bound with all the strength of our souls. Society is a benefactor as well as a master. Whatever increases the vitality of the society increases our vitality. It is not therefore surprising that the society and its members should attach value to the same things.

But, thus understood, a sociological theory of values raises in its turn certain grave difficulties. These are, moreover, not peculiar to it in that the same objections may be directed against the preceding psychological theory.

There are different types of value. Economic, moral, religious, aesthetic and speculative values are all different. The attempts to reduce the one to the other, ideas of goodness, beauty, truth and utility, have always proved abortive. If what determines value is only the way in which things affect the working of the social life, the diversity of values becomes hard to explain. If the same cause is at work in every case, whence arise effects so specifically different?

Again, if the value of a thing is determined by the degree of its social (or individual) utility, the system of human values would be shaken and changed from top to bottom. The place given to luxury would from this point of view become unjustified and incomprehensible. By definition what is superfluous is not useful or is less useful than what is necessary. Surplus in any form may be lacking without the vital functions being seriously disturbed. In a word, luxuries are by nature costly and cost more than they return. We find doctrinaire spirits who despise them and who try to reduce them to a more congruous position, but in fact there is nothing that has more value in the eyes of man. All art is a luxury; aesthetic activity is not subordinated to any useful end; it is released for the sole pleasure of the release. What is pure speculation if not thought exercising itself quite free from any utilitarian goal? Yet who can deny that humanity has always esteemed artistic and speculative values much more highly than economic? Like the intellect, the moral sphere has an aesthetic peculiar to itself. The highest virtue consists not in the strict and regular performance of those acts immediately necessary to the well-being of the social order, but rather in those free and spontaneous movements and sacrifices which are not demanded and are sometimes even contrary to the principles of a sound economy. There is virtue that is folly, and it is in its folly that its grandeur consists. Spencer has shown that philanthropy is often not in the best interests of society. His demonstration will not prevent men from esteeming the virtue he condemns very highly. Economic life itself does not always follow closely the rules of economics. If luxuries are those things that cost most, it is not only because they are often the most rare; it is because they are also the most esteemed. Life as man at all times has conceived it is not simply a precise arrangement of the budget of the individual or social organism, the reaction with the least possible expense to the outside stimulus, the careful balance between debit and credit. To live is above all things to act, to act without counting the cost and for the pleasure of acting. If the evidence demands that we do not discount economy, as man must amass in order to expend, nevertheless that expenditure is his end, and to expend is to act.

Let us go further and examine all these theories for the fundamental principle underlying them. We find that all equally presuppose that the value of a thing is inherent in, and expresses the nature of, that thing. This postulate is, however, contrary to the facts. There are many instances in which no such relation exists between the characteristics of an object and the value attributed to it.

An idol is a very sacred object and sacredness the highest value ever recognized by man. An idol is often, however, nothing but a block of stone or a piece of wood, things which in themselves have no value. There is no order of being, however humble or commonplace, that has not at some time in our history inspired sentiments of religious respect. The most useless or harmless animals, lacking any kind of attraction, have been worshipped. The current theory that the things which have become the objects of a cult are those that have most forcibly impressed the mind of man is contradicted by history. The incomparable value attributed to such objects has nothing to do with their intrinsic character. There is no active faith, however secular, that has not its fetishes where the same striking disproportion can be observed. A flag is only a bit of cloth; nevertheless a soldier will die to save it. Morality is no less rich in contrasts of this sort. Between a man and an animal the differences from the point of view of anatomy, physiology and psychology are only differences of degree, and yet man has a high moral dignity and an animal none. From the point of view of values they are separated by an abyss. Men are unequal in physical strength and in talent, and yet we tend to regard all as having equal moral value. No doubt moral equality is an ideal never to be realized, but we are drawing constantly nearer its realization. A postage stamp is a thin square of paper, lacking for the most part all artistic character, and yet it may be worth a fortune. Obviously it is not the intrinsic nature of pearls, diamonds, furs or laces that make the value of these different articles of dress vary at the caprice of fashion.

II

If value is not in the thing, not inherent in some characteristic of the empirical reality, does it follow that the source of value lies beyond experience and the empirically verifiable? This, in fact, is a theory maintained more or less explicitly by a line of thinkers whose doctrine derives *via* Ritschl from Kantian morality. They have supposed in man a *sui generis* faculty for transcending experience and for conceiving an extra-empirical reality—in a word, the ability to create ideals. This faculty of representation has been conceived in a more or less intellectual form by some and in a sentimental form by others, but always as quite distinct from the faculty exercised in scientific thought. Thus there is one way of considering the real and another, quite different, of considering the ideal. It is from the relation between reality and these ideals that values are estimated. Things are said to have value when they express or reflect, in any way whatsoever, an aspect of the ideal and to have more or less value according to the ideal and according to the degree to which they embody it.

Thus while in the preceding theories value judgments were offered as another form of judgments of reality, here the heterogeneity of the two is radical. The objects to which they refer are as distinct as the faculties they presuppose. The objections that we made to the first explanations will not apply to the second. It is easy to understand that the value and the nature of an object may to a certain extent be distinct and independent if the value is dependent upon causes exterior to the object. Further, the privileged place always given to the value of luxury is easily justified, since the ideal is not subordinate to the real; it exists for itself and therefore will not be measured by the interests of reality.

However, the value thus attributed to the ideal, while it explains much, does not explain itself. It is postulated but it is not, nor can it be, accounted for. If the ideal does not depend upon the real it would be impossible to find in the real the conditions and causes which would make it intelligible. But beyond the real where can the material for a satisfactory explanation be found? There is, in fact, something profoundly empiricist in this kind of idealism. It is a fact that men love a goodness, beauty and truth that are never adequately realized in action. But that itself is a fact unjustifiably exalted as a sort of absolute, beyond which we are forbidden to go. Further, we should wish to know how it comes about that we have both the need and the means for surpassing the real and imposing upon the world of matter a different world which the best of us make our home.

To this question the theological hypothesis makes a sort of answer. It postulates the existence of the world of ideals as a supra-experimental, but none the less objective, reality from which our empirical reality derives and depends. Thus we are joined to the ideal as the source of our being. Quite apart from other difficulties raised by this explanation, once the ideal has been hypostatized in this way it has at the same time become immobile, and all means of explaining its infinite variability are lost

to us. We know today that not only is the ideal different in different groups, but also that it *should* vary. The ideal of the Romans was not, and cannot be, ours, and the scale of values varies accordingly. These changes are not due to human blindness but are based in the nature of the facts. How may they be explained if the ideal is one unassailable reality? We should be forced to admit that the Divinity varies in space and in time, and how can this be explained? The changing condition of God could only be intelligible if He had to realize an ideal beyond Himself, and anyhow this merely shifts the problem but does not change it.

By what reasoning can the ideal be said to be beyond nature and science? It manifests itself in nature and surely, then, depends upon natural causes. In order that it may be more than a mere possibility for speculation it must be desired, and must therefore have a force capable of swaying our wills. Our wills alone can make it a living reality. Since this force must ultimately be translated in terms of muscular movement it cannot differ essentially from the other forces of the universe. Why should it not be possible to analyse it, to resolve it into its elements and find those causes that determine the synthesis from which it results? We already have instances in which it is possible to measure it. Each human group at each moment in its history has a respect of a certain intensity for human dignity. It is this sentiment, varying among different people and at different times, that is at the root of the moral ideal of contemporary societies. Now accordingly as it is more or less strong, the number of criminal assaults against the person will be low or high. In the same way the number of adulteries, divorces and separations expresses the relative force with which the conjugal ideal makes itself felt. No doubt these are clumsy devices, but what measurement of any physical force can be more than an approximation? In fact, the relation of the one to the other shows that there are only differences of degree between them.

Furthermore there is an order of values that cannot be separated from reality without losing all significance; these are economic values. It is generally accepted that these express and imply no faculty of the supra-experimental. For this reason Kant refused to consider them as real values; he preferred to reserve this term solely for facts of the moral order. (He says that things in the economic sphere have a price [*einen Preis, einen Marktpreis*] not an intrinsic value [*einen inneren Werth*]. 5th ed., Hartenstein, VII, 270 et seq. and 614.) This exclusion is unjustified. Certainly there are different types of value, but they are all species of the same genus. All correspond to an evaluation of things even though evaluation be made from different points of view. The progress that the theory of values has made of late lies in the establishment of the generality and unity of this notion. If, then, the various types of value are related, and if certain of them are so closely bound to our empirical existence, the others cannot be independent of that existence.

III

To sum up; if the value of a thing cannot be, and has never been, estimated except in relation to some conception of the ideal, the latter needs explanation. To understand how value judgments are possible it is not enough to postulate a certain number of ideals. Their origins, the way in which they are related to, yet transcend, experience, and the nature of their objectivity must be accounted for.

Since ideals and their corresponding value systems vary with various human groups, does this not suggest a collective origin for both? It is true that we have already disposed of one sociological theory of value which seemed insufficient, but that was because it rested upon misconception of the real nature of society. There society was presented as a system of organs and functions, maintaining itself against outside forces of destruction just like a physical organism whose entire life consists in appropriate reactions to external stimuli. Society is, however, more than this, for it is the centre of a moral life (*le foyer d'une vie morale*) of which the strength and independence have not always been fully recognized.

When individual minds are not isolated but enter into close relation with and work upon each other, from their synthesis arises a new kind of psychic life. It is clearly distinguished by its peculiar intensity from that led by the solitary individual. Sentiments born and developed in the group have a greater energy than purely individual sentiments. A man who experiences such sentiments feels himself dominated by outside forces that lead him and pervade his milieu. He feels himself in a world quite distinct from that of his own private existence. This is a world not only more intense but also qualitatively different. Following the collectivity, the individual forgets himself for the common end and his conduct is orientated in terms of a standard outside himself. At the same time, and owing to their theoretical nature, these forces are not easily controlled, canalized and adjusted to closely determined ends. They need to overflow for the sake of overflowing, as in play without any specific objective, at one time in the form of stupid destructive violence or, at another, of heroic folly. It is in a sense a luxurious activity since it is a very rich activity. For all these reasons this activity is quali-

tatively different from the everyday life of the individual, as is the superior from the inferior, the ideal from the real.

It is, in fact, at such moments of collective ferment that are born the great ideals upon which civilizations rest. The periods of creation or renewal occur when men for various reasons are led into a closer relationship with each other, when reunions and assemblies are most frequent, relationships better maintained and the exchange of ideas most active. Such was the great crisis of Christendom, the movement of collective enthusiasm which, in the twelfth and thirteenth centuries, bringing together in Paris the scholars of Europe, gave birth to Scholasticism. Such were the Reformation and Renaissance, the revolutionary epoch and the Socialist upheavals of the nineteenth century. At such moments this higher form of life is lived with such intensity and exclusiveness that it monopolizes all minds to the more or less complete exclusion of egoism and the commonplace. At such times the ideal tends to become one with the real, and for this reason men have the impression that the time is close when the ideal will in fact be realized and the Kingdom of God established on earth. This illusion can never last because the exaltation cannot maintain itself at such a pitch; it is too exhausting. Once the critical moment has passed, the social life relaxes, intellectual and emotional intercourse is subdued, and individuals fall back to their ordinary level. All that was said, done and thought during this period of fecund upheaval survives only as a memory, a memory no doubt as glorious as the reality it recalls, but with which it is no longer at one. It exists as an idea or rather as a composition of ideas. Between what is felt and perceived and what is thought of in the form of ideals there is now a clear distinction. Nevertheless these ideals could not survive if they were not periodically revived. This revivification is the function of religious or secular feasts and ceremonies, all public addresses in churches or schools, plays and exhibitions—in a word, whatever draws men together into an intellectual and moral communion. These moments are, as it were, minor versions of the great creative movement. But these means have only a temporary effect. For a short time the ideal comes to life and approaches reality, but it soon becomes differentiated from it.

If man conceives ideals, and indeed cannot help conceiving and becoming attached to them, it is because he is a social being. Society moves or forces the individual to rise above himself and gives him the means for achieving this. Through the very awareness of itself society forces the individual to transcend himself and to participate in a higher form of life. A society cannot be constituted without creating ideals. These ideals are simply the ideas in terms of which society sees itself and exists at a culminating point in its development. To see society only as an organized body of vital functions is to diminish it, for this body has a soul which is the composition of collective ideals. Ideals are not abstractions, cold intellectual concepts lacking efficient power. They are essentially dynamic, for behind them are the powerful forces of the collective. They are collective forces—that is, natural but at the same time moral forces, comparable to the other forces of the universe. The ideal itself is a force of this nature and therefore subject to scientific investigation. The reason why the ideal can partake of reality is that it derives from it while transcending it. The elements that combine to form the ideal are part of reality, but they are combined in a new manner and the originality of the method of combination produces the originality of the synthesis itself. Left alone, the individual could never find in himself the material for such a construction. Relying upon his own powers, he could never have the inclination or the ability to surpass himself. His personal experience might enable him to distinguish ends already realized from those to be desired, but the ideal is not simply something which is lacking and desired. It is not simply a future goal to which man aspires; it has its own reality and nature. It is to be thought of rather as looming impersonally above the individual wills that it moves. If it were the product of the individual will, how could it be impersonal? If in answer to this question the impersonal reason of humanity is appealed to, the question is again only shifted and not resolved. This latter impersonality is scarcely different from the first and must itself be accounted for. If minds are at one to this degree, it is, surely, because they derive their homogeneity from a common source and, in fact, participate in a common reason.

In order to explain value judgments it is not necessary either to lose the concept of value by reducing them to judgments of reality or to relate them to some faculty or other by which man enters into relations with the transcendental world. Certainly value derives from the relation of things to different aspects of the ideal, but the ideal is not "cloud cuckoo land"; it is *of* and *in* nature. It is subject to examination like the rest of the moral or physical universe. The intellect can no more exhaust the ideal than it can any other aspect of reality, but it can be applied in the hope of a progressive understanding without assigning in advance a limit to this indefinite progress. From this point of view we can the more easily understand that the nature and the value of a thing can be distinct. Collective

ideals can only be manifested and become aware of themselves by being concretely realized in material objects that can be seen by all, understood by all, and represented to all minds. Drawings, symbols of all sorts, formulae, whether written or spoken, animate or inanimate objects, provide examples of such concrete realizations. No doubt it may occur that the characteristics of certain objects have a natural affinity with the ideal, and thus it may seem, wrongly, that their intrinsic characteristics are themselves the cause of the value attached to the whole. But the ideal can, and does, attach itself where it will. All sorts of contingent circumstances determine the manner of its embodiment, and the object once chosen, however commonplace, becomes unique. In this way a rag achieves sanctity and a scrap of paper may become extremely precious. Two beings may be essentially different or from certain points of view unequal, but if they embody the same ideal they appear equal. In such a situation the ideal appears to be their most important common characteristic and overshadows their dissimilarities. In this way collective thought changes everything that it touches. It throws down the barriers of the realms of nature and combines contraries; it reverses what is called the natural hierarchy of being, makes disparity equal, and differentiates the similar. In a word, society substitutes for the world revealed to us by our senses a different world that is the projection of the ideals created by society itself.

IV

What finally is the relation between value judgments and judgments of reality?

From the foregoing we have seen that there is no difference in nature. A value judgment expresses the relation of a thing to an ideal. The ideal is, like the thing, a given reality itself although of different order. The relation expressed unites two given terms as in a judgment of reality. No distinction arises here because of the bringing into play of ideals, for this is, in fact, common to both kinds of judgment. Concepts are equally constructions of the mind, and consequently ideals. It would not be difficult to demonstrate that these concepts are collective ideals, since concepts are formed in and through language, which is a collective thing. The elements of judgment are then the same on both sides. This is not to say that they can be reduced to each other; they are similar because they are the products of the same faculty. There is not one way of thinking and judging for dealing with existence and another for estimating value. All judgment is necessarily based upon given fact; even judgments of the future are related materially to the present or to the past. On the other hand, all judgment brings ideals into play. There cannot then be more than one faculty of judgment.

We have, nevertheless, indicated a difference that still persists. If all judgments involve ideals we have different species of ideals. The function of some is to express the reality to which they adhere. These are properly called concepts. The function of others is, on the contrary, to transfigure the realities to which they relate, and these are the ideals of value. In the first instance the ideal is a symbol of a thing and makes it an object of understanding. In the second the thing itself symbolizes the ideal and acts as the medium through which the ideal becomes capable of being understood. Naturally the judgments vary according to the ideals involved. Judgments of the first order are limited to the faithful analysis and representation of reality, while those of the second order express that novel aspect of the object with which it is endowed by the ideal. This aspect is itself real, but not real in the same way that the inherent properties of the object are real. An object may lose its value or gain a different one without changing its nature; only the ideal need change. A value judgment, then, adds to the given fact in a sense, even though what is added has been borrowed from another fact of a different order. Thus the faculty of judgment functions differently according to the circumstances, but these differences do not impair the essential unity of the function.

Positive sociology has been accused of having a fetish for fact and a systematic indifference to the ideal. We can see now the injustice of such an accusation. The principal social phenomena, religion, morality, law, economics and aesthetics, are nothing more than systems of values and hence of ideals. Sociology moves from the beginning in the field of ideals—that is its starting-point and not the gradually attained end of its researches. The ideal is in fact its peculiar field of study. But (and here the qualification "positive" is perhaps justified if such an adjective were not otiose before the word "science") sociology cannot deal with the ideal except as a science. It does not set out to construct ideals, but on the contrary accepts them as given facts, as objects of study, and it tries to analyse and explain them. In the faculty of ideation (*faculté d'idéal*), sociology sees a natural faculty for which conditions and causes can be found for the purpose, if possible, of giving man a greater control of it. The aim is to bring the ideal, in its various forms, into the sphere of nature, with its distinctive attributes unimpaired. If to us, as sociologists, the task does not seem impossible, it is because society itself fulfils all the necessary conditions for presenting an account of these opposing chracteristics. Society is also of nature and yet dominates it. Not only do all the forces of the universe converge in society, but they also form a new synthesis which surpasses in richness, complexity and power of action all that went to form it. In a word, society is nature arrived at a higher point in its development, concentrating all its energies to surpass, as it were, itself.

5. *The Principle of Immanent Change*

BY PITIRIM A. SOROKIN

Some Implications of the Principle of Immanent Change

A. PRINCIPLE OF IMMANENT GENERATION OF CONSEQUENCES

THE FIRST implication of the principle of immanent change may be formulated as follows: *As long as it exists and functions, any sociocultural*

Reprinted from Pitirim Sorokin, *Social and Cultural Dynamics* (Boston: Porter Sargent, 1957), pp. 639–646, with the permission of the publisher and the author.

system incessantly generates consequences which are not the results of the external factors to the system, but the consequences of the existence of the system and of its activities. As such, they must be imputed to it, regardless of whether they are good or bad, desirable or not, intended or not by the system. One of the specific forms of this immanent generation of consequences is an incessant change of the system itself, due to its existence and activity. Let us have a sociocultural system X (individual, family, State, any social organization, any cultural system). Since it exists, it incessantly works or acts. Let it, at a given moment, in a milieu B, perform act A (the performance of some act, as explained, is inevitable to any going concern or system as long as it exists). The very performance of the act—inevitable in some form—generates a series of infinitesimal or great changes in the milieu, as well as in the system itself. After its performance, and due to it, the system ceases to be what it was before: it greatly or infinitesimally changes. Thus, among other consequences of the discharge of the act, there is the consequence of a modification of the system itself.

Since the system is changed, it will react in the same milieu B (identical with the first) in a somewhat different way compared with the first reaction. Thus, the milieu (theoretically) remains the same; meanwhile the system changes and its reactions change. For the same reason, its third reaction in the same milieu B will again be different from the first and second reactions. And so on. Thus the milieu or the stimuli remaining constant, the system and its reactions to the milieu incessantly change. As some actions have to be performed incessantly by any sociocultural system so long as it exists, the incessant generation of the change of the system itself becomes immanent in it.

In the preceding case I took the milieu B as constant (which, in many experiments with the biological or sociocultural systems, we can have, with some approximation). Factually, the situation is somewhat different and the principle of the immanent generation of the consequences becomes still more important. The point is that outside the experimental laboratory conditions, the discharge of the act A by the system changes not only the system but also the milieu, infinitesimally or greatly. The changes in the milieu produced by the act of the system now begin to react upon the system in a different way than before. Therefore, the system now has to act differently, not only because it is changed itself, but also because by its act it has changed the milieu, and these changes force the system to act differently than did the pressure of the milieu B, before it was changed by the act of the system. A given state declares war against another state. The act of warfare changes not only the first state but introduces a series of important consequences in the world external to it. Among these changes, the other state is forced to enter the warfare. In the process of war, the second state becomes victorious, invades and subjugates the first state. Thus the act of the first state immanently generated a series of changes in itself; a series of changes in the external world; internal and external changes in their turn have reacted forcibly upon the state and have led to its profound transformation, up to

the loss of its sovereignty and independence. In this sense, any system not only bears in itself the seeds of its change, but generates the change incessantly, with every act, every reaction, every activity it discharges.

B. PRINCIPLE OF IMMANENT SELF-DETERMINATION OF THE SYSTEM'S DESTINY (Existence Career).

The second fundamental implication of the principle of immanent change is the principle of immanent self-determination of the potentially given course of the existence of a sociocultural system. It may be formulated as follows: *As soon as a sociocultural system emerges, its essential and "normal" course of existence, the forms, the phases, the activities of its life career or destiny are determined mainly by the system itself, by its potential nature and the totality of its properties. The totality of the external circumstances is relevant, but mainly in the way of retarding or accelerating the unfolding of the immanent destiny; weakening or reinforcing some of the traits of the system; or facilitating a realization of the immanent potentialities of the system; finally, in catastrophic changes, destroying the system; but these external circumstances cannot force the system to manifest what it potentially does not have; to become what it immanently cannot become; to do what it immanently is incapable of doing. Likewise, the external conditions can crush the system or terminate an unfolding of its immanent destiny at one of the earliest phases of its development (its immanent life career), depriving it of a realization of its complete life career; but they cannot fundamentally change the character and the quality of each phase of the development; nor can they, in many cases, reverse or fundamentally change the sequence of the phases of the immanent destiny of the system.*[1]

This proposition is a mere result of the principle of immanent change and immanent generation of the consequences. With all the traits at a given moment (T^1), the system acts in the form of A; A introduces changes in the milieu and in the system itself. Therefore, for the next moment, T^1, the system's total situation is determined by the external consequences of the act A. This situation at T^1 is thus determined by the system's properties and ac-

---

1. A. Comte, in spite of his externalistic tendencies, well understood this. "This human being cannot be modified indefinitely by exterior circumstances; such modifications can affect only the degrees of phenomena, without at all changing their nature; and again, when the disturbing influences exceed their general limits, the organism is no longer modified, but destroyed. All this is . . . more eminently true of the social than of the individual organism, on account of its higher complexity and position." A. Comte, *The Positive Philosophy,* translated by M. Martineau (New York, 1853), Vol. II, p. 117.

tivities at the moment T^1. The same is true for the moment T^2, T^3 ... T^n, up to the end of the existence of the system. This means that any sociocultural system, as soon as it emerges as a system, bears in itself its future destiny. To use Aristotle's example an acorn as soon as it emerges bears in itself its destiny, namely the unfolding destiny of an oak and of nothing else. So with the initial system of any plant or animal organism. The same is still truer of a sociocultural system: a moronic family cannot unfold itself into the Great Christian Church or develop the properties of the Royal Scientific Society; from an emerged contractual business concern one cannot expect the properties, functions, and life career of the early Christian monastery; from a Sensate "Society of Conoisseurs of Wines and Women" the characteristics and destiny of an ascetic society; from the State, the functions and destiny of a sentimental philanthropic society; from a real university, the functions, behavior and life career of a criminal gang; and so on. As soon as a sociocultural system emerges, with all its properties and *modus vivendi* and *modus agendi,* it contains in itself its "normal" future. At any moment of its existence and activity it creates it, controls it, determines it, and molds it. In this sense, to use the proverb, any sociocultural system is the molder of its own future.[2]

This does not deny the role of the external circumstances. But as mentioned, it specifies their functions. The external agencies may crush the system and in this way prevent it from a realization of its immanent destiny. Earthquake, fire, plague, inundation, war, and other agencies external to a given system—the family, the artistic society, the religious or political sect—can kill all or a part of its members; can destroy its property and other instrumentalities of its activities; can disperse the members; can destroy the scientific libraries and laboratories, art museums and churches, means of transportation and communication, food supply; and in hundreds of forms may put an end to the existence of the system. Still more frequently, the external circumstances many accelerate or retard, facilitate or hinder, reinforce or weaken a realization of the immanent potentialities of the system and therefore of its destiny. All this is granted as self-evident. And yet, all this does not determine funda-

mentally the "normal" career and phases of the development of the system. All this does not and cannot force the system A (oak, man, criminal gang), destined to have a life career B to have a life career fundamentally different, for which A does not have any potentiality: for instance, for a female to become a male; for a criminal gang to change into a society of the real saints; for the State to become a night club; and so on. This "normal" career or destiny is an unfolding of the immanent potentialities of the system given at the moment of its emergence.

C. IMMANENT SELF-DETERMINISM AS SYNTHESIS OF DETERMINISM AND INDETERMINISM.

The preceding analysis raises the question: *What is the relationship of the immanent principle to the problem of determinism-indeterminism?* Is the immanent principle of change a variety of determinism or is it that of indeterminism? *The answer is: neither or both.* So far as the immanent principle implies that the normal course and the essential traits of the system are greatly determined by the potentialities of the system at the moment of its emergence, it is deterministic. It is also deterministic so far as the influence of external factors is concerned, when it reaches beyond the margin of the system's autonomy. Considering, however, that the determining potentialities of the system are *the system itself* and are its immanent properties, *the determinism of the system turns into self-determinism. Self-determinism is the equivalent of freedom.* When we ourselves determine something, we feel ourselves free; and especially when this self-determination flows spontaneously from us as something quite natural to us and emanating from our very nature. The self-determination of a system is exactly this: it is rooted in the system; it expresses its very nature and its most essential potentialities; it flows spontaneously from the system and cannot do otherwise. For all these reasons the principle of immanent self-determination is equivalent to indeterminism. It is indeterministic also in the sense that the very notion of the potentialities of the system, as we shall see in the next paragraph, contains an element of indeterminacy on its fringes and in no way means a rigid necessity, as has been shown above. In all these aspects, the principle of immanent change of a system is indeterministic and implies a considerable margin of autonomy from all the agencies that are external to the system; and also some amount of indeterminacy within the system itself, so far as realization of its potentialities is concerned.

Such is the definite and precise answer to the question raised. The answer appears to be more adequate and sound than the half-truths of pure

2. Compare Aristotle's "Natural things are exactly those which do move continuously, by virtue of a principle inherent in themselves, towards a determined goal." "The final development reached from any one principle (*e.g.,* human seed) is neither exactly the same for every individual (for no two men are exactly alike) nor yet is it any random result (*e.g.,* dog or horse). There is, however, in each species always a tendency towards an identical result if nothing interferes." Aristotle, *The Physics,* Bk. II, 199b, pp. 176–77, quoted edition.

determinism and indeterminism.[3] The stated principle organically and logically unites in itself the valid parts of either of these principles and is free from the fallacies of either. It clearly indicates in what sense and to what degree the sociocultural system is indeterministic or free, and in what respects it is deterministic. In application to man and man's sociocultural world it synthesizes the doctrine of "free will" with the doctrine of determinism and "predestination." The next paragraph will specify still more fully the conclusion reached.

D. PRINCIPLE OF DIFFERENTIAL DEGREES OF SELF-DETERMINATION AND DEPENDENCE FOR VARIOUS SOCIOCULTURAL SYSTEMS.

If any sociocultural system bears in itself the reason of its change and determination of its destiny, three questions arise: 1. In the unfolding of the potentialities of the system in its life career, is there only one quite rigid and definite course for the system, or are there several possibilities or routes to be traveled? 2. Is the margin of self-determination of the system and its dependence upon the external conditions the same for all sociocultural systems or is it different for different systems? 3. If so, upon what conditions does the relative portion of self-determination and dependence upon external agencies in the systems depend?

These are the three questions to be answered. Turn to the first problem. Put in a more definite way, the first problem asks whether the destiny or the future life career of any sociocultural system is quite rigidly predetermined in one definite course, from the moment of the emergency of the system. If the question is answered positively, this would mean that any system is devoid of any possibility of deviating from its predetermined course, and becomes what it shall become. Such an answer cannot be accepted in this rigid form. First, because it entirely ignores the role of the external conditions of the system. We have seen that though the external circumstances cannot fundamentally modify the "normal" destiny of any system, nevertheless,

they can crush it, can accelerate and retard, favor and disfavor the development of the "native potentialities" of the system, and in this way can exert of considerable influence upon its life career. In some respects they play a role similar to the row of tracks at the railroad station: the train (the system) remains the same, but where it will go and what will be its destination depends upon what track it follows. Sometimes when it is shifted on to a wrong track, the result is a collision and catastrophe. *In other words, the very existence of the external conditions of a system makes its life career not absolutely predetermined at the moment of the emergence of the system.* The immanent potentialities of the system (at the moment of its emergence) can actualize in somewhat different life careers if the external conditions are different (for the same system) or when they change differently during the life career of the system. Second, the very conception of the immanent potentialities of a system (at the moment of its emergence) hardly entitles us to interpret their totality as something absolutely rigid, devoid of any elasticity. "Potentiality" is only an approximately marked course of career or direction of development. It implies some leeway of variation in most of its detailed "curves" and "turns" and "byways." It is not one highway which a driver has to follow (though even on such a highway the actual trajectories of the cars passing upon it are also somewhat different and never absolutely the same), but reminds us rather of several different routes to the point of destination, which the drivers can take and do take indeed: 3, 3A, 3B, 3C, each leading in the same direction, but each being a different route from the others. *Potentiality has always a margin for variations, especially on its fringes.* These variations are never rigidly determined or excluded. They are always the given datum. Otherwise, "potentiality" would not be "potentiality" but absolutely determined actuality or necessity, which conception contradicts that of potentiality.[4] In empirical sociocultural reality, the leeway of variations of potentiality is rather considerable for most of the sociocultural systems. Even when we are reasonably certain that a given child is gifted, we never can tell exactly what his accomplishments will be. The same is still truer of a given family, state, business corporation, religious current, literary movement, or a fighting army, or what not. Considering the potentialities of each of these systems, we can expect roughly, that their course, under given conditions, would be approximately such and such, but only a

---

3. It seems also more consistent and less self-contradictory than some theories of the modern physicists, like Sir Arthur Eddington, who extends the law of chance or indeterminacy over the inorganic world but exempts from it the realm of life, consciousness and spirit, as governed in a considerable part by the "objective law of direction"; or like Max Planck, who extends the "dynamic and statistical" determinism over the inorganic phenomena but exempts from it the region of "Ego" and "free will." Such a mechanical division can hardly be satisfactory and consistent, not to mention the conspicuous contradiction of the theories of Eddington and Planck, confronted with each other. See Sir Arthur Eddington, *The Philosophy of Physical Science* (New York, 1939), pp. 61, 89–90, 180–181, 220–21; Max Planck, *Where Science Is Going* (New York, 1932), pp. 145–169.

4. Compare Aristotle's "There are different stages of potentiality. The learner is a potential thinker in any given science, in a different sense from that in which he is a potential thinker in it, when he has learned its principles but is not thinking about it." *Physics*, 255b; also 199c.

fool or a charlatan can forecast all the details of this course.

Even in regard to the biological systems this leeway of a given potentiality is considerable. Having an acorn, we can reasonably expect the growth of an oak from it. But, how long actually the oak will live, what will be its shape, strength, height, size, the exact patterns of its branches, number of its leaves, and hundreds of other detailed characteristics, we cannot foresee.

Thus, the role of the external milieu and the nature of the immanent potentialities of any sociocultural system force us to admit a margin of indetermined possibilities in the development of the life career of the system. I say a "margin," not the complete indeterminacy. Such a margin means the rejection of a fatalistic and absolutely determined course of development of the system. Put in symbolic form, this thesis means that a given system A has an immanent potentiality B, which has to be unfolded in the course of its existence. But, granting even similar external circumstances, this B in one case will actualize into Ba, in another into Bb, in the third into Bc, and so on, up to Bn. In different external milieus, the difference between the actualizations of this B will be still greater.

Turn now to the second question: *Is the margin of self-determination of the future career of the system the same for all sociocultural systems?* Phrased in different form this question means: Are all the social and cultural systems equally dependent upon or independent of the external conditions in shaping their own destiny?

This destiny is shaped, as we have seen, by the immanent forces of the system itself and by the milieu in which it exists. Are the shares of both "molders" constant for any system?

It seems almost axiomatic that the share of the immanent factor of self-determination and that of the external circumstances is different for different systems. Some social and cultural systems seem to be conditioned by external circumstances much more than others. In our daily observation we notice the individuals who are the playthings of circumstances and the individuals who are to a much greater degree the builders of their own destiny, often contrary to the most inimical conditions. There are "soft and weak" persons and the persons with "an iron will power and determination." Likewise, we all know strong and weak families, unions, associations, states, governments. The strong weather many storms and stand firmly against many attacks, misfortunes, perturbations, while the weak fundamentally change or go to pieces after a slight inimical pressure of circum-

stances. The same is true about many systems of culture mentality (in religion, science, philosophy, art, law, literature, etc.). Some systems rise quickly, carried on by the wave of favorable circumstances, and as quickly decline when the luck of the circumstances changes; or rapidly change their character and individuality, adapting themselves to the external milieu and soon lose their identity, turning into a kind of formless and skeletonless protoplasma. Other systems persist and hold their identity, regardless of external circumstances. They remain equal to themselves under both adverse and favorable conditions; they display much less elasticity and versatility than the former; they ride the same ship in all weathers. Thus they show themselves much more immune to and independent from, the external conditions than the former. Facts of this kind are daily observations. They mean that the amount of self-determination of their own destiny or the amount of the dependence upon the external conditions is not constant for various sociocultural systems.

Logically, such a conclusion is also comprehensible. In order that all sociocultural systems shall be equally dependent on or independent of the external conditions in molding their own destiny, we should require: first, that all the systems be identical in all their potential nature, and therefore in their capacity to resist the influence of the external circumstances, or that all systems have the same immunity in this respect. To accept such an assumption would be a logical as well as a factual fallacy. A logical fallacy, because we here ascribe an identity to the systems which otherwise we recognize as different from one another. Since they are different in other respects they can hardly be equally immune to be dependent upon, the external conditions. Observationally, we know that various mechanical (*e.g.,* automobile), organic (different organisms), psychosocial (human individuals), and sociocultural systems have a different amount of "immunity" in regard to many external conditions. A good automobile can continue to function on a poor road without difficulty, while an old and poor automobile would break down or have trouble. Some organisms are more immune to several kinds of germs, or weather or food conditions than many others. Many minds are influenced by the current fads and fashions much less than many others. Likewise, as mentioned, some married couples get divorced after some slight quarrel or "incompatibility," while some others remain married up to their death. Some societies and unions persist for decades and even centuries, amidst most different environmental circumstances; while others quickly die, after meeting the first adverse outside conditions. Thus logically and observationally, the degree of self-determination (or dependence upon the external conditions) in molding their own destiny is different for different systems.

Is it possible to indicate a few more or less general conditions upon which depends the amount of self-determination of its destiny by the system?

First of all, it depends upon the *kind of social or cultural system*. Different social and cultural systems, like different mechanical or organic systems are likely to have different degrees of dependence upon external conditions in unfolding their immanent potentialities. However, this does not get us far: the proposition does not answer exactly which traits and properties make the systems differently immune to the forces of the environment. Until these properties are pointed out, the answer is useless.

Second, the amount of self-determination of various systems depends also upon the *kind of milieu*. We have seen that the milieu may be favorable or unfavorable to the unfolding of the potentialities of the system. Sometimes it may even crush it and end its existence. This again does not lead us far: to be a real answer, the proposition must indicate what properties of the milieu are favorable or unfavorable.

Third, we must distinguish farther between *the total and the specific immunity* of the system from its environment, in the molding of its own destiny. An organism, for instance, may possess a specific immunity in regard to typhus or diphtheria forces of the environment; and yet, as a whole, be more dependent upon the milieu than another organism which does not have this specific immunity, but, as a whole, stands better all the shocks of the environment, lives longer, and unfolds its potentialities better than the first. Farther on, different organisms may have different specific immunities: one in regard to diphtheria, another in regard to tuberculosis, a third in regard to venereal disease. A similar situation is thinkable in regard to the social and cultural systems. Some of them may have a high specific immunity and low total immunity; some others may have a high total immunity and a low specific immunity. Some of them may be immune in regard to one set of specific forces of the environment, while others are immune in regard to different agencies of the milieu. For instance, a business firm may be very sensitive towards the economic conditions of its environment (have a low immunity) and quite insensitive towards the artistic or philosophical or family agencies of its milieu. An art association or a philosophical society may, on the contrary, be very immune towards the economic

forces of the environment, and greatly dependent upon the nature of its artistic or philosophical atmosphere.

These preliminary remarks show all the complexity of the problem discussed and warn against its simplification. Before laying down the propositions answering the question, we must specify as exactly as possible under what conditions they can be valid and what kind of self-determination— general or special—they mean.

Let us assume, first, that we have social and cultural systems *of the same kind:* say, the family, or the State, or the business firm; or a philosophical school or an art system.

E. OTHER CONDITIONS BEING EQUAL (INCLUDING THE MILIEU), IN THE SOCIAL AND CULTURAL SYSTEMS OF THE SAME KIND, THE GREATER AND BETTER IS THEIR INTEGRATION, THE GREATER IS THEIR SELF-DETERMINATION (AND AUTONOMY FROM THE ENVIRONMENT) IN MOLDING THEIR OWN DESTINY

By the greater and better integration of a social and cultural system or group is meant first, the existence and the degree of the causal and meaningful interdependence between its components; second, and this is very important, the solidary (familistic, or at least, contractual) character of the relationship between the members or human agents; third, consistency between other components of the system.

Such is probably the most important condition of the amount of self-determination of the system, in unfolding its potentiality during its life career.

Unfolded, the proposition implies:

(1) *Other conditions being equal, of the social and cultural complexes, the least amount of self-determination is found in unorganized social groups and in cultural congeries.* An unorganized group of individuals (unintegrated social congeries) or an unintegrated cultural congeries is a mere collection of the elements of the social and cultural system. As such, it does not have any causal and meaningful cohesion and unity; any unified direction of its activities; any unified efforts towards a fuller unfolding of its potentialities; any unified end; and respectively, any unified system of forces directed towards the preservation of its identity and a realization of its destiny. Therefore, it cannot successfully oppose the adverse pressure of environmental forces, cannot press unifiedly against the agencies of the milieu and overcome their resistance. It is like a collection of individuals not organized into a disciplined army and therefore incapable of resisting the attack of the same number of individuals

unified into a well-integrated military body. Such social and cultural congeries have only the atomized and divergent self-determination of each of its elements, but no unified and therefore more powerful system of self-determination. Respectively, it is much more a plaything in the hands of the environmental forces than an integrated system of the same elements.

(2) Other conditions being equal, *the highest amount of self-determination belongs to those social and cultural systems which are most perfectly integrated, causally and meaningfully,* where the causal interdependence of the components and elements of the system is the greatest; and their relationship is the most solidary (among human agents) and most consistent among the components, where, neither actually nor potentially, is there any contradiction, any *Spannung,* any inner tension, antagonism or conflict. Out of similar families or states—the family or state which is perfectly integrated, where the relationships are solidary, where all members spontaneously and deliberately strive towards the same ends; have the same mentality and objectives; have a unified system of aims, efforts, and activities—such a family or state is a builder of its own future much more than the family or state with lower causal and meaningful integration, where the causal interdependence of the members is loose, relationships less solidary, and where heterogeneous aims, conflicts, and antagonisms exist.

Finally, *between these types stand the intermediate systems, which are neither congeries nor perfectly integrated systems.* Such are the social systems where only the causal interdependence is found but where relationships are not quite solidary; or the cultural systems where relationships of the elements of the system are somewhat eclectic, not quite consistent, and actually or latently conflicting between and in each of its components. In such systems there always is found what Max Weber, M. Scheler and E. Barthel style, *Spannung,* a kind of tension or latent antagonism; a hidden split or crack, which flares into an open split of the system as soon as the respective adverse interference of the external conditions takes place. For this reason, it is less capable of standing the modifying and breaking influence of the environmental forces, and depends upon them more than the systems with perfect integration. This again concerns a person, a social and cultural system. Fanatics, Don Quixotes, persons with deep convictions and consistent systems of mentality, are examples of strongly integrated personalities. We all know that they are much more immune towards all the currents of fashions and fads in art and science, philosophy

and religion, ideology and so forth, than the persons whose mentality is a kind of elastic attic, where side by side lie traditional religion and progressive diluted atheism; enthusiasm for American democracy and the Soviet paradise; parrot-like eulogy of Bach, and enjoyment of crooning and jazz; admiration of each succeeding best-seller, be it Papini's *Life of Christ,* Strachey's psychoanalytic biography, *Trader Horn, Anthony Adverse,* Thurman Arnold's *Folklore of Capitalism,* or what not. They follow any fad and fashion and are continually being passively molded—in their mentality and behavior—by the passing currents of their environment. They have little selective function: within their capacity they ingest all that environment gives to them, and therefore are playthings of the external forces.

The same, with a proper variation, can be said of the social and cultural systems. Any eclectic pseudo system of philosophy, art, religion, or law is similar to the above "eclectic" and "open-minded" persons. They seem to accept almost anything. As a result, they are always being changed by the passing currents of thought of their environment. As such, they seldom have any real individuality and remind us of something formless and shapeless, passively plastic, molded principally by their milieu and little by their own potentialities. This is the reason why the eclectic pseudo systems of culture mentality—in all the compartments of culture—do not last long, as an eclectic system of a *definite* sort (as endlessly varying complexes the eclecticism, like other congeries, is a perennial phenomenon). They leave faint traces in the annals of history. They come and go, while any consistent cultural systems, such as idealism and materialism, eternalism and temporalism, realism and nominalism, in philosophy; the visual and ideational styles in art; the classic, the Gothic, the baroque and other styles in architecture; the unified systems of religious beliefs or ethical teachings, persist for centuries and dominate for centuries. Even when they are on the decline, they still exist and are distinguishable; and—what is more—sooner or later they again ascend and become dominant (see Volumes One and Two). It is not incidental that, whether it be in the history of philosophy, art, ethical systems, scientific theories, religions, or law—in all such histories very little can be found about innumerable eclectic theories which existed, and still exist. The bulk of the histories deal with only the more or less perfectly integrated systems of philosophy of the great "integrating minds," or with the integrated systems of art, ethics, science, or religion. The greater the integration of the system, the more space is given to it, and the longer it persists, and often the greater the influence it exerts upon the destiny not only of its own but other cultural systems of mankind.

The same is true of the social systems. Unintegrated armies have always been beaten by integrated ones. Unintegrated states have always been short-lived compared with the integrated ones. A poorly integrated family, or business organization, or any "eclectic social organization" has always been more dependent upon external forces and external "good or bad luck," and, as a rule, more quickly and frequently has come to an end (divorce, separation, disorganization and loss of independence, bankruptcy or dissolution) than similar but better integrated social systems.

One word of caution: *integration and lack of it should not be mixed with fashionable terms like "plasticity," "capacity of adjustment to environment," "progressiveness," and the like.* These terms are not equivalent to good or poor integration. A system may be well integrated, and yet may possess a high plasticity and versatility in its functioning activities and "adjustment of the environment" to itself (in contradistinction to the contemporary passive: "adjustment to the environment"). And vice versa, a system may be poorly integrated and yet be very rigid and unchangeable; for instance, in its vehicles, agents, and activities, in the perennial presence of antagonisms among its members, in its use of antiquated ways and means for a discharge of its functions, in the ossification of its activities and so on.

Well-integrated systems may be both elastic and rigid in their structure and tactics, according to the conditions; the same is true of the poorly integrated systems. In passing, it is to be noted that nowadays what is so widely extolled as the virtue of plasticity and "capacity of adjustment" is often, in fact, a cult of a lack, or of a poor integration in a system, be it an individual or social body. If we are to believe the partisans of this theory, we all, it seems, should ingest all the best-sellers; follow all the fashions and fads; praise simultaneously democracy and fascism and communism, religion and atheism, capitalism and communism; if others become obsessed with cross-word puzzles, or bridge, or "Information, Please," we should "adjust" ourselves by sharing the obsession; open widely all the organizations to everybody who wants to join them; follow simultaneously quite opposite and conflicting policies in our organizations; join quite unrelated movements; in brief, be spineless, skeletonless, unintegrated eclectics, passively "adjusting ourselves" to everything from the last-minute conception of God, to the last-minute current fad of the artistic, scientific, philosophical, political, culinary, and

what-not movement or organization.[5] Such a triumph of unintegrated eclecticism and unintegrated passivity is in accordance with our super-ripe Sensate culture and society. But, as has been shown above, it is not the way of self-determination and control of one's own or the nation's or mankind's future destiny, as the partisans of this backboneless eclecticism and passive environmentalism often claim. It is the most hopeless road to that end.

Of other conditions relevant to the amount of self-direction of a system in molding its own destiny, the following ones can be mentioned:

(3) *Other conditions being equal (including the identical environment and the perfection of integration), the greater the power of the system, the greater its autonomy from the social, biological and cosmic environment, and the greater its self-control and self-direction.* Put in that form, the proposition is almost axiomatic. The more powerful system naturally has the greater chance to resist, overcome, and therefore to carry on its aims and potentialities, in its environment, than a less powerful system. The weakness of the proposition consists in the indeterminacy of the term "power." Left at that, it is valid, but fairly indefinite. What is the power of a sociocultural system? How can it be measured? And measured it must be, in order that we can say which system is more powerful.

I do not know any satisfactory device for a measurement as well as for a clear definition of the power of a social or cultural system. All that one can do is to indicate a few rough criteria which are somewhat measurable, and which can give at least a very rough, but nevertheless hardly misleading, "index" of the power of the system.

Other conditions being equal, (*a*) *the greater the membership of a social system;* (*b*) *the better their biological and mental and social qualities;* (*c*) *the greater the sum total of real knowledge, experience, and wisdom at its disposal;* (*d*) *the more efficient its*

5. See P. Sorokin, "Tragic Dualism of Sensate Culture," *Science, Philosophy and Religion. Symposium* (New York, 1941). K. Horney accurately sees in such self-contradictory eclecticisms the tensions of our culture; in such tensions the source of many contemporary neuroses, and in such persons the neurotics of our time. Among tensions of our culture she emphasizes such contradictions as: the ideal of competition and success, on the one hand; on the other, the ideal of brotherly love and humility; the stimulation of needs, and their frustrations in hundreds of ways; the freedom of the individual (in Sensate meaning) and his progressive limitation. Such eclecticisms and contradictory tensions breed poorly integrated neurotics. See K. Horney, *The Neurotic Personality of Our Time* (New York, 1937). And their number is far greater than the official statistics of the *Patients in Hospitals for Mental Diseases* give. Factually, all the enormous masses of the eclectics of the type described are potential neurotics. Their name is millions. *Cf.* A. J. Toynbee's theory of "Syncretism" and "Promiscuity" in the periods of disintegration of civilizations. *A Study of History*, quoted, Vol. V, pp. 376–569.

organization in the sense of the distribution of rights-duties-functions among its members (including the distribution to everybody according to his talent and ability); (*e*) *the greater the sum total of the means and instruments of influencing human conduct as well as of modifying biological and cosmic nature; and finally,* (*f*) *the better its solidary integration* (discussed above); *the greater is the power of the group—the more independent it is from the external conditions in the realization of its potentialities.*

A few comments will make each of these conditions clear.

(*a*) That the power and influence of any social system depends upon its membership is self-evident: an army of one hundred soldiers will be beaten by one of ten thousand soldiers of similar quality. A labor union with a membership of one hundred can exert much less pressure upon the employers and other groups than a union with one million members. And so in regard to any social group. The mere number of the members of a system is always a relevant component of its influence and power.

(*b*) Besides the quantity, the quality of the members plays an important role in the influence, power, and realization of the system's ends. It is also evident that of the groups of equal size, the group consisting of the mentally talented, morally integrated, biologically healthy persons can do much more than a group whose members are either morons, or biologically weak, or morally disintegrated persons.

(*c*) Likewise, the important role of knowledge, experience, and wisdom that are in the possession of the system or group also needs no lengthy comment. This condition is specifically mentioned, because a group may be composed of good human material but, due to various conditions, may be deprived of an actual possession of knowledge, experience, and wisdom at a given moment. In such a case, for a given moment, the influence of the group would be less than that of another similar group in actual possession of the knowledge and experience. Military history furnishes many cases of this kind: the invaders (in the past or in the present) often have been little, if at all, superior to the nation invaded. But they had in their actual possession the knowledge of the military technique and the perfect military weapons which were lacking among the invaded people. As a result, even though not being superior either morally, mentally, or biologically, the invaders have often been able to subjugate the people of the invaded country and become victorious over them. It is not enough to be potentially talented; it is no less important

actually to have the necessary knowledge and experience.

(*d*) The next important condition is the technical organization of the system; its social differentiation and stratification; the manner of distribution of rights, duties, functions among its members; and the kind of persons to whom these rights, duties, and functions are given. It must be evident, to begin with the simplest case, that, of two groups, the one where military command is given to an inborn Napoleon or Caesar; where moral and religious leadership is likewise entrusted to inborn moral and religious leaders; and where the governmental and other, including the humblest, functions are given to those who are most fitted for them—such a group will evidently be more efficient and powerful than a similar one where a potential Beethoven is made a captain of finances; an idiotic strategist, the commander-in-chief; an inborn slave, a ruler; a stupid person, a captain of science.

No less important, however, is the existence or nonexistence of the social stratification and differentiation, with their division of labor; and what kind of social organization is found in all these respects. Generally, division of functions of the members of the system increases the system's efficiency and power. Likewise, these greatly depend upon what kind of division of functions, or social organization, is carried through in the system: for instance, whether it is "democratic," or "fascist," or "monarchical"; a system with masters and slaves; highly hierarchical or equalitarian; "capitalistic" or "communistic," and so on. There is hardly any definite form of social organization which is most efficient for all the systems, at all times, and in all conditions and circumstances. On the contrary, the difference in the nature of the systems and their objectives makes certain that for widely different systems widely different forms of social organization are most efficient and best: the form of social organization of an army is little suited to a monastery of ascetics or a university or even a business corporation. And vice versa, the best form of organization of a preparatory school will be disastrous for an army. But for the same systems of the same kind, there are more and less fit, more and less perfect forms of organization. What they are for different groups is out of place to discuss here. The important fact is that the power and efficiency of the group depends greatly upon how fitted is its social organization to its nature and to its environment. Hence, its mention among other conditions.

(*e*) By means of influencing human behavior and of controlling the social, biological, and cosmic milieu in conformity with the ends of the system, is meant any instrumentality that serves the purpose: the total sum of the technical instruments and tools; machines, arms, weapons, factories, mills; wealth and money; means of communication and contact; army; police; prisons; electric chairs; and finally, the total sum of the talents mentioned above: preachers; teachers; orators; inventors; researchers; in brief, anything and anybody that helps to influence the human behavior of the members and outsiders to overcome the obstacles of the social, biological, and cosmic external world.

(*f*) Finally, the important role of perfect solidary integration of the system has been already discussed.[6]

With a slight modification, the same criteria are applicable to the comparative power of cultural systems. *The greater the number of the human agents of the system (of art, religion, philosophy, science, etc.); the better their biological, mental, moral, and social qualities; the greater the wisdom, knowledge, and value it incorporates* (value or system of meanings: religious, scientific, artistic, ethical, etc.); *the better it fits the social organization of its followers; the greater is its logico-causal integration* (within the system of meanings and between all its components); *the greater the sum total of means or vehicles for its unfolding, broadcasting, and maintenance at its disposal; the greater the power of the cultural system—the more independent it is from its environmental forces.*

Here, however, a greater emphasis is to be put upon the value (the system of meanings) the system incorporates and the consistency of the integration of its elements and components (see above, Chapter Two) than in the social system.

The rest of the conditions are in a sense derivative from these properties of the system. If the value it incarnates is great; and if this value is integrated perfectly into a system, the system is likely to have a large number of followers; be fitted to their social

organization (because it incorporates a great value); and get an abundance of vehicles—means for its objectification, broadcasting, maintenance, and functioning.

Each of these conditions is unquestionably a basic constituent of the power of a social or cultural system. Taken separately, each condition cannot be an index of the power of the system. Taken together, they give a very approximate, but hardly misleading, indicator of that power.

This proposition then sums up, if not all, then probably the most essential uniform conditions of the comparative autonomy of the system (in building its destiny) from the external conditions, and explains the relative share of the system's self-control and self-regulation in molding its own destiny.

Summary

1. The reason or cause of a change of any sociocultural system is in the system itself, and need not be looked for anywhere else.

2. Additional reason for change of a system is its milieu, which is again composed mostly of the immanently changing systems.

3. Any sociocultural system changing immanently, incessantly generates a series of immanent consequences, which change not only the milieu of the system but also the system itself.

4. Bearing the seeds of its change in itself, any sociocultural system bears also in itself the power of molding its own destiny or life career. Beginning with the moment of emergence, each sociocultural system is the main factor of its own destiny. This destiny, or the system's subsequent life career, represents mainly an unfolding of the immanent potentialities of the system in the course of its existence.

5. The environmental forces are not negligible, but their role consists essentially in retardation or acceleration; facilitation or hindrance; reinforcement or weakening, of the realization of the immanent potentialities of the system. Sometimes they can crush the system and put an end to its existence; or stop the process of unfolding the immanent potentialities at one of the early phases. They cannot, however, change fundamentally the immanent potentialities of the system and its normal destiny in the sense of making the life career of an unfolding acorn that of a cow, or vice versa.

6. So far as the system, since the moment of its emergence, bears in itself its future career, it is a determinate system and in this sense deterministic. So far as the future of the system is determined mainly not by external agents, but by the system itself, such a determinism is indeterministic or free,

---

6. On the power of social systems and its criteria see further details in P. Sorokin, *Sistema Soziologii* (Petrograd, 1920), Vol. II, pp. 45 ff., 83 ff. The problem of the comparative powerfulness of social systems has been studied very little. Of the the previous attempts to roughly elucidate it and even to give the definite index of powerfulness, the theory of A. Coste is probably most notable, but entirely unsatisfactory. (See P. Sorokin, *Contemporary Sociological Theories*, pp. 364 ff.)

The recent attempt of Bertrand Russell according to whom, "The power of a community depends not only upon its numbers and its economic resources and its technical capacity, but also upon its beliefs," plus upon a kind of organization, practically repeats (independently), in a vaguer and less systematic and complete way, the above criteria of mine, set forth in my Russian work. In other respects, the analysis of power given by Russell is rather patchy, superficial, and far from being "A New Social Analysis" as the book claims to be. Bertrand Russell, *Power, A New Social Analysis* (New York, 1938), pp. 145, 158, *et passim*.

as flowing spontaneously, in accordance with its nature, from the system itself.

7. The process of unfolding the immanent potentialities of the emerged system is somewhat predetermined by the system, but this predetermination leaves a considerable margin for variations. In this sense it is not absolutely and narrowly preconditioned. Only the main direction and the main phases of the unfolding are predetermined; the rest, including most of the details, are "free" and become an unforeseen and unpredictable matter of chance, environment, and free choice of the system.

8. Since the destiny or life career of any system is the result of the system's self-control and of the influence of the environmental forces, the relative share of each of these two factors in molding the system's career is not constant for all sociocultural systems. The share of the self-control of the system is the greater, the more perfectly the system is integrated and the more powerful it is.

9. As a rough indicator of the elusive concept of the power of a sociocultural system, the following less elusive combination of the criteria is offered: the greater the membership of the system; the better the members biologically, mentally, morally and socially; the greater the actual wisdom, knowledge and experience the system has at its disposal; the better it is organized; the greater the total sum of means of influencing human behavior and forces of nature at its disposal; the more solidarily (or consistently) the system is integrated; the more powerful it is; the more independent from the forces of the environment,—the greater is the share of its own control in molding its destiny.

6. On Configurations of Culture Growth

BY ALFRED L. KROEBER

IT IS CLEAR that aesthetic and intellectual endeavors resulting in higher values preponderantly realize themselves in temporary bursts, or growths, in all the higher civilizations examined. The same sort of bursts or growths tend to characterize nationalistic development, as expressed in successful political organization and expansion. Whether the phenomenon holds also for wealth and population, is a separate question, which I have not gone into because the data are of a different order and seem much more difficult to acquire over continuous long ranges of history. It seems possible that the behavior of wealth and population may prove different, because these phenomena are naturally expressible quantitatively, whereas the index for those considered is essentially qualitative through the medium of genius. At any rate, genius is one way in which the degree of aesthetic and intellectual achievement can be expressed. The world has, however, never been ready to admit any strong correlation between genius and wealth accumulation; and the peculiarly quantitative consideration of population size is obviously also a distinct matter.

Reprinted from Alfred L. Kroeber, *Configurations of Culture Growth* (Berkeley: University of California Press, 1944), pp. 838–46, with the permission of the University of California Press.

It is entirely conceivable that there may be a connection between growth of population and wealth and the achievement growths which have been analyzed. It would certainly be somewhat difficult to imagine highly cultural achievements reaching their culmination among a population whose size and wealth were consistently declining. No serious long-range and comparative studies appear, however, to have been undertaken on this problem, and it seems wise to defer opinion until they shall have been made.

The tracing of the degree or quality of value growths has been made on the assumption that genius is a fair representative of cultural value. It is the clustering of recognized genius in time and space and common speech which is the basis of the value-growth appraisals which have been outlined in this book.

This implies a definition of genius supplementary to the customary or popular one that a genius is an individual who is eminently superior in his mental endowment. A social definition of genius may also be offered. Geniuses are the indicators of the realization of coherent pattern growths of cultural value.

A corollary is that most of the potential geniuses born are never realized, so far as history or human values are concerned. The supply of genius, physiologically or psychologically speaking, ought to remain essentially constant in any one race within any period which is not unduly long. However, inasmuch as even the peoples possessing higher civilization have produced cultural products of value only intermittently, during relatively small fractions of their time span, it follows that more individuals born with the endowment of genius have been inhibited by the cultural situations into which they were born than have been developed by other cultural situations.

The reason for the transience of high-value patterns is not altogether clear. It is evident that such patterns must be selective and somehow differentiated or specialized. This in turn necessitates that any such pattern fairly early takes a particular direction. The pattern is then gradually pushed to its limits in that direction. These limits may be the limitations of the physical world. But they need not be such. The very selection which at the outset is necessary if a distinctive pattern is to be produced, is almost certain later on to become a limitation. It is then often or normally too late to go back and widen the scope of the pattern without undoing the entire growth which it has achieved. It seems to be historically almost as difficult to reconstitute a pattern fundamentally, or to widen greatly the scope of a growth, as at an earlier stage it is difficult to get a distinctive pattern growth or pattern value started. Not infrequently, when a pattern has attained realization or reached saturation, its limitations appear to be felt and efforts are made to alter or enlarge it. If these efforts take the form of a pause in activity, there may be a reconstitution of energy and direction, with the result that, after a lull, growth is resumed along somewhat new and broader lines. The early eighteenth-century pause in the growth of European science is an illustration of this type of phenomenon.

More often, perhaps, there is no such abatement or recession once a peak of pattern realization has been attained. Endeavors become evident toward strain and rupture of the pattern. The impulses toward change and growth persist, but take the form of extravagance, flamboyance, or alteration for the sake of novelty. At other times these endeavors are repressed, with the result that, change, or at any rate important change, being no longer tolerated, there is no recourse for activity other than in essential repetition, which necessarily brings with it deterioration of quality. This is the condition familiar as Byzantinism. Such Byzantinism need not be permanent, nor need it involve the whole of a civilization. If it remains sufficiently brief, it may behave somewhat like one of the temporary lulls and be followed by a period of renewed activities with more or less

reconstituted patterns. If the interval is not too long, and the reconstituted growth reaches higher values than the original one, the type is that of a lull followed by the second phase of a greater growth. If, on the other hand, the interval is longer, and especially if the second-growth pulse fails to reach as high an achievement as the first, the later effort is of the type of an attenuated renaissance episode in a Byzantine decline.

Particular attention has been paid both to these lulls and to the pulses or phases which they separate. Latin literature, with its three or four pulses separated by definite time intervals, is a case in point. So is Egyptian art in a very much longer time span.

In well-unified and well-defined civilizations the configuration of growth and decline may be clean-cut even though marked by several crests. In a multinational civilization like that of Europe, each nation shows its own crests, and at the same time the several culminations replace each other, like instruments in an orchestra, so that there is a larger polyphonic configuration for the supernational civilization as a whole.

There are a number of configurations with several crests, of which the middle one is clearly the highest. In them, the first and last growth pulses partake of the nature of prologue and epilogue; or, prodromal and aftermath efforts may be better designations. The total culture history of Spain, and again that of ancient Greece, seem to fall into this form.

The growth curves are sometimes symmetrical like a normal variability curve; sometimes skew, the crest appearing either before or after the middle of the duration. Skew curves are, if anything, more frequent for single activities. The curves for total cultures show somewhat more of a tendency toward symmetry, presumably because they are a composite of curves for several activities. There is enough variability to make it uncertain whether growth is typically expressible by a symmetrical normal curve.

The duration is also extremely variable, ranging from as little as thirty or forty years to as much as five hundred or a thousand. On the whole, it can be said that growths tend to be longer in proportion as they produce what posterity has recognized as great values. There are, however, large differences in duration, apart from this consideration. Thus the Sanskrit drama took several times as long to develop and decline as the Elizabethan, even with the Restoration drama counted in as part of the latter. There do seem to be significant national differences. Irrespective of kind of activity, all datable growths in India are slow.

There is no clear evidence of a tendency toward acceleration of growth as we pass from ancient to modern times. Of course, in this connection, comparison would be illegitimate between a culture like that of France, which is only one strand of the larger European culture, and, say, that of India or China, which, culturally speaking, are continental rather than national. Occidental culture as a whole has already developed about as long as ancient and Asiatic ones.

I do not set a norm of duration for the growths of larger civilizations, though the usual estimates of a thousand to fifteen hundred years are probably approximately right as an average. It seems doubtful whether any absolute figure can have much meaning: it would be only the doubtfully significant statistical average of a small number of instances. That is, it is uncertain whether duration values *per se* are significant of anything inherent. It seems reasonable that conditions of area, population, and kind of culture developed, which are almost necessarily variable, would be of sufficient influence to prevent any standard duration. The similarity between instances is probably less in tempo than in configuration; and this suggests that the real constants lie in the growth processes involved.

There is an evident tendency for growths in distinct activities to be associated in time, but no clear indication that a successful growth in one activity must be accompanied by growths in other activities. In other words, successful activity growths in one culture may be few or solitary; and many civilizations have failed to attain high achievement in one or another activity. That, on the contrary, growths tend to occur associated may be attributed to the fact that distinctive success in one activity presupposes a high degree of cultural energy, and once this is aroused it is unlikely to remain restricted to a single activity. But again, there is no reason to believe that once such cultural energy is aroused it must necessarily spread to all possible fields of cultural activity, since it is notorious that civilizations differ in their interests and emphases. The most marked example toward close clustering in time of the culminations in diverse activities is furnished by Greek civilization. Here the unusually small population involved may have been the cause; not only the number in any one city-state, but the total number of Greeks, was small. Our familiarity with Greek history has, then, served to set up this case as a type. Actually, it is almost unique in its degree of simultaneity of activity developments.

There is no marked evidence of an inherent order of succession in which the several cultural activities develop. So far as there is a tendency for sculpture to precede painting, the cause lies not in anything cultural, but in the fact that sculpture is the physically simpler art. The tendency toward sequence, if there is one, lies in the laws of nature rather than

in some law of culture. Science possesses certain inherent relations with philosophy, and philosophy again with religion, and religion again with art. But these relations have been worked out quite diversely in their cultural manifestations. Science, philosophy, and religion impinge on one another psychologically, but their expressions in cultural growth do have manifold, and may have minimal, relations.

Religion, however, in general precedes aesthetic and intellectual developments of note, and a history of the arts is frequently one of gradual emancipation from religion as they attain their culminations. This relation appears to inhere in the definition of the concepts. We hardly recognize philosophy and science as such until they have reached a certain level of development and organization. Below this threshold, which we do not avow but nevertheless recognize, we tend to treat these activities as nonexistent. Somewhat similarly for the arts, though there the threshold is a certain degree of quality attainment. Religion, on the other hand, is more or less omnipresent. At any rate, we tend to deal with it as if there were no corresponding threshold. The result is that when we begin our consideration of florescences in art, science, or philosophy, it is against a background of preëxisting religion, which has inevitably had relation with the formative or prethreshold stages of the other activities. Nevertheless, the criterion of emancipation of these activities from religious influence has a certain empirical value of defining their degree of development.

To the question whether there may be national florescences without accompanying cultural ones, or vice versa, the answer must be yes, although such happenings are rare in history. It is evident that ethnic or national energy and cultural energy are related but are not the same thing. Ethnic energy may be conceived of as potential cultural energy, or as cultural energy expressed in simple and immediate forms, with more emphasis on specifically social than on specifically cultural ends.

Of some importance is the relation of cultural content, which is fairly readily expressible quantitatively through descriptive enumeration, and cultural forms or patterns, which we apperceive qualitatively and which seem quantitatively expressible only by the indirect method of estimating the rating of genius. The difficulty of dealing with the relation lies in the fact that culture content and culture form occur only in association with each other, and are therefore imperfectly distinguishable. Here is a fundamental problem of anthropology which still awaits most of its solution. It will probably be conceded that more growth of value can be attained on a larger body of content or material. Content tends to grow cumulatively, whereas forms are more or less predetermined by their origins. The result is that a certain set of forms may be realized or fulfilled while the content of the culture is still growing. In that event, the consequence is a partial dissolution with reconstitution on an ampler scale; after which the patterns may proceed in a new growth or pulse. Fourteenth- and fifteenth-century transalpine Europe is an example of such an interval between pattern growths, while culture content was rapidly expanding.

The more insular cultures, like those of Japan and England, seem to possess a somewhat retarded growth, which, however, is steadier and less intermittent than that of corresponding mainland cultures exposed to more numerous and sharper competitive contacts.

Geographically, a radiating spread of culture growth can usually be traced from a first hearth or focus over the larger area finally occupied. This is in accord with what anthropologists have again and again noted in regard to specific diffusions. They have, it is true, mostly dealt with items of culture content; but the same process of spread seems to apply more or less to culture patterns and values. The spread is perhaps most often from the center outward; but the original focus may be situated on a geographical margin and the spread therefore be fanwise rather than radiating. If so, the focus is likely to lie on a frontier exposed to foreign stimulation. It is also possible for much of the periphery to develop first, and the remaining spread then to be centripetal.

Another type of centripetal change sometimes occurs during the decline of a large civilization: it then shrinks upon itself; as Mediterranean or Classic civilization, after having spread from the Hellenic area to include the Roman West, retracted later within its original Greek limits, the West relapsing into barbarism.

Cultural death has here been construed only as the death of particular cultures or forms of culture; that is, as the replacement of particular patterns, which may be of higher value, by other patterns. The question whether a whole culture can die of itself through internal causes or inherent aging is not answered.

A final review listing of such genius as has occurred in isolation shows such occurrence to be definitely rare, and justly to be designated as exceptional. The methodological assumption on which this volume rests seems therewith to be vindicated, at any rate approximately. A derivative corollary is that we human beings are, at least so far as our accomplishments go, the products of our cultures much more than we ordinarily recognize.

As for findings that are universal, or such as might express a general sociology of human history, this investigation has attained only to approximations, though some of these may stimulate further inquiry. My own feeling is that the growth-configuration approach results rather in a multiplicity of specific historic findings. These are occasionally new, more frequently a shifted emphasis or realigned interpretation. And the endless events of history are lifted out of their level of near-uniformity into organized relief, by an attitude which consciously recognizes pattern-growth configurations in their space-time relations as well as in their value relations.

7. On Conflict

BY GEORG SIMMEL

MAN'S NEED FOR ACCENTUATION

WHEN a historical development occurs in the form of a continuous rhythmical change be-

Reprinted from Georg Simmel, *Conflict,* trans. Kurt A. Wolff, in *Conflict* and *The Web of Group Affiliations* (Glencoe, Ill.: The Free Press, 1955), pp. 107–10, with the permission of The Free Press.

tween two recurring periods, each of them as important as the other and attaining its own meaning only through its relation and contrast with it, then the consistent image we form of such a process rarely reflects the objective regularity and the persistent level on which its elements alternate. Instead, we almost inevitably bestow on the change of these elements a teleological accent so that one of them is always the point of origin, which is objectively primary, while the other develops out of it; and the renewed transition of the second to the first appears to us as a kind of regression.

For instance, we represent the world-process as an eternal change between the qualitative homogeneity of fused masses of matter and their differentiated dispersion. We may well be convinced that always the one comes out of the other and then again the reverse takes place. Yet because of the way in which our conceptual categories happen to function, we think of the undifferentiated state as of the first. That is, our need for explanation requires us to derive variety from unity much more than vice versa. Even so, objectively it would perhaps be more correct to posit neither as first but to assume an infinite rhythm where we cannot stop at any stage we have calculated but where we must always derive that stage from an earlier, opposite one. It is similar in regard to the principles of rest and motion. The two follow each other endlessly—whether we look at the whole of being or at particular sequences of it. Nevertheless, we usually feel the state of rest to be the original, or definitive, state, which itself needs no derivation, as it were. Thus whenever we look at a pair of periods together, one of them always seems to be the explanatory and the other the derived one; it is only in such a rank ordering that we believe to grasp the meaning of their dynamic process. We are not satisfied with their mere alternation, as it actually shows itself, without designating one of its elements as primary and the other as secondary. Man is too much of a discriminating, valuing, purposive being not to articulate the uninterrupted flow of alternating periods by means of such accents; not to interpret them in analogy to domination and submission, or preparation and fulfillment, or transitory and definitive states.

THE TRANSITION FROM CONFLICT TO PEACE AND FROM PEACE TO CONFLICT

This also applies to conflict and peace. Both in the succession and in the simultaneity of social life, the two are so interwoven that in every state of peace the conditions of future conflict, and in every conflict the conditions of future peace, are formed. If one follows historical developments back in time from this standpoint, one cannot stop anywhere. In historical reality, each of the two conditions uninterruptedly relates itself to the other. Nevertheless, we "feel" an inner difference into this sequence of the links of the chain: conflict appears as preliminary, with peace and its contents as the purpose of it. While from an objective viewpoint, the rhythm of the two elements pulsates evenly on the same level, our valuation articulates, as it were, iambic periods, with war as thesis, and peace as arsis. Thus, in the oldest constitution of Rome, the king must ask the citizens for their consent when he wants to start a war, but he needs no such consent—which is thus presupposed as a matter of course—when he wants to make peace.

This example by itself is enough to suggest that the transition from war to peace constitutes a more serious problem than does the reverse. For the transition from peace to war really needs no particular examination: in peace, the situations out of which open conflict develops themselves are conflict in a diffuse, imperceptible, or latent form. For instance, the economic superiority (because of their slave economy) of the Southern American states before the Civil War over the Northern states was itself the reason for that war. Yet as long as such a situation causes no antagonism but is a matter of the internal conditions of the two territories, it remains outside the specific question of war and peace. The moment, however, the situation took on the color of war, it itself turned out to be an accumulation of antagonisms, of attitudes of hatred, newspaper polemics, frictions between private persons, frictions at the borders, and reciprocal moral suspicions in areas outside the central point of conflict. The end of peace thus is not signaled by a specific sociological situation. Antagonism, though not at once in its most explicit or strongest form, rather develops directly out of whatever the objective conditions of peace may be.

It is different with the opposite sequence. Peace does not follow conflict with the same directness. The ending of conflict is a specific enterprise. It belongs neither to war nor to peace, just as a bridge is different from either bank it connects. The sociology of conflict thus requires, at least as an appendix, an analysis of the forms in which a fight terminates. These forms constitute interactions not to be observed under any other circumstances.

Section C

Patterns of Change and Development

Editorial Foreword, BY KASPAR D. NAEGELE   *1329*

1. *On the Three Stages of Social Evolution*, BY AUGUSTE COMTE   *1332*
2. *On the Style-Patterns of Culture*, BY OSWALD SPENGLER   *1343*
3. *The Disintegrations of Civilizations*, BY ARNOLD TOYNBEE   *1355*
4. *The Reality of Social Evolution*, BY ROBERT M. MAC IVER   *1364*
5. *Diffusion*, BY RALPH LINTON   *1371*
6. *Cycles of Interdependence*, BY VILFREDO PARETO   *1381*
7. *The Social Psychology of the World Religions*, BY MAX WEBER   *1385*

Patterns of Change and Development

by Kaspar D. Naegele

THIS FINAL SECTION ASSEMBLES some discussions of the old question: Can one discern and demonstrate a directionality to the succession of transformations that mark the histories of societies?

Many different answers have been given. Searching for the directionality of change on the several planes of cultural, social, or personal tranformation is always accompanied by complementary questions concerning meaning of, and in, human phenomena. On virtually every page, it is demonstrated that the discovery of regularities within the domain of human affairs must somehow take into account the fact that, amid the patterns of institutional arrangements or personal actions, however automatic these may appear, questions of meaning always arise. Their way of arising varies; the way they are studied also varies. For some purposes, it could be useful to confront overt interactions in a small group, the patterns behind bank robberies, or fluctuations in the birthrate, for instance, with a model, borrowed from mechanics or biology, where meaning as such does not directly arise.

The experience of directionality, as entailed in experiencing one's self as a personality, is by no means sufficient for understanding social change and historic causation, even though one cannot absolutely divorce these matters. Yet some concept of directionality is necessary for dissecting the problems in this dimension of social systems. Concern with directionality is usually an inhibiting compound of quite different considerations—growth, differentiation, progress—which all tend to overlap one another.

Moreover, empirical and non-empirical, as well as existential and normative, matters have a tendency to converge in discussions of social change.

The progressive disclosure of some divine purpose, the relentless unfolding of some equally divine (if not benign) fate, an interval before the establishment of a qualitatively different realm either on this earth or elsewhere—these modes of belief become both the object of explanation and the grounds from which explanations are generated. Concern with the directionality of human arrangements indicates concern with the intentions with which people confront themselves and with the ends that they seek to attain.

Calculation, confrontation, and attainment all imply standards, which are, in turn, prerequisites of choice. Standards of action always involve both cognitive matters concerning the character of the world in which one acts here and now, and also normative matters implying commitment to alternative ideals. These issues are all the more prominent when—as is increasingly the case—deliberate social change, even on a large scale, becomes both the object of men's consideration and the subject of sociological investigation.

In other words, the search for directionality is often not far removed from the wish for mastery. The wish can be passive—resignation, when the discovery of pattern persuades one that history as well as personal development are the fateful outgrowths of forces ultimately beyond any deliberate management. The several selections of this section, among them, contain virtually the full range of moral points of view as these inform the study of change. They also contain rival proposals about the directionality of the broad sweep of the history of Western society, or even of civilizations in general. As selections, however, they converge on several questions.

(1) If societies are taken as one's minimal unit

of study, and civilizations possibly are seen as the largest intelligible units of study, what patterns of development are discernible and demonstrable?

(2) Are there similar patterns between otherwise different societies?

The apprehension of the directionality of human change is still partly paralyzed by the dichotomies and associations which the end of the nineteenth and the beginning of the twentieth centuries instilled in our intellectual tradition in this connection.

The world has shrunk, yet our skepticism about seeing it in the large over a long period has increased. Beliefs in progress and steady human betterment have given way to more pessimistic ideas and to the insistence that a variety of distinctions be made between short- and long-range changes, which would take different forms in different spheres of the human enterprise.

The opening selection below provides an example of the belief that a single line of progression along which to order the succession of events, at least in the West, can be simply stated. Comte is even bold enough to call his proposal a law. Although this model now has dire shortcomings, it indicates the process of rationalization that, in much more complex and relativistic ways, is again considered in the last selections culled from the works of Max Weber.

Since the end of the nineteenth century, those wishing boldly to outline the most comprehensive social changes have converged on the idea of the increased rationalization of human arrangements. As an idea, this raises many problems concerning the pre-conditions, wider causes, and associated consequences of this process. Besides, even Comte, and especially Max Weber, acknowledge a certain dialectic between the spread of an emphasis on calculation, rationality, impersonal rules, and technical competence, and the cultivation of complementary modes of personalness, privacy, and belief. Still, the relative contraction of the sphere of kinship and of general ascriptive considerations, and the expansion of impersonal arrangements requiring technical competence and leading to a wide web of increasingly large organizations through which the majority must earn its livelihood—these seem broad themes of change, progressively elaborated and refined by those who want to combine an interest in social change with fairly concrete attempts at documenting their claims.

Spengler's famous attempt to regard history as closely analogous to the life cycle of organisms is almost in opposition to Comte's line of increased mastery and rational enlightenment over earlier forms of philosophic, magical, or theological irrationality. Spengler documents the need and limitations of analogies in the study of human affairs.

Descriptions of people's experiences, and of their reactions to the social institutions by which and in which they live, are always a compound of circumscribing their variously clear ideas with the help of more or less explicit analogies from a physical and non-human world; and of formulating proposals about the physical world by abstracting from the terms appropriate to the flux of the experience of human relations and private reactions.

In spite of its gloom and severe limitation, Spengler's attempt is noteworthy for its wish to see the larger coherence on the plane of civilization and culture, its attempt to classify the types of such coherence, and its willingness to assert a cycle of ascendancy and decline. Spengler complements Comte's emphasis on increased rationality with a reminder of the relevance of biological analogies, as well as of biological determinants, in the realm of human affairs; Toynbee complements him by a greater respect for the religiosity permanently associated with the conditions of social stability and the resources for human participation. Toynbee's contribution combines a theological position and a concomitant emphasis on the moral necessities of permanence and change, with an elaborate set of distinctions acknowledging the complexity of the courses of the several civilizations that he studies. His views align a sensitivity to the character of inner resources with a parallel awareness of the interaction, within given civilizations, between technical, technological, economic, environmental, and collective arrangements. Social categories and groupings—e.g., majorities, minorities, proletariats, etc.—here hold their balance with a view of the several directions of human action implied by, e.g., withdrawal and return, challenge and response.

The selections from MacIver, Linton, and Pareto represent less global scope and less fervent moral commitment. Pareto's emphasis on equilibrium, on the virtually mechanical mutual interdependence of the several elements of institutional arrangements —e.g., interests, rationalizations, types of functionaries, and a continuing tendency for the restoration of a state of equilibrium—is in interesting contrast to the more dramatic analyses of Spengler and Toynbee. MacIver and Linton, fully committed not to lose sight of the characteristic features of culture as a product and condition of human consciousness, assert between them the continuous transformation and diffusion, where geography permits, that institutional arrangements and all other human accomplishments must generate.

Max Weber returns us to the beginning. He regards history as the battleground between the demands of tradition, the sporadic arrival of charismatic authorities, and the growth of rational legal authority associated with the routinization of charisma itself. He evaluates, in different ways, the world of social institutions and individual participation as a whole, and makes it, as such, subject to normative and psychological modes of acceptance and rejection. These have counterparts in various solutions to the problem of meaning and the concomitant questions of pleasure and pain. One can hardly summarize Weber's extraordinary discussions of the antinomies between an ethic of particularistic brotherhood and one of universalistic concern, between acceptance and mastery of the world, between mystic and esthetic modes of discipline, or between the religious roots of progressive rationalization and the ultimate demands of all religion for the sacrifice of one's intellect.

The conclusion of this Reader is taken from Weber's Introduction to his comparative essays on religion, which was written after the study of Protestantism and its bearing on the rise of modern capitalism. This Introduction concerns itself with explicating the notion of an economic ethic and its relation to the world religions. Weber began this series of essays shortly before the beginning of World War I. Weber read much of these beginnings to friends—a practice that changes in the academic life have probably removed from contemporary modes of procedure, at least within the university. Originally, Weber had intended to elaborate the theoretical aspects of his various empirical studies of the religions of India, China, and ancient Judaism. The war intervened, and the essays were printed without the intended extensions. Weber explained this: he considered it impossible to return to earlier, if unfinished, lines of thought after an interval of some years (which included his military service and political activity). Moreover, he regarded World War I as the "end of an epoch," and was certain that everyone regarded it as such. In this way, social change intimately helps constitute intellectual history, with its characteristic patterns of discontinuity and continuity.

In this selection, Weber describes various proposals concerning the conditions and consequences of social change. Schematically, in virtually his own words, they can be listed as follows:

1) For every religion, a change in the socially decisive strata has usually been profoundly important.

2) The evaluation of *suffering* in religious ethics has been subject to a typical change.

3) The development of a rational religious ethic occurred among unprivileged strata; its positive roots were in their inner conditions.

4) The demand that the world in its totality is, could, and should somehow be a meaningful "cosmos"—the core of genuine religious rationalism—has been carried by strata of intellectuals.

5) Men are differently qualified religiously: this empirical fact stands at the beginning of the history of religion.

6) The sacred values that have been most cherished —the ecstatic and visionary capacities of shamans, sorcerers, ascetics, and pneumatics of all sorts, could not be attained by everyone. The possession of such faculties is a charisma, which might be awakened in some, but not in all. It follows from this that all intensive religiosity tends toward a sort of *status qualification,* in accordance with differences in the charismatic qualifications.

These are but a few generalizations, proposing directions and regularities of social change and differentiation, contained in this rich introductory essay. They are part of a huge, if fragmentary, effort. They imply persistent distinctions and ideas: charisma, rationality, strata, classes, virtuosi, masses. With their help, Weber, with his characteristic qualifications and scholarly circumspection, formulates the proposition that religion has become transferred into what, in his special sense, is the irrational realm. He explains this shift through a long list of considerations. Among these is the idea that religious phenomena have become subject to a division—facilitated by the influence of genteel and intellectual groups. This would make us the possessors of rational cognition and masters over nature; and also—since there is always a residue left—subjects of mystic experiences, or at least acceptors of imponderable given qualities. Moreover, differences in social position and function contribute to religious differences, even if the latter also contain—especially in their doctrine—an "autonomous" history. Professional preoccupation with cult or myth, for instance, tends to monopolize the administration of religious values. It leads to notions of corporate grace whose bestowal is contingent on a (professional) priesthood, rather than accessible to individual attainment. Chivalrous warriors, on the other hand, pursued both worldly interests and the belief in an irrational fate, while peasants "have been inclined towards magic." Civic strata usually are religiously ambiguous, though among them there is a tendency toward practical rationalism as well as a possibility of "letting an ethical and rational regulation of life arise."

If there is a concrete and historic sense of the complexity of society, the study of social change is likely to move forward precisely as it strains toward propositions of this kind. Thus they are listed here, even though the listing only represents to the reader what he can find directly in the original.

Concluding with such suggestive fragments should help to make this Reader the gateway to its larger original sources, where many buried treasures await contemporary discoveries.

1. On the Three Stages of Social Evolution

BY AUGUSTE COMTE

WE HAVE INDICATED the general direction of the human evolution, its rate of progress, and its necessary order. We may now proceed at once to investigate the natural laws by which the advance of the human mind proceeds. The scientific principle of the theory appears to me to consist in the great philosophical law of the succession of the three states—the primitive theological state, the transient metaphysical, and the final positive state—through which the human mind has to pass, in every kind of speculation. This seems to be the place in which we should attempt the direct estimate of this fundamental law, taking it as the basis of my historical analysis, which must itself have for its chief object to explain and expand the general notion of this law by a more and more extended and exact application of it in the review of the entire past of human history. I hope that the frequent statement and application of this law throughout the preceding part of my work will enable me to condense my demonstration of it here, without impairing its distinctness, or injuring its efficacy in such ulterior use as we shall have to make of it.

LAW OF THE THREE PERIODS

The reader is by this time abundantly familiar with the interpretation and destination of the law. All thoughtful persons can verify for themselves its operation in individual development, from infancy to manhood, as I pointed out at the beginning of this work. We can test it, as we have tested other laws, by observation, experiment, and comparison. I have done so through many years of meditation; and I do not hesitate to say that all these methods of investigation will be found to concur in the complete establishment of this historical proposition, which I maintain to be as fully demonstrated as any other law admitted into any other department of natural philosophy. Since the discovery of this law of the three periods, all positive philosophers have agreed on its special adaptation to the particular science in which each was interested, though all have not made the avowal with equal openness. The only objections that I have encountered have re-

lated merely to the universality of its application. I hold it to be now implicitly recognised with regard to all the sciences which are positive: that is, the triple evolution is admitted in regard to all cases in which it is accomplished. It is only in regard to social science that its application is supposed to be impossible: and I believe the objection to signify nothing more than that the evolution is in this case incomplete. Social science has, with all its complexity, passed through the theological state, and has almost everywhere fully attained the metaphysical; while it has nowhere yet risen to the positive, except in this book. I shall leave the assertion of the law in regard to sociology to the demonstration which my analysis will afford: for those who can not perceive in this volume, as a whole, the nascent realization of this last philosophical process could not be convinced by argument. Leaving the historical verification of the law, therefore, to the reader, I invite attention to its philosophical explanation. It is not enough that the succession of the three states is a general fact. Such generality would go for more in any other science than in sociology, because, as we have seen, our biological philosophy enables us to conceive of all the main relations of social phenomena à priori, independently of their direct investigation, and we need confirmation of our conceptions by a direct knowledge of human nature and experience. An à-priori conception of a law so important as this is of the deepest interest in the study of social dynamics; and, to confirm it, we must carefully mark the general grounds, derived from an exact knowledge, which have rendered indispensable on the one hand, and inevitable on the other, that succession of social phenomena which take their course under the operation of this law. The logical grounds have already been assigned, at the outset of the work, and repeatedly since: and it is with the moral and social that we now have to do, and we can review them without subjecting ourselves to the reproach of severing the parts of a philosophical demonstration which are in their nature bound up together.

THE THEOLOGICAL PERIOD

The necessity of the intellectual evolution I assert lies in the primary tendency of Man to transfer

Reprinted from Auguste Comte, *The Positive Philosophy,* freely trans. and condensed by Harriet Martineau (London: George Bell & Sons, 1896), II, 522–40.

the sense of his own nature into the radical explanation of all phenomena whatever. Philosophers tell us of the fundamental difficulty of knowing ourselves; but this is a remark which could not have been made till human reason had achieved a considerable advance. The mind must have attained to a refined state of meditation before it could be astonished at its own acts—reflecting upon itself a speculative activity which must be at first incited by the external world. If, on the one hand, Man must begin by supposing himself the centre of all things, he must, on the other hand, next set himself up as a universal type. The only way that he can explain any phenomena is by likening them, as much as possible, to his own acts—the only ones whose mode of production he can suppose himself, by the accompanying sensations, to understand. We may therefore set up a converse statement, and say that Man knows nothing but himself; and thus, his philosophy, in his earliest stage, consists principally in transferring this spontaneous unity, more or less fortunately, into all subjects which may present themselves to his nascent attention. It is the highest proof of his philosophical maturity when he can, at length, apply the study of external nature to his own. When I laid this down as the basis of biological philosophy, I intimated the extreme rarity of such an attainment. At the outset, under the inverse process, the universe is always subordinated to Man, in speculative as well as in active respects. We shall not have attained a truly rational position till we can reconcile these two great philosophical views, at present antagonistic, but admitting of being made mutually complementary, and, in my opinion, prepared for being so, from this time forward. Such a harmony is even now barely conceivable in the brightest insight of philosophical genius, and there could have been no choice between the two courses in the earliest days of human development. The starting-point must have been that which alone was naturally possible. This was the spontaneous origin of the theological philosophy, the elementary spirit of which consists in explaining the intimate nature of phenomena, and their mode of production, and in likening them, as much as possible, to the acts of human will, through our primary tendency to regard all beings as living a life analogous to our own, and often superior, from their greater habitual energy. This procedure is so eminently exclusive, that men are unable to emancipate themselves from it, even in the most advanced stages of evolution, except by abandoning altogether these inaccessible researches, and restricting themselves to the study of the laws of phenomena, apart from their causes. Whenever, at this day, the human mind attempts to pass these inevitable limits, it in-

voluntarily falls again into the primary errors, even in regard to the simplest phenomena, because it recurs to an aim and point of view essentially analogous, in attributing the production of phenomena to special volitions, internal, or more or less external. One case presents itself as an example, of the simplest scientific character—that of the memorable philosophical error of the illustrious Malebranche in regard to the explanation of the mathematical laws of the elementary collision of solid bodies. If such a mind, in such an age, could explain such a theory in no other way than by an express recurrence to the continuous activity of a direct and special providence, we can not doubt the tendency of our reason toward a radically thelogical philosophy whenever we attempt to penetrate, on any ground whatever, the intimate nature of phenomena.

INTELLECTUAL INFLUENCE OF THE THEOLOGICAL PHILOSOPHY

This inevitableness of the theological philosophy is its most radical property, and the first cause of its long ascendency. We have seen before that it was necessary, as the only possible beginning of our intellectual evolution; for the facts which must form the basis of a positive theory could not be collected to any purpose without some preliminary theory which should guide their collection. Our understanding can not act without some doctrine, false or true, vague or precise, which may concentrate and stimulate its efforts, and afford ground for enough speculative continuity to sustain our mental activity. Our meteorological *observations*, as we call them, show us how useless may be vast compilations of facts, and how really unmeaning, while we are destitute of any theory whatever. Those who expect that the theory will be suggested by the facts, do not understand what is the course necessarily pursued by the human mind, which has achieved all real results by the only effectual method,—of anticipating scientific observations by some conception (hypothetical in the first instance) of the corresponding phenomena. Such a necessity has already been shown to be especially marked in the case of social speculations, not only from their complexity, but from the peculiarity that a long preparatory development of the human mind and of society constitutes the phenomena of the case, independently of all preparation of observers, and all accumulation of observations. It may be worth observing, that all the partial verifications of this fundamental proposition that we meet with in the different sciences confirm each other, on account of our tendency to unity of method and homogeneousness of doctrine, which would incline us to extend the theological philosophy from one class of speculations to another, even if we should not so treat each one of them separately.

The original and indispensable office of the theological philosophy is then to lead forth the human mind from the vicious circle in which it was confined by the two necessities of observing first, in order to form conceptions, and of forming theories first, in order to observe. The theological philosophy afforded an issue by likening all phenomena whatever to human acts; directly, in the first instance, by supposing all bodies to have a life more or less like our own, and indirectly afterward, by means of the more durable and suggestive hypothesis which adds to the visible system of things an invisible world, peopled by superhuman agents, who occasion all phenomena by their action on matter, otherwise inert. The second stage is especially suitable to the human mind which begins to feel its difficulties and its needs; for every new phenomenon is accounted for by the supposition of a fresh volition in the ideal agent concerned, or, at most, by easy creation of a new agent. However futile these speculations may now appear, we must remember that, in all times and everywhere, they have awakened human thought by offering to it the only material which it could at first accept. Besides that there was no choice, the infant reason can be interested by nothing but sublime solutions, obtained without any deep and sustained conflict of thought. We, at this day, find ourselves able, after suitable training, to devote ourselves to the study of the laws of phenomena, without heed to their first and final causes; but still we detect ourselves occasionally yielding to the infantine curiosity which pretends to a power of knowing the origin and the end of all things. But such severity of reason as we are capable of has become attainable only since the accumulation of our knowledge has yielded us a rational hope of finally discovering the natural laws that were altogether out of reach, in the early states of the human mind; and the only alternative from total inactivity was, in those days, in the pursuit of the inaccessible subject which are represented by the theological philosophy.—The moral and social grounds of this philosophy were as necessary as the intellectual. Its moral influence was to inspire Man with confidence enough for action, by animating him with a sense of a position of supremacy. There is something astonishing in the contrast between the actual powers of Man in an infant state and the indefinite control which he aspires to exercise over external nature; just as there is in his expectation of understanding matters which are inaccessible to reason. The practical and the speculative expectation alike belong to the theological philosophy. Supposing all phenomena to be regulated by superhuman will, Man may hope to modify the universe by his desires; not by his personal resources, but by the access which he believes himself to have to the imaginary beings whose power is unlimited: whereas, if he was aware from the beginning that the universe is subject to invariable laws, the certainty that he could no more influence than understand them would so discourage him that he would remain for ever in his original apathy, intellectual and moral. We find ourselves able to dispense with supernatural aid in our difficulties and sufferings, in proportion as we obtain a gradual control over Nature by a knowledge of her laws: but the early races of men were in an opposite condition. They could obtain confidence, and therefore courage, only from above, and through the illusion of an illimitable power residing there, which could, on any occasion, afford them irresistible aid. I am not referring now to any hope of a future life. We shall see presently that it was not till a much later period that that hope exercised any important social influence: and even in more recent times, we shall find that the effect of the religious spirit on the conduct of human life proceeds much more from belief in actual and special immediate aid than from the uniform perspective of a remote future existence. This seems to me the leading aspect of the remarkable state which is produced in the human brain by the important intellectual and moral phenomenon of prayer; the admirable properties of which, when it has attained its full physiological efficacy, are very manifest in the earliest stage of progress. After a long decline of the religious spirit, the notion of *miracle* was naturally formed, to characterize the events which had become exceptional, and were attributed to divine intervention: but the very conception shows that the general principle of natural laws had become familiar, and even preponderant, because the only sense of *miracle* was a transient suspension of natural laws.

While the theological philosophy was all in all, there were no miracles, because everything was equally marvellous, as we see by the artless descriptions of ancient poetry, in which the commonest incidents are mixed up with the most monstrous prodigies, and undergo analogous explanations. Minerva intervenes to pick up the whip of a warrior in military games, as well as to protect him against a whole army: and in our own time, the devotee is as importunate in praying for his smallest personal convenience as for the largest human interests. In all ages, the priest has been more occupied with the solicitations of his flock about immediate favors of Providence than with their care for their eternal state. However this may be, we see that it is a radical property of the theological philosophy to be the sole support and stimulus of Man's moral courage, as well as the awakener and director of his intellectual activity.—To this we must add, as another attraction of Man to this philosophy, that the affective influence comes in to fortify the speculative. Feeble as are the intellectual organs, relatively considered, the attractive moral perspective of an unbounded power of modifying the universe, by the aid of supernatural protectors, must have been most important in exciting mental action. In our advanced state of scientific progress, we can conceive of the perpetual pursuit of knowledge for the sake of the satisfaction of intellectual activity, joined to the tranquil pleasure which arises from the discovery of truth: yet it is doubtful whether such natural stimulus as this would always suffice without collateral instigations of glory, of ambition, or of lower and stronger passions, except in the case of a very few lofty minds; and with them, only after training in the requisite habits. And nothing of this kind can be supposed possible in the early days, when the intellect is torpid and feeble, and scarcely accessible to the strongest stimulus; nor yet afterward, when science is so far advanced as to have attained some speculative success. In the working out of such speculation, the mental activity can be sustained by nothing short of the fictions of the theological philosophy about the supremacy of man and his unbounded empire over external nature; as we have seen in regard to astrology and alchemy. In our own time, when there are enlightened men who hold such delusions in regard to social speculations alone, we see how irrationally they expect to modify at will the whole course of political phenomena, in which they could not take any adequate scientific interest without such an expectation. What we see of the influence of this view in maintaining the old polities may give us some faint idea of its power when it pervaded every part of the intellectual system, and illusion beset the reason of Man, whichever way he turned. Such then was the moral operation of the theological philosophy,—stimulating Man's active energy by the offer, in the midst of the troubles of his infantine state, of absolute empire over the external world, as the prize of his speculative efforts.

SOCIAL INFLUENCES OF THE THEOLOGICAL PHILOSOPHY

The social evidences under this head will be fully treated in the following chapters, so that we may dismiss them now with a very short notice, impor-

tant as they are; and the more easily, because this class of evidences is the most indisputable of the three. There are two views which must be considered, in relation to the high social office of the theological philosophy: first, its function in organizing society; and next, its provision for the permanent existence of a speculative class.—As to the first, we must perceive that the formation of any society, worthy to be so called, supposes a system of common opinions, such as may restrain individual eccentricity; and such an influence, if needful now, when men are connected together by such a concurrence of obligations as high civilization introduces, must be absolutely indispensable in the infancy of society, when families adhere to each other so feebly, by means of relations as precarious as they are defective. No concurrence of interests, nor even sympathy in sentiment, can give durability to the smallest society, if there be not intellectual unanimity enough to obviate or correct such discordance as must inevitably arise. It has been shown that, indolent as our intellectual faculties are in comparison with the others, reason must rule, not domestic but social, and yet more political life: for through it alone can there be any organization of that reaction of society on the individual which appoints the function of government, and absolutely requires a system of common opinions about nature and Man. Such a system, then, is a political necessity; and especially in the infancy of society. But, on the other hand, we must admit that the human mind, having thus furnished a basis for social organization, must depend for its further development on society itself, whose expansion is really inseparable from that of human intelligence. Here we see that society is in a vicious circle in a political, as well as a logical view, through the opposition of two equal necessities; and here, again, the only possible issue is afforded by the theological philosophy. It directs the first social organization, as it first forms a system of common opinions, and by forming such a system. Because we see it now in such a state of decomposition that its advocates lose sight of the unity of opinions that it once secured and are themselves involved in intellectual discordance, we must not forget how, in those days of vigor by which it must be judged, it established an intellectual communion which constituted its most remarkable political function. The police consideration of a future life is wrongly attributed to this period of human society. It arose long after, and was of very inferior importance to the intellectual agreement which preceded it: and its operation would not be so erroneously exaggerated, but that religion has so far faded out of men's minds as to leave no other strong habitual remembrance than of its grossest impressions.

INSTITUTION OF A SPECULATIVE CLASS

Another way in which the theological philosophy was politically indispensable to human progress was by instituting in the midst of society, a special class regularly devoted to speculative activity. In this view, the social supremacy of the theological philosophy has lasted to our own time. It is scarcely possible for us to form any but an indirect idea of the difficulty of establishing, in the earliest period of society, any permanent division between theory and practice, such as is effected by the existence of a class regularly occupied with speculation. Even now, amidst all the refinement of our mental habits, we find extreme difficulty in duly estimating any new operation which has no immediate practical bearing: and by this we may imperfectly understand how impossible it was, in the remotest ages, to institute among populations of warriors and slaves a corporation that should be disengaged from military and industrial employments, and whose activity should be mainly of an intellectual kind. Such a class could, in those times, have been neither established nor tolerated if it had not been introduced in the natural course of social movement, and invested with authority beforehand by the influence of the theological philosophy. The political function of that philosophy thus was to establish a speculative body whose social existence not only admitted of no preparatory discussion, but was itself an indispensable preparation for the regular organization of all other classes. Whatever might have been the confusion of intellectual labor, and the inanity of the leading investigations of the sacerdotal orders, it is not the less true that the human mind owes to them the first effectual separation between theory and practice, which could take place in no other manner. Mental progress, by which all other progress is directed, would certainly have been destroyed at its birth, if society had continued to be composed of families engaged in the cares of material existence, or, as the only alternative, in the excitement of a brutal military activity. Any spiritual expansion supposes the existence of a privileged class, enjoying the leisure indispensable to intellectual culture, and at the same time urged, by its social position, to develop to the utmost the kind of speculative activity compatible with the primitive state of humanity; and this description is answered by the sacerdotal institution established by the theological philosophy. Though, in the decrepitude of the old philosophy, we see the theological class sunk in mental lethargy, we must not forget that, but for their activity in the days of its prime, human society would have remained in a condition much like that of a company of superior monkeys. By forming this speculative class, then, the theological philosophy fulfilled the political conditions of a further progression of the human mind.

Such are the qualities, intellectual, moral and social, which secured the supremacy of the theological philosophy, at the outset of human progress. This is the only part of my sociological demonstration which is at all open to dispute; and this is one reason why I have dwelt so long upon it: but it is not the only reason. Another and a greater is that this view contains the radical principle of the whole demonstration, the remainder of which will not detain us long.

THE POSITIVE PERIOD

If this starting-point of human development has been placed beyond dispute, the final or positive stage does not admit of it. We have seen enough of the establishment of the positive philosophy in other departments to be satisfied of its destined prevalence in sociology. For the same reasons which explain and justify the early supremacy of the theological philosophy, we see that it must be a provisional state, for its supremacy was owing to its aptitude to meet the needs of a primitive state of humanity; and those needs are not the same, nor requiring the same philosophy to satisfy them, as those which arise in a more advanced stage of the human evolution. After having awakened human reason, and superintended its progress, in the absence of a more real philosophy, theology began to repress the human mind from the first moment of its coming into direct antagonism with the positive philosophy. And in the same way, in its moral relations, it imparted at first a consolatory confidence and active energy, which have become transmuted, by too long a duration, into oppressive terror and a faint apathy which have been too common a spectacle since it has been driven to struggle to retain its hold, instead of extending its dominion. There is no more question of the moral than of the intellectual superiority and final supremacy of the positive philosophy, capable as it is of developing in us an unshaken vigor and a deliberate steadfastness, directly derived from our own nature, without any external assistance, or any imaginary hinderance. And again, in regard to its social bearings, though the ascendency of the theological philosophy lasted longer on this ground than on the other two, it is evident enough at present that, instead of uniting men, which was its proper function at first, it now divides them, so that, after having created speculative activity, it has ended with radically hindering it. The function of reuniting, as of stimulating and directing, belongs more and more, as religious belief declines, to the conceptions of positive philosophy, which alone can establish that intellectual community all over the world on which the great future political organization is to be grounded. The intellectual destination of the two philosophies has been sufficiently established in our review of all the departments of natural philosophy. Their moral and social destination will be illustrated in succeeding chapters of this work. My historical analysis will explain to us the continuous decline of the one and the corresponding rise of the other, from the earliest period of human progression. It may appear paradoxical to regard the theological philosophy as in a steadily-declining state intellectually, at the very time that it was fulfilling its most exalted political mission; but we shall find satisfactory scientific evidence that Catholicism, its noblest social work, must necessarily be its last effort, on account of the germs of disorganization which must thenceforth grow more and more rapidly. We need here, therefore, only assign the general principle of the inevitable tendency of the human mind toward an exclusive positive philosophy, throughout the whole range of the intellectual system.

ATTEMPTED UNION OF THE TWO PHILOSOPHIES

The general, like the individual human mind, is governed by imagination first, and then, after a sufficient exercise of the faculties at large, more and more by reason. The same grounds on which the process takes place in the individual case determine that of the whole species; and with the more certainty and power on account of the greater complexity and perpetuity of the social organism. Supreme as the theological philosophy once was, it is certain that such a method of philosophizing was resorted to only because no other was possible. Wherever there has been a choice, in regard to any subject whatever, Man has always preferred the study of the laws of phenomena to that of their primary causes, though prior training, which there has been no rational education adapted to counteract, has often occasioned lapse into his old illusions. Theological philosophy has, however, never been absolutely universal. That is, the simplest and commonest facts in all classes of phenomena have always been supposed subject to natural laws, and not to the arbitrary will of supernatural agents. (Adam Smith made the remark that there never was, in any age or country, a god of Weight). In more complex cases, if only the relations of phenomena are seen to be invariable, the most superficial observer recognizes the presence of law. Even among moral and social phenomena, where the

entrance of positive philosophy has been interdicted, we are all obliged to act daily on the supposition of natural laws, in order to conduct the common affairs of life, for all forecast would be impossible if we supposed every incident to be ascribable to supernatural agency, and no other resource therefore possible than prayer, for influencing the course of human actions. It is even noticeable that the principle of the theological philosophy itself lies in the transference to the phenomena of external nature of the first beginnings of the laws of human action; and thus the germ of the positive philosophy is at least as primitive as that of the theological philosophy itself, though it could not expand till a much later time. This idea is very important to the perfect rationality of our social theory; because, as human life can never present any real creation, but only a gradual evolution, the final spread of the positive spirit would be scientifically incomprehensible, if we could not trace its rudiments from the very beginning. From that scarcely-appreciable presence at the beginning, the rise of the positive spirit has been recognisable, in proportion to the extension and generalization of our observations, and the theological philosophy has been slowly but steadily driven back within the narrowing limits of phenomena whose natural laws were still unknown. Thus was the function of the old philosophy clearly a provisional one—to maintain our mental activity by the only exercise open to it, till the positive philosophy should usher it into the wide field of universal knowledge, made accessible to the whole race. This destination has only recently exhibited itself in an unquestionable way since the disclosure of natural laws in phenomena, so numerous and so various as to suggest the necessary existence of analogous laws in all other departments, however remote their actual discovery may be.

It does not follow, from anything that I have said, that the two philosophies were always visibly opposed to each other. On the contrary, the physical study must have succumbed to the theological spirit if they had seemed at the outset to be incompatible. In fact the study of the laws of phenomena appeared, for a long course of time, to agree very well with the investigation into their causes. It was only when observations became more connected, and disclosed important relations, that the radical opposition of the two doctrines began to be felt. Before the antagonism was avowed, the positive spirit manifested its repugnance to the futile absolute explanations of the theological philosophy; and the theological spirit lavished its disdain on the circumspect march and modest investigations of the new school; while still there was no idea that the study of real laws was irreconcilable with that of essential causes. When natural laws of considerable scope were at length discovered, the incompatibility became clear between the preponderance of imagination and that of reason, between the absolute spirit and the relative; and, above all, between the ancient hypothesis of the sovereign direction of events by any arbitrary will, and the growing certainty that we can foresee and modify them by the rational access of human wisdom. It is only in our own time that the antagonism has been extended to all parts of the intellectual field; and even up to the last moment, the students of special subjects have believed that by confining themselves to the investigation of natural laws, and paying no attention to the nature of beings and mode of production of phenomena, they might find physical researches compatible with the explanations of theology; while theology made its own concessions in the form of a provisional notion of a universal providence, combined with special laws which it had imposed on itself. The conduct of Catholicism, in interdicting the habitual use of miracle and prophecy, which prevailed so largely in ancient times, seems to me to present, in religious affairs, a transient situation analogous to that which is exhibited by what is called the institution of constitutional monarchy in the political world; each being, in its own way, an indisputable symptom of decline. However this may be, the insufficiency of the theological philosophy manifests itself to popular observation in that form of popular evidence which can alone reach the majority of mankind,—in its comparison with its opponent in the application of means. The positive philosophy enables us to foresee and to modify natural events, and thus satisfies, more and more, as it advances, the most urgent intellectual needs of humanity, while the ancient philosophy remains barren; so that its fanciful explanations are more and more neglected, while the new philosophy obtains a perpetually firmer hold on the public reason. Those who have remained faithful in their attachment to the theological philosophy make no practical use of it in their daily life, and ground their predilection for it on its characteristic generality: so that when its antagonist shall have become systemized as fully as it is destined to be, the ancient philosophy will have lost the last attribute which has ever entitled it to social supremacy.

THE METAPHYSICAL PERIOD

We have now only to take a cursory survey of the intermediate state. I have pointed out more than once before, that any intermediate state can be judged of only after a precise analysis of the two extremes. The present case is a remarkable illustration of this necessity; for if it is once admitted that the human mind must set out from the theological state, and arrive certainly at the positive, we may easily understand how it must pass through the metaphysical, which has no other destination than to afford a transition from the one to the other. The bastard and mobile character of the metaphysical philosophy fits it for this office, as it reconciles, for a time, the radical opposition of the other two, adapting itself to the gradual decline of the one, and the preparatory rise of the other, so as to spare our dislike of abrupt change, and to afford us a transition almost imperceptible. The metaphysical philosophy takes possession of the speculative field after the theological has relinquished it, and before the positive is ready for it: so that in each particular case, the dispute about the supremacy of any of the three philosophies is reduced to the mere question of opportuneness, judged by a rational examination of the development of the human mind. The method of modification consists in substituting gradually the entity for a deity when religious conceptions become so generalized as to diminish perpetually the number of supernatural agents, as well as their active intervention, and at length arrive, professedly if not really, at rigorous unity. When supernatural action loses its original speciality, it consigns the immediate direction of the phenomenon to a mysterious entity, at first emanating from itself, but to which daily custom trains the human mind to refer more and more exclusively the production of each event. This strange process has favored the withdrawal of supernatural causes, and the exclusive consideration of phenomena; that is, the decline of the theological and the rise of the positive spirit. Beyond this, the general character of this philosophy is that of the theological, of which it is only a modification, though the chief. It has an inferior intellectual consistency, and a much less intense social power; so that it is much better adapted for a critical function than for any real organization: and it is those very qualities which disable it for resistance to the growth of the positive spirit. On the one hand the increasing subtilty of metaphysical speculations is for ever reducing their characteristic entities to mere abstract denominations of the corresponding phenomena, so as to render their own impotence ridiculous when they attempt explanations: a thing which would not have been possible, in an equal degree, with purely theological forms. On the other hand, its deficiency of organizing power, in consequence of its radical inconsistency, must prevent its maintaining any such political struggle as theology maintained against the spread of positive social philosophy. However, it obtains a respite by its own equivocal and mobile nature, which enables it to escape from rational discussion even more than the theological philosophy itself, while the positive spirit is as yet too imperfectly generalized to be able to attack the only substantial ground of their common authority,—the universality which they can boast, but which it has not. However this may be, we must admit the aptitude of metaphysics to sustain, provisionally, our speculative activity on all subjects till it can receive more substantial aliment; at the same time carrying us over from the theological *régime* farther and farther in the direction of the positive. The same aptitude appears in its political action. Without overlooking the serious intellectual and moral dangers which distinguish the metaphysical philosophy, its transitional quality accounts to us for the universal ascendency which it has provisionally obtained among the most advanced societies, which can not but have an instinctive sense of some indispensable office to be fulfilled by such a philosophy in the evolution of humanity. The irresistible necessity of this temporary phase is thus, on all grounds, as unquestionable as it could be prior to the direct analysis to which it will be subjected in the course of our historical review.

COEXISTENCE OF THE THREE PERIODS

During the whole of our survey of the sciences, I have endeavoured to keep in view the great fact that all the three states, theological, metaphysical, and positive, may and do exist at the same time in the same mind in regard to different sciences. I must once more recall this consideration, and insist upon it; because in the forgetfulness of it lies the only real objection that can be brought against the grand law of the three states. It must be steadily kept in view that the same mind may be in the positive state with regard to the most simple and general sciences; in the metaphysical with regard to the more complex and special; and in the theological with regard to social science, which is so complex and special as to have hitherto taken no scientific form at all. Any apparent contradiction must certainly arise, even if it could be shown to exist, from the imperfection of our hierarchical arrangement, and not from the law of evolution itself. This once fully understood, the law itself becomes our guide in further investigation, as every proved theory does, by showing us by anticipation, what phenomena to look for, and how to use those which arise: and it supplies the place of direct exploration, when we have not the means of investiga-

tion. We shall find that by this law alone can the history of the human mind be rendered intelligible. Having convinced ourselves of its efficacy in regard to all other sciences, and in interpreting all that has yet come to pass in human history, we must adhere to it steadily, in analyzing the present, and in forming such anticipation of the future as sociology, being a real science, enables us to rely upon.

To complete my long and difficult demonstration, I have only now to show that material development, as a whole, must follow a course, not only analogous, but perfectly correspondent with that of intellectual development, which, as we have seen, governs every other.

CORRESPONDING MATERIAL DEVELOPMENT

All political investigation of a rational kind proves the primitive tendency of mankind, in a general way, to a military life; and to its final issue in an industrial life. No enlightened mind disputes the continuous decline of the military spirit, and the gradual ascendency of the industrial. We see now, under various forms, and more and more indisputably, even in the very heart of armies, the repugnance of modern society to a military life. We see that compulsory recruiting becomes more and more necessary, and that there is less voluntary persistence in that mode of life. Notwithstanding the immense exceptional development of military activity which was occasioned by anomalous circumstances at the beginning of the present century, our industrial and pacific instincts have returned to their regular course of expansion, so as to render us secure of the radical tranquillity of the civilized world, though the peace of Europe must often appear to be endangered through the provisional deficiency of any systematic organization of international relations; a cause which, though insufficient to produce war, keeps us in a state of frequent uneasiness. We need not then go over again the proof of the first and last terms of the evolution: which will be abundantly illustrated by the historical analysis that I shall offer. We have only to refer the facts of human experience to the essential laws of human nature, and the necessary conditions of social development:—a scientific procedure which has never yet been attempted.

PRIMITIVE MILITARY LIFE

As long as primitive Man was averse from all regular toil, the military life alone furnished a field for his sustained activity. Apart from cannibalism, it offered the simplest means of subsistence. However deplorable the necessity, its universal prevalence and continuous development, even after subsistence might have been obtained by other means, proves that the military *régime* must have had some indispensable, though provisional office to fulfil in the progression of the race. It was indeed the only one under which human industry could make a beginning; in the same way that the scientific spirit could not have arisen without the protection of the religious. The industrial spirit supposed the existence of a considerable social development, such as could not have taken place till isolated families had been connected by the pursuits of war. The social, and yet more the political properties of military activity are, in their early stages, perfectly clear and decisive, and, in short, fully appropriate to the high civilizing function which they had to fulfil. It was thus that habits of regularity and discipline were instituted, and the families of men were brought into association for warlike expeditions, or for their common defence. The objects of association could not possibly be more obvious or urgent, nor the elementary conditions of concurrence more irresistible. In no other school could a primitive society learn order; as we may see at this day in the case of those types of ancient humanity,—the exceptional individuals who can not now be made amenable to industrial discipline. This ascendency of the military spirit was indispensable, not only to the original consolidation of political society, but yet more to its continuous extension, which could not otherwise have taken place but with excessive slowness; and such extension was, to a certain degree, indispensable to the final development of human industry. Thus, then, we find humanity involved in the same kind of vicious circle with regard to its temporal as we saw it to be with its spiritual progress; and in both cases an issue was afforded by the fortunate expansion of a preliminary tendency. In fact, the necessary basis of the military *régime* has everywhere been the individual slavery of the producing class, by which warriors were allowed the full and free development of their activity. We shall see hereafter that the great social operation which was to be accomplished, in due time, by the continuous progression of a military system, powerfully instituted and wisely carried out, must have failed in its earliest stages. We shall also see how this ancient slavery was the necessary preparation for the final prevalence of the industrial life, by imposing on the majority of the race, irresistibly and exclusively, that toil to which Man is constitutionally averse, though an ultimate condition of laborious perseverance was in store for all. To view the case without prejudice, we must transport ourselves to those primitive times, and not regard the slavery of that age with the just horror with which we view that of

modern times,—the colonial slavery of our day, which is truly a social monstrosity, existing as it does in the heart of an industrial period, subjecting the laborer to the capitalist in a manner equally degrading to both. The ancient slavery was of the producer to the warrior; and it tended to develop their respective energies, so as to occasion their final concurrence in the same social progression.

THE MILITARY RÉGIME PROVISIONAL

Necessary as this military *régime* was, it was not the less merely provisional. While industrial activity has the fine quality of bearing the most energetic extension among all individuals and nations without making the rise of the one irreconcilable with that of the other, it is evident that the exaltation of the military life among any considerable portion of the race must occasion the restriction of all the rest; this being, in fact, the proper function of the *régime* in regard to the whole field of civilization. Thus, while the industrial period comprehends the whole term of human progress under natural laws—that is, the whole future that we can conceive of—the military period could last no longer than the formation of those preparatory conditions which it was its function to create. This end was attained when the chief part of the civilized world was at length united under the same rule; that is, in regard to Europe, when Rome had completed its conquests. From that time forward, military activity had neither object nor aliment; and from that time forward, therefore, it declined, so as no longer to disguise that gradual rise of the industrial spirit, which had been preparing during the interval. But, notwithstanding this connection, the industrial state was so radically different from the military as to require an intermediate term; and in the same way that, in the spiritual evolution, an intermediate term was required between the theological and the positive spirit. In both cases, the middle phase was fluctuating and equivocal. We shall see hereafter that, in the temporal case, it consisted, first, in a substitution of a defensive for an offensive military organization, and afterward in an involuntary general subordination, more and more marked, of the military spirit to the instinct of production. This transitory phase being the one in which we live, its proper nature, vague as it is, can be estimated by direct intuition.

Such is the temporal evolution, briefly surveyed in its three periods. No philosophical mind can help being struck by the analogy between this indisputable progression and our primary law of succession of the three states of the human mind. But our sociological demonstration requires that we should

establish the connection between them by exhibiting the natural affinity which has always existed,
first between the theological and the military spirit,
and afterward between the scientific and the industrial; and, consequently, between the two transient
functions of the metaphysicians and the legists. This
elucidation will impart the last degree of precision
and consistency to my demonstration, and will thus
establish it as the rational basis of the entire historical analysis which will follow.

AFFINITY BETWEEN THE THEORETICAL AND MILITARY RÉGIME

The occasional rivalry between the theological
power and the military, which history presents, has
sometimes their radical affinity, even the eyes of
philosophers. But, if we consider, there can be no
real rivalry but among the different elements of
the same political system, in consequence of that
spontaneous emulation which, in all cases of human concurrence, must become more earnest and
extensive as the end is more important and indirect,
and therefore the means more distinct and independent, without the participation, voluntary or
instinctive, being thereby prevented. When two
powers, equally energetic, rise, increase, and decline together, notwithstanding the difference of
their natures, we may be assured that they belong
to the same *régime,* whatever may be their habitual
conflicts. Conflict indicates radical incompatibility
only when it takes place between two elements employed in analogous functions, and when the gradual growth of the one coincides with the continuous
decline of the other. As to the present case, it is
evident that, in any political system, there must
be an incessant rivalry between the speculative and
the active powers, which, through the imperfection
of our nature, must often be inclined to ignore their
necessary co-ordination, and to disdain the general
limits of their reciprocal attributes. Notwithstanding the social affinity between science and industry,
we must look for similar conflict between them
hereafter, in proportion to the political ascendency
which they will obtain together. We see signs of
it already in the intellectual and moral antipathy of
Science to the natural inferiority of these labors
of Industry which yet are the means of wealth, and
in the instinctive repugnance of Industry to the
abstraction which characterizes Science, and to
the just pride by which it is animated.

Having despatched these objections, we may
now contemplate the strong bond which united the
theological and military powers, and which has in
all ages been felt and honored by all enlightened

men who have borne a part in either, notwithstanding the passions of political rivalry. It is plain that
no military system could arise and endure without
the countenance of the theological spirit, which
must secure for it the complete and permanent subordination essential to its existence. Each period
imposes equal exigencies of this sort in its special
manner. At the outset, when the narrowness and
nearness of the aim required a less absolute submission of mind, social ties were so weak that nothing
could have been done but for the religious authority
with which military chiefs were naturally invested.
In more advanced times the end became so vast and
remote, and the participation so indirect, that even
long habits of discipline would not have secured
the necessary co-operation without the aid of theological convictions occasioning blind and involuntary confidence in military superiors. It was in
very ancient times that the military spirit had its
great social function to fulfil; and it was in those
ancient times that the two powers were usually
found concentrated in the same chiefs. We must
observe also that it was not every spiritual authority
whatever that would have sufficiently suited the
foundation and consolidation of military government, which, from its nature, required the concurrence of the theological philosophy, and no other:
for instance, though natural philosophy has rendered eminent service in modern times to the art of
war, the scientific spirit, which encourages habits
of rational discussion, is radically incompatible
with the military spirit; and we know that the subjection of their art to the principles of science has
always been bitterly deplored by the most distinguished soldiers, on the introduction of every
change, as a token of the decline of the military
system. On this ground, then, the affinity of temporal military powers for spiritual theological
powers is sufficiently accounted for. At the first
glance we might suppose the converse relation to
be less indispensable, since purely theocratic societies have existed, while an exclusively military one
has never been known. But a closer examination
will always show the necessity of the military system to consolidate, and yet more to extend, the
theological authority, developed in this way by a
continual political application, as the sacerdotal instinct has always been well aware. We shall see
again that the theological spirit is as hostile to the
expansion of industry as the military. Thus the two
elements of the primitive political system have not
only a radical affinity, but common antipathies and
sympathies, as well as general interests; and it must
be needless to enlarge further in this place on the
sociological principle of the concurrence of these
powers, which my historical analysis will present

as constantly engaged in consolidating and correcting each other.

AFFINITY BETWEEN THE POSITIVE AND THE INDUSTRIAL SPIRIT

The latest case of political dualism is even more unquestionable than the earliest, and we are favorably circumstanced for observing it—the two elements not having yet attained their definite ascendency, though their social development is sufficiently marked. When the time arrives for their political rivalry, it may be more difficult than now to exhibit that resemblance in origin and destination, and that conformity of principles and interests, which could not be seriously disputed as long as their common struggle against the old political system acts as a restraint upon their divergencies. The most remarkable feature that we have to contemplate in their case is the aid which each renders to the political triumph of the other, by seconding its own efforts against its chief antagonist. I have already noticed, in another connection, the secret incompatibility between the scientific spirit and the military. There is the same hostility between the industrial spirit, when sufficiently developed, and the theological. The most zealous advocates of the old *régime* are very far removed from the old religious point of view; but we can transport ourselves to it for a moment, and see how the voluntary modification of phenomena by the rules of human wisdom must thence appear as impious as the rational prevision of them, as both suppose invariable laws, finally irreconcilable with all arbitrary will. According to the rigorous though barbarous logic of the least-civilized nations, all human intervention to improve the economy of nature is an injurious attack upon providential government. There is no doubt, in fact, that a strong preponderance of the religious spirit benumbs the industrial, by the exaggerated feelings of a stupid optimism, as has been abundantly clear on many decisive occasions. That this disastrous effect has not been more fatal is owing to priestly sagacity, which has so managed this dangerous power as to educe its civilizing influence, while neutralizing its injurious action by constant and vigilant effort, in a way which I shall presently exhibit. We can not, then, overlook the political influence by which the gradual expansion of human industry must aid the progressive ascendency of the scientific spirit, in its antagonism to the religious; to say nothing of the daily stimulus which industry and science impart to each other, when once strong enough for mutual action. Thus

far their office has chiefly been to substitute themselves for the ancient political powers which are yielding up their social influence; and our attention is necessarily drawn chiefly to the aid they have afforded to each other in this operation. But it is easy to perceive what force and what efficacy must reside in their connection, when it shall have assumed the organic character, in which it is at present deficient, and shall proceed to the final reorganization of modern society.

Now that we have examined the two extreme states, the intermediate dualism requires little notice. The interconnection of the convergent powers, spiritual and temporal, which constitutes the transitory *régime,* is a necessary consequence of all that we have been observing. Indeed, we need but look at the labors of metaphysicians and legists to see what their affinity is, amidst their rivalries; an affinity which stakes the philosophical ascendency of the one class on the political preponderance of the other. We may, then, regard as now complete the necessary explanation required by our fundamental law of human evolution, in order to its direct application to the study of this great phenomenon. That study will be guided by the consideration of the three dualisms which I have established as the only basis of sound historical philosophy. It is worth noticing the conformity of this law of succession, at once intellectual and material, social and political, with the historical order which popular reason has instinctively established by distinguishing the ancient and the modern world, separated and reunited by the Middle Ages. The sociological law which I have propounded may be found to have for its destination to take up a vague empirical notion, hitherto barren, and render it rational and prolific. I hail this spontaneous coincidence, as giving a sanction to my speculative labors; and I claim this confirmation, in virtue of that great aphorism of positive philosophy which I have quoted so often, which enjoins upon all sound scientific theories to start from a point sufficiently accordant with the spontaneous indications of popular reason, of which true science is simply a special prolongation.

The series of views of social dynamics sketched out in this chapter has established the fundamental law of human development, and therefore the bases of historical philosophy. We had before ascertained the spirit and method of that philosophy; and we may now therefore proceed to apply this great sociological conception to the analysis of the history of mankind.

2. *On the Style-Patterns of Culture*

BY OSWALD SPENGLER

THAT which is expressed by the soul of the West in its extraordinary wealth of media—words, tones, colours, pictorial perspectives, philosophical systems, legends, the spaciousness of Gothic cathedrals and the formulæ of functions—namely its world-feeling, is expressed by the soul of Old Egypt (which was remote from all ambitions towards theory and literariness) almost exclusively by the immediate language of *Stone*. Instead of spinning word-subtleties around its form of extension, its "space" and its "time," instead of forming hypotheses and number-systems and dogmas, it set up its huge symbols in the landscape of the Nile in all silence. Stone is the great emblem of the Timeless-Become; space and death seem bound up in it. "Men have built for the dead," says Bachofen in his autobiography, "before they have built for the living, and even as a perishable wooden structure suffices for the span of time that is given to the living, so the housing of the dead for ever demands the solid stone of the earth. The oldest cult is associated with the stone that marks the place of burial, the oldest temple-building with the tomb-structure, the origins of art and decoration with the grave-ornament. Symbol has created itself in the graves. That which is thought and felt and silently prayed at the grave-side can be expressed by no word, but only hinted by the boding symbol that stands in unchanging grave repose." The dead strive no more. They are no more Time, but only Space—something that stays (if indeed it stays at all) but does *not* ripen towards a Future; and hence it is stone, the abiding stone, that expresses how the dead is mirrored in the waking consciousness of the living. The Faustian soul looks for an immortality to follow the bodily end, a sort of marriage with endless space, and it disembodies the stone in its Gothic thrust-system (contemporary, we may note, with the "consecutives" in Church music[1]) till at last nothing remained visible but the indwelling

depth- and height-energy of this self-extension. The Apollinian soul would have its dead burned, would see them annihilated, and so it remained averse from stone building throughout the early period of its Culture. The Egyptian soul saw itself as moving down a narrow and inexorably-prescribed life-path to come at the end before the judges of the dead ("Book of the Dead," cap. 125). That was its *Destiny-idea*. The Egyptian's existence is that of the traveller who follows one unchanging direction, and the whole form-language of his Culture is a translation into the sensible of this one theme. And as we have taken *endless space* as the prime symbol of the North and *body* as that of the Classical, so we may take the word *way* as most intelligibly expressing that of the Egyptians. Strangely, and for Western thought almost incomprehensibly, the one element in extension that they emphasize is that of direction in depth. The tomb-temples of the Old Kingdom and especially the mighty pyramid-temples of the Fourth Dynasty represent, not a purposed organization of space such as we find in the mosque and the cathedral, but a rhythmically ordered *sequence* of spaces. The sacred way leads from the gate-building on the Nile through passages, halls, arcaded courts and pillared rooms that grow ever narrower and narrower, to the chamber of the dead, and similarly the Sun-temples of the Fifth Dynasty are not "buildings" but a path enclosed by mighty masonry. The reliefs and the paintings appear always as rows which with an impressive compulsion lead the beholder in a definite direction. The ram and sphinx avenues of the New Empire have the same object. For the Egyptian, the depth-experience which governed his world-form was so emphatically directional that he comprehended space more or less as a continuous process of actualization. There is nothing rigid about distance as expressed here. The man must move, and so become himself a symbol of life, in order to enter into relation with the stone part of the symbolism. "Way" signifies both Destiny and third dimension. The grand wall-surfaces, reliefs, colonnades past which he moves are "length and breadth"; that is, mere perceptions of the senses, and it is the forward-driving life that *extends* them into "world." Thus the Egyptian experienced space, we may say, in and by the processional march

---

Reprinted from Oswald Spengler, *The Decline of the West*, trans. Charles F. Atkinson (New York: Alfred A. Knopf, 1929), I, 188–207, 214–16, by permission of Alfred A. Knopf, Inc., and George Allen & Unwin Ltd.

1. This refers to the diaphonic chant of Church music in the eleventh and twelfth centuries. The form of this chant is supposed to have been an accompaniment of the "plain chant" by voices moving parallel to it at a fourth, fifth, or octave.—*Tr.*

along its distinct elements, whereas the Greek who sacrificed *outside* the temple did not feel it and the man of our Gothic centuries praying in the cathedral let himself be immersed in the quiet infinity of it. And consequently the art of these Egyptians must aim at *plane* effects and nothing else, even when it is making use of solid means. For the Egyptian, the pyramid over the king's tomb is a *triangle,* a huge, powerfully expressive *plane* that, whatever be the direction from which one approaches, closes off the "way" and commands the landscape. For him, the columns of the inner passages and courts, with their dark backgrounds, their dense array and their profusion of adornments, appear entirely as vertical strips which rhythmically accompany the march of the priests. Relief-work is—in utter contrast to the Classical—carefully restricted in one plane; in the course of development dated by the Third to the Fifth dynasties it diminishes from the thickness of a finger to that of a sheet of paper, and finally it is *sunk* in the plane. The dominance of the horizontal, the vertical and the right angle, and the avoidance of all foreshortening support the two-dimensional principle and serve to insulate this directional depth-experience which coincides with the way and the grave at its end. It is an art that admits of no deviation for the relief of the tense soul.

Is not this an expression in the noblest language that it is possible to conceive of what all our space-theories would like to put into words? Is it not a metaphysic in stone by the side of which the written metaphysics of Kant seems but a helpless stammering?

There is, however, another Culture that, different as it most fundamentally is from the Egyptian, yet found a closely-related prime symbol. This is the Chinese, with its intensely directional principle of the Tao. But whereas the Egyptian treads to the end a way that is prescribed for him with an inexorable necessity, the Chinaman *wanders* through his world; consequently, he is conducted to his god or his ancestral tomb not by ravines of stone, between faultless smooth walls, but by friendly Nature herself. Nowhere else has the *landscape* become so genuinely the material of the architecture. "Here, on religious foundations, there has been developed a grand lawfulness and unity common to all building, which, combined with the strict maintenance of a north-south general axis, always holds together gate-buildings, side-buildings, courts and halls in the same homogeneous plan, and has led finally to so grandiose a planning and such a command over ground and space that one is quite justified in saying that the artist builds and reckons with the land-

scape itself."[2] The temple is not a self-contained building but a lay-out, in which hills, water, trees, flowers, and stones in definite forms and dispositions are just as important as gates, walls, bridges and houses. This Culture is the only one in which the art of gardening is a grand religious art. There are gardens that are reflections of particular Buddhist sects. It is the architecture of the landscape, and only that, which explains the architecture of the buildings, with their flat extension and the emphasis laid on the roof as the really expressive element. And just as the devious ways through doors, over bridges, round hills and walls lead at last to the end, so the paintings take the beholder from detail to detail whereas Egyptian relief masterfully points him in the one set direction. "The whole picture is *not* to be taken at once. Sequence in time presupposes a sequence of space-elements through which the eye is to wander from one to the next."[3] Whereas the Egyptian architecture dominates the landscape, the Chinese espouses it. But in both cases it is direction in depth that maintains the *becoming* of space as a continuously-present experience.

All art is *expression-language.* Moreover, in its very earliest essays—which extend far back into the animal world—it is that of one active existence speaking for itself only, and it is unconscious of witnesses even though in the absence of such the impulse to expression would not come to utterance. Even in quite "late" conditions we often see, instead of the combination of artist and spectator, a crowd of art-makers who *all* dance or mime or sing. The idea of the "Chorus" as sum total of persons present has never entirely vanished from art-history. It is only the higher art that becomes decisively an art "before witnesses" and especially (as Nietzsche somewhere remarks) before God as the supreme witness.[4]

---

2. O. Fischer, *Chinesische Landmalerei* (1921), p. 24. What makes Chinese—as also Indian—art so difficult a study for us is the fact that all works of the early periods (namely, those of the Hwangho region from 1300 to 800 B.C. and of pre-Buddhist India) have vanished without a trace. But that which we now call "Chinese art" corresponds, say, to the art of Egypt from the Twentieth Dynasty onward, and the great schools of painting find their parallel in the sculpture schools of the Saïte and Ptolemaic periods, in which an antiquarian preciosity takes the place of the living inward development that is no longer there. Thus from the examples of Egypt we are able to tell how far it is permissible to argue backwards to conclusions about the art of Chóu and Vedic times.

3. Glaser, *op. cit.,* p. 43.

4. The monologue-art of very lonely natures is also in reality a conversation with self in the second person. But it is only in the intellectuality of the megalopolitan stages that the impulse to express is overcome by the impulse to communicate which gives rise to that tendencious art that seeks to instruct or convert or prove views of a politico-

This expression is either *ornament* or *imitation*. Both are *higher* possibilities and their polarity to one another is hardly perceptible in the beginnings. Of the two, imitation is definitely the earlier and the closer to the producing race. Imitation is the outcome of a physiognomic idea of a second person with whom (or which) the first is involuntarily induced into resonance of vital rhythm (mitschwingen in Lebenstakte); whereas ornament evidences an ego conscious of its own specific character. The former is widely spread in the animal world, the latter almost peculiar to man.

Imitation is born of the secret rhythm of all things cosmic. For the waking being the One appears as discrete and extended; there is a Here and a There, a Proper and an Alien something, a Microcosm and a Macrocosm that are polar to one another in the sense-life, and what the rhythm of imitation does is to bridge this dichotomy. Every religion is an effort of the waking soul to reach the powers of the world-around. And so too is Imitation, which in its most devoted moments is wholly religious, for it consists in an identity of inner activity between the soul and body "here" and the world-around "there" which, vibrating as one, become one. As a bird poises itself in the storm or a float gives to the swaying waves, so our limbs take up an irresistible beat at the sound of march-music. Not less contagious is the imitation of another's bearing and movements, wherein children in particular excel. It reaches the superlative when we "let ourselves go" in the common song or parade-march or dance that creates out of many units one unit of feeling and expression, a "we." But a "successful" picture of a man or a landscape is also the outcome of a felt harmony of the pictorial motion with the secret swing and sway of the living opposite; and it is this actualizing of physiognomic rhythm that requires the executant to be an adept who can reveal the idea, the *soul*, of the alien in the play of its surface. In certain unreserved moments we are all adepts of this sort, and in such moments, as we follow in an imperceptible rhythm the music and the play of facial expression, we suddenly look over the precipice and see great secrets. The aim of all imitation is effective simulation; this means effective assimilation of ourselves into an alien something—such a transposition and transubstantiation that the One lives henceforth in the Other that it describes or depicts—and it is able to awaken an intense feeling of unison over all the range from silent absorption and acquiescence to the most abandoned laughter and down into the last depths

of the erotic, a unison which is inseparable from creative activity. In this wise arose the popular circling-dances (for instance, the Bavarian *Schuhplattler* was originally imitated from the courtship of the woodcocks) but this too is what Vasari means when he praises Cimabue and Giotto as the first who returned to the imitation of "Nature"—the Nature, that is, of springtime men, of which Meister Eckart said: "God flows out in all creatures, and therefore all created is God." That which in this world-around presents itself to our contemplation—and therefore contains meaning for our feelings—as movement, we render by movement. Hence all imitation is in the broadest sense dramatic; drama is presented in the movement of the brush-stroke or the chisel, the melodic curve of the song, the tone of the recitation, the line of poetry, the description, the dance. But everything that we *experience* with and in seeings and hearings is always an alien soul to which we are uniting ourselves. It is only at the stage of the Megalopolis that art, reasoned to pieces and de-spiritualized, goes over to naturalism as that term is understood nowadays, viz., imitation of the charm of visible appearances, of the stock of sensible characters that are capable of being scientifically fixed.

Ornament detaches itself now from Imitation as something which does not follow the stream of life but rigidly *faces it*. Instead of physiognomic traits overheard in the alien being, we have established motives, *symbols*, which are impressed upon it. The intention is no longer to pretend but to conjure. The "I" overwhelms the "Thou." Imitation is only a *speaking with* means that are born of the moment and unreproduceable—but Ornament *employs a language* emancipated from the speaking, a stock of forms that possesses duration and is not at the mercy of the individual.

Only the *living* can be imitated, and it can be imitated only in movements, for it is through these that it reveals itself to the senses of artists and spectators. To that extent, imitation belongs to Time and Direction. All the dancing and drawing and describing and portraying for eye and ear is irrevocably "directional," and hence the highest possibilities of Imitation lie in the copying of a destiny, be it in tones, verses, picture or stage-scene.[5] Ornament, on the

---

social or moral character, and provokes the antagonistic formula of "Art for Art's sake"—which is itself rather a view than a discipline, though it does at least serve to recall the primitive significance of artistic expression.

5. Imitation, being life, is past in the very moment of accomplishment. The curtain falls, and it passes either into oblivion or, if the product is a durable artifact, into art-history. Of the songs and dances of old Cultures nothing remains, of their pictures and poems little. And even this little contains, substantially, only the ornamental side of the original imitation. Of a grand drama there remains only the text, not the image and the sound; of a poem only the words, not the recital; and of all their music the notes at most, not the tone-colours of the instruments. The essential is irrevocably gone, and every "reproduction" is in reality something new and different.

contrary, is something taken away from Time: it is pure extension, settled and stable. Whereas an imitation expresses something by *accomplishing itself,* ornament can only do so by presenting itself to the senses as a finished thing. It is Being as such, wholly independent of origin. Every imitation possesses beginning and end, while an ornament possesses only duration, and therefore we can only imitate the destiny of an *individual* (for instance, Antigone or Desdemona), while by an ornament or symbol only the generalized destiny-idea itself can be represented (as, for example, that of the Classical world by the Doric column). And the former presupposes a talent, while the latter calls for an acquirable knowledge as well.

All strict arts have their grammar and syntax of form-language, with rules and laws, inward logic and tradition. This is true not merely for the Doric cabin-temple and Gothic cottage-cathedral, for the carving-schools of Egypt and Athens and the cathedral plastic of northern France, for the painting-schools of the Classical world and those of Holland and the Rhine and Florence, but also for the fixed rules of the Skalds and Minnesänger which were learned and practised as a craft (and dealt not merely with sentence and metre but also with gesture and the choice of imagery[6]), for the narration-technique of the Vedic, Homeric and Celto-Germanic Epos, for the composition and delivery of the Gothic sermon (both vernacular and Latin), and for the orators' prose in the Classical, and for the rules of French drama. In the ornamentation of an art-work is reflected the inviolable causality of the macrocosm as the man of the particular kind sees and comprehends it. Both have system. Each is penetrated with the religious side of life—*fear* and love. A genuine symbol can instil fear or can set free from fear; the "right" emancipates and the "wrong" hurts and depresses. The imitative side of the arts, on the contrary, stands closer to the real race-feelings of *hate* and love, out of which arises the opposition of *ugly* and *beautiful.* This is in relation only with the living, of which the inner rhythm repels us or draws us into phase with it, whether it be that of the sunset-cloud or that of the tense breath of the machine. An imitation is beautiful, an ornament *significant,* and therein lies the difference between direction and extension, organic and inorganic logic, life and death. That which we think beautiful is "worth copying." Easily it swings with us and draws us on to imitate, to join in the singing, to repeat. Our hearts beat higher, our limbs twitch, and we are stirred till our spirits overflow. But as it belongs to

Time, it "has its time." A symbol endures, but everything beautiful vanishes with the life-pulsation of the man, the class, the people or the race that feels it as a specific beauty in the general cosmic rhythm.[7] The "beauty" that Classical sculpture and poetry contained for Classical eyes is something different from the beauty that they contain for ours—something extinguished irrecoverably with the Classical soul—while what we regard as beautiful in it is something that only exists for us. Not only is that which is beautiful for one kind of man neutral or ugly for another—e.g., the whole of our music for the Chinese, or Mexican sculpture for us. For *one and the same life* the accustomed, the habitual, owing to the very fact of its possessing duration, cannot possess beauty.

And now for the first time we can see the opposition between these two sides of every art in all its depth. Imitation spiritualizes and quickens, ornament enchants and kills. The one becomes, the other is. And therefore the one is allied to love and, above all—in songs and riot and dance—to the *sexual love,* which turns existence to face the future; and the other to care of the past, to recollection[8] and to the *funerary.* The beautiful is longingly pursued, the significant instils dread, and there is no deeper contrast than that between the house of the living and the house of the dead. The peasant's cottage and its derivative the country noble's hall, the fenced town and the castle are mansions of life, unconscious expressions of circling blood, that no art produced and no art can alter. The idea of the family appears in the plan of the protohouse, the inner form of the stock in the plan of its villages—which after many a century and many a change of occupation still show what race it was that founded them[9]—the life of a nation and its social ordering in the plan (*not* the elevation or silhouette) of the city. On the other hand, Ornamentation of the high order develops itself on the stiff symbols of death, the urn, the sarcophagus, the stele and the temple of the dead, and beyond these in gods' temples and cathedrals *which are Ornament through and through,* not the expressions of a race but the language of a world-view. They are pure art through and through—just what the castle and the cottage are not.

6. K. Burdach, *Deutsche Renaissance,* p. 11. The pictorial art of the Gothic period also has its strict typism and symbolism.

7. The translation is so far a paraphrase here that it is desirable to reproduce the German original. "Alles Schöne vergeht mit dem Lebenspulsschlag (dessen) der es aus dem kosmischen Takt heraus als solches empfindet."

8. Hence the ornamental character of script.

9. E.g., the Slavonic round-villages and Teutonic street-villages east of the Elbe. Similarly, conclusions can be drawn as to many of the events of the Homeric age from the distribution of round and rectangular buildings in ancient Italy.

For cottage and castle *are buildings in which* art, and, specifically, imitative art, is *made and done,* the home of Vedic, Homeric and Germanic epos, of the songs of heroes, the dance of boors and that of lords and ladies, of the minstrel's lay. The cathedral, on the other hand, *is* art, and, moreover, the only art by which *nothing* is imitated; it alone is pure tension of persistent forms, pure three-dimensional logic that expresses itself in edges and surfaces and volumes. But the art of villages and castles is derived from the inclinations of the moment, from the laughter and high spirit of feasts and games, and to such a degree is it dependent on Time, so much is it a thing of occasion, that the troubadour obtains his very name from finding, while Improvisation—as we see in the Tzigane music to-day—is nothing but race manifesting itself to alien senses under the influence of the hour. To this free creative power all spiritual art opposes the strict *school* in which the individual—in the hymn as in the work of building and carving—is the servant of a logic of timeless forms, and so in all Cultures the seat of its style-history is in its early cult architecture. In the castle it is the life and not the structure that possesses style. In the town the plan is an image of the destinies of a people, whereas the silhouette of emergent spires and cupolas tells of the *logic in the builders' world-picture,* of the "first and last things" of their universe.

In the architecture of the living, stone *serves a* worldly *purpose,* but in the architecture of the cult *it is a symbol.* Nothing has injured the history of the great architectures so much as the fact that it has been regarded as the history of architectural techniques instead of as that of architectural ideas which took their technical expression-means as and where they found them. It has been just the same with the history of musical instruments, which also were developed on a foundation of tone-language. Whether the groin and the flying buttress and the squinch-cupola were imagined specially for the great architectures or were expedients that lay more or less ready to hand and were taken into use, is for art-history a matter of as little importance as the question of whether, technically, stringed instruments originated in Arabia or in Celtic Britain. It may be that the Doric column was, as a matter of workmanship, borrowed from the Egyptian temples of the New Empire, or the late-Roman domical construction from the Etruscans, or the Florentine court from the North-African Moors. Nevertheless the Doric peripteros, the Pantheon, and the Palazzo Farnese belong to wholly different worlds—they subserve the artistic expression of the prime-symbol in three different Cultures.

In every springtime, consequently, there are two definitely ornamental and non-imitative arts, that of building and that of decoration. In the longing and pregnant centuries before it, elemental expression belongs exclusively to Ornamentation in the narrow sense. The Carolingian period is represented only by its ornament, as its architecture, for want of the *Idea,* stands between the styles. And similarly, as a matter of art-history, it is immaterial that no buildings of the Mycenæan age have survived.[10] But with the dawn of the great Culture, *architecture as ornament* comes into being suddenly and with such a force of expression that for a century mere decoration-as-such shrinks away from it in awe. The spaces, surfaces and edges of stone speak *alone.* The tomb of Chephren is the culmination of mathematical simplicity—everywhere right angles, squares and rectangular pillars, nowhere adornment, inscription or desinence—and it is only after some generations have passed that Relief ventures to infringe the solemn magic of those spaces and the strain begins to be eased. And the noble Romanesque of Westphalia-Saxony (Hildesheim, Gernrode, Paulinzella, Paderborn), of Southern France and of the Normans (Norwich and Peterborough) managed to render the whole sense of the world with indescribable power and dignity in *one* line, *one* capital, *one* arch.

When the form-world of the springtime is at its highest, and not before, the ordained relation is that architecture is lord and ornament is vassal. And the word "ornament" is to be taken here in the widest possible sense. Even conventionally, it covers the Classical *unit*-motive with its quiet poised symmetry or meander supplement, the *spun surface* of arabesque and the not dissimilar surface-patterning of Mayan art, and the "Thunder-pattern"[11] and others of the early Chóu period which prove once again the landscape basis of the old Chinese architecture without a doubt. But the warrior figures of Dipylon vases are also conceived in the spirit of ornament, and so, in a far higher degree still, are the statuary *groups* of Gothic cathedrals. "The figures were composed pillarwise from the spectator, the figures of the pillar being, with reference to the spectator, ranked upon one another like rhythmic figures in a symphony that soars heavenward and and expands its sounds in every direction."[12] And besides draperies, gestures, and figure-types, even

10. The same applies to the architecture of Thinite Egypt and to the Seleucid-Persian sun and fire temples of the pre-Christian area.

11. The combination of scrolls and "Greek keys" with the Dragon or other emblem of storm-power.—*Tr.*

12. Dvorák, *Idealismus und Naturalismus in der got. Skulptur u. Malerei (Hist. Zeitschrift,* 1918, pp. 44 et seq.).

the structure of the hymn-strophe and the parallel motion of the parts in church music are ornament in the service of the all-ruling architectural idea.[13] The spell of the great Ornamentation remains unbroken till in the beginning of a "late" period architecture falls into a *group* of civic and worldly special arts that unceasingly devote themselves to pleasing and clever imitation and become *ipso facto* personal. To Imitation and Ornament the same applies that has been said already of time and space. Time gives birth to space, but space gives death to time. In the beginning, rigid symbolism had petrified everything alive; the Gothic statue was not permitted to be a living body, but was simply a set of lines disposed in human form. But now Ornament loses all its sacred rigour and becomes more and more decoration for the architectural setting of a polite and mannered life. It was purely as this, namely *as a beautifying* element, that Renaissance taste was adopted by the courtly and patrician world of the North (and by it alone!). Ornament meant something quite different in the Egyptian Old Kingdom from what it meant in the Middle; in the geometric period from what it meant in the Hellenistic; at the end of the 12th Century from what it meant at the end of Louis XIV's reign. And architecture too becomes pictorial and makes music, and its forms seem always to be trying to imitate something in the picture of the world-around. From the Ionic capital we proceed to the Corinthian, and from Vignola through Bernini to the Rococo.

At the last, when Civilization sets in, true ornament and, with it, great art as a whole are extinguished. The transition consists—in every Culture—in Classicism and Romanticism of one sort or another, the former being a sentimental regard for an Ornamentation (rules, laws, types) that has long been archaic and soulless, and the latter a sentimental Imitation, not of life, but of an older Imitation. In the place of architectural style we find architectural taste. Methods of painting and mannerisms of writing, old forms and new, home and foreign, come and go with the fashion. The inward

necessity is no longer there, there are no longer "schools," for everyone selects what and where it pleases him to select. *Art becomes craft-art* (*Kunstgewerbe*) in all its branches—architecture and music, poetry and drama—and in the end we have a pictorial and literary stock-in-trade which is destitute of any deeper significance and is employed according to taste. This final or industrial form of Ornament—no longer historical, no longer in the condition of "becoming"—we have before us not only in the patterns of oriental carpets, Persian and Indian metal work, Chinese porcelain, but also in Egyptian (and Babylonian) art as the Greeks and Romans met it. The Minoan art of Crete is pure craft-art, a northern outlier of Egyptian post-Hyksos taste; and its "contemporary," Hellenistic-Roman art from about the time of Scipio and Hannibal, similarly subserves the habit of comfort and the play of intellect. From the richly-decorated entablature of the Forum of Nerva in Rome to the later provincial ceramics in the West, we can trace the same steady formation of an unalterable craft-art that we find in the Egyptian and the Islamic worlds, and that we have to presume in India after Buddha and in China after Confucius.

Now, Cathedral and Pyramid-temple are different in spite of their deep inward kinship, and it is precisely in these differences that we seize the mighty phenomenon of the Faustian soul, whose depth-impulse refuses to be bound in the prime symbol of a way, and from its earliest beginnings strives to transcend every optical limitation. Can anything be more alien to the Egyptian conception of the State—whose tendency we may describe as a noble sobriety—than the political ambitions of the great Saxon, Franconian and Hohenstaufen Emperors, who came to grief because they overleapt all political actualities and for whom the recognition of any bounds would have been a betrayal of the idea of their rulership? Here the prime symbol of infinite space, with all its indescribable power, entered the field of active political existence. Beside the figures of the Ottos, Conrad II, Henry VI and Frederick II stand the Viking-Normans, conquerors of Russia, Greenland, England, Sicily and almost of Constantinople; and the great popes, Gregory VII and Innocent III—all of whom alike aimed at making their visible spheres of influence coincident with the whole known world. This is what distinguishes the heroes of the Grail and Arthurian and Siegfried sagas, ever roaming in the infinite, from the heroes of Homer with their geographically modest horizon; and the Crusades, that took men from the Elbe and the Loire to the limits of the known world, from

13. And, finally, ornament in the highest sense includes *script,* and with it, the Book, which is the true associate of the cult-building, and as an art-work always appears and disappears with it. (See Vol. II, pp. 182 et seq., pp. 298 et seq.) In writing, it is understanding as distinct from intuition that attains to form: it is not essences that those signs symbolize but notions abstracted therefrom by words, and as for the speech-habituated human intellect rigid space is the presented objective, the writing of a Culture is (after its stone-building) the purest of all expressions of its prime-symbol. It is quite impossible to understand the history of Arabesque if we leave the innumerable Arabian scripts out of consideration, and it is no less impossible to separate Egyptian and Chinese style-history from the history of the corresponding writing-signs and their arrangement and application.

the historical events upon which the Classical soul built the "Iliad" and which from the style of that soul we may safely assume to have been local, bounded, and completely appreciable.

The Doric soul actualized the symbol of the corporal-present individual thing, while deliberately rejecting all big and far-reaching creations, and it is for this very good reason that the first post-Mycenæan period has bequeathed nothing to our archæologists. The expression to which this soul finally attained was the Doric temple with its purely outward effectiveness, set upon the landscape as a massive image but denying and artistically disregarding the space within as the $\mu\dot{\eta}\delta\nu$, that which was held to be incapable of existence. The ranked columns of the Egyptians carried the roof of a hall. The Greek in borrowing the motive invested it with a meaning proper to himself—he turned the architectural type inside out like a glove. The outer column-sets are, in a sense, relics of a denied interior.[14]

The Magian and the Faustian souls, on the contrary, built high. Their dream-images became concrete as vaultings above significant inner-spaces, structural anticipations repectively of the mathematic of algebra and that of analysis. In the style that radiated from Burgundy and Flanders rib-vaulting with its lunettes and flying buttresses emancipated the contained space from the sense-appreciable surface[15] bounding it. In the Magian interior "the window is merely a negative component, a utility-form in no wise yet developed into an art-form—to put it crudely, nothing but a hole in the wall."[16] When windows were in practice indispensable, they were for the sake of artistic impression concealed by galleries as in the Eastern basilica. The *window as architecture,* on the other hand, is peculiar to the Faustian soul and the most significant symbol of its depth-experience. In it can be felt the will to emerge from the interior into the boundless. The same will that is immanent in contrapuntal music was native to these vaultings. The incorporeal world of this music was and remained that of the first Gothic, and even when, much later, polyphonic music rose to such heights as those of

the Matthew Passion, the Eroica, and Tristan and Parsifal, it became of inward necessity *cathedral-like* and returned to its home, the stone language of the Crusade-time. To get rid of every trace of Classical corporeality, there was brought to bear the full force of a deeply significant Ornamentation, which defies the delimiting power of stone with its weirdly impressive transformations of vegetal, animal and human bodies (St. Pierre in Moissac), which dissolves all its lines into melodies and variations on a theme, all its façades into many-voiced fugues, and all the bodiliness of its statuary into a music of drapery-folds. It is this spirituality that gave their deep meaning to the gigantic glass-expanses of our cathedral-windows with their polychrome, *translucent and therefore wholly bodiless,* painting—and art that has never and nowhere repeated itself and forms the completest contrast that can be imagined to the Classical fresco. It is perhaps in the Sainte-Chapelle at Paris that this emancipation from bodiliness is most evident. Here the stone practically vanishes in the gleam of the glass. Whereas the fresco-painting is co-material with the wall on and with which it has grown and its colour is effective as material, here we have colours dependent on no carrying surface but as free in space as organ notes, and shapes poised in the infinite. Compare with the Faustian spirit of these churches—almost wall-less, loftily vaulted, irradiated with many-coloured light, aspiring from nave to choir—the Arabian (that is, the Early-Christian Byzantine) cupola-church. The pendentive cupola, that seems to float on high above the basilica or the octagon, was indeed also a victory over the principle of natural gravity which the Classical expressed in architrave and column; it, too, was a defiance of architectural body, of "exterior." But the very absence of an exterior emphasizes the more the unbroken coherence of the wall that shuts in the Cavern and allows no look and no hope to emerge from it. An ingeniously confusing interpenetration of spherical and polygonal forms; a load so placed upon a stone drum that it seems to hover weightless on high, yet closing the interior without outlet; all structural lines concealed; vague light admitted, through a small opening in the heart of the dome only the more inexorably to emphasize the walling-in—such are the characters that we see in the masterpieces of this art, S. Vitale in Ravenna, Hagia Sophia in Constantinople, and the Dome of the Rock in Jerusalem. Where the Egyptian puts reliefs that with their flat planes studiously avoid any foreshortening suggestive of lateral depth, where the Gothic architects put their pictures of glass to draw in the world of space without, the Magian clothes his walls with sparkling, predominantly

---

14. Certainly the Greeks at the time when they advanced from the Antæ to the Peripteros were under the mighty influence of the Egyptian *series*-columns—it was at this time that their sculpture in the round, indisputably following Egyptian models, freed itself from the relief manner which still clings to the Apollo figures. But this does not alter the fact that the motive of the Classical column and the Classical application of the rank-principle were wholly and peculiarly Classical.

15. The surface of the space-volume itself, not that of the stone. Dvorák, *Hist. Ztschr.,* 1918, pp. 17 et seq.

16. Dehio, *Gesch. der deutschen Kunst,* I, p. 16.

golden, mosaics and arabesques and so drowns his cavern in that unreal, fairly-tale light which for Northerners is always so seductive in Moorish art.

The phenomenon of the *great style*, then, is an emanation from the essence of the Macrocosm, from the prime-symbol of a *great* culture. No one who can appreciate the connotation of the word sufficiently to see that it designates not a form-aggregate but a form-history, will try to aline the fragmentary and chaotic art-utterances of primitive mankind with the comprehensive certainty of a style that consistently develops over centuries. Only the art of great Cultures, the art that has ceased to be only art and has begun to be an effective unit of expression and significance, possesses style.

The organic history of a style comprises a "pre—," a "non—" and a "post—." The bull tablet of the First Dynasty of Egypt is not yet "Egyptian." Not till the Third Dynasty do the works acquire a style—but then they do so suddenly and very definitely. Similarly the Carolingian period stands "between-styles." We see different forms touched on and explored, but nothing of inwardly necessary expression. The creator of the Aachen Minster "thinks surely and builds surely, but does not feel surely."[17] The Marienkirche in the Castle of Würzburg (c. 700) has its counterpart in Salonika (St. George), and the Church of St. Germigny des Près (c. 800) with its cupolas and horseshoe niches is almost a mosque. For the whole of West Europe the period 850–950 is almost a blank. And just so to-day Russian art stands between two styles. The primitive wooden architecture with its steep eight-sided tent-roof (which extends from Norway to Manchuria) is impressed with Byzantine motives from over the Danube and Armenian-Persian from over the Caucasus. We can certainly feel an "elective affinity" between the Russian and the Magian souls, but as yet the prime symbol of Russia, the plane without limit,[18] finds no sure expression either in religion or in architecture. The church roof emerges, hillockwise, but little from the landscape and on it sit the tent-roofs whose points are coifed with the "koskoshniks" that suppress and would

abolish the upward tendency. They neither tower up like the Gothic belfry nor enclose like the mosque-cupola, but *sit,* thereby emphasizing the horizontality of the building, which is meant to be regarded merely from the outside. When about 1760 the Synod forbade the tent roofs and prescribed the orthodox onion-cupolas, the heavy cupolas were set upon slender cylinders, of which there may be any number and which sit on the roof-plane. It is not yet a style, only the promise of a style that will awaken when the real Russian religion awakens.

In the Faustian West, this awakening happened shortly before A.D. 1000. In one moment, the Romanesque style was there. Instead of the fluid organization of space on an insecure ground plan, there was, suddenly, a strict dynamic of space. From the very beginning, inner and outer construction were placed in a fixed relation, the wall was penetrated by the form-language and the form worked into the wall in a way that no other Culture has ever imagined. From the very beginning the window and the belfry were invested with their meanings. The form was irrevocably assigned. Only its development remained to be worked out.

The Egyptian style began with another such creative act, just as unconscious, just as full of symbolic force. The prime symbol of the Way came into being suddenly with the beginning of the Fourth Dynasty (2930 B.C.). The world-creating depth-experience of this soul gets it substance from the direction-factor itself. Spatial depth as stiffened Time, distance, death. Destiny itself dominate the expression, and the merely sensuous dimensions of length and breadth become an escorting plane which restricts and prescribes the Way of destiny. The Egyptian flat-relief, which is designed to be seen at close quarters and arranged serially so as to compel the beholder to pass along the wall-planes in the prescribed direction, appears with similar suddenness about the beginning of the Fifth Dynasty.[19] The still later avenues of sphinxes and statues and the rock- and terrace-temples constantly intensify that tendency towards the one distance that the world of Egyptian mankind knows, the grave. Observe how soon the colonnades of the early period come to be systems of huge, close-set pillars that *screen off* all side-view. This is some-

---

17. Frankl, *Baukunst des Mittelalters* (1918), pp. 16 et seq.

18. The lack of any vertical tendency in the Russian life-feeling is perceptible also in the saga-figure of Ilya Murometz (see Vol. II, p. 231). The Russian has not the smallest relation with a *Father*-God. His ethos is not a filial but purely a *fraternal* love, radiating in all directions along the human plane. Christ, even, is conceived as a Brother. The Faustian, wholly vertical, tendency to strive up to fulfilment is to the real Russian an incomprehensible pretension. The same absence of all vertical tendency is observable in Russian ideas of the state and property.

19. The disposition of Egyptian and that of Western history are so clear as to admit of comparison being carried right down to the details, and it would be well worth the expert's while to carry out such an investigation. The Fourth Dynasty, that of the strict Pyramid style, B.C. 2930–2750 (Cheops, Chephren), corresponds to the Romanesque (980–1100), the Fifth Dynasty (2750–2625, Sahu-rê) to the early Gothic (1100–1230), and the Sixth Dynasty, prime of the archaic portraiture (2625–2475, Phiops I and II), to the mature Gothic of 1230–1400.

thing that has never reproduced itself in any other architecture.

The grandeur of this style appears to us as rigid and unchanging. And certainly it stands beyond the passion which is ever seeking and fearing and so imparts to subordinate characters a quality of restless personal movement in the flow of the centuries. But, vice versa, we cannot doubt that to an Egyptian the Faustian style (which *is* our style, from earliest Romanesque to Rococo and Empire) would with its unresting persistent search for a Something, appear far more uniform than we can imagine. It follows, we must not forget, from the conception of style that we are working on here, that Romanesque, Gothic, Renaissance, Baroque and Rococo are only *stages of one and the same style,* in which it is naturally the variable that we and the constant that men of other eyes remark. In actual fact, the inner unity of the Northern Renaissance is shown in innumerable reconstructions of Romanesque work in Baroque and of late Gothic work of Rococo that are not in the least startling. In peasant art, Gothic and Baroque have been identical, and the streets of old towns with their pure harmony of all sorts of gables and façades (wherein definite attributions to Romanesque or Gothic Renaissance or Baroque or Rococo are often quite impossible) show that the family resemblance between the members is far greater than they themselves realize.

The Egyptian style was purely architectural, and remained so till the Egyptian soul was extinguished. It is the only one in which Ornamentation as a decorative supplement to architecture is entirely absent. It allowed of no divergence into arts of entertainment, no display-painting, no busts, no secular music. In the Ionic phase, the centre of gravity of the Classical style shifted from architecture to an independent plastic art; in that of the Baroque the style of the West passed into music, whose form-language in its turn ruled the entire building art of the 18th Century; in the Arabian world, after Justinian and Chosroes-Nushirvan, Arabesque dissolved all the forms of architecture, painting and sculpture into style-impressions that nowadays we should consider as craft-art. But in Egypt the sovereignty of architecture remained unchallenged; it merely softened its language a little. In the chambers of the pyramid-temple of the Fourth Dynasty (Pyramid of Chephren) there are unadorned angular pillars. In the buildings of the Fifth (Pyramid of Sahu-rê) the plant-column makes its appearance. Lotus and papyrus branches turned into stone arise gigantic out of a pavement of transparent alabaster that represents water, enclosed by purple walls. The ceiling is adorned with birds and stars. The sacred way from the gate-buildings to the tomb-chamber, the picture of life, is a stream—it is the Nile itself become one with the prime-symbol of direction. The spirit of the mother-landscape unites with the soul that has sprung from it.

In China, in lieu of the awe-inspiring pylon with its massy wall and narrow entrance, we have the "Spirit-wall" (yin-pi) that conceals the way in. The Chinaman slips into life and thereafter follows the Tao of life's path; as the Nile valley is to the up-and-down landscape of the Hwang Ho, so is the stone-enclosed temple-way to the mazy paths of Chinese garden-architecture. And just so, in some mysterious fashion, the Euclidean existence is linked with the multitude of little islands and promontories of the Ægean, and the passionate Western, roving in the infinite, with the broad plains of Franconia and Burgundy and Saxony.

The Egyptian style is the expression of a *brave* soul. The rigour and force of it Egyptian man himself never felt and never asserted. He dared all, but said nothing. In Gothic and Baroque, on the contrary, the triumph over heaviness became a perfectly conscious motive of the form-language. The drama of Shakespeare deals openly with the desperate conflict of will and world. Classical man, again, was weak in the face of the "powers." The κάθαρσις of fear and pity, the *relief and recovery* of the Apollinian soul in the moment of the περιπέτεια was, according to Aristotle, the effect deliberately aimed at in Attic tragedy. As the Greek spectator watched *someone whom he knew* (for everyone knew the myth and its heroes and lived in them) senselessly maltreated by fortune, without any conceivable possibility of resistance to the Powers, and saw him go under with splendid mien, defiant, heroic, his own Euclidean soul experienced a marvellous uplifting. If life was worthless, at any rate the *grand gesture* in losing it was not so. The Greek willed nothing and dared nothing, but he found a stirring beauty in *enduring.* Even the earlier figures of Odysseus the patient, and, above all, Achilles the archetype of Greek manhood, have this characteristic quality. The moral of the Cynics, that of the Stoics, that of Epicurus, the common Greek ideals of σωφροσύνη and ἀταρξία, Diogenes devoting himself to θεωρία in a tub—all this is masked cowardice in the face of grave matters and responsibilities, and different indeed from the pride of the Egyptian soul. Apollinian man goes below ground out of life's way, even to the point of suicide, which *in this Culture alone* (if we ignore certain related Indian ideals) ranked as a high ethical act and was treated with the solemnity of a ritual symbol.[20] The Dionysiac intoxication seems a sort of furious drowning of uneasiness that to the Egyptian soul were utterly unknown. And consequently the Greek Culture is that of the small, the easy, the simple. Its technique is, compared with Egyptian or Babylonian, a clever nullity. No ornamentation shows such a poverty of invention as theirs, and their stock of sculptural positions and attitudes could be counted on one's fingers. "In its poverty of forms, which is conspicuous even allowing that at the beginning of its development it may have been better off than it was later, the Doric style pivoted everything on proportions and on measure."[21] Yet, even so, what adroitness in avoiding! The Greek architecture with its commensuration of load and support and its peculiar smallness of scale suggests a persistent evasion of difficult architectural problems that on the Nile and, later, in the high North were literally looked for, which moreover were known and certainly not burked in the Mycenæan age. The Egyptian loved the strong stone of immense buildings; it was in keeping with his self-consciousness that he should choose only the hardest for his task. But the Greek avoided it; his architecture first set itself small tasks, then ceased altogether. If we survey it as a whole, and then compare it with the totality of Egyptian or Mexican or even, for that matter, Western architecture, we are astounded at the feeble development of the style. A few variations of the Doric temple and it was exhausted. It was already closed off about 400 when the Corinthian capital was invented, and everything subsequent to this was merely modification of what existed.

The result of this was an almost bodily standardization of form-types and style-species. One might choose between them, but never overstep their strict limits—that would have been in some sort an admission of an infinity of possibilities. There were three orders of columns and a definite disposition of the architrave corresponding to each; to deal with the difficulty (considered, as early as Vitruvius, as a conflict) which the alternation of triglyphs and metopes produced at the corners, the nearest inter-columniations were narrowed—no one thought of imagining new forms to suit the case. If greater dimensions were desired, the requirements were met by superposition, juxtaposition, etc., of additional elements. Thus the Colosseum possesses three rings, the Didymæum of Miletus three rows of columns in front, and the Frieze of the Giants of Pergamum an

endless succession of individual and unconnected motives. Similarly with the style-species of prose and the types of lyric poetry, narrative and tragedy. Universally, the expenditure of powers on the basic form is restricted to the minimum and the creative energy of the artist directed to detail-fineness. It is a statical treatment of static genera, and it stands in the sharpest possible contrast to the dynamic fertility of the Faustian with its ceaseless creation of new types and domains of form.

We are now able to see the *organism* in a great style-course. Here, as in so many other matters, Goethe was the first to whom vision came. In his "Winckelmann" he says of Velleius Paterculus: "with his standpoint, it was not given to him to see all art as a living thing ($\zeta\tilde{\omega}o\nu$) that must have an inconspicuous beginning, a slow growth, a brilliant moment of fulfilment and a gradual decline like every other organic being, though it is presented in a set of individuals." This sentence contains the entire morphology of art-history. Styles do not follow one another like waves or pulse-beats. It is not the personality or will or brain of the artist that makes the style, but the style that makes the *type* of the artist. The style, like the Culture, is a prime phenomenon in the strictest Goethian sense, be it the style of art or religion or thought, or the style of life itself. It is, as "Nature" is, an ever-new experience of waking man, his alter ego and mirror-image in the world-around. And therefore in the general historical picture of a Culture there can be but one style, *the style of the Culture*. The error has lain in treating mere style-phases—Romanesque, Gothic, Baroque, Rococo, Empire—as if they were styles on the same level as units of quite another order such as the Egyptian, the Chinese (or even a "prehistoric") style. Gothic and Baroque are simply the youth and age of one and the same vessel of forms, the style of the West as ripening and ripened. What has been wanting in our art-research has been detachment, freedom from prepossessions, and the will to abstract. Saving ourselves trouble, we have classed any and every form-domain that makes a strong impression upon us as a "style," and it need hardly be said that our insight has been led astray still further by the Ancient-Mediæval-Modern scheme. But in reality, even a masterpiece of strictest Renaissance like the court of the Palazzo Farnese is infinitely nearer to the arcade-porch of St. Patroclus in Soest, the interior of the Magdeburg cathedral, and the staircases of South-German castles of the 18th Century than it is to the Temple of Pæstum or to the Erechtheum. The same relation exists between Doric and Ionic, and hence Ionic columns can be

---

20. That which differentiates the Japanese harakiri from this suicide is its intensely purposeful and (so to put it) active and demonstrative character.—*Tr.*

21. Koldewey-Puchstein, *Die griech. Tempel in Unter-Italien und Sizilien,* I, p. 228.

as completely combined with Doric building forms as late Gothic is with early Baroque in St. Lorenz at Nürnberg, or late Romanesque with late Baroque in the beautiful upper part of the West choir at Mainz. And our eyes have scarcely yet learned to distinguish within the Egyptian style the Old Kingdom and Middle Empire elements corresponding to Doric and Gothic youth and to Ionic and Baroque maturity, because from the Twelfth Dynasty these elements interpenetrate in all harmony in the form-language of all the greater works.

The task before art-history is to write the *comparative biographies of the great styles,* all of which as organisms of the same genus possess structurally cognate life histories.

In the beginning there is the timid, despondent, naked expression of a newly-awakened soul which is still seeking for a relation between itself and the world that, though its proper creation, yet is presented as alien and unfriendly. There is the child's fearfulness in Bishop Bernward's building at Hildesheim, in the Early-Christian catacomb-painting, and in the pillar-halls of the Egyptian Fourth Dynasty. A February of art, a deep presentiment of a coming wealth of forms, an immense suppressed tension, lies over the landscape that, still wholly rustic, is adorning itself with the first strongholds and townlets. Then follows the joyous mounting into the high Gothic, into the Constantinian age with its pillared basilicas and its domical churches, into the relief-ornament of the Fifth-Dynasty temple. *Being* is understood, a sacred form-language has been completely mastered and radiates its glory, and the Style ripens into a majestic symbolism of directional depth and of Destiny. But fervent youth comes to an end, and contradictions arise within the soul itself. The Renaissance, the Dionysiac-musical hostility to Apollinian Doric, the Byzantine of 450 that looks to Alexandria and away from the overjoyed art of Antioch, indicate a moment of resistance, of effective or ineffective impulse to destroy what has been acquired. It is very difficult to elucidate this moment, and an attempt to do so would be out of place here.

And now it is the manhood of the style-history that comes on. The Culture is changing into the intellecuality of the great cities that will now dominate the country-side, and *pari passu* the style is becoming intellectualized also. The grand symbolism withers; the riot of superhuman forms dies down; milder and more worldly arts drive out the great art of developed stone. Even in Egypt sculpture and fresco are emboldened to lighter movement. The *artist* appears, and "plans" what formerly grew out of the soil. Once more existence becomes self-conscious and now, detached from the land and the dream and the mystery, stands questioning, and wrestles for an expression of its new duty—as at the beginning of Baroque when Michelangelo, in wild discontent and kicking against the limitations of his art, piles up the dome of St. Peter's—in the age of Justinian I which built Hagia Sophia and the mosaic-decked domed basilics of Ravenna—at the beginning of that Twelfth Dynasty in Egypt which the Greeks condensed under the name of Sesostris—and at the decisive epoch in Hellas (c. 600) whose architecture probably, nay certainly, expressed that which is echoed for us in its grandchild Æschylus.

Then comes the gleaming autumn of the style. Once more the soul depicts its happiness, this time conscious of self-completion. The "return to Nature" which already thinkers and poets—Rousseau, Gorgias and their "contemporaries" in the other Cultures—begin to feel and to proclaim, reveals itself in the form-world of the arts as a sensitive longing and *presentiment of the end.* A perfectly clear intellect, joyous urbanity, the sorrow of a parting—these are the colours of these last Culture-decades of which Talleyrand was to remark later: "qui n'a pas vécu avant 1789 ne connaît pas la douceur de vivre." So it was, too, with the free, sunny and superfine art of Egypt under Sesostris III (c. 1850 B.C.) and the brief moments of satiated happiness that produced the varied splendour of Pericles's Acropolis and the works of Zeuxis and Phidias. A thousand years later again, in the age of the Ommaiyads, we meet it in the glad fairyland of Moorish architecture with its fragile columns and horseshoe arches that seem to melt into air in an iridescence of arabesques and stalactites. A thousand years more, and we see it in the music of Haydn and Mozart, in Dresden shepherdesses, in the pictures of Watteau and Guardi, and the works of German master-builders at Dresden, Potsdam, Würzburg and Vienna.

Then the style fades out. The form-language of the Erechtheum and the Dresden Zwinger, honey-combed with intellect, fragile, ready for self-destruction, is followed by the flat and senile Classicism that we find in the Hellenistic megalopolis, the Byzantium of 900 and the "Empire" modes of the North. The end is a sunset reflected in forms revived for a moment by pedant or by eclectic—semi-earnestness and doubtful genuineness dominate the world of the arts. We to-day are in this condition—playing a tedious game with dead forms to keep up the illusion of a living art.

*   *   *

The idea of the Macrocosm, then, which presents itself in the style-problem as simplified and capable of treatment, poses a multitude of tasks for the future to tackle. To make the form-world of the arts available as a means of penetrating the spirituality of entire Cultures—by handling it in a thoroughly physiognomic and symbolic spirit—is an undertaking that has not hitherto got beyond speculations of which the inadequacy is obvious. We are hardly as yet aware that there may be a psychology of the metaphysical bases of all great architectures. We have no idea what there is to discover in the change of meaning that a form of *pure extension* undergoes when it is taken over into another Culture. The history of the column has never yet been written, nor have we any notion of the deeply symbolic significances that reside in the means and the instruments of art.

Consider mosaic. In Hellenic times it was made up of pieces of marble, it was opaque and corporeal-Euclidean (e.g., the famous Battle of Issus at Naples), and it adorned the floor. But with the awakening of the Arabian soul it came to be built up of pieces of glass and set in fused gold, and it simply covered the walls and roofs of the domed basilica. This Early-Arabian Mosaic-picturing corresponds exactly, as to phase, with the glass-picturing of Gothic cathedrals, both being "early" arts ancillary to religious architectures. The one by letting in the light enlarges the church-space into world-space, while the other transforms it into the magic, gold-shimmering sphere which bears men away from earthly actuality into the visions of Plotinus, Origen, the Manichæans, the Gnostics and the Fathers, and the Apocalyptic poems.

Consider, again, the beautiful notion of *uniting the round arch and the column;* this again is a Syrian, if not a North-Arabian, creation of the third (or "high Gothic") century.[22] The revolutionary importance of this motive, which is specifically Magian, has never in the least degree been recognized; on the contrary, it has always been assumed to be Classical, and for most of us it is even representatively Classical. The Egyptians ignored any deep relation between the roof and the column; the latter was for them a plant-column, and represented not stoutness but growth. Classical man, in his turn, for whom the monolithic column was the mightiest symbol of Euclidean existence—all body, all unity, all steadiness—connected it, in the strictest proportions of vertical and horizontal, of strength and load, with his architrave. But here, in this union of arch and column which the Renaissance

in its tragicomic deludedness admired as expressly Classical (though it was a notion that the Classical neither possessed nor could possess), the bodily principle of load and inertia is rejected and the arch is made to spring clear and open out of the slender column. The idea actualized here is at once a liberation from all earth-gravity and a capture of space, and between this element and that of the dome which soars free but yet encloses the great "cavern," there is the deep relation of like meaning. The one and the other are eminently and powerfully Magian, and they come to their logical fulfilment in the "Rococo" stage of Moorish mosques and castles, wherein ethereally delicate columns—often growing out of, rather than based on, the ground—seem to be empowered by some secret magic to carry a whole world of innumerable notched arcs, gleaming ornaments, stalactites, and vaultings saturated with colours. The full importance of this basic form of Arabian architecture may be expressed by saying that the combination of column and architrave is the Classical, that of column and round arch the Arabian, and that of pillar and pointed arch the Faustian Leitmotiv.

Take, further, the history of the Acanthus motive. In the form in which it appears, for example, on the Monument of Lysicrates at Athens, it is one of the most distinctive in Classical ornamentation. It has body, it is and remains individual, and its structure is capable of being taken in at one glance. But already it appears heavier and richer in the ornament of the Imperial Fora (Nerva's, Trajan's) and that of the temple of Mars Ultor; the organic disposition has become so complicated that, as a rule, it requires to be studied, and the tendency to *fill up* the surfaces appears. In Byzantine art—of which Riegl thirty years ago noticed the "latent Saracenic character" though he had no suspicion of the connexion brought to light here—the acanthus leaf was broken up into endless tendril-work which (as in Hagia Sophia) is disposed quite inorganically over whole surfaces. To the Classical motive are added the old-Aramæan vine and palm leaves, which have already played a part in Jewish ornamentation. The interlaced borders of "Late-Roman" mosaic pavements and sarcophagus-edges, and even geometrical plane-patterns are introduced, and finally, throughout the Persian-Anatolian world, mobility and *bizarrerie* culminate in the Arabesque. *This* is the genuine Magian motive—anti-plastic to the last degree, hostile to the pictorial and to the bodily alike. Itself bodiless, it disembodies the object over which its endless richness of web is drawn. A masterpiece of this kind—a piece of architecture completely opened out into Ornamentation—is the façade of the Castle of Mashetta in Moab built by

---

22. The relation of column and arch spiritually corresponds to that of wall and cupola, and the interposition of the drum between the rectangle and the dome occurs "simultaneously" with that of the impost between the column and the arch.

the Ghassanids.[23] The craft-art of Byzantine-Islamic style (hitherto called Lombard, Frankish, Celtic or Old-Nordic) which invaded the whole youthful West and dominated the Carolingian Empire, was largely practised by Oriental craftsmen or imported as patterns for our own weavers, metal-workers and armourers. Ravenna, Lucca, Venice, Granada, Palermo were the efficient centres of this then highly-civilized form-language; in the year 1000, when in the North the forms of a new Culture were already being developed and established, Italy was entirely dominated by it.

Take, lastly, the changed point of view towards the human body. With the victory of the Arabian world-feeling, men's conception of it underwent a complete revolution. In almost every Roman head of the period 100–250 that the Vatican Collection contains, one may perceive the opposition of Apollinian and Magian feeling, and of muscular position and "look" as different bases of expression. Even in Rome itself, since Hadrian, the sculptor made constant use of the drill, an instrument which was wholly repugnant to the Euclidean feeling towards stone—for whereas the chisel brings out the

limiting surfaces and *ipso facto* affirms the corporeal and material nature of the marble block, the drill, in breaking the surfaces and creating effects of light and shade, denies it; and accordingly the sculptors, be they Christian or "pagan," lose the old feeling for the phenomenon of the naked body. One has only to look at the shallow and empty Antinous statues—and yet these were quite definitely "Classical." Here it is only the head that is physiognomically of interest—as it never is in Attic sculpture. The drapery is given quite a new meaning, and simply dominates the whole appearance. The consul-statues in the Capitoline Museum are conspicuous examples. The pupils are bored, and the eyes look into the distance, so that the whole expression of the work lies no longer in its body but in that Magian principle of the "Pneuma" which Neo-Platonism and the decisions of the Church Councils, Mithraism and Mazdaism alike presume in man.

The pagan "Father" Iamblichus, about 300, wrote a book concerning statues of gods in which the divine is substantially present and working upon the beholder. Against this idea of the image—an idea of the Pseudomorphosis—the East and the South rose in a storm of iconoclasm, and the sources of this iconoclasm lay in a conception of artistic creation that is nearly impossible for us to understand.

---

23. The Ghassanid Kingdom flourished in the extreme North-west of Arabia during the sixth century of our reckoning. Its people were essentially Arab, and probably came from the south; and an outlying cousinry inhabited Medina in the time of the Prophet.—*Tr.*

3. *The Disintegrations of Civilizations*

BY ARNOLD TOYNBEE

The Nature of Disintegration

A GENERAL SURVEY

IN PASSING from the breakdowns of civilizations to their disintegrations we have to face a question like that which confronted us when we passed from the geneses of civilizations to their growths. Is disintegration a new problem on its own account or can we take it for granted as a natural and inevitable sequel to breakdown? When we con-

Reprinted from Arnold Toynbee, *A Study of History*, abridged and edited by D. C. Somervell (New York: Oxford University Press, 1946), I, 360–61, 363–68, 403–7, 422–28, with the permission of Oxford University Press.

sidered the earlier question, whether growth was a new problem, distinct from the problem of genesis, we were led to answer the question in the affirmative by discovering that there were, in fact, a number of "arrested" civilizations which had solved the problem of genesis, but had failed to solve the problem of growth. And now again, at this later stage in our Study, we can meet the analogous question with the same affirmative answer by pointing to the fact that certain civilizations, after breakdown, have suffered a similar arrest and entered on a long period of petrifaction.

The classic example of a petrified civilization is presented by a phase in the history of the Egyptiac

Society which we have already had occasion to consider. After the Egyptiac Society had broken down under the intolerable burden that was imposed on it by the Pyramid-builders, and when thereafter it had passed through the first and the second into the third of the three phases of disintegration—a "time of troubles," a universal state and an interregnum—this apparently moribund society then departed unexpectedly and abruptly, at a moment when it was apparently completing its life course, from what we may provisionally regard as the standard pattern if we take for our norm the Hellenic example in which these three phases first came under our notice. At this point the Egyptiac Society refused to pass away and proceeded to double its life-span. When we take the time-measure of the Egyptiac Society from the moment of its galvanic reaction against the Hyksos invaders in the first quarter of the sixteenth century before Christ down to the obliteration of the last traces of an Egyptiac culture in the fifth century of the Christian Era, we find that this span of two thousand years is as long as the combined span of the birth, growth, breakdown and almost complete disintegration of the Egyptiac Society, reckoning back from the date of its passionate reassertion of itself in the sixteenth century before Christ to its first emergence above the primitive level at some unknown date in the fourth millennium B.C. But the life of the Egyptiac Society during the second half of its existence was a kind of life-in-death. During those supernumerary millennia, a civilization whose previous career had been so full of movement and of meaning lingered on inert and arrested. In fact it survived by becoming petrified.

Nor does this example stand alone. If we turn to the history of the main body of the Far Eastern Society in China, in which the moment of breakdown may be equated with the break-up of the T'ang Empire in the last quarter of the ninth century of the Christian Era, we can trace the subsequent process of disintegration following its normal course through a "time of troubles" into a universal state, only to be pulled up in the course of this stage by a reaction of the same abrupt and passionate kind as the Egyptiac reaction to the Hyksos invaders. The Southern Chinese revolt, under the leadership of the founder of the Ming dynasty, Hung Wu, against a Far Eastern universal state which had been established by the barbarian Mongols, is strongly reminiscent of the Theban revolt, under the leadership of the founder of the Eighteenth Dynasty, Amosis, against the "successor-state" which had been erected on part of the derelict domain of the defunct Egyptiac universal state (the so-called "Middle Empire") by the barbarian

Hyksos. And there has been a corresponding similarity in the sequel. For the Far Eastern Society has prolonged its existence in a petrified form instead of passing expeditiously through disintegration into dissolution by way of a universal state running out into an interregnum.

We may add to these two examples the various fossilized fragments of otherwise extinct civilizations which have come to our notice: the Jains in India, the Hinayanian Buddhists in Ceylon, Burma, Siam and Cambodia, and the Lamaistic Mahayanian Buddhists of Tibet and Mongolia, all of them fossilized fragments of the Indic Civilization, and the Jews, Parsees, Nestorians and Monophysites, who are fossilized fragments of the Syriac Civilization.

*   *   *

In studying the growths of civilizations we found that they could be analysed into successions of performances of the drama of challenge-and-response and that the reason why one performance followed another was because each of the responses was not only successful in answering the particular challenge by which it had been evoked but was also instrumental in provoking a fresh challenge, which arose each time out of the new situation that the successful response had brought about. Thus the essence of the nature of the growths of civilizations proved to be an *élan* which carried the challenged party through the equilibrium of a successful response into an overbalance which declared itself in the presentation of a new challenge. This repetitiveness or recurrence of challenge is likewise implied in the concept of disintegration, but in this case the responses fail. In consequence, instead of a series of challenges each different in character from a predecessor which has been successfully met and relegated to past history, we have the same challenge presented again and again. For example, in the history of the international politics of the Hellenic World, from the time when the Solonian economic revolution first confronted the Hellenic Society with the task of establishing a political world order, we can see that the failure of the Athenian attempt to solve the problem by means of the Delian League led on to Philip of Macedon's attempt to solve it by means of the Corinthian League, and Philip's failure to Augustus's attempt to solve it by the *Pax Romana,* upheld by a Principate. This repetition of the same challenge is in the very nature of the situation. When the outcome of each successive encounter is not victory but defeat, the unanswered challenge can never be disposed of, and is bound to present itself again and again until it either receives some tardy and imperfect answer or else brings about the destruction of the society which has shown itself inveterately incapable of responding to it effectively.

Can we say, then, that the alternative to petrifaction is total and absolute extinction? Before answering in the affirmative we may remind ourselves of the process of apparentation-and-affiliation which we noticed at an early stage of this Study. The Solonian *Respice finem* and a suspension of judgment may be for the present our wisest course.

In our study of the process of the growths of civilizations we began by looking for a criterion of growth before we attempted to analyse the process, and we will follow the same plan in our study of disintegrations. One step in the argument, however, we may spare ourselves. Having decided that the criteria of growth were not to be found in an increasing command over the human or the physical environment, we may fairly assume that loss of such command is not among the causes of disintegration. Indeed, the evidence, so far as it goes, suggests that an increasing command over environments is a concomitant of disintegration rather than of growth. Militarism, a common feature of breakdown and disintegration, is frequently effective in increasing a society's command both over other living societies and over the inanimate forces of nature. In the downward course of a broken-down civilization's career there may be truth in the Ionian philosopher Heracleitus's saying that "war is the father of all things," and, since the vulgar estimates of human prosperity are reckoned in terms of power and wealth, it thus often happens that the opening chapters of a society's tragic decline are popularly hailed as the culminating chapters of a magnificent growth. Sooner or later, however, disillusionment is bound to follow; for a society that has become incurably divided against itself is almost certain to "put back into the business" of war the greater part of those additional resources, human and material, which the same business has incidentally brought into its hands. For instance, we see the money-power and man-power won through Alexander's conquests being poured into the civil wars of Alexander's successors, and the money-power and man-power won by the Roman conquests of the second century B.C. being poured into the civil wars of the last century B.C.

Our criterion for the process of disintegration has to be sought for elsewhere; and the clue is given to us in the spectacle of that division and discord within the bosom of a society to which an increase in its command over its environment can so often be traced back. This is only what we should expect; for we have found already that the ultimate criterion and the fundamental cause of the breakdowns which precede disintegrations is an outbreak of internal discords through which societies forfeit their faculty of self-determination.

The social schisms in which this discord partially reveals itself rend the broken-down society in two different dimensions simultaneously. There are vertical schisms between geographically segregated communities and horizontal schisms between geographically intermingled but socially segregated classes.

So far as the vertical type of schism is concerned, we have already seen how frequently a reckless indulgence in the crime of inter-state warfare has been the main line of suicidal activity. But this vertical schism is not the most characteristic manifestation of the discord by which the breakdowns of civilizations are brought about; for the articulation of a society into parochial communities is, after all, a feature which is common to the whole genus of human societies, civilized and uncivilized, and inter-state warfare is merely an abuse of a potential instrument of self-destruction which is within the reach of any society at any time. On the other hand, the horizontal schism of a society along lines of class is not only peculiar to civilizations but is also a phenomenon which appears at the moment of their breakdowns and which is a distinctive mark of the periods of breakdown and disintegration, by contrast with its absence during the phases of genesis and growth.

We have already come across this horizontal type of schism. We encountered it when we were exploring the extension of our own Western Society backwards in the time-dimension. We found ourselves led back to the Christian Church and a number of barbarian war-bands which had come into collision with the Church in Western Europe inside the northern frontiers of the Roman Empire; and we observed that each of these two institutions—the war-bands and the Church—had been created by a social group which was not, itself, an articulation of our own Western body social and which could only be described in terms of another society, antecedent to ours: the Hellenic Civilization. We described the creators of the Christian Church as the internal proletariat, and the creators of the barbarian war-bands as the external proletariat, of this Hellenic Society.

Pursuing our inquiries farther, we found that both these proletariats had arisen through acts of secession from the Hellenic Society during a "time of troubles" in which the Hellenic Society itself was manifestly no longer creative but was already in decline; and pushing our inquiry yet another stage back, we further found that these secessions had been provoked by an antecedent change in the character of the ruling element in the Hellenic body social. A "creative minority" which had once evoked a voluntary allegiance from the uncreative mass, in virtue of the gift of charm which is the privilege of creativity, had now given place to a "dominant minority" destitute of charm because it was uncreative. This dominant minority had retained its privileged position by force, and the secessions which had ultimately resulted in the creation of the war-bands and the Christian Church had been reactions to this tyranny. Yet this defeat of its own intentions—through the disruption of a society which it was attempting, by perverse methods, to hold together—is not the only achievement of the dominant minority that came to our notice. It has also left a monument of itself in the shape of the Roman Empire; and the Empire not only took shape earlier than either the Church or the war-bands; its mighty presence in the world in which these proletarian institutions grew up was a factor in the growth of both of them which cannot be left out of account. This universal state in which the Hellenic dominant minority encased itself was like the carapace of a giant tortoise; and, while the Church was reared under its shadow, the barbarians trained their war-bands by sharpening their claws on the tortoise-shell's outer face.

Finally, at a later point in this Study, we tried to obtain a clearer view of the nexus of cause and effect between the loss of the leading minority's faculty for creation and the loss of the faculty for attracting the majority by charm rather than by force. And here we put our finger on the creative minority's expedient of social drill—as a short cut for bringing the uncreative mass into line—in which we had already found the weak spot in the relation between minority and majority in the growth stage. On this showing, the estrangement between minority and majority which eventually comes to a head in the secession of the proletariat is the consequence of the breaking of a link which, even in the growth phase, had only been maintained by playing upon the well-drilled faculty of mimesis; and it is not surprising to find that mimesis fails when the leaders' creativity gives out, considering that, even in the growth phase, this link of mimesis has always been precarious by reason of a treacherous duality—the revenge of an unwilling slave—which is part of the nature of any mechanical device.

These are the threads of inquiry into the horizontal type of schism that are already in our hands; and perhaps the most promising way of pursuing our inquiry farther will be to draw these threads together and then spin out our strand.

Our first step will be to take a closer and wider survey of the three fractions—dominant minority and internal and external proletariats—into which

it appears from the Hellenic example, as also from other examples at which we have glanced at earlier points in this Study, that a broken-down society splits when a horizontal schism rends its fabric. After that we will turn, as we did in our study of growths, from the macrocosm to the microcosm, and there we shall discover a complementary aspect of disintegration in the increasing distraction of the soul. Both these lines of search will lead us to the, at first sight, paradoxical discovery that the process of disintegration works out, in part at least, to a result which is logically incompatible with its nature—works out, that is to say, to a "recurrence of birth" or "palingenesia."

When we have completed our analysis we shall find that the qualitative change which disintegration brings with it is exactly opposite in character to that which is the outcome of growth. We have seen that, in the process of growth, the several growing civilizations become increasingly differentiated from one another. We shall now find that, conversely, the qualitative effect of disintegration is standardization.

This tendency towards standardization is the more remarkable when we consider the extent of the diversity which it has to overcome. The broken-down civilizations bring with them, when they enter on their disintegration, the extremely diverse dispositions—a bent towards art or towards machinery or whatever the bent may be—that they have severally acquired during their growth. And they are also further differentiated from one another by the fact that their breakdowns overtake them at widely different ages. The Syriac Civilization, for example, broke down after the death of Solomon, *circa* 937 B.C., at a date probably less than two hundred years removed from the original emergence of this civilization out of the post-Minoan interregnum. On the other hand the sister Hellenic Civilization, which emerged out of the same interregnum coevally, did not break down till five hundred years later, in the Atheno-Peloponnesian War. Again, the Orthodox Christian Civilization broke down at the outbreak of the great Romano-Bulgarian War in A.D. 977, while the sister civilization, which is our own, was unquestionably growing for several centuries longer and—for all we yet know—may not have broken down even yet. If sister civilizations can run to such different lengths of growth-span, it is manifest that the growths of civilizations are not predestined to any uniform duration; and indeed we have failed to find any reason *a priori* why a civilization should not go on growing indefinitely, once it has entered on this stage. These considerations make it plain that the differences between growing civilizations are extensive and profound. Nevertheless, we shall find that the process of disintegration tends to conform in all cases to a standard pattern—a horizontal schism splitting the society into the three fractions already mentioned, and the creation, by each of these three fractions, of a characteristic institution: universal state, universal church and barbarian war-bands.

We shall have to take note of these institutions, as well as of their respective creators, if our study of the disintegrations of civilizations is to be comprehensive. But we shall find it convenient, so far as it may prove possible, to study the institutions for their own sake in separate parts of the book; for these three institutions are something more than products of the disintegration process. They may also play a part in the relations between one civilization and another; and when we examine the universal churches we shall find ourselves compelled to raise the question whether churches can really be comprehended in their entirety in the framework of the histories of the civilizations in which they make their historical appearances, or whether we have not to regard them as representatives of another species of society which is at least as distinct from the species "civilizations" as these latter are distinct from primitive societies.

This may prove to be one of the most momentous questions that a study of history can suggest to us, but it lies near the farther end of the inquiry we have just been sketching out.

*   *   *

EXTERNAL PROLETARIATS

The external, like the internal, proletariat brings itself into existence by an act of secession from the dominant minority of a civilization that has broken down, and the schism in which the secession results is in this case palpable; for, whereas the internal proletariat continues to be geographically intermingled with the dominant minority from which it is divided by a moral gulf, the external proletariat is not only morally alienated but is also physically divided from the dominant minority by a frontier which can be traced on the map.

The crystallization of such a frontier is indeed the sure sign that such a secession has taken place; for, as long as a civilization is still in growth, it has no hard and fast boundaries except on fronts where it happens to have collided with another civilization of its own species. Such collisions between two or more civilizations give rise to phenomena which we shall have occasion to examine in a later part of this Study, but at present we will leave this contingency out of account and confine our

attention to the situation in which a civilization has for its neighbour not another civilization but societies of the primitive species. In these circumstances we shall find that, as long as a civilization is in growth, its frontiers are indeterminate. If we place ourselves at the focus of growth in a growing civilization and proceed to travel outwards until we find ourselves sooner or later in an environment which is unmistakably and completely primitive, we shall not be able, at any point on such a journey, to draw a line and say: "Here civilization ends and we enter the Primitive World."

In fact, when a creative minority successfully performs its role in the life of a growing civilization, and the spark which it has kindled "gives light unto all that are in the house," the light, as it radiates outward, is not arrested by the walls of the house, for in fact there are no walls and the light is not hid from the neighbours outside. The light shines as far as, in the nature of things, it can carry until it reaches vanishing-point. The gradations are infinitesimal, and it is impossible to demarcate the line at which the last glimmer of twilight flickers out and leaves the heart of darkness in undivided possession. In fact, the carrying-power of the radiation of growing civilizations is so great that, although civilizations are relatively a very recent achievement of mankind, they have long ago succeeded in permeating, at least in some degree, the whole array of surviving primitive societies. It would be impossible anywhere to discover a primitive society which had entirely escaped the influence of some civilization or other. In 1935, for example, a society previously quite unknown was discovered in the interior of Papua, and this society possessed a technique of intensive agriculture which must, at some unknown date, have been acquired from some unidentified civilization.

This all-pervasiveness of the influence of civilizations in what remains of the Primitive World strikes us forcibly when we regard the phenomenon from the point of view of the primitive societies. If, on the other hand, we look upon it from the standpoint of a civilization, we shall be no less forcibly struck by the fact that the strength of the influence radiated wanes as the range increases. As soon as we have recovered from our astonishment at detecting the influence of Hellenic art in a coin that was struck in Britain in the last century before Christ or on a sarcophagus carved in Afghanistan in the first century of the Christian Era, we observe that the British coin looks like a caricature of its Macedonian original and that the Afghan sarcophagus is a shoddy product of "commercial art." At this remove mimesis has passed into travesty.

Mimesis is evoked by charm; and we can now

see that the charm which is exercised, during the growth of a civilization, by a succession of creative minorities preserves the house not only from being divided against itself but also from being attacked by its neighbours—in so far, at least, as these neighbours are primitive societies. Wherever a growing civilization is in contact with primitive societies, its creative minority attracts their mimesis as well as the mimesis of the uncreative majority in its midst. But, if this is the normal relation between a civilization and the primitive societies round about so long as the civilization is in growth, a profound change sets in if and when the civilization breaks down and goes into disintegration. The creative minorities which have won a voluntary allegiance by the charm which their creativity exerts are replaced by a dominant minority which, lacking charm, relies on force. The surrounding primitive peoples are no longer charmed but are repelled; these humble disciples of the growing civilization then renounce their discipleship and become what we have called an external proletariat. Though "in" the now broken-down civilization they are no longer "of" it.[1]

The radiation of any civilization may be analysed into three elements—economic, political and cultural—and, so long as a society is in a state of growth, all three elements seem to be radiated with equal power or, to speak in human rather than physical terms, to exercise an equal charm. But, as soon as the civilization has ceased to grow, the charm of its culture evaporates. Its powers of economic and political radiation may, and indeed probably will, continue to grow faster than ever, for a successful cultivation of the pseudo-religions of Mammon and Mars and Moloch is eminently characteristic of broken-down civilizations. But, since the cultural element is the essence of a civilization and the economic and political elements are relatively trivial manifestations of the life that it has in it, it follows that the most spectacular triumphs of economic and political radiation are imperfect and precarious.

If we look at the change from the standpoint of the primitive peoples, we shall express the same truth by saying that their mimesis of the broken-down civilization's arts of peace comes to an end, but that they continue to imitate its improvements—its technical gadgets—in the arts of industry, war and politics, not in order that they may become one with it—which was their aspiration so long as it charmed them—but in order that they may the more effectively defend themselves against the violence which is by now its most conspicuous characteristic.

In our foregoing survey of the experiences and reactions of internal proletariats we have seen how the path of violence has allured them, and also how, in so far as they have yielded to this temptation, they have only brought disaster on themselves. The Theudases and Judases inevitably perish with the sword; it is only when it follows a prophet of gentleness that the internal proletariat has a chance of taking its conquerors captive. The external proletariat, if it chooses (as it almost certainly will) to react with violence, is at no such disadvantage. Whereas the whole of the internal proletariat lies, *ex hypothesi*, within the dominant minority's reach, some part at any rate of the external proletariat is likely to be beyond the effective range of the dominant minority's military action. In the contest that now ensues the broken-down civilization radiates force instead of attracting mimesis. In these circumstances the nearer members of the external proletariat are likely to be conquered and added to the internal proletariat, but a point will be reached where the dominant minority's qualitative superiority in military power is counterbalanced by the length of its communications.

When this stage is reached it brings with it the completion of a change in the nature of the contact between the civilization in question and its barbarian neighbours. So long as a civilization is in growth, its home territory, where it prevails in full force, is screened, as we have seen, from the impact of unreclaimed savagery by a broad threshold or buffer zone across which civilization shades into savagery in a long series of fine gradations. On the other hand, when a civilization has broken down and fallen into schism and when the consequent hostilities between the dominant minority and the external proletariat have ceased to be a running fight and have settled down into trench warfare, we find that the buffer zone has disappeared. The geographical transition from civilization to barbarism is now no longer gradual but is abrupt. To use the appropriate Latin words, which bring out both the kinship and the contrast between the two types of contact, a *limen* or threshold, which was a zone, has been replaced by a *limes* or military frontier, which is a line that has length without breadth. Across this line a baffled dominant minority and an unconquered external proletariat now face one another under arms; and this military front is a bar to the passage of all social radiation except that of military technique—an article of social exchange which makes for war and not for peace between those who give and take it.

---

1. When we say "in it," we do not mean geographically within it—for that, being "external," they obviously are not—but "in it" inasmuch as they continue willy-nilly to be in a state of active relationship with it.

The social phenomena which follow when this warfare becomes stationary along a *limes* will occupy our attention later. Here it is sufficient to mention the cardinal fact that this temporary and precarious balance of forces inevitably tilts, with the passage of time, in favour of the barbarians.

* * *

Dominant Minorities and External Proletariats.— We have seen that universal states are usually provided by dominant minorities indigenous to the society for which they perform this high-handed service. These indigenous empire-builders may be frontiersmen from the outer edge of the world upon which they confer the blessing of peace through the imposition of political unity; but this origin does not in itself convict them of having any alien tinge in their culture. We have, however, also noted cases in which the moral débâcle of the dominant minority has been so rapid that, by the time when the disintegrating society has been ripe for entering a universal state, there has no longer been any remnant of the dominant minority still possessed of the empire-building virtues. In such cases the task of providing a universal state is not usually allowed to remain unperformed. Some alien empire-builder steps into the breach and performs for the ailing society the task that ought to have been performed by native hands.

All universal states, alien and indigenous alike, are apt to be accepted with thankfulness and resignation, if not with enthusiasm; they are at any rate an improvement, in a material sense, upon the time of troubles that has preceded them. But as time passes "a new king" arises "who knew not Joseph"; in plain language, the time of troubles and the memory of its horrors recedes into a forgotten past, and the present—in which the universal state extends over the entire social landscape—comes to be judged as a thing in itself irrespective of its historical context. At this stage the fortunes of indigenous and alien universal states diverge. The indigenous universal state, whatever its real merits, tends to become more and more acceptable to its subjects and is more and more regarded as the only possible social framework for their life. The alien universal state, on the other hand, becomes more and more unpopular. Its subjects are more and more offended by its alien qualities and shut their eyes more and more firmly to the useful service which it has performed and perhaps still is performing for them.

An obvious pair of universal states for the illustration of this contrast is the Roman Empire which provided an indigenous universal state for the Hellenic World and the British Rāj which has provided the second of two alien universal states for the Hindu Civilization. Many quotations could be collected to illustrate the love and veneration with which the latter-day subjects of the Roman Empire regarded that institution, even after it had ceased to perform its task with tolerable efficiency and when it was in manifest dissolution. Perhaps the most striking of these tributes in a passage in the poem *De Consulatu Stilichonis* written in Latin hexameters by Claudian of Alexandria in A.D. 400.

> She—prouder boast than other conquerors knew—
> Gently her captives to her bosom drew;
> Mother not mistress, made the thrall her kin
> And 'neath her wing called all the nations in.
> Who owns, and owes not to her parent sway,
> His civick rights in utmost lands to-day?[2]

It would be easy to prove that the British Rāj has been in many respects a more benevolent and also perhaps a more beneficent institution than the Roman Empire, but it would be hard to find a Claudian in any of the Alexandrias of Hindustan.

If we look at the history of other alien universal states, we shall observe the same mounting tide of hostile feeling among their subjects as we find in British India. The alien Syriac universal state imposed by Cyrus on the Babylonic Society was so bitterly hated by the time it had completed the second century of its existence that in 331 B.C. the Babylonian priests were prepared to give an effusive welcome to the equally alien conqueror Alexander of Macedon, as in our day certain extreme nationalists in India might have been prepared to welcome Clive from Japan. In Orthodox Christendom the alien *Pax Ottomanica* had been welcomed in the first quarter of the fourteenth century of the Christian Era by the Greek adherents of the founder of the Ottoman commonwealth on the Asiatic shores of the Sea of Marmara had become an object of loathing to the Greek nationalists of A.D. 1821. The passage of five centuries had produced among Greeks a change of sentiment which was the exact inverse of the change in Gaul from the Romano-phobia of a Vercingetorix to the Romano-philia of a Sidonius Apollinaris.

Another prominent example of the hatred aroused by empire-builders of an alien culture is the animosity of the Chinese towards the Mongol conquerors who provided a distracted Far Eastern World with a sorely needed universal state, and this animosity might appear to present a curious contrast to the tolerance with which the same society accepted two-and-a-half centuries of Manchu domination at a later period. The explanation is to be found in the fact that the Manchus were back-

---

2. Translation by R. A. Knox, in *The Making of Western Europe*, by C. R. L. Fletcher, p. 3.

woodsmen of the Far Eastern World who were not contaminated by any alien culture, whereas the Mongols' barbarism was mitigated, however slightly, by a tincture of Syriac culture derived from Nestorian Christian pioneers and by an open-minded readiness to enlist the services of able and experienced men whatever their provenance. That this is the real explanation of the unpopularity of the Mongol régime in China is made plain by Marco Polo's account of explosive contacts between the Chinese subjects and the Orthodox Christian soldiers and Muslim administrators of the Mongol Khāqān.

It was perhaps a tincture of Sumeric culture that made the Hyksos intolerable to their Egyptiac subjects, whereas the subsequent intrusion of the completely barbarian Libyans was accepted without resentment. In fact, we can venture to formulate something like a general social law to the effect that barbarian invaders who present themselves free from any alien cultural taint are apt to make their fortunes, while those who, before their Völkerwanderung, have acquired either an alien or a heretical tinge must go out of their way to purge themselves of it if they are to escape the otherwise inevitable doom of being either ejected or exterminated.

To take undiluted barbarians first: the Aryas and the Hittites and the Achaeans, each of whom invented a barbarian pantheon of their own during their sojourn on the threshold of a civilization, and who persisted in this barbarian worship after they had broken through and made their conquests, each also succeeded, notwithstanding this "invincible ignorance," in founding new civilizations: the Indic, the Hittite and the Hellenic. Again, the Frankish and English and Scandinavian and Polish and Magyar converts from a native paganism to Western Catholic Christianity secured the opportunity to play full, and even leading, parts in the building up of Western Christendom. On the other hand the Hyksos worshippers of Set were evicted from the Egyptiac World and the Mongols were evicted from China.

An exception to our rule would seem to be presented by the Primitive Muslim Arabs. Here was a group of barbarians, belonging to the external proletariat of the Hellenic Society, who achieved a high degree of success in the Völkerwanderung which accompanied the dissolution of that society in spite of the fact that they clung to their own barbarian travesty of Syriac religion instead of adopting the Monophysite Christianity of their subjects in the provinces that they wrested from the Roman Empire. But the historic role of the primitive Muslim Arabs was altogether exceptional. Through their incidental conquest of the whole Sassanian Empire

in the course of their victorious assault upon the Oriental provinces of the Roman Empire, the barbarian successor-state of the Roman Empire which the Arabs founded on Syrian soil transformed itself into a restoration of the Syriac universal state which had been prematurely destroyed, a thousand years before, when the Achaemenidae had been overthrown by Alexander; and the vast new political mission with which the Muslim Arabs were thus, almost accidentally, endowed opened up a new horizon for Islam itself.

It would seem, therefore, that the history of Islam is a special case which does not invalidate the general results of our inquiry. In general we are justified in concluding that, for external proletariats and dominant minorities alike, an alien inspiration is a handicap because it is a fruitful source of friction and frustration for them in their dealings with the other two of the fractions into which a disintegrating society splits up.

Internal Proletariats.—In contrast with these findings about dominant minorities and external proletariats we shall find that for internal proletariats an alien inspiration is not a curse but a blessing which confers on those who receive it an apparently superhuman power of taking their conquerors captive and of attaining the end to which they have been born. This thesis can best be tested by an examination of those "higher religions" and universal churches which are the internal proletariat's characteristic works. Our survey of these has shown that their potency depends on the presence, and varies in proportion to the strength, of an alien spark of vitality in their spirit.

For example the worship of Osiris, which was the "higher religion" of the Egyptiac proletariat, can be traced back tentatively, as we have seen, to an alien origin in the Sumeric worship of Tammuz; and the manifold and competing "higher religions" of the Hellenic internal proletariat can all be traced back to various alien origins with certainty. In the worship of Isis the alien spark is Egyptiac; in the worship of Cybele it is Hittite; in Christianity and Mithraism it is Syriac; in the Mahāyāna it is Indic. The first four of these "higher religions" were created by Egyptic, Hittite and Syriac populations which had been conscripted into the Hellenic internal proletariat through Alexander's conquests, and the fifth was created by an Indic population likewise conscripted, in the second century B.C., through the Euthydemic Bactrian Greek princes' conquests in the Indic World. Profoundly though they differ from one another in their inward spiritual essence, all five of them have in common at least this superficial feature of being alien in their origin. Our conclusion will not be shaken by a consideration of certain cases in which an attempt to conquer a society has been made by a higher religion without success. There is, for example, the abortive attempt of the Shī'ah sect of Islam to become the universal church of Orthodox Christendom under the Ottoman régime, and the abortive attempt of Catholic Christianity to become the universal church of the Far Eastern Society—in China during the last century of the Ming and the first century of the Manchu dynasties and in Japan at the moment of transition from the time of troubles to the Tokugawa Shogunate. The Shī'ah in the Ottoman Empire and Catholicism in Japan were both cheated of their prospective spiritual conquests by being exploited —or at any rate suspected of being exploited—for illegitimate political ends. The failure of Catholicism in China was due to the refusal of the Papacy to allow the Jesuit missionaries to carry on their work of translating an alien Catholic religious idiom into the traditional language of Far Eastern philosophy and ritual.

We may conclude that an alien spark is a help and not a hindrance to a "higher religion" in winning converts; and the reason for this is not far to seek. An internal proletariat, alienated from the broken-down society from which it is in process of secession, is seeking a new revelation, and this is what the alien spark supplies; it is its newness which makes it attractive. But, before it can become attractive, the new truth has to be made intelligible; and, until this necessary work of exposition has been performed, the new truth will be inhibited from making its potential appeal. The victory of the Christian Church in the Roman Empire could not have been won if the Fathers of the Church, from St. Paul onwards, had not exerted themselves, during the first four or five centuries of the Christian era, to translate the Christian doctrine into terms of Hellenic philosophy; to build up the Christian ecclesiastical hierarchy on the pattern of the Roman civil service; to mould the Christian ritual on the model of the Mysteries; and even to convert pagan into Christian festivals and replace pagan cults of heroes by Christian cults of saints. It was an undertaking of this kind which was nipped in the bud by the Vatican's instructions to the Jesuit missionaries in China; and the conversion of the Hellenic World would have been as fatally arrested after the first excursions of Christian missionaries on to Gentile ground, if the Judaizing Christian opponents of St. Paul had been victorious in the conferences and conflicts described in The Acts of the Apostles and in the earlier Pauline epistles.

Our muster of "higher religions" which appear to have had an indigenous inspiration will include Judaism and Zoroastrianism and Islam—three religions which have found their field in the Syriac World and have drawn their inspiration from the same quarter—and also Hinduism, which is clearly Indic both in its inspiration and in its field of operations. Hinduism and Islam must be regarded as exceptions to our "law," but Judaism and Zoroastrianism will turn out on examination to be, after all, illustrations of it. For the Syriac populations among which Judaism and Zoroastrianism came to birth, between the eighth and the sixth century before Christ, were broken peoples which had been forcibly conscripted into the internal proletariat of the Babylonic Society by the Assyrian armies of the Babylonic dominant minority. It was this Babylonic aggression that evoked the Jewish and Zoroastrian religious responses from the Syriac souls that were subjected to the ordeal. On this showing we clearly ought to classify Judaism and Zoroastrianism as religions which were introduced by Syriac conscripts into the internal proletariat of the Babylonic Society. Judaism actually took shape "by the waters of Babylon," as the Christian Church took shape in the Pauline congregations in the Hellenic World.

If the disintegration of the Babylonic Civilization had been as long drawn out as that of the Hellenic Civilization and had passed through all the same stages, then the birth and growth of Judaism and Zoroastrianism would present themselves, in historical perspective, as events in a Babylonic story— as the birth and growth of Christianity and Mithraism do, in fact, present themselves as events in Hellenic history. Our perspective has been thrown out by the fact that Babylonic history came to a premature close. The Chaldaean attempt at a Babylonic universal state collapsed; and the Syriac conscripts in its internal proletariat were able not only to throw off their chains but to turn the tables on their Babylonic conquerors by taking them captive in body as well as in spirit. The Iranians became converts to the Syriac and not to the Babylonic culture, and the Achaemenian Empire founded by Cyrus came to play the part of a Syriac universal state. It is in this perspective that Judaism and Zoroastrianism take on their present appearance of being Syriac religions with an indigenous inspiration. We can now see that they were, in their origin, religions of a Babylonic internal proletariat to which their Syriac inspiration was alien.

If a "higher religion" has an alien inspiration— and we have found that this is a rule with only two notable exceptions—then obviously the nature of that religion cannot be understood without taking into account the contact of at least two civilizations: the civilization in whose internal proletariat the new religion arises and the civilization (or civilizations) from which its alien inspiration (or inspirations) is derived. This fact requires us to make a radical new departure; for it requires us to relinquish the basis on which this Study has so far been built up. So far we have been dealing in terms of civilizations; and we have assumed that any single civilization will afford a practicable "field of study" in virtue of being a social whole, intelligible in isolation from whatever social phenomena might present themselves outside the spatial and temporal limits of this particular society. But now we find ourselves entangled in the same net as that in which, in our opening pages, we so confidently entangled those historians who believed that they could "make sense" of an isolated national history. Henceforth we shall have to transcend the limits within which we have hitherto found ourselves able to work.

4. *The Reality of Social Evolution*

BY ROBERT M. MacIVER

Misleading Trails

SKEPTICISM REGARDING SOCIAL EVOLUTION

CAN SOCIETY or its forms properly be said to have passed through evolutionary stages in the sense in which the species of organism have evolved? It has been fashionable in the last decade or two for American anthropologists and sociologists to abandon the concept of social evolution. Some have declared it an advance that sociologists generally speak of social change instead. One school of anthropologists is constantly attacking the doctrine of "unilineal evolution" and tends to disparage the evolutionary method altogether. These tendencies may signify revulsions from oversimple and sweeping formulations of the elementary hypothesis, from the school of Spencer and Ward and Giddings. With increasing knowledge we learn the endless diversities of social systems. Primitive peoples as well as civilized exhibit a myriad of different patterns in their social systems. But it is equally true that there are endless diversities in the species of life, which fact does not prevent the biologist from discovering the evolutionary stages to which they belong. There can be vast differences between societies at the same evolutionary level, and in fact at any of the higher levels there must be—for this itself is part of the significance of evolution—great variations of one from another. If the ambiguous phrase "unilineal evolution," means a sequence in which specific institutions of the simpler societies pass by similar processes into specific institutions of the more advanced societies, then it is certainly to be rejected. But we have no reason to interpret evolution in this way. Differentiation, the emergence of more distinct organs to fulfill more distinct functions, may take a multitude of forms. The system of law differs widely in, say, the United States and in France, but in both countries it has a character which entitles us to call it more evolved than the corresponding system in Melanesia.

One reason for the neglect of the study of social evolution is that social change is, as we have seen, often confused with technological and cultural change and thus, embracing everything that happens to human beings, is regarded as too complex and many-sided to reveal an evolutionary process. Another reason is that the evolutionary principle is often itself misunderstood. Cats do not evolve from dogs, but both dogs and cats are products of evolution. The patriarchal family may not have evolved from the matriarchal family, but both types have undergone evolutionary change. What we mean by social evolution, which has nothing to do with what is called "unilineal" evolution, should be clear from our earlier discussions. But there is one frequent misunderstanding with which we have not dealt and which deserves some attention. It is a mistaken search for the *origins* of things.

THE PROBLEM OF ORIGINS

The question of origins has always been an engrossing one for the human mind, and the mythology of all peoples contains crude answers to it. But the question itself, in most of its forms, belongs to pre-evolutionary thought. People used to ask—and answer—the question, How and when did society begin? That particular question has grown obsolete, and the answers to it, such as that of the "social contract" theory, have been discarded. The seed of society is in the beginnings of life, and if there were such beginnings in any absolute sense we know nothing of them. But we still raise similar questions regarding the family, the state, the church, the law, and other social formations, though the quest for their origins may be as vain as that of the social contractualists. It seems at first sight a reasonable enough question. There was certainly a time when there was not a state or a church, therefore, we argue, they must have had a historical beginning. So we have various theories of origin, that the state, for example, was the result of war and conquest and slavery or of the establishment of a dominant class or even of some convention or constitution on which people all at once agreed. But all these theories are misleading because they misconceive the naure of an evolutionary process. There was a time when there was no state, and yet the state has no beginning in time, no point of origin. This is a paradox but not a contradiction, as it would have seemed to pre-evolutionary thought. We recognize now that even salient or revolutionary social changes need have no absolute moment of origination. When, for example, did the "Industrial Revolution" begin?

WHEN AND HOW DID THE STATE BEGIN?

Let us take one theory of the origin of the state to show how such theories mislead us. Franz Oppenheimer in his book, *The State,* gives the following version of the well-known Marxist doctrine of its origin.[1] There are, he points out, two fundamental and fundamentally opposed means whereby man seeks to supply his needs. One is work, the other robbery, or exploitation of the work of others. The former is the economic, the latter the political means, and the state arose when the political means was organized. There are peoples who possess no vestige of the state, primitive grubbers and huntsmen. They have a social structure but no political structure. The latter originates among herdsmen and among vikings, the first groups to exploit others or rob them of the rewards of their toil. Among these arise class distinctions based on wealth and poverty, on privilege and the denial of privilege. The most decisive of these distinctions is that between the slaveowner and the slave. It was the warrior nomad who invented slavery, the seeding of the state. The grubbing peasant who toils for his own would never have discovered it. When he is subjected to the warrior and pays tribute, the land state begins. Similarly, through coastal raids and robberies the vikings created the maritime state.

Now if Oppenheimer had set out to show the importance of the role played by robbery and exploitation in the early making of the state, it would have been a valid enterprise. It would have involved a study of the relation of this factor to other factors and a close and difficult historical investigation which he avoids only by making certain dogmatic assumptions. It is, in the first place, arbitrary to *define* the political means as robbery, from which it follows all too simply that the state, being the organization of the political means, was established in the manner he describes. On this definition a pirate band would be a state, and not because it is organized but because it is organized to rob. Since the organization of the state certainly serves other ends, since it is concerned to establish some principle of internal justice so that the disputes between man and man are settled by a tribunal and not by violence, since the economic factor is only one of its interests, only one of the ways in which from early times the solidarity of the group was maintained by the state, to identify the political means with exploitation is the simplification of an inadequate psychology. Significant as that motive was, it did not work alone. The authority of the elders over the younger kin was not exploitation, but it played a part in the making of the state. The tribal sense of justice evoked agencies of jurisdiction, and they too were conditions of the emerging state. And many factors contributed to create the kind of political loyalty without which the state could never have grown to maturity.

We are thus thrown back on the question, What does the state, *once it has clearly evolved,* mean? It implies, we may say, a territory over which a unified order is maintained by means of law, involving some kind of coercion of those who violate the order and therefore some kind of authority to which appeal can be made. This is the objective fact, the expression, surely, of more than one aspect of human nature. Now, there seems to be no people among which there are not rudiments of this order, a foreshadowing of the state. There may be no settled government, but there are always some elements of organization out of which such government may evolve. There will be elders, or an individual headman or medicine man who wields some

---

1. English translation, New York, 1926. The exploitation theory is not peculiar to Marxist writers; it is also put forward by authors of quite different schools, such as L. Gumplowicz in his *Soziologische* (2nd ed., Innsbruck, 1902).

sort of authority. This authority will be ostensibly based on age or birth or prowess or religious lore or magical power, but the authority is not wholly without a political aspect. In a small group, say of Andaman Islanders, there is no state as we define the term, but there are already germs of the state organization, custom which prevails by social sanction over a locality, and skilled or aged men who have prestige and win respect and obedience.

EMERGENCE, NOT BEGINNING

We should speak then of the emergence of the state rather than of its origin. It is a structure which in a certain process grows more distinct, more elaborate, more permanent. Its organization becomes distinguished from the organization of kinship. Custom passes into law. The patriarch becomes the political chief, the judge becomes the king. Following this process historically, we can better understand the statement that though there was a time before the state was, the state itself has no beginning in time. Its birth is a logical fact, only its evolution belongs to history. The idea of historical origins is here related to that of specific creation, in the pre-evolutionary sense. There is no state among the Yurok Indians or the Andamanese, yet in some degree these are political beings, just as in some degree they are religious beings, though they have no church.

We pointed out in another context that our application to earlier social stages of terms indicative of later and more evolved conditions is apt to confuse our understanding of this fact. Sometimes a term is sufficiently generic to comprehend the less evolved and the more evolved types of the social form referred under it. The term "family" is an example. But in other instances our modern terms denote specializations which did not exist as such in earlier stages. Of these the term "state" and the related terms "sovereignty," "government," and "law" are examples. The specific forms and functions so denoted are lacking not only in primitive tribes such as the Melanesians and the Eskimos, but also under much more advanced conditions. And even when political institutions are themselves highly evolved, as in classical Greece, it is often doubtful whether we should use our term "state" concerning them. As we shall show presently, specific institutions evolve earlier than specific associations. The people of Athens or of Sparta had themselves no separate term for the state. Their word "polis" did not distinguish the state from the community.

Every community, no matter how primitive, contains germinal elements of the state. We think of

primitive communities, in contrast to modern ones, as based on kinship. But this does not mean that the general bases of community, the common living and the common earth, were absent from their consciousness of solidarity. In some degree they were both present and determinative. R. H. Lowie well brings out the point that in the ostensibly kin-based community locality also served as a social bond.[2] If the sense of contiguity had not also been active, the social cohesion of the kin-group would have been dissipated. It is in part at least because of this sense of contiguity that the tribe exercises jurisdiction over the differences between families within its area, that it adopts strangers into the kin, and so forth. And other bonds, such as that of religion, merged with the bond of kinship. In fact, under the aegis of kinship were half concealed all the grounds of social relationship, including the rudiments of the state.

What we have shown concerning the state, that the search for specific origins is vain, could also be shown concerning the other significant elements of the social structure. We have already seen how unsatisfactory has been the attempt to find an original specific form of the family. And we shall presently see, when studying the emergence of the church, how that process precludes the idea that it had a specific historical beginning. In this context it is permissible to speak of origins only if we mean thereby a process of formation which itself has no *precise starting point*.

WHAT KINDS OF SOCIAL PHENOMENA HAVE DEFINITE BEGINNINGS AND ENDINGS?

But surely, it may be said, some social phenomena have beginnings and endings. Have not many institutions disappeared and others come into being? Is history not strewn with accounts of the passing of organizations, from empires to outworn sects? We answer that we are dealing with social types, not with individual embodiments of the type which, of course, are always appearing and disappearing. But the type itself is a different category, and is revealed only as process. Here again it may be objected that type-forms also disappear at historical moments. Has not slavery passed away or, if it lingers in some parts of the earth, is not its total abolition practicable? Have not totemism and the classificatory system of kinship disappeared in the more advanced societies? If things have an end, have they not also an origin?

Let us take the last two cases first. It is not indeed necessary to our argument that no social types

2. *The Origin of the State*, Chap. IV. Cf. also A. Goldenweiser, *Early Civilization*, Chap. XII.

should vanish altogether. In the same way the doctrine of the continuity of species is not affected by the disappearance of some forms of life. Nor does the argument hold that what ends in a historical moment also begins in a historical moment. For what ends is a specialized form, and it does not begin as such but only grows into specificity. Even so, the social type-forms which we think of as dead are remarkably persistent. Totemism in its full significance **as a** basis of social identification and classification is absent in civilized society while characteristic of a wide range of primitive peoples. But the type-form of totemism is present vestigially among ourselves, as Goldenweiser points out, in the use of animal mascots, the emblems of political parties, badges and crests and other tokens, in such symbols as the flag and the college colors, in such orders as the Elks, the Lions, and so forth.

The names and things that are thus used as classifiers and symbols habitually rest on a background of emotion. In the case of regimental banners, the emotions may reach great violence, while in the instance of animal and bird mascots there arises a complex of attitudes and rites so curiously exotic as to invite an exaggerated analogy with primitive totemism. The fact remains that the supernaturalistic as well as the social tendencies of totemic days live on in modern society. But in our civilization these tendencies, in the absence of a crystallization point, remain in solution, whereas in primitive communities the same tendencies . . . function as a highly distinctive vehicle of culture.[3]

Conversely it may be said that many tendencies which "remain in solution" in primitive society are "crystallized" in our own civilization. Again, the classificatory system which is seemingly so alien to us has its paler analogues among ourselves. We apply the terms "brother" and "sister" to the members of various social orders, and, as Goldenweiser also points out, we even use for classificatory purposes some kinship terms, such as "uncle" and "aunt," which were not so employed in primitive groups.

Finally, let us take the case of slavery, since it illustrates a further distinction. Slavery was abolished from among us at a precise moment of history. It was an ancient institution of mankind. We need not pause to consider whether the surviving use of the term, in such expressions as "wage slave" and "white slave," are significant or fanciful, for certainly the definite type of economic relationship properly called "slavery" has disappeared. What has here happened is that a once socially accepted system has been legally or constitutionally disestablished. Since slavery involved an essentially coercive relationship, it could exist in a complex society only if legally established. Modes of social regulation can be set up and can be discarded. All specific institutions which depend for their existence on convention or prescriptive law have an hour of birth and may have an hour of death. But the great social forms are more deeply rooted. Regulation may modify them, but it neither creates nor destroys them.

Social relationships are subject to an endless process of transformation, of growth and decay, of fusion and separation. Since they are all expressions of human nature, the social relationships of the present are found in germ at least in the past, and those of the past survive, if only as relics, in the present. We distinguish social stages, not by the sheer presence or absence of social factors, but by their prominence, their relation to others, their organizing function.[4] (Even abolished institutions, like slavery, may be present "in solution," ready to "crystallize" again if an opportunity is given.) The most significant social changes are not those which bring an entirely new thing into being, but those which alter the relations of eternal or omnipresent or universal factors. The pattern is always changing but the threads endure. What is new is the emphasis, rather than the factor emphasized. Thus, for example, democracy is not a kind of rule—or a mode of life—wholly apart from oligarchy or dictatorship. The elements of all are present together—the difference is the degree of dominance of one over the other.

Continuity, then, is an essential character of the evolutionary process. Continuity is the union of change and permanence, and when in this union we move in the direction of social differentiation we are following the road of evolution. The general nature of this road will occupy us next.

PRIMITIVE SOCIETY AS FUNCTIONALLY UNDIFFERENTIATED

The functional interdependence of the groups and organizations of an advanced social system is almost totally lacking in primitive society. The main divisions of the latter—families, clans, exogamous groups, totem groups—are segmentary or compartmental. It may have a fairly elaborate system of ceremonial offices, and a more elaborate system of kin-distinctions than is characteristic of an evolved society. But there are few groupings or categories into which, for the practical purposes of co-operative living, the members fall. The kin-

---

3. Goldenweiser, *Early Civilization*, Chap. XIII.

4. We may distinguish technological, as distinct from social, stages by the presence or absence of particular devices or inventions, as F. Müller-Lyer, for example, constantly does in his *History of Social Development* Eng. tr., London, 1923).

grouping is usually predominant and inclusive. To be a member of the kin is *ipso facto* to share the common and inclusive rights and obligations, the customs, the rituals, the standards, the beliefs of the whole. These are, of course, certain "natural" groupings, particularly those of age and sex. There may be prestige groups, perhaps a simple system of classes or castes, though these latter are not found under the most primitive conditions. There may be some rudimentary occupational distinctions, but the division of labor is narrow and usually follows "natural" lines, such as that between the sexes or between the older and the younger. The great associations do not yet exist. There is no seperate organization of religion—still less of religions; there are no schools, no distinct cultural associations; there is little specialization of economic productivity and exchange. The only clearly associational groups, other than temporary partnerships in trading ventures and so forth, are usually "secret societies," not specifically functional, and the very fact that they are "secret" is significant, implying that the group has not yet found a way to incorporate them effectively within its unity.

The undifferentiated character of primitive society is seen in the prevalence of a simple form of communism. The kin is a larger family and exhibits something of the communistic character of the family. The tribe devises a system of participation in the booty of the chase and the products of the earth. Where private or family rights are admitted, it is in the usufruct, not in the ownership, of the land. Even what are to us the most intimate or personal of rights were then rights pertaining to the blood brotherhood. The lending of wives to tribal guests, common to American Indians and many tribes of Africa, Polynesia, and Asia, may be regarded as a mode of admission to the "freedom" of the tribe. It may be, as Julius Lippert interprets it, that thus "the guest enters into all the rights of the tribal members, and the special sanctity of the relationship revives the ancient rights of the latter."[5] The sanctioned license at primitive marriage feasts, the institution among some African peoples of the "bride-hut" where the bride was free to the men of the tribe, the premarriage prostitution established as a Babylonian temple rite, may be interpreted as survivals of sexual communism or at least as the assertion, before their alienation through marriage, of rights regarded as belonging intrinsically to the tribe.

Such a communism typifies the simple solidarity of an undifferentiated community. Such differentiations as exist are based on the natural distinctions

---

5. *Evolution of Culture* (tr. Murdock, New York, 1931), p. 217.

of youth and age, of man and woman, of different aptitudes such as that for leadership, and on a few socially acquired distinctions, such as the inheritance of ceremonial office or of magical lore. The myriad aspects of differentiation belonging to a civilized society are latent. The divergent interests, aptitudes, capacities which may appear in rudimentary forms have no opportunity to develop within the restricted range of the communal life. The social heritage is too rude to afford them selective stimulation. The mores appropriate to that narrow heritage tend to be repressive of such differences, as endangering the solidarity of like-mindedness, the only solidarity of which the group as a whole is yet capable.

The civilizations of the past and of the present emerged from that early stage. How they emerged, through what blind forces of conquest and subjection and expansion, creating differences of wealth and of class, through what nurture of the arts, through what clashes of customs and faiths leading to some liberation of the mind, through what increments of scientific knowledge and its application, is the main theme of human history. For us here it is enough to point the contrast. It is characteristic of our own stage that we have a vast multiplicity of organizations of such a nature that to belong to one has no implication of belonging to the rest, that every kind of interest has created its correspondent association, that nearly every kind of attitude can find some social corroboration, and that thus the greater social unity to which we belong is conceived of as multiform, not uniform. This is the necessary intellectual feat demanded of the participants in the "great society," and the many who still cannot achieve it belong to it in form but not in spirit.

THE ROLE OF DIFFUSION IN SOCIAL EVOLUTION

Long and difficult as the evolutionary process may seem in historical perspective, it has been remarkably rapid if we take the larger perspective of organic evolution. We have already commented on the relative rapidity of social change; we may now add that social evolution has likewise moved at a pace vastly quicker than that of evolution in the biological order. No primitive type of animal evolves into an advanced type in so short a period as that comprised by recorded human history—the very idea seems absurd. But in that period one primitive society after another has moved to a stage that at least by comparison reveals a highly evolved structure. Social evolution is liberated in a sense from organic evolution because human beings can use for their purposes instruments that are not part of their own physical structure and because in using them they are in a measure guided by intelligence and not merely by instinct. Thus equipped, they can rapidly increase their social heritage and transmit its evolutionary potentialities to their descendents and communicate them to others over the whole face of the earth.

Sometimes diffusion and evolution are regarded as opposing principles in the interpretation of social change. But in truth there is no need for this opposition. Diffusion should be regarded as one of the most important factors in social evolution. The great societies of the past all reveal, in so far as records remain, the formative and challenging influence of cultural intercourse. The civilization that arose on the Nile penetrated as far as India. The thought-systems of India reached into China and later contributed elements to the awakening civilizations of the West. The Greeks built on the heritage of Mycenae, Crete, and Egypt. Rome from its earliest days began to feel the impact of the cultural forces already full-grown in Greece. And so it has been down to our own days.

ANTI-EVOLUTIONARY INFLUENCES

Needless to say, the establishment of this present stage of differentiation was the task of many centuries, and pressures emanating from the older conception of solidarity have been strongly directed against it and are still in some measure operative. In the making of modern society it has usually been the state—though sometimes the church—which has sought to prevent further differentiation by making all other organizations a part of its own structure and subject to the conformity it imposed. Hobbes in the seventeenth century had denounced free associations as being like "worms in the entrails of the natural man," and as late as the end of the eighteenth the French Revolution had sought in the name of liberty to abolish all corporate bodies. Rousseau no less than Burke, the philosopher of revolution as much as the philosopher of reaction—so slowly do our minds perceive the growing social fact—could still not admit the separate organization of state and church, still believed in the "universal partnership" or the "total surrender" which made the membership of a society culturally inclusive. Even today partial attempts are made to re-establish great societies on the basis of the simpler solidarity, as seen in some of the manifestations of both the fascist and the communist principles and still more in the policies of national socialist Germany. But whatever the claims of these opposing principles—and again it should be clear that we are speaking of social evolution and not of social progress—it is significant that the attempts in question have succeeded only in countries which had experienced to a lesser extent or for a shorter period the diversifying conditions of modern industrialism, the cultural variations revealed in divergent faiths, and the conflict over the issue of free association; that they have succeeded only by establishing a coercive control suppressive of the differentiations which would otherwise arise; and that they have occurred as the sudden sequel of catastrophic and abnormal events, not in the more orderly course of social change.

THE MAIN LINE OF SOCIAL EVOLUTION

We cannot attempt to trace the historical process by which these various grades of differentiation have come about, but if we turn to our primitive societies we can see the generic lines which that process follows. Since the social structure exists only as the creation of mentality, behind the differentiated form lies always the differentiating mind. Before institutions come attitudes and interests. As these grow distinct they become reflected in customs which assume a more and more institutional character. The continuum of social thought is interrupted by the spur of special interests which experience and circumstance detach from the undifferentiated sense of solidarity. There is thus a constant deflection of the social being from the uniformity of the social path, to be ignored, winked at, or suppressed by the guardians of the tribal ways. But if the deflection occurs repeatedly and in the same direction, aided by changing circumstance or opportunity, it may gain recognition, creating a zone of indifference within the older institution or establishing a new one beside it. Thus the ways of the group are diversified without loss of unity. Moreover, by slow accretion lores and skills are increased and particular members of the group become their repositories and acknowledged practitioners. Specific modes of procedure, specific taboos, specific approaches to the mysterious powers of nature or to the *sacra* of the tribe, are thus developed—in other words, new institutions are formed.

The formation of institutions usually precedes, and often by a very long interval, the formation of associations. In fact, in relatively primitive societies the step from institutions to associations is seldom taken at all. For the associational phase implies an elasticity of the social structure which primitive conditions and primitive mentality can hardly admit; it implies the more difficult unity which difference combines with likeness to create. Social evolution must be already well advanced, the scale of society expanded and the pressure of the common mores lightened, the diversification of interests enlarged through the advance of knowledge and the specialization of the economic life, before the right of free association becomes effective. Only under these conditions does the family detach itself sufficiently from the social matrix to become an autonomous unit, dependent for its creation and for its maintenance on the will of the consenting parties. Only under these conditions does the uniformity of communal education break into the variety of particular schools, and other educational associations. And finally the great politico-religious system which claimed to control all the rest reveals the internal disharmonies of its enforced unity, and in their different ways the associations of the state and of the church are formed.

Schematically this process may be presented as follows:

I. Communal Customs
   The fusion of political-economic-familial-religious-cultural usages, which pass into
II. Differentiated Communal Institutions
   The distinctive forms of political, economic, familial, religious, cultural procedures, which become embodied in
III. Differentiated Associations
   The state, the economic corporation, the family, the church, the school, etc.

The passage from the second to the third of these stages means a momentous transformation of the social structure. There may, of course, be some minor incidental associations under primitive social conditions, but the great permanent forms of association, as we define that term, are as yet unthinkable. Primitive solidarity requires that if you belong to the tribe you belong also to—or are adopted into—the kin, that if you share its life you share also its gods. The diversity of institutions, as they unfold themselves, is at first only the diversity of the aspects of communal life. In that growing diversity is hidden the germ of a new order, but it takes ages to develop. For the new order means a new freer diversity. In our second stage there is one set of political institutions for the whole community. In our third stage there is still one state, but there are also political organizations embodying diverse ideas concerning the state. In our second stage there is one set of religious institutions recognized by the community, and these are bound up with its political institutions. In our third stage not only have they become detached from the state, culturally autonomous, but they have in consequence created a variety of religious associations. This freedom of association admits an indefinite multiplicity of contingent forms, with endless pos-

sibilities of interrelationship and independence, based on the general foundations of a community life, the obligatory aspects of which are now safeguarded by the state.

The differentiation of the great associations from one another is accompanied by vast differentiations within their respective structures, responsive to the same forces which bring about the former. To deal in any detail with this whole process would occupy a large volume in itself. All we can do in the present work is to offer, in rather brief compass, a single illustration of it, so as to bring out more clearly the main principle. For this purpose we shall examine the process by which the organization of religion has evolved.

HOW THE EVOLUTIONARY CLUE HELPS US
TO UNDERSTAND SOCIETY

Before we turn to this illustration, it may be well to point out the way in which the evolutionary clue helps us to understand society. While there are many social changes which may seem as undirected and inconsequential as the waves of the sea, there are others which clearly fall within an evolutionary process. And in tracing these the student gets a firmer grip on the social reality and learns that there are great persistent forces underlying many movements which at first he apprehends as mere events in the historical flux. More particularly, the evolutionary clue, where it can be traced, has the following advantages.

In the first place, we see the nature of a system better as it "unfolds" itself. Evolution is a principle of internal growth. It shows us not merely what happens to a thing, but what happens within it. Since in the process latent characters or attributes emerge, we may say that the very nature of the system emerges, that, in Aristotelian phrase, it becomes more fully itself. Suppose, for example, that we are seeking to understand the nature of custom or morality, things we are still very apt to confuse. We understand each the better by seeing how the two, fully merged in primitive society, have grown distinct as the range of conduct over which custom rules has diminished. And so with many another distinction, such as that between religion and magic, or crime and sin, or justice and equity, or right and privilege, or economic and political power.

Again, the evolutionary clue enables us to set a multitude of facts in significant order, giving them the coherence of successive stages instead of tying them on the purely external thread of chronology. For the historical record presents us with a confusing multitude of events, a mere chaos of change until we find some principle of selection. Inevitably we seek to discover the type or type-situation which these events indicate in a particular frame of time and space, and then to relate that type to earlier and later ones. The latter aim is realized if we discover an evolutionary character in the series of changes. Take, for example, the endless changes of the family. In studying them we discover that within a certain area of modern history the functions of the family have become more limited to those essentially arising out of its foundations in sex; in short, a significant time-succession is revealed. Just as biological science achieved order by following the evolutionary clue, so here at least does social science. And the evolutionary principle, where discernible, is of far-reaching significance because it relates whole successive situations, no matter what their magnitude, to one another and consequently has proved serviceable in every field of science. So universal a clue must lead us nearer to the very nature of reality than any more partial one. It is surely a primary order of change that is revealed alike in the history of Rome and of Japan and of America, alike in the record of the snake and of the bird, of the horse and of man, alike in the brief story of each organic being and in the inconceivably immense record of the cosmos itself.

Again, the evolutionary principle provides us with a simple means of classifying and characterizing the most diverse social systems. If we tried to classify all societies on the basis of the kind of customs they followed or creeds the accepted, or of their diverse ways of making pottery or pictures or the like, our classifications would be elaborate, cumbrous, difficult, and limited. When, on the other hand, we classify them according to the degree and mode of differentiation shown by their customs and creeds and techniques, we are taking as our basis a structural character applicable to society as such, and one with which the endlessly variant manifesta-

tions of customs and creeds are integrally bound.

Finally, the evolutionary clue spurs us to the quest of causes. Where we discover direction in change we know that there are persistent forces cumulatively at work. Some of these are indeed sufficiently obvious. We can trace, for example, the differentiation of the professions, and it is easy to see how the principle of efficiency or economy—which is one form of the expression of intelligence—would, given the conditions for its exercise, such as greater economic resources, a wider market, and better technological equipment, lead to this result. As early as the days of Hesiod it was said of a man that "he had skill in many things, but little skill in any." In its degree this is true of every nonspecialist. The following quotation from an American historian illustrates the condition out of which the differentiated professions arose:

In the Boston *Gazette,* February 6, 1738, Peter Pelham advertised that he taught "Dancing, Writing, Reading, painting upon Glass, and all kinds of needle work"; he was a painter, an engraver and also gave instruction on the harpsichord and in the elements of psalmody. . . . Really, that society of 1738 did not have sufficient occasion for him in all these varied forms of competence to keep him alive and he had to piece out as a merchant of tobacco. Eventually there would be engravers, dancing masters, painters, musicians, various teachers of elementary subjects including manual training, who could track back the converging lines of their respective developments to such an unforked stem of their general branch.[6]

This particular development is readily explained but the broader trends of social evolution, like those of organic evolution, raise profoundly interesting and difficult questions of causation.

6. From an article by Dixon Ryan Fox, "A Synthetic Principle in American Social History," *The American Historical Review,* Vol. 35 (1930), 256–266.

5. *Diffusion*

BY RALPH LINTON

WE HAVE SEEN in the previous chapter how the particular culture within which any inventor works directs and circumscribes his efforts

Reprinted from Ralph Linton, *The Study of Man: An Introduction* (New York: Appleton-Century-Crofts, 1936), pp. 324–46, with the permission of Appleton-Century-Crofts.

and determines whether his inventions will be socially accepted. Because of this the number of successful inventions originating within the confines of any one linked society and culture is always small. If every human group had been left to climb upward by its own unaided efforts, progress would have been so slow that it is doubtful whether any society by now would have advanced beyond the level of the Old Stone Age. The comparatively rapid growth of human culture as a whole has been due to the ability of all societies to borrow elements from other cultures and to incorporate them in their own. This transfer of culture elements from one society to another is known as *diffusion*. It is a process by which mankind has been able to pool its inventive ability. By diffusion an invention which has been made and socially accepted at one point can be transmitted to an ever-widening group of cultures until, in the course of centuries, it may spread to practically the whole of mankind.

Diffusion has made a double contribution to the advance of mankind. It has stimulated the growth of culture as a whole and at the same time has enriched the content of individual cultures, bringing the societies which bore them forward and upward. It has helped to accelerate the evolution of culture as a whole by removing the necessity of every society to perfect every step in an inventive series for itself. Thus a basic invention which has been made at one point will ultimately be brought to the attention of a great number of inventors and its potentialities for use and improvement thoroughly explored. As more minds are put to work upon each problem the process of culture advance is accelerated. The rapidity of progress during the past century is certainly due in large part to the development of means for easy and rapid communication plus techniques for ensuring to the inventor the economic rewards of his labors. Patents have made secrecy unnecessary. They impose a temporary tax upon the use of inventions but make the idea available to all. Any invention which is made at the present time is promptly diffused over a wide area and becomes part of the store of knowledge available to hundreds of inventors. Prior to the development of the present conditions it took centuries for any new element of culture to diffuse over the same territory to which it is now extended in a few months or years.

The slow cultural advance of societies which are left to their own abilities is well illustrated by the conditions in isolated human groups. Perhaps the outstanding example is the Tasmanians. These people were cut off from the rest of mankind at least 20,000 years ago. When they reached their island they seem to have had a culture which, in its material development at least, corresponds roughly to that of Europe during the Middle Paleolithic. They were still in this stage when Europeans first visited them during the eighteenth century. During the long period of isolation they had no doubt made some minor advances and improvements, but their lack of outside contacts was reflected in a tremendous culture lag. To cite a much less extreme example, the culture of some of our own isolated mountain communities still corresponds in many respects to that of the pioneers of a century ago. The first settlers of these isolated regions brought this culture with them, and their unaided efforts have contributed little to it. In general, the more opportunities for borrowing any society has the more rapid its cultural advance will be.

The service of diffusion in enriching the content of individual cultures has been of the utmost importance. There is probably no culture extant today which owes more than 10 per cent of its total elements to inventions made by members of its own society. Because we live in a period of rapid invention we are apt to think of our own culture as largely self-created, but the rôle which diffusion has played in its growth may be brought home to us if we consider the beginning of the average man's day. The locations listed in the following paragraphs refer only to the origin points of various culture elements, not to regions from which we now obtain materials or objects through trade.

Our solid American citizen awakes in a bed built on a pattern which originated in the Near East but which was modified in Northern Europe before it was transmitted to America. He throws back covers made from cotton, domesticated in India, or linen, domesticated in the Near East, or wool from sheep, also domesticated in the Near East, or silk, the use of which was discovered in China. All of these materials have been spun and woven by processes invented in the Near East. He slips into his moccasins, invented by the Indians of the Eastern woodlands, and goes to the bathroom, whose fixtures are a mixture of European and American inventions, both of recent date. He takes off his pajamas, a garment invented in India, and washes with soap invented by the ancient Gauls. He then shaves, a masochistic rite which seems to have been derived from either Sumer or ancient Egypt.

Returning to the bedroom, he removes his clothes from a chair of southern European type and proceeds to dress. He puts on garments whose form originally derived from the skin clothing of the nomads of the Asiatic steppes, puts on his shoes made from skins tanned by a process invented in ancient Egypt and cut to a pattern derived from the classical civilizations of the Mediterranean, and ties around his neck a strip of bright-colored cloth which is a vestigial survival of the shoulder shawls worn by the seventeenth-century Croatians. Before going out for breakfast he glances through the window, made of glass invented in Egypt, and if it is raining puts on overshoes made of rubber discovered by the Central American Indians and takes an umbrella, invented in southeastern Asia. Upon his head he puts a hat made of felt, a material invented in the Asiatic steppes.

On his way to breakfast he stops to buy a paper, paying for it with coins, an ancient Lydian invention. At the restaurant a whole new series of borrowed elements confronts him. His plate is made of a form of pottery invented in China. His knife is of steel, an alloy first made in southern India, his fork a medieval Italian invention, and his spoon a derivative of a Roman origin. He begins breakfast with an orange, from the eastern Mediterranean, a cantaloupe from Persia, or perhaps a piece of African watermelon. With this he has coffee, an Abyssinian plant, with cream and sugar. Both the domestication of cows and the idea of milking them originated in the Near East, while sugar was first made in India. After his fruit and first coffee he goes on to waffles, cakes made by a Scandinavian technique from wheat domesticated in Asia Minor. Over these he pours maple syrup, invented by the Indians of the Eastern woodlands. As a side dish he may have the egg of a species of bird domesticated in Indo-China, or thin strips of the flesh of an animal domesticated in Eastern Asia which have been salted and smoked by a process developed in northern Europe.

When our friend has finished eating he settles back to smoke, an American Indian habit, consuming a plant domesticated in Brazil in either a pipe, derived from the Indians of Virginia, or a cigarette, derived from Mexico. If he is hardy enough he may even attempt a cigar, transmitted to us from the Antilles by way of Spain. While smoking he reads the news of the day, imprinted in characters invented by the ancient Semites upon a material invented in China by a process invented in Germany. As he absorbs the accounts of foreign troubles he will, if he is a good conservative citizen, thank a Hebrew deity in an Indo-European language that he is 100 per cent American.

The foregoing is merely a bit of antiquarian virtuosity made possible by the existence of unusually complete historic records for the Eurasiatic area. There are many other regions for which no such records exist, yet the cultures in these areas bear similar witness to the importance of diffusion in establishing their content. Fairly adequate techniques have been developed for tracing the spread of individual traits and even for establishing their origin points, and there can be no doubt that diffusion has occurred wherever two societies and cultures have been brought into contact.

In view of the tremendous importance of this mechanism for the enrichment of culture, it is rather surprising that so little is still known about the actual dynamics of the diffusion process. Most of the students who have been interested in this field have considered the study of diffusion little more than a preliminary to historic reconstruction. They have spent much time and effort in tracing the distribution of culture elements, but have been content with the formulation of two or three basic principles of diffusion which were immediately applicable to their historic studies. Such studies are by no means the mere satisfactions of idle curiosity which some of their opponents would have them to be. The content of a culture at any point in its history can only be explained in terms of its past, and any light which can be thrown upon that past contributes to our understanding of the present. Even the study of the functions of the various elements within a culture becomes largely meaningless unless we can determine the factors to which these elements owe their form and consequently their potentialities for function. This matter will be discussed at length in a later chapter. For the present we need only point out that the more exact our knowledge of the dynamics of the diffusion process the greater will be the possibility of making valid historic reconstructions from trait distributions.

A real understanding of the dynamics of diffusion can be arrived at only by observing the process in actual operation. A thorough study of the current spread of any new culture element, the factors responsible for this spread, the reactions which the new element has evoked in different societies, and the adaptations which the acceptance of the new trait into various cultures has entailed would do more to put diffusion studies on a sound basis than twenty studies of trait distributions at a given point in time. Unfortunately there is hardly a single study of this sort extant. In the discussion which follows we must, therefore, raise far more questions than we can answer. Nevertheless, there are a few generally recognized principles of diffusion, and we may begin our investigation with these.

The first of these is that, *other things being equal, elements of culture will be taken up first by societies which are close to their points of origin and later by societies which are more remote or which have less direct contacts*. This principle derives from the fact that the diffusion of any element obviously requires both contact and time. It is impossible for any trait to spread to a culture unless there is contact with some other culture which already has it. Thus if we have three tribes, A, B, and C, with the territory of B intervening between that of A and C and preventing any direct contact between them, no new culture trait which A may develop can reach C until after it has been accepted by B. From this it also follows that the trait will be received later by C than by B.

There is abundant historic evidence of the general validity of this principle. Thus the alphabet, which seems to have been invented in the general region of the Sinai peninsula, was taken up first by the Semitic groups which immediately adjoined this area and transmitted by them to the Phoenicians. These carried it by sea to the Greeks and Romans, from whom it was diffused into northern Europe. It did not appear in Scandinavia until about 2,000 years after its invention and reached this region by way of a series of intermediary cultures each of which had had certain effects on the alphabet's development.

From this principle of the diffusion of traits to more and more remote localities a second principle emerges, that of *marginal survivals*. Let us suppose that a new appliance has been developed by a particular society and is spreading to the neighboring societies in an ever-widening circle. At the same time it may very well be undergoing changes and improvements at its point of origin. These improvements will, in turn, be diffused to the neighboring societies, but since this diffusion will begin at a later point in time, the improved appliance will have a tendency to lag behind the original one in its spread. Long after the new appliance has completely supplanted the ancestral one at its point of origin, the ancestral one will continue in use about the margins of the diffusion area. This principle may be illustrated by the present distribution of telephone types in the United States. The earliest telephones had cranks for calling central. At the present time the crank telephone is still used in the more remote rural districts but has completely disappeared in the cities. The desk type of telephone, with automatic call, is used over an intermediate zone, while the hand telephone, first used in New York in 1927, is still largely confined to city use. Lastly, dial telephones are making rapid headway in the larger cities, but are only beginning to spread to the smaller ones and have not reached any rural districts. The example may not be considered a perfect one, since the diffusion of the telephone has obviously been influenced by such atypical factors as the monopoly of telephone service and desire of the company to use old equipment already in existence, but it does serve to illustrate the principle.

The simile most commonly applied to the diffusion process is that of the ripples sent out by dropping a stone into still water. The last ripples will still be moving outward when the center has once more become quiet. While such a constant and uniform spread of traits from a single center in order of their development may be used as a hypothetical case to illustrate the principle, actual historic records show that it never occurs in fact. Even traits which originate in the same center spread irregularly and travel at different speads. A few examples will make this clear.

Everything indicates that the cultivation of maize in America was a culture trait which originated in Mexico. From there it spread widely over the Mississippi Valley and eastern United States and also took firm root in the Southwest. While in the East it reached New England, the Dakotas and the peninsula of Michigan, in the West it barely penetrated southern California. This in spite of the fact that this region was in fairly close touch with the Southwest, where maize culture was highly developed and where there were adequate techniques for growing the crop under semi-arid conditions. Again, the California Indians, outside a small area in the south, failed to take over pottery although they were close to an area of high pottery development and although the rather sedentary life of most California tribes would have given it great utility. Our present fairly accurate knowledge of Southwestern time sequences proves that tribes on the margin of the California area must have been exposed to both maize and pottery for at least 1,500 years, yet they failed to accept either.

Such reluctance to accept new elements of culture slows down their rate of speed even when it does not completely inhibit their diffusion in certain directions. A group which is reluctant to take over a new trait interposes a bar between the origin point of that trait and more remote groups which might be quite willing to accept it if given the opportunity. Even if the reluctance of the intermediary culture is finally broken down, much time will have been lost. Because of this varying coefficient of receptivity, traits always spread from their origin points irregularly and certain traits may be diffused with amazing speed while others diffuse slowly, if at all. One of the most striking examples of extremely rapid diffusion is that afforded by the spread of certain New World food crops, especially maize, during the first 300 years following Columbus's discovery. By the end of this period these crops had penetrated practically all areas of Europe, Asia, and Africa in which they could be raised and in many places had profoundly altered the patterns of native life. Thus the Betsimisaraka of Madagascar, who could scarcely have received maize before 1600, have a myth that it was given to them by the Creator at the same time that he gave rice to the Plateau tribes of the island. They meet any suggestion that it might be a fairly recent introduction by the simple statement that it cannot be, since the people could not live without it.

The spread of tobacco after the discovery of the New World is a still more striking example of rapid diffusion and has the advantage of being well documented. For once, popular traditions seem to be correct in their ascription of the introduction of smoking into England to Sir Walter Raleigh. At least the first mention of it there is in connection with the return of his Virginia colonists, and we know that Ralph Lane, the first governor, presented Raleigh with an Indian pipe in 1586 and instructed him in its use. This launched the custom of smoking in court circles, and from there it spread to the common people with amazing speed. It should be noticed that tobacco had also been introduced into Spain by Francisco Fernandez in 1558, but it came in the guise of a medicine and there was considerable delay in its acceptance for purely social purposes.

These two points of introduction became, in turn, centers for the diffusion of tobacco over the Old World. England was the main donor to northern Europe. Smoking was introduced into Holland in 1590 by English medical students, and the English and Dutch together spread the new habit by sea into the Baltic countries and Scandinavia and overland through Germany into Russia. By 1634, forty-eight years after its first appearance in northern Europe, it had become a nuisance in Russia and laws were enacted against it. Nevertheless its spread eastward continued unchecked, and within 200 years it had crossed the steppes and mountains of Siberia and was reintroduced into America at Alaska. This rapid diffusion is the more remarkable since in much of this northern region the plant had to be obtained by trade over great distances.

From Spain and Portugal tobacco was diffused throughout the Mediterranean countries and into the near East. The dates here are less certain, but Sultan Murad of Turkey passed laws against its use in 1605. The Dutch and Portuguese together carried it to Africa and southeastern Asia. In far-off Japan it was accepted so quickly that by 1605 it was found necessary to limit the amount of ground which could be devoted to its cultivation. In South Africa tobacco became the regular medium of exchange between the Dutch and the natives, a cow being valued at its over-all length in tobacco leaves. In spite of frequent official opposition and drastic laws, the new element of culture spread almost as fast as men could travel.

It has been observed that while elements of culture may be diffused alone they are more likely to travel in groups of elements which are functionally related. This point is also illustrated by the spread of tobacco, since with the plant there were diffused various methods of using it. The linking of these

methods with the various lines of diffusion can be traced back even to the New World. The Indians used tobacco in different ways in different regions. Those of the eastern coast of North America smoked it in elbow pipes, which became the prototypes of the modern English briars. Although this form of pipe underwent various modifications along the northern route of diffusion, all the people who derived their tobacco habit by way of England have remained predominant pipe-smokers. The Indians of Brazil, with whom the Portuguese had most contact, preferred cigars, as did some of the Antillean groups. The Mexicans, on the other hand, preferred the cigarette and gave it to the Spaniards. From them it passed to the other Mediterranean cultures, a fact reflected in our own preference for Turkish and Egyptian cigarettes. Since the Portugese and Dutch acted simultaneously in the diffusion of tobacco to southeastern Asia, that region received both the pipe and the cigar, and the two still exist side by side there in many localities. Some tribes even preserve complete neutrality by rolling their tobacco into cigars and then smoking these in pipes. In Africa, where the Dutch won in the struggle against the Portuguese, the pipe became the regular appliance.

In the course of its diffusion tobacco even developed two new methods of use, the water-pipe and snuff. The water-pipe originated in the Near East and never diffused far beyond that region. Snuff seems to have originated in Spain and grew out of the medicinal application of tobacco. It had no prototype in America. Some of the Antillean and South American tribes did use snuff, but it was not made from tobacco. On the other hand snuffs of one sort or another had been used in Europe for centuries. Apparently this was a result of a mistaken attempt to reach the brain through the nasal passages. The first tobacco sent from Portugal to France was in the form of snuff, and the habit to taking tobacco in this way became established at the French court and spread from there to the whole of European polite society. In fact, it seems for a time to have threatened the existence of smoking in higher social circles. Toward the close of the eighteenth century the high tide of snuff began to recede, and it now survives only in marginal areas and even there is at a social disadvantage.

The last chapter in the diffusion of methods of smoking is curious enough to deserve special mention. The cigarette, in spite of its general acceptance in the Mediterranean area, did not spread to northern Europe or the United States until very recent times. It was not introduced into England until after the close of the Crimean War, when the custom of cigarette smoking was brought back by officers who had learned it from their Turkish allies. It reached the United States still later, within the memory of many persons now alive, and there encountered vigorous opposition. Although there seems to be no proof that the cigarette is any more harmful than the virile corn-cob or the chewing tobacco which was the American pioneer's special contribution to the tobacco complex, laws against its use are still to be found on many statute books. It was considered not only harmful but also effeminate, and traces of the latter attitude survive even to-day. He-men who enjoy their cigarette can console themselves with the knowledge that many a "hard-boiled" Aztec priest must have indulged in one before beginning his "daily dozen" of human sacrifices.

It should be plain from the foregoing that no simple mechanistic interpretation of diffusion will prove adequate to the needs of even the rather limited field of historic reconstruction. Diffusion required not only a donor but also a receiver, and the rôle of this receiver is certainly the more important. As we have seen in the case of the California Indians with regard to maize and pottery, exposure to a culture trait is not necessarily followed by acceptance. Diffusion really includes three fairly distinct processes: presentation of the new culture element or elements to the society, acceptance by the society, and the integration of the accepted element or elements into the preëxisting culture. Each of these is influenced by a large number of variable factors most of which still require study.

The presentation of new elements to a society always presupposes contact. The society with which this contact is established may, of course, be either the originator of the new culture element or simply an intermediary in its spread. This factor can have little influence on the process. However, the nature of the contact is of tremendous importance. Such contacts vary from those in which two societies and cultures are brought into a close relationship as wholes to sporadic trade contacts of those in which a single individual from one society settles in another society. Complete contacts are decidedly rare. It is difficult to find examples of them except in the case of conquering groups who settle among and exploit the conquered or in that of immigrant groups such as we still have in many parts of America. Such contacts have a somewhat different quality from those involved in the ordinary diffusion process, and the process of culture change under these conditions is usually termed *acculturation*. Apparently the use of this term, which was first applied to the study of changes in immigrant groups, is based on the rather naïve belief that one of the societies thus brought into contact completely abandons its former culture and completely accepts that of the others. Actually such close and complete contacts always result in an exchange of culture elements. In the long run both the originally diverse societies and their cultures will fuse to form a new society and culture. In this final product elements from both will be represented, although they may be represented in widely varying proportions. Thus the Italians in America usually lose their identity as a distinct society by the third or fourth generation and accept the culture in which they then find themselves. At the same time this culture is not the same which their ancestors encountered on arrival. It has been enriched by the American acceptance of such originally Italian elements as a popular interest in grand opera, spaghetti dinners, and superior techniques for racketeering.

Taking the world as a whole, the type of contact which makes acculturation possible is more likely to arise through conquest and the settlement of the conquering groups among the vanquished than through anything else. In such cases the normal numerical superiority of the conquered is likely to be balanced to a considerable extent by the superior prestige of the conquerors, so that the two cultures stand on fairly equal terms in their contribution to the new culture which always arises under such conditions. Such hybrid cultures usually present the aspects of a chemical rather than a mechanical mixture. In addition to traits drawn from both the parent cultures they possess qualities foreign to both. However, we must return to the more normal forms of culture contact and the dissemination of culture elements which these make possible.

It goes without saying that contacts between cultures can only be established through the medium of individuals. We have pointed out in a previous chapter that no individual participates completely in the culture of his own society. This means that under ordinary conditions the full culture of the donor society is never offered to the receiving society. The only elements made available to them are those with which the contact individuals are familiar. Thus if a trade relation exists between two tribes, the trade being carried on by men, the product of the women's industries in one tribe may become familiar to the other tribe, but the techniques will not be transmitted with it. The men who do the trading, even if they do not guard these techniques as valuable commercial secrets, will have only a vague idea of how the things are made. If the receiving tribe becomes accustomed to the use of this product and then finds the supply suddenly cut off, it may develop quite different techniques for the manufacture of equivalent articles. It is interesting to conjecture whether the extreme diversity of techniques of pottery manufacture in the

Melanesian region may not have arisen in this way. There are many tribes here who regularly use pottery without manufacturing it, and it is easy to imagine the members of such a group working out a method of making the familiar and necessary pots if their normal source was removed.

The differential which is introduced into diffusion by this varying participation of individuals in their own culture is just as strongly operative when the contact-individuals from the donor group settle among the receiving group. The trader, missionary, or government official can transmit no more of his culture than he himself knows. If the contact-individual is a male, he usually can transmit very little from the female half of his own culture, and the female elements which he can transmit are likely to be heterogeneous and to bear little functional relation to each other. I knew a French official who was the envy of all his colleagues because he had been able to teach his native mistress how to starch and iron his white shirts. His knowledge of this technique had been acquired by accident, and he knew no more about other aspects of housekeeping than the average male. Conversely, if the contact-individual is a female she can transmit female techniques but is most unlikely to pass on such purely masculine items as a new form of metalworking or a new war magic. It is easy to imagine situations in which, due to this contact differential, many elements from certain sections of a culture will have been presented and even accepted while few or none have been presented from other sections. Thus the natives on an island which has been a regular port of call for whaling vessels may have absorbed a good many of the cultural elements connected with the industry and even a fair number of the habits and attitudes of whalemen. They may learn to build whaleboats and dress in European garments gotten from the whalers, while they still have no idea that drawing-rooms exist, still less of the behavior appropriate to them. To cite a less extreme case, a native group might have had close contact with half a dozen missionaries and their wives without receiving any inkling of the evolutionary theories which now influence so much of European thought or of modern European trends in dress and interior decoration.

When two societies are in long-continued contact, as in the case of two tribes who live side by side and are generally on friendly terms, sooner or later the entire culture of each will be made available to the other. The long series of contacts with individuals, each of whom is a partial participant, will have a cumulative effect. When, on the other hand, the contacts of one society are exclusively with selected groups of individuals from the other society, the receiving group may never be exposed to the totality of the donor group's culture. This situation holds true to a very large extent for regions to which whites come as traders or administrators, but never as artisans or laborers.

A second factor which exercises a strong influence upon diffusion is what, for lack of a better term, may be called the inherent communicability of the culture elements themselves. This has nothing to do with the attitudes of the receiving group or with its preëxisting culture configurations. Although this aspect of the diffusion problem has never been studied, it seems probable that we are dealing here with something which is fairly constant. In a previous chapter we have pointed out that culture is itself a socio-psychological phenomenon and that the various forms of behavior which we are able to observe and record are simply its overt expressions. Certain elements of culture can be much more readily expressed than others, whether this expression takes the form of ordinary acts or verbalizations. Since it is only through the observation of these overt expressions that culture elements can be transmitted from one individual to another or from one society to another, it follows that those cultural elements which can be most readily and completely expressed will be those which are the most readily available for acceptance. Among the varied elements which go to make up the totality of a culture, the techniques for food-getting and manufacturing take precedence in this respect. These can be made clear to a bystander without the medium of speech. If he wishes to acquire such techniques, all he has to do is to imitate the worker's movements carefully and exactly. Although he may lack the proper muscular control at first, this can be acquired through practice. The same holds for manufactured objects. Even when the techniques have not been observed, the members of the receiving culture can fix the details of the object firmly in their memory and proceed to reproduce it at leisure. The tendency which the Japanese still show to study and reproduce imported objects would be a case in point.

As soon as we pass from such simple culture elements as techniques and their material products, we encounter increasing difficulties in communication. Although it is quite possible to describe such an element of culture as the ideal pattern for marriage and even to express it in non-verbal behavior, this expression is much less complete than that which is possible with regard to such a culture element as basket-making. The most thorough verbalization has difficulty in conveying the series of associations and conditioned emotional responses which are attached to this pattern and which give it meaning and vitality within our own culture configuration. In all our overt expressions of such a pattern these things are taken for granted, but the individual to whom we are attempting to convey a sense of the pattern can know nothing of them. Even when language difference has ceased to be a serious barrier to the conveyance of such patterns, it is extremely difficult to put them across. This is even more true of those concepts which, while a part of culture, find no direct expression in behavior aside from verbalizations. There is a story of an educated Japanese who was trying to understand the nature of the Trinity and after a long discussion with a European friend burst out with: "Oh, I see now. It is a committee." Such a remark gives a shock to any good Christian. The Trinity certainly is not a committee, but it may bring the point home to the reader if he pictures himself as trying to explain to this Japanese student just how and why he was in error.

Lastly, we have in all cultures those vital attitudes and values which lie largely below the level of individual consciousness and which the average member of a society rarely tries to verbalize even to himself. The practical impossibility of making such elements available for borrowing by the members of some other society is obvious. This part of any culture simply is not susceptible to diffusion. It can never be presented in sufficiently concrete and objective terms. Such things as religious or philosophical concepts can be communicated after a fashion, although probably never in their entirety. Patterns of social behavior can also be transmitted in the same uncertain way, but the associations which give them genuine potentialities for function cannot be transmitted. A borrowing group may imitate their outward forms, but it will usually be found that it has introduced new elements to replace those which could not be genuinely communicated to it. The institution of marriage as it exists among our own Southern Negroes would be a good example of such incomplete transmission of a pattern and its consequent modifications. As a matter of fact, the material techniques and their products are probably the only elements of culture which can be completely communicated, and it is significant that it is usually these elements which are accepted most readily and retained in most nearly their received form. It is obvious that such inherent differences in communicability must be of tremendous importance in diffusion, especially through their influence upon completeness of transmission and rate of transmission.

Our discussion hitherto has dealt with donor cultures and the qualities of culture elements. Let us turn now to what is the real core of the problem

of diffusion, the reaction of the accepting group to the elements presented to it. In its acceptance or rejection of these elements a society exercises free will. There may be a few exceptions to this in cases in which a socially dominant group seeks to impose its culture forcibly upon a subject society, but these are less important than they might appear. In the first place, such a dominant group rarely, if ever, attempts to impose its culture as a whole. It is content with the imposition of a few selected elements, such as outward adherence to its religion or the custom of wearing trousers. Obviously no amount of force can introduce into another culture any element which is not constantly and directly reflected in overt behavior. The conquered can be forced to attend church regularly, and it may even become a habit with them, something which produces no emotional response, but they cannot be forced to accept the new faith emotionally or be prevented from praying to their own gods alone and in private. At the same time, the very use of force makes the proscribed elements of the native culture symbols of revolt and this inspires a stronger attachment to them. Under a veil of superficial compliance a persecuted group can maintain its own ideals and values intact for generations, modifying and reinterpreting the superficial elements of culture which are forced upon it in such a way that they will do these no violence.

With very few exceptions, therefore, every new element which a society incorporates into its culture, it accepts of its own free will. This acceptance, in turn, is controlled by a large number of variable factors. The only constant in the situation is that such elements are always taken at their face value. A society can apprehend only those parts of a total complex which can be communicated to it plainly and directly. Thus a woman from one tribe who copies the design which she has seen on a basket made by some other tribe does so simply because its esthetic qualities appeal to her. She knows nothing of the symbolism which may surround this design or of what the original makers consider appropriate or inappropriate uses for it. Similarly when a new appliance, say a rifle, is presented to any group, they accept or reject it not on the basis of its associations and functions in the donor culture but on the potentialities for use which they perceive for it in their own. This perception never extends beyond the limits of immediate utility. There is no perception of the modifications in preëxisting patterns which the adoption of the new element will entail. In fact it is doubtful whether any mind is ever able to foresee any but the most immediate of these. Even in our own culture no one could have foretold the profound changes which have come in the wake of the acceptance of the automobile, changes which have affected our social patterns even more deeply than they have affected our economic ones.

The factors which control the receptivity of a society toward any new element of culture are, after all, very much the same whether this element originates inside or outside of their culture, i.e., whether it comes to them through invention or through diffusion. The main difference between these two processes lies in the fact that, if society rejects an invention, that addition to the sum total of culture is permanently lost, while if it rejects an element presented by diffusion this element is not lost but remains in the hands of the donor culture and may crop up at a later time when the society's reaction to it may be quite different.

New traits are accepted primarily on the basis of two qualities, utility and compatibility: in other words, on the basis of what they appear to be good for and how easily they can be fitted into the existing culture configuration. Both these qualities are, of course, relative to the receiving culture and are influenced by such a long series of factors that an outsider can hardly ascertain all of them. We have mentioned elsewhere that culture change is mainly a matter of the replacement of old elements by new ones and that every culture normally includes adequate techniques for meeting all the conscious needs of the society's members. When a new trait presents itself its acceptance depends not so much on whether it is better than the existing one as on whether it is enough better to make its acceptance worth the trouble. This in turn must depend upon the judgment of the group, their degree of conservatism, and how much change in existing habits the new appliance will entail. Even in the simplest form of diffusion, that of mechanical appliances, superiority cannot be judged simply in terms of increased output. There are pleasant and unpleasant forms of work, and even such a simple change as that from the use of adzes to axes for tree-felling entails a change in muscular habits which is unpleasant for the time being. In many parts of Oceania the natives have been receptive to European plane irons, which they could haft and use like their original stone adzes, but have refused to accept the vastly more efficient axe simply because they did not like to work with it.

Very much the same situation holds with regard to the problem of compatibility. The acceptance of any new culture element entails certain changes in the total culture configuration. Although the full extent of these changes can never be forecast, certain of them are usually obvious. If the new trait is of such a sort that its acceptance will conflict directly with important traits already present in the culture, it is almost certain to be rejected. One cannot conceive of techniques of mass production being accepted by a culture which had a pattern of uniqueness. There actually are societies which believe that no two objects should ever be the same and never make any two things exactly alike.

One very good example of such a conflict is afforded by the reactions of the Apache to peyote, a narcotic cactus used by many Indian tribes to induce visions and through these to put the individual in closer touch with the supernatural. The Apache attach as much importance to visions as any other tribe, but each individual hoards the power which comes to him through his supernatural experiences, and such power can be stolen by other medicine men. The regular pattern of peyote use is that of eating it in a group ceremonial. After a tentative and partial acceptance of the new idea the Apache rejected it. The opportunities for stealing power which contact in the assembly would provide, especially if an individual were under the influence of the drug and thus off guard, were too dangerous. It was felt that a man was likely to lose more power than he could gain. As a result, the use of peyote in this tribe has become infrequent and even then is limited to men of no importance who have little power to lose.

Most conflicts between new elements and preexisting elements are less direct and obvious. In the matter of compatibility as in that of utility there is a broad zone of uncertainty. There are new elements which may be recognized as slightly superior to existing ones and other elements which may be seen to be somewhat incompatible, but not enough so as to make their acceptance impossible. Very often the advantages and disadvantages are so evenly balanced that the acceptance of the new trait may seem desirable to certain members of the society and undesirable to others. The ultimate acceptance or rejection of elements which fall within this zone is controlled by still another series of variable factors about which we know very little. One of the most important of these is certainly the particular interests which dominate the life of the receiving group. A new trait which is in line with these interests will be given more serious consideration and has a better chance of adoption than one which is not. A slight gain along the line of these interests is felt to be more important than a larger one in some other line in which the group takes little interest. Thus the Hindus have always been highly receptive to new cults and new philosophic ideas as long as these did not come into too direct conflict with their existing patterns, but have shown an almost complete indifference to improved techniques of manufacture. The material world was felt to be of so little importance that minor advances in its control were not considered worth the trouble of changing established habits.

There are other factors beside those of the receiving group's interests and evaluations which may help to weight the scales for or against a new element of culture. One of the most important of these is the prestige of the donor group. There are many different grades and kinds of prestige. Occasionally one encounters a society which seems to have a genuine inferiority complex with regard to some other and to consider everything which this admired society has superior to the corresponding elements in its own culture. Such a group will borrow almost anything from its model that it has an opportunity to borrow. An example of this would be the indiscriminate acceptance of elements of European culture by the Japanese during the latter half of the nineteenth century. Such an attitude usually ends either in thorough disillusionment or in the disappearance of the borrowing society as a distinct cultural entity.

Such a condition is unusual. Donor prestige is usually of a much more limited type, referring only to certain aspects of culture. The average society believes in its general superiority to the rest of mankind, but at the same time admits that some other society or societies are superior in particular respects. Thus although Americans feel a certain condescension toward French culture as a whole, it has become almost an article of faith that the French are superior to us in the designing of women's wear. When an American woman is called upon to choose between a Paris model and a Chicago model, this feeling is strong enough to give the Paris model a distinct advantage. Conversely, a style which was advertised as originating in Germany would get less consideration than even the Chicago one, since we believe that dress-designing is not along the line of Germany's best efforts. In other words, Paris styles are aided in their American diffusion by French prestige, while Berlin styles are hampered in their American diffusion by a lack of prestige. Even in primitive society there are always neighboring tribes who are admired in certain respects and other tribes who are despised. Any trait which comes from the admired source will at least be given serious consideration, while one which comes from the despised source must be markedly advantageous to win acceptance.

A further factor which influences the acceptance of new culture elements is the prestige of the individuals under whose auspices the new thing is presented to the society. In diffusion as in invention, acceptance of a new trait begins with a single individual or at most a small group of individuals. It makes a great deal of difference who these innovators happen to be. If they are persons whom the society admires and is accustomed to imitate, the way for the general acceptance of the new trait is smoothed from the start. If the innovators happen to be personally unpopular or of low social status, the new element immediately acquires undesirable associations which may outweigh any intrinsic advantages. Thus in our own society no one would try to launch a new and daring style through the cheap dress shops. It would not take even in the social group which patronizes these shops, since the wearing of the new style would then be a mark of a social status about which its holders were not enthusiastic. The same style launched from the highest point in the social ladder which its designers could reach would be eagerly accepted by the cheap-shop patrons.

Lastly, there is the factor of what can only be termed "faddism." It is an observed fact that certain new elements of culture will be eagerly accepted by groups when there are no discernible reasons of either utility or prestige. Major elements are unlikely to be introduced into any culture in this way, but a whole series of minor ones may be. We ourselves have witnessed the arrival and departure of such items as the ankle watch, sunburn initials, etc. Moreover, such fads are by no means limited to effete civilizations. Primitive tribes also have their changes of fashion and their borrowing of intrinsically useless items of culture which happen to catch their fancy. Thus among the Bara of Madagascar the past twenty years have witnessed the introduction of fantastic haircuts among the men, while prior to this time there was a rather simple uniform mode of tribal hairdressing. The style is said to have owed its origin to an enterprising Imerina barber who settled in the Bara territory and sought an outlet for his professional gifts. The young men who accepted it were severely ridiculed at first, but once done it could not be undone and they thus had a strong incentive to make converts to the new idea. Beginning with no utility and a rather negative prestige, it has now become firmly established as a part of Bara culture.

All this will indicate the great number of variable factors which enter into both the presentation and the acceptance of new culture elements. Until we know more about the operation of these factors we can have only a very imperfect understanding of the diffusion process. The last step in this process, that of the changes and readjustments which inevitably follow the adoption of any new trait, will be treated in the next chapter.

6. Cycles of Interdependence

BY VILFREDO PARETO

2202. BUT AT THIS POINT a question arises of its own accord: Why have certain governments used force and others not? And it is evident that on the step that we have taken above in explaining things other steps must now follow. And it is further evident that we are not strictly exact when we say, as we have just said, that this or that government fell "because" it did not use force; for if there should prove to be facts on which the failure to use force depended, those facts more properly would be the "cause" of the outcome, the failure to use force being merely the apparent cause. It might also be that those facts in their turn depended, in part at least, upon the failure to use force, and so our relationships of cause and effect would have to be amended into broader relationships of independence. Nor is that all. If it is true that governments which are incompetent or unable to use force fall, it is also true that no government endures by depending entirely upon force. From all of which it is apparent that we have examined only one side of the situation and must therefore broaden the scope of our researches and look at it in a much more general way. Suppose we do that.

2203. *Cycles of Interdependence.* Let us go back and think once more of the elements upon which the social equilibrium depends; and since, unfortunately, we cannot consider them all and take their interdependences into account in all strictness, suppose we follow the course suggested in earlier sections, and consider a restricted group of elements, to be selected, naturally, from among the more important, gradually enlarging the groups thereafter so as to have them include as many elements as possible....

2204. An element of a given group acts upon elements in other groups, either apart from the other elements in its own group or in conjunction with them. Suppose we call the effect it has when considered apart from the other elements in its group the *direct* effect; the effect it has in virtue of its combination with other elements in its group, the *indirect* effect. In so doing we shall be continuing the analysis we began in a previous section. There we divided facts into two categories: 1. The fact of the existence of a society. 2. The facts observable in that society, in other words, the elements from which the fact of its existence results. Let us now first divide this second category into groups, and then go on to select one element from each group and try to determine the effect that it has, as a distinct unit, upon the elements in other groups (*direct* effect) as well as the effect it has upon them when it is considered as operating in conjunction with the other elements in its own group (*indirect* effect).

2205. And now let us turn to the matter of interdependence among the groups. To be as brief as possible, suppose we indicate the following elements by letters of the alphabet: Residues, *a;* interests, *b;* derivations, *c;* social heterogeneity and circulation, *d.* If one could use mathematical logic, the interdependence of the elements could be expressed in equations; but since that cannot be done in the present state of knowledge and we are compelled to use ordinary language, we have nothing left but to consider the interdependence in another form—in the form of actions and reactions among the elements—and to follow the course indicated in §2104.

2206. We may say, accordingly: (I) That *a* acts upon *b, c, d;* (II) that *b* acts upon *a, c, d;* (III) that *c* acts upon *a, b, d;* (IV) that *d* acts upon *a, b, c.*

From what we have been saying in the previous chapter, it is evident that Combination I yields a very considerable portion of the social phenomenon; and those writers who have regarded ethics as the foundation of society may have had a remote and inadequate perception of that fact. In it also lies the modicum of truth that is to be found in metaphysical doctrines which make facts dependent upon "concepts," since "concepts" reflect, though very confusedly, residues and sentiments corresponding to residues. It is Combination I also that assures continuity in the history of human societies, since the category *a* varies slightly or slowly.

Combination II also yields a very considerable portion of the social phenomenon, and it too varies but slightly and slowly and contributes to the continuity of human societies. The importance of Com-

Reprinted from Vilfredo Pareto, *The Mind and Society,* ed. Arthur Livingston, trans. Andrew Bongiorno and Arthur Livingston. (New York: Harcourt, Brace & Co., 1935), Vol. IV, §§ 2202–21, with the permission of The Pareto Fund.

bination II was noticed by the followers of "economic determinism"; but they fell into the error of substituting the part for the whole and disregarding the other combinations. Combination III is the least important of all. Failure to perceive that fact has rendered the lucubrations of humanitarians, "intellectuals," and worshippers of the goddess Reason, erroneous, inconclusive, fatuous. However, to a greater degree than any of the others it is known to us through literature, and a far greater importance is commonly attached to it than it really has in society. Combination IV is of no mean importance, a fact remarked of old by Plato and Aristotle, to say nothing of other ancient writers. In our day the studies of Lapouge, Hamon, and others, incomplete and marred by errors as they may be, have had the great merit of throwing that very important relation into relief, while failure to take account of it fundamentally vitiates so-called democratic theories.

2207. It must not be forgotten that actions and reactions follow one on another indefinitely and, as it were, in a circle: that is to say, beginning with Combination I one goes on to Combination IV and from IV back again to I. In Combination I the element a was acting upon d; in IV the element d is acting upon a; then one goes back again to Combination I, so that a is again acting upon d, and so on. In virtue, therefore, of Combination I a variation in a causes variations in the other elements, b, c, d; and just to make the situation more manageable in language, we will give the variations in a, b, c, d that are effected in virtue of Combination I the name of *immediate effects*. But in virtue of the other combinations, variations in b, c, d also effect variations in a; and because of the circular movement this variation reacts upon Combination I and gives rise to new variations in a, b, c, d. To these variations we will, again for mere purposes of convenience, give the name of *mediate effects*. Sometimes it is necessary to consider two or more combinations simultaneously. Farther along we shall see an example of great significance in which effects are so intertwined that we are obliged to study Combinations II and IV together. The state of concrete equilibrium observable in a given society is a resultant of all these effects, of all these actions and reactions. It is therefore different from a state of theoretical equilibrium obtained by considering one or more of the elements a, b, c, d instead of considering all. Political economy, for instance, deals with category b, and one of its branches is pure economics. Pure economics yields a theoretical equilibrium that is different, still within category b, from another theoretical equilibrium yielded by applied economics; and different from other theoretical equilibria

that could be obtained by combining b with some of the elements a, c, d; and different, again, from the theoretical equilibrium that most nearly approximates the concrete and is obtained by combining all the elements a, b, c, d.

2208. This will all be clearer if we give a less abstract form to what we have just been saying, and at the same time proceed from particular cases to more general ones, following the inductive method. Suppose we locate the protection of industries by import duties in the group b. We first get its economic effects, direct and indirect; and these are the concern primarily of economics, which is the science of the group b. We shall not go into them here, but merely note certain effects that we find it necessary to consider for our purposes. Among these we shall have to consider economic effects that have so far been more or less neglected by the science of economics. As a rule, champions of free trade have considered low prices, implicitly at least, as an advantage to a population at large, whereas champions of protection have regarded low prices as an evil. The first view is readily acceptable to anyone thinking chiefly of consumption, the latter to anyone thinking chiefly of production. From the scientific standpoint they are both of little or no value, since they are based on an incomplete analysis of the situation. A forward step along the scientific path was taken when the theories of mathematical economics supplied a proof that, in general, the direct effect of protection is a destruction of wealth. If one were free to go on and add an axiom, which is implicitly taken for granted by many economists, that any destruction of wealth is an "evil," one could logically conclude that protection is an "evil." But before such a proposition can be granted the indirect economic effects and the social effects of protection have to be known. Keeping to the former for the moment, we find that protection transfers a certain amount of wealth from a part, A, of the population to a part B, through the destruction of a certain amount of wealth, q, the amount representing the costs of the operation. If, as a result of this new distribution of wealth, the production of wealth does not increase by a quantity greater than q, the operation is economically detrimental to a population as a whole; if it increases by a quantity greater than q, the operation is economically beneficial. The latter case is not to be barred *a priori*; for the element A contains the indolent, the lazy, and people, in general, who make little use of economic combinations; whereas the element B comprises the people who are economically wide-awake and are always ready for energetic enterprise—people who know how to make effective use of economic combinations. Going on, then, to consider in general not only economic but social effects, one has to distinguish between dynamic effects, which ensue for a brief period of time after protection has been established, and static effects, which ensue after protection has been established for a certain length of time. A distinction must further be drawn between the effects on productions that are readily susceptible of increase, such as manufactures in general, and the effects on productions not so susceptible of increase, such as the agricultural. The dynamic effect is more considerable in the case of the manufacturer than in the case of the farmer. When protection is established those manufacturers who already own factories for protected goods, and persons who are shrewd enough to anticipate protection or to go out and get it, enjoy temporary monopolies, and these come to an end only when new manufacturers enter the field to compete with established firms—that takes time, and often not a short time. Farmers, on the other hand, have little to fear from new enterprise, and for them, therefore, the dynamic effect is not so very different from the static. Furthermore, protection may encourage new industries and so increase, if not the profits, at least the numbers, of manufacturers. That may also happen in agriculture, though on a very much smaller scale, and the ordinary effect of agricultural protection is merely to replace one kind of acreage with another. The static effect, on the other hand, is less considerable on the profits of manufacturers than on the profit of the farmer. It increases the earnings of the farmer, while competition cuts down the earnings of the manufacturer from his temporary monopoly. For that very reason industrial protection usually destroys more wealth than agricultural protection, for with the latter the new earnings, which represent a mere transfer of wealth, are saved from destruction.

2209. Let us look at the *immediate* effects on the other groups.

Combination II. The most perceptible effects are on *d,* that is to say, on social heterogeneousness. The dynamic effects of industrial protection enrich not only individuals who are endowed with technical talents, but especially individuals who have talents for financial combinations or gifts for manipulating the politicians who confer the benefits of protection. Some individuals possess such endowments in conspicuous degree. They grow rich and influential, and come to "run the country." The same is true of politicians who are clever at selling the benefits of protection. All such persons possess Class I residues in high intensities, and Class II residues in fairly low intensities. On the other hand, people in whom endowments of character are more notable than technical or financial talents, or who lack the

gift for clever political manoeuvring, are pushed down the ladder. Deriving no benefit from protection, they are the ones who pay its costs. The static effects are not identical—they are analogous in that, though they enrich far fewer persons, they nevertheless open new fields for the activities of individuals who have endowments of talent and cunning, and they increase the industrial population, often at the expense of the agricultural. In short, to put the situation briefly, when account is taken, in making up the governing class, of the imaginary examinations that we used for illustration in an earlier section, the higher grades have to be given to individuals in whom Class I residues are numerous and intense and who know how to use them in garnering the fruits of protection; and the lower grades, to individuals in whom Class I residues are few and feeble, or, if they are numerous and strong, are not skilfully exploited. So it results that industrial protection tends to strengthen Class I residues in the governing class. Class-circulation, furthermore, is accelerated. In a country where there is little industry an individual born with a good assortment of combination-instincts finds far fewer opportunities for using them than an individual born in a country where there are many industries and where new enterprises are starting every day. The very art of manipulating protectionist favours offers a wide field of activity for people whose talents lie in that direction, even though they do not use them directly in industry. Carrying on the analogy suggested, one may say that the examinations for purposes of discovering the candidate best equipped with Class I residues are held more frequently and attract larger numbers of aspirants.

2210. No very appreciable effects are apparent on residues, *a,* if only for the reason that residues change but slowly. On the other hand, effects upon derivations, *c,* are very considerable, and one notes a rank florescence of economic theories in defence of protection, many of which are comparable to the dedications and sonnet sequences that were addressed to wealthy feudal lords in a day gone by as bids for pensions.

2211. *Combination III.* Derivations act feebly, or not at all, upon residues, *a,* feebly upon interests, *b,* a little more potently upon social heterogeneity, *d,* for in any society persons who have the knack for praising people in power find ready admission to the governing class. Schmoller might never have been named to the Prussian House of Lords had he been a free-trader; on the other hand English free-traders win favours from a so-called "Liberal" government. That gives us an indirect effect outside our categories: the interest, *b,* acting upon derivations, *c*, and they in turn upon social heterogeneity, *d*.

2212. *Combination* IV. Here again we get effects of great importance, not so much in the influence of heterogeneity upon residues—in view, as usual, of their relative stability—as in the influence of interests.

2213. Indeed, considering Combination IV in general, the indirect, or "mediate," influence of interests on residues is far from negligible and if continued over long periods of years, may even be very considerable. In a country that concentrates almost exclusively on economic interests, combination-sentiments are stimulated, exhilarated, and sentiments corresponding to group-persistences are attenuated. In those two classes of residues, certain genera, and especially the forms in which residues are expressed, are modified, and therefore also derivations. Perfection is located in the future instead of in the past. The god Progress is enthroned on Olympus. Humanitarianism triumphs because interests are now better safe-guarded by chicanery than by force. It becomes a habit and a principle to circumvent obstacles instead of pushing them aside by brute force. In the long run such practices sap strength of character, and cunning in all its forms comes to reign supreme.

2214. Such things have been perceived in all periods of history, but the writers whom they have chanced to interest have as a rule soon deviated from the study of facts to turn to ethical considerations, to praise or to blame; and to discovering some way of realizing this or that ideal.

2215. Going back now to the particular case of protection: After interests have, thanks to protection, brought into the governing class individuals richly endowed with Class I residues, those individuals in their turn influence interests and stimulate the whole country in the direction of economic pursuits and industrialism. The thing is so noticeable that it has not escaped even casual observers, or people who wear the blinders of mistaken theories, and it has often been described as an "increase in capitalism" in modern societies. Then going on, arguing as usual *post hoc, propter hoc,* the "increase in capitalism" has been taken as the cause of a decline in moral sentiments (group-persistence).

2216. That, really, is a case of an indirect, a mediate, effect: interests, in other words, have influenced heterogeneity; the latter, in its turn, now reacts upon interests; and through a sequence of actions and reactions, an equilibrium is established in which economic production and class-circulation become more intense, and the composition of the governing class is profoundly modified.

2217. The increase in economic production may be great enough to exceed the destruction of wealth caused by protection; so that, sum total, protection may yield a profit and not a loss in wealth; it may therefore prove (though not necessarily so) that the economic prosperity of a country has been enhanced by industrial protection.

2218. That, notice, is a *mediate* effect, coming about through the influence of industrial protection upon social heterogeneity and class-circulation, which go on in turn to react upon the economic situation. It is possible for that reason to suppress the first link in the chain; and so long as the second is kept, the effect will follow just the same. For that reason, again, if protection were to act in a different wise upon social heterogeneity and class-circulation, the effect also would be different; and that is what actually happens, as a rule, with agricultural protection. Halting, therefore, at the point in the cycle where we now stand, we may say that it will be possible to get the indirect, the *mediate,* effect of an increase in economic prosperity either through industrial protection or through a free trade that removes a burdensome agricultural protection. This latter is, roughly, what took place in England at the time of Cobden's League. Abolition of agricultural protection had strong effect; an effect much less strong was the abolition of industrial protection, for at that time English industry led the world, and the effects were especially due to the first measure. In England, furthermore, class-circulation was already intense and became more so through a number of political measures. On the other hand, when Germany turned to protectionism class-circulation was sluggish and largely came about for other than economic considerations. Agricultural protectionism could have had little if any effect upon a circulation already slow in itself; whereas industrial protectionism stimulated it marvellously. The effects therefore were effects largely of industrial protectionism. Observable in England also were effects depending upon the abolition of agricultural protection, and the country moved rapidly forward towards a state of demagogic industrialism, which cannot prevail in Germany so long as the Junker element remains strong and vigorous under the shelter of agricultural duties. In Italy, after the establishment of the new kingdom protectionism in finance and public works had already exerted upon social heterogeneity the influence that we have elsewhere seen attaching to industrial protection; so that when the latter was established, along with a strong dosage of agricultural protection, it had indirect, *mediate,* effects of slight importance—with some exceptions perhaps in Northern Italy, whereas in the South agricultural protection was virtually the only kind that had any effect. As a consequence, the mediate effects were on the whole almost un-noticeable, the economic effects of the destruction of wealth alone striking the eye, until, as time went on, they were obscured by a coating of beneficial effects resulting from a period of prosperity general throughout the civilized world.

2219. Knowledge of the causes of these various effects, which are none the less economic, could not have been supplied by political economy alone. That science had to be combined with another more general science that would show how to throw off the spell of the derivations on which mistaken theories were commonly erected, and emphasize the multiplicity and great variety of the forces that were really determining phenomena which, though strictly economic to all appearances, actually depended upon other social phenomena.

2220. It must not be forgotten that so far we have been very roughly sketching a first picture of the situation. A great deal still remains to be done in filling in the secondary details. This is not just the place to do that; but we are obliged to eliminate one other imperfection in it that is due to our stopping at a certain point in the cycle, whereas actually we have to go on and look at further mediate effects that are quite different.

2221. If no counter-forces stood in the way, and the cycle of actions and reactions were to go on indefinitely, economic protection and its effects ought to go on becoming progressively greater; and that is what is actually observable in many countries during the nineteenth century. But as a matter of fact counter-forces do develop, and increasingly so. Speaking now not of the particular case of protection, but in general, such forces may be noted in the modifications that the *élite* undergoes, and in variations in the circumstances that make the cyclical movements possible. History shows that when the proportions between Class I and Class II residues in the *élite* begin to vary, the movement does not continue indefinitely in one direction, but is sooner or later replaced by a movement in a counter-direction. Such counter-movements often result from wars, as was the case in the conquest of Greece by Rome, Greece at the time possessing Class I residues in very great abundance, while in Rome the advantage lay with the residues of group-persistence (Class II). Then again, the counter-movement to a movement that has been in progress for a fairly long time has resulted from internal revolutions, a striking case being the change from the Republic to the Empire in Rome, which was primarily a social revolution and profoundly altered proportions of residues in the ruling class. Considering the two processes together we may say, in general and roughly, that when the counter-movement does not come from wars, it comes from revolutions, much as when the fruit is ripe on the tree either it is plucked by a human hand or it falls naturally to the ground, but in either event is removed from the tree. The cause just mentioned—modifications in the *élite*—is among the major ones determining the undulating form that the movement assumes, and of that we shall see notable examples as we proceed.

7. *The Social Psychology of the World Religions*

BY MAX WEBER

BY WORLD RELIGIONS, we understand the five religions or religiously determined systems

Reprinted from *From Max Weber: Essays in Sociology,* trans. and eds. Hans A. Gerth and C. Wright Mills (New York: Oxford University Press, 1946), pp. 267–301, with the permission of Oxford University Press.
"Die Wirtschaftsethik der Weltreligionen," *Gesammelte Aufsaetze zur Religionssoziologie* (Tübingen, 1922–3), vol. I, pp. 237–68. This is a translation of the Introduction to a series of studies which Weber published as articles in the *Archiv für Sozialforschung* under the title "Die Wirtschaftsethik der Weltreligionen" (The Economic Ethic of the World Religions). The Introduction and the first parts on Confucianism and Taoism were written in 1913. They were not published until September 1915, in the 41st volume of the *Archiv.*

of life-regulation which have known how to gather multitudes of confessors around them. The term is used here in a completely value-neutral sense. The Confucian, Hinduist, Buddhist, Christian, and Islamist religious ethics all belong to the category of world religion. A sixth religion, Judaism, will also be dealt with. It is included because it contains historical preconditions decisive for understanding Christianity and Islamism, and because of its historic and autonomous significance for the development of the modern economic ethic of the Occident —a significance, partly real and partly alleged, which has been discussed several times recently

References to other religions will be made only when they are indispensable for historical connections.

What is meant by the "economic ethic" of a religion will become increasingly clear during the course of our presentation. This term does not bring into focus the ethical theories of theological compendia; for however important such compendia may be under certain circumstances, they merely serve as tools of knowledge. The term "economic ethic" points to the practical impulses for action which are founded in the psychological and pragmatic contexts of religions. The following presentation may be sketchy, but it will make obvious how complicated the structures and how many-sided the conditions of a concrete economic ethic usually are. Furthermore, it will show that externally similar forms of economic organization may agree with very different economic ethics and, according to the unique character of their economic ethics, how such forms of economic organization may produce very different historical results. An economic ethic is not a simple "function" of a form of economic organization; and just as little does the reverse hold, namely, that economic ethics unambiguously stamp the form of the economic organization.

No economic ethic has ever been determined solely by religion. In the face of man's attitudes towards the world—as determined by religious or other (in our sense) "inner" factors—an economic ethic has, of course, a high measure of autonomy. Given factors of economic geography and history determine this measure of autonomy in the highest degree. The religious determination of life-conduct, however, is also one—note this—only one, of the determinants of the economic ethic. Of course, the religiously determined way of life is itself profoundly influenced by economic and political factors operating within given geographical, political, social and national boundaries. We should lose ourselves in these discussions if we tried to demonstrate these dependencies in all their singularities. Here we can only attempt to peel off the directive elements in the life-conduct of those social *strata* which have most strongly influenced the practical ethic of their respective religions. These elements have stamped the most characteristic features upon practical ethics, the features that distinguish one ethic from others; *and,* at the same time, they have been important for the respective economic ethics.

By no means must we focus upon only one stratum. Those strata which are decisive in stamping the characteristic features of an economic ethic may change in the course of history. And the influence of a single stratum is never an exclusive one. Nevertheless, as a rule one may determine the strata whose styles of life have been at least predominantly decisive for certain religions. Here are some examples, if one may anticipate:

Confucianism was the status ethic of prebendaries, of men with literary educations who were characterized by a secular rationalism. If one did not belong to this *cultured* stratum he did not count. The religious (or if one wishes, irreligious) status ethic of this stratum has determined the Chinese way of life far beyond the stratum itself.

Earlier Hinduism was borne by a hereditary caste of cultured literati, who, being remote from any office, functioned as a kind of ritualist and spiritual advisers for individuals and communities. They formed a stable center for the orientation of the status stratification, and they placed their stamp upon the social order. Only Brahmans, *educated* in the Veda, formed, as bearers of tradition, the fully recognized religious status group. And only later a non-Brahman status group of ascetics emerged by the side of the Brahmans and competed with them. Still later, during the Indian Middle Ages, Hinduism entered the plain. It represented the ardent [*Inbrünstige*] sacramental religiosity of the savior, and was borne by the lower strata with their plebeian mystagogues.

Buddhism was propagated by strictly contemplative, mendicant monks, who rejected the world and, having no homes, migrated. Only these were full members of the religious community; all others remained religious laymen of inferior value: objects, not subjects, of religiosity.

During its first period, Islamism was a religion of world-conquering warriors, a knight order of disciplined crusaders. They lacked only the sexual asceticism of their Christian copies of the age of the Crusades. But during the Islamic Middle Ages, contemplative and mystical Sufism attained at least an equal standing under the leadership of plebeian technicians of orgiastics. The brotherhoods of the petty bourgeoisie grew out of Sufism in a manner similar to the Christian Tertiarians, except they were far more universally developed.

Since the Exile, Judaism has been the religion of a civic "pariah people." We shall in time become acquainted with the precise meaning of the term. During the Middle Ages Judaism fell under the leadership of a stratum of intellectuals who were trained in literature and ritual, a peculiarity of Judaism. This stratum has represented an increasingly quasi-proletarian and rationalist petty-bourgeois intelligentsia.

Christianity, finally, began its course as a doctrine of itinerant artisan journeymen. During all periods of its mighty external and internal development it has been a quite specifically urban, and above all a civic, religion. This was true during Antiquity, during the Middle Ages, and in Puritanism. The city of the Occident, unique among all other cities of the world—and citizenship, in the sense in which it has emerged only in the Occident—has been the major theatre for Christianity. This holds for the pneumatic piety of the ancient religious community, for the mendicant monk orders of the high Middle Ages, and for the [Protestant] sects of the reformation up to pietism and methodism.

It is not our thesis that the specific nature of a religion is a simple "function" of the social situation of the stratum which appears as its characteristic bearer, or that it represents the stratum's "ideology," or that it is a "reflection" of a stratum's material or ideal interest-situation. On the contrary, a more basic misunderstanding of the standpoint of these discussions would hardly be possible.

However incisive the social influences, economically and politically determined, may have been upon a religious ethic in a particular case, it receives its stamp primarily from religious sources, and, first of all, from the content of its annunciation and its promise. Frequently the very next generation reinterprets these annunciations and promises in a fundamental fashion. Such reinterpretations adjust the revelations to the needs of the religious community. If this occurs, then it is at least that religious doctrines are adjusted to *religious needs*. Other spheres of interest could have only a secondary influence; often, however, such influence is very obvious and sometimes it is decisive.

For every religion we shall find that a change in the socially decisive strata has usually been of profound importance. On the other hand, the type of a religion, once stamped, has usually exerted a rather far-reaching influence upon the life-conduct of very heterogeneous strata. In various ways people have sought to interpret the connection between religious ethics and interest-situations in such a way that the former appear as mere "functions" of the latter. Such interpretation occurs in so-called historical materialism—which we shall not here discuss—as well as in a purely psychological sense.

A quite general and abstract class-determination of religious ethics might be deduced from the theory of "resentment," known since Friedrich Nietzsche's brilliant essay and since then spiritedly treated by psychologists. As is known, this theory regards the moral glorification of mercy and brotherliness as a "slave revolt in morals" among those who are disadvantaged, either in their natural endowments or in their opportunities as determined by life-fate. The ethic of "duty" is thus considered a product of "repressed" sentiments for vengeance on the part of banausic men who "displace" their sentiments be-

cause they are powerless, and condemned to work and to money-making. They resent the way of life of the lordly stratum who live free of duties. A very simple solution of the most important problems in the typology of religious ethics would obviously result if this were the case. However fortunate and fruitful the disclosure of the psychological significance of resentment as such has been, great caution is necessary in estimating its bearing for social ethics.

Later we shall have to discuss the motives that have determined the different forms of ethical "rationalization" of life conduct, *per se*. In the main, these have had nothing whatsoever to do with resentment. But that the evaluation of *suffering* in religious ethics has been subject to a typical change is beyond doubt. If properly understood, this change carries a certain justification for the theory first worked out by Nietzsche. The primeval attitude towards suffering has been thrown into relief most drastically during the religious festivities of the community, especially in the treatment of those haunted by disease or other cases of obstinate misfortune. Men, permanently suffering, mourning, diseased, or otherwise unfortunate, were, according to the nature of their suffering, believed either to be possessed by a demon or burdened with the wrath of a god whom they had insulted. To tolerate such men in the midst of the cultic community could result in disadvantages for it. In any case, they were not allowed to participate in cultic feasts and sacrifices, for the gods did not enjoy the sight of them and could be incited to wrath by it. The sacrificial feasts were occasions for rejoicing—even in Jerusalem during times of siege.

In treating suffering as a symptom of odiousness in the eyes of the gods and as a sign of secret guilt, religion has psychologically met a very general need. The fortunate is seldom satisfied with the fact of being fortunate. Beyond this, he needs to know that he has a *right* to his good fortune. He wants to be convinced that he "deserves" it, and above all, that he deserves it in comparison with others. He wishes to be allowed the belief that the less fortunate also merely experience his due. Good fortune thus wants to be "legitimate" fortune.

If the general term "fortune" covers all the "good" of honor, power, possession, and pleasure, it is the most general formula for the service of legitimation, which religion has had to accomplish for the external and the inner interests of all ruling men, the propertied, the victorious, and the healthy. In short, religion provides the theodicy of good fortune for those who are fortunate. This theodicy is anchored in highly robust ("pharisaical") needs of man and is therefore easily understood, even if sufficient attention is often not paid to its effects.

In contrast, the way in which this negative evaluation of suffering has led to its religious glorification is more complicated. Numerous forms of chastisement and of abstinences from normal diet and sleep, as well as from sexual intercourse, awaken, or at least facilitate, the charisma of ecstatic, visionary, hysterical, in short, of all extraordinary states that are evaluated as "holy." Their production therefore forms the object of magical asceticism. The prestige of these chastisements has resulted from the notion that certain kinds of suffering and abnormal states provoked through chastisement are avenues to the attainment of superhuman, that is magical, powers. The ancient prescriptions of taboo and abstinences in the interest of cultic purity, which follow from a belief in demons, has worked in the same direction. The development of cults of "redemption" has been added to these prescriptions, abstinences, and interests. In principle, these cults have occupied an independent and new position in the face of individual suffering. The primeval cult, and above all, the cult of the political associations, have left all individual interests out of consideration. The tribal and local god, the gods of the city and of the empire, have taken care only of interests that have concerned the collectivity as a whole. They have been concerned with rain and with sunshine, with the booty of the hunt and with victory over enemies. Thus, in the community cult, the collectivity as such turned to its god. The individual, in order to avoid or remove evils that concerned himself—above all, sickness—has not turned to the cult of the community, but as an individual he has approached the sorcerer as the oldest personal and "spiritual adviser." The prestige of particular magicians, and of those spirits or divinities in whose names they have performed their miracles, has brought them patronage, irrespective of local or of tribal affiliation. Under favorable conditions this has led to the formation of a religious "community," which has been independent of ethnic associations. Some, though not all, "mysteries" have taken this course. They have promised the salvation of individuals *qua* individuals from sickness, poverty, and from all sorts of distress and danger. Thus the magician has transformed himself into the mystagogue; that is, hereditary dynasties of mystagogues or organizations of trained personnel under a head determined in accordance with some sort of rules have developed. This head has either been recognized as the incarnation of a superhuman being or merely as a prophet, that is, as the mouthpiece and agent of his god. Collective religious arrangements for individual "suffering" *per se,* and

for "salvation" from it, have originated in this fashion.

The annunciation and the promise of religion have naturally been addressed to the masses of those who were in need of salvation. They and their interests have moved into the center of the professional organization for the "cure of the soul," which, indeed, only therewith originated. The typical service of magicians and priests becomes the determination of the factors to be blamed for suffering, that is, the confession of "sins." At first, these sins were offenses against ritual commandments. The magician and priest also give counsel for behavior fit to remove the suffering. The material and ideal interests of magicians and priests could thereby actually and increasingly enter the service of specifically *plebeian* motives. A further step along this course was signified when, under the pressure of typical and everrecurrent distress, the religiosity of a "redeemer" evolved. This religiosity presupposed the myth of a savior, hence (at least relatively) of a *rational* view of the world. Again, suffering became the most important topic. The primitive mythology of nature frequently offered a point of departure for this religiosity. The spirits who governed the coming and going of vegetation and the paths of celestial bodies important for the seasons of the year became the preferred carriers of the myths of the suffering, dying, and resurrecting god to needful men. The resurrected god guaranteed the return of good fortune in this world or the security of happiness in the world beyond. Or, a popularized figure from heroic sagas —like Krishna in India—is embellished with the myths of childhood, love, and struggle; and such figures became the object of an ardent cult of the savior. Among people under political pressure, like the Israelites, the title of "savior" (Moshuach name) was originally attached to the saviors from political distress, as transmitted by hero sagas (Gideon, Jephthah). The "Messianic" promises were determined by these sagas. With this people, and in this clear-cut fashion only among them and under other very particular conditions, the suffering of a people's *community,* rather than the suffering of an individual, became the object of hope for religious salvation. The rule was that the savior bore an individual and universal character at the same time that he was ready to guarantee salvation for the *individual* and to every individual who would turn to him.

The figure of the savior has been of varying stamp. In the late form of Zoroastrianism with its numerous abstractions, a purely constructed figure assumed the role of the mediator and savior in the economy of salvation. The reverse has also occurred: a historical person, legitimized through miracles and visionary reappearances, ascends to the rank of savior. Purely historical factors have been decisive for the realization of these very different possibilities. Almost always, however, some kind of theodicy of suffering has originated from the hope for salvation.

The promises of the religions of salvation at first remained tied to ritualist rather than to ethical preconditions. Thus, for instance, both the worldly and the other worldly advantages of the Eleusinian mysteries were tied to ritual purity and to attendance at the Eleusinian mass. When law gained in significance, these special deities played an increasing role, and the task of protecting the traditional order, of punishing the unjust and rewarding the righteous, was transferred to them as guardians of juridical procedure.

Where religious development was decisively influenced by a prophecy, naturally "sin" was no longer a mere magical offense. Above all, it was a sign of disbelief in the prophet and in his commandments. Sin figured as the basic cause of all sorts of misfortunes.

The prophet has not regularly been a descendant or a representative of depressed classes. The reverse, as we shall see, has almost always been the rule. Neither has the content of the prophet's doctrine been derived preponderantly from the intellectual horizon of the depressed classes. As a rule, however, the oppressed, or at least those threatened by distress, were in need of a redeemer and prophet; the fortunate, the propertied, the ruling strata were not in such need. Therefore, in the great majority of cases, a prophetically announced religion of redemption has had its permanent locus among the less-favored social strata. Among these, such religiosity has either been a substitute for, or a rational supplement to, magic.

Wherever the promises of the prophet or the redeemer have not sufficiently met the needs of the socially less-favored strata, a secondary salvation religion of the masses has regularly developed beneath the official doctrine. The rational conception of the world is contained in germ within the myth of the redeemer. A rational theodicy of misfortune has, therefore, as a rule, been a development of this conception of the world. At the same time, this rational view of the world has often furnished suffering as such with a "plus" sign, which was originally quite foreign to it.

Suffering, voluntarily created through mortification, changed its meaning with the development of ethical divinities who punish and reward. Originally, the magical coercion of spirits by the formula of prayer was increased through mortification as a source of charismatic states. Such coercion was preserved in mortification by prayer as well as in cultic prescriptions of abstinence. This has remained the case, even after the magical formula for coercing spirits became a supplication to be heard by a deity. Penances were added as a means of cooling the wrath of deities by repentance, and of avoiding through self-punishment the sanctions that have been incurred. The numerous abstinences were originally attached to the mourning for the dead (with special clarity in China) in order to turn away their jealousy and wrath. These abstinences were easily transferred to relations with the appropriate divinities; they made self-mortification, and finally, unintentional deprivation as such, appear more pleasing to the gods than the naive enjoyment of the goods of this earth. Such enjoyment, indeed, made the pleasure-seeking man less accessible to the influence of the prophet or the priest.

The force of all these individual factors was tremendously enhanced under certain conditions.

The need for an ethical interpretation of the "meaning" of the distribution of fortunes among men increased with the growing rationality of conceptions of the world. As the religious and ethical reflections upon the world were increasingly rationalized and primitive, and magical notions were eliminated, the theodicy of suffering encountered increasing difficulties. Individually "undeserved" woe was all too frequent; not "good" but "bad" men succeeded—even when "good" and "bad" were measured by the yardstick of the master stratum and not by that of a "slave morality."

One can explain suffering and injustice by referring to individual sin committed in a former life (the migration of souls), to the guilt of ancestors, which is avenged down to the third and fourth generation, or—the most principled—to the wickedness of all creatures *per se*. As compensatory promises, one can refer to hopes of the individual for a better life in the future in this world (transmigration of souls) or to hopes for the successors (Messianic realm), or to a better life in the hereafter (paradise).

The metaphysical conception of God and of the world, which the ineradicable demand for a theodicy called forth, could produce only a few systems of ideas on the whole—as we shall see, only three. These three gave rationally satisfactory answers to the questioning for the basis of the incongruity between destiny and merit: the Indian doctrine of Kharma, Zoroastrian dualism, and the predestination decree of the *deus absconditus*. These solutions are rationally closed; in pure form, they are found only as exceptions.

The rational need for a theodicy of suffering and of dying has had extremely strong effects. As a matter of fact, this need has molded important traits of such religions as Hinduism, Zoroastrism, and Judaism, and, to a certain extent, Paulinian and later Christianity. Even as late as 1906, a mere minority among a rather considerable number of proletarians gave as reasons for their disbelief in Christianity conclusions derived from modern theories of natural sciences. The majority, however, referred to the "injustice" of the order of this world—to be sure, essentially because they believed in a revolutionary compensation in this world.

The theodicy of suffering can be colored by resentment. But the need of compensation for the insufficiency of one's fate in this world has not, as a rule, had resentment as a basic and decisive color. Certainly, the need for vengeance has had a special affinity with the belief that the unjust are well off in this world only because hell is reserved for them later. Eternal bliss is reserved for the pious; occasional sins, which, after all, the pious also commit, ought therefore to be expiated in this world. Yet one can readily be convinced that even this way of thinking, which occasionally appears, is not always determined by resentment, and that it is by no means always the product of socially oppressed strata. We shall see that there have been only a few examples of religion to which resentment contributed essential features. Among these examples only one is a fully developed case. All that can be said is that resentment *could* be, and often and everywhere has been, significant as one factor, among others, in influencing the religiously determined rationalism of socially disadvantaged strata. It has gained such significance, in highly diverse and often minute degrees, in accordance with the nature of the promises held out by different religions.

In any case, it would be quite wrong to attempt to deduce "asceticism" in general from these sources. The distrust of wealth and power, which as a rule exists in genuine religions of salvation, has had its natural basis primarily in the experience of redeemers, prophets, and priests. They understood that those strata which were "satiated" and favored in this world had only a small urge to be saved, regardless of the kind of salvation offered. Hence, these master strata have been less "devout" in the sense of salvation religions. The development of a rational religious ethic has had positive and primary roots in the inner conditions of those social strata which were less socially valued.

Strata in solid possession of social honor and power usually tend to fashion their status-legend in such a way as to claim a special and intrinsic quality of their own, usually a quality of blood; their sense of dignity feeds on their actual or alleged being. The sense of dignity of socially repressed strata or of strata whose status is negatively (or at least not positively) valued is nourished most easily on the belief that a special "mission" is entrusted to them; their worth is guaranteed or constituted by an *ethical imperative,* or by their own functional *achievement.* Their value is thus moved into something beyond themselves, into a "task" placed before them by God. One source of the ideal power of ethical prophecies among socially disadvantaged strata lies in this fact. Resentment has not been required as a leverage; the rational interest in material and ideal compensations as such has been perfectly sufficient.

There can be no doubt that prophets and priests through intentional or unintentional propaganda have taken the resentment of the masses into their service. But this is by no means always the case. This essentially negative force of resentment, so far as is known, has never been the source of those essentially metaphysical conceptions which have lent uniqueness to every salvation religion. Moreover, in general, the nature of a religious promise has by no means necessarily or even predominantly been the mere mouthpiece of a class interest, either of an external or internal nature.

By themselves, the masses, as we shall see, have everywhere remained engulfed in the massive and archaic growth of magic—unless a prophecy that holds out specific promises has swept them into a religious movement of an ethical character. For the rest, the specific nature of the great religious and ethical systems has been determined by social conditions of a far more particular nature than by the mere contrast of ruling and ruled strata.

In order to avoid repetition, some further comments about these relationships may be stated in advance. For the empirical student, the sacred values, differing among themselves, are by no means only, nor even preferably, to be interpreted as "otherworldly." This is so quite apart from the fact that not every religion, nor every world religion, knows of a "beyond" as a locus of definite promises. At first the sacred values of primitive as well as of cultured, prophetic or non-prophetic, religions were quite solid goods of this world. With the only partial exception of Christianity and a few other specifically ascetic creeds, they have consisted of health, a long life, and wealth. These were offered by the promises of the Chinese, Vedic, Zoroastrian, ancient Hebrew, and Islamite religions; and in the same manner by the Phoenician, Egyptian, Babylonian, and ancient Germanic religions, as well as by the promises of Hinduism and Buddhism for the devout laymen. Only the religious virtuoso, the ascetic, the monk, the Sufi, the Dervish strove for sacred values, which were "other-worldly" as compared with such solid goods of this world, as health, wealth, and long life. And these other-worldly sacred values were by no means only values of the *beyond*. This was not the case even where it was understood to be so by the participants. Psychologically considered, man in quest of salvation has been primarily preoccupied by attitudes of the here and now. The puritan *certitudo salutis,* the permanent state of grace that rests in the feeling of "having proved oneself," was psychologically the only concrete object among the sacred values of this ascetic religion. The Buddhist monk, certain to enter Nirvana, seeks the sentiment of a cosmic love; the devout Hindu seeks either Bhakti (fervent love in the possession of God) or apathetic ecstasy. The Chlyst with his radjeny, as well as the dancing Dervish, strives for orgiastic ecstasy. Others seek to be possessed by God and to possess God, to be a bridegroom of the Virgin Mary, or to be the bride of the Savior. The Jesuit's cult of the heart of Jesus, quietistic edification, the pietists' tender love for the child Jesus and its "running sore" [*Wundbruehe*], the sexual and semi-sexual orgies at the wooing of Krishna, the sophisticated cultic dinners of the Vallabhacharis, the gnostic onanist cult activities, the various forms of the *unio mystica,* and the contemplative submersion in the All-one—these states undoubtedly have been sought, first of all, for the sake of such emotional value as they directly offered the devout. In this respect, they have in fact been absolutely equal to the religious and alcoholic intoxication of the Dionysian or the soma cult; to totemic meat-orgies, the cannibalistic feasts, the ancient and religiously consecrated use of hashish, opium, and nicotine; and, in general, to all sorts of magical intoxication. They have been considered specifically consecrated and divine because of their psychic extraordinariness and because of the intrinsic value of the respective states conditioned by them. Even the most primitive orgy has not entirely lacked a meaningful interpretation, although only the rationalized religions have imputed a metaphysical meaning into such specifically religious actions, in addition to the direct appropriation of sacred values. Rationalized religions have thus sublimated the orgy into the "sacrament." The orgy, however, has had a pure animist and magical character; it has contained only small or, indeed, no beginnings of the universalist, cosmic pragmatism of the holy. And such pragmatism is peculiar to all religious rationalism.

Yet even after such a sumblimation of orgy into sacrament has occurred, the fact remains, of course, that for the devout the sacred value, first and above all, has been a psychological state in the *here and now.* Primarily this state consists in the emotional attitude *per se,* which was directly called forth by the specifically religious (or magical) act, by methodical asceticism, or by contemplation.

As extraordinary attitudes, religious states can be only transient in character and in external appearance. Originally this, of course, was everywhere the case. The only way of distinguishing between "religious" and "profane" states is by referring to the extraordinary character of the religious states. A special state, attained by religious means, can be striven for as a "holy state" which is meant to take possession of the entire man and of his lasting fate. The transition from a passing to a permanent holy state has been fluid.

The two highest conceptions of sublimated religious doctrines of salvation are "rebirth" and "redemption." Rebirth, a primeval magical value, has meant the acquisition of a new soul by means of an orgiastic act or through methodically planned asceticism. Man transitorily acquired a new soul in ecstasy; but by means of magical asceticism, he could seek to gain it permanently. The youth who wished to enter the community of warriors as a hero, or to participate in its magical dances or orgies, or who wished to commune with the divinities in cultic feasts, had to have a new soul. The heroic and magical asceticism, the initiation rites of youths, and the sacramental customs of rebirth at important phases of private and collective life are thus quite ancient. The means used in these activities varied, as did their ends: that is, the answers to the question, "For what should I be reborn?"

The various religious or magical states that have given their psychological stamp to religions may be systematized according to very different points of view. Here we shall not attempt such a systematization. In connection with what we have said, we merely wish to indicate quite generally the following.

The kind of empirical state of bliss or experience of rebirth that is sought after as the supreme value by a religion has obviously and necessarily varied according to the character of the stratum which was foremost in adopting it. The chivalrous warrior class, peasants, business classes, and intellectuals with literary education have naturally pursued different religious tendencies. As will become evident, these tendencies have not by themselves determined the psychological character of religion; they have, however, exerted a very lasting influence upon it. The contrast between warrior and peasant classes, and intellectual and business classes, is of special importance. Of these groups, the intellectuals have always been the exponents of a rationalism which in their case has been relatively theoretical. The business classes (merchants and artisans) have been at least possible exponents of rationalism of a more practical sort. Rationalism of either kind has borne very different stamps, but has always exerted a great influence upon the religious attitude.

Above all, the peculiarity of the intellectual strata in this matter has been in the past of the greatest importance for religion. At the present time, it matters little in the development of a religion whether or not modern intellectuals feel the need of enjoying a "religious" state as an "experience," in addition to all sorts of other sensations, in order to decorate their internal and stylish furnishings with paraphernalia guaranteed to be genuine and old. A religious revival has never sprung from such a source. In the past, it was the work of the intellectuals to sublimate the possession of sacred values into a belief in "redemption." The conception of the idea of redemption, as such, is very old, if one understands by it a liberation from distress, hunger, drought, sickness, and ultimately from suffering and death. Yet redemption attained a specific significance only where it expressed a systematic and rationalized "image of the world" and represented a stand in the face of the world. For the meaning as well as the intended and actual psychological quality of redemption has depended upon such a world image and such a stand. Not ideas, but material and ideal interests, directly govern men's conduct. Yet very frequently the "world images" that have been created by "ideas" have, like switchmen, determined the tracks along which action has been pushed by the dynamic of interest. "From what" and "for what" one wished to be redeemed and, let us not forget, "could be" redeemed, depended upon one's image of the world.

There have been very different possibilities in this connection: One could wish to be saved from political and social servitude and lifted into a Messianic realm in the future of this world; or one could wish to be saved from being defiled by ritual impurity and hope for the pure beauty of psychic and bodily existence. One could wish to escape being incarcerated in an impure body and hope for a purely spiritual existence. One could wish to be saved from the eternal and senseless play of human passions and desires and hope for the quietude of the pure beholding of the divine. One could wish to be saved from radical evil and the servitude of sin and hope for the eternal and free benevolence in the lap of a fatherly god. One could wish to be saved from peonage under the astrologically conceived determination of stellar constellations and long for the dignity of freedom and partaking of the substance of the hidden deity. One could wish to be redeemed from the barriers to the finite, which express themselves in suffering, misery and death, and the threatening punishment of hell, and hope for an eternal bliss in an earthly or paradisical future existence. One could wish to be saved from the cycle of rebirths with their

inexorable compensations for the deeds of the times past and hope for eternal rest. One could wish to be saved from senseless brooding and events and long for the dreamless sleep. Many more varieties of belief have, of course, existed. Behind them always lies a stand towards something in the actual world which is experienced as specifically "senseless." Thus, the demand has been implied: that the world order in its totality is, could, and should somehow be a meaningful "cosmos." This quest, the core of genuine religious rationalism, has been borne precisely by strata of intellectuals. The avenues, the results, and the efficacy of this metaphysical need for a meaningful cosmos have varied widely. Nevertheless, some general comments may be made.

The general result of the modern form of thoroughly rationalizing the conception of the world and of the way of life, theoretically and practically, in a purposive manner, has been that religion has been shifted into the realm of the irrational. This has been the more the case the further the purposive type of rationalization has progressed, if one takes the standpoint of an intellectual articulation of an image of the world. This shift of religion into the irrational realm has occurred for several reasons. On the one hand, the calculation of consistent rationalism has not easily come out even with nothing left over. In music, the Pythagorean "comma" resisted complete rationalization oriented to tonal physics. The various great systems of music of all peoples and ages have differed in the manner in which they have either covered up or bypassed this inescapable irrationality or, on the other hand, put irrationality into the service of the richness of tonalities. The same has seemed to happen to the theoretical conception of the world, only far more so; and above all, it has seemed to happen to the rationalization of practical life. The various great ways of leading a rational and methodical life have been charaterized by irrational presuppositions, which have been accepted simply as "given" and which have been incorporated into such ways of life. What these presuppositions have been is historically and socially determined, at least to a very large extent, through the peculiarity of those strata that have been the carriers of the ways of life during its formative and decisive period. The *interest* situation of these strata, as determined socially and psychologically, has made for their peculiarity, as we here understand it.

Furthermore, the irrational elements in the rationalization of reality have been the *loci* to which the irrepressible quest of intellectualism for the possession of supernatural values has been compelled to retreat. That is the more so the more denuded of irrationality the world appears to be. The unity of the primitive image of the world, in which everything was concrete magic, has tended to split into rational cognition and mastery of nature, on the one hand, and into "mystic" experiences, on the other. The inexpressible contents of such experiences remain the only possible "beyond," added to the mechanism of a world robbed of gods. In fact, the beyond remains an incorporeal and metaphysical realm in which individuals intimately possess the holy. Where this conclusion has been drawn without any residue, the individual can pursue his quest for salvation only as an individual. This phenomenon appears in some form, with progressive intellectualist rationalism, wherever men have ventured to rationalize the image of the world as being a cosmos governed by impersonal rules. Naturally it has occurred most strongly among religions and religious ethics which have been quite strongly determined by genteel strata of intellectuals devoted to the purely cognitive comprehension of the world and of its "meaning." This was the case with Asiatic and, above all, Indian world religions. For all of them, contemplation became the supreme and ultimate religious value accessible to man. Contemplation offered them entrance into the profound and blissful tranquillity and immobility of the All-one. All other forms of religious states, however, have been at best considered a relatively valuable *Ersatz* for contemplation. This has had far-reaching consequences for the relation of religion to life, including economic life, as we shall repeatedly see. Such consequences flow from the general character of "mystic" experiences, in the contemplative sense, and from the psychological preconditions of the search for them.

The situation in which strata decisive for the development of a religion were active in practical life has been entirely different. Where they were chivalrous warrior heroes, political officials, economically acquisitive classes, or, finally, where an organized hierocracy dominated religion, the results were different than where genteel intellectuals were decisive.

The rationalism of hierocracy grew out of the professional preoccupation with cult and myth or—to a far higher degree—out of the cure of souls, that is, the confession of sin and counsel to sinners. Everywhere hierocracy has sought to monopolize the administration of religious values. They have also sought to bring and to temper the bestowal of religious goods into the form of "sacramental" or "corporate grace," which could be ritually bestowed only by the priesthood and could not be attained by the individual. The individual's quest for salvation or the quest of free communities by means of contemplation, orgies, or asceticism, has been considered highly suspect and has had to be regulated ritually and, above all, controlled hierocratically.

From the standpoint of the interests of the priesthood in power, this is only natural.

Every body of *political* officials, on the other hand, has been suspicious of all sorts of individual pursuits of salvation and of the free formation of communities as sources of emancipation from domestication at the hands of the institution of the state. Political officials have distrusted the competing priestly corporation of grace and, above all, at bottom they have despised the very quest for these impractical values lying beyond utilitarian and worldly ends. For all political bureaucracies, religious duties have ultimately been simply official or social obligations of the citizenry and of status groups. Ritual has corresponded to rules and regulations, and, therefore, wherever a bureaucracy has determined its nature, religion has assumed a ritualist character.

It is also usual for a stratum of *chivalrous* warriors to pursue absolutely worldly interests and to be remote from all "mysticism." Such strata, however, have lacked—and this is characteristic of heroism in general—the desire as well as the capacity for a rational mastery of reality. The irrationality of "fate" and, under certain conditions, the idea of a vague and deterministically conceived "destiny" (the Homeric *Moira*) has stood above and behind the divinities and demons who were conceived of as passionate and strong heroes, measuring out assistance and hostility, glory and booty, or death to the human heroes.

Peasants have been inclined towards magic. Their whole economic existence has been specifically bound to nature and has made them dependent upon elemental forces. They readily believe in a compelling sorcery directed against spirits who rule over or through natural forces, or they believe in simply buying divine benevolence. Only tremendous transformations of life-orientation have succeeded in tearing them away from this universal and primeval form of religiosity. Such transformations have been derived either from other strata or from mighty prophets, who, through the power of miracles, legitimize themselves as sorcerers. Orgiastic and ecstatic states of "possession," produced by means of toxics or by the dance, are strange to the status honor of knights because they are considered undignified. Among the peasants, however, such states have taken the place that "mysticism" holds among the intellectuals.

Finally, we may consider the strata that in the western European sense are called "civic," as well as those which elsewhere correspond to them: artisans, traders, enterprisers engaged in cottage industry, and their derivatives existing only in the modern Occident. Apparently these strata have been the most ambiguous with regard to the religious stands open to them. And this is especially important to us.

Among these "civic" strata the following religious phenomena have had especially strong roots: the institutional and sacramental grace of the Roman church in the medieval cities—the pillars of the popes; the mystagogic and sacramental grace in the ancient cities and in India; the orgiastic and contemplative Sufi, and Dervish religion of the Middle Eastern Orient; the Taoist magic; the Buddhist contemplation; the ritualist appropriation of grace under the direction of souls by mystagogues in Asia; all the forms of love for a savior; the beliefs in redemption the world over, from the cult of Krishna to the cult of Christ; the rational ritualism of the law and the sermon of the synagogue denuded of all magic among Jewry; the pneumatic and ancient as well as the asceticist medieval sects; the grace of predestination and the ethical regeneration of the Puritan and the Methodist; as well as all sorts of individual pursuits of salvation. All of these have been more firmly rooted among "civic" strata than among any other.

Of course, the religions of all strata are certainly far from being unambiguously dependent upon the character of the strata we have presented as having special affinities with them. Yet, at first sight, civic strata appear, in this respect and on the whole, to lend themselves to a more varied determination. Yet it is precisely among these strata that elective affinities for special types of religion stand out. The tendency towards a *practical* rationalism in conduct is common to all civic strata; it is conditioned by the nature of their way of life, which is greatly detached from economic bonds to nature. Their whole existence has been based upon technological or economic calculations and upon the mastery of nature and of man, however primitive the means at their disposal. The technique of living handed down among them may, of course, be frozen in traditionalism, as has occurred repeatedly and everywhere. But precisely for these, there has always existed the possibility—even though in greatly varying measure—of letting an *ethical* and rational regulation of life arise. This may occur by the linkage of such an ethic to the tendency of technological and economic rationalism. Such regulation has not always been able to make headway against traditions which, in the main, were magically stereotyped. But where prophecy has provided a religious basis, this basis could be one of two fundamental types of prophecy which we shall repeatedly discuss: "exemplary" prophecy, and "emissary" prophecy.

Exemplary prophecy points out the path to salvation by exemplary living, usually by a contemplative and apathetic-ecstatic life. The emissary type of prophecy addresses its *demands* to the world in the name of a god. Naturally these demands are ethical; and they are often of an active ascetic character.

It is quite understandable that the more weighty the civic strata as such have been, and the more they have been torn from bonds of taboo and from divisions into sibs and castes, the more favorable has been the soil for religions that call for action in this world. Under these conditions, the preferred religious attitude could become the attitude of active asceticism, of God-willed *action* nourished by the sentiment of being God's "tool," rather than the possession of the deity or the inward and contemplative surrender to God, which has appeared as the supreme value to religions influenced by strata of genteel intellectuals. In the Occident the attitude of active asceticism has repeatedly retained supremacy over contemplative mysticism and orgiastic or apathetic ecstasy, even though these latter types have been well known in the Occident. Active asceticism, however, has not been confined to civic strata. Such an unambiguous social determination has not in any way existed. The prophecy of Zoroaster was directed at the nobility and the peasantry; the prophecy of Islam was directed to warriors. These prophecies, like the Israelite and the early Christian prophecy and preaching, have had an active character, which stands in contrast with the propaganda of Buddhism, Taoism, Neo-Pythagorism, Gnosticism, and Sufism. Certain specific conclusions of emissary prophecies, however, have been drawn precisely on "civic" grounds.

In the missionary prophecy the devout have not experienced themselves as vessels of the divine but rather as instruments of a god. This emissary prophecy has had a profound elective affinity to a special conception of God: the conception of a supra-mundane, personal, wrathful, forgiving, loving, demanding, punishing Lord of Creation. Such a conception stands in contrast to the supreme being of exemplary prophecy. As a rule, though by no means without exception, the supreme being of an exemplary prophecy is an impersonal being because, as a static state, he is accessible only by means of contemplation. The conception of an active God, held by emissary prophecy, has dominated the Iranian and Mid-Eastern religions and those Occidental religions which are derived from them. The conception of a supreme and static being, held by exemplary prophecy, has come to dominate Indian and Chinese religiosity.

These differences are not primitive in nature. On the contrary, they have come into existence only by means of a far-reaching sublimation of primitive conceptions of animist spirits and of heroic deities which are everywhere similar in nature. Certainly the connection of conceptions of God with religious states, which are evaluated and desired as sacred values, have also been strongly influential in this process of sublimation. These religious states have simply been interpreted in the direction of a different conception of God, according to whether the holy states, evaluated as supreme, were contemplative mystic experiences or apathetic ecstasy, or whether they were the orgiastic possession of god, or visionary inspirations and "commands."

At the present time, it is widely held that one should consider emotional content as primary, with thoughts being merely its secondary expression. Of course, this point of view is to a great extent justified. From such a standpoint one might be inclined to consider the primacy of "psychological" as over against "rational" connections as the only decisive causal nexus, hence to view these rational connections as *mere* interpretations of the psychological ones. This, however, would be going much too far, according to factual evidence. A whole series of purely historical motives have determined the development toward the supra-mundane of the immanent conception of God. These conceptions, in turn, have decisively influenced the way in which experiences of salvation have been articulated. This definitely holds for the conception of the supra-mundane God, as we shall see again and again. If even Meister Eckhart occasionally and expressly placed Martha above Mary, he did so ultimately because he could not realize the pantheist experience of God, which is peculiar to the mystic, without entirely sacrificing all the decisive elements of Occidental belief in God and creation.

The rational elements of a religion, its "doctrine," also have an autonomy: for instance, the Indian doctrine of Kharma, the Calvinist belief in predestination, the Lutheran justification through faith, and the Catholic doctrine of sacrament. The rational religious pragmatism of salvation, flowing from the nature of the images of God and of the world, have under certain conditions had far-reaching results for the fashioning of a practical way of life.

These comments presuppose that the nature of the desired sacred values has been strongly influenced by the nature of the external interest-situation and the corresponding way of life of the ruling strata and thus by the social stratification itself. But the reverse also holds: wherever the direction of the whole way of life has been methodically rationalized, it has been profoundly determined by the ultimate values toward which this rationalization has been directed. These values and positions were thus *religiously* determined. Certainly they have not always, or exclusively, been decisive; however, they have been decisive in so far as an *ethical* rationalization held sway, at least so far as its influence reached. As a rule, these religious values have been also, and frequently absolutely, decisive.

One factor has been very important in determining the nature of the mutual inter-relations between external and internal interest-situations. The "supreme" sacred values, which are promised by religion and have been discussed above, have not necessarily been the most universal ones. Not everybody had entree to Nirvana, to the contemplative union with the divine, the orgiastic or the ascetic possession of God. In a weakened form, the transposition of persons into religious states of frenzy or into the trance may become the object of a universal cult of the people. But even in this form such psychic states have not been elements of everyday life.

The empirical fact, important for us, that men are *differently qualified* in a religious way stands at the beginning of the history of religion. This fact had been dogmatized in the sharpest rationalist form in the "particularism of grace," embodied in the doctrine of predestination by the Calvinists. The sacred values that have been most cherished, the ecstatic and visionary capacities of shamans, sorcerers, ascetics, and pneumatics of all sorts, could not be attained by everyone. The possession of such faculties is a "charisma," which, to be sure, might be awakened in some but not in all. It follows from this that all intensive religiosity has a tendency toward a sort of *status stratification*, in accordance with differences in the charismatic qualifications. "Heroic" or "virtuoso" religiosity is opposed to mass religiosity. By "mass" we understand those who are religiously "unmusical"; we do not, of course, mean those who occupy an inferior position in the secular status order. In this sense, the status carriers of a virtuoso religion have been the leagues of sorcerers and sacred dancers; the religious status group of the Indian Sramana and of the early Christian "ascetics," who were expressly recognized in the congregation as a special "estate"; the Paulinian, and still more the Gnostic, "pneumatics," the pietist *ecclesiola;* all genuine "sects"—that is, sociologically speaking, associations that accept only religiously qualified persons in their midst; and finally, monk communities all over the world.

Now, every hierocratic and official authority of a "church"—that is, a community organized by officials into an institution which bestows gifts of grace—fights principally against all virtuoso-religion and against its autonomous development. For the church, being the holder of institutionalized grace, seeks to organize the religiosity of the masses and to put its own officially monopolized and mediated sacred values in the place of the autonomous and religious status qualifications of the religious virtuosos. By its nature, that is, according to the interest-situation of its officeholders, the church must be "democratic" in the sense of making the sacred values generally accessible. This means that the church stands for a universalism of grace and for the ethical sufficiency of all those who are enrolled under its institutional authority. Sociologically, the process of leveling constitutes a complete parallel with the political struggles of the bureaucracy against the political privileges of the aristocratic estates. As with hierocracy, every full-grown political bureaucracy is necessarily and in a quite similar sense "democratic"—namely, in the sense of leveling and of fighting against status privileges that compete with its power.

The most varied compromises have resulted from this struggle between officialdoms and the virtuosos. These struggles have not always been official but they have always existed at least covertly. Thus, the religiosity of the Ulema stood against the religiosity of the Dervishes; the early Christian bishops against the pneumatics and heroist sectaries as well as against the power of The Key of asceticist charisma; the Lutheran preacher's office and the Anglican and priestly church stood against asceticism in general; the Russian state church was opposed to the sects; and the official management of the Confucian cult stood against Buddhist, Taoist, and sectarian pursuits of salvation of all sorts. The religious virtuosos saw themselves compelled to adjust their demands to the possibilities of the religiosity of everyday life in order to gain and to maintain ideal and material mass-patronage. The nature of their concessions have naturally been of primary significance for the way in which they have religiously influenced everyday life. In almost all Oriental religions, the virtuosos allowed the masses to remain stuck in magical tradition. Thus, the influence of religious virtuosos has been infinitely smaller than was the case where religion has undertaken ethically and generally to rationalize everyday life. This has been the case even when religion has aimed precisely at the masses and has cancelled however many of its ideal demands. Besides the relations between the religiosity of the virtuosos and the religion of the masses, which finally resulted from this struggle, the peculiar nature of the concrete religiosity of the virtuosos has been of decisive importance for the development of the way of life of the masses. This virtuoso religiosity has therefore also been important for the economic ethic of the respective religion. The religion of the virtuoso has been the genuinely "exemplary" and practical religion. According to the way of life his religion prescribed to

the virtuoso, there have been various possibilities of establishing a rational ethic of everyday life. The relation of virtuoso religion to *workaday life* in the locus of the economy has varied, especially according to the peculiarity of the sacred values desired by such religions.

Wherever the sacred values and the redemptory means of a virtuoso religion bore a contemplative or orgiastic-ecstatic character, there has been no bridge between religion and the practical action of the workaday world. In such cases, the economy and all other action in the world has been considered religiously inferior, and no psychological motives for worldly action could be derived from the attitude cherished as the supreme value. In their innermost beings, contemplative and ecstatic religions have been rather specifically hostile to economic life. Mystic, orgiastic, and ecstatic experiences are extraordinary psychic states; they lead away from everyday life and from all expedient conduct. Such experiences are, therefore, deemed to be "holy." With such religions, a deep abyss separates the way of life of the laymen from that of the community of virtuosos. The rule of the status groups of religious virtuosos over the religious community readily shifts into a magical anthropolatry; the virtuoso is directly worshipped as a Saint, or at least laymen buy his blessing and his magical powers as a means of promoting mundane success or religious salvation. As the peasant was to the landlord, so the layman was to the Buddhist and Jainist bhikshu [mendicant friar]; ultimately, mere sources of tribute. Such tribute allowed the virtuosos to live entirely for religious salvation without themselves performing profane work, which always would endanger their salvation. Yet the conduct of the layman could still undergo a certain ethical regulation, for the virtuoso was the layman's spiritual adviser, his father confessor and *directeur de l'âme*. Hence, the virtuoso frequently exercises a powerful influence over the religiously "unmusical" laymen; this influence might not be in the direction of his (the virtuoso's) own religious way of life; it might be an influence in merely ceremonious, ritualist, and conventional particulars. For action in this world remained in principle religiously insignificant; and compared with the desire for the religious end, action lay in the very opposite direction.

In the end, the charisma of the pure "mystic" serves only himself. The charisma of the genuine magician serves others.

Things have been quite different where the religiously qualified virtuosos have combined into an ascetic sect, striving to mould life in this world according to the will of a god. To be sure, two things were necessary before this could happen in a genuine way. First, the supreme and sacred value must not be of a contemplative nature; it must not consist of a union with a supra-mundane being who, in contrast to the world, lasts forever; nor in a *unia mystica* to be grasped orgiastically or apathetic-ecstatically. For these ways always lie apart from everyday life and beyond the real world and lead away from it. Second, such a religion must, so far as possible, have given up the purely magical or sacramental character of the *means* of grace. For these means always devalue action in this world as, at best, merely relative in their religious significance, and they link the decision about salvation to the success of processes which are *not* of a rational everyday nature.

When religious virtuosos have combined into an active asceticist sect, two aims are completely attained: the disenchantment of the world and the blockage of the path to salvation by a flight from the world. The path to salvation is turned away from a contemplative "flight from the world" and towards an active ascetic "work in this world." If one disregards the small rationalist sects, such as are found all over the world, this has been attained only in the great church and sect organizations of Occidental and asceticist Protestantism. The quite distinct and the purely historically determined destinies of Occidental religions have co-operated in this matter. Partly, the social environment exerted an influence, above all, the environment of the stratum that was decisive for the development of such religion. Partly, however—and just as strongly—the intrinsic character of Christianity exerted an influence: the supra-mundane God and the specificity of the means and paths of salvation as determined historically, first by Israelite prophecy and the thora doctrine.

The religious virtuoso can be placed in the world as the instrument of a God and cut off from all magical means of salvation. At the same time, it is imperative for the virtuoso that he "prove" himself before God, as being called *solely* through the ethical quality of his conduct in this world. This actually means that he "prove" himself to himself as well. No matter how much the "world" as such is religiously devalued and rejected as being creatural and a vessel of sin, yet psychologically the world is all the more affirmed as the theatre of God-willed activity in one's worldly "calling." For this inner-worldly asceticism rejects the world in the sense that it despises and taboos the values of dignity and beauty, of the beautiful frenzy and the dream, purely secular power, and the purely worldly pride of the hero. Asceticism outlawed these values as competitors of the kingdom of God. Yet precisely because of this rejection, asceticism did not fly from the world, as did contemplation. Instead, asceticism

has wished to rationalize the world ethically in accordance with God's commandments. It has therefore remained oriented towards the world in a more specific and thoroughgoing sense than did the naive "affirmation of the world" of unbroken humanity, for instance, in Antiquity and in lay-Catholicism. In inner-worldly asceticism, the grace and the chosen state of the religiously qualified man prove themselves in everyday life. To be sure, they do so not in the everyday life as it is given, but in methodical and rationalized routine-activities of workaday life in the service of the Lord. Rationally raised into a vocation, everyday conduct becomes the locus for proving one's state of grace. The Occidental sects of the religious virtuosos have fermented the methodical rationalization of conduct, including economic conduct. These sects have not constituted valves for the longing to escape from the senselessness of work in this world, as did the Asiatic communities of the ecstatics: contemplative, orgiastic, or apathetic.

The most varied transitions and combinations are found between the polar opposites of "exemplary" and "emissary" prophecy. Neither religions nor men are open books. They have been historical rather than logical or even psychological constructions without contradiction. Often they have borne within themselves a series of motives, each of which, if separately and consistently followed through, would have stood in the way of the others or run against them head-on. In religious matters "consistency" has been the exception and not the rule. The ways and means of salvation are also psychologically ambiguous. The search for God of the early Christian monk as well as of the Quaker contained very strong contemplative elements. Yet the total content of their religions and, above all, their supra-mundane God of creation and their way of making sure of their states of grace again and again directed them to the course of action. On the other hand, the Buddhist monk was also active, but his activities were withdrawn from any consistent rationalization *in this world;* his quest for salvation was ultimately oriented to the flight from the "wheel" of the rebirths. The sectarians and other brotherhoods of the Occidental Middle Ages spearheaded the religious penetration of everyday life. They found their counter-image in the brotherhoods of Islam, which were even more widely developed. The stratum typical of such brotherhoods in the Occident and in Islam were identical: petty bourgeois and especially artisans. Yet the spirit of their respective religions were very different. Viewed externally, numerous Hinduist religious communities appear to be "sects" just as do those of the Occident. The sacred value, however, and the manner in which values were mediated pointed in radically different directions.

We shall not accumulate more examples here, as we wish to consider the great religions separately. In no respect can one simply integrate various world religions into a chain of types, each of them signifying a new "stage." All the great religions are historical individualities of a highly complex nature; taken all together, they exhaust only a few of the possible combinations that could conceivably be formed from the very numerous individual factors to be considered in such historical combinations.

Thus, the following presentations do not in any way constitute a systematic "typology" of religion. On the other hand, they do not constitute a purely historical work. They are "typological" in the sense that they consider what is typically important in the historical realizations of the religious ethics. This is important for the connection of religions with the great contrasts of the *economic* mentalities. Other aspects will be neglected; these presentations do not claim to offer a well-rounded picture of world religions. Those features peculiar to the individual religions, in contrast to other religions, but which at the same time are important for our interest, must be brought out strongly. A presentation that disregards these special accents of importance would often have to tone down the special features in which we are interested. Such a balanced presentation would almost always have to add other features and occasionally would have to give greater emphasis to the fact that, of course, all qualitative contrasts in reality, in the last resort, can somehow be comprehended as purely quantitative differences in the combinations of single factors. However, it would be extremely unfruitful to emphasize and repeat here what goes without saying.

The features of religions that are important for economic ethics shall interest us primarily from a definite point of view: we shall be interested in the way in which they are related to economic rationalism. More precisely, we mean the economic rationalism of the type which, since the sixteenth and seventeenth centuries, has come to dominate the Occident as part of the particular rationalization of civic life, and which has become familiar in this part of the world.

We have to remind ourselves in advance that "rationalism" may mean very different things. It means one thing if we think of the kind of rationalization the systematic thinker performs on the image of the world: an increasing theoretical mastery of reality by means of increasingly precise and abstract concepts. Rationalism means another thing if we think of the methodical attainment of a definitely given and practical end by means of an increasingly precise calculation of adequate means. These types of rationalism are very different, in spite of the fact that ultimately they belonged inseparably together. Similar types may be distinguished even within the intellectual comprehension of reality; for instance, the differences between English Physics and Continental Physics has been traced back to such a type difference within the comprehension of reality. The rationalization of life conduct with which we have to deal here can assume unusually varied forms.

In the sense of the absence of all metaphysics and almost all residues of religious anchorage, Confucianism is rationalist to such a far-going extent that it stands at the extreme boundary of what one might possibly call a "religious" ethic. At the same time, Confucianism is more rationalist and sober, in the sense of the absence and the rejection of all non-utilitarian yardsticks, than any other ethical system, with the possible exception of J. Bentham's. Yet Confucianism, in spite of constantly actual and apparent analogies, nevertheless differs extraordinarily from Bentham's as well as from all other Occidental types of practical rationalism. The supreme artistic ideal of the Renaissance was "rational" in the sense of a belief in a valid "canon," and the view of life of the Renaissance was rational in the sense of rejecting traditionalist bonds and of having faith in the power of the *naturalis ratio*. This type of rationalism prevailed in spite of certain elements of Platonizing mysticism.

"Rational" may also mean a "systematic arrangement" [*Planmassig-Keil*]. In this sense, the following methods are rational: methods of mortificatory or of magical asceticism, of contemplation in its most consistent forms—for instance, in *yoga*—or in the manipulations of the prayer machines of later Buddhism.

In general, all kinds of practical ethics that are systematically and unambiguously oriented to fixed goals of salvation are "rational," partly in the same sense as formal method is rational, and partly in the sense that they distinguish between "valid" norms and what is empirically given. These types of rationalization processes are of interest to us in the following presentations. It would be senseless to try to anticipate the typologies of these presentations here, for they aim to make a contribution to such typology.

In order to make this attempt, the author must take the liberty of being "unhistorical," in the sense that the ethics of individual religions are presented systematically and essentially in greater unity than has ever been the case in the flux of their actual development. Rich contrasts which have been alive in individual religions, as well as incipient developments and ramifications, must be left aside; and the features that to the author are important must often be presented in greater logical consistency and less historical development than was actually the case. If it were done arbitrarily, this simplification would be a historical "falsification." This, however, is not the case, at least not intentionally. The author has always underscored those features in the total picture of a religion which have been decisive for the fashioning of the *practical* way of life, as well as those which distinguish one religion from another.

Finally, before going into the subject matter, some remarks by way of explaining terminological peculiarities which frequently recur in the presentation may be advanced.

When fully developed, religious associations and communities belong to a type of corporate authority. They represent "hierocratic" associations, that is, their power to rule is supported by their monopoly in the bestowal or denial of sacred values.

All ruling powers, profane and religious, political and apolitical, may be considered as variations of, or approximations to, certain pure types. These types are constructed by searching for the basis of *legitimacy,* which the ruling power claims. Our modern "associations," above all the political ones, are of the type of "legal" authority. That is, the legitimacy of the power-holder to give commands rests upon rules that are rationally established by enactment, by agreement, or by imposition. The legitimation for establishing these rules rests, in turn, upon a rationally enacted or interpreted "constitution." Orders are given in the name of the impersonal norm, rather than in the name of a personal authority; and even the giving of a command constitutes obedience toward a norm rather than an arbitrary freedom, favor, or privilege.

The "official" is the holder of the power to command; he never exercises this power in his own right; he holds it as a trustee of the impersonal and "compulsory institution" [*Anstalt*]. This institution is made up of the specific patterns of life of a plurality of men, definite or indefinite, yet specified according to rules. Their joint pattern of life is normatively governed by statutory regulations.

The "area of jurisdiction" is a functionally delimited realm of possible objects for command and thus delimits the sphere of the official's legitimate power. A hierarchy of superiors, to which officials may appeal and complain in an order of rank, stands opposite the citizen or member of the association. Today this situation also holds for the hierocratic association that is the church. The pastor or priest has his definitely limited "jurisdiction," which is fixed by rules. This also holds for the supreme head of the church. The present concept of [papal] "in-

fallibility" is a jurisdictional concept. Its inner meaning differs from that which preceded it, even up to the time of Innocent III.

The separation of the "private sphere" from the "official sphere" (in the case of infallibility: the *ex cathedra* definition) is carried through in the church in the same way as in political, or other, officialdoms. The legal separation of the official from the means of administration (either in natural or in pecuniary form) is carried through in the sphere of political and hierocratic associations in the same way as is the separation of the worker from the means of production in capitalist economy: it runs fully parallel to them.

No matter how many beginnings may be found in the remote past, in its full development all this is specifically modern. The past has known other bases for authority, bases which, incidentally, extend as survivals into the present. Here we wish merely to outline these bases of authority in a terminological way.

1. In the following discussions the term "charisma" shall be understood to refer to an *extraordinary* quality of a person, regardless of whether this quality is actual, alleged, or presumed. "Charismatic authority," hence, shall refer to a rule over men, whether predominantly external or predominantly internal, to which the governed submit because of their belief in the extraordinary quality of the specific *person.* The magical sorcerer, the prophet, the leader of hunting and booty expeditions, the warrior chieftain, the so-called "Caesarist" ruler, and, under certain conditions, the personal head of a party are such types of rulers for their disciples, followings, enlisted troops, parties, et cetera. The legitimacy of their rule rests on the belief in and the devotion to the extraordinary, which is valued because it goes beyond the normal human qualities, and which was originally valued as supernatural. The legitimacy of charismatic rule thus rests upon the belief in magical powers, revelations and hero worship. The source of these beliefs is the "proving" of the charismatic quality through miracles, through victories and other successes, that is, through the welfare of the governed. Such beliefs and the claimed authority resting on them therefore disappear, or threaten to disappear, as soon as proof is lacking and as soon as the charismatically qualified person appears to be devoid of his magical power or forsaken by his god. Charismatic rule is not managed according to general norms, either traditional or rational, but, in principle, according to concrete revelations and inspirations, and in this sense, charismatic authority is "irrational." It is "revolutionary" in the sense of not being bound to

the existing order: "It is written—but I say unto you . . . !"

2. "Traditionalism" in the following discussions shall refer to the psychic attitude-set for the habitual workaday and to the belief in the everyday routine as an inviolable norm of conduct. Domination that rests upon this basis, that is, upon piety for what actually, allegedly, or presumably has always existed, will be called "traditionalist authority."

Patriarchalism is by far the most important type of domination the legitimacy of which rests upon tradition. Patriarchalism means the authority of the father, the husband, the senior of the house, the sib elder over the members of the household and sib; the rule of the master and patron over bondsmen, serfs, freed men; of the lord over the domestic servants and household officials; of the prince over house- and court-officials, nobles of office, clients, vassals; of the patrimonial lord and sovereign prince (*Landesvater*) over the "subjects."

It is characteristic of patriarchial and of patrimonial authority, which represents a variety of the former, that the system of inviolable norms is considered sacred; an infraction of them would result in magical or religious evils. Side by side with this system there is a realm of free arbitrariness and favor of the lord, who in principle judges only in terms of "personal," not "functional," relations. In this sense, traditionalist authority is irrational.

3. Throughout early history, charismatic authority, which rests upon a belief in the sancity or the value of the extraordinary, and traditionalist (patriarchical) domination, which rests upon a belief in the sanctity of everyday routines, divided the most important authoritative relations between them. The bearers of charisma, the oracles of prophets, or the edicts of charismatic war lords alone could integrate "new" laws into the circle of what was upheld by tradition. Just as revelation and the sword were the two extraordinary powers, so were they the two typical innovators. In typical fashion, however, both succumbed to routinization as soon as their work was done.

With the death of the prophet or the war lord the question of successorship arises. This question can be solved by *Kürung,* which was originally not an "election" but a selection in terms of charismatic qualification; or the question can be solved by the sacramental substantiation of charisma, the successor being designated by consecration, as is the case in hierocratic or apostolic succession; or the belief in the charismatic qualification of the charismatic leader's sib can lead to a belief in hereditary charisma, as represented by hereditary kingship and hereditary hierocracy. With these routinizations, *rules* in some form always come to govern. The

prince or the hierocrat no longer rules by virtue of purely personal qualities, but by virtue of acquired or inherited qualities, or because he has been legitimized by an act of charismatic election. The process of routinization, and thus traditionalization, has set in.

Perhaps it is even more important that when the organization of authority becomes permanent, the staff supporting the charismatic ruler becomes routinized. The ruler's disciples, apostles, and followers became priests, feudal vassals and, above all, officials. The original charismatic community lived communistically off donations, alms, and the booty of war: they were thus specifically alienated from the economic order. The community was transformed into a stratum of aids to the ruler and depended upon him for maintenance through the usufruct of land, office fees, income in kind, salaries, and hence, through prebends. The staff derived its legitimate power in greatly varying stages of appropriation, infeudation, conferment, and appointment. As a rule, this meant that princely prerogatives became *patrimonial* in nature. Patrimonialism can also develop from pure patriarchalism through the disintegration of the patriarchical master's strict authority. By virtue of conferment, the prebendary or the vassal has as a rule had a personal *right* to the office bestowed upon him. Like the artisan who possessed the economic means of production, the prebendary possessed the means of administration. He had to bear the costs of administration out of his office fees or other income, or he passed on to the lord only part of the taxes gathered from the subjects, retaining the rest. In the extreme case he could bequeath and alienate his office like other possession. We wish to speak of *status* patrimonialism when the development by appropriation of prerogatory power has reached this stage, without regard to whether it developed from charismatic or patriarchical beginnings.

The development, however, has seldom stopped at this stage. We always meet with a *struggle* between the political or hierocratic lord and the owners or usurpers of prerogatives, which they have appropriated as status groups. The ruler attempts to expropriate the estates, and the estates attempt to expropriate the ruler. The more the ruler succeeds in attaching to himself a staff of officials who depend solely on him and whose interests are linked to his, the more this struggle is decided in favor of the ruler and the more the privilege-holding estates are gradually expropriated. In this connection, the prince acquires administrative means of his own and he keeps them firmly in his own hands. Thus we find political rulers in the Occident, and progressively from Innocent III to Johann XXII, also hierocratic rulers who have finances of their own, as well as secular rulers who have magazines and arsenals of their own for the provisioning of the army and the officials.

The *character* of the stratum of officials upon whose support the ruler has relied in the struggle for the expropriation of status prerogatives has varied greatly in history. In Asia and in the Occident during the early Middle Ages they were typically clerics; during the Oriental Middle Ages they were typically slaves and clients; for the Roman Principate, freed slaves to a limited extent were typical; humanist literati were typical for China; and finally, jurists have been typical for the modern Occident, in ecclesiastical as well as in political associations.

The triumph of princely power and the expropriation of particular prerogatives has everywhere signified at least the possibility, and often the actual introduction, of a rational administration. As we shall see, however, this rationalization has varied greatly in extent and meaning. One must, above all, distinguish between the *substantive* rationalization of administration and of judiciary by a patrimonial prince, and the *formal* rationalization carried out by trained jurists. The former bestows utilitarian and social ethical blessings upon his subjects, in the manner of the master of a large house upon the members of his household. The trained jurists have carried out the rule of general laws applying to all "citizens of the state." However fluid the difference has been—for instance, in Babylon or Byzantium, in the Sicily of the Hohenstaufen, or the England of the Stuarts, or the France of the Bourbons—in the final analysis, the difference between substantive and formal rationality has persisted. And, in the main, it has been the work of *jurists* to give birth to the modern Occidental "state" as well as to the Occidental "churches." We shall not discuss at this point the source of their strength, the substantive ideas, and the technical means for this work.

With the triumph of *formalist* juristic rationalism the legal type of domination appeared in the Occident at the side of the transmitted types of domination. Bureaucratic rule was not and is not the only variety of legal authority, but it is the purest. The modern state and municipal official, the modern Catholic priest and chaplain, the officials and employees of modern banks and of large capitalist enterprises represent, as we have already mentioned, the most important types of this structure of domination.

The following characteristic must be considered decisive for our terminology: in legal authority, submission does not rest upon the belief and devotion to charismatically gifted persons, like prophets and heroes, or upon sacred tradition, or upon piety toward a personal lord and master who is defined by an ordered tradition, or upon piety toward the possible incumbents of office fiefs and office prebends who are legitimized in their own right through privilege and conferment. Rather, submission under legal authority is based upon an *impersonal* bond to the generally defined and functional "duty of office." The official duty—like the corresponding right to exercise authority: the "jurisdictional competency"—is fixed by *rationally established* norms, by enactments, decrees, and regulations, in such a manner that the legitimacy of the authority becomes the legality of the general rule, which is purposely thought out, enacted, and announced with formal correctness.

The differences between the types of authority we have sketched pertain to all particulars of their social structure and of their economic significance. Only a systematic presentation could demonstrate how far the distinctions and terminology chosen here are expedient. Here we may emphasize merely that by approaching in this way, we do not claim to use the only possible approach nor do we claim that all empirical structures of domination must correspond to one of these "pure" types. On the contrary, the great majority of empirical cases represent a combination or a state of transition among several such pure types. We shall be compelled again and again to form expressions like "patrimonial bureaucracy" in order to make the point that the characteristic traits of the respective phenomenon belong in part to the rational form of domination, whereas other traits belong to a traditionalist form of domination, in this case to that of estates. We also recognize highly important forms that have been universally diffused throughout history, such as the feudal structure of domination. Important aspects of these structures, however, cannot be classified smoothly under any one of the three forms we have distinguished. They can be understood only as combinations involving several concepts, in this case the concepts of "status group" and "status honor." There are also forms that have to be understood partly in terms of principles other than those of "domination," partly in terms of peculiar variations of the concept of charisma. Examples are: the functionaries of *pure* democracy with rotations of honorific offices and similar forms, on the one hand, and plebiscitarian domination, on the other hand, or certain forms of notable rule that are special forms of traditional domination. Such forms, however, have certainly belonged to the most important ferments for the delivery of political rationalism. By the terminology suggested here, we do not wish to force schematically the infinite and multifarious historical life, but simply to create concepts useful for special purposes and for orientation.

The same qualifications hold for a final terminological distinction. We understand by "status" situation the probability of certain social groups receiving positive or negative social *honor.* The chances of attaining social honor are primarily determined by differences in the *styles of life* of these groups, hence chiefly by differences of *education.* Referring to the preceding terminology of forms of authority, we may say that, secondarily, social honor very frequently and typically is associated with the respective stratum's legally guaranteed and monopolized claim to sovereign rights or to income and profit opportunities of a certain kind. Thus, if all these characteristics are found, which, of course, is not always the case, a "status group" is a group societalized through its special styles of life, its conventional and specific notions of honor, and the economic opportunities it legally monopolizes. A status group is always somehow societalized, but it is not always organized into an association. *Commercium,* in the sense of "social intercourse," and *connubium* among groups are the typical characteristics of the *mutual esteem* among status equals; their absence signifies status differences.

By "class situation," in contrast, we shall understand the opportunities to gain sustenance and income that are primarily determined by typical, *economically* relevant, situations; property of a certain kind, or acquired skill in the execution of services that are in demand, is decisive for income opportunities. "Class situation" also comprises the ensuing general and typical living conditions, for instance, the necessity of complying with the discipline of a capitalist proprietor's workshop.

A "status situation" can be the cause as well as the result of a "class situation," but it need be neither. Class situations, in turn, can be primarily *determined by markets,* by the labor market and the commodity market. The specific and typical cases of class situation today are ones determined by markets. But such is not necessarily the case: class situations of landlord and small peasant may depend upon market relations only in a negligible way. In their differing situations, the various categories of "rentiers" depend on the market in greatly varying senses and extents, according to whether they derive their rents as landlords, slave-holders, or as owners of bonds and effects.

One must therefore distinguish between "propertied classes" and primarily market-determined "income classes." Present-day society is predominantly stratified in classes, and to an especially high degree in income classes. But in the special *status* prestige of the "educated" strata, our society contains a very tangible element of stratification by status. Externally, this status factor is most obviously represented by economic monopolies and the preferential social opportunities of the holders of degrees.

In the past the significance of stratification by status was far more decisive, above all, for the economic structure of the societies. For, on the one hand, status stratification influences the economic structure by barriers or regulations of consumption, and by status monopolies which from the point of view of economic rationality are irrational, and on the other hand, status stratification influences the economy very strongly through the bearing of the status *conventions* of the respective ruling strata who set the example. These conventions may be in the nature of *ritualist* stereotyped forms, which to a large extent has been the case with the status stratification of Asia.

EPILOGUE

The Calling of Sociology

BY EDWARD SHILS

THE ESTABLISHMENT AND RECEPTION OF SOCIOLOGY

From Heterogeneity to Unity

AFTER THE FIRST WORLD WAR, intellectual seismologists could detect the tremors in psychoanalysis. The ground under the Tree of Knowledge was shaking. The trunk resisted, but the branches shook and the leaves fluttered. The source of the shock was clear and definite and had a namable author. Since the Second World War, another vibration has been felt. It has not been experienced so startlingly as psychoanalysis; it does not, at first sight, seem to challenge inherited ethical ideas so sharply. It sometimes seems a fitter subject for intellectual meteorology than seismology; it is more like a cloud that envelops than a startling, bodily felt shock. It has crept in like a fog and appeared in our midst without plan and without visible intention. It has no single locatable, namable source. It was innocuously in our midst all the time, and grew upon us without announcement. It is not, however, a subject of the upper atmosphere. The entry of sociology is something as fundamental as the ground we stand on; the changes that have accompanied its formation are fundamental changes in the relationships of human beings with each other and with the things they regard as important. Before it spread among us and became part of our outlook, it had been in long and diverse preparation.

The concerns of counselors to princes, of philosophers who would be kings, of disenchanted moralists, of rueful critics of conquest and revolution provided the rudiments of the sociological outlook. They provided that detachment in intimate participation which is the platform of sociological observation. Distinct families of tradition began to be formed, linking with each other and then drawing away again. The coalescence of those preacademic traditions of thought and observation, which retrospectively may now be seen as the sources of sociology, has occurred only recently—certainly no earlier than the present century. The heterogeneous rudiments of sociology took shape before the emergence of universities; but sociology could not have become the comprehensively open and unitary sensibility that it is now, without having become a subject of the modern university syllabus. The relatively unified theoretical orientation that now dominates sociological inquiry, even among those sociologists who believe that they are its antagonists, could not have emerged had it not been for the assimilation of sociology into the universities. It had to become a university subject before it could come into the possession of its present, larger public; it had to become a university subject, first and foremost. It had to become academic—academic in its home, academic in its style—to acquire such unity as it now possesses and to develop the aspiration toward a greater unity.

The scatter of concrete sociological interests was, for a long time, the bane of thoughtful sociologists and the butt of its critics. Assembled into a single university faculty, the diversity of the traditions that have gone into its making revealed its motleyness. It was not a motleyness that went deep; the instinct of the university professors and administrators who brought those apparently random things together was a sound one. For a time, it appeared that sociology was just a collection of the rejects and sweepings cast off by the other, older academic

1405

social sciences—which were also not academic in their origins. It is not, however, in the nature of the best academic minds to tolerate randomness indefinitely—even though many accept it, some glory in it, and many more are incapable of overcoming it.

The establishment of sociology as a coherent subject, the creation of the general theory that is now in its beginnings, and the nurture of the comprehensive sociological sensibility that is its product and its source, all owe a tremendous amount —as does almost everything in the modern learned world—to the great age of the German university. It is not that sociology prospered in the German universities. For the most part of its history in the German universities—which coincided mainly with a period of decline of those institutions from their once great condition—sociology was an arid subject. It was a thing of definitions and classifications, as dry as dust and as lifeless. There was, however, a valid impulse in these efforts. They were an attempt to make sociology systematic—that is, to make it into a coherent body of thought, unified around certain fundamental problems and the fundamental concepts that were entailed in these problems. The problem was the formation of a coherent order, of the concert of actions and their disaggregation. The effort was not very successful. The greatest mind of German sociology did not teach sociology. The academic German sociologists never succeeded in going beyond the taxonomic into the dynamic. The impetus the German university tradition gave to the unification of concepts exhausted itself with the attainment of classification. They did not know how to go further; but, more important, they did not have the impetus to go further. They lacked the curiosity about particular actions and about man and society in general to go further. The quality of imagination and the contemplative intensity of those scholars who had sociology in their care were too slight. The empirical achievement of sociology was still too meager, the scope of sociological interest still too narrow, to give the sociological sensibility the substantial and differentiated stimulation it needed.

Nonetheless, the German tradition of the systematic treatise and textbook that orders a whole body of knowledge—although it was often performed with scholastic pedantry and was regarded by some sociologists as the end state of sociological development—was one source of the movement to bring into a single complex discipline, with a central outlook, the wide diversity of scattered traditions that have gone into the making of sociology. The mere coexistence, within a single faculty of a characteristic American university of the twentieth century, of criminology, family studies, human ecology,

and urban sociology, the study of social status, political sociology, rural sociology, and the many other small dominions of the academic sociological empire, would, in the course of time, by an imperceptible osmotic process, have drawn them into a somewhat greater unity. But independent of this possibility, and more important, was the effort to systematize the subject as a whole that arose from the Germanic university tradition of comprehensive textbooks and systematic treatises. For many decades, the efforts, although persistent, were unavailing. The sociological outlook—that vision of society as an incessant interplay of creativity, discipline, refusal, and revolt against a shifting scene of primordial, civil, sacred, and personal objects— had not yet become articulate.

By the late 1930's, sociology presented a picture of disarray. In the United States, there was already in existence a disconnected mass of particular inquiries, with practically nothing in common except their lively curiosity about contemporary America and their aspiration toward observational discipline. In Britain, the output was far smaller; on a microscopic scale, the situation was as in the United States. In other countries, empirical studies were rare. Analytically, the coherent sociological standpoint we now know made an occasional muffled appearance in the inquiries of the pupils of Park, and in the work of Mayo, Roethlisberger, Warner, Lazarsfeld, Dollard, and others. It was hesitant and uncertain, and its movements were unco-ordinated. The promulgation of a substantive sociological theory had made scarcely any progress since Weber and Durkheim. In Germany, in France, in Italy and Great Britain, the theoretical movement of the first part of the century came practically to a halt. In the United States, exertions were more deliberate, but the results were not impressive. False starts, from psychoanalysis and the behaviorist theory of learning, ran into the ground or evaporated into the air.

The Structure of Social Action was the turning point. It was this work that brought the greatest of the partial traditions into a measure of unity. It precipitated the sociological outlook that had been implicit in the most interesting of the empirical inquiries; it made explicit the affinities and complementarity of the sociological traditions that had arisen out of utilitarianism, idealism, and positivism. It redirected sociology into its classical path, and, in doing so, it began the slow process of bringing into the open the latent dispositions that had underlain the growth of sociological curiosity. Abstract and complicated though its argument was, *The Structure of Social Action* laid out the main lines of the concrete sociological outlook that has come forward in academic study and in the public appreciation of sociology since its appearance.

From the University to a Wider Public

In its largely inchoate state, sociology in the 1920's scarcely engaged the public mind. *Middletown* was, perhaps, the first work of academic sociology that aroused and partially satisfied the need for self-understanding. It left no lasting impact, other than the awareness that such efforts were possible and would be welcomed. *Recent Social Trends* and *The American Dilemma,* in the 1930's, refreshed the memory of *Middletown* and prepared the way for a more general reception of sociology.

Except, however, for the occasional trajectory of an isolated report across the field of public attention, sociology lived mainly within the walls of the university, emerging only for material and then returning to digest and assimilate the facts of the outer world into an academic discipline. In the United States, it led a quiet, crudely respectable life, largely confined to the universities, where it was popular among students and diseesteemed among the practitioners of the other academic disciplines. In Britain, it hardly found academic tolerance until the end of the Second World War, and its infiltration into the larger public occurred much later. In Germany, too, in the universities, sociology—after the First World War and until the beginning of the Nazi regime, when it went into exile—led a fruitlessly solitary, usually neglected, sometimes dimly stormy career. The seed of German sociology ripened only when it was transplanted to America. The seed of sociological theory could not grow without being fertilized by empirical research and by the diversification of its objects; the German universities offered little opportunity or motive for this kind of research. In France, its establishment was still scant and scattered; but, in so far as it existed at all, it was in universities.

So, for many years, sociology lived its life, despised and scarcely tolerated by publicists, amateurs and professors of philosophy, economists, and students of literature. Even when it obtained academic establishment, its lot was not a happy one. Its intellectual right to existence was often denied, even when it was allowed academic survival. Many were the debates in Germany about the possible existence of sociology—debates which often ended in negative conclusion. Sociologists themselves felt the pressure of this contempt and expended much energy in attempting to justify their existence—not by works, but by the demonstration that they had a proper place in the hierarchy of the sciences, that they were practitioners of a branch of learning that had an important subject matter and a logically defensible claim to respect. They spent much time in the assertion of methodological principles that received neither reinforcement nor guidance from a matrix of experience.[1]

Even in pragmatic America, the country of legendary theorylessness, sociology could not resist the feeling of obligation to prove itself by the argument that the fully assembled family of the sciences necessarily required the existence of sociology. No one was convinced by these arguments—the sociologists no more than the professors of other subjects with a longer history and more glorious achievements, in the strength of which their own mediocre efforts could seek protection. By an obdurate tenacity, sociologists finally found their vocation in research. In Britain and then in the United States, utilitarian and humanitarian concerns with the poor opened the way to empirical sociological inquiries. The roaring flood of immigrants to the large cities of the United States disturbed a Victorian calm. Humanitarian social workers were alarmed by squalor and delinquency, and sociologists came to share this alarm, which they tempered with curiosity and the pleasure of concrete discovery. At the end of the second decade of the twentieth century, the crisis in the relations between Negroes and whites—which had been uncovered and aggravated by the northward urban movement—gave sociologists a further extension of their domain. It also gave them a parochial self-confidence, which muted their larger intellectual uncertainties. Within the universities of America— nothing much was happening in Europe—a sympathetic skepticism replaced disparagement among the neighboring disciplines: the conventional humanistic departments took abhorrent note of the sociological goings-on, and the real sciences showed a patient condescension.

In the 1930's, American sociology underwent a marked expansion at its peripheries. Its population grew, and so did its output. It was helped by the Great Depression, by the influx of German and Austrian refugees, and by the coming of intellectual age of the first generation of offspring of the Eastern European immigrants of thirty years before. Research became more sophisticated, through the development of a new statistical discipline, and through the improvement in interviewing techniques under the influence of psychoanalysis and the public opinion polling industry. Substance became a little more sophisticated under the impact

1. It was at this stage of sociological development that Henri Poincaré said that sociology was a science that produced a new methodolgy every year but never produced any results. Because there was so little substance, theory remained empty and directionless. Because there were no results, the methodological self-justifications of sociology remained empty and, quite naturally, possessed no persuasive powers.

of psychoanalysis, Marxism, and a greater knowledge of Emile Durkheim's and Max Weber's writings. These owed much to the influence of the Central European refugees and to indigenous developments in American intellectual life.

The Second World War gave sociologists the evidence they desired for their usefulness. Their employment, in many military and civilian roles, as sociologists, conferred on them the conviction of full-fledged intellectual citizenship that they had hitherto lacked. To this growth of a sense of belonging to the central circle of the intellectual cosmos, there corresponded a growing belief, among public and civic officials, publicists, and the educated public at large, that sociology had something to contribute to the national life.

Sociology has moved forward in the academic hierarchy. Its spokesmen are often among the leading lights of their universities. The other disciplines have become deferential or have at least suspended their derogation and replaced it by attentive distrust, furtive curiosity, or sheer resignation. Political science is eager to learn from sociology. Anthropology, solid in its knowledge of facts and linked with the real sciences through physical anthropology, is ready to assimilate a little of it. Even the proud economists are willing to concede its right of existence and to allow that it might have something to say. A few American sociologists are known and respected throughout the academic world. A few sociologists have become public figures in America, prophets on the same order as famous scientists and publicists; their fame has spread to England, Germany, and Italy—and even France, intellectually self-satisfied but discontented, has heard of them.

The improvised sociology of the war years, increased attention to American intellectual affairs after the War, and—probably most important—the change in fundamental sensibility, opened the way for the admission of sociology into the theater of public intellectual life.

The simple fact of the prominence of sociology in the United States would have made it, willy-nilly, a presence in Europe, with its preoccupation with American things. But the force comes not merely— nor even primarily—from the outside. Within each of the European countries, a wave of deeper opinion carries sociology forward toward academic establishment and public attention and appreciation.

Thus, sociology—which was once an earnest, uncouth subject, a subject of the American Middle West, a dreary scholastic classificatory scheme of the German universities—has invaded the parlors of the most refined intellectuals of the United States and Europe. In England, it is a rallying cry of the young who denounce their elders for the obscurantism that stands in the way of its academic establishment. It has become a proper subject for the intellectual reviews and the superior Sunday papers. It has become an instrument for the sober criticism of government policies and for contemplating, appreciating, and criticizing the qualities of social classes. It has become an organ for discovering one's fellow-man.

In France, too, it has become the vehicle of public intellectual discourse, and disillusioned Marxists seek it in the solace for a lost faith. The French government, with unprecedented beneficence, offers funds for sociological investigations—of a combination of concreteness, contemporaneity. and curiosity that has been unknown in France since Diderot went to the workshops to study the technology of his time. In Italy and Germany, sociology has already begun to make its way in private and public administration and in its claims on the public purse and attention. Intellectual awakening, commercial enterprise, and youthful spirits combine to explore the contemporary environment, rigorously, studiously, enthusiastically. In Poland, in the most inhospitable environment, what was once a proper academic discipline has become the breath of life, the cord that binds to a fresh reality. In Poland, the claim of sociology to an ample place in the modern *Weltanschauung* has an especial force and poignancy. The grounds for a reception that has extended sociology from an academic subject into a part of the universal dialogue are more transparent in Poland than anywhere else in the world. In Poland, sociology—whatever the limitations of its intellectual achievement—is a critique of lifeless dogma; it is a declaration of the will to live and live in conviviality with one's fellow-man.

The criticism of sociology from the outside has dwindled very markedly. There is still criticism, usually neither friendly nor understanding. It is not what it once was—neither in volume, in acerbity of tone, nor in the objects criticized. Thirty years ago, sociology was belittled for not being scientific. It was scorned because it could not make its case for a place in some problematical classification of the sciences. It was accused of gathering "mere" facts without regard to their meaning. It was charged with only rediscovering what every intelligent man already knew—and doing so only with great effort and high cost. It was derided for its preoccupation with the trivial. It was ridiculed for its propensity to cumbersome terminology of sometimes obscure and sometimes too obvious reference. It was abhorrent to humanists, who were apprehensive that its "scientific" procedures would destroy what is essential in the human being, would falsify his nature and degrade him. Sociology was accused of abolishing individuality, of degrading man by an inhumane determinism. It was charged that it aspired to the erection of a Machiavellian regime of scientists. The poverty of its historical knowledge and imagination was underscored; its excessive and unthinking readiness to obliterate the uniqueness of historical events by cramping them in general categories was often bemoaned.

Somehow, for no good reason—since what was valid in the criticisms still retains some validity—these accusations have evaporated. It is not that sociologists confronted these criticisms and refuted them by reasoned argument, or that the actual development of sociology rendered them completely nonsensical. They simply faded away. The critics and those who accepted their criticisms ordinarily were not very knowledgeable about sociology or perceptive of its deficiencies; the silence of their heirs is no more reasonable than the volubility of the preceding generation of critics. Sociology, by the magnitude of its exertions and the grand scale of its establishment, by some of its achievements, and especially by the groping discovery of its true vocation, has simply succeeded in imposing itself on its critics. Only a few echoes of the older arguments still resounded after the Second World War, and they were faint.

A rear-guard action expresses apprehension about the literary inelegance of sociology and its imperialistic relationship with the treasuries of foundations and governments. Sociologists are now accused—and often rightly so—of not presenting their thought in readily intelligible and grammatically correct language. But their intellectual right to do what they are doing, and the interest and value of their results, go, on the whole, unchallenged. Only among the dwindling old guard does it still encounter the otherwise long-expired complaints that sociology has not properly defined its subject matter and its boundaries vis-à-vis other academic disciplines, that it is not really a science after all, that it is too concerned with the contemporary, or that it is one of the madnesses in which rich, enthusiastic, and juvenile America might well indulge itself, but which sober countries would do well to eschew.

Most of these external complaints belong to the past. They did not help sociology to outgrow its faults when the faults were more obvious and the criticisms more harsh and numerous. The criticism sociology receives from outside the circle of its practitioners is still, because of the limitations imposed by ignorance and ill-will, bound to be of limited helpfulness in the movement toward improvement. Improvements are necessary in every

aspect of sociology, and not just because it is a science and, as such, committed to the postulate of progress. Its improvement, however, will have to be generated from the inside of the sociological enterprise, because only long exposure to and permeation by the sociological outlook can provide the preconditions for its deepening, differentiation, and extension, for the transformation it requires.

Intellectual Discipline and Moral Sentiment

Sociology has, thus, withstood the contumely of intellectual reactionaries. It has outlived them and come to enjoy the acceptance of a new generation, more open in sentiment than its predecessors and certainly not less intelligent. How has sociology, after all the sterile travail of its deliberate search for citizenship in the intellectual community, and despite its own present uncertainties and imperfections, succeeded in gaining its now nearly unchallenged reception?

The first, most obvious, and most rational of the explanations is the actual improvement of sociology. Sociology has progressed, and not just in its institutional prominence and financial prosperity. It has, in fact, progressed intellectually. Even one whom present-day sociology often appals by naïveté and crudity cannot evade the evidence of improvement. Sociology is now richer in its perception of possibilities and in its estimates of why one rather than another is realized. The accumulation of systematic inquiries on particular phenomena—such as the structure of the middle-class family in Western industrial societies—and the widened perspective of possibilities that growing intellectual friendships with history and anthropology have engendered, have made for more subtlety in interpretation.

This age of the Big Lie is also the age of a greater truthfulness about sentiments; perhaps the Big Lie has made many reasonable people suspicious of high-flown allegations of motives. Psychoanalysis has certainly done so. Whatever the cause, sociologists are now more able and more apt to include, in their observations, the experience of situations as they appear to those who live in them, and to heed the actual experience and the sentiments it evokes. This alone would constitute a tremendous advance over the sociology of half a century ago; and it represents, by its concentration and discipline, an advance even over the understanding of the classics.

Sociology has also greatly increased its sophistication in observation and in the analysis of observation. Its ties with the more advanced disciplines of mathematics and statistics have become more intimate. It has, furthermore, come out of dull isolation, which it once thought it needed for its self-respect, and mingled with the subject matters of other fields, with the more weighty topics of politics and religion.

Sometimes hand-in-hand with this more refined and more realistic understanding and this more complex technology, sometimes moving at its own self-determined pace, theoretical reflection has moved forward. Whereas, a quarter of a century ago, there were a scatter of brilliant propositions and the implicit standpoint of the sociological outlook, a powerful effort is constantly being made now to unify these scattered propositions and to articulate and differentiate the outlook that provides unity. Many sociologists squirm over the *medicina forte* that this theoretical undertaking imposes, and hostile critics find in it a ground for ribaldry. The fact remains, however, that inferiors, however much they scoff, know their betters; and the theory goes on imposing itself, even on those who believe they are rejecting it.

These are some of the intellectual grounds for the reception of sociology. There are others, some less admirable, some more so. The popularity of sociology as an undergraduate subject in many American universities must in part be a function of the very modest demands made on intelligence and diligence by much of the pedagogy of sociology—and this, in turn, has increased the professional sociological population and expanded the public for a better kind of sociology. For another— a smaller, but intellectually far more significant— part of the youth of America and of Europe as well, sociology is a substitute or complement of Marxism. The world of practical affairs, because of fantasies of scientific omnipotence, or excessive affluence, or a humble desire to understand better the situation in which decisions are made and actions taken, has also encouraged the development of sociology. It has invoked its aid and counsel, supported its inquiries, and endowed its study.

Sociology has, in short, been accepted, in varying degrees and ways, throughout the educated world. The retreating rear guard of its enemies might still contend that its acceptance is one feature of a general decay of intelligence and of moral discipline, manifesting itself in the loss of respect for elders, the unwillingness to do an honest day's work, sexual promiscuity, hedonism, and the other alleged vices of this age. And others, who give a little more thought to it—but not much more thought—might argue that it expresses the mental disarray that besets those who forsake the idols of tribe, class, and church, and set out on their own in the uncharted wilderness of the universe.

We see the matter rather differently. The scientific, the practical, the political explanations of the reception of sociology are all part of the picture. We think, however, that the recent reception of sociology is a historically unique phenomenon, which corresponds to a great progress of the human race. Sociology has found its reception because it is an organ of the experience of a broader life, a life that reaches out toward other human beings. It is one major manifestation of the current of life, in a society in which the sense of affinity of men with each other has passed from the thoughts of philosophers into actual existence, however fragmentary. Sociology has arrived by becoming an organ of the ties that form modern society in its most recent phase. Sociology has come into its present estate because its own development bears a rough correspondence to the development of the consciousness of mankind in its moral progress. The latest phase of modern society—called, by its derogators, "mass society"—has some dreadful features in which sociology shares. It has some tendency toward a scientistic technocracy, and sociology is not entirely unconnected with this. Its vulgarity is more rampantly visible than in the more hierarchical societies of the past; and sociology shares in this vulgarity. It has its profound and violent alienations in the Communist, Fascist, and National Socialist parties, and their fellow-travelers; sociology has certainly shared in this alienation, glories in it, and even contributes to it.

Nonetheless, this is far from the whole story. Modern society, especially in its latest phase, is characteristically a consensual society; it is a society in which personal attachments play a greater part than in most societies in the past, in which the individual person is appreciated, in which there is concern for his well-being—not just in a veterinary sense, but as a moral personality. The humanitarianism of the present age, which extends beyond the boundaries of national societies; the growing acknowledgment as well as demand for the moral equality of races; the welfare policies and dreams of states; the very desire to please; the greater concern for the claims of the living than for the claims of the dead—all of these features of contemporary Western, and increasingly of the modern sector of non-Western, societies disclose a concern with the happiness of the individual human being and an appreciation of the moral dignity of his interior life.

Sociology in its development runs closely parallel to this deep and broad flow of the river of modern life. From a distant and almost police-like concern with the "condition of the poor," from a concern with numbers as clues to national wealth and power, from a desire to "unmask" and discredit the hopes and fantasies of the race, sociology has advanced to a fundamental orientation—incipiently present in the classics, and now tentatively elaborated in the prevailing direction of sociological theory—that appreciates not just the animality or mechanical properties of man, but his cognitive, moral, and appreciative humanity. This has corresponded to the developments, in these categories, throughout the morally and intellectually sensitive sections of the human race. Sociology is a part of this growth in humanity.

This orientation is manifested both in the technique of sociology and in its theoretical orientation. The popularity of the interview is not simply a product of scientific necessity. It is also an act of human conviviality. In both of these, there is an appreciation of the profound fellowship of human beings—what, long ago, Franklin Giddings, without quite knowing what he was talking about, called the "consciousness of kind." The basic technique of sociological research—the interview—despite all its distortions and corruptions in market research, is one of the ways in which this fellowship is expressed. The books that come forth from this kind of research are collaborative in a sense much more important than the widely practiced team research. The elaboration of the theory of action is an affirmation of the bases of conviviality. It accepts the human being as an object of sociological study through an act of communion between object and subject. This act of communion is acknowledged through the promulgation of categories of person, society, and culture, which are as applicable to the analyst as to the object analyzed, as applicable to the act of analysis as to the actions analyzed.

Sociology as it stands today is the confluence of a variety of traditions, intellectual and social. It stems from the empirical inventory first developed in Great Britain from the seventeenth to the nineteenth centuries. It stems from German idealism, from French positivism, and from British utilitarianism. It would not have been possible without the pedantic systematizing tradition of the German university and the open, adventurous helter-skelter of the American university. It could not exist without the humanitarian humanism of modern society, without the fundamental moral revolution which asserted that "the poorest he that is in England hath a life to live as the greatest he." It could not have come into existence without the empirical inquiries that so often seemed to lead nowhere, and that nonetheless played a great part in sharpening

our sense of social reality and in preparing our sensibility for new experiences.

The ungainly ill-assortment of sociology and its academic isolation were, in a sense, the preconditions of its present improvement. The former gave it a variety of experience and such an anomalous heterogeneity that a need for unity was generated. The latter placed it in the stream of tradition in which unity was a prized object of striving.

In Germany, it was only in the schematic work of Max Weber that this unifying intention was even partially successful. It was as successful as it was in his case because it arose from that matrix of actual intellectual experience of empirical and historical research, and was guided by the judgment and sensibility of one of the most powerful minds and one of the most passionate personalities of his age.

Sociology is now beginning to realize some of the possibilities laid open by Max Weber, Durkheim, and Freud. The outlook and disposition on which a more unified and realistic sociological theory depends are gradually taking a clearer form. They are still imperfect. In the attempts at explicit formulation, in the repeated efforts to cope with the empirical observations it inspires, in the interstices and at the margins of these formulations, the general orientation is being precipitated. The present vitality of sociology, and the hope for its progress, lie in this orientation. They exist in the proto-system of insights, partial propositions, and hard-won and often painfully elaborated categories, and, above all, the cultivated sensibilities from which all these derive. The ratiocinative achievement up to the present moment, important though it is, is as nothing compared to this.

The shaping of this orientation is the major achievement of sociology thus far. Its rigorously scientifically established general truths are still very few, and they are not at the center of sociological thought. The achievements of sociology in concrete descriptive research are, likewise, more important for the general orientation, which they exemplify in increasingly nuanced form, than for the particular details that convey it, which are themselves often only of transient interest.

The general orientation is not the goal of sociological theory; but it is its most important by-product and precondition. Sociological theory could not, in its present or in any foreseeable future condition, dispense with it. At the same time, one of the most fertile methods of enriching and stabilizing this general and inarticulate orientation is the strenuous effort to be systematically and articulately theoretical.

SOCIOLOGY AND SCIENCE

..iology was born in the scientific age, but it ..ot been a creation of the scientific spirit. The ..lems of sociology are old problems; at least the ..damental problems are older than the scientific .. They were perceived and promulgated without thought of being scientific in the contemporary .ense of the word—although the scientific metaphors of the time of their origin did enter into their formulation. The fundamental problems of the conditions of the establishment and mutability of order, of the conditions of the effectiveness of authority, of the assimilation of the individual organism into culture and collectivity, are all much older than the modern scientific outlook. They have remained the proper problems of sociology into the scientific age. The effort to elicit general principles or laws from particular observations and concrete experience, and to do so within an intellectual tradition, are, of course, older than scientific research as we now understand it.

Nonetheless, sociology has been tremendously influenced by the scientific model, to its advantage and disadvantage. The advantages it has gained from the scientific environment in modern culture in general, and in the universities in particular, have been priceless. From science, it has learned the virtue of discipline. It has learned to criticize the quality of its observations. It has learned to control and order its observation—it has learned not only the specific techniques, but even more, the ideal of detached, dispassionate observation. It has learned to be painstaking in selecting the objects of its inquiries; it has learned the advantages of specifying the categories of events it would investigate and to stabilize the procedures of investigation. It has learned the fruitfulness of disciplined, routinized assessment of the data gathered through rule-directed observation.

From science, sociology has acquired the ideal of a theory intimately, dialectically, and systematically related to its observations. These are all tremendous acquisitions; and, to the extent that sociology has become a science, it has done so by conforming with the standards learned and adapted from the prevailing sciences.

In so far as a science is a coherent body of empirically supported propositions, which retain their stability within a particular theoretical framework and which sustain that framework, sociology is not a science today. The empirically verified propositions at a level of low particularity are many; as they rise toward generality, they become fewer—not because the structure of any science requires it, but because of the deficient coherence of the analytical scheme that explicitly or implicitly guides these inquiries, and because the techniques of research have still not been sufficiently well adapted to the observation of more abstractly formulated variables.

Nor, for that matter, has theory become sufficiently articulated and explicit. The gap between general theory and actual observation is still considerable, although the sociological outlook inherent in the theory runs beyond the limits of the explicit theoretical formulation and has entered increasingly into research activity. The sociological outlook, however, is at least as ambiguous as the existing theory; and the task of establishing a firm correspondence of "index-terms" and "concept-terms" has still some considerable distance to go before it will have been accomplished.

Thus, sociology has begun to approximate the condition of science with respect to its observational and "processing" procedures, although—even on the level of particularity—results are too often indeterminate and problems are deformed by excessive technical preoccupations. It is in its relations to theory that sociological research is least satisfactory scientifically. Sociological theory itself is not scientific, in either the sense of guiding research by precise direction, or the sense of being itself precisely guided by the results of research. In its internal constitution, too, sociological theory is not very scientific; and this applies equally to the general theory and to those theories of middle principles which some of the critics of general theory suggest as the best way toward science.

Despite these critical remarks, it must be acknowledged that sociology has become more scientific over the years, and in a way that not only gratifies a scientistic idol, but that represents a genuine intellectual advance. Every decade of the past half-century has seen an improved solidity. Observations are better made; new and better techniques of observation are devised and applied; theory becomes more comprehensive and more differentiated; particular inquiries are more dominated by the sociological outlook, which is being fostered by theoretical reflection. The progress is not simply a quantitative increase, decade by decade, in scientific properties.

Continuity too is growing, and the sources of inspiration are becoming more consolidated and more preponderant. Sociology has become increasingly a collective enterprise. We refer not to the fact of organized team research, but to the sense that sociologists, theorists as much as investigators of particular problems, have come to have of themselves as members of a community, engaged in a great common effort. No sociologist nowadays believes that he starts from scratch or that his work is the final word on the subject he treats. There are *virtuosi,* but they accept their place in the tradition of their subject. Their achievement lies in deepening its interpretation, in extending it, in fortifying it—but not in any entirely disjunctive act of creation. Their sense of responsibility to the future of a subject, growing from its past, is a quality that brings sociology closer to science than it was in its period of isolated individual achievement, when there were many starts—some false, some true, but most of which ran off into nothingness. Cumulativeness of a self-revising, self-deepening sort is essential to science; and this has now become characteristic of sociology. It is partly a result of the location of its center in the world of the university, which lays heavy emphasis on disciplined continuity. It is also the result of a broadening of interest and sympathy, and of a more intense need for unity at the center of this greater breadth. The traditions of sociology are now less discretely heterogeneous than they have ever been before. Sociology is at once more catholic and less eclectic than in the past. There is by no means a complete consensus among the most creative workers in the field and their most productive followers; but the formation of the loose consensus necessary to define a true scientific community is well under way, and its potential for growth has undoubtedly not been exhausted.

There is nothing in the nature of the subject matter of sociology that would prevent it from becoming more scientific than it is now. The very fact that sociology has made such progress toward the condition of science in the past half-century is evidence that the subject matter does permit an increase in the scientific component of its treatment. What has been achieved in the past half-century renders it reasonably probable that, in the next half-century, the scientific features of sociology will become more important in the enterprise. Whether they will also become more central is another matter.

Let us suppose that, in the course of time, sociology does succeed in formulating and demonstrating laws of universal validity—the like of which it does not know at present. Would this place sociology among the natural sciences and cut off any links it has with the humanistic disciplines? On the contrary, it would show that the conventional distinction between scientific and humanistic disciplines is ill conceived. The discernment of universal regularities has gone further in linguistics than in sociology. Does this make linguistics less humanistic than sociology? It would be so only if the nature of the subject matter is irrelevant, and if the logical

structure of the system of propositions and the degree of their confirmation are the decisive criteria distinguishing scientific and humanistic disciplines. Sociology can never become simply a natural science like physics or astronomy, even if its logical structure were to become indistinguishable from that of physics or astronomy. The nature of the basic categories of action precludes the *complete* identification, though it does not stand in the way of an identity of logical structure, or even an approximately equal measure of reliability of demonstration.

In purely cognitive respects, sociology could be a science like any other science, and it might well become such. Sociology is not, however, a purely cognitive undertaking. It is also a moral relationship between the human beings studied and the student of the human beings. This is easily evident in the situation of the field worker who must establish a relationship of trust with his interviewees and informants, who must call forth sentiments like friendship and affection in them and in himself. Naturally, a considerable element of detachment too must be present; otherwise the cognitive interest would be suppressed by the inevitable conviviality. Problems are raised by this relationship that sociologists have not yet resolved but which they cannot lightly disregard.

This is true not only of the procedure of sociological inquiry, but of the results of inquiry as well. The communication of the results of research is an opinion-affecting action. It naturally is intended to affect the opinion of other sociologists; whether intended or not, it also is likely to affect the opinion and the action of other persons, including the classes of persons with whom the inquiry deals. Now, this does not, as some writers have said, invalidate the proposition communicated. That proposition remains true, if it was true when first enunciated. It does, however, raise a question about the appropriate forms of sociological discourse about living persons and about contemporaneous events.

The logical structure of a sociological proposition might not be affected by these observations. Sociology is not only science; it is rhetoric at the same time, directed to an open situation. The rhetoric of sociology, in a very serious sense, does, however, require more circumspection than it has yet been accorded. The positive outcome of such reflection is obscure; but I am quite confident that the rhetoric of the natural sciences, which are not in communication with the data of their inquiries, will have to be considerably revised for the purposes of sociology. This applies equally to reports on the most concrete research and to abstract

theoretical treatises, and no less to theories of the
middle range.

SOCIOLOGY AND THE HUMANISTIC
STUDY OF MAN

The relations between sociologists and those who
have taken in their charge the scholarly custody of
man's past and his achievements in the objectiva-
tion of symbols have been neither amicable nor intelligent in the past. Mutual distrust, derogation, and
avoidance have been the common traits of the
relationship. Defensive ignorance has played a
larger part in engendering this relationship than
awareness of each other's procedures and objects.
A genuine desire to understand the other side has
been rare. The situation has been at its worst in
America because, until quite recently, it was only
there that sociology was prominent enough to be
noticed by the practitioners of the humanistic disciplines. In Europe, for the most part, the mention
of sociology merely called forth a response of
unsympathetic blankness. There, sociologists have
more often had the traditional humanistic education, and this made them more tolerable. In
America, sociologists have wished to see themselves
as scientists—which means being tough-minded,
"objective," and skeptical of "intuition" with its
overtones of effeminacy and mysticism. Sociologists have usually been unsympathetic with existing
religious institutions, and they have not had much
religious imagination. They have usually been
poorly educated in history.

An important current of sociological opinion has
been "progressive," and had looked upon the past
as in error, superstitious, and, in any case, dead.
Sociologists have not been much interested in traditions except in a negative way, with an emphasis on
their breakdown; whereas traditions are very much
of the stock-in-trade of the humanistic disciplines.
The "progressive" attitude of sociology toward the
past has been reinforced by the increased prominence of field work, of the interview of living persons as a major sociological activity. Humanistic
scholarship has, up until quite recently, studiously
avoided the contemporary. Sociologists have recognized the relevance of statistical procedures, which
humanistic scholars associate with science and
which only a few humanistic scholars apply in their
research. Sociologists have thought of the humanists as antiquarians, moralists, or aesthetes, in
contrast with their own unsentimental, evaluatively
neutral selves. To these more intellectual differences, sociologists have added a few others. They
were uncouth in their literary style at a time when

the humanistic disciplines had not yet sunk to the
same level of jargon and prolixity. Then, too, feeling inferior, sociologists were aggressive against disciplines they regarded as even more vulnerable than
their own to the criticism of being insufficiently
scientific. Some of the animus of sociologists
against the humanistic academic disciplines has
arisen from the inherent necessities of sociology at
a particular stage of its career. Others have derived
from the less admirable social and cultural qualities
of sociologists themselves.

The academic humanists have been not a bit
better from their side. They have been eager to see
sociology, in its pride and its superficial worldly
success, cast down in humiliation. The very indifference, if not animosity, of sociologists toward the
past and its works, the sociologists' ignorance of
literary and artistic achievements with which the
academic humanists dealt, were an affront to the
dignity of their disciplines. Humanists live in an
atmosphere of dusty books and footnotes citing
recondite German monographs; while many sociologists seldom read a book published earlier than
a few years ago. Books are not so often regarded by
them as part of the apparatus of their science, and
humanists exaggerate this and feel aggrieved about
it. Besides, sociology, despite all its imperfections—
which have been real enough—has prospered in the
most obvious ways. Its population has increased,
and its wealth even more, while the humanistic disciplines have had to yield preponderance of place
and influence. The humanistic departments of the
universities have seen increasing proportions of
students turn toward the natural sciences and the
social sciences. Sociology has attracted many students who, in the past, would have concentrated
their academic attentions on English literature and
history. Sociology has become a major beneficiary
of the reallocation of university funds, while the
humanistic departments have suffered a measure
of attrition. Funds from private foundations and
from governments have gone in great sums to the
social sciences, while the humanistic disciplines
have been relatively neglected. Even though humanistic research is not as costly as scientific research—including research in the social sciences—
still, the indulgence enjoyed by sociology has made
it a plausible object for resentment, especially when
there appeared to be so many substantive grounds
for denying the legitimacy of its intellectual claims
and its financial enjoyments.

It cannot be said that this episode of the academic
history of the twentieth century adds to the credit
of anyone. The acrimony and vanity of the discussion have obscured the genuine affinities and differences of these two domains of intellectual work.

There are real differences in the activities of sociologists and humanistic scholars. There will continue to be real differences: the techniques of humanistic research—such as paleography, the establishment of critical editions of literary texts, the establishment of the authenticity of manuscripts, the dating of paintings by chemical analysis and of archaeological finds by the use of radioactive carbon, the decipherment of hitherto unknown scripts, archaeological excavation, the establishment of detailed biographical accounts of individuals—will probably never become part of the techniques of sociology.

Sociology is concerned with the establishment of the validity of observations, but the immediate objects observed are rather different. Sociology in its latest phase—ever since it became convinced that it would have to occupy itself with primary observation—has been concerned with living persons. The humanistic disciplines draw their objects from the whole range of human history and even prehistory. Let us omit, for the moment, the far greater attention of the humanistic disciplines to the objectivations of man's creative powers, which makes it more feasible to extend backward the span of historical interest. The technical preoccupations of the humanistic studies correspond to a substantive preoccupation with the concrete individualities of persons and works.

This difference is almost a historical accident. The conditions that gave rise to sociology were conditions in which the existence of the "nameless masses" had been discovered; the humanistic disciplines arose out of a stream of traditions that included the practice of hagiography and the celebration of greatness. Although humanistic biography has largely freed itself from the burden of its origins, it has nonetheless concentrated on the understanding of the thematic coherence and the inner diversity of a career and a personality. Sociological theory is concerned with the same kind of phenomena in the structure of the individual's life.

There is another aspect of the difference, which is not a historical accident but constitutional to sociology. Sociology is concerned with classes of individuals and not with a particular individual. Therein lies one major difference. Sociology has an abstractness of interest, a determination to see particular events as instances of classes of events, or as variants or composites of classes, or as subclasses. Sociologists do conduct case studies; but they do so to illustrate the operation of more general classes of variables. They assemble many case studies, in each of which justice is done to individual uniqueness; but they do so with the intention of establishing the distribution of individual variations and the connections between several distributions.[2]

There is nothing in the constitution of sociology that would prohibit the writing of a biography of a person, living or dead; and, if the sociologist were literarily talented, scholarly, and empathic, he could write a book that would be much like the standard biography. In so far, however, as he remained a sociologist, there would inevitably be a tendency to adduce general propositions to explain particular or recurrent events in the life history of the subject, or to cite particular events or sequences of events as illustrative of general propositions. Indeed, this tendency would most likely dominate the work as a whole.

The fundamental disposition of an intelligent and sympathetic sociological biographer would necessarily approximate, in practice, the orientation that underlies and arises from the theory of action. It would resemble too the disposition of the intelligent and sympathetic nonsociological biographer, except that it would be somewhat more articulately sensitive to factors in the social situation of the subject. Each of them would have to be guided by an outlook common to both—assuming, of course, that they were both realistically empathic. The fact that the biographer is interested in a particular man—one with a name and fame, who is often a marked, although always imperfect, individuality—does not represent any fundamental departure from the paths of sociology. Individuality, creativity, strength and force of character, are just as much the proper themes and problems of sociological inquiry as they are of humanistic study—even if sociology does not usually express the same intensity of interest in biographical particularity.

Sociology does not often, however, take upon itself the description and explanation of the individuality of one particular human being or the task of giving a causal explanation of his creative achievement. The description and causal explanation of the action and creation of a particular indi-

---

2. This distinction should not be regarded as one that makes a profound disjunction between sociology and the humanistic disciplines. Humanistic scholars treat general categories, such as landscape paintings or allegories or naturalistic novels or epic poems. Furthermore, the enunciation of a judgment with respect to a particular work of literature or art involves—in different ways—the use of general categories and standards, and their application, through judgment, to particular instances. It is very similar to sociological analysis in this regard. Moreover, the effort of sociology progressively to translate its orientation into an articulate theory, and its occasionally and relatively greater self-consciousness in the deployment of its general categories, do not distinguish it from one of the greatest fields of humanistic achievement, namely, linguistics. Its rhythmic movement into abstraction is not a criterion that separates it from philosophy, which is far more self-containedly abstract and less frequently in contact with the particular and the concrete.

vidual are less often the concern—and are, therefore, less likely to be the successful achievement—
of the sociologist.[3]

Much more important, sociology does not share
the deeply rooted tradition of the appreciation and
contemplation of greatness of an individual life or
creation that dominates the humanistic disciplines.
This is a tradition that survives in great strength—
even though humanistic research frequently falls
far short and into a pit of particular triviality, as in
much literary-historical scholarship, or goes off into
the quite different direction of scientific generalization, as in contemporary linguistics.

Sociology too has its contemplative, appreciative
inclination. It is one that enjoys the contemplation
of collective entities rather than of a great life or a
great work. The concept of the "ideal-type" was in
part a product of this contemplative-appreciative
inclination of sociology. It involved the construction of a "whole," of the image of some collectivity
or process—either representative of a historical
epoch or trans-historical and free of any epochal
particularity. Even when sociology leaves behind
the contemplative appreciation of the ideal-type,
and goes forward toward scientific generalization,
there remains an element of contemplative appreciation. The appreciated object is, however, a
process or a proposition that refers to a process. It
is something abstract, divorced from concrete individuality. It might arouse the same delight as any
great and true scientific proposition about a phenomenon central to the nature of the universe; but
the object contemplated differs from the object
contemplated and appreciated by a humanistic
scholar. It is an abstraction, a general rule or law,
and not a concrete particular constellation of events
or symbols.

The contemplative appreciation of concrete and
particular actions, persons, or symbolic creations,
and the cognitive interest in establishing universally
valid general propositions about collectivities, are
not rigorously and mutually exclusively divided between the humanistic disciplines and sociology.
Each of the latter does some of each of the former.

3. In so far as it has been, sociologists have not been
any more successful than humanists—indeed, rather less
so. General sociological categories are still too nebulous and
unstable, their explanatory powers are still too indeterminate, for this task to be carried out better by a sociologist
than by a very superior nonsociological biographer with a
sure touch. Even if our categories and hypotheses were better than they are, the task of passing from general categories
and propositions to the description and explanation of a
particular individual event or to an individual constellation
of events would still require an act of practiced judgment,
which a good theoretical orientation can support but cannot supply or compel. There is a tradition of biography
that a writer of biography must accept to be effective; a
sociologist might supplement this tradition, but he could
not replace it or dispense with it.

Nevertheless, there is a significant difference in
concentration here.

There are parallel differences in techniques of
inquiry associated with the concern with events
of the past as against the concern with recent
events and still-living persons, with the valid establishment of particular details for the purpose of
constructing a unique whole as against the valid
establishment of details for the purpose of constructing a general proposition. There is another
difference between the humanistic disciplines and
sociology. The former are very largely interested in
the symbolic objectivations of man's creative
powers: language, science, art, philosophy, religious
belief, literature. Sociology has been more concerned with the systems of human action, the networks formed by human beings in their actions with
and against each other. Of course, this dividing line
is only an analytical one. History, political history,
the history of religious and educational institutions,
and even social history, are regarded as within the
humanities; and they certainly deal with the networks and structure of human actions. Biography
does the same. On its side, sociology—and particularly the sociology that grows from the traditions
portrayed and exemplified in these volumes—includes the cultural sphere as a major element in its
analysis of action. Its interest turns more toward
the institutional matrix of these symbolic objectivations and toward the penetration of these symbolic
objectivations in actions and institutions. One of
the most impressive consequences of the cultivation
of the traditions of sociological analysis leading to
the theory of action is that cultural systems, and the
institutions that maintain and are formed by cultural
systems, have come more and more into the foreground of attention. Sociologists formed under the
inspiration of Max Weber and Emile Durkheim are
giving themselves increasingly to the study of the
achievements of the more conventionally humanistic disciplines of the history of art, of science, of
literature, of religious beliefs, and even of languages. They are doing so, furthermore, not within
the utilitarian and evolutionist schemes of analysis
that treated the subject matters of these disciplines
as epiphenomena. They do not any longer regard it
as their task to "explain" religious ideas or scientific conceptions as products of the "relationships
of production" or of the conflict of classes or the
like. Their task now is to understand them—their
constitution and functioning—within the mutual
interpenetration of the tripartite system of culture,
person, and society.

The present sociological theory and the orientation that underlies and grows from it embrace the
humanistic subject matter; and they acknowledge

the partial autonomy of the cultural sphere. They are now more open to the sociological analysis of the institutions of the cultural sphere and their determination by the standards and internal necessities of the various systems of culture. Thus, while accepting the differences of technique, intention, and interest, the central tradition of sociological theory now coming increasingly into articulation has promoted a very considerable rapprochement with the humanistic disciplines.

The unification will never be complete. There is no good reason why it should be. Different tasks require different techniques; different interests require different logical structures. Substantive specialization will stand in the way of complete unification too, and that is unlikely ever to be overcome completely. The persistence of these differences and this specialization certainly does not, however, entail any necessary conflict between sociology and the humanistic disciplines, other than that arising from the jealousies, vanities, and hypersensitivities of human beings. Progress in the construction of theory in sociology has now gone far enough, and the defensive parochialism that characterized sociology in the early part of the century has now been sufficiently alleviated, to enable us to see that sociology and the humanistic disciplines are bound together by an indissoluble tie. This is the tie of their common subject matter and the shared appreciation of the human qualities of the moral, intellectual, and aesthetic powers that constitute the humanity of their subject matter.

Certainly, there will be sociologists in the future who will work on human beings outside these categories—just as there will be humanistic scholars who will be either extremely specialized or extremely technical, and marginal to the human qualities of their subject matter. This will not damage our re-established awareness of the humanism of sociology.[4]

Sociology is humanistic because it attempts to understand whatever man does, in categories that acknowledge his humanity: his need for cognitive orientation; his capacity for rational judgment and action, for affectionate attachment, for aesthetic expression and response, for moral decision. Naturally, there is not a complete consensus among sociologists in this respect. There are sociologists who deny or disregard it, just as there are philologists and archaeologists and historians who lose sight of the connections between the objects they hold in their hands or before their minds and the humanity of the creators, recipients, and users of

those objects. The great traditions of sociology are humanistic; and the general sociological theory and the sociological orientation that represent the present phase of those traditions continue and make more articulate their humanism. Behaviorism and experimentalism, although they have not been without a following and have contributed valuably to sociological theory and research, have not moved to the center of sociology. The fact that sociology attempts to observe precisely, and to express with precision, events that by their nature have imprecise boundaries does not diminish the essentially humanistic orientation of sociology. The fact that sociology is often and increasingly quantitative does not diminish its humanistic component—which is necessitated by the task it takes upon itself—any more than does the fact that it seeks, with growing frequency but still relatively rarely, to express its theoretical constructions in mathematical form. The more refined rhetoric that sociology might come to use, as and if it becomes more mathematical, will not change the nature of the variables with which sociology deals or of the concepts that refer to them. Man does not have to be reduced to a biological organism or to an electronic mechanism for the regularities of his action to be described mathematically. The efforts of sociology to attain determinate laws in its propositions no more deprive it of that status than the regularities of linguistics or the uniformities discerned by comparative religious studies deprive these of their status as humanistic disciplines.

The humanistic orientation is not a function of busying one's self with books containing novels, poems, or philosophical ideas. It is not bookishness. The humanistic orientation is not inevitably associated with preoccupation with the past, with avoidance of rigorous analytical procedures; it does not call for lucubrative compilation or undisciplined impressionism. These qualities, alone or in combination, are found in both sociological and humanistic faculties; and they are neither decisive nor constitutive of the nature of the intellectual disciplines in which they are found.

SOME PHILOSOPHICAL-
ANTHROPOLOGICAL OBSERVATIONS

The Self-Interpretation of Man:
The Extension of the Tradition
of Self-Interpretation

Sociological analysis is a continuation in a contemporary idiom of the great efforts of the human

---

4. The issue is a relatively new one. It is the product of academic faculties and the struggle for academic existence. It did not exist for the heroic figures of the sociological tradition.

mind to render judgment on man's vicissitudes on earth. It springs from an aspiration ultimately as profound as, if less far-reaching than, theology. Agnostic in a theological sense, it is more modest in its intention than that grandiose fusion of eschatology and the diagnosis of contemporaneity that has come down to us under the name of philosophy of history. It does not aspire to go beyond the boundaries of historical time. On the other side, sociological theory would be unfaithful to its traditions, its tasks, and possibilities if it were to confine itself to the diagnosis of the contemporary situation. Sociology and the diagnosis of our time are, when they are decently conducted, very intimate with each other. They are not identical. Sociology is much the larger, because it attempts to transcend the role of *laudator temporis acti* that tradition has rendered an almost inevitable standpoint for the analysis of the present. Sociology has suffered from the conceptual limitations arising from preoccupation with its own society and its own epoch. Despite this temporal and territorial particularism, its aspirations are, however, always broader. "Ethnocentrism" is a pejorative among sociologists; to be "culture-bound" is to be inferior. The dominant sociological theory of the present century has sought to transcend the local and periodic and to enter into a more trans-historical stratum of being.

Is this not what the moral philosophers have sought to do? Is the oracular "know thyself" a recommendation to understand one's self as a particular bundle of motives and powers, alive in a Greek polis; or did it command those who read it to understand themselves as men? Cicero's reflections on friendship might well have been insufficiently catholic and too much preoccupied with the claims and weaknesses of friendship in Rome when the dangers of life in the dying Republic placed such strains on loyalty and affection. It was not, however, his intention to speak only of his age and country; he sought to speak of man, and if he failed, it was more a result of the narrowness of his knowledge than of the narrowness of his intention.

The situation of sociology is similar in many respects. Even the sociological theory that would confine itself to middle principles is aware of the possibility of more general principles, less restricted in the historical and territorial range of their validity. It recommends middle principles because it does not yet feel itself ready to ascend to the loftier heights of a translocal, transperiodic generality. This more self-limiting theory, like the more abstract general theory, appreciates the aspiration of sociology to attain a coherent view of man's nature, of the meaning of the society given

by man's nature and the exigencies of coexistence, and of the transformations these can undergo within the scope of limited potentialities so far known in the course of evolution and history.

Sociology is a continuation and elaboration of the permanent and necessary effort of man to understand himself and his species. It goes beyond the classical moralists, by directing the exertion of self-interpretation to the trans-individual, trans-historical network as well as to the earlier task of individual self-interpretation.

Sociology is an address to the task of understanding of man as a collective entity—of man's capacities that make him into a political animal, and of the network of human actions and creations linking the present and the past and the spatially dispersed into a reality as real as concrete individual biological existence. Sociology attempts to cast the results and procedures of this collective self-interpretation into the form of science. In so far as it is a science—which at present is not very much—it differs from the sciences of the external world and large parts of the biological sciences, not just in the sense that its subject matter is different and human, but also in the sense that it has taken upon itself a task different from the natural sciences of physics, chemistry, and even biology. It is part of the vast, unorganized collective effort of the human mind to understand itself as a collectivity. To understand itself, it needs to know the temptations to which it yields, the resistances it can erect against temptation, the sources of its weaknesses and strengths, of its impulses and its disciplines. These are the good reasons for being as scientific as possible.

Sociological self-understanding—which is an elaboration of old traditions that are not accidents in the life of our species—does not stand in a continuous line of the tradition from classical ethical philosophy, through Renaissance humanism and the French moralists from Montaigne to Tocqueville. It is inspired by these, but its sources are more heterogeneous. It has, for example, received a powerful impetus from Darwinism, and it will in the future derive much from neurology and the theory of servomechanisms. Nonetheless, the very constitution of the impulse that generates sociological exertion compels adherence to the basic task of self-understanding of man as an organism with moral and rational propensities.

Sociology enters the endless stream of man's effort to assess himself at a point where the stream has broadened and somewhat changed its course. Sociology, traditionally, is agnostic; and it proceeds, even at its best, muted on the religious side. By virtue of this noncommittal attitude on the reality of a relationship between divinity and man, it refuses certain traditional currents in the self-understanding of man. Except for this refusal, however, it has absorbed the main substance of traditional self-interpretation, adding to it the knowledge of the animal in man. It has immensely enriched and complicated the inheritance through its openness to the Darwinian increment and by its assimilation of the general lines of psychoanalytical interpretation —itself a fusion of the classical and the Darwinian traditions.

Through its receptivity to the Hegelian variant of idealism, it has widened its range tremendously. This is what has made the self-interpretation of man sociological. The traditional self-interpretation of man saw man as an instance of a category, but not as a knot in a network. To the extent that it saw man as a member of a collectivity, it saw him as a beneficiary of the advantages and a victim of the disadvantages of that membership. Society did not quite come into the picture of the objects of self-interpretation. Sociology has partially closed the gap left by Aristotle between the *Ethics* and the *Politics*. It was only natural that it should do so, because, in the age in which it has flourished, the consensual capacities of man have grown proportionately with his individuality. With this growth, the problems of self-interpretation have been complicated and deepened.

The strivings and writhings of collective humanity; the accumulation, transmission, assimilation, and transformation of the fruits and by-products of these movements, transcending generations and localities; and the precipitation of multitudinous individual actions into determinate social systems—these have become integral to our conception of man. Man is not simply an organism bounded by an epidermis. He is not just an intelligence and a moral capacity formed into an individuality. He is also an essence beyond the boundaries of skin and person; he is a system of such organisms over space and through time. He has a memory, and he has the capacity to incorporate the images of others into an opened self. These form an entity with an extension beyond the individual life-span and beyond the experiences of particular individuals. Its observations, concrete and particular, abstract and general, on man in this broader view, are what sociology adds to the traditional self-interpretation of man.

The Self-Interpretation of Man: Self-Control and Technological Sociology

Sociology is not simply the traditional self-interpretation of man, broadened by modern sensi-

bility. It also shares in the modern scientific movement, and it attempts to act accordingly.

Disciplined, detached observation, emancipation from prejudice, the intellectual control of arbitrariness in judgment, the desire for a generalized picture of the world, the postulate of regularity in the sequence of events—these are all parts of the constitution of the scientific community; and, by virtue of acceptance of these rules, sociology becomes one of the dominions of the community. But the scientific community is a federal system. Not all the intellectual dominions need adhere rigorously or absolutely to the same rules. They can vary their conduct within the framework of the constitution of the community, according to their own traditions and the tasks that these traditions set.

There is one feature of the more specialized constitutions of some of the other dominions that sociology cannot share, although within it there are parties contending that it is the right policy. This is the technological aspiration that would put sociology to use in the way in which the knowledge of genetics is put to use in animal and plant breeding, or chemical knowledge, in industry, or physiology and pharmacology, in the practice of the profession of medicine. The Comtian maxim, *Savoir pour prévoir pour pouvoir*, drew its inspiration from a tradition at least as old as Francis Bacon; and it did not run into the ground with Auguste Comte. It has continued to be part of the platform of sociology ever since—even though, for the most part, there is precious little prediction and even less provision. Sociology has not succeeded in becoming a technological discipline. This is not just because it has not yet advanced sufficiently in a scientific sense—although that is a factor—but because, in its essential character, sociology cannot ever become a science like the sciences of the world external to man, or like the sciences that deal with man's physical or biological organism. The tradition in which it is working, the very nature of the enterprise, and the sociological outlook that is emerging in the course of the theoretical elaboration of this theory, are all ill adapted to the technological application of sociology. To be technological means to be manipulative; it means treating the events to be controlled as having no affinity with the manipulator, as being incapable of exercising rational judgment or of possessing or discriminating valid empirical knowledge.

Concrete empirical research of a descriptive sort can, of course, serve to make more exact and differentiated the knowledge with which those who exercise authority confront their tasks of decision and management. At this level, the problem of manipulation does not yet exist—or at least the potential contribution of sociology to a more effective manipulation is not yet visible. When sociology ascends from concrete description to a more general theory, the conception of human action that is either suppressed or peripheral in descriptive portrayal moves much more into the foreground. To be technological entails the acceptance of a mechanistic, conventionally behavioristic conception of man as incapable of valid reasoning, of choice guided by standards, responding to persuasion that is more than instigation in a simple stimulus-response model. Sociological theory cannot make any serious progress in this direction; although it has gained much from the past assimilation of considerable features of the behavioristic tradition and will gain from the assimilation of the knowledge of thought processes from research on computers, it is most unlikely to be forced to renounce its central conception of action in favor of a more mechanistic model—that is, one that does not allow for intellectual, moral, and aesthetic creativity. Not only the great intellectual traditions that have gone into the formation of sociology, but also the immanent necessities of present-day sociological research, the sheer need to do justice to the subject matter, require a movement toward one or another form of the theory of action. Any particular form of this theory will certainly undergo continuous revision, and bit by bit the whole thing as it now stands will be modified. The general conception of man that underlies it will, however, remain.

Now, this theory is a self-interpretation in the sense that it includes the act of theory-construction itself as part of its data. Its categories for describing man's nature must include the capacity for the construction of a theory about man and society. This itself is an acknowledgment of the continuity between the theorist and the subject matter of the theory. It is a construction that acknowledges in rational self-consciousness, the rational powers of man (even if it does not accord them a monopoly or disregard their limitations). It acknowledges man's need for a cognitive order in the universe that is more than an instrument of biological adaptation. The theory of action sees itself as part of what it is trying to understand. Thus, sociological theory is not just a theory like any other theory; it is a social relationship between the theorist and the subject matter of his theory. It is a relationship formed by the sense of affinity.

The sociological theory that grows from the theory of action is simply a more forward part of a widespread consensual collectivity. Its cognitive elaboration is certainly richer and profounder than the consensual sensibility of the ordinary intelligent, educated person; its scope is broader; it is more

articulate. But it is a development from the same matrix and, in its elaboration, it does not renounce its origins.

The sociological theory that is self-interpretive has its correlate in the practice of collective self-control. The technological counterpart of sociological theory is not the manipulation of others, but the illumination and discipline of the self—individual and collective. Of course, it is impossible to commend or practice manipulation while asserting adherence to the theory of action. It is even possible to point to parts of the theory of action that can be interpreted to fit the scheme that underlies the manipulative relationship, for example, the paradigm of interaction that asserts the dependence of response on anticipated reward. It does violence to the theory as a whole to take the paradigm out of its context of the patterns of choice and the categories of orientation. In any case, it most assuredly does not commit those who espouse it to a manipulative relationship with the subjects of the theory—as does the conventional behavioristic theory.

Manipulation entails the perception of the object of the manipulation as a discrete entity having no social relationship with the manipulator except with regard to the manipulative actions themselves. It excludes the object's perception of the manipulating person, and it thus denies the mutuality inherent in the theory of action. This does not mean that manipulative actions are not intelligible to the theory of action—they are. What it does mean is that manipulative actions involve the suppression of certain of the features of the relationship between manipulator and manipulated that are fundamental to the theory of action, namely, the identities of theorist and the subject of the theory.

Nonetheless, the sociological theory of action is not a purely cognitive product with no bearing on action. It can and does affect action; but it does so through a process of illumination that modifies the disposition of the actor who shares it. Its efficacy necessitates the sharing of its insights with those whom it would affect. The understanding of the social system that it conveys, heightening, as it does, the awareness of the unity that binds (as well as the discreteness that separates!), will, when it is "applied," work through *collective* self-transformations. Collective self-transformations are those which are decided upon consensually, by tacit understanding, and by deliberation, and in which the adaptations of the actions of individual to individual are made within the context of a perceived affinity.

It is unlikely that, in the foreseeable future, mankind will dispense entirely with coercion in the internal life of its societies; it is also unlikely that deception or manipulation will disappear in the relationships of adults. Indeed, the latter are rendered more probable because modern knowledge of pharmacology and communication make them more easily feasible. It is imperative intellectually for the theory of action to comprehend these deceptive and manipulative actions and to find a place for them in its schema of action. The theory of action, however, even though it finds a place for these elements in its analytical scheme, does not itself—either in its underlying disposition, or as a comprehensive theory—provide the legitimation or the motivation for them. The scientific rationale of manipulative actions can derive only from distorted or, rather, partial "application" of the sociological theory of action.

The sociological theory of action—both on the level of relatively concrete middle principles and on that of more abstract analysis—is not a discipline capable of technological application; nor is it capable of becoming a technological science. It is not a discipline the propositions of which, if they are articulated, may be simply reformulated from: "If, under conditions A, B, and C, D changes into D_1, then E will change into E_1," to the form: "If A, B, and C exist, and we wish to produce E_1 from E, then we must change D into D_1." Technological propositions in this latter form assume that *we* and D belong to different classes of events. Sociology based on the theory of action asserts, on the contrary, that the relationships between *ourselves* and D are as much of the same class as the relationships among A, B, C, D, E, and so on. The relationship between D and ourselves must, therefore, be, in at least some measure, a consensual relationship. It can also contain coercive or manipulative elements as well, although probably not to the exclusion of the consensual element. In any case, a large part of the relationship we undertake for the transformation of our collective situation will be one in which the consensual element will be very weighty.

The assertion of the nontechnological character of sociological knowledge infused with the outlook of the theory of action does not imply that such knowledge is incapable of contributing to the improvement of man's condition and a greater efficacy in the management of man's practical affairs. The positivistic and the instrumentalist-pragmatist traditions that have guided the opinion of sociologists have made it appear as if a technological application of sociology, like the technological applications of the physical and biological sciences, is indispensable to its contribution to the welfare of human beings.[5]

This view is probably not wholly incorrect: there are undoubtedly human situations that can be ameliorated only by manipulation, or coped with only by coercion; and the scientific improvement of sociology might well make these actions more efficacious. The technological application of sociology, quite apart from its distortion and partiality, can hardly claim to be fitting for a democratic liberal society that respects the dignity of individual existence. Sociology would be a moral monstrosity if, after its decent and even noble childhood, it were in its maturity to develop into a tool for technocrats to rule the human race—presumably for its benefit.

The danger is not great. For one thing, sociological knowledge at present is not in such a condition that it could be technologically applied. More important is the fact that the substance of the emerging sociological outlook is hostile to the technological orientation, and the variables with which it concerns itself are resistant to manipulation. Its benefits, in addition to the dignity inherent in any cognitive achievement, will come through the enlightenment of opinion, in the furtherance of collective self-knowledge and the self-transformation which that better understanding of one's self can produce.

Sociology and the Critique of Society

Sociology is not a normative science according to the sensible but simplistic view that distinguishes between "norm" and "fact." It has, however, the greatest ethical—and therewith political—implications, by virtue of its construction of the elements of human action. Man's existence as a moral and rational being is a fact of a different order from his existence as a biological entity. Our perception of these properties in him is possible only through organs involving our own moral and rational powers. These qualities that we perceive in man call to the like qualities in ourselves and demand the recognition of an affinity that has ethical and political implications. Sociology also possesses ethical and political dispositions, by virtue of its ancestral traditions.

It is the fruition of some of the traditions of sociological theory, in their confluence with the growing humanity of this still so distressing age, that leads toward the attenuation of the alienation that has long been characteristic of sociology.

The traditions from which the theory of action

5. Even among those who started from this standpoint, an originally manipulative instrumentalist viewpoint has been forced more and more, by cognitive as well as by moral imperatives, toward a more consensual practice—if not

toward a more self-aware acknowledgment of the theoretical implications of this practice. I refer here to the sociological theory and practice that derive from the work of Kurt Lewin.

springs are not all equally oriented toward the more consensual position of contemporary theory. The powerful impulsion given by Hobbes and the utilitarianism that came from it contained an alienative tendency, which the moderate political views of its nineteenth-century proponents did not eradicate. Nor did Durkheim fully overcome such elements in his inheritance from St. Simon and Comte. For many years, sociology was viewed by its adherents as something outside the existing social order and as necessarily at odds with it. Sociology conceived of itself as a necessarily dissensual factor in society; its observations emphasized the dissensual processes, toward which it took a tone of severe disapproval.

It is still a proud boast of some sociologists that sociology is an "oppositional" science. Some of those who take pride in the oppositional character of sociology are former or quasi-Marxists—who, without giving their allegiance to Marxism, wish nonetheless to retain its original disposition.

It is, however, not only the Marxian influence in sociological analysis that has sustained this alienated standpoint. It came into sociology much earlier than the first contacts of sociology with Marxism. Marxism and late nineteenth-century German sociology both drank from the wells of inspiration provided by German Romanticism and by the radical Hegelian version of alienation. Rationalism and scientism, from Bacon to Descartes, although not producing a substantive influence on sociology, helped to create the still prevailing culture of sociology.

The original association of sociological research with poverty and the miseries of the poor left a precipitate that has lasted long after these subjects have ceased to preoccupy sociologists. After first focusing attention on the miserable, the homeless, the parentless, the insulted, and the injured, sociologists later generalized this particular condition into one which was put forward as representative of all of modern society. While the subject matter of sociology was extended and even shifted from the poor into the other sections of society, and to problems other than the description of poverty and its attendant troubles, the original conception remained more or less intact. The great efflorescence of empirical inquiry took place in America in the 1930's, during the Great Depression and at the time of the awakening interest, among American sociologists, in Marxism, psychoanalysis, and German sociology. Very few of the investigators of that period underwent all these influences simultaneously, and not many bore them directly; but they permeated the intellectual atmosphere and could not be avoided. They increased the sophistication of

American social science; but they also raised to a more abstract level the orientation that had, at least in urban sociological studies, already been very much alive, albeit in a more callow form. The great efflorescence of empirical inquiry in the second half of the 1930's—in industrial sociology, in the study of race relations, in the interest in mass communications, and in the introduction of psychoanalytic conceptions—differentiated but did not otherwise change the basic attitude toward contemporary society.

The movement toward theory that accompanied this lively activity in empirical research had no difficulty in giving a more elaborate expression to this "oppositional" science. The theory that came forth has been largely constituted by "middle principles." It has not aspired to reach the level of abstraction and scope of the sociological theory of action, and for this reason the fundamental divergences of the two orientations in sociology have not come to a full confrontation.

The numerous investigations into industrial sociology, mass communications, criminality and delinquency, educational institutions, elites, urban communities, adolescents, and the aged, are conducted in a radically iconoclastic mood. This iconoclasm is not merely the realistic dissipation of erroneous views; it is almost always directed against authority. There is often an overtone to the effect that those in authority have acted wrongly, out of incompetence, blindness, or disregard for the common good. This is frequently not a result of a personal attitude; it is a product of the setting of the problem and of the establishment of a certain set of subject matters as the appropriate ones for investigation. The power of the tradition in which sociologists work dominates their own not especially strong or clearly defined moral and intellectual impulses.

The result is an outlook that radically distrusts the inherited order of society. It is an outlook that has much to recommend it on the moral side and many intellectual achievements to its credit. It is nonetheless defective intellectually, and it will not sustain juxtaposition with experience or systematic theoretical reflection. Society is not just a "congeries of atomized individuals"; nor has bourgeois society "reduced the family relation to a mere money relation." Contemporary society does not consist of anonymous faces in the crowd; political life is not just a scene in which self-interested pressure groups determine every policy. Yet these are notions that many sociologists have believed until quite recently and many still believe. To the extent to which they have given up believing in them, they have done so out of submission to the pressure of a wider experience and of the theory of action, which has undermined the extremer utilitarian and romantic assumptions of this alienated sociology. Much of the resistance against the theory of action comes from this obstinately alienated sociology, which contends that the theory of action purports to see consensus where there is only a concert of interests or an equilibrium of coercive powers. The sociological theory of action is, moreover, charged with an unjustifiable attachment to the status quo, and with a conservatism that denies the reality of revolutionary social change because it is ethically and politically unsympathetic with such change.

The criticism, from the standpoint of the theory of action, of the alienated outlook of much of the sociological work of recent years does not rest on political grounds. The primary reason for criticizing the oppositional conception and outlook is that they provide a distorted picture of contemporary society and of society in general. They greatly overestimate the extent to which the Hobbesian state of nature prevails in society; they overestimate correspondingly the role of deception, manipulation, and coercion, and the degree of deliberate concerting of action by the elites against the rest of society. It is not that these observations are entirely without foundation; but they do not merit the preponderance that "oppositional science" accords to them.

There is another reason for rejecting this standpoint. In so far as it is not entirely contemplative, it is manipulative because it does not accept the possibility of a consensual modification of conduct through self-control. It is not necessarily committed to a manipulative attitude by its analytical schema. That is too seldom sufficiently well worked out to impel commitment, and often its inclinations are in the direction of the theory of action. The manipulative orientation is a product of a political and ethical attitude that has little to do with the fundamental sociological orientation.

The argument for the alienated standpoint, aside from the allegation of the correctness of the results it produces, is twofold. First, it is alleged that it is the most fruitful point of departure for understanding a society; and second, it is alleged that the main and inescapable function of sociology is to be the critic of its society. The first argument need not detain us here. The second is more germane to our consideration of the calling of sociology. One may grant its correctness and yet deny that the critical attitude necessarily entails the kind of criticism that has implicitly and explicitly been associated with this standpoint in sociology during the past century.

If the theory of action is capable of integration with certain ethical standpoints and not with others, then it stands to reason that it also affords a range of alternative points of view from which to criticize the performance of any particular society. If the sociological theory of action is an act of self-interpretation, it also carries with it the possibility of self-criticism, individual and collective. In neither case does it provide either the sole foundation of criticism or a single determinate standpoint. It simply leaves open the possibility. Indeed, if by "criticism" is meant rational criticism, which is intended to be effective through appeal to the cognitive and ratiocinative powers of those to whom it is addressed, it might be said that only a theory having much in common with the theory of action is in a position to criticize. Otherwise, criticism must take the form of manipulation, subversion, etc.

A NOTE ON MARXISM, SOCIOLOGY, AND THE CRITIQUE OF SOCIETY

The greatest popularity of sociology in Europe has fallen in the years since the Second World War, and it has coincided with the erosion of Marxism, as a result of the moral discredit of its association with tyranny and of its intellectual insufficiency in dealing with the history of the last thirty years. Lively young men and women who have been, or who would otherwise have been, drawn to Marxism have turned to sociology. The failure of Marxism to satisfy, and the readiness to replace it by sociology, testify to an aspiration to enter into serious contact with contemporary society, and to the capacity of sociology to provide a critical self-assessment of contemporary society. The appeal of Marxism and of a sociology inspired by it had lain in part in its critical attitude, and in part in its purely cognitive comprehension, in its scope and differentiatedness, in its grand scale. It facilitated the location of the self, in one's own epoch and society, on the largest map available to the mind of its time. It provided a standard for criticizing that society and one's own conduct in it. Sociology continues both these themes. It, after all, grew out of some of the same sources as Marxism; and it was, as a contemporary of Marxism, a competing response to the same yearning. Marxism has failed to hold the imagination of morally sensitive and intelligent young people because its political implications became too rigid and simplistic, and because its present embodiment and its chief exponents were too obviously contradictory to its enduring critical dispositions.

Sociology, both in its theory and in concrete analyses, possesses, in contrast with Marxism, a critical potentiality all the greater for the flexibility which its implicitness confers on it. It appeals more to the mind of the contemporary intellectual by the freedom of experience it permits; it allows a man to make his own personal contact with reality, to test it by his own experience, and to criticize it in a way that does more justice, as he sees it, to that experience. This is especially true of concrete sociological research on particular topics.

Can the same be said for sociological theory? Would a theory that is not just a theory of *contemporary Western* society be equally attractive for those who wish to make contact with their society and to criticize it realistically? Sociological theory as it stands today is, to too large an extent, an abstraction of concepts formed in the historical context of the second half of the European nineteenth century, and extended by the assimilation—in part—of the experience of the United States in the twentieth century. As such, it has the possibility, often realized, of illuminating major trends of contemporary and recent society. It is a sort of shorthand description of the chief features of "modern society," with occasional extensions to non-Western and nonmodern societies. It is the aim of general theory to become genuinely universal and transhistorical, and there is nothing in principle that would obstruct the attainment of this aim. If sociological theory attains a generality of scope and a differentiation that render it equally applicable to all societies of the past and present, will it still retain the potentiality of criticism and self-location that makes it so attractive today?

With respect to the former, it might well be that the more genuinely *general* and abstract the propositions of sociology become, the less they will contain of a genuinely critical response to any contemporary situation. Criticism that is not just a grim hopelessness about the condition of man is always particular and concrete. It is directed against particular persons, particular classes of persons, and particular institutions; it is about things that exist *at present* and that have a prospect of being made *not to exist in the future*. The terms for referring specifically to such conditions are rather concrete—in any case, more concrete than the abstract language that a well-founded sociology of universal scope would be likely to employ. The key words that are crucial in a critique of society have not only a relatively particular reference; they also have a tone that they share with current opinion and that they lose when they are replaced by terms of greater generality, of greater historical and territorial inclusiveness.

These observations refer only to a general theory of sociological analysis. They do not apply to a theory of "middle principles." The latter kind of theory will undoubtedly still exist even under conditions of a higher theoretical achievement. There is no necessary incompatibility between these two kinds of theory, which will, in any case, as they already do in their present very imperfect forms, overlap and intertwine with each other.

The "theories of the middle range" will be the vehicles of the critical outlook that is essential to sociology. In its function as a critique of any contemporary society, Marxism will be replaced by middle principles and not by a general sociological theory. As the theories of "the middle range" become more general and abstract, the critical element will become more attenuated and more generalized. An element of ethical or moral orientation will always remain, by virtue of the fundamental categories of intellectual orientation that are integral to sociology; but it will be in the same relationship to the concrete critical disposition as serious publicistic analysis bears to moral and political philosophy.

What, then, of the value of sociology as self-interpretation, as "self-location," which is so closely related to the critical function of sociological theory? A similar process will be at work. Sociological theory, as it becomes more abstract and general, will be more significant as the location of man in general. Its value in the location of particular and more concrete, historically sigular variants of the human possibility will diminish as it turns its attention toward the determinants of human possibilities on a more universal scale. It will then provide the instrument of self-location of the sort that "philosophical anthropology" presents, and more differentiatedly and less nebulously than that considerable intellectual achievement at present permits.

D. *Sociology, Tradition, Authority*

The critical potentiality of sociology in the face of tradition and authority comes from a more serious source than mere rebelliousness or antinomianism. The myth-making needs of man are too great, his excitation by authority is too pronounced, for him to be able to picture things as they appear to an observer disciplined by training and experience to view certain major events sympathetically and yet without the passions they arouse in the untrained. Despite the countertendencies of philistinism, there are strong inclinations to transfigure, glorify, or denigrate. Some men much of the time, many men some of the time, must be awestruck or sacrilegious. Those who have power over others are compelled to paint for themselves a picture of their constituents that is almost always at variance with the facts. Those who are subordinated to authority are under similar compulsions to distort and obscure, out of self-abasing submissiveness or resentment. There are naturally great variations in the capacity of the agents and patients of authority to perceive truthfully the reality in which they live, just as all human beings, however disciplined, have difficulties in understanding themselves and others. The justification for sociology, when it is at its best, is that it aspires to assimilate and advance the best understanding that human beings can acquire in the course of their intelligent and sympathetic confrontation of life's tasks. Whatever else sociology might be, it is the cultivation of detachment. A detachment that has no appreciation of attachments to sacred objects would be worse than useless for sociology; and sociology furthermore must work with categories that are just to these attachments. This empathic detachment is bound to keep sociology, however consensual it is fundamentally, in a less than perfect consensus with much of the human race. Sociology is forced by this detachment to have somewhat strained relations with the belief-ful sections of the race and with those who enjoy or who are sensitive to authority.

It is not that sociology irritates by its detachment from what men think is sacred in the universe or in their own lives, but rather that its results must diverge cognitively from what many of the best intelligences and spirits among human beings can produce. It is the divergence from the established view of authority and tradition that generates a certain measure of isolation of sociology from the rest of the culture and the institutions that carry it. Some of this strain is at present historically accidental. It is an inheritance of earlier strains between the traditions that have brought sociology to its present position and the beliefs against which the forerunners of sociology had at one time had to contend. Some of the present disposition against tradition and authority is a result of sociology's historical share in a tradition of intellectual development much broader than sociology; another part is inherent in the sociological enterprise proper.

It is certainly reasonable to expect the historically adventitious part of the strain to be eliminated or reduced over the next decades. It is of a piece with that phase and outlook of sociology that caused it to be designated as an "oppositional science." As an orientation more sympathetic, or at least more open, to the constitution of society comes to the fore, this factor will diminish. It is legitimate, moreover, to expect the rhetoric and mood of sociology to become more compassionate and less impelled by the bitterness of a disappointed rationalism in its contemplation of the poor human race. This too will aid in the diminution of the extraneous sources of strain.

Can sociology ever cease to be an implicit criticism of traditional beliefs and authorities? Can it ever give up its implicit critique of the vanity of princes and the magic of priests? The answer to these questions can be put in a single and extreme form: if ever the time should come when the results of sociological analysis will be identical—for whatever cause—with what is believed by adult human beings in that society in which sociology so prospers, then sociology will no longer maintain the distance or imply at least some measure of distrust toward beliefs and institutions that most people share and on behalf of which authorities speak. This condition is unlikely ever to occur, because of both the nature of men and the nature of any concentrated intellectual activity. The sociological enterprise would make no sense whatever if sociology could not in some way transcend the knowledge that the widest human experience and the most discriminating sifting of tradition render available. Even now, when sociology is still a rather feeble subject, filled with prejudices and vague notions, it competes at its peaks quite impressively with the best that the sober judgment and mature wisdom of the age can bring forth. There is no ground to think that it cannot, from the nature of things, do better in the future. Even if ordinary human understanding improves—which is by no means a hopeless prospect—sociological analysis, as its better traditions become consolidated and as it attracts better minds to their cultivation, is likely to improve disproportionately.

As long as this gap exists, then, the observations, insights, and generalizations of sociology will inevitably assert that things are not what they seem. They will impugn the grounds human beings adduce to justify their conduct. They will disclose an image of the world different in some important respects from what the ordinary, and even the very intelligent, unsociological man sees. Some of these disenchanting insights will be absorbed by many people, and the gap will be narrowed thereby.

A gap will remain, however. If one thinks, as I do, that authority—exercising it, submitting to it, or being fascinated by it—is one of the most mind-disturbing things in all human experience; if one thinks that authority upsets the mind, affects one's inmost image of one's self, of man, and of the world; then the very difference between the states of mind induced by attachment to or repulsion from authority and the detached and dispassionate states of mind induced by the exercise of sociological analysis means that different images of man, the world, and the authoritative self will almost inevitably persist.

Sociology can and almost certainly will divest itself of the quasi-Marxist, populistic, rationalistic, anti-authoritarianism and the blindness to the nature and working of tradition that it has inherited. It will, on the whole, gain considerably thereby. It will in that event also find the idiom, just as it has already found the analytical categories, that can give expression to a closer sense of affinity with those who exercise authority or generally receive traditional beliefs. Fundamentally, however, the problem confronting sociology here is the problem of its relationship to religion, since authority and tradition are at bottom, although not entirely, religious phenomena. They are religious phenomena in the sense that they claim validity through the embodiment of, or through contact with, something ultimately, irreducibly, and transcendently important. They contain the vital and touch on the source of the vital. There is much more to authority and tradition than this religious element—expediency, convenience, pig-headed complacency, vain self-esteem—but neither would be the profound force in the world that it has been and continues to be if it were not affected with this sense of the ultimately vital. The cleavage between sociological analysis and the religious belief, whether it be theological, political, or traditional, seems unbridgeable—and it might well remain a permanent gap.

Sociological analysis still has forward steps to make in the appreciation of religious phenomena and the diversity of their manifestations. Sociologists can become much more religiously musical than they have ever been, except for Max Weber. Sociologists might even become genuinely religious persons. Sociological analysis, as long as it remains within the most general outlines of its present fundamental framework, excludes the reality of miracles and revelations. It has no place at present for divine intervention in the affairs of man. These are hypotheses with which it can at present dispense. This refusal, which is seldom avowed because it is so much taken for granted, is the barrier between sociological analysis and the religious interpretation of events. Sociological analysis can make peace with rational natural law or with the natural law based on the theory of moral sentiments, but it cannot make a home with natural law based on a religion of revelation. It need not war with it, it need not carry on polemics, it need not regard it as its task to make men acknowledge the illusory nature of religious beliefs. It can coexist with a religion based on revelation, but there will always be a gap between them; and for genuinely religious persons, and not just stick-in-the-mud religious philistines, there must be some awareness of the sociological denial of the final claims of religion in general or of any of the great world religions of revelation.

The same obtains for the relations between socio-logical analysis and the outlook of the politician at the pinnacle of authority or of the revolutionary outsider preoccupied with the subversion of the prevailing system of authority and with his own accession to its seat. The experience of such perceptions partakes of the nature of religious experience. It is a contact with the weightiest determinants of man's life. It is a confrontation reaching toward the order that intrigues and excites. Although the idiom in which modern politicians and revolutionaries speak is not the cognitive idiom of religion—and this makes it appear easier to bridge the gap—the experience is of the same family as the religious experience. It makes claims, and estimates the nature and value of self and others, similar to the claims and estimates of religious experience. Sociological analysis can try to penetrate these states of mind by empathy, but it cannot easily accredit them according to their own standards. Sociology is agnostic vis-à-vis the order of being with which religions, authorities, and traditions purport to be in contact. The ultimate grounds of their validity are events that do not have the same reality to sociology as they have for those who espouse them. Their cognitive claims go beyond what sociology can acknowledge, however sympathetic it wishes to be.

These, then, are the outer limits of the extent to which sociological theory can become incorporated into society or can take an affirmative position with respect to traditional beliefs and authorities. The development of sociological theory will only make this fundamental difference more explicit, in a way in which particular empirical inquiries need not do. Theories of the middle range, because they avoid fundamentals, can enter into a more harmonious relationship with the thoughts of those who accept traditional beliefs or who exercise or seek to exercise authority. When, however, sociology ascends, even in a much more religious cultural climate, to a higher level of abstraction and thus touches more openly on the more fundamental features of man's existence, the persistent potentiality of the sociological criticism of tradition and authority will still lie open to the compassionate, dispassionate mind.

Past and Present

THE SENSE OF THE PAST

The interest in the past is not merely the product of contact between man's cognitive powers and the "stock" of events that are available to the play of those powers and that happen to have occurred in the past. It is the expression of a need to be in contact with the past, to feel continuous with it, to be in its presence. The need is a part of the need for the cognitive map that "locates" the self in the universe. It is more than that. It is the sense that the existing self is only a fragment or stage in a larger being, which might be familial, ethnic, national, or human. This larger being has a past that is as much a part of it as anything contemporary. Many human beings believe that in the past resides a value that is not exhausted by the virtue of having been the parent of the present. Of course, historians study the past to understand why the present is as it is, but they also study it, and many are fascinated by the results of their studies because for them the past has a value of its own. Of course, many professional historians do not have this sense, any more than newspaper vendors have the great journalist's eagerness to be in the center of important events, or than many professional sociologists possess a consensual disposition, or than clergymen have a vivid sense of the divinely numinous. The writing of history has, however, been sustained by the great historians who do, and by the readers of their works who, in varying degrees, act under the same fascination. Even the least traditional societies possess, very unevenly distributed within the population, some attachment to the past, and the belief that vital matters, of great concern to the present, occurred there.

On the whole, it may be said that neither concrete empirical sociology nor theoretical sociology has been especially well endowed with a "sense of the past." Neither in the mental constitution of sociologists nor in their assessment of the societies they have studied have the power and fascination of the past been prominent. The predominant conception of modern society as cut loose from tradition gives adequate evidence of this deficient appreciation of pastness. A very extraordinary feature of almost all of contemporary sociological literature is the pervasive absence of any analysis of the nature and mechanisms of tradition. This omission only confirms the insensateness of sociologists to the significance of the past to other human beings, and their own deficient sense of the past.

The "oppositional" traditions of sociology, its friendliness toward the scientific spirit, its association with progressivistic ideas, are closely associated with this blindness to tradition. Exposure to the influence of Romanticism encouraged the devaluation of modern society; it led to an idealization of "traditional" societies. Nonetheless, even this did not promote an analysis of traditional attachments, perhaps because the animus was directed against the modern society, and traditionality was only a stick with which to beat the modern dog. The fundamental distinction between *Gemeinschaft* and *Gesellschaft,* which still underlies so much of

sociological analysis, called for a more direct consideration of the nature of tradition and the mechanisms of its transmission and reception. It never became more than a residual category employed for purposes of delineating a problematical picture of modern society.

It is not so difficult to understand why American, French, and British sociology managed to avoid the issue. Their empiricism, their rationalism, and their commitment to enlightened improvement help to account for their failure. It is more difficult to understand the failure of German sociology to do more than it did. The profound influence of Romanticism on German intellectual life, and the predominance of historical scholarship in the circles in which the fledgling sociology moved, should have been conducive to a greater appreciation of tradition and the traditional disposition. Even Max Weber's grandiose analysis of traditional authority leaves the question little advanced beyond where he found it, at least as far as fundamentals are concerned.

Will the prospective development of sociological theory overcome this deficiency? As long as the theory of middle principles preponderates, and as long as the preponderant concern of that theory is modern or contemporary Western—and, above all, contemporary American—society, then this lack is not very likely to be made good. The traditional sense is not tangible enough in these situations to impose itself on the techniques of inquiry now in use, and the theory in question will operate only in a matrix of concrete observation.

As the theory of middle principles moves beyond Western societies into the African and Asian cultures, which are more overt in their attachment to the past and in their acknowledgment of the validity of sheer pastness, then some improvement might be expected. As long, however, as the focus is on the process of modernization—as it is likely to be—then the decay of tradition, rather than its maintenance and reproduction, will be accorded primacy. Mankind's attachment to the past will thus continue unstudied.

The root of the deficiency goes very deep into the constitution of contemporary sociology. It is impossible that it will yield readily. Sociological propositions are largely synchronic. Where they are not, it is by virtue of the interest in personality structure (mainly of Freudian inspiration); and they therefore extend themselves at most to a two-generational relationship occurring within the lifetime of a single generation. Those who find the situation intellectually unsatisfactory take refuge in more uncritical historicism, adducing "history" as a residual explanatory factor.

Pastness as the property of an object, of an individual action, of a symbol, or of a collectivity, has not yet been accorded a place in sociological theory. It need not remain so; and the correction of the foundations of the theory of action in a way that would do it justice should not be a hard task. The adaptation of the larger theory will be harder. Like much in the general theory, it will depend as much on a matrix of sensibility as on the deductive powers.

The study of history is not the therapy that sociology needs, although it is an important part of the cure. It is not facts about the past that sociology needs, but a better sense of the past and a better sympathy with the sense of the past as it occurs in daily life and on exalted occasions. In the century-long *querelle des anciens et modernes,* there is so much that was right and humane on the modern side that one is reluctant to criticize its results. But one of these results is an allegedly unbridgeable gap between the old and the modern. This has produced the disjunction between the archaic and the modern that has coincided with the equally deep disjunction between *Gemeinschaft* and *Gesellschaft,* which came from a very different source. The outcome is a distortion of the nature of the past and of the present.

This brings us once more to the phenomena of primordiality and sacredness. Sociology will not come to grips with man's attachment to the past, and therewith of one of the most massive determinants of the continuity and stability of any order of society, until it has acquired a better, more empathic relationship with the phenomena of age, kinship, and religion. This is where the inherited conception of modern society has had disastrous results. The notion of a society that is disjunctive with past human experience—of an individuated society, in which the family has shrunk down to its nuclear minimum and in which "secularism" is universal and all pervasive—is an exaggeration of certain tendencies in modern society. But, as a set of middle principles for the interpretation of society, it reveals the best arguments against the claims of those who place the theory of middle principles so high on the present-day agenda of sociology. As long as these middle principles confine thought to their own explicit framework, sociological analysis will be able to avoid the recognition of the improbable character of its description of modern society. The growth of a general sociological theory will make sociologists more aware that, human beings being what they are, the historicism inherent in a doctrine of self-sufficient middle principles exaggerates and absolutizes certain tendencies in modern Western society that can never be completely fulfilled.

The myth-building generated by attachment to the past, the cosmological constructions that arise from the need to locate and objectivize the sacred, the morally irrational and repulsive emanations that come from attachment to the primordial properties of objects—these are all contrary to the agnostic, individualistic, liberal, and humane postulates of sociology. It is difficult, if not impossible, for an educated sociologist to share completely these images and attachments. They are contrary to his best traditions. He must, however, come closer to them than he has hitherto. He must come at least close enough to discern and appreciate their effectiveness in the lives of those who regard them as real.

To recognize the mythogenic propensities of man without believing in the literal, cognitive truthfulness of the imagery of the myths; to appreciate man's propensity to attach himself transfiguringly to the past of his collectivity, without sharing that attachment; to prize the achievement and cultivation of moral, intellectual, and aesthetic individuality, while understanding how rare it is in human history—these and similarly demanding tasks lie as great burdens on the sociologists of the present day and the future. A complete consensus with those we study would bring with it the cessation of our sociological activity; inadequate consensus will condemn that activity to intellectual insignificance. The general sociological theory now taking form makes possible a greater approximation to this optimal consensus of student and studied. Before it can do so, however, it will require reformulation, and that will require a concurrent enrichment of sensibility.

SOCIOLOGY AND CONTEMPORANEITY

The past lives in us, but we live in the present. The present is experience. It is the moment of sensation—all else is memory or anticipation. In a culture in which experience and sensation are prized, contemporaneity is also prized. Contemporaneity acquires a value of its own, independently, but derivatively, of sensation and experience. Being up to date in knowledge, in association, not losing contact with oncoming generations that have been born later than one's own, the sensations of the extended self—these are valuable in themselves.

Man's need for conviviality is not just a need for co-operation or protection; it is not merely a need for "company," or a response to the threat of loneliness. Our convivial need goes beyond personal relationships, beyond the enlivening presence of other human beings loved or enjoyed. We need to be members of a society larger than our own associations and contacts—and for other than ecological, economic, or other functional grounds. There is a need to be in contact with persons and events. This is part of what Aristotle meant when he said that man was a "political animal."

The growth of consensuality in contemporary Western society has brought with it this increased need for contemporaneity. It is a merit and a motive of contemporary sociology that it is an organ of the need for contemporaneity. The practice of sociological inquiry and the reception of its results are equally gratifying to this need. The more abstract and general sociology becomes, the less it satisfies this need directly. General sociological theory, apart from its intellectual merits and the enjoyment of an intellectual exercise that it affords, leaves unsatisfied this need for contemporaneity—at least to the extent that it is truly general and transhistorical.

It would be a genuine loss to our cultural life and a crippling of our moral existence if sociology were to become exclusively concentrated on the construction of a general theory, however scientific. The diagnosis of the age, *Zeitdiagnostik,* has always been the concern of the moral and aesthetically sensitive, who are aware of the flow of time. *Zeitdiagnostik*—of which our own time offers so many so melancholy and so ridiculous instances—has always been the device for criticizing one's contemporaries and for being in contact with them at the same time. It has almost always, except for a fairly short span of time between the seventeenth and nineteenth centuries and in limited areas, been a means of derogating the present and mourning the past. It has, however, always testified to the acuteness of the sensation of contemporaneity and the need to give expression to it. Historicism corresponded exactly to this need, and this remains one of the grounds for its persistence.

General sociological theory is a turning away from this preoccupation with presentness. It is that, however, only in its logical structure and intention. Its function need not be so unsatisfying to the need for contact with the present. As long as it is capable of evocation—that is, as long as it expresses and arouses a fresh sensibility to the particular events it is qualified to explain—it will keep our minds open to the present and make it meaningful to us. Once general sociological theory has been fully established and is no longer a mixture of ad hoc insights into the present and general categories and hypotheses, it will be less of a substitute for the diagnosis of the age than it is at present. It will fulfill a different need. The maps we need must be maps that chart the world in which we stand; but

maps themselves need intellectual location on a larger trans-historical map. That is the responsibility of general sociological theory.

Sociology and the Growth of "The Larger Mind"

Contemporary Western society does not enjoy a good press in the world today. Nor is it only among intellectuals, or those who praise the Communist societies or the wisdom of the East, that its name is darkened. Juvenile delinquency and criminality are on the minds of those who never heard of the "sickness" of mass society. The faithlessness of the age is on the lips of those ill-educated clergymen who speak to empty churches, and of those zealots who speak in no church but would stir the Western societies to a more active opposition to Communist zealotry. The decay of morals, atomization, lovelessness, the rupture with the past, the loneliness of man, are the worn-out coins of an inflated intellectual currency.

It is not really as bad as it is made out to be. Contemporary Western societies certainly are not completely integrated societies. The very notion of complete integration is an utter impossibility as well as a very undesirable state. But it should also be said that contemporary Western societies, with all those deficiencies detected by the sensitive moral conscience and the sharpened sociological eye, are probably more decently integrated than any societies that have preceded them in world history or are contemporaneous with them in other parts of the world. They are more integrated in the sense that there is more mutual awareness, more perception of others, more imaginative empathy about the states of mind and motivations of others, more fellow feeling. How else can we explain the still small, but nonetheless real and growing, respect for the rights of Negroes, African and American; the increased responsiveness to the human claims of women and children—indeed, the very idea of the welfare state and the right of every miserable creature among us to such happiness as this vale of tears allows? These represent a new stage in human existence—a stage in which consensus rests on individuality and on the bonds that can exist between individualities; not a consensus that assumes the absence of individuality and crushes its first manifestations. It is a consensus constructed out of the affectional ties of one individual perceiving the individuality of another, out of a civility that perceives and attaches to the mere humanity of another person, out of a sense of nationality that perceives in the other the element of a shared territoriality.

Although it is better than what has gone before, it is all rather meager so far. The discrepancies between what is and what ought to be are painful to contemplate—partly because our standards as to what ought to be have become more elevated and more demanding of observance.

The progress of humanity toward a more liberal, more rational, more humane consensus is slow, and the ascent is only just beginning. And every step forward faces a new danger. Every new virtue that renders it possible can all too readily become a vice that will undo it. Perceptiveness of the state of mind of another can become a maliciously prying destruction of privacy. Love can turn to tyranny and then to hatred. The sense of nationality can become a monstrous exclusiveness. Civility can become a harshly self-righteous Puritanism, uncomprehending toward peccadillos and mean toward small pleasures.

And still, and nonetheless, the forward movement is a real thing, unprecedented in human history. Sociological analysis, no less unique and no less without a great preparatory tradition, is part of this movement. Without this movement, there would be no sociological analysis as we know it. There was no sociology in antiquity or the Middle Ages, and there has been no sociology in the great civilizations of Asia or in the lesser ones of Africa. There have been sages and shrewd observers, but they were not sociologists. There have been preparers of the way, sometimes greater than most of those who have recently followed that way; sociology is nonetheless a new thing. It is no derogation of the past achievements of the mind of man to say that the realistic novel, as it appeared first and intermittently in the eighteenth century and then with greater density in the nineteenth century, depicting the shape of a human life and taking its place among the greatest genres of artistic creation, did not exist in Western antiquity or the Middle Ages, or that it did not exist in India or Africa, or even in China or Japan (although approximations thereto did exist in these countries). Nor is it a derogation of human greatness in the Western past or outside the West to insist that the vivid, curious, empathic appreciation of the details of the pattern of man's action and relationship with other human beings is part of this new phase of more intimate, more appreciative, more civil—more human—relationships on an emergently universal scale.

In this "growth of the larger mind," as Charles Horton Cooley named it, sociology is intimately involved. It is its product and it contributes to it, not only by its enactment but also by its consequences. In fact, aside from the prospective intellectual achievement of sociology, its greatest value

lies in its share in the enrichment of awareness, in the play of the moral sentiments, and in the expansion of the range of sympathy.

Sociology takes the other man as he is; it tries to find out what he does, what he thinks and feels. It is an acknowledgment of his right to an independent moral existence. In trying to learn of his own past as he sees it and in his own words, the interviewed-partner who is at the center of sociological inquiry is introduced into science as a morally meaningful being.

Sociological inquiry is a social relationship, but it can scarcely be a relationship of love or friendship. The detachment that it demands from the investigator deprives it of the symmetry and spontaneity required for affection. Rudiments of a personal relationship are formed and then restricted by detachment and by the limitations of time. Within the limits imposed by the passionately impelled primacy of the cognitive element in the relationship between sociologist and interviewee, the relationship offers the opportunity of the opening outward of the minds of men of all types toward other men, through the sociologist as an intermediary.[6]

The content of a human life flows outward into other minds and lives through the medium of sociology. The "larger mind" is extended and deepened through the program of the sociology that moves in the direction of the theory of action. The oppositional impetus and the drive toward a critical assessment existed earlier. They still exist and will necessarily always exist, from the very nature of sociological analysis, as long as sociology continues. The consensual impetus to sociological inquiry is, however, something new in the world, and a positive addition to the moral progress of the race.

The consensual orientation did not create the present-day techniques of sociological inquiry. It found many of them ready to hand in the social survey that came out of heterogeneous traditions. The traditions of political arithmetic, scientific and concerned with national power, and those of the more humanitarian, if inequalitarian, poverty-line survey, were much improved by the development of the technique of participant-observation. Psychoanalysis has contributed the prolonged intensive interview. These two latter techniques, less scientific than the more recent survey procedures, are major sources of the deepened sensibility and the sociological disposition. The techniques of inquiry developed under the inspiration of experi-

---

6. Of course, this is a danger to privacy; but the dialectic of the creation and expansion of individuality always involves the creation of the possibility of privacy and the risk of its infringement—two incompatibles that are mutually dependent and that could not exist without each other.

mental psychology, although more rigorous, are less conducive to the sociological orientation.

There are risks that are run in the flow of eagerness to be in human contact. The more rigorous scientific techniques that discipline this eagerness also suppress it to some extent. They certainly narrow its receptivity and make it more superficial. There is a mixture of motives associated with contemporary social inquiry. The cognitive, the consensual, and the alienative dispositions are in a tense equilibrium; and it sometimes happens that the first and the last impulses get the better of the consensual components. None of these can be avoided, and each alone would be insufficient. The task is to find the optimal combination. In this combination, the consensual element, as expressed in technique of investigation, in general orientation, and in abstract theory, must be central. It is only through the consensual that the cognitive interest will be provided with the substratum necessary for its fruitfulness. This proposition applies equally to concrete inquiry into particular situations and to the most abstract theoretical construction. The cultivation of the alienative approach to human action, and its organization in institutions and systems, would obstruct the *further* growth of sociology both as a cognitive undertaking and as a part of the life of its age. One is no less important than the other, one is indispensable to the other. Should the academic practice of sociology refuse to acknowledge its rootedness in consensual experience and stress instead the manipulative and, by virtue of that, the alienative, dispositions, it will dry up the springs of its own recent vitality.

General sociological theory is not yet, and will probably not be for some time to come, a rigorously deductive theory. It still rests, and it should rest for its truthfulness, on a rich matrix of concrete knowledge of many societies and of many parts of these societies. The full range of experience necessary for the construction of a universally applicable general theory of society is certainly beyond the capacities of any one man. No one could himself do the systematic research or acquire the experience of life that must underlie such a theoretical construction. It must rest on the work of many men, and that work must be concrete and based on firsthand experience and intimate confrontation with the human beings with whom it is concerned. Such research must be consensual. The collation of information gathered for administrative and commercial purposes, useful though it is in the context of consensually impelled inquiry, cannot produce that enriched matrix of sensibility necessary for the guidance of sociological theory. Organized manipulative research, conducted by techniques adapted

from experimental psychology, cannot produce it either—even though, within marked limits, that type of research does have definite cognitive value. The reason that they cannot produce it is that they are not conducted in the medium of empathy, which is the essential constituent of consensus and which can grow only from direct human contact.

The more exact techniques of sociological research, in their present state and probably rather far into the future, produce results that are indeterminate without the support of empathically acquired knowledge. In fact, most of the rigorous research conducted at present is interesting because of the results of empathy that accumulate in their interstices. Without that "supplement" of empathy, the results would be of little intellectual consequence.

The results of concrete sociological inquiry would be unusable in the construction of sociological theory if they did not have this effluvium of perception, which influences the direction of mind of the theorist. This effluvium is the unarticulated knowledge that grows from the experiencing of other human beings, from experiencing them in all the fullness of consensual contact. If the concepts of sociology were perfectly explicit and precise, and if rules of deduction could be established to govern their elaboration and interconnection, there would probably be no need for this primitive dependence. Such a development does not, however, seem to be immediately on the schedule of progress of sociological theory. And as long as sociology remains sociology and does not become absorbed into or subjugated to neurology or cybernetics, the fact that it is continuous with the experiencing of human beings will incessantly engender a condition in which much of our understanding will be penumbral around the zone we can make explicit. Even if human relationships and mutual understanding lose something or even much of their present opacity, there will always be a zone of shadows. This is said here not just because the postulate of the possibility both of permanent progress and of never-ending ignorance is basic to our conception of the relationship between our scientific efforts and the nature of the universe. This would be true even if sociology were to cease to be sociology and become an application of neurology and information theory. Such a culmination will probably never happen, even though sociology will benefit greatly from the instruction provided by these branches of science and new ones yet to come. As long as sociology retains its present partial autonomy, so long will its theory rest—although perhaps not so heavily as at present—on the recurrently renewed and enlivened matrix of experience. And as long as this is so, the consensual element in sociological knowledge will continue to be indispensable.

If, as is not inconceivable, human relationships become freer and the interior of one individuality becomes more accessible to another individuality, then there will be a proportional increment to concrete sociological inquiry and to sociological theory. If, on the other hand, there is a renewal of ethnic tribalism or puritanism on a grand scale, so that human beings seal themselves off from each other or inhibit their individuality, then the incipient consensual society will stop dead in its tracks, and the scarcely born civility of the human race will shrivel and die. We shall then return to the sparse and dessicated condition of humanity before the present age. If this occurs, then sociological theory, made more sophisticated by advances in mathematics and neurology, will resume its earlier aridity in a more sophisticated form.

If it does not, then the richness of experience will always be a bit beyond our capacities for articulation. Our articulations will always be challenged to extend themselves into the zone of the still unarticulated. To seek this extension will require the kind of contact with the object of inquiry—even when the inquiry is pursued at the levels of highest abstraction—that only consensuality can furnish.

Sociology is slowly entering into the broader current of opinion. It is doing so very unequally. As the subject becomes established in the universities, and as larger proportions of the population enter into universities or orient themselves toward the higher culture formed by universities (not toward American collegiate football or the Cambridge-Oxford Boat Race!), so sociology will pass beyond the condition of an academic speciality, practiced and thought about only in academic environments. It will become part of educated opinion. It has in fact already begun to become integral to the opinion of the more curious and the more reflective sections of society. This educated opinion even now receives reinforcement from the creation of a body of sociological literature capable of being read and appreciated and even sought out by the educated public outside the universities.

Sociology, not always of the sort that nourishes the medium of consensus and the consensual sensibility, has already found its way into the circles of industrial and administrative management. It may be expected that, as it infuses medical practice and education, it will have a pronounced moral impact, and not just contribute to the manipulation of human beings "for their own good."

Sociology could play the role that psychoanalysis did during one phase of its earlier popular recep-tion. It could be employed to "unveil" base motives and discredit their bearers. It could encourage—as it seems to do in the instance of the problematic domain of "motivational research"—an immoral manipulativeness. This is no more inevitable than it is desirable. Concrete research disclosing the motivations of human beings and the institutions in which those motivations operate can bring the persons described, and the whole class they exemplify, closer to those whom it informs. The readers and students of concrete sociology can be brought into a more empathic, still unilateral relationship with their subjects. A section of humanity newly laid open, with due respect for individual privacy (which is always *particular* to an individual) is another opportunity for the extension of a genuine, multilateral consensus. Its function would not be merely cognitive, although it would be that at first. Concrete sociology, which has learned the art of exposition, heightens identification and renders sadly plausible the odd deeds of human beings, introducing into them an evidence that issues from the actor's standpoint.

As sociologists spread their activities over the surface of the earth, they widen the consensual network, they thicken its strands, in a way in which the literature of travel, geography, and even social anthropology seldom did. Our knowledge of the "nature and causes of things" would change the structure of our relationships with the human beings we study and with the species at large.

SOCIOLOGY AND POLICY

The Philosopher-King and Counselor of Princes

The line of thought from which contemporary sociology has come forth was occupied with problems of public policy in a way that became less prominent in the nineteenth and twentieth centuries. The great figures of classical social philosophy considered the fundamental problems of policy from the point of view of men who had to exercise authority and to make practical decisions. Even where they themselves lived in remoteness from practical affairs, the clarification of the standards for the judgment and guidance of public policy was always close to the center of their attention. The politicians' problems, reduced to fundamentals, were their problems. The problem of maintaining order through the exercise of princely authority was the point of departure of classical political philosophy; in the age of mercantilism, it was concerned with the maintenance and extension of the power of the state; and it was extended, by modern liberalism, to the maintenance of liberty in a framework of order. Political philosophy was regarded, by those who professed it, as a means of enlightening rulers—and citizens —regarding their right ends and the appropriate means. One of the greatest ancestors of modern empirical sociology, Sir William Petty, viewed his task as the quantitative inventory of what existed. This inventory was justified because it would enable the prince to know the resources at his disposal to safeguard and maximize his power. Early economic theory accepted the same task. Even after mercantilism gave way to liberalism, economic theory was still intended to be a guide to policy.

A rather fundamental change occurred in the course of the nineteenth century. The coming forward of the "oppositional science," and the academic establishment of the embryonic sociology at the turn of the century, decreased this readiness to take the standpoint of the ruler. The study of politics adulterated its preoccupation with policy by concrete recipes of administration and the aproblematic description of governmental processes. In America, an important antecedent of urban sociology—the muckraking movement— was strongly antipolitical, and it left a lasting impact on sociological studies there. The "survey movement" in America and the poverty-line survey in Britain were not intended so much for the use of administrators or legislators as they were intended to prod the leaders of public opinion into a more serious attitude toward the hardships of the poor. The prevailing liberalism of the age replaced princes and legislators by the leaders of public opinion. Except in Germany, where the "socialists of the chair" sought to keep the social sciences in the service of the state, the forerunners of sociology at the end of the century wished to separate social science and social policy. The greatest of modern social scientists, Max Weber, wrote one of his most powerful methodological essays to justify that separation.

This general tendency toward de-politicization might in part have resulted from the "separation" of the various spheres of life in the liberal society of the nineteenth century. The relative autonomy of the spheres fostered a belief in the possibilities of separate fields of inquiry, with the resultant expulsion of political elements from sociological and economic studies. (The academic separation of political science, sociology, and economics from one another, and their consequent de-politicization, never went so far in Germany as it did in

the Western countries where liberalism flourished.) Moreover, the nature of the ideal social order "prescribed" by the liberal economic theory, which was the most impressive product of this intellectual division of labor, minimized the importance of large, central decisions. It dispersed decisions into a great multitude of organs and attributed to them an automatic character. The intellectual preponderance of economic theory among the social sciences in the English-speaking world thus reinforced this tendency of each social science to rid itself of any political traces in content and especially in its conception of its calling.

The development of the universities of the nineteenth century and their relations with the world of affairs also appear to be important factors in the de-politicization of the social sciences. The great schemes of interpretation and judgment formulated by the masters who formed the traditions from which sociology has emerged grew up outside the universities and in a fairly close connection with politics and practical affairs. Except for Adam Smith, no major figure of social science outside Germany, until the latter part of the nineteenth century, was primarily a university teacher. Germanic social science—which in Germany at least had some connection with the theory of the state as the embodiment of the highest values— was introduced into the American universities by men who had had their training in Germany in the 1870's and 1880's. In the United States, the German theory of the state found no echo; while the administrative recipes that formed a large part of the remainder of the syllabus of the *Staatswissenschaften* were accepted as useful by teachers who thought that the main problems of life and of public policy could be resolved by the reform of the civil service.

This period of university history in the United States coincided with a period of severe alienation of the educated from politics. The corruption of government at all levels attendant on industrial and urban expansion revolted the intellectuals. Except for a guerrilla war of intermittent urban reform and scholarly journalistic exposure of the "malefactors of great wealth" and their political confederates, the American academic social scientist lost the feeling of kinship with the mighty, and even the yearning for such a kinship.

This was the milieu into which sociology came. It was unaware of the breadth and depth of its great traditions, and all around itself it saw its social science colleagues in opposition. (There were exceptions in the Middle West, especially in Wisconsin, where the Progressive opposition formed the government, and the academic social scientists

1434   *Epilogue*

were, once more, for a time the counselors of princes.) Without a clear perception of the civil values to which it could be relevant, political science became a morally directionless and scientifically sterile descriptive discipline. Political theory, too, fell victim to intradepartmental specialization and the moral temper of the age. It degenerated into the history of doctrine, losing contact with the greatness of its past and failing to establish contact with the new, descriptively realistic political science of the present.

Sociology, which set out to fill the empty spaces left by contemporary political science, did nothing to compensate for the political abdication of political science. In order to prove their rights to existence, sociologists sought to find a sphere of events left untouched by the already accredited social sciences. The inherited distinction between the state and civil society fitted this need very well. Even though they found a justification for their independent existence in the numerous "social problems" that had arisen in connection with urbanization and immigration, they seldom expected them to be solved by governmental action. Such theory as they then possessed was often accented toward the view that political decisions were impotent to affect "social processes." The persistence of evolutionary, biologistic, instinctivist theories in French, British, and American sociology (even in Sumner and Park) obstructed the formulation of a sociological theory in which knowledge and decision were important categories, and even distorted the interpretation of those sociologists whose theoretical orientation was more adequate intellectually and politically. Neither in substance nor in its general theoretical scheme did sociology concern itself much with politics, with political decisions, or with decision-making in other spheres. The "new history" to which sociologists felt akin was a revolt from political history— it was a denial of the relevance of political decisions in social life; it was a denial of their worthiness as objects of study.

This tendency to withhold themselves from the problems of policy, as they appear to the makers of the highest policies, was furthered by the desire of social scientists, and especially sociologists, to be scientific. The vastly superior prestige of the natural sciences, and the inferiority feelings of the social sciences in the face of the contumely they received from both the scientific and the humanistic disciplines, led sociologists to the conviction that their own salvation lay in becoming scientific. "Scientific" meant being "objective," totally cut off from the object by any tie of sympathy, deliberately indifferent to the fate of the object. To be

scientific meant other things as well, but these are the aspects that concern us here.

The program of "ethical neutrality" involved not simply abstention from the belief that recommendations for policy could be based exclusively on statements of fact. It involved, for many social scientists, a belief that an utter detachment in matters of policy was incumbent on a social scientist, beyond even the boundaries of his scientific role. For such social scientists—and there were certainly sociologists among them—it involved renunciation of the role of the citizen. There was no uniformity and much confusion about this, and men were often better in their conduct than a strict adherence to their doctrine would have caused them to be.

Logically, the proposition asserting that judgments of fact alone cannot give rise to judgments of value is correct; what was incorrect was the deduction that, because empirical knowledge alone can offer no ineluctible imperative in the determination of the ultimate ends of individual conduct or social policy, social scientists are not only not qualified to discuss questions of value and policy, but their very profession as social scientists forbade their serious involvement in evaluative problems in any way—and particularly in the selection of problems.

Social scientists did, nonetheless, serve on government commissions, testify before congressional committees, and participate in various political reform movements; but on the whole, they were exceptions to the mood of their professions. Woodrow Wilson, as Professor of Political Science and President of the United States, was the great exception to the prevalent attitude among American university social scientists that rejected politics as unclean. Even among those who participated in reform politics, the improvement of politics consisted in their elimination—*viz.*, the city-manager movement. This contemptuous and fearful alienation from the holders of power and the makers of public decisions brought about a situation in which sociologists—and their associates in political science—neither studied political action realistically on the hoof nor strove toward a theory that could enter into the improvement of policy.

The Return to Policy

Of course, sociology and the sociological part of the social sciences had much less to offer at that time to policy-makers, administrators, and those concerned with the public good than they have at present. It was the First World War that showed, particularly in the United States, that academic social scientists could serve governments and all organizations interested in controlling and modifying human behavior. The important work of psychologists in the United States Army during the First World War gave rise to a new conception of the relevance of the scientific study of man to the exercise of authority. This wartime experience promoted the development of psychology toward personnel selection and industrial psychology. Places were found for political scientists, historians, and geographers in "political warfare" and in the fumbling organization of the peace. After the War, psychologists, inspired by their acceptance, extended their skills in testing, selection, and counseling: and many powers, private and public, sought to employ them. The great extension of advertising and propaganda after the First World War, and the increased prestige of psychologists in associated activities, gave many opportunities in the world of affairs to academically trained social scientists. The turning by enterprisers toward personnel management—which was also accentuated by the war and particularly by the disturbances in industrial relations following the war—was another stimulus to the increasingly mature science of psychology and an additional invitation for the social sciences to think manipulatively about society.

Today governments, political parties, military, private business, civic, and economic organizations compete with universities and endowed research institutes as employers of social scientists. Naturally, the process has gone farther in the United States than elsewhere, but Great Britain, France, Germany, Italy, and Poland—in short, all the countries where sociology is moderately well established—have moved along the same path. It is a trend that is unlikely to be reversed. Truth is always useful to those who exercise authority, regardless of whether they wish to share that truth with those over whom their power is exercised, or whether they wish to bring about particular patterns of behavior in others, to reach their own ends. It is desired because of its prestige, even by those who will not heed it. As governments incline more and more toward intervention into the economy and comprehensive economic planning, and as the welfare state progresses, a more specific knowledge of the human beings over whom authority plays appears desirable.

The growth of the mass communications industries and the advertisement of consumers goods have generated a great demand for sociologists in private employment. Nowadays, almost any organization with a claim to respectability believes it needs a sociologist to help it with the tasks it

has taken on itself. Mental hospitals, housing authorities, institutions for the aged, scientific institutions, churches—these are only a few of the bodies that think they can gain from the labors of the sociologist. Social scientists, after many decades of abstention from the executive influence on human affairs, are now involved in it more numerously and more intricately than ever before.

They work primarily as consultants and advisors, at more exalted levels. At lower levels, they are providers of intelligence; not secret or military intelligence, but intelligence nonetheless—or, in other words, information gathered by the techniques of contemporary social research.

Three Types of Orientation to Policy

Sociologists have, in the course of time, taken three types of attitude toward authority. They have sought to serve it as unquestioning servants; they have felt repelled by it and resisted any identification with it or subordination to it; and they have regarded themselves as equal to it and equally part of the same society. These three attitudes correspond to three modes of use of sociological knowledge: (1) the use of sociology as a part of the manipulative action performed by the powerful over those they control; (2) the use of sociology as criticism from the outside; (3) the use of sociology as part of the process of transformation of the relationship of authority and subject through the enhancement of self-understanding and of the sense of affinity. These three modes may be summarized as manipulation, alienation, and consensuality. Each has its characteristic research procedures, its own conception of what sociological science would be like at the height of its development, and its characteristic conception of the calling of sociology. Each has its own intellectual tradition, somewhat separate from the others' but also sometimes overlapping. Different though they are from each other in tone, emphasis, and feeling about what the world is and ought to be, they are also capable of joining with each other. One sometimes adapts the techniques of another—for example, the knowledge gained by the techniques associated with manipulative use and intentions might also be applied consensually.

MANIPULATIVE SOCIOLOGY IN THE
SERVICE OF POLICY

Social scientists are not drawn upon for their wisdom as counselors in the clarification of fundamental alternatives, nor as guides in the choice from among these alternatives once discovered. Nor, in the main, are they looked to for basic truths about human behavior derived either from rigorous scientific research or from the slow accretion of wisdom. Social scientists are, rather, viewed as instruments for descriptive reporting and for the provision of recipes concerning the most effective way to implement a given policy. For the most part, they provide estimates, more or less accurate, of the magnitude of different variables, inventories of activities and beliefs. They tell of the attitudes of subordinates toward various kinds of conduct by their superiors. They report on the frequency of alleged intentions to perform particular actions, such as voting, changing residence, sowing a certain number of acres, and so on. This type of knowledge is of interest to executives, allegedly because they will be able, on the basis of it, to adapt their actions more realistically to their goals. They will be able to elicit more co-operation or arouse less resistance from the subjects of their authority, and thus attain their goals more easily. In their very role as exercisers of authority, they are concerned with the future and with the consequences of particular changes in their own behavior on the behavior of others. Their decisions, incorporated in legislation or administrative orders, as to whether so and so many policemen or soldiers should be dispatched to a particular point, or whether such and such housing should be provided for a given group, take into account the probability that certain particular events will occur if they act in one way, and other particular events will occur if they act in another.

The point of departure of these predictions is an approximate description of the present and recently past situation. The inventories, the estimates of magnitude, with which sociological research workers furnish policy-makers are used by the policy-makers as data for *their own* predictions or "interpretations." The social scientist may, indeed, accompany his inventory with *his* own estimate of the way in which one course of action or another, working on these magnitudes, will affect the fulfillment of the ostensible goals of the policy; he might even present some data that show, on the basis of a contrived test, how the population in question responds to one kind of measure as compared with another.[7] Here, the social scientist

does not merely determine isolated magnitudes; he analyzes the causal relations of the variables. His result is on an elementary level, a "theory of the middle range." Because of the far from determinate character of presumably demonstrated causal connections in present-day sociological research, this part of the report is usually not entirely persuasive to anyone who does not already incline toward persuasion; it is also likely to be less compelling to the mind of the policy-maker who examines it. The description of *what* happened is more likely to be accepted than the explanation of *why* it happened.

Yet there is nothing forever fixed in this situation. Research techniques are improving. There is, despite all the intellectual squalor of much of sociology, a gradual improvement in skill and realism in interpretation of the observations made by these improved techniques. There will undoubtedly come a time when the interpretation of data made by the sociologist will increase its persuasiveness, even to a hard-headed administrator or politician, so that he will give it a heavier weighting in forming his judgment than is usually the case nowadays.

There is no doubt that "sociology" will then be more "useful" to authority than it has been through most of the present century. Throughout the earlier part of this century, it was barely competent to ascertain either an existing state of affairs or the interconnections between two or more series of particular events. As it improved in technique, its "poverty" with respect to policy became more apparent. The long process of dilapidation of the classical standpoint collected its tribute. Sociologists were called to the performance of menial, even if costly, "intelligence functions." The executive used them to supplement his capacities in an important function but still a relatively peripheral one. Sociologists were to help him to "size up" the situation, but they were to enter into nothing more fundamental in the formation of policy. Given the technically underdeveloped condition of sociological research, its theoretical backwardness,

---

7. The significant difference between applied sociological research and other types of sociological research lies neither in the logical structure of the propositions with which an investigation concludes, in their subject matter, nor even in the aims of the investigator. The term "applied research" in the social sciences refers to investigations performed for policy-makers who use or intend to take the resulting propositions into account in their decisions. It is simply research, the results of which are to be applied in some way in practice by those who have in their charge the care of practical affairs. It is not applied research in the sense of the application, of scientifically tested general

principles obtained in "basic" or "pure" research, to the explanation of concrete and particular situations or to the management or construction of concrete and particular constellations of actions. Applied social research of the latter type might indeed develop in the course of time, when there is a body of basic propositions, rigorously tested by systematic empirical procedures and systematically integrated into general theory. Since there are practically no such propositions in social science today, this type of social applied research cannot exist for the time being.

The difference from applied research in the better-established sciences, therefore, consists (a) in the absence of rigorously tested general propositions; and (b) in the absence of rigorous intellectual controls over the results of the manipulations introduced in accordance with those hypotheses.

and the incivility of so much of the culture of the sociologist, there was little to regret. There would not have been any great advantage to policy had it been otherwise. Sociology, for its part, has benefited from its menial offices.

The progress of research techniques, which has been such a considerable feature of the development in sociology in the past quarter of a century, owes much to the interest and patronage of government and commerce. The development of public opinion surveys, with the concomitant improvement of sampling and interviewing, owe very much to the support of governmental bodies and commercial enterprises; without this experience and the accumulation of material, the capacity of sociologists to deal with large masses of data and their facility in resorting to extensive data in order to test hypotheses would not be so advanced as they are. Content analyses, sociometric tests, attitude scaling, latent structure analyses, and small group studies are only a few of the devices for which some credit must go to a sociology in the service of authority and the market place.

What of the future? Can sociology, in its relations with authority, rest content with the extension and sharpening of the eye of the ruler in our polity and in our economy? Is the only alternative the continuation of the great tradition of the "oppositional science"?

A sociology that is drawn to the former alternative will become more scientific. It will have great resources at its disposal, and it will be able to provide employment for many gifted young men and women. The increasing intellectual complexity of research techniques will challenge acute intelligences; and the brilliant minds that are now attracted to mathematics, physics, econometrics, and linguistics will see, in sociology, an equally demanding and equally rewarding field for their talents. These talents will not be content to work in the sphere of research techniques alone, nor will they be satisfied with the improvement of the methods of description. They will inevitably push forward into the analysis of the interconnections of the events before them. They will go beneath the surface of events. They will produce a science of middle principles, theories of middle range; and they will go even more deeply into general theory. Sociology will at last become the science of which some of its great nineteenth-century forerunners dreamed.

As a science, sociology will permit the application of which sciences are capable. Carrying on the scientistic tradition, its application will entail the manipulation of its objects in the light of the scientific knowledge it has created. The scientific

and the scientistic traditions that will guide this development will impel it into a manipulative course. The nature of its patronage will have the same tendency. The existing division of labor between policy-making and intelligence will be maintained. Sociologists, when they come into advisory roles, will naturally not confine themselves to the sphere of their scientific expertise any more than physical scientists at the higher levels of defense policy do today. They will spill over the limits of their inevitably fragmentary knowledge and will offer counsel on matters on which, as citizens, they have an interest. The counsel they will offer is likely to be of the sort for which their traditions, their experience, and the formation of their minds by their scientific roles will qualify them.

The scientistic tradition is a tradition of alienation. It is not the romantic revolutionary tradition of alienation; but it is a tradition of alienation nonetheless. The tradition of scientism, not the practice of science, is a tradition of tidiness, of planned and ordered progress, of continuous improvement along clearly defined lines. It is impatient of inefficiency, of a plurality of ends, of compromise and slovenliness. It wants its principles to be clear and their application to be prompt and efficient. It likes comprehensiveness and the long-range view.

There is nothing in this view of the world that renders it logically compelling on those who practice the human sciences. There is, however, an inner affinity between the scientistic ideology and the practice of the physical sciences, which makes their adhesion in the course of modern history more than adventitious. By no means all physical scientists share the scientistic outlook, but it is not an accident that it is prominent among those who extend their activities into the public sphere. In sociology, it has a long and respected history in French positivism and Marxism. The very fact that the enlivenment of sociology in the past two decades in a number of countries, including the United States, stems from a disillusionment with Marxism, means that, even among those who found Marxian scientism insufficient for the needs of their intelligence and morals, undercurrents of scientism are still flowing.

It is not merely the extrascientific culture of the scientific movement that causes me to think that the technical development of sociology under the patronage of the mighty will take a scientistic turn. The internal life of the science will also play an influential part. The chief source of technical progress in sociology has come hitherto from psychology—the most scientific of the various branches of the study of man. The fields of sociology that have benefited from these advances have been those closest to psychology—for example, attitude studies, public opinion polling, small groups, and industrial relations. As sectors of sociology farther from psychology have undergone technical improvement, they too have been "psychologized."

For better or for worse, the experimental tradition of psychology and its early invitation to help in the tasks of personnel selection, propaganda, and advertising, and the increase in the efficiency of learning processes have strengthened the manipulative orientation. Despite occasional efforts in a contrary direction by the followers of Lewin in Britain and America, improvement of the condition of man and the increase in the efficiency of institutions through manipulation continue as a basic article in the program of psychology. The sociology that is inspired by that psychology shares the belief in that article.

The "terms of employment" exert a similar pressure. The large-scale occupation of sociologists in market research, or in inquiries resembling market research, on behalf of civic, political, and governmental organizations usually delimits the sphere of competence of the sociologist. There are situations in which he is invited to discuss the fundamental issues of policy, or in which chance and intention enable him to discuss these issues as one who shares the responsibility for decision. On the whole, this is not so; and sociologists become used to accepting this division of functions. Sometimes it is because they conceive of themselves as scientists who have no special qualifications for discussing questions of value; sometimes they regard these questions as falling outside their responsibility as experts called upon by their employers only for a certain kind of judgment and no other. Then, too, there are many social scientists of the younger generation whose alienation from authority comes from the broader romantic revolutionary stream; and they find the service of authority so distasteful that they eagerly immerse themselves in technical considerations so as not to confront their service for ends with which they are out of sympathy. The less tolerable they deem the ends they serve, the more they confine themselves to technical problems and to theories of a very low order of generality.

Not all research done for government or private corporate bodies is designed to facilitate manipulation. The sociologists are not always, despite their intentions, able to design an inquiry so that the manipulable variable and the independent variable coincide. It happens not infrequently that their separation from policy-making has been so long

and so great that, even though they would wish to make a policy more effective, they are unable to design their inquiries in a way that will produce the necessary recipes. Nor is all manipulatively oriented research done outside the universities. It is not just a function of the "terms of employment"; the general cultural tradition of the natural sciences and the aura of experimental psychology can produce similar results within universities.

The inventories, middle range theories, and practical recipes emerging from this kind of research should not be considered as adding a new danger to human dignity. Social science in the service of authority, even if it produces knowledge that is used for deception of the subjects of authority, only comes upon an already sullied scene. It would not be social science that has brought about the degradation of man—that has been going on for a long time. Sociological research might make deception more skillful, it might make it more effective—just as developments in electronics make intrusions into privacy more effective and, perhaps, more tempting.

The sociology used in this way shares the immorality of its use and therefore merits our moral condemnation—but only in so far as the use or the intention is immoral. Not all manipulation is immoral—*vide* the education of children—and the sociology that serves this purpose is not immoral either.

ALIENATED SOCIOLOGY AND POLICY

The real deficiency of manipulative sociology, which remains despite its scientific rigor and its moral innocence, is its failure to answer to the true calling of sociology—which is to contribute to the self-improvement of society rather than to the manipulated improvement of society. An alternative to this subservience to manipulation—to which, at present, sociology does not contribute very markedly, because it still offers too little—is the refusal to submit to authority. This alternative also involves attempting to remain outside the system of social relationships being analyzed. It entails a moral condemnation of the society it analyzes; it entails in particular the rejection of the prevailing system of authority and the refusal to co-operate with it either in its self-transformation or in its manipulation of others. In some instances, this refusal may take the form of a detached "scientific" analysis; in others, it may take the form of a revolutionary critique.[8]

The alienated outlook was not confined to the

8. Marxism combined the second of these possibilities with the intention that its insights be used by the revolutionary party to coerce the ruling classes.

European revolutionary tradition. It has been profoundly influential in American sociology, among scholars who had nothing of the revolutionary in their makeup and who, in fact, were generally liberal or conservative in their politics. The most formative figures of American sociology before the great upsurge that preceded the Second World War were William Graham Sumner, Robert E. Park, William I. Thomas, and Charles H. Cooley. With the exception of Sumner, who expected nothing reasonable from any society and demanded only individual freedom—and who, therefore, found himself quite at home in the freebooting capitalistic America of the turn of the century—all of these men practiced a sociological analysis that was severely critical of the American society taking form during their lifetime. They were liberals who regarded Western, and particularly their American, times as "out of joint." The age of the "trusts," of the malefactors of great wealth, the great flood of immigration, and the anxiety these called up in intellectual circles, gave an imprint to their work. They were liberal men, warm-hearted and empathic with a genuine feeling for the other man— Sumner perhaps less so than the others. They were not populists. They were certainly not Marxists. They were, however, the children of their age and, at a time when the names of politics and politicians stank in the nostrils of sensitive Americans, their noses too were wrinkled. Of course, as children of their age, they came under the almost cosmic weight of the Darwinian influence. They therefore believed in natural processes of evolutionary growth. Darwinism and liberalism combined to persuade them that governments, like the owl of Minerva, take their flight only when the shade of night has fallen. Their alienation was a rustic one, like that of the upright Romans who mourned the decline of Republican virtue.

The coming of the Great Depression gave a stronger impulsion to the native American sociological critique. A variety of currents of Marxism began to flow through the intellectual classes in the United States in the second half of the 1930's. In the youngest generation, Stalinist sociologists, fellow-traveling sociologists, Trotskyite sociologists, ex-Trotskyite sociologists, and others who were none of these were attracted by the large perspectives and the humanitarian pretensions of Marxism. By the end of the Second World War, dissident Marxism, renewed and reclothed by Max Weber, was ready to take up where liberal and populist alienation had left off. Psychoanalysis was added to the armament of criticism, especially through the writings of Horney and Fromm.

This broad current of sociological research and analysis continues the great oppositional tradition. It thinks that, on the whole, contemporary society is on the wrong track and there is nothing that can put it right. Romanticism, Marxism, psychoanalysis, Darwinism, populism have coalesced to form a point of view that sees modern, and especially contemporary, society as a theater of a mad struggle for power, of a war of each against all, saved from absolute chaos by fear and repression. How can men of honor serve such a society and, above all, how can they serve those who rule it? Of course, in fact, the temptations of employment and readiness of those in positions of authority do bring the exponents of this kind of sociology into the service of policy. Community studies, studies of class and industrial conflict, of bureaucracies and professions, all find sponsors who believe that sociology offers information and insight that will make their actions more effective, their policies more consistent and more far-reachingly conceived. This kind of sociology, although it does not usually have the precision of the microsociological techniques, is capable of a more scientific form. For one thing, the techniques in question are adaptable to different standpoints. Then, too, the manipulative and the alienated standpoints are not so alien to each other, and the boundaries between them are not in any case so clearly defined.

Nor should it be thought that such research, well done, cannot have a salutary effect on the making of policy, despite its hostility toward authority and its repugnance for the age and society in which it lives. There are various reasons for this partial self-negation of alienated sociology. Most important is the fact that its inheritance includes the tradition of field work, extended interviews, and participant observation. This is the very kernel of consensual sociology, historically and at present. The sociological research with which it was associated was alienated; but it was a populistic alienation, and hence not so radical or comprehensive as the more theoretical quasi-Marxist alienation of the later phase. This research did have a small inclination toward policy: it sought to influence public opinion and thus, in accordance with its Darwinian postulates, to influence legislation, which inevitably moved in the wake of custom and opinion. The alienated sociology of the period since the Second World War has inherited this tradition, although it does not always acknowledge either the substantive or the political contents of that inheritance. The alienated orientation in sociology, in so far as it conducts empirical research on the kinds of subject matter that interest it, is inevitably forced into dependence on the research techniques developed by the alienated liberal sociology. The European "oppositional science" and Marxism were not research disciplines. They had no specific techniques other than conventional research in libraries. When they tried to become sociological in procedures as well as in substance, they had to turn toward the available body of techniques. Those closest to their needs, which were not always, fortunately, unalloyedly the needs of the oppositional critique, were those developed by American sociology in the first quarter of the century in connection with urban sociology and the community study.

For these reasons, even the alienated kind of sociological inquiry is not incompatible with the service of policy—even though its spirit is repelled by that service.

CONSENSUAL SOCIOLOGY, POLICY, AND OPINION

Both the manipulative and the alienated forms of sociological research, and theories associated with them, are afflicted by intellectual deformity. Neither is capable, given their traditions and present dispositions, of producing a coherent and comprehensive sociological theory. Neither can meet the requirements of a polity that respects human dignity and is, therefore, adequate to aspirations of universal validity. Consensual sociology is alone capable of satisfying the requirements of an adequate theory and of a proper relationship with policy.

Sociological research conducted by publicly avowable techniques, which can take place only with the voluntary and conscious co-operation of the subjects of the inquiry, at present represents a considerable part of the total product of this discipline. Even among the inquiries intended to serve purposes of manipulation or the alienated critique, a substantial part of many of them meets the ethical standards of consensual observation. Its procedures are equally open to the observers and the observed; it does nothing that it will not disclose to the subjects of its studies. It does not humiliate, embarrass, or deceive them. It avows its ends and the uses to which its results will be put.

Such knowledge, in the more generalized form or in the particular detail in which it is obtained, can be employed in manipulation. The manipulation need not be malicious; it might be only the conventional procedure of persons in positions of power who do what they have to do to carry on with their job. Much of ordinary executive procedure involves manipulation, and some of it is indispensable to the effective conduct of the affairs of any organization. It is one of the prices mankind must pay for seeking to achieve ends through

organization. There is no reason why sociology should not place itself at the disposal of a manipulation that is in principle accepted as legitimate.

It is, however, a much higher calling for sociology to be able to participate in those forms of co-ordinated activity that involve insight, reasonable persuasion, loyalty, and mutual attachment. These are morally better modes of concerting the actions of human beings, and it would be a serious defect of sociology if it were not competent to take its part in that process.

The sociology built around the theory of action is competent to do so. Its competence derives in part from the tradition of the political philosophy that regards events of political life from the standpoint of one who must take responsible action in them. It derives also from the more specific tradition that regards not only the prince as a rational being with moral powers, but the entire population as so endowed. In consequence of these two traditions, one of which is an extension of the other, the place of sociology in the formation of policy requires its sharing with both ruler and ruled. In relationship to ruler and ruled, the sociologist does not, therefore, stand as a supplier of intelligence about the consequences of actions initiated by the self but intended to produce a sequence of action among other persons. The function of sociological research and of sociological theory in the working of society is to enrich the empathic element in opinion, to provide insight into the self as well as others, and to unite the self and others through a better appreciation of the ties that bind them.

The intelligence function of sociological research for manipulative executive action has many limitations. Like military intelligence, except in immediate tactical situations, it tends to become out of date by the time it is gathered, processed, and communicated. The situation it reports changes in its particulars by the time it has been reported. The meticulous precision of observation is thus something of a wasted effort as far as the guidance of policy is concerned. More valuable is a general picture of the situation, a general set of expectations that permits a realistic and empathic interpretation of the particular events encountered in the course of the execution of policy. The value of detailed research that precisely portrays a real situation is that it disciplines and trains the imagination of the prince—who, in a democracy, is the citizen as well as the civil servant, the chief of the executive, the judge, and the legislator. Its value lies in giving him a richer intellectual and moral appreciation of his society and of his own powers and role within it. Its task is the education of opinion.

The proper calling of sociology today is the illumination of opinion. Having its point of departure in the opinion of the human beings who make up the society, it is its task to return to opinion, clarified and deepened by dispassionate study and systematic reflection. To return effectively to opinion, to persuade by evidence and argument, to aid journalists, politicians, civil servants, and citizens to see in the light switched on by systematic observation and analysis, presupposes, however, a state of affinity between the sociologist and the bearers and guides of opinion whom he addresses. The bearers of opinion and makers of policy are his fellow men, whom he studies, whose actions and thoughts are the data of his inquiries. He learns about them through the application of exact methods of observation in the matrix of a sense of affinity with them. He need not obviously believe all they believe or perform the same actions as they perform in order to feel them to be of the same vital substance as himself. He must see their beliefs as variant elaborations of the same fundamental propensities and possibilities as his own. This is in the nature of consensual inquiry—even in situations in which the investigator accepts the task of serving a manipulative authority.

To exercise consensual influence effectively and properly is to return to the sphere of unformed opinion, which was the field of observation, a better formed, more enlightened, more realistic opinion. This means making opinion more sociological. To make this sociological opinion a part of policy requires reasonable persuasion. This in its turn needs a relationship of mutual respect and trust between the person who seeks to persuade by reasoned argument and the person who is to be persuaded by reasoned argument. The politician or citizen must feel trust and confidence in the good will of the sociologist who confronts him; the sociologist must feel the same way about the good will of the politician and citizen. Mutual respect is a *sine qua non;* but neither the outlook of the sociologist nor the substantive content of his sociology has yet realized the potentialities inherent in the sociology being formed today.[9]

There are numerous instances of progress to-

ward this realization. On the whole, however, the relationships between sociologists and the central institutions of American society have not been happy. They share in the wider tradition of the relationship between the intellectuals and the powers in the West, with some additional complications arising from the American situation. Experience and necessity since the Second World War have imposed some improvement, and mutual dependence has enforced a measure of mutual tolerance that is not by any means wholly stable. As the relationship improves, so the contribution of sociology to policy will improve—although it must guard against the temptations of a consensus mere intense with rulers than with ruled. In important respects, this expanding consensus will also improve the realism of sociology, because it will also open the society more widely to the exploration of the sociologist.

Sociologists will then come into their own as the contemporary equivalents of the *philosophes.* The liberality and empiricism of the *philosophes,* their action on behalf of *les lumières,* only more comprehensive, more deep-going, will be the inheritance of the sociologists, and society will benefit accordingly. Like the *philosophes,* sociologists will be the commentators and illuminators of the current scene. They will be able, proportionately to their talents, to do the job better than the *philosophes,* since they will be better informed, their penetration will extend more widely throughout society and the world, the procedures of observation will be better, and they will have a theory that will have assimilated the best in the ideas of the Enlightenment and strengthened it by the progress of a great variety of disciplines cultivated since the eighteenth century. Some sociologists might feel that this definition of the calling of sociology is one that undoes the progress of the subject. On the contrary, it shows the right direction for a subject that is at once a science, a moral discipline, and a body of opinion.

THE PROSPECT OF
SOCIOLOGICAL THEORY

The Agenda

Sociological theory will certainly not remain for very long in its present state. The theory as it now stands has too many imperfections for powerful and lively minds, which are certainly going to be attracted to sociology in the coming decades, to

---

9. The popularity among sociologists of the alienated "highbrow" literature of sociology and political science testifies to the powerful appeal of this outlook. It is usually contained in works that are quite "unscientific" according to the prevailing canons; but the scientific and scientistic dispositions of the sociologists offer a resistance that is frequently overcome. When a work like *The Authoritarian Personality* meets both the "scientific requirements" and the requirements of the alienated, dissensually oriented ideology, it receives top marks.

allow it to stand as it is. Some of these imperfections are imperfections of form, of rhetoric. These are unpleasant but minor. Other, more important imperfections arise from the historical accidents of the intellectual and institutional traditions in which sociological theory has grown, and the vastness of its undertaking in contrast with the narrowness of the academic disciplines in which its practitioners have been formed. These imperfections seem relatively easily remediable. There are, finally, the imperfections inherent in any intellectual activity, capable of growth, when confronted with the reality it seeks to encompass. The advancement of sociological theory encounters the inherent difficulties of any task of intellectual discovery. Nothing can alleviate this difficulty.

It is most likely that, in the coming half-century, sociology will attract a larger number of highly gifted young persons who will be attracted by the quality of its subject matter and its challenge to their intellects. The enlarged scope and higher intellectual rigor will engage them more demandingly and will satisfy them and elicit greater exertions. This process might not go on indefinitely. Theology once attracted the best minds of every country that had a complex written culture. It has long since ceased to do so, because the best minds found other ways of reaching out toward contact with the vital, with the center of creativity. The epoch now emerging is more sociocentric and more concerned with the individual human being as a morally valuable entity. If it should become less intensely preoccupied with these values, sociology might become as idle and empty as much theological thought is to us today.

Until it does, we have before us the prospect of progress. In which directions should this progress be sought?

One of the simplest of the tasks before sociological theory—and not a very easy one—is the clarification of its conceptual vocabulary. This is not just a stylistic matter of reformulating ideas already in existence. The clarification of numerous ambiguous terms will involve, inevitably, a transformation in their meanings. Already intended, even if inadequately expressed, meanings will be elucidated; what are now only dimly apprehended in an apparently inextricable involvement will undoubtedly turn out to be several different things. In this process of elucidation, connections that are now not suspected or only crudely perceived will become more evident. Certain ostensible connections between analytically elementary concepts and more complex, more concrete concepts will evaporate. The result will be a more coherent, more unitary, and more differentiated image of society.

The dynamic properties of the variables will have to be made more explicit, so that the classificatory aspect will be less misleadingly prominent than it is at present. The emphasis, accordingly, will shift from concept to proposition, and the explanatory intention will become more overt. Correspondingly, the process of deductive theory-construction will move from more abstract to more particular proposition, rather than from more abstract to more particular concept—as is the case today.

As our present concepts become more explicit and as facility in their utilization becomes greater, they will become more adequately assimilated into our effective sociological outlook. They will be brought closer to its articulated surface, they will become more useful in research and in self-interpretation. They will, in other words, be more intimately and more spontaneously evocative of concreteness, while they remain abstract or become even more abstract than they are at present.

The easier relationship between the concrete and the abstract should contribute to the alleviation of another fault in contemporary sociology, namely, the tendency of our abstract theory to hypostatize the particular situation of our own modern Western society. When abstract concepts can become properly abstract and free of the concrete elements they now contain, we might be able to see more clearly how they overgeneralize the particularity of time and place.

This advance should coincide with another, of closely related intention. Recent years have witnessed a growing historical cultivation among sociologists and the extension of the geographical scope of sociological interests. These changes have in part come about from the increased attention to the writings of Max Weber, from the immanent necessities of the subject, and, in the newer generation of sociologists, from the extension of the moral horizon of the educated classes of the West. These changes and another immanent necessity of sociological analysis have brought whole societies increasingly into the purview of sociologists.

In the situation of sociological analysis for quite a long time, this has not been the case. The imposition on American sociology of a choice of concrete subjects not dealt with by the other social sciences, and the tendency in Britain as well as in America to deal with concrete, directly investigatable problems of practical interest, precluded for many years the emergence of the larger comparative macrosociology from within the academic discipline of sociology. The situation is now changing, partly from external pressure, partly because of the obvious limitations of the fragmentary particularities of empirical sociology as we have known it. Until this deficiency is remedied, propositions about subsystems within any particular society will be insufficiently particularized, because there is too little awareness of the systematic particularity of the society as a whole. At present, the propositions of sociological theory, in so far as they are concrete enough to have a particular referent, tend to be more particular in substance than their formulation acknowledges. The important macrodeterminants of human action that are constitutive of the particular society as a whole fail to be noticed or are misattributed to the properties of subsystems.[10] In consequence, there is a disposition to universalize what is, in fact, particular to one society and one epoch, and to support this unjustified universalization by the adduction of fragmentary observations of other societies and other epochs.

Such a development will not inevitably condemn sociology to historicism. Historicism is inevitable only for those who choose it in advance. It is not given in the nature of either social reality, historical experience, or sociological analysis. Macrosociology and the sociological theory of subsystems within the context of macrosociological theory are not compelled, by their acknowledgment of the uniqueness of societies, cultures, and epochs, to deny the applicability of a general theory. Indeed, only through the application of such a general theory and the categories and concepts it uses can uniqueness be perceived, understood, and analyzed. The very assertion of uniqueness presupposes general categories of comparison. The so-called "historical explanation" involves, willy-nilly, the adduction of canons of explanation and categories of description that are general in their reference. It is the task of macrosociology to develop these canons and categories for the characterization and explanation of those features that are constitutive of a social system as a society.

It is difficult to decide at present just how this construction of macrosociological theory is to be undertaken. It is quite unlikely to be done deductively from the existing body of concepts, since these concepts, apart from their limitations arising from ambiguity and particularity, have been largely formed with regard to patterns of individual action and action in social subsystems. It will, perhaps, have to move in the other direction, although not

exclusively or for always. The study of non-Western societies and of societies removed in time from the modern age—heretofore the preserve of historians, social anthropologists, Sinologists, Indologists, travelers, and the like—might well afford the best point of departure. Novelty and distance, both, will permit the perspective required to see, at least in first approximation, the most general constitution of a whole society and those properties that make it a single, whole society. As our familiarity grows through the enrichment of our universe of discourse—an enrichment that must surely follow from the heightened awareness produced by political events, literature, travel, and personal encounter—so will our sense of the wholeness of societies, of the variety of their types of wholeness, of the different relationships of center and periphery.

A second item on the agenda of sociological theory is the analysis of change. It is recurrently charged against the sociological theory of action, with its emphasis on systemic equilibrium, that it has no place for change. What is presumably meant is that it does not theoretically encompass enduring shifts of a whole society from one state to another state. There is truth in this charge.

The Marxian theory of change is in part a shorthand summary of the course of history from its origin to its culmination, coupled with an extremely inadequate explanation of the decline of each of the types of society intermediate between the beginning and the end of history. The "theory of change" that attributes causal primacy to technological innovation is even less satisfactory than the "theory" that explains everything by changes in the "relations of production." The latter at least sought to explain why one type of society gave way to another type, whereas the "technological theory" did not reach that far.

There are some reasonable explanatory hypotheses in sociology concerning why a given subsystem goes into a state of disequilibrium—for example, why a family or an army unit breaks up; and there are a few that attempt to explain why a given subsystem—for instance, a religious body—changes from one state of equilibrium to another, from a system of charismatic to one of bureaucratic authority. These are steps in the right direction; and, as the classificatory heritage falls away from our present theoretical orientation, its proper dynamic intention will come to the fore, and progress will be made in this type of analysis of change. There are also propositions of a very loose sort about the instigation of change in general. These have the same logical structure as the conventional "technological theory": that is, they

---

10. This is another, no less important, consequence of our failure to deal sufficiently with "whole societies," of our being too microsociological. Sociology has not seen with enough clarity that there are properties of societies as a whole that have repercussions on the subsystems. Thus, the subsystems cannot be realistically analyzed because their position with respect to the center of society is not taken enough into account.

explain, on an entirely *ad hoc* basis, by referring to particular technological innovations, why changes in X occur, but they do not explain why X changes into X¹ rather than anything else. One cannot predict a fruitful life, or wish a long one, for this kind of theoretical program.

What is most obviously lacking in the present situation of sociology is a theory as to why and how one type of society yields place to another, or why one type of society passes through one, rather than another, of alternative sets of sequences. This, however, has no chance of realization until the focus of the theory of action is widened to a macrosociological scope. The construction of a realistically differentiated typology of societies is thus once more thrust upon the agenda of sociological theory.

This cannot be done until the macrosociological problem itself is better treated. At present, there are overtures toward macrosociology in the study of power, of class structure, of values; but they are not put together. The co-ordination of a territorially extensive society, which is the proper subject of macrosociology, has entered into neither empirical sociology nor the theory of middle principles, and it is just now coming onto the horizon of the general theory. It gets no assistance from field research. It cannot proceed deductively, since the problem is too far from the foundations. The existing models of an integrated society and of the state of nature are too unrealistic and too remote from each other; reality lies scattered between them, and it is difficult to bring the criteria of classification into focus. For this reason, the macrosociological theory of change is impeded.

An associated reform is called for. Except when it commits itself to historicism in principle, and particular historical analysis in practice, contemporary sociology avoids the temporal. Its concepts have little time depth. Except for a few recent developments in the theory of action, there is an inclination to treat the complex of actions that go into the constitution of a subsystem as simultaneous; even where occasional and intermittent features of subsystems are allowed for, the tendency is to treat them as instantaneous. The temporal structure of an action or event has not yet been grasped. To bring the temporal structure of action more visibly into the field of our attention would, of course, contribute to the understanding of the mechanism of equilibrium—which is not thought to be a very important thing by the party that demands the production of a theory of change. In truth, however, this "natural history" of the components of an equilibrated system is likely to open the way to a better insight into the failure of re-

establishment of equilibrium and, thus, into the mechanism of change. This bringing forward of the temporal dimension—not concrete narrative history—would be no satisfaction of the need for a macrosociological classification of types of societies. Both are among the tasks that must be accepted for the construction of a theory of change.

A further necessity for the progress of sociological theory is an increased sophistication in the analysis of culture. Two decades of concern with "personality and culture" have passed with little consolidation of advantage. Now the danger is that what was once an object of passionate enthusiasm will fall into that oblivion into which disagreeable and scantily fruitful experiences are consigned, and that nothing will remain of either the interest or the task it posited. There was a real, if misformulated, problem at the bottom of that interest of the 'thirties and 'forties of the present century. One of the reasons for the failure to do justice to the task was the incapacity of sociologists to deal with the phenomenon of culture and to draw the line between it and the personality system. The need to analyze the phenomena of culture remains, quite apart from the problem of "culture and personality."

The internal coherence of symbol systems is only now beginning to be taken seriously by sociologists. Yet, until some progress is made in this matter, macrosociology and the study of change will be stunted. The inherent potentialities of symbolic systems, and the limits given by their substance, affect every sphere of social life. Sociology has thus far not assimilated—although strivings are already apparent—the conventional *geisteswissenschaftliche* analysis of the realm of symbolic forms, of the "objectivations" of culture. The dynamic properties of symbolic systems must be understood, not only for the study of the spheres of cultural creation, more narrowly conceived, such as the development of painting or music or theology, but for the wider reaches of culture, such as moral standards and religious belief.

It is hard for sociologists, with the long tradition of studying "real factors," to appreciate the autonomy of cultural systems and their capacities for autonomous development. In part, this might be a result of a too narrow education, of a lack of sympathy with the proper subject matter of academic rivals. It is also at least in part a function of the sheer difficulty of learning and formulating the problem and observing the phenomena to which it refers. The tradition of tough-mindedness, the humanitarian tradition, the oppositional tradition of sociological analysis, all stand in the way of the analysis of cultural systems. The rudimentary possibilities are already available in the theory of action; but, like the macrosociological typology, it is not likely to make great strides forward by strictly deductive procedures. Much more concentrated study of the various cultural systems is imperative.

The study of cultural systems runs off into several directions, all of them capable of illuminating the stability and change of societies. One of these directions is the study of tradition.

The present historical moment, in which the leaders of so many "traditional" societies desire to bring them into modernity, coincides with the immanent development of the theory of action. Both of these will press sociologists to consider afresh the meaning of "tradition," which is surprisingly one of the most neglected subjects in sociology. Its neglect has various causes—oppositional rationalism and progressivism, the swallowing up of the subject latterly in a psychoanalytically oriented conception of "socialization," and the subtle and far-flung character of the phenomenon itself. The intensity of adherence to traditional beliefs and standards, the degrees and varieties of consensus in a society, the motives and conditions of its reception, are all involved in the sociological analysis of cultural systems and in the macrosociological interest in the stability and transformation of societies.

Finally, the agenda of sociological theory must find a place for religion. I do not mean the study of ecclesiastical institutions, or of the influence of beliefs about God's intentions on daily conduct, of church attendance, or attitudes toward priests. These are all interesting subjects, and there are many more like them in the sociological study of religion. What I have in mind is a much more elusive and much more fundamental matter.

Sociologists are accustomed to and take for granted the distinction between sacred and secular. It is an inheritance from our Western religious and political traditions and, more specifically, of our sociological tradition. It has been accepted without question; but it is now time to re-examine it. The re-examination should not be regarded as an attempt to establish a theocracy or a state church, to argue on behalf of the truth of any theology, or even to argue that the piety of the masses is conducive to social order. These arguments vary from the obnoxious to ridiculous, and they have nothing whatsoever to do with the proposal that sociology concern itself with the ways in which man's need for being in contact with sacred or charismatic things manifests itself in politics, in the legal system, in education and learning, as well as in the churches. Both Durkheim and Max Weber had a wonderful sense of this phenomenon, but this aspect of their understanding of society has not been taken up. The time is now ripe.

The Future Validity of Sociological Theory

Sociological theory has begun, in the middle of the twentieth century, to transcend both the historicism of the preceding one hundred years and the hypostatization of an image of Western society into a prototype of all societies. It has also begun to breach the wall between "archaic" and "modern" man, between traditional societies and advanced societies. It has begun to see all hitherto known human societies within a comprehensive and diversified kinship chart, in which affinities and identities are no less appreciated than differences and disjunctions.

The intellectual growth of these years is not confined to sociology. Never more prominently has the smallness of man in the universe been put before our minds than in this part of our century. The exploration of outer space, by radioastronomy and by the launching of rockets and satellites, has deepened our consciousness of the infinite spaces and of extension of time. It has made us more aware than our earthbound existence and our Christian heritage have hitherto permitted us to be of the brief moment that our telluric history represents in the history of the universe and of the brief moment that our human history represents in the history of the earth. The development of genetics and the possibility of genetic variations arising from increasing radioactivity in the atmosphere cause us to reflect on the special situation of man in the universe and on the delicate poise on which his short career has thus far rested.

What is the impact of all this on sociological theory? Hitherto it has been negligible, and there is no reason to think that it can be much otherwise in the near future. It might, in the end, turn out that the sociological theory based on the theory of action is only one possibility, of limited scope, within a far more general theory of organisms or mechanisms of which we on earth still have only a very limited experience. In a sense, this is already very tentatively and incipiently apparent, in connection with the emergence of ethology. Such developments do not invalidate the great aspirations and small achievements of sociological theory; they merely locate and circumscribe their location more definitely in the cosmos.

The possible transformation of man in the future would not do more than render sociological theory historically specific to the stage of *homo sapiens* in telluric and cosmic history. In so far as man's moral powers, his physiological needs and capacities, remain approximately as they are, and as long as he possesses the moral, cognitive, and expressive orientations he has possessed throughout our human history, the achievements of sociological theory will retain their validity, in the way in which any scientific theory about a constant universe retains its validity. Technological developments, such as the extension of the life span, can, however great in the future, only add thus far unforeseen variants within the already established pattern.

Thus, although very fundamental changes in human powers might produce a situation that could be envisaged within the framework of a cosmic historicism, such changes would not enhance the claims of historicism as an alternative to sociological theory within the limits of man's existence as he has been known hitherto or is likely to be in the foreseeable future.

This acceptance of the limitations of the scope of sociological theory, and the simultaneous denial of the claims of historicism, do not imply that we regard the possibilities of man's development as unmodifiably confined within the boundaries already experienced. It is not inevitable that any future society must, as long as genetic endowment remains more or less as it has, be a reproduction of some previously existent society. Any classification of types of society, or of types of kinship structure, or the like, does not necessarily foreclose the possibility of the emergence of some previously unenvisaged type.

All that we would contend here is that such novel emergents will have to fit into the then existing general theory, or that the then existing general theory will have to be revised to comprehend those events for which there was no previous analytical provision.

Sociological theory is about the society, the culture, and the personality of *homo sapiens*. The society with which it deals is not a directly and immediately determined consequence of his genetic properties; but the range of its variety is circumscribed by these genetic properties. The theory that attempts to deal with these societies makes no direct derivations from genetic propensities, but its main categories must have the same trans-historical stability as the genetic properties themselves. The types of fundamental human powers remain the same through time. The fundamental alternatives remain the same—attachment to life and the fear of death, dependence on authority and hostility against authority, and, above all, the constrictions of scarcity, are permanent conditions of human existence. Their intensity can and does vary, em-

phases shift from one basic alternative to another; but until man no longer fears death or cares about life, until he loses his capacity for moral judgment and no longer feels the burden of guilt or the appreciation of virtue, until justice and injustice lose their meanings and authority becomes nonexistent, and above all until scarcity of time, strength, and love have disappeared from the lives of men and women—until then, the range of variation of societies will be limited.

This is the postulate of our effort to advance sociological theory. The limits of sociological theory can never be finally or conclusively known until the cessation of our species. It compels no self-restriction of our exertions to deepen our understanding. It requires no refusal to acknowledge things we have not known before. It does not contend that experience has come to an end or that its variety is exhausted. Nor does it contend that our knowledge of the nature of our existence is ever exhaustible. The endless possibility of a deeper knowledge is just as important a postulate of sociological theory as the postulate that asserts the stability of the fundamental determinants of human society.

The Progress of Sociological Theory and the Permanent Relevance of the Classics

Sociology is not a science in its achievement, but it has many of the features of science. In one most important respect it is scientific: it makes cumulative progress, revising and clarifying its foundations, extending its scope, unifying discrete observations into coherent patterns of observation. If one reads almost any significant sociological work of the past decade and contrasts it with works of preceding decades or centuries, one cannot deny the greater approximation to reality, the greater subtlety of interpretation of motives and causes, the greater richness of the categories. Sociology, with all its insufficiencies—technical and substantive—is definitely making progress.

What, then, is the present value of the classics of social and political analysis, and what is likely to be their value in the future, when progress will probably be more marked than it now is? The question must be answered in two stages. The first part of the answer is that progress is still insufficient, and the improvement of sociology in the past one hundred years has still not brought it up to the level of the great classics of political and social thought. The classics, according to this view, have not been sufficiently drawn upon by sociologists; and their unaided efforts, although acknowledged to be improving, are still below the level of great peaks of earlier thought. There is a little truth in this argument, but not enough to count. The main line of sociological thought runs in a direct line from the problems of the classics. The ideas of Max Weber and Durkheim elaborate and improve the deeper insights of the classics; and, although much of contemporary sociological analysis does not live up to the tradition they offer, the heights do not fall away from the standard they set.

This first part of our answer to the question would appear to put the classics into a somewhat more secondary position. If sociology makes the progress we predict it will make, the classics should be overtaken and then left behind, even by the more mediocre among sociologists. In physics, a great work of the past, like Newton's *Principia,* is no longer a scientific necessity to the young physicist. Its germinal quality has already fulfilled itself, in the continuing movement of science; its scientific creative power has been exhausted. Its surviving interest is historical and aesthetic. It is the precipitate of a great mind in contact with the constitution of the universe; its contemplation exhilarates. It has become a monument celebrating a great event in the history of the subject, but it no longer has anything to offer to the scientist that a first-class contemporary manual or treatise cannot offer in better form.

In literature or in art, a great work of the past allows no supersession. It might lose its hold over the taste of a period, but it cannot be transcended by a progress that assimilates what is valid in it and goes beyond it. Its aesthetic quality, its moral sensitivity, its understanding of profoundly important things, remain permanently valid acquisitions of the human race as long as men are capable of aesthetic judgment and as long as moral problems retain their validity.

A classic is not a monument. It is a continuous opportunity for contact with an enduring problem, with a permanently important aspect of existence, as disclosed through the greatness of a mind. It never becomes archaic, even if its stylistic idiom is out of fashion. It remains a classic as long as the problems with which it deals remain problematic, relevant, and insoluble in any definitive way. It becomes a monument of a great human achievement once the problem ceases to be relevant to contemporary concerns, or when its solution is permanently transcended by a better solution.

The great works that are the antecedents of modern sociology—Aristotle's *Politics* and *Ethics,* Thucydides on the Peloponnesian War, Polybius on Roman history, Machiavelli's *Il Principe* and *Discorsi,* Hobbes's *Leviathan,* Adam Smith's *Theory of the Moral Sentiments,* Hegel's *Philoso-*

phie des Rechts, Comte's *Philosophie positive—* retain their importance because they treat fundamental phenomena that are not better treated by contemporary sociology, because they analyze experiences that are basic in human existence, and because the centrality they accord to these experiences keeps them unfailingly before our attention. Robertson Smith's *Lectures on the Early Religion of the Semites,* Tocqueville's *Democratie en Amérique,* Harnack's *Dogmengeschichte,* and Sohm's *Kirchenrecht* are not works of the same order. They are works of analytical scholarship and reflective observation; they retain a freshness and pertinence to contemporary sociological analysis—despite the corrections and improvements that later scholars can bring to them—for the same reasons that the great classics of social and political philosophy retain their power. The classics of recent sociology—the writings of Max Weber, Durkheim, Toennies, Max Scheler, for example— will continue to be interesting and significant to sociologists because they have focused on categories of events that are at the root of our social existence.

In some measure, all these great sociologists retain their pertinence for us because we have not exceeded them. They had more insight and understanding of fundamental things than practically any living sociologist, and their ideas have not yet been widely absorbed. The recognition of the need for their study is an acknowledgment of our contemporary deficiencies—although they are not necessarily criticism of our present virtues, which are, in some respects, the virtues inseparable from contemporaneity and, in other respects, the merits of meticulousness and other smaller distinctions.

If contemporary sociologists had been better educated, and had studied and assimilated into their perspective and their observational capacities the truths of the classics, would these works then have had a status different from the classics of the natural sciences? We have a test in economic theory, which is one of the fields of the social sciences in which genuine progress has been achieved. Is David Ricardo's *Principles of Political Economy and Taxation* still as relevant to the economic theorist as certain works of the same order are to sociologists? The general opinion seems to be that it is not. The cause of this discrepancy lies in the assimilation of what was valid in this work, its differentiation and deepening, and the critical replacement of what was insufficient by what is more adequate to the understanding of the workings of an economic system. In certain branches of psychology, progress on another level of concreteness has been made: better techniques and more systematic inquiry have enabled psychologists to go on from the conclusions of earlier psychologists, refining and differentiating older propositions, locating and correcting them within a more complex system of analysis. But this is not true of sociology today. Sociologists today still have much to learn, in a substantive way, from the works of their ancestors, in a way that is unnecessary for scientists. Is this condition, however, simply a consequence of the ramshackle nature of contemporary sociological development? Is there not something inherent in sociological thought that will render the classics of the subject long-enduring sources of renewal in a way that Newton's *Principia* or Harvey's *De Motu Cardis et Sanguinis* are no longer? We are now ready for the second stage of the answer to the question we asked at the beginning of this section.

It is not just because sociological theory has not yet matured that the classics are still alive to us. Nor do they earn their vitality just from the personal grandeur of the achievements they constitute. There is, however, a personal element that is decisive. Sociological analysis, however much we succeed in systematizing, codifying, routinizing it—however close we bring it to the natural sciences in rigor of procedures, in the reliability of observation, and in refinement of demonstration—will always retain an important element of the personal. By this, we mean that the most elementary categories, the most fundamental variables, will have to be apprehended through an experience, through a kind of secular revelation. The "operational" definition of terms will be useful in the design of research; but what is defined will never be learned from handbooks, nor will it be learned ordinarily from the study of concrete investigations. The best of sociological theory will encompass these variables; but the theory itself will need the guidance of the "experience," or of the "vision," of authority, and the refusal of order, of scarcity, of loving attachment, and of hatred. Even the possible mathematization of sociological theory will not evade this necessity of recurrent refreshment of the experience of the fundamental variables of sociological theory. The fundamental terms of sociological theory are "primitive" terms. Their meanings are apprehended in "personal" experience and through the secondary experience of contact with the "vision," which expresses the deepest experiences of the greatest minds of the race.

This brings us back to the classics. The classics are revelations of fundamental experiences of human existence. They are not revelations of divine intention. They are revelations forced from life and the world by the exertions of uniquely powerful minds. Their greatness is a personal achievement; and contact with it discloses to others, with the force of direct personal experience, a vision of what is of enduring significance to those who would understand the nature of society.

This does not mean that the classics are sufficient and that sociological inquiry and theory are superfluous, that they have nothing to add. They have a tremendous lot to add, and they add it by empirical inquiry, by interviews and surveys and historical research, and by analytical reasoning. The progress of sociology and sociological theory consists in improving on the classics—in being more disciplined, more differentiated, and more intimate in the penetration into particular situations, in being more systematic in comprehending historical and territorial variations, in greater systematic rigor of formulation and greater reliability of particular propositions. The particular propositions of the classics are, in fact, usually far below the level of their grasp of vital issues; the range of their historical comprehension is too limited; the rigor of their systematic architectonic is too feeble. What commends them to us is their perception and preoccupation with certain elementary facts, like the fear of death, the need for attachment to a polity, the creativity of authority, the horror of and desire for disorder, the pressure of scarcity, the propensity to rank. These are some of the ultimate phenomena of social life, and our primitive experience of them must be constantly renewed for the effective guidance of research and theory.

This does not condemn sociology to a permanent imprisonment within the postulates of classical political and social analysis. These too are subject to revision. Their permanently enigmatic quality is a challenge and invitation to such revision. Their inexhaustibility does not arise from an inevitable ambiguity of formulation. Enhanced precision will not make them less demanding of recurrent attention or less fruitful of development. Their study will remain, for the foreseeable future, among the chief conditions of the progress of the subject that does so much to render them antiquated and, at the same time, to give evidence of their continuing indispensability.

BIBLIOGRAPHY

Bibliography

JOHN EMERICH EDWARD DALBERG ACTON, FIRST BARON ACTON (1834–1902)

BRITISH HISTORIAN

Lectures on Modern History, ed. J. N. Figgis and R. V. Laurence. London: Macmillan & Co., 1896.

Letters of Lord Acton to Mary Gladstone, ed. H. Paul. New York: Macmillan, 1904.

The History of Freedom and Other Essays, ed. J. N. Figgis and R. V. Laurence. London: Macmillan & Co., 1907.

Historical Essays and Studies, ed. J. N. Figgis and R. V. Laurence. London: Macmillan & Co., 1907.

Lectures on the French Revolution, ed. J. N. Figgis and R. V. Laurence. London: Macmillan & Co., 1910.

Essays on Freedom and Power, selected by G. Himmelfarb. Boston: Beacon Press, 1948.

Essays on Church and State, ed. D. Woodruff. London: Hollis & Carter, 1952.

CHESTER IRVING BARNARD (1886–1961)

AMERICAN BUSINESS AND FOUNDATION EXECUTIVE

Mind in Everyday Affairs; an Examination into Logical and Non-Logical Thought Processes. Princeton: The Guild of Brackett Lectures, 1936.

The Functions of the Executive. Cambridge, Mass.: Harvard University Press, 1938.

Dilemmas of Leadership in the Democratic Process. Princeton: University Extension Fund, 1939.

The Nature of Leadership. Cambridge, Mass.: Harvard University Press, 1940.

Organization and Management, Selected Papers. Cambridge, Mass.: Harvard University Press, 1948.

SIR CHARLES BELL (1774–1842)

SCOTTISH ANATOMIST

The Anatomy of the Brain. London: Longman, 1802.

The Anatomy and Physiology of the Human Body. 3 vols. London: Longman, 1802–1804. 7th ed., 1829.

Essays on the Anatomy of Expression in Painting. London: Longman, 1806.

A System of Operative Surgery. 2 vols. London: Longman, 1814.

An Essay on the Forces Which Circulate the Blood. London: Longman, 1819.

An Exposition of the Natural System of the Nerves of the Human Body. London: Spottiswood, 1824.

The Hand, Its Mechanism and Vital Endowments, as Evincing Design. London: Pickering, 1833.

Institutes of Surgery. Philadelphia: Waldie, 1840.

The Anatomy and Philosophy of Expression as Connected with Fine Arts. London: Murray, 1847. 7th rev. ed., 1890.

Letters. Selected by George J. Bell. London: Murray, 1870.

Expression: Its Anatomy and Philosophy. New York: Wells, 1873.

RUTH BENEDICT (1887–1948)

AMERICAN ANTHROPOLOGIST

The Concept of the Guardian Spirit in North America. Menasha, Wis.: The American Anthropological Association, 1923.

Tales of the Cochiti Indians. Washington: Government Printing Office, 1931.

Patterns of Culture. Boston and New York: Houghton Mifflin Co., 1934.

Zuni Mythology. New York: Columbia University
	Press, 1935.
Race: Science and Politics. New York: Modern
	Age Books, 1940.
*Race and Cultural Relations; America's Answer to
	the Myth of a Master Race*. Washington: Na-
	tional Council for the Social Studies, 1942.
*The Chrysanthemum and the Sword: Patterns of
	Japanese Culture*. Boston: Houghton Mifflin,
	1946.
In Henry's Backyard; the Races of Mankind (with
	Gene Weltfish). New York: Schuman, 1947.
	2nd rev. ed.: *The Races of Mankind*. New
	York: Public Affairs Committee, 1951.
*Thai Culture and Behavior: An Unpublished War-
	time Study dated September 1943*. Ithaca,
	N.Y.: Cornell University, Department of Far
	Eastern Studies, 1952.

MARC LÉOPOLD BENJAMIN BLOCH
(1886–1944)

FRENCH HISTORIAN

WORKS IN FRENCH

L'Isle-de-France (les pays autour de Paris). Paris:
	Cerf, 1913.
Rois et serfs; un chapitre d'histoire capétienne
	Paris: Champion, 1920.
Les rois thaumaturges. Strasbourg: Librairie Istra;
	London: Oxford University Press, 1924.
*Les caractères originaux de l'histoire rurale fran-
	çaise*. Oslo: Aschehoug; Cambridge, Mass.:
	Harvard University Press, 1931. New ed.,
	Paris: Colin, 1956.
La société féodale; la formation de dépendence.
	Paris: Michel, 1939.
*La société féodale; les classes et le gouvernement
	des hommes*. Paris: Michel, 1940.
Apologie pour l'histoire; ou, Métier d'historien.
	Paris: Colin, 1949.
Esquisse d'une histoire monétaire de l'Europe.
	Paris: Colin, 1954.
La France sous les derniers Capétiens, 1223–1328.
	Paris: Colin, 1958.

WORKS IN ENGLISH TRANSLATION

*Strange Defeat; a Statement of Evidence Written
	in 1940*. Translated by G. Hopkins. London:
	Oxford University Press, 1949.

The Historian's Craft. Translated by P. Putnam.
	New York: Knopf, 1953.

FRANZ BOAS (1858–1942)

AMERICAN ANTHROPOLOGIST

The Central Eskimo. Washington: U. S. Bureau of
	American Ethnology, 1888.
Chinook Texts. Washington: Government Printing
	Office, 1894.
*The Social Organization and the Secret Societies of
	the Kwakiutl Indians*. Washington: U. S. Na-
	tional Museum, 1897.
Kathlamet Texts. Washington: Government Print-
	ing Office, 1901.
The Measurement of Variable Quantities. New
	York: The Science Press, 1906.
Kwakiutl Texts (with George Hunt). 2 vols. Lei-
	den: Brill; New York: Stechert, 1906.
The Kwakiutl of Vancouver Island. Leiden: Brill;
	New York: Stechert, 1909.
Kwakiutl Tales. Leiden: Brill; New York: Colum-
	bia University Press, 1910.
The Mind of Primitive Man. New York: Macmil-
	lan, 1911.
Handbook of American Indian Languages. Wash-
	ington: Government Printing Office, 1911.
Tsimshian Mythology. Washington: Bureau of
	American Ethnology, 1916.
Kutenai Tales. Washington: Government Printing
	Office, 1918.
Ethnology of the Kwakiutl. Washington: U. S.
	Bureau of American Ethnology, 1921.
Contributions to the Ethnology of the Kwakiutl.
	New York: Columbia University Press, 1925.
Primitive Art. Oslo: Aschehoug; Cambridge,
	Mass.: Harvard University Press, 1927.
Materials for the Study of Inheritance in Man. New
	York: Columbia University Press, 1928.
Anthropology and Modern Life. New York: Nor-
	ton, 1928.
Bella Bella Tales. New York: Columbia University
	Press, 1928.
The Religion of the Kwakiutl Indians. 2 vols. New
	York: Columbia University Press, 1930.
*Aryan and Semite; with Particular Reference to
	Nazi Racial Dogmas*. Cincinnati: B'nai B'rith,
	1934.
Kwakiutl Culture as Reflected in Mythology. New
	York: Stechert, 1935.
Race, Language and Culture. New York: Macmil-
	lan, 1940.

KARL BÜCHER (1847–1930)

GERMAN ECONOMIC HISTORIAN

WORKS IN GERMAN

Die Aufstände der unfreien Arbeiter 143–128 v. Chr. Frankfurt am Main: Sauerländer, 1874.
Die Frauenfrage im Mittelalter. Tübingen: Laupp, 1882. 2nd ed.: 1910.
Die Arbeiterfrage im Kaufmannstande. Berlin: Habel, 1883.
Die Bevölkerung von Frankfurt am Main im XIV. und XV. Jahrhundert. Tübingen: Laupp, 1886.
Basels Staatseinnahmen und Steuervertheilung 1878–1887. Basel: Baur, 1888.
Die Wohnungsenquête in der Stadt Basel. Basel: Georg, 1891.
Die Entstehung der Volkswirtschaft. Tübingen: Laupp, 1893. 17th rev. ed. in 2 vols. 1926.
Arbeit und Rhythmus. Leipzig: Hirzel, 1896. 6th rev. ed.: Leipzig: Reinicke, 1924.
Die Wirtschaft der Naturvölker. Dresden: Zahn & Jaensch, 1898.
Der deutsche Buchhandel und die Wissenschaft. Leipzig: Teubner, 1903. 3rd rev. and enl. ed.: 1904.
Hochschulfragen. Leipzig: Wörner, 1912.
Unsere Sache und die Tagespresse. Tübingen: Mohr (Siebeck), 1915.
Die Sozialisierung. Tübingen: Laupp, 1919.
Beiträge zur Wirtschaftsgeschichte. Tübingen: Laupp, 1922.
Gesammelte Aufsätze zur Zeitungskunde. Tübingen: Laupp, 1926.

WORKS IN ENGLISH TRANSLATION

Industrial Evolution. Translated by S. Morley Wickett. New York: Holt, 1901.

KENNETH BURKE (1897–   )

AMERICAN CRITIC

Permanence and Change; An Anatomy of Purpose. New York: New Republic, 1935.
Attitudes Toward History. New York: The New Republic, 1937; 2nd ed. Los Altos, Cal.: Hermes, 1959.
The Philosophy of Literary Form; Studies in Symbolic Action. Baton Rouge, La.: Louisiana State University Press, 1941.
A Grammar of Motives. New York: Prentice-Hall, 1945.
A Rhetoric of Motives. New York: Prentice-Hall, 1950.
Counter-Statement. Chicago: University of Chicago Press, 1957.

ERNST CASSIRER (1874–1945)

GERMAN PHILOSOPHER

WORKS IN GERMAN

Descartes' Kritik der mathematischen und naturwissenschaftlichen Erkenntnis. Marburg: Preuss, 1899.
Leibniz' System in seinen wissenschaftlichen Grundlagen. Marburg: Elwert, 1902.
Das Erkenntnisproblem in der Philosophie und Wissenschaft der neueren Zeit. 2 vols. Berlin: Cassirer, 1906–1907. 2nd ed. in 3 vols. 1922–1923.
Substanzbegriff und Funktionsbegriff. Berlin: Cassirer, 1910.
Heinrich von Kleist und die Kantische Philosophie. Berlin: Reuther & Reichard, 1919.
Zur Einsteinschen Relativitätstheorie; erkenntnistheoretische Betrachtungen. Berlin: Cassirer, 1920.
Kants Leben und Lehre. Berlin: Cassirer, 1921.
Idee und Gestalt. Goethe/ Schiller/ Hölderlin/ Kleist. Berlin: Cassirer, 1921.
Die Begriffsform im mythischen Denken. Leipzig, Berlin: Teubner, 1922.
Freiheit und Form. Studien zur deutschen Geistesgeschichte. Berlin: Cassirer, 1922.
Philosophie der symbolischen Formen. 4 vols. Berlin: Cassirer, 1923–1931.
Sprache und Mythos. Leipzig, Berlin: Teubner, 1925.
Individuum und Kosmos in der Philosophie der Renaissance. Leipzig, Berlin: Teubner, 1927.
Die Platonische Renaissance in England und die Schule von Cambridge. Leipzig, Berlin: Teubner, 1932.
Die Philosophie der Aufklärung. Tübingen: Mohr, 1932.
Goethe und die geschichtliche Welt. Berlin: Cassirer, 1932.
Determinismus und Indeterminismus in der modernen Physik. Göteborg: Elander, 1937.
Descartes; Lehre — Persönlichkeit — Wirkung. Stockholm: Berman-Fischer, 1939.
Die Philosophie im XVII. und XVIII. Jahrhundert. Paris: Herman & Cie., 1939.

Axel Hägerström; eine Studie zur schwedischen Philosophie der Gegenwart. Göteborg: Elander, 1939.

Zur Logik der Kulturwissenschaften. Göteborg: Elander, 1942.

Vom Mythus des Staates. Zürich: Artemis, 1949.

WORKS IN ENGLISH

Substance and Function, and Einstein's Theory of Relativity. Translated by W. C. Swabey and M. C. Swabey. Chicago, London: The Open Court Publishing Co., 1923.

An Essay on Man, an Introduction to a Philosophy of Human Culture. New Haven: Yale University Press, 1944.

Rousseau, Kant, Goethe. Translated by J. Gutmann, P. O. Kristeller, and J. H. Randall, Jr. Princeton: Princeton University Press, 1945.

Language and Myth. Translated by S. K. Langer. New York: Harper, 1946.

The Myth of the State. New Haven: Yale University Press, 1946.

The Renaissance Philosophy of Man. Selections in Translation. Ed. Ernst Cassirer and others. Chicago: University of Chicago Press, 1948.

The Problem of Knowledge; Philosophy, Science, and History since Hegel. Translated by W. H. Woglom and C. W. Hendel. New Haven: Yale University Press, 1950.

The Philosophy of the Enlightenment. Translated by F. C. A. Koelln and J. P. Pettegrove. Boston: Beacon Press, 1951.

The Platonic Renaissance in England. Translated by J. P. Pettegrove. Austin: University of Texas Press, 1953.

The Philosophy of Symbolic Forms. 3 vols. Translated by R. Manheim. New Haven: Yale University Press, 1953–1957.

The Question of Jean-Jacques Rousseau. Translated and edited by P. Gay. New York: Columbia University Press, 1954.

Determinism and Indeterminism in Modern Physics. Translated by O. T. Benfey. New Haven: Yale University Press, 1956.

AUGUSTE COMTE (1798–1857)

FRENCH PHILOSOPHER AND SOCIOLOGIST

WORKS IN FRENCH

Cours de philosophie positive. 6 vols. Paris: Bachelier, 1830–1842.

Traité élémentaire de géometrie analytique à deux et à trois dimensions. Paris: 1843.

Traité philosophique d'astronomie populaire. Paris: Carilian-Goeury, 1844.

Discours sur l'esprit positif. Paris: Carilian-Goeury, 1844.

Discours préliminaire sur l'ensemble du positivisme. Paris: Mathias, 1848.

Système de politique positive; ou, Traité de sociologie instituant la religion de l'humanité. 4 vols. Paris: Mathias, 1851–1854.

Catéchisme positiviste; ou, Sommaire exposition de la religion universelle. Paris: Carilian-Goeury, 1852.

Calendrier positiviste; ou, Système général de commémoration publique. Paris: Mathias, 1852.

Appel aux conservateurs. Paris: Dalmont, 1855.

La synthèse subjective; ou, Système universel des conceptions propres à l'état normal de l'humanité. Paris: Chez l'auteur, 1856.

Lettres d'Auguste Comte à M. Valat, 1815–1844. Paris: Dunod, 1870.

Essais sur la philosophie des mathématiques. Paris: La Revue Occidentale, 1879.

Opuscules de philosophie sociale, 1819–1828. Paris: Leroux, 1883.

Lettres d'Auguste Comte à divers. 2 vols. Paris: Fonds typographiques de l'Exécution testementaire d'Auguste Comte, 1902–1905.

Correspondance inédite. 4 vols. Paris: Société Positiviste, 1903–1904.

Nouvelles lettres inédites. Paris: Costes, 1939.

WORKS IN ENGLISH TRANSLATION

The Philosophy of Mathematics. Translated by W. M. Gillespie. New York: Harper, 1851.

The Catechism of Positive Religion. Translated by R. Congreve. London: Chapman, 1858.

The General View of Positivism. Translated by J. H. Bridges. London: Trubner & Co., 1865.

The Positive Philosophy of Auguste Comte. Translated and condensed by H. Martineau. London: Chapman, 1868.

System of Positive Polity. 4 vols. Translated by J. H. Bridges. London: Longmans, Green & Co., 1875–1877.

Appeal to Conservatives. Translated by T. C. Donkin and R. Congreve. London: Trubner & Co., 1889.

Passages from the Letters of Auguste Comte. Selected and translated by J. K. Ingram. London: Black, 1901.

Early Essays on Social Philosophy. Translated by H. D. Hutton. London: Routledge, 1911.

CHARLES HORTON COOLEY (1864–1929)

AMERICAN SOCIOLOGIST

The Theory of Transportation. Baltimore: American Economic Association, 1894.
Genius, Fame and the Comparison of Races. Philadelphia: American Academy of Political and Social Sciences, 1897.
Personal Competition. New York: Macmillan, 1899.
Human Nature and the Social Order. New York: Scribner's, 1902. Rev. ed. 1922.
Social Organization; a Study of the Larger Mind. New York: Scribner's, 1909.
Social Process. New York: Scribner's, 1918.
Life and the Student. New York: Knopf, 1927.
Sociological Theory and Social Research. New York: Holt, 1930.
Introductory Sociology (with Robert C. Angell and Lowell J. Carr). New York: Scribner's, 1933.

CHARLES ROBERT DARWIN (1809–1882)

ENGLISH NATURALIST

The Zoology of the Voyage of H. M. S. Beagle. 5 vols. in 3. London: Smith, Elder & Co., 1839–1843.
The Structure and Distribution of Coral Reefs. New York: Appleton, 1842.
Journal of Researches into the Natural History and Geology of the Countries Visited during the Voyage of H. M. S. Beagle round the World. 2 vols. New York: Harper, 1846.
Geological Observations on South America. London: Smith, Elder & Co., 1846.
On the Origin of Species by Means of Natural Selection, or the Preservation of Favoured Races in the Struggle for Life. London: Murray, 1859. 6th ed., 1878.
Queries about Expression for Anthropological Inquiry. Washington, D.C.: Smithsonian Institution, 1868.
The Variation of Animals and Plants under Domestication. 2 vols. New York: Orange Judd, 1868.
The Descent of Man, and Selection in Relation to Sex. New York: Appleton, 1871. 2nd rev. ed., 1906.

Emotional Expressions of Man and the Lower Animals. London: Murray, 1872.
The Movements and Habits of Climbing Plants. London: Murray, 1875.
The Effects of Cross and Self Fertilization in the Vegetable Kingdom. London: Murray, 1876. 2nd ed., 1888.
The Different Forms of Flowers on Plants of the Same Species. New York: Appleton, 1877.
The Various Contrivances by Which Orchids Are Fertilized by Insects. New York: Appleton, 1877.
The Power of Movement in Plants. New York: Appleton, 1888.
The Formation of Vegetable Mould, through the Action of Worms. New York: Appleton, 1883.
Insectivorous Plants. London: Murray, 1884.
The Life and Letters of Charles Darwin, ed. Francis Darwin. 2 vols. London: Murray, 1887.
The Voyage of the Beagle. New York: Collier, 1907.
Autobiography, ed. Sir Francis Darwin. New York: Schuman, 1950.

WILLIAM JOHN DICKSON (1904–   )

AMERICAN MANAGEMENT EXPERT

Understanding and Training Employees (with others). New York: American Management Association, 1938.
Management and the Worker (with Fritz J. Roethlisberger). Cambridge, Mass.: Harvard University Press, 1939.

EMILE DURKHEIM (1858–1917)

FRENCH SOCIOLOGIST

WORKS IN FRENCH

De la division du travail social. Paris: Alcan, 1893. 2nd ed., 1902.
Les règles de la méthode sociologique. Paris: Alcan, 1895. 2nd rev. ed., 1901.
La suicide. Paris: Alcan, 1897.
Les formes élémentaires de la vie religieuse. Paris: Alcan, 1912.
Education et sociologie. Paris: Alcan, 1922.

Sociologie et philosophie. Paris: Alcan, 1924.

L'éducation morale. Paris: Alcan, 1925.

Le socialisme; sa définition, ses débuts, la doctrine saint-simonienne. Paris: Alcan, 1928.

L'évolution pédagogique en France. 2 vols. Paris: Alcan, 1938.

Leçons de sociologie: physique des moeurs et du droit. Paris: Presses universitaires de France, 1950.

Montesquieu et Rousseau, précurseurs de la sociologie. Paris: Riviere, 1953.

Pragmatisme et sociologie. Paris: Vrin, 1955.

WORKS IN ENGLISH TRANSLATION

The Elementary Forms of Religious Life. Translated by J. W. Swain. London: Allen & Unwin, 1915.

The Division of Labor in Society. Translated by G. Simpson. New York: Macmillan, 1933.

The Rules of Sociological Method. Translated by S. A. Solovay and J. H. Mueller, ed. G. E. G. Catlin. Chicago: University of Chicago Press, 1938.

Suicide. Translated by J. A. Spaulding and G. Simpson. Glencoe, Ill.: The Free Press, 1951.

Sociology and Philosophy. Translated by D. F. Pocock. Glencoe, Ill.: The Free Press, 1953.

Education and Sociology. Translated by S. D. Fox. Glencoe, Ill.: The Free Press, 1956.

Professional Ethics and Civic Morals. Translated by C. Brookfield. London: Routledge & K. Paul, 1957.

Socialism and Saint-Simon, ed. A. W. Gouldner. Translated by Charlotte Sattler. Yellow Springs, Ohio: Antioch Press, 1958.

Montesquieu and Rousseau: Forerunners of Sociology. Translated by Ralph Mannheim. Ann Arbor: University of Michigan Press, 1960.

SIR JAMES GEORGE FRAZER (1854–1941)

BRITISH ANTHROPOLOGIST

The Golden Bough: A Study in Comparative Religion. 2 vols. London: Macmillan, 1890. 3rd ed. in 12 vols., 1911–1915.

Pausanias and Other Greek Sketches. London: Macmillan, 1900.

Lectures on the Early History of Kingship. London: Macmillan, 1905.

Adonis, Attis, Osiris; Studies in the History of Oriental Religion. London: Macmillan, 1906.

Psyche's Task. London: Macmillan, 1909. 2nd rev. ed., 1913.

Totemism and Exogamy. 4 vols. London: Macmillan, 1910.

The Belief in Immortality and the Worship of the Dead. 3 vols. London: Macmillan, 1913–1924.

Folk-lore in the Old Testament. 3 vols. London: Macmillan, 1918.

The Worship of Nature. London: Macmillan, 1926.

Myths of the Origin of Fire. London: Macmillan, 1930.

The Growth of Plato's Ideal Theory. London: Macmillan, 1930.

Garnered Sheaves; Essays, Addresses, and Reviews. London: Macmillan, 1931.

The Fear of the Dead in Primitive Religion. 3 vols. London: Macmillan, 1933–1936.

Creation and Evolution in Primitive Cosmogonies. London: Macmillan, 1935.

Aftermath; a Supplement to the Golden Bough. London: Macmillan, 1936.

Greece and Rome, ed. S. G. Owen. London: Macmillan, 1937.

Anthologia Anthropologica. The Native Races of Africa and Madagascar. London: Lund, Humphries & Co., 1938.

SIGMUND FREUD (1856–1939)

FOUNDER OF PSYCHOANALYSIS

WORKS IN GERMAN

Gesammelte Schriften. 12 vols. Leipzig: Internationaler Psychoanalytischer Verlag, 1924–1934.

Gesammelte Werke. 18 vols. London: Imago, 1940–1952.

Zur Auffassung der Aphasien. Leipzig: Deuticke, 1891.

Die infantile Cerebrallähmung. Wien: Holder, 1897.

Die Traumdeutung. Leipzig, Wien: Deuticke, 1900. 4th ed., 1914.

Der Witz und seine Beziehung zum Unbewussten. Leipzig, Wien: Deuticke, 1905.

Drei Abhandlungen zur Sexualtheorie. Leipzig, Wien: Deuticke, 1905. 3rd ed., 1915.

Sammlung kleiner Schriften zur Neurosenlehre. 3 vols. Leipzig, Wien: Deuticke, 1906–1913.

Zur Psychopathologie des Alltagslebens. Berlin: Karger, 1907. 4th ed., 1912.

Über Psychoanalyse. Leipzig, Wien: Deuticke, 1912.

Totem und Tabu. Leipzig, Wien: Heller, 1913.
Vorlesungen zur Einführung in die Psychoanalyse. Leipzig, Wien: Heller, 1918.
Jenseits des Lustprinzips. Leipzig: Internationaler Psychoanalytischer Verlag, 1921.
Massenpsychologie und Ich-Analyse. Leipzig: Internationaler Psychoanalytischer Verlag, 1921.
Psychoanalytische Studien an Werken der Dichtung und Kunst. Leipzig: Internationaler Psychoanalytischer Verlag, 1924.
Die Frage der Laienanalyse. Leipzig: Internationaler Psychoanalytischer Verlag, 1926.
Hemmung, Symptom und Angst. Leipzig: Internationaler Psychoanalytischer Verlag, 1926.
Die Zukunft einer Illusion. Wien: Internationaler Psychoanalytischer Verlag, 1927.
Das Unbehagen in der Kultur. Wien: Internationaler Psychoanalytischer Verlag, 1930.
Neue Folge der Vorlesungen zur Einführung in die Psychoanalyse. Wien: Internationaler Psychoanalytischer Verlag, 1933.
Der Mann Moses und die monotheistische Religion. Amsterdam: Lange, 1939.

WORKS IN ENGLISH TRANSLATION

The Standard Edition of the Complete Psychological Works of Sigmund Freud, ed. James Strachey. 24 vols. London: Hogarth Press, 1953.
Collected Papers. 5 vols. Authorized translation under supervision of Joan Riviere. London: Hogarth Press and Institute of Psychoanalysis, 1948–1950.
Selected Papers on Hysteria and Other Psychoneuroses. Translated by A. A. Brill. New York: The Journal of Nervous and Mental Disease Pub. Co., 1909.
Three Contributions to the Sexual Theory. Translated by A. A. Brill. New York: The Journal of Nervous and Mental Disease Pub. Co., 1910.
The Interpretation of Dreams. Translated by A. A. Brill. London: Allen, 1913.
On Dreams. Translated by M. D. Eder. New York: Rebman, 1914.
Psychopathology of Everyday Life. Translated by A. A. Brill. New York: Macmillan, 1914.
Leonardo da Vinci; a Psychosexual Study of an Infantile Reminiscence. Translated by A. A. Brill. New York: Moffat, Yard & Co., 1916.
Wit and its Relation to the Unconscious. Translated by A. A. Brill. New York: Moffat, Yard & Co., 1916.
Delusion and Dream. Translated by H. M. Downey. New York: Moffat, Yard & Co., 1917.

The History of the Psychoanalytic Movement. Translated by A. A. Brill. New York: The Journal of the Nervous and Mental Disease Pub. Co., 1917.
Reflection on War and Death. Translated by A. A. Brill and A. B. Kuttner. New York: Moffat, Yard & Co., 1918.
Totem and Taboo. Translated by A. A. Brill. New York: Moffat, Yard & Co., 1918.
A General Introduction to Psychoanalysis. Translated by G. S. Hall. New York: Boni & Liveright, 1920.
Dream Psychology. Translated by M. D. Eder. New York: McCann, 1920.
Beyond the Pleasure Principle. Translated by C. J. M. Hubback. London, Vienna: The International Psychoanalytical Press, 1922.
Group Psychology and the Analysis of Ego. Translated by J. Strachey. London, Vienna: The International Psychoanalytical Press, 1922.
Introductory Lectures on Psychoanalysis. London: Allen & Unwin, 1922.
The Ego and the Id. Translated by J. Riviere. London: Hogarth Press and Institute of Psychoanalysis, 1927.
Future of an Illusion. Translated by W. D. Robson-Scott. London: Hogarth Press and Institute of Psychoanalysis, 1928.
Civilization and its Discontents. Translated by J. Riviere. New York: Cape & Smith, 1930.
New Introductory Lectures on Psychoanalysis. Translated by W. J. H. Sprott. London: Hogarth Press, 1933.
Autobiography. Translated by J. Strachey. New York: Norton, 1935.
Inhibition, Symptom and Anxiety. Translated by A. Strachey. London: Hogarth Press, 1936.
The Problem of Anxiety. Translated by H. A. Bunker. New York: The Psychoanalytic Quarterly Press and W. W. Norton, 1936.
Civilization, War and Death, ed. John Rickman. London: The Hogarth Press and the Institute of Psychoanalysis, 1939.
Moses and Monotheism. Translated by K. Jones. London: The Hogarth Press, 1939.
The Question of Lay Analysis. Translated by N. Procter-Gregg. London: Imago Publishing Co., 1947.
An Outline of Psychoanalysis. Translated by J. Strachey. New York: Norton, 1949.
On Aphasia. Translated by E. Stengel. New York: International Universities Press, 1953.
The Origins of Psychoanalysis, ed. M. Bonaparte, A. Freud and E. Kris. Translated by E. Mosbacher and J. Strachey. New York: Basic Books, 1954.

Letters, ed. Ernst L. Freud. Translated by Tania and James Stern. New York: Basic Books, 1960.

NUMA DENIS FUSTEL DE COULANGES
(1830–1889)

FRENCH HISTORIAN

WORKS IN FRENCH

Polybe, ou la Grèce conquise par les Romains. Amiens: Jennet, 1858.
La cité antique. Paris: 1864.
Recherches sur quelques problèmes d'histoire. Paris: Hachette, 1885.
Histoire des institutions politiques de l'ancienne France. 6 vols. Paris: Hachette, 1888–1892.
Nouvelles recherches sur quelques problèmes d'histoire. Paris: Hachette, 1891.
Questions historiques. Paris: Hachette, 1893.
Leçons à l'impératrice sur les origines de la civilisation française. Paris: Hachette, 1930.

WORKS IN ENGLISH TRANSLATION

Aryan Civilization. Translated by T. C. Barker. London: Parker, 1871.
The Ancient City. Translated by W. Small. Boston: Lee & Shepard. 1874.
The Origin of Property in Land. Translated by M. Ashley. London: Sonnenschein, 1892.

ARNOLD VAN GENNEP (1872–1957)

BELGIAN ANTHROPOLOGIST

WORKS IN FRENCH

Tabou et totémisme à Madagascar. Paris: Leroux, 1904.
Mythes et légendes d'Australie. Paris: Guilmoto, 1906.
Religions, mœurs et légendes. 5 vols. Paris: Mercure de France, 1908–1914.
Les rites de passage. Paris: Nourry, 1909.
La formation des légendes. Paris: Flammarion, 1910.
En Algérie. Paris: Mercure de France, 1914.
Le génie de l'organisation. Paris: Payot, 1915.
L'état actuel du probleme totémique. Paris: Leroux, 1920.

Traité comparatif des nationalités. Paris: Payot, 1922.
Le folklore; croyances et coutumes populaires françaises. Paris: Stock, 1924.
Le folklore du Dauphiné. 2 vols. Paris: Maisonneuve, 1932–1933.
Le folklore de la Bourgogne (Côte-d'Or). Gap: L. Jean, 1934.
Le folklore de la Flandre et du Hainaut français. 2 vols. Paris: Maisonneuve, 1935–1936.
Manuel de folklore française contemporain. 2 vols. Paris: Picard, 1937.
Le folklore de l'Auvergne et du Velay. Paris: Maisonneuve, 1942.
Le folklore des Hautes-Alpes. 2 vols. Paris: Maisonneuve, 1946.

WORK IN ENGLISH TRANSLATION

The Rites of Passage. Translated by M. B. Vizedom and G. L. Caffee. Chicago: The University of Chicago Press, 1960.

OTTO FRIEDRICH VON GIERKE
(1841–1921)

GERMAN LEGAL HISTORIAN

WORKS IN GERMAN

Das deutsche Genossenschaftsrecht. 4 vols. Berlin: Weidmann, 1868–1913.
Johannes Althusius und die Entwicklung der naturrechtlichen Staatstheorien. Breslau: Marcus, 1880. 2nd ed., 1902.
Die Genossenschaftstheorie und die deutsche Rechtsprechung. Berlin: Weidmann, 1887.
Der Entwurf eines bürgerlichen Gesetzbuchs und das deutsche Recht. Leipzig: Duncker und Humblot, 1889.
Deutsches Privatrecht. 2 vols. Leipzig: Duncker & Humblot, 1895–1905.
Das Wesen der menschlichen Verbände. Berlin: Francke, 1902.
Schuld und Haftung im älteren deutschen Recht. Breslau: Marcus, 1910.
Die Grundbegriffe des Staatsrechts und die neuesten Staatstheorien. Tübingen: Mohr (Siebeck), 1915.

WORKS IN ENGLISH TRANSLATION

Political Theories of the Middle Ages. Translated by F. W. Maitland. Cambridge: Cambridge University Press, 1900.

Natural Law and the Theory of Society, 1500–1800. Translated by E. Barker. Cambridge: Cambridge University Press, 1934.

The Development of Political Theory. Translated by B. Freyed. London: Allen & Unwin, 1939.

EDMOND GOBLOT (1858–1935)

FRENCH PHILOSOPHER

Essai sur la classification des sciences. Paris: Alcan, 1898.

Le vocabulaire philosophique. Paris: Colin, 1901.

Justice et liberté. Paris: Alcan, 1902.

Traité de logique. Paris: Colin, 1918.

Le système des sciences. Paris: Colin, 1922.

La barrière et le niveau; étude sociologique sur la bourgeoisie française moderne. Paris: Alcan, 1925.

La logique des jugements de valeur. Paris: Colin, 1927.

MARCEL GRANET (1884–1940)

FRENCH SINOLOGIST

WORKS IN FRENCH

Fêtes et chansons anciennes de la Chine. Paris: Leroux, 1919.

La polygynie sororale et le sororat dans la Chine féodale. Paris: Leroux, 1920.

La religion des Chinois. Paris: Gauthier-Villars, 1922.

Danses et légendes de la Chine ancienne. Paris: Alcan, 1926.

La civilisation chinoise. Paris: La Renaissance du Livre, 1929.

La pensée chinoise. Paris: La Renaissance du Livre, 1934.

Catégorie matrimoniales et relations de proximité dans la Chine ancienne. Paris: Alcan, 1939.

La féodalité chinoise. Oslo: Aschehoug; Cambridge, Mass.: Harvard University Press, 1952.

Etudes sociologiques sur la Chine. Paris: Presses universitaires de France, 1953.

WORKS IN ENGLISH TRANSLATION

Chinese Civilization. Translated by K. E. Innes and M. R. Brailsford. London: K. Paul, Trench, Trubner; New York: Knopf, 1930.

Festivals and Songs of Ancient China. London: Routledge; New York: Dutton, 1932.

ADOLF VON HARNACK (1851–1930)

GERMAN CHURCH HISTORIAN

WORKS IN GERMAN

Das Mönchtum. Giessen: Ricker, 1881. 6th ed., 1903.

Die Überlieferung der griechischen Apologeten des 2. Jahrhunderts. Leipzig: Hinrichs, 1882.

Die Lehre der zwölf Apostel. Leipzig: Hinrichs, 1884.

Die Apostellehre und die jüdischen beiden Wege. Leipzig: Hinrichs, 1886.

Lehrbuch der Dogmengeschichte. 3 vols. Freiburg: Mohr, 1886–1890. 4th rev. ed., 1909–1910.

Grundriss der Dogmengeschichte. 2 vols. Freiburg: Mohr (Siebeck), 1889–1891.

Das apostolische Glaubensbekenntnis. Berlin: Haack, 1892.

Geschichte der altchristlichen Literatur bis Eusebius. 2 vols. Leipzig: Hinrichs, 1893–1904.

Dogmengeschichte. Freiburg: Mohr, 1898. 5th rev. ed., 1914.

Geschichte der königlich preussischen Akademie der Wissenschaften. 3 vols. Berlin: Reichsdruckerei, 1900.

Das Wesen des Christentums. Leipzig: Hinrichs, 1900.

Diodor von Tarsus. Leipzig: Hinrichs, 1901.

Die Mission und Ausbreitung des Christentums in den ersten drei Jahrhunderten. Leipzig: Hinrichs, 1902. 4th rev. ed. in 2 vols., 1924.

Reden und Aufsätze. 2 vols. Giessen: Ricker, 1904. New ed. in 5 vols., 1911–1930.

Lukas der Arzt, der Verfasser des dritten Evangeliums und der Apostelgeschichte. Leipzig: Hinrichs, 1906.

Beiträge zur Einleitung in das neue Testament. 7 vols. Leipzig: Hinrichs, 1906–1916.

Sprüche und Reden Jesu. Leipzig: Hinrichs, 1907.

Die Apostelgeschichte. Leipzig: Hinrichs, 1908.

Entstehung und Entwicklung der Kirchenverfassung und des Kirchenrechts in den zwei ersten Jahrhunderten. Leipzig: Hinrichs, 1910.

Aus Wissenschaft und Leben. Giessen: Töpelmann, 1911.

Die Entstehung des Neuen Testaments und die wichtigsten Folgen der neueren Schöpfung. Leipzig: Hinrichs, 1914.

Aus der Friedens- und Kriegsarbeit. Giessen: Töpelmann, 1916.

Der kirchengeschichtliche Ertrag der exegetischen Arbeiten des Origenes. Leipzig: Hinrichs, 1918.

Marcion: das Evangelium vom fremden Gott. Leipzig: Hinrichs, 1921.

Erforschtes und Erlebtes. Giessen: Töpelmann, 1923.

Einfuhrung in die alte Kirchengeschichte. Leipzig: Hinrichs, 1929.

Studien zur Geschichte des Neuen Testaments und der alten Kirche. Berlin: Gruyter, 1931.

WORKS IN ENGLISH TRANSLATION

Outlines of the History of Dogma. Translated by F. K. Mitchell. New York: Funk & Wagnalls, 1893.

History of Dogma. 7 vols. Translated by N. Buchanan. London: Williams & Norgate, 1894–1899.

Monasticism: its Ideals and its History. Translated by C. R. Gillett. New York: Christian Literature Co., 1895.

Christianity and History. Translated by T. B. Saunders. London: Black, 1896.

Thoughts on the Present Position of Protestantism. Translated by T. B. Saunders. London: Black, 1899.

The Apostles' Creed. Translated by S. Means and T. B. Saunders. London: Black, 1901.

What Is Christianity? Translated by T. B. Saunders. London: Williams & Norgate, 1901.

Essays on the Social Gospel. Translated by G. M. Craik, ed. M. A. Canney. London: Williams & Norgate, 1907.

Luke the Physician. Translated by J. R. Wilkinson. London: Williams & Norgate, 1907.

The Mission and Expansion of Christianity in the First Three Centuries. 2 vols. Translated by J. Moffatt. London: Williams & Norgate, 1908.

The Sayings of Jesus, the Second Source of St. Matthew and St. Luke. Translated by J. R. Wilkinson. London: Williams & Norgate, 1908.

The Acts of Apostles. Translated by J. R. Wilkinson. London: Williams & Norgate, 1909.

The Constitution and Law of the Church in the First Two Centuries. Translated by F. L. Pogson, ed. H. D. A. Major. London: Williams & Norgate, 1910.

Bible Reading in the Early Church. Translated by J. R. Wilkinson. London: Williams & Norgate, 1912.

The Origin of the New Testament. Translated by J. R. Wilkinson. London: Williams & Norgate, 1925.

GEORG WILHELM FRIEDRICH HEGEL (1770–1831)

GERMAN PHILOSOPHER

WORKS IN GERMAN

Werke. Complete edition. 18 vols. Berlin: Duncker & Humblot, 1832–1845.

Differenz des Fichteschen und Schellingschen Systems der Philosophie. Jena: Seidler, 1801.

Phänomenologie des Geistes. Bamberg: Goebhardt, 1807.

Wissenschaft der Logik. 2 vols. Nürnberg: Schrag, 1812–1816.

Grundlinien der Philosophie des Rechts. Berlin: Nicolai, 1821.

Encyclopädie der philosophischen Wissenschaften im Grundrisse. Heidelberg: Osswald, 1827.

Vorlesungen ueber die Geschichte der Philosophie. ed. K. L. Michelet. Berlin: Duncker & Humblot, 1833.

Vorlesungen über die Philosophie der Geschichte, ed. E. Gans. Berlin: Duncker & Humblot, 1837.

Vorlesungen über die Philosophie der Religion, ed. P. Marheineke. 2 vols. Berlin: Duncker & Humblot, 1840.

Vorlesungen über die Aesthetik. 3 vols. Berlin: Duncker & Humblot, 1842–1843.

Philosophische Abhandlungen, ed. C. L. Michelet. Berlin: Duncker & Humblot, 1845.

Kritik der Verfassung Deutschlands, ed. G. Mollat. Kassel: Fischer, 1893.

System der Sittlichkeit, ed. G. Mollat. Osterwieck: Zickfeldt, 1893.

Hegels theologische Jugendschriften, ed. H. Nohl. Tübingen: Mohr, 1907.

WORKS IN ENGLISH TRANSLATION

Philosophy of History. Translated by J. Sibree. New York: Collier, 1861.

The Philosophy of Art. Translated by W. M. Bryant. New York: Appleton, 1879.

The Introduction to Hegel's Philosophy of Fine Art. Translated by B. Bosanquet. London: K. Paul, Trench & Co., 1886.

The Logic of Hegel. Translated by W. Wallace. Oxford: Clarendon Press, 1892.

Lectures on the History of Philosophy. 3 vols. Translated by E. S. Haldane and F. H. Simson. London: K. Paul, Trench, 1892–1896.

Philosophy of Mind. Translated by W. Wallace. Oxford: Clarendon Press, 1894.

Lectures on the Philosophy of Religion. 3 vols. Translated by E. B. Speirs and J. B. Sanderson. London: K. Paul, 1895.

Philosophy of Right. Translated by S. W. Dyde. London: Bell, 1896.

The Philosophy of Fine Art. 4 vols. Translated by F. P. B. Osmaston. London: Bell, 1920.

Hegel's Logic of World and Idea. Translated by H. S. Macran. Oxford: Clarendon Press, 1929.

Hegel's Science of Logic. Translated by W. H. Johnston. London: Allen & Unwin, 1929.

The Phenomenology of Mind. Translated by J. B. Baillie. London: Allen & Unwin, 1931. 2nd ed., 1949.

Early Theological Writings. Translated by T. M. Knox. Chicago: University of Chicago Press, 1948.

Reason in History. Translated by R. S. Hartman. New York: Liberal Arts Press, 1953.

THOMAS HOBBES (1588–1679)

BRITISH PHILOSOPHER

The English Works, ed. Sir William Molesworth. 11 vols. London: Bohn, 1839–1845.

Elementa philosophica de cive. Amsterdam: Elzevir, 1647.

De corpore politico. Or, The Elements of Law, Moral and Politick. London: Martin & Ridley, 1650.

Human Nature: or, The Fundamental Elements of Policie. London: Bowman, 1650.

Leviathan, or, The Matter, Form, and Power of a Common-wealth Ecclesiastical and Civil. London: Crooke, 1651.

Philosophicall Rudiments Concerning Government and Society. London: Royston, 1651.

Elements of Philosophy, the First Section, Concerning Body. London: Crooke, 1656.

Elementorum philosophiae sectio secunda de homine. London: Crooke, 1658.

Decameron physiologicum: or, Ten Dialogues of Natural Philosophy. London: Crooke, 1678.

Behemoth; or, An Epitome of the Civil Wars of England from 1640 to 1660. London: 1679.

The Art of Rhetoric. London: Crooke, 1681.

HENRI HUBERT (1872–1927)

FRENCH ANTHROPOLOGIST

WORKS IN FRENCH

Mélanges d'histoire des religions (with Marcel Mauss). Paris: Alcan, 1909.

Les Celtes et l'expansion celtique jusqu'à l'époque de la Tène. Paris: Renaissance du Livre, 1932.

Les Celtes depuis l'époque de la Tène et la civilisation cultique. Paris: Renaissance du Livre, 1932.

Les Germains. Paris: Michel, 1952.

WORKS IN ENGLISH TRANSLATION

The Rise of the Celts. Translated by M. R. Dobie. London: K. Paul, 1934.

The Greatness and Decline of the Celts. Translated by M. R. Dobie. London: K. Paul, 1934.

CLARK L. HULL (1884–1952)

AMERICAN PSYCHOLOGIST

Aptitude Testing. Yonkers-on-Hudson, New York and Chicago: World Book, 1928.

Hypnosis and Suggestibility, An Experimental Approach. New York: Appleton-Century, 1933.

Hull's Psychological Seminars, 1936–1938; notices and abstracts of proceedings, by Clark L. Hull and O. H. Mowrer. New Haven: Yale University Press, 1938.

Mathematico-Deductive Theory of Rote Learning. New Haven: Yale University Press, 1940.

Principles of Behavior: An Introduction to Behavior Theory. New York and London: Appleton-Century, 1943.

Essentials of Behavior. New Haven: Yale University Press, 1951.

A Behavior System. New Haven: Yale University Press, 1952.

DAVID HUME (1711–1776)

SCOTTISH PHILOSOPHER

A Treatise of Human Nature. 2 vols. London: Noon, 1739.

Essays, Literary, Moral, and Political. London: Millar, 1748.

Philosophical Essays Concerning Human Under-
standing. London: Millar, 1748.
An Enquiry Concerning the Principles of Morals.
London: Millar, 1751.
Insecurity of the British Funds; Essay on Public
Credit. London: Keyes, 1752.
Political Discourses. Edinburgh: Kincaid & Don-
aldson, 1752.
The History of England from the Invasion of Julius
Caesar to the Revolution in 1688. 6 vols. Lon-
don: Millar, 1754–1762. New ed. in 8 vols.,
1763.
Four Dissertations. I. The Natural History of Reli-
gion. II. Of the Passions. III. Of Tragedy. IV.
Of the Standard of Taste. London: Millar,
1757.
Dialogues concerning Natural Religion. London:
1779.
The Letters of David Hume, ed. J. Y. T. Greig.
Oxford: Clarendon Press, 1932.

JOHN MAYNARD KEYNES (1883–1946)

BRITISH ECONOMIST

Indian Currency and Finance. London: Macmillan,
1913.
The Economic Consequences of the Peace. Lon-
don: Macmillan, 1919.
A Treatise on Probability. London: Macmillan,
1921.
A Revision of the Treaty. London: Macmillan,
1922.
A Tract on Monetary Reform. London: Macmillan,
1923.
The End of Laissez-faire. London: Woolf, 1926.
Laissez-faire and Communism. New York: New
Republic, 1926.
A Treatise on Money. 2 vols. London: Macmillan,
1930.
Essays in Persuasion. London: Macmillan, 1931.
The Essays in Biography. London: Macmillan,
1933.
The General Theory of Employment, Interest and
Money. London: Macmillan, 1936.
Two Memoirs. London: Rupert Hart-Davis, 1949.

FRANK HYNEMAN KNIGHT (1885–   )

AMERICAN ECONOMIST

Risk, Uncertainty and Profit. Boston, New York:
Houghton Mifflin, 1921.

The Economic Organization. Chicago: University
of Chicago Press, 1933.
The Ethics of Competition. New York: Harper,
1935.
The Economic Order and Religion (with T. W.
Merriam). New York: Harper, 1945.
Freedom and Reform. New York: Harper, 1947.
On the History and Method of Economics. Chi-
cago: University of Chicago Press, 1956.
Intelligence and Democratic Action. Cambridge,
Mass: Harvard University Press, 1960.

WOLFGANG KÖHLER (1887–

GERMAN-AMERICAN PSYCHOLOGIST

WORKS IN GERMAN

Intelligenzprüfungen an Menschenaffen. Berlin:
Springer, 1921.
Die physischen Gestalten in Ruhe und im Station-
ären Zustand. Erlangen: Philosophische Aka-
demie, 1924.
Psychologische Probleme. Berlin: Springer, 1933.

WORKS IN ENGLISH

The Mentality of Apes. Translated by E. Winter.
New York: Harcourt, 1926.
Gestalt Psychology. New York: Liveright, 1929.
The Place of Value in a World of Facts. New York:
Liveright, 1938.
Dynamics in Psychology. New York: Liveright,
1940.

ALFRED LOUIS KROEBER (1876–1960)

AMERICAN ANTHROPOLOGIST

The Arapaho. New York: Knickerbocker Press,
1902.
Zuñi Kin and Clan. New York: The Trustees, 1917.
People of the Philippines. New York: American
Museum Press, 1919.
Source Book in Anthropology (with T. T. Water-
man). Berkeley: University of California
Press, 1920. Rev. ed., 1931.
Anthropology. New York: Harcourt, 1923. Rev.
ed., 1948.
Handbook of the Indians of California. Washing-
ton: Government Printing Office, 1925.

Cultural and Natural Areas of Native North America. Berkeley: University of California Press, 1939.

Configurations of Culture Growth. Berkeley: University of California Press, 1944.

World Renewal, a Cult System of Native Northwest California (with E. W. Gifford). Berkeley: University of California Press, 1949.

Culture; a Critical Review of Concepts and Definitions (with Clyde Kluckhohn). Cambridge, Mass.: The Museum, 1952.

The Nature of Culture. Chicago: University of Chicago Press, 1952.

Proto-Lima; a Middle Period Culture of Peru. Chicago: Chicago Natural History Museum, 1954.

Style and Civilizations. Ithaca, N.Y.: Cornell University Press, 1957.

SUZANNE KATHERINA (KNAUTH) LANGER (1895–   )

AMERICAN PHILOSOPHER

The Practice of Philosophy. New York: Holt, 1930.

An Introduction to Symbolic Logic. London: Allen & Unwin, 1937; 2d ed. (rev.) New York: Dover Publications, 1953.

Philosophy in a New Key; a Study in the Symbolism of Reason, Rite, and Art. Cambridge, Mass.: Harvard University Press, 1942. 3rd ed., 1957.

Feeling and Form: A Theory of Art. New York: Scribner, 1953.

The Problems of Art: Ten Philosophical Lectures. New York: Scribner, 1957.

Reflections on Art. Baltimore: Johns Hopkins Press, 1958.

NICOLAI (VLADIMIR IL'JICH) LENIN (1870–1924)

RUSSIAN SOCIAL PHILOSOPHER

Works (in Russian). 35 vols. Moscow, Leningrad: Gosudarstvennoe izdatel'stvo, 1926–1932. 4th ed., 1951–

Werke (in German). 35 vols. Berlin: Dietz Verlag, 1954–

WORKS TRANSLATED INTO ENGLISH

Selected Works. 12 vols. New York: International Publishers, n.d.

The Collapse of the Second International. Translated by A. Sirnis. Glasgow: The Socialist Labour Press, 1915.

The State and Revolution. London: Allen & Unwin, 1919.

"Left Wing" Communism, an Infantile Disorder. London: The Communist Party of Great Britain, 1920.

The Proletarian Revolution and Kautsky the Renegade. New York: International Publishers, 1920.

Imperialism, the Latest Stage in the Development of Capitalism. Translated by J. T. Kozlowski. Detroit: The Marxian Educational Society, 1924.

Materialism and Empirio-Criticism. Translated by D. Kvitko. London: Lawrence & Wishart, 1927.

The Revolution of 1917. Translated by J. Kunitz and M. J. Olgin. New York: 1929.

What Is to Be Done? New York: International Publishers, 1929.

The Revolution of 1905. New York: International Publishers, 1931.

Imperialism and Imperialist War. New York: International Publishers, 1935.

Marx, Engels, Marxism. New York: International Publishers, 1935.

Two Tactics of Social Democracy in the Democratic Revolution. New York: International Publishers, 1935.

From the Bourgeois Revolution to the Proletarian Revolution. New York: International Publishers, 1936.

Theory of the Agrarian Question. New York: International Publishers, 1938.

One Step Forward, Two Steps Back. London: Lawrence & Wishart, 1941.

The Development of Capitalism in Russia. Moscow: Foreign Languages Publishing House, 1956.

Against Revisionism. Moscow: Foreign Languages Publishing House, 1959.

PIERRE GUILLAUME FRÉDÉRIC LE PLAY (1806–1882)

FRENCH SOCIOLOGIST

WORKS IN FRENCH

Les ouvriers européens. Paris: Imprimerie impériale, 1855. 2nd ed. in 6 vols., Tours: Mame, 1877–1879.

La réforme sociale en France. 3 vols. Paris: Dentu, 1864–1867.

L'organisation du travail. Tours: Mame, 1870.

L'organisation de la famille. Paris: Téqui, 1871. 4th ed., Tours: Mame, 1895.

Le paix sociale. Tours: Mame, 1876.

La réforme en Europe et le salut en France. Tours: Mame, 1876.

La constitution essentielle de l'humanité. Tours: Mame, 1881.

WORKS IN ENGLISH TRANSLATION

The Organization of Labor. Translated by G. Emerson. Philadelphia: Claxton, 1872.

Family and Society by Carle Clark Zimmerman contains Le Play's "European Studies." It is an abridged adaptation of Volume 1 of "Les ouvriers européens" translated by S. Dupertuis. New York: Van Nostrand, 1935.

KURT LEWIN (1890–1947)

GERMAN-AMERICAN PSYCHOLOGIST

WORKS IN GERMAN

Der Begriff der Genese in Physik, Biologie und Entwicklungsgeschichte. Berlin: Springer, 1922.

Vorsatz, Wille und Bedürfnis. Berlin: Springer, 1926.

Die Entwicklung der experimentellen Willenspsychologie und die Psychotherapie. Leipzig: Hirzel, 1929.

Die psychologische Situation bei Lohn und Strafe. Leipzig: Hirzel, 1931.

WORKS IN ENGLISH

A Dynamic Theory of Personality. Translated by D. K. Adams and K. E. Zeuner. New York: McGraw-Hill, 1935.

Principles of Topological Psychology. Translated by F. Heider and G. M. Heider. New York: McGraw-Hill, 1936.

The Conceptual Representation and Measurement of Psychological Forces. Durham, N.C.: Duke University Press, 1938.

Resolving Social Conflicts, ed. G. V. Lewin. New York: Harper, 1948.

Field Theory in Social Science, ed. D. Cartwright. New York: Harper, 1951.

Studies in Topological and Vector Psychology. Iowa City: Iowa University Press, 1940.

RALPH LINTON (1893–1953)

AMERICAN ANTHROPOLOGIST

The Material Culture of the Marquesas Islands. Honolulu: Bishop Museum, 1923.

Archeology of the Marquesas Islands. Honolulu: The Museum, 1925.

The Tanala, a Hill Tribe of Madagascar. Chicago: Field Museum of Natural History, 1933.

The Study of Man. New York: Appleton, 1936.

Acculturation in Seven American Indian Tribes (ed.). New York: Appleton, 1940.

The Cultural Background of Personality. New York: Appleton, 1945.

The Tree of Culture. New York: Knopf, 1955.

Culture and Mental Disorders, ed. G. Devereux. Springfield, Ill.: Thomas, 1956.

JOHN LOCKE (1632–1704)

BRITISH PHILOSOPHER

An Essay Concerning Human Understanding. London: Basset, 1690. 5th ed., 1706.

Two Treatises of Government. London: Churchill, 1690.

Some Thoughts Concerning Education. London: Churchill, 1693. 4th ed., 1699.

The Reasonableness of Christianity as delivered in the Scriptures. London: Awnsham, 1695.

Several Papers Relating to Money, Interest and Trade. London: Churchill, 1696.

A Common-place Book to the Holy Bible. London: Churchill, 1697.

A Second Vindication of the Reasonableness of Christianity. London: Churchill, 1697.

Posthumous Works. London: Churchill, 1706.

Elements of Natural Philosophy. Berwick upon Tweed: Taylor, 1754.

Letters Concerning Toleration. London: Millar, 1765.

The Conduct of the Understanding. Cambridge: Nicholson, 1781.

On Civil Government and Toleration. London: Cassel, 1895.

Essays on the Law of Nature. Oxford: Clarendon Press, 1954.

ROBERT HARRY LOWIE (1883–1957)

AMERICAN ANTHROPOLOGIST

The Assiniboine. New York: The Trustees, 1909.
Social Life of the Crow Indians. New York: The Trustees, 1912.
Societies of the Crow, Hidatsa and Mandan Indians. New York: The Trustees, 1913.
Culture and Ethnology. New York: McMurtrie, 1917.
Myths and Tradition of the Crow Indians. New York: The Trustees, 1918.
Primitive Society. New York: Boni & Liveright, 1920.
The Religion of the Crow Indians. New York: The Trustees, 1922.
Primitive Religion. New York: Boni & Liveright, 1924.
The Origin of the State. New York: Harcourt, 1927.
Are We Civilized? New York: Harcourt, 1929.
An Introduction to Cultural Anthropology. New York: Farrar & Rinehart, 1934.
The Crow Indians. New York: Farrar & Rinehart, 1935.
The History of Ethnological Theory. New York: Farrar, 1937.
The German People, a Social Portrait to 1914. New York: Farrar, 1945.
Social Organization. New York: Rinehart, 1948.
Indians of the Plains. New York: McGraw-Hill, 1954.
Toward Understanding Germany. Chicago: University of Chicago Press, 1954.
Selected Papers in Anthropology, ed. Cora du Bois. Berkeley: University of California Press, 1960.

NICCOLO MACHIAVELLI (1469–1527)

ITALIAN POLITICAL PHILOSOPHER

WORKS IN ITALIAN

Opere di Niccolò Machiavelli. 10 vols. Firenze: Conti, 1818–1821.
Discorsi sopra la prima deca di Tito Livio. Roma: Blado, 1531.
Historie Fiorentine. Firenze: Ciunta, 1532.
Il principe. Venezia: 1537.
L'arte della guerra. Venezia: Zanetti, 1538.

WORKS IN ENGLISH TRANSLATION

The Works of Nicholas Machiavel. 2 vols. Translated by E. Farnesworth. London: Davies, 1762.
The Historical, Political, and Diplomatic Writings. Translated by C. E. Detmold. 4 vols. Boston: Osgood, 1882.
The Art of War. Translated by P. Whitehorne. London: Wight, 1573.
The Florentine History. Translated by T. Bedingfield. London: Ponsoby, 1595.
Florentine History. Translated by W. K. Marriott. London: Dent, 1922.
Discourses upon the First Decade of Titus Livius. Translated by E. Dacres. London: Hills & Pakeman, 1636.
Discourses. 2 vols. Translated by L. J. Walker. New Haven: Yale University Press, 1950.
The Prince. Translated by E. Dacres. London: Hills, 1640.
The Prince. Translated by N. H. Thomson. 3rd ed., Oxford: Clarendon Press, 1913.

WILLIAM McDOUGALL (1871–1938)

BRITISH-AMERICAN PSYCHOLOGIST

Physiological Psychology. London: Dent, 1905.
An Introduction to Social Psychology. London: Methuen, 1909. Rev. ed., Boston: Luce, 1926.
Body and Mind. London: Methuen, 1911.
Psychology. New York: Holt, 1912.
The Group Mind. Cambridge: Cambridge University Press; New York: Putnam, 1920.
Is America Safe for Democracy? New York: Scribner, 1921.
Ethics and Some Modern World Problems. New York: Putnam, 1924.
The Indestructible Union. Boston: Little, Brown & Co., 1925.
Outlines of Abnormal Psychology. New York: Scribner, 1926.
Character and the Conduct of Life. New York: Putnam, 1927.
Janus: the Conquest of War. New York: Dutton, 1927.
Modern Materialism and Emergent Evolution. London: Methuen, 1929.
The Energies of Men. London: Methuen, 1932.
Religion and the Sciences of Life. London: Methuen, 1934.
The Frontiers of Psychology. New York: Appleton, 1935.

Psychoanalysis and Social Psychology. London: Methuen, 1936.

The Riddle of Life. London: Methuen, 1938.

ROBERT MORRISON MACIVER (1882–   )

BRITISH-AMERICAN SOCIOLOGIST

Community. London: Macmillan, 1917.

Labor in the Changing World. New York: Dutton, 1919.

The Elements of Social Science. New York: Dutton, 1921.

The Modern State. Oxford: Clarendon Press, 1926.

The Contribution of Sociology to Social Work. New York: Columbia University Press, 1931.

Society; its Structure and Changes. New York: Long & Smith, 1931.

Leviathan and the People. University, La.: Louisiana State University Press, 1939.

Social Causation. Boston, New York: Ginn, 1942.

Towards an Abiding Peace. New York: Macmillan, 1943.

The Web of Government. New York: Macmillan, 1947.

The More Perfect Union. New York: Macmillan, 1948.

Society, an Introductory Analysis (with Charles H. Page). New York: Rinehart, 1949.

The Ramparts We Guard. New York: Macmillan, 1950.

Academic Freedom in Our Time. New York: Columbia University Press, 1955.

The Pursuit of Happiness. New York: Simon & Schuster, 1955.

SIR HENRY JAMES SUMNER MAINE
(1822–1888)

BRITISH LEGAL HISTORIAN

Ancient Law. London: Murray, 1861.

Village Communities in the East and West. London: Murray, 1871.

Lectures on the Early History of Institutions. New York: Holt, 1875.

Dissertations on Early Law and Custom. London: Murray, 1883.

Popular Government. London: Murray, 1885.

International Law. London: Murray, 1888.

FREDERIC WILLIAM MAITLAND
(1850–1906)

BRITISH LEGAL HISTORIAN

Justice and Police. London: Macmillan, 1885.

The Court Baron. London: Quaritch, 1891.

The History of English Law Before the Time of Edward I (with Sir Frederick Pollock). 2 vols. Cambridge: Cambridge University Press, 1895.

Domesday Book and Beyond. Cambridge: Cambridge University Press, 1897.

Roman Canon Law in the Church of England. London: Methuen, 1898.

Township and Borough. Cambridge: Cambridge University Press, 1898.

English Law and the Renaissance. Cambridge: Cambridge University Press, 1901.

The Life and Letters of Leslie Stephen. London: Duckworth, 1906.

The Constitutional History of England. Cambridge: Cambridge University Press, 1908.

The Collected Papers of Frederic William Knowland, ed. H. A. L. Fisher. 3 vols. Cambridge: Cambridge University Press, 1911.

Equity, ed. A. H. Chaytor and W. S. Whittaker. Cambridge: Cambridge University Press, 1936.

Selected Essays, ed. H. D. Hazeltine *et al.* Cambridge: Cambridge University Press, 1936.

BRONISLAW MALINOWSKI (1884–1942)

BRITISH ANTHROPOLOGIST

The Family Among the Australian Aborigines. London: University of London Press, 1913.

Argonauts of the Western Pacific. London: Routledge, 1922.

Crime and Custom in Savage Society. London: K. Paul, Trench, Trubner, 1926.

Myth in Primitive Psychology. London: K. Paul, Trench, Trubner, 1926.

The Father in Primitive Psychology. London: K. Paul, Trench, Trubner, 1927.

Sex and Repression in Savage Society. London: K. Paul, Trench, Trubner, 1927.

The Sexual Life of Savages in North-Western Melanesia. London: Routledge, 1929.

Coral Gardens and Their Magic. 2 vols. London: Allen & Unwin, 1935.

The Foundations of Faith and Morals. London: Oxford University Press, 1936.

Freedom and Civilization. New York: Roy, 1944.

A Scientific Theory of Culture. Chapel Hill: The University of North Carolina Press, 1944.

Magic, Science and Religion. Selected by Robert Redfield. Boston: Beacon Press, 1948.

THOMAS ROBERT MALTHUS (1766–1834)

BRITISH ECONOMIST

An Essay on the Principle of Population. London: Johnson, 1798. 2nd ed., 1803.

An Inquiry into the Nature and Progress of Rent. London: Murray, 1815.

Observation on the Effects of Corn Laws. London: Murray, 1814.

Principles of Political Economy. London: Murray, 1820. 2nd rev. ed., London: Pickering, 1836.

The Measure of Value stated and illustrated. London: Murray, 1823.

Definitions of Political Economy. London: Murray, 1827.

KARL MANNHEIM (1893–1947)

GERMAN SOCIOLOGIST

WORKS IN GERMAN

Die Strukturanalyse der Erkenntnistheorie. Berlin: Reuther & Reichard, 1922.

Ideologie und Utopie. Bonn: Cohen, 1921. 3rd ed., 1952.

Die Gegenwartsaufgaben der Soziologie. Tübingen: Mohr (Siebeck), 1932.

Mensch und Gesellschaft im Zeitalter des Umbaus. Leiden: Sijthoff, 1935.

WORKS IN ENGLISH

Ideology and Utopia. Translated by L. Wirth and E. Shils. New York: Harcourt, 1936.

Man and Society in an Age of Reconstruction. Translated by E. Shils. London: K. Paul, Trench, Trubner, 1940.

Diagnosis of Our Time. London: K. Paul, Trench, Trubner, 1943.

Freedom, Power, and Democratic Planning. London: Oxford University Press, 1950.

Essays on the Sociology of Knowledge, ed. P. Kecskemeti. London: Oxford University Press, 1952.

Essays on Sociology and Social Psychology, ed. P. Kecskemeti. London: Oxford University Press, 1953.

Essays on the Sociology of Culture, ed. E. Manheim. London: Oxford University Press, 1956.

Systematic Sociology, ed. J. S. Eros and W. A. C. Stewart. London: Routledge & K. Paul, 1957.

ALFRED MARSHALL (1842–1924)

BRITISH ECONOMIST

The Economics of Industry. London: Macmillan, 1879.

Principles of Economics. London: Macmillan, 1890. Enlarged ed., 1920.

Elements of Economics of Industry. London: Macmillan, 1892.

Industry and Trade. London: Macmillan, 1919.

Money, Credit and Commerce. London: Macmillan, 1923.

Official Papers. London: Macmillan, 1924.

KARL MARX (1818–1883)

GERMAN ECONOMIST AND SOCIAL PHILOSOPHER

Karl Marx, Friedrich Engels; Historisch-kritische Gesamtausgabe: Werke-Schriften-Briefe. Moscow: Marx-Engels-Archiv, 1927– .

Karl Marx and Friedrich Engels. Works (in Russian). Moscow: Gosudarstvennoe Izdatel'stvo politicheskoi literatury, 1955–

Ausgewählte Schriften in zwei Bänden. Berlin: Dietz Verlag, 1955.

Die Frühschriften, ed. Siegfried Landshut. Stuttgart: Kröner, 1953.

Misère de la philosophie. Paris: Frank, 1847.

Das kommunistische Manifest. London: 1848.

Der achtzehnte Brumaire des Louis Bonaparte. London: 1852.

Zur Kritik der politischen Ökonomie. Berlin: Duncker, 1859.

Herr Vogt. London: Petsch, 1860.

Das Kapital. 3 vols. Hamburg: Meissner, 1867, 1885–1894.

Der Bürgerkrieg in Frankreich. Leipzig: Genossenschaftsdruckerei, 1876.

Die Klassenkämpfe in Frankreich 1848–1850. Berlin: Glocke, 1895.

Theorien über den Mehrwert, ed. Karl Kautsky. 3 vols. Stuttgart: Dietz, 1905.

Die deutsche Ideologie (1845/1856). Moscow: Marx-Engels-Archiv, 1938.

WORKS IN ENGLISH TRANSLATION

Manifesto of the Communists. New York: Schaerr & Frantz, 1883.

Capital: A Critique of Political Economy. 3 vols. complete. Vol. I, A Critical Analysis of Capitalist Production, translated by Samuel Moore and Edward Aveling. Vol. II, The Process of Circulation of Capital, translated by E. Untermann. Vol. III, The Process of Capitalist Production as a Whole, translated by E. Untermann, Chicago: Kerr, 1887, 1907, 1909.

Revolution and Counter-Revolution, or Germany in 1848, ed. Eleanor Marx Aveling. Chicago: Kerr, 1896.

The Eighteenth Brumaire of Louis Bonaparte. Translated by D. DeLeon. New York: International Publishers, 1898.

Value, Price, and Profit, ed. E. Marx Aveling. London: Sonnenschein, 1898.

The Poverty of Philosophy. Translated by H. Quelch. London: Twentieth Century Press, 1900.

A Contribution to the Critique of Political Economy. Translated by N. I. Stone. New York: International Library, 1904.

The Civil War in France. Translated by E. B. Bax. Chicago: Kerr, 1920.

The Class Struggles in France, 1848–1850. Translated by H. Kuhn. New York: New York Labor News Co., 1924.

Capital. 2 vols. Translated by E. and C. Paul. London: Dent, 1930.

The Correspondence of Marx and Engels, 1846–1895. Ed. and translated by Dona Torr. New York: International Publishers, 1934.

The German Ideology, ed. R. Pascal. London: Lawrence & Wishart, 1938.

Selected Works in Two Volumes. London: Lawrence & Wishart, 1942.

Economic and Philosophic Manuscripts of 1844. Translated by Martin Milligan. London: Lawrence and Wishart, 1959.

MARCEL MAUSS (1872–1950)

FRENCH ANTHROPOLOGIST

WORKS IN FRENCH

Mélanges d'histoire des religions (with Henri Hubert). Paris: Alcan, 1909.

"Essai sur le don, forme archaique de l'échange," *Année sociologique,* N. S., vol. I, 1923–1924.

"Les variations saisonnières dans les sociétés eskimo," *Année sociologique,* N. S., vol. I, 1923–1924.

Les Celtes depuis l'époque de la Tène et la civilisation celtique (with Henri Hubert). Paris: La Renaissance du Livre, 1932.

Manuel d'éthnographie. Paris: Payot, 1947.

Sociologie et anthropologie, ed. C. Lévi-Strauss. Paris: Presses universitaires de France, 1950.

WORKS IN ENGLISH TRANSLATION

The Gift; Forms and Functions of Exchange in Archaic Societies. Translated by J. Cunnison. London: Cohen & West; Glencoe, Ill.: The Free Press, 1954.

GEORGE HERBERT MEAD (1863–1931)

AMERICAN PHILOSOPHER

The Philosophy of the Present, ed. A. E. Murphy. Chicago: Open Court Publishing Co., 1932.

Mind, Self and Society. Chicago: University of Chicago Press, 1934.

Movements of Thought in the Nineteenth Century, ed. M. H. Moore. Chicago: University of Chicago Press, 1936.

The Philosophy of the Act, ed. C. W. Morris. Chicago: University of Chicago Press, 1938.

ANTOINE MEILLET (1866–1936)

FRENCH PHILOLOGIST

Du genre animé en vieux-slave. Paris: Bouillon, 1897.

Etudes sur l'étymologie et le vocabulaire du vieux slave. 2 vols. Paris: Bouillon, 1902–1905.

Esquisse d'une grammaire comparée de l'arménien classique. Vienne: 1903. 2nd rev. ed., 1936.

Introduction à l'étude comparative des langues indoeuropéens. Paris: Hachette, 1903. 7th rev. ed., 1934.

Les dialectes indo-européens. Paris: Champion, 1908.

Aperçu d'une histoire de la langue grecque. Paris: Hachette, 1913.

Caractères géneraux des langues germaniques. Paris: Hachette, 1917. 4th rev. ed., 1930.

Les langues dans l'Europe moderne. Paris: Payot, 1918.

Linguistique historique et linguistique génerale. 2 vols. Paris: Champion, 1921–1938.

Le slave commun. Paris: Champion, 1924. 2nd rev. ed., 1934.

La méthode comparative en linguistique historique. Oslo: Aschehoug, 1925.

Traité de grammaire comparée des langues classique (with J. Vendryes) Paris: Champion, 1927.

Esquisse d'une histoire de la langue latine. Paris: Hachette, 1928. 2nd rev. ed., 1931.

Soziologie als Gesellschaftswissenschaft. Berlin: Mauritius, 1926.

Storia critica del movimento socialista Italiano. Firenze: La voce, 1926.

Bedeutende Männer. Leipzig: Quelle & Meyer, 1927.

Corso di sociologia politica. Milano: Instituto editoriale scientifico, 1927.

Francia contamporanea. Milano: Corbaccio, 1927.

Sittlichkeit in Ziffern? München: Duncker & Humblot, 1928.

Die Verelendungstheorie. Leipzig: Kröner, 1928.

Der Patriotismus. München: Duncker & Humblot, 1929.

Italien von heute. Zürich: Orell Füssli, 1930.

Das psychologische Moment im Welthandel. Leipzig: Deutsche wissenschaftliche Buchhandlung, 1931.

Intoduzione alla storia delle dottrine economiche e politiche. Bologna: Zanichelli, 1932.

Il boicottaggio. Torino: Einaudi, 1934.

Umschichtungen in den herrschenden Klassen nach dem Kriege. Stuttgart: Kohlhammer, 1934.

ROBERT MICHELS (1876–1936)

GERMAN-ITALIAN SOCIOLOGIST

WORKS IN GERMAN AND ITALIAN

Il proletariato e la borghesia nel movimento socialista italiano. Torino: Bocca, 1908.

Die Grenzen der Geschlechtsmoral. München: Frauenverlag, 1911.

Zur Soziologie des Parteiwesens in der modernen Demokratie. Leipzig: Klinkhardt, 1911. 2nd ed., Stuttgart: Kröner, 1925.

Saggi economico-statistici sulle classi popolari. Milano: Sandron, 1913.

L'imperialismo italiano. Milano: Società editrice libraria, 1914.

Probleme der Sozialphilosophie. Leipzig: Teubner, 1914.

Economia e felicità. Milano: Vallardi, 1918.

Problemi di sociologia applicata. Torino: Bocca, 1919.

Le colonie italiane in Svizzera durante la guerra. Roma: Alfieri, 1922.

La teoria di C. Marx, sulla miseria crescente. Torino: Bocca, 1922.

Fattori e problemi della espansione commerciale. Torino: Bocca, 1924.

Lavoro e razza. Milano: Vallardi, 1924.

Sozialismus und Fascismus in Italien. 2 vols. München: Meyer & Jessen, 1925.

WORKS IN ENGLISH TRANSLATION

Sexual Ethics. London: Walter Scott Publishing Co., 1914.

Political Parties. Translated by E. and C. Paul. New York: Hearst, 1915; Glencoe, Ill.: The Free Press, 1949.

First Lectures in Political Sociology. Translated by A. de Grazia. Minneapolis: University of Minnesota Press, 1949.

JOHN STUART MILL (1806–1873)

BRITISH ECONOMIST AND PHILOSOPHER

A System of Logic, Ratiocinative and Inductive. 2 vols. London: Parker, 1843.

Essays on Some Unsettled Questions of Political Economy. London: Parker, 1844.

Principles of Political Economy. 2 vols. London: Parker, 1848. 5th ed., 1862.

On Liberty. London: Parker, 1859.

Considerations on Representative Government. London: Parker, 1861.

Utilitarianism. London: Parker, 1863.

Dissertations and Discussions: Political, Philosophical, and Historical. 4 vols. Boston: Spencer, 1865–1868.

An Examination of Sir William Hamilton's Philosophy. London: Longmans, 1865.

Auguste Comte and Positivism. Philadelphia: Lipincott, 1866.

The Subjection of Women. London: Longmans, 1869.

Autobiography. London: Longmans, 1873.

Three Essays on Religion. New York: Holt, 1874.

Socialism, ed. W. D. P. Bliss. New York: Humboldt, 1891.

LEWIS HENRY MORGAN (1818–1881)

AMERICAN ANTHROPOLOGIST

League of the Ho-dé-no-sau-nee or Iroquois, ed. H. M. Lloyd. Rochester, N. Y.: Sage, 1851. Rev. ed., New York: Dodd, Mead & Co., 1904.

The American Beaver and His Works. Philadelphia: Lippincott, 1868.

Systems of Consanguinity and Affinity of the Human Family. Washington: Smithsonian Institution, 1870.

Ancient Society. New York: Holt, 1877.

Houses and House-Life of the American Aborigines. Washington: Government Printing Office, 1881.

Government and Institutions of the Iroquois. Rochester, N. Y.: New York State Archeological Association, 1928.

Abstracts of Lewis Henry Morgan's European Travel Journal, ed. Leslie White. Rochester, N. Y.: Rochester Historical Society, 1937.

GAETANO MOSCA (1858–1941)

ITALIAN POLITICAL PHILOSOPHER

WORKS IN ITALIAN

Appunti di diritto constituzionale. Milano: Societa editrice libraria, 1921.

Elementi di scienza politica. Torino: Bocca, 1896. 2nd ed., 1923.

Storia delle dottrine politiche. Bari: Laterza, 1937. 5th ed., 1945. (Translated into French by G. Bouthoul as *Histoire des doctrines politiques.* Paris: Payot, 1936.)

Partiti e sindacati nella crisi del regime parlamentare. Bari: Laterza, 1949.

TRANSLATED INTO ENGLISH

The Ruling Class. Translated by H. D. Kahn. Ed. A. Livingston. New York: McGraw-Hill, 1939.

WILLIAM FIELDING OGBURN (1886–1959)

AMERICAN SOCIOLOGIST

Progress and Uniformity in Child-Labor Legislation. New York: Columbia University Press, 1912.

Social Change. New York: Huebsch, 1922. New ed., New York: Viking Press, 1950.

American Marriage and Family Relationships (with E. Groves). New York: Holt, 1928.

The Economic Development of Post-War France (with William Jaffé). New York: Columbia University Press, 1929.

Social Characteristics of Cities. Chicago: International City Managers Association, 1937.

Sociology (with Meyer F. Nimkoff). Boston, New York: Houghton Mifflin, 1940. 3rd ed., 1958.

The Social Effects of Aviation. Boston: Houghton Mifflin, 1946.

Technology and the Changing Family (with Meyer F. Nimkoff). Boston: Houghton Mifflin, 1955.

VILFREDO PARETO (1848–1923)

ITALIAN ECONOMIST AND SOCIOLOGIST

WORKS IN FRENCH AND ITALIAN

Cours d'économie politique. 2 vols. Lausanne: Rouge; Paris: Pichon, 1896–1897.

La liberté économique et les événements d'Italie. Lausanne: Rouge, 1898.

Les systèmes socialistes. 2 vols. Paris: Giard & Brière, 1902–1903.

Manuale di economia politica. Milano: Società editrice libraria, 1906.

Le mythe vertuiste et la littérature immorale. Paris: Riviere, 1911.

Trattato di sociologia generale. 2 vols. Firenze: Barbéra, 1916. Authorized French edition, *Traité de sociologie génerale.* 2 vols. Lausanne, Paris: Payot, 1917–1919.

Fatti e teorie. Firenze: Vallecchi, 1920.

Trasformazione della democrazia. Milano: Corbaccio, 1921.

Scritti teorici. Milano: Malfasi, 1952.

WORKS IN ENGLISH TRANSLATION

The Mind and Society. 4 vols. Translated by A. Bongiorno and A. Livingston. New York: Harcourt, 1935.

The Ruling Class in Italy before 1900. New York: Vanni, 1950.

ROBERT EZRA PARK (1864–1944)

AMERICAN SOCIOLOGIST

Masse und Publikum. Berlin: Lack & Grunau, 1904.

Introduction to the Science of Sociology (with Ernest W. Burgess). Chicago: University of Chicago Press, 1921.

Old World Traits Transplanted (with H. A. Miller). New York: Harper, 1921.

The Immigrant Press and Its Control. New York: Harper, 1922.

The City (with Ernest W. Burgess and R. D. McKenzie). Chicago: University of Chicago Press, 1925.

Race and Culture. Glencoe, Ill.: The Free Press, 1950.

Human Communities. Glencoe, Ill.: The Free Press, 1952.

Society. Glencoe, Ill.: The Free Press, 1955.

IVAN PETROVICH PAVLOV (1849–1936)

RUSSIAN PHYSIOLOGIST

WORKS IN ENGLISH TRANSLATION

The Work of the Digestive Glands. Translated by W. H. Thompson. London: Griffin, 1902.

Conditioned Reflexes. Translated by G. V. Anrep. London: Oxford University Press, 1927.

Lectures on Conditioned Reflexes. 2 vols. Translated by W. H. Gantt. New York: International Publishers, 1928–1941.

Selected Works, ed. K. S. Koshtoyants. Translated by S. Belsky. Moscow: Foreign Languages Publishing House, 1955.

Experimental Psychology and Other Essays. New York: Philosophical Library, 1957.

JEAN PIAGET (1896–   )

SWISS PSYCHOLOGIST

WORKS IN FRENCH

Le jugement et le raisonnement chez l'enfant. Neuchâtel, Paris: Delachaux & Niestlé, 1924.

Le réprésentation du monde chez l'enfant. Paris: Alcan, 1926.

La causalité physique chez l'enfant. Paris: Alcan, 1927.

La naissance de l'intelligence chez l'enfant. Neuchâtel, Paris: Delachaux & Niestlé, 1936.

La construction du réel chez l'enfant. Paris: Delachaux & Niestlé, 1937.

Classes, relations et nombres. Paris: Vrin, 1942.

La développement de la notion de temps chez l'enfant. Paris: Presses universitaires de France, 1946.

Traité de logique. Paris: Colin, 1949.

Introduction à l'épistémologie génétique. 3 vols. Paris: Presses universitaires de France, 1950.

La genèse de l'idée de hasard chez l'enfant (with B. Inhelder). Paris: Presses universitaires de France, 1951.

Essai sur les transformations des opérations logiques. Paris: Presses universitaires de France, 1952.

WORKS IN ENGLISH TRANSLATION

The Language and Thought of the Child. Translated by M. Warden. London: K. Paul, Trench, Trubner, 1926.

Judgement and Reasoning in the Child. Translated by M. Warden. London: K. Paul, Trench, Trubner, 1928.

The Child's Conception of the World. Translated by J. and L. Tomlinson. London: K. Paul, Trench, Trubner, 1929.

The Child's Conception of Physical Reality. Translated by M. Gabain. London: K. Paul, Trench, Trubner, 1930.

The Moral Judgement of the Child. Translated by M. Gabain. London: K. Paul, Trench, Trubner, 1932.

The Psychology of Intelligence. Translated by M. Piercy and D. E. Berlyne. New York: Harcourt, 1950.

Play, Dreams, and Imitation in Childhood. Translated by C. Gattegno and F. M. Hodgson. New York: Norton, 1951.

The Child's Conception of Hunger. Translated by C. Gattegno and F. M. Hodgson. London: Routledge & K. Paul, 1952.

The Origins of Intelligence in Children. Translated by M. Cook. New York: International Universities Press, 1952.
The Construction of Reality in the Child. Translated by M. Cook. New York: Basic Books, 1954.
The Child's Conception of Space (with B. Inhelder). Translated by F. J. Langsdon and J. L. Lunzer. London: Routledge & K. Paul, 1956.

SIR FREDERICK POLLOCK (1845–1937)

BRITISH LEGAL HISTORIAN

Principles of Contract. London: Stevens, 1876. 10th ed., 1936.
A Digest of the Law of Partnership. London: Stevens, 1877. 13th ed., 1937.
Spinoza, His Life and Philosophy. London: C. K. Paul, 1880.
Essays in Jurisprudence and Ethics. London: Macmillan, 1882.
The Land Laws. London: Macmillan, 1883.
The Law of Torts. London: Stevens, 1887. 13th ed., 1929.
An Essay on Possession in the Common Law. Oxford: Clarendon Press, 1888.
An Introduction to the History of the Science of Politics. London: Macmillan, 1890.
Oxford Lectures and Other Discourses. London: Macmillan, 1890.
The History of English Law Before the Time of Edward I (with Frederic W. Maitland). 2 vols. Cambridge: University Press, 1895.
A First Book of Jurisprudence. London: Macmillan, 1896. 6th ed., 1929.
The League of Nations. London: Stevens, 1920.
Essays in the Law. London: Macmillan, 1922.

ALFRED REGINALD RADCLIFFE-BROWN (1881–1955)

BRITISH ANTHROPOLOGIST

The Andaman Islanders. Cambridge: The University Press, 1922.
The Social Organization of Australian Tribes. London: Macmillan, 1931.
Structure and Function in Primitive Society. London: Cohen & West; Glencoe, Ill.: The Free Press, 1952.

A Natural Science of Society. Glencoe, Ill.: The Free Press, 1957.

FRITZ JULES ROETHLISBERGER (1898–   )

AMERICAN INDUSTRIAL SOCIOLOGIST

Management and the Worker (with William J. Dickson). Cambridge, Mass.: Harvard University Press, 1939.
Management and Morale. Cambridge, Mass.: Harvard University Press, 1941.

JEAN JACQUES ROUSSEAU (1712–1778)

FRENCH PHILOSOPHER

WORKS IN FRENCH

Collection complète des oeuvres de J.-J. Rousseau. 33 vols. Ed. P. A. Du Peyrou. Genève: Moulton, 1782–1789.
Oeuvres complètes. Ed. B. Gagnebin and M. Raymond. Paris: Galimard, 1959.
Discours sur les sciences et les arts. Genève: Barillot, 1750.
Discours sur l'origine et les fondements de l'inégalité parmi les hommes. Amsterdam: Rey, 1755.
Julie, ou, La nouvelle Heloise. 6 vols. Amsterdam: Rey, 1761.
Émile; ou, De l'éducation. Amsterdam: Néaulme, 1762.
Du Contrat social; ou, Principes du droit politique. Amsterdam: Rey, 1762.
Pensées. Amsterdam, 1763.
Traités sur la musique. Genève, 1781.
Mélanges. 6 vols. Paris: Cazin, 1782.
Considérations sur le gouvernement de Pologne et sur la réformation projettée. Paris: Cazin, 1782.
Les Confessions, suivies des Rêveries du promeneur solitaire. 4 vols. Genève, 1782–1789.
Lettres élementaires sur la botanique. 2 vols. Paris, 1789.
Corréspondance générale, ed. Théophile Dufour. 20 vols. Paris: Colin, 1924–1934.

WORKS IN ENGLISH TRANSLATION

A Discourse upon the Origin and Foundation of Inequality among Mankind. London: Dodsley, 1761.

Thoughts on Different Subjects. 2 vols. London: Crowder, 1768.

Eloisa. 4 vols. London: Beckett, 1776.

Letters on the Elements of Botany. Translated by Thomas Martyn. London: White, 1787.

A Dissertation on Political Economy. Albany: Barber & Southwick, 1797.

Original Letters of Jean Jacques Rousseau. London: Symonds, 1799.

Émile. Translated by Barbara Foxley. London: Dent, 1911.

The Social Contract and the Discourses. Translated by G. D. H. Cole. London: Dent, 1913.

The Political Writings of Jean Jacques Rousseau, ed. C. E. Vaughan. 2 vols. Cambridge: The University Press, 1915.

A Lasting Peace through the Federation of Europe and the State of War. Translated by C. E. Vaughan. London: Constable, 1917.

The Confessions. An eighteenth-century translation. London: Dent, 1935.

Politics and the Arts: Letter to D'Alembert. Translated by Allan Bloom. Glencoe: The Free Press, 1960.

EDWARD SAPIR (1884–1939)

AMERICAN ANTHROPOLOGIST

Takelma Texts. Philadelphia: The University Museum, 1909.

Wishram Texts. Leyden: Brill, 1909.

Yana Texts. Berkeley: University of California Press, 1910.

Time Perspective in Aboriginal American Culture. Ottawa: Government Printing Bureau, 1916.

Language. New York: Harcourt, 1921.

Selected Writings in Language, Culture and Personality, ed. D. G. Mandelbaum. Berkeley: University of California Press, 1949.

Native Accounts of Nootka Ethnography (with M. Swadesh). Bloomington, Ind.: University of Indiana Press, 1955.

HERMAN SCHMALENBACH (1885–1950)

GERMAN SOCIOLOGIST

WORKS IN GERMAN

Leibniz. München: Drei Masken Verlag, 1921.

Mittelalter, sein Begriff und Wesen. Leipzig: Quelle & Meyer, 1926.

Kants Religion. Berlin: Funker & Dünnhaupt, 1929.

Das Ethos und die Idee des Erkennens. Tübingen: Mohr (Siebeck), 1933.

Geist und Sein. Basel: Haus zum Falken, 1939.

JOSEPH ALOIS SCHUMPETER (1883–1950)

AUSTRIAN-AMERICAN ECONOMIST

WORKS IN GERMAN

Das Wesen und der Hauptinhalt der theoretischen Nationalökonomie. Leipzig: Duncker & Humblot, 1908.

Theorie der wirtschaftlichen Entwicklung. Leipzig: Duncker & Humblot, 1912. 5th ed., 1952.

Vergangenheit und Zukunft der Sozialwissenschaften. München: Duncker & Humblot, 1915.

Aufsätze zur ökonomischen Theorie. Tübingen: Mohr, 1952.

Aufsätze zur Soziologie. Tübingen: Mohr, 1953.

Dogmenhistorische und biographische Aufsätze. Tübingen: Mohr, 1954.

WORKS IN ENGLISH

The Theory of Economic Development. Translated by R. Opie. Cambridge, Mass.: Harvard University Press, 1934.

Business Cycles. 2 vols. New York: McGraw-Hill, 1939.

Capitalism, Socialism, and Democracy. New York: Harper, 1942.

Essays, ed. R. V. Clemence. Cambridge, Mass.: Addison-Wesley, 1951.

Imperialism and Social Classes, ed. P. M. Sweezy. Translated by H. Norded. New York: Kelley, 1951.

Ten Great Economists, from Marx to Keynes. London: Allen & Unwin, 1952.

Economic Doctrine and Method. Translated by R. Aris. London: Allen & Unwin, 1954.

History of Economic Analysis, ed. E. B. Schumpeter. New York: Oxford University Press, 1954.

GEORG SIMMEL (1858–1918)

GERMAN PHILOSOPHER AND SOCIOLOGIST

WORKS IN GERMAN

Über sociale Differenzierung. Leipzig: Duncker & Humblot, 1890.

Einleitung in die Moralwissenschaft. 2 vols. Berlin: Hertz, 1892–1893.

Die Probleme der Geschichtsphilosophie. Leipzig: Duncker & Humblot, 1892. 2nd rev. ed., 1905.

Philosophie des Geldes. Leipzig: Duncker & Humblot, 1900. 2nd ed., 1907.

Kant. Leipzig: Duncker & Humblot, 1904. 6th ed., 1924.

Kant und Goethe. Berlin: Marquardt, 1906.

Die Religion. Frankfurt am Main: Rütten & Loening, 1906. 2nd ed., 1912.

Schopenhauer und Nietzsche. Leipzig: Duncker & Humblot, 1907.

Soziologie. Leipzig: Duncker & Humblot, 1908.

Hautprobleme der Philosophie. Leipzig: Göschen, 1910.

Philosophische Kultur. Leipzig: Kröner, 1911. 2nd ed., 1919.

Goethe. Leipzig: Klinkhardt, 1913.

Grundfragen der Soziologie. Berlin: Göschen, 1917.

Rembrandt. Leipzig: Wolff, 1917.

Lebensanschauung. München: Duncker & Humblot, 1918.

Zur Philosophie der Kunst. Potsdam: Kiepenheuer, 1922.

Fragmente und Aufsätze aus dem Nachlass, ed. G. Kantorowicz. München: Drei Masken Verlag, 1923.

Brücke und Tür, ed. M. Landmann and M. Susman. Stuttgart: Koehler, 1957.

WORKS IN ENGLISH TRANSLATION

The Sociology of Georg Simmel. Edited and translated by Kurt H. Wolff. Glencoe, Ill.: The Free Press, 1950.

Conflict. The Web of Group Affiliations. Translated by K. H. Wolff and R. Bendix. Glencoe, Ill.: The Free Press, 1955.

ADAM SMITH (1723–1790)

SCOTTISH PHILOSOPHER AND ECONOMIST

The Theory of Moral Sentiments. London: Millar, 1759. 5th ed., London: Strahan & Rivington, 1781.

An Inquiry into the Nature and Causes of the Wealth of Nations. 2 vols, London: Strahan & Cadell, 1776. 5th ed. in 3 vols., 1789.

Essays on Philosophical Subjects. London: Cadell & Davies, 1795.

Lectures on Justice, Police, Revenue and Arms, ed. E. Cannan. Oxford: Clarendon Press, 1896.

WILLIAM ROBERTSON SMITH (1846–1894)

BRITISH HISTORIAN OF RELIGION

The Old Testament in the Jewish Church. London: Black, 1881.

The Prophets of Israel and their Place in History. Edinburgh: Black, 1882.

Kinship and Marriage in Early Arabia. Cambridge: University Press, 1885.

Lectures on the Religion of the Semites. Edinburgh: Black, 1889.

Lectures and Essays, ed. J. S. Black and G. Chrystal. London: Black, 1912.

PITIRIM ALEKSANDROVICH SOROKIN (1889–   )

RUSSIAN-AMERICAN SOCIOLOGIST

WORKS IN ENGLISH

Leaves from a Russian Diary. New York: Dutton, 1924.

The Sociology of Revolution. Philadelphia: Lippincott, 1925.

Social Mobility. New York: Harper, 1927.

Contemporary Sociological Theories. New York: Harper, 1928.

Principles of Rural-Urban Sociology (with Carle C. Zimmerman). New York: Holt, 1929.

Social and Cultural Dynamics. 4 vols. New York: American Book Co., 1937–1941.

Time Budgets of Human Behavior (with C. Q. Berger). Cambridge, Mass.: Harvard University Press, 1939.

The Crisis of Our Age. New York: Dutton, 1941.

Man and Society in Calamity. New York: Dutton, 1942.

Sociocultural Causality, Space, Time. Durham: Duke University Press, 1943.

Russia and the United States. New York: Dutton, 1944.

Society, Culture, and Personality. New York: Harper, 1947.

The Reconstruction of Humanity. Boston: Beacon Press, 1948.

Altruistic Love. Boston: Beacon Press, 1950.
Social Philosophies of An Age of Crisis. Boston: Beacon Press, 1950.
The American Sex Revolution. Boston: Sargent, 1956.
Fads and Foibles in Modern Sociology and Related Sciences. Chicago: Regnery, 1956.
The Ways and Power of Love. Boston: Beacon Press, 1957.
Power and Morality; Who Shall Be the Guardians? (with Walter A. Lunden). Boston: Sargent, 1959.

HERBERT SPENCER (1820–1903)

BRITISH PHILOSOPHER AND SOCIOLOGIST

Essays. 3 vols. London: Longmans, 1858–1874.
A System of Synthetic Philosophy. 10 vols. (I. First Principles, II–III. Principles of Biology, IV–V. Principles of Psychology, VI–VIII. Principles of Sociology, IX–X. Principles of Ethics). London: Appleton, 1862–1896.
Education: Intellectual, Moral, and Physical. London: Manwaring, 1861.
The Classification of Sciences. London: Williams & Norgate, 1864.
Illustrations of Universal Progress. London: Appleton, 1864.
Social Statics. London: Appleton, 1865.
Philosophy of Style. London: Appleton, 1871.
Descriptive Sociology. 8 vols. London: Williams & Norgate, 1873–1885.
The Study of Sociology. London: Appleton, 1874.
The Man versus State. London: Appleton, 1884.
Facts and Comments. London: Appleton, 1902.
An Autobiography. 2 vols. New York: Appleton, 1904.

OSWALD SPENGLER (1880–1936)

GERMAN PHILOSOPHER OF HISTORY

WORKS IN GERMAN

Der Untergang des Abendlandes. 2 vols. München: Beck, 1919–1922.
Preussentum und Sozialismus. München: Beck, 1920.
Neubau des Deutschen Reiches. München: Beck, 1924.

Der Mensch und die Technik. München: Beck, 1931.
Jahre der Entscheidung. München: Beck, 1933.
Politische Schriften. München: Beck, 1933.
Reden und Aufsätze. München: Beck, 1938.
Gedanken. München: Beck, 1941.

WORKS IN ENGLISH TRANSLATION

The Decline of the West. 2 vols. Translated by C. F. Atkinson. New York: Knopf, 1926–1928.
Man and Technics. Translated by C. F. Atkinson. New York: Knopf, 1932.
The Hour of Decision. Translated by C. F. Atkinson. New York: Knopf, 1934.

WILLIAM GRAHAM SUMNER (1840–1910)

AMERICAN SOCIOLOGIST

A History of American Currency. New York: Holt, 1874.
Andrew Jackson. Boston: Houghton Mifflin, 1882.
What Social Classes Owe to Each Other. New York: Harper, 1883.
Problems in Political Economy. New York: Holt, 1884.
Collected Essays in Political and Social Science. New York: Holt, 1885.
Protectionism. New York: Holt, 1885.
Alexander Hamilton. New York: Dodd, Mead & Co., 1890.
The Financier and the Finances of the American Revolution. 2 vols. New York: Dodd, Mead & Co., 1892.
Robert Morris. New York: Dodd, Mead & Co., 1892.
Folkways. Boston: Ginn, 1906.
War and Other Essays, ed. Albert G. Keller. New Haven: Yale University Press, 1911.
Earth Hunger and Other Essays, ed. Albert G. Keller. New Haven: Yale University Press, 1913.
The Challenge of Facts, ed. Albert G. Keller. New Haven: Yale University Press, 1914.
The Forgotten Man, ed. Albert G. Keller. New Haven: Yale University Press, 1918.
The Science of Society (with Albert G. Keller). 4 vols. New Haven: Yale University Press, 1927–1928.
Essays, ed. Albert G. Keller and Maurice R. Davie. 2 vols. New Haven: Yale University Press, 1934.

WILLIAM ISAAC THOMAS (1863–1947)

AMERICAN SOCIOLOGIST

Sex and Society. Chicago: University of Chicago Press, 1907.
Source Book for Social Origins. Chicago: University of Chicago Press, 1909.
Race Psychology. Chicago: University of Chicago Press, 1912.
The Polish Peasant in Europe and America (with Florian Znaniecki). 5 vols. Chicago: University of Chicago Press, 1918–1920.
The Unadjusted Girl. Boston: Little, Brown & Co., 1923.
The Child in America. New York: Knopf, 1928.
Primitive Behavior. New York: McGraw-Hill, 1937.
Social Behavior and Personality, ed. Edmund H. Volkart. New York: Social Science Research Community, 1951.

EDWARD LEE THORNDIKE (1874–1949)

AMERICAN PSYCHOLOGIST

Animal Intelligence. New York: Macmillan, 1898.
The Human Nature Club. New York: Longmans, 1901.
Notes on Child Study. New York: Macmillan, 1901.
Educational Psychology. New York: Lemcke & Buechner, 1903. Rev. ed. in 3 vols., New York: Teachers College, Columbia University, 1913–1914.
An Introduction to the Theory of Mental and Social Measurements. New York: The Science Press, 1904. 2nd rev. ed., 1913.
The Elements of Psychology. New York: Seiler, 1905. 2nd ed., 1907.
The Principles of Teaching. New York: Seiler, 1906.
Education. New York: Macmillan, 1912.
The New Methods in Arithmetic. New York: Rand, McNally, 1921.
The Teachers Word Book. New York: Columbia University Press, 1921. Rev. ed., 1944.
The Psychology of Arithmetic. New York: Macmillan, 1922.
The Psychology of Algebra. New York: Macmillan, 1923.

Algebra. Chicago, New York: Rand, McNally & Co., 1927.
The Measurement of Intelligence. New York: Columbia University Press, 1927.
Adult Learning. New York: Macmillan, 1928.
Elementary Principles of Education (with A. I. Gates). New York: Macmillan, 1929.
Human Learning. New York: The Century Co., 1931.
The Fundamentals of Learning. New York: Columbia University Press, 1932.
Comparative Psychology. New York: Prentice-Hall, 1934.
Prediction of Vocational Success. New York: The Commonwealth Fund, 1934.
Adult Interests. New York: Macmillan, 1935.
The Psychology of Wants, Interests and Attitudes. New York: Appleton, 1935.
Your City. New York: Harcourt, 1939.
Human Nature and the Social Order. New York: Macmillan, 1940.
Man and His Works. Cambridge, Mass.: Harvard University Press, 1943.
Selected Writings from a Connectionist's Psychology. New York: Appleton, 1949.

FREDERIC MILTON THRASHER (1892–   )

AMERICAN SOCIOLOGIST

The Gang. Chicago: University of Chicago Press, 1926. 2nd rev. ed., 1936.

FERDINAND TOENNIES (1855–1936)

GERMAN SOCIOLOGIST

WORKS IN GERMAN

Gemeinschaft und Gesellschaft. Leipzig: Fues's Verlag, 1887. 8th ed., Leipzig: Buske, 1935.
Hobbes Leben und Lehre. Stuttgart: Frommann, 1896. 3rd ed., 1925.
Der Nietzsche-Kultus. Leipzig: Reisland, 1897.
Philosophische Terminologie in psychologischer Ansicht. Leipzig: Thomas, 1906.
Die Entwicklung der sozialen Frage. Leipzig: Göschen, 1907.
Die Sitte. Frankfurt am Main: Rütten & Loening, 1909.

Der Englische Staat und der deutsche Staat. Berlin: Curtius, 1917.

Marx, Leben und Lehre. Jena: Lichtenstein, 1921.

Kritik der öffentlichen Meinung. Berlin: Springer, 1922.

Soziologische Studien und Kritiken. 3 vols. Jena: Fischer, 1925–1929.

Fortschritt und soziale Entwicklung. Karlsruhe: Braun, 1926.

Der Selbstmord in Schleswig-Holstein. Breslau: Hirt, 1927.

Einführung in die Soziologie. Stuttgart: Enke, 1931.

Geist der Neuzeit. Leipzig: Buske, 1935.

WORKS IN ENGLISH TRANSLATION

Warlike England as Seen by Herself. New York: Dillingham, 1915.

Fundamental Concepts of Sociology (Gemeinschaft und Gesellschaft). Translated by C. P. Loomis. New York: American Book Co., 1940.

EDWARD CHASE TOLMAN (1886–1959)

AMERICAN PSYCHOLOGIST

A Self-recording Maze with an Automatic Delivery Table (with R. C. Tryon and L. A. Jeffres). Berkeley: University of California Press, 1929.

Degrees of Hunger, Reward and Non-reward, and Maze Learning In Rats (with C. H. Honzik). Berkeley: University of California Press, 1930.

The Effect of Degrees of Hunger Upon the Order of Elimination of Long and Short Blinds (with C. H. Honzik and E. W. Robinson). Berkeley: University of California Press, 1930.

"Insight" in Rats (with C. H. Honzik). Berkeley: University of California Press, 1930.

Introduction and Removal of Reward and Maze Performance in Rats (with C. H. Honzik). Berkeley: University of California Press, 1930.

Purposive Behavior in Animals and Men. New York: The Century Co., 1932.

Drives Toward War. New York: Appleton, 1942.

Collected Papers in Psychology. Berkeley: University of California Press, 1951.

ARNOLD JOSEPH TOYNBEE (1889–   )

BRITISH HISTORIAN

Armenian Atrocities. London: Hodder & Stoughton, 1915.

Nationality and the War. London: Dent, 1915.

The German Terror in Belgium. London: Hodder & Stoughton, 1917.

The German Terror in France. London: Hodder & Stoughton, 1917.

The Western Question in Greece and Turkey. London: Constable, 1922.

Turkey (with K. P. Kirkwood). London: Benn, 1926.

The Islamic World Since the Peace Settlement. London: Oxford University Press, 1927.

The Conduct of British Empire Foreign Relations Since the Peace Settlement. London: Oxford University Press, 1928.

A Journey to China. London: Constable, 1931.

A Study of History. 12 vols. London: Oxford University Press, 1934–1961.

Civilization on Trial. London: Oxford University Press, 1948.

The World and the West. London: Oxford University Press, 1953.

An Historian's Approach to Religion. London: Oxford University Press, 1956.

Christianity among the Religions of the World. New York: Scribner's, 1957.

Hellenism; the History of a Civilization. London: Oxford University Press, 1959.

ERNST TROELTSCH (1865–1923)

GERMAN HISTORIAN

WORKS IN GERMAN

Vernunft und Offenbarung bei Johann Gerhard und Melanchton. Göttingen: Vandenhoeck & Ruprecht, 1891.

Die Bedeutung des Protestantismus für die Entstehung der modernen Welt. München: Oldenbourg, 1911.

Gesammelte Schriften. 4 vols. Tübingen: Mohr (Siebeck), 1912–1925.

Die Soziallehren der christlichen Kirchen und Gruppen. Tübingen: Mohr (Siebeck), 1912.

Augustin, die christliche Antike und das Mittelalter. München: Oldenbourg, 1915.

Deutsche Zukunft. Berlin: Fischer, 1916.

Der Historismus und seine Probleme. Tübingen: Mohr (Siebeck), 1922.

Der Historismus und seine Überwindung. Berlin: Heise, 1924.

Spektator-Briefe, ed. H. Baron. Tübingen: Mohr (Siebeck), 1924.

Deutscher Geist und Westeuropa, ed. Hans Baron. Tübingen: Mohr (Siebeck), 1925.

Glaubenslehre. München: Duncker & Humblot, 1925.

WORKS IN ENGLISH TRANSLATION

Protestantism and Progress. Translated by W. Montgomery. London: Williams & Norgate, 1912.

Christian Thought, its History and Application, ed. F. von Hügel. London: University of London Press, 1923; New York: Meridian Books, 1957.

The Social Teaching of the Christian Churches. Translated by O. Wyon. New York: Macmillan, 1931. New ed. in 2 vols., Glencoe, Ill.: The Free Press, 1949.

THORSTEIN VEBLEN (1857–1929)

AMERICAN ECONOMIST

The Theory of the Leisure Class. New York: Macmillan, 1899.

The Theory of Business Enterprise. New York: Scribner, 1904.

The Instinct of Workmanship. New York: Macmillan, 1914.

Imperial Germany and the Industrial Revolution. New York: Macmillan, 1915.

The Higher Learning in America. New York: Huebsch, 1918.

An Inquiry into the Nature of Peace and the Terms of its Perpetuation. New York: Huebsch, 1919.

The Place of Science in Modern Civilization. New York: Huebsch, 1919.

The Vested Interests and the Common Man. New York: Huebsch, 1920.

The Engineer and the Price System. New York: Huebsch, 1921.

Absentee Ownership and Business Enterprise in Recent Times. New York: Huebsch, 1923.

Essays in Our Changing Order, ed. Leon Ardzrooni. New York: Viking Press, 1934.

JOHN BROADUS WATSON (1878–1958)

AMERICAN PSYCHOLOGIST

Animal Education. Chicago: University of Chicago Press, 1903.

Behavior. New York: Holt, 1914.

Psychology, from the Standpoint of a Behaviorist. Philadelphia: Lippincott: 1919. 3rd rev. ed., 1929.

Behaviorism. New York: Norton, 1925. Rev. ed., 1958.

The Battle of Behaviorism (with William McDougall). London: K. Paul, Trench, Trubner, 1928.

Psychological Care of Infant and Child. New York: Norton, 1928.

The Ways of Behaviorism. New York: Harper, 1928.

ALFRED WEBER (1868–1958)

GERMAN SOCIOLOGIST

WORKS IN GERMAN

Über den Standort der Industrien. Tübingen: Mohr (Siebeck), 1909.

Gedanken zur deutschen Sendung. Berlin: Fischer, 1915.

Die Krise des modernen Staatsdenkens. Stuttgart: Deutsche Verlagsanstalt, 1925.

Ideen zur Staats- und Kultursoziologie. Karlsruhe: Braun, 1927.

Kulturgeschichte als Kultursoziologie. Leiden: Sijthoff, 1935. 2nd ed., München: Piper, 1950.

Das Tragische und die Geschichte. Hamburg: Govert, 1943.

Abschied von der bisherigen Geschichte. Bern: Francke, 1946.

Prinzipien der Geschichts- und Kultursoziologie. München: Piper, 1951.

Der dritte oder der vierte Mensch. München: Piper, 1953.

Einführung in die Soziologie (with others). München: Piper, 1955.

WORKS IN ENGLISH TRANSLATION

Theory of the Location of Industries. Translated by C. J. Friedrich. Chicago: University of Chicago Press, 1929.

Farewell to European History. Translated by R. F. C. Hull. New Haven: Yale University Press, 1948.

MAX WEBER (1864–1920)

GERMAN ECONOMIST AND SOCIOLOGIST

WORKS IN GERMAN

Zur Geschichte der Handelsgesellschaften im Mittelalter. Stuttgart: Enke, 1889.

Die römische Agrargeschichte in ihrer Bedeutung fur das Staats- und Privatrecht. Stuttgart: Enke, 1891.

Parlament und Regierung im neugeordneten Deutschland. München: Duncker & Humblot, 1918.

Politik als Beruf. München, Leipzig: Duncker & Humblot, 1919.

Gesammelte Aufsätze zur Religionssoziologie. 3 vols. Tübingen: Mohr (Siebeck), 1920–1921.

Gesammelte politische Schriften. München: Drei Masken Verlag, 1921.

Gesammelte Aufsätze zur Wissenschaftslehre. Tübingen: Mohr (Siebeck), 1922.

Wirtschaft und Gesellschaft. 2 vols. Tübingen: Mohr (Siebeck), 1922.

Wirtschaftsgeschichte, ed. S. Hellman and M. Palyi. München: Duncker & Humblot, 1923.

Gesammelte Aufsätze zur Soziologie und Sozialpolitik. Tübingen: Mohr (Siebeck), 1924.

Gesammelte Aufsätze zur Sozial- und Wirtschaftsgeschichte. Tübingen: Mohr (Siebeck), 1924.

Jugendbriefe. Tübingen: Mohr (Siebeck), 1936.

WORKS IN ENGLISH TRANSLATION

General Economic History. Translated by Frank H. Knight. London: Allen & Unwin, 1927; Glencoe, Ill.: The Free Press, 1950.

The Protestant Ethic and the Spirit of Capitalism. Translated by Talcott Parsons. London: Allen & Unwin, 1930.

From Max Weber: Essays in Sociology. Translated and edited by Hans H. Gerth and C. Wright Mills. New York: Oxford University Press, 1946.

The Theory of Social and Economic Organization. Translated by A. M. Henderson and Talcott Parsons. New York: Oxford University Press, 1947.

Max Weber on the Methodology of the Social Sciences. Translated and edited by Edward A. Shils and H. A. Finch. Glencoe, Ill.: The Free Press, 1949.

The Hindu Social System. Translated by Hans Gerth and Don Martindale. Minneapolis: University of Minnesota Sociology Club, 1950.

The Religion of China: Confucianism and Taoism. Translated by H. H. Gerth. Glencoe, Ill.: The Free Press, 1951.

Ancient Judaism. Translated by H. H. Gerth and Don Martindale. Glencoe, Ill.: The Free Press, 1952.

Max Weber on Law in Economy and Society. Translated and edited by Edward Shils and Max Rheinstein. Cambridge, Mass.: Harvard University Press, 1954.

The City. Translated by Gertrud Neuwirth and Don Martindale. Glencoe, Ill.: The Free Press, 1958.

Rational and Social Foundations of Music, edited and translated by J. Riedel and Don Martindale. Carbondale, Ill.: Southern Illinois University Press, 1958.

The Religion of India. Translated by Don Martindale and H. H. Gerth. Glencoe, Ill.: The Free Press, 1958.

LOUIS WIRTH (1897–1952)

AMERICAN SOCIOLOGIST

The Ghetto. Chicago: University of Chicago Press, 1938.

Community Life and Social Policy, ed. E. Wirth Marvick and Albert J. Reiss, Jr. Chicago: University of Chicago Press, 1956.

FLORIAN ZNANIECKI (1882–1957)

POLISH-AMERICAN SOCIOLOGIST

The Polish Peasant in Europe and America (with William I. Thomas). 5 vols. Chicago: University of Chicago Press, 1918–1920.

Cultural Reality. Chicago: University of Chicago Press, 1919.

The Laws of Social Psychology. Chicago: University of Chicago Press, 1925.

The Method of Sociology. New York: Farrar & Rinehart, 1934.

Social Actions. New York: Farrar & Rinehart, 1936.

The Social Role of the Man of Knowledge. New York: Columbia University Press, 1940.

Modern Nationalities. Urbana, Ill.: University of Illinois Press, 1952.

Cultural Sciences, their Origin and Development. Urbana, Ill.: University of Illinois Press, 1952.

Index

Abel (Old Testament), 1242
Abraham (Old Testament), 697, 845, 1136
Abraham, K., 731
Accursius, 620
Acton, Lord, 268, 392–404, 1451
Adam (Old Testament), 1250
Adams, D. K., 794, 1464
Addams, Jane, 316, 742
Addington, Rev., 1232
Adler, Alfred, 915
Adorno, T. W., 692
Aeschylus (Greek dramatist), 1353
Agobard (Catholic reformer), 1119
Aikin, Dr., 1243, 1246, 1247
Aldricus, 614, 624
Alexander, 1035, 1157, 1357, 1362
Alexander of Macedon, 1361
Alexander II (czar), 1041
Althusius, 544
Amosis (Founder of the Eighteenth Dynasty), 1356
Andemar, Mlle., 831
Anderson, A., 1240, 1247
Anderson, James, 1232, 1233, 1240
Andreas-Salomé, Lou, 841, 842
Angell, Robert C., 40, 1455
Anne (Engish queen), 1045
Anrep, G. V., 764, 1471
Antinous, 1355
Antony, Mark, 597
Appian, 1232
Aquinas, Thomas, 673, 1139
Arber, 1229
Archilochos, 1130
Ardzrooni, Leon, 1478
Arendt, Hannah, 151
Arensberg, Conrad, 245
Aris, R., 1473
Aristophanes (Athenian dramatist), 1200
Aristotle (Greek philosopher), 21, 147, 471, 544, 573,
    616, 713, 1109, 1172, 1173, 1175, 1182, 1204,
    1210, 1254, 1313, 1314, 1351, 1382, 1419, 1447
Arkwright, Sir R., 77

Arnim, Count, 603
Arnold, Gottfried, 666
Arnold, Thurman, 1317
Ashley, M., 1458
Aspasia of Pericles, 551, 1130
Athanasius (Greek church father), 1133
Atkinson, C. F., 1343, 1475
Atkinson, John W., 697, 1266
Augier, Marie, 1247
Augustine, St., 670, 1118, 1119
Augustus, 597, 1143, 1356
Austin, 88, 433
Aveling, Eleanor Marx, 1468
Aveling, Edward, 1226, 1468
Azo, 614, 618, 620, 624

Babbage, 482
Baboeuf, 394
Bach, J., 398, 1317
Bacon, Francis, 1229, 1419, 1422
Bagehot, Walter, 91
Baillie, J. B., 1461
Baldus, 612
Baldwin, J. M., 155, 821, 831
Bales, Robert, 31, 76, 694, 696, 699, 707
Banbury, T. C., 1230
Barber, Bernard, 991
Barber, Elinor, 262
Barker, E., 1459
Barker, T. C., 1458
Barnard, Chester I., 64, 580, 632–641, 1451
Baron, Hans, 1478
Barrister, P., 1237
Barthel, E., 1317
Barton, R. F., 365
Basianus, Johannes, 614, 620
Bastian, 1093
Baudelaire, C. P., 1125, 1202
Bauer, Raymond A., 78
Bax, E. B., 1468
Baxter, R., 725, 727, 728, 1262, 1264

Beaurepaire, Commandant, 217
Bebel, August, 581, 604
Bedingfield, T., 1465
Beecher-Stowe, Harriet, 1234
Beethoven, Ludwig van, 988
Belin, 554
Bell, Charles, 1166, 1167–1168, 1451
Bell, Daniel, 1211
Bell, George J., 1451
Bellah, Robert N., 78, 241, 963, 985, 987, 993
Belsky, S., 1471
Benedict, Ruth, 675, 999, 1033, 1047–1050, 1451
Benfey, O. T., 1454
Bentham, J., 88, 89, 433, 1061, 1202, 1204, 1216, 1398
Bergson, H., 1204, 1212
Berlyne, D. E., 1471
Bernard of Clairvaux, 672
Bernheim, 900
Bernini, G., 1348
Bernward, Bishop, 1353
Berthold of Ratisbon, 673
Bertillon, A., 922
Bethmann-Hollweg, von, 603
Bexton, W. H., 692
Bichat, 131
Bickford-Smith, L., 1176
Binet, A., 864
Bismarck, 329, 542
Black, E. C., 256
Black, J. S., 1474
Black, Max, 79
Blakey, R., 1230
Blanqui, August, 609
Bleuler, 816
Bliss, W. D. P., 1470
Bloch, Herbert, 709
Bloch, Marc, 268, 385–392, 1452
Bloom, Allan, 1473
Blumenbach, 1024
Boas, Franz, 240, 998, 999, 1024–1032, 1034, 1452
Bodin, 120
Bodio, 917
Boeckh, 786
Bogen, H., 798
Bonaparte, M., 1457, 1467, 1468
Bonaventura, Saint, 673
Bongiorno, Andrew, 551, 589, 780, 1061, 1288, 1381, 1471
Borgoras, 369
Bosanquet, B., 1460
Bosquet, Amélie, 1082
Bossuet, J., 402, 647, 1157
Boulton, 480
Bouthoul, G., 1470
Boutroux, 679
Boyer, 1015

Bracke, 581
Bracton, 424, 425, 427, 428, 429
Brailsford, M. R., 1459
Bréal, 1015
Bridges, J. H., 1454
Bright, John, 1242
Brill, A. A., 887, 892, 1457
Brodbeck, A. J., 35
Brookfield, C., 1456
Brougham, Henry, 1247
Brunswick, Ruth Mack, 858, 904
Bryant, W. M., 1460
Buchanan, David, 1233, 1234
Buchanan, N., 1460
Bücher, Karl, 409, 493–504, 571, 1453
Buckez, 1239
Buddha, 1136, 1147, 1152, 1348
Bunker, Henry A., 799, 1457
Bunyan, John, 725
Burckhardt, Jacob, 1274
Burdach, K., 1346
Burdick, E., 35
Burgess, Ernest W., 1471
Burke, Edmund, 395, 402, 1166, 1167, 1231, 1247, 1369
Burke, Kenneth, 970, 971, 987, 988, 1200–1204, 1453
Burrow, 1202
Busch, 889

Caesar, Julius, 249, 317, 554, 597, 1024, 1117, 1127, 1319, 1462
Caffee, G. L., 1458
Cailliet, Emile, 1181
Cain (Old Testament), 102, 1242
Calvin, J., 22, 86, 725, 726, 727, 1259
Camberlege, Geoffrey, 1170
Campanella, 393
Camper, 1024
Cannan, E., 1474
Canney, M. A., 1460
Cannon, W. B., 37, 1166
Cantillon, 413
Carducci (the poet), 551
Carey (a great Russophile), 1242
Carlyle, Thomas, 606, 1107, 1216
Carr, Lowell J., 1455
Cartwright, D., 1464
Cary, H., 1234
Cassirer, Ernest, 997, 1004–1008, 1166, 1167, 1170–1178, 1453, 1454
Catlin, George E. G., 1456
Cato, M. P., 217
Cesari, E., 556
Chapelier, 1255

Charcot, J. M., 812
Charlemagne, 389, 401, 1232
Charles I, 1229, 1230
Charles V, 1237
Charles X, 597, 1231
Charles XI, 1231
Charles Albert (Austrian king), 398
Charles the Great, 402, 496
Charlevoix, P. de, 1078
Chaytor, A. H., 1466
Chéon, 1016
Cheops (King of Egypt), 1350
Chephren, 1347, 1350, 1351
Child, Irvin L., 697
Child, J., 1247
Chosroes-Nushirvan, 1351
Chrystal, G., 1474
Cicero, M. T., 554, 675, 1063, 1304, 1418
Clark, Russell A., 697
Claudian (of Alexandria in A.D. 400), 1361
Claudius (of Turin), 1119
Cleisthenes (Athenian statesman), 364
Clemence, R. V., 1473
Cloward, R. A., 709
Cobbett, William, 1230, 1244, 1245
Cobden, R., 1384
Codrington, R. H., 1081, 1089
Coghill, 778
Cohen, A. K., 709
Coke, Sir E., 422
Colbert, J. B., 1245
Cole, G. D. H., 1473
Colins, 1252
Commodus, L. A., 1141
Comte, Auguste, 16, 23, 24, 25, 26, 90, 91, 92, 93, 95,
    96, 97, 125–136, 147, 241, 645, 646–656, 686,
    966, 985, 1312, 1330, 1332–1342, 1419, 1422,
    1447, 1454, 14470
Comte, Charles, 1243
Conant, James B., 32
Condé, Prince de, 1140
Condorcet, Marquis de, 90, 130, 985
Confucius (Chinese philosopher), 657, 658, 955, 1348
Congreve, R., 1454
Conrad II (Italian emperor), 389, 1348
Conrad, J., 839
Constantine (Roman emperor), 1113
Cook, J., 1024
Cook, M., 1472
Cooley, Charles Horton, 96, 155, 240, 268, 315–318,
    331, 821, 822–829, 931, 945, 1430, 1439, 1455
Cooper, Goodman, 1240
Copernicus (Polish astronomer), 985
Cornwallis, Lord, 376, 378
Corre, 929
Cortegiano, 1131

Coste, A., 1320
Craik, G. M., 1460
Crocker, Roger, 1229
Cromwell, Oliver, 597, 727, 1126, 1229, 1230, 1242,
    1303
Culler, 748
Culpeper, T., 1247
Cummings, E. E., 1204
Cunnison, Ian, 169
Cunnison, J., 1468
Curr, E. M., 1084
Curtius, G., 1174, 1176
Cyrus (King of Persia), 1361, 1363

Dacres, E., 1465
Dalhousie, Earl of, 1235
Damon, Timothy Williams, 763
Dante, 17, 399, 594, 673, 878
Darwin, Charles Robert, 25, 89, 90, 94, 599, 826, 1024,
    1166, 1168–1169, 1171, 1204, 1209, 1266, 1455
Darwin, Francis, 1455
Davie, Maurice R., 1475
Dawson, J., 1084
D'Alembert, 120, 125
D'Arezzo, Lionardo, 98
De Bonald, 92
De Bourgoigne, 1240
De Coulanges, Fustel, 602, 645, 659–660, 1458
D'Este, Renate, Duchess, 1107
Defoe, 1264
De Grazia, Alfred, 603, 1469
De la Court, Pieter, 1263
De la Vega, Garcilasso, 103
De Leon, D., 1468
De Lupus, Hugo, 483
De Maistre, Count, 92, 397
De Melisso, 1175
Demosthenes (Athenian orator), 323, 1130
Deniker, J., 1084
Descartes, R., 1422
De Schlieffen, Count, 603
De Staël, Mme., 828
De Thoraine, Jacques, 1240
Detmold, Christian E., 98, 1465
Deuteronomy (Old Testament), 1157
Deutsch, Helene, Dr., 858
Devereux, G., 1464
Dewey, John, 1184
De Witt, J., 1245
Dickens, Charles, 9
Dickson, William John, 219, 348–356, 714, 1455, 1472
Diderot, D., 1408
Diesmann, 1145
Dilthey, Wilhelm, 91, 94, 989, 999

Diocletian (Roman emperor), 1113
Diogenes (Greek philosopher), 1351
Dobie, M. R., 1461
Dollard, John, 691, 697, 1406
Donkin, T. C., 1454
Doob, Leonard W., 691
Dostoevsky, F., 1160
Dowden, E., 1263
Downey, H. M., 1457
Doyle, A. C., 1262
Dubin, Robert, 79
Du Bois, Cora, 1465
Duffy, C. G., 1253
Dufour, Théophile, 1472
Dunning, P. J., 1247
Dupertuis, S., 1464
Du Prel, 1011
Durkheim, Emile, 6, 15, 18, 19, 20, 21, 22, 23, 25,
    26, 31, 39, 44, 55, 57, 59, 66, 87, 91, 92, 96, 97,
    149, 151, 154, 155, 184, 186, 187, 188, 189, 190,
    208–218, 241, 243, 249, 251, 268, 281, 292, 295,
    356–363, 408, 436–440, 645, 646, 677–682, 686,
    687, 688, 691, 699, 707, 708, 713, 719, 720–724,
    821, 822, 860–865, 869, 870, 871, 872–875, 916–
    928, 951, 952, 959–960, 972, 975, 982, 983, 985,
    990, 993, 997, 998, 1008–1009, 1032, 1054, 1055,
    1065, 1068–1070, 1093, 1166, 1167, 1187, 1210,
    1211, 1212, 1214, 1216, 1217, 1220, 1221, 1287,
    1288, 1305–1311, 1406, 1408, 1411, 1416, 1422,
    1445, 1447, 1455
Dvořák, A., 1156, 1347, 1349
Dyde, S. W., 112, 1461

Eckart, Meister, 1345, 1395
Eckstein, Harry, 1225
Eddington, Sir Arthur, 1314
Eden, Sir F. M., 1230, 1233, 1246, 1247
Eder, M. D., 1457
Edman, Irwin, 945, 946
Edward I, 1472
Edward III, 1237
Edward VI, 1236
Eggan, Fred, 290, 291, 295
Einstein, A., 985, 1076, 1219
Eisenstadt, S. N., 694
Eisler, Robert, 911
Elijah (Old Testament), 662, 663, 664
Elizabeth I (Queen of England), 1230, 1236, 1237,
    1238
Ellis, Sir H., 372
Ellis, Havelock, 839, 850
Emerson, G., 1464
Emerson, Ralph Waldo, 147, 1216

Engels, Frederick, 581, 585, 1209, 1226, 1249, 1463,
    1467, 1468
Ensor, George, 1234
Epicurus (Greek philosopher), 1174, 1351
Erikson, Eric H., 699, 987
Erman, A., 1082
Eroféeva, Dr., 769
Eros, J. S., 1467
Euclid (Greek geometer), 782
Evans-Pritchard (British anthropologist), 1034
Ezra (first scriptural scholar), 1157

Farnsworth, E., 1465
Fawcett, 1242
Fechner, T., 333
Fénelon, F., 394
Fenichel, Otto, 697, 750, 751
Ferenczi, 803, 909, 915
Fernandez, Francisco, 1375
Fielden, John, 1246
Figgis, J. N., 1451
Finch, H. A., 993, 1479
Firth, Raymond, 267, 1034, 1055
Fischer, Eugen, 1025
Fischer, O., 1344
Fisher, H. A. L., 1466
Fison, Lorimer, 1084
Flannigan, Edward, 931
Fletcher (of Saltoun Scotland), 1230
Fletcher, C. R. L., 594, 1361
Forbes, D., 1078
Forbes, Wilhelm, 838, 915
Ford, Henry, 572
Forde, 1034
Forster, E., 1232
Fortescue, Chancellor, 1228, 1229
Fournière, E., 573
Fox, Dixon Ryan, 1371
Fox, George, 1259
Fox, S. D., 1456
Foxley, Barbara, 1473
Franck, Sebastian, 666, 727
Frankfort, Henri, 987
Frankl, 1350
Franklin, Benjamin, 727, 1109, 1264
Franz, 778
Frazer, Sir James George, 678, 951, 952, 953, 958,
    1055, 1065, 1077–1088, 1093, 1190, 1456
Frederick II (German emperor), 1040, 1041, 1228,
    1235, 1240, 1241, 1348
Frederick William I, 392
Freeman, D., 372
Frere, W. H., 1186
Freud, Anna, 698, 911, 912, 1457

Freud, Ernst L., 1458
Freud, Sigmund, 6, 21, 25, 26, 27, 31, 62, 63, 76, 96,
    97, 154, 155, 189, 240, 241, 278, 687, 688, 689,
    692, 693, 697, 698, 703, 719, 720, 729–738, 747,
    750, 749, 751, 799–808, 821, 822, 838–852, 852–
    860, 869, 870, 871, 887–895, 896–903, 903–916,
    940–944, 968, 988, 998, 1010–1012, 1093, 1166,
    1167, 1202, 1210, 1211, 1212, 1216, 1221, 1225,
    1265–1270, 1411, 1456, 1457
Freyed, B., 1459
Friedrich, C. J., 45, 1478
Fromm, Erich, 1439

Gabain, M., 1471
Gagnebin, B., 1472
Galileo (Italian astronomer), 26, 985
Galsworthy, John, 878
Galton, Francis, 757
Gans, E., 1460
Gantt, W. H., 1471
Garfinkel, Harold, 714
Garofalo, M., 874
Gason, 1084
Gatschet, A. S., 1178
Gattegno, C., 1471
Gay, E. F., 420
Gay, P., 1454
Geertz, Clifford, 984, 988, 993
George II, 1238
George III, 1238
George, Stefan, 17, 331
Gerth, Hans H., 21, 1101, 1120, 1385, 1479
Giddings, Franklin, 1364, 1411
Gideon, 1388
Gierke, Otto von, 580, 611–626, 1458
Gifford, E. W., 281, 295, 368, 1463
Gilbert, Wm. H., Jr., 295
Giles, 424
Gillen, 317, 1084
Gillespie, W. M., 1454
Gillett, C. R., 1460
Giotto (Florentine painter), 673
Gisborne, 1246
Gladstone, Mary, 1451
Gladstone, Wm., 1238
Glueck, Eleanor, 714
Glueck, Sheldon, 714
Goblot, Edmond, 517, 535–540, 1459
Godunof, Boris, 1231
Godwin, William, 89, 92, 95, 106, 107, 108, 109, 111,
    415, 416, 417, 418.
Goethe, 17, 823, 907, 912, 1007, 1133, 1174, 1264,
    1352, 1453, 1454, 1474

Goffman, Erving, 716
Goldenweiser, A. A., 1057, 1366, 1367
Goldwin, 1242
Gorer, G., 698
Gorgias, 1174, 1175, 1353
Görres, 397
Gossen, 513
Gouldner, A. W., 1456
Goya (Spanish painter), 1219
Granet, Marcel, 1055, 1098–1100, 1459
Graves, 587
Gregory VII (the pope), 79, 1348
Greig, J. Y. T., 1462
Grimaldi (Genoese family), 383
Grimm, Jacob, 1174, 1177
Groot, Jeanne Lamplde, 858
Grosz, George, 1201
Grotius, St., 119 ,124
Groves, E. T., 1470
Grube, W., 1104
Guardi, 1353
Guieysse, 1016
Gülich, 1244
Gumplowics, 599, 600, 1365
Gutmann, J., 1454
Guyan, 863

Haakon V (King of Norway), 186
Hadrian (Pope), 1355
Haeckel, E., 1024
Hahn, Eduard, 1025
Haldane, E. S., 1461
Halévy, Elie, 87, 579
Halifax, Somers, 1231
Hall, G. S., 1457
Halle, Morris, 973, 974, 975
Haller, J., 1169
Hallowell, 1034
Hamilton, William, 1470
Hamon, 1382
Handel, G., 988
Hannibal (Carthaginian general), 1348
Harbord, James G., Major-general, 633, 635
Harnack, Adolf von, 646, 670–676, 1055, 1111–1120,
    1139, 1158, 1447, 1459
Harris, Seymour E., 992
Harrison, B., 1228, 1239
Harrison, Jane, 1186, 1188, 1189
Hartland, E. S., 1077
Hartenstein, 1308
Hartley, E. L., 701
Hartmann, Eduard von, 333
Hartmann, H., 698
Hartmann, R. S., 1461

Harvey, G., 1448
Hastings, Warren, 1243
Hawthorn, H. B., 20
Haydn, N., 1353
Hazael (Old Testament), 663
Hazeltine, H. D., 1466
Hebb, D. O., 692
Hegel, George W. F., 87, 88, 90, 91, 92, 93, 94, 95,
    112, 116, 147, 1216, 1217 1447, 1454, 1460, 1461
Heider, F., 1464
Heider, G. M., 1464
Heisenberg, Werner, 779, 1076
Hendel, C. W., 1454
Henderson, A. H., 219, 443, 470
Henderson, A. M., 173, 229, 418, 446, 460, 573, 626,
    1063, 1297, 1479
Henderson, L. J., 32–37
Henry II (English King), 424
Henry VI (English King), 1348
Henry VII (English King), 1229, 1236
Henry VIII (English King), 1229, 1236
Heracleitus (Ionian philosopher), 1357
Herder, J. von, 1024
Herodotus (Greek historian), 1024, 1045, 1189
Heron, W., 692
Hervé, Gustave, 604
Herzog, E., 1014
Hesiod (Greek poet), 1062, 1063, 1371
Hettner, 1030
Hewitt, 1091
Hi Ts'en, 1098
Hildebrand (Pope Gregory VI), 670
Himmelfarb, G., 1451
Hirshman, C. F., 1274
Hitler, A., 1035
Hobbes, Thomas, 26, 27, 86, 87, 90, 91, 92, 94, 95,
    99–100, 147, 183, 279, 543, 579, 1369, 1422, 1447,
    1461
Hobhouse, L. P., 747
Hodgskin, Th., 1243
Hodgson, F. M., 1471
Hohenstaufen, 675
Holinshed, 1228
Hollin, 235, 628
Hollingshead, A. B., 708
Holmes, Oliver Wendell, Jr., 429
Homer (Greek poet), 317, 497, 660, 1044, 1174, 1189,
    1348
Honzik, C. H., 1477
Hopkins, G., 1452
Horn, 1016
Horner, Francis, 1246
Horney, K., 1318, 1439
Hosea (Old Testament), 663
Howard, H., 316

Howitt, A. W., 1079, 1084
Howitt, William, 1242
Hsün Tse, 955
Hubback, C. J. M., 1457
Hubert, Henri, 1055, 1088–1090, 1461, 1468
Hügel, F. von, 1478
Hughes, Everett C., 157
Hugolinus, 612, 613, 617, 624
Hull, Clark L., 690, 691, 748, 749, 770–772, 1461
Hull, R. F. C., 1478
Humboldt, Baron von, 397, 1177
Hume, David, 278, 645, 646, 656–658, 957, 1219, 1461,
    1462
Hung Wu (Founder of Ming dynasty), 1356
Hunt, George, 1452
Hunter, Dr., 1229
Hus, J., 393
Hutcheson (Scottish philosopher), 606
Hutton, H. D., 1454
Hutton, J. H., 365, 367
Huxley, T. H., 90, 1024, 1026
Hyades, P., 1084
Hymes, Dell W., 975

Iamblichus (pagan Father), 1355
Ibn Batuta, 1024
Ibn Khaldun, 1210
Ibsen, H., 1011
Immermann, 496
Ingram, J. K., 1454
Inkeles, A., 78, 698
Innes, K. E., 1459
Innocent III (pope), 79, 249, 1348, 1399, 1400

Jackson, Andrew, 1475
Jaffé, William, 1470
Jakobson, Roman, 973, 974, 975
James I, 1229, 1230, 1236, 1238
James, William, 678, 757, 822, 1212
Janet, P., 831, 832
Jannaeus, Alexander, 1151
Jaspers, Karl, 21
Janrès, Jean, 604
Jeffres, L. A., 1477
Jenghiz, Kahn, 1035
Jephthah, 1388
Jevons, F. B., 1080
Joan of Arc, 722
Job (Old Testament Book of), 1151, 1155, 1156
Johann XXII, 1400
John, King, 1237

Johnston, W. H., 1461
Jones, Ernest, 21, 697, 887
Jones, Katherine, 1265, 1457
Jones, Peter, 1078
Jorio, Andrea de, 1172
Joseph II (German emperor), 1041
Josephus, Flavius, 911
Jowett, B., 471
Joyce, J., 1201
Julian (Roman emperor), 1141
Jung, C., 1202
Justinian I (Byzantine emperor), 617, 1351, 1353

Kahn, Hannah D., 598, 1470
Kant, I., 17, 152, 158, 548, 1007, 1200, 1217, 1219,
    1278, 1279, 1281, 1308, 1344, 1454, 1474
Kantorowicz, G., 1474
Kardiner, A., 698
Karl, 603
Kassel, 1460
Kaulbach (a painter), 738
Kautsky, Karl, 1463, 1468
Kaysen, Carl, 992
Kayser, Christine, 1138
Kecskemeti, P., 1467
Keller, Albert G., 1475
Kennet, 1229
Kent, J., 1232
Kepler, J., 985
Kerr, Charles F., 529
Keynes, John Maynard, 408, 447–454, 1210, 1462,
    1473
Kierkegaard, Sören, 726
Kirkwood, K. P., 1477
Kirtko, D., 1463
Klatt, B., 1025
Klemm, 1024
Kluckhohn, Clyde, 73, 78, 983, 1034, 1463
Kluge, G. von, 1016
Knight, Frank Hyneman, 408, 434, 1462, 1479
Knowland, Frederic Wm., 1466
Knox, R. A., 1361
Knox, T. M., 1461
Koch, Sigmund, 34
Koelln, F. C. A., 1454
Kohl, J. G., 1078
Köhler, B. W., 1175
Kohler, J., 281, 282, 292, 296, 691, 749
Köhler, Wolfang, 748, 772–776, 778, 1462
Kolabinska, 551, 552, 553
Koldewey-Puchstein, 1352
Kolegar, Ferdinand, 296, 305, 611
Koshtoyants, K. S., 1471

Kozlowski, J. T., 1463
Kraepelin, 816
Kreemer, J., 1078
Krestovnikov, Dr., 768
Kris, E., 698, 1457
Krishna (Hindu deity), 1391, 1394
Kristeller, P. O., 1454
Kroeber, Alfred L., 33, 267, 271, 275, 283, 284, 296,
    365, 366, 984, 985, 995, 1032–1036, 1209, 1218,
    1219, 1288, 1321–1324, 1462
Kropotkins, P., 587
Kuhn, H., 1468
Kunity, J., 1463
Kuttner, A. B., 1457

Lafendel, 831
Lagrange, J., 131
Laïnez, 1154
La Marck, Comte de, 600
Lamarck (biologist), 1024
Landes, David S., 256, 993
Landmann, Michael, 1474
Landshut, Siegfried, 1467
Lane, Ralph, 1375
Lange, G., 1204
Langer, Suzanne, 1166, 1179–1189, 1454, 1463
Langsdon, F. J., 1472
Lao-tse, 1109, 1153
Lapouge, 1382
La Rochefoucauld, N., 1204
Lasalle, Ferdinand, 225, 581, 584, 585, 603
Lashley, Karl, 778
Laud, W., 1264
Laurence, R. V., 1451
Law, John, 506
Lawrence, 1204
Lazarsfeld, Paul F., 1406
Lazarus (New Testament), 1152
Le Bon, Gustave, 174
Lecoeur, J., 1082
Le Dantec (French biologist and philosopher), 690
Lee, D. D., 701
Legoyt, 918
Leibniz, 1006, 1007, 1176, 1204
Lenin, Nicolai, 95, 579, 580–588, 1220, 1463
Le Play, Frédéric, 408, 457–459, 556, 1463, 1464
Lepidus, M., 597
Leroy, 1014
Lersch, L., 1174
Levasseur, P., 357, 358
Levi, Leone, 1235
Levine, D., 18
Levinson, D. J., 692, 698

Index

Lévi-Strauss, C., 52, 267
Levy, D. M., 692
Lévy-Bruhl, Lucien, 1053, 1056, 1057
Lewin, G. V., 1464
Lewin, Kurt, 749, 779, 794–798, 1421, 1438, 1464
Lightwood, 428
Lincoln, Abraham, 709
Lindner (Hungarian pediatrician), 839
Lindzev, G., 698
Linguet, 1237
Linnaeus, C., 1024
Linton, Ralph, 185, 186, 190, 202–208, 309, 1034, 1216, 1330, 1371, 1464
Lipmann, O., 798
Lippert, Julius, 1368
Lippincott, B. E., 475
Littleton, 428
Livingston, Arthur, 551, 589, 780, 1061, 1288, 1381, 1470
Lloyd, H. H., 1470
Locke, John, 87, 88, 89, 90, 91, 93, 96, 101–103, 147, 579, 1464
Louis VI, 1237
Louis XIV (French king), 256, 551
Louis XV (French king), 551
Louis XVI (French king), 556, 592, 595, 597
Louis Philippe, 598, 1304
Lowell, Edgar L., 697
Lowenstein, R., 698
Lowie, Robert H., 268, 364–369, 572, 1034, 1366, 1465
Loyola, Ignatius, 675
Lucca, 99
Lucretius (Roman poet), 554
Lunden, Walter A., 1475
Lunzer, J. L., 1472
Luther, Martin, 22, 86, 393, 676, 725, 726, 1127, 1139
Lyall, A. C., 1080
Lycurgus (Spartan lawgiver), 786, 1040
Lysicrates, 1354

Macaulay, Thomas B., 554, 1228, 1230
McClelland, David, C., 697
MacCulloch, 411, 1232
McDougall, William, 696, 747, 749, 751–758, 778, 779, 1465, 1478
Machiavelli, Niccolo, 15, 27, 85, 86, 87, 98, 147, 1254, 1447, 1465
MacIver, Robert M., 1219, 1330, 1364–1371, 1466
McKenzie, R. D., 1471
M'Lennan, John F. M., 278, 279, 296
Macran, H. S., 1461

Macrobius, 784
Maeder, A., 887
Magnus, Albertus, 673
Maine, Henry Sumner, 91, 139, 147, 184, 267, 364, 365, 367, 369, 370–408, 429,–436, 1217, 1466
Maintenon, F., 551
Maitland, Frederic W., 253, 408, 422, 1458, 1466, 1472
Malebranche, 1333
Malinowski, Bronislaw, 52, 169, 170, 245, 267, 276–278, 369, 572, 700, 871, 947–949, 952, 957, 991, 1053, 1054, 1055, 1056–1060, 1091–1095, 1166, 1189–1191, 1466
Mallery, G., 1172
Mallinkrodt, 603
Malthus, Thomas R., 25, 27, 89, 90, 94, 96, 106–112, 147, 407, 415–418, 1209, 1467
Mamiani, Terenzio, 605
Mancini, Stanislas, 605
Mandelbaum, O. G., 1473
Manin, 399
Mann, H., 1040
Mannhardt, 1093
Mannheim, Karl, 989, 991, 992, 993, 1004, 1054, 1070–1076, 1467
Mannheim, Ralph, 1170, 1454, 1456
Manteuffel, 398
Marco Polo, 414, 1024, 1362
Marcus Aurelius, 1117
Marheineke, P., 1460
Marquardt, 602
Marriott, W. K., 1465
Marshall, Alfred, 31, 372, 379, 407, 409–410, 454, 478–492, 1467
Martel, Charles, 389
Martha (New Testament), 1395
Martindale, Don, 380, 1479
Martineau, Harriet, 125, 646, 1332, 1454
Martineau, M., 1312
Martinus, 624
Martyn, Thomas, 1473
Marvick, E. Wirth, 1479
Marx, Karl, 25, 27, 91, 92, 93, 94, 95, 96, 97, 136–139, 147, 184, 255, 263, 407, 517, 529–534, 575, 581, 582, 583, 584, 585, 587, 686, 989, 990, 1200, 1202, 1209, 1211, 1212, 1214, 1217, 1225, 1226–1253, 1463, 1467, 1468, 1473
Mary, Virgin, 1391
Mary (New Testament), 1395
Maspero, G., 1082
Mathew, J., 1084
Matthews, Washington, 1078
Maudsley, 1009
Maunier, R., 572
Maurras, Charles, 606

Mauss, Marcel, 156–157, 169–172, 1054, 1055, 1065–1068, 1088–1090, 1461, 1468
Maximilian (Holy Roman emperor), 1078
Maxwell, Clerk, 985
Mayer, 887
Mayo, Elton, 1406
Mazzini, Giuseppe, 394, 399
Mead, George Herbert, 15, 96, 149, 152, 154, 155, 156, 163–168, 240, 686, 688, 713, 720, 739–740, 750, 751, 821, 829–830, 869, 876–886, 979, 997, 999–1004, 1034, 1166, 1167, 1468
Mead, Margaret, 292, 296
Means, S., 1460
Medici, Cosimo, 98
Medici, Gian Angelo, 1046
Medici, Giovanni, 98
Meeson, 426
Mehemet, Ali, 600
Meillet, Antoine, 998, 1013–1018, 1468
Meinhold, 1157
Meninger, 1015
Menno, 1259
Meringer, 887
Merivale, 1251
Merriam, T. W., 1462
Merton, Robert K., 18, 20, 75, 95, 706, 991
Metternick, K. von, 398
Meyer, A., 778
Michelangelo (Italian sculptor), 17, 1353
Michelet, C. L., 1460
Michelet, K. L., 1460
Michels, Robert, 579, 603–610, 633, 1220, 1469
Michelson, A., 982
Milford, Humphrey, 1091
Mill, John Stuart, 88, 89, 92, 117, 118, 399, 506, 598, 1216, 1242, 1469
Miller, H. A., 697, 1471
Miller, Neal E., 691
Miller, Walter B., 709
Milligan, Martin, 1468
Mills, C. Wright, 1120, 1385, 1479
Mills, Theodore M., 18, 20, 21
Mirabeau, H. de, 600, 1228, 1235, 1241, 1246
Misch, George, 987
Mitchell, F. K., 1460
Mithras, 1157
Mo Ti, 955
Moffatt, J., 1460
Mohammed (Arab prophet), 1140
Mohammed II, 600
Molesworth, Wm., 1461
Molinari, 1251, 1252
Mollatt, G., 1460
Moltke, H. von, 17
Monteil, Alexis, 1240

Montesquieu, 15, 430, 554, 1245, 1456
Moore, M. H., 1468
Moore, Samuel, 1226, 1468
More, Thomas, 393, 1229, 1236
Morgan, Lewis H., 267, 269, 271, 278, 279, 280, 281, 282, 283, 284, 287, 296, 364, 365, 367, 369, 529, 1470
Morgan, Lloyd, 1032
Morgan, W., 1232
Morley, J., 982
Morris, Charles W., 829, 999, 1468
Morrison, Elting, 73
Mosbacher, E., 1457
Mosca, Gaetano, 579, 598–602, 608, 1220, 1470
Moses (Old Testament), 662, 1040, 1042, 1139, 1269
Mowrer, O. H., 692, 1461
Moyses, 613
Mozart, W., 988, 1353
Müeller, John, 1002
Mueller, J. H., 872, 1456
Müller, F., 397
Müller, Max, 997
Müller-Lyer, F., 1367
Murad, Sultan (of Turkey), 1375
Murdock, George P., 242, 268, 691, 1034, 1368
Murphy, A. E., 1468
Murray, Gilbert, 1187, 1188
Murray, H. A., 63, 697
Musset, Alfred de, 927
Mussolini, Benito, 604
Myres, J. L., 1057

Näcke, P., 731
Nadel, S. F., 1034
Naegele, Kaspar D., 147–157, 183–190, 331, 1207–1222, 1225–1226, 1287–1288, 1329–1331
Napoleon, 380, 392, 397, 398, 552, 597, 609, 742, 1035, 1040, 1304
Napoleon II, 1302
Napoleon III, 592, 598, 1063, 1304
Nasse, Prof., 379, 380
Nauck, 786
Neiderhoffer, Arthur, 709
Nerva, M., 1348, 1354
Nesselrode, Count C., 397
Nestor, 431
Nestroy, Johann, 908
Neuwirth, Gertrud, 380, 1479
Newcomb, T. M., 701
Newman, F. W., 1231, 1233
Newton, Sir I., 25, 26, 410, 782, 985, 1006, 1219, 1447, 1448

Nietzsche, Friedrich, 17, 25, 154, 548, 815, 1150, 1210, 1216, 1344, 1387, 1474
Nightingale, Florence, 742
Nimkoff, Meyer F., 1470
Nohl, H., 1460
Norded, H., 1473
Numa, 125, 1040

Octavius, Caesar, 597
Ogburn, William F., 1219, 1226, 1270–1273, 1470
Ohlin, L. E., 709
Oldenberg, H., 1080, 1081, 1884
Olds, James, 62, 66, 692, 693, 968
Olgin, Moissaye J., 580, 1463
Opie, R., 1473
Opler, M. E., 296
Oppenheimer, Franz, 245, 1365
Origen (Greek writer), 1354
Orkney, Lady, 1231
Osmaston, F. P. B., 1461
Otto (Holy Roman emperor), 1348
Ovid (Roman poet), 1078
Owen, S. G., 1456
Oxford, Earl of, 1231

Page, Charles H., 1466
Paley (archdeacon), 111
Palow, von, 603
Papini, G., 1317
Pareto, Vilfredo, 15, 21, 31, 37, 240, 517, 518, 551–558, 573, 579, 589–598, 606, 608, 610, 686, 749, 780–786, 1054, 1061–1063, 1210, 1214, 1215, 1216, 1217, 1220, 1287, 1288–1292, 1330, 1381–1385, 1470
Park, Robert E., 240, 695, 709, 870, 944–946, 1406, 1434, 1439, 1471
Parker, 1264
Parmenides (Greek philosopher), 1207
Parsons, Talcott, 11, 32, 34, 62, 65, 75, 76, 79, 86–97, 173, 219, 229, 239–264, 267–268, 407–408, 418, 443, 446, 460, 470, 517–518, 573, 579–580, 626, 645–646, 694, 695, 696, 697, 699, 706, 707, 708, 709, 712, 724, 750, 751, 870, 963–993, 997–998, 1053–1056, 1063, 1165–1167, 1253, 1297, 1479
Pascal, R., 1468
Pasteur, L., 742, 1203
Paul, B. D., 991
Paul, C., 1468, 1469
Paul, H., 1451
Paulhan, 1014
Pavlov, Ivan P., 690, 747, 748, 764–770, 1471
Pearson, Harry, 245

Peel, Robert, 1246, 1249, 1250, 1253
Pelham, Peter, 1371
Penn, William, 1133
Pericles (Athenian statesman), 1353
Peristiany, J. G., 1305
Peter (New Testament), 672, 674, 1117, 1353
Peter the Great, 1040, 1041
Petronius (Roman satirist), 957, 1200
Pettegrove, J. P., 1454
Petty, William, 1264, 1433
Pharaoh (Old Testament), 661, 1267
Phidias (Greek sculptor), 1353
Philine, 789
Philip (of Macedon), 1356
Phiops I, 1350
Phiops II, 1350
Piaget, Jean, 15, 18, 24, 698, 821, 830–834, 835–837, 1471
Piercy, M., 1471
Pigou, A. C., 452, 509
Pillius, 612, 624
Pinchot, Gifford, 1272
Pisano, Nicholas, 1147
Pitts, Jesse R., 262, 457, 535, 685–715, 719–720, 747–750, 821–822, 860, 869–871, 950, 1013, 1065, 1088
Pius IX (pope), 1118
Placentinus, 613, 618, 624
Planck, Max, 1314
Plantagenet (ruling family of England), 483
Plato (Greek philosopher), 147, 393, 478, 544, 548, 554, 573, 675, 945, 1007, 1104, 1131, 1172, 1210, 1382, 1456
Plautus, T., 435
Plotinus (Roman philosopher), 393, 1188, 1354
Pocock, D. F., 1305, 1456
Poggio (Italian historian), 98
Pogson, F. L., 1460
Poincaré, Henri, 1407
Polanyi, Karl, 245
Pollock, Sir Frederick, 253, 408, 422–428, 429, 1466, 1472
Polybius (Greek historian), 1447
Pompey (Roman general), 1157
Poseidon, 1061, 1062
Preuss, 678, 1009
Prezzolini, 556
Price, Dr., 107, 1232
Proctor-Gregg, N., 1457
Prynne (Puritan), 1264
Putnam, P., 1452
Pythagoras (philosopher), 131, 653, 1147

Quelch, H., 1468

Radcliffe-Brown, A. R., 267, 278–296, 871, 951–958, 986, 1166, 1191–1199, 1472
Radin, Paul, 1034
Raffles, Thomas Stamford, 1243
Raleigh, Sir Walter, 1375
Ramon (Indian chief), 1047
Randall, J. H., Jr., 1454
Rank, Otto, 802
Rathgen, 385
Ratzel, 1009
Raumer, Friedrich von, 609
Ray, P. Orman, 605
Raymond, M., 1472
Redfield, Robert, 1034, 1216, 1467
Redlech, F. C., 708
Reid, L. A., 1182
Reinach, S., 786
Reiss, Albert J., Jr., 1479
Rembrandt (Dutch painter), 17, 1474
Rheinstein, Max, 1479
Ribot, T., 696, 747, 753, 755
Ricardo, David, 90, 94, 136, 1246, 1447
Rickert, Heinrich, 94
Rickman, John, 698, 1457
Riedel, J., 1479
Riegl, 1354
Riesman, David, 73
Riggs, 274, 275
Rivers, W. H. R., 279, 281, 283, 284, 287, 293, 296
Riviere, Joan, 729, 903, 940, 1457
Roberto, George, 1230
Robespierre, M. de, 1303
Robinson, E. W., 136
Robinson, G., 1229
Robson-Scott, W. D., 1457
Rodbertus, 300, 461
Rodin, F., 17
Roethlisberger, Fritz Jules, 219, 348–356, 714, 1406, 1455, 1472
Roffredus of Benevant, 616, 618
Rogers, Prof., 1230, 1242
Roosevelt, Theodore, 1272
Roscher, 486
Rosegger, P. K., 498
Rostow, W. W., 74
Rousseau, Jean Jacques, 16, 88, 91, 92, 93, 95, 96, 97, 119–124, 136, 394, 402, 554, 606, 844, 1024, 1156, 1217, 1241, 1353, 1369, 1454, 1456, 1472, 1473
Roux, 1239
Royère, Jean, 1202
Rückert, 818
Rümelin, Max, 232
Russell, Bertrand, 1320
Russell, John, Lord, 1231

Sachs, Hanns, 888
Sahu-rê, 1351
Salmeron, 1154
St. Bartholomew, 727
St. Francis of Assissi, 572, 673, 675, 676, 1136
Saint Hilaire, Geoffrey, 1240
St. Luke, 1460
St. Matthew, 1123, 1460
St. Paul, 1117, 1118, 1119, 1148, 1157, 1158, 1268, 1269, 1363
Saint-Simon, 15, 90, 604, 1422, 1456
Sanderson, J. B., 1461
Santayana, George, 871, 945, 946
Sapir, Edward, 286, 998, 1018, 1473
Sappho (Greek poet), 1130
Sattler, Charlotte, 1456
Saunders, Thomas Bailey, 1111, 1460
Savigny, 426
Say, J. B., 505
Schaeffle, Otto, 15
Scheler, Max, 989, 1167, 1317, 1447
Schelting, Alexander von, 989
Schiller, J. von, 1024, 1207, 1220, 1453
Schmalenbach, Herman, 268, 331–347, 1473
Schmidt, Father, 278
Schmoller (Prussian House of Lords), 1383
Schneidewin, 786
Schopenhauer, A., 17, 1474
Schumpeter, E. B., 1473
Schumpeter, Joseph A., 64, 95, 255, 262, 409, 505–513, 1473
Schwab, A., 1016
Schwartz, Morris S., 710
Schwarzenberg, 398
Scipio (Roman general), 1348
Scott, T. H., 692
Scupin, 832
Sears, Robert, 691, 692
Seligman, Brenda Z., 281, 296
Sering, 303
Servius, 125
Sesostris (Egypt), 1353
Shakespeare, William, 823, 1131, 1169, 1351
Shand, A. F., 747, 755
Shein, E. H., 692
Shils, Edward, 11, 27, 31, 964, 993, 1405–1448, 1467, 1479
Shrewsbury, Duke of, 1231
Sibree, J., 1460
Sidonius, Apollinaris, 1361
Siebeck, Paul, 296
Siebert, 1084
Simmel, Georg, 15, 17, 19, 20, 21, 22, 23, 25, 152, 153, 154, 155, 156–162, 268, 318–330, 340, 517, 540–551, 749, 787–794, 945, 1167, 1210, 1214, 1288, 1324–1325, 1473, 1474

Simpson, George, 208, 213, 356, 362, 436, 1456
Simson, F. H., 1461
Sirach, 1157
Sirnis, A., 1463
Sismondi, J., 1248
Skeat, W. W., 1078
Small, Willard, 1458
Smelser, Neil J., 31, 65, 76, 77, 255
Smith, Adam, 15, 25, 88, 104, 136, 104–105, 407, 409,
    114–414, 415, 416, 479, 494, 518–528, 606, 1226,
    1233, 1234, 1237, 1242, 1247, 1337, 1433, 1447,
    1474
Smith, Elliot, 278
Smith, W. Robertson, 249, 278, 645, 646, 661–664,
    952, 1055, 1093, 1096–1097, 1166, 1266, 1447,
    1474
Snigge, Sergeant, 1230
Socrates (Greek philosopher), 875, 1200
Sohm, Rudolf, 235, 628, 1447
Solomon, 1358
Solovay, Sarah, 872, 1456
Sombart, Werner, 91, 94, 989
Somers, Robert, 1234, 1235
Somervell, D. C., 1355
Somló, F., 572
Sophocles (Greek dramatist), 786, 891, 987
Sorel, Georges, 592, 605, 610, 1210, 1216
Sorokin, Pitirim A., 570–572, 1216, 1219, 1288, 1311–
    1321, 1474
Spaulding, John A., 213, 362, 916, 1456
Speirs, E. B., 1461
Spence, 426
Spencer, Herbert, 24, 26, 33, 89, 90, 91, 139–143, 147,
    152, 184, 241, 317, 436, 437, 441, 442, 686, 786–
    794, 985, 998, 999, 1021–1023, 1032, 1084, 1209,
    1216, 1364, 1475
Spener, 727, 1109
Spengler, Oswald, 94, 946, 1036, 1200, 1216, 1217,
    1218, 1219, 1330, 1343–1355, 1475
Spéranski, 1015
Spier, L., 1034
Spinoza, B., 1204, 1472
Spiridonova, Maria, 742
Spitz, René, 693
Sprott, W. J. H., 852, 1457
Ssu-ma Ch'ien, 1106
Stafford, William, 1240
Stammler, Rudolf, 230, 231
Stanley, Hiram M., 822
Stanton, Alfred H., 710
Starcke, C. N., 283, 296
Statius, P., 957
Stein, Freiherr vom, 397
Stein, Gertrude, 15
Steinthal, 1174
Stekel, W., 891

Stengel, E., 1457
Stephen, Sir Leslie,, 1466
Stern, James, 832, 1458
Stern, Tania, 1458
Steuart, Sir James, 1228, 1233, 1240
Stewart, Dugald, 278, 296
Stewart, W. A. C., 1467
Stoddart, Cyril, 930
Stoll, 1046
Stone, Gregory P., 331
Stone, N. I., 136, 1468
Stonequist, Everett V., 709, 944, 945
Stouffer, S. A., 700
Strachey, A., 1317, 1457
Strachey, James, 838, 1010, 1457
Stradivarius, A., 410
Strype, 1236
Stuarts, the, 1230, 1264
Stutz, U., 1301
Sturzo, Don, 607
Styles, Dr., 107
Sulla, L., 592, 597
Sullivan, Harry S., 699
Sully, T., 862
Sumner, William Graham, 944, 999, 1037–1046, 1211,
    1434, 1439, 1475
Sunderland, 1231
Susman, Margaret, 1474
Sutherland, Alex, 755
Sutherland, Duchess of, 1234
Sutherland, Edwin H., 705
Sutton, Francis X., 992
Swabey, M. C., 1454
Swabey, W. C., 1454
Swadeah, M., 1473
Swain, Joseph Ward, 677, 959, 1009, 1068, 1456
Swan, Joseph, 720
Sykes, G. M., 712
Symonds, J., 1046

Tacitus (Roman historian), 1024, 1140, 1301
Taine, H., 554
Talleyrand, C. de, 397, 1353
Tamerlane (Mongol conqueror), 886
Tancredus, 625
Tarde, Gabriel, 174, 210, 606, 685, 1032
Tauler, 673
Taussig, F. W., 572
Tax, Sol, 288, 289, 290, 296
Tchernoff, 586
Teuber, E., 775
Thales (Greek philosopher), 131, 1188
Theocritus (Greek poet), 519, 1078
Theotokos, 1147

Thomas, William I., 96, 240, 686, 688, 697, 720, 741–744, 748, 870, 930, 932, 934–940, 1287, 1292–1297, 1439, 1476, 1479
Thompson, W. H., 1471
Thomson, N. H., 1465
Thoreau, H., 1216
Thorndike, A., 690, 747, 748, 749
Thorndyke, Edward Lee, 762–764, 795, 1476
Thornton, W., 1229
Thrasher, Frederic M., 870, 929–934, 1476
Thucydides (Greek historian), 1254, 1447
Thurnwald, R., 369, 572
Tietz, 603
Timasheff, N. S., 226
Tito, Marshal, 6
Titus Livius, 1465
Tobin, James M., 992
Tocqueville, Alexis de, 1418, 1447
Toennies, Ferdinand, 183, 184, 185, 186, 187, 190, 191–201, 219, 268, 331, 332, 333, 343, 1216, 1447, 1476
Tolman, Edward C., 692, 694, 696, 748, 749, 777–779, 1477
Tolstoy, L., 1035, 1112, 1160, 1216
Tomlinson, J., 1471
Tomlinson, L., 1471
Torr, Dona, 1468
Tournefort, 1061
Toynbee, A. J., 1216, 1219, 1318, 1330, 1355–1364, 1477
Trajan (Roman emperor), 1117, 1354
Troeltsch, Ernst, 332, 579, 645, 646, 664–670, 1055, 1120, 1220, 1274, 1477
Tryon, R. C., 1477
Tseretelli, 586
Tucker, Rev., 1247
Tuckett, J. D., 1230, 1242
Tugan-Baranowsky, 585
Tweed, W., 1464
Tylor, E. B., 33, 91, 287, 368, 948, 997, 1032, 1093

Uexküll, von, 794, 795
Ulysses, 431
Untermann, E., 1468
Urban (pope), 1141
Urquhart, David, 1241, 1242

Vallabha, 1143
Vanderbilt, Cornelius, 706
Van Emden, J. E. G., 894
Van Gnnep, Arnold, 871, 950–951, 1458
Vasari, G., 1345
Vaughan, C. E., 1473

Veblen, Thorstein, 517, 518, 558–570, 742, 1225, 1478
Velleius, Paterculus, 1352
Vendryes, J., 1469
Vercingetroix, 1361
Vergniaud, 395
Vernon, Secretary, (Eng.), 1231
Vico, Giambattista, 609
Victor-Emmanuel (King of Italy), 917
Vierkandt, Alfred, 1185
Vignola, G. da, 1348
Villeneuve, Admiral, 217
Villon (French poet), 1016, 1219
Vinci, Leonardo da, 1457
Vincke, von, 603
Virgil, P., 1078
Vischer, Th., 890
Visconti, Filippo, 98
Vitruvius, M., 1352
Vizedom, M. B., 1458
Volkart, Edmund H., 741, 934, 1476
Voltaire, F., 554

Waitz, 1024
Wakefield, E. G., 1249, 1250, 1251, 1252, 1253
Walker, L. J., 1465
Wallace, W., 1209, 1460, 1461
Walton, John B., 758–762
Ward, Lester F., 1364
Warden, M., 1471
Warner, C., 1406
Washington, George, 709
Waterman, T. T., 1462
Watson, J. B., 690, 741, 747, 748, 749, 1001, 1478
Watt, J., 480
Watteau, J., 1353
Weber, Alfred, 94, 989, 1219, 1226, 1274–1283, 1478
Weber, Max, 6, 15, 19, 21, 23, 25, 26, 27, 28–31, 50, 77, 78, 92, 93, 94, 97, 149, 151, 152, 155, 156, 173–179, 183, 185, 189, 190, 219–235, 241, 246, 249, 253, 255, 268, 296–308, 331, 332, 343, 344, 345, 346, 347, 380–384, 407, 408, 418, 443–446, 460–478, 518, 573–576, 580, 603, 608, 626–632, 645, 646, 686, 687, 705, 719, 724–729, 970, 983, 984, 985, 986, 989, 991, 992, 993, 1054, 1055, 1056, 1063–1065, 1075, 1093, 1100–1110, 1129–1137, 1138–1161, 1167, 1210, 1211, 1212, 1214, 1215, 1216, 1217, 1219, 1220, 1221, 1225, 1253–1265, 1274, 1277, 1287, 1297–1304, 1317, 1330, 1331, 1385–1402, 1406, 1408, 1411, 1416, 1426, 1427, 1433, 1439, 1442, 1445, 1447, 1479
Webster, J., 1100
Weiss, 778
Welsby, 426
Weltfish, Gene, 1452

Weltner, G. H., 1274
Wertham, Frederick, 714
Wesley, John, 1109, 1259, 1262, 1263
Westermann, D., 1176
Westermarck, E., 316
Westphal, W., 1076
White, Leslie, 1032, 1470
Whitefield, S., 1106
Whitehead, A. N., 32, 148, 964, 1204, 1210
Whitehorne, P., 1465
Whiting, John, 691
Whittaker, W. S., 1466
Whorf, Benjamin Lee, 701, 974
Whyte, William Foote, 712
Wickett, S. Morley, 493, 1453
Wiedemann, A., 1082
Wilberforce, Bishop William, 1045
William (King), 1231
William I (King of Prussia), 542, 1063
William II (German King), 605
William the Conqueror, 483, 555
William of Orange, 1231
Wilkinson, J. R., 1460
Wilson, Woodrow, 1434
Windelband, Wilhelm, 94

Winter, Ella, 1462
Wirth, Louis, 268, 309–314, 1467
Wise, G. M., 692
Wittvogel, Karl, 50
Woglom, W. H., 1454
Wolff, Kurt H., 318, 540, 787, 1324, 1474
Woodruff, D., 1451
Wright, Thomas, 429, 1232
Wundt, Wilhelm, 747, 947, 1017, 1171, 1172, 1173
Wycliffe, John, 393
Wyon, Olive, 664, 1478

Yves-Guyot, 603

Zeldich, Morris, Jr., 699
Zeuner, K. E., 794, 1464
Zeuxis (Greek painter), 1353
Zimmerman, Carle Clark, 1464, 1474
Znaniecki, Florian, 870, 934–940, 1292–1297, 1476, 1479
Zoroaster, 1040, 1139, 1140, 1143

DATE DUE